Eastern
Europe

Brhris Deliso,
Petesna Maric,
Tom Masters, Marika McAdam, Leif Pettersen, Brandon Presser,
Robert Reid, Tim Richards, Simon Richmond

RĪGA (p443)
Shimmering church spires, devilish art nouveau gargoyles, and cobbled lanes secreted behind gingerbread trim

BELAVEZHSKAYA PUSHCHA NATIONAL PARK (p90)
Step into one of Europe's last wildernesses and spot a rare zoobr (European bison)

LVIV (p926)
This baroque beauty boasts a gorgeous Unesco-protected Old Town that cannot fail to enchant

HIGH TATRAS (p851)
Scale the peaks and shoosh the alpine slopes in the Carpathians' tallest mountains

KRAKÓW (p608)
The former royal capital of Poland is a blend of splendid historic architecture and vibrant nightlife

CURONIAN SPIT (p495)
A sliver of shifting pine-scented sand that separates the Baltic Sea from the Curonian Lagoon

KURSHSKAYA KOSA (p794)
An impressive national park with drifting sand dunes and a 'dancing forest' of wind-twisted pines

OLOMOUC (p315)
A thriving university town with all the history of Prague but a fraction of the tourists

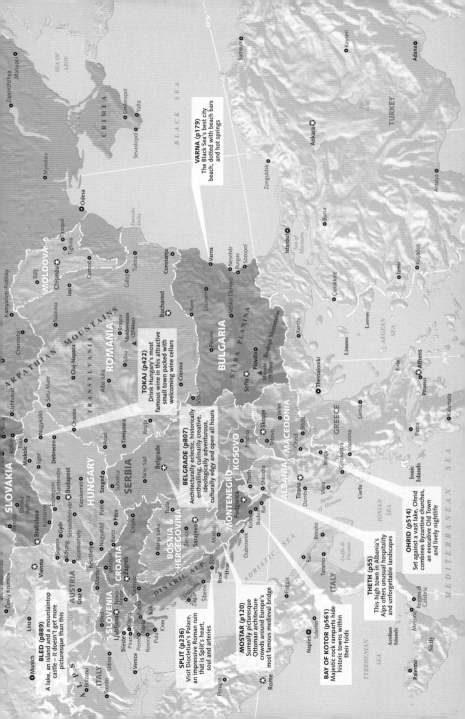

BLED (p889)
A lake, an island and a mountaintop castle – it doesn't get more picturesque than this

SPLIT (p236)
Visit Diocletian's Palace, an impressive Roman ruin that is Split's heart, soul and arteries

MOSTAR (p120)
Surreally picturesque Ottoman architecture crowds around Europe's most famous medieval bridge

BAY OF KOTOR (p561)
Majestic rock ramparts hide historic towns within their folds

THETH (p55)
This high town in Albania's Alps offers unusual hospitality and unforgettable landscapes

OHRID (p514)
Set against a vast lake, Ohrid combines Byzantine churches, an evocative Old Town and lively nightlife

BELGRADE (p807)
Architecturally eclectic, historically enthralling, culinarily creative, ideologically adventurous, culturally edgy and open all hours

TOKAJ (p422)
Drink Hungary's most famous wine in this attractive small town packed with welcoming wine cellars

VARNA (p179)
The Black Sea's best city beach, dotted with beach bars and hot springs

Eastern Europe Highlights

For years Eastern Europe was the undiscovered half of the continent, where architectural gems, wonderful landscapes and buzzing cities saw only a fraction of the number of visitors heading to Western Europe. Things have changed, with Eastern Europe now drawing travellers by the trainload, but the diversity and appeal of the region's highlights remain the same. Whether you're discovering them for the first time or coming back for a second dose, you won't be disappointed.

GRANT DI

1 VRŠIČ PASS, SLOVENIA

More often than not, even serial visitors to Slovenia like myself just stop and stare, mesmerised by the sheer beauty of this land. With so much splendour strewn across the country, it's nigh on impossible to choose a *številka ena* (that's 'number one' to you) absolute favourite top place. OK, OK, it's the Vršič Pass (p894), which stands head and shoulders above the rest, and leads me past Mt Triglav, and down to sunny Primorska province and the bluer-than-blue Soča River in one hair-raising, spine-tingling hour.

Steve Fallon, Lonely Planet Author

SARAJEVO, BOSNIA & HERCEGOVINA

Sarajevo (p106) was the place where WWI got started when Gavrilo Princip assassinated Archduke Franz Ferdinand in 1914, and seeing the spot where it happened was the whole reason we first visited 25 years ago. Back then concrete 'footprints' marked the spot from which Princip had pounced. Returning in 2008 I found that those footprints had been removed (as had the traffic from the now pedestrianised Latin Bridge opposite), but there's now a great little museum there that tells the whole story.

Mark Elliott, Lonely Planet Author

MLJET ISLAND, CROATIA

Seventy per cent of Mljet (p248) is a natural park; there are three salt lakes in the middle of the island, remote sandy beaches and only one conventional hotel; and the food – consisting of fresh fish, octopus and goat, all baked under hot coals – is magnificent. Need I say more?

Vesna Maric, Lonely Planet Author

TALLINN, ESTONIA

All you've heard about the chocolate-box Old Town of Tallinn (p334) is true – but in July you're appreciating its medieval magic alongside thousands of others. We legged it to leafy Kadriorg Park for some elbow room, a breath of fresh air and prime people-watching – wedding parties having their photos taken, kids squealing in the playground, locals and tourists wandering and admiring. A coffee by the pond followed by a stroll around the artworks of KUMU was completely reenergising.

**Carolyn Bain,
Lonely Planet Author**

© DAN BACHMANN / ALAMY

JONATHAN SA

4

ORHEIUL VECHI, MOLDOVA

Every time I stumble up the ridge at Orheiul Vechi (p542), I feel compelled to stop every few steps and take a dozen photos. Never mind that I already have countless photos from every conceivable angle. Each time it feels as if I'm seeing it under more favourable light, or from a slightly better perspective. Comparing the nearly identical pictures now, I've realised that Orheiul Vechi is one of those places that enthrals each time anew. It's just wonderful.

Leif Pettersen, Lonely Planet Author

5

JOHN ELK

6

LOKET, CZECH REPUBLIC

In the pretty West Bohemian town of Loket (p299), all of the Czech Republic's different attractions come together. The town sits improbably on a serpentine bend in the Ohře River, and is crowned by a dramatic castle. It's a good starting-off point for river adventures or a day hike to the spa scene at nearby Karlovy Vary. And when you come back from tasting the spa town's mineral-laden waters, Loket's Pivovar Sv Florian microbrewery is one of the country's best.

Brett Atkinson, Lonely Planet Author

ŽDIAR, SLOVAKIA

Whether snow is lying quietly on the hillsides or heather is blooming in the fields, there's something so tranquil about Ždiar (p856), a traditional Slovak village snuggled beneath the High Tatra mountain peaks. Is it the hand-painted designs on the log cottages, the fire burning in each of the handful of restaurants, or the nature surrounding you on every side? Yes – all of the above.

**Lisa Dunford,
Lonely Planet Author**

CRAIG PERSHOUSE

7

WAYNE WALTON

8

TORUŃ, POLAND

Whenever I arrive in Toruń (p651), I start to relax. This beautiful Gothic city has a great vibe, and just the right balance between sightseeing and chilling. I like to grab a *zapiekanka* (toasted roll topped with mushrooms, cheese and tomato sauce) from the window of the milk bar just off the main square, then saunter past the locals to check out the curious statuary around the square's edge, waving hello to my old friend Copernicus on his plinth. To finish a warm summer's day in one of the fancy beer garden decks perched on the cobblestones is perfection itself.

Brett Atkinson, Lonely Planet Author

BRUCE BI

9

RĪGA, LATVIA

The art nouveau architecture in Rīga (p443) is some of the most beautiful in the world. It also exemplifies the vibrant, often contradictory spirit of the city: elaborate, lovingly restored buildings stand next to crumbling facades, still elegant in their decay. And interspersed throughout the art nouveau district, Riga's wooden houses have met a similar fate: some are falling apart, others have been carefully refurbished. The old and the new, the refined and the grit, the effort and the neglect – much of Riga's personality can be seen through its architecture.

Ellie Schilling, Riga Resident

10 MINSK, BELARUS

Wandering down the grandiose main thoroughfare in Minsk (p76), where the ghost of Stalinism still lurks amid the monolithic architecture bequeathed to the city by Uncle Joe, is an experience unlike any other. But don't be fooled – Minsk has much more to offer than just its dark past. Good restaurants, cosy coffee shops and rocking nightclubs are all evidence that the city has cautiously moved into the 21st century.

Tom Masters, Lonely Planet Author

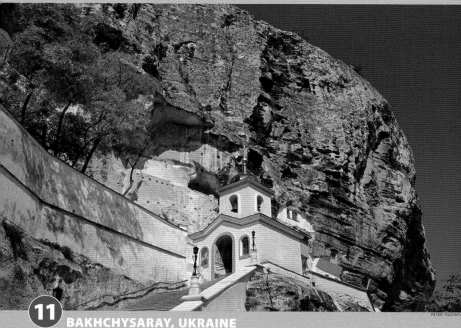

11 BAKHCHYSARAY, UKRAINE

On this most Russian of peninsulas, it's nothing short of astounding to come across the ancient Tatar Crimean capital of Bakhchysaray (p950), where the wonderful Khan's Palace and majestic mountain landscapes are the perfect antidote to the bucket-and-spade resorts elsewhere in Crimea.

Tom Masters, Lonely Planet Author

VISEGRÁD, HUNGARY

I remember looking over the Danube at Visegrád (p394), thinking how remarkable it was that I was gazing at the ancient border of the Roman Empire. Just for a moment, I had an overwhelming sense of all the kingdoms and people who'd come and gone since that distant time in the past.

Tim Richards, Lonely Planet Author

12

STEPHEN SAKS

ST PETERSBURG, RUSSIA

The Yusupov Palace is my favourite of the grand homes of St Petersburg (p771) – but not because of its kitsch Rasputin-murder waxwork tableaux. I love the succession of grand rooms, each more ornate than the last, culminating in an adorable gilded theatre in which intimate dance and opera performances are still held.

Simon Richmond, Lonely Planet Author

© CUBOIMAGES SRL / ALAMY

13

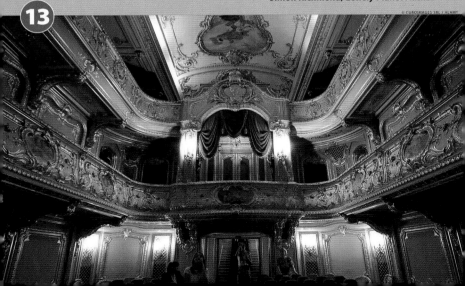

TONY WHE

(14) ALBANIA'S CASTLES

Being spooked in castles ain't unusual in Albania (p39); Robert Carver wrote about it years ago in *The Accursed Mountains*. Being on your own with practically unrestricted access to isolated historical monuments does bring up some 'skin crawl' moments, but just emphasises how fresh to tourism this country is.

Jayne D'Arcy, Lonely Planet Author

PATRICK HOR

(15) PRISTINA, KOSOVO

In the 1990s, foreign correspondent Robert D Kaplan said 'Defeat…has a name: Prishtina.' I wished Kaplan was there with me as my taxi drove through this newly self-proclaimed capital (p434); the streets were pretty much the mess he described (but with more buildings on their way up than down), but now, a few months after independence was declared, blood red Albanian flags were flapping a new name: change.

Marika McAdam, Lonely Planet Author

NORTHWEST BULGARIA

I like Bulgaria's northwest 'pinkie' (p191) – a forgotten little slice of Bulgaria where you'll see lifelike rock formations sticking out of an ancient fortress at Belogradchik. I spent a couple of days undergoing DIY adventures to Bulgaria's northernmost point with locals who were happy to lead me on fruitless hikes to see Roman ruins and an old factory now serving as a mental-health asylum.

Robert Reid, Lonely Planet Author

ROBERTO GEROMETTA

16

ZLATIBOR, SERBIA

I was told I would find a monument commemorating victims of Nazi brutality on top of a hill in the centre of Zlatibor (p826). The monument was there, but so were extraordinary panoramas of Zlatibor's rolling plains, and groups of friends who had gathered with picnic lunches. I sat on the grass and quietly decided that this heartbreakingly lovely patch of the country was my favourite.

Marika McAdam, Lonely Planet Author

© DIOMEDIA / ALAMY

17

CURONIAN SPIT, LITHUANIA

I'd been told that meeting wild boar on the cycle path of the Curonian Spit (p495) was a daily occurrence, but I didn't believe it until I rounded the bend and almost cycled straight into a full-grown male. He appeared totally unfazed by my sudden appearance, and continued to go about his business. By the time I organised my camera, his entire family had magically appeared from the undergrowth. I snapped a few of shots and went on my way, wondering if I'd be lucky enough to also see some elusive elk.

**Neal Bedford,
Lonely Planet Author**

19

© PICTORIUM / AI

© DIOMEDIA / ALAMY

18

TARA RIVER, MONTENEGRO

The Tara River (p576) slices deeply through the Durmitor range, creating one of the world's most dramatic rafting routes and the nation's most popular active attraction.

Peter Dragicevich, Lonely Planet Author

DIANA MAYF

20 MARAMUREŞ, ROMANIA

As I was asked to omit details of indulgent wine binges and achingly beautiful women, my third-favourite Romanian highlight is the bucolic paradise of Maramureş (p716). This veritable conga line of increasingly captivating villages starts just after the last painted monastery of Bucovina and ends at the Ukrainian border. The occasional villager armed with a pitchfork in one hand and a mobile phone in the other is about the only thing jarring the time-travel sensation that characterises most visits here.

Leif Pettersen, Lonely Planet Author

Contents

914
7
VOR

7/3/11

Contents

Regional Map Contents

Estonia p328
Russia p746
Latvia p440
Lithuania p468
Kaliningrad Region p787
Belarus p73
Poland p590
Czech Republic p264
Slovakia p832
Ukraine pp912–13
Hungary p366
Moldova p530
Slovenia p874
Romania p672
Croatia pp200–1
Bosnia & Hercegovina p100
Serbia p805
Montenegro p556
Kosovo p432
Bulgaria p142
Macedonia p502
Albania p40

Destination Eastern Europe

It seems like a simple concept: it's Europe, but it's the eastern part. Eastern Europe.

Well, yes, but… It is not geography that defines Eastern Europe. If it were, this book would include countries such as Finland and Greece, which are at the eastern edge of the continent.

Language is not a binding factor either, for some of these countries use the Latin alphabet, while others use Cyrillic; most speak Baltic, Romance or Slavic languages, but Estonian and Hungarian are indecipherable anomalies of the Finno-Ugric family.

Religion does not unite the region (if we may be forgiven the understatement). The region's population is Catholic, Orthodox, Muslim and Lutheran. In recent years, religion and ethnicity sparked the worst violence Europe had seen since WWII, busting the former Yugoslavia into seven independent countries. It's fair to say that Eastern Europeans are still working out their religious differences.

Culturally the region is an art nouveau mosaic, each country a tile with its own colour, shape and texture. On display are southern hospitality and northern reserve, EU-approved transparency and post-Soviet haze, provincial modesty and big-city audacity, flabbergasting prosperity and heart-rending poverty.

So what is the unifying factor that defines Eastern Europe? What do these 21 countries have in common?

Their only universal commonality is a little piece of shared history: the 40-odd years that they spent under communist rule. The Iron Curtain so split the continent that even now – two decades after it was ripped from its dictatorial rod – it still divides Europe in popular imagination. (Only the former East Germany has completely discarded its 'eastern' label.)

These days, the communist legacy endures in different ways. Every city has a relic or two – a Lenin monument or a KGB museum that remembers the bad old days. Bits of Soviet-era bureaucracy linger on in visa and registration requirements, and standing in an orderly queue is still a skill that evades many Eastern Europeans. But throughout the region, the grey, bleak uniformity is long gone.

Eager young democracies are queuing up to join the new Europe. Ten of the countries covered in this book are already members of the European Union, with two candidates and five 'potential' candidates in the works. This leaves only four countries – Russia, Belarus, Ukraine and Moldova – with no EU prospects. It explains a lot about why the Russian administration might feel a bit isolated.

Politics aside, these countries are embracing the 21st century with more gusto than anyone would have guessed. From Albania to Ukraine, their citizens are breaking down the barriers of generations past and exploring the possibilities of consumerism, creativity and career. Fusion food and edgy art, high-tech hot spots and high-life nightspots – this is not your parents' Eastern Europe.

Getting Started

It has been 20 years since the Iron Curtain was pulled down, opening up an entire region for discovery by intrepid travellers. While much has changed in the course of two decades, Eastern Europe remains an intriguing destination – a region that mingles rich cultures, wild natural beauty and incongruous postcommunist quirks.

If this is your first trip to Eastern Europe, you may be surprised by a few bureaucratic hurdles that still plague travellers, especially as you move further east. If it's not your first trip, you will be surprised at how easy things have become. There are 10 Eastern European countries that are already in the EU, and two more vying for membership in the near future, thereby simplifying border crossing, moneychanging and life in general. (That said, other entities continue to declare themselves to be independent countries, so there are still plenty of national boundaries to deal with.)

Don't forget, visas are still required to enter Belarus and Russia. Even when visas are available at the point of entry, you must obtain an invitation in advance – so you'll want to plan ahead, even if you normally prefer to fly by the seat of your pants.

At the time of publication, Bulgaria, the Czech Republic, Estonia, Hungary, Latvia, Lithuania, Poland, Romania, Slovakia and Slovenia were members of the EU. Croatia and Macedonia were candidates for membership.

WHEN TO GO

In deciding when to go to Eastern Europe, the most obvious factors to consider are climate and crowds, but festivals and other events may also influence when you want to travel (see p29).

The high tourist season generally runs from May until September. However, the peaks vary from place to place: the snowy season attracts skiers to mountain destinations; in Catholic countries, festive pre-Lenten carnivals draw revellers in early spring; 'white nights' make June a popular month in St Petersburg and the Baltics; sun worshippers and seafarers flock to the Adriatic coast and the Black Sea in late summer.

Unless you are angling for a specific event or activity, the best time to visit is either side of the summer peak: May, June and September stand out for pleasant weather and manageable crowds.

July and August are sunny and warm, and filled with lively festivals (p30), but they are also jammed with backpackers, bus tours and beachcombers. Any place with a coastline draws massive crowds in late summer. You may also want to avoid July and August if you're going to any of the 'big three' – Prague, Budapest and Kraków – as they can be unbearably crowded at this time.

See Climate Charts (p963) for more information.

Travelling out of season, you might discover some bargains in accommodation. However, beach towns and other places where tourism is the main industry may resemble ghost towns during the low season.

Winter is cold, especially in the Baltics, Belarus, Russia and Ukraine, where temperatures dip to -10°C and below between November and February. Still, the snow-covered landscapes and long dark nights can be enticing for the well-equipped traveller. In the southern reaches of the region, winter is not nearly so formidable.

COSTS & MONEY

Gone are the days when you can travel east, sell one pair of blue jeans and live like a king for a week. Long gone. First of all, nobody wants your blue jeans. Secondly, if you want to live like a king you have to pay for it.

Generally speaking, Eastern Europe is still cheaper than Western Europe. But the cost of living has surged in Prague, Warsaw, Bratislava and Bucharest;

DON'T LEAVE HOME WITHOUT...

- Checking the visa situation, especially for Belarus (p95) and Russia (p797)
- Notifying your bank and your credit card companies to expect charges and withdrawals from Eastern European countries; see p968
- Brushing up on your Cyrillic (p1009): a little bit goes a long way!
- Your European Health Insurance Card or other proof of medical insurance (p988)
- Flip-flops to wear indoors
- A Swiss Army knife with a bottle opener
- A torch for dark streets (Albania) and stairwells (Russia)
- A headscarf, worn by women upon entering Orthodox churches
- Painkillers: at least one hangover is practically guaranteed!

at the time of publication, Moscow is the most expensive city in the world for expatriates.

Budget travellers can expect to pay €10 to €15 for a dorm bed in cheaper cities such as Sofia or Tirana, while similar accommodation in Moscow or Prague is between €20 and €25. By self-catering and eating fast food, you might get by on €20 to €30 per day for food.

Midrange travellers will pay about €50 for a private room in most parts of the region, but you'll fork out about €80 in Prague and more than €100 in Moscow or St Petersburg. Expect to pay €10 to €20 per head to dine in a decent restaurant in the major cities.

Of course, Eastern Europe is a vast region with widely ranging costs. You'll need far less in the countryside than in the city, and your euro will go further in winter than in summer. Museums, excursions and transportation are extra costs that will increase your expenses.

Students and seniors are often eligible for discounts, especially if you have an EU passport or ISIC card (see p966).

Nobody would have thought it a decade ago, but these days you can use your ATM card to obtain money in any Eastern European city. All major credit and debit cards are accepted by ATMs, including those on the Cirrus/Maestro system. Credit cards are also widely accepted by hotels, restaurants and shops.

It's always useful to have a back-up plan in case of emergencies: most major banks will do cash advances on credit cards. Travellers cheques are still the safest way to carry large sums of money, but they are a pain in the proverbial, especially if you try to change them outside major cities.

XE (www.xe.com) is an up-to-the-second online currency-exchange calculator. Find out the rates for all Eastern European currencies, and see exactly how much your trip is going to cost you.

If you are carrying cash, both euros and US dollars are easy to exchange throughout the region. In many places you can even pay for hotel accommodation in euros, although never count on this. The days of currency controls in Eastern Europe are gone, so you can freely exchange your extra local currency for 'hard' currency before you depart. That said, it may be difficult to exchange the local currency once you leave the country in question. You are better off spending it or changing it, even if this means getting bad exchange rates at the border.

TRAVELLING RESPONSIBLY

Most Eastern European countries lag behind their Western European counterparts when it comes to awareness of ecological issues. But that does not mean that you're off the hook. Here are some ways that you can minimise the environmental impact of your trip.

Getting There & Away

Air travel is the worst form of transportation for emitting greenhouse gases (or best, if your goal is to give off as much carbon dioxide as possible). It should come as no surprise that your ability to avoid air travel to Eastern Europe will be directly related to your place of origin.

The good news is that if you are coming from Western Europe, there is no shortage of overland routes. All of the Eastern European capitals (with the exception of Tirana) are connected to Western Europe by train, as are many of the smaller cities (see p978). Cheap buses also ply the most popular tourist routes (p978). Ferries cross the Baltic and Adriatic, dropping passengers on their eastern shores (p979).

Even if you are coming from Asia, you might travel overland if you have some time to spare. (Trans-Siberian Railway, anyone?) Intercontinental travellers will have a tougher time of it, though.

> On the 'Day of the Tree', hundreds of thousands of Macedonian volunteers planted two million trees in a single day in March 2008, and another six million on one day in November.

Slow Travel

Once you arrive, the entirety of Eastern Europe is at your disposal. You may wish to pop in for a weekend on a low-cost carrier, but you'll experience only a tiny fraction of this riveting region. Why not take some time and explore by extended overland travel? Not only is it more environmentally sound, it also allows you to see more, do more and learn more.

Most major cities in Eastern Europe are well served by public transportation, so you might as well use it. Many of these towns are already choked with traffic, which you'll want to avoid, so hop on the metro, bus or tram instead of driving. Even outside the cities, you'll find that buses and trains will get you almost everywhere you wish to go.

> If you must fly, consider offsetting your carbon emissions; see www .climatecare.org and www.carbonneutral.com.

While parts of the region still suffer from industrial pollution, you will be amazed by the extensive network of national parks and nature preserves, often protecting spectacular mountain scenery, gorgeous coastline or primeval forest. Head out to these green sanctuaries and explore by bicycle, on horseback or by foot!

Accommodation & Food

'Biodegradable' and 'organic' may not be widespread in Eastern Europe, but we came across a few establishments that are doing their part to go green (see the boxed text, p26).

Shopping at local markets is an easy way to eat healthy and cheap. There's a good chance you are buying locally grown produce, which benefits the environment and your wallet! Plus, the local market often provides a chance to interact with vendors and to sample local foods (sometimes homemade) – a great cultural experience.

Guest houses and hostels are an appealing, intimate alternative to hotels. These days, most small, private properties offer the same professional service that you'll find at a larger hotel. But they are often family-run operations with much more character, sometimes at a fraction of the price – again, this benefits the local economy.

> Ethical Traveller (www .ethicaltraveller.org) has selected Bulgaria, Croatia and Estonia for its list of the 'Developing World's 10 Best Ethical Destinations', based on criteria such as environmental protection, social welfare and human rights.

Responsible Travel Organisations

Biljana Tourist Association (www.beyondohrid.com) An excellent resource for independent travellers who wish to explore Macedonia 'Beyond Ohrid'.

Black Mountain (www.montenegroholiday.com) A Montenegro tour operator that is committed to protecting the environment while organising activities such as birdwatching, mountain biking and white-water rafting.

Blue World (www.blue-world.org) This NGO is dedicated to research and conservation in the Adriatic. Also sponsors 'ecovolunteers' to participate in 12-day research missions.

GOOD FOR THE BODY, GOOD FOR THE SOUL

These are our top picks for ecofriendly accommodation and organic eateries in Eastern Europe:

- **Aed** (p344), Tallinn, Estonia – An organic 'garden' of Estonian Eden.
- **Kauno Arkivyskupijos Svečių Namai** (p490), Kaunas, Lithuania – A church-run guest house with an ecoconscious approach.
- **Morkų Šėlsmas** (p490), Kaunas, Lithuania – You're invited to a Carrot Party! Homemade vegetarian goodies, made with organic ingredients and lots of love.
- **National Eco Restaurant** (p577), Durmitor National Park, Montenegro – Is it 'eco' because it's in the national park or because the menu features local game and produce? Both, of course!
- **Natyral & Organik** (p52), Tirana, Albania – Stocks organic goodies from local producers and advocates for environmental awareness.
- **Soline 6** (p249), Mljet Island, Croatia – A rustic and ecofriendly lodge in the midst of Mljet National Park.

Caput Insulae – Beli (www.supovi.hr) This Croatian organisation works to protect the Eurasian griffon. Travellers can volunteer on a weekly basis to clean up the endangered bird species' habitat on the island of Cres.

Centre for Scientific Tourism (www.csts.sk) Tours in Slovakia that allow travellers to learn about natural history, geology and ecology.

Centre for Sustainable Tourism Initiatives (www.cstimontenegro.org) An NGO that promotes sustainable tourism in Montenegro. Its commercial wing, Montenegro Adventures (www.montenegro-adventures.com) organises tours, accommodation and the like.

European Centre for Eco Agro Tourism (www.eceat.org) A network of more than 1000 small-scale lodges and farms that provide rural, ecofriendly lodging. Also certifies environmentally friendly establishments throughout Europe.

Skype – the software that allows you to make free international phone calls over the internet – was invented in 2003 by two Estonian software engineers.

Green Key (www.green-key.org) It's a Scandi initiative, but the Baltic states are also signing up. The search engine includes hotels, hostels and restaurants that have fulfilled numerous environmental criteria.

Green Visions (www.greenvisions.ba) Offers ecofriendly tours and activities, engages in community development and lobbies for environmental protective measures in Bosnia and Hercegovina.

Heritage Trails (www.heritage-trails.cz) A Czech company that offers walking and cycling tours all around Central Europe.

Organic Agriculture Association (www.organic.org.al) An organisation of farmers in Albania that promotes the use of organic practices and principles.

Pro Natura (www.pronatura.ro) Administers protected areas and works to reduce the impact of tourism in Romania.

Responsible Travel (www.responsibletravel.com) A fantastic search engine that allows you to search for environmentally and socially responsible tour operators in your country and city of interest. All operators are screened for certain 'responsible travel' criteria.

Transylvania Ecological Club (www.greenagenda.org) Grass-roots environmental group that focuses on ecotravel in Romania.

Travelling Balkans (www.travellingthebalcans.net) Advocates for cultural and natural awareness as a means of promoting ethical and responsible travel throughout the Balkans.

Worldwide Opportunities on Organic Farms (www.wwoof.org) Work at an organic farm in exchange for food, accommodation and some hands-on experience in organic farming. WWOOF has representative organisations in Bulgaria, the Czech Republic, Estonia and Romania, but there are also 'independent' farms offering work opportunities in other countries.

TRAVEL LITERATURE

The most pertinent titles for each country are listed in the individual country chapters. The following books provide an interesting introduction to the complexities and idiosyncrasies of Eastern Europe as a region.

- *Stalin's Nose* (Rory Maclean) Immediately following the collapse of the Berlin Wall, Rory Maclean set out on a journey in a Trabant from Berlin to Moscow, accompanied by his aunt and her pet pig. His hilarious account captures the quirks of postcommunist Europe at an exceptional time in history – after the wall but before the mall.
- *Café Europa: Life after Communism* (Slavenka Drakulic) This book, by a Croat journalist, comments on the rush for Eastern Europe to become Western Europe. Born of a communist father, married to a Swede and now living in Vienna, Drakulic has a unique perspective on the changes sweeping the region in the 1990s. This book follows on her earlier collection of essays, *How We Survived Communism and Even Laughed*, published in 1992.
- *The Zookeeper's Wife* (Diane Ackerman) A well-documented account of one Polish family's heroic efforts to shelter Jews fleeing the Warsaw ghetto. The biographical account also shares Ackerman's own impressions as she returns to Poland 50 years after her story transpired.
- *Guerrilla Radio* (Matthew Collin) This is a riveting, informative account of the music-lovers turned political rebels who ran an independent radio station during the Milošević era in Serbia. Collin's personal interactions and interviews with the founders of the station make this a fascinating read.
- *Bury Me Standing* (Isabel Fonseca) Eastern Europe's culturally rich Roma people are explored in this history, travelogue and cultural guide. It's a deeply moving account of Roma trying to retain their culture in postcommunist, nationalist Eastern Europe.
- *Eastern Approaches* (Fitzroy Maclean) The wry wit and derring-do of Fitzroy Maclean is on display in this firsthand account of his adventures as a British diplomat and dynamite in Stalin's Soviet Union and Nazi-occupied Yugoslavia. Maclean plays the role of diplomat, soldier, spy and all-around adventurer; some claim he inspired Ian Fleming's character of Bond, James Bond.
- *Black Lamb and Grey Falcon* (Rebecca West) This is a huge, unclassifiable look at the Balkans on the eve of WWII through the eyes of Brit Rebecca West as she makes her way through Bosnia, Serbia, Kosovo, Albania and Croatia in 1937. This fascinating, poetic account is still considered a travel literature classic.
- *Another Fool in the Balkans* (Tony White) Sixty years after Rebecca West's journey, White retraces her footsteps, paying tribute to her in this collection of essays. He explores the region's history and cultures in attempt to make sense of the contemporary conflict.
- *Hidden Macedonia* (Christopher Deliso) This engaging travelogue records a journey around the great Macedonian lakes of Ohrid and Prespa, and the three countries that share them: Greece, Albania and Macedonia.
- *To the Baltic with Bob* (Griff Rhys Jones) For a light-hearted read, try this account of sailing from the UK to St Petersburg via the canals of Eastern Europe. Written by British TV comedian Griff Rhys Jones, it's eccentric and grumpy but good fun.

For a laugh, read *Molvania: A Land Untouched by Modern Dentistry* (Santo Cilauro et al), a faux-guidebook to a fictitious Eastern European country that's the 'next big thing'. Hilarious!

Several Western writers turned their surreal postcommunist travel experiences into funny and insightful novels. *Everything is Illuminated* is Jonathan Safran Foer's fictionalised account of the retracing of his roots in Ukraine. Gary Shteyngart wrote *The Russian Debutante's Guide* about expat life in the fictitious city of Prava.

INTERNET RESOURCES

Whether you're planning a weekend in Prague or an odyssey around the entire region, you'll find plenty of information on the web.

Balkan Travellers (www.balkantravellers.com) News and musings from the Balkans. Articles feature off-the-beaten-track destinations, active adventures and cultural discoveries, plus there is a route planner to help you plan your trip.

Baltic Times (www.baltictimes.com) News from Estonia, Latvia and Lithuania, as well as travel stories in the region and cultural listings from the capital cities.

Flycheapo (www.flycheapo.com) This brilliant website saves you the hassle of checking every budget airline's website for routes to wherever you want to go. Flycheapo monitors the flights of all these airlines and tells you who flies to where you want to go.

In Your Pocket (www.inyourpocket.com) This Vilnius-based desktop-publishing company has enjoyed incredible success. The formula is simple: it produces frequently updated booklets about scores of destinations within Eastern Europe, which are financially supported by advertising. You can download a huge amount of information in PDF form from the website – all for free!

Rail Europe (www.raileurope.com) Gives lots of information on timetables, routes and prices for most of the region (but not the former Soviet Union). For detailed information about the entire former Soviet Union's trains, check out www.poezda.net.

Southeast European Times (www.setimes.com) A source of news and information about business, politics and society in Southeast Europe, offered in 10 different languages.

Thorn Tree (http://thorntree.lonelyplanet.com) The Lonely Planet interactive travellers' message board. There's a dedicated section for posts relating to Eastern Europe and a huge number of travellers able to give up-to-the-minute advice.

Multilingual, multi-national and multimedia: Cafe Babel (www.cafebabel.com) is the magazine for the new Europe, an interactive forum commenting on current affairs across the continent.

MUST-SEE MOVIES

Most people think Eastern European film means slow-paced psychological dramas in black and white, but that stereotype couldn't be less true these days. Against all odds, Eastern Europe has a small but creatively dynamic film industry, as well as a long history of classic (erm, slow-paced, black-and-white) films. Here are some recent releases that offer good entertainment and insight on the region:

- *California Dreamin'* (2007) A train bound for Kosovo gets delayed in a small Romanian village, much to the chagrin of Polish and American soldiers who are guarding the cargo on board. Some local officials attempt to entertain their unexpected guests, while others attempt to profit from them.
- *Kráska v nesnázich* (Beauty in Trouble; 2006) This delightful and insightful drama follows three generations of a Czech family as they try to navigate the tumultuous transition from communism. Their troubled existence is disrupted when they cross paths with a kind-hearted and wealthy émigré who has returned to settle his dead mother's estate.
- *Grbavica* (2006) Set in the area of Sarajevo of the same name, *Grbavica* is a Bosnian film about the realities of Serb rape camps during the Bosnian War. The harrowing story shocked Bosnians and outraged Serbs, and it won the Golden Bear for best film at the Berlin Film Festival in 2006.
- *Lost and Found* (2005) Six short films produced in Estonia, Bulgaria, Bosnia and Hercegovina, Hungary, Romania and Serbia, and Montenegro. All offer poignant peeks into the hearts and minds of young Eastern Europeans in the generation since the fall of the Berlin Wall.
- *Cesky Sen* (Czech Dream; 2004) A documentary about two students who undertake the hoax of launching a huge new supermarket. A clever and compelling film full of observations on consumer society in the Czech Republic after the fall of communism.
- *The Pianist* (2002) Roman Polański's film vividly depicts the Warsaw ghetto during the Nazi occupation. The true story is based on the autobiography of musician Władysław Szpilman.

Events Calendar

KUKERI   Sun before Lent
Masked dancers in Shiroka Lâka (p194; Bulgaria) ward off evil spirits in this (hairy) festival.

KURENTOVANJE   10 days leading up to Lent
This rite of spring in Ptuj (p905; Slovenia) is celebrated for 10 days before Shrove Tuesday; it's the most popular Mardi Gras celebration in Slovenia.

RIJEKA CARNIVAL   2 weeks leading up to Lent
Held in Rijeka (p227; Croatia), this carnival's two weeks of partying involves pageants, street dances, concerts, masked balls, exhibitions and an international parade.

VITRANC CUP   late Feb-early Mar
Men's slalom and giant slalom competitions in Kranjska Gora (p894; Slovenia).

MARTENITSA   Mar
Bulgarian custom (see p194) dictates that locals exchange red-and-white figures, which they wear until they see a stork.

SKI-JUMPING WORLD CUP CHAMPIONSHIPS   3rd weekend in Mar
This competition in Planica (p894; Slovenia) was the site of a world-record jump of 239m in 2005.

ZAGREB BIENNALE   3rd week in Apr
Held since 1961, the Zagreb Biennale (p214) is Croatia's most important classical-music event; it takes place in odd years only.

FESTIVAL OF SACRED MUSIC   2 weeks leading up to Easter
Six thematic concerts in the solemn setting of Petrov Cathedral in Brno (p313; Czech Republic).

INTERNATIONAL LABOUR DAY   1 May
Still celebrated as a major holiday in the former Soviet Union (p955); bigger cities have fireworks, concerts and other performances.

PRAGUE SPRING   12 May-3 Jun
This international classical-music festival kicks off summer in Prague (p281; Czech Republic).

KHAMORO   last week in May
An annual festival of Roma music, dance and culture in Prague (p281; Czech Republic).

DRUGA GODBA   late May-early Jun
A festival of alternative and world music held at the Križanke in Ljubljana (p883; Slovenia).

VILNIUS FESTIVAL   late May-early Jul
Throughout June, performances in Vilnius (p480; Lithuania) highlight Lithuanian composers and music from different eras, including early baroque and contemporary jazz.

WROCŁAW NON STOP   Jun
Movies, music, theatre, dance and art are exhibited throughout the month at venues around Wrocław (p635; Poland).

OPERA FESTIVAL   Jun
An annual event that showcases the best of Rīga's (p451; Latvia) opera season.

OLD TOWN DAYS   early Jun
Held in the photogenic 14th-century Old Town of Tallinn (p342; Estonia), this week-long festival features dancing, concerts, costumed performers and plenty of medieval merrymaking.

BALTICA INTERNATIONAL FOLK FESTIVAL   early–mid-Jun
A week of music, dance and displays focusing on folk traditions. It's shared between the Baltic capitals; it will be in Rīga (Latvia) in 2009, Tallinn (p342; Estonia) in 2010, and in Vilnius (p497; Lithuania) in 2011.

ROSE FESTIVAL   1st weekend in Jun
Three-day celebration of roses in Kazanlâk (p168; Bulgaria) that culminates in the crowning of a festival queen.

VIP INMUSIC FESTIVAL   3-4 Jun
Zagreb (p214; Croatia) hosts a two-day music extravaganza on the island in Jarun Lake.

**MALTA INTERNATIONAL
THEATRE FESTIVAL**   3rd week in Jun
A prestigious international theatre festival in Poznań (p639; Poland).

UNITED ISLANDS   3rd weekend in Jun
World-music festival in Prague (p281; Czech Republic).

**FIVE-PETALLED
ROSE FESTIVAL**   3rd weekend in Jun
Knights, jugglers, musicians and artists roam Český Krumlov (p307; Czech Republic), celebrating the Renaissance period.

**ST JOHN'S EVE
& ST JOHN'S DAY**   23 & 24 Jun
The Baltic region's biggest annual night out is a celebration of midsummer. It's best experienced out in the country, where huge bonfires flare for all-night revellers. See p363 and p463 for details.

WHITE NIGHTS   late Jun
St Petersburg (p781; Russia) celebrates the summer solstice with all-night parties and a packed cultural calendar.

**LENT INTERNATIONAL
SUMMER FESTIVAL**   late Jun-early Jul
A two-week festival of folklore and culture in Maribor (p904; Slovenia).

ROCK OTOČEC   late Jun or early Jul
Slovenia's biggest open-air rock concert takes place in Novo Mesto (p907; Slovenia).

KALIAKRA ROCK FEST   last weekend in Jun
This festival in Kavarna (p184; Bulgaria) kick-starts the Black Sea summer with well-known heavy-metal bands.

JULY

RĪGAS RITMI   Jul
This international music festival in Rīga (p451; Latvia) highlights rhythms from around the world, including world beat, nu jazz and Afro-Cuban music.

WARSAW SUMMER JAZZ DAYS   Jul
This summer concert series in Warsaw (p601; Poland) attracts international artists such as Wynton Marsalis and Natalie Cole, as well as Polish performers.

LJUBLJANA FESTIVAL   Jul-Aug
Slovenia's premier cultural event (p883) includes music, dance and theatre.

JEWISH CULTURE FESTIVAL   1st week in Jul
Kraków (p614; Poland) hosts a week of music, art exhibitions and lectures celebrating Jewish culture.

**KARLOVY VARY INTERNATIONAL
FILM FESTIVAL**   early Jul
A renowned event in Karlovy Vary (p296; Czech Republic) that shows hundreds of films and attracts international celebrities.

**BALKAN FESTIVAL OF FOLK
DANCES & SONGS**   early Jul
A five-day festival in Ohrid (p517; Macedonia) that captivates audiences with performances by folkloric groups from around the region.

EXIT FESTIVAL   2nd weekend in Jul
Europe's edgiest annual music festival, held in Novi Sad (p820; Serbia), pulls in an international audience and a star-studded line-up.

GALIČNIK WEDDING   12 & 13 Jul
A beloved traditional event in gorgeous Mavrovo National Park (p514; Macedonia).

**MEDIEVAL FESTIVAL OF
THE ARTS**   mid-Jul
Sighişoara (p701; Romania) hosts open-air concerts, parades and ceremonies, all glorifying medieval Transylvania.

SLAVYANSKY BAZAAR   mid-Jul
Dozens of singers and performers from Slavic countries come together for a week of concerts and parties in Vitsebsk (p92; Belarus).

MARAMUZICAL FESTIVAL   mid-Jul
A lively four-day international folk music-festival in Vadu Izei (p719; Romania).

**INTERNATIONAL
MUSIC FESTIVAL**   mid-Jul–mid-Aug
Thousands of music lovers congregate in Český Krumlov (p307; Czech Republic) for classical concerts, as well as jazz, rock and folk music.

CROATIA SUMMER
FESTIVALS   mid-Jul–mid-Aug
Dubrovnik, Pula, Split and Zagreb host month-long events (p256), with music, dance and theatre performances at venues around the towns.

OHRID SUMMER
FESTIVAL   mid-Jul–mid-Aug
Held in Ohrid (p517), Macedonia's biggest cultural event features classical music, opera, theatre and dance.

BALTIC
BEACH PARTY   3rd weekend in Jul
A weekend of music and drinking in Liepāja (p459; Latvia), along with volleyball and football competitions on the beach, and a sand-sculpture exhibition.

SEA FESTIVAL   late Jul
Celebrations in the port city of Klaipėda (p493; Lithuania).

AUGUST

DON CHENTO
JAZZ FESTIVAL   1st weekend in aug
A newish jazz event in Kaliningrad (p791; Russia) that already attracts performers from across Europe.

SARAJEVO
FILM FESTIVAL   mid-Aug
Globally acclaimed festival screening commercial and art-house movies in Sarajevo (p113; Bosnia and Hercegovina).

SZIGET
MUSIC FESTIVAL   mid-Aug
A week-long world-music bash in Budapest (p382; Hungary) that features bands from around the world playing at more than 60 venues.

SEPTEMBER

DVOŘÁK AUTUMN   Sep
A festival of classical music in honour of the Czech Republic's favourite composer. Held in Karlovy Vary (p298; Czech Republic).

PRAGUE AUTUMN   12 Sep-1 Oct
This festival of orchestral music, held in Prague (Czech Republic; p281), hosts conductors and symphony orchestras from around the world.

COWS' BALL   mid-Sep
A weekend of folk dancing, music, eating and drinking in Bohinj (p893; Slovenia) to mark the return of the cows from their high pastures.

OCTOBER

ADVENTURE RACE MONTENEGRO   early Oct
A two-day fundraising challenge (p578) that incorporates kayaking, mountain biking, trekking and orienteering.

WINE FESTIVAL   2nd Sun in Oct
Winemakers, wine tasting, wine buying and wine-enriched folkloric performances in Moldova (p550).

NOVEMBER–DECEMBER

INTERNATIONAL
JAZZ FESTIVAL   2nd week in Nov
Held in Sarajevo (p113; Bosnia and Hercegovina), this festival showcases local and international jazz musicians.

PRAGUE INTERNATIONAL
JAZZ FESTIVAL   late Nov-early Dec
This festival in Prague (p281) attracts the Czech Republic's top jazz musicians, as well as a few international performers.

Itineraries
CLASSIC ROUTES

EASTERN EUROPE 101
Four Weeks / Prague to Budapest

Begin your trip in magical **Prague** (p270), spending several days absorbing the city and nearby towns, such as beer lovers' mecca **Plzeň** (p300) and beautiful **Kutná Hora** (p291).

Head into Poland to **Kraków** (p608), with its gobsmacking Old Town. This is a great base for visiting the **Tatra Mountains** (p629) and for the harrowing trip to **Oświęcim** (p618).

Travel south to Slovakia, where you can enjoy magnificent scenery in the **High Tatras** (p851) before pursuing more-urban activities in delightful **Bratislava** (p836).

Journey up the Danube to **Budapest** (p373). From here visit the picturesque Hungarian countryside – try the baroque city of **Eger** (p419), with its ancient castle, or **Pécs** (p410), stuffed full of relics from the Turkish occupation.

Now plunge into Romania. Use **Cluj-Napoca** (p706) as your base for visiting the region of **Maramureş** (p716), then head for the medieval superlatives of **Sibiu** (p702) and **Braşov** (p694) before heading on to the **Danube Delta** (p735), where you can ogle birds, dine on fish and enjoy some of the quietest beaches in Europe. Finish in **Bucharest** (p677) for excellent food and nightlife, and a taste of megalomaniac architecture.

If you are a first-timer, consider Eastern Europe 101, which covers the region's 'big five'. It begins in the Czech Republic and wends its way through Poland, Slovakia, Hungary and Romania, providing a fantastic introduction to a region in transition.

EAST OF EAST TOUR
Four Weeks / Warsaw to Warsaw

Begin in bustling **Warsaw** (p595), where you can see the reconstructed Old Town and learn about its dark history. From here, head by train to **Lviv** (p926), Ukraine's most beautiful city, and spend a few days here before crossing the country to graceful **Kyiv** (p916), the Jerusalem of East Slavonic culture.

After a few days enjoying the sights in the Ukrainian capital, take the sleeper train to the megalopolis **Moscow** (p753), Europe's biggest city and a place of striking extremes. Travel around the **Golden Ring** (p769) to get a sense of the Russian countryside. Next on the agenda is the beautiful baroque architecture and rich cultural life of **St Petersburg** (p771). You can easily spend three or four days in the city itself, although there are abundant sights outside St Petersburg, such as the tsarist palace at **Petrodvorets** (p786).

In Estonia, you'll love medieval **Tallinn** (p334) and the rural delights of **Saaremaa** (p359). The Latvian capital at **Rīga** (p443) boasts Europe's finest collection of art nouveau architecture. But don't ignore the country's other highlights, such as the medieval castles and caves of **Sigulda** (p460) and the breathtaking Baltic coastline around **Ventspils** (p459). In Lithuania, enjoy charming **Vilnius** (p472) and the amazing **Curonian Spit** (p495) before re-entering Poland and heading back to Warsaw.

Plan ahead to get your Russian visa. Once armed with the appropriate *dokumenty*, you'll make a grand loop, starting in westward-looking Poland, traversing the Ukrainian countryside, dipping into Mother Russia and circling back to sample the feisty Baltic countries.

THE BALKANS & BEYOND   Four Weeks / Ljubljana to Varna

Begin in lively little Slovenia, with a cheap flight to charming **Ljubljana** (p877). Indulge in superb scenery and adrenaline-rush mountain sports in the **Julian Alps** (p889) before heading south to the Croatian coast and working your way through the beaches along the **Dalmatian coast** (p232). Stop in **Dubrovnik** (p249) to explore the Old Town and the surrounding islands. Take a side trip to Bosnia – perhaps a day trip to **Mostar** (p120) to see the legendary bridge, or a night or two in bustling **Sarajevo** (p106).

Then continue south into Montenegro, one of Europe's youngest countries. Visit the historic walled city of **Kotor** (p563) and enjoy some of the country's beautiful beaches around **Sveti Stefan** (p567) before heading over into Albania.

From the northern city of **Shkodra** (p53) take a bus straight on to **Tirana** (p46), a mountain-shrouded ramshackle capital on the rise. Make an excursion to **Kruja** (p55) and gorgeous **Berat** (p59) before taking a bus through the mountains into little-explored Macedonia, ending up in **Ohrid** (p514). Spend at least two days here, enjoying the multitude of sights and swimming in the beautiful eponymous lake. Make your way to **Skopje** (p507), Macedonia's fun capital, from where you can head overland into Bulgaria.

Your obvious first stop is **Sofia** (p145), Europe's cheapest capital and best hidden gem. But don't tarry too long before continuing east to **Veliko Târnovo** (p169), the awesome ancient capital and university town. From here it's an easy bus to the beach at **Varna** (p179), complete with marvellous museums, Roman ruins and open-air nightclubs.

Beginning in the Slovenian capital, this itinerary winds down the spectacular coastline of the former Yugoslav states and Albania, visiting some of Europe's newest nations along the way.

ROADS LESS TRAVELLED

ON THE EDGE
Four Weeks / Timişoara or Cluj-Napoca to Warsaw

Begin with a cheap flight from Western Europe to **Timişoara** (p713) or **Cluj-Napoca** (p706), the best budget gateway cities for the far reaches of Eastern Europe. Then get medieval in **Sibiu** (p702) and/or **Braşov** (p694) before a run to lively **Iaşi** (p720), near the Moldovan border.

Here the real adventure starts – cross into Moldova and head for the entertaining capital, **Chişinău** (p534), where partying is a way of life and wine is plentiful and cheap, as it's made in the local vineyards, including **Cricova** (p541). Travel into Transdniestr, a country that doesn't officially exist, to go back in time in **Tiraspol** (p545).

Entering Ukraine, make a beeline for the ethnic melting pot at **Odesa** (p936) and enjoy the relaxed pace of the Black Sea. If you want to check out the Crimean peninsula, head to **Simferopol** (p945), the peninsula's transport hub. From here you can make a loop around the peninsula to admire the palaces near **Yalta** (p947), and the fantastic Khan's Palace and monastery at **Bakhchysaray** (p950).

When you have had your fill of sun and sea, head north to **Kyiv** (p916), which demands several days' attention. Be one of the few people in the world to make the grim but fascinating trip to the abandoned towns near **Chornobyl** (p926); consider the risks before you sign up, however.

Your last stop is Belarus. Have a blast in monolithic **Minsk** (p76). Heading west, stop at **Brest** (p86) on the border and use it as a base to visit **Belavezhskaya Pushcha National Park** (p90) before circling back to **Warsaw** (p595).

This region is on the edge in more ways than one: geographically, for sure, but also culturally. You'll find these off-the-beaten-track destinations to be nearly tourist-free, but still replete with fascinating history, amazing architecture and glorious fresh air.

THE IONIAN TO THE BALTIC   Four Weeks / Saranda to Kaliningrad

Arrive in Albania at **Saranda** (p63), then stay the night and try to see the glorious ruins of **Butrint** (p64) before travelling up the **Ionian Coast** (p61) to **Tirana** (p46).

Spend a day or two in the Albanian capital before taking the bus to Kosovo. Revel in the freedom at **Pristina** (p434), Europe's newest capital. Then head north to **Belgrade** (p807), now vibrant and rejuvenated. Continue north to **Novi Sad** (p819) – if you come in July you might catch the Exit Festival, held annually in the city's historic hilltop fortress.

Cross into Hungary at pretty **Szeged** (p416) and head for **Lake Balaton** (p403). Keep surging north into Slovakia, aiming for **Bratislava** (p836), before going on to the incredible scenery of **Slovenský raj** (p861).

Crossing the **Tatra Mountains** (p629) into Poland, travel via **Kraków** (p608) to unsung gem **Wrocław** (p633), spending a few days in both before dropping in on beautifully restored **Poznań** (p638). From here, the Baltic is yours. Try any of the towns along the coast: **Hel** (p650) and **Łeba** (p655) are both recommended for beaches, wildlife and water sports; **Malbork** (p651) is famed for Europe's biggest Gothic castle; while **Gdańsk** (p643) is the thriving port city where Solidarity was born.

Finally, for true adventure (and that's just getting your Russian visa) head for **Kaliningrad** (p786) – about as far from the beaten track as anyone can get in Europe!

From Albania's magnificent Ionian Coast, weave your way north across the continent, covering Kosovo, Serbia, Hungary, Slovakia and Poland. End your journey in Russian Kaliningrad.

TAILORED TRIPS

WORLD HERITAGE SITES

Eastern Europe is flush with history, culture and natural wonders, so it is no surprise that it contains numerous **World Heritage sites** (http://whc.unesco.org). Start in the historic centres of **Prague** (p270), **Kraków** (p608) and **Budapest** (p373), then kick off the Baltic countries with the capitals' extraordinary Old Towns: art nouveau **Rīga** (p447), baroque **Vilnius** (p478) and medieval **Tallinn** (p339). Moscow earns acclaim for **Red Square** (p758) and the **Kremlin** (p759).

But there are scores of sites outside the capitals. Sites in the Czech Republic include the historic centres of **Kutná Hora** (p291), **Český Krumlov** (p305) and **Telč** (p318). In Slovakia, Spišské Podhradie is home to the remarkable **Spiš Castle** (p860).

In Poland, medieval **Zamość** (p624) boasts an incredible architectural ensemble. The Lithuanian archaeological site of **Kernavė** (p486) is a world gem, as is the extraordinary **Curonian Spit** (p495).

In Belarus, stop at **Mir Castle** (p86) and **Belavezhskaya Pushcha National Park** (p90).

In Hungary, don't miss the wine-producing region of **Tokaj** (p422). The jewel in Croatia's glittering cultural crown is **Dubrovnik** (p251).

Montenegro's World Heritage sites are natural wonders: the fjords of the **Bay of Kotor** (p561), and the icy peaks of **Durmitor National Park** (p575).

Over in Albania, **Berat** (p59) and **Gjirokastra** (p65) earn Unesco attention. In Bulgaria, **Nesebâr** (p185) evokes ancient Byzantium with its churches.

JEWISH HERITAGE TRIP

Begin in Rīga and learn about the deportation of Latvia's Jewish population at the **Jews in Latvia** (p450) museum, then visit the haunting memorial to the **Salaspils concentration camp** (p450) before going south to Lithuania.

Vilnius has plenty of sites of interest, including the **Holocaust Musuem** (p481), while **Trakai** (p485) is still home to some 360 Karaite Jews, a fascinating example of cultural continuity. Stop in Kaunas for a visit to the chilling **Ninth Fort** (p490) and the **Sugihara House & Foundation** (p489).

In Poland, head for Warsaw, taking in the wealth of museums and memorials, including the **Warsaw Rising Museum** (p600). In Lublin, you can walk the Jewish heritage trail and visit the remains of one of the Nazis' largest death camps at **Majdanek** (p622). Your last stop in Poland is Kraków, where the Jewish quarter **Kazimierz** (p613) was made famous by the movie *Schindler's List*. Use Kraków as your base to make the harrowing trip to **Oświęcim** (p618) for a shocking firsthand glimpse of human evil.

In the Czech Republic, **Josefov** (p277) was Prague's original Jewish quarter; it's jam-packed with Jewish history.

End in **Budapest** (p373), where you'll find a flourishing Jewish population of 80,000 and some 25 active synagogues – a hopeful and positive end to a sometimes harrowing trip.

Albania

Alps sprout in the background, vast plains and lakes surround the central mountain ranges, and coastal areas provide the traveller to Albania (or Shqipëria, as the locals call it) with a huge variety of experiences in this country of dramatically different cultural and geographical landscapes. Head up into the isolated mountains, stay in luxury accommodation on peaceful beaches, or visit historic homes in equally historic towns where the main streets are lined with Roman pillars. City slickers can down coffee after coffee in busy, always surprising Tirana before heading out to an exhibition, free art-house cinema night or a buzzing nightclub.

Albanians, after years of government-enforced isolation, welcome travellers with sincere hospitality. There are signs of a lack of infrastructure, though the upgraded roads that swirl past new houses and bar/restaurant/hotel developments is evidence of newfound prosperity.

Summer, particularly August, sees quiet seaside spots morph into loud disco-laden towns where every day is a thumping weekend. In contrast, head north and you'll find locals in traditional dress and shepherds guiding flocks in the otherwise inhospitable mountains.

The unique sights of Albania are hard to forget: donkeys tethered to concrete bunkers, houses crawling up each other to reach the top of hills in the Unesco World Heritage–listed Ottoman towns of Berat and Gjirokastra, and pockets of isolated beaches.

Like a good meat-and-three-veg dish, Albania is affordable, filling and ready to eat.

FAST FACTS

- **Area** 28,748 sq km
- **Capital** Tirana
- **Currency** lekë; €1 = 131 lekë; US$1 = 96 lekë; UK£1 = 140 lekë; A$1 = 67 lekë; ¥100 = 101 lekë; NZ$1 = 54 lekë
- **Famous for** cool flag, concrete bunkers, international diaspora
- **Official language** Albanian
- **Phrases** *miredita* (hello/good day); *lamtumirë* (goodbye); *ju lutem* (please); *ju falem nderit* (thank you); *më fal* (excuse me/sorry)
- **Population** 3.62 million
- **Telephone codes** country code ☎ 355; international access code ☎ 00
- **Visas** no visa needed for citizens of the EU, Australia, New Zealand, the US and Canada; see p68

ALBANIA

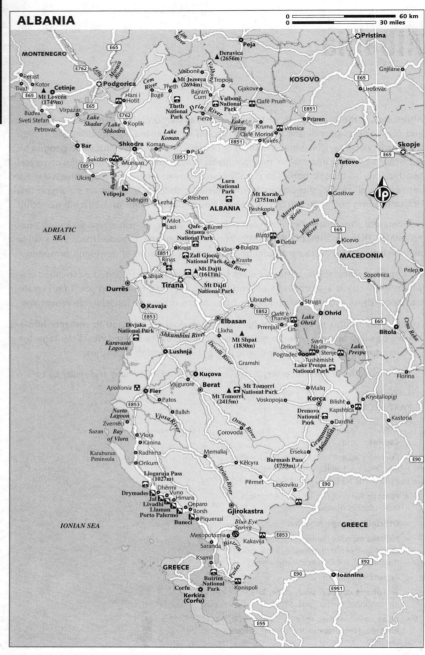

0 — 60 km
0 — 30 miles

MONTENEGRO

Perast
Kotor
Tivat
Cetinje
Mt Lovćen (1749m)
Budva
Sveti Stefan
Petrovac
Bar

Podgorica
Hani i Hotit
Bogë
Koplik
Shkodra
Koman

Peja
Đeravica (2656m)
Valbonë
Mt Jezerca (2694m)
Tropoja
Theth
Bajram Curri
Theth National Park
Valbonë National Park
Qafë Prush
Fierzë
Lake Fierza
Kruma
Qafë Morina
Vrbnica
Kukës

Pristina
Gnjilane
Uroševac
Gjakove
Prizren

KOSOVO

Skopje

Lake Skadar
Lake Shkodra
Lake Koman
Puka

Sukobin
Muriqan
Ulcinj

Velipoja
Shëngjin
Lezha

Rreshen

Lura National Park
Mt Korab (2751m)
Peshkopia

Gostivar
Tetovo

ADRIATIC SEA

ALBANIA

Milot
Laci
Kruja
Rinas
Shijak

Qafe Shtama National Park
Burrel
Klos
Zall Gjocaj National Park
Kraste
Bulqiza
Blato
Debar

Kicevo

MACEDONIA

Sopotnica
Prilep

Durrës
Kavaja

Tirana
Mt Dajti (1611m)
Mt Dajti National Park

Librazhd
Struga
Elbasan
Lixha
Prrenjasi
Qafë e Thanës
Lin
Lake Ohrid
Ohrid

Bitola

Divjaka National Park
Shkumbini River
Mt Shpat (1830m)
Devolli River

Karavasta Lagoon
Lushnja
Gramshi

Drilon
Sveti Naum
Stenje
Pogradec
Tushëmisht
Lake Prespa
Lake Prespa National Park

Florina

Apolonia
Fier
Patos
Narta Lagoon
Zvernëci
Sazan
Bay of Vlora
Vlora
Kanina

Kuçova
Vajgurore
Berat
Mt Tomorri National Park
Mt Tomorri (2415m)
Osumi River
Voskopoja
Maliq
Korça
Drenova National Park
Bilisht
Kapshtica
Dardhë
Krystallopigi
Kastoria

Radhima
Orikum
Karaburun Peninsula

Ballsh
Vjosa River
Çorovoda
Memaliaj
Këlcyra
Erseka
Barmash Pass (1759m)
Gramozi Mountains

Llogaraja Pass (1027m)
Drymades
Dhërmi
Jal
Vuno
Himara
Livadhi
Llaman
Porto Palermo
Qeparo
Borsh
Piqerasi
Buneci

Përmet
Leskoviku

Drinos River
Gjirokastra

GREECE

IONIAN SEA

Mesopotamia
Blue Eye Spring
Kakavija
Bistrica River

Ksamil
Saranda

Butrint National Park

Corfu
Kerkira (Corfu)
Konispoli

GREECE

Ioannina

E65
E762
E65
E762
E851
E851
E851
E851
E853
E853
E852
E65
E65
E65
E90
E90
E90
E853
E92
E951
E55

Lim River
Zeta River
Moraca River
Cem River
Valbonë River
Drin River
Mat River
Ishm River
Erzeni River
Mavrovska River
Ladorska River
Crna Reka

ALBANIA

HIGHLIGHTS

- Feast your eyes on the wild colour schemes and experience the hip Blloku cafe culture in **Tirana** (p46).
- Explore the Unesco World Heritage–listed museum cities of calm **Berat** (p59) and slate-roofed **Gjirokastra** (p65).
- Catch some sun along the south's dramatic Ionian Coast and its wonderful beaches, including **Dhërmi** (p62).
- Travel back in time to the ruins of **Butrint** (p64), hidden in the depths of the forest in a serene lakeside setting.
- Make your way to the hard-to-reach village of **Theth** (p55), high in the northern Alps.

ITINERARIES

- **Three days** Drink frappé at Tirana's trendy Blloku cafes, then spend the night dancing in nightclubs and get some morning mountain time on the Djati Express before heading to the Ottoman-era town of Berat to explore the town's old quarters. Kruja is a good airport detour; check out one of the country's best ethnographic museums and buy your souvenirs in its authentic little bazaar.
- **One week** Spend two days in Tirana then trek south via the scenic Llogaraja Pass. Take on beachside Dhërmi before making a pit stop at Saranda to prepare for a stroll around Butrint's ruins. Pause at the Blue Eye Spring en route to the Ottoman-era town of Gjirokastra.

CLIMATE & WHEN TO GO

Coastal Albania has a pleasant Mediterranean climate. Summer is the peak tourist season, when people from the sweltering interior escape temperatures that can reach the high 30s in July. In August, the temperature is high, accommodation is very tight in coastal regions and most hotels will only take bookings for stays of one week or more. The high mountains can experience heavy snow between November and March, and the road to Theth can be blocked as late as June. The best time to visit Albania is spring or autumn.

HISTORY

Albanians call their country Shqipëria, and trace their roots to the ancient Illyrian tribes. Their language is descended from Illyrian, making it a rare survivor of the Roman and Slavic influxes and a European linguistic oddity on a par with Basque. The Illyrians occupied the western Balkans during the 2nd millennium BC. They built substantial fortified cities, mastered silver and copper mining and became adept at sailing the Mediterranean. The Greeks arrived in the 7th century BC to establish self-governing colonies at Epidamnos (now Durrës), Apollonia and Butrint. They traded peacefully with the Illyrians, who formed tribal states in the 4th century BC.

Roman, Byzantine & Ottoman Rule

Inevitably the expanding Illyrian kingdom of the Ardiaei, based at Shkodra, came into conflict with Rome, which sent a fleet of 200 vessels against Queen Teuta in 229 BC. A long war resulted in the extension of Roman control over the entire Balkan area by 167 BC.

Under the Romans, Illyria enjoyed peace and prosperity, though the large agricultural estates were worked by slaves. The Illyrians preserved their own language and traditions despite Roman rule. Over time the populace slowly replaced their old gods with the new Christian faith championed by Emperor Constantine. The main trade route between Rome and Constantinople, the Via Egnatia, ran from the port at Durrës.

When the Roman Empire was divided in AD 395, Illyria fell within the Eastern Empire, later known as the Byzantine Empire. Three early Byzantine emperors (Anastasius I, Justin I and Justinian I) were of Illyrian origin. Invasions by migrating peoples (Visigoths,

> **CONNECTIONS: MOVING ON FROM ALBANIA**
>
> Albania is a mere hop from Greece's Corfu, and there are daily ferries heading each way (p64). It's a longer journey to Italy (up to 12 hours) and ferries leave from Vlora (p62) and Durrës (p58) frequently. Mainland Greece is easily reached via bus from almost every town in Albania and especially from the southern coast. Travel via the Koman River ferry (p55) to Kosovo is popular, as is simply walking to the Macedonian border near Pogradec. Shkodra (p55) has daily buses to Montenegro, and Tirana (p52) has buses to Kosovo and Macedonia.

ALBANIA

HOW MUCH?

- **Shot of mulberry raki** 100 lekë
- **Bottle of good Albanian wine** 600 lekë
- **Short taxi ride** 300 lekë
- **English translation of an Ismail Kadare novel** 1800 lekë
- **Pizza** 300 lekë

LONELY PLANET INDEX

- **1L petrol** 120 lekë
- **1L bottled water** 50 lekë
- **Beer (Tirana)** 150 lekë
- **Souvenir T-shirt** 800 lekë
- **Street snack (byrek)** 30 lekë

Huns, Ostrogoths and Slavs) continued through the 5th and 6th centuries.

In 1344 Albania was annexed by Serbia, but after the defeat of Serbia by the Turks in 1389 the whole region was open to Ottoman attack. The Venetians occupied some coastal towns, and from 1443 to 1468 the national hero Skanderbeg (Gjergj Kastrioti) led Albanian resistance to the Turks from his castle at Kruja. Skanderbeg won all 25 battles he fought against the Turks, and even Sultan Mehmet-Fatih, the conqueror of Constantinople, could not take Kruja. After Skanderbeg's death the Ottomans overwhelmed Albanian resistance, taking control of the country in 1479, 26 years after Constantinople fell.

Ottoman rule lasted 400 years. Muslim citizens were favoured and were exempted from the janizary system, whereby Christian households had to give up one of their sons to convert to Islam and serve in the army. Consequently many Albanians embraced the new faith.

Independent Albania

In 1878 the Albanian League at Prizren (in present-day Kosovo) began a struggle for autonomy that the Turkish army put down in 1881. Further uprisings between 1910 and 1912 culminated in a proclamation of independence and the formation of a provisional government led by Ismail Qemali at Vlora in 1912. These achievements were severely compromised when Kosovo, roughly one-third of Albania, was ceded to Serbia in 1913. The Great Powers tried to install a young German prince, Wilhelm of Wied, as ruler, but he wasn't accepted and returned home after six months. With the outbreak of WWI, Albania was occupied in succession by the armies of Greece, Serbia, France, Italy and Austria-Hungary.

In 1920 the capital city was moved from Durrës to less vulnerable Tirana. A republican government under the Orthodox priest Fan Noli helped to stabilise the country, but in 1924 it was overthrown by the interior minister, Ahmed Bey Zogu. A northern warlord, he declared himself King Zogu I in 1928, but his close collaboration with Italy backfired in April 1939 when Mussolini ordered an invasion of Albania. Zogu fled to Britain with his young wife, Geraldine, and newborn son, Leka, and used gold looted from the Albanian treasury to rent a floor at London's Ritz Hotel.

On 8 November 1941 the Albanian Communist Party was founded with Enver Hoxha as first secretary, a position he held until his death in April 1985. The communists led the resistance against the Italians and, after 1943, against the Germans.

The Rise of Communism

In January 1946 the People's Republic of Albania was proclaimed, with Hoxha as president and 'Supreme Comrade'.

In September 1948 Albania broke off relations with Yugoslavia, which had hoped to incorporate the country into the Yugoslav Federation. Instead, it allied itself with Stalin's USSR and put into effect a series of Soviet-style economic plans – raising the ire of the USA and Britain, which made an ill-fated attempt to overthrow the government.

Albania collaborated closely with the USSR until 1960, when a heavy-handed Khrushchev demanded that a submarine base be set up at Vlora. Breaking off diplomatic relations with the USSR in 1961, the country reoriented itself towards the People's Republic of China.

From 1966 to 1967 Albania experienced a Chinese-style cultural revolution. Administrative workers were suddenly transferred to remote areas and younger cadres were placed in leading positions. The collectivisation of agriculture was completed and organised religion banned.

Following the Soviet invasion of Czechoslovakia in 1968, Albania left the

Warsaw Pact and embarked on a self-reliant defence policy. Some 60,000 igloo-shaped concrete bunkers (see p44) serve as a reminder of this policy. Under the communists, some malarial swamps were drained, hydroelectric schemes and railway lines were built, and the literacy level was raised.

With the death of Mao Zedong in 1976 and the changes that followed in China after 1978, Albania's unique relationship with China also came to an end, and the country was left isolated and without allies. The economy was devastated and food shortages became more common.

Post-Hoxha

Hoxha died in April 1985 and his associate Ramiz Alia took over the leadership. Restrictions loosened but people no longer bothered to work on the collective farms, leading to food shortages in the cities. Industries began to fail and Tirana's population tripled as people took advantage of being able to freely move to the city.

In June 1990, inspired by the changes that were occurring elsewhere in Eastern Europe, around 4500 Albanians took refuge in Western embassies in Tirana. After a brief confrontation with the police and the Sigurimi (secret police), these people were allowed to board ships for Brindisi in Italy, where they were granted political asylum.

Following student demonstrations in December 1990, the government agreed to allow opposition parties, and the Democratic Party, led by heart surgeon Sali Berisha, was formed.

The March 1992 elections ended 47 years of communist rule, with parliament electing Sali Berisha president. Former president Alia was later placed under house arrest for writing articles critical of the Democratic government, and the leader of the Socialist Party, Fatos Nano, was also arrested on corruption charges.

During this time Albania switched from a tightly controlled communist regime to a rambunctious free-market free-for-all. A huge smuggling racket sprang up, in which stolen Mercedes-Benzes were brought into the country and the port of Vlora became a major crossing point for illegal immigrants from Asia and the Middle East into Italy.

In 1996, 70% of Albanians lost their savings when private pyramid-investment schemes, believed to have been supported by the government, collapsed. Riots ensued, elections were called, and the victorious Socialist Party under Nano – who had been freed from prison by a rampaging mob – was able to restore some degree of security and investor confidence.

In 1999 a different type of crisis struck when 465,000 Kosovars fled to Albania as a result of a Serbian ethnic-cleansing campaign. The influx had a positive effect on Albania's economy, and strengthened the relationship between Albania and Kosovo, which has historically been close. In 2008, songs sung by Albanian pop stars celebrating Kosovo's independence hit the top of the charts in both countries.

Since 2002 Albania has found itself in a kind of miniboom, with much money being poured into construction projects and infrastructure renewal. The general election of 2005 saw a return of Berisha's Democratic Party to government, and since then Albanian politics and the economy have been stable; however, work still has to be done to ensure that there is an end to electricity shortages and other infrastructure deficiencies that plague the country.

Albania signed NATO accession protocols in 2008, and EU membership beckons.

PEOPLE

In July 2008 the population was estimated to be 3.62 million, of which approximately 95% is Albanian, 3% Greek and 2% 'other' – comprising Vlachs, Roma, Serbs, Macedonians and Bulgarians.

Albanians are generally kind, helpful and generous. If you ask for directions, don't be surprised if you're guided all the way to your destination. The majority of young people speak some English, but speaking a few words of Albanian will be useful. Italian and Greek speakers are also widespread.

Albanians shake their heads sideways to say yes (po) and usually nod and 'tsk' to say no (jo). Albanians working with tourists usually take on the nod-for-yes way, which is even more confusing.

The Ghegs in the north and the Tosks in the south have different dialects, music, dress and the usual jokes about each other's weaknesses.

RELIGION

Albanians are nominally 70% Muslim, 20% Christian Orthodox and 10% Catholic, but

ALBANIA

BUNKER LOVE

On the hillsides, beaches and generally most surfaces in Albania, you will notice small concrete domes with their rectangular slits. Meet the bunkers: Enver Hoxha's concrete legacy, built from 1950 to 1985. Weighing in at five tonnes of concrete and iron, these little mushrooms are almost impossible to destroy. They were built to repel an invasion and can resist full tank assault – a fact proved by their chief engineer, who vouched for his creation's strength by standing inside one while it was bombarded by a tank. The shell-shocked engineer emerged unscathed, and tens of thousands were built. Some are creatively painted, but most are just eyesores with no further use; that said, quite a few Albanians will admit to losing their virginity in the security of one, and the bunkers also seem to make handy public toilets.

more realistic statistics estimate that up to 75% of Albanians are nonreligious. Religion was ruthlessly stamped out by the 1967 cultural revolution, when all mosques and churches were taken over by the state. By 1990 only about 5% of Albania's religious buildings were left intact. The rest had been turned into cinemas, army stores or were destroyed. Albania remains a very secular society, and it is difficult to assess how many followers each faith has.

The Muslim faith has a branch called 'Bektashism', similar to Sufism, and its world headquarters were in Albania from 1925 to 1945. Bektashi followers go to *teqe* (temple-like buildings without a minaret), which are usually found on hilltops in towns where those of the faith fled persecution. Most Bektashis live in the southern half of the country.

ARTS
Literature

One Albanian writer who is widely read outside Albania is Ismail Kadare (1936–). In 2005 he won the inaugural Booker International Prize for his body of work. His books are a great source of information on Albanian traditions, history and social events, and exquisitely capture the atmosphere of the country's towns, as in the lyrical descriptions of Kadare's birthplace, Gjirokastra, in *Chronicle in Stone* (1971). *Broken April* (1990), set in the northern highlands before the 1939 Italian invasion, describes the life of a village boy who is next in line in a desperate cycle of blood vendettas.

There is no substantial body of Albanian literature before the 19th century besides some Catholic religious works. Poetry that drew on the great tradition of oral epic poetry was the most popular literary form during the period leading up to Albanian independence in 1912. A group of romantic patriotic writers at Shkodra, including Migjeni (1911–38) and

Martin Çamaj (1925–92), wrote epics and historical novels.

Perhaps the most interesting writer of the interwar period was Fan Noli (1880–1965). Educated as a priest in the US, Noli became premier of Albania's Democratic government until it was overthrown in 1924, when he returned to head the Albanian Orthodox Church in the US. Although many of his books have religious themes, the introductions he wrote to his own translations of Cervantes, Ibsen, Omar Khayyám and Shakespeare established him as Albania's foremost literary critic.

Cinema

During Albania's isolationist years the only Western actor approved by Hoxha was UK actor Sir Norman Wisdom (he became quite a cult hero). However, with so few international movies to choose from, the local film industry had a captive audience. While much of its output was propagandist, by the 1980s this little country was turning out an extraordinary 14 films a year. Despite a general lack of funds, two movies have gone on to win awards at international film festivals. Gjergj Xhuvani's comedy *Slogans* (2001) is a warm and touching account of life during communist times. This was followed in 2002 by *Tirana Year Zero,* Fatmir Koci's bleak look at the pressures on the young to emigrate.

Another film worth seeing is *Lamerica* (1995), a brilliant and stark look at Albania around 1991. Woven loosely around a plot about a couple of Italian scam artists and Albanians seeking to escape to Italy, the essence of the film is the unshakeable dignity of the ordinary Albanian in the face of adversity.

Vdekja e Kalit (1995) covers the harrowing 1980s and the change of regime in 1992, and is the only film that includes Albania's Roma.

ALBANIA

Renowned Brazilian director Walter Salles (*Central Station*) adapted Ismail Kadare's novel *Broken April*: keeping the novel's main theme, he moved the action to Brazil in *Behind the Sun* (2001).

Music

There's pop aplenty in Albania, and artists like Sinan Hoxha manage to merge traditional instrumental polyphony with new beats. Others you may hear include the band The Dream, and Erion Korini.

Polyphony, the blending of several independent vocal or instrumental parts, is a southern Albanian tradition dating from ancient Illyrian times. Choirs perform in a variety of styles, and the songs, usually with an epic-lyrical or historical theme, may be dramatic to the point of yodelling, or slow and sober, with alternate male and female voices combining in harmony. Instrumental polyphonic *kabas* (a sedate style, led by a clarinet or violin alongside accordions and lutes) are played by small Roma ensembles. One well-known group that often tours outside Albania is the Lela Family of Përmet (www.kabarecords.com).

Visual Arts

The art scene in Albania is on the rise. One of the first signs are the multicoloured buildings of Tirana, a project organised by the capital's mayor, Edi Rama, himself an artist. The building's residents don't get a say in the colour or design, but some of the more inventive work includes paintings of silhouettes of laundry hanging to dry under windowsills.

Remnants of socialist realism still adorn the walls and gardens of some galleries and museums, although most were destroyed after the fall of the communist government in protest against against the old regime.

One of the most delicious Albanian art treats is to be found in Berat's Onufri Museum (p60). Onufri was the most outstanding Albanian icon painter of the 16th and 17th centuries, and his work is noted for its unique intensity of colour, derived from natural dyes that are as fresh now as the day he painted with them.

Churches around the country also feature amazing and original frescos.

ENVIRONMENT
The Land

The diversity of Albania's land is visually stunning; the country consists of 30% vast interior plains, over 300km of coastal region and the mountainous spine that runs its length. Mt Korab, at 2764m, is Albania's highest peak. Forest covers just under 40% of Albania, with Mediterranean shrubs at up to 600m, an oak forest belt between 600m and 1000m, and beech and pine forests between 1000m and 1600m.

The country's large and beautiful lakes include the Balkans' biggest, Lake Shkodra, which borders Montenegro in the north, and the ancient Lake Ohrid in the east (one-third Albanian, two-thirds Macedonian). Albania's longest river is the Drin (280km), which originates in Kosovo and is fed by melting snow from mountains in Albania's north and east. Hydroelectricity has changed Albania's landscape: Lake Koman was once a river, and the blue water from the Blue Eye Spring near Saranda travels to the coast in open concrete channels via a hydroelectricity plant. Agriculture makes up a small percentage of land use, but citrus and olive trees spice up the coastal plains while most rural householders grow their own food.

Wildlife

Snakes, turtles, bats, toads and a huge variety of birds are easy to spot all over Albania, but for those after something more glamorous, the northern Alps impress with its collection of brown bear, wolf, otter, marten, wild cat, wild boar and deer. Falcons and grouse are also alpine favourites, and birdwatchers can also flock to the country's wetlands at Lake Butrint, Karavasta Lagoon and Lake Shkodra (though the wetlands aren't pristine).

Lake Ohrid's trout is endangered (but still eaten), and endangered loggerhead turtles nest on the Ionian Coast and on the Karaburun Peninsula, where there have also been sightings of critically endangered Mediterranean monk seals.

National Parks

The number of national parks in Albania has risen from six to 15 since 1966 and include Mt Dajti, Butrint, Mt Tomorri, Valbone and Theth. Most are protected only by their remoteness, and tree-felling and hunting still take place. Hiking maps of the national parks are available, though they can be hard to find, and more guest houses and camping grounds are popping up. Llogaraja Pass has an established accommodation scene and is suitable

ALBANIA

for shorter hikes. Mt Tomorri near Berat is becoming popular with hikers; local organisations in Berat operate guided tours, and plenty of experienced hikers are taking on the Valbone–Theth route with the assistance of local guides. The Karaburun Peninsula near Vlora is a nature reserve protected largely, again, by its isolation.

Independent camping is not advisable as the mountains are almost completely uninhabited and have no cellphone coverage; in case of an injury, help would be impossible to find.

Environmental Issues

During communism, there were around 2000 cars in the country; the number of roaring automobiles has since risen to Western European levels. Many of them are old diesel Mercedes-Benzes stolen from Western Europe. As a consequence of the explosion, air pollution levels in Tirana are five to 10 times higher than in Western European countries.

Illegal logging and fishing reached epidemic proportions during the 1990s, and there are signs of it today; fishing for the endangered *koran* trout in Lake Ohrid continues, as does fishing with dynamite along the coast.

Badly maintained oilfields around Fier continue to leak sludge into the surrounding environment, and plans for an oil pipeline and hydrocarbon terminal are opposed by local environmentalists. Several coastal regions discharge raw sewage into seas and rivers. The rapid development of beach areas has compounded the issue, though projects are in place to improve waste disposal in sensitive environmental areas, including Lake Ohrid.

There is rubbish everywhere. Albania was practically litter-free until the late '90s; everything was reused or recycled. The change seems to be a result of both novelties like nonbiodegradable plastic bags and a reaction against the harsh communist-era rules on littering. Even household garbage is an issue: walk around the outside of a picturesque hotel and you are likely to come across its very unpicturesque dumping ground. Some Albanians are doing their bit to improve these conditions, and there is considerable Western investment in aiding this process. The **Organic Agriculture Association** (www.organic.org.al) is one group trying to make a difference.

FOOD & DRINK

Foodwise, the only thing you're likely to be lacking in Albania is *mëngjes* (breakfast), which tends to consist of a shot of the spirit raki or an espresso. If you're desperate, most shops sell packet croissants, or ask your hotel for some *bukë* and *mjaltë* (bread and honey) to go with your espresso. Albanians make excellent coffee and bread, and the local honey (usually sold by the side of the road) is delicious.

Patate të skuqura (potato chips) are served everywhere, and all meals come with bread. In coastal areas the calamari, mussels and fish will knock your socks off, while mountain areas like Llogaraja have roast lamb worth climbing a mountain for.

Offal is popular; *fërgesë Tiranë* is a traditional Tirana dish of offal, eggs and tomatoes cooked in an earthenware pot. If the *biftek* (beef) you ordered looks suspiciously like veal, take heart that it's likely to have been reared in a more humane way than it is elsewhere.

Italian influences mean vegetarians will probably become vegitalians, and most restaurants serve pizza, pasta or grilled vegetables.

Raki is very popular. The two main types are grape raki (the most common) and *mani raki* (mulberry raki). Ask for homemade if possible *(raki ë bërë në shtëpi)*. If raki is not your cup of tea, try a glass of wine from the Rilindja region, which produces a sweet white and a medium-bodied red. Wine aficionados should seek out the Çobo winery near Berat. Local beers include Tirana, Norga (from Vlora) and Korça.

Restaurants, cafes and bars are usually open from 8am and stay open until midnight or later. Most restaurants allow smoking, though some may have designated nonsmoking areas.

TIRANA

☎ 04 / pop 600,000

Lively, colourful Tirana has changed beyond belief in the last decade from the dull, grey city it once was (see the old Albanian movies for evidence). It's amazing what a lick of paint can do – it covers one ugly tower block with horizontal orange and red stripes, another with concentric pink and purple circles, and plants perspective-fooling cubes on its neighbour.

Trendy Blloku buzzes with the well-dressed nouvelle bourgeoisie hanging out in bars or zipping between boutiques. Quite where their money comes from is the subject of much speculation in this economically deprived nation, but thankfully you don't need much of it to have a fun night out in the city's many bars and clubs.

The city's grand central boulevards are lined with fascinating relics of its Ottoman, Italian and communist past – from delicate minarets to socialist murals – guarded by bored-looking soldiers with serious automatic weaponry. The traffic does daily battle with both itself and pedestrians in a constant scene of unmitigated chaos.

Loud, crazy, colourful, dusty – Tirana is simply fascinating.

ORIENTATION
Running through Tirana is Blvd Zogu I, which becomes Dëshmorët e Kombit as it crosses the Lana River. At its northern end is Tirana train station, and the south section ends at Tirana University. The main sites of interest are on or very close to this large blvd, including, roughly halfway along, the orientation point of Sheshi Skënderbej (Skanderbeg Square).

Most of the eating and drinking action is at Blloku, a square of 10 blocks of shops, restaurants, cafes and hotels situated one block west of Dëshmorët and along the Lana River in south Tirana. Mt Dajti (1612m) rises in the distant east.

Incoming buses will probably drop you off at the bus and train station at the north end of Blvd Zogu I, a five-minute walk from Sheshi Skënderbej. *Furgons* (shared minibuses) can also drop you at various points around the city, and it's easy and reasonably cheap to catch a waiting taxi to your destination.

INFORMATION
Bookshops
Adrion International Bookshop (☎ 2235 242; Palace of Culture, Sheshi Skënderbej; ⏰ 9am-9pm Mon-Sat) Stocks Penguin classics, maps of Tirana and Albania, foreign magazines and newspapers and an excellent selection of books on the region.

Internet Access
More and more of Tirana's Blloku cafes offer free wi-fi to go with your frappé, but if you didn't bring your own laptop expect to pay 100 lekë per hour.

Internet Café (Rr Presidenti George W Bush; ⏰ 9am-11pm)
Top Net (Rr Vasco Pasha; ⏰ 8.30am-11pm) In the thick of Blloku.

Laundry
Drycleaner and laundry (☎ 068 216 8268; Rr Hoxha Tahsim; ⏰ 8am-8pm Mon-Sat, 9am-1pm Sun) Charges 200 lekë per kilo of washing.

Medical Services
ABC Clinic (☎ 2234 105; Rr Qemal Stafa 260; ⏰ 9am-1pm Mon-Fri) Has English-speaking doctors and a range of services, including regular (€50) and emergency (€80) consultations.

Money
Tirana has plenty of ATMs linked to international networks. The main ATM chains are Alpha Bank, Tirana Bank, Pro Credit Bank, Raiffeisen Bank and the American Bank of Albania.

Independent money exchangers operate directly in front of the main post office and on Sheshi Skënderbej and offer the same rates as the banks. Changing money here is not illegal or dangerous, but do count the money you receive before handing yours over. Travellers cheques are near impossible to exchange outside Tirana, so if you're relying on them (our advice is, don't), try one of the following:
American Bank of Albania (☎ 2276 000; Rr Ismail Qemali 27; ⏰ 9.30am-3.30pm Mon-Fri) A reliable, secure place to cash your travellers cheques (2% commission). Also an Amex representative.
National Savings Bank (☎ 2235 035; Blvd Dëshmorët e Kombit; ⏰ 10.30am-5pm Mon-Fri) Located in the Rogner Hotel Europapark Tirana, it offers MasterCard advances and currency exchange and cashes US-dollar, euro and sterling travellers cheques for 1% commission.

Post
DHL (☎ 2227 667; fax 2233 934; Rr Ded Gjo Luli 6).
Main post office (☎ 2228 262; Rr Çameria; ⏰ 8am-8pm) On a street jutting west from Sheshi Skënderbej. There's an Albtelecom office next door.

Tourist Information
Tirana does not have an official tourist office, but travel agencies can help. *Tirana in Your Pocket* (www.inyourpocket.com) lists what's going on and can be downloaded free or bought at bookshops, hotels and some of the larger kiosks for 400 lekë.

ALBANIA

TIRANA

0 ————— 500 m
0 ————— 0.3 miles

A **B** **C** **D**

INFORMATION
ABC Clinic..............................1 D3
Adrion International Bookshop......(see 30)
American Bank of Albania............2 C6
Avis....................................(see 43)
DHL.....................................3 C4
Drycleaner & Laundry.................4 D4
Dutch Embassy.........................5 D6
French Embassy.......................6 B4
German Embassy......................7 B4
Greek Embassy........................8 B4
Internet Café..........................9 D5
Italian Embassy.......................10 C6
Macedonian Embassy................11 B4
Main Post Office.......................12 C5
National Savings Bank...........(see 43)
Serbian Embassy......................13 C6
Top Net................................14 C6
UK Embassy...........................15 B4
US Embassy............................16 D6

SIGHTS & ACTIVITIES
Albanian Experience..................17 C6
Archaeological Museum..............18 C6
Clock Tower..........................19 C4
Congress Building....................20 C6
Equestrian Statue of Skanderbeg...21 C4

Et'hem Bey Mosque...................22 C4
Former Residence of Enver Hoxha...23 C6
Fortress of Justinian.................24 C5
Lincoln Centre........................25 C6
Luna Park.............................26 D5
National Art Gallery..................27 C5
National Museum of History.........28 C4
Outdoor Albania......................29 B5
Palace of Culture....................30 C4
Prime Minister's Residence.........31 C6
Pyramid...............................32 C5
Statue of the Unknown Partisan....33 C4
Tanners' Bridge......................34 D5

SLEEPING
Firenze Hotel.........................35 C4
Freddy's Hostel......................36 C4
Hotel Endri...........................37 C6
Hotel Nirvana.........................38 B4
Hotel Nobel...........................39 C4
Lana River's Last House Standing...40 A6
Luna Hotel............................41 C6
Pension Andrea.......................42 D5
Rogner Hotel Europapark Tirana....43 C6
Tirana Backpacker Hostel...........44 D5

EATING
Anais.................................45 B6
Era..................................46 B6
Green House.........................47 C5
Pasticeri Française..................48 C5
Villa Ambassador/Chocolate........49 D6

DRINKING
Buda Bar.............................50 B6
Charl's..............................51 C6
Sky Club Bar.........................52 C5

ENTERTAINMENT
Academy of Arts.....................53 C6
Kinema Millennium 2.................54 C5
Living Room..........................55 C4
Theatre of Opera & Ballet...........56 C4

SHOPPING
National Museum of History ......(see 28)
Natyral & Organik...................57 C6

TRANSPORT
Bus Stand............................58 C3
Buses to Airport.....................59 C4
Drita Travel & Tours.................60 C4
Europcar.............................61 A3
Hertz................................62 C4
Pollogu Travel Agency...............63 C3
Sixt.................................64 B4

To MARUBI Film &
Multimedia School (6km);
Mt Dajti (25km)

Train Station
58

To Airport
(26km)

To Martyrs'
Cemetery (2km)

To Tirana
University

Parku
Kombëtar

Parku
Rinia

Blloku

Selman
Stërmasi
Stadium

Lana River

Sheshi Nënë
Tereza

Sheshi
Italia

Sheshi
Skënderbej

Sheshi Avni
Rustemi

Rr Jeronim
de Rada

TIRANA IN TWO DAYS

Start your day with croissants in **Pasticeri Française** (p51) and stroll up to **Sheshi Skënderbej** (below) to explore the **National Museum of History** (right). Look around **Et'hem Bey Mosque** (below) and march down to the **National Art Gallery** (right). Admire the stunning views of Tirana at sunset as you have a beer, wine or sundae at the **Sky Club Bar** (p51). Drink and party the night away in the trendy **Blloku** (p50) area.

On day two catch a lbus up to the **Martyrs' Cemetery** (p50), then dine at **Villa Ambassador/Chocolate** (p51) for a mouthwatering meal in regal surrounds.

Travel Agencies

Travel agencies and airlines of all descriptions and destinations abound on Rr Mine Peza northwest of Sheshi Skënderbej. Nearly all sell tickets to leave Albania.

DANGERS & ANNOYANCES

Tirana is a very safe city with little petty crime. The streets are badly lit and there are a few massive potholes, though, so mind your step and arm yourself with a pocket torch at night to light your way. There are occasional power cuts in the city so the torch idea stretches further. Crossing the street is not for the fainthearted – don't assume the traffic automatically stops at a red light.

SIGHTS
North of the River

Sheshi Skënderbej is the best place to start witnessing the daily goings-on. Until it was pulled down by an angry mob in 1991, a 10m-high bronze statue of Enver Hoxha stood here, watching over a mainly carless square. Now only the **equestrian statue of Skanderbeg** remains, deaf to the cacophony of screeching horns as cars four lanes deep try to shove their way through the battlefield below.

If you stop to examine Skanderbeg's emblematic goat's-head helmet, the minaret of the 1789–1823 **Et'hem Bey Mosque** will catch your eye. The small and elegant mosque is one of the oldest buildings left in the city, spared from destruction during the atheism campaign of the late '60s because of its status as a cultural monument. Take your

shoes off to look inside at the beautifully painted dome.

Behind the mosque is the tall **Clock Tower** (Kulla e Sahatit; Rr Luigi Gurakqi; admission 50 lekë; ☉ 9am-1pm Mon, 9am-1pm & 4-6pm Thu), which you can climb for views of the square. Further on, the socialist realist **Statue of the Unknown Partisan** attracts day labourers waiting for work, some with their own jackhammers – a fitting image of the precarious position of the postcommunist Albanian worker.

To the east of Sheshi Skënderbej is the white stone **Palace of Culture** (Pallate Kulturës; Sheshi Skënderbej), which has a theatre, shops and art galleries. Construction of the palace began as a gift from the Soviet people in 1960 and was completed in 1966, years after the 1961 Soviet-Albanian split. The entrance to the National Library is on the south side of the building.

On the northwestern side of the square, beside the 15-storey Tirana International Hotel, is the **National Museum of History** (Muzeu Historik Kombëtar; Sheshi Skënderbej; admission 300 lekë; ☉ 9am-1pm & 4-7pm Tue-Sat, 9am-noon Sun). This, the largest museum in Albania, holds most of the country's archaeological treasures and a replica of Skanderbeg's massive sword. The fantastic mosaic mural entitled *Albania* adorning the museum's facade shows Albanians victorious and proud from Illyrian times through to WWII. In case you thought everyone had erased the Hoxha era from their minds, a sombre gallery devoted to its miseries is on the top floor. Its walls are covered with the names of those killed from 1941 to 1985 – and there are many, many names. Even the guides seem to find the exhibit confronting. The museum's better with a guide (around 100 lekë), and they speak English, French and Italian. There's a good souvenir shop on site. Note that you won't be let in if you arrive half an hour or less before closing time.

Stroll down the spacious tree-lined Blvd Dëshmorët e Kombit to Tirana's **National Art Gallery** (Galeria Kombëtare e Arteve; Blvd Dëshmorët e Kombit; admission 100 lekë; ☉ 9am-1pm & 5-8pm Tue-Sun), whose garden is adorned with statues of proud partisans. See the astonishing exhibition of icons inside by Onufri, the renowned 16th-century master of colour. If you're lucky you'll catch some modern work by Albanian-born artists in the ground-floor temporary exhibition area.

If you turn up Rr Murat Toptani, you'll pass the 6m-high walls of the **Fortress of Justinian**

ALBANIA

(Rr Murat Toptani), the last remnants of a Byzantine-era castle. Strangely, half a cinema overflows over the top. East from here, on the corner of Rr Presidenti George W Bush and the Lana River is **Tanners' Bridge**, a small 19th-century slippery-when-wet stone bridge.

South of the River

It's hard not to notice the sloping white-marble and glass walls of the 1988 **Pyramid** (Blvd Dëshmorët e Kombit), formerly the Enver Hoxha Museum, designed by Hoxha's daughter and son-in-law. Now used as a disco and conference centre, the building never really took off as a museum, but makes a good slide. Nearby is the **Prime Minister's Residence** (Blvd Dëshmorët e Kombit), where Enver Hoxha and cronies would stand and view military parades from the balcony.

Another creation of the dictator's daughter and son-in-law is the square **Congress Building** (Blvd Dëshmorët e Kombit), just a little down the blvd. Follow Rr Ismail Qemali two streets north of the Congress Building and enter the once totally forbidden but now totally trendy **Blloku** area. This former communist party elite hang-out was opened to the general public for the first time in 1991. Security still guards the **former resi-**

dence of Enver Hoxha (cnr Rr Dëshmorët e 4 Shkurtit & Rr Ismail Qemali).

The **Archaeological Museum** (Muzeu Arkeologik; Sheshi Nënë Tereza; admission 200 lekë; ☉ 10.30am-2.30pm Mon-Fri) houses an extensive collection close to Tirana University. The foyer displays maps and information about current archaeological digs in Albania.

At the top of Rr Elbasanit is the **Martyrs' Cemetery**, where some 900 partisans who died in WWII are buried. The views over the city and surrounding mountains (including Mt Dajti to the east) are excellent, as is the sight of the immense, beautiful and strangely androgynous Mother Albania statue (1972). Hoxha was buried here in 1985, but was exhumed in 1992 and interred in an ordinary graveyard on the other side of town. Catch any municipal bus heading up Rr Elbasanit; the grand driveway is on your left.

TOURS

Get off the beaten track or discover Albania's tourist attractions with the following Tirana-based tour companies:

Albanian Experience (☎ 2266 389; Sheraton Hotel, Sheshi Italia; ☉ 8.30am-7pm Mon-Fri, 8.30am-5pm Sat) Organises tours of Albania with knowledgeable guides.

Outdoor Albania (☎ 069 218 8845, 2227 121; www .outdooralbania.com; Metropol Bldg, Rr Sami Frashëri; ☉ 8am-8pm Mon-Fri) Excellent trailblazing adventure tour agency offering trekking, rafting, ski touring, sea and white-water kayaking and, in summer, hikes through the Alps.

SLEEPING
Budget

our pick **Tirana Backpacker Hostel** (☎ 068 216 7357; www.tiranahostel.com; Rr Elbasanit 85; dm €12) Albania's first hostel opened in 2005 in a 70-year-old villa close to the city centre. The 25 beds are spread over four rooms with shared bathrooms. It has big balconies, a great garden with a cosy outdoor kitchen, a summer cinema in the basement and friendly, helpful young managers. Head east along Rr Ismail Qemali until it meets Rr Elbasanit; it's over the road on your left.

Freddy's Hostel (☎ 068 203 5261; www.freddyshostel .com; Rr Bardhok Biba 75; dm/r €12/30) Freddy's has a bunch of clean, basic rooms in different configurations and in two different buildings in the same area. To find the main apartment block, walk north of Tirana International Hotel and look for the suburban street parallel to Blvd Zogu I. The hostel is past Hestia restaurant (a great place for a snack and a beer), on the left.

Pension Andrea (☎ 069 290 4915; Rr Jeronim de Rada 103; s/d €20/30) Gina runs this homey, quiet pension. All rooms have TVs and a couple also have air-con. There's a safe storage area for bicycles. On Rr Jeronim de Rada take the first right down the court; it's on your right.

Hotel Endri (☎ 2244 168, 2229 334; Rr Vaso Pasha 27; r €30; ⊠) The Endri is good value and located south of Blloku, where all the action is. The 'hotel' is basically a couple of clean rooms in a building next to owner Petrit Alikaj's apartment. It's on the left at the end of Rr Vaso Pasha, but call Petrit for directions.

Midrange

Hotel Nobel (☎ 2256 444; www.hotelnobeltirana.com; Blvd Zogu I; s/d €40/50; ⊠) Albania's two Nobel Peace Prize winners are Mother Teresa and Prof Ferid Murad, the inventor of Viagra. It's good to see a hotel getting into the spirit of things, and charismatic owner Edmond has done a great job giving his hotel some Nobel personality (although the stick of dynamite in his drawer is curious). The six rooms are clean and bright, there's wi-fi and an Italian restaurant downstairs, and it's central (next to VEVE Business Centre).

Luna Hotel (☎ 2272 950; www.hotels-tirana.com; Rr Sami Frashëri 4; s/d €50/60; ⊠) Just south of Blloku, off Sami Frasheri, this modern hotel has had the power of Zen through its rooms and bathrooms. Gigantic stencilled flowers decorate the hall's lime-green walls, and everything's been thought of, down to hairdriers in the bathrooms.

Firenze Hotel (☎ 2249 099; firenzehotel@albania online.net; Blvd Zogu I 72; s/d €50/70; ⊠) This cheerful and colourful little hotel between the railway station and Sheshi Skënderbej has seven cosy, clean rooms with TV and minibar and a great 'magazine corner' in the breakfast room.

Hotel Nirvana (☎ 2235 270; Rr e Kavajës 96/2; s/d €60/80; ⊠) With its ostentatious marble staircase and walls dripping in art (apparently this is nothing compared with the owner's house), this hotel may have delusions of grandeur, but thankfully the price remains reasonably humble and the staff friendly and helpful.

Top End

Rogner Hotel Europapark Tirana (☎ 2235 035; www .hotel-europapark.com; Blvd Dëshmorët e Kombit; s €210-240, d €250-290, ste €320-350; ⊠ 🖳 🕑) With an unbeatable location in the heart of the city, the Rogner is a peaceful oasis with a huge garden, tennis court, free wi-fi in the lobby, banks, car rental and travel agencies. The rooms are spacious and comfortable and have flat-screen TVs.

EATING

If you thought that cuisine in Tirana's restaurants might be monotonous or that eating out would be a downmarket experience, you were wrong.

Era (☎ 2266 662; Rr Ismail Qemali; mains from 200 lekë; 🕑 11am-midnight) Serves traditional Albanian and Italian fare in the heart of Blloku. Be warned: it's hard to move on once you've eaten here. Also does delivery and takeaway.

Pasticeri Française (☎ 2251 336; Rr Dëshmorët e 4 Shkurtit 1; breakfasts from 300 lekë; 🕑 8am-10pm) One of the few breakfast spots in Tirana, this French-owned cafe has red walls, high ceilings and a huge selection of sweet pastries.

Green House (☎ 2222 632; Rr Jul Varibova 6; mains from 700 lekë; 🕑 9am-11pm) This quite formal restaurant is a modern and friendly expat hangout with a varied menu (including non-Albanian fare like gnocchi gorgonzola) and a huge wine list. It offers boutique-style accommodation (single/double €100/110) upstairs, too.

Villa Ambassador/Chocolate (☎ 069 206 6257; Rr Asim Zeneli 2; mains 700-1500 lekë; 🕑 8am-midnight) Located in the former Romanian Ambassador's residence, this well-regarded restaurant has a great team creating and serving up tasty Albanian dishes for carnivores and vegetarians alike. Crêpes and pastries make it a good spot for breakfast, too.

Anais (☎ 2246 624; Rr Sami Frashëri 20; mains 1000-1200 lekë; 🕑 11am-11pm) Quite expensive by local standards, the Ottoman cuisine served here by a chef who worked in Turkey is utterly superb. The selection of mezes is tremendous: puréed eggplant, spicy beans and mushrooms and rich kebabs.

DRINKING

Most of Tirana's nightspots let you party on to the wee hours.

Sky Club Bar (☎ 2221 666; Sky Tower, Rr Dëshmorët e 4 Shkurtit; 🕑 8am-midnight) Start your night here for spectacular city views from the revolving bar on top of one of the highest buildings in town. If you're just going up for a look, it's cheaper to buy a beer up there than pay the 250-lekë charge that reception may request.

ALBANIA

Living Room (☎ 2274 837; Rr Presidenti George W Bush 16; ☼ 7.30pm-late) This is the hippest place to drink and dance in Tirana, with eclectic DJs, a good crowd, cool lampshades and '70s sofas for you to lounge on when you're danced (or drunk) off your feet. The terrace is airy and fun.

Charl's (☎ 2253 754; Rr Pjetër Bogdani 36; ☼ 8am-late) Charl's is a consistently popular bar with Tirana's students because of its ever-varying live music, with bands coming from places as diverse as Cuba and Serbia. The relaxed vibe is enhanced by the bar's open-air garden.

Buda Bar (☎ 068 205 8825; Rr Ismail Qemali; ☼ 4.30pm-late) This place is all about a relaxed atmosphere, with subdued lighting, incense burning, chaise longues and armchairs abounding with cushions.

ENTERTAINMENT

There is a good choice of entertainment options in Tirana, in the form of bars, clubs, cinema, performances, exhibitions and even ten-pin bowling. For the low-down on events and exhibitions, check out the free fortnightly *Planet Albania* (www.planet-albania.com) guide as well as the monthly leaflet *ARTirana* (a free supplement in *Gazeta Shqiptare*) and the weekly *Tirana Times*.

MARUBI Film & Multimedia School (www.afmm .edu.al; Rr Aleksander Moisiu 76; admission free; ☼ 7pm Thu) shows free art-house movies during the semester. It's near the last Kino Studio bus stop in the city's northeast.

Kinema Millennium 2 (☎ 2253 654; www.ida-millennium.com; Rr Murat Toptani; tickets 200-500 lekë) Current-release movies that are cheaper the earlier in the day you go.

Theatre of Opera & Ballet (☎ 2224 753; Sheshi Skënderbej; tickets from 300 lekë; ☼ performances from 7pm, from 6pm winter) Check the listings and posters outside this theatre for performances. You can buy tickets half an hour before the show for 200 lekë.

Academy of Arts (☎ 2257 237; Sheshi Nënë Tereza) Classical music and other performances take place throughout the year in either the large indoor theatre or the small open-air faux-classical amphitheatre; both are part of the university. Prices vary according to the program.

SHOPPING

Natyral & Organik (☎ 2250 575; Rr Vaso Pasha) This wonderful store in Blloku not only supports small village producers by stocking organic olive oil, honey, herbs, tea, eggs, spices, raki and cognac (these make great gifts, but be aware of customs regulations in the countries you're travelling through); it's also a centre for environmental activism.

Find souvenir shops on Rr Durrësit and Blvd Zogu I or try the National Museum of History (p49). They all sell the same things: red Albanian flags, red T-shirts, red lighters, bunker ashtrays and lively traditional textiles.

GETTING THERE & AWAY

Air

Nënë Tereza International Airport (Mother Teresa Airport, Rinas airport) is at Rinas, 26km northwest of Tirana. Its new passenger terminal opened in 2006. There's a €10 entry fee to enter Albania by air.

For a list of airlines flying to Albania, see p69.

Bus

You have the option of buses or *furgons* (minibuses). Since there are few actual bus stations in Tirana, it's impossible to pin down where the buses and *furgons* actually leave from. It's best to jump in a taxi and say '*Dua të shkoj në...*', meaning 'I want to go to...'. Taxi drivers always know the latest departure points and, given Albania's unique attitude to assisting travellers, will often secure the next part of the trip for you as well.

See below for costs, distances and durations of domestic departures from Tirana. *Furgons* are usually 20% to 30% more expensive than buses.

Buses for Pristina (€30, 10 hours, 343km, three daily) leave from behind the museum

BUSES FROM TIRANA			
Destination	**Cost**	**Duration**	**Distance**
Berat	400 lekë	2½hr	122km
Durrës	100 lekë	1hr	38km
Elbasan	300 lekë	1½hr	54km
Fier	300 lekë	2hr	113km
Gjirokastra	1000 lekë	7hr	232km
Korça	800 lekë	4hr	181km
Kruja	200 lekë	30min	32km
Pogradec	700 lekë	3½hr	150km
Saranda	1200 lekë	8hr	284km
Shkodra	400 lekë	2hr	116km
Vlora	500 lekë	3hr	147km

near Sheshi Skënderbej. To Macedonia, there are buses via Struga (€10, five hours) to Tetovo (€15, seven to eight hours), and Skopje (€25, eight hours). If you're heading to Greece, buses go daily to Thessaloniki (11 hours) and Athens (17 hours).

The **Pollogu travel agency** (☎ 2235 000, 069 209 4906; Pall 103 Blvd Zogu I) sells tickets for the Macedonian bus company Polet, which has services at 9am and 9pm daily from the train station. The Pollogu office is upstairs in a modern apartment building at the top end of Zogu I. **Drita Travel and Tours** (☎ 2251 277; www .dritatravel.com) has offices at the train station and behind the museum, and runs an evening service to Skopje.

Train

The run-down train station is at the northern end of Blvd Zogu I. Albania's trains range from sort of OK to very decrepit. Albanians travel by train if they can't afford to travel by bus. Six trains daily go to Durrës (70 lekë, one hour, 36km). Trains also depart for Elbasan (190 lekë, four hours, two daily), Pogradec (2km out of town; 295 lekë, seven hours, once a day at 5.55am), Shkodra (150 lekë, 3½ hours, once a day at 1.15pm) and Vlora (250 lekë, 5½ hours, once a day at 2.50pm). Check timetables at the station the day before travelling. You can't buy tickets in advance, however; purchase them just before hopping on the train.

GETTING AROUND
To/From the Airport

The Rinas airport bus operates an hourly (6am to 6pm) service from the western side of the National Museum at Sheshi Skënderbej for 250 lekë. The going taxi rate is €20. It usually takes 20 to 25 minutes to get to or from the airport, but plan for traffic delays.

Car & Motorcycle

Driving around Albania is not as hard as it once was, although there are bound to be hair-raising moments.

Major car-hire companies in Tirana include the following:

Avis (☎ 2235 011; Rogner Hotel Europapark, Blvd Dëshmorët e Kombit)

Europcar (☎ 2227 888; Rr Durrësit 61)

Hertz (☎ 2255 028; Tirana Hotel International, Sheshi Skënderbej)

Sixt (☎ 2259 020; Rr e Kavajës 116)

Taxi

Taxi stands dot the city, and taxis charge 400 lekë for a ride inside Tirana and 600 lekë at night and to destinations outside the CBD area. Make sure you reach an agreement with the driver before setting off. **Radio Taxi** (☎ 377 777), with 24-hour service, is particularly reliable.

AROUND TIRANA

Just 25km east of Tirana is **Mt Dajti National Park** (1611m). It is the most accessible mountain in the country, and many Tiranans go there to escape the city rush and have a spit-roast lamb lunch. A cable car, **Dajti Express** (www.dajtiekspres .com; 500 lekë return), plies the route, cutting the time it takes to chug up the hill down to 15 minutes. Check first if it's operating.

If you're driving, there's a checkpoint where you pay a park admission fee of 200 lekë per car. Put your sturdy shoes on for a gentle hike in the lovely, shady beech and pine forests and then have a coffee and enjoy the spectacular views from the wide terrace of the **Panorama Restaurant** (☎ 361 124; meals 800 lekë; ☻ 9am-11pm).

To get to the Dajti Express departure point, take the public bus from outside Tirana's Clock Tower to 'Porcelain' (20 lekë), then walk uphill, following the signs, for around 10 minutes. Taxis seem to charge what they want to the Express, but the 6km trip should only cost 600 lekë. A taxi from the city to the top takes about 45 minutes, and you can arrange to phone the driver to pick you up when you want to go back. The road to the park starts on Tirana's Rr Qemal Stafa.

NORTHERN ALBANIA

The northern Albanian landscape has rich wildlife, swamps and lagoons around Shkodra and Lezha and high mountains around Theth in the northeast (named the Accursed Mountains, Bjeshkët e Namuna, in Albanian). Blood feuds may occupy the locals' minds, but pose little risk to tourists (see p54).

SHKODRA
☎ 022 / pop 91,300
Shkodra (Shkodër), the traditional centre of the Gheg cultural region, is one of the oldest

cities in Europe. Rozafa Fortress is beautiful, and the Marubi permanent photography exhibition is small but fascinating. A section of town (between the mosque and cathedral) has benefited from sensitive renovations of most of its older houses and storefronts, and Shkodra's locals are more likely to ride a bicycle than drive a car. Out of the centre, tatty grey apartment buildings lend it a rather sombre air.

Travellers pass through here on the way between Tirana and Ulcinj in Montenegro, but more are beginning to use the town as a base for forays into the alpine area of Theth and the isolated wonder of Lake Koman.

As the Ottoman Empire declined in the late 18th century, Shkodra became the centre of a semi-independent *pashalik* (region governed by a pasha, an Ottoman high official), which led to a blossoming of commerce and crafts. In 1913 Montenegro attempted to annex Shkodra (it succeeded in taking Ulcinj), a move not approved of by the international community, and the town changed hands often during WWI. Badly damaged by an earthquake in 1979, Shkodra was subsequently repaired and is Albania's fourth-largest town. The communist-era Hotel Rozafa in the town centre does little to welcome guests, but it makes a good landmark: restaurants, transport to Montenegro, and most of the town's sights are close by.

Sights

Three kilometres southwest of Shkodra, near the southern end of Lake Shkodra, is the **Rozafa Fortress** (admission 200 lekë; ☺ 8am-10pm), founded by the Illyrians in antiquity and rebuilt much later by the Venetians and Turks. The fortress derives its name from a woman named Rozafa, who was allegedly walled into the ramparts as an offering to the gods so that the construction would stand. The story goes that Rozafa asked that two holes be left in the stonework so that she could continue to breastfeed her baby. There's a spectacular wall sculpture of her near the entrance of the castle's **museum** (admission 150 lekë; ☺ 8am-7pm). Some nursing women come to the fortress to smear their breasts with the milky water that seeps from the wall and appears annually in January and February. A return (with waiting time) taxi from Shkodra is 800 lekë, or, if you're up for a steep walk through a poor part of town, municipal buses stop near the turn-off to the castle.

Hidden behind a building that looks like a block of flats, the **Marubi Permanent Photo Exhibition** (Rr Muhamet Gjollesha; admission 100 lekë; ☺ 8am-4pm Mon-Fri) has fantastic photography by the Marubi 'dynasty', Albania's first and foremost photographers. The first-ever photograph taken in Albania is here, taken by Pjetër Marubi in 1858. The exhibition shows fascinating portraits, places and events. Not only is this a rare insight into what things looked like in old Albania, it is also a small collection of mighty fine photographs. To get here, go northeast of the clock tower to Rr Çlirimi; Rr Muhamet Gjollesha darts off to the right. The exhibition is on the left in an unmarked building, but locals will help you find it if you ask. Postcards of some of the images are for sale for 100 lekë.

FAMILY FEUD WITH BLOOD AS THE PRIZE

The *Kanun* (Code) was formalised in the 15th century by powerful northern chieftain Lekë Dukagjin. It consists of 1262 articles covering every aspect of daily life: work, marriage, family, property, hospitality, economy and so on. Although the *Kanun* was suppressed by the communists, there has been a revival of its strict precepts in northern Albania. How much so is uncertain, as dramatic incidents may have been overplayed by the media.

According to the *Kanun*, the most important things in life are honour and hospitality. If a member of a family (or one of their guests) is murdered, it becomes the duty of the male members of that clan to claim their blood debt by murdering a male member of the murderer's clan. This sparks an endless cycle of killing that doesn't end until either all the male members of one of the families are dead, or reconciliation is brokered through respected village elders.

Hospitality is so important in these parts of Albania that the guest takes on a godlike status. There are 38 articles giving instructions on how to treat a guest – an abundance of food, drink and comfort is at his or her disposal, and it is also the host's duty to avenge the murder of his guest, should this happen during their visit.

WORTH THE TRIP: THETH

Heading north to Theth is truly heading into Albania's unknown. Wooden watermills, fast-flowing rivers, great hiking trails and lock-in towers (where men waited, protected, during a blood feud) are features of this small town and, with foreign nongovernment investment assisting the locals to move into the B&B industry, the three-hour hair-raising journey is rewarded with fully catered homestay accommodation. Theth's snowed out much of the year (outside June to September).

Petrit Imeraj (☎ 069 206 5205) is a Shkodra-based mountain man who offers a variety of tours around the region.

Harusha Family Home (☎ 069 277 0294; per person 2500 lekë) is a friendly homestay in Theth's 'centre'. The Harushas are the biggest family in the village, so look out for a bunch of (English-speaking) children and you're close. The house is on the left, over the bridge.

A *furgon* (shared minibus; 500 lekë, three hours) is supposed to make a daily trip, departing at 7am from outside Shkodra's Café Rusi.

Sleeping & Eating

Hotel Kaduku (HK; ☎ 42 216; Sheshi 5 Heronjtë; r €30) This popular and clean hotel is behind Raiffeisen Bank on the roundabout near Hotel Rozafa. The two wings have been renovated, and staff and other guests are great information providers. Breakfast is an extra €4.

Piazza Park (Rr 13 Dhjetori; mains 250-1000 lekë) Where the locals return to, night after night, day after day. Once you get past security, people-watch (or be watched) next to the fountains.

G&T Tradita (tradita Gegë dhe Toskë; Rr Skenderbeu; meals 1100 lekë) Serves great food (fresh fish is a speciality) in what could be an ethnographic museum. You can watch grills and pita being cooked on the huge hearth. It's really dim inside, but no doubt that's part of the Gheg and Tosk's atmosphere.

Getting There & Away

There are frequent *furgons* to and from Tirana (350 lekë, 2½ hours). From Shkodra, *furgons* depart from Radio Shkodra near Hotel Rozafa. The train station is a fair walk away, but *furgons* meet arriving trains.

Furgons to Ulcinj and Bar in Montenegro leave at 9am and 3pm (500 lekë) from outside the Hotel Rozafa. They fill quickly, so get in early. Taxis to Han i Hotit on the way to Podgorica charge about 2500 lekë; you can also catch a *furgon* to Koplik (the turn-off to Theth) and a taxi from there.

Buses also depart Shkodra for Lake Koman (400 lekë, two hours, 6.30am and 9.30am), dropping you at the ferry terminal for the wonderful ferry trip across the lake to Fierza (400 lekë), located near the border with Kosovo.

CENTRAL ALBANIA

Central Albania crams it all in. Just an hour or two from Tirana and you can be Ottoman house-hopping in brilliantly alive Berat, or musing over ancient ruins in deserted Apollonia or bubbly beachside Durrës. Don't forget to bargain for antiques under the gaze of Skanderbeg in Kruja, and to take time out on the cable car to Mt Dajti National Park.

KRUJA

☎ 0511 / pop 20,000

From the road below, Kruja's houses appear to sit in the lap of a mountain. An ancient castle juts out to one side, and the massive Skanderbeg Museum juts out of the castle itself. The local plaster industry is going strong, so, sadly, expect visibility-reducing plumes of smoke to cloud views of the Atlantic.

Kruja is Skanderbeg's town. Yes, Albania's hero was born here, and although it was over 500 years ago, there's still a great deal of pride in the fact that he and his forces defended Kruja until his death. As soon as you get off the *furgon* you're face to knee with a statue of Skanderbeg wielding his mighty sword with one hand, and it just gets more Skanderdelic after that.

At a young age Kastrioti, the son of an Albanian prince, was handed over as a hostage to the Turks, who converted him to Islam and gave him a military education at Edirne in Turkey. There he became known as Iskander (after Alexander the Great) and Sultan Murat II promoted him to the rank of *bey* (governor), thus the name Skanderbeg.

In 1443 the Turks suffered a defeat at the hands of the Hungarians at Niš in present-day

Serbia, and nationally minded Skanderbeg took the opportunity to abandon the Ottoman army and Islam and rally his fellow Albanians against the Turks. Skanderbeg made Kruja his seat of government between 1443 and 1468. Among the 13 Turkish invasions he subsequently repulsed was that led by his former commander Murat II. Pope Calixtus III named Skanderbeg the 'captain general of the Holy See' and Venice formed an alliance with him. The Turks besieged Kruja four times. Though beaten back in 1450, 1466 and 1467, they took control of Kruja in 1478 (after Skanderbeg's death).

Kruja's sights can be covered in a few hours, making this an ideal town to visit en route to Tirana's international airport, which is only 16km away. The main sight in Kruja is the **castle** (admission 100 lekë; ☽ 24hr) and its peculiar **Skanderbeg Museum** (admission 200 lekë; ☽ 9am-1pm & 4-7pm Tue-Sun). Designed by Enver Hoxha's daughter and son-in-law, it opened in 1982, and its spacious seven-level interior displays replicas of armour and paintings depicting Skanderbeg's struggle against the Ottomans. The museum is something of a secular shrine, and takes itself very seriously indeed, with giant statues and dramatic battle murals.

The **Ethnographic Museum** (admission 100 lekë; ☽ 9am-7pm) in the castle complex below the Skanderbeg Museum is one of the best in the country. Set in an original 19th-century Ottoman house that belonged to the affluent Toptani family, this museum shows the level of luxury and self-sufficiency the household maintained by producing its own food, drink, leather and weapons. They even had their very own mini-*hammam* (Turkish bath) and watermill. The walls are lined with original frescos from 1764. The English-speaking guide's detailed explanations are excellent; offer a tip if you can.

A short scramble down the cobblestone lane are the remains of a small *hammam* as well as a functioning *teqe* – a small place of worship for those practising the Bektashi branch of Islam. This beautifully decorated *teqe* has been maintained by successive generations of the Dollma family since 1789. Skanderbeg himself reputedly planted the knotted and ancient olive tree in front.

The bazaar is the country's best place for souvenir shopping and has WWII medical kits, antique gems and quality traditional ware, including beautifully embroidered tablecloths, copper coffee pots and plates. You can watch women using looms to make *kilims* (rugs) and purchase the results.

Kruja is 32km from Tirana. A cab from Tirana to Kruja and back with two hours' waiting time costs around 4000 lekë, while a *furgon* one way costs 200 lekë. It is very easy to reach the airport (100 lekë, 30 minutes) by *furgon* or taxi from here, and there are direct links by bus and *furgon* to Durrës (200 lekë, one hour).

DURRËS
☎ 052 / pop 114,000

Durrës is an ancient city and was, until 1920, Albania's capital. Its 10km-long beach begins a few kilometres southeast of the city (past the port and tangle of overpasses and roundabouts). Here families take up position under rented umbrellas and sun lounges, and the brave cool down in its shallow, and frequently red-flagged, section of the Adriatic Sea. The beaches are something of a lesson in unplanned development; hundreds of hotels stand side by side, barely giving breathing space to the beach and contributing to the urban waste problem that has caused outbreaks of skin infections in swimmers.

Away from the beach, Durrës is a relaxed, amiable city with some gracious early-20th-century buildings, centrally located ancient ruins, a unique museum and an abundance of fun waterfront eating options.

Orientation

The town centre is easily covered on foot. The **Great Mosque** (Xhamia e Madhe Durrës; Sheshi i Lirisë) serves as a point of orientation: the archaeological attractions are immediately around it, and the train and bus stations are a kilometre to the northeast. The former palace of King Zogu I and the lighthouse are to the west, on the ridge.

Information

There are plenty of ATMs near the station, on Rr Tregtare, and a branch of the American Bank of Albania is on Sheshi Mujo Ulqinaku.
Century 91 Internet (Rr Tregtare; per hr 60 lekë; ☽ 1pm-midnight) Down a lane near the Great Mosque.
Dea Lines (☎ 30 386; dealines@dealines.com; Rr Tregtare 102; ☽ 8.30am-8pm) Trustworthy travel agency that will help you find up-to-date information on ferries and flights.
Post office (Blvd Kryesor) One block west of the train and bus stations.

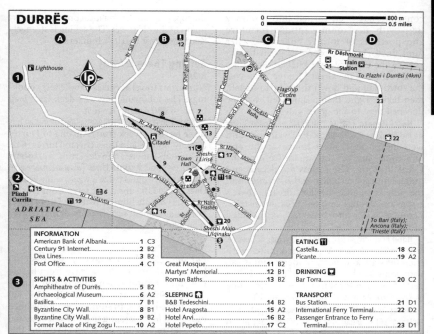

DURRËS

0 _____ 800 m
0 _____ 0.5 miles

INFORMATION	
American Bank of Albania	1 C3
Century 91 Internet	2 B2
Dea Lines	3 B2
Post Office	4 C1
SIGHTS & ACTIVITIES	
Amphitheatre of Durrës	5 B2
Archaeological Museum	6 A2
Basilica	7 B1
Byzantine City Wall	8 B1
Byzantine City Wall	9 B2
Former Palace of King Zogu I	10 A2

Great Mosque	11 B2
Martyrs' Memorial	12 B1
Roman Baths	13 B2
SLEEPING	
B&B Tedeschini	14 B2
Hotel Aragosta	15 A1
Hotel Arvi	16 B2
Hotel Pepeto	17 C2

EATING	
Castella	18 C2
Picante	19 A2
DRINKING	
Bar Torra	20 C2
TRANSPORT	
Bus Station	21 D1
International Ferry Terminal	22 D2
Passenger Entrance to Ferry	
Terminal	23 D1

Sights

The **Archaeological Museum** (Muzeu Arkeologik; Rr Taulantia; admission 200 lekë; 9am-3pm Tue-Sun), on the waterfront, is well laid out and has an impressive collection of artefacts from the Greek, Hellenistic and Roman periods. Highlights include engraved Roman funeral stelae and some big carved-stone sarcophagi. Back in the day when it was called Epidamnos, Durrës was a centre for the worship of Venus, and the museum has a cabinet full of little busts of the love goddess.

North of the museum, beginning at the Torra and following Rr Anastas Durrsaku, are the 6th-century **Byzantine city walls**, built after the Visigoth invasion of AD 481 and supplemented by round Venetian towers in the 14th century.

The **Amphitheatre of Durrës** (Rr e Kalasë; admission 500 lekë; 8am-7pm) was built on the hillside inside the city walls in the early 2nd century AD. In its prime it had the capacity to seat 15,000 spectators, but these days a few inhabited houses occupy the stage, a reminder of its recent rediscovery and excavation. The Byzantine chapel in the amphitheatre has several mosaics.

Ruins of **Roman baths** are just off the main square at the back of the Alexsandër Moisiu Theatre. Across the road a large circular **basilica** still has some columns standing. Also intriguing are the Roman columns located in front of the shopfronts, palm trees and road lights on Rr Tregtare.

Durrës' attractions are not all ancient. There are some fine socialist-realist monuments, including the **Martyrs' Memorial** (Rr Shefget Beja) by the waterfront.

On the hilltop west of the amphitheatre stands the decaying **former palace of King Zogu I** (Rr Anastas Durrsaku). It's a 15-minute climb up from the town centre to what was a grand palace (marble staircases, carved wooden ceilings and the like), but it's slightly derelict now and closed to the public.

Sleeping

Durrës has a variety of accommodation options in the city itself, but most line the beach to the east.

B&B Tedeschini (24 343, 068 224 6303; ipmcrsp@icc.al.eu.org; Rr Dom Nikoll Kaçorri 5; s/d €15/30) This gracious 19th-century former Italian consulate has been turned into a homey B&B with airy rooms, antique furniture and portraits of former consuls. Owner (and doctor) Alma prepares great breakfasts in the country-style kitchen. From the square fronting the Great Mosque, walk past the town hall and down the alley to its left, then take a right, then a quick left. Use the doorbell next to the green gates.

Hotel Pepeto (☎ 24 190; Rr Mbreti Monun 3; s/d/ste incl breakfast €20/30/50; ❄) A well-run (and well-signposted) guest house at the end of a court, just off the square fronting the Great Mosque. The rooms are decent and quiet, some have baths and balconies and the suite is an attic-dweller's dream. There's a spacious lounge and bar area downstairs. Laundry is €5 and breakfast is included in rates.

Hotel Arvi (☎ 30 403; www.hotelarvi.com; Rr Taulantia; d/ste €60/80; ❄ 🖥) A polished hotel with friendly staff and neat, modern rooms (all with some kind of sea view), it's also in the perfect location for watching or participating in the Durrës waterfront *xhiro* (walk).

Hotel Aragosta (☎ 26 477; www.aragosta.al; Rr Taulantia; s/d €60/100; ❄ 🖥) With carpet so cushy you can't walk straight, this new beachfront hotel is close to good restaurants and has one of its own, while staff boast that its private beach is the cleanest beach in town. Its name means 'lobster' and you can guess the colour scheme of the modern rooms (some with wonderful spa baths). Totally nonsmoking – and proud of it.

Eating & Drinking

Castella (Rr Grigor Durrsaku; mains 200-400 lekë; ❄ 10am-4pm Mon-Sat) Popular with locals who prefer a good feed rather than being seen, this casual restaurant has bargain-priced homestyle lunches.

Picante (Rr Taulantia; mains 700-4000 lekë) Upping the trendiness ante is this stark white restaurant on the promenade. The red-chilli motif may indicate how hot this place is; it's certainly where the young locals are spending their disposable income. The music's good, the furniture is white and minimalist, and the meals are priced to stretch the budget.

Bar Torra (Sheshi Mujo Ulqinaku) Housed inside a fortified Venetian tower at the beginning of the city walls, this was one of the first private cafes in Albania, opened by a team of local artists. After you've had a peek at the view from

the top, you can drink a local brew in the cosy nooks of the old tower. The ceiling is strangely reminiscent of Hoxha's bunkers.

Getting There & Away
BOAT
Numerous travel agencies handle ferry bookings. The following one-way deck fares leap by up to €30 during August.

Adria Ferries (☎ 220 105; booking@adriaferries.al) has three ferries a week from Ancona to Durrës (€90, 17 hours), and from Bari to Durrës (€42, eight hours); there's a €6 departure fee. **Agemar** (☎ 25 154) and **Azzurra Lines** (www.azzurraline.com) ply the same routes twice a week, while **Venezia Lines** (☎ 30 383) runs a fast ferry from Durrës to Bari (€60, 3½ hours). **Ventouris Ferries** (☎ 25 338) has a frequent service from Bari to Durrës (€56, eight hours).

BUS
Furgons (150 lekë, one hour) and buses (100 lekë, one hour) to Tirana leave from beside the train station when they're full. Buses leave for Shkodra at 7.30am and 1.30pm (300 lekë, three hours). In summer, long-distance buses and *furgons* going to and from Saranda, Gjirokastra, Fier and Berat tend to bypass this station, picking up and dropping off passengers at the end of Plazhi i Durrësi, to the far east of the harbour. A taxi there costs 500 lekë, or catch the orange municipal bus to 'Plepa' for 20 lekë (10 minutes).

In July and August there are additional services to ethnic Albanian towns in Macedonia.

TRAIN
Albania's 720km railway network centres on Durrës. There are six trains a day to Tirana (70 lekë, one hour), one to Shkodra at 1pm (160 lekë, 3¾ hours) via Lezha, one to Pogradec at 7.07am (300 lekë, 5½ hours) via Elbasan (2½ hours), and one to Vlora at 4.05pm (260 lekë, four hours) via Fier. Times and services change, so check the station noticeboard beforehand to confirm. They sometimes depart slightly before schedule. If your train plans fall through, there are plenty of buses at the adjacent bus station.

APOLLONIA
The ruined city of ancient **Apollonia** (admission 700 lekë; ❄ 9am-5pm) is 12km west of Fier, which is 90km south of Durrës. Apollonia is

set on rolling hills among olive groves, and the plains below stretch for miles. Apollonia (named after the God Apollo) was founded by Greeks from Corinth and Corfu in 588 BC and quickly grew into an important city-state, which minted its own currency and benefited from a robust slave trade. Under the Romans (from 229 BC) the city became a great cultural centre with a famous school of philosophy.

Julius Caesar rewarded Apollonia with the title 'free city' for supporting him against Gnaeus Pompeius Magnus (Pompey the Great) during the civil war in the 1st century BC, and sent his nephew Octavius, the future Emperor Augustus, to complete his studies here.

After a series of military and natural disasters (including an earthquake in the 3rd century AD that turned the river into a malarial swamp), the population moved southward into present-day Vlora, and by the 5th century AD only a small village with its own bishop remained at Apollonia.

There is far less to see at Apollonia than there is at Butrint, but there are some picturesque ruins within the 4km of city walls, including a small original theatre and the elegant pillars on the restored facade of the city's 2nd-century-AD administrative centre. The 3rd-century-BC House of Mosaics is closed off to the public, and its mosaics have been covered with sand to protect them from the elements.

Inside the Museum of Apollonia complex is the Byzantine monastery and church of St Mary, which has fascinating gargoyles on the outside pillars. Many of the rooms inside the complex are not open for display yet, but interesting and ancient statues are displayed in the church garden and cloisters and labelled in Albanian. Much of the site remains to be excavated, but more recent discoveries include a necropolis outside the castle walls with graves from the Bronze and Iron Ages.

Apollonia is best visited on a day trip from Tirana, Durrës, Vlora or Berat, as there's nothing of interest in the nearby industrial centre of Fier. From Fier, *furgons* head to Durrës (200 lekë, 1½ hours), Tirana (300 lekë, two hours), Berat (500 lekë, one hour) and Vlora (200 lekë, one hour). The train from Tirana (175 lekë, 4½ hours) comes via Durrës. Once in Fier there's no public transport to the site, so expect to pay around 2500 lekë for a return taxi journey (15 minutes each way, including an hour's waiting time.)

BERAT
☎ 032 / pop 45,500

A highlight of any trip to Albania is a visit to beautiful Berat. Its most striking feature is the collection of white Ottoman houses climbing up the hill to its castle, earning it the title of 'town of a thousand windows' and helping it join Gjirokastra on the list of Unesco World Heritage sites in 2008. Its rugged mountain setting is particularly evocative when the clouds swirl around the tops of the minarets, or break up to show the icy top of Mt Tomorri.

The old quarters are lovely ensembles of whitewashed walls, tile roofs and old stone walls guarding grapevine-shaded courtyards. Surrounding the town, olive and cherry trees decorate the gentler slopes, while pine woods stand on the steeper inclines. In true Albanian style, an elegant mosque with a pencil minaret is partnered on the main square by a large new Orthodox church. The centre of town and the newer outlying areas along the river flats are less attractive ensembles of rectilinear concrete housing blocks, but the Osum River and its bridges (especially the 1780 seven-arched stone footbridge) help redeem it.

In the 3rd century BC an Illyrian fortress called Antipatrea was built here on the site of an earlier settlement. The Byzantines strengthened the hilltop fortifications in the 5th and 6th centuries, as did the Bulgarians 400 years later. The Serbs, who occupied the citadel in 1345, renamed it Beligrad, or 'White City'. In 1450 the Ottoman Turks took the town. After a period of decline, in the 18th and 19th centuries the town began to thrive as a crafts centre specialising in woodcarving.

For a brief time in 1944 Berat was the capital of liberated Albania.

Sights

Berat is in the midst of a tourism transformation: audioguides to the sights are available for hire from the **Medieval Centre** (behind the King's Mosque).

KALA

Start by taking a 15-minute walk up to the impressive 14th-century **Kalasa** (Citadel; admission 100 lekë; ☉ 24hr). The neighbourhood inside the walls, Kala, still lives and breathes; you'll see old Mercedes-Benz cars struggling to get up the cobblestone roads to return locals home. If you walk around this busy, ancient

ALBANIA

neighbourhood for long enough you'll invariably stumble into someone's courtyard thinking it's a church or ruin (no one seems to mind, though). In spring and summer the fragrance of chamomile is in the air (and underfoot), and other wildflowers seem to burst from every gap between the stones.

Kala was traditionally a Christian neighbourhood, but fewer than a dozen of the 20 churches remain. The quarter's biggest church, **Church of the Dormition of St Mary** (Kisha Fjetja e Shën Mërisë), is the site of the **Onufri Museum** (Muzeu Onufri; ☎ 32 248; admission 200 lekë; ⊙ 9am-1pm & 4pm-7pm Apr-Sep, 9am-4pm Oct-Mar, closed Mon). The church itself dates from 1797 and was built on the foundations of a 10th-century church. Onufri's spectacular 16th-century artworks are displayed on the ground level along with a beautifully gilded iconostasis.

Ask at the Onufri Museum if you can see the other churches and tiny chapels in Kala, including **St Theodore** (Shën Todher), close to the citadel gates; the substantial and picturesque **Church of the Holy Trinity** (Kisha Shën Triades), below the upper fortress; and the little chapels of **St Mary Blachernae** (Shën Mëri Vllaherna) and **St Nicholas** (Shënkolli). Some of the churches date back to the 13th century. Also keep an eye out for the **Red Mosque**, which was the first in Berat and dates back to the 15th century.

The rest of Berat and the Osum valley look quite spectacular from Kala. The highest point of the citadel is occupied by the **Inner Fortress**, where ruined stairs lead to a Tolkien-esque water reservoir (take a torch). Perched on a cliff ledge below the citadel is the artfully positioned little chapel of **St Michael** (Shën Mihell), best viewed from the Gorica quarter.

Down from the castle is Berat's **Ethnographic Museum** (Muzeu Etnografik; ☎ 32 224; admission 200 lekë; ⊙ 9am-1pm & 4-7pm Tue-Sat, 9am-2pm Sun Apr-Sep, 9am-4pm Tue-Sat, 9am-2pm Sun Oct-Mar). It's in an 18th-century Ottoman house that is as interesting as the exhibits. The ground floor has displays of traditional clothes and the tools used by silversmiths and weavers, while the upper storey has kitchens, bedrooms and guest rooms decked out in traditional style. Check out the *mafil*, a kind of mezzanine looking into the lounge where the women of the house could keep an eye on male guests (and see when their cups needed to be filled). Brochures are available, but to get the most out of it, ask for a guided tour and give a tip.

MANGALEM
Down in the traditionally Muslim Mangalem quarter, there are three grand mosques. The 16th-century **Sultan's Mosque** (Xhamia e Mbretit) is one of the oldest in Albania. The **Helveti teqe** behind the mosque has a beautiful carved ceiling and was specially designed with acoustic holes to improve the quality of sound during meetings. The Helveti, like the Bektashi, are a dervish order, or brotherhood, of Muslim mystics. Staff at the neighbouring Medieval Centre should have the keys.

The big mosque on the town square is the 16th-century **Lead Mosque** (Xhamia e Plumbit), so named because of the lead coating its sphere-shaped domes. The 19th-century **Bachelors' Mosque** (Xhamia e Beqarëvet) is down by the Osum River; look for the enchanting paintings on its external walls. This mosque was built for unmarried shop assistants and junior craftsmen and is perched between some fine Ottoman-era shopfronts.

GORICA
Gorica has tremendous views of the Kala and the Mangalem quarter. It's tucked under a steep hillside and never sees the sun in the winter (it's also one of the coolest places to be in summer). It's a tough, unmarked walk up to the negligible remains of an old **Illyrian fortress** in the woods above Gorica.

Sleeping
Berat Backpackers (☎ 069 306 4429; www.beratbackpackers.com; Gorica; dm €12; ⊙ summer) This English-run hostel with dorm rooms and camping spots (€6) is next to the Monastery of St Spyridon and has wonderful views of Berat's thousand windows and castle.

   Hotel Mangalemi (☎ 32 093, 068 242 9803; Rr e Kalasë; s/d €17/25) Tomi Mio (the hotel is known locally as Hotel Tomi) and his family run a great hotel in a sprawling Ottoman house with a restaurant on the ground floor and a clutch of warm, cosy rooms upstairs, plus a terrace with great views across Berat over to Mt Tomorri. It's on the street that runs from the main square up to Kala.

Getting There & Away
Buses and *furgons* run between Tirana and Berat (400 lekë, 2½ hours) hourly until 4pm. From Tirana, buses leave from the 'Kombinati' station (catch the municipal bus from Sheshi Skënderbej to Kombinati

for 30 lekë). In Berat, all buses depart from and arrive at the bus station next to the Lead Mosque. From Berat there are buses to Vlora (300 lekë, 2½ hours, nine daily), Saranda via Gjirokastra (1000 lekë, six hours, three daily at 8am, 9.30am and 1.30pm) and Gjirokastra (700 lekë, five hours, one daily).

SOUTHERN COAST

With rough mountains falling headfirst into bright blue seas, this area is wild and ready for exploration. Some of the beaches are jam-packed in August, yet there's plenty of space, peace and happy-to-see-you faces in low season. With careful government planning, the southern coast could shine. In the meantime, if the rubbish lying next to you on the beach gets you down, you only have to bend your neck a bit to see the snowcapped mountain peaks and wide green valleys zigzagged by rivers around you. There are still untouched beaches here.

VLORA

☎ 033 / pop 124,000

It's here in sunny Vlora (the ancient Aulon) that the Adriatic Sea meets the Ionian. The beaches are muddy and grubby, but it's a bustling little port city. A long (1.5km) palm-lined avenue runs through the centre of town from the port and Independence Museum, ending at the mosque, bus station and grand Independence Monument. The outstanding museums deserve a few hours' exploration, and a quick hike up the hill to Kuzum Babai behind the bus station is rewarded with good views. The road out to Zvernëci passes through some of the Vlora neighbourhoods that harboured illegal immigrants during the 1990s – speedboats laded with Kurds, Chinese and marijuana used to zip across the 75km Straits of Otranto to Italy almost nightly. The 1997 revolution after the collapse of the pyramid schemes started here, and it took several years for the authorities to crack down on local gangs.

Information

Everything you'll need in Vlora is on Rr Sadik Zotaj, including ATMs, the post office and telephone centre. The best place to get online is **Internet Café Studenti** (Rr Kullat Skele 2; per hr 100 lekë; ☺ 7am-midnight), just off Rr Sadik Zotaj.

The helpful **Colombo Travel Agency** (☎ 27 659; www.colomboalb.com; Hotel Sazani, Sheshi i Flamurit; ☺ 8am-7pm), on Hotel Sazani's ground floor (near Muradi Mosque), runs tours and sells ferry tickets to Italy.

Sights

Start at **Sheshi i Flamurit** (Flag Square), near the top of Sadik Zotaj. The magnificent socialist-realist **Independence Monument** stands proud against the sky with the flag bearer hoisting the double-headed eagle into the blue. Near the base of the monument lies the grave of local Ismail Qemali, the country's first prime minister.

On the other side of the avenue is the **Muzeu Historik** (History Museum; Sheshi i Flamurit; admission 100 lekë; ☺ 8am-2pm & 5-8pm), displaying a collection of items dating from the 4th century BC up to WWII. Opposite, behind an inconspicuous metal fence, is the home that houses the excellent **Ethnographic Museum** (Sheshi i Flamurit; admission 100 lekë; ☺ 9am-2pm Mon-Sat).

Walk down towards the 16th-century **Muradi Mosque**, a small elegant structure made of red and white stone and with a modest minaret; its exquisite design is attributed to one of the greatest Ottoman architects, Albanian-born Sinan Pasha. Overlooking the town is the Bektashi shrine of Kuzum Baba. Walk up the steps behind Hotel Alpin to see the well-kept gardens, bars and restaurants and take in the great views over the Bay of Vlora. Narta Lagoon is in the distance.

Down by the harbour the **National Museum of Independence** (admission 200 lekë; ☺ 9am-1pm & 5-8pm Mon-Sat, 9am-noon & 5-8pm Sun) is housed in the villa that became the headquarters of Albania's first government in 1912. If you're lucky you'll get a passionate pro-independence guided tour; otherwise the preserved offices, historic photographs and famous balcony still make it an interesting place to learn about Albania's short-lived, but long-remembered, 1912 independence.

Vlora's main beaches stretch south from the harbour, and the further south you go, the better they get. Turn left before the harbour to reach Plazhi i Ri, a long public beach that can get quite crowded. Apparently new sand is trucked in each year. A good 2km walk away, **Uji i Ftohtë** (meaning 'cold water') is a better beach choice. It has open-air bars and discos during summer, and plenty of private beaches (ie someone actually picks up the rubbish). You'll need to hire a sunbed and umbrella for 200 lekë per person. Orange municipal buses

ALBANIA

run from Sadik Zotaj to the Uji i Ftohtë post office (20 lekë, 10 minutes, every 15 minutes from 7am to 9pm).

Sleeping & Eating

Hotel Konomi (☎ 29 320; Rr e Uji i Ftohtë; r 2000 lekë) Set on top of a hill with views of the party end of town, this stark former workers' camp is good for the socialist idealism experience. It's a short hike up from the last bus stop along the beach road.

Hotel Alpin (☎ 069 224 1198; r 2500 lekë) This new hotel next to the bus station is named after its owner's passion: climbing Albania's Alps. The rooms are spotless and modern, with large bathrooms and excellent beds.

Hotel Vlora International (☎ 24 408; www.vlorainter national.com; Rr Sadik Zotaj; s/d €50/60; 🖢) Perched by the port, this luxury hotel has modern, comfortable rooms with flat-screen TVs, a fitness centre, indoor pool and restaurant.

Xhokla (Plazhi i Ri; mains 200-1000 lekë) Attentive staff, great Italian food and a good variety of wines make this the best restaurant in town. Being on Vlora's beachfront *xhiro* route makes for great people-watching, too.

Getting There & Away

Buses (500 lekë, three hours) and *furgons* (600 lekë, two hours) to Tirana and to Durrës (bus/ *furgon* 500 lekë, three hours) whiz back and forth in the morning hours. Buses to Saranda (1000 lekë, six hours) and on to Gjirokastra (1300 lekë, seven hours) leave at 5am, 7am, 1pm and 2pm. There are nine buses a day to Berat (300 lekë, two hours).

Buses leave from Rr Rakip Malilaj, although departures to Athens (€40) and all major cities in Italy (€60 to €80) leave from near the Muradi Mosque.

There's one train a day from Tirana to Vlora at 2.50pm and from Vlora to Tirana at 5.40am (250 lekë, five hours).

Ferries from Vlora to Brindisi, Italy, take around six hours. From Monday to Saturday, there are departures from Brindisi at 11pm and Vlora at noon (deck tickets €35 to €70). Buy tickets at Colombo Travel Agency (p61).

LLOGARAJA PASS NATIONAL PARK

Reaching the pine-tree-clad Llogaraja Pass National Park (1025m) is one of the special moments of Albanian travel. If you've been soaking up the sun on the southern coast's beaches, it seems impossible that after a

steep hairpin-bend climb you're up in the mountains tucking into spit-roasted lamb and homemade wine. There's great scenery up here, including the *pisha flamur* (flag pine) – a tree resembling the eagle design on the Albanian flag. Watch clouds descending onto the mountain, shepherds on the plains guiding their herds, and thick forests where deer, wild boar and wolves roam. Check out the resident deer at the Tourist Village before heading across the road to the cute family-run cabins at **Hotel Andoni** (☎ 068 240 0929; cabins 4000 lekë). The family do a wonderful lamb roast (800 lekë) here, too.

DHËRMI & DRYMADES

As you zigzag down the mountain from the Llogaraja Pass National Park, the white crescent-shape beaches and azure waters lure you from below. **Dhërmi** (Dhërmiu) is under the tourist trance and ferryloads of Italians arrive in the beach town almost daily in summer, while Tirana-based Albanians and expats pack the beaches, bars and restaurants on the weekends.

Just after the beginning of the walk down to Dhërmi beach is the dirt road to **Drymades beach**. Turn right, and a 45-minute walk through olive groves brings you to **Drymades Hotel** (☎ 068 228 5637; sites 500 lekë, cabins 4000 lekë), a quiet accommodation option where a white virgin beach (albeit with bunkers) stretches before you. A constellation of cabins and rooms under the shade of pine trees is just a step away from the blue sea. You can stay indoors, camp or simply sleep under the stars on the beach. There's a bar, restaurant and shaded playground, plus a classic beach bar with a straw roof.

The best place to stay and eat is **Hotel Luciano** (☎ 069 209 1431; Dhërmi Beach; r per person 1000 lekë; 🖢). The water is metres away, the views are sublime, rooms simple but comfortable and staff busy but helpful. There's a popular waterfront restaurant here too, with plenty of pasta choices and good wood-fired pizzas (300 lekë). To get here, turn left at the bottom of the hill.

Hotel Riviera (☎ 068 263 3333; Dhërmi Beach; d €40-60; 🖢) has had a leopard-skin-curtain makeover and is now truly focussed on too-cool-for-school, with orange, lime green and brown walls. The new futon-style beds and flat-screen TVs make it all acceptable. An ubercool bar is perched on the water's edge.

The beach is about 2km below the Vlora–Saranda road, so ask the conductor to stop at the turn-off on the Llogaraja side of the village. From here it's an easy 10-minute walk downhill (not so easy on the way back though).

HIMARA
☎ 0393 / pop 4500

This sleepy town has fine beaches, a couple of great Greek seafood tavernas, some hi-tech, good-looking hotels and an interesting Old Town high on the hill. Most of the ethnic Greek population left in the 1990s, but many have returned. The lower town comprises three easily accessible rocky beaches, the town's hotels and restaurants. The main Vlora–Saranda road passes the entrance to the hilltop castle and, like the one in Berat, many residents still call it home. A taxi there from Himara costs 300 lekë. From the top you can take in the superb views of Livadhi beach and check out some frescos in the old churches. Try Albania's best top-end resort, **Rapos Resort** (☎ 22 856; www.raposresorthotel.com; d €65-90; 🏊), or the very cool **Manolo** (☎ 22 375; d €50) near the port.

Buses towards Saranda and Vlora pass through town in the morning only; check with locals exactly when.

SARANDA
☎ 0852 / pop 32,000

Skeletal high-rises crowd around the horseshoe shape of Saranda, a result of the past few years' astounding level of development. Barring blackouts, a night view of the town shows just how few of the buildings are actually occupied. Despite this massive development, Saranda is still a really pleasant town that is increasingly drawing mostly Albanian tourists into its sea. To make things interesting, a daily stream of Corfu holidaymakers take the 45-minute ferry trip to Albania, add the Albanian stamp to their passports and hit Butrint and Blue Eye Spring before heading back.

The town's name comes from Ayii Saranda, an early monastery dedicated to 40 saints; its bombed remains (including some preserved frescos) are still high on the hill above the town. The town was called Porto Edda for a period in the 1940s, after Mussolini's daughter.

Saranda's stony beaches are quite decent for a town of this size, and the section near the port even has built-in starting blocks and lanes for swimmers. Apart from the beach,

Saranda has other attractions: a well-preserved mosaic floor bizarrely housed in what looks like an office complex on Rr Flamurit, as well as a central 5th-century synagogue. The other sights are a bus or taxi trip out of the town itself: the mesmerising ancient archaeological site of Butrint and the hypnotic Blue Eye Spring. Between Saranda and Butrint, the lovely beaches and islands of Ksamil are perfect for a dip after a day of exploring.

Orientation & Information

Four main streets arc around Saranda's bay, including the waterfront promenade that becomes prime *xhiro* territory in the evening. There are six banks with ATMs along the sea road (Rr 1 Maji) and the next street inland (Rr Skënderbeu). The incredibly helpful **information centre** (ZIT; Rr Skënderbeu; 🕙 8am-4pm Mon-Fri) provides bus timetables and maps. **Sipa Tours** (☎ 66 75; Rr 1 Maji; www.sipatours.com) arranges tours to Butrint for around €30.

Sleeping & Eating

Hairy Lemon (☎ 069 355 9317; dm €13) This backpackers hostel is in an orange-and-yellow apartment block. It's a 10-minute walk from the port (turn left as you exit).

Hotel Palma (☎ 22 929; Rr Mithat Hoxha; s/d/apt incl breakfast €20/30/120; 🏊) Right next to the port, this hotel has carpets that don't fit, but some rooms have great views with large balconies and the location is handy. If you're up for it, guests get free entry into the on-site disco. Breakfast and wi-fi are free.

Hotel Republica (☎ 22 240; Rr 1 Maji; s/d €25/30) This is a central hotel with character, and the restaurant on the top floor (there's a lift with a view) comes to life in summer. The bar underneath will bemuse history lovers; you drink coffee at tables wedged between the ruins of the town's ancient walls.

Hotel Grand (☎ 25 574; Rr Saranda-Butrint 1; d incl breakfast €40; 🏊) This hotel takes up a fair whack of Saranda's eastern foreshore with its swimming pool, playground, bar and restaurant. Rooms are spacious and rates include wi-fi access and breakfast.

Castle of Lekursi (Kalaja e Lëkurësit; ☎ 25 555; mains 250-1200 lekë; 🕙 11am-midnight) This restaurant sits inside the reconstructed castle above Saranda and serves traditional Albanian cuisine (grills and fish) plus Italian dishes. Sit back on the wrought-iron thrones and check out the tremendous views of Saranda and

Butrint lagoon. A taxi costs about 1000 lekë return; arrange a time for the driver to pick you up. The cheaper Piceri Lekursi (pizza restaurant) operates from the castle's lower tier between May and September.

Pupi (Rr Saranda-Butrint; seafood dishes around 650 lekë; ☻ 9am-midnight) Pupi has an unfortunate name but serves good seafood dishes in a terrace setting with pine trees. It's about 50m from Hotel Grand towards Butrint. Check out the great wall mosaic inside, and in summer take a swim at its private beach.

Getting There & Away

In a stroke of genius, the information centre gives out up-to-date bus timetables. The main bus station is uphill from the synagogue on Rr Vangjel Pando, and taxis wait for customers here and opposite Central Park on Rr Skënderbeu.

Nine regular municipal buses go to Butrint via Ksamil (100 lekë, about 40 minutes), leaving from the information centre and opposite Hotel Butrinti.

Buses to Tirana (1200 lekë, eight hours) leave at 5am, 6.30am, 8.30am, 9.30am and 10.30am, and buses to Gjirokastra (300 lekë, 1½ hours) depart at 6am, 8am, 11am and 1pm; there's one bus to Durrës (900 lekë, seven hours) at 7.30am. Buses to Himara leave at 5.30am, 6am and 2pm, and daily services to Korça leave at 5.30am (1200 lekë, eight hours).

Furgons to Gjirokastra (300 lekë, one hour) and Vlora (via Himara; 600 lekë, six hours) usually leave between 5.30am and 10am.

A taxi to the Greek border at Kakavija will cost 4000 lekë, while a cab to the border near Konispoli will cost around 5000 lekë.

Finikas (☎ 60 57; finikaslines@yahoo.com; Rr Mithat Hoxha) has two boats a day, at 10.30am and 4pm, to Corfu (one way €17.50, including the €2.50 port tax). From Corfu it's €15 for the 90-minute boat trip to Saranda, which leaves at 9am. **Ionian Cruises** (www.ionian-cruises.com) operates a faster, Dolphin boat that departs Corfu at the same time (€17.50, 45 minutes). There's a one-hour time difference between Greece and Albania.

AROUND SARANDA
Butrint

The ancient ruins of **Butrint** (www.butrint.org; admission 700 lekë; ☻ 8am-dusk), 18km south of Saranda, are renowned for their size, beauty and tran-

quillity. They're in a fantastic natural setting and are part of a 29-sq-km national park. Set aside at least three hours to lose yourself and explore this fascinating place.

Although the site had been inhabited long before, Greeks from Corfu settled on the hill in Butrint (Buthrotum) in the 6th century BC. Within a century Butrint had become a fortified trading city with an acropolis. The lower town began to develop in the 3rd century BC, and many large stone buildings had already been built by the time the Romans took over in 167 BC. Butrint's prosperity continued throughout the Roman period, and the Byzantines made it an ecclesiastical centre. The city subsequently went into decline and was abandoned until 1927, when Italian archaeologists arrived. These days Lord Rothschild's UK-based Butrint Foundation helps maintain the site.

As you enter the site the path leads to the right, to Butrint's 3rd-century-BC **Greek theatre**, secluded in the forest below the acropolis. Also in use during the Roman period, the theatre could seat about 2500 people. Close by are the small **public baths**, whose geometric mosaics are buried under a layer of mesh and sand to protect them from the elements.

Deeper in the forest is a wall covered with crisp Greek inscriptions, and the 6th-century palaeo-Christian **baptistery** decorated with colourful mosaics of animals and birds, again under the sand. Beyond are the impressive arches of the 6th-century **basilica**, built over many years. A massive **Cyclopean wall** dating back to the 4th century BC is further on. Over one gate is a relief of a lion killing a bull, symbolic of a protective force vanquishing assailants.

The top of the hill is where the **acropolis** once was. There's now a castle here, housing an informative **museum** (☻ 8am-4pm). The views from the museum's courtyard give you a good idea of the city's layout, and you can see the Vivari Channel connecting Lake Butrint to the Straits of Corfu. There's a community-run shop inside the gates where you can buy locally produced souvenirs.

The local bus from Saranda to Butrint costs 100 lekë. A taxi to Butrint from Saranda will cost around 2000 lekë, and you can usually negotiate to get there and back and see the Blue Eye Spring for 4000 lekë. Saranda-based **Sipa Tours** (☎ 66 75; Rr 1 Maji; www.sipatours.com) arranges local tours for around €30 and can include a

---

WORTH THE TRIP: GJIROKASTRA

Like something from a vampire movie, it's hard to imagine a creepier setting than the stone city of Gjirokastra, shrouded in clouds on its rocky perch and surrounded by savage mountains. Above it all a gloomy, dark castle with a blood-chilling history watches over everything, perpetually guarded by black crows. It's the sort of place where dictators are raised (Enver Hoxha) and young boys dream up dramatic stories and become famous writers (Ismail Kadare, whose *Chronicle in Stone* is set here). In short, it's a thrilling place to spend a day absorbing the life of its steep cobbled streets, where the pace is slow and suspended in the past.

our pick **Hotel Kalemi** (☎ 63 724; draguak@yahoo.com; Lagjia Palorto; r 4000 lekë) is the spot to go an authentic experience of Ottoman Albania. It's a cross between a hotel and an ethnographic museum, with original carved wooden ceilings and stone fireplaces.

Gjirokastra is located 70km northeast of Saranda; the bus here takes 90 minutes and costs 300 lekë.

---

translator, which is useful to get the whole gist of Butrint. Make sure you pick up a written guide to the site from the ticket booth.

Ksamil

Ksamil, 17km south of Saranda, has three small, dreamy islands within swimming distance and dozens of beachside bars and restaurants that open in the summer. To get to the beach, head past the church and take the second right, then first left. You'll pass **Hotel Jon** (☎ 069 209 1554; s/d 1000/1500 lekë) near the roundabout, which is the bar and hotel of choice.

Blue Eye Spring

About 25km east of Saranda, the **Blue Eye Spring** (Syri i Kaltër; admission 50 lekë) is a hypnotic pool of deep-blue water surrounded by electric-blue edges like the iris of an eye. It feeds the Bistrica River and its depth is still unknown. It's a pleasant spot; blue dragonflies dash around the water, and the surrounding shady oak trees make a good picnic spot. If you don't mind a 3km walk, any bus heading between Saranda and Gjirokastra can drop you off at the turn-off to Blue Eye Spring. Otherwise it's only accessible by taxi or on a private tour.

ALBANIA DIRECTORY

ACCOMMODATION

Albania's budget accommodation (doubles €15 to €50) is usually decent and clean; breakfast is sometimes included in the price. Finding people who've partly converted their homes into private accommodation is possible, and backpacker-style hostels are sprouting up in

Tirana, Saranda and Berat. Midrange hotels (doubles €50 to €100) are a notch up, with wi-fi, telephones and evidence of attempts to spruce up the rooms. Top-end hotels (doubles €100 to €270) are mostly on a par with modern European hotels in terms of price, comfort and facilities, and offer fitness centres, satellite TV, internet access and swimming pools.

Hotels line the beaches in Saranda, Durrës and Vlora, while homestays abound in Theth. Most towns have at least a few good hotel or B&B options in most price categories. The local hotel booking company **Albania-hotel .com** (www.albania-hotel.com) is a reliable resource for new lodgings.Camping is possible in the south and sometimes on deserted beaches.

Prices given in this chapter include private bathroom unless otherwise stated.

ACTIVITIES

The further south you get, the better the swimming is. South of Vlora the sandy Adriatic gives it up for its rockier Ionian counterpart, but it's much more picturesque. You can go birdwatching around Lezha, Velipoja and the Drin delta and hiking in Mt Dajti National Park. For challenging hiking, find a local guide and try Theth. Hiking and adventure sports are in their infancy in Albania, and the leaders are the team at Outdoor Albania (p50). A few Berat operatives run hiking tours to Mt Tomorri National Park. Cyclists: get motivated. There are more than a few two-wheeled adventurers carving up the countryside.

BOOKS

For a helpful list of Albanian words and phrases, check out the *Mediterranean Europe Phrasebook* from Lonely Planet. *Colloquial*

Albanian (2007) by Isa Zymberi is a good teach-yourself language course accompanied by a CD.

The Albanians: A Modern History (1999), by Miranda Vickers, is a comprehensive and very readable history of Albania from the time of Ottoman rule to the restoration of democracy after 1990.

James Pettifer's *Albania and Kosovo Blue Guide* (2001) is a thoroughly informed source for Albanian history and a good guide of things to see.

Albania: From Anarchy to a Balkan Identity (1999) by Miranda Vickers and James Pettifer covers the tumultuous 1990s in great detail, while managing to convey a sense of the confusion Albania faced as it shed its communist past.

Biografi (1993) by New Zealander Lloyd Jones (also author of *Mr Pip*) is a rather arresting story set in post-1990 Albania: a semi-factual account of the writer's quest to find the alleged double of former communist dictator Enver Hoxha.

Rumpalla: Rummaging Through Albania (2002) by Peter Lucas is a personal account of Albania before and after the revolution by this American journalist of Albanian descent.

The Best of Albanian Cooking (1999) by Klementina Hysa and R John Hysa is one of scant few books on Albanian cuisine and contains a wide range of family recipes.

High Albania (published in 1909 and reprinted in 2000), written by Albania's 'honorary citizen' Edith Durham, recounts the author's experiences in northern Albania in the early 20th century.

The Accursed Mountains (1999) is written by a seemingly miserable Robert Carver, who doesn't have many nice things to say about his journey through Albania in 1996.

Black Lambs and Grey Falcons (1991; edited by John B Allcock and Antonia Young) is a collection of stories by women writers who travelled through the Balkans.

BUSINESS HOURS

Most offices open at 8am and close around 5pm. Shops usually open at 8am and close around 7pm, though some close for a siesta from noon to 4pm, and then stay open till 8pm. Banking hours are shorter (generally 9am to 3.30pm). Restaurants, cafes and bars are usually open from 8am and stay open until midnight or later.

COURSES

The **Lincoln Centre** (Map p48; ☎ 2230 880; www.lincoln-intl.org; Rr Qemal Stafa 184, Tirana) runs Albanian language courses. Private tutorial is another way of picking up the language, so if you're keen, stop by the secretariat office of the University of Europe on the Lana River and ask for students who can teach Albanian.

DANGERS & ANNOYANCES

Albania is a relatively safe country to travel around, although locals suggest it's best to travel with a local guide to Bajram Curri and Tropoja in the far north, and in the area around Theth. There are still landmines near the northern border with Kosovo, though these are being removed.

There isn't a hard-core drinking culture here so it's almost unheard of to be bailed up by drunks after dark. Take the usual precautions of avoiding rowdy demonstrations, and beware of pickpockets on crowded city buses. The most serious risk is on the roads – Albania has a high traffic accident rate. Other dangers are the ripped-up pavements, ditches and missing manhole covers – watch your step! Packs of dogs are an issue; take particular care around castles.

To avoid being overcharged, travellers who've just entered Albania from Montenegro should know the real price for a *furgon* trip to Tirana is 400 lekë. Sometimes it pays to show taxi drivers how much you will pay, as mysterious things can happen with the number '0', and a taxi ride may cost 3000 instead of the 300 you thought you had negotiated (and even, perhaps, written down).

As Albania was closed off for so long, black travellers may encounter some curious stares; in fact, most visitors to Albania can expect a certain amount of curiosity.

There are risks in drinking tap water and local milk; plenty of bottled water and imported UHT milk is available. The standard of health care in Albania is variable: local hospitals and clinics are understaffed and underfunded, but pharmacies are good.

EMBASSIES & CONSULATES

There are no Australian, New Zealand or Irish embassies in Albania. The following embassies and consulates are in Tirana (Map p48; area code ☎ 042):

France (☎ 2234 054; ambafrance.tr@adanet.com.al; Rr Skënderbej 14)

Germany (☎ 2274 505; www.tirana.diplo.de; Rr Skënderbej 8)
Greece (☎ 2274 670; gremb.tir@mfa.gr; Rr Frederik Shiroka 3)
Italy (☎ 2275 900; www.ambtirana.esteri.it; Rr Lek Dukagjini 2)
Macedonia (☎ 2230 909; makambas@albnet.net; Rr e Kavajës 116)
Netherlands (☎ 2240 828; www.mfa.nl/tir; Rr Asim Zeneli 10)
Serbia (☎ 2232 091; www.tirana.mfa.gov.yu; Rr Donika Kastrioti 9/1)
UK (☎ 2234 973; www.uk.al; Rr Skënderbej 12)
USA (☎ 2247 285; http://tirana.usembassy.gov; Rr Elbasanit 103)

GAY & LESBIAN TRAVELLERS

Gay and lesbian life in Albania is alive and well but is not yet organised into out clubs or organisations. It's no problem to be foreign and affectionate with your same-sex partner in the street, but keep in mind that no couples are overly demonstrative in public in Albania so any public sexual behaviour beyond holding hands and kissing will be a spectacle. Gaydar will serve gay and lesbian visitors well here: you'll have to ask on the street where the parties are. The alternative music and party scene is queer friendly.

HOLIDAYS

New Year's Day 1 January
Summer Day 14 March
Nevruz 22 March
Catholic Easter March or April
Orthodox Easter March or April
May Day 1 May
Bajram i Madh September
Mother Teresa Day 19 October
Bajram i Vogël November
Independence Day 28 November
Liberation Day 29 November
Christmas Day 25 December

MEDIA

A diverse range of newspapers is printed in Tirana; *Shekulli* is the largest daily paper.

The *Albanian Daily News* is a fairly dry English-language publication that has useful information on happenings around Albania. It's generally available from major hotels for 300 lekë.

The weekly *Tirana Times* is 350 lekë from central street kiosks. Despite many of the articles being about the same topic

(with a different perspective), it has some interesting features.

Foreign newspapers and magazines, including the *Times,* the *International Herald Tribune* and the *Economist,* are sold at most major hotels and some central street kiosks, though they tend to be a few days old.

The BBC World Service can be picked up in and around Tirana on 103.9FM, while the Voice of America's mainly music program is on 107.4FM.

MONEY
ATMs

A variety of ATMs can be found in most towns and cities, except for villages like Theth and Dhërmi. ATMs frequently offer currency in euros or lekë. The main networks are Alpha Bank, Raiffeisen Bank, American Bank of Albania, Pro Credit Bank and Tirana Bank.

Credit Cards

Credit cards are accepted only in the larger hotels and travel agencies, and in only a handful of establishments outside Tirana. Major banks can offer credit-card advances.

Currency

Albanian banknotes come in denominations of 100, 200, 500, 1000 and 5000 lekë. There are five, 10, 20, 50 and 100 lekë coins. In 1964 the currency was revalued 10 times; prices on occasion may still be quoted at the old rate (3000 lekë instead of 300). Happily, if you hand over 3000 lekë you will probably be handed 2700 lekë in change.

Everything in Albania can be paid for with lekë, but most of the hotel prices are quoted in euros. Day trippers from Corfu can rely on euros, though they won't get a good exchange rate.

You will not be able to change Albanian lekë outside of the country, so exchange them or spend them before you leave.

Moneychangers

Every town has its free-currency market, which usually operates on the street in front of the main post office or state bank. Such transactions are not dangerous or illegal and it all takes place quite openly, but make sure you count the money twice before tendering yours. The advantages are that you get a good rate and avoid the 1% bank commission. Currency-exchange businesses in major

ALBANIA

towns are usually open 8am to 6pm and closed on Sundays.

Travellers Cheques

Travellers cheques are about as practical and useful here as a dead albatross, though you can change them at Rogner Hotel Europapark Tirana and at major banks in Tirana. Some banks will change US-dollar travellers cheques into US cash without commission. Travellers cheques (euro and US dollar) can be used at a few top-end hotels, but cash (euro or lekë) is preferred everywhere.

POST

Outside of main towns there are few public postboxes, but there is an increasing number of post offices around the country where you can hand in your mail directly (whether they have stamps is another matter). Sending a postcard overseas costs around 60 lekë, while a letter costs 80 to 160 lekë. The postal system is fairly rudimentary – there are no postcodes, for example – and it does not enjoy a reputation for efficiency. Don't rely on sending or receiving parcels through Albapost.

RESPONSIBLE TRAVEL

You'll get fed up with the amount of active littering that you'll see, and litter you have to negotiate around, whether on the beach or walking down the street. Lead by example. Lake Ohrid trout is endangered, and travellers should resist buying it. Buying locally produced beer and wine supports the local economy.

TELEPHONE & FAX

Long-distance telephone calls made from main post offices (Albtelecom) are cheap, costing about 90 lekë a minute to Italy. Calls to the USA cost 230 lekë per minute. Calls from private phone offices are horribly expensive, though – 800 lekë per minute to Australia, for example. Albania's country phone code is ☎ 355. For domestic directory enquiries call ☎ 124; international directory assistance is ☎ 12. Faxing can be done from the main post office in Tirana for the same cost as phone calls, or from major hotels, though they will charge more.

Mobile Phones

The three established mobile-phone providers are Vodafone, AMC and Eagle, and a fourth

EMERGENCY NUMBERS

- Ambulance ☎ 127
- Fire ☎ 128
- Police ☎ 129

licence has been promised. Nearly all populated areas of the country are covered, though the networks can become congested. Prepaid SIM cards cost around 1000 lekë and usually include credit. Mobile tariffs are roughly 45 to 60 lekë a minute nationally, and 200 to 245 lekë a minute to Zone 4 areas (including USA, Australia and Japan). International texts are 20 lekë. You can also check to see if a roaming agreement exists with your home service provider. Numbers begin with ☎ 067, ☎ 068 or ☎ 069. To call an Albanian mobile number from abroad, dial ☎ 355 then either ☎ 67, ☎ 68 or ☎ 69 (ie drop the 0).

TOILETS

Carry toilet paper with you and expect the occasional squat toilet.

TOURIST INFORMATION

Tourist information offices operate in Saranda, Gjirokastra, Berat and Korça, and hotel reception or travel agencies also assist with information. You can buy city maps of Tirana in bookshops, and maps of Vlora, Saranda, Gjirokastra, Durrës and Shkodra from the respective town's travel agencies or hotels.

TRAVELLERS WITH DISABILITIES

There are few special facilities for travellers in wheelchairs, and footpaths are not wheelchair friendly. Tirana's top hotels cater to people with disabilities, however. The roads and castle entrances in Gjirokastra, Berat and Kruja are cobblestone, although taxis can get reasonably close to the action.

VISAS

No visa is required by citizens of EU countries or nationals of Australia, Canada, New Zealand, Japan, South Korea, Norway, South Africa or the USA. Travellers from other countries should check www.mfa.gov.al. Citizens of all countries – even those entering visa-free – will be required to pay €1 to enter the country, or €10 if arriving at Tirana Airport. Israeli citizens pay €30.

WOMEN TRAVELLERS

Albania is quite a safe country for women travellers, but outside Tirana it is mainly men who go out and sit in bars and cafes in the evenings. While they are not threatening, it may feel strange to be the only woman in a bar. It's extremely unlikely that you'll be involved, but be aware that Albania is a source country for people trafficking.

TRANSPORT IN ALBANIA

GETTING THERE & AWAY
Air

Albania's international airport is the recently renovated **Nënë Tereza International Airport** (Mother Teresa Airport or Rinas airport), 26km northwest of Tirana. There are no domestic flights within Albania. The following airlines fly to and from Albania:

Adria Airways (JP; ☎ 04-2272 666; www.adri.si)
Bulgaria Air (FB; ☎ 04-2230 410; www.air.bg)
Jat Airways (JU; ☎ 04-2251 033; www.jat.com)
Malév Hungarian Airlines (MA; ☎ 04-2234 163; www.malev.hu)

Land

There are no passenger trains into Albania, so your border-crossing options are buses, *furgons*, taxis or walking to a border and picking up transport on the other side.

BUSES

From Tirana, regular buses head to Pristina, Kosovo; to Struga, Tetovo and Skopje in Macedonia; and to Athens and Thessaloniki in Greece (p52). *Furgons* and buses leave Shkodra (p55) for Montenegro and Kosovo, and buses head to ethnic Albanian towns in Macedonia from Durrës and southern coastal towns in July and August. Buses travel to Greece from most Albanian towns; buses to Italy leave from Vlora (p62).

CAR & MOTORCYCLE

To enter Albania, you'll need a Green Card (proof of third-party insurance, issued by your insurer); check that your insurance covers Albania.

The two main crossings between Albania and Kosovo are at Qafë Morina between Kukës and Prizren, and Qafë Prush. The popularity of the Lake Koman car ferry means you're unlikely to be alone on the drive to Qafë Prush.

For Macedonia, the two best crossings are on either side of Lake Ohrid. The southern crossing is at Tushëmisht/Sveti Naum, 29km south of Ohrid; the northern crossing is at Qafë e Thanës, between Struga and Pogradec. However, there are sometimes delays at Qafë e Thanës due to trucks.

At the time of writing there are two border crossings between Albania and Macedonia, one at Han i Hotit (between Shkodra and Podgorica) and another at Muriqan (between Ulcinj and Shkodra).

TAXI

Heading to Macedonia, taxis from Pogradec will drop you off just before the border at Tushëmisht/Sveti Naum. Alternatively, it's an easy 4km to the border from Pogradec.

Sea

A few ferries a day ply the route between Saranda and Corfu (p64), and frequent ferries leave for Italy from Vlora (p62) and Durrës (p58).

GETTING AROUND
Bicycle

Cycling in Albania is tough but certainly doable. Expect lousy road conditions including open drains, some abysmal driving from fellow road-sharers and roads that are not really roads (eg the road to Theth). Organised groups head north for mountain biking, and cyclists are even spotted cycling the long and tough Korça–Gjirokastra road. Shkodra is one of the few places you'll see the locals embracing the two-wheeled beast.

Bus

Albanians travel around their country in private minivans called *furgons* or in buses. These run fairly frequently throughout the day, though peak time is in the morning, and services are usually a distant memory by 2pm. Buses to Tirana depart from towns all around Albania at the crack of dawn. The fares are low (eg Tirana–Durrës costs 150 lekë), and you pay the conductor on board (don't expect a ticket).

Municipal buses operate in Tirana, Durrës, Shkodra and Vlora, and trips usually cost 30 lekë. Watch your possessions.

Car & Motorcycle

Albania's drivers are not the best in the world, mostly due to the communist era, when car ownership required a permit from the government, and only two were issued to nonparty members. As a result, the government didn't invest in new roads, and most Albanians were inexperienced motorists. Nowadays the road infrastructure is improving, especially on the routes from the Macedonian border to Dhërmi; from Durrës to Korça, and on the stretch from Fier to Gjirokastra.

If you're keen to drive, spend a few hours in a taxi first so you can see what conditions to expect. Off the main routes a 4WD is a good idea. Driving at night is particularly hazardous, and driving on mountain 'roads' at any time is a whole new field of extreme sport. Cars, *furgons,* trucks and buses *do* go off the edge.

There is no national automobile association in Albania as yet.

DRIVING LICENCE

Foreign driving licences are permitted, but it is recommended to have an International Driving Permit as well. Car-hire agencies usually require that you have held a full licence for one year.

FUEL & SPARE PARTS

There are plenty of petrol stations in the cities and increasing numbers in the country. Unleaded fuel is available along all major highways, but fill up before driving into the mountainous regions. A litre of unleaded petrol costs 170 lekë, while diesel costs 160 lekë. There isn't yet a highly developed network of mechanics and repair shops capable of sourcing parts for all types of vehicles, but if you're driving an old Mercedes-Benz there will be parts galore.

HIRE

There are four car-hire companies operating out of Tirana: Avis, Europcar, Hertz and Sixt (see p53). Hiring a small car costs from €35 per day.

ROAD RULES

Drinking and driving is forbidden, and there is zero tolerance for blood-alcohol readings. Both motorcyclists and passengers must wear helmets. Speed limits are as low as 30km per hour in built-up areas and 35km per hour on the edges. Keep your car's papers with you as police are active paper-checkers.

Train

Albanians prefer bus and *furgon* travel, and when you see the speed and the state of the (barely) existing trains, you'll know why. However, the trains are dirt cheap and travelling on them is an adventure. Daily passenger trains leave Tirana (p53) for Durrës, Shkodra, Fier, Vlora, Elbasan and a few kilometres out of Pogradec. Check timetables at the station in person, and buy your ticket 10 minutes before departure.

Belarus Беларусь

Europe's outcast, Belarus lies at the edge of Eastern Europe and seems determined to avoid integration with the rest of the continent at all costs; taking its lead from the Soviet Union rather than the European Union. Yet this lies at the heart of its appeal – while the rest of Eastern Europe has charged headlong into capitalism, Belarus offers a chance to visit a Europe with almost no advertising, litter or graffiti. Far more than just the 'last dictatorship in Europe' – Condoleezza Rice's phrase has come to haunt Alexander Lukashenko's democratically challenged country – Belarus is a land of earthy humour, friendly people and courage in the face of bleak political adversity. Outside the capital, Belarus offers a simple yet pleasing landscape of cornflower fields, thick primeval forests and picturesque villages. While travellers will always be subject to curiosity, they'll invariably also be on the receiving end of extremely warm hospitality.

While the country's flattening in WWII means that there's relatively little of historic interest to see, Belarus' three most appealing cities – Minsk, Brest and Vitsebsk – offer a surprising amount to visitors – from nightlife and cosmopolitan spark in the capital, to the tragic remnants of the Brest Fortress, and the childhood home of painter Marc Chagall in Vitsebsk. The country also offers two excellent national parks, both well worth a visit. Europe's largest mammal, the zoobr, or European bison, can be seen at Belavezhskaya Pushcha National Park, while the Pripyatsky National Park, the 'lungs of Europe', offers great birdwatching in its vast wetlands.

FAST FACTS

- **Area** 207,600 sq km
- **Capital** Minsk
- **Currency** Belarusian rouble (BR); €1 = BR3780; US$1 = BR2773; UK£1 = BR4012; A$1 = BR1916; ¥100 = BR2894; NZ$1 = BR1555
- **Famous for** president Lukashenko, bearing the brunt of Chornobyl, being a 'Soviet time capsule'
- **Official languages** Belarusian and Russian
- **Phrases** dobry dzyen (hello); kalee laska (please); dzyahkooee (thanks)
- **Population** 10 million
- **Telephone codes** country code ☎ 375; international access code ☎ 810
- **Visa** required by nearly all visitors; see p95

BELARUS

HIGHLIGHTS

- Enjoy 'communism with cappuccino' in the trendy cafes of **Minsk** (p76).
- Spot a European bison, a brown bear or a wolf while deep inside the primeval **Belavezhskaya Pushcha National Park** (p90).
- Stroll through the mellow pedestrian streets of cosmopolitan Brest to the epic WWII memorial that is **Brest Fortress** (p88).
- Discover the charming childhood home of painter Marc Chagall in the old city of **Vitsebsk** (p91).

ITINERARIES

Belarusian cities and towns are not packed with tourist attractions, so you can count on each of these itineraries feeling rather leisurely.

- **Three days** Spend two days getting to know Minsk and then take a day trip to Dudutki and Mir to get a feel for the countryside.
- **One week** Begin with two nights in Brest, including a day trip to the Belavezhskaya Pushcha National Park, then take a train to Minsk and follow the three-day itinerary there before continuing on to historic Vitsebsk.

CLIMATE & WHEN TO GO

Belarus has a continental climate. Average January temperatures are between -4°C and -8°C, with frosts experienced for five to six months of the year. The warmest month is July, when temperatures can reach up to 30°C, but the average temperature is 18°C. June and August are the wettest months.

Since Belarus is not visited by many tourists, you won't have to worry about when to go to beat the crowds. If you don't mind cold

---

CONNECTIONS: MOVING ON FROM BELARUS

Belarus has excellent overland links to all its neighbouring countries. Daily trains from Minsk serve Moscow, St Petersburg, Vilnius, Warsaw (via Terespol) and Kyiv; see p85 for more detail. Bus services, which tend to be less comfortable, connect Minsk to Moscow, St Petersburg, Kyiv, Warsaw and Vilnius; Vitsebsk (p93) to Moscow and St Petersburg; and Brest to Terespol in Poland.

HOW MUCH?

- Ride on the Minsk metro BR600
- 500mL Belavezhskaya (herbal firewater) BR6000
- Straw doll BR6000 to BR14,000
- Plate of draniki (potato pancakes) BR4000
- Souvenir Lukashenko poster BR1000

LONELY PLANET INDEX

- 1L petrol BR2230
- 1L bottled water BR600
- Beer (Krynitsa) BR1000
- Street snack (hot dog) BR6000

---

weather, the snowy winters can be very pretty, especially on sunny days.

HISTORY
Arrival of the Slavs

Evidence of a human presence in Belarus goes back to the early Stone Age. Eastern Slavs from the Krivichi, Dregovichi and Radimichi tribes arrived here in the 6th to 8th centuries AD. The principalities of Polatsk (first mentioned in 862), Turau (980), Pinsk and Minsk were formed, all falling under the suzerainty of Prince Vladimir's Kyivan Rus by the late 10th century. The economy was based on slash-and-burn agriculture, honey farming and river trade, particularly on the Dnyapro River (Dnepr in Russian), a vital link between Byzantium and the Nordic Varangians.

Lithuanian & Polish Control

Belarus means 'White Russia', a name determined by the fact that it is the one part of Rus that, while conquered by the Mongols in 1240, was never settled by them. The term 'white' refers therefore to the purity of the people, who unlike their Muscovite cousins, never intermarried.

In the 14th century, the territory of modern-day Belarus became part of the Grand Duchy of Lithuania. It was to be 400 years before Belarus came under Russian control, a period in which Belarusians became linguistically and culturally differentiated from the Russians to their east and the Ukrainians to their south.

After Lithuania became Roman Catholic following the uniting of its crown with Poland's in 1386, the Belarusian peasantry remained Orthodox but were reduced to serf status. Lithuania nonetheless permitted its subjects a fair degree of autonomy, even using Belarusian as its state language during the early 15th century – an important fact for patriotic Belarusians today as proof of their historical legitimacy. All official correspondence, literature, doctrines and statutes at the time were written in Belarusian.

In 1596 the Polish authorities arranged the Union of Brest, which set up the Uniate Church (also known as Ukrainian Catholic or Greek Catholic), bringing much of the Orthodox Church in Belarus under the authority of the Vatican. The Uniate Church insisted on the pope's supremacy and Catholic doctrine, but permitted Orthodox forms of ritual.

Over the next two centuries of Polish rule, Poles and Jews controlled trade and most Belarusians remained peasants. Only after the three Partitions of Poland (1772, 1793 and 1795–96) was Belarus absorbed into Russia.

Tsarist Rule

Under Russian rule, a policy of Russification was pursued, and in 1839 the Uniate Church was abolished, with most Belarusians returning to Orthodoxy. The Russian rulers and the Orthodox Church regarded Belarus as 'western Russia' and tried to obliterate any sense of a Belarusian nationality. Publishing in the Belarusian language was banned.

The economy slowly developed in the 19th century with the emergence of small industries such as timber-milling, glass-making and boat-building. However industrial progress lagged behind that of Russia, and poverty in the countryside remained at such a high level that 1.5 million people – largely the wealthy or educated – emigrated in the 50 years before the Russian Revolution in 1917, mostly to Siberia or the USA.

During the 19th century, Belarus was part of the Pale of Settlement, the area where Jews in the Russian Empire were required to settle. The percentage of Jews in many Belarusian cities and towns before WWII was between 35% and 75%. The vast majority of Belarusians remained on the land, poor and illiterate. Due to their cultural stagnation, their absence from positions of influence and their historical domination by Poles and Russians, any sense among Belarusian speakers that they were a distinct nationality was very slow to emerge. Nonetheless, Belarusian intellectuals were part of a wave of nationalism across Europe and it was in the 19th century that the concept of Belarusians as a distinct people first emerged.

World Wars & the Soviet Union
In March 1918, under German occupation during WWI, a short-lived independent Belarusian Democratic Republic was declared, but the land was soon under the control of the Red Army, and the Belarusian Soviet Socialist Republic (BSSR) was formed. The 1921 Treaty of Rīga allotted roughly the western half of modern Belarus to Poland, which launched a program of Polonisation that provoked armed resistance by Belarusians. The eastern half was left to the Bolsheviks, and the redeclared BSSR was a founding member of the USSR in 1922.

In the 1920s the Soviet regime encouraged Belarusian literature and culture, but in the 1930s under Stalin, nationalism and the Belarusian language were discouraged and their proponents ruthlessly persecuted. The 1930s also saw industrialisation, agricultural collectivisation, and purges in which hundreds of thousands were executed – most in the Kurapaty Forest, outside Minsk.

In September 1939 the Red Army seized western Belarus from Poland. When Nazi Germany invaded Russia in 1941, Belarus was on the front line and suffered greatly.

German occupation was savage and partisan resistance widespread until the Red Army drove the Germans out in 1944, with massive destruction on both sides. Hundreds of villages were destroyed, and barely a stone was left standing in Minsk. At least 25% of the Belarusian population (over two million people) died between 1939 and 1945. Many of them, Jews and others, died in 200-plus concentration camps; the third-largest Nazi concentration camp was set up at Maly Trostenets, outside Minsk, where over 200,000 people were executed.

Western Belarus remained in Soviet hands at the end of the war, with Minsk developing into the industrial hub of western USSR and Belarus becoming one of the Soviet Union's most prosperous republics.

The 1986 Chornobyl disaster (p926), just over the border in Ukraine, was most profoundly felt by the people of Belarus. The radiation cloud released left about a quarter of the country seriously contaminated, and its effects are still felt today, particularly in the southeastern regions of the country.

Post-Soviet Belarus
On 27 July 1990, the republic issued a declaration of sovereignty within the USSR. On 25 August 1991 a declaration of full national independence was issued. With no history whatsoever as a politically or economically independent entity, the country of Belarus was one of the oddest products of the disintegration of the USSR.

Since July 1994 Belarus has been governed by Alexander Lukashenko, a former collective-farm director, from which his derogatory nickname, Kolkhozni (a member of a collective farm owned by the communist state), is derived; his favourable nickname is Bat'ka (Papa). His presidential style has been seen by many as autocratic and authoritarian, and the country was declaimed an 'outpost of tyranny' by US Secretary of State Condoleezza Rice. Lukashenko has on several occasions altered the constitution (using referenda widely regarded in the West as illegitimate), rendering the parliament essentially toothless and extending both his term and the number of times he can campaign for president. Media distribution is handled by the state, so independently produced publications are easily quashed. Online publications are all that is left for independent Belarusian media, and even those are on shaky ground as internet access remains state controlled, and antigovernment sites are easily blocked.

On 19 March 2006, Lukashenko officially won another five-year term as president, with 83% of the vote and 98% voter turnout. However, newspapers such as the *Guardian* have claimed that his opponents – the most popular being European-styled Alexander Milinkevich – were harassed and deprived of public venues throughout the campaign. On the night of the 19th, thousands of protesters turned out on the city's main square for what was being termed as the Denim Revolution – a 'mini-maydan' echoing what happened in Kyiv 1½ years earlier. A peaceful tent city started, and hundreds of people, mostly students, withstood freezing temperatures for almost a week. But once the international media left the scene to cover Ukrainian parliamentary elections, protesters were beaten and arrested by riot police.

Since then, Lukashenko has tightened his grip on power, and Amnesty International reports that democracy activists continue to be harassed and arrested. Many Belarusians reject foreign criticism of their political system, however, citing the stability and relative economic prosperity that Belarus has enjoyed compared with many post-Soviet states.

Yet Russian hikes in the historically low gas prices it sets for Belarus are likely to change things in the near future. Putin and Lukashenko, rumoured to hate each other on a personal level, have nevertheless enjoyed a useful anti-European partnership for the past decade. But as the cheap gas supplies dry up, Lukashenko has been courting the EU in a bid to increase its bargaining position with Russia.

Despite some nearly miniscule reforms in Minsk, such as the release of certain political prisoners designed to placate the EU in 2008, parliamentary elections held shortly afterwards saw all 110 seats going to Lukashenko loyalists. The elections were again declared unfair by observers and, for the time being at least, Belarus remains isolated on the edge of the EU.

PEOPLE

There are approximately 10 million people in Belarus, of which 81.2% are Belarusian, 11.4% Russian, 4% Polish and 2.4% Ukrainian, with the remaining 1% consisting of other groups. This results in a rather homogeneous population. Prior to WWII, 10% of the national population was Jewish, and in cities like Minsk, Hrodna and Brest Jews made up between one-third and three-quarters of the population. They now make up about 0.3% of the country's population.

Generally speaking, Belarusians are quiet, polite and reserved people. Because they tend to be shy, they seem less approachable than Russians and Ukrainians, but they are just as friendly and generous (probably more so) once introductions are made.

RELIGION

Atheism is widespread. Of believers, 80% are Eastern Orthodox and 20% are Roman Catholic (about 15% of the Catholics are ethnic Poles). During the early 1990s the Uniate Church (an Orthodox sect that looks to Rome, not Moscow) was re-established and now it has a following of over 100,000 members. There's also a small Protestant minority, the remnant of a once-large German population.

ARTS

Assumed by many to be Russian or French, surrealist painter Marc Chagall (1887–1985) was actually born and grew up in Belarus and is by far the country's best known artist. Born to a Jewish family in a village near Vitsebsk in 1887, Chagall lived and trained there before moving to St Petersburg aged 20 and then Paris in the 1930s to set the world alight with his surrealist images and trademark flying people. His family home is now a small museum (see p91), although there are very few Chagalls in evidence anywhere in Belarus today – the Soviet government clearly didn't think much of his work, refusing multiple offers of canvases from the artist during his lifetime.

The hero of early Belarusian literary achievement was Francysk Skaryna. Born in Polatsk but educated in Poland and Italy, the scientist, doctor, writer and humanist became the first person to translate the Bible into Belarusian. He also built the first printing press in the country. In the late 16th century the philosopher and humanist Symon Budny printed a number of works in Belarusian. The 19th century saw the beginning of modern Belarusian literature with works by writers

BELARUS

and poets such as Maxim Bohdanovich, Janka Kupala and Jakub Kolas.

The band Pesnyary have been extremely popular since the 1960s for putting a modern twist on traditional Belarusian folk music. Acclaimed Belarusian rock bands include Lyapis Trubetskoi and NRM. The Soviet Union's answer to Elton John, Boris Moiseev, was born in a prison in Mogilev, Belarus, even though, like most modern Belarusian acts, he sings in Russian. There's a surprisingly strong vein of Belarusian rap that came to prominence in the 1990s, with underground crew Udar Bandy. Their decade-long silence was broken in 2007 when they came back under the name Da Joint.

ENVIRONMENT

It's safe to say that Belarus does not enjoy a wildly exciting geography. It's a flat country, consisting of low ridges dividing broad, often marshy lowlands with more than 11,000 lakes. In the south are the Pripet Marshes, Europe's largest marsh area, dubbed locally the 'lungs of Europe' because air currents passing over it are re-oxygenated and purified by the swamps. Around 6.4% of Belarusian land is protected.

Because of the vast expanses of primeval forests and marshes, Belarusian fauna abounds. The most celebrated animal is the zoobr (European bison), the continent's largest land mammal. It was hunted almost to extinction by 1919, but was fortunately bred back into existence from 52 animals that had survived in zoos. Now several hundred exist, mainly in the Belavezhskaya Pushcha National Park (p90), a Unesco World Heritage site. It is the oldest wildlife refuge in Europe, the pride of Belarus and the most famous of the country's five national parks. The *pushcha* (wild forest) went from obscurity to the front page in late 1991 as the presidents of Belarus, Russia and Ukraine signed the death certificate of the USSR – a document creating the Commonwealth of Independent States (CIS) – at the Viskuli dacha here.

Trips to Belarusian national parks and biosphere reserves, including arranged activities and camping or hotel stays, are possible; contact a tourist agency (p79) in Minsk for all but the Belavezhskaya, which is best arranged with Brest agencies (p87).

The 1986 disaster at Chornobyl has been the defining event for the Belarusian environment. The dangers of exposure to radiation for travellers, particularly in the areas covered in this guide, are almost nonexistent. Ironically, the exclusion zone has proved a boon for nature – the absence of human habitation seems to have done more to improve biodiversity than a nuclear explosion appears to have done to damage it. For more about Chornobyl, see p926.

FOOD & DRINK

Belarusian cuisine rarely differs from Russian cuisine (see p752), although there are a few uniquely Belarusian dishes. *Draniki* are the Belarusian version of *olad'i* (potato pancakes); *kolduni* are potato dumplings stuffed with meat; and *kletsky* are dumplings stuffed with mushrooms, cheese or potato. *Manchanka* are pancakes served with meat gravy.

Belavezhskaya is a bitter herbal alcoholic drink. Of the Belarusian vodkas, Charodei is probably the most esteemed (but can be hard to find). Other popular souvenir-quality vodkas are Belarus Sineokaya and Minskaya. Beer is a much-loved drink in Belarus too. Local brews are decent, although most bars now serve imported lager from the EU.

Although the cuisine is largely meat-based, and although the concept of vegetarianism is not exactly widespread, it is possible to find some dishes without meat, although eating vegan will be considerably more difficult.

Restaurants and bars usually open around 10am and, with unfortunately few exceptions, close between 10pm and midnight. There is no nationwide ban on smoking, though most bars and restaurants have nonsmoking areas.

MINSK МIHCK

☎ 017 / pop 1.73 million

Minsk will almost certainly surprise you. The capital of Belarus is, despite its thoroughly dreary-sounding name, an amazingly progressive and modern place. Here fashionable cafes, wi-fi-enabled restaurants and crowded bars and nightclubs vie for your attention. Sushi bars and art galleries have taken up residence in a city centre totally remodelled to the tastes of Stalin. Despite the strong police presence and obedient citizenry, scrape the surface and you'll find that there's more than a whiff of rebellion in the air.

Totally razed to the ground in WWII, Minsk is an ideological statement wrought in stone and cement. With almost no buildings remaining from the pre-war years, there are relatively few traditional sights in the city. Instead though, there are myriad places of interest for anyone fascinated by the Soviet period, and plenty of cosmopolitan pursuits to keep you entertained come the evening.

ORIENTATION

Minsk's main thoroughfare, pr Nezalezhnastsi, stretches over 11km from the train station to the outer city limits. The most interesting section is between the stubbornly austere and huge pl Nezalezhnastsi and pl Peramohi – this strip forms the city centre. The Svislach River wends its way across the city from the northwest to the southeast.

INFORMATION
Bookshops
Tsentralnaya Kniharnya (☎ 227 4918; pr Nezalezhnastsi 19) Large and central, this bookshop offers the city's best range of books, including a small section in English.

Internet Access
Free wi-fi can be had in top-end hotels (buy a coffee in the lobby and try to look like a guest) or at X-Ray (p83) and News Café (p83). The best internet cafes include the following:
Internet Café (3rd fl, Train Station; ☽ 9am-7am) Usefully located club in the city's new railway station.
Soyuz Online (☎ 226 0279; www.soyuzoline.by; 2nd fl, vul Krasnaarmeyskaya 3; prices vary; ☽ 24hr) Large internet cafe in the centre of town. Food and drinks available. Go up the steps to the Dom Ofitserov and enter the far door near the tank monument.
Virus Internet Club (cnr pr Masherava & vul Chirvonaya; per hr BR3000; ☽ 24hr)

Internet Resources
Minsk in Your Pocket (inyourpocket.com) Has a free Minsk guide download, which is regularly updated; it's also available in hard copy from many hotels.

What's on in Minsk (www.whatsoninminsk.com) A new English-language website devoted to the city, with useful listings and tonnes of insider information.

Laundry
Most hotels offer laundry services; if you're renting an apartment, most places will have a machine. Cheap laundry service is available at **Prachechnaya** (vul Berestyanskaya 1; ☽ 9am-5.30pm Mon-Fri).

Left Luggage
Hotels will hold your baggage for several hours after you check out.
Train station (lockers BR500, luggage room BR1000; ☽ 24hr) Downstairs is a well-signed place, with a fiendishly complex system. To use the lockers, put your stuff in an empty one, select a code on the inside of the door, put a token in, shut the door. Use your second token to open the locker again. Ask staff to help if you're confused (you probably will be) – or pay a little extra to use the luggage room.

Medical Services
24-hour Pharmacy (☎ 227 4844; pr Nezalezhnastsi 16)
EcoMedservices (☎ 207 7474; www.ems.by; vul Tolstoho 4; ☽ 8am-9pm) The closest thing to a reliable, Western-style clinic. Dental services are offered here too.

Money
ATMs can be found throughout the city. Many but not all ATMs offer US dollars or euros, if for some reason you need foreign currency (don't take out dollars or euros just to change them to roubles though; you'll pay the exchange rate twice). Hotels all have exchange bureaus, and a handful cash travellers cheques.

Post
DHL and UPS have offices based in the major hotels, including Hotel Yubileiny (p81) and Hotel Oktyabrsky (p81).

MINSK IN TWO DAYS

Take in Minsk's extraordinary architectural heritage by strolling down Stalinist pr Nezalezhnastsi, stopping to see the **Museum of the Great Patriotic War** (p80) and finishing up at **Gurman** (p82) for the best *pelmeni* (Russian-style ravioli) you'll probably ever eat. Walking back into the city centre, stop off to visit the **Traetskae Pradmestse** (p80) and the **Island of Courage & Sorrow** (p80). That evening, enjoy some excellent traditional Belarusian fare at **Strawnya Talaka** (p82), then cross the street to **Rakovsky Brovar** (p82) for some killer home brews.

On day two, leave the city and visit **Dudutki** (p85) for its open-air interactive museum and traditional meals, and **Mir** (p86) for its fairy-tale castle and a taste of real life in small-town Belarus.

BELARUS

MINSK

0 ——————— 1 km
0 ——————— 0.5 miles

INFORMATION
24-hour Pharmacy.....................1 B5
Alatan Tour...............................2 C4
Belintourist.............................3 A4
Central Post Office...................4 B5
EcoMedservices.......................5 A6
French Embassy........................6 B5
German Embassy.......................7 D4
Internet Café...........................8 B6
Moldovan Embassy...................9 C6
Prachechnaya.........................10 D4
PVU Main Office......................11 B5
Russian Consulate...................12 A3
Soyuz Online..........................13 C5
Tsentralnaya Kniharnya...........14 B5
UK Embassy............................15 C5
Ukrainian Consulate................16 B3
US Embassy............................17 B3
Virus Internet Club..................18 D3
Vokrug Sveta..........................19 B5

SIGHTS & ACTIVITIES
Belarusian Government Building.20 B6
Belarusian Popular Front
  Headquarters........................21 D3
Belarusian State University.......22 B6
Bust of Felix Dzerzhinsky.........23 D4
Church of St Aleksandr Nevsky..24 D4
Church of Sts Simon & Elena...25 B5
Dom Ofitserov.................(see 13)
Former Bernardine Church.......(see 27)
Former Residence of Lee Harvey
  Oswald.................................26 C4
Holy Spirit Cathedral...............27 B4

Island of Courage and Sorrow..........28 B4
KGB Headquarters.....................29 B5
Museum of the Great Patriotic War..30 C5
Palats Respubliki.....................31 C5
Presidential Administrative Building..32 C5
Ratusha..................................33 B5
Sts Peter & Paul Church............34 B4
Trade Unions' Culture Palace....35 C5
Traetskae Pradmestse...............36 B4
Victory Obelisk........................37 D4
Viktor Tsoi Monument..............38 C5
Zaslavsky Jewish Monument.....39 A4

SLEEPING
40 Let Pobedy.........................40 D5
Hotel Belarus..........................41 B3
Hotel Europe...........................42 B5
Hotel Minsk............................43 B5
Hotel Oktyabrsky....................44 C5
Hotel Planeta..........................45 A3
Hotel Yubileiny.......................46 B4
Juravinka...............................47 C4

EATING
Byblos....................................48 B5
Casa Agustin López..................49 D4
Gurman..................................50 C4
Lido.......................................51 D3
Mirsky Zamak.........................52 B5
Pizza Tempo............................53 B5
Planeta Sushi..........................54 C5
Strawnya Talaka......................55 B4
Sushi Vysola............................56 A3
Tsentralny Magazin..................57 C5

DRINKING
Drozhzhi United.......................58 B5
London...........................(see 54)
My English Granny............(see 59)
News Café...............................59 C5
Rakovsky Brovar......................60 B5
Stary Mensk...........................61 B5
U Ratushi................................62 B4
Upteka...................................63 B5

ENTERTAINMENT
Bela Vezha.....................(see 65)
Belarusian State Circus.............64 C5
Bronx.....................................65 C3
Central Ticket Office................66 B5
National Academic Opera & Ballet
  Theatre.................................67 C4
X-Ray.....................................68 C4

SHOPPING
GUM......................................69 B5
Minsky Vernisazh.....................70 C5
Podzemka...............................71 D4
Stolitsa Shopping Centre..........72 B6
TsUM.....................................73 D3

TRANSPORT
Avis.............................(see 41)
Belavia...................................74 B5
Domestic Train Ticket Office.....75 B5
Europcar......................(see 43)
International Train Ticket Office..76 B6
Tari Transcom.................(see 45)
Tsentralny Bus Station.............77 B6

WHERE AM I?

Between the Soviet, post–Soviet Russian and Belarusian names for streets and places in Belarus things can get confusing. In this chapter we use Belarusian street and place names, as this is almost universally how they are written on signposts (in Cyrillic of course – so you'll still have to transliterate; see p1009 for a guide to deciphering the Cyrillic alphabet). However, almost everyone will tell you the Russian names for streets, so there's room for real confusion. When giving addresses we use the abbreviations vul *(vulitsa)*, pr *(praspekt)* and pl *(ploshcha)* to denote street, avenue and square. Russian speakers will call these *ulitsa, prospekt* and *ploshchad* respectively, but again, the Belarusian versions are used on street signs in most cases.

Minsk is particularly confusing in this respect. To honour the great Belarusian renaissance man, the city's main thoroughfare was once called pr Francyska Skaryny, but in 2005 Lukashenko changed it to 'Independence Avenue': pr Nezalezhnastsi (pr Nezavisimosti in Russian). Similarly pl Peramohi (Victory Sq) is often referred to as its Russian variant, pl Pobedy.

Metro stop and town square pl Lenina also goes by its post-Soviet name, which switches 'Lenin' for 'Independence': ploshcha Nezalezhnastsi (pl Nezavisimosti in Russian). Metro change station and main town square Oktyabrskaya pl (its Russian name) is sometimes called pl Kastrychnitskaya (the Belarusian version of the same name). Enjoy!

Central post office (☎ 227 8492; pr Nezalezhnastsi 10; ☸ 7am-11pm) In the centre of town.

Tourist Information
Travel agencies can provide information but of course want you to book tours.
Minsk Tourist Information (☎ 203 3995/3981) The official tourism authority, although it did not at the time of writing have an office.

Travel Agencies
Alatan Tour (☎ 227 7417; www.welcomebelarus.com; vul Yanki Kupaly 21) Offers visa support, hotel bookings, guide services and drivers.
Belarus Tour Service (☎ 200 5675; www.hotels belarus.com; vul Rozi Lyuksemburg 89) Visa support, hotel bookings and transfers.
Belintourist (☎ 226 9971; www.belintourist.by; pr Peramozhtsau 19a) The state-run tourist agency does visa support, city tours and trips to Mir, Dudutki, Nyasvizh and Belavezhskaya Pushcha National Park – as well as offering the intriguingly named Eight Wonders of Belarus tour.
Top Tour (☎ 281 7047; www.toptour.by; vul Ya Kolasa 40) Visa support, hotels, interpreters and tours.
Vokrug Sveta (☎ 226 8392; vokrugsveta.by; vul Internatsyanalnaya 10) Another good agency offering visa support, accommodation, excursions and interpreters.

SIGHTS
Razed to the ground in WWII, Minsk retains almost nothing from the prewar period, and was built anew in the late 1940s and 1950s as a flagship Stalinist city. The result is a remarkably uniform conurbation that is actually strangely attractive, the Stalinist style being far grander and more colourful than the later Soviet architecture of the 1960s and 1970s.

The city's central square is pl Nezalezhnastsi (also called pl Lenina), which is dominated by the **Belarusian Government Building** (behind the Lenin statue) on its northern side, and the equally proletarian **Belarusian State University** on the south side. The red-brick Catholic **Church of Sts Simon & Elena** built in 1910 is also here. Its tall, gabled bell tower and attractive detailing are reminiscent of many brick churches in the former Teutonic north of Poland. Beneath the square lies Stolitsa Shopping Centre (p84), a modern three-storey mall where you'll find much of Minsk's best shopping.

Heading northeast from pl Nezalezhnastsi is the main part of pr Nezalezhnastsi and the bustling heart of Minsk, including Soviet GUM (p84). An entire block at No 17 is occupied by a yellow neoclassical building with an ominous, temple-like Corinthian portal – the **KGB headquarters**. On the other side of the street is a long, narrow park with a **bust of Felix Dzerzhinsky**, the founder of the KGB's predecessor (the Cheka) and a native of Belarus.

Between vul Enhelsa and vul Yanki Kupaly is a square that is still referred to by its Russian name, Oktyabrskaya pl (in Belarusian, it's pl Kastrychnitskaya). This is where opposition groups gather to protest against Lukashenko from time to time, and it's where they attempted the Denim Revolution in March 2006. Here you'll find the impressive, severe **Palats Respubliki** (Palace of the Republic), a concert

---

QUIRKY MINSK

Just across the bridge over the Svislach River, on the west bank, is the **former residence of Lee Harvey Oswald** (vul Kamyunistychnaya 4); it's the bottom left apartment. The alleged assassin of former US president John F Kennedy lived here for a couple of years in his early 20s. He arrived in Minsk in January 1960 after leaving the US Marines and defecting to the USSR. Once here, he truly went native: he got a job in a radio factory, married a Minsk woman, had a child – and even changed his name to Alek. But soon he returned to the United States and…you know the rest.

Lovers of old coins should stop in at the train station's **left-luggage area**, where there are lockers that (surprise, surprise) date back to the Soviet days – and they still only work with Soviet coins. Pay BR550 and get in exchange two locker 'tokens' – 15-kopek coins from the USSR, some dating back to the 1960s.

There are impromptu monuments and shrines to him all over the former USSR, but the **Viktor Tsoi monument** (1962–1990) on vul Internatsyanalnaya opposite the Juravinka Hotel serves as a much-needed focal point for disaffected youth in this most conformist of cities. Wander along to see how much the half-Russian, half-Korean Kino front man, the Soviet Jim Morrison who died in a car crash when he fell asleep at the wheel, still means to young Minsk residents.

---

hall. Also on this square is the classical, multi-columned **Trade Unions' Culture Palace**, and next to this, the excellent **Museum of the Great Patriotic War** (☎ 277 7635; pr Nezalezhnastsi 25A; admission BR5000; ☻ 10am-6pm Tue-Sun), where Belarus' horrors and heroism during WWII are exhibited in photographs, huge dioramas and other media. Particularly harrowing are the photographs of partisans being executed in recognisable central Minsk locations. The big sign above the building (ПОДВИГУ НАРОДА ЖИТЬ В ВЕКАХ) means 'The Feats of Mankind Will Live On for Centuries'. For an extra BR2000, you can visit the open-air display behind the museum where tanks, anti-aircraft guns and missiles are on display, as well as a huge Lisunov Li-2 bomber, which can sadly only be entered on a guided tour (BR20,000; call ahead to reserve a tour in English).

Across the street is Tsentralny Skver (Central Square), a small park on the site of a 19th-century marketplace. The dark-grey building is **Dom Ofitserov** (Officer's Building), which has a tank memorial in front, devoted to the soldiers who freed Minsk from the Nazis. Beyond this is the lifeless-looking, seriously guarded **Presidential Administrative Building**, from where Alexander Lukashenko rules.

Further north on pr Nezalezhnastsi, across the narrow Svislach River is pl Peramohi, marked by a giant **Victory Obelisk** and its eternal flame.

In lieu of any real remaining Old Town is **Traetskae Pradmestse**, a pleasant – if tiny – recreation of Minsk's pre-war buildings on a pretty bend of the river downstream from

pl Peramohi. It's worth strolling through for its little cafes, restaurants and shops. At the end of a little footbridge nearby is the evocative Afghan war memorial, **Island of Courage & Sorrow**, more commonly called the Island of Tears. Standing on a small island connected by a walking bridge, it's built in the form of a tiny church, with four entrances, and is surrounded by towering gaunt statues of sorrowful mothers and sisters of Belarusian soldiers who perished in the war between the Soviet Union and Afghanistan (1979–89). Look for the small statue of the crying angel, off to the side – it is the guardian angel of Belarus.

Another extremely moving sight is the **Zaslavsky Jewish Monument**, rather hidden away in an amphitheatre amid some trees off vul Melnikayte. It commemorates the savage murder of 5000 Jews from Minsk at the hands of the Nazis on 2 March 1942, and is made up of sculptures of scared men, women and children lining up to be shot, one person even playing the violin for the last time.

Between vul Internatsyanalnaya and the river is the charming pl Svabody, which contains the baroque, twin-towered Orthodox **Holy Spirit Cathedral**, which was built in 1642 and stands confidently on a small hill. It was once part of a Polish Bernardine convent, along with the **former Bernardine Church** next door, which now houses city archives.

Across the vul Lenina overpass is the attractively restored 17th-century **Sts Peter & Paul Church** (vul Rakovskaya 4), the city's oldest church (built in 1613, looted by Cossacks in

1707 and restored in 1871). Now it is awkwardly dwarfed by the surrounding morose concrete structures.

Another red-brick church is the **Church of St Aleksandr Nevsky** (vul Kazlova 11). Built in 1898, it was closed by the Bolsheviks, opened by the Nazis, closed by the Soviets and now it's open again. It's said that during WWII, a bomb crashed through the roof and landed plum in front of the altar, but never detonated.

For a taste of post-Soviet Belarus, head north of the centre to the new **National Library of Belarus** (☎ 266 3737; www.nlb.by; pr Nezalezhnastsi 116; 10am-9pm Mon-Fri, 10am-6pm Sat & Sun, closed Sun Jun-Aug; M Vostok), a ghastly piece of Lukashenko-approved hubris. The building is a giant rhombicuboctahedron (look it up!) that is lit up at night and contains over two million records as well as art galleries and a **viewing platform** (admission BR4000; 1-9pm Tue-Fri, 10am-6pm Sat & Sun) on the 22nd floor.

SLEEPING

To put it bluntly, Minsk's accommodation scene is decidedly unexciting. You're generally limited to fusty old Soviet hotels or overpriced four- and five-star places geared to business travellers. A much better option if you're in the city for more than a few days is to rent an apartment. Several agencies offer this service, although the best option is **Belarus Rent** (www.belarusrent.com). Rates range from €40 to €90 per night. Another option is **Belarus Apartment** (www.belarusapartment.com).

40 Let Pobedy (☎ 294 7963; vul Azgura 3; dm from BR51,000, s/d from BR80,000/160,000) This rather out-of-the-way, dated place offers decent and good-value rooms, and friendly service. Even the name, which means '40 Years of Victory', is dated as it's now been more than 60 years since the end of WWII, which is what 'victory' always refers to in Belarus.

Hotel Turist (☎ 295 4031; Partizansky pr 81; s/d from BR110,000/165,000) Out of the city centre, but handily located for the Partizanskaya metro station, this old Soviet place has been partially remodelled. The economy-class rooms, all with bathrooms, are basic but good value for money.

Hotel Oktyabrsky (☎ 222 3289; www.hotel-oktyabr .by; vul Enhelsa 13; s/d/ste incl breakfast BR116,500/144,000/260,000) There's nowhere safer in the city to bed down than this elite Soviet place, overlooking the heavily guarded presidential administration. Managed by the Hotel Minsk, the hotel

has totally standard Soviet-style rooms with TV, phone and fridge.

Hotel Planeta (☎ 226 7855; www.hotelplaneta.by; pr Peramozhtsau 31; s/d incl breakfaast from BR122,900/BR142,600;) On a hill a fair walk from the centre of the city, the Hotel Planeta nevertheless offers good value for money, with all rooms having been remodelled and the standard of service surprisingly high. An endearing Soviet air remains and there's free lobby wi-fi.

Hotel Yubileiny (☎ 226 9024; fax 226 9171; pr Peramozhtsau 19; unrenovated s/d BR125,000/167,000, renovated s/d BR170,000/225,000, all incl breakfast;) Another cookie-cutter Soviet place, the Yubileiny is located across the road from Minsk's main athletics stadium, right in the city centre. Most of the rooms have been done up, but rooms on the 5th, 7th, 8th and 13th floors have not and are cheaper as a result. The staff are friendly and there's free lobby wi-fi.

Hotel Belarus (☎ 209 7693/7537; www.hotel-belarus .com; vul Starazhouskaya 15; s/d from BR145,000/195,000;) Just when you thought Minsk couldn't get any more Soviet, along comes the monolithic Hotel Belarus. Set in parkland amid plenty of open space, but just an easy walk into the city centre, this Soviet-era place has undergone little change since it was built, although free lobby wi-fi and a swimming pool with a waterslide set it apart from other hotels of this standard.

Hotel Minsk (☎ 209 9062; www.hotelminsk.by; vul Nezalezhnastsi 11; s/d BR390,000/450,000, ste BR650,000-2,440,000, all incl breakfast;) Excellently located, the city's long-standing hotel of choice has now been eclipsed by newer five-star hotels, but it's still a solid option. The rooms are of good four-star standard and service is friendly. There's free wi-fi in the lobby only.

Juravinka (☎ 328 6900; www.juravinka.by; vul Yanki Kupaly 25; s/d/ste incl breakfast BR400,000/580,000/2,550,000;) The 18-room Juravinka has a great location and very comfortable rooms, some with small kitchens, although in many the interior design sums up everything bad about the '90s. The hotel attracts the nouveau riche who like to hang out in the casino. The presidential suite is ginormous and has its own swimming pool.

Hotel Europe (☎ 229 8333; www.hoteleurope.by; vul Internatsyanalnaya 28; s/d from BR800,000/930,000, ste from BR1,400,000, all incl breakfast;) The first five-star hotel in Belarus opened to great

BELARUS

fanfare in 2006, and while there are some horrific crimes against taste being perpetrated in the lobby, the flouncy, spacious rooms can't really be faulted. Service is excellent, and extras such as a fitness centre and a small pool give this place the edge on all other top-end hotels in town.

EATING

Minsk has a decent eating scene and plenty of choice – don't believe the hype about food in Belarus; in the capital, at least, you'll eat well. Consider reserving tables at weekends.

Lido (☎ 284 8264; pr Nezalezhnastsi 49/1; mains BR4000-10,000; ☽ 8am-11pm Mon-Fri, 11am-11pm Sat & Sun) This excellent place is a real lifesaver for a quick, decent meal. The large cafeteria has all the food on display, so it's easy for non-Russian speakers: just point at what you want. Lunchtime is packed, but staff will help you find a seat.

Gurman (☎ 290 6774; vul Kamyunistychnaya 7; mains BR8000-25,000; ☽ 8am-11pm) This Minsk institution specialises in many varieties of delicious, freshly made *pelmeni* (Russian-style ravioli) and also offers a wide selection of pastas and even curries. The light and airy premises and friendly staff make this well worth a detour, even though it's not particularly atmospheric.

Pizza Tempo (☎ 292 1111; www.pizzatempo.by; vul Karla Marksa 9; mains BR10,000-25,000; ☽ 8am-11pm) This chain of pizzerias is spread across the city, with each restaurant stylishly decorated and enjoying a relaxed vibe. Citywide delivery is available and the pizza is excellent.

Byblos (☎ 289 1218; vul Internatsyanalnaya 21; mains BR10,000-25,000; ☽ noon-midnight) What this Lebanese-style place lacks in authenticity it makes up for in value, quick service and an English menu. Great for an easy lunch, the kebabs and hummus are decent enough, given that you're in Belarus.

Sushi Vyosla (☎ 321 0000, 872 7777; pr Masherova 78; sushi boxes BR10,000-30,000; ☽ 10am-10pm) Sushi Vyosla is Minsk's sushi delivery service and while you can drop in to pick it up, there's no space to eat in. The sushi and sashimi here is generally of a better quality than at Planeta Sushi.

Planeta Sushi (☎ 210 5645; pr Nezalezhnastsi 18; mains BR10,000-35,000) This Russian chain has a popular outlet in the centre of town, and while you shouldn't expect anything amazing,

there's surprisingly decent fare on offer here, including other Japanese dishes (udon, tempura etc) beyond sushi. The pictorial menu helps non-Russian speakers.

ourpick Strawnya Talaka (☎ 203 2794; vul Rakovskaya 18; mains BR15,000-30,000; ☽ 10am-6am Thu-Sat, 10am-last customer Sun-Wed) Hands down the best place in Minsk for an authentic local meal in intimate, cosy surroundings. Try hare in bilberry sauce or just a plate of the fabulous *deruni* (potato pancakes). Take a table inside for cosy, traditional decor, or during the summer eat on the summer terrace across the road. Reservations are required for the evenings.

Casa Agustin López (☎ 233 9584; vul Zakharava 31; mains BR20,000-45,000; ☽ noon-3am) Despite its unlikely location, this popular Spanish restaurant is a winner, with pleasant outdoor seating and a darker, more atmospheric interior. Authentic Spanish food from tapas to seafood paella and a decent selection of Torres wine are all on offer.

Mirsky Zamak (☎ 323 5347; Haradsky Val 9; mains BR20,000-75,000; ☽ noon-midnight Sun-Thu, to 2am Fri & Sat) The 'Mir Castle' is a friendly place, which is as traditionally decked out as possible given its location in a Soviet residential block to one side of the KGB. Hearty, meaty Belarusian dishes are served up and loud live music is performed each evening from 8pm.

Tsentralny Magazin (☎ 227 8876; 2nd fl, pr Nezalezhnastsi 23) A large, Western-style grocery store with plenty of supplies for self-caterers.

DRINKING
Bars

It's not advisable to drink alcohol on the streets, as it's illegal and may lead to a police shakedown.

Rakovsky Brovar (☎ 328 6404; vul Vitsebskaya 10; ☽ noon-midnight) Minsk's first microbrewery is housed in an enormous central venue and shows no sign of losing its popularity more than a decade since it opened. There's a full menu here too (mains BR15,000 to BR45,000), although most people come here for after-work drinks and stay late in the raucous atmosphere.

U Ratushi (☎ 226 0643; vul Gertsena 1; ☽ 10am-2am) Formerly called 'Nul Pyat', referring to the standard serving of beer (a half-litre), this multilevel pub-style restaurant, right across from the *ratusha* (town hall), is packed with a raucous, fun-loving crowd on weekends (there is often a small cover charge for live bands). Book ahead for weekends, or come really early.

Drozhzhi United (☎ 200 5456; vul Sverdlova 2; ☽ 9am-2am) Centrally located, Minsk's Irish pub is instantly recognisable to anyone who has ever been an expat, anywhere. There's good food, Guinness on tap, and a friendly atmosphere.

Upteka (☎ 203 1137; vul Internatsyanalnaya 9; ☽ 9am-11pm) This surprisingly sleek cafe-bar is tucked away unobtrusively in central Minsk. Its entire interior is done out like a pharmacy, so, for example, you can check your eyes while you visit the bathroom. It's much cooler than it sounds.

Cafes

The best cafes in Minsk are **News Café** (☎ 103 1111; vul Karla Marksa 34; ☽ 8am-midnight), where free wi-fi, good coffee and plenty of English-language magazines and newspapers make for a great hang-out, and the bizarre next-door **My English Granny** (☎ 227 2224; vul Karla Marksa 36; ☽ 9am-11pm), a cafe that has pulled off the incredible feat of making kitschy Victoriana look trendy, but where you'll get a lovely pot of tea and some good cakes, as well as full meals. Two other good options are sister cafes **Stary Mensk** (☎ 289 1400; pr Nezalezhnastsi 14; ☽ 10am-11pm) and **London** (☎ 289 1529; pr Nezalezhnastsi 18; ☽ 10am-11pm), which both serve coffee, tea and a mean hot chocolate.

ENTERTAINMENT
Performing Arts

A pleasant hangover from Soviet times is that performing arts are of very good quality and tickets are priced to make them accessible to the proletariat.

To buy advance tickets or to find out what's on, head to the **central ticket office** (pr Nezalezhnastsi 13; ☽ 9am-7pm). There are more places for tickets in the underground crossing in the centre. Same-day tickets are sometimes available only from the performance venues.

Don't miss the highly respected **National Academic Opera & Ballet Theatre** (☎ 234 8074; pl Parizhskoy Kamunni 1; ☽ ticket office 9am-1pm & 2-6pm Mon-Fri), where there are several different operas performed each month; performances take place at 7pm on Thursday, Saturday and Sunday. The **Belarusian State Circus** (☎ 226 1008; pr Nezalezhnastsi 32) also comes highly recommended for younger audiences.

CIRCLE 16

There is little graffiti on the streets of Minsk, but you may come across the circled number '16' spray-painted in somewhat obscure places. This is a sign of solidarity with Belarusian political prisoners, disappeared oppositionists and independent journalists. At 8pm on the 16th of each month, participants turn off their lights and put a candle in their window for 15 minutes.

Live Music

our pick **Graffiti** (☎ 029 179 9918; www.graffiti.by; per Kalinina 16; cover BR10,000-20,000; ☽ 11am-11pm, to 1am Fri & Sat) For something more contemporary and underground, Graffiti offers nightly concerts from local bands (many of whom are anti-Lukashenko and have trouble getting gigs elsewhere). Come early to ensure you get in – it's a 10-minute walk from the Park Chelyuskintsev metro station.

Nightclubs

If you read Russian, a great website for clubs and events is www.mixtura.org/minsk/clubs .html. And if you don't there's plenty going on in town to keep night owls busy.

X-Ray (☎ 203 9355; vul Internatsyanalnaya 27; cover free-BR35,000; ☽ 9am-4am Mon-Fri, noon-4am Sat & Sun) This retro-styled colourful bar-restaurant-club hosts some of Minsk's best parties and is popular with the city's in-crowd. The furniture comes from the Jetsons, while the funky antique knick-knacks are all Soviet.

6A (Partizansky Pr 6a; cover BR5,000; ☽ 10pm-3am; Ⓜ Proletarskaya) The only gay club in Minsk is a curious but friendly Soviet throwback in a building where time appears to have stood still since the 1970s. A unique experience.

Bela Vezha (☎ 284 6922; pr Masherava 17; cover approx BR40,000; ☽ 11pm-5am Tue-Sun) Minsk's most exciting nightclub has a space-aged theme, excellent DJs and lots of live acts. Its labyrinthine corridors contain a huge 24-hour casino, an expensive restaurant and a cutting-edge dance floor.

Bronx (☎ 288 1061; pr Masherava 17/1; cover BR10,000-50,000; ☽ noon-5am Thu-Sat, noon-2am Sun-Wed) Without a doubt, Bronx is the hippest nightclub in town and prices inside match the glam crowd. Special guest bands and DJs from abroad show up at the sleek, ultramodern warehouse-style space, where there are billiards, dance floors and fashion shows.

BELARUS

SHOPPING

Minsk's shopping scene is far from mind-blowing, although things have improved vastly in the past few years. If you want a general browse, a good place to start is the **Stolitsa Shopping Centre** (pl Nezalezhnastsi; ⏰ 10am-10pm), a three-level subterranean mall housing much of the capital's best shopping.

Souvenirs from Belarus tend to be alcoholic, but there are other options beyond buying vodka. At many grocery shops you'll find candies with old-fashioned wrappers steeped in nostalgia for a Soviet childhood. Belarus is also known for its straw crafts, which include dolls and wooden boxes intricately ornamented with geometric patterns of the stuff. Linens and other woven textiles unique to Belarus are also popular handicrafts. These are easily found in city department stores, hotel lobbies and at **Minsky Vernisazh** (Oktyabrskaya pl; ⏰ 8am-6pm), a typical souvenir market right next to the Museum of the Great Patriotic War where you can haggle for local art, folk crafts and other traditional items. Other recommended shops include **Podzemka** (☎ 288 2036; www.podzemka.org; pr Nezalezhnastsi 43; ⏰ 10am-8pm Mon-Sat, 11am-6pm Sun), an underground bohemian shop-cum-art-gallery that sells all sorts of goodies you won't find anywhere else; for example, 'Women of the War' calendars, funky artistic pieces, photographs and handmade jewellery.

The Belarusian company **Milavitsa** (www.milavitsa.by) sells stylish lingerie for a fraction of what Westerners pay. Check the department stores, such as **GUM** (Government All-Purpose Store; ☎ 226 1048; pr Nezalezhnastsi 21) and **TsUM** (☎ 284 8164; pr Nezalezhnastsi 54) for souvenirs and Milavitsa products. There are no dressing rooms here.

GETTING THERE & AWAY
Air
International flights entering and departing Belarus do so at the **Minsk-2 international airport** (☎ 006, 279 1300; www.airport.by), about 40km east of Minsk. Some domestic flights as well as those to Kyiv, Kaliningrad and Moscow depart from the smaller **Minsk-1 airport** (☎ 006; vul Chkalova 38), only a few kilometres south of the city centre.

Bus
There are three main bus stations, and you can buy tickets for anywhere at any of them.

At the time of writing the Tsentralny bus station next to the train station was being rebuilt and all the Tsentralny routes were being run from the Vostochny bus station, about 2km southeast of the city. Ask locals for the current situation on arrival. To ask which station you're departing from in Russian is 'v ka-*kom* av-toh-vak-*za*-le ot-prav-*lye*-ni-ye'. The excellent **MinskTrans** (www.minsktrans.by) website also gives full timetable information in English.

Moskovsky bus station (☎ 219 3622; vul Filimonava 63) Near Maskouskaya metro station, about 4km east of the city.

Tsentralny bus station (☎ international 225 2256, CIS destinations 227 3725; vul Bobruyskaya 6) By the train station, though under reconstruction at the time of writing.

Vostochny bus station (☎ 248 5821; vul Vaneeva 34) To get here from the train station (or metro Pl Lenina), take bus 8 or trolley 20 or 30; get off at 'Avtovokzal Vostochny'.

From Minsk, international services include buses to Vilnius, Warsaw, Kyiv, Moscow and St Petersburg.

Car & Motorcycle
You can hire cars from the following places:
Avis (☎ 334 7990; www.avis.by; Hotel Belarus, vul Storozhevskaya 15)
Europcar (☎ 209 9009; www.europcar.by; Hotel Minsk, pr Nezalezhnastsi 11)
Tari Transcom (☎ 226 7383; Hotel Planeta, pr Peramozhtsau 31)

Train
The capital's busy but modern train station is pretty easy to deal with. Basic food and left-luggage services are available here, as well as an internet cafe on the 3rd floor. You can buy tickets at the train station, but the ticket offices have shorter lines. At the station, there are ATMs and exchange offices, but the lines are often long.

The nearest metro station is Pl Nezalezhnastsi.

Domestic train ticket office (☎ 225 6271; pr Nezalezhnastsi 18; ⏰ 9am-8pm Mon-Fri, 9am-7pm Sat & Sun) Tickets for domestic and CIS (Commonwealth of Independent States) destinations.

International train ticket office (☎ 213 1719; vul Bobruyskaya 4; ⏰ 9am-8pm) Advance tickets for non-CIS destinations; located to the right of the train station.

Minsk train station (☎ 005, 596 5410) Domestic and CIS tickets.

There are two daily trains to Vilnius (BR45,000, four hours), multiple trains to Moscow (BR170,000, 11 hours), one overnight train to Kyiv (BR178,000, 12 hours), and there are also three to four daily trains to St Petersburg (BR168,000, 13 to 15 hours). There are three direct trains to Warsaw (BR135,000, 10 hours), as well as numerous indirect services involving a change of trains in Brest or Terespol.

GETTING AROUND
See opposite for information on car rentals.

To/From the Airport
From Minsk-2 airport, a 40-minute taxi ride into town should cost anywhere between BR50,000 to BR100,000, depending on your bargaining skills. There are buses (BR3000, 90 minutes, hourly) that bring you to the Tsentralny bus station, not far from the centre and Pl Lenina metro station. There are also about eight daily minibuses that make the trip in a little over an hour and cost BR5000. From Minsk-1 airport, take bus 100 to the centre; it goes along pr Nezalezhnastsi.

Public Transport
Minsk's metro is simple: just two lines with one transfer point at the Kastrychnitskaya–Kupalauskaya interchange on pr Nezalezhnastsi – and operates until just after midnight. One token (zheton) costs BR600.

Buses, trams, trolleybuses and the metro operate from 5.30am to 1am. Minibuses (marshrutki) cost about BR1000 to BR1500 per ride and are quicker than overground transport methods. Popular bus 100 comes every five to 15 minutes and plies pr Nezalezhnastsi as far as Moskovsky bus station. You can buy a ticket from the person on board wearing a bright vest. Once you get the ticket, punch it at one of the red buttons placed on the poles.

Taxis
For taxis, ☎ 081 is the state service and almost always has cars available, while ☎ 007 is private, the cheapest and has the best service (less likely to rip off foreigners) but cars are sometimes not available during peak times. You can also hail one from the street. Unlike in Russia, private cars don't usually stop for passengers.

AROUND MINSK

Leave Minsk for an easy taste of the gently appealing Belarusian countryside, to a world where instead of mobile phone shops and sushi bars, the few stores you'll will have names like 'Bread' and 'Shoes', dating from a bygone era of no choice. Don't miss the fairytale castle at Mir or your chance to taste a slice of traditional village life at Dudutki.

To really immerse yourself in rural life, consider trying **Rural & Ecotourism** (☎ 251 0076; www .ruralbelarus.by), a nonprofit association of B&Bs that offers dozens of homestays throughout the country.

When using public transport to visit towns around Minsk, bear in mind that Sunday evenings are often booked in advance for the return trip to Minsk, as people are returning from their dachas. Alternatively, you could visit all these places in one day if you hire a car or a taxi for the day.

DUDUTKI ДУДУТКІ
☎ 01713
Tasting delicious farm-made sausages, cheese and bread is only a small part of the experience of a visit to the **open-air interactive museum** (☎ 137 2525; www.dudutki.by; adult/child incl tastings BR20,000/6000; ☑ 10am-4pm Tue-Wed, 10am-5pm Thu-Sun) of Dudutki, located 40km south of Minsk. This completely self-sufficient farm offers horse riding, sleigh rides, demonstrations of ceramic making, blacksmithing and more. You'll be offered fresh salo (tallow) with garlic, salt and rye bread; pickles dipped in honey; and homemade moonshine – even the ficklest eater should try them, as they are all scrumptious.

There are three daily buses (one hour, BR9000 each way) to/from Dudutki from Minsk's Tsentralny bus station. Otherwise, contact Valeria's **Dudutki Tur** (☎ 017-251 0076; dudutki@telecom.by).

NYASVIZH НЯСВІЖ
☎ 01770 / pop 15,000
The magical old buildings of Nyasvizh make it a great place to get in touch with Belarus' past – one that elsewhere has all too often been destroyed as military campaigns flattened the country. This quiet but green and attractive town 120km southwest of Minsk is one of the oldest sites in the country, dating

from the 13th century. It reached its zenith in the mid-16th century while owned by the mighty Radziwill magnates.

The **Farny Polish Roman Catholic Church** was built between 1584 and 1593 in early baroque style and features a splendidly proportioned facade. Inside, the frescos have been restored to their former elaborate glory.

Just beyond the church is the red-brick arcaded **Castle Gate Tower**. Constructed in the 16th century, the tower was originally part of a wall and gateway controlling the passage between the palace and the town. Here there's an **excursion bureau** (☎ 53 067; vul Leninskaya 19; ☼ 8am-5pm Mon-Fri) where you pay to enter the fortress grounds (BR5000). Guided tours (BR48,000) for one to 25 people last about 1½ hours and are available in either Russian or Belarusian.

Further on is a causeway leading to the beautiful **Radziwill Palace Fortress** (1583), the main sight in Nyasvizh. In Soviet times it was unfortunately turned into a sanatorium and was closed for a full restoration at the time of research. There are English and Japanese gardens to stroll in here, as well as an eternal flame in the attractive lakeside park, commemorating those who died in WWII.

From Minsk's Tsentralny bus station, there are approximately hourly buses to/from Nyasvizh (BR14,730, 2½ hours).

MIR МІР
☎ 01596 / pop 2500
The charming small town of Mir, 85km southwest of Minsk, is dominated by the impossibly romantic 16th-century **Mir Castle** (☎ 23 035; admission BR10,660; ☼ 10am-5pm) that overlooks a small lake at one end of the town. It was once owned by the powerful Radziwill princes and has been under Unesco protection since 1994. Sadly, today the exterior is the highlight of the castle as almost all the original contents have been removed. Even though it's worth a walk around the small areas open to visitors, there's little to see here. Guided tours in Russian are offered (BR42,610 for one to 10 people). The town of Mir itself is a delightful backwater.

The small, friendly **Hotel Mir** (☎ 23 851; pl 17ogo Sentyabrya 2; s/d BR77,000/118,000) is the only place to stay in town. You'll find it on the charming town square, across the way from the bus station. Breakfast is not included,

but there is a cafe here and a restaurant on the other side of the square.

From Minsk's Tsentralny bus station, buses to Navahrudak (Novogrudok in Russian), Lida, Svitsiaz and Zel'va stop in Mir (BR13,800, 2½ hours, hourly).

KHATYN ХАТЫНЬ
☎ 01774
The hamlet of Khatyn, 60km north of Minsk, was burned to the ground by Nazis on 22 March 1943. Of a population of 149 (including 85 children), only one man, Yuzif Kaminsky, survived. The site is now a sobering **memorial** (☎ 55 787; ☼ 9am-5pm Tue-Sat); tours are offered in Russian. More information can be found at www.khatyn.by. There's also an exhibit of photographs (admission BR2000).

There's no public transport to Khatyn from Minsk, but a taxi will cost around BR80,000 for the return journey. Pricey trips are organised by **Belintourist** (p79).

SOUTHERN BELARUS

Leave Minsk and you're quickly in another world – the concrete landscape gives way to pastoral scenes and undulating flat green plains rich in simple bucolic beauty – a river wending its way gently past thick forests, fields of cornflowers in bloom, and small villages populated entirely by pensioners. It's not dramatic, but this is the 'real' Belarus.

The south of Belarus is dominated by Brest, a lively and attractive border town with a far more progressive feel than Minsk. The star attraction nearby is of course the wonderful Belavezhskaya Pushcha National Park, which can be visited in a day trip from Brest, or – even better – on an overnight trip staying in the park itself. There's also the excellent Pripyatsky National Park for those *really* wanting to get off the beaten path.

BREST БРЭСТ
☎ 0162 / pop 312,000
After visiting Minsk you'd be forgiven for thinking you'd arrived in another country when you get off the train in Brest. This prosperous and cosmopolitan border town looks far more to the neighbouring EU than to Minsk or Moscow. It has plenty of rowdy

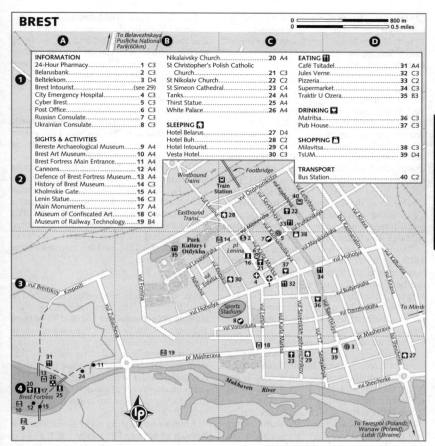

BREST

0 _____ 800 m
0 _____ 0.5 miles

INFORMATION
24-Hour Pharmacy.........................1 C3
Belarusbank.................................2 C3
Beltelekom..................................3 D4
Brest Intourist.........................(see 29)
City Emergency Hospital.................4 C3
Cyber Brest................................5 C3
Post Office..................................6 C3
Russian Consulate........................7 C3
Ukrainian Consulate......................8 C3

SIGHTS & ACTIVITIES
Bereste Archaeological Museum......9 A4
Brest Art Museum.......................10 A4
Brest Fortress Main Entrance.........11 A4
Cannons....................................12 A4
Defence of Brest Fortress Museum..13 A4
History of Brest Museum...............14 C3
Kholmskie Gate..........................15 A4
Lenin Statue..............................16 C3
Main Monuments........................17 A4
Museum of Confiscated Art...........18 C4
Museum of Railway Technology......19 B4

Nikalaivsky Church.......................20 A4
St Christopher's Polish Catholic
   Church....................................21 C3
St Nikolaiv Church.......................22 C2
St Simeon Cathedral....................23 C4
Tanks.......................................24 A4
Thirst Statue..............................25 A4
White Palace..............................26 A4

SLEEPING 🛏
Hotel Belarus.............................27 D4
Hotel Buh..................................28 C2
Hotel Intourist...........................29 C4
Vesta Hotel...............................30 C3

EATING 🍴
Café Tsitadel.............................31 A4
Jules Verne................................32 C3
Pizzeria....................................33 C2
Supermarket..............................34 C3
Traktir U Ozera..........................35 B3

DRINKING 🍷
Matritsa...................................36 C3
Pub House................................37 C3

SHOPPING 🛍
Milavitsa...................................38 C3
TsUM......................................39 D4

TRANSPORT
Bus Station...............................40 C2

BELARUS

---

charm that only looks set to increase as the city completes the massive DIY job it has been performing on itself over the past few years.

The city's main sight is the Brest Fortress, a moving WWII memorial where Soviet troops held out far longer than expected against the Nazi onslaught in the early days of Operation Barbarossa. If you have time, pay a visit to the nearby primeval forests of Belavezhskaya Pushcha National Park – where you'll be able to see the endangered zoobr or European bison, the largest mammal on the continent.

Orientation

Central Brest fans out southeast from the train station to the Mukhavets River. Vul Savetskaya is the main drag and has several pedestrian sections. Brest Fortress lies where the Buh and Mukhavets Rivers meet, about 2km southwest of the centre down pr Masherava.

Information

24-hour pharmacy (☎ 23 80 28; vul Hoholya 32)
Belarusbank (pl Lenina) Currency exchange, Western Union and a nearby ATM.
Beltelekom (☎ 22 13 15; pr Masherava 21; internet per hr BR1500; ☉ 7am-10.30pm) You can make long-distance calls here, as well as use the internet cafe. There's also a free wi-fi zone for those with laptops.
Brest Intourist (☎ 22 19 00; www.brest-intourist .com; pr Masherava 15; ☉ 9am-6pm Mon-Fri) Inside Hotel Intourist; the superfriendly English-speaking staff can arrange city tours including 'Jewish Brest' and trips to Belavezhskaya Pushcha National Park.

City Emergency Hospital (☎ 23 58 38; vul Lenina 15)
Cyber Brest (☎ 20 03 00; 3rd fl, vul Kamsamolskaya 36; per hr BR2000; ⏰ 9am-11pm) Internet access at your choice of 50 computers.
Post office (pl Lenina)

Sights
BREST FORTRESS
Very little remains of **Brest Fortress** (Brestskaya kre-post; ☎ 20 03 65; pr Masherava; admission free) – certainly don't come here expecting a medieval turreted affair – this is a Soviet WWII memorial to the devastating battle that resulted when German troops advanced into the Soviet Union in the early days of Operation Barbarossa in 1941. The large complex occupies a beautiful spot at the confluence of the Buh and Mukhavets Rivers, a 20-minute walk from the centre; the hourly bus 17 travels between here and Hotel Intourist, although it's usually more convenient to walk.

The fortress was built between 1838 and 1842, but by WWII it was used mainly for housing soldiers. The two regiments bunking here when German troops launched a surprise attack in 1941 defended the fort for an astounding month and became venerated as national legends thanks to Stalin's propaganda machine.

The **Brest Fortress main entrance** is its most iconic building – a huge socialist star formed from concrete. Sombre music accompanies you through the tunnel, and as you leave it, on the left and past a small hill, you'll see some **tanks** and, straight ahead, the stone **Thirst statue**, which depicts a water-starved soldier crawling for a drink. After you cross a small bridge, to your right are the brick ruins of the **White Palace**, where the 1918 Treaty of Brest-Litovsk – which marked Russia's exit from WWI – was signed. Further to the right is the **Defence of Brest Fortress Museum** (☎ 20 03 65; adult/student BR5500/2750; ⏰ 9am-6pm, closed last Tue of the month). Its extensive and dramatic exhibits demonstrate the plight of the defenders. There's also a small collection of weaponry from 18th- to 20th-century warfare for which a separate ticket is required (BR3500).

Behind the museum is Café Tsitadel (opposite), the only eating option here.

On the other side of the fortress is a collection of **cannons**. Behind this area is the entrance to the new **Brest Art Museum** (☎ 20 08 26; admission BR2500; ⏰ 10am-6pm Tue-Sun), which holds art done by Brest citizens, and some local crafts.

Heading to the **main monuments** – a large stone soldier's head projecting from a massive rock, entitled *Valour*, and a skyscraping obelisk – you'll see an eternal flame and stones bearing the names of those who died (several are marked 'unknown'). Sombre orchestral music is played here too to ensure you are suitably moved.

Behind the Valour rock is the attractive, recently renovated Byzantine **Nikalaivsky Church**, the oldest church in the city, which dates from when the town centre occupied the fortress site. It holds regular services.

To the south is **Kholmskie Gate**; its bricks are decorated with crenulated turrets and its outer face is riddled with hundreds of bullet and shrapnel holes. Beyond the Kholmskie Gate is the **Bereste Archaeological Museum** (☎ 20 55 54; admission BR2500; ⏰ 9am-6pm), a large covered archaeological site where peasant and artisan huts from the 12th to 14th centuries have been uncovered.

OTHER SIGHTS
There are a couple of excellent museums in the city centre. The most interesting is the **Museum of Confiscated Art** (☎ 20 41 95; vul Lenina 39; admission BR2500; ⏰ 10am-5.15pm Tue-Sun), where there's an extraordinary display of icons, paintings, jewellery and other valuables that were seized from smugglers trying to get them across the border to Poland during the 1990s. Items on display are of unknown origin, hence their display in a museum rather than a return to their rightful owners.

Another interesting sight is the outdoor **Museum of Railway Technology** (☎ 27 47 64; pr Masherava 2; admission BR6000; ⏰ 9am-6pm Wed-Sun May-Oct, 9am-5pm Wed-Sun Nov-Apr), where there's a superb collection of locomotives and carriages dating from 1903 (the Moscow–Brest Express with shower rooms and a very comfy main bedroom) to 1988 (far more proletarian Soviet passenger carriages). You can go inside many of them, so train enthusiasts and children love this place.

With its gold cupolas and yellow-and-blue facades, the breathtakingly detailed 200-year-old Orthodox **St Nikolaiv Church** (cnr vul Savetskaya & vul Mitskevicha) is one of many lovely churches in Brest. On pl Lenina, a **Lenin statue** points east towards Moscow, but it appears more to be pointing across the street accusingly at the 1856 **St Christopher's Polish Catholic Church**. The peach-and-green **St Simeon Cathedral** (cnr pr Masherava & vul Karla Marksa) was built in 1865 in Russian-Byzantine style (the gold on the cupolas was added in 1997).

In an unassuming white building, the two-storey **History of Brest Museum** (☎ 23 17 65; vul Levaneiskaha 3; admission BR2580; ☼ 10am-6pm Tue-Sat) has a small exhibit on the city in its different guises throughout history, including an excellent model of the Brest Fortress in its heyday.

Sleeping

There are four almost identical Soviet-era hotels serving Brest. Don't lose any sleep choosing between them.

Hotel Buh (☎ 23 64 17; vul Lenina 2; s/d/ste from BR60,000/95,000/120,000) The cheapest and oldest of Brest's hotels is also the best choice for some character – the Stalin-era building is run by a group of bawdy ladies who don't speak a word of English but are very accommodating. Some rooms share facilities, although there are plenty with private bathrooms too.

Hotel Belarus (☎ 22 16 48; bresttourist@tut.by; bulvar Shevchenko 6; s/d incl breakfast BR102,000/126,000) This large block on a busy avenue leading out of the city centre is a little further out than the other hotels, and its rooms overlooking the main road can be very loud at night. Other than that, it's fine – simple but clean rooms with basic bathrooms contain TV, fridge and phone.

Vesta Hotel (☎ 23 71 69; hotelvesta@tut.by; vul Krupskoi 16; s/d BR108,000/156,000, ste BR210,000-430,000) Identical to its sister Soviet hotels in town, the Vesta does however boast a side-street location making it far more peaceful than the other options. Its rooms are also somewhat more spacious, but largely identical, with TV and phones in them.

Hotel Intourist (☎ 20 05 10; int@brest.by; pr Masherava 15; s/d BR114,020/177,200, ste BR224,800-320,000, all incl breakfast) A slightly better location than Hotel Belarus, the Intourist nevertheless has distinctly less friendly reception staff and its cavernous reception remains determinedly dark. Rooms are passable, though, with modernised facilities on almost every floor, and there are good city views.

Eating

Pizzeria (vul Pushkinskaya 20; pizzas BR9000-15,000) It's not well signed, but you can pretty much follow your nose into the building and down the stairs. Surprisingly excellent thin-crust pizzas are made to order and consumed in this basement place while dubbed Mexican soap operas entertain the diners. Salads and fries are available as well.

Traktir U Ozera (☎ 23 57 63; Park Kultury i Otdykha; mains BR12,000-45,000) This old Russian inn (*traktir*) by the lake in Brest's main park has plenty of charm, although it's perhaps better for an evening meal than a daytime one, as it rather squanders its lakeside position and is surprisingly dark inside. That said, the food is good, although the menu is only available in florid Russian and incomprehensible even to decent speakers. Dishes range from steaks and kebabs to sushi and grills. For something simpler in equally pleasant surroundings, there's an open-air cafe serving up kebabs and beer outside.

ourpick **Jules Verne** (☎ 23 67 17; vul Hoholya 29; mains BR18,000-26,000; ☼ noon-midnight) It's almost a miracle that such a great restaurant exists in Brest. Decked out like a gentleman's club and with a travel theme, this dark, atmospheric joint manages to be refined without being stuffy. It serves up cracking dishes – from mouth-watering curries to sumptuous desserts and the best coffee in town – don't miss it.

Brest has plenty of takeaways and fast food on offer, particularly around the pedestrianised area of vul Savetskaya. There's also a decent **supermarket** (vul Savetskaya 48; ☼ 8am-8pm Mon-Sat, 10am-8pm Sun) in the centre. At the fortress itself there's only the decidedly mediocre **Café Tsitadel** (☼ 9am-6pm) to cater for you – it's best to bring a packed lunch if you want to eat while you visit.

Drinking

Pub House (☎ 21 93 46; vul Hoholya; ☼ 9am-11pm) This friendly and rustic old-style wooden bar offers up a selection of beers from all over Europe, as well as showing sports events and serving decent food too. It's by far the most pleasant place for a drink in town.

Matritsa (☎ 23 82 39; vul Savetskaya 73; ☼ 9pm-5am) Bowling, billiards, bars and babes – it's all here. There's dancing too. The cover varies depending on what's on, but this is Brest's busiest and best club.

Shopping

Souvenirs can be bought on the 1st floor of the city's **TsUM** (☎ 20 57 44; pr Masherava 17; ☼ 9am-9pm Mon-Sat, 9am-7pm Sun), although there are not tonnes of goodies to choose from. Just in case

BELARUS

you missed your bra-purchasing opportunity in Minsk, there's a branch of **Milavitsa** (☎ 26 64 69; www.milavitsa.by; vul Pushkinskaya 21) in Brest as well.

Getting There & Around

The **train station** (☎ 005) has on-site customs. Trains leave for Minsk (BR25,000, four hours) several times daily. When taking a train from Brest, note that the platform nearest the city centre is for eastbound trains; the next one is for trains heading west. To get to the city from the train station, you'll have to mount a steep flight of steps from the platform; once you're up, go right on the overpass. If you're exhausted or have a lot of luggage, a taxi into town should be no more than BR10,000.

The **bus station** (☎ 004, 114) is in the centre of town. There are five daily buses between Minsk and Brest (BR25,000 to BR29,500, five hours).

For a taxi, call ☎ 061 or have your hotel call for you. Count on spending between BR5000 and BR10,000 for a taxi from the centre to Brest Fortress.

AROUND BREST

A Unesco World Heritage site some 60km north of Brest, **Belavezhskaya Pushcha National Park** (☎ 01631-56 370, 01631-56 242) is the oldest wildlife refuge in Europe and is the pride of Belarus. Half the park's territory lies in Poland, where it's called Białowieża National Park (p607).

Some 1300 sq km of primeval forest survives here. It's all that remains of a canopy that eight centuries ago covered northern Europe. Some oak trees here are over 600 years old and some pines at least 300 years old.

At least 55 mammal species, including deer, lynx, boars, wild horses, wolves, elks, ermines, badgers, martens, otters, mink and beavers, call this park home, but the area is most celebrated for its 300 or so European bison, the continent's largest land mammal. These free-range zoobr – slightly smaller than their American cousins – were driven to near extinction (the last one living in the wild was shot by a hunter in 1919) and then bred back from 52 animals that had survived in zoos. Now a total of about 3000 exist, of which over 300 are wild in the Belavezhskaya Pushcha. Amazingly you can pay to shoot them – '300 is enough' according to park wardens, who want to control their numbers due

to the vast amount of foliage these enormous beasts consume.

There's a **nature museum** (☎ 01631-56 398; admission BR3000; ☽ 9am-5pm) that gives a great introduction to the species living in the park and *volerei* (enclosures; admission BR3000), where you can view bison, deer, bears, boars and other animals (including the rare hybrid Tarpan horse, a crossbreed of a species that was also shot into near extinction).

There are a few different options for overnight stays, all of which are best arranged through Brest Intourist (p87). Camping requires permission but costs only about BR15,000 per person. The **Kamyanyuki Hotel Complex** (☎ 01631-56 497; Kamyanyuki; s/d incl breakfast BR56,000/66,000) includes a serviceable hotel next to the nature museum in the eponymous village just outside the national park. Rooms are remodelled, have bathrooms and balconies and include breakfast. Other options include Dom Grafa Tushkevicha, a guest house better for families or other small groups, and the historical Viskuli Hotel, where Lukashenko often stays. Book these through Brest Intourist as they aren't used to people just turning up. There's a restaurant in the Kamyanyuki Hotel Complex, as well as a couple of other cafes serving up simple *shashlyk* (meat kebabs) and bliny.

It's entirely possible (and a great deal cheaper) to see the national park without taking a guided tour, although if you don't speak Russian you may miss some interesting commentary on trips through the woods and in the museum. From Brest take one of the six daily *marshrutkas* or buses to Kamyanyuki (BR14,800, one hour 20 minutes) and walk from the village to the clearly visible reserve buildings. Once there you can walk around the park yourself, or even better, hire a bike from the museum (BR3000 per hour). On some days individuals with private cars or taxis are allowed to drive along the set route for tours in the reserve, although usually you'll have to join a tour bus, which runs one to three times a day from the museum (BR12,000, 1½ hours) depending on demand.

An altogether easier option is to book a day trip with Brest Intourist (see p87). This includes transport and the services of an English-speaking guide, although you'll have to pay your own entry fees on top of the BR235,000 fee for one to three people.

WORTH THE TRIP: PRIPYATSKY NATIONAL PARK

One of the best-kept secrets in Belarus is the excellent **Pripyatsky National Park** (☎ 02353-75 644, 75 173; www.npp.by in Russian; vul Leninskaya 127, Turau), a relatively untouched swath of marshes, swampland and floodplains known locally as 'the lungs of Europe'. Flora and fauna particular to wetlands are found here, including more than 800 plant species, some 50 mammal species and more than 200 species of birds.

At the park headquarters and museum you can tour a great display of the flora and fauna specific to the area, and make all the arrangements you need. Excursions range from one day to a week, and can include extended fishing, hunting and boating expeditions deep into the marshlands. Cruises on the river are particularly recommended.

Park staff can also put you up at one of their guest houses in town, arrange accommodation in a private home or, even better, put you up in the middle of the park's nature itself. Several comfy cottages have been kitted out with kitchens and saunas and are set in sublimely peaceful settings. The park organises winter ice-fishing expeditions (followed by vodka and a sauna, of course) and many summer activities. Prices vary, but generally a person need only spend about €75 per day, including accommodation, three meals and guided tours.

From the UK, **Nature Trek** (www.naturetrek.co.uk) offers a well-regarded eight-day guided bird-watching trip to the park each May that costs £1200 all-inclusive from London.

From Minsk there are at least two daily buses to Turau (BR18,000, four to seven hours), plus one daily *marshrutka* (buses), (BR30,000, four hours) from Minsk's Vostochny bus station.

NORTHERN BELARUS

In the north of the country, Vitsebsk is the most obviously appealing destination to travellers, with its dramatic river, a clutch of lovely churches and the artistic heritage bequeathed to it by Marc Chagall. Also of interest is lovely Hrodna, one of the few towns in the country not destroyed in WWII.

VITSEBSK
ВІЦЕБСК
☎ 0212 / pop 365,000

The historic city of Vitsebsk (known universally outside Belarus by its Russian name, Vitebsk) lies a short distance from the Russian border and almost 300km from Minsk. Unlike the Belarusian capital, Vitsebsk has survived the whippings of history to some degree, making it one of the country's most historically and culturally significant places.

Clustered around the steep banks of the Dvina River, the city is today most famous for being the childhood home of the painter Marc Chagall, who grew up and studied here before moving to St Petersburg where his career began. With its relaxed atmosphere, attractive centre and diverting museums, Vitsebsk makes for a pleasant side trip or stopover on the way into Russia.

Orientation

Coming into Vitsebsk, you may be inclined to turn around and leave again, as the grey suburbs and heavy industry on the city's outskirts are particularly unappealing. The main drag, inventively named vul Lenina, runs parallel to the Dvina River, while the perpendicular Kirovsky Bridge crosses the river and leads via vul Kirova to the train and bus stations.

Information

There are ATMs on vul Lenina, although there always seems to be a queue for their services.
Internet Centre (☎ 362 090; vul Mayakovskaya 3; per hr BR1860; 🕙 10am-10pm) On a small square off vul Lenina and behind the Svyato-Voskresenesky Church.
Post office (vul Lenina) Offers international phone calls and internet access.

Sights

The first museum on every itinerary should be the excellent **Chagall Museum** (☎ 36 03 87, tours 36 34 68; www.chagall.vitebsk.by; vul Punta 2; admission BR5000, tours BR20,000; 🕙 11am-7pm Tue-Sun Mar-Sep, 11am-7pm Wed-Sun Oct-Feb), which was established in 1992 and displays collections of Chagall lithographs – his illustrations for the Bible (1956–60), designs to accompany Gogol's *Dead Souls* (1923–25) and graphic representations of the 12 tribes of Israel (1960). Downstairs there's a space for temporary exhibits.

Across the river a good 20-minute walk away is the **Marc Chagall House Museum** (☎ 36 34 68; vul Pokrovskaya 11; admission BR5000; ☙ 11am-7pm Tue-Sun), where the artist lived as a child for 13 years between 1897 and 1910 – a period beautifully evoked in his autobiography, *My Life*. The simple, small house contains photographs of Chagall and his family, various Jewish knick-knacks and some period furniture, and leads out into a garden. It's very evocative of a simple Jewish-Russian childhood.

The grand halls of the **Art Museum** (☎ 36 22 31; vul Lenina 32; admission BR500; ☙ 11am-6pm Wed-Sun) are decked out with mainly local art, both old and new. There are numerous 18th- to 20th-century works, including those by Repin and Makovsky. A highlight is the collection of very moving realist scenes of early-20th-century Vitsebsk street life by Yudel Pyen. Of the 793 paintings he donated to the city before he died, only 200 have survived, most of them held here.

While Vitsebsk does not have many churches of note, there is a pair of very different **Orthodox churches** on the eastern bank of the Dvina, near the main bridge on vul Zamkovaya. Nearby too is the lovely **Svyato-Voskresensky Church**, on the corner of vul Lenina and vul Zamkovaya, a reconstruction of a magnificent 18th-century church with gorgeous frescos on its facade and golden onion domes.

Festivals & Events

The immensely popular **Slavyansky Bazaar** (Slavic Bazaar; www.festival.vitebsk.by) is held in mid-July, and brings together dozens of singers and performers from Slavic countries for a week-long series of concerts. The annual event attracts tens of thousands of visitors, creating a huge citywide party.

Sleeping

Hotel Vitebsk (☎ 35 92 80; vul Zamkovaya 5/2a; s BR62,000-116,000, d BR82,000-155,000) This is the standard-issue Soviet hotel block option. While it won't win any prizes for charm or subtlety, the hotel is decent value and centrally located by the Kirovsky Bridge. The cheaper rooms need to be booked in advance. There's also a popular nightclub in the building.

Hotel Luchesa (☎ 29 85 00; pr Stroiteley 1; s/d incl breakfast from BR86,000/172,000; ☒) The new top hotel in town is the four-star Luchesa. A modern building some way south of the city centre, the place is well run and has comfy – if

fairly standard – modern rooms in varying shades of brown.

our pick **Hotel Eridan** (☎ 36 24 56; vul Savetskaya 21/17; s/d/ste incl breakfast BR152,000/198,000/249,000; ☒ ▯) This reliable establishment is handy for the Chagall Museum and well located in the middle of the Old Town. With pleasant wooden furniture, high ceilings, free wi-fi and well-equipped rooms (albeit done out rather gaudily), this place has just the charm so lacking in the standard-issue Soviet hotels you'll stay in elsewhere.

Eating & Drinking

Vitebsky Traktir (☎ 37 01 07; vul Suvorova 4; mains BR6000-18,000) What else would you expect to find in a dark cellar oozing centuries of Slavic tradition? Why, sushi of course. This decent place has lots of charm, even if it is a little too dark for its own good. A traditional menu is also available.

Zolotoy Drakon (☎ 23 63 00; vul Krylova 8; mains BR10,000-20,000; ☙ noon-midnight) The golden dragon is a surprisingly good Chinese restaurant complete with a Chinese chef (a true rarity in these parts), a relaxed atmosphere and a full menu with some dodgy English translations.

our pick **Zolotoy Lev** (☎ 35 81 11; vul Suvorova 20/13; mains BR10,000-25,000; ☙ noon-midnight) The smartest place in town is the expansive golden lion. There's a charming interior (when the TV is off), a large menu offering traditional Belarusian cuisine and a spacious outdoor area serving up *shashlyk* (meat kebabs) and beer. Live music is thankfully relegated to the 2nd floor each night (entry BR5000), meaning you can dine in relative peace.

Kofeynya (vul Suvorova 2) This minute coffeehouse next door to the Vitebsky Traktir serves up the best coffee in town, as well as a large selection of teas and cake.

Café Melody (☎ 35 81 36; vul Lenina 65; ☙ 10am-11pm) Vitebsk's answer to the Hard Rock Café is a surprisingly cool place, even if instead of Hendrix's guitar it only has a worn copy of Macca's *Flowers in the Dirt* LP carefully displayed. During the day a young crowd drinks coffee and eats cake to a rocking soundtrack, while at night cocktails are served up and there's often live music.

Getting There & Away

Vitsebsk is on one of the major railway lines heading south from St Petersburg into

---

WORTH THE TRIP: HRODNA

If you're entering Belarus from northern Poland, or if you have extra time in the country, think about visiting Hrodna (Grodno in Russian). It was one of the few Belarusian cities that *wasn't* bombed during WWII, so it's rife with old wooden homes and, although it's a major city, it definitely has a 'big village' sort of feel to it. The city's best hotel by far is the privately run, superfriendly **Semashko** (☎ 152-75 02 99; www.hotel-semashko.ru/en; vul Antonova; s/d BR180,000/200,000; 🖳), which you should reserve in advance due to its immense popularity. Trains between Minsk and Hrodna leave five times a day (BR15,000, six hours), although *marshrutky* (buses) from Minsk's Vostochny bus station do the trip much faster and far more regularly (BR30,000, three hours).

Ukraine. There are two or three daily trains to Minsk (BR30,000 to BR40,000, 4½ to six hours) and one to St Petersburg (BR188,000, 13 hours). On even-numbered days of the month trains run to Kyiv (BR105,000, 16 hours). There's also a daily train to both Moscow (BR95,000, 11 hours) and Brest (BR61,000, 16 hours).

There are approximately hourly to two-hourly buses or *marshrutky* to Minsk (BR30,000, four to five hours). Four times a week Ecolines buses head to Moscow (BR85,000, 8½ hours) and St Petersburg (BR100,000, 11 hours).

Getting Around
While Vitsebsk is larger than most other regional centres, the city is pleasant to explore on foot. Buses ply the 1.5km main drag from the bus and train stations into town; get off just after crossing the Dvina and you'll be just 500m from the Art Museum.

BELARUS DIRECTORY

ACCOMMODATION
Farmers and villagers are usually generous about allowing campers to pitch a tent on their lot for an evening. If you do this it would be polite to offer to pay a small amount, but do not insist as in many cases locals will be delighted to accommodate you on their land; in this case, a small gift such as flowers or chocolate would be appropriate. Outside national parks you may camp pretty much anywhere, although camping in or near a city is asking for trouble from the police.

While budget and midrange accommodation standards in Belarus tend to be lower than in the West, they are still generally acceptable and often better than in Russia or Ukraine. Top-end places, of which there are a few in Minsk, are for the most part equal to what you would expect from a top-end place in the West.

A fledgling B&B association, **Rural & Ecotourism** (☎ 017-251 0076; www.ruralbelarus.by), was started by the woman who runs Dudutki and offers the chance to do homestays all over the country.

All rooms in this chapter have private bathrooms unless otherwise indicated; prices given are for the high season. Smoking in hotel rooms usually occurs in Belarus; in Minsk, four- or five-star hotels will usually offer non-smoking rooms, but these usually don't exist in lower price ranges.

ACTIVITIES
Belarus is flat, but it's not so flat that you can't find some places to enjoy skiing. About 20km from Minsk is the Raubichy Olympic Sports Complex, where you can enjoy some great cross-country skiing, while downhill skiing and snowboarding are possible at **Logoisk** (☎ 01774-53 758, 53 000; www.logoisk.by) and the newer **Silichy** (☎ 01774-50 285), both about 30km from Minsk. Belintourist (p79) does skiing and other activity- related tours.

BUSINESS HOURS
Offices are generally open from 9am to 6pm during the work week, with banks closing at 5pm. Shops are open from about 9am or 10am to about 9pm Monday to Saturday, closing on Sunday around 6pm (if they're open at all that day). Some businesses will close for lunch, which is usually for an hour and occurs anytime between noon and 2pm.

Restaurants and bars usually open around 10am and, with unfortunately few exceptions, close between 10pm and midnight.

EMBASSIES & CONSULATES

There is no representation for Canada, Australia, New Zealand or the Netherlands in Belarus.

France (Map p78; ☎ 017-210 2868; www.ambafrance -by.org; pl Svabody 11, Minsk)

Germany (Map p78; ☎ 017-217 5900; www.minsk .diplo.de; vul Zakharava 26, Minsk)

Moldova (Map p78; ☎ 017-289 1441; vul Belarusskaya 2, Minsk)

Romania (off Map p78; ☎ 017-203 8097; per Moskvina 4, Minsk)

Russia Minsk (Map p78; ☎ 017-222 4985; fax 222 4980; vul Gvardeiskaya 5a, Minsk); Brest (Map p87; ☎ 0162-23 78 42; fax 0162-21 0473; brestcons@brest.by; vul Pushkin-skaya 10, Brest)

UK (Map p78; ☎ 017-210 5920; www.ukinbelarus.fco .gov.uk; vul Karla Marksa 37, Minsk)

Ukraine Minsk (Map p78; ☎ /fax 017-283 1990; vul Staravilenskaya 51, Minsk); Brest (Map p87; ☎ 0162-22 04 55; vul Vorovskaha 19, Brest)

USA (Map p78; ☎ 017-210 1283; http://minsk.usem bassy.gov; vul Staravilenskaya 46, Minsk)

FESTIVALS & EVENTS

The night of 6 July is **Kupalye**, a celebration with pagan roots when young girls gather flowers and throw them into a river as a method of fortune-telling, while everyone else sits by lake or riverside fires drinking beer.

Belarus' best-loved cultural event is the Slavyansky Bazaar, held in Vitsebsk; see p92 for details.

GAY & LESBIAN TRAVELLERS

Homophobia is rife in Belarus, even though officially gay sex acts were legalised in 1994. Despite this, Slavic laissez-faire attitudes mean that you don't have to look hard to find gay life, the details of which flourish on the internet, and at Minsk's one gay club, 6A (p83), and a handful of other ever-changing venues that are gay friendly or have gay nights. As travellers, gay and lesbian couples are unlikely to horrify locals by asking for a double room, but otherwise discretion is advisable. Websites to check out include www.gay.by and pride.by.

HOLIDAYS

New Year's Day 1 January
Orthodox Christmas 7 January
International Women's Day 8 March
Constitution Day 15 March
Catholic & Orthodox Easter March/April
Unity of Peoples of Russia and Belarus Day 2 April
International Labour Day (May Day) 1 May
Victory Day 9 May
Independence Day 3 July
Dzyady (Day of the Dead) 2 November
Day of the October Revolution 7 November
Catholic Christmas 25 December

Note that Independence Day is the date Minsk was liberated from the Nazis, not the date of independence from the USSR, which is not celebrated.

INSURANCE

All visitors to Belarus are required to possess medical insurance from an approved company to cover the entire period of their stay. It is often unlikely you will ever be asked for it, but you may have to purchase the official policy at border posts if you don't have documentation to prove you're not insured. This is relatively cheap; see www.belarusconsul. org for costs and details. Note that medical coverage is not required for holders of transit visas (see p96).

LANGUAGE

Despite the fact that almost all signage (especially anything official, such as road signs) is in Belarusian, you'll almost never hear Belarusian used on the street. There is now a small but strong and growing group of student nationalists who are working to support the use of Belarusian, and it is now considered to be the country's language of the intellectual elite. However, at nearly all levels of society, Russian – which enjoys equal status with Belarusian as the country's official language – is the language of choice, creating a rather strange dichotomy between what you see and hear. This means you'll ask the name of the street and be told it's ulitsa Krasnaya, only to find that the street sign calls it vulitsa Chyrvonaya. Confused? You will be. In this guide we've used the Belarusian names for streets, to match the local signage. See boxed text, p79, for more details on this thorny issue.

MONEY

The Belarusian rouble (BR) is the national currency, and the money's wide spectrum of bill denominations is overwhelming to the newcomer. There are BR10, BR20, BR50, BR100, BR500, BR1000, BR5000, BR10,000, BR20,000,

BR50,000 and BR100,000 notes. You'll quickly acquire a thick wad of largely worthless notes. Thank god there are no coins. Ensure you change any remaining roubles before leaving Belarus, as it's almost impossible to exchange the currency outside the country.

ATMs and currency-exchange offices are not hard to find in Belrusian cities. Major credit cards are accepted at many of the nicer hotels, restaurants, and supermarkets in Minsk, but travellers cheques are not worth the effort. Some businesses quote prices in euros or US dollars (using the abbreviation YE), but payment is only accepted in roubles.

POST

The word for post office is *pashtamt*. Posting a 20g letter to anywhere in the world costs BR480. The best way to mail important, time-sensitive items is with the Express Mail Service (EMS), offered at most main post offices.

TELEPHONE

Numbers listed in this chapter are all landlines, unless they have a three-digit number before them, which indicate that they are mobile phone numbers. The mobile-phone market is divided between four companies, of which Velcom (www.velcom.by) and MTS (www.mts.by) are the dominant players. Anyone with an unlocked mobile-phone handset can buy a SIM card for next to nothing, although some vendors will be wary of selling a SIM card to foreigners.

Avoid using payphones in Belarus; they require special phonecards and are a hassle. It's better to find the local Beltelekom, a state-run company that opens late. You can access the internet, place international and domestic calls, and send and receive faxes at these offices.

To dial a Minsk landline number from a Minsk landline number, just dial the number; from a local mobile phone, press ☎ 8 017 or ☎ 375 17 and then dial the number.

To dial from one Minsk mobile number to another, dial ☎ 8 029 for Velcom, MTS and Dialtog (the most common providers) or ☎ 8 025 for BeST.

To make an intercity call from a land phone, dial ☎ 8 (wait for the tone), the city's area code (including the 0) and the number; from a mobile, do the same, and if it doesn't work, try dialling ☎ +375 and the area code without the 0, then the number.

> ### EMERGENCY NUMBERS
> - Ambulance ☎ 03
> - Fire ☎ 01
> - Police ☎ 02

To make an international call from a landline phone, dial 8 (wait for the tone), 10, then the country code, area code and number; from a mobile, press + then dial the country code, area code and number.

If your local mobile phone is on roaming, call a Belarusian landline by dialling ☎ +375 and the area code without the 0; to call a Belarusian mobile, dial ☎ +375 29 and the number (or ☎ +375 25 for calls to BeST phones).

To phone Belarus from abroad, dial ☎ 375 followed by the city code (without the first zero) and number.

For operator enquiries, call ☎ 085 (it's serviced 24 hours); a few of the staff speak English.

VISAS

Belarusian visa regulations change frequently, so check with your nearest Belarus embassy for the latest details (most embassies have visa information on their websites, although be aware that they are not always up to date). All Western visitors need a visa, and arranging one before you arrive is essential. Point-of-entry visas are only issued at the Minsk-2 international airport (p84), but you still need to get an invitation in advance, and some carriers may not be prepared to let you fly without a visa in your passport, so for peace of mind we advise arranging a visa before you travel.

Applications

To get a visa, you will need a photograph; an invitation from a private person or a business; or a confirmation of reservation from a hotel, and your passport. There are three main types of visas: tourist, issued if you have a tourist invitation or hotel reservation voucher; visitor (guest), if your invitation comes from an individual in Belarus; and business, if your invitation is from a business. There are also transit visas, if you are passing through and won't be in the country for more than 48 hours, for which no invite or voucher is necessary. Visitor and tourist visas are issued for 30 days (tourist visas can be multientry); business visas are for 90 days and can also be multientry.

By far the simplest – although the most expensive – way to get a visa is to apply through a visa agency. Alternatively, you can take a faxed confirmation from your hotel to the nearest Belarusian embassy and apply for one yourself.

Tallinn, Rīga and Vilnius have numerous travel agencies specialising in Belarusian visas.

Getting an invitation from an individual can be a long, complex process. Your friend in Belarus needs a *zaprashenne* (official invitation) form from their local passport and visa office and should then send it to you. With this, you apply at the nearest Belarusian embassy.

Visa costs vary depending on the embassy you apply at and your citizenship. Americans pay more, but typically single-entry visas cost about €90 for five-working-days service and €160 for next-day service; double-entry visas usually cost double that. Business visas are more expensive than tourist visas. Transit visas typically cost from €65 to €85, more if needed the next day.

Registration

If you are staying in the country for more than 72 hours, you must have your visa officially registered. Hotels do this automatically, sometimes for a small fee. They'll give you small pieces of paper with stamps on them, which you keep to show to customs agents upon departure if asked. In theory you'll be fined if you don't provide proof of registration for every day of your stay; in practice, proof of one day is good enough. If you're staying at a short-term let apartment, the owner will usually have a connection at a local hotel and will organise your registration for you.

If you've received a personal invitation, you'll need to find the nearest *passportno-vizovoye upravleniye* (passport and visa department; PVU, formerly OVIR) or try to convince hotel staff to register your visa for the cost of one night's stay. The **PVU main office** (Map p78; ☎ 017-231 9174; pr Nezalezhnastsi 8, Minsk) is in Minsk.

Transit Visas

All persons passing through Belarusian territory are required to possess a transit visa, which can be obtained at any Belarusian consulate upon presentation of travel tickets clearly showing the final destination as being outside of Belarus. The possession of a valid Russian visa is not enough to serve as a transit visa. Transit visas are not available at the border.

TRANSPORT IN BELARUS

GETTING THERE & AWAY
Air

There is no departure tax in Belarus. See p84 for information on Minsk's airports. Belarus' national airline is **Belavia** (B2; Map p78; ☎ 017-210 4100; www.belavia.by; vul Nyamiha 14, Minsk) with flights to London, Paris, Frankfurt, Berlin, Vienna, Rome and Milan, as well as connections to Manchester, Shannon, Tel Aviv and many Eastern European capitals.

The following are the main international airlines that fly to Minsk:

Aeroflot (SU; ☎ 017-227 2887; www.aeroflot.com/eng)

Austrian Airlines (OS; ☎ 017-288 2535/55; www.aua.com)

El Al (LY; ☎ 017-211 2606; www.elal.co.il)

LOT Polish Airlines (LO; ☎ 017-226 6628; www.lot.com)

Lufthansa (LH; ☎ 017-284 7129; www.lufthansa.com)

Land

Long queues at border crossings are not uncommon.

BUSES

The most frequently used international bus services are the quick four-hour trip between Vilnius (Lithuania) and Minsk, and the seven-hour trip between Minsk and Bialystok (Poland). Buses stop at the border for customs and passport controls. See p84 for details on bus services from Minsk, and p93 for services from Vitsebsk.

CAR & MOTORCYCLE

If you're driving your own vehicle, there are 10 main road routes into Belarus via border stations through which foreigners can pass. International driving permits are recognised in Belarus. Roads in Belarus are generally very good and main motorways are wonderfully light on traffic, although the main M1/E30 motorway gets busy with long-distance trucks travelling between Russia and the EU in both

AT YOUR OWN RISK

There is effectively no border between Russia and Belarus. In theory, it's possible to enter Belarus by train and leave it for Russia – or go to Russia and back from Belarus – without going through passport control, and therefore without needing a visa for the country you're sneaking into. However, a hotel won't take you without a visa, so you'd have to stay with friends or rent an apartment, and if your visa-less documents are checked on the street (unlikely unless you're a troublemaker or a person of colour), you will be deported.

If you do not receive a migration card when entering Russia, contact your embassy immediately upon arrival to find out how to get one. If you do not receive an entry stamp, go to the local OVIR (Visa and Registration) office in Russia – but bring a full supply of patience.

A much better option if you plan to travel from Belarus into Russia is to ensure you have a valid visa for Russia as well. This will be stamped by Belarusian control on entry to Belarus and, under the terms of the Russian–Belarusian 'one state' agreement, is valid as an entry stamp for Russia. Keep your immigration card from Belarus and use it when you leave Russia, as they are valid in both countries.

BELARUS

directions. Signage is excellent throughout the country, although usually only in Cyrillic. On intercity road trips, fill up with fuel when exiting the city; fuel stations may be scant before you hit the next big town.

TRAIN

Trains are usually a more comfortable but slightly slower way to travel than bus. From Minsk there are services to Russia, Lithuania and Poland, plus connections to the rest of Europe via Brest; see p85 for details. You can also get to Russia or Ukraine from Vitsebsk; see p92 for more.

GETTING AROUND

Train and bus are the most common ways to travel around Belarus. Bus is a little faster and cheaper, but trains are generally more comfortable.

Hitching is practised by young locals quite a bit. But it's never entirely safe in any country in the world, and Lonely Planet doesn't recommend it.

Car

It's perfectly possible to hire a car in Minsk (see p84), and, if you can read Cyrillic, it's surprisingly easy to drive in Belarus. In general cars are old and badly maintained. Look them over carefully and check the spare tyre before you drive off.

The Brest–Minsk highway (Brestskoye shosse; E30/M1) is an excellent two-laner, but there are frequent tollbooths (they only charge cars with foreign licence plates).

Drivers from the USA or EU can use their own country's driving licence for six months. Cars drive in the right-hand lane, children 12 and under must sit in a back seat, and your blood-alcohol level should be 0%. Fuel is usually not hard to find, but try to keep your tank full, and it would even be wise to keep some spare fuel as well.

You will be instructed by signs to slow down when approaching GAI (road police) stations, and not doing so is a sure-fire way to get a substantial fine. You may see GAI signs in Russian (ГАИ) or in Belarusian (ДАЙ).

Bosnia & Hercegovina

Bosnia and Hercegovina (BiH) describes itself as the 'heart-shaped land'. Geographically the allusion is surprisingly anatomically accurate. Emotionally too, the deep yet unimposing human warmth of this craggily beautiful land fits the bill. And despite some lingering scars, the heartbreaking societal haemorrhaging of the 1990s has been completely stemmed (if not forgotten). The BiH of today has regained its once-famed religious tolerance. Rebuilt churches, mosques and synagogues huddle closely, rekindling that intriguing East-meets-West atmosphere born of Bosnia's fascinatingly blended Ottoman and Austro-Hungarian histories.

Socialist urban planning and war damage still combine to give certain post-industrial cityscapes all the charm of a Molvanian nightmare. But such scenes are surprisingly rare blots on a beautiful, largely rural landscape. Meanwhile the reincarnated Austro-Ottoman centres of Sarajevo and especially Mostar are unexpected delights. And the majority of Bosnian towns are lovably small, wrapped around medieval castles and surrounded by mountain ridges, verdant hills or merrily cascading river canyons. Few places in Europe offer better rafting or such accessible and excellent-value skiing.

Fashionable bars and wi-fi-equipped cafes abound but employment concerns remain as the fledgling state finally comes to terms with postcommunist realities that were masked for years by more pressing war worries. Roads remain slow and winding but they're extremely scenic, mostly well surfaced and relatively quiet, making for delightful random adventures, especially if you're driving. Indeed, however you travel, BiH offers a great sense of discovery, of real personal interaction and of very fair value for money that's all too rare in the heart of 21st-century Europe.

BOSNIA & HERCEGOVINA

FAST FACTS

- **Area** 51,129 sq km
- **Capital** Sarajevo
- **Currency** convertible mark (KM, BAM); €1 = 1.96KM; US$1= 1.43KM; UK£1 = 2.08KM; A$1 = 0.99KM; ¥100 = 1.50KM; NZ$1 = 0.80KM
- **Famous for** 1984 Sarajevo Winter Olympics, the bridge at Mostar
- **Official languages** Bosnian, Croatian, Serbian
- **Phrases** *zdravo* (hello); *hvala* (thanks); *molim* (please)
- **Population** 4 million (estimate)
- **Telephone codes** country code ☎ 387; international access code ☎ 00
- **Visas** not required for most visitors, see p138

BOSNIA & HERCEGOVINA

HIGHLIGHTS

- Nose about Mostar's delightful Old Town seeking ever-new angles from which to photograph young men throwing themselves off the magnificently rebuilt **Stari Most** (Old Bridge; p122).
- Explore waterfall-fronted **Jajce** (p131), one of BiH's most appealing fortress towns, which hides some compelling historical curiosities and makes an ideal base for visiting the stunning mountain lakes nearby.
- Raft dramatic canyons down one of BiH's fast-flowing rivers – whether from **Foča** (p129), **Bihać** (p134) or **Banja Luka** (p133) – or even start with a quad-bike 'safari' through the wild upland villages behind the ski resort of **Bjelašnica** (p119).
- Potter around the timeless Turkish- and Austrian-era pedestrian lanes of **Sarajevo** (p106), sample its fashionable cafes and eclectic nightlife or gaze down on the mosque-dotted, red-roofed cityscape from the Park Prinčeva restaurant.

ITINERARIES

- **Six days** Arriving from Dubrovnik (coastal Croatia), roam Mostar's Old Town and join a day-tour visiting Počitelj, Blagaj and Kravice Waterfalls. After two days in Sarajevo head for Jajce then bus down to Split (Croatia). Or visit Višegrad en route to Mokra Gora and Belgrade (Serbia).

CONNECTIONS: MOVING ON FROM BOSNIA & HERCEGOVINA

Regular buses link the Croatian coast to Mostar (p126) and Sarajevo (p118), and there's one little-publicised Trebinje–Dubrovnik bus (p128). A new Sarajevo–Zagreb sleeper train (p117) offers an inexpensive and comfortable westward exit. Connections to Serbia and Montenegro are easiest from the Republika Srpska, with a direct night train from Banja Luka to Belgrade (p134) and various useful bus links from Višegrad (p129) and Trebinje (p128). Connecting to Hungary is now limited to one poorly timed all-day train from Sarajevo (p117).

■ **Two weeks** As above, but add quaint Trebinje and historic Stolac between Dubrovnik and Mostar, ski or go quad-biking around Bjelašnica near Sarajevo, visit the controversial Visoko pyramid and old-town Travnik en route to Jajce, and consider adding in some high-adrenaline rafting from Banja Luka, Bihać or Foča.

CLIMATE & WHEN TO GO

Winters are cold and snowy, albeit milder in Hercegovina, where summers are baking hot. On spring nights you'll need a light sweater but days are gently warm with dazzling blossoms and lush meadow greenery. Rafting in April is high-adrenaline, world-quality stuff but by July white water calms down, making rivers less taxing for novices.

In spring and autumn tourists are rare but in summer accommodation can be stretched in Sarajevo and Mostar as diaspora Bosnians come 'home'. The peak ski season is mid-December to mid-March but prices fall considerably in later March if you're prepared to gamble on snow conditions (often excellent but much less predictable at that time).

HISTORY

Be aware that much of BiH's 'history' remains highly controversial and is seen very differently according to one's ethno-religious viewpoint.

In AD 9 ancient Illyrian Bosnia was conquered by the Romans. Slavs arrived from the late 6th century and were dominant by 1180, when Bosnia first emerged as an independent entity under former Byzantine governor Ban Kulina. BiH had a patchy 'golden age' between 1180 and 1463, especially in the late 1370s when Bosnia's King Tvtko gained Hum (future Hercegovina) and controlled much of Dalmatia.

But for the next 80 years Turkish raids whittled away at the country. By the 1460s most of Bosnia was under Ottoman control. Within a few generations, Islam became dominant among townspeople and landowners, though a sizeable proportion of the serfs *(rayah)* remained Christian. Bosnians also became particularly prized soldiers in the Ottoman army, many rising eventually to high rank with the imperial court. The broad-minded early Ottoman era also produced great advances in infrastructure, with fine mosques and bridges built by charitable bequests. However, the Ottomans failed to follow the West's Industrial Revolution.

By the 19th century the empire's economy was archaic, and all attempts to modernise the feudal system in BiH were strenuously resisted by the entrenched Bosnian-Muslim elite. In 1873 İstanbul's banking system collapsed under the weight of the high-living sultan's debts. To pay these debts the sultan demanded added taxes. But in 1874 BiH's harvests failed, so paying those taxes would have meant starving. With nothing left to lose the mostly Christian Bosnian peasants kicked off a wave of revolts that snowballed into a tangle of pan-Balkan wars.

BOSNIA & HERCEGOVINA

HOW MUCH?

- **Short taxi ride** 5KM
- **Internet access per hour** 1.50KM to 3KM
- **Espresso coffee** 0.50KM to 2KM
- **Shot of šljia (plum brandy)** 1.50KM
- **Movie ticket** 3KM to 5KM

LONELY PLANET INDEX

- **1L petrol** 1.51KM
- **1L bottled water** 0.90KM
- **500mL beer (in a bar)** 3KM
- **Souvenir T-shirt** 15KM
- **Street snack (burek)** 2KM

Austro-Hungarian Rule

These pan-Balkan wars ended with the farcical 1878 Congress of Berlin, at which the Western powers carved up the western Ottoman lands. Austria-Hungary was 'invited' to occupy BiH, which was treated like a colony even though theoretically remaining Ottoman under sovereignty. An unprecedented period of development followed. Roads, railways and bridges were built and coal mining and forestry became booming industries. Education encouraged a new generation of Bosnians to look increasingly towards Vienna.

But new nationalist feelings were simmering: Bosnian Catholics increasingly identified with neighbouring Croatia (itself within Austria-Hungary) while Orthodox Bosnians sympathised with recently independent Serbia's dreams of a greater Serbian homeland. In between lay Bosnia's Muslims (40%), who belatedly started to develop a distinct Bosniak 'ethnic' consciousness.

While Turkey was busy with the 1908 Young Turk revolution, Austria-Hungary annexed BiH. This was a slap in the face for all those who dreamed of a pan-Slavic or greater Serbian future. The resultant scramble for the last remainders of Ottoman Europe kicked off the Balkan Wars of 1912 and 1913. No sooner had these been (unsatisfactorarily) resolved than the heir to the Austrian throne was shot dead while visiting Sarajevo. One month later Austria declared war on Serbia and WWI swiftly followed.

World Wars, Communism & Political Tension

WWI killed an astonishing 15% of the Bosnian population. It also brought down both the Turkish and Austro-Hungarian empires, leaving BiH to be absorbed into proto-Yugoslavia.

During WWII BiH was occupied partly by Italy, partly by Germany, then absorbed into the newly created fascist state of Croatia. Croatia's Ustaše decimated Bosnia's Jewish population, and they also persecuted Serbs and Muslims. Meanwhile a pro-Nazi group of Bosnian Muslims committed their own atrocities against Bosnian Serbs while Serb Četniks and Tito's Communist Partizans put up some stalwart resistance to the Germans (as well as fighting each other). The BiH mountains proved ideal territory for Tito's flexible guerrilla army, whose greatest victories are still locally commemorated with vast memorials. At Jajce (p132) in 1943, Tito's antifascist council famously formulated a constitution for an inclusive postwar, socialist Yugoslavia.

After WWII, BiH was granted republic status within Tito's initially anti-religious Yugoslavia. After Tito fell out with the USSR in 1954 and became prominent in the 'non-aligned movement', Yugoslavia's alliances with countries like Egypt meant that having 'token' Muslim Bosnians on the diplomatic staff suddenly became a useful cachet. However, up until 1971, 'Muslim' was not considered an 'ethnic group' so Bosniaks had had to register as Croat, Serb or 'Other/Yugoslav'.

Despite considerable mining development in the northeast and the economic boost of the 1984 Sarajevo Winter Olympics, Bosnia remained one of the least developed Yugoslav republics.

The 1990s Conflict

In the post-Tito era, as Yugoslavia imploded, 'ethnic' tensions were ratcheted up by the ultranationalist Serb leader Slobodan Milošević and equally radical Croat leader Franjo Tuđman. Although these two leaders were at war by spring 1991, they reputedly came up with a de facto agreement in which they

---

WHAT'S IN A NAME?

Geographically Bosnia and Hercegovina (BiH) comprises Bosnia (in the north) and Hercegovina (pronounced Her-tse-GO-vina, in the south), although the term 'Bosnian' refers to anyone from BiH, not just from Bosnia-proper. Politically, however, BiH is divided into two entirely different political entities. Southwest and central BiH falls mostly within the Federation of Bosnia and Hercegovina, usually shortened to 'the Federation'. Meanwhile most areas bordering Serbia, Montenegro and the northern arm of Croatia are within the Serb-dominated Republika Srpska (abbreviated RS). The entities were once at war, but these days you'll sometimes struggle to know which one you're in. The biggest giveaway is the use of the Cyrillic alphabet in the RS, but a few minor practicalities are also different, notably stamps and phonecards.

THE TWO ENTITIES OF BOSNIA & HERCEGOVINA

planned to divide BiH between breakaway Croatia and rump Yugoslavia.

Under president Alija Izetbegović, BiH declared independence from Yugoslavia on 15 October 1991. Bosnian Serb parliamentarians wanted none of this and withdrew to set up their own government at Pale, 20km east of Sarajevo. BiH was recognised internationally as an independent state on 6 April 1992 but Sarajevo was already under siege both by Serb paramilitaries and by parts of the Yugoslav army (JNA).

Over the next three years a brutal and extraordinarily complex civil war raged. Best-known is the campaign of ethnic cleansing in northern and eastern BiH creating the 300km 'pure'-Serb Republika Srpska (RS). But *there were terrible criminals on our side too* as locals of each religion will readily admit. In western Hercegovina the Croat population armed itself with the help of neighbouring Croatia, eventually ejecting Serbs from their villages in a less-reported but similarly brutal war.

Perhaps unaware of the secret Tuđman–Milošević understanding, Izetbegović had signed a formal military alliance with Croatia in June 1992. But by early 1993 fighting had broken out between Muslims and Croats, creating another war front. Croats attacked Muslims in Stolac and Mostar, bombarding their historic monuments and blasting Mostar's famous medieval bridge into the river. Muslim troops, including a small foreign mujahedin force, desecrated churches and attacked Croat villages, notably around Travnik.

With atrocities on all sides, the West's reaction was confused and erratic. In August 1992, pictures of concentration-camp and rape-camp victims (mostly Muslim) found in northern Bosnia spurred the UN to send a Protection Force (Unprofor) of 7500 peacekeeping troops. They secured the neutrality of Sarajevo airport well enough to allow the delivery of humanitarian aid, but overall proved notoriously impotent.

Ethnic cleansing of Muslims from Foča and Višegrad led the UN to declare 'safe zones' around the Muslim-majority towns of Srebrenica, Župa, and Goražde. But rarely has the term 'safe' been so misused. When NATO belatedly authorised air strikes to protect these areas, the Serbs responded by capturing 300 Unprofor peacekeepers and chaining them to potential targets to keep the planes away.

In July 1995 Dutch peacekeepers could only watch as the starving, supposedly 'safe area' of Srebrenica fell to a Bosnian Serb force led by the infamous Ratko Mladić. An estimated 8000 Muslim men were slaughtered in Europe's worst mass killings since WWII. Somewhat miraculously, Goražde held out, albeit in ruins, thanks to sporadically available UN food supplies.

By this stage, Croatia had renewed its own internal offensive, expelling Serbs from the Krajina region of Croatia in August 1995. At least 150,000 of these dispossessed people then moved to the Serb-held areas of northern Bosnia.

Finally, another murderous Serb mortar attack on Sarajevo's Markale Market kick-started a shift in UN and NATO politics. An ultimatum to end the Serbs' siege of Sarajevo was made more persuasive through two weeks of NATO air strikes in September 1995. US president Bill Clinton's proposal for a peace conference in Dayton, Ohio was accepted soon after.

The Dayton Agreement

While maintaining BiH's pre-war external boundaries, Dayton divided the country into today's pair of roughly equally sized 'entities' (see the boxed text, opposite), each with limited autonomy. Finalising the border between the Federation of Bosnia & Hercegovina (the Muslim and Croat portion including central Sarajevo) and the Republika Srpska (RS; the Serb part) required considerable political and cartographic creativity. The process was only

BOSNIA & HERCEGOVINA

finally completed in 1999 when the last sticking point, Brčko, was belatedly given a special self-governing status all of its own. Meanwhile BiH's curious rotating tripartite overall presidency has been kept in check by the EU's powerful 'High Representative' (www.ohr.int).

For refugees (1.2 million abroad, and a million displaced within BiH), the Dayton Agreement emphasised the right to return to (or to sell) their pre-war homes. International agencies donated very considerable funding to restore BiH's infrastructure, housing stock and historical monuments.

An embarrassing problem post-Dayton was the failure to find and try as war criminals Ratko Mladić and the Bosnian Serb leader Radovan Karadžić (president of the RS until July 1996). Despite $5 million dollar rewards offered for their arrest, Karadžić was only apprehended in 2008, while Mladić remains at large, probably protected by supporters who perceive him to be an honest patriot.

Bosnia & Hercegovina Today

Nonnationalist politicians now run the RS, while under EU and American pressure BiH has centralised considerably in a movement away from the original Dayton 'separate powers' concept. BiH now has a unified army and common passports. Both entities now have indistinguishable car licence plates and use the same currency, albeit with banknotes in two somewhat different designs. Many (though by no means all) refugees have returned and rebuilt their pre-war homes.

Today it's economics more than nationalism that is the great concern for most Bosnians. Those few socialist-era factories that weren't destroyed in the 1990s conflicts have downsized to fit tough 21st-century global realities. New 'business-friendly' government initiatives, including a recent wave of privatisations, are eyed with suspicion; the populace fears growing corruption. People assume that one day BiH will join the EU, though for many, nearby Slovenia's experience suggests that EU membership will just push up prices and make life harder. 'Life's tough' one war-widowed homestay hostess told us, 'but at least there's peace'.

PEOPLE

Bosniaks (Bosnian Muslims), Bosnian Serbs (Orthodox) and Bosnian Croats (Catholics) are all Southern Slavs. Physically they are indistinguishable. The pre-war population was mixed, with intermarriage common in the cities. Stronger divisions have inevitably appeared since the 'ethnic cleansing' of the 1990s. The war resulted in massive population shifts, changing the size and linguistic balance of many cities. Notably the population of Banja Luka grew by over 100,000 as it absorbed Serb refugees from Croatia.

Bosniaks now predominate in Sarajevo and central BiH, Bosnian Croats in western and southern Hercegovina, and Bosnian Serbs in the RS, which includes Istochno (East) Sarajevo. Relations between the three groups have virtually normalised on a human level, though politically contacts remain limited.

RELIGION

Blurring the borderline between Europe's Catholic west and Orthodox east, sparsely populated medieval Bosnia had its own independent church. This remains the source of many historical myths, but the long-popular idea that it was 'infected' by the Bulgarian Bogomil heresy is now largely discounted.

Following their conquest by the Ottoman Turks, many Bosnians converted to the easy-going Ottoman brand of Sufi-inspired Islam, as much to gain civil privileges as for spiritual enlightenment. The Ottoman Empire was much more religiously open minded than Western Europe at that time and offered refuge to the Sephardic Jews evicted en masse from Spain in 1492. While conditions varied, Bosnian Jews mostly prospered up until WWII, when most of the 14,000-strong community fled or were murdered by Nazis.

Bosnian Muslims also suffered horribly during WWII, with at least 756 mosques destroyed. Postwar Yugoslavia's Stalinist initially anti-religious line softened when Tito repositioned the country as a 'nonaligned' state, resulting in the growing status of Islam within 1950s Yugoslavia.

Today, about 40% of the population is Muslim, 31% is Orthodox (mostly Bosnian Serbs), 15% Roman Catholic (mostly Bosnian Croats) and 4% Protestant. There are around 500 Jews. Religion is taken seriously as a badge of ethnicity but spiritually most people are fairly secular.

ARTS

Bosnia's best-known writer, Ivo Andrić (1892–1975) won the 1961 Nobel Prize in

Literature. With astonishing psychological agility, his epic novel, the classic *Bridge over the Drina*, retells 350 years of Bosnian history as seen through the eyes of unsophisticated townsfolk in Višegrad. His *Travnik Chronicles* (aka Bosnian Chronicle) is also rich with human insight, though its portrayal of Bosnia is through the eyes of somewhat jaded 19th-century foreign consuls in Travnik.

Many thought-provoking essays, short stories and poems explore the prickly subject of the 1990s conflict, often contrasting horrors against the victims' enduring humanity. Quality varies greatly but recommended collections include Miljenko Jergović's *Sarajevo Marlboro* and Semezdin Mehmedinović's *Sarajevo Blues*.

The relationship between two soldiers, one Muslim, one Serb, caught alone in the same trench during the Sarajevo siege was the theme for Danis Tanović's Oscar-winning 2002 film *No Man's Land*. The movie *Go West* takes on the deep taboo of homosexuality as a wartime Serb-Bosniak gay couple become latter-day Romeo and Juliet. *Gori Vatra* (aka Fuse) is an irony-packed dark comedy set in the pretty Bosnian castle town of Tešanj just after the war, parodying efforts to hide corruption and create a facade of ethnic reintegration for the sake of a proposed visit by US President Bill Clinton.

Sevdah (traditional Bosnian music) typically uses heart-wrenching vocals to recount tales of unhappy amours. Meanwhile Sarajevo has an annual jazz festival (p113) and the post-industrial city of Tuzla has vibrant rap and metal scenes.

Medieval Bosnian craftsmen created unique oversized gravestones called *stećci* (singular *stećak*). The best-known examples are found at Radimlja near Stolac (p127). However, those collected outside Sarajevo's National Museum (p112) are finer, while a group near Umoljani (p120) has a much more visually satisfying setting.

BiH crafts from *kilims* (woollen flat-weaves) to copperware and decoratively repurposed bullet casings are widely sold in Mostar's Kujundžiluk (p125) and Sarajevo's Baščaršija (p117).

ENVIRONMENT

BiH is predominantly mountainous. Some 30 peaks rise between 1700m and 2386m, while only 8% of BiH's 51,129 sq km are below 150m. Just a toe of land tickles the Adriatic Sea at Neum. The arid south (Hercegovina) gives way to limestone uplands carved with grey craggy caves and deep canyons. The mountain core then descends again through green rolling hills further north, finally flattening out altogether but only in the very northeasternmost corner.

BiH's highest mountains are divided by breathtaking canyons, waterfalls and alpine valleys in the magnificent Sutjeska National Park.

Hercegovina's Hutovo Blato wetlands provide a prime sanctuary for migratory birds.

Environmental worries include landmines, wrecked building-stock and unexploded ordnance still left over from the 1990s war, plus rubbish disposal difficulties and air pollution from metallurgical plants.

FOOD & DRINK

Popular all across the Balkans, Bosnia's archetypal dishes are made of grilled minced meat formed into cylindrical little *ćevapi* (*ćevapčići*) or patty-shaped *pljeskavica*. Either are typically served in spongy *somun* bread, ideally with an added scoop of *kajmak* (local curd-butter). *Čevabdžinica* are *ćevapi* specialist-eateries but almost all restaurants serve them along with *šnicla* (steak/schnitzel), *kotleti* (normally veal), *ražnjići* (shish kebab), *pastrmka* (trout) and *ligne* (squid). Pizza and pasta are also ubiquitous.

Aščinica (usually downmarket local canteens) are most likely to serve pre-prepared traditional dishes like *dolme* (cabbage leaves or vegetables stuffed with minced meat) and hearty stews including *bosanski ionac* (cabbage and meat hotpot).

Buregdžinica eateries serve *burek* (meat stuffed filo pastry) or equivalent meat-free *sirnica* (filled with cheese), *krompiruša* (with potato) or *zeljanica* (with spinach). Pre-cooked versions of the same dishes are sold by weight at many a *pekara* (bakery shop).

Vegetarians might also consider side dishes of stewed beans or courgettes (zucchinis), though meaty traces can't be discounted.

Typical desserts include sugar-soaked baklava, excellent stuffed *palačinci* (pancakes), *hurmastica* (syrup-soaked sponge fingers) and *tufahije* (baked apple stuffed with walnut paste and topped with whipped cream). Bosnian cakes and ice creams are divine.

Tap water is almost always drinkable. Alcohol is readily available in both Muslim and Christian areas. Hercegovina produces some excellent wines. Good local beers cost as little as 1.50KM per 300ml glass. Shots (*pića*) of *šljiva* (plum brandy) or *loza* (local grappa) make great aperitifs or digestives.

Coffee (*kava*) is the main social lubricant. Traditional *bosanski* coffee is served, grinds-and-all, in a *džezva* (small long-handled brass pot) then carefully decanted into thimble-sized cups (*fildžan*). Excellent espressos are widely available.

Cafes open from around 9am and restaurants from around 11.30am; they generally close around midnight if there's custom, and much earlier when there isn't.

SARAJEVO

☎ 033 / pop 737,000

In the 1990s Sarajevo was on the edge of annihilation. Today it's a cosy, vibrant capital whose humanity, wonderful cafe scene, attractive contours and East-meets-West ambience are increasingly making it a favourite summer traveller destination. Meanwhile in winter it's brilliantly handy for some of Europe's best-value skiing.

HISTORY

Romans had bathed at Ilidža's sulphur springs a millennium earlier, but Sarajevo was officially 'founded' by 15th-century Turks. It rapidly grew wealthy as a silk-importing entrepôt and developed considerably during the 1530s when Ottoman governor Gazi-Husrevbey lavished the city with mosques and built the covered bazaar that still bears his name (see p108). In 1697 the city was burnt by Eugene of Savoy's Austrian army. When rebuilt, Sarajevo cautiously enclosed its upper flank in a large, fortified citadel whose remnants still dominate the Vratnik area.

The Austro-Hungarians were back more permanently in 1878 and erected many sturdy central European–style buildings. However their rule was put on notice by Gavrilo Princip's fatal 1914 pistol shot that killed Archduke Franz Ferdinand, plunging the world into WWI.

Seventy years later, Sarajevo hosted the 1984 Winter Olympics. Then from 1992 to 1995 the infamous siege of the city grabbed headlines and horrified the world. Sarajevo's heritage of six centuries was pounded into rubble and its only access to the outside world was via a metre-wide, 800m-long tunnel under the airport (p112). Over 10,500 Sarajevans died and 50,000 were wounded by Bosnian Serb shelling and sniper fire. Endless white-stoned graveyards on Kovači (Map pp110–11) and up near Koševo Stadium (Map p107) are a moving testimony to those terrible years.

ORIENTATION

Sarajevo is tightly wedged into the steep, narrow valley of the modest Miljacka River. Attractive Austro-Hungarian era avenues Maršala Tita/Ferhadija and Obala Kulina Bana converge at the very atmospheric Baščaršija 'Turkish Town'. North, east and south a pretty fuzz of red-roofed Bosnian houses dotted with uncountable minarets climbs the valley sides towards remarkably rural green-mountain ridges. Westward, however, Sarajevo sprawls for over 10km through Novo Sarajevo and dreary Dobrinja past contrasting dismal ranks of bullet-scarred apartment blocks. Park-filled Ilidža, beyond the airport, marks the end of the city's tramway spine with a parkland flourish.

INFORMATION
Bookshops
For maps, guidebooks, magazines and English-language books on ex-Yugoslavia try:

BuyBook (Map pp110-11; ☎ 716450; www.buybook.ba; Radićeva 4; ☻ 9am-10pm Mon-Sat, 10am-6pm Sun)

Šahinpašić (Map pp110-11; ☎ 667210; www.btcsahin pasic.com; Vladislava Skarića 8; ☻ 9am-8pm Mon-Sat)

Sejtarija (Map pp110-11; ☎ 205233; www.sejtarija .com; Maršala Tita 19; ☻ 9am-8pm Mon-Sat)

Internet Access
Click (Map pp110-11; Kundurdžiluk 1a; per hr 3KM; ☻ 9am-11pm) Nonsmoking.

Cyber (Map pp110-11; Pehlivanuša 2; per hr 3KM; ☻ 10am-11pm Mon-Sat, noon-7pm Sun)

Internet Caffe Baščaršija (Map pp110-11; Aščiluk bb; per hr 1.5KM; ☻ 24hr) Take the steps marked Sultan Caffe.

Laundry
Askos Laundry (Map pp110-11; Halilbašića 2; ☻ 9am-5pm Mon-Fri, 9am-3pm Sat)

Left Luggage
Luggage can be left at the main bus station (p117) It costs 2KM for the first hour and then 1KM for subsequent hours.

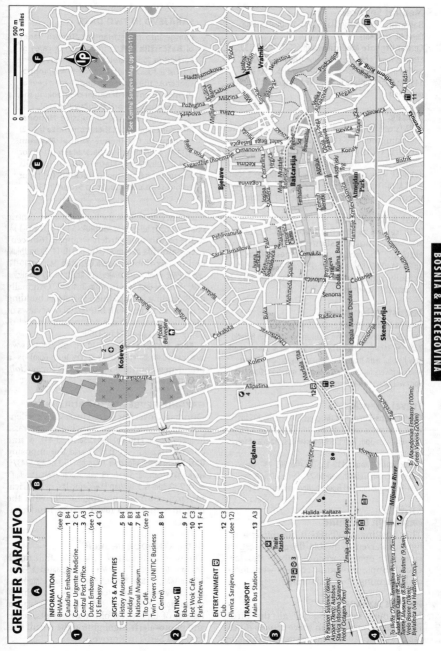

GREATER SARAJEVO

INFORMATION
BHMAC	(see 6)
Canadian Embassy	1 B4
Centar Urgente Medicine	2 C1
Central Post Office	3 A3
Dutch Embassy	(see 1)
US Embassy	4 C3

SIGHTS & ACTIVITIES
History Museum	5 B4
Holiday Inn	6 B3
National Museum	7 B4
Tito Café	(see 5)
Twin Towers (UNITIC Business Centre)	8 B4

EATING 🍽
Biban	9 F4
Hot Wok Café	10 C3
Park Prinčeva	11 F4

ENTERTAINMENT 🎭
Club	12 C3
Pivnica Sarajevo	(see 12)

TRANSPORT
Main Bus Station	13 A3

BOSNIA & HERCEGOVINA

Medical Services

Baščaršija Pharmacy (Map pp110-11; Obala Kulina Bana 40; ☻ 24hr)

Centar Urgente Medicine (Map p107; ☎ 297330; Stepana Tomića bb; ☻ 24hr) Emergency assistance section of the vast Koševo Hospital complex. Take bus 14 from Dom Armije to Hotel Belvedere then walk 300m northwest.

Money

ATMs are sprinkled all over the city centre, including outside the bus station and in the airport. Oddly there's nowhere to change money at the stations. **Turkish Ziraat Bank** (Map pp110-11; www.ziraatbosnia.com; Ferhadija 10; ☻ 8.30am-8pm Mon-Fri, 9am-3pm Sat) cashes travellers cheques if you show the original receipt.

Post & Telephone

The **central post office** (Map p107; ☻ 7am-8pm Mon-Sat) for poste restante is beside the bus station. The gorgeous **main post office** (Map pp110-11; Obala Kulina Bana 8; ☻ 7am-8pm Mon-Sat) is actually much more central. Counters 17 to 19 are for stamps.

Tourist Information

Tourist information centre (Map pp110-11; ☎ 220724; www.sarajevo-tourism.com; Zelenih Beretki 22a; ☻ 9am-6pm Mon-Fri, 9am-3pm Sat & Sun) Remarkably helpful with maps, bus timetables, brochures and ready answers for many an awkward question. Open to 9pm weekdays in summer.

Travel Agencies

Centrotrans-Eurolines (Map pp110-11; ☎ 205481; www.centrotrans.com; Ferhadija 16; ☻ 8.30am-8.30pm Mon-Fri, 9am-3pm Sat) International bus, train and ferry tickets.

Relax Tours (Map pp110-11; ☎ /fax 263 330; www .relaxtours.com; Zelenih Beretki 22; ☻ 8.30am-8pm Mon-Fri, 9am-5pm Sat) Books airline and ferry tickets.

SIGHTS
Baščaršija & Around

This bustling old Turkish quarter is a delightful warren of marble-flagged pedestrian lanes with open courtyards full of cafes, jewellery shops, mosques, copper workshops and charming little restaurants.

PIGEON SQUARE

Nicknamed Pigeon Sq for all the birds, Baščaršija's central open space centres on the **Sebilj** (Map pp110-11), an ornate 1891 drinking

---

SARAJEVO IN TWO DAYS

Plunge into pedestrianised 'Turkish' lanes of **Baščaršija** (left) and the street cafes of **Ferhadija** (opposite). From the spot where a 1914 assassination kicked off WWI (opposite) cross the cute Latin Bridge for a beer at **Pivnica HS** (p116) or dinner overlooking the city rooftops at **Park Prinčeva** (p115).

Next day see the impressive **National Museum** (opposite), then from **Ilidža** (p112) bus-hop to the unique **Tunnel Museum** (p112). A drink at laid-back **Mash** (p116) or delightfully Gothic **Zlatna Ribica** (p116) sets you up for a feisty gig at **Bock/FIS** (p116) or an old-style party night at **Sloga** (p116).

fountain. It leads past the lively if tourist-centric coppersmith alley, **Kazandžiluk** (Map pp110–11), to the picturesque garden-wrapped 16th-century **Baščaršija mosque** (Map pp110-11; Bravadžiluk) and the six-domed **Bursa Bezistan** (Map pp110-11; ☎ 239590; www.muzejsarajeva.ba; Abadžiluk 10; admission 2KM; ☻ 10am-6pm Mon-Fri, 10am-3pm Sat). Originally a silk trading bazaar, this 1551 stone building is now a museum with bite-sized overviews of the city's history and a compelling model of Sarajevo as it looked in 1878.

Kuća Sevdaha (Map pp110-11; ☎ 239943; www .artkucasevdaha.ba/en/; Halači 5; ☻ 10am-6pm) is a brand-new multimedia showcase for *sevdah*, traditional Bosnian music.

GAZI-HUSREVBEY VAKUF BUILDINGS

Ottoman Governor Gazi-Husrevbey's splendid 16th-century complex includes a **madrassa** (religious school; Map pp110-11; Sarači 33-49), a fine covered bazaar (see p117) and the imposing **Gazi-Husrevbey Mosque** (Map pp110-11; ☎ 534375; www.vakuf-gazi.ba; Sarači 18; admission 2KM; ☻ 9am-noon, 2.30-4pm & 5.30-7pm May-Sep). Its cylindrical minaret contrasts photogenically with the elegant stone **clock tower** across Mudželeti Veliki alley.

OLD ORTHODOX CHURCH

This outwardly austere little 1740 stone **church** (Map pp110-11; ☎ 571065; Mula Mustafe Bašeskije 59; admission 1KM; ☻ 8am-8pm summer, 8am-4pm winter) has an impressive gilded iconostasis and a three-room **cloister-museum** (admission 2KM; ☻ 9am-3pm Tue-Sun) of tapestries, old manuscripts, icons and photo-alerts highlighting the recent suffering of Serbs in Kosovo.

Bjelave & Vratnik

These lived-in neighbourhoods have their share of dreary apartment blocks but also feature a few intimidating Catholic edifices like **Vrhbosnanska Bogoslovija Seminary** (Map pp110-11; Josipa Štadlera bb) and Moorish masterpieces like the fabulous **Islamic Science Faculty building** (Map pp110-11; Ćemerlina 54). Of several traditionally Turkish-styled houses retaining courtyards and *doksat* (overhanging box-windows), the most impressive example is the brilliantly restored 18th-century **Svrzo House** (Svrzina Kuća; Map pp110-11; ☎ 535264; Glođina 8; admission 2KM; ☺ 10am-6pm Mon-Fri, 10am-3pm Sat). For great views over town continue up towards the once-vast **Vratnik Citadel** (Map pp110–11), built in the 1720s and reinforced in 1816. Its **Kula Ploče tower** (Map pp110-11; Ploča bb; admission free; ☺ 10am-6pm Mon-Fri, 10am-3pm Sat) houses a fascinating little museum to BiH's first president, Alija Izetbegović. But the best panoramas are from the grassy-topped **Yellow Bastion** (Map pp110-11; Žuta Tabija; Jekovac bb). Minibus 55 runs to Vratnik.

Ferhadija & Around

Summer street-cafes fill every open space around pedestrianised Ferhadija, lined with the city's Austro-Hungarian era main thoroughfare. The city's harmonious pre-1990s past is illustrated by the close proximity of three places of worship. The 1889 neo-Gothic **Catholic Cathedral** (Katedrala; Map pp110-11; Trg Fra Grge Martića 2; ☺ 9am-4pm) is where Pope John Paul II served mass during his 1997 visit. The large 1872 **Orthodox Cathedral** (Saborna Crkva; Map pp110-11; Trg Oslobođenja), built in Byzantine-Serb style, is artfully lit at night. And the atmospheric 1581 Sephardic Synagogue is still active at Rosh Hashana (Jewish New Year), though otherwise doubles as the interesting **Jewish Museum** (Map pp110-11; ☎ 535688; Mula Mustafe Bašveskije 40; admission 2KM; ☺ 10am-6pm Mon-Fri, 10am-1pm Sun).

Further west, several fine if somewhat triumphalist early-20th-century architecture lines Maršala Tita beyond an **eternal flame** (Vječna vatra; Map pp110-11; Maršala Tita 62) that commemorates victims of WWII.

The Riverbank

Intricately decorated with story-book Moorish arched balconies, Bosnia's once-glorious **National Library** (Map pp110–11) started life as the 1892 City Hall. In 1992 it was deliberately hit by a Serb incendiary shell and its unique collection of Bosnian books and irreplaceable manuscripts was destroyed. Restoration work has stalled and the building remains a stabilised partial-ruin.

The **Sarajevo 1878–1918 Museum** (Map pp110-11; ☎ 533288; Zelenih Beretki 2; admission 2KM; ☺ 10am-6pm Mon-Fri, 10am-3pm Sat) is a one-room exhibition on Sarajevo's Austro-Hungarian era focusing on the infamous 1914 assassination of Franz Ferdinand that happened right outside (ultimately triggering WWI). Further west, Obala Kulina Bana is patchily flanked with fine Austro-Hungarian era buildings. The grand **main post office** (Map pp110-11; Obala Kulina Bana 8; ☺ 7am-8pm Mon-Sat) has a soaring interior and old-fashioned brass counter-dividers. Next door, the **University Rectorate** (Map pp110-11; Obala Kulina Bana 7) is similarly grand. Across the river the splendid Gothic Revival style **Academy of Arts** (Map pp110-11; www.unsa.ba/eng/pregled.php; Obala Maka Dizdara) looks like a miniature version of Budapest's magnificent national parliament building.

Novo Sarajevo

During the 1992–95 siege, the wide road in from the airport (Zmaja od Bosne) was dubbed 'sniper alley' because Serb gunmen in surrounding hills could pick off civilians as they tried to cross it. The distinctive, custard-and-pudding-coloured **Holiday Inn** (Map p107; ☎ 288000; www.holidayinn.com/sarajevo; Zmaja Od Bosne 4) famously housed most of the embattled journalists covering the war and Sarajevo's **Twin Towers** next door spent much of the post-civil-war period as burnt-out wrecks, a sad symbol of the city's devastation. Today they're gleamingly reconstructed as the UNITIC Business Centre.

NATIONAL MUSEUM

Large and very impressive, the **National Museum** (Zemaljski Muzej Bosne-i-Hercegovine; Map p107; ☎ 668026; www.zemaljskimuzej.ba; Zmaja od Bosne 3; adult/student 5/1KM; ☺ 10am-5pm Tue-Fri, 10am-2pm Sat & Sun) is a quadrangle of four splendid neoclassical buildings purpose-built in 1913. The ancient history section displays fine Illyrian and Roman carvings in a room that looks dressed for a toga party. Upstairs, peep through the locked, high-security glass door of room 37 to glimpse the world-famous **Sarajevo Haggadah**, a 14th century Jewish codex estimated to be worth around a billion US dollars. Geraldine

BOSNIA & HERCEGOVINA

CENTRAL SARAJEVO

A · **B** · **C** · **D**

INFORMATION
Askos Laundry	1 F4
Australian Consulate	2 C6
Baščaršija Pharmacy	3 E5
BuyBook	4 A6
Centrotrans-Eurolines	5 D5
Click	6 E5
Croatian Embassy	7 B4
Cyber	8 D4
French Embassy	9 A4
German Embassy	10 B4
Internet Caffè Baščaršija	11 E5
Japanese Embassy	12 E6
Main Post Office	13 D5
Montenegrin Embassy	14 F5
Relax Tours	15 D5
Šahinpašić	16 C5
Sartour	17 E4
Sejtarija	18 B5
Serbian Embassy	19 A6
Slovenian Embassy	20 G5
Tourist Information Centre	21 D5
Turkish Ziraat Bank	22 D5
UK Consulate	23 C4

SIGHTS & ACTIVITIES
Academy of Arts	24 A6
Baščaršija Mosque	25 F5
Bursa Bezistan	26 E5
Catholic Cathedral	27 D5
Clock Tower	28 E5
Eternal Flame	29 C5
Gazi-Husrevbey Madrassa	30 E5

Gazi-Husrevbey Mosque	31 E5
Islamic Science Faculty Building	32 F4
Jewish Museum	33 E4
Kazandžiluk	34 F5
Kula Ploče Tower	35 G3
Kuća Sevdaha	36 F5
Ljubičica	37 E5
National Library	38 F5
Old Orthodox Church	39 E4
Orthodox Cathedral	40 D5
Sarajevo 1878-1918 Museum	41 E5
Sebilj	42 F5
Svrzo House	43 E3
University Rectorate	44 B6
Vratnik Citadel	45 H4
Vrhbosnanska Bogoslovija Seminary	46 D4
Yellow Bastion	47 H4

SLEEPING
Ada Hotel	48 F4
Guest House Halvat	49 F4
Hecco Deluxe	50 C5
Hostel City Center	51 E5
Hostel Marko Polo	52 E4
Hostel Posillipo	53 E4
Hostel Sebilj	54 F5
Hotel Astra	55 D5
Hotel Europa Garni	56 D5
Hotel Gaj	57 A6
Hotel Hecco	58 F2
Hotel Michele	59 C4
Hotel Safir	60 F4
Hotel Unica	61 B6

Identico	62 F5
Kod Keme	63 E5
Ljubičica Hostel	(see 37)
Motel Sokak	64 D4
Pansion Lion	65 F5
Pansion Stari Grad	66 F4
Pansion Vijećnica	67 F5
Sartour Hostel	68 G3
Villa Wien	69 E5

EATING
Amko	70 B5
Bosanska Kuća	71 F5
Butik-Badem	72 E5
Ćevabdžinica Petica	73 F5
DM	74 D5
Dveri	75 F5
Gradska Tržnica	76 C5
Hoše	77 B4
Inat Kuća	78 G5
Karuzo	79 C4
Konsum	80 F4
Markale Market	81 C4
Metropolis	82 B5
Michele	83 C5
Pekara Edin	84 F4
Pekara Nina	85 C5
Sara	86 C5
To Be or Not to Be	87 F5
Urban Grill	88 B4
Vinoteka	89 A6
Željo 1	90 E5
Željo 2	91 E5

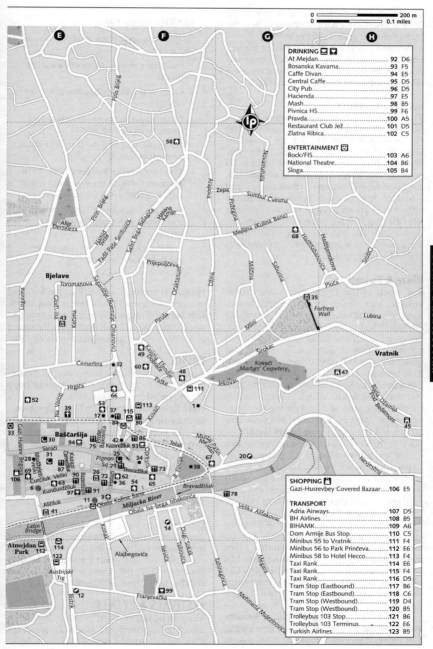

0 — 200 m
0 — 0.1 miles

DRINKING 🍺 🍷
At Mejdan.............................92 D6
Bosanska Kavarna...................93 F5
Caffe Divan..........................94 E5
Central Caffe........................95 D5
City Pub..............................96 D5
Hacienda.............................97 E5
Mash..................................98 B5
Pivnica HS............................99 F6
Pravda...............................100 A5
Restaurant Club Jež................101 D5
Zlatna Ribica........................102 C5

ENTERTAINMENT 🎭
Bock/FIS.............................103 A6
National Theatre....................104 B6
Sloga................................105 B4

SHOPPING 🛍
Gazi-Husrevbey Covered Bazaar.....106 E5

TRANSPORT
Adria Airways.......................107 D5
BH Airlines..........................108 B5
BIHAMK..............................109 A6
Dom Armije Bus Stop...............110 C5
Minibus 55 to Vratnik..............111 F4
Minibus 56 to Park Prinčeva........112 E6
Minibus 58 to Hotel Hecco.........113 F4
Taxi Rank...........................114 E6
Taxi Rank...........................115 F4
Taxi Rank...........................116 D5
Tram Stop (Eastbound).............117 B6
Tram Stop (Eastbound).............118 C6
Tram Stop (Westbound)............119 D4
Tram Stop (Westbound)............120 B5
Trolleybus 103 Stop................121 B6
Trolleybus 103 Terminus...........122 E6
Turkish Airlines.....................123 B5

Brooks' 2007 historical novel *People of the Book* is a part-fictionalised drama of how the Nazis failed to grab it during WWII.

Across a peaceful botanical garden are sections on natural history, minerals, Roman mosaics and Bosnian textiles. Out front are some fabulous medieval *stećci* grave-markers.

HISTORY MUSEUM

The small but engrossing **History Museum** (Map p107; ☎ 210418; Zmaja od Bosne 5; admission 2KM; ☼ 9am-4pm Mon-Fri, 9am-1pm Sat & Sun) 'nonideologically' charts the course of the 1990s conflict. Affecting personal exhibits include ID cards of 'lost' medics, examples of food aid, stacks of Monopoly-style 1990s dinars and a makeshift siege-time 'home'. Behind the museum is an amusingly tongue-in-cheek **Tito Café** (Map p107; beer/coffee 2/1KM; ☼ 7am-3am), replete with Tito busts, stormtrooper-helmet lampshades and a garden-terrace of Jeep seats and old artillery pieces.

Ilidža & Butmir

For much of the 1990s war, Sarajevo was virtually surrounded by hostile Serb forces. Butmir was the last Bosniak-held part of the city still linked to the outside world. However, between Butmir and Sarajevo was the airport runway. Although supposedly neutral and under tenuous UN control, crossing it would have been suicidal. The solution, in extremis, was a hand-dug 800m tunnel beneath the runway that proved just enough to keep Sarajevo supplied with arms and food during the three-year siege. Most of the tunnel has since collapsed, but the unmissable **Tunnel Museum** (off Map p107; ☎ 061-213760; Tuneli 1, Butmir; admission 5KM; ☼ 9am-4pm) gives visitors just a glimpse of its hopes and horrors. Photos and construction equipment are displayed around the shell-pounded house that hid the tunnel entrance (still visible) and there's a 20-minute video of the wartime tunnel experience.

The museum features in many Sarajevo city tours. Alternatively take tram 3 to its western terminus, Ilidža (30 minutes, 11km from Baščaršija) then switch to Kotorac bus 68A (10 minutes, at least twice-hourly). Get off at the last stop, walk across the bridge then turn immediately left down Tuneli for 600m.

While in Ilidža you could soak at **Termalna Rivijera** (off Map p107; ☎ 771 000; www.terme-ilidza.ba; Butmirska Cesta 18, Ilidža; adult/child weekday 10/8KM, weekends

14/12KM; ☼ 9am-10pm), a complex of indoor and outdoor swimming pools. Some 3km south, **Vrelo Bosne** (off Map p107) park is a pretty patchwork of lush mini-islands near where the source of the Bosna River gushes out of a rocky cliff.

TOURS

Assuming a minimum group size, all the following offer city tours, often fascinatingly accompanied by siege survivors:

Green Visions (off Map p107; ☎ 717290; www.greenvisions.ba; opposite Radnička 66; ☼ 9am-5pm Mon-Fri) Also offers a wide range of set-departure and tailor-made hiking trips into the Bosnian mountains and villages.

Ljubičica (Map pp110-11; ☎ 232109, 061-131813; www.hostelljubicica.net; Mula Mustafe Bašeskije 65; ☼ 8am-10pm Oct-Apr, 7am-11pm May-Sep) Helpful and popular.

Sartour (Map pp110-11; ☎ 238680; Mula Mustafe Bašeskije 63; ☼ 9am-7pm)

Ljubičica's popular €15 tour includes the Tunnel Museum (and transport). The tourist information centre (p108) lists private guides and is the starting point for the €10 **Sarajevo Discovery** (☎ 061-190591; www.sarajevo-discovery.com) walking tour (3pm daily, summer only).

FESTIVALS & EVENTS

The tourist information centre (p108) has a monthly *Programme of Cultural Events*; check www.sarajevoarts.ba as well.

Baščaršijske Noći (Baščaršija Nights; www.bascarsijske noci.ba) A whole range of international events in July covering dance, music and street theatre performed at various open-air stages around town.

Futura (October) Electronic music.

International Jazz Festival (www.jazzfest.ba) Week-long event in November showcasing local and international performers.

Sarajevo Film Festival (☎ 209411; www.sff.ba; Zelenih Beretki 12/1; tickets 3–6KM) Globally acclaimed festival held in August screening commercial and art-house movies, almost all with English subtitles.

SLEEPING
Budget
Tour agencies (p108) can arrange hostel and homestay accommodation. Beware that many budget hostels have much less central 'over-flow' locations.

AutoKamp Oaza (off Map p107; ☎ 636141; www.hotel iilidza.ba/site/oaza; sites per person 10KM, per tent/car/camper-van 7/8/12KM) Tree-shaded camping and caravan hook-ups (electricity 3KM extra) tucked behind the Hotel Izmit, 1.5km west of Ilidža terminus (ie 12km from Baščaršija). Youthful, international vibe.

Sartour Hostel (Map pp110-11 ☎ office 238680; www .sartour-hostel-sarajevo.ba; Hadžisabanovića 15; dm €7-13, tw €24-30) Obliging Sartour (opposite) acts as agent for various homestays, *pansions* and hostels but also has its own house-hostel with a pleasant if sloping garden (camping from €5) and fine views from some windows. Linen costs €3 extra per person so bring your own sleeping bag. Lockout is between 11am and 5pm.

Ljubičica Hostel (Map pp110-11; ☎ 232109; Mula Mustafe Bašeskije 65; dm/homestay/apt from €10/15/20; ☒ 8am-10pm winter, 7am-11pm summer) The mixed bag of simple homestay rooms here can be decent value if you score a relatively central one. The hostel is contrastingly dingy, with tight-packed bunk-beds and battered old bathrooms, but it's superbly central and free transfers from the stations ensure a steady flow of takers.

Hostel City Center (HCC; Map pp110-11; ☎ 503294; www .hcc.ba; 3rd fl, Saliha Muvekita 2; dm/s/d/tr/q €12/18/32/45/54) Head and shoulders above most Bosnian hostels, the brand new HCC has new bunk rooms, an appealing chill-out space, kitchen and free internet access. Ring the bell marked HCC at a doorway beyond downmarket shot-bar Bife Velež.

Hostel Posillipo (Map pp110-11; ☎ 061-778603; amassko@hotmail.com; Besarina Čikma 5; s/d from €15/30)

Tucked away up a tiny lane in central Baščaršija, the three small, clean rooms here share a decent bathroom. The three-bed apartment (€20 per person) has a bar area, leather sofas and its own bathroom. The overflow sister building is close by. The helpful if slightly chaotic owners speak good English.

Hostel Sebilj (Map pp110-11; ☎ 573500; www.pansion sebilj.com.ba; Bravadžiluk bb; dm/s/d/tr from €15/15/30/45) Around a decent-sized if unsophisticated barn-like sitting area, most rooms at this hostel share his-or-hers bathrooms, though the €20 four-bed dorms have private facilities.

Kod Keme (Map pp110-11; ☎ 531140; Mali Ćurčiluk 15; s/d from €20/40) This place has neat, unfussy rooms, two of which are surreally pierced by a Corinthian column. Most share bathrooms. Nera, the charming Bosnian-Aussie owner, will soon open a full hotel at Mali Ćurčiluk 11.

Pansion Lion (Map pp110-11; ☎ 236137, 061-268150; www.lion.co.ba; Bravadžiluk 30; dm/s/d/tr/q 30/50/100/120/200KM) Warm antique effects, teddies on some beds, dried flowers and hairdriers in bathrooms all take this 10-room *pansion* up a notch above most hostels, though the five- and eight-bed dorms are windowless and less cutesy. No real lounge area.

Other options:

Hostel Marko Polo (Map pp110-11; ☎ 535000, 061-245620; www.hostel-markopolo.com; 1st fl, Logavina 6; dm/d €10/30) Unexceptional but decently located family flat-hostel with tight-packed beds and no common area. Emina speaks minimal English.

Identico (Map pp110-11; ☎ 233310; Halači 3; dm/s/d with shared bathroom from €15/15/20, s/d with private bathroom €20/40) Unspectacular rooms, minuscule shower booths but perfect old-city location.

Motel Sokak (Map pp110-11; ☎ 570355; www.sokak -motel.com; Mula Mustafe Bašeskije 24; s/d/tr €42/68/93) The 11 fairly plain rooms have limited natural light but there's a decent communal sitting area.

Midrange
Pansion Suljović (off Map p107; ☎ 627670; www.sul jovic.com; Kurta Schorka 22; s/d 50/90KM) Functional rooms above a pizzeria beside the EP petrol station, 1.5km from the airport, 10 minutes' (unpleasant) walk from Stup tram stop. Cheaper budget rooms (35KM per person) share bathrooms.

Pansion Vijećnica (Map pp110-11; ☎ 233433; www .pansionvijecnica.co.ba; Mustaj-Pašin Mejdan 5; s/d €30/50) This four-bedroom mini-hotel has period furniture, suave little lobby, attractive lilac interiors and excellent private showers.

BOSNIA & HERCEGOVINA

It's slightly more sophisticated than sister-property Pansion Stari Grad (Map pp110–11; ☎ 239898; www.sgpansion.co.ba; Bjelina Čikma 4; singles/doubles from €35/50).

Hotel Hecco (Map pp110–11; ☎ 273730; www.hotel-hecco.net; Medresa 1; s/tw/d/tr 80/110/130/150KM; 🖳) Twenty-nine bright, airy modern rooms with strong rectilinear lines lead off an artfully designed warren of corridors dotted with armchairs, pot plants and even a weight-training machine. Staff are delightful but there's no lift and only the top floor has air-con. Minibus 58 stops outside.

Guest House Halvat (Map pp110–11; ☎ /fax 237714; www.halvat.com.ba; Kasima Efendije Dobraće 5; s/d/tr 90/121/152KM; 🖳) Homely, five-room family-run guest house with a friendly, supertalkative hostess still mourning her beloved Dalmatian.

Ada Hotel (Map pp110–11; ☎ 475870; www.adahotel.ba; Abdesthana 8; s/d/tr/apt 90/140/170/200KM) Popular with embassy guests, this eight-room hideaway has lots of loveable touches. Corridor surprises include a fake fireplace that opens to reveal secret cabinets. Old teapots and a guitar await in the attractive breakfast room. Rooms in peach or pastel green are a little less characterful but pleasant and calm.

Hotel Safir (Map pp110–11; ☎ 475040; www.hotelsafir.ba; Jagodića 3; s/d 98/140KM) The ultrawhite rooms have artistic flashes in sunny colours, stylish conical basins and a kitchenette. Great value.

Hotel Gaj (Map p107; ☎ 445200; www.hotel-gaj.co.ba; Skenderija 14; s/d/apt €60/90/120) The bright, modern-coloured rooms here have polished wood floors and some have antique-style bedsteads and gilt-framed pictures. All have great clean shower booths. Take breakfast in the half-timbered restaurant or on the garden verandah.

Hotel Octagon (off Map p107; ☎ 471105; www.hotel-octagon.com; Akifa Šeremeta 48; s/d 120/150KM) This place tries overly hard to look upmarket but staff are friendly and it's just a short stroll from the airport, albeit well hidden.

Top End

Villa Orient (Map pp110–11; ☎ 232702; http://hotel-villa-orient.com; Oprkanj 6; s/d 153/206KM; 🖳) The great location, neo-Ottoman exterior and soothing modern water features in the stylish lobby set expectations high, so the very ordinary rooms and worn carpets prove sadly disappointing. However, when occupancy is low, significant discounts are possible.

Hotel Astra (Map pp110–11; ☎ 252100; www.hotel-astra.com.ba; Zelenih Beretki 9; s/d 153/206KM) Behind a striking Austro-Hungarian era facade, the minimalist reception booth is hidden within a '40s-retro cafe. Rooms are impressively spacious and elegantly trendy, sporting over-bed 'flying' drapes. Three rooms have jacuzzi-showers.

Hotel Unica (Map pp110–11; ☎ 555225; www.hotel-unica.ba; Hamdije Kreševljakovića 42; s/d 156/195KM) Tan and brown tones of boutiquey Modernisme are reflected even in the receptionists' suits. The stylish breakfast room has reverse ceiling beams, 1940s-style square seats and walls partly decorated with old newspapers.

Hotel Europa Garni (Map pp110–11; ☎ 232855; www.europa-garni.ba; Ferhadija 30a; s/d/apt 183/236/306KM) Behind a discordantly uninteresting facade, this invitingly modern, supercentral hotel has warm peach-toned rooms with polished pine floors draped in Persian rugs. Some have computers. Ask about the Villa Wein annexe (Ćurčiluk Veliki 3), which is cosier and more stylish yet slightly cheaper.

Hecco Deluxe (Map pp110–11; www.hotel-hecco.net/deluxe.html; 9th-12th fl, Ferhadije 2; s/d/tr 195/254/279KM) Plonked atop a misleadingly scraggy apartment block, the 12 oddly shaped but stylishly appointed modern rooms have unsurpassed views of the city centre.

our pick **Hotel Michele** (Map pp110–11; ☎ 560310; www.hotelmichele.ba; Ivana Cankara 27; d/apt €100/150) Looking at the building's unrefined contemporary exterior, nothing prepares you for the eccentric, lavish luxury of this marvellously offbeat boutique hotel. Most rooms are vast, exotically furnished apartments. Celebrity guests have included Bono and Richard Gere.

EATING

There's plenty of choice, but some of Sarajevo's real gems are so small that you might need to book ahead.

Restaurants

Bosanska Kuća (Map pp110–11; Bravadžiluk 3; mains 6–9KM; ☼ 24hr) Colour-picture menus make choosing a meal here easy and among the Bosnian standards are a couple of vegie options.

Biban (Map p107; ☎ 232026; Hošin Brijeg 95a; grills 6–12KM, wine from 20KM per litre) The comparatively rustic Biban offers superbly panoramic views similar to those from Park Prinčeva, without the latter's scurrying army of waistcoated waiters. Walk 600m uphill from Park Prinčeva and turn left after Nalina 15.

Karuzo (Map pp110-11; ☎ 444647; Dženetića Čikma 2; mains 6-18KM; ☟ noon-3pm & 6-11pm Mon-Fri, 6-11pm Sat) This tiny, friendly one-man (ie slow service) restaurant is styled like a yacht's interior. Some dishes, like the Indian-influenced vegetarian chickpea pockets, are successful – however, the strange 'sushi' uses 'tuna' that tastes more like watery beef than *maguro*.

Inat Kuća (Spite House; Map pp110-11; ☎ 447867; Velika Alifakovac 1; mains 7-12KM, steaks 18KM) This Sarajevo institution is a veritable museum-piece, an Ottoman house with great views of the National Library from a perfect riverside terrace. The menu tells its odd history but much of the typical Bosnian food (stews, *dolme*) is pre-prepared and slightly lacklustre. The *sirnica* (cheese pie) is fresh and might suit vegetarians. Beer costs 4KM to 6KM.

Hot Wok Café (Map p107; ☎ 203322; Maršala Tita 12; meals 10-15KM; ☟ 8am-midnight) Hot Wok's puntastic menu of southeast-Asian fusion meals is full of unexpected flavour combinations that confuse the palate but leave you wanting to lick the plate. Stylish decor recalls a scene from *Kill Bill*. High stool–seating puts fashion before comfort.

Dveri (Map pp110-11; ☎ 537020; www.dveri.co.ba; Prote Bakovića 10; meals 10-16KM; ☟ 11am-11pm Mon-Fri, 8am-11pm Sat & Sun; ☒) This charming 'country cottage' is hung with loops of garlic, corn cobs and gingham-curtained windows. Inky risottos, vegie-stuffed eggplant or plum goulash all wash down a treat with 5KM glasses of the house red, a truly excellent Hercegovinian Blatina. But beware when offered 'homemade bread': it's good but costs 5KM extra.

To Be or Not to Be (Map pp110-11; ☎ 233205; Čizmedžiluk 5; meals 10-22KM; ☟ noon-11pm) Arched metal shutters creak open to reveal a tiny two-table room lovably decorated in traditional Bosnian style. Try the daring, tongue-tickling steak in chilli chocolate (18KM). The name's crossed-out 'or Not' bit dates from the war years when not surviving was not an option.

Park Prinčeva (Map p107; ☎ 222708; www.park princeva.ba; Iza Hidra 7; meals 12-23KM; ☟ 9am-late) Like Bono and Bill Clinton before you, gaze down from this picture-perfect ridge-top perch for fabulous views of Sarajevo's rooftops, mosques and twinkling lights. Wine starts at 30KM a bottle. Get there by minibus 56 from Latin Bridge.

Vinoteka (Map pp110-11; ☎ 214996; Skenderija 12; mains 18-32KM; ☟ 11am-3pm & 7-11pm Mon-Sat, wine bar 7pm-1am) This expat favourite has an appealing rafter room up top, a mini rainforest effect on the ground floor, and a basement wine bar. The menu changes weekly and includes such delights as venison in forest fruits and John Dory with roast vegies.

Quick Eats
BAKERIES
Inexpensive bakeries with sit-in tables include **Pekara Edin** (Map pp110-11; Mula Mustafe Bašeskije 69; ☟ 5am-midnight) facing the Sebilj, and the unremarkable but all-night **Pekara Nina** (Map pp110-11; Mula Mustafe Bašeskije; ☟ 24hr).

CAKE-SHOP CAFES
Indulgent coffee-and-cake paradises include fashionably relaxed **Metropolis** (Map pp110-11; Maršala Tita 21; cakes 3.50KM; ☟ 8am-11pm Mon-Fri, 9am-11pm Sat, 11am-10pm Sun), the supercentral **Sara** (Map pp110-11; Baščaršija 22; cakes from 1.50KM) and the ever-popular **Michele** (Map pp110-11; ☎ 444484; Ferhadija 15; coffee 2KM, cakes 3KM, pizzas 7-11KM; ☟ 8am-10.30pm) with its period drawing-room interior, Arabian Nights basement and great people-watching street-terrace.

ĆEVABDŽINICAS
Željo (Map pp110-11; ☎ 441200; ćevapi 3-7KM; ☟ 8am-10pm) Željo 1 (Kundurdžiluk 17); Željo 2 (Kundurdžiluk 20) These twin eateries are not as sexy as many surrounding restaurants but they're veritable institutions famous for offering Sarajevo's best *ćevapi*. They deliver too, and at sensible prices. Don't shirk on the 1KM dollop of *kajmak*.

For similar fare in a more stylish, contemporary setting try **Ćevabdžinica Petica** (Bravadžiluk 29; ćevapi 3-6KM) or **Urban Grill** (www.urbangrill.ba; Pruščakova 8; ćevapi 3.50-5.50KM).

Self-Catering
Markale market (Map pp110-11; Mula Mustafe Bašeskije; ☟ 7am-5pm Mon-Sat, 7am-2pm Sun) Facing off across a busy road, Markale comprises a huddle of vegetable stalls and the covered 1894 Gradska Tržnica (Map pp110–11) market hall selling meat and dairy goods. Market-goers were massacred here on several occasions by Serb mortar attacks in the 1990s, including a 1995 assault that proved a 'last straw', triggering NATO air strikes against the forces besieging Sarajevo.

Butik-Badem (Map pp110-11; Abadžiluk 12) This super little health-food shop sells caramelised nuts, luscious Turkish delight and a variety of tempting snack foods by weight. There's another branch at Maršala Tita 34.

Handy central supermarkets include **Konsum** (Map pp110-11; Safvet Basagica; 🕑 7am-10pm), **DM** (Map pp110-11; Ferhadija 25; 🕑 9am-9pm Mon-Sat), **Amko** (Map pp110-11; Maršala Tita; 🕑 7am-10pm Mon-Sat, 8am-6pm Sun) and **Hoše** (Map pp110-11; Mejtaš 5; 🕑 7am-10pm Mon-Sat, 7am-3pm Sun).

DRINKING

As chilly April melts into sunny May, street-terraces blossom and central Sarajevo becomes one great cafe.

Bars

Pivnica HS (Map pp110-11; Franjevačka 15; 🕑 10am-1am) This fabulous Willy Wonka–meets–Las Vegas beer hall is the only place to be sure of finding excellent Sarajevskaya dark beer: it's brewed next door! Superb food too (mains 12MK to 22KM).

Mash (Map pp110-11; 1st fl, Branilaca Sarajeva 20; beer 2KM; 🕑 8am-1am Mon-Thu, 9am-3am Fri & Sat, 10am-midnight Sun) Within an outwardly unpromising 1970s concrete building, Mash offers a brilliantly chaotic stylistic mishmash of colours, old furniture and bric-a-brac attracting a studenty clientele.

Hacienda (Map pp110-11; www.placetobe.ba; Bazerdzani 3; 🕑 10am-very late) The not-quite Mexican food could be spicier. Not so the ambience at 2am, by which time this cosy, cane-ceilinged cantina has metamorphosed into one of the Old Town's most happening nightspots.

ourpick Zlatna Ribica (Map pp110-11; Kaptol 5; 🕑 9am-late) This marvellously Gothic cafe-bar serves wine in delightful little potion-bottle carafes with complimentary nibbles and dried figs. The uniquely stocked toilet will have you laughing out loud. Unmissable.

City Pub (Map pp110-11; Despićeva bb; 🕑 8am-late) Despite a could-be-anywhere pub interior, this friendly place is a very popular meeting point, with occasional live music.

Restaurant Club Jež (Map pp110-11; ☎ 650312; Zelenih Beretki 14; 🕑 6pm-late) Atmospheric, under-lit, pseudo-olde basement bar that's a packed-full late-night hot spot with a varying program of themed events and parties.

Cafes

The choice in Sarajevo is simply phenomenal.

Bosanska Kavarna (Map pp110-11; Oprkanj 9; coffee 0.50KM; 🕑 8.30am-6pm Mon-Sat) Copper bra-pad

lamps, tick-tocking wall-clocks and not-so-saucy Islamic pin-ups adorn this downmarket, very authentic coffee house whose primary clientele are wizened old local men.

Caffe Divan (Map pp110-11; Morića Han, Saraći 77; coffee 1.50-3KM; 🕑 8am-10pm) Relax in wicker chairs beneath the wooden beams of a gorgeous *caravanserai* (inn) courtyard whose stables now contain a fine Iranian carpet shop.

Pravda (Map pp110-11; www.pravdasarajevo.com; Radićeva 4c; coffee 2-5KM, cocktails 7-14KM; 🕑 8am-midnight) Choose from marigold-patterned chill-out sofas or angular perch-stools, then strike your pose amid Sarajevo's gilded youth. Oh no, don't say they've all gone next door to the Nivea?!

Central Caffe (Map pp110-11; Strosmayerova 1; 🕑 7.30am-3am) Pure '70s retro with beam-me-up-Scottie ceiling effects and hip youthful clientele. The whole street outside becomes one long cafe in summer.

At Mejdan (Map pp110-11; Atmejdan Park; coffee 3KM, beer 3-5KM; 🕑 9am-11pm Mon-Sat, 10am-11pm Sun) Like a Middle Eastern pagoda, this open-sided wooden pavilion has curls of communal sofa seating upstairs and oodles of upmarket summer terrace-space. Fresh fruit juices and wines are served, but there's no food.

ENTERTAINMENT
Nightclubs & Live Music

Sloga (Map pp110-11; Mehmeda Spahe 20; beer from 2.50KM) Downstairs the taverna-style bar Club Gandeamus (open 7pm to midnight) has live Bosnian folk music on Thursday nights around 10pm. Upstairs, much bigger blood-red Seljo-Sloga (open 8pm to 4am) is a cavernous 1990s-style concert/disco/music bar drawing an excitable, predominantly student crowd.

Bock/FIS (Map pp110-11; ☎ 063-943431; www.bock.ba; Musala bb; 🕑 6pm-2am) There's no easy-to-spot sign for this wonderfully intimate zebra-striped venue for live alternative and 'urban' music. Uncompromisingly real. Dress in black.

Behind gruffly humourless bouncers, the subterranean trio of stone cavern rooms called **Club** (Map p107; ☎ 550550; www.theclub.ba; Maršala Tita 7; beer 4KM; 🕑 10am-late) contains a highly esteemed DJ bar (live concerts too), a plush chill-out space and a surprisingly decent late-night restaurant. If you arrive too early, the **Pivnica Sarajevo** (Map p107; coffee/beer 2/2.50KM; 🕑 8am-midnight) behind the same building also offers alternative cavern rooms, plus a plushly cushioned garden terrace.

Performing Arts

National Theatre (Narodno Pozorište; Map pp110-11; ☎ 221682; www.nps.ba; Obala Kulina Bana 9; tickets from 10KM; ☒ box office 9am-noon & 4pm-7.30pm) Classically adorned with fiddly gilt mouldings, this proscenium-arched theatre hosts a ballet, opera, play or philharmonic concert (www.sarf .com.ba) virtually every night in season (mid-September to mid-June).

SHOPPING

Baščaršija's pedestrian lanes are full of jewellery stalls and wooden-shuttered souvenir shops flogging slippers, Bosnian flags, carpets, archetypal copperware and wooden spoons, though if you're heading to Mostar, you might find prices better there. The attractive, one-street, stone-domed **Gazi-Husrevbey Covered Bazaar** (Map pp110-11; ☎ 534375; www.vakuf-gazi.ba; ☒ 8am-8pm Mon-Fri, 9am-2pm Sat) sells relatively inexpensive souvenirs, fake bags and sunglasses (from 5KM).

CDs of highly suspect legality cost 3KM from stalls filling a hidden yard behind the Hecco Deluxe hotel (p114).

GETTING THERE & AWAY
Air

Sarajevo's modest international **airport** (off Map p107; ☎ 234841; www.sarajevo-airport.ba; Kurta Šchorka 36) is about 12km southwest of Baščaršija. For flight details see p138.

Bus

Sarajevo's **main bus station** (Map p107; ☎ 213100; Put Života 8) primarily serves locations in the Federation, Croatia and Western Europe, while most services to the RS and Serbia leave from the **Autobus Stanica Istochno Sarajevo** (Автобус Станица Источно Сарајево; off Map p107; ☎ 057-317377; Nikole Tesle bb). It's commonly, if misleadingly, nicknamed 'Lukavica bus station', and lies way out in the Dobrinja suburb, 400m beyond the western terminus of trolleybus 103. Buses to some destinations – Banja Luka, Belgrade, Pale, Srebrenica – leave from both stations.

Buses to the mountain villages of Bjelašnica and to Butmir start from behind the Ilidža tram terminus.

The 10pm bus to Novi Pazar (€15, eight hours) 'secretly' continues to Pristina (around 12 hours) and Prizren in Kosovo, for which

you'll pay an extra €5 fare once you reach Novi Pazar.

For services to Serbia, Croatia and Montenegro, see p118. Other international destinations include Amsterdam (206KM, four weekly), Berlin (167KM, three weekly), Brussels (206KM, Sunday), Dortmund (209KM, Saturday to Thursday), Cologne (235KM, Saturday to Thursday), Ljubljana (74KM, four weekly), Munich (190KM, daily), Paris (260KM, Thursday), Stockholm (280KM, daily) and Vienna (92KM, twice daily).

Train

The **train station** (Map p107; ☎ 655330; Put Života 2) is close to the main bus station. Two daily services connect Ploče (on the Croatian coast) via Mostar (9.90KM, three hours) at 6.45am and 6.18pm. Both either continue on to Zagreb or connect with trains heading there. The overnight Sarajevo–Zagreb section (56.60KM, 9½ hours, 9.20pm) has one carriage of comfortable six-berth couchettes (19.60KM supplement).

The Budapest train (96KM, 12 hours) leaves Sarajevo at 7.14am, routed via Doboj, Šamac and Osijek (Croatia). It returns from Budapest-Keleti at 9.25am.

From Sarajevo to Belgrade (46KM, nine hours), take the Budapest train, changing in Strizivojna-Vrpolje (Croatia) with 1½ hours' wait. Or take the 9.20pm Zagreb-bound service and change at Doboj (13.60KM) around midnight; that will get you onto the Banja Luka–Belgrade train (eight hours), which runs overnight eastbound (departing Banja Luka at 10.30pm).

GETTING AROUND
To/From the Airport

There's no direct airport–centre bus. Blue bus 36 departs from directly opposite the terminal to Nedžarići on the Ilidža–Baščaršija tram line, but it only runs twice an hour. Much more frequent is trolleybus 103, which picks up around 700m away. To find the stop turn right out of the airport then take the first left. Shimmy right/left/right past the Hotel Octagon, then turn right at the Panda car wash (Braće Mulića 17). Just before the Mercator Hypermarket (Mimar Sinana 1) cross the road and take the bus going back the way you've just come.

Metered airport taxis charge around 7KM to Ilidža and 25KM to Baščaršija.

BOSNIA & HERCEGOVINA

BUSES FROM SARAJEVO

Destination	Station	Price (KM)	Duration (hr)	Departures
Banja Luka (via Jajce)	M	29	5	5am, 7.45am, 9.15am, 2.30pm, 3.30pm & 4.30pm
	L	31	5	9.30am & 11.30am
Bihać	M	41	6½	7.30am, 1.30pm & 10pm
Belgrade (via Zvornik)	M	55	10	6am
	L	55	10-11	6.15am, 8am, 9.45am, 11am, 12.30pm, 3pm & 10pm
Dubrovnik	M	30-44	5-7	7.15am & 10am (plus 2.30pm & 10.30pm summer)
Foča	L	9	1½	11am, 4.35pm & 6.25pm; Trebinje & Višegrad services also stop here
Goražde	M	11	2¼	six daily, four Sunday
Gradačac (via Srebrenik)	M	31	4¼	8.30am & 5pm
Herceg Novi	M	38	7½	11am year-round, 10.30pm summer only
Jahorina (in ski season)	M	10	1	9am Fri, Sat & Sun
Mostar	M	16	2½	15 daily
Niš	L	40	11	8.40am & 6pm
Novi Pazar	M	30	7-8	9am, 3pm, 6pm, 9pm & 10pm
Pale	L	3.50	40min	14 daily Mon-Fri (but 3.15pm only weekends)
	M	4	25min	7am, 10am, 2pm
Podgorica	L	31	6	8.15am & 2pm
Split (via Čapljina)	M	41	7½	10am & 9pm
Split (via Livno)			7¼	6am & 11pm
Split (via Imotski)			6¾	2.30pm
Srebrenica	M	32	3½	7.10am
	L	27.50	3¾	8.40am & 3.30pm
Tešanj	M	23	3	7am, 1.15pm & 5.15pm
Travnik	M	15	2	nine daily
Trebinje (via Sutjeska National Park)	L	23	5	7.45am, 1pm & 4.05pm
Tuzla	M	20	3¼	hourly 10am-4pm plus 6.50pm
Visoko	M	5.70	50min	at least hourly by Kakanj bus
Zagreb	M	54	9½	6.30am, 9.30am, 12.30pm & 10pm

Note: M = main bus station, L = Autobus Stanica Istochno Sarajevo

Car

Sarajevo is not driver-friendly. One-way systems are awkward and Baščaršija is largely pedestrianised with minimal parking. However, renting a car makes it much easier to reach the surrounding mountain areas. Most major car-hire agencies have offices at Sarajevo airport including **Budget** (☎ 766670), **Hertz** (☎ 235050), **Avis** (☎ 469933), **Sixt** (☎ 622200) and **National** (☎ 267590), but booking ahead (online) is advisable.

Public Transport

Tram 3 runs every four to seven minutes from Ilidža, passing the Holiday Inn then looping anticlockwise around Baščaršija. Tram 1 (every eight to 20 minutes) does the same but starting from the main bus station (but note that it's only seven minutes' walk from the Tram 3 line to the stations).

Handy for the Lukovica bus station and the airport, usefully frequent trolleybus 103 runs along the southern side of the city from Austrijski Trg to Dobrinja (30 minutes), with stops near Hotel Unica, the Skenderija Center and Green Visions en route.

From Dom Armije, bus 16B runs past the US embassy to the Koševo area.

Many lines (including tram 3, trolley 103, minibus 56) operate 6am to 11pm daily, but some stop after 7pm, and all have reduced services on Sundays. Full timetables are available in Bosnian on www.gras.co.ba. Click 'Redove Voznje' then select mode of transport.

Single-ride tickets cost 1.60/1.80KM from kiosks/drivers and must be stamped in a special machine once aboard the bus/tram; inspectors have no mercy on 'ignorant foreigners'. Some major kiosks (with red-on-yellow signs) sell good-value 5.30KM day passes, valid for almost all trams, buses and trolleybuses.

Taxi

Charges usually start at 2KM plus about 1KM per kilometre. While all of Sarajevo's taxis have meters, **Žuti Taxis** (Yellow Cab; ☎ 663555) actually turn them on.

There are handy central taxi ranks near Latin Bridge, Hotel Kovači and outside Zeleni Beretki 5.

AROUND SARAJEVO

Tempting moutains rise straight up behind the city, making access to winter skiing or summer rambles in the highland villages very convenient. But don't forget the dangers of landmines – stick to well-used paths.

JAHORINA JAXOPUHA
☎ 057

This purpose-built **ski resort** (ski pass per day 30KM, ski rentals per day 24-50KM) offers world-class pistes designed for the 1984 Winter Olympics. In summer there's mountain biking, hiking and **AeroKlub Trebević** (☎ 065-350201; per hr €25; ☼ Jun-Sep) offers paragliding.

Jahorina's single main road wiggles 2.5km up from a little seasonal shopping 'village' where cheaper pansions open only during the ski season. It passes the Termag Hotel (300m), s-bending past the Dva Javora (1.5km), the post office and the still-ruined Hotel Jahorina, tunnelling beneath Rajska Vrata before dead-ending at the top of the long Skočine Lift.

Sleeping & Eating

All accommodation is within 300m of one of Jahorina's six main ski lifts. Beware that most hotels won't take bookings for less than seven-day stays. You can always turn up hoping for a cancellation. Lowest (summer) and highest (New Year) prices are quoted but several shoulder pricings exist within the main December to March ski season.

Pansion Sport (☎ 270333; s/d 80/160KM; ☼ 20 Dec-10 Apr) Pleasant Swiss chalet–style guest house at the bottom 'village area' of the resort.

Hotel Club Dva Javora (☎ 270481; www.dvajavora .com; s/d/apt 47.50/65/125KM, peak season 118/150/300KM) Above a seasonal shopping centre, the refreshingly modern lobby bar feels like a trendy London coffee house. Rooms are less hip but very presentable.

Hotel Bistrica (☎ 270020; www.oc-jahorina.com; s/d with half-board 71.50/123KM, peak season 160/214KM; ☻) This vast, unsophisticated 1984 resort complex feels somewhat dated but there are lovely views and many family-style facilities in season. It's set back 300m from the Dva Javora.

Termag Hotel (☎ 270422; www.termaghotel.com; per person from 96KM Apr-Nov, 132KM Dec-Mar; ☒ ☐ ☻) Within an oversized mansion built in Scooby Doo Gothic style, the Termag is a beautifully designed fashion statement where traditional ideas and open fireplaces are given a stylish, Modernisme twist. Sumptuous rooms have glowing bedside tables and high headboards.

Rajska Vrata (☎ 272020; www.jahorina-rajskavrata .com; beer 2.50-3.50KM, mains 7-14KM) Beside the longest piste, this perfect alpine ski-in cafe-restaurant has rustic sheepskin benches around a centrally flued real fire. In summer, lovely fully equipped bedrooms (doubles/triples €50/75) are available.

Getting There & Away

Ski-season-only buses depart from Pale (3KM, 25 minutes) at 6.15am, 2.15pm and 8pm, returning 7am, 3.15pm and 11pm. From Sarajevo's main bus station there's a direct bus on winter Fridays, Saturdays and Sundays at 9am, returning at 3.45pm. There are no summer buses. A taxi from Pale costs 30KM.

BJELAŠNICA
☎ 033

Sarajevo's second Olympic ski field has only one hotel (as yet) but **Eko Planet** (☎ 579035; www .touristbiro.ba) can organise year-round apartment rental (100KM to 200KM) and offers exciting summer quad-bike trips that can take you cross country through bracing upland scenery to **Lukomir**, Bosnia's most traditional surviving mountain village. Sarajevo's ecotourism outfit Green Visions (p112) organises hikes in this lovely area.

Fronted by what looks like a giant Plexiglas pencil, the aging **Hotel Maršal** (☎ 279100;

WARNING

Stay on the groomed ski runs and hiking paths around Jahorina and Bjelašnica as there are mines in the vicinity of both resorts.

WORTH THE TRIP: UMOLJANI

If you're driving consider driving randomly to the web of villages tucked away in the grassy uplands above Bjelašnica. All suffered severely in the war, so traditional architecture is very limited, but the settings are truly lovely. **Umoljani village** (16km from Bjelašnica) is a particularly interesting choice with *stećci* above the beautiful approach lane and more in **Šabići** (11km), a junction village you'll pass part way. In Šabići, there's cheap accommodation at the very rustic **Hojta Hostel** (☎ 437874; emina2708@yahoo.com; Šabići Village; dm 20KM, dinner 6KM), run by a gruff, Bosnian Basil Fawlty. Its front room forms the de facto village pub attracting a wonderfully genuine cross-section of farming folk for a beer and a chat. No English is spoken.

---

www.hotel-marsal.ba; s/d €46/62, s/d winter €59/78; 🖥) is very friendly but haphazardly patched-up and somewhat lacklustre. In season seven-day minimum bookings apply.

Minibus 85 from Ilidža bound for Sinanovići runs just four times a week and drives via Bjelašnica and Šabići. Consider renting a car to come up here.

HERCEGOVINA

Hercegovina is the part of BiH that no one in the West ever mentions, if only because they can't pronounce its name. Its arid, Mediterranean landscape has a distinctive beauty punctuated with barren mountain ridges and photogenic river valleys. Famed for its fine wines and sun-packed fruits, Hercegovina is sparsely populated, but it has several intriguing historic towns and the Adriatic coast is just a short drive away.

MOSTAR
☎ 036 / pop 94,000
At dusk the lights of numerous mill-house restaurants twinkle delightfully across gushing streamlets. The impossibly quaint Kujundžiluk 'gold alley' bustles joyously with trinket sellers. And in between, the Balkans' most celebrated bridge forms a truly majestic stone arc between reincarnated medieval towers. It's a magical scene.

Meanwhile, behind the delightful cobbled lanes of the attractively restored Ottoman quarter, a less palatable but equally unforgettable 'attraction' lies in observing the devastating urban scars that still recall the brutal 1990s conflict all too vividly.

Add in a selection of fascinating day trips for which Mostar makes an ideal base and it's not surprising that this fascinating little city is starting to attract a growing throng of summer visitors. Visit in low season and you'll have it much to yourself.

History
Mostar means 'bridge-keeper' and the crossing of the Neretva River here has always been its raison d'être. In the mid-16th century, Mostar boomed as a key transport gateway within the powerful, expanding Ottoman Empire. Some 30 *esnafi* (craft guilds) included the tanners for whom the Tabahana was built, and goldsmiths (hence Kujundžiluk, 'gold alley'). In 1557, Suleyman the Magnificent ordered a fine stone arch to replace the suspension bridge whose wobbling had previously terrified tradesmen as they gingerly crossed the fast-flowing Neretva River. The beautiful Stari Most (Old Bridge) that resulted was finished in 1566 and came to be appreciated as one of the world's engineering marvels. It survived the Italian occupation of WWII, but after standing for 427 years the bridge was destroyed in November 1993 by Bosnian Croat artillery. That was one of the most poignant, pointless and depressing moments of the whole Yugoslav civil war.

Ironically Muslims and Croats had initially fought together against Serb and Montenegrin forces who had started bombarding Mostar in April 1992. However on 9 May 1993 a bitter conflict erupted between the former allies. Bosnian Croat forces expelled many Bosniaks from their homes: some were taken to detention camps, others fled to the very relative 'safety' of the Muslim east bank of the Neretva. For two years the two sides swapped artillery fire and the city was pummelled into rubble.

By 1995 Mostar resembled Dresden after WWII with all its bridges destroyed and all but one of its 27 Ottoman-era mosques utterly ruined. Vast international assistance efforts have since rebuilt almost all of the Unesco-listed old city core. By 2004 the Stari Most had been painstakingly reconstructed using

MOSTAR

0 ————— 500 m
0 ————— 0.3 miles

INFORMATION

Almira Travel	**1**	C5
Barbados	**2**	C4
BuyBook	**3**	B6
Europa Club	**4**	C4
Fortuna Travel	(see 31)	
Fortuna Travel	**5**	B6
Fortuna Travel	**6**	C3
GPO & Telephone Centre	**7**	B4
Post Office	**8**	C4
Tourist Information Centre	**9**	B6

SIGHTS & ACTIVITIES

Biščevića Ćošak	**10**	C5
Crooked Bridge	**11**	B6
Gutted Apartments	**12**	B3
Gymnasium	**13**	B4
Hotel Neretva	**14**	C4
Kajtaz House	**15**	D5
Koski Mehmed Paša Mosque	**16**	C5
Ljubljanska Banka Tower	**17**	B4
Museum of Hercegovina	**18**	D5
Music School	**19**	C4
Muslibegović House	**20**	C4
Old Bridge Museum	**21**	B6
Orthodox Church	**22**	D5
Roznamedži Ibrahimefendi Madrassa	**23**	C4
Roznamedži Ibrahimefendi Mosque	**24**	C4
Stari Most	**25**	B6
Tabahana	**26**	B6
Tara Gunpowder Tower	**27**	B6

— — — Former Front Line

SLEEPING

Apartments Konak	**28**	C6
Hostel Nina	**29**	D6
Hotel Bevanda	**30**	A5
Hotel Ero	**31**	B3
Hotel Old Town	**32**	B6
Hotel Pellegrino	**33**	C4
Kriva Ćuprija	**34**	B6
Kriva Ćuprija 2	**35**	D6
Majda's Rooms	**36**	B5
Motel Deny	**37**	B6
Muslibegović House	(see 20)	
Pansion Aldi	**38**	C3
Pansion Armin	**39**	C6
Pansion Emen	**40**	C6
Pansion Oscar	**41**	B6
Vila Sara	**42**	C4

EATING

ABC	**43**	C4
Dan-i-Noć	**44**	C4
Dvije Pecine	**45**	B6
Grill Centar	**46**	C4
Mercur Supermarket	**47**	C4
MM Restaurant	**48**	C4
Restaurant Bella Vista	**49**	B6
Šadrvan	**50**	B6
Tepa Market	**51**	C5
Urban Grill	**52**	B6

DRINKING

Ali Baba Bar	**53**	B6
Bijeli Bar	**54**	B6
Caffe Marshall	**55**	B6
Coco Loco Bar	**56**	B4
Koščela	**57**	B6
OKC Abrašević	**58**	B4
Villa Neretva	**59**	C4

ENTERTAINMENT

Club Oxygen	**60**	C4
Dom Kultura Herceg Stjepan Kosača	**61**	B4
Pavarotti Music Centre	**62**	D6

SHOPPING

Ismet Kurt	**63**	B6

TRANSPORT

BH Airlines	(see 43)	
Bus Station	**64**	C3
Bus Stop for Medugorje	**65**	A5
Helax	(see 31)	
Lučki Bridge Bus Stop for Blagaj	**66**	D6
MaxLine	**67**	C3
Mostar Bus Stop	**68**	C3

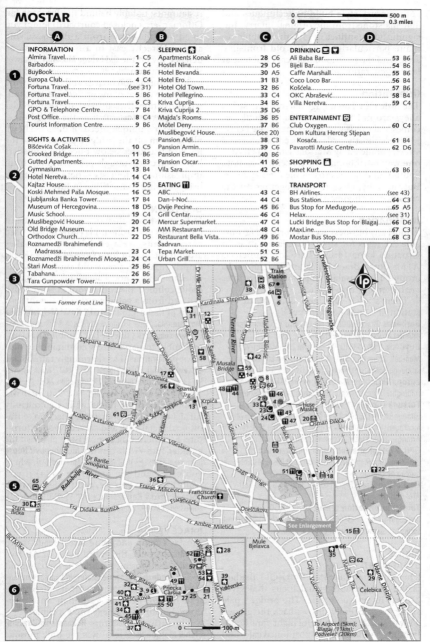

BOSNIA & HERCEGOVINA

16th-century-style building techniques and Tenelija stone from the original quarry. But significant quantities of ghostlike rubble remain, particularly along the old front-line area. And the psychological scars will take at least a generation to heal.

Orientation

The little Old Town hugs narrow pedestrian alleys around Stari Most. Kujundžiluk becomes Mala Tepa which becomes Braće Fejića, Mostar's mostly pedestrianised commercial street, paralleled by Maršala Tita, which runs one way northbound for its central section. Southbound traffic crosses the river and uses Bulvar or bypasses town altogether on the considerably higher M17.

Information

Almost any business accepts euros (at favourable 2:1 rates for small purchases) or even Croatian kuna (4:1). There are numerous ATMs down Braće Fejića and several banks around Trg Musala change money, but rates are better at the post office.

There's a left-luggage facility in the bus station; it's 2KM per item per day.

Barbados (Braće Fejića 26; per hr 2KM; ☺ 9am-11pm) Internet access; upstairs, enter by side door.

BuyBook (☎ 558810; Onešcukova 24; ☺ 9am-9pm Mon-Sat, 10am-6pm Sun) A useful array of English-language books, guidebooks and CDs.

Europa Club (Huse Maslića 10; per hr 1KM; ☺ 7am-midnight) Internet access; beneath a stationery shop.

Fortuna Travel (☎ 552197; www.fortuna.ba; Rade Bitange 34; ☺ 8am-4.30pm Mon-Fri, 9am-1pm Sat) Major local agency with sub-offices on Mala Tepa and at Hotel Ero. Arranges guided tours, accommodation and car hire.

GPO & Telephone Centre (Dr Ante Starčevića bb; ☺ 7am-7pm Mon-Sat, 8am-noon Sun) Poste restante; bureau de change.

Post office (Braće Fejića bb; ☺ 8am-8pm Mon-Sat) ATM outside.

Tourist information centre (☎ 397350; www .hercegovina.ba; Onešcukova bb; ☺ 9am-9pm) Useful but subject to sporadic closures out of season.

Sights

STARI MOST

The world-famous **Stari Most** (Old Bridge) is the indisputable visual focus that gives Mostar its unique magic. The bridge's pale stone magnificently throws back the golden glow of sunset or the tasteful night-time floodlighting. Numerous well-positioned cafes and restaurants, notably behind the **Tabahana** (an Ottoman-era enclosed courtyard) tempt you to admire the scene from a dozen varying angles. Directly east in a five-storey stone defence tower, the **Old Bridge Museum** (admission 5KM; ☺ 11am-2pm winter, 10am-6pm summer) has historical information boards and slow-moving 15-minute videos of the bridge's destruction/ reconstruction. Directly west, the semicircular **Tara Gunpowder Tower** is now the 'club house' for Mostar's unique breed of divers. They'll plunge 21m off the bridge's parapet into the icy Neretva River below once their hustlers have collected enough photo money from impressionable tourists. There's an annual bridge-diving competition in July.

OLD TOWN

Delightful footpath-stairways linking quaint old houses and stone mills (now mostly used as restaurants) are layered down a mini-valley around the quaint little **Crooked Bridge** (Kriva Ćuprija). Above, pretty old shopfronts line Prječka Čaršija and **Kujundžiluk**, the picturesque cobbled alleys that join at Stari Most. Entered from a gated courtyard, the interior decor of the originally 1618 **Koski Mehmed Paša Mosque** (Mala Tepa 16; mosque/mosque & minaret 3/5KM; ☺ 9am-6pm) lacks finesse but climbing its claustrophobic minaret offers commanding old-town panoramas. The charmingly ramshackle **Bišćevića Ćošak** (Turkish House; ☎ 550677; www.biscevica kuca.bravehost.com; Bišćevića 13; admission 2KM; ☺ 9am-3pm Nov-Feb, 8am-8pm Mar-Oct) is a 350-year-old Ottoman-Bosnian home with a colourfully furnished interior sporting a selection of traditional metalwork and carved wooden furniture. For interesting comparisons also visit the grander 18th-/19th-century **Muslibegović House** (admission 3KM; ☺ 10am-8pm mid-Apr–mid-Oct), where you can spend the night (see p124) if you really like what you see, and the less-central, 16th-century **Kajtaz House** (☎ 550913; Gaše Ilića 21; admission 2KM; ☺ unpredictable).

BRAĆE FEJIĆA

Mostar's main shopping street leads up to **Trg Musala**, once the grand heart of Austro-Hungarian Mostar, passing the large, rebuilt 1557 **Karađozbeg Mosque** (Braće Fejića; mosque/minaret 3/2KM; ☺ 9am-6pm Sat-Thu) with its distinctive lead-roofed wooden verandah and four-domed madrassa annexe (now a clinic).

The early-17th-century **Roznamedži Ibrahim-efendi Mosque** (Braće Fejića) was the only mosque to survive the 1993–95 shelling relatively unscathed. Its associated **madrassa** has just been rebuilt, the original having been demolished in 1960.

BAJATOVA

The little **Museum of Hercegovina** (☎ 551602; Bajatova 4; admission 1.50KM; 🕒 9am-2pm Mon-Fri, 10am-noon Sat) is housed in the former home of Džemal Bijedić, an ex-head of the Yugoslav government who died in mysterious circumstances in 1978. A well-paced 10-minute film features pre- and post-1992 bridge-diving plus war footage that shows the moment Stari Most was blown apart.

Stairway-lane Bajatova climbs on towards the M17 with an underpass leading towards the site of a once imposing **Orthodox church** almost totally destroyed by Croat shelling in 1993. From amidst the rubble there are superb city views.

WAR DAMAGE

Along the thought-provoking and intensely moving **former front line**, many buildings remain shockingly burned-out wrecks, including the once-stately 1896 **Gymnasium** (High School; Spanski Trg), now under slow reconstruction; the once-beautiful 1898 **Hotel Neretva** (www.cinv.co.ba/en/neretva.htm); and the 1920s **Music School**. The bombed-out nine-storey former **Ljubljanska Banka Tower** (Kralja Zvonimira bb) and the **gutted apartments** on Aleske Šantića seem even more heart-rendingly poignant being so comparatively modern.

Tours

With French- and English-speaking guides, **Almira Travel** (☎ /fax 551873; www.almira-travel.ba; Mala Tepa 9; 🕒 9am-5pm Mon-Sat, later in season) offers a vast range of imaginative tour options including wine-tasting tours. It can arrange guided tours, accommodation and car hire, and sells decent BiH–Croatia maps (€7).

Homestay owners can also organise tours, and the trips organised through Madja's Rooms (right) are particularly good value.

Sleeping

If you're stumped for accommodation the tourist information centre (opposite) and travel agencies can help you find a bed. Almira Travel (above) also offers rural village homestays. Note that mid-summer prices can rise 20% to 50%.

BUDGET

All places listed are effectively glorified homestays. None have full-time receptionists so calling ahead is wise, especially in low season when some are virtually dormant (and unheated). At such times you'll probably get a whole room for the dorm price. All but the Armin have shared bathrooms.

Hostel Nina (☎ 061-382743; www.hostelnina.ba; Čelebica 18; dm/s/d with shared bathroom €10/15/20; 💻) Good-value homestay-style accommodation with three rooms per neat bathroom run by a very obliging English-speaking lady. Her overflow-annexe is out near the Rondo.

Pansion Oscar (☎ 061-823649; Oneščukova 33; per person €10-20, breakfast €5; ❄) Six very presentable rooms, some with balconies, share two bathrooms in a truly unbeatable location near the Stari Most. Seid speaks good English, and washing machines are available (€5 per load), but there's no communal sitting area.

Vila Sara (☎ 555940; www.villasara-mostar.com; Sasarogina 4; dm/s/d/tr with shared bathroom 20/30/40/60KM) Crammed-together new beds with fresh duvets share a decent kitchen and cramped but piping-hot showers. Phone ahead in low season. Checkout is a yawny 10am.

Pansion Aldi (☎ 552185, 061-273457; www.pansion-aldi.com; Laćina 69a; dm/d/apt with shared bathroom €10/20/42) This no-frills hostel has 13 beds in five spacious if simple rooms (two air-conditioned) sharing a kitchenette and riverside garden terrace but only one shower and two squat toilets. It's unmarked but very handy for the bus station. No heating, limited English.

Majda's Rooms (☎ 061-382940; 1st fl, Franje Milicevica 39; dm/d with shared bathroom €11/24; ❄) By sheer force of personality, and a very human awareness of traveller needs, sharp-witted Bata and his surreally delightful mother have turned a once-dreary tower-block apartment into Mostar's cult hostel. Most rooms are eight-bed dorms. Bata's regional tours are superb value.

Pansion Armin (☎ 552700; Kalkhanska 3; s/d from €15/30) Excellent-value en suite rooms in a bright-yellow new house with trellis frontage facing the eerie ruin of a bombed-out school.

MIDRANGE & TOP END

Apartments Konak (☎ 551105; http://apartmani-konak.com/; Maršala Tita 125; d/tr/q €30/45/60; ❄) Good-value homely apartments, central and fairly well set back from the noisy main road up a little stairway.

Motel Deny (☎ 578317; www.mdmostar.com; Kapetanovina 1; s/d 53/86KM, high season 63/106; ⚄) This modern mini-hotel overlooks the mill area of the Old Town and has a charming lobby decked out with flickering candles. Rooms are slightly plain in comparison but well furnished and clean.

Pansion Emen (☎ 581120, 061-848734; www.motel-emen .com; Oneščukova 32; ; s/d/tr from €30/50/60; ⚄ 💻) More a fashionable mini-hotel than a pansion, the Emen is one of old Mostar's most prized addresses, with understated chic and a remarkably reasonable price tag. It features wonderful sitting areas, two shared internet computers and angular bath fittings straight from a design magazine.

Kriva Ćuprija (☎ 550953; www.motel-mostar.ba; s/d/ apt from €30/55/65; ⚄) Soothe yourself with the sounds of gushing streams in new, impeccably furnished (if not necessarily large) rooms ranged above this charming stone mill-house restaurant overlooking the Crooked Bridge. Don't be palmed off to Kriva Ćuprija 2, a new annexe on the main road across Lučki Bridge.

our pick Muslibegović House (☎ 551379; Osman Đikća 41; www.muslibegovichouse.com; s/d €40/70; ⚄) In summer tourists pay to visit this superbly restored 18th-century Ottoman courtyard house (p122). But it's simultaneously an extremely convivial 15-room homestay-hotel. Room sizes and styles vary significantly, mixing excellent modern bathrooms with elements of traditional Bosnian-Turkish design. Room 2 is especially atmospheric.

Hotel Pellegrino (☎ 061-480784; Faladjica 1c; www .hotel-pellegrino.ba; s/d/tr 90/130/150KM; ⚄) Above a surprisingly spacious neo-Tuscan restaurant/lounge, expansive rooms have excellent anti-allergenic bedding and kitchenette. Each room has its own oddity, be it a giant black lacquer vase, a bundle-of-twigs lamp or a whole-cow mat.

Hotel Old Town (☎ 558877; www.oldtown.ba; Oneščvćukova 30; d/tr/ste from €90/120/150) This delightful supercentral boutique hotel is full of specially designed handmade furniture, uses energy-saving waste-burning furnaces for water-heating and has ecofriendly air-circulation to save on air-conditioning wastage.

Hotel Ero (☎ 386777; www.ero.ba; Dr Ante Starčevića bb; s/d/apt 99/166/215KM; ⚄ 💻) The 165 solidly renovated rooms have balconies and peachy-cream new decor, though rickety doors and abandoned floor-lady areas faintly recall its previous Tito-era incarnation.

Hotel Bevanda (☎ 332332; www.hotelbevanda.com; Stara Ilićka 1; s/d/ste 199/255/425KM; ⚄) The over-shiny little atrium does little to support the Bevanda's illusions of grandeur, though rooms are perfectly comfortable and the very plush suites come with a waiting decanter of brandy.

Eating

Cafes and restaurants with divine views of the river cluster along the western riverbank near Stari Most. Although unapologetically tourist-oriented, their meal prices are only a *maraka* or two more than any ordinary dive, though wine can get comparatively costly.

Šadrvan (☎ 579057; Jusovina 11; dishes 6-17KM) On a quaint corner where the pedestrian lane from Stari Most divides, this appealing, gently upmarket restaurant has tables set around a trickling fountain made of old Turkish-style metalwork, shaded by the spreading tentacles of a kiwi-fruit vine. The menu covers all Bosnian bases. Several other streamside mill-restaurants nearby are every bit as good: simply pick the atmosphere that suits.

Restaurant Bella Vista (☎ 061-656421; Tabahana; pizzas 7-10KM, mains 7-17KM) Along with the almost indistinguishable Restaurants Babilon and Teatr next door, the Bella Vista has stupendous terrace views across the river to the Old Town and Stari Most. The food is less impressive than the views, but some of the set 'tourist menus' are excellent value.

ABC (☎ 194656; Braće Fejića 45; pizza & pasta 6-9KM, mains 12-15KM; ☷ 8am-11pm Mon-Sat, noon-11pm Sun) Downstairs is Mostar's most popular cake shop and a narrow see-and-be-seen pavement cafe. Upstairs is a relaxed pastel-toned Italian restaurant. Pizzas are rather bready but the plate-lickingly creamy Aurora tortellini comes with an extra bucketful of parmesan.

Also recommended:

Urban Grill (www.urbangrill.ba; Mala Tepa; ćevapi 3.50-5.50KM) Can *ćevapi* ever be cool? They think so here.

Grill Centar (Braće Fejića 13; grills 5KM; ☷ 8am-11pm) Unsophisticated *ćevadžinica* attached to an old Bosnian courtyard house.

MM Restaurant (Mostarskog Bataljona 11; meals 6-12KM; ☷ 8am-10pm Mon-Sat) Easy to use buffet-style feeding station.

For self-caterers, **Mercur Supermarket** (Braće Fejića 51; ☷ 7am-10pm) is a sizeable, central grocery store, while **Dan-i-Noć** (Mostarskog Bataljona 8; ☷ 24hr) is an all-night bakery.

Some of the gnarled characters working at **Tepa market** (Braće Fejića bb; ☾ 6.30am-2pm), a modest fruit-and-veg market, look like they've been here for centuries. Great views from the parapet behind.

Drinking

Ali Baba Bar (Kujundžiluk; ☾ summer only) Remarkable, seasonal bar-club tucked into the cliff-face that looms directly above Kujundžiluk.

our pick OKC Abrašević (☎ 561107; www.okcabrasevic.org; Alekse Šantića 25; beer 2KM; ☾ variable) This uncompromising yet understatedly intellectual bar offers Mostar's most vibrantly alternative 'scene', and has an attached venue for offbeat gigs. You'll need the guts to seek it out, as it's hidden away between the prison and the city's most daunting burnt-out war ruins.

Bijeli Bar (Stari Most 2; coffee 2KM, beer 4KM; ☾ 7am-11pm) The ubercool main bar zaps you with a wicked white-on-white Clockwork Orange decor. Meanwhile, around the corner the same bar owns an utterly spectacular perch-terrace from which the old bridge and towers appear from altogether new angles. The latter is entered from Maršala Tita, through a wrought-iron gate marked Atelje Novalić: cross the Japanese-style garden and climb the stone roof-steps.

Košćela (Kujundžiluk; coffee 2KM; ☾ 10am-7pm) Bridge views are almost as perfect as from the Bijeli Bar terrace and Bosnian coffee (2KM) comes in full traditional copper regalia, complete with Turkish delight. Light grill-meals are served but there's no alcohol.

Caffe Marshall (Oneščukova bb; beer 3KM; ☾ 8am-midnight) Minuscule but appealing box-bar draped with musical instruments.

Villa Neretva (Trg Musala; ☾ 7am-11pm) This spacious, modern cafe attracts a calm, literate crowd, while the attached Monkey Bar has a livelier music vibe that pumps harder as the evening progresses.

Coco Loco Bar (Kralja Zvonimira bb; ☾ 8am-late) With minimal decor and wafting, questionable vapours, this place is nonetheless packed to the gunnels at weekends for deafening DJ-parties.

Entertainment

Club Oxygen (☎ 512244; www.biosphere.ba/biosfere-stranice-oxigen-en.html; Braće Fejića bb; ☾ variable) Oxygen has movie nights, DJ-discos and Mostar's top live gigs. In summer its rooftop SkyBar takes over as the place to party.

Dom Kultura Herceg Stjepan Kosača (☎ 323501; Rondo; ☾ variable) Large cultural centre offering diverse shows, concerts and exhibitions. Visiting opera, ballet and theatre companies from Croatia show up occasionally.

OKC Abrašević (left) and the **Pavarotti Music Centre** (☎ 550750; Maršala Tita 179) also host occasional concerts.

Shopping

The stone-roofed shop-houses of Kujundžiluk throw open metal shutters to sell agreeably colourful, inexpensive if somewhat trashy Turkish souvenirs from amulets to glittery velveteen slippers (€7), pashmina-style wraps (from €5), fezzes (€5), *boncuk* (evil-eye) pendants and Russian-style nested dolls. Many stalls sell pens fashioned from old bullets, while master coppersmith **Ismet Kurt** (☎ 550017; Kujundžiluk 5) hammers old mortar-shell casings into works of art while you watch.

Getting There & Away

AIR

Mostar airport (OMO; ☎ 350992) is 6km south of town off the Čapljina road. **BH Airlines** (☎ 551820; Braće Fejića 45; ☾ 9am-5pm Mon-Fri) flies to İstanbul on Sunday mornings for €180.

BUS

From the main **bus station** (☎ 552025; Trg Ivana Krndelja), tickets for most services are pre-sold through **Autoprevoz-bus** (☎ 551900). See p126 for details of services.

Yellow **Mostar Bus** (☎ 552250; www.mostarbus.ba/linije.asp) services to Blagaj and Podvelež depart from opposite the station and also pick up from the Lučki Most stop.

For Međugorje (4KM, 45 minutes) buses pick up outside the Bevanda Hotel at 6.30am, 11.30am, 1.10pm, 2.30pm, 3.30pm, 6.10pm and 7.30pm on weekdays. The 6.30am, 11.30am, 6.10pm and 7.30pm services operate on Saturdays, and only the 7.30pm bus runs on Sundays.

CAR

Vehicle rentals are available at travel agencies, from **Helax** (☎ 382114; Hotel Ero, Dr Ante Starčevića bb; from 490KM per week; ☾ 8am-5pm Mon-Fri, 8am-noon Sat) and **MaxLine** (☎ 551525; www.maxline.ba; Station Sq; from €45/245 per day/week; ☾ 8am-6pm Mon-Fri, 9am-3pm Sat).

BUSES FROM MOSTAR

Destination	Price (KM)	Duration (hr)	Departures
Banja Luka (via Jajce)	25	6	1.30pm
Belgrade	48	11	7.30pm
Čapljina	6	40min	twice-hourly weekdays, only six daily Sun
Dubrovnik	27	3½	7am, 10.15am & 2.30pm
Sarajevo	16	2½-3	hourly 6am-3pm plus 6.15pm & 8.30pm
Split	25	4½	9.30am, 10.45am, 12.50pm, 5.30pm & midnight
Stolac	4	1	6.15am, 3.30pm & 8.15pm
Tešanj	34	6	5.30pm
Trebinje (via Nevesinje)	19	3	5.30pm
Trebinje (via Stolac)	19	3	6.15am & 3.30pm
Visoko	20	3¾	6.30pm
Zagreb	43	9½	9am

TRAIN

The **train station** (☎ 552198) is beside the bus station. Two daily services run to Sarajevo (9.90KM, 2¾ hours) at 7.38am and 6.40pm, puffing alongside fish farms in the pea-green Neretva River's magnificent dammed gorge before struggling up a series of switchbacks behind Konjic to reach Sarajevo after 65 tunnels.

AROUND MOSTAR

By joining a tour or sharing a hire-car you can combine into a single day visits to Blagaj, Počitelj, Međugorje and the brilliant but awkward-to-reach Kravice Waterfalls. Maybe visit a winery or two en route: look for the white-on-brown Vinska Cesta road-signs or consult www.wine route.ba.

Blagaj

☎ 036 / pop 4000

Pretty Blagaj village culminates at the very picturesque, half-timbered **Tekija** (Dervish monastery; ☎ 573221; admission 3KM; ⏱ 8am-10pm), whose charmingly wobbly carved wooden interior entombs two Tajik 15th-century dervishes. Outside, the green Buna River gushes out of a gaping cave backed by soaring cliffs topped way above by the **Herceg Stjepan Fortress** ruins.

Walking to the Tekija takes 10 minutes from the seasonal **tourist information booth** (⏱ 10am-7pm in season), passing the delightful **Oriental House** (Velagomed, Velagic House; ☎ 572712; www.velagomed.ba; Velagicevina bb; admission 2KM; ⏱ 10am-7pm), an artistically appointed 18th-century Ottoman ensemble with fabulous island-meadow gardens and even a couple of simple rooms to rent (double €30). Near the 1892 octagonal **Sultan Sulejman Mosque**, the

friendly unmarked **Kayan Pansion** (☎ 572299; nevresakajan@yahoo.com; tw €20) offers well-kept homestay rooms and Merima (☎ 061-346969) speaks English.

Mostar Bus lines 10, 11 and 12 run patchily to or near Blagaj (1.80KM, 30 minutes), but check www.mostarbus.ba/linije.asp for the frequently changing schedule. There's no public transport from Blagaj to Podveluž or Počitelj.

Međugorje

☎ 036 / pop 4300

Since the Holy Virgin spoke to six local teenagers on 24 June 1981, **Međugorje** (www .medjugorje.hr) has been transformed from poor winemaking backwater to BiH's pilgrim central. The odd blend of honest faith and cash-in tackiness is reminiscent of Lourdes (France) or Fatima (Portugal). Pilgrim numbers just keep growing, even though the Catholic Church has not officially acknowledged the visions' legitimacy.

There are countless hotels and *pansions*, but for many nonpilgrims a two-hour visit often proves plenty long enough to get the idea. The town's focus is double-towered 1969 **St James' Church** (Župna Crkva), 200m behind which is the mesmerising **Resurrected Saviour** (Uskrsli Spasitej). This masterpiece of Modernisme sculpture shows a gaunt 5m-tall metallic Christ standing crucified yet cross-less, his manhood wrapped in scripture. Erected in 1998, the statue 'miraculously' weeps a colourless liquid from its right knee, with pilgrims queuing to dab a drop of this holy fluid onto specially inscribed pads.

A 3km (5KM) taxi ride away is **Podbrdo** village from which streams of faithful climb **Brdo Ukazanja** (Apparition Hill) to a white statue of the Virgin Mary at the site of the original 1981 visions. The red-earth paths are studded with sharp stones and some pilgrims make the 15-minute walk barefoot in deliberately painful acts of penitence.

Download artist's-eye town maps from the **tourist association** (www.tel.net.ba/tzm-medju gorje/1%20karta100.jpg).

Počitelj
☎ 036 / pop 350

This stepped Ottoman-era fortress village is one of the most picture-perfect architectural ensembles in BiH. Cupped in a steep rocky amphitheatre, it was systematically despoiled in the 1990s conflicts but its finest 16th-century buildings are now rebuilt, including the **Šišman Ibrahim Madrassa**, the 1563 **Hadži Alijna Mosque** and the 16m **tower** (Sahat Kula). The upper village culminates in the still part-ruined **Gavrakapetan Tower**.

There's a basic cafe but no accommodation. Počitelj is right beside the main Split–Mostar road, 5km north of Čapljina. Mostar–Split and Mostar–Čapljina buses pass by, but southbound only the latter (roughly hourly on weekdays) will usually accept Počitelj-bound passengers. In summer arrive early to avoid the heat and the Croatian tour groups.

Kravice Waterfalls

In spring this stunning mini-Niagara of **25m cascades** pounds itself into a dramatic, steamy fury. In summer the falls themselves are less impressive but surrounding pools become shallow enough for swimming. The site is 4km down a dead-end road that turns off the Čapljina–Ljubuški road at km42.5. There's no public transport.

NEUM

Driving between Split and Dubrovnik, don't forget your passport, as you'll pass through BiH's tiny toe-hold of Adriatic coastline. The one resort here, **Neum** (www.neum.ba), is crammed with concrete apartment-hotels for holidaying locals and the water isn't as inviting as in parts of neighbouring Croatia. For most travellers the brief refreshment break taken on the Neum bypass by Split–Dubrovnik buses is ample.

STOLAC
☎ 036 / pop 12,000

Guarding an impressive craggy canyon, the attractive castle town of Stolac was the site of Roman Diluntum (3rd century AD), then a prominent 15th-century citadel. Stolac suffered serious conflict in 1993 but the displaced population has returned and reconstruction of the shattered town continues apace. From the bus station, cross the river to the pretty main street, Hrvatske-Brante (aka Ada), which arcs around the base of overgrown **Vidoški Grad** (the castle hill). After 600m in the town centre, the fine 1735 **Šarić House** faces memorable mural-fronted **Čaršija Mosque**, rebuilt to look just like the 1519 original. Upstream are several delightfully picturesque if partly ruined 17th-century stone **mill-races**. Beside the Mostar road 3km west of Stolac, **Radimlja Necropolis** is a famous if somewhat disappointing collection of around 110 *stećci* grave-markers (see p104). Stolac's only hotel, **Villa Ragusa** (☎ 853700; s/d/tr 35/70/105KM), offers worn if mostly clean rooms across a small bridge from the town centre.

Weekday buses run approximately hourly to Čapljina (5KM, 45 minutes, last departure at 5pm), with five services on Saturdays and none on Sunday. Weekdays only, buses run to Mostar at 6.30am and 12.30pm. Mostar–Trebinje buses pass through twice daily but oddly bypass Stolac's bus station.

EASTERN BOSNIA & HERCEGOVINA

To get quickly yet relatively easily off the main tourist trail, try linking Sarajevo or Mostar to Dubrovnik via Trenbinje, possibly visiting the gorgeous Sujeska National Park. You'll pass through the 'other half' of BiH, the Republika Srpska, where's it's fascinating to hear about the nation's traumas from the 'other side'.

TREBINJE ТРЕБИЊЕ
☎ 059 / pop 36,000

A beguiling quick stop between Dubrovnik (28km) and Višegrad (or Mostar), Trebinje has a small, walled **Old Town** (Stari Grad) where inviting, unpretentious cafes offer a fascinating opportunity to meet friendly local residents and hear Serb viewpoints on divisive recent history. Old-town ramparts back onto the riverside near a 19th-century former Austro-Hungarian barracks which now houses the eclectic **Hercegovina Museum** (Музеј Херцеговине; ☎ 271060; Stari Grad 59; admission 1KM; ⏰ 8.30am-2pm). Lovely stone-flagged **Trg Svobode** is ringed with chestnut trees, street cafes and old buildings with wrought-iron overhangs. It's reminiscent of rural France and hosts a lively Saturday market.

Trebinje's 1574 **Arslanagić Bridge** (Perovića Most) is a unique, double-backed structure sadly let down by the unexotic suburban location (700m northeast of Hotel Leotar) to which it was moved in the 1970s.

For phenomenal views take the 2km winding lane leading east of Motel Etage to hilltop **Hercegovacka Gracanica**, where the compact but eye-catching **Presvete Bogorodice Church** was erected in 2000 to rehouse the bones of local hero Jovan Dučić. Its design is based on the 1321 Gračanica monastery (p435) in Kosovo, a building that's symbolically sacred to many Serbs.

For town maps visit www.trebinje.info/trebinje/mape or the **tourist office** (☎ 273122; www.trebinjeturizam.com; Preobraženska 10; ⏰ 8am-3pm Mon-Fri). The latter is hidden in an unlikely apartment building behind the very central **Balkan Investment Bank** (☎ Preobraženska 6; ⏰ 8am-4pm Mon-Fri), which changes money and has an ATM.

Sleeping

Hotel Leotar (☎ 261086; www.hotelleotar.com; Obala Luke Vukalovića bb; old s/d 51.50/83KM, deluxe 81.50/113KM) This growling four-storey socialist-era remnant faces the old-town ramparts across the river. So far 35 deluxe rooms have been attractively upgraded, but twice that many are sorry old affairs with all the glamour of a 1960s hospital ward.

Motel Etage (☎ 261443; Dušanova 9; s/d/tr incl breakfast €30/45/55) Bright, colourful but not over-large rooms with a decent buffet breakfast included. Cross the river east of the tourist office then turn left at the T-junction.

Motel Viv (☎ 273500; www.hotelviv-trebinje.com; Dušanova 11; s/d/tr 60/90/120KM) Slightly more prone to road noise, this joint is marginally smarter than its next-door neighbour Motel Etage.

Hotel Platani (☎ 225134; www.hotelplatani.com; Trg Svobode; s/d/tr 79/115/135KM; 🖳) Perfectly located above the town's top street-cafe, this cosy 12-room hotel is gently upmarket but the tiny reception can take a bit of finding.

Eating & Drinking

Pizza Castello (☎ 223192; Trg Travunije 3; pizzas 6.50-7.50KM; ⏰ 7.30am-midnight) Castello's three-table terrace is great for people-watching. Jovial host Snezhan speaks great English and the thin-crust pizza is excellent. Several other relatively downmarket eateries share this same Old Town square.

Galerija Veritas (Stari Grad 17; beer 2.50KM; ⏰ 9am-11pm) This eccentric brick-domed cavern cafe is dotted with antique TV sets. Check out the beamed upper level. It's hidden on an alley between the museum and Kameni Bridge.

Azzovo (Stari Grad 114; beer 2KM; ⏰ 8am-11pm Mon-Sat, 10am-11pm Sun) Cosy, Old Town blues-oriented bar with ceilings of bamboo and vine-stems. Nearby several others have similarly great summer terraces, while Kafe Serbia and Bajica Caffe are built right into the old-town ramparts.

Getting There & Away

Since 2007, the '**bus station**' (Vojvode Stepe Stepanovića) is an unmarked parking area west of the centre through the park behind large Saborna church.

BUSES FROM TRENBINJE

Destination	Price (KM)	Duration (hr)	Departures
Belgrade (via Foča & Višegrad)	40	11	8am & 6pm
Dubrovnik	5	¾	10am Mon-Sat (returns at 1.30pm)
Herceg Novi (via Risan)	13	1¾	6am
Ljubinje	9	1½	2.10pm Mon-Fri, 7pm daily
Mostar (via Nevesinje)			10am
Mostar (via Stolac)	19	3	6.15am & 2.30pm
Pale (via Foča)	22	4½	5am
Podgorica (via Nikšič)	20	3½	8.30am, 3pm & 4.30pm
Sarajevo (via Foča)	20	4	5am, 7.30am & 11am

TREBINJE TO VIŠEGRAD

Trebinje–Belgrade and Trebinje–Sarajevo buses pass through the glorious **Sutjeska National Park** (www.npsutjeska.srbinje.net in Bosnian), where magnificent wooded canyon-lands open out near an impressively vast concrete **Partizans' Memorial** commemorating the classic WWII battle of **Tjentište**. Further north, war-battered **Foča** is a centre for world-class **rafting** on the Tara River that cascades out of Europe's deepest canyon (across the Montenegrin border) then thunders over 21 rapids (class III to class IV in summer, class IV to class V in April). Foča's very professional extreme sports outfit **Encijan** (☎ 211220; www.pkencijan.com; Kraljapetra-I 1; ☒ 9am-5pm) can organise everything.

VIŠEGRAD ВИШЕГРАД

☎ 058 / pop 20,000

Višegrad is internationally famous for its 10-arch 1571 **Mehmet Paša Sokolović Bridge** (www .pbase.com/vmarinkovic/the_bridge_on_the_drina) immortalised in Andrić's classic *Bridge on the Drina*. In early July there's a very popular Mostar-style **bridge-diving competition** from this Unesco World Heritage Site. The town is otherwise architecturally unexotic, but it's set between some of Bosnia's most impressive river canyons. The ultrahelpful **tourist office** (☎ 620821; www.visegradturizam.com; Užičkog 11; ☒ 8am-3pm Mon-Fri) operates a summer-only information kiosk right by the south end of the old bridge. Its website has a town map.

The central, garishly coloured **Hotel Višegrad** (☎ 620378) is under reconstruction. Until it reopens, the best accommodation is **Motel Aura** (☎ 631021; auravgd@teol.net; Kraljapetpui bb; s/d from 45/65KM) behind the AutoGas LPG station, 1km northeast of the old bridge. Adequate but lacking style, **Motel Okuka** (☎ 065-998761; s/d/tr 50/80/120KM) is a similar distance upstream but on the other bank. Many longer-distance buses conveniently stop outside. Useful departures include Sarajevo (8am), Mostar (4am), Foča (7am) and Trebinje (10am) via Foča and Sutjeska National Park. Buses to Belgrade (9.30am and 1.30pm) and to Užice (7.30am, 11.30am and 6pm) pass the historic **Dobrun Monastery** (11km east) and Mokra Gora (Serbia). From 2009 a newly reconstructed narrow-gauge railway should start operating from Dobrun to Mokra Gora, connecting with the popular **Šargan 8 tourist train**

(see p826). The Dobrun–Višegrad section is slated to open in 2010.

CENTRAL & WESTERN BOSNIA

West of Sarajevo lies a series of gently historic towns, green wooded hills, rocky crags and dramatic rafting canyons. The area offers ample opportunities for exploration and adrenaline-rush activities.

VISOKO

☎ 032 / pop 17,000

Once the capital of medieval Bosnia and the spiritual centre of the controversial Bosnian Church, this unremarkable leather-tanning town had been largely forgotten in the 20th century. Then, Bosnian archaeologist Semir Osmanagic hatched a bold theory that Visoko's 250m high Visočica Hill is in fact the **World's Greatest Pyramid** (Sun Pyramid; www .piramidasunca.ba), built around 12,000 years ago by a long disappeared superculture. Initial **archaeological excavations** (admission free) have revealed what seem to be 'paving' and 'tunnel entrances' and tourists have flocked here to take a look. The forested hill does indeed have a remarkably perfect pyramidal shape when viewed from some angles. However, a long ridge at the back rather spoils the idea.

The site is 15 minutes' walk from Visoko bus station. Cross the river towards the Motel Piramida-Sunca tower, turn immediately left down Visoko's relatively attractive main street, passing the **museum** (Alije Izetbegovića 29), **tourist office** (☎ 733189; Alije Izetbegovića 29; ☒ 9am-4pm Mon-Fri) and **post office** (Čaršijska 75; ☒ 8am-8pm Mon-Fri, 8am-3pm Sat). Then after the bazaar merge left into Tvrtka/Mule Hodžić. Opposite Mule Hodžić 25 climb steeply up winding Pertac, then turn left at the top.

Sleeping & Eating

Motel Piramida-Sunca (☎ 731460; www.motelpiramida sunca.co.ba; 6th fl, Musala 1; s/d/tr/q 50/80/100/120KM; ☒) Good, unfussy new rooms aren't nearly as wacky as you'd expect from the triangular key-fobs, crazy nozzle lamps and acid-trip colours in the corridors.

ourpick **Hotel Centar** (☎ 730030; www.hotelcentar .ba; Alaudina 1; d/apt 156/206KM; ☒) This design-book, high-fashion boutique hotel has dark-wood interiors, top quality linens and an excellent, city-centre location above Volksbank (Alije Izetbegovića 37). Apartment 301 has pyramid views and the remarkable basement restaurant is designed like an old Bosnian village courtyard.

Caffe Fashion (Čaršijska 14; coffee 1KM, beer 2.50KM; 7am-10pm) Curious little multilevel cafe near the bazaar with unexplained stove-doors, token beams and a ribbon-wrapped piano.

Getting There & Away

Buses stop here twice hourly until 8.30pm, running between Sarajevo (5.50KM, 50 minutes) and Kakanj (4.40KM, 35 minutes). For Travnik (10.50KM, 1¼ hours) buses leave at 8.10am, 9.50am, 2.10pm, 4.10pm and 10.30pm, or change in Zenica (14 buses on weekdays).

TRAVNIK
☎ 030 / pop 27,500

Once the seat of Bosnia's Turkish viziers (Ottoman governors), Travnik's sizeable castle ruin and patchily attractive old architecture makes it a good half-day stop between Sarajevo and Jajce. The town wiggles along the deep Lavša Valley, the M5 highway roughly paralleled by main street Bosanska. From the **bus station** (☎ 792761), west of the centre, exit through the yellow fencing and walk past the **post office** (☎ 547102; Prnjavor) to emerge on Bosanska near the Lipa Hotel. Here, the **Viziers' turbe** is the best known of several Travnik tombs. Turn right for the **tourist office** (☎ 511588; www.tzsbk.com; Bosanska 75; 8am-4pm Mon-Fri). Or turn left and walk 400m east to reach the mural-fronted **Many Coloured Mosque** (Bosanska 203), remarkable for the *bezistan* (mini-bazaar) built into the arches beneath the main prayerhouse.

Readers who enjoyed *Bosnian Chronicle* should visit the **Ivo Andrić museum** (☎ 518140; Zenjak 19; admission 2KM; 10.30am-5pm Thu-Tue) in an old-style house designed to simulate Andrić's birthplace. Labels are in Bosnian but the enthusiastic curator speaks English. The museum is one block off Bosanska (between 171 and 169). If it's locked, request the key from the somewhat stuffy **Regional Museum** (Zavičajni Muzej Travnik; ☎ 518140; adult/child 1.50/1KM; 9am-3pm Mon-Fri, 10am-2pm Sat & Sun) opposite Bosanska 145.

Using a pedestrian underpass beneath the M5, climb up Varoš to reach the impressive **medieval castle ruins** (Stari Grad; admission 2KM; 9am-6pm Oct-Apr, 8am-8pm May-Sep) then descend further east at **Plava Voda** (Blue Water), where a rushing mountain stream is criss-crossed by small stone bridges and overlooked by several delightful restaurants.

Sleeping

Central hotels suffer somewhat from road noise. There are six other motels within 10km along the eastbound M5.

Motel Aba (☎ 511462; www.aba.ba; Šumeća 166a; s/d/tr/q 30/40/50/70KM) Central Travnik's best yet cheapest option offers highly acceptable, unfussy en suite rooms at excellent prices; breakfast costs 10KM. But it's not really a motel: getting a car to this area near Plava Voda can prove modestly challenging given the one-way system.

Hotel Lipa (☎ 511604; Lažajeva 116; s/d 52/84KM) Entering from Bosanska, the Lipa's zinc-wrap retro-trendy cafe creates a misleadingly hip image. In fact its renovated rooms are uninspired and the corridors dingy. But at least the showers are good and the location's handy.

Motel Consul (☎ 514195; www.consultravnik.20fr.com; s/d 52/84KM) With a private orchard, sepia photos of Old Travnik, big double beds and an art-filled dining-room, this peaceful new eight-room retreat is the town's most comfortable option. However it's inconveniently situated 1.5km west of the centre, overlooking the industrial zone.

CASTLE CAPERS

Dotted among the faceless industrial towns of virtually untouristed northeastern Bosnia are several very photogenic medieval castle ruins.

- **Srebrenik** Truly dramatic crag-top setting 6km east of Srebrenik town.
- **Vrandux** Small ruins set in BiH's most idyllic castle village, around 10km north of Zenica.
- **Tešanj** Powerful ruins rise above a loveable Old Town square.
- **Doboj** The city is an ugly railway junction but the castle hosts costumed festivals and there's a great little cafe-tower.
- **Gradačac** Dominating Gradačac town centre, the partly reconstructed castle now hosts a unique hotel (www.zebed.com.ba).

BUSES FROM TRAVNIK

Destination	Price (KM)	Duration (hr)	Departures
Bihać	28-31	6	6.50am, 9.30am, 3.30pm, 4.20pm & 11.50pm
Guča Gora	2.30	30min	approx hourly, weekdays only (Maline bus)
Jajce	8-12	1½	nine daily
Sarajevo	15	2	hourly in morning, plus 3.40pm, 6.20pm & 7.10pm
Split	28-36	4½	up to six daily via Bugojno
Vranduk	7.50	1¼	8.40am, noon or 3.30pm (Tuzla bus)
Zenica	4.50-7	1	25 daily

Eating

Along Bosanska self-caterers will find super-markets, bakeries, a decent market and several shops selling Travnik's trademark white cheese.

Čevabdžinica Asko (ćevapi 3.50-6KM; 7am-10pm) Just 30m south of the Many Coloured Mosque, Asko's streamside terrace is the best central cheapy for warm sitting-out evenings.

Restaurant Divan (061-786471; Zenjak 19; meals 5-17KM; 8am-11pm) Dine on fish, squid or Bosnian grills around the piano in thick-walled, timber-beamed rooms beneath the Ivo Andrić museum.

Konoba Plava Voda (512171; Šumeće bb; meals 5.50-12KM) Three restaurants, all called Plava Voda, each have lovely summer terraces over-looking the attractive springs area.

Getting There & Away

Travnik's **bus station** (792761) is off Sehida (the M5 highway), set back one block behind Bosanska. For bus services, see above.

AROUND TRAVNIK

Three-lift ski resort **Vlašić** (www.babanovac.net; ski passes 26KM; lifts 9am-4pm in season) at **Babanovac Village** has a wide selection of accommoda-tion. The homely **Hotel Central** (540165; www.hotel-central-vlasic.net; s/d 35/70KM, peak season 70/140KM), facing the ski jump, is rare for not demanding five-day minimum stays. Buses from Travnik (4KM, 40 minutes) leave at 10am and 3.10pm in summer, or at 7.15am, 11.30am and 6pm in winter, returning around 90 minutes later.

JAJCE
030 / pop 30,000

Above an impressive waterfall, Jajce's forti-fied Old Town climbs a steep rocky knoll to the powerful, ruined castle where Bosnia's medieval kings were once crowned. The sur-rounding array of glorious mountains, lakes and canyons make Jajce a great exploration base, while curious catacombs and a Mithraic temple will intrigue fans of mysterious 'lost' religions.

Information

Several central, moneychanging banks also have ATMs.

Eko Kuća (Eco House; 654100; www.plivatourism.ba; Pijavice bb; 8am-3pm Mon-Fri, 8am-1pm Sat) Regional ecotourism and rural self-help group selling local biological produce.

Kantonal tourist office (1st fl, Sadije Softića 1; 8am-3pm Mon-Fri, 8am-1pm Sat) Within the historic Omirbegović House. Brochures but minimal English spoken.

Network Internet (Trg Jajačkih Branitelja; per hr 1.50KM; 9am-midnight)

Tourist information kiosk (065-323782; 9am-8pm with various breaks May-Sep) Helpful Alida arranges homestay accommodation and has the key for closed attractions.

Sights

Old-town Jajce's attractions can be seen in a two-hour ramble, assuming you can locate the sites' various key-holders: the tourist booth can help.

CATACOMBS

Built around 1400, the **catacombs** (Svetog Luke bb; admission 1KM) are unique for their boldly sculpted interior featuring a sun and crescent moon de-sign considered one of the best surviving me-morials to the independent Bosnian Church. Tito is said to have hidden here during 1943 and the small, half-lit subterranean space is very atmospheric. Request the key from the little cafe/hairdresser opposite, built onto the side of the sturdy round **Bear Tower** (Medvjed Kula).

Other attractive buildings on Svetog Luke (Ademovića) include an 1880 **schoolhouse** and the fine, 15th-century campanile **Tower of St Luke**.

FORTRESS

From the Tower of St Luke, a stairway leads past the small **Dizdar Mosque** (Women's Mosque) to the stone **fortress entry portal** of the sturdy main **fortress** (Tvrđava; admission 1KM), whose ramparts enclose mostly bard grass but offer sweeping views of surrounding valleys and crags. Get the key from Mediha at the second house on the right before the entry portal.

From the **Velika Tabija** (Gornja Mahala) descend a further section of citadel wall to the **Midway Tower** (Mala Tabija) facing the attractively renovated **Old Kršlak House**.

WATERFALLS

Jajce's impressive 21m-high **waterfalls** mark the confluence of the Pliva and Vrbas Rivers.

For the classic tourist-brochure-view photo, cross the big Vrbas bridge and turn left on the Banja Luka road. After walking 500m, at the third lay-by on the left climb over the low crash-barrier and double back 150m down a footpath through the pine-woods to the viewpoint.

AVNOJ MUSEUM

In 1943 the second congress of AVNOJ (Antifascist Council of the People's Liberation of Yugoslavia) formulated Yugoslavia's postwar socialist constitution in a building that's now the small **AVNOJ-a Museum** (☎ 657712; admission 2KM; ☉ 8am-6pm). Peep in to see a large brooding statue of partisan Tito in gold-painted polystyrene.

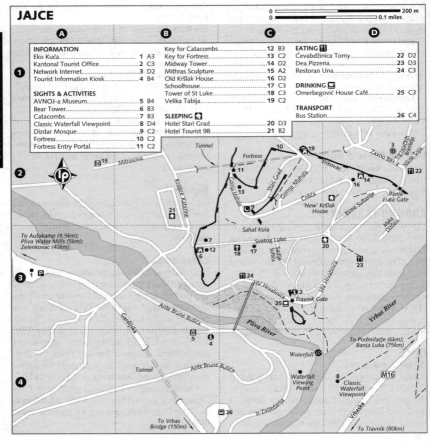

JAJCE

0 ━━━━━━━━ 200 m		
0 ━━━━━━━━ 0.1 miles		

INFORMATION
Eko Kuća...1 A3
Kantonal Tourist Office....................2 C3
Network Internet...............................3 D2
Tourist Information Kiosk................4 B4

SIGHTS & ACTIVITIES
AVNOJ-a Museum.............................5 B4
Bear Tower...6 B3
Catacombs...7 B3
Classic Waterfall Viewpoint............8 D4
Dizdar Mosque...................................9 C2
Fortress...10 C2
Fortress Entry Portal......................11 C2

Key for Catacombs.........................12 B3
Key for Fortress...............................13 C2
Midway Tower..................................14 D2
Mithras Sculpture............................15 A2
Old Kršlak House.............................16 D2
Schoolhouse.....................................17 C3
Tower of St Luke.............................18 C3
Velika Tabija.....................................19 C2

SLEEPING
Hotel Stari Grad...............................20 D4
Hotel Tourist 98...............................21 B2

EATING
Ćevabdžinica Tomy.........................22 D2
Dea Pizzeria......................................23 D3
Restoran Una....................................24 C3

DRINKING
Omerbegović House Café...............25 C3

TRANSPORT
Bus Station..26 C4

BUSES FROM JAJCE

Destination	Price (KM)	Duration (hr)	Departures
Banja Luka	9.50	1½	7.30am, 9.15am, 1pm, 4.40pm & 5.30pm
Bihać	23.50	3½	8.30am, 11.15am, 12.40pm & 5.25pm
Jezero	2.50	¼	nine daily, last return at 5.30pm
Mostar	18.50	3	2.20pm
Sarajevo	23.50	3½	7am, 9.15am, 10.20am & 5.20pm
Split	30.50	4½	6am (from Split departs at 12.30pm)
Zenica	14	2¼	8.15am, 1.45pm & 3.15pm

MITHRAS SCULPTURE

In an unassumingly house-like building, remnants of a 4th-century **sculpture** (Mitrasova 12; admission 1KM) feature Mithras fighting a bull for an audience of ladies and centurions. Once worshipped in a now-mysterious, forgotten religion, Mithras was a pre-Zoroastrian Persian sun God 'rediscovered' by mystical Romans. You can get the key from the tourist booth.

Sleeping

The tourist booth can arrange old-city **homestays** (s/d 30/50KM), while Eko Kuća can find rooms in rural village homes from 30KM per person.

Hotel Stari Grad (☎ 654006; hotel.stari.grad@tel.net.ba; Svetog Luke 3; s/d/apt 55/80/160KM; ⌗) Although it's not actually old, beams, wood-panelling and a heraldic fireplace give this comfortable little hotel a look of suavely modernised antiquity. Unbeatably central, it's the ideal address as long as you can manage the stairs. An added curiosity is the lobby restaurant's glass floor beneath, which are the excavations of an Ottoman-era *hammam* (Turkish bath).

Hotel Tourist 98 (☎ 658151; Kraljice Katerine bb; s/d/tr/q/apt 57/84/106/135/120KM; ⌗) This bright-red box beside Jajce's big hypermarket offers new, very straightforward rooms that are clean and mostly spacious.

For lakeside alternatives see right.

Eating & Drinking

The Hotel Stari Grad serves decent Bosnian and Italian food in its appealing little lobby **restaurant** (mains 9-14KM; ◷ 7am-9pm). Several potentially intriguing cafe-bars are cut out of the cliff-face on HV Hrvatnica. However, only the lovably incompetent **Restoran Una** (mains 4-12KM; ◷ 10am-9pm) serves full meals and even here most items were unavailable when we tried to dine. **Dea Pizzeria** (☎ 657173; pizzas 6-8KM; ◷ 8am-11pm) opposite the Hotel Stari Grad bakes acceptable pizzas. **Ćevabdžinica Tomy** (grills from 3KM; ◷ 8am-3pm Mon-Sat) offers fast(ish) food from a cube of an ancient stone building.

The unpretentiously local **Omerbegović House Café** (coffee/beer 0.50/2KM; ◷ 7am-11pm) is intriguingly hidden in the bare stone former guard house of the medieval Travnik Gate. Enter via the stairway of the Kantonal tourist office.

Getting There & Away

See above for services from the **bus station** (☎ 659202; Il-Zasjedanja AVNOJ-a).

For Travnik (8KM to 12KM) take Zenica or Sarajevo buses.

AROUND JAJCE

Wooded mountains reflect idyllically in the two picture-perfect **Pliva Lakes** (Plivsko Jezero) and a park between the two contains a superquaint collection of 17 miniature **watermills**. Take Jezero-bound buses to km92 on the M5 (4km from Jajce), then walk 800m via the **Autokamp** (per child/adult 5/10KM; site without/with electricity 8/12KM; ◷ mid-Apr–Sep). A kilometre beyond, the lakeside lane rejoins the M5 beside waterfront **Plaža Motel** (☎ 647200; s/d 40/70KM) and the plusher **Hotel Plivsko Jezero** (☎ 654090; www.hoteljajce.bet.net.ba; s/d/tr/q/apt 57/84/106/135/120KM).

BANJA LUKA БАЊА ЛУКА
☎ 051 / pop 232,000

Probably Europe's least-known 'capital' (of the Republik Srpska since 1998), Banja Luka was devastated by a 1969 earthquake and its 15 mosques were subsequently dynamited during the civil war. Today just two blocks of impressive old architecture remain around the iconic **Orthodox Church of Christ Saviour** (Crkva Hrista Spasitelja), whose brick bell tower looks like a Moroccan minaret on Viagra. It's 300m north up the main thoroughfare, Kralja Petra,

BUSES FROM BANJA LUKA

Destination	Price (KM)	Duration (hr)	Departures
Belgrade	35	7	15 daily
Bihać	20	3	5.30am, 7.30am (Mon-Sat only), 1pm & 2pm
Jajce	11.50	1½	6.40am, 7.45 (Mon-Sat only), 2.25pm, 1pm, 2pm & 4pm
Sarajevo	31	5	6.30am, 7.45am, 2.30pm, 4pm, 5pm & midnight
Zagreb	24	7	8.45am, 9.10am, 4.10pm & 5.30pm

from the **tourist office** (☎ 232760; www.banjaluka
-tourism.com; Kralja Petra 87; ⏰ 8.30am-5.45pm Mon-Fri, 9am-
2pm Sat). Directly southeast of the tourist office
the chunky walls of a large, squat 16th-century
castle (Kaštel) enclose riverside parkland where
in summer there's a well-reputed arts festival
that encompasses open-air plays, Thursday-
night folklore displays and the **Demofest** (www.
demofest.org), at which up-and-coming raw garage
bands blare out their new music.

Sleeping & Eating

Prenoćište vl Marija C (☎ 218673; Solunska 21; s/d with
shared bathroom 27/54KM) Four slightly spartan
rooms share a decent bathroom in this inexpensive family homestay. Turn diagonally
right at the south end of Kralja Petra and enter
from the rear.

Hotel Palace (Хотел Палас; ☎ 218723; Kralja Petra
60; www.hotelpalasbl.com; s/d/tr/ste from 63.50/117/
130.50/147KM; 🖳) Almost elegant behind its copious street cafe, the Palace's 1933 building's
lobby uses hypnotic new art deco–inspired
design. Rooms are straightforward, midrange international standard, while cheaper
singles are small and built into the sloping
roof.

Vila Vrbas (☎ 433840; Brace Potkonjaka 1; s/d/ste
70/110/120KM) Excellent-value boutique hotel
peering through the plane trees at the castle ramparts from across the river. Some
rooms have a computer, internet access and
a wraparound shower pod. For dining, the Sur
Sedra next door has a terrace that's cheaper
and less pretentious than the Vila Vrbas'
well-known restaurant.

Running parallel to Kralja Petra, Veselina
Maslaše offers a wide range of tempting street-cafes, bars, pastry shops and
ice-cream vendors.

Getting There & Away

The **main bus station** (☎ 315555; Prote N Kostića 38)
and train station are together, 3km north by
buses 6, 8 or 10 from near Hotel Palace.

Useful rail connections include Zagreb
(4¼ hours, 3.30pm) and Sarajevo (five hours,
1.15pm). The Banja Luka–Belgrade train (eight
hours) runs overnight eastbound (departing
10.30pm) but don't expect much sleep: you'll
be woken twice for both Croatian and Serbian
border crossings. The westbound train returns
by day, departing Belgrade at 1.20pm.

AROUND BANJA LUKA
Vrbas Canyons

Between Jajce and Banja Luka the Vrbas River
descends in a wonderful series of lakes and
gorges that together form one of BiH's foremost adventure-sport playgrounds. Based at
Ada, near Karanovac, **Kanjon Rafting** (☎ 065-
420000; www.kanjonraft.com) is a reliable, well-
organised adventure outfit offering guided
canyoning (€25, no minimum group number)
and rafting (€25 per person for three hours including transport, four person minimum). At
Krupa (26km), a pretty set of cascades tumbles
down between little wooden mill-huts, mountaineers scale the canyon sides nearby and
limestone grottoes attract cavers. The canyon
beyond offers top-class rafting and the Jajce
road winds steeply on past a high dam into the
long, beautiful Bočac Reservoir gorge.

BIHAĆ
☎ 037 / pop 80,000

A closely clumped **church tower**, **turbe** and
16th-century stone **tower-museum** (☎ 223214;
admission 2KM; ⏰ 9am-4pm Mon-Fri, 9am-2pm Sat) look
very photogenic viewed across gushing rapids
in central Bihać. But that's about all there is
to see here apart from nearby **Fethija Mosque**,
converted from a rose-windowed medieval
church in 1595. If you're driving, Bihać could
make a decent staging post for reaching the
marvellous Plitvice Lakes (p236) in Croatia,
30km away. Otherwise grab a map-brochure
from Bihać's **tourist booth** (Bosanska 1; ⏰ 8am-4pm)
then head out into the lovely Una Valley,
preferably on a raft!

Sights & Activities

In the **Una Valley**, the adorable **Una River** gushes through lush green gorges, over widely fanned rapids and down pounding cascades most dramatically at **Kostela** and **Štrcački Buk**. There are lovely watermill restaurants at **Otoka Bosanska** and **Bosanski Krupa** and spookily Gothic **Ostrožac Fortress** (☎ 061-236841; www.ostrozac.com; admission 1KM; ☯ 8am-6pm by phoning caretaker) is the most inspiring of several castle ruins.

Several adventure-sports companies offer rafting (€25 to €40, six person minimum), kayaking and climbing. Each has its own campsites and provides transfers from Bihać. Try **Una Kiro Rafting** (☎ /fax 223760; www.una-kiro-rafting .com; Golubić), **Sport Bjeli** (☎ 388555; www.una-rafting.ba; Klokot) or **Limit** (☎ 061-144248; www.limit.co.ba; Džanića Mahala 7, Bihać). The **Una Regatta** in late July is festive but very busy, with hundreds of kayaks and rafts following a three-day course from Kulen-Vakuf to Bosanska Krupa, via Bihać.

Sleeping & Eating
CENTRAL BIHAĆ

Villa Una (☎ /fax 311393; Bihaćkih Branilaca 20; s/d/tr 50/70/90KM) This friendly homestay-style *pansion* behind a jewellery shop, halfway between the bus station and the Una Bridge, suffers somewhat from road noise.

Hotel Park (☎ 226394; www.aduna.ba; ul 5-Korpusa bb; s/d/apt 69/125/160KM; ♿) This very central hotel looks dated but thoroughly renovated rooms have good new bathrooms and wheelchair access. Singles are pretty small. Reception can help with information if the nearby tourist info booth is closed.

Restaurant River Una (☎ 310014; Džemala Bijedića 12; mains 7-15KM, beer 2KM; ☯ 7am-11pm) Of several riverside eateries facing central Bihać's pretty rapids, River Una has the most appealing wooden-rustic interior, with stone platforms, giant hooks and 'flying' fish.

UNA VALLEY

Motel Estrada (☎ 531320; Ostrožac; s/d 30/60KM) Homely en suite rooms in the fifth unmarked house on the left up the Prečići road; 300m southwest of the castle.

Pansion Kostelski Buk (☎ 302340; www.kostelski -buk.co.ba; M14 hwy, Kostela; s/d 60/90KM; ♿) Lavishly equipped great-value rooms and an excellent-view-restaurant overlooking some dramatic waterfall-rapids. It's 9km from Bihać towards Banja Luka.

Getting There & Away

Bihać's **bus station** (☎ 311939) is 1km west of the centre, just off Bihaćkih Branilaća. Buses run to Zagreb (25KM, 2½ hours, 4.45am, 10.20am, 2pm and 4.45pm) and Banja Luka (20KM, three hours, 5.30am, 7.30am, 1pm and 3pm) via Bosanska Krupa and Otoka Bosanska. Sarajevo buses (40.50KM, seven hours, 12.45am, 7.30am, 2.30pm and 10pm) drive via Travnik. Cazin-bound buses (5.50KM, 11 daily except Sundays) pass through Kostela (10 minutes) and Ostražac (25 minutes). **Super-Matrix** (☎ 061-257098; Zagreb Hwy) rents cars.

BOSNIA & HERCEGOVINA DIRECTORY

ACCOMMODATION

Prices quoted are for the low season, which is October to May generally, but April to November in ski resorts. In Mostar and Sarajevo summer prices rise 20% to 50% and touts appear at the bus stations. These cities also have a wide selection of home-hostels bookable via international hostel-booking sites.

Pansions range from glorified homestays to sophisticated little boutique hotels. Very widespread new suburban motels are ideal for those with cars, though occasionally the term 'motel' is confusingly used to simply imply a lower midrange hotel. Don't assume there's parking.

Many hotels inhabit the husk of old Tito-era concrete monsters. Although some of these have been elegantly remodelled, others remain gloomy and a little forbidding.

Slip-on shoes and plentiful clean socks are a boon if you're sleeping in homestays, since it's normal courtesy to remove shoes on entering a private house. Hosts will provide slippers.

Breakfast is usually included for *pansions*, motels and hotels. Unless stated, all rooms have private bathroom (except in hostels).

ACTIVITIES

BiH is an outdoor wonderland. For inexpensive yet world-class skiing visit Jahorina (p119), Bjelašnica (p119) or Vlašić (p131). Superb rafting reaches terrifyingly difficult class V in April/May but is more suitable for beginners in summer. Top spots are around Foča (p129), Bihać (p135) and Banja Luka (p134).

Hiking and mountain biking have been compromised since the 1990s by the presence of landmines, but many upland areas and national parks now have safe, marked trails. Expat-run ecotourism organisation Green Visions (p112) offers regular hiking excursions from Sarajevo.

BOOKS

Noel Malcolm's very readable *Bosnia: A Short History* is a great introduction to the complexities of Bosnian history. Joe Sacco's deeply humane comic-strip books give moving, personal insights into the sufferings of the 1990s. Nobel Prize–winning Ivo Andrić's epic historical-fiction *Bridge over the Drina* is a must-read, especially if you go to Višegrad. Time Out publishes the excellent, annual *Sarajevo and Bosnia-Herzegovina for Visitors* magazine-guide (15KM), available locally. Babić and Bozja's *Mountaineering Tourist Guide* (35KM) is a great resource for hikers with detailed topographic maps and many photos. **BuyBook** (www.buybook.ba) produce several regional guides.

Tim Clancy's photo-book *Bosnia and Hercegovina: People and Places* makes a great gift for people back home. Some Sarajevo bookshops (p106) still stock the darkly humorous *Sarajevo Survival Guide* (23KM), originally published during the 1992–93 siege.

BUSINESS HOURS

Official hours are 8am to 4pm Monday to Friday; banks open Saturday mornings. Shops open longer, usually 8am to 6pm, including Sundays. Restaurants typically serve food from 11.30am till around 10.30pm in winter, 11.30pm in summer, but whatever their signs say, actual closing time depends more on cusom than fixed schedules. Note that restaurants that claim to open in the morning usually operate as a cafe till 11.30am or noon, only starting to serve food from lunchtime.

DANGERS & ANNOYANCES

An estimated million landmines and fragments of unexploded ordnance are spread over around 4% of BiH's area, causing around 40 mine casualties per year. That's only a twentieth of the number in Cambodia, but caution remains the key. Stick to asphalt/concrete surfaces or well-worn paths and don't enter war-damaged buildings. Sarajevo's Mine Action Centre, **BHMAC** (Map p107; ☎ 033-209762; www.bhmac.org; Zmaja od Bosne 8; ⊙ 8am-4pm Mon-Fri) has more information.

EMBASSIES & CONSULATES

The nearest embassies for Ireland and New Zealand are found in Ljubljana (p877) and Rome respectively. Representation in Sarajevo:

Australia (Map pp110-11; ☎ 033-206167; Obala Kulina Bana 15/1) Honorary Consulate.
Canada (Map p107; ☎ 033-222033; Grbavička 4/2)
Croatia (Map pp110-11; ☎ 033-444331; Mehmeda Spahe 16)
France (Map p107; ☎ 033-282050; Mehmed-bega Kapetanovica Ljubusaka 18)
Germany (Map pp110-11; ☎ 033-275000; Buka bb)
Hungary (☎ 033-208353; www.hungemb.ba; Splitska 2)
Japan (Map pp110-11; ☎ 033-209580; Bistrik 2)
Macedonia (off Map p107; ☎ 033-206004; Splitska 57)
Montenegro (Map pp110-11; ☎ 033-239925; Talirovića 4)
Netherlands (Map p107; ☎ 033-562600; www.netherlandsembassy.ba; Grbavička 4/1)
Serbia (Map pp110-11; ☎ 033-260080; Obala Maka Dizdara 3a)
Slovenia (Map pp110-11; ☎ 033-271251; Bentbaša 7)
UK (Map pp110-11; ☎ 033-208229; Petrakijina 11)
USA Sarajevo (Map p107; ☎ 033-445700; Alipašina 43); Banja Luka (☎ 051-211500; Jovana Dučića 5)

GAY & LESBIAN TRAVELLERS

Although homosexuality was decriminalised per se in 1998 (2000 in the RS), attitudes are very conservative. **Logos** (www.logos.org.ba/cont) focuses on combating discrimination against sexual minorities, while **Association Q** (www.queer.ba) attempts to empower the self-reliance of the gay community in BiH. The English-language **Gay Romeo** (www.gayromeo.com) chat site reportedly has around 400 Sarajevo members and www.queer.ba (in Bosnian) organises occasional local meet-ups.

HOLIDAYS

Major Islamic festivals are observed in parts of the Federation, their dates changing annually according to the Muslim lunar calendar. The Feast of Sacrifice is known locally as Kurban Bajram, while the end of Ramadan celebration is called Ramazanski Bajram. Orthodox Easter (variable) and Christmas (6 January) are observed in the RS. Western Easter (variable) and Christmas (25 December) are celebrated in the Federation. The following are national holidays celebrated across the whole of BiH:

New Year's Day 1 January
Independence Day 1 March
May Day 1 May
National Statehood Day 25 November

INTERNET RESOURCES

BiH Ministry of Foreign Affairs (www.mvp.gov.ba) Visa and embassy details.
BiH Tourism (www.bhtourism.ba)
Bosnian Institute (www.bosnia.org.uk) Bosnian cultural affairs.
Grad Sarajevo (www.sarajevo.ba) City site.
Herceg-Bosna (www.hercegbosna.org) BiH seen from a Croat angle.
Hidden Bosnia (www.hiddenbosnia.com) Useful if commercial overview.
InsideBosnia (www.insidebosnia.com) Events and interesting links.
Office of the High Representative (www.ohr.int) BiH's EU overseers.

LANGUAGE

Notwithstanding different dialects, the people of BiH basically speak the same language. However, it's referred to as 'Bosnian' (Bosanski) in Muslim parts, 'Croatian' (Hrvatski) in Croat-controlled areas and 'Serbian' (Српски) in the RS. The Federation uses the Latin alphabet. The RS uses predominantly Cyrillic (ћирилица) but Latin (Latinica) is gaining wider parallel usage there too. Brčko uses both alphabets equally.

MAPS

Freytag & Berndt's very useful 1:250,000 BiH road map costs 12KM in Sarajevo bookshops (p106). City maps are patchily available from bookshops, kiosks or tourist information centres. Many cities post town plans on their .ba websites.

MONEY

Bosnia's convertible mark (KM or BAM) is pronounced *kai-em* or *maraka* and divided into 100 fenig. It's tied to the euro at approximately €1=1.96KM. Many establishments (shops, restaurants and especially hotels) unblinkingly accept euros though this is slightly rarer in the RS. In Mostar even Croatian kuna are also accepted without fuss. ATMs accepting Visa and MasterCard brands are ubiquitous.

Travellers cheques can be readily changed at Raiffeisen and Zagrebačka Banks but you'll usually need to show the original purchase receipt.

POST

Post and telephone offices are usually combined. Poste restante is available for a small fee but only at main cities' central post offices. BiH's complex postal history makes it fascinating for philatelists and three postal organisations still issue their own stamps. The Cyrillic lettering makes RS **Srpske Poste** (www.filatelija.rs.ba) stamps obviously distinctive. Those from Mostar-based **HP Post** (www.post.ba) and Sarajevo's **BH Post** (www.bhp.ba) have their own designs but are both marked 'Bosnia i Hercegovina' in Latin.

TELEPHONE

BiH's country code is ☎ 387. Of the three mobile-phone companies here, BH Mobile (☎ 061- and ☎ 062-) is most widely used in the Federation. Its prepaid 'Ultra' SIM cards cost 15KM including 10KM credit. Alternatives are ☎ 063- (HT/EroNet), and ☎ 065- (M-Tel), with marginally cheaper call costs. All have virtually nationwide coverage.

Phonecards for public telephones can be purchased at post offices or from some street kiosks for 10KM but beware that different cards are required for the Federation and for RS.

Dial ☎ 1201 for the international operator, ☎ 1188 for local directory information.

EMERGENCY NUMBERS

- Ambulance ☎ 124
- Fire ☎ 123
- Police ☎ 122
- Roadside assistance ☎ 1282, 1288

TOURIST INFORMATION

All BiH cities and many smaller towns have tourist offices. The typically underemployed staff are generally delighted to see travellers, dispensing maps, brochures and advice and sometimes helping with accommodation. However, don't be surprised by unexplained office closures.

TRAVELLERS WITH DISABILITIES

Most of Bosnia's most appealing town- and village-cores are based around steep, rough streets and stairways. It's visually charming but very awkward if you're disabled. A few places have wheelchair ramps in response to all the war-wounded, but smaller hotels won't have lifts and disabled toilets are still extremely rare.

VISAS

EU nationals don't need visas. Nor do citizens of Andorra, Australia, Brunei, Canada, Croatia, Japan, Kuwait, Liechtenstein, Macedonia, Malaysia, Monaco, Montenegro, New Zealand, Norway, Qatar, Russia, San Marino, Serbia, Switzerland, the Vatican, Turkey and the USA.

For other nationals, single-/multi-entry visas cost from €31/57. Visa applications must be accompanied by one photograph and either a letter of invitation or a tourist agency voucher. For full details see www.mvp .gov.ba.

TRANSPORT IN BOSNIA & HERCEGOVINA

GETTING THERE & AWAY
Air

Even BiH's main airport, **Međunarodni Aerodrom Sarajevo** (SJJ; ☎ 033-289100; www.sarajevo-airport .ba) is decidedly modest, served by just the following airlines:

Adria Airways (JP; Map pp110-11; ☎ 033-232125; www.adria-airways.com; Ferhadija 23)
Austrian Airlines (OS; ☎ 033-202059; www.aua.com)
BH Airlines (JA; Map pp110-11; ☎ 033-218605; www .bhairlines.ba; Branilaca Sarajeva 15; ⏱ 9am-5pm Mon-Fri, 9am-2pm Sat)
British Airways (BA; www.ba.com)
Croatia Airlines (OU; ☎ 033-666123; www.croatia airlines.hr)
JAT (JU; ☎ 033-259750; www.jat.come)

Lufthansa (LH; ☎ 033-278590; www.lufthansa.com; Mula Mustafe Bašeskije 2)
Malév Hungarian Airlines (MA; ☎ 473200; www .malev.hu)
Turkish Airlines (TK; Map pp110-11; ☎ 033-666092; www.thy.com; Branilaca Sarajeva)

Between them, all of BiH's other airports have only seven scheduled flights a week on three routes: Mostar–İstanbul (p125), Banja Luka–Zürich and Banja Luka–Belgrade.

The national carrier, BH (pronounced 'Bay-Ha') Airlines flies inexpensively from Sarajevo to Frankfurt, Cologne/Bonn, İstanbul, Skopje, Stuttgart and Zürich. Phone in reservations then pay at the airport immediately before departure.

If prices to Sarajevo seem high, consider taking budget flights to Dubrovnik, Split or Zagreb in Croatia, then connecting to BiH by bus or train.

Land

Crossing borders is generally hassle free. By bus or train just wait: either a border guard gets on board to check documents or the driver collects passports and takes them to the guard post. Don't panic, this is normal.

When driving simply queue up and flash your passport and car documents.

BUS
Most towns in the Federation have daily buses to Zagreb and/or Split (Croatia). RS towns usually have links to Serbia and Montenegro. Most bigger BiH cities have weekly services to Germany/Scandinavia. See p117 for details on Sarajevo's international bus services.

CAR & MOTORCYCLE
Drivers need to ensure that they have Green Card insurance for their vehicle and an EU or International Driving Permit. Petrol (95 and 98 octane) and diesel are readily available in any town, though many service stations close between 11pm and 7am.

TRAIN
Two daily services connect Ploče (on the Croatian coast) via Mostar to Sarajevo. There are also services from Banja Luka to Belgrade and Sarajevo–Belgrade. A service from Sarajevo to Budapest goes via Doboj, Šamac and Osijek (Croatia); see p117 for details.

GETTING AROUND
Bicycle
Roads are very hilly, but for tough cyclists BiH's calm secondary routes can prove a delight. Several mountain areas now have suggested off-road trails for mountain bikers but beware of straying off-route into minefields (see p136).

Bus
Slow if usually on time, BiH's buses can be annoyingly infrequent. At weekends local shorter-hop buses drastically reduce services, often stopping altogether on Sundays. Bus stations pre-sell tickets but it's normally easy enough to wave down any bus en route. Advance reservations might be necessary for overnight routes or during peak holiday times.

Fares vary between different companies but average around 7KM per hour travelled. A return ticket is usually significantly cheaper than two singles, but inconveniently limits you to a specific company. Add 2KM per stowed bag.

Car & Motorcycle
Given the minimal transport to BiH's most spectacular remote areas, having wheels can really transform your trip. Bosnian roads are winding, lightly trafficked and almost unanimously beautiful, a delight for driving as long as you aren't in a hurry. Flowers and graves litter sharper bends where haste proved fatal. Luckily most local drivers are reasonably calm and the main frustration can be getting past slow trucks, tractors or occasional horse-carts. Some country roads are not asphalted.

EU or International Driving Permits are accepted.

AUTOMOBILE ASSOCIATIONS
BIHAMK (Automobile Association of Bosnia & Hercegovina; Map pp110-11; ☎ 033-212771; www.bihamk.ba; Skenderija 23, Sarajevo; annual membership 25KM; ☺ 8am-4.30pm Mon-Fri, 9am-noon Sat) offers road assistance and towing services for members.

HIRE
Most bigger towns in BiH offer car hire starting at around €43/245 per day/week with unlimited mileage and basic insurance. Before signing, check car condition, insurance excess and whether the 17% VAT costs extra.

ROAD RULES
Driving is on the right, seatbelts must be worn and headlights must be kept on day and night. The maximum tolerated blood-alcohol level is 0.05% (roughly 0.5g/l). Speed limits are 80km/h for rural roads, dropping to 60km/h or less in town, often without reminder signs for many kilometres. Police spot-checks are very common. Parking is awkward in Mostar and Sarajevo, where tow-away trucks are ruthless. However, elsewhere parking is usually contrastingly easy; in town centres expect to pay 1KM per hour to an attendant.

Train
Trains depart much less frequently than buses but they're generally 30% cheaper. **RS Railways** (www.zrs-rs.com/red_voznje.php?pageNum_vozovi=4&totalRows_vozovi=105) has full, up-to-date timetables.

BOSNIA & HERCEGOVINA

Bulgaria България

The EU has arrived at Eastern Europe's last stop to the south, but other than its mountains and Black Sea beaches, much of the appeal of Bulgaria is linked with a far-distant past. You can't dig a metre down anywhere and not stumble onto a Thracian tomb or Roman road, evident in sights around Kazanlâk or off-the-radar Kârdzhali. Whole cobblestone towns, like Koprivshtitsa, are filled with 19th-century revival-era homes, built in a frenzy as the Ottoman Empire lost its grip on the country that introduced Cyrillic to Russia. And when you raise a goblet of Bulgaria's tasty 'hangover-free' wines, you're sipping a tradition that dates back at least 3000 years.

Most visitors start in Sofia, then dart to lively Varna on the Black Sea; the more ambitious add visits to the former capital Veliko Târnovo or Plovdiv's Old Town. Try to see more. Veliko, for instance, offers the nation's cheapest car rental, where you can day-trip on your own to woodcutter villages or abandoned UFO-shaped buildings. Meanwhile, the unheralded northwest – and Belogradchik's dreamlike mountain fortress – can be toured on an alternate route to Serbia or Romania. The Alps-like southwest has good skiing, hikes from the famous Rila Monastery, and local wine made in mountain-carved wineries in wee Melnik. With patience, you can find still-undeveloped beaches, protected from the hordes by (very) bumpy roads.

Bulgaria is surrounded by well-known legends (eg Greece's togas, old Constantinople, Dracula's Transylvania) and sometimes the truth of 'what is Bulgaria' remains elusive even for locals. Finding out the truth – in a land that still shakes its head 'yes' – well, that's what travel is supposed to be, isn't it?

FAST FACTS

- **Area** 110,910 sq km
- **Capital** Sofia
- **Currency** leva (lv); €1 = 1.95lv; US$1 = 1.43lv; UK£1 = 2.08lv; A$1 = 0.99lv; ¥100 = 1.49lv; NZ$1 = 0.80lv
- **Famous for** Black Sea beaches, monasteries, yoghurt
- **Official language** Bulgarian
- **Phrases** *zdrasti* (hello); *blagodarya* (thank you); *imati li?* (do you have?); *kolko struva?* (how much?); *oshte bira molya* (another beer please)
- **Population** 7.26 million
- **Telephone codes** country code ☎ 359; international access code ☎ 00
- **Visas** not required for citizens of Australia, Canada, the EU, New Zealand, USA and several other nations; see p195 for details

BULGARIA

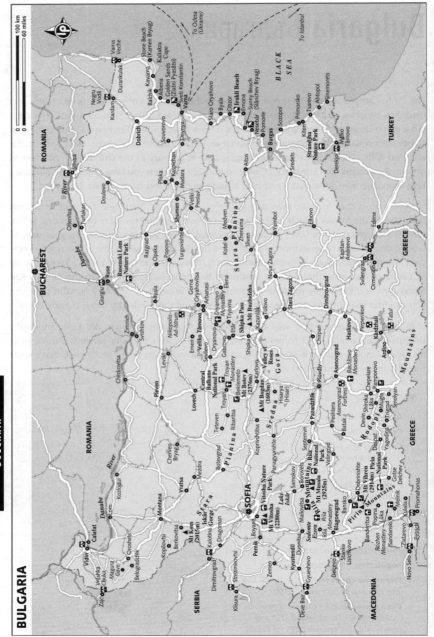

HIGHLIGHTS

▪ Look across a river gorge and up to the tsar-sized citadel at hilly **Veliko Târnovo** (p169).

▪ Visit the Black Sea's busiest hub, **Varna** (p179), where the museums and open-air clubs would be worth visiting even without the sea.

▪ Channel *The Lord of the Rings* in the animated peaks that surround **Belogradchik** (p191).

▪ Check out Roman theatres and revival-era taverns in **Plovdiv** (p159), Bulgaria's most relaxing city.

▪ Blaze new trails to the recently discovered Thracian/Roman city of **Perperikon** (p166) carved from mountain-top rocks.

ITINERARIES

▪ **One week** Start in Varna for a couple of beach days, then bus to Veliko Târnovo for a few days more for monastery hikes. For the last two, walk Plovdiv's Old Town and day-trip to nearby Asenovgrad Fortress.

▪ **Two weeks** After a couple of days in Sofia, train through the Iskâr Gorge to Vidin for a night, then day-trip to Belogradchik's unreal fortress, and back to Sofia. Take the bus to Melnik for wine and hikes. After two nights, bus to Plovdiv for two days. Bus on to hilly Veliko Târnovo for four relaxed days of hikes, then head to Varna's beach bars for two days, and finish in ancient Sozopol.

CLIMATE & WHEN TO GO

Bulgaria has a temperate climate with cold, damp winters and hot, dry summers. From mid-July to August, Bulgaria swarms with tourists, particularly at Black Sea resorts. Try to go in September, when it's still hot, but quieter (and a bit cheaper). The ski slopes fill from mid-December to March or mid-April, when much of the country's attractions trim their hours.

If you're not beach-bumming or skiing, spring or autumn are great times to visit (particularly May) as there are very few tourists, and theatres and other cultural venues awake from hibernation.

HISTORY
Becoming Bulgaria

Thracians moved into the area in the 4th millennium BC, and by AD 100 Romans controlled the lands. The first Slavs migrated here from the north in the 5th century, and the first Bulgarian state was formed in 681.

The fierce Turkic Bulgars – whose name later became Bulgarians – first reached these areas from their expansive territories between the Caspian and Black Seas. By the time the Byzantine Empire conquered Bulgaria in 1014 (after blinding 15,000 Bulgarian troops in one bloody poke-fest), the first state had created a language, the Cyrillic alphabet, a church and – spurred on by enforced conversion to Christianity – a people (a mix of Slavs, Proto-Bulgarians and a few Thracians).

Bulgaria's second kingdom, based in Veliko Târnovo, lasted from 1185 until the Ottoman army took control in 1396.

Life with the Ottomans

The next 500 years were spent living 'under the yoke' of Ottoman rule. The Orthodox Church persevered by quietly holing up in monasteries. Higher taxes for Christians saw many convert to Islam.

During the 18th and 19th centuries, many 'awakeners' are credited with reviving Bulgarian culture. By the 1860s several revolutionaries (including Vasil Levski – something akin to Bulgaria's Che Guevara – and Hristo Botev) organised *cheti* (rebel) bands for the (failed) April Uprising of 1870. With Russia stepping in, the Ottoman army was defeated in 1878, and Bulgaria became independent again.

Nazis & Soviets

With eyes on lost Macedonia, following a series of painful Balkan Wars (including WWI), Bulgaria surprisingly aligned with Nazi Germany in WWII with hopes to expand

---

CONNECTIONS: MOVING ON FROM BULGARIA

Although Sofia has international bus (p154) and train (p154) connections, it's not necessary to backtrack to the capital if you're heading to Bucharest or İstanbul. From central Veliko Târnovo (p173), for example, there are daily trains both ways – and much of the country offers overnight buses to İstanbul. Heading to Greece or Belgrade by train means going through Sofia; for Skopje, you'll need to catch a bus from there too.

BULGARIA

its borders. Famously, Tsar Boris III said 'no' to Hitler, refusing to send Bulgaria's Jewish population to concentration camps, sparing up to 50,000 lives (though losing his own).

As the war drew to a close, Bulgaria did a final flip-flop over to the Soviet side, but that did little to smooth relations with the West or the USSR following WWII. Bulgaria embraced communism wholeheartedly (even proposing in 1973 to join the Soviet republics).

Modern Bulgaria

After making friends with the USA, and being accepted by NATO in 2004 and the EU in 2007, Bulgarians are hopeful of the new EU-funded projects but worried over new regulations. Some, pessimistically, wonder how long the EU will last. As one local joke goes: 'We were little brother to the Ottoman Empire for 500 years; they collapsed. Then the Nazis and Soviets, and they collapsed. NATO, USA and EU, watch out!'

PEOPLE

The population of Bulgaria is 7.26 million (slightly shrinking recently), with Bulgarians and Slavs constituting 84%. The largest minorities are Turks (9.4%) and Roma (4.7%).

A few famous Bulgarians include Christo, an environmental artist famous for putting up the orange gates in New York's Central Park in 2005; and Hristo Stoichkov, the country's favourite footballer.

RELIGION

During the communist era Bulgaria was officially atheist. These days, about 83% of the population are Orthodox and 12% are Muslim (almost all of these are Sunni).

ARTS
Music

The currently popular and controversial 'wedding music', aka *chalga,* is a vaguely Indian-sounding synth-pop (picked up from Turkey and Serbia) with less-than-intellectual lyrics. (One sample: 'We win, we lose…either way we get drunk, we're Bulgarians!') Essentially no one in the country admits to liking Azis, a seriously flamboyant, sexually ambiguous *chalga* performer, who has sold more CDs than nearly any Bulgarian artist.

Traditional music – played with *gaida* (bagpipes), *tambura* (four-stringed lute) and *tâppan* (drum) – is widespread. Turn on a TV and you'll see it on several channels nightly.

Architecture

Bulgaria's 19th-century revival saw many town makeovers with quaint, traditionally styled *kâshta* buildings (with whitewashed walls, wood shutters, woodcarved ceilings and hand-woven carpets) built close alongside cobbled streets. This massive source of Bulgarian pride is evident in many towns, such as Koprivshtitsa.

Visual Arts

Bulgaria's most treasured art is on the walls of medieval monasteries and churches, such as Boyana Church (p156) near Sofia, Arbanasi's Nativity Church (p174) and the paintings by Zahari Zograf (1810–53) at Rila Monastery (p157).

ENVIRONMENT

Bulgaria lies in the heart of the Balkan Peninsula, stretching 502km from the Serbian border to the 378km-long Black Sea coast.

Bulgaria is one-third mountains. The Stara Planina (also known as the Balkan Mountains) stretch across central Bulgaria. In the southwest are three higher ranges: the Rila Mountains, south of Sofia (home to the country's highest point, Mt Musala, 2925m); the Pirin Mountains, just south towards Greece; and the Rodopi Mountains to the east.

Although Bulgaria has some 56,000 kinds of living creature – including 400 bird species and one of Europe's largest bear popu-

---

HOW MUCH?

- **Night in Sofia hostel** from 18lv
- **Sofia–Varna bus ticket** 29lv
- **Museum admission** 2lv to 10lv
- **Varna city map** 3lv
- **Day car rental** 25lv to 60lv

LONELY PLANET INDEX

- **1L petrol** 1.73lv
- **1L bottled water** 0.80lv
- **Beer (Kamenitza)** 1lv
- **Souvenir T-shirt** 5lv to 10lv
- **Street snack (banitsa)** 0.80lv

lations – most visitors see little wildlife, unless venturing deep into the thickets and mountains. Popular birdwatching spots near the Black Sea include Burgas Lakes, west of Burgas, and Durankulak Lake, near the Romanian border.

Bulgaria has three national parks (Rila, Pirin and Central Balkan) and 10 nature parks, all of which offer some protection to the environment (and have tourist potential). The EU has funded a number of projects to offer more protection, particularly along the Black Sea Coast and the Rodopi Mountains. Also see www.bulgariannationalparks.org.

FOOD & DRINK
Staples & Specialities

There are two kinds of Bulgarian food: Bulgarian food and pizza. The former comprises many light dishes, with Turkish or Greek influences. Bulgarians have a more intimate relationship with salads than most people. Salads, one local told us, 'are solely for drinking' and you'll find many locals downing the ever-present *shopska* (tomatoes, onions, cucumbers and cheese) with a guttingly strong shot of *rakia* brandy.

Main dishes are mostly grilled beef, pork, lamb and chicken – such as the *kebabche* (spicy meat sausages) – or heavier stews such as *kavarma*. Side dishes (such as boiled potatoes or cheese-covered chips) are ordered separately. In summer, it's hard to beat starting a meal with a refreshingly cold *tarator* (yoghurt soup with cucumber).

Vegetarians are not at a loss. As well as salads, most restaurants serve yoghurt- or vegetable-based soups and several egg dishes. Well-made pizza, served by slice or whole, is everywhere.

Breakfast for most Bulgarians is espresso, cigarettes (plural intended) and a hot cheese-filled *banitsa* pastry, available at small bakeries (often named *zakuska*, 'breakfast').

Where to Eat & Drink

Evocative Bulgarian restaurants, it must be said, don't differ from one another much, but can be quite good. A 10% tip is expected at sit-down restaurants, though sometimes it's included with the *smetka* (bill). By law, all restaurants must set aside 'nonsmoking' areas, often a lone table surrounded by 'smoking' ones.

Cafes also act as de facto bars, serving local beer, wine and brandies.

Most restaurants are open roughly 10am or 11am to midnight daily. Cafes generally open early enough for an early-morning java buzz.

SOFIA СОФИЯ

☎ 02 / pop 1.39 million

Don't expect to uncover the 'new Prague' in the mostly modern city at the base of towering Mt Vitosha. Filling fast with more and more cars, Sofia is an energetic little place – far more 20th-century than most Eastern European capitals. But you'll find its charm not with quaint bridges or evocative baroque squares, but with random encounters in arty nooks of south-central neighbourhoods, the golden-brick roads around the centre, or the delirious nightlife scene.

Settled perhaps 7000 years ago by a Thracian tribe, and later called Serdica by Romans, Sofia

BULGARIA

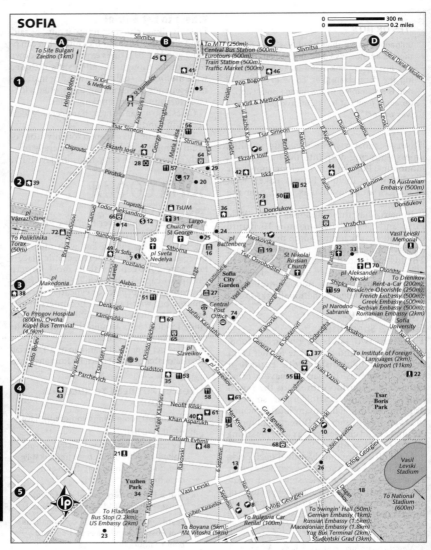

(Greek for 'wisdom') was an outpost of 1200 residents when it became the nation's unlikely fourth capital in 1879. In the decades thereafter, much planned or aesthetic development was curbed by war and communism.

Some visitors come for a night just to 'tick Bulgaria off the list'. Fine. But if you want to get a better sense of Bulgaria – and only have a couple of days – consider the more historic, laid-back Veliko Târnovo or Plovdiv instead.

ORIENTATION

Sofia's main bus and train station are across bul Maria Luisa from each other, about 500m north of the centre. Thoroughfares bul Maria Luisa and Vitosha meet at central pl Sveta Nedelya.

INFORMATION
Bookshops
Book Market (pl Slaveikov) This daily open-air market sells some English secondhand novels.
Booktrading (ul Graf Ignatiev 50; 🕙 8.30am-8.30pm Mon-Sat, 10am-8pm Sun) Super selection of English-language books.

Internet Access
There's a couple of free internet stands in the central bus station, and free wi-fi access in many cafes.
BTC (ul General Gurko; per hr 0.80lv; 🕙 8am-8pm Mon-Fri, 10am-4pm Sat)
Site (bul Vitosha 45; per hr 4.20lv; 🕙 24hr) Also makes international calls for 0.20lv per minute for the USA and Australia, from 0.60lv for the UK.

Left Luggage
Central bus station (per small/big bag per day 5/7lv; 🕙 24hr)
Central train station (per bag per day 2-3lv; 🕙 6am-11pm) At the south end of the main floor; electronic lockers are in the basement.

Media
Look out for the excellent free quarterly *Sofia: In Your Pocket. Sofia Echo* is an English-language paper that comes out every Friday (2.40lv). There are a few freebie publications also available including the quarterly *Sofia Inside & Out,* the monthly *Sofia City* (www.cityinfoguide.net) and the weekly *Programata* (in Bulgarian only; however, its website www.programata.bg has an English version).

Medical Services
Pirogov Hospital (☎ 915 4111; bul General Totleben 21; 🕙 24hr) Finding an English-speaker's a gamble.
Poliklinika Torax (☎ 91285; www.thorax.bg; bul Stamboliyski 57; 🕙 24hr) Good private clinic west of the centre.

Money
Most foreign-exchange booths along bul Vitosha, bul Maria Luisa and bul Stamboliyski run nonstop.
Unicredit Bulbank (ul Lavele & ul Todor Aleksandrov; 🕙 8.30am-6pm Mon-Fri) Changes travellers cheques in euros or US dollars for 4% commission (minimum €1).

Telephone
BTC (ul General Gurko; 🕙 8am-8pm Mon-Fri, 10am-4pm Sat) It's 0.32lv per minute for international calls.

BULGARIA

SOFIA IN TWO DAYS

Walk! Start at the **Aleksander Nevski Church** (right). Wander south on side streets – lunch at **Krâchme Divaka** (p152) – and then salute the **Monument to the Soviet Army** (p150); then head to the **NDK** (p150) for deck views. Head back along bul Vitosha to **Sveta Nedelya Cathedral** (p150) to fill up your bottle at the **spring wells** (p150) and wander the **Ladies Market** (p153). A second day is well spent hiking or skiing at **Vitosha** (p155).

Tourist Information

National Tourism Information & Advertising Centre (☎ 933 5811; www.bulgariatravel.org; ul Sveta Sofia; ✆ 9am-5.30pm Mon-Fri) English-speaking staff hand out national maps and brochures; you can call for bus times.

Travel Agencies

Eurotours (Evroturs; ☎ 0878 258 468; Traffic Market, office 61; ✆ 6.30am-7pm Mon-Fri, 6.30am-5pm Sat & Sun) This bus station agent can find basic apartments with shared bathrooms (€25); it also has an office in the train station basement.

Usit Colours (☎ 981 1900; www.usitcolours.bg; ul Vasil Levski 35; ✆ 9.30am-6.30pm Mon-Fri) Sells ISIC cards (10lv) and offers discounted airfares for students.

Zig Zag/Odysseia-In (☎ 980 5102; www.zigzagbg.com; bul Stamboliyski 20V; ✆ 8.30am-7.30pm Mon-Fri, Sat summer) Superhelpful English-language staff charge a 5lv 30-minute consultation fee on priceless hiking tips. Also can book rooms, sell trail maps (6lv) and offer a host of day trips (to Rila Monastery, Vitosha or Seven Rila Lakes for about €75 to €86 per person). Note that Zig Zag handles individual travellers (and most walk-ins), Odysseia-In handles bigger groups of over six. Enter from ul Lavele.

DANGERS & ANNOYANCES

The days of pickpockets on bul Vitosha seem to be passing. As for annoyances, fines are issued to new arrivals who don't punch a tram ticket for both themself *and* their bag. Some people report being ripped off by taxi drivers; use recommended companies only. Some moneychangers advertise one rate outside, then a worse one in tiny print inside the changing booth. Watch out for dog pooh, too.

SIGHTS

The modern capital's lure can be elusive – try roaming its most atmospheric streets, particularly the tight lanes between ul Graf Ignatiev and bul Vitosha north of the NDK and Doctor's Garden near Sofia University.

Ploshad Aleksander Nevski

Gold-domed and massive, Sofia's premier focal point is the deliberately Russian-style **Aleksander Nevski Church** (pl Aleksander Nevski; admission free; ✆ 7am-7pm), constructed between 1882 and 1916. It's named after a Swedish-born Russian warrior in honour of the Russian liberators (including the 200,000 who died fighting the Ottomans). Inside, giant brass chandeliers hang from the smoky ceilings high above where God (and his beard) look over daily worshippers.

On the church's northwestern corner, a door leads down to the pricey **Aleksander Nevski Crypt** (☎ 981 5775; adult/student 6/3lv; ✆ 10.30am-5.30pm Wed, Fri-Sun, 10am-6.30pm Tue & Thu). Originally planned for tombs, the wide, well-lit area houses many national icons stretching back to the 5th century.

To the west (with an eternal flame burning outside), **Sveta Sofia Church** (admission free; ✆ 7am-7pm summer, 7am-6pm winter) is responsible for the city's name. Inside the red-brick church, smashed by earthquakes over the years, you can see Sofia in all its incarnations – Serdica-era tombs from the 3rd century AD, and church walls from the later Sredets period, both visible through glass-panel floors; an EU-funded basement exhibit may open

---

IT'S NOT A RUSSIAN ALPHABET

The two scholar brothers Kiril (Cyril) and Metodii (Methodius) were born in Thessaloniki in the early 9th century to a noble Byzantine family of Slavic-Bulgarian origins.

They are revered here for developing, in 863, the first Bulgarian alphabet, called Glagolitic, which was later simplified as the Cyrillic alphabet. They also helped spread Orthodox Christianity throughout the Balkans by promoting the use of Slavic as the fourth accepted language of the Church (after Latin, Greek and Hebrew).

The Cyrillic alphabet is now used in Bulgaria, Russia, Macedonia, Ukraine, Belarus, Serbia and Mongolia, and some parts of Bosnia. Bulgarians celebrate Cyrillic Alphabet Day on 24 May.

BULGARIA

BULGARIAN WINE

Since the fall of communism, Bulgaria has seen an explosion of privatised wineries, producing often excellent bottles for €2 to €25 or more that many locals with extra stotinki swirl and sip in wine bars across the country. It's not a new thing though. The god of wine Dionysus was actually a Thracian linked with these lands, and Homer wrote fondly of the area's wine (though most Greeks were flabbergasted how locals drank it without watering it down!).

All the hubbub has led to a recent crisis in identity. Bigger wineries, including some run by Western European vintners, are focused on recreating the West, with some excellent merlots and cabernet sauvignons (particularly the small-scale Chateau de Val near Vidin), while smaller, family-run wineries focus on local grapes, like the mavrud or rubin on the north slopes of the Rodopis, or melnik in the southwestern Pirins (which produced Winston Churchill's favourite wine).

The owner of Sofia's Vinopolis (p153) told us 'wines like the mavrud are horrible', shaking his head in disgust, while Melnik's six-fingered vintner Mitko Manolev (p157) said, 'People making those wines act like we are all robots – it's the same grape as France!'

Wine tourism here is still in its infancy. Some high-end wineries – who often buy grapes rather than grow them – have new restaurant-hotels for tastings *for groups only*. We were turned away at several wineries, as facilities sat empty. Smaller wineries, like one near Byala on the Black Sea, offer no distribution. 'If people want to try, they can come here.' Try asking for advice at wine shops like Vinopolis, or Bendida (p163) in Plovdiv.

soon. Behind the church is the **tomb of Ivan Vazov**, a famous Bulgarian writer (and street nomenclature inspirateur).

Sofia City Garden

This fountain-filled park a couple of blocks southwest of pl Aleksander Nevski is lined with cafes and surrounded by a – bring your tin outfit – **yellow-brick road**.

The best sight here, Oz fans, is the super **Archaeological Museum** (adult/student 10/2lv; 10am-6pm May-Oct, 10am-5pm Tue-Sun Nov-Apr), housed in a former mosque and surrounded by a jumble of Roman ruins. It's worth the ticket, for many of the finest finds nicked, er, relocated from Thracian and Roman sights across the country. Facing the entry is a century-old reproduction of the Madara horseman (p176). In other rooms, there's exhibits showing how Bulgaria may have been home to the 'first Europeans' 1.1 million years ago, and various treasures like the stunningly lifelike bust of a 4th-century-BC Thracian king's head (with unsettling ivory eyeballs) found near Shipka in 2004.

Across the street is the unmistakable giant white **Party House** and the **President's Building** (both closed to the public), the site of the **changing of the guards**, where three feather-capped guys ceremoniously slap boot soles on the pavement (on the hour during daylight hours).

To the north is the former Royal Palace, now home to two museums. The squeaky-floored **National Art Gallery** (980 0093; ul Tsar Osvoboditel; adult/student 6/3lv; 10am-5.30pm Wed & Fri-Sun, 10am-6.30pm Tue & Thu) does a good job of orienting the half-heartedly interested observer into the transition of Bulgarian art from icons to abstract, focusing chiefly on derivative oils from the 1880s to the 1930s.

Sharing the palace, the good **Ethnographical Museum** was closed for renovations for 'at least six months' at the time of research.

On the south side of the park, the **Sofia City Art Gallery** (ul General Gurko 1; admission free; 10am-7pm Tue-Sat, 11am-6pm Sun) is well worth ducking

FREE THRILLS

Some of Sofia's most endearing attractions are free to see:

- Visit **Aleksander Nevski Church** (opposite), Bulgaria's most famous church and a Sofia centrepiece.
- Take a day trip north of town for hiking or skiing on **Mt Vitosha** (p155).
- Peek into the ever-changing **Sofia City Art Gallery** (above).
- Browse through the atmospherically scrappy and long-running **Ladies Market** (p153).
- Sneak up to the top deck of the **NDK** (p150) for a huge view of central Sofia.

BULGARIA

A LION'S TALE

Sofia's landmark Lion's Bridge (corner of bul Maria Luisa and bul Slivnitsa), careful observers may note, is marked by four lions – but only one with a (recently replaced) black tail. One went missing in the years of freedom, and was finally replaced. But not before the art for a new 20-lev note was drawn by an artist, who faithfully drew a lion without its tail.

---

in to for a mix of local art, ranging from dated oils to contemporary video installations.

Ploshad Sveta Nedelya & Around

In the heart of pl Sveta Nedelya (a big block west of the President's Building) is well-lit, ornate **Sveta Nedelya Cathedral**, built between 1856 and 1863. Colourful murals line the inside top of the dome (if you can see through the candle smoke). Communists bombed the church in 1925 to kill Tsar Boris III, but failed.

Just north, accessed via an underpass, the **Sveta Petka Samardjiska Church** (admission 3lv; ☻ 7.30am-7.30pm) is a small church that pokes up its 14th-century steeple from the underpass amid a sea of traffic. Some say iconic hero Vasil Levski is buried here; the attendant told us, 'Levski? Maybe no'.

North on bul Maria Luisa, you'll see the ornate red-and-gold **mineral baths** (aka Turkish baths) in the back of a small square. They've long been closed but at research time they were, supposedly, due to reopen as the long-homeless **Sofia History Museum**. If not, you can get an idea of its interiors from the renovated **Tsentralni Hali** (a mall across the street, which dates from 1909), or see mineral water in action just across ul Ekzarh Iosif, where locals fill bottles from modern **spring wells**.

Nearby is the unmistakable 16th-century **Banya Bashi Mosque** (admission free; ☻ dawn-dusk). A block west is the **Sofia Synagogue** (ul Ekzarh Iosif 16; ☻ 9am-4pm Mon-Fri, 10am-2pm Sun), the largest Sephardic synagogue in Europe.

Bulevard Vitosha & Yuzhen Park

Extending south of Sveta Nedelya, towards its towering namesake, Mt Vitosha, bul Vitosha is now a car-free strip with Sofia's ritziest shops, plus more than a handful of chances for coffee or pizza slices. A kilometre south it reaches **Yuzhen Park** (Youth Park), aptly named considering the number of skateboarders.

Facing the scene is the legendary **Monument to the Bulgarian State**. Now walled off, the 1981 glob of socialist sculpture has been steadily falling apart for years. ('Be careful there', one local warned. 'You can still get hurt by communist society!') Beyond is the gigantic **NDK** (Palace of Culture) complex, popular with trade fairs and cheap boutiques. Take the lift up to access the usually open **viewing deck**.

Borisova Gradina & Around

A few blocks south of pl Nevski, or east of NDK, a giant **Monument to the Soviet Army** conjures a different era. Built in 1954 to celebrate Russia's (second) liberation of Bulgaria – this time from the Germans in 1944 – the monument guards the entrance, more or less, of the massive **Borisova Gradina Park**, with more socialist remnants, a couple of football stadiums and good open-air bars.

A block north, the **Red House** (☎ 988 8188; www.redhouse-sofia.bg; ul Lyuben Karavelov 15) is a fun art house–cafe buzzing with Sofia intellects. Many events – including lectures on the ongoing transition from communism – are given by regional experts in English, with Bulgarian translations.

COURSES

Sofia University's **Institute of Foreign Languages** (☎ 871 0069; www.deo.uni-sofia.bg; ul Lulchev 27) offers Bulgarian-language courses (private tutors for 17lv per hour, three-week courses for 510lv).

SLEEPING

New hotels and hostels are constantly appearing. We've focused on more-intimate ones – no chains – that are within walking distance of central sights. Prices shift seasonally and business hotels often cut prices at weekends.

Some travel agents find private accommodation.

Budget

Sofia Guesthouse (☎ 403 0100; www.sofiaguest.com; ul Patriarkh Evtimii 27; dm/r incl breakfast €9/30; ✖ ▣) Filling a little house off the busy street, this friendly hostel has a travel agent, but a rather clinical feel inside with cheap flooring. Private rooms have their own bathrooms, but are tiny.

Kervan Hostel (☎ 983 9428; www.kervanhostel.com; ul Rositza 3; dm incl breakfast €10) Cute and grandma-clean, the Kervan has an entry lined with

BULGARIA

antique radios, a 'Spanish' tiled kitchen and three dorms and a single bathroom.

Be My Guest Hostel (☎ 989 5092; www.bemyguest -hostel.com; ul Ivan Vazov 13; dm incl breakfast €10-12, s/d incl breakfast €15/30; 🖳) Oodles of homey style in this house-turned-hostel on a graffitied side street near many student hang-outs. Lots of unexpected details; one dorm has loft bunks with bamboo, TV, kitchen and private bathroom. Wi-fi throughout.

Hostel Mostel (☎ 0889 223 296; www.hostelmostel .com; ul Makedoniya 2; dm incl breakfast €10-13, s €25, d €30-39; 🖳) The lovingly run Mostel fills the sweeping 1st floor of an old roadside tavern with sofas, tables, a pool table, wi-fi access and a shoes-off TV pit. It's not a party pad though – drinking is forbidden after 9pm. The six- and eight-bed rooms upstairs have an adjoining shower in most. Rila Monastery day trips are €20 per person; pasta-and-beer dinner is free. Private rooms are in a satellite pad five minutes away. It's just west of pl Makedoniya.

Sofia Hostel (☎ 989 8582; hostel-sofia@yahoo.com; ul Pozitano 16; dm incl breakfast €10) Bulgaria's first hostel has family decorations giving the small place a kindergarten feel, but it's starting to wear a little. Two big dorm rooms share a lone bathroom, so it can get tight.

Art Hostel (☎ 987 0545; www.art-hostel.com; ul Angel Kânchev 21a; dm incl breakfast €11, s/d incl breakfast €14/28; 🖳) 'Let it be' with a roar, this Boho hang-out has a back garden, dark TV area and less attention paid to rooms than the cool basement bar. Dorms get tight with triple bunks. A ground-floor room with four beds is sold as a private; better are the upstairs doubles.

Rooms (☎ 983 3508; theroomshostel@yahoo.com; ul Pop Bogomil 10; dm/s/d incl breakfast 20/34/46lv; 🖳) A purple-and-gold house on a grey street, this seven-room guest house offers tidy but tiny themed rooms with some funny antiques and wi-fi access. Breakfast's served in a tiny nook; the lone dorm has three beds and its own bathroom. No TVs.

Hotel Enny (☎ 983 4395; www.enyhotel.com; ul Pop Bogomil 46; s/d 30/40lv) A back-up in the centre, the Enny has simple rooms (some small, all without air-con or fan) that can get you to the next day OK.

Midrange

Hotel Iskâr (☎ 986 6750; ul Iskâr 11; r 50-59lv) For a simple but welcoming midrange deal, the Iskâr's 11 rooms are tough to beat. They're a bit small though, and a few have private

bathrooms across the hall. Breakfast is 6lv in the small cafe.

Knyaz Boris Hotel (☎ 931 3142; ul Knyaz Boris 188; r 53-59lv) Part of Iskâr's family, this pleasant 21-room hotel has clean, welcoming rooms with tiny TVs. Breakfast available; no internet.

Red House (☎ 988 8188; www.redbandb.com; ul Lyuben Karavelov 15; s/d incl breakfast €30/40; 🖳) This cultural house keeps three basic, but pleasant wood-floored rooms (all with shared bathroom) upstairs, with wi-fi and breakfast in the snazzy cafe-restaurant downstairs.

Hotel Niky (☎ 952 3058; www.hotel-niky.com; ul Neofit Rilski 16; s/d incl breakfast from €35/40; 🍴 🖳) It's chiefly about business travellers, but an English-speaking staff keeps it cheerful. The 22 rooms aren't huge but are superclean, with full-wall headboards, blue carpet and coffee-makers to use. Room 203 has a big balcony. Cheapest rooms always seem to be full though.

Top End

Scotty's Boutique (☎ 953 0110; www.scottyshotel.eu; ul Ekzarh Iosif 11; s €45, d €70-100; 🍴 🖳) Across from the Sofia Synagogue, this gay-friendly splash of modernity has 16 colourful rooms named for cities – 'Paris' is particularly bright; the orange 'San Francisco' gets a small balcony. All have TV, wi-fi and great old wood floors, though some furnishings look like they are from Ikea. The cheapest are a bit tight.

Hotel Diter (☎ 989 8998; www.diterhotel.com; ul Khan Asparukh 65; s incl breakfast weekday/weekend €72/60, d €92/82; 🍴 🖳) Built in 1895, this sky-blue house was once home to Bulgarian writer Todor Vlaykov – and now his descendants have opened the doors for a simple, very friendly business-type hotel, with a nice restaurant.

Residence Oborishte (☎ 814 4888; www.residence -oborishte.com; ul Oborishte 63; r/apt incl breakfast from €80/110; 🍴 🖳) A bright-red '30s-era home with its own bistro on a ritzy side street, the Residence pleases picky parents with its nine classy options, wall mouldings, choice fabrics and balconies.

Hotel Anel (☎ 911 9900; www.hotelanel.com; bul Todor Aleksandrov 14; r incl breakfast weekday/weekend €140/80; 🍴 🖳) Despite the unfortunate name (it's pronounced 'a-NELL,' Beavis), this business hotel has great monthly rates that dip below €100, with a slick, art deco ambience in the rooms – soft lights, wood-panel walls, thick carpeting (in a good way) and leather armchairs.

Arte Hotel (☎ 402 7100; www.artehotelbg.com; bul Dondukov 5; s/d €110/120; 🍴 🖳) A stone's throw

BULGARIA

from the President's House (don't test it), this 25-room hotel has smart rooms with standard modern-business sense – carpet, orange-and-burgundy colour schemes, and an overpriced €10 breakfast.

EATING

Sofia has the country's most dynamic and stylin' dining. Appealing new places are popping up constantly – try between bul Vitosha and ul Rakovski.

Trops Kâshta (ul General Gurko 38; mains from 2.50lv; ☺ 8am-8.30pm) For cheap, fast, fresh, point-and-eat cafeteria-style food, Trops is your new comrade. It's 30% off after 8pm. There is another branch at bul Maria Luisa 26.

ourpick Dream House (ul Alabin 50a; mains 3.90-7.80lv; ☺ 11am-10pm) Offering Sofia's best meatless dining, this cool-mint restaurant, upstairs from the tram lines, shifts its menu seasonally, with tons of inspired vegie and vegan choices you won't find outside the capital, plus a Sunday buffet from 11am to 4pm (7lv).

Chaina (☎ 0887 051 080; ul Benkovski 11; mains 4.20-7lv; ☺ 10am-11pm Mon-Sat) This arty tea-house doubles as a vegetarian restaurant, with a changing menu with nods to salads, wholewheat spinach and tomato pastas and all-day breakfasts.

Krâchme Divaka (☎ 986 6971; ul 6 Septemvri 41a; mains 4.30lv; ☺ 24hr) In a great old home on a south-central backstreet, this quick-filling four-room restaurant is an appealing place for a Bulgarian beer and some nicely prepared meats (a wine-soaked kebab with mashed potatoes is 4.30lv, or the filling cream soup in a bun is 3.20lv). A bigger, far less intimate, four-room location is at ul Gladston 54.

ourpick Site Bulgari Zaedno (All Bulgarians Together; ☎ 931 5161; ul Stoletov 37; mains from 5lv; ☺ 10am-midnight) For a wild, very Bulgarian night out, this slick, place is all-out joy. Packed on weekends, with a live traditional band and 47 framed portraits of heroes along the walls. Get *rakia* with your salads and grill, and don't resist invitations to join the circle *khoro* dancing. It's a few blocks west of the train station.

Ugo (ul Khan Krum 2; pizza from 5lv; ☺ 24hr) Twenty-something couples meet up at this slick, modern pizza mini-chain. Its location is great, with soft hanging lights and seats looking out on a quiet side street.

Victoria (ul Tsar Osvoboditel 7; pizza 7.60-11.50lv; ☺ 24hr) Set in a grand neoclassical building just off pl Nevski – and with its own Ottoman-era building used to, uh, store patio seats – Victoria serves great pizzas conveniently near many central attractions. Best seating is on the back-facing deck.

Gara Za Dvama (☎ 989 7675; ul Benkovski 18; mains 12.50-18.50lv; ☺ noon-midnight) This tiny Russian restaurant has super food and is set up like a train compartment, with old photos and Russian tunes (and vodkas) in the air. They don't make kitchens like this on the Trans-Siberian.

A refurbished covered market, **Tsentralni Hali** (cnr bul Maria Luisa & ul Ekzarh Iosif; ☺ 7am-midnight) has three floors busy with fresh produce, baked goods, sausage, Swiss chocolate, beer, ice cream, wine and cheap meals (kebabs are 2.20lv).

DRINKING

Look for *Programata*'s free annual *Club Guide* for listings in English. Those wanting to search on their own can find a student scene around ul Tsar Sushman; ritzier drinkers go for open-air cafes along ul Vitosha.

Bilkovata (ul Tsar Shushman 22; ☺ 10am-2am) In an area trolled by Sofia University students, see if you can't squeeze into this unpretentious, unsigned (other than 'Heineken') basement bar with couples and a welcoming vibe.

Hambara (ul 6 Septemvri 22; ☺ 8pm-late) Located in a century-old grain-storage building, where a WWII antifascist press was based, this low-key, candlelit place is unsigned, and down a dark path.

Adam's Bar (ul Vrabcha 28; ☺ 10am-2am) Hole-in-the-wall heavy-metal bar with Pantera and Motorhead banners, *five* foosball tables, the HQ of the 'Storm Riders Table Soccer Club', bartenders with circa-'87 Slayer haircuts (that is, women bartenders), a mixed crowd and 2lv Zagorkas. Could this be the best bar of all time?

Apartment (☎ 088 665 5093; ul Neofit Rilski 68; ☺ 10am-2am) A century-old apartment as a bar is a tad boho. You're certainly not lost for comfort here with its soft lighting and stylishly lazy sofas resting beneath chandeliers. There's a mix of rooms with free internet, and the occasional cosy couple.

ENTERTAINMENT

If you're keen to hear traditional Bulgarian music, eat/drink/dance at Site Bulgari Zaedno (left).

Odeon (☎ 989 2469; bul Patriarkh Evtimii 1; tickets 4lv) is a great art-house cinema with cafe and

---

STUDENTSKI GRAD NIGHTS

The wind sweeping off towering Mt Vitosha first greets Sofia in Studentski Grad, a scrappy student-filled remnant of communist times, with drab Stalin-era housing blocks, cracked sidewalks and an abandoned building or two. Yet once darkness falls, nowhere in Sofia is more alive than this 'Student Town', where non-Sofian students have for generations huddled in dorms, and now – as freedom's bells ring – old libraries and cafeterias are being transformed into some of the city's most lively, cheap and welcoming bars and clubs you can find. Options vary. Here are a few:

our pick **Strozha** (☎ 962 5977; www.stroeja.com; Block 23b) Local indie rockers sip cheap beers and cocktails in a dive bar fashioned to look like a construction site.

Avenue (☎ 0898 553 086; www.complexavenue.com; ul Atanas Manchev 1a) At least half of the Grad rolls their eyes over *chalga*, others cram in this fairly mellow dance hall with hip-shaking, finger-snapping dances on tabletops.

Maskata (☎ 868 8079; Block 19) Filling a dorm ground floor, this fun raucous club kicks off the week loudly and late with well-attended Monday-night karaoke, and has bands scheduled most other nights.

Take minibus 7 from bul Maria Luisa or minibus 8 along ul Rakovski (1.5lv one way). A taxi is about 6lv.

---

many unexpected old films shown, while **Dom na Kinoto** (☎ 980 7838; ul Ekzarh Iosif 37; tickets 6-8lv) sticks with new releases.

Sofia's big kids' favourite central disco is **Escape** (☎ 0887 990 000; www.clubescape.bg; ul Angel Kânchev 1; cover 10lv; ☼ 10pm-late Thu-Sun). **Exit Club** (☎ 0888 140 133; ul Lavele 16; ☼ 6pm-late) is a gay-friendly club with house music and food.

Swingin' Hall (☎ 963 0696; bul Dragan Tsankov 8; ☼ Tue-Sun) is probably Sofia's best live-music venue, with jazz, blues and rock shows taking over the cellar-styled club.

Opera is taken seriously in this country and the **National Opera House** (☎ 987 1366; www.operasofia.com; ul Vrabcha 1; ☼ ticket office 9.30-6.30pm Mon-Fri, 10.30-6pm Sat & Sun) features Sofia's best.

Levski (☎ 982 2156; www.levski.bg) and **CSKA** (☎ 963 3477; www.cska.bg) are Sofia's most popular football teams. The season runs from August through May. **National Stadium** (☎ 930 0666; Borisova Gradina) is the main venue.

SHOPPING

Souvenir shop (ul Tsar Osvoboditel; ☼ 10am-6pm) At the Ethnographical Museum, this (pricey) shop has traditional music, attire and masks.

Cohort (ul Denkoglu 40; ☼ 11am-7pm Mon-Fri) The place to find particularly good communist-era antiques.

Stenata (☎ 980 5491; www.stenata.com; ul Bratya Miladinovi 5; ☼ 10am-7pm Mon-Fri, 10am-6pm Sat) A great outfitter for the woods-bound, with a two-floor selection of camping, hiking and rock-climbing gear.

Vinopolis (☎ 987 7796; ul Bacho Kiro 8; ☼ 10am-11pm) One of the country's best wine stores,

Vinopolis has a huge collection of Bulgarian wines and occasional tastings.

our pick **Ladies Market** (ul Sv Stambolov; ☼ dawn-dusk) A lively, messy market has been here for ages and still draws a colourful crew of old-timers, both Bulgarian and Turkish. It's food on the south half (barrels of wine to fill your bottle) and clothes on the north half.

The year-round daily **fleamarket** (pl Aleksander Nevski) is a classic for a mix of actual antiques and touristy junk – good for communist-era vinyl, Soviet cameras and icons.

GETTING THERE & AWAY
Air

Sofia airport's new terminal 2 receives most flights; some charter flights still use terminal 1. In terminal 2's arrival hall there's an **information booth** (☎ 937 2211; www.sofia-airport.bg), ATM, foreign exchange and car rental.

See p195 for information on airlines.

SQUAT SHOPS

In the can-do capitalist fervour that followed the fall of communism, Sofia saw an outbreak of the *klek* (squat shop), a basement-level window that sells coffee, beer, snacks and the like. Despite the explosion of Western-style boutiques, these legacies of the transition – when expanding a basement window was cheaper and quicker than overhauling a ground-floor apartment – remain across Sofia. Just look for Sofians bent over and holding their backs in pain.

BULGARIA

Bus

DOMESTIC BUSES

Navigating the mass of stands at Sofia's modern **central bus station** (☎ 0900 21000; www .centralnaavtogara.bg; bul Maria Luisa; ☽ 24hr), next to the train station, is confusing, but there's a 24-hour information centre to help you. The OK Taxi stand outside is dependable. Many international buses, and a few domestic ones, leave from the wilder Traffic Market, between the station and train station (an info centre is on hand at the south end of the parking lot).

Following are sample bus fares. All go from the central bus station and times are frequent (generally every hour) unless otherwise noted. Some Black Sea towns have less-frequent service outside of summer:

Bansko (13–14lv, three hours) Also from Ovcha Kupel.
Belogradchik (15lv, four hours, one or two daily)
Blagoevgrad (10lv, two hours)
Burgas (30lv, six hours)
Kârdzhali (20lv, four hours)
Kazanlâk (16lv, three hours)
Koprivshtitsa (10lv, two hours, in summer every two hours from 8am to 8pm) Traffic Market.
Melnik (12lv, three hours, once daily)
Plovdiv (13lv, two hours)
Ruse (15lv, 4½ hours)
Shumen (27lv, five hours)
Sinemorets (35lv, seven hours, one daily)
Smolyan (21lv, 4½ hours)
Sozopol (28lv, six hours, five daily)
Varna (29lv, six hours)
Veliko Târnovo (17lv, 3½ hours)
Vidin (18lv, 4½ hours)

Those heading to Borovets must transfer in Samokov. Minibuses leave for Samokov (4.50lv, one hour) from Sofia's **Yug bus terminal** (☎ 872 2345) half-hourly between 7am and 7pm. Tram 18 goes within a few hundred metres of the station.

Two buses connect Sofia with the Rila Monastery (10lv, 2½ hours), leaving at 10.20am and 6.20pm from the **Ovcha Kupel bus terminal** (Zapad; ☎ 955 5362; bul Tsar Boris III). Reach the station by tram 5 from pl Makedoniya, west of the centre on ul Alabin (it's a 20-minute ride).

INTERNATIONAL BUSES

Most international buses are handled by the stands at the Traffic Market, between the bus station and train station. **Matpu** (☎ 981 5653; www.matpu.com; office 58, Traffic Market) sells tickets for Skopje (24lv, six hours, three daily) and Belgrade (54lv, eight hours, two daily) with a change in Nish. Other stands sell tickets for Budapest, Bratislava and Prague.

Up the street a few hundred metres, **MTT** (bul Maria Luisa; ☽ 8.30am-5.30pm Mon-Fri, 8.30am-4.30pm Sat) sends at least one daily bus to Thessaloniki, Greece (48lv, 6½ hours) and five weekly to Athens (108lv, 12 to 13 hours).

Several companies go daily to İstanbul (40lv to 50lv, eight to 10 hours) from the central station, leaving at 1pm, 8pm and 10.30pm.

Macedonia-bound buses cross at Gyueshevo–Deve Bair; Belgrade-bound buses from Sofia cross at Kalotina-Dimitrovgrad, Serbia (most travellers prefer the train on this route).

Train

Sofia's **central train station** (☎ 931 1111; www.bdz.bg; bul Maria Luisa) is a bit confusing, though departures and arrivals are listed in English on a large computer screen on the main floor, where there's an information booth (but usually no English). You buy same-day tickets for Vidin, Ruse and Varna on the main floor, and all other domestic destinations downstairs. Advance tickets are available at another office downstairs.

DOMESTIC

Sample 2nd-class train fares for direct routes:

Blagoevgrad (6.80lv, 2½ to three hours, six daily)
Burgas (17.20lv, 6½ to 7½ hours, six daily) Nondirect trains change in Karnobat.
Gorna Oryakhovitsa (13.40lv, 4½ hours, 10 daily) Near Veliko Târnovo.
Plovdiv (8.10lv, 2½ hours, 12 daily)
Ruse (17.20lv, 6½ hours, four daily)
Varna (21.90lv, eight to nine hours, six daily)
Vidin (12.60lv, 5½ hours, four daily)

Reaching **Veliko Târnovo** (14.10lv, about 6½ hours) requires a change (usually in Gorna Oryakhovitsa), sometimes getting onto an ordinary train, which may be late; about six times a day trains are timed to link for easy transfers.

The train to **Koprivshtitsa** (4.70lv, 2½ hours, six daily) isn't ideal, as the station is 10km north of town, and transfers are unreliable.

INTERNATIONAL

Two daily trains go to Bucharest (sleeper 57lv, 10½ hours); the *Trans Balkan* (No 462) leaves in the morning, the *Bulgaria Express* (No 382) at night, and on to Kiev and Moscow. The *Trans Balkan* also heads in the opposite direction to Thessaloniki. The night train to Athens (sleeper 95lv, 15 hours) leaves daily at 5pm.

The *Balkan Express* (No 491) leaves at night for İstanbul (82lv, 12 hours). At the time of research, the same train going in the reverse direction went during the day to Belgrade (58lv, eight hours) only on Saturday and Sunday – but this should become daily. Otherwise, the Sofia–Belgrade Train (No 292) leaves nightly.

International tickets can be purchased at the **Rila Bureau** (☎ 932 3346; ☽ 24hr) in the northern part of the station's main floor, or at its **centre office** (☎ 987 0777; ul General Gurko 5; ☽ 7am-7.30pm Mon-Fri, 7am-6.30pm Sat).

GETTING AROUND
To/From the Airport
An **OK Taxi** (☎ 973 2121) booth in the arrivals hall arranges metered cabs to the centre (about 8lv or 10lv). Outside is a bus stop, where bus 284 leaves for a stop along bul Vasil Levski, near Sofia University (a bookshop in the arrival hall sells bus tickets). Minibus 30 travels between bul Maria Luisa and the airport.

Car & Motorcycle
Parking garages are available, but most drivers park on the sidewalks. Watch for speed traps if entering Sofia from the east.

The big car-rental names are here, but local companies are usually cheaper. The literally named **Bulgaria Car Rental** (☎ 400 1060; www.bulgariacarrent.com; ul Orfei 9) rents cars from 30lv per day outside the July and August period (when they rise to 50lv).

Another reliable local company is **Drenikov Rent-a-Car** (☎ 944 9532; www.drenikov.com; ul Oborishte 55; ☽ 9am-6pm Mon-Fri, 10am-2pm Sat & Sun), which has several classes of cars from €28 per day, or €24 if you rent two to six days, €20 for over seven days – there's a 10% discount for cash payments.

Most travel agents rent out cars too.

Public Transport
Sofia's trams, buses and metro line run from 5.30am to 11pm and use the same ticket system. A single ride is 1lv and a day pass 4lv. There are no transfers. Blue ticket booths are near most stops. Single-ride tickets must be validated once you board; disguised officials fine those without them. You *must* punch a separate ticket for a big bag.

Trams 1 and 7 connect the bus station and train station with the centre. Minibuses ply many useful city routes at 1.50lv per ride.

Sofia's expanding metro line currently goes to western suburbs. By late 2009, supposedly, a southwest line will open, meaning a useful connection with Sofia University from the 'Serdica' stop by TsUM.

Taxi
Sofia's taxis have a reputation for overcharging foreigners. **OK Taxi** (☎ 973 2121) runs on the meter; check the telephone number on cars, as there are fake 'OK Taxis' too.

AROUND SOFIA

In addition to the following, many visitors go to Rila Monastery (p156) as a day trip.

VITOSHA ВИТОША
The feather in Sofia's cap is this 23km by 13km mountain range (part of Vitosha Nature Park, www.park-vitosha.org), just south of the city. At summer weekends, many Sofians come to hike, picnic and pick berries. In winter, it's the nearest skiing to the capital.

Activities
The mountain is home to dozens of well-marked **hiking trails**. It's worth paying 5lv for the Cyrillic trail map *Vitosha Turisticheska Karta* (1:50,000), available in Sofia. Popular ones include the steep 90-minute trip up Mt Cherni Vrâh (2290m) from Aleko; a three-hour trek east of Mt Sredets (1969m) from Aleko past Goli Vrâh (1837m) to Zlatni Mostove; and a three-hour hike from Boyana Church past a waterfall to Zlatni Mostove.

The **skiing**, from mid-December to April, covers 29km of the mountain; it's generally cheaper here than ski resorts (about 30lv for a lift ticket) and you can ski higher (the peak is 1800m). Rental equipment is available; try to avoid busy weekends.

Most people reach the mountain by a couple of chairlifts. **Dragalevtsi** has two chairlifts, located a few kilometres up from the village bus stop (walk via the creekside) – one lift goes to Bai Krâstyo, the second to Goli Vrâh (1837m). The other option is the six-person gondola at **Simeonovo**, which runs Friday through Sunday (closed in April), and goes to Aleko, a popular hike/ski hub. It's possible to go up either Dragalevtsi or Simeonovo, hike 30 minutes, and return down the other.

Getting There & Away

About 2km south of NDK in Sofia, the useful **Hladilnika bus stop** (ul Srebârna), just east of bul Cherni Vrâh, has several Vitosha-bound buses. Bus 122 leads directly to the Simeonovo chairlift. Bus 64 goes to Dragalevtsi centre and on to Boyana. Get to Hladilnika bus stop by tram 9, just east of NDK.

BOYANA БОЯНА

Once a separate village (now officially a part of Sofia), hillside Boyana has a couple of interesting attractions. The **National Historical Museum** (☎ 955 4280; www.historymuseum.org; bul Vitoshko Lale 16; adult/student 10/1lv, combined ticket with Boyana Church 20lv; 🕙 9.30am-6pm Apr-Oct, 9am-5.30pm Nov-Mar) is housed in a 1970s presidential palace. Its collection gives an exhaustive look at Bulgaria's past from Thracian towns to EU signatures. Unfortunately there are many, many copies of original pieces and a disappointing lack of context to themes of the past.

Built between the 11th and 19th centuries, the colourful, Unesco-protected **Boyana Church** (☎ 959 0939; adult/student 10/1lv, combined ticket with National Historical Museum 12lv, guide 10lv; 🕙 9.30am-5.30pm Apr-Dec, 9am-5pm Jan-Mar), located 1.5km south of the historical museum, is a three-part, mural-filled medieval church that only allows 10-minute visits. At parts of the colourful walls you can see two layers, from when – in 1259 – the original Byzantine-styled murals were covered over in a more Bulgarian style.

It's tricky reaching these sights from the centre. Tram 9 goes down ul Hristo Botev from the centre to Hladilnika bus stop, where bus 64 goes past the museum to the east then within 200m of the church. One way to do it is taxi to the church, then walk down the steps, then left to ul Puskhin and around to the right to the museum entrance (1.5km in all).

RILA & PIRIN MOUNTAINS

These buddy mountain chains snuggle up to the Greek border south of Sofia, and are made of serious Alps-like rocky-topped peaks full of rewarding hikes. It's here that one of Bulgaria's most famous sites, Rila Monastery, stands guarded by mountains, while Melnik is a favourite spot for wining weekends.

Activities

Most hiking paths are well signed. For Rila hikes, the monastery is a possible starting point, with four trails meeting others higher up. Day hikes are certainly possible and *hizhas* (mountain huts) are spaced three to nine hours apart. For longer hikes, it's best to start up at Malîovitsa (southwest from Samokov), where you can reach the Sedemte Ezera (Seven Lakes).

Pirin hikes are generally tougher than Rila ones, with more abrupt slopes. In summer it's better to end walking down to (hot) Melnik.

Also see www.rilanationalpark.org and www.pirin-np.com.

RILA MONASTERY
РИЛСКИ МАНАСТИР
☎ 07054

Bulgaria's most famous **monastery** (admission free; 🕙 6am-9pm), set in a towering forested valley 120km south of Sofia, is a popular destination for day trippers from around the region. The murals here, painted by Zahari Zograf, are of Bulgaria's finest, and many hikes are in the nearby Rila Mountains.

Day trips to Rila from Sofia range from about €20 to €80 or more. There are usually direct buses from Sofia, but it sometimes requires a change.

First built in 927, and heavily restored in 1469, the monastery helped keep Bulgarian culture and language alive during Ottoman rule. A fire engulfed most buildings in 1833, but they were rebuilt shortly thereafter.

The entrance to the monastery is from the west at Dupnitsa Gate, and around the east side at Samokov Gate. **Rila village**, 21km away, has a hotel, ATM and an information centre.

Sights

The 300 monks' cells fill four levels of colourful balconies overlooking the large misshapen courtyard. Built in the 1830s, the **Nativity Church** (Church of Rozhdestvo Bogorodichno) contains 1200 magnificent murals. **Tsar Boris III's tomb** – actually his heart only – is to the right when you enter; it's believed he was poisoned by the Nazis after clamouring to save Bulgaria's Jewish population during WWII. Nearby, the 23m stone **Hrelyu Tower** is all that remains from the 14th century.

The **Ethnographic Museum** (admission 8lv; ☼ 8am-5pm) houses many ornate woodwork pieces, including the double-sided Rila Cross, with 140 tiny biblical scenes.

If you have time, hike up the **Tomb of St Ivan** (Grobyat na Sv Ivan Rilski). To reach the start of the 15-minute hike up the clearly marked trail, walk about 3.7km east on the road, behind the monastery.

Sleeping

You can stay in the **monastery's rooms** (☎ 2208; r about €15); the attendant often leaves midafternoon. There are also a couple of nearby hotels, plus camping and bungalows at riverside **Zodiak** (☎ 2291; camp sites 10lv, d from 30lv), 2km past the monastery.

The nearest *hizha* is about a six-hour walk up.

Getting There & Away

Two daily direct buses connect the monastery with Sofia's Ovcha Kupel bus terminal (10lv, 2½ hours), with one returning at 3pm. There are also five daily buses to nearby Rila village (2lv, 30 minutes), where you can catch hourly buses to Blagoevgrad (1.70lv, 25 minutes).

MELNIK МЕЛНИК
☎ 07437 / pop 275

Wee and happy with itself, Melnik – hidden by jutting pyramid-style clay-sand mountains at the dramatic southwest end of the Pirins – is one of the country's most famous wine centres, with great day hikes too. Family-run *mehanas* (tavern restaurants) boast their own barrels of blood-red Melnik – the local varietal that locals swear is 'hangover-free' – which are sold in emptied plastic jugs on the dirt streets.

A century ago, Melnik was home to 20,000 – mostly Greeks – until much of it burned down during the 1912–13 Balkan Wars.

From the bus stop, roads run on either side of a (mostly dry) creek into town. There's no ATM.

Sights

Follow the main road east, and up, to the **Mitko Manolev Winery** (☎ 0887 545 795; admission incl tasting 1lv; ☼ 9am-dusk), a 250-year-old winery. The manager – nicknamed 'Shestaka' for his six-fingered hand – is happy to talk wine (in English) and sell glasses of his red and white wine for 1.50lv, on a nice setting with wood stools overlooking Melnik.

Located to the south is **Kordopulov House** (admission 2lv; ☼ 9am-6pm), a giant revival-period home with high-ceilinged rooms.

Activities

The best half-day hike is the trip to (or better yet, back from) the hilltop **Rozhen Monastery**, 10km east by road (or about 4km by hiking trail). Built in 1217 and redone in the mid-18th century, the monastery has a mural-filled church and is connected by a trail through the mountains with Melnik (about one hour downhill).

Consider taking one of the few daily buses up to Rozhen village (or a share taxi for about 6lv), then walk 800m up to the monastery and back down to Melnik. Signs point west, going behind the monastery. The trail gets slippery after rains.

More exploring can be done closer to Melnik too. Framing the village to the south is **Nikolova Gora**, a flat-top hill scattered with ruins. A sign points up from across the Rodina Hotel. About 15 minutes up, signs point left and right. To the right, you'll pass the battered 13th-century **St Nicola Church**, and further on, the dramatic cliffside, 13th-century **Despot Slav Fortress**. Back the other way, the trail looks over Melnik, reaching the **St Mary Spileotisa Monastery** (which draws pilgrims on 31 August); the trail heading back on the opposite side of the hill goes to another monastery. You'll need about two hours in all.

Sleeping

Most of the traditional-style private homes let out simple rooms with shared bathroom from 10lv or 12lv per person.

Mehana Barbekyu (☎ 088 866 6047; r incl breakfast 30lv) By the post office, this small tavern has six plain but clean rooms, open all year.

Hotel Despot Slav (☎ 248; s/d incl breakfast 48/60lv) On the main strip heading towards the winery, this hotel has nice, modern rooms with wood floors and TV.

Eating
One popular *mehana* is **Mencheva Kâshta** (dishes 7-20lv; ✆ 8am-10pm), a homey tavern, halfway to the winery. It's tasty *vreteno* (12lv) is something like a pork kayak stuffed with onions and mushrooms, and with fries on the side. Desserts include ice yoghurt with honey and walnuts served in a clay cup (4lv).

Getting There & Away
One daily direct bus connects Melnik with Sofia (13lv, 4¼ hours), leaving Sofia at 2pm, returning from Melnik at 6am. If you want to take an extended loop, take the Sofia–Melnik bus, then – brace for this – take one of the four daily buses to nearby Sandanski (1.50lv, 30 minutes), catch one of the frequent buses to Blagoevgrad (5lv, 1¼ hours), where there are frequent connections from its two neighbouring bus stations to Sofia, Rila village and Bansko (7lv). From Bansko you can bus to Plovdiv.

Yellow share taxis sometimes are around the Melnik bus stop, offering rides to Sandanski for 3lv.

BOROVETS & AROUND БОРОВЕЦ
Once Bulgaria's premier ski grounds, Borovets (70km south of Sofia) is steaming over how Bansko has recently stolen its thunder – and is attempting to steal it back. An ongoing €600-million overhaul (funded by the likes of the Sultan of Oman) will transform Borovets to, drum roll…, Super Borovets, including a controversial road and lifts to the revered Sedemte Ezera (Seven Lakes) region.

Many activists have protested this part of the plan, for its tree-clearing roads, traffic and lifts that would penetrate a protected area – now reached by tough trails; in early 2008 there were reported death threats given by a few men at the scene to journalists reporting the controversy.

The draw of the popular **Seven Lakes hike** may fade with all the changes. If you go, there's a daily bus from Sofia to **Maliovitsa** (25km southwest of Samokov), where you can reach the glittering turquoise lakes via well-marked trails below Mt Maliovitsa, after an eight-hour hike. The Rilski Esera *hizha* is like a hotel, with en suite doubles (about 20lv per person). Serious hikers can continue on to Rila Monastery (eight hours), or north to Paniciste (four hours), where the new lifts will be based.

If you go for skiing, **Samokov** (8km west of Borovets) is where you change buses from Sofia and is a far cheaper base than Borovets' resort-burg; friendly **Relax Hotel** (✆ 0722 24284; www.relaxhotel-bg.com; d incl breakfast €20) is across from a central museum.

Minibuses reach Samokov (4.50lv, one hour) regularly from Sofia's Yug bus terminal; from Samokov frequent buses (or taxis) go on to Borovets or four times daily to Maliovitsa.

BANSKO БАНСКО
☎ 0749 / pop 9200
A once quaint, historic mountain town, Bansko has recently gotten pudgy from tacky modern resorts cozying up to Mt Vihren (2914m) and its ski slopes and hiking trails. Bansko lost its hopes to host the 2014 Olympics to Suchi, Russia, but roars forward with new construction anyway. If you come, eat out at Bansko's famously festive *mehanas*.

Orientation & Information
Buses and trains stop about 300m north of the central pl Nikola Vaptsarov, reached along ul Todor Aleksandrov. From the square ul Pirin goes south to pl Vûzhrazhdane and on to the ski lifts and, 2km further, the Pirin National Park entrance.

Pick up maps at the **tourist information centre** (✆ 88580; www.bansko.bg; pl Nikola Vaptsarov; ✆ 9am-5pm), which naughtily defies its advertised hours.

Sights
The **Kâshta-Museum of Nikola Vaptsarov** (✆ 88304; pl Nikola Vaptsarov; admission 3lv; ✆ 9am-noon, 2-6pm) is dedicated to an appealing local poet who was executed for antifascist poems in 1942 at the same age as Jesus, a fact not lost on the curators here.

Built in the 1830s, the **Sveta Troitsa Church** (pl Vûzhrazhdane; ✆ 8am-6pm) is particularly striking for its woodcarved interior and gloomy, faded murals – currently undergoing a €100,000 renovation.

Activities
The ski season in Bansko lasts from mid-December to April, though the first snows tickle the mountains in late September. And it's good skiing. There are two major mountains – the lower Chalin Valog and the bigger Shiligarnika, higher up – with 26km of runs (7km of night skiing, too).

A lift pass for all four lifts is 50lv for a day, ski rental is 30lv per day, snowboard gear is 50lv. For old-school lifts, and shorter lines, bus 6km east to **Dobrinishte**, which at some point may merge with Bansko's lifts into one mega-slope.

Paths to the Pirin Mountains are accessed just south of town. In summer minibuses go to Banderitsa (about 4lv, three daily) to access trails to lakes and *hizhas*.

Festivals & Events
Bansko celebrates its folk dances and music during the **Celebration of Bansko Traditions** (mid-May). The **Pirin Sings Folk Festival** is staged nearby in August every four years (scheduled for 2009 and 2013); annually in August is the **International Jazz Festival**.

Sleeping
Hotels are everywhere, as are options for private rooms. Book way ahead during ski season, when prices are sometimes 50% higher.

Hotel Tipik (☎ 88185; ul Tudor Aleksandrov 15; r per person summer/winter 15/25lv) A happy little budget hotel with small but clean rooms a block south of the stations.

Hotel Avalon (☎ 88399; www.avalonhotel-bulgaria .com; ul Eltepe 4; s/d €18/25, winter €33/49; ☻ closed Apr, May & late Nov; ☐) This friendly, Brit-run hotel offers nicely arranged rooms and is big with the budget crowd. Staff can arrange day trips.

Dvata Smarcha (☎ 82632; ul Velyan Ognev 2; s/d 20/30lv, winter r 55lv) One of many *mehanas* that offer rooms, this one is 50m southeast of pl Vûzhrazhdane and has eight welcoming rooms.

DETOUR: NARROW-GAUGE TRAIN RIDE

Few visitors come or go from Bansko by train, but if you have the time, the ride to Septemvri (5.60lv, five hours, three daily) on a wonderful narrow-gauge line offers one of the country's most unusual, scenic rides. Bring snacks. The little carriage goes slo-o-wly north towards the Sofia–Plovdiv track line at the unglamorous Septemvri, offering some great glimpses of local life both in and out of the carriage. If bored, count tunnels and stops (for our last tally, tunnels beat stops 31 to 18).

Eating
The most appealing *mehanas* – with wood-beamed ceilings, hanging vines and live bands – are just north of the square, including **Kasapinova Kâshta** (ul Sandanski 4; mains from 5lv; ☻ noon-midnight).

Getting There & Away
From the **bus station** (☎ 88420; ul Patriarh Evtimii), frequent buses go to Sofia (14lv, three hours) and Blagoevgrad (7lv, one hour), while one or two go to Plovdiv (12lv, 3½ hours).

The **train station** (ul Akad Yordan Ivanov) is next to the bus station.

THRACIAN PLAIN & THE RODOPIS

Sitting in the wide-open Thracian plain, Plovdiv lies just within the cusp of the thickly forested Rodopi Mountains rising to the south. Like the Pirin and Rila, the Rodopis have good hikes, and offer culturally rich villages to top it all off. Smolyan is a key Rodopi hub, near the Pamporovo ski resort, where you can bus further into Rodopi or east to wayward Kârdzhali to see the Thracian/Roman city Perperikon.

Activities
Shiroka Lâka, 24km northwest of Smolyan, is a good base for hikes. A popular one is the five-hour hike south to Golyam Perelik (where there's a *hizha*) or there's a two-day hike from Shiroka to Trigrad via Mugla (a mountain village with accommodation). The international trail E8 plies the Rodopis.

Trail maps (5lv each) split the Rodopis into the western and eastern ranges.

PLOVDIV ПЛОВДИВ
☎ 032 / pop 375,000
Despite its sprawl, Bulgaria's second city lives more like a town, particularly around its legendary cafe-lined ped malls from the laid-back, cobbled, hilltop 'Old Town'. It's got a lot to take in – student life, Roman theatres still in use, cobbled 19th-century revival-era taverns, local wines galore, and landmark hills that look like forlorn grapes spilled from a bigger pile from the nearby Rodopi Mountains.

Ask proud locals what they think of Sofia to get a colourful conversation. One reason why, perhaps, is how much more history is found

BULGARIA

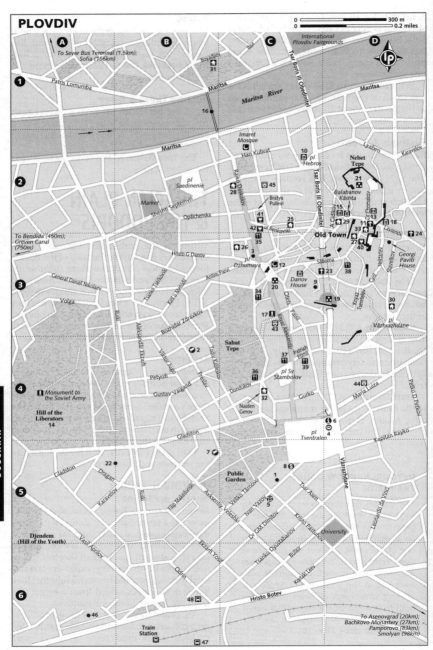

PLOVDIV

0   300 m
0   0.2 miles

To Sever Bus Terminal (1.5km);
Sofia (156km)

Boyadziev
31

Patris Lomumba

Maritsa

Maritsa   River

16

Maritsa

International
Plovdiv
Fairgrounds

Imaret
Mosque

Han Kubrat

10 pl
Hebros

Nebet
Tepe

21

pl
Saedinenie

Rayko Daskalov

28

45

Bratya
Pulievi

Balabanov
Kâshta

15
29
13

Tsar Boris III Obedinitel

18

Lyaben

Karavelov

Market

Sheshti Septemvri

Opâlchenska

41

25

Il Benkovski

42

35

A Chipov

11

33

27

Old Town

40

24

Georgi
Paviti
House

To Bendida (450m);
Greven Canal
(750m)

Hristo G Danov

26

3

pl
Dzhumaya

12

Saborna

23

38

Lavrenov

Netzarov

General Danail Nikolaev

Tsanko Tserkovski

Kiril u Metodi

Antim Parvi

Otets Paisii

Danov
House

9

Knyaz Tsereteley

Georgi

Volga

34

20

19

Botzhidar Zdravkov

Todor Kableshov

Viktor Iuho

Pesta

17

43

Iosif Aleksandsi

30

pl
Vâzrazhdane

Sahat
Tepe

Patriah
Evtimi

2

37

39

pl Sv
Stambolov

Petyofi

36

44

Monument to
the Soviet Army

Gustav Vaigand

Dondukon

Gurko

Maria Luiza

Petko D Petkov

Hill of the
Liberators
14

Naiden
Gerov

32

Gladston

7

pl
Tsentralen

6

4

Kapitan Rayko

Gladston

22

Karavelov

Dragan

Filip Makedonski

Avksenti Velishki

Veliko Târnovo

Ivan Vazov

8

Public
Garden

1

5

Tsar Asen

Vâzrazhdane

Leonardo da Vinci

Djendem
(Hill of the Youth)

Vasil Aprilov

Odrin

Elizaft Yosif

Tsanko Dyudzabanov

Dr GM Dimitov

Krista Pastuhov

Bufair

University

Kosiak Lesv

46

48

Hristo Botev

To Asenovgrad (20km);
Bachkovo Monastery (27km);
Pamporovo (83km);
Smolyan (98km)

Train
Station

47

BULGARIA

here. Plovdiv was known as Philippopolis to the Romans in the 3rd century AD, but was settled thousands of years before by Thracians.

Orientation

Plovdiv's train station and (main) Yug Bus Terminal are about 600m southwest of the central pl Tsentralen. From the square, the main pedestrian mall, ul Knyaz Aleksandâr, stretches 500m north to pl Dzhumaya, near Old Town just east.

Information

Foreign-exchange offices and ATMs abound along the pedestrian mall (ul Knyaz Aleksandâr) and also on ul Ivan Vazov.

The train station has 24-hour luggage storage (3lv per piece per day); the Yug and Rodopi bus stations both hold bags for 1lv per day.

Five of the sights in the Old Town have a discount combination ticket; see p162 for details.

Esperansa (☎ 260 653, 0897 944 951; travel_plovdiv@ abv.bg; ul Ivan Vazov 14; s/d 25/50lv, apt from 80lv; ☯ 10am-8pm) A nine-minute walk from the main stations. Can help you find accommodation; email ahead or go in and look through its photo book. Language can be a barrier unless you speak Russian or German. It's at the back of the building.

Helikon (ul Raiko Daskalov; ☯ 9am-8pm Mon-Sat, 10am-8pm Sun) Sells guidebooks and maps.

Main post office (pl Tsentralen; ☯ 7am-7pm Mon-Sat, 7-11am Sun) Also has several computers with online access, and phone booths on the ground floor (open 7am to 10pm daily).

Phone stand (ul Ivan Vazov & ul Kristo Pastuhov; ☯ 8am-8pm) A covered sidewalk stand a few blocks from the train station.

Penguin Travel (☎ 622 432; www.plovdivguest.com; Plovdiv Guesthouse, ul Sâborna 20) Offers day trips and rents cars.

Tourist information centre (☎ 656 794; www .plovdiv-tour.info; pl Tsentralen; ☯ 9am-6pm Mon-Fri, 10am-2pm Sat & Sun) Next to the post office, this newish tourist information centre hands out local maps and can help find private accommodation.

Unicredit Bulbank (ul Ivan Vazov 4; ☯ 8am-6pm Mon-Fri)

Sights

Most of Plovdiv's main attractions can be seen in a day.

OLD TOWN

Revival-era wood-shuttered homes lean over wee cobbled lanes (and galleries and often excellent antique shops) in this hilly neighbourhood, which is practically a free, living museum. About a dozen *kâshta* (traditional homes) are well signed and open to see too,

BULGARIA

> **OLD TOWN COMBO TICKET**
>
> Five Old Town sights have signed onto a combo ticket (adult/student 15/3lv), which works out a bit cheaper than going to each individually. The combo-ticket sights include Balabanov Kâshta (ul Stoilov 57), Hindliyan Kâshta (below), Nedkovich Kâshta (ul Lavrenov), the Roman Amphitheatre (below) and Zlatyu Boyadjiev Kâshta (ul Sâborna 18).

for a price; some double as museums, and not all are equally rewarding.

Seeing the 22 rooms inside the Old Town's most striking building (built in 1847) is an added bonus to the country's finest **Ethnographical Museum** (☎ 625 654; ul Dr Chomakov 2; adult/student 5/1lv; ⏰ 9am-noon & 2-5pm). It has many traditional outfits upstairs, including the masked *kukeri* costumes from the Rodopi region, with pointed noses and bell-belts.

Just past the nearby fortress gate, the **Museum of History** (☎ 629 409; pl Saedinenie 1; admission 2lv; ⏰ 9am-noon, 1-5.30pm Mon-Sat, closed Sat winter) occupies the lovely gold Georgiadi House, home to this interesting three-floor exhibit (with English descriptions) on Bulgaria's ebbing revival in the late 1800s, concluding rather gruesomely with murals of decapitations from the Batak massacre in 1876.

Of the other 'baroque' homes open to see, probably the most rewarding is the **Hindliyan Kâshta** (☎ 628 998; ul Artin Gidikov 4; adult/student 3/1lv; ⏰ 9am-5pm), an 1835 two-storey home that really evokes the period. Ask at nearby Balabanov Kâshta for entry if it's locked.

The area has more than 19th-century architecture. Past the Ethnographical Museum, the path reaches the **Ruins of Eumolpias** (ul Dr Chomakov; admission free; ⏰ 24hr), scattered upon Nebet Tepe hilltop, that date from a Thracian settlement from about 5000 BC.

A more impressive site, and one of Plovdiv's landmarks, is the amazing **Roman Amphitheatre** (admission 3lv; ⏰ 10am-5pm). It's easily seen from the cafe set up outside the gates, but entry lets you tread on worn steps approaching their 2000th birthday. The theatre holds various events from June to August.

A few Old Town churches have played big roles in the emergence of the Bulgarian Orthodox separation from the Greek Orthodox

religion in 1870. One of the most active, with swarms of worshippers on occasions like Easter, is the 19th-century **Sveta Bogoroditsa** (ul Sâborna 40), with a huge pink clock tower; note the murals of Turkish soldiers harassing chained Bulgarians on the right entry wall.

Near the Ethnographical Museum, the mural-filled **Church of St Constantine & Elena** (ul Sâborna 24), tucked behind walls, is Plovdiv's oldest, dating from the 4th century when it was built over a Roman church. Much of what you see, though, was rebuilt in 1832.

OTHER SIGHTS

Fresh from a recent renovation (the last one never filled the cracks from a 1928 earthquake), the **Dzhumaya Mosque** (Friday mosque; pl Dzhumaya; admission free; ⏰ dawn-dusk) is not your typical centrepiece attraction in a Bulgarian city. Once the largest of Plovdiv's 50 mosques, this one may date from as far back as 1368, making it one of the first in the Balkans. Outside, a shiny **statue of Philip II** (Alexander the Great's dad) looks over the **Roman stadium ruins**, providing a bizarre peek to the past from below the ped walkway.

A short walk northwest of Old Town, the appealing **Banya Starinina/Centre for Contemporary Art** (☎ 638 868; www.arttoday.org; ul Shesthi Septemvri 179; adult/student 2/1lv; ⏰ during exhibitions 1-6pm Tue-Sun) frequently houses modern art in the nooks and crannies of late-16th-century Turkish baths.

It ain't Florence's Ponte Vecchio, but Plovdiv's modern, recently fixed-up **Maritsa Bridge** is a pedestrian link to the north side of the river; it's lined with boutiques selling *chalga* disco–ready outfits and there's a cafe.

The nation's biggest canal, the impressive 2.5km **Greven Canal**, is about 1km west of the centre. It carries the honour of being Bulgaria's last communist-built project and features rowing races. It's surrounded by shady Loven Park. Take bus 10 or 15 west as far as it goes on ul Sheshti Septemvri, then walk 200m northwest.

Courses

It's possible to enrol in folk singing or traditional Bulgarian instrument classes at Plovdiv's **Art Academy** (www.artacademyplovdiv.com, ul Todor Samoudomov 2), near the Roman amphitheatre.

Sleeping

It's worth calling ahead; Plovdiv hosts many trade fairs, when hotels fill (and rates rise).

PBI Hostel (☎ 326 384; www.pbihostel.com; ul Naiden Gerov 13; dm/r €10/15; 🖳) Outside of high season PBI seems to mean 'problems being in', as the staff often aren't around to let travellers in. It's clean and central, if lacking much spirit, with a few dorms and a couple of bathrooms.

Gusto Hostel (☎ 625 258; www.gustohostel.com; ul Petko Karavelov 2; dm/d incl breakfast €10/25; 🖳) Taking over a floor of a side-street apartment building, this simple new hostel has six- and eight-bunk dorms, a private double and two bathrooms.

Plovdiv Guesthouse (☎ 622 432; www.plovdivguest .com; ul Sâborna 20; dm/s/d incl breakfast €10/28/36; 🔀 🖳) Home to Penguin Travel, this all-pink house is still sussing out whether it's a guest house or hostel (all dorms have private bathroom, kept clean if clinical), but offers comfort, rental bikes and DIY laundry (4lv).

ourpick **Hiker's Hostel** (☎ 0885 194 553, www.hikers -hostel.org; ul Sâborna 53; tent/dm incl breakfast 14/22lv, d 52-60lv; 🖳) Plovdiv's top backpacker stop occupies a cosy little house in Old Town. The staff is laid-back, and happy to join in on nights out or sit in the stone deck area (with blankets in winter). They keep a couple of tents to use in the courtyard; the claustrophobic private room is a converted storage space. There's also a less atmospheric satellite apartment in summer.

Hotel Elite (☎ 624 537; www.hotel-elite.eu; ul Raiko Daskalov 53; r from 39lv) A simple corner hotel allows 'two-hour couples' during the day only, so it should be pretty quiet after hours. Rooms vary, but are clean with views of Imaret Mosque. There's a TV but no breakfast or internet.

Hotel Renaissance (☎ 266 966; www.renaissance -bg.com; pl Vâzhrazhdane 1; s/d incl breakfast from €59/69; 🔀 🖳) Ignore the name, this cosy place in a slightly removed pocket of south Old Town is tiny – just a five-room guest house with modern takes on revival-era rooms, with plenty of colour and wood floors. The helpful English-speaking manager runs a restaurant and cafe next door.

Dafi Hotel (☎ 620 041; www.hoteldafi.com; ul Benkovski 23; s/d incl breakfast from 85/105lv; 🔀 🖳) The modern Dafi's 20 rooms offer nice midrange, carpeted comfort with flowing curtains to push back so you can look over the cobbled lane near several bars.

ourpick **Hotel Hebros** (☎ 260 180; www.hebros -hotel.com; ul Stoilov 51; s/d incl breakfast €99/119; 🔀 🖳) Those looking for a classic Old Town sleep should opt for this inviting 10-room inn fully decked out in 19th-century style. There's a

---

> ### CITY OF SEVEN, UH, SIX HILLS
>
> Proud locals and even tourist brochures proudly link their city with Rome as 'the city of seven hills'. It'd be a snazzy slogan if it were still true. During the early communist era, one hill – about 100m south of the Hill of the Liberators – was blasted to pieces to re-pave Old Town. Other hills, including its one-time neighbour, have partially chipped sides from the same purpose.
>
> For the past couple of years, the former seventh-hill site has been fenced off – a (slow-going) construction site for a new mall.
>
> Of Plovdiv's six hills, Old Town covers three, while the most prominent, the **Hill of the Liberators** (Bunardjika Park), is topped by the statue of 'Alyosha', a Russian soldier – a fun one to climb.

back courtyard, spa, sauna and free wi-fi, plus one of Plovdiv's best restaurants.

Novotel (☎ 934 444; www.novotel.com; ul Boyadjiev 2; r from €109; 🔀 🖳 🐾) A swank makeover of a drab communist-era tower on the north side of the river is a big scene for business travellers coming for trade-fair cocktail meetings. Novotel has two pools and a few good, if impersonal, restaurants.

Eating

Dreams (pl Sv Stambolov; sandwiches from 2.80lv; ⏱ 8am-midnight) Plovdiv goes ga-ga for this inside-and-out cafe for its desserts, sandwiches, cocktails or a dream-fulfilling Coke-and-coffee combo (2.70lv).

Dayana (ul Dondukov; dishes from 2.80lv, grills from 8lv; ⏱ 24hr) Aside the rocky walls of Sahat Tepe hill, this sprawling spot goes with the usual Bulgarian grill items plus egg dishes (2.80lv), skewers of meats (from 8lv) and vegetables (4.90lv).

Gradzhanski Klub (ul Chalkov; dishes 5-12lv; ⏱ 8.30am-midnight) A local hang-out in an old home below a gallery, with the sign in Cyrillic, the Grad is a three-room smoky spot with students yapping over coffee, Kamenitza beers or shopska salads as a little R&B pumps gently.

ourpick **Bendida** (☎ 640 771; bndidawine@abv.bg; ul Druzhba 15; ⏱ 4-10pm Mon-Sat) A simple wine shop–restaurant in way west Plovdiv. The lovely English-speaking family may sit with you as you eat their delicious 'home-style' food (pumpkin *banitsas*, lasagne-style casseroles

PLOVDIV CHARACTERS

Notice that big-eared bloke on the main drag of ul Knyaz Aleksandâr? The seated statue on the central steps is a tribute to wisecracker **Milyu**, a legendary *zavek* (wanderer) from the early '70s of Plovdiv. Milyu, who died in 1974, was famous for coming to unsubtly 'listen in' to various conversations and pass on things he heard.

Another new cult character popular these days is the bearded '**Stefchu Avtografa**', who is trying to get into the Guinness Book of World Records for most autographs. Don't be surprised if he finds you. To quote one local: 'He's not exactly normal, but we love him'.

with egg and potato) along with wine tastings of local rubin and mavrud wines. Take bus 10 or 15 west along ul Shesti Septemvri to just past ul Vasil Aprilov; ul Druzhba is a block south.

Gusto (ul Otets Paisii 26; pizza from 6lv; ⏰ 9am-1am) For good sit-down pizza, loungey Gusto has some 'tude to go along with crispy, delicious pies. Skip the basement bar (where staff may forget you) and go for green-leather booths in the main floor – or sidewalk seats.

Hotel Hebros (☎ 260 180; ul Stoilov 51; mains 9-21lv; ⏰ 11am-midnight) Even if you can't spring for the rooms, Hebros' cosy basement (and courtyard) is one of Old Town's best dining spots, with live music and a delicious daily menu going from gamey faves like roasted rabbit with plums, duck, plus pumpkin soup and at least one vegie option.

North of pl Dzhumaya, you'll find a popular **banitsa stand** (ul Daskalov; banitsa 0.80lv). The best spot for kebabs or falafel is **Alaeddin** (ul Knyaz Aleksandâr; kebabs 1.60lv, falafel 2lv; ⏰ 24hr).

Drinking

Marmalad (ul Bratya Pulievi 3; cocktails 3lv; ⏰ 9am-2am) On a side lane, the ultramod Marmalad has cream leather booths and stools on old wooden floors popular with local dress-uppers who sip to house music only, please. There's a basement nightclub that gets going after 9pm or so.

King's Stable (ul Sâborna; cocktails 3.40lv; ⏰ 8.30am-2am Apr-Sep) This great open-air bar – behind a host of Old Town buildings – serves drinks and snacks at a leisurely pace.

our pick Nylon (ul Benkovski 8; ⏰ noon-4am) Across the street from Marmalad, the Nylon (aka

Naylona) offers the flipside. A crusty local dive, with a fair share of grey-haired guys, Thom Yorke lookalikes and a lesbian couple or two… it's certainly welcoming to all. The plain entry has a leaky ceiling; in back, ancient trumpets hang over the long wood bar and a DJ occasionally spins music from the analogue era.

Entertainment

Much of the nightlife lingers around the Kapana district, around ul Benkovski north of Dzhumaya Mosque. Look around for club, restaurant and cinema listings in *Programata*, *Navigator* and *Plovdiv Guide* (all free).

Petnoto (ul Yoakim Gruev 36) It claims an underground status and earns it with local bands and DJs mixing things up in a mod setting geared for *chalga*-haters.

Paparazi (bul Maria Luiza 43) Speaking of which, the eternally popular, and ginormous Paparazi gives up one of three halls to *chalga*, fitting in house and hip hop in the other two.

Caligula (ul Knyaz Aleksandâr 30) Off the main strip, Plovdiv's only gay club appeals to folks of all stripes.

Getting There & Away

BUS

Plovdiv has three bus stations: the main **Yug bus terminal** (☎ 626 916; ul Hristo Botev), 100m northeast of the train station; the fancy lil' **Rodopi bus terminal** (☎ 657 828), reached by underground passageway from the train station; and the **Sever bus terminal** (☎ 935 705), 1.5km north of the river.

Sample fares follow; buses leave/arrive at Yug unless otherwise noted:

Asenovgrad (3lv, 30 minutes, at least hourly from 6.50am to 6.20pm)

Bansko (12lv, four hours, one daily) Departs 3pm.

Burgas (20lv, four hours, four daily)

İstanbul (35lv, six hours, at least six daily)

Kârdzhali (12lv, 2½ hours, every two hours) From Rodopi.

Kazanlâk (8lv, two hours, three daily) From Sever.

Koprivshtitsa (10lv, two hours, one daily) Departs 4.30pm; from Sever bus terminal.

Pamporovo (8.50lv, two hours, hourly 6am to 7pm except noon) Departs from Rodopi terminal.

Smolyan (9lv, 2½ hours, hourly 6am to 7pm except noon) Departs from Rodopi terminal.

Sofia (13lv, two hours, once or twice hourly 6am to 8pm)

Varna (26lv, seven hours, two daily)

Veliko Târnovo 1(4lv, 4½ hours, four daily) Departs Sever.

Buses to Athens go via Sofia.

TRAIN

Plovdiv's **train station** (☎ 622 729; bul Hristo Botev) serves the Sofia–Burgas line.

A dozen or so daily trains go to Sofia (8.10lv, three hours); avoid the morning one arriving from İstanbul, which is often an hour or more late.

There are also direct services to Burgas (13.40lv, 4½ to four hours, five daily), Veliko Târnovo (11lv, five hours, one daily) and Varna (16.70lv, 6½ hours, four daily). Other destinations may mean a change in Stara Zagora.

A nightly train to İstanbul (49lv, 11 hours) leaves at 9.35pm. The train to Belgrade requires a change in Sofia. For international tickets, go to nearby **Rila Bureau** (☎ 643 120; bul Hristo Botev 31a; ☼ 7.30am-7.30pm Mon-Fri, 8am-6pm Sat summer, 7.30am-5.30pm Mon-Fri, 8am-5pm Sat winter).

Getting Around

It's easy to get around Plovdiv's centre by foot. On arrival, take bus 7, 20 or 26 in front of the train station (0.80lv; buy ticket on board) and exit on ul Tsar III Obedinitel past the tunnel to reach Old Town.

AROUND PLOVDIV

Plovdiv is a bit too stranded in the Thracian plain to catch much Rodopi action by day. The closest and most rewarding trip combines a couple of sights on the highway to Smolyan.

About 20km south of Plovdiv is the **Asenovgrad Fortress**, a renovated mountaintop fortress built in the 11th century. It's about 4km south of the humble town of Asenovgrad's bus station on the road to Smolyan.

Another 7km south (past the Chepelarska Gorge), **Bachkovo Monastery** (admission free; ☼ 6am-10pm) is Bulgaria's second biggest and is a nice stop-off. Founded in 1083 and restored in the 17th century, Bachkovo's central courtyard is filled with a 12th-century **Archangel Church** and a larger 17th-century **Church of the Assumption of Our Lady**. Nearby are several hikes, labelled by a signboard.

All the above is a relatively easy DIY day trip. Catch a nearly hourly bus to Smolyan and ask to be dropped off near the Bachkovo entrance (there are a couple of restaurants). Afterwards, hitch back to the Asenovgrad Fortress, or wait for a Plovdiv bus (again, nearly hourly) and ask to get dropped off by the fortress, where you'll have to hike up.

Buses to Asenovgrad leave from Plovdiv's Yug Bus Terminal.

PAMPOROVO ПАМПОРОВО
☎ 3021

Guarded by resorts, this popular ski resort 83km south of Plovdiv has eight ski runs and 25km of cross-country trails in a pine-thick mountaintop location. Rental equipment is about 30lv and a lift ticket 48lv. A bus connects the centre (near the T-junction of the roads to Smolyan, Plovdiv and Shiroka Lâka and Devin, where the bus stop is) to the lifts. It's quiet in low season, though you can hike up **Mt Perelik** (2190m) from here.

Most people book tours, or book way ahead, to stay in resort hotels. An information centre can point out nearby hotels.

Buses travelling between Plovdiv and Smolyan stop here, as do regular buses between Smolyan and Chepelare.

SMOLYAN СМОЛЯН
☎ 0301 / pop 32,800

A convenient Rodopi hub in a stunning, sweeping valley, Smolyan could be Bulgaria's most beautiful town – but its streets are spread out, and modern buildings are, to quote one local, 'lacking harmony with nature'. It does, though, have a couple of interesting attractions, and all-important bus links into deeper, more rewarding Rodopi villages.

Orientation & Information

Buses arrive near the west end of long bul Bulgaria (at the 'old centre'). About 250m east it becomes a pedestrian mall, where you'll find ATMs.

Another 1km east on bul Bulgaria, near the museums, is a superb **tourist office** (☎ 62 530; www .smolyan.com; bul Bulgaria 5; ☼ 9am-5.30pm Mon-Fri), with handouts on hikes and accommodation.

Sights

The **Planetarium** (☎ 83 074; admission 6lv, minimum 5 visitors; ☼ English shows 2pm), open since 1975, features a domed-ceiling show of outer space (about 40 minutes, also in French and German) that conjures the age of cosmonauts despite its updated soundtrack. The best part is watching the stars for real via the mega-telescope at 8pm Wednesday if the sky's clear (admission 3lv).

The interesting **Historical Museum** (☎ 62 770; pl Bulgaria 3; adult/student 5/3lv; ☼ 9am-noon & 1-5pm Tue-Sun), a five-minute walk up the steps just east of the tourist office, fills three floors outlining Bulgaria's ethnographical past, including full-bodied, hairy *kukeri* costumes.

Sleeping & Eating

The tourist office has a partial list of private accommodation available (about 20lv per person). Ask about camping areas in the hills outside town.

our pick **Three Fir-Tree House** (☎ 63 862; www .trieli.hit.bg; ul Srednogorec 1; s/d 30/40lv) The motherly owner of this lovely hotel is as proud of her homemade meals (giant breakfasts for 5lv, plus tasty four-course dinners) as of ensuring homely comfort in her nicely furnished rooms. She speaks German and English and arranges interesting tours. It's down the steps at the start of bul Bulgaria's pedestrian mall.

Hotel Kiparis A (☎ 64 040; www.hotelkiparis.eu; bul Bulgaria 3a; s/d incl breakfast €30/40; 🍴 🖳) Near the tourist office, this modern hotel has nice rooms and helpful staff, plus a restaurant, a gym and hookah pipes in the lobby bar (!).

Getting There & Around

Hourly buses leave Smolyan's **bus station** (☎ 63 104) to Plovdiv (9lv, 2½ hours), stopping in Pamporovo. Smolyan has less-frequent links into the mountains, including half a dozen buses to Shiroka Lâka (about 4lv, 40 minutes).

Buses to Kârdzhali (10lv, two hours) leave twice daily from the **Ustov bus station** (☎ 64 585), in east Smolyan, reached by city bus 3.

City buses 1 and 2 go from the bus station past the pedestrian mall and museums.

SHIROKA LÂKA & AROUND ШИРОКА ЛЪКА

☎ 03030 / pop 1501

Cute Shiroka Lâka, 24km west of Smolyan, is a streamside town of Roman bridges and 19th-century whitewashed villas, which give a very other-era vibe (maybe it's the dung heaps). The best time to visit is the first Sunday in March, when locals adorn full-bodied animal-like costumes during the *kukeri* festival.

The **tourist office** (☎ 2233; www.rhodope.net; ul Kapitan Petko Voivoda 48; 🕑 8.30am-5pm Tue-Sat), 100m east of the bus stop, sells maps and books private rooms.

Hikes – overnight or day – loom in the green forested hills. One goes a few hours up to **Gela village**. Another goes up **Mt Perelik**.

About 36km east, **Trigrad** is a fun end-of-the-road village that's past the lovely Trigrad gorge, where there's a cave to see. You can hike a few hours to **Yagodina** village, home to the Rodopis' longest cave. Buses to Trigrad go via Devin.

It's possible to study traditional music (or sit in on a recital) at the revered **National School of Folk Music & Instruments** (☎ 2333; nufi_shirokaluka@ abv.bg); it's closed in summer.

There are several nice guest houses around offering rooms and meals. **Kâshta James** (☎ 0887 136 207 www.shirokalaka.com; s/d incl breakfast 40/60lv) is run by a South African, with modernised traditional Rodopi-style rooms and tips on regional activities.

Buses between Devin and Smolyan stop here, or you can hail a group taxi.

KÂRDZHALI & AROUND КЪРДЖАЛИ

☎ 0361 / pop 45,000

A spread-out industrial town with two dammed lakes, a diverse mix of Turks and Bulgarians, and absolutely stunning natural and archaeological attractions, Kârdzhali (named for a 17th-century Turkish general) remains far removed from most itineraries. That could change. The border with Greece, about 55km south, may open in 2009 or 2010, giving a new overland route option.

Sights

Housed in a grand 1930s building designed to be a Muslim *madrasa* (Islamic school), the artful and well-arranged **Regional History Museum** (☎ 63 584; ul Renublikanska 4; adult/student 2/1lv; 🕑 9am-noon & 1-5pm Tue-Sun) has an interesting collection of Perperikon relics (and others from Thracian and Roman sites), plus some ethnographical and geological exhibits – most are signed in English.

PERPERIKON ПЕРПЕРИКОН

The recently rediscovered (and expanding) excavation site of **Perperikon** (www.perperikon.bg; admission free) is about 20km east of town (brown signs lead the way). Atop a rocky bluff (a 15-minute walk up) are stunning indications of Thracian (and later Roman) life dug out of a rock mountain that was first inhabited up to 7000 years ago. There's much to see: dug-out water tanks and grooves where doors were pivoted open, tombs and church walls – all supposedly part of the Temple of Dionysus and the location where Alexander the Great learned his prophecy. Note the larger hill looking back to the southwest – covered in brush and trees – is an extension of the town (still unexcavated), and what this one looked like only a decade past.

You can go by a couple of daily buses to the nearby Turkish village of Gorna Krepost, where it's a 2km walk south to the turn-off, and 750m up to the parking lot. The bus returns at 2pm and 5.30pm.

TATUL ТАТУЛ
About 27km southwest (east of Momchilgrad town) is the recent find of **Tatul**, an arched Thracian above-grown tomb reached by a short dung-splattered trail (there are lots of shepherds here). Apparently the first settlement here was around 6000 years ago. It's very hard bussing here.

WEST OF KÂRDZHALI
The drives overlooking the **Kârdzhali Dam**, just west of the city, take in hilltop Turkish villages such as Enchets and Dâzhdovnitsa. But be careful if you swim. It's believed a 500kg catfish roams the lake's depths – grown in size after swallowing a boy whole. A couple of years ago, a diver supposedly glimpsed it and resurfaced with white hair from fear!

If heading towards Smolyan with your own wheels, detour to the lovely stone **Devil's Bridge**, arching over a small gorge 10km northeast of Ardino town. Some locals like to call it Roman, but it dates from the Ottoman Empire.

Sleeping
Rodopi Smile (☎ 85 581, 0898-665 581; www.rodopismile .com; Gorna Gledka 5; dm/r incl breakfast 18/20lv; 🖥) A hostel here? Staying at this couple's simple home is like hanging with your Bulgarian friends – and they soon will be. It's a bit raw still, but the duo can help you see Perperikon, do rock-climbing trips, or visit many attractions not listed here. It's remote, about 4km south of the bus station, and about 500m east of Uspenie Bogorodichno monastery (reached by bus 6 or 26).

Across from the bus station, about 1km south of the centre, **Hotel Kârdzhali** (☎ 82 354; www.hotel-kardjali.com; bul Belomorski 68; s/d incl breakfast 45/75; 🆒 🖥) has simple, modern rooms and friendly staff.

Getting There & Around
From the Kârdzhali bus station, buses go every two hours to Plovdiv (12lv, 2½ hours) and a couple of daily to Smolyan (12lv, three hours).

The **car-rental agency** (☎ 0896 346 046; Hotel Kârdzhali; ⏰ 9am-6pm Mon-Sat) doesn't always have cars (from 60lv per day). A taxi to Perperikon with a 90-minute wait is about 35lv.

CENTRAL BALKANS

Crossing Bulgaria's belly, this broad swipe of lovely mountains – called the Stara Planina – is striped with hiking trails and dotted with towns in 19th-century revival style. Some hiking paths can also be cross-country skied or cycled. Historic Veliko Târnovo is the most convenient stop, while windswept hubs (Kazanlâk and Shumen) are more off the beaten track. Check www .staraplanina.org for more information.

Some travellers find themselves changing trains or buses in the Stara Planina's outer reaches at Stara Zagora, where there's a nice central garden and little else to see.

KOPRIVSHTITSA КОПРИВЩИЦА
☎ 07184 / pop 2680
Two-and-a-half hours east of Sofia, Koprivshtitsa is a quaint, quiet setting of revival-era taverns, horse-carts clacking on cobbled streets and nearby hiking trails. It tends to mean more for weekender Sofians escaping summer heat than some foreigners, and it isn't exactly the easiest place to get to by public transport, but it's certainly a fine setting for a kick-back day.

It's also historic. Koprivshtitsa was the setting for a key early revolt against the Turks: the 20 April 1876 uprising. Its re-enactment (curiously held on 1 May or 2 May) and the **Folklore Days Festival** (mid-August) are popular annual events.

Orientation & Information
The town spreads north–south for 1km along a small creek. The bus stop is about 100m south of the centre, which is at pl 20 April.

The **tourist information centre** (☎ 2191; www .koprivshtitsa.com; pl 20 April; ⏰ 10am-7pm summer, 9am-6pm winter) arranges horse-riding trips, offers internet access (per hour 1lv) and sells town and hiking maps (3.50lv).

There's an ATM next to the bus station.

Sights
Six of Koprivshtitsa's traditional homes are now 'house museums', and a supervalue

BULGARIA

combo ticket (adult/student 5/2lv) will get you into them all; otherwise it's 2/1lv each. All are open 9am to 5.30pm summer, 9am to 5pm winter, with Monday or Tuesday off (see listings). The six pack is as follows:

Benkovski House (ul Georgi Benkovski 5; ☺ closed Tue) Exhibits on the cavalier who continued the 1876 uprising in surrounding areas.

Debelyanov House (ul Dimcho Debelyanov 6; ☺ closed Mon) The 'tender poet' who lived here was not as short as the ceiling suggests (the floors were raised for renovation).

Kableshkov House (ul Todor Kableshkov 8; ☺ closed Mon) The home of the intriguing chairman of the revolutionary committee, with a wavy facade and many interesting old photos.

Karavelov House (ul Hadzhi Nencho Palaveev 39; ☺ closed Tue) Three-section home where the brothers Karavelov grew up.

Lyutov House (Topalov House; ul Nikola Belovezhdov 2; ☺ closed Tue) The most colourful of the homes, with vibrant walls and ceilings.

Oskelov House (ul Gereniloto 4; ☺ closed Mon) Detailed home of one of the town's 19th-century tax collectors.

Sleeping

The tourist office can help arrange private rooms (30lv to 45lv).

Voivodenets Hostel (☎ 2145; ul Vekilova 5; dm 12lv) An old home with a nice sitting area downstairs but mostly cramped rooms with two to 10 beds in each.

Hotel Trayanova Kâshta (☎ 3057; ul Gereniloto 5; d 45lv) Off a cobbled lane, this four-room home often fills its huge, traditionally decked-out rooms early.

Hotel Panorama (☎ 2035; www.panoramata.com; ul Georgi Benkovski 40; s/d incl breakfast 45/60lv) A friendly English-speaking family runs this quickly filled hotel with nice views of the southern part of town (worth the 300m walk from the bus stop).

Eating

Traditional *kâshtas* serve meaty meals and are found on side streets, some keeping seasonal hours. One good choice is **Dyado Liben** (ul Hadzhi Nencho Palaveev; dishes from 3lv; ☺ 11am-midnight), occupying a wonderful 1852 home.

Getting There & Away

The **bus station** (☎ 3044) sends buses every couple of hours to Sofia's Traffic Market (10lv, 2½ hours). At research time, a 6.30am bus (2pm on Sunday) left for Plovdiv (10lv, 2½ hours).

Because of the unpredictability of local bus or taxi transfers to town from Koprivshtitsa's train station, 9km north, arriving by train is a bit of a gamble. There are normally four daily trains to Sofia (two hours) and one to Burgas (five hours); for Plovdiv, you have to change in Karlovo.

KAZANLÂK & AROUND КАЗАНЛЪК
☎ 0431 / pop 82,500

It's not exactly lipstick on a pig, but the otherwise haggard little town sure benefits, PR-wise, from the presence of the surrounding 'Valley of Roses' (and the towering Stara Planina a few kilometres north). The June bloom ushers in the annual three-day **Rose Festival** (www.rose-festival.com; finishing the 1st Sun in Jun) – not to mention some tour groups to see the crowning of the festival queen, sip rose liquor and endure doubled hotel rates. At other times it can feel forgotten – and it shouldn't. Kazanlâk's most rewarding draws are the nearby Thracian sites, including 40 tombs.

If you stay, nearby **Shipka village** is a more atmospheric base.

Kaz's central pl Sevtopolis is about 400m north of the train and bus stations (via ul Rozova Dolina), with banks, an internet cafe and the **tourist information centre** (☎ 62817; ul Iskra 4; ☺ 8am-1pm & 2-6pm Mon-Fri).

Sights
IN KAZANLÂK

A couple of blocks north of pl Sevtopolis, the **Iskra Museum & Art Gallery** (☎ 63762; ul Slaveikov 8; adult/student 3/1.5lv; ☺ 9am-5pm) has plenty of Bulgarian art and neolithic pieces from 6000 BC, but best is the Thracian room, which gives an excellent overview of area sites (in English). Staff can help you visit some area tombs (not listed here) otherwise locked up.

Kazanlâk's **Tyulbe Park** (about 300m northeast of the centre) houses the small, 3rd- or 4th-century, domed **Tomb of Kazanlâk** (admission 20lv; ☺ 9am-5pm), a remarkably well-preserved Unesco World Heritage site with ceiling paintings; only 20 people per day can visit. Frankly, the fluorescent lighting and carpeted walkways hardly evoke the age, so consider just visiting the **tomb copy** (admission 3lv; ☺ approximately 9am-5pm), which feels identical to the untrained eye. Entering the park go up the steps then right; the cashier (and keys) are at the tomb copy.

At the north end of Kazanlâk, 2km towards Shipka, you can stop by the **Museum of the Rose** (admission 2lv; ☻9am-5pm Apr-Oct), a small exhibit on rose cultivation (and festival queens!) in the basement of an institute.

VALLEY OF THRACIAN KINGS

Outside town lie 1500 Thracian *mogila* (burial mounds), though only a few have been excavated. The only one keeping regular hours is **Kosmatka** (Shipka village; admission 3lv; ☻9am-5pm), with three chambers where the 5th-century tomb of Sevt III was found in 2004. A replica of Sevt's gold bust is here; the remarkable original is now at Sofia's Archaeological Museum (p149). Contact the Iskra Museum about getting a guide (and keys) to visit other less-excavated tombs in the area, such as **Ostrusha** ('sharp one'), which contains pre-Christian paintings.

The nearby Thracian town of **Sevtopolis** was only briefly studied before a communist-era dam buried it in water. In recent years, there's been extravagant talk of building a wall and emptying the site – to be visited by boat.

Sleeping & Eating

In town, there are a couple of good choices near Tyulbe Park, including **Chiflika** (☎81411; www.chiflika-bg.com; ul Knyaz Mirskia 38; r 44lv), a lively traditional restaurant with six rooms, and **Hotel Teres** (☎64272; www.hotelteres.com; ul Nikola Petkov; s/d incl breakfast 48/64lv; ✗▢).

our pick Hotel IT Shipka (☎42112; www.shipkaithotel.com; ul Kolyo Adzhara 12; s/d 37/42lv; ✗▢▣), 13km north in Shipka village, is run by a cuddly English-speaking couple of former musicians – Ivan occasionally interrupts discussions to ponder the greatest song of all time, 'Hotel California' ('where does such greatness come from?' – pauses – 'only God knows'). Their seven-room home has modern rooms, courtyard deck and pool, and good meals.

You can find pizzerias and cafes around pl Sevtopolis in Kazanlâk, including **New York Bar & Grill** (pl Sevtopolis; pizza from 4lv; ☻10am-midnight).

Getting There & Away

Kazanlâk's little **bus station** (☎63200) sends a handful of daily buses to Sofia (16lv, 3½ hours), Veliko Târnovo (15lv to 20lv, three

hours) and Plovdiv (8lv, two hours). City bus 6 goes to Shipka village.

Across the street, Kazanlâk's **train station** (☎62012) sends seven daily trains to Sofia (10.40lv, 3½ hours) and three to Burgas (10.40lv, three hours).

VELIKO TÂRNOVO
ВЕЛИКО ТЪРНОВО
☎ 062 / pop 72,000

Clinging to a sharp S-shaped gorge split by a snaking river, Veliko Târnovo is too convenient and lovely to miss. The former capital (1185–1393) and busy student hub is easygoing (despite the occasional traffic jams on its narrow winding roads) and filled with days of potential, including hill hikes, hill towns, hill climbs and the best ruined citadel in the country.

The twenty-second of March is Veliko's (and a certain Lonely Planet author's) birthday, when a big festival is staged around town.

Orientation

Sloping ul Hristo Botev leads north from the Yug Bus Terminal to pl Maika Bulgaria, where ul Vasil Levski heads west and the main crawl, ul Nezavisimost, heads east for 1km.

Information

The main streets winding through town have many foreign-exchange offices.
Main post office (ul Nezavisimost) There is also a telephone centre.
Navigator (ul Nezavisimost 3; per hr 0.90-1.20lv; ☻24hr) Internet cafe in basement of corner mall.
Tourist information centre (☎622 148; www .velikotarnovo.info; ul Hristo Botev 5; ☻9am-6pm Mon-Fri, Mon-Sat summer) Helpful English-speaking staff will call for accommodation reservations, rent cars (30lv to 40lv per day) and sell regional maps (from 3lv).
United Bulgarian Bank (ul Hristo Botev; ☻8.30am-4.30pm) Cashes travellers cheques.
Usit Colours (☎601 751; pl Slaveikov 7; ☻9.30am-6pm Mon-Fri) Sells student cards for 10lv.
Wash & Dry (ul Nezavisimost 3; per load 6.50lv; ☻8.30am-7pm) Laundry drop-off service.

Sights

Veliko has many attractions, but watch out! Museum admin folks are flirting with increasing the prices for museums and churches to a hefty 6lv each (a bit much for a three-minute peek into a church, by our estimation).

BULGARIA

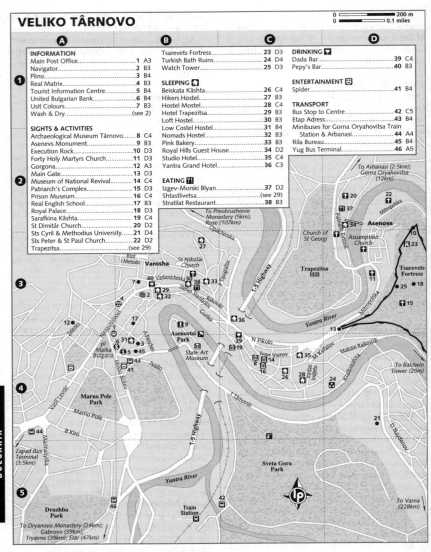

VELIKO TÂRNOVO

INFORMATION
Main Post Office.....................1 A3
Navigator................................2 B3
Plino.....................................3 B4
Real Matrix.............................4 B3
Tourist Information Centre........5 B4
United Bulgarian Bank..............6 B4
Usit Colours...........................7 B3
Wash & Dry.......................(see 2)

SIGHTS & ACTIVITIES
Archaeological Museum Târnovo......8 C4
Asenevs Monument...................9 B3
Execution Rock.....................10 D3
Forty Holy Martyrs Church.......11 D3
Gorgona..............................12 A3
Main Gate............................13 D3
Museum of National Revival....14 C4
Patriarch's Complex...............15 D3
Prison Museum......................16 C4
Real English School...............17 D3
Royal Palace........................18 D3
Sarafkina Kâshta...................19 D2
St Dimitâr Church..................20 D2
Sts Cyril & Methodius University...21 D4
Sts Peter & St Paul Church......22 D2
Trapezitsa.......................(see 29)

Tsarevets Fortress.................23 D3
Turkish Bath Ruins.................24 D4
Watch Tower........................25 D3

SLEEPING
Beiskata Kâshta....................26 C4
Hikers Hostel.......................27 B3
Hostel Mostel.......................28 C4
Hotel Trapezitsa...................29 B3
Loft Hostel..........................30 B3
Low Costel Hostel.................31 B4
Nomads Hostel.....................32 B3
Pink Bakery.........................33 B3
Royal Hills Guest House..........34 D2
Studio Hotel.........................35 C4
Yantra Grand Hotel................36 C3

EATING
Izgev-Morski Blyan................37 D2
Shtastlivetsa...................(see 29)
Stratilat Restaurant...............38 B3

DRINKING
Dada Bar.............................39 C4
Pepy's Bar...........................40 B3

ENTERTAINMENT
Spider.................................41 B4

TRANSPORT
Bus Stop to Centre................42 C5
Etap Adress.........................43 B4
Minibuses for Gorna Oryahovitsa Train Station & Arbanasi......44 A4
Rila Bureau..........................45 B4
Yug Bus Terminal..................46 A5

Fun walks are free though. A great one goes up to the nearby village of Arbanasi (p173). In town, be sure to walk along **ul Gurko**, Veliko's best-preserved street, which twists its way along the gorge. Across from it – reached by a bridge from near the Etap Adress bus stop – is the huge 1985 **Asenevs Monument** (aka Four Bulgarian Kings Monument, for

Assen, Petâr, Ivan Shishman and Kaloyan), with great views looking back. Meanwhile, up from the main road **ul Stambolov** in the centre, ul Rakovski is lined with cobblers, woodcarvers and blacksmiths.

Also, along the old road south of the Tsarevets gate, there are interesting **Turkish bath ruins**, a mound of brick covered in brush and vegetation. You can enter and see original details. One Turkish local told us, 'When I was a kid 40 years ago, we used to go down into the tunnels that connected with another bath and the fortress – but it was too scary to go far'. They're not accessible now.

TSAREVETS FORTRESS

About a kilometre from the centre, this mammoth **fortress** (admission 4lv; 8am-7pm Apr-Sep, 9am-5pm Oct-Mar) sits stoically, sprawling on a site shared over the centuries by Thracians, Romans and Byzantines. What's seen now – a triangular, high-walled fortress with the remains of more than 400 houses and 18 churches – was largely built between the 5th and 12th centuries.

From the **main gate,** follow the left wall past a **watch tower** to the northern end where you can see **execution rock,** from where convicted souls were pushed. Back south, the giant Bulgarian flag flies from the ruined **Royal Palace.** Its high-up neighbour is the renovated **patriarch's complex.** Inside are surprisingly modern murals and a suspended altar. Back near the main gate, you can follow the south wall to **Baldwin Tower.**

The after-dark, half-hour **sound and light show** (636 952), a slightly silly but worthwhile show of colourful lights and music lighting up the full fortress, is arranged frequently for group tours. It costs around €300 for the group, and you can watch for free. It's held most nights in summer; listen for the warning bells after sunset.

Buses 20, 400 and 110 make the trip between the centre and the site.

MUSEUMS

Sarafkina Kâshta (635 802; ul Gurko 88; adult/student 4/2lv; 9am-5pm Mon-Fri Dec-Mar, 9am-6pm Tue-Sun Apr-Nov) is a two-storey former banker's home from 1861 with a sitting room set up upstairs, including traditional objects and interesting photos.

Further east along ul Gurko, past the Golemuyat monument, the zigzag steps to the left lead up to the **Archaeological Museum Târnovo** (601 528; ul Ivan Vazov; admission 4lv; 9am-6pm Tue-Sun). The 2nd floor is best, with a fun 1961 mural of Veliko in its capital life and an excellent new collection of locally found Roman objects.

Next door, the interesting **Museum of National Revival** (629 821; ul Ivan Vazov; adult/student 4/2lv;

9am-6pm Wed-Mon) occupies the 1872 National Assembly, where the country's first constitution was penned (and leaders picked Sofia as the post-Ottoman capital).

Just behind is the little **Prison Museum** (Zatvor; ul Ivan Vazov; adult/student 4/2lv; 9am-5.30pm Tue-Sat), where Liberation-era hero Vasil Levski spent a few of his last days in 1873. Torture is never funny, but the staff's straight-faced demonstrations of beatings and piped-in wails on cassette tempt a chuckle.

CHURCHES & MONASTERIES

Veliko is home to numerous churches, particularly in the Asenova quarter. Walking there from the Tsarevets gate, you first pass the **Forty Holy Martyrs Church** (ul Mitropolska; adult/student 5/1lv; 9am-5.30pm). It dates from 1230, and King Kaloyan's tomb (apparently) was found here in 2004, but so much is reconstructed that feeling the history takes imagination.

Probably most rewarding for most is the **St Peter & St Paul Church** (ul Mitropolska; adult/student 4/2lv; 9am-6pm), past the bridge. Inside are fragments of many old frescos from the 14th to 17th centuries. Across the pedestrian bridge, you can reach the often-closed, Byzantine-influenced **St Dimitâr Church** (ul Patriarh Evtimii), Veliko's oldest church, and where the Assen brothers declared rebellion in 1185. Ask at the Tsarevets gate about unlocking churches if they're closed.

Activities

Trapezitsa (635 823; www.trapezitca1902.com; ul Stefan Stambolov 79; 9am-6pm Mon-Fri), which (true to its website) dates from 1902, arranges **rock-climbing** trips, sells a climbing guide (6lv) and can point you to local climbing or biking clubs. Nearby climbs include St Trinity Monastery and Usteto (2km south).

For biking options, **Gorgona** (601 400; www .gorgona-shop.com, in Bulgarian; ul Zelenka 2; 10am-1pm & 2-7pm Mon-Fri, 10am-2pm Sat) rents out mountain bikes (10lv per day) and helmets (2lv per day) and knows good trails to ride. Head up the steps across ul Nezavisimost from the post office.

Nomads Hostel (p172) offers biking tours too.

Ask at the tourist centre about **horse riding** in Arbanasi and other **hiking** trails in the area.

Courses

Real English School (605 749; www.realenglish school.eu; ul Hadzhi Dimitâr 21) offers individual or group Bulgarian classes; an individual class is 20lv per hour, a group course with three students is 45lv per week. **Sts Cyril & Methodius University** (☎ 600 362, 623 670; www.cet-vtu.com; ul Teodosi Tarnovski 2) also offers Bulgarian-language courses.

Sleeping

Touts offering abundant private rooms (around 12lv or 15lv per person) usually await buses and trains at the stations, though some travellers end up at hostels the next day complaining about so-so rooms far from the centre.

Hikers Hostel (☎ 0889 691 661; www.hikers-hostel .org; ul Rezevoarska 91; camp sites/dm/r incl breakfast €7/10/26; 💻) Way up a cobbled path, this nice, smallish hostel is a hike to reach but has superb views – the upstairs sitting room, with Mexican blankets and a wall mural one guest painted, looks onto the fortress's light show.

Hostel Mostel (☎ 0897 859 359; www.hostel mostel.com; ul Iordan Indjeto 10; camp sites/dm/s/d incl breakfast €9/11/23/30; 💻) Bulgaria's best hostel resides in a transformation of an old Turkish home, with sitting areas on two decks, under vines or in a cushions-on-the-floor TV room; it's roomy and its en suite private rooms are nicer than most hostels' private choices. Free breakfast and dinner (with beer) is served in a stone-wall dining room downstairs. There are three dorms and four private choices.

Nomads Hostel (☎ 603 092; www.nomadshostel.com; ul Gurko 27; dm incl breakfast 20-22lv, d 50-54lv; ❄ 💻) Veliko's only air-conditioned hostel, Nomads sits on the historic Gurko with straight-on looks at the gorge. Nine- and four-bunk dorms have their own bathrooms, and staff lead biking trips and tours to Dryanavo Monastery and Kazanlâk (40lv per person if two or three go).

Hotel Trapezitsa (☎ 635 823; www.trapezitca1902 .com; ul Stefan Stambolov 79; s/d 30/40lv) The one-time lone budget choice is a bit worn out these days (manifesto-brown carpets and faded furnishings don't help), but most rooms look right over the gorge.

Pink Bakery (☎ 633 339; www.the-pink-bakery .com; ul Rezervoarska 5; r 45-55lv) On a cobbled side street, this lovely dollhouse-style cheapie with shared bathrooms mixes colourful themes in a grab-bag of six rooms (eg orange-slice bedspreads); some come with terraces.

Yantra Grand Hotel (☎ 958 2843; www.yantrabg .com; pl Velchova Zavera 2; s/d incl breakfast from 90/120lv;

❄ 💻 🛁) Off Veliko's main strip, this 71-room, eight-floor hotel is popular for valley views directly onto the fortress; it's all nice, if a bit typical business-standard. The spa and indoor pool help.

Royal Hills Guest House (☎ 0889 210 707; royal _hills@mail.bg; ul Tsar Ivan Assen II 3a; house 95lv; ❄) In the quiet Asenova quarter, an Ikea shopping spree filled this pleasant stream-side house with two rooms, full kitchen/TV room and barbecue area out back. Comfy for four, snug for five or six.

Beiskata Kâshta (☎ 602 480; www.beiskata.com; ul Chitalishtna 4; s/d incl breakfast from 98/138lv May-Sep, from 78/114 Oct-Apr; ❄ 💻 🛁) Fronted by a *mehana* eatery, this cute seven-room guest house has 19th-century-style rooms with modern touches like TVs and wi-fi.

Studio Hotel (☎ 604 010; www.studiohotel-vt.com; ul Todor Lefterov 4; s/d incl breakfast 140/180lv; ❄ 💻) The 13-room Studio lives the city life, with surprisingly slick rooms with black carpet and bold wallpaper. Best are the fortress views (room 7 is best) and getting your free breakfast on the outside terrace.

Other reliable choices:

Low Costel Hostel (☎ 0885 726 733; www.lowcostel hostel.com; ul Assen Ruskov 6; dm/d 16/40lv; 💻) Compact and colourful British-run hostel, with two clean dorms, a private double and a lounge area. No breakfast, but there's a kitchen to use.

Loft Hostel (☎ 0877 323 255; www.thelofthostel.com; ul Kapitan Diado Nikola 2a; dm 18-20lv, d 44lv, incl breakfast; 💻) Overlooking the main drag, bunking at the American-run Loft feels like living in a stylish little Bulgarian home – because it is. Owners live upstairs. Only one shared bathroom.

Eating

Many eateries can be found along ul Hristo Botev and ul Nezavisimost, though many aren't particularly inspiring.

Stratilat Restaurant (ul Rakovski 11; sandwiches & pizza from 3.50lv; ⏰ 8am-midnight) Named 'the lucky one', perhaps because it's hard to get a seat at the outside tables, the Stratilat can be a bit snooty, but irresistible for its sandwiches, cakes and coffee.

Shtastlivetsa (☎ 600 656; ul Stefan Stambolov 79; mains from 4.50lv; ⏰ 10am-11pm) If you're into detail, allow an hour to look over the two giant menus (for Bulgarian or Italian food) in the two-storey spot overlooking the gorge that's long been Veliko's most popular eating place. There are nine 'diet pizzas' made of rye flour (5.50lv to 7.90lv), plus a 28lv 'Gypsy' family-sized meal and a mere 82 salads.

Izgev-Morski Blyan (ul Patraiarh Evtimii 6; mains from 5lv; ☏ 6-11.45pm Mon, 11.30am-2pm & 6-11.45pm Tue-Sat) A quiet local hang-out across the ped bridge in the Asenova quarter, this deck restaurant serves nicely grilled fish dishes – Bulgarian menu only.

Drinking

Pepy's Bar (ul Veneta Boteva 5; ☏ 8am-11pm) A laid-back, softly lit bar with mixed ages, big windows and a grab-bag decor (Jackie O photos, Bulgarian 78s).

Dada Bar (ul Stefan Stambolov; beer 2lv; ☏ 6pm-1am) A few steps down from the street, this pocket-sized dive plays imported rock 'n' roll (Kinks, White Stripes) for mostly locals chatting at the bar. Small deck in back.

Entertainment

Follow students to the latest clubs, such as **Spider** (ul Hristo Botev; admission 2-3lv), a two-floor dance club with dance areas around a barstool centre; access through a plain brown door next to the City Pub, near the Etap bus stand.

Getting There & Away
BUS

Veliko has three bus stations. **Yug Bus Terminal** (☏ 620 014; ul Hristo Botev), a 15-minute walk downhill from the centre, and the glorified bus stand of **Etap Adress** (☏ 630 564; Hotel Etâr, ul Ivailo 2) serve most bigger, long-distance destinations. For buses to Sofia (17lv, 3½ hours) or Varna (17lv, 3½ hours), it's easiest to catch one of the 10 daily stopping at Etap Adress, which also sends buses to Shumen (14lv, two hours). Yug serves these destinations, plus Burgas (18lv to 23lv, four hours) four times daily, a midday bus with a quick transfer in Ruse to Bucharest (28lv) and a night bus to İstanbul (40lv, seven hours).

Yug also sends a morning bus to Ruse (8lv, 2½ hours) and Plovdiv (14lv, four hours); otherwise other buses to these two towns leave from the **Zapad Bus Terminal** (☏ 640 908), located 4km west of the centre, which also has buses to regional destinations including Tryavna and Gabrovo. Bus 10, among others, heads west to the terminal from ul Vasil Levski.

CAR
The tourist information centre and most hostels can arrange rental cars from 25lv per day, the best deal in the country.

TRAIN
Veliko's small **train station** (☏ 622 130, 620 065) sends about five direct trains a day to Ruse (6.80lv, about three hours), one to Plovdiv (11lv, five hours) and eight to Tryavna (3.80lv, 45 minutes). There are five daily trains to Sofia (15.40lv, five to six hours), and four to Varna (12.50lv, four or five hours) require a change at the busier **Gorna Oryakhovitsa train station** (☏ 0618-26 118), 13km north of town. Minibuses along ul Vasil Levski, or bus 10 east from the centre, head there every 10 or 15 minutes; a taxi is about 15lv.

An overnight train to İstanbul (couchette/ sleeper 58/72lv, 13¾ hours) and mid-morning train to Bucharest (29lv, six hours) stop in Veliko. Buy international tickets at **Rila Bureau** (☏ 622 2042; ul Tsar Kolyan; ☏ 7.30am-6pm Mon-Sat Jul & Aug, 8am-4pm Mon-Sat Sep-Jun), in the alley behind the information centre.

There's a walkway from the train platform (away from station) that connects to an underpass leading to ul Hristo Botev. Catch bus 4, 5, 13, 30 or 70 heading south from outside the station to reach the centre. Frankly a taxi (about 4lv or 5lv) is a better deal if you're not alone.

AROUND VELIKO TÂRNOVO
Nowhere in Bulgaria has better day-trip potential than Veliko. And because car rental here is so cheap, it's worth buddying up and making a DIY adventure for a day or two. Interesting places besides those already mentioned here include the lovely, historic hill town of **Elena** (37km southeast), the empty Roman ruins of **Nikopolis-ad-Istrum** (admission 4lv; 20km north) and the valley hiking trails (and eerie caves) at **Emen** (27km northwest).

Nomads Hostel and Hostel Mostel (opposite) offer interesting biking or swimming-hole day trips.

Arbanasi Арбанаси
☏ 062 / pop 1500
In Veliko's glory years, the walled villas of high-on-a-hill Arbanasi (4km northeast of Veliko) housed much of the king's royal entourage. It's still mostly for the privileged, as you'll see many sports cars with Sofia plates pulling into private villas.

The one site most worth seeking out is the 16th-century **Nativity Church** (☎ 604 323; adult/student 4/2lv; ☺ 9am-5pm), 200m west of the bus stop. Outside, it's a ho-hum building, built that way to fool Ottomans from guessing its religious purposes. Inside, it bursts with colourful, ceiling-to-floor murals depicting 2000 scenes, including the evocative 'wheel of life'.

Perhaps the best thing about Arbanasi is getting here via the 90-minute **hiking trail**. Walk through the Asenova Quarter on the west side of Tsarevets then cross a ped bridge; the trail begins below the bridge.

Panorama (☎ 623 421; d 40-50lv; ☒) is a friendly, simple and daringly nontraditional hillside hotel, located about 400m west of the bus stop. It has a few rooms and hilariously large ice-cream portions at its cafe overlooking Veliko.

It's about 5lv to reach Arbanasi by taxi from Veliko. Some Gorna Oryakhovitsa–bound minibuses from ul Vasil Levski in Veliko stop in Arbanasi (all come within a 700m walk of the centre).

Preobrazhenski Monastery
Приображенски Манастир

Dating from 1360, this hilltop **monastery** (admission 2lv) can be reached via the Ruse road, 6km north of the centre, or by a 90-minute hike beginning near the Hikers Hostel (turn right on a path going through a small playground). Its location – on a cliff below a higher wall – is gorgeous, as are the murals by Zahari Zograf (of Rila Monastery fame). The giant boulders strewn around the compound are narrow misses from a 1991 earthquake. Looking west, you can see hilltop **Sveta Troitsa convent** – a nunnery dramatically separated by the valley below.

Dryanovo Monastery Дряновски Манастир
☎ 0676

Top-heavy cliffs stoop over this charming stream-side **monastery** (☎ 72 332), 24km south of Veliko. Built in the 12th century, the monastery has been destroyed once or twice, and was last rebuilt in the early 18th century. Behind is the **Bacho Koro cave** (short/long tour 2/4lv; ☺ 9am-6pm Apr-Oct, 10am-4pm Nov-Mar), a damp 12-degree cave that has evidence of life from 40,000 BC.

Above is a **hiking trail** that links Dryanovo with nearby village Bozhentsite (15km). For a superfun 45-minute loop, go left upstream from the monastery, past the trashed-out 'EU

toilet' to a dark swimming hole, and up some *steep* steps to an overview near some Roman roads; it continues on to the cave entrance.

There are bungalows and a small hotel nearby, and along the river a leafy open-air *mehana* serving Bulgarian food. Gabrovo-bound buses will stop at the turn-off (if requested), about 5km south of the town of Dryanovo, from where it's a 1.5km walk to the monastery.

Tryavna Трявна
☎ 0677 / pop 12,000

Bulgaria's cute woodcarving capital, revival-era Tryavna – reached by a web of backroads (39km south of Veliko) – is a bit like an Arbanasi without (so many) tourists, or an Etâr without the ticket price.

From the neighbouring bus and train stations, walk along ul Angel Kânchev 400m (over the creek) to the centre, where you'll find a **tourist information centre** (☎ 2247; www.tryavna.bg; ul Angel Kânchev 33; ☺ 9am-noon & 2-5pm Mon-Fri). Several hikes and bike trails loop to nearby villages; you can **rent bikes** from **Hotel Tryavna** (☎ 3448) for 5lv.

The town has about a dozen signed museums, traditional homes and churches to see. All are allegedly open 9am to 7pm May to September, 9am to 5pm October to April, and most cost 2lv. West of the tourist office, you'll find **St Archangel Michael Church** (admission 1lv), with a two-storey collection of icons, and **Shkolo**, a school-turned-art-museum next to the chiming clock tower.

Over the arched bridge to ul Slaveikov, 150m past antiques shops, is the **Daskalov House** (1808; ul Slaveikov 27), dedicated to woodcarving.

In the centre, **Trevnenski Kât** (☎ 2033; ul Kânchev 8; s/d from 20/30lv) is a buzzing tavern-restaurant with a few simple rooms.

From Veliko, it's best taking the train (3.80lv, 45 minutes). Otherwise there are frequent buses from Gabrovo (2.90lv, 25 minutes).

Etâr Етър
☎ 066

Played up by many tour operators, **Etâr Ethnographic Village Museum** (☎ 801 838; adult/student 4/1lv; ☺ 8.30am-6pm May-Sep, 9am-4.30pm Oct-Apr), 8km south of the large town of Gabrovo, is an open-air museum with water-powered mills and workshops showing how life was in the 19th century. You can get traditional hats

(36lv) and snacks, then hike 3km uphill to the pleasant **Sokolski Monastery**.

Buses go to/from Gabrovo every 20 to 45 minutes.

Shipka Pass Шипченски проход

Capping one of Bulgaria's loveliest drives, the Shipka Pass (about 60km south of Veliko) is home to a six-storey **Freedom Monument** (admission 2lv; ⊗ 9am-5pm summer, 9am-4.30pm Sat & Sun winter), the scene of a decisive battle of the Russian-Turkish War in 1877. This monument has exhibits and superb 360-degree views of the Valley of Roses.

It's a Shipka tradition to finish a visit with **buffalo yoghurt** (birosko mlyako; cup 1.70lv) at the roadside stands.

With wheels, head along the mountaintop, 12km to **Mt Buzludzha** (aka 'the UFO building'), a menacing, spaceship-styled building that marks the place where the Bulgarian Communist Party was founded in 1891. The copper exterior was stripped bare in recent years, and its front stairs are now used as a defecating spot for apparently hundreds of horses, sheep and cows. There are creepy ways in to see faded tile mosaics (take a torch and a friend).

Buses between Kazanlâk and Gabrovo will drop you off at the pass if you ask, or you could make a long hike up from Shipka village, near Kazanlâk.

SHUMEN ШУМЕН

☎ 054 / pop 103,000

Freedom's bells didn't ring evenly across this great land, and Shumen (among other places) keeps up a rather grim vibe with the ol' housing blocks, sadly bereft of much of the quaint cobbled-lane punch of other historic towns. It's on the travel map chiefly for nearby attractions (forts, monuments, ancient capitals), plus a fresh bottle of Bulgaria's best beer, Shumensko.

It's old though. It's been around since before Bulgaria's first empire began in nearby Veliki Preslav in the 7th century.

Orientation & Information

The main square, pl Osvobozhdenie, is about 1km west of the neighbouring bus and train stations on bul Slavyanksi. Here you'll find ATMs, cafes, a post office and a **tourist information centre** (☎ 853 773; bul Slavyanski 17; ⊗ 8.30am-5pm Mon-Fri).

Sights

Viewed from afar, it's an enigmatic grey mass overlooking town, but up close the super **Creators of the Bulgarian State Monument** (admission 3lv; ⊗ 24hr) welcomes those who climb the 1.3km from the centre (or take a taxi). Its incredible cubist-style horseback figures peer down from between crevices like stone Don Quixotes. The monument (ambitiously described as 'Europe's largest triptych mosaic') was built in 1981 to commemorate Bulgaria's 1300th birthday. There's rarely anyone around to sell you a ticket.

On a hilltop 6km west of the centre, **Stariyat Grad** (Shumen Fortress; adult/student 3/1lv; ⊗ 9am-5pm Apr-Oct, 9am-3pm Nov-Mar) is a spread-out site lived in by Thracians, Romans and Byzantines; it peaked in the 10th century. A road marked 'Pametnik Sâzdateli na Bâlgarskata Dârzhava' meanders 5km to the Creators monument.

Everything in the impressive 18th-century (and still active) **Tombul Mosque** (☎ 802 875; ul Rakovski 21; admission 2lv; ⊗ 9am-6pm), 500m southwest of pl Osvobozhdenie, is original – much of the paint has been atmospherically lost to the ages.

Sleeping & Eating

Solo Hotel (☎ 981 571; www.hotelsolo-bg.com; ul Volov 2; s/d 40/50lv; 🞨 🖳) Just off the pedestrian crawl in the centre (next to a popular Chinese restaurant), the Solo keeps seven spatial room with mixed designs.

Zamâka (☎ 800 049; www.zamakbg.com; ul Vasil Levski 17; s/d incl breakfast 40/60lv; 🞨 🖳) This comfy 12-room hotel (150m west of the post office, towards the mosque) has a good restaurant downstairs.

There are a couple of *mehana* restaurants on ul Tsar Osvoboditel.

Getting There & Away

Numerous buses en route to Sofia (27lv, five hours) and Varna (10lv, 1½ hours) stop in Shumen. Also, at least four buses daily go to Ruse (8lv, 2½ hours) and Veliko Târnovo (14lv, two hours).

Around nine daily direct trains leave for Varna (6.20lv, 1¾ hours), five for Sofia (17.70lv, 6½ hours), one for Plovdiv (16.70lv, 7½ hours) and one to Veliko Târnovo (8.10lv, 2½ hours). Trains to Ruse (8.50lv, 3½ hours) require a change in Kaspichan.

BULGARIA

MADARA МАДАРА

☎ 05313 / pop 1300

Off the main highway between Shumen and Varna, Madara is a simple village that's home to the cute horseman that brands many of Bulgaria's stotinki coins: the **Madara National Historical & Archaeological Reserve** (☎ 2095; admission 4lv; ⊙ 8am-7.30pm summer, 8am-5pm winter). The enigmatic 23m bas-relief on a sheer rock wall depicts a horseman running over a lion. It's believed to date from the 8th century, though some argue it's much older.

Afterwards follow a trail north and up 378 steps to a mountaintop **fortress**.

From Shumen, 16km west, buses reach Madara village (2lv, 30 minutes) five times daily, the last returning at 6.30pm. You can also take the train (1.40lv, five daily). From Madara village follow the road towards the mountain (just east), and take the left fork; it's a 2km walk slightly uphill.

RUSE РУСЕ

☎ 082 / pop 175,00

Confident and thriving, Ruse (pronounced roo-*say*) boasts a Habsburg-era centre with enough ornate buildings on central leafy squares to offer a little pomp not often found in Bulgaria. The museums here are good, and the often overlooked Rusenski Lom Nature Park potentially offers a couple of days of sightseeing.

Ruse's **March Days Music Festival** is held in the last two weeks of March.

Orientation

From the bus and train stations, ul Borisova leads 2km north to the central pl Svoboda and pedestrian mall ul Aleksandrovska. The Danube is several blocks further north from pl Svoboda.

Information

Bulbank (pl Sveta Troitsa 5; ⊙ 8.30am-4.30pm) Just southeast of pl Svoboda (next to the red opera house).
Internet Dexter (ul Duhovno Vûzrazhdane 10; per hr 1.20lv; ⊙ 24hr)
Left luggage (train station; per day 2lv; ⊙ 24hr)
Post office (pl Svoboda)
Telephone centre (ul Panov 14; ⊙ 8am-midnight) A block south of pl Svoboda, to the left as you enter the pedestrian mall from the south.
Tourist information centre (☎ 824 704; ul Aleksandrovska; ⊙ 9am-6pm Mon-Fri, 9.30am-12.30pm & 1-6pm Sat & Sun) Tons of free brochures, cheerful English-spoken help (and *banitsa* tips) and a great city map with suggested walking tours. Just northeast of pl Svoboda.

Sights

Ruse is proud to be called 'Little Vienna' – even if no one outside it knows of its reputation. Its Danube locale meant many Viennese architects floated down to rebuild a city razed during the war for liberation in the 1870s, evident all over the centre with fine buildings like the lovely **Drama Theatre** (pl Svoboda) or ones surrounding the lovely **pl Batemberg**.

On pl Batemberg, a few blocks west of the centre, you'll find the newly opened **History Museum** (☎ 825 002; www.museumruse.com; pl Batemberg 3; adult/student 4/0.50lv; ⊙ 8.30am-5.30pm Tue-Sat), which occupies a lovely 1882 building. Chronological exhibits start way back, with prehistoric 'boomerangs' from 4500 BC found in the area and an unreal collection of silver Thracian wine goblets.

Sadly much of Ruse seems to turn its back to the Danube (or Romania), but there is a **promenade** that gets views of both, and you can access the shore at various points. Also here, across from the grey communist-era Riga Hotel, the fun lil' **Museum of the Urban Lifestyle in Ruse** (☎ 820 997; ul Tsar Ferdinand 39; adult/student 4/1lv; ⊙ 9am-noon & 1-5.30pm Mon-Sat) is essentially a two-fer – the ground floor is all about women (early 1900s attire, protest, feminism) and the 2nd floor is a faithful recreation of a rich town house.

Heading about 400m east from pl Svoboda along the pedestrian mall, you'll reach the **Soviet Army Monument**, at the start of the **Youth Park**.

About 300m southwest, via ul Saedinenie, you'll reach the rather bizarre gold-domed **Pantheon of the National Revival** (☎ 820 998; ul Tsar Osbvoboditel; admission 1lv; ⊙ 9am-noon, 1-5.30pm Mon-Sat), dedicated to those who fought the Ottomans in 1878, with a collection of swords under a bizarre gold-mosaic tile. Just outside (to the right, as you exit) is **Paniot Ivanov Kitov's tomb**, a fighter from the period. He was apparently a remarkably moustached man.

Sleeping

OUR PICK **English Guest House** (☎ 823 100; babatonka@gmail.com; ul Baba Tonka 28; s/d 35/50lv; ✖ 💻) Run by a hilarious Brit in love with his new city, this six-room spot, a couple of blocks northwest of pl Svoboda, buzzes with activity, as travellers

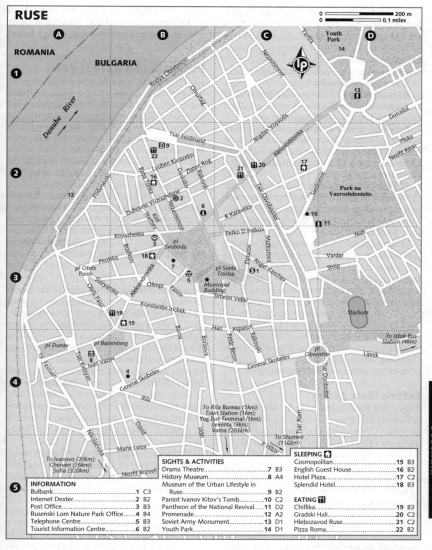

RUSE

BULGARIA

and property buyers mingle in the common room. Shared bathroom, wi-fi access, and big plans for regional trips and a restaurant complex outside town.

   Hotel Plaza (☎ 820 008; ul Bolyarska 15; s 35-49lv, d 69lv; ☒ ☐) On a residential strip just east of the central square, the Plaza has comfortable, clinically clean, tiled rooms.

   Splendid Hotel (☎ 825 972; splendid@rousse.bg; ul Aleksandrovska 51; s/d 53/64lv; ☒ ☐) Off the main square, the Splendid has average modern rooms and a rather serious vibe.

   Cosmopolitan (☎ 805 063; www.cosmopolitan hotelbg.com; ul Dobri Nemirov 1-3; s/d incl breakfast 80/150lv; ☒ ☐ ☒) Spa hotel and business mecca, the Cosmo is urban chic all the way – a bit at odds with the century-old buildings it faces. But rooms are carpeted and cool, and there are two pools.

Eating

There are plenty of open-air cafes and snacks to find on ul Aleksandrovska.

Hlebozavod Ruse (ul Aleksandrovska; banitsa 0.70lv; ☉ 6.30am-7.30pm Mon-Fri, 6.30am-2pm Sat) Ruse's best take-away *banitsa* draws locals all day.

Pizza Roma (ul Nezavisimost 16; pizza from 5lv; ☉ noon-midnight) Nothing fancy here, just the best pizzas in Ruse. Green tables spill outside a basement eatery by modern buildings, half a block from the river.

ourpick **Chiflika** (ul Otets Paisii 2; mains 5-12lv; ☉ 11am-2am) Ruse's top Bulgarian restaurant, just north of pl Batemberg, has richly traditional rooms and a stone-floor mezzanine for tasty local fare in a buzzing spot.

Leventa (☎ 867 115; www.leventa-bg.net; ul General Kutuzov; mains from 10lv; ☉ 11am-midnight) Splurgers can make it up south of the train station, under the hilltop TV tower, where a 19th-century Turkish fort has been transformed into a geared-for-groups winery and restaurant.

For groceries, head northwest on ul Aleksandrovska 200m from pl Svoboda to **Gradski Hali** (ul Aleksandrovska 93; ☉ 8am-10pm). Just behind it to the north is residential street ul Omurtag, which leads four blocks to a couple of open-air restaurants with river views.

Getting There & Away

Ruse's **Yug Bus Terminal** (ul Pristanishtna; www.auto gararuse.org) has frequent daily buses heading to Sofia (15lv to 20lv, five hours) and Veliko Târnovo (8lv, two hours). There are also a few buses to Varna (16lv, 3½ hours), stopping in Shumen (6lv, 1½ hours). A couple of companies send buses to İstanbul (40lv, 13 hours), including **Ozbatu** (☎ 874 777), which also sends an early-morning bus to Bucharest (20lv, three hours).

Two or three daily buses to Cherven and Ivanovo in Rusenski Lom Nature Park leave from **Iztok Bus Terminal** (☎ 845 064), 4.5km east of the centre; taxi there or take bus 2 or 13 from near the pl Oborishte roundabout.

The **train station** (☎ 820 222), next to Yug, has two daily trains to Sofia (17.20lv, seven hours), four to Veliko Târnovo (6.80lv, 2½ to 3½ hours) and two to Varna (11lv, four hours). International tickets are sold from the Rila Bureau here. Trains leave for Bucharest

(23lv, three hours) at the unreasonable hour of 3.15am or the perfectly reasonable 3pm. The daily train for İstanbul (60lv) leaves at 3.15pm.

RUSENSKI LOM NATURE PARK
ПРИРОДЕН ПАРК РУСЕНСКИ ЛОМ

Trompe l'œil lives in the Danube plain southwest of Ruse. What first appears like ho-hum rolling countryside suddenly dips to this under-rated 3400-hectare park of winding rivers, cliffside hiking paths, cave monasteries, 192 bird species and other-era villages. There are plans to expand the park (apparently) by 10 times, to more than 33,000 hectares.

Before going out, drop by Ruse's **Rusenski Lom Nature Park Office** (☎ 872 397; www.lomea.org; ul General Skobelev 7; ☉ 9am-5pm Mon-Fri). Helpful staff can point out camping grounds and hikes, and sell useful maps (3lv). Ask about **canoe trips**, in the works at the time of research.

Sights

Four kilometres east of Ivanovo (where there's a hokey info centre with brochures; see www .ivanovo.bg), the park's most famous attraction is the **Ivanovo Rock Monastery** (St Archangel Michael; ☎ 0889 370 006; adult/student 4/1lv; ☉ 9am-noon & 1-6pm Tue-Sun), a centuries-old sanctuary cut into cliffs with colourful, well-preserved 14th-century murals. Afterwards, there's a nice little loop trail that goes out over **Panorama Rock**.

From the village Bozhichen, 4km northeast of Ivanovo, there's a new 6km **hiking trail** that hugs the river on a two-hour walk back to Ivanovo. Get a trail map from the office in Ruse.

In the lovely valley village of **Cherven**, about 14km southeast of Ivanovo, the spread-out remains of the 6th-century **citadel** (adult/student 4/0.5lv) sit atop a cliff at a sharp bend in the river.

About 22km southeast of Ivanovo, the 13km long **Orlova Chuka Cave** is filled with a huge bat colony (with 25 bat species); visitors can make a 1.5km loop, though it's usually closed when bats are birthing (around May and June).

Sleeping

Many villages offer homestays, including Ivanovo and the nicer villages of Cherven and Koshov. In a red building next to the Ivanovo train station, **Kladenitsa** (☎ 0899 773 288; www.hotel

-kladeneca.com; r per person 20lv) offers simple rooms with shared bathroom and meals.

Getting There & Away

It's easiest to visit with your own wheels. Buses from Ruse's Iztok bus terminal go a few times daily to Cherven via Ivanovo and Koshov, while eight trains from Ruse reach Ivanovo (2.80lv, 25 minutes). Hiking trails link villages throughout the park.

BLACK SEA COAST

Every summer brings the annual race to the 378km coastline, the Black Sea's best expanse of golden sand on blue water, and one of Bulgaria's main draws. The package tourists fly to the sea's western shores on charter flights into (nice) Varna or (disappointing) Burgas to reach crassly overdeveloped resort 'towns' like Sunny Beach or Golden Sands; most indie travellers train or bus into Varna.

There's more to see, of course, but it takes time – or a car. If you depend on local transport, the ancient towns of Nesebâr and Sozopol follow matching plans (cobbled streets on tiny peninsula, with nearby beaches) and are easily reached by microbuses, but they're touristy. For pockets of untouched sand, head north of central Byala or make your way to Sinemorets, near the Turkish border.

VARNA ВАРНА

☎ 052 / pop 357,000

Bulgaria's second city – with Roman ruins and shady cosmopolitan streets – would be a highlight even without the Black Sea at its lip – but it's sure nice having its long beach, beach clubs and water-slide park as a bonus. Briefly called 'Stalin' after WWII, Varna's roots date to the Thracians from 4000 BC until it got refashioned as Odessos by heel-clicking Greek sailors in the 6th century BC.

Information

For entertainment listings check the free seasonal guide *Varna In Your Pocket* (www.inyourpocket.com), the annual English-language *Varna Guide* or weekly Bulgarian-language *Programata*.

Bulbank (ul Slivinitsa; ☽ 8am-6pm Mon-Fri)

Frag (pl Nezavisimost; per hr 0.50-1lv; ☽ 24hr) Get online down the spiral stairs from a back door of the Opera House.

Global Tours (☎ 601 085; www.globaltours-bg.com; ul Knyaz Boris I 67; ☽ 8am-8pm Mon-Fri, 10am-6pm Sat & Sun Jun-Sep, 9am-6pm Mon-Fri Oct-May) This travel agent books private apartments (from €25 in summer), rents cars and offers group bus tours to Balchik and Kaliakra Cape (82lv) or yacht trips (72lv).

Left luggage (main bus terminal; bul Vladislav Varenchik; per day 5lv; ☽ 7am-7pm)

Main post office (ul Sâborna 36)

Municipal tourist information centre (☎ 602 907; office@vct-bg.org; ul Batenberg; ☽ 9am-7pm Mon-Sat May-Sep, 9am-6pm Mon-Sat Oct-Apr) Drop by for area tips, plus homestay hook-ups (singles 30lv, doubles 40lv).

Peralnya (ul Voden; per load 6lv; ☽ 9am-7pm Mon-Sat) Drop-off laundry service.

Pinginivite (ul 27 Juli 13; ☽ 9am-7pm Mon-Fri, 10am-6pm Sat & Sun) This bookshop stocks maps and some English-language titles.

Sea Shadow (☎ 0887 364 711; www.guide-bg.com) One-man operation of Patrick Perev, an engaging local

---

WHY *BLACK* SEA?

Anyone who looks onto the Black Sea's turquoise blue waters may wonder about how it got its macho name. No one's sure. The ancient Greeks called the sea that Jason and the Argonauts crossed Pontus Axeinus, or 'inhospitable sea' (for its storms and mean locals); meanwhile, an old Turkish word for 'north' is Kara (or 'Black') apparently used to differentiate it from the 'south' Mediterranean. Some locals tell of tales when the ocean was on fire – undersea gases rising and taking to flame!

'Dead' was taken, or it might have worked. The sea – which is only half as salty as other seas, as Mediterranean beach-hoppers may note – is biologically dead at depths of 70m below – so no Great Whites will surface for beach snacks.

Nomenclature aside, there's a bit of debate about how the sea formed. Some scientists believe that a massive flooding, following the ice age, pushed sea water through the Bosphorus River into a previously glacially made freshwater lake around 5600 BC. The event, they say, may have inspired the flood of flood stories, including Noah's little tale. Others don't doubt such a rise, but felt it did so in a less ark-requiring 2000-year period.

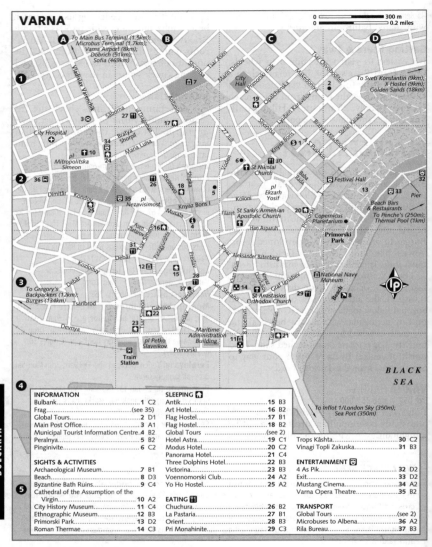

VARNA

who leads nationwide trips or day trips to Kaliakra Cape and around the coast. Charges from €80 for a day (including car, not petrol), from €50 per day for longer trips. Ask about obscure Thracian sites – one locals fear.

Dangers & Annoyances
Every summer visitors lose cameras and bags left on the beach; go in groups and have someone keep an eye on them. The area around the Cathedral of the Assumption becomes a seedy drug and prostitution zone after-hours. Taxis are known to con visitors; be cautious. Your hotel or hostel will be able to direct you to reliable ones that don't overcharge visitors.

Sights
BEACHES
You have a couple of choices – sticking in town (good enough if you have just a day) or bussing to join the resort crowd further north (p184).

Starting just steps from the train station, the Varna city **beach** is 8km long and has three essential parts: the south beach (with its pool, water slides and pirate-ship restaurant) has a nice, but quite popular stretch; the central beach has thinner sand patches and is dominated by clubs; beyond is the north beach, with nicer patches of sand, some rocky parts and a great old-school **thermal pool** with year-round hot water and some old codgers taking a dip daily all year.

All along, of course, are beach bars renting chairs and umbrellas (5lv).

Just in from the beach is the 8km-long, Vienna-inspired **Primorski Park**, a lovely strolling ground freckled with a monument or two, plus kiddie rides, open-air cafes and popcorn vendors.

ARCHAEOLOGICAL MUSEUM
Housed in a grand old two-storey building (a former girls' school), this large **museum** (☎ 681 030; ul Maria Luisa 41; adult/student 10/2lv; ☼ 10am-5pm Tue-Sun Apr-Sep, 10am-5pm Tue-Sat Oct-Mar) is a contender for Bulgaria's best. It's filled with more than 100,000 pieces from some 6000 years of local history, all remarkably well explained in English.

In the first room, a wall display posts finds of chronological periods (Stone Age, Bronze Age, Roman, Ottoman etc) to show how art evolved. Highlights include the gold and copper pieces from the Varna Eneolithic Necropolis, dating from 4500 BC and excavated in the 1970s.

OTHER SIGHTS
At the greatest of Varna's churches (and the city symbol), the towering, gold onion-domed **Cathedral of the Assumption of the Virgin** (pl Mitropolitska Simeon) is often an awkward clash of tourists in shorts, souvenir stands and local worshippers coming to light a candle. It was built in the 1880s.

Varna's second-best museum, housed in an 1860 revival building, is the **Ethnographic Museum** (☎ 630 588; ul Panagyurishte 22; adult/student 4/2lv; ☼ 10am-5pm Tue-Sun Apr-Sep, 10am-5pm Tue-Fri Oct-Mar), a complex of traditional buildings on a rising pedestrian alley. Look for an elaborately decorated town house, rooms c 1900, and camel costumes, traditionally used at new year's to ward off evil spirits.

You'll get more out of the three-floor **City History Museum** (ul 8 Noemvri 5; adult/student 4/2lv; ☼ 10am-5pm Tue-Sun) if you get the free, often funny, guide to lead you around (in an all-orange outfit, no less). The vine-covered building, just behind a pit of **Byzantine bath ruins**, focuses on the city's past, with plenty of century-old photos and souvenirs from its early resort days. The building itself has been a Belgian consulate, a hotel, and – the typical result of both – a prison.

Wedged impossibly between the St Anastasios Orthodox Church and modern housing, the leftovers of the 2nd-century-AD **Roman Thermae** (cnr ul Khan Krum & ul San Stefano; adult/student 4/2lv; ☼ 10am-5pm May-Oct, 10am-5pm Tue-Sat Nov-Apr) are easily seen from outside if you're feeling cheap.

Festivals & Events
The **Varna Summer International Festival**, which dates from 1926, features all sorts of music between May and October.

Sleeping
During high season (from June through to September), there are endless opportunities for private accommodation. Check www.accommodatebg.com for homestays from 20lv per person. There are agents in the main bus and train stations finding rooms from the same price.

Other places that can help:

Global Tours (☎ 601 085; www.globaltours-bg.com; ul Knyaz Boris I 67; ☼ 8am-8pm Mon-Fri, 10am-6pm Sat & Sun Jun-Sep, 9am-6pm Mon-Fri Oct-May) Finds apartments from 50lv per day.

Victorina (☎ 603 541; http://victorina.borsabg.com; Tsar Simeon 36; r with family from 30lv, private apt from 40lv; ☼ 7am-9pm Jun-Sep, 10am-6pm Mon-Fri Oct-May) Operates a window bureau across from the train station.

BUDGET
The Varna area has the only hostels on the Black Sea.

Gregory's Backpackers (☎ 379 909; www.hostelvarna.com; 42 Fenix St, Zvezditsa village; camp site/dm/d incl breakfast €6.50/11/28; ☐ ☒) Run by Brits, Gregory's is a great kick-back hostel base, but it's a 15-minute ride outside Varna. Staff offer one daily drop-off and pick-up ride; or bus 36 makes its way hourly. The TV room with sofas and beanbags gets busy with its DVD catalogue and the bar. Open April to October only.

Flag Hostel (☎ 089 740 8115; www.varnahostel.com; 2nd fl, ul Sheinovo 2; dm incl breakfast €10; 🖳) Also run by a Brit, the all-year Flag is a toaster's paradise – free beer in the evening, free toast-and-vodka breakfasts. At research time, it was in the process of moving to a new location (ul Maria Luisa 35) with a garden; the present location offers private rooms (a bit tight as is).

Yo Ho Hostel (☎ 088 760 1691; 088 793 3340; www .yohohostel.com; ul Ruse 23; dm/r 22/28lv; 🖳) Nothing pirate about the place; the laid-back Bulgarian guys running this urban-style hostel are more into surfing and anime-style art. Staff offer interesting regional day trips (35lv to 45lv per person).

X Hostel (☎ 054-361 881; www.xhostel.eu; Evksinograd 19, 16th Rd, Sveti Konstantin; dm/d €11/32; 🖳) About 10km north of Varna, the X is in an unreal '70s-style party pad hostel on a hill (and a 15-minute walk from a resort beach). It has lots of public spaces, including a wading pool, garden and bar. Exit the bus 1km south of the main Sveti Konstanti stop (by the Opet gas station), then follow the signs 600m to 'Villa Waikiki'.

Voennomorski Club (☎ 617 965; ul Vladislav Varenchik 2; s 21-31lv, d 42-46lv; 🍴) Filling the top two floors of the sky-blue building, rooms at the 'BNK' can be a little musty and the staff grumpy, but it'll work if the hostels are full.

MIDRANGE

Art Hotel (☎ 657 600; www.arthotelbg.com; ul Preslav 59; s/d 50/70lv; 🍴 🖳) Just off the main square, the Art Hotel is a functional hotel with hip hop on in the lobby and 11 small tiled rooms with just enough space to set your suitcase down. Rates drop by 10lv in low season.

Antik (☎ 632 167; www.galia-online.com/antik; ul Ohrid 10; r from 50lv; 🍴 🖳) On a cobbled shady lane, the friendly Antik has a mix of rooms – 60lv doubles get more space plus a balcony – in a convenient locale between the train station and central pedestrian zone. Breakfast is 5lv.

Three Dolphins Hotel (☎ 600 911; three_dolphins@ abv.bg; ul Gabrovo 27; s incl breakfast 51-60lv, d incl breakfast 61-76lv; 🍴 🖳) Set on a leafy street near the train station, the 10 recently renovated rooms mix up aquatic and Victorian motifs.

TOP END

Hotel Astra (☎ 630 524; hotel_astra@abv.bg; ul Opolchenska 9; s/d 60/84lv; 🍴 🖳) Quirky, roomy old-fashioned rooms in a 10-room turquoise building on a leafy central street. Rooms have funny brass-frame sofas and wi-fi access – rates drop by 12lv outside summer.

Panorama Hotel (☎ 687 300; www.panoramabg.com; bul Primorski 31; s/d incl breakfast 150/185lv; 🍴 🖳) This comfy, five-floor hotel is just across from the south beach, with nice carpeted rooms, huge beds and little sofas, plus extras including a gym.

Modus Hotel (☎ 660 910; www.modushotel.com; ul Stefan Stambolov 46; r from 220lv; 🍴 🖳) Varna's candidate for swank boutique hotel, this new mod choice has stylish rooms with flat-screen TVs and slick lobby restaurant. Rates drop by up to 40lv Friday through Sunday nights.

Eating

In summer, try the outdoor seats and front bar-restaurants along ul Knyaz Boris I and (a bit more upmarket) bul Slivnitsa, leading to Primorski Park, where at least a couple of waterfront bars keep hours in winter.

Vinagi Topli Zakuska (cnr ul Tsar Simeon & ul Debâr; banitsa 0.90lv; ⏰ 6am-7pm Mon-Fri, 6am-2pm Sat & Sun) The walk-up stand – its name means 'always warm breakfast' – draws lines for warm or outright hot *banitsas*.

Trops Kâshta (bul Knyaz Boris I 48; dishes 2-5lv; ⏰ 8.30am-11pm) This bright pick-and-point chain offers fresh, cheap and fast Bulgarian staples.

Chuchura (☎ 0889 213 519; ul Dragoman 11; dishes 3-12lv; ⏰ 11am-midnight) A traditional *mehana* off the main square, with nice grilled meats prepared on fire by gruff staff who become softies if you persevere.

our pick **Orient** (☎ 602 380; ul Tsaribrod 1; dishes from 4lv; ⏰ 8am-11pm) This atmospheric Turkish eatery spills onto a bench-seat, shaded passageway and fills with locals coming for lamb kebab (7lv), hummus (3.80lv), *lavash* bread (0.60lv) and stuffed vine leaves (3.50lv) – all well priced and fresh.

Pri Monahinite (☎ 611 830; ul Primorski 47; salads 4-5lv, mains 6-22lv; ⏰ 10am-11pm) For a bit more class, follow nicely dressed locals who opt for this one-time nunnery's courtyard seats. It's big on grilled meats (lots of fish and lamb) that come with more aplomb than your average tavern.

La Pastaria (☎ 632 060; ul Dragoman 25; pizza 5.90-8.90lv, seafood 12-20lv; ⏰ 11am-11pm Mon-Sat, 5-11pm Sun) This inviting Italian place with chequered tablecloths and crispy pies, also has heaps of vegie and pasta options (from 6lv) and a back deck.

Drinking

In summer, a beach nightlife zone – mostly grouped about 400m north along the beach – opens doors on the beach. At last pass, a few good 'chill-out' bars clustered near the south end.

Entertainment

Just north of the beach nightlife zone, in a long old seaside complex, you'll find clubs like **Exit** (🕙 10pm-4am), a long-standing pick. Another 100m or 200m north, you'll pass popular club 4 As Pik, and on the inland side, the classic frat-friendly Pench's, supposedly the Guinness World Record–holder for the biggest cocktail list. Check for the latest listings in *Programata* or *Varna In Your Pocket.*

If you can't handle another techno beat (or drink), the **Varna Opera Theatre** (☎ 650 555; www.operavarna.bg; pl Nezavisimost 1) stages regular shows.

The screens at **Mustang Cinema** (☎ 610 333; ul Bratya Shorpil 33; tickets 6lv) show many English-language films.

Getting There & Away

AIR

Varna airport (☎ 573 323; www.varna-airport.bg), 8km northwest of the centre, sees charter flights in summer and all-year flights to Sofia (about 210lv one way). Bus 409 goes from the bus station; a taxi is about 15lv.

BOAT

From the sea port, **Inflot 1/London Sky** (☎ 692 099, 617 577; www.londonsky-bg.com; ul Shishman 20) sends direct ferries to Odesa (from €95, nine hours) on Monday, via Constanţa, Romania (from €30, four hours) on Friday from early June through early September.

BUS

The **main bus terminal** (☎ 748 349; www.autogaravn .com; bul Vladislav Varenchik 158), 2km north of the city centre, is three stops north of the main cathedral on bus 409 or 148. A simple booth on the back platform marked 'information' can help you decipher the maze of ticket booths and overlapping bus services.

Direct domestic bus destinations:

Balchik (5lv, 50 minutes, hourly)
Burgas (12lv, 2½ hours, 10 daily)
Durankulak (9lv, 1½ hours, two daily)
Plovdiv (26lv, six hours, two daily)
Ruse (16lv, four hours, five daily)

Shumen 6lv, 1½ hours, hourly.
Sofia 30lv, seven to eight hours, half-hourly.
Veliko Târnovo 17lv, four hours, half-hourly.

International schedules are likely to change, but at our last pass, **Orlan** (☎ 500 795) sent buses to Bucharest (70lv, about 6½ hours) daily in July and August, otherwise just Monday and Friday; **Nisikli** (☎ 601 175) sent buses to İstanbul (50lv, 10 hours) at 10.30am and 9pm; and **Eurolines** (☎ 503 427) sent buses to Athens (141lv, 26 hours) Thursday through Sunday, and to Odesa (89lv, 20 hours) three days weekly.

MICROBUS

The **microbus terminal** (Avtogara Mladost; ☎ 500 039; ul Knyaz Cherkazki), 200m west of the bus station (cross the street via an underpass and go left 50m, then right past the next block), sends microbuses hourly to Burgas (12lv), and to Albena and Balchik (5lv) from about 7am to 7pm. Less-frequent services go to Nesebâr (via Sunny Beach, 10v).

Microbuses also leave for Albena (5lv) from the more convenient stop at ul Maria Luisa.

TRAIN

Direct train services from the **main train station** (☎ 630 444; bul Primorski) link Varna to Sofia (25.20lv, eight to nine hours, six daily), Plovdiv (16.70lv, 6½ to 7½ hours, four daily), Ruse (11lv, 3¾ hours, two daily), and Gorna Oryakhovitsa (for Veliko Târnovo; 14.10lv, 3½ hours, five daily).

Direct trains to Bucharest (41lv, 13 hours) are available on an overnight Russia-bound Russian train from mid-June to early September only. The rest of the year there are two options: a day train to Bucharest requiring a 2¾-hour wait in Ruse, and a night train requiring a five-hour wait in Ruse in the middle of the night. International tickets must be purchased at **Rila Bureau** (☎ 632 348; ul Preslav 13; 🕙 8am-7.30pm Mon-Fri, 8am-3.30pm Sat), a few minutes' walk from the station.

Getting Around

Local bus routes are listed on the Domino city map; tickets are sold on the bus for 1lv. Some taxi drivers overcharge – make sure the meter is on.

Global Tours (☎ 601 085; www.globaltours-bg.com; ul Knyaz Boris I 67; 🕙 8am-8pm Mon-Fri, 10am-6pm Sat & Sun Jun-Sep, 9am-6pm Mon-Fri Oct-May) rents out cars from €35 per day.

BULGARIA

NORTH COAST

Much of the coast extending 110km north of Varna to Romania is zipped through by fancy cars with Romanian or Bulgarian licence plates. The south half is mountainous, with sandy beaches and resorts, then after historic Balchik it opens up into a steppe of farmland that meets rocky seashores and less-visited villages such as Kamen Bryag.

Varna to Balchik

Just 9km north of Varna, **Sveti Konstantin** is a lovely area of elms, pines and oaks, with a nice monastery, and, of course, a beach crammed with better-than-usual '80s and '90s-era midrange resorts. From Varna, take bus 8 from ul Maria Luisa. See p182 for information about X Hostel, located here.

Another 9km north is **Golden Sands** (Zlatni Pyasâtsi), a tackier resort-burg with a busy 4km beach lined with kebab stands and a fake Eiffel Tower. In the nearby hills, the interesting **Aladzha Monastery** (☎ 052-355 460; adult/student 5/2lv; ☼ 9am-6pm May-Oct, 9am-4pm Tue-Sat Nov-Apr) is a 13th-century rock monastery with a pleasant forest hike to interesting catacombs, 600m away.

Buses 109, 209, 309 and 409 pass near Golden Sands. It might be worth taking a taxi to the monastery, then following the blue or gold signs marking trails down to Golden Sands; otherwise hop off the bus just past the monastery turn-off and walk up (about one hour).

Another 15km north, the road winds past **Albena**, a high-end resort with a far more thoughtful plan of development, and a shady camping area Gorska Feya, 500m south.

Microbuses leave hourly for Albena from Varna (5lv, 30 minutes), continuing on to Balchik.

Balchik Балчик

☎ 0579 / pop 12,000

Snuggled into white-chalk bluffs, historic Balchik is a nice English, uh, Bulgarian town (ie lots of 'new Bulgarians', aka Brits buying local homes, in the area) with good access to north-coast attractions without that resort aftertaste.

The bus stop is 1km above the historic centre, by the small beach, where you'll find ATMs, waterside restaurants, car-rental agents and a free map at the **tourist information centre** (☎ 76951; www.balchik.bg; ul Ribarski; ☼ 8am-8pm summer, 8am-5.30pm 'most days' winter).

In the 1920s, when the region was part of Romania, King Ferdinand built the **Summer Palace Queen Marie & Botanical Gardens** (Dvoretsa; ☎ 76854; mandatory separate admission each 5lv; ☼ 8am-8pm May–mid-Oct, 8.30am-6.30pm mid-Oct–Apr) for his wife because she wanted something 'small and romantic'. The palace shows off Marie's eccentric tastes, mixing Islamic and Bulgarian revival styles. It's a nice 2km walk south from the centre along the promenade.

An English couple runs **JJ's** (☎ 0887 844 953; jayjaysbalchik@yahoo.co.uk; ul Primorska 33; s/d 35/40lv), a modest five-room guest house and pub by the beachside mill.

At the south end of the waterfront, **Jupiter** (☎ 76470; www.hotel-jupiter-bg.info; ul Primorska 1a; r incl breakfast 50-60lv; ☒ ☒) has simple rooms and a pool.

The **bus station** (☎ 74069) sends frequent minibuses to Varna (5lv, one hour). Two daily buses leave at 11am and 5.30pm for Kaliakra Cape (5lv, 45 minutes), returning at 1pm and 7pm.

Kaliakra Cape & Around Нос Калиакра

The area's most arresting scene is at this 2km-long, 70m-high headland topped by the **Kaliakra Nature Reserve** (admission 3lv; ☼ 24hr) poking into the Black Sea about 30km northeast of Balchik. The crux of the site are ruins dating from the 4th-century-BC Thracian town Thirisi, which was rebuilt as Kaliakra (or 'Beautiful') in the 13th century. A couple of kilometres north (past the whirling wind-power mills) is a small beach at **Bolata**.

Kaliakra is 12km east of **Kavarna** (aka 'Heavy Metal Capital of the World'), which has done up its housing blocks with murals of Uriah Heep and Billy Idol, and hosts the annual butt-kicking Kaliakra Rock Fest on the last weekend of June. A ticket is 50/70/90lv for one/two/three nights. Kavarna's waterfront is a little sad.

About 2km east (towards Kaliakra) a small blue sign points to the legendary **Dâlbolka** (☎ 0899 911 377; dishes 5-30lv), a seaside mussels eatery huge with locals.

Two daily buses go from Balchik to Kaliakra, many more go to Kavarna, where there are a few more buses to Kaliakra during the day.

Kamen Bryag (Stone Beach) & Around

Камен Бряг

North of Kaliakra, a beachside road continues (apart from the main highway), taking in a few mostly undeveloped towns (and the un-remarkable resort at Rusalka) along the rocky seashore stretching north to Romania.

The highlight, 18km north, is Kamen Bryag, a quiet town along cliffs and the seaside site **Yailata** (admission 1.50lv), featuring 2nd- to 5th-century tombs and bigger caves along accessible waters. Some rock climbers come to the area for rope-free climbs above the water.

There's a guest house and restaurant, and many homes offer private rooms. You'll need your own transport to get here.

The lake in **Durankulak**, 33km north (on the main highway), is popular for bird-watching. From here, you can taxi to the 24-hour Romanian border (about 5lv), and walk to the hippie outpost of Vama Veche, Romania.

CENTRAL COAST

Dominating the coastal strip between Varna and Burgas – often a mountainous ride, generally inland away from the water – is the tacky resort Sunny Beach and its worthwhile ancient neighbour, the evocative Nesebâr. A few surprises can be found via out-of-the-way rough roads too.

Varna to Burgas

Byala, about 54km south of Varna, is a basic town of 2100 people, set on the rising hills above an OK beach. It's worth stopping to taste local merlot or chardonnay wines from **roadside wineries**, and go 4km north – on a dirt road past rolling hills of vineyards – to the long, gorgeous, undeveloped **Karadere beach**. Varna–Burgas buses pass by Byala.

About 13km south (past the not-bad beach town Ozbor, where buses stop), a road heads east a couple of kilometres towards the largely untouched **Irakli beach**, with a guest house and a couple of bungalows.

For the best views, a (very) rough road rambles from Irakli a long 8km up to the hill-side **Emona**, a scrambling village atop Emine Cape. The trans-Bulgarian Mt Kom/Emine Cape hike (E3) ends here, and a very rough dirt road leads down to a small beach, where you can flip off the hordes at Sunny Beach. **Villa Emona** (☎ 0556-37093; r 40lv) has rooms and a restaurant. No buses serve Irakli or Emona.

The road curves inland, bypassing Sunny Beach and Nesebâr, and continues on 31km into Burgas.

Nesebâr Несебър

☎ 0554 / pop 9360

The saving grace of the overdeveloped mess of nearby Sunny Beach – a zone of pastel-coloured resorts, water parks and a nice 8km-long beach – Nesebâr is a peninsular piece of ancient history protected by Unesco that gets rocked by visitors shopping for handicrafts and naughty postcards in summer. It is nice, though, dating back to 3000 BC when Thracians settled Mesembria here. It's loveliest at night, when the Sunny tour groups leave and the cobblestone alleys are lit up.

INFORMATION

Unicredit Bulbank (ul Mesembria; ☑ 8.30am-5pm Mon-Fri) has an ATM. The **tourist information centre** (☎ 42611; www.visitnessebar.org; ul Mesembria 10; ☑ 9am-5.30pm May-Oct) has a few brochures. Internet access is available in summer at the **White House Hotel** (ul Tsar Simeon 2; per hr 5lv).

SIGHTS

Nesebâr is famous for its handful of **Byzantine-influenced churches** built between the 6th and 14th centuries – some just ruins (and free), others locked up, others tackily filled with galleries or guarded by admission prices of 3lv.

The best to see is the 6th-century **Basilica**, a ruin of a towering frame that makes up the centre – and often fields local kids' football games. Facing the south, the earthquake-battered **St John Aliturgetos Church** (ul Mena) is set on a cliff overlooking the harbour. One of the best-preserved churches is the 14th-century **Pantrokrator Church** (ul Mesembria), sadly dominated by an art gallery.

Nesebâr's surprisingly interesting **Archaeological Museum** (☎ 46019; www.ancient-nessebar.org; ul Mesembria 2; admission 4lv; ☑ 9am-7pm Mon-Fri, 9am-6pm Sat & Sun summer, 9am-noon & 12.30-5pm Mon-Sat winter) has many Mesembrian-era pieces including little figures of guys with Billy Joel haircuts from the 3rd century BC.

A simple **promenade** runs along the rocky coast (and a small beach on the east end), with great views looking back at Sunny Beach.

To reach Sunny's 8km stretch of sand – where it's said the capacity of the hotel rooms is three times the capacity of the sand! – it's an hour walk; also, every 20 minutes, **boat taxis** ride around Nesebâr then reach Sunny Beach (15lv).

BULGARIA

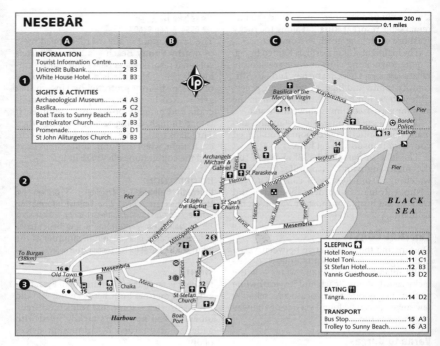

NESEBÂR

0 _____ 200 m
0 _____ 0.1 miles

INFORMATION
Tourist Information Centre......1 B3
Unicredit Bulbank......................2 B3
White House Hotel.....................3 B3

SIGHTS & ACTIVITIES
Archaeological Museum...........4 A3
Basilica...................................5 C2
Boat Taxis to Sunny Beach......6 A3
Pantrokrator Church................7 B3
Promenade.............................8 D1
St John Aliturgetos Church.......9 B3

SLEEPING
Hotel Rony...........................10 A3
Hotel Toni.............................11 C1
St Stefan Hotel......................12 B3
Yannis Guesthouse................13 D2

EATING
Tangra.................................14 D2

TRANSPORT
Bus Stop...............................15 A3
Trolley to Sunny Beach..........16 A3

To Burgas
(38km)

BLACK SEA

SLEEPING

Some hotels operate only from May through October; high-season July and August prices (listed here) are often about 75% higher than other periods.

Hotel Toni (☎ 42403, 0889 268 004; ul Kraybrezhna 20; r 50lv; ✶) Half of the 12 clean and cosy rooms have balconies facing Sunny Beach, the others look over the back courtyard and cafe. The owner speaks English. Laundry is 10lv.

Hotel Rony (☎ 44001; ul Chaika 1; s/d 65/75lv; ✶) Just in from the gates, the Rony's 11 basic rooms – up from a sprawling cafe – are fine; prices drop to 40lv in low season.

Yannis Guesthouse (☎ 45041; www.ianis.hit.bg; ul Emona 20; r 70lv; ✶ ▣) The sun-drenched deck and the simple modern rooms' balconies peer onto water.

St Stefan Hotel (☎ 43603; hotel-stefan@gmail.com; ul Ribarska 11; s 85-105lv, d 110lv Apr-Sep; ✶) This classier 17-room hotel has balconies and overlooks its namesake church.

EATING

Avoid the places with touts trying to reel in passersby for an in/out/see-you-later so-so meal. The further from the gates, the better it gets. One good choice open all year, just in from the water, is **Tangra** (ul Neptun; fish 6-20lv), with many Black Sea fish options.

GETTING THERE & AWAY

From outside the Nesebâr gate, buses go to Burgas (5lv, 40 minutes) every 40 minutes. Six minibuses head to Varna (10lv, two hours). Most Varna–Burgas buses stop 2km west on the main highway.

Bus 1 goes regularly to Sunny Beach (1lv), or if you don't mind looking goofy, there's a colourful trolley along the water (3lv).

BURGAS БУРГАС
☎ 056 / pop 229,000

Cheap flights are the great perfume for this industrial port town, with an OK beach but hardly the appeal of Varna or Sozopol.

Hilariously, the rivalry between Varna and Burgas led the Varnese founder of national chain Happy Bar & Grill to ban expansion here.

Touts around the train station sometimes offer too-good-to-be-true exchange rates.

Information

Look around for free copies of *Burgas in Your Pocket* (www.inyourpocket.com) for many listings of the south coast.

Bulbank (ul Aleksandrovska; ⏰ 8am-6pm Mon-Fri)

Dim-ant (☎ 840 779; dimant91@abv.bg; ul Tsar Simeon 15; ⏰ 8am-9pm summer, 8am-5.30pm Mon-Fri winter) Finds homestay rooms in Burgas and along the coast.

Internet Klub Nonstop (cnr ul Slavyanska & Bogoridi; per hr 1lv; ⏰ 8am-midnight) 'Nonstop' until midnight, that is.

Left luggage (per bag 2lv; ⏰ 6am-10.30pm) By the bus station.

Post office (ul Tsar Petâr; ⏰ 7.30am-7pm Mon-Fri, 8am-noon & 1-5pm Sat, 8am-1pm Sun)

Tourist Service Agency (☎ 840 601; Hotel Bulgaria, ul Aleksandrovska 21; ⏰ 7.30am-7pm Mon-Fri, 7.30am-5pm Sat & Sun) English-speaking staff book bus tickets or help with rental cars.

Sights

Rimmed by the pleasant **Maritime Park**, Burgas' 2km-long **beach** is far from the Black Sea's best, but was nice enough for MTV Europe, who held a 2008 festival here. It's lined with many umbrella spots, open-air lounges and fish restaurants, getting a bit nicer the further north you go.

Probably the best of the handful of museums in town is the **Ethnographical Museum** (☎ 842 587; ul Slavyanska 69; adult/student 2/1lv; ⏰ 9am-12.30pm & 1.30-5.40pm), with two floors of 100-year-old traditional clothing, or the pink **Archaeological Museum** (☎ 843 541; ul Bogoridi 21; adult/student 2/1lv;

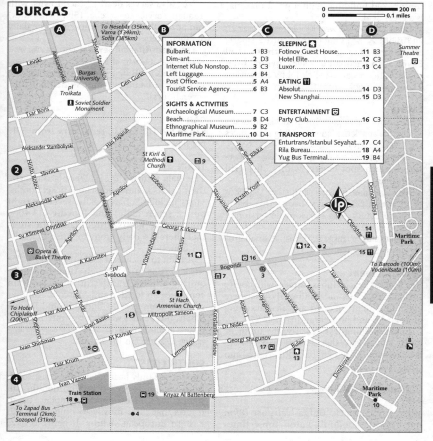

⊙ 10am-7pm Mon-Fri, 10am-6pm Sat), with various Thracian and Roman pieces.

Sleeping

Hotel Elite (☎ 845 780; ul Morska 35; s/d incl breakfast 45/50lv) In a pleasant location off ul Bogodini, the Elite has comfortable rooms – some with balcony, all with phone. Avoid the cramped attic room. No internet.

Fotinov Guest House (☎ 0879-834 130; www.hotel fotinov.com; ul Konstantin Fotinov 22; s/d 50/60lv; ✖) This 11-room boutique-inspired hotel has rust-coloured shaggy carpet, colourful bedspreads, small work desks and TVs.

Hotel Chiplakoff (☎ 829 325; www.chiplakoff.com; ul Ferdinandova 88; s/d incl breakfast 60/75lv; ✖ 🖳) If you don't mind the 10-minute walk west of the centre, this cheerful 15-room hotel in a century-old building (with a good pizzeria) is a great deal.

Luxor (☎ 847 670; www.luxor-bs.com; ul Bulair 27; s/d 95/105lv; ✖ 🖳) One of the centre's smartest options – though on a busy street – is all Egypt, with Cleopatra images, pyramid-tan colour schemes and a slick lobby restaurant a couple of blocks from the beach.

Eating

Walk up busy ul Bogoridi or ul Aleksandrovska to find the snack that suits you (big pizza slices are 1.50lv or 2lv).

Vodenitsata (Water Mill; mains from 3.50lv; ⊙ 10am-1am) A beach-spot tavern, with a busy grill in summer.

New Shanghai (ul Bogoridi 61; mains 4.90-7.90lv; ⊙ 11am-midnight) Always busy, this basic 'Chinese' eatery does a reasonable version of rice and noodles.

Absolut (ul Demokratskiya 22; ⊙ 24hr) A small grocery near the beach.

Entertainment

The hippest beach club is **Barcode**, with comfy sofas and cocktails and visiting DJs. Elsewhere you'll find plenty of open-air cafe-bars along ul Bogoridi and ul Aleksandrovska.

For something less beach-y, the unfortunately named **Party Club** (ul Bogoridi 36; ⊙ 5pm-late) is a cavernous basement bar with original and cover rock bands.

Getting There & Away

AIR

Wizz Air connects Burgas' airport (8km north) with London's Luton three times weekly. Bus 15 (1lv, 15 minutes) heads to/from Yug Bus Terminal every half-hour from 6am to 11pm.

BUS

Most buses and microbuses leave from and arrive at the convenient **Yug Bus Terminal** (☎ 842 692; near cnr ul Aleksandrovska & ul Bulair). However, Varna-bound buses from central Bulgaria usually drop off Burgas passengers at the **Zapad Bus Terminal** (☎ 831 429), 2km west of the centre. City bus 4 connects the two.

Buses from Yug go to Varna (12lv, 2½ hours) half-hourly from 6.30am to 7pm. About eight buses go daily to Sofia (25lv to 30lv, 6¼ hours), most of which stop in Plovdiv (20lv to 26lv, four hours), several go to Ruse (28lv, 4¾ hours) and two to Veliko Târnovo (26lv, 4½ hours).

Yug also serves nearby beach towns, with frequent service to Nesebâr (5lv, 45 minutes) and Sozopol (4lv, 40 minutes) and one daily to Sinemorets.

Enturtrans/Istanbul Seyahat (☎ 844 708; www .istanbulseyahat.com.tr; ul Bulair 22; ⊙ 6.30am-1am) sells tickets for Bulgaria destinations and the 1am bus to İstanbul (adult/student 50/40lv, seven hours).

CAR

Balkan Net (☎ 820 182) rents cars from 50lv per day.

TRAIN

The **train station** (☎ 845 022) sells domestic train tickets behind old-school ticket booths. Links include Sofia (18.80lv, seven to eight hours, seven daily) and Plovdiv (13.40lv, four to five hours, three daily). In summer there's a daily train to Ruse (15.50lv, 6½ hours).

A train to Bucharest (53lv, 11 hours, twice weekly) runs June through August only, requiring a quick transfer in Ruse; the train continues on to Kiev and Moscow. Another summer train goes to Budapest and Prague (283lv, three times weekly); buy international tickets at **Rila Bureau** (☎ 845 242; ⊙ 8am-4pm Mon-Fri, 8am-2.30pm Sat) in the station.

SOUTH COAST

The finest sandy beaches dot the coast south from Sozopol to the Turkish border, though some come with less-appealing modern beach resorts that cater mostly to Bulgarians and Eastern European visitors. It helps to have wheels, but you can reach more-rewarding spots (like Sinemorets) by bus too.

Sozopol Созопол
☎ 0550 / pop 4650

A jutting peninsula of cobbled streets, beaches and Greek roots, touristy Sozopol is a Bulgarian favourite summer destination. But unlike its rival cousin to the north, Nesebâr, it misses that crass Sunny Beach package-trip beat.

ORIENTATION & INFORMATION

The town, 31km southeast of Burgas, has two parts: the peninsular (old) and inland Harmanite (new). In Old Town, you'll find foreign-exchange offices and a couple of

banks including **Investbank** (ul Apollonia), and **Unicredit Bulbank** (ul Republikanska) in New Town. Get info at www.sozopol.com. Agents like **Enigma Tours** (☎ 22693; ul Kulata 5) find private accommodation from 35lv.

The 10-day **Apollonia Festival** (www.apollo nia.bg), brings music and theatre, beginning on 1 September.

SIGHTS

Sozopol has two good beaches, though the water is sometimes a little rough. The smaller **town beach**, about 500m long, and the much longer **Harmanite Beach** are lined with cafes with umbrellas to rent. **Gradina Beach**, arcing to the north towards Chernomorets, has more room (along with a fewer cafes) and calmer

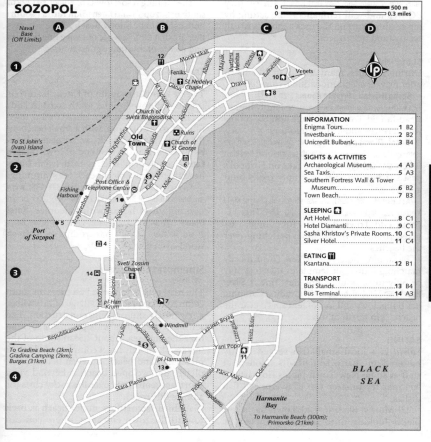

SOZOPOL

INFORMATION	
Enigma Tours	1 B2
Investbank	2 B2
Unicredit Bulbank	3 B4

SIGHTS & ACTIVITIES	
Archaeological Museum	4 A3
Sea Taxis	5 A3
Southern Fortress Wall & Tower Museum	6 B2
Town Beach	7 B3

SLEEPING	
Art Hotel	8 C1
Hotel Diamanti	9 C1
Sasha Khristov's Private Rooms	10 C1
Silver Hotel	11 C4

EATING	
Ksantana	12 B1

TRANSPORT	
Bus Stands	13 B4
Bus Terminal	14 A3

BULGARIA

conditions; get there after the first stop on a north-bound bus.

Another popular summer attraction is hiring sea taxis to reach swimming spots offshore, and the 6.6-sq-km **St John's (Ivan) Island**, just offshore, with a 19th-century lighthouse and 70 species of birds. From July through to early September there are regular hour-long **night cruises** (per person 10lv) at 7pm and 8.15pm. Boat day trips to Nesebâr cost 45lv per person. To hire a boat, look for 'sea taxis' at the port.

In Old Town, there are several churches and museums, all of which tend to be closed in the low season. The most in-depth is the **Archaeological Museum** (ul Han Krum 2; admission 3lv; ⊙ 8am-5pm, closed Sat & Sun winter).

The newer **Southern Fortress Wall & Tower Museum** (ul Milet 40; adult/student 4/3lv; ⊙ 9.30am-8pm Jul & Aug, 9.30am-5pm May-Oct) has a 4th-century BC well and wall remnants – the setting by the crashing surf on the rocky shore is worth seeing (and free to see).

SLEEPING

During summer, many houses in Old Town offer private accommodation (from 20lv).

Sasha Hristov's Private Rooms (☎ 23434; ul Venets 17; r with shared bathroom 25lv) A nice family homestead in Old Town with four homely rooms with terraces and a kitchen to use.

Hotel Diamanti (☎ 22640; www.hoteldiamanti .com; ul Morski Skali; r without/with sea view incl breakfast 70/80lv; ⊠ 🖳) This modern take on Sozopol's past sits looking over an empty rocky bluff at the sea.

Art Hotel (☎ 24081; www.arthotel-sbh.com; ul Kiril i Metodii 72; r incl breakfast 70-100lv; ⊠ 🖳) This 11-room Old Town deal has functional, carpeted rooms with balconies watching over the beaches.

By far most hotels are in New Town, mostly matching four-floor templates that cost 40lv or 50lv for a double; one new one is **Silver Hotel** (☎ 22764; ul Lozengrad 10). Gradina Camping has bungalows and lots of tent space near the beach, 2km north of town.

EATING

Safrid is a local small fish served lightly battered in many restaurants. Note that staff at some New Town places (in particular) may try to steer you to overpriced fish dishes.

Ul Morksi Skali in Old Town has a few places looking onto the sea with terrific

food, including **Ksantana** (ul Morski Skali 7; mains from 7lv; ⊙ 11am-11pm).

GETTING THERE & AWAY

Buses and minibuses leave the **bus terminal** (☎ 22 239; ul Han Krum) for Burgas (5lv, 40 minutes, half-hourly 6am to 9pm) all year. In summer buses go to Primorsko (3.50lv) and Kiten (4lv) to the south. Stands in New Town sell tickets (with a quick change in Burgas) to Plovdiv and Veliko Târnovo, as well as direct buses to Sofia (28lv, seven hours).

Sozopol to Tsarevo

Just south of Sozopol, an inland road rambles past undeveloped **Stork Beach** (Alepu), a protected beach backed by marsh that sees thousands of storks in August.

The bustling resort towns of **Primorsko** (22km south of Sozopol) and **Kiten** (5km further south) both aspire to be Sunny Beach's little bro; neither are that atmospheric but have fine beaches and plenty of midrange guest houses.

Tsarevo царево
☎ 0590

Twelve kilometres south of Kiten, Tsarevo is the 'realest' town on the south coast. A laidback, friendly, uncommercialised fishing town filling a rocky outcrop, with a small beach on its north side, and rocky water access from below a park at the east end of town. **Arapya Cape**, a couple of kilometres north (some buses head there), has a nicer beach for swimming.

In town, **Sunhouse** (☎ 0899 371 008; www .sunhouse.hit.bg; ul Krai Morska 2; r 34-45lv; ⊠) is an inviting guest house with balconies. **Hotel Diana** (☎ 54 855; hoteldiana@abv.bg; ul Hristo Botev 2; s/d 30/40lv; ⊠ 🖳) has rooms and fresh wood-oven pizzas.

Sinemorets Синеморец
☎ 0590

The road gets bumpier as you press on south 20km to this spread-out village of new villas, a few hotels and ongoing construction. The setting's lovely, on a wide peninsula looking over the blue sea. About 1.5km south of the bus stand, an ugly hotel complex overlooks a nice gold-sand beach; an even better, completely undeveloped beach is beyond via a short, gorgeous walk over the rocky cliffs (or along a dirt road).

A third (sometimes nude) beach is back toward the town entrance, where you can take boat trips into the marshy riverway of the **Strandzha Nature Park**. A 90-minute ride on the Veleka River is 15lv, including a walk up a bluff south of town.

Casa Domingo (☎ 0888 744 019; 66 093; www .casadomingo.info; r 22-35lv) is a simple hotel with pool, restaurant and English-speaking staff.

NORTHWEST BULGARIA

Bulgaria's little horn – jutting up between Romania and Serbia – sees few foreign travellers, and it's surprising. 'Yes', one local sighed to us. 'We're underestimated.' Curved to the northeast by the Danube, it's seen plenty of military struggles, and prehistoric forces that forged stunning rock formations and gorges that make for great hiking and rock climbing. The train from Sofia goes past impressive **Iskâr Gorge**, south of Mezdra.

VIDIN ВИДИН
☎ 094 / pop 68,000

No place in Bulgaria embraces the Danube like Vidin, a historic city with a laid-back pedestrian-oriented centre with 300-year-old walls, a long, leafy park extending along the riverside dotted with floating fish restaurants, as well as communist monuments with erect genitalia spray-painted on stern heroes.

There are ATMs near pl Bdin, two blocks north of the stations.

Sights
About 1km north of the centre, past a nice riverside walkway, the interesting **Baba Vida Museum-Fortress** (☎ 601 705; admission 2lv; ☒ 8.30am-5pm Mon-Fri, 9.30am-5pm Sat & Sun) was built in the 10th century atop a 1st-century Roman fort called Bononia ('good fort') and redone by Turks in the 17th century. Inside the squat, (dry) moat-surrounded structure are a few exhibits (eg executioner's chamber, a decapitated dummy playing chess). The fort's commonly used for movie settings.

On the way back to the centre, watch for the ruins of an 1897 **synagogue** to the right. It was disassembled in the '80s to be a theatre hall but funds dried up.

A block more inland, you'll reach the white cross-shaped **Krastata Kazarma** (ul Knyaz Boris 1; admission 2lv; ☒ 9am-noon & 2-5pm Mon-Sat), a former Turkish barracks built in 1801, now an ethnographical museum.

Sleeping
Hotel Bononia (☎ 606 031; moira_bg200@yahoo.com; ul Bdin 2; s/d 33/40lv; ☒ ▣) This scrubbed-up commie leftover does a good job with new paint jobs and Danube prints in boxy rooms. Breakfast is 4lv.

ourpick **Anna-Kristina Hotel** (☎ 606 038; ul Baba Vida 2; www.annakristinahotel.com; ul Baba Vida 2; d incl breakfast 70-100lv; ☒ ▣ ☒) Made from a century-old Turkish bath and topped in a faux blue terracotta tile, this nice 21-room hotel goes all mod in the rooms, but best is the resort-worthy pool outside.

Getting There & Away
Ten or more daily buses connect Vidin's bus station with Sofia (15lv to 18lv, four hours); the best company is **Aleksiev** (☎ 606 190). Also four or five go to Belogradchik (4lv, 1¼ hours), the first at 7.30am. A couple of buses daily head for Bregova, at the Serbia border; you can walk across and catch the train for Belgrade.

Three fast trains leave from the train station, across from the bus station, to Sofia (13lv, 5½ hours) at 6.05am, 12.40pm and 4.15pm.

A bridge to Calafat, Romania may be completed by 2011; meanwhile a ferry leaves every hour or two from 3km north of town. Passengers cost €3, cars are €18 to €22.

BELOGRADCHIK БЕЛОГРАДЧИК
☎ 0936 / pop 5640

Reached by side roads, Belogradchik is a scene too out there for *Lord of the Rings:* jagged stone figures, carved by prehistoric seas, stand atop a rising mountain, looking like petrified giants – angry ones – way above a toy fort built by Romans, then Bulgarians, then Turks. It is real, though, part of the 50-sq-km collection of **Belogradchiski Stali**, lifelike red-rock peaks named for people.

The main highlight is 1km past the central square (where ATMs are found) at **Kaleto Fortress** (admission 3lv; ☒ 9am-6pm), surrounded by Turk-built walls. Up above, it feels less like a fort than a windswept rock-climbing haven, with steps going up rounded rocks with far-off views. Romans first built here from the 1st to 3rd centuries AD.

One **hiking trail** goes from the village central square past many formations and up around the fort above.

About 25km north, **Magura Cave** (☎ 0894 481 955; admission 4lv; ☒ 10am-3pm) is worth a trip for a memorable, hour-long, unguided walk past

BULGARIA

stalagmites on sometimes slippery walkways. When we were there, its prize possessions (4500-year-old rock paintings) were closed off for restoration, but was due to reopen soon. Drakite Guesthouse arranges rides here (about 25lv); taxis are about 10lv more.

Sleeping

our pick **Drakite Guesthouse** (☎ 3930; www.drak ite.com; ul Treti Mart 37; s/d from 20/30lv) is run by a superhelpful English-speaking local (who will pick you up from the train station). It has five nice rooms with views over mountains. Follow the signs to the fort, then follow the orange sign pointing right 400m just past the internet cafe.

There are plenty of small guest houses with cafes around, including **Hotel Rai** (☎ 3735; r per person 15lv), across from the bus station.

In the centre, a midrange makeover of old stand-by Hotel Skalite was set to open at research time.

Eating

A few places are around, but it's worth following the road between the central square 1.5km to **Hanche Madona** (☉ 10am-2am), a friendly spot built into a giant boulder. It serves typical Bulgarian barbecue dishes.

Getting There & Away

Four or five daily buses connect Belogradchik with Vidin (4lv, 1¼ hours). From Sofia, the Vidin-bound train stops at nearby **Gara Oroshets** (☎ 09322-382), 15km east, where a bus for Belogradchik (1.5lv) meets most oncoming trains daily (except Saturday). The train leaves Oroshets for Sofia at 7.04am, 1.40pm and 5.22pm.

BULGARIA DIRECTORY

ACCOMMODATION

Accommodation listings in this guide have been ordered by price from cheapest to most expensive. You'll find a budget room for under 50lv a double; midrange doubles will cost somewhere between 50lv and 80lv, while top-end places tend to cost more than 80lv. Prices listed in this chapter are for the high season, and include private bathroom unless otherwise stated.

In addition to the following options, most active monasteries have basic rooms

for as little as 10lv per night (no drinking binges, kids).

Camping & Huts

Generally, 'camping' here refers to rather lifeless areas where bungalows sit side by side in a small thicket of woods. Camp sites can be cheap though (about 5lv). Discreet camping outside the camping ground is, as one local says, 'No problem – just don't have a loud party – and say you have permission if anyone asks'. In other words, it's not technically legal and you probably shouldn't do it.

Hizhas (mountain huts) dot the high country and range in quality. Many are now privately run (and cost about 10lv to 30lv per person); some more remote ones are free. Most Bulgaria maps show these. In July and August, you may wish to reserve ahead at an agency such as Zig Zag (p148) in Sofia.

Hostels

Only five places have hostels: Bulgaria's big four – Sofia, Plovdiv, Veliko Târnovo and Varna – and the unlikely Kârdzhali. Expect to pay 18lv to 24lv per person in a dorm, including free breakfast and internet use; many have private rooms as well.

Hotels

Generally hotels have private bathrooms (sometimes down the hall), in-room TV, heating and a fan if not air-conditioned, and about half of them offer free breakfast. All entries in this chapter have private bathrooms and TV unless otherwise noted. Most double rooms have two twin beds. Average rates for a cheapie are around 30lv for a single and 40lv for a double. In some tourist locations this rate can drop by 10lv in the off season.

Many hotels do not have smoke-free rooms, but the trend is for more to set aside nonsmoking rooms.

Watch out for hotels advertising *pochivka* ('rest') rates, which means two-hour slots used by makeshift couples (ie guys with prostitutes) seeking privacy. They're not necessarily dangerous, but walls don't always block out 'noise'.

Private Rooms

Travellers on a budget can rent private rooms *(stai pod naem)*, often offered by agencies, signed homes or English-speaking touts at train and bus stations. Rates range from 10lv or 15lv per person in smaller towns, to 35lv or more in places such as Sofia, Plovdiv and Varna. We've found many to be rather clinical and uninspired modern flats with shared bathroom.

ACTIVITIES

Bulgaria's mountains have more than 37,000km of hiking trails, some of which can be cross-country skied or cycled; nearly all lead to *hizhas* with dorm or private rooms and cafes. Before setting out, drop by the expert consultants at Zig Zag (p148) in Sofia for tips and maps (particularly Kartografia's excellent trail maps).

We list some popular hikes in introductions for the Rila and Pirin Mountains in the southwest (p156) and Rodopi Mountains (p159). Veliko Târnovo (p171, p173), meanwhile, is a good hub for hikes or rock climbing in the central Stara Planina. There's also good rock climbing at Kamen Bryag (p185) and at Vratsa, between Sofia and Vidin. The mother of all Bulgarian hikes is the 20-plus day E3, crossing the Balkan Mountain spine of Bulgaria from Mt Kom (near the Serbian border, at Berkovitsa, about 85km north of Sofia) to Emine Cape on the Black Sea.

Bulgaria's reputation as a cheap downhill skiing (and snowboarding) destination is outliving its deals. Its three main resorts – Borovets (p158), Bansko (p158) and Pamporovo (p165) – all charge about 50lv for a one-day lift ticket, not including snowboard or ski rental. Sofia's Mt Vitosha (p155) is cheaper, as are older lifts at Malîovitsa (near Borovets) or Dobronishte (near Bansko). The ski season runs from mid-December to mid-April. Check www.bulgariaski.com for loads of information.

Caving tours such as those near Belogradchik (p191) and Trigrad (p166) are another drawcard.

BOOKS

Lonely Planet's *Bulgaria* offers more comprehensive coverage of the country. Ivan Ilchev's *The Rose of the Balkans* is a recent historical overview of Bulgaria translated into English, available in Sofia. The communist-era KGB world is uncovered in Alexenia Dimitrova's *The Iron Fist: Inside the Archives of Bulgaria's Secret Police*.

BUSINESS HOURS

Banks and most public offices are open Monday to Friday, roughly 8.30am to 5pm or 6pm, sometimes with an hour off for lunch. Many shops and all foreign-exchange booths are open daily. Many post offices are open daily. Most restaurants are open from around 10am or 11am to midnight daily.

Hours for many Bulgarian museums and shops drift. It can depend on the season (in winter, some museums may close for a few weeks unexpectedly, while summer sees longer hours). Hours in this chapter reflect the official line, but brace yourself for changes.

'Summer' and 'winter' refer to either side of daylight savings.

COURSES

It's possible to study Bulgarian language in Sofia (p150) and Veliko Târnovo (p171). You can also learn traditional Bulgarian music or dance at heralded schools in Plovdiv (p162) and Shiroka Lâka (p166).

DANGERS & ANNOYANCES

You're unlikely to have problems in Bulgaria. Pickpocketing or beach grab-and-runs can happen in summer, particularly on Varna's beach. You will be warned by some Bulgarians that Roma people will rob you blind (example: 'You'll be lucky to keep your pants'), which is incorrect and an annoyance in itself.

DISCOUNT CARDS

Most museums offer up to 75% discounts for students. **Usit Colours** (www.usitcolours.bg; Sofia Map p146; ☎ 02-981 1900; ul Vasil Levski 35; ◷ 9.30am-6.30pm Mon-Fri; Veliko Târnovo Map p170; ☎ 062-601 751; pl Slaveikov 7; ◷ 9.30am-6pm Mon-Fri) issues student cards for 10lv.

EMBASSIES & CONSULATES

New Zealanders can turn to the UK Embassy for assistance, or contact their **consulate general** (☎ 210-6924 136; 76 Kifissias Ave, Ambelokipi) in Athens.

All of the below are in Sofia unless stated:
Australia (off Map p146; ☎ 02-946 1334; ul Trakia 37) Main office in Athens.
Canada (Map p146; ☎ 02-969 9710; ul Moskovska 9)
France (off Map p146; ☎ 02-965 1100; www.ambafrance-bg.org; ul Oborishte 27-29)
Germany (off Map p146; ☎ 02-918 380; www.sofia.diplo.de; ul Frederic Joliot-Curie 25)
Greece Plovdiv (Map p160; ☎ 032-632 003; ul Preslav 10); Sofia (off Map p146; ☎ 02-946 1750; ul San Stefano 33)
Hungary (Map p146; ☎ 02-963 1135; ul 6 Septemvri 57)
Ireland (Map p146; ☎ 02-985 3425; ul Bacho Kiro 26-28)
Macedonia (Map p146; ☎ 02-870 5098; ul Frederic Joliot-Curie 17)

Poland (Map p146; ☎ 02-987 2610; ul Han Krum 46)
Romania (off Map p146; ☎ 02-973 3081; ul Sitnyakovo 4)
Russia (off Map p146; ☎ 02-963 0914; www.bulgaria
.mid.ru; bul Dragan Tsankov 28)
Serbia (off Map p146; ☎ 02-946 1633; ul Veliko Târnovo 3)
Turkey Plovdiv (Map p160; ☎ 032-632 309; ul Filip
Makedonski 10); Sofia (Map p146; ☎ 02-935 5500; bul
Vasil Levski 80)
UK (Map p146; ☎ 02-933 9222; www.british-embassy
.bg; ul Moskovksa 9)
USA (off Map p146; ☎ 02-937 5100; www.usembassy
.bg; ul Kozyak 16)

FESTIVALS & EVENTS

In February or March, the *kukeri* festival –
famous in Shiroka Lâka (p166) – is held on the
first Sunday before Lent, when masked dancers in hairy costumes ward off evil spirits.

All March you can take part in the national
custom of Martenitsa, when Bulgarians exchange red-and-white figures and wear them
until they see a stork, after which they tie the
figure to a tree.

GAY & LESBIAN TRAVELLERS

Homosexual sex is legal in Bulgaria, and the
age of consent is 16, but Bulgaria is far from
openly tolerant (a 2008 poll found 80% of
the nation had 'negative attitudes' towards
homosexuality). A few gay events, however,
are starting to appear, including Varna's Gay
Week in September. Some gay clubs are listed
in this chapter; also check www.gay.com. The
Sofia-based **Bulgarian Gay Organization Gemini**
(www.bgogemini.org) covers political issues.

HOLIDAYS

Official public holidays:
New Year's Day 1 January
Liberation Day (National Day) 3 March
Orthodox Easter Sunday & Monday March/April; one
week after Catholic/Protestant Easter
St George's Day 6 May
Cyrillic Alphabet Day 24 May
Unification Day (National Day) 6 September
Bulgarian Independence Day 22 September
National Revival Day 1 November
Christmas 25 and 26 December

INTERNET RESOURCES

A few helpful sites:
www.bdz.bg Train schedule and fares.
www.bulgariatravel.org Official tourist site, with
detailed background and photos.

www.inyourpocket.com Online guides to Sofia, Burgas
and Varna.
www.cityinfoguide.net Monthly publication's website
for Sofia, Burgas and Varna.
www.sofiaecho.com English-language paper that
has national coverage, travel tips and extensive
archives.

LANGUAGE

Most signs are written in Cyrillic (even
'*kseroks*' for Xerox), though increasingly
highway signs and hip cafes go Roman
too. Most Bulgarians in their early 30s
and older know a fair bit of Russian, but
English is the vogue second language of
choice these days. Remember that Cyrillic
is a Bulgarian invention – it's the Russians
who borrowed it.

MONEY

Bulgaria lists many prices in euros, which is
roughly 2:1 to the lev; prices in this chapter
reflect local quotes. Note that all businesses
accept either. Despite Bulgaria's recent integration into the EU, prices have remained
relatively stable for the past handful of years
except for bus and train fares, which seem to
go up by 25% every couple of years. Bulgaria
won't be adopting the euro during the life
of this book.

ATMs

ATMs (cash points) are ubiquitous and
compatible with foreign cards (ask your
bank).

Cash

The local currency, the lovely lev (lv), comprises 100 stotinki. It's been pegged to the euro
(roughly 2:1) since January 2002. Banknotes
come in denominations of one, two, five, 10,
20 and 50 leva, and coins in one, two, five,
10, 20 and 50 stotinki. The little horse guy
on the coins is from a bas-relief made in the
8th century at Madara. And, your eyes don't
deceive you, the lion on the 20lv note *is* missing a tail (see p150).

Exchanging Money

Foreign-exchange offices are abundant across
Bulgaria. Note that some occasionally post
more-attractive rates outside, then put the
real rates in tiny print inside a booth. Ask
before handing over cash. US dollars, UK

pounds and euros are the best currencies to carry.

Travellers Cheques

American Express and Thomas Cook cheques in US dollars and euros can be cashed at many banks.

POST

Sending a postcard or letter costs 1lv to Europe, and 1.40lv to elsewhere.

TELEPHONE

In most cities and towns you'll find a Bulgarian Telecommunications Centre (BTC) inside, or next to, the main post office, from where you can make local or international calls. Some telephone stands use Net cards and are as cheap as 0.20lv per minute to call overseas.

Nearly all Mobika and BulFon telephone booths use phonecards (*fonkarta*), available at news-stands for 5lv to 25lv, for local or international calls.

GSM mobile phones can be used in nearly all places in Bulgaria. M-tel, Globul and Vivatel are the three operators. Numbers have different codes (eg ☎ 087 and ☎ 088).

To ring Bulgaria from abroad, dial the international access code then ☎ 359, followed by the area code (minus the first zero) then the number.

To call direct from Bulgaria, dial ☎ 00 followed by the country code.

TOURIST INFORMATION

Information centres vary. Little places like Smolyan or Shiroka Lâka have two, while Sofia or Burgas lack any city-oriented one. Generally English-speaking staff hand out brochures, help you find accommodation or a rental car.

VISAS

Citizens of Australia, Canada, Israel, Japan, New Zealand and the USA can stay in Bulgaria visa-free for up to 90 days. If you need to extend, it may be easier to hop across the border than deal with the headaches of Sofia's **Immigration Office** (☎ 982 3316; bul Maria Luisa 48; ☺ foreigner services 12.15-1.30pm Mon-Fri). EU citizens can stay for up to five years by registering for a permit.

TRANSPORT IN BULGARIA

GETTING THERE & AWAY

Air

Bulgaria's chief airports are in Sofia, Varna and Burgas. No additional departure tax is levied outside the price of your ticket. Airlines flying to/from Bulgaria (all addresses are for Sofia):

Aeroflot (SU; ☎ 02-943 4489; www.aeroflot.ru; ul Oborishte 23)

Air France (AF; ☎ 02-939 7010; www.airfrance.com; ul Sâborna 5)

Alitalia (AZ; ☎ 02-981 6702; www.alitalia.com; ul Kânchev 5)

Austrian Airlines (AUA; ☎ 02-806 000;www.aua.com; bul Zlaten rog 12)

British Airways (BA; ☎ 02-945 7000; www.britishair ways.com; bul Patraiarh Evtimii 49)

Bulgaria Air (FB; ☎ 02-402 0406; www.air.bg; NDK underpass)

ČSA (OK; ☎ 02-981 5408; www.czechairlines.com; ul Sâborna 9)

easyJet (EZY; www.easyjet.com) Flies daily to London's Gatwick airport.

LOT Polish Airlines (LO; ☎ 02-987 4562; www.lot. com; bul Aleksandâr Stamboliski 27a)

Lufthansa (LH; ☎ 02-930 4242; www.lufthansa.com; ul Bacho Kiro 26-30)

Malév (MA; ☎ 02-981 5091; www.malev.com; bul Patriarh Evtimii 19)

Sky Europe (NE; www.skyeurope.com) Flies to Prague.

Turkish Airlines (TK; ☎ 02-988 3596; www.turkishair lines.com; ul Sâborna 11a)

Wizz Air (8Z; ☎ 960 3888; www.wizzair.com) Flies daily to London's Luton airport and a couple of times weekly to Brussels, Rome and Barcelona.

Land

It's possible to walk across to Vama Veche, Romania on the Black Sea coast.

> ### EMERGENCY NUMBERS
>
> ■ Ambulance ☎ 150
> ■ Fire ☎ 160
> ■ Police ☎ 166
> ■ Roadside Assistance ☎ 146

BULGARIA

BUS

International tickets to the region (and beyond) are available at practically any bus station in the country. There's not one set price, so it's worth checking a couple of companies.

Sofia has buses to international destinations including the Czech Republic, Greece, Macedonia, Romania, Serbia, Slovenia and Turkey (see p154).

You can also head to Romania from towns including Veliko Târnovo (p173) and Varna (p183) via Ruse (p178). There are buses to İstanbul from towns throughout the country, including Plovdiv (p164), Veliko Târnovo (p173), Varna (p183) and Ruse (p178).

Other international options include buses to Macedonia from Blagoevgrad, and buses to Athens and Odesa from Varna (p183). It's possible to reach the Serbian border at Bregovo by bus from Vidin and then walk to the nearby train station.

CAR & MOTORCYCLE

Drivers bringing cars into Bulgaria are asked to pay a 'road fee' of €5 per week.

TRAIN

There are a number of international trains from Bulgaria, including services to Romania, Greece and Turkey. Sofia (p154) is the main hub, although trains stop at other towns. The daily *Trans Balkan,* running between Budapest and Thessaloniki, stops at Ruse, Gorna Oryakhovitsa (near Veliko Târnovo) and Sofia. The *Balkan Express* normally goes daily between Belgrade and İstanbul, with stops in Sofia and Plovdiv. The *Bulgaria Express* to Bucharest leaves from Sofia.

Tickets for international trains can be bought at any government-run **Rila Bureau** (www.bdz-rila.com; most closed Sun) or at some stations' dedicated ticket offices (most open daily) at larger stations with international connections.

River

You can ferry across the Danube River from Vidin (p191).

Sea

Ferries connect Varna (p183) with Odesa (Ukraine) and Constanţa (Romania) in summer.

GETTING AROUND

Prices for buses and trains in Bulgaria tend to rise a little every year, but are still relatively cheap.

Air

Bulgaria Air (www.air.bg), which merged with Hemus Air in 2007, flies between Sofia and Varna daily (about 210/350lv one way/return); it also flies to Burgas.

Bicycle

Traffic is relatively light outside the cities, but winding curves in the mountains and/or potholes everywhere can be obstacles.

Bulgaria has few bike-rental options: you can rent wheels at Zig Zag (p148) and some hostels in Sofia, and at Gorgona and Nomads Hostel in Veliko Târnovo (p171). Trains and buses will carry your bike for an extra 2lv or so.

Boat

Sadly there's no regular boat service down the Danube River, though some folks in Ruse were talking of starting a cruise.

Bus

Buses (public and private) and minibuses connect all cities and major towns. Routes that are more popular – such as Sofia–Varna – have nice, modern buses; the older ramshackle varieties are being phased out these days. The best web source is www.avtogari .info (in Bulgarian only); also try www.cen tralnaavtogara.bg for international routes.

Anywhere you go, centralised information is difficult to find, as stations have a confusing array of private bus booths advertising overlapping destinations. Generally buses leave roughly from 7am to 7pm only. Most bus stations have a left-luggage service with long (but not 24-hour) opening hours.

This chapter lists prices, duration for trips and number of buses daily, but these are particularly prone to change.

Car & Motorcycle

Bulgaria is a great country to explore on your own wheels. The best place, by far, to rent is Veliko Târnovo, which rents from 25lv per day all year. Prices are double that or more in Sofia and the Black Sea Coast in summer. A car rental will include unlimited kilometres and should include some car insurance, but

---

SCENIC ROUTES

Best-looking views from the window:

- **Bansko–Septemvri by train** Narrow-gauge train clanks (slowly), with smokers and chatters admiring mountain scenery.

- **Shipka Pass** Best by car, the route from Veliko Târnovo and Kazanlâk is a classic, twisting and turning over the 1306m pass.

- **Sofia–Burgas highway** Of all the main highways this is the nicest – a smooth road running where the Thracian plain meets the towering mountain wall of the Stara Planina.

- **Sofia–Vidin train** Passes the narrow Iskâr Gorge south of Vratsa.

---

check on how extensive the policy is. Most companies charge for drop-offs in select cities (from €50 to €80).

To rent, you normally need to be 21 and have a driving licence from your own country. Generally prices should include the 20% VAT. If not, ask about paying in cash to waive it.

Most road conditions are pretty good and traffic reasonably light. Most roads are well signed in Cyrillic and Roman alphabets. On smaller roads, you may have to negotiate big bumps (but nothing like Romanian bumps). Passing through some larger towns isn't always a breeze, as signs sometimes go on unwieldy circuits around the housing blocks and industrial zones of a town (passing Varna from the south to north comes to mind); sometimes it's easier to go through the centre.

If oncoming cars flick their lights, it's likely a police speed trap is around the corner (the west-bound entry to Sofia is notorious for police traps). Speed limits are well signed: usually 130km/h on main highways and 90km/h on smaller ones. Town speed limits are 50km/h unless otherwise noted.

Train

Trains – all run by the Bulgarian State Railways (BDZh) – are generally cheaper but take a little longer than buses. Some offer great views (including the pretty Bansko–Septemvri route). *Ekspresen* (express) and *bârz* (fast) trains way out-speed the slow *pâtnicheski* (passenger, or ordinary) trains, which don't offer much savings for their time loss (eg Sofia–Plovdiv 2nd-class fast train is 8.10lv, as opposed to 7.10lv on a passenger train – and makes the trip in 2½ hours rather than 3½). You can buy tickets on board, but prices are more expensive (about 50% on some routes).

All prices in this chapter are for 2nd-class seats (with eight seats per cabin); 1st-class seats (only a few leva more) have six seats per cabin, and for some routes see far fewer people.

Most Europe-wide rail passes can be purchased in Bulgaria, but will not be good value for getting around the country.

Bring what food or water you'll need for the trip. Many train stations are signposted in Cyrillic only, and no announcements are made on board.

All train stations should have a left-luggage service (about 2lv per bag for 24 hours).

An extra daily train or two run on some routes in summer, particularly serving the Black Sea coast.

BULGARIA

Croatia

Touted as the 'new this' and the 'new that' for years since its re-emergence on the world tourism scene, it is now clear that Croatia is a unique destination that can hold its own and then some: this is a country with a glorious 1778km-long coast and a staggering 1185 islands. The Adriatic coast is a knockout: its limpid sapphirine waters draw visitors to remote islands, hidden coves and traditional fishing villages, all while touting the glitzy beach and yacht scene. Istria is captivating, thanks to its gastronomic delights and wines, and the bars, clubs and festivals of Zagreb, Zadar and Split remain little-explored gems. Eight national parks protect pristine forests, karstic mountains, rivers, lakes and waterfalls in a landscape of primeval beauty. Punctuate all this with breathtaking Dubrovnik in the south and a country couldn't wish for a better finale.

Sitting on a see-saw between the Balkans and central Europe, Croatia has suffered from having something of a love-hate-love affair with the European Union. Statistics show that the support for joining the vast EU – once palpable – is lately hovering around the 50% mark, thanks to the already seemingly elusive joining date (Is it 2010? Or 2011? Or even 2012?) becoming snagged on a number of hurdles. Developers and investors are increasing by the year, but despite this the country has, with few exceptions, managed to keep (massive) development at bay and maintain the extraordinary beauty of the coast – the very thing that keeps the punters coming back for more.

FAST FACTS

- **Area** 56,538 sq km
- **Capital** Zagreb
- **Currency** kuna (KN); €1 = 7.42KN; US$1 = 5.44KN; UK£1 = 7.87KN; A$1 = 3.76KN; ¥100 = 5.66KN; NZ$1 = 3.05KN
- **Famous for** neckties, Slaven Bilić, Tito
- **Official language** Croatian
- **Phrases** *bog* (hello); *doviđenja* (goodbye); *hvala* (thanks); *pardon* (sorry)
- **Population** 4.5 million
- **Telephone codes** country code ☎ 385; international access code ☎ 00
- **Visas** unnecessary for citizens of the EU, USA, Australia and Canada; see p258 for details

CROATIA

CROATIA

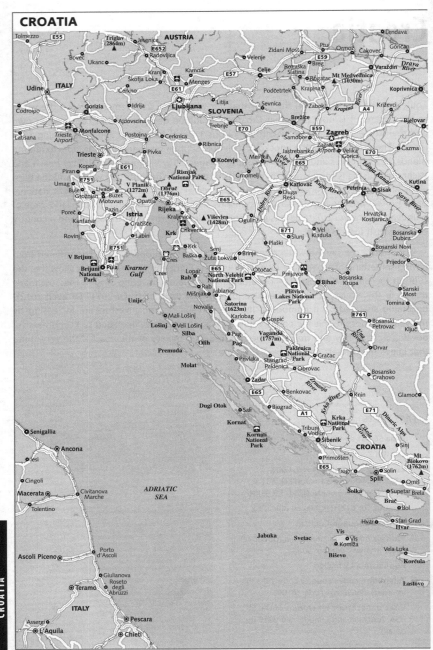

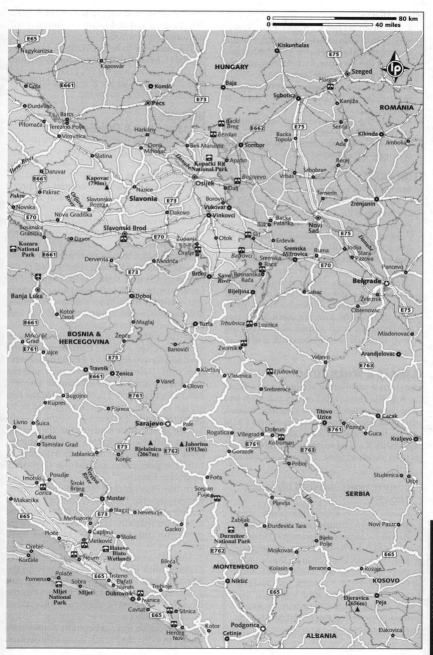

HIGHLIGHTS

- Gape at **Dubrovnik's** (p249) Old Town wall, which surrounds luminous marble streets and finely ornamented buildings.
- Admire the Venetian architecture and vibrant nightlife of **Hvar Town** (p244).
- Indulge in the incredible, lively and historic delights of Diocletian's Palace in **Split** (p236).
- Explore the lakes, coves and island monastery of **Mljet** (p248).
- Stroll the cobbled streets and unspoiled fishing port of **Rovinj** (p221).

ITINERARIES

- **One week** After a day in dynamic Zagreb head down to Split for day and night at Diocletian's Palace. Then take a ferry to Hvar, windsurf in Brač and end with two days in Dubrovnik, taking a day trip to Mljet or the Elafiti Islands.
- **Two weeks** After two days in Zagreb, head to Rovinj for a three-day stay, taking day trips to Pula and Poreč. Head south to Zadar for a night and then go on to Split for a night. Take ferries to Hvar, Brač, and then Vis or Korčula, spending a day or three on each island before ending with three days in Dubrovnik and a day trip to Mljet.

CLIMATE & WHEN TO GO

The climate varies from Mediterranean along the Adriatic coast, with hot, dry summers and mild, rainy winters, to continental inland, with cold winters and warm summers. You can swim in the sea from mid-June until late September. Coastal temperatures are slightly warmer south of Split. The peak tourist season runs from mid-July to the end of August. Prices are highest and accommodation scarcest during this period.

The best time to be in Croatia is June. The weather is beautiful, the boats and excursions are running often and it's not yet too crowded. May and September are also good, especially if you're interested in hiking.

HISTORY
Romans, Slavs & Christianity

In 229 BC the Romans began their conquest of the indigenous Illyrians by establishing a colony at Solin (Salona), close to Split in Dalmatia. Emperor Augustus then extended the empire and created the provinces of Illyricum (Dalmatia and Bosnia) and Pannonia (Croatia). In AD 285 Emperor Diocletian decided to retire to his palace fortress in Split, today the greatest Roman ruin in Eastern Europe.

Around 625, Slavic tribes migrated from the Caucasus and the Serbian tribe settled in the region that is now southwestern Serbia. The Croatian tribe moved into what is now Croatia and occupied two former Roman provinces: Dalmatian Croatia along the Adriatic, and Pannonian Croatia to the north.

By the early part of the 9th century both settlements had accepted Christianity but the northern Croats fell under Frankish domination, while Dalmatian Croats came under the nominal control of the Byzantine Empire. The Dalmatian duke Tomislav united the two groups in 925 in a single kingdom that prospered for nearly 200 years.

Late in the 11th century the throne fell vacant and the northern Croats, unable to agree upon a ruler, united with Hungary in 1102 for protection against the Orthodox Byzantine Empire.

In the 14th century the Ottomans began pushing into the Balkans, defeating the Serbs in 1389 and the Hungarians in 1526. Northern Croatia turned to the Hapsburgs of Austria for protection and remained part of their empire until 1918.

Some Dalmatian cities changed hands repeatedly until Venice imposed its rule on the Adriatic coast in the early 15th century and occupied it for nearly four centuries. Only the Republic of Ragusa (Dubrovnik) maintained its independence.

After Venice was shattered by Napoleonic France in 1797, the French occupied southern

CONNECTIONS: MOVING ON FROM CROATIA

Croatia is a convenient transport hub for southeastern Europe and the Adriatic. Zagreb is connected by train (p217) and/or bus (p217) to Venice, Budapest, Belgrade and Ljubljana, and Sarajevo. Down south there are easy bus connections from Dubrovnik (p254) to Mostar and Sarajevo, and to Kotor. There are a number of ferries linking Croatia with Italy, including from Dubrovnik to Bari (p254), and Split to Ancona (p241).

Croatia, abolishing the Republic of Ragusa in 1808. Napoleon merged Dalmatia, Istria and Slovenia into the 'Illyrian Provinces', but following his defeat at Waterloo in 1815, Austria-Hungary occupied the coast.

Push for Independence

It wasn't long before Croatia began itching for independence from the Austrian empire and for the unification of Dalmatia and Slavonia. When an uprising in Hungary threatened Austrian rule, Croatia seized the opportunity to intervene in return for greater autonomy. The Croatian commander Josip Jelačić set out to fight the rebels but his campaign was unsuccessful and Croatian hopes were crushed. Disillusionment spread after 1848, and deepened when the monarchy placed Croatia and Slavonia within the Hungarian administration, while Dalmatia remained within Austria.

The river of discontent running through late-19th-century Croatia forked into two streams that dominated the political landscape for the next century. On the one side was Bishop Josif Juraf Strossmayer, who believed that *Jugoslavenstvo* (south-Slavic unity), unified by a common language, was the only way forward for the aspirations of the southern Slavs. His opponent, the militantly anti-Serb Ante Starčević, envisaged an independent Croatia made up of Slavonia, Dalmatia, the Krajina, Slovenia, Istria and part of Bosnia and Hercegovina.

South Slavic Unity

The first organised resistance against the Austro-Hungarian empire formed in Dalmatia. Croat representatives in Rijeka and Serb representatives in Zadar joined together in 1905 to demand the unification of Dalmatia and Slavonia with a formal guarantee of Serbian equality as a nation. The spirit of unity mushroomed, and by 1906 Croat-Serb coalitions had taken over local government in Dalmatia and Slavonia, forming a serious threat to the Hungarian power structure.

Similar resistance was going on in the neighbouring Bosnia and Hercegovina (BiH) and with the outbreak of WWI, the idea that only Slavic unity could check Great Power ambitions in the region was cemented. With the collapse of the Austro-Hungarian empire in 1918, the Kingdom of Serbs, Croats and

Slovenes was established. Italy seized Pula, Rijeka and Zadar in November 1918.

Problems with the kingdom began almost immediately, with the abolishment of Croatia's Sabor (Parliament) and the centralisation of power in Belgrade. The new electoral districts under-represented the Croats and the new government gave away Istria, Zadar and a number of islands to Italy.

One of the main opposition leaders was Stjepan Radić, who, together with Svetozar Pribićević, advocated a federal democracy within the Kingdom and tried to promote the idea of an egalitarian state. He formed HSS (The Croatian Peasant Party), a political party that remains influential to this day. Following a number of heated debates in the parliament, Radić was assassinated, along with two other party members. Exploiting fears of civil war, on 6 January 1929 King Aleksandar in Belgrade proclaimed a royal dictatorship, abolished political parties and suspended parliamentary government.

Ustaše, Chetniks & Partisans

One day after the coup d'état, a Bosnian Croat, Ante Pavelić, set up the Ustaše Croatian Liberation Movement in Zagreb with the stated aim of establishing an independent state by force if necessary. Fearing arrest, he fled to Sofia in Bulgaria and then to Italy. There, he established training camps for his organisation, favoured by Mussolini. Pavelić succeeded in assassinating King Aleksandar in Marseilles in 1934 and Italy responded by closing down the training camps and imprisoning Pavelić and many of his followers.

When Germany invaded Yugoslavia on 6 April 1941, the Nazis installed the exiled Ustaše with the support of the Italians. In return, Pavelić agreed to cede a good part of Dalmatia to Italy, which left him with the Lika region southwest of Zagreb and western Hercegovina as his political base.

Within days the Independent State of Croatia (NDH), headed by Pavelić, issued a range of decrees designed to persecute and eliminate Serbs, Jews, Roma and antifascist Croats. Villages conducted their own personal pogroms against Serbs and extermination camps were set up, most notoriously at Jasenovac (south of Zagreb). The extermination program was carried out with appalling brutality. The exact number of Serb victims is uncertain and controversial, with Croatian historians tending to minimise the figures and Serbian historians tending to maximise them. The number of Serb deaths range from 60,000 to 600,000, but the most reliable estimates settle somewhere between 80,000 to 120,000. Whatever the number, it's clear that the NDH and its supporters made a diligent effort to eliminate the entire Serb population.

Armed resistance to the regime took the form of Serbian 'Chetniks' led by General Draža Mihajlović, which began as an antifascist rebellion but soon degenerated into massacres of Croats in eastern Croatia and Bosnia.

In the meantime, Josip Broz, himself of Croat-Slovene parentage, the leader of the outlawed Yugoslavian Communist Party, fronted the partisans, who consisted of leftwing Yugoslav intellectuals, Croats disgusted with Chetnik massacres, Serbs disgusted with Ustaše massacres, and antifascists of all kinds.

Although the Allies initially backed the Serbian Chetniks, it became apparent that the partisans were waging a far more focused and determined fight against the Germans. On 20 October 1944 Tito entered Belgrade with the Red Army and was made prime minister. When Germany surrendered in 1945, Pavelić and the Ustaše fled and the partisans entered Zagreb.

The remnants of the NDH army, desperate to avoid falling into the hands of the partisans, attempted to cross into Austria at Bleiburg. A small British contingent met the 50,000 troops and promised to intern them outside Yugoslavia in exchange for their surrender. Tricked, the troops were forced into trains that headed back into Yugoslavia where the partisans claimed the lives of at least 30,000 men (although the exact number is in doubt).

Tito's Yugoslavia

Tito's attempt to retain control of the Italian city of Trieste and parts of southern Austria faltered in the face of Allied opposition, but Dalmatia and most of Istria were made a permanent part of postwar Yugoslavia. Tito was determined to create a state in which no ethnic group dominated the political landscape. Croatia became one of six republics – Macedonia, Serbia, Montenegro, BiH and Slovenia – in a tightly configured federation. Tito effected this delicate balance by creating a one-party state and stamping out opposition.

During the 1960s, the concentration of power in Belgrade became an increasingly testy issue as it became apparent that money from the more prosperous republics of Slovenia and Croatia was being distributed to the poorer regions, such as BiH, Kosovo and Montenegro. Serbs in Croatia were overrepresented in the government, armed forces and the police – this was, allegedly, partly because state service offered financial certainty and career opportunities among the poorer Yugoslavs.

The dissatisfaction with Tito's government manifested itself in many student and other demonstrations across Yugoslavia during the late '60s, but Croatia's unrest reached a crescendo in 1971, during the 'Croatian Spring'. Led by reformers within the Communist Party of Croatia, intellectuals and students first called for greater economic autonomy and then constitutional reform to loosen Croatia's ties to Yugoslavia. Tito's crackdown meant that leaders of the movement were either jailed or expelled from the party. Serbs viewed the movement as the Ustaše reborn, and jailed reformers blamed the Serbs for their troubles. The stage was set for the later rise of nationalism and war that followed Tito's death in 1980, even though his 1974 constitution afforded the republics more autonomy.

Independence

After Tito's death, Yugoslavia was left with a large external debt. The country was unable to service the interest on its loans and inflation soared. The authority of the central government sank along with the economy, and mistrust among Yugoslavia's ethnic groups resurfaced.

In 1989 the repression of the Albanian majority in Serbia's Kosovo province sparked renewed fears of Serbian hegemony and heralded the end of the Yugoslav Federation. With political changes sweeping Eastern Europe, many Croats felt the time had come to separate from Yugoslavia and the elections of April 1990 saw the victory of Franjo Tuđman's Croatian Democratic Union (HDZ; Hrvatska Demokratska Zajednica). On 22 December 1990 a new Croatian constitution was promulgated, changing the status of Serbs in Croatia from that of a 'constituent nation' to a national minority.

The constitution's failure to guarantee minority rights, and mass dismissals of Serbs from the public service, stimulated the 600,000-strong ethnic Serb community within Croatia to demand autonomy. In early 1991 Serb extremists within Croatia staged provocations designed to force federal military intervention. A May 1991 referendum (boycotted by the Serbs) produced a 93% vote in favour of independence, but when Croatia declared independence on 25 June 1991, the Serbian enclave of Krajina proclaimed its independence from Croatia.

War & Peace

Under pressure from the EC (now EU), Croatia declared a three-month moratorium on its independence, but heavy fighting broke out in Krajina, Baranja (the area north of the Drava River opposite Osijek) and Slavonia. The Serb-dominated Yugoslav People's Army intervened in support of Serbian irregulars, under the pretext of halting ethnic violence.

When the Croatian government ordered a blockade of 32 federal military installations in the republic, the Yugoslav navy blockaded the Adriatic coast and laid siege to the strategic town of Vukovar on the Danube. During the summer of 1991, a quarter of Croatia fell to Serbian militias and the Yugoslav People's Army.

In early October 1991 the federal army and Montenegrin militia moved against Dubrovnik to protest the blockade of their garrisons in Croatia, and on 7 October the presidential palace in Zagreb was hit by rockets fired by Yugoslav air-force jets in an unsuccessful assassination attempt on President Tuđman. When the three-month moratorium on independence ended, Croatia declared full independence. On 19 November the city of Vukovar fell after a bloody three-month siege. During six months of fighting in Croatia 10,000 people died, hundreds of thousands fled and tens of thousands of homes were destroyed.

To fulfil a condition for EC recognition, in December the Croatian Sabor (which was re-established under Tito) belatedly amended its constitution to protect minority groups and human rights. A UN-brokered ceasefire from 3 January 1992 generally held. The federal army was allowed to withdraw from its bases inside Croatia and tensions diminished. In January 1992 the EC, succumbing to strong pressure from Germany, recognised Croatia. This was followed three months later by US recognition and in May 1992 Croatia was admitted to the UN.

In January 1993 the Croatian army launched an offensive in southern Krajina, pushing the Serbs back and recapturing strategic points. In June 1993 the Krajina Serbs voted overwhelmingly to join the Bosnian Serbs (and eventually Greater Serbia). Meanwhile, continued 'ethnic cleansing' left only about 900 Croats in Krajina out of an original population of 44,000.

On 1 May 1995 the Croatian army and police entered occupied western Slavonia, east of Zagreb, and seized control of the region within days. The Krajina Serbs responded by shelling Zagreb in an attack that left seven people dead and 130 wounded. As the Croatian military consolidated its hold in western Slavonia, some 15,000 Serbs fled the region, despite assurances from the Croatian government that they were safe from retribution.

Belgrade's silence throughout this campaign showed that the Krajina Serbs had lost the support of their Serbian allies, encouraging Croats to forge ahead. On 4 August the military launched a massive assault on the rebel Serb capital of Knin and, vastly outnumbered, the Serb army fled towards northern Bosnia and into Serbia. An estimated 150,000 civilians fled and many were murdered. The military operation ended in days, but was followed by months of terror. Widespread looting and burning of Serb villages, and attacks upon the remaining Serbs cemented the huge population shift. The Dayton Accord signed in

Paris in December 1995 recognised Croatia's traditional borders and provided for the return of eastern Slavonia, which was effected in January 1998. The transition proceeded relatively smoothly, but the two populations still regard each other with suspicion.

Although the central government in Zagreb has made the return of Serb refugees a priority in accordance with the demands of the international community, its efforts have been less than successful. Serbs intending to reclaim their property face an array of legal impediments.

Franjo Tuđman's combination of authoritarianism and media control, and tendency to be influenced by the far Right, no longer appealed to the postwar Croatian populace. By 1999 opposition parties united to work against Tuđman and the HDZ. Tuđman was hospitalised and died suddenly in late 1999, and planned elections were postponed until January 2000. Still, voters turned out in favour of a centre-left coalition, ousting the HDZ and voting the centrist Stipe Mesić into the presidency.

The country gradually began welcoming foreign tourists again, and the economy opened up to foreign competition. General Mirko Norac turned himself in to the Hague in 2001 and General Ante Gotovina was arrested in 2005 for crimes against the Krajina's Serb population. Gotovina's handover was one of the conditions for the EU to start discussing Croatia's eventual membership. The arrests of both men were accompanied with some nationalist protest. A spate of suspected mafia-related murders in late 2008 – of 26-year-old Ivana Hodak, the daughter of a prominent Croat lawyer, and Ivo Pukanic, editor of political weekly *Nacional* – triggered nationwide protests and a political crackdown, as well as further doubts over the date of Croatia joining the EU. The discussions with the EU have been slowed down by various hurdles and the proposed joining date is anywhere between 2010 and 2012.

PEOPLE

Croatia has a population of roughly 4.5 million people. Before the war Croatia had a population of nearly five million, of which 78% were Croats and 12% were Serbs. Bosnians and Hercegovinians, Hungarians, Italians, Czechs, Roma and Albanians made up the remaining 10%. Today Croats constitute 89% of the population and slightly less than

5% of the populations are Serb, followed by 0.5% Bosnians and about 0.4% each of Hungarians and Italians. Most Serbs live in eastern Croatia (Slavonia). The largest cities in Croatia are Zagreb (780,000), Split (188,700), Rijeka (144,000), Osijek (114,600) and Zadar (72,700).

RELIGION

Croats are overwhelmingly Roman Catholic, while the Serbs belong to the Orthodox Church. Catholicism is undergoing a strong resurgence in Croatia. Pope John Paul II visited Croatia several times before his death, though Benedict XVI had not visited at the time of writing. Muslims make up 1.2% of the population and Protestants 0.4%, with a small Jewish population in Zagreb.

ARTS
Literature

Croatia's towering literary figure is 20th-century novelist and playwright Miroslav Krleža (1893–1981). His most popular novels include *The Return of Philip Latinovicz* (1932), which has been translated into English.

Some contemporary writers worth reading are expat writer Dubravka Ugrešić (www.dubravkaugresic.com), best known for her novels *The Culture of Lies* and *The Ministry of Pain*. Slavenka Drakulić's *Café Europa – Life After Communism* is an excellent read, while Miljenko Jergović's *Sarajevo Marlboro* and *Mama Leone* powerfully conjure up the atmosphere and the life in pre-war Yugoslavia.

Music

Although Croatia has produced many fine classical musicians and composers, its most original musical contribution lies in its rich tradition of folk music. The instrument most often used in Croatian folk music is the *tamburica*, a three- or five-string mandolin that is plucked or strummed. Translated as 'group of people', *klapa* is an outgrowth of church-choir singing. The form is most popular in rural Dalmatia and can involve up to 10 voices singing in harmony.

There's a wealth of homegrown talent on Croatia's pop and rock music scene. Some of the most prominent pop, fusion and hip-hop bands are *Hladno Pivo* (Cold Beer), *Pips Chips & Videoclips*, *TBF*, *Edo Maajka*, *Vještice* (The Witches), *Gustafi* and the deliciously insane *Let 3*.

Visual Arts

Vlaho Bukovac (1855–1922) was the most notable Croatian painter in the late 19th century. Important early-20th-century painters include Miroslav Kraljević (1885–1913) and Josip Račić (1885–1908). Post-WWII artists experimented with abstract expressionism but this period is best remembered for the naive art that was typified by Ivan Generalić (1914–92). Recent trends have included minimalism, conceptual art and pop art. Contemporary art that is attracting notice include the multimedia works of Andreja Kulunči and the installations of Sandra Sterle.

ENVIRONMENT

The Land

Croatia is half the size of both Serbia and Montenegro in area and population. The republic swings around like a boomerang from the Pannonian plains of Slavonia between the Sava, Drava and Danube Rivers, across hilly central Croatia to the Istrian Peninsula, then south through Dalmatia along the rugged Adriatic coast.

The narrow Croatian coastal belt at the foot of the Dinaric Alps is only about 600km long as the crow flies, but it's so indented that the actual length is 1778km. If the 4012km of coastline around the offshore islands is added to the total, the length becomes 5790km. Most of the 'beaches' along this jagged coast consist of slabs of rock sprinkled with naturists. Don't come expecting to find sand, but the waters are sparkling clean, even around large towns.

Croatia's offshore islands are every bit as beautiful as those off the coast of Greece. There are 1185 islands and islets along the tectonically submerged Adriatic coastline, 66 inhabited.

Wildlife

Deer are plentiful in the dense forests of Risnjak, as well as brown bears, wild cats and *ris* (lynx). Occasionally a wolf or wild boar may appear, but only rarely. Plitvice Lakes National Park, however, is an important refuge for wolves. A rare sea otter is also protected in Plitvice, as well as in Krka National Park.

The griffon vulture, with a wing span of 2.6m, has a permanent colony on Cres Island, and Paklenica National Park is rich in peregrine falcons, goshawks, sparrow hawks, buzzards and owls. Krka National Park is an important migration route and winter habitat for marsh birds such as herons, wild duck, geese, cranes, rare golden eagles and short-toed eagles.

National Parks

The eight national parks occupy nearly 10% of the country. Brijuni near Pula is the most carefully cultivated park, with well-preserved Mediterranean holm oak forests. The mountainous Risnjak National Park near Delnice, east of Rijeka, is named after one of its inhabitants – the *ris*.

Dense forests of beech and black pine in the Paklenica National Park near Zadar are home to a number of endemic insects, reptiles and birds. The abundant plant and animal life, including bears, wolves and deer, in the Plitvice Lakes National Park between Zagreb and Zadar has warranted its inclusion on Unesco's list of World Natural Heritage sites. Both Plitvice Lakes and Krka National Parks (near Šibenik) feature a dramatic series of cascades and incredible turquoise lakes.

Environmental Issues

The lack of heavy industry in Croatia has left the country largely free of industrial pollution, but its forests are under threat from acid rain from neighbouring countries. The dry summers and brisk *maestral* winds pose substantial fire hazards along the coast. Waste disposal is a pressing problem in Croatia, with insufficient and poorly regulated disposal sites.

FOOD & DRINK

Croatian food is a savoury smorgasbord of taste, echoing the varied cultures that have influenced the country over the course of its history. You'll find a sharp divide between the Italian-style cuisine along the coast and the flavours of Hungary, Austria and Turkey in the continental parts.

Staples & Specialities

Zagreb and northwestern Croatia favour the kind of hearty meat dishes you might find in Vienna. Juicy spit-roasted and baked meat features *janjetina* (lamb), *svinjetina* (pork) and *patka* (duck), often accompanied by *mlinci* (baked noodles) or *pečeni krumpir* (roast potatoes).

CROATIA

Coastal cuisine is typically Mediterranean, using a lot of olive oil, garlic, fresh fish and shellfish, and herbs. Along the coast, look for lightly breaded and fried *lignje* (squid) as a main course. For a special appetiser, try *paški sir*, a pungent hard cheese from the island of Pag. Dalmatian *brodet* (stewed mixed fish served with polenta; also known as *brodetto*) is another regional treat, but it's often only available in two-person portions.

Istrian cuisine has been attracting international foodies for its long gastronomic tradition, fresh foodstuffs and unique specialities. Typical dishes include *maneštra*, a thick vegetable-and-bean soup, *fuži*, hand-rolled pasta often served with truffles or game meat, and *fritaja* (omelette often served with seasonal vegies). Istrian wines and olive oil are highly rated.

It's customary to have a small glass of brandy before a meal and to accompany the food with one of Croatia's many wines. Croatians often mix their wine with water, calling it *bevanda*. *Rakija* (brandy) comes in different flavours. The most commonly drunk are *loza* (grape brandy), *šljivovica* (plum brandy) and *travarica* (herbal brandy).

Zagreb's Ožujsko *pivo* (beer) is very good but Karlovačko *pivo* from Karlovac is even better. You'll probably want to practise saying *živjeli!* (cheers!).

Where to Eat & Drink

Most restaurants cluster in the middle of the price spectrum – few are unbelievably cheap and few are exorbitantly expensive. A restaurant *(restauracija* or *restoran)* is at the top of the food chain, generally presenting a more formal dining experience. A *gostionica* or *konoba* is usually a traditional family-run tavern. A *pivnica* is more like a pub, with a wide choice of beer. A *kavana* is a cafe. Self-service cafeterias are quick, easy and inexpensive, though the quality of the food tends to vary.

Restaurants are open long hours, often noon to midnight, with Sunday closings outside of peak season.

Smoking is a widespread activity in Croatia, and nonsmoking establishments are few and far between. You'll find bars and nightclubs permanently clouded in smoke, while some restaurants have nonsmoking sections.

Vegetarians & Vegans

Outside of major cities like Zagreb, Rijeka, Split and Dubrovnik, vegetarian restaurants are few but Croatia's vegetables are usually locally grown and quite tasty. *Blitva* (swiss chard) is a nutritious side dish often served with potatoes. The hearty *štrukli* (baked cheese dumplings) are a good alternative too.

ZAGREB

☎ 01 / pop 780,000

Everyone knows about Croatia, its coast, beaches and islands, but a mention of the country's capital still draws confused questions of whether it's nice or worth going to for a weekend. Well, here it is, once and for all: yes, Zagreb is a great destination, weekend or week-long. There's lots of culture, arts, music, architecture, nightlife, gastronomy and all the other things that make a quality capital. Admittedly, it doesn't register highly on a nightlife Richter scale, but it does have an ever-developing art and music scene and a growing influx of fun-seeking travellers.

Zagreb is made for strolling, drinking coffee in almost permanently full cafes, popping into museums and galleries and enjoying theatres, concerts, cinema and music. It's a year-round outdoor city; in spring and summer everyone scurries to Lake Jarun in the southwest to swim, boat or dance the night away in a lakeside disco, and in autumn and winter the Zagrebians go skiing at Mt Medvednica, only a tram ride away, or hiking in nearby Samobor.

HISTORY

Medieval Zagreb developed from the 11th to the 13th centuries in the twin villages of Kaptol and Gradec, which make up the city's hilly Old Town. Kaptol grew around St Stephen's Cathedral (now renamed the Cathedral of the Assumption of the Blessed Virgin Mary) and Gradec centred on St Mark's Church. The two hilltop administrations were bitter and often warring rivals until a common threat in the form of Turkish invaders emerged in the 15th century. The two communities merged and became Zagreb, capital of the small portion of Croatia that hadn't fallen to the Turks in the 16th century. As the Turkish threat receded in the 18th century, the town expanded and the population grew. It was the centre of intellectual and political life under the Austro-Hungarian empire and became capital of the Independent State of Croatia in 1941 after the German invasion. The 'independent state' was in fact a Nazi puppet regime in the hands of Ante Pavelić and the Ustaša movement, even though most Zagrebians supported Tito's partisans.

In postwar Yugoslavia, Zagreb took second place to Belgrade but continued expanding. The area south of the Sava River developed into a new district, Novi Zagreb, replete with the glum residential blocks that were a hallmark of postwar Eastern European architecture. Zagreb has been capital of Croatia since 1991, when the country became independent.

ORIENTATION

The city is divided into Lower Zagreb, where most shops, restaurants, hotels and businesses are located, and Upper Zagreb, defined by the two hills of Kaptol and Gradec. As you come out of the train station, you'll see a series of parks and pavilions directly in front of you and the twin neo-Gothic towers of the cathedral in Kaptol in the distance. Trg Jelačića, beyond the northern end of the parks, is the main city square of Lower Zagreb. There is a bus that runs from the airport to the bus station (see p218). The bus station is 1km east of the train station. Trams 2 and 6 run from the bus station to the train station, with tram 6 continuing to Trg Jelačića.

INFORMATION
Bookshops

Algoritam (Gajeva 1; ⏲ 8am-7pm Mon-Fri, 9am-5pm Sat) A wide selection of books and magazines to choose from in English, French, German, Italian and Croatian.

Discount Cards

Zagreb Card (www.zagrebcard.fivestars.hr/page_hr_on linecatalogue.htm; 24/72hr 60/90KN) Provides free travel on all public transport, a 50% discount on museum and gallery entries, plus discounts in some bars and restaurants, car rental etc. The card is sold at the main tourist office and many hostels, hotels, bars and shops.

Emergency

Police station (☎ 45 63 311; Petrinjska 30) Assists foreigners with visa problems.

Internet Access

Sublink (☎ 48 11 329; Teslina 12; per hr 15KN; ⏲ 9am-10pm Mon-Sat, 3-10pm Sun) It was the city's first cybercafe and it remains its best.

Laundry

If you're staying in private accommodation you can usually arrange with the owner to do your laundry, which would be cheaper than the two options listed below. Expect to pay about 65KN to do 5kg of laundry.
Petecin (☎ 48 14 802; Kaptol 11; ⏲ 8am-8pm Mon-Fri)
Predom (☎ 46 12 990; Draškovićeva 31; ⏲ 7am-7pm Mon-Fri)

Left Luggage

Garderoba bus station (per hr 1.20KN; ⏲ 5am-10pm Mon-Sat, 6am-10pm Sun); train station (per hr 1.20KN; ⏲ 24hr)

Medical Services

Dental Emergency (☎ 48 28 488; Perkovčeva 3; ⏲ 24hr)
KBC Rebro (☎ 23 88 888; Kišpatićeva 12; ⏲ 24hr) East of the city, it provides emergency aid.
Pharmacy (☎ 48 16 159; Trg Jelačića 2; ⏲ 24hr)

Money

There are ATMs at the bus and train stations and the airport, as well as numerous locations around town. Exchange offices at the

---

ZAGREB IN TWO DAYS

Start your day with a stroll through Strossmayerov Trg, Zagreb's oasis of greenery. While you're there, take a look at the **Strossmayer Gallery of Old Masters** (p213) and then walk to Trg Josipa Jelačića, the city's centre. Head up to **Kaptol** (p212) for a look at the **Cathedral of the Assumption of the Blessed Virgin Mary** (p213), the centre of Zagreb's (and Croatia's) spiritual life. While you're in the Upper Town, pick up some fruit at the **Dolac fruit and vegetable market** (p212). Then, get to know the work of Croatia's best sculptor at **Meštrović Atelier** (p213) and take in a contemporary art exhibition at **Galerija Klovićevi Dvori** (p213). See the lay of the city from the top of **Lotrščak Tower** (p213). Enjoy a drink at **Škola** (p216) or bar-crawling along Tkalčićeva (p216).

On the second day, tour the Lower Town museums, reserving a good two hours for the **Museum Mimara** (p213), then have lunch at **Tip Top** (p216). Early evening is best at **Trg Petra Preradovića** (p216) before dining at one of the **Lower Town restaurants** (p215) and sampling some of Zagreb's nightlife.

CROATIA

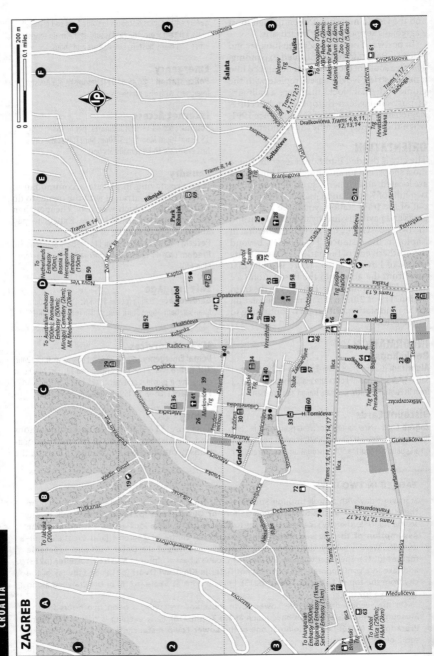

ZAGREB

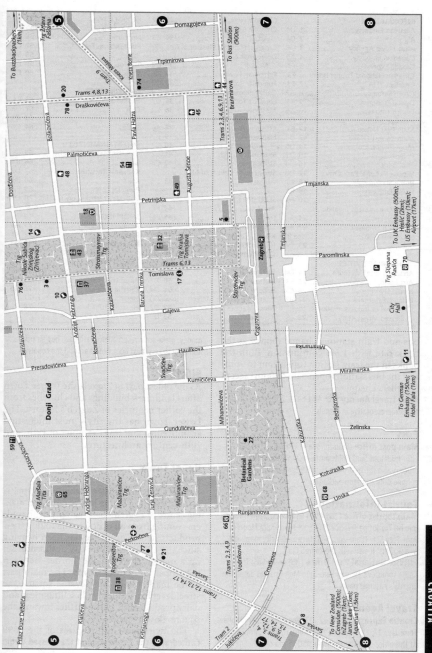

bus and train stations change money at the bank rate with 1.5% commission. Both the banks in the train station (open 7am to 9pm) and the bus station (open 6am to 8pm) accept travellers cheques.

Atlas Travel Agency (☎ 48 13 933; Zrinjevac 17) The Amex representative in Zagreb.

Post

Main post office (Branimirova 4; ⏰ 24hr Mon-Sat, 1pm-midnight Sun) Holds poste-restante mail. This post office is also the best place to make long-distance telephone calls and send packages.

Tourist Information

Main tourist office (☎ 48 14 051; www.zagreb-tourist info.hr; Trg Josipa Jelačića 11; ⏰ 8.30am-8pm Mon-Fri, 9am-5pm Sat, 10am-2pm Sun) Distributes city maps and free leaflets. It also sells the Zagreb Card.

Plitvice National Park Office (☎ 46 13 586; Trg Kralja Tomislava 19; ⏰ 9am-5pm Mon-Fri) Has details on Croatia's national parks.

Travel Agencies

Croatia Express (☎ 49 22 237; www.zug.hr; Trg Kralja Tomislava 17; ⏰ 9.30am-7pm Mon-Fri, 9am-3pm Sat) At this office opposite the train station you can change

money, make train reservations, rent cars, buy air tickets and ferry tickets, plus book hotels around the country.

SIGHTS

As the oldest part of Zagreb, the Upper Town offers landmark buildings and churches from the earlier centuries of Zagreb's history. The Lower Town has the city's most interesting art museums and fine examples of 19th- and 20th-century architecture.

Upper Town
KAPTOL

Zagreb's colourful **Dolac** (Market; ⏰ 6am-3pm) is just north of Trg Josipa Jelačića. It's the buzzing centre of Zagreb's daily activity, with traders coming from all over Croatia to flog their products here. The Dolac has been heaving since the 1930s when the city authorities set up a market space on the 'border' between the Upper and Lower towns. The main part of the market is on an elevated square; the street level has indoor stalls selling meat and dairy products and a little further towards the square, flower stands.

The twin neo-Gothic spires of the 1899 **Cathedral of the Assumption of the Blessed Virgin**

Mary (Katedrala Marijina Uznešenja; formerly known as St Stephen's Cathedral) are nearby. Elements of the medieval cathedral on this site, destroyed by an earthquake in 1880, can be seen inside, including 13th-century frescos, Renaissance pews, marble altars and a baroque pulpit. The baroque **Archbishop's Palace** surrounds the cathedral, as do 16th-century fortifications constructed when Zagreb was threatened by the Turks.

GRADEC

From Radićeva 5, off Trg Jelačića, a pedestrian walkway called stube Ivana Zakmardija leads to the **Lotrščak Tower** (Kula Lotrščak; ☎ 48 51 768; admission 10KN; ☺ 11am-7pm Tue-Sun) and a **funicular railway** (one way 3KN; ☺ 6.30am-9pm) built in 1888, which connects the Lower and Upper Towns. The tower has a sweeping 360-degree view of the city. To the east is the baroque **St Catherine's Church** (Crkva Svete Katarine), with Jezuitski trg beyond. The **Galerija Klovićevi Dvori** (☎ 48 51 926; Jezuitski trg 4; adult/student 40/20KN; ☺ 11am-7pm Tue-Sun) is Zagreb's premier exhibition hall, where superb art shows are staged. Further north and to the east is the 13th-century **Stone Gate**, with a painting of the Virgin, which escaped the devastating fire of 1731.

Gothic **St Mark's Church** (Crkva Svetog Marka; ☎ 48 51 611; Markovićev trg; ☺ 11am-4pm & 5.30-7pm) marks the centre of Gradec. Inside are works by Ivan Meštrović, Croatia's most famous modern sculptor. On the eastern side of St Mark's is the Croatia's 1908 **National Assembly** (Sabor).

FREE THRILLS

Though you'll have to pay to get into most of Zagreb's galleries and museums, there are some gorgeous parks and markets to be enjoyed for nowt – and there's always window shopping!

- Taste bits of food for free at **Dolac** (opposite) – but don't be too cheeky!
- Smell the herbs at the **Botanical Gardens** (p214).
- Enjoy the long walks around **Maksimir Park** (p214).
- See the magnificent **Mirogoj cemetery** (p214).
- Pop inside the gorgeous baroque **St Catherine's Church** (above) and the ever-renovated **cathedral** (above).

West of the church is the 18th-century **Banski Dvori**, the presidential palace, with guards at the door in red ceremonial uniform. Between April and September there is a changing of the guard ceremony at noon at the weekend.

Not far from the palace is the former **Meštrović Atelier** (☎ 48 51 123; Mletačka 8; adult/concession 30/15KN; ☺ 10am-6pm Tue-Fri, to 2pm Sat), now housing an excellent collection of some 100 sculptures, drawings, lithographs and furniture created by the artist. There are several other museums nearby. The best is the **City Museum** (Muzej Grada Zagreba; ☎ 48 51 364; Opatička 20; adult/concession 20/10KN; ☺ 10am-6pm Tue-Fri, to 1pm Sat & Sun), with a scale model of old Gradec, atmospheric background music and interactive exhibits that fascinate kids. Summaries in English and German are in each room of the museum, which is in the former Convent of St Claire (1650). There's also the lively and colourful **Croatian Museum of Naive Art** (Hrvatski Muzej Naivne Umjetnosti; ☎ 48 51 911; Ćirilometodska 3; adult/concession 10/5KN; ☺ 10am-6pm Tue-Fri, to 1pm Sat & Sun).

Lower Town

Zagreb really is a city of museums. There are four in the parks between the train station and Trg Jelačića. The yellow **exhibition pavilion** (1897) across the park from the station presents changing contemporary art exhibitions. The second building north, also in the park, houses the **Strossmayer Gallery of Old Masters** (Strossmayerova Galerija Starih Majstora; ☎ 48 95 115; www.mdc.hr/strossmayer; Zrinjevac 11; adult/concession 10/5KN; ☺ 10am-1pm & 5-7pm Tue, 10am-1pm Wed-Sun). When it's closed you can still enter the interior courtyard to see the Baška Slab (1102) from the island of Krk, one of the oldest inscriptions in the Croatian language.

The fascinating **Archaeological Museum** (Arheološki Muzej; ☎ 48 73 101; www.amz.hr; Trg Nikole Šubića Zrinjskog 19; adult/concession 20/10KN; ☺ 10am-5pm Tue-Fri, to 1pm Sat & Sun) has a wide-ranging display of artefacts from prehistoric times through to the medieval period. Behind the museum is a garden of Roman sculpture that is turned into a pleasant open-air cafe in the summer.

The **Modern Gallery** (Moderna Galerija; ☎ 49 22 368; Andrije Hebranga 1; adult/concession 20/10KN; 10am-6pm Tue-Sat, to 1pm Sun) presents temporary exhibitions that offer an excellent chance to catch up with the latest in Croatian painting.

The **Museum Mimara** (Muzej Mimara; ☎ 48 28 100; Rooseveltov trg 5; adult/concession 20/15KN; ☺ 10am-5pm

CROATIA

Tue, Wed, Fri & Sat, to 7pm Thu, to 2pm Sun) houses a diverse collection amassed by Ante Topić Mimara and donated to Croatia. Housed in a neo-Renaissance palace, the collection includes icons, glassware, sculpture, Oriental art and works by renowned painters such as Rembrandt, Velázquez, Raphael and Degas.

The neobaroque **Croatian National Theatre** (☎ 48 28 532; Trg Maršala Tita 15; ☿ box office 10am-1pm & 5-7.30pm Mon-Fri, to 1pm Sat, 30min before performances Sun) dates from 1895 and has Ivan Meštrović's sculpture *Fountain of Life* (1905) in front. The **Botanical Gardens** (Mihanovićeva; admission free; ☿ 9am-7pm Tue-Sun), laid out in 1890, has 10,000 species of plant, including 1800 tropical flora specimens. The landscaping has created restful corners and paths that seem a world away from bustling Zagreb.

Out of Town

A 20-minute ride north of the city centre on bus 106 from the cathedral takes you to **Mirogoj** (Medvednica; ☿ 6am-10pm), one of the most beautiful cemeteries in Europe. The cemetery was designed in 1876 by one of Croatia's finest architects, Herman Bollé, who also created numerous buildings around Zagreb. The sculpted and artfully designed tombs lie beyond a majestic arcade topped by a string of cupolas.

Another suburban delight is **Maksimir Park** (Maksimirska; ☿ 9am-dusk), a peaceful wooded enclave covering 18 hectares; it is easily accessible by trams 4, 7, 11 and 12. Opened to the public in 1794, it was the first public promenade in southeastern Europe. There's also a modest **zoo** (adult/child under 8yr, 20/10KN; ☿ 9am-8pm).

TOURS

The main tourist office sells tickets for two-hour walking tours (95KN) that operate Monday through Thursday, leaving from Trg Jelačića, as well as three-hour bus and walking tours (150KN) that operate Friday through Sunday, leaving from the Arcotel Allegra hotel.

FESTIVALS & EVENTS

During odd-numbered years in April there's the **Zagreb Biennale** (www.biennale-zagreb.hr), Croatia's most important classical music event. Zagreb also hosts the gay **Queer Zagreb FM Festival** (www.queerzagreb.org). Zagreb's highest profile music event is **Vip INmusic Festival** (www.vipinmusicfestival.com), a two-day extravaganza on

3 and 4 June, taking place on Jarun Lake's island. In July and August the **Zagreb Summer Festival** presents a cycle of concerts and theatre performances on open stages in the upper town. For a complete listing of Zagreb events, see www.zagreb-convention.hr.

SLEEPING

Zagreb's accommodation scene has been undergoing a small but noticeable change with the arrival of some of Europe's budget airlines: the budget end of the market (so far rather fledgling) has started to get a pulse. Although the new hostels cater mainly to the backpacker crowd, it's a good beginning. For midrangers and those wanting more privacy and a homely feel, there are private rooms and apartments, arranged through agencies.

Prices stay the same in all seasons, but be prepared for a 20% surcharge if you arrive during a festival, especially the autumn business fair (16 to 21 September).

If you intend to stay in a private house or apartment, try not to arrive on Sunday, because most of the agencies will be closed. Prices for doubles run from about 300KN and apartments start at 400KN per night for a studio. Some agencies:

Evistas (☎ 48 39 554; evistas@zg.htnet.hr; Augusta Šenoe 28; s from 200KN, d 250KN; ☿ 9am-1.30pm & 3-8pm Mon-Fri, 9.30am-5pm Sat) Recommended by the tourist office.
InZagreb (☎ 65 23 201; www.inzagreb.com; Remetinečka 13; apts from €65-86) Great, centrally located apartments with a minimum two-night stay. The price includes bike rental and pick-up and drop-off from the train and/or bus station.
Nemoj Stati/Never Stop (☎ 48 73 225; www.nest.hr; Boškovićeva 7a; ☿ 9am-5pm Mon-Fri) Has apartments in the centre of town, but note the minimum three-night stay. Contact for prices.

Fulir Hostel (☎ 48 30 882; www.fulir-hostel.com; Radićeva 3a; dm 100-140KN; ⌨) Right in the centre of town and seconds away from the bustle of Jelačića and bars on Tkalčićeva, the Fulir has 16 beds, friendly owners, self-catering facilities (perfect for its proximity to Dolac market), a DVD-packed common room, satellite TV and free internet. Opened in summer 2006, it's a popular spot for shoestring travellers, so book in advance.
Omladinski Hostel (☎ 48 41 261; www.hfhs .hr; Petrinjska 77; 6-/3-bed dm per person 103/113KN, s/d 193/256KN) A bit of a sad place, which, although recently refurbished, maintains the old gloomy

feel. The rooms are sparse and clean, it's relatively central and the cheapest in town.

Buzzbackpackers (☎ 23 20 267; www.buzzbackpackers.com; Babukićeva 1b; dm from 120KN; d from 400KN; ☒ 🖳) More slick and bright than Fulir, but a bit further out, Buzzbackpackers is another great-value newcomer. It's clean, the rooms are bright, there's wi-fi access, free internet, a shiny kitchen, laundry service (for a fee), and a BBQ area for the summer months. Take tram 4 or 9 from the main train station to Heinzelova stop, it's a short walk from there (check the website for detailed directions).

Krovovi Grada (☎ 48 14 189; Opatovina 33; s/d/tr 200/300/400KN) Possibly the most charming of Zagreb's central options, this place is right in the Upper Town. The restored old house is set back from the street and has creaky-floor rooms with pieces of vintage furniture and grandma blankets. There are two large apartments with shared bathrooms that can sleep eight.

Hotel Ilica (☎ 37 77 522; www.hotel-ilica.hr; Ilica 102; s/d/tr/apt 399/499/599/849KN; ☒) A great central option, with rooms ranging from super kitsch to lushly decorous – there are gilded motifs, plush beds, wall-long paintings and lots of reds. The bathrooms are well-equipped and the setting is quiet. Trams 6, 11 and 12 stop right outside the entrance, or walk down buzzy Ilica for 15 minutes.

ourpick Arcotel Allegra (☎ 46 96 000; www.arcotel.at/allegra; Branimirova 29; d €152-162; ☒ 🖳) The Arcotel Allegra is Zagreb's first designer hotel, with airy, elegant rooms and a plush, marble-and-exotic-fish reception. The bed linen is covetable and soft and the bed throws are printed with the faces of Kafka, Kahlo, Freud, Lorca and numerous other iconic personalities. There's a DVD player in each room and the hotel has movies you can borrow. The top floor has a gym, sauna and great views of the city. The on-site Radicchio restaurant is good and Joe's Bar's hot on Latino music.

EATING
You'll have to love Croatian and (below par) Italian food to enjoy Zagreb's restaurants, but new places are branching out to include Japanese and other world cuisines. The biggest move is towards elegantly presented haute cuisine at haute prices.

Upper Town
Rubelj (☎ 48 18 777; www.rubelj-grill.hr; Tržnica Mala Terasa; mains from 25KN) One of the many Rubeljs

across town, this Dolac branch is a great place for a quick portion of ćevapi (spicy beef or pork meatballs). And though none are as tasty as those in neighbouring Bosnia and Hercegovina (the spiritual home of the ćevap), these are Zagreb's best.

Vallis Aurea (☎ 48 31 305; Tomićeva 4; mains from 30KN) This is a true local eatery that has some of the best home cooking you'll find in town, so it's no wonder that it's chock-a-block at lunchtimes. Taste the Dalmatian staple, the paštacida (beef stew) or the slightly spicy beans, and accompany either with some house red. Right by the lower end of the funicular.

Ivica i Marica (☎ 48 17 321; Tkalčićeva 70; mains from 40KN) Based on the Brothers Grimm story of Hansel and Gretel, this little restaurant–cake shop is made to look like the 'food house' from the tale, with waiting staff clad in traditional costume. It's not exactly vegie, but it does have a decent range of vegie and fish dishes plus meatier fare. The ice creams and cakes are good too.

ourpick Kerempuh (☎ 48 19 000; Kaptol 3; mains 50-70KN) Overlooking Dolac market, this is a fabulous place to taste a) Croatian cuisine cooked well and simply, and b) the market's ingredients on your plate. The daily set menu changes, well, daily, and the dishes are decided in the morning, when the chef gets that day's freshest ingredients from Dolac. Get an outside table and enjoy the excellent food and market views.

Pod Gričkim Topom (☎ 48 33 607; Zakmardijeve Stube 5; mains from 90KN) Tucked away by a leafy path below the Upper Town, this restaurant has a somewhat self-conscious charm, but it has an outdoor terrace and good Croatian meat-based specialities. It's a great place to hole up on a snowy winter evening or dine under the stars in the summer months.

Baltazar (☎ 46 66 999; www.restoran-baltazar.hr; Nova Ves 4; mains from 120KN; ✍ Mon-Sat) Meat – duck, lamb, pork, beef and turkey – is grilled and prepared the Zagorje and Slavonia way in this upmarket old-timer with a good choice of local wines. The summer terrace is a great place to dine under the stars.

You can pick up excellent fresh produce at Dolac market (p212).

Lower Town
Nocturno (☎ 48 13 394; Skalinska 4; mains 20-50KN) Right on the sloping street underneath the Cathedral, this place is very popular for its

Italian menu and lively outdoor terrace. There are all the usual pizzas, plus some good salads, which will gladden vegetarian hearts. The risottos are pretty huge, so order one of those if you're starving.

our pick Tip Top (☎ 48 30 349; Gundulićeva 18; mains from 35KN) Oh, how we love Tip Top and its wait staff, who still sport old Socialist uniforms and scowling faces that eventually turn to smiles. But how we mostly love the excellent Dalmatian food. Every day has its own set menu (in addition to à la carte) but Thursdays are particularly delicious, with the octopus *brodet* (octopus stewed in red wine, garlic and herbs). Owned and run by Korčulans, you'll find that island's wines on offer – the wines that were no doubt enjoyed by Tin Ujević, Tip Top's once most loyal customer.

Boban (☎ 48 11 549; Gajeva 9; mains 40-60KN) Italian is the name of the game in this cellar restaurant that's owned by the Croatian World Cup star Zvonimir Boban. Devised by an Italian chef (who hasn't quite instilled the concept of *pasta al dente* into the local chefs), the menu is a robust range of pastas, salads and meats. It's a popular lunch and dinner spot; the upstairs cafe's terrace attracts Zagreb's youngsters.

Konoba Čiho (☎ 48 17 060; Pavla Hatza 15; mains from 55KN; Mon-Sat) Another old-school Dalmatian *konoba,* where downstairs you can get fish and seafood grilled or stewed just the way the regulars like it. Try the wide range of *rakija*.

Makronova (☎ 48 47 115; www.makronova.com; Ilica 72; mains 80-120KN; Mon-Sat) This macrobiotic restaurant is elegant and peaceful and more than welcoming for those of the vegan persuasion. It's part of a whole healthy emporium – there's a health-food shop downstairs, shiatsu treatment, yoga classes and feng-shui courses.

There's also a **fruit and vegetable market** (7am-3pm) on Britanski Trg.

DRINKING

In the Upper Town, the chic Tkalčićeva is throbbing with bars. In the Lower Town, Trg Petra Preradovića is the most popular spot for street performers and occasional bands in mild weather. One of the nicest ways to see Zagreb is to join in on the *špica* – the Saturday morning and pre-lunch coffee drinking on the many terraces along Preradovićeva and Tkalčićeva.

our pick Booksa (☎ 46 16 124; www.booksa.hr; Martićeva 14D; 9am-11pm Tue-Sun) Bookworms and poets, writers and performers, oddballs and artists, and anyone on the creative side of things in Zagreb come to chat and drink coffee, buy books and hear readings at this lovely bookshop. There are English-language readings here too, so check the website.

Eli's Café (☎ 091 527 9990; www.eliscaffe.com; Ilica 63; 8am-9pm Mon-Sat, 9am-3pm Sun) You'll see why this tiny place was awarded the 'Best Coffee in Croatia' in 2008, when you try the excellent espresso or smooth cappuccino. There are also breakfast pastries for dipping.

our pick Škola (☎ 48 28 197; www.skolaloungebar.com; Bogovićeva 7) This has to be the best designed bar in the whole of Zagreb with its huge, differently themed rooms, lounge sofas, an olive tree in the middle of the main room, and notebook-style menus (it's called School, you see?). There are DJ nights, various 'afterschool' parties and it's packed with the trendiest of people (and, of course, students).

Cica (Tkalčićeva 18) It's the size of an East London bedsit, with a similar vibe to match: an underground place with a massive choice of *rakija* in all flavours – herbal, nutty, fruity – you think it, they have it. Lovers of hedonistic pleasures, Cica is your place.

ENTERTAINMENT

Zagreb is definitely a happening city. Its theatres and concert halls present a great variety of programs throughout the year. Many (but not all) are listed in the monthly brochure *Zagreb Events & Performances*, which is available from the main tourist office.

Nightclubs

The dress code is relaxed in most Zagreb clubs. It doesn't get lively until near midnight.

KSET (☎ 61 29 999; www.kset.org; Unska 3; 8pm-midnight Mon-Fri, to 3am Sat) Zagreb's best music venue, with everyone who's anyone performing here.

Aquarius (☎ 36 40 231; Jarun Lake) A truly fab place to party, this enormously popular spot has a series of rooms that open onto a huge terrace on the lake.

Boogaloo (☎ 63 13 021; www.boogaloo.hr; OTV Dom, Vukovarska 68) A great venue that hosts DJ nights and live music.

Purgeraj (☎ 48 14 734; Park Ribnjak) Live rock, blues, rock-blues, blues-rock, country rock and avant-garde jazz.

Jabuka (☎ 48 34 397; Jabukovac 28) An old-time favourite, with 1980s hits played to a thirty-something crowd that reminisces about the good old days.

Gay & Lesbian Venues

The gay and lesbian scene in Zagreb is finally becoming more open than it had previously been, although 'free-wheeling' it isn't. Many gays discreetly cruise the south beach around Jarun Lake and are welcome in most discos. **David** (☎ 091 533 7757; Marulićev Trg 3) is a sauna, bar and video room, popular on Zagreb's gay scene.

Sport

Football (soccer) games are held every Sunday afternoon at the **Maksimir Stadium** (Maksimirska 128), on the eastern side of Zagreb; catch tram 4, 7, 11 or 12 to Bukovačka. If you arrive too early for the game, Zagreb's zoo is just across the street.

Performing Arts

It's worth making the rounds of the theatres in person to check their programs. Tickets are usually available for performances, even for the best shows. A small office marked 'Kazalište Komedija' (look out for the posters) also sells theatre tickets; it's in the Oktogon, a passage connecting Trg Petra Preradovića to Ilica 3.

The neobaroque Croatian National Theatre (p214) was established in 1895. It stages opera and ballet performances.

Komedija Theatre (☎ 48 14 566; Kaptol 9) Near the cathedral, the Komedija Theatre stages operettas and musicals.

Vatroslav Lisinski Concert Hall (☎ ticket office 61 21 166; Trg Stjepana Radića 4; ⏾ 9am-8pm Mon-Fri, to 2pm Sat) Just south of the train station, this concert hall is a prestigious venue where symphony concerts are held regularly.

SHOPPING

Ilica is Zagreb's main shopping street.

our pick Prostor (☎ 48 46 016; www.multiracional nakompanija.com; Mesnička 5; ⏾ noon-8pm Mon-Fri; 10am-3pm Sat) A fantastic little shop that's an art gallery and a clothes shop at the same time, featuring some of the city's best independent artists and young designers.

Rukotvorine (☎ 48 31 303; Trg Josipa Jelačića 7) Sells traditional Croatian handicrafts such as dolls, pottery and red-and-white embroidered tablecloths.

MARKET DAYS

The Sunday **antiques market** (⏾ 9am-2pm) on Britanski Trg is one of central Zagreb's joys, but to see a flea market that's un-matched in the whole of Croatia, you have to make it to **Hrelić** (⏾ 7am-3pm). It's a huge space that's packed with anything – and we mean anything – from car parts, cars, antique furniture to clothes, records, kitchenware, you name it. Apart from the shopping it's a great place to experience the truly Balkan part and chaotic fun of Zagreb – Roma, music, bartering, grilled meat smoke and general gusto. If you're going in the summer months, take a hat and put on some sunscreen – there's no shade. Take bus 295 to Sajam Jakuševac from behind the train station.

GETTING THERE & AWAY
Air

For information about international flights to and from Croatia, see p258.

Bus

Zagreb's big, modern **bus station** (☎ 61 57 983; www.akz.hr, in Croatian) has a large waiting room and a number of shops. You can buy most international tickets at windows 17 to 20.

Buses depart from Zagreb for most parts of Croatia, Slovenia and places beyond; see p218 for domestic services. There is a service between Sarajevo (BiH) and Zagreb (€18, eight hours, three daily), as well as a service from Zagreb to Belgrade (€20, six hours, six daily; at Bajakovo on the border, a Serbian bus takes you on to Belgrade). There are buses from Ljubljana (Slovenia) to Zagreb (110KN, three hours, two daily).

Train

Domestic trains depart from **Zagreb train station** (☎ 060 33 34 44; www.hzn et.hr); see p218 for services. All daily trains to Zadar stop at Knin. Reservations are required on fast InterCity (IC) trains and there's a supplement of 5KN to 15KN for fast or express trains.

For destinations outside Croatia, there's a daily train service to Zagreb from Sarajevo (BiH) each morning (260KN, eight hours), five daily trains between Zagreb and Belgrade (Serbia; €25, seven hours), and up to 11 trains daily between Zagreb and Ljubljana

BUSES FROM ZAGREB

Destination	Fare (KN)	Duration (hr)	Daily services
Dubrovnik	250	11	7-8
Korčula	224	11	1
Krk	160-190	4-5	4
Mali Lošinj	260-280	6½	2
Osijek	125-160	4	8
Plitvice	80	2½	19
Poreč	170-210	5	6
Pula	170-230	4-5	6
Rab	195	5	2
Rijeka	125-150	2½-3	14
Rovinj	170-190	5-8	8
Šibenik	165	6½	15
Split	195	5-9	27
Zadar	120-140	3½-5	20

(Slovenia; €16, 2¼ hours). There are also four daily trains from Zagreb to Budapest (€60, 5½ to 7½ hours). Between Venice and Zagreb (€60, 6½ to 7½ hours) there are two daily direct connections and several more that run through Ljubljana.

GETTING AROUND

Zagreb is a fairly easy city to navigate, whether by car or public transport. Traffic isn't bad, there's sufficient parking and the efficient tram system should be a model for other polluted, traffic-clogged European capitals.

To/From the Airport

The Croatia Airlines bus to Pleso airport leaves from the bus station every half-hour or hour from about 4am to 8.30pm, depending on flights, and returns from the airport on about the same schedule (50KN one way). A taxi would cost about 300KN.

Car

Of the major car-hire companies, you could try **Budget Rent-a-Car** (☎ 45 54 936; Kneza Borne 2) in the Hotel Sheraton and **Hertz** (☎ 48 46 777; Vukotinovićeva 4). Prices start at 300KN per day. Bear in mind that local companies will usually have the lower rates. Try **H&M** (☎ 37 04 535; www.hm-rentacar.hr; Grahorova 11), which also has an office at the airport.

Zagreb is relatively easy to navigate by car, but remember that the streets around Trg Jelačića and up through Kaptol and Gradec are pedestrian only. Watch out for trams sneaking up on you.

The **Hrvatski Autoklu** (HAK, Croatian Autoclub; ☎ 46 40 800; Derenčinova 20) information centre helps motorists in need. It's just east of the centre.

Public Transport

Public transport is based on an efficient network of trams, though the city centre is compact enough to make them unnecessary. Buy tickets at newspaper kiosks for 8KN. Each ticket must be stamped when you board. You can use your ticket for transfers within 90 minutes but only in one direction.

A *dnevna karta* (day ticket), valid on all public transport until 4am the next morning, is 25KN at most Vjesnik or Tisak news outlets. (See p209 for details of the Zagreb Card.) Controls are frequent on the tram system, with substantial fines for not having the proper ticket.

Taxi

Zagreb's taxis ring up 8KN per kilometre after a flag fall of 25KN. On Sunday and during the hours of 10pm to 5am there's a 20% surcharge.

TRAINS FROM ZAGREB

Destination	Fare (KN)	Duration (hr)	Daily services
Osijek	113	4	5
Pula	131	6½	2
Rijeka	96	5	5
Šibenik	149	6½-10	3
Split	160	6-8½	6
Zadar	156	7-9¾	5

ISTRIA

☎ 052

Continental Croatia meets the Adriatic in Istria (Istra to Croatians), the heart-shaped 3600-sq-km peninsula just south of Trieste in Italy. While the bucolic interior of rolling hills and fertile plains has been attracting artists and visitors to its hilltop villages, rural hotels and farmhouse restaurants, the verdant in-dented coastline is enormously popular with the sun 'n' sea set. Vast hotel complexes line much of the coast and its rocky beaches are not Croatia's best, but the facilities are wide-ranging, the sea is clean and secluded spots still aplenty.

The northern part of the peninsula belongs to Slovenia. Just across the water is Italy, but the pervasive Italian influence makes it seem much closer. Italian is, in fact, a sec-ond language in Istria, many Istrians have Italian passports, and each town name has an Italian counterpart. Perhaps they dream of the days when the string of Istrian resorts belonged to Italy. Italy seized Istria from Austria-Hungary in 1918, then gave it up to Yugoslavia in 1947. Tito wanted Trieste (Trst) as part of Yugoslavia too, but in 1954 the Anglo-American occupiers returned the city to Italy so that it wouldn't fall into the hands of the 'communists'.

Visit Poreč, Rovinj and Pula on the coast and then move on to the interior, known for its hilltop towns and acclaimed gastronomy, starring prime truffles, wild asparagus, top olive oil and award-winning wines.

POREČ

pop 17,000

Poreč (Parenzo in Italian) sits on a low, nar-row peninsula halfway down the western coast of Istria. The ancient Roman town is the centrepiece of a vast system of resorts that stretch north and south, entirely devoted to summer tourism. While this is not the place for a quiet getaway (unless you come out of season), there is a World Heritage–listed ba-silica, well-developed tourist infrastructure, a strip of rocky beaches nearby and the pristine Istrian interior within easy reach.

Orientation

The compact Old Town, called Parentium by the Romans, is based on a rectangular street plan. The ancient Decumanus with its polished stones is still the main street running through the peninsula's middle, lined with shops and restaurants. Hotels, travel agencies and excursion boats are on the quay, Obala Maršala Tita, which runs from the small-boat harbour to the tip of the peninsula. The bus station is just outside the Old Town, behind Rade Končara.

Information

You can change money at any of the many travel agencies or banks. There are ATMs all around town.

Atlas Travel Agency (☎ 434 933; www.atlas-croatia .com; Eufrazijeva 63; ☯ 9am-2pm & 6-9pm) Books excursions.

CyberM@c (☎ 427 075; Mire Grahalića 1; per hr 42KN; ☯ 8am-10pm) A full-service computer centre.

Di Tours (☎ 432 100; www.di-tours.hr; Prvomajska 2; ☯ 9am-10pm Jul & Aug, to 9pm Jun & Sep) Finds private accommodation.

Garderoba (per day 22KN; ☯ 7am-9pm daily) Left-luggage facilities at the bus station.

Main post office (Trg Slobode 14; ☯ 8am-noon & 6-8pm Mon-Sat)

Poreč Medical Centre (☎ 451 611; Maura Gioseffija 2)

Sunny Way (☎ 452 021; Alda Negrija 1; sunnyway@ pu.t-com.hr; ☯ 9am-9pm Jul & Aug) Specialises in boat tickets and excursions to Italy and around Croatia.

Tourist office (☎ 451 293; www.to-porec.com; Zagrebačka 9; ☯ 8am-10pm Mon-Sat, 9am-1pm & 6-10pm Sun Jul & Aug, 8am-4pm Mon-Sat rest of the year)

Sights

The main reason to visit Poreč is the 6th-century **Euphrasian Basilica** (☎ 431 635; Eufrazijeva bb; admission free, belfry 10KN; ☯ 7am-8pm Apr–mid-Oct or by appointment), one of Europe's finest intact examples of Byzantine art. What packs in the crowds are the glittering wall mosaics in the apse, veritable masterpieces featuring biblical scenes, archangels and martyrs. The belfry affords an invigorating view of the Old Town. Worth a visit is the adjacent **Bishop's Palace** (admission 10KN; ☯ 9am-7pm Apr–mid-Oct or by appointment) which contains a display of ancient stone sculptures, religious paintings and 4th-century mosaics from the original oratory.

The numerous historic sites in the Old Town include the ruins of two **Roman tem-ples**, between Trg Marafor, once the site of the Roman forum, and the western end of the peninsula. There's also a medley of Gothic and Romanesque buildings to look out for, as well as the baroque Sinčić Palace, which houses the

Regional Museum (Decumanus 9; www.muzejporec.hr), under renovation at the time of research but due to re-open at the end of 2009.

From May to October there are passenger boats (15KN) travelling to **Sveti Nikola**, the small island that lies opposite Poreč harbour. They depart every 30 minutes to an hour from the wharf on Obala Maršala Tita.

Activities

Nearly every activity you might want to enjoy is outside the town in either Plava Laguna or Zelena Laguna. For details, pick up the yearly *Poreč Info* booklet from the tourist office, which lists all the recreational facilities in the area.

From March to early October a tourist train operates regularly from Šetalište Antuna Štifanića by the marina to Plava Laguna (10KN) and Zelena Laguna (15KN). There's an hourly passenger boat that makes the same run from the ferry landing (25KN).

The well-marked paths make **cycling** and **hiking** a prime way to explore the region. The tourist office issues a free map of roads and trails. You can rent a bike at many places around town; try the outlet just below the **Hotel Poreč** (☎ 098 335 838) for 70KN per day.

There is good diving in and around shoals and sandbanks in the area, as well as to the nearby *Coriolanus*, a British Royal Navy warship sunk in 1945. At **Plava Laguna Diving Center** (☎ 098 367 619; www.plava-laguna-diving.hr) boat dives start at 100KN (more for caves or wrecks).

Sleeping

Accommodation in Poreč is plentiful but gets booked ahead of time, so advance reservations are essential if you come in July or August.

If you want to find private accommodation consult Poreč's travel agencies (see p219). Expect to pay between 200KN and 250KN for a double room in high season (up to 350KN for a two-person apartment), plus a 30% surcharge for stays of less than four nights. There are a limited number of rooms in the Old Town, where there's no parking. Look for the *Domus Bonus* certificate of quality in private accommodation.

Camp Zelena Laguna (☎ 410 700; www.plavalaguna.hr; per adult/site 55/75KN; Apr-Sep) Well equipped for sports, and with access to many beaches, this camping ground is only 5km from the Old Town.

Camp Bijela Uvala (☎ 410 551; www.plavalaguna.hr; per adult/site 55/75KN; Apr-Sep) It can be crowded, as it houses up to 6000, but there are two outdoor pools and the facilities of Zelena Laguna a stone's throw away.

Hotel Poreč (☎ /fax 451 811; www.hotelporec.com; Rade Končara 1; s 285-495KN; d 395-730KN;) While the rooms inside this concrete box have uninspiring views over the bus station, they're acceptable and an easy walk from the Old Town. It's open all year.

our pick Hotel Hostin (☎ 408 800; www.hostin.hr; Rade Končara 4; s 300-650KN, d 395-920KN;) Each of the well-equipped rooms comes with balconies, in verdant parkland. An indoor swimming pool, fitness room, Turkish bath and sauna are nice perks, as is the pebble beach 70m away.

Eating

A large supermarket and department store are situated next to Hotel Poreč, near the bus station.

Nono (☎ 435 088; Zagrebačka 4; pizzas 45-80KN) Nono serves the best pizza in town, with puffy crust and toppings such as truffles. Other dishes are tasty too.

Barilla (☎ 452 742; Eufrazijeva 26; mains from 45KN) Comforting Italian concoctions in all shapes and forms. There are tables on the square and a quieter patio in the back. Try the spaghetti with seashells (170KN for two).

our pick Dva Ferala (☎ 433 416; Obala Maršala Tita 13a; mains from 50KN) Savour well-prepared Istrian specialties, such as Istarski Tris for two – a copious trio of homemade pastas (110KN) – on the terrace of this pleasant *konoba*.

Drinking

Lapidarium (Svetog Maura 10) Gorgeous bar with a large courtyard in the back of the regional museum and a series of antique-filled inner rooms. Wednesday is jazz night in the summer, with alfresco live music.

Torre Rotonda (Narodni Trg 3a) Take the steep stairs to the top of the historic Round Tower and grab a table at the open-air cafe to watch the action on the quays.

Entertainment

Byblos (www.byblos.hr; Zelena Laguna bb) Celeb guest DJs like David Morales and Eric Morillo crank out house tunes at this humongous open-air club, one of Croatia's hottest places to party.

Getting There & Away

There are daily buses from the **bus station** (☎ 432 153; Rade Končara 1) to Rovinj (38KN, 40 minutes, seven daily), Zagreb (217KN, five hours, seven daily), Rijeka (81KN, two hours, 11 daily) and Pula (50KN, one to 1½ hours, 11 daily).

The nearest train station is at Pazin, 37km to the east. There are about 10 buses daily from Poreč (34KN, 30 minutes).

Sunny Way (☎ 452 021; sunnyway@pu.t-com.hr; Alda Negrija 1; ⊗ 9am-9pm Jul & Aug) runs a fast catamaran to Venice daily in season (one way/return 430/520KN). **Ustica Lines** (www.usticalines.it) has ferries to Trieste (one way/return 150/280KN, two hours), which run daily except Monday.

ROVINJ

pop 14,200

Rovinj (Rovigno in Italian) is coastal Istria's star attraction. While it can get over-run with tourists in the summer months and residents are developing a sharp eye for maximising their profits (by upgrading the hotels and restaurants to four-star status), it remains one of the last true Mediterranean fishing ports. Fishermen haul their catch into the harbour in the early morning, followed by a horde of squawking gulls, and mend their nets before lunch. The massive Cathedral of St Euphemia, with its 60m-high tower, punctuates the peninsula. Wooded hills and low-rise hotels surround the Old Town webbed by steep, cobbled streets and piazzas. The 13 green, offshore islands of the Rovinj archipelago make for a pleasant afternoon away, and you can swim from the rocks in the sparkling water below the Old Town.

Orientation

The Old Town of Rovinj is contained within an egg-shaped peninsula, with the bus station just to the southeast. There are two harbours – the northern open harbour and the small, protected harbour to the south.

Information

There's an ATM next to the bus station entrance, and banks all around town. Most travel agencies will change money.

Futura Travel (☎ 817 281; www.futura-travel.hr; Matteo Benussi 2; ⊗ 8.30am-9pm Mon-Sat, 8.30am-1pm & 5-9pm Sun May-Sep) Private accommodation, excursions and transfers.

Garderoba (per hr 1.40KN; ⊗ 6.30am-8.15pm Mon-Fri, 7.45am-7.30pm Sat & Sun) Left luggage at bus station. Note the three 30-minute breaks, at 9.15am, 1.30pm and 4.30pm.

Globtour (☎ 814 130; www.globtour-turizam.hr; Alda Rismonda 2; ⊗ 9am-10pm Jul & Aug, reduced hr rest of year) Excursions, private accommodation and bike rental (60KN per day).

Kompas (☎ 813 211; www.kompas-travel.com; Trg Maršala Tita 5; ⊗ 9am-10pm Jul & Aug, reduced hr rest of year) Daily excursions.

Main post office (Matteo Benussi 4; ⊗ 7am-8pm Mon-Fri, to 2pm Sat)

Medical Centre (☎ 813 004; Istarska bb)

Planet (☎ 840 494; Svetog Križa 1; per 10min 6KN; ⊗ 9am-10pm Mon-Sat, 9am-1pm & 5-9pm Sun) Travel agency with an internet terminal.

Tourist office (☎ 811 566; www.tzgrovinj.hr; Pina Budicina 12; ⊗ 8am-10pm Jul & Aug, to 9pm Sep & Jun) Just off Trg Maršala Tita, it has plenty of brochures, maps and materials.

Sights

The town's showcase is the imposing **Church of St Euphemia** (Sveta Eufemija; ☎ 815 615; Petra Stankovića; ⊗ 10am-6m Jul & Aug, 11am-3pm Sep-Jun) that dominates the Old Town from its hilltop location. Built in 1736, it's the largest baroque building in Istria, reflecting the period during the 18th century when Rovinj was its most populous town, an important fishing centre and the bulwark of the Venetian fleet.

Inside the church behind the right-hand altar, don't miss the marble tomb of St Euphemia, Rovinj's patron saint martyred in AD 304, whose body mysteriously appeared in Rovinj according to legend. On the anniversary of her martyrdom (16 September), devotees congregate here. The mighty 60m tower is topped by a copper statue of St Euphemia, which shows the direction of the wind by turning on a spindle. You can climb it for 10KN.

The **Heritage Museum** (☎ 816 720; www.muzej-rovinj.hr; Trg Maršala Tita 11; adult/concession 15/10KN; ⊗ 9am-3pm & 7-10pm Tue-Fri, 9am-2pm & 7-10pm Sat & Sun mid-Jun–mid-Sep, 9am-3pm Tue-Sat rest of year) in a baroque palace contains a collection of contemporary art and old masters from Croatia and Rovinj, as well as archaeological finds and a maritime section.

Nearby is the elaborate **Balbi Arch**, built in 1679 on the location of the former town gate. The cobbled street of **Grisia** leads uphill from behind the arch to St Euphemia, lined with galleries where local artists sell their work. On the second Sunday in August each year, narrow Grisia becomes an open-air **art exhibition** with anyone from children to professional painters displaying their work. The winding narrow backstreets that spread around Grisia are an attraction in themselves. Windows, balconies, portals and squares are a pleasant confusion of styles – Gothic, Renaissance, baroque and neoclassical.

On the harbour, **Batana House** (☎ 812 593; www.batana.org; Pina Budicina 2; admission free, with guide 15KN; ☷ 10am-1pm & 7-10pm Tue-Sun May-Sep, 10am-1pm Tue-Sun rest of year) is a multimedia museum dedicated to the *batana*, a flat-bottomed fishing boat that stands as a symbol of Rovinj's seafaring and fishing tradition.

When you've seen enough of the town, follow the waterfront on foot or by bike past Hotel Park to the verdant **Golden Cape Forest Park** (Zlatni Rt, or Punta Corrente) about 1.5km south. Covered in oak and pine groves and boasting 10 species of cypress, the park was established in 1890 by Baron Hütterott, an Austrian admiral who kept a villa on Crveni Otok. Here you can swim off the rocks or just sit and admire the offshore islands.

Activities

Most people hop aboard a boat for swimming, snorkelling and sunbathing. A trip to Crveni Otok or Sveti Katarina is easily arranged. In summer, there are 18 boats daily to Sveta Katarina (15KN, five minutes) and on to Crveni Otok (15KN return, 15 minutes). They leave from just opposite Hotel Adriatic and also from the Delphin ferry dock near Hotel Park.

Diver Sport Center (☎ 816 648; www.diver.hr; Villas Rubin) is the largest operation in Rovinj, offering boat dives from 210KN, with equipment rental. The main dive attraction is the wreck of the *Baron Gautsch*, an Austrian passenger-steamer sunk in 1914 by a mine.

Biking around Rovinj and the Golden Cape Park is a superb way to spend an afternoon. You can rent bicycles at many agencies around town, from 60KN per day. The cheapest bike rental (5KN per hour) is at the town entrance, by the Valdibora parking lot and the market.

Tours

Most travel agencies (p221) sell day trips to Venice (450KN to 520KN), Plitvice (580KN) and Brijuni (380KN to 420KN). There are also fish picnics (250KN), panoramic cruises (100KN) and trips to Limska Draga Fjord (150KN). These trips can be slightly cheaper if booked through one of the independent operators that line the waterfront; **Delfin** (☎ 813 266) is reliable.

Sleeping

Rovinj has become Istria's destination of choice for hordes of summertime tourists, so reserving in advance is strongly recommended.

If you want to stay in private accommodation, there is little available in the Old Town, plus there is no parking and the cost is higher. Double rooms start at 180KN in the high season, with a small discount for single occupancy; two-person apartments start at 380KN. You can book directly through www .inforovinj.com or one of the listed agencies.

The surcharge for a stay of less than three nights is 50% and guests who stay only one night are punished with a 100% surcharge. Outside summer months, you should be able to bargain the surcharge away.

Except a few private options, most hotels and camping grounds in the area are managed by **Maistra** (www.maistra.com).

Porton Biondi (☎ 813 557; www.portonbiondi.hr; per person/tent 40/23KN; ☷ Apr-Oct) This camping ground that sleeps 1200 is about 700m from the Old Town.

Vila Lili (☎ 840 940; www.hotel-vilalili.hr; Mohorovičića 16; s 333-385KN, d 505-730KN; ⊠ ☐) Bright rooms with all the three-star perks, including air-con and minibars in a small modern house a short walk out of town.

Hotel Adriatic (☎ 815 088; www.maistra.hr; Pina Budicina bb; s 392-589KN, d 522-784KN; ⊠ ☐) The location right on the harbour is excellent and the rooms spick-and-span and well equipped, albeit on the kitschy side. The sea-view rooms are more spacious.

our pick **Casa Garzotto** (☎ 811 884; www.casa -garzotto.com; Via Garzotto 8; s 510-760KN, d 650-1015KN; ⊠ ☐) Each of the four nicely outfitted studio apartments have original detail, a stylish touch and up-to-the-minute amenities. The historic townhouse can't be better placed. Bikes are complimentary.

Hotel Villa Angelo D'Oro (☎ 840 502; www.angelo doro.hr; Vladimira Švalbe 38-42; s 619-990KN, d 1005-1762KN; ⊠) In a renovated Venetian townhouse, the 24 plush rooms and (pricier) suites of this boutique hotel have lots of antiques plus mod perks aplenty. There's sauna, jacuzzi and a lush interior terrace, a great place for a drink amid ancient stone.

Eating

Most of the restaurants that line the harbour offer the standard fish and meat mainstays at similar prices. For a more gourmet experience, you'll need to bypass the water vistas. Note that many restaurants shut their doors between lunch and dinner. For an evening snack of local cheese, cured meats and tasty small bites, head to **Ulika** (Vladimira Švalbe 34; ☺ dinner only), a tiny tavern a few doors down from Angelo d'Oro.

Veli Jože (☎ 816 337; Svetog Križa 3; mains from 35KN) Graze on good Istrian standards, either in the eclectic interior crammed with knick-knacks or on the outdoor tables with water views.

Trattoria Dream (☎ 830 613; Joakima Rakovca 18; mains from 75KN) Tucked away in the maze of narrow streets, with its two earthy-coloured outdoor terraces, this stylish trattoria does flavourful dishes such as salt-baked sea bass and some global favourites such as chilli con carne and chicken curry.

La Puntuleina (☎ 813 186; Svetog Križa 38; mains 100-160KN) Sample creative Med cuisine on three alfresco terraces – from traditional recipes like žgvacet (a sauce made from chicken, beef and venison, and served with pasta) to revamped ones like truffle-topped fish fillet. Pastas are more affordable (from 55KN). At night, grab a cushion and sip a cocktail on the rocks below this converted townhouse. Reservations recommended.

Picnickers can get supplies at the supermarket next to the bus station or at one of the Konzum stores around town.

Drinking

Havana (Aldo Negri bb) Tropical cocktails, Cuban cigars, straw parasols and the shade of tall pine trees make this open-air cocktail bar a popular spot to chill and watch the ships go by.

Zanzibar (☎ 813 206; Pina Budicina bb) Indonesian wood, palms, wicker lounge chairs and subdued lighting on the huge outdoor terrace of this cocktail bar create a tropical and definitely upscale vibe.

Getting There & Away

Eurostar Travel (☎ 813 144; Pina Budicina 1; ☺ 9am-9pm Mon-Sat, 9am-1pm & 5-8pm Sun) has schedules and tickets for boats to Venice and Trieste.

There are buses from Rovinj to Pula (35KN, 40 minutes, 13 daily), Dubrovnik (593KN, 16 hours, one daily), Poreč (37KN, one hour, eight daily), Rijeka (112KN, 3½ hours, four daily), Zagreb (173KN to 255KN, five hours, four daily) and Split (417KN, 11 hours, one daily). For Slovenia, there is one weekday bus that runs between Rovinj and Koper (87KN, three hours) stopping at Piran, Poreč and Portorož (41KN, 1½ hours), as well as a daily bus from Rovinj to Ljubljana (94KN, 5½ hours).

The closest train station is at Kanfanar, 20km away on the Pula–Divača line.

PULA

pop 65,000

The wealth of Roman architecture makes the otherwise workaday Pula (ancient Polensium) a standout among Croatia's larger cities. The star of the Roman show is the remarkably well-preserved Roman amphitheatre, which dominates the streetscape and doubles as a venue for summer concerts and performances. Historical attractions aside, Pula is a busy commercial city on the sea that has managed to retain a friendly small-town appeal. A series of beaches and good nightlife are just a short bus ride away at the resorts that occupy the Verudela Peninsula to the south. Further south along the indented shoreline, the Premantura Peninsula hides a spectacular nature area, the protected cape of Kamenjak.

Orientation

The oldest part of the city follows the ancient Roman plan of streets circling the central citadel. Most businesses are clustered in and around the Old Town, as well as on Giardini, Carrarina, Istarska and Riva, which runs along the harbour. The bus station is 500m northeast of the town centre. The harbour is west of the bus station. The train station is near the sea, less than a kilometre north of town.

Information

You can exchange money in travel agencies, banks or at the post offices. There are numerous ATMs around town.

Arenaturist (☎ 529 400; www.arenaturist.hr; Splitska 1a; ☺ 8am-8pm Mon-Fri, to 6pm Sat) In the Hotel Riviera, it books rooms in the network of hotels it manages. It also offers guide services and excursions.

Garderoba (per hr 2.20KN; ☺ 4am-10.30pm Mon-Sat, 5am-10.30pm Sun) Left luggage at bus station.

Hospital (☎ 376 548; Zagrebačka 34)

Istra Way (☎ 214 868; www.istraway.hr; Riva 14; ☺ 9am-9pm Jul–mid-Sep) On the harbour, it books private accommodation, offers excursions to Brijuni, Rovinj and Lim and has bikes for rent (100KN per day).

CROATIA

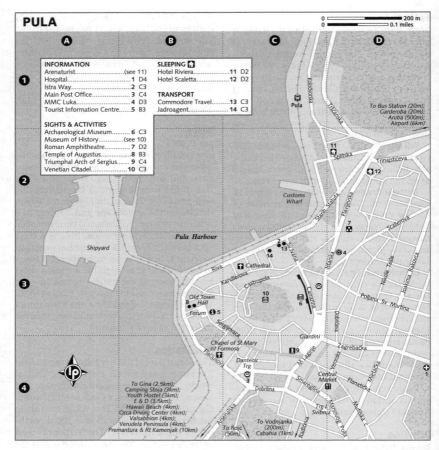

PULA

0 — 200 m
0 — 0.1 miles

INFORMATION
Arenaturist.....................(see 11)
Hospital.............................**1** D4
Istra Way............................**2** C3
Main Post Office.................**3** C4
MMC Luka..........................**4** D3
Tourist Information Centre...**5** B3

SIGHTS & ACTIVITIES
Archaeological Museum........**6** C3
Museum of History............(see 10)
Roman Amphitheatre............**7** D2
Temple of Augustus............**8** B3
Triumphal Arch of Sergius....**9** C4
Venetian Citadel.................**10** C3

SLEEPING
Hotel Riviera.....................**11** D2
Hotel Scaletta..................**12** D2

TRANSPORT
Commodore Travel..........**13** C3
Jadroagent......................**14** C3

Pula

To Bus Station (20m);
Garderoba (20m);
Aruba (500m);
Airport (6km)

Customs Wharf

Pula Harbour

Shipyard

Cathedral

Old Town Hall
Forum

Chapel of St Mary of Formosa

Danteov Trg

Central Market

Giardini

To Gina (2.5km);
Camping Stoja (3km);
Youth Hostel (3km);
E & D (3.5km);
Hawaii Beach (4km);
Orca Diving Center (4km);
Valsabbion (4km);
Verudela Peninsula (4km);
Premantura & Rt Kamenjak (10km)

To Vodnjanka (200m);
Cabahia (1km)

To Roje (50m)

Main post office (Danteov Trg 4; 7.30am-7pm Mon-Fri, to 2.30pm Sat) You can make long-distance calls here. Check out the cool staircase inside!

MMC Luka (224 316; Istarska 30; per hr 20KN; 8am-midnight Mon-Fri, to 3pm Sat) Internet access.

Tourist information centre (212 987; www.pula info.hr; Forum 3; 8am-9pm Mon-Fri, 9am-9pm Sat & Sun summer, 8am-7pm Mon-Fri, 9am-7pm Sat, 10am-4pm Sun winter) Knowledgeable and friendly, it provides heaps of maps and brochures. Pick up the useful *Domus Bonus* booklet, which lists the best-quality private accommodation in Istria.

Sights
ROMAN RUINS
Pula's most imposing sight is the 1st-century **Roman amphitheatre** (219 028; Flavijevska bb; adult/concession 40/20KN; 8am-9pm summer, 9am-8pm spring

& autumn, 9am-5pm winter) overlooking the harbour. Built entirely from local limestone, the amphitheatre, with seating for up to 20,000 spectators, was designed to host gladiatorial contests. In the chambers downstairs is a small museum with a display of ancient olive oil equipment. Every summer, Pula Film Festival is held here, as are pop and classical concerts.

The **Archaeological Museum** (Arheološki Muzej; 218 603; Carrarina 3; adult/concession 20/10KN; 9am-8pm Mon-Sat, 10am-3pm Sun May-Sep, 9am-2pm Mon-Fri Oct-Apr) presents archaeological finds from all over Istria. Even if you don't enter the museum, be sure to visit the large sculpture garden around it, and the **Roman theatre** behind. The garden, entered through 2nd-century twin gates, is the site of concerts in summer.

CROATIA

Along Carrarina are **Roman walls**, which mark the eastern boundary of old Pula. Follow these walls south and continue down Giardini to the **Triumphal Arch of Sergius** (27 BC). The street beyond the arch winds right around old Pula, changing names several times. Follow it to the ancient **Temple of Augustus** (☎ 218 603; Forum; adult/concession 10/5KN; ☼ 9am-8pm Mon-Fri, 10am-3pm Sat & Sun summer, by appointment otherwise), erected from 2 BC to AD 14 and now housing a small historical museum with captions in English.

BEACHES

Pula is surrounded by a half-circle of rocky beaches, each one with its own fan club. The most tourist-packed are undoubtedly those surrounding the hotel complex on the **Verudela Peninsula** although some locals will dare to be seen at the small turquoise-coloured **Hawaii Beach** near the Hotel Park.

For more seclusion, head out to the wild **Rt Kamenjak** (www.kamenjak.hr, in Croatian; pedestrians & cyclists free, cars 20KN, scooters 10KN; ☼ 7am-10pm) on the Premantura Peninsula 10km south of town. Istria's southernmost point, this gorgeous, entirely uninhabited cape has wild flowers, including 30 species of orchid, 30km of virgin beaches and coves, and a delightful beach bar, **Safari** (snacks 25-50KN; ☼ Easter-Sep), half-hidden in the bushes near the beach. Watch out for strong currents if swimming off the southern cape. Take city bus 26 (15KN) from Pula to Premantura and rent a bike to get inside the park from **Windsurf Bar** (☎ 091 512 3646; Camping Village Stupice; www.windsurfing.hr) near the bus top (50KN to 100KN per day).

OTHER SIGHTS

The 17th-century **Venetian citadel**, on a high hill in the centre of the Old Town, is worth the climb for the view if not for the meagre maritime-related exhibits in the tiny **Museum of History** (Povijesni Muzej Istre; ☎ 211 566; Gradinski Uspon 6; adult/concession 15/7KN; ☼ 8am-9pm Jun-Sep, 9am-5pm Oct-May) inside.

Activities

There are several diving centres around Pula. At **Orca Diving Center** (☎ 224 422; www.orcadiving .hr; Hotel Histria) on the Verudela Peninsula you can arrange for boat dives, wreck dives and introductory dives.

In addition to windsurfing courses, Windsurf Bar (above) in Premantura

offers biking (250KN) and kayaking (300KN) excursions.

Sleeping

Pula's peak tourist season runs from the second week of July to the end of August. During this period it's wise to make advance reservations. The tip of the Verudela Peninsula, 4km southwest of the city centre, has been turned into a vast tourist complex, replete with hotels and apartments.

Any travel agency can give you information and book you into one of the hotels, or you can contact Arenaturist (p223). The travel agencies listed find private accommodation but there is little available in the town centre. Count on paying from 250KN to 490KN for a double room (up to 535KN for a two-person apartment).

Camping Stoja (☎ 387 144; www.arenaturist.hr; Stoja 37; per person/tent 52/30KN; ☼ Apr-Oct) The closest camping ground to Pula, 3km southwest of the centre, has lots of space on the shady promontory, with a restaurant, diving centre and swimming possible off the rocks. Take bus 1 to Stoja.

Youth Hostel (☎ 391 133; www.hfhs.hr; Valsaline 4; dm 85-114KN, mobile home 103-134KN; 🖳) This hostel overlooks a beach in Valsaline bay, 3km south of central Pula. There are dorms and mobile homes split into two tiny four-bed units, each with bathroom and air-con on request (15KN per day). There's bike rental (80KN per day) and camp sites (per person/tent 70/15KN). Take bus 2 or 3 to the 'Piramida' stop, walk back to the first street, then turn left and look for the sign.

Hotel Riviera (☎ 211 166; www.arenaturist.hr; Splitska 1; s 283-354KN, d 464-600KN) There's plenty of old-world elegance at this grand 19th-century building but the rooms need a thorough overhaul and the carpets a serious scrub. On the plus side, it's in the centre and the front rooms have water views.

ourpick Hotel Scaletta (☎ 541 599; www.hotel-scal etta.com; Flavijevska 26; s 398-498KN, d 598-718KN) There's a friendly family vibe, the rooms have tasteful decor and a bagful of trimmings, such as minibars, plus the restaurant serves good food. It's just a hop from town.

Eating

There are a number of decent eating places in the city centre, although most locals head out of town for better value and fewer tourists.

Vodnjanka (☎ 210 655; Vitezića 4; mains from 30KN; ☾ closed Sun & dinner Sat) Locals swear by the home cooking here. It's cheap, casual, cash-only and has a small menu that concentrates on simple Istrian dishes. To get here, walk south on Radićeva to Vitezića.

our pick Gina (☎ 387 943; Stoja 23; mains from 60KN) Istrian mainstays like *maneštra* and *fritaja* are prepared with care, pastas are handmade, and vegies picked from the garden. This stylish but low-key eatery near Camping Stoja draws in a local crowd. Try the semifreddo with a hot sauce of figs, pine nuts and lavender.

Valsabbion (☎ 218 033; www.valsabbion.hr; Pješčana Uvala IX/26; mains 95-175KN) The creative Croatian cuisine conjured up at this award-winning restaurant, one of Croatia's best, is an epicurean delight. The decor is showy but stunning and the menu gimmicky in its descriptions but the food is tops. Sampling menus range from 395KN to 555KN. It doubles as a plush 10-room hotel (doubles 860KN) with a top-floor spa. It's in upscale Pješčana Uvala, south of the city.

Drinking

Although most of the nightlife is out of the town centre, in mild weather the cafes on the Forum and along the pedestrian streets, Kandlerova, Flanatička and Sergijevaca, are lively people-watching spots.

our pick Cabahia (Širolina 4) An artsy hideaway in Veruda, with cosy wood-beamed interior, eclectic decor of old objects, dim lighting, South American flair and a great garden terrace in the back. It hosts concerts and gets packed on weekends.

E&D (☎ 894 2015; Verudela 22) Lounge just above Umbrella beach on Verudela, on the lush outdoor terrace with several levels of straw-chair seating interspersed with small pools and waterfalls. The sunset views are great and weekend nights spiced with live DJ tunes.

Entertainment

You should definitely try to catch a concert in the spectacular amphitheatre; the tourist office has schedules.

For the most underground experience, check the program at **Rojc** (Gajeva 3; www.rojc net.hr), a converted army barracks that now houses a multimedia art centre and art studios with occasional concerts, exhibits and other events.

Getting There & Away

BOAT

Jadroagent (☎ 210 431; www.jadroagent.hr; Riva 14; ☾ 7am-3pm Mon-Fri) has schedules and tickets for boats connecting Istria with Italy and the islands. They also represent Jadrolinija.

Commodore Travel (☎ 211 631; www.commodore-travel.hr; Riva 14, ☾ 8am-8pm Jun-Sep) sells tickets for a catamaran between Pula and Zadar that runs five times weekly from July through early September (100KN, five hours) and twice weekly in June and September. There's a weekly boat to Venice between June and September (370KN, 3½ hours).

BUS

From the Pula **bus station** (☎ 500 012; Trg 1 Istarske Brigade bb) there are buses heading to Rijeka almost hourly (86KN to 91KN, two hours). In summer, reserve a seat a day in advance and be sure to sit on the right-hand side of the bus for a stunning view of the Kvarner Gulf.

Other destinations you can reach by bus include: Rovinj (35KN, 45 minutes, 15 daily), Poreč (54KN to 65KN, one to 1½ hours, 13 daily), Zagreb (210KN, four to five hours, 18 daily), Zadar (249KN to 257KN, seven hours, three daily), Split (360KN to 396KN, 10 hours, three daily) and Dubrovnik (568KN, 10½ hours, one daily).

TRAIN

There are two daily trains to Ljubljana, with a change in Buzet (133KN, two hours), and four to Zagreb (125KN to 148KN, 6½ hours), but you must board a bus for part of the trip, from Lupoglav to Rijeka.

Getting Around

The city buses of use to visitors are bus 1, which runs to the Autocamp Stoja, and bus 2 and 3 to Verudela. Tickets are sold at *tisak* (newsstands) for 6KN, or 10KN from the driver.

KVARNER REGION

☎ 051

The Kvarner Gulf (Quarnero in Italian) covers 3300 sq km between Rijeka and Pag Island in the south, protected by the Velebit Range in the southeast, the Gorski Kotar in the east and the Učka massif in the northwest. Covered with luxuriant forests, lined with beaches and dotted with islands, the region has a mild gentle climate and a wealth of vegetation.

The metropolitan focus is the busy commercial port of Rijeka, Croatia's third-largest city, only a few kilometres from the aristocratic Opatija Riviera. The islands of Krk, Rab, Cres and Lošinj offer picture-perfect old towns just a ferry ride away, as well as plenty of beaches for scenic swimming.

RIJEKA
pop 147,700

While Rijeka (Fiume in Italian) doesn't quite fit the bill as a tourist destination, it does offer an insightful glimpse into the workaday life of Croatia's largest port. Most people rush through en route to the islands or Dalmatia but for those who pause, a few assets await. Blend in with the coffee-sipping locals on the bustling Korzo pedestrian strip, stroll along the tree-lined promenade that fronts the harbour, and visit the imposing hilltop fortress of Trsat. Rijeka also boasts a burgeoning nightlife, and every year it hosts Croatia's biggest and most colourful Carnival celebration.

Much of the centre contains the ornate, imposing public buildings you would expect to find in Vienna or Budapest, evidence of the strong Austro-Hungarian influence. The industrial aspect is evident from the boats, cargo and cranes that line the waterfront but there's a seedy beauty to it. As one of Croatia's most important transportation hubs, Rijeka has buses, trains and ferries that connect Istria and Dalmatia with Zagreb.

Orientation
Korzo runs through the city centre, roughly parallel to Riva (seafront), towards the Rječina River in the east. The intercity bus station is at the western edge of Riva. The train station is a five-minute walk west of the intercity bus station, along Krešimirova.

Information
There are two ATMs at the train station and a number of them along Korzo and around the city centre. The exchange offices adjacent to the train and bus stations keep long hours.

There's free wireless internet access along Korzo and in parts of Trsat.

Blitz (Krešimirova 3a; small load 51KN; ☑ 7am-8pm Mon-Fri, to 2pm Sat) Laundry facilities.

Cont (☎ 371 630; Andrije Kačića Miošića 1; per hr 15KN; ☑ 7am-10pm) This cafe inside Hotel Continental has a full bank of computers.

Hospital (☎ 658 111; Krešimirova 42)
Garderoba intercity bus station (per day 13KN; ☑ 5.30am-10.30pm); train station (per day in locker 15KN; ☑ 4.30am-10.30pm) The bus station left-luggage facility is at the cafe next door to the ticket office.
Main post office (Korzo 13; ☑ 7am-8pm Mon-Fri, to 2pm Sat) Has a telephone centre and an exchange office.
Tourist information centre (☎ 335 882; www .tz-rijeka.hr; Korzo 33a; ☑ 8am-8pm Mon-Sat, 9am-2pm Sun summer, 8am-8pm Mon-Fri, 8am-2pm Sat rest of year) This spiffy centre has plentiful free materials and info about private accommodation.

Sights
Rijeka's main orientation point is the distinctive yellow **City Tower** (Korzo), originally a gate from the seafront to the city and one of the few monuments to have survived the devastating earthquake of 1750.

Just up from the Korzo on the 2nd floor of the University Library is the **Museum of Modern & Contemporary Art** (Muzej Moderne i Suvremene Umjetnosti; ☎ 334 280; www.mmsu.hr; Dolac 1; adult/ student 10/5KN; ☑ 10am-1pm & 6-9pm Tue-Sun summer, 10am-1pm & 5-8pm rest of year) in an L-shaped space that puts on rotating shows. The **Maritime & History Museum** (Pomorski i Povijesni Muzej Hrvatskog Primorja; ☎ 553 666; www.ppmhp.hr; Muzejski Trg 1; adult/ student 10/5KN; ☑ 9am-8pm Tue-Fri, to 1pm Sat) gives a vivid picture of life among seafarers, with model ships, sea charts, navigation instruments and portraits of captains. A five-minute walk to the east is the **Natural History Museum** (Prirodoslovni Muzej; ☎ 553 669; Lorenzov Prolaz 1; adult/student 10/5KN; ☑ 9am-7pm Mon-Sat, to 3pm Sun), devoted to the geology and botany of the Adriatic, inside a 19th-century villa.

Also worth a visit is the **Trsat Castle** (☎ 217 714; adult/student 15/5KN; ☑ 9am-8pm May-Oct, to 5pm Nov-Apr), a 13th-century hill fortress that houses two galleries and great vistas from the open-air cafe. During the summer, the fortress features concerts, theatre performances and fashion shows. The other hill highlight is the **Church of Our Lady of Trsat** (Crkva Gospe Trsatske; ☎ 452 900; Frankopanski Trg; ☑ by appointment only), a centuries-old magnet for believers that showcases an apparently miraculous icon of Virgin Mary.

Festivals & Events
The **Rijeka Carnival** (www.ri-karneval.com.hr) is the largest and most elaborate in Croatia, with two weeks of partying that involves pageants, street dances, concerts, masked balls, exhibitions and an international parade. Check out

CROATIA

RIJEKA

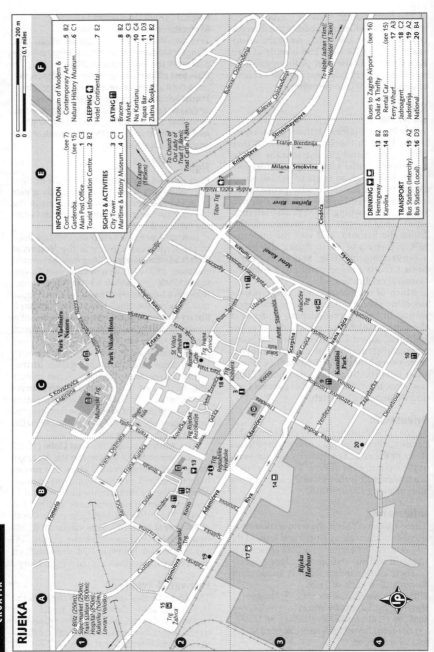

CROATIA

INFORMATION
Cont.	(see 7)
Garderoba	(see 15)
Main Post Office	1 C3
Tourist Information Centre	2 B2

SIGHTS & ACTIVITIES
City Tower	3 C3
Maritime & History Museum	4 C1
Museum of Modern & Contemporary Art	5 B2
Natural History Museum	6 C1

SLEEPING
Hotel Continental	7 E2

EATING
Bracera	8 B2
Market	9 C3
Na Kantunu	10 C4
Tapas Bar	11 D3
Zlatna Školjka	12 B2

DRINKING
Hemingway	13 B2
Karolina	14 B3

TRANSPORT
Bus Station (Intercity)	15 A2
Bus Station (Local)	16 D3
Buses to Zagreb Airport	(see 16)
Dollar & Thrifty	(see 15)
Rental Car	17 A3
Ferry Wharf	18 C2
Jadroagent	19 A2
Jadrolinija	20 B4
National	

0   200 m
0   0.1 miles

the *zvončari*, masked men clad in animal skins who dance and ring loud bells to frighten off evil spirits. The festivities take place anywhere between late January and early March, depending on when Easter falls.

Sleeping

Prices in Rijeka hotels generally stay the same year-round, except at popular Carnival time, when you can expect to pay a surcharge. There are few private rooms in Rijeka itself; the tourist office lists these on its website. Opatija (see p231) is a much better choice for accommodation.

Youth Hostel (☎ 406 420; rijeka@hfhs.hr; Šetalište XIII Divizije 23; dm/s/d 130/235/310KN; 🖳) Five bus stops east of the centre (bus 2) in the leafy residential area of Pečine, this renovated 19th-century villa has clean and snug units and a communal TV room. Breakfast is available (15KN) and reservations advisable in the summer.

Hotel Continental (☎ 372 008; www.jadran-hoteli.hr; Andrije Kačića Miošića 1; s/d 384/449KN; 🖳) At the time of writing, more than half of the rooms inside this grand building were being revamped. Once they're primped up, the rating will go up to three stars and the prices by 15%. The location is prime, just northeast of the centre.

our pick **Hotel Jadran** (☎ 216 600; www.jadran -hoteli.hr; Šetalište XIII Divizije 46; s/d 672/793KN; 🐾 🖳) The four-star upgrade of this long-standing hotel produced airy rooms with huge glass windows or balconies offering sea vistas. Perks include a restaurant, a small gym and a private beach below. Worth the 1km trip east of the city centre.

Eating

If you want a meal on a Sunday, you'll be relegated to either fast food, pizza or a hotel restaurant, as nearly every other place in Rijeka is closed.

Tapas Bar (☎ 315 313; Pavla Rittera Vitezovića 5; tapas around 25KN) This small and stylish spot churns out Croatian-inspired tapas. Delicious *bruschette* are topped with anchovies, truffles, fresh tuna…at 9KN per piece. Portions are small and the bill adds up.

our pick **Na Kantunu** (☎ 313 271; Demetrova 2; mains from 35KN) If you're lucky enough to grab a table at this tiny lunchtime spot on an industrial stretch of the port, you'll be treated to a superlative daily catch.

Zlatna Školjka (☎ 213 782; Kružna 12; mains 65-95KN) Savour the superbly prepared seafood

and choice Croatian wines at this classy maritime-themed restaurant. The mixed fish starter Conco d'Oro is pricey (100KN) but worth it.

The adjacent Bracera, by the same owners, serves crusty pizza, even on Sunday.

Kukuriku (☎ 691 417; Trg Matka Laginje 1a, Kastav; 6-course meal 370-510KN; 🕑 closed Mon winter) Among the pioneers of the slow-food movement in Croatia, this gastronomic destination in the Old Town of Kastav, Rijeka's hilltop suburb, offers delectable meals amid lots of rooster-themed decoration. It's worth the splurge and the trek on bus 18.

For self-caterers, there's a large supermarket between the bus and train stations, and a **city market** (btwn Vatroslava Lisinskog & Trninina) open till 2pm daily (till noon Sunday).

Drinking

With several recent openings, Rijeka's nightlife got a boost of energy. Bar-hoppers cruise the bars and cafes along Riva and Korzo for the liveliest social hubbub. Many of the bars double as clubs on weekends.

Hemingway (☎ 211 696; Korzo 28) This stylish venue for coffee-sipping, cocktail-drinking and people-watching pays homage to the bar's namesake, with the hero's large black and white photos and eponymous drinks. It's part of a fashionable chain.

Karolina (☎ 211 447; Gat Karoline Riječke bb) Trendy but not self-conscious about it, this waterfront bar-cafe is a relaxed place for a daytime coffee. At night, crowds spill out onto the wharf in a huge outdoor party.

Getting There & Away
BOAT

Jadrolinija (☎ 211 444; www.jadrolinija.hr; Riva 16; 🕑 8am-8pm Mon-Fri, 9am-5pm Sat & Sun) sells tickets for the large coastal ferries that run all year between Rijeka and Dubrovnik on their way to Bari in Italy, via Split, Hvar and Korčula. Other ferry lines include Rijeka–Cres–Mali Lošinj and Rijeka–Rab–Pag. All ferries depart from Rijeka's **wharf** (Adamićev Gat).

Jadroagent (☎ 211 626; www.jadroagent.hr; Trg Ivana Koblera 2) has information on all boats around Croatia.

BUS

If you fly into Zagreb, there is a Croatia Airlines van directly from Zagreb airport to Rijeka (145KN, two hours, 3.30pm and 9pm) and back from Rijeka (5am and 11am).

CROATIA

BUSES FROM RIJEKA

Destination	Fare (KN)	Duration (hr)	Daily services
Baška	71	2¼	4-8
Dubrovnik	340-485	12-13	2-3
Krk	50	1-2	14
Poreč	72-114	1-3	7-11
Pula	78-88	2¼	8-10
Rab	125	3	2
Rovinj	81-112	2-3	4-5
Split	241-327	8	6-7
Zadar	153-202	4-5	6-7
Zagreb	95-174	2½-3	13-17

There are six daily buses from the **intercity bus station** (☎ 060 302 010; Trg Žabica 1) to Trieste (Italy; 60KN, 2½ hours) and one daily bus to Plitvice, with a change in Otočac (130KN, four hours). There's a service between Sarajevo (BiH) and Rijeka too (€35, 10 hours, daily) and a bus between Ljubljana (Slovenia) and Rijeka (84KN, 2½ hours, one daily).

See above for popular domestic routes.

CAR
Dollar & Thrifty Rental Car (☎ 325 900; www.subrosa .hr) with a booth inside the intercity bus station has rental cars from 466KN per day (2500KN per week) with unlimited kilometres. You can also try **National** (☎ 212 452; www.nationalcar .hr; Demetrova 18b).

TRAIN
The **train station** (☎ 213 333; Krešimirova 5) is a five-minute walk from the city centre. Seven trains daily run to Zagreb (96KN, 3½ to five hours). There's a daily train to Split that changes at Ogulin, where you wait for two hours (160KN, 10 hours). Reservations are compulsory on some *poslovni* (executive) trains. For Slovenia, there are four trains daily between Rijeka and Ljubljana (93KN, three hours).

OPATIJA
pop 9070

Opatija stretches along the coast, just 13km west of Rijeka, its forested hills sloping down to the sparkling sea. It was this breathtaking location and the agreeable all-year climate that made Opatija the most fashionable seaside resort for the Viennese elite during the Austro-Hungarian empire. The grand residences of the wealthy have since been revamped and turned into upscale hotels, with a particular accent on spa and health holidays. Foodies have been flocking from afar too, for the clutch of fantastic restaurants in the nearby fishing village of Volosko.

Orientation & Information
Opatija sits on a narrow strip of land sandwiched between the sea and the foothills of Mt Učka. Ulica Maršala Tita is the main road that runs through town; it's lined with travel agencies, ATMs, restaurants, shops and hotels.

Da Riva (☎ 272 990; www.da-riva.hr; Ulica Maršala Tita 170; ☼ 8am-8pm Jun–mid-Sep, reduced hr rest of year) Finds private accommodation and offers excursions around Croatia.

Linea Verde (☎ 701 107; www.lineaverde-croatia.com; Andrije Štangera 42, Volosko; ☼ 8am-10pm Mon-Sat, to 9pm Sun summer, to 4pm Mon-Sat rest of year) Hiking excursions to Risnjak, gourmet tours to Istria and shepherd's picnics to Učka.

Tourist office (☎ 271 310; www.opatija-tourism.hr; Ulica Maršala Tita 101; ☼ 8am-10pm Mon-Sat, 5-9pm Sun Jul & Aug, 8am-7pm Mon-Sat Apr-Jun & Sep, 8am-4pm Mon-Sat Mar & Oct) Distributes maps, leaflets and brochures.

Sights & Activities
Visit the exquisite **Villa Angiolina** (Park Angiolina 1), which houses the **Croatian Museum of Tourism** (admission free; ☼ 9am-1pm & 4.30-9.30pm Tue-Sun summer, reduced hr rest of year) with the collection of old photographs, postcards, brochures and posters tracing the history of travel. Admission was free at the time of research, but due to increase to 20KN later. Don't miss a stroll around the park, overgrowing with gingko trees, sequoias, holm oaks and Japanese camellia, Opatija's symbol.

The pretty **Lungomare** is the region's showcase. Lined with plush villas and ample gardens, this shady promenade winds along

CROATIA

the sea for 12km, from Volosko to Lovran. Along the way are innumerable rocky outgrowths on which to throw down a towel and jump into the sea from – a better option than Opatija's concrete beach.

Opatija and the surrounding region offer some wonderful opportunities for hiking and biking around the **Učka** mountain range (the tourist office has maps and information).

Sleeping & Eating
There are no real budget hotels in Opatija, but the midrange and top-end places offer surprisingly good value for money considering Opatija's overall air of chic. Maršala Tita is lined with serviceable restaurants that offer pizza, grilled meat and fish. The better restaurants are away from the main strip.

Private rooms are abundant and reasonably priced. The travel agencies listed opposite find private accommodation. In high season, rooms cost between 80KN and 115KN per person, depending on the amenities. A 30% surcharge applies for stays under three nights.

Camping Opatija (☎ 704 836; www.rivijera-opatija.hr; Liburnijska 46, Ičići; per adult/site 36/27KN; Apr-Oct) In a pine forest 5km south of town before you reach Lovran.

Hotel Residenz (☎ 271 399; www.liburnia.hr; Ulica Maršala Tita 133; s 293-524KN, d 354-816KN) While rooms boast no frills – unless you pay extra for a unit with a balcony – the building is a classic right on the seafront, with a private beach below.

Hotel Mozart (☎ 718 260; www.hotel-mozart.hr; Ulica Maršala Tita 138; s 660-920KN, d 1095-1530KN;) Light-flooded rooms feature old-school style and Secessionist furniture, the stars add up to five, and the spiffy new spa offers saunas and steam baths. Most rooms come with sea-facing balconies.

Istranka (☎ 271 835; Bože Milanovića 2; mains from 45KN) Graze on flavourful Istrian mainstays like *maneštra* and *fuži* at this rustic-themed tavern in a small street just up from Maršala Tita.

Bevanda (☎ 493 888; Zert 8; mains from 80KN) It recently switched the ownership that built its reputation but this elegant restaurant on the Lido still delivers terrific fresh fish and shellfish. Get a table at the all-white terrace right on the sea.

Entertainment
An **open air-cinema** (Park Angiolina) screens films nightly and presents occasional concerts at 9.30pm from May to September. There are some bars around the harbour, although Rijeka has a much more dynamic scene.

Getting There & Away
Bus 32 stops in front of the train station in Rijeka (15KN, 20km) and runs along the Opatija Riviera west of Rijeka to Lovran every 20 minutes until late in the evening.

KRK ISLAND
pop 16,400
Croatia's largest island, 409-sq-km Krk (Veglia in Italian) is also one of the busiest in the summer. It may not be the most beautiful or lush island in Croatia – in fact, it's largely overdeveloped and stomped over – but its decades of experience in tourism make it an easy place to visit, with good transport connections and a well-organised infrastructure.

GETTING THERE & AROUND
The Krk toll bridge links the northern part of the island with the mainland, and a regular car ferry links Valbiska with Merag on Cres (17KN/113KN passenger/car, 30 minutes). Another ferry by Split Tours operates between Valbiska and Lopar (37KN, 1½ hours) on Rab four times daily.

Krk is also home to **Rijeka airport** (www.rijeka-airport.hr), the main hub for flights to the Kvarner region, which consist mostly of low-cost and charter flights during summer.

About 14 buses per weekday travel between Rijeka and Krk Town (50KN, one to two hours). There are 10 daily buses to Baška from Krk Town (27KN, 45 minutes). All services are reduced on weekends.

Six daily buses run from Zagreb to Krk Town (163KN to 183KN, three to four hours). Note that some bus lines are more direct than others, which will stop in every village en route.

Krk Town
The picturesque Krk Town makes a good base for exploring the island. Baška, on a wide sandy bay at the foot of a scenic mountain range, is the island's prime beach destination. It clusters around a medieval walled centre and, spreading out into the surrounding coves and hills, a modern development that includes a port, beaches, camping grounds and hotels. From the 12th to 15th centuries, Krk Town and the surrounding region remained semi-independent

CROATIA

under the Frankopan Dukes of Krk, an indigenous Croatian dynasty, at a time when much of the Adriatic was controlled by Venice. This history explains the various medieval sights in Krk Town, the ducal seat.

ORIENTATION & INFORMATION

The **seasonal tourist office** (☎ 220 226; www.tz-krk .hr, in Croatian; Obala Hrvatske Mornarice bb; ☼ 8am-9pm Jun-Sep) distributes brochures and materials, including a map of hiking paths. Out of season, go to the **main tourist office** (☎ 220 226; Vela Placa 1; ☼ 8am-3pm Mon-Fri) nearby. You can change money at any travel agency (there are 13 in town) and there are numerous ATMs around town.

The bus from Baška and Rijeka stops at the station (no left-luggage office) by the harbour, a few minutes' walk from the Old Town.

SIGHTS

Sights include the Romanesque **Cathedral of the Assumption** and the fortified **Kaštel** (Trg Kamplin) facing the seafront on the northern edge of the Old Town. The narrow cobbled streets that make up the pretty old quarter are worth a wander.

SLEEPING & EATING

There is a range of accommodation in and around Krk, but many hotels only open between April and October. Private rooms can be organised through any of the agencies, including **Autotrans** (☎ 222 661; www.autotrans-turizam .com; Šetalište Svetog Bernardina 3; ☼ 8am-9pm Mon-Sat, 9am-1.30pm & 6-9pm Sun) in the bus station. You can expect to pay between 210KN and 250KN for a double room in the high season.

Autocamp Ježevac (☎ 221 081; camping@val amar.com; Plavnička bb; per adult/site 44/56KN; ☼ mid-Apr–mid-Oct) The beachfront ground offers shady sites and places to swim. It's the closest camping ground to town, a 10-minute walk southwest.

Bor (☎ /fax 220 200; www.hotelbor.hr; Šetalište Dražica 5; s 152-369KN; d 231-564KN) The rooms are modest and without trimmings at this low-key hotel, but the seafront location amid pine forests makes it a worthwhile stay.

Marina (☎ 221 357; www.hotelikrk.hr; Obala Hrvatske Mornarice 6; s 760KN; d 1168KN; ⛱ 🖵) The most recent overhaul boosted this Old Town hotel to four-star. Now each of the 10 deluxe units sports sea vistas and modern trappings like LCD TV.

Konoba Nono (☎ 222 221; Krčkih Iseljenika 8; mains from 40KN) Savour local specialities like *šurlice* (homemade noodles) topped with goulash or scampi, just a hop and a skip from the Old Town.

Casa del Padrone (Šetalište Svetog Bernardina bb) Krk partygoers crowd the two floors of this faux-Renaissance bar-club, which hosts DJs on summer weekends. Daytime fun consists of lounging on the seaside tables as you nibble on cakes and sip espresso.

Baška

At the southern end of Krk Island, Baška has its most beautiful beach, a 2km-long crescent set below a dramatic, barren range of mountains. There's one caveat should you visit in summer – tourists are spread towel-to-towel and what's otherwise a pretty pebble beach turns into a fight for your place under the sun. The 16th-century core of Venetian townhouses is pleasant enough for a stroll but what surrounds it is a bland tourist development of apartment blocks and restaurants.

The bus stops at the top of a hill on the edge of the Old Town, between the beach and the harbour. The main street is Zvonimirova, which overlooks the harbour; the beach begins at the western end of the harbour, continuing southwards past a big sprawling hotel complex. The **tourist office** (☎ 856 817; www.tz-baska .hr; Zvonimirova 114; ☼ 7am-9pm Mon-Sat, 8am-1pm Sun Jun–mid-Sep, 8am-3pm Mon-Fri mid-Sep–May) is just down the street from the bus station.

Popular trails include an 8km walk to **Stara Baška**, a restful little village on a bay surrounded by stark, salt-washed limestone hills.

Most hotels and the two camps are managed by **Hoteli Baška** (☎ 656 111; www.hotelibaska .hr). Private accommodation can be arranged by most agencies in town, such as **PDM Guliver** (☎ /fax 856 004; www.pdm-guliver.hr; Zvonimirova 98; ☼ 7am-9pm Mon-Sat, 8am-1pm Sun Jun–mid-Sep, reduced hr rest of year). There's a four-night minimum stay in summer (or a hefty surcharge).

DALMATIA

Roman ruins, spectacular beaches, old fishing ports, medieval architecture and unspoilt offshore islands make a trip to Dalmatia (Dalmacija) unforgettable. Occupying the central 375km of Croatia's Adriatic coast, Dalmatia offers a matchless combination of hedonism and historical discovery. The jagged

CROATIA

coast is speckled with lush offshore islands and dotted with historic cities.

Split is the largest city in the region and a hub for bus and boat connections along the Adriatic, as well as home to the late-Roman Diocletian's Palace. Nearby are the early Roman ruins in Solin (Salona). Zadar has yet more Roman ruins and a wealth of churches. The architecture of Hvar and Korčula recalls the days when these places were outposts of the Venetian empire. None can rival majestic Dubrovnik, a cultural and aesthetic jewel.

ZADAR

☎ 023 / pop 72,700

It's hard to decipher the mystery of why Zadar (ancient Zara), the main city of northern Dalmatia, is an under-rated tourist destination. Is it because it has a compact, marble, traffic-free Old Town that follows the old Roman street plan and contains Roman ruins and medieval churches? Or could it be that it's recently been dubbed as Croatia's 'city of cool' for its clubs, bars and festivals run by international music stars?

Zadar is a city to behold on the Dalmatian coast – its cultural and entertainment offers are growing by the year, and with one of Europe's biggest budget airlines (Ryanair) starting to fly into its airport, it's safe to say that Zadar is not going to remain off-the-beaten track for much longer.

History

In the past 2000 years Zadar has escaped few wars. Its strategic position on the Adriatic coast made it a target for the Romans, the Byzantine, Venetian and Austro-Hungarian empires and Italy. Although it was damaged by Allied bombing raids in 1943–44 and Yugoslav rockets in 1991, this resilient city has been rebuilt and restored, retaining much of its old flavour. Don't forget to sample Zadar's famous maraschino-cherry liqueur.

Orientation

The train station and the bus station are adjacent and are 1km southeast of the harbour and Old Town. From the stations, Zrinsko-Frankopanska leads northwest to the town and harbour. Buses marked 'Poluotok' run from the bus station to the harbour. Narodni trg is the heart of Zadar.

Information

Aquarius Travel Agency (☎ /fax 212 919; www .jureskoaquarius.hr; Nova Vrata bb) Books accommodation and excursions.

Garderoba (per day 15KN) bus station (☼ 7am-9pm Mon-Fri); Jadrolinija dock (☼ 7am-8pm Mon-Fri, to 3pm Sat); train station (☼ 24hr)

Hospital (☎ 315 677; Bože Peričića 5) Emergency services are available 24 hours.

Main post office (Poljana Pape Aleksandra III) You can make phone calls here.

Miatours (☎ /fax 212 788; www.miatours.hr; Vrata Sveti Krševana) Books accommodation and excursions. Vrata Sveti Krševana is an extremely tiny passage through the walls that contains little more than the travel agency.

Internet Spot (Varoška 3; per hr 30KN)

Tourist office (☎ 316 166; www.tzzadar.hr; Mihe Klaića 5; ☼ 8am-8pm Mon-Sat, to 1pm Sun Jun-Sep, to 6pm Mon-Sat Oct-May)

Sights & Activities

Most attractions are near **St Donatus Church** (Sveti Donat; ☎ 250 516; Šimuna Kožičića Benje; admission 10KN; ☼ 9.30am-1pm & 4-6pm Mar-Oct), a circular 9th-century Byzantine structure built over the Roman forum. Slabs for the ancient forum are visible in the church and there is a pillar from the Roman era on the northwestern side. In summer, ask about the musical evenings here (featuring Renaissance and early baroque music). The outstanding **Museum of Church Art** (Trg Opatice Čike bb; adult/student 20/10KN; ☼ 10am-12.30pm daily, 6-8pm Mon-Sat), in the Benedictine monastery opposite St Donatus, offers three floors of elaborate gold and silver reliquaries, religious paintings, icons and local lacework.

The 13th-century Romanesque **Cathedral of St Anastasia** (Katedrala Svete Stošije; Trg Svete Stošije; ☼ Mass only) has some fine Venetian carvings in the 15th-century choir stalls. The **Franciscan Monastery** (Franjevački Samostan; Zadarskog Mira 1358; admission free; ☼ 7.30am-noon & 4.30-6pm) is the oldest Gothic church in Dalmatia (consecrated in 1280), with lovely interior Renaissance features and a large Romanesque cross in the treasury, behind the sacristy.

The most interesting museum is the **Archaeological Museum** (Arheološki Muzej; Trg Opatice Čike 1; adult/student 10/5KN; ☼ 9am-1pm & 6-9pm Mon-Fri, 9am-1pm Sat), across from St Donatus, with an extensive collection of artefacts, from the Neolithic period through the Roman occupation to the development of Croatian culture under the Byzantines. Some captions are in

CROATIA

English and you are handed a leaflet in English when you buy your ticket.

Less interesting is the **National Museum** (Narodni Muzej; Poljana Pape Aleksandra III; admission 10KN; 9am-1pm & 5-7pm Mon-Fri), just inside the sea gate, featuring photos of Zadar from different periods, and old paintings and engravings of many coastal cities. The same admission ticket will get you into the **Art Gallery** (Galerija; Smiljanića; 9am-noon & 5-8pm Mon-Fri, 9am-1pm Sat). One church worth a visit is **St Šimun Church** (Crkva Svetog Šime; Šime Budinića; 8am-1pm & 6-8pm Jun-Sep), which has a 14th-century gold chest.

Zadar's incredible (and world's only) **Sea Organ** (Morske Orgulje), designed by local architect Nikola Bašić, is bound to be one of the more memorable sights you'll see in Croatia. Set within the perforated stone stairs that descend into the sea is a system of pipes and whistles that exudes wistful sighs when the movement of the sea pushes air through the pipes.

Right next to it is the newly built **Sun Salutation** (Pozdrav Suncu), another wacky and wonderful Bašić creation. It's a 22m circle, cut into the pavement and filled with 300 multilayered glass plates that collect the sun's energy during the day and, powered by the same wave energy that makes the sound of the Sea Organ, produces a trippy light show from sunset to sunrise, meant to simulate the solar system.

You can swim from the steps off the promenade and listen to the sound of the Sea Organ. There's a **swimming area** with diving boards, a small park and a cafe on the coastal promenade off Zvonimira. Bordered by pine trees and parks, the promenade takes you to a beach in front of Hotel Kolovare and then winds on for about a kilometre up the coast.

Tours

Any of the many travel agencies around town can supply information on tourist cruises to the beautiful **Kornati Islands** (Kornati Islands National Park is an archipelago of 147 mostly uninhabited islands), river-rafting and half-day excursions to the Krka waterfalls.

Sleeping

Most visitors head out to the 'tourist settlement' at Borik, 3km northwest of Zadar, on the Puntamika bus (6KN, every 20 minutes from the bus station). Here there are hotels, a hostel, a camping ground, big swimming pools, sporting opportunities and numerous *sobe* (rooms) signs; you can arrange a private room through a travel agency in town. Expect to pay from €22 to €50 for a room, depending on the facilities.

Autocamp Borik (☎ 332 074; camp sites per adult 36-53KN, per site low/high season 90/135KN; ✆ May-Oct) Steps away from Borik beach, this camping ground is shaded by tall pines and has decent facilities.

Zadar Youth Hostel (☎ 331 145; zadar@hfhs.hr; Obala Kneza Trpimira 76; dm €13; ⌨) A great option for backpackers, with plain but clean rooms – some have wooden floors that creak comfortingly. Borik beach is minutes away. There's internet access at 5KN for 15 minutes.

Venera Guest House (☎ 214 098; www.hotel-venera -zd.hr; Šime Ljubića 4a; d 300-450KN) Venera – also known as the Jović Guesthouse – is the centre's only option. Although the rooms are miniscule, have oversized wardrobes and no numbers on the doors, all have private bathrooms, the beds are good and the atmosphere is pretty relaxed.

our pick **Villa Hrešć** (☎ 337 570; www.villa-hresc.hr; Obala Kneza Trpimira 28; s 550-650KN, d 750-850KN; ▣ ▣) Zadar's plushest choice is in a cheery pink building on a bay. The stylish rooms are in pastel colours, the beds are luxurious dreaming spots, and as you lounge by the swimming pool you can admire views of the Old Town.

Eating

Zalogajnica Ljepotica (☎ 311 288; Obala Kneza Branimira 4b; mains from 35KN) The cheapest place in town prepares three to four dishes a day at knock-out prices in a setting that would fit well in a Kaurismaki movie – you know, a rugged, lonesome diner and a pot-bellied chef/waiter who brings you a steaming dish with a somnolent look on his face. The food is great and home cooked, and the dishes are usually squid-ink risotto, tomato and seafood pasta, plus something meaty.

Trattoria Canzona (☎ 212 081; Stomorića 8; mains 40KN) A great little trattoria in the Old Town, with red-and-white chequered tablecloths, friendly waiters and tons of locals who love the menu of daily specials. Try the delicious *pašticada* that comes with a bunch of juicy gnocchi, and accompany it with a crunchy green salad.

our pick **Kornat** (☎ 254 501; Liburnska Obala 6; mains from 80KN) This is without a doubt Zadar's best restaurant. It's elegant, with wooden floors and modern furnishings, and the service is excellent, but it's the food that's the real knockout. There's the smooth Istrian truffle monkfish, a creamy squid and salmon risotto (70KN), and the fresh fish (around 350KN per kilogram) is prepared with simple ingredients to maximum deliciousness.

Zadar's morning **market** (✆ 6am-3pm) is one of Croatia's best.

Entertainment

In summer the many cafes along Varoška and Klaića place their tables on the street; it's great for people-watching.

Arsenal (☎ 253 833; www.arsenalzadar.com; Trg Tri Bunara 1) A large renovated shipping warehouse now hosts this brilliant cultural centre, with a large lounge bar-restaurant–concert hall in the centre, that has a small stage for live music and shows.

our pick **Garden** (☎ 450 907; www.thegardenzadar .com; Bedemi Zadarskih Pobuna; ✆ late May-Oct) One of the reasons many of Croatia's youngsters rate Zadar as 'a really cool place' is basically because it has the Garden. It's owned and run by UB40's producer Nick Colgan and drummer James Brown. Daytime here is relaxed, while night-time is when the fun really begins. Don't miss it if you're in town.

Getting There & Away
AIR

Zadar's airport, 12km east of the city, is served by **Croatia Airlines** (☎ 250 101; Poljana Natka Nodila 7) and **Ryanair** (www.ryanair.com). A Croatia Airlines bus meets all flights and costs 15KN; a taxi into town costs around 175KN.

CROATIA

WORTH THE TRIP: PLITVICE LAKES NATIONAL PARK

Midway between Zagreb and Zadar, **Plitvice Lakes National Park** (☎ 053 751 015; www.np-plitvicka -jezera.hr; adult/student Apr–Oct 110/50KN, Nov–Mar 70/35KN; ☉ 7am-8pm) is 19.5 hectares of wooded hills and 16 turquoise lakes, all connected by a series of waterfalls and cascades. The mineral-rich waters carve new paths through the rock, depositing tufa (new porous rock) in continually changing formations. Wooden footbridges follow the lakes and streams over, under and across the rumbling water for an exhilaratingly damp 18km. Swimming is not allowed. Your park admission (prices vary by season) is valid for the entire stay and also includes the boats and buses you need to use to see the lakes. There is hotel accommodation only on-site, and private accommodation just outside the park. Check the options with the National Parks information office in Zagreb (see p212).

The Zagreb–Zadar buses that don't use the new motorway road (ie the ones that drive between Zagreb and Zadar in over three hours) stop at Plitvice (check www.akz.hr for more details). The journey takes three hours from Zadar (80KN) and 2½ hours from Zagreb (60KN). Luggage can be left at the **tourist information centres** (☎ 053 751 015; www.np-plitvice.com; ☉ 7am-8pm), located at each entrance to the park.

BOAT

The office of **Jadrolinija** (☎ 254 800; www.jadrolinija.hr) is on the harbour and has tickets for all local ferries, or you can buy ferry tickets from the Jadrolinija stall on Liburnska Obala. The company runs car ferries from Ancona, Italy (€49.50, six to eight hours, daily). Ferries are less frequent during winter months.

BUS

The **bus station** (☎ 211 035; www.liburnija-zadar.hr, in Croatian) is a 10-minute walk from the centre and has daily buses to Zagreb (100KN to 140KN, 3½ to seven hours, 20 daily).

TRAIN

The **train station** (☎ 212 555; www.hznet.hr; Ante Starčevića 3) is adjacent to the bus station. There are five daily trains to Zagreb: two fast trains (150KN, seven hours) and three slower ones (134KN, 9¾ hours).

SPLIT

☎ 021 / pop 188,700

The second-largest city in Croatia, Split (Spalato in Italian), is a great place to see Dalmatian life as it's really lived. Free of mass tourism and always buzzing, this is a city with just the right balance of tradition and modernity. Just step inside Diocletian's Palace – a Unesco World Heritage site and one of the world's most impressive Roman monuments – and you'll see dozens of bars, restaurants and shops thriving amid the atmospheric old walls where Split life has been going on for thousands of years. Split's unique setting and exuberant nature make it one of the most delectable cities in Europe. The dramatic coastal mountains are the perfect backdrop to the turquoise waters of the Adriatic and you'll get a chance to appreciate the gorgeous Split cityscape when making a ferry journey to or from the city.

History

Split achieved fame when Roman emperor Diocletian (AD 245–313) had his retirement palace built here from 295 to 305. After his death the great stone palace continued to be used as a retreat by Roman rulers. When the neighbouring colony of Salona was abandoned in the 7th century, many of the Romanised inhabitants fled to Split and barricaded themselves behind the high palace walls, where their descendants continue to live to this day.

Orientation

The bus, train and ferry terminals are adjacent on the eastern side of the harbour, a short walk from the Old Town. The seafront promenade, Obala Hrvatskog Narodnog Preporoda, better known as Riva, is the best central reference point.

Information

BOOKSHOPS

Algoritam (Map p238; Bajamontijeva 2) A good English-language bookshop.

DISCOUNT CARDS

Split Card (1 day 36KN) Not a bad deal at all – get the Split Card for one day and you can use it for three days without

CROATIA

SPLIT

INFORMATION	
KBC Firule.....................1	F3
SIGHTS & ACTIVITIES	
Archaeological Museum........2	C1
Stairway to Marjan Hill.......3	A3
EATING 🍴	
Buffet Fife......................4	B3
Makrovega....................5	C2
TRANSPORT	
Ferry Terminal.................6	D4
Jadroagent...................(see 6)	
Jadrolinija....................(see 6)	
Local Bus Station.............7	D1
SEM Agency..................(see 6)	
SNAV........................(see 6)	

CROATIA

CENTRAL SPLIT

0 ——————— 200 m
0 ——————— 0.1 miles

INFORMATION
Algoritam..................................**1** B4
Atlas Travel Agency....................**2** B5
Daluma Travel............................**3** C6
Main Post Office........................**4** B4
Mriža..**5** B4
Turist Biro.................................**6** B5
Turistička Zajednica...................**7** C5

SIGHTS & ACTIVITIES
Basement Halls..........................**8** B5
Cathedral..................................**9** C5
East Palace Gate.......................**10** C4
North Palace Gate.....................**11** B4
Old Town Hall...........................**12** B4
Peristyle..................................**13** C5

Statue of Gregorius of Nin.........**14** C4
Temple of Jupiter.....................**15** B5
Town Museum..........................**16** C4
Vestibule...........................(see 13)
West Palace Gate.....................**17** B4

SLEEPING
B&B Kaštel 1700.......................**18** B5
Hostel Split Mediterranean House..**19** D3
Hotel Adriana...........................**20** B5
Split Hostel Booze & Snooze......**21** B4

EATING
Galija......................................**22** A4
Konoba Trattoria Bajamont........**23** B4
Market.....................................**24** C5
Supermarket.............................**25** A3

DRINKING
Café Puls/Café Shook................**26** B5
Le Porta..................................**27** C4

ENTERTAINMENT
Croatian National Theatre **28** A3

TRANSPORT
Buses to Airport.......................**29** C5
Buses to Solin (Salona)..............**30** B3
Croatia Airlines........................**31** B5
Ferry Terminal (Passenger Lines)..**32** B6
Jadrolinija Stall.........................**33** C6
Main Bus Station......................**34** D6
Touring...................................**35** C6

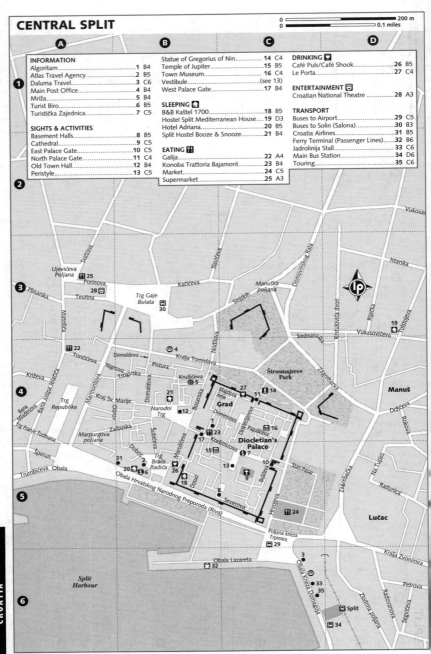

paying anything extra. You get free access to most of the city museums, half-price discounts to many galleries, and tons of discounts on car rental, restaurants, shops and hotels.

INTERNET ACCESS

Mriža (Map p238; ☎ 321 320; Kružićeva 3; per hr 20KN)

LEFT LUGGAGE

Garderoba (per hr/day 2.20/20KN) bus station (☺ 6am-10pm); train station (Obala Kneza Domagoja 6; ☺ 7am-9pm) The train station's left-luggage office is about 50m north of the station.

MEDICAL SERVICES

KBC Firule (Map p237; ☎ 556 111; Spinčićeva 1) Split's hospital. Emergency services are available 24 hours.

MONEY

Change money at travel agencies or the post office. You'll find ATMs around the bus and train stations.

POST

Main post office (Map p238; Kralja Tomislava 9; ☺ 7.30am-7pm Mon-Fri, 8am-noon Sat) There's also a telephone centre (open 7am to 9pm Monday to Saturday) here.

TOURIST INFORMATION

Turist Biro (Map p238; ☎ /fax 342 142; turist-biro -split@st.t-com.hr; Obala Hrvatskog Narodnog Preporoda 12) This office arranges private accommodation and sells guidebooks and the Split Card (€5, offers free and dis-counted admission to Split attractions).

Turistička Zajednica (Map p238; ☎ /fax 342 606; www .visitsplit.com; Peristile; ☺ 9am-8.30pm Mon-Sat, 8am-1pm Sun) Has information on Split; sells the Split Card.

TRAVEL AGENCIES

Atlas Travel Agency (Map p238; ☎ 343 055; Nepotova 4) The town's Amex representative.

Daluma Travel (Map p238; ☎ /fax 338 484; www .daluma.hr; Obala Kneza Domagoja 1) Finds private accom-modation and has information on boat schedules.

Sights

DIOCLETIAN'S PALACE

The Old Town is a vast open-air museum and the new information signs at the important sights explain a great deal of Split's history. **Diocletian's Palace** (Map p238; entrance Obala Hrvatskog Narodnog Preporoda 22), facing the harbour, is one of the most imposing Roman ruins in ex-istence. It was built as a strong rectangular fortress, with walls measuring 215m from east to west, 181m wide at the southernmost

point and reinforced by square corner tow-ers. The imperial residence, mausoleum and temples were south of the main street, now called Krešimirova, connecting the east and west palace gates.

Enter through the central ground floor of the palace. On the left are the excavated **Basement Halls** (Map p238; ☺ 10am-6pm), which are empty but impressive. Go through the passage to the **Peristyle** (Map p238), a picturesque col-onnaded square, with a neo-Romanesque ca-thedral tower rising above. The **Vestibule** (Map p238), an open dome above the ground-floor passageway at the southern end of the peri-style, is overpoweringly grand and cavernous. A lane off the peristyle opposite the cathedral leads to the **Temple of Jupiter** (Map p238), which is now a baptistry.

On the eastern side of the peristyle is the **Cathedral** (Map p238), originally Diocletian's mausoleum. The only reminder of Diocletian in the cathedral is a sculpture of his head in a circular stone wreath, below the dome which is directly above the baroque white-marble altar. The Romanesque wooden doors (1214) and stone pulpit are notable. For a small fee you can climb the tower.

In the Middle Ages the nobility and rich merchants built their residences within the old palace walls; the Papalic Palace is now the **Town Museum** (Gradski Muzej; Map p238; ☎ 341 240; Papalićeva ul 5; adult/concession 10/5KN; ☺ 9am-noon & 5-8pm Tue-Fri, 10am-noon Sat & Sun Jun-Sep, 10am-5pm Tue-Fri, 10am-noon Sat & Sun Oct-May). It has a tidy collection of artefacts, paintings, furniture and clothes from Split; captions are in Croatian.

OUTSIDE THE PALACE WALLS

The **East Palace Gate** (Map p238) leads to the market area. The **West Palace Gate** (Map p238) opens onto medieval Narodni Trg, dominated by the 15th-century Venetian Gothic **Old Town Hall** (Map p238).

Go through the **North Palace Gate** (Map p238) to see Ivan Meštrović's powerful 1929 **statue of Gregorius of Nin** (Map p238), a 10th-century Slavic religious leader who fought for the right to perform Mass in Croatian. Notice that his big toe has been polished to a shine; it's said that touching it brings good luck.

OUTSIDE CENTRAL SPLIT

The **Archaeological Museum** (Arheološki Muzej; Map p237; ☎ 318 720; Zrinjsko-Frankopanska 25; adult/student 20/10KN; ☺ 9am-2pm Tue-Fri, to 1pm Sat & Sun), north

CROATIA

of town, is a fascinating supplement to your walk around Diocletian's Palace, and to the site of ancient Salona. The history of Split is traced from Illyrian times to the Middle Ages, in chronological order, with explanations in English.

The finest art museum in Split is **Meštrović Gallery** (Galerija Meštrović; ☎ 358 450; Šetalište Ivana Meštrovića 46; adult/student 30/15KN; ☼ 9am-9pm Tue-Sun Jun-Sep, 9am-4pm Tue-Sat, 10am-3pm Sun Oct-May). You'll see a comprehensive, well-arranged collection of works by Ivan Meštrović, Croatia's premier modern sculptor.

From the Meštrović Gallery it's possible to hike straight up **Marjan Hill** (Map p237). Go up Tonča Petrasova Marovića on the western side of the gallery and continue straight up the stairway to Put Meja. Turn left and walk west to Put Meja 76. The trail begins on the western side of this building. Marjan Hill offers trails through the forest to lookouts and old chapels.

Festivals & Events
February Carnival This traditional carnival is presented in the Old Town.
Feast of St Duje 7 May.
Split Summer Festival Mid-July to mid-August. Features open-air opera, ballet, drama and musical concerts.

Sleeping
Split is quite thin on the ground when it comes to good budget accommodation, unless you're looking to sleep in dorms. Private accommodation is again the best option and in the summer you may be deluged at the bus station by women offering *sobe* (rooms available). Make sure you are clear about the exact location of the room or you may find yourself several bus rides from the town centre. The best thing to do is to book through the **Turist Biro** (Map p238; ☎ /fax 342 142; www.turistbiro-split.hr; Obala Hrvatskog Narodnog Preporoda 12; ☼ 9am-7pm Mon-Fri, to 4pm Sat). Expect to pay between 145KN to 220KN for a double room where you will probably share the bathroom with the proprietor.

Hostel Split Mediterranean House (Map p238; ☎ 098 987 1312; www.hostel-split.com; Vukasovićeva 21; dm from 100KN; ❂) It's a 10-minute walk from the Northern Gate to this friendly, family-run hostel set in a lovely old stone building. There are two six-bed dorms and some newer ensuite three-bed dorms.

Split Hostel Booze & Snooze (Map p238; ☎ 342 787; www.splithostel.com; Narodni Trg 8; dm 110-180KN; ❂)

A great new addition to Split's backpacker scene, this hostel is run by Aussie Croats and does exactly what it says on the tin – it's a party place, with 23 beds to snooze in, a nice terrace and it's right in the centre of town.

our pick **B&B Kaštel 1700** (Map p238; ☎ 343 912; www.kastelsplit.com; Mihovilova Širina 5; s 290-510KN, d 400-660KN; ❂ 💻) Among Split's best value for money places, it's near the bars, overlooks Radićev Trg and has sweet and tidy rooms and friendly, efficient service.

Hotel Adriana (Map p238; ☎ 340 000; www.hotel-adriana.com; Obala Hrvatskog Narodnog Preporoda (Riva) 9; s 550-650KN, d 750-900KN; ❂) Good value, excellent location. The rooms are not massively exciting, with their navy curtains and beige furniture, but some have sea views, which is a real bonus in Split's Old Town.

Eating
Galija (Map p238; Tončićeva 12; pizzas from 26KN) Galija has been the most popular place on Split's pizza scene for several decades now. It's the sort of joint that the locals take you to for an unfussy but good lunch or dinner, and where everyone relaxes on the wooden benches with the leftovers of a *quattro staggioni* or a *margharita* in front of them.

Makrovega (Map p237; ☎ 394 440; www.makrovega.hr; Leština 2; mains from 40KN; ☼ 9am-7pm Mon-Fri, to 4pm Sat) A meat-free haven with a clean, spacious (nonsmoking!) interior and delicious buffet and à la carte food that alternates between macrobiotic and vegetarian.

Buffet Fife (Map p237; ☎ 345 223; Trumbićeva Obala 11; mains around 40KN) Dragomir presides over a motley crew of sailors and misfits who drop in for the simple, home-cooking (especially the *pašticada*) and his own brand of grumpy but loving hospitality.

our pick **Konoba Trattoria Bajamont** (Map p238; ☎ 091 253 7441; Bajamontijeva 3; mains from 50KN) A one-room joint with four or five tables on one side and a heavily leaned-on bar on the other; there's no sign above the door and the menu is written out in marker pen and stuck in an inconspicuous spot by the entrance. The food is excellent and the menu usually features things such as small fried fish, squid-ink risotto, *brujet* (fish/seafood stew with wine, onions and herbs, served with polenta) and octopus salad.

The delicatessen at the **supermarket** (Map p238; Svačićeva 1) has a wide selection of meat and cheese for sandwiches. The **market** (Map p238; ☾ 6am-2pm), outside the east palace gate, has a wide array of fresh local produce.

Drinking

Split is great for nightlife, especially (or more so) in the spring and summer months. The palace walls are generally throbbing with loud music on Friday and Saturday nights.

Le Porta (Map p238; Majstora Jurja) Next door to Teak Caffe, Le Porta is renowned for its cocktails. On the same square – Majstora Jurja – are Kala, Dante, Whisky Bar and Na Kantunu, all of which end up merging into one when the night gets busy.

Café Puls (Map p238; Mihovilova Širina) and **Café Shook** (Map p238; Mihovilova Širina) are pretty much indistinguishable late on Friday or Saturday night, when the dozen steps that link these two bars are chock-a-block with youngsters.

Entertainment

Croatian National Theatre (Map p238; Trg Gaje Bulata; best seats about 60KN) During winter, opera and ballet are presented here. Erected in 1891, the theatre was fully restored in 1979 in its original style; it's worth attending a performance for the architecture alone.

Getting There & Away

AIR

The country's national air carrier, **Croatia Airlines** (Map p238; ☎ 062-777 777; Obala Hrvatskog Narodnog Preporoda 8), operates flights between Zagreb and Split (170KN to 350KN, 45 minutes) up to four times every day. Rates are lower if you book in advance. There's also **easyJet** (www.easyjet.com).

BOAT

The following companies have ferries to/from Italy:

Jadrolinija (www.jadrolinija.hr) Croatia's national boat line runs car ferries from Ancona to Split (€51, nine or 10 hours, six weekly), as well as a route from Bari to Dubrovnik (€51, eight hours, six weekly), which continues on to Rijeka, Stari Grad and Split. Ferries are less frequent during winter months.

SNAV (Map p237; ☎ 322 252; www.snav.com) Has a fast car ferry that travels from Ancona to Split (4½ hours, daily), and another from Pescara to Hvar (3½ hours, daily) and on to Split (6½ hours).

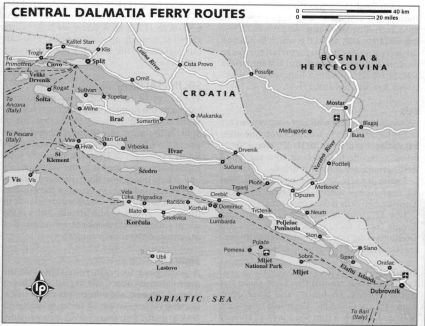

CENTRAL DALMATIA FERRY ROUTES

CROATIA

BUSES FROM SPLIT			
Destination	**Fare (KN)**	**Duration (hr)**	**Daily services**
Dubrovnik	105–166	4½	12
Ljubljana*	310	10½	1
Makarska	60	1½	every 30min
Međugorje**	120	3	5
Mostar**	120	2–4	4
Pula	331	10	1
Rijeka	250–380	7½	10
Sarajevo**	200	7	5
Zadar	120	3	8
Zagreb	195	5–9	27

*Slovenia
**Bosnia & Hercegovina

Split Tours (www.splittours.hr) Connects Ancona and Split (nine hours), continuing on to Stari Grad (Hvar, 12 hours). In summer, ferries leave twice daily Saturday to Monday and daily on other days. In winter, they travel three times a week, and only as far as Split.

You can buy tickets for passenger ferries at the **Jadrolinija stall** (Map p238; Obala Kneza Domagoja). There are also several agents in the large ferry terminal (Map p237) that can assist with boat trips from Split, including **Jadroagent** (Map p237; ☎ 338 335); **Jadrolinija** (Map p237; ☎ 338 333), which handles all car-ferry services that depart from the docks around the ferry terminal; and **SEM agency** (Map p237; ☎ 060 325 523), which handles tickets between Ancona, Split and Hvar.

BUS
Advance bus tickets with seat reservations are recommended. There are buses from the main **bus station** (Map p238; ☎ 060 327 327; www.ak-split.hr, in Croatian) beside the harbour to a variety of destinations; see above for details.

Touring (Map p238; ☎ 338 503; Obala Kneza Domagojeva 10), near the bus station, represents Deutsche Touring and sells tickets to German cities.

Bus 37 going to Solin, Split airport and Trogir leaves from a local bus station on Domovinskog, 1km northeast of the city centre (see Map p237).

TRAIN
From the train station there are three fast trains (138KN, six hours) and three overnight trains (138KN, 8½ hours) between Split and Zagreb. From Monday to Saturday there are six trains a day between Šibenik and Split (33KN, two hours) and four trains on Sunday.

Getting Around
There's an airport bus stop at Obala Lazareta 3 (Map p238). The bus (30KN, 30 minutes) leaves about 90 minutes before flight times, or you can take bus 37 from the bus station on Domovinskog (11KN for a two-zone ticket).

Buses run about every 15 minutes from 5.30am to 11.30pm. A one-zone ticket costs 9KN for one trip in central Split. You can buy tickets on the bus and the driver can make change.

SOLIN (SALONA)
The ruin of the ancient city of Solin (known as Salona by the Romans), among the vineyards at the foot of mountains 5km northeast of Split, is the most interesting archaeological site in Croatia. Salona was the capital of the Roman province of Dalmatia from the time Julius Caesar elevated it to the status of colony. It held out against the barbarians and was only evacuated in AD 614 when the inhabitants fled to Split and neighbouring islands in the face of Avar and Slav attacks. Solin is the site of a summer **Ethnoambient** (www.ethnoambient .net) music festival each August.

Sights
A good place to begin your visit is at the main entrance, near Caffe Bar Salona. There's a small **museum and information centre** (admission 10KN; ☯ 9am-6pm Mon-Sat Jun-Sep, to 1pm Mon-Sat Oct-May) at the entrance, which also provides

a helpful map and some literature about the complex.

Manastirine, the fenced area behind the car park, was a burial place for early Christian martyrs before the legalisation of Christianity. Excavated remains of the cemetery and the 5th-century basilica are highlights, although this area was outside the ancient city itself. Overlooking Manastirine is **Tusculum**, with interesting sculptures embedded in the walls and in the garden.

The Manastirine-Tusculum complex is part of an archaeological reserve that can be freely entered. A path bordered by cypress trees runs south towards the northern **city wall** of Salona. Note the **covered aqueduct** along the inside base of the wall. The ruins in front of you as you stand on the wall were the early Christian cult centre, which include the three-aisled, 5th-century **cathedral** and a small **baptistry** with inner columns. **Public baths** adjoin the cathedral on the eastern side.

Southwest of the cathedral is the 1st-century east city gate, **Porta Caesarea**, later engulfed by the growth of Salona in all di-

rections. Grooves in the stone road left by ancient chariots can be seen at this gate.

Walk west along the city wall for about 500m to **Kapljuč Basilica** on the right, another martyrs' burial place. At the western end of Salona you'll find the huge 2nd-century **amphitheatre**, which was destroyed in the 17th century by the Venetians to prevent it from being used as a refuge by Turkish raiders.

Getting There & Away

The ruins are easily accessible on Split city bus 1 direct to Solin every half-hour from the city bus stop at Trg Gaje Bulata.

From the amphitheatre at Solin it's easy to continue to Trogir by catching a westbound bus 37 from the nearby stop on the adjacent new highway. If, on the other hand, you want to return to Split, use the underpass to cross the highway and catch an eastbound bus 37 (buy a four-zone ticket in Split if you plan to do this).

Alternatively, you can catch most Sinj-bound buses (15KN, 10 daily) from Split's main bus station to take you to Solin.

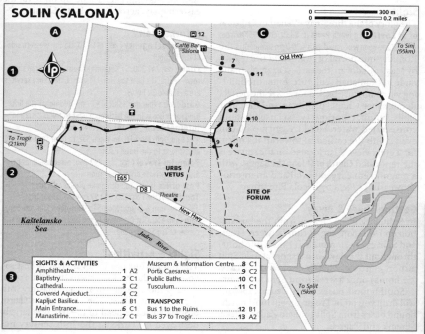

SOLIN (SALONA)

SIGHTS & ACTIVITIES
Amphitheatre..........................1 A2
Baptistry..................................2 C1
Cathedral................................3 C2
Covered Aqueduct..................4 C2
Kapljuč Basilica.......................5 B1
Main Entrance.........................6 C1
Manastirine.............................7 C1
Museum & Information Centre....8 C1
Porta Caesarea........................9 C2
Public Baths...........................10 C1
Tusculum................................11 C1

TRANSPORT
Bus 1 to the Ruins..................12 B1
Bus 37 to Trogir.....................13 A2

CROATIA

TROGIR

☎ 021 / pop 600

Gorgeous and tiny Trogir (formerly Trau) is beautifully set within medieval walls, its streets knotted and maze-like. It's fronted by a wide seaside promenade lined with bars and cafes and luxurious yachts docking in the summer. Trogir is unique among Dalmatian towns for its profuse collection of Romanesque and Renaissance architecture (which flourished under Venetian rule), and this, along with its magnificent cathedral, earned it the status as a World Heritage site in 1997.

Trogir is an easy day trip from Split and a relaxing place to spend a few days, taking a trip or two to nearby islands.

Orientation & Information

The heart of the Old Town is a few minutes' walk from the bus station. After crossing the small bridge near the station, go through the north gate. Trogir's finest sights are around Narodni Trg to the southeast.

Atlas travel agency (☎ 881 374; www.atlas-trogir .com; Zvonimira 10) finds private accommodation, books hotels and runs excursions.

Sights

The glory of the three-nave Venetian **Cathedral of St Lovre** (Trg Ivana Pavla II; adult/child 15KN/free; ⏰ 9.30am-noon year-round, plus 4.30-7pm summer) is the Romanesque portal of *Adam and Eve* (1240) by Master Radovan, the earliest example of the nude in Dalmatian sculpture. Enter the building via an obscure back door to see the perfect Renaissance Chapel of St Ivan and the choir stalls, pulpit, ciborium (vessel used to hold consecrated wafers) and treasury. You can even climb the cathedral tower, if it's open, for a great view. Also located on the square is the renovated **Church of St John the Baptist** with a magnificent carved portal and an interior showcasing a *Pietá* by Nicola Firentinac.

Getting There & Away

In Split, city bus 37 leaves from the bus station on Domovinskog. It runs between Trogir and Split every 20 minutes (15KN, one hour) throughout the day, with a short stop at Split airport en route. There's also a ferry (11KN, 2½ hours) once a week from Split to Trogir.

Southbound buses from Zadar (130km) will drop you off in Trogir, as will most northbound buses from Split going to Zadar, Rijeka, Šibenik and Zagreb.

HVAR ISLAND

☎ 021 / pop 12,600

Hvar is the number-one carrier of Croatia's superlatives: it's the most luxurious island, the sunniest place in the country (2724 sunny hours each year) and, along with Dubrovnik, the most popular tourist destination. Hvar is also famed for its verdancy and its lilac lavender fields, as well as other aromatic herbs such as rosemary and heather.

The island's hub and busiest destination is Hvar Town, estimated to draw around 30,000 people a day in the high season. It's odd that they can all fit in the small bay town, but fit they do. Visitors wander along the main square, explore the sights on the winding stone streets, swim on the numerous beaches or pop off to nudist Pakleni Islands. There are several good restaurants and a number of great hotels, as well as a couple of hostels.

Orientation

Car ferries from Split deposit you in Stari Grad but local buses meet most ferries in summer for the trip to Hvar Town. The town centre is Trg Sv Stjepana, 100m west of the bus station. Passenger ferries tie up on Riva, the eastern quay, across from Hotel Slavija.

Information

Atlas travel agency (☎ 741 670) On the western side of the harbour.

Clinic (☎ 741 300; Sv Katarina) About 200m from the town centre, it's past the Hotel Pharos. Emergency services are available 24 hours.

Garderoba (per day 15KN; ⏰ 7am-midnight) The left-luggage office is in the bathroom next to the bus station.

Internet Leon (☎ 741 824; Riva; per hr 42KN; ⏰ 8am-9pm Mon-Fri, to 10pm Sat, to 6pm Sun) Internet access next to the Hotel Palace.

Pelegrini Travel (☎ /fax 742 250; pelegrini@inet.hr) Also finds private accommodation.

Post office (Riva) You can make phone calls here.

Tourist office (☎ /fax 742 977; www.tzhvar.hr; ⏰ 8am-1pm & 5-9pm Mon-Sat, 9am-noon Sun Jun-Sep, 8am-2pm Mon-Sat Oct-May) In the arsenal building on the corner of Trg Sv Stjepana.

Sights & Activities

The full flavour of medieval Hvar is best savoured on the backstreets of the Old Town. At each end of Hvar Town is a monastery with a prominent tower. The Dominican **Church of St Marko** at the head of the bay was largely destroyed by Turks in the 16th century but you can visit the local **Archaeological Museum** (admission 10KN; ☽ 10am-noon Jun-Sep) in the ruins. If it is closed you'll still get a good view of the ruins from the road just above, which leads up to a stone cross on a hilltop offering a picture-postcard view of Hvar.

At the southeastern end of Hvar you'll find the 15th-century Renaissance **Franciscan Monastery** (☽ 10am-noon & 5-7pm Jun-Sep, Christmas week & Holy Week), with a wonderful collection of Venetian paintings in the church and adjacent **museum** (admission 15KN; ☽ 10am-noon & 5-7pm Mon-Sat Jun-Sep), including *The Last Supper* by Matteo Ingoli.

Smack in the middle of Hvar Town is the imposing Gothic **arsenal**, and upstairs is Hvar's prize, the first **municipal theatre** in Europe (1612) – both under extensive renovations at the time of research. On the hill high above Hvar Town is a **Venetian fortress** (1551), and it's worth the climb up to appreciate the lovely, sweeping panoramic views. The fort was built to defend Hvar from the Turks, who sacked the town in 1539 and 1571.

Sleeping

Accommodation in Hvar Town is extremely tight in July and August: a reservation is highly recommended. For private accommodation, try Pelegrini Travel (see opposite). Expect to pay from 160/280KN per single/double with bathroom in the town centre.

Green Lizard Hostel (☎ 742 560; www.greenlizard.hr; Lučića bb; dm 110KN, d per person 135KN; ☽ Apr-Nov) This privately run hostel is a welcome and most necessary budget option on Hvar. Rooms are simple and immaculately clean, there's a communal kitchen and a few doubles with private and shared facilities.

Jagoda & Ante Bracanović Guesthouse (☎ 741 416, 091 520 3796; www.geocities.com/virgilye/hvar-jagoda.html; Poviše Škole; s 100-120KN, d 190-220KN) The Bracanović family has turned a traditional stone building into a small *pensione*. Rooms come with balconies, private bathrooms and access to a kitchen, and the family goes out of its way for guests.

Hotel Croatia (☎ 742 400; www.hotelcroatia.net; Majerovica bb; per person 245-575KN;) Only a few steps from the sea, this medium-size, rambling 1930s building is among gorgeous, peaceful gardens. The rooms are simple and fresh, many with balconies overlooking the gardens and the sea.

ourpick Hotel Riva (☎ 750 750; www.suncanihvar .hr; Riva bb; s €176-380, d €187-391; 🐕 💻) Now the luxury veteran on the Hvar Town hotel scene, the Riva is a 100-year-old hotel that's a picture of modernity. The location is right on the harbour, perfect for watching the yachts glide up and away.

Eating

Konoba Menego (☎ 742 036; mains from 70KN) This is a rustic old house where everything is decked out in Hvar antiques and the staff wears traditional outfits. Try the cheeses and vegetables, prepared the old-fashioned Dalmatian way.

Luna (☎ 741 400; mains from 70KN) Climb the 'stairway to heaven' (you have to guffaw) to the rooftop terrace. Luna has dishes such as gnocchi with truffles, and seafood and wine pasta.

Yakša (☎ 277 0770; www.yaksahvar.com; mains from 80KN) A top-end restaurant where many come not just for the food but also for its reputation as the place to be seen in Hvar. There is a lovely garden at the back and the food is excellent, with lobster being a popular choice (250KN).

The pizzerias along the harbour offer predictable but inexpensive eating. The **grocery store** (Trg Sv Stjepana) is a viable restaurant alternative, and there's a morning market next to the bus station.

Drinking

Hvar has some of the best nightlife on the Adriatic coast, and it's mainly famous for **Carpe Diem** (☎ 742 369; www.carpe-diem-hvar.com; Riva), the mother of all Dalmatian clubs. The music is smooth, the drinks aplenty and there's lots of dancing on the tables in bikinis.

Veneranda (☽ from 9.30pm), a former fortress on the slope above Hotel Delfin, alternates star DJs with live bands while the punters dance on a dance floor surrounded by a pool.

Getting There & Away

The Jadrolinija ferries between Rijeka and Dubrovnik stop in Stari Grad before continuing to Korčula. The Jadrolinija agency sells boat tickets. Car ferries from Split call at Stari Grad (42KN, one hour) three times daily (five daily in July and August). The speedy catamaran goes five times a day between Split and Hvar Town in the summer months (22KN, one hour). The **Jadrolinija agency** (☎ 741 132; www .jadrolinija.hr; Riva) is beside the landing in Stari

Grad. There are at least 10 shuttle ferries (less in the low season) running from Drvenik, on the mainland, to Sućuraj on the tip of Hvar island (13KN, 25 minutes).

It's possible to visit Hvar on a (hectic) day trip from Split by catching the morning Jadrolinija ferry to Stari Grad, a bus to Hvar town, then the last ferry from Stari Grad directly back to Split.

Ferries to/from Italy:

Jadrolinija (www.jadrolinija.hr) Runs car ferries from Bari to Dubrovnik (€51, eight hours, six weekly), continuing on to Rijeka, Stari Grad and Split.

SNAV (www.snav.com) Has a car ferry that travels from Pescara to Hvar (3½ hours, daily) and on to Split (6½ hours).

Split Tours (www.splittours.hr) Connects Ancona to Split (nine hours) and Stari Grad (12 hours). In summer, ferries leave twice daily Saturday to Monday and daily on other days.

Getting Around

Buses meet most ferries that dock at Stari Grad in July and August, but if you come in the low season it's best to check at the tourist office or at Pelegrini to make sure the bus is running. A taxi costs from 150KN to 200KN. **Radio Taxi Tihi** (☎ 098 338 824) is cheaper if there are a number of passengers to fill up the minivan. It's easy to recognise the photo of Hvar painted on the side.

KORČULA ISLAND
☎ 020 / pop 16,200

Rich in vineyards and olive trees, the island of Korčula was named Korkyra Melaina (Black Korčula) by the original Greek settlers because of its dense woods and plant life. As the largest island in an archipelago of 48, it provides plenty of opportunities for scenic drives, particularly along the southern coast.

Swimming opportunities abound in the many quiet coves and secluded beaches, while the interior produces some of Croatia's finest wine, especially dessert wines made from the *grk* grape cultivated around Lumbarda. Local olive oil is another product worth seeking out.

On a hilly peninsula jutting into the Adriatic sits Korčula Town, a striking walled town of round defensive towers and red-roofed houses. Resembling a miniature Dubrovnik, the gated, walled Old Town is criss-crossed by narrow stone streets designed to protect its inhabitants from the winds swirling around the peninsula.

Orientation

The big Jadrolinija car ferry drops you off either in the west harbour next to the Hotel Korčula or the east harbour next to Marko Polo Tours. The Old Town lies between the two harbours. The large hotels and main beach lie south of the east harbour, and the residential neighbourhood Sveti Nikola (with a smaller beach) is southwest of the west harbour. The town bus station is 100m south of the Old Town centre.

Information

There are ATMs in the town centre at HVB Splitska Banka and Dubrovačka Banka. You can change money there, at the post office or at any of the travel agencies. The post office is hidden next to the stairway up to the Old Town. The post office also has telephones.

Atlas travel agency (☎ 711 231; Trg Kralja Tomislava) Represents Amex, runs excursions and finds private accommodation. There's another office nearby.

Eterna (☎ 716 538; eterno.doo@du.t-com.hr; Put Sv. Nikola bb) Finds private accommodation and offers internet access (per hour 25KN).

Hospital (☎ 711 137; Ul 59, Kalac) It's south of the Old Town, about 1km past the Hotel Marko Polo. Emergency services are available 24 hours.

Marko Polo Tours (☎ 715 400; marko-polo-tours@ du.t-com.hr; Biline 5) Finds private accommodation and organises excursions.

Tino's Internet (☎ 091 50 91 182; ul Tri Sulara; per hr 30KN) Tino's other outlet is at the ACI Marina; both are open long hours.

Tourist office (☎ 715 701; tzg-korcule@du.t-com.hr; Obala Franje Tudjmana bb; ☻ 8am-3pm & 5-9pm Mon-Sat, 8am-3pm Sun Jun-Sep, 8am-1pm & 5-9pm Mon-Sat Oct-May) An excellent source of information, located on the west harbour.

Sights

Other than following the circuit of the former city walls or walking along the shore, sightseeing in Korčula centres on Trg Sv Marka. The Gothic **St Mark's Cathedral** (Katedrala Svetog Marka; ☻ 10am-noon & 5-7pm Jul & Aug, Mass only rest of year) features two paintings by Tintoretto (*Three Saints* on the altar and *Annunciation* to one side).

The **Town Museum** (Gradski Muzej; ☎ 711 420; Trg Sv Marka Statuta; admission 10KN; ☻ 10am-1pm Nov-Mar, 10am-2pm Apr & May, 10am-2pm & 7-9pm Jun & Oct, 10am-9pm Jul & Aug) in the 15th-century Gabriellis Palace opposite the cathedral has exhibits of Greek pottery, Roman ceramics and home furnishings, all

CROATIA

with English captions. The **treasury** (☎ 711 049; Trg Sv Marka; admission 15KN; ☾ 9am-2pm & 5-8pm May-Oct), in the 14th-century Abbey Palace next to the cathedral is also worth a look. It's said that Marco Polo was born in Korčula in 1254; you can visit what is believed to have been his **house** (Depolo; admission 10KN; ☾ 10am-1pm & 5-7pm Mon-Sat Jul & Aug) and climb the tower.

There's also an **Icon Museum** (Trg Svih Svetih; admission 7.50KN; ☾ 9am-2pm & 5-8pm May-Oct) in the Old Town. It isn't much of a museum, but visitors are let into the beautiful old **All Saints Church**.

In the high summer season, water taxis at the east harbour collect passengers to visit various points on the island, as well as to **Badija Island**, which features an historic 15th-century Franciscan Monastery in the process of reconstruction, plus **Orebić** and the nearby village of **Lumbarda**, which both have sandy beaches.

Tours

Both Atlas travel agency and Marko Polo Tours offer a variety of boat tours and island excursions.

Sleeping & Eating

The big hotels in Korčula are overpriced, but there are a wealth of guest houses that offer clean, attractive rooms and friendly service. Atlas and Marko Polo Tours arrange private rooms, charging from 200KN to 220KN for a room with a bathroom, and starting at about 400KN for an apartment. Or you could try one of the following options.

Autocamp Kalac (☎ 711 182; fax 711 146; per person/ site €5.40/8.20) This attractive camping ground is behind Hotel Bon Repos, about 4km from the west harbour, in a dense pine grove near the beach.

Pansion Marinka (☎ 712 007, 098 344 712; marinka .milina-bire@du.t-com.hr; d 150-230KN) This is a working farm and winery situated in Lumbarda, in a beautiful setting within walking distance of the beach. The owners turn out excellent wines and liqueurs, catch and smoke their own fish and are happy to explain the processes to their guests.

Villa DePolo (☎ /fax 711 621; tereza.depolo@du.t -com.hr; d 240/290KN; ☒) In the residential neighbourhood close to the Old Town and 100m west of the bus station, this guest house has four modern, clean rooms, some with sea views. Note that there is a 30% extra charge for one-night stays.

Fresh (☎ 091 799.2086; www.igotfresh.com; 1 Kod Kina Liburne; snacks from 20KN) Right across from the bus station, Fresh is fab for breakfast smoothies, lunch wraps or beers and cocktails in the evening.

Planjak (☎ 711 015; Plokata 19 Travnja; mains from 50KN) Meat lovers should head here for the mixed grill and proper Balkan dishes, served on a covered terrace.

Konoba Marinero (☎ 711 170; Marka Andrijića; mains from 50KN) Right in the heart of the medieval Old Town, the family-run and marine-themed Marinero has the sons catch the fish and the parents prepare it according to a variety of traditional recipes.

Konoba Maslina (☎ 711 720; Lumbarajska cesta bb; mains from 50KN) It's well worth the walk out here for the authentic Korčulan home-cooking. The multibean soup is a standout. It's about a kilometre past the Hotel Marko Polo on the road to Lumbarda, but you can often arrange to be picked up or dropped off in town.

Entertainment

Between June and October there's **moreška sword dancing** (tickets 100KN; ☾ show 9pm Thu) by the Old Town gate; performances are more frequent during July and August. The clash of swords and the graceful movements of the dancers/fighters make an exciting show. Atlas, the tourist office and Marko Polo Tours sell tickets.

Getting There & Away

Transport connections to Korčula are good. There's one bus every day to Dubrovnik (87KN, three hours), one to Zagreb (195KN, 12 hours), and one a week to Sarajevo (165KN, eight hours).

There's a **Jadrolinija office** (☎ 715 410) about 25m up from the west harbour.

There's a regular afternoon car ferry between Split and Vela Luka (35KN, three hours), on the island's western end, that stops at Hvar most days. Six daily buses link Korčula town to Vela Luka (28KN, one hour), but services from Vela Luka are reduced at the weekend.

The daily fast boat running from Split to Hvar and Korčula is great for locals working in Split but not so great for tourists who find themselves leaving Korčula at 6am. Nevertheless, you can go quickly from Korčula to Hvar (33KN, 1½ hours) and to Split (55KN, 2¾ hours). Get tickets at Marko Polo.

CROATIA

WORTH THE TRIP: OREBIĆ

Orebić, on the southern coast of the Pelješac Peninsula between Korčula and Ploče, offers better beaches than those found at Korčula, 2.5km across the water. The easy access by ferry from Korčula makes it the perfect place to go for the day. The best beach in Orebić is Trstenica cove, a 15-minute walk east along the shore from the port.

In Orebić the ferry terminal and the bus station are adjacent to each other. Korčula buses to Dubrovnik, Zagreb and Sarajevo stop at Orebić.

From Orebić, look for the passenger launch (15KN, 15 minutes, at least five times daily on weekdays), which will drop you off near Hotel Korčula. There's also a car ferry to Dominče (10KN, 15 minutes), which stops near the Hotel Bon Repos, where you can pick up the bus from Lumbarda (10KN) a few times a day or a water taxi to Korčula town.

Next to Marko Polo, **Rent a Đir** (☎ 711 908; www.korcula-rent.com) hires autos, scooters and small boats.

MLJET ISLAND
☎ 020 / pop 1110

Of all the Adriatic islands, Mljet (Meleda in Italian) may be the most seductive. Over 72% of the island is covered by forests and the rest is dotted by fields, vineyards and villages. Created in 1960, Mljet National Park occupies the western third of the island and surrounds two saltwater lakes, Malo Jezero and Veliko Jezero. Most people visit the island on excursions from Korčula or Dubrovnik, but it is now possible to take a passenger boat from Dubrovnik or come on the regular ferry from Dubrovnik and stay a few days for hiking, cycling and boating.

Orientation & Information

The island is 37km long, and has an average width of about 3km. The main points of entry are Pomena and Polače, two tiny towns about 5km apart. Tour boats from Korčula and the Dubrovnik catamarans arrive at Polače wharf in the high season. Pomena is the site of the island's only conventional hotel, Hotel Odisej. There's a good map of the island posted at the wharf. Jadrolinija ferries stop only at Sobra but catamarans from Dubrovnik and Korčula stop at Polače.

Goveđari, the national park's entry point, is just between Pomena and Polače. The **national park** (adult/concession 90/30KN) measures 54 sq km and the entry price includes a bus and boat transfer to the Benedictine monastery. If you stay overnight on the island you only pay the park admission once.

The **tourist office** (☎ 744 186; www.mljet.hr; ⏱ 8am-8pm Mon-Sat, 8am-1pm Sun Jun-Sep, 8am-1pm & 5-8pm Mon-Fri Oct-May) is in Polače and there is an ATM next door. There's another ATM at the Hotel Odisej in Pomena.

The administrative centre of the island is at Babino Polje, 18km east of Polače, where there is another **tourist office** (☎ /fax 745 125; www.mljet .hr; ⏱ 9am-5pm Mon-Fri) and a post office.

Sights & Activities

From Pomena it's a 15-minute walk to a jetty on **Veliko Jezero**, the larger of the two lakes. Here you can board a boat to a small lake islet and have lunch at a 12th-century **Benedictine monastery**, which now houses a restaurant.

You can catch an early boat back to the main island and spend a couple of hours walking along the lakeshore before taking the late-afternoon excursion boat back to Korčula or Dubrovnik. There's a small landing on the main island opposite the monastery where the boat operator drops off passengers upon request. It's not possible to walk right around Veliko Jezero because there's no bridge over the channel that connects the lakes to the sea.

Mljet is good for cycling; several restaurants along the dock in Polače and the Odisej Hotel in Pomena hire bicycles (10/100KN per hour/day). If you plan to cycle between Pomena and Polače be aware that the two towns are separated by a steep mountain. The bike path along Veliko Jezero is an easier pedal but it doesn't link the two towns.

The island offers some unusual opportunities for **diving**. There's a Roman wreck dating from the 3rd century in relatively shallow water. The remains of the ship, including amphorae, have calcified over the centuries and this has protected them from pillaging. There's also a German torpedo boat from WWII and several walls to dive. Contact **Kronmar diving** (☎ 744 022; Hotel Odisej).

Sleeping & Eating

The Polače tourist office arranges private accommodation at 200KN per double room in summer but it is essential to make arrangements before arrival in peak season. There are more *sobe* signs around Pomena than Polače, but practically none at all in Sobra.

Stermasi (☎ 098 939 0362; Saplunara; per apt €30-45; 🌃) An excellent choice for those wanting to self-cater and get away from it all – seven well-equipped, bright apartments sleep two to four people. Saplunara is pretty isolated, though, on the eastern side of the island, but you are near the only sandy beaches on Mljet. There's a good restaurant here too.

Soline 6 (☎ 744 024; www.soline6.com; Soline; d €45-75) This is the only accommodation within the national park and is designed with waterless toilets, solar heating and organic waste composting. You'll have to do without electricity though.

Odisej (☎ 744 022; Pomena; s/d from €62/88; 🌃) Rooms are pleasant enough here, plus you are right on the port and can hire bicycles, snorkelling equipment etc.

Melita (☎ 744 145; www.mljet-restoranmelita.com; St Mary's Island, Veliko Jezero; mains from 60KN) A more romantic (and touristy) spot can't be found on the island – this is the restaurant attached to the church on the little island in the middle of the big lake.

Getting There & Away

Jadrolinija ferries stop only at Sobra (32KN, two hours) but the **Melita catamaran** (☎ 313 119; www.gv-line.hr; Vukovarska 34) goes to Polače (70KN) after Sobra (50KN) in the summer months, leaving Dubrovnik at 9.45am daily and returning from Polače at 4.55pm, making it ideal for a day trip from Dubrovnik. From Sobra, you can get to Pomena on a bus (1½ hours) and from Polače you can either cycle or walk there.

Tickets are sold in the **tourist office** (Map p250; ☎ 417 983; Obala Stjepana Radića 27) in Gruž or on board, but it's wise to buy in advance as the boat fills up quickly.

DUBROVNIK
☎ 020 / pop 43,800

No matter whether you are visiting Dubrovnik for the first time or if you're returning again and again to this marvellous city, the sense of awe and beauty when you set eyes on the Stradun never fades. It's hard to imagine anyone, even the city's inhabitants, becoming jaded by its marble streets and baroque buildings, or failing to be inspired by a walk along the ancient city walls that once protected a

civilised, sophisticated republic for five centuries and that now look out onto the endless shimmer of the peaceful Adriatic.

History

Founded 1300 years ago by refugees from Epidaurus in Greece, medieval Dubrovnik (Ragusa until 1918) shook off Venetian control in the 14th century, becoming an independent republic and one of Venice's more important maritime rivals, trading with Egypt, Syria, Sicily, Spain, France and later Turkey. The double blow of an earthquake in 1667 and the opening of new trade routes to the east sent Ragusa into a slow decline, ending with Napoleon's conquest of the town in 1806.

The deliberate shelling of Dubrovnik by the Yugoslav army in 1991 sent shockwaves through the international community but, when the smoke cleared in 1992, traumatised residents cleared the rubble and set about repairing the damage. Reconstruction has been extraordinarily skilful.

After a steep postwar decline in tourism, Dubrovnik has become a major tourist destination once again.

Orientation

The Jadrolinija ferry terminal and the bus station are next to each other at Gruž, several kilometres northwest of the Old Town, which is closed to cars. The main street in the Old Town is Placa (better known as Stradun). Most accommodation is on the leafy Lapad Peninsula, west of the bus station.

Information

You can change money at any travel agency or post office. There are numerous ATMs in town, near the bus station and near the ferry terminal.

Algoritam (Map p252; Placa) Bookshop with a good selection of English-language books, including guidebooks.

Atlas Travel Agency Obala Papa Ivana Pavla II (Map p250; ☎ 418 001; Obala Papa Ivana Pavla II 1); Sv Đurđa (Map p250; ☎ 442 574; Sv Đurđa 1) In convenient locations, this agency is extremely helpful for general information, as well as finding private accommodation. All excursions are run by Atlas.

Garderoba (Map p250; 🕐 5.30am-9pm) Left luggage; at the bus station.

Hospital (Map p250; ☎ 431 777; Dr Roka Mišetića bb) Emergency services are available 24 hours.

Lapad post office (Map p250; Šetalište Kralja Zvonimira 21)

CROATIA

CROATIA

DUBROVNIK

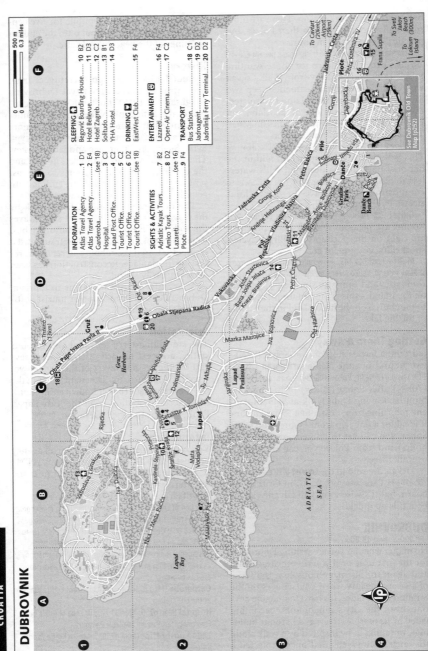

0 — 500 m
0 — 0.3 miles

INFORMATION
Atlas Travel Agency.....................1 D1
Atlas Travel Agency.....................2 E4
Garderoba...............................(see 18)
Hospital..................................3 C3
Lapad Post Office.......................4 C2
Tourist Office............................5 C2
Tourist Office............................6 D2
Tourist Office............................(see 18)

SIGHTS & ACTIVITIES
Adriatic Kayak Tours...................7 B2
Amico Tours.............................8 D2
Lazareti.................................(see 16)
Ploce...................................9 F4

SLEEPING 🏠
Begović Boarding House..............10 B2
Hotel Bellevue.........................11 D3
Hotel Zagreb...........................12 C2
Solitudo...............................13 B1
YHA Hostel............................14 D3

DRINKING 🍷
EastWest Club.........................15 F4

ENTERTAINMENT 🎭
Lazareti...............................16 F4
Open-Air Cinema......................17 C2

TRANSPORT
Bus Station............................18 C1
Jadroagent.............................19 D2
Jadrolinija Ferry Terminal.............20 D2

See Dubrovnik Old Town
Map (p252)

ADRIATIC
SEA

Lapad
Bay

Gruž
Harbour

Main post office (Map p252; cnr Široka & Od Puča)
Netcafe (Map p252; ☎ 321 125; www.netcafe.hr; Prijeko
21; per hr 30KN; ⏰ 9am-11pm) A wonderfully friendly
cafe with a fast connection and good services.
Tourist office (www.tzdubrovnik.hr) Bus Station (Map
p250; ☎ 417 581; Obala Pape Ivana Pavla II 24; ⏰ 8am-
8pm Jun-Sep, 8am-3pm Mon-Fri, 9am-2pm Sat, closed
Sun Oct-May); Gruž Harbour (Map p250; ☎ 417 983; Obala
Stjepana Radića 27; ⏰ 8am-8pm daily Jun-Sep, 8am-3pm
Mon-Fri, 9am-2pm Sat, closed Sun Oct-May); Lapad (Map
p250; ☎ 437 460; Šetalište Kralja Zvonimira 25; ⏰ 8am-
8pm daily Jun-Sep, 8am-3pm Mon-Fri, 9am-2pm Sat,
closed Sun Oct-May); Old Town (Map p252; ☎ 323 587;
Široka 1; ⏰ 8am-8pm daily Jun-Sep, 8am-3pm Mon-Fri,
9am-2pm Sat, closed Sun Oct-May); Pile Gate (Map p250;
☎ 427 591; Dubrovačkih Branitelja 7; ⏰ 8am-8pm daily
Jun-Sep, 8am-3pm Mon-Fri, 9am-2pm Sat, closed Sun Oct-
May) Maps, information and the indispensable *Dubrovnik
Riviera* guide.

Sights
OLD TOWN

You will probably begin your visit of
Dubrovnik's World Heritage–listed Old Town
at the city bus stop outside **Pile Gate** (Map
p252). As you enter the city, Dubrovnik's
wonderful pedestrian promenade, Placa, extends before you all the way to the **clock tower**
(Map p252) at the other end of town.

Just inside Pile Gate is the huge 1438 **Onofrio
Fountain** (Map p252) and **Franciscan Monastery**
(Muzej Franjevačkog Samostana; Map p252; ☎ 321 410; Placa
2; adult/concession 20/10KN; ⏰ 9am-6pm) with a splendid cloister and the third-oldest functioning
pharmacy (Map p252; ⏰ 9am-5pm) in Europe; it's
been operating since 1391. The **church** (Map
p252; ⏰ 7am-7pm) has recently undergone a long
and expensive restoration to startling effect.
The **monastery museum** (Map p252; adult/concession
20/10KN; ⏰ 9am-5pm) has a collection of liturgical
objects, paintings and pharmacy equipment.

In front of the clock tower at the eastern
end of Placa (on the square called Luža) is
the 1419 **Orlando Column** (Map p252) – a favourite meeting place. On opposite sides of
the column are the 16th-century **Sponza Palace**
(Map p252) – originally a customs house,
later a bank, and which now houses the
State Archives (Državni Arhiv u Dubrovniku; ☎ 321 032;
admission 15KN; ⏰ 8am-3pm Mon-Fri, 8am-1pm Sat) –
and **St Blaise's Church** (Map p252), a lovely
Italian baroque building built in 1715 to replace an earlier church destroyed in the 1667
earthquake. At the end of Pred Dvorom, the
wide street beside St Blaise, is the baroque

Cathedral of the Assumption of the Virgin (Map
p252). Located between the two churches,
the 1441 Gothic **Rector's Palace** (Map p252;
☎ 321 437; Pred Dvorom 3; adult/student 35/15KN, audio
guide 30KN; ⏰ 9am-6pm) houses a museum with
furnished rooms, baroque paintings and historical exhibits. The elected rector was not
permitted to leave the building during his
one-month term without the permission of
the senate. The narrow street opposite opens
onto Gundulićeva Poljana, a bustling **morning
market** (Map p252). Up the stairs south of
the square is the 1725 **Jesuit Monastery** (Map
p252; Poljana Ruđera Boškovića).

As you proceed up Placa, make a detour
to the **Museum of the Orthodox Church** (Muzej
Pravoslavne Crkve; Map p252; ☎ 323 283; Od Puča 8;
adult/concession 10/5KN; ⏰ 9am-2pm Mon-Sat) for a
look at a fascinating collection of 15th- to
19th-century icons.

By now you'll be ready for a leisurely
walk around the **city walls** (Gradske Zidine; Map
p252; adult/child 50/20KN; ⏰ 9am-7.30pm Apr-Oct, 10am-
3.30pm Nov-Mar), which has entrances just inside Pile Gate, across from the Dominican
monastery and near Fort St John. Built between the 13th and 16th centuries, these
powerful walls are the finest in the world
and Dubrovnik's main claim to fame. They
enclose the entire city in a protective veil
over 2km long and up to 25m high, with
two round and 14 square towers, two corner fortifications and a large fortress. The
views over the town and sea are great –
this walk could be the high point of your
visit.

Whichever way you go, you'll notice
the 14th-century **Dominican Monastery** (Muzej
Dominikanskog Samostana; Map p252; ☎ 322 200; off
Svetog Dominika 4; adult/child 20/10KN; ⏰ 9am-5pm) in
the northeastern corner of the city, whose
forbidding fortress-like exterior shelters a
rich trove of paintings from Dubrovnik's
finest 15th- and 16th-century artists.

Dubrovnik has many other sights, such
as the unmarked **synagogue** (Sinagoga; Map p252;
☎ 321 028; Žudioska 5; admission 10KN; ⏰ 9am-3pm Mon-
Fri Oct-May, 10am-8pm daily Jun-Sep) near the clock
tower, which is the second-oldest synagogue
in Europe. The uppermost streets of the Old
Town below the north and south walls are
pleasant to wander along.

One of the better photography galleries
you're likely to come across, **War Photo Limited**
(Map p252; ☎ 326 166; www.warphotoltd.com; Antuninska 6;

CROATIA

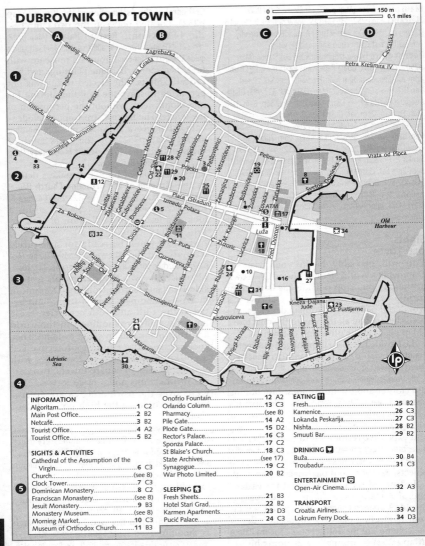

DUBROVNIK OLD TOWN

admission 30KN; ⏰ 9am-9pm daily May-Sep, 10am-4pm Tue-Sat, 10am-2pm Sun Oct & Apr, closed Nov-Apr) has changing exhibitions that are curated by the gallery owner and former photojournalist Wade Goddard. It's open summer only, and has up to three exhibitions over that period, relating to the subject of war and seen from various perspectives.

BEACHES
Ploče (Map p250), the closest beach to the Old Town, is just beyond the 17th-century **Lazareti** (Map p250; a former quarantine station) outside **Ploče Gate** (Map p252). Another nearby, good, local beach is **Sveti Jakov**, a 20-minute walk down Vlaho Bukovac or a quick ride on bus 5 or 8 from the northern end of the Old

Town. There are also hotel beaches along the **Lapad Peninsula** (Map p250), which you are able to use without a problem.

An even better option is to take the ferry that shuttles half-hourly in summer to lush **Lokrum Island** (return 40KN), a national park with a rocky nudist beach (marked FKK), a botanical garden and the ruins of a medieval Benedictine monastery.

Activities
Adriatic Kayak Tours (Map p250; ☎ 312 770; www .kayakcroatia.com; Frankopanska 6) offers a great series of kayak tours for experienced and beginner kayakers.

Tours
Amico Tours (Map p250; ☎ 418 248; www.amico-tours .com; Od Skara 1) offers day trips to Mostar and Međugorje (390KN), Montenegro (390KN), Albania (990KN), Korčula and Pelješac (390KN), and the Elafiti Islands (250KN), as well as numerous kayaking, rafting and jeep safari day trips (590KN).

Festivals & Events
Feast of St Blaise 3 February
Carnival February
Dubrovnik Summer Festival Mid-July to mid-August. A major cultural event, with over 100 performances at different venues in the Old Town.

Sleeping
Private accommodation is generally the best option in Dubrovnik, but beware of the scramble of private owners at the bus station or Jadrolinija wharf. Some offer what they say they offer, others are rip-off artists. Expect to pay about €28 to €50 a room in high season.

OLD TOWN
Fresh Sheets (Map p252; ☎ 091 799 2086; beds@igotfresh .com; Sv Šimuna 15; per person €25; 🖳) A brand new place, this is a collection of four individually decorated apartments – Lavender, Rainforest, Sunshine, Heaven – each sleeping two to four people (plus a sofa), and one double room. The location is excellent – in the heart of Old Town – you get free internet and wi-fi and, when the Fresh bar's kitchen is open, a free smoothie.

ourpick Karmen Apartments (Map p252; ☎ 323 433, 098 619 282; www.karmendu.com; Bandureva 1; apt €55-145; 🞨) Set inside an old stone house in the middle of the Old Town, the four apartments are

beautifully decorated with original artwork and imaginative use of recycled materials. There are small, one- to two-person apartments, as well as two for three and four people. Book well in advance because it all gets snapped up by June.

Hotel Stari Grad (Map p252; ☎ 322 244; www.hotel starigrad.com; Palmotićeva; s 650-1180KN, d 920KN-1580KN; 🞨) Staying in the heart of the Old Town in a lovingly restored stone building is an unmatchable experience. The eight rooms are elegantly and tastefully furnished to feel simple and luxurious at the same time.

Pucić Palace (Map p252; ☎ 326 222; www.thepucic palace.com; Od Puča 1; s €206-315, d €290-505; 🞨) Right in the heart of the Old Town and inside what was once a nobleman's mansion, this five-star hotel is Dubrovnik's most exclusive and hottest property. There are only 19 rooms, all exquisitely decorated and featuring Italian mosaics, Egyptian-cotton linen and baroque beds.

OUTSIDE THE OLD TOWN
Solitudo (Map p250; ☎ 448 200; Vatroslava Lisinskog 17; per person/site €5.40/10.20) This pretty and renovated camping ground is within walking distance of the beach.

YHA Hostel (Map p250; ☎ 423 241; dubrovnik@hfhs .hr; Vinka Sagrestana 3; B&B per person 85-120KN) Basic in decor, the YHA Hostel is clean and, as travellers report, a lot of fun. The best dorms are rooms 31 and 32, for their 'secret' roof terrace.

Begović Boarding House (Map p250; ☎ 435 191; http://begovic-boarding-house.com; Primorska 17; dm €14-19, s €25-32, d €32-40) A long-time favourite with our readers, this friendly place in Lapad has three rooms with shared bathroom and three apartments. There's a terrace out the back with a good view. Breakfast is an additional 30KN.

Hotel Zagreb (Map p250; ☎ 430 930; www.hotels -sumratin.com; Šetalište Kralja Zvonimira 27; s 400-660KN, d 700-1060KN; 🞨) Under the same ownership as Hotel Sumratin, Hotel Zagreb is a more stylish sister, set inside a lovely, salmon-coloured 19th-century building. The rooms are large, with marine motifs and large bathrooms.

ourpick Hotel Bellevue (Map p250; ☎ 330 000; www .hotel-bellevue.hr; Petra Čingrije 7; d from €250; 🞨🖳🖳) Although not within the borders of the Old Town, but a five-minute walk west from Pile Gate, Hotel Bellevue's location – on a cliff that overlooks the open sea and the lovely bay underneath – is pretty much divine. The rooms are beautifully designed, and the balconies overlook the said sea and bay.

Eating

Weed out tourist traps and choose carefully, and you'll find fabulous food in the Old Town.

Smuuti Bar (Map p252; ☎ 091 896 7509; Palmotićeva 5; smoothies 18-25KN) Perfect for breakfast smoothies and nice big mugs of coffee (at a bargain 10KN).

Fresh (Map p252; ☎ 091 896 7509; www.igotfresh.com; Vetranićeva 4; wraps from 20KN) A mecca for young travellers who gather here for the smoothies, wraps and other healthy snacks, as well as drinks and music in the evening.

Nishta (Map p252; ☎ 091 896 7509; Prijeko 30; mains from 30KN) Head here for a refreshing gazpacho, a heart-warming miso soup, thai curries, vegies and noodles, and many more vegie delights.

Kamenice (Map p252; ☎ 421 499; Gundulićeva Poljana 8; mains from 40KN) It's been here since the 1970s and not much has changed: the socialist-style waiting uniforms, the simple interior, the massive portions of mussels, grilled or fried squid and griddled anchovies, and *kamenice* – oysters – too.

our pick **Lokanda Peskarija** (Map p252; ☎ 324 750; Ribarnica bb; mains from 40KN) Located on the Old Harbour right next to the fish market, this is undoubtedly one of Dubrovnik's best eateries. The quality of the seafood dishes is unfaltering, the prices are good, and the location is gorgeous.

Drinking

our pick **Buža** (Map p252; Ilije Sarake) The Buža is just a simple place on the outside of the city walls, facing out onto the open sea, with simple drinks and blissful punters.

EastWest Club (Map p250; ☎ 412 220; Frana Supila bb) By day this outfit on Banje Beach rents out beach chairs and umbrellas and serves drinks to the bathers. When the rays lengthen, the cocktail bar opens.

Troubadur (Map p252; ☎ 412 154; Bunićeva Poljana 2) A legendary Dubrovnik venue; come here for live jazz concerts in the summer.

Entertainment

Lazareti (Map p250; ☎ 324 633; www.lazareti.du-hr.net; Frana Supila 8) Dubrovnik's best art and music centre, Lazareti hosts cinema nights, club nights, live music, masses of concerts and pretty much all the best things in town.

Open-Air Cinema (Lapad Map p250; Kumičića; Old Town Map p252; Za Rokom) In two locations, it is open nightly in July and August with screenings starting after sundown (9pm or 9.30pm); ask at Sloboda Cinema for the schedule.

Getting There & Away

AIR

Daily flights to/from Zagreb are operated by **Croatia Airlines** (Map p252; ☎ 413 777; Brsalje 9). The fare runs from 400KN one way, higher in peak season; the trip takes about an hour.

There are also nonstop flights to Rome, London and Manchester between April and October.

BOAT

In addition to the **Jadrolinija** (Map p250; ☎ 418 000; Gruž) coastal ferry north to Hvar, Split and Rijeka (Rijeka–Split 12½ hours, Split–Hvar 1¾ hours, Hvar–Korčula 3¾ hours, Korčula–Dubrovnik 3¼ hours), there's a local ferry that leaves from Dubrovnik for Sobra on Mljet Island (50KN, 2½ hours) throughout the year. There are several ferries a day year-round to the outlying islands of Šipanska, Suđurađ, Lopud and Koločep. See also the Central Dalmatia Ferry Routes map (p241).

Jadroagent (Map p250; ☎ 419 009; fax 419 029; Radića 32) handles ticketing for most international boats from Croatia.

For international connections:

Azzurra Lines (www.azzurraline.com) Sails from Bari, Italy to Dubrovnik (€65).

Jadrolinija (www.jadrolinija.hr) Runs car ferries from Bari to Dubrovnik (€51, eight hours, six weekly), which continue on to Rijeka, Stari Grad and Split. Ferries are less frequent during winter months.

BUS

In a busy summer season and at weekends buses out of Dubrovnik can be crowded, so book a ticket well before the scheduled departure time.

Internationally there are daily bus connections from Sarajevo (€18, five hours, daily), Međugorje (€18, three hours, two daily) and Mostar (€15, three hours, two daily) in Bosnia and Hercegovina to Dubrovnik, plus a daily bus from Kotor (Montenegro) to Dubrovnik (120KN, 2½ hours) that starts at Bar and stops at Herceg Novi.

BUSES FROM DUBROVNIK			
Destination	**Fare (KN)**	**Duration (hr)**	**Daily services**
Korčula	95	3	1
Orebić	80	2½	1
Rijeka	400	13	2
Split	120	4½	14
Zadar	250	8	7
Zagreb	250	11	7-8

Getting Around

Čilipi international airport is 24km southeast of Dubrovnik. The Croatia Airlines airport buses (25KN, 45 minutes) leave from the main **bus station** (Map p250; ☎ 357 088) 1½ hours before flight times. Buses meet Croatia Airlines flights but not all others. A taxi costs around 200KN.

Dubrovnik's buses run frequently and generally on time. The fare is 10KN if you buy from the driver but only 8KN if you buy a ticket at a kiosk.

CROATIA DIRECTORY

ACCOMMODATION

Budget accommdation in this chapter includes camping grounds, hostels and some guest houses, and costs up to 500KN (€70) for a double. Midrange accommodation costs 500KN to 900KN (€125) a double, while top-end places start at 900KN and can go as high as 4000KN (€550) a double. Unless otherwise stated, all rooms in this chapter include private bathroom.

Accommodation listings in this guide have been arranged in order of price. Many hotels, rooms and camping grounds issue their prices in euros but some places to stay have stuck with the kuna. Although you can usually pay with either currency, we have listed the primary currency the establishment uses in setting its prices.

Along the Croatian coast accommodation is priced according to three seasons, which tend to vary from place to place. Generally October to May are the cheapest months, June and September are mid-priced, but count on paying top price for the peak season, which runs for a six-week period in July and August. Price ranges quoted in this chapter are from the cheapest to the most expensive (ie low to high season) and do not include 'residence tax' (7.50KN per person per night). Note that prices for rooms in Zagreb are pretty much constant all year and that many hotels on the coast close in winter. Some places offer half-board, which is bed and two meals a day, usually breakfast and one other meal.

Most hotels have smoking and nonsmoking rooms.

Camping

Nearly 100 camping grounds are scattered along the Croatian coast. Opening times of camping grounds generally run from mid-April to September, give or take a few weeks. The exact times change from year to year, so it's wise to call in advance if you're arriving at either end of the season.

Nudist camping grounds (marked FKK) are among the best, as their secluded locations ensure peace and quiet. However, bear in mind that freelance camping is officially prohibited. A good site for camping information is www.camping.hr.

Hostels

The **Croatian YHA** (Map pp210-11; ☎ 01-48 47 472; www.hfhs.hr; Dežmanova 9, Zagreb) operates youth hostels in Dubrovnik, Zadar, Zagreb and Pula. Nonmembers pay an additional 10KN daily for a stamp on a welcome card; six stamps entitles you to a membership. Prices in this chapter are for high season during July and August; prices fall the rest of the year. The Croatian YHA can also provide information about private youth hostels in Krk, Zadar, Dubrovnik and Zagreb.

Hotels

Hotels are ranked from one to five stars with most in the two- and three-star range. Features, such as satellite TV, direct-dial phones, high-tech bathrooms, minibars and air-con, are standard in four- and five-star hotels, and one-star hotels have at least a bathroom in the room. Many two- and three-star hotels offer satellite TV but you'll find better decor in the higher categories. In August, some hotels may demand a surcharge for stays of less than four nights, but this is usually waived during the rest of the year, when prices drop steeply. In Zagreb prices are the same all year.

Breakfast is included in the prices quoted for hotels in this chapter, unless stated otherwise.

CROATIA

Private Rooms

Private rooms or apartments are the best accommodation in Croatia. Service is excellent and the rooms are usually extremely well kept. You may very well be greeted by offers of *sobe* as you step off your bus and boat, but rooms are most often arranged by travel agencies or the local tourist office. Booking through an agency will ensure that the place you're staying in is officially registered and has insurance.

It makes little sense to price-shop from agency to agency, since prices are fixed by the local tourist association. Whether you deal with the owner directly or book through an agency, you'll pay a 30% surcharge for stays of less than four nights and sometimes 50% or even 100% more for a one-night stay, although you may be able to get them to waive the surcharge if you arrive in the low season. Prices for private rooms in this chapter are for a four-night stay in peak season.

ACTIVITIES

The clear waters and varied underwater life of the Adriatic have led to a flourishing dive industry along the coast. Cave diving is the real speciality in Croatia; night diving and wreck diving are also offered and there are coral reefs in some places, but they are in rather deep water. Most of the coastal resorts mentioned in this chapter have dive shops. See **Diving Croatia** (www.diving-hrs.hr) for contact information.

If you're interested in hiking, Risnjak National Park at Crni Lug, 12km west of Delnice between Zagreb and Rijeka, is a good area in summer. Hiking is advisable only from late spring to early autumn.

There are countless possibilities for anyone carrying a folding sea kayak, especially among the Elafiti and Kornati Islands. Lopud makes a good launch point from which to explore the Elafiti Islands; there's a daily ferry from Dubrovnik.

BOOKS

Lonely Planet's *Croatia* is a comprehensive guide to the country.

As Croatia emerges from the shadow of the former Yugoslavia, several writers of Croatian origin have taken the opportunity to rediscover their roots. *Plum Brandy: Croatian Journeys* by Josip Novakovich is a sensitive exploration of his family's Croatian background. *Croatia: Travels in Undiscovered Country* by Tony Fabijančić recounts the life of rural folks in a new Croatia.

BUSINESS HOURS

Banking and post office hours are 7.30am to 7pm on weekdays and 8am to noon on Saturday. Many shops are open 8am to 7pm on weekdays and until 2pm on Saturday. Along the coast life is more relaxed; shops and offices frequently close around noon for an afternoon break and reopen around 4pm. Restaurants are open long hours, often noon to midnight, with Sunday closings outside of peak season.

EMBASSIES & CONSULATES

The following addresses are in Zagreb (area code ☎ 01):

Albania (Map pp210–11; ☎ 48 10 679; Jurišićeva 2a)

Australia (off Map pp210–11; ☎ 48 91 200; www.auembassy.hr; Kaptol Centar, Nova Ves 11) North of the centre.

Bosnia & Hercegovina (off Map pp210–11; ☎ 46 83 761; Torbarova 9) Northwest of the centre.

Bulgaria (off Map pp210–11; ☎ 48 23 336; Novi Goljak 25) Northwest of the centre.

Canada (Map pp210–11; ☎ 48 81 200; zagreb@dfait-maeci.gc.ca; Prilaz Đure Deželića 4)

Czech Republic (Map pp210–11; ☎ 61 77 239; Savska 41)

France (Map pp210–11; 48 93 680; consulat@ambafrance.hr; Hebrangova 2)

Germany (off Map pp210–11; ☎ 61 58 105; www.deutschebotschaft-zag reb.hr in German; ul grada Vukovara 64) South of the centre.

Hungary (off Map pp210–11; ☎ 48 22 051; Pantovčak 128/I) Northwest of the centre.

Ireland (Map pp210–11; ☎ 66 74 455; Turinina 3)

Netherlands (off Map pp210–11;Map pp210–11; ☎ 46 84 880; nlgovzag@zg.t-com.hr; Medveščak 56)

New Zealand (off Map pp210–11; ☎ 61 51 382; Trg Stjepana Radića 3) Southwest of the centre.

Poland (Map pp210–11; ☎ 48 99 444; Krležin Gvozd 3)

Romania (off Map pp210–11; ☎ 45 77 550; roamb@zg.t-com.hr; Mlinarska ul 43) North of the centre.

Serbia (off Map pp210–11; ☎ 45 79 067; Pantovčak 245) Northwest of the centre.

Slovakia (Map pp210–11; ☎ 48 48 941; Prilaz Đure Deželića 10)

Slovenia (Map pp210–11; ☎ 63 11 000; Savska 41)

UK (off Map pp210–11; ☎ 60 09 100; I Lučića 4)

USA (off Map pp210–11; ☎ 66 12 200; www.usembassy.hr; Ul Thomasa Jeffersona 2) South of the centre.

FESTIVALS & EVENTS

In July and August there are summer festivals in Dubrovnik, Split, Pula and Zagreb.

Dubrovnik's summer music festival emphasises classical music, with concerts in churches around town, while Pula hosts a variety of pop and classical stars in the Roman amphitheatre and also hosts a film festival. Mardi Gras celebrations have recently been revived in many towns with attendant parades and festivities, but nowhere is it celebrated with more verve than in Rijeka.

GAY & LESBIAN TRAVELLERS

Homosexuality has been legal in Croatia since 1977 and is tolerated, but public displays of affection between members of the same sex may be met with hostility, especially outside major cities. Exclusively gay clubs are a rarity outside Zagreb, but many of the large discos attract a mixed crowd.

On the coast, gays gravitate to Rovinj, Hvar, Split and Dubrovnik and tend to frequent naturist beaches. In Zagreb, the last Saturday in June is Gay Pride Zagreb day, an excellent opportunity to connect with the local gay scene.

Most Croatian websites devoted to the gay scene are in Croatian only, but a good starting point is the English-language www.touristinfo .gay.hr which has articles on the gay scene and links to other relevant websites.

HOLIDAYS

New Year's Day 1 January
Epiphany 6 January
Easter Monday March/April
Labour Day 1 May
Corpus Christi 10 June
Day of Antifascist Resistance 22 June; marks the outbreak of resistance in 1941
Statehood Day 25 June
Victory Day and National Thanksgiving Day 5 August
Feast of the Assumption 15 August
Independence Day 8 October
All Saints' Day 1 November
Christmas 25 and 26 December

INTERNET RESOURCES

Croatia Homepage (www.hr.hr) Hundreds of links to everything you want to know about Croatia.
Croatia Traveller (www.croatiatraveller.com) All ferry schedules, flights, forums, accommodation, sightseeing and travel planning.
Dalmatia Travel Guide (www.dalmacija.net) All about Dalmatia, including reservations for private accommodation.

MONEY
Credit Cards

Amex, MasterCard, Visa and Diners Club cards are widely accepted in large hotels, stores and many restaurants, but don't count on cards to pay for private accommodation or meals in small restaurants. You'll find ATMs accepting MasterCard, Maestro, Cirrus, Plus and Visa in most bus and train stations, airports, all major cities and most small towns. Many branches of Privredna Banka have ATMs that allow cash withdrawals on an Amex card.

Currency

The currency is the kuna. Banknotes are in denominations of 500, 200, 100, 50, 20, 10 and five. Each kuna is divided into 100 lipa in coins of 50, 20 and 10. Many places exchange money, all with similar rates.

Tax

A 22% VAT is imposed upon most purchases and services, and is included in the price. If your purchases exceed 500KN in one shop you can claim a refund upon leaving the country. Ask the merchant for the paperwork, but don't be surprised if they don't have it.

Tipping

If you're served well at a restaurant, you should round up the bill, but a service charge is always included. Bar bills and taxi fares can also be rounded up. Tour guides on day excursions expect to be tipped.

POST

Mail sent to Poste Restante, 10000 Zagreb, Croatia, is held at the **main post office** (Branimirova 4; ☽ 24hr Mon-Sat, 1pm-midnight Sun) next to the Zagreb train station. A good coastal address to use is c/o Poste Restante, Main Post Office, 21000 Split, Croatia. If you have an Amex card, most Atlas travel agencies will hold your mail.

TELEPHONE
Mobile Phones

Croatia uses GSM 900/1800. If your mobile is unlocked, SIM cards are widely available.

Phone Codes

To call Croatia from abroad, dial your international access code, ☎ 385 (Croatia's country code), the area code (without the initial zero) and the local number. When calling from one region to another within Croatia, use the initial zero. Phone numbers with the prefix 060 are sometimes free and other times charged at a premium rate, while numbers that begin with 09 are mobile numbers (and are quite expensive). When in Croatia, dial ☎ 00 to speak to the international operator.

Phonecards
To make a phone call from Croatia, go to the town's main post office. You'll need a phonecard to use public telephones, but calls using a phonecard are about 50% more expensive. Phonecards are sold according to *impulsa* (units), and you can buy cards of 25 (15KN), 50 (30KN), 100 (50KN) and 200 (100KN) units. These can be purchased at any post office and most tobacco shops and newspaper kiosks.

TOURIST INFORMATION
The **Croatian National Tourist Board** (Map pp210-11; ☎ 45 56 455; www.htz.hr; Iblerov Trg 10, Importanne Gallerija, 10000 Zagreb) is a good source of information with an excellent website. There are regional tourist offices that supervise tourist development and municipal tourist offices that have free brochures and good information on local events. Some arrange private accommodation.

TRAVELLERS WITH DISABILITIES
Because of the number of wounded war veterans, more attention is being paid to the needs of disabled travellers. Public toilets at bus stations, train stations, airports and large public venues are usually wheelchair accessible. Large hotels are wheelchair accessible but very little private accommodation is. The bus and train stations in Zagreb, Zadar, Rijeka, Split and Dubrovnik are wheelchair accessible but the local Jadrolinija ferries are not. Note that the steep streets in the Old Towns, such as in Dubrovnik, are restrictive for travellers with walking difficulties and those in wheelchairs. For further information, get in touch with **Savez Organizacija Invalida Hrvatske** (☎ /fax 01-48 29 394; Savska cesta 3, 10000 Zagreb).

VISAS
Visitors from Australia, Canada, New Zealand, the EU and the USA do not require a visa for stays of less than 90 days. For other nationalities, visas are issued free of charge at Croatian consulates.

EMERGENCY NUMBERS

- Ambulance ☎ 94
- Fire ☎ 93
- Police ☎ 92
- Roadside Assistance ☎ 987

TRANSPORT IN CROATIA

GETTING THERE & AWAY
Connections into Croatia are in a constant state of flux, with new air and boat routes opening every season. Following is an overview of the major connections into Croatia.

Air
The major airports in the country are as follows:
Dubrovnik (☎ 020-773 377; www.airport-dubrovnik.hr)
Pula (☎ 052-530 105; www.airport-pula.com)
Rijeka (☎ 051-842 132; www.rijeka-airport.hr)
Split (☎ 021-203 506; www.split-airport.hr)
Zadar (☎ 023-313 311; www.zadar-airport.hr)
Zagreb (☎ 01-62 65 222; www.zagreb-airport.hr)

The following airlines fly to Croatia:
Adria Airways (JD; ☎ 01-48 10 011; www.adria-airways.com)
Aeroflot (SU; ☎ 01-48 72 055; www.aeroflot.ru)
Air Canada (AC; ☎ 01-48 22 033; www.aircanada.ca)
Air France (AF; ☎ 01-48 37 100; www.airfrance.com)
Alitalia (AZ; ☎ 01-48 10 413; www.alitalia.it)
Austrian Airlines (OS; ☎ 062 65 900; www.aua.com)
British Airways (BA; www.british-airways.com)
Croatia Airlines (OU; ☎ 01-48 19 633; www.croatiaairlines.hr; Zrinjevac 17, Zagreb)
ČSA (OK; ☎ 01-48 73 301; www.csa.cz)
Delta Airlines (DL; ☎ 01-48 78 760; www.delta.com)
Easyjet (EZY; www.easyjet.com)
Germanwings (GWI; www.germanwings.com)
Hapag Lloyd Express (HLX; www.hlx.com)
KLM-Northwest (KL; ☎ 01-48 78 601; www.klm.com)
LOT Polish Airlines (LO; ☎ 01 48 37 500; www.lot.com)
Lufthansa (LH; ☎ 01-48 73 121; www.lufthansa.com)
Malév Hungarian Airlines (MA; ☎ 01-48 36 935; www.malev.hu)
SNBrussels (SN; www.flysn.com)
Turkish Airlines (TK; ☎ 01-49 21 854; www.turkishairlines.com)
Wizzair (W6; www.wizzair.com)

Land
BUS
Bosnia & Hercegovina
See p254 for details on transport between Dubrovnik and Sarajevo, Međugorje and Mostar. See p242 for details on connections between Sarajevo and Split (via Mostar); p217 for buses between Sarajevo and Zagreb; and p230 for buses between Sarajevo and Rijeka.

Italy
There are bus connections between Rijeka and Trieste (p230).

Montenegro
The border between Montenegro and Croatia is open to visitors, allowing Americans, Australians, Canadians and Brits to enter visa-free. See p254 for details of the bus between Kotor and Dubrovnik.

Serbia
See p217 for details of the bus between Zagreb and Belgrade.

Slovenia
Slovenia is well connected with the Istrian coast; see p223 for details on connections with Rovinj. There are also connections between Ljubljana and Zagreb (p217), Rijeka (p230) and Split (p242).

CAR & MOTORCYCLE
The main highway entry/exit points between Croatia and Hungary are Goričan (between Nagykanisza and Varaždin), Gola (23km east of Koprivnica), Terezino Polje (opposite Barcs) and Donji Miholjac (7km south of Harkány). There are dozens of crossing points to/from Slovenia, too many to list here. There are 23 border crossings into Bosnia and Hercegovina and 10 into Serbia and Montenegro, including the main Zagreb to Belgrade highway. Major destinations in Bosnia and Hercegovina, such as Sarajevo, Mostar and Međugorje, are accessible from Zagreb, Split and Dubrovnik.

Motorists require vehicle registration papers and the green insurance card to enter Croatia. Bear in mind that if you hire a car in Italy, many insurance companies will not insure you for a trip into Croatia. Border officials know this and may refuse you entry unless permission to drive into Croatia is clearly marked on the insurance documents. Most car-hire companies in Trieste and Venice are familiar with this requirement and will furnish you with the stamp. Otherwise, you must make specific inquiries.

See p260 for road rules and further information.

TRAIN
Bosnia & Hercegovina
See p217 for details on connections between Sarajevo and Zagreb. There's also a daily train to Osijek (113KN, 8½ hours), and a daily service to Ploče (310KN, 10 hours), near Dubrovnik via Mostar, Sarajevo and Banja Luka.

Hungary
There are services from Budapest to Zagreb; see p218.

Italy
Trains run between Venice and Zagreb; see p218.

Serbia
See p217 for details on connections between Belgrade and Zagreb.

Slovenia
See p217 for details on connections between Ljubljana and Zagreb, and p230 for details on trains between Rijeka and Ljubljana.

Sea
Regular boats from several companies connect Croatia with Italy from towns including Poreč (p221), Pula (p226), Rijeka (p229), Zadar (p236), Split (p241), Stari Grad (p246) on Hvar Island, and Dubrovnik (p254).

GETTING AROUND
Air
Croatia Airlines is the one and only carrier for flights within Croatia. The price of flights depends on the season and you get better deals if you book ahead. Seniors and people aged under 26 get discounts.

Bicycle
Cycling is a great way to see the islands, and bikes are fairly easy to hire in most tourist spots. Many tourist offices have helpful maps of cycling routes. However, bike lanes are nearly unknown in Croatia; you'll need to exercise extreme caution on the many narrow two-lane roads.

CROATIA

Boat

Year-round Jadrolinija car ferries operate along the Bari–Rijeka–Dubrovnik coastal route, stopping at Zadar, Split and the islands of Hvar, Korčula and Mljet. Services are less frequent in winter. The most scenic section is Split to Dubrovnik, which all Jadrolinija ferries cover during the day. Ferries are a lot more comfortable than buses, though somewhat more expensive. From Rijeka to Dubrovnik the deck fare is €26/31 in low/high season, with high season running from about the end of June to the end of August; there's a 20% reduction on the return portion of a return ticket. With a through ticket, deck passengers can stop at any port for up to a week, provided they notify the purser beforehand and have their ticket validated. This is much cheaper than buying individual sector tickets but is only good for one stopover. Cabins should be booked a week ahead, but deck space is usually available on all sailings.

Deck passage on Jadrolinija is just that: *poltrone* (reclining seats) are about €6 extra and four-berth cabins (if available) begin at €48.50/58 in low/high season from Rijeka to Dubrovnik. You must buy tickets in advance at an agency or the Jadrolinija office, as they are not sold on board. Cabins can be arranged at the reservation counter aboard the ship, but advance bookings are recommended if you want to be sure of a place. Bringing a car means checking in at least two hours in advance, more in the summer.

Bus

Bus services are excellent and relatively inexpensive. There are often a number of different companies handling each route so prices can vary substantially, but the prices in this book should give you an idea of costs (and unless otherwise noted, all bus prices are for one-way fares). Generally, the cheaper fares are on overnight buses.

It's generally best to call or visit the bus station to get the complete schedule but the following companies are among the largest:

Autotrans (☎ 051-660 360; www.autotrans.hr) Based in Rijeka with connections to Istria, Zagreb, Varaždin and Kvarner.

Brioni Pula (☎ 052-502 997; www.brioni.hr, in Croatian) Based in Pula with connections to Istria, Trieste, Padua, Split and Zagreb.

Contus (☎ 023-315 315; www.contus.hr) Based in Zadar with connections to Split and Zagreb.

FLIGHT-FREE TRAVEL

To learn how to get to Zagreb from London without having to fly, log on to www.seat61.com and search 'Croatia'. You'll get instructions on how to get to Zagreb from the UK capital via bus and rails (it gives you departure times and all!).

At large stations bus tickets must be purchased at the office; book ahead to be sure of a seat. Tickets for buses that arrive from somewhere else are usually purchased from the conductor. Buy a one-way ticket only or you'll be locked into one company's schedule for the return

On schedules, *vozi svaki dan* means 'every day' and *ne vozi nedjeljom ni praznikom* means 'not Sunday and public holidays'. Check www.akz.hr (in Croatian) for information on schedules and fares to and from Zagreb.

Car & Motorcycle

You have to pay tolls on the motorways around Zagreb, to use the Učka tunnel between Rijeka and Istria, the bridge to Krk Island, as well as the road from Rijeka to Delnice and from Zagreb to Split. Tolls can be paid in foreign currencies. The motorway connecting Zagreb and Split has cut travel time to the coast to around four hours. Tolls add up to about 160KN. Over the next few years, look for completion of the final leg running from Split to Dubrovnik. For general news on Croatia's motorways and tolls, see www.hac.hr.

DRIVING LICENCE

Any valid driving licence is sufficient to legally drive and hire a car; an International Driving Permit is not necessary. **Hrvatski Autoklub** (HAK; Croatian Auto Club; www.hak.hr) offers help and advice, plus there's the nationwide **HAK road assistance** (vučna služba; ☎ 987).

FUEL

Petrol stations are generally open 7am to 7pm and often until 10pm in summer. Petrol is Eurosuper 95, Super 98, normal or diesel. See www.ina.hr for up-to-date fuel prices.

HIRE

The large car-hire chains represented in Croatia are Avis, Budget, Europcar and Hertz. Throughout Croatia, Avis is allied with the Autotehna company, while Hertz is often represented by Kompas.

Independent local companies are often much cheaper than the international chains, but Avis, Budget, Europcar and Hertz have the big advantage of offering one-way rentals that allow you to drop the car off at any one of their many stations in Croatia free of charge.

Prices at local companies begin at around €40 a day with unlimited kilometres.

ROAD RULES
Unless otherwise posted, the speed limits for cars and motorcycles are 50km/h in the urban zones, 90km outside urban zones, 110km/h on main highways and 130km/h on motorways. The maximum permitted amount of alcohol in the blood is – none at all! It is also forbidden to use a mobile phone while driving.

Hitching
Hitching is never entirely safe, and we don't recommend it. Hitchhiking in Croatia is unreliable. You'll have better luck on the islands, but in the interior cars are small and usually full.

Local Transport
Zagreb has a well-developed tram system as well as local buses, but in the rest of the country you'll only find buses. In major cities such as Rijeka, Split, Zadar and Dubrovnik buses run about every 20 minutes, and less often on Sunday.

Taxis are available in all cities and towns, but they must be called or boarded at a taxi stand. Prices are rather high (meters start at 25KN).

Train
Train travel is about 15% cheaper than bus travel and often more comfortable, although slower. The main lines run from Zagreb to Rijeka, Zadar and Split and east to Osijek. There are no trains along the coast. Local trains usually have only unreserved 2nd-class seats. Reservations may be required on express trains. 'Executive' trains have only 1st-class seats and are 40% more expensive than local trains.

On posted timetables in Croatia, the word for arrivals is *dolazak* and for departures it's *odlazak* or *polazak*. For train information check out **Croatian Railway** (www.hzn et.hr).

Czech Republic

Two decades after the fall of the Berlin Wall, an atlas-full of Eastern European countries and cities are touted to travellers as the 'new Prague', or the 'next Czech Republic'. The focus may have shifted slightly to other up-and-coming destinations, but the original Prague and Czech Republic remain essential stops on any European sojourn.

Prague's inevitable transition from communist capital to modern metropolis is now complete, as centuries of history and architectural overachievement compete with energy and impetus. And now, more than ever, is the time to explore the Czech Republic beyond Prague.

Elsewhere, castles and chateaux abound, illuminating the stories of powerful families and individuals whose influence was felt well beyond the nation's current borders. Unravel the history of Bohemia and Moravia and you're delving into the legacy of Europe itself.

Beautifully preserved Renaissance towns that withstood ravages of the communist era link the centuries, and idiosyncratic landscapes provide a stage for active adventures.

Highlights include the audacious cliff-top chateau at Český Krumlov, the discreetly confident university town of Olomouc, and Brno's cosmpolitan buzz. Venture further to quieter gems such as Loket, Telč, Mikulov and Slavonice to uncover the true essence of the Czech Republic.

You'll discover the Czech Republic is more than a match for any new challengers.

FAST FACTS

- **Area** 78,864 sq km
- **Capital** Prague
- **Currency** Czech crown (Kč); €1 = 27Kč; US$1= 20Kč; UK£1 = 28Kč; A$1 = 14Kč; ¥100 = 20Kč; NZ$1 = 11Kč
- **Famous for** beer, ice hockey, Kafka, supermodels
- **Official Language** Czech
- **Phrases** *dobrý den/ahoj* (hello/hi); *na shledanou* (goodbye); *děkuji* (thank you); *promiňte* (excuse me)
- **Population** 10.2 million
- **Telephone codes** country code ☎ 420; international access code ☎ 00
- **Visas** citizens of Australia, Canada, Israel, Japan, New Zealand, South Korea, the USA and 23 other countries can stay for up to 90 days without a visa; see p324 for details

CZECH REPUBLIC

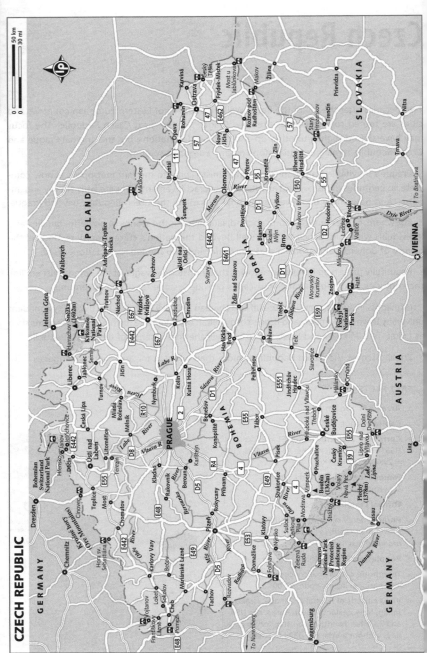

HIGHLIGHTS

- Experience the glorious old-world heritage of **Prague** (p270), but also dive into the emerging arts, music, and nightlife scenes in hip neighbourhoods like Vinohrady and Žižkov.
- Savour the tasty future of Czech beer at the best of the country's **microbreweries** (p270).
- Spend a lazy day on the Vltava River around **Český Krumlov**, (p305) before getting active in the **Šumava** (p309) region.
- Explore the spectacular rock formations and sinuous river valleys of the **Bohemian Switzerland National Park** (p295).
- Relax in the beautiful town square in **Olomouc** (p315) and try and keep its easygoing vibe to yourself.

ITINERARIES

- **One week** Experience Prague's exciting combination of a tumultuous past and an energetic present. Take an essential day trip to Terezín, and then head south to Český Krumlov for a few days of riverside R&R.
- **Two weeks** Begin in Prague before heading west for the spa scenes at Mariánské Lázně or Karlovy Vary. Balance the virtue and vice ledger with a few Bohemian brews in Plzeň before heading south for relaxation and rigour around Český Krumlov. Head east through České Budějovice en route to the Renaissance grandeur of Telč and Brno's cosmpolitan galleries and museums. Use the Moravian capital as a base for exploring the Moravian Karst caves and Mikulov's wine country, before continuing to under-rated Olomouc to admire the Holy Trinity Column. From Olomouc it's an easy trip back to Prague, or on to Poland.

CLIMATE & WHEN TO GO

The Czech climate has cool, humid winters, warm summers and distinct spring and autumn seasons. July and August are very busy so try and visit in May, June or September. Easter, Christmas and New Year are also busy. During the Prague Spring festival (in May), accommodation in Prague can be scarce.

HISTORY

Czech history is the story of a people surviving occupation, and Czechs are more interested in their rebels and heretics than the kings, emperors and dictators who oppressed them.

Located in central Europe, the Czechs have been invaded by the Habsburgs, the Nazis and the Soviets. The country's location has meant domestic upheavals have not stayed local for long. Their rejection of Catholicism in 1418 resulted in the Hussite Wars. The 1618 revolt against Habsburg rule ignited the Thirty Years' War, and the German annexation of the Sudetenland in 1938 helped fuel WWII. The liberal reforms of 1968's Prague Spring led to tanks rolling in from across the Eastern Bloc, and the peaceful ousting of the government during 1989's Velvet Revolution is a model for freedom-seekers everywhere.

Bohemian Beginnings

Ringed by hills, the ancient Czech lands of Bohemia and Moravia have formed natural territories since earliest times. A Celtic tribe called the Boii gave Bohemia its name, while Moravia comes from the Morava River, a Germanic name meaning 'marsh water'.

Slavic tribes from the east settled these territories, and they united from 830 to 907 in the Great Moravian Empire. Christianity was adopted after the arrival in 863 of the Thessalonian missionaries Cyril and Methodius, who created the first Slavic (Cyrillic) alphabet.

In the 9th century, the first home-grown dynasty, the Přemysls, erected some huts in what was to become Prague. This dysfunctional clan gave the Czechs their first martyred saints – Ludmila, killed by her daughter-in-law in 874,

---

CONNECTIONS: MOVING ON FROM THE CZECH REPUBLIC

The Czech Republic is a convenient hub for exploring neighbouring countries. Prague (p288) is well connected to Berlin, Nuremberg and Hamburg, and Plzeň (p302) is on the main train line from Nuremberg via Prague to Munich. From Český Krumlov (p309) it's a short distance to Linz in Austria, with connections to Vienna, and Budapest in Hungary. For travel to Poland, Olomouc (p318) is a key transit point for trains to Warsaw and Kraków, and the eastern city of Brno (p314) has regular bus and train services to Vienna and the Slovakian capital, Bratislava.

HOW MUCH?

- **Night in hostel** 400Kč
- **Double room in pension** 1100Kč
- **Oplátky (spa wafer)** 10Kč
- **Two hours' rafting** 250Kč
- **Postcard home** 15Kč

LONELY PLANET INDEX

- **1L petrol** 25Kč
- **1L bottled water** 45Kč
- **500mL beer** 35Kč
- **Souvenir T-shirt** 250Kč
- **Street snack (sausage & mustard)** 30Kč

and her grandson, the pious Prince Václav (or Good 'King' Wenceslas; r 921–29), murdered by his brother Boleslav the Cruel.

The Přemysls' rule ended in 1306, and in 1310 John of Luxembourg came to the Bohemian throne through marriage, and annexed the kingdom to the German empire. The reign of his son, Charles IV (1346–78), who became Holy Roman Emperor, saw the first of Bohemia's two 'Golden Ages'. Charles founded Prague's St Vitus Cathedral, built Charles Bridge, and established Charles University. The second was the reign of Rudolf II (1576–1612), who made Prague the capital of the Habsburg Empire and attracted artists, scholars and scientists to his court. Bohemia and Moravia remained under Habsburg dominion for almost four centuries.

Under the Habsburg Thumb

In 1415 the Protestant religious reformer Jan Hus, rector of Charles University, was burnt at the stake for heresy. Hus led a movement that espoused letting the congregation taste the sacramental wine as well as the host. He inspired the nationalist Hussite movement which plunged Bohemia into civil war (1419–34).

When the Austrian and Catholic Habsburg dynasty ascended the Bohemian throne in 1526, the fury of the Counter-Reformation was unleashed when Protestants threw two Habsburg councillors from a Prague Castle window. This escalated into the Catholic–Protestant Thirty Years' War (1618–48), which devastated much of central Europe.

The defeat of the Protestants at the Battle of White Mountain in 1620 marked the start of a long period of forced re-Catholicisation, Germanisation and oppression of Czech language and culture. The baroque architectural style of the time symbolised the Catholic victory.

National Reawakening

The Czechs starting rediscovering their linguistic and cultural roots at the start of the 19th century, during the so-called Národní obrození (National Revival). Overt political activity was banned, so the revival was culturally based. Important figures included historian Josef Palacký and composer Bedřich Smetana.

An independent Czech and Slovak state was realised after WWI, when the Habsburg empire's demise saw the creation of the Czechoslovak Republic on 28 October 1918. The first president was Tomáš Garrigue Masaryk. Three-quarters of the Austro-Hungarian empire's industrial power was inherited by Czechoslovakia, as were three million Germans, mostly in the border areas of Bohemia (the pohraniči, known in German as the Sudetenland).

The Czechs' elation was to be short-lived. Under the Munich Pact of September 1938, Britain and France accepted the annexation of the Sudetenland by Nazi Germany, and in March 1939 the Germans occupied the rest of the country (calling it the Protectorate of Bohemia and Moravia).

Most of the Czech intelligentsia and 80,000 Jews died at the hands of the Nazis. When Czech paratroopers assassinated the Nazi governor Reinhardt Heydrich in 1942, the entire town of Lidice was wiped out in revenge.

Communist Coup

After the war, the Czechoslovak government expelled 2.5 million Sudeten Germans – including antifascists who had fought the Nazis – from the Czech borderlands and confiscated their property. During the forced marches from Czechoslovakia many were interned in concentration camps and tens of thousands died. In 1997 Czech Prime Minister Václav Klaus and German chancellor Helmut Kohl signed a declaration of mutual apology, but many Sudeten Germans are still campaigning for the restitution of lost land and houses.

In 1947 a power struggle began between the communist and democratic forces, and in early 1948 the Social Democrats withdrew from the postwar coalition. The result was the Soviet-backed coup d'état of 25 February 1948, known as *Vítězný únor* (Victorious February). The new communist-led government established the dictatorship of the proletariat.

The 1950s were repressive years and thousands of noncommunists fled the country. Many were imprisoned and hundreds were executed or died in labour camps.

Prague Spring & Velvet Revolution

In April 1968 the new first secretary of the Communist Party, Alexander Dubček, introduced liberalising reforms to create 'socialism with a human face' – known as the 'Prague Spring'. Censorship ended, political prisoners were released, and economic decentralisation began. Moscow was not happy, but Dubček refused to buckle and Soviet tanks entered Prague on 20 August 1968, closely followed by 200,000 Soviet and Warsaw Pact soldiers.

Many Communist Party functionaries were expelled and 500,000 party members lost their jobs after the dictatorship was re-established. Dissidents were summarily imprisoned and educated professionals were made manual labourers.

The 1977 trial of the rock group the Plastic People of the Universe inspired the formation of the human-rights group Charter 77. (The communists saw the musicians as threatening the status quo, but others viewed the trial as an assault on human rights.) Charter 77's group of Prague intellectuals, including the playwright/philosopher Václav Havel, continued their underground opposition throughout the 1980s.

By 1989 Gorbachev's perestroika and the fall of the Berlin Wall on 9 November raised expectations of change. On 17 November an official student march in Prague was smashed by police. Daily demonstrations followed, culminating in a general strike on 27 November. Dissidents led by Havel formed the Anti-Communist Civic Forum and negotiated the resignation of the Communist government on 3 December, less than a month after the fall of the Berlin Wall.

A 'Government of National Understanding' was formed, with Havel elected president on 29 December. With no casualties, the days after 17 November became known as *Sametová revoluce* (the 'Velvet Revolution').

Velvet Divorce

Following the end of communist central authority, antagonisms between Slovakia and Prague re-emerged. The federal parliament granted both the Czech and Slovak Republics full federal status within a Czech and Slovak Federated Republic (ČSFR), but this failed to satisfy Slovak nationalists. The Civic Forum split into two factions: the centrist Civic Movement and the more right-wing Civic Democratic Party (ODS).

Elections in June 1992 sealed Czechoslovakia's fate. Václav Klaus' ODS took 48 seats in the 150-seat federal parliament; while 24 went to the Movement for a Democratic Slovakia (HZDS), a left-leaning Slovak nationalist party led by Vladimír Mečiar.

In July, goaded by Mečiar's rhetoric, the Slovak parliament declared sovereignty. Compromise couldn't be reached, and on 1 January 1993 Czechoslovakia ceased to exist for the second time. Prague became capital of the new Czech Republic, and Havel was elected its first president.

A New Country

Thanks to booming tourism and a solid industrial base, the Czech Republic started strongly. Unemployment was negligible, shops were full and, by 2003, Prague enjoyed Eastern Europe's highest living standards. Capitalism also meant a lack of affordable housing, rising crime and a deteriorating health system.

Since then the Czech Republic has continued as one of the economic success stories from the communist bloc, and in 2006 it was awarded the status of 'Developed Country' by the World Bank, the only former Comecon (an organisation of communist states from 1949 to 1991) nation to achieve this.

Annual growth in GDP is around 6%, and for a few years economic growth occurred despite government instability. In 2003, Václav Havel was replaced as president by former prime minister Václav Klaus; it took three elections for Czechs to confirm this appointment. Further government instability followed inconclusive elections in June 2006, which left the Czech Republic's lower house equally divided between the left and the right. The country's next general election is planned for 2009, and at the time of writing, Mirek Topolánek of the ODS was prime minister.

MIND YOUR MANNERS

It's customary to say *dobrý den* (good day) when entering a shop, cafe or quiet bar, and *na shledanou* (goodbye) when leaving.

The Czech Republic became a member of NATO in 1999, and joined the EU on 1 May 2004. With EU membership, greater numbers of younger Czechs are now working and studying abroad, seizing opportunities their parents didn't have. The Czech Republic is currently scheduled to adopt the euro in 2012.

PEOPLE

The population of the Czech Republic is 10.2 million; 95% of the population are Czech and 3% are Slovak. Only 150,000 of the three million Sudeten Germans evicted after WWII remain. A significant Roma population (0.3%) is subject to hostility and racism, suffering from poverty and unemployment. There are an estimated 55,000 Vietnamese in the Czech Republic, the biggest ethnic minority, at around 0.5% of the total population.

RELIGION

Most Czechs are atheist (39.8%) or nominally Roman Catholic (39.2%), but church attendance is low. There are small Protestant (4.6%) and Orthodox (3%) congregations. The Jewish community (1% in 1918) today numbers only a few thousand. Religious tolerance is accepted and the Catholic Church abstains from political interference.

ARTS
Literature

Franz Kafka and other German-speaking Jewish writers strongly influenced Prague's literary scene in the early 20th century.

After WWI Jaroslav Hašek devoted himself to lampooning the Habsburg empire. His folk masterpiece *The Good Soldier Švejk* is a riotous story of a Czech soldier during WWI.

Bohumil Hrabal (1914–97), one of the finest Czech novelists of the 20th century, wrote *The Little Town Where Time Stood Still,* a gentle portrayal of the machinations of small-town life.

Milan Kundera (b 1929) is the most renowned Czech writer internationally, with

his novel *The Unbearable Lightness of Being* being adapted as a film. His first work *The Joke* explores the communist era's paranoia.

Jáchym Topol is the contemporary rock-lyricist author of *Sister City Silver,* an exhilarating exploration of post-communist Prague.

Cinema

The films of Jan Hrebejk (b 1967), *Musíme si pomáhat* (Divided We Fall, 2000), *Pupendo* (2003), and *Horem pádem* (Up and Down, 2004) all cover different times in the country's tumultuous 20th-century history.

Jiří Menzel's take on writer Bohumil Hrabal's *I Served the King of England* (2006) enjoyed art-house success, and *Občan Havel* (Citizen Havel, 2008) is a documentary about Václav Havel that enjoyed huge domestic support.

Buy Czech films on DVD at Kino Světozor (p288).

Music

Bedřich Smetana (1824–84), an icon of Czech pride, incorporated folk songs and dances into his classical compositions. His best-known pieces are the operas *Prodaná Nevěsta* (The Bartered Bride) and *Dalibor a Libuše* (Dalibor and Libuše), and the symphonic-poem cycle *Má vlast* (My Homeland).

Antonín Dvořák's (1841–1904) most popular works include the symphony *From the New World,* his *Slavonic Dances* of 1878 and 1881, the operas *The Devil & Kate* and *Rusalka,* and his religious masterpiece *Stabat Mater.*

More recently the Plastic People of the Universe influenced 1989's Velvet Revolution in 1989 and still play the occasional live gig. Jaromír Nohavica is a Dylanesque singer-songwriter, and Traband integrate Jewish klezmer music and Roma styles.

In recent years, Czech musician Markéta Irglová won an Academy Award for Best Song for the movie *Once* (2006).

Visual Arts

Though he is associated with the French art-nouveau movement, Alfons Mucha's (1860–1939) heart remained at home in Bohemia. Much of his work reflects themes of Slavic suffering, courage and cross-nation brotherhood. Most outstanding are 20 large cinematic canvasses called the *Slav Epic* (see p278), and his interior decoration in Prague's Municipal House (p277).

David Černý (b 1967) is a contemporary Czech sculptor. His controversial work includes the statue of St Wenceslas riding an upside-down horse in Prague's pasáž Lucerna and the giant babies crawling up the Žižkov TV tower in Prague; see p277.

ENVIRONMENT
The Land

The landlocked Czech Republic is bordered by Germany, Austria, Slovakia and Poland. The land is made up of two river basins: Bohemia in the west, drained by the Labe (Elbe) River flowing north into Germany; and Moravia in the east, drained by the Morava River flowing southeast into the Danube. Each basin is ringed by low, forest-clad hills, notably the Šumava range along the Bavarian-Austrian border in the southwest, the Krušné hory (Ore Mountains) along the northwestern border with Germany, and the Krkonoše mountains along the Polish border east of Liberec. The country's highest peak, Sněžka (1602m), is in the Krkonoše. Interspersed with farmland, spruce, oak and beech forests cover one-third of the country.

South Bohemia has hundreds of linked fishponds and artificial lakes, including the 4870-hectare Lake Lipno. East Bohemia is home to the striking 'rock towns' of the Adršpach-Teplice Rocks.

National Parks

National parks and protected landscape areas cover 15% of the country, with the emphasis on both visitor use and species and landscape protection. Key areas include the Bohemian Switzerland and Šumava national parks, and the Adršpach-Teplice Protected Landscape Area.

Environmental Issues

Now regenerating, the forests of northern Bohemia and Moravia were devastated by acid rain created by the burning of brown coal. Industrial emissions have been cleaned up in recent years following the adoption of EU environmental codes.

In 2008, the Czech environmental group Friends of the Earth made a formal complaint to the EU that German and Austrian clear-felling of forest just across the border from the Šumava national park, was also threatening forests in the Czech Republic.

FOOD & DRINK

Czech food is similar to German or Polish food, with lots of meat served with *knedlíky* (dumplings) and cabbage. A few differences make Czech food special though. Have *svíčková* (roast beef with a sour-cream sauce and spices) with fluffy *knedlíky* and you'll be wondering why you haven't heard more about this cuisine.

Staples & Specialities

Traditional Czech cuisine is strong on meat, *knedlíky* and gravy and weak on fresh vegetables. The classic Bohemian dish is *knedlo-zelo-vepřo* – bread dumplings, sauerkraut and roast pork. Also look out for *cesneková* (garlic soup), *svíčková na smetaně* (roast beef with sour-cream sauce and cranberries), and *kapr na kmíní* (fried or baked carp with caraway seed). *Ovocné knedlíky* (fruit dumplings) are a delicious dessert served with cottage cheese or crushed poppy seeds and melted butter.

One of the first words of Czech you'll learn is *pivo* (beer). The most famous brands are Budvar (see p302) and Pilsner Urquell (see p300), but beyond the 'Big Two' there's a whole hoppy world of other regional and local brews to be discovered.

The South Moravian vineyards (p320) produce improving *bílé víno* (white wines).

Where to Eat & Drink

A *bufet* or *samoobsluha* is a self-service, cafeteria with *chlebíčky* (open sandwiches), salads, *klobásy* (spicy sausages), *špekačky* (mild pork sausages), *párky* (frankfurters), *guláš* (goulash) and of course *knedlíky*. Some of these places are tucked to the side of *potraviny* (food shops). A *bageteria* serves made-to-order sandwiches and baguettes.

A *pivnice* is a pub without food, while a *hospoda* or *hostinec* is a pub or beer hall serving basic meals. A *vinárna* (wine bar) has anything from snacks to a full-blown menu. The occasional *kavárna* (cafe) has a full menu but most only serve snacks and desserts. A *restaurace* is any restaurant.

Restaurants open as early as 11am and carry on till midnight; some take a break between lunch and dinner. Main dishes may stop being served well before the advertised closing time, with only snacks and drinks after that.

Fearing public disapproval, the Czech Republic goverment has been slow to ban smoking in bars and restaurants. Despite this,

CZECH REPUBLIC

TOP FIVE CZECH MICROBREWERIES

Czech beer is not just about Pilsner Urquell and Budvar. There are an increasing number of excellent microbreweries also worth investigating. Buy the 'Good Beer Guide to Prague & the Czech Republic' by longtime Prague resident Evan Rail. It's available at Prague's Big Ben Bookshop (right), the Globe Café & Bookstore (opposite) or Shakespeare & Sons (opposite). Online, see www.amazon.com or www.amazon.co.uk.

- Pivovarský Dům, Prague (p285)
- Pivnice Dačický, Kutná Hora (p293)
- Pivovar Sv Florian, Loket (p300)
- Pivnice Pegas, Brno (p314)
- Moritz, Olomouc (p318)

a growing number of food and drink outlets are establishing special nonsmoking areas. Look out for signs saying *Kouření zakázano*.

Vegetarians & Vegans

In Prague and other main cities, you'll find vegetarian restaurants, but smaller towns remain limited. Vegans will find life difficult. There are a few standard *bezmasá jídla* (meatless dishes) served by most restaurants. The most common are *smažený sýr* (fried cheese) and vegetables cooked with cheese sauce.

Habits & Customs

Most beer halls have a system of marking everything you eat or drink on a small piece of paper that is left on your table, then totted up when you pay (say *zaplatím, prosím* – I'd like to pay, please).

In a pub, always ask if a chair is free before sitting down *(Je tu volno?)*. The standard toast involves clinking together first the tops, then the bottoms of glasses, then touching the glass to the table. Most people say *Na zdraví* (To health).

PRAGUE

pop 1.22 million

It's the perfect irony of Prague. You are lured there by the past, but compelled to linger by the present and the future. Fill your days with its artistic and architectural heritage – from Gothic and Renaissance to art nouveau and cubist – but after dark move your focus to the here and now in the lively restaurants, bars and clubs in emerging neighbourhoods like Vinohrady and Žižkov. And if Prague's seasonal army of tourists sometimes wears you down, that's OK. Just drink a glass of the country's legendary Bohemian lager, relax and be reassured that quiet moments still exist: a private dawn on Charles Bridge, a chilled beer in Letná as you gaze upon the glorious cityscape of Staré Město or getting reassuringly lost in the intimate lanes of Malá Strana or Josefov. Everyday you'll uncover plenty of reasons to reinforce Prague's reputation as one of Europe's most exciting cities.

ORIENTATION

Central Prague nestles on the Vltava River, separating Hradčany (the medieval castle district) and Malá Strana (Little Quarter) on the west bank, from Staré Město (Old Town) and Nové Město (New Town) on the east.

Prague Castle overlooks Malá Strana, while the twin Gothic spires of Týn Church dominate Old Town Sq (Staroměstské nám). The broad avenue of Wenceslas Sq (Václavské nám) stretches southeast from Staré Město towards the National Museum and main train station.

Walk from Praha-hlavní nádraží (Prague's main train station) to Old Town Sq in 10 minutes. Some international trains stop at Praha-Holešovice, where it is 10 minutes by metro to Old Town Sq. From Florenc bus station take Line B (yellow) to Můstek for the city centre.

Prague's up-and-coming neighbourhoods include leafy Vinohrady with good cafes and restaurants, and the grungier, more energtic after dark scene of Žižkov.

Maps

Good maps include Marco Polo's *Praha – centrum* (1:5000) and SHOCart's GeoClub *Praha – plán města* (1:15,000), both available from city bookshops. The Prague Information Service (p273) offers maps of the city centre on request.

INFORMATION
Bookshops

Anagram (Map pp274-5; ☎ 224 895 737; www .anagram.cz; Týn 4, Staré Město; ◷ 10am-8pm Mon-Sat, to 7pm Sun) History and culture books. Another branch at Prague's Ruzyně airport.

Big Ben Bookshop (Map pp274-5; ☎ 224 826 565; www.bigbenbookshop.com; Malá Štupartská 5, Staré

Město; ⏰ 9am-7pm Mon-Fri, 10am-6pm Sat, noon-5pm Sun) English-language books, magazines and newspapers. Also carries *Provokátor*, a free magazine listing Prague events.

Globe Café & Bookstore (Map pp274-5; ☎ 224 934 203; www.globebookstore.cz; Pštrossova 6, Nové Město; ⏰ 9.30am-midnight) Books in English and German, international magazines and newspapers.

Kiwi (Map pp274-5; ☎ 224 948 455; Jungmannova 23, Nové Město; ⏰ 9am-6.30pm Mon-Fri, 10am-2pm Sat) Maps and guidebooks.

Neo Luxor (Map pp274-5; ☎ 221 111 364; Václavské nám 41, Nové Město; ⏰ 8am-8pm Mon-Fri, 9am-7pm Sat, 10am-7pm Sun) Books and magazines in English, German and French and internet access (1Kč per minute). Another branch in Prague's main train station.

Shakespeare & Sons (Map pp272-3; ☎ 271 740 839; www.shakes.cz; Krymská 12; ⏰ 10am-7pm) More than books with a cafe, poetry readings and live jazz.

Emergency
If your passport or valuables are stolen, obtain a police report and crime number from the **Prague 1 Police Station** (Map pp274-5; ☎ 224 222 558; Jungmannovo nám 9, Nové Mesto; ⏰ 24hr). You'll need this for an insurance claim. There's usually an English-speaker on hand. The emergency phone number for the police is ☎ 158.

Internet Access
Many hotels, bars, fast-food restaurants and internet cafes provide wi-fi hotspots.

Globe Café & Bookstore (Map pp274-5; ☎ 224 934 203; www.globebookstore.cz; Pštrossova 6, Nové Město; per min 1.50Kč; ⏰ 9.30am-midnight) Weekly (800Kč) and monthly (2250Kč) rates with your own laptop.

Mobilarium (Map pp274-5; ☎ 221 967 327; Rathova Pasaž, Na příkopě 23, Nové Město; per min 1.50Kč; ⏰ 10am-7pm Mon-Fri, 11am-6pm Sat) Also cheap international phone calls.

Planeta (Map pp272-3; ☎ 267 311 182; Vinohradská 102, Vinohrady; per min 0.45-1Kč; ⏰ 8am-11pm) Also CD photo downloads and Skype.

Internet Resources
Dopravní podnik (www.dpp.cz) Information about public transport in Prague. Includes section for disabled travellers.

Prague Information Service (www.pis.cz) Official tourist office site.

Prague Post (www.praguepost.cz) News, events and visitor information.

Prague TV (www.prague.tv) Events, arts and nightlife.

Laundry
Laundrettes charge around 250Kč to wash and dry a 9kg load of laundry.

Laundryland (Map pp274-5; ☎ 221 014 632; Na příkopě 12, Nové Město; ⏰ 9am-8pm Mon-Fri, 9am-7pm Sat, 11am-7pm Sun) On the 1st floor of Černá Růže shopping centre, above the Panská entrance. Last wash two hours before closing.

Prague Cyber Laundromat (Map pp274-5; ☎ 222 510 180; Korunní 14, Vinohrady; ⏰ 8am-8pm) Near Náměsti Míru metro station. Friendly place with internet cafe (20Kč per 30 minutes) and kids' play area.

Left Luggage
Florenc bus station (per bag per day 35Kč; ⏰ 5am-11pm) Upstairs on the left beyond the main ticket hall.

Main train station (per small/large bag per day 15/30Kč; ⏰ 24hr) On Level 1. Also lockers (80Kč).

Medical Services
Canadian Medical Care (off Map pp272-3; ☎ 235 360 133, after hr 724 300 301; www.cmcpraha.cz; Veleslavín-ská 1, Veleslavín; ⏰ 8am-6pm Mon, Wed & Fri, to 8pm Tue & Thu) Expat centre with English-speaking doctors, 24-hour medical aid and pharmacy.

Na Homolce Hospital (off Map pp272-3; ☎ 257 271 111, after hr 257 272 527; www.homolka.cz; 5th fl, Foreign Pavilion, Roentgenova 2, Motol) Prague's main casualty department.

Polyclinic at Národní (Map pp274-5; ☎ 222 075 120; 24hr emergencies 720 427 634; www.poliklinika.narodni.cz; Národní třída 9, Nové Město; ⏰ 8.30am-5pm Mon-Fri) English-, French- and German-speaking staff.

PRAGUE IN TWO DAYS

Beat the tourist hordes with an early-morning stroll across **Charles Bridge** (p281) and continue uphill to Hradčany and the glories of **Prague Castle** (p278). Head back down to the **Franz Kafka Museum** (p281), and cross the river again to the **Charles Bridge Museum** (p278).

On day two, explore **Josefov** (p277), Prague's original Jewish quarter, and then pack a hilltop picnic for the view-friendly fortress at **Vyšehrad** (p281). Make time for a few Czech brews, either at the relaxed beer garden at **Letenské sady** (p286), or at the excellent **Pivovarský Klub** (p285), before kicking on for robust Czech food at **Kolkovna** (p284) or **Na Verandách** (p284). For a nightcap head to an effortlessly cool late-night bar like **Hapu** (p285) or **Bukowski's** (p285).

GREATER PRAGUE

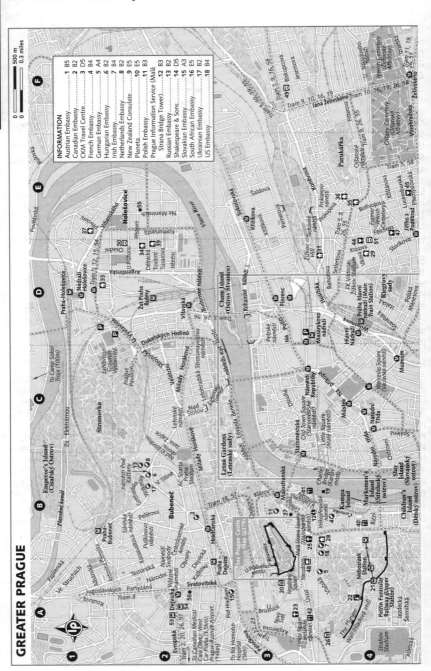

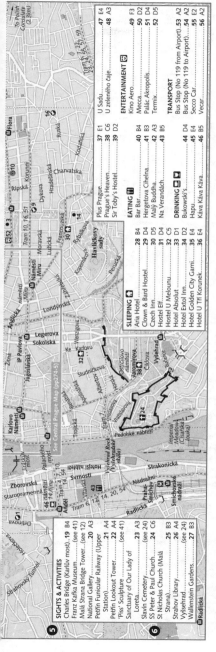

SIGHTS & ACTIVITIES

Charles Bridge (Karlův most)...19	B4
Franz Kafka Museum.............(see 41)	
Malá Strana Bridge Tower.....(see 12)	
National Gallery.....................20	A3
Petřín Funicular Railway (Upper	
Station)...............................21	A4
Petřín Lookout Tower.............22	A4
'Piss' Sculpture...................(see 41)	
Sanctuary of Our Lady of	
Loreta.................................23	A3
Slavín Cemetery..................(see 24)	
SS Peter & Paul Church.........24	C6
St Nicholas Church (Malá	
Strana)...............................25	B3
Strahov Library.....................26	A4
Vyšehrad..........................(see 24)	
Wallenstein Gardens............27	B3

...47	E4
...48	A3
ENTERTAINMENT	
Kino Aero..........................49	F3
Mecca...............................50	D2
Palác Akropolis..................51	D4
Termix...............................52	D5
TRANSPORT	
Bus Stop (No 119 from Airport)..53	A2
Bus Stop (No 119 to Airport)....54	A2
Secco Car..........................55	E2
Vecar...............................56	A4

U Sadu.............................37	E1
U zeleného čaje..................38	C6
	...39	D2

SLEEPING	
Aria Hotel.........................28	B4
Clown & Bard Hostel...........29	D4
Czech Inn.........................30	D5
Hostel Elf.........................31	D4
Hostel U Melounu...............32	C5
Hotel Absolut.....................33	D1
Hotel Extol Inn....................34	D2
Hotel Golden City Garni.......35	E4
Hotel U Tří Korunek............36	E4

...40	B4
Hergetova Cihelna.............41	B3
Malý Buddha.....................42	A3
Na Verandách....................43	B5

EATING	
Bar Bar.............................	

DRINKING	
Bukowski's........................44	D4
Hapu...............................45	E4
Káva Káva Káva................46	B5

Plus Prague.......................(see 41)	
Prague's Heaven................(see 41)	
Sir Toby's Hostel................(see 41)	

Praha lékárna (Map pp274-5; ☎ 224 946 982; Palackého 5, Nové Město) A 24-hour pharmacy; for emergency service after business hours, ring the bell.

Money

The major banks are best for changing cash, but using a debit card in an ATM gives a better rate of exchange. Avoid *směnárna* (private exchange booths), which advertise misleading rates and have exorbitant charges.

Česká spořitelna (Map pp274-5; Václavské nám 16, Nové Město)

ČSOB (Map pp274-5; Na příkopě 14, Nové Město)

Komerční banka (Map pp274-5; Václavské nám 42, Nové Město)

Živnostenská banka (Map pp274-5; Na příkopě 20, Nové Město)

Post

At the **main post office** (Map pp274-5; Jindřišská 14, Nové Město; ☽ 2am-midnight), collect a ticket from the automated machines outside the main hall (press 1 for stamps and parcels, 4 for Express Mail Service – EMS). Wait until your *lístek číslo* (number) comes up on the electronic boards inside and go to the window indicated.

Pick up poste-restante mail at window 1 and buy phonecards at window 28. International and EMS parcels, are sent from window 7 to 10 (closed from noon Saturday and all day Sunday).

Telephone

There's a 24-hour telephone centre to the left of the right-hand entrance to the central post office. Most internet cafes have Skype.

Tourist Information

The **Prague Information Service** (Pražská informační služba, PIS; ☎ 12 444, in English & German 221 714 444; www.pis.cz) provides free tourist information with good maps and detailed brochures including accommodation.

There are three PIS offices:

Czech Tourism (Map pp274-5; www.czechtourism.com; Staroměstské nám, Staré Město; ☽ 9am-5pm Mon-Fri) Has an office in Prague's Old Town Sq.

Main train station (Praha hlavní nádraží; Map pp274-5; Wilsonova 2, Nové Město; ☽ 9am-7pm Mon-Fri, to 6pm Sat & Sun)

Malá Strana Bridge Tower (Map pp272-3; Charles Bridge; ☽ 10am-6pm Apr-Oct)

Old Town Hall (Map pp274-5; Staroměstské nám 5, Staré Město; ☽ 9am-7pm Mon-Fri, to 6pm Sat & Sun Apr-Oct, to 6pm Mon-Fri, to 5pm Sat & Sun Nov-Mar) The main branch.

CZECH REPUBLIC

CENTRAL PRAGUE

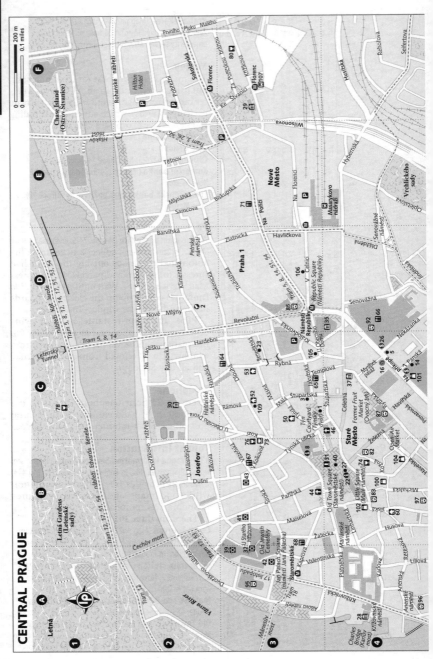

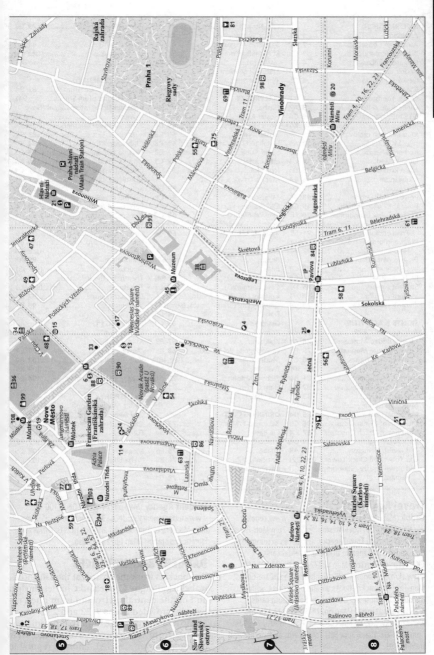

Travel Agencies

Čedok (Map pp274–5; ☎ 800 112 112; www.cedok
.cz; Na příkopě 18, Nové Město; 🕐 9am-7pm Mon-Fri,
9.30am-1pm Sat) Travel agency; also books accommodation, concert and theatre tickets and rental cars.

CKM Travel Centre (Map pp272–3; ☎ 222 721 595;
www.ckm.cz; Mánesova 77, Vinohrady; 🕐 10am-6pm
Mon-Thu, to 4pm Fri) Books air and bus tickets, with
discounts for those aged under 26. Sells youth cards.

GTS International (Map pp274–5; ☎ 222 119 700;
www.gtstravel.cz; Ve Smečkách 33, Nové Město; 🕐 9am-
6pm Mon-Fri, 10am-3pm Sat) Youth cards and air, bus and
train tickets.

Student Agency (Map pp274–5; ☎ 0800 100 1300;
www.studentagency.cz; Ječná 37, Vinohrady; 🕐 9am-
6pm Mon-Fri, to 1pm Sat) Air and bus tickets. Office at
Florenc bus station (Map pp274–5) also.

DANGERS & ANNOYANCES

Pickpockets work the crowds at the astronomical clock, Prague Castle and Charles Bridge,
and on the central metro and tram lines, especially crowded trams 9, 22 and 23.

Most taxi drivers are honest, but some operating from tourist areas overcharge their
customers (even Czechs). Phone a reputable

taxi company (see p291), or look for the red and yellow signs for the 'Taxi Fair Place' scheme, indicating authorised taxi stands.

The park outside the main train station is a hang-out for dodgy types and worth avoiding late at night. Slightly less dodgy, but often as drunk, are occasional groups of stag-party boozers around Wenceslas Sq and the Old Town.

Scams
Bogus police sometimes approach tourists and ask to see their money, claiming they're looking for counterfeit notes. They then run off with the cash. If in doubt, just ask the 'policeman' to accompany you to the nearest police station.

SIGHTS
All the main sights are in the city centre, and are easily reached on foot. You can take in the Castle, Charles Bridge and Old Town Sq in a couple of days.

Staré Město
Kick off in Prague's **Old Town Square** (Staroměstské nám), dominated by the twin Gothic steeples of **Týn Church** (Map pp274–5; 1365), the baroque **St Nicholas Church** (Map pp274–5; 1730s; not to be confused with the more famous St Nicholas Church in Malá Strana) and the **Old Town Hall clock tower** (Map pp274–5; ☎ 224 228 456; Staroměstské nám 12; adult/child 60/40Kč; ◷ 11am-6pm Mon, 9am-6pm Tue-Sun). From the top spy on the crowds below watching the **astronomical clock** (Map pp274–5; 1410), which springs to life every hour with assorted apostles and a bell-ringing skeleton. Don't be too surprised to hear random mutterings of the 'Is that it?' variety. In the square's centre is the **Jan Hus Monument**, erected in 1915 on the 500th anniversary of the religious reformer's execution.

The shopping street of Celetná leads east to the art-nouveau **Municipal House** (Obecní dům; Map pp274–5; www.obecni-dum.cz; nám Republiky 5; guided tours adult/child 190/140Kč; ◷ 11am-5pm), decorated by the early 20th century's finest Czech artists. Included in the guided tour are the impressive Smetana Concert Hall and other beautifully decorated rooms.

To the south of the Old Town Sq is the neoclassical **Estates Theatre** (Stavovské divadlo; Map pp274–5; 1783), where Mozart's *Don Giovanni* was premiered on 29 October 1787, with the maestro himself conducting.

North and northwest of the Old Town Sq, **Josefov**, was Prague's Jewish Quarter. Six monuments form the **Prague Jewish Museum** (☎ 221 711 511; www.jewishmuseum.cz; adult/child 300/200Kč; ◷ 9am-6pm Sun-Fri Apr-Oct, to 4.30pm Nov-Mar). The museum's collection exists only because in 1942 the Nazis gathered objects from 153 Jewish communities in Bohemia and Moravia, planning a 'museum of an extinct race' after completing their extermination program.

Part of the museum, the **Klaus Synagogue** (Map pp274–5; U Starého hřbitova 1) features an exhibition on Jewish customs and traditions, and the **Pinkas Synagogue** (Map pp274–5; Široká 3) is now a memorial to the Holocaust. Its walls are inscribed with the names of 77,297 Czech Jews, including Franz Kafka's three sisters. A few blocks northeast is the **Spanish Synagogue** (Map pp274–5; Dušní 12), built in a Moorish style in 1868. Now the ornate interior is used occasionally for concerts.

The oldest still-functioning synagogue in Europe, the early Gothic **Old-New Synagogue** (Map pp274–5; Červená 1; adult/child 200/140Kč; ◷ 9.30am-5pm Sun-Thu, 9am-4pm Fri), dates from 1270. Opposite is the Jewish town hall with its picturesque 16th-century clock tower. A combined ticket (adult/child 480/320Kč) is available for entry to the Prague Jewish Museum and the Old-New Synagogue.

The **Old Jewish Cemetery** (Map pp274–5; entered from the Pinkas Synagogue) is Josefov's most evocative corner. The oldest of its 12,000 graves date from 1439. Use of the cemetery ceased in 1787 as it was becoming so crowded that burials were up to 12 layers deep.

Tucked away in the northern part of Staré Město's narrow streets is one of Prague's oldest Gothic structures, the magnificent **Convent of St Agnes** (Map pp274–5; ☎ 221 879 111; www.ngprague.cz; U Milosrdných 17; adult/child 150/80Kč; ◷ 10am-6pm Tue-Sun), now housing the National Gallery's collection of Bohemian and Central European medieval art, dating from the 13th to the mid-16th centuries.

THE CHALLENGING MR CĚRNÝ

David Cěrný is the kind of artist whose work polarises people. In the art-nouveau Lucerna pasáž, (p278), he's hung St Wenceslas and his horse upside down, and across the river, Cěrný's 'Piss' sculpture (p281) invites contributions by SMS. Rising above the city, like a faded relic from *Star Wars*, is the Žižkov Tower with Cěrný's giant babies crawling up the exterior.

More contemporary is the **Museum of Czech Cubism** (Map pp274-5; ☎ 221 301 003; www.ngprague.cz; Ovocný trh 19; adult/child 100/50Kč; 10am-6pm Tue-Sun). Located in Josef Gočár's House of the Black Madonna, the angular collection of art and furniture is yet another branch of Prague's National Gallery. On the ground floor is the Grand Café Orient (p286).

Nové Město

Dating from 1348, Nové Město (New Town) is only 'new' when compared with the even older Staré Město. The sloping avenue of **Wenceslas Sq** (Václavské nám; Map pp274–5), lined with shops, banks and restaurants, is dominated by a **statue of St Wenceslas** (Map pp274–5) on horseback. Wenceslas Sq has always been a focus for demonstrations and public gatherings. Beneath the statue is a shrine to the victims of communism, including students Jan Palach and Jan Zajíc, who burned themselves alive in 1969 protesting against the Soviet invasion.

The nearby **Lucerna pasáž** (Map pp274–5; Lucerna Passage) is an art-nouveau shopping arcade now graced with David Černý's (p277) 'Horse' sculpture; a sly upside-down reflection of the statue of St Wenceslas in the square.

At the uphill end of the square is the imposing **National Museum** (Map pp274-5; ☎ 224 497 111; www.nm.cz; Václavské nám 68; adult/child 100/50Kč; 10am-6pm May-Sep, to 5pm Oct-Apr, closed 1st Tue of month). The ho-hum collections cover prehistory, mineralogy and stuffed animals, but the grand interior is worth seeing for the pantheon of Czech historical luminaries. In 2009, a new annex was due to open across the street; in 2011 the museum is scheduled to close for five years for major renovations.

Fans of artist Alfons Mucha, renowned for his art-nouveau posters of garlanded Slavic maidens, can admire his work at the **Mucha Museum** (Map pp274-5; ☎ 221 451 333; www.mucha.cz; Panská 7; adult/child 120/60Kč; 10am-6pm), including an interesting video on his life and art. Mucha also painted the magnificent *Slav Epic*, a monumental series of paintings the size of billboards depicting Slavic history and mythology. The canvases were due to be moved from the small Moravian town of Moravský Krumlov to a purpose-built space somewhere in Prague sometime after 2009. Ask at the Mucha Museum for an update.

The **City of Prague Museum** (Map pp274-5; ☎ 224 227 490; www.muzeumprahy.cz; Na Poříčí 52; Karlin; adult/child 100/40Kč; 9am-6pm Tue-Sun), housed in a grand, neo-Renaissance building near Florenc metro station, charts Prague's evolution from prehistory to the 19th century, culminating in a huge scale model of Prague in 1826–37.

The **Museum of Communism** (Map pp274-5; ☎ 224 212 966; www.muzeumkomunismu.cz; Na příkopě 10; Nové Město; adult/child 180/140Kč; 9am-9pm) is tucked (ironically) behind McDonald's. The exhibition is fascinating through its use of simple everyday objects to illuminate the restrictions of life under communism. Unfortunately, 1989's momentous Velvet Revolution is given a once-over-lightly treatment.

Before or after strolling across Charles Bridge (p281), examine the history of the Vltava's most famous crossing at Prague's newest museum, the **Charles Bridge Museum** (Map pp274-5; ☎ 739 309 551; www.muzeumkarlovamostu.cz; Křížovnické nám; Staré Město; adult/child 150/100Kč; 10am-8pm). When you know the bridge's tumultuous 650-year history, it's surprising it's still standing.

FREE THRILLS

Prague's great for walking, and some of the city's best sights seen on two legs are also free of charge:

- Stroll through the gardens and courtyards at **Prague Castle** (below).
- Visit **Charles Bridge** (p281) at dawn.
- Wander through the **Wallenstein Gardens** (p281).
- Wait patiently under the **astronomical clock** (p277).
- Explore the fortess at **Vyšehrad** (p281).

Entry to the National Museum (left) is free on the first Monday of every month, and the varied locations of the **National Gallery** (www.ngprague.cz) have free admission from 3pm to 8pm on the first Wednesday of every month.

Prague Castle

The biggest castle complex in the world, **Prague Castle** (Pražský hrad; Map p279; ☎ 224 373 368; www.hrad.cz; castle 9am-5pm Apr-Oct, 9am-4pm Nov-Mar, grounds 5am-midnight Apr-Oct, 9am-11pm Nov-Mar) feels more like a small town. It's the seat of Czech power, housing the president's office and the ancient Bohemian crown jewels.

The **long tour** (adult/child 350/175Kč) includes the Old Royal Palace, the Story of Prague Castle exhibit, Basilica of St George, Convent of St George and Golden Lane with Daliborka Tower. The **short tour** (adult/child 250/125Kč) omits a visit to the Old Royal Palace. Buy tickets at the **Castle Information Centre** in the Second Courtyard. Most areas are wheelchair accessible. Count on about three hours for the long tour and two hours for the short tour. Tickets are valid for two days, but you can only visit each attraction once. DIY audio guides can also be rented. Entry to the castle courtyards and the gardens is free.

The main entrance is at the western end. The **changing of the guard**, with stylish uniforms created by Theodor Pištek (costume designer for the film *Amadeus*) takes place every hour, on the hour. At noon a band plays from the windows above.

The **Matthias Gate** leads to the Second Courtyard and the **Chapel of the Holy Cross** (concert tickets on sale here). On the north side is the **Prague Castle Picture Gallery** (adult/child 150/80Kč; ⊙ 9am-5pm Apr-Oct, to 4pm Nov-Mar), with a collection of European baroque art.

The Third Courtyard is dominated by **St Vitus Cathedral**, a French Gothic structure begun in 1344 by Emperor Charles IV, but not completed until 1929. Stained-glass windows created by early-20th-century Czech artists illuminate the interior, including one by Alfons Mucha (third chapel on the left as you enter the cathedral) featuring SS Cyril and

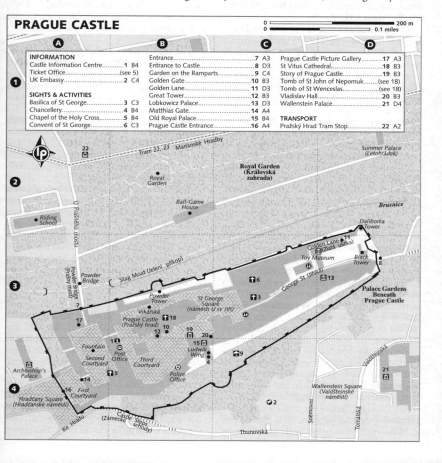

PRAGUE CASTLE

0 ——— 200 m
0 ——— 0.1 miles

INFORMATION
Castle Information Centre............1 B4
Ticket Office.............................(see 5)
UK Embassy................................2 C4

SIGHTS & ACTIVITIES
Basilica of St George..................3 C3
Chancellery................................4 B4
Chapel of the Holy Cross............5 B4
Convent of St George.................6 C3

Entrance....................................7 A3
Entrance to Castle......................8 D3
Garden on the Ramparts............9 C4
Golden Gate.............................10 B3
Golden Lane.............................11 D3
Great Tower.............................12 B3
Lobkowicz Palace.....................13 D3
Matthias Gate..........................14 A4
Old Royal Palace......................15 B4
Prague Castle Entrance............16 A4

Prague Castle Picture Gallery..........17 A3
St Vitus Cathedral.........................18 B3
Story of Prague Castle...................19 B3
Tomb of St John of Nepomuk......(see 18)
Tomb of St Wenceslas...................(see 18)
Vladislav Hall.............................20 B3
Wallenstein Palace.......................21 D4

TRANSPORT
Pražský Hrad Tram Stop................22 A2

Methodius. In the apse is the **tomb of St John of Nepomuk** – two tons of baroque silver watched over by hovering cherubs.

The 14th-century chapel on the cathedral's southern side with the black imperial eagle on the door contains the **tomb of St Wenceslas**, the Czechs' patron saint and the Good King Wenceslas of Christmas carol fame. Wenceslas' zeal in spreading Christianity and his submission to the German King Henry I saw him murdered by his brother, Boleslav I. According to legend he was stabbed to death clinging to the Romanesque lion's-head handle that graces the chapel door. The smaller door on the far side, beside the windows, leads to the Bohemian crown jewels (not open to the public). On the other side of the transept, climb the 287 steps of the **Great Tower** (adult/child 50/25Kč; 9am-4.15pm Apr-Oct).

On the southern side of the cathedral's exterior is the **Golden Gate** (Zlatá brána) a triple-arched doorway topped by a 14th-century mosaic of the Last Judgment.

Also on the southern side is the **Story of Prague Castle** (www.story-castle.cz; adult/child 140/70Kč, incl with long tour tickets) exhibition. This multimedia take on history includes a 40-minute **documentary** (in English 9.45am, 11.14am, 12.45pm, 2.15pm & 3.45pm). The exhibit is a good way to get a handle on Prague Castle's sprawling location and history before or after you go exploring.

Opposite is the entrance to the **Old Royal Palace** (included with long and short tour tickets) with the elegantly vaulted **Vladislav Hall**, built between 1486 and 1502. Horsemen used to ride into the hall up the ramp at the far end for indoor jousts. Two Catholic councillors were thrown out the window of the adjacent **Chancellery** by irate Protestant nobles on 23 May 1618. This infamous Second Defenestration of Prague ignited the Thirty Years' War.

Leaving the palace, the Romanesque **Basilica of St George** (1142; included with long and short tour tickets), and the nearby **Convent of St George** (adult/child 100/50Kč; www.ngprague.cz; 1am-6pm Tue-Sun) has an extensive Renaissance art collection administered by the National Gallery.

Beyond, the crowds surge into the **Golden Lane** (included with long and short tour tickets), a 16th-century tradesmen's quarter of tiny houses in the castle walls. Kafka lived and wrote at his sister's place at No 22 from 1916 to 1917.

On the right, before the castle's exit, is the **Lobkowicz Palace** (admission free; 10.30am-6.30pm), a 16th-century mansion with paintings by

Brueghel and Canaletto, and manuscripts from Beethoven and Mozart. From the castle's eastern end, the Old Castle Steps lead to Malostranská metro station, or turn sharp right to wind through the **Garden on the Ramparts**.

There are two main routes to the castle. Either catch the metro to Malostranská or tram 12, 20, 22 or 23 to Malostranska nám and look forward to a brisk walk up Nerudova. Alternatively take tram 22 or 23 to the Pražský hrad stop, where you can enter at the Second Courtyard.

Hradčany

The Hradčany area west from Prague Castle is mainly residential, with shops and restaurants on Loretánská and Pohořelec. In 1598, Hradčany was almost levelled by Hussites and fire, and the 17th-century palaces were built on the ruins.

The 18th-century Šternberg Palace outside the castle entrance houses the **National Gallery** (Map pp272-3; 220 514 598; www.ngprague.cz; adult/child 150/80Kč; 10am-6pm Tue-Sun) with the country's principal collection of 14th- to 18th-century European art.

A passage at Pohořelec 8 leads to the **Strahov Library** (Map pp272-3; 233 107 718; www.strahovskyklaster .cz; adult/child 80/50Kč; 9am-noon & 1-5pm), the country's largest monastic library, built in 1679. The Philosophy and Theological Halls feature gorgeous frescoed ceilings.

The baroque **Sanctuary of Our Lady of Loreta** (Map pp272-3; 220 516 789; www.loreta.cz; Loretánské nám 7; adult/child 110/90Kč; 9.15am-4.30pm Tue-Sun) showcases precious religious artefacts, and the cloister houses a 17th-century replica of the Santa Casa from the Italian town of Loreta, reputedly the Virgin Mary's house in Nazareth, and transported to Italy by angels in the 13th century.

Malá Strana

Downhill are the baroque backstreets of Malá Strana (Little Quarter), built in the 17th and 18th centuries by victorious Catholic clerics and nobles on the foundations of their Protestant predecessors' Renaissance palaces.

Near the cafe-crowded main square of Malostranské nám is the beautiful baroque **St Nicholas Church** (Map pp272-3; www.psalterium.cz; adult/child 70/35Kč; 9am-5pm Mar-Oct, to 4pm Nov-Feb). Take the stairs to the gallery to see the 17th-century

Passion Cycle paintings. From April to October the church is used for **classical music concerts** (adult/child 490/300Kč; 6pm Wed-Mon).

East along Tomášská, is the **Wallenstein Palace** (Map p279; Valdštejnský palác; admission free; 10am-4pm Sat & Sun), built in 1630 and now home to the Czech Republic's Senate. Albrecht von Wallenstein, a notorious general in the Thirty Years' War, defected from the Protestants to the Catholics and built this palace with his former comrades' expropriated wealth. In 1634 the Habsburg Emperor Ferdinand II learned that Wallenstein was about to switch sides again and had him assassinated.

The **Wallenstein Gardens** (Map pp272-3; admission free; 10am-6pm Apr-Oct) boast a Renaissance loggia and bronze (replica) sculptures by Adrian de Vries (the Swedish army looted the originals in 1648 and they're in Stockholm).

Malá Strana is linked to Staré Město by **Charles Bridge** (Karlův most; Map pp272-3). Built in 1357, and graced by 30 18th-century statues, until 1841 it was the city's only bridge. Climb the **Malá Strana bridge tower** (Map pp272-3; adult/child 50/30Kč; 10am-6pm Apr-Nov) for excellent views. In the middle of the bridge is a bronze statue (1683) of St John of Nepomuk, a priest thrown to his death from the bridge in 1393 for refusing to reveal the queen's confessions to King Wenceslas IV. Visit the bridge at dawn before the tourist hordes arrive. An after-dark crossing with an illuminated Prague Castle is also an essential Prague experience. From 2006 to 2010, Charles Bridge has undergone significant reconstruction. Visit the **Charles Bridge Museum** (p278) to understand why, after 650 years of history, a makeover was overdue.

North of Charles Bridge is the **Franz Kafka Museum** (Map pp272-3 257 535 507; www.kafkamuseum.cz; Cihelná 2b; adult/child 120/60Kč; 10am-6pm). Kafka's diaries, letters and first editions provide a poignant balance to the T-shirt cliché the writer has become in tourist shops.

In front is the **'Piss' sculpture** by Czech artist David Černý (p277) with two animatronic figures piddling in a puddle shaped like the Czech Republic. Interrupt the flow of famous Prague literary quotations by sending your own message via SMS to 420 724 370 770.

Escape the tourist throngs on the **funicular railway** (Map pp272-3; tram ticket 26Kč; every 10-20 min 9.15am-8.45pm) from Újezd to the rose gardens on **Petřín Hill**. Cimb 299 steps to the top of the view-friendly iron-framed **Petřín Lookout Tower**

(Map pp272-3; adult/child 50/40Kč; 10am-10pm May-Sep, to 7pm Apr & Oct, to 5pm Sat & Sun Nov-Mar), built in 1891 in imitation of the Eiffel Tower. Behind the tower a staircase leads to lanes winding back to Malostranské nám.

Vyšehrad
Pack a picnic and take the metro (Vyšehrad station) to the ancient clifftop fortress **Vyšehrad** (Map pp272-3; www.praha-vysehrad.cz; admission free; 9.30am-6pm Apr-Oct, to 5pm Nov-Mar), perched above the Vltava. Dominated by the towers of **SS Peter & Paul Church** (Map pp272–3) and founded in the 11th century, Vyšehrad was rebuilt in the neo-Gothic style between 1885 and 1903. Don't miss the art-nouveau murals inside. The adjacent **Slavín Cemetery** (Map pp272–3), contains the graves of many Czechs, including the composers Smetana and Dvořák. The view from the citadel's southern battlements is superb.

TOURS
Prague Tours (777 816 849; www.praguer.com; per person 300-450Kč) Including an Old Town Pub Tour and Ghost Trail.
Prague Walks (608 339 099; www.praguewalks.com; per person 300-450Kč) From Franz Kafka to microbreweries, communism, and a 'Fashion Tour' (300Kč).
Pražské Benátky (776 776 749; www.prazskebenatky.cz; adult/child 350/175Kč; 10.30am-11pm Jul & Aug, to 8pm Mar-Jun, Sep & Oct, to 6pm Nov-Feb) Runs 45-minute cruises under the arches of Charles Bridge.
Wittmann Tours (603 426 564; www.wittmann-tours.com; per person from 750Kč) Specialises in tours of Jewish interest, including day trips (1150Kč) to the Museum of the Ghetto at Terezín.

To explore Prague on two wheels, see p289.

FESTIVALS & EVENTS
Prague Spring (www.festival.cz) From 12 May to 3 June, classical music kicks off summer.
Prague Fringe Festival (www.praguefringe.com) Eclectic action in late May.
Khamoro (www.khamoro.cz) Late May's annual celebration of Roma culture.
United Islands (www.unitedislands.cz) World music in mid-June.
Prague Autumn (www.pragueautumn.cz) Celebrates summer's end from 12 September to 1 October.
Prague International Jazz Festival (www.jazzfestivalpraha.cz) Late November.
Christmas Market 1 to 24 December in the Old Town Sq.
New Year's Eve Castle fireworks.

CZECH REPUBLIC

SLEEPING

At New Year, Christmas or Easter, or from May to September, book in advance. Prices quoted are for the high season, generally April to October. Rates can increase up to 15%, notably at Christmas, New Year, Easter and during the Prague Spring festival. Some hotels lower rates in July and August. Rates normally decrease by 20% to 40% from November to March. Consider an apartment for stays longer than a couple of nights.

Accommodation agencies include the following:

Ave Hotels (☎ 800 046 385; www.avehotels.cz; ☺ 8am-6pm) Online and telephone booking service.
Hostel.cz (☎ 415 658 580; www.hostel.cz) Around 60 hostels with online booking.
Mary's Travel & Tourist Service (Map pp274-5; ☎ 222 254 007; www.marys.cz; Italská 31, Vinohrady; ☺ 9am-9pm) Private rooms, hostels, apartments and hotels.
Prague Apartments (☎ 224 990 900; www.prague-apartments.com) Web-based offering of furnished apartments.

Budget

Camp Sokol Troja (off Map pp272-3; ☎ 233 542 908; www.camp-sokol-troja.cz; Trojská 171a, Troja 102, camp sites per person/car 130/90Kč; ☑) Riverside campground with kitchen and laundry in Troja, 15 minutes north of the centre on tram 5, 14 or 17.
Czech Inn (Map pp272-3; ☎ 267 267 600; www.czech-inn.com; Francouzská 76, Vinohrady; dm 295-545Kč, s/d/tw from 990/1320/1320Kč, apt from 1650Kč; ☑) From dorms to private apartments, everything's covered at this designer hostel with good transport links. There are no kitchen facilities, but Vinohrady's restaurants and cheap eats are minutes away. Breakfast costs an additional 140Kč.
Clown & Bard Hostel (Map pp272-3; ☎ 222 716 453; www.clownandbard.com; Bořivojova 102, Žižkov; dm 300-380Kč, d 1000-1160Kč; ☑) Party hard in the basement bar and recharge at the all-you-can-eat breakfast any time until 2pm. Double rooms offer (slightly) more seclusion.
Prague's Heaven (Map pp272-3; ☎ 603 153 617; www.hostelpraha.eu; Jaromírova 8, Vyšehrad; dm 320-350Kč, s/d/tr/q from 850/1300/1500/1980; ☑) This quieter spot in Vyšehrad is ideal for travellers not interested in Prague's reputation as a party town. Apartment-style rooms and shiny new bathrooms huddle around a central lounge. It's a 15-minute journey to central Prague on tram 7, 18 or 24. Credit cards not accepted.
Hostel Elf (Map pp272-3; ☎ 222 540 963; www.hostelelf.com; Husitská 11, Žižkov; dm 320-390Kč, s/d/tr 750/950/1450Kč;

☑) Have the best of both worlds at this hip hostel near Žižkov's bars. Swap tales in the beer garden or grab quiet time in the hidden nooks and crannies. More expensive rooms have private bathrooms.
Hostel AZ (Map pp274-5; ☎ 246 052 409; www.hostel-az.com; Jindřišská 5, Nové Město; dm 320-350Kč, s/d/tr/q 950/1000/1450/1600Kč; ☑) This smaller, homely hostel enjoys a central location near Wenceslas Sq, an in-house laundromat, and seven-bed dorms. It's down a shopping arcade so is relatively quiet after dark. Breakfast is an extra 80Kč.
Sir Toby's Hostel (Map pp272-3; ☎ 283 870 635; www.sirtobys.com; Dělnická 24, Holešovice; dm 330-470Kč, s/d/tw/tr 1150/1400/1600/1800Kč; ☑) In an up-and-coming suburb a 10-minute tram ride from the city centre, Sir Toby's is in a refurbished apartment building on a quiet street. The staff is friendly and knowledgeable and there is a shared kitchen and lounge.
Plus Prague (Map pp272-3; ☎ 246 052 409; www.plusprague.com; Přívozní 1, Holešovice; dm 350-520Kč; ☑ ☒) The rooms are a bit clinical and it's a preferred stop of backpacker tour groups, but this 540-bed place in Holešovice includes a pool, on-site bar and restaurant, and separate accomodation for women. Recommended for the younger, social traveller.
Hostel U Melounu (Map pp272-3; ☎ 224 918 322; www.hostelumelounu.cz; Ke Karlovu 7, Vinohrady; dm/s/d 400/750/1200Kč; ☑) An attractive hostel in an historic building on a quiet street, U Melounu features a sunny barbecue area, plus shared kitchen and laundry facilities. A few pricier rooms have private bathrooms.
Hostel Týn (Map pp274-5; ☎ 224 808 333; www.tyn.prague-hostels.cz; Týnská 19, Staré Město; dm/s/d/tr 420/1240/1240/1410Kč; ☑) In a quiet lane metres from Old Town Sq, you'll struggle to find better-value central accommodation. Look forward to occasional church bells.
Hostel Rosemary (Map pp274-5; ☎ 222 211 124; www.praguecityhostel.cz; Růžová 5, Nové Město; dm 450-500Kč, s/tw/tr from 900/1400/1650Kč; ☑) Hostel Rosemary enjoys a quiet location near Wenceslas Sq and Prague's main railway station. Rooms are light and airy with high ceilings; some include a private bathroom and kitchen.

Midrange

Miss Sophie's (Map pp274-5; ☎ 296 303 530; www.miss-sophies.com; Melounova 3; dm 560Kč, s/d from 1790/2050Kč, apt from 2290Kč; ☑) 'Boutique hostel' sums up this converted apartment building. Polished concrete blends with oak flooring, and the basement lounge is all bricks and black leather. Good restaurants await outside.

Hotel Extol Inn (Map pp272-3; ☎ 220 876 541; www .extolinn.cz; Přístavní 2, Holešovice; s/d from 820/1400Kč; 🖳) The reader-recommended rooms here are all excellent value. The cheapest rooms with shared bathrooms are no-frills but spick-and-span, while the three-star rooms with private bathroom include use of the sauna and spa. Breakfast is included, and the city is 10 minutes by tram.

Pension Březina (Map pp274-5; ☎ 296 188 888; www .brezina.cz; Legerova 39-41; Nové Město; s/d economy 1400/1600Kč, luxury 2700/2900Kč) A friendly pension in a converted art-nouveau apartment block with a small garden. Ask for a quieter room at the back. The economy rooms are great value for budget travellers.

Hotel Golden City Garni (Map pp272-3; ☎ 222 711 008; www.goldencity.cz; Táboritská 3, Žižkov; s/d/tr 1900/2700/2900Kč, apts 3100-4100Kč; 🖳) This 19th-century apartment block has clean Ikea-furnished rooms, buffet breakfasts and easy access to the city centre on tram 5, 9 or 26. Family apartments with small kitchenettes are also on offer.

Dasha (Map pp274-5; ☎ 602 210 716; www.accommoda tion-dasha.cz; Jeruzalémská 10; Nové Město; s/d from €30/40, apt €70-90) A restored apartment building 200m from the main train station has private rooms and apartments for up to 10 people. With kitchen facilities the apartments are a good choice for larger groups or families. Advance bookings are essential.

Old Prague Hotel (Map pp274-5; ☎ 224 211 801; www .pragueexpreshotel.cz; Skořepka 5, Staré Město; s/d from 1800/3000Kč; 🖳) The decor's chintzy, but a central location amid winding lanes and hidden squares maximises Prague's reputation as a walking city. Cheaper rooms with shared bathrooms are also available (single/double 1200/1600Kč).

Penzión u Medvídků (Map pp274-5; ☎ 224 211 916; www.umedvidku.cz; Na Perštýně 7, Staré Město; s/d 1950/3000Kč) 'At the Little Bear' is a pub and restaurant with attractive rooms upstairs. Romantic types should choose an historic attic room with exposed wooden beams. Just mind your head after having a few in the microbrewery downstairs.

Hotel Antik (Map pp274-5; ☎ 222 322 288; www.antik hotels.com; Dlouhá 22; Staré Město; s/d 2590/2990Kč) A recent makeover has given the popular Antik a modern tinge, but heritage fans can still cele-brate its 15th-century building (no lift) beside an antique shop. It's a great area for bars and restaurants, so ask for a quieter back room. Breakfast is served in a garden courtyard.

Hotel Absolut (Map pp272-3; ☎ 221 634 100; www.ab soluthotel.cz; Jablonského 639; Vinohrady; d from €100; 🖳) This smart new opening combines modern bathrooms, wi-fi and cosmopolitan style. The area's a bit characterless, but there's an excellent on-site restaurant, and trams and the Holešovice metro are just 200m away.

Hotel 16 U sv Kateřiny (Map pp274-5; ☎ 224 920 636; www.hotel16.cz; Kateřinská 16, Nové Město; s/d incl breakfast from 2900/3700Kč; 🖳) Near the Botanic Gardens and five minutes' walk from Karlovo nám metro station; most days you'll wake up to birdsong at this family-run spot with a quiet garden and cosy bar.

Hotel U Tří Korunek (Map pp272-3; ☎ 222 781 112; www .three-crowns-hotel-prague.com; Cimburkova 28; Žižkov; s/d/tr from €85/105/130) The 'Three Crowns' rambles across three buildings. It's worth upgrading to a superior room with wooden floors and de-signer furniture (around €20 extra). Up-and-coming Žižkov is a good area for bars, and the city centre is just a few tram stops away.

Top End

Savic Hotel (Map pp274-5; ☎ 233 920 118; www.hotelsavic .cz; Jilská 7; Staré Město; d €149-159; 🖳) Looking for somewhere romantic and central? Originally a Dominican convent, the Savic's combi-nation of 14th-century heritage and 21st-century amenities avoids the chintzy overkill of other top-end places. Rooms are cheaper from Sunday to Thursday.

Hotel Josef (Map pp274-5; ☎ 221 700 111; www.hoteljosef .cz; Rybná 20, Staré Město; s/d from €153/174; 🖳) Sleekly modern in old-world Staré Město, this bou-tique hotel combines top-class linen, a newly completed massage room and massive shower-heads for effortless luxury.

our pick Icon Hotel (Map pp274-5; ☎ 221 634 100; www .iconhotel.eu; V jámě 6; Nové Město; d €165-210; 🖳) Here's design-savvy cool concealed down a quiet laneway. The handmade beds are extra-wide, and the crew at reception is unpretentious and hip. Linger in the downstairs bar before exploring Prague's nightlife.

Aria Hotel (Map pp272-3; ☎ 225 334 111; www.ariahotel .net; Tržiště 9, Malá Strana; d from €215; 🖳) Choose your favourite composer or musician and stay in a luxury themed room with a selection of their tunes in a music database. Check online for interesting packages.

EATING

Prague has many cuisines and price ranges. Choose from good-value beer halls with no-nonsense fare, or enjoy a chic riverside restaurant with a high-flying clientele and prices to match. Increasing numbers of ethnic restaurants makes the cloistered days of communism a fading memory.

Eating in Prague's tourist areas is pricey, but cheaper eats are available just a block or two away. Pubs offer both snacks and full meals, and there are stands in Wenceslas Sq selling street snacks such as *párek* (hot dog) or *bramborák* (potato pancake). A late night/early morning plate of *smažený sýr* (fried cheese) is an essential Prague experience.

Prague has good vegetarian restaurants, and most restaurants have a few vegie options. Most restaurants open from 11am to 11pm.

Staré Město

Country Life Nové Město (Map pp274-5; ☎ 224 247 280; Jungmannova 1; ⏰ 9.30am-6.30pm Mon-Thu, 9am-6pm Fri); Staré Město (Map pp274-5; ☎ 224 213 366; Melantrichova 15; mains 75-150Kč; ⏰ 9am-8.30pm Mon-Thu, 9am-6pm Fri, 11am-8.30pm Sat & Sun) This all-vegan cafeteria features inexpensive salads, sandwiches, soy drinks and sunflower-seed burgers.

Kolkovna (Map pp274-5; ☎ 224 819 701; Kolkovně 8, Staré Město; meals 160-400Kč) Kolkovna's contemporary spin on the traditional beer hall serves up classy versions of Czech dishes like *guláš* and roast pork. Try Pilsner Urquell's delicious unpastuerised *tankovna* beer.

Dahab (Map pp274-5; ☎ 224 837 375; Dlouhá 33, Staré Město; mains 200-400Kč; ⏰ noon-1am) Morocco meets the Middle East amid Dahab's softly lit souk-like ambience. Relax with a mint tea and a hookah (water pipe) before diving into tagines and couscous. There's also takeaway falafel and shawarma wraps for on-the-go dining.

Tucked away in an Old Town courtyard, **Beas** (Map pp274-5; ☎ 608 035 727; Týnská 19, Staré Město; mains 90-120Kč; ⏰ 11am-10pm Mon-Sat, 11am-6pm Sun) dishes up good-value Indian vegetarian food. There's another good-value incense-infused **branch** (Map pp274-5; ☎ 608 035 727; Bělehradská 90, Vinohrady; ⏰ 11am-9pm Mon-Fri, noon-8pm Sat, noon-6pm Sun) near the IP Pavlova metro station.

Nové Město

Café Vesmírna (Map pp274-5; ☎ 222 212 363; Ve Smečkách 5, Nové Město; snacks 30-70Kč; ⏰ 9am-10pm Mon-Fri, noon-8pm Sat) Vesmírna provides training and opportunities for people with special needs. There's

healthy snacks like savoury crêpes and a 'how do I choose?' selection of teas and coffees.

Velryba (Map pp274-5; ☎ 224 912 484; Opatovická 24, Nové Město; mains 80-150Kč; ⏰ closed Sun) Good salads, pasta and vegetarian dishes feature at this student fave with an attached art gallery. Dig out your black polo-neck jumper for the back-streets-of-Prague bohemian vibe.

Pizzeria Kmotra (Map pp274-5; ☎ 224 934 100; V Jirchářích 12; Nové Město; pizza 100-150Kč) More than 30 varieties feature at this cellar pizzeria that gets superbusy after 8pm.

Giallo Rossa (Map pp274-5; ☎ 604 898 989; Jabuská 2; mains 100-180Kč; 💻) Dine in on rustic pizza and pasta or duck next door to the takeaway window and grab a few late night/early morning slices (from 30Kč) of Neapolitan-style pizza. Another deal you can't refuse is free internet with your pizza.

Café FX (Map pp274-5; ☎ 224 254 776; Bělehradská 120, Vinohrady; mains 120-230Kč; ⏰ 11.30am-2am) Café FX is chiffon and chandelier chic, with Prague's best vegetarian flavours from Mexico, India and Thailand. The kitchen stays open until the wee small hours. Relax at weekend brunch and lose yourself in the adjacent CD store.

Modrý Zub (Map pp274-5; ☎ 222 212 622; Jindřišská 5, Nové Město; mains 120-280Kč) Sometimes all you want is healthy Asian food. The 'Blue Tooth' turns out authentic versions of pad Thai and satay you'll recall from your favourite Asian food hall back home.

Kogo (Map pp274-5; ☎ 224 451 259; Slovanský dům; Na příkopě 22, Nové Město; pizzas 150-250Kč, mains 200-450Kč) Concealed in a leafy garden behind a ritzy shopping arcade, Kogo's classy pizza, pasta, steak and seafood are favourites of Prague's business elite.

Na Verandách (Map pp272-3; ☎ 257 191 200; Nádražní 84, Smichov; meals 150-300Kč) Across the river in Smichov, the Staropramen brewery's restaurant is a modern spot crowded with locals enjoying superior versions of favourite Czech dishes, and an 'it could be a long night' selection of different brews. Na Verandách is a short walk from Anděl metro station.

Pastička (Map pp272-3; ☎ 222 253 228; Blanikcá 24, Vinohrady; mains 150-350Kč; ⏰ 11am-midnight Mon-Fri, from 5pm Sat & Sun) Vinohrady's emerging dining scene around Mánesova now features the unpretentious 'Mousetrap'. Locals come for excellent Bernard beer, eat huge meaty meals, and feel good about living in the funky part of town.

Siam Orchid (Map pp274–5; ☎ 222 319 410; Na poříčí 21; Nové Město; mains 160–280Kč) The waiter's Cambodian, but that doesn't stop this tiny Thai restaurant from being Prague's most authentic Asian eatery.

La Bodeguita del Medio (Map pp274–5; ☎ 224 813 922; Kaprova 5, Staré Město; mains 200–550Kč; ⏰ 10am–2am) Crammed energetically into a heritage space near Old Town Sq, this Cuban-themed place includes the mojito-fuelled bar you've only dreamed about, and zesty food like chilli prawns.

Hradčany & Malá Strana

Malý Buddha (Map pp272–3; ☎ 220 513 894; Úvoz 46, Hradčany; mains 70–220Kč) Malý ('Little') Buddha is an incense-infused haven atop Hradčany hill. When the castle's crowds wear you down, restore your chi with restorative wines, healing tea and pan-Asian food. Credit cards are not accepted.

Bar Bar (Map pp272–3; ☎ 257 312 246; Všhrdova 17, Malá Strana; mains 120–240Kč) Despite the double-barrelled name, this spot – a pleasant riverside walk from Malá Strana's tourist bustle – is actually a good-value local restaurant. Look forward to rustic comfort food such as risotto and savoury crêpes.

Hergetova Cihelna (Map pp272–3; ☎ 257 535 534; Cihelná 2b, Malá Strana; mains 220–550Kč; ⏰ 9am–2am) A restored *cihelná* (brickworks) is now a hip space with a riverside terrace looking back to Charles Bridge and Staré Město. Come for steak, seafood or pizza, and linger for the sublime view.

DRINKING

Bohemian beers are among the world's best. The most famous brands are Budvar, Plzeňský Prazdroj (Pilsner Urquell), and Prague's own Staropramen. An increasing number of independent microbreweries also offer a more unique drinking experience.

Avoid the tourist areas, and you'll find local bars selling half-litres for 35Kč or less. Traditional pubs open from 11am to 11pm. More stylish modern bars open from noon to 1am, and often stay open till 3am or 4am on Friday and Saturday.

Bars & Pubs

our pick **Pivovarský Dům** (Map pp274–5; ☎ 296 216 666; cnr Ječná & Lipová, Nové Město) The 'Brewery House' microbrewery conjures everything from a refreshing wheat beer to coffee and banana-

flavoured styles – even a beer 'champagne'. The classic Czech lager is a hops-laden marvel. Really keen beer fans are directed to their associated Pivovarský Klub (see below).

Pivovarský Klub (Map pp274–5; ☎ 222 315 777; Křižíkova 17, Karlín) Submit to your inner hophead at this pub-restaurant–beer shop with interesting limited-volume draught beers, and bottled brews from around the Czech Republic. Come for lunch, as it gets full of loyal regulars later on. It's right beside Florenc metro station.

Čili Bar (Map pp274–5; Kozná 10, Staré Město; ⏰ from 5pm) This raffish bar is more Žižkov than Staré Město, with cool cocktails and a grungy tinge in welcome contrast to the crystal shops and Russian dolls around the corner.

Kozička (Map pp274–5; ☎ 224 818 308; Kozí 1, Staré Město) The 'Little Goat' rocks in standing-room-only fashion until well after midnight in a buzzing basement bar. Your need for midnight munchies will be answered by the late-night kitchen.

U Medvídků (Map pp274–5; ☎ 296 216 666; Na Perštýně 7, Staré Město; ⏰ beer museum noon–10pm) A microbrewery with the emphasis on 'micro', this place specialises in X-Beer, an 11.8% 'knocks-your-socks-off' dark lager.

Bukowski's (Map pp272–3; Bořvojova 86, Žižkov; ⏰ from 6pm) This new late-night cocktail bar is driving grungy Žižkov's inevitable transformation into Prague's hottest after-dark neighbourhood. Leave the Old Town English pubs to the easyJet masses, and sip on cool concoctions here instead.

U Sadu (Map pp272–3; ☎ 222 727 072; Škroupovo nám, Žižkov) Escape the overpriced tyranny of central Prague at this neighbourhood pub in up-and-coming Žižkov. With its ragtag collection of memorabilia, including communist-era posters of forgotten politicians, nothing's really changed here in a few decades. An essential stop before or after gigs at the Palác Akropolis (p287).

Hapu (Map pp272–3; 222 720 158 Orlická 8; Vinohrady; ⏰ from 6pm) 'Pop round for a drink after work.' Well, that's what it feels like at this shabby but chic basement bar that's a dead ringer for a friend's front room. That's if you had mates with superb mixologist skills.

U Sudu (Map pp274–5; ☎ 222 232 20; Vodičkova 10, Nové Město) Moravian wines are growing in reputation and this labyrinth of cellar bars and lounges is a good spot to fast-track your knowledge of the local wine scene.

Letenské sady (Map pp274-5; Letna Gardens, Bubeneč) This garden bar has views across the river of the Old Town and southwest to the castle. In summer it's packed with a young crowd enjoying cheap beer and grilled sausages. Sometimes the simple things in life are the best.

Cafes

Prague's summer streets are crammed with outdoor tables, and good-quality tea and coffee are widely available.

Grand Café Orient (Map pp274-5; ☎ 224 224 240; Ovocný trh 19, Nové Město; ☽ 9am-10pm Mon-Fri, from 10am Sat & Sun) In the 'House of the Black Madonna', Josef Gočár's cubist gem, the reborn Grand Café Orient also features Gočár-designed lampshades and furnishings. He had nothing to do with the coffee, but it's also pretty good.

Káva.Káva.Káva (Map pp274-5; ☎ 224 228 862; Národní třída 37, Nové Město; ☽ 7am-10pm Mon-Fri, 9am-10pm Sat & Sun; ☐) In the Platýz courtyard, this cafe offers huge smoothies and tasty nibbles such as chocolate brownies. Access the internet (2Kč per minute or 15 minutes free with a purchase) or hitch your laptop to the wi-fi hot spot. There's another branch in Smichov (Map pp272-3; ☎ 257 314 277; Lidicka 42).

Bakeshop Praha (Map pp274-5; ☎ 224 329 060; Kozí 1; snacks 40-180Kč; ☽ 7am-7pm) Bakeshop's corner spot offers innovative salads, superior pies and almost healthy quiche. Service can be hit or miss, but it's worth grabbing a coffee and watching Prague's cinematic scroll outside.

Kaaba (Map pp274-5; ☎ 224 254 021; Mánesova 20; Vinohrady; snacks 50-80Kč; ☽ 8am-10pm Mon-Sat, 10am-10pm Sun) Vinohrady's hipsters park themselves on 1950s-style furniture and recharge with snappy espressos, beer, wine and tasty snacks. The decor may be retro, but the cool staff are definitely not old-school surly.

U zeleného čaje (Map pp272-3; ☎ 257 530 027; Nerudova 19, Malá Strana) Linger at this tiny wooden-floored tea-haven on the way to the castle, or grab a speciality tea to go for the final push up the hill. Sandwiches and wine are also available.

ENTERTAINMENT

From clubbing to classical music, puppetry to performance art, Prague offers plenty of entertainment. It's an established centre of classical music and jazz, and is now also famed for its dance and rock scenes. For current listings, see *Culture in Prague* (available from PIS offices; see p273), www.prague.tv, or the monthly free *Provokátor* magazine (www.provokator.org), from clubs, cafes, and art-house cinemas.

For classical music, opera, ballet, theatre and some rock concerts – even the most 'sold-out' *vyprodáno* (events) – you can often find tickets on sale at the box office around 30 minutes before the performance starts. Ticket agencies sell the same tickets with a high commission.

Tickets can cost as little as 100Kč for standing-room only to over 1000Kč for the best seats; the average price is about 600Kč. Be wary of touts selling concert tickets in the street. You may end up sitting on stacking chairs in a cramped hall listening to amateur musicians, rather than in the grand concert hall that was implied.

Try the following ticket agencies:

Bohemia Ticket International (☎ 224 227 832; www.ticketsbti.cz) Nové Město (Map pp274-5; Na příkopě 16, ☽ 10am-7pm Mon-Fri, to 5pm Sat, to 3pm Sun); Staré Město (Map pp274-5; Malé nám 13; ☽ 9am-5pm Mon-Fri, to 1pm Sat)

FOK Box Office (Map pp274-5; ☎ 222 002 336; www.fok.cz; U obecního domu 2, Staré Město; ☽ 10am-6pm Mon-Fri) For classical concert tickets.

Ticketpro (Map pp274-5; ☎ 296 333 333; www.ticketpro.cz; Lucerna pasáž, Štěpánská 61, Nové Město; ☽ 9am-12.30pm & 1-5pm Mon-Fri) Also has branches in PIS offices (p273).

Ticketstream (www.ticketstream.cz) Online bookings for events in Prague and the Czech Republic.

Performing Arts

You'll see fliers advertising concerts for tourists. It's a good chance to relax in old churches and historic buildings, but performances can be of mediocre quality. Prices begin around 400Kč.

Rudolfinum (Map pp274-5; ☎ 227 059 352; www.rudolfinum.cz; nám Jana Palacha, Staré Město; ☽ box office 10am-12.30pm & 1.20-6pm Mon-Fri plus 1hr before performances) One of Prague's main concert venues is the Dvořák Hall in the neo-Renaissance Ruldolfinum, and home to the Czech Philharmonic Orchestra.

Smetana Hall (Obecní dům; Map pp274-5; ☎ 222 002 101; www.obecni-dum.cz; nám Republiky 5, Staré Město; ☽ box office 10am-6pm Mon-Fri) Another main concert venue is Smetana Hall in the art-nouveau Municipal House. A highlight is the opening of the Prague Spring festival.

Prague State Opera (Státní opera Praha; Map pp274-5; ☎ 224 227 266; www.opera.cz; Legerova 75, Nové Město; ☽ box office 10am-5.30pm, 10am-noon & 1-5pm Sat & Sun) Opera, ballet and classical drama (in Czech) are performed at this neo-Renaissance theatre. The box office is at Wilsonova 4.

National Theatre (Národní divadlo; Map pp274-5; ☎ 224 901 377; www.narodni-divadlo.cz; Národní třída 2, Nové Město; ☼ box office 10am-6pm) Classical drama, opera and ballet.

Laterna Magika (Map pp274-5; ☎ 224 931 482; www .laterna.cz; Nová Scéna, Národní třída 4, Nové Město; tickets 540-680Kč; ☼ box office 10am-8pm Mon-Sat) A multimedia show combining dance, opera, music and film.

Estates Theatre (Stavovské divadlo; Map pp274-5; ☎ 224 902 322; www.estatestheatre.cz; Ovocný trh 1, Staré Město; ☼ box office 10am-6pm) Every night from mid-July to the end of August Opera Mozart (☎ 271 741 403; www.mozart-praha.cz) performs *Don Giovanni*, which premiered here in 1787.

Divadlo Hybernia (Hybernia divadlo; Map pp274-5; ☎ 221 419 420; www.divadlo-hybernia.cz; nám Republiky 4, Nové Město; ☼ box office 10am-7pm Mon-Sat, to 3pm Sun) Originally a 17th-century church for Irish monks, the Hybernia now showcases musical theatre with tourist-friendly themes like the Jewish legend of Golem.

Black Theatre of Jiří Srnec (Map pp274-5; ☎ 257 921 835; www.blacktheatresrnec.cz; Reduta Theatre, Národní 20, Nové Město; tickets 620Kč; ☼ box office 3-7pm Mon-Fri, shows at 9.30pm) Prague is awash in 'black light theatre' shows combining mime, ballet, animated film and puppetry. Jiří Srnec's Black Theatre is the original and the least touristy.

Theatre on the Balustrade (Divadlo na zábradlí; Map pp274-5; ☎ 222 868 868; www.nazabradli.cz; Anenské nám 5, Staré Město; ☼ box office 2-8pm Mon-Fri, 2hr before show Sat & Sun) Plays by former president Václav Havel are often staged (in Czech) here.

Divadlo Minor (Map pp274-5; ☎ 222 231 351; www.minor .cz; Vodičkova 6, Nové Město; ☼ box office 9am-1.30pm & 2.30-8pm Mon-Fri, 11am-6pm Sat & Sun) Kid-friendly shows including puppets and pantomime.

Nightclubs

Mecca (Map pp272-3; ☎ 283 870 522; www.mecca.cz; U Průhonu 3, Holešovice; admission 100-400Kč; ☼ 10pm-6am Wed-Sat) Prague's most fashionable dance club attracts film stars, fashionistas and fab types, plus occasional gigs by name DJs.

Club Radost FX (Map pp274-5; ☎ 224 254 776; www .radostfx.cz; Bělehradská 120, Vinohrady; admission 120-280Kč; ☼ 10pm-6am) Prague's most stylish, self-assured club remains hip for its bohemian-boudoir decor and its popular Thursday hip-hop night FXBounce (www.fxbounce.com).

Roxy (Map pp274-5; ☎ 224 826 296; www.roxy.cz; Dlouhá 33, Staré Město; admission 120-280Kč; ☼ 10pm-6am) In a resurrected old cinema, the Roxy presents innovative DJs and the occasional global act. 'Free Mondays' will give you more money for beer.

Live Music

Prague has jazz clubs varying in style from traditional to avant-garde.

Lucerna Music Bar (Map pp274-5; ☎ 224 217 108; www.musicbar.cz; Lucerna pasaž, Vodičkova 36, Nové Město; ☼ 8pm-3am) Lucerna features local bands and almost-famous international acts. Jettison your musical snobbery at the wildy popular '80s and '90s nights (admission 100Kč; Friday and Saturday).

Palác Akropolis (Map pp272-3; ☎ 296 330 911; www .palacakropolis.cz; Kubelikova 27, Žižkov; ☼ club 7pm-5am) Get lost in the labyrinth of theatre, live music, clubbing, drinking and eating that makes up Prague's coolest venue. Hip hop, house, reggae, or rocking Roma bands from Romania – anything goes. Kick your night off nearby at the quirky U Sadu pub (p285).

Reduta Jazz Club (Map pp274-5; ☎ 224 912 246; www .redutajazzclub.cz; Národní třída 20, Nové Město; ☼ 9pm-3am) Founded in 1958 and one of the oldest jazz clubs in Europe. Bill Clinton jammed here in 1994.

USP Jazz Lounge (Map pp274-5; ☎ 603 551 680; www .jazzlounge.cz; Michalská 9, Staré Město; ☼ 8pm-3am) A less traditional venue with modern jazz from 10pm. DJs kick on from midnight.

AghaRTA Jazz Centrum (Map pp274-5; ☎ 222 221 275; www.agharta.cz; Železná 16, Staré Město; admission 200Kč; ☼ 6pm-1am) Rock up early for a table in the medieval cellar or book online the day before.

Gay & Lesbian Venues

The inner suburb of Vinohrady is developing as a gay quarter, and the city enjoys a relaxed scene.

Prague Saints (Map pp274-5; ☎ 222 250 326; www .praguesaints.cz; Polska 32; Vinohrady) Online information on Prague's gay scene. The on-site Saints Bar (open from 5pm to 4am) is a good intro to what's happening. Thursdays from 8pm is lesbian night.

Termix (Map pp272-3; ☎ 222 710 462; www.club-termix .cz; Třebízckého 4A, Vinohrady; ☼ 8pm-5am Wed-Sun) A friendly mixed gay-and-lesbian scene with an industrial/high-tech vibe. Wednesdays are good fun with retro Czech pop.

Valentino (Map pp274-5; ☎ 222 513 491; www.club -valentino.cz; Vinohradská 40, Vinohrady; ☼ from 11am)

CZECH REPUBLIC

Welcome to Prague's gay superclub, with three floors concealing two dance areas, four bars, and other rooms with exceedingly low lighting. Weekends get interestingly busy.

Cinemas

Most films are screened in their original language with Czech subtitles (*české titulky*), but Hollywood blockbusters are often dubbed into Czech (*dabing)*; look for the labels 'tit.' or 'dab.' on listings. Tickets are around 180/140Kč for adult/child.

Kino Aero (Map pp272-3; ☎ 271 771 349; www.kinoaero .cz; Biskupcova 31, Žižkov) An art-house cinema, with themed weeks and retrospectives; often with English subtitles.

Kino Světozor (Map pp274-5; ☎ 224 946 824; www.kino svetozor.cz; Vodičkova 41, Nové Město) Your best bet for Czech films with English subtitles; under the same management as Kino Aero but more central, plus it includes a cool DVD and movie poster shop.

Palace Cinemas (Map pp274-5; ☎ 257 181 212; www .palacecinemas.cz; Slovanský dům, Na příkopě 22, Nové Město) A 10-screen multiplex showing current Hollywood films.

SHOPPING

Prague's main shopping streets are in Nové Město – Wenceslas Sq, Na příkopě, 28.října and Národní třída – and there are many tourist-oriented shops on Celetná, the Old Town Sq, Pařížská and Karlova in Staré Město. Local souvenirs include Bohemian crystal, ceramics, marionettes and garnet jewellery.

Crystal

Moser (Map pp274-5; ☎ 224 211 293; Na příkopě 12, Nové Město; ⊙ 10am-8pm Mon-Fri, to 7pm Sat & Sun) Top-quality Bohemian crystal.

Rott Crystal (Map pp274-5; ☎ 224 229 529; Malé nám 3, Staré Město; ⊙ 10am-8pm) Housed in a neo-Renaissance building that's worth a look even if you're just browsing.

Department Stores

The **Tesco Department Store** (Map pp274-5; ☎ 222 003 111; Národní třída 26, Nové Město; ⊙ 8am-9pm Mon-Fri, 9am-8pm Sat, 10am-7pm Sun) has clothes, electrical and household goods, plus a **supermarket** (⊙ 7am-10pm Mon-Fri, 8am-8pm Sat, 9am-7pm Sun).

Handicrafts, Antiques & Ceramics

Manufaktura (Map pp274-5; ☎ 221 632 480; www.manu faktura.biz; Melantrichova 17, Staré Město) Sells traditional Czech handicrafts, wooden toys and handmade cosmetics.

Near the Old Town Sq, explore the antique shops of Týnská and Týnská ulička. For traditional Moravian folk cermaics, see **Tupesy lidová keramika** (Map pp274-5; ☎ 224 210 728; Havelská 21, Staré Město)

Music

Bontonland (Map pp274-5; ☎ 224 473 080; Václavské nám 1, Nové Město; ⊙ 9am-8pm Mon-Sat, 10am-7pm Sun) A megastore stocking all genres, including lots of contemporary Czech music.

GETTING THERE & AWAY

See also p324.

Bus

The main terminal for international and domestic buses is **Florenc Bus Station** (ÚAN Florenc; Map pp274-5; ☎ 12 999; Křižíkova 4, Karlín), 600m northeast of the main train station (ÚAN is short for *Ústřední autobusové nádraží*, or 'central bus station'). Some regional buses depart from near metro stations Anděl, Dejvická, Černý Most, Nádraží Holešovice, Smíchovské Nádraží and Želivského. Check timetables and departure points at www.idos.cz.

At Florenc get information at **windows 6 to 21** (⊙ 6am-9pm), or use the touch-screen computer.

Short-haul tickets are sold on the bus. Long-distance domestic tickets are sold at the station from AMS windows 1 to 4 in the central hall, or direct from the nearby Student Agency (www.studentagency.cz) or Megabus (www.megabus.cz) offices.

More buses depart in the mornings. Buses sometimes leave early, so be there at least 10 minutes before departure time. If you're not seated five minutes before departure, you could lose your reservation. Many services don't operate at weekends, so trains can often be a better option.

There are direct services from Florenc to Brno (180Kč, 2½ hours, hourly), České Budějovice (130Kč, 2¾ hours, four daily), Karlovy Vary (130Kč, 2¼ hours, eight daily) and Plzeň (90Kč, 1½ hours, hourly). Student Agency's bus from Florenc to Karlovy Vary travels via Prague's Ruzyně airport.

International services from Florenc include Amsterdam (14 to 16 hours), Bern (12 hours), Berlin (five hours), Dusseldorf (12 hours), Frankfurt (seven to eight hours), Hamburg

(12 hours), Munich (six hours), London (20 hours), Geneva (15 hours), Oslo (11 hours), Paris (15 hours), Rotterdam (16 hours), Salzburg (7½ hours), Stockholm (12 hours) and Vienna (five hours). In summer, these buses run at least daily, while service may be less frequent at other times of year. Most of these routes originate in Brno. There are also buses that go to Naples (24 hours) via Venice, Florence and Rome.

Other buses from Prague to České Budějovice (130Kč, 2½ hours, 16 daily) and Český Krumlov (140Kč, three hours, seven daily) depart from Ná Knížecí bus station, at Anděl metro's southern entrance, or from outside Roztyly metro station.

Companies include the following:

Eurolines (Map pp274–5; ☎ 245 005 245; www.bei.cz; ÚAN Florenc Bus Station; ⏰ 8am-7pm Mon-Fri) Buses to all over Europe.

Megabus Central Prague (Map pp274–5; ☎ 234 704 977; Shop 12, Můstek metro station, Nove Město; ⏰ 8.30am-7pm Mon-Fri) Florenc (☎ 777 320 102; www.megabus.cz; ⏰ 7am-7pm Mon-Fri) Linking Prague with Karlovy Vary, Plzeň and Brno. Also has a branch at Ruzyně airport.

Student Agency Central Prague (Map pp274–5; ☎ 224 999 666; Ječná 37; Nove Město ⏰ 9am-6pm Mon-Fri); Florenc (☎ 224 894 430; www.studentagency.cz; ⏰ 9am-6pm Mon-Fri) Linking major Czech cities and services throughout Europe. Also has a branch at Ruzyně airport.

Train

Prague's main train station is **Praha-hlavní nádraží** (Map pp274–5; ☎ 221 111 122; Wilsonova, Nové Město). Domestic tickets and seat reservations are sold on level 2 at even-numbered windows from 10 to 24 to the right of the stairs leading up to level 3. International tickets are sold on level 3 at windows 26 to 36. At the time of writing Praha-hlavní nádraží was undergoing major redevelopment and the station layout may be different when you read this.

Some international trains stop at Praha-Holešovice station on the northern side of the city, while some domestic services terminate at Praha-Masarykovo in Nové Město, or Praha-Smíchov south of Malá Strana. Also buy train tickets and get timetable information from **ČD Centrum** (⏰ 6am-7.30pm) at the southern end of level 2 in Praha-hlavní nádraží.

There are direct trains from Praha-hlavní nádraží to Brno (314Kč, three hours, eight daily), České Budějovice (211Kč, 2½ hours, hourly), Karlovy Vary (292Kč, three hours, three daily), Kutná Hora (95Kč, 55 minutes, seven daily) and Plzeň (145Kč, 1½ hours, eight

daily). There are also SC Pendolino (high-speed) daily departures to Brno (514Kč) from Praha-Holešovice.

Sample one-way fares to Prague from other European cities include the following:

Basel €113, 14 hours
Berlin €51, five hours
Bratislava €20, 4¾ hours
Budapest €88, seven hours
Hamburg €106, 7½ hours
Frankfurt €78, 7½ hours
Kraków €29, 8½ hours
Munich €66, six hours
Salzburg €44, eight hours
Vienna €38, 4½ hours
Warsaw €43, 9½ hours

Check train timetables and depature points online at www.idos.cz.

GETTING AROUND
To/From the Airport

Prague's Ruzyně airport is 17km west of the city centre. To get into town, buy a ticket from the public transport (Dopravní podnik; DPP) desk in arrivals and take bus 119 (26Kč, 20 minutes, every 15 minutes) to the end of the line (Dejvická), then continue by metro into the city centre (another 10 minutes; no extra ticket needed). You'll also need a half-fare (13Kč) ticket for your backpack or suitcase if it's larger than 25cm by 45cm by 70cm.

Alternatively, the **Airport Express** (adult/child 45/25Kč; ⏰ 5am-9pm) bus service goes direct to the Holešovice metro station. Luggage is free on this service; buy your ticket from the driver.

The **Cedaz minibus** (☎ 221 111 111; www.cedaz.cz) leaves from outside arrivals (20 minutes, every half-hour from 6am to 9pm). Buy your ticket from the driver. The minibus stops at the **Czech Airlines** (Map pp274–5; V Celnici 5) office near the Hilton around nám Republiky (120Kč) or further out at the Dejvická metro station (90Kč). You can also get a Cedaz minibus from your hotel or any other address (480Kč for one to four people, 960Kč for five to eight).

Prague Airport Taxis, with airport-regulated prices, charge 650Kč into central Prague. Drivers speak good English. **AAA Taxis** (☎ 14 014; www.aaataxi.cz) is also reputable.

Bicycle

City Bike (Map pp274–5; ☎ 776 180 284; www.citybike-prague .com; Královská 5, Staré Město; ⏰ 9am-7pm May-Sep)

CZECH REPUBLIC

Two- to three-hour tours cost 540Kč, departing at 10.30am, 1.30pm and 4.30pm. Independent hire is 300Kč for the first two hours and 500Kč for all day.

Praha Bike (Map pp274-5; ☎ 732 388 880; www.praha bike.cz; Dlouhá 24, Staré Město; ☺ 9am-8pm) A range of different tour routes including rail and bike combos to Karlštejn Castle.

Car & Motorcycle

Challenges to driving in Prague include cobblestones, trams and one-way streets. Try not to arrive or leave on a Friday or Sunday afternoon or evening, when Prague folk are travelling to and from their weekend houses.

Central Prague has many pedestrian-only streets, marked with Pěší Zoná (Pedestrian Zone) signs, where only service vehicles and taxis are allowed; parking can be a nightmare. Meter time limits range from two to six hours at around 50Kč per hour. Parking in one-way streets is normally only allowed on the right-hand side. Traffic inspectors are strict, and you could be clamped or towed. There are several car parks at the edges of Staré Město, and Park-and-Ride car parks around the outer city (most are marked on city maps), close to metro stations.

Public Transport

All public transport is operated by **Dopravní podnik hl. m. Prahy** (DPP; ☎ 800 191 817; www.dpp .cz), with information desks at **Ruzyně airport** (☺ 7am to 7pm) and in four metro stations – **Muzeum** (☺ 7am to 9pm), **Můstek** (☺ 7am to 6pm), **Anděl** (☺ 7am to 6pm) and **Nádraží Holešovice** (☺ 7am to 6pm) – where you can get tickets, directions, a multilingual system map, a map of Noční provoz (night services) and a detailed English-language guide to the whole system.

Buy a ticket before boarding a bus, tram or metro. Tickets are sold from machines at metro stations and major tram stops, at newsstands, Trafiky snack shops, PNS and other tobacco kiosks, hotels, all metro station ticket offices and DPP information offices.

A jízdenka (transfer ticket) is valid on tram, metro, bus and the Petřín funicular and costs 26Kč (half-price for six- to 15-year-olds); large suitcases and backpacks (anything larger than 25cm by 45cm by 70cm) also need a 13Kč ticket. Kids under six ride free. Validate (punch) your ticket by sticking it in the little yellow machine in the metro station lobby or on the bus or tram the first time you board; this stamps the time and date on it. Once validated, tickets remain valid for 75 minutes from the time of stamping, if validated between 5am and 10pm on weekdays, and for 90 minutes at other times. Within this period, you can make unlimited transfers between all types of public transport (you don't need to punch the ticket again).

There's also a short-hop 18/9Kč adult/child ticket, valid for 20 minutes on buses and trams, or for up to five metro stations. No transfers are allowed with these, and they're not valid on the Petřín funicular or on night trams (51 to 58) or night buses (501 to 512). Being caught without a valid ticket entails a 400Kč on-the-spot fine (100Kč for not having a luggage ticket). The inspectors travel incognito, but will show a badge when they ask for your ticket. A few may demand a higher fine from foreigners and pocket the difference, so insist on a doklad (receipt) before paying.

Tickets for 24 hours (100Kč) and three/five days (330/500Kč) are also available. If you're staying for longer and will be travelling a lot, consider a monthly pass (550Kč). All passes must be validated on first use only. If a ticket is stamped twice, it becomes invalid. Before shelling out on a pass, note much of central Prague can be explored on foot.

On metro trains and newer trams and buses, an electronic display shows the route number and the name of the next stop, and a recorded voice announces each station or stop. As the train, tram or bus pulls away, it says: Příští stanice (or zastávka)… meaning 'The next station (or stop) is…', perhaps noting that it's a přestupní stanice (transfer station). At metro stations, signs point you towards the výstup (exit) or to a přestup (transfer to another line).

The metro operates from 5am to midnight daily. Line A runs from northwest Prague at Dejvická to the east at Depo Hostivař; line B runs from the southwest at Zličín to the northeast at Černý Most; and line C runs from the north at Letňany to the southeast at Háje. Line A intersects line C at Muzeum, line B intersects line C at Florenc and line A intersects line B at Můstek.

After the metro closes, night trams (51 to 59) and buses (501 to 512) travel about every 40 minutes. Check if one of these services passes near where you're staying.

Taxi

Try to avoid getting a taxi in tourist areas such as Wenceslas Sq. To avoid being ripped off, phone a reliable company such as **AAA** (☎ 14 014; www.aaa.radiotaxi.cz) or **City Taxi** (☎ 257 257 257; www.citytaxi.cz). Both companies also offer online bookings.

Prague recently introduced the 'Taxi Fair Place' scheme, with authorised taxis in tourist areas. Drivers can charge a maximum of 28Kč/km and must announce the estimated price in advance. Look for the yellow and red signs.

If you do feel cheated, keep the receipt and email the details to taxi@cityofprague.cz.

AROUND PRAGUE

Visit the following places on day trips using public transport.

KARLŠTEJN

Erected by the Emperor Charles IV in the mid-14th century, **Karlštejn Castle** (☎ 274 008 154; www.hradkarlstejn.cz; Karlštejn; 🕑 9am-6pm Tue-Sun Jul & Aug, to 5pm May, Jun & Sep, to 4pm Apr & Oct, to 3pm Mar & Nov, closed Jan, Feb & Dec), crowns a ridge above Karlštejn village. It's a 20-minute walk from the train station.

The highlight is the **Chapel of the Holy Rood**, where the Bohemian crown jewels were kept until 1420. The 55-minute guided tours (in English) on Route I costs 200/120Kč for adult/child tickets. Route II, which includes the chapel (June to October only), are 300/150Kč adult/child and must be prebooked.

Trains from Praha-hlavní nádraží station to Beroun stop at Karlštejn (46Kč, 45 minutes, hourly).

KONOPIŠTĚ

The assassination of the heir to the Austro-Hungarian throne, Archduke Franz Ferdinand d'Este, sparked off WWI. For the last 20 years of his life he hid away southeast of Prague in **Konopiště Chateau**, his country retreat.

Three guided tours are available. **Tour III** (adult/child 300/200Kč) is the most interesting, visiting the archduke's private apartments, unchanged since the state took over the chateau in 1921. **Tour II** (adult/child 190/110Kč) takes in the **Great Armoury**, one of Europe's most impressive collections.

The castle is a testament to the archduke's twin obsessions of hunting and St George. Having renovated the massive Gothic and Renaissance building in the 1890s, Franz Ferdinand decorated his home with some of his 300,000 hunting kills. About 100,000 of them adorn the walls, marked with when and where it was slain. The **Trophy Corridor** and **Chamois Room** (both on Tour III) are truly bizarre.

His collection of St George–related artefacts includes 3750 items, many displayed in the **Muzeum sv Jiří** (adult/child 30/15Kč) at the front of the castle. From June to September weekend concerts are sometimes held in the castle's grounds.

There are direct trains from Prague's hlavní nádraží to Benešov u Prahy (66Kč, 1¼ hours, hourly). Buses depart from Florenc or the Roztyly metro station to Benešov on a regular basis (48Kč, 1¼ hours)

Konopiště is 2.5km west of Benešov. Local bus 2 (11Kč, six minutes, hourly) runs from a stop on Dukelská, 400m north of the train station (turn left out of the station, then first right on Tyršova and first left) to the castle car park. Otherwise it's a 30-minute walk. Turn left out of the train station, go left across the bridge over the railway, and follow Konopištská street west for 2km.

KUTNÁ HORA

In the 14th century, the silver-rich ore under Kutná Hora gave the now-sleepy town an importance in Bohemia second only to Prague. The local mines and mint turned out silver *groschen* for use as the hard currency of central Europe. The silver ore ran out in 1726, leaving the medieval townscape largely unaltered. Now with several fascinating and unusual historical attractions, the Unesco World Heritage–listed town is a popular day trip from Prague.

Orientation & Information

Kutná Hora hlavní nádraží (the main train station) is 3km northeast of the Old Town centre. The bus station is more conveniently located on the Old Town's northeastern edge.

To visit Kutná Hora on a day trip, arrive on a morning train from Prague, then make the 10-minute walk from Kutná Hora hlavní nádraží to Sedlec Ossuary. From there it's another 2km walk or a five-minute bus ride into town. A bus leaves Prague Florenc at 8.10am for an early start.

CZECH REPUBLIC

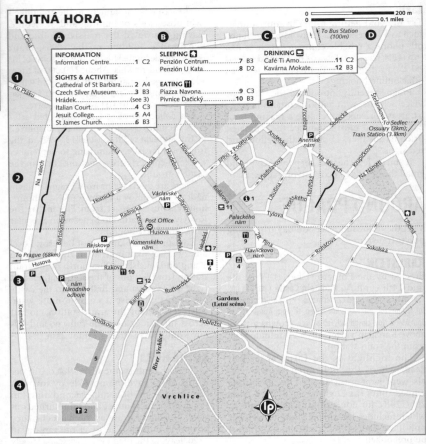

KUTNÁ HORA

0 ——— 200 m
0 ——— 0.1 miles

To Bus Station (100m)

INFORMATION
Information Centre..............**1** C2

SIGHTS & ACTIVITIES
Cathedral of St Barbara.......**2** A4
Czech Silver Museum.........**3** B3
Hrádek..........................(see 3)
Italian Court.....................**4** C3
Jesuit College..................**5** A4
St James Church..............**6** B3

SLEEPING 🛏
Penzión Centrum.............**7** B3
Penzión U Kata................**8** D2

EATING 🍴
Piazza Navona................**9** C3
Pivnice Dačický..............**10** B3

DRINKING 🍷
Café Ti Amo...................**11** C2
Kavárna Mokate.............**12** B3

To Sedlec Ossuary (3km); Train Station (3.8km)

To Prague (68km)

Gardens (Letní scéna)

Vrchlice

The **information centre** (☎ 327 512 378; www
.kutnahora.cz; Palackého nám 377; ☯ 9am-6pm Apr-Sep,
9am-5pm Mon-Fri, 10am-4pm Sat & Sun Oct-Mar) books
accommodation, provides internet access
(1Kč per minute), and rents bicycles (220Kč
per day).

In early June, the town hosts an **International
Music Festival** (www.mfkh.cz), with chamber-music
recitals in venues, including the soaring
Cathedral of St Barbara.

Sights

Walk 10-minutes south from Kutná Hora
hlavní nádraží to the remarkable **Sedlec
Ossuary** (Kostnice; ☎ 327 561 143; www.kostnice.cz;
adult/child 50/30Kč; ☯ 8am-6pm Apr-Sep, 9am-noon &
1-5pm Oct & Mar, 9am-noon & 1-4pm Nov-Mar). When

the Schwarzenberg family purchased Sedlec
monastery in 1870, a local woodcarver got
creative with the bones of 40,000 people
from the centuries-old crypt. Skulls and fe-
murs are strung from the vaulted ceiling,
and the central chandelier contains at least
one of each bone in the human body. Four
giant pyramids of stacked bones squat in the
corner chapels, and crosses of bone adorn
the altar.

From the Kutná Hora bus station catch
bus 1B and get off at the 'Tabak' stop. From
Sedlec it's another 2km walk (or five-minute
bus ride) to central Kutná Hora.

The Old Town lies south of **Palackého nám**,
the main square. From the square's western
end, Jakubská leads to **St James Church** (1330).

Further east is the **Italian Court** (Vlašský dvůr; ☎ 327 512 873; Havlíčkovo nám 552; adult/child 100/80Kč; ♘ 9am-6pm Apr-Sep, 10am-5pm Mar & Oct, 10am-4pm Nov-Feb), the former Royal Mint. Florentine craftsmen began stamping silver coins here in 1300. It houses a mint museum and a 15th-century **Audience Hall** with 19th-century murals depicting the election of Vladislav Jagiello as King of Bohemia in 1471 and the Decree of Kutná Hora being proclaimed by Wenceslas IV and Jan Hus in 1409.

From the southern side of St James Church, Ruthardská leads to the **Hrádek** (Little Castle), a 15th-century palace housing the **Czech Silver Museum** (České Muzeum Stříbra; ☎ 327 512 159; www .cms-kh.cz; adult/child 60/30Kč, English-speaking guide 400Kč; ♘ 10am-6pm Jul & Aug, 9am-6pm May, Jun & Sep, 9am-5pm Apr & Oct, 10am-4pm Sat & Sun Nov, closed Mon year-round). Don a miner's helmet to join the 1½-hour 'Way of Silver' tour (adult/child 110/70Kč) through 500m of medieval mine shafts beneath the town. Kids need to be at least seven for this tour. A combination ticket for the museum and the mine tour (adult/child 130/80Kč) is also available.

Beyond the Hrádek is a 17th-century former **Jesuit college**, with a terrace featuring 13 baroque sculptures of saints, inspired by those on Prague's Charles Bridge. The second one along of a woman holding a chalice is St Barbara, the patron saint of miners and Kutná Hora.

At the terrace's far end is the Gothic **Cathedral of St Barbara** (☎ 327 512 115; adult/child 50/30Kč; ♘ 9am-5.30pm Tue-Sun, 10am-4pm Mon May-Sep, 10am-4pm Oct-Apr). Rivalling Prague's St Vitus in magnificence, its soaring nave culminates in elegant, six-petalled ribbed vaulting. The ambulatory chapels preserve original 15th-century frescos, some showing miners at work. Outside there are fine views.

Sleeping

Penzión U Kata (☎ 327 515 096; www.ukata.cz; Uhelná 596; s/d/tr 500/760/1140Kč) You won't lose your head over the rates at this good-value family hotel called 'The Executioner'. Bikes can be rented for 200Kč per hour and it's a short stroll from the bus station.

Penzión Centrum (☎ 327 514 218; Jakubská 57; d incl breakfast 800Kč) A quiet, central location with snug rooms – what more could you want? How about pancakes and coffee in the grassy courtyard? Just around the corner are the best of Kutná Hora's galleries.

Eating & Drinking

Pivnice Dačický (☎ 327 512 248; Rakova 8; mains 90-240Kč) Try Kutná Hora's dark beer at this traditional beer hall. Rustle up three drinking buddies and order the Gamekeepers Reserve, a huge platter that demands at least a second beer. There are six different brews available, so try not to miss your bus back to Prague.

Piazza Navona (☎ 327 512 588; Palackého nám 90; mains 100-140Kč) Have authentic pizza by an authentic Italian on Kutná Hora's main square. Finish with gelati in summer and hot chocolate in winter.

Café Ti Amo (Kollárova 9; snacks 65-70Kč) This cosmopolitan cafe with outdoor tables, excellent coffee and wine is a popular meeting spot for locals. It's a couple of blocks from the main square tourist hubbub.

Kavárna Mokate (Baborská 7; coffee & cake 70-80Kč; ♘ 8.30am-9.30pm Mon-Thu, 9am-midnight Fri & Sat, noon-7pm Sun) It's not just good coffee at this place with rustic tiled floors, and mismatched furniture from your last student flat. A global array of teas complements yummy cakes.

Getting There & Away

There are direct trains from Prague's hlavní nádraží to Kutná Hora hlavní nádraží (98Kč, 55 minutes, seven daily).

Buses to Kutná Hora from Prague (62Kč, 1¼ hours, hourly) depart Florenc bus station; services are less frequent at weekends.

BOHEMIA

The ancient land of Bohemia makes up the western two-thirds of the Czech Republic. The modern term 'bohemian' comes to us via the French, who thought that Roma came from Bohemia; the word *bohémien* was later applied to people living an unconventional lifestyle. The term gained currency in the wake of Puccini's opera *La Bohème* about poverty-stricken artists in Paris.

TEREZÍN

The massive fortress at Terezín (Theresenstadt in German) was built by the Habsburgs in the 18th century to repel the Prussian army, but the place is better known as a notorious WWII prison and concentration camp. Around 150,000 men, women and children, mostly Jews, passed through en route to the extermination camps of Auschwitz-Birkenau: 35,000 of them died here of hunger, disease or suicide, and only 4000 survived. From 1945 to 1948 the fortress served as an internment camp for the Sudeten Germans, who were expelled from Czechoslovakia after the war.

Ironically, Terezín played a tragic role in deceiving the world of the ultimate goals of the Nazi's 'Final Solution'. Official visitors were immersed in a charade, with Terezín being presented as a Jewish 'refuge', complete with shops, schools and cultural organisations – even an autonomous Jewish 'government'. As late as April 1945, Red Cross visitors espoused positive reports.

The **Terezín Memorial** (☎ 416 782 225; www .pamatnik-terezin.cz) consists of the Museum of the Ghetto in the Main Fortress, and the Lesser Fortress, a 10-minute walk east across the Ohře River. Admission to one part costs 160/130Kč; a combined ticket is 200/150Kč. At the ticket office, ask about historical films in the museum's cinema.

The **Museum of the Ghetto** (Muzeum ghetta; 9am-6pm Apr-Oct, to 5.30pm Nov-Mar) records daily life in the camp during WWII, through moving displays of paintings, letters and personal possessions. Entry to the Museum of the Ghetto includes entry to the Magdeburg Barracks and vice versa.

Around 32,000 prisoners, many of them Czech partisans, were incarcerated in the **Lesser Fortress** (Malá pevnost; 8am-6pm Apr-Oct, to 4.30pm Nov-Mar). Take the grimly fascinating self-guided tour through the prison barracks, workshops, morgues and mass graves, before arriving at the bleak execution grounds where more than 250 prisoners were shot.

At the **Magdeburg Barracks** (Magdeburská kasárna; cnr Tyršova & Vodárenská; 9am- 6pm Apr-Oct, to 5.30pm Nov-Mar), the former base of the Jewish 'government', are exhibits on the rich cultural life – music, theatre, fine arts and literature – that flourished against this backdrop of fear. Most poignant are the copies of *Vedem* ('In the Lead') magazine, published by 100 boys from 1942 to 1944. Only 15 of the boys survived the war.

Terezín is northwest of Prague and 3km south of Litoměřice. Buses between Prague and Litoměřice stop at both the main square and the Lesser Fortress. There are frequent buses between Litoměřice bus station and Terezín (10Kč, 10 minutes). Many Prague tour companies offer day trips to Terezín.

LITOMĚŘICE
pop 25,100

Founded by German colonists in the 13th century, Litoměřice prospered in the 18th century as a royal seat and bishopric. The town centre features picturesque buildings and churches, some designed by the locally born baroque architect Ottavio Broggio.

The Old Town lies across the road to the west of the train and bus stations, guarded by the remnants of the 14th-century town walls. Walk along Dlouhá to the central square, Mírové nám.

The **information centre** (☎ 416 732 440; www .litomerice.cz; Mírové nám 15/7; 8am-6pm Mon-Sat, 9.30am-4pm Sun May-Sep, 8am-4pm Mon-Fri, 8-11am Sat Oct-Apr) in the town hall books accommodation and runs **walking tours** (adult/child 60/40Kč; 9am-4.30pm Mon-Sat, 9.30am-3.30pm Sun, May-Sep, 8.30am-3.30pm Mon-Fri Apr & Oct).

Internet Club Centrum (1st Flor, Mírové nám 25; noon-midnight Mon-Sat, 2-8pm Sun) is down an arcade opposite the information centre.

Sights

The main square is lined with Gothic arcades and facades dominated by the tower of **All Saints Church**, the step-gabled **Old Town Hall** and the distinctive **House at the Chalice** (Dům U Kalicha), housing the present town hall. Sprouting from the roof is a copper chalice, the traditional symbol of the Hussite church. The slim baroque facade at the square's elevated end is the **House of Ottavio Broggio**.

Along Michalská on the square's southwest corner is another Broggio design, the **North Bohemia Fine Arts Gallery** (☎ 416 732 382; Michalská 7; adult/child 32/18Kč; 9am-noon & 1-6pm Tue-Sun Apr-Sep, 9am-noon & 1-5pm Oct-Mar) with the priceless Renaissance panels of the Litoměřice Altarpiece.

Turn left on Michalská and follow Domská to Domské nám on Cathedral Hill, passing the baroque **St Wenceslas Church**, on a side street to the right. Atop the hill is the town's oldest church, the 11th-century **St Stephen Cathedral**.

Follow the arch on the cathedral's left and descend down steep and cobbled Máchova. At the foot of the hill turn left then first right, up the zigzag steps to the **Old Town walls**. Follow the walls right to the next street, Jezuitská, then turn left back to the square.

Sleeping

Autocamp Slavoj (☎ 416 734 481; kemp.litomerice@post
.cz; per tent/bungalow 80/220Kč; ☺ May-Sep; ☐)
South of the train station is this rudimentary camping ground on Střelecký ostrov
(Marksmen Island).

U Svatého Václava (☎ 416 737 500; www.upfront
.cz/penzion; Svatovaclavská 12; s/d incl breakfast 700/1200Kč)
Beside St Wenceslas Church, this popu-
lar haven has well-equipped rooms, hearty
cooked breakfasts, and owners whose English
is better than they think.

Pension Prislin (☎ 416 735 833; www.prislin.cz; Na
Kocandě 12; s/d/tr/q incl breakfast 750/1260/1570/1880Kč)
Pension Prislin has a friendly dog called
Baltimore and a switched-on owner who's dec-
orated his pension in bright colours. The spa-
cious apartments take up to five travellers.

Hotel Salva Guarda (☎ 416 732 506; www.salva
-garda.cz; Mírové nám 12; s/d 1220/1750Kč) With old
maps in reception, it's a shame they keep the
lights so low. However, the spotless rooms
are well lit in this classy hotel that's housed
in a *sgraffito* building from 1566. Breakfast
is 140Kč.

Eating

U Štěpána Pizzeria (☎ 728 928 804, Dlouhá 43;
pizza 45-145Kč) At the downhill end of the
square, this spot has a monk as a logo, but
there's definitely nothing frugal about the
pizza toppings.

Music Club Viva (☎ 606 437 783; Mezibrani; mains
100-235Kč) Shared wooden tables ensures conversation flows as naturally as the drinks in
this hip spot in the Old Town bastion.

Radniční sklípek (☎ 416 731 142; Mírové nám 21;
mains 110-250Kč) Keep your head down in this underground labyrinth that does great grills accompanied by a good wine list. In summer, the
meaty action spills onto the main square.

Gurmănie (☎ 416 532 305; Novobranská 14; mains
110-250Kč; ☺ 9am-5pm Mon-Fri, 9am-3pm Sat) At the
top end of the square, Gurmănie has tasty
ciabatta sandwiches for on-the-go dining,
and salads and pasta. Say *ahoj* to Litoměřice's
best coffee.

Pekárna Kodys & Hamele (Novobranská 18) has all
your favourite baked goodies in one place.

Getting There & Away

Direct buses from Prague to Litoměřice (75Kč,
one hour, hourly) depart from station 17 at
Florenc bus station (final destination Ústí
nad Labem).

BOHEMIAN SWITZERLAND NATIONAL PARK

The main road and rail route between Prague
and Dresden follows the fast-flowing Labe
(Elbe) River, gouging a sinuous, steep-sided
valley through a sandstone plateau on the
border between the Czech Republic and
Germany. The landscape of sandstone pinnacles, giddy gorges, dark forests and high meadows is the Bohemian Switzerland National
Park (Národní park České Švýcarsko), named
after two 19th-century Swiss artists who
settled here.

Sights & Activities

Just south of the German border, **Hřensko**
is a cute village of half-timbered houses
crammed into a sandstone gorge where the
Kamenice River joins the Labe. It's overrun with German day trippers on summer
weekends, but upstream peaceful hiking
trails begin.

A signposted 16km (five to six hours) circular hike explores the main sights. From
Hřensko's eastern end a trail leads via ledges,
walkways and tunnels through the mossy
chasms of the **Kamenice River Gorge**.

Two sections — **Edmundova Soutěska**
(Edmund's Gorge; ☺ 9am-6pm May-Aug, Sat & Sun only
Apr, Sep & Oct) and **Divoká Soutěska** (Savage Gorge;
☺ 9am-5pm May-Aug, Sat & Sun only Apr, Sep & Oct) —
have been dammed. Continue by punt and
a ferryman through a canyon 5m wide
and 50m to 150m deep. Each ferry trip
costs 60/30Kč per adult/child.

The **Hřensko information office** (☎ 414 554 286;
www.ceskosaske-svycarsko.cz; ☺ 9am-6pm Apr-Oct) on
the road from Děčín organises canoeing trips
(per person €20).

A kilometre beyond the end of the second
boat trip, a blue-marked trail leads uphill to
the Hotel Mezní Louka. Across the road, a red-
marked trail continues through the forest to
the spectacular rock formation **Pravčická Brána**
(www.pbrana.cz; adult/child 75/25Kč; ☺ 10am-6pm Apr-Oct,
to 4pm Sat & Sun Nov-Mar), the largest natural arch in
Europe. Crouched beneath is the **Falcon's Nest**, a
19th-century chateau housing a national park
museum and restaurant. From here the red
trail descends westward back to Hřensko.

The area is also popular with climbers.
Ask at the Hřensko information office about
climbing day trips, and hire gear from **Hudy
Sport** (☺ 9am-5.30pm) around 400m up the
Kamenice River Gorge road.

Sleeping & Eating

Pension Lugano (☎ 412 554 146; www.hrensko-lugano
.cz; Hřensko; s/d incl breakfast 500/1000Kč) A cheerful
place in the centre of Hřensko serving terrific
breakfasts at a riverside restaurant.

In the hills, **Hotel Mezní Louka** (☎ 412 554 220;
www.mezni-louka.cz; Mezní Louka 71; s/d 900/1450Kč) is
a 19th-century hiking lodge with a decent
restaurant (mains 90Kč to 170Kč). Across the
road is **Camp Mezní Louka** (☎ 412 554 084; r.kolarova@
npcs.cz; camp sites per tent/bungalow 110/510Kč).

With your own car, base yourself in either
Janov or Jetřichovice. In Janov **Pension Pastis**
(☎ 142 554 037; www.pastis.cz; Janov 22; s/d incl breakfast
540/1080Kč; ☐) has an excellent restaurant; in
Jetřichovice try **Pension Dřevák** (☎ 412 555 015; s/d
incl breakfast 700/1050Kč), housed in a 19th-century
wooden building. Bookings can be made at
www.ceskosaske-svycarsko.cz.

Getting There & Away

From Prague, take a bus from Florenc (120Kč,
1¾ hours, five daily) to Děčín, then another to
Hřensko (18Kč, 25 minutes, four daily).

Alternatively, catch a Dresden-bound train
and get off at Bad Schandau (280Kč, two hours,
eight daily), in Germany, and then a local train
back to Schöna (€1.80, 12 minutes, every half-
hour) on the German bank of the river opposite Hřensko. From the station, a ferry (20Kč,
three minutes, from 6am to 10pm April to
September and from 8am to 6pm October to
March) crosses to Hřensko on demand.

On weekdays there are three buses a day
(year-round) between Hřensko and Mezní
Louka (8Kč, 10 minutes), and two a day at weekends (July to September only). In summer, keep
an eye out for the big red **Nationalpark Express**, a
heritage double-decker bus that crosses over
from Germany and provides regular transport
to Pravčická Brána and Mezní Louka.

If you're heading on to Germany, either do
the river crossing to Schöna described above
and catch a local train to Bad Schandau,
or catch a local bus from Hřensko back to
Děčín and then catch a direct train to Dresden
(110Kč, 50 minutes, 10 daily). Most of these
trains also carry on to Berlin or Hamburg.
See ww.idos.cz.

KARLOVY VARY
pop 60,000

According to legend, Emperor Charles IV
discovered Karlovy Vary's hot springs ac-
cidentally in 1350 when one of his hunting

dogs fell into the waters. Now the fashionable
town is the closest the Czech Republic has to a
glam resort, but Karlovy Vary is definitely glam
with a small 'g'. Well-heeled hypochondriacs
from Germany, Austria and (especially) Russia
make the pilgrimage for courses of lymphatic
drainage, hydrocolonotherapy, and other
treatments that sound more like weapons of
mass destruction. Preferred form is to sip on
the mineral-laden waters from a dainty porcelain cup, but the caffeine-laden offerings from
the town's cafes are actually much tastier.

The **Karlovy Vary International Film Festival** in
early July is well worth attending. More than
200 films are shown, tickets are easy to get, and
a funky array of concurrent events, including
buskers and world-music concerts, gives the
genteel town an annual energy transfusion. It's
also your chance to spy international visitors
such as Robert De Niro and John Malkovich.

Orientation

Karlovy Vary has two train stations: Dolní
nádraží (Lower Station), beside the main bus
station, and Horní nádraží (Upper Station),
across the Ohře River the the north.

Trains from Prague arrive at Horní nádraží.
Take bus 11, 12 or 13 (12Kč) from across the
road to the Tržnice station; 11 continues to
Divadelni nám in the spa district.

Alternatively, it's 10 minutes on foot: cross
the road outside the station and go right,
then first left on a path that leads downhill
under the highway. At its foot, turn right on
U Spořitelny, then left at the far end of the
big building and head for the river bridge.

The Tržnice bus stop is three blocks east
of Dolní nádraží, in the middle of the town's
modern commercial district. Pedestrianised
TG Masaryka leads east to the Teplá River;
from here the old spa district stretches
upstream for 2km along a steep-sided valley.

Information

Infocentrum Dolní nádraží (☎ 353 232 838; www
.karlovyvary.cz; Západni; ☼ 9am-5pm Mon-Fri, 10am-
4pm Sat & Sun); Lázeňska (☎ 353 224 097; Lázeňska
1; ☼ 10am-6pm Mon-Fri, to 5pm Sat & Sun) Loads of
information on the town, plus maps, accommodation help
and pricey internet (per minute 2Kč).
Main post office (TG Masaryka 1)
Moonstorm Internet (TG Masaryka 31; per min 1Kč;
☼ 9am-9pm)

There's free wi-fi at Kino Panasonic (p299).

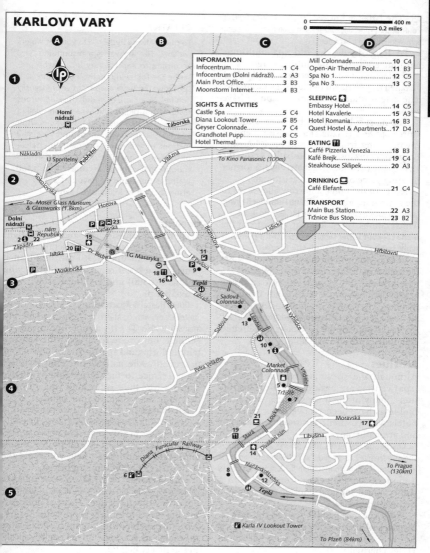

KARLOVY VARY

INFORMATION	
Infocentrum	1 C4
Infocentrum (Dolní nádraží)	2 A3
Main Post Office	3 B3
Moonstorm Internet	4 B3

SIGHTS & ACTIVITIES	
Castle Spa	5 C4
Diana Lookout Tower	6 B5
Geyser Colonnade	7 C4
Grandhotel Pupp	8 C5
Hotel Thermal	9 B3

Mill Colonnade	10 C4
Open-Air Thermal Pool	11 B3
Spa No 1	12 C5
Spa No 3	13 C3

SLEEPING ⌂	
Embassy Hotel	14 C5
Hotel Kavalerie	15 A3
Hotel Romania	16 B3
Quest Hostel & Apartments	17 D4

EATING 🍴	
Caffé Pizzeria Venezia	18 B3
Kafé Brejk	19 C4
Steakhouse Sklipek	20 A3

DRINKING 🍷	
Café Elefant	21 C4

TRANSPORT	
Main Bus Station	22 A3
Tržnice Bus Stop	23 B2

Sights

At the central spa district is the neoclassi-cal **Mill Colonnade** (Mlýnská Kolonáda), with occasional summer concerts. Other elegant colonnades and 19th-century spa buildings are scattered along the Teplá River, with the 1970s concrete **Hotel Thermal** spoiling the effect slightly.

Purchase a *lázenské pohár* (spa cup) and some *oplátky* (spa wafers; p298) and sample the various hot springs (free). Infocentrum has a leaflet describing the 12 springs in the 'drinking cure', ranging from the **Rock Spring** (Skalní Pramen), which dribbles just 1.3L per minute, to the robust **Geyser** (Vřídlo), which spurts 2000L per minute in a 14m-high

CZECH REPUBLIC

jet. The latter is housed in the 1970s **Geyser Colonnade** (Vřídelní Kolonáda; admission free; 🕑 10am-6pm Mon-Fri, to 4pm Sat & Sun).

To look inside the old spa buildings without enduring the dubious rigours of *proktologie* and *endoskopie*, nip into **Spa No 3** (Lázně III) just north of the Mill Colonnade. The cafe upstairs is a good reason to have a look.

The most splendid spa building is the restored **Spa No 1** (Lázně I) at the south end of town, dating from 1895 and once housing Emperor Franz Josef's private baths. Across the river is the baroque **Grandhotel Pupp**, a former meeting place of European aristocrats.

North of the hotel, a narrow alley leads to the bottom station of the **Diana Funicular Railway** (adult one-way/return 36/60Kč; child 18/30Kč; 🕑 9am-6pm), which climbs 166m to great views from the **Diana Lookout Tower** (admission free). It's a pleasant walk back down through the forest.

Just out of town, the newly expanded **Moser Glass Museum** (Sklářské muzeum Moser; ☎ 353 416 242; www.moser-glass.com; Kpt Jaroše 19; adult/child 80/50Kč; 🕑 9am-5pm) has more than 2000 items on display. Afterwards get hot under the collar at the adjacent **glassworks** (adult/child 120/70Kč; 🕑 9am-2.30pm). Combined tickets (adult/child 180/100Kč) are also available.

Activities

Although the surviving traditional *lázně* (spa) centres are basically medical institutions, many of the town's old spa and hotel buildings have been renovated as 'wellness' hotels with cosmetic treatments, massages and aromatherapy.

Castle Spa (Zámecké Lázně; ☎ 353 222 649; http://english.edenhotels.cz; Zámechý vrch; treatments from €25; 🕑 7.30am-7.30pm Mon-Fri, from 8.30am Sat & Sun) is a modernised spa centre, complete with a subterranean thermal pool. It still retains a heritage ambience.

For a cheaper paddle head to the **open-air thermal pool** (per hr 80Kč; 🕑 8am-8pm Mon-Sat, to 9pm Sun). Follow the 'Bazén' signs up the hill behind Hotel Thermal.

Festivals & Events

Karlovy Vary International Film Festival (www.kviff.com) Early July.
International Student Film Festival (www.freshfilmfest.net) Late August.
Karlovy Vary Folklore Festival Early September.
Dvořák Autumn September; classical music festival.

OPLÁTKY

To quote Monty Python: 'Do you get wafers with it?' The answer is a resounding 'yes' according to Karlovy Vary locals, who prescribe the following method of taking your spring water: have a sip from your *lázenský pohárek* (spa cup), then dull the sulphurous taste with a big, round sweet wafer called *oplátky*. *Oplátkly* are sold for 10Kč each at spa hotels, speciality shops and at a stall in front of the Hotel Thermal. Steer clear of the fancy chocolate or hazelnut flavours though; they're never as crunchily fresh and warm as the standard flavour. *Oplátkly* are also a big hit in Mariánské Lázně.

Sleeping

Accommodation is pricey, and can be tight during weekends and festivals; definitely book ahead. Infocentrum (p296) can find hostel, pension and hotel rooms. Consider staying in Loket (p300) and visiting Karlovy Vary as a day trip.

Quest Hostel & Apartments (☎ 353 820 030; www.hostel-karlovy-vary.cz; Moravská 44; dm from 410Kč, s/tw from 845/1090Kč; 🖳) It's a long uphill walk to get here, but you're rewarded with well-run budget dorms and apartments with two, four or six beds. Alternatively catch bus 8 (12Kč) from Tržnice to the Černý Kůn stop (five stops). Cross the road behind you and walk down the steps 100m to your right.

Hotel Kavalerie (☎ 353 229 613; www.kavalerie.cz; TG Masaryka 43; s/d incl breakfast from 950/1225Kč) Friendly staff abound in this cosy spot above a cafe. It's located near the bus and train stations, and nearby eateries can help you avoid the spa district's high restaurant prices.

Hotel Romania (☎ 353 222 822; www.romania.cz; Zahradni 49; s/d incl breakfast 1950/1650Kč) Don't be put off by the ugly Hotel Thermal dominating the views from this good-value, reader-recommended spot. Just squint a little, because the rooms are spacious and the English-speaking staff very helpful.

Embassy Hotel (☎ 353 221 161; www.embassy.cz; Nová Luka 21; s/d incl breakfast from 2260/3130Kč; 🖳) KV's not short of top-end hotels, but most lack the personal touch inherent in the Embassy's family-owned combination of a riverside location and perfectly pitched heritage rooms. Downstairs the Embassy Pub has seen visits from a DVD store full of Film Fest luminaries.

Eating & Drinking

Caffé Pizzeria Venezia (☎ 353 229 721; Zahradní 43; pizza 95-120Kč) After an espresso and pizza, blur your eyes through your designer sunnies and see if you can spot any gondoliers from this pretty-in-pink spot looking out on the Teplá River.

Steakhouse Sklipek (☎ 353 229 197; Zeyerova 1; meals 140-180Kč) Red-checked tablecloths and an emphasis on good steaks, fish and pasta give this place an honest, rustic ambience missing from the more expensive chichi spots down the hill in the spa district.

Also recommended:

Café Elefant (☎ 353 223 406; Stará Louka 30; coffee 50Kč) Classy old-school spot for coffee and cake. A tad touristy, but still elegant and refined.

Kafé Brejk (Stará Louka 62; coffee 45Kč; baguettes 60Kč; 🕘 9am-5pm) Trendy new-school spot for takeaway coffees and design-your-own baguettes.

Entertainment

Kino Panasonic (☎ 353 233 933; www.kinopanasonic.cz; Vítězná 48; 🖳) This compact art-house cinema showcases Karlovy Vary's film-festival credentials year-round. The coffee's good, and there's free wi-fi access.

Getting There & Around

Student Agency (www.studentagency.cz) and **Megabus** (www.megabus.cz) run frequent buses to/from Prague Florenc (130Kč, 2¼ hours, eight daily) departing from the main bus station beside Dolní nádraží train station. There are direct buses to Plzeň (84Kč, 1½ hours, hourly).

There are direct (but slow) trains from Karlovy Vary to Prague Holešovice (288Kč, three hours). Heading west from Karlovy Vary to Nuremberg, Germany (4½ hours, two a day), and beyond, you'll have to change at Cheb (Eger in German). Check online at www.idos.cz and www.bahn.de.

Buses to/from Loket, a recommended base for visiting Karlovy Vary, run throughout the day (26Kč, 20 minutes).

LOKET

Nestled in a bend of the Ohře River, Loket is a gorgeous little place that's attracted many famous visitors from nearby Karlovy Vary. A plaque on the facade of the Hostinec Bílý Kůň on the chocolate-box town square commemorates Goethe's seven visits. Loket even scored a cameo role in the 2006 James Bond movie, *Casino Royale*.

Most people visit Loket as a day trip from Karlovy Vary, but it's also a sleepy place to ease off the travel accelerator for a few days, especially when the day trippers have all departed. Loket also makes a good base for visiting Karlovy Vary.

The bus arriving from Karlovy Vary stops across the bridge from the Old Town. Walk across the bridge to reach the castle, accommodation and **Infocentrum** (☎ 352 684 123; www.loket.cz; TG Masaryka 12; 🕘 10.30am-5pm). The Hrnčírna Galerie Café (see p300) has internet access.

In the second half of July, the annual **Loket Summer Cultural Festival** (www.loketfestival.info) features classical music and opera on an outdoor stage near the river with the castle as a dramatic backdrop.

WORTH THE TRIP: MARIÁNSKÉ LÁZNĚ & CHODOVÁ PLANÁ

For a more relaxed Bohemian spa experience than bustling Karlovy Vary, consider Mariánské Lázně. Perched at the southern edge of the Slavkov Forest (Slavkovský Les), the spa town formerly known as Marienbad drew luminaries such as Goethe, Thomas Edison and King Edward VII. Even old misery-guts Franz Kafka was a regular visitor, enjoying the pure waters and getting active on the walking trails that criss-cross the rolling forest. In contemporary times the appeal of spa services, heritage hotels and gentle exercise is complemented by a busy summertime cultural program, including mid-August's **Chopin Music Festival** (www.chopinfestival.cz). You can also catch a local bus (18Kč, 20 minutes) to nearby Chodová Planá and bath in giant hoppy tubs of lager in the Czech Republic's only **beer spa** (www.chodovar.cz).

From Prague, Mariánské Lázně can be reached by train (390Kč, five hours) via Cheb from Prague's main train station (Praha-hlavní nádraží). Buses (160Kč, three hours) run from platform 18 at Prague's Florenc bus station. There are also trains (98Kč, 1½ hours, eight per day) and buses (69Kč, one hour, four daily) to/from Plzeň. From the adjacent bus and train stations at the southern end of Mariánské Lázně, catch trolleybus 5 to the spa area's main bus stop. The **information office** (www.marianskelazne.cz) is 200m uphill on the left.

CZECH REPUBLIC

Sights & Activities

Perched above the river, the **castle** (☎ 352 684 104; adult/child with English guide 90/60Kč, with English text 80/45Kč; ◷ 9am-4.30pm Apr-Oct, to 3.30pm Nov-Mar) has a museum dedicated to locally produced porcelain. The nearby **Black Gate Tower** (Černá Věž; TG Masaryka; admission 20Kč; ◷ 11am-5pm Jul & Aug, Fri-Sun only May, Jun & Sep) provides great views.

Ask at Infocentrum about short walks in the surrounding forests. You can also walk from Karlovy Vary to Loket along a 17km (three hours) blue-marked trail, starting at the Diana lookout (p298).

Karlovy Vary is the destination for one-day rafting trips along the Ohře River with either **Dronte** (☎ 274 779 828; www.dronte.cz) or **Petr Putzer** (☎ 606 902 310; www.putzer.cz). Rafting on the Ohře is a quieter alternative to Český Krumlov and the Vltava River. Costs including transport are around 1200Kč per person. Ask at Infocentrum.

Sleeping & Eating

Lazy River Hostel (☎ 352 684 587; www.lazyriverhostel .com; Kostelní 61; dm/d/tr 300/750/1125Kč) Friendly expat owner Doug is a long-term Loket resident, and his new, more spacious digs for Lazy River have a heritage ambience with ancient wooden floors and Old Town views. He's got a castle-full of ideas for day trips, so look forward to staying longer than planned.

Penzion Ve Skalé (☎ 352 624 936; www.penzion veskale.cz; Nádražní 232; 61; s/d 650/1200Kč) Spacious and romantic rooms feature at this new pension just up the hill from the train station. You're forgoing an Old Town location, but the excellent-value rooms more than compensate. Discounts kick in on your second night.

Pizzeria na Růžka (☎ 606 433 282; cnr TG Masaryka & Kostelní; pizza 130Kč) Has a sunny Mediterranean ambience and excellent thin-crust wood-fired pizzas.

Hrnčírna Galerie Café (☎ 352 684 459; TG Masaryka 32; ◷ 2pm-6pm Mon-Fri, 10am-6pm Sat & Sun; 🖳) This funky main-square cafe conceals an art space for local artists and a cosy garden. Loket's best coffee and internet access comes as standard.

Pivovar Sv Florian (☎ 352 225 959; TG Masaryka 81) In the basement of the restored Hotel Císař Ferdinand, a few enthusiastic locals brew what could be Bohemia's best beer. Well, that's according to in-depth research by one guidebook writer anyway.

Getting There & Away

Buses run frequently from Karlovy Vary to Loket (26Kč, 20 minutes).

PLZEŇ

pop 175,000

Plzeň (Pilsen in German) is the hometown of Pilsner Urquell (Plzeňský prazdroj), the world's original lager beer. 'Urquell' (in German; *prazdroj* in Czech) means 'original source' or 'fountainhead', and the local style is now imitated across the world.

Pilsner Urquell is now owned by international conglomerate SAB-Miller, and some beer buffs claim the brew's not as good as before. One taste of the town's tasty *nefiltrované pivo* (unfiltered beer) will have you disputing that claim, and the original brewery is still an essential stop for beer aficionados.

The capital of West Bohemia is a sprawling industrial city, but has an attractive Old Town wrapped in tree-lined gardens. Plzeň's industrial heritage includes the massive Škoda Engineering Works. These armament factories were bombed heavily during WWII and now make machinery and locomotives.

Plzeň is an easy day trip from Prague, but the buzzing pubs of this university town also reward an overnight stay.

Orientation

The main bus station is west of the centre on Husova. Plzeň-hlavní nádraží, the main train station, is on the eastern side of town, 10 minutes' walk from nám Republiky, the Old Town square. Tram 2 (12Kč) goes from the train station through the centre of town and on to the bus station.

Information

There are left-luggage facilities at the **bus station** (per small/large bag 15Kč/25Kč; ◷ 6am-8pm) and the **train station** (per small/large bag 12/23Kč; ◷ 7am-7pm). Lockers at the train station are 30Kč per 2 hours.

City Information Centre (www.plzen.eu) nám Republik (městské informační středisko; ☎ 378 035 330; nám Republiky 41; ◷ 9am-6pm); train station (☎ 972 524 313; ◷ 9am-7pm Apr-Sep, to 6pm Oct-Mar) Arranges accommodation.

Main post office (Solní 20)

Matrix Internet (Sedláčkova, per hr 40Kč; ◷ 8.30am-8pm Mon-Thu, 10am-8pm Fri, noon-10pm Sat & Sun) Down the arcade beside Oberbank.

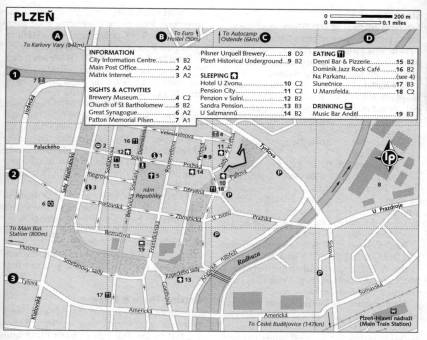

PLZEŇ

0   200 m
0   0.1 miles

INFORMATION
City Information Centre..........**1** B2
Main Post Office....................**2** A2
Matrix Internet.....................**3** A2

SIGHTS & ACTIVITIES
Brewery Museum....................**4** C2
Church of St Bartholomew.....**5** B2
Great Synagogue...................**6** A2
Patton Memorial Pilsen...........**7** A1

Pilsner Urquell Brewery...........**8** D2
Plzeň Historical Underground....**9** B2

SLEEPING
Hotel U Zvonu......................**10** C2
Pension City.........................**11** C2
Penzion v Solní.....................**12** B2
Sandra Pension.....................**13** B3
U Salzmannů.........................**14** B2

EATING
Denní Bar & Pizzerie..............**15** B2
Dominik Jazz Rock Café..........**16** B2
Na Parkanu.........................(see 4)
Slunečnice...........................**17** B3
U Mansfelda........................**18** C2

DRINKING
Music Bar Anděl....................**19** B3

To Karlovy Vary (84km)
To Euro Hostel (50m)
To Autocamp Ostende (6km)
Palackého
Veleslavínova
Jiráska
Sedláčkova
Riegrova
Bedřicha Smetany
Presovska
Zbrojnická
Bezručova
Františkánská
Smetanovy sady
Kopeckého sady
Anglické nábřeží
Americká
Tylova
Klatovská
Husova
To Main Bus Station (800m)
Dřevěná
nám Republiky
Pražská
Perlová
Sady 5. května
Tyršova
Pallova
U zvonu
Pražská
Radbuza
Šírková
Šumavská
U Prazdroje
To České Budějovice (147km)
To Karlovy Vary
Americká
Plzeň-Hlavní nádraží
(Main Train Station)

Sights

In summer people congregate at the outdoor beer bar in nám Republiky, the sunny Old Town square, beneath the Gothic **Church of St Bartholomew** (adult/child 20/10Kč; 10am-6pm Wed-Sat Apr-Sep, to 6pm Wed-Fri Oct-Dec). Inside the 13th-century structure there's a Gothic *Madonna* (1390) on the high altar and fine stained-glass windows. Climb the 102m church **tower** (adult/child 30/10Kč; 10am-6pm, weather dependent), the highest in Bohemia, for great views of Plzeň's rugged sprawl. Ask at the city information centre about guided tours of the church.

The **Brewery Museum** (☎ 377 235 574; www.prazdroj.cz; Veleslavínova 6; guided tour adult/child 120/100Kč, with text 100/60Kč; 10am-6pm Apr-Dec, to 5pm Jan-Mar) is in a medieval malt house. A combined entry (adult/child 250/130Kč) including the Pilsner Urquell Brewery is also available.

In previous centuries beer was brewed, stored, and served in the tunnels beneath the Old Town. The earliest were dug in the 14th century and the latest date from the 19th century. Take a 30-minute guided tour through 500m of tunnels at the **Plzeň Historical Underground** (☎ 377 225 214; Perlová 4; adult/child 55/35Kč; 9am-5pm Tue-Sun Jul-Sep, Wed-Sun Apr-Jun, Oct & Nov). The temperature is a chilly 10°C, so wrap up and bring a torch (flashlight).

The **Great Synagogue** (☎ 377 223 346; Sady Pětatřicátníků 11; adult/child 55/35Kč; 10am-6pm Mon-Sun Apr-Oct), west of the Old Town, is the third-largest in the world – only those in Jerusalem and Budapest are bigger. It was built in the Moorish style in 1892 by the 2000 Jews who lived in Plzeň at the time. English guides cost 50Kč extra. The building is often used for concerts and art and photography exhibitions.

North of the Great Synagogue is the **Patton Memorial Pilsen** (☎ 377 320 414; Podřežni 10; adult/child 45/30Kč; 9am-1pm & 2-5pm Tue-Sun), with an interesting and poignant display on the liberation of Plzeň in 1945 by the American army under General George Patton. Look for the jeep parked outside.

Beer fans should make the pilgrimage east across the river to the famous **Pilsner Urquell Brewery** (☎ 377 062 888; www.prazdroj.cz; guided tour adult/child 150/80Kč; 10am-6pm). A combined entry (adult/child 250/130Kč) including the Brewery Museum is also available.

Sleeping

Autocamp Ostende (☎ 377 520 194; www.ostende-web node.cz; per tent/bungalow per person 100/300Kč; ☒ May-Sep) On Velký Bolevecký rybník, a lake about 6km north of the city centre, and accessible by bus 20 from near the train station.

Euro Hostel (☎ 377 373 729; www.eurohostel.cz; Na Roudne 1; dm €14, s/d/tr €39/39/57) Housed in a grand old corner building 400m from Plzeň's Old Town. It's pretty basic and lacking in atmosphere, but the location is good. Walk north on Rooseveltova across the river and veer right on Luční.

U Salzmannů (☎ 377 235 855; www.usalzmannu .cz; Pražská 8; s 550-1350Kč, d 700-1900Kč) Right above one of Plzeň's most historic pubs is a range of rooms from budget to midrange. Should you go for the cheaper rooms to have more to spend downstairs on the beer and hearty food? Decisions, decisions.

Penzion v Solní (☎ 377 236 652; www.volny.cz/pension solni; Solní 8; s/d 600/1020Kč) The best deal in town is this friendly spot sandwiched between a butcher and a clothes shop. With only three rooms, it's essential to book ahead.

Sandra Pension (☎ 377 325 358; sandra.101@seznam .cz; Kopeckého sady 15; s/d incl breakfast 990/1260Kč) This pension has three clean rooms above a friendly parkside restaurant with off-street parking. Family rooms for four people are 2200Kč.

Pension City (☎ 377 326 069; www.pensioncityplzen .cz; Sady 5 kvetna 52; s/d incl breakfast 1050/1450Kč) On a quiet street near the river, the City is popular with both local and overseas guests. The welcoming English-speaking staff are a good source of local information.

Hotel U Zvonu (☎ 378 011 855; www.hotel-uzvonu .cz; Pražská 27; s/d 1850/2710Kč; ⌨) Owned by Czech ice-hockey legend Martin Straka, the four-star U Zvonu is at the edge of the Old Town and has modern rooms and facilities galore for business travellers. The flash 'Apartment 31' (3950Kč) is decorated with memorabilia from the owner's 18 seasons in the NHL.

Eating & Drinking

Na Parkanu (Veleslavínova 4; mains 100-150Kč) Attached to the Brewery Museum, Na Parkanu lures a mix of tourists and locals with good-value meals and a summer garden. Don't leave without trying the *nefiltrovaně pivo* (unfiltered beer). It's not our fault if you stay for another.

U Mansfelda (☎ 37 333 844; cnr Dřevěna & Křížíkovy sady; mains 110-160Kč) Sure, it's a pub – remember

you're in Plzeň now – but it's also more refined and with more interesting food than other places. Try Czech cuisine like wild boar *guláš* (spicy meat and potato soup).

Denní Bar & Pizzerie (☎ 377 237 965; Solní 9; pizza 110Kč) Come for the interesting photographs of old Plzeň and stay for the pizza and pasta in this restaurant just off the main square.

Dominik Jazz Rock Café (☎ 377 323 226; Dominikánská 3; mains 120Kč; ☒ 10am-11pm Mon-Wed, to 2am Thu, to 4am Fri, 1pm-2am Sat, 1pm-10pm Sun) Get lost in the nooks and crannies of this vast student hang-out. There's cool beats all day everyday and good-value salads and sandwiches at lunchtime. Downstairs they've added a nicely grungy beer garden.

By day **Music Bar Anděl** (☎ 377 323 226; Bezručova 7) is a hip cafe, but after dark it's a live venue featuring the best of touring Czech bands.

Also recommended is **Slunečnice** (Jungmanova 10; baguettes 60Kč; ☒ 7.30am-6pm) for its fresh sandwiches, self-service salads and vegetarian dishes. For around 100Kč you can buy a plate-full.

Getting There & Away

All trains travelling from Munich and Nuremberg to Prague stop at Plzeň. There are fast trains that run to/from Plzeň and Prague Smíchov (140Kč, 1½ hours, eight daily) and České Budějovice (172Kč, two hours, five daily).

If you're heading for Karlovy Vary, take a bus (80Kč, 1¾ hours, five daily). There are express buses to Prague (90Kč, 1½ hours, hourly), and trains (98Kč, 1½ hours, eight daily) and buses (69Kč, one hour, four daily) to/from Mariánské Lázně .

ČESKÉ BUDĚJOVICE

pop 100,000

After Plzeň, conduct the ultimate Bohemian beer taste test at České Budějovice (Budweis in German), the home of Budvar lager. The regional capital of South Bohemia is also a picturesque medieval city. Arcing from the town square are 18th-century arcades leading to bars that get raffishly rowdy on weekends – most fuelled by the town's prized export, of course.

Orientation

From the train station it's a 10-minute walk west down Lannova třída, then Kanovnická, to nám Přemysla Otakara II, the main

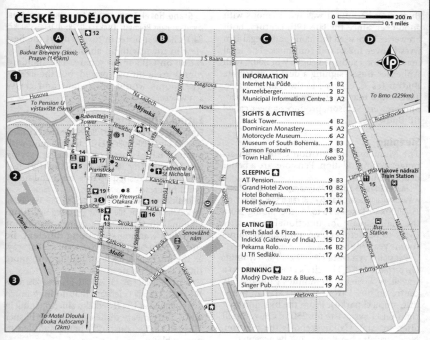

ČESKÉ BUDĚJOVICE

square. České Budějovice's flash new bus station is 300m southeast of the train station above the Mercury Central shopping centre on Dvořákova.

Information

Internet Na Půdě (Krajinská 28; ⏰ 8am-10pm)
Kanzelsberger (☎ 386 352 584; Hroznová 17) English-language books.
Left luggage (per small/large bag 12/25Kč) bus station (⏰ 6am-8pm); train station (⏰ 2.30am-11pm)
Municipal Information Centre (Městské Informařní Centrum; ☎ 386 801 413; www.c-budejovice.cz; nám Přemysla Otakara II 2; ⏰ 8.30am-6pm Mon-Fri, 8.30am-5pm Sat, 10am-4pm Sun May-Sep, 9am-5pm Mon-Fri, to 1pm Sat Oct-Apr) Books tickets, tours and accommodation, and has free internet.

Sights

The broad expanse of **Nám Přemysla Otakara II**, centred on the **Samson Fountain** (1727) and surrounded by 18th-century arcades, is one of the largest town squares in Europe. On the western side stands the baroque **town hall** (1731), topped with figures of the cardinal virtues: Justice, Wisdom, Courage and Prudence.

On the square's opposite corner is the 72m-tall **Black Tower** (adult/child 25/15Kč; ⏰ 10am-6pm daily Jul & Aug, closed Mon Apr-Jun, Sep & Oct, closed Nov-Mar), dating from 1553.

The streets around the square, especially Česká, are lined with old burgher houses. West near the river is the former **Dominican monastery** (1265) with a tall tower and a splendid pulpit. Adjacent is the **Motorcycle Museum** (☎ 723 247 104; Piaristické nám; adult/child 50/20Kč; ⏰ 10am-6pm Tue-Sun), with a fine collection of Czech Jawas and WWII Harley-Davidsons. The **Museum of South Bohemia** (Jihočeské muzeum; ☎ 387 929 328; adult/child 60/30Kč; ⏰ 9am-12.30pm & 1-5.30pm Tue-Sun) showcases history, books, coins, weapons and wildlife.

The **Budweiser Budvar Brewery** (☎ 387 705 341; www.budvar.cz; cnr Pražská & K Světlé; adult/child 100/50Kč; ⏰ 9am-4pm) is 3km north of the main square. Group tours run every day and the 2pm tour (Monday to Friday only) is open to individual travellers. The highlight is a glass of real-deal Budvar deep in the brewery's chilly cellars. Catch bus 2 to the Budvar stop (12Kč).

In 1876, the founders of US brewer Anheuser-Busch chose the brand name

Budweiser because it was synonymous with good beer. Since the late 19th century, both breweries have used the name and a legal arm wrestle over the brand continues. The legal machinations subsided slightly in 2007, with Anheuser-Busch signing a deal to distribute Budvar (as 'Czechvar') in the United States. To confuse matters, České Budějovice's second brewery Samson, produces a beer called BB Budweiser.

Sleeping

The Municipal Information Centre can arrange accommodation. Pensions are a better deal than hotels.

Motel Dlouhá Louka Autocamp (☎ 387 203 601; www.dlouhalouka.cz; Stromovka 8; camp sites per tent/s/d 75/750/1000Kč) Take bus 6 to 'Autocamping' from the main square for functional camp sites (May to September), or uninspiring motel rooms year-round.

Pension U výstaviště (☎ 387 240 148; U výzstaviště 17; r per person 270Kč) The city's closest thing to a travellers' hostel is 20 minutes from the city centre on bus 1 from the bus station to the fifth stop (U parku). From the bus stop veer right on U výstaviště for 250m. On your left after crossing Čajkovského is the pension. New arrivals after 9pm won't be accepted.

AT Pension (☎ 603 441 069; www.atpension.cz; Dukelská 15; s/d 490/750Kč) In a quiet riverside neighbourhood a leafy stroll from the Old Town, this great-value spot still has the Czech Republic's biggest breakfasts (50Kč). Don't go making plans for a big lunch.

Penzión Centrum (☎ 387 311 801; www.penzion centrum.cz; Biskupská 130/3; s/d incl breakfast 1000/1400Kč) Huge rooms with queen-size beds and crisp linen make this an excellent reader-recommended spot near the main square. Right next door there's a good organic restaurant.

Hotel Savoy (☎ 387 201 719; www.hotel-savoy -cb.cz; B Smetany; s/d/tr 1350/1850/2350Kč; 🖳) Newly opened, the Savoy is already making an impression with spacious, modern rooms decorated with art deco–style furniture – trust us, the combination works – and a quiet location just outside the Old Town.

Hotel Bohemia (☎ 386 360 691; www.bohemiacb .cz; Hradební 20; s/d incl breakfast 1490/1790Kč) Carved wooden doors open to a restful interior in two old burghers' houses down a quiet street. The restaurant comes recommended by the tourist information office.

Grand Hotel Zvon (☎ 387 311 384; www.hotel -zvon.cz; nám Přemysla Otakara II 28; d 1800-3900Kč; 🖳) The best hotel in town enjoys the best view in town with an absolute ringside location on CB's main square. The standard rooms are a bit overpriced, but the executive rooms would be elegant and classy anywhere.

Eating & Drinking

Fresh Salad & Pizza (☎ 387 200 991; Hroznová 21; salads 70-90Kč, pizza 100-130Kč) This lunch spot with outdoor tables does exactly what it says on the tin; healthy salads and (slightly) less healthy pizza dished up by a fresh and funky youthful crew.

Indická (Gateway of India; ☎ 386 359 355; 1st fl, Chelčického 11; mains 100-150Kč; 🕑 closed Sun) From Chennai to České, here comes respite for travellers wanting something different. Be sure to request spicy if you want it that way, as the kitchen is used to dealing with more timid Czech palates.

U Tří Sedláku (☎ 387 222 303; Hroznová 488; mains 101-170Kč) Locals celebrate that nothing much has changed at U Tří Sedláku since opening in 1897. Tasty meaty dishes go with the Pilsner Urquell that's constantly being shuffled to busy tables.

Pekarna Rolo (Dr Stejskala 7; 🕑 7.30am-6pm Mon-Fri, 7am-noon Sat) Superb baked goods, open sandwiches and fresh fruit cover all the bases for an on-the-go combination of eating and strolling.

Singer Pub (Česká 55) With Czech and Irish beers, plus good cocktails, don't be surprised if you get the urge to rustle up something on the Singer sewing machines on every table. If not, challenge the regulars to a game of *foosball* with a soundtrack of noisy rock.

modrý dveře jazz & blues (☎ 386 359 958; Biskupská 1) By day modrý dveře is a welcoming bar-cafe with vintage pics of Sinatra. At dusk the lights dim for regular jazz piano gigs on Wednesdays (from 7pm) and live blues and jazz on Thursdays (from 8pm). Tell them Frank sent you.

Getting There & Away

There are trains from České Budějovice to Prague (211Kč, 2½ hours, hourly) and Plzeň (172Kč, two hours, five daily). Frequent trains trundle to Český Krumlov (44Kč, 45 minutes).

WORTH THE TRIP: TÁBOR

The Old Town of Tábor was a formidable natural defence against invasion. Six centuries ago, the Hussite religious sect founded Tábor as a military bastion in defiance of Catholic Europe. Based on the biblical concept that 'nothing is mine and nothing is yours, because everyone owns the community equally', all Hussites participated in communal work, and possessions were allocated equally in the town's main square. This exceptional nonconformism gave the word 'bohemian' the connotations we associate with it today. Religious structures dating from the 15th century line the town square and it's possible to visit the 650m stretch of underground tunnels the Hussites used for refuge in times of war.

Penzión Alfa (☎ 381 256 165; www.pensionalfa.zde.cz; Klokotská; s/d/tr 570/900/1300Kč) occupies a cosy corner just metres from the main square. Downstairs get your Geronimojo back at the funky Native American–themed cafe.

The annual **Tabor Meetings Festival** is held on the second weekend in September. Expect medieval merriment with lots of food, drink and colourfully dressed locals celebrating their Hussite heritage. See www.tabor.cz for more information.

Travel to Tábor by bus, either from Prague Florenc (86Kč, 1½ hours, eight daily) or České Budějovice (62Kč, one hour, 15 daily).

Heading for Vienna (620Kč, four hours, two daily) you'll have to change at Gmünd, or take a direct train to Linz (420Kč, 2¼ hours, one daily) and change there.

The bus to Brno (194Kč, 3½ to 4½ hours, four daily) travels via Telč (92Kč, two hours). Buses regularly shuttle south to Český Krumlov (32Kč, 45 minutes).

HLUBOKÁ NAD VLTAVOU

Hluboká nad Vltavou's neo-Gothic **chateau** (☎ 387 843 911; www.zamek-hluboka.eu; 9am-5pm Jul & Aug, to 5pm Tue-Sun May-Jun, to 4.30pm Apr, Sep & Oct), was rebuilt by the Schwarzenberg family in 1841–71 with turrets and crenellations inspired by England's Windsor Castle. The palace's 144 rooms remained in use up to WWII.

There are three English-language tours available. Tour 1 (adult/child 220/150Kč) focuses on the castle's public areas, while Tour 2 (adult/child 230/150Kč) goes behind the scenes in the castle apartments. Tour 3 (adult/child 170/80Kč) explores the kitchens. Tours in Czech are 90Kč cheaper. The park is open throughout the year (no admission charge). The **information centre** (☎ 387 966 164; www.visithluboka.cz; Masarykova 35) can help with accommodation, but Hluboká is an easy day trip from České Budějovice by local bus (18Kč, 20 minutes, two hourly).

ČESKÝ KRUMLOV

pop 14,600

Crowned by a stunning castle, and centred on an elegant Old Town square, Český Krumlov's Renaissance and baroque buildings enclose the meandering arc of the Vltava river.

During summer, countless photographic memory cards are filled as pigeons dart through busloads of day-tripping tourists exploring the town's narrow lanes and footbridges. Either side of July and August, the town is (slightly) more subdued and secluded. Come in winter to experience the castle blanketed in snow.

The town's original Gothic fortress was rebuilt as an imposing Renaissance chateau in the 16th century. Since the 18th century the town's appearance is largely unchanged, and careful renovation and restoration has replaced the architectural neglect of the communist era. In 1992 Český Krumlov was granted Unesco World Heritage status.

For too many travellers, Český Krumlov is just a hurried day trip, but its combination of glorious architecture and watery fun on the Vltava deserve more attention. Add in the rugged attractions of the nearby Šumava region, and you can easily fill three days.

Orientation

The bus station is east of the town centre, but if you're arriving from České Budějovice get off at the Špičák bus stop (the first in the town centre, just after you pass beneath a road bridge). The train station is 1.5km north of the town centre; buses 1, 2 and 3 go from the station to the Špičák bus stop. From the bridge over the main road beside the bus stop, Latrán leads south into town.

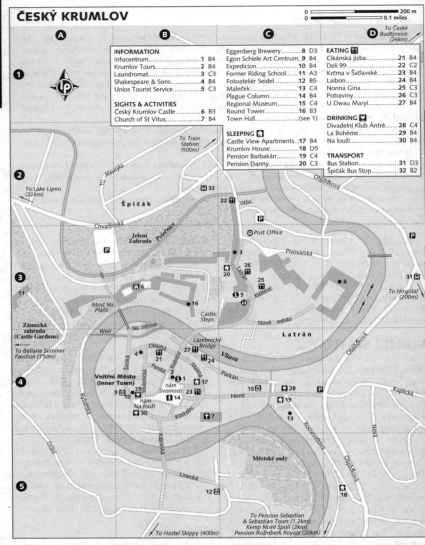

ČESKÝ KRUMLOV

| 0 | 200 m |
| 0 | 0.1 miles |

INFORMATION
Infocentrum	1	B4
Krumlov Tours	2	B4
Laundromat	3	C3
Shakespeare & Sons	4	B4
Unios Tourist Service	5	C3

SIGHTS & ACTIVITIES
Český Krumlov Castle	6	B3
Church of St Vitus	7	B4
Eggenberg Brewery	8	D3
Egon Schiele Art Centrum	9	B4
Expedicion	10	B4
Former Riding School	11	A3
Fotoateliér Seidel	12	B5
Maleček	13	C4
Plague Column	14	B4
Regional Museum	15	C4
Round Tower	16	B3
Town Hall	(see 1)	

SLEEPING
Castle View Apartments	17	B4
Krumlov House	18	D5
Pension Barbakán	19	C4
Pension Danny	20	C3

EATING
Cikánská jizba	21	B4
Deli 99	22	B4
Krčma v Šatlavské	23	B4
Laibon	24	B4
Nonna Gina	25	C3
Potraviny	26	C3
U Dwau Maryí	27	B4

DRINKING
Divadelní Klub Antré	28	C4
La Bohème	29	B4
Na louži	30	B4

TRANSPORT
| Bus Station | 31 | D3 |
| Špičák Bus Stop | 32 | B2 |

Don't take a car into the centre of the Old Town; use one of the car parks around the perimeter. The Chvalšinská car-park, north of the Old Town, is most convenient.

Information
There is wi-fi at Egon Schiele Art Centrum cafe (opposite) and Deli 99 (p308).

Infocentrum (☎ 380 704 622; www.ckrumlov.cz; nám Svornosti 1; ⏰ 9am-6pm) Transport and accommodation info, maps, internet access (5Kč per five minutes) and audio guides (100Kč per hour). A guide for disabled visitors is available. A good source of information on the Šumuva region.
Krumlov Tours (☎ 723 069 561; www.krumlovtours .com; nám Svornosti; per person 200-250Kč) Has walking tours with regular departure times; good for solo travellers

Laundromat (☎ 380 713 153; Pension Lobo, Latrán 73; per load 140Kč; ☺ 9am-noon & 1-4pm Mon-Fri, 9-11am Sat)

Oldřiška Baloušková (oldriskab@gmail.com) Offers tailored tours (per hr 450Kč).

Shakespeare & Sons (☎ 380 711 203; Soukenická 44; ☺ 11am-7pm) Good for English-language paperbacks.

Unios Tourist Service (☎ 380 725 110; www.visit ceskykrumlov.cz; Zámek 57; ☺ 9am-6pm) Accommodation and an internet cafe with international calling.

Sights

The Old Town, almost encircled by the Vltava River, is watched over by **Český Krumlov Castle** (☎ 380 704 721; www.castle.ckrumlov.cz; ☺ 9am-6pm Tue-Sun Jun-Aug, to 5pm Apr, May, Sep & Oct) and its ornately decorated **Round Tower** (45/30Kč). Three different guided tours are on offer: **Tour I** (adult/child 230/130Kč) takes in the Renaissance and baroque apartments that the aristocratic Rožmberk and Schwarzenberg families called home; **Tour II** (adult/child 180/100Kč) visits the Schwarzenberg apartments used in the 19th century; and the **Theatre Tour** (adult/child 350/200Kč; ☺ 10am-4pm Tue-Sun May-Oct) explores the chateau's remarkable rococo theatre, complete with original stage machinery. Wandering through the courtyards and gardens is free.

The path beyond the fourth courtyard leads across the spectacular **Most ná Plášti** to the castle gardens. A ramp to the right leads to the **former riding school**, now a restaurant. The relief above the door shows cherubs offering the head and boots of a vanquished Turk – a reference to Adolf von Schwarzenberg, who conquered the Turkish fortress of Raab in the 16th century. From here the Italian-style **Zámecká zahrada** (castle gardens) stretch away towards the **Bellarie summer pavilion**.

Across the river is nám Svornosti, the Old Town square, overlooked by the Gothic **town hall** and a baroque **plague column** (1716). Above is the striking Gothic **Church of St Vitus** (1439), and nearby is the **Regional Museum** (☎ 380 711 674; Horní 152; adult/child 50/25Kč; ☺ 10am-6pm Jul & Aug, 10am-5pm May, Jun & Sep, 9am-4pm Tue-Fri, 1-4pm Sat & Sun, Mar, Apr & Oct-Dec), with an interactive model of the town c 1800.

The **Egon Schiele Art Centrum** (☎ 380 704 011; www.schielartcentrum.cz; Široká 70-72; adult/child 120/700Kč; ☺ 10am-6pm) is an excellent gallery showcasing the Viennese painter Egon Schiele (1890–1918). The attached **cafe** (☺ 10am-7pm) is appropriately arty and has a good selection of Moravian wines.

Newly opened in 2008, the **Fotoateliér Seidel** (☎ 380 704 611; Linecká 272; www.seidel.ckrumlov.cz; admission 130Kč; ☺ 9am-6pm) presents a retrospective of the work of local photographers Josef Seidel and his son František. Especially poignant are the images recording early-20th-century life in nearby mountain villages.

The **Eggenberg Brewery** (☎ 380 711 225; www .eggenberg.cz; Latrán 27; tours with/without tasting 130/100Kč; ☺ tours 11am) is also where most canoeing and rafting trips end. Relive your experiences on the Vltava's gentle rapids in the brewery's beer garden. Book brewery tours at Infocentrum.

Activities

Rent canoes, rafts and rubber rings from **Maleček** (☎ 380 712 508; http://en.malecek.cz; Rooseveltova 28; ☺ 9am-5pm). A half-hour splash in a two-person canoe costs 350Kč, or you can rent a canoe for a full day trip down the river from Rožmberk (850Kč, six to eight hours). Maleček also has sedate river trips through Český Krumlov on giant wooden rafts seating up to 36 people (290Kč, 45 minutes).

Sebastian Tours (☎ 607 100 234; www.sebastianck -tours.com; 5 Května Ul, Plešivec; per person 450Kč) can get you discovering southern Bohemia on guided tours including stops at Hluboká nad Vltavou and České Budějovice.

Expedicion (☎ 607 963 868; www.expedicion.cz; Soukenická 33; ☺ 9am- 7pm) rents bikes (280Kč a day), arranges horse-riding (250Kč an hour) and operates action-packed day trips (1680Kč including lunch) incorporating horse-riding, fishing, mountain biking and rafting in the nearby Šumava region.

Festivals & Events

Infocentrum sells tickets to most festivals.
Five-Petalled Rose Festival In mid-June; features two days of street performers, medieval games.
Chamber Music Festival Late June to early July.
Český Krumlov International Music Festival (www .festivalkrumlov.cz) July to August.
Jazz at Summer's End Festival (www.jazz-krumlov .cz) Mid-September.

Sleeping

Kemp Nové Spolí (☎ 380 728 305; www.kempkrumlov.cz; camp sites per person 70Kč; ☺ Jun-Aug) Located on the Vltava River about 2km south of town, with basic facilities and an idyllic location. Take bus 3 from the train or bus station to the Spolí mat. šk. stop, otherwise it's a half-hour walk from the Old Town.

CZECH REPUBLIC

Krumlov House (☎ 380 711 935; www.krumlovhostel .com; Rooseveltova 68; dm/d 300/650Kč) Perched above the river, Krumlov House is friendly and comfortable and has plenty of books, DVDs and local info to feed your inner backpacker. Lots of day trips are also on offer.

Hostel Skippy (☎ 380 728 380; www.skippy.wz.cz; Plesivecka 123; dm/d 300/650Kč) Smaller and less boisterous than some other CK hostels, Skippy is more like staying at a friend's place. The creative owner, 'Skippy', is an arty muso type, so you might be surprised with an impromptu jam session in the front room.

our pick Pension Sebastian (☎ 608 357 581; www .sebastianck.com; 5 Května Ul, Plešivec; s/d/tr incl breakfast 790/990/1490Kč; ☼ Apr–Oct) An excellent option just 10 minutes' walk from the Old Town, and therefore slightly cheaper. Larger four-bed rooms (1780Kč) are good for families and there's a pretty garden for end-of-day drinks and diary writing. The well-travelled owners also run tours of the surrounding region (p307).

Pension Rožmberk Royale (☎ 380 727 858; www .pensionroyale.cz; Rožmberk nad Vltavou; s/d 800/1300Kč) This new pension has an absolute riverfront location in the sleepy village of Rožmberk nad Vltavou. A castle looms above the village, and it's a short, scenic bus ride from Český Krumlov (28Kč, 35 minutes, seven daily). A pleasant stroll just around the river reveals a good fish restaurant.

Pension Danny (☎ 380 712 710; www.pensiondanny .cz; Latrán 72; d incl breakfast from 990Kč) Exposed timber beams and refurbished bathrooms add up to a good-value Old Town location. Have breakfast in your room and enjoy views of romantic CK at the same time.

Pension Barbakán (☎ 380 717 017; www.barbakan.cz; Horní 26; s/d incl breakfast from 1700Kč; ☐) Originally the town's gunpowder arsenal, Barbakán now creates fireworks of its own, with supercomfy rooms featuring bright and cosy wooden decor. Sit in the grill restaurant (mains 140Kč to 210Kč) and watch the tubing and rafting action below.

Castle View Apartments (☎ 731 108 677; http:// accommodation-cesky-krumlov.castleview.cz; Satlavska; d incl breakfast 2900-3500Kč) Furnished apartments are better value than top-end hotels in Český Krumlov. Castle View has seven apartments with spacious bathrooms and decor combining sophistication and romance in equal measure. Five of the apartments can sleep up to five people.

Infocentrum can also recommend other furnished apartments, easily Krumlov's best option for romantic couples.

Eating

Booking for dinner in July and August is recommended.

our pick Laibon (☎ 728 676 654; Parkán 105; mains 90-180Kč) Candles and vaulted ceilings create a great boho ambience in the best little vegetarian teahouse in Bohemia. The riverside setting's pretty fine as well. Order the blueberry dumplings for dessert and don't miss the special 'yeast beer' from the Bernard brewery. Ask David, the well-travelled owner, where he's headed next.

Nonna Gina (☎ 380 717 187; Klášteriní ul 52; pizza 90-155Kč) Authentic Italian flavours from the authentic Italian Massaro family feature in this pizzeria down a quiet lane. Grab an outdoor table and pretend you're in Naples.

Krčma v Šatlavské (☎ 380 713 344; Horní 157; mains 100-150Kč) Nirvana for meat-lovers, this medieval barbecue cellar serves sizzling platters in a funky labyrinth illuminated by candles and the flickering flames of open grills.

U Dwau Maryí (☎ 380 717 228; Parkán 104; mains 100-200Kč) The 'Two Marys' medieval tavern recreates old recipes and is your best chance to try dishes made with buckwheat and millet; all tastier than they sound. Wash the food down with a goblet of mead (a drink made with honey) or a 21st-century Pilsner. In summer it's a tad touristy, but the stunning riverside castle views easily compensate.

Cikánská jizba (☎ 380 717 585; Dlouhá 31; mains 120-210Kč; ☼ 3pm–midnight Mon-Sat) At 'The Gypsy Room' there's live Roma music at the weekends to go with the menu of meaty Czech favourites.

Also recommended:

Deli 99 (Latrán 106; snacks 50-80Kč; ☼ 7am-7pm Mon-Sat, 8am-5pm Sun) Bagels, sandwiches, organic juices and wi-fi internet all tick the box marked 'Slightly Homesick Traveller'.

Potraviny (supermarket; Latrán 55) Self-catering central, especially if you're going rafting.

Drinking

Na louži (☎ 380 711 280; Kájovská 66) Nothing's changed in this wood-panelled *pivo* parlour for almost a century. Locals and tourists pack Na louži for huge meals and tasty dark beer from the Eggenberg brewery.

La Bohème (Soukenická 34; ☼ from 5pm) With art-deco styling, La Bohème is your best bet for a quieter spot with good cocktails. It's a favourite for locals avoiding the tourist rush. From 5pm to 8pm, there's a 30% 'Happy Hour' discount.

Divadelní Klub Ántré (☎ 602 336 320; Horní Braná 2; www.klubantre.cz) This arty cafe-bar in the town theatre has a sprawling terrace overlooking the river. There's free wi-fi, and it's always worth dropping by to see if any music gigs are scheduled.

Getting There & Away

Buses depart from Prague Florenc to Český Krumlov (160Kč, three hours, daily) via České Budějovice. **Student Agency** (www.student agency.cz) leaves from Prague Ná Knížecí (140Kč). In July and August this route is very popular and booking a couple of days ahead is recommended.

Local buses (32Kč, 50 minutes, seven daily) and trains (46Kč, one hour, eight daily) run to České Budějovice, for onward travel to Brno or Plzeň.

The most straighforward way to Austria are the direct shuttle buses offered by several Český Krumlov companies. Stiff competition keeps prices relatively low; Vienna (1100Kč), Salzburg (1100Kč) and Linz (350Kč). From Linz there are regular trains to Vienna, Salzburg and Munich. Public transport to Austria involves heading to north to České Budějovice and catching a train to Linz (two hours).

ŠUMAVA

The Šumava region's forested hills stretch for 125km along the border with Austria and Germany. The highest summit is Plechý (1378m), west of Horní Planá. Before 1989 the range was divided by the Iron Curtain, a line of fences, watchtowers, armed guards and dog patrols between Western Europe and the communist East. Many Czechs made a bid for freedom by creeping through the forests at night. In a different era, the hills are popular for hiking, cycling and cross-country skiing.

The **Povydří trail** along the Vydra (Otter) River in the northern Šumava is one of the national park's most popular walk. It's an easy 7km hike along a deep, forested river valley between Čeňkova Pila and Antýgl. Buses run between Sušice and Modrava, stopping at Čeňkova Pila and Antýgl. Plenty of pension accommodation is available.

Around the peak of **Boubín** (1362m), the 46-hectare *prales* (virgin forest) is the only part of the Šumava forest that is largely untouched by human activity. The trailhead is 2km north-east of the zastávka Zátoň train stop (not Zátoň town train station) at Kaplice, where there is car parking as well as basic camping facilities. From here it's an easy 2.5km to U pralesa Lake on a blue and green marked trail. Remain on the blue trail for a further 7.5km to reach the summit of Boubín. Return by following the trail southwest. The complete loop takes about five hours.

If you'd rather use wheels, the **Šumava Trail** is a weeklong bike ride through dense forests and past mountain streams from Český Krumlov to Domažlice.

If lying in the sun sounds more fun, head to **Lake Lipno**, a 30km-long reservoir south of Český Krumlov. Known as 'the Czech Riviera', it's lined with camping grounds, swimming areas and water-sports centres; there's even a yacht marina at Lipno nad Vltavou.

Infocentrum (p306) in Český Krumlov has a wall-full of Šumava suggestions.

A nightly train runs from České Budějovice (121Kč, three hours) and Český Krumlov (83Kč, one hour 40 minutes), to Volary, calling at Horní Planá and Nová Pec on Lake Lipno. From May to August, buses cover a similar route (80Kč, two hours).

From Volary, trains continue north to Strakonice via Zátoň (28Kč, 30 minutes, four daily).

The Povydří trail is best approached from Sušice, which can be reached by direct bus from Prague Ná Knížecí (121Kč, 2½ hours, two daily). Another bus links Sušice with Čeňkova Pila and Antýgl (46Kč, one hour, two or three daily).

See Infocentrum (p306) in Český Krumlov for detailed transport information.

ADRŠPACH-TEPLICE ROCKS

The Czech Republic's most extraordinary scenery lies near Poland, in a protected landscape region known as the Adršpach-Teplice Rocks (Adršpašsko-Teplické skály). Thick layers of stratified sandstone have been eroded and fissured by water and frost to form giant towers and deep, narrow chasms. Discovered by mountaineers in the 19th century, the region is popular with rock climbers and hikers. Sandy trails lead through pine-scented forests and loop through the pinnacles, assisted occasionally by ladders and stairs.

Two main formations – **Adršpach Rock Town** (Adršpašské skalní město) and **Teplice Rock Town** (Teplické skalní město) – comprise a single nature reserve. At each entrance there's a **ticket booth** (adult/child 60/30Kč; ☺ 8am-6pm Apr-Nov) with handy 1:25,000 trail maps on offer. Outside the official opening hours, enter for free. It's an additional 25Kč for a boat trip on a compact lake secreted in the rocks. Buy tickets on the boat.

There's a small **information office** (☎ 491 586 012; www.skalyadrspach.cz; ☺ 8am-12.30pm & 1-5pm Apr-Oct) near Adršpach train station. In summer the trails are busy; book accommodation at least a week ahead. In winter – snow lingers to mid-April – you'll have the area mainly to yourself but some trails may be closed. Try and avoid weekends, when Polish busloads visit on day trips.

If you're pushed for time, walk the green loop trail (1½ hours), starting at Adršpach and progressing through deep mossy ravines and soaring rock towers to the **Great Lookout** (Velké panorama). Admire the view of pinnacles escalating above the pines, before threading through the **Mouse Hole** (Myší díra), a vast vertical fissure barely a shoulder-width wide.

The blue loop trail (2½ hours), starting at Teplice, passes a metal staircase leading strenuously to **Střmen**, a rock tower once occupied by an outlaw's timber castle, before continuing through the area's most spectacular pinnacles to the chilly ravine of **Siberia** (Sibiř). An excellent day hike (four to five hours), taking in the region's highlights, links the head of the Teplice trail, beyond Sibiř, to Adršpach via the **Wolf Gorge** (Vlčí rokle). Return from Adršpach to Teplice by walking along the road (one hour) or by train (10 minutes).

To experience the rock towns more closely, contact Tomas Pycha at **Tomadventure** (☎ 775 158 838; www.tomadventure.org, climbing per hr 200Kč). Climbing instruction for beginners to advanced is available, and Tomas also rents out bicycles for 250Kč per day.

Sleeping & Eating

In Teplice nad Metují-Skály, the **Hotel Orlík** (☎ 491 581 025; www.orlik.hotel-cz.com; s/d incl breakfast 450/900Kč) is a good place to recharge with a popular bar. Nearby **Pension Skály** (☎ 491 581 174; www.adrspach-skaly.cz; Střmenské Podhradi 132; s/d incl breakfast 500/1000Kč) has cosy rooms for post-hike relaxation.

Eating at the rock towns is limited to a few over-priced fast-food emporia, and you're better off to eat where you're staying.

In Adršpach, the new **Hotel Javor** (☎ 491 586 182; www.hotel-adrspach.cz; s/d incl breakfast 850/1700Kč; ☐) has 41 smart rooms decked out in modern furniture with skylights galore. Downstairs the restaurant also achieves a lighter touch with good salads and pasta. If you're really hungry after hiking, they can also whistle you up a meaty mixed grill.

In a quiet setting between Teplice and Adršpach, the **Skalní Mlýn** (☎ 491 586 961; www .skalni-mlyn.cz; s/d incl breakfast 500/1000Kč) has rustic rooms and friendly dogs in a restored river mill. It's best if you have your own transport to get here.

Getting There & Away

There are direct buses from Prague's Černý Most metro station to Trutnov (152Kč, 2¾ hours, hourly).

Trains (eight daily) rattle from Trutnov to Adršpach (40Kč, one hour) and Teplice nad Metují (46Kč, 1¼ hours).

MORAVIA

Away from the tourist commotion of Prague and Bohemia, Moravia provides a quietly authentic experience. Olomouc and Telč are two of the country's prettiest towns, and bustling Brno serves up Czech urban ambience, without the tourists. Mildly active travellers can explore the stunning landscapes of the Moravian Karst region and everyone can celebrate with a good vintage from the Moravian wine country.

BRNO
pop 387,200

The attractions of Brno may not seem that obvious after the showy buzz of Prague, but after a short stay you'll see the traditional Moravian reserve melting away in the Old Town's bars and restaurants. Leave the touristy commotion back west in the capital – you'll have a stellar array of museums and galleries almost to yourself. Despite having a population of less than 400,000, Brno behaves just like the confident, cosmopolitan capital (ie of Moravia) that it is.

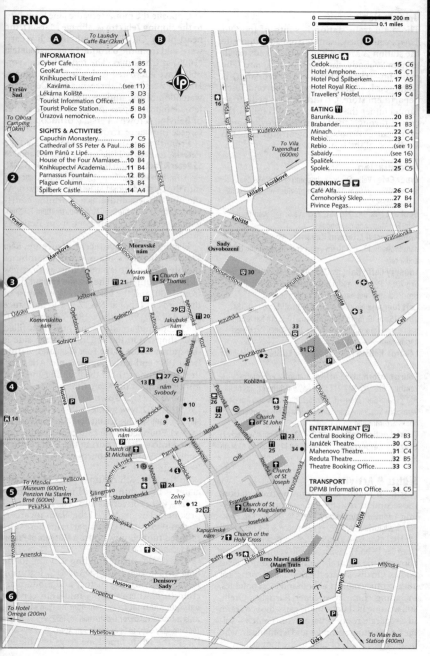

BRNO

0 — 200 m
0 — 0.1 miles

INFORMATION
Cyber Cafe.....................................1 B5
GeoKart...2 C4
Knihkupectví Literární
 Kavárna.................................(see 11)
Lékárna Koliště.............................3 D3
Tourist Information Office...........4 B5
Tourist Police Station...................5 B4
Úrazová nemocnice.....................6 D3

SIGHTS & ACTIVITIES
Capuchin Monastery.....................7 C5
Cathedral of SS Peter & Paul......8 B6
Dům Pánů z Lipé...........................9 B4
House of the Four Mamlases......10 B4
Knihkupectví Academia.............11 B4
Parnassus Fountain......................12 B5
Plague Column............................13 B4
Špilberk Castle............................14 A4

SLEEPING
Čedok..15 C6
Hotel Amphone..........................16 C1
Hotel Pod Špilberkem...............17 A5
Hotel Royal Ricc........................18 B5
Travellers' Hostel.......................19 C4

EATING
Barunka.......................................20 B3
Brabander....................................21 B3
Minach..22 C4
Rebio...23 C4
Rebio.....................................(see 1)
Sabaidy.................................(see 16)
Špaliček......................................24 B5
Spolek...25 C5

DRINKING
Café Alfa.....................................26 C4
Černohorský Sklep......................27 B4
Pivnice Pegas.............................28 B4

ENTERTAINMENT
Central Booking Office..............29 B3
Janáček Theatre..........................30 C3
Mahenovo Theatre......................31 C4
Reduta Theatre...........................32 B5
Theatre Booking Office.............33 C3

TRANSPORT
DPMB Information Office...........34 C5

To Laundry Caffe Bar (2km)
Tyršův Sad
To Obora Camping (10km)
To Vila Tugendhat (600m)
Moravské nám
Sady Osvobození
Church of St Thomas
Komenského nám
Jakubské nám
nám Svobody
Dominikánská nám
Church of St Michael
Church of St John
Church of St Joseph
To Mendel Museum (600m); Penzion Na Starém Brně (600m)
Šilingrovo nám
Zelný trh
Church of St Mary Magdalene
Kapucínské nám
Church of the Holy Cross
Denisovy Sady
Brno hlavní nádraží (Main Train Station)
To Hotel Omega (200m)
To Main Bus Station (400m)

Orientation

The main train station is south of the Old Town, with a busy tram stop outside. Opposite the station is Masarykova, which leads north to nám Svobody, the city's main square. The main bus station (Brno ÚAN Zvonařka) is 800m south of the train station, beyond Tesco department store. Go through the pedestrian tunnel under the train tracks, and follow the crowd through the Galerie Vaňkovka shopping centre. Brno's Tuřany airport is 7.5km southeast of the train station.

Information

Cyber Cafe (Velký Spalicek shopping centre, Mečova 2; per hr 60Kč; 9am-11pm) Also provides wi-fi access for laptop toters.

Geokart (542 216 561; Vachova 8; 9am-6pm Mon-Fri) Maps and guidebooks.

Knihkupectví Literární Kavárna (542 217 954; nám Svobody 13; 10am-7pm) English-language books and a cafe.

Laundry Caffe Bar (775 602 167; Skřivanova 1; per 6kg 70Kč; 2pm-midnight) Catch tram 6 or 7 to the Hrnčířská stop and have a drink while you wait.

Left luggage bus station (per day small/big bag 9/18Kč; 5.15am-10.15pm Mon-Fri, 6am-10.15pm Sat & Sun); train station (ground fl; lockers per 24hr 90Kč; closed 11pm-4am)

Lékárna Koliště (545 424 811; Koliště 47) A 24-hour pharmacy.

Tourist information office (Kulturní a Informační Centrum; KIC; 542 211 090; www.ticbrno.cz; Radnická 8; 8am-6pm Mon-Fri, 9am-5.30pm Sat & Sun Apr-Sep, 9am-5pm Sat, 9am-3pm Sun Nov-Mar) Sells maps and books accommodation.

Tourist police station (974 626 100; nám Svobody 7)

Úrazová nemocnice (545 538 111; Ponávka 6) Main hospital.

Sights & Activities

North on Masarykova from the train station, the second turn on the left leads to the compelling **Capuchin Monastery** (542 213 232; Kapucínské nám 5; adult/child 60/30Kč; 9am-noon & 2-4.30pm Mon-Sat, 11-11.45am & 2-4.30pm Sun May-Sep, closed Mon Oct-Apr, closed Dec 15-Jan 31), with a well-ventilated crypt allowing the natural mummification of dead bodies. On display are the desiccated corpses of 18th-century monks, abbots and local notables, including chimney-sweeper Barnabas Orelli, still wearing his boots. In the glass-topped coffin in a separate room is Baron von Trenck – soldier, adventurer, gambler and womaniser, who bequeathed loads of cash to the monastery.

Opposite the monastery, the lane leads into to the sloping **Zelný trh** (Cabbage Market), the heart of the Old Town, and where live carp were sold from the baroque **Parnassus Fountain** (1695) at Christmas. The fountain is a symbolic cave encrusted with allegorical figures. Hercules restrains three-headed Cerberus, watchdog of the underworld, and the three female figures represent the ancient empires of Babylon (crown), Persia (cornucopia) and Greece (quiver of arrows).

From the top of the Cabbage Market take Petrská to Petrov Hill, site of the **Cathedral of SS Peter & Paul**. Climb the **tower** (adult/child 35/30Kč; 11am-6pm Mon-Sat, from 11.45am Sun) or descend into the **crypt** (adult/child 20/10Kč; as per tower). At the foot of the cathdral is a charming courtyard **cafe** (11am-9pm Mon-Thu, to 10pm Fri-Sun), which serves excellent beer from Prague's Strahov monastery.

Having survived a recent spruce up, **Nám Svobody**, the city's main square, combines mainly 19th-century buildings with a few older monuments. The **plague column** dates from 1680, and the **Dům Pánů z Lipé** (House of the Lords of Lipé) at No 17 is a Renaissance palace (1589–96) with a 19th-century *sgraffito* facade and arcaded courtyard (now filled with shops). On the square's eastern side is the quirky **House of the Four Mamlases**, dating from 1928 and with four moronic 'Atlas' figures struggling to hold the building and their loincloths up at the same time.

Above the Old Town looms **Špilberk Castle** (542 215 012; www.spilberk.cz; 9am-6pm Tue-Sun May-Sep, 9am-5pm Tue-Sun Oct-Apr, 10am-5pm Wed-Sun Nov-Mar). Founded in the 13th century and converted into a citadel during the 17th century, opponents of the Habsburgs were imprisoned here until 1855.

In the late 18th century, parts of the **casemates** – brick tunnels within the fortifications – were converted into cells for political prisoners. During WWII the Nazis incarcerated and executed Czech partisans here. The restored tunnels now house a **Museum of Prison Life** (adult/child 70/35Kč).

The castle's main building is home to the **Brno City Museum** (adult/child 120/60Kč), featuring Renaissance art, city history and modern architecture. There's also a mid-18th-century **baroque pharmacy** (9am-6pm Tue-Sun May-Sep), and a **lookout tower** (adult/child 30/15Kč; 9am-6pm Tue-Sun May-Sep, to 5pm Sat & Sun Apr-Oct). Try and locate the white limestone crags of Mikulov on the southern horizon. A combined ticket (adult/child 120/60Kč) allows admission to the casemates, museum and tower.

Gregor Mendel (1822–84), the Augustinian monk whose studies of peas and bees at Brno's Abbey of St Thomas established modern genetics, is commemorated in the **Mendel Museum** (☎ 543 424 043; www.mendel-museum.org; Mendlovo nám 1; adult/child 60/30Kč; ⊙ 10am-6pm Tue-Sun Apr-Oct, to 5pm Nov-Mar), housed in the Abbey itself. In the garden are the foundations of Mendel's original greenhouse.

Fans of modern architecture will love Brno's cubist, functionalist and internationalist styles. The finest is the functionalist **Vila Tugendhat** ☎ 545 212 118; www.tugendhat-villa.cz; Černopolni 45; adult/child 120/60Kč; ⊙ 10am-6pm Wed-Sun), north-east of town, and designed by Mies van der Rohe in 1930. Catch tram 3, 5 or 11 to the Dětská nemocnice stop. Advance booking is essential.

Ask at the tourist information office about Brno's many other museums and art galleries.

Festivals & Events
During Easter, there's the **Festival of Sacred Music** (www.mhf-brno.cz). The noisiest event is mid-August's **Moto Grand Prix** (www.motogp.com), when the city packs out with motorbike fans. The race circuit is off the D1 road to Prague, 10km west of Brno. Accommodation can be difficult to find on race weekend.

Only slightly less noisy is the **Ignis Brunensis Fireworks Festival** (www.ignisbrunensis.cz; ⊙ late May-early Jun) with fireworks geeks from around the world.

Sleeping
Accommodation increases in cost and demand when major trade fairs are on, especially IBF (mid-April) and MSV (mid-September). See www.bvv.cz for a calendar of events.

Čedok (☎ 542 321 267; Nádražní 10/12) Books accommodation in student dormitories during July and August.

Obora Camping (☎ 546 223 334; www.autocamp obora.cz; per tent/bungalow per person 80/230Kč; ⊙ May-Sep) At the Brněnská přehrada (Brno dam), northwest of the city centre. Take tram 1 from the train station to the zoo and change to bus 103 alighting at the seventh stop.

Travellers' Hostel (☎ 542 213 573; www.travellers.cz; Jánská 22; dm incl breakfast 290Kč; ⊙ Jul & Aug) Set in the heart of the Old Town, this place provides the

most central cheap beds in the city – for July and August anyway.

Hotel Omega (☎ 543 213 876; www.hotelomega.cz; Křídloviská 19b; s/d incl breakfast 950/1450Kč; ▯) In a quiet neighbourhood, 1km from the centre, this tourist information favourite has spacious rooms with modern pine furniture. A couple of three- and four-bed rooms cater to travelling families. Catch tram 1 from the railway station to the Václavská stop.

Penzion Na Starém Brně (☎ 543 247 872; www .pension-brno.com; Mendlovo nám 1a; s/d incl breakfast 960/1290Kč) An atmospheric Augustinian monastery conceals five compact rooms that come reader-recommended. Just metres away there's a Moravian wine bar.

Hotel Amphone (☎ 545 428 310; www.amphone.cz; třída kpt Jaroše 29; s/d incl breakfast from 990/1390Kč; ▯) On an elegant tree-lined street, the friendly Amphone has bright and airy rooms around a garden. New carpet and a lick of paint wouldn't go amiss though.

Hotel Pod Špilberkem (☎ 543 235 003; www .hotelpodspilberkem.cz; Pekařská 10; s/d incl breakfast 1400/1550Kč) Tucked away near the castle are quiet rooms clustered around a central court-yard. The secure car-park is a good option for self-drive travellers.

Hotel Royal Ricc (☎ 542 219 262; www.romantichotels .cz; Starobrněnská 10; s/d incl breakfast from 3500/3900Kč; ▧ ▯) An utterly captivating mix of traditional and modern, this intimate Old Town hotel with 29 rooms would be right at home in Paris or Venice. Rates fall by around 25% on weekends.

Eating
Rebio (☎ 542 211 110; Orli 16; mains 70-100Kč; ⊙ 8am-8pm Mon-Fri, 10am-3pm Sat) Healthy risottos and vegie pies stand out in this self-service spot. There's another all-veg branch (open 9am to 9pm Monday to Friday, 10am to 10pm Saturday and Sunday) on the 1st floor of the Velký Spalicek shopping centre.

Spolek (☎ 542 213 002; Orli 22; mains 70-100Kč; ⊙ closed Sun) The service is unpretentious at this coolly bohemian – yes, we are in Moravia – haven with interesting salads, soups, pasta and wine.

Sabaidy (☎ 545 428 310; třída kpt Jaroše 29; mains 100-220Kč; ⊙ 5pm-11pm Mon-Fri) With decor incorporating Buddhist statues and a talented Lao chef delivering authentic flavours, Sabaidy delivers both 'ommm' and 'mmmm'. After lots of 'same same' Czech food, this really is different.

Špaliček (☎ 542 215 526; Zelný trh 12; mains 140–300Kč)
Brno's oldest (and just maybe its meatiest)
restaurant sits on the edge of the Cabbage
Market. Ignore the irony and dig into the huge
Moravian meals.

Brabander (☎ 542 211 922; Joštova 4; mains 150–340Kč)
This cellar restaurant serves up innovative
food – on a Brno scale anyway – with a lighter
Mediterranean and Asian touch. A good wine
list adds to the appeal of one of Brno's best.

Also recommended:

Barunka (Běhounská 20; snacks 15–25Kč; ⏰ 7am–7pm
Mon–Fri, 8am–noon Sat) A sunny spot for open sandwiches,
salads, coffee, beer and wine.

Minach (Poštovská 6; per chocolate 13Kč; ⏰ 10am–7pm
Mon–Sat, from 2pm Sun) More than 50 kinds of handmade
chocolates and bracing coffee make this an essential mid-
morning or mid-afternoon detour.

Drinking

Pivnice Pegas (Jakubská 4) *Pivo* melts that old
Moravian reserve as the locals become pleasantly noisy. Don't miss the wheat beer with a
slice of lemon. Good luck finding a table, or
grab a spot at Brno's longest bar.

Café Alfa (Poštovská 6; ⏰ 8am–midnight Mon–Sat,
3–11pm Sun) This groovy spot has an arty vibe,
but also welcomes the not-so-hip. Start the
day with coffee and return for Alfa's nocturnal
transformation into a funky bar.

Černohorský Sklep (nám Svobody 5; ⏰ closed Sun)
Try the Black Hill aperitif beer or the honey-
infused Kvasar brew at the Black Mountain
Brewery's Brno outpost.

Entertainment

Brno offers excellent theatre and classical
music. Find entertainment listings in the
free monthly *Metropolis*, ask at the tourist information office or see the website
of the Národni' Divadlo Brno (National
Theatre Brno; www.ndb.cz).

Theatre Booking Office (předprodej; ☎ 542 321 285;
www.ndb.cz; Dvořákova 11; ⏰ 8am–5.30pm Mon–Fri, 9am–
noon Sat) Sells tickets for performances at the
Reduta, Mahenovo and Janáček Theatres.

Central Booking Office (Centrální předprodej; ☎ 542
210 863; Běhounská 17; ⏰ 10am–6pm Mon–Fri) Tickets to
rock, folk and classical concerts.

Janáček Theatre (Janáčkovo divadlo; Sady Osvobození)
Opera and ballet are performed at the
modern theatre.

Mahenovo Theatre (Mahenovo divadlo; Dvořákovo 11)
The neo-baroque Mahenovo Theatre presents
classical drama in Czech, and operettas.

Reduta Theatre (Reduta divadlo; Zelný trh 4) The
restored Reduta showcases Mozart's work (he
played there in 1767).

Getting There & Away

There are frequent buses from Brno to Prague
(130Kč, 2½ hours, hourly), Bratislava (110Kč,
2¼ hours, hourly) and Vienna (200Kč, 2½
hours, two daily). The departure point is either the bus station or near the railway station opposite the Grand Hotel. Check your
ticket. Private companies **Student Agency** (www
.studentagency.cz) and **Megabus** (www.megabus.cz)
both leave from their ticket booths opposite
the Grand Hotel.

There are trains to Prague (160Kč, three
hours) every two hours. Direct Eurocity trains
from Brno to Vienna (5725Kč, 1¾ hours, five
daily) arrive at Vienna's Südbahnhof. There
are frequent trains to Bratislava in Slovakia
(188Kč, two hours), and direct trains to Berlin
(€72, 7½ hours), Dresden (€43, five hours) and
Hamburg (€120, 10½ hours) in Germany. See
www.idos.cz for bus and train information.

ČSA (www.csa.cz) flies from Prague and **Ryan
Air** (www.ryanair.com) flies daily from London.
Smart Wings (www.smartwings.net) flies to Moscow
twice a week.

Getting Around

Buy public transport tickets from vending machines, news-stands or at the **DPMB Information
Office** (☎ 543 174 317; www.dpmb.cz; Novobranská 18;
⏰ 6am–6pm Mon–Fri, 8am–3.30pm Sat). Tickets are
valid for 60/90 minutes, cost 15/21Kč, and
allow unlimited transfers; 24-hour tickets are
60Kč. A 10-minute, no-transfer ticket is 10Kč.
For taxis, try **City Taxis** (☎ 542 321 321).

AROUND BRNO
Slavkov u Brna

Slavkov u Brna is better known in history by
its Austrian name, **Austerlitz**. On 2 December
1805 the Battle of the Three Emperors was
fought here, when Napoleon Bonaparte's
Grande Armée defeated the combined
forces of Emperor Franz I (Austria) and
Tsar Alexander I (Russia). During lulls in the
fighting, Napoleon stayed at **Slavkov Chateau**
(zámek Slavkov; ☎ 544 221 204; www.zamek-slavkov.cz;
tours adult/child 60/40Kč, in English 105/85Kč; ⏰ 9am–
5pm Jun–Aug, Tue–Sun May & Sep, to 4pm Tue–Sun Apr,
Oct & Nov).

The battle was decided at **Pracký kopec**, 12km
west of Slavkov, now marked by the **Cairn of**

Peace (Mohyla míru; adult/child 75/35Kč; 9am-6pm Jul & Aug, to 5pm May, Jun & Sep, Tue-Sun Apr, to 3.30pm Tue-Sun Oct-Mar) with a museum on the conflict which claimed 20,000 lives. Annual re-enactments take place around 2 December.

Slavkov is 21km east of Brno and reached by bus (29Kč, 25 minutes) or train (40Kč, 35 minutes). Pracký kopec is awkward by public transport. Take a local train from Brno to Ponětovice (26Kč, 20 minutes) and walk 3.5km southeast through Prace.

Moravian Karst

A good day trip from Brno, the limestone plateau of the Moravian Karst (Moravský kras) is riddled with caves and canyons carved by the subterranean Punkva River. There's a car park at Skalní Mlýn with an information desk and ticket office. A **mini-train** (adult/child return 70/60Kč; Apr-Sep) travels along the 1.5km between the car park and the caves. Otherwise it's a 20-minute stroll through forest.

The **Punkva Caves tour** (Punkevní jeskyně; 516 418 602; www.smk.cz; adult/child 150/70Kč; 8.40am-3.50pm Apr-Sep, 8.40am-2pm Mon-Fri, 8.40am-3.40pm Sat & Sun Oct, 8.40am-2pm Nov-Mar) involves a 1km walk through limestone caverns to the bottom of the **Macocha Abyss**, a 140m-deep sinkhole. Small, electric-powered boats then cruise along the underground river back to the entrance. On weekends and in July and August tickets for cave tours can sell out in advance, so book ahead.

Beyond the Punkva Caves entrance, a **cable car** (adult/child return 80/70Kč, combined tourist train & cable-car ticket 120/100Kč) travels to the upper rim of the Macocha Abyss. Afterwards, wander down on the blue-marked trail (2km).

Kateřinská Cave (Kateřinská eskyně; 516 413 161; adult/child 60/50Kč; 8.20am-4pm Apr-Sep, to 2pm Oct, 10am, noon & 2pm Feb-Mar) is 300m from the Skalní Mlýn car park. Usually less crowded, the 30-minute tour explores two massive chambers.

From Brno trains run to Blansko (33Kč, 30 minutes, hourly). Bus 226 departs from platform 742 at Blansko bus station (across the bridge from the train station) to Skalní Mlýn (16Kč, 15 minutes, five daily April to September).

Get an early start from Brno and catch one of the two buses (9.15am and 11.15am) departing to Blansko before noon, and you can easily visit the caves as a day trip. You can also hike an 8km trail from Blansko to Skalní Mlýn (two hours).

OLOMOUC
pop 105,000

While show-offs Prague, Karlovy Vary and Český Krumlov are constantly praised, Olomouc (pronounced olla-moats) goes quietly about its authentically Moravian business, and emerges as the Czech Republic's most under-rated destination.

An Old Town square rivalling Prague's Old Town Sq combines with the graceful campus of the country's second-oldest university. Moravia's most impressive religious structures play host to a thrilling history and one of the Czech Republic's best museums. And, with tourist numbers at a relative trickle, Olomouc is a great-value destination.

Orientation

The main train station (hlavní nádraží) is 2km east of the Old Town, over the Morava and Bystřice rivers (tram 2 or 6). The bus station is 1km further east (tram 4).

The Old Town comprises the two linked squares of Horní (Upper) and Dolní (Lower) nám. The Přemysl Palace is along Ostružinická and třída 1 máje.

Information

Internet U Dominika (Slovesnská 12; per min 1Kč; 9am-9pm Mon-Fri, from 10am Sat & Sun) Includes wi-fi for laptop travellers.

Knihy Dobrovský (585 393 252; Horní nám) Bookshop with English-language paperbacks and good maps.

Main tourist information office (Olomoucká informační služba; 585 513 385; www.olomouc-tourism.cz; Horní nám; 9am-7pm) Sells maps and makes accommodation bookings. Audio guides (150Kč for three hours) include a map detailing 28 points of interest.

Olomouc Tours (775 345 570; www.olomouctours.com; by donation Jul & Aug, rest of year 200Kč) Two-hour walking tours with the guys from Poet's Corner Hostel leave from the astronomical clock daily at 10am from July to August. During other months you'll need to book. Cycling tours (350Kč, two hours) are also available.

Sights & Activities
HORNÍ NÁM & AROUND

The splendid **town hall** was built in 1378, though its present appearance and **tower** (věž; admission 15Kč; tours 11am & 3pm Mar-Oct) date from 1607. Don't miss the **astronomical clock** on the north side, remodelled in communist style, so that each hour is announced by ideologically pure workers instead of pious saints. The best display is at

OLOMOUC

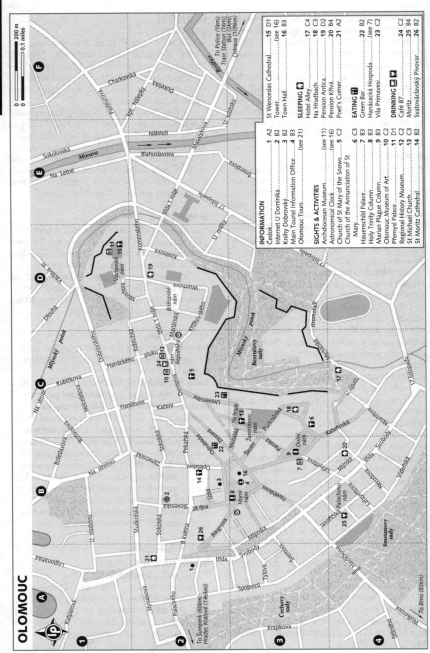

INFORMATION
Cedok..	1	A2
Internet U Dominika.....................	2	B2
Knihy Dobrovský..........................	3	B2
Main Tourist Information Office......	4	B3
Olomouc Tours.............................	(see 21)	

SIGHTS & ACTIVITIES
Archdiocesan Museum...................	(see 11)	
Astronomical Clock......................	(see 16)	
Church of St Mary of the Snows.....	5	C2
Church of the Annunciation of St		
Mary..	6	C3
Hauenschild Palace.......................	7	B3
Holy Trinity Column.....................	8	B3
Marian Plague Column.................	9	C2
Olomouc Museum of Art...............	10	C2
Přemysl Palace.............................	11	D1
Regional History Museum.............	12	C2
St Michael Church........................	13	C3
St Moritz Cathedral......................	14	B2
St Wenceslas Cathedral................	15	D1
Tower...	(see 16)	
Town Hall...................................	16	B3

SLEEPING 🛏
Hotel Alley..................................	17	C4
Na Hradbach...............................	18	C3
Pension Antika............................	19	D2
Pension Křiva..............................	20	B4
Poet's Corner..............................	21	A2

EATING 🍴
Green Bar....................................	22	B2
Hanácacká Hospoda.....................	(see 7)	
Vila Primavesi.............................	23	C2

DRINKING 🍷
Café 87......................................	24	C2
Moritz.......................................	25	B4
Svatováclavský Pivovar.................	26	B2

noon. In front of the town hall, a brass model of Olomouc will help you get your bearings.

Across the square is the Unesco World Heritage–listed **Holy Trinity Column** (Sousoší Nejsvětější trojice). Built between 1716 and 1754, the baroque structure is reminiscent of the Buddhist stupa. During summer, a friendly nun explains the meaning of the interior sculptures. The square is ringed by historic facades and features two of the city's six baroque fountains. The tourist information office has a good brochure about the distinctive fountains.

Down Opletalova is the immense, Gothic **St Moritz Cathedral** (chrám sv Mořice), built slowly from 1412 to 1530. The cathedral's peace is shattered every September with an International Organ Festival; the cathedral's own organ is Moravia's mightiest.

DOLNÍ NÁM

The 1661 **Church of the Annunciation of St Mary** (kostel Zvěstování Panny Marie) has a beautifully sober interior. In contrast is the opulent 16th-century Renaissance **Hauenschild Palace** (not open to the public), and the **Marian Plague Column** (Mariánský morový sloup).

Picturesque lanes thread northeast to the green-domed **St Michael Church** (kostel sv Michala). The baroque interior includes a rare painting of a pregnant Virgin Mary. Draped around the entire block is an active Dominican seminary (Dominikánský klášter).

NÁM REPUBLIKY & AROUND

The original Jesuit college complex, founded in 1573, stretched along Universitní and into nám Republiky, and includes the **Church of St Mary of the Snows** (kostel Panny Marie Sněžné), with many fine frescos.

Opposite is the **Regional History Museum** (Vlastivědné muzeum; ☎ 585 515 111; www.vmo.cz; nám Republiky 5; adult/child 40/20Kč; ⏱ 9am-6pm Tue-Sun Apr-Sep, 10am-5pm Wed-Sun Oct-Mar) with historical, geographical and zoological displays. Adjacent is the **Olomouc Museum of Art** (Olomoucký muzeum umění; ☎ 585 514 111; www.olumart.cz; Denisov 47; adult/child 50/25Kč; ⏱ 10am-6pm Tue-Sun), with an excellent collection of 20th-century Czech painting and sculpture. Admission includes entry to the Archdiocesan Museum (see right).

PŘEMYSL PALACE & ST WENCESLAS CATHEDRAL

To the northeast, the pocket-sized Václavské nám has Olomouc's most venerable buildings, now converted into one of the Czech Republic's finest museums.

The early-12th-century **Přemysl Palace** (Přemyslovský palác) is now the **Archdiocesan Museum** (☎ 585 514 111; www.olumart.cz; Václavské nám 3; adult/child 50/25Kč; ⏱ 10am-6pm Tue-Sun) with treasures from the 12th to the 18th centuries, when Olomouc was the Moravian capital. A thoughtful makeover showcases the site's diverse architecture from several centuries and many of the ecclesiastical treasures are superb. Don't miss the magnificent Troyer Coach, definitely the stretch limo of the 18th century. Admission includes entry to the Olomouc Museum of Art.

Originally a Romanesque basilica first consecrated in 1131, the adjacent **St Wenceslas Cathedral** (dóm sv Václava) was rebuilt several times before having a 'neo-Gothic' makeover in the 1880s.

Sleeping

The information office can book private and hotel rooms.

Poet's Corner (☎ 777 570 730; www.hostelolomouc .com; 3rd fl, Sokolská 1; dm/tw/tr/q 350/900/1200/1600Kč) Aussie owners Greg and Francie are a wealth of local information at this friendly and well-run hostel. Bicycles can be hired for 100Kč per day. In summer there's a two-night minimum stay, but Olomouc's definitely worth it.

Na Hradbach (☎ 585 233 243; nahradbach@quick .cz; Hrnčířská 3; s/d 600/800Kč) On a pretty street sits Olomouc's best-value pension, with two good restaurants across the lane. Be sure to book ahead.

Pension Křivá (☎ 585 209 204; www.pension-kriva .cz; Křivá 8; s/d 1450/1950Kč) This new opening gets a lot of things right: spacious rooms with cherrywood furniture, flash bathrooms with even flasher toiletries, plus a cosy cafe downstairs. The quiet laneway location doesn't hurt either.

Pension Antica (☎ 731 560 264; www.pension .antica.cz; Wurmova 1; apt 1450-2000Kč) With antique furniture, crisp white duvets and Oriental rugs on wooden floors, the Antica is a spacious and splurge-worthy romantic getaway. Catch bus 2 or 6 from the train station or bus 4 from the bus station. Get off at the U Domú stop.

Hotel Alley (☎ 585 209 204; www.hotel-alley.cz; Křivá 8; s/d 2800/3100Kč) The preferred digs of rock stars – well, Suzanne Vega stayed here anyway – the Hotel Alley combines solid four-star business cred and an in-house spa-massage centre. Slightly characterless, but the best digs in town. From Friday to Sunday there's a 30% discount.

Eating & Drinking

Café 87 (Denisova 87; chocolate pie 40Kč, coffee 40Kč; 8am-9pm) Locals flock to this funky cafe beside the Museum of Art for coffee and the famous chocolate pie. Some locals still prefer the dark chocolate to the white chocolate. When will they learn? It's a top spot for breakfast too.

our pick **Hanácacká Hospoda** (582 237 186; Dolní nám 38; mains 70-100Kč) In the same building as the Hauenschild palace; the menu lists everything in the local Haná dialect. It's worth persevering though, as the huge Moravian meals are tasty and supreme value. They've got an English menu if you're still coming up to speed with Haná.

Green Bar (777 749 274; Ztacená 3; meals 100Kč; 10am-5pm Mon-Fri, to 2pm Sat) Around 100Kč will get you a feast of salads, couscous and veg lasagna at this self-service vegetarian cafe. It's popular with a cosmoplitan mix of overseas students.

Moritz (585 205 560; Nešverova 2; mains 100-180Kč) This microbrewery and restaurant quickly became a local favourite after opening in 2007. We reckon it's a combination of the terrific beers, good-value food and a praise-worthy 'No smoking' policy.

Svatováclavský Pivovar (585 203 641; Riegrova 22; meals 140-200Kč) Another new microbrewery – what's in the water in Olomouc? – the Svatováclavský has a buzzy beerhall ambience. Try the zingy wheat beer with the stinky Olomouc cheese.

Vila Primavesi (777 749 288; Universtiní 7; mains 180-250Kč) In an art-nouveau villa that played host to Austrian artist Gustav Klimt in the early 20th century, the Vila Primavesi is Olomouc's newest eatery. On summer evenings enjoy meals such as tuna steak and risotto in the lovely gardens.

Getting There & Away

From Brno, there are 15 buses (83Kč, 1¼ hours) and five direct fast trains (120Kč, 1½ hours) daily. Trains from Prague (324Kč, 3¼ hours) leave from Praha-hlavní nádraží. Faster SC Pendolino trains (634Kč, 2¼ hours) stop at Olomouc en route from Praha-Holešovice to Ostrava. See www.idos.cz.

From Olomouc to Poland there is one direct train to Warsaw at 12.57pm daily (750Kč, six hours), and one to Kraków at 4.57pm (430Kč, 4½ hours).

Direct trains link Olomouc to Košice at 1.57pm (538Kč, 5½ hours) in Slovakia, but for Bratislava you'll need to change at Břeclav.

TELČ
pop 6000

Telč is a quiet town, with a gorgeous old centre ringed by medieval fish ponds and unspoilt by modern buildings. Unwind with a good book and a glass of Moravian wine at one of the local cafes.

The bus and train stations are a few hundred metres apart on the eastern side of town. A 10-minute walk along Masarykova leads to nám Zachariáše z Hradce, the Old Town square.

The **information office** (567 243 145; www .telc-etc.cz; nám Zachariáše z Hradce 10; 8am-5pm Mon-Fri, 10am-5pm Sat & Sun) books accommodation in private homes (around 350Kč to 400Kč per person). Internet access is 1Kč per minute.

Sights

In a country full of gorgeous Old Town squares, Telč's Unesco World Heritage–listed and cobblestoned **nám Zachariáše z Hradce** may outshine the lot. When the day trippers have departed, the Gothic arcades and elegant Renaissance facades are a magical setting.

At the square's northwestern end is the **Water Chateau** (567 243 943; www.zamek-telc.cz). **Tour A** (1hr adult/child90/45Kč, in English 180Kč; 9am-5pm Tue-Sun May-Sep, to 4pm Apr & Oct) visits the Renaissance halls, while **Tour B** (45min adult/child 80/40Kč; 9am-5pm Tue-Sun May-Sep) visits the private apartments, inhabited by the aristocratic owners until 1945. A new exhibition focuses on the chateau's **portrait gallery** (adult/child 40/20Kč; 9am-5pm Tue-Sun May-Sep, to 4pm Apr & Oct, to 3pm Nov-Mar).

At the castle's entrance is the **Chapel of All Saints**, where trumpeting angels guard the tombs of Zacharias of Hradec, the castle's founder, and his wife. The **historical museum** (adult/child 30/15Kč; 9am-5pm Tue-Sun May-Sep, to 4pm Apr & Oct), in the courtyard, has a model of Telč from 1895. More than a century later, not much has changed.

Sleeping & Eating

Penzión u Rudolfa (567 243 094; nám Zachariáše z Hradce 58; s/d 300/600Kč; Jul & Aug) A pretty

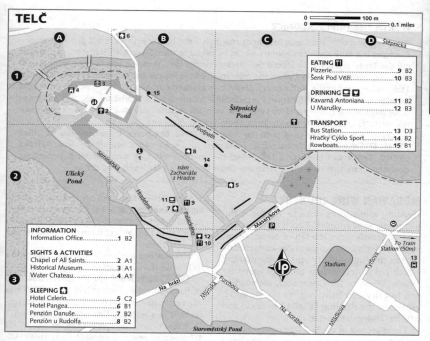

TELČ

merchant's house on the main square conceals a friendly pension with shared kitchen facilities.

Penzión Danuše (☎ 567 213 945; www.telc-etc.cz/cz/privat/danuse; Hradebni 25; s/d 450/900Kč, 4-bed apt 2000Kč) Discreet wrought-iron balconies and wooden window boxes provide a touch of class just off the main square.

Hotel Celerin (☎ 567 243 477; www.hotelcelerin.cz; nám Zachariáše z Hradce 43; s/d incl breakfast from 980/1530Kč; 🖥) Three-star charm showcases 12 romantic rooms wth decor varying from cosy wood to wedding-cake kitsch. Have a look before you hand over your passport.

Hotel Pangea (☎ 567 213 122; www.pangea.cz; Na Baště 450; s/d incl breakfast 1200/1600Kč; 🍴 🖥 🐕) Huge buffet breakfasts and loads of facilities make the functional Pangea good value. Ask the friendly hotel dog for a discount outside of July and August.

Kavarná Antoniana (☎ 605 519 903; nám Zachariáše z Hradce; coffee & cake 70Kč; 🕐 8am-2am) Documentary-style photography from around the world will get you planning your next trip at this modern refuge from the Renaissance glories outside. Have a coffee or something stronger.

Šenk Pod Věži (☎ 603 526 999; Palackého 116; mains 100-200Kč; 🕐 11am-3pm & 6-9pm Mon-Sat, 11am-4pm Sun) Sizzling grills and live music are the big drawcards at this cosy restaurant under the tower.

U Marušky (☎ 605 870 854; Palackého) Telč's hipper younger citizens crowd this buzzy bar for cool jazz and tasty eats.

Order in pizza from **Pizzerie** (☎ 567 223 246; nám Zachariáše z Hradce 32; pizza 75-140Kč) just across the square.

Getting There & Away
Five buses daily travel from Prague Roztyly to Telč (124Kč, 2½ hours). Buses running between České Budějovice and Brno also stop at Telč (92Kč, two hours, two daily). Trains rumble south to the beautiful village of Slavonice.

Getting Around
Hračky Cyklo Sport (nám Zachariáše z Hradce 23; per day 100Kč; 🕐 8am-5pm Mon-Fri, 9am-noon Sat) rents bicycles.

Rent **rowboats** (per 30min 20Kč; 🕐 10am-6pm Jul & Aug) from outside the East gate.

WORTH THE TRIP: SLAVONICE

Barely hanging onto the Czech Republic's coat-tails – the border with Austria is just 1km away – Slavonice is a little town any country would be proud to own. Slavonice's initial prosperity during the Thirty Years' War produced two squares dotted with stunning Renaissance architecture. Economic isolation followed when the main road linking Prague and Vienna was diverted in the 18th century, and in the 20th century, Slavonice's proximity to the Cold War border with Austria maintained its isolation. The town's architectural treasures were spared the socialist makeover other parts of the country endured and now, once the Austrian day trippers have left, Slavonice resurrects its compellingly moody atmosphere like nowhere else.

Slavonice is on a little-used train line from Telč (43Kč, one hour). The sleepy **tourist office** (☎ 384 493 320; www.mesto-slavonice.cz) is on the main square, nám Miru. Just off nám Miru, **Besídka** (☎ 606 212 070; www.besidka.cz; d 1290-1490Kč) has spacious loft-style rooms and a cosmopolitan downstairs cafe that might just serve the Czech Republic's best wood-fired pizzas.

MORAVIAN WINE COUNTRY

Heading south from Brno to Vienna is the Moravian wine country. Czech wine has improved greatly since the fall of communism in 1989, with small producers concentrating on the high-quality end of the market. Czech red wines, such as the local speciality Svatovavřinecké (St Lawrence), are mediocre, but dry and fruity whites can be good, especially the Riesling (*Vlašský Ryzlink*) and Müller-Thurgau varietals.

There are lots of *vinné sklepy* (wine cellars), *vinoteky* (wine shops) and *vinárny* (wine bars) to explore, as well as spectacular chateaux. The terrain is relatively flat, so cycling is a leisurely way to get around.

Mikulov

Described by Czech poet Jan Skácel as a 'piece of Italy moved to Moravia by God's hand', Mikulov is an excellent base to explore the neighbouring Lednice-Valtice Cultural Landscape. The nearby Palava Hills are a mecca for hiking and cycling. If you're travelling from Brno to Vienna, Mikulov is a good stopping-off point.

The **tourist information office** (☎ 519 510 855; www.mikulov.cz; Nám 30; ☺ 8am-6pm Mon-Fri, 9am-6pm Sat & Sun Jun-Sep, 8am-noon & 12.30-5pm Mon-Fri, 9am-4pm Sat & Sun Apr, May & Oct, 8am-noon & 1-4pm Mon-Fri Nov-Mar) is beneath the impressive Renaissance **chateau** (☎ 519 510 255; adult/child 70/35Kč; ☺ 9am-5pm Tue-Sun May-Sep, 9am-4pm Apr & Oct), seat of the Dietrichstein and Liechtenstein families.

Bicycles and cycle-touring information are available from **Půjčovna Kol** (Husova 42; per day 120Kč). If no-one's around, ask at the Hotel Templ next door.

Spend the afternoon wine-tasting at the **Vinařské Centrum** (☎ 519 51 368; www.obchodsvinem .cz; Nám 11, per tasting glass 15-25Kč; ☺ 10am-5.30pm Sun-Thu, to 8pm Fri & Sat). Wines from across the region are available.

Mikulov has some excellent boutique hotels in the old Jewish quarter.

our pick **Hotel Templ** (☎ 519 323 095; www.templ .cz; Husova 50; s/d incl breakfast from 1390/1650Kč) has discreetly furnished rooms and a stylish restaurant in a restored Renaissance mansion.

A few doors up, **Pension Reisten** (☎ 519 324 327; www.pensionreisten.cz; Husova 44; d incl breakfast 1400-2400Kč) effortlessly combines modern furniture with beautifully resurrected rooms with exposed brick walls and wooden floors.

More affordable is the **Fajka Vinárna & Pension** (☎ 732 833 147; www.fajka-mikulov.cz; Alfonse Mucha 18; s/d 400/800Kč), with comfortable rooms above a cosy wine bar. Out back is a garden restaurant if you really, really like the local wine.

There are regular buses from Brno to Mikulov (55Kč, one hour, 14 daily), and less frequent buses between Mikulov and Vienna (180Kč, two hours, two daily).

Lednice & Valtice

A few kilometres east, the **Lednice-Valtice Cultural Landscape** consists of 200 sq km of woodland, artificial lakes and tree-lined avenues dotted with baroque, neoclassical and neo-Gothic chateaux. Effectively Europe's biggest landscaped garden, it was created over several centuries by the dukes of Liechtenstein and is now a Unesco World Heritage site.

The massive neo-Gothic **Lednice Chateau** (☎ 519 340 128; www.lednice.cz; ☺ 9am-6pm Tue-Sun May-Aug, to 5pm Tue-Sun Sep, to 4pm Sat & Sun only Apr & Oct), was the Liechtensteins' summer palace.

Studded with battlements, pinnacles and gargoyles, it gazes across an island-dotted artificial lake. **Tour 1** (adult/child 80/40Kč, 45 min) visits the major rooms, while **Tour 2** (adult/child 100/50Kč, 45 min) concentrates on the Liechtenstein apartments. Visit the gardens for free, or cruise on a **pleasure boat** (☉ 9.30am-5pm Jul & Aug, Tue-Sun May, Jun & Sep, Sat & Sun Apr & Oct). Routes include between the chateau and an incongruous minaret (adult/child 80/40Kč) and between the minaret and nearby Janův castle (adult/child 120/60Kč).

During summer the **Birds of Prey show** (www .zayferus.cz; adult/child 90/45Kč) presents birds soaring and hunting above Lednice's meadows.

Valtice's huge baroque chateau houses the **National Wine Salon** (Národní salon vín; ☎ 519 352 072; www.salonvin.cz; Zámek 1; ☉ 9.30am-5pm Tue-Thu, 10.30am-6pm Fri & Sat, 10.30am-5pm Sun Jun-Sep), with wine-tasting sessions from 120Kč to 399Kč per person (minimum five people).

There are five buses daily from Mikulov to Lednice (31Kč, 40 minutes), and one daily at 11am from Brno (68Kč, 1¾ hours). Regular buses shuttle the short distance between Lednice and Valtice (14Kč, 15 minutes).

CZECH REPUBLIC DIRECTORY

ACCOMMODATION

Accommodation reviews in this chapter are listed in order of price, from cheapest to most expensive. Budget means less than 1400Kč for a double, midrange is 1400Kč to 3500Kč, and top end is more than 3500Kč. Unless otherwise stated, rooms in this chapter include private bathroom.

You usually have to show your passport when checking in at accommodation in the Czech Republic. There is no law banning smoking in rooms, but a growing number of midrange and top-end options can provide nonsmoking accommodation.

There are several hundred camping grounds spread around the country; most are open from May to September only and charge around 70Kč to 100Kč per person. Camping on public land is prohibited.

Klub mladých cestovatelů (KMC Young Travellers Club; Map pp274-5; ☎ 222 220 347; Karolíny Světlé 30, Prague 1) is the HI affiliate in Prague, and can book hostel accommodation throughout the country. In July and August many student dormitories become temporary hostels, and some in Prague are also year-round backpacker hostels. Prague and Český Krumlov are the only places with a solid choice of backpacker-oriented hostels. Dorm beds costs around 400Kč in Prague and 300Kč to 350Kč elsewhere; it's best to book ahead. An HI-membership card is not usually needed, although it will often get you a reduced rate. An ISIC, ITIC, IYTC or Euro26 card may also get you a discount.

Another category of hostel accommodation is *turistické ubytovny* (tourist hostels), which provide very basic dormitory accommodation (200Kč to 300Kč); rooms can usually be booked through the local tourist information office or KMC branch. Look for signs advertising private rooms (*privát* or *Zimmer frei* – like B&Bs without the breakfast). Most tourist information offices can book them for you. Expect to pay from 400Kč to 550Kč per person outside Prague. Some have a three-night minimum-stay requirement.

Pensions *(penzióny)* are a step up: small, homely, often family-run, but offering rooms with private bathroom, often including breakfast. Rates range from 900Kč to 1500Kč for a double room (1800Kč to 2500Kč in Prague).

Hotels in central Prague, Český Krumlov and Brno can be expensive, but smaller towns are usually significantly cheaper. Two-star hotels offer reasonable comfort for 900Kč to 1000Kč for a double, or 1100Kč to 1500Kč with private bathroom (50% higher in Prague).

ACTIVITIES

There is good hiking among the hills of the Šumava (p309) south of Český Krumlov, in the forests around Karlovy Vary, in the Moravian Karst and in the Adršpach-Teplice Rocks (p309). Climbing is also excellent in these last two. Canoeing and rafting are popular on the Vltava River around Český Krumlov (p307) and the whole country is ideal for cycling and cycle touring. Especially good for cycling are the Šumava region (p309) and the Moravian Wine Country. A recent introduction are beer and wine tours.

The following companies provide activities-based tours:

Ave Bicycle Tours (☎ 251 551 011; www.bicycle-tours .cz) Cycle touring specialists.

E-Tours (☎ 572 557 191; www.etours.cz) Nature, wildlife and photography tours.

Greenways Travel Club (☎ 519 511 572; www.visit greenways.com) From cycling and walking to beer and wine, Czech glass and Czech music tours.

Top Bicycle (☎ 519 513 745; www.topbicycle.com) Biking and multisport tours.

BUSINESS HOURS

Outside Prague, almost everything closes on Saturday afternoon and all day Sunday. Most restaurants are open every day; most museums, castles and chateaux are closed on Mondays year-round. Banks open from 8am to 4.30pm Monday to Friday, while post office operate from 8am to 6pm Monday to Friday and to noon Saturdays. Shops are generally open from 8.30am to 5pm or 6pm Monday to Friday and to noon or 1pm Saturday. Restaurant opening hours are 11am to 11pm daily; bars operate from 11am to midnight daily.

COURSES

The **Institute for Language & Preparatory Studies** (Ústav jazykové a odborné přípravy; ☎ 224 990 411; www .ujop.cuni.cz) runs six-week Czech language courses for foreigners (€610). The **London School of Modern Languages** (☎ 226 096 140; www .londonschool.cz) offers one-on-one Czech language tuition (350Kč per 45 minutes), while the **Prague School** (☎ 257 534 013; www.filmschool.cz) runs four-week intensive film-making workshops in summer.

DANGERS & ANNOYANCES

Pickpocketing can be a problem in Prague's tourist zone and there are occasional reports of robberies on overnight international trains. There is racism towards the local Roma population, but Prague's increasingly cosmopolitan society means that abuse directed at darker-skinned visitors is rapidly becoming less prevalent.

EMBASSIES & CONSULATES

Most embassies and consulates are open at least 9am to noon Monday to Friday.

Australia (Map pp274-5; ☎ 296 578 350; www.embassy .gov.au/cz.html; 6th fl, Klimentská 10, Nové Město) Honorary consulate for emergency assistance only; nearest Australian embassy is in Vienna.

Austria (Map pp272-3; ☎ 257 090 511; www.austria.cz, in German & Czech; Viktora Huga 10, Smíchov)

Bulgaria (Map pp274-5; ☎ 222 211 258; bulvelv@mbox .vol.cz; Krakovská 6, Nové Město)

Canada (Map pp272-3; ☎ 272 101 800; www.canada.cz; Muchova 6, Bubeneč)

France (Map pp272-3; ☎ 251 171 711; www.france.cz, in French & Czech; Velkopřerovské nám 2, Malá Strana)

Germany (Map pp272-3; ☎ 257 113 111; www.deutsch land.cz, in German & Czech; Vlašská 19, Malá Strana)

Hungary (Map pp272-3; ☎ 233 324 454; huembprg@ vol.cz; Českomalínská 20, Bubeneč)

Ireland (Map pp272-3; ☎ 257 530 061; www.embassyof ireland.cz; Tržiště 13, Malá Strana)

Netherlands (Map pp272-3; ☎ 233 015 200; www .netherlandsembassy.cz; Gotthardská 6/27, Bubeneč)

New Zealand (Map pp272-3; ☎ 222 514 672; egermayer@ nzconsul.cz; Dykova 19, Vinohrady) Honorary consulate providing emergency assistance only (eg stolen passport); the nearest NZ embassy is in Berlin. Visits only by appointment.

Poland consulate (off Map pp272-3; ☎ 224 228 722; konspol@mbox.vol.cz; Vúžlabině 14, Strašnice); embassy (Map pp272-3; ☎ 257 099 500; www.ambpol.cz; Valdštejnská 8, Malá Strana) Go to the consulate for visas.

Russia (Map pp272-3; ☎ 233 374 100; rusembas@ bohem-net.cz; Pod Kaštany 1, Bubeneč)

Slovakia (Map pp272-3; ☎ 233 113 051; www .slovakemb.cz, in Slovak; Pod Hradbami 1, Dejvice)

South Africa (Map pp272-3; ☎ 267 311 114; www .saprague.cz; Ruská 65, Vršovice)

UK (Map p279; ☎ 257 402 111; www.britain.cz; Thunovská 14, Malá Strana)

Ukraine (Map pp272-3; ☎ 233 342 000; emb_cz@mfa .gov.ua; Charlese de Gaulla 29, Bubeneč)

USA (Map pp272-3; ☎ 257 022 000; www.usembassy.cz; Tržiště 15, Malá Strana)

GAY & LESBIAN TRAVELLERS

Homosexuality is legal in the Czech Republic (the age of consent is 15), but Czechs are not yet used to seeing public displays of affection; it's best to be discreet. In July 2006 same-sex civil unions became legal. **Prague Saints** (www.prague saints.cz) has comprehensive English-language information, and links to gay-friendly accommodation and bars. Also worth checking out are www.gay.cz and www.prague.gayguide.net.

HOLIDAYS

New Year's Day 1 January; also anniversary of the founding of the Czech Republic.

Easter Monday March/April

Labour Day 1 May

Liberation Day 8 May

SS Cyril and Methodius Day 5 July

Jan Hus Day 6 July

Czech Statehood Day 28 September

Republic Day 28 October

Struggle for Freedom and Democracy Day 17 November

Christmas 24 to 26 December

INTERNET RESOURCES

ABC Prague (www.abcprague.com) English-language news.
Czech Tourism (www.czechtourism.com) Official tourist information.
Czech.cz (www.czech.cz) Informative government site on travel and tourism, including visa requirements.
IDOS (www.idos.cz) Train and bus timetables.
Mapy (www.mapy.cz) Online maps.
Prague Information Service (www.prague-info.cz) Official tourist site for Prague.
PragueTV (www.praguetv.cz) Prague events and entertainment listings.
Radio Prague (www.radio.cz) Dedicated to Czech news, language and culture (in English, French, German, Spanish and Russian).

MONEY
Currency

Czech crown (Koruna česká, or Kč) banknotes come in denominations of 20, 50, 100, 200, 500, 1000, 2000 and 5000Kč, and coins in one, two, five, 10, 20 and 50Kč.

Keep small change handy for use in public toilets, telephones and tram-ticket machines, and try to keep some small denomination notes for shops, cafes and restaurants. Changing larger notes from ATMs can be a problem.

The Czech crown (Koruna česká) has appreciated against other currencies in recent years and Prague is no longer a budget destination.

Some businesses quote prices in euros; prices in this chapter conform to quotes of individual businesses.

Exchanging Money

There is no black market, and anyone who offers to change money in the street is a thief.

There's a good network of *bankomaty* (ATMs). The main banks are the best places to change cash and travellers cheques or get a cash advance on Visa or MasterCard.

EMERGENCY NUMBERS

- Ambulance ☎ 155
- Fire ☎ 150
- Motoring Assistance (ÚAMK) ☎ 1230
- Municipal Police ☎ 156
- State Police ☎ 158

American Express (Amex) and Travelex offices change their own cheques without commission. Credit cards are widely accepted in petrol stations, midrange and top-end hotels, restaurants and shops.

Beware of *směnárna* (private exchange offices), especially in Prague – they advertise misleading rates, and often charge exorbitant commissions or 'handling fees'.

Tipping

Tipping in restaurants is optional, but increasingly expected in Prague. If there is no service charge you should certainly round up the bill to the next 10 or 20Kč (5% to 10% is normal in Prague). The same applies to tipping taxi drivers. When you're a buying a beer, it's customary to leave leftover small change as a tip.

POST

General delivery mail can be addressed to Poste Restante, Pošta 1, in most major cities. For Prague, the address is Poste Restante, Jindřišská 14, 11000 Praha 1, Czech Republic. International postcards cost 15Kč.

TELEPHONE

All Czech phone numbers have nine digits – you have to dial all nine for any call, local or long distance. Make international calls at main post offices or directly from phonecard booths. The international access code is ☎ 00. The Czech Republic's country code is ☎ 420.

Payphones are widespread, some taking coins and some phonecards. Buy phonecards from post offices, hotels, news-stands and department stores for 150Kč or 1000Kč.

Mobile-phone coverage (GSM 900) is excellent. If you're from Europe, Australia or New Zealand, your own mobile phone should be compatible. It's best to purchase a Czech SIM card from any mobile-phone shop for around 500Kč (including 300Kč of calling credit) and make local calls at local rates. In this case you can't use your existing mobile number.

Local mobile phone numbers start with the following numbers; 601 to 608 and 720 to 779.

TOURIST INFORMATION

Czech Tourism (www.czechtourism.com) offices provide information about tourism, culture and business in the Czech Republic.

TRAVELLERS WITH DISABILITIES

Ramps for wheelchair users are becoming more common, but cobbled streets, steep hills and stairways often make getting around difficult. Public transport is still problematic, but a growing number of trains and trams have wheelchair access. See www.dpp.cz for more information (listed under 'Barrier Free'). Major tourist attractions such as Prague Castle also offer wheelchair access. Anything described as *bezbarierová* is 'barrier-free'.

Czech Tourism (Map pp274-5 ☎ 221 580 111; www .czechtourism.com; Vinohradská 46; Vinohrady; ⌚ 8.30am-noon & 1-4pm) can supply 'Wheeling the Czech Republic' brochure with a list of wheelchair-friendly accommodation and attractions. See also the 'Holidays Suitable for the Disabled' section on www.czechtourism.com

Prague Wheelchair Users Organisation (Map pp274-5; Pražská organizace vozíčkářů; ☎ 224 827 210; www.pov .cz, in Czech; Benediktská 6, Staré Město) has a CD-ROM guide 'Prague for the Disabled' in Czech, English and German.

VISAS

Everyone requires a valid passport (or identity card for EU citizens) to enter the Czech Republic.

Since March 2008, the Czech Republic has been part of the Schengen Agreement, and citizens of EU and EEA countries do not need visas. Citizens of Australia, Canada, Israel, Japan, New Zealand, Singapore, the USA and 23 other countries can stay for up to 90 days in a six-month period without a visa. If you are also travelling in other Schengen Agreement countries, you can still only stay for a maximum of 90 days in any six-month period.

For travellers from other countries, a Schengen Visa is required. You can only do this from your country of residence. Most Schengen Agreement countries will honour Schengen Visas issued by other member countries. Visa regulations change from time to time, so check www.czech.cz for the latest information.

TRANSPORT IN THE CZECH REPUBLIC

GETTING THERE & AWAY
Air

The Czech Republic's main international airport is **Prague-Ruzyně** (☎ 220 113 314; www.csl.cz/en).

The national carrier, **Czech Airlines** (ČSA; Map pp274-5; ☎ 239 007 007; www.csa.cz; V celnici 5, Nové Město), has direct flights to Prague from many European cities.

The main international airlines serving Prague:

Aer Lingus (EI; ☎ 224 815 373; www.aerlingus.com)
Aeroflot (SU; ☎ 227 020 020; www.aeroflot.ru)
Air France (AF; ☎ 223 090 933; www.airfrance.cz)
Alitalia (AZ; ☎ 224 194 150; www.alitalia.com)
Austrian Airlines (OS; ☎ 227 231 231; www .aua.com)
bmibaby (WW; www.bmibaby.com)
British Airways (BA; ☎ 239 000 299; www .ba.com)
Brussels Airlines (SN; ☎ 220 114 323; www .flysn.com)
Croatia Airlines (OU; ☎ 222 222 235; www .croatiaairlines.com)
Czech Airlines (OK; ☎ 239 007 007; www.csa.cz)
Delta (DL; www.delta.com)
easyJet (EZY; www.easyjet.com)
El Al (LY; ☎ 224 226 624; www.elal.co.il)
germanwings (4U; www.germanwings.com)
JAT Airways (JU; ☎ 224 942 654; www.jat.com)
Jet2.com (LS; www.jet2.com)
KLM (KL; ☎ 233 090 933; www.klm.com)
LOT (LO; ☎ 222 317 524; www.lot.com)
Lufthansa (LH; ☎ 234 008 234; www.lufthansa.com)
Malev (MA; ☎ 841 182 182; www.malev.com)
Ryanair (FR; www.ryanair.com)
SAS (SK; ☎ 220 116 031; www.flysas.com)
SkyEurope (NE; ☎ 246 096 096; www.skyeurope .com)
SmartWings (QS; ☎ 900 166 565; www.smart wings.net)
Turkish Airlines (TK; ☎ 234 708 708; www.thy.com)

Land

If you're travelling overland into the Czech Republic, note that under the Schengen Agreement there's no border control between the Czech Republic and surrounding countries.

BUS

Prague's main international bus terminal is Florenc Bus Station, 600m north of the main train station. The peak season for bus travel is mid-June to the end of September, with daily buses to major European cities. Outside this season, frequency falls to two or three a week. See p288 for services from Prague. Other international services include shuttle buses to Austria from Český Krumlov (p309), and buses from Brno (p314) to Austria and Slovakia.

CAR & MOTORCYCLE

Motorists can enter the country at any of the many border crossings marked on most road maps; see the map on p264 for all major 24-hour crossings.

You will need to buy a *nálepka* (motorway tax coupon) – on sale at border crossings, petrol stations and post offices – in order to use Czech motorways (220/330Kč for one week/month). See www.ceskedalnice.cz for more information.

TRAIN

International trains arrive at Prague's main train station (Praha-hlavní nádraží, or Praha hl. n.), or the outlying Holešovice (Praha Hol.) and Smíchov (Praha Smv.) stations. See p289 for further information on services.

Trains between Prague and Germany stop at Plzeň (p302), while Brno (p314) has services to Austria, Slovakia and Germany. Other international services include trains to Poland and Slovakia from Olomouc (p318).

You can buy tickets in advance from Czech Railways (České dráhy, or ČD) ticket offices and various travel agencies. Seat reservations are compulsory on international trains. International tickets are valid for two months with unlimited stopovers. Inter-Rail (Zone D) passes are valid in the Czech Republic, and in 2009 the country became part of the Eurail network.

GETTING AROUND
Bicycle

The Czech Republic offers good opportunities for cycle touring. Cyclists should be careful as minor roads are often narrow and potholed. In towns, cobblestones and tram tracks can be a dangerous combination, especially after rain. Theft is a problem, especially in Prague and other large cities, so always lock up your bike.

It's fairly easy to transport your bike on Czech trains. First purchase your train ticket and then take it with your bicycle to the railway luggage office. There you fill out a card, which will be attached to your bike; on the card you should write your name, address, departure station and destination.

The cost of transporting a bicycle is 60Kč to 80Kč, depending on the length of the journey. You can also transport bicycles on most buses if they are not too crowded and if the bus driver is willing.

Czech Railway also provides a handy bicycle hire service in areas best explored on two wheels. See www.cd.cz/static/eng /bikehireservice.htm.

Bus

Within the Czech Republic buses are often faster, cheaper and more convenient than trains, though not as comfortable. Many bus routes have reduced frequency (or none) at weekends. Buses occasionally leave early, so get to the station at least 15 minutes before the official departure time.

Most services are operated by the national bus company **ČSAD** (☎ information line 900 144 444). Check bus timetables and prices at www.idos .cz. Ticketing at main bus stations is computerised, so you can often book a seat ahead and be sure of a comfortable trip. Other stations are rarely computerised and you must line up and pay the driver.

Private companies include **Student Agency** (www.studentagency.cz), with destinations including Prague, Brno, České Budějovice, Český Krumlov, Karlovy Vary and Plzeň, and **Megabus** (www.megabus.cz), linking Prague with Karlovy Vary, Brno and Plzeň.

The footnotes on printed timetables may drive you crazy. Note the following: crossed hammers means the bus runs on *pracovní dny* (working days; ie Monday to Friday only); a Christian cross means it runs on Sundays and public holidays; and numbers in circles refer to particular days of the week (1 is Monday, 2 Tuesday etc). *Jede* means 'runs', *nejede* means 'doesn't run' and *jede denne* means 'runs daily'. *V* is 'on', *od* is 'from' and *do* is 'to' or 'until'.

Fares are very reasonable; expect to pay around 80Kč for a 100km trip.

Car & Motorcycle
DRIVING LICENCE

Foreign driving licences are valid for up to 90 days. Strictly speaking, licences that do not include photo identification need an International Driving Permit as well, although this rule is rarely enforced. Ordinary UK licences without a photo are normally accepted without comment.

FUEL

There are plenty of petrol stations, many open 24/7. Leaded petrol is available as *special*

(91 octane) and *super* (96 octane), and un-leaded as *natural* (95 octane) or *natural plus* (98 octane). The Czech for diesel is *nafta* or just *diesel*. *Autoplyn* (LPG gas) is available in every major town but at very few outlets.

HIRE

The main international car-rental chains all have offices in Prague. Small local companies offer better prices, but are less likely to have fluent, English-speaking staff. It's often easier to book by email than by phone. Typical rates for a Škoda Fabia are around 800Kč a day including unlimited kilometres, collision-damage waiver and value-added tax (VAT). Reputable local companies include the following:

Secco Car (Map pp272-3; ☎ 220 802 361; www .seccocar.cz; Přístavní 39, Holešovice)

Vecar (Map pp272-3; ☎ 224 314 361; www.vecar.org; Svatovítská 7, Dejvice)

West Car Praha (off Map pp272-3; ☎ 235 365 307; www.westcarpraha.cz, in Czech; Veleslavínská 17, Veleslavín)

ROAD RULES

Road rules are the same as the rest of Europe. A vehicle must be equipped with a first-aid kit, a red-and-white warning triangle and a nationality sticker on the rear; the use of seat belts is compulsory. Drinking and driving is strictly forbidden – the legal blood-alcohol level is zero. Police can hit you with on-the-spot fines of up to 2000Kč for speeding and other traffic offences (be sure to insist on a receipt).

Speed limits are 30km/h or 50km/h in built-up areas, 90km/h on open roads and 130km/h on motorways; motorbikes are limited to 80km/h. At level crossings over railway lines the speed limit is 30km/h. Beware of speed traps.

You need a motorway tax coupon to use the motorways. This is included with most rental cars.

Local Transport

City buses and trams operate from around 4.30am to midnight daily. Tickets must be purchased in advance – they're sold at bus and train stations, news-stands and vending machines – and must be validated in the time-stamping machines found on buses and trams and at the entrance to metro stations. Tickets are hard to find at night, on weekends and out in residential areas, so carry a good supply.

Taxis have meters – ensure they're switched on.

Train

Czech Railways provides efficient train services to almost every part of the country. Fares are based on distance: one-way, 2nd-class fares cost around 80/150/275/500Kč for 50/100/200/400km. For travel within the Czech Republic only, the Czech Flexipass is available (from US$112 to US$268 for three to eight days travel in a 15-day period). The sales clerks at ticket counters outside of Prague may not speak English, so write down your destination with the date and time you wish to travel. If you're paying by credit card, let them know *before* they issue the ticket.

Train categories include the following:

EC (EuroCity) Fast, comfortable international trains, stopping at main stations only, with 1st- and 2nd-class coaches; supplementary charge of 60Kč, reservations recommended. Includes 1st-class only SC Pendolino trains which run from Prague to Olomouc, Brno and Ostrava, with links to Vienna and Braitslava.

Ex (express) As for IC, but no supplementary charge.

IC (InterCity) Long-distance and international trains with 1st- and 2nd-class coaches; supplement of 40Kč, reservations recommended.

Os (*osobní*) Slow trains using older rolling stock that stop in every one-horse town; 2nd-class only.

R (*rychlík*) The main domestic network of fast trains with 1st- and 2nd-class coaches and sleeper services; no supplement except for sleepers; express and *rychlík* trains are usually marked in red on timetables.

Sp (*spěšný*) Slower and cheaper than *rychlík* trains; 2nd class only.

If you need to purchase a ticket or pay a supplement on the train, advise the conductor *before* they ask for your ticket or you'll have to pay a fine. Some Czech train conductors may try to intimidate foreigners by pretending there's something wrong with their ticket. Don't pay any 'fine', 'supplement' or 'reservation fee' unless you first get a *doklad* (written receipt).

Estonia

These are heady days for Estonia. In the space of one generation Estonia has had its prayers answered and dreams realised, and is now scarcely recognisable in its new incarnation. After some hiccups in the early days, this diminutive country has politically and economically shaken off the dead weight of the Soviet era, and has turned its focus very much to the West. Since the turn of the millennium, Estonia has gained both NATO and EU membership, plus one of Europe's fastest-growing economies, and the country is now celebrating its return to the world stage – independent, economically robust, tech savvy and pretty damn satisfied.

And why wouldn't it be? There's certainly much to be proud of, and the world is slowly tuning in to the low-key and lovely Estonian charms, an appealing blend of Eastern European and Nordic flavours. Revelling in Tallinn's long white nights and medieval history, and exploring the country's coastline, studded with 1521 islands, are joys to be savoured. National parks provide plenty of elbow room, and are home to wildlife long gone in Western Europe. Quaint villages evoke a sense of history, while uplifting song-and-dance festivals celebrate age-old traditions.

The last century has been full of twists and turns for the country, but it's now anxious to emphasise what distinguishes it from the rest of Europe. Estonia's primped and primed, and waiting to shine in the spotlight.

FAST FACTS

- **Area** 45,226 sq km
- **Capital** Tallinn
- **Currency** kroon (EEK); €1 = 15.65EEK; US$1 = 11.47EEK; UK£1 = 16.62EEK; A$1 = 7.94EEK; ¥100 = 11.93EEK; NZ$1 = 6.44EEK
- **Famous for** song festivals, Skype, Kazaa, saunas, forest
- **Official language** Estonian
- **Phrases** *tere* (hello); *vabandage* (excuse me); *palun* (please); *aitäh* (thanks)
- **Population** 1.3 million
- **Telephone codes** country code ☎ 372; international access code ☎ 00
- **Visa** no visa needed for citizens of the EU, USA, Canada and Australia for stays of up to 90 days; see p364

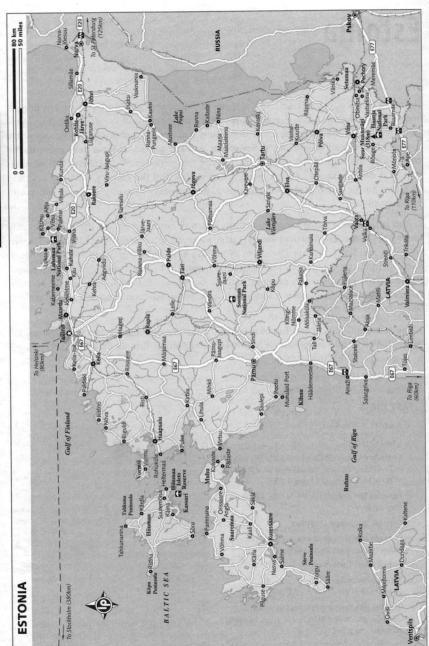

ESTONIA

HIGHLIGHTS

- Find medieval bliss exploring Old Town in **Tallinn** (p334), then unwind among the artistic eye candy at leafy, lovely Kadriorg Park.
- Get sand in your shorts in **Pärnu** (p355), Estonia's beachy-keen summertime mecca.
- Escape to the island of **Saaremaa** (p359) for castles, coastlines and spas.
- Have a natural encounter worth writing home about in **Soomaa National Park** (p359).
- Further your local education among the bars and cafes of **Tartu** (p350), Estonia's second city.

ITINERARIES

- **Five days** Hit Tallinn at a weekend to get in your sightseeing and partying, then head east to Lahemaa National Park or west to the island of Saaremaa – two wheels will offer the chance to really explore.
- **Two weeks** There'll be time to explore Tallinn more deeply; a retreat to Lahemaa National Park or Saaremaa could also be on your agenda. If the weather's fine, opt for fun in the sun in Pärnu, then get back to nature at Soomaa National Park.

CLIMATE & WHEN TO GO

Between May and September is the best time of the year to visit Estonia as there's better weather and longer days. White nights, when the skies darken slightly for only a few hours each night, peak in late June, but the sun rarely sets for long from mid-May to mid-August. June can still be cool; the warmest temperatures come in July and August. Winter is temperate, dark and damp, but has a special magic. Slushy, drizzly March is the only really depressing month.

HISTORY
Early History

It's commonly held that in the mid-3rd millennium BC Finno-Ugric tribes came from either the east or south to the territory of modern-day Estonia and parts of Latvia, and mixed with the tribes who had been present from the 8th millennium BC. They were little influenced from outside until German traders and missionaries, followed by knights, were unleashed by Pope Celestinus III's 1193 crusade against the 'northern heathens'. In 1202

the bishop of Rīga established the Knights of the Sword to convert the region by conquest; southern Estonia was soon subjugated, and the north fell to Denmark.

Foreign Rule

After a crushing battle with Alexander Nevsky in 1242 on the border of present-day Estonia and Russia, the Knights of the Sword were subordinated to a second band of German crusaders, the Teutonic Order, which by 1290 ruled the eastern Baltic area as far north as southern Estonia, as well as most of the Estonian islands. Denmark sold northern Estonia to the Livonian Order (a branch of the Teutonic Order) in 1346, placing Estonians under servitude to a German nobility that lasted till the early 20th century. Although Sweden and Russia would later rule the region, German nobles and land barons maintained great economic and political power. The Hanseatic League (a mercantile league of medieval German towns bound together by trade) encompassed many towns on the routes between Russia and the west, which prospered under the Germans, although many Estonians in rural areas were forced into serfdom.

By 1620 Estonia had fallen under Swedish control. The Swedes consolidated Estonian Protestantism and aimed to introduce universal education; however, frequent wars were devastating. After the Great Northern War (1700–21), Estonia became part of the Russian Empire. Repressive government from Moscow and economic control by German powers

CONNECTIONS: MOVING ON FROM ESTONIA

Estonia is well connected for visiting the neighbours. It's an easy northern addition to Eastern European roaming, as plenty of daily buses connect with destinations in Latvia and Lithuania, with Rīga–Tallinn buses particularly plentiful; see p347 for details. There's the option of following the white nights to Scandinavia – Tallinn has daily ferry connections to/from Stockholm (p347) and Helsinki (p347). Or if you're hearing the siren call of Russia, nightly trains connect Tallinn and Moscow (p348), and half-a-dozen daily buses run between Tallinn and St Petersburg (p347). You can also reach St Petersburg by bus from Tartu (p354).

ESTONIA

slowly forged a national self-awareness among native Estonians. Serfs were freed in the 19th century, and their improved education and land-ownership rights also helped promote national culture and welfare.

Independence

With the Treaty of Brest-Litovsk, the Soviets abandoned the Baltic countries to Germany in March 1918, although Estonian nationalists had originally declared independence on 24 February. The resulting War of Independence led to the Tartu Peace Treaty on 2 February 1920, in which Russia renounced territorial claims to Estonia, supposedly forever.

Damaged by the war and hampered by a world slump and disruptions to trade with the USSR, independent Estonia suffered economically even as it bloomed culturally. Prime Minister Konstantin Päts declared himself president in 1934 and ruled Estonia as a relatively benevolent dictator while also quietly safeguarding the USSR's interests.

Soviet Rule & WWII

The Molotov–Ribbentrop Pact of 23 August 1939, a nonaggression pact between the USSR and Nazi Germany, secretly divided Eastern Europe into Soviet and German spheres of influence. Estonia fell into the Soviet sphere and by August 1940 was under occupation. Estonia was 'accepted' into the USSR after fabricated elections and within a year more than 10,000 people in Estonia had been killed or deported. When Hitler invaded the USSR in 1941, many saw the Germans as liberators, but during their occupation about 5500 people died in concentration camps. Some 40,000 Estonians joined the German army to prevent the Red Army from reconquering Estonia; nearly twice that number fled abroad.

Russia annexed Estonia after WWII. Between 1945 and 1949 agriculture was collectivised, industry was nationalised and 60,000 more Estonians were killed or deported. An armed resistance led by the Metsavennad (Forest Brothers) fought Soviet rule until 1956.

With postwar industrialisation, Estonia received an influx of migrant workers from Russia, Ukraine and Belarus, all looking for improved living conditions but having little interest in local language and customs. Resentment among Estonians grew as some of these immigrants received prized new housing and top job allocations. In the second half of the 20th century, within the USSR, Estonia developed the reputation of being the most modern and European of all the republics, mainly due to its proximity to Finland, and enjoyed a relatively high standard of living.

New Independence

On 23 August 1989, on the 50th anniversary of the Molotov–Ribbentrop Pact, an estimated two million people formed a human chain across Estonia, Latvia and Lithuania, calling for secession from the USSR. Independence came suddenly, however, in the aftermath of the Moscow putsch against Gorbachev. Estonia's declaration of complete independence on 20 August 1991 was recognised by the West immediately, and by the USSR on 6 September.

In October 1992 Estonia held its first democratic elections, which brought to the presidency the much loved Lennart Meri, who oversaw the removal of the last Russian troops in 1994. The decade after independence saw the government focusing on radical reform policies, and on gaining membership to the EU and NATO. The sweeping transformations on all levels of society saw frequent changes of government, however, and no shortage of scandal and corruption charges. Yet despite this, the country came to be seen as *the* post-Soviet economic miracle. In 2004, Estonia officially entered both NATO and the EU, although troubled relations with its big easterly neighbour are of ongoing concern.

HOW MUCH?

- **Coffee** 35EEK
- **Taxi fare (10 minutes)** 100EEK
- **Bus ticket (Tallinn to Tartu)** 150EEK
- **Bicycle hire (per day)** 150EEK to 200EEK
- **1L bottle of Vana Tallinn** 180EEK

LONELY PLANET INDEX

- **1L petrol** 13EEK
- **1L bottled water** 14EEK to 20EEK
- **500mL beer (Saku) in a bar** 35EEK to 50EEK
- **Souvenir T-shirt** 200EEK
- **Street snack (packet of roasted nuts)** 40EEK

LAND OF DREAMS

Estonia is a land of young talent and crea-tive, dynamic entrepreneurs who have changed the world or are waiting to do so – usually, they're well under 25. The coun-try's biggest success stories are Skype and Kazaa, two of the planet's most downloaded programs in history; indeed, there are 300 million Skype user accounts and counting.

An overheated economy and high inflation rates saw the 2007 adoption of the euro post-poned, but Estonia plans to adopt the currency some time in the coming years. The global financial crisis of 2008, which saw Estonia's economy enter recession and the bursting of the Baltic-wide real-estate bubble, was the big news at the time of research. Time will tell if this plucky country can ride out the turmoil.

PEOPLE

In the 1930s native Estonians composed more than 90% of the population. This began to change with the Soviet takeover; migration from other parts of the USSR occurred on a mass scale from 1945 to 1955. Today only 69% of the people living in Estonia are ethnic Estonians. Russians make up 26% of the popu-lation, with 2% Ukrainian, 1% Belarusian, 1% Finnish. Ethnic Russians are concentrated in the industrial cities of the northeast, where in some places (such as Narva) they make up around 95% of the population. Russians also have a sizeable presence in Tallinn (37%). While much is made of tension between Estonians and Russians, the two communities live together in relative harmony, with only occasional flare-ups, such as the violence that followed the decision to move a Soviet war memorial from the centre of Tallinn in 2007.

Estonians are closely related to the Finns, and more distantly to the Sami (indigenous Laplanders) and Hungarians; they're unrelated to the Latvians and Lithuanians, however, who are of Indo-European heritage. Estonians are historically a rural people, cautious of out-siders and stereotypically most comfortable when left alone. Women are less shy and more approachable than men, though both exude a natural reticence and cool-headed distance in social situations. In general, the younger the Estonian, the more relaxed, open and friendly they'll be.

RELIGION

Historically Estonia was Lutheran from the early 17th century, though today only a minority of Estonians profess religious be-liefs, and there's little sense of Estonia as a religious society. The Russian community is largely Orthodox, and beautiful brightly domed churches are sprinkled around eastern Estonia. There are approximately 10,000 Muslims in Estonia, and about 2500 Jews. In 2007 the Jewish community cele-brated the opening of its first synagogue (in Tallinn) since the Holocaust.

ARTS

Most travellers are likely to notice paintings and ceramics of bright pastel colours and fan-ciful animal compositions, especially works by one-man industry Navitrolla (www.navitrolla .ee), whose playful world adorns postcards, coffee mugs, posters and cafe walls. The arts-and-crafts world in Estonia is much wider than that, however.

Literature

Estonian was traditionally considered a mere 'peasants' language' rather than one with full literary potential, and as a result the history of written Estonian is little more than 150 years old.

Estonian literature grew from the poems and diaries of Kristjan Jaak Peterson, who died when he was but 21 years old in 1822. His lines 'Can the language of this land/carried by the song of the wind/not rise up to heaven/and search for its place in eternity?' are engraved in stone in Tartu, and his birthday (14 March) is celebrated as Mother Tongue Day.

Until the mid-19th century, Estonian culture had been preserved only by way of an oral folk tradition among the peasants. Many of these stories were collected around 1861 to form the national epic *Kalevipoeg* (The Son of Kalev), by Friedrich Reinhold Kreutzwald, which was inspired by Finland's *Kalevala*. The *Kalevipoeg* relates the adventures of the mythical hero, and ends in his death, his land's conquest by foreigners and a promise to restore freedom. The epic played a major role in fostering the national awakening of the 19th century.

Lydia Koidula (1843–86), the face of the 100EEK note, was the poet of Estonia's national awakening, and first lady of literature.

Anton Hansen Tammsaare (1878–1940) is considered the greatest Estonian novelist for

ESTONIA

KIIKING – WHAT THE?

Is it only the Estonians who could turn the gentle pleasure of riding a swing into an extreme sport (though, frankly, we're surprised the New Zealanders didn't think of it first)? From the weird and wacky world of Estonian sport comes kiiking, invented in 1997. Kiiking sees competitors stand on a swing and attempt to complete a 360-degree loop around the top bar (with their feet fastened to the swing base and their hands to the swing arms). The inventor of kiiking, Ado Kosk, observed that the longer the swing arms, the more difficult it is to complete a 360-degree loop. Kosk then designed swing arms that can gradually extend, for an increased challenge. In competition, the winner is the person who completes a loop with the longest swing arms – the current record stands at a fraction over 7m! If this concept has you scratching your head, head to **Eesti Kiikingi Liti** (www.kiiking.ee) to get a visual version of the whole thing and find out where you can see it in action (or even give it a try yourself).

his *Tõde ja Õigus* (Truth and Justice), written between 1926 and 1933. Eduard Vilde (1865–1933) was a controversial early-20th-century novelist and playwright who wrote with sarcasm and irony about parochial mindsets.

Jaan Kross (1920–2007) is the best-known Estonian author abroad, and several of his most renowned books, including *The Czar's Madman* and *The Conspiracy and Other Stories,* have been translated into English. Tõnu Õnnepalu and Mati Unt are two important figures in modern Estonian literature.

Cinema

The first 'moving pictures' were screened in Tallinn in 1896, and the first theatre opened in 1908. The nation's most beloved film is Arvo Kruusement's *Kevade* (Spring; 1969), an adaptation of Oskar Luts' country saga. Grigori Kromanov's *Viimne Reliikvia* (The Last Relic; 1969) is a brave, unabashedly anti-Soviet film that has been screened in some 60 countries.

A number of recent feature films have been shown at international film festivals, garnering recognition and minor awards. Notable among them is *Sügisball* (Autumn Ball; 2007), based on the novel by Mati Unt and directed by Veiko Õunpuu, which follows 'fragments of six lonely lives, stuck in the humdrum world of Soviet-era tower blocks', and *Klass* (The Class; 2007), a disturbing drama about high-school students who take revenge on bullies.

Music

Estonia has a strong and internationally well-respected classical-music tradition, and is most notable for its choirs. The Estonian Boys Choir has been acclaimed the world over. Hortus Musicus is Estonia's best-known

ensemble, performing mainly medieval and Renaissance music.

The three main Estonian composers of the 20th century are Rudolf Tobias, Mart Saar and Eduard Tubin. Veljo Tormis writes striking music based on old runic chants. Composer Arvo Pärt is among the world's most renowned living composers for his haunting sonic blend of tension and beauty, creating outwardly simple but highly complex musical structures.

Hard rock thrives in Estonia, with groups such as Vennaskond, The Tuberkuloited and the U2-style Mr Lawrence (very popular in the 1990s). Also popular is Metsatöll, whose song titles and lyrics make use of archaic Estonian language and imagery; the music is heavy, but timelessly Estonian. The more approachable Ultima Thule, Genialistid and Smilers are among the country's longest-running and most beloved bands.

The pop and dance-music scene is strong in Estonia, exemplified by the country's performances in that revered indicator of true art, Eurovision (it won the competition in 2001). The tough-girl band Vanilla Ninja became a hot ticket throughout central Europe early in the millennium, while Koit Toome, Maarja-Liis Ilus and Tanel Padar are also popular pop singers. Hedvig Hanson blends jazz and rock with surprising results. Exciting names in electronica are the mesmerisingly talented Paf and house kings Rulers of the Deep.

See **estmusic.com** (www.estmusic.com) for detailed listings and streaming samples of Estonian musicians of all genres; it's a worthwhile site, despite not being particularly up to date.

Theatre

Modern Estonian theatre is considered to have begun in 1870 in Tartu, where Lydia

Koidula's *Saaremaa Onupoeg* (The Cousin from Saaremaa) became the first Estonian play performed in public.

Many of the country's theatres were built solely from donations by private citizens, which gives an indication of the role theatre has played in Estonian cultural life. The popularity of theatre is also evidenced by statistics: in 2007 the Eurobarometer found 93% of Estonians go to concerts, the theatre and watch cultural content on TV (the EU average is 78%). Travellers, however, will have trouble tapping into the scene without knowledge of the local language.

SPORT

Basketball and football are Estonia's most popular sports, while the country's reigning sporting heroes are Gerd Kantler, who won a gold medal at the 2008 Olympics for discus, and Kristina Šmigun, recipient of two gold cross-country skiing medals at the 2006 Winter Olympics. Another well-known name in the sports world is Erki Nool, the decathlon gold-medal winner at the 2000 Olympics, who is now a parliamentarian; up-and-comers include tennis player Kaia Kanepi, who reached the quarter finals of the French Open in 2008.

ENVIRONMENT

With an area of 45,226 sq km, Estonia is only slightly bigger than Denmark or Switzerland. It is part of the East European Plain, and is extremely flat, though it's marked by extensive bogs and marshes. At 318m, Suur Munamägi (Great Egg Hill) is the highest point in the country – a mere molehill for those of you from less height-challenged terrain. There are more than 1400 lakes, the largest of which

is Lake Peipsi (3555 sq km), straddling the Estonian–Russian border. Swamps, wetlands and forests make up half of Estonia's territory. There are more than 1500 islands along the 3794km-long, heavily indented coastline, and they make up nearly 10% of Estonian territory.

The Baltic Glint is Estonia's most prominent geological feature. These 60-million-year-old limestone banks extend 1200km from Sweden to Lake Ladoga in Russia, forming impressive cliffs along Estonia's northern coast; at Ontika the cliffs stand 50m above the coast.

Most of the population of Estonia's rare or protected species can be found in one of the several national parks, nature reserves and parks. There are beavers, otters, flying squirrels, lynxes, wolves and brown bears in these areas. White and black storks are common in southern Estonia.

Estonia's western islands and national parks boast some of the most unspoilt landscapes in Europe, and with the exception of the country's northeast (where Soviet-era industry is concentrated), Estonian levels of air pollution are low by European standards. Almost 20% of Estonia's lands (more than double the European average) are protected to some degree. Thus far, the country's only Unesco World Heritage site is Tallinn's Old Town.

Since independence there have been major clean-up attempts to counter the effects of Soviet-era industrialisation. Toxic emissions in the industrialised northeast of Estonia have been reduced sharply, and new environmental-impact legislation aims to minimise the effects of future development. However, heavy oil-shale burning in the northeast keeps air-pollution levels there high.

WWOOF-ING

If you don't mind getting your hands dirty, an economical and enlightening way of travelling around Estonia involves doing some voluntary work as a member of **Worldwide Opportunities on Organic Farms** (WWOOF, Willing Workers on Organic Farms; ☎ 5342 2378; www.wwoof.ee). Membership of this popular, well-established international organisation (which has representatives around the globe) provides you with access to the WWOOF Estonia website, which at the time of research listed 17 organic farms and other environmentally sound cottage industries throughout the country. Bear in mind, however, that WWOOF only got started here in 2007, so this number should increase. In exchange for daily work at these farms, the owner will provide food, accommodation and some hands-on experience in organic farming. You must contact the farm owner or manager beforehand to arrange your stay; don't turn up at a farm without warning. Check the website for more information.

ESTONIA

FOOD & DRINK

Did someone say 'stodge'? Baltic gastronomy has its roots planted firmly in the land, with livestock and game forming the basis of a hearty diet. The Estonian diet relies on *sealiha* (pork), other red meat, *kana* (chicken), *vurst* (sausage), *kapsa* (cabbage); potatoes add a generous dose of winter-warming carbs to a national cuisine often dismissed as bland, heavy and lacking in spice. Sour cream is served with everything but coffee, it seems. *Kala* (fish), most likely *forell* (trout) or *lõhe* (salmon), appears most often as a smoked or salted starter. *Sült* (jellied meat) is likely to be served as a delicacy as well. At Christmas time *verivorst* (blood sausage) is made from fresh blood and wrapped in pig intestine (joy to the world indeed!). Those really in need of a culinary transfusion will find blood sausages, blood bread and blood dumplings available in most traditional Estonian restaurants year-round.

Though the idea that a meal can actually be spicy or vegetarian has taken root, you'll need to hit one of Tallinn's or Tartu's ethnic restaurants for exotic spices or mains that don't include meat. Delicious and inexpensive freshly baked cakes, breads and pastries are available everywhere.

Õlu (beer) is the favourite alcoholic drink in Estonia and the local product is very much in evidence. The best brands are Saku and A Le Coq, which come in a range of brews. *Viin* (vodka) and *konjak* (brandy) are also popular drinks. Vana Tallinn, a seductively pleasant, sweet and strong (40% to 50% alcohol) liqueur of unknown extraction, is an integral part of any Estonian gift pack.

DRINKING WATER

Official travel advisories detail the need to avoid tap water in the Baltic countries and drink only boiled or bottled water, but locals insist the tap water is safe. Some visitors may wish to buy bottled water simply because they prefer the taste. If this is you, please consider the environment – buy locally sourced and bottled water, rather than imports. In Estonia you can return recyclable bottles to vending machines at supermakets for the return of a deposit (usually 0.50EEK or 1EEK) – it won't make you rich, but it will help the environment.

At mealtimes, seek out a *restoran* (restaurant) or *kohvik* (cafe); both are plentiful. In addition, a *pubi* (pub), *kõrts* (inn) or *trahter* (tavern) will usually serve hearty, traditional meals. Nearly every town has a *turg* (market), where you can buy fresh produce. Many Estonians have their main meal at lunchtime, and accordingly most establishments have excellent-value set lunches. The main cities burst with sophisticated restaurants, funky eateries, cool bars and cosy cafes; while they often command Western European city prices, eating in the provinces is cheap.

Restaurants are generally open from noon to midnight; cafes often open at 8am or 9am and close by 10pm. Bars are open from noon to midnight Sunday to Thursday, and noon to 2am on Friday and Saturday. Food shops and supermarkets are open until 10pm every day. Unless otherwise noted, listings in this chapter follow these general rules.

Since 2007 smoking is not permitted in restaurants, bars, nightclubs and cafes, although it is permitted on outdoor terraces or in closed-off smoking rooms.

TALLINN

pop 400,000

Today's Tallinn fuses the medieval and the cutting edge to come up with an energetic new mood all of its own – an intoxicating mix of ancient church spires, glass-and-chrome skyscrapers, cosy wine cellars inside 15th-century basements, sun-filled Raekoja plats (Town Hall Sq), and bike paths to beaches and forests – with a few Soviet throwbacks for added spice.

The jewel in Tallinn's crown remains two-tiered Old Town, a 14th- and 15th-century jumble of turrets, spires and winding streets. Most tourists see nothing other than this cobblestoned labyrinth of intertwining alleys and picturesque courtyards, but Tallinn's modern dimension – its growing skyline, shiny shopping malls, cutting-edge art museum, the wi-fi that bathes much of the city – is a cool surprise and harmonious counterbalance to the city's old-world allure.

HISTORY

In 1219 the Danes set up a castle and installed a bishop on Toompea (the origin of the name Tallinn is thought to be from *Taani linn*, Estonian for 'Danish town'). German traders arrived and Tallinn joined the Hanseatic League in 1285, becoming a vital link between

TALLINN IN TWO DAYS

Get your bearings by heading to **Raekoja plats** (p339) to climb up the **town hall tower** (p339). Follow this by an in-depth exploration of the streets down below – museums, shops, churches, courtyards, whatever takes your fancy. That night treat yourself to a medieval feast at **Olde Hansa** (p345).

On the second day, do what most tourists don't – step out of Old Town. Explore the neighbourhood of **Kadriorg** (p341), with its old homes, sprawling park and superb museums. Or go on a **cycling tour** (p342) with the folks from the Travellers Info Tent or City Bike. Hit a **nightclub** (p346) or go **bar-hopping** (p345) before calling it a day.

east and west. The Danes sold northern Estonia to the German knights and by the mid-14th century Tallinn was a major Hanseatic town. The merchants and artisans in the lower town built a fortified wall to separate themselves from the bishop and knights on Toompea.

Prosperity faded in the 16th century as Swedes, Russians, Poles and Lithuanians all fought over the Baltic region. The city grew in the 19th century and by WWI had a population of 150,000. In 1944 Soviet bombing destroyed several central sectors, including a small section on Old Town's fringes. After WWII, industry developed and Tallinn expanded quickly, with much of its population growth due to immigration from Russia. Politically and economically, Tallinn is the driving force of modern Estonia.

ORIENTATION

Tallinn spreads south from the edge of Tallinn Bay on the Gulf of Finland. Just south of the bay is Old Town (Vanalinn), the city's heart. It divides neatly into Upper Town and Lower Town. Upper Town on Toompea hill was the medieval seat of power, and it still features the parliament buildings. Lower Town spreads around the eastern foot of Toompea, and a 2.5km defensive wall still encircles much of it. The centre of Lower Town is Raekoja plats.

A belt of green parks around Old Town follows the line of the city's original moat defences. Radiating from this old core is New Town, dating from the 19th and early 20th centuries.

The airport lies 4km southeast of the centre on the Tartu road. It's best reached by bus 2.

The passenger port lies just 350m from the edge of Old Town, reachable on foot, or by tram or bus. For more details on getting into town, see p348.

INFORMATION
Bookshops
Apollo (☎ 683 3400; Viru 23)
Rahva Raamat (☎ 644 6655; 3rd & 4th fl, Viru Keskus, Viru väljak 4) Inside Viru Keskus shopping centre; it's well stocked and home to two excellent cafes.

Discount Cards
Tallinn Card (www.tallinncard.ee; 1-/2-/3-day card 350/400/450EEK) Offers free rides on public transport, admission to museums, free excursions and discounts at restaurants. It can be purchased from any of the information desks of the Tallinn tourist information centre (p338).

Internet Access
There are numerous wi-fi hot spots in Tallinn, but if you're not packing a laptop, you'll find the city light on internet cafes. Most hostels and hotels will offer a computer for guests to connect to the internet, or try the following:
Bookingestonia.com (☎ 712 2102; 2nd fl, Voorimehe 1; per hr 45EEK) Booking agency with computers; hidden just off Raekoja plats.
Estonian National Library (☎ 630 7611; Tõnismägi 2; per hr 40EEK; ⏰ 10am-8pm Mon-Fri, noon-7pm Sat Sep-Jun, noon-6pm Mon-Fri Jul-Aug)
Metro Internet Café (☎ 610 1519; basement, Viru Keskus, Viru väljak 4; per hr 40EEK) By the bus terminal.

Laundry
Sauberland (☎ 661 2075; Maakri 23; self-service wash & dry 5kg 75EEK) Wash and wait; there's also a pick-up service.

Media
Tallinn in Your Pocket (www.inyourpocket.com) The king of the region's listings guides has up-to-date information on everything to do with arriving, staying and having fun in Tallinn and other cities in Estonia. Its booklets are on sale at bookshops or can be downloaded free from its website.

Medical Services
Apteek 1 (☎ 627 3607; Aia 7; ⏰ 9am-8.30pm Mon-Fri, 9am-8pm Sat, 9am-6pm Sun) One of many well-stocked *apteek* (pharmacies) in town.
First-Aid hotline (☎ 697 1145) English-language advice on treatment, hospitals and pharmacies.
Tallinn Central Hospital (☎ 620 7070, emergency department 620 7040; Ravi 18) Has a full range of services and a 24-hour emergency room.

ESTONIA

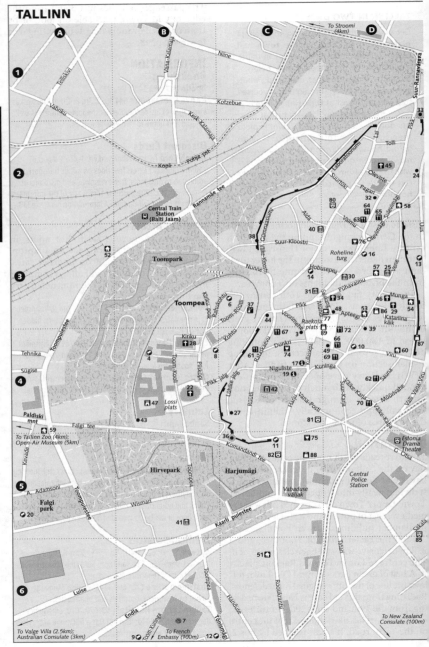

TALLINN

To Stroomi (4km)

Central Train Station (Balti Jaam)

Toompark

Toompea

Kiriku

Lossi plats

Paldiski mnt

To Tallinn Zoo (4km); Open-Air Museum (5km)

Hirvepark

Harjumägi

Falgi park

Vabaduse väljak

Central Police Station

Estonia Drama Theatre

To Valge Villa (2.5km); Australian Consulate (3km)

To French Embassy (100m)

To New Zealand Consulate (100m)

Roheline turg

Hobusepea

Raekoja plats

Niguliste

Katariina käik

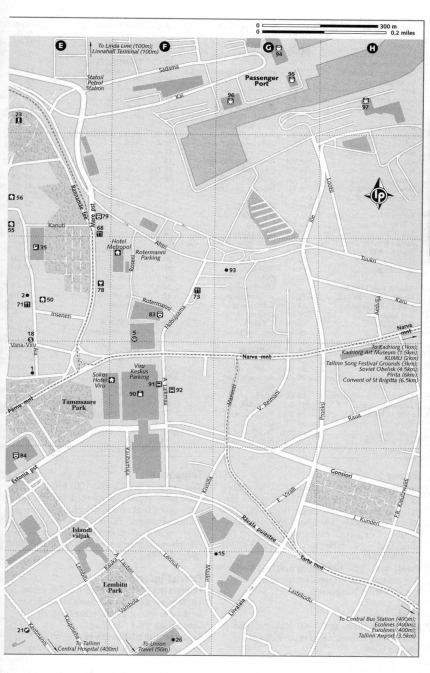

ESTONIA

0   300 m
0   0.2 miles

To Linda Line (100m);
Linnahall Terminal (100m)

Sadama

Statoil
Petrol
Station

Passenger
Port

Kai

96

95

94

97

Mere pst

Rannamäe tee

Kanuti

56

55

35

79

68

78

Hotel
Metropol

Rotermanni
Parking

Ahtri

Roseni

93

Rotermanni

73

Ateena

2

71

50

18

Inseneri

83

5

Vana-Viru

1

Aia

Tammsaare
Park

Sokos
Hotel
Viru

Viru
Keskus
Parking

91

90

92

Lootsi

Joe

Tuukri

Karu

Aedvilja

Narva-mnt

To Kadriorg (1km);
Kadriorg Art Museum (1.5km);
KUMU (2km);
Tallinn Song Festival Grounds (3km);
Soviet Obelisk (4.5km);
Pirita (6km);
Convent of St Brigitta (6.5km)

Narva-mnt

Maneeзi

V. Reimani

Pronksi

Raua

A. Laikmaa

Pärnu-mnt

84

Estonia pst

Kaubamaja

Gonsiori

E. Vilde

FR. Kreutzwaldi

J. Kunderi

Islandi
väljak

Lembitu

A. Lauteri

Kauka

Lennuki

Maakri

Rävala puiestee

Kuizilli

Tartu-mnt

Lastekodu

Lembitu
Park

Vambola

Liivalaia

15

21

Kentmanni

Kaupmehe

To Tallinn
Central Hospital (400m)

To Union
Travel (50m)

26

To Central Bus Station (400m);
Ecolines (400m);
Eurolines (400m);
Tallinn Airport (3.5km)

Money
Foreign-currency exchange is available at any large bank *(pank)*, transport terminals, exchange bureaux, the post office and major hotels, but check the rate of exchange. For better rates, steer clear of the small Old Town exchanges. Banks and ATMs are widespread.

Tavid (☎ 627 9900; Aia 5) Reliably good rates. A nighttime exchange window is open 24 hours, but rates aren't as good as during business hours.

Post
Central post office (☎ 661 6616; Narva mnt 1) Full postal services. Note that stamps can be purchased from any kiosk in town.

Telephone
You can buy 50EEK and 100EEK chip cards from news-stands to use for local and international calls at any of the blue phone boxes scattered around town. Otherwise, post offices, supermarkets and some kiosks sell mobile-phone starter kits with prepaid SIM cards (from 50EEK).

Tourist Information
Ekspress Hotline (☎ 1182; www.1182.ee; per min 14EEK) Pricey English-speaking service has telephone numbers, transport schedules, theatre listings etc. The website is also useful – and free.

Tallinn tourist information centre (☎ 645 7777; www.tourism.tallinn.ee; cnr Kullassepa & Niguliste;

9am-7pm Mon-Fri, 10am-5pm Sat & Sun May-Jun, 9am-8pm Mon-Fri, 10am-6pm Sat & Sun Jul-Aug, 9am-6pm Mon-Fri, 10am-5pm Sat & Sun Sep, 9am-5pm Mon-Fri, 10am-3pm Sat Oct-Apr) A block south of Raekoja plats, the main tourist office has a full range of services. Note there are also small information desks at the port (Terminal A), and inside Viru Keskus shopping centre.

Traveller Info Tent (☎ 5814 0442; www.traveller -info.com; Niguliste; 🕙 9am-9pm or 10pm Jun–mid-Sep) Stop by this fabulous source of information, which has been set up by young locals in a tent opposite the official tourist information centre. It produces an invaluable map of Tallinn with loads of recommended places (plus similar maps to Tartu and Pärnu), dispenses lots of local tips, keeps a 'what's on' board that's updated daily, and operates entertaining, well-priced walking and cycling tours (see p342).

Travel Agencies

Bookingestonia.com (☎ 712 2102; www.booking estonia.com; 2nd fl, Voorimehe 1) Hidden just off Raekoja plats, this small, helpful agency can book bus, train and ferry tickets (no commission), and help arrange accommodation and car rental. Also offers internet access (per hour 45EEK).

Union Travel (☎ 627 0627; Lembitu 14) Close to the Reval Hotel Olümpia. Can help arrange visas to Russia, but these take 10 working days to process and there are restrictions on who can apply outside of their country of residence.

SIGHTS

There are loads of sights inside Old Town to keep you occupied, but only a fraction of visitors make it outside the medieval town walls. Chart-topping drawcards to get you out of Old Town include leafy Kadriorg Park and the stunning KUMU art museum.

Old Town

RAEKOJA PLATS & AROUND

Raekoja plats has been the pulsing heart of Tallinn life since markets began here in the 11th century. Throughout summer, outdoor cafes implore you to sit and people-watch; come Christmas, a huge pine tree stands in the middle of the square. Whether bathed in sunlight or sprinkled with snow, it's always a photogenic spot.

The square is dominated by the only surviving Gothic **town hall** (☎ 645 7900; adult/student 40/25EEK; 🕙 10am-4pm Mon-Sat Jul-Aug, by appointment Sep-Jun) in northern Europe. Built between 1371 and 1404, the town hall is faced by pretty pastel-coloured buildings from the 15th to 17th centuries. Old Thomas, Tallinn's symbol and guardian, has been keeping watch from his

perch on the weathervane atop the town hall since 1530. You can climb the **town hall tower** (adult/student 30/15EEK; 🕙 11am-6pm Jun-Aug) for fine Old Town views.

The **Town Council Pharmacy** (Raeapteek; Raekoja plats 11; 🕙 9am-5pm Tue-Sat), on the northern side of Raekoja plats, is another ancient Tallinn institution; there's been a pharmacy or apothecary's shop here since at least 1422, though the present facade is from the 17th century. Duck through the arch beside it into the narrow Saiakang (White Bread Passage), which leads to the striking 14th-century Gothic **Holy Spirit Church** (☎ 644 1487; adult/concession 15/7.50EEK; 🕙 9am-5pm Mon-Sat May-Sep, 10am-2pm Mon-Fri Oct-Apr). Its luminous blue-and-gold clock (on the facade, just to the right of the entry) is the oldest in Tallinn. The lavish carvings inside the church date from 1684 and the tower bell was cast in 1433.

VENE & AROUND

Several 15th-century warehouses and merchant residences surround Raekoja plats, notably when heading towards the street of Vene (meaning 'Russian' in Estonian, and named for the Russian merchants who traded here centuries ago). Vene is home to some gorgeous passageways and courtyards – the loveliest being **Katariina käik** (Vene 12), home to artisans' studios (p346) and a decent Italian restaurant, and **Masters' Courtyard** (Vene 6), a cobblestoned delight partially dating from the 13th century that's filled with craft stores (p347) and a sweet chocolaterie (p345).

A medieval merchant's home houses the **City Museum** (☎ 644 6553; www.linnamuuseum.ee; Vene 17; adult/student 35/10EEK; 🕙 10.30am-6pm Wed-Mon Mar-Oct, to 5pm Wed-Mon Nov-Feb), which traces Tallinn's development from its beginnings through to 1940 with some quirky displays and curious artefacts.

Also on Vene is the whitewashed 1844 **Sts Peter & Paul's Catholic Church** (Vene 16; 🕙 7-10am & 5-7pm Mon, Wed, Fri & Sat, 5-7pm Tue, Thu & Sun), looking like it belongs in Spain. A door in the courtyard leads into the **Dominican Monastery** (☎ 515 5489; www.kloostri.ee; Vene 16; adult/concession 90/45EEK; 🕙 10am-6pm mid-May–Aug, by appointment Aug–mid-May), founded in 1246 as a base for Scandinavian monks. Today the monastery complex houses Estonia's largest collection of stone carvings; there are also often summertime concerts and medieval-tinged activities taking place here.

ESTONIA

PIKK & LAI

From the Holy Spirit Church you can stroll along Pikk (Long Street), which runs north to the **Great Coast Gate** – the medieval exit to Tallinn's port. Pikk is lined with the 15th-century houses of merchants and gentry, as well as the buildings of several old Tallinn guilds.

The **Estonian History Museum** (☎ 641 1630; www.eam.ee; Pikk 17; adult/student 25/15EEK; ☺ 11am-6pm daily May-Aug, closed Wed Sep-Apr) is set in the 1440 building of the Great Guild, to which the most important merchants belonged. The museum's exhibits feature Estonian history up to the 18th century, and contain ceramics, jewellery and archaeological delights. Nearby is the 1911 **Draakoni Gallery** (☎ 646 4110; Pikk 18; ☺ 10am-6pm Mon-Fri, 10am-5pm Sat), which has a fabulous sculpted facade.

At the northern end of Pikk stands an important Tallinn landmark, the gargantuan **St Olaf's Church** (Pikk 48; ☺ 10am-2pm). Anyone unafraid of a bit of sweat should head up to the **observation tower** (☎ 621 2241; adult/student 30/15EEK; ☺ 10am-6pm Apr-Oct), halfway up the church's 124m structure; it offers the city's best views of Old Town. First built in the early 13th century, the church was once the world's tallest building (it used to tower 159m before several fires and reconstructions brought it down to its present size). The church is dedicated to the 11th-century King Olav II of Norway, but is linked in local lore with another Olav (Olaf), the church's architect, who fell to his death from the tower.

Just south of the church is the **former KGB headquarters** (Pikk 59), whose basement windows were sealed to conceal the sounds of interrogations.

The Great Coast Gate is joined to **Fat Margaret**, a rotund 16th-century bastion that protected this entrance to Old Town. Inside the bastion is the **Maritime Museum** (☎ 641 1408; Pikk 70; adult/student 40/20EEK; ☺ 10am-6pm Wed-Sun). The exhibits are ho-hum, but there are nice views from the rooftop.

Just beyond the bastion stands the **broken line monument**, a black, curved slab in memory of victims of the *Estonia* ferry disaster. In September 1994, 852 people died when the ferry sank en route from Tallinn to Stockholm.

While Pikk was the street of traders, Lai, running roughly parallel, was the street of artisans, whose traditions are recalled in the **Museum of Applied Art & Design** (☎ 627 4600; Lai 17;

FREE THRILLS

You certainly don't have to put your hand in your pocket to enjoy the best of Tallinn. Following are some of our favourite ways to enjoy the capital for free:

- Absorb the medieval magic while wandering **Old Town** (p339).
- Get a breath of fresh air at **Kadriorg Park** (opposite).
- Hit the beach at **Pirita** (opposite).
- Browse the artists' studios of **Katariina käik** (p346) and **Masters' Courtyard** (p347).

---

adult/student 40/20EEK; ☺ 11am-6pm Wed-Sun). You'll find an excellent mix of historical and contemporary ceramics, glass, rugs, and metal-and leatherwork.

Suur-Kloostri leads to a long and photogenic stretch of the **Lower Town Wall**, which has nine towers along Laboratooriumi.

NIGULISTE MUSEUM & CONCERT HALL

The Gothic St Nicholas' Church (Niguliste Kirik) is another of the city's medieval treasures. Dating from the 13th century, St Nicholas' is now known as the **Niguliste Museum & Concert Hall** (☎ 631 4330; Niguliste 3; adult/concession 35/20EEK; ☺ 10am-5pm Wed-Sun) and houses artworks from medieval Estonian churches. The acoustics are first-rate, and organ recitals are held most weekends (beginning at 4pm Saturday and Sunday).

TOOMPEA

A regal approach to Toompea hill is through the red-roofed 1380 **Pikk jalg gate tower** at the western end of Pikk in Lower Town, and then heading uphill along Pikk jalg (Long Leg). The 19th-century Russian Orthodox **Alexander Nevsky Cathedral** (Lossi plats; ☺ 8am-8pm) greets you at the top. It was built as a part of Alexander III's policy of Russification, and is sited strategically across from **Toompea Castle**, Estonia's traditional seat of power. The Riigikogu (National Council) meets in a pink baroque-style building, an 18th-century addition to the castle. Nothing remains of the original 1219 Danish castle; three of the four corner towers of its successor, the Knights of the Sword's Castle, are still standing. The finest of these towers is the 14th-century **Pikk Hermann** (Tall

Hermann) at the southwestern corner, from which the state flag flies. A path leads down from Lossi plats through an opening in the wall to the **Danish King's Courtyard**, where in summer artists set up their easels.

Nearby **Kiek in de Kök** (☎ 644 6686; Komandandi tee; adult/student 25/8EEK; ☼ 10.30am-5pm Tue-Sun), a tall tower built in about 1475, is a museum that holds weapons, models of old Tallinn, and a photographic gallery. Its name is Low German for 'Peep into the Kitchen' – from the upper floors of the tower, medieval voyeurs could see into Old Town kitchens.

The Lutheran **Dome Church** (Toomkirik; ☎ 644 4140; Toom-Kooli 6; ☼ 9am-4pm Tue-Sun) is Estonia's oldest church. Positioned on the site of a 1219 Danish church, it dates from the 14th century. Inside the impressive, austere and damp church are finely carved tombs and coats of arms. From the Dome Church, follow Kohtu to the city's favourite **lookout** over Lower Town.

The **Museum of Occupation & Fight for Freedom** (☎ 668 0250; www.okupatsioon.ee; Toompea 8; adult/concession 20/10EEK; ☼ 11am-6pm Tue-Sun), just downhill from Toompea, has a worthwhile display on Estonia's 20th-century occupation. Photos and artefacts illustrate five decades of oppressive rule, under both the Nazis and the Soviets. Displays are good, but it's the videos (lengthy but enthralling) that leave the greatest impression – and the joy of a happy ending. Head to the basement toilets to check out the graveyard of Soviet-era monuments.

Kadriorg

To reach the lovely, wooded **Kadriorg Park**, 2km east of Old Town along Narva mnt, take tram 1 or 3 to the last stop. The park and its centrepiece, Kadriorg Palace (1718–36), were designed for Peter the Great's wife Catherine I (Kadriorg means 'Catherine's Valley' in Estonian). Kadriorg Palace is now home to the **Kadriorg Art Museum** (☎ 606 6403; www.ekm.ee; Weizenbergi 37; adult/student 55/30EEK; ☼ 10am-5pm Tue-Sun May-Sep, 10am-5pm Wed-Sun Oct-Apr). The 17th- and 18th-century foreign art is mainly unabashedly romantic, and the palace unashamedly splendid.

The grand new showpiece of Kadriorg (and Tallinn) is **KUMU** (Kunstimuuseum, Art Museum of Estonia; ☎ 602 6000; www.ekm.ee; Weizenbergi 34; adult/student 80/45EEK; ☼ 11am-6pm Tue-Sun May-Sep, 11am-6pm Wed-Sun Oct-Apr). It opened in this futuristic Finnish-designed seven-storey building

to rave reviews in early 2006, and in 2008 won the title European Museum of the Year from the European Museum Forum. It's a spectacular structure of limestone, glass and copper, nicely integrated with the landscaping, and it contains the largest repository of Estonian art, plus constantly changing contemporary exhibitions.

Towards Pirita

Jutting north of Kadriorg alongside the sea coast towards Pirita is **Pirita tee**, Tallinn's seaside promenade. Summer sunsets around midnight are particularly romantic from here, and it's a nice cycling and rollerblading area.

North of Kadriorg you come to **Tallinn Song Festival Grounds** (Lauluväljak; Narva mnt), an impressive amphitheatre that hosts song festivals and big-name concerts. Heading further north, you pass the foreboding **Soviet obelisk**, locally dubbed 'the Impotent's Dream'. It's the focal point of a 1960 Soviet war memorial that's now more crumbling than inspiring.

Just before Pirita tee crosses the Pirita River, a side road leads to **Pirita Yacht Club** and the **Tallinn Olympic Yachting Centre**, near the mouth of the river. This was the base for the sailing events of the 1980 Moscow Olympics, and international regattas are still held here.

North of the bridge is long, clean **Pirita beach**, which is *the* place to shed your clothes in Tallinn summertime. On the other side of Pirita tee are the ruins of the 15th-century **Convent of St Brigitta** (☎ 605 5044; Kloostri tee; adult/student 20/10EEK; ☼ 10am-6pm Apr-May & Sep-Oct, 9am-7pm Jun-Aug, noon-4pm Nov-Mar), which are the perfect place for a ramble. Atmospheric concerts are occasionally held here in summer.

Buses 1A, 8, 34A and 38 all run between the city centre and Pirita, stopping on Narva mnt near Kadriorg Park.

Southwest of Old Town

About 4.5km southwest from Old Town, **Tallinn Zoo** (☎ 694 3300; www.tallinnzoo.ee; Paldiski mnt 145; adult 50-90EEK; child 25-45EEK; ☼ 9am-5pm Mar-Apr & Sep-Oct, 9am-7pm May-Aug, 9am-3pm Nov-Feb) boasts the world's largest collection of mountain goats and sheep(!), plus around 350 other species of feathered, furry and four-legged friends. It's best reached by bus 22 or trolleybus 6.

North of the zoo is the Rocca al Mare neighbourhood and its **Open-Air Museum** (☎ 654 9100; www.evm.ee; Vabaõhumuuseumi tee 12; adult 35-80EEK; child

20-35EEK; ⏱ buildings 10am-6pm May-Sep, grounds 10am-8pm May-Sep, 10am-5pm Oct-Apr). Most of Estonia's oldest wooden structures, mainly farmhouses but also a chapel (1699) and a windmill, are preserved here. Every Saturday and Sunday morning from June to August there are folk song-and-dance shows; if you find yourself in Tallinn on midsummer eve, come here to witness the traditional celebrations, bonfire and all. There's also an old wooden tavern serving traditional Estonian cuisine. Bus 21 runs here.

ACTIVITIES

Water parks are all the rage in Estonia; the biggest in Tallinn is the **Kalev Spa Waterpark** (☎ 649 3370; www.kalevspa.ee; Aia 18; 2½hr visit adult/family 150/405EEK; ⏱ 6.45am-10.30pm Mon-Fri, 8am-10.30pm Sat & Sun). For serious swimming there's an Olympic-size indoor pool, but there are also plenty of other ways to wrinkle your skin, including water slides, jacuzzis, saunas and a kids' pool. There's also a gym and day spa.

Saunas are an Estonian institution and come close to being a religious experience. If you're looking to convert, splurge at **Club 26** (☎ 631 5585; 26th fl, Reval Hotel Olümpia, Liivalaia 33; per hr before/after 3pm 300/600EEK; ⏱ 8am-11pm), located on the top floor of the Reval Hotel Olümpia and with correspondingly outstanding views. There are two private saunas here, each with plunge pool and tiny balcony. Food and drink can be ordered to complete the experience.

The most popular beaches are at **Pirita** (p341) and **Stroomi** (4km due west of the centre, or a 15-minute ride on bus 40 or 48). You can hire rowing boats and canoes at **Pirita Rowboat Rental** (☎ 621 2175; Kloostri tee 6, Pirita; per hr from 150EEK; ⏱ 10am-10pm Jun-Aug), located beside the bridge over the river.

TOURS

City Bike (☎ 683 6383; www.citybike.ee; Uus 33; ⏱ 9am-7pm May-Sep, 9am-5pm Oct-Apr) has a great range of Tallinn tours, by bike or on foot, as well as tours to Lahemaa National Park. Two-hour cycling tours (250EEK) of the capital run year-round and cover 16km, heading out towards Kadriorg and Pirita.

The guys behind the **Traveller Info Tent** (☎ 5814 0442; www.traveller-info.com; Niguliste; ⏱ 9am-9pm or 10pm Jun–mid-Sep) also run walking and cycling city tours. Three-hour bike tours (150EEK to 200EEK) take in the town's well-known eastern attractions (Kadriorg, Pirita etc), or more off-beat areas to the west. There's also a pub crawl (200EEK, including drinks). From June to August, the tours run daily from the tent itself; the rest of the year they start from Euphoria hostel (opposite) and need to be booked in advance via email, phone or through the hostel. Winter tours are weather dependent.

FESTIVALS & EVENTS

For a complete list of Tallinn's festivals, visit **culture.ee** (www.culture.ee) and the Events page of **Tallinn** (www.tourism.tallinn.ee). Expect an extra-full calendar of events in 2011 as Tallinn celebrates its status as a European City of Culture; check **Tallinn 2011** (www.tallinn2011.ee). Big-ticket events include the following:

Jazzkaar (www.jazzkaar.ee) Jazz greats from around the world converge on Tallinn in mid-April for this excellent two-week festival; there are also smaller events in autumn and around Christmas.

Old Town Days (www.vanalinnapaevad.ee) Week-long fest in early June featuring dancing, concerts, costumed performers and plenty of medieval merrymaking on nearly every corner of Old Town.

Õllesummer (Beer Summer; www.ollesummer.ee) Popular ale-guzzling, rock-music extravaganza over five days in early July at the Song Festival Grounds.

Black Nights Film Festival (www.poff.ee) Films and animations from all over the world. Estonia's biggest film festival brings life to cold winter nights from mid-November to mid-December.

Estonian Song & Dance Celebration (www.laulupidu .ee) Convenes every five years and culminates in a 30,000-strong traditional choir; due in Tallinn in 2009 and 2014.

Baltica International Folk Festival A week of music, dance and displays focusing on Baltic and other folk traditions, this festival is shared between Rīga, Vilnius and Tallinn; it's Tallinn's turn to play host in 2010.

SLEEPING

Tallinn has a wide range of accommodation, from charming guest houses to lavish five-star hotels. Old Town undoubtedly has the top picks, with plenty of atmospheric rooms set in beautifully refurbished medieval houses – though you'll pay a premium for them. Midrange and budget hotels are scarcer in Old Town, though apartment-rental agencies have the best deals. In recent times there's been an explosion of hostels competing for the attention of backpackers. Most of them are small, friendly and full of laid-back charm; they're largely found in Old Town, but few offer private rooms. The website **Tallinn** (www .tourism.tallinn.ee) has a full list of options.

The capital has dozens of apartments for rent – a great alternative for those who prefer privacy and self-sufficiency. Try the following agencies:

Ites Apartments (☎ 631 0637; www.ites.ee; Harju 6; per night 1100-2500EEK) Friendly and efficient bunch offering several too-good-to-be-true apartments in Old Town and its surrounds. There are discounts for stays of more than one night, and car rental can be arranged.

Old House (☎ 641 1464; www.oldhouse.ee; Uus 22; per night 1100-3900EEK) As well as a guest house and hostel, Old House has 16 beautifully furnished apartments scattered through Old Town, including two spectacular three-bedroom options.

Whatever your preference, be sure to book in advance in summer. As ever, look for good deals on the internet.

Budget

Euphoria (☎ 5837 3602; www.euphoria.ee; Roosikrantsi 4; dm/d with shared bathroom 200/600EEK; 🖳) So laid-back it's almost horizontal, this new backpacker hostel, just south of Old Town, has adopted some very '60s hippie vibes and given them a modern twist. It's a fun place to stay, with a sense of traveller community – especially if you like hookah pipes, bongo drums, jugglers, musos, artists and impromptu late-night jam sessions (pack earplugs if you don't).

Tallinn Backpackers (☎ 644 0298; www.tallinnbackpackers.com; Olevimägi 11; dm 200-225EEK; 🖳) In a perfect Old Town location and staffed by backpackers who are more than happy to go drinking with guests, this place has a good global feel and a roll-call of traveller-happy features: free wi-fi and internet, lockers, free sauna, snazzy bathrooms, big-screen movies in the common room, a foosball table and day trips to nearby attractions. The second option run by the guys behind Tallinn Backpackers is the Monk's Bunk (☎ 644 0818; Müürivahe 33–15; dorms 200EEK to 225EEK), while private rooms are available at the offshoot Viru Backpackers (☎ 644 6050; 3rd fl, Viru 5; singles/doubles/twins/triples 350/600/600/825EEK), which has less atmosphere but a central location.

Old House Hostel (☎ 641 1464; www.oldhouse.ee; Uus 26; d/s/tw 290/550/690EEK; 🖳) More like its sister establishment (Old House Guesthouse, right) than the party-oriented places listed above, this 34-bed place has a mature feel: wooden floors and old-world decor, plus normal beds (no bunks), and a choice of private rooms. In

summer it expands into a nearby local school. Kitchen, living room, wi-fi and parking are good extras.

Old House Guesthouse (☎ 641 1464; www.oldhouse.ee; Uus 22; s/tw/q with shared bathroom incl breakfast 490/690/1300EEK; 🖳) This cosy six-room guest house with wooden floors and tasteful old-world furnishings offers warm, friendly hospitality in a low-key Old Town neighbourhood that's close to everything. There's a guest kitchen and TV room, plus free wi-fi.

Midrange

Valge Villa (☎ 654 2302; www.white-villa.com; Kännu 26/2; r 790-1190EEK) A villa in more than name only, this three-storey, 10-room home in a quiet residential area 3km south of the centre is a great option that's somewhere between a B&B and a hotel. All rooms boast antiques or wooden furniture, coffee machine, fridge and wi-fi, and some have fireplace, balcony, kitchenette and bath-tub. Take trolleybus 2, 3 or 4 from the centre to the Tedre stop.

Hotel Schnelli (☎ 631 0100; www.gohotels.ee; Toompuiestee 37; r incl breakfast 800-1625EEK; 🖳) The modern hotel at the train station isn't just for train travellers. The block-boring building is home to small but fresh and functional rooms, and offers decent value a short walk from Old Town; rates include buffet breakfast, parking and wi-fi. Nontrainspotters should opt for a room in the Green Wing, with views to the park opposite and Old Town beyond; Blue Wing rooms overlook the station.

Bern Hotel (☎ 680 6630; www.bern.ee; Aia 10; s/d from 1173/1330EEK; ❌) One of a rash of new hotels on the outskirts of Old Town, Bern is named after the Swiss city to indicate 'hospitality and high quality'. It's nothing special from the outside, but rooms are petite and modern, with great attention to detail for the price – nice extras include robes and slippers, air-con, minibar, hairdryer and toiletries. And traveller reports indicate that the service is living up to the ideal.

Uniquestay Hotel Tallinn (☎ 660 0700; www.uniquestay.com; Toompuiestee 23; s/d from 1565/1956EEK; 🖳) Here local traditions and folk elements merge with Japanese sparsity, quirky eccentricity and modern furnishings to create an excellent midrange place to lay your head. The pricier 'Zen' doubles are worthwhile for the extra harmony (whirlpool baths, antigravity NASA-designed chairs). All rooms come with their own computer and internet connection.

ESTONIA

Check the website for deals; in high season rooms were going for 1175EEK.

Top End

Hotel Telegraaf (☎ 600 0600; www.telegraafhotel.com; Vene 9; s/d/ste from 3455/3943/6489EEK; 🛋) Opened in 2007, this hotel in a converted 19th-century former telegraph station delivers style in spades. It boasts a spa and a small swimming pool, gorgeous black-and-white decor, a pretty courtyard, an acclaimed restaurant, parking (an Old Town rarity!) and smart, efficient service.

Schlössle Hotel (☎ 699 7700; www.schlossle-hotels .com; Pühavaimu 13/15; d/ste from 4000/7700EEK) The individually designed rooms are nothing less than breathtaking in this five-star medieval complex in the heart of Old Town. The lovingly restored hotel features details from the original 17th-century building, such as original wooden beams and old stone walls, and its sumptuously decorated rooms are among the country's finest.

EATING

Headquartered in Old Town, Tallinn's restaurant scene has unbeatable atmosphere: whether you want to dazzle a date or just soak up the medieval digs alfresco, you'll find plenty of choices. There aren't many bargains, however – expect to pay the kind of prices you'd pay in any European capital. A word to the wise: lunchtime specials offer the best deals.

Budget

Bonaparte Café (☎ 646 4444; Pikk 45; pastries 14-20EEK, meals 55-130EEK; 🕑 8am-10pm Mon-Fri, 9am-10pm Sat, 10am-6pm Sun) Flaky croissants and raspberry mousse cake are just a few of the reasons why Bonaparte ranks as Tallinn's best patisserie. It's also a supremely civilised lunch stop, with the likes of French onion soup and salad Niçoise on the menu. And the quiches – *très magnifique!*

Pizza Grande (☎ 641 8718; Väike-Karja 6; small pizzas 39-70EEK) The local students we polled voted this their favourite pizza spot. Enter from the courtyard and check the lengthy menu, where some left-of-centre topping combos (chicken, shrimps, blue cheese and peach?) stand alongside the tried-and-true. It's a good budget option, with salads and pasta dishes all coming in under 70EEK.

Kompressor (☎ 646 4210; Rataskaevu 3; pancakes 50-55EEK) Under an industrial ceiling you can plug any holes in your stomach with cheap pancakes of the sweet or savoury persuasion. The smoked cheese and bacon is a treat, but don't go thinking you'll have room for dessert. By night, this is a decent detour for a drink.

our pick **Vapiano** (☎ 682 9010; Hobujaama 10; pizza & pasta 50-125EEK) Choose your pasta or salad from the appropriate counter and watch as it's prepared in front of you. If it's pizza you're after, you'll receive a pager to notify you when it's ready. This is 'fast' food done healthy, fresh and cheap (without sacrificing quality). The restaurant itself is big, bright and buzzing, with huge windows, high tables and shelves of potted herbs. We like.

For first-rate picnic fodder, stock up at **Bonaparte Deli** (☎ 646 4024; Pikk 47; 🕑 10am-7pm Mon-Sat). Otherwise, try **Rimi** (Aia 7), a grocery store on the outskirts of Old Town; or **Tallinna Kaubamaja** (basement, Viru Keskus, Viru väljak 4), located in the basement of Viru Keskus shopping centre.

Midrange

Angel (☎ 641 6880; Sauna 1; mains 70-160EEK; 🕑 noon-2am Mon & Tue, noon-late Wed-Fri, 2pm-late Sat, 2pm-1am Sun) One of Tallinn's most diverse crowds gathers at this stylish 2nd-floor restaurant, upstairs from Tallinn's best gay nightclub (p346). Exposed brickwork, great B&W photography and a loungelike feel provide a warm setting for the small but eclectic menu (salads, pastas and an unbeatable cheeseburger). Best of all, the kitchen stays open until late – perfect for those craving chicken curry or a fruity cocktail at 3am some Wednesday night.

Aed (☎ 626 9088; Rataskaevu 8; mains 85-280EEK; 🕑 noon-10pm Mon-Sat, 3-9pm Sun) From the pots of herbs framing the doorway to the artwork screens on the walls, a lot of care has gone into creating this beautiful, plant-filled restaurant (the name means 'Garden'). The menu of complex dishes (all organic produce) wins fans by noting gluten-, lactose- and egg-free options, and there are creative vegetarian choices too. We like the weekday lunchtime dish of the day – great value at 95EEK.

Kaerajaan (☎ 615 5400; Raekoja plats 17; mains 135-325EEK) Named after a traditional song and dance, this new place on the main square has quirky decor and an intriguing menu of modern Estonian cuisine that takes traditional dishes and gives them an international, 21st-century twist – try gravlax with cucumber-lemon sorbet and forest cranberries, or pork tenderloin marinated with juniper berries. The jury's out on herring lasagne, however!

Troika (☎ 627 6245; Raekoja plats 15; soup or pelmeni 70-100EEK, mains 154-594EEK) Tallinn's most cheerful Russian restaurant is an experience in itself, with wild hunting-themed murals, live accordion music and an old-style country tavern upstairs. Even if you don't opt for a plate of delicious *pelmeni* (Russian-style ravioli stuffed with meat), bliny or a bowl of heavenly borsch, make sure you stop in for an ice-cold shot of vodka.

Top End

Olde Hansa (☎ 627 9020; www.oldehansa.ee; Vana turg 1; mains 155-365EEK) With peasant-garbed servers labouring beneath large plates of wild game in candlelit rooms, medieval-themed Olde Hansa is the place to indulge in a gluttonous feast. Juniper cheese, forest-mushroom soup and exotic meats such as wild boar and elk are among the delicacies available. And if the medieval music, communal wooden tables, and thick fragrance of red wine and roast meats sound a bit much, take heart – the chefs have done their research in producing historically authentic fare. It may sound a bit cheesy and touristy, but even the locals rate this place.

Chedi (☎ 646 1676; www.chedi.ee; Sulevimägi 1; main dishes 195-450EEK) If you can't get a booking at London's top Asian restaurants, console yourself at sleek and sexy Chedi. UK chef Alan Yau (of London's Michelin-starred Hakkasan and Yauatcha) consulted on the menu, and some of his trademark dishes are featured here. The pan-Asian food is exemplary – try the delicious crispy duck salad or sublime roasted silver cod.

Ö (☎ 661 6150; Mere pst 6e; www.restoran-o.ee; mains 310-395EEK) No, we can't pronounce it either, but award-winning Ö has carved a unique space in Tallinn's culinary world. With angelic chandelier sculptures, and charcoal-and-white overtones, the dining room is an understated work of art – as are the plates of modern Estonian cuisine coming out of the kitchen. The result is something quite special; bookings are advised.

DRINKING
Bars & Pubs

Whether you seek a romantic wine cellar, a chic locals-only lounge or a raucous pub full of pint-wielding punters, you'll find plenty to choose from.

Gloria Wine Cellar (☎ 640 6804; Müürivahe 2) This mazelike cellar has a number of nooks and crannies where you can secrete yourself with a date and/or a good bottle of shiraz. The dark wood, antique furnishings and flickering candles add to the allure

our pick **Hell Hunt** (☎ 681 8333; Pikk 39) See if you can score a few of the comfy armchairs out the back of this trouper of the pub circuit, beloved by discerning locals of all ages. It boasts an amiable air and reasonable prices for local-brewed beer and cider, plus decent pub grub. Don't let the menacing-sounding name put you off – it actually means 'Gentle Wolf'.

Beer House (☎ 644 2222; Dunkri 5) Tallinn's only microbrewery offers up the good stuff (seven house brews) in a huge, tavernlike space where, come evening, the German oom-pah-pah music can rattle the brain into oblivion. Fun and sometimes raucous, it's for those who have had an overdose of cosy at other venues.

Scotland Yard (☎ 653 5190; Mere pst 6e) As themed pubs go, this is actually quite well done, right down to the electric-chair toilets and staff dressed as English bobbies. There's a big menu of all-day pub grub, clubby leather banquettes and a small outdoor terrace, plus live bands on weekends.

Cafes

Tallinn's Old Town is so packed with absurdly cosy cafes that you can spend your whole trip wandering from one coffee house to the next. In most the focus is on coffee, tea, cakes and pastries – and the latest craze, handmade chocolates. There's usually considerably less effort put into savoury snacks, but these places often stay open until midnight dispensing postdinner sweets and treats.

Kehrwieder (☎ 505 258; Saiakang 1; 🕙 11am-midnight) Sure there's seating on Raekoja plats, but inside the city's cosiest cafe is where ambience is found in spades – you can stretch out on a couch, read by lamplight and bump your head on the arched ceilings.

Café-Chocolaterie de Pierre (☎ 641 8061; Masters' Courtyard, Vene 6; 🕙 8am-midnight) Nestled inside the picturesque Masters' Courtyard, this snug cafe feels like you're hiding away at your granny's place. Filled with antiques, it's renowned for its delectable handmade chocolates – they're impossible to resist.

Park Café (☎ 601 3040; A Weizenbergi 22; 🕙 10am-8pm Tue-Sun) At the western entrance to Kadriorg

Park is this sweet slice of Viennese cafe culture. If the sun's shining, the alfresco tables by the pond might just be our favourite place in town.

ENTERTAINMENT

Tallinn is small as capitals go and the pace is accordingly slower than in other big cities, but there's lots to keep yourself stimulated, whether in a nightclub, laid-back bar or concert hall. Buy tickets for concerts and main events at **Piletilevi** (www.piletilevi.ee; Viru Keskus, Viru väljak 4), which has a number of central locations. Events are posted on city centre walls and advertised on flyers found in shops and cafes.

Nightclubs

Club Hollywood (☎ 627 4770; www.club-hollywood.ee; Vana-Posti 8; ☼ from 11pm Wed-Sat) A multilevel emporium of mayhem, this is the nightclub that draws the largest crowds, especially of foreigners. Plenty of tourists and Tallin's young party crowd mix it up to international and local DJs. Wednesday night is ladies' night (free entry for women), so expect to see loads of guys anticipating some eye candy.

Bon Bon (☎ 661 6080; www.bonbon.ee; Mere pst 6e; ☼ 11pm-5am Fri & Sat) With enormous chandeliers and a portrait of Bacchus overlooking the dance floor, Bon Bon is renowned for its chichi attitude. It attracts a 25- to 30-something A-list clientele who want to party in style. Frock up to fit in.

Club Privé (☎ 631 0545; www.clubprive.ee; Harju 6; cover 150-200EK; ☼ 11pm-5am Wed-Sat) Tallinn's most progressive club gets busiest on Saturdays. Despite the high prices, good DJs attract a club-savvy local and foreign crowd that is after something more cutting edge than the likes of Club Hollywood.

Angel (☎ 641 6880; www.clubangel.ee; Sauna 1; ☼ 11pm-5am Wed, Fri, Sat) Open to all sexes and orientations, this mainly gay club has become one of the liveliest spots in town for fun of all kinds; there is strict door control, however, and women may struggle to get in on Friday and Saturday. Check the website for party nights, and see www.gay.ee for more on the (small) gay scene in Tallinn.

Performing Arts

The places listed tend to stage performances in Estonian only, save of course for modern dance shows or the rare show in English or other languages. *Tallinn in Your Pocket* (www.inyourpocket.com) lists major shows; other good sources of information are **culture.ee** (www.culture.ee), **Eesti Kontsert** (www.concert.ee) and **Eesti Teatri Agentuur** (www.teater.ee).

Estonia Concert Hall & National Opera (☎ concert hall 614 7760, opera 683 1201; www.concert.ee & www.opera.ee; Estonia pst 4) The city's biggest concerts are held in this double-barrelled venue. It's Tallinn's main theatre, and also houses the Estonian national opera and ballet.

City Theatre (Tallinna Linnateater; ☎ 665 0800; www.linnateater.ee; Lai 23) The most beloved theatre in town always stages something memorable. Watch for its summer plays on an outdoor stage or different Old Town venues.

Teater No99 (☎ 660 5051; www.no99.ee; Sakala 3) More experimental productions happen here, but come by on Friday and Saturday evenings for the jazz bar downstairs.

Cinemas

Films are shown in their original language, subtitled in Estonian and Russian. Nighttime and weekend tickets cost around 100EEK to 120EEK (daytime sessions are cheaper).

Kino Sõprus (☎ 644 1919; Vana-Posti 8) Set in a magnificent Stalin-era theatre, this art-house cinema has an excellent repertoire of European, local and independent productions.

Coca-Cola Plaza (☎ 1182; www.superkinod.ee; Hobujaama 5) Modern 11-screen cinema playing the latest Hollywood releases. Located behind the post office.

SHOPPING

Inside Old Town, you'll be tripping over handicraft stores – look for signs for *käsitöö* (handicrafts). Dozens of small shops sell Estonian-made handicrafts, linen, leatherbound books, ceramics, jewellery, silverware, stained glass and objects carved from limestone, or made from juniper wood. These are all traditional Estonian souvenirs – as is a bottle of Vana Tallinn, of course! In summer a souvenir market sets up daily on Raekoja plats.

Katariina Gild (Katariina käik, Vene 12) This lovely laneway is home to a number of artisans' studios where you can happily browse and potentially pick up some beautiful pieces, including stained glass, ceramics, textiles, patchwork quilts, hats, jewellery and beautiful leather-bound books.

ESTONIA

Knit Market (Müürivahe) Along the Old Town wall there are a dozen or so vendors praying for cool weather and selling handmade linens, scarves, sweaters, mittens, beanies and socks.

Masters' Courtyard (Vene 6) Rich pickings here, with the courtyard not only home to a cosy cafe (p345), but also small stores selling quality ceramics, jewellery, knitwear, candles, and wood and felt designs.

Nu Nordik (☎ 644 9392; Vabaduse väljak 8) Unafraid of the avant-garde, this small boutique has youthful, edgy creations from up-and-coming local designers. Stock includes a small range of men's and women's clothes, plus bags, ceramics, CDs of local artists and homewares.

Tallinn's showpiece shopping mall **Viru Keskus** (☎ 610 1400; www.virukeskus.com; Viru väljak 4; ☻ 9am-9pm), aka Viru Centre, lies just outside Old Town.

GETTING THERE & AWAY
Air
For information on international flights to Estonia, see p364. Year-round, **Avies Air** (U3; ☎ 605 8022; www.avies.ee) flies daily from Tallinn to the island of Hiiumaa, while **Estonian Air** (OV; ☎ 640 1163; www.estonian-air.ee) connects Tallinn and Saaremaa.

Tallinn airport (TLL; ☎ 605 8888; www.tallinn-airport .ee) is just 4km southeast of the city centre on Tartu mnt. See p348 for details on getting to/from the airport.

Boat
See p348 for details on getting to/from the ferry terminals.

FINLAND
A fleet of ferries carries more than two million people annually across the 85km separating Helsinki and Tallinn. There are dozens of crossings made every day (ships two to 3½ hours; hydrofoils approximately 1½ hours). Note that in high winds or bad weather, hydrofoils are often cancelled; they operate only when the sea is free from ice (generally around late March/April to late December), while larger ferries sail year-round.

All companies provide concessions, allow pets and bikes (for a fee) and charge higher prices for weekend travel. Expect to pay around the price of an adult ticket extra to take a car. There's lots of competition, so check the companies for special offers and packages.

Operators include the following:
Eckerö Line (☎ 664 6000; www.eckeroline.ee; Terminal A) Sails once daily back and forth year-round (adult 300EEK to 390EEK, three to 3½ hours).
Linda Line (☎ 699 9333; www.lindaliini.ee; Linnahall Terminal) Small, passenger-only hydrofoils up to seven times daily late March to late December (adult 295EEK to 455EEK, 1½ hours).
Nordic Jet (☎ 613 7000; www.njl.info; Terminal C) Runs seven daily crossings with jet catamarans, generally from May to September (adult from 440EEK, 1½ hours).
Tallink (☎ 640 9808; www.tallinksilja.com; Terminal D) At least five services daily in each direction. The huge *Baltic Princess* takes 3½ hours; brand-new high-speed ferries take two hours and operate year-round. One-way adult prices start at 360EEK.
Viking Line (☎ 666 3966; www.vikingline.ee; Terminal A) Operates a giant car ferry, with two departures daily (adult from 300EEK, 2½ hours).

SWEDEN
Tallink (☎ 640 9808; www.tallinksilja.com) sails every night between Tallinn's Terminal D and Stockholm (cabin berth from 2250EEK, 16 hours). Book ahead.

Bus
For bus information and advance tickets for Estonian and international destinations, go to the **Central Bus Station** (Autobussijaam; ☎ 680 0900; Lastekodu 46), about 2km southeast of Old Town. Tram 2 or 4 will take you there, as will bus 17, 23 or 23A. **Ecolines** (www.ecolines.net) and **Eurolines** (☎ 680 0909; www.eurolines.ee) have offices here, but **Bookingestonia.com** (☎ 712 2102; www .bookingestonia.com; 2nd fl, Voorimehe 1) in Old Town will book and issue your international bus tickets for no commission.

Eurolines connects Tallinn with several cities in Germany and Poland, and from there to cities throughout Europe. Direct services connect Tallinn with Rīga (190EEK to 295EEK, 4½ hours, seven daily) and Vilnius (465EEK to 570EEK, 9½ to 12 hours, six daily via Rīga). Buses leave Tallinn for St Petersburg seven or eight times daily (495EEK, eight hours), passing through border-town Narva en route.

The excellent website **Bussi Reisid** (www.bussi reisid.ee) has times, prices and durations for all national bus services.

Car & Motorcycle
There are 24-hour fuel stations at strategic spots within the city, and on major roads leading to and from Tallinn.

ESTONIA

Car rental in Tallinn can often be arranged by your hotel, or try the following:

Bulvar (☎ 503 0222; www.bulvar.ee) Will deliver cars to you; from 500EEK daily.

Hansarent (☎ 627 9080; www.hansarent.eu) Will deliver cars to you; from 600EEK daily.

Hertz (www.hertz.ee) city centre (☎ 611 6333; Ahtri 12; ☎ 9am-6pm Mon-Fri); Tallinn airport (☎ 605 8923; Tallinn Airport; ☒ 9am-6pm)

Train

The **Central Train Station** (Balti Jaam; ☎ 615 6851; www.baltijaam.ee, in Estonian; Toompuiestee 35) is on the northwestern edge of Old Town, a short walk from Raekoja plats via Nunne, or three stops on tram 1 or 2, heading north from the Mere pst stop.

Train travel is not as popular as bus travel in Estonia, so domestic routes are quite limited.

The on-again, off-again Tallinn–St Petersburg service was off at the time of research. An overnight train runs every evening in either direction between Moscow and Tallinn (1500EEK in a four-berth compartment, 14 hours) operated by **GO Rail** (☎ 631 0044; www.gorail.ee).

GETTING AROUND
To/From the Airport

Bus 2 runs every 20 to 30 minutes (6am to around 11pm) from A Laikmaa, next to Viru Keskus; the bus stop is opposite, not out front of, the Tallink Hotel. From the airport, bus 2 will take you to the centre. Tickets are 20EEK from the driver (or cheaper from a kiosk, see right); journey time depends on traffic but rarely takes more than 20 minutes.

A taxi between the airport and the city centre should cost about 100EEK to 120EEK.

To/From the Ferry Terminals

Tallinn's sea-passenger terminal is at the end of Sadama, a short, 1km walk northeast of Old Town. Bus 2 runs every 20 to 30 minutes between the bus stop by Terminal A and A Laikmaa in the city centre; if you're heading to the terminal, the bus stop is out the front of the Tallink Hotel. Also from the heart of town (around the Viru Keskus transport hub), trams 1 and 2, and bus 3 go to the Linnahall stop, by the Statoil Petrol Station, five minutes' walk from terminals A, B and C. Terminal D is at the end of Lootsi, better accessed from Ahtri; bus 20 runs every hour or two along Narva mnt and Pärnu mnt to/from Terminal D.

A taxi between the city centre and any of the terminals will cost about 60EEK.

Bicycle

As well as offering hostels and tours (p342), **City Bike** (☎ 683 6383; www.citybike.ee; Uus 33; rental per hr/day/week 35/200/765EEK; ☒ 9am-7pm May-Sep, 9am-5pm Oct-Apr) can take care of all you need to get around by bike, whether it's within Tallinn, around Estonia or throughout the Baltic region.

Public Transport

Tallinn has an excellent network of buses, trams and trolleybuses that usually run from 6am to midnight. The major local bus station is on the basement level of Viru Keskus shopping centre; local buses may also terminate their route on the surrounding streets, just east of Old Town. All local public transport timetables are online at **Tallinn** (www.tallinn.ee).

The three modes of local transport all use the same ticket system. Buy *piletid* (tickets) from street kiosks (13EEK, or a book of 10 single tickets for 90EEK) or from the driver (20EEK). Validate your ticket using the hole puncher inside the vehicle – watch a local to see how this is done. One-/three-/10-day tickets are available for 40/70/125EEK, but can only be bought from kiosks. The Tallinn Card (p335) gives you free public transport in the city.

Taxi

Taxis are plentiful in Tallinn. Oddly, taxi companies set their own rates, so flag fall and per-kilometre rate vary from cab to cab – prices should be posted in each taxi's right rear window. If you merely hail a taxi on the street, there's a chance you'll be overcharged. To save yourself the trouble, order a taxi by phone: try **Krooni Takso** (☎ 1212, 638 1111) and **Tulika Takso** (☎ 1200, 612 0000).

NORTHEASTERN ESTONIA

This region has received much less attention by tourists than more-popular destinations such as Pärnu and Tartu, but shows a different side of Estonia. As you head east from Lahemaa, the vast majority of the population is Russian-speaking, which adds another flavour to the Estonian cultural mosaic, and some places feel like Soviet relics. Time to explore!

LAHEMAA NATIONAL PARK

The perfect country retreat from the capital, Lahemaa takes in a stretch of coast deeply indented with peninsulas and bays, plus 475 sq km of pine-fresh forested hinterland. Visitors are well looked after: there are cosy guest houses, restored manor houses, remote camp sites along the sea and an extensive network of pine-scented forest trails.

Information

Lahemaa National Park visitor centre (☎ 329 5555; www.lahemaa.ee; ◷ 9am-7pm May-Aug, 9am-5pm Sep, 9am-5pm Mon-Fri Oct-Apr) is in Palmse, 8km north of Viitna in the park's southeast, next door to Palmse Manor. Here you'll find the essential map of Lahemaa, as well as information on accommodation, hiking trails, island exploration and guide services.

Sights & Activities

There is an unlimited amount of sightseeing, hiking, cycling and boating to be done here; remote islands can also be explored. The park has several well-signposted nature trails and cycling paths winding through it. The small coastal towns of **Võsu**, **Käsmu** and (to a lesser extent) **Loksa** are popular seaside spots in summer. Käsmu is a particularly enchanting village, one of Estonia's prettiest.

Lahemaa also features historic manor houses. Park showpiece **Palmse Manor** (☎ 324 0070; www.svm.ee; adult/concession 60/30EEK; ◷ 10am-7pm May-Sep, 10am-6pm Wed-Sun Oct-Apr), next to the visitors centre, was once a wholly self-contained Baltic German estate, while the pink-and-white neoclassical **Sagadi Manor** (☎ 676 7878; www.sagadi.ee; adult/concession 35/15EEK; ◷ 10am-6pm May-Sep, by appt Oct-Apr) was built in 1749. There are also other manor houses at **Kolga** and **Vihula**.

Sleeping & Eating

Both Palmse Manor and Sagadi Manor have good sleeping and eating options on the estates.

ourpick **Toomarahva Turismitalu** (☎ 325 2511; www.zone.ee/toomarahva; Altja; camp sites per person 25EEK; d incl breakfast 450-800EEK) A farmstead with thatch-roofed wooden outhouses, and a garden full of flowers and sculptures, this gem of a place offers a gorgeous taste of rural Estonia. There's a yard for camping, a barn full of beds serving as a summer dorm for groups, plus rooms with private bathrooms (the 'suite' also has kitchen facilities). There is a rustic sauna, and bikes for rent; the friendly owner also offers catering. Signage is minimal – it's located opposite the yard of the Altja Kõrts (Altja Inn), which is well worth a visit for its rustic interior and traditional home cooking (mains 65EEK to 190EEK).

Sagadi Manor Hotel & Restaurant (☎ 676 7888; www.sagadi.ee; dm 250EEK, s/d from 900/1200EEK) With its whitewashed exterior and hanging flower baskets, this hotel on the Sagadi estate offers a cheerful welcome. On the ground floor are fresh new rooms opening onto small patios and a courtyard. Upstairs rooms are older and marginally cheaper. Sagadi also has a 35-bed hostel in the old steward's house. The hotel's 2nd-floor restaurant (mains 95EEK to 235EEK) offers a menu ranging from Caesar salad to elk stew. Bike rental is available.

Getting There & Away

Hiring a car is a good way to reach and explore the areas inside the park; alternatively you can take a tour from Tallinn. Daily in summer (and four times a week from mid-October to mid-May), **City Bike** (Map pp336-7; ☎ 683 6383; www.citybike.ee; Uus 33, Tallinn; ◷ 9am-7pm May-Sep, 9am-5pm Oct-Apr) runs a minibus tour of Lahemaa (759EEK) that takes in Palmse, Sagadi, Altja, Võsu and Käsmu villages. If you feel like getting closer to nature, it also offers bus transport to the park and supply of a bike and maps, plus the option of guided (920EEK) or self-guided (759EEK) exploration. Talk to the staff about itinerary building and transfers if you fancy spending a few days discovering the park by bike.

Otherwise, for public transport exploration you'll need patience and plenty of time up your sleeve. The best starting points for buses to destinations within the park are Tallinn, Viitna and Rakvere (most Tallinn–Rakvere buses stop in Viitna).

From May to September, a bus runs (only once daily) from Tallinn to Kasmu, Vosu and Altja. Rakvere has the most frequent services to the most villages inside the park. From Rakvere buses run year-round, but services are curtailed in winter. We highly recommend your own wheels or a tour.

ESTONIA •

NARVA & AROUND
pop 67,000

Estonia's easternmost town is separated from Ivangorod in Russia only by the thin Narva River and is almost entirely populated by Russians. Although the most outstanding architecture was destroyed in WWII, Estonia's third-largest city is an intriguing place to wander, as you'll find no other place in Estonia quite like it. The centre has a melancholy, downtrodden air; the prosperity evident in other parts of the country is harder to find here (though it does exist in some pockets, most notably the brash shopping centres along Tallinna mnt). Narva's a place that will have you scratching your head at times: is it a Russian city on the wrong side of the border? Is it Estonia (and Europe's) easternmost point, or is it Russia's westernmost town?

Orientation & Information

The **tourist information centre** (☎ 356 0184; http://tourism.narva.ee; Pushkini 13; 🕙 10am-6pm Mon-Fri, 10am-3pm Sat & Sun mid-May–mid-Sep, 10am-5pm Mon-Fri mid-Sep–mid-May) is in the city centre; it has an ATM and currency exchange as neighbours. The bus and train stations are located together at Vaksali 2, opposite the Russian Orthodox Voskresensky Cathedral. Walk north up Pushkini to the castle (500m) and the centre.

Sights

Restored after WWII, imposing **Narva Castle**, guarding the Friendship Bridge over the river to Russia, dates from Danish rule in the 13th century. It faces Russia's matching Ivangorod Fortress across the river, creating a picturesque face-off that's best captured from the **Swedish Lion monument**, in a small park behind the Narva Hotel at Pushkin 6. The castle houses the **Town Museum** (☎ 359 9245; adult/concession 60/35EEK; 🕙 10am-6pm).

About 13km north of Narva is the resort of **Narva-Jõesuu**, popular since the 19th century for its long golden-sand beach backed by pine forests. There are impressive early-20th-century wooden houses and villas here, as well as spa hotels.

Sleeping & Eating

Hostel & Restoran Lell (☎ 354 9009; www.narvahotel .ee; Partisani 4; s 275EEK, d 550-750EEK) If you're after budget digs, don't be put off by the grey concrete exterior of this option. The rooms are well worn but decent; the cheaper options share shower facilities. It's about 20 minutes' walk west of the centre, south of Astri Keskus shopping centre.

Pansionaat Valentina (☎ 357 7468; keeping@hot.ee; Aia 49, Narva-Jõesuu; s 400-500EEK, d 600-800EEK) Behind the slick new Meresuu Spa & Hotel in Narva-Jõesuu, and just metres from the beach, is this handsome, salmon-coloured guest house in immaculate grounds. It's family friendly, with plenty of facilities, including bike rental, tennis courts, sauna, barbecue and cafe. Be sure to admire the breathtaking intricacy of the historic villa right next door.

King Hotel (☎ 357 2404; www.hotelking.ee; Lavretsovi 9; s/d 690/890EEK; 🖵) Not far north of the centre (and with a few sleeping and eating options in the immediate vicinity) is Narva's best hotel choice, which has snug modern rooms and an excellent on-site restaurant (mains 109EEK to 249EEK). For something different, try the lamprey (a local fish from the Narva River), or the tasty trout kebab with bacon.

Getting There & Away

Narva is 210km east of Tallinn on the road to St Petersburg, which is a further 150km away. Around 25 daily buses travel between Tallinn and Narva (135EEK to 170EEK, three to four hours), and one train (100EEK, 3½ hours) runs daily. There are also up to 10 daily Tartu–Narva buses (125EEK to 160EEK, 3½ hours). All Tallinn–St Petersburg buses pass through town.

Bus 31 runs about hourly to connect Narva with Narva-Jõesuu (25EEK, 20 minutes), as do numerous *marshrutkas* (minibuses) without set timetables.

SOUTHEASTERN ESTONIA

Set with rolling hills, picturesque lakes and vast woodlands, the southeast sings with some of Estonia's prettiest countryside. It also contains one of the country's most important cities: the vibrant university centre of Tartu.

TARTU
pop 102,000

If Tallinn is Estonia's head, Tartu may well be its heart (and possibly its university-educated

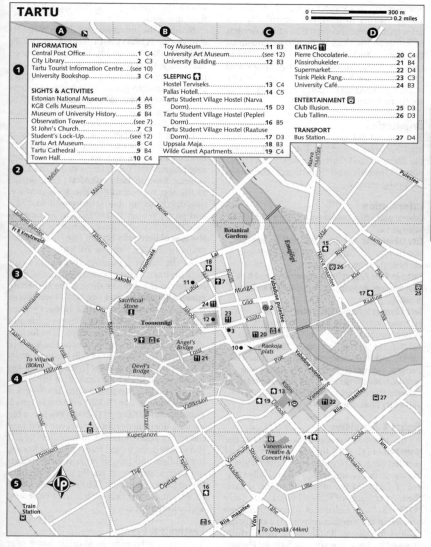

TARTU

INFORMATION
Central Post Office.........................1 C4
City Library....................................2 C3
Tartu Tourist Information Centre....(see 10)
University Bookshop.......................3 C4

SIGHTS & ACTIVITIES
Estonian National Museum.............4 A4
KGB Cells Museum..........................5 B5
Museum of University History........6 B4
Observation Tower......................(see 7)
St John's Church............................7 C3
Student's Lock-Up......................(see 12)
Tartu Art Museum..........................8 C4
Tartu Cathedral 9 B4
Town Hall....................................10 C4

Toy Museum.................................11 B3
University Art Museum...............(see 12)
University Building.......................12 B3

SLEEPING
Hostel Terviseks..........................13 C4
Pallas Hotell................................14 C5
Tartu Student Village Hostel (Narva
    Dorm)....................................15 D3
Tartu Student Village Hostel (Pepleri
    Dorm)....................................16 B5
Tartu Student Village Hostel (Raatuse
    Dorm)....................................17 D3
Uppsala Maja...............................18 B3
Wilde Guest Apartments...............19 C4

EATING
Pierre Chocolaterie.......................20 C4
Püssirohukelder............................21 B4
Supermarket.................................22 D4
Tsink Plekk Pang...........................23 C3
University Café.............................24 B3

ENTERTAINMENT
Club Illusion................................25 D3
Club Tallinn..................................26 D3

TRANSPORT
Bus Station...................................27 D4

ESTONIA

brains trust, too). Tartu lays claim to being Estonia's spiritual capital – locals talk about a special Tartu *vaim* (spirit), created by the time-stands-still, 19th-century feel of many of its wooden-house-lined streets, and by the beauty of its parks and riverfront.

Small and provincial, with the Emajõgi River quietly flowing through it, Tartu is

also Estonia's premier university town, with students making up nearly one-fifth of the population. This injects a boisterous vitality into the leafy, historic setting and grants it a surprising sophistication for a city of its size.

Tartu was the cradle of Estonia's 19th-century national revival and it escaped

Sovietisation to a greater degree than Tallinn. Today visitors to Estonia's second city can get a more authentic depiction of the rhythm of Estonian life than in its glitzier cousin to the north (and accompanied by far fewer tourists, too). In addition to galleries and cafes, there are good museums here; the city is also a convenient gateway to exploring southern Estonia.

Orientation
Toomemägi hill and the area of older buildings between it and the Emajõgi River are the focus of 'old' Tartu. Its heart is Raekoja plats. Ülikooli and Rüütli are the main shopping streets.

Information
Central post office (Vanemuise 7; ⏰ 8am-7pm Mon-Fri, 9am-4pm Sat)

City Library (☎ 736 1379; Kompanii 3; ⏰ 9am-8pm Mon-Fri, 10am-4pm Sat Sep-late Jul, 9am-6pm Mon-Fri late Jul-Aug) Free internet upstairs.

Tartu in Your Pocket (www.inyourpocket.com) More great info from this listings guide; available in bookshops or online.

Tartu tourist information centre (☎ 744 2111; www.visittartu.com; town hall, Raekoja plats; ⏰ 9am-6pm Mon-Fri, 10am-5pm Sat, 10am-3pm Sun mid-May–mid-Sep, 9am-5pm Mon-Fri, 10am-3pm Sat mid-Sep–mid-May) This friendly office has local maps and brochures, and loads of other city info. It can also book accommodation and tour guides, sell you souvenirs and get you online (free internet access available).

University Bookshop (☎ 744 1102; Ülikooli 1)

Sights & Activities
At the town centre on Raekoja plats is the **town hall** (1782–89), topped by a tower and weathervane, and fronted by a statue of lovers kissing under an umbrella – an apt, jolly symbol of Tartu. At the other end of the square, the former home of Colonel Barclay de Tolly (1761–1818), an exiled Scot who distinguished himself in the Russian army's 1812 campaign against Napoleon. Today it's a wonderfully crooked building housing the **Tartu Art Museum** (☎ 744 1080; Raekoja plats 18; adult/student 30/20EEK; ⏰ 11am-6pm Wed-Sun).

The university was founded in 1632 by the Swedish king; the main **university building** (☎ 737 5100; www.ut.ee; Ülikooli 18) dates from 1804. It houses the **University Art Museum** (☎ 737 5384; adult/child 10/5EEK; ⏰ 11am-5pm Mon-Fri) and **Student's Lock-Up** (admission 5EEK; ⏰ 11am-5pm Mon-Fri),

where 19th-century students were held for their misdeeds.

North of the university stands the magnificent Gothic **St John's Church** (Jaani Kirik; ☎ 744 2229; Jaani 5; ⏰ 10am-7pm Tue-Sat). This brick church dates back to at least 1323, and is noteworthy for its rare terracotta sculptures in niches around the main portal. Climb the 135 steps of the 30m **observation tower** (adult/child 25/15EEK; ⏰ 12.30-7pm Tue & Fri, 11am-7pm Wed, Thu & Sat) for a great bird's-eye view of Tartu.

Rising to the west of Raekoja plats is the splendid Toomemägi (Cathedral Hill), landscaped in the manner of a 19th-century English park and perfect for a stroll. The 13th-century Gothic **Tartu cathedral** (Toomkirik) at the top was rebuilt in the 15th century, despoiled during the Reformation in 1525, and partly rebuilt in 1804–07 to accommodate the university library, which is now the **Museum of University History** (☎ 737 5674; adult/student 25/15EEK; ⏰ 11am-5pm Wed-Sun).

As the major repository of Estonia's cultural heritage, Tartu has an abundance of first-rate museums. Among them is the absorbing **Estonian National Museum** (☎ 742 1311; www.erm.ee; Kuperjanovi 9; adult/student 20/15EEK, Fri free; ⏰ 11am-6pm Wed-Sun), which traces the history, life and traditions of the Estonian people. The former KGB headquarters now houses the sombre and highly worthwhile **KGB Cells Museum** (☎ 746 1717; Riia mnt 15b; adult/student 12/8EEK; ⏰ 11am-4pm Tue-Sat); you'll find the entrance on Pepleri.

The best place to pass a rainy few hours is the **Toy Museum** (☎ 736 1550; www.mm.ee; Lutsu 8; adult/concession 25/20EEK; ⏰ 11am-6pm Wed-Sun), a big hit with the under-eight crowd (you won't see too many adults anxious to leave, either). It showcases dolls, model trains, rocking horses, toy soldiers and tons of other desirables dating back a century or so. Be sure to wander through the adjacent TEFI House, home to an outstanding collection of theatre and animation puppets.

Festivals & Events
Tartu regularly dons its shiniest party gear and lets its hair down – good events to circle in your calendar include the following. Check out **kultuuriaken.tartu.ee** (http://kultuuriaken.tartu.ee) for more.

Tartu Ski Marathon (www.tartumaraton.ee) The city hosts this 63km race in mid-February, drawing around 4000 competitors to the region's cross-country tracks. The same organisation hosts a range of sporting events (such as cycling road races, mountain-bike races and running races) in and around Tartu throughout the year.

Tartu Student Days (www.studentdays.ee, in Estonian) Catch a glimpse of modern-day student misdeeds at the end of April, when they take to the streets to celebrate term's end. A second, smaller version occurs in mid-October.

Hansa Days Festival (www.hansapaevad.ee) Crafts, markets, family-friendly performances and more commemorate Tartu's Hanseatic past over three days in mid-July.

Sleeping

Hostel Terviseks (☎ 5353 1153; www.hostelterviseks .blogspot.com; apt 6, 4th fl, Ülikooli 1; dm 200-250EEK; ☐) Run by an Australian and a Canadian, this is a real travellers hostel that's best described as staying at your mate's place (albeit a mate with quite a few bunks in their apartment). There are 14 beds spread over two dorm rooms, plus a decent kitchen and cosy, orange-coloured lounge, but only one bathroom. It can be a little tricky to find – check directions on the website, or call if you're lost.

Tartu Student Village Hostels (☎ 740 9955; www .tartuhostel.eu; s/d from 350/600EEK) Narva dorm (**Narva mnt 27**); Pepleri dorm (**Pepleri 14**); Raatuse dorm (**Raatuse 22**) These student dorms offer accommodation that's cheap, clean and central (only Pepleri is south of the river). The Raatuse dorm is newest but somewhat institutional; it's the cheapest, as every three rooms share a kitchen and bathroom. The Narva option has two rooms sharing a kitchen and bathroom. The Pepleri dorm is the best pick – it's older but a bit cosier, and there's a private kitchenette and bathroom in each room. There are also larger suites at Pepleri that are excellent value. Advance reservations are a must.

Uppsala Maja (☎ 736 1535; www.uppsalamaja.ee; Jaani 7; s/d incl breakfast from 535/1020EEK; ☐) Maintained by the Swedish city of Uppsala (Tartu's sister city), this effortlessly pretty guest house in the town's old quarter features five warm, light-filled guestrooms ranging from two single rooms sharing a bathroom and lounge to a two-room suite (room 3). There's a kitchen for guest use. This place is deservedly popular, so book ahead.

Pallas Hotell (☎ 730 1200; www.pallas.ee; Riia mnt 4; s/d/ste 1060/1375/2100EEK) Set on the top three floors of a renovated central building that used to house a famous art school, the Pallas has some of the most flamboyantly decorated rooms in Estonia, with vibrantly colourful walls and decent furnishings. Some rooms boast floor-to-ceiling windows that give sweeping views over

the city. Request a city-facing room on the 3rd floor for space, size and artworks, or one of the six art-filled suites and deluxe doubles.

Wilde Guest Apartments (☎ 511 3876; www.wilde apartments.ee; Vallikraavi 4; apt d 1120-1500EEK, extra person 310EEK) This company rents four beautiful apartments with old-world details; two have sauna and balcony. All can sleep four.

Eating & Drinking

University Café (Ülikooli Kohvik; ☎ 737 5405; www.koh vik.ut.ee; Ülikooli 20; buffet per 100g 13EEK, snacks & meals from 50EEK; ☒ cafeteria 7.30am-7pm Mon-Fri, 10am-4pm Sat & Sun, 2nd-fl cafe 11am-11pm Mon-Thu, 11am-1am Fri & Sat, 11am-9pm Sun) Some of the most economical meals in town are waiting at the ground-floor cafeteria, which serves up decent breakfasts and a simple daytime buffet. Upstairs is a labyrinth of elegantly decorated rooms, both old-world grand and embracingly cosy, where deliciously artfully presented dishes are served.

our pick **Tsink Plekk Pang** (☎ 730 3415; Küütri 6; dishes 50-150EEK) Behind Tartu's funkiest facade (look for the stripy paintwork) and set over three floors (plus a rooftop sun terrace) is this cool Chinese-flavoured restaurant-lounge, named after the zinc buckets that are suspended from the ceiling as lampshades. You may need some time to peruse the huge, veg-friendly menu – there are plenty of well-priced noodles and soups, plus a decent Indian selection and even a handful of Japanese dishes. Or simply stop by to enjoy drinks with a DJ-spun soundtrack on weekends.

Pierre Chocolaterie (☎ 730 4680; www.pierre.ee; Raekoja plats 12; meals 65-195EEK; ☒ 8am-11pm Mon-Thu, 8am-1am Fri, 10am-1am Sat, 10am-11pm Sun) From Pierre, Tallinn's favourite choc-meister, comes a new branch on the main square of Tartu. There's the same refined atmosphere, old-world decor and all-ages crowd – plus the all-important truffles. This is a prime spot for coffee and a sugar fix at any time of day, or, for something more filling, there's a surprising range of salads, plus heftier mains.

Püssirohukelder (☎ 730 3555; Lossi 28; mains 70-260EEK) Set in a cavernous old gunpowder cellar under a soaring, 10m-high vaulted ceiling, this is both a boisterous pub and a good choice for tasty meat and fish dishes. When the regular live music kicks in later in the night (sometimes with a cover charge), you'll find the older crowd withdrawing to the more secluded wine cellar, which serves tapas-style snacks.

ESTONIA

The most central **supermarket** (Tartu Kaubamaja, Riia 1; 9am-10pm Mon-Sat, 9am-7pm Sun) is in the basement of the Kaubamaja shopping centre.

Entertainment

Wednesday is the traditional party night for students. Admission at the following places ranges from 40EEK to 150EEK, depending on the event.

Club Tallinn (740 3157; www.clubtallinn.ee, in Estonian; Narva mnt 27; Wed-Sat) Tartu's (and possibly Estonia's) best nightclub is a multifloored dancefest with many nooks and crannies. Top-notch DJs spin here, drawing a fashionable, up-for-it crowd. It's open only during the school year; during the summer, Club Tallinn relocates to Pärnu (p358).

Club Illusion (742 4341; www.illusion.ee; Raatuse 97; Wed-Sat) Close to the student dorms and built into an ex–movie theatre, Illusion has a lavish interior and first-class DJs drawing a stylish, club-savvy crowd. Themed nights include retro grooves, R'n'B, hip hop and house – check the website for info.

Getting There & Away

From the **bus station** (Autobussijaam; 733 1277; Turu 2), daily buses run to/from Tallinn (125EEK to 160EEK, 2½ to 3½ hours) about every 15 to 30 minutes from 6am to 9pm. Three daily trains also make the journey (95EEK to 140EEK, 2¼ hours).

Tartu is the main hub for destinations in south and southeastern Estonia, and has frequent connections with all other towns, including some 10 buses a day to Pärnu (135EEK to 150EEK, 2¾ hours).

There is one daily bus connecting Tartu with St Petersburg (370EEK, eight hours).

OTEPÄÄ
pop 2100

The small hilltop town of Otepää, 44km south of Tartu, is the centre of a scenic area beloved by Estonians for its hills and lakes, and thus its endless opportunities for sports – hiking, cycling and swimming in summer, and cross-country skiing in winter.

Orientation & Information

The point where Valga mnt and Tartu mnt meet is the epicentre of the town, with the bus station here, alongside the new **tourist information centre** (766 1200; www.otepaa.ee; Tartu mnt 1; 9am-6pm Mon-Fri, 10am-3pm Sat & Sun mid-May–mid-Sep, 9am-5pm Mon-Fri, 10am-3pm Sat mid-Sep–mid-May).

Behind the tourist info centre is the triangular main 'square', Lipuväljak; in this area you'll find the main town services.

Sights & Activities

Otepää's pretty 17th-century **church** (10am-4pm mid-May–Aug) is on a hilltop about 300m northeast of the bus station. It was in this church in 1884 that the Estonian Students' Society consecrated its new blue, black and white flag, which later became the flag of independent Estonia. The former vicar's residence now houses two museums, one dedicated to the story of the flag, and the other to local skiing.

The tree-covered hill south of the church is **Linnamägi** (Castle Hill), a major stronghold from the 10th to 12th centuries. There are traces of old fortifications on top, and good views of the surrounding country.

The best views, however, are along the shores of the 3.5km-long **Pühajärv** (Holy Lake), just southwest of town. A 12km nature trail and a bike path encircle the lake, making it a lovely spot for a walk. It's a 30-minute (2.3km) walk from Otepää township (via Pühajärve tee) to the northern tip of the lake, where there a **beach park** that's popular with summer swimmers. The lake was blessed by the Dalai Lama and a monument on the eastern shore commemorates his visit in 1991.

It would be a shame not to take advantage of some of the excellent outdoor activities the region has to offer. To rent bikes, rollerblades, skis and snowboards, or to take a fun bike or canoe tour, contact **Fan Sport** (767 7537; www .fansport.ee), which has three offices inside the larger hotels in Otepää. **Toonus Pluss** (505 5702; www.toonuspluss.ee) specialises in canoeing trips in the area; tailor-made trips can combine canoeing with hiking and mountain biking. Ask at the tourist office for more options.

Sleeping & Eating

Low season here is April to May and September to November; at this time hotel prices are about 10% to 15% cheaper.

Edgari (766 6550; karnivoor@hot.ee; Lipuväljak 3; s/d with shared bathroom from 250/400EEK) One of the cheapest places to stay right in town, this guest house feels like a hostel, with its thin walls, shared kitchen and communal lounge. The 2nd-floor rooms are like miniapartments, with kitchenette and private bathroom. Downstairs is a tavern and a small food shop.

Pühajärve Spa Hotel (☎ 766 5500; www.pyhajarve .com; Pühajärve tee; s/d/ste weekdays 750/900/1550EEK, weekends 900/1200/1790EEK; 🏊) With its 85 rooms and sprawling lakeside grounds, this is not somewhere you're likely to feel the personal touch. Sports and recreation facilities are laid on thick; there is a day spa, indoor pool, boat trips, beach, bowling alley, gym, tennis courts and bike rental. Modern rooms are nothing flash; the activities and on-site eating options go a long way towards compensating for this, however. Best of all is the pub (mains 90EEK to 250EEK); its sunny outdoor terrace is the place to be, but the brick-lined interior, with pool tables and an open fire, is not a bad wet-weather option.

Getting There & Away
Buses connect Otepää with Tartu (35EEK to 50EEK, 45 minutes to 1½ hours, 10 daily) and Tallinn (175EEK, 3½ hours, one daily).

SETUMAA
In the far southeast of Estonia lies the area of Setumaa (Setomaa in the local language). Unlike the rest of Estonia, this part of the country never came under the control of the Teutonic and German tribes, but instead fell under the subjugation of Novgorod and later Pskov. The Setu people, originally Finno-Ugric, then became Orthodox, not Lutheran. The whole of Setumaa was contained within independent Estonia between 1920 and 1940, but the greater part of it is now in Russia. There are only approximately 4000 Setu left in Estonia (with about another 3000 in Russia), half the population of the early 20th century.

Aside from the large, silver breastplate that is worn on the women's national costume, what sets the Setu aside is their singing style. Information on the region can be found online at **Setomaa Valdade Liit** (www.setomaa.ee). Museums worth visiting include the **Setu Museum House** (☎ 785 4190; adult/concession 15/10EEK; 🕙 10am-5pm Mon-Fri year-round, plus 11am-5pm Sat & Sun mid-May–mid-Sep) in the village of Obinitsa, which has a few folk costumes, tapestries, cookware and old photos. It also functions as a tourist information centre.

The **Setu Farm Museum** (☎ 505 4673; Pikk 40; adult/ concession 30/15EEK; 🕙 10am-5pm mid-May–mid-Sep, 10am-4pm Tue-Sat mid-Sep–mid-May) in Värska is a re-created 19th-century farmhouse complex. Its rustic log-cabin restaurant is worth a stop, and there are some very good handicrafts.

There are four to five buses daily between Tartu and Värska (85EEK, 1½ to two hours). To reach Obinitsa from Tartu, you'll need to travel via Võru (60EEK to 75EEK, one to 1½ hours, 16 buses daily). From Võru, four to six buses run to Obinitsa (20EEK to 36EEK, 45 minutes).

WESTERN ESTONIA
As well as a summer-magnet coastline, the western half of the country houses Estonia's most popular resort town, sweet country villages, a vast national park and a handful of islands – developed or remote and windswept, take your pick.

PÄRNU
pop 44,000
Local families, young party-goers, and German and Finnish holidaymakers join together in a collective prayer for sunny weather while strolling the golden-sand beaches, sprawling parks and picturesque historic centre of Pärnu (*pair*-nu), Estonia's premier seaside resort.

Come summer, the town acts as a magnet for party-loving Estonians – its name alone is synonymous with fun in the sun in these parts (one local described it to us as 'Estonia's Miami' – we think he was being tongue-in-cheek!). Yet

ESTONIA

WORTH THE TRIP: SETOMAA TURISMOTALU

One of this area's highlights is the **Setomaa Turismotalu** (Tourist Farm; ☎ 508 7399; www.setotalu .ee; per person camp sites/r with shared bathroom 50/400EEK). With your own wheels, this makes a great base for exploring the southeast region, and the owners will help you plan your explorations and tap into the Setu culture. It's possible to take part in traditional Setu arts and crafts in idyllic surrounds, have a smoke sauna, and stay in a log house decorated with natural textiles. The food's great (dinner 90EEK to 120EEK), the staff friendly and you can partake in tradition without feeling touristy. You'll need to book, as this place is popular with groups. It's 1.7km from the village of Meremäe, towards Vatseliina castle ruins.

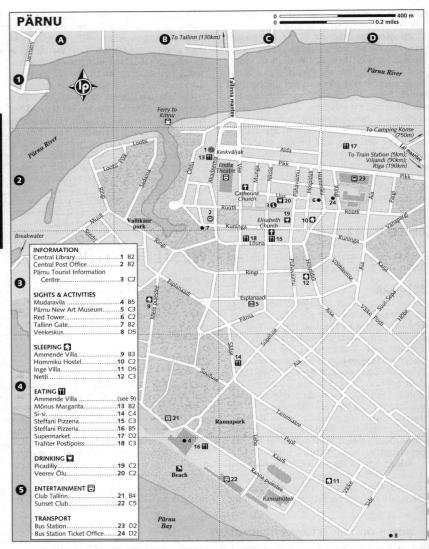

PÄRNU

To Tallinn (130km)

Pärnu River

Pärnu River

Ferry to Kihnu

To Camping Konse (750m)

To Train Station (5km); Viljandi (90km); Riga (190km)

Keskväljak

Aida

Pikk

Pikk

Endla Theatre

Catherine Church

Vallikäär park

Elisabeth Church

Breakwater

Esplanaadi

Ringi

Esplanaadi

Pärna

Rannapark

Beach

Rannahotell

Pärnu Bay

INFORMATION
Central Library....................1 B2
Central Post Office...............2 B2
Pärnu Tourist Information
 Centre............................3 C2

SIGHTS & ACTIVITIES
Mudaravila.........................4 B5
Pärnu New Art Museum........5 C3
Red Tower..........................6 C2
Tallinn Gate.......................7 B2
Veekeskus..........................8 D5

SLEEPING
Ammende Villa.....................9 B3
Hommiku Hostel..................10 C2
Inge Villa..........................11 D5
Netti................................12 C3

EATING
Ammende Villa.................(see 9)
Mõnus Margarita................13 B2
Si-si................................14 C4
Steffani Pizzeria.................15 C3
Steffani Pizzeria.................16 B5
Supermarket......................17 D2
Trahter Postipoiss...............18 C3

DRINKING
Picadilly...........................19 C2
Veerev Õlu........................20 C2

ENTERTAINMENT
Club Tallinn.......................21 B4
Sunset Club.......................22 C5

TRANSPORT
Bus Station........................23 D2
Bus Station Ticket Office.......24 D2

youth and bacchanalia aren't the only spirits moving through town. Most of Pärnu is
actually quite docile, with leafy streets and
expansive parks intermingling with turn-of-
the-century villas that reflect the town's past as
a resort capital of the Baltic region. Pärnu is still
a popular health resort for older visitors from
the Baltics, Finland and Eastern Europe, who
come seeking rest, amelioration and Pärnu's
vaunted mud treatments, which are available in
both old-school Soviet-style sanatoriums and
more modern, glitzier spa resorts.

Orientation & Information
Pärnu lies on either side of the Pärnu River
estuary, which empties into Pärnu Bay. The

southern half of the town contains the major attractions, including Old Town (beginning a few blocks south of the river), and the beach, which lies half a kilometre further on the far southern end. Between Old Town and the shoreline is a series of parks.

Central Library (☎ 445 5706; Akadeemia 3; ⏰ 10am-6pm Mon-Fri, 10am-4pm Sat) Free internet.

Central post office (Akadeemia 7)

Pärnu in Your Pocket (www.inyourpocket.com) More great info from this listings guide; available in bookshops or online.

Pärnu tourist information centre (☎ 447 3000; www.visitparnu.com; Rüütli 16; ⏰ 9am-6pm Mon-Fri, 10am-4pm Sat, 10am-3pm Sun Jun-Aug, 9am-5pm Mon-Fri Sep-May) Pick up maps and brochures. Helpful staff will book accommodation for a 25EEK fee.

Sights & Activities

The wide, golden-sand beach and Ranna pst, whose buildings date from the early 20th century, are among Pärnu's finest attractions. Note especially the handsome 1927 neoclassical **Mudaravila** (Ranna pst 1), a symbol of the town's history. The legendary mud baths that once operated here have closed; new owners are planning to restore the building and add an adjacent new spa hotel. (Does Pärnu need another one?) Stay tuned.

A fine beach promenade was opened in 2006, with a curving path lined with fountains and park benches stretching along the sand. At the far end, Estonia's largest water park, **Veekeskus** (☎ 445 1166; www.terviseparadiis.ee; Side 14; adult 115-290EEK, concession 75-205EEK; ⏰ 10am-10pm), beckons with pools, slides, tubes and other slippery fun. It's a big family-focused draw, especially when bad weather ruins beach plans. It's part of the huge Tervise Paradiis hotel complex.

The main thoroughfare of the historic centre is Rüütli. Just off the main street is the **Red Tower** (Punane Torn; Hommiku 11; ⏰ 10am-5pm), the city's oldest building, which dates from the 15th century; despite its name, it's actually white. Parts of the 17th-century Swedish moat and ramparts remain at the western end of Rüütli; the tunnel-like **Tallinn Gate** (Tallinna Värav), which once marked the main road to Tallinn, pierces the point where the rampart meets the western end of Kuninga.

The **Pärnu New Art Museum** (☎ 443 0772; www.chaplin.ee; Esplanaadi 10; adult/concession 25/15EEK; ⏰ 9am-9pm), southwest of the centre, is among Estonia's cultural highlights with its exhibitions that always push the cultural envelope. It also holds a cafe and bookshop, and hosts the annual **Pärnu International Film Festival**, which showcases documentary and anthropology films in early July.

Sleeping

There's loads of accommodation here, from hostels to apartments and everything in between. In summer, however, it's well worth booking ahead; outside of high season you should be able to snare yourself a good deal. Prices listed below are for high season (websites will list off-season rates, which can be up to 40% lower).

Camping Konse (☎ 5343 5092; www.konse.ee; Suur-Jõe 44a; camp sites 60EEK plus per person 60EEK, r with shared/private bathroom 550/700EEK) Perched on a spot by the river only 1km from Old Town, Konse offers camp sites and a variety of rooms (half with private bathroom, half with shared facilities, all with kitchen access). There's a sauna, and bike and rowing-boat. It can get crowded, but that makes it easier to meet people. Open year-round.

Hommiku Hostel (☎ 445 1122; www.hommikuhostel.ee; Hommiku 17; dm/s/d/tr/q 300/600/900/1200/1400EEK) You'll do well to snare a room at Hommiku, which is far more like a hotel than a hostel (except for its prices). This modern place has handsome rooms with private bathrooms, TV and kitchenettes; some also have old beamed ceilings. It's in a prime in-town position, with good eateries as its neighbours.

Inge Villa (☎ 443 8510; www.ingevilla.ee; Kaarli 20; s/d/ste 1000/1250/1450EEK) In a prime patch of real estate not far back from the beach you'll find the low-key and lovely Inge Villa, a 'Swedish-Estonian villa hotel'. Its 11 rooms are simply decorated in muted tones with Nordic minimalism at the fore. The garden, lounge and sauna seal the deal.

Netti (☎ 516 7958; www.nettihotel.ee; Hospidali 11-1; ste 1200-1600EEK) Anni, your host at Netti, is a ray of sunshine, and her three-storey guest house, comprising four two-room suites (all with kitchenette) positively gleams under her care. The suites sleep three, are bright and breezy (reminiscent of the '80s), and the downstairs sauna area is a lovely place to unwind after a hard day at the beach.

Ammende Villa (☎ 447 3888; www.ammende.ee; Mere pst 7; r/ste from 3500/4800EEK) If money's no object, this is where to spend it. Class and luxury abound in this exquisitely refurbished

1904 art nouveau mansion, which lords over handsomely manicured grounds. The gorgeous exterior is matched by an elegant lobby, individually antique-furnished rooms and top-notch service.

Eating & Drinking

Mõnus Margarita (☎ 443 0929; Akadeemia 5; mains 69-310EEK) Huge, colourful and decidedly upbeat, as all good Tex-Mex places should be – but if you're looking for heavy-duty spice, you won't find it here. Fajitas, burritos and quesadillas all score goals, plus there are margaritas and tequilas for the grown-ups, and a play area for the kids.

Steffani Pizzeria (☎ 443 1170; Nikolai 24; pizzas 75-105EEK) The queue out front should alert you – this is a top choice for thin-crust and pan pizzas, particularly in summer when you can dine alfresco on the big, flower-filled terrace. In a smart business move, a second summertime branch opens near the beach at Ranna pst 1.

Si-si (☎ 447 5612; Supeluse 21; mains 75-220EEK) The beachside dining is disappointingly bland, but a walk up Supeluse presents some good options, including this brand-spanking-new Italian restaurant-lounge. Inside is smart white-linen dining, outside is a stylishly relaxed terrace peopled by equally stylish holidaymakers. There's a good selection of pizzas (topped by Parma ham, gorgonzola and the like), plus mains including wild boar stew and osso bucco.

Trahter Postipoiss (☎ 446 4864; Vee 12; mains 98-320EEK) One of Pärnu's highlights, this converted 17th-century postal building houses a rustic Russian tavern, with excellent Russian cuisine, a convivial crowd (especially after a few vodka shots) and imperial portraits watching over the proceedings. The spacious patio opens during summer, and there's live music on weekends.

Ammende Villa (☎ 447 3888; Mere pst 7; breakfast buffet 150EEK, mains 120-350EEK; 🕑 breakfast 7-10am Mon-Fri, 8-11am Sat & Sun, restaurant noon-11pm) Nonguests can get a taste of life at this art nouveau gem by joining in the morning breakfast buffet – a splendid spread of salmon, fresh fruit and Champagne. Otherwise, various salons and the beautiful garden terrace are great spots to dine, or you can simply stop by for a glass of bubbles and a cheese platter. To help unleash your inner sophisticate, weekly classical concerts are held on the lawn in summer.

Picadilly (☎ 442 0085; Pühavaimu 15) The city's only wine bar–cafe offers down-tempo bliss in plush surroundings, plus a top wine selection, and an extensive range of coffee, tea and hot choc. Savoury food begins and ends with quiche – here it's all about the sweeties, including moreish cheesecake (25EEK) and handmade chocolates.

Veerev Õlu (☎ 442 9848; Uus 3a) The 'Rolling Beer' (named after the Rolling Stones) wins the award for friendliest and cosiest pub by a long shot – it's a tiny rustic space with lots of good vibes, cheap beer and the occasional live rock-folk band (with compulsory dancing on tables, it would seem).

The most central **supermarket** (🕑 9am-10pm) is inside the Port Artur 2 complex, off Pikk and opposite the bus station.

Entertainment

Club Tallinn (www.clubtallinn.ee; Mere pst 22; 🕑 Wed-Sat Jun-Aug) This summertime-only club is held in one section of the beachside Kuursaal beer hall. It's the city's hottest spot, with excellent DJs and an eager young crowd.

Sunset Club (☎ 443 0670; www.sunset.ee; Ranna pst 3; 🕑 Fri & Sat) In a grandiose seafront building dating from 1939, Pärnu's biggest and most famous nightclub has an outdoor beach terrace and a sleek multifloor interior with plenty of cosy nooks for when the dance floor gets crowded. Imported DJs and bands, plus a wild young crowd, keep things cranked until the early hours.

Getting There & Away

About 30 daily buses connect Pärnu with Tallinn (115EEK to 125EEK, two hours), and 10 services connect Pärnu with Tartu (135EEK to 150EEK, 2½ to three hours). Tickets for a multitude of other destinations, including Rīga and beyond, are available at the Pärnu **bus station ticket office** (☎ 447 1002; Ringi; 🕑 6.15am-7.30pm), across from the bus station.

There are also two daily Tallinn–Pärnu trains (75EEK, 2¾ hours), though the train station is an inconvenient 5km east of the town centre, down Riia mnt.

VILJANDI & AROUND

pop 20,000

One of Estonia's most charming towns, Viljandi, 90km east of Pärnu, is a relaxed place to stop for a day or more. It's a good spot to use as a base for exploring the country' largest flood plain and bog area (no laughing!), and the town itself, settled since the 12th century, has a gentle 19th-century flow to it. The **tourist information centre** (☎ 433 0442; www.viljandi.ee; Vabaduse plats 6) is one of Estonia's finest, with local maps and information in loads of languages; it also has info on Soomaa National Park.

A highlight is visiting **Castle Park** (Lossimäed), which sprawls out from behind the tourist information office. A picturesque green area with spectacular views over Lake Viljandi, the park contains the ruins of a 13th- to 15th-century castle founded by the German Knights of the Sword, which are open for all to muck about in. The excellent **Kondase Keskus** (☎ 433 3968; www.kondase.ee; Pikk 8; adult/student 15/5EEK; 10am-5pm Wed-Sun) is the country's only art gallery devoted to naive art.

Easily the biggest event on the calendar is the hugely popular four-day **Viljandi Folk Music Festival** (www.folk.ee/festival), held in late July, and renowned for its friendly relaxed vibe and impressive international line-up. It's the country's biggest music festival and sees Viljandi's population double in size.

On one of Viljandi's loveliest streets, the small six-room **Hostel Ingeri** (☎ 433 4414; www.hostelingeri.ee; Pikk 2c; s350EEK; d 500-600EEK) offers seriously good value with its bright, comfortable rooms, all with TV and bathroom. Plant life and a kitchen for guest use make it a good home from home, while the parkside location couldn't be better.

The terrace overlooking the park is the big drawcard of the tavern-style **Tegelaste Tuba** (☎ 433 3944; Pikk 2b; mains 45-80EEK), but so are the comfy interiors on cold, rainy days. Estonian handicrafts enliven the walls, and a diverse crowd enjoys the wide-ranging menu of soups, salads, omelettes and meaty mains.

Around 12 daily buses connect Viljandi with Tallinn (140EEK to 150EEK, two to 2½ hours). There are about 10 daily buses to/from Pärnu (90EEK, 1½ to two hours), up to 16 to/from Tartu (70EEK to 85EEK, 1½ hours). There is no public transport to Soomaa National Park. Rent a car locally at **Unistar Auto** ☎ 435 5921; unistar@unistar-auto.ee; Tallinna 86).

SOOMAA NATIONAL PARK

Some 40km west of Viljandi is **Soomaa National Park** (☎ 445 7164; www.soomaa.ee), a rich land of bogs, marsh, criss-crossing rivers and iron-rich black pools of water, perfect for a quick summer dip. Much more interesting than what the word 'bog' implies, this 37,000-hectare park is full of quirky opportunities, from a walk through the swampland landscape to a single-trunk canoe trip down one of the rivers to an unforgettable sauna atop a floating raft.

The **Soomaa National Park visitor centre** (☎ 435 7164; www.soomaa.ee; 10am-6pm May-Sep, 10am-4pm Oct-Apr) is 22km west of the village of Kõpu, itself 20km west of Viljandi. You can also call into the Viljandi **tourist office** (☎ 433 0442; www.viljandi.ee; Vabaduse plats 6; 9am-6pm Mon-Fri, 10am-3pm Sat & Sun mid-May–mid-Sep, 10am-5pm Mon-Fri, 10am-2pm Sat mid-Sep–mid-May) to pick up maps and brochures.

The best way to explore the park is with **Soomaa.com** (☎ 506 1896; www.soomaa.com), a local company promoting ecotourism and sustainable development. It offers a fabulous range of year-round activities; transfers from Pärnu are available. The Discover Soomaa National Park day trip includes river canoeing and walking on peat bog (782EEK from Soomaa, 1095EEK from Pärnu; runs from May to September). There are also guided and self-guided canoeing, beaver-watching, bog-shoeing and mushroom-picking experiences and, in winter, kick-sledding, cross-country-skiing and snow-shoeing excursions. Independent adventurers can rent gear such as tents and sleeping bags, as well as canoes. Accommodation in an old farmhouse can be arranged (from 156EEK per night), as can the rental of our favourite Soomaa treat, the floating sauna atop the Raudna River. You'll need to contact Soomaa .com in advance to arrange your itinerary; check the website for all the options.

There is no public transport to Soomaa National Park.

SAAREMAA
pop 36,000

For Estonians, Saaremaa (literally 'Island Land') is synonymous with space, spruce, peace and fresh air – and killer beer. Estonia's largest island (roughly the size of Luxembourg) still lies covered in thick pine and spruce forests, and juniper groves, while old windmills, slender lighthouses and tiny villages appear unchanged by the passage of time. There's also a long history of beer home-brewing, and a large beer festival, **Õlletoober** (www.olletoober.ee), takes place here in mid-July.

During the Soviet era, the entire island was off limits (due to a radar system and rocket base). This unwittingly resulted in a minimum of industrial build-up and the protection of the island's rural charm.

Orientation & Information

To reach Saaremaa you must first cross Muhu, the small island where the ferry from the mainland docks, which is connected to Saaremaa by a 2.5km causeway. Kuressaare, the capital of Saaremaa, is on the south coast and is a natural base for visitors.

Kuressaare's **tourist information office** (☎ 453 3120; www.kuressaare.ee; Tallinna 2; ☻ 9am-7pm Mon-Fri, 9am-5pm Sat, 9am-3pm Sun May-Sep, 9am-5pm Mon-Fri Oct-Apr) can help you make the best of your stay.

More information is online at **Saaremaa** (www.saaremaa.ee).

Sights & Activities

The island's most distinctive landmark is the fantastic **Bishop's Castle** (1338–80), located at the southern end of Kuressaare and ringed by a moat. It looks like it was plucked from a fairy tale, and now houses the **Saaremaa Museum** (☎ 455 7542; www.saaremaamuuseum.ee; adult/concession 50/25EEK; ☻ 10am-6pm May-Aug, 11am-6pm Wed-Sun Sep-Apr).

At Angla, 40km from Kuressaare, just off the road to the harbour on the Leisi road, is a photogenic group of five **windmills**. Two kilometres away, along the road opposite the windmills, is **Karja Church**, a striking 14th-century German Gothic church.

At Kaali, 18km from Kuressaare, is a 110m-wide, water-filled **crater** formed by a meteorite at least 3000 years ago. In ancient Scandinavian mythology the site was known as the sun's grave. It's Europe's largest and most accessible meteorite crater, but looks mighty tiny up close!

Saaremaa's magic can really be felt along the **Sõrve Peninsula**, jutting out south and west

of Kuressaare. This sparsely populated strip of land saw some of the heaviest fighting in WWII, and some bases and antitank defence lines still stand. A bike or car trip along the coastline provides some of the most spectacular sights on the island; several daily buses from Kuressaare bus station also head down the coast of the peninsula. But a trip anywhere on this island is likely to be memorable – particularly the sparsely populated, wilder northwestern section.

Pärimusmatkad Heritage Tours (☎ 526 9974; www .parimusmatkad.ee) is a recommended company that arranges a raft of year-round Saaremaa excursions and activities, including berry and mushroom picking, horse riding, birdwatching, bog walks and jeep safaris.

Sleeping

The tourist information office (left) can organise beds in private apartments throughout the region; farm stays are also available across the island. Hotel prices are up to 40% cheaper from September through to April.

Mändjala Kämping (☎ 454 4193; www.mandjala .ee; camp sites/cabins per person 60/220EEK; ☻ May-Sep; ▣) Heaving in high summer (and with a capacity for 1000 people), this camping ground 10km west of Kuressaare offers rustic wooden cabins and camp sites amid lots of pine-filled greenery. It's a short walk to the beach, and water sports are available, as is a sauna, bike rental, bar, restaurant etc. In summer, half-a-dozen buses from Kuressaare to Salme, Torgu or Sääre stop at the Mändjala bus stop.

SYG Hostel (☎ 455 4388; www.syg.edu.ee; Kingu 6, Kuressaare; s/d/q with shared bathroom 300/420/640EEK; ▣) A comfy and well-priced hostel about 600m from the city centre; it's attached to a school, so there's a small gym and internet room, plus a cafeteria doling out cheap meals. On the minus side, there hasn't been much

WORTH THE TRIP: HIIUMAA

Hiiumaa, Estonia's second-biggest island, is a quiet, sparsely populated haven, rich in bird life and encompassing some great stretches of empty coastline. The 'capital' of the island is Kärdla, where you'll find the tourist information centre and most services. Get island information from **Matkamine Hiiumaal** (http://turism.moonsund.ee) or **Hiiuaa.ee** (http://hiiumaa.ee).

Hiiumaa is perfect for a cycling trip – you'll find picturesque lighthouses and eerie old Soviet bunkers scattered about. If the weather's good, laid-back **Surf Paradiis** (☎ 5625 1015; www.paap .ee/eng/suvi/; ☾ mid-May–Sep), on the far west of the island (no public transport), is an unexpected treat. Set on a stretch of sandy beach, it overflows with activity options: windsurfing, kitesurfing, parasailing, sea kayaking, jet-skiing, scuba diving, ATV (all-terrain vehicle) safaris, waterskiing etc. It's a good idea to call ahead, as all activities are weather dependent, and the place is sometimes booked solid by groups. A day pass for the 'water park' costs 600EEK, and includes use of boogie boards, water trampoline, kayaks, skimboards, zip lines (from the roof of the sauna into the sea), snorkelling, sauna and sun lounges.

There are also a number of kooky overnight options, including camping (25EEK per person), tepees (from 300EEK per person), beachfront bungalows (500EEK) – even sleeping in a surfboard bag, or on the sand under an upturned boat (100EEK). There are traditional rooms too, for those after creature comforts. BYO food.

Ferries operate daily between Rohuküla on the Estonian mainland and Heltermaa on Hiiumaa, or between northern Saaremaa and southern Hiiumaa; see **Saaremaa Laevakompanii** (www .laevakompanii.ee) for details. Two buses daily run from Tallinn to Kärdla (185EEK, 4½ hours). **Avies Air** (U3; ☎ 605 8022; www.avies.ee) flies daily from Tallinn to Hiiumaa.

renovation here in ages, there's no kitchen, and the place is not exactly overflowing with backpacker cheer.

Arensburg Boutique Hotel & Spa (☎ 452 4700; www.arensburg.eu; Lossi 15, Kuressaare; s/d/ste from 1250/1550/3950EEK; ☒) With a split personality and severe case of old versus new, central Arensburg is almost two hotels in one. Our vote goes to the bold and sexy charcoal-painted rooms in the slick 2007 extension to the historic hotel; standard rooms in the old wing are OK but unremarkable. A new spa and two restaurants round things out nicely.

Eating & Drinking

Chameleon (☎ 668 2212; Kauba 2, Kuressaare; meals 50-140EEK) Newly opened Chameleon is indeed a changing creature, effortlessly morphing from daytime cafe to night-time restaurant to late-night cocktail bar. The sleek black-and-grey decor (with pink lighting) adds an air of city slickness, but it's not too cool to offer a kids' menu and playroom.

La Perla (☎ 453 6910; Lossi 3, Kuressaare; mains 65-245Kr) A pearl of a menu makes dining at this popular Italian restaurant a warming Mediterranean treat. Swing from bruschetta to tiramisu via all manner of pizza, pasta and grilled meats, preferably accompanied by a glass of cheeky Italian red.

Veski Trahter (☎ 453 3776; Pärna 19, Kuressaare; mains 105-250EEK) Without being too touristy, this place inside an 1899 windmill emphasises quality and ambience, with plenty of hearty local fare such as wild-boar hotpot, cabbage soup and Saaremaa cheeses.

John Bull Pub (☎ 453 9988; Pärgi 4, Kuressaare) In the park suurounding the castle, this pub (not particularly English, despite its name) has a great moatside deck, a menu of cheap'n'cheerful pub classics, and our favourite feature – a bar made from an old Russian bus.

RAE Supermarket (Raekoja 10, Kuressaare; ☾ 9am-10pm) is the best grocery store. It's located behind the tourist information centre.

Getting There & Around

A year-round vehicle ferry runs throughout the day from Virtsu on the mainland to the island of Muhu, which is joined by cause-way to Saaremaa; see **Saaremaa Laevakompanii** (www.laevakompanii.ee) for ferry schedules and prices.

Around 12 direct buses travel daily between Tallinn and Kuressaare (205EEK to 250EEK, four to 4½ hours, 220km), via the ferry. There are three buses daily to/from Tartu (250EEK, six to 6½), and to/from Pärnu (200EEK, 3¼ hours).

Estonian Air (OV; ☎ 640 1163; www.estonian-air
.ee) flies up to eight times a week year-round
between Tallinn and Kuressaare (484EEK,
45 minutes).

ESTONIA DIRECTORY

ACCOMMODATION

Places are listed in our Sleeping sections in
order of ascending price. In the budget category (double rooms under 800EEK), you'll
find backpackers' lodgings, hostels, and
basic guest houses and hotels (many with
shared bathrooms). A dorm bed generally
costs 150EEK to 200EEK. Midrange listings
(800EEK to 2000EEK) run the gamut from
family-run guest houses to large hotel rooms
(private bathroom and breakfast generally
included). Top-end listings (over 2000EEK)
comprise historic hotels, spa resorts and
charming places offering something particularly special (such as antique-filled rooms or
ocean views). All prices listed in this chapter
are high-season prices and for rooms that have
private bathroom, unless otherwise stated.

There are a few *kämpingud* (camping
grounds; open from mid-May to September)
that allow you to pitch a tent, but most consist
of permanent wooden huts or cabins, with
communal showers and toilets. Farms and
homestays offer more than a choice of rooms;
in many cases meals, a sauna and a range of
activities are available. There's a search engine
at **Visitestonia.com** (www.visitestonia.com) for all types
of accommodation throughout the country.

The peak tourist season is from June
through August. If you come then, you should
book well in advance. This is essential in
Tallinn, and in popular summertime destinations such as the islands and Pärnu.

In 2007 Estonia introduced legislation
outlawing smoking in public areas such as
restaurants and bars. Some smaller hotels and
most hostels are 100% nonsmoking; larger
establishments will offer nonsmoking and
smoking rooms.

ACTIVITIES

Many travel agencies can arrange a variety of
activity-based tours of Estonia. A detailed list
of companies keeping tourists active can be
found at **Turismiweb.ee** (www.turismiweb.ee).

For energetic, ecofriendly activities, contact **Reimann Retked** (☎ 511 4099; www.retked.ee). The

---

company offers a wide range of sea-kayak-
ing excursions, including overnight trips and
four-hour paddles out to Aegna island, 14km
offshore from Tallinn (450EEK). Other possibilities include diving, rafting, bog walking and
snowshoeing, as well as kick sledding on sea ice,
frozen lakes or in snowy forest; most arrangements need a minimum of eight to 10 people,
but smaller groups should enquire as you may
be able to tag along with another group.

As well as offering Tallinn hostels and
tours, **City Bike** (Map pp336–7; ☎ 683 6383; www
.citybike.ee; Uus 33, Tallinn; ☒ 9am-7pm May-Sep, 9am-
5pm Oct-Apr) can take care of all you need to get
around by bike.

BUSINESS HOURS

Banks are open from 9am to 4pm Monday to
Friday, while post offices open from 8am to
6pm Monday to Friday, and 9am to 3pm on
Saturday. Shops are generally open every day,
from 9am or 10am to 6pm or 7pm Monday to
Friday, and 10am to 4pm Saturday and Sunday.
Food shops and supermarkets are open until
10pm every day. Restaurants are generally open
from noon to midnight; cafes often open at 8am
or 9am and close by 10pm, but in the larger cities
some stay open until midnight dispensing coffee and after-dinner sweet treats. Bars are open
from noon to midnight Sunday to Thursday,
and noon to 2am on Friday and Saturday, while
clubs are generally open Thursday to Saturday
from 10pm to 4am or later.

Only exceptions to these general rules are
listed in the text.

DISCOUNT CARDS

There are frequent student, pensioner and
group discounts on transport, in museums
and in some shops upon presentation of
accredited ID.

EMBASSIES & CONSULATES

For up-to-date contact details of Estonian
diplomatic organisations, as well as foreign
embassies and consulates in Estonia, check the
website of the **Estonian Foreign Ministry** (☎ 637
7000; www.v m.ee).

All the following embassies and consulates are in Tallinn unless otherwise indicated.

Australia (off Map pp336–7; ☎ 650 9308; mati@standard.ee; Marja 9)

Canada (Map pp336–7; ☎ 627 3311; tallinn@canada.ee; 2nd fl, Toom-Kooli 13)

Finland (Map pp336–7; ☎ 610 3200; www.finland.ee; Kohtu 4)

France (Map pp336–7; ☎ 631 1492; www.ambafrance-ee.org; Toom-Kuninga 20)

Germany (off Map pp336–7; ☎ 627 5300, www.tallinn.diplo.de; Toom-Kuninga 11)

Ireland (Map pp336–7; ☎ 681 1888; tallinnembassy@dfa.ie; 2nd fl, Vene 2)

Japan (Map pp336–7; ☎ 631 0531; www.japemb.ee; Harju 6)

Latvia (Map pp336–7; ☎ 627 7860; embassy.estonia@mfa.gov.lv; Tõnismägi 10)

Lithuania (Map pp336–7; ☎ 616 4991; http://ee.mfa.lt; Uus 15)

Netherlands (Map pp336–7; ☎ 680 5500; www.netherlandsembassy.ee; Rahukohtu 4i)

New Zealand (off Map pp336–7; ☎ 627 2020; toomas.luman@nordecon.ee; Liivalaia 13/15)

Russia Narva (☎ 356 0652; narvacon@narvacon.neti.ee; Kiriku 8); Tallinn (Map pp336–7; ☎ 646 4166; www.rusemb.ee; Lai 18)

Sweden (Map pp336–7; ☎ 640 5600; www.sweden.ee; Pikk 28)

UK (Map pp336–7; ☎ 667 4700; www.britishembassy.ee; Wismari 6)

USA (Map pp336–7; ☎ 668 8100; www.usemb.ee; Kentmanni 20)

FESTIVALS & EVENTS

Estonia has a busy festival calendar celebrating everything from religion to music, art to film, beer to ghosts. Peak festival fun is in summer, with a highlight being midsummer festivities. A good list of upcoming major events nationwide can be found at **culture.ee** (www.culture.ee). See also p342.

The biggest occasion in Estonia is **Jaanipäev** (St John's Day; 24 June), a celebration of the pagan midsummer or summer solstice. Celebrations peak on the evening of 23 June, and are best experienced far from the city along a stretch of beach, where huge bonfires are lit for all-night parties.

GAY & LESBIAN TRAVELLERS

While open displays of same-sex affection are infrequent in Estonia, the overall attitude is more of openness than antagonism. For more information, contact the **Gay and Lesbian**

Infocenter (GLIK; ☎ 645 4545; glik@gay.ee; 2nd fl, Rüütli 16, Tallinn). The website **Gei ja Lesbi Infokeskus** (www.gay.ee) lists Tallinn's gay venues and events.

HOLIDAYS

New Year's Day 1 January
Independence Day 24 February
Good Friday & Easter March/April
Spring Day 1 May
Whitsunday Seventh Sunday after Easter; May/June
Victory Day (1919; Battle of Võnnu) 23 June
Jaanipäev (St John's Day; Midsummer's Night) 24 June
Day of Restoration of Independence 20 August
Christmas Eve 24 December
Christmas Day 25 December
Boxing Day 26 December

INTERNET ACCESS

There are more than 1170 wi-fi areas throughout Estonia, with 372 in Tallinn alone; many of these are free. Visit **wifi.ee** (www.wifi.ee) for a complete list of locations.

MONEY

Estonia currency is the kroon (EEK; pronounced krohn), which is pegged to the euro (€1 = 15.65EEK). The kroon comes in 2, 5, 10, 25, 50, 100 and 500EEK notes. One kroon is divided into 100 senti (cents), and there are coins of 5, 10, 20 and 50 senti, as well as 1EEK and 5EEK coins. The euro is expected to be introduced some time between 2010 and 2013.

The best foreign currencies to bring into Estonia are euros and US dollars, although all Western currencies are readily exchangeable.

Credit cards are widely accepted. Most banks (but not stores and restaurants) accept travellers cheques, but commissions can be high.

Tipping in service industries has become the norm, but generally no more than 10% is expected.

POST

Mail service in and out of Estonia is highly efficient. To post a letter up to 50g anywhere in the world costs 9EEK.

There is a poste restante bureau, where mail is kept for up to one month, at Tallinn's **central post office** (Map pp336–7; Narva mnt 1).

TELEPHONE

There are no area codes. All landline numbers have seven digits; mobile numbers have seven or eight digits, and begin with ☎ 5.

Estonia's country code is ☎ 372.

ESTONIA

EMERGENCY NUMBERS

- Ambulance ☎ 112
- Fire ☎ 112
- Police ☎ 110
- Roadside assistance ☎ 1888

VISAS

Citizens of EU countries, Australia, Canada, Japan, New Zealand, the USA and many other countries can enter Estonia visa-free for a maximum 90-day stay over a six-month period. For more information, check out the website of the **Estonian Foreign Ministry** (www.vm.ee).

TRANSPORT IN ESTONIA

GETTING THERE & AWAY
Air

The national carrier **Estonian Air** (OV; ☎ 640 1163; www.estonian-air.ee) links Tallinn with some 20 cities in Europe and Russia. Other airlines serving **Tallinn airport** (TLL; ☎ 605 8888; www.tallinn-airport.ee) include **airBaltic** (BT; ☎ 640 7750; www.airbaltic.com), which has flights to Vilnius and Rīga, and **Finnair** (AY; ☎ 626 6309; www.finnair.com), with flights to Helsinki.

Land
BUS

Buses are the cheapest way of reaching the Baltics; see p347 and p354 for further details on international buses.

CAR & MOTORCYCLE

From Finland, put your vehicle on a Helsinki–Tallinn ferry; see p347 for details. If approaching Estonia from the south or Western Europe, make sure to avoid crossing through Kaliningrad or Belarus – you'll need hard-to-get visas for these countries, and are likely to face hassles from traffic police and encounter roads in abominable conditions!

TRAIN

There are international trains between Tallinn and Russia; see p348 for details.

Sea

Ferries run to Finland and Sweden from Tallinn; see p347 for details.

GETTING AROUND
Air

Avies Air (☎ 605 8022; www.avies.ee) and **Estonian Air** (☎ 640 1163; www.estonian-air.ee) provide domestic flights.

Bicycle

The flatness and small scale of Estonia, and the light traffic on most roads, make it good cycling territory. On the islands you will see cyclists galore in summer. Most bring their own bicycles, but there are plenty of places where you can rent a bicycle, including Tallinn's **City Bike** (Map pp336-7; ☎ 683 6383; www.citybike.ee; Uus 33; ☺ 9am-7pm May-Sep, 9am-5pm Oct-Apr).

Bus

Buses are a good option, as they're more frequent and faster than trains, and cover many destinations not serviced by the limited rail network. For detailed bus information and advance tickets, contact Tallinn's **Central Bus Station** (off Map pp336-7; Autobussijaam; ☎ 680 0900; Lastekodu 46). The website **Bussi Reisid** (www.bussireisid.ee) has schedules and prices for all national bus services.

Car & Motorcycle

An International Driving Permit (IDP) is useful; otherwise, carry your national licence bearing a photograph. It's compulsory to carry your vehicle's registration papers and accident insurance, which can be bought at border crossings. Fuel and service stations are widely available.

Traffic drives on the right-hand side of the road, and driving with any alcohol in your blood is illegal. Seatbelts are compulsory, and headlights must be on at all times while driving. Speed limits in built-up areas are 50km/h; limits outside urban areas vary from 70km/h to 110km/h. Be on the lookout for signs, as these limits are often strictly enforced.

Train

Trains are slower and rarer than buses; the most frequent trains service the suburbs of Tallinn and aren't much use to travellers. Regional train schedules are listed at **Edelaraudtee** (www.edel.ee), though it's only in Estonian (on the Estonian-language page, click on Sõiduplannid ja hinnad to access the timetables and prices).

Hungary

Where else but Hungary can you laze about in an open-air thermal spa while snow patches glisten around you, then head to a local bar where a Romani band yelps while a crazed crowd whacks its boot heels, as commanded by Hungarian tradition? And where else could you go clubbing in an ancient bathhouse, where everyone dances in swimsuits, waist-deep in the healing waters?

If these pursuits don't appeal, there are always Roman ruins, ancient castles, and Turkish minarets in baroque cities such as Pécs and Eger. In the countryside you can experience the joy of seeing cowboys riding astride five horses, storks nesting on streetlamps, and a sea of apricot trees blooming.

Not that urban pleasures are neglected. Cosmopolitan Budapest is replete with world-class operas, monumental historical buildings, and the mighty Danube River flowing through its centre. Prices here are somewhere in the middle: not nearly as high as in Austria nor as inexpensive as in Ukraine. However, the focus is slowly turning from quantity to quality. Boutique hotels are popping up in Budapest and Balaton; world-class restaurants are spreading out from the capital to smaller enclaves; and superior thermal retreats are replacing dated communist-era eyesores.

Despite the rising tide of commericalism, Hungary has held onto the one factor that makes it special – being Hungarian. Having established itself as a state in the year 1000, Hungary has a long history, a rich culture and strong folk traditions that are well worth exploring.

FAST FACTS

- **Area** 93,000 sq km
- **Capital** Budapest
- **Currency** forint (Ft); €1 = 306Ft; US$1 = 225Ft; UK£1 = 325Ft; A$1 = 155Ft; ¥100 = 234Ft; NZ$1 = 126Ft
- **Famous for** paprika, Bull's Blood and *csárda* music
- **Official language** Hungarian (Magyar)
- **Phrases** *jo napot kivanok* (good day); *szia* (hi/bye); *köszönöm* (thank you)
- **Population** 10 million
- **Telephone codes** country code ☎ 36; international access code ☎ 00; intercity access code ☎ 06
- **Visa** no visa needed for most nationalities if you stay less than 90 days; see p428

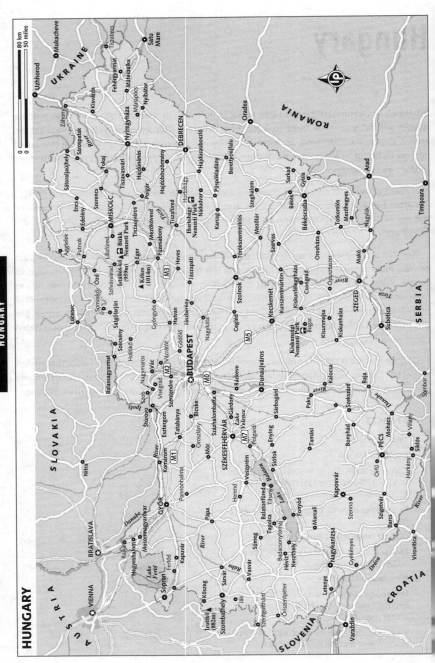

HIGHLIGHTS

- Ease your aching muscles in the warm waters of Budapest's **thermal baths** (p378), and try a spa treatment for good measure.
- Learn about the defiance **Eger** (p419) showed to Turkish invaders, and how the city's Bull's Blood wine got its name.
- Watch the cowboys ride at Bugac in **Kiskunsági Nemzeti Park** (p416), in the heart of the Hungarian *puszta* (plain).
- Absorb the Mediterranean climate and historic architecture of the southern city of **Pécs** (p410), including its intriguing Mosque Church.
- Take a pleasure cruise across (or a dip in) Central Europe's largest body of fresh water, **Lake Balaton** (p403).

ITINERARIES

- **One week** Make sure that you spend at least four days in Budapest, checking out the sights, museums and pavement cafes. On your fifth day take a day trip to a Danube Bend town: see the open-air museum in Szentendre or the cathedral at Esztergom. Day six can be spent getting a morning train to Pécs and seeing the lovely Turkish remains, and checking out the many galleries in town. Let your hair down on day seven and try some local wine in Eger, a baroque town set in red-wine country.
- **Two weeks** If you're here in summer, make sure you spend some time exploring the towns around Lake Balaton, or just chill out on the beach by the side of this popular lake. Tihany is a rambling hillside village filled with craftsmen's houses, set on a peninsula that is a protected nature zone. Keszthely is an old town with a great palace in addition to a beach. Alternatively, head south to Pécs and see more of the Great Plain. Szeged is on the Tisza River, and Kecskemét is further north. Finish your trip in Tokaj, home of Hungary's most famous wine.

CLIMATE & WHEN TO GO

Hungary has a temperate continental climate. July and August are the warmest months, and when the thermometer hits 27°C it can feel much hotter, given that most places don't have air-con. Spring is unpredictable, but usually arrives in April. November is already rainy and chilly; January and February are the coldest, dreariest months, with temperatures dropping below 0°C. September, with loads of sunshine, mild temperatures and grape-harvest festivals in the countryside, may be the best time to visit. May, with a profusion of flowers and sunshine, is a close second. See p963 for climate charts.

The busiest tourist season is July and August (Lake Balaton is especially crowded), but hotels quote high-season prices from April to October. In provincial and smaller towns, attractions are often closed, or have reduced hours, from October to May.

HISTORY
Pre-Hungarian Hungary

The plains of the Carpathian Basin attracted waves of migration, from both east and west, long before the Magyar tribes decided to settle there. The Celts occupied the area in the 3rd century BC, but the Romans conquered and expelled them just before the Christian era. The lands west of the Danube (Transdanubia) in today's Hungary became part of the Roman province of Pannonia, where a Roman legion was stationed at the town of Aquincum (now called Óbuda). The Romans brought writing, planted the first vineyards and built baths near some of the region's many thermal springs.

A new surge of nomadic tribespeople, the Huns, who lent Hungary its present-day name, arrived on the scene with a leader who would become legendary in Hungarian history. By AD 441, Attila and his brother Bleda had conquered the Romans and acquired a reputation as great warriors. This reputation

---

CONNECTIONS: MOVING ON FROM HUNGARY

Hungary's landlocked status ensures plenty of possibilities for onward travel overland. There are direct train connections (p389) from Budapest to major cities in all of Hungary's neighbours, including Vienna, Bratislava, Bucharest, Kyiv (continuing to Moscow), Zagreb, Belgrade and Ljubljana. International buses head in all directions (p389), including localities across the border in Serbia, Croatia and Romania. And in the warmer months, you can take a ferry along the Danube to reach Bratislava or Vienna (p388).

HOW MUCH?

- **Cheap bottle of wine in a supermarket** 750Ft
- **Bed in a private room outside Budapest** from 3000Ft
- **Cup of coffee in a cafe** 250Ft to 500Ft
- **Local English-language newspaper** 400Ft to 600Ft
- **Dinner for two at a good restaurant in Budapest** 15,000Ft

LONELY PLANET INDEX

- **1L petrol** 257Ft
- **1L bottled water** 100Ft
- **Beer** 400Ft to 700Ft
- **Souvenir T-shirt** 2000Ft
- **Street snack (lángos)** 300Ft to 500Ft

still runs strong and you will notice that many Hungarians carry the name Attila, even though the Huns have no connection with present-day Hungarians and the Huns' short-lived empire did not outlast Attila's death (453), when remaining tribespeople fled back from whence they came. Many tribes filled the vacuum left by the Huns and settled in the area, such as the Goths, Longobards and the Avars, a powerful Turkic people who controlled parts of the area from the 5th to the 8th centuries. The Avars were subdued by Charlemagne in 796, leaving space for the Franks and Slavs to move in.

The Conquest

Magyar (Hungarian) tribes are said to have moved in around 896, when Árpád led the alliance of seven tribes into the region. The Magyars, a fierce warrior tribe, terrorised much of Europe with raids reaching as far as Spain. They were stopped at the Battle of Augsburg in 955 and subsequently converted to Christianity. Hungary's first king and its patron saint, István (Stephen), was crowned on Christmas Day in 1000, marking the foundation of the Hungarian state.

Medieval Hungary was a powerful kingdom that included Transylvania (now in Romania), Transcarpathia (now in Ukraine), modern-day Slovakia and Croatia. Under King Matthias Corvinus (1458–90), Hungary expe-

rienced a brief flowering of Renaissance culture. However, in 1526 the Ottomans defeated the Hungarian army at Mohács and by 1541 Buda Castle had been seized and Hungary sliced in three. The central part, including Buda, was controlled by the Ottomans, while Transdanubia, present-day Slovakia, and parts of Transcarpathia were ruled by Hungarian nobility based in Pozsony (Bratislava) under the auspices of the Austrian House of Habsburg. The principality of Transylvania, east of the Tisza, prospered as a vassal state of the Ottoman Empire.

Habsburg Hegemony & the Wars

After the Ottomans were evicted from Buda in 1686, the Habsburg domination of Hungary began. The 'enlightened absolutism' of the Habsburg monarchs Maria Theresa (r 1740–80) and her son Joseph II (r 1780–90) helped the country leap forward economically and culturally. Rumblings of Hungarian independence surfaced off and on, but it was the unsuccessful 1848 Hungarian revolution that really started to shake the Habsburg oligarchy. After Austria was defeated in war by Prussia in 1866, a weakened empire struck a compromise with Hungary in 1867, creating a dual monarchy. The two states would be self-governing in domestic affairs, but act jointly in matters of common interest, such as foreign relations. The Austro-Hungarian monarchy lasted until WWI.

After WWI and the collapse of the Habsburg Empire in November 1918, Hungary was proclaimed a republic. But she had been on the losing side of the war. The 1920 Treaty of Trianon stripped the country of more than two-thirds of its territory – a hot topic of conversation to this day.

In 1941 Hungary's attempts to recover lost territories saw the nation in war, on the side of Nazi Germany. When leftists tried to negotiate a separate peace in 1944, the Germans occupied Hungary and brought the fascist Arrow Cross Party to power. The Arrow Cross immediately began deporting hundreds of thousands of Jews to Auschwitz. By early April 1945, all of Hungary was liberated by the Soviet army.

Communism

By 1947 the communists assumed complete control of the government and began nationalising industry and dividing up large estates among the peasantry. On 23 October 1956, student demonstrators demanding the withdrawal of Soviet troops were fired upon. The next day Imre Nagy, the reformist minister of agriculture, was named prime minister. On 28 October Nagy's government offered an amnesty to all those involved in the violence and promised to abolish the hated secret police, the ÁVH (known as ÁVO until 1949). On 4 November Soviet tanks moved into Budapest, crushing the uprising. By the time the fighting ended on 11 November, some 25,000 people were dead. Then the reprisals began: an estimated 20,000 people were arrested; 2000 were executed, including Nagy; another 250,000 fled to Austria.

By the 1970s Hungary had abandoned strict central economic control in favour of a limited market system, often referred to as 'Goulash Communism'. In June 1987 Károly Grósz took over as premier and Hungary began moving towards full democracy. The huge numbers of East Germans who were able to slip through the Iron Curtain by leaving via Hungary contributed to the eventual crumbling of the Berlin Wall.

The Republic

At their party congress in February 1989 the Hungarian communists agreed to surrender their monopoly on power. The Republic of Hungary was proclaimed in October, and democratic elections were scheduled for March 1990. Hungary changed its political system with scarcely a murmur, and the last Soviet troops left the country in June 1991.

The painful transition to a full market economy resulted in declining living standards for most people and a recession in the early 1990s, but the early years of the 21st century saw astonishing growth. Hungary became a fully fledged member of NATO in 1999. In a national referendum during April 2003, the Hungarian people voted to join the European Union (EU), and the country became a member on 1 May 2004.

In April 2006 the Socialist-led coalition won the parliamentary elections, becoming the first government to win two consecutive terms in office since the restoration of democracy in 1990. The incoming prime minister, multimillionaire businessman Ferenc Gyurcsány, was chosen by the Socialist Party to succeed the former prime minister, Peter Medgyessy. His efforts to rein in Hungary's large budget deficit by introducing austerity measures caused riots on the streets later that year.

In December 2007 Hungary joined the Schengen zone of European countries, abandoning border controls with its EU neighbours Austria, Slovakia and Slovenia. Late in 2008, reeling from the fallout of the global financial crisis, Hungary was forced to approach the International Monetary Fund for economic assistance. Hungary originally aimed to adopt the euro by 2010, but the effects of the crisis have since obliged the government to delay adoption until at least 2012.

PEOPLE
Some 10.2 million people live within the national borders, and another five million Hungarians and their descendants are abroad. The estimated 1.45 million Hungarians in Transylvania constitute the largest ethnic minority in Europe, and there are another 530,000 in Slovakia, 293,000 in Serbia, 156,000 in Ukraine and 40,500 in Austria.

Ethnic Magyars make up approximately 93% of the population. Many minority groups estimate their numbers to be significantly higher than official counts. There are 13 recognised minorities in the country, including Germans (2.6%), Serbs and other South Slavs (2%), Slovaks (0.8%) and Romanians (0.7%). The number of Roma is officially put at 1.9% of the population, though some sources place the figure as high as 4%.

RELIGION
Of those Hungarians declaring religious affiliation, about 52% are Roman Catholic, 16% Reformed (Calvinist) Protestant, 3% Evangelical (Lutheran) Protestant, and 2.6% Greek Catholic and Orthodox. Hungary's Jews number around 100,000, down from a prewar population of nearly eight times that amount.

ARTS
Budapest is Hungary's artistic heart, but the provinces resound with the arts too. The country (and the capital in particular) is known for its traditional culture, with a strong emphasis on the classical – and for good reason. The history of Hungarian arts and literature includes world-renowned

HUNGARY

composers such as Béla Bartók and Franz Liszt, and the Nobel prize–winning writer Imre Kértesz and his innovative contemporary Peter Esterházy. Hungary's proximity to classical music hub Vienna, as well as the legacy of the Soviet regard for the 'proper arts', means that opera, symphony and ballet are high on the entertainment agenda, and even provincial towns have decent companies.

For the more contemporary branches of artistic life, Budapest is the focus, containing many art galleries and theatre and dance companies. The capital is also a centre for folk music and crafts that have grown out of village life or minority culture.

Literature

Hungary has some excellent writers, both of poetry and prose. Sándor Petőfi (1823–49) is Hungary's most celebrated poet. A line from his work *National Song* became the rallying cry for the War of Independence between 1848 and 1849, in which he fought and is commonly thought to have died. His comrade-in-arms, János Arany (1817–82), wrote epic poetry. The prolific novelist and playwright Mór Jókai (1825–1904) gave expression to heroism and honesty in works such as *The Man with the Golden Touch*. Lyric poet Endre Ady (1877–1919) attacked narrow materialism; poet Attila József (1905–37) expresses the alienation felt by individuals in the modern age; and novelist Zsigmond Móricz (1879–1942) examines the harsh reality of peasant life in Hungary.

Contemporary Hungarian writers whose work has been translated into English and are worth a read include Tibor Fischer, Péter Esterházy and Sándor Márai. The most celebrated Hungarian writer is the 2002 Nobel prize winner Imre Kertész. Among his novels available in English are *Fatelessness* (1975), *Detective Story* (1977), *Kaddish for an Unborn Child* (1990) and *Liquidation* (2003). Another prominent contemporary writer, who died in 2007 at age 90, was Magda Szabó (*Katalin Street*, 1969; *The Door*, 1975).

Music

As you will no doubt see from the street names in every Hungarian town and city, the country celebrates and reveres its most influential musician, composer and pianist, Franz (or Ferenc) Liszt (1811–86). The eccentric Liszt described himself as 'part Gypsy', and in his *Hungarian Rhapsodies,* as well as in other works, he does indeed weave Romani motifs into his compositions.

Ferenc Erkel (1810–93) is the father of Hungarian opera, and his stirringly nationalist *Bánk Bán* is a standard at the Hungarian State Opera House in Budapest. Béla Bartók (1881–1945) and Zoltán Kodály (1882–1967) made the first systematic study of Hungarian folk music; both integrated some of their findings into their compositions.

Hungarian folk musicians play violins, zithers, hurdy-gurdies, bagpipes and lutes on a five-tone diatonic scale. Look out for Muzsikás; Marta Sebestyén; Ghymes, a Hungarian folk band from Slovakia; and the Hungarian group Vujicsics, which mixes in elements of southern Slav music. Another folk musician with eclectic tastes is the Paris-trained Bea Pálya, who combines such sound as traditional Bulgarian and Indian music with Hungarian folk.

Romani music, found in restaurants in its schmaltzy form (best avoided), has become a fashionable thing among the young with Romani bands playing 'the real thing' in trendy bars till the wee hours: a dynamic hopping mix of fiddles, bass and cymbalom (a stringed instrument played with sticks). An instrument a Romani band would never be seen without is the tin milk bottle used as a drum, which gives Hungarian Roma music its characteristic sound. It's reminiscent of traditional Indian music, an influence that perhaps harks back to the Roma's Asian roots. Some modern Romani music groups – Kalyi Jag (Black Fire) from northeastern Hungary, Romano Drom (Gypsy Road) and Romani Rota (Gypsy Wheels) – have added guitars, percussion and even electronics to create a whole new sound.

Klezmer music (traditional Eastern European Jewish music) has also made a comeback in the playlists of the young and trendy.

Pop music is as popular here as anywhere; indeed, Hungary has one of Europe's biggest pop spectacles, the annual Sziget Music Festival (p382). It has more than 1000 performances over a week and attracts an audience of up to 385,000 people. Popular Hungarian musical artists to look for include pop singers Magdi Rúzsa and Laci Gáspár, and pop/folk band Nox.

Visual Arts

Favourite painters from the 19th century include realist Mihály Munkácsy (1844–1900), the so-called painter of the plains, and Tivadar Kosztka Csontváry (1853–1919). Győző Vásárhelyi (1908–97), who changed his name to Victor Vasarely when he emigrated to Paris, is considered the 'father of op art'. Contemporary painters to keep an eye out for include Árpád Müller and the late Endre Szász (1926–2003).

In the 19th and early 20th centuries, the Zsolnay family created world-renowned decorative art in porcelain. Ceramic artist Margit Kovac (1902–1977) produced a large number of statues and ceramic objects during her career. The traditional embroidery, weavings and ceramics of the nation's *népművészet* (folk art) endures, and there is at least one handicraft store in every town.

SPORT

The Hungarian Formula One Grand Prix, held in mid-August, is the year's biggest sporting event. The **Hungaroring** (www.hungaroring.hu) track is 19km north of Budapest, in Mogyórod, but hotels in the capital fill up and prices skyrocket during the event.

ENVIRONMENT
The Land

Hungary occupies the Carpathian Basin to the southwest of the Carpathian Mountains. Water dominates much of the country's geography. The Duna (Danube River) divides the Nagyalföld (Great Plain) in the east from the Dunántúl (Transdanubia) in the west. The Tisza (597km in Hungary) is the country's longest river, and historically has been prone to flooding. Hungary has hundreds of small lakes and is riddled with thermal springs. Lake Balaton (596 sq km, 77km long), in the west, is the largest freshwater lake in Europe outside Scandinavia. Hungary's 'mountains' to the north are merely hills, with the country's highest peak being Kékes (1014m) in the Mátra Range.

Wildlife

There are a lot of common European animals in Hungary (deer, hares, wild boars and foxes), as well as some rare species (wild cat, lake bat and Pannonian lizard), but most of the country's wildlife comes from the avian family. Hungary is a premier European spot for birdwatching. Around 75% of the country's 480 known vertebrates are birds, for the most part waterfowl attracted by the rivers, lakes and wetlands. The rare black stork, a smaller, darker version of its common cousin, also spends time in Hungary on its migration from Africa to Europe.

National Parks

There are 10 national parks in Hungary. Bükk Nemzeti Park, north of Eger, is a mountainous limestone area of forest and caves. Kiskunsági Nemzeti Park and Bugac, near Kecskemét, and Hortobágy Nemzeti Park (www.hnp.hu) in the Hortobágy Puszta (a World Heritage site), outside Debrecen, protect the unique grassland environment of the plains.

Environmental Issues

In the past decade there has been a marked improvement in both the public's awareness of environmental issues and the government's dedication to environmental safety. Air pollution has long been a problem due to emissions from inefficient coal-fired power plants and the nation's ancient car fleet. Many of the plants have been shut down in recent years, resulting in the reduction of the country's sulphur dioxide emissions by a third. Additionally, the government has forced many polluting autos off the road and introduced lead- and sulphur-free petrol.

To cut down your carbon emissions, consider travelling to Hungary by train (p429) or bus (p428), rather than flying.

FOOD & DRINK
Staples & Specialities

The omnipresent seasoning in Hungarian cooking is paprika, a mild red pepper that appears on restaurant tables as a condiment beside the salt and black pepper, as well as in many recipes. *Pörkölt*, a paprika-infused stew, can be made from different meats, including *borju* (veal), and usually it has no vegetables. *Galuska* (small, gnocchi-like dumplings) are a good accompaniment to soak up the sauce. The well-known *paprikas csirke* (chicken paprikash) is stewed chicken in a tomato-cream-paprika sauce (not as common here as in Hungarian restaurants abroad). *Töltött káposzta* (cabbage rolls stuffed with meat and rice) is cooked in a roux made with paprika, and topped with sour cream, as is *székelygulyás* (stewed pork and sour cabbage). Another local favourite is *halászlé* (fisher's soup), a rich mix of several kinds of poached freshwater fish, tomatoes, green peppers and (you guessed it) paprika.

Leves (soup) is the start to any main meal in a Hungarian home; some claim that you will develop stomach disorders if you don't eat a hot, daily helping. *Gulyás* (goulash), although served as a stew outside Hungary, is a soup here, cooked with beef, onions and tomatoes. Traditional cooking methods are far from health-conscious, but they are tasty. Frying is a nationwide obsession, and you'll often find fried turkey, pork and veal schnitzels on the menu.

For dessert you might try the cold *gyümölcs leves* (fruit soup) made with sour cherries and other berries, or *palincsinta* (crêpes) filled with jam, sweet cheese or chocolate sauce. A good food-stand snack is *lángos*, fried dough that can be topped with cheese and/or *tejföl* (sour cream).

Two Hungarian wines are known internationally: the sweet, dessert wine Tokaji Aszú and Egri Bikavér (Eger Bull's Blood), the full-bodied red, high in acid and tannin. But the country produces a number of other eminently drinkable wines. Hungarian beers sold nationally include Dreher and Kőbanyai; Borosodi is a decent amber brew. For the harder stuff, try *pálinka*, a strong, firewater-like brandy distilled from a variety of fruits, but most commonly plums or apricots. Zwack distillery produces Unicum, a bitter aperitif that has been around since 1790; it tastes a bit like the medicine doctors give you to induce vomiting – but it's popular.

Where to Eat & Drink

An *étterem* is a restaurant with a large selection, formal service and formal prices. A *vendéglő* is smaller, more casual and serves homestyle regional dishes. The overused term *csárda*, which originally meant a rustic country inn with Romani music, can now mean anything – including 'tourist trap'. To keep prices down, look for *étkezde* (a tiny eating place that may have a counter or sit-down service), *önkiszolgáló* (a self-service canteen), *kinai gyorsbüfé* (Chinese fast food), *grill* (which generally serves gyros or kebabs and other grilled meats from the counter) or a *szendvicsbar* (which has open-faced sandwiches to go).

There are still a number of stuffy Hungarian restaurants with condescending waiters, for-

mal service and Romani music from another era. For the most part, avoiding places with tuxedoed waiters is a good bet.

Wine has been produced in Hungary for thousands of years, and you'll find it available by the glass or bottle everywhere. There are plenty of pseudo-British/Irish/Belgian pubs, smoky *sörözök* (Hungarian pubs, often in a cellar, where drinking is taken very seriously), *borozók* (wine bars, usually a dive) and nightclubs, but the most pleasant place to imbibe a cocktail or coffee may be in a cafe. A *kávéház* may primarily be an old-world dessert shop, or it may be a bar with an extensive drinks menu; either way they sell alcoholic beverages in addition to coffee. In spring, pavement tables sprout up alongside the new flowers.

Restaurants generally open from 11am to 11pm, and bars and cafes open from 11am to midnight.

Though Hungarian bars and restaurants are required to have separate smoking and nonsmoking sections, their often compact size means that passive smoking is inevitable. However, at the time of research the government was bravely set on introducing a total ban on smoking in public places.

Vegetarians & Vegans

Traditional Hungarian cuisine and vegetarianism are definitely not a match made in heaven. However, things are changing and there are places even in the provinces that serve good vegetarian meals. Where there are no vegetarian restaurants, you'll have to make do with what's on the regular menu or shop for ingredients in the markets.

Some not very light, but widely available dishes for vegetarians to look for are *rántot sajt* (fried cheese), *gombafejek rántva* (fried mushroom caps), *gomba leves* (mushroom soup) and *túrós* or *káposzta csusza* (short wide pasta with cheese or cabbage). *Bableve* (bean soup) usually contains meat.

Habits & Customs

The Magyar are a polite people and their language is filled with courtesies. To toast someone's health before drinking, say *egéségér* (egg-eh-shaig-eh-ray), and to wish them a good appetite before eating, *jo étvágat* (yo ate-vad-yaht). If you're invited to someone's home, always bring a bunch of flowers and/or a bottle of good local wine.

BUDAPEST

☎ 1 / pop 1.7 million

There's no other Hungarian city like Budapest in terms of size and importance. Home to almost 20% of the national population, Hungary's capital (*főváros*, or main city) is the nation's administrative, business and cultural centre; everything of importance starts or finishes here.

But it's the beauty of Budapest – both natural and constructed – that makes it stand apart. Straddling a gentle curve in the Danube, the city is flanked by the Buda Hills on the west bank and the beginnings of the Great Plain to the east. Architecturally, it is a gem, with enough baroque, neoclassical, eclectic and art nouveau elements to satisfy anyone.

In recent years, Budapest has taken on the role of the region's party town. In the warmer months outdoor entertainment areas called *kertek* (gardens) are heaving with party-makers, and the world-class Sziget Music Festival in August is a cultural magnet. And you need not venture out for fun; the city's scores of new hostels offer some of the best facilities and most convivial company in Europe.

Budapest does have an ugly side, with organised crime, pollution, ubiquitous fast-food chain eateries, and mindless graffiti covering much of its gorgeous architecture. But come dusk on a fine day, cross the Danube on foot and you'll see why unique, passionate, vibrant Budapest remains unmissable.

HISTORY

Strictly speaking, the story of Budapest begins only in 1873 with the administrative union of three cities that had grown together: Buda, west of the Danube; Óbuda (Buda's oldest neighbourhood) to the north; and Pest on the eastern side of the river. But the area had already been occupied for thousands of years.

The Romans built a settlement at Aquincum (Óbuda) during the first centuries of the Common Era. In the 1500s, the Turks arrived uninvited and stayed for almost 150 years. The Habsburg Austrians helped kick the invaders out, but then made themselves at home for 200 more years.

In the late 19th century, under the dual Austro-Hungarian monarchy, the population of Budapest soared. Many notable buildings date from that boom period. The city suffered some damage in the two world wars, and the 1956 revolution left structures pockmarked with bullet holes. Today many of the city's grand buildings have been restored, and Budapest is the sophisticated capital of a proud nation with a distinctive heritage.

ORIENTATION

The city's aquatic artery, the Danube, is spanned by nine bridges that link hilly, residential Buda with bustling, commercial and very flat Pest. Two ring roads link three of the bridges across the Danube and essentially define central Pest. Important boulevards such as Rákóczi út and leafy Andrássy út fan out from these, creating large squares and circles. The most central square in Pest is Deák tér, where the three metro lines meet. Buda is dominated by Castle and Gellért Hills; its main square is Moszkva tér.

Budapest is divided into 23 *kerület* (districts). The Roman numeral appearing before each street address signifies the district. Central Buda is district I; central Pest is district V, and fans out to districts VI and VII. You can also tell the district by reading its postal code:

BUDAPEST IN TWO DAYS

The best way to start your day in Budapest is to have an early-morning soak alfresco at **Széchenyi Baths** (p379). Then stroll down Andrássy út and grab a late breakfast or coffee at **Lukács** (p387), next to the infamous and ever-popular spy museum, the **Terror House** (p381). Take an afternoon tour around the grand **Hungarian State Opera House** (p381) and have cake at the legendary **Gerbeaud** (p387), before hitting the shops on **Váci utca** (p381). Then go dancing at **Merlin** (p388).

On day two grab breakfast at **Centrál Kávéház** (p387), before getting the funicular to **Castle Hill** (p377) in Buda. Tour **Matthias Church** (p377) and explore the many museums, including the **Budapest History Museum** (p378). In the evening, back in Pest, walk along the waterfront and have a meal at any of the boat restaurant-pubs, before going Hungarian dancing at **Fonó Budai Zeneház** (p388).

HUNGARY

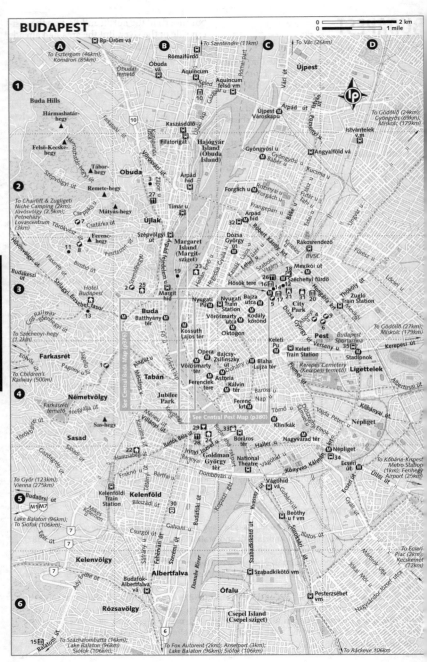

BUDAPEST

HUNGARY

the two numbers after the initial one signify the district (ie H-1114 is in the XI district).

INFORMATION
Bookshops
Bestsellers (Map p380; V Október 6 utca 11; ☺ 9am-5.30pm Mon-Fri, 10am-5pm Sat, 10am-4pm Sun) The best English-language bookshop in town.

Írók Boltja (Map p380; VI Andrássy út 45; ☺ 10am-7pm Mon-Fri, to 1pm Sat) Good selection of Hungarian writers in translation.

Red Bus Second-hand Bookstore (Map p380; V Semmelweiss utca 14; ☺ 11am-6pm Mon-Fri, 10am-2pm Sat) Sells used English-language books.

Treehugger Dan's Bookstore (Map p380; VI Csengery utca 48; ☺ 10am-7pm Mon-Fri, 10am-5pm Sat) New kid on the block sells thousands of secondhand English-language books, does trade-ins and serves organic fair trade coffee.

Discount Cards
See p426 for details on the Hungary Card.
Budapest Card (☎ 266 0479; www.budapestinfo.hu; 48/72hr card 6500/8000Ft) Offers access to many museums; unlimited public transport; and discounts on tours and other services. Buy it at hotels, travel agencies, large metro station kiosks and tourist offices.

Emergency
For emergency numbers, see p428.
District V Police Station (Map p380; ☎ 373 1000; V Szalay utca 11-13) Pest's most central police station.

Internet Access
The majority of hostels offer internet access, often free of charge. Among the most accessible internet cafes in Budapest are the following:

Electric Café (Map p380; VII Dohány utca 37; per hr 400Ft; ☺ 9am-midnight) Huge place, very popular with travellers.

Plastic Web (Map p380; V Irány utca 1; per hr 390Ft; ☺ 9.30am-11.30pm) This friendly place is about as central as you'll find in Pest.

Medical Services
FirstMed Centers (Map p376; ☎ 224 9090; I Hattyú utca 14, 5th fl; ☺ 8am-8pm Mon-Fri, 9am-2pm Sat) On call 24/7 for emergencies.

SOS Dent (Map p380; ☎ 269 6010; VI Király utca 14; ☺ 24hr) Around-the-clock dental care.

Teréz Patika (Map p380; ☎ 311 4439; VI Teréz körút 41; ☺ 8am-8pm Mon-Fri, 8am-2pm Sat) Pharmacy.

Money
You'll find ATMs everywhere.
K&H Bank (Map p380; V Váci utca 40) Quite central.
OTP Bank (Map p380; V Deák Ferenc utca 7-9) Favourable rates.

Post
Main post office (Map p380; V Petőfi Sándor utca 13-15; ☺ 8am-8pm Mon-Fri, to 2pm Sat) Just minutes from Deák Ferenc tér.

Tourist Information
Tourinform main office (Map p380; ☎ 438 8080; V Sütő utca 2; ☺ 8am-8pm); Castle Hill (Map p376; ☎ 488 0475; I Szentháromság tér; ☺ 9am-7pm May-Oct, 10am-6pm Nov-Apr); Liszt Ferenc Square (Map p380; ☎ 322 4098; VI Liszt Ferenc tér 11; ☺ 10am-6pm Mon-Fri)

Travel Agencies
Discover Budapest (Map p380; ☎ 269 3843; VI Lázár utca 16; ☺ 9.30am-6.30pm Mon-Fri, 10am-4pm Sat & Sun) Visit this one-stop shop for helpful tips and advice, accommodation bookings, internet access, and cycling and walking tours.

Express (Map p380; ☎ 327 7298; www.express-travel.hu; VII Dohány utca 30/a & Kazinczy utca 3/b; ☺ 8.30am-5pm Mon-Fri, 9am-1pm Sat) The main office of this

HUNGARY

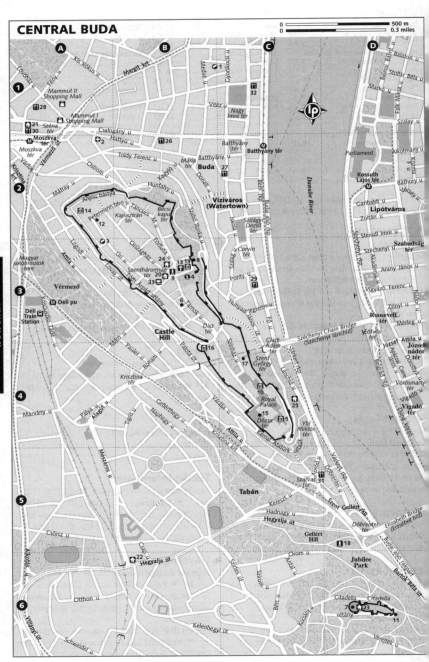

INFORMATION
Canadian Embassy....1 B1
FirstMed Centers....2 A2
German Embassy....3 A3
Tourinform (Castle Hill)....4 B3

SIGHTS & ACTIVITIES
Budapest History Museum....5 C4
Castle Hill....6 B3
Citadella....7 D6
Fishermen's Bastion....8 B3
Holy Trinity Statue....9 B3
Hungarian National Gallery....10 C4
Liberty Monument....11 D6
Magdalene Tower....12 A2
Matthias Church....13 B3
Military History Museum....14 A2
Royal Palace....15 C4
Royal Wine House & Wine Cellar Museum....16 B4
Sikló....17 C4
St Gellért Statue....18 D5
St Stephen Statue....19 B3

SLEEPING
Burg Hotel....20 B3
Büro Panzió....21 A1
Charles Hotel & Apartments....22 B6
Hotel Citadella....23 D6
Hotel Kulturinnov....24 B3
Lánchíd 19....25 C4

EATING
Csalogány 26....26 B2
Éden....27 C2
Fény Utca Market....28 A1
Le Jardin de Paris....29 C3
Szent Jupát....30 A1
Tabáni Terasz....31 C5
Új Lanzhou....32 C1

DRINKING
Ruszwurm Cukrászfa....33 B3

youth-oriented agency can book accommodation in Budapest, particularly in hostels and colleges, and sells transport tickets.

Ibusz (Map p380; ☎ 501 4910; www.ibusz.hu; V Ferenciek tere 10; ⌚ 9am-6pm Mon-Fri, to 1pm Sat) The main branch of this national agency has an exchange office, sells transport train tickets and books accommodation.

DANGERS & ANNOYANCES

Overall, Hungary is a very safe country with little violent crime, but scams can be a problem in the capital. Those involving attractive young women, gullible guys, expensive drinks in nightclubs and a frogmarch to the nearest ATM accompanied by in-house security have been all the rage in Budapest for well over a decade now, so be aware. Overcharging in taxis is also not unknown.

Watch out for pickpockets: the usual method is for someone to distract you (by running into you, or dropping something) while an accomplice makes off with your goods. Pickpocketing is most common in markets, the Castle District, Váci utca and Hősök tere, near major hotels, and on certain popular buses (eg 7) and trams (2, 4, 6, 47 and 49).

As for personal security, some locals now avoid Margaret Island after dark during the low season, and both residents and visitors give the dodgier parts of the VIII and IX districts (areas of prostitution activity) a wide berth.

SIGHTS & ACTIVITIES

Budapest is an excellent city for sightseeing, especially on foot. The Castle District in Buda contains a number of museums, both major and minor, but the lion's share is in Pest. Think of Margaret Island as a green buffer between the two – short on things to see, but a great place for a breather.

Buda

CASTLE HILL

Surfacing at the M2 metro station of the Socialist-style Moszkva tér, continue left up Várfok utca, or board bus 16A to reach **Castle Hill** (Várhegy; Map p376) where most of Budapest's remaining medieval buildings are clustered. Castle Hill is high above the glistening Danube, and wandering the old streets and enjoying the city views is part of the attraction, so get off at the first stop after the Vienna Gate and walk.

Magdalene Tower (Magdolona toronye; Map p376; Kapisztrán tér) is all that's left of a Gothic church destroyed here during WWII. The white neoclassical building facing the square is the **Military History Museum** (Hadtörténeti Múzeum; Map p376; I Tóth Árpád sétány 40; adult/concession 700/350Ft; ⌚ 10am-6pm Tue-Sun Apr-Sep, to 4pm Tue-Sun Oct-Mar).

For a peek into the life of the Budapest bourgeoisie, check out the mansions of the Buda Hills to the south of the ramparts promenade. Follow the third alleyway to your left and you reach Szentháromság tér and the **Holy Trinity statue** (Szentháromság szobor; Map p376) at its centre.

Don't miss the gorgeous, neo-Gothic **Matthias Church** (Mátyás Templom; Map p376; www.matyas-templom.hu; I Szentháromság tér 2; adult/concession 700/480Ft; ⌚ 9am-5pm Mon-Sat, 1-5pm Sun), with a colourful tiled roof and lovely murals inside. Franz Liszt's *Hungarian Coronation Mass* was played here for the first time at the coronation of Franz Joseph and Elizabeth in 1867.

Step across the square, under the gaze of Hungary's first king, immortalised in the equestrian **St Stephen statue** (Szent István szobor; Map p376). Behind the monument, walk along **Fishermen's Bastion** (Halászbástya; Map p376; I Szentháromság tér; adult/concession 330/160Ft; ⌚ 8.30am-11pm). The fanciful, neo-Gothic arcade built on the fortification wall is prime picture-taking territory, with views of the river and the parliament beyond.

Tárnok utca runs southeast to Dísz tér, past which is the entrance for the **Sikló** (Map p376; I Szent György tér; one way/return adult 800/1400Ft, child 500/900Ft; 🕙 7.30am-10pm, closed 1st & 3rd Mon of month), a funicular railway. The views from the little capsule, across the Danube and over to Pest, are glorious. The Sikló takes you down the hill to Clark Ádám tér. The massive **Royal Palace** (Királyi Palota; Map p376) occupies the far end of Castle Hill; inside are the **Hungarian National Gallery** (Nemzeti Galéria; www.mng.hu; I Szent György tér 6; adult/concession 800/400Ft; 🕙 10am-6pm Tue-Sun) and the **Budapest History Museum** (Budapesti Történeti Múzeum; www.btm.hu; I Szent György tér 2; adult/concession 900/450Ft; 🕙 10am-6pm daily mid-Mar–mid-Sep, 10am-4pm Wed-Mon mid-Sep–mid-Mar).

Nearby is the **Royal Wine House & Wine Cellar Museum** (Borház és Pincemúzeum; Map p376; www.kiralyi borok.com; I Szent György tér, Nyugati sétány; adult/concession 900/500Ft; 🕙 noon-8pm), situated in what were once the royal cellars, dating back to the 13th century. Tastings cost 1350/1800/2700Ft for three/four/six wines. You can also elect to try various types of Hungarian champagne and *pálinka* (fruit brandy).

GELLÉRT HILL

The 'other peak' overlooking the Danube, south of Castle Hill, is Gellért Hill. The **Liberty Monument** (Szabadság szobor; Map p376), a gigantic statue of a lady with a palm frond proclaiming freedom throughout the city, sits at its top and is visible from almost anywhere in town. The monument was erected as a tribute to the Soviet soldiers who died liberating Hungary in 1945, but the victims' names in Cyrillic letters that used to adorn the plinth, as well as the memorial statues of Soviet soldiers, were removed in 1992.

West of the monument is the **Citadella** (Map p376; www.citadella.hu; admission free; 🕙 24hr). Built by the Habsburgs after the 1848 revolution to 'defend' the city from further Hungarian insurrection, it was never used as a fortress. Excellent views, exhibits, a restaurant and a hotel can be enjoyed here. Take tram 19 along the riverfront from Clark Ádám tér and climb the stairs behind the waterfall and **St Gellért statue** (Szent Gellért szobor; Map p376), then follow the path through the park opposite the entrance to the Danubius Hotel Gellért. Or take bus 27, which runs almost to the top of the hill from XI Móricz Zsigmond

körtér, a square located southwest of the Gellért Hotel and accessible using trams 18, 19, 47 or 49.

Bellow Gellért Hill is the city's most famous thermal spa, the **Gellért Baths** (Gellért Fürdő; Map p380; ☎ 466 6166; Danubius Hotel Gellért, XI Kelenhegyi út; admission 3400Ft; 🕙 6am-7pm May-Sep, 6am-7pm Mon-Fri & 6am-5pm Sat & Sun Oct-Apr), where majestic domes hang above healing waters. This art nouveau palace has dreamy spas where you can soak for hours while enjoying its elegant and historic architecture.

MEMENTO PARK

In Buda's southwest is **Memento Park** (Map p374; www.mementopark.hu; XXII Balatoni út 16; adult/concession 1500/1000Ft; 🕙 10am-dusk), a kind of historical dumping ground for socialist statues deemed unsuitable since the early '90s. It's a major tourist attraction and there's a direct bus from Deák tér in Pest at 11am daily (adult/concession return 3950/2450Ft, including admission). To go independently, take tram 19 from Clark Ádám tér to the XI Etele tér Terminus, then catch bus 150 to the park.

AQUINCUM

Seven kilometres north of Buda's centre, in Óbuda, is the **Aquincum Museum** (Aquincumi Múzeum; Map p374; www.aquincum.hu; III Szentendre út 139; adult/concession 900/450Ft; 🕙 10am-6pm May-Sep, 10am-5pm Tue-Sun Oct-Apr), containing the most complete ruins of a 2nd-century Roman civilian town left in Hungary. Take the HÉV from the Batthyány tér metro stop.

BUDA HILLS

With 'peaks' up to 500m, a comprehensive system of trails and no lack of unusual conveyances to get you around, the **Buda Hills** (Map p374) are the city's playground and are a welcome respite from hot, dusty Pest in summer.

Heading for the hills is more than half the fun. From Moszkva tér metro station on the M2 line in Buda, walk westward along Szilágyi Erzsébet fasor for 10 minutes (or take tram 18 or 56 for two stops) to the circular Hotel Budapest at Szilágyi Erzsébet fasor 47. Directly opposite is the terminus of the **Cog Railway** (Fogaskerekű vasút; Map p374; www.bkv.hu; Szilágyi Erzsébet fasor 14-16; admission 270Ft; 🕙 5am-11pm). Built in 1874, the cog climbs for 3.6km in 14 minutes three or four times an hour to Széchenyi-hegy (427m), one of the prettiest residential areas in Buda.

At Széchenyi-hegy, you can stop for a picnic in the attractive park south of the old-time station or board the narrow-gauge **Children's Railway** (Gyermekvasút; off Map p374; www .gyermekvasut.hu; adult/child section 450/250Ft; entire line 600/300Ft; closed Mon Sep-Apr), two minutes to the south on Hegyhát út. The railway, with eight stops, was built in 1951 by Pioneers (socialist Scouts) and is now staffed entirely by schoolchildren aged 10 to 14 – the engineer excepted. The little train chugs along for 12km, terminating at Hűvösvölgy. Departure times vary widely depending on the day or the week and the season – but count on one every hour or so between 9am or 10am and 5pm or 6pm.

There are walks fanning out from all of the stops along the Children's Railway line, or you can return to Moszkva tér on tram 56 from Hűvösvölgy. A more interesting way down, however, is to get off at János-hegy, the fourth stop on the Children's Railway and the highest point (527m) in the hills. About 700m to the east is a **chairlift** (libegő; off Map p374; adult/child 500/400Ft; 9.30am-5pm mid-May–mid-Sep, 10am-4pm mid-Sep–mid-May, closed 2nd & 4th Monday each month), which will take you down to Zugligeti út. From here, bus 291 returns to Moszkva tér.

Margaret Island

Neither Buda nor Pest, 2.5km-long **Margaret Island** (Margit-sziget; Map p374) in the middle of the Danube was the domain of one religious order or another until the Turks came and turned what was then called the Island of Rabbits into – of all things – a harem. It's been a public park since the mid-19th century. Like the Buda Hills, the island is a recreational rather than educational experience.

Cross over to Margaret Island from Pest or Buda via trams 4 or 6. Bus 26 covers the length of the island as it makes the run between Nyugati train station and Árpád Bridge bus station. Cars are allowed on Margaret Island from Árpád Bridge only as far as the two big hotels at the northeastern end; the rest is reserved for pedestrians and cyclists.

You can hire a bicycle from one of several stands, including **Sétacikli** (Map p374; 06 30 966 6453; per hr 650Ft; 9am-dusk), which is on the western side just before the athletics stadium as you walk from Margaret Bridge.

Pest
HŐSÖK TERE & AROUND

The leafy Andrássy út, Pest's northeastern artery, is the best place to start your sightseeing. From Deák tér, Bajcsy-Zsilinszky ut becomes Andrássy út, which ends at the wide, tiled **Hősök tere** (Heroes' Sq; Map p374). This public space holds a sprawling monument constructed to honour the millennial anniversary (in 1896) of the Magyar conquest of the Carpathian Basin.

Continental Europe's oldest underground – Budapest's M1 yellow line metro, constructed in the 19th century – runs beneath Andrássy út. Start your Hősök tere sightseeing from the metro station of the same name. The tall green monument on the square showcases statues of important moustachioed tribal leaders, kings and statesmen. Across the street, the **Museum of Fine Arts** (Szépművészeti Múzeum; Map p374; www .mfab.hu; XIV Dózsa György út 41; adult/concession 1200/600Ft; 10am-5.30pm Tue, Wed & Fri-Sun, 10am-10pm Thu) houses a collection of foreign art, including an impressive number of El Grecos. Don't miss the **Palace of Art** (Műcsarnok; Map p374; www.mucsarnok .hu; XIV Hősök tere; adult/concession 1200/600Ft; 10am-6pm Tue-Wed & Fri-Sun, to 8pm Thu), a large contemporary-art gallery, opposite the museum.

Adjacent is the oasis of **City Park** (Városliget; Map p374), which has boating on a small lake in the summer, ice skating in winter, and duck-feeding year round. The park's schizophrenic **Vájdahunyad Castle** (Vájdahunyad Vár; Map p374) was built in varied architectural styles typical of historic Hungary, including baroque, Romanesque, Gothic and Tudor. Nearby, the varied exhibits of the **Transport Museum** (Közlekedési Múzeum; Map p374; XIV Városligeti körút 11; adult/concession 800/400Ft; 10am-5pm May-Sep, to 4pm Oct-Apr) make it one of the most enjoyable museums in Budapest, and a great place for kids. In the park's northern corner is **Széchenyi Baths** (Széchenyi Fürdő; Map p374; 363 3210; XIV Állatkerti út 11; admission 2600Ft; 6am-10pm), its cupola visible from anywhere in the park. Built in 1908, this place has a dozen thermal baths and five swimming pools. The peaceful atmosphere of the indoor thermal baths, saunas and massage area contrasts with the buzzing atmosphere of the main pool.

Walk southwest from Hősök tere on Andrássy út to see many grand, World Heritage–listed 19th-century buildings. Stop for coffee and cake at Lukács (p387), the old haunt of the dreaded secret police, whose headquarters have now been turned into the **Terror**

HUNGARY

CENTRAL PEST

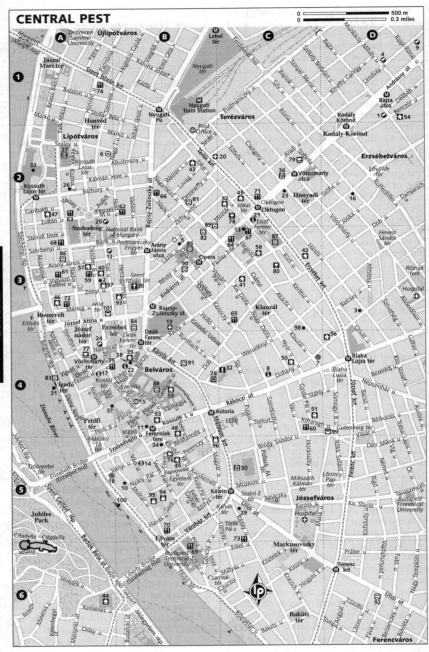

HUNGARY

INFORMATION
Austrian Embassy......................**1** D1
Bestsellers..............................**2** A3
Centre of Rural Tourism...........**3** D3
Croatian Embassy.....................**4** D1
Discover Budapest....................**5** B3
District V Police Station..............**6** A2
Electric Café...........................**7** C4
Express..................................**8** C4
French Embassy........................**9** D1
Hungarian Youth Hostels
  Association...........................**10** B5
Ibusz....................................**11** B4
Irish Embassy..........................**12** A3
Írók Boltja.............................**13** C3
K&H Bank..............................**14** B5
Main Post Office......................**15** B4
National Federation of Rural &
  Agrotourism.........................**16** D2
OTP Bank...............................**17** A4
Plastic Web............................**18** A5
Red Bus Second-hand
  Bookstore.......................(see 55)
SOS Dent...............................**19** B3
Teréz Patika...........................**20** B2
Tourinform (Liszt Ferenc
  Square)..............................**21** C2
Tourinform (Main Office)..........**22** B4
Treehugger Dan's Bookstore.....**23** C2
UK Embassy............................**24** A4
US Embassy............................**25** A2

SIGHTS & ACTIVITIES
Debrecen Summer University
  Branch...............................**26** A2
Ethnography Museum...............**27** A2
Gellért Baths....................(see 44)
Great Synagogue.....................**28** B4
Hungarian Equestrian Tourism
  Association...........................**29** C5
Hungarian National Museum...**30** C5
Hungarian State Opera House..(see 85)
Mahart PassNave.....................**31** A4

Memorial of the Hungarian Jewish
  Martyrs..............................**32** C4
Parliament..............................**33** A2
Pegazus Tours.........................**34** B5
St Stephen's Basilica................**35** B3
Terror House...........................**36** C2
Váci utca...............................**37** A4
Yellow Zebra Bikes..................**38** B4

SLEEPING
Best Hotel Service....................**39** B4
Central Backpack King Hostel..**40** A3
Connection Guest House.........**41** C3
Corinthia Grand Hotel Royal....**42** C3
Cotton House..........................**43** B2
Danubius Hotel Gellért............**44** A6
Erzsébet Hotel........................**45** B5
Four Seasons Gresham Palace
  Hotel................................**46** A3
Garibaldi Guesthouse..............**47** A2
Gingko Hostel.........................**48** B4
Home-Made Hostel..................**49** C2
Hostel Marco Polo **50** C4
Hotel Anna.............................**51** C4
Hotel Medosz.........................**52** C2
Leo Panzió..............................**53** B4
Radio Inn...............................**54** D1
Red Bus Hostel........................**55** B4
Soho Hotel.............................**56** D4
To-Ma Travel Agency...............**57** A3
Unity Hostel...........................**58** C3

EATING
Első Pesti Rétesház..................**59** A3
Fülemüle................................**60** C4
Govinda.................................**61** A3
Hold utca Market....................**62** B2
Iguana..................................**63** A2
Klassz...................................**64** C3
Köleves.................................**65** C3
Marquis de Salade...................**66** B2
Menza..................................**67** C3
Momotaro Ramen...................**68** A3

Nagycsarnok...........................**69** B6
Pireus Rembetiko Taverna.........**70** B5
Rothschild Supermarket............**71** C2
Salaam Bombay.......................**72** A3
Soul Café..............................**73** C5
Szeráj...................................**74** A1
Vapiano................................**75** A4

DRINKING
Centrál Kávéház......................**76** B5
Gerbeaud..............................**77** A4
Kiadó Kocsma.........................**78** C2
Lukács..................................**79** C2
Szimpla.................................**80** C3

ENTERTAINMENT
Alter Ego...............................**81** B2
Café Eklektika........................**82** B3
Columbus Jazzklub..................**83** A4
Gödör Klub............................**84** B3
Hungarian State Opera House...**85** B3
Kalamajka Táncház..................**86** A3
Liszt Ferenc Zeneakadémia.......**87** C3
Merlin...................................**88** B4
Symphony Ticket Office............**89** B2
Ticket Express.........................**90** B3
Ticket Pro..............................**91** B4
Trafó Bár Tangó......................**92** D6

SHOPPING
Bortársaság **93** B3
Folkart Centrum......................**94** B5
Intuita..................................**95** B5
Központi Antikvárium...............**96** B5
Mester Pálinka........................**97** A3

TRANSPORT
BKV Office.............................**98** C3
Kenguru.................................**99** D4
Mahart PassNave................(see 31)
Mahart PassNave Ticket Office.**100** B5
MÁV-Start Passenger Service
  Centre..............................**101** A3

House (Terror Háza; Map p380; www.terrorhaza.hu; VI Andrássy út 60; adult/concession 1500/750Ft; 10am-6pm Tue-Fri, to 7.30pm Sat & Sun), almost next door. The museum focuses on the crimes and atrocities committed by Hungary's fascist and Stalinist regimes. The years leading up to the 1956 uprising get the lion's share of the exhibition space.

Further down on Andrássy út, the opulence of the 1884 neo-Renaissance **Hungarian State Opera House** (Magyar Állami Operaház; Map p380; 332 8197; www.operavisit.hu; VI Andrássy út 22; tours adult/concession 2800/1400Ft; 3pm & 4pm) is a real treat; try to make it to an evening performance here. **Váci utca**, in Pest's touristy centre, is an extensive pedestrian shopping street. It begins at the southwest terminus of the yellow line, Vörösmarty tér.

PARLIAMENT & AROUND
The huge, riverfront **Parliament** (Parlament; Map p380; 441 4904; www.parlament.hu; V Kossuth Lajos tér 1-3; adult/concession 2520/1260Ft; 8am-6pm Mon & Wed-Fri, 8am-4pm Sat, 8am-2pm Sun May-Sep, 8am-4pm Mon & Wed-Sat, 8am-2pm Sun Oct-Apr) dominates Kossuth Lajos tér. English-language tours are at 10am, noon and 2pm daily.

Across the park is the **Ethnography Museum** (Néprajzi Múzeum; Map p380; www.neprajz.hu; V Kossuth Lajos tér 12; adult/concession 800/400Ft; 10am-6pm Tue-Sun), which has an extensive collection of national costumes among the permanent displays on folk life and art. Look for the mummified right hand of St Stephen in the chapel of the colossal **St Stephen's Basilica** (Szent István Bazilika; Map p380; V Szent István tér; adult/concession 400/300Ft; 9am-5pm Apr-Sep, 10am-4pm Oct-Mar) near Bajcsy-Zsilinszky út.

JEWISH QUARTER
Northeast of the Astoria metro stop is what remains of the Jewish quarter. The twin-towered,

1859 **Great Synagogue** (Nagy Zsinagóga; Map p380; VII Dohány utca 2; synagogue & museum adult/concession 1600/750Ft; ☺ 10am-6.30pm Mon-Thu, to 2pm Fri, to 5.30pm Sun mid-Apr–Oct, 10am-3pm Mon-Thu, to 2pm Fri, to 4pm Sun Nov–mid-Apr) has a museum with a harrowing exhibit on the Holocaust, and behind the synagogue is the **Memorial of the Hungarian Jewish Martyrs** (p380) in the shape of a weeping willow. Funded by the actor Tony Curtis, it's dedicated to those who perished in the death camps. A few blocks south along the *kis körút* (little ring road) is the **Hungarian National Museum** (Magyar Nemzeti Múzeum; Map p380; www.hnm .hu; VIII Múzeum körút 14-16; adult/concession 1000/500Ft; ☺ 10am-6pm Tue-Sun), with its historic relics, from archaeological finds to coronation regalia.

TOURS

To tour the Danube, hop on one of the cruises operated by **Mahart PassNave** (Map p380; ☎ 484 4005; www.mahartpassnave.hu; Vigadó tér Pier; ☺ Apr–Oct). There are regular two-hour sightseeing cruises (adult/concession 2900/1490Ft), and lunch- and dinner-buffet cruises (adult/concession 5990/2990Ft). Tickets can be purchased at the pier before departure.

For a fun way to tour Budapest, day or night, **Yellow Zebra Bikes** (Map p380; ☎ 266 8777; www .yellowzebrabikes.com; V Sütő utca 2, courtyard; ☺ 8.30am- 8pm Apr–Oct, 10am-6pm Nov–Mar) offers cycling tours (adult/concession 5000/4500Ft) of the city. The same company runs **Absolute Walking Tours** (☎ 266 8777; www.absolutetours.com), whose repertoire includes an entertaining 3½-hour city walking tour (adult/concession 4000/3500Ft), the Hammer & Sickle Tour (adult/concession 5000/4500 Ft), the 1956 Revolution Walk (6000/3000Ft) and the Absolute Hungaro Gastro Tour (7000/3500Ft).

FESTIVALS & EVENTS

Many festivals and events are held in and around Budapest. Look out for the tourist board's annual *Events Calendar* for a complete listing.

Budapest Spring Festival (www.springfestival.hu) In March.

Sziget Music Festival (www.sziget.hu) On Óbudai hajógyári-sziget (Óbuda Shipbuilding Island), from late July to early August.

Hungarian Formula One Grand Prix (www.hungaro ring.hu) At Mogyoród, 24km northeast of Budapest, in mid-August.

Budapest International Wine Festival (www .winefestival.hu) Held in September.

Budapest International Marathon (www.budapest marathon.com) In October.

SLEEPING

Accommodation prices and standards are pretty reasonable in Budapest. Many year-round hostels occupy middle floors of old apartment buildings (with or without a lift) in central Pest. Come summer (July to late August), student dormitories at colleges and universities open to travellers. The travel agency Express (p375) can help book these rooms.

Private rooms in Budapest homes generally cost 6000Ft to 7500Ft for a single, 7000Ft to 8500Ft for a double, and 9000Ft to 13,000Ft for a small apartment. Ibusz (p377) has the most extensive listings in town (some with photos on its website). Two other private-room brokers:

Best Hotel Service (Map p380; ☎ 318 4848; www .besthotelservice.hu; V Sütő utca 2; ☺ 8am-8pm)

To-Ma Travel Agency (Map p380; ☎ 353 0819; www .tomatour.hu; V Október 6 utca 22; ☺ 9am-noon & 1-8pm Mon-Fri, 9am-5pm Sat & Sun)

Buda

BUDGET

Zugligeti Niche Camping (off Map p374; ☎ 200 8346; www.campingniche.hu; XII Zugligeti út 101; camp sites per person 1800Ft, small/big tents 1500/2000, campervans 3200Ft) An excellent option for mixing a city break with a hiking holiday: the camp's in the Buda Hills at the bottom station of a chairlift. Take bus 158 from Moszkva tér to the terminus.

our pick **Back Pack Guesthouse** (Map p374; ☎ 385 8946; www.backpackbudapest.hu; XI Takács Menyhért utca 33;

beds in yurt 2500Ft, large/small dm 3000/3500Ft, d 9000Ft; 🖥) A hippyish, friendly place, though relatively small, with just 50 beds. There's a lush garden in the back with a hammock stretched invitingly between trees. Take bus 7 (from Erzsébet híd or Keleti train station in Pest), tram 49 from the *kis körút* in central Pest, or tram 19 from Batthyány tér in Buda.

Hotel Citadella (Map p376; ☎ 466 5794; www.citadella.hu; XI Citadella sétány, Gellért Hill; dm 3200Ft, r from 10,500Ft) What could be better than sleeping in a historic old fortress? Well, OK, this hotel in the fortress atop Gellért-hegy is pretty threadbare, though the dozen guestrooms are extra large, retain some of their original features and each has its own shower. Take bus 27 from XI Móricz Zsigmond körtér in Buda, then hike about 500m uphill from the stop near the Búsuló Juhász restaurant on Kelenhegyi út.

Martos Hostel (Map p374; ☎ 209 4883; http://hotel.martos.bme.hu; XI Sztoczek utca 5-7; s/d/tr/q/apt from 4000/6000/9000/12,000/15,000Ft; 🖥) Primarily student accommodation, Martos is open year-round to all. It's a few minutes' walk from Petőfi Bridge (or take tram 4 or 6).

MIDRANGE & TOP END
Papillon Hotel (Map p374; ☎ 212 4750; www.hotelpapillon.hu; II Rózsahegy utca 3/b; s/d/tr/apt from €31/41/56/72; 🅿 🖥 🛌) This small 20-room hotel in Rózsadomb has a delightful back garden with a small swimming pool, and some rooms have balconies. There are also four apartments available in the same building, one of which has a lovely roof terrace.

Büro Panzió (Map p376; ☎ 212 2929; www.buropanzio.hu; II Dékán utca 3; s/d/tr/q from €42/56/72/82; 🅿 🖥) This pension looks basic from the outside, but its 10 compact rooms are comfortable and have TV and telephone. The central Moszkva tér transportation hub – metro stop, tram stations – is seconds away.

Charles Hotel & Apartments (Map p376; ☎ 212 9169; www.charleshotel.hu; I Hegyalja út 23; d/tr/apt from €45/60/75; 🖥) Somewhat on the beaten track (a train line runs right past it), the Charles has 70 inexpensive 'studios' (larger-than-average rooms) with tiny kitchens and weary-looking furniture, as well as two-room apartments. Bike hire is available for 2000Ft per day.

Hotel Kulturinnov (Map p376; ☎ 224 8102; www.mka.hu; I Szentháromság tér 6; s/d/tr €60/75/100; 🅿) A small hotel sitting in the belly of the grandiose Hungarian Culture Foundation, a neo-Gothic structure dating back to 1904. The rooms are unimpressive, but you can't beat the scenic locale, on top of Castle Hill.

Danubius Hotel Gellért (Map p380; ☎ 889 5500; www.danubiusgroup.com/gellert; XI Szent Gellért tér 1; s/d/ste from €67/135/233; 🅿 🖥 🛌) Peek through the doors of this turn-of-the-20th-century grand dame, even if you don't choose to stay here. The 234-room, four-star hotel has loads of character, and its famous thermal baths (p378) are free for guests. Prices depend on your room's view and the quality of its bathroom.

Burg Hotel (Map p376; ☎ 212 0269; www.burghotelbudapest.com; I Szentháromság tér 7-8; s/d/ste from €85/99/109; 🅿 🖥) The affordable Burg is at the centre of Castle Hill, just opposite Matthias Church. Ask for a room overlooking Matthias Church for a truly historic wake-up view. The 26 partly refurbished rooms are fairly ordinary, but location is everything here.

ourpick Lánchíd 19 (Map p376; ☎ 419 1900; www.lanchid19hotel.hu; I Lánchíd utca 19; s/d/ste from €120/140/300; 🅿 🖥) This new boutique number facing the Danube won the European Hotel Design Award for Best Architecture in 2008. Its facade features images created by special sensors that reflect the movement of the Danube, and its rooms are equally impressive, containing distinctive artwork and unique chairs designed by art students.

Pest
BUDGET
Home-Made Hostel (Map p380; ☎ 302 2103; www.homemadehostel.com; VI Teréz körút 22; dm/d/q from €8/40/56; 🖥) This cosy, extremely welcoming hostel has unique decor, with recycled tables hanging upside down from the ceiling, and old valises serving as lockers. The old-style kitchen is also a blast from the past.

Hostel Marco Polo (Map p380; ☎ 413 2555; www.marcopolohostel.com; VII Nyár utca 6; dm/s/d/tr/q from 3000/10,000/12,000/15,000/18,000; 🖥) Very central flagship hostel with swish, powder-blue rooms. All rooms other than dorms have telephones and TVs, and there's a lovely courtyard.

Unity Hostel (Map p380; ☎ 413 7377; www.unityhostel.com; VI Király utca 60; dm/d from €12/36; 🖥) Hostel located in the heart of party town, with a roof terrace taking in breathtaking views of the Liszt Music Academy. There are 24 beds in five rooms over two levels.

Gingko Hostel (Map p380; ☎ 266 6107; www.gingko.hu; V Szép utca 5; dm/d/q 3500/11,000/18,000Ft; 🖥) This very green hostel is one of the best kept in town and the fount-of-all-knowledge manager keeps it so clean you could eat off the floor. There are books to share, bikes to hire (per day 2500Ft) and a positively enormous double giving on to Reáltanoda utca.

Red Bus Hostel (Map p380; ☎ 266 0136; www .redbusbudapest.hu; V Semmelweiss utca 14; dm/s/d/tr 3900/9900/9900/13,000Ft; 🖥) Red Bus is a central and well-managed place, with large and airy dorms as well as five private rooms. It's a quiet spot with a fair number of rules – the full 16 are listed in reception – so don't expect to party here.

Central Backpack King Hostel (Map p380; ☎ 06 30 200 7184; centralbpk@freemail.hu; V Október 6 utca 15; dm/d/tr/q from €15/54/66/84; 🖥) This upbeat place has dorm rooms with between seven and nine beds on one floor, and doubles, triples and quads on another. There's a small but scrupulously clean kitchen, and a large and very bright common room.

Boat Hotel Fortuna (Map p374; ☎ 288 8100; www .fortunahajo.hu; XIII Szent István Park, Pesti alsó rakpart; s/d/tr from €20/30/40; 🌣 🖥) Sleeping on this one-time river ferry anchored in the Danube is a unique experience. The best choices on this 'boatel' are the air-conditioned rooms with shower and toilet at water level.

MIDRANGE
Garibaldi Guesthouse (Map p380; ☎ 302 3457; garibaldi guest@hotmail.com; V Garibaldi utca 5; s/d €28/36, apt per person €25-45) This old building belongs to a gregarious owner who has many apartments available over several floors, as well as private rooms in apartments with shared bathroom and kitchen.

Connection Guest House (Map p380; ☎ 267 7104; www.connectionguesthouse.com; VII Király utca 41; s/d from €45/50; 🖥) This central gay-friendly pension above a leafy courtyard attracts a young crowd due to its proximity to nightlife venues. Three of the seven rooms share bathroom facilities.

Hotel Medosz (Map p380; ☎ 3753 1700; www.medosz hotel.hu; VI Jókai tér 9; s/d/tr/ste from €49/59/69/89) Well priced for its central location, the Medosz is opposite the restaurants and bars of Liszt Ferenc tér. Its rooms are well worn but slated for a revamp at the time of research.

Leo Panzió (Map p380; ☎ 266 9041; www.leopanzio.hu; V Kossuth Lajos utca 2/a; s/d from €49/76; 🌣) Just steps from Váci utca, this B&B with a lion motif is in the middle of everything. A dozen of its 14 immaculate rooms look down on busy Kossuth Lajos utca, but they all have double glazing and are quiet.

Radio Inn (Map p380; ☎ 342 8347; www.radioinn.hu; VI Benczúr utca 19; s/d/apt from €65/78/80) Spacious apartments with full kitchens, sitting areas and one or two bedrooms are the drawcard here, perfect for a longer stay. Embassies are your neighbours on the quiet, tree-lined street near Bajza utca metro stop (M1 yellow line).

Hotel Anna (Map p380; ☎ 327 2000; www.anna hotel.hu; VIII Gyulai Pál utca; s/d/ste from €66/82/88) Anna has 42 fairly basic rooms scattered over three floors of two 18th-century buildings that surround an enormous courtyard and garden. It's not the greatest value for money in town, but the rooms are quiet and the location is great.

Cotton House (Map p380; ☎ 354 2600; www.cotton house.hu; Jókai utca 26; r €70-150; 🖥) This 23-room guest house has a jazz/speakeasy theme, complete with old radios and vintage telephones that actually work. Prices vary, depending on the season and whether there's a shower, tub or spa in the bathroom.

Erzsébet Hotel (Map p380; ☎ 889 3700; www.danubius group.com/erzsebet; V Károlyi Mihály utca 11-15; s/d from €72/84; 🌣 🖥) The Erzsébet is in a very good location in the centre of the university district, within easy walking distance of the pubs and bars of Ráday utca. The 123 rooms – mostly twins – are spread across eight floors. They tend to be small and somewhat dark, but they're comfortable enough.

TOP END
Soho Hotel (Map p380; ☎ 872 8292; www.sohohotel .hu; VII Dohány utca 64; s/d/ste from €99/109/169; 🌣 🖥) This delightfully stylish boutique hotel sports a foyer bar in eye-popping reds, blues and lime greens. The nonallergenic rooms have bamboo matting on the walls, parquet floors and a music/film theme throughout (check out the portraits of Bono, George Michael and Marilyn).

Corinthia Grand Hotel Royal (Map p380; ☎ 479 4000; www.corinthia.hu; VII Erzsébet körút 43-49; r/ste from €179/310; 🌣 🖥 🕭) Decades in the remaking, this five-star beauty has been carefully reconstructed in the Austro-Hungarian style of heavy drapes, sparkling chandeliers and large, luxurious ballrooms. Its restored Royal Spa, dating from 1886 but now as modern as tomorrow, is a legend reborn.

Four Seasons Gresham Palace Hotel (Map p380; ☎ 268 6000; www.fourseasons.com; V Roosevelt tér 5-6;

s/d/ste from €305/340/1090; 🛇 🛋) Restored to its bygone elegance, with mushroom-shape windows, whimsical ironwork and glittering gold decorative tiles on the exterior, the Four Seasons inhabits the art nouveau Gresham Palace (1907) and provides superb views of the Danube through Roosevelt Park.

EATING

Very roughly, a cheap two-course sit-down meal for one person with a glass of wine or beer in Budapest costs 3000Ft, while the same meal in a midrange eatery would be 6500Ft. An expensive meal ranges up to 10,000Ft. Unless otherwise stated, restaurants listed below are open from 10am or 11am to 11pm or midnight. It's always best to arrive by 9pm or 10pm at the latest, though, to ensure being served. It is advisable to book tables at medium-priced to expensive restaurants, especially at the weekend.

Ráday utca and Liszt Ferenc tér are the two most popular traffic-free streets. The moment the weather warms up, tables and umbrellas spring up on the pavements and the people of Budapest crowd the streets. Both areas have oodles of cafes, restaurants, snack shops and bars.

International fast-food places are a dime a dozen in Budapest, but old-style self-service restaurants, the mainstay of both white- and blue-collar workers under the old regime, are disappearing fast. As everywhere else, pizzerias are on an upward spiral.

Buda

Éden (Map p376; ☎ 06 20 337 7575; I Iskola utca 31; mains 790-990Ft; 🕑 8am-9pm Mon-Thu, 8am-6pm Fri, 11am-9pm Sun) Located in an 1811 town house just below Castle Hill, this self-service place offers solid but healthy vegetarian fare.

Új Lanzhou (Map p376; ☎ 201 9247; II Fő utca 71; mains 1190-3290Ft; 🕑 noon-11pm) Many diners think this is the most authentic Chinese restaurant in Budapest. Make up your own mind while sampling the excellent soups, the relatively large choice of vegetarian dishes, and the stylish surrounds.

Szent Jupát (Map p376; ☎ 212 2923; II Dékán utca 3; mains 1490-3380Ft; 🕑 noon-2am Sun-Thu, to 4am Fri & Sat) This is the classic late-night choice for solid Hungarian fare, and there's half a dozen vegetarian choices too. It's just north of Moszkva tér and opposite the Fény utca market – enter from II Retek utca 16.

Kisbuda Gyöngye (Map p374; ☎ 368 6402; III Kenyeres utca 34; mains 1880-4680Ft; 🕑 noon-midnight Mon-Sat) A traditional and very elegant Hungarian restaurant in Óbuda, with an antique-cluttered dining room evoking a fin de siècle atmosphere.

Marcello (Map p374; ☎ 466 6231; XI Bartók Béla út 40; mains 2000Ft; 🕑 noon-10pm Mon-Sat) Popular with students from the nearby university for over two decades, this family-owned eatery has good Italian fare at affordable prices.

Le Jardin de Paris (Map p376; ☎ 201 0047; II Fő utca 20; mains 2200-4700Ft; 🕑 noon-midnight) A regular haunt of staff from the French Institute across the road, the Parisian Garden is located in a wonderful old town house abutting an ancient castle wall. The back garden is a delight in the warmer months. Set lunch is 1500Ft.

Tabáni Terasz (Map p376; ☎ 201 1086; I Apród utca 10; mains 2600-4900Ft; 🕑 noon-midnight) This delightful terrace and cellar restaurant at the foot of Castle Hill has a modern take on Hungarian cuisine, with lighter dishes and an excellent wine selection. Set lunch is a snip at under 1200Ft.

Csalogány 26 (Map p376; ☎ 201 7892; I Csalogány utca 26; mains 2800-4000Ft; noon-3pm & 7pm-midnight Tue-Sat) One of the best restaurants in Budapest turns out superb international dishes. Try the tenderloin of *mangalica* (a kind of pork) with puy lentils (2800Ft). A three-course set lunch is 1400Ft.

For self-catering in Buda, visit the **Fény utca market** (Fény utcai piac; Map p376; II Fény utca; 🕑 6am-6pm Mon-Fri, 6am-2pm Sat), just next to the Mammut shopping mall.

Pest
BUDGET

Govinda (Map p380; ☎ 269 1625; V Vigyázó Ferenc utca 4; mains 230-490Ft; 🕑 11.30am-8pm Mon-Fri, noon-9pm Sat) This basement restaurant northeast of the Chain Bridge serves wholesome salads, soups and desserts as well as a daily set menu for 1550/1850Ft (small/large).

Első Pesti Rétesház (Map p380; V Október 6 utca 22; strudels 240-290Ft; 🕑 9am-11pm Mon-Fri, 11am-11pm Sat & Sun) The decor may resemble a Magyar Disneyland, with olde-worlde counters, painted plates on the walls and curios embedded in plexiglass washbasins. However, the First Strudel House of Pest is just the place to taste this Hungarian pastry filled with apple, cheese, poppy seeds or sour cherries.

Szeráj (Map p380; ☎ 311 6690; XIII Szent István körút 13; mains 450-1400Ft, 🕑 9am-4am Mon-Thu, to 5am Fri &

Sat, to 2am Sun) A very inexpensive self-service Turkish place for *lahmacun* (or 'Turkish pizza'), falafel and kebabs, with up to a dozen varieties on offer.

Vapiano (Map p380; ☎ 411 0864; V Bécsi utca 5; mains 1200-1950Ft) A very welcome addition is this pizza and pasta bar where everything is prepared on site. You'll be in and out in no time, but the taste will pleasantly linger.

Köleves (Map p380; ☎ 322 1011; Kazinczy utca 35 & Dob utca 26; mains 1280-3680Ft; ⏰ noon-midnight) Always buzzing, 'Stone Soup' attracts a young crowd with its delicious matzo-ball soup, tapas, lively decor and reasonable prices. It's a great place to first try Hungarian food.

Iguana (Map p380; ☎ 331 4352; V Zoltán utca 16; mains 1390-3990Ft; ⏰ 11.30am-12.30am) Iguana serves decent-enough Mexican food, but it's hard to say whether the pull is the enchilada and burrito combination plates, the fajitas or the frenetic party atmosphere.

A self-catering option is the **Hold utca market** (Map p380; V Hold utca 11; ⏰ 6am-5pm Mon, 6.30am-6pm Tue-Fri, 6.30am-2pm Sat) near Szabadság tér. The **Nagycsarnok** (Great Market; Map p380; IX Vámház körút 1-3; ⏰ 6am-5pm Mon, to 6pm Tue-Fri, to 2pm Sat) is a vast market built of steel and glass. Head here for fruit, vegetables, deli items, fish and meat.

A nonstop supermarket in Pest is the **Rothschild Supermarket** (Map p380; VI Teréz körút 19; ⏰ 24hr), near Oktogon.

MIDRANGE

our pick **Klassz** (Map p380; ☎ 413 1545; www.klassz.eu; VI Andrássy út 41; mains 1490-3490Ft; ⏰ 11.30am-11pm Mon-Sat, 11.30am-6pm Sun) Klassz is focused on wine, but the food is also of a high standard. Varieties of foie gras and native *mangalica* pork are permanent stars on the menu, with dishes such as Burgundy-style leg of rabbit and lamb trotters with vegetable ragout playing cameo roles.

Momotaro Ramen (Map p380; ☎ 269 3802; V Széchenyi utca 16; mains 1500-3600Ft; ⏰ 11am-10pm) This is a favourite pit stop for Chinese and Japanese noodles and dumplings when the *pálinka* has been a-flowing the night before. But it's also good for more-substantial dishes.

Menza (Map p380; ☎ 413 1482; VI Liszt Ferenc tér 2; mains 1890-2490Ft; ⏰ 10am-1am) This stylish restaurant on Budapest's most lively square takes its name from the Hungarian for a drab school canteen – something it is anything but. It's always packed with diners who come for its simply but perfectly

cooked Hungarian classics with a modern twist. Weekday two-course set lunches are just 890Ft.

Pireus Rembetiko Taverna (Map p380; ☎ 266 0292; V Fővám tér 2-3; mains 1890-4990Ft; ⏰ noon-midnight) Overlooking the Nagycsarnok (Great Market) at the foot of Liberty Bridge, this place serves reasonably priced and pretty authentic Greek fare.

Fülemüle (Map p380; ☎ 266 7947; VIII Kőfaragó utca 5; mains 1900-4800Ft; ⏰ noon-10pm Sun-Thu, noon-11pm Fri & Sat) Quaint Hungarian restaurant that seems frozen in time in the interwar period. Dishes mingle Hungarian and international tastes with some old-style Jewish favourites.

Soul Café (Map p380; ☎ 217 6986; IX Ráday utca 11-13; mains 1990-4390Ft; ⏰ noon-11.30pm) One of the better choices along a street heaving with so-so restaurants and iffy cafes, the Soul has inventive European cuisine and decor and a great terrace on both sides of the street.

Salam Bombay (Map p380; ☎ 411 1252; V Mérleg utca 6; mains 2190-3990Ft; ⏰ noon-3pm & 6-11pm) If you hanker after a fix of authentic curry or tandoori in a bright, upbeat environment, look no further than this attractive eatery just east of Roosevelt tér. As would be expected, there's a wide choice of vegetarian dishes.

TOP END

Marquis de Salade (Map p380; ☎ 302 4086; VI Hajós utca 43; mains 2400-3400Ft; ⏰ noon-midnight) Taking its cue from its odd name, this basement restaurant is a strange hybrid of a place, with dishes from Russia and Azerbaijan as well as Hungary. There are lots of quality vegetarian choices on the menu.

Bagolyvár (Map p374; ☎ 468 3110; XIV Állatkerti út 2; mains 2850-4250Ft; ⏰ noon-11pm) Serving imaginatively reworked Hungarian classics, the 'Owl's Castle' attracts the Budapest foodie cognoscenti. It's staffed entirely by women – in the kitchen, at table, and front of house.

DRINKING

One of Budapest's ceaseless wonders is the number of bars, cellars, cafes, clubs and general places to drink.

Budapest in the 19th century rivalled Vienna in its cafe culture, though cafe numbers waned under communism. The majority of the surviving traditional cafes are in Pest, but Buda can still lay claim to a handful.

HUNGARY

Budapest is also loaded with pubs and bars, and there's enough variation to satisfy all tastes. In summer the preferred drinking venues are the *kerteks*, outdoor entertainment zones.

The best places to drink are in Pest (Buda's too sleepy to stay up all night), especially along Liszt Ferenc tér and Radáy utca, which have a positively festive feel during the summer.

Buda

Kisrabló (Map p374; XI Zenta utca 3; ☽ 11am-2am Mon-Sat) Attractive and well-run pub that's very popular with students. Take tram 19 or 49 one stop past Danubius Hotel Gellért.

Ruszwurm (Map p376; I Szentháromság utca 7; ☽ 10am-7pm) This is the perfect place for coffee and cake in the Castle District, though it can get pretty crowded.

Pest

Kiadó Kocsma (Map p380; VI Jókai tér 3; ☽ 10am-2am Mon-Fri, noon-2am Sat & Sun) The 'Pub for Rent' is a great place for a swift pint and a quick bite (salads and pasta), and is just a stone's throw away from Liszt Ferenc tér.

Szimpla (Map p380; VII Kertész utca 48; ☽ 10am-2am Mon-Fri, noon-2am Sat, noon-midnight Sun) This distressed-looking, very unflashy place remains one of the most popular drinking venues south of Liszt Ferenc tér. There's live music in the evenings from Tuesday to Thursday.

Centrál Kávéház (Map p380; V Károlyi Mihály utca 9; ☽ 8am-midnight) One of the finest coffee houses in the city, with high, decorated ceilings, lace curtains, pot plants, elegant coffee cups and professional service. You can have an omelette breakfast here, eat a full-on meal, or just sit down with a coffee or beer and enjoy the atmosphere.

For more coffee in exquisite art nouveau surroundings, two places are particularly noteworthy. **Gerbeaud** (Map p380; V Vörösmarty tér 7; ☽ 9am-9pm; ✷), Budapest's cake-and-coffee-culture king, has been serving since 1870. Or station yourself where Hungary's dreaded ÁVH secret police once had its HQ, at **Lukács** (Map p380; VI Andrássy út 70; ☽ 8.30am-8pm Mon-Fri, 9am-8pm Sat, 9.30am-8pm Sun).

ENTERTAINMENT

Budapest has a nightlife that can keep you up for days on end – and not just because the techno beat from the club next to your hotel is keeping you awake. There are nightclubs, bars,

live concerts (classical and folk), Hungarian traditional dancing nights, opera treats, ballet, DJ bars and random **Cinetrip** (www.cinetrip.hu) club nights at the thermal spas. It's usually not difficult getting tickets or getting in; the hard part is deciding what to do.

To find out what's on, check out the free **Budapest Funzine** (www.funzine.hu) published every second Thursday and available at hotels, bars, cinemas and various tourist spots. More comprehensive is the freebie **PestiEst** (www.est.hu, in Hungarian) and the ultrathorough **Pesti Műsor** (Budapest Program; www.pestimusor.hu, in Hungarian; 295Ft), with everything from clubs and films to art exhibitions and classical music. Both appear every Thursday.

The free *Koncert Kalendárium*, published monthly (bimonthly in summer), covers the performing arts, including classical concerts, opera and dance. A hip little publication with all sorts of insider's tips is the *Budapest City Spy Map*. It's available free at pubs and bars.

Gay & Lesbian Venues

Alter Ego (Map p380; www.alteregoclub.hu; VI Dessewffy utca 33; ☽ 10pm-5am Fri & Sat) Budapest's premier gay club, with the coolest crowd (think attitude) and the best dance music.

Café Eklektika (Map p380; V Semmelweiss utca 21; ☽ noon-midnight) This lesbian-owned cafe and restaurant (lunch buffet 990Ft) in stunning new digs is a great place for a meal and a little LGBT information gathering. Attracts a youthful, arty crowd.

Performing Arts

Magyar Állami Operaház (Hungarian State Opera House; Map p380; ☎ 331 2550; www.opera.hu; VI Andrássy út 22) Take in a performance while admiring the incredibly rich interior decoration. The ballet company performs here as well.

Liszt Ferenc Zeneakadémia (Liszt Academy of Music; Map p380; ☎ 342 0179; VI Liszt Ferenc tér 8) You can hear the musicians practising from outside this magnificent concert hall, which hosts classical music performances.

Classical concerts are held regularly in the city's churches, including Matthias Church (p377) on Castle Hill in Buda.

A useful ticket broker, with outlets across town, is **Ticket Express** (Map p380; ☎ 312 0000; www.tex.hu; VI Andrássy út 18; ☽ 10am-6.30pm Mon-Fri, to 3pm Sat). **Ticket Pro** (Map p380; ☎ 555 5155; www.ticketpro.hu; VII Károly körút 9; ☽ 9am-9pm Mon-Fri, 10am-2pm Sat) also sells tickets to plays, concerts and

HUNGARY

sporting events, while the **Symphony Ticket Office** (Szimfonikus Jegyiroda; Map p380; ☎ 302 3841; VI Nagymező utca 19; ۞ 10am-6pm Mon-Fri, 10am-2pm Sat) specialises in classical-music events.

Live Music

Kalamajka Táncház (Map p380; ☎ 354 3400; V Arany János utca 10; ۞ 8.30pm-midnight Sat) The Kalamajka is an excellent place to hear authentic Hungarian music, especially on its dance nights, when everyone gets up and takes part.

Fonó Budai Zeneház (Map p374; ☎ 206 5300; www .fono.hu; XI Sztregova utca 3; ۞ 2-10pm Wed-Fri, 7-10pm Sat) The best place in Budapest for folk music of any kind, including the diverse sounds of Hungarian, Transylvanian, Balkan, Romani, klezmer and tango. You might even strike a didgeridoo night.

Columbus Jazzklub (Map p380; ☎ 266 9013; www .majazz.hu; V Pesti alsó rakpart at Lánchíd bridgehead; ۞ 4pm-midnight) Jazz venue located on a boat moored in the Danube, just off the northern end of V Vigadó tér, hosting big-name local and international performers. Music starts at 8pm nightly.

Nightclubs

Not all clubs and music bars in Budapest levy a cover charge, but those that do will ask for between 1000Ft and 2500Ft at the door. Nightclubs usually open from 4pm to 2am Sunday to Thursday and until 4am on Friday and Saturday; some only open on weekends.

Merlin (Map p380; www.merlinbudapest.org; V Gerlóczy utca 4; ۞ 10am-midnight Sun-Thu, to 5am Fri & Sat) One of those something-for-everyone places, with everything from jazz and breakbeat to techno and house. It's most visitors' first port of call in Budapest.

Gödör Klub (Map p380; V Erzsébet tér; ۞ 9am-late) This large underground club is a real mixed bag, offering a mix of folk, world, rock and pop, played to an audience of all ages.

Trafó Bár Tangó (Map p380; IX Lilliom utca 41; ۞ 6pm-4am) An arty crowd makes the scene beneath this cultural house and exhibition space, enjoying some of the best DJs in town.

SHOPPING

As well as the usual folk arts, wines, spirits, food and music, Budapest has more distinctive items such as hand-blown glassware and antique books. But there are those who consider the city's flea markets their shopping

highlight – and they certainly are a distinctive Budapest experience. Shops are generally open from 9am or 10am to 6pm during the week, and till 1pm on Saturday.

Folkart Centrum (Map p380; ☎ 318 4697; V Váci utca 58; ۞ 10am-7pm) Everything Magyar – whether made here or in China – is available here, from embroidered waistcoats and tablecloths to painted eggs and plates.

Intuita (Map p380; ☎ 266 5864; V Váci utca 67; ۞ 11am-6pm) Purveyor of modern Hungarian crafted items such as hand-blown glass, jewellery, ceramics and bound books.

Központi Antikvárium (Map p380; ☎ 317 3514; V Múzeum körút 13-15) For antique and secondhand books, try the Central Antiquarian, which was established in 1885.

There's an excellent selection of Hungarian wines at **Bortársaság** (Map p380; ☎ 328 0341; V Szent István tér 3; ۞ noon-8pm Mon-Fri, 10am-4pm Sat) in Pest, and you can pick up the Hungarian fruit-flavoured brandy *pálinka* at **Mester Pálinka** (Map p380; ☎ 374 0388; V Zrínyi utca 18).

Two major flea markets take place in Budapest during the week. The closest to the city centre is **Városligeti Bolhapiac** (Map p374; ۞ 7am-2pm Sat & Sun) in City Park. There's junk and antiques, and the best things are to be found early in the morning. The real market mamma, though, is the **Ecseri Piac** (off Map p374; XIX Nagykőrösi út 156; ۞ 8am-4pm Mon-Fri, 6am-3pm Sat, 8am-1pm Sun), on the edge of town. International antiques dealers come to scout on Saturdays, so things can get pricey. Take bus 54 from Boráros tér in Pest or, for a quicker journey, the red-numbered express bus 84E, 89E or 94E from the Határ utca stop on the M3 metro line and get off at the Fiume utca stop. Then follow the crowds over the pedestrian bridge.

GETTING THERE & AWAY
Air

The main international carriers fly in and out of Terminal 2 at Budapest's **Ferihegy airport** (www.bud.hu), 24km southeast of the centre on Hwy 4; low-cost airlines use the older Terminal 1 next door. For carriers flying to Hungary, see p428.

Boat

Mahart PassNave (Map p380; www.marhartpassnave.hu; Belgrád rakpart ☎ 484 4010; Vigadó tér Pier ☎ 484 4005), with two docks, runs ferries and hydrofoils from Budapest. A hydrofoil service on the Danube River between Budapest and Vienna

(5½ to 6½ hours) operates daily from late April to early October; passengers can disembark at Bratislava with advance notice (four hours). Adult one-way/return fares for Vienna are €89/109 and for Bratislava €79/99. Students with ISIC cards receive a €10 discount, and children between two and 14 years of age travel for half-price. Boats leave from the Nemzetközi hajóállomás (International Ferry Pier).

There are ferries departing at 10.30am daily for Szentendre (one way/return 1490/2235Ft, 1½ hours) from May to September, decreasing to 9am departures on weekends only in April and October.

Vác (one way/return 1990/2990Ft, 40 minutes), Visegrád (one way/return 2690/3990Ft, one hour) and Esztergom (one way/return 3290/4990Ft, 1½ hours) can be reached by fast hydrofoil from Budapest at 9.30am on weekends between May and September (and also on Friday from June to August). There are also slower daily ferries at 8am from Budapest to Vác (one way/return 1490/2235Ft, 2½ hours), Visegrád (one way/return 1590/2385Ft, 3½ hours) and Esztergom (one way/return 1990/2985Ft, 5½ hours) between June and August. Services run on Friday and weekends in May, and weekends only in September.

When day-tripping to the Danube Bend by ferry, remember to check the return departure time when you arrive at your destination. Most sail to Budapest between 4.30pm and 6.45pm.

Bus

Volánbusz (☎ 382 0888; www.volanbusz.hu), the national bus line, has an extensive list of destinations from Budapest. All international buses and some buses to/from southern Hungary use **Népliget bus station** (Map p374; IX Üllői út 131). **Stadionok bus station** (Map p374; XIV Hungária körút 48-52) generally serves places to the east of Budapest. Most buses to the northern Danube Bend arrive at and leave from the **Árpád híd bus station** (Map p374; off XIII Róbert Károly körút). All stations are on metro lines, and all are in Pest. If the ticket office is closed, you can buy your ticket on the bus.

Buses depart from Budapest for Vienna (5900Ft, 3½ hours, five daily); Bratislava, Slovakia (in Hungarian, Pozsony; 3700Ft, four hours, one daily); Subotica in Serbia (in Hungarian, Szabadka; 3900Ft, 4½ hours, one daily); Rijeka in Croatia (9900Ft, 8¼ hours,

one weekly), Prague in the Czech Republic (9900Ft, 7½ hours, two weekly); and Sofia in Bulgaria (12,500Ft, 13½ hours, three weekly). Other countries serviced include Belgium, Denmark, France, Germany, Great Britain, Italy, Netherlands, Sweden and Switzerland; sample destinations include Frankfurt (22,900Ft, 18 hours, daily), Munich (14,900Ft, 10 hours, four weekly), Paris (24,900Ft, 21 hours, three weekly), London (30,900Ft, 27 hours, four weekly) and Rome (24,900Ft, 22½ hours, twice weekly) via Florence (19,900Ft, 19 hours, twice weekly).

Car & Motorcycle

Car rental is not recommended if you are staying in Budapest. The public transport network is extensive and cheap, whereas parking is scarce and road congestion is high.

If you want to venture into the countryside, travelling by car is an option. Daily rates start at around €60 per day with unlimited kilometres included. If the company does not have an office at the airport, it will usually provide free pick-up and delivery within Budapest or at the airport during office hours. All the major international chains have branches in Terminal 2 at Ferihegy airport.

Two good options are:

Anselport (☎ 362 6080; www.anselport.hu; ⏰ 9am-6pm) Reliable outfit.

Fox Autorent (☎ 382 9000; www.foxautorent.com; ⏰ 8am-6pm) Another good bet.

Train

The Hungarian State Railways, **MÁV** (☎ 06 40 494949; www.mav.hu) covers the country well and has its schedule online. The **MÁV-Start passenger service centre** (Map p380; ☎ 512 7921; www.mav-start.hu; V József Attila utca 16) provides information and sells domestic and international train tickets and makes seat reservations (though you can also buy tickets at the busy stations).

Keleti train station (Eastern; Map p374; VIII Kerepesi út 2-4) handles international trains from Vienna and most other points west, plus domestic trains to/from the north and northeast. For some Romanian destinations, as well as domestic ones to/from the northwest and the Danube Bend, head for **Nyugati train station** (Western; Map p380; VI Nyugati tér). For trains bound for Lake Balaton and the south, go to **Déli train station** (Southern; Map p376; I Krisztina körút 37). All three train stations are on metro lines.

Some direct train connections from Budapest include Vienna (€26, three hours), Austria; Bratislava (€16, 2½ hours), Slovakia; Bucharest (€82, 13 to 15 hours), Romania; Csop (4½ hours) and Kyiv (€96, 24 hours), Ukraine, continuing to Moscow (37 hours); Berlin (€58, 12 hours), Frankfurt (€78, 15 hours) and Munich (€58, seven to nine hours), Germany; Ljubljana (€39, 8½ hours), Slovenia; Prague (€38, seven hours), Czech Republic; Warsaw (€58, 12 hours), Poland; Zürich (€78, 12 hours), Switzerland; Venice (€55, 14 hours), Italy; Sofia (€77, 18 hours), Bulgaria; and Thessaloniki, Greece (23 hours).

GETTING AROUND

To/From the Airport

The simplest way to get to town is to take the **Airport Minibus** (☎ 296 8555; www.airportshuttle.hu; one way/return 2990/4990Ft) directly to the place you're staying. Buy tickets at the clearly marked stands in the arrivals halls.

An alternative is travelling with **Zóna Taxi** (☎ 365 5555), which has the monopoly on picking up taxi passengers from the airport. Fares to most central locations range from 5100Ft to 5700Ft. Of course, you can take any taxi *to* the airport, and several companies offer a flat fare (between 4600Ft and 5100Ft) to/from Ferihegy.

The cheapest (and slowest) way to get into the city centre from Terminal 2A and 2B is to take city bus 200 (270Ft, or 350Ft on the bus), which terminates at the Kőbánya-Kispest metro station. Look for the stop on the footpath between terminals 2A and 2B. From its final stop, take the M3 metro into the city centre. The total cost is 540Ft to 620Ft.

Bus 93 runs from Terminal 1 to Kőbánya-Kispest metro station. Trains also link Terminal 1 with Nyugati station. They run between one and six times an hour between 4am and 11pm and cost 300Ft (or 520Ft if you board the hourly IC train). The journey takes 20 minutes.

Boat

From May to August, the **BKV passenger ferry** (Map p374; ☎ 461 6500; www.bkv.hu) departs from Boráros tér Terminus beside Petőfi Bridge, south of the centre, and heads for III Pünkösdfürdő in Óbuda, a 2¼-hour trip with 14 stops along the way. Tickets (adult/concession 900/450Ft from end to end) are sold on board. The ferry stop closest to the Castle District is Batthyány tér, and Petőfi tér is not far from Vörösmarty tér, a convenient place to pick up the boat on the Pest side.

Public Transport

Public transport is run by **BKV** (☎ 461 6500; www.bkv.hu). The three underground metro lines (M1 yellow, M2 red, M3 blue) meet at Deák tér in Pest. The HÉV above-ground suburban railway runs north from Batthyány tér in Buda. A *turista* transport pass is only good on the HÉV within the city limits (south of the Békásmegyer stop). There's also an extensive network of buses, trams and trolleybuses. Public transport operates from 4.30am until 11.30pm, and 35 night buses run along main roads.

A single ticket for all forms of transport is 270Ft (60 minutes of uninterrupted travel on the same metro, bus, trolleybus or tram line *without* transferring/changing). A transfer ticket (420Ft) is valid for one trip with one validated transfer within 90 minutes. The three-day *turista* pass (3400Ft) or the seven-day pass (4000Ft) make things easier, allowing unlimited travel inside the city limits. Keep your ticket or pass handy; the fine for 'riding black' is 6000Ft on the spot, or 12,000Ft if you pay later at the **BKV Office** (Map p380; ☎ 461 6800; VII Akácfa utca 22; 🕒 6am-8pm Mon-Fri, 8am-1.45pm Sat).

Taxi

Taxi drivers overcharging foreigners in Budapest has been a problem for some time. Never get into a taxi that lacks an official yellow licence plate, the logo of the taxi firm, and a visible table of fares. If you have to take a taxi, it's best to call one; this costs less than if you flag one down. Make sure you know the number of the landline phone you're calling from, as that's how the dispatcher establishes your address (though you can call from a mobile as well). Dispatchers usually speak English. **City** (☎ 211 1111), **Fő** (☎ 222 2222) and **Rádió** (☎ 377 7777) are reliable companies.

THE DANUBE BEND

North of Budapest, the Danube breaks through the Pilis and Börzsöny Hills in a sharp bend before continuing along the Slovak border. The Roman Empire had its northern border here, and medieval kings ruled Hungary from majestic palaces overlooking the river at Esztergom and Visegrád. East of Visegrád

HUNGARY

the river divides, with Szentendre and Vác on different branches. Today the easy access to historic monuments, rolling green scenery – and vast numbers of souvenir craft shops – lure many day trippers from Budapest.

SZENTENDRE
☎ 26 / pop 24,000

Once an artists colony, now a popular day trip 19km north of Budapest, pretty little Szentendre (*sen*-ten-dreh) has narrow, winding streets and is a favourite with souvenir-shoppers. The charming old centre has plentiful cafes and art-and-craft galleries, and there are several Orthodox churches that are worth a peek. Expect things to get crowded in summer and at weekends. Outside town is the largest open-air village museum in the country.

Orientation & Information

From the HÉV train and bus stations, walk under the subway and up Kossuth Lajos utca to Fő tér, the centre of the Old Town. The Duna korzó and the river embankment is a block east of this square. The Mahart ferry pier

is about 1km northeast on Czóbel sétány, off Duna korzó. There are no left-luggage offices at the HÉV train or bus stations.

Tourinform (☎ 317 965; szentendre@tourinform.hu; Dumtsa Jenő utca 22; ☟ 9.30am-4.30pm Mon-Fri year-round, 10am-2pm Sat & Sun mid-Mar–Oct) has information about the numerous small museums and galleries in town. The **OTP Bank** (Dumtsa Jenő utca 6) is just off Fő tér, and the **main post office** (Kossuth Lajos utca 23-25) is across from the bus and train stations. **Silver Blue** (Dunakanyar Körút 14; per hr 400Ft; ☟ 10am-8pm Mon-Sat) is an internet cafe near the train and bus terminals.

Sights

Begin your sightseeing at the colourful Fő tér, the town's main square. Here you'll find many structures from the 18th century, including the 1763 **Memorial Cross** (Emlékkereszt) and the 1752 Serbian Orthodox **Blagoveštenska Church** (Blagoveštenska Templom; Fő tér; admission 250Ft; ☟ 10am-5pm Tue-Sun), which is small but stunning.

All the pedestrian lanes surrounding the square burst with shops, the merchandise spilling out into displays on the streets. Downhill to the east, off a side street on the way to the

HUNGARY

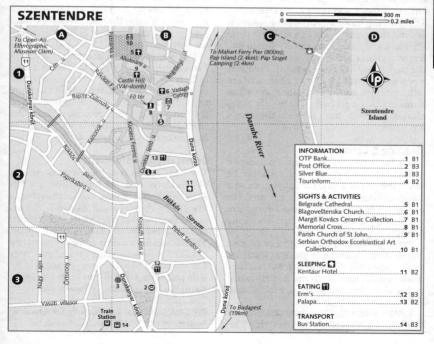

SZENTENDRE

0   300 m
0   0.2 miles

To Open-Air Ethnographic Museum (3km)
To Mahart Ferry Pier (800m); Pap Island (2.4km); Pap Sziget Camping (2.4km)

Szentendre Island
Danube River
Bükkös Stream
To Budapest (19km)

INFORMATION	
OTP Bank	1 B1
Post Office	2 B3
Silver Blue	3 B3
Tourinform	4 B2

SIGHTS & ACTIVITIES	
Belgrade Cathedral	5 B1
Blagoveštenska Church	6 B1
Margit Kovács Ceramic Collection	7 B1
Memorial Cross	8 B1
Parish Church of St John	9 B1
Serbian Orthodox Ecclesiastical Art Collection	10 B1

SLEEPING 🏠	
Kentaur Hotel	11 B2

EATING 🍴	
Erm's	12 B3
Palapa	13 B2

TRANSPORT	
Bus Station	14 B3

Danube, is the **Margit Kovács Ceramic Collection** (Kovács Margit Kerámiagyüjtemény; Vastagh György utca 1; adult/concession 700/350Ft; 🕙 10am-6pm). Kovács (1902–77) was a ceramicist who combined Hungarian folk, religious and modern themes with a hint of Gothic to create her figures. Uphill to the northwest, a narrow passageway leads up from between Fő tér 8 and 9 to Castle Hill (Vár-domb) and the **Parish Church of St John** (Szent Janos Plébánia Templom; Várhegy), rebuilt in 1710, from where you get great views of the town and the Danube. Nearby, the tall red tower of the Serbian **Belgrade Cathedral** (Belgradi Székesegyház; Pátriárka utca 5; 🕙 10am-4pm Fri-Sun Jan & Feb, 10am-4pm Tue-Sun Mar, Apr & Oct-Dec, 10am-6pm Tue-Sun May-Sep), from 1764, casts its shadow. You can hear beautiful chanting wafting from the open doors during services. The **Serbian Orthodox Ecclesiastical Art Collection** (Szerb Ortodox Egyháztörténeti Gyüjtemény; Pátriárka utca 5; adult/concession 500/250Ft; 🕙 10am-6pm Tue-Sun Mar-Sep, 10am-4pm Tue-Sun Oct-Dec, 10am-4pm Fri-Sun Jan & Feb) is in the courtyard.

Don't miss the extensive **Open-Air Ethnographic Museum** (Szabadtéri Néprajzi Múzeum; www.skanzen.hu; Sztaravodai út; adult/concession 1000/500Ft; 🕙 9am-5pm Tue-Sun late Mar-Oct), 3.5km outside town. Walking through the fully furnished ancient wooden and stone homes, churches and working buildings brought here from around the country, you can see what rural life was – and sometimes still is – like in different regions of Hungary. In the centre of the park stand Roman-era ruins. Frequent weekend festivals give you a chance to see folk costumes, music and dance, as well as home crafts. To get here, take hourly buses marked 'Skansen' from stop 7 at the town's bus station.

Sleeping & Eating

Seeing Szentendre on a day trip from Budapest is probably your best bet. The town can be easily covered in a day, even if you spend a couple of hours at the open-air museum. For private rooms in town, visit the Tourinform office. Being a tourist town, there are plenty of places to grab a bite to eat.

Pap-sziget Camping (☎ 310 697; www.pap-sziget.hu; camp sites per adult/concession 1000/600Ft, tents 2920Ft, bungalows from 8200Ft; 🕙 May–mid-Oct; 🖳) Has large shady trees, a sandy beach and numerous tent and caravan sites. Bungalows are fairly basic. Take bus 11 from Szentendre.

Kentaur Hotel (☎ 312 125; www.hotels.hu/kentaur; Marx tér 3; s/d 11,700/14,500Ft) After receiving a recent makeover, this hotel is a fine choice close to the action. Rooms are neat and tidy, and staff are eager to please.

Erm's (☎ 303 388; Kossuth Lajos utca 22; mains around 2000Ft) Unpretentious spot serving Hungarian specialities, and even some vegetarian choices. The simple wooden tables dressed in lacy cloth are reminiscent of yesteryear.

For a change from Hungarian cuisine, try the varied dishes of **Palapa** (☎ 302 418; Batthyány utca 4; mains 1500-3000Ft; 🕙 5pm-midnight Mon-Fri, noon-midnight Sat & Sun).

Getting There & Away

The most convenient way to get to Szentendre is to take the commuter HÉV train from Buda's Batthyány tér metro station to the end of the line (one way 370Ft, 45 minutes, every 10 to 15 minutes).

For ferry services from Budapest, see p389.

VÁC

☎ 27 / pop 33,300

Lying on the eastern bank of the river, Vác is an unpretentious town with interesting historic relics, from its collection of baroque town houses to its vault of 18th-century mummies. It's also the place to view glorious sunsets over the Börzsöny Hills, reflected in the Danube.

Vác is an old town. Uvcenum – the town's Latin name – is mentioned in Ptolemy's 2nd-century *Geographia* as a river crossing on an important road. The town's medieval centre and Gothic cathedral were destroyed during the Turkish occupation; reconstruction under several bishops in the 18th century gave Vác its present baroque appearance.

Orientation & Information

The train station is at the northeastern end of Széchenyi utca, the bus station is a few steps southwest. Following Széchenyi utca towards the river for about 500m will take you across the ring road (Dr Csányi László körút) and down to Március 15 tér, the main square. The Mahart ferry pier is at the northern end of Liszt Ferenc sétány; the car and passenger ferry to Szentendre Island is just south of it.

Main post office (Posta Park 2) Off Görgey Artúr utca.

Matrix (Rév köz; per hr 280Ft; 🕙 9am-1pm Mon-Fri) Small internet cafe.

OTP Bank (Dunakanyar shopping centre, Széchenyi utca)

Tourinform (☎ 316 160; www.tourinformvac.hu;

THE AQUATIC HIGHWAY

No other river in Europe is as evocative as the Danube. It has been immortalised in legends, tales, songs, paintings, and movies through the ages, and has played an essential role in the cultural and economic life of millions of people since the earliest human cultures settled along its banks.

Originating in Germany's Black Forest, the river cuts an unrelenting path through – or along the border of – 10 countries, and after 2800km, empties itself into the Black Sea in Romania. It is second only in length to the Volga in Europe (although, at 6400km, the Amazon dwarfs both), and contrary to popular belief, is green-brown rather than blue. Around 2400km of its length is navigable, making it a major transport route across the continent.

Even though only 12% of the river's length is located in its territory, Hungary is greatly influenced by the Danube. The entire country lies within the Danube river basin, and being so flat, it is highly prone to flooding. As early as the 16th century, massive dyke systems were built for flood protection. However, it's hard to stop water running where it wants to – as recently as 2006 the river burst its banks, threatening to fill Budapest's metro system and putting the homes of 32,000 people in danger.

Despite the potential danger the river is much beloved, and has even been awarded its own day. On 29 June every year cities along the Danube host festivals, family events and conferences in honour of the mighty waterway. If you'd like to join in, visit www.danubeday.org for more information.

Március 15 tér 17; 10am-7pm Mon-Fri, 10am-2pm Sat mid-Jun–Aug, 9am-5pm Mon-Fri, 10am-noon Sat Sep–mid-Jun) On the main square.

Sights

Március 15 tér, the main square, has the most colourful buildings in Vác. Here you'll find a **crypt** (Március 15 tér; admission 240Ft; 9am-5pm May-Sep), the only remnant of the medieval St Michael's Church. It contains a brief history of the church and town in the Middle Ages.

Dominating the square is the **Dominican church** (Fehérek temploma; Március 15 tér 19; admission free), below which you can meet some fascinating mummies (see boxed text, p394). Also of note is another baroque masterpiece, the **Town Hall** (1764; Március 15 tér 11). Opposite is the former **Bishop's Palace** (Március 15 tér 6). Next door, the **Vác Diocesan Museum** (Március 15 tér 4; adult/concession 500/200Ft; 2-6pm Wed-Fri, 10am-6pm Sat & Sun) displays a tiny portion of the treasures the Catholic Church amassed in Vác over the centuries.

North of the main square is the **Triumphal Arch** (Diadalív-kapu), the only such structure in Hungary. It was built by Bishop Migazzi in honour of a visit by Empress Maria Theresa and her husband Francis of Lorraine in 1764. From here, dip down one of the narrow side streets (such as Molnár utca) to the west for a stroll along the Danube. The **old city walls** and Gothic **Pointed Tower**

(now a private home) are near Liszt Ferenc sétány 12.

Tree-lined Konstantin tér to the southeast is dominated by colossal **Vác Cathedral** (Váci székesegyház; admission free; 10am-noon & 1.30-5pm Mon-Sat, 7.30am-7pm Sun), which dates from 1775 and was one of the first examples of neoclassical architecture in Hungary.

If you continue walking south along Budapesti főút, you'll reach the small stone **Gombás Stream Bridge** (Gombás-patak hídja; 1757), lined with the statues of seven saints – Vác's modest response to Charles Bridge in Prague.

Sleeping & Eating

Vác is an easy day trip from Budapest, but here are some accommodation and dining options if you want to stay over.

Alt Gyuláné (316 860; altvendeghaz@invitel .hu; Tabán utca 25; s/d 5000/12,000Ft;) Staying at this small pension is like staying with (nice) family. Rooms are kitschy but very cosy, and there's a fully equipped kitchen and private garden.

Fónagy & Walter (310 682; www.fonagy.hu; Budapesti főút 36; r 8500Ft) Fónagy & Walter is a pension from the 'homely' mould – rooms are lovingly prepared, and the wine selection from the private cellar is outstanding.

Vörössipka (501 055; okktart@netelek.hu; Honvéd utca 14; s/d 9000/14,000Ft) If the previous two are full, consider this plain hotel located away from

THE MUMMIES OF VÁC

Between 1731 and 1801 the original crypt of the Dominican church functioned as a place of burial for the general public, but it was later bricked up and forgotten. The microclimatic conditions underground were perfect for mummification – a cool temperature and minimal ventilation allowed the bodies of the deceased to remain in exceptional condition for centuries. When renovation work on the church began in 1994, the crypt was rediscovered. Of the 262 bodies exhumed over the ensuing months, 166 were easily identified through church records. It was a goldmine for historians; the clothing, jewellery and general appearance of the corpses helped to shed light on the burial practices and the local way of life in the 18th century.

The majority of mummies now reside in the vaults of the Hungarian National Museum (p382) in Budapest but three are on display in the **Memento Mori exhibition** (Március 15 tér 19; adult/concession 800/400Ft; ☯ 10am-6pm Tue-Sun) below the church. It also showcases some colourfully painted coffins, clothes and jewellery of the deceased, a registry of those buried, and a brief history of the church and its crypt.

the centre. Rooms lack character, but they're clean and definitely adequate for a night.

Barlang Bar (☎ 501 760; Március 15 tér 12; mains 1000-2800Ft; ☯ 11am-11pm Sun-Thu, to 1am Fri & Sat) With its fluorescent lighting and red booths, this cellar restaurant/bar looks like it would be more at home in New York. Its international menu is appealing, and there's outdoor seating on the square in summer.

Váci Remete (☎ 302 199; Fürdő utca; mains 1800-2600Ft) This eatery impresses with views of the Danube from its terrace, a top-notch wine selection, and a fine choice of Hungarian specialities.

Duna Presszó (Március 15 tér 13) Duna is the quintessential cafe: dark-wood furniture, chandeliers, excellent cake and ice cream, and the occasional resident drunk. Good for coffee during the day and something stronger at night.

Entertainment

Imre Madách Cultural Centre (☎ 316 411; Dr Csányi László körút 63) This circular centre can help you with what's on in Vác, such as theatre, concerts and kids' shows.

Getting There & Away

Car ferries (1200/400/400/330Ft per car/bicycle/adult/concession, hourly 6am to 8pm) cross over to Szentendre Island; a bridge connects the island's west bank with the mainland at Tahitótfalu. From there hourly buses run to Szentendre. You can also catch half-hourly buses (450Ft, 50 minutes) and trains (525Ft, 40 minutes) from Vác to Budapest.

For ferry services from Budapest, see p389.

VISEGRÁD

☎ 26 / pop 1700

The spectacular vista from the ruins of Visegrád's (*vish*-eh-grahd) 13th-century citadel, high on a hill above a curve in the Danube, is what pulls visitors to this sleepy town. The first fortress here was built by the Romans as a border defence in the 4th century. Hungarian kings constructed a mighty citadel on the hilltop, and a lower castle near the river, after the 13th-century Mongol invasions. In the 14th century a royal palace was built on the flood plain at the foot of the hills, and in 1323 King Charles Robert of Anjou, whose claim to the local throne was being fiercely contested in Buda, moved the royal household here. For nearly two centuries Hungarian royalty alternated between Visegrád and Buda.

The destruction of Visegrád came first at the hands of the occupying Turks and then at the hands of the Habsburgs, who destroyed the citadel to prevent Hungarian independence fighters from using it. All trace of the palace was lost until 1934 when archaeologists, by following descriptions in literary sources, uncovered the ruins that you can visit today.

The small town has two distinct areas: one to the north around Mahart ferry pier and another, the main town, about 1km to the south.

Sights & Activities

The partial reconstruction of the **Royal Palace** (Királyi Palota; Fő utca 29; adult/concession 1000/500Ft; ☯ 9am-5pm Tue-Sun), 400m south of the Mahart pier, only hints at its former magnificence.

Inside, a small museum is devoted to the history of the palace and its excavation and reconstruction.

The palace's original Gothic fountain, along with town-history exhibits, is in the museum at **Solomon's Tower** (Salamon Torony; adult/concession 600/300Ft; 9am-5pm Tue-Sun May-Sep), a few hundred metres north of the palace. The tower was part of a lower castle controlling river traffic. From here you can climb the very steep path uphill to the **Visegrád Citadel** (Visegrád Cittadella; adult/concession 1400/700Ft; 9.30am-5.30pm daily mid-Mar–mid-Oct, 9.30am-5.30pm Sat & Sun mid-Oct–mid-Mar) directly above. While the citadel (1259) ruins themselves are not as spectacular as their history, the view of the Danube Bend from the walls is well worth the climb. From the town centre a trail leads to the citadel from behind the Catholic church on Fő tér; this is less steep than the arduous climb from Solomon's Tower.

Sleeping & Eating

As with the other towns in the Danube Bend, Visegrád is an easy day trip from Budapest, so it's not necessary to stay over if you don't want to. **Visegrád Tours** (398 160; Rév utca 15; 8am-5.30pm), a travel agency in the town centre, provides information and books private rooms for around 5000Ft per person per night.

Jurta Camping (398 217; camp sites per adult/concession/tent 800/500/650Ft; May-Sep) On Mogyoróhegy (Hazelnut Hill), about 2km northeast of the citadel, this camping ground is pretty and green. There's a taxi-van service (2500Ft for up to six passengers) between the Mahart ferry pier and the citadel via the Nagymaros ferry pier and Jurta Camping, available on request from April to September.

Hotel Honti (398 120; www.hotelhonti.hu; Fő utca 66; s/d from €40/55;) Honti is a friendly pension filled with homey rooms. Its large garden and table tennis are available for guest use, and bicycles can be hired for 2000Ft per day.

Reneszánsz (398 081; Fő utca 11; mains 2000-4000Ft) Step through this restaurant's doors to be greeted by a medieval banquet and men in tights with silly hats. In the right mood, it can be quite a hoot.

Kovács-kert (398 123; Rév utca 4; mains 1300-2500Ft) A more down-to-earth dining option close to the Nagymaros ferry. The large menu covers a fine array of Hungarian standards, and its terrace seating is a welcome relief in the warmer summer months.

Getting There & Away

Frequent buses go to Visegrád from Budapest's Árpád híd bus station (525Ft, 1¼ hours, hourly), the Szentendre HÉV station (375Ft, 45 minutes, every 45 minutes) and Esztergom (375Ft, 40 minutes, hourly).

For ferry services from Budapest, see p389.

ESZTERGOM

 33 / pop 29,800

It's easy to see the attraction of Esztergom, even from a distance. The city's massive basilica, sitting high above the town and Danube River, is an incredible sight, rising magnificently from its rural setting.

The significance of this town is greater than its architectural appeal. The 2nd-century Roman emperor-to-be Marcus Aurelius wrote his famous *Meditations* while he camped here. In the 10th century, Stephen I, founder of the Hungarian state, was born and crowned at the cathedral. From the late 10th to the mid-13th centuries Esztergom served as the Hungarian royal seat. In 1543 the Turks ravaged the town and much of it was destroyed, only to be rebuilt in the 18th and 19th centuries. Nowadays it's an attractive riverside town, with much spiritual and temporal attraction for both Hungarians and international visitors.

Orientation & Information

The train station is on the southern edge of town, about a 15-minute walk (1.2km) south of the bus station. From the train station, walk north on Baross Gábor út, then along Ady Endre utca to Símor János utca, past the bus station to the town centre.

OTP Bank (Rákóczi tér 2-4) does foreign-exchange transactions. The **post office** (Arany János utca 2) is just off Széchenyi tér. **Gran Tours** (502 001; Rákóczi tér 25; 8am-5pm Mon-Fri, 9am-noon Sat Jun-Aug, 8am-4pm Mon-Fri Sep-May) is the best source of information in town.

Sights & Activities

Hungary's largest church is the **Esztergom Basilica** (Esztergomi Bazilika; www.bazilika-esztergom.hu; Szent István tér 1; 6am-6pm). Perched on Castle Hill, its 72m-high central dome can be seen for many kilometres around. Reconstructed in the neoclassical style, much of the building dates from the 19th century; the oldest section is the red-marble **Bakócz Chapel** (Bakócz

HUNGARY

ESZTERGOM

Kápolna; 1510). The **treasury** (kincsház; adult/concession 600/300Ft; 9am-4.30pm Mar-Oct, 11am-3.30pm Sat & Sun Nov-Dec) contains priceless objects, including ornate vestments and the 13th-century Hungarian coronation cross. Among those buried in the **crypt** (altemplom; admission 150Ft; 9am-4.45pm) under the cathedral is the controversial Cardinal Mindszenty, who was imprisoned by the communists for refusing to allow Hungary's Catholic schools to be secularised (see boxed text, opposite).

At the southern end of the hill is the **Castle Museum** (Vár Múzeum; adult/concession 800/400Ft; 10am-6pm Tue-Sun Apr-Oct, 10am-4pm Tue-Sun Nov-Mar), inside the reconstructed remnants of the medieval royal palace (1215), which was built upon previous castles. The earliest exca-

vated sections on the hill date from the 2nd to 3rd centuries.

Southwest of the cathedral along the banks of the Little Danube, narrow streets wind through the Víziváros (Watertown) district, home to the **Watertown Parish Church** (Víziváros Plébánia Templom; 1738) at the start of Berényi Zsigmond utca. The **Christian Museum** (Keresztény Múzeum; www.christianmuseum .hu; Berényi Zsigmond utca 2; adult/concession 700/350Ft; 10am-6pm Wed-Sun May-Oct, 11am-3pm Tue-Sun Nov, Dec, Mar & Apr) is in the adjacent Primate's Palace (1882). The stunning collection of medieval religious art includes a statue of the Virgin Mary from the 11th century.

Cross the bridge south of Watertown Parish Church, and about 100m further down is **Mária**

Valéria Bridge. Destroyed during WWII, it again connects Esztergom with Slovakia and the city of Štúrovo. Just east of the Little Danube are **outdoor thermal pools** (Kis-Duna sétány 1; adult/concession 1100/800Ft; 9am-7pm May-Sep) and stretches of grass 'beach'. You can use the **indoor pool** (6am-6pm Mon-Sat, 8am-4pm Sun) year-round.

Sleeping & Eating

Although frequent transportation connections make Esztergom an easy day trip from Budapest, you might want to stop a night if you are going on to Slovakia. Contact Gran Tours (p395) about private rooms (3000Ft to 4000Ft per person) or apartments (from 9000Ft).

Gran Camping (402 513; www.grancamping-fort anex.hu; Nagy-Duna sétány 3; camp sites per adult/concession/tent/tent & car 1500/750/1000/1600Ft, bungalows 12,000-16,000Ft, dm/d/tr 1900/8500/9500Ft; May-Sep;) Small but centrally located, this camping ground has space for 500 souls in various forms of accommodation, as well as a good-size swimming pool. It's a 10-minute walk along the Danube from the cathedral.

Alabárdos Panzió (312 640; www.alabardospanzio .hu; Bajcsy-Zsilinszky utca 49; s/d 7500/11,500Ft) Alabárdos isn't flashy but it does provide neat, tidy and sizeable accommodation. The breakfast is big, as is the friendly guard dog. The location is great if you want to be close to the cathedral: the hotel is at the base of Castle Hill.

Ria Panzió (313 115; www.riapanzio.com; Batthyány Lajos utca 11; s/d 9000/12,000Ft;) This is a family-run place in a converted town house just down from the basilica. Relax on the terrace or arrange an adventure through the owners: you can rent a bicycle or take a waterskiing trip on the Danube in summer.

Padlisán (311 212; Pázmány Péter utca 21; mains 1500-3000Ft) With a sheer rock face topped by a castle bastion as its backdrop, Padlisán has a dramatic setting. Thankfully its menu doesn't let the show down, featuring modern Hungarian dishes and imaginative salads.

Csülök Csárda (412 420; Batthyány Lajos utca 9; mains 1800-3900Ft) The Pork Knuckle Inn – guess the speciality here – is a charming eatery popular with visitors and locals alike. It serves up good home cooking (try the bean soup), with huge portions.

Múzeumkert (Batthyány Lajos utca 1; 9am-midnight Apr-Oct, 9am-10pm Nov-Mar) For a drink, alcoholic or otherwise, head to this modern cocktail lounge serving the best cakes and pastries in Esztergom.

Self-caterers can shop at the **Match** (Bajcsy-Zsilinszky utca; 6.30am-8pm Mon-Fri, 6.30am-6pm Sat, 8am-noon Sun), next to the OTP Bank, or the small town **market** on Simor János utca.

Getting There & Away

Buses run to/from Budapest's Árpád híd bus station (675Ft, 1½ hours) and to/

HUNGARY

CARDINAL MINDSZENTY

Born József Pehm in 1892, Mindszenty was politically active from the time of his ordination in 1915. Imprisoned under the short-lived regime of communist Béla Kun in 1919 and again when the fascist Arrow Cross came to power in 1944, Mindszenty was made archbishop of Esztergom – and thus primate of Hungary – in 1945, and cardinal the following year.

In 1948, when he refused to secularise Hungary's Roman Catholic schools under the new communist regime, Mindszenty was arrested, tortured and sentenced to life imprisonment for treason. Released during the 1956 Uprising, he took refuge in the US Embassy on Szabadság tér when the communists returned to power. He remained there until September 1971.

As relations between the Kádár regime and the Holy See began to improve in the late 1960s, the Vatican made several requests for the cardinal to leave Hungary, which he refused to do. Following the intervention of US President Richard Nixon, Mindszenty left for Vienna, where he continued to criticise the Vatican's relations with the regime in Hungary. He retired in 1974 and died the following year. But as he had vowed not to return to his homeland until the last Soviet soldier had left Hungarian soil, Mindszenty's remains were not returned until May 1991. This was actually several weeks before the last soldier had been repatriated.

If you wish to know more about one of Hungary's most controversial figures, visit the **Mindszenty Memorial Museum** (Mindszenty Emlékmúzeum; Szent István tér 4; adult/concession 400/200Ft; 9am-5pm Wed-Sun May-Dec), northeast of the basilica, which displays a handful of his personal items and shows a short film on his life and times.

from Visegrád (375Ft, 45 minutes) at least hourly. Hourly buses also link Esztergom to Szentendre (750Ft, 1½ hours).

The most comfortable way to get to Esztergom from Budapest is by rail. Trains depart from Budapest's Nyugati train station (900Ft, 1½ hours) at least hourly. Cross the Mária Valéria Bridge into Štúrovo, Slovakia, and you can catch a train to Bratislava, which is an hour and a half away.

For ferry services from Budapest, see p389.

NORTHWESTERN HUNGARY

A visit to this region is a boon for anyone wishing to see remnants of Hungary's Roman legacy, medieval heritage and baroque splendour. This swath of land was fortunate in largely avoiding the Ottoman destruction wrought on the country in the 16th and 17th centuries. Its seminal towns – Sopron and Győr – managed to save their medieval centres from total devastation, and exploring their cobbled streets and hidden courtyards is a magical experience. They also house a cornucopia of baroque architecture, something rare in Hungary. Equally rewarding are reminders of Roman settlement, and the region's natural beauty.

GYŐR

☎ 96 / pop 128,000

Not many tourists make the effort to stop at Győr (German: Raab), which is all the more reason to visit. This large city with the tricky name (pronounced *jyeur*) is a surprisingly splendid place, with a medieval heart hidden behind a commercial facade.

Midway between Budapest and Vienna, Győr sits at the point where the Mosoni-Danube, Rábca and Rába Rivers meet. This was the site of a Roman town named Arrabona. In the 11th century, Stephen I established a bishopric here, and in the 16th century a fortress was erected to hold back the Turks. The Ottomans captured Győr in 1594 but were able to hold on to it for only four years. For that reason Győr is known as the 'dear guard', watching over the nation through the centuries.

Orientation & Information

The large neobaroque City Hall (1898) is the prominent structure opposite the train station. Baross Gábor utca, which leads to the Old Town and the rivers, lies diagonally opposite this building. Much of central Győr is pedestrianised, making walking easy.

Main post office (Bajcsy-Zsilinszky út 46; ☿ 8am-6pm Mon-Fri)

Mandala (Sarkantyú köz 7; per hr 300Ft; ☿ 10am-10pm Mon-Thu, 10am-11pm Fri & Sat, 2-9pm Sun) Internet access on one computer.

OTP Bank (Baross Gábor 16)

Tourinform (☎ 311 771; www.gyortourism.hu; Árpad út 32; ☿ 9am-6pm Jun-Aug, 9am-5pm Mon-Fri, 9am-1pm Sat Sep-May) Small but helpful tourist office.

Sights & Activities

The enchanting 1725 **Carmelite Church** (Karmelita Templom; Bécsí kapu tér) and many fine baroque palaces line riverfront Bécsí kapu tér. On the northwestern side of the square are the fortifications built in the 16th century to stop the Turks. A short distance to the east is **Napoleon House** (Napoleon-ház; Király utca 4), named after the French dictator (see p400). Walk the old streets and stop in at a pavement cafe or two.

North up Káptalan-domb (Chapter Hill), in the oldest part of Győr, is the solid baroque

---

WORTH THE TRIP: PANNONHALMI ABBEY

Take half a day and make the short trip to the ancient and impressive **Pannonhalma Abbey** (Pannonhalmi Főapátság; ☎ 570 191; www.bences.hu; Vár utca 1; foreign-language tours adult/student/family 2400/1500/6000Ft; ☿ 9am-4pm Tue-Sun Apr & Oct–mid-Nov, 9am-4pm Jun-Sep, 10am-3pm Tue-Sun mid-Nov–Mar), now a Unesco World Heritage site. Most buildings in the complex date from the 13th to the 18th centuries; highlights include the Romanesque basilica (1225), the Gothic cloister (1486) and the impressive collection of ancient texts in the library. Because it's an active monastery, the abbey must be visited with a guide. English and German tours leave at 11.20am and 1.20pm from April to September, with an extra tour at 3.20pm from June to September. Between October and March, foreign-language tours must be booked in advance.

There are frequent buses to/from Győr (375Ft, 30 minutes, 21km, half-hourly).

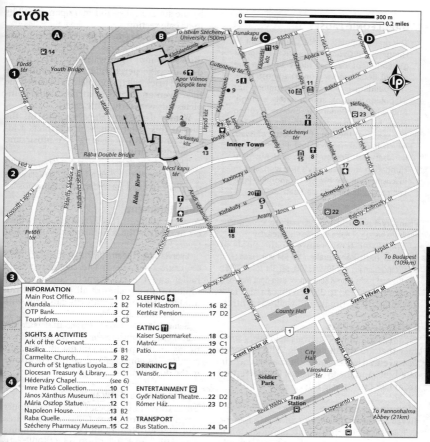

Basilica (Bazilika; Apor Vilmos püspök tere; 8am-noon & 2-6pm). Situated on the hill, it was originally Romanesque, but most of what you see inside dates from the 17th and 18th centuries. Don't miss the Gothic **Hédervary Chapel** (Hédervary-kápolna) on the southern side of the cathedral, which contains a glittering 15th-century bust of King (and St) Ladislas.

East of the Basilica is the **Diocesan Treasury & Library** (Egyházmegyei Kincstár és Kkönyvtár; adult/concession 700/400Ft; 10am-4pm Tue-Sun Mar-Oct). Of particular value in its collection are the Gothic chalices and Renaissance mitre embroidered with pearls, but stealing the show is the precious library, containing almost 70,000 volumes printed before 1850. At the bottom of the hill on Jedlik Ányos utca is the **Ark of the Covenant**

(Frigyláda), a statue dating from 1731. From here you can head north to a bridge overlooking the junction of the city's three rivers.

In Széchenyi tér, the heart of Győr, is the fine **Church of St Ignatius Loyola** (Szent Ignác Templom; 1641) and the **Column of the Virgin Mary** (Mária-ozlop; 1686). Cross the square to the **Xántus János Múzeum** (János Xántus Museum; Széchenyi tér 5; adult/concession 650/300Ft; 10am-6pm Tue-Sun Apr-Sep, 1-5pm Tue-Sun Oct-Mar), built in 1743, to see exhibits on the city's history. Next door is the **Patkó Imre Gyűjtemény** (Imre Patkó Collection; Széchenyi tér 5; adult/concession 550/300Ft; 10am-6pm Tue-Sun Apr-Sep, 1-5pm Tue-Sun Oct-Mar), a fine small museum in a 17th-century house. Collections include 20th-century Asian and African art. Look out for the highly decorated baroque ceiling at the **Szécheny**

NAPOLEONIC PAUSE

The great Napoleon once spent a night in Hungary – in Győr to be precise. The great general slept over at Király utca 4, due east of Bécsi kapu tér, on 31 August 1809. The building is now called Napóleon-ház (Napoleon House), appropriately enough. And why did Bonaparte choose Győr to make his grand entrée into Hungary? The city was near the site of the Battle of Raab, which had taken place just 11 weeks earlier, between Franco-Italian and Austrian-Hungarian armies. Boney's side won, and an inscription on the Arc de Triomphe in Paris still recalls 'la bataille de Raab'.

Pharmacy Museum (Szécheny Patikamúzeum; Széchenyi tér 9; admission free; ☽ 7.40am-4pm Mon-Fri) nearby.

The water temperature in the pools at thermal bath **Rába Quelle** (☎ 514 900; Fürdő tér 1; adult/concession per day 1950/1350Ft, per 3hr 1550/1100Ft; ☽ thermal baths 9am-8.30pm, pool 8am-8pm Mon-Sat) ranges from 29°C to 38°C. You can also take advantage of its fitness and wellness centres.

Festivals & Events

Győr has a couple of festivals held every summer that are worth catching. The **Hungarian Dance Festival** (www.magyartancfesztival.hu) is held in late June, and the **Győr Summer Cultural Festival** from late June to late July.

Sleeping & Eating

István Széchenyi University (☎ 503 447; Hédervári út 3; dm 3100Ft) Dormitory accommodation is available year-round at this huge academic institution north of the town centre.

Kertész Pension (☎ 317 461; www.kertesz-panzio.hu; Iskola utca 11; s/d/tr/q 7000/11,000/14,000/16,000Ft) The Gardener has very simple rooms on offer, but it's well located in downtown Győr and staff couldn't be friendlier.

Hotel Klastrom (☎ 516 910; www.klastrom.hu; Zechmeister utca 1; s/d/tr 14,700/18,700/21,400Ft; ▣) This delightful three-star hotel occupies a 300-year-old Carmelite convent south of Bécsi kapu tér. Rooms are charming and bright, and extras include a sauna, a solarium, a pub with a vaulted ceiling, and a restaurant with seating in a leafy and peaceful garden.

Patio (☎ 310 096; Baross Gábor utca 12; mains 1000-2000Ft) This restaurant's dining area serves up Hungarian dishes, which are overshadowed by the superb cakes and marzipan creations in its cafe section.

our pick Matróz (☎ 336 208; Dunakapu tér 3; mains 1080-1700Ft) Matróz makes the best damn fish dishes around, from warming carp soup to delicate pike-perch fillets. The handsome vaulted brick cellar, complete with dark-blue tiled oven and nautical memorabilia, completes this wonderful little eatery.

Wansör (Lépcső köz) Have a night on the tiles at this cellar pub, which attracts a jovial crowd with occasional live music and inexpensive drinks.

The massive **Kaiser supermarket** (Arany János utca 16; ☽ 7am-7pm Mon-Fri, 6.30am-3pm Sat, 8am-1pm Sun) is the place to head for self-catering purposes.

Entertainment

A good source of information for what's on in Győr is the free fortnightly magazine *Győri Est*.

Győr National Theatre (Győri Nemzeti Színház; ☎ 520 600; Czuczor Gergely utca 7) The celebrated Győr Ballet and the city's opera company and philharmonic orchestra all perform at this modern venue. Tourinform can help with performance schedules.

Rómer Ház (☎ 550 850; www.romerhaz.eu; László Teleki utca 21) One-stop shop for entertainment, featuring an independent cinema upstairs, and regular live concerts and club nights down in the dungeon.

Getting There & Away

Buses travel to Budapest (2040Ft, two hours, hourly), Pannonhalma (375Ft, 30 minutes, half-hourly), Esztergom (1770Ft, 2½ hours, one daily) and Balatonfüred (1500Ft, 2½ hours, six daily).

Győr is well connected by express train to Budapest's Keleti and Déli train stations (2040Ft, 1½ hours, half-hourly), and ten daily trains connect Győr with Vienna's Westbahnhof (2750Ft, 1½ hours).

SOPRON

☎ 99 / pop 56,400

It's true – many visitors to Sopron (*shop-ron*) are Austrians seeking inexpensive dental work and cheap haircuts. However, Sopron is also one of Hungary's most beautiful towns, with a Gothic town centre enclosed by medieval walls, narrow streets and mysterious passages. Many have called it 'little Prague', and rightly so. Once you've strolled through its

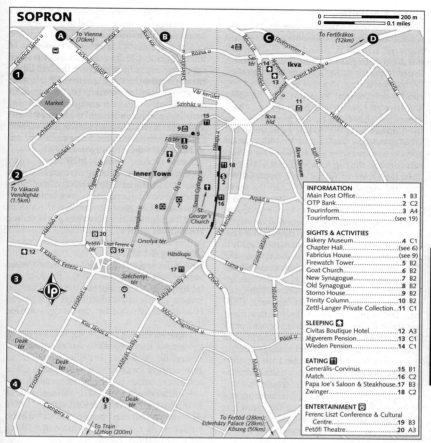

SOPRON

quiet backstreets, you can opt for a glass or two of the local wine, or head out of town and enjoy nature's offerings.

The Mongols and Turks never got this far, so unlike many Hungarian cities, numerous medieval buildings remain in use. The town sits on the Austrian border, only 69km south of Vienna. In 1921 the town's residents voted in a referendum to remain part of Hungary, while the rest of Bürgenland (the region to which Sopron used to belong) went to Austria. The region is known for producing good red wines such as Kékfrancos, which you can sample in local cafes and restaurants.

Sopron Festival Weeks (www.prokultura.hu) run from late June to mid-July.

Orientation & Information

From the main train station, walk north on Mátyás Király utca, which becomes Várkerület, part of a loop following the line of the former city walls. Előkapu (Front Gate) and Hátsókapu (Back Gate) are the two main entrances in the walls. The bus station is northwest of the Old Town on Lackner Kristóf utca.

Main post office (Széchenyi tér 7-10)
OTP Bank (Várkerület 96/a)
Tourinform main branch (☎ 517 560; sopron@tourinform.hu; Liszt Ferenc utca 1; ⏰ 9am-6pm daily mid-Jun–Aug, 9am-5pm Mon-Fri, 9am-noon Sat Sep–mid-Jun); southern branch (☎ 505 438; Deák tér 45; ⏰ 9am-5pm Mon-Fri, 9am-noon Apr-Oct) Both branches offer free internet access and a plethora of tourist information.

Sights & Activities

Fő tér is the main square in Sopron; there are several museums, monuments and churches scattered around it. Above the Old Town's northern gate rises the 60m-high **Firewatch Tower** (Tűztorony; Fő tér; adult/concession 700/350Ft; 10am-8pm May-Aug, 10am-6pm Tue-Sun Apr, Sep & Oct), run by the Soproni Múzeum. The building is a true architectural hybrid: the 2m-thick square base, built on a Roman gate, dates from the 12th century, the middle cylindrical and arcaded balcony was built in the 16th century and the baroque spire was added in 1680. You can climb to the top for views of the Alps.

In the centre of Fő tér is the **Trinity Column** (Szentháromság Ozlop; 1701). On the north side of the square is **Storno House** (Storno Ház; Fő tér 8; adult/concession 1000/500Ft; 10am-6pm Tue-Sun Apr-Sep, 2-6pm Tue-Sun Oct-Mar), where King Mátyás stayed in 1482 while his armies lay siege to Vienna. Today it houses a so-so local history exhibition, with an impressive art collection on the floor above. Upstairs at **Fabricius House** (Fabricius Ház; Fő tér 6; adult/concession 700/350Ft; 10am-6pm Tue-Sun Apr-Sep, 10am-2pm Tue-Sun Oct-Mar), walk through rooms re-created to resemble those in 17th- and 18th-century homes. In the basement see stone sculptures and other remains from Roman times. The back rooms of the ground floor are dedicated to an archaeology exhibit.

Beyond the square is the 13th-century **Goat Church** (Kecske Templom; Templom utca 1; admission free; 8am-9pm mid-Apr-Sep, 8am-6pm Oct-mid-Apr), whose name comes from the heraldic animal of its chief benefactor. Below the church is the **Chapter Hall** (Káptalan Terem), part of a 14th-century Franciscan monastery, with frescos and stone carvings.

The **New Synagogue** (Új Zsinagóga; Új utca 11) and **Old Synagogue** (Ó Zsinagóga; Új utca 22; adult/concession 600/300Ft; 10am-6pm Tue-Sun May-Oct), both built in the 14th century, are reminders of the town's once substantial Jewish population. The latter contains a museum of Jewish life.

There are many other small museums in town. Two in the Ikva district, northeast of the centre, are quite interesting: the **Zettl-Langer Private Collection** (Zettl-Langer Gyűjtemény; Balfi út 11; admission 500Ft; 10am-noon Tue-Sun Apr-Oct, 10am-noon Fri-Sun Nov-Jan & Mar), containing antiquities, ceramics, paintings and furniture; and the **Bakery Museum** (Pék Múzeum; 311327; Bécsi út 5; adult/concession 400/200Ft; 2-6pm Tue-Sun Apr-Sep), in a house and shop used by bakers' families from 1686 to 1970.

Avid cyclists should pick up a copy of the brochure *Cycling Around Sopron* from Tourinform. Alternatively, the pamphlet *Green Sopron*, also available from Tourinform, suggests a number of walks in the hills, along with horse riding and sailing possibilities nearby.

Sleeping & Eating

Vákáció Vendégház (338 502; www.vakacio-vendeghazak.hu; Ady Endre út 31; dm 2800Ft) Cheap, cheerful lodgings not far west of the town centre. Rooms are clean and furnished with two to 10 beds; bus 10 will drop you off right outside the door.

Jégverem Pension (510 113; www.jegverem.hu; Jégverem utca 1; s/d 6900/8900Ft) An excellent and central bet, with five suitelike rooms in an 18th-century ice cellar in the Ikva district. The restaurant comes highly recommended.

Wieden Pension (523 222; www.wieden.hu; Sas tér 13; s/d/tr from 7700/10,900/12,900Ft, apt from 11,900Ft;) Sopron's loveliest pension is located in an attractive old town house within easy walking distance of Inner Town.

Civitas Boutique Hotel (788 228; www.civitashotel.com; s/d/apt from €40/63/80;) A thoroughly modern hotel within easy striking distance of

---

WORTH THE TRIP: ESTERHÁZY PALACE

Don't miss **Esterházy Palace** (Esterházye Kasthély; Joseph Haydn utca 2; Palace Museum tour adult/concession 1500/750Ft, Great Palace tour 2500/2000Ft; 10am-6pm Tue-Sun mid-Mar–Oct, 10am-4pm Fri-Sun Nov–mid-Mar), a magnificent, Versailles-style baroque extravaganza 28km outside town in Fertőd. Built in 1766, this 126-room palace was owned by one of the nation's foremost families. You have to put on felt booties and slip around the marble floors under gilt chandeliers with a Hungarian guide, but information sheets in various languages are on hand. The Haydn Festival of the Budapest Strings happens here in July, followed by the Haydn Festival in late August/early September. The Tourinform (p398) office in Győr can help you with performance schedules.

Fertőd is easily accessible from Sopron by bus (450Ft, 45 minutes, hourly); the town is dominated by the palace and its grounds.

the centre. Rooms feature smart furniture and flat-screen TVs.

Generális-Corvinus (☎ 505 035; Fő tér 7-8; mains 990-2100Ft; ☯ 9am-11pm) This large restaurant is in reality two eateries – one serving decent Hungarian cuisine and guarded by a very camp general, the other dishing up pizzas under the gaze of a black crow. In summer its tables on the main square are *the* place to dine.

Papa Joe's Saloon & Steak House (☎ 340 933; Várkerület 108; mains 2000Ft; ☯ 11am-midnight Sun-Wed, 11am-2am Thu-Sat) If you insist on dining at a Wild West–themed pub/restaurant while in Hungary, this is the one to choose.

Zwinger (Várkerület 92; ☯ 8am-7pm) Sidling up to the old city walls down a narrow alleyway is this old-fashioned cafe. Its pink, purple and flowery decor may not be to everyone's liking, but its winter garden and homemade cakes are a different matter.

For self-catering supplies, head for **Match** (Várkerület 100; ☯ 6.30am-7pm Mon-Fri, 6.30am-3pm Sat) supermarket.

Entertainment

Ferenc Liszt Conference & Cultural Centre (Liszt Ferenc Kulturális Központ; ☎ 517 517; Liszt Ferenc tér) A concert hall, cafe and exhibition space all rolled into one. The information desk has the latest on classical music and other cultural events in town.

Petőfi Theatre (☎ 517 517; www.prokultura.hu; Petőfi tér 1) This beautiful building with mosaics on its facade is Sopron's leading theatre.

Getting There & Away

There are two buses a day to Budapest (3010Ft, 3¾ hours), and seven to Győr (1350Ft, two hours). Trains run to Budapest's Keleti train station (3390Ft, 2¾ hours, eight daily) via Győr. You can also travel to Vienna's Südbahnhof station (3750Ft, 1¼ hours, up to 15 daily).

LAKE BALATON

Central Europe's largest expanse of fresh water is Lake Balaton, covering 600 sq km. Hungarians flock here to enjoy the obvious activities – swimming, sailing, sunbathing, fishing and relaxing.

The southern shore is mostly a forgettable jumble of tacky resorts, with the exception of party town Siófok. The northern shore, however, is yin to the southern's yang. Here the pace of life is more gentle and refined, and the forested hills of the Balaton Uplands National Park create a wonderful backdrop. Historical towns such as Keszthely and Balatonfüred dot the landscape, while Tihany, a peninsula cutting the lake almost in half, is home to an important historical church.

But the best thing about the Lake Balaton region is the lake itself. Spend some time here, and before you know it you'll have fallen under its spell, like so many artists and holiday-makers have over the centuries.

SIÓFOK
☎ 84 / pop 23,900
Siófok is officially known as 'Hungary's summer capital' – unofficially it's called 'Hungary's Ibiza'. In July and August, nowhere in the country parties as hard or stays up as late as this lakeside resort, which attracts an ever-increasing number of international DJs and their avid followers. Outside the summer months Siófok returns to relative normality, and is largely undistinguishable from the other resorts on the southern shore.

Orientation & Information
Greater Siófok stretches for some 17km, as far as the resort of Balatonvilágos (once reserved exclusively for communist honchos) to the east and Balatonszéplak to the west. Szabadság tér, the centre of Siófok, is to the east of the Sió Canal and about 500m southeast of the ferry pier. The bus and train stations are in Millennium Park just off Fő utca, the main drag.

Main post office (Fő utca 186)
OTP Bank (Szabadság tér 10/a)
Tourinform (☎ 310 117; tourinform@siofokportal.hu; Szabadság tér; ☯ 8am-7pm Mon-Fri, 10am-7pm Sat & Sun mid-Jun–mid-Sep, 8am-4pm Mon-Fri, 9am-noon Sat mid-Sep–mid-Jun) Based in the old *víztorony* (water tower).

Sights & Activities
There's not a whole lot to see of cultural or historical importance in a place where hedonism rules the roost. However, if you walk north on narrow Hock János köz, you'll reach the **Imre Kálmán Museum** (Kálmán Imre sétány 5; adult/concession 300/150Ft; ☯ 9am-4pm Tue-Sun). It's devoted to the life and works of a composer of popular operettas who was born in Siófok in 1882.

For an overview of the town and lake beyond, climb the wooden **water tower** (víztorony; Szabadság tér; adult/concession 200/100Ft; ☺ 8am-7pm Mon-Fri, 10am-7pm Sat & Sun mid-Jun–mid-Sep, 8am-4pm Mon-Fri, 9am-noon Sat mid-Sep–mid-Jun). It was built in 1912.

Nagy Strand (adult/concession 750/500Ft), Siófok's 'Big Beach', is centre stage on Petőfi sétány; free concerts are often held here on summer evenings. There are many more managed swimming areas along the lakeshore which cost around the same as Nagy Strand.

There are rowing boats and sailing **boats** for hire at various locations along the lake, including Nagy Strand. **Lake cruises** run from late May to mid-September, generally daily at 10am, 11.30am, 1pm, 2.30pm, 4pm, and 5.30pm. There are additional cruises at 11am, 2pm and 4pm daily from late April to late May.

Siófok's newest attraction, **Galerius** (☎ 506 580; www.galerius-furdo.hu, in Hungarian; Szent László utca 183; swimming pools adult/concession 2000/1300Ft, sauna & swimming pools adult 2300Ft; ☺ 9am-9pm), is 4km west of downtown Siófok. It offers a plethora of indoor thermal pools, saunas and massages.

Sleeping & Eating

Prices quoted below are for the high season in July and August. Tourinform can help find you a private room (€12 to €20 per person), or an apartment for slightly more.

Siófok Város College (☎ 312 244; www.siofokvaros kollegiuma.sulinet.hu; Petőfi sétány 1; dm 2530Ft) Close to the action in central Siófok, it's hard to beat this basic college accommodation for price and location.

Hotel Yacht Club (☎ 311 161; www.hotel -yachtclub.hu; Vitorlás utca 14; s/d €58/92; ⚅ 🖳 🍽) Overlooking the harbour is this excellent little hotel with cosy rooms, some of which have balconies overlooking the lake, and a new wellness centre. Bicycles can be hired.

our pick **Mala Garden** (☎ 506 687; www.mala garden.hu; Petőfi sétány 15/a; r 18,900-26,900Ft; ⚅) Most of Siófok's accommodation options pale in comparison with this gorgeous boutique hotel. It's reminiscent of Bali, with Indonesian art lining the walls, a small manicured flower garden at the rear of the hotel, and a quality restaurant serving Asian cuisine.

Roxy (☎ 506 573; Szabadság tér; mains 990-3000Ft) This pseudo-rustic restaurant-pub on busy Szabadság tér attracts diners with its wide range of international cuisine and surprisingly imaginative Hungarian mains. Don't arrive too late in the evening or you'll be hard-pressed to find a table.

Entertainment

South Balaton Cultural Centre (☎ 311 855; Fő tér 2), Siófok's main cultural venue, stages concerts, dance performances and plays. However, most visitors to Siófok are interested in more-energetic entertainment. Turnover of bars and clubs is high, but the following manage to attract punters year after year:

Flört (www.flort.hu; Sió utca 4) Well-established club with trippy light shows.

Palace (www.palace.hu; Deák Ferencutca 2) Hugely popular club. Accessible by free bus from outside Tourinform between 9pm and 5am daily from May to mid-September.

Renegade (Petőfi sétány 9) Wild pub near the beach where table dancing and live music are common.

Getting There & Away

From April to October, four daily Mahart ferries run between Siófok and Balatonfüred (1280Ft, 55 minutes), two of which carry on to Tihany. Up to eight ferries follow the same route in July and August.

Buses serve a lot of destinations from Siófok, but you'll find the more frequent train connections of more use. Trains to Nagykanizsa pass through all the resorts on the southern edge of the lake, and there are eight daily train connections to and from Budapest (1770Ft, two hours).

BALATONFÜRED

☎ 87 / pop 13,000

Walking the hillside streets, you'll catch glimpses of the easy grace that 18th- and 19th-century Balatonfüred (*bal*-ah-tahn fuhr-ed) enjoyed. In those days the wealthy and famous built large villas on its tree-lined streets, hoping to take advantage of the health benefits of the town's famous thermal waters. In more recent times, the lake frontage has received a massive makeover and now sports the most stylish marina on the lake. The hotels here are a bit cheaper than those on the neighbouring Tihany peninsula, making this a good base for exploring.

Orientation & Information

The adjacent bus and train stations are on Dobó István utca, 1km from the lake.

BALATONFÜRED

HUNGARY

OTP Bank (Petőfi Sándor utca 8)
Post office (Zsigmond utca 14; 8am-4pm Mon-Fri)
Tourinform (580 480; balatonfured@tourinform.hu; Kisfaludy utca 1; 9am-7pm Mon-Fri, to 6pm Sat, to 1pm Sun Jul & Aug, 9am-5pm Mon-Fri, to 1pm Sat Jun & Sep, 9am-4pm Mon-Fri Oct-May) Helpful tourist office.

Sights & Activities

The park along the central shore, near the ferry pier, is worth a promenade. You can take a one-hour **pleasure cruise** (342 230; www.balatonhajozas.hu; Mahart ferry pier; adult/concession 1250/625Ft) five times a day, from late May to mid-September. The **disco boat** (disco hajo; 342 230; www.balatonihajozas.hu; Mahart ferry pier; cruise 1600Ft), a two-hour cruise with music and drinks, leaves at 9pm Tuesday, Wednesday, Friday and Saturday in July and August.

Kisfaludy Strand (Aranyhíd sétány; adult/concession 375/275Ft; 8am-6pm mid-May–mid-Sep), along the footpath 800m northeast of the pier, is a relatively sandy beach. You can explore the waterfront by bike (see p406).

North of the pier is the renovated 1846 **Round Church** (Kerek Templom; cnr Jókai Mór & Honvéd utca). **Mór Jókai Museum** (Jókai Mór Múzeum; Honvéd utca 1) commemorates the life of the acclaimed novelist in what was once his summer house (1871), though at the time of research it was closed for renovation. The heart of the old spa town is Gyógy tér, where **Kossuth Forrásvíz** (Kossuth Spring, 1853) dispenses slightly sulphurous water that people actually drink for health. Don't stray far from a bathroom afterwards.

On the lake, sprawling the length of Zákonyi Ferenc utca, is Balatonfüred's biggest development in years. Explore the sparkling new **marina** and its stylish cafes, fashionable restaurants and boutique shops.

Sleeping

Prices fluctuate throughout the year and usually peak between early July and late August; high-season prices are quoted below.

As elsewhere around Lake Balaton, private room prices are rather inflated. **Sun City Tours** (☎ 06 30 947 2679; Csokonai utca 1) can help with finding you a place, as can **Fontaine Room Service** (☎ 343 673; Honvéd utca 11). There are lots of houses with rooms for rent on the streets north of Kisfaludy Beach.

Füred Camping (☎ 580 241; fured@balatontourist.hu; Széchenyi utca 24; camp sites per adult/concession/tent 1600/1200/5500Ft, bungalows/caravans from 17,000/23,000Ft; ☺ mid-Apr–early Oct) Sprawling beachfront complex 1km west of the centre, with water-sport rentals, swimming pools, tennis courts, a restaurant and a convenience store.

Villa Balaton (☎ 06 30 223 6453; www.villabalaton.hu; Deák Ferenc utca 38; s/d 6000/12,000Ft) The large, bright rooms of this pastel-yellow villa uphill from the lake are available for rent. Each has its own balcony overlooking a sunny garden and grapevines, and guests can make use of the well-equipped kitchen.

Hotel Blaha Lujza (☎ 581 210; www.hotelblaha.hu; Blaha Lujza utca 4; s/d €37/50) This was once the holiday home of the much-loved 19th-century Hungarian actress-singer Blaha Lujza. Its rooms are a little compact but very comfy.

Eating & Drinking

Balaton (☎ 481 319; Kisfaludy utca 5; mains 1000-3000Ft) This cool, leafy oasis amid all the hubbub is set back from the lake in a shaded park area. It serves generous portions and, like so many restaurants in town, has an extensive fish selection.

Bazsalikom (☎ 06 30 538 0690; Zákonyi Ferenc sétány 4; mains 1500-3000Ft) Taking pride of place on the new marina's waterfront is Bazsalikom, a restaurant that combines fine dining and a relaxed atmosphere. Pasta and pizza are the mainstays of the menu, but don't overlook the daily blackboard specials.

Stefánia Vitorlás (☎ 343 407; Tagore sétány 1; mains 1500-3000Ft) Enormous wooden eatery sitting right on the lake's edge at the foot of the pier. Watch the yachts sail in and out of the harbour while enjoying Hungarian cuisine and local wine.

our pick Karolina (Zákonyi Ferenc sétány 4) Karolina is a sophisticated cafe-bar that serves excellent coffee, teas and local wines.

Getting There & Around

Buses to Tihany (250Ft, 30 minutes) leave every 30 minutes or so throughout the day. Seven buses daily head to the northwestern lakeshore towns including Keszthely (1050Ft, 1½ hours).

Budapest-bound buses (2040Ft) depart from Balatonfüred four times daily and take between two and three hours to get there. Trains (1690Ft, three daily) take about as long. There are a number of towns on the train line with 'Balaton' or 'Füred' somewhere in their name, so double-check which station you're getting off at.

From April to September, four daily ferries ply the water from Balatonfüred to Tihany (930Ft, 20 minutes) and Siófok (1280Ft, 55 minutes).

A good way to explore the waterfront is to rent a bike from **Tempo 21** (☎ 06 20 924 4995; Deák Ferenc utca 56; per hr/day 350/2400Ft; ☺ 9am-7pm mid-May–mid-Sep).

TIHANY
☎ 87 / pop 1500

The place with the greatest historical significance on Lake Balaton is Tihany, a peninsula jutting 5km into the lake. Activity here is centred on the tiny town of the same name, which is home to the celebrated Abbey Church. Contrasting with this are the hills and marshy meadows of the peninsula's nature reserve, which has an isolated, almost wild feel to it.

The peninsula has beaches on both its eastern and western coasts, and a big resort complex on its southern tip. However, you can easily shake off the tourist hordes by going hiking. Birdwatchers, bring your binoculars: the trails have abundant avian life.

Orientation & Information

The harbour where ferries heading to and from Balatonfüred dock is a couple of kilometres downhill from the village of Tihany. Buses pull up in the heart of town, outside the post office on Kossuth Lajos utca.

Tourinform (☎ 448 804; tihany@tourinform.hu; Kossuth Lajos utca 20; ☺ 9am-7pm Mon-Fri, 10am-6pm Sat

& Sun mid-Jun–mid-Sep, 9am-5pm Mon-Fri, 10am-4pm Sat mid-Apr–mid-Jun & late Sep, 10am-4pm Mon-Fri Oct–mid-Apr) sells hiking maps and film, and provides tourist information.

Sights & Activities

You can spot Tihany's twin-towered **Abbey Church** (Apátság Templom; adult/concession 700/300Ft; 9am-6pm May-Sep, 10am-5pm Apr & Oct, 10am-3pm Nov-Mar), dating from 1754, from a long way off. Entombed in the church's crypt is the abbey's founder, King Andrew I. The admission fee includes entry to the attached **Abbey Museum** (Apátsági Múzeum). The path behind the church leads to outstanding views.

Follow the pathway along the ridge north from the church in the village to reach the tiny **Open-air Folk Museum** (Szabadtéri Néprajzi Múzeum; Pisky sétány 10; adult/concession 350/250Ft; 10am-6pm May-Sep).

Back at the clearing in front of the church, there's a large hiking map that has all of Tihany's trails marked. Following the green trail northeast of the church for an hour will bring you to a Russian well (oroszkút) and the ruins of the Old Castle (Óvár), where Russian Orthodox monks, brought to Tihany by Andrew I, hollowed out cells in the soft basalt walls.

Sleeping & Eating

Tihany is an easy day trip from Balatonfüred, so there's no reason to stay over unless you're hiking. If you are looking for lodgings, one option is to look for a 'Zimmer frei' (German for 'room for rent') sign on the small streets north of the church.

Adler (538 000; www.adler-tihany.hu; Felsőkopaszhegyi utca 1/a; r €41-52, apt €68-95;) Features large, whitewashed rooms with balconies, and there's a spa bath, sauna and restaurant on the premises.

our pick **Ferenc Pince** (448 575; Cser-hegy 9; mains from 1500Ft; noon-11pm Wed-Mon) Ferenc is a wine and food lover's dream. During the day, its open terrace offers expansive views of the lake, while at night the twinkling lights of the southern shore are in full view. It's about 2km south of the abbey church.

Rege Cafe (Kossuth Lajos utca 22; 10am-6pm) From its high vantage point near the Benedictine abbey, this modern cafe has an unsurpassed panoramic view of Lake Balaton. On a sunny day, there is no better place to enjoy coffee, cake and the sparkling waters.

Getting There & Away

Buses travel along the 14km of mostly lakeside road between Tihany village and Balatonfüred's train and bus stations (250Ft, 30 minutes) at least 13 times a day.

Passenger ferries sail between Tihany and Balatonfüred from April to September (930Ft, 20 minutes, seven daily). You can follow a steep path up to the village from the pier to reach the Abbey Church.

KESZTHELY

83 / pop 21,800

At the very western end of the Balaton sits Keszthely (kest-hey), a place of grand town houses and a gentle ambience far removed from the lake's tourist hot spots. Its small, shallow beaches are well suited to families, and there are enough accommodation options to suit most holidaymakers. Of its handful of museums and historical buildings, nothing tops the Festetics Palace, a lavish baroque residence. The town lies just over 1km northwest of the lake and with the exception of a few guest houses, almost everything stays open year-round. If you visit in May, you might catch the town's annual Balaton Festival.

Orientation & Information

The bus and train stations, side by side at the end of Mártírok útja, are fairly close to the ferry pier. Walk northeast on Kazinczy utca and you'll see the water to your right in a few hundred metres. To get to town, turn left and head towards Kossuth Lajos utca.

Tourinform (314 144; keszthely@tourinform.hu; Kossuth Lajos utca 28; 9am-8pm Mon-Fri, to 6pm Sat mid-Jun–mid-Sep, 9am-5pm Mon-Fri, to 12.30pm Sat mid-Sep–mid-Jun) has information on the whole Lake Balaton area.

There's a huge **OTP Bank** (Kossuth Lajos utca) facing the park south of the church, and close by is the **main post office** (Kossuth Lajos utca 48).

Sights & Activities

The glimmering white, 100-room **Festetics Palace** (Festetics Kastély; 312 190; Kastély utca 1; adult/concession 1650/800Ft; 9am-6pm Jul-Aug, 10am-4pm Sep-Jun) was first built in 1745; the wings were extended out from the original building 150 years later. About a dozen rooms in the one-time residence have been turned into a museum. Many of the decorative arts in the gilt salons were imported from England in the mid-1800s. The **Helikon Library** (Helikon

HUNGARY

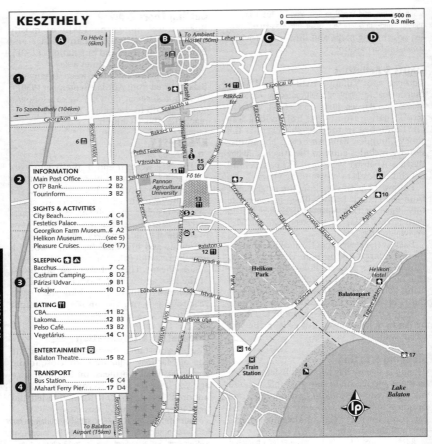

KESZTHELY

INFORMATION
Main Post Office...............1 B3
OTP Bank.........................2 B2
Tourinform......................3 B2

SIGHTS & ACTIVITIES
City Beach........................4 C4
Festetics Palace................5 B1
Georgikon Farm Museum...6 A2
Helikon Museum............(see 5)
Pleasure Cruises.............(see 17)

SLEEPING
Bacchus............................7 C2
Castrum Camping.............8 D2
Párizsi Udvar....................9 B1
Tokajer.............................10 D2

EATING
CBA..................................11 B2
Lakoma.............................12 B3
Pelso Café........................13 B2
Vegetárius.......................14 C1

ENTERTAINMENT
Balaton Theatre...............15 B2

TRANSPORT
Bus Station.......................16 C4
Mahart Ferry Pier.............17 D4

Könyvtár), in the baroque south wing, is known for its 100,000 volumes and its hand-carved furniture, crafted by a local artisan. To reach the palace, follow Kossuth Lajos utca, the long pedestrian street in the centre of the Old Town.

In 1797 Count György Festetics, an uncle of the reformer István Széchenyi, founded Europe's first agricultural institute, the Georgikon, in Keszthely. Part of the original school is now the **Georgikon Farm Museum** (Georgikon Major Múzeum; Bercsényi Miklós utca 67; adult/concession 500/250Ft; 10am-5pm Tue-Sun May-Sep, 10am-5pm Mon-Fri Apr & Oct).

The lakeside area centres on the long Mahart ferry pier. From March to October you can take a one-hour **pleasure cruise** (312 093; www.balatoni

hajozas.hu; Mahart ferry pier; adult/concession 1250/625Ft) on the lake at 11am, 1pm, 3pm and 5pm daily. If you're feeling like a swim, **City Beach** (Városi Strand) is not far west of the pier, near plenty of beer stands and food booths. There are other beaches you can explore further afield; some hotels have private shore access.

Sleeping

Tourinform can help find private rooms (from 3000Ft per person). Otherwise, strike out on your own (particularly along Móra Ferenc utca) and keep an eye out for 'szoba kiadó' or 'Zimmer frei' signs (Hungarian and German, respectively, for 'room for rent').

Castrum Camping (312 120; www.castrum-group .hu; Móra Ferenc utca 48; camp sites per adult/concession/

tent 1200/900/1800Ft; Apr-Oct;) North of the stations, this large camping ground is green and spacious, but the management seems to prefer caravans to tents. Unfortunately you have to cross the railway tracks to reach the lake.

Ambient Hostel (06 30 460 3536; hostel-accommodation.fw.hu; Sopron utca 10; dm/d from 2900/6800Ft;) Only a short walk north of the palace is this new hostel with basic, cheap dorms, each of which comes with its own bathroom. Laundry service is available 3pm to 5pm, from Monday to Friday.

Tokajer (319 875; www.pensiontokajer.hu; Apát utca 21; s/d/apt from €33/50/58;) Spread over four buildings in a quiet area of town, Tokajer has slightly dated rooms, but they're still in good condition. Extras include a mini–wellness centre and free use of bicycles.

Párizsi Udvar (311 202; parizsiudvar@freemail.hu; Kastély utca 5; d/tr/apt 9400/11,400/15,000Ft) Large basic rooms share kitchen facilities in what was once part of the Festetics Kastély complex. The central courtyard adds to the quiet of the place.

Bacchus (510 450; www.bacchushotel.hu; Erzsébet királyné utca 18; s/d/apt 12,300/16,500/24,800Ft) Bacchus' central position and immaculate rooms make it a popular choice with travellers. Equally pleasing is its atmospheric cellar, which is divided between a fine restaurant and a wine museum (admission free, open 11am to 11pm) where tastings are available.

Eating

Pelso Café (Fő tér; coffee & cake from 290Ft; 9am-9pm) This modern two-level cafe at the southern end of the main square does decent coffee, cake and cocktails, has a selection of teas from around the world, and attracts both young and old.

Vegetárius (311 023; Rákóczi tér 3; mains 800-1000Ft; 11am-4pm Mon-Fri) This small vegetarian restaurant down the hill from the palace has a good vibe and plenty of healthy choices during the midweek lunch-hour rush.

Lakoma (313 129; Balaton utca 9; mains 1000-2600Ft) With a good fish selection, grill/roast specialities and a back garden that transforms itself into a leafy dining area in the summer months, it's hard to go wrong with Lakoma.

If you need groceries, shop while admiring the beautiful stained-glass windows of the **CBA** (Kossuth Lajos utca 35) supermarket on the main street.

Entertainment

The biweekly *ZalaEst* booklet, available from Tourinform, is a good source of information on entertainment activities in Keszthely.

Balaton Theatre (515 230; www.balatonszinhaz.hu, in Hungarian; Fő tér 3) Catch the latest in theatre performances at this venue on the main square.

Getting There & Away

Balaton airport (354 256; www.flybalaton.hu), 15km southwest of Keszthely at Sármellék, receives Ryanair flights from Düsseldorf, Frankfurt and London Stansted. There's no public transport between the airport and Keszthely, but transfers can be arranged with **FlyBalaton Airport Transfer** (554 055; www.balatonairporttransfer.com; one way/return €6/10).

Back on the ground, buses from Keszthely to Hévíz (200Ft, 15 minutes) leave at least every 30 minutes during the day. Other places served by buses include Balatonfüred (1050Ft,

HUNGARY

WORTH THE TRIP: HÉVÍZ

Just 6km northwest of Keszthely is the spa town of Hévíz. People have utilised the warm mineral water here for centuries, first for tanning in the Middle Ages and later for curative purposes (it was developed as a private resort in 1795). One of Europe's largest thermal lakes, the 5-hectare **Gyógytó** (Thermal Lake; www.spaheviz.hu; day pass 2900Ft; 8am-6pm May-Sep, 9am-4pm Oct-Apr) gurgles up in the middle of town. The hot spring is a crater some 40m deep that disgorges up to 80 million litres of warm water a day. The surface temperature here averages 33°C and never drops below 26°C, allowing bathing year-round. You can rent towels, inner tubes and even swimsuits. Both the water and the bottom mud are slightly radioactive; the minerals are said to alleviate various medical conditions.

To get here, take the bus from Keszthely station (200Ft, 15 minutes, half-hourly). The lake park is across Deák tér from the Hévíz bus station. Walk right around the park to get to the closest year-round entrance in the east.

1½ hours, seven daily) and Budapest (2780Ft, three hours, seven daily).

Keszthely is on a railway branch line linking the lake's southeastern shore with Budapest (2780Ft, four hours, six daily). To reach towns along Lake Balaton's northern shore by train, you have to change at Tapolca (375Ft, 30 minutes, hourly). A more extravagant rail option is the vintage steam train operated by **MÁV Nostalgia** (www.mavnosztalgia.hu) from Keszthely to Badacsonytomaj (one way 1170Ft, 1¾ hours) from late June to late August at 9.50am every Tuesday, Thursday and Saturday, returning at 2.53pm.

From April to September, **Mahart ferries** (www.balatonihajozas.hu) link Keszthely with Badacsonytomaj (1430Ft, two hours, four daily) and other, smaller lake towns.

SOUTH CENTRAL HUNGARY

Southern Hungary is a region of calm, a place to savour life at a slower pace. It's only marginally touched by tourism, and touring through the countryside is like travelling back in time. Passing through the region, you'll spot whitewashed farmhouses whose thatched roofs and long colonnaded porticoes decorated with floral patterns seem unchanged over the centuries.

Historically, the area bordering Croatia and Serbia has often been 'shared' between Hungary and these countries, and it's here that the remnants of the 150-year Turkish occupation can be most strongly felt.

The region is bounded by the Danube River to the east, the Dráva River to the south and west, and Lake Balaton to the north. Generally flat, the Mecsek and Villány Hills rise up in isolation from the plain. The weather always seems to be a few degrees warmer here than in other parts of the country; the sunny clime is great for grape growing, and oak-aged Villány reds are well regarded, if highly tannic.

PÉCS
☎ 72 / pop 156,000

Blessed with a mild climate, an illustrious past and a number of fine museums and monuments, Pécs (pronounced *paich*) is one of the most pleasant and interesting cities to visit in Hungary. For those reasons and more – a handful of universities, the nearby Mecsek Hills, a lively nightlife – many travellers put it second only to Budapest on their Hungary must-see list.

Lying equidistant from the Danube to the east and the Dráva to the south, Pécs enjoys a microclimate that lengthens the summer and is ideal for viticulture and fruit production (especially almonds). An especially fine time to visit is during a warm *indián nyár* (Indian summer), when the light seems to take on a special quality.

History has far from ignored Pécs. The Roman settlement of Sopianae on this site was the capital of the province of Lower Pannonia for 400 years. Christianity flourished here in the 4th century and in 1009 Stephen I made Pécs a bishopric. The first Hungarian university was founded here in the mid-14th century. City walls were erected after the Mongol invasion of 1241, but 1543 marked the start of almost a century and a half of Turkish domination. In the 19th century the manufacture of Zsolnay porcelain and other goods, such as Pannonia sparkling wine, helped put Pécs back on the map.

Orientation & Information
The train station is a little over 1km south of the old town centre. Walk up Jókai Mór utca to the town centre. The bus station is a few blocks closer, next to the market. Follow Bajcsy-Zsilinszky utca north to get to the centre.

Tourinform (☎ 213 315; baranya-m@tourinform.hu; Széchenyi tér 9; ✆ 8am-6pm Mon-Fri, 10am-8pm Sat & Sun Jun-Aug, 8am-5.30pm Mon-Fri, 10am-2pm Sat May, Sep & Oct, 8am-4pm Mon-Fri Nov-Apr) has internet access (100Ft per hour) and tons of local info, including a list of museums. The **main post office** (Jókai Mór utca 10) is in a beautiful art nouveau building (1904) with a colourful Zsolnay porcelain roof. There are plenty of banks and ATMs scattered around town. The **Ibusz** (☎ 211 011; www.ibusz.hu; Király utca 11; ✆ 8am-5pm Mon-Fri, 8am-noon Sat) travel agency offers a currency-exchange booth, rents private rooms and books transport tickets.

Sights & Activities
The curiously named **Mosque Church** (Mecset Templom; Széchenyi tér; ✆ 10am-4pm Mon-Sat, 11.30am-4pm Sun mid-Apr–mid-Oct, 10am-noon Mon-Sat, 11.30am-2pm Sun mid-Oct–mid-Apr) dominates the city's central square. It has no minaret and has

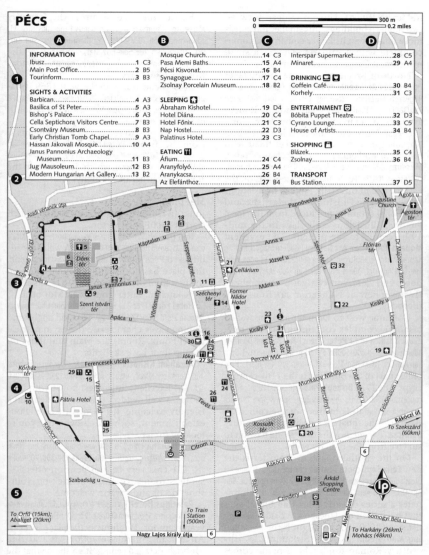

PÉCS

HUNGARY

been a Christian place of worship for a long time, but the Islamic elements inside, such as the mihrab on the southeastern wall, reveal its original identity. Constructed in the mid-16th century from the stones of an earlier church, the mosque underwent several changes of appearance over the years – including the addition of a steeple. In the

late 1930s the building was restored to its medieval form.

West along Ferencesek utcája, you'll pass the ruins of the 16th-century Turkish **Pasa Memi Baths** (Memi Pasa Fürdője) before you turn south on Rákóczi utca to get to the 16th-century **Hassan Jakovali Mosque** (Hassan Jakovali Mecset; adult/concession 500/250Ft; 9.30am-5.30pm

Wed-Sun late Mar-Oct). Though wedged between two modern buildings, this smaller mosque is more intact than its larger cousin and comes complete with a minaret. There's a small museum of Ottoman history inside.

North of Széchenyi tér, the minor **Janus Pannonius Archaeology Museum** (Janus Pannonius Régészeti Múzeum; Széchenyi tér 12; adult/concession 350/180Ft; ☺ 10am-2pm Tue-Sat) contains Roman artefacts found in the area. From here, climb Szepessy Ignéc utca and turn left (west) on Káptalan utca, which is a street lined with museums and galleries. The **Zsolnay Porcelain Museum** (Zsolnay Porcélan Múzeum; Káptalan utca 2; adult/concession 700/350Ft; ☺ 10am-5pm Tue-Sun) is on the eastern end of this strip. English translations provide a good history of the artistic and functional ceramics produced from this local factory's illustrious early days in the mid-19th century to the present. The excellent **Modern Hungarian Art Gallery** (Modern Magyar Képtár; Káptalan utca 4; adult/concession 460/230Ft; ☺ noon-6pm Tue-Sun Apr-Oct, 10am-4pm Tue-Sun Nov-Mar) is next door, and here you can get a comprehensive overview of Hungarian art from 1850 till today.

Continue west to Dóm tér and the walled bishopric complex containing the four-towered **Basilica of St Peter** (Szent Péter Bazilika; Dóm tér; adult/concession 800/500Ft; ☺ 9am-5pm Mon-Sat, 1-5pm Sun Apr-Oct, 10am-4pm Mon-Sat, 1-4pm Sun Nov-Mar). The oldest part of the building is the 11th-century crypt. The 1770 **Bishop's Palace** (Püspöki Palota; adult/concession 1500/700Ft; ☺ tours 2pm, 3pm & 4pm Thu late Jun–mid-Sep) stands in front of the cathedral. Also near the square is a nearby 15th-century **barbican** (barbakán), the only stone bastion to survive from the old city walls.

On the southern side of Dom tér is the new **Cella Septichora Visitors Centre** (Janus Pannonius utca; adult/concession 1500/800Ft; ☺ 10am-6pm Tue-Sun Apr-Oct, 10am-4pm Tue-Sun Nov-Mar), which illuminates a series of early-Christian burial sites that have been on Unesco's World Heritage list since 2000. The highlight is the so-called **Jug Mausoleum** (Korsós Sírkamra), a 4th-century Roman tomb whose name comes from a painting of a large drinking vessel with vines.

Across Janus Pannonius utca from the centre, the **early Christian tomb chapel** (Ókeresztény sírkápolna; Szent István tér 12; adult/concession 400/200Ft; ☺ 10am-6pm Tue-Sun Apr-Oct, 10am-4pm Tue-Sun Nov-Mar) dates from about AD 350 and has frescos of Adam and Eve, and Daniel in the lion's den.

East of the mausoleum is the **Csontváry Museum** (Csontváry Múzeum; Janus Pannonius utca 11; adult/concession 700/350Ft; ☺ 10am-6pm Tue-Sun Apr-Oct, 10am-4pm Tue-Sun Nov-Mar), exhibiting the works of master 19th-century painter Tivadar Kosztka Csontváry.

Pécs' beautifully preserved 1869 **synagogue** (zsinagóga; Kossuth tér; adult/concession 500/300Ft; ☺ 10am-noon & 12.45-5pm Sun-Fri May-Oct) is south of Széchenyi tér.

An easy way to see the city's highlights is from the mobile **Pécs Little Train** (Pécsi Kisvonat; ☎ 06 70 454 5610; www.pecsikisvonat.hu; adult/concession 950/500Ft; ☺ 10am-5pm), which departs from the southeast corner of Széchenyi tér.

Sleeping

Ibusz (p410) arranges private rooms, which start at 3500Ft per person.

Nap Hostel (☎ 950 684; www.naphostel.com; Király utca 23-25; dm/d from 2400/9600Ft; 🖵) A welcome addition to Pécs' budget accommodation scene, this place has dorms and a double room on the first floor of a former bank. There's also a large kitchen. Enter from Szent Mór utca.

Hotel Főnix (☎ 311 682; www.fonixhotel.hu; Hunyadi János út 2; s/d 7790/12,590Ft; 🅿 🖵) Odd angles and sloping eaves characterise the asymmetrical Hotel Főnix. Rooms are plain and those on the top floor have skylights.

Ábrahám Kishotel (☎ 510 422; www.abrahamhotel .hu; Munkácsy Mihály utca 8; s/d/tr 9100/12,000/14,000Ft; 🅿 🖵) Excellent little guest house with blue rooms, a well-tended, peaceful garden and a friendly welcome. It's owned by a religious establishment, so head elsewhere if you're looking for a party.

Hotel Diána (☎ 328 594; www.hoteldiana.hu; Tímár utca 4/a; s/d/tr/q from 9500/13,000/18,300/20,000Ft; 🅿 🖵) This very central pension offers 20 spotless rooms, comfortable kick-off-your-shoes decor and a warm welcome.

Palatinus Hotel (☎ 889 400; www.danubiushotels .com; Király utca 5; s/d from €60/80; 🅿 🖵) For art nouveau glamour, Palatinus is the place in Pécs. An amazing, marble reception has a soaring Moorish-detailed ceiling. It's a shame that the rooms are not as luxurious, but still, in Pécs, it's as good as it gets.

Eating & Drinking

Pubs, cafes and fast-food eateries line pedestrian-only Király utca.

Aranyfolyó (☎ 212 269; Váradi Antal utca 9; mains 450-750Ft; ☺ 11.30am-10pm) The two Chinese dragons guarding the door of this restaurant are a hint about the in-house cuisine. Rice and noodle dishes are a snip at 450Ft to 2100Ft.

Minaret (☎ 311 338; Ferencesek utcája 35; mains 1200-2100Ft; ☽ noon-4pm Sun-Mon, to 9pm Tue-Thu, to 11pm Fri & Sat) Boasting one of the loveliest gardens in the city, this eatery in the shadow of the Pasa Memi Baths serves tasty Hungarian favourites.

our pick Áfium (☎ 511 434; Irgalmasok utca 2; mains 1400-1900Ft; ☽ 11am-1am) With Croatia and Serbia so close, it's a wonder that more restaurants don't offer cuisine from south of the border. Don't miss the bean soup with trotters. Set lunch is 520Ft during the week.

Az Elefánthoz (☎ 216 055; Jókai tér 6; mains 1600-2100Ft) With its enormous terrace and quality Italian cuisine, this place is a sure bet for first-rate food in the centre of town. It has a wood-burning stove for making pizzas.

Aranykacsa (☎ 518 860; Teréz utca 4; mains 1620-3240Ft; ☽ 11.30am-10pm Tue-Thu, to midnight Fri & Sat, to 3pm Sun) This stunning wine restaurant takes pride in its silver service and beautiful venue. The menu offers at least eight duck dishes, including such memorables as duck ragout with honey and vegetables.

Korhely (Boltív köz 2; ☽ 11am-midnight) This outrageously popular *csapszék* (tavern) has peanuts on the table, shells on the floor, a half-dozen beers on tap and a sort of 'retro socialist meets Latin American' decor. It works.

Coffein Café (Széchenyi tér 9; ☽ 8am-midnight Mon-Thu, 8am-2am Fri & Sat, 10am-10pm Sun) For the best views across Széchenyi tér to the Mosque Church and Király utca, find a perch at this cool cafe done up in the warmest of colours.

Get self-catering supplies at the **Interspar supermarket** (Bajcsy-Zsilinszky utca 11; ☽ 7am-9pm Mon-Thu & Sat, 7am-10pm Fri, 8am-7pm Sun) in the basement of the Árkád shopping centre.

Entertainment

Pécs has well-established opera and ballet companies as well as a symphony orchestra. Tourinform has schedule information. The free biweekly *Pécsi Est* also lists what's on around town.

House of Artists (Művészetek Háza; ☎ 522 834; www.pmh.hu; Széchenyi tér 7-8) This is a cultural venue that hosts classical-music performances. A schedule is posted outside.

Bóbita Puppet Theatre (Bóbita Bábszínház; ☎ 210 301; www.bobita.hu; Mária utca 18) Somewhere John Malkovich would be proud to perform, the Bóbita is not just for kids.

Cyrano Lounge (Czindery utca 6; ☽ 8pm-5am Fri & Sat) A big nightclub, popular with the in crowd, next to the big Árkád shopping centre.

Shopping

Pécs has been known for its leatherwork since Turkish times, and you can pick up a few bargains around the city. Try **Blázek** (☎ 332 460; Teréz utca 1), which deals mainly in handbags and wallets. **Zsolnay** (☎ 310 220; Jókai tér 2) has a porcelain outlet south of Széchenyi tér.

Getting There & Away

Buses for Harkány (900Ft, 1½ hours) leave regularly throughout the day. At least five buses a day connect Pécs with Budapest (3010Ft, 4½ hours), three with Siófok (2040Ft, three hours) and eight with Szeged (3010Ft, 4½ hours).

Pécs is on a main rail line with Budapest's Déli train station (3230Ft, 3½ hours, nine daily). Three daily trains run from Pécs to Osijek (two hours) in Croatia, with one continuing to the Bosnian capital, Sarajevo (nine hours).

AROUND PÉCS

The hot springs at **Harkány** (www.harkany.hu, in Hungarian), 26km south of Pécs, have medicinal waters with the richest sulphuric content in Hungary. The indoor and outdoor baths and pools of **Gyógyfürdő** (Thermal Baths; ☎ 480 251; www.harkanyfurdo.hu; Kossuth Lajos utca 7; adult/concession 2250/1590Ft; ☽ 9am-8pm) range in temperature from 26°C to 33°C in summer and from 33°C to 35°C in winter. Consider booking a spa service, mud bath or massage. The town is basically the thermal bath complex in a 12-hectare park surrounded by hotels and restaurants. Buses between Harkány and Pécs (900Ft, 1½ hours) depart at least half-hourly. The Harkány bus station is at the southeast corner of the park.

SOUTHEASTERN HUNGARY

Like the Outback for Australians or the Old West for Americans, the Nagyalföld (Great Plain) holds a romantic appeal for Hungarians. Images of shepherds guiding their flocks with moplike *puli* dogs and cowboys riding across the *puszta* are scattered throughout the nation's poetry and painting. The Great Plain covers some 45,000 sq km east and southeast of Budapest. Beyond its big sky country appeal, the Great Plain is also home to cities of graceful architecture, winding rivers and easygoing afternoons.

KECSKEMÉT
☎ 76 / pop 103,000

Located about halfway between Budapest and Szeged, Kecskemét (*kech*-kah-mate) is a green, pedestrian-friendly city with interesting art nouveau architecture. Colourful buildings, fine small museums and the region's excellent *barackpálinka* (apricot brandy) beckon. And Kiskunsági Nemzeti Park, the *puszta* of the Southern Plain, is right at the back door. Day-trip opportunities include hiking in the sandy, juniper-covered hills, a horse show at Bugac, or a visit to one of the area's many horse farms.

Orientation & Information

Central Kecskemét is made up of squares that run into one another, and consequently it's hard to tell them apart. The main bus and train stations are opposite each other

in József Katona Park. A 10-minute walk southwest along Nagykőrösi utca brings you to the first of the squares, Szabadság tér.

Datanet Internet Café (Kossuth tér 6-7; per hr 300Ft; ☻ 9am-10pm) Internet access.

Ibusz (☎ 486 955; Malom Centre, Korona utca 2; ☻ 8am-5pm Mon-Fri Sep-Jun, 8am-5pm Mon-Fri, 9am-1pm Sat Jul-Aug) Arranges private rooms.

Main post office (Kálvin tér 10)

OTP Bank (Malom Centre, Korona utca 2)

Tourinform (☎ 481 065; kecskemet@tourinform.hu; Kossuth tér 1; ☻ 8am-7pm Mon-Fri, 10am-8pm Sat & Sun Jul-Aug, 8am-6pm Mon-Fri Sep-Jun) In the northeastern corner of the large Town Hall.

Sights

Walk around the parklike squares, starting at Szabadság tér, and admire the eclectic buildings, including the Technicolor art nouveau style of the 1902 **Ornamental Palace** (Cifrapalota; Rákóczi út 1), recently refurbished and covered in multicoloured majolica tiles. Check out the wonderful interiors of the **Kecskemét Gallery** (Kecskeméti Képtár; Rákóczi út 1; adult/concession 300/150Ft; ☻ 10am-5pm Tue-Sat, 1.30-5pm Sun) here. Across the street, the Moorish building is the

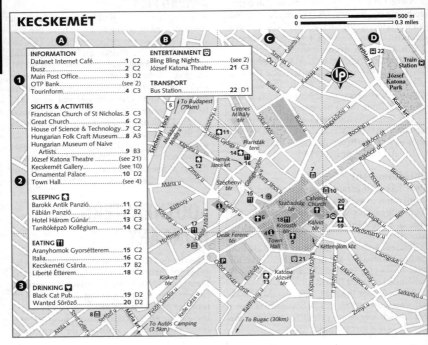

KECSKEMÉT

0 ————— 500 m
0 ————— 0.3 miles

INFORMATION
Datanet Internet Café.............1 C2
Ibusz.................................2 C2
Main Post Office....................3 D2
OTP Bank..........................(see 2)
Tourinform..........................4 C3

SIGHTS & ACTIVITIES
Franciscan Church of St Nicholas.5 C3
Great Church.......................6 C2
House of Science & Technology...7 D2
Hungarian Folk Craft Museum....8 A3
Hungarian Museum of Naïve
    Artists.............................9 B3
József Katona Theatre ....(see 21)
Kecskemét Gallery..............(see 10)
Ornamental Palace................10 D2
Town Hall.........................(see 4)

SLEEPING
Barokk Antik Panzió................11 C2
Fábián Panzió.......................12 B2
Hotel Három Gúnár.................13 C3
Tanítóképző Kollégium.............14 C2

EATING
Aranyhomok Gyorsétterem.......15 C2
Italia.................................16 C2
Kecskeméti Csárda................17 B2
Liberté Étterem....................18 C2

DRINKING
Black Cat Pub......................19 D2
Wanted Söröző....................20 D2

ENTERTAINMENT
Bling Bling Nights................(see 2)
József Katona Theatre.........21 C3

TRANSPORT
Bus Station........................22 D1

To Budapest (79km)

Train Station

József Katona Park

To Bugac (30km)

To Autós Camping (3.5km)

House of Science & Technology (Tudomány és Technika Háza; Rákóczi út 2; adult/concession 200/100Ft; ⊙ 8am-4pm Mon-Fri). This former synagogue is now an exhibition hall.

Kossuth tér is dominated by the massive 1897 art nouveau **Town Hall** (Városháza), which is flanked by the baroque **Great Church** (Nagytemplom; Kossuth tér 2; ⊙ 9am-noon & 3-6pm Tue-Sun May-Sep, 9am-noon Tue-Sun Oct-Apr) and the earlier **Franciscan Church of St Nicholas** (Szent Miklós Templom), dating from the 13th century. Nearby is the magnificent 1896 **József Katona Theatre** (Katona József Színház; ☎ 483 283; Katona József tér 5), a neobaroque performance venue with a statue of the Trinity (1742) in front of it.

The town's museums are scattered around the main squares' periphery. Go first to the **Hungarian Museum of Naive Artists** (Magyar Naiv Müvészek; Gáspár András utca 11; adult/concession 200/100Ft; ⊙ 10am-5pm Tue-Sun mid-Mar–Oct), in the Stork House (1730) northwest off Petőfi Sándor utca. It has an impressive small collection. Further to the southwest, the **Hungarian Folk Craft Museum** (Népi Iparmüvészeti Múzeum; Serfőző utca 19/a; adult/concession 300/150Ft; ⊙ 10am-5pm Tue-Sat Feb-Nov) has a definitive collection of regional embroidery, weaving and textiles, as well as some furniture, woodcarving and agricultural tools. A few handicrafts are for sale at the entrance.

Sleeping

Tourinform can help you locate the numerous colleges that offer dormitory accommodation in July and August, and the Ibusz agency arranges private rooms (see opposite).

Autós Camping (☎ 329 398; Csabay Géza körút 5; camp sites per person/tent 800/700Ft; bungalows 5000-8000Ft; ⊙ May-Sep) Neat rows of tents and bungalows (with kitchen and bathroom, but no hot water) line this camping ground near the Aqua Park, 3km from centre. Don't expect much shade. Take bus 1 to get southwest of town.

Tanítóképző Kollégium (Teachers' College; ☎ 486 977; loveikollegium@tfk.kefo.hu; Piaristák tere 4; s/d 2500/5000Ft; ⊙ mid-Jun–Aug) A good choice among the academic accommodation options, with a central location.

Barokk Antik Panzió (☎ 260 3215; www.barokk antik-panzio.hu; Fráter György utca 17; s/d 7500/10,500Ft) A sombre painting or two lends a bit of an old-world feel, but we wouldn't say the rooms have actual antiques. Thankfully, they do have minibars and very modern bathrooms.

our pick **Fábián Panzió** (☎ 477 677; www.panzio fabian.hu; Kápolna utca 14; s/d from 8800/11,000Ft; ⊠ ⌨) The world-travelling family that owns this pretty-in-pink guest house knows how to treat a visitor well. Friendly staff help their guests plan each day's excursions, teapots are available for in-room use, wireless internet is free, and bikes are available for hire. Simply luvverly.

Hotel Három Gúnár (☎ 483 611; Batthyány utca 1; s/d 10,500/13,800Ft; ⊠) Four multihued town houses – flowerboxes and all – have been transformed to contain 49 smallish rooms (the best are Nos 306 to 308). Simple veneer furnishings in the rooms are less cheery than the exterior facade. There's an on-site restaurant.

Eating & Drinking

Aranyhomok Gyorsétterem (☎ 503 730; Kossuth tér 3; mains 300-600Ft; ⊙ 24hr) Locals love this quick and tasty self-service cafeteria on the ground floor of the city's ugliest hotel. The staff keep the food fresh, despite being open round the clock.

Italia (☎ 484 627; Hornyik János körút 4; mains 1200-1400Ft) Italia is a little short on atmosphere but does a roaring trade with students from the nearby Teachers' College. Order pizza, pasta or any fried-pork variation you can imagine.

our pick **Liberté Étterem** (☎ 509 175; Szabadság tér 2; mains 1200-2000Ft) Artistic presentations come with your order, whether it's the traditional stuffed cabbage or the mixed sautéed chicken with aubergine. This is modern Hungarian done well. Its outside tables have the best seats in town for people-watching.

Kecskeméti Csárda (☎ 488 686; Kölcsey utca 7; mains 1500-2000Ft) Restaurant trading on folksy charm. It goes over the top with rustic fishing gear on the walls and Romani music at weekends.

For drinkies, the Western-themed pub **Wanted Söröző** (Csányi János körút 4; ⊙ 10am-midnight Mon-Sat, from 4pm Sun) sits handily across from the more alternative **Black Cat Pub** (Csányi János körút 6; ⊙ 11am-midnight Sun-Thu, to 2am Fri & Sat), making for quite the convivial corner.

Entertainment

Tourinform has a list of what concerts and performances are on, or check out the free weekly magazine *Kecskeméti Est*.

József Katona Theatre (Katona József Színház; ☎ 483 283; www.katonaj.hu; Katona József tér 5) Experience operettas and symphony performances in this grand 19th-century building.

HUNGARY

Bling Bling Nights (www.blingblingnights.hu; Malom, Korona tér 2) Hip hop, house, R&B – the nightclub atop Malom Shopping Centre is definitely eclectic. DJs host most nights, but there are occasional live concerts.

Getting There & Away

Frequent buses depart for Budapest (1350Ft, 1½ hours, hourly) and for Szeged (1350Ft, 1¾ hours, hourly). A direct rail line links Kecskemét to Budapest's Nyugati train station (1770Ft, 1½ hours, hourly) and Szeged (1350Ft, one hour, hourly).

KISKUNSÁGI NEMZETI PARK

Totalling 76,000 hectares, **Kiskunsági Nemzeti Park** (Kiskunság National Park; www.knp.hu) consists of half a dozen 'islands' of protected land. Much of the park's alkaline ponds and sand dunes are off limits. Bugac (*boo*-gats) village, about 30km southwest of Kecskemét, is the most accessible part of the park.

From the village, walk, drive, or ride a **horse-driven carriage** (adult/concession incl horse show 2900/1700Ft; ☺ 11.15pm & 12.15pm May–Oct) along the 1.5km-long sandy track to the **Herder Museum** (admission free; ☺ 10am–5pm May–Oct), a circular structure designed to look like a horse-driven dry mill. The highlight of the museum is the popular **horse show** (admission 1400Ft; ☺ 12.15pm & 1.15pm May–Oct, extra show 3.15pm Jun–Aug). Once the show starts, the horse herders crack their whips, race one another bareback and ride 'five-in-hand', a breathtaking performance in which one *csikós* (cowboy) gallops five horses at full speed while standing on the backs of the rear two.

Afterwards, the food is surprisingly good at the kitschy **Bugaci Karikás Csárda** (☎ 575 112; Nagybugac 135; mains 1600–2100Ft; ☺ 8am–8pm May–Oct), next to the park entrance. The *gulyás* is hearty and the accompanying folk-music ensemble will get your feet tapping on the terrace.

The best way to get to Bugac is by bus from Kecskemét (600Ft, 50 minutes). The 11am bus from the main terminal gets you to the park entrance around noon. A bus returns directly from Bugac to Kecskemét at 3.50pm on weekdays. Otherwise catch a bus to Kiskunfélegyháza or Jakabszállás, and change there for Kecskemét (approximately hourly).

SZEGED

☎ 62 / pop 177,000

It's hard to decide what's most appealing about Szeged (*seh*-ged). Perhaps it's the shady green main square, perhaps the abundant sidewalk cafe seating in its pedestrian zone that seems to stretch on forever or perhaps it's the stimulating architecture of its attractive palaces. But it could also be its lively vibe – a product of year-round cultural performances and its energetic student population.

Szeged sits astride the Tisza River, which almost wiped the city off the map in 1879 via a major flood. However, the town bounced back with a vengeance and an eye for uniform architecture.

Orientation & Information

The train station is south of the city centre on Indóház tér; from here, tram 1 takes you along Boldogasszony sugárút into the centre of town. The bus station, on Mars tér, is west of the centre within easy walking distance via pedestrian-only Mikszáth Kálmán utca.

Tourinform (☎ 488 699; http://tip.szegedvaros.hu; Dugonics tér 2; ☺ 9am–5pm Mon–Fri, to 1pm Sat) Tourist office hidden in a courtyard.

Cyber Arena (Híd utca 1; per hr 400Ft; ☺ 24hr) Internet access with Skype set-ups and cheap international phonecards.

Main post office (Széchenyi tér 1)

OTP Bank (Klauzál tér 4)

Sights & Activities

East of Széchenyi tér, the huge, neoclassical **Ferenc Móra Museum** (Móra Ferenc Múzeum; www.mfm.u-szeged.hu; Roosevelt tér 1; adult/concession 600/300Ft; ☺ 10am–5pm Tue-Sun) overlooks the Tisza River. The museum contains a colourful collection of folk art from Csongrád County with descriptions in several languages and an exhibit of 7th-century gold work by the Avar, a mysterious people who are thought to have originated somewhere in Central Asia. But the best exhibit showcases an even more obscure group, the Sarmatians, who originated in present-day Iran.

To the west, the **New Synagogue** (Új Zsinagóga; www.zsinagoga.szeged.hu; Gutenberg utca 13; adult/concession 300/150Ft; ☺ 10am–noon & 1-5pm Sun-Fri Apr-Sep, 10am-2pm Sun-Fri Oct-Mar) is the most beautiful Jewish house of worship in Hungary and is still in use. An ornate blue and gold-painted interior graces the 1903 art nouveau building. The nearby **Old Synagogue** (Ó Zsinagóga; Hajnóczy utca 12) was built in 1843.

The **Szeged Open-Air Festival** (☎ 541 205; www.szegediszabadteri.hu) is held in Dom tér from mid-July to late August. Running along three sides

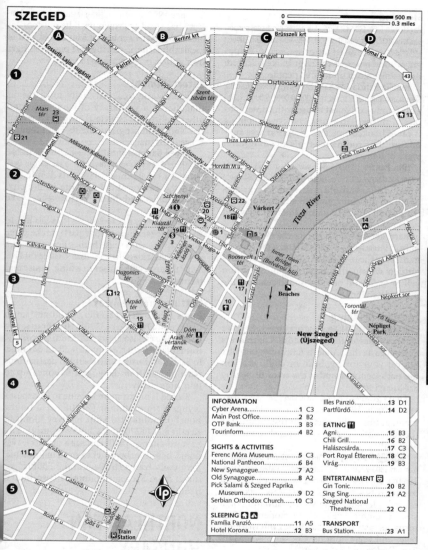

SZEGED

INFORMATION
Cyber Arena	1	C3
Main Post Office	2	B2
OTP Bank	3	B3
Tourinform	4	B2

SIGHTS & ACTIVITIES
Ferenc Móra Museum	5	C3
National Pantheon	6	B4
New Synagogue	7	A2
Old Synagogue	8	A2
Pick Salami & Szeged Paprika Museum	9	D2
Serbian Orthodox Church	10	C3

SLEEPING
Família Panzió	11	A5
Hotel Korona	12	B3
Illes Panzió	13	D1
Partfürdő	14	D2

EATING
Agni	15	B3
Chili Grill	16	B2
Halászcsárda	17	C3
Port Royal Étterem	18	C2
Virág	19	B3

ENTERTAINMENT
Gin Tonic	20	B2
Sing Sing	21	A2
Szeged National Theatre	22	C2

TRANSPORT
Bus Station	23	A1

HUNGARY

of the square is the **National Pantheon** (Nemzeti Emlékcsarnok), with statues and reliefs of 80 Hungarian notables. One block northeast, inside the **Serbian Orthodox Church** (Szerb Ortodox Templom; adult/concession 200/150Ft; 8am-4pm), have a look at the fantastic iconostasis – a central gold 'tree' with 60 icons hanging off its branches.

Just north of the Old Town ring road is the **Pick Salami & Szeged Paprika Museum** (Pick Szalámi és Szegedi Paprika Múzeum; Felső Tisza-part 10; adult/concession 3 50/250Ft; 3-6pm Mon, 9am-5pm Tue-Fri, 9am-noon Sat). Two floors of exhibits show traditional methods of salami production. There's a small gift stand in the museum and a butcher shop around the corner in this factory building.

Sleeping

Partfürdő (☎ 430 843; Közép-kikötő sor; camp sites per person/tent 990/350Ft; r 4600-6900Ft; bungalows 8,000-12,000Ft; ☼ mid-May–Sep; ☻) This green, grassy camping ground is across the river in New Szeged. Bungalows sleep up to four people.

Família Panzió (☎ 411 122; www.familiapanzio.hu; Szentháromság utca 71; s/d/tr 8000/10,000/15,000Ft; ☻) This family-run guest house with contemporary furnishings in a great Old Town building is often booked up. The reception area may be dim, but rooms have high ceilings and loads of light.

Illes Panzió (☎ 315 641; www.illespanzio-vadaszterem.hu; Maros utca 37; r 9900-12,900Ft; ☻ ☐ ☻) This refurbished old mansion 10 minutes north of the centre has fresh, clean rooms with wood panels, cool tiled floors, TVs and polished woodwork.

Hotel Korona (☎ 555 787; www.hotelkoronaszeged.hu; Petőfi Sándor sgt 4; s/d 13,800/18,000Ft; ☻) You can hardly see the original 1883 building outlines hidden within this modern hotel. Lemon yellow walls and blond wood accentuate the up-to-date vibe.

Eating & Drinking

Chili Grill (☎ 317 344; Nagy Jenő utca 4; mains 600-1000Ft; ☼ 11am-10pm Mon-Fri, 11am-6pm Sat) There *are* a few tables at this modern takeaway, but why not eat your turkey, bean or chilli wrap on the park benches under the trees of nearby Széchenyi tér?

Agni (☎ 477 739; Tisza Lajos körút 76; mains 1000-1300Ft) Daily lunch specials round out the menu at this little vegetarian restaurant. Try the substantial paprika-and-mushroom stew with millet.

our pick **Port Royal Étterem** (☎ 547 988; Stefánia 4; mains 1300-2200Ft; ☼ 11am-midnight Mon-Thu, 11am-2am Fri & Sat, 11am-11pm Sun) Tropical plants and live parrots are enough reason to make this eatery's pleasant patio your destination on a steamy summer evening. The modern kitchen turns out tasty traditional dishes, international faves and vegie options. Cocktails served till 2am Friday and Saturday.

Halászcsárda (☎ 555 980; Roosevelt tér 14; mains 2000-3500Ft) An institution that knows how to prepare the best fish dish in town – whole roasted pike with garlic, accompanied by pan-fried frog legs and fillet of carp soup. Although there are white tablecloths and waiters are dressed to the nines, the outdoor terrace is pretty casual.

Since 1922, cafe-bar **Virág** (Klauzál tér 1; ☼ 8am-10pm) has steadily grown until its outdoor tables have taken over half of Klauzál tér. Lots of locals think this is still the best place to linger over coffee, or something harder.

Entertainment

Szeged's status as a university town means that there's a vast array of bars, clubs and other nightspots, especially around Dugonics tér. Nightclub programs are listed in the free *Szegedi Est* magazine.

Szeged National Theatre (Szegedi Nemzeti Színház; ☎ 479 279; www.szinhaz.szeged.hu, in Hungarian; Deák Ferenc utca 12-14) Since 1886, this venue has been the centre of cultural life in the city. Opera, ballet and drama performances take to its stage.

Sing Sing (Mars tér C pavilion; ☼ 11pm-5am Wed, Fri & Sat) Huge warehouse rave parties take place here, replete with sexy themes and dancers.

Gin Tonic (Széchenyi tér 1; ☼ 10pm-4am Wed-Fri) This central dance club pulses to a funk, house and techno beat.

Getting There & Away

Buses run to Pécs (2780Ft, 4¼ hours, seven daily) and Debrecen (3230Ft, five hours, two daily). Buses also head for Arad, across the Romanian border, daily at 6.30am Monday to Saturday. Buses run to Serbian destinations Novi Sad at 4pm daily, and Subotica up to four times daily.

Szeged is on the main rail line to Budapest's Nyugati train station (2780Ft, 2¾ hours, hourly); trains also stop halfway along in Kecskemét (1770Ft, 1¼ hours, hourly). You have to change in Békéscsaba (1500Ft, two hours, half-hourly) to get to Arad in Romania. Two daily trains (6.50am and 12.30pm) go direct from Szeged to Subotica (two hours) in Serbia.

NORTHEASTERN HUNGARY

If ever a Hungarian wine were world-famous, it would be tokay. And this is where it comes from, a region of Hungary containing microclimates conducive to wine production. The chain of wooded hills in the northeast constitutes the foothills of the Carpathian Mountains, which stretch along the Hungarian border with Slovakia. Though you'll definitely notice the rise in elevation, Hungary's highest peak of Kékes is still only a proverbial bump in the road at 1014m. The highlights here are wine towns Eger and Tokaj, and Szilvásvárad – the Hungarian home of the snow-white Lipizzaner horse.

EGER

☎ 36 / pop 58,300

Filled with wonderfully preserved baroque architecture, Eger (*egg*-air) is a jewel box of a town containing gems aplenty. Explore the bloody history of Turkish conquest and defeat at its hilltop castle, climb a Turkish minaret, hear an organ performance at the ornate basilica…but best of all, go from cellar to cellar in the Valley of Beautiful Women (yes, it's really called that), tasting the celebrated Bull's Blood wine where it's made.

It was here in 1552 that Hungarian defenders temporarily stopped the Turkish advance into Western Europe and helped preserve Hungary's identity (see boxed text, p421). However, the persistent Ottomans returned in 1596 and finally captured Eger Castle. They were evicted in 1687.

In the 18th century, Eger played a central role in Ferenc Rákóczi II's attempt to overthrow the Habsburgs, and it was then that a large part of the castle was razed by the Austrians. Eger has some of Hungary's finest architecture, especially examples of Copf (Zopf in Hungarian), a transitional style between late baroque and neoclassicism found only in central Europe.

Orientation & Information

The main train station is a 15-minute walk south of town, on Vasút utca, just east of Deák Ferenc utca. Egervár train station, which serves Szilvásvárad and other points north, is a five-minute walk north of the castle along Vécseyvölgy utca. The bus station is west of Széchenyi István utca, Eger's main drag.

Egri Est Café (Széchenyi István utca 16; per hr 300Ft; ☽ 11am-midnight Sun-Thu, to 2am Fri & Sat) Cafe-bar with internet access.

OTP Bank (Széchenyi István utca 2)

Post office (Széchenyi István utca 22; ☽ 8am-8pm Mon-Fri, to 1pm Sat)

Tourinform (☎ 517 715; eger@tourinform.hu; Bajcsy-Zsilinszky utca 9; ☽ 9am-5pm Mon-Fri, to 1pm Sat & Sun mid-Jun–mid-Sep, closed Sun mid-Sep–mid-Jun)

Sights & Activities

The most striking attraction and the best views of town are from **Eger Castle** (Egri Vár; www.egrivar .hu; Vár 1; adult/concession incl museum 1200/600Ft; ☽ 9am-5pm Tue-Sun Apr-Oct, 10am-4pm Tue-Sun Nov-Mar), a huge walled complex at the top of the hill off Dósza tér. First fortified after an early Mongol invasion in the 13th century, the earliest ruins on site are the foundations of St John's Cathedral, built in the 12th century and destroyed by the Turks. The excellent **István Dobó Castle Museum** (Dobó István Vármuzeum), inside the Bishop's Palace (1470) within the castle grounds, explores the history and development of the castle and the town. Other on-site exhibits such as the **Waxworks** (Panoptikum; adult/concession 400/300Ft) and the **Minting Exhibit** (Éremverde; adult/concession 400/300Ft) cost extra. Even on days when the museums are closed, you can walk around the grounds and battlements and enjoy the views if you buy a *sétaljegy* (strolling ticket, adult/concession 400/200Ft).

A surprise awaits you west of the castle hill: a 40m-high **minaret** (Knézich Károly utca; admission 200Ft; ☽ 10am-6pm Apr-Oct), minus the mosque, is allegedly Europe's northernmost remains of the Ottoman invasion in the 16th century. The **Minorite Church** (Minorita Templom; Dobó István tér; admission free; ☽ 9am-5pm Tue-Sun), built in 1771, is a glorious baroque building. In the square in front are statues of national hero István Dobó and his comrades-in-arms routing the Turks in 1552.

The first thing you see as you come into town from the bus or train station is the neoclassical **Eger Basilica** (Egri Bazilika; Pyrker János tér 1), built in 1836. Directly opposite is the Copf-style **Lyceum** (Líceum; Esterházy tér 1; admission free; ☽ 9.30am-3.30pm Tue-Sun Apr-Sep, 9.30am-1pm Sat & Sun Oct-Mar), dating from 1765, with a 20,000-volume frescoed **library** (könyvetár; adult/concession 700/350Ft) on the 1st floor and an 18th-century observatory in the **Astronomy Museum** (Csillagászati Múzeum; adult/concession 800/650Ft) on the 6th floor. Climb three more floors up to the observation deck for a great view of the city and to try out the camera obscura, the 'eye of Eger', designed in 1776 to entertain the locals.

The Archbishop's Garden was once the private reserve of papal princes, but today the park is open to the public. Inside the park, the **City Thermal Baths** (Városi Térmalfürdő; ☎ 413 356; Fürdő utca 1-3; adult/concession 1250/1050Ft; ☽ 6am-8pm Apr-Oct, 9am-7pm Nov-Mar) has both open-air and

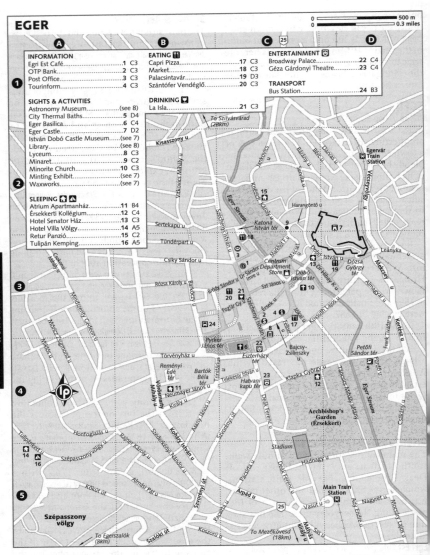

EGER

covered pools with different temperatures and mineral contents. From June to August you can pay 700Ft extra to get into the modern 'adventure' complex with bubbling massage pools and a castle-themed kids' pool. By the time you read this, the 1617 Turkish Bath (Török Fürdő) should have reopened after a total reconstruction.

To sample Eger's wine, visit the extravagantly named **Szépasszony völgy** (Valley of the Beautiful Women; off Király utca), home to dozens of small wine cellars that truck in, store and sell Bull's Blood and other regional red and white wines. Walk the horseshoe-shaped street through the valley and stop in front of one that strikes your fancy and ask ('*meg-*

AS STRONG AS A BULL

The story of the Turkish attempt to take Eger Castle is the stuff of legend. Under the command of István Dobó, a mixed bag of 2000 soldiers held out against more than 100,000 Turks for a month in 1552. As every Hungarian kid in short trousers can tell you, the women of Eger played a crucial role in the battle, pouring boiling oil and pitch on the invaders from the ramparts.

If we're to believe the tale, it seems that Dobó sustained his weary troops with a ruby-red vintage of the town's wine. When they fought on with increased vigour – and stained beards – rumours began to circulate among the Turks that the defenders were gaining strength by drinking the blood of bulls. The invaders departed, and the legend of Bikavér (Bull's Blood) was born.

---

kosztólhatok?') to taste their wares (100Ft per decilitre). If you want wine to go, you can bring an empty bottle and have it filled for about 350Ft per litre. The cellar's outdoor tables fill up on a late summer afternoon as locals cook *gulyás* in the park and strains from a gypsy violinist float up from the restaurants at the valley's entrance. A taxi back to the centre costs about 1000Ft.

Sleeping

Tourinform has a glossy booklet of accommodation, including private rooms, for the city and the surrounding area.

Tulipán Kemping (☎ 410 580; Szépasszony völgy utca 71; camp sites per person 1450Ft, bungalows 6000Ft; 🖭) Many of the camping sites here are in an open, shadeless field, but you're surrounded by vineyards and are stumbling distance from the valley wine cellars. The bungalows are simple cabins, without bathrooms or kitchens.

Érsekkerti Kollégium (Archbishop's Garden College; ☎ 520 432; Klapka György utca 12; dm 3000Ft) A number of colleges offer dormitory accommodation from June to August; this is the most central option, in an Old Town building full of character.

our pick **Retur Panzió** (☎ 416 650; www.returven deghaz.hu; Knézich Károly utca 18; s/d 4000/6000Ft) You couldn't find sweeter hosts than the daughter and mother who own this pension. It's in a central location and has a cheery shared kitchen/eating area and a huge garden with tables and fire pit at your disposal.

Atrium Apartmanház (☎ 418 427; www.atriumapart ment.eu; Neumayer János út 8; s/d/tr apt 6500/10,000/12,500Ft; 🖭 🖳) Your home in the city. Each loft apartment has at least one bedroom, a kitchenette, and cool tile floors.

Hotel Villa Völgy (☎ 321 664; www.hotelvillavolgy hu; Tulipánkert utca 5; s/d 12,900/17,500Ft; 🖭) Awaken to a view of the vineyards in this classy, modern-design villa situated in the wine valley. Neoclassical columns surround the glass-enclosed pool.

Hotel Senator Ház (☎ 320 466; www.senatorhaz.hu; Dobó István tér 11; s/d 15,000/19,000Ft; 🖭) Warm and cosy rooms with traditional white furnishings fill the upper floors of this delightful 18th-century inn on Eger's main square. The ground floor is shared by a quality restaurant and a reception area that could easily moonlight as a history museum.

Eating & Drinking

At the base of Szépasszony völgy utca there are numerous small terrace *büfé* (snack bars) that resemble food stands but employ a waiter to serve you at your picnic table. There are also lots of restaurants and cafes along pedestrianised Széchenyi István utca in town. The area is known for its *pistrang* (trout) dishes.

Capri Pizza (☎ 410 877; Bajcsy-Zsilinszky utca 4; mains 550-1100Ft) Beans feature on a surprising number of the pizzas at this hole-in-the-wall eatery. White pizzas (sans sauce) and vegetarian options available.

our pick **Palacsintavár** (☎ 413 986; Dobó István utca 9; mains 1400-1600Ft) Pop art lines the walls, and groovy music provides the soundtrack to this eclectic eatery. Entrée-sized *palacsintak* (crêpelike pancakes) are served with an abundance of fresh vegetables and range in flavour from Asian to Italian.

Szántófer Vendéglő (☎ 517 298; Bródy utca 3; mains 1400-1800Ft; 🕐 8am-10pm) The best choice in town for hearty, homestyle Hungarian food. Farming equipment and cooking utensils hang on the walls, and the covered courtyard out back is perfect for escaping the heat.

La Isla (cnr Széchenyi & Foglár utca; 🕐 10am-midnight Sun-Thu, to 2am Fri & Sat) As much a Latin cocktail bar as a cafe, this is a fine place to kick back after a hard day's sightseeing.

Head to the covered **market** (piac; Katona István tér; 6am-6pm Mon-Fri, to 1pm Sat, to 10am Sun) to buy fruit, vegetables, meat and bread.

Entertainment

The Tourinform office can tell you what concerts and musicals are on. The free *Egri Est* magazine has nightlife listings.

Géza Gárdonyi Theatre (Gárdonyi Géza Színház; 310 026; Hatvani kapu tér 4) Dance, opera and drama are staged at this theatre.

Broadway Palace (Pyrker János tér 3; 10pm-6am Wed, Fri & Sat) This bizarre, cavernous dance club beneath the cathedral's steps parties hard on weekends.

Getting There & Away

Hourly buses make the trip from Eger to Szilvásvárad (450Ft, 45 minutes). Other destinations include Kecskemét (2060Ft, 4½ hours, three daily) and Szeged (3220Ft, 5¾ hours, two daily). To get to Tokaj by bus, you have to go past it to Nyíregyháza and get another bus back.

Up to seven direct trains a day head to Budapest's Keleti train station (2290Ft, 2½ hours). Otherwise, Eger is on a minor train line linking Putnok and Füzesabony, so you have to change at the latter for Debrecen (1770Ft, three hours). You can also catch infrequent trains to Szilvásvárad (525Ft, one hour, six daily), but at the time of research this service was threatened with discontinuation.

SZILVÁSVÁRAD

36 / pop 1750

Home to graceful white stallions, carriage races, a narrow-gauge train and forest trails, Szilvásvárad makes an excellent day's excursion from Eger, 28km to the south. The town hides in the Bükk Hills, most of which fall within the 43,000-hectare **Bükk Nemzeti Park**. The village has an **information stand** (www.szil vasvarad.hu; Szalajka-völgy; 10am-6pm Jun-Oct) in high season; at other times, check with the Tourinform office in Eger (p419).

The bus from Eger will drop you off in the centre on Egri út. You get off the train at Szilvásvárad-Szalajkavölgy, the first of the town's two stations. Follow Egri út east and then north for about 10 minutes into town. At the turn, if you go right instead, you'll get to the valley.

Learn more about the famous Lipizzaner horses at the **Lipcsai Múzeum** (355 135; Park utca 8; adult/concession 400/200Ft; 9am-noon & 1-4pm Thu-Sun). Exhibits focus on bloodlines, but the real sight is the breeding mares who live here in an 18th-century stable.

Call a day ahead to arrange a carriage (from 5000Ft per hour) or a horseback ride at the **Lipizzaner State Stud Farm** (Lipicai Állami Ménesgazdaság; 564 400; www.menesgazdasag.hu; Fenyves utca; adult/concession 300/200Ft; 10am-noon & 2-4pm Thu-Sun).

At the entrance of Szalajka völgy there are restaurants, souvenir shops and tracks where Lipizzaner coaches race some summer weekends. You can park here for 100Ft per hour. Hike from here further into the valley, or take a ride on the **narrow-gauge railway** (keskeny nyomtávú vasút; Szalajka-völgy 6; adult/concession one-way 300/150Ft; Apr-Oct). The train makes the journey seven times daily from May to September (10 times daily on the weekend). Departures in April and October leave when enough people gather.

Hourly buses connect Szilvásvárad and Eger (405Ft, 45 minutes), but there's been talk of discontinuing service on the rail line from Eger (525Ft, one hour). At the time of research, there were six trains a day, but none between 10am and 2pm.

TOKAJ

47 / pop 5100

The sweet and sultry wines produced here have been around for centuries, thanks to the area's volcanic soil and unique microclimate, which promotes the growth of *Botrytis cinerea* (noble rot) on the grapes. The result is Tokaji Aszú, a world-class dessert wine.

Today Tokaj is a picturesque little town of old buildings, wine cellars and nesting storks. The 66-sq-km Tokaj-Hegyalja wine-producing region, a microclimate along the southern and eastern edges of the Zemplén Hills, was declared a World Heritage site in 2002.

Orientation & Information

Trains arrive 1200m south of the town centre; walk north on Baross Gábor utca and turn left on Bajcsy-Zsilinszky út, which turns into Rákóczi út, the main thoroughfare. The bus station is much more convenient, in town on Seráz utca. **Tourinform** (552 070; www.tokaj .hu; Serház utca 1; 9am-6pm Mon-Fri, 10am-7pm Sat & Sun Jun-Aug, 9am-5pm Mon-Fri Sep-May) is just off Rákóczi út.

Sights & Activities

Start at the **Tokaj Museum** (Tokaji Múzeum; Bethlen Gábor utca 13; adult/concession 400/200Ft; ☽ 10am-4pm Tue-Sun), which leaves nothing unsaid about the history of Tokaj, the region and its wines. After you're thoroughly knowledgeable, head to the 600-year-old **Rákóczi Cellar** (Rákóczi Pince; Kossuth tér 15; ☽ 11am-7pm) for a tasting and a tour. Bottles of wine mature underground in the long cavelike corridors (one measures 28m by 10m). A flight of six Tokaj wines costs about 2600Ft. The correct order of sampling Tokaj wines is: Furmint, dry Szamorodni, sweet Szamorodni and then the Aszú wines, moving from three to six *puttony*, the measurement used for sweetness. Six, by the way, is the sweetest.

Smaller cellars line Hegyalja utca, off Bajcsy-Zsilinszky utca at the base of the vine-covered hill above the train station. A small, wheeled **wine train** (per ride 500Ft; ☽ May-Oct) departs from Tourinform at varying hours and rolls around town, allowing time to visit cellars.

Other town attractions include the 19th-century eclectic **Great Synagogue** (Nagy Zsinagóga; Serház utca 55). Having been used as a German barracks during WWII, it's once again gleaming after a thorough renovation.

Sleeping & Eating

Private rooms on offer along Hegyalja utca are convenient to the train station and are surrounded by vineyards.

Tutajos Beach Camping (☎ 06 20 969 1088; Honfoglalas 24; per person camp sites/bungalows 300/2200Ft; ☽ Apr-Oct) Shady tent sites and basic bungalows are adjacent to a beach with boat rental. Showers cost 100Ft for four people.

Huli Panzió (☎ 352 791; www.hulipanzio.hu; Rákóczi út 16; s/d 4000/8000Ft; ☒) Bright pension with 12 down-to-earth rooms. Enjoy breakfast (800Ft) at the ground-floor restaurant.

Vaskó Panzió (☎ 352 107; http://vaskopanzio.fw.hu; Rákóczi út 12; r 8000Ft) The supremely central Vaskó has eight cute rooms, and windowsills bedecked with flowerpots. It's above a private wine cellar and the proprietor can organise tastings.

Millennium Hotel (☎ 352 247; www.tokajmillennium.hu; Bajcsy-Zsilinszky utca 34; s/d 13,000/15,900Ft; ☒ ▣) Equidistant from the train station and town centre, the only drawback to this hotel's location is the busy road out front. Pleasant beer garden, though.

Huli Panzió Grill Büfé (☎ 352 791; Rákóczi út 16; mains 1100-1600Ft; ☽ 8am-10pm) When everything in Tokaj seems touristy and over the top, step into this simple counter-service eatery for a hot breakfast or grilled meat meal.

our pick **Degenfeld** (☎ 553 050; Kossuth tér 1; mains 1650-2500Ft) Experts' wine pairings accompany each exquisite dish, such as the pork loin medallions with wild mushroom stew, on this restaurant's two set menus.

Shopping

You can buy wine at any of the places mentioned for tasting, or stop at the **Furmint Vinotéka** (☎ 353 340; Bethlen Gábor utca 12; ☽ 9am-6pm) wine shop for a large local selection.

Getting There & Away

No direct buses connect Tokaj with Budapest or Eger; train travel is your best option here. Up to 16 trains a day head west to Budapest Keleti (3750Ft; 2½ hours), and east to Debrecen (1480Ft, two hours).

DEBRECEN

☎ 52 / pop 215,000

Flanked by the golden Great Church and historic Aranybika Hotel, the main square of Hungary's second city is quite pretty; a surprise given the unattractive industrial zones and apartment blocks you pass when arriving by bus or train. During summer, street festivals fill the pedestrian core with revellers, and the city's array of museums and its town thermal baths will keep you busy for a day or two. The Debrecen Flower Carnival happens in late August; Debrecen Jazz Days, in September.

The area around Debrecen has been settled since the earliest times. Debrecen's wealth, based on salt, the fur trade and cattle-raising, grew steadily through the Middle Ages and increased during the Turkish occupation. Debrecen played a pivotal role in the 1848 revolt, and it experienced a major building boom in the late 19th and early 20th centuries.

Orientation & Information

A ring road, built on the city's original earthen walls, encloses the Belváros, or Inner Town. This is bisected by Piac utca, which runs northward from the train station (Petőfi tér) to Kálvin tér, site of the Great Church and Debrecen's centre. The bus station (Külső-Vásártér) is on the 'outer marketplace' at the western end of Széchenyi utca.

Data Net Cafe (Kossuth utca 8; per hr 900Ft; ☒ 9am-midnight) Internet and cheap international calls.

Ibusz (☎ 415 555; Révész tér 2; ☒ 8am-5pm Mon-Fr, 9am-1pm Sat) Travel agency renting private apartments.

Main post office (Hatvan utca 5-9)

OTP Bank (Piac utca 16 & 45) Both have ATMs.

Tourinform (☎ 412 250; www.gotodebrecen.hu) town hall office (Piac utca 20; ☒ 9am-8pm Mon-Fri, 9am-5pm Sun Jun-Aug, 9am-5pm Mon-Fri Sep-May); summer booth (Kossuth tér; ☒ 10am-6pm daily Jun-Sep)

Sights & Activities

Many of the town's big sights are at the northern end of Piac utca, including the yellow neoclassical **Great Church** (Kálvin tér; adult/concession 300/200Ft; ☒ 9am-4pm Mon-Fri, 9am-1pm Sat, noon-4pm Sun Apr-Oct, 10am-1pm Mon-Sat, 11.30am-1pm Sun Nov-Mar). Built in 1821, it has become so synonymous with Debrecen that mirages of its twin clock towers were reportedly seen on the Great Plain early last century. Climb the 210 steps to the top of the west clock tower for grand views over the city.

North of the church stands the 1816 **Reformed College** (Református Kollégium; Kálvin tér 16; adult/concession 500/200Ft, English-language tours 3000Ft; ☒ 10am-4pm Tue-Sat, to 1pm Sun), the site of a prestigious secondary school and theological college since the Middle Ages. It houses exhibits on religious art and sacred objects (including a 17th-century chalice made from a coconut) and on the school's history.

Folklore exhibits at the **Déri Museum** (Déri tér 1; adult/concession 1000/500Ft; ☒ 10am-4pm Tue-Sun Nov-Mar, to 6pm Apr-Oct), a short walk west of the Reformed College, offer excellent insights into the lives of both the proletarian and bourgeois citizens of Debrecen up to the 19th century. The museum's entrance is flanked by four superb bronzes by sculptor Ferenc Medgyessy (1881–1958), a local boy who merits his own **Medgyessy Museum** (Péterfia utca 28; adult/concession 500/250Ft; ☒ 10am-4pm Tue-Sun) in an old burgher house to the northeast.

Just walking along Piac utca and down some of the side streets, with their array of neoclassical, baroque and art nouveau buildings, is a treat. Kossuth utca and its continuation, Széchenyi utca, are especially interesting. Check out the baroque Calvinist **Little Church** (Révész tér 2; admission free; ☒ 9am-noon Mon-Fri & Sun), completed in 1726, with its bastion-like tower.

You can wander along leafy trails and rent a **paddle boat** (per hr 1000Ft; ☒ 9am-8pm Jun-Aug) in **Nagyerdei Park**, north of the centre. But the main attraction here is **Aquaticum** (www.aquaticum.hu; adult/concession 2100/1600Ft; ☒ 10am-10pm), a complex of 'Mediterranean Enjoyment Baths' offering all manner of slides and waterfalls, spouts and grottoes within its pools.

Sleeping

Loads of dormitory accommodation is available in July and August; ask at Tourinform for details.

Maróthi György College (☎ 502 780; Blaháné utca 15; s/d 3000/6000Ft) Right across from the Votive Church, this is a central place to stay. Rooms are fairly basic (containing just a bed and a desk), and facilities are shared. There are simple kitchens available, along with a courtyard and a basketball court for guest use.

our pick **Szí Panzió** (☎ 322 200; www.szivpanzio.hu; Szív utca 11; s/d 6000/7800Ft) Guest house on a tree-lined street not far from the train station. Warm colours enliven the simple, fresh rooms with low-slung beds (and well-stocked minibars).

Centrum Panzió (☎ 442 843; www.panziocentrum.hu; Péterfia utca 37/a; s/d 8500/10,500Ft; ☐) A bit like your grandmother's apartment, if she collected Victorian bric-a-brac. All rooms have fridges and microwaves.

Aranybika (☎ 508 600; www.civishotels.hu; Piac utca 11-15; s/d from €60/85; ☒ ☐) This landmark art nouveau hotel has been *the* place to stay in Debrecen since construction in 1915. Superior rooms have a bit more space than standard, as well as reproduction antique furnishings.

Aquaticum Wellness Hotel (☎ 514 111; www.aquaticum.hu; Nagyerdei park 1; s/d €80/95; ☒ ☐ ☒) Kids' programs, babysitting, bike rental, spa services, a swimming pool, and loads of other amenities make Aquaticum attractive to both adults and children.

Eating & Drinking

Klári Salátabár (☎ 412 203; Bajcsy-Zsilinszky utca 3; per 100g 100-300Ft; ☒ 9am-7pm Mon-Fri) Broccoli egg rolls, fried mushrooms, peas and white rice – the dishes at this self-service storefront are mostly vegetarian.

Pompeji Étterem (☎ 416 988; Batthyány utca 4; mains 1300-1800Ft) Despite the Italian name and murals, the menu is a delicious smorgasbord. Sautéed chicken might be topped with mozzarella and tomato sauce, or with

Greek yoghurt dip and olives. The wood-fired pizzas are great, too.

Csokonai Söröző (☎ 410 802; Kossuth utca 21; mains 1600-2000Ft) Medieval decor, sharp service and excellent Hungarian specialities all help to create one of Debrecen's best eating experiences. This cellar pub-restaurant also serves the odd international dish, like turkey enchiladas with beans.

Teaház a Vörös Oroszlánhaz (Bajcsy-Zsilinszky utca 14; ☽ 1-11pm Mon-Sat, 3-11pm Sun) Hushed conversations and the smell of incense rises from this esoteric teahouse, which has dozens of cold and hot choices.

There's a **grocery shop** (Piac utca 75; ☽ 24hr) within walking distance of the train station and a small covered **fruit and vegetable market** (Csapó utca; ☽ 5am-3pm Mon-Sat, to 11am Sun) right in the centre.

Entertainment
Pick up a copy of the biweekly entertainment freebie *Debreceni Est* (www.est.hu) for music listings.

Csokonai Theatre (☎ 455 075; www.csokonaiszinhaz.hu; Kossuth utca 10) Three-tiered gilt balconies, ornate ceiling frescos, and elaborate chandeliers: the Csokonai is everything a 19th-century theatre should be. Musicals and operas are staged here.

Club Silence (Bajcsy-Zsilinszky utca 3-5; cover charge 1000Ft) DJs spin house and techno tunes here most weekends, but some Saturdays see theme parties.

Getting There & Away
Buses are quickest if you're going directly to Eger (2040Ft, 2½ hours) or Szeged (3220Ft, five hours, three daily). Frequently departing trains will get you to Budapest (3750Ft, 3¼ hours) and Tokaj (1350Ft, 1½ hours).

Trains also depart Debrecen to Satu Marie (2½ hours) in Romania at 3.30pm daily. The night train from Budapest to Moscow stops here at 9pm.

HUNGARY DIRECTORY

ACCOMMODATION
Budapest has the widest variety of lodging prices, but even in provincial towns you can find camping grounds, hostels and private rooms in the budget range (under 7500Ft per double per night in the provinces; under 13,500Ft in Budapest); *panziók* (pensions), guest houses and small hotels in the mid-range (between 7500Ft and 15,500Ft in the country; 13,500Ft and 30,000Ft in Budapest); and multiamenity hotels at the top end (over 16,000Ft outside Budapest; over 30,000Ft in Budapest). Reviews in this chapter are ordered according to price. Unless otherwise stated, rooms in this chapter include private bathroom.

Hungary's more than 400 camping grounds are listed in Tourinform's *Camping Hungary* map/brochure (www.camping.hu). Facilities are generally open May to October and can be difficult to reach without a car.

The **Hungarian Youth Hostels Association** (MISZSZ; www.miszsz.hu) keeps a list of year-round hostels throughout Hungary. In general, year-round hostels have a communal kitchen, laundry and internet service, and sometimes a lounge; a basic bread-and-jam breakfast may be included. Having an HI card is not required, but it may get you a 10% discount. Useful websites with online booking include www.youthhostels.hu and www.hiho stels.hu.

From July to August, students vacate college and university dorms, and administration opens them to travellers. Facilities are usually – but not always – basic and shared. Local Tourinform offices can help you locate such places.

Renting a private room in a Hungarian home is a good budget option and can be a great opportunity to get up close and personal with the culture. You generally share a bathroom with the family. Prices outside Budapest run from 3000Ft to 6000Ft per person per night. Tourinform offices can usually help with finding these; otherwise look for houses with signs reading *'szoba kiadó'* or *'Zimmer frei'*.

Midrange accommodation may or may not have a private bathroom, satellite TV and in-room phone, but all top-end places do. A cold breakfast buffet is usually included in the price at pensions, and there are hot breakfasts included at hotels. A reasonable place might bill itself as a *kishotel* (small hotel) because it has satellite TV and a minibar. Air-conditioning is scarce nationwide, but you're more likely to find it at higher-priced establishments.

An engaging alternative is to stay in a rural village or farmhouse, but only if you have wheels: most of these places are truly remote. Contact Tourinform, the **National**

Federation of Rural & Agrotourism (FATOSZ; Map p380; ☎ 1-352 9804; VII Király utca 93) or the **Centre of Rural Tourism** (Map p374; ☎ 1-321 2426; www.falutur .hu; VII Dohány utca 86) in Budapest.

ACTIVITIES

Hungary has more than 100 thermal baths open to the public, and many are attached to hotels with well-being packages. For locations, ask Tourinform for the *Spa & Wellness* booklet. For more about Budapest spas, check out www.spasbudapest.com.

There's also a helpful HNTO *Riding in Hungary* booklet on equestrian tourism, or you could contact the **Hungarian Equestrian Tourism Association** (Map p380; MLTSZ; ☎ 1-456 0444; www.equi.hu; IX Ráday utca 8, Budapest). **Pegazus Tours** (Map p380; ☎ 1-317 1644; www.pegazus.hu; V Ferenciek tere 5, Budapest) organises horse-riding tours, and occasionally bicycle tours as well.

Hiking enthusiasts may enjoy the trails around Tihany at Lake Balaton, the Bükk Hills north of Eger or the plains at Bugac Puszta south of Kecskemét. Hiking maps usually have yellow borders. Birdwatchers could explore these same paths or take a tour with **Birding Hungary** (www.birdinghungary.com).

Hungary's flat terrain makes it ideal for cycling. **Velo-Touring** (☎ 1-319 0571; www.velo -touring.hu) has a great selection of seven-night trips in all regions, from a senior-friendly Danube Bend tour (€690) to a bike ride between spas on the Great Plain (€750).

For canoeists, **Ecotours** (☎ 1-361-0438; www.eco tours.hu) leads seven day Danube River canoe-camping trips (tent rental and food extra) for about €500, as well as shorter Danube Bend and Tisza River trips.

BUSINESS HOURS

With some rare exceptions, opening hours (*nyitvatartás*) are posted on the front door of establishments; *nyitva* means 'open' and *zárva* is 'closed'. Grocery stores and supermarkets open from about 6am or 7am to 6pm or 7pm Monday to Friday and 7am to 3pm Saturday; an ever-increasing number also open 7am to noon Sunday. Smaller ones, especially in Budapest, may be open on Sunday or holidays as well. Most towns have a 'nonstop' convenience store, and many have 'hyper-markets', such as Tesco, which are open 24 hours. Main post offices are open 8am to 6pm weekdays, and to noon Saturday. Banks are

generally open from 8am to 4pm weekdays. Most restaurants open from 11am to 11pm, and bars and cafes open from 11am to midnight. Nightclubs usually open from 4pm to 2am Sunday to Thursday and until 4am on Friday and Saturday; some only open on weekends.

COURSES

The granddaddy of all Hungarian language schools, **Debreceni Nyári Egyetem** (Debrecen Summer University; ☎ 52-532 594; www.nyariegyetem.hu; Egyetem tér 1, Debrecen), in eastern Hungary, is the most well known and the most respected. It organises intensive two- and four-week courses during July and August and 80-hour, two-week advanced courses during winter. The **Debrecen Summer University Branch** (Map p380; ☎ 1-320 5751; www.nyariegyetem.hu/bp; V Báthory utca 4) in Budapest puts on regular and intensive courses.

DISCOUNT CARDS

Those planning extensive travel in Hungary might consider the **Hungary Card** (☎ 1-266 3741; www.hungarycard.hu; 6540Ft), which gives 50% discounts on six return train fares and some bus and boat travel; free entry to many museums; up to 20% off selected accommodation; and 50% off the price of the Budapest Card (p375). It's available at Tourinform offices.

EMBASSIES & CONSULATES

Embassies in Budapest (phone code ☎ 1) include the following. Most embassies are open to the public from 9am to 4pm on weekdays, though some only open in the morning.

Australia (Map p374; ☎ 457 9777; XII Királyhágó tér 8-9)

Austria (Map p380; ☎ 413 0240; VI Benczúr utca 16)

Canada (Map p376; ☎ 392 3360; II Ganz utca 12-14)

Croatia (Map p380; ☎ 269 5657; VI Munkácsy Mihály utca 15)

France (Map p380; ☎ 374 1100; VI Lendvay utca 27)

Germany (Map p376; ☎ 488 3505; I Úri utca 64-66)

Ireland (Map p380; ☎ 301 4960; V Szabadság tér 7-9)

Netherlands (Map p374; ☎ 336 6300; II Füge utca 5-7)

Romania (Map p374; ☎ 220 1666; XIV Thököly út 72)

Serbia (Map p374; ☎ 322 1436; VI Dózsa György út 92/a)

Slovakia (Map p374; ☎ 273 3500; XIV Gervay utca 44)

Slovenia (Map p374; ☎ 438 5600; II Csatárka köz 9)

South Africa (Map p374; ☎ 392 0999; II Gárdonyi Géza út 17)

UK (Map p380; ☎ 266 2888; V Harmincad utca 6)

Ukraine (Map p374; ☎ 422 4122; XIV Stefánia út 77)

USA (Map p380; ☎ 475 4164; V Szabadság tér 12)

GAY & LESBIAN TRAVELLERS

There is little openly antigay sentiment in Hungary, but neither is there a large openly gay population. The organisations and nightclubs that do exist are generally in Budapest, though the Budapest-biased freebie pamphlet **Na Végre!** (At Last!; www.navegre.hu) lists a handful of venues in the countryside. For up-to-date information on venues, events, groups etc, contact **Budapest gayguide.net** (☎ 06 30 932 3334; ✆ 4-8pm Mon-Fri).

HOLIDAYS

Hungary's public holidays:

New Year's Day 1 January
1848 Revolution Day 15 March
Easter Monday March/April
International Labour Day 1 May
Whit Monday May/June
St Stephen's Day 20 August
1956 Remembrance Day 23 October
All Saints' Day 1 November
Christmas Holidays 25 and 26 December

MEDIA

Budapest has three English-language weeklies: the expat-oriented *Budapest Sun* (399Ft), with a useful arts and entertainment supplement; the *Budapest Business Journal* (1250Ft); and the *Budapest Times* (580Ft), containing interesting reviews and opinion pieces.

MONEY

The unit of currency is the Hungarian forint (Ft). Coins come in denominations of five, 10, 20, 50 and 100Ft, and notes are denominated in 200, 500, 1000, 2000, 5000, 10,000 and 20,000Ft. ATMs accepting most credit and cash cards are everywhere in Hungary, even in small villages. Some businesses quote prices in euros, as reflected in this chapter. Hungary is a very tip-conscious society, and everyone routinely tips waiters, hairdressers and taxi drivers approximately 10% of the bill.

POST

Postcards and letters up to 30g sent within Hungary cost 70Ft (100Ft for priority mail), while to the rest of Europe letters up to 20g cost 200Ft (230Ft priority) and postcards 150Ft (170Ft priority). To addresses outside Europe, expect to pay 220Ft (250Ft priority) for letters up to 20g, and 170Ft (190Ft priority) for postcards.

Mail addressed to poste restante in any town or city will go to the main post office (*főposta*). When collecting poste-restante mail, look for the sign *'postán maradó küldemények'*.

TELEPHONE & FAX

Hungary's country code is ☎ 36. To make an outgoing international call, dial ☎ 00 first. To dial city-to-city (and all mobile phones) within the country, first dial ☎ 06, wait for the second dial tone and then dial the city code and phone number. All localities in Hungary have a two-digit city code, except for Budapest, whose code is ☎ 1.

In Hungary you must always dial ☎ 06 when ringing mobile telephones, which have specific area codes depending on the telecom company: **Pannon GSM** (☎ 06 20; www.pgsm.hu), **T-Mobile** (☎ 06 30; www.t-mobile.hu) or **Vodafone** (☎ 06 70; www.voda fone.hu).

If you have a GSM mobile phone, check with your service provider about using it in Hungary, and beware of calls being routed internationally. If you're going to spend more than just a few days here, consider buying a rechargeable SIM card. Pannon offers prepaid SIMs for 2600/3900Ft with 1300/2500Ft worth of credit; T-Mobile 4000Ft with 2500Ft worth of credit; and Vodafone 1680Ft with 500Ft worth of credit. Recharge cards, available from mobile phone stores and supermarkets, come in denominations of 900Ft, 1800Ft and 3600Ft. Local calls using a local SIM card cost between 25Ft and 40Ft per minute.

There's also a plethora of phonecards on offer, including T-Com's **Barangoló**, which come in denominations of 1000Ft and 5000Ft; **NeoPhone** (www.neophone.hu), with cards also valued at 1000Ft and 5000F; and **Pannon**, offering cards for 1000Ft, 3000Ft and 5000Ft. It can cost as little as 8Ft per minute to call the USA, Australia and New Zealand using such cards. Telephone boxes with a black-and-white arrow and red target on the door and the word *'Visszahívható'* display a telephone number, so you can be phoned back.

TOURIST INFORMATION

The **Hungarian National Tourist Office** (HNTO; www.hungarytourism.hu) has a chain of over 140 **Tourinform** (☎ hotline 30 30 30 600; www.tourinform.hu) information offices across the country. These are the best places to ask general questions and pick up brochures.

EMERGENCY NUMBERS

- Ambulance ☎ 104
- Fire ☎ 105
- Police ☎ 107
- Roadside assistance ☎ 188

If your query is about private rooms, flights or international train travel, you could ask a commercial travel agency. The oldest, **Ibusz** (www.ibusz.hu), is arguably the best for private accommodation.

TRAVELLERS WITH DISABILITIES

Hungary has made great strides in recent years in making public areas and facilities more accessible to people with disabilities. Wheelchair ramps and toilets fitted for people with disabilities do exist, though not as commonly as in Western Europe, and audible traffic signals are becoming commonplace in cities. For more information, contact the **Hungarian Federation of Disabled Persons' Associations** (MEOSZ; Map p374; ☎ 1-388 5529; www.meoszinfo.hu; III San Marco utca 76) in Budapest.

VISAS

EU citizens do not need visas to visit Hungary and can stay indefinitely. Citizens of the USA, Canada, Israel, Japan, New Zealand and Australia do not require visas to visit Hungary for stays of up to 90 days.

However, since Hungary's entry into the Schengen zone of European nations in December 2007, the 90-day visa-free entry period includes stays in all Schengen countries; so if travelling from Hungary through Austria and Germany, for example, you can't exceed 90 days in total. Once your 90 days is up, you must leave the Schengen zone for a minimum of 90 days before you can once again enter it visa-free.

South Africans do still require a visa. Check with the **Ministry for Foreign Affairs** (www.mfa.gov.hu) for an up-to-date list of which country nationals require visas.

Visas are issued at Hungarian consulates or missions, most international highway border crossings, Ferihegy airport and the International Ferry Pier in Budapest. However, visas are never issued on trains and rarely on international buses.

TRANSPORT IN HUNGARY

GETTING THERE & AWAY

Air

The vast majority of international flights land at **Ferihegy International Airport** (☎ 1-296 7000; www.bud.hu) on the outskirts of Budapest. **Balaton airport** (☎ 83-354 256; www.flybalaton.hu) receives Ryanair flights from Düsseldorf, Frankfurt and London Stansted, and is 15km southwest of Keszthely near Lake Balaton. Hungary's national carrier is **Malév Hungarian Airlines** (MA; ☎ 06 40 212121; www.malev.hu).

Major airlines, aside from Malév, servicing Hungary:

Aeroflot (SU; ☎ 1-318 5955; www.aeroflot.com)
Air Berlin (AB; ☎ 06 800 17 110; www.airberlin.com)
Air France (AF; ☎ 1-483 8800; www.airfrance.com)
Alitalia (AZ; ☎ 1-483 2170; www.alitalia.it)
Austrian Airlines (OS; ☎ 1-296 0660; www.aua.com)
British Airways (BA; ☎ 1-777 4747; www.ba.com)
CSA (OK; ☎ 1-318 3045; www.csa.cz)
easyJet (EZY; www.easyjet.com)
El Al (LY; ☎ 1-266 2970; www.elal.co.il)
EgyptAir (MS; www.egyptair.com)
Finnair (AY; ☎ 1-296 5486; www.finnair.com)
germanwings (4U; ☎ 1-526 7005; www.germanwings.com)
LOT Polish Airlines (LO; ☎ 1-266 4771; www.lot.com)
Lufthansa (LH; ☎ 1-411 9900; www.lufthansa.com)
Ryanair (FR; www.ryanair.com)
SAS (SK; www.flysas.com)
Tarom (RO; www.tarom.ro)
Turkish Airlines (TK; ☎ 1-266 4291; www.thy.com)
Wizz Air (W6 ☎ 06 90 181 181; www.wizzair.com)

Land

Hungary's entry into the Schengen zone means that there are no border controls with Austria, Slovakia and Slovenia.

There are excellent land transport connections with Hungary's neighbours. Most of the departures listed are from Budapest, though other cities and towns closer to the various borders can also be used as springboards.

BUS

Most international buses arrive at the Népliget bus station in Budapest. **Eurolines** (www.eurolines.com), in conjunction with its Hungarian affiliate, **Volánbusz** (☎ 1-382 0888; www.volanbusz.hu), is the international bus company of Hungary.

Useful international buses include those from Budapest to Vienna; Bratislava, Slovakia; Subotica in Serbia; Rijeka in Croatia; Prague in the Czech Republic; and Sofia in Bulgaria. For more details, see p389.

CAR & MOTORCYCLE

Foreign driving licences are valid for one year after entering Hungary. Drivers of cars and riders of motorbikes also need the vehicle's registration papers. Third-party insurance is compulsory for driving in Hungary. If your car is registered in the EU, it's assumed you have it. Other motorists must show a Green Card or buy insurance at the border.

TRAIN

The Hungarian State Railways, **MÁV** (☎ 1-371 9449; www.mav.hu) links up with international rail networks in all directions, and its schedule is available online.

Inter-Rail (www.interrailnet.com) Global Passes cover much of Europe and can be purchased by nationals of European countries (or residents of at least six months). A pass offers 1st- and 2nd-class travel for five days within a 10-day period (€329/249), 10 days within a 22-day period (€489/359), 22 continuous days (€629/469), or one month (€809/599). Discounts are available for those aged under 26.

Eurail passes are also valid, but not sold, in Hungary. EuroCity (EC) and Intercity (IC) trains require a seat reservation and payment of a supplement. Most larger train stations in Hungary have left-luggage rooms open from at least 9am to 5pm. There are three main train stations in Budapest, so always note the station when checking a schedule online.

Some direct train connections from Budapest include Austria, Slovakia, Romania, Ukraine (continuing to Russia), Croatia, Serbia, Germany, Slovenia, the Czech Republic, Poland, Switzerland, Italy, Bulgaria and Greece. See p389 for details.

For tickets or more information about passes and discounts, ask at the MÁV Ticket Office in Budapest.

River

A hydrofoil service on the Danube River between Budapest and Vienna operates daily from late April to early October; passengers can disembark at Bratislava with advance notice. See p388 for more details.

GETTING AROUND
Air

Hungary does not have any scheduled internal flights.

Boat

In summer there are regular passenger ferries on Lake Balaton and on the Danube from Budapest to Szentendre, Vác, Visegrád and Esztergom. Details of the schedules are given in the relevant destination sections.

Bus

Domestic buses, run by **Volánbusz** (☎ 1-382 0888; www.volanbusz.hu) cover an extensive nationwide network.

Timetables are posted at stations and stops. Some footnotes you could come across include *naponta* (daily), *hétköznap* (weekdays), *munkanapokon* (on work days), *munkaszüneti napok kivételével naponta* (daily except holidays), and *szabad és munkaszüneti napokon* (on Saturday and holidays). A few large bus stations have luggage rooms, but these generally close by 6pm.

Car & Motorcycle

Many cities and towns require that you 'pay and display' when parking. The cost averages about 200Ft an hour in the countryside, and up to 400Ft on central Budapest streets.

AUTOMOBILE ASSOCIATIONS

The so-called 'Yellow Angels' of the Hungarian Automobile Club do basic breakdown repairs for free if you belong to an affiliated organisation such as AAA in the USA or AA in the UK. You can telephone 24 hours a day on ☎ 188 nationwide.

FUEL & SPARE PARTS

Ólommentes benzin (unleaded petrol 95/98 octane) is available everywhere. Most stations also have *gázolaj* (diesel).

HIRE

In general, you must be at least 21 years old and have had your licence for at least a year to rent a car. Drivers under 25 sometimes have to pay a surcharge.

ROAD RULES

The most important rule to remember is that there's a 100% ban on alcohol

HUNGARY

when you are driving, and this rule is *very* strictly enforced.

Using a mobile phone while driving is prohibited in Hungary. *All* vehicles must have their headlights switched on throughout the day outside built-up areas. Motorcyclists must have their headlights on at all times.

Hitching

In Hungary, hitchhiking is legal except on motorways. Hitchhiking is never an entirely safe way to travel and we don't recommend it, but if you're willing, **Kenguru** (Map p380; ☎ 1-266 5837; www.kenguru.hu; VIII Kőfaragó utca 15, Budapest; ⏱ 10am-2pm Mon-Fri) is an agency that matches riders with drivers.

Local Transport

Public transport is efficient and extensive, with city bus and, in many towns, trolleybus services. Budapest and Szeged also have trams, and there's an extensive metro and a suburban commuter railway in Budapest. Purchase tickets at news-stands before travelling and validate them once aboard. Inspectors do check tickets, especially on the metro lines in Budapest.

Train

MÁV (☎ 06 40 494 949; www.mav.hu) operates reliable train services on its 8000km of tracks. Schedules are available online, and computer information kiosks are popping up at rail stations around the country. Second-class domestic train fares range from 125Ft for a journey of less than 5km, to 3830Ft for a 300km trip. First-class fares are usually 25% more. IC trains are express trains, the most comfortable and modern. *Gyorsvonat* (fast trains) take longer and use older cars; s*zemélyvonat* (passenger trains) stop at every village along the way. Seat reservations *(helyjegy)* cost extra and are required on IC and some fast trains; these are indicated on the timetable by an 'R' in a box or a circle (a plain 'R' means seat reservations are available but not required).

In all stations a yellow board indicates departures *(indul)* and a white board arrivals *(érkezik)*. Express and fast trains are indicated in red, local trains in black. In some stations, large black-and-white schedules are plastered all over the walls.

Most train stations have left-luggage offices that are open at least from 9am to 5pm.

You might consider purchasing the Hungary pass from Eurail, available to non-European residents only, before entering the country. It costs US$104/147 for five/10 days of 1st-class travel in a 15-day period, and US$79/99 for youths in 2nd-class. Children aged five to 11 pay half-price. You would, however, need to use it a lot to get your money's worth.

KOSOVO

Kosovo doesn't leap to mind as a travel destination; it has the weakest economy in Europe, half the population is unemployed, and the innards of hollow buildings still lay strewn across smashed-up footpaths. But though the wounds of the past are still visible, the future is coming on quickly. In towns set against a backdrop of snow-capped mountains and endless green fields lush with promise, buildings are being transformed from tired grey blocks into shiny new shopping centres, and apartment blocks are shooting up from the razed earth. Though not universally recognised, Kosovo claimed ownership of all this activity by declaring itself independent in early 2008.

The capital, Pristina, is a montage of everywhere that has had a hand in its past and vies to play a role in its future. The centre is a *Who's Who* of international organisations, and tucked between them are understated and underrated restaurants with cosmopolitan waiters who offer you a choice of languages with the wine list. Incongruous images abound: American diners on Bulevardi Bil Klinton, İstanbul hair salons, Turkish rugs hanging from Balkan balconies, and blood red Albanian flags flapping next to the benign blue ones of the UN and EU.

Nothing is more than a couple of hours by car or public transport from Pristina; it's possible to visit Unesco-recognised Serbian Orthodox monasteries in Prizren or barter for goat's cheese in Peja's Turkish-style bazaar, and be back in Pristina in time for dinner.

Kosovo is a complicated country, but interesting places are rarely simple.

FAST FACTS

- **Area** 10,887 sq km
- **Capital** Pristina
- **Currency** euro (€); US$1 = €0.73; UK£1 = €1.06; A$1 = €0.50; ¥100 = €0.76; NZ$1 = €0.41
- **Famous for** being the world's newest self-declared country
- **Official language** Albanian
- **Phrases** *tungjatjeta* (hello); *mirupafshim* (goodbye); *ju lutem* (please); *faleminderit* (thank you); *me falni* (excuse me), *më vjen keq* (I'm sorry)
- **Population** 1.8 million to 2.4 million
- **Telephone codes** country code ☎ 381; international access code ☎ 00
- **Visas** not required; see p438

KOSOVO

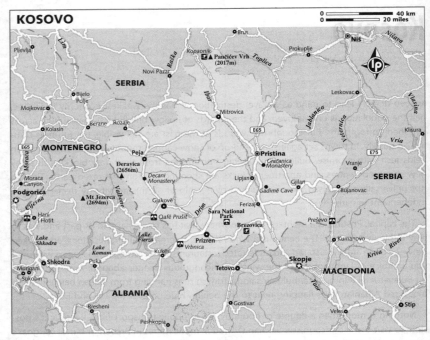

HIGHLIGHTS

- Admire the fine views from the **Kalaja** (fort; p437) over the former medieval capital, Prizren.
- Feast on culinary cosmopolitanism in newly declared capital **Pristina** (p436).
- Explore labyrinthine **Gadimë Cave** (p435).
- Sample goat's cheese of every texture and tang in Peja's **farmers market** (p436).
- Light a candle at the **Patriachate of Peć** (p436), close to the Montenegro border.

ITINERARIES

- **Two to three days** Fine dining and sightseeing in Pristina and a visit to Gračanica Monastery.
- **One week** After two or three days in the capital, loop to Prizren for mosques and churches, and Peja for monasteries and markets.

CLIMATE & WHEN TO GO

Ski season stretches from December until the end of April. Summer daytime maximum temperatures sit comfortably in the mid-20°Cs. Winters can hover around 0°C.

HISTORY

In the 12th century Kosovo was the heart of the Serbian empire, until Turkish triumph at the pivotal 1389 Battle of Kosovo ushered in 500 years of Ottoman rule.

TRAVEL ADVISORY

Government travel advisories strongly warn against visiting certain areas of Kosovo. At the time of writing, some northern municipalities were no-go zones after a spate of Serb–Albanian conflict due to the fact that Serbia did not recognise Kosovo's declaration of independence. Unrest in border areas between Serbia and Kosovo also made travelling overland between them ill-advised. Check the situation before attempting to do so.

There is heavy KFOR (Kosovo Force) presence in Serbian enclaves and sites of potential tension (border areas and heritage buildings at risk of vandalism). Carry your passport to present to KFOR when asked.

HOW MUCH?

- **Short taxi ride** €2
- **One-hour bus trip** €1
- **Internet access per hour** €1
- **Coffee** €1
- **Independent Republic of Kosovo passport cover** €2

LONELY PLANET INDEX

- **1L petrol** €0.98
- **1L bottled water** €0.30
- **Beer (Peja)** €0.50 to €1
- **Souvenir T-shirt** €5
- **Street snack (burek)** €0.50 to €1

Serbia regained control in the 1912 Balkan War. In WWII the territory was incorporated into Italian-controlled Albania and liberated in October 1944 by Albanian partisans. After decades of neglect, Yugoslavia granted Kosovo de facto self-government status in 1974.

In 1989 the autonomy Kosovo enjoyed under the 1974 constitution was suspended by Slobodan Milošević. Ethnic Albanian leaders declared independence from Serbia in 1990. War broke out in 1992 – that same year, Ibrahim Rugova was elected as the first president of the self-proclaimed Republic of Kosovo. Ethnic conflict heightened and the Kosovo Liberation Army (KLA) was formed in 1996.

In March 1999 a US-backed plan to return Kosovo's autonomy was rejected by Serbia, which moved to empty the province of its non-Serbian population. Nearly 850,000 Kosovo Albanians fled to Albania and Macedonia. After Serbia refused to desist, NATO unleashed a bombing campaign on 24 March 1999. In June, Milošević agreed to withdraw troops, air strikes ceased, the KLA disarmed and the NATO-led KFOR (Kosovo Force; the international force responsible for establishing security in Kosovo) took over. From June 1999, Kosovo was administered as a UN–NATO protectorate.

Kosovo caught the world's attention again in 2004 when violence broke out in Mitrovica; 19 people were killed, 600 homes were burnt and 29 monasteries and churches were destroyed in the worst ethnic violence since 1999.

UN-sponsored talks on Kosovo's status began in February 2006. Hasim Thaçi became president in November 2007 and declared Kosovo independent on 17 February 2008. Many countries have recognised Kosovo's independence, but the Serbian prime minister, Vojislav Koštunica, stated that 'As long as the Serb people exist, Kosovo will be Serbia.'

In June 2008 a new constitution transferred power from the UN to the government of Kosovo. Kosovo Serbs established their own assembly in Mitrovica.

PEOPLE

Population estimates range between 1.8 and 2.4 million; 88% are Albanian and 7% Serbs (mostly living in KFOR-protected enclaves). The remaining 5% comprises Bosniaks, Gorani, Roma, Turks, Ashkali and Egyptians.

RELIGION

Muslims are mostly Albanians, and Orthodox Christians mostly ethnic Serbs. There is a Roman Catholic minority.

ARTS

Former president Ibrahim Rugova was a significant figure in Kosovo's literary scene; his presidency of the Kosovo Writers' Association was a step towards presidency of the nation.

Kosovar music bears the imprint of five centuries of Turkish rule; high-whine flutes carry tunes above goat-skin drumbeats. Architecture also shows Islamic influence, mixed with Byzantine and vernacular styles.

The visual-arts scene is re-emerging after troubled times; visit Kosovo Art Gallery (p435) to check it out.

ENVIRONMENT

Kosovo is broadly flat but surrounded by impressive mountains, the highest being Đeravica

KOSOVO

CONNECTIONS: MOVING ON FROM KOSOVO

Kosovo has surprisingly good overland bus connections; a few hours from Pristina you can be in Macedonia, Montenegro, Albania or Serbia, or take a long-haul bus to central Europe or as far east as İstanbul. See p436 for international bus trips between Kosovo and various destinations.

(2656m). Most of Kosovo's protected area is in Šara National Park, created in 1986.

Among the estimated 46 species of mammal in Kosovo are bears, lynx, deer, weasels and the endangered river otter. Around 220 bird species live in or visit Kosovo, including eagles and falcons. Waterbird numbers have declined in recent decades.

Pollutants emitted from infrastructure hit by NATO bombs have impacted on Kosovo's biodiversity. Industrial pollution, rapid urbanisation and over-harvesting of wood threaten ecosystems.

FOOD & DRINK

'Traditional' food is generally Albanian – most prominently, stewed and grilled meat and fish. *Kos* (goat's-cheese yoghurt) is eaten alone or with almost anything. Turkish kebabs and *duveč* (baked meat and vegetables) are common. The local beer is Peja (from Peja). International presence has brought world cuisines to the capital. Outside Pristina, however, waiters respond to vegetarian requests with thigh-slapping laughter. Requests for nonsmoking areas will be met with the same reaction.

Restaurants generally open at around 7am or 8am, and shut at around midnight (or maybe later on weekends).

PRISTINA

☎ 038 / pop 200,000

Pristina looks like a torn-apart town crudely reassembled by differences of opinion, but look closer and you'll notice its pride at being a newly declared capital. It's one of the most raw and eclectic cities in Europe, and also makes a great base for day trips to Peja and Prizren.

ORIENTATION

The main artery is Bul Nëna Terezë, which converges with Agim Ramadani near the National Theatre. Parallel is Rr Luan Haradinaj. Bul Bil Klinton runs southwest past the bus station and airport (18km from the centre) towards Peja.

INFORMATION

Air Kosova (☎ 246 510; Rr UÇK 54; ⏰ 8am-7pm Mon-Sat) Travel agency.

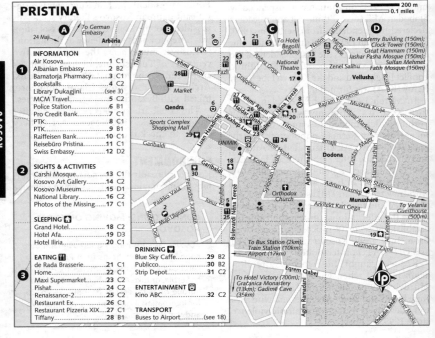

PRISTINA

| 0 | 200 m |
| 0 | 0.1 miles |

INFORMATION
Air Kosova................................1 C1
Albanian Embassy.....................2 B2
Barnatorja Pharmacy.................3 C1
Bookstalls.................................4 C2
Library Dukagjini...................(see 3)
MCM Travel...............................5 C1
Police Station...........................6 B1
Pro Credit Bank........................7 C1
PTK...8 C1
PTK...9 B1
Raiffeisen Bank......................10 C1
Reisebüro Pristina..................11 C1
Swiss Embassy........................12 D2

SIGHTS & ACTIVITIES
Carshi Mosque........................13 C1
Kosovo Art Gallery..................14 C1
Kosovo Museum......................15 D1
National Library.......................16 C1
Photos of the Missing.............17 C1

SLEEPING
Grand Hotel.............................18 C2
Hotel Afa.................................19 D3
Hotel Iliria..............................20 C1

EATING
de Rada Brasserie....................21 C1
Home.......................................22 C1
Maxi Supermarket...................23 C2
Pishat......................................24 C2
Renaissance-2.........................25 C2
Restaurant Ex..........................26 C1
Restaurant Pizzeria XIX..........27 C1
Tiffany.....................................28 B1

DRINKING
Blue Sky Caffe........................29 B2
Publico....................................30 B2
Strip Depot..............................31 C2

ENTERTAINMENT
Kino ABC.................................32 C2

TRANSPORT
Buses to Airport..................(see 18)

To German Embassy
Arbëria
To Hotel Begolli (300m)
To Academy Building (150m);
Clock Tower (150m);
Great Hammam (150m);
Jashar Pasha Mosque (150m);
Sultan Mehmet Fatih Mosque (150m)
24 Maji
UÇK
Tirana
Fehmi Agani
Fazli
Craigevci
Andrej Gropa
National Theatre
Nazim Gafuri
Mitra Vokshi
Idriz Hadi
Zenel Salihu
Vellusha
Market
Qendra
Fehmi Agani
Haxhi Qamili
Rexhep Luci
Bulevardi Nëna Terezë
Tringe
Bajram Kelmendi
Mustafa Kruja
Svetozar Markovic
Sports Complex Shopping Mall
Luan Haradinaj
UNMIK
Qamil Hoxha
Smajli
Dodona
Gustav Majer
Hamzi Jashari
Garibaldi
Garibaldi
Pashko Vasa
Perandori Justinian
Bulevardi Nëna Terezë
I Korriku
Sylejman Vokshi
Rrustem Statovci
Adrian Krasniqi
Arkitekt Kari Gega
Munxherë
To Velania Guesthouse (500m)
Pajko Vasa
Mujo Ulqinaku
Robert Doll
Jonuz Zendeli
Orthodox Church
Agim Ramadani
Al Kelmendi
Gazmend Zajmi
To Bus Station (2km);
Train Station (10km);
Airport (17km)
To Hotel Victory (700m);
Gračanica Monastery (13km); Gadimë Cave (35km)
Eqrem Qabej
Agim Ramadani
Yhedain Bakalli
Enver Maloku

KOSOVO

WORTH THE TRIP: GRAČANICA MONASTERY & GADIMË CAVE

Explore beyond Pristina by heading southeast to Gračanica Monastery or south to Gadimë Cave. Dusty fingers of sunlight pierce the darkness of **Gračanica Monastery** (6am-5pm), completed in 1321 by Serbian King Milutin. The enchanting monastery is guarded by KFOR soldiers. Take a Gjilan-bound bus (€0.50, 15 minutes, every 30 minutes).

Famed for helictites, **Gadimë Cave** (admission €2.50; 9am-7pm) is visited with a guide who enthusiastically points out shapes like a hand, an elephant head, and various body parts (which only the most active imagination can see).

Buses go to Gadimë (€1, 30 minutes, every half-hour) via Lipjan. Or take a Ferizaj-bound bus, get dropped at the Gadimë turn-off and walk the 3km to town.

Barnatorja Pharmacy (☎ 224 245; Bul Nëna Terezë; 7.30am-8pm Mon-Sat, 9am-5pm Sun)

Bookstalls (Bul Nëna Terezë) Just north of the Grand Hotel.

Library Dukagjini (☎ 248 143; Bul Nëna Terezë 20; 8am-8pm Mon-Sat) Maps, language, history and novels.

MCM Travel (☎ 242 424; www.mcmtravel.net; Bul Nëna Terezë; 9am-8pm) Airline agent.

Police (☎ 504 604 6666, emergency 92; www.kosovopolice.com; Rr Luan Haradinaj)

ProCredit Bank (Rr Skenderbeu; 9am-5.30pm Mon-Fri, 9am-2pm Sat)

PTK (www.ptkonline.com) Rr UÇK (Rr UÇK 66; 8am-8pm Mon-Sat); Agim Ramadani (Agim Ramadani; 8am-10pm Mon-Sat) Post and phone services.

Raiffeissen Bank (Rr UÇK 51; 8am-5pm Mon-Fri, 10am-2pm Sat)

Reisebüro Pristina (Turist Kosovo; ☎ 232 999, 237 777; Bul Nëna Terezë 25a; 8am-7pm Mon-Fri, 8am-1pm Sat) Travel agent.

SIGHTS
Bazaar Area

Reminiscent of a Turkish bazaar, the area is home to some key attractions. The **Kosovo Museum** (☎ 249 964; Sheshi Adam Jashari; admission €1; 9.30am-5.30pm Tue-Fri, 11am-3pm Sun) has an Austro-Hungarian exterior, which may be all you'll see if the museum doesn't open when it says it will. In front is the 15th-century **Carshi Mosque**. Nearby, the **Sultan Mehmet Fatih Mosque** (the 'Big Mosque') was built by its namesake around 1461, converted to a Catholic church during the Austro-Hungarian era and refurbished again during WWII.

Nearby is a 26m **clock tower** and the **Great Hammam**, currently being renovated. Next to the clock tower, the **Jashar Pasha Mosque** has vibrant interiors that exemplify Turkish baroque style. The lovely *konak* (19th-century Ottoman building with a protruding 2nd floor) **Academy Building** is occupied by the Academy of Science and Arts.

Centre

The **National Library** (www.biblioteka-ks.org; 8am-8pm), completed in 1982 by Croatian Andrija Mutnjakovic, must be seen to be believed (think gelatinous eggs wearing armour). East towards Agin Ramadani, **Kosovo Art Gallery** (www.kosovoart.com; vary) shows works of local artists.

The gates of the government buildings at the northern end of Bul Nëna Terezë bear **photos of the missing** locals – a stark reminder of how recently Pristina was in turmoil.

SLEEPING

Velania Guesthouse (Guesthouse Professor; ☎ 531 742, 044 167 455; www.guesthouse-ks.com; Velania 4/34; s/d €13/18;) Run by a jovial professor, this is the choice for anyone missing hostel socialising or their granddad. The communal kitchens have complimentary coffee. Private rooms have TVs and cable internet.

our pick **Hotel Begolli** (☎ 044 308 093, 049 308 093; www.hotelbegolli.com; Rr Maliq Pash Gjinolli 8; s/d €30/35, ste €50-60, apt €80-100;) Begolli offers twice what you need and charges half what it could (the catch: no internet, and dull breakfast). Some suites have jacuzzis. Opt for front rooms rather than the smaller, windowless rear ones.

Also recommended:

Hotel Afa (☎ 225 226; www.hotelafa.com; Ali Kelmendi 15; s/d €65/75;) Spacious rooms, free soft drinks, and a breakfast buffet stretching further than most.

Hotel Iliria (☎ 224 275; Bul Nëna Terezë; s/d with shared bathroom €20/40, with private bathroom €25/50) Dated but central.

Hotel Victory (☎ 543 267/277; www.hotel-victory.com; Bul Nëna Terezë; s/d/ste €80/100/120;) Even standard rooms offer stretch-out space. Look for the 6m-high rooftop Statue of Liberty.

Reviewed only so you don't get lured here, the poor old **Grand Hotel** (☎ 220 210; www.grandhotel-pr.com; Bul Nëna Terezë; s €50-90, d €120, ste €300-1000;)

KOSOVO

is mocked by the irony of its name. Rooms are adequately furnished but scream for an upgrade, starting with the carpets. The miserable brown bathrooms are nothing that a quick whack with a wrecking ball wouldn't fix.

EATING

Catering to an international community, Pristina offers a smorgasbord of cuisines. For local fare, try Bul Nëna Terezë, south of Garibaldi.

Pishat (☎ 245 333; Rr Qamil Hoxha 11; mains €6; 8am-11pm Mon-Sat, noon-11pm Sun) Sample Albanian dishes (€5) at this spot, popular with expats and discerning locals.

our pick de Rada Brasserie (☎ 222 622; Rr UÇK 50; mains €7; 8am-midnight Mon-Sat, 6pm-midnight Sun) The sort of place you wish you could afford in Paris. Start with gorgonzola-stuffed mushrooms (€3.70).

Other popular choices:
Restaurant Pizzeria XIX (☎ 044 300 022; www.xix online.com; Rr Luan Haradinaj 2; meals €2-5; 7am-midnight Sun-Thu, 7am-2am Fri & Sat) Rugged, with a hard-working pizza oven.
Home (☎ 244 041; home@Pristinanet.com; mains €6; 7am-11pm Mon-Sat, 11am-11pm Sun) A veal-laden menu, plus an eggplant tower for vegetarians.
Restaurant Ex (☎ 044 157 039; Rr Fehmi Agani 3/8; mains €6; 8am-11pm Mon-Sat, 4-11pm Sun) Regularly changing menu.
Tiffany (☎ 244 040; mains €6; 8am-11pm Mon-Sat, 6-11pm Sun) Off Fehmi Agani, opposite the sports stadium. No menu, but chefs grill up a treat.
Renaissance-2 (☎ 044 118 796; meals €15; 6-11pm) Opposite Radio Kosovo. Pay for your spot at the table, then enjoy whatever the chef brings you.

Head to **Maxi Supermarket** (Rr Rexhep Luci; 7am-midnight) for groceries.

DRINKING

The **Strip Depot** (Rr Rexhep Luci; 8am-midnight Mon-Sat, 9am-midnight Sun) has nothing to do with stripping but lots to do with cocktails and conversation.

Staff at **Blue Sky Caffe** (Rr Luan Haradinaj; 9am-midnight) have as much fun as the patrons. Sleek **Publicco** (www.gizzigroup.com/publico; Rr Garibaldi 7; 8am-1am) is a suave option.

ENTERTAINMENT

Kino ABC (☎ 243 117; www.kinoabc.info; Rr Rexhep Luci 1; 8am-midnight) shows blockbusters in English.

GETTING THERE & AROUND

The major **bus station** (Stacioni I Autobusëve; ☎ 550011; Rr Lidja e Pejes) is 2km southwest of the centre off Bul Bil Klinton. From the airport, there are supposedly buses (€3, 30 minutes, every two hours) to and from the Grand Hotel, but the timetable is unreliable. Official taxis charge €20 to €25, unofficial taxis (blokes with cars) €10 to €12.

Sample international bus fares from Pristina include Serbia's Belgrade (€19, six hours) and Novi Pazar (€5, three hours), also reachable from Peja (€5, three hours) and Prizren (€10, six hours). Other international destinations include Skopje, Macedonia (€5, 1½ hours); Linz, Austria (€50, 14 hours); Podogorica, Macedonia (€15, seven hours); and İstanbul (€30, 20 hours).

Trains run to Peja (€3, 1½ hours, 5.30pm) and, internationally, Skopje (€4, three hours, 6.24pm).

Kombis (minibuses; €0.30 to €0.50) can be pulled over anywhere. Local taxi trips cost a few euro; the meter starts at €1.50. Operators include **Radio Taxi** (☎ 044 111 999) and **VIP Taxi** (☎ 044 333 444). Fares for unofficial taxis must be negotiated.

AROUND PRISTINA

Not far in distance, but worlds away from the chaotic capital, the smaller towns of Peja and Prizren offer a different pace and a new perspective. The easy journey through the countryside is an experience in itself.

PEJA (PEĆ)
☎ 039
Peja is flanked by sites vital to Orthodox Serbians, with a Turkish-style bazaar beating at its heart. Lumbardhi River torrents through town.

The bustling bazaar makes you feel like you've turned left into İstanbul. Farmers gather here on Saturday mornings with wooden barrels of goat's cheese. Follow your nose from Bajrakli Mosque.

The **Patriachate of Peć** (☎ 044 15 07 55; 9am-6pm) is a slice of Serbian Orthodoxy. Multilingual Mrs Dobrilla (☎ 044 15 07 55) may be able to show you around. Taxis cost €2, or follow the river until the road bends inland to the KFOR checkpoint.

Another Orthodox oasis is **Decani Monastery** (☎ 377 44 158 326; decani@gmx.net; Rr Ul St Manastirit;

⊙ 11am-1pm & 4-6pm), 15km south of Peja. Several buses go to Decani (€0.80, 30 minutes, every 20 minutes) on their way to destinations such as Gjakovë. It's a pleasant 2km walk to the monastery from the bus stop. Keep to the roads – KFOR warns of UXO (unexploded ordnance) in the area.

If you want to stay overnight, try the well-furnished **Hotel Gold** (☎ 434 571; Rr Eliot Engl 122/2; s/d €40/50; ▣) or cosy **Hotel Peja** (☎ 044 406 777; hotel_peja@hotmail.com; Pjetro Marko; s/d €30/40; ⊠). Enjoy sky-high views (but average food) at the rooftop restaurant of the **Semitronix Centre** (☎ 432 754; semitronix3@yahoo.com; Mbretëresha Teutë; meals €4; ⊙ 7am-11pm).

Frequent buses run to Peja (€3, 90 minutes, every 15 to 20 minutes) from Pristina.

PRIZREN

☎ 029 / pop 70,000

Picturesque Prizren shines with postindependence euphoria, but burnt-out buildings hang over the macchiato-sipping centre like a bad conscience.

Prizren's centrepiece, the 15th-century **Ottoman bridge**, has been superbly restored. Nearby is **Sinan Pasha Mosque** (1561), which renovations are resurrecting as a central landmark in Prizren. The **Gazi Mehmed Pasha Baths** were also closed at the time of writing, but their exteriors feature frequently on postcards.

The **Orthodox Church of the Virgin of Leviša** is barbed with wire and warnings to dissuade would-be vandals.

The **Ethnological Museum** (admission €1; ⊙ 11am-7pm Tue-Sun) building is where the Prizren League (for Albanian autonomy) organised itself in 1878.

There is naught to see at the 11th-century **Kalaja**, but the 180-degree views over Prizren from this fort are well worth the walk. On the way, KFOR-guarded **Saint Savior church** hints at the fragility of Prizren's remaining relics.

One of few central sleeping options is **Hotel Tirana** (☎ 230 818; tirana_hotelpz@yahoo.com; Rr Adem Jashari 14; s/d/tr €30/30/45). Upstream is a vibrant strip of bars and eateries (near the ugly bridge). The Shadrvan is popular for food and people-watching.

Prizren is well connected to Pristina (€3, 90 minutes, every 10 to 25 minutes), Peja (€3, 90 minutes, six daily) and Gjakovë (€2, 40 minutes, every 30 minutes).

KOSOVO DIRECTORY

ACCOMMODATION

Accommodation options in Kosovo rarely qualify as either top-enders or hostels, but the midrange category spans a wide variety of standards and options. Budget rooms come in under €30, while midrange rooms will cost somewhere between €30 and €90; all rooms include private bathroom unless otherwise stated. Nonsmoking hotel rooms do not yet exist.

Don't be lured into timeworn hotels on main roads; newer gems hide down laneways.

BUSINESS HOURS

Banks are open from 8am to 5pm Monday to Friday, and 8am to 2pm Saturday; shops are open for around an hour longer. Restaurants close at around midnight, while bars will often stay open for the last man standing.

DANGERS & ANNOYANCES

Check government travel advisories before travelling to and within Kosovo; see boxed text, p432. Keep an eye out for signs warning of unexploded ordnance (UXO) in more remote areas; seek KFOR advice before venturing off beaten tracks.

Make sure your insurance covers you for travel in Kosovo.

EMBASSIES & CONSULATES

In the absence of consular representation, contact embassies in Skopje (p524).

Albania (Map p432; ☎ 038-248 208; www.mfa.gov.al; Qyteza Pejton, Rr Mujo Ulqinaku 18)

Germany (off Map p432; ☎ 038-254 500; www.kon sulate.de; Azem Jashanica 17)

Switzerland (Map p432; ☎ 038-248 088/089, visas 038-248 090; www.eda.admin.ch; Adrian Krasniqi 11; ⊙ 8.15am-noon & 2-3pm Mon-Fri)

UK (☎ 038-254 700; www.british embassy.gov.uk; Ismail Qemajli 6; ⊙ 8.30am-5pm Mon-Thu, 8.30am-1.30pm Fri)

USA (☎ 038-59 59 3000; http://pristina.usembassy.gov; Arberia, Nazim Hikmet 30; ⊙ 8am-5pm Mon-Fri)

HOLIDAYS

Kosovo's declaration of independence may earn 17 February holiday status. Flag Day is traditionally marked on 28 November, but this may change. Traditional Islamic holidays will probably be marked.

KOSOVO

INTERNET RESOURCES

Pristina in Your Pocket (www.inyourpocket.com/city/pristina.html) is a downloadable guide; it's also available at Library Dukagjini (p435).

MONEY

Kosovo's currency is the euro; arrive with small denominations. ATMs are common and established businesses accept credit cards.

POST

The ubiquitous PTK overseas post and tele-communications (including Vala mobile-phone coverage) throughout Kosovo.

Sending international postcards costs €0.50, letters between €0.70 and €2.50.

TELEPHONE

Kosovo's country code is ☎ 381.

Small offices offer competitive calling rates, but internet calls are cheaper. **Vala** (www.vala mobile.com) SIM cards are effectively free; the €5 fee includes €5 worth of credit. Recharge cards are available from PTK and street vendors.

VISAS

Kosovo has no visa requirements. Upon arrival, you get a 90-day entry stamp; longer stays require police permission. There is no problem entering as a tourist.

If you wish to travel between Serbia and Kosovo, it may be advisable to enter Kosovo from Serbia first; see the boxed text, below.

TRANSPORT IN KOSOVO

GETTING THERE & AWAY
Air

Pristina International Airport (☎ 5958 123; www.airportpristina.com) is 18km from the centre of Pristina.

Adria Airways (JP; ☎ 038-543 411/285; www.adria-airways.com)

EMERGENCY NUMBERS

- Ambulance ☎ 94
- Emergency ☎ 541 644
- Emergency (from Vala phones) ☎ 112
- Fire ☎ 93
- Police ☎ 92

Albanian Airlines (LV; ☎ 038-542 056; www.albanianairlines.com)
Austrian Airlines (OS; ☎ 038-548 435, 038-502 456; www.aua.com)
British Airways (BA; ☎ 038-548 661; www.britishairways.com)
Germania Airlines (ST; www.gexx.de)
Germanwings (4U; www.germanwings.com)
Kosova Airlines (KOS; ☎ 038-249 185; www.kosovaairlines.com)
Malév (MA; ☎ 038-535 535, 038-260 026 www.malev.hu)
Meridiana (IG; ☎ 038-5859 123; www.meridiana.it)
SAS (SK; www.flysas.com)
Turkish Airlines (TK; ☎ 038-247 711/696; www.turkishairlines.com)

Land

See p436 for sample fares of international bus trips between Kosovo and various destinations. There's also a train to Skopje from Pristina (€4, three hours, 6.24pm).

GETTING AROUND
Bus

Services linking towns and villages are generally frequent and efficient, and completely comfortable for the distances between towns. Buses stop at distinct blue signs, but can be flagged down anywhere.

A 90-minute bus trip in Kosovo will cost you around €90.

Car

Rental-car agencies include **Europcar** (☎ 381-38 59 41 01; www.auto-shkodra.com). Hard-to-spot potholes make road conditions far from safe. It's unwise to bring Serbian-plated cars into Kosovo.

Train

The train system is stretching itself to routes including Pristina–Peja (€3, 1½ hours, 5.30pm) and Pristina–Skopje (€4, three hours, 6.24pm). Locals generally catch buses.

TRAVELLING BETWEEN SERBIA & KOSOVO

Because Serbia doesn't consider Kosovo's entry and exit points to be official international borders, attempts to enter Serbia from Kosovo may be futile unless you initially entered Kosovo from Serbia. See also p829 for further details.

Latvia

Tucked between Estonia to the north and Lithuania to the south, Latvia is the meat in the Baltic sandwich. We're not implying that the neighbouring nations are slices of white bread, but Latvia is the savoury middle, loaded with colourful fixings. Thick greens take the form of Gauja Valley pine forests peppered with castle ruins. Onion-domed Orthodox cathedrals cross the land from salty Liepāja to sweet Cēsis. And spicy Rīga adds an extra zing as the country's cosmopolitan nexus, and unofficial capital of the entire Baltic region.

Latvians often wax poetic about their country, calling it 'the land that sings'. It seems to be in the genes; locals are blessed with unusually pleasant voices, and their canon of traditional tunes is the power source for their indomitable spirit. Latvians (along with their Baltic brothers) literally sang for their freedom from the USSR in a series of dramatic protests known as the 'Singing Revolution' and today the nation holds the Song and Dance Festival, which unites thousands upon thousands of singers from across the land in splendid harmony.

Travellers who manage to tear themselves away from enchanting Rīga will discover a second spin on the singing metaphor – the land itself provides a feast of sounds. Frigid waves pound the desolate coasts like a drum, choirs of cicadas cut the muggy midsummer air with melodic chirping, and soft seagull coos accent the rhythmic clopping of roving horses.

The next few years will be interesting as this hinterland approaches its 20th birthday. No more are the days of teenage growing pains – big things are in store for this little country...

FAST FACTS

- **Area** 64,589 sq km
- **Capital** Rīga
- **Currency** lats (Ls); €1 = 0.70Ls; US$1 = 0.52Ls; UK£1 = 0.75Ls; A$1 = 0.36Ls; ¥100 = 0.54Ls; NZ$1 = 0.29Ls
- **Famous for** ballet dancer Mikhail Barishnikov, the jaw-dropping Song and Dance Festival, Rīga's Black Balsam
- **Official language** Latvian
- **Phrases** *labdien* (hello); *paldies* (thank you); *lūdzu* (please/you're welcome)
- **Population** 2.25 million
- **Telephone codes** country code ☎ 371; international access code ☎ 00
- **Visas** none required for stays of up to 90 days for Australian, Canadian, EU, New Zealand and US citizens; see p464

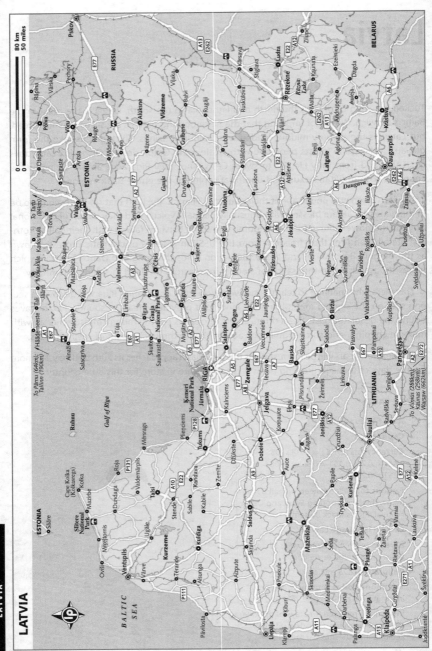

HIGHLIGHTS

- Click your camera at shimmering church spires, devilish art nouveau gargoyles, and crooked cobbled lanes secreted behind gingerbread trim in **Rīga** (p443).
- Trek through never-never land in **Sigulda** (p460), chronicling its vivid history with stops at rambling Livonian castles and top-secret Soviet bunkers.
- Close your eyes and listen to the pounding waves along the stunning **Kurzeme coast** (p458), studded with surfer towns and crowned by the awesomely remote Cape Kolka.
- Sneak away from the capital and indulge in aristocratic decadence at **Rundāle Palace** (p457).
- Hobnob with Russian jetsetters in the heart of **Jūrmala**'s (p456) swanky spa scene.

ITINERARIES

- **Three days** Fill your first two days with a feast of Rīga's architectural eye candy, and spend your third day hiking betwixt Sigulda's castles, sunbathing in scintillating Jūrmala, or snapping photos of Rundāle's opulent palace.
- **One week** After a few days in the capital, swing by Jūrmala on your way up the horn of Cape Kolka for saunas, sunsets and solitude. Glide through western Latvia comparing its ultrabucolic townships to Rundāle's majestic grounds, then blaze a trail across eastern Latvia for a rousing trip back in time spiced with adrenaline sports.

CLIMATE & WHEN TO GO

Latvia experiences relatively harsh, long winters and warm, short summers. Winter is a great time to visit Rīga, as the crowds thin, although daylight is minimal and thermals are a must. Beer gardens, sunbathing and superlong days are compelling reasons to visit in the summer. The average summer temperature is 15.8°C, and in winter it's a brisk -4.5°C.

HISTORY

The first signs of modern man in the region date back to the Stone Age, although Latvians descended from tribes that migrated to the region around 2000 BC. Eventually, four main Baltic tribes evolved: the Selonians, the Letts (or Latgals), the Semigallians and the Cours.

From the latter three derived the names of three of Latvia's four principal regions: Latgale, Zemgale and Kurzeme. The fourth region, Vidzeme (Livland), derived its name from the Livs, a Finno-Ugric people unrelated to the Balts.

In 1201, at the behest of the pope, German crusaders, led by Bishop von Buxhoevden of Bremen, conquered Latvia and founded Rīga. Von Buxhoevden also founded the Knights of the Sword, who made Rīga their base for subjugating Livonia. Colonists from northern Germany followed, and during the first period of German rule Rīga became the major city in the German Baltic, thriving from trade between Russia and the West, and joining the Hanseatic League (a medieval merchant guild) in 1282.

The 15th, 16th and 17th centuries were marked with battles and disputes about how to divvy up what would one day become Latvia. After a period of Swedish rule, the Russians conquered the area during the Great Northern War (1700–21).

The idea of a cohesive national identity began around the 17th century and by the mid-19th century the sentiment grew stronger as the first newspapers printed Latvian editions and the Song and Dance Festival started up.

Out of the post-WWI confusion and turmoil arose an independent Latvian state, declared on 18 November 1918. By the 1930s, Latvia had achieved one of the highest standards of living in all of Europe. Initially, the Soviets were the first to recognise Latvia's independence, but the honeymoon didn't last long. Soviet occupation began in 1939 with the Molotov-Ribbentrop Pact. Nationalisation, killings and mass deportations to Siberia followed. Latvia was occupied partly or wholly

---

CONNECTIONS: MOVING ON FROM LATVIA

Latvia is the link in the Baltic chain, making Rīga a convenient connecting point between Tallinn and Vilnius. Long-distance buses also connect the capital to St Petersburg and Warsaw. Rīga is the hub of AirBaltic, which offers direct service to an array of European cities, including Berlin, Baku, Moscow, İstanbul, Kaliningrad, Minsk, Vienna and Kyiv. See p455 for more info.

LATVIA

HOW MUCH?

- **Small bottle of Black Balsam** 2.89Ls
- **Big bowl of pelmeņi** 2Ls
- **Sauna session** 7Ls
- **Dorm bed in Rīga** from 7Ls
- **Public transport ticket** 0.40Ls

LONELY PLANET INDEX

- **1L petrol** 0.63Ls
- **1L bottled water** 0.34Ls
- **Pint of beer** 2Ls
- **Souvenir T-shirt** 5Ls to 15Ls
- **Street snack (blintz)** 0.65Ls

by Nazi Germany from 1941 to 1945, during which time an estimated 175,000 Latvians were killed or deported.

When WWII ended, the Soviets marched back in claiming to 'save' Latvia from the Nazis. A series of deportations and mass killings began anew as the nation was forced to adapt to communist ideologies. The first public protest against Soviet occupation was on 14 June 1987, when 5000 people rallied at Rīga's Freedom Monument to commemorate the 1941 Siberia deportations. On 23 August 1989, two million Latvians, Lithuanians and Estonians formed a 650km human chain from Vilnius, through Rīga, to Tallinn, to mark the 50th anniversary of the Molotov-Ribbentrop Pact. Although an all-important Moscow coup failed in 1991, the attempt rocked the Soviet just enough so that Latvia could break free.

The country declared independence on 21 August 1991 and on 17 September 1991 Latvia, along with its Baltic brothers, joined the UN. After a game of prime minister roulette and a devastating crash of the country's economy, Vaira Vīķe-Freiberga, a Latvian by birth who spent most of her life in Canada, won the election in 1999 with the promise of propelling the country towards EU membership. It was a tough uphill battle as the nation shook off its antiquated Soviet fetters, but on 1 May 2004 the EU opened its doors to the fledgling nation. Long the Baltic laggard, Latvia registered the highest economic growth in the EU in 2004, 2005, 2006 and 2007. The nation's current president is Valdis Zatlers, a

surgeon and former member of the Popular Front of Latvia in the late 1980s.

PEOPLE

Casual hellos on the street aren't common, but Latvians are a friendly and welcoming bunch. Some will find that there is a bit of guardedness in the culture, but this caution, most likely a response to centuries of foreign rule, has helped preserve the unique language and culture through changing times. As Latvia opens up to the world, this slight xenophobia is quickly melting away. Citizens are growing secure with their nation's freedom and the younger generations have access to a more cosmopolitan culture (especially since youths are almost always trilingual, speaking Latvian, Russian and English).

Of Latvia's 2.25 million citizens, only 58.8% are ethnically Latvian. Russians account for 28.7% of the total population, and Belarusians (3.8%), Ukrainians (2.6%), Poles (2.5%) and a small Jewish community (0.4%) help round out the rest of the pack. Latvians make up less than 50% of the population in Jūrmala, Liepāja, Ventspils and the capital, Rīga, where 43% are Russian and 41% Latvian.

RELIGION

Today, most Latvians are members of the Lutheran Church (Russian citizens are mostly Roman Catholics, Orthodox and Old Believers), although ancient pagan traditions still influence daily life and are readily embraced around the nation. These pre-Christian beliefs are centred on nature-related superstition and although they seem incongruous when juxtaposed with Christian ideals, Latvians have done a good job of seamlessly uniting the two. Midsummer's Day, or Jāņi as it's commonly known, is the most popular holiday in Latvia. The solstice was once a sunlit night of magic and sorcery, and today everyone flocks to the countryside for an evening of revelry.

ARTS

The traditional importance of song as Latvia's greatest art form is shown in the 1.4 million *dainas* (folk songs) identified and collected by Krišjānis Barons (1835–1923). In 2003 the Song and Dance Festival (p463), held every five years, was inscribed on Unesco's list of 'Oral and Intangible Heritage of Humanity' masterpieces.

Of Latvia's spectrum of visual arts, visitors will be most awestruck by the collection of art nouveau architecture in Rīga (p448). The capital has more Judengstil buildings than any other European city – 750 buildings and counting (as renovations continue).

ENVIRONMENT

Latvia is 64,589 sq km in area – a little smaller than Ireland. Unlike its relatively compact Baltic neighbours, Latvia is a lot wider from east to west than from north to south. A good half of its sweeping 494km coast faces the Gulf of Rīga, a deep inlet of the Baltic Sea shielded by the Estonian island of Saaremaa.

Latvians love nature, so it's no surprise that almost half of the nation is covered with thick patches of forest. Much of this leafy terrain falls under protected jurisdiction, which continues to grow as Soviet industrial relics are eradicated.

The Latvian Sustainable Development Strategy, conceived in 2002, is a broad-reaching scheme uniting environmental, social and economic structures to increase the longevity and viability of the Latvian land.

FOOD & DRINK

Attention foodies: pack a sandwich if you don't want to pack an artery – food in Latvia is (to put it nicely) very hearty. For centuries, eating has been but a utilitarian task rather than an art and a pleasure, and although things are starting to change, one should still expect greasy menus governed by the almighty pig and ubiquitous potato.

A walk through a Latvian market, such as Rīga's Central Market (p449) will quickly reveal the local faves: roasted meats, smoked fish, fried potatoes, boiled vegies, curdled cheeses and loads of pork grease.

Not to be missed is Latvia's famous Black Balsam, a jet-black, 45% proof concoction which Goethe called 'the elixir of life'. We like to mix it with a glass of cola. *Alus* (beer) is also a traditional favourite, and for such a small country Latvia has more than its share of breweries.

Most bars and restaurants open around 11am and close around 11pm. On weekends these establishments stay open until 2am or later.

Latvia adopted a smoking ban on 1 July 2008, prohibiting smoking in indoor public venues and restaurants.

RĪGA

pop 717,400

'The Paris of the North', 'The Second City that Never Sleeps' – everyone's so keen to tack on qualifying superlatives to Latvia's capital, but regal Rīga does a hell of a job of holding its own. For starters, the city has the largest and most impressive showing of art nouveau architecture in Europe. Nightmarish gargoyles and praying goddesses adorn over 750 buildings along the stately boulevards radiating out from Rīga's castle core. The heart of the city – Old Town – is a fairy-tale kingdom of winding wobbly lanes and gingerbread trim that beats to the sound of a bumpin' discotheque.

Although some Latvians may lament the fact that they are an ethnic minority in their own capital, others will be quick to point out that Rīga was never a 'Latvian' city. Founded in 1201 by the German Bishop Albert von Buxhoevden (say that three times fast) as a

---

RĪGA IN TWO DAYS

Start in the heart of the city, getting lost amid twisting cobbled alleys that snake through medieval **Old Rīga** (p447). For lunch, clog your arteries with some traditional Latvian cuisine at **LIDO Atpūtas Centrs** (p453) or binge on *pelmeņi* (Russian-style ravioli stuffed with meat) at **Pelmeņi XL** (p453) and walk off the calories in the afternoon with a stroll through the eye-popping **art nouveau district** (p448). After sunset, bar-hop your way through Old Rīga (don't forget to try Black Balsam) and end the night with a well-deserved cocktail at **Skyline Bar** (p454) overlooking the twinkling urban lights below.

On day two, fine-tune your bargaining skills (and your Russian) with an early-morning visit to the **Central Market** (p449). Then, for something truly offbeat, try firing a round with an AK47 in a former **Soviet fallout shelter** (p451). In the evening grab tickets for an evening at the **opera** (p454) and treat yourself to some of the finest classical music in Europe.

RĪGA

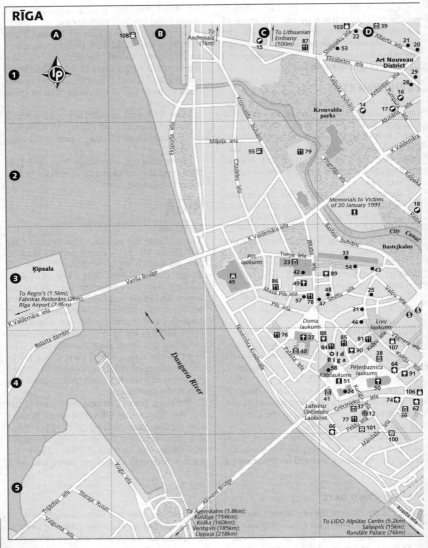

bridgehead for the crusade against the northern 'heathens', Rīga became a stronghold for the Knights of the Sword and the newest trading junction between Russia and the West. When Sweden snagged the city in 1621, it grew into the largest holding of the Swedish Empire (even bigger than Stockholm). Soon the Russians snatched Latvia from Sweden's grip and added an industrial element to the bustling burg. By the mid-1860s Rīga was the world's biggest timber port and Russia's third city after Moscow and St Petersburg. The 20th century also saw the birth of cafes, salons, dance clubs and a thriving intellectual culture, which was bombed to high hell in WWI, and captured by the Nazis during

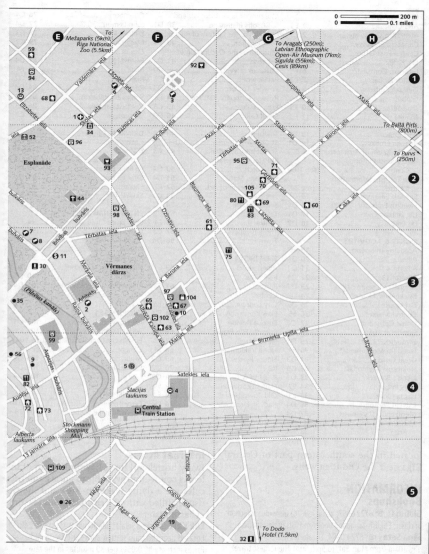

WWII. Somehow, Rīga's indelible international flavour managed to rise up from the rubble, and even as a part of the USSR Rīga was known for its forward thinking and thriving cultural life.

Today, Rīga's cosmopolitan past has enabled the city to effortlessly adjust to a global climate, making it more than just the capital of Latvia – it's the cornerstone of the Baltic.

ORIENTATION

Old Rīga (Vecrīga), which straddles the Daugava River, is separated from Central Rīga (Centrs) by an emerald necklace of lush parkland. The bus and train stations are

located in the southeastern part of Central
Rīga near the Old Rīga walls.

INFORMATION
Bookshops
Globuss (☎ 6722 6957; Vaļņu iela 26) Generous selection
of classic English-language books and lots of newspapers.
Jāņa Sēta (☎ 6724 0894; Elizabetes iela 83-85;
🕙 10am-7pm Mon-Sat, to 5pm Sun) The largest travel
bookstore in the Baltics overflows with a bounty of maps,
souvenir photo books, and Lonely Planet guides.

Discount Cards
Rīga Card (☎ 6721 7217; www.rigacard.lv; 1-/2-/3-day
card 10/14/18Ls) The useful Rīga Card is a discount card
for sights, museums and accommodation. It's available for
purchase at the Rīga tourism information centres (opposite).

Internet Access
Every hostel and hotel has some form of internet connection available to guests. Internet
cafes are a dying breed in Rīga and they're
usually filled with 12-year-old goons blasting
cybermonsters.
Elik Kafe (Merķeļa iela 1; per 30min 0.35Ls; 🕙 24hr)
Located near the train station above the McDonalds.
Prices increase by 0.05Ls per 30 minutes in the late
evening.
net.café (Peldu iela 17; per hr 1Ls; 🕙 24hr) A chill spot
to update your blog. Full-service bar.

Media
City Spy (www.cityspy.info) Pocket-sized City Spy was
the best map we found in town. Available at most budget
accommodation.

WI-FI ACCESS

Rīga is covered in a virtual blanket of wireless internet access. Lattelecom, the main service provider, has set up wi-fi beacons at every payphone around the city. Users can access the internet from within a 100m radius of these phone booths. Almost every hotel and hostel has wireless access (usually free of charge), as do a large percentage of restaurants (including the dozens of Double Coffee cafes peppered around the city).

To register for a Lattelecom password and username, call ☎ 9000 4111, or send a text message with the word 'WiFi' to ☎ 1188. One hour of internet costs 0.94Ls. Prepaid user cards are also available for purchase at most of the establishments with a wireless hook-up. Visit www .wifi.lv for more information (although at the time of research the site was predominantly in Latvian and Russian).

Riga in Your Pocket (www.inyourpocket.com/latvia /city/riga.html) Handy city guide published every other month. Download a PDF version or pick up a copy (2 Ls) at most hotels and tourist offices.

Riga this Week (www.rigathisweek.lv) An excellent (and free) city guide available at virtually every sleeping option in town. Published every second month.

Medical Services

ARS Clinic (☎ 6720 1001, emergency 6720 1003; Skolas iela 5; ☯ 24hr) English-speaking service and an emergency home service.

Money

There are scores of ATMs scattered around the capital. Withdrawing cash is easier than trying to exchange travellers cheques or foreign currencies; exchange bureaux often have lousy rates and most do not take travellers cheques. For detailed information about Latvian currency and exchange rates visit www.ba nk.lv.

Marika (Brīvības bulvāris 30) Offers 24-hour currency exchange services with reasonable rates.

Post

Those blue storefronts with 'Pasta' written on them aren't Italian restaurants – they're post offices.

Central post office (Stacijas laukums 1; ☯ 7am-9pm Mon-Fri, 9am-8pm Sat, 10am-8pm Sun) Convenient location near the train station. International calling and faxing services available.

Post office (Elizabetes iela 41/43; ☯ 7.30am-9pm Mon-Fri, 8am-4pm Sat)

Tourist Information

Rīga tourism information centre (www.rigatourism .com) main office (☎ 6703 7900; Rātslaukums 6; ☯ 10am-7pm); bus station (☎ 6722 0555; ☯ 9am-7pm); train station (☎ 6730 7900; ☯ 10am-6.30pm) Gives out free maps and has loads of information. It can

arrange accommodation and book walking, bus or boat tours from a variety of operators. Its website has great Old Town walking tour suggestions.

Telephone hotline (☎ 2203 3000; ☯ 24hr) English-speaking hotline offering information and assistance for tourists.

SIGHTS
Old Rīga (Vecrīga)
RĀTSLAUKUMS

Touristy Rātslaukums is home to the picture-worthy **Blackheads' House** (Melngalvju House; Rātslaukums 6; admission 1.50Ls; ☯ 10am-5pm, closed Mon), built in 1344 as a veritable fraternity house for the Blackheads guild of unmarried German merchants. The house was destroyed in 1941, and flattened by the Soviets seven years later. Somehow the original blueprints survived and an exact replica was constructed in 2001 for Rīga's 800th birthday.

Once the home of a wealthy merchant, the 17th-century **Mentzendorff's House** (Mencendorfa nams; www.mencendorfanams.com; Grēcinieku iela 18; admission 1.50Ls; ☯ 10am-5pm Wed-Sun), right behind the Blackheads' House, continues Rīga's history of mercantile excess.

Facing the Blackheads' House across the square is the **Town Hall**, also rebuilt from scratch in recent years. A statue of Rīga's patron saint **St Roland** stands between the two buildings. It's a replica of the original, erected in 1897, which now sits in St Peter's (p448).

The **Museum of the Occupation of Latvia** (Latvijas okupācijas muzejs; www.occupationmuseum.lv; Latviesu Strēlnieku laukums 1; admission free; ☯ 11am-6pm May-Sep, to 5pm Tue-Sun Oct-Apr) ironically inhabits a Soviet bunker, and carefully details Latvia's Soviet and Nazi occupations between 1940 and 1991. Audioguides are available for supplemental information.

LATVIA

ART NOUVEAU IN RĪGA

If you ask any Rīgan where to find the city's world-famous art nouveau architecture, you will always get the same answer: 'Look up!' Over 750 buildings in Rīga (more than any other city in Europe) boast this flamboyant and haunting style of decor; and the number continues to grow as myriad restoration projects get under way. Art nouveau is also known as Jugendstil, meaning 'youth style', named after a Munich-based magazine called *Die Jugend*, which popularised the design on its pages.

Art nouveau's early influence was Japanese print art disseminated throughout Western Europe, but as the movement gained momentum, the style became more ostentatious and freeform – design schemes started to feature mythical beasts, screaming masks, twisting flora, goddesses and goblins. The turn of the 20th century marked the height of the art nouveau movement, as it swept through every major European city from Porto to Petersburg.

The art nouveau district is centred around **Alberta iela** (check out **2a, 4** and **13** in particular), but you'll find fine examples throughout the city. Don't miss the renovated facades of **Strēlnieku 4a** and **Elizabetes 10b** and **33**. In Old Rīga, Jugendstil crops its head up (quite literally) at many addresses, including **Teātra 9** and **Smilšu 2** and **8**.

PĒTERBAZNĪCA LAUKUMS

Rīga's skyline centrepiece is Gothic **St Peter's Lutheran Church** (Sv Pētera baznīca; www.peterbaznica.lv; Skārņu iela 19; admission 2Ls; 10am-5pm, closed Mon), thought to be around 800 years old. Don't miss the view from the spire, which has been rebuilt three times in the same baroque form. Legend has it that in 1667 the builders threw glass from the top to see how long the spire would last. A greater number of shards meant a very long life. The glass ended up landing on a pile of straw and didn't break – a year later the tower was incinerated. When the spire was resurrected after a bombing during WWII, the ceremonial glass chucking was repeated, and this time it was a smash hit. The spire is 123.25m high, but the lift only whisks you up to 72m.

Behind St Peter's church sits another impressive religious structure – the former **St George's Church** – which is now the **Museum of Decorative & Applied Arts** (Dekoratīvi lietišķās mākslas muzejs; www.dlmm.lv; Skārņu iela 10/20; admission 0.70Ls; 11am-5pm, to 7pm Wed, closed Mon), highlighting Latvia's impressive collection of woodcuts, tapestries and ceramics. The building's foundations date back to 1207, when the Livonian Brothers of the Sword erected their castle here.

KALĒJU IELA & MĀRSTAĻU IELA

Zigzagging Kalēju iela and Mārstaļu iela are dotted with poignant reminders of the city's legacy as a wealthy northern European trading centre. There are several merchants' manors that are now museums, including the **Latvian**

Photography Museum (Latvijas fotogrāfijas muzejs; Mārstaļu iela 8; admission 1.40Ls; 10am-5pm Wed, Fri & Sat, noon-7pm Thu). Don't forget to look up at the curling vines and barking gargoyles adorning several **art nouveau facades** (above).

LĪVU LAUKUMS

This bustling square is lined by a colourful row of 18th-century buildings – most of which have been turned into rowdy restaurants and beer halls. The 19th-century Gothic exterior of the **Great Guild** (Lielā ģilde; Amatu iela 6) encloses a sumptuous merchants' meeting hall, built during the height of German power in the 1330s. The fairy-tale castle next door is the **Small Guild** (Mazā ģilde; Amatu iela 5), founded during the 14th century as the meeting place for local artisans.

Don't miss the **Cat House** (Miestaru iela 10), named for the spooked black cat sitting on the roof. According to legend, the owner was rejected from the local Merchants' Guild across the street, and exacted revenge by placing a black cat on the top of his turret with its tail raised towards the esteemed Great Guild hall.

DOMA LAUKUMS

The centrepiece of expansive Doma Laukums is Rīga's enormous **Dome Cathedral** (Doma baznīca; admission 0.50Ls; 11am-6pm Tue-Fri, 10am-2pm Sat). Founded in 1211 as the seat of the Rīga diocese, it is still the largest church in the Baltics. The floor and walls of the huge interior are dotted with old stone tombs. In 1709, the cholera and typhoid outbreak that killed a third of Rīga's population was blamed on a flood that inundated the crypt. The cathedral's pulpit dates from 1641 and the huge, 6768-pipe organ was the world's largest when it was completed in 1884 (it's now the fourth largest). Mass is held at noon on Sundays, and at 8am every other day of the week.

The **Museum of the History of Rīga & Navigation** (Rīgas vēstures un kuǵniecības muzejs; www.rigamuz.lv; Palasta iela 4; admission 2.50Ls; 11am-5pm Wed-Sun), the Baltics' oldest museum, is situated in the monastery's cloister at the back of the Dome Cathedral complex. Founded in 1773, the exhibition space features a permanent collection of artefacts from the Bronze Age all the way up to WWII.

Located behind Doma Laukums, away from the cathedral, are the **Three Brothers** (Trīs brāļi; Mazā Pils iela 17, 19 & 21), exemplifying Old Rīga's diverse collection of old architectural styles. Number 19 (built in the 17th century) is now the **Rīga Museum of Architecture** (Latvijas arhitektūras muzejs; www.archmuseum.lv; admission free; 10am-6pm Mon-Fri). Note the tiny windows on the upper levels – Rīga's property taxes during the Middle Ages were based on the size of one's windows.

Latvia's first Lutheran services were held in nearby **St Jacob's Cathedral** (Sv Jēkaba katedrāle; Klostera iela), which has an interior dating back to 1225. Today it is the seat of Rīga's Roman Catholic archbishopric.

PILS LAUKUMS
In the far corner of Old Rīga near the Vanšu bridge, verdant **Pils Laukums** sits at the doorstep of **Riga Castle** (Rīgas pils; Pils laukums 3). Originally built as the headquarters for the Livonian Order, the foundation dates to 1330 and served as the residence of the order's grand master. This canary yellow bastion boasts an art and history museum, and is also home to Latvia's president.

The **Arsenāls Museum of Art** (Mākslas muzejs Arsenāls; Torņa iela 1; adult/child 0.70/0.40Ls; 11am-5pm Tue, Wed & Fri-Sun, to 7pm Thu), sits just east of Pils Laukums, and shares a block with Latvia's **Parliament** (Saeima; Jēkaba iela 11), a Florentine Renaissance structure originally commissioned as the Knights' House of the German landlords.

TORŅA IELA
The entire north side of handsome Torņa iela is flanked by the custard-coloured **Jacob's Barracks** (Jēkaba Kazarmas; Torņa iela 4), built as an enormous warehouse in the 16th century. Tourist-friendly

cafes and boutiques now inhabit the refurbished building. On the other side of the street, find **Trokšnu iela**, Old Rīga's narrowest *iela* (street), and the **Swedish Gate** (Zviedru vārti; Torņa iela 11), which was built in 1698 while the Swedes were in power. The cylindrical **Powder Tower** (Pulvera Tower; Smilšu iela 20) dates back to the 14th century, and is the only survivor of the 18 original towers that punctuated the old city wall. In the past it served as a prison, torture chamber and frat house. Today it is the **Museum of War** (Kara muzejs; www.karamuzejs.gov.lv; Smilšu iela 20; admission free; 10am-6pm Wed-Sun May-Sep, to 5pm Wed-Sun Oct-Apr).

Central Rīga (Centrs)
FREEDOM MONUMENT
Affectionately known as 'Milda', Rīga's **Freedom Monument** (Brīvības bulvāris) was erected in 1935 where a statue of Russian ruler Peter the Great once stood. A copper female Liberty tops the soaring monument, holding three gold stars representing the original cultural regions of Latvia; Kurzeme, Vidzeme and Latgale. Two soldiers stand guard at the monument throughout the day and perform a modest changing of the guard every hour on the hour from 9am to 6pm.

A second spire, the **Laima Clock**, sits between Milda and the entrance to Old Rīga. Built in the 1920s as a gentle way to encourage Rīgans not to be late for work, the clock is now used as the preferred meeting place for young Latvians.

CENTRAL MARKET
Haggle for your huckleberries at the **Central Market** (Centrāl tirgus; www.centraltirgus.lv; Nēǵu iela 7; 7am-5pm Sun-Mon, to 6pm Tue-Sat), housed in a series of mammoth zeppelin hangars. Myriad vendors peddle their wares from golf visors to pickled herring. It's a fantastic spot to assemble a picnic lunch and ogle some seriously outdated hairdos (more like hair-don'ts).

Just beyond the market in the heart of Akadēmijas Laukums, the **Academy of Science** (Zinātņu Akadēmija; www.lza.lv; Turgeņeva iela; 9am-8pm), also called 'Stalin's Birthday Cake', is Rīga's Russified Empire State Building. Those with an eagle eye will spot hammers and sickles hidden in the convoluted facade. A mere 1.50Ls grants you admission to the observation deck on the 17th floor.

Don't miss the moving **Holocaust Memorial** nearby. A large synagogue once occupied this street corner until it was burned to the ground

---

FREE THRILLS

Five fun (and free) things to do in the capital that will save you lots of lats:

■ Go click-crazy at the hundreds of **art nouveau facades** (p448).

■ View the cityscape on a 26-floor elevator ride up to **Skyline Bar** (p454).

■ Snoop around the zeppelin hangars in the **Central Market** (p449).

■ Breathe in the heady mix of revellers and street musicians in **Livu Laukums** (p448).

■ Watch the mini 'changing of the guard' at the **Freedom Monument** (p449).

---

during WWII with the entire congregation trapped inside. No one survived.

ART NOUVEAU DISTRICT

Just when you thought that Old Rīga was the most beautiful neighbourhood in town, the city's audacious art nouveau district swoops in to vie for the prize. Check out p448 for more info.

Stop by the neighbourhood's **Museum of Janis Rozentāls and Rūdolfs Blaumanis** (www.rtmm .lv; Alberta iela 12; admission 1Ls; 🕑 11am-6pm Wed-Sun) to explore the interior of one of the lavish art nouveau buildings. The nearby **Jews In Latvia** (www.rtmm.lv; Skolas iela 6; admission free; 🕑 noon-5pm Sun-Thu) museum recounts the city's history of Jewish life until 1945 through artefacts and photography.

ESPLANADE

The **State Museum of Art** (Valsts mākslas muzejs; K Valdemāra iela 10a; admission 1-3Ls; 🕑 11am-5pm Wed-Mon) sits within leafy grounds and features pre-WWII Russian and Latvian art displayed among the Soviet grandeur of ruched net curtains, marble columns and red carpets.

At the other end of the park, the stunning 19th-century **Russian Orthodox Cathedral** (Pareiztīcīgo katedrāle; Brīvības bulvāris), with its gilded cupolas, majestically rises off Brīvības. During the Soviet era the church was used as a planetarium.

Outlying Neighbourhoods

Those who venture beyond Rīga's inner sphere of cobbled alleyways and over-the-top

art nouveau will uncover a handful of other neighbourhoods that help paint a full picture of this cosmopolitan capital.

If you don't have time to visit the heart of the Latvian countryside, then a stop at the **Latvian Ethnographic Open-Air Museum** (Latvijas etnogrāfiskais brīvdabas muzejs; www.muzejs.lv; Brīvības gatve 440; adult/child 1/0.50Ls; 🕑 10m-5pm mid-May– mid-Oct) is a must. This vast stretch of forest contains over 100 wooden buildings from all over Latvia. Take bus 1 from the corner of Merķeļa iela and Tērbatas iela to the 'Brīvdabas muzejs' stop.

Woodsy **Mežaparks** (literally 'Forest Park' in Latvian), 7km outside the centre, is Europe's oldest planned suburb. Built by the Germans in the 20th century, this 'garden city' was the go-to neighbourhood for wealthy merchants looking to escape the city's grimy industrial core. The suburb is home to the **Rīga National Zoo** (Zoologiskais dārz; www.rigazoo.lv; Meža prospekts 1; adult/child 4/3Ls; 🕑 10am-6pm), which offers the usual cast of Noah's ark.

Other interesting suburban districts include **Andrejsala**, with its burgeoning artists' colony, **Āgenskalns**, which sports loads of wooden architecture and a Russified market, and **Salaspils**, further afield, featuring a haunting memorial where a Nazi concentration camp once stood.

ACTIVITIES
Saunas & Spas

You don't have to run all the way to Jūrmala to see some serious spa action. Rīga has a few standout places to get pampered in the traditional Latvian style: getting whipped by dried birch branches while sweating it out in temperatures beyond 40°C. Sounds relaxing…

Taka Spa (☎ 6732 3150; www.takaspa.lv; Kronvalda bulvāris 3a; cleansing 'rituals' from 29Ls; 🕑 11am-9pm Mon-Wed, 9am-9pm Thu & Fri, 10am-7pm Sat, 10am-5pm Sun) is a high-end relaxation centre offering massages, wraps, scrubs and sauna treatments. Try the signature 'opening ritual', in which clients move between saunas and plunge pools while drinking herbal teas. Yoga classes, Pilates courses and exercise facilities are also available.

Baltā Pirts (White Birch; ☎ 6727 1733; www.balta pirts.lv; Tallinas iela 71; sauna 7Ls; 🕑 8am-8pm Wed-Sun), frequented mostly by locals rather than tourists, combines traditional Latvian relaxation techniques with a subtle, oriental design scheme.

Shooting Range

The ambience at **Regro's** (☎ 6760 1705; Daugavgrīvas iela 31; bullets 0.80-2Ls; ⏰ 10am-5pm Mon-Sat, by appointment Sun) is reason enough to visit: a dingy Soviet fallout shelter adorned with posters of rifle-toting models wearing fur bikinis. Choose from a large selection of retro firearms (including Kalashnikovs) to aim at your paper cut-out of James Bond. You pay by the bullet. Take the Vanšu bridge across the river, pass Kīpsala, and take your first right until you hit a petrol station. Also accessible by tram 13. Don't forget your passport.

FESTIVALS & EVENTS

Rīga hosts loads of yearly events, such as the **Opera Festival** (www.music.lv/opera) and **Rīgas Ritmi** (www.rigasritmi.lv).

SLEEPING

If you're only in town for a short period of time, go for a room in the heart of Old Rīga. Those who are more concerned with getting the biggest bang for their buck will find the best deals along Central Rīga's grand boulevards. The summer months are quite busy, so it's best to book in advance. All accommodation here offers wi-fi.

Hostelworld (www.hostelworld.com) has become Rīga's unofficial go-to website for choosing budget digs.

Old Rīga (Vecrīga)

Naughty Squirrel (☎ 2614 7214; www.naughtysquirrel backpackers.com; Kalēju iela 50; dm/d from 7/28Ls; 🖥️) Five years ago this hostel (previously called Argonauts) was undoubtedly the coolest spot to hang your hat. Today, the rooms feel a bit worn out, but the staff are superfriendly and the couch-strewn common room is still a great spot to chill with new friends.

Old Town Hostel (☎ 6722 3406; www.rigaoldtown hostel.lv; Valņu iela 43; dm/d 7/35Ls; 🖥️) The bricklined pub on the ground floor doubles as the hostel's hang-out space, and if you can manage to lug your suitcase up the narrow, twisting staircase, you'll find spacious dorms with chandeliers and plenty of sunlight. Private rooms are located in another building near the train station.

Friendly Fun Franks (☎ 6722 0040; www.franks.lv; Novembra Krastmala 29; dm/d from 7/40Ls; 🖥️) If you want to party, look no further than this bright orange stag-magnet, where every backpacker is greeted with a hearty hello and a complimentary pint of beer. The staff offer guided tours of Old Rīga and frequent trips to the beach (5Ls).

Radi un Draugi (☎ 6782 0200; www.draugi.lv; Mārstaļu iela 1; s/d/ste 42/52/58Ls; 🖥️) Despite recent renovation attempts, this old-timer is starting to show its age. We're not a huge fan of puke-green shag carpeting, but if you can turn your expectations down a notch, then Radi provides good bang for your buck if you want to stay in the heart of Old Rīga.

Ekes Konventas (☎ 6735 8393; www.ekeskonvents.lv; Skārņu iela 22; s/d incl breakfast 55/60Ls; 🖥️) Not to be confused with Konventa Sēta next door, the 600-year-old Ekes Konventas oozes wobbly medieval charm from every crooked nook and cranny. Curl up with a book in the adorable stone alcoves on the landing of each storey.

Centra (☎ 6722 6441; www.centra.lv; Audēju iela 1; s/d 77/84Ls; 🖥️) Centra is a great choice for comfort in the heart of Old Rīga. Recently renovated rooms are spacious and sport loads of designer details such as swish LCD monitors, porcelain sinks and minimalist art on the walls. The hotel is completely nonsmoking.

Central Rīga (Centrs)
BUDGET

House Hostel (☎ 2649 1235; www.comehome.lv, www.riga-hostels.com; K Barona iela 44; dm/d from 7/28Ls; 🖥️) Warning: if you stay at the House, you probably won't see any of Rīga's sights – the ultrachill common space is both effortlessly stylish and a veritable black hole for backpackers. The hostel doubles as the office for Riga Out There, a reputable tour operator. Enter from Lāčplēša iela.

Barons (☎ 2910 5939; www.baronshostel.com; K Barona iela 25; dm/s/d 11/30/35Ls; 🖥️) Perched high on the top floor (sorry, no elevator), Barons has a bit more personality than the other low-key hostels in Central Rīga. Guests can save a lats or two and cook in the spacious kitchen, or relax in front of the plasma TV with a DVD.

ourpick City Lounge (☎ 2935 8958; www.citylounge .lv; Alfrēda Kalniņa iela 4; dm/d from 11/36Ls; 🖥️) Rumour has it that it's building an elevator, but until then guests should hire a sherpa to climb the 128 stairs. Once you get to the top, however, you'll find a fantastic hostel that's both hip and spotless. Guests staying in the London room can store their luggage in the iconic red telephone booth, and in the Rīga room there's a giant city map on the ceiling so you can plan

LATVIA

tomorrow's itinerary while lying in bed. Book nooks and electrical outlets are conveniently found beside every pillow.

Dodo Hotel (☎ 6724 0220; www.dodohotel.com; Jersikas iela 1; r from 27Ls; 🖳) Hidden deep in the Maskavas neighbourhood (east of the Central Market), this new cheapie is a fantastic find if you don't mind being slightly removed from the action. Savvy designers have feng shui-ed the small rooms with stylish details such as a scarlet accent wall, a mini plasma TV and teeny bucket sink in the bathroom.

KB (☎ 6731 2323; www.kbhotel.lv; K Barona iela 37; s/d/tr from 27/32/38Ls; 🖳) One of the only non-hostels in the budget category, this great B&B is located in a rather opulent building with a sweeping marble staircase taking travellers up to the top-floor hotel. The rooms are simple but well-appointed and there's a modern communal kitchen.

MIDRANGE

Krišjānis & Ģertrūde (☎ 6750 6604; www.kg.lv; K Barona iela 39; s/d/tr incl breakfast from 30/40/60Ls; 🖳) Step off the bustling intersection into this quaint, family-run B&B adorned with still lifes of fruit and flowers. It's best to book ahead since there are only six cosy rooms. Enter from Ģertrūdes iela.

B&B Rīga (☎ 2652 6400; www.bb-riga.lv; Ģertrūdes iela 43; s/d from 35/46Ls; 🖳) Snug, apartment-style accommodation comes in different configurations (suites with lofted bedrooms are particularly charming), and are scattered throughout the otherwise residential building. Streetside rooms can be a bit noisy.

Albert Hotel (☎ 6733 1717; www.alberthotel.lv; Dzirnavu iela 33; s/d incl breakfast 51/56Ls; 🖳 🖳) The boxy, metallic facade starkly contrasts with the surrounding art nouveau gargoyles, but the interior design is undeniably hip, paying tribute to the hotel's namesake, Albert Einstein. The patterned carpeting features rows of atomic energy symbols, and the 'do not disturb' doorknob danglers have been replaced with red tags that read 'I'm thinking'.

Hotel Valdemārs (☎ 6733 4462; www.valdemars.lv; Valdemāra iela 23; s/d incl breakfast from 63/88Ls; 🖳 🖳) Modern Hotel Valdemārs is a great find geared towards the Scandinavian market – rooms feel efficient yet homey, in an upmarket Ikea kind of way. Don't forget to give away the flower adorning the bureau in your room – it's a Latvian tradition! Online bookings yield cheaper rates.

TOP END

Europa Royale (☎ 6707 9444; www.europaroyale.com; K Barona iela 12; s/d/ste incl breakfast from 83/94/105Ls; 🖳 🖳) Once the home of media mogul Emilija Benjamiņa (Latvia's version of Anna Wintour), this ornate manse retains much of its original opulence with sweeping staircases and stately bedrooms. In fact, when Latvia regained its independence, the house was initially chosen to be president's digs but the government didn't have enough funds for the restoration. There are 60 large rooms, yet guests will feel like they're staying at their posh aunt's estate.

our pick Hotel Bergs (☎ 6777 0900; www.hotelbergs .lv; Elizabetes iela 83/85; r/ste incl breakfast from 123/173Ls; 🖳 🖳) Hotel Bergs' manor house-meets-spaceship exterior will grab you before you walk in the door. The lobby's mix of sharp lines, rococo portraits and tribal imagery seems to click, while spacious suites are lavished with monochromatic furnishings that feel avant garde yet remarkably comfortable. Countless other treats await, including our favourite – the 'pillow service' – which allows guests to choose from an array of different bed pillows based on material and texture.

EATING

For centuries in Latvia, food equalled fuel, energising peasants as they worked the fields, and warming their bellies during bone-chilling Baltic winters. Today, the era of boiled potatoes and pork gristle has begun to fade, as food becomes more than a necessary evil. Although it will be a while before globetrotters stop qualifying local restaurants as being 'good by Rīga's (mediocre) standards', the cuisine scene has improved by leaps and bounds over the last decade.

Lately the Slow Food movement has taken the city's high-end dining scene by storm. Seasonal menus feature carefully prepared, environmentally conscious dishes using organic produce grown across Latvia's ample farmland. Beyond the sphere of up-market eats, most local joints embrace the literal sense of the term 'slow food', with tortoise-speed service.

As Rīga's dining scene continues to draw its influence from a clash of other cultures, tipping is evolving from customary to obligatory. A 10% gratuity is common in the capital, and many restaurants are now tacking the tip onto the bill.

LATVIA

Old Rīga (Vecrīga)

Šefpavārs Vilhelms (Chef William; Šķūņu iela 6; pancake rolls 0.65Ls) Each time we visited, customers of every ilk were eagerly queuing for a quick nosh. Three blintze-like pancakes smothered in sour cream and jam equals the perfect backpacker's breakfast.

Pelmeņi XL (Kaļķu iela 7; dumpling bowls 0.90-2.50Ls) A Rīga institution for backpackers and undiscerning drunkards, this extra-large cafeteria stays open extra-late serving up huge bowls of *pelmeņi* (Russian-style ravioli stuffed with meat) to hungry mobs.

John Lemon (Peldu iela 21; mains 2.50-5Ls) This trendy spot attracts bleary-eyed partiers from Pulkvedis (across the street) for cheap, late-night munchies. Take your pick of three stylish rooms: an orange realm with '60s space station seating, the trellis-lined courtyard or a small nook drenched in lipstick reds.

Vecmeita ar kaki (The Spinster & Her Cat; Mazā Pils iela 1; mains 3-7.50Ls) This cosy spot across from the president's palace specialises in cheap Latvian cuisine. Menus have been crafted from old-school newspaper clippings, and patrons dine on converted sewing machine tables.

Ķiploka krogs (Garlic Bar; Jēkaba iela 3/5; mains 4-11Ls) Vampires beware – *everything* at this joint contains garlic, even the ice cream. The menu is pretty hit-and-miss, but no matter what, it's best to avoid the garlic pesto spread – it'll taint your breath for days (trust us). The entrance is from Mazā Pils.

Rozengrāls (Rozena iela 1; meals 9-15Ls) Remember 500 years ago when potatoes weren't the heart and soul of Latvian cuisine? We don't, but Rozengrāls does – this candlelit haunt takes diners back a few centuries offering medieval game (sans spuds) served by costume-clad waiters.

Gutenbergs (Doma laukums 1; meals 9.90-19.90Ls) At the Hotel Gutenbergs' rooftop restaurant you don't look down on the spires of Old Rīga, you sit among them. Potted plants, cherubic statues and trickling fountains contribute to a decidedly Florentine vibe, although the menu focuses on local favourites.

If you're self-catering, **Rimi** (www.rimi.lv; Audēju iela 16; 9am-10pm) is a high-quality supermarket in Old Rīga's Galerija Centrs shopping mall.

Central Rīga (Centrs)

Meta Kafe (Kronvalda bulvāris 2b; soups & salads 3Ls) Safely tucked away from those who are not in the know, this hipster hang-out is an inconspicuous prefab at the tennis club in Kronvalda Garden. The staff serves light, mostly vegie options on concrete tables as loiterers mess around on their laptops. Weekend poetry slams and DJ-ed dance parties usually last until sunrise. Wi-fi available.

LIDO Atpūtas Centrs (LIDO Recreation Centre; Krasta iela 76; mains 3-7Ls) If Latvia and Disney World had a love child it would be the LIDO Atpūtas Centrs – an enormous wooden palace dedicated to the country's coronary-inducing cuisine. Servers dressed like Baltic milkmaids bounce around as patrons hit the rows of buffets for classics like pork tongue, potato pancakes and cold beet soup. Take tram 3, 7 or 9, or bus 17E, and get off at the 'LIDO' stop. There are a handful of miniature LIDO restaurants dotted around the city centre for those who don't have time to make it out to the mothership.

Osiriss (K Barona iela 31; mains 3-7Ls) Despite Rīga's wishy-washy cafe culture, where establishments come and go like the seasons, Osiriss continues to be a local mainstay. The green faux-marble tabletops haven't changed since the mid-'90s and neither has the clientele: angsty artsy types scribbling in their Moleskines over a glass of red wine. Wi-fi available.

Charlestons (Čarlstons; Blaumaņa iela 38/40; mains 5-11Ls) If you're up to your elbows in pork tongue, Charlestons is a sure bet to get rid of the meat sweats. Lounge around the terraced courtyard in the heart of a residential block and feast on delicious platters like Norwegian salmon, sautéed duck and the best Caesar salad in the Baltics. Wi-fi available.

our pick Aragats (Miera iela 15; meals 6-9Ls) Ignore the plastic shrubbery – this place is all about sampling some killer cuisine from the Caucasus. Start with an appetiser of pickled vegetables – the perfect chaser for your home-brewed *chacha* (Georgian vodka). Then, make nice with the matronly owner as she dices up fresh herbs at your table to mix with the savoury lamb stew. At the end of the meal be a gentleman and pay for the ladies at the table, especially since the women's menus don't have any of the prices listed!

Fabrikas Restorāns (Balasta dambis 70; meals 8-18Ls) Once a crumbling gypsum factory, this chic dining option is now the preferred address for switched-on Russian jetsetters. Located on the banks of the Daugava River across from the city centre, Fabrikas serves up some of the best views in town. Live music on Friday evenings.

Vincents (Elizabetes iela 19; meals 16-22Ls) Ask any Rīgan – they'll all tell you that Vincents is the best restaurant in town. So, it's no surprise that it's also the most expensive. Apparently when Queen Elizabeth spent a day in town, she ate both her lunch and dinner here, and other world figures have followed suit. The head chef is a stalwart of the Slow Food movement, and crafts his ever-changing menu amid eye-catching van Gogh-inspired decor (hence the name).

Self-caterers can head to **Rimi** (www.rimi.lv; K Barona iela 46; 🕙 9am-10pm), a supermarket in Central Rīga's Barona Centrs shopping mall; fresh produce can also be purchased at the Central Market (p449).

DRINKING

If you want to party like a Latvian, assemble a gang of friends and pub-crawl your way through the city, stopping at colourful haunts for rounds of beers, belly laughter, and, of course, Black Balsam. On summer evenings, nab a spot at one of the beer gardens in rowdy Līvu Laukums.

Old Rīga (Vecrīga)

Cuba Cafe (Jauni iela 15) An authentic mojito and a table overlooking Doma laukums is just what the doctor ordered after a long day of sightseeing. On colder days, swig your caipirinha inside amid dangling Cuban flags, wobbly stained-glass lamps, and the murmur of trumpet jazz. Wi-fi available.

Orange Bar (Jāņa sēta 5) An alternative spot slathered in jet-black paint and splashes of neon orange light, this edgy alternative joint attracts hipsters of every ilk for some late-night carousing on the bar top.

La Belle Epoque (French Bar; Mazā Jaunavu iela 8) Students flock to this basement bar to power down its trademark 'apple pie' shots (go for their '10 shots for nine lats' deal if you're with friends.) The Renoir mural and kitsch *Moulin Rouge* posters seem to successfully ward off stag parties.

I Love You (Aldaru iela 9) The three words everyone loves to hear is a chill joint tucked away down one of Old Rīga's wobbly streets. Sneak downstairs for a sea of comfy couches. DJs spin alternative beats on Thursday nights.

Central Rīga (Centrs)

our pick Skyline Bar (Elizabetes iela 55) A must for anyone visiting Rīga, glitzy Skyline Bar sits on the 26th floor of the Reval Hotel Latvija. The sweeping views are the city's best, and the mix of glam spirit-sippers makes for great people-watching under the retro purple lighting.

Sarkans (Stabu iela 10) Safely removed from Old Rīga's mix of backpackers and stag fests, 'Red' lures party animals of all ages, with three fantastic levels of lounges and dance floors.

D'vine (Elizabetes iela 55) This cleverly named wine bar in the Reval Hotel Latvija could easily be mistaken for a Scandinavian space station (even the toilets look futuristic). Spanish tapas accompanies the laundry list of imported wines and champagnes.

ENTERTAINMENT
Nightclubs

Club Essential (www.essential.lv; Skolas iela 2) Rīga's hottest club is a spectacle of beautiful people boogying to some of Europe's top DJ talent. Overzealous security aside, there's no safer bet if partying till dawn is your mission.

Pulkvedim Neviens Neraksta (No-one Writes to the Colonel; www.pulkvedis.lv; Peldu iela 26/28; cover weekends/weekdays 3Ls/free) There's no such thing as a dull night at Pulkvedis. The atmosphere is 'warehouse chic', with pumping '80s tunes on the ground floor, and trance beats down below.

Nautilus (Kungu iela 8; cover 4-10Ls) Nautilus is a throbbing hot spot inside a faux submarine. There's a chill-out room with plush red couches, a frantic dance floor and a tad too much uniformed security. It's not worth showing up before midnight.

Performing Arts

The **National Opera House** (☎ 6707 3777; www.opera .lv; Aspazijas bulvāris 3; tickets 5-30Ls; box office 🕙 10am-7pm) is the pride of Latvia, boasting some of the finest opera in all of Europe (and for the fraction of the price in other countries). Mikhail Baryshnikov got his start here. Rīga's ballet, opera and theatre season breaks for summer holidays (between June and September).

The acoustics and massive organ make the **Dome Cathedral** (☎ 6721 3213; www.hbf.lv; Doma laukums; box office 🕙 noon-6pm Tue-Sat) a must for music lovers. Twice-weekly evening organ concerts (Wednesday and Friday) and well worth attending.

The **Great Guild** (☎ 6722 7105; www.hbf.lv; Amatu iela 6; box office ✆ noon-6pm Tue-Sat) is home to the acclaimed Latvian National Symphonic Orchestra. Classical music and jazz scats are often heard from the window.

Cinemas
Catching a movie is a great way to spend a rainy day in Rīga (trust us, there are many). Tickets cost between 2Ls and 4Ls.

Kino Rīga (Elizabetes iela 61) The Baltics' first cinema now specialises in European films and hosts several film festivals, including the international Future Shorts (www.futureshorts.lv).

K Suns (www.kinogalerija.lv; Elizabetes iela 83/85, Bergs Bazārs) An artsy cinema that projects mostly indie films on its one screen.

Live Music
Bites Blues Club (www.bluesclub.lv; Dzirnavu iela 34a; cover 3-5Ls) Friday nights see most of the live music action during the summer; in winter expect tunes on Thursday and Saturday as well.

City Jazz Club (www.cityjazzclub.lv; Ģertrūdes iela 34; cover 10Ls) A swank affair with claret-coloured tablecloths, a lengthy wine list and an international menu.

Gay & Lesbian Venues
If you're looking for a thriving gay scene, pick another city.

Purvs (Matīsa iela 60/62; cover free-5Ls) Believe it or not, Purvs isn't short for 'pervert'; it's Latvian for 'swamp'. Behind the unmarked entrance lies pumping club music, go-go dancers and the occasional tranny show.

XXL (Kalniņa iela 1; cover 1-10Ls) 'Tom of Finland' porno adorns the walls and disco music blares on weekends. A dark labyrinth and video screening room are also available.

SHOPPING
The mall has boomed in the last decade, with scores of plazas around Old and Central Rīga. Street sellers peddle their touristy wares outside St Peter's church. Keep an eye out for the beautiful Namēju rings worn by Latvians around the world as a way to recognise one another.

Art Nouveau Riga (Strēlnieku iela 9) Purchase a variety of art nouveau–related souvenirs, from guidebooks to postcards and stone gargoyles.

Latvijas Balzams (Audēju iela 8) A chain of liquor stores selling the trademark Latvian Black Balsam.

Upe (Vāgnera iela 5) Classical Latvian music wafts through the air as customers peruse traditional instruments and CDs of local folk, rock and experimental artists.

Istaba (K Barona iela 31a) A wee gallery displaying the works of local artisans mixed with kitsch trinkets and souvenirs. The lofted 2nd floor doubles as a trendy cafe.

The following shops are located in **Berga Bazārs** (www.bergabazars.lv; Dzirnavu iela 84), a maze of upmarket boutiques orbiting the five-star Hotel Bergs:

Emihla Gustava Shokolahde (www.sokolade.lv) Latvia's finest chocolate shop doubles as a chic cafe. The fruit-stuffed truffles are divine.

Garage (www.garage.lv) A gallery and souvenir shop featuring upmarket handicrafts designed by Latvian artists.

GETTING THERE & AWAY
Air
Riga airport (Lidosta Rīga; ☎ 6720 7009; www.riga-airport.com, Marupes pagast) is in the suburb of Skulte, 13km southwest of the city centre. See p464 for info on airlines flying into the capital.

airBaltic (☎ 6720 7886; www.airbaltic.com) offers flights twice daily (Monday to Friday) to/from Ventspils and five daily (all week) to/from Liepāja. One-way tickets start at 1Ls if purchased in advance.

Boat
Rīga's outdated passenger **ferry terminal** (☎ 6703 0800; www.rop.lv; Eksporta iela 3a), located about 900m downstream (north) of Akmens Bridge, offers service to Stockholm aboard **Tallink** (☎ 6709 9700; www.tallink.lv). **DFDS Tor Line** (☎ 2735 3523; www.dfdstorline.lv; Zivju iela 1), near the mouth of the Daugava River, goes to/from Lübeck, Germany (from 45Ls, 34 hours, two weekly).

Bus
Buses to other towns and cities leave from Rīga's **international bus station** (Rīgas starptautiskā autoosta; www.autoosta.lv; Prāgas iela 1), located behind the railway embankment just beyond the southeastern edge of Old Town. **Ecolines** (☎ 6721 4512; www.ecolines.lv; ✆ 7am-9.30pm) and **Eurolines Baltic** (☎ 6721 4080; www.eurolines.lv) have offices at the bus station. International destinations include Warsaw, Amsterdam, Berlin, Brussels, Kyiv, London, Moscow, St Petersburg, Paris and Prague.

LATVIA

Domestic services departing from Rīga include the following:

Bauska (1.90Ls, 1¼ hours, three or four per hour from 6.15am to 11.20pm)

Cēsis (2.50Ls, around 2 hours, two or three per hour from 6.15am to 10.20pm)

Kolka (3.85Ls to 4.85Ls, 3½ to 4½ hours, five daily from 7.20am to 5.15pm)

Kuldīga (2.50Ls, 2½ to 3¼ hours, 15 daily from 7am to 8pm)

Liepāja (4.50Ls to 5.40Ls, 3½ to 4½ hours, two or three per hour from 6.45am to 8.30pm)

Sigulda (1Ls, 70 minutes, twice-hourly from 8.10am to 10.15pm)

Ventspils (4.55Ls, 2¾ to 4 hours, hourly from 7am to 10.30pm)

Train

Rīga's **Central Train Station** (Centrālā stacija; ☎ 6723 1181, 1188; Stacijas laukums) is located around the corner, near the Central Market in a glass-encased complex. Rīga is linked by direct train to Moscow (from 20Ls, 17 hours, twice daily) and St Petersburg (from 16Ls, 13 hours, daily). Visit www.ldz.lv and www.1188.lv for international train schedules and info on domestic buses.

GETTING AROUND
To/From the Airport

There are three means of transport connecting the city centre to the airport. The cheapest option is bus 22, which runs every 15 minutes and stops at several points around town. Tickets (0.40Ls) are sold by the bus drivers; exact change is preferred. AirBaltic runs lime green vans from the airport to the hotel of your choice (so long as it's in Central Rīga – those staying in Old Rīga will be dropped off on the outskirts of the medieval neighbourhood and will have to walk the last five to 10 minutes to their hotel). Taxis should not cost more than 7Ls.

Car & Motorcycle

Latvians joke that the traffic is so bad in Rīga that it takes longer to drive across the city than it does to drive across the entirety of Latvia. For information on car rentals, see p465. Motorists must pay 5Ls per hour to enter Old Town.

Public Transport

If you weren't born in Rīga, then you don't have the gene that innately enables you to understand the city's horribly convoluted network of buses, trams and trolleybuses. Fortunately, most of the main tourist attractions are within walking distance of one another, so you might never have to use any of Rīga's 11 tramlines, 23 trolleybus paths or 39 bus routes. Tickets cost 0.40Ls (0.50Ls if you buy your tram or trolleybus ticket from the driver – exact change is necessary). Tram and trolleybus tickets can also be purchased at Narvesen superettes. City transport runs daily from 5.30am to midnight. Some routes have an hourly night service. For Rīga public transport routes and schedules visit www.rigass atiksme.lv.

Taxi

Officially, taxis charge 0.30Ls per kilometre (0.40Ls between 10pm and 6am), but don't be surprised if you get ripped off. Insist on having the meter on before you set off. Meters usually start running at 0.50Ls to 1.50Ls. Don't pay more than 3Ls for short journeys. There are taxi ranks outside the bus and train stations, at the airport and in front of the major hotels in Central Rīga.

AROUND RĪGA

It's hard to believe that long stretches of flaxen beaches and shady pine forests lie just 20km from Rīga's metropolitan core. The highway connecting Rīga to Jūrmala (Latvia's only six-lane road) was known as '10 Minutes in America' during Soviet times, because locally produced films set in the USA were always filmed on this busy asphalt strip.

JŪRMALA
pop 55,600

The Baltics' version of the French Riviera, Jūrmala is a long string of townships with stately wooden beach estates belonging to Russian oil tycoons and their supermodel trophy wives. Even during the height of communism, Jūrmala was always a place to *sea* and be seen. Today, on summer weekends, vehicles clog the roads when jetsetters and day-tripping Rīgans flock to the resort town for some serious fun in the sun.

If you don't have a car or bicycle, you'll want to head straight to the heart of the action – the townships of Majori and Dzintari. A 1km-long pedestrian street, Jomas iela, connects these two districts and is considered

---

WORTH THE TRIP: RUNDĀLE PALACE

If you only have time for one day trip out of Rīga, make it **Rundāle Palace** (Rundāles pils; ☎ 6396 2197; www.rundale.net; garden 1Ls; palace adult/child 2.50/2Ls, combined ticket adult/child 5/4.30Ls, guided group tour 32Ls; ☽ 10am-7pm Jun-Aug, to 6pm Sep-Oct, to 5pm Nov-Apr), 75km south of the capital near the tiny town of Bauska. The architect of this sprawling monument to aristocratic ostentatiousness was the Italian baroque genius Bartolomeo Rastrelli, best known for designing the Winter Palace in St Petersburg. About 40 of the palace's 138 rooms are open to visitors, as are the wonderfully landscaped gardens.

To reach the palace, take a bus from Rīga to Bauska (1.90Ls, 70 minutes to 1½ hours), then switch to one of the nine daily buses (0.35Ls) connecting Bauska to the palace, 12km away.

---

to be Jūrmala's main drag. The **tourism information centre** (☎ 6714 7902; www.jurmala .lv; Lienes iela 5; ☽ 9am-7pm Mon-Fri, 10am-5pm Sat, 10am-3pm Sun), located across from Majori train station, has scores of brochures outlining walks and bike routes. Staff can assist with accommodation bookings.

Sights & Activities
NOTABLE BUILDINGS
Besides its beach, Jūrmala's main attraction is its colourful **art nouveau wooden houses**, distinguishable by frilly awnings, detailed facades and elaborate towers. There are over 4000 wooden structures (most are lavish summer cottages) found throughout Jūrmala, but you can get your fill of wood by taking a leisurely stroll along Jūras iela, which parallels Jomas iela between Majori and Dzintari. The houses are in various states of repair; some are dilapidated and abandoned, some are beautifully renovated and others are brand new. The tourism information office has a handy booklet called *The Resort Architecture of Jūrmala City*, which features several self-guided walking tours. Ask about bicycle rentals (5Ls per day).

At the other end of the architectural spectrum are several particularly gaudy beachfront Soviet-era sanatoriums. No specimen glorifies the genre quite like the **Vaivari sanatorium** (Asaru prospekts 61), on the main road 5km west of Majori. It resembles a giant, beached cruise ship that's been mothballed since the Brezhnev era. Surprisingly it still functions, catering to an elderly clientele who have been visiting regularly since, well, the Brezhnev era.

ĶEMERI NATIONAL PARK
After Jūrmala's chic stretch of celebrity homes and seaside bar huts lies a verdant hinterland called **Ķemeri National Park** (☎ 6714 6819; www .kemeri.gov.lv; ☽ Jun-Aug). Today, the park features sleepy fishing villages tucked between protected bogs, lakes and forests, but at the end of the 19th century Ķemeri was known for its curative mud and spring water, attracting visitors from as far away as Moscow.

SPAS
Jūrmala's first spa opened in 1838, and since then, the area has been known far and wide as the spa capital of the Baltic countries. Treatments are available at a variety of big-name hotels and hulking Soviet sanatoriums further along the beach towards Ķemeri National Park. Many accommodation options offer combined spa and sleeping deals.

our pick **Baltic Beach Spa** (☎ 6777 1400; www .balticbeach.lv; Jūras iela 23-25; massages 60/90mins 25/35Ls; ☽ 8am-10pm) is the largest treatment centre in the Baltic, with three rambling storeys full of massage rooms, saunas, yoga studios, swimming pools and Jacuzzis. The 1st floor is themed like a country barn and features invigorating hot-and-cold treatments in which one takes regular breaks from the steam room by pouring buckets of ice water over their head à la Jennifer Beals in *Flashdance*.

Sleeping & Eating
Jūrmala has a wide selection of lodging options – very few of them are good value. If penny pinching's your game, do a day trip to Jūrmala and sleep in Rīga. Summertime prices are listed below; room rates fall dramatically during the low-season months.

Kempings Nemo (☎ 6773 2350; www.nemo.lv; Atbalss iela 1; cottages 8-32Ls, per camp site/person 2/2Ls, parking 2Ls; ☒) Bright yellow-and-blue banners welcome guests to this popular camping ground, located right beside Nemo Water Park on the beach in Vaivari township. Don't miss the home-cooked Latvian breakfasts (3.90Ls).

LATVIA

Villa Joma (☎ 6777 1999; www.villajoma.lv; Jomas iela 90; s 52-97Ls, d 55-100) This inviting boutique hotel sports 15 immaculate rooms that come in quirky configurations. Try for a room with a skylight. Sample the fantastic food (lunch mains 6Ls to 8Ls; dinner mains 9Ls to 17Ls) served at the airy ground-floor restaurant.

our pick **Hotel MaMa** (☎ 6776 1271; www.hotel mama.lv; Tirgonu iela 22; d from 90Ls) The bedroom doors have thick, mattress-like padding on the interior (psycho-chic?) and the suites themselves are a veritable blizzard of white drapery. A mix of silver paint and pixie dust accent the ultramodern furnishings and amenities. If heaven had a bordello, it would probably look something like this. The in-house restaurant has a special menu for dogs (no joke), and check out the techni-coloured bathroom with a fun surprise on the ceiling.

Crystalbar (Klavu iela 14; mains 5-10Ls) Located well off the tourist track, this slick hang-out is a popular pick among young locals who come for cocktails on the patio and fresh homemade pasta. It's across the street from a hard-to-miss bright blue Orthodox church.

Seaside Lounge (www.seasidelounge.lv; Jomas iela 57) This 2nd-storey nightclub, above the popular Slāvu restaurant, rocks late into the night with a spacious dance floor and a host of local DJs.

Getting There & Away

Two to three trains per hour link Central Rīga to the sandy shores of Jūrmala (0.65Ls); disembark at Majori station (30 to 35 minutes). Minibuses (1Ls) are also a common mode of transportation between Rīga and Jūrmala. Minibuses also connect Jūrmala to Rīga airport (2Ls). Motorists driving the 15km in Jūrmala must pay a 1Ls toll per day, even if they are just passing through. Keep an eye out for the self-service toll stations sitting at both ends of the resort town.

WESTERN LATVIA

Just when you thought that Rīga was the only star of the show, in comes western Latvia from stage left, dazzling audiences with a whole different set of talents. While the capital wows the crowd with intricate architecture and metropolitan majesty, Kurzeme (Courland in English) takes things in the other di-

rection: miles and miles of jaw-dropping natural beauty.

It's hard to believe that desolate Kurzeme was once the bustling Duchy of Courland. During the 1600s, Duke Jakob, Courland's ruler, flexed his imperial muscles by colonising Tobago and Gambia. He even had plans to colonise Australia! (Needless to say, that didn't quite work out…)

CAPE KOLKA (KOLKASRAGS)

Enchantingly desolate and hauntingly beautiful, a journey to Cape Kolka (Kolkasrags) feels like a trip to the end of the earth. During Soviet times the entire peninsula was zoned off as a high-security military base – the dirt road between Ventspils and Kolka was a giant aircraft runway. The region's development was subsequently stunted, and today the string of desolate coastal villages has a distinct anachronistic feel – as though they've been locked away in a time capsule.

The village of **Kolka** is nothing to write home about, but the windswept moonscape at the waning edge of the cape (just 500m away) could have you daydreaming for days. It's here that the Gulf of Rīga meets the Baltic Sea in a very dramatic fashion. A **monument** to those claimed by treacherous waters marks the entrance to the beach near a small **information centre** (☎ 2914 9105). The poignant stone slab, with its haunting anthropomorphic silhouette, was erected in 2002. If you plan to stay the night, **Ūši** (☎ 2947 5692; www.kolka.info; s/d incl breakfast 26/38Ls) has simple but prim rooms, and a spot to pitch tents in the garden.

The easiest way to reach Cape Kolka is by private vehicle (adventurous types can bike), but buses are also available. To reach the town of Kolka, buses either follow the Gulf Coast Rd through Roja, or they ply the route through Talsi and Dundaga (inland). Either way, there are five buses that link Rīga and Kolka town per day between 4.30am and 5.15pm (3.85Ls to 4.85Ls, 3½ to 4¾ hours).

KULDĪGA
pop 13,010

If adorable Kuldīga were a tad closer to Rīga it would be crowded with day-tripping camera-clickers. Fortunately, the town is located deep in the heart of rural Kurzeme, making it just far enough to be the perfect reward for more-intrepid travellers. In its heyday, Kuldīga served as the capital of the Duchy of Courland (1596–1616) and was known as the 'city where salmon fly' – during spawning season, salmon would swim upstream, and when they reached **Ventas Rumba** (the widest waterfall in Europe) they would jump through the air attempting to surpass it.

Kuldīga was badly damaged during the Great Northern War and was never quite able to regain its former lustre. Today, this blast from the past is a favourite spot to shoot Latvian period-piece films – 29 movies and counting…

Stop by the **tourist information centre** (☎ 6332 2259; www.kuldiga.lv; Baznīcas iela 5; 🕑 9am-6pm Mon-Sat, 10am-2pm Sun mid-May–mid-Sep, 9am-5pm Mon-Fri rest of year) in the old town hall for a handy brochure explaining the history of this adorable town and its signature **Livonian Order Castle** ruins.

Kuldīga's best hotel, **Hotel Metropole** (☎ 6335 0588; Baznīnas iela 11; d/ste incl breakfast from 40/100Ls; 🖳), rolls out the red carpet (literally) up its mod concrete stairwell to charming double-decker bedrooms overlooking the town's main drag, pedestrian **Liepājas iela**. The slightly spartan **Jāņa Nams** (☎ 6332 3456; www.jananams .lv; Liepājas iela 36; s/d incl breakfast 27/29Ls) is a solid second choice.

At **Dārziņš Bakery** (Baznīcas iela; snacks 0.10-2Ls) the cashier calculates your bill with an amber abacus. Try the *sklandu rausis* (0.12Ls), an ancient Cour carrot cake. **Pagrabiņš** (Baznīcas iela 5; mains 4Ls) lurks in the cellar beneath the information centre in what used to be the town's prison.

From the **bus station** (Stacijas iela 2), buses run to/from Rīga (3.90Ls to 4.45Ls, 2½ to 3½ hours, 12 daily), Liepāja (2Ls to 2.40Ls, 1¾ hours, eight daily), Ventspils (1.75Ls to 1.90Ls, 1¼ hours, seven daily), and Talsi (2Ls to 2.25Ls, 1½ to 2¼ hours, four daily).

VENTSPILS
pop 43,300

Fabulous amounts of oil and shipping money have turned Ventspils into one of Latvia's most beautiful and dynamic cities. And although locals coddle their Užavas beer and claim that there's not much to do, tourists will find a weekend's worth of fun in the form of brilliant beaches, interactive museums and winding Old Town streets dotted with the odd boutique and cafe.

The folks at the **tourism information centre** (☎ 6362 2263; www.tourism.ventspils.lv; Dārza iela 6; 🕑 8am-7pm Mon-Fri, 10am-5pm Sat, 10am-3pm Sun May-Sep, 8am-5pm Mon-Fri, 10am-3pm Sat & Sun Oct-Apr) can point you in the direction of the state-of-the-art museum in the 13th-century **Livonian Order Castle** (☎ 6362 2031; Jana iela 17; adult/child 1/0.50Ls; 🕑 9am-6pm May-Oct, 10am-5pm Tue-Sun Nov-Apr), as well as the **House of Crafts** (☎ 6362 0174; Skolas iela 3; adult/child 0.60/0.30Ls; 🕑 11am-7pm Tue-Fri, 10am-7pm Sat, 11am-3pm Sun).

Our favourite spot to spend the night, **Kupfernams** (☎ 6362 6999; Kārļa iela 5; s/d 25/35Ls) sits in an inviting wooden house at the centre of Old Town. The cheery rooms with slanted ceilings sit above a fantastic restaurant and a trendy hair salon (which doubles as the front desk). Penny-pinchers should try **Piejūras Kempings** (☎ 6362 7925; www.camping.ventspils.lv; Vasarnicu iela 56; camp sites per person 2Ls, cottages 18-45Ls; 🖳). Grab a bite at **Melanis Sivēns** (Jāņa iela 17; meals 4-12Ls), a medieval-style restaurant on the castle grounds.

During the week, two flights per day connect Ventspils' **airport** (☎ 6362 4262; www.airport .ventspils.lv; Ganibu iela 103) with Rīga. Ventspils is served by buses to/from Rīga (4.55Ls, 2¾ to four hours, hourly), Liepāja (3.30Ls, 2¼ to three hours, seven daily) and Kuldīga (1.85Ls, 1¼ hours, seven daily).

Scandlines (☎ 6360 0173; www.scandlines.lt) runs seasonal ferries five times weekly from the **ferry terminal** (Dārza iela 6) to Nynashamn, Sweden (60km from Stockholm) and Rostock, Germany. **SSC Ferries** (☎ 6360 7184; www.sscf.lv) runs a ferry service four to five times per week to Montu habour on Saaremaa in Estonia.

LIEPĀJA
pop 85,050

For the last decade, Liepāja has been searching for its identity like an angsty teenager. The city's growing pains are evident in the visual clash of gritty warehouses stacked next to swish hipster bars and tricked-out nightclubs. The local tourist office markets Liepāja as 'the place where wind is born', but we think the city's rough-around-the-edges garage-band scene is undoubtedly the city's biggest draw. Liepāja lures revellers for the annual **Baltic Beach Party** (www.balticbeachparty.lv) and the **Amber of Liepāja** (www.liepajas dzintars.lv).

The **tourist information centre** (☎ 6348 0808; www.liepaja.lv/turisms; Rožu laukums 3/5; 🕑 9am-7pm Mon-Fri, to 4pm Sat, 10am-3pm Sun Jun-Aug, 9am-5pm

LATVIA

Mon-Sat Sep-May) offers maps for walking tours and has details on getting to Liepāja's one must-see attraction, **Karosta Prison** (Karostas cietums; ☎ 2636 9470; www.karostascietums.lv; Invalīdu iela 4; tours 2Ls, 2hr shows 5Ls, sleepovers 10Ls; ✆ 10am-6pm May-Sep, by appointment Oct-Apr), 4km north of the centre. Daily multilingual tours detail the history of the prison, which was strictly used to punish disobedient soldiers in the Russian army. Sign up to become a prisoner for the night and subject yourself to regular bed checks and verbal abuse by guards in period garb. For those only wanting a pinch of masochism, there are abridged two-hour 'reality shows'.

You'll either adore or abhor spending a night at **Hotel Fontaine** (☎ 6342 0956; www.fontaine .lv; Jūras iela 24; r from 20Ls; 🖳), a funky hostelry that feels like a secondhand store with its kitschy knick-knack shop used as the reception, and the 20-some rooms stuffed to the brim with rock memorabilia, dusty oriental rugs, bright tile mosaics, Soviet propaganda and anything else deemed appropriately offbeat. Tighter budgets should try **Traveller's Hostel** (☎ 2869 0106; www.liepajahostel.com; Republikas iela 25; dm 10Ls; 🖳), a friendly spot with five bright rooms and oodles of common space.

Fontaine Palace (Dzirnavu iela 4) is a never-closing rock house luring loads of live acts and crowds of sweaty fanatics. The attached **Delisnack** (mains 1.40-7.50Ls) was designed with the inebriated partier in mind: the American-style burgers are a foolproof way to sop up some of those vodka shots done earlier in the evening.

Restaurants, billiards and a rooftop beer garden are all rolled into the massive, pseudo-industrial mega-complex known as **Latvia's 1st Rock Café** (Stendera iela 18/20; www.pablo .lv; cover free-5Ls). Pablo, the roaring basement club, features live music every night, and rave parties on the weekends. Don't forget to buy your Hard Rock Café T-shirt…er…we mean…1st Rock Café.

The city's **airport** (☎ 6340 7592; www.liepaja -airport.lv; Lidosta iela 8) offers five daily flights to/from Rīga. Buses run to/from Kuldīga (2.20Ls, 1¼ hours, eight daily) and Ventspils (3.40Ls, two hours, seven daily), and there are several buses (4.30Ls, 3¼ hours) and one early-morning train (3.40Ls, 3¼ hours) to/from Rīga. At the time of research, ferries were no longer operating in and out of Liepāja.

EASTERN LATVIA

When Rīga's urban hustle fades into a pulsing hum of chirping crickets, you've entered eastern Latvia. Known as Vidzeme, or 'the Middle Land', to locals, the country's largest region is an excellent sampler of what Latvia has to offer. Most tourists head to **Gauja National Park** (Gaujas nacionālais parks; www .gnp.gov.lv, admission free), the country's oldest preserve, where forest folks hike, bike or paddle through the thicketed terrain, and history buffs ogle at the generous sprinkling of castles throughout.

SIGULDA
pop 10,700

With a name that sounds like a mythical ogress, it comes as no surprise that the gateway to the Gauja is an enchanting little spot with delightful surprises tucked behind every dappled tree. Locals proudly call their pine-peppered town the 'Switzerland of Latvia', but if you're expecting the majesty of a mountainous snowcapped realm, you'll be rather disappointed. Instead, Sigulda mixes its own exciting brew of scenic trails, extreme sports and 800-year-old castles steeped in colourful legends.

Information

The **Gauja National Park Visitors Centre** (☎ 6780 0388; www.gnp.gov.lv; Baznīcas iela 7; ✆ 9.30am-7pm Apr-Oct, 10am-4pm Nov-Mar) can arrange tours, back-country camping and other accommodation. Cycle and hiking trail maps also available. The **Sigulda tourism information centre** (☎ 6797 1335; www.sigulda.lv; Valdemāra iela 1a; ✆ 10am-7pm Jun-Sep, to 5pm Oct-May) has an internet kiosk and stocks mountains of help information about activities and accommodations. Ask about the *Sigulda Spiekis* discount card.

Sights

If you just arrived from the train or bus station, walk down Raina iela to linden-lined Pils iela until you reach **Sigulda New Castle**, built in the 18th-century during the reign of German aristocrats. Check out the ruins of **Sigulda Medieval Castle** around back, which was constructed in 1207 by the Order of the Brethren of the Sword, but now lies mostly in ruins after being severely damaged in the 18th century during the Great Northern War. Follow Ainas

---

WORTH THE TRIP: THE PENSION

Deep in the heart of the Gauja National Park, the little town of Līgatne is a twilight zone of extremes. The town's collection of hideous industrial relics sprouts up from a patchwork of picturesque pine forests and cool blue rivulets. Despite the unsightly Soviet reminders, it's worth stopping by a top-secret lair fit for a James Bond film.

After entering Līgatne, wind your way up a small hill until you reach a dreary rehabilitation centre. This is no ordinary rehab hospital; hidden underneath the bland '60s architecture lies a clandestine Soviet bunker, known by its code name, the **Pension** (☎ 6416 1915; www.rehcentrsligatne .lv; Skaļupes; admission per person 2Ls). When Latvia was part of the USSR, 'the Pension' was one of the most important strategic hideouts during a time of nuclear threat. In fact, the bunker's location was so tightly guarded that it remained classified information until 2003. Almost all of the bunker's 2000 sq metres still look as it did when it was in operation. Multilanguage tours must be booked in advance and last up to 1½ hours.

Two buses per hour trundle along the Cēsis–Sigulda route, stopping in Līgatne along the way (1Ls). If you have your own transportation, it's a quick 20-minute drive from either Sigulda or Cēsis.

---

iela to the rocky precipice and take the **cable car** (☎ 6797 2531; www.lgk.lv; Poruka iela 14; one-way 1Ls; ⏰ 10am-7.30pm Jun-Aug, to 5pm Sat & Sun May-Sep) over the scenic river valley to **Krimulda Manor**, an elegant estate currently used as a rehabilitation clinic. After exploring the grounds, check out the crumbling ruins of **Krimulda Medieval Castle** nearby, then follow the serpentine road down to **Gūtmaņa Cave**. Immortalised by the legend of the Rose of Turaida (learn about her heartbreaking story at Turaida), it's the largest erosion cave in the Baltic. Take some time to read the myriad inscriptions carved into the cave walls then up to the **Turaida Museum Reserve** (Turaidas muzejrezervats; ☎ 6797 1402; www .turaida-muzejs.lv; admission 3Ls; ⏰ 10am-9pm May-Oct, to 5pm Nov-Apr). The medieval castle was erected in the 13th century for the Archbishop of Rīga over the site of an ancient Liv stronghold. The sprawling grounds also include the sculpture-festooned **Dainu Hill Song Garden**.

Activities

If you're looking to test your limits with a bevy of adrenalin-pumping activities, then you've come to the right place. Those looking for something more subdued will enjoy hiking and cycling trails through the national park's shady pines, or canoeing down the lazy Gauja River.

EXTREME SPORTS

Sigulda's 1200m artificial **bobsled track** (☎ 6797 3813; Sveices iela 13) was built for the former Soviet bobsleigh team. In winter you can fly down the 16-bend track at 80km/h in a five-person **Vučko tourist bob** (rides per person 6Ls; ⏰ noon-7pm Sat & Sun Oct-Mar), or try the real Olympian experience on the hair-raising **winter bob** (rides per person 35Ls). Summer speed fiends can ride a wheeled **'summer sled'** (rides per person 6Ls; ⏰ 11am-6pm Sat & Sun May-Sep) without booking in advance.

If the bobsled wasn't enough to make you toss your cookies, take your daredevil shenanigans to the next level and try a 43m **bungee jump** (☎ 2644 0660; www.bungee.lv; Poruka iela 14; Fri/weekend jumps 20/25Ls; ⏰ 7.30pm to last jump Fri-Sun May-Sep) from the cable car that glides high over the Gauja River. The one-of-a-kind **aerodium** (☎ 2838 4400; www.aerodium.lv; 2min weekday/weekend 15/18Ls; additional min weekday/weekend 5/6Ls; ⏰ 4-10pm Mon-Fri, noon-8pm Sat & Sun May-Sep) is a giant wind tunnel that propels participants up into the sky as though they were flying.

HIKING, CYCLING & CANOEING

Sigulda is prime hiking territory, so bring your walking shoes. A popular (and easy) route is the 40-minute walk from Krimulda Medieval Castle to Turaida Museum Reserve via Gūtmaņa Cave and Viktors' Cave. Or you can head south from Krimulda and descend to **Little Devil's Cave** and **Big Devil's Cave**. Try the well-marked loop (east of town) that leads to **Artists' Hill** for a beautiful panoramic view of Turaida Castle and the Gauja River valley. Many outfitters around Sigulda offer daily bicycle and mountain-bike rentals for around 7Ls to 10Ls per day.

Makars Tourism Agency (☎ 2924 4948; www.makars .lv; Peldu iela 1) arranges one- to three-day water tours around the park. For the less intrepid paddler, Makars rents out canoes and rubber boats seating between two and six people starting at 10Ls per day.

Sleeping & Eating

Check out Sigulda's official website www.tourism.sigulda.lv for additional lodging info.

Kempings Siguldas Pludmale (☎ 2924 4948; www.makars.lv; Peldu iela 2; camp sites per person/tent/car/caravan 3/1.50/1.50/6Ls; ♥ 15 May-15 Sep) Pitch your tent in the grassy camping ground beside the sandy beach along the Gauja. The location is perfect; however, there's only one bathroom for each sex.

Līvkalns (☎ 6797 0916; www.livkalns.lv; Pēteralas iela; s/d from 25/30Ls) No place is more romantically rustic than this idyllic retreat next to a pond on the forest's edge. The rooms are pine-fresh and sit among a campus of adorable thatch-roof manors. The cabin-in-the-woods-style restaurant is fantastic.

Segevold (☎ 2647 6652; www.hotelsegevold.lv; Mālpils iela 4b; s/d 40/55Ls; 🖳) After entering the swankified lobby, you'll immediately forget that Segevold is bizarrely located in the heart of an industrial park – the futuristic lighting and giant tentacle-like reliefs starkly contrast with the grungy Soviet tractors around the corner. Upstairs, the rooms are noticeably less glam, but they're in mint condition and kept pathologically clean.

Kaķu Māja (Pils iela 8; mains from 2Ls) The 'Cat House' is the top spot around town for a cheap bite. In the bistro, point to the ready-made dishes that tickle your fancy, and hunker down on one of the inviting picnic tables outside. For dessert, visit the attached bakery to try out-of-this-world pastries, pies and cakes. On Friday and Saturday nights, the restaurant in the back busts out the disco ball until the wee hours of the morning.

Getting There & Around

Buses also run from Sigulda to Līgatne (0.40Ls, 10 minutes) and Cēsis (0.90Ls, 40 minutes).

Sigulda's attractions are quite spread out; bus 12 links all of the sights, and plies the route seven times daily (more on weekends). Bus times are posted at the stations and on the info centre's official website.

CĒSIS

pop 18,260

Cēsis' unofficial moniker, 'Latvia's most Latvian town', pretty much holds true,
and day trippers will be treated to a mosaic of quintessential country life – a stunning Livonian castle, soaring church spires, cobbled roads and a lazy lagoon – all wrapped up in a bow like an adorable adult Disneyland.

Pick up a map, check email or arrange bike rentals at the **Cēsis tourist information centre** (☎ 6412 1815; www.tourism.cesis.lv; Pils laukums 2; ♥ 9am-7pm Jun-Aug, to 6pm Sep-May). Note that there are plans to move the information centre across the square to Pils laukums 5.

In 1209 the Knights of the Sword founded the fairy-tale-like **Cēsis Castle** (Cēsu pils). Its dominant feature is two stout towers at the western end. To enter, visit **Cēsis History & Art Museum** (Cēsu Vēstures un mākslas muzejs; Pils laukums 9; adult/child 2/1Ls; ♥ 10am-5pm Tue-Sun), in the adjoining 18th-century 'new castle', painted salmon pink. The castle's western tower has a viewpoint overlooking serene **Castle Park**, which sits along a scene lake with lily pads.

Housed in a grubby Soviet-style building, **Hostel Putiņkrogs** (☎ 6412 0290; www.cdzp.lv; Saules iela 23; s/d with shared bathroom 9/18Ls) has shockingly cheery (not to mention very tidy) rooms – even the once-sterile lobby is warmed with a mural of technicolour flowers. **Province** (☎ 6412 0849; www.provincecesis.viss.lv; Niniera iela 6; s/d 30/38Ls), a cute celery-green guest house, pops out from the dreary Soviet-block housing nearby. The five rooms are simple, spotless and sport funky bedspreads.

Sleek **Sarunas** (Rīgas iela 4; pizzas 2.50-4Ls) dishes out decent pizzas to a mix of young locals and older tourists. Grab a booth on the outdoor terrace for excellent views of the central square and Cēsis' charming wooden architecture.

LATVIA DIRECTORY

ACCOMMODATION

Cheap airfares and warmer weather lures the crowds during summer, so it's best to book your bed ahead of time. Prices are known to drop by more than 30% in the colder months. Visit www.hotels.lv for detailed accommodation information for Rīga and the rest of Latvia.

Backpackers should check out **Hostelworld** (www.hostelworld.com), which has become Rīga's unofficial go-to website for choosing budget digs. You'll pay up to 33Ls for a budget double room; figure between 6Ls and 12Ls for a dorm bed. There are loads of places to pitch a tent as well. Expect to spend around 35Ls to 88Ls for a midrange double room; those with a bit more bling will drop more than 89Ls on a top-end room.

All rooms in this chapter have private bathrooms unless otherwise stated. Most hotels in Latvia have a mix of smoking and nonsmoking rooms.

ACTIVITIES
Latvia's miles and miles of forested acreage are tailor-made for nature enthusiasts. For an intense adrenalin fix, such as bungee jumping, bobsledding, mountain biking and skydiving, head to the town of Sigulda (p461). Water sports and spa enthusiasts should spend the day in Jūrmala (p457).

BUSINESS HOURS
Most bars and restaurants open around 11am and close around 11pm. On weekends these establishments stay open until 2am or later. Nightclubs usually go all night between Thursday and Sunday. Shops tend to be open from 11am to 7pm and post offices are generally open between 7.30am and 8pm. Banks operate from 9am to 5pm, but 24-hour ATMs are available all over the country.

EMBASSIES & CONSULATES
The following embassies are in Rīga:
Australia (Map pp444-5; ☎ 6722 4251; australia@ apollo.lv; Arhitektu iela 1-305)
Canada (Map pp444-5; ☎ 6781 3945; www.dfait -maeci.gc.ca/canada-europa/baltics; Baznīcas laukums 4)
Estonia (Map pp444-5; ☎ 6781 2020; www.estemb .lv; Skolas iela 13)
France (Map pp444-5; ☎ 6703 6600; www.amba france-lv.org; Raiņa bulvāris 9)
Germany (Map pp444-5; ☎ 6708 5100; www.riga .diplo.de; Raiņa bulvāris 13)
Lithuania (off Map pp444-5; ☎ 6732 1519; lt@apollo .lv; Rūpniecības iela 24)
Russia (Map pp444-5; ☎ 6733 2151; www.latvia.mid .ru; Antonijas iela 2)
Spain (Map pp444-5; ☎ 6732 0281; Elizabetes iela 11)
Sweden (Map pp444-5; ☎ 6768 6600; www.sweden abroad.com/riga; Pumpura iela 8)
UK (Map pp444-5; ☎ 6777 4700; www.britain.lv; Alunāna iela 5)
USA (Map pp444-5; ☎ 6703 6200; www.usembassy.lv; Raiņa bulvāris 7)

FESTIVALS & EVENTS
Latvians enjoy any excuse to party, and during the midsummer **Līgo** celebration on the night of 23 June (St John's Eve), the entire country retreats to the countryside for a white night of revelry. Latvia's biggest event, the **Song and Dance Festival**, is held every five years. The 24th festival occurred in 2008.

HOLIDAYS
The website of the **Latvia Institute** (www.li.lv) has a page devoted to special Latvian remembrance days. Latvian national holidays:
New Year's Day 1 January
Easter in accordance with the Western Church calendar
Labour Day 1 May
Restoration of Independence of the Republic of Latvia 4 May
Mothers' Day second Sunday in May
Whitsunday a Sunday in May or June in accordance with the Western Church
Līgo Eve (midsummer festival) 23 June
Jāņi (St John's Day & Summer Solstice) 24 June
National Day 18 November; anniversary of proclamation of Latvian Republic, 1918
Christmas (Ziemsvētki) 25 December
Second Holiday 26 December
New Year's Eve 31 December

INTERNET ACCESS
Almost every hotel and hostel in Rīga offers some form of internet access, whether it's a wi-fi connection or a computer terminal. Hotels in smaller cities have been doing a good job of following suit. Internet cafes are a dying breed, as many restaurants, cafes, bars and even clubs are installing wireless connections. See p447 for detailed information about wireless access.

MONEY
Latvia's currency, the lats, was introduced in March 1993. The lats (Ls) is divided into 100 santīms. Lats come in coin denominations of 1Ls and 2Ls and notes of 5Ls, 10Ls, 20Ls, 50Ls, 100Ls and 500Ls; and santīms come in coins of 1, 2, 5, 10, 20 and 50. The national bank **Latvijas Bankas** (Latvian Bank; www.bank.lv) posts the lats' daily exchange rate on its website.

POST
Latvia's official postal service website (www .post.lv) can answer any of your mail-related questions, including shipping prices. Stamps for international postcards cost between 0.36Ls

LATVIA

EMERGENCY NUMBERS

- Ambulance ☎ 03
- Fire ☎ 01
- Police ☎ 02

---

and 0.58Ls depending on the destination. Standard letters (20g) to international destinations cost 0.50Ls to 0.55Ls, and increase with weight. Mail to North America takes about 10 days, and to Europe about a week.

TELEPHONE

Latvian telephone numbers have eight digits; all landlines start with '6'. To make any call within Latvia, simply dial the eight-digit number. To call a Latvian telephone number from abroad, dial the international access code, then the country code for Latvia (371) followed by the subscriber's eight-digit number. Telephone rates are posted on the website of the partly state-owned **Lattelekom** (www.lattelekom .lv), which enjoys a monopoly on fixed-line telephone communications in Latvia.

Two, three or four digit numbers are directory and emergency numbers, where English, Latvian and Russian are spoken. Eight-digit numbers starting with '80' are toll-free, and numbers starting with '90' are fee-based.

Calls on a public phone are made using cardphones called *telekarte*, which come in different denominations and are sold at post offices, newspaper stands and superettes.

Mobile telephones have eight numbers and always start with the digit '2'. Mobile phones are available for purchase at most shopping malls around Rīga and other major Latvian cities. If your own phone is GSM900-/1800-compatible, you can purchase a SIM-card package from one of Latvia's mobile telephone operators, available at any Narvesen superette or Rimi grocery store.

Okarte (www.lmt.lv), Latvijas Mobilais Telfons's prepaid starter kit, will set you back 3Ls, and comes with 3Ls worth of phone credit. To add credit to your prepaid plan, simply stop by a Narvesen or Rimi and purchase a recharge card. **Tele2** (www.tele2.lv), pronounced 'tele-divi', has a comparable plan.

VISAS

Holders of EU passports do not need a visa to enter Latvia; nor do Australian, Canadian, New Zealand and US citizens, if staying for less than 90 days. For information on obtaining visas (and seeing if you need one), please visit www.mfa.gov.lv/e n/service/visas.

TRANSPORT IN LATVIA

GETTING THERE & AWAY
Air

Rīga airport (Lidosta Rīga; ☎ 6720 7009; www.riga-airport .com), about 13km southwest of the city centre, houses Latvia's national carrier, **airBaltic** (BT; ☎ 6720 7886; www.airbaltic.com), which offers direct flights to over 50 international destinations (most in Europe).

Other carriers with direct flights to Rīga include the following:

Aeroflot (SU; ☎ 6724 0228; www.aeroflot.lv)
Czech Airlines (OK; ☎ 6720 7636; www.czech -airlines.lv)
Finnair (AY; ☎ 6720 7010; www.finnair.com)
KLM (KL; ☎ 6766 1305; www.klm.lv)
LOT (LO; ☎ 6720 7113; www.lot.com)
Lufthansa (LH; ☎ 6750 7711; www.lufthansa.com)
Norwegian (DY; ☎ 900 6200; www.norwegian.no)
Ryanair (FR; www.ryanair.com)
Turkish Airlines (TK; ☎ 6735 94444; www.turkish airlines.com)

Latvia does not have departure tax.

Land

In 2007 Latvia acceded to the Schengen Agreement (p978), which removed all border control between both Estonia and Lithuania.

BUS

Ecolines (☎ 6721 4512; www.ecolines.lv; ☒ 7am-9.30pm) has an office at the bus station in Rīga and additional offices in Daugavpils and Liepāja. **Eurolines Baltic** (☎ 6721 4080; www.eurolines.lv) is also based at Rīga bus station. See p455 for more.

CAR

Rental cars are allowed to travel around the Baltic at no extra fee.

TRAIN

See p456 for more details about train travel to/from the capital from Russia.

Sea

Latvia is connected to a number of destinations by sea. See p455 for details of services between Rīga, Sweden and Germany, and p459 for details of services to/from Ventspils.

GETTING AROUND
Air
AirBaltic (BT; ☎ 6720 7886; www.airbaltic.com) offers government-subsidised domestic flights from Rīga to Ventspils and Liepāja.

Bus
Buses are much more convenient than trains. Updated timetables are available at www.1188.lv.

Car & Motorcycle
Driving is the best way to get around the Latvian countryside. However, in 2008, an article in the *Baltic Times* stated that Latvia was the country with the highest percentage of car-accident-related fatalities in the EU. If you are planning to rent a car, keep in mind that local drivers tend to be aggressive.

Several small businesses in Rīga offer rentals, usually at a cheaper price than the international companies at the airport (expect cash-only transactions). Rentals range from 20Ls to 50Ls per day, depending on the type of car and time of year. The number of automatic cars in Latvia is limited. Companies usually allow you to drive in all three Baltic countries, but not beyond.

Driving is on the right-hand side. Headlights must be on at all times while driving. Be sure to ask for *'benzene'* when looking for a petrol station – *gāze* means 'air'.

Train
Most Latvians live in the large suburban ring around Rīga, commuting into the city for work. The city's network of handy suburban train lines help facilitate the commute and makes day-tripping to nearby Jūrmala (0.65Ls, 30 minutes, two hourly), Sigulda (1.11Ls, one hour, hourly) and Cēsis (1.72Ls, 1¾ hours, five daily) quite convenient for tourists too. Beyond the sphere of suburban rails, Latvia's further destinations are easier to access by bus or by plane. All train schedule queries can be answered at www.1188.lv.

Lithuania

The Baltic countries have a reputation for their dour ways, but this image fades when you enter rebellious Lithuania, a country blessed with boundless energy and studded with reminders of its colourful history.

It may be a dot on Europe's map, but that hasn't stopped Lithuania making big waves on the continent. Outside the country it's a little-known fact that in the 1400s Lithuania extended beyond Kursk in the east and all the way to the Black Sea in the south. This giant empire didn't last long, but even today Lithuanians brim with pride and confidence befitting their mighty heritage. More recently – and most notably – the Baltic's most southern nation became the first state to formally declare its independence from the Soviet Union.

In a country favoured by Mother Nature, where pagan roots run deep and Catholic passion lives on, there's plenty to attract the traveller. For starters there's effortlessly charming Vilnius and its skyline of baroque spires. The eerie Hill of Crosses near Šiauliai is a truly unique experience. In the west, thousands of migratory birds make Curonian Spit their primary destination, while to the north lies Aukštaitija National Park, a lake land blanketed in dense pine forests and dotted with tiny rural villages. More and more tourists are making Lithuania a port of call, but don't let that scare you away – there are enough delights to go around in this Baltic beauty.

FAST FACTS

- **Area** 65,303 sq km
- **Capital** Vilnius
- **Currency** litas (Lt); €1 = 3.45Lt; US$1 = 2.53Lt; UK£1 = 3.67Lt; A$1 = 1.75Lt; ¥100 = 2.64Lt; NZ$1 = 1.42Lt
- **Famous for** causing the USSR to collapse, baroque churches, *cepelinai* (dough shaped like zeppelins, stuffed with meat and potato)
- **Official language** Lithuanian
- **Phrases** *labas* (hello); *ačiū* (thanks); *prašau* (please/you're welcome); *taip* (yes); *ne* (no); *viso gero* (goodbye)
- **Population** 3.4 million
- **Telephone codes** country code ☎ 370; international access code ☎ 00
- **Visa** most nationalities don't need one; see p498 for more information

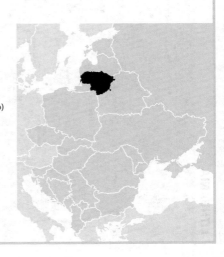

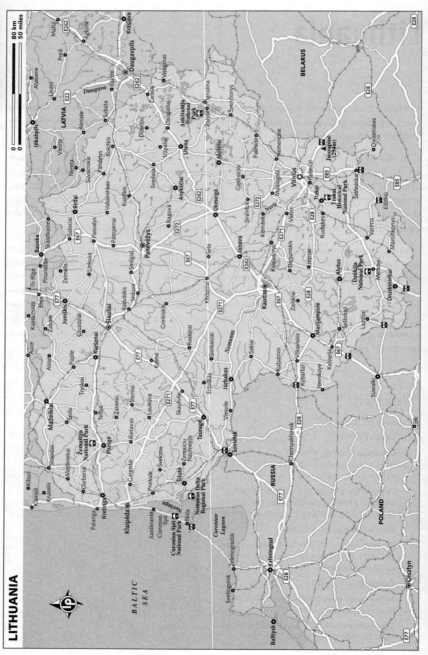

HIGHLIGHTS

- Explore beautiful baroque **Vilnius** (p472), with its cobbled streets, skyline of church spires, and bars and bistros.
- Breathe the pure air within the fragrant pine forests and high sand dunes of enchanting **Curonian Spit** (p495).
- Hear the wind breathe between the thousands of crosses on the eerie **Hill of Crosses** (p491) in Šiauliai.
- Wander wonderful **Trakai** (p485), home of the rare Karaite people and a stunning island castle.
- Berry-pick, bathe, and boat in **Aukštaitija National Park** (p487).

ITINERARIES

- **Three days** Devote two days to exploring the baroque heart of Vilnius, then day-trip to Trakai for its spectacular island castle and the homesteads of the Karaite people, stopping off at Paneriai on the way.
- **One week** Spend four nights in Vilnius, with day trips to both Trakai and the Soviet sculpture park near Druskininkai. Travel cross-country to Šiauliai and the Hill of Crosses, then spend two or three days exploring some serious nature on Curonian Spit. Head back east via Klaipėda and Kaunas.

CLIMATE & WHEN TO GO

Lithuania tends to have a beautiful but short summer, a crisp autumn, a long winter and a dreary spring. Summer is the ideal time for forays to coastal areas and inland national parks. Vilnius is enchanting any time of the year, but is much less crowded in winter.

HISTORY

Lithuania's history is a story of riches to rags and then back to riches again. It all started when ancient tribes fanned out across the Baltics to take advantage of the region's plentiful amber deposits. In 1009 those tribes were sufficiently assimilated for Lithuania to be mentioned for the first time in writing.

By the 12th century Lithuania's peoples had split into two tribal groups: the Samogitians (lowlanders) in the west and the Aukštaitiai (highlanders) in the east and southeast. In the mid-13th century Aukštaitiai leader Mindaugas unified Lithuanian tribes to create the Grand Duchy of Lithuania, of which he was crowned king in 1253 at Kernavė.

It was the mighty Lithuanian leader Gediminas who pushed Lithuania's borders south and east between 1316 and 1341. In 1386 marriage forged an alliance with Poland against the Teutonic Order – Germanic crusaders who were busy conquering much of the region – that lasted 400 years. The alliance defeated the German knights in 1410 at the battle of Grünwald in Poland, ushering in a golden period during which Vilnius was born and Lithuania became one of Europe's largest empires.

But Lithuania was destined to disappear off the maps of Europe. In the 18th century, the Polish-Lithuanian state was so weakened by division that it was carved up by Russia, Austria and Prussia (successor to the Teutonic Order) in the partitions of Poland (1772, 1793 and 1795–96).

Vilnius was a bastion of Polish culture in the 19th century and a focus of uprisings against Russia. It also became an important Jewish centre; Jews made up almost half of its 160,000-strong population by the early 20th century (see p481).

Lithuanian nationalists declared independence on 16 February 1918, with Kaunas proclaimed the capital, as Polish troops had annexed Vilnius from the Red Army in 1920. Lithuania's first president, Antanas Smetona, ruled the country with an iron fist during this time.

In 1940, after the Molotov-Ribbentrop Pact, Lithuania was forced into the USSR. Within a year, 40,000 Lithuanians were killed or deported. Up to 300,000 more people, mostly

CONNECTIONS: MOVING ON FROM LITHUANIA

Trains, buses and ferries provide travel options to Lithuania's neighbouring countries. From Vilnius (p484), buses travel to Kaliningrad, Poland, Latvia and Belarus; from Kaunas there are buses to Kaliningrad, Latvia and Estonia (p491); and Klaipėda (p495) and Curonian Spit (p495) also have services to Kaliningrad. Trains serve Kaliningrad, Poland and Belarus from the capital (p484), but there are no connections to Rīga or Tallinn. Denmark, Sweden and Germany can be reached by ferry from Klaipėda (p495), Lithuania's international port.

HOW MUCH?

- **Cup of coffee** 3Lt to 7Lt
- **Taxi fare** 3Lt/km
- **Public transport ticket** 1.40Lt to 2Lt
- **Bicycle hire (per day)** 35Lt
- **Sauna** 100Lt to 200Lt

LONELY PLANET INDEX

- **1L petrol** 3.28Lt
- **1.5L bottled water** 2Lt to 2.50Lt
- **Beer (50cL bottle of Švyturys)** 2.40Lt
- **Souvenir T-shirt** 20Lt to 50Lt
- **Street snack (pancake)** 5Lt to 10Lt

Jews, died in concentration camps and ghettos during the 1941–44 Nazi occupation, many of them at Paneriai.

The USSR ruled again between 1945 and 1991. An estimated 250,000 people were murdered or deported to Siberia while armed partisans resisted Soviet rule from the forests. This bloody period of resistance, which petered out in 1953, is chronicled in Vilnius' Museum of Genocide Victims (p479) and a number of smaller museums around the country.

In the late 1980s Lithuania led the Baltic push for independence. The popular front, Sajūdis, won 30 seats in the March 1989 elections for the USSR Congress of People's Deputies. Lithuania was the first Soviet state to legalise noncommunist parties. In February 1990 Sajūdis was elected to form a majority in Lithuania's new Supreme Soviet (now the parliament), which on 11 March declared Lithuania independent.

Moscow marched troops into Vilnius and cut off Lithuania's fuel supplies. On 13 January 1991, Soviet troops stormed key buildings in Vilnius. Fourteen people were killed at Vilnius' TV tower and Lithuanians barricaded the Seimas (their parliament). In the wake of heavy condemnation from the West, the Soviets recognised Lithuanian independence on 6 September 1991, bringing about the first of the Baltic republics.

The last Soviet troops left the country on 31 August 1993. Lithuania replaced the rouble with the litas, joined NATO in April 2004, and entered the EU a month later. True to form, bold Lithuania forthrightly ratified the EU constitution in November 2004, becoming the first of the 25 EU member countries to do so.

Lithuania's enthusiasm for the EU continues unabated. In a mid-2008 poll, 70% of the population still viewed EU membership optimistically. Many are gagging for the euro, but the EU currency won't be introduced here until at least 2010. As with everything, EU membership has its downside: the country's younger generation are leaving in droves for the greener pastures of the UK and Ireland. Yet Lithuania still remains a country of optimism.

PEOPLE

Easily the most ethnically homogeneous population of the three Baltic countries, Lithuanians account for 85% of the total population. Poles form 6.3% and Russians 5.1%. The remaining 3.6% comprises various nationalities from Eastern Europe and further afield.

Compared with their reticent neighbours in Latvia and Estonia, Lithuanians are an outgoing, cheeky bunch. That has led some to call them the 'Spanish of the Baltics'. Others call them the 'Italians of the Baltics', citing their fierce pride – a result of the many brutal attempts to eradicate their culture and the memories of their long-lost empire.

RELIGION

Lithuania was the last pagan country in Europe, explaining why so much of its religious art, national culture and traditions have raw pagan roots. Today the country is 70% to 80% Roman Catholic by most estimates, with strong Lutheran and Russian Orthodox minorities.

ARTS

Lithuania's best-known national artist will always be Mikalojus Konstantinas Čiurlionis (1875–1911), a depressive painter who also composed symphonic poems and piano pieces. The best collection of his paintings are in the National Čiurlionis Art Museum in Kaunas (p489).

Lithuania has a thriving contemporary art scene. Vilnius artists created the tongue-in-cheek Užupis Republic (p480), which hosts alternative art festivals, fashion shows and exhibitions in its breakaway state. Other home-grown artists can be seen at **Europas Parkas Sculpture Park** (www.europosparkas.lt) at the geographical centre of Europe (19km from Vilnius; ask a tourist office for details).

Music is at the heart of the Lithuanian spirit, and Lithuania is the jazz giant of the Baltics, with its highlight the Kaunas International Jazz Festival (p489).

Lithuanian fiction began with the late-18th-century poem 'Metai' (The Seasons) by Kristijonas Donelaitis. Antanas Baranauskas' 1860 poem 'Anykščiai Pine Forest' uses the forest as a symbol of Lithuania. Literature suffered persecution from the tsarist authorities, who banned the use of the Latin alphabet between 1864 and 1904.

Several major Polish writers grew up in Lithuania and regarded themselves as partly Lithuanian, most notably Adam Mickiewicz (1798–1855), the inspiration of 19th-century nationalists, whose great poem 'Pan Tadeusz' begins 'Lithuania, my fatherland…'

ENVIRONMENT

Lush forests and more than 4000 lakes mark the landscape of Lithuania, a country that is largely flat with a 100km-wide lowland centre. Forest covers a third of the country and contains creatures such as wild boar, wolves, deer and elk. Aukštaitija National Park is one place where these beasts roam, although you are unlikely to encounter them without a guide. You're more likely to spot a stork – Lithuania has Europe's highest concentration of storks, and their nests crop up in the unlikeliest places.

A huge amount of EU money is being sunk into cleaning up Lithuania's environment, which continues to suffer from years of Soviet mismanagement and indifference.

For years the hot potato has been the Ignalina Nuclear Power Plant, 120km north of Vilnius. One of two reactors similar in design to Chornobyl was closed in December 2004, and the final shutdown of the plant is scheduled for 2009 at a massive cost of €3.2 billion.

Other problems Lithuania faces include the threat of large-scale pollution from a recently discovered arsenal of decomposing chemical weapons. About 40,000 bombs and mines lie on the seabed 70 nautical miles off Klaipėda, where Soviet forces sank German ships, and the cargo from these ships could threaten the fragile coastline of Curonian Spit. The spit is also threatened by the D-6 oil field in the Kaliningrad region, 22km from the coast and 500m downstream from the Lithuania–Russia border. Oil rigs are currently being operated by Lukoil in the area.

Greenhouse gases have been on the rise in recent years. Among the main sources of air pollution are city transport and industrial sites. Additionally, the delicate biodiversity of Lithuania's forests are under threat due to mismanagement and illegal logging.

To do your part for the environment, camp only in designated areas and, when required, keep to the marked trails on the sand dunes of Curonian Spit and in other national parks.

FOOD & DRINK

Unbuckle your belts for the gastronomic delights of good, hearty Lithuanian cooking. The food was tailor-made for peasants out working the fields, so it's seriously stodgy comfort eating rather than delicate morsels. Based on potatoes, meat and dairy goods, it's not ideal for vegetarians, so we've highlighted options for those who shun the pleasures of pigs trotters and pork knuckles.

The national dish is the hearty, jiggle-when-they-wiggle *cepelinai* (zeppelins): airship-shaped parcels of thick potato dough stuffed with cheese, *mesa* (meat) or *grybai* (mushrooms). It comes topped with a rich sauce made from onions, butter, sour cream and bacon bits. Another artery-hardening favourite is sour cream–topped *kugelis*, a dish that bakes grated potatoes and carrots in the oven. *Koldūnai* are hearty ravioli stuffed with meat or mushrooms, and *virtiniai* are stodgy dumplings.

Lithuanians drink their share of *alus* (beer) and it's all pretty good. The most popular brand is Švyturys, but try Utenos, Kalnapilis and Gubernija as well. No beer is complete without the world's most fattening bar snack, *kepta duona* (deep-fried black bread with garlic).

Midus (mead) originated in the Middle Ages but is making a comeback these days. It's made of honey boiled with water, berries and spices, then fermented with hops.

Restaurants tend to open around noon and close around 11pm, but many stay open much later on weekends, especially in cities. Bars tend to be open from 11am to midnight from Sunday to Thursday, and 11am to 2am Friday and Saturday.

Since January 2007 there has been a total countrywide ban on smoking in restaurants and bars.

VILNIUS

☎ 5 / pop 542,800

Vilnius, the baroque bombshell of the Baltics, is a city of immense allure. As beautiful as it is bizarre, it easily tops the country's best attraction bill, drawing tourists to it like moths to a flame with a confident charm and warm, golden glow that makes one wish for long, midsummer evenings every day of the year.

At its heart is Europe's largest baroque Old Town, so precious that Unesco added it to its World Heritage list in 1994. Its skyline, pierced by (almost) countless Orthodox and Catholic church steeples, appears like a giant bed of nails from the basket of a hot-air balloon. Adding to the intoxicating mix is a combination of cobbled alleys, hilltop views, breakaway states, and traditional artists' workshops.

Vilnius feels tiny, but that's a bit deceptive because the sprawling suburban jacket that surrounds Old Town is a fairly typical Soviet-style mess of snarled traffic, car shops and concrete.

HISTORY

Legend has it that Vilnius was founded in the 1320s when Lithuanian grand duke Gediminas dreamt of an iron wolf that howled with the voices of 100 wolves – a sure sign to build a city as mighty as their cry. In fact, the site had already been settled for 1000 years.

Despite the threat of attacks from the Teutonic Knights and Tatars, Vilnius prospered during the Middle Ages and by the end of the 16th century it was among Eastern Europe's biggest cities. It became a key Jewish city in the 19th century and an isolated pocket of Poland after WWI, but WWII rang the death knoll for its Jewish population (p481). Soviet rule scarred Vilnius' skyline with residential high-rises, but since independence it has fast become a European city. In 1994 its Old Town became a Unesco World Heritage site.

ORIENTATION

Most of the action in Vilnius takes place in Old Town. Vokiečių gatvė is the most commercial street in Old Town; Pilies gatvė is the most touristy. Old Town's northern border merges with New Town at Gedimino prospektas, a wide, part-time pedestrianised avenue that runs west–east from parliament to Cathedral Sq (Katedros aikštė), the spiritual, if not geographical, heart of Vilnius.

> **VILNIUS IN TWO DAYS**
>
> Spend your first day taking in the magic of **Old Town** (p478). Start off at the **Gates of Dawn** (p479), then spend a few hours snaking your way towards **Cathedral Square** (opposite). Climb **Gediminas Hill** (opposite) for sunset, and crown the day with a home brew at **Avilys** (p483).
>
> On day two, devote some time to the **Museum of Genocide Victims** (p479) and take in another museum or two near Cathedral Sq. Then either explore the old **Jewish quarter** (p481) or cross the Vilnia River into bohemian **Užupis** (p480), where another fine sunset panorama beckons at **Tores** (p483).

INFORMATION

Bookshops

Akademinė Knyga (Map pp476-7; Universiteto gatvė 4) Some translated Lithuanian works, and Lonely Planet travel guides.

Littera (Map pp476-7; Šv Jono gatvė 12) University bookshop.

Internet Access

A growing number of cafes, restaurants and hotels have free wi-fi zones; check www.wifi.lt for more information.

Collegium (Map pp476-7; Pilies gatvė 22-1; per hr 5Lt; ⏰ 8am-midnight)

Interneto Kavinė (Map pp476-7; Pylimo gatvė 21; per hr 4Lt; ⏰ 9am-midnight)

Taškas (Map pp476-7; Jasinskio gatvė; per hr 5Lt; ⏰ 24hr)

Internet Resources

Vilnius in Your Pocket (www.inyourpocket.com) Quality city guide, available as PDF download or in bookshops, tourist offices and newspaper kiosks (5Lt).

Left Luggage

Ask for the *bagažinė* (left-luggage room).

Bus station (Map pp474-5; per bag per 24hr 3Lt; ⏰ 5.30am-9.45pm Mon-Sat, 7am-8.45pm Sun)

Train station (Map pp474-5; per bag per 24hr 4-6Lt; ⏰ 24hr)

Medical Services

24-hour pharmacy (Map pp476-7; Gedimino Vaistinė, Gedimino prospektas 27)

Baltic-American Medical & Surgical Clinic (off Map pp474-5; ☎ 234 2020; www.bak.lt; Nemenčinės gatvė

54a; 24hr) English-speaking health care inside Vilnius
University Antakalnis hospital, northeast of town.

Money

Vilnius is littered with ATMs and banks,
and most offer the usual exchange, money
transfer, travellers cheques and cash-advance
services. Many are concentrated on Vokiečių
gatvė (Map pp476–7).

Keitykla Exchange (Map pp474-5; Parex Bankas;
☎ 213 5454; www.keitykla.lt; Geležinkelio gatvė 6;
24hr) Currency exchange with ATM near the train station. Parex Bankas is Lithuania's Amex representative.

Post

Branch post office (Map pp476-7; Vokiečių gatvė 7)
Central post office (Map pp476-7; Gedimino prospektas 7)

Tourist Information

Vilnius tourist information centre (www.vilnius
-tourism.lt; 9am-6pm Mon-Fri, 10am-4pm Sat &
Sun) Town Hall (Map pp476-7; ☎ 262 6470; Didžioji
gatvė 31); train station (Map pp474-5; ☎ 269 2091);
Vilniaus gatvė (Map pp476-7; ☎ 262 9660; Vilniaus gatvė
22) Friendly centres with a wealth of glossy brochures
and general information. They also arrange tour guides
and book accommodation (hotel reservation fee of 6Lt
applies).

SIGHTS

Vilnius is a compact city, and most sights
are easily reached on foot. Those visiting for
a couple of days will scarcely move out of
Old Town, where souvenir stalls, folk-artist
workshops and design boutiques jostle for
attention with a treasure trove of architectural gems. Stay a couple more days and New
Town – with its museums, shops and riverside
action – beckons.

Gediminas Hill & Cathedral Square

Vilnius was founded on 48m-high Gediminas
Hill, topped since the 13th century by the oft-
rebuilt **Gediminas Tower** (Map pp476–7). There
are spectacular views of Old Town from the
top of the tower, which houses the **Upper Castle
Museum** (Map pp476-7; adult/child 4/2Lt; 10am-7pm
May-Oct, 11am-5pm Tue-Sun Nov-Apr), reached by **funicular** (Map pp476-7; adult/child 2/1Lt; 10am-7pm daily
May-Oct, 10am-5pm Nov-Apr) located at the rear of
the Museum of Applied Arts. From here you'll
also see the white **Three Crosses** (Map pp476–7)
on a hill to the east, erected in memory of
three crucified monks.

The **Museum of Applied Arts** (Map pp476-7; www
.ldm.lt; Arsenalo gatvė 3a; admission 6Lt; 11am-6pm Tue-
Sat, 11am-4pm Sun), in the old arsenal at the foot of
Gediminas Hill, houses temporary exhibitions
alongside a permanent collection showcasing
15th- to 19th-century Lithuanian sacred art.
Much of it was only discovered in Vilnius
cathedral in 1985 after being hidden in the
walls by Russian soldiers in 1655.

Sitting stoically next door, the **National
Museum of Lithuania** (Map pp476-7; www.lnm.lt;
Arsenalo gatvė 1; adult/child 4/2Lt; 10am-5pm Tue-Sat,
10am-3pm Sun) is guarded by a proud statue
of Mindaugas, the first and only king of
Lithuania. Inside are exhibits looking at everyday Lithuanian life from the 13th century
to WWII.

At the base of Gediminas Hill sprawls
Cathedral Sq (Katedros aikštė), dominated by
Vilnius Cathedral (Map pp476-7; admission free; 7am-
7.30pm, Sunday mass at 9am, 10am, 11am & 7pm) and its
57m-tall **belfry** (Map pp476–7), a Vilnius landmark. The square buzzes with local life, especially during Sunday-morning mass. Amuse
yourself by hunting for the secret *stebuklas*
(miracle) tile; if found it can grant you a wish
if you stand on it and turn around clockwise.
It marks the spot where the Tallinn–Vilnius
human chain ended in 1989.

The first wooden cathedral, built here in
1387–88, was in Gothic style but has been rebuilt many times since then. The most important restoration was completed from 1783 to
1801, when the outside was redone in today's
classical style. The interior retains more of its
original aspect. Its showpiece is the baroque
St Casimir's Chapel (Map pp476–7), with white
stucco sculptures and frescos depicting the
life of St Casimir (Lithuania's patron saint),
whose silver coffin lies within.

At the square's eastern end is an **equestrian
statue of Gediminas** (Map pp476–7), built on
an ancient pagan site. Behind it stands the
Royal Palace (Valdovų rumai; Map pp476–7),
which buzzed with masked balls, gay banquets
and tournaments in the 16th century. But in
1795 the Russians occupied Lithuania and
demolished the palace along with the Lower
Castle and city defence wall.

Currently being rebuilt red brick by red
brick, this palace of incredible dimensions
should have risen from the ashes by the time
you read this to mark the millennium anniversary of the first mention of Lithuania
in writing. Inside will be a museum with

LITHUANIA

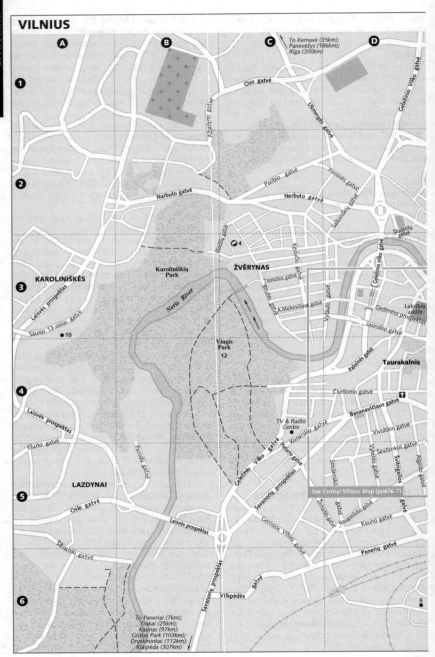

VILNIUS

To Kernavė (35km);
Panevėžys (186km);
Rīga (300km)

Ozo gatvė

Antakalnio gatvė

Ukmergės gatvė

Geležinio Vilko gatvė

Paribio gatvė

Pieninės gatvė

Narbuto gatvė

Narbuto gatvė

Saltoniškių gatvė

Studentų gatvė

Blindžių gatvė

Krėslio gatvė

Karoliniškių Park

ŽVĖRYNAS

⊘ 4

KAROLINIŠKĖS

Treniotos gatvė

Geležinio vilko gatvė

Laisvės prospektas

Birutės gatvė

A Mickevičiaus gatvė

Vytauto gatvė

Lukiškių aikštė

Gedimino prospektas

Sausio 13-osios gatvė

● 10

Nerts River

Jasinskio gatvė

Pakalnės gatvė

Taurakalnis

Vingis Park
12

Čiurlionio gatvė

Basanavičiaus gatvė

H

Laisvės prospektas

Vivulskio gatvė

Efurto gatvė

Paroolų gatvė

TV & Radio Centre ●

Geležinio Vilko gatvė

Pietario gatvė

Konarskio gatvė

Vytanio gatvė

Ševčenkos gatvė

Švitrigalos gatvė

Algirdo gatvė

Savanorių prospektas

Smolensko

See Central Vilnius Map (pp476-7)

LAZDYNAI

Oslo gatvė

Laisvės prospektas

Gerosios Vilties gatvė

Žemaitės gatvė

Naugarduko gatvė

Kauno gatvė

Siltnamių gatvė

Panerių gatvė

Savanorių prospektas

gatvė

Vilkpėdės

5
●

To Paneriai (7km);
Trakai (25km);
Kaunas (97km);
Grūtas Park (103km);
Druskininkai (112km);
Klaipėda (307km)

A   B   C   D

1   2   3   4   5   6

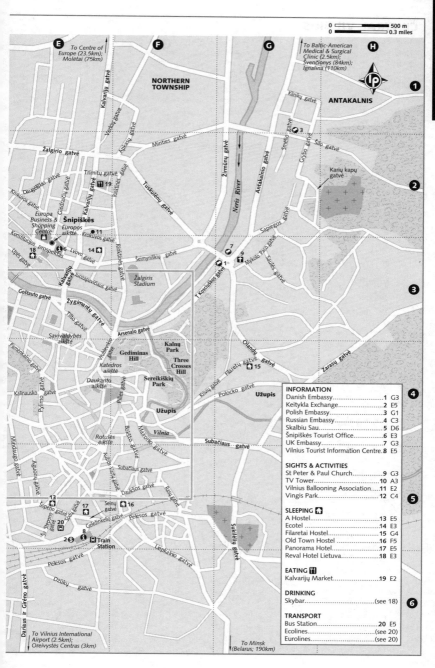

LITHUANIA

CENTRAL VILNIUS

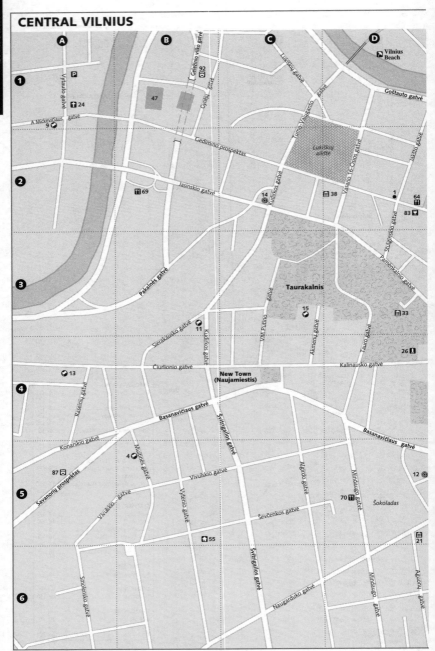

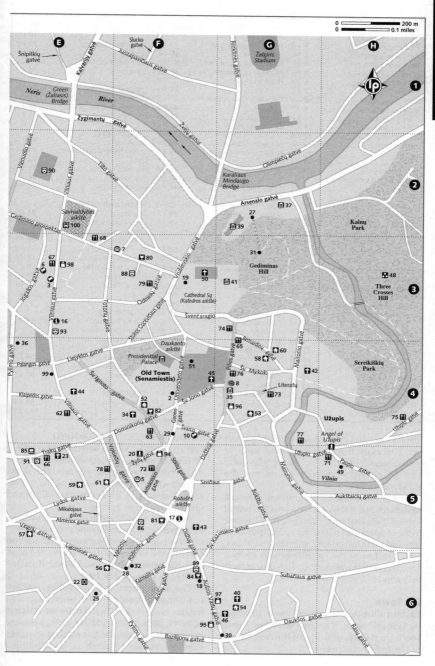

displays detailing the reconstruction project and a treasure trove of Gothic and baroque archaeological finds – ceramics, glassware and jewellery, – discovered during the excavation work.

East of Cathedral Sq, magnificent **St Peter & Paul Church** (Map pp474–5; Antakalnio gatvė 1) is one of Vilnius' finest baroque churches. It's a treasure trove of sparkling white stucco sculptures of real and mythical people, animals and plants, with touches of gilt, paintings and statues. The decoration was done by Italian sculptors between 1675 and 1704.

Old Town

Eastern Europe's largest old town deserves its Unesco status. The area stretches 1.5km south from Cathedral Sq and the eastern end of Gedimino prospektas.

VILNIUS UNIVERSITY & AROUND

The students of **Vilnius University** (Map pp476–7; ☎ 268 7001; www.vu.lt; Universiteto gatvė 3; adult/child 5/1Lt; ⏱ 9am–6pm Mon-Sat) attend school on a spectacular campus featuring 13 courtyards framed by 15th-century buildings and splashed with 300-year-old frescos.

Founded in 1579 during the Counter-Reformation, Eastern Europe's oldest university was run by Jesuits for two centuries and became one of the greatest centres of Polish learning before being closed by the Russians in 1832. It reopened in 1919.

The library here, with five million books, is Lithuania's oldest. The university also houses the world's first **Centre for Stateless Cultures** (Map pp476–7; ☎ 268 7293; www.state lesscultures.lt), established for those cultures that lack statehood, such as Jewish, Roma and Karaimic (Karaite) cultures, in its history faculty.

You need to go through the university entrance on Universiteto gatvé (and pay the admission fee) to access Littera bookshop (p472) and **St John's Church** (Map pp476-7; 🕑 10am-5pm Mon-Sat), a baroque gem. Founded in 1387 – well before the university arrived – its 17th-century bell tower is the highest structure in Old Town.

Cobbled **Pilies gatvé** (Map pp476–7) – the hub of tourist action and the main entrance to Old Town from Cathedral Sq – buzzes with buskers, souvenir stalls and the odd beggar. At No 26 stands the **House of Signatories** (Map pp476-7; admission free; 🕑 10am-5pm Tue-Sat & 10am-3pm Sun May-Oct, 10am-5pm Tue-Sat Nov-Mar), where the act granting Lithuania independence in 1918 was signed.

GATES OF DAWN

Located at the southern border of Old Town, the 16th-century **Gates of Dawn** (Aušros Vartai; Map pp476–7) is the only one of the town wall's original nine gates still intact. The gate houses the **Chapel of the Blessed Virgin Mary** (Map pp476-7; admission free; 🕑 6am-7pm, mass 9am Mon-Sat & 9.30am Sun) and the black-and-gold 'miracle-working' **Virgin Mary icon**. A gift from the Crimea by Grand Duke Algirdas in 1363, it is one of the holiest icons in Polish Catholicism, and the faithful arrive in droves to offer it whispered prayer. Look up as you're exiting Old Town and you can spot the icon through the window of the chapel.

There are four stunning churches in the immediate vicinity of the Gates of Dawn. Catholic **St Teresa's Church** (Map pp476-7; Aušros Vartų gatvé 14) is early baroque (1635–50) outside and more-elaborate late baroque inside. Roughly behind it is the big, pink, domed 17th-century **Orthodox Church of the Holy Spirit** (Map pp476-7; Aušros Vartų gatvé 10), Lithuania's chief Russian Orthodox church and another fine baroque specimen. Directly across the street, through a late baroque archway known as the **Basilian Gates** (Map pp476-7; Aušros Vartų gatvé 7), is the dilapidated **Holy Trinity Church** (Map pp476–7). And further up Aušros Vartų gatvé, on the eastern side, is ravishing **St Casimir's Church** (Map pp476-7; Aušros Vartų gatvé), the oldest of Vilnius' baroque masterpieces. It was built by Jesuits (1604–15) and under Soviet rule was a museum of atheism.

VOKIEČIŲ GATVĖ & AROUND

Vokiečių gatvė, Old Town's main commercial street, makes a good jumping-off point for explorations of the old Jewish quarter (p481); it offers fine views of several churches. Peering north from Vokiečių you'll spot **St Catherine's Church** (Vilniaus gatvė 30), displaying Vilnius' trademark peach baroque style.

The **Holy Spirit Church** (Dominikonų gatvė 8) is Vilnius' primary Polish church (1679) and has one of the most elaborate baroque interiors you'll find anywhere. The reconsecrated **Church of the Assumption** (Trakų gatvė 9/1) is symbolic of the incredible wave of renovations sweeping through Old Town.

New Town

Vilnius' 19th-century New Town boasts a true European boulevard in Gedimino prospektas. It's a grand road with Vilnius Cathedral (p473) at one end and the silver-domed **Church of the Saint Virgin's Apparition** (Map pp476-7; A Mickevičiaus 1) at the other. Much of Gedimino becomes a pedestrian street outside working hours, when fashionable types flock here to see, be seen and peruse the sundry Western brands on display in the shop fronts.

A statue of Lenin once stood on Lukiškių Aikštė, a square that used to bear the name; the statue is now displayed in Druskininkai's Soviet sculpture park, Gruto Parkas (p487).

The building facing the square was the notorious KGB headquarters and prison, but is now the **Museum of Genocide Victims** (Map pp476-7; ☎ 249 6264; www.genocid.lt; Aukų gatvė 2a; adult/child 4/1Lt; 🕑 10am-5pm Tue-Sat, to 3pm Sun). Called the 'KGB Museum' by locals, it is Vilnius' most important and most popular museum. It is best taken in with a headphone audio tour (8Lt).

Names of those who were murdered in the prison are carved into the stone walls outside – note how young many victims were. Inside, inmate cells and the execution cell where prisoners were shot or stabbed in the skull between 1944 and the 1960s can be visited. Two exhibits document the post-WWII Lithuanian resistance movement and the gulags.

At the west end of Gedimino prospektas is the **Seimas** (parliament; Map pp476–7) building. Further along lies pleasant **Vingis Park** (Map pp474–5), and beyond that the 326m-tall **TV Tower** (Map pp474-5; www.lrtc.lt; Sausio 13-osios gatvė 10; adult/child 21/9Lt; 🕑 observation deck 10am-10pm), where wooden crosses remember the victims of 13 January 1991.

LITHUANIA

Užupis

The cheeky streak of rebellion that pervades Lithuania flourishes in this district, located just east of Old Town. In 1998 the resident artists, dreamers, squatters and drunks declared the district a breakaway state known as the **Užupis Republic** (Map pp476–7). The state has its own tongue-in-cheek president, anthem, flags and a 41-point **Užupis Republic constitution** (Map pp476–7) that, among other things, gives inhabitants the right to cry, the right to be misunderstood and the right to be a dog. Read the entire thing in English, French or Lithuanian on a wall on Paupio gatvė.

The best time to visit Užupis is April Fool's Day. Mock border guards set up at the main bridge into town and stamp visitors' passports and a huge party rages all day and all night. However, it's worth visiting any time of year for its galleries, craft workshops and bohemian vibe.

Just over Užupis' northern bridge you'll find baroque **Bernardine Church** (Map pp476–7) and pint-sized Gothic **St Anne's Church** (Map pp476–7), essentially fused together like mismatched Siamese twins.

FESTIVALS & EVENTS

A comprehensive list of festivals is at www.vilniusfestivals.lt.

Lygiadienis Pagan carnival marking spring equinox, March.

Vilnius Festival Classical music, jazz and folk music concerts in Old Town courtyards, June.

Capital Days Music and performing arts festival, end of August to the beginning of September.

SLEEPING

For tips on booking accommodation in Vilnius, see p497.

Budget

Filaretai Hostel (Map pp474–5; ☎ 215 4627; www.filaretaihostel.lt; Filaretų gatvė 17; dm from 34Lt, s/d with shared bathroom 70/100Lt; 🖳) This chilled-out hostel occupies a quaint old villa in Užupis. It's clean and quiet, and there's a laundry and kitchen for guest use. Take bus 34 from the bus station to the Filaretų stop.

Old Town Hostel (Map pp474–5; ☎ 262 5357; old townhostel@lha.lt; Aušros Vartų gatvė 20-15a; dm 35Lt, d/tr with shared bathroom 110/144Lt; 🖳) It's nothing special by world standards, but it sticks out in Vilnius because of its perfect location, five minutes from both Old Town and the train station. You'll have few problems finding a drinking buddy here.

our pick **VB Sleep Inn** (Map pp476–7; ☎ 8 638 32818; www.vb-sleep-inn.lt; Mikalojaus gatvė 3; dm 39-42Lt, tw 110Lt; 🖳) Friendly, accommodating and not averse to its guests having a shindig in the inner courtyard, this great little hostel is a grand choice for travellers. There's free internet access, tea, coffee and lockers, but no breakfast (there is a kitchen). Location couldn't be better, just off Vokiečių gatvė.

Litinterp (Map pp476–7; ☎ 212 3850; www.litinterp.lt; Bernardinų gatvė 7-2; s/d/tr with shared bathroom 80/140/180Lt, with private bathroom 100/160/210Lt, apt 210Lt) This bright, clean, and friendly establishment has a wide range of options in the heart of Old Town. Rooms with shared bathroom can be a little cramped, but those with en suite are generously large.

FREE THRILLS

There's plenty to see and do in Vilnius without having to empty the wallet:

- Wander the baroque **Old Town** (p478), taking in the likes of Pilies gatvė and the **Gates of Dawn** (p479), or explore the green of **Vingis Park** (p479).

- Take in splendid views of the city from **Gediminas Tower** (p473), **Three Crosses** (p473), **Panorama Hotel** (opposite) and **Skybar** (p483).

- Visit **Vilnius Cathedral** (p473), **St Peter & Paul Church** (p478), and the **Chapel of the Blessed Virgin Mary** (p479) – every church in Vilnius is free to enter.

- Check out the **House of Signatories** (p479), centre of Lithuania's post-WWI push for independence.

- Peruse Vilnius' statues – don't pass over the chance to see the world's first **Frank Zappa memorial** (Map pp476–7; Kalinausko gatvė 1) or the oversized **egg statue** (Map pp476–7; cnr Šv Stepono & Raugyklos gatvė) on a nest of real twigs.

JEWISH VILNIUS

Dubbed by Napoleon as the 'Jerusalem of the north', Vilnius had one of Europe's most prominent Jewish communities until Nazi brutality wiped it out (with assistance from the Soviets).

The old Jewish quarter lay in the streets west of Didžioji gatvė, including present-day Žydų gatvė (Jews St) and Gaono gatvė, named after Vilnius' most famous Jewish resident, Gaon Elijahu ben Shlomo Zalman (1720–97), a sage who could recite the entire Talmud by heart at the age of six.

A good place to start your tour is the **Centre for Tolerance** (Map pp476-7; ☎ 266 9666; www .jmuseum.lt; Naugarduko gatvė 10; adult/child 5/2Lt; 🕒 10am-6pm Mon-Thu, 10am-4pm Sun), the nerve centre for the rebuilding of Vilnius' Jewish community. It also houses thought-provoking historical displays. The **Holocaust Museum** (Map pp476-7; ☎ 262 0730; Pamėnkalnio gatvė 12; adult/child 5/2Lt; 🕒 9am-5pm Mon-Thu, 10am-4pm Sun), in the so-called 'Green House', is a moving museum detailing the horror suffered by Lithuanian Jews in an 'unedited' display of horrific images and words. Nearby, the **Jewish Community of Lithuania** (Map pp476-7; ☎ 261 3003; www.litjews.org; Pylimo gatvė 4; admission free; 🕒 10am-5pm Mon-Fri) is another source of information – pick up a copy of the country's only Jewish newspaper, *Jerusalem of Lithuania*, here.

Vilnius' only remaining synagogue, the **Choral Synagogue** (Map pp476-7; Pylimo gatvė 39; donations welcome; 🕒 10am-2pm Sun-Fri), was built in 1894 for the wealthy and survived only because the Nazis used it as a medical store.

For a more casual glimpse of Jewish life, walk down Žydų gatvė to the memorial **bust of Gaon Elijahu** (Map pp476-7; Žydų gatvė 3), imagining how life once was. There's a **map** of the two main Jewish ghettos during WWII at Rūdninkų gatvė 18, which used to be the single gate to the largest ghetto.

Office hours are 8.30am to 7pm Monday to Friday, 9am to 3pm Saturday; guests can check in after office hours providing they give advance notice.

Šauni Vietelė (Map pp476-7; ☎ 212 4110; sauni .vietele@takas.lt; Pranciškonai gatvė 3/6; s/d 80/150Lt) This three-room guest house above a crumbling courtyard cafe is great value for money, with large, old fashioned en suites. Breakfast isn't included, but the cafe offers pancakes and such.

Other recommended hostels:

Arts Academy Hostel (Map pp476-7; ☎ 212 0102; Latako gatvė 2; dm 20-22Lt, s/d/tr 60/100/110Lt Apr-Sep, 50/90/100Lt Sep-Mar) Very cheap, basic and central.

A Hostel (Map pp474-5; ☎ 8 680 18557; www .ahostel.lt; Šv Stepono gatvė 15; 4-/8-bed dm 48/34Lt; 🖳) Modern, squeakier than squeaky-clean hostel near train station.

Midrange

our pick **Domus Maria** (Map pp476-7; ☎ 264 4880; www .domusmaria.lt; Aušros Vartų gatvė 12; s 100-289Lt, d150-349Lt, tr/q 329/369Lt; 🖳) Positively unique and immensely popular, this guest house within a monastery captures the soul of Vilnius without capturing too much of your hard-earned cash. It stays true to its monastic origins with wide-arched corridors and spartan white rooms.

E-Guest House (Map pp476-7; ☎ 266 0730; www .e-guesthouse.lt; Ševčenkos gatvė 16; s/d/tr from 190/220/260Lt; 🖳) This professional hotel with bold blue exterior and free internet connection throughout runs a handy rent-a-laptop service (50Lt per day). It's a little out of the centre but real value for money. Breakfast is an extra 5Lt, and guests receive a 20% discount at the restaurant next door.

Ecotel (Map pp474-5; ☎ 210 2700; www.ecotel.lt; Slucko gatvė 8; s/d/tr 179/199/255Lt; 🍴 🖳) Ecotel is a steal, with simple but smart furnishings filling its squeaky-clean rooms, in which bathrooms have heated towel rails. There is a computer with free internet access in the lobby as well.

Panorama Hotel (Map pp474-5; ☎ 273 8011; www .hotelpanorama.lt; Sodų gatvė 14; s/d from 235/269Lt; 🖳) The Soviet-era chocolate-brown tiled facade of this hotel near the train station hides a bright, stylish, and airy interior. An added bonus is the fabulous views of Old Town.

Hotel Rinno (Map pp476-7; ☎ 262 2828; www.rinno .lt; Vingrių gatvė 25; s/d from 240/280Lt; 🍴 🖳) Rinno is tops – its staff is exceptionally helpful and polite; its rooms are first rate; its location, between Old Town and train and bus stations, is handy; and its price is a bargain. Breakfast is served in the pleasant, and private, backyard.

LITHUANIA

Apia Hotel (Map pp476-7; ☎ 212 3426; www.apia
.lt; Sv Ignoto gatvé 12; s/d/tr 280/321/382Lt) This smart,
fresh, and friendly hotel occupies some prime
real estate in the heart of Old Town. Choose
from courtyard or cobble-street views, but if
you're after a balcony, reserve room 3 or 4.

Top End

Shakespeare (Map pp476-7; ☎ 266 5885; www.shake
speare.lt; Bernardinų gatvé 8/8; s/d from 360/600Lt; ✗ ☐)
Striving to be the best of boutique hotels,
Shakespeare is a refined Old Town gem that
evokes a cultured, literary feel with its abundance of books, antiques and flowers. Each
room pays homage to a different writer – in
name and design.

Reval Hotel Lietuva (Map pp474-5; ☎ 272 6272; www
.revalhotels.com; Konstitucijos prospektas 20; s/d/ste from
380/449/794Lt; ✗ ☐) The burly, bustling Reval
is the antidote to Vilnius' plethora of quaint
boutique hotels, with well-appointed business-class rooms, the best casino in Vilnius
and a rare fitness centre that's worthy of the
name. The top-floor Skybar (opposite) has the
city's best views.

Grotthuss (Map pp476-7; ☎ 266 0322; www.grot
thusshotel.com; Ligoninés gatvé 7; r/ste from 442/863Lt;
✗ ☐) Step through the red-canopied en-
trance of this buttercup-yellow town house
to find Villeroy & Boch bathtubs, 19th-
century Titanic-style fittings, and Italian-
made furniture. Substantial discounts are
available on weekends.

EATING

Whether it's curry, *cepelinai* (gut-busting
meat and potato zeppelins) or *kepta duona*
(fried bread sticks oozing garlic) you want,
Vilnius has a mouth-watering selection of
local and international cuisine.

Coffee Inn (Map pp476-7; Vilniaus gatvé 17) This
Lithuanian-owned cafe chain offers freshly
made wraps (8Lt), sandwiches (6.50Lt), cookies
(3.50Lt) and cheesecake (arguably the best in
town). Eat in or pick up something to go; there
are also branches at Trakų gatvé 7 (Map pp467-
7), Gedimino prospektas 9 (Map pp476-7) and
Pilies gatvé 10 (Map pp476-7).

Balti Drambliai (Map pp476-7; Vilniaus gatvé 41; mains
10-17Lt) The 'White Elephant' whips up a vegan
and vegie storm, offering pancakes, pizzas,
Indian curries, and tofu-based dishes to hungry non-meat-eaters. Its lively courtyard is
also good for a drink, while winter dining is
in its cavernous basement.

René (Map pp476-7; Antokolskio gatvé 13; mains 20-35Lt)
René bases its cuisine on beer, Belgian beer
no less. Everything on the menu, from pots
of mussels to homemade oven-fried sausages
and chilli con carne, features the amber brew.
And eating here won't break the budget, if you
time it right – lunch menus and afternoon
discounts are offered on weekdays.

our pick Bistro 18 (Map pp476-7; Stiklių gatvé 18;
mains 20-40Lt) Bistro 18 is a breath of fresh air
in Vilnius' restaurant scene. The service is
friendly, polite and attentive, the decor minimalist yet comfortable, the food imaginative,
international and flavoursome, and the wine
list featuring bottles from as far away as the
Antipodes. At around 20Lt, the lunch menu
is an absolute bargain.

Zoe's Bar & Grill (Map pp476-7; Odminių gatvé 3; mains
20-50Lt) Often when a restaurant tries to cover
too many culinary bases, it all ends up tasting like cat food. Zoe's, however, manages to
pull it off, with the likes of fabulous homemade meatballs and sausages (26Lt), tender
steaks (20Lt to 50Lt) and spicy Thai stir-fries
and soups (20Lt to 30Lt). Grand views of
the cathedral.

Žemaičių Smuklé (Map pp476-7; Vokiečių gatvé 24;
mains 20-60Lt) Of the many brick-walled, old-style
Lithuanian themed restaurants in Vilnius, this
institution, famous for its pigs trotters, offers
the most authentic Lithuanian experience.

Saint Germain (Map pp476-7; Literatų gatvé; mains 30-
50Lt) Paris is the inspiration behind this idyllic
wine bar–cum-restaurant inside a convivial century-old house on a quiet Old Town street. Of
particular importance: the service is fit for the
best restaurants on the continent, and advance
reservations for its street terrace are essential.

Pizza and pasta often come cheap in this
city. Two worthy options for both are **Čili
Pica** (Map pp476-7; Gedimino prospektas 23; mains 15-30Lt;
🕑 7.30am-3am Sun-Wed, 7.30am-6am Thu-Sat), the
ubiquitous pizza chain spread far and wide in
Lithuania, and **Trattoria Da Antonio** (Map pp476-7;
Pilies gatvé 20; mains 20-30Lt), which wins local votes
for its Italian cuisine and prime position on
busy Pilies.

For those with a sweet tooth, also worth
recommending is **Soprano** (Map pp476-7; Pilies gatvé
3). Get lickin' with fruit-topped *gelato Italiano*
by the cone (3Lt).

Fresh fruit, honey, smoked eel and cheap
staples can all be found at **Kalvarijų market** (Map
pp474-5; Kalvarijų gatvé 16; 🕑 7am-noon Tue-Sun), located north of the Neris River. Supermarkets

---

EATING IN UŽUPIS

There are few eateries in bohemian Užupis, but most of them are noteworthy. Mountain lodge–style **Tores** (Map pp476–7; Užupio gatvė 40; mains 25-50Lt) has good food and atmosphere, but the main reason to come is for the stunning panorama of Gediminas Castle and the cathedral across the Vilnia River valley. You can take it all in from the outdoor patio while sipping Švyturys pints (7Lt).

Užupio Kavinė (Map pp476–7; Užupio gatvė 2; mains 15-40Lt), right on the river as you enter Užupis, is a legendary spot known for its arty clientele and good cheap breakfasts. Ask the bartender for a copy of the Užupis constitution in English. Lastly, **Prie Angelo Kavinė** (Map pp476–7; Užupio gatvė 9; pizzas 20Lt), on the main square, fires up what may be Vilnius' best pizzas.

---

are everywhere: **Iki** (Map pp476-7; Jasinskio gatvė 16) and **Maxima** (Map pp476-7; Mindaugo gatvė 11; 24hr) are leading chains.

DRINKING

Vilnius' riotous party culture centres on clubs in the cold months and outdoor cafes in the summer. On weekends, many cafes turn into clubs and many restaurants turn into raucous bars.

our pick Cozy (Map pp476-7; Dominikonų gatvė 10; 9am-2am Mon-Wed, 9am-4am Thu & Fri, 10am-4am Sat, 10am-2am Sun) Cozy has been a hot address in Vilnius for years, and will probably continue to be so for years to come. It welcomes all comers and has something for everyone; street level is a lounge-style cafe/restaurant with a chef who cooks until late, while local DJs spin tunes downstairs to a discerning crowd Thursday to Saturday (9am to 4am).

In Vino (Map pp476-7; Aušros Vartų gatvė 7) This is the bar of the moment, with one of the loveliest courtyards in the city. Excellent wines, expensive tapas (20Lt to 40Lt) and a few mains. Arrive early in summer to secure a table, then watch the place fill to overflowing.

Contemporary Art Centre (Map pp476-7; Vokiečių gatvė 2) This art centre has a smoky hideout bar filled with arty Lithuanian luvvies and one of the most simple but hip summer terraces in town.

Skybar (Map pp474-5; Konstitucijos prospektas 20; 4pm-1am Sun-Thu, to 2.30am Fri & Sat) It may look – and feel – like an airport lounge, but nothing can beat the panoramas of this sky-blue bar on the 22nd floor of the Reval Hotel Lietuva. DJs spin tunes Friday and Saturday.

Skonis ir Kvapas (Map pp476-7; Trakų gatvė 8) Heaven for tea connoisseurs, this stylish courtyard cafe knows how to make a great cuppa. Choose from around 100 teas from across the globe and a sublime array of creamy homemade cakes, cucumber sandwiches and breakfasts.

Avilys (Map pp476-7; Gedimino prospektas 5; beer 7-8Lt) 'Beehive' draws a refined crowd to sample its excellent home brew – the dark and honey beers especially – and a variety of dishes cooked in beer. There's even nonalcoholic beer ice cream (12Lt).

Double Coffee (Map pp476-7; Gedimino prospektas 26; 24hr) Starbucks-inspired chain with coffee in all shapes and sizes. Six locations in town.

ENTERTAINMENT

In Your Pocket (www.inyourpocket.com) publishes a list of movie theatres as well as listings for opera, theatre, classical music and other big events. Most such venues break for the summer. The tourist offices also post events listings. Check www.cinema.lt (in Lithuanian) for movie listings.

The tourist office publishes events listings, as does the **Baltic Times** (www.baltictimes.com), a local English-language paper.

Cinemas

Films are screened in English at the 12-screen **Coca-Cola Plaza** (Map pp476-7; 1567; www.forum cinemas.lt; Savanorių prospektas 7) and are usually dubbed in Lithuanian elsewhere.

Performing Arts

Opera & Ballet Theatre (Map pp476-7; 262 0727; www.opera.lt; Vienuolio gatvė 1) Classical productions in a grand, gaudy building near the river.

National Philharmonic (Map pp476-7; 266 5233; www.filharmonija.lt; Aušros Vartų gatvė 5) The country's most renowned orchestras perform here.

Lithuanian National Drama Theatre (Map pp476-7; 262 9771; www.teatras.lt; Gedimino Prospektas 4) This theatre stages national and international productions in Lithuanian.

Nightclubs

Vilnius has a thriving, if small, nightlife. Expect cover charges most nights and gorillas on the doors.

Woo (Map p476-7; www.woo.lt; Vilniaus gatvė 22) Escape the mainstream at Woo, a basement club below Radvilos' Palace. Resident DJs spin drum'n'bass, techno and house to a backdrop of VJ art, and jazz sessions occasionally fill the space.

Pacha Vilnius (Map pp476-7; www.pachavilnius.lt; Gyneju gatvė 14) Part of the legendary Pacha club franchise, this massive club is arguably the best spot in town to shake it. Expect to find quality DJs and a happy crowd upon entering.

Pablo Latino (Map pp476-7; Trakų gatvė 3) This sultry-red club specialises in sweet Latino tunes and strong cocktails. Put on your dancing shoes (Wednesday night for lessons), fortify your liver, and be prepared for a fun night out.

Brodvéjus (Map pp476-7; www.brodvejus.lt; Mėsinių gatvė 4) The place to come for live bands and cheesy tunes. It's hugely popular with expats, students, local lookers, and travel-guide writers.

Men's Factory (Map pp476-7; www.gayclub.at; Švencenkos gatvė 16/10) This wildly popular gay club west of Old Town draws plenty of straight club-goers, too.

SHOPPING

Amber (often described as 'Baltic gold') and linen are two commodities worth tracking down in Lithuania. Old Town's main thoroughfare, running from Pilies gatvė to Aušros Vartų gatvė, is something of a bustling craft market/tourist trap, depending on your perspective, with its fair share of stores selling both. Of particular note are **Lino ir Gintaro Studija** (www.lgstudija.lt; Aušros Vartų Map p476-7; Aušros Vartų gatvė 12; Pilies Map p476-7; Pilies gatvė 38) and **Lino Namai** (Map p476-7; www.siulas.lt; Vilniaus gatvė 12); the former stands out for its amber and linen, the latter for its table and bedlinen.

Folk art is alive and kicking in the capital. **Jonas Bugailiškis** (Map p476-7; Aušros Vartų gatvė 17-10) produces a menagerie of wooden creations at this workshop, while **Aldona Mickuvienė** (Map pp476-7; Žydų gatvė 2-10) and **Bronė Daškevičienė** (Map pp476-7; Žydų gatvė 2-9) weave colourful wedding sashes in their neighbouring workshops. Buy a ready-made sash (50Lt) or order one with your name on it (70Lt). Each sash takes a full day or more to weave.

GETTING THERE & AWAY
Air

For information on air transport to/from Lithuania, see p498.

Bus

The **bus station** (Map pp474-5; ☎ 216 2977; Sodų gatvė 22) is across the street from the train station, south of Old Town.

Eurolines (Map pp474-5; ☎ 233 6666; www.eurolines .lt), **Ecolines** (Map pp474-5; ☎ 213 3300; www.ecolines .net) or one of a few smaller carriers have services between Vilnius and the following destinations in Eastern Europe: Rīga (55Lt, five hours, at least four daily), Kaliningrad (110Lt, seven hours, two daily), Tallinn (from 108Lt, 10½ hours, up to five daily), Warsaw (106Lt, nine hours, three daily), Moscow (150Lt, 15 hours, daily) and St Petersburg (from 150Lt, 18½ hours, four daily). A few of these bus services continue westward to Kaunas and/ or Klaipėda; some northbound buses stop in Šiauliai.

There are a couple of weekly buses from Vilnius to Kyiv and a handful of Western European cities, including London and several German cities. There are also daily services to Berlin (around 270Lt, 16 hours).

For travel within Lithuania, you can get to/from Vilnius by bus.

Car & Motorcycle

The big international car-rental agencies are well represented at Vilnius airport. Try **Avis** (☎ 232 9316; www.avis.lt), **Budget** (☎ 230 6708; www .budget.lt) or **Hertz** (☎ 232 9301; www.hertz.lt). You'll save a ton of money by renting from a local operator. Charismatic **Rimas** (☎ 277 6213, 8 698 21662; rent-car-rimas.w3.lt) rents older cars at the lowest rates in town and just might invite you ice fishing.

Train

The **train station** (Map pp474-5; ☎ 233 0088; Geležinkelio gatvė 16) is a five-minute walk south of Old Town.

Vilnius is linked by regular direct trains to Moscow (from 170Lt, 15 to 18 hours, up to five daily), St Petersburg (from 130Lt, 13½ hours, daily), Kaliningrad (from 77Lt, 6½ hours, up to seven daily) and Minsk (65Lt, 4½ hours, up to eight daily). You'll need a Belarus visa for the Moscow train. There are also sporadic services to Lviv and Kyiv in Ukraine, but these also go through Belarus. For Warsaw (from

120Lt, eight to 10 hours, one daily), a change in Šeštokai is required.

You can lumber from Vilnius to a few domestic destinations on Lithuania's clunky suburban trains. Destinations include Kaunas (12Lt, 1¼ hours, up to 17 daily), Klaipėda (42.10Lt, five hours, three daily), Šiauliai (28.70Lt, 2½ to three hours, three daily), Ignalina (13.10Lt, two hours, eight daily) and Trakai (3.40Lt, 40 minutes, up to 10 daily).

GETTING AROUND
To/From the Airport

Vilnius International Airport (☎ 273 9305; www.vno .lt; Rodūnė kelias 2) lies 5km south of the centre. Bus 1 runs between the airport and the train station; bus 2 runs between the airport and the northwestern suburb of Šeškinė via the Žaliasis bridge across the Neris and on to Lukiškių aikštė.

A taxi from the airport to the city centre should cost between 40Lt and 50Lt.

Bicycle

Hawaii Express (☎ 261 1617; www.hawaii.lt in Lithuanian; Vilniaus gatvė 37) rents bicycles for 8/35Lt per hour/day, plus 200Lt deposit.

Car & Motorcyle

There are numerous guarded paid car parks around town. Avoid parking on unlit streets overnight; car break-ins are on the increase. See opposite for car-hire companies.

Public Transport

Unless you're heading well out of Old Town, you won't have much need for public transport in Vilnius, although the route from the train station to New Town via Pylimo gatvė is handy. It is serviced by trolleybuses 2 and 5, and by buses 26, 26a and 53.

Tickets cost 1.10Lt at news kiosks and 1.40Lt direct from the driver; punch tickets on board in a ticket machine or risk a 20Lt on-the-spot fine.

Taxi

Taxis officially charge 3Lt per kilometre and must have a meter. Drivers often try to rip tourists off, especially if flagged down on the street. You can phone a **taxi** (☎ 261 6161, 240 0004, 239 5539), or queue up at one of numerous taxi ranks. Popular spots are outside the train station and at the southern end of Vokiečių gatvė.

BUSES FROM VILNIUS			
Destination	**Cost (Lt)**	**Duration (hr)**	**Frequency**
Druskininkai	25	2	10 daily
Kaunas	20	1¾	2-3 hourly
Klaipėda	59	4-5½	15 daily
Palanga	63	4¼-6	7 daily
Šiauliai	41	3-4½	6 daily

AROUND VILNIUS

A fairy-tale castle and ancient castle mounds lie within easy reach of the capital. Or there is the trip to Paneriai.

PANERIAI

During WWII the Nazis, aided by Lithuanian accomplices, exterminated three-quarters of Vilnius' 100,000-strong Jewish population at this site, 10km southwest of central Vilnius.

From the entrance a path leads to the small **Paneriai Museum** (Agrastų gatvė 15; ☒ 11am-6pm Wed-Sat Jun-Sep, by appointment Oct-May), near which there are two monuments – one Jewish (marked with the Star of David), the other one Soviet (an obelisk topped with a Soviet star).

Paths lead from here to grassed-over pits where the Nazis burnt the exhumed bodies of their victims to hide the evidence of their crimes.

There are over two dozen trains daily from Vilnius to Paneriai station (1.30Lt, 12 to 15 minutes). From the station, it is a 1km walk southwest along Agrastų gatvė to the site.

TRAKAI
☎ 528 / pop 5400

With its red-brick fairy-tale castle, Karaite culture, quaint wooden houses and pretty lakeside location, Trakai is a must-see within easy reach of the capital.

The Karaite people are named after the term *Kara*, which means 'to study the scriptures' in both Hebrew and Arabic. The sect originated in Baghdad and practises strict adherence to the Torah (rejecting the rabbinic Talmud). Grand Duke of Lithuania Vytautas brought about 380 Karaite families to Trakai from Crimea, in around 1400, to serve as bodyguards. Only 60 remain in Trakai today and their numbers – about 280 in Lithuania – are dwindling rapidly.

This area has protected status as the **Trakai Historical National Park** (www.seniejitrakai.lt). The **tourist information centre** (☎ 51 934; www.trakai.lt; Vytauto gatvė 69; 🕑 9am-5pm Mon, to 6pm Tue-Fri, to 3pm Sat & Sun May-Sep, 8am-5pm Mon-Thu, to 3.45pm Fri Oct-Apr) sells maps, books accommodation, and has information on fishing, sailing, scuba diving, horse riding and a range of other activities.

Sights

Trakai's trophy piece is the fairy-tale **Island Castle**, occupying a small island in Lake Galvė. The painstakingly restored, red-brick Gothic castle dates from the late-14th century when Prince Kęstutis, father of Vytautas, once ruled the area. Vytautas completed what his father started in the early 1400s and died in the castle in 1430.

A footbridge links the Island Castle to the shore. Inside the castle is a branch of the **Trakai History Museum** (www.trakaimuziejus.lt; adult/student & child 12/5Lt; 🕑 10am-7pm May-Sep, 10am-6pm Tue-Sun Oct, Mar & Apr, 10am-5pm Tue-Sun Nov-Feb), in which the history of the castle is charted. In summer the castle courtyard is a magical stage for concerts and plays.

The museum has two other branches in town: a **Sacral Art Exhibition** (Kestučio gatvė 4; adult/ student & child 4/2Lt; 🕑 10am-6pm Wed-Sun) and the **Karaite Ethnographic Exhibition** (Karaimų etnografinė paroda; ☎ 55 286; Karaimų gatvė 22; adult/student & child 4/2Lt, camera 4Lt, guided tour 20Lt; 🕑 10am-6pm Wed-Sun). The latter provides a good introduction to the fascinating Karaite culture, while the former houses a small but very fine collection of precious reliquaries and monstrances. Karaimų gatvė 30 is a beautifully restored early-19th-century **Kenessa** (prayer house) of the Karaites.

The ruins of Trakai's **Peninsula Castle**, built from 1362 to 1382 by Kęstutis and destroyed in the 17th century, are near the Sacral Art Exhibition.

Sleeping & Eating

Kempingas Slėnyje (☎ 53 380; www.camptrakai.lt; Slėnio gatvė 1; adult/car/tent 18/8/9Lt, summer house for 3 people 90Lt, d/tr/q with shared bathroom 70/90/100Lt, cottage for 2-6 people 220-300Lt, d in guest house 140Lt) This sublime complex is 5km out of Trakai on the northern side of Lake Galvė. Pitch your tent by the lake or stay in wooden cabins or the spectacular guest house with lakeside balconies. Activities include horse riding, canoeing and hot-air balloon rides. Bicycles are available for hire.

Trakai National Sports & Health Centre (Trakų Poilsio ir pramogų centras; ☎ 55 501; sportocentras@mail .lt; Karaimų gatvė 73; s/d 110/130Lt) Rooms here are basic but big and clean, and half have wonderful lakeside views. There's also a decent eatery with huge terrace attached overlooking the lake. As the name implies, it doubles as a mighty fine activity centre.

There are two good options for trying out Karaite food – especially *kibinai*, meat-stuffed pastries that are similar to empanadas. Prices at both will seem refreshing after Vilnius. **Kibininė** (Karaimų gatvė 65; kibinai 3.80-5Lt) has a dreamy location right on the lake, while **Kybynlar** (Karaimų gatvė 29; mains 15-30Lt) has a more Turkic feel. The writing on the wall is in the endangered Karaim language.

Buy picnics at **Iki** (Vytauto gatvė 56) opposite the tourist office.

Getting There & Away

Up to 10 daily trains (3.40Lt, 40 minutes) travel between Trakai and Vilnius.

KERNAVĖ

Deemed an 'exceptional testimony to some 10 millennia of human settlements in this region' by Unesco, which made it a World Heritage site in 2004, Kernavė is the 'Pompeii of Lithuania' and a must-see. Thought to have been the spot where Mindaugas (responsible for uniting Lithuania for the first time) celebrated his coronation in 1253, the rural cultural reserve comprises four old castle mounds and the archaeological remains of a medieval town.

The fascinating heritage of the **Kernavė Cultural Reserve** (Kernavės kultūrinio rezervato; www .kernave.org; admission free; 🕑 dawn-dusk) can be explored in the **Archaeological & Historical Museum** (Archeologijos ir istorijos muziejus; ☎ 382-47 385; Kerniaus gatvė 4a) after spring 2010, when it reopens following extensive renovations. **Guided tours** (per person 12Lt; 🕑 9am-5pm Tue-Sat Apr-Oct) of the area are still available by prior arrangement, otherwise the area is free to explore at your leisure.

Medieval fun and frolics – axe throwing, catapulting, mead making, medieval fights, music making and so on – fill Kernavė with festivity on 23 June and during the three-day International Festival of Experimental Archaeology (lots of fun despite the deadly name) in mid-July.

To reach Kernavė, 35km northwest of Vilnius in the Neris Valley, follow the road through Dūkštos from Maisiagala on the main road north to Ukmergė.

EASTERN & SOUTHERN LITHUANIA

The mythical forests and famous spas of eastern and southern Lithuania make easy day trips from Vilnius – although outdoor enthusiasts should not hesitate to spend more time here camping, cross-country skiing, canoeing, hiking, birdwatching or berry-picking.

AUKŠTAITIJA NATIONAL PARK
☎ 386

Lithuania's first national park (founded in 1974) is a 400-sq-km wonderland of rivers, lakes, centuries-old forests and tiny villages still steeped in rural tradition. Around 70% of the park comprises pine, spruce and deciduous forests, inhabited by elk, deer, wild boar, storks, and white-tailed and golden eagles. Its highlight is a labyrinth of 126 lakes, the deepest being Lake Tauragnas (60.5m deep).

The park is mainly for outdoor lovers, but there are also some cultural attractions, including several settlements that are protected ethnographic centres. For those interested in getting deeper under the skin of this enchanting area, the **Aukštaitija National Park Office** (☎ 53 135, 47 478; www.anp.lt; ⏰ 9am-6pm Mon-Sat) in Palūšė has everything you need to know, including park maps (15Lt) and free internet access. The **tourist office** (☎ 52 597; www.ignalina.lt/tic; Ateites gatvė 23; ⏰ 8am-6pm Mon-Fri, 10am-3pm Sat Jun-Aug, 8am-5pm Mon-Fri, 8am-3.45pm Sat Sep-May) in Ignalina, the main gateway town to the park, can also help with information and accommodation.

To get here jump on a train from Vilnius to Ignalina (13.10Lt, two hours, eight daily), from where three buses daily travel to Palūšė (2.50Lt).

DRUSKININKAI
☎ 313 / pop 16,500

Druskininkai, 130km south of Vilnius, is Lithuania's most famous health resort. In recent years it has gained notoriety as the home of the somewhat controversial Soviet sculpture museum known as Grūto Parkas.

People have been taking in the incredibly salty waters in this leafy riverside town since the 18th century. Today there's a mix of both Soviet-style and more modern treatments to

be had if you're in the mood for pampering. The magical powers of local mineral water can be tested at the Dzūkija Fountain inside the **Mineralinio Vandems Biuvetė** near the Nemunas River, or not far north at the **Fountain of Beauty** (Grožio šaltinis) – one slurp of the shockingly salty water promises eternal beauty.

The **Tourist information centre** (www.info.drus kininkai.lt; former train station building ☎ 60 800; Gardino gatvė 3; ⏰ 8.30am-12.15pm & 1-5.15pm Mon-Fri; town centre ☎ 51 777; Čiurlionio gatvė 65; ⏰ 10am-1pm & 1.45-6.45pm Mon-Sat, 10am-5pm Sun) can help you out with accommodation and information on the town's dozens of spas, including the brand-new **Aqua Park** (www.akvapark.lt). An excellent camping ground with tepees (40Lt) and cabins (120Lt) is next door to the train station information centre.

But chances are you are here to see **Grūto Parkas** (www.grutoparkas.lt; adult/6-15yr 15/7Lt, audioguide 40Lt; ⏰ 9am-8pm), 8km west of town in the village of Grūtas. The park has been an enormous hit since it opened to much fanfare in 2001. The sprawling grounds contain dozens of statues of Soviet heroes, exhibits on Soviet history and loudspeakers bellowing Soviet anthems. The statues once stood confidently in parks or squares across Lithuania.

There are up to 10 daily buses between Druskininkai and Vilnius, and hourly buses to/from Kaunas (both 25Lt, two hours). If you're going straight to Grūto Parkas, ask to be let off at the park turn-off, then walk the final 1km to the park.

CENTRAL LITHUANIA

Most view Lithuania's nondescript interior as little more than something you must cross to get to the west coast or Latvia, but it does offer a few worthwhile diversions, including the country's signature tourist attraction, the Hill of Crosses in Šiaulia.

KAUNAS
☎ 37 / pop 358,000

Kaunas, a sprawling city on the banks of the Nemunas River, has a compact Old Town, a menagerie of artistic and educational museums, and a rich history all of its own. Its sizeable student population provides it with plenty of vibrant, youthful energy, and its rough edges give it that extra bit of spice lacking in many of Lithuania's provincial towns and urban expanses.

LITHUANIA

KAUNAS

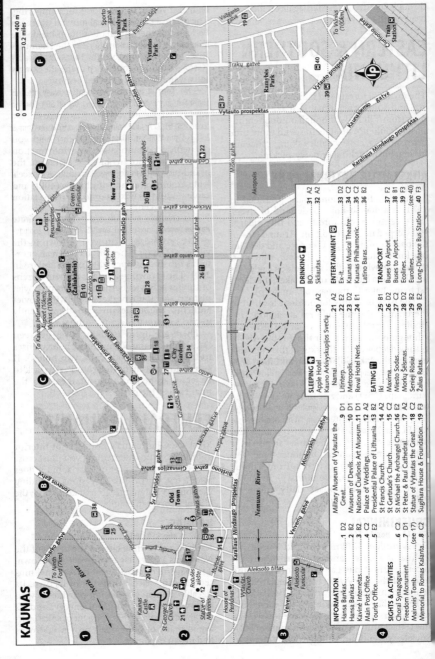

INFORMATION	
Hansa Bankas	1 D2
Hansa Bankas	2 B2
Kavinė Internetas	3 B2
Main Post Office	4 C2
Tourist Office	5 E2

SIGHTS & ACTIVITIES	
Choral Synagogue	6 C2
Freedom Monument	7 D1
Maironis' Tomb	(see 7)
Memorial to Romas Kalanta	8 C2
Military Museum of Vytautas the Great	9 D1
Museum of Devils	10 D1
National Čiurlionis Art Museum	11 D1
Palace of Weddings	12 A2
Presidential Palace of Lithuania	13 B2
St Francis Church	14 A2
St Gertrude's Church	15 C2
St Michael the Archangel Church	16 E2
St Peter & Paul Cathedral	17 A2
Statue of Vytautas the Great	18 C2
Sugihara House & Foundation	19 F3

SLEEPING	
Apple Hotel	20 A2
Kauno Arkivyskupijos Svečių Namai	21 A2
Litinterp	22 E2
Metropolis	23 D2
Reval Hotel Neris	24 E1

EATING	
Iki	25 B1
Maxima	26 D2
Miesto Sodas	27 C2
Morkų Šėlsmas	28 D2
Senieji Rūsiai	29 B2
Žalias Ratas	30 E2

DRINKING	
BO	31 A2
Skliautas	32 A2

ENTERTAINMENT	
Ex-it	33 D2
Kaunas Musical Theatre	34 C2
Kaunas Philharmonic	35 C2
Latino Baras	36 B2

TRANSPORT	
Buses to Airport	37 F2
Buses to Airport	38 B1
Ecolines	39 F3
Eurolines	(see 40)
Long-Distance Bus Station	40 F3

The capital of Lithuania in the dark days between the two world wars, Kaunas is enjoying a renaissance of sorts as Ryanair has made the city its Lithuanian hub. But its hotels and restaurants need to improve if it is to lure more than a fraction of those who use its airport, most of whom head straight to Vilnius.

Kaunas is a convenient overnight stopover and, in the warmer months, a decent place to experience the real Lithuania away from the crowds of Vilnius. A great time to visit is in April, when the city comes alive during the four-day **International Jazz Festival** (www.kaunasjazz.lt).

Information

Casinos have 24-hour currency exchanges. All major banks cash travellers cheques and have ATMs.

Hansa Bankas Old Town (Vilniaus gatvé 13); New Town (Laisvés aléja 79) Both branches have an ATM.

Kaunas in Your Pocket (www.inyourpocket.com) Annual city guide sold in hotels, art galleries and news kiosks for 5Lt.

Kavinė Internetas (www.cafenet.ot.lt; Vilniaus gatvé 24; per hr 5Lt; 🕒 9am-9pm) Old Town internet cafe.

Main post office (Laisvés aléja 102)

Tourist office (☎ 323 436; www.kaunastic.lt; Laisvés aléja 36; 🕒 9am-7pm Mon-Fri, 10am-1pm & 2-6pm Sat & 10am-3pm Sun Jun-Aug, 9am-6pm Mon-Fri & 10am-3pm Sat May & Sep, 9am-6pm Mon-Fri Oct-Apr) Books accommodation, sells maps and guides; arranges bicycle rental (50Lt per day plus 5Lt for lock) and guided tours of Old Town (35Lt, 4pm Thursday mid-May to September).

Sights

OLD TOWN

Start by wandering through the lovely little Old Town, where most streets lead to Rotušés aikšté (Central Sq). Surrounding the square are 15th- and 16th-century German merchants' houses. The 18th-century, white, baroque former city hall is now the **Palace of Weddings**. The southern side of the square is dominated by the 18th-century twin-towered **St Francis church**.

St Peter & Paul Cathedral (Vilniaus gatvé 1) on the northeastern corner of the square owes much to baroque reconstruction, but its early-15th-century Gothic-shaped windows remain. **Maironis' tomb** is outside the cathedral's south wall. Near the eastern edge of Old Town is the former **Presidential Palace of Lithuania** (Vilniaus gatvé 33; adult/student 3/1.50Lt; 🕒 11am-5pm Tue-Sun, gardens 8am-9pm daily), from where the country was run between 1920 and 1939.

NEW TOWN

Kaunas expanded east from Old Town in the 19th century, giving birth to the modern centre and its striking 1.7km-long pedestrian street, Laisvés aléja, which today is lined with trees, bars, shops and restaurants.

Near the western end you'll find City Garden (Miestos Sodas), where a **memorial to Romas Kalanta** – a Kaunas student who set himself on fire on 14 May 1972 in protest at tyrannical communist rule – takes the form of several stone slabs. Nearby stands a **statue** of Vytautas the Great.

Tucked away in a courtyard off Laisvés aléja is **St Gertrude's Church** (Laisvés aléja 101a), a Gothic gem of a church, while not far north of New Town's main artery is the pale-blue **Choral Synagogue** (Ožeškienés gatvé 17; admission free; 🕒 5.45pm-6.30pm Mon-Fri, 10am-noon Sat), a functioning house of worship.

The blue, neo-Byzantine **St Michael the Archangel Church** (1893) dominates the eastern end of Laisvés aléja from its position on the adjacent Nepriklausomybés aikšté (Independence Sq). On the same square, the **statue of man**, modelled on Nike the Greek god of victory, caused a storm of controversy when his glorious pose exposing his manhood was unveiled.

East of here, the **Sugihara House & Foundation** (☎ 423 277; Vaižganto gatvé 30; admission free; 🕒 10am-5pm Mon-Fri & 11am-4pm Sat & Sun May-Oct, 11am-3pm Mon-Fri Nov-Apr) tells the story of Chiune Sugihara, the Japanese consul to Lithuania (1939–40), known as 'Japan's Schindler'. He saved 12,000 lives by issuing visas (against orders) to Polish Jews who faced the advancing Nazi terror.

North of Laisvés aléja, Vienybés aikšté (Unity Sq) contains the **Freedom Monument**, which honours 16 February 1918, the day Lithuania declared independence. It was erected in 1928. It was hidden during the Stalin era, and put back in place on 16 February 1989.

Two museums share the large building on the north side of the square. The **Military Museum of Vytautas the Great** (Donelaičio gatvé 64; adult/child 4/2Lt; 🕒 11am-5pm Tue-Sun) recounts Lithuania's history from prehistoric times to the present day. The **National Čiurlionis Art Museum** (Putvinskio gatvé 55; adult/child 5/2.50Lt; 🕒 11am-5pm Tue-Sun) has an extensive collection of the romantic symbolic paintings of Mikalojus Konstantinas Čiurlionis (1875–1911), Lithuania's beloved artist and composer.

Nearby is the bizarre **Museum of Devils** (Putvinskio gatvė 64; adult/child 5/2.50Lt; ☺ 10am-5pm Tue-Sun), which contains more than 2000 devil statuettes. Note the satanic figures of Hitler and Stalin, formed from tree roots and performing a deadly dance over Lithuania.

Leaving town, the 19th-century **Ninth Fort** (Žemaičių plentas 73; adult/child old museum 2/1Lt, new museum 2/1Lt; ☺ 10am-6pm Wed-Mon Mar-Nov, 10am-4pm Wed-Sun Dec-Feb), 7km north of Kaunas, was used by the Russians in WWI to defend their western frontier against Germany. During WWII the Nazis murdered an estimated 80,000 people, mostly Kaunas Jews, here. Take bus 38 from the bus station to the Mega Shopping & Leisure Centre, from where it's a 1km walk west to the fort.

Sleeping

our pick **Kauno Arkivyskupijos Svečių Namai** (☎ 322 597; kaunas.lcn.lt/sveciunamai; Rotušės aikštė 21; s/d/tr from 50/80/110Lt; 🖳) This charming guest house, run by the Lithuanian Catholic Church, couldn't have a better location, sitting smugly between centuries-old churches over looking Old Town square. Rooms are spartan but spacious, and management employ a number of ecofriendly practices, including energy-saving light bulbs, recycling, and changing towels only once for guests. Breakfast is not included.

Metropolis (☎ 205 992; www.greenhillhotel.lt; Daukanto gatvė 21; s/d/tr/q 90/120/165/220Lt) This graceful old dame is looking a bit frayed these days, but she still displays strong overtones of past grandeur. Sculpted-stone balconies overlook a leafy street, a hefty wooden turnstile door sweeps guests into a lobby with moulded ceiling, and age-old furnishings only add to the charm.

Litinterp (☎ 228 718; www.litinterp.lt; Gedimino gatvė 28/7; s/d/tr from 120/160/210Lt) Not a lot of character, but rooms are cheap, clean, and highly functional, and the staff is superfriendly and knowledgeable about the town. Office hours are 8.30am to 7pm Monday to Friday, 9am to 3pm Saturday.

Apple Hotel (☎ 321 404; www.applehotel.lt; Valančiaus gatvė 19; s 150-170Lt; d 210-230Lt; 🖳) Fans of minimalism will crave a stay at the quirky Apple. Spot the green-apple motif on your pillows and on the silk wall hangings that add a splash of colour to the otherwise white rooms.

Reval Hotel Neris (☎ 306 100; www.revalhotels.com; Donelaičio gatvė 27; s/d from 260/330Lt; 🖳) This smart business hotel fills eight floors of a recently renovated building in New Town. Service is slick and professional, and rooms are standard business class, with a few extras such as heated bathroom floors, and free tea and coffee.

Eating

It's no Vilnius, but Kaunas' restaurant scene is gradually improving, and food tends to be cheaper than in the capital.

Žalias Ratas (Laisvės alėja 36b; mains 7-30Lt) Tucked away behind the tourist office is this pseudo-rustic inn where staff don traditional garb and bring piping-hot Lithuanian fare to eager customers.

our pick **Morkų Šėlsmas** (Laisvės alėja 78b; mains 10-12Lt; ☺ 8am-7pm Mon-Fri, 11am-7pm Sat, 11am-5pm Sun) 'Carrot Party' specialises in imaginative vegetarian mains, tasty salads, home-baked muffins, and carrot-based smoothies – all using local organic produce when available. Look for the tiny patio tucked away in a private courtyard.

Senieji Rūsiai (Vilniaus gatvė 34; mains 18-40Lt) Easily the tastiest street terrace at which to dine, drink and soak up Old Town. Its candlelit 17th-century cellar has great grilled meats and a wide selection that includes frogs legs, trout, and the ubiquitous potato pancakes.

Miesto Sodas (Laisvės alėja 93; mains 20-30Lt; ☺ 11am-midnight) Kaunas' trendiest eatery has more than passable steaks and, rarity of all rarities, a salad bar. Service can be snail-slow. Siena nightclub in the basement is a great place to watch Žalgiris basketball games.

Central supermarkets include **Iki** (Jonavos gatvė 3) and **Maxima** (Kęstučio gatvė 55).

Drinking

BO (Muitinės gatvė 9) This laid-back bar attracts an alternative student set and gets rammed to overflowing on weekends. Its own brew is a tasty offering, but rather potent.

Skliautas (Rotušės aikštė 26) Skliautas bursts with energy most times of the day and night, and in summer its crowd basically takes over the small alley it occupies off Rotušės aikštė. Also good for coffee and cake.

Entertainment

Ex-it (www.exit.lt; Maironio gatvė 19; ☺ Tue-Sat) Arguably the best club in town, with a thumping sound system, huge dance floor, and quality DJs.

Latino Baras (Vilniaus gatvė 22) Latin music, occasional dance lessons, multiple rooms, and beautiful young things combine to make Latino Baras a standout club for many locals.

Kaunas Philharmonic (☎ 222 558; www.kaunofilhar monija.lt; Sapiegos gatvė 5) This is the main concert hall for classical music.

Kaunas Musical Theatre (☎ 200 933; www.muzik inisteatras.lt; Laisvės alėja 91) This 1892 building hosts operettas from September to June.

Getting There & Away
AIR
For information on international flights, see p498).

BUS
Major international services to/from Kaunas are operated by **Eurolines** (☎ 322 222; www.euro lines.lt) and **Ecolines** (☎ 202 022; www.ecolines.net). International routes to/from the **long-distance bus station** (☎ 409 060; Vytauto prospektas 24) include St Petersburg (150Lt, 18 hours, daily), Kaliningrad (123Lt, five hours, daily), Rīga (42Lt, five hours, daily) and Tallinn (106Lt, nine hours, daily).

Domestic routes include Vilnius (20Lt, 1¾ hours, up to three per hour), Druskininkai (25Lt, two to three hours, hourly), Klaipėda (44Lt, 2¾ hours, over 20 daily), Palanga (48Lt, 3¼ hours, about 14 daily) and Šiauliai (30Lt, three hours, 23 daily).

TRAIN
From the **train station** (☎ 221 093; Čiurlionio gatvė 16) there are up to 17 trains daily to/from Vilnius (12Lt, 1¼ to 1¾ hours).

Getting Around
Kaunas International Airport (☎ 399 307; www.kaunas air.lt; Savanorių prospektas) is 10km north of Old Town in the suburb of Karmėlava. To get there take minibus 120 from the big stop at Šv Gertrūdos gatvė or bus 29 from the stop on Vytauto prospektas (1.50Lt).

ŠIAULIAI
☎ 41 / pop 128,400

Lithuania's fourth-largest city is a work in progress. Formerly a shabby place on the outskirts of a massive Soviet military airfield, Šiauliai has been cleaning up its act (and its main street) in the recent past and transform-ing into a city with a buzz. Its biggest draw-card is the incredible Hill of Crosses, 10km to the north.

Get your bearings at the **tourism informa-tion centre** (☎ 523 110; www.tic.siauliai.lt; Vilniaus gatvė 213; ☺ 9am-6pm Mon-Fri, 10am-4pm Sat, 10am-3pm Sun), which sells maps and guides, including cycling itineraries to the Hill of Crosses, and makes accommodation bookings.

Sights & Activities
HILL OF CROSSES
Lithuania's most incredible, awe-inspiring sight is the legendary **Hill of Crosses** (Kryžių kalnas). It is a two-hump hillock blanketed by thousands of crosses. The sound of the evening breeze tinkling through the crosses, which appear to grow on the hillock, is in-describable and unmissable. Each and every cross represents the amazing spirit, soul-fulness and quietly rebellious nature of the Lithuanian people.

Legend says the tradition of planting crosses began in the 14th century. The crosses were bulldozed by the Soviets, but each night people crept past soldiers and barbed wire to plant yet more, risking their lives or freedom to express their national and spiritual fer-vour. Today the Hill of Crosses is a place of national pilgrimage.

Some of the crosses are devotional, others are memorials (many for people deported to Siberia) and some are finely carved folk-art masterpieces.

This strange place lies 10km north of Šiauliai – head north up highway A12, then travel 2km east from a well-marked turn-off (the sign says 'Kryžių kalnas 2'). You can rent a bike from the tourist information centre (5Lt per hour) and pedal out here, or take one of seven buses (2.50Lt). The bus schedule is in the tourist centre. A round-trip taxi with a half-hour to see the crosses should cost 40Lt.

OTHER SIGHTS
Vilniaus gatvė is the city's main drag and a great place to stroll or plop down in a streetside cafe and watch the world go by. It's also a free wi-fi zone.

The city's quirky symbol is a bizarre golden **sundial** (cnr Salkausko gatvė & Ežero gatvė), topped by a gleaming statue of an archer. It stands on the edge of the city's peaceful cemetery, about five minutes' walk north from the centre.

Šiauliai's list of eccentric museums is im-pressive. In the centre you'll find the **Radio &**

LITHUANIA

TV Museum (Vilniaus gatvė 174; adult/child 2/1Lt; ☺ 10am-6pm Tue-Fri, 11am-5pm Sat & Sun), **Photography Museum** (Vilniaus gatvė 140; adult/child 4/2Lt; ☺ 10am-6pm Tue-Fri, 11am-5pm Sat & Sun) and **Bicycle Museum** (Vilniaus gatvė 139; adult/child 6/3Lt; ☺ 10am-6pm Tue-Fri, 11am-5pm Sat & Sun). A little east of central Šiauliai is the **Museum of Cats** (Žuvininkų gatvė 18; adult/child 4/2Lt; ☺ 10am-5pm Tue-Sat), which houses feline memorabilia and one live cat.

Sleeping & Eating

Šiauliai College Youth Hostel (☎ 523 764; www.jnn .siauliukolegija.lt; Tilžės gatvė 159; s/d/tr 50/70/90Lt; reception ☺ 7am-11pm) This former college has been renovated with EU funds to create a spanking-clean and sparkling hostel with kitchen and TV room. None of the staff at reception (which is open 7am to 11pm) speaks English, but they do their very best to help.

Šiauliai (www.hotelsiauliai.lt; Draugystės prospektas 25; s/d/tr from 95/170/195) The town's old 14-storey Soviet hotel has enjoyed recent renovations both inside and out, leaving it with pleasant rooms dressed in pale yellow and brown. The views are still as great as ever.

Juonė Pastuogė (Aušros 31a; mains 10-30Lt) A country-and-western style music club/tavern with an enormous garden and an imaginative menu including the likes of ostrich steak, hearty country stews, and vegetarian pancakes.

Getting There & Away

Šiauliai is roughly 140km from both Kaunas and Rīga. With your own wheels you could feasibly visit the Hill of Crosses as a day trip from either.

Services from the **bus station** (☎ 525 058; Tilzes gatvė 109) include Vilnius (41Lt, three hours, six daily), Kaunas (30Lt, three hours, 23 daily), Klaipėda (30Lt, 3½ hours, five daily) and Rīga (28Lt, 2½ hours, four daily).

From the **train station** (☎ 430 652; Dubijos gatvė 44) there are trains to Vilnius (28.70Lt, 2½ hours, three daily) and Klaipėda (from 18.60Lt, two to three hours, five daily).

WESTERN LITHUANIA

Lithuania's lively left coastline is only 99km long but it packs plenty of firepower, with a thriving port city, a thumping party town and its crown jewel, the starkly beautiful, sand dune-infested Curonian Spit – a Unesco World Heritage site. Toss in a few fine fes-

tivals, add a dollop of German history and there will be plenty to keep you occupied in this wonderful part of the world.

PALANGA
☎ 460 / pop 17,600
Downright dull by winter, beachside Palanga, just 25km north of Klaiepėda, explodes into Lithuania's undisputed party capital in the summer months.

The **tourist information centre** (☎ 48 811; www .palangatic.lt; Kretingos gatvė 1; ☺ 9am-7pm Mon-Fri & 10am-4pm Sat & Sun mid-Jun–Aug, 1-5pm Mon & 10am-5pm Tue-Sat Sep–mid-Jun) adjoins the tiny bus station, east of Palanga's lengthy main artery, pedestrian Basanavičiaus gatvė.

For a peaceful escape from the crowds of Basanavičiaus gatvė, walk or cycle south along Meilės alėja, the main beachfront path, to Palanga's **Botanical Park**, where you'll discover lush greenery and swans gliding on still lakes. The park's highlight is the **Amber Museum** (Vytauto gatvė 17; adult/child 5/2.50Lt; ☺ 10am-8pm Tue-Sat & to 7pm Sun Jun-Aug, 11am-5pm Tue-Sat & 11am-4pm Sun Sep-May), inside the sweeping former palace of the noble Polish Tyszkiewicz family.

Sleeping & Eating
Room rates change by the week in summer. Litinterp (opposite) in Klaipėda can arrange B&Bs in Palanga. For cheap digs try haggling with one of the dozens of locals who stand at the eastern end of Kretingos gatvė touting *nuomojami kambariai* (rooms for rent). Expect to pay 30Lt to 100Lt per head.

Seklytėlė (☎ 57 415; Jūratės gatvė 18; r 100-150Lt) Above the restaurant of the same name are large rooms going for a song in summer. The furniture and bedding may be mismatched but that doesn't distract from their homely feel.

Ema (☎ 48 608; www.ema.lt; Jūratės gatvė 32; r from 135Lt) This basic guest house has stripped-back rooms in every pastel colour known to man. A cactus marks the spot.

Palanga Hotel (☎ 41 414; www.palangahotel.lt; Birutės gatvė 60; d 600-700Lt, 1-/2-room apt 1200/1600Lt; ❄ ⌨ ⌘) If you want to do it in style, look no further than this swish hotel of glass and wood wrapped inside 80-year-old pine trees.

There are scores of eating options along Basanavičiaus gatvė. One that stands out is rustic **1925 Baras** (Basanavičiaus gatvė 4; mains 20-40Lt), which has a less carnival atmosphere than many Palanga restaurants.

Getting There & Away

There are regular daily buses to Vilnius (63Lt, 4¼ hours, seven daily), Kaunas (48Lt, 3¼ hours, about 14 daily), Klaipėda (4.50Lt, 45 minutes, every 20 minutes) and Šiauliai (29.50Lt, three hours, eight daily).

KLAIPĖDA

☎ 46 / pop 186,000

Gritty Klaipėda is Lithuania's main port city and gateway to the lush natural beauty of Curonian Spit. It boasts a fascinating history as the East Prussian city of Memel, and many Germans enjoy visiting to dig into Klaipėda's Prussian past and waltz among the few buildings still standing from that era.

Information

The **tourist office** (☎ 412 186; www.klaipedainfo.lt; Turgaus gatvė 7; ☯ 9am-7pm Mon-Fri & 10am-4pm Sat & Sun Jun-Aug, 9am-6pm Mon-Fri & 10am-4pm Sat May & Sep, 9am-6pm Mon-Fri Oct-Apr) is exceptionally efficient, selling maps, arranging accommodation and renting bicycles (10/40Lt per hour/day plus €100/300Lt deposit). There's also free internet here. **Krantas Travel** (☎ 395 111; www.krantas.lt; Teatro gatvė 5) sells ferry tickets to Kiel and Karlshamn.

Sights

What little remains of Klaipėda's **Old Town** (most of it was destroyed in WWII) is wedged between the Danė River and Turgaus gatvė. There are several well-preserved old German half-timbered buildings in the vicinity of Teatro aikštė (Theatre Sq), which is Klaipėda's spiritual heart.

The square's dominant building is the **Drama Theatre** (Teatro aikštė 2), where in 1939 Hitler stood on the balcony and announced the incorporation of Memel into Germany. Occupying the middle of the square is the much-loved **statue of Ännchen von Tharau** – a character from a love poem thought to be written by the 17th-century German poet Simon Dach. The statue is a replica of the original destroyed during the war.

West of Old Town are the remains of Klaipėda's moat-protected **castle**. The **Klaipėda Castle Museum** (www.mlimuziejus.lt; Pilies gatvė 4; adult/child 4/2Lt; ☯ 10am-6pm Tue-Sat) inside the one remaining tower tells the castle's story from the 13th to 17th centuries. To get to the museum, walk through the Klaipėda State Sea Port Authority building and a ship-repair yard.

The city celebrates its nautical heritage each July with a flamboyant **Sea Festival** (www.juros.svente.lt) that draws crowds for a weekend of concerts, parties, exhibitions and nautical manoeuvres.

Sleeping

Klaipėda Travellers Hostel (☎ 211 879; www.lithuanianhostels.org; Butkų Juzės gatvė 7/4; dm/d 44/88Lt; ☐) This friendly hostel close to the bus station looks terrible from the outside but is very homely and pleasant inside.

Litinterp Guesthouse (☎ 410 644; www.litinterp.lt; Puodžių gatvė 17; s/d/tr with shared bathroom 80/140/180Lt, with private bathroom 100/160/210Lt; ☯ 8.30am-7pm Mon-Fri, 10am-3pm Sat) This accommodation agency arranges B&B in and around Klaipėda. The 16 rooms in its own guest house are plain, clean and nonsmoking.

Preliudija Guesthouse (☎ 310 077; www.preliudija.com; Kepėjų gatvė 7; s/d from 180/210Lt; ☐) Snug in an Old Town house dating to 1856, this guest house – a rare breed in Klaipėda – is charming. Despite its history, rooms are minimalist and modern; each has a single fresh flower in a vase, and sparkling bathroom.

Hotel Klaipėda (☎ 404 372; www.klaipedahotel.lt; Naujoji Sodo gatvė 1; s/d/ste/apt from 320/400/540/1000Lt; ☯ ☐) Choose from sturdy and comfortable rooms in the 12-storey red-brick monstrosity or their newer yet shabbier cousins in the celebrated 'K' building next door. The latter has the best views (rooms reside on floors six to 17).

Eating & Drinking

Pėda (Turgaus gatvė 10; mains 10-20Lt) A stylish cellar adjoining an art gallery (entrance around the corner), this spot is ideal for light evening snacks and live jazz at weekends.

our pick Kurpiai (Kurpių gatvė 1a; mains 20-40Lt; ☯ noon-3am) Kurpiai's cobbled terrace and dark old-world interior are not only the best place in town to catch live jazz, but also to sample ostrich steak, fresh trout and a wide range of pork, beef and vegetarian dishes. Service is also well above par. Arrive before 9.30pm on weekends (entrance Friday/Saturday 10/15Lt) or you'll be fighting for standing space.

Memelis (Žvejų gatvė 4) This red-brick brewery-restaurant by the river has been in operation since 1871. Interior is old-style beer hall; outside is industrial-feel riverside terrace.

our pick Vivalavita (Naujojo Sodo 1; ☯ noon-3am) Occupying the 20th floor of the 'K' building, Vivalavita has spectacular views of the swath

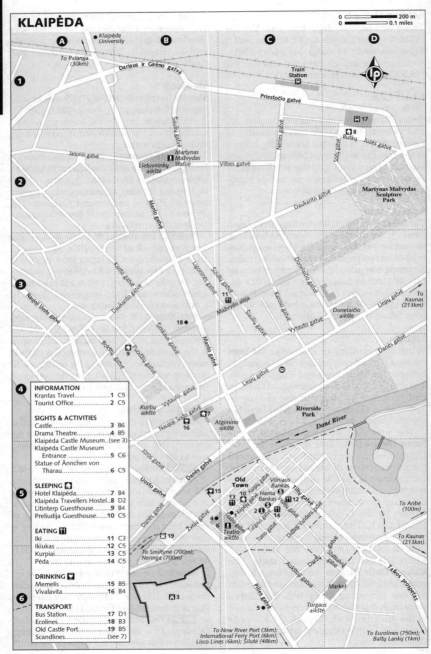

KLAIPĖDA

Klaipėda University

To Palanga (30km)

Dariaus ir Girėno gatvė

Train Station

Priestočio gatvė

17

8 Butkų

Juzės gatvė

Šaulių gatvė

Netiés gatvė

Sodų gatvė

Janonio gatvė

Martynas Mažvydas Statue

Lietuvninkų aikštė

Vilties gatvė

Daukanto gatvė

Martynas Mažvydas Sculpture Park

Manto gatvė

Kanto gatvė

Daukanto gatvė

Naujoji Uosto gatvė

Ligonines gatvė

Šaulių gatvė

Mažvydo aleja

Karoso gatvė

Šaulių gatvė

Vytauto gatvė

Donelaičio gatvė

Donelaičio aikštė

Liepų gatvė

To Kaunas (213km)

Danės gatvė

11

18

Bokštu gatvė

Puodžių gatvė

9

Sinkaus gatvė

Manto gatvė

Liepų gatvė

Vytauto gatvė

Kuršių aikštė

Naujoji Sodo gatvė

7

16

Atgimimo aikštė

Riverside Park

Danė River

Jūros gatvė

Uosto gatvė

Danės gatvė

Old Town

10 Kurpių gatvė

Vilniaus Bankas

Hansa Bankas

Tiltų gatvė

Kepéjų gatvė

Turgaus gatvė

Vežėjų gatvė

To Aribė (100m)

To Kaunas (213km)

13

15

12

2

14

4

6

Teatro aikštė

Tomo gatvė

Didžioji Vandens gatvė

Žvejų gatvė

19

To Smiltyné (700m); Neringa (700m)

Aukštoji gatvė

Darzų gatvė

Bažnyčių gatvė

Taikos prospektas

3

Pilies gatvė

5

Turgaus aikštė

Market

To Euroliny (750m); Balty Lanky (1km)

To New River Port (3km); International Ferry Port (6km); Lisco Lines (6km); Šilute (48km)

0 — 200 m
0 — 0.1 miles

INFORMATION
Krantas Travel.................1 C5
Tourist Office..................2 C5

SIGHTS & ACTIVITIES
Castle.............................3 B6
Drama Theatre................4 B5
Klaipėda Castle Museum..(see 3)
Klaipėda Castle Museum
  Entrance 5 C6
Statue of Ännchen von
  Tharau..........................6 C5

SLEEPING
Hotel Klaipėda.................7 B4
Klaipėda Travellers Hostel..8 D2
Litinterp Guesthouse.........9 B4
Preliudija Guesthouse......10 C5

EATING
Iki 11 C3
Ikiukas..........................12 C5
Kurpiai..........................13 B5
Pėda 14 C5

DRINKING
Memelis 15 B5
Vivalavita......................16 B4

TRANSPORT
Bus Station....................17 D1
Ecolines........................18 B3
Old Castle Port...............19 B5
Scandlines.....................(see 7)

A   B   C   D

1

2

3

4

5

6

LITHUANIA

of docks along Klaipėda's waterfront, the spit's northern point, and the Baltic Sea beyond.

Self-caterers can head for **Iki** (Mažvydo alėja 7/11) and **Ikiukas** (Turgaus gatvė) supermarkets.

Getting There & Away

Klaipėda **bus station** (☎ 411 547; Priestočio gatvė) welcomes daily buses from Vilnius (59Lt, four to 5½ hours, up to 15 daily), Kaunas (44Lt, 2¾ hours, over 20 daily), Liepāja (18Lt, 2¾ hours, daily), Šiauliai (30Lt, 3½ hours, five daily), Palanga (4.50Lt, 45 minutes, every 20 minutes) and Kaliningrad via Nida (40Lt, 4½ hours, daily). The major operators are **Eurolines** (☎ 415 555) and **Ecolines** (☎ 310 103; www.ecoli nes.net).

From the **train station** (☎ 313 677; Priestočio gatvė 1), 150m from the bus station, there are three trains daily to/from Vilnius (42.10Lt, 4½ to five hours) and five trains to/from Šiauliai (from 18.60Lt, two to three hours).

Ferries to the Smiltynė ferry landing on Curonian Spit lead from the **Old Castle Port** (www .keltas.lt; Žvejų gatvė 8), near Klaipėda Castle west of Old Town. Ferries leave every half-hour in the high season and cost 2Lt return (10 minutes). Vehicles must use the **New River Port** (Nemuno gatvė 8; per car 32Lt), 3km south of the passenger terminal. Services depart at least hourly.

The **International Ferry Port** (☎ 395 051; www .lisco.lt; Perkėlos gatvė 10) is another 3km south of the New Ferry Terminal. **Scandlines** (☎ 310 561; www.scandlines.lt; Naujoji Sodo gatvė 1) sails to Aarhus and Aabenraa (Denmark; with cabin, both €148, twice weekly); and **Lisco Lines** (☎ 395 051; www.lisco.lt; Perkėlos gatvė 10) runs passenger ferries to/from Kiel (Germany; from €46, six weekly), Sassnitz (Germany; from €46, twice weekly) and Karlshamn (Sweden; from €52, daily). Tickets on Lisco Lines can be booked through Krantas Travel (p493).

Take bus 1 (2Lt) to both the New Ferry Terminal (10 minutes) and the International Ferry Port (30 minutes).

CURONIAN SPIT

pop 3100

This magical pigtail of land, dangling off the western rump of Lithuania, hosts some of Europe's most precious sand dunes and a menagerie of elk, deer and avian wildlife. Just 3.8km at its widest point, the spit looks positively brittle on a map, but in person it seems much sturdier, thanks to the pine forests that cover 70% of its surface. A few dunes rise high above those forests, creating a surreal effect.

The fragile spit, which Unesco recognised as a World Heritage site in 2000, has faced a number of environmental threats over the years, beginning with the clear-felling of its forests in the 16th century. Lately the dunes have been eroding rapidly and tourism is exacerbating the problem. When observing the dunes, stick to the marked paths.

The entire Curonian Spit was Prussian territory until WWI. These days the spit is divided roughly evenly between Lithuania and Russia's Kaliningrad region in the south. Lithuania's share of the spit is protected as **Curonian Spit National Park** (www.nerija.lt), which has two **visitors centres** (Smiltynė ☎ 46-402 257; info@nerija.lt; Smiltynės plentas 11; ⌚ 9am-noon & 1-6pm Mon-Fri, 9am-6pm Sat & 9am-4pm Sun Jun-Aug, 8am-noon & 1-5pm Mon-Fri Sep-May; Nida (☎ 469-51 256; nidainfo@nerija.lt; Naglių gatvė 8; ⌚ 9am-noon & 1-5pm Mon-Thu, to 6pm Fri & Sat, to 4pm Sun May-Sep) with abundant information on walking, cycling, boating and lazing activities.

Administratively, the Lithuania side is divided into two regions: the township of Smiltynė, which is part of Klaipėda; and the Neringa municipality, which contains the townships Juodkrantė, Pervalka, Preila and touristy Nida.

GETTING THERE & AWAY

To get to the spit you need to take a ferry or bus from Klaipėda or take the Kaliningrad–Klaipėda bus (see left).

From Smiltynė, buses and microbuses (9Lt, one hour) run regularly to/from the **Nida bus station** (☎ 469-54 859; Naglių gatvė 20) via Juodkrantė (4Lt, 15 to 20 minutes).

Smiltynė

☎ 46

Smiltynė is where the ferries from Klaipėda dock. The **visitor centre** (☎ 402 257; info@nerija .lt; Smiltynės plentas 11; ⌚ 9am-noon & 1-6pm Mon-Fri, 9am-6pm Sat & 9am-4pm Sun Jun-Aug, 8am-noon & 1-5pm Mon-Fri Sep-May) here is a good place to plot strategies for forays south and has a small nature museum.

On summer weekends Klaipėda residents cram Smiltynė, flocking to its beaches and to the **Lithuanian Sea Museum** (☎ 469-490 754; www.juru.muziejus.lt; adult/student Jun-Aug 12/6Lt, Sep-May 10/5Lt, dolphin show Jun-Aug 18/9Lt, Apr-May 14/7Lt, camera 5Lt; ⌚ 10.30am-6.30pm Tue-Sun Jun-Aug, 10.30am-6pm Wed-Sun May & Sep–mid-Oct, 10.30am-5pm Sat & Sun mid-Oct–Apr), which contains an aquarium with seal and sea-lion shows.

LITHUANIA

Neringa
☎ 469

South of Smiltynė the crowds begin to thin and you enter Neringa, which slinks majestically southward to the Russian border. The fresh air and scent of pine grow headier as you get further and further away from civilisation.

JUODKRANTĖ

Juodkrantė is a quiet settlement with everything a traveller needs. The most popular activity in the village is one of Neringa's trademark activities: buying and tasting freshly caught and smoked fish, which is sold from several wooden houses along the main road, Rėzos gatvė.

Top of the strange sights list is **Raganų Kalnas** (Witches' Hill), a spooky sculpture trail through gorgeous forest with large, fairy-tale Lithuanian wooden carvings.

Less than 1km south of Juodkrantė is one of Neringa's must-see attractions, a massive **colony of grey herons and cormorants**. Wooden steps lead from the road to a viewing platform where the panorama of thousands of nests amid pine trees – cormorants to the north, herons to the south – is breathtaking. In March and April the air is thick with birds carrying huge sticks to build their nests, in May the cacophony rises to a deafening crescendo as the chicks are born.

In Juodkrantė stay at the marvellously rustic **Vila Flora** (☎ 53 024; www.vilaflora.lt; Kalno gatvė 7a; s/d 200/260Lt), which also serves up some of the best food on the spit (mains cost 20Lt to 40Lt). For an adventurous mealtime, board **Kogas** (Liudviko Rėzos gatvė 1; mains 20-40Lt), a pseudo pirate ship moored in the harbour.

NIDA

Neringa's southernmost settlement is Nida, a charming resort town that slumbers much of the year but in summer becomes Neringa's tourist nerve centre.

Bankas Snoras (Naglių gatvė 27) has a currency exchange and ATM opposite the bus station. The **tourist information centre** (☎ 52 345; www .visitneringa.lt; Taikos gatvė 4; 10am-8pm Mon-Sat & 10am-3pm Sun Jun-Aug, 9am-5pm Mon-Fri Sep-May) books accommodation (5Lt fee) and stocks loads of useful information on walks, bike rides, fishing boat trips etc.

Sights & Activities

An excellent way to see the spit is by bicycle. A flat **cycling trail** runs all the way from Nida to Smiltynė, and you stand a good chance of seeing wild boar or other wildlife at any point along the path. There are bicycles for hire (around 35Lt per 24 hours) on almost every street corner in Nida; some allow you to leave your bike in Smiltynė and bus it back to Nida.

Curonian Spit's awe-inspiring sand dunes are on full display from the smashed granite sundial atop the 52m-high **Parnidis Dune**. The panorama of coastline, forests and the spit's most stunning dune extending into Kaliningrad to the south is unforgettable. You can walk up here from town on a **nature trail** (ask at the tourist information centre for a map) or drive via Taikos gatvė.

Back in Nida, check out the **Ethnographic Museum** (Naglių gatvė 4; adult/child 2/1Lt; 10am-6pm May-Sep, 10am-5pm Tue-Sat Sep-May), the **Thomas Mann Memorial Museum** (☎ 52 260; www.mann .lt; adult/child 3/1Lt; 10am-6pm Jun-Aug, 10am-5pm Tue-Sat Sep-May) in the Nobel Prize–winning German writer's former summer house, and the **Neringa History Museum** (Pamario gatvė 53; adult/child 2/1Lt; 10am-6pm Jun–mid-Sep, 10am-5pm Mon-Sat mid-Sep–May).

Another of Nida's many highlights is its **architecture**, a mix of classic German half-timbered construction and quaint wooden houses with frilly eaves and intricate facades.

Sleeping & Eating

The tourist information centre can help arrange accommodation in private houses, but contact the centre weeks in advance for summer bookings. In winter expect steep discounts on prices listed here.

Nidos Kempingas (☎ 52 045; www.kempingas.lt; Taikos gatvė 45a; per tent 10-15Lt, per person 15-20Lt, per car 10-15Lt, d from 230Lt, 4-/6-bed studios with garden 350/490Lt;) Set in pine forest at the foot of a path that leads to Parnidis Dune, this spruced-up camping ground has accommodation to suit all budgets. There are also bikes for hire.

Naglis (☎ 51 124; www.naglis.lt; Naglių gatvė 12; d/apt 250/300Lt) This beautiful wooden guest house has immaculate rooms, most of which face the table-clad, tree-shaded garden. There's a dining room and kitchen for guests to share too.

Miško Namas (☎ 52 290; www.miskonamas.com; Pamario gatvė 11-2; r from 250Lt;) Another charmer – every room here has its own fridge, sink and kettle and a couple have balconies. Self-cater in the cosy communal kitchen. Take note of the 180-year-old twisting wooden staircase.

LITHUANIA DIRECTORY

ACCOMMODATION

Vilnius has a serious room crunch so book ahead in high season. The tourist information offices (p473) can help, but they tend to utilise unexceptional midrange hotels. Coastal locations such as Palanga and Curonian Spit are popular with Lithuanians as well as foreigners, and rooms fill up months ahead in summer. **In Your Pocket** (www.inyourpocket.com) has hotel listings for Vilnius, Kaunas, Šiauliai, Klaipėda and Curonian Spit.

Vilnius has no shortage of excellent top-end lodgings. Good budget accommodation is hard to come by in Vilnius and most other cities; the few deals that exist are highlighted prominently in this book. Vilnius only sports a few hostels, but the numbers are slowly growing. Outside of Vilnius hostels are scarce, but in rural areas you can find perfectly fine hotel rooms at hostel prices. Most camping grounds are cheap and basic (5Lt to 20Lt for a camp site), but they are gradually improving.

For a double room in Vilnius from May to September you'll pay around 150Lt for budget lodgings, 300Lt for a midrange room, and more than 600Lt at the top end. Prices in regional areas are gradually increasing, too – expect to pay around 100Lt for a budget double, 250Lt for a midrange double, and around 450Lt for a top-end room. Prices in this chapter include private bathroom unless otherwise stated.

Smoking is still generally accepted in Lithuania, but this is slowly changing, particularly in the hotel business. Expect most hotels to offer a handful of nonsmoking rooms.

ACTIVITIES

Lithuania is conducive to any activity revolving around its gazillion forests: hiking, mushrooming, berry-picking, picnicking and birdwatching are at the top of the list. Lakes are also abundant, especially in the wilderness of Aukštaitija National Park, where both hiking and boating activities abound.

Cycling is becoming more popular in flat Lithuania. Most towns have outlets that rent out bikes. Good places for day rides include Curonian Spit (opposite), and Druskininkai.

BUSINESS HOURS

Most shops open at 9am or 10am and close around 7pm on weekdays and a little earlier on Saturdays. Banks are generally open between 9am and 5pm on weekdays. Restaurants tend to open around noon and close around 11pm, but many stay open much later on weekends, especially in cities.

EMBASSIES & CONSULATES

The following embassies and consulates are in Vilnius:

Australia (Map pp476-7; ☎ 5-212 3369, emergency 8-687 11117; australia@consulate.lt; Vilniaus gatvė 23)

Belarus (Map pp476-7; ☎ 5-213 2255; www.belarus.lt; Muitinės gatvė 41)

Canada (Map pp476-7; ☎ 5-249 0950; www.canada .lt; Jogailos gatvė 4)

Denmark (Map pp474-5; ☎ 5-264 8760; www.amb vilnius.um.dk; T Kosciuškos gatvė 36)

Estonia (Map pp476-7; ☎ 5-278 0200; www.estemb.lt; A Mickevičiaus gatvė 4a)

France (Map pp476-7; ☎ 5-212 2979; www.amba france-lt.org; Švarco gatvė 1)

Germany (Map pp476-7; ☎ 5-210 6400; www.deut schebotschaft-wilna.lt; Sierakausko gatvė 24/8)

Latvia (Map pp476-7; ☎ 5-213 1260; www.latvia.lt; Čiurlionio gatvė 76)

Poland (Map pp474-5; ☎ 5-270 9001; www.wilno .polemb.net; Smėlio gatvė 20a)

Russia (Map pp474-5; ☎ 5-272 1763; www.rusemb.lt; Latvių gatvė 53/54)

UK (Map pp474-5; ☎ 5-246 2900; www.britain.lt; Antakalnio gatvė 2)

USA (Map pp476-7; ☎ 5-266 5500; www.usembassy.lt; Akmenų gatvė 6)

FESTIVALS & EVENTS

There's no better time to observe Lithuanian culture than during its stupendous Unesco-honoured **national song festival**, held every four years in July in Vilnius. The next one is scheduled for 2011.

The pan-Baltic **Baltica International Folk Festival** takes place all over Lithuania every three years. Lithuania is due to host the festival in 2011.

SPLURGE

There's no better way to see Lithuania than from a hot-air balloon. Of course, it's not cheap (around 450Lt for a one-hour flight), but the experience is unforgettable. Contact the **Vilnius Ballooning Association** (Map pp474-5; ☎ 8-676 00050; www.oreivis.lt; Krokuvos gatvė 11-29) for more information.

HOLIDAYS

New Year's Day 1 January
Independence Day 16 February; anniversary of 1918 independence declaration
Lithuanian Independence Restoration Day 11 March
Easter Sunday March/April
Easter Monday March/April
International Labour Day 1 May
Mothers Day First Sunday in May
Feast of St John (Midsummer) 24 June
Statehood Day 6 July; commemoration of coronation of Grand Duke Mindaugas
Assumption of Blessed Virgin 15 August
All Saints' Day 1 November
Christmas 25 & 26 December

INTERNET ACCESS

Internet use has developed at a staggering pace in Lithuania's urban areas – free wi-fi hot spots can be found all over Vilnius and in ever-increasing numbers in other cities. However the drawback of this is fewer internet cafes. Saying that, most reasonably sized provincial towns have at least one place to log on.

MONEY

The Lithuanian litas (the plural is litai; Lt) will remain firmly in place until at least 2010, when Lithuania could possibly trade in its litas for the euro. The litas is divided into 100 centai. It is pegged to the euro at the rate of 3.45Lt per euro.

All but the smallest Lithuanian towns usually have at least one bank with a functional ATM. Most big banks cash travellers cheques and exchange most major currencies. Credit cards are widely accepted.

POST

Sending a postcard/letter abroad costs at least 2.45/2.95Lt. Mail to North America takes about 10 days, and to Europe about a week.

TELEPHONE

Lithuania's digitalised telephone network is run by **TEO** (www.teo.lt).

EMERGENCY NUMBERS

- Ambulance ☎ 03
- Fire ☎ 01
- Police ☎ 02

To call other cities within Lithuania, dial ☎ 8 followed by the city code and phone number. To make an international call dial ☎ 00 before the country code.

To call Lithuania from abroad, dial ☎ 370 then the city code, followed by the phone number.

Picking up a local prepaid SIM card allows for pain-free and relatively cheap calling and texting. Mobile companies **Bitė** (www.bite.lt), **Omnitel** (www.omnitel.lt) and **Tele 2** (www.tele2.lt) sell prepaid SIM cards; Tele2 is the only one to offer pan-Baltic roaming with prepaid cards.

To call a mobile phone within Lithuania, dial ☎ 8 followed by the three-digit code and mobile number; to call a mobile from abroad dial ☎ 370 instead of ☎ 8.

Public telephones, which are increasingly rare given the widespread use of mobiles, are blue and only accept phonecards, which are sold in denominations of 9/13/16/30Lt at newspaper kiosks.

VISAS

Citizens from the EU, Australia, Canada, Israel, Japan, New Zealand, Switzerland and the US do not require visas for entry into Lithuania if staying for less than 90 days. South African nationals are required to obtain a visa. For information on other countries and obtaining a visa, visit www.migr acija.lt.

TRANSPORT IN LITHUANIA

GETTING THERE & AWAY

Air

The Europe-wide budget-airline explosion hasn't left Lithuania untouched. Kaunas, not Vilnius, is the destination for budget flights, but most tourists landing there immediately hop in a car or bus for the one-hour drive to Vilnius. Flights to Kaunas land at **Kaunas International Airport** (☎ 37-399 307; www.kaunasair .lt; Savanorių prospektas), about 12km north of the centre. Its website has updated timetables.

Most international traffic to Lithuania still goes through **Vilnius International Airport** (☎ 5-230 6666; www.vno.lt; Rodūnios gatvė 2); see the airport website for updated timetables and a full list of airlines flying to/from Vilnius. **SAS** (SK; ☎ 5-235 6000; www.flysas.com) flies to **Palanga airport** (☎ 460-52 020; www.palanga-airport.lt;

Liepojos plentas 1), 6km north of the centre, from Copenhagen.

airBaltic (☎ 5-235 6000/1; www.airbaltic.com) runs direct flights between Vilnius and about a dozen Western European destinations.

Major international carriers with direct flights to Vilnius:

Aer Lingus (EI; ☎ 5-265 2690; www.aerlingus.com)

Austrian Airlines (OS; ☎ 5-210 5030; www.aua.com)

ČSA (Czech Airlines; OK; ☎ 5-215 1503; www.czech-airlines.com)

Estonian Air (OV; ☎ 5-235 6001; www.estonian-air.com)

Finnair (AY; ☎ 5-261 9339; www.finnair.com)

LOT (LO; ☎ 5-273 9000; www.lot.com)

Lufthansa (LH; ☎ 25-329 290; www.lufthansa.com)

SAS (SK; ☎ 5-235 6000; www.flysas.com)

Land

Now that Lithuania is part of the Schengen zone, crossing the border into Latvia and Poland is generally a breeze; border-control points do exist, but they are rarely staffed. For all land crossings into Russia (Kaliningrad) or Belarus, see the boxed text, p97.

BUS

The main international bus companies operating in Lithuania are **Eurolines** (www.eurolines.lt) and **Ecolines** (www.ecolines.net). Buses serve destinations across Eastern Europe, including Rīga, Kaliningrad, Tallinn, Warsaw, St Petersburg, and as far away as London. See p484 and p491 for details of major services.

CAR & MOTORCYCLE

Coming from the south, you're looking at a 30-minute to one-hour wait at the two Polish border crossings (Ogrodniki and Budzisko). Lines at the Latvian border are generally non-existent. Have your passport, insurance and registration documents ready.

If you're planning on crossing into Russia (Kaliningrad) or Belarus in a rental car, check your rental conditions very carefully – most rental companies forbid this.

See p484 for car-hire companies in Vilnius.

TRAIN

Vilnius is linked by regular direct trains to Moscow, St Petersburg, Kaliningrad and Minsk. You'll need a Belarus visa for the Moscow train. See p484 for details on departures from Vilnius.

Sea

International ferry services depart from Klaipėda. Destinations include Denmark, Germany and Sweden. See p495 for details.

GETTING AROUND
Air

At the time of research, there were no domestic flights serving Lithuania.

Bicycle

Get everything you need to know about bike touring in Lithuania from the website of **BaltiCCycle** (www.bicycle.lt). Lithuania is flat and its once-disastrous roads are gradually improving.

Bus

Timetables for local buses are displayed prominently in most stations.

Car & Motorcycle

You can drive from any one point in Lithuania to another in a couple of hours. Modern four-lane highways link Vilnius with Klaipėda (via Kaunas) and Panevėžys.

The speed limit in Lithuania is 50km/h in cities and 90km/h to 110km/h outside the city and on highways. Headlights must be switched on at all times and winter tyres must be fitted between 1 November and 1 March. It is useful to have an International Driving Permit (IDP), but usually your home-country licence will suffice as long as it has a photograph of the licence holder.

See p484 for car-hire companies in Vilnius.

Local Transport

Lithuanian cities are generously covered by networks of buses, trolleybuses and mini-buses. Tickets are sold at news kiosks and from drivers, but buying them from drivers will cost you more. Punch your ticket in one of the punch boxes inside the vehicle; in most towns you must punch your bus ticket or you'll risk a fine.

Train

You can get to Kaunas, Klaipėda, Šiauliai, Ignalina and Trakai from Vilnius by suburban train. See p485 for more details.

Macedonia Македонија

With vast lakes ringed by Byzantine churches, thickly forested mountains, inexhaustible archaeological riches and endless vineyards bursting with grapes, Macedonia is truly a land of plenty. Still largely unexplored, it's also somewhat mysterious for outsiders. Yet, as the locals fondly attest, Macedonia is a little country with a big heart. This is felt in its gracious hospitality, the merry creativity of its carnivals and feasts, and in Macedonians' close ties to their faith, family and traditions. Indeed, being relatively ignored by outsiders, the country has happily retained an authenticity missing elsewhere in Europe.

Aside from Skopje and some small cities, Macedonia is all natural. Bountiful agricultural plains are intersected with rugged mountain ranges, many peaks topping 2500m. Rivers and ancient tectonic lakes dot this country where the Continental and Mediterranean climate zones merge. Diverse ecosystems, with endemic flora and fauna, enhance its natural beauty.

The other main draw is history: Macedonia boasts everything from Ottoman mosques, Roman ruins and antique theatres to traditional village stone houses, medieval castles and awe-inspiring monasteries. The country's most-visited destination, Ohrid, has numerous historical attractions and an atmospheric Old Town, all set against a sublime and unforgettable lake.

Of course, not everything's perfect – the economy is sluggish, while littering, reckless drivers and insufficient flights to important destinations still vex. Nevertheless, curious and open-minded visitors will be amply rewarded here.

FAST FACTS

- **Area** 25,713 sq km
- **Capital** Skopje
- **Currency** Macedonian denar (MKD); €1 = 65MKD; US$1 = 47MKD; UK£1 = 69MKD; A$1 = 33MKD; ¥100 = 49MKD; NZ$1 = 27MKD
- **Famous for** Lake Ohrid, Byzantine monasteries, name dispute with Greece
- **Official language** Macedonian
- **Phrases** *zdravo* (hello); *blagodaram/fala* (thanks); *molam* (please); *prijatno* (goodbye)
- **Population** 2 million
- **Telephone codes** country code ☎ 389; international access code ☎ 00
- **Visas** unnecessary for many visitors; see p525

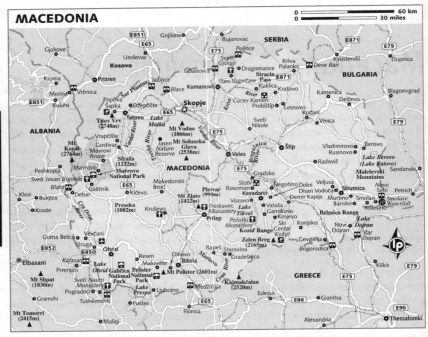

HIGHLIGHTS

- Dive into Macedonia's spiritual heart in **Ohrid** (p514), a town that is rich in cultural treasures and overlooks a magnificent lake.
- Enjoy culture and nightlife in **Skopje** (p507), which combines Ottoman architecture, Byzantine flourishes and Yugoslav concrete excess.
- Admire the atmospheric Ottoman-era architecture and sip coffee at chic cafes in **Bitola** (p519), below Pelister National Park.
- Head to **Mariovo** (p521), in Macedonia's southern-border badlands, for legends, mountain rivers and ghost villages.
- Treat yourself to winery tours, historical sites and outdoor activities in the **Tikveš wine region** (p522).

ITINERARIES

- **Three days** Enjoy Skopje's Old Town and cafe culture, before heading to Ohrid the next day, with its history, nature and magnificent lake.
- **One week** Explore Skopje for two days, continuing to Ohrid for the Old Town

sites and swimming. Continue to fashionable Bitola, visiting Heraclea Lyncestis and traditional villages. While returning to Skopje, quaff wine at a Tikveš winery or visit ancient Stobi.

CLIMATE & WHEN TO GO

Macedonia's hot, dry summers, sustained by warm Aegean winds, exceed 40°C. In winter, temperatures sink to -30°C (in the mountains). Snowfall there continues from November until May.

Macedonia's best between May and September. It's hectic (in Ohrid especially) in summer.

HISTORY

The historical or geographical Macedonia is now divided between the Republic of Macedonia (38%), Greek Macedonia (51%) and Bulgaria's Pirin Macedonia (11%). For its people, their history's a source of great pride but also a heavy burden. The post-Yugoslav experience has seen existential pressure from neighbours, constantly challenging their right to an identity. Macedonia's history is too complex for simple truths or answers; remember that many people have strong opinions.

Ancient Macedonians & Romans

As a powerful Macedonian dynasty emerged, King Philip II (r 359–336 BC) compelled the Greeks and other powers to submit. His son, Alexander the Great, spread the empire to India before dying in 323 BC. The empire soon dissolved amid infighting. In 168 BC, Rome conquered Macedonia; its position on key trade routes (the Via Egnatia from Byzantium to the Adriatic, and the Axios from Thessaloniki up the Vardar Valley) kept cities prosperous.

With the preaching of the Apostle Paul, Christianity arrived in Macedonia and soon expanded. With the Roman Empire's division in AD 395, Macedonia came under Constantinople and Greek-influenced Orthodox Christianity.

The Coming of the Slavs & the Macedonian Cars

The 7th-century Slavic migrations intermingled with Macedonia's various peoples. In 862, two Thessaloniki-born monks, St Cyril and St Methodius, were dispatched by the Byzantine emperor to spread orthodoxy and literacy among the Slavs of Moravia (in modern-day Czech Republic). Their disciple, St Kliment of Ohrid, would modify their Glagolitic script, creating the Cyrillic alphabet. With St Naum, he propagated literacy in Ohrid (the first Slavic university) in the late 9th century.

Byzantium and the Slavs shared a religion, but sharing political power was impossible. Numerous wars unfolded between Constantinople and an expansionist Bulgarian state of Car Simeon (r 893–927) and subsequently Car Samoil (r 980–1014). Prespa and Ohrid in Macedonia became their strong-

> ### HOW MUCH?
>
> - **Hotel room in Skopje** 2750MKD
> - **Ohrid-area private accommodation** 500MKD
> - **Loaf of bread** 25MKD
> - **Souvenir icon** 800MKD
> - **Shot of rakija** 60MKD
>
> ### LONELY PLANET INDEX
>
> - **1L petrol** 51MKD
> - **1L bottled water** 20MKD
> - **Beer in shop/bar (Skopsko)** 35/100MKD
> - **Souvenir T-shirt** 450MKD
> - **Street snack (burger, pizza or toasted sandwich)** 90MKD

holds, until Byzantine emperor Basil II defeated Samoil at the Battle of Belasica (near today's Strumica, in eastern Macedonia) in 1014. According to legend (probably only that), he blinded 14,000 of Samoil's men.

After Belasica, the Byzantines annexed Macedonia. The sacking of Constantinople by Latin knights in 1204, and the rise of the Serbian Nemanjid dynasty, allowed Serbia to briefly expand into Macedonia. However, after Emperor Stefan Dušan (r 1346–55) died, Serbian power waned. The Ottoman Turks soon arrived, and Macedonia would remain theirs until 1913.

Ottoman Rule & The Macedonian Question

The Ottomans introduced Islam and Turkish settlers to Macedonia. Skopje became a trade centre, and the Turks built beautiful mosques, *hammams* and castles. However, even though the Turks were ruling, Greeks wielded considerable power. In 1767, Greek intriguing caused the abolition of the seven-centuries-old Ohrid archbishopric. Greek priests started opening schools and building churches in Macedonia, to the resentment of the Macedonians. Bulgaria and Serbia also sought Macedonia. The lines were drawn.

In Macedonia, Western European ethnic nationalism collided violently with the Ottomans' organisation of citizens by religion, not ethnicity. Europe's great powers intervened

> ### CONNECTIONS: MOVING ON FROM MACEDONIA
>
> Macedonia is well-connected internationally. From Skopje (p513), buses reach cities including Sofia, Belgrade, Pristina, Tirana, İstanbul and Thessaloniki. Thessaloniki is also the origin point for an international train (p512) running through Skopje and continuing on to Belgrade, Zagreb and Ljubliana.

after the Russo-Turkish War of 1877–78, when the Treaty of San Stefano awarded Macedonia to Bulgaria. However, with Western powers fearful of Russia, the ensuing Treaty of Berlin reversed the decision; the enmities this inspired fuelled 40 years of conflict.

After Berlin, Macedonia remained Ottoman, but the 'Macedonian question' persisted. With the Turks' days in Europe numbered, various Balkan powers sponsored revolutionary groups. Greek rebels emerged and, in 1893, the Internal Macedonian Revolutionary Organisation (in Macedonian, Vnatrešna-Makedonska Revolucionerna Organizacija, or VMRO) was formed. VMRO was fatally divided, however, between 'Macedonia for the Macedonians' propagandists and a pro-Bulgarian wing.

In the Ilinden St Elijah's Day Uprising (2 August 1903), Macedonian revolutionaries declared the first Balkan republic, in Kruševo; the Turks crushed it 10 days later. Although nationalist leader Goce Delčev had died months earlier, he's considered Macedonia's national hero today.

In 1912 the Balkan League (Greece, Serbia, Bulgaria and Montenegro) declared war on Turkey: in this, the First Balkan War, Macedonia was the prime battleground. The Turks were expelled, but Bulgarian dissatisfaction led Sofia to declare war on its former allies in 1913 (the Second Balkan War). Bulgaria was soon defeated, but quickly allied with Germany and Austria in WWI and then reoccupied Macedonia. Macedonia's population was again beset by rivals demanding their allegiance, and further divided.

The Yugoslav Experience
The end of WWI saw Bulgaria defeated and Macedonia divided between Greece and the new Kingdom of Serbs, Croats and Slovenes (Royalist Yugoslavia). The Belgrade authorities banned the Macedonian name and language. Disgruntled VMRO elements helped Croat nationalists assassinate Serbian king Aleksandar in 1934. During WWII, resistance to the Bulgarian-German occupation was led by Josip Broz Tito's Partisans. He promised Macedonians republican status within a communist Yugoslavia but had little interest in the Macedonian people or their goals – Macedonian Partisans pushing to fight for Greek-controlled Macedonia were shot as an example to the rest. Nevertheless, the Greek communists got many Macedonians there to fight the Royalists in the 1946–49 Greek Civil War. Their defeat forced thousands of Macedonians, many of them children (known as the *begalci*, or refugees) to flee Greece.

After WWII the communists redistributed Macedonia's wealth, as in other Yugoslav republics. Nationalisation of property and industry ruined villages, with farmers soon deprived of their flocks. Tito's concrete monstrosities sheltered the newly urbanised populations. Nevertheless, some nation-building overtures were made: a Macedonian grammar was released in 1952 and the Macedonian Orthodox Church was created in 1967 – the 200th anniversary of the Ohrid archbishopric's abolition.

Macedonia After Independence
In a referendum on 8 September 1991, 74% of Macedonians voted to split from Yugoslavia. In January 1992 the Republic of Macedonia declared independence. President Kiro Gligorov negotiated a peaceful withdrawal of the Yugoslav army – the only such withdrawal in any former Yugoslav republic.

The Greeks, however, were enraged. Macedonia's first flag bore the Vergina star – the ancient Macedonian royal symbol – and Greece argued that use of the Macedonian name implied territorial claims on northern Greece, something the Macedonian side has continually denied.

Vigorous Greek lobbying thus forced Macedonia to accept a 'provisional' name, the Former Yugoslav Republic of Macedonia (FYROM), to gain UN admission in April 1993. When the USA (following six EU countries) recognised the country as FYROM in February 1994, Greece retaliated with an economic embargo. In November 1995 Greece relented when Macedonia changed its flag and agreed to further name negotiations.

As in other 1990s-era 'transition' countries, an oligarchical system arose in Macedonia amid shady privatisations, deliberate bankrupting of state-owned firms and dubious pyramid schemes. Worse, tensions were simmering with Macedonia's ethnic Albanians, who complained of ill treatment. During the 1999 NATO bombing of Serbia, Macedonia sheltered over 400,000 Kosovo Albanian refugees; despite this, emboldened separatist leaders from the Ushtria Člirimtare Kombetare (UČK; National Liberation Army) attacked it in early 2001. The conflict lasted six months, until the Ohrid Framework Agreement was signed, granting more minority rights for languages and national symbols, along with quota-based public-sector hiring.

Implementing the Framework Agreement proved difficult, though, especially concerning power decentralisation and municipal rezoning. The agreement stipulated more rights for local minorities comprising 20% of the population; the artfully created new municipal boundaries rewarded Albanians more than other ethnic groups, critics claimed. This 'solution' might eventually lead to a biethnic (not multiethnic) Macedonia.

Towards Europe

Macedonia is enacting EU-membership reforms and has restructured its army to NATO standards, participating in peace-keeping missions abroad. However, Greece blocked Macedonia's NATO invitation in April 2008, citing the unresolved name issue – a stance that frustrated Macedonians and many foreign leaders. Greece pledged to block Macedonia's future NATO – and EU – memberships, and nationalism surged in both countries. Western countries pressured both sides to resolve their differences.

Through all of this turbulence, Macedonians today try to keep optimistic. Although the economy remains slow, things are improving. Ethnic tensions have lessened. While EU membership seems distant, many Macedonians simply perceive joining the EU as a means to travel and work abroad without visas.

PEOPLE

Macedonia's population of 2,022,547 people (in 2004) was divided thus: Macedonians (66.6%), Albanians (22.7%), Turks (4%), Roma (2.2%), Serbs (2.1%) and others (2.4%). Most Serbs live near the Serbian border, while most Albanians live in the northern and western towns nearest to Kosovo and Albania. The Vlachs, descendents of ancient Romans but long assimilated into Macedonianness, hail from the Bitola region. Turks also remain, in Skopje, western Macedonia and elsewhere. The disadvantaged Roma are mostly urban, surviving through begging and odd jobs.

RELIGION

Most Macedonians are Orthodox Christians, with a few Macedonian-speaking Muslims (the so-called Torbeši and Gorani, in western Macedonia). Turks are Muslim, as are most Albanians; however, Catholic Albanians exist (Mother Theresa, who grew up here as Agnes Gonxha Bojaxhiu, is the most famous example). A Jewish community of about 200 people descends from Sephardic Jews who fled Spain after 1492. Sadly, approximately 98% of the Jewish population – over 7200 people – were deported to the Treblinka concentration camp during the WWII Bulgarian occupation. The community holds a Holocaust commemoration ceremony every 11 March.

The Macedonian Orthodox Church was created in 1967 and, despite not being recognised by neighbouring Orthodox countries, is active in church building and restoration work. Although Macedonians don't attend church services often, you'll see them stop by church to light a candle, kiss icons and pray.

ARTS
Cinema

Macedonia's leading film-maker, Milčo Mančevski, highlighted interethnic relations in the Oscar-nominated *Before the Rain* (1994). Mančevski's next film, *Dust* (2001), was an Ilinden Uprising–era cowboy classic that riled the Greeks (see p503). In 2007, Mančevski released *Semki* (Shadows) a racy urban love story with supernatural overtones. In it, an elderly female speaking an 'Aegean' Macedonian dialect intones the film's recurring line – 'give back what is not yours'. The Greeks were infuriated; Mančevski insisted it was not a nationalistic reference.

Music & Dance

Macedonian folk instruments include the *gajda*, a single-bag bagpipe, played solo, or accompanied by a large drum, the *tapan*, which is played with different sticks for different tones. The *kaval* (flute) and/or *tambura* (small lute with two pairs of strings) are other instruments, as is the Turkish-inherited *zurla* (a double-reed horn, also accompanied by the *tapan*). The Čalgija music form, involving clarinet, violin, *darabuk* (hourglass-shaped drum) and *đoumbuš* (banjo-like instrument) is representative. Macedonian music employs the 7/8 time signature.

Macedonian traditional folk dancing includes the *oro*, a simple Balkan circle dance. The male-only *Teškoto oro* (difficult dance) is accompanied by the *tapan* and *zurla* and performed in traditional costume. The *Komitsko oro* symbolises the anti-Turkish struggle, while the *Tresenica* is a dance for women.

The **Ministry of Culture** (www.culture.in.mk) lists dates and venues for performances. Try to see the national folk-dance ensemble, **Tanec** (☎ 02-461 021; www.tanec.com.mk; Vinjamin Macukovski 7, Skopje).

Although several Macedonian musicians have won international acclaim, such as pianist Simon Trpčevski and opera singer Boris Trajanov, the favourite of many is Toše Proeski. When this charismatic singer with a booming voice and seductive smile died tragically at the age of 26 (on 16 October 2007), Macedonians were devastated. Toše was beloved not only for his music, but also for his frequent humanitarian work for children. Today, you'll hear his music played everywhere.

ENVIRONMENT
The Land
Macedonia's 25,713 sq km is mostly plateau (600m to 900m above sea level), though over 50 mountain peaks top 2500m. It's also where the Continental and Mediterranean climate zones converge, and alpine climates exist. The Vardar River passes Skopje and runs into the Aegean near Thessaloniki. Ohrid and Prespa Lakes, in the southwest, are two of the oldest tectonic lakes (around three million years old); at 300m, Ohrid is the Balkans' deepest lake. Lining the borders are mountains, including Šar Planina, near Kosovo in the northwest; Mt Belasica, in the southeast, bordering Greece; and the Osogovski and Maleševski ranges, in the east, abutting Bulgaria. Macedonia's highest peak, Mt Korab (Golem Korab; 2764m), borders Albania in the Mavrovo National Park.

Wildlife
Macedonia belongs to the eastern Mediterranean and Euro-Siberian vegetation region. Upper slopes are pine clad, while the lower mountains feature beech and oak. Vineyards dominate the central plains. Endemic fauna includes the molika tree, a subalpine pine unique to Mt Pelister, and the rare *foja* tree on Golem Grad island in Lake Prespa.

Macedonia's alpine and low Mediterranean valley zoological zones contain forest fauna such as bears, wild boars, wolves, foxes, chamois and deer. The rare lynx inhabits Šar Planina. Blackcaps, grouse, white Egyptian vultures, royal eagles and forest owls inhabit woodlands, while lake birds include Dalmatian pelicans, herons and cormorants. Storks (and their huge nests) are visible. Macedonia's national dog, the *šar planinec,* is a 60cm tall sheepdog that will fight bears and wolves.

Lakes Ohrid, Prespa and Dojran are separate fauna zones, due to territorial and temporal isolation. Ohrid, which boasts 146 endemic species, is a living museum of the fossil age. Ohrid's endemic trout predates the last ice age. Ohrid also has whitefish, gudgeon and roach, plus a 30-million-year-old snail genus, and the mysterious Ohrid eel, which arrives from the Sargasso Sea to live for 10 years before returning to breed and die; its offspring restart the cycle.

National Parks
Macedonia's national parks are Pelister (near Bitola), Galičica (between Lakes Ohrid and Prespa) and Mavrovo (between Debar and Tetovo). Pelister and Galičica are part of a tri-border protected area involving Albania and Greece. Hiking in summer and skiing at Mavrovo in winter are fantastic. All parks are accessible by road; none requires tickets or permits.

Environmental Issues
Lake Ohrid's endemic trout is a severely endangered species and, while commonly found in restaurants, is supposedly illegal to fish. Do the right thing and try any of three other trout varieties *(mavrovska, kaliforniska* or *rekna)* instead – they're just as tasty, and cheaper.

Despite strict new laws, littering continues and recycling is rare.

FOOD & DRINK
Macedonia's specialities combine Ottoman flavours with central European tastes. Condiments include *ajvar,* a sweet red-pepper sauce and *lutenica,* similar to *ajvar* but with hot peppers and tomatoes. The national salad, *šopska salata,* features tomatoes and cucumbers topped with *sirenje* (white cheese). *Čorba* (soup) is popular, as is *tavče gravče* (oven-cooked white beans).

Skara (grilled meat) includes spare ribs, beef *kebapci* (kebabs) and *uviač* (rolled chicken or pork stuffed with yellow cheese), and remains Macedonia's definitive food, though 'international' cuisine is definitely well established too.

For breakfast, try *burek* (cheese, spinach or minced meat in filo pastry) accompanied by drinking yoghurt or *kiselo mleko* (sour milk, like yoghurt).

Bitter Skopsko Pivo is Macedonia's leading beer. The national firewater, *rakija*, is a strong grape spirit, delicious when served hot with sugar in winter. *Mastika*, like ouzo, is also popular. Macedonians enjoy making homemade brandies from cherries and plums. The Tikveš region produces excellent wines.

All restaurants and bars operate until midnight (1am on weekends), with the exception of nightclubs that have paid for late licenses. Although smoking is still widespread, most larger places have nonsmoking sections. Still, you can expect a smoky reception in most crowded bars and clubs.

SKOPJE СКОПЈЕ

☎ 02 / pop 640,000

Don't let the drab Yugoslav-era architecture fool you – Skopje's a lively town, and one with more to it than meets the eye. It's both an outgoing place where shopkeepers shout greetings across cobbled lanes and lithe young in-line skaters blaze by, and a conspiratorial one where political apparatchiks and foreign diplomats crouch over their coffees – a place where everyone knows something about everyone else.

While much of what makes Skopje tick will be lost on the first-time visitor, there's also much to enjoy. Crossing the Vardar River on the 15th-century Stone Bridge (Kamen Most) leads into the Čaršija (old Turkish bazaar), with its enduring Ottoman attractions. Despite the city-wide destruction caused by a great earthquake in 1963 (which ushered in an age of Yugoslav concrete), here, handsome mosques and Turkish baths renovated into art galleries still stand. They are interspersed with shops where skilled craftsmen fashion silver, gold and clothing. Above it all looms Tvrdina Kale (the city fort), still yielding up archaeological treasures.

Skopje also offers great cafes and nightlife. Its clubs are pumping and there's always something on, from jazz and classical to opera, theatre and rock. It might not make many lists of top European capitals, but then again, Skopje might surprise you.

ORIENTATION

The Vardar River, spanned by the Stone Bridge and other bridges, divides Skopje. North of it is the Čaršija and south is the new town, where a pedestrianised central zone spans main square Ploštad Makedonija, the Gradski Trvgovki Centar city mall, and ul Makedonija, featuring many cafes. The adjoining train and bus stations are a 10-minute walk from the square.

Maps

Get the Trimaks *New Skopje City Map* (200MKD) at Kultura Bookstore on Ploštad Makedonija bb.

INFORMATION
Bookshops

Ikona Bookstore (☎ 3065 312; Dimitrije Čupovski) Travel guides and novels.

Kultura Bookstore (☎ 3235 862; Ploštad Makedonija bb) Maps, guides and Macedonia-related books.

World Press Shop (Vasil Glavinov 3) Has English- and European-language newspapers.

Internet Access

Skopje has many wi-fi hot spots and internet cafes, including at the train station.

Contact Café (Gradski Trgovski Centar; per hr 120MKD; ⏰ 9am-10pm) Central but pricier.

Medical Services

City hospital (☎ 3130 111; 11 Oktomvri 53; ⏰ 24hr)

Neuromedica private clinic (☎ 3133 313; 11 Oktomvri 25; ⏰ 24hr)

Money

ATMs and *menuvačnici* (exchange offices) abound.

Menuvačnica Euro (Gradski Trgovski Centar; ⏰ 9am-8.30pm Mon-Sat)

Post & Telephone

Post offices exist opposite the train station, in the Gradski Trgovski Centar and in Ramstore mall.

The train-station branch houses the telephone centre. Kiosks (newsagents) have private telephones, and sell cards for public phones.

Main post office (☎ 3141 141; Orce Nikolov 1; ⏰ 7am-7.30pm Mon-Sat, 7.30am-2.30pm Sun) About 75m northwest of Ploštad Makedonija.

Tourist Information

City of Skopje Bureau for Tourism and Information (070 812882; www.skopje.mk; Vasil Adzilarski bb; ⏰ 8.30am-4.30pm Mon-Fri) The friendly official city tourism office offers free info on Skopje and the country.

SKOPJE

0 — 500 m
0 — 0.3 miles

INFORMATION
Atlantis Travel.....................................1 D6
Bulgarian Embassy...............................2 A5
Canadian Embassy................................3 A4
City Hospital..4 B5
City of Skopje Bureau for Tourism and
 Information.......................................5 C5
Contact Café.................................(see 57)
Dutch Embassy.....................................6 A5
Greek Embassy.....................................7 A4
Ikona Bookstore...................................8 B5
Kultura Bookstore.................................9 B5
Macedonia Travel...............................10 A4
Main Post Office.................................11 B4
Menuvačnica Euro.........................(see 57)
Neuromedica Private Clinic................12 C6
Post Office..13 D5
Russian Embassy.................................14 A4
UK Embassy..15 A5
World Press Shop................................16 B5

SIGHTS & ACTIVITIES
Bit Pazar..17 C4
Čifte Amam..18 C4
City Art Gallery..................................19 C4
City Museum......................................20 B6
Daud Paša Baths...........................(see 19)
Kuršumli An.......................................21 C4
Museum of Contemporary Art.........22 B3

Museum of Macedonia........................23 C4
Mustafa Paša Mosque..........................24 C4
Soboren Hram Sveti Kliment
 Ohridski...25 A4
Sultan Murat Mosque..........................26 C4
Sveti Dimitrija......................................27 C4
Sveti Spas...28 C4
Trvdina Kale Fortress...........................29 B4

SLEEPING
Art Hostel...30 B6
Hotel Ambasador................................31 A4
Hotel Dal Met Fu................................32 A4
Hotel Jadran.......................................33 B5
Hotel Square......................................34 B5
Hotel Stone Bridge..............................35 B5
Hotel TCC Plaza.................................36 B5
Tim's Apartments................................37 A4

EATING
Amici Miei..38 A5
Dal Met Fu Restaurant...................(see 32)
Destan..39 C4
Idadija..40 A4
Kapan An..41 C4
Papu...42 A4
Pivnica An...43 C4

DRINKING
Bastion...44 A4
Café di Roma......................................45 B5
Café Trend..46 B5
La Bodeguito Del Medio......................47 B5
Lezet..48 A4
Mr Jack..49 B5

ENTERTAINMENT
Colosseum (Summer Location)............50 A3
Colosseum (Winter Location)..............51 D6
Element..(see 50)
Hard Rock..52 C5
Kino Milenium...............................(see 57)
Macedonian National Theatre.............53 C4
Multimedia Centre Mala Stanica.........54 A5
Universal Hall.....................................55 A3

SHOPPING
Beershop..56 A5
Gradski Trgovski Centar......................57 B5
Ikona..58 B5
Lithium Records............................(see 57)
Ramstore Mall....................................59 A4
Trgovski Centar Bunjakovec................60 A4

TRANSPORT
Budget Car Rental..............................61 B6
Bus Station...62 D6

Travel Agencies

Atlantis Travel (☎ 2400 941; skopje@atlantis.com.mk; Bojmija 1, lok l7m; ☺ 9am-5pm) City maps, accommodation information and in-country tours. Opposite the train station, 50m east of Cosmofon Building.

Go Macedonia (☎ 3232 273; www.gomacedonia.com .mk; Trgovski Centar Beverly Hills lok 32, Naroden Front 19) Arranges hiking, cycling, caving and winery tours.

Macedonia Travel (☎ 3112 408; www.macedonia travel.com; Orce Nikolov 109/1, lok 3) Tours, including trips to the hard-to-access Jasen Nature Reserve, and discounted air tickets.

SIGHTS

Ploštad Makedonija & the South Bank

Ploštad Makedonija is Skopje's main orientation point. Stroll the south bank along the riverside path, or relax in one of numerous river-facing cafes jutting from the Gradski Trgovski Centar. More cafes line pedestrianised ul Makedonija, which crosses ul Dimitrije Cupovski, ending at the **City Museum** (☎ 3114 742; Mito Hadživasilev Jasmin bb; admission free; ☺ 9am-3pm Tue-Sun), which has interesting temporary exhibitions. It's in the old train station; the fingers of its stone **clock** were frozen in time at 5.17am on 27 July 1963, the moment the great earthquake struck.

The austere **Soboren Hram Sveti Kliment Ohridski** (bul Sveti Kliment Ohridski bb; admission free; ☺ 7am-8pm) is Skopje's main Orthodox cathedral. It's full on holidays and sees daily visitors who light candles in its dark, icon-rich confines. Cross over to **Debar Maalo**, with its tree-lined streets and old architecture. Follow bul Ilindenska to the **city park**, where kids can run around and chase the strutting ducks and geese.

North Bank & Čaršija

From the Ploštad Makedonija cross the **Stone Bridge** and enter the **Čaršija**, where Skopje's Ottoman past lingers in the form of architecture and a largely Muslim Albanian and Turkish population. On the left is **Sveti**

Dimitrija (☺ 9am-6pm), a handsome, three-aisled Orthodox church from 1886. Across from it rise the double domes of the **Daud Paša Baths** (1466), once the Balkans' largest Turkish bath. The building houses the **City Art Gallery** (☎ 3133 102; Kruševska 1a; admission 100MKD; ☺ 9am-3pm Tue-Sun), where modern art occupies seven rooms. Also check out the neighbourhood's other old bath-turned–art gallery, **Čifte Amam** (admission 50MKD; ☺ 9am-4.45pm Mon-Fri, to 3pm Sat, to 1pm Sun).

From the Čaršija's small shops and tea houses, take ul Samoilova to the church of **Sveti Spas** (admission 100MKD; ☺ 8am-3pm Tue-Sun). It was built underground, as the Turks didn't allow churches to be taller than mosques. The wood-carved iconostasis is 10m wide and 6m high, built by early-19th-century master craftsmen Makarije Frčkovski and the brothers Petar and Marko Filipovski. See the **Tomb and Museum of Goce Delčev**, leader of VMRO and national hero, killed by Turks in 1903.

Back in Čaršija, the **Museum of Macedonia** (☎ 3116 044; Čurčiska 86; admission 50MKD; ☺ 9am-3pm Tue-Sun) documents Neolithic through communist times. The ethnographical exhibition has old costumes and traditional house models. The museum's highlights, however, are its icons and wood-carved iconostases. Archaeological items decorate the lovely **Kuršumli An** (1550), once an Ottoman *caravanserai* (inn).

The Čaršija ends at **Bit Pazar**, a big, busy vegetable market also selling bric-a-brac and household goods. Across bul Goce Delčev from Bit Pazar, **Sultan Murat mosque** (1436) features a distinctive, red-tipped

MACEDONIA

SKOPJE IN ONE DAY

Catch the morning sun while sipping an espresso at **Café di Roma** (p511) on pedestrianised ul Makedonija, before crossing the **Stone Bridge** (above) into the Old Town. See modern paintings at the **Daud Paša Baths** (above) and **Čifte Amam** (above). Wander the **Čaršija** (above) and savour beef kebabs at **Destan** (p511). Next, see the magnificent wood-carved iconostasis at the church of **Sveti Spas** (above) and visit **Mustafa Pasa Mosque** (p510). Climb Ottoman **Tvrdina Kale fortress** (p510) for panoramic views. Back in the new town, watch the action at **Dal Met Fu Restaurant** (p511). By night, tackle a whiskey bar like **Mr Jack** (p511), or go Cuban at **La Bodeguito Del Medio** (p511).

MACEDONIA

FREE THRILLS

Free thrills? Skopje's full of 'em:

- Saunter up to the Ottoman fortress **Tvrdina Kale** (below) for panoramic views.
- Shop with locals at the garrulous open market, **Bit Pazar** (p509).
- Stroll the Ottoman Old Town, **Čaršija** (p509).
- Roller-blade and relax in summer at the expansive **city park** (p509).
- Flock with stylish sorts to cafes along the grand **Ploštad Makedonija** (p509) and the adjacent, pedestrianised **ul Makedonija** (p509).

---

clock tower and Ottoman *madrassa* (Islamic school) remains.

Kale & Around

Above Sveti Spas, the 1492 **Mustafa Paša mosque** (Samoilova bb) exemplifies magnificent Ottoman architecture, also boasting a lovely lawn, garden and fountain.

Opposite it, ascend the Ottoman **Tvrdina Kale fortress**. Restoration and archaeological investigations continue; six layers of civilisation have been discovered in artefacts dating from Neolithic times onwards. There are great views, too.

Further on, the **Museum of Contemporary Art** (☎ 3117 735; Samoilova bb; admission 100MKD; ☾ 9am-3pm Tue-Sun) displays works by Macedonian artists and world-famous masters too.

Mt Vodno

Framing Skopje to the south, **Mt Vodno** is popular with hikers and picnickers. Topping it is the 66m-high **Millenium Cross** (2002), the world's largest, illuminated at night. Taxis drive to Sredno (Middle) Vodno (about 120MKD).

Further west along Vodno, in the Gorno Nerezi suburb-village, the **Sveti Pantelejmon monastery** (1164) has important Byzantine frescos. Some, such as the *Lamentation of Christ*, depict a pathos and realism that pre-date the Renaissance by two centuries. The church is 20 minutes by taxi (120MKD).

FESTIVALS & EVENTS

The **Skopje Jazz Festival** (☎ 3131 090; www.skopjejazzfest.com.mk; Maksim Gorki 5), held in October, is fun and always features a world-renowned head-liner. The organisers do the **Off-Fest** (www.offest.com.mk) in May, combining world music and DJ events. There's also the **May Opera Evenings** (☎ 3114 691).

In December, the ever-more-popular **Taxirat Festival** (☎ 2775 430; www.lithiumrecords.com.mk, in Macedonian; Gradski Trgovski Centar) rocks Skopje. Art exhibitions, performances and concerts compose the summertime **Skopsko Leto** (☎ 3165 064; www.dku.org.mk; bul Sveti Kliment Ohridski 58) festival.

SLEEPING

Online resources like www.allmacedonia hotels.com do hotel bookings. Macedonia Travel (p509) offers good-value flight–hotel combos.

Budget

Art Hostel (☎ 070 233336; www.art-hostel.com.mk; Tome Arsovski 14; dm/s/d €12/25/40) There are slightly cramped six-bed dorms and small private rooms at this hostel, a 20-minute walk from both the central square and the bus/train stations. The shared bathrooms are clean and new. The relaxed vibe is enhanced by a billiards table and low-lit outdoor balcony with couches. A similar feel (with the same prices) prevails at smaller sister Hostel Hostel (☎ 3222 321; Ognjen Pricev 18), a five-minute walk away.

Hotel Bimbo (☎ 321 4517; 29 Noemvri 63; s/d incl breakfast €35/50) Rooms are basic but clean, and there's a cosy breakfast nook. It's in a residential area near the centre.

Hotel Square (☎ 3225 090; 6th fl, Nikola Vapcarov 2; s/d/tr incl breakfast €45/50/75) Well-situated overlooking the square, this place offers great value for the location. The cosy rooms are well-kept and modern, and the balcony cafe offers lovely views.

Hotel Ambasador (☎ 3215 510; Pirinska 36; s/d incl breakfast €57/84) Skopje's only place for lava mud–wrap massages, the Ambasador has slightly dated but pleasant rooms. The staff is well informed and helpful.

Midrange

Hotel Jadran (☎ 3118 427; 27 Mart bb; s/d €45/75) Service is a bit gruff and some of the fixtures antiquated, but the Jadran is very central and the rooms have an old-style charm, with high, lengthy ceilings.

our pick **Hotel Dal Met Fu** (☎ 3239 584; www.dal metfu.com.mk; Ploštad Makedonija; s/d/apt from €59/65/85) A trendy, discreet boutique hotel above the eponymous restaurant, this very central address offers well-designed modern rooms with flair.

Tim's Apartments (☎ 3237 650; Orce Nikolov 120; s/d/apt €69/89/110) Near the park, friendly Tim's has 10 classy rooms and seven apartments with kitchenettes.

Hotel Aristocrat Palace (☎ 3133 978; www.aristocratpalace.com.mk; Elisie Popovski 59; d/apt €80/99) This relaxing and friendly new hotel is a 15-minute walk from downtown, in the posh Vodno neighbourhood. The handsome rooms feature all mod cons, including jacuzzis in the spotless bathrooms. There's a restaurant, bar and terrace too.

Top End

Hotel TCC Plaza (☎ 3111 807; Vasil Glavinov 12; s/d/ste €95/115/144) This central five-star hotel offers spacious, nicely lit rooms and suites; the spa centre includes swimming pool, fitness and massage (from 600MKD).

Hotel Stone Bridge (☎ 324 900; Kej Dimitar Vlahov 1; s/d/apt €138/159/259) Near the bridge, this deluxe hotel has sophisticated rooms with stylised Ottoman furnishings – great if you can afford it.

EATING

Idadija (Rade Koncar 1; mains 180-250MKD; ☯ 8am-12am) In Debar Maalo's *skara* corner, Idadija has been serving excellent grills for 80 years.

Papu (Djuro Djakovic 63; mains 220-400MKD) The tastes and decor of old Kruševo are preserved with style at this lovely place in Debar Maalo, studded with stone arches, antiques and the sounds of cascading water.

Dal Met Fu Restaurant (Ploštad Makedonija; mains 280-350MKD; ☯ 7.30am-midnight) It might strike tourists as, well, touristy, but Dal Met Fu is appreciated by locals for its light pastas, cheerful waitresses and preening position behind big windows.

Pivnica An (☎ 3212 111; Čaršija; mains 300-500MKD; ☯ 9am-midnight) You're paying for the ambience, primarily, at this 'beerhouse' located in a restored Ottoman building's sumptuous courtyard (while tasty, the food is overpriced).

Amici Miei (Nikola Trimpare 6; mains 350-500MKD; ☯ 11am-midnight) Before opening, owner Alessio Zuccarini imported his Tuscan parents to train the chefs; the frequent visits of Italian diplomats attest to the results.

Restaurant Imes (☎ 3061 367; Ilindenska 138a; mains 350-520MKD; ☯ 9am-midnight) Visit this banquet-hall restaurant specifically during the Macedonian Wine Club's monthly tastings (see p512).

The Čaršija has *kebapčilnici* – the classic is **Destan** (ul 104 6; kebabs 120MKD; ☯ 7am-11pm), with Skopje's best kebabs, accompanied by seasoned grilled bread – Turkish doner kebab and *lahmacan* (a spicy sort of pizza) places, plus fancier joints. Several eateries are tucked inside the shaded Old Town courtyard of **Kapan An** (Čaršija; mains 160-400MKD), behind Čifte Amam; it's good for *kebapci* and alfresco dining. Ploštad Makedonija has both fast-food and chic eateries, while leafy Debar Maalo is clustered with good *skara* spots.

DRINKING

Cafes and bars work until 1am on Friday and Saturday night, and till midnight other days. After that, only late-licence nightclubs can operate.

⬛ our pick La Bodeguito Del Medio (Kej 13 Noemvri; ☯ 9am-1am) Known as 'the Cuban', this gregarious riverfront place does do Cuban food – but it's best at night, when the long bar's lined with carousels and cocktails.

Café di Roma (Makedonija; ☯ 8am-1am) This place has Skopje's best espresso and a stylish clientele.

Lezet (Nikola Trimpere 8a; ☯ 9am-1am) Cluttered with amphorae, curtains and gurgling fountains, this Ottomanesque cafe exudes atmosphere.

Bastion (Pirinska 43; ☯ 8am-1am) Bohemian Bastion is a Skopje classic, popular day and night.

Café Trend (Ploštad Makedonija; ☯ 8am-1am) Aspiring socialites mix with (and gossip about) local celebrities at this slick Ploštad Makedonija place.

Mr Jack (bul Partizanski Odredi 3; ☯ 8am-1am) This rockin' night bar with 50 whiskys, draught Guinness and live bands has a mixed Macedonian–international clientele.

ENTERTAINMENT

Skopje gets many international DJs; see www.skopjeclubbing.com.mk.

Colosseum (www.colosseum.com.mk; City Park summer, under train station winter) This venue is Skopje's biggest and most popular club, along with Element (www.element.com.mk; City Park). When major international DJs appear, tickets run 250MKD to 500MKD.

Multimedia Center Mala Stanica (Zheleznička 18; ☯ 9am-midnight) Featuring arty, ornate decor, the cafe of the National Art Gallery hosts temporary exhibitions, and live music.

Club Castro (train station; 🕙 8pm-4am) This student favourite under the train station gets going late with live rock, reggae and ska.

Hard Rock (Kej Dimitar Vlahov bb; 🕙 10pm-4am) A popular late-night place, Hard Rock features DJ parties and sometimes live bands.

Macedonian Wine Club (mwc.org.mk; Ilindenska 138a; tastings 400MKD) Drop in to Restaurant Imes for the MWC's monthly wine tastings, accompanied by live music and a *skara*-and-salads buffet– Skopje's cheapest gourmet experience. All are welcome, but dress smart; you'll be rubbing shoulders with foreign diplomats.

Universal Hall (🕿 3224 158; bul Partizanski Odredi bb; tickets 100-200MKD) Classical, jazz, pop and kids' performances happen here.

Macedonian National Theatre (🕿 3114 060; Kej Dimitar Vlahov bb; tickets 100-400MKD) In a communist-era building, the theatre hosts opera, ballet and classical music.

Kino Milenium (🕿 3111 111; Gradski Trgovski Centar; tickets 60-120MKD) The Kino is Skopje's largest cinema; Ramstore shopping mall has another.

SHOPPING

Ikona (🕿 3215 330; Luj Paster 19; 🕙 9am-9pm Mon-Fri, 9am-4pm Sat; gifts 300-7000MKD) 'Traditional' souvenirs, including Orthodox icons, archaeological replicas, pottery, painted boxes and folk dolls are available here.

Lithium Records (Gradski Trgovski Centar; 🕙 8.30am-8pm Mon-Sat) Lithium sells all kinds of music (Macedonian and international) plus concert and festival tickets, including Serbia's Exit Festival.

Makedonska Vinoteka (Ilindenska 138a; 🕙 9am-6pm) The Macedonian Wine Club's official shop, in Restaurant Imes.

Beershop (Teodosije Gologanov 42; 🕙 noon-8pm, closed Sun) Has one of the Balkans' biggest beer selections (more than 100 different brews!)

The Čaršija sells jewellery, traditional carpets, dresses and more, while Bit Pazar sells fruit, vegetables and anything random. The **Gradski Trgovski Centar** (11 Oktomvri; 🕙 9am-8pm) is a modern mall, like the slicker **Ramstore** (Mito Hadživasilev Jasmin bb; 🕙 8am-8pm) by the City Museum. **Trgovski Centar Bunjakovec** (bul Partizanski; 🕙 9am-7pm), and **Trgovski Centar Beverly Hills** (Naroden Front; 🕙 9am-7pm) are smaller, containing clothing boutiques, banks, pharmacies, hairdressers, cafes and so on.

GETTING THERE & AWAY
Air
Aleksandar the Great Airport (Aerodrom Aleksandar Veliki; 🕿 3148 333; www.airports.com.mk) is 21km east of Skopje and handles flights from major European cities. Flying into Thessaloniki with a budget carrier and then getting a train, bus or vehicle transfer into Macedonia is often cheaper.

Bus
Skopje's **bus station** (bul Jane Sandanski; 🕿 2466 011) adjoins the train station. English is spoken, and there's an exchange office.

Buses to Ohrid go via Kičevo (three hours, 167km) or Bitola (four to five hours, 261km). In summer, book ahead. For details of domestic and international routes, see below.

Train
The **train station** (Zheleznička Stanica, bul Jane Sandanski; 🕿 3164 255) serves Negotino (135MKD, two hours, three daily), Prilep (170MKD, three hours, three daily), Bitola (200MKD, four hours, three daily), Gevgelija (185MKD, 2½ hours, three daily), Kumanovo (60MKD, 40 minutes, four daily) and Kičevo (150MKD, two hours, three daily).

The international north–south train line serving Macedonia starts in Thessaloniki. Two daily Thessaloniki–Skopje trains (700MKD, five hours) run, continuing through Serbia to Belgrade (1300MKD, eight to 10 hours, two daily), and then Zagreb (Croatia) and Ljubljana (Slovenia). Another international line unites Skopje and Pristina (Kosovo).

GETTING AROUND
To/From the Airport
There's no airport bus. Taxi prices should be signposted; they're around 800MKD.

Bus
Skopje city buses cost 25MKD to 35MKD.

DOMESTIC BUSES FROM SKOPJE

Destination	Cost (MKD)	Duration (hr)	Frequency
Bitola	430	2½	10 daily
Kavadarci	240	1½	9 daily
Mavrovo	170	1½	4 daily Mon-Fri
Negotino	310	2	5 daily
Ohrid	450	3-4	11 daily
Vevčani	450	4	2 daily

INTERNATIONAL BUSES FROM SKOPJE			
Destination	Cost (MKD)	Duration (hr)	Frequency
Belgrade	1400	9	13 daily
İstanbul	2560	12	5 daily
Ljubljana	3770	14	1 daily
Pristina	350	2	8 daily
Sofia	850	5½	3 daily
Thessaloniki	1280	4	Mon, Wed & Fri
Tirana	1300	7	2 daily
Zagreb	3150	12	1 daily

Car

Daily rental prices start at 26000MKD. Try **Budget Car Rental** (☎ 3290 222; Mito Hadživasilev Jasmin bb; ⏱ 9am-5pm).

Taxi

Skopje's taxi base rate is 50MKD, and drivers use their meters. Central destinations cost 50MKD to 100MKD. **Pulstar** (☎ 15177) and **Vardar** (☎ 15165) are two fair and reliable taxi companies, but any cab displaying a five-digit number starting with 151 is OK.

Taxis at the bus/train station have been known for rip-offs; if you take one, remember the above-cited average rates, and ensure the driver uses the meter.

AROUND SKOPJE

Possible day trips from Skopje are numerous; they include ancient Roman **Stobi**, and perhaps a **wine tasting** at one of several wineries near it (see p522).

The closest getaway (30 minutes by car), however, is tranquil **Lake Matka**. Sitting beneath the steep Treska Canyon amidst verdure, Matka offers hiking, rock climbing, boating and caving (€10). Restaurants serving excellent fish include **Manastirska Pestera** (Monastery Cave; ☎ 02-2052 512; mains 350-600MKD), dug into the rock.

Matka means 'womb'; the link with the Virgin Mary is accentuated by grotto shrines like **Sveta Bogorodica**, below the wall. From here a steep path reaches **Sveti Spas**, **Sveti Trojica** and **Sveta Nedela** – the last, a 90-minute walk away. In these caves hermits once meditated and revolutionaries hid from Turks.

The **Church of Sveti Nikola** is beyond the dam, across the bridge, followed by the frescoed **Church of Sveti Andrej** (1389). Next door, the mountaineering hut **Matka** (☎ 02-3052 655;

per bed 500MKD) offers guides, climbing gear and accommodation.

From Skopje drive, take a taxi (350MKD), or catch bus 60 along bul Partizanski Odredi (50MKD, 40 minutes, hourly).

WESTERN MACEDONIA

Western Macedonia gets the lion's share of travellers to the country, and no wonder – its spectacular mountain ranges provide a stunning backdrop running south from the Šar Planina range to the gentler Jablanica range. Yet the major draw is at the road's end; here the 34km Lake Ohrid lies outstretched, flanked by the lovely old town of Ohrid.

MAVROVO NATIONAL PARK МАВРОВО НАЦИОНАЛЕН ПАРК
☎ 042

Mavrovo is best known for its ski resort (Macedonia's biggest), though the rarefied air and stunning vistas make it great year-round. It comprises 730 sq km of birch and pine forest, gorges, karst fields and waterfalls, plus Macedonia's highest peak, Mt Korab (2764m). The park, located up a winding road southwest of Gostivar, contains the must-see Sveti Jovan Bigorski monastery and Galičnik, famous for its traditional village wedding.

Sights & Activities

The **Zare Lazarevski ski centre** (☎ 489 002; www.zarelaz.com) is Macedonia's top ski resort. Average snow cover is 70cm and slopes run from 1860m to 2255m. Ski rental is 600MKD, lift tickets 800MKD/3500MKD per day/week). There's also a ski school. The Hotel Bistra (p514) runs the show. Mavrovo's also a good base for summer **hiking**, when hotel prices drop.

Sveti Jovan Bigorski monastery, off the Debar road, was built in 1020 where an icon of Sveti Jovan Bigorski (St John the Forerunner, ie St John the Baptist) miraculously appeared. Since then, the monastery has been rebuilt often – the miraculous icon occasionally reappearing. The impressive church also boasts the alleged forearm of the saint himself.

However, the main draw here is the monastery's awe-inspiring iconostasis. The final of just three such iconostases carved by 19th-century local master craftsmen Makarije Frčkovski and the brothers Filipovski between 1829 and 1835, this colossal work depicting biblical scenes is

MACEDONIA

enlivened with 500 tiny human and 200 animal figures. Gazing up at this enormous, intricate masterpiece will take your breath away. After finishing it, the carvers allegedly flung their tools into the nearby Radika River – ensuring that the secret of their artistic genius would be washed away forever.

Lying 17km southwest of Mavrovo, up a winding, tree-lined road ending in rocky moonscape, almost depopulated **Galičnik** survives, its traditional houses rising from the mountainside. Galičnik's once-wealthy sheep-herding residents were ruined by Tito's nationalisation program, and most emigrated.

Galičnik's national significance survives with the traditional **Galičnik Wedding** (12 to 13 July), for which prospective couples must enter a lottery. Everyone's welcome: attending unites you with 3000 happy Macedonians (and a few bemused foreigners) and involves much eating, drinking, traditional folk dancing and music.

Sleeping & Eating

For Galičnik Wedding visits, book early for Mavrovo hotels. Alternatively, Go Macedonia (see p509) arranges Galičnik Wedding trips including transport, guided activities, local accommodation and monastery tours.

Sveti Jovan Bigorski (☎ 478 675; per person €5) The monastery has dormitories with self-catering facilities.

Hotel Srna (☎ 388 083; s/d/apt €20/40/60; Mavrovo) The smaller Srna, 400m from the chairlifts, has a cosy ambience and breezy, clean rooms. Apartments have balconies.

Hotel Bistra (☎ 489 002; s/d €65/90; Mavrovo) The big Bistra has comfortable, clean rooms and everything required (restaurant, bar, pool, fitness centre, sauna) to cultivate that ski-lodge glow, including jacuzzis in the deluxe rooms. Prices fall in summer. In high season, the Bistra also runs the simpler Hotel Ski Škola and Hotel Mavrovski (singles/doubles €20/40); guests can use the Bistra's facilities.

Getting There & Away

Buses pass through Mavrovo Anovi (2km away) heading south to Debar (120MKD, seven daily), or north to Tetovo (140MKD, five daily) and Skopje (180MKD, three daily).

To reach Sveti Jovan Bigorski Monastery, drive; alternatively, if busing in from Skopje or Tetovo, any bus transiting Debar for Ohrid or Struga will stop by the monastery's entrance point.

OHRID ОХРИД

☎ 046 / pop 55,749

Sublime Ohrid is Macedonia's most popular destination, and deservedly so. It boasts an atmospheric Old Town with beautiful churches stacked up a graceful hill, all topped by a medieval castle overlooking serene, 34km-long Lake Ohrid. Nearby, mountainous Galičica National Park offers pristine nature, while secluded beaches dot the lush eastern shore.

In summer, the town and big beaches are packed, and there's great nightlife and a popular summer festival. For more tranquillity, but still warm weather, try June or September.

WORTH THE TRIP: VEVČANI

Off-beat Vevčani, famed for its costumes-and-grog winter carnival, is a Macedonian village 14km northwest of Struga. Vevčani has a long tradition of independence: locals even declared their own republic following Macedonia's independence from Yugoslavia. Although secession was never actually attempted, villagers did have some fun with it, creating their own flag, passports and currency (the *ličnici*), available as souvenirs.

Vevčani's relaxed atmosphere, clear air and traditional architecture are enhanced by its icon-rich 18th-century **Church of Sveti Nikola** (🕑 8am-5pm), and wooded **mountain springs**, criss-crossed by bridges and steps. The **Vevčani Carnival**, held annually from 12 to 14 January (over Orthodox New Year), attracts over 3000 people, who gape as some fairly lit villagers don elaborate costumes, ride livestock and pontificate from home-grown floats.

There are several neat eating and sleeping spots, including the upper-town **Pansion Kutmičevica** (☎ 046-798 399, 070 249197; kutmicevica@yahoo.com.mk; d €30), a relaxing, family-run B&B with traditional decor, views to Lake Ohrid, and hearty rustic meals. There are just two rooms, so call ahead.

An hourly bus connects Vevčani with Struga (30MKD, 20 minutes), itself easily accessible from Ohrid. A direct taxi from Ohrid to Vevčani costs 600MKD.

MACEDONIA

OHRID

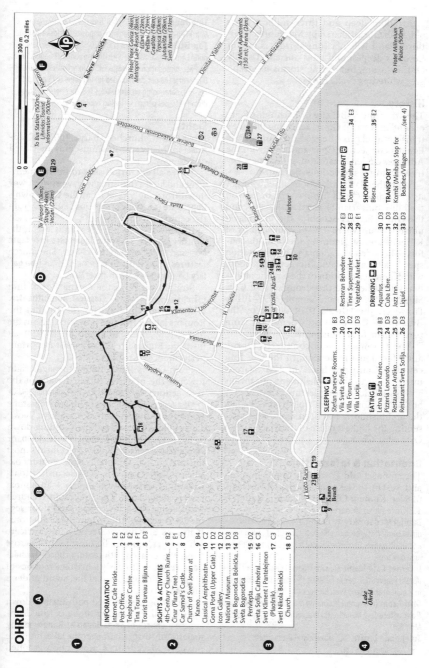

INFORMATION
Internet Cafe Inside............1 E2
Post Office..........................2 E2
Telephone Centre................3 E2
Tina Tours..........................4 F1
Tourist Bureau Biljana.........5 D3

SIGHTS & ACTIVITIES
4th-Century Church Ruins....6 B2
Cinar (Plane Tree)...............7 E1
Car Samoil's Castle.............8 C2
Church of Sveti Jovan at
Kaneo...............................9 B4
Classical Amphitheatre......10 C2
Gorna Porta (Upper Gate)..11 D2
Icon Gallery......................12 D2
National Museum...............13 D3
Sveta Bogorodica Bolnička..14 D3
Sveta Bogorodica
Perivlepta.......................15 D2
Sveta Sofija Cathedral.......16 C3
Sveti Kliment I Pantelejmon
(Plaošnik).......................17 C3
Sveti Nikola Bolnički
Church............................18 D3

SLEEPING
Stefan Kanevče Rooms.......19 B3
Vila Sveta Sofija................20 D3
Villa Forum.......................21 D2
Villa Lucija.......................22 D3

EATING
Letna Bavča Kaneo.............23 B3
Pizzeria Leonardo..............24 D3
Restaurant Antiko..............25 D3
Restaurant Sveta Sofija......26 D3

Restoran Belvedere............27 E3
Tinex Supermarket.............28 E3
Vegetable Market...............29 E1

DRINKING
Aquarius...........................30 D3
Cuba Libre........................31 D3
Jazz Inn............................32 D3
Liquid...............................33 D3

ENTERTAINMENT
Dom na Kultura..................34 E3

SHOPPING
Bisera...............................35 E2

TRANSPORT
Kombi (Minibus) Stop for
Beaches/Villages.........(see 4)

At 300m deep and three million years old, Lake Ohrid, shared by Macedonia (two-thirds) and Albania (one-third), is one of Europe's deepest and most ancient. Usually Ohrid is calm, but during storms its steely-grey whitecaps evoke the sea.

History

The 4th-century-BC city of Lychnidos ('city of light' in Ancient Greek, reflecting the lake's translucent quality) hugged the Roman Via Egnatia connecting Constantinople with the Adriatic. Under Byzantium, it became a key trade, cultural and ecclesiastic centre.

With the Slavic migrations, the town got its new name, Ohrid (from *vo rid*, or 'city on the hill'). Bulgarian Slavs arrived in 867, and the Ohrid literary school – the first Slavic university anywhere – was established by St Kliment and St Naum in the late 9th century. This aided Macedonia's Christianisation specifically, and Slavic literacy in general, with Kliment's creation of the Cyrillic alphabet. Ohrid became the stronghold of Cars Simeon (r 893–927) and Samoil (r 997–1014). However, the latter's 1014 defeat by the Byzantines led to Ohrid's demotion from patriarchate to archbishopric.

The Ottoman Turks conquered Ohrid, and Macedonia in general, in the late 14th century. Centuries later, in 1767, Greek intrigue led to the abolishment of Ohrid's archbishopric – a long-lasting grievance for both Macedonians and Bulgarians. Today, the archbishopric has been restored, representing the highest office of the Macedonian Orthodox Church.

Orientation & Information

The compact Old Town is hemmed in south and west by the lake and the pedestrian mall, ul Sveti Kliment Ohridski. The bus station is 1.5km east of centre.

Danijel Medaroski (☎ 070 836074; dmedaroski@ gmail.com) Witty, erudite philologist, certified tour guide and Ohrid native, Danijel leads city tours (€10) and Ohrid-area day trips.

Internet Café Inside (Amam Trgovski Centar, bul Makedonski Prosvetiteli; per hr 60MKD; ☺ 9am-1am) Located in a mall near Ploštad Sveti Kliment Ohridski.

Ohrid.com (www.ohrid.com.mk) Municipal website.

Post office (bul Makedonski Prosvetiteli; ☺ 7am-8pm Mon-Sat)

Telephone centre (bul Makedonski Prosvetiteli; ☺ 7am-8pm Mon-Sat)

Tina Tours (☎ 254 665; bul Turisticka 66; ☺ 9am-6pm) Full-service travel agency opposite Ohridska Banka.

Tourist Bureau Biljana (☎ 070 684428; www.beyond ohrid.com; Car Samoil 38; ☺ 10am-midnight) General info and accommodation help. Specialises in activities: mountain-bike rental (€8 per day); guided hiking tours (€25 per person); paragliding on Mt Galičica (€80 per person); scuba diving (€60 per person including equipment).

Sights

Most Ohrid churches charge 100MKD admission. Many sites and museums are closed on Monday.

To see all of Ohrid's sites in the most efficient and least exhausting way, work your way down from the top. Start at the Old Town's **Upper Gate** (Gorna Porta) about 80MKD from the centre by taxi.

Just inside it to the left stands the 13th-century church of **Sveta Bogorodica Perivlepta** (admission 100MKD; ☺ 9am-1pm & 4-8pm). The church features vivid biblical frescos and an **icon gallery** (☺ 9am-2pm & 5-8pm, closed Mon).

Straight on from the Gorna Porta, find Ohrid's impressive **Classical Amphitheatre**. It was originally built for theatre, but the Romans later retrofitted it by yanking out the first 10 rows to accommodate the gladiators. It hosts the Summer Festival's most important performances (see opposite).

From Gorna Porta, follow the signs right towards the massive, turreted walls of the 10th-century **Car Samoil's Castle** (admission 30MKD; ☺ 9am-6pm, closed Mon). Ascend the narrow stone stairways to the ramparts for fantastic views. Then follow the wooded path leading down to the church of **Sveti Kliment i Pantelejmon**, or **Plaošnik** (admission free; ☺ 9am-6pm), Ohrid's most unusual church. Originally a 5th-century basilica, it was restored in 2002 according to its Byzantine architectural design – an almost unprecedented feat. This multidomed church with facing clock tower has glass floor segments revealing the original foundations. It houses St Kliment's relics, and intricate 5th-century mosaics lie outside. Just across from the church, **4th-century church foundations**, replete with early Christian mosaics of flora and bird and animal life, stand under a protective roof.

Following the wooded path further down opens to the stunning sight of the 13th-century **Church of Sveti Jovan at Kaneo**, rising majestically from a cliff over the lake. It's quite possibly Macedonia's most photographed structure, and a wonderful place to relax. Peer down into the azure waters and you'll see why medieval monks found spiritual inspiration here. The small church has some original frescos behind the altar.

Continuing on from this church up the straight road running from it parallel with the lake brings you through the lovely houses of old Ohrid and, after five minutes, down a long stone staircase leading to Ohrid's grandest church – the 11th-century **Sveta Sofija Cathedral** (Car Samoil bb; ☼ 10am-8pm) lined with columns and decorated with elaborate Byzantine frescos. The church's superb acoustics mean that it's also used for concerts.

Continuing from the cathedral along ul Car Samoil brings you past the 1827 **National Museum** (Car Samoil 62; admission 50MKD; ☼ 9am-4pm & 7-11pm Tue-Sun), marked by distinctive Ohrid white-and-brown architecture. The **Robev Residence** houses an archaeological display including ancient epigraphy, and the **Urania Residence** opposite has an ethnographic display.

Finally, you'll pass two other frescoed 14th-century churches in the old quarter, **Sveta Bogorodica Bolnička** and **Sveti Nikola Bolnički**. *Bolnica* means hospital in Macedonian; during plagues, visitors faced 40-day quarantines here.

Exiting the Old Town on ul Car Samoil, turn left onto the pedestrian mall, ul Sveti Kliment Ohridski, lined with cafes and shops. Follow it to the end, where stands an enormous, 900-year-old plane tree, the **Činar**.

Festivals & Events

July's five-day **Balkan Festival of Folk Dances & Songs** draws regional folkloric groups. The mid-July to mid-August **Ohrid Summer Festival** (☎ 262 304; www.ohridsummer.com.mk) features classical and opera concerts, theatre and dance. Ohrid's **swimming marathon** is a 30km race from Sveti Naum to Ohrid, usually in June.

Each August, a three-week **Macedonian language course** (€850) attracts international students. It includes language lessons, cultural excursions and accommodation and is, by all accounts, great fun. See the SS Cyril & Methodius University website (www.ukim.ed u.mk/smjlk).

Sleeping

Private rooms or apartments (per person €5-10) are available anywhere you see the sign *sobi* (rooms) –

search, or ask at Tourist Bureau Biljana (opposite), which finds private accommodation.

Stefan Kanevče Rooms (☎ 234 813; apostolanet@yahoo.co.uk; Kočo Racin 47; per person €10) Near Kaneo beach, this atmospheric 19th-century house boasts carved wooden ceilings and good hospitality.

Mimi Apartments (☎ 250 103; mimioh@mail.com.mk; Strašo Pinđur 2; r incl breakfast 800MKD) These centrally located private rooms are spacious and equipped with fridge and satellite TV.

Villa Lucija (☎ 265 608; lucija@mtnet.mk; Kosta Abraš 29; s/d/apt €15/25/40) The Old Town Lucija has fantastic ambience and lovingly decorated, breezy rooms with balconies right over the lake.

Vila Sveta Sofija (☎ 254 370; www.vilasofiya.com.mk; Kosta Abraš 64; s/d €35/60, ste €80-120) This opulent getaway combines traditional furnishings with chic modern bathrooms. It's in an old Ohrid mansion near Sveta Sofija church. Book ahead.

Villa Forum (☎ 267 060; www.villaforumohrid.com.mk; Kuzman Kapidan 1; s/d/apt €45/60/80) New and luxurious, this Upper Gate hotel has well-furnished, comfortable rooms with sparkling bathrooms. Book ahead.

Hotel Millenium Palace (☎ 263 361; www.milleniumpalace.com.mk; Kej Maršal Tito bb; s/d/ste/apt €49/70/99/149) This southern waterfront hotel has business-class rooms, gym, sauna and an indoor swimming pool with a cocktail bar. Suites have lake-view terraces.

Eating

The Old Town has Ohrid's best restaurants.

our pick **Letna Bavča Kaneo** (Kočo Racin 43; fish 100-300MKD; ☼ 8am-midnight) The 'summer terrace' on Kaneo beach is inexpensive and great. A fish fry-up of diminutive plasnica, plus salad, feeds two people. Swim from the restaurant's dock.

Pizzeria Leonardo (Car Samoil 31; pizzas 200-350MKD; ☼ 9am-midnight) This Old Town joint has Ohrid's best pizza.

Restoran Belvedere (Kej Maršal Tito 2; mains 300MKD; ☼ 8am-2am) Excellent *skara* is the speciality here, where outdoor tables extend under a leafy canopy.

Restoran Sveta Sofija (Car Samoil 88; mains 300-500MKD; ☼ 9am-midnight) This upscale restaurant opposite Sveta Sofija has great traditional dishes and over 100 Macedonian wines.

Restaurant Antiko (Car Samoil 30; mains 350-600MKD; ☼ 9am-midnight) Set in an old Ohrid mansion,

MACEDONIA

the famous Antiko has great traditional ambience and (pricey) food.

Self-caterers have **Tinex supermarket** (bul Makedonski Prosvetiteli) and the **vegetable market** (Kliment Ohridski).

Drinking

our pick **Jazz Inn** (☎ 070 304737; Kosta Abraš 74; ⏲ 10.30pm-4am) This low-lit, jazzy hipster hangout gets roaring after midnight.

Liquid (Kosta Abraš 17; ⏲ 9am-1am) This hip, chill-out place has a lakefront patio.

Aquarius (Kosta Abraš bb; ⏲ 10am-1am) Near Liquid, always-popular Aquarius was Ohrid's original lake-terrace cafe and it remains cool.

Cuba Libre (Kosta Abraš; ⏲ 10pm-4am) This festive bar-cum-club is perennially popular.

Entertainment

Arena (cnr Jane Sandanski & Karpoš Vojvoda; ⏲ 10pm-4am) Sweaty, packed pop-rock nightclub Arena is 1.5km out of town.

Dom na Kultura (Grigor Prličev; admission 50-100MKD) The house of culture holds cultural events and is home to Ohrid's movie theatre.

Shopping

Bisera (Kliment Ohridski 60; ⏲ 9am-1pm & 6-10pm; pearls from €25) From his little shop, friendly Vane Talev continues a family tradition started in 1924: making the unique Ohrid pearls with local formulas. Prices range from €25 for a simple piece to €600 for an elaborate necklace.

Getting There & Away

AIR

Four airlines serve Ohrid's **St Paul the Apostle Airport** (☎ 252 820; www.airports.com.mk), 10km north. JAT flies to Belgrade via Skopje on Monday and Friday. Charter flights operate in summer. Take a taxi (300MKD).

BUS

From the **bus station** (☎ 260 339; 7 Noemvri bb), 1.5km east of the centre, buses serve Skopje, either via Kičevo (450MKD, three hours, seven daily) or (the longer route) via Bitola; for Bitola itself, 10 daily buses run (300MKD, 1¼ hours). Buses to Struga (50MKD, 14km) leave every 30 minutes. Book ahead for Skopje buses in summer. Some *kombi* and taxis wait outside Tina Tours for intercity destinations.

International buses serve Belgrade (Serbia), at 1pm (via Bitola, 2050MKD, 12 hours) and 5.30pm (via Kičevo, 1820MKD, 10 hours).

BUSES & TAXIS FROM OHRID		
Destination	**Bus fare (MKD)**	**Taxi fare (MKD)**
Elšani	40	300
Gradište	60	400
Lagadin	30	200
Ljubaništa	90	600
Sveti Naum	110	900
Trpejca	70	500

A daily bus at 7pm serves Sofia (Bulgaria; 1450MKD, eight hours). For Albania, take a bus to Sveti Naum (110MKD, 29km). Cross the border and take a cab (€5) 6km to Pogradeci. Ohrid to Sveti Naum by taxi costs 900MKD.

AROUND OHRID

☎ 046

South of Ohrid town, a long and wooded coast conceals several lovely (if mostly pebbly) beaches, historic churches and villages, plus camping spots and Galičica National Park. In summer, the big resort-style hotels and their beaches are packed, but beyond them things become more pacific.

In summer, frequent buses and *kombi* serve everything up to Gradište; further destinations like Trpejca, Ljubaništa and Sveti Naum are served less frequently.

Sights & Activities

People-watch and sunbathe with cocktail at **Cuba Libre Beach** or **Corali** (one of the 10 **Lagadin** beaches), 2km from Ohrid. Water clarity improves at **Peštani** (12km from Ohrid), the last coastal village, with an ATM, health centre, police station and night bars, but no sights.

Around 2km further, **Gradište** is an expansive, wooded camping ground with popular beaches for young hedonists. Days spent sunbathing are followed by beachside DJ parties at night. There's also a new **Neolithic Settlement Museum** with artefacts from a 4000-year-old settlement.

TRPEJCA ТРПЕЈЦА

Further along the coastal road lies **Trpejca**, cupped between a sloping hill and tranquil bay. The last traditional Ohrid fishing village, it features clustered houses with terracotta roofs and a white-pebble beach with very clear water. At night, the sounds of crickets and frogs fill the air.

Trpejca has limited services and public transport. Nevertheless, the superb waters offer excellent swimming, and the forested Mt Galičica's just opposite. The **Church of Sveti Nikola** here has great views.

Another church, **Sveta Bogorodica Zahumska** (usually called simply Sveti Zaum) requires water access (arrange boats locally or via an Ohrid travel guide). It's 2.5km south of Trpejca on a wooded beach. The church's unusual frescos date from 1361.

SVETI NAUM СВЕТИ НАУМ

Splendid **Sveti Naum monastery**, 29km south of Ohrid, lies before the Albanian border above a sandy beach. Built by Naum, a contemporary of Sveti Kliment's, the monastery became an educational centre. Naum built the Church of the Holy Archangels (AD 900), replaced by the 16th-century **Church of Sveti Naum**; this multidomed, Byzantine-style structure set on a cliff and surrounded by roses and peacocks boasts fine 16th- and 19th-century **frescos**.

Inside, drop an ear to the **tomb of Sveti Naum** to hear his muffled heartbeat. Outside, there's a deep **wishing well** for spare denars.

GALIČICA NATIONAL PARK

The rippling, rock-crested Mt Galičica separates Lake Ohrid from Lake Prespa. A national park since 1958, Galičica's peaks top 2000m. It comprises 228 sq km of territory, and features endemic plants and trees; it's great for outdoor activities, like hiking and paragliding.

Galičica's best village, idyllic **Elšani**, is 10km from Ohrid. Elšani makes a great hiking base. The lake views alone make it worthwhile, as from the 19th-century **Church of Sveti Ilias**, set on a high bluff atop the village.

Sleeping & Eating

Most coastal accommodation and restaurants close after summer – in low season, call ahead. In summer, **private accommodation** (per person 300-600MKD) is plentiful, and you can usually just turn up. Since quality varies, shop around.

Camping Ljubaništa (☎ 283 240; per tent 800MKD; ♥ May-Oct) Families and solitude-seekers might like this place, 27km from Ohrid on a sandy beach, though facilities here are quite dated.

Gradište Camping (☎ 285 920; Gradište; per tent 1000MKD; ♥ May-Oct) Party-minded campers head to the waterfront Gradište Camping, 14km from Ohrid. Both camping grounds have shops and eateries.

ourpick **Risto's Guest House** (☎ 285 464, 075 977930; elshani@mt.net.mk; Elšani; s/d/tr incl breakfast €15/24/32) Friendly young couple Risto and Anita Stojoski run this relaxing place on Mt Galičica. Ring for free pick-up from Ohrid. Rooms are spacious and clean. Most have shared bathrooms; all have lake-view balconies. The excellent home-cooked meals cost €12 per person.

Vila DeNiro (☎ 070 212518; Trpejca; d/apt €25/50) Trpejca's only modern place is this yellow mansion, located exactly where the main walkway downhill branches off. The DeNiro has three doubles, plus an apartment with gleaming kitchenette.

Hotel Sveti Naum (☎ 283 080; Sveti Naum; s/d/ste from €37/74/116) This fancy hotel with restaurant in the Sveti Naum monastery works year-round. The rooms are luxurious; note lake-view rooms cost €20 extra.

Restoran Ribar (Trpejca; fish per person 300-600MKD; ♥ 9am-midnight) Right on Trpejca's waterfront, Ribar is one of the coast's best fish restaurants.

Getting There & Away

Frequent buses and *kombi* ply the Ohrid–Sveti Naum route in summer, as far as Gradište. Services are less frequent to Trpejca, Ljubaništa and Sveti Naum further on. In Ohrid, wait for *kombi* by Tina Tours (p516), opposite Ohridska Banka. These operate in summer until 2am.

Taxis are expensive. During summer they may charge bus-ticket rates when filling up fast (check with the driver).

For bus and regular taxi fares from Ohrid, see the boxed text, opposite. Boat travel from Ohrid includes the daily 30km tour to Sveti Naum on a big cruising vessel (350MKD return). Rates for boat trips from villages vary.

CENTRAL MACEDONIA

Macedonia's diverse central region is one of its wildest, most unexplored areas, full of mountains, canyons, vineyards and caves. Yet it also boasts plenty of culture, and some of Macedonia's most important historical sites.

BITOLA БИТОЛА

☎ 047 / pop 95,385

With some of Macedonia's most elegant buildings and most beautiful people, elevated Bitola (660m) has a taste for sophistication inherited from its days as the Ottoman 'City of

MACEDONIA

Consuls'. Its colourful 18th- and 19th-century townhouses, Ottoman mosques, and cafe culture make it the most intriguing and liveable of Macedonia's big towns.

Orientation & Information

The adjoining train and bus stations stand beside the park; from here, it's a 15-minute walk downtown. Cafes and neoclassical architecture line the major pedestrian street, ul Maršal Tito, known as Širok Sokak (Wide Street in Turkish).

Širok Sokak is a wi-fi hotspot, and internet cafes are nearby.

Baloyannis Tours (☎ 220 204, 075 207273; Solunska 118; 🕙 8am-6pm Mon-Sat) Provides city tours and adventure trips in wild nature.

Biosfera (☎ 234 973; biosfera.org.mk; Dimo Hadzi Dimov 3) An ecotourism NGO that arranges local hiking and birdwatching trips.

Tourist information centre (☎ 241 641; bitola-tourist-info@t-home.mk; Sterio Georgiev 1; 🕙 9am-6pm Mon-Sat) Friendly, informative info centre.

Sights & Activities

Bitola's 16th-century **Yeni mosque**, **Isak mosque** and **Yahdar-Kadi mosque**, all between the Dragor River and the Stara Čaršija (Old Bazaar), testify to its Ottoman past, as does the enormous **Clock Tower** (Saat Kula) nearby.

Bitola is distinguished too by great neoclassical architecture. The tourist information centre arranges three-hour **architecture sightseeing tours** (per group €30).

During Ottoman times, the **Stara Čaršija** boasted around 3000 clustered artisans' shops; though much smaller today, about 70 different trades are still conducted, and cheaply (250MKD for shoe repairs).

The **Church of Sveti Dimitrij** (11 Oktomvri bb; 🕙 7am-6pm), near the Clock Tower, dates from 1830 and has rich frescos, ornate lamps and huge iconostasis. Bitola's **Catholic church** is staid but is strikingly conspicuous amid the multicoloured facades of the Širok Sokak. Enjoying the **cafe life** on this street, while the beautiful people promenade past, is an essential Bitola experience.

Festivals & Events

The **Bit Fest** (June to August) features concerts, literary readings and art exhibits. The **Ilinden Festival** (2 August), honouring the Ilinden Uprising of 1903, is celebrated with food and music.

The **Manaki Brothers Film Festival** (www.manaki.com.mk), from late September to early October, screens independent foreign films. It honours Milton and Ianachia Manaki, the Balkans' first film-makers (1905). It's followed by the **Inter Fest**, with classical-music performances in the Centar na Kultura and Bitola Museum.

Sleeping & Eating

Chola Guest House (☎ 224 919; guesthouse_chola@hotmail.com; Stiv Naumov 80; s/d €12/20) Bitola's best budget option is this quiet place in an old mansion. The pretty rooms are clean and well kept, with colourful modern bathrooms. Ask the taxi driver for Video Club Dju (directly opposite the Chola).

Hotel Šumski Feneri (☎ 293 030; sfeneri@mt.net.mk; Trnovo; s/d/apt €30/45/60) In Mt Pelister's Trnovo village, 4km from Bitola, the hotel has snug rooms and four good-sized apartments. The restaurant has a nice outdoor terrace. A taxi from Bitola costs 250MKD.

Hotel De Niro (☎ 229 656; www.hotel-deniro.com; Kiril i Metodij 5; s/d/ste €35/50/80) The central yet discreet De Niro has two locations: one has snazzy, old Bitola–style rooms and an Italian restaurant, while the other has slick minimalist fixtures and a happening pub below.

Hotel Milenium (☎ 241 001; Marsal Tito 48; h.milenium@t-home.mk; s/d/ste/apt €39/66/80/99) Atriums with splashes of stained glass, smooth marble opulence and historical relics channel old Bitola. The spacious rooms have all mod cons and sparkling bathrooms. Great value for quality, and right on the Širok Sokak too.

Hotel Epinal (☎ 224 777; www.hotelepinal.com; Maršal Tito bb; s/d €49/69) The ageing Epinal rises unpromisingly over central Bitola but is actually quite nice – especially considering the swimming pool, jacuzzi and gym.

El Greko (cnr Maršal Tito & Elipda Karamandi; mains 180-320MKD; 🕙 10am-1am) This Sokak taverna and pizzeria has great beer-hall ambience.

Drinking

Simbol Café (Maršal Tito 65; 🕙 8am-midnight) Situated on the Sokak, this place has an old-Bitola feel.

Art Gallery-Café Van (Dalmatinska 29; 🕙 10am-11pm) Over in the Čaršija, this cafe has eclectic decor such as Orthodox icons, oil paintings and photos of old Bitola to complement the coffee.

Basa (🕙 10pm-2am) Get your groove on at this dark-lit bar on a side street off ul Leninova, behind Centar na Kultura. Plays house music, local and Western pop.

Porta Jazz (Maršal Tito; ☒ 8am-midnight) is popular, and the Hotel De Niro's subterranean bar, **Pivnica** (Hotel De Niro, Kiril i Metodij 5; ☎ noon-1am), is a fun nightspot.

Entertainment
Nightclub Rasčekor (☒ 10pm-4am) The best Bitola nightclub is the smooth, sleek and trendy Rasčekor, near the train station.

Getting There & Away
The **bus station** (☎ 231 420; Nikola Tesla) and the **train station** (☎ 237 110; Nikola Tesla) are adjacent, about 1km south of the centre. Buses serve Skopje (480MKD, four hours, 10 daily) via Prilep (120MKD, one hour); Kavadarci (280MKD, two hours, four daily); Strumica (480MKD, four hours, one daily); and Ohrid (300MKD, 1¼ hours,10 daily).

For Greece, take a taxi to the border (450MKD) and find a Greek cab to Florina, or find a Bitola cab driver who will take you all the way to Florina (3000MKD).

Three daily trains (3.49am, 1.39pm and 5.50pm) serve Skopje (210MKD) via Prilep (66MKD) and Veles (154MKD).

AROUND BITOLA
Heraclea Lyncestis (admission 100MKD, photos 500MKD; ☒ 9am-3pm winter, to 5pm summer), 1km south of Bitola (70MKD by taxi), is one of Macedonia's best archaeological sites. Founded by Philip II of Macedon, Heraclea became an important commercial city. The Romans conquered it in 168 BC, but Heraclea's position on the Via Egnatia kept it prosperous. In the 4th century it became an episcopal seat, but Goths and then Slavs sacked it during the next two centuries.

The Roman baths, portico and amphitheatre are remarkable, but the most striking are ruins of an early Christian basilica and episcopal palace, with beautiful, well-preserved floor mosaics. They're unique in depicting trees and animals endemic to the area.

The 830m-high mountainside hamlet of **Dihovo** is only 5km from Bitola, and a good base for Pelister hikes. See Dihovo's stone houses, its icon-rich **Church of Sveti Dimitrije** (1830), and jump into its outdoor **swimming pool** – basically, a very large conduit for ice-cold mountain-spring waters. For guided **hiking trips**, find Petar Cvetkovski of Villa Dihovo (p522). Alternatively, Petar can explain local trails you can tackle independently.

From Bitola, a taxi costs 150MKD.

PELISTER NATIONAL PARK
Macedonia's oldest national park (1948) covers 125 sq km of forest on its third-highest mountain range, the quartz-filled Baba massif. Eight peaks top 2000m, crowned by Mt Pelister (2601m). Two glacial lakes, known as Pelisterski Oči (Pelister's Eyes), provide chilly refreshment.

Pelister's 88 tree species include the rare five-leafed Molika pine. The mountain also hosts endemic Pelagonia trout, deer, wolves, chamois, wild boars and eagles. Bears frequently travel, apparently without visas, across the mountain to Greece.

Down in the foothills, the old Vlach village of **Malovište** has great rustic ambience and well-preserved traditional architecture. However, it has neither restaurants nor guest houses. The cobblestone laneways require good shoes. The **Church of Sveta Petka** (1856) is

---

WORTH THE TRIP: MARIOVO
If there's one place-name in Macedonia that still connotes mystery, it's Mariovo. The southern-border badlands region hums with the disconcerting energy of another time, still resonating in its rugged mountains, deep river-canyons and strange plateaus dotted with deserted villages. The entire region is characterised by its breathtaking and pristine nature. Mariovo boasts the fearsome Kajmakčalan peak (2520m), on the Greek border; its major river, the Crna, meanders across it into Lake Tikveš.

Now sparsely inhabited, the 25 Mariovo villages were once wealthy sheep-herding centres. If coming by road (paved/good dirt) from Bitola, enjoy pretty **Rapeš**, **Staravina** and five-centuries-old **Gradesnica**, the largest today, with 80 inhabitants.

Various hiking trips, jeep safaris, village tours and mountain-climbing trips to Kajmakčalan's peak are organised by Bitola's **Baloyannis Tours** (☎ 047-220 204, 047-075 207273; Solunska 118, Bitola; ☒ 8am-6pm Mon-Sat) or environmental NGO **Biosfera** (☎ 047-234 973; biosfera.org.mk; Dimo Hadzi Dimov 3, Bitola).

MACEDONIA

WORTH THE TRIP: TRESKAVEC MONASTERY

The 13th-century Treskavec Monastery, located 10km above Prilep on remote Mt Zlato (1422m), is one of Macedonia's spiritual and artistic treasures. Its vivid frescos, including a rare depiction of Christ as a boy, line the 14th-century **Church of Sveta Bogorodica**, itself built over a 6th-century basilica. Earlier Roman remains are visible, along with graves, inscriptions and monks' skulls.

Although the monastery has suffered from neglect, the Macedonian government is investing some €320,000 to repair damaged structures.

Treskavec offers basic **accommodation** (☎ 070 918339; per person 200MKD) and food.

To get there, a paved road is planned; till then, drive from Prilep to the end of the paved road, unless you have a 4WD for the final few rocky kilometres. If going by jeep, start from Prilep's cemetery and look for the sign marked 'Manastir Sveta Bogorodica, Treskavec'. Head straight up.

Alternatively, to hike there, drive or take a taxi to Dabnica village and follow the cobbled track up towards Mt Zlato; after the fountain, continue on a straight path, and you'll arrive (two hours total).

---

brimming with frescos and icons; a 30-minute hike leads to the **Church of Sveta Ana**, in a secluded beech forest.

The extraordinary **Villa Dihovo** (☎ 070 544744; persafizicko@yahoo.com; Dihovo; pay as you like) offers three perfectly decorated traditional rooms in the 80-year-old home of Petar Cvetkovski and family. It's inside the first long driveway after the village centre's restaurant, and has a big flowering lawn that's great for kids. The only fixed prices are for the homemade wine and *rakija*; all else, room price included, is your choice.

Villa Patricia (☎ 239 977; Dihovo; s/d 900/1440MKD), a friendly family guest house with spacious and well-maintained rooms, is a 10-minute walk from Dihovo centre towards the pool.

Hotel Molika (☎ 229 406; Pelister National Park; s/d €28/46), up at 1420m, is 12km from Bitola. The setting is great, the facilities worn. Still, despite the cramped rooms and uninventive cuisine, watching the stars glimmer on a snowy winter's night here is perfect. A taxi from Bitola costs 400MKD.

The nourishing **Restoran Idela** (☎ 293 033; Dihovo; mains 250-400MKD; ☺ 6am-midnight) has a hunting-lodge feel and does great local food.

To reach Malovište from Bitola, drive 4km west towards Resen, and turn off at Kazani. Take the first left, and then another left through a tunnel and proceed straight.

TIKVEŠ WINE REGION

Macedonia's winery heartland, Tikveš features rolling vineyards, serpentine lakes, deep caves and mountains, as well as world-class archaeological sites and churches. It's especially beautiful at dusk in summer, when the fading sunlight suffuses soft hills laden with millions and millions of grapes.

The region has continuously produced wine since the 4th century BC. Vintners both local and foreign venerate its unique soil, with apocryphal tales of Frenchmen sighing in despair over not having such fertile earth back home. In any case, the climatic conditions mean that very little rain is necessary. Tikveš local grapes generally retain an ideal sugar concentration (17% to 26%).

Skopje travel agencies arrange tastings; alternatively, contact the wineries (in advance).

Kavadarci КАВАДАРЦИ
☎ 043 / pop 38, 741

While nearby Negotino is conveniently located on the railway and highway, Kavadarci just west is arguably a better base. Fittingly dusty and agricultural, the Tikveš region's hub is starting to improve its services and attractions – chiefly, wine tastings. Yet it's also near some intriguing monasteries and meandering Lake Tikveš, good for boating and birdwatching.

SIGHTS & ACTIVITIES

The **Kavadarci Museum** (☎ 413 470; 7 Septembri 58; admission free; ☺ 8.30am-4.30pm, closed Sun) contains ancient finds, some depicting divine wine bacchanalia.

Massive **Tikveš Winery** (☎ 414 304; www.tikves .com.mk; 29 Noemvri 5), southeastern Europe's biggest, was created in 1885 and produces 29 quality wines. Winery tours involve seeing the facilities, followed by a tasting.

Central **Vinoteka David** (cnr Cano Pop Ristov & Ilindenska; ⏲ 8am-1pm & 5-7pm) has regional wines.

Visit during the **Kavadarci Wine Carnival** (5 to 7 September) to enjoy a costumed parade, public wine tasting and merrymaking.

SLEEPING & EATING

our pick **Hotel Uni Palas** (☎ 419 600; Edvard Kardelj bb; s/d incl breakfast €36/56) This comfortable modern hotel has well-appointed rooms with hydro-massage showers, and a popular cafe-bar.

Restoran Exclusive (☎ 411 561; bul Makedonija 66; ⏲ 8am-midnight) About 100m from the hotel, Kavadarci's best wine restaurant serves Macedonian and international dishes.

GETTING THERE & AWAY

From Kavadarci buses serve Skopje (eight daily, 240MKD), Prilep (190MKD, one hour, two daily) and Bitola (300MKD, four daily). For Negotino, use local buses (30MKD, 15 minutes, six daily), or take a taxi (200MKD).

Around Kavadarci

Lying 3km southwest of Kavadarci, past **Vataša**, the **Monastery of Sveti Nikola** sits amid forests alongside a river. Its tiny church boasts rare 16th-century frescos. In Vataša itself, stop for homemade wine at **Badev Winery** (☎ 071 250693; Blažo Itsev 10, Vataša). Call ahead for planned organised tours and accommodation.

Created in 1968 by damming the Crna River, nearby **Lake Tikveš** is surrounded by scrubland and stark cliffs, dotted with medieval hermitage frescos, and circled by eagles and hawks. Being artificial, it has no endemic species, though it seems the monster catfish – weighing in at up to 200kg – have gotten pretty territorial since Comrade Tito first dispatched them into the 100m depths.

The 32km-long lake lies 11km southwest of Kavadarci; turn south at **Vozarci** to reach the small beach.

Check in Kavadarci at the Hotel Uni Palas or call **Saško Atanasov** (☎ 071 250810; atanasov.sasko@yahoo.com) to arrange half-day **boat trips** with skippers and an English-speaking guide. Large groups use the 40-seater boat (4000MKD per group), while small groups use a regular fisherman's caique (1800MKD).

The tour navigates the lake's widest stretches for 20km, visiting the 14th-century **Pološki Monastery** (also called Polog Monastery). The monastery's **Church of Sveti Gjiorgji** is a single-nave construction built by Serbian emperor Stefan Dušan (r 1331–55), featuring expressive **frescos** of saints as well as of the Emperor Dušan and his wife, Empress Jelena.

Ringed by rugged cliffs, the lake is good for **bird-watching** (look for the royal eagle, bearded vulture and white Egyptian vulture). Sometimes **fishing** is possible, though reeling in the obese catfish from the muddy depths might require a hydraulic lift. You can try **swimming**, from boat or shore, though be mindful of the strong currents.

Vataša's Monastery of Sveti Nikola has basic rooms (100MKD per person) set amid forest. Staying at Lake Tikveš's Pološki Monastery requires advance preparations – consult ahead with your trip organiser.

Other Wineries

Grkov Winery (☎/fax 400 565; pericajovevski@urbaninvest.com.mk; Krnjavo) enjoys a spectacular vineyard setting in **Krnjavo** (26km south of Kavadarci). Organised tours and tastings are held – call ahead to see if accommodation is available. It's challenging to reach; after **Garnikovo** village, turn at the large yellow road sign with many printed destinations onto the small left-hand road. Continue straight, and turn on a dirt road leading uphill to the winery. If you reach the settlement below, you've missed this road.

Bovin Winery (☎ 365 322; Industriska bb; www.bovin.com.mk) in Negotino has won numerous awards. Tours include extensive tastings.

Winery Dudin (☎ 368 506; www.dudinwinery.com.mk; Aco Adzi Ilov 5, Krivolak), 7km east of Negotino in Krivolak, offers tastings. To get here, you'll cross the main E75 highway; turning south here leads to Demir Kapija, located near the magnificent **Demir Kapija Gorge**.

At Demir Kapija, visit **Elenov Winery** (☎ 02-367 232; vinarija_elenov@t-home.mk; Ivo Lola Ribar bb, Demir Kapija), on the right-hand side before entering the village. Dating from 1928, it was Serbian king Aleksandar's official wine cellar. Elenov also organises tastings.

Also in Demir Kapija is **Popova Kula Winery** (☎ 02-3228 781; Demir Kapija; d/ste €60/120), with great views over vineyards and the gorge from a traditionally decorated tasting room. Call ahead to reserve the brand-new traditionally accentuated rooms. Entering town, turn right past the cemetery up an 800m dirt road to get there.

Around 5km south of Negotino, **Disan Hills Winery** (☎ 362 520, 070 384325; ristov@mt.net.mk;

Dolni Disan) is set amid vineyards and is run by people who put heart and soul into crafting limited quantities of high-quality wine. There are fantastic views to lively little **Dolni Disan**, sustained by its large-scale grape collective, and run by wine-dark elders. Call to see if Disan Hills' planned traditional-style rooms are ready; alternatively, the winery can find private rooms in Dolni Disan.

Stobi СТОБИ

The ruins of Roman Stobi occupy a valley beside the E75 highway, 9km northwest of Negotino. The **site** (admission 100MKD; ⏰ 9am-5pm), discovered in 1861, is organised, with running descriptions of the major ruins. There's a snack bar and gift shop selling replicas and wines.

Stobi dates from the 7th century BC, and grew under the Macedonians and Romans. An ancient Jewish population is attested by synagogue foundations beneath remnants of a Christian basilica. Although Stobi became a Byzantine archbishopric, the Goths sacked it in 479, an earthquake in 518 further dooming the city.

Start at the **Roman amphitheatre** (on the left) and clamber up past it; from here, you'll see Stobi's best **mosaics**. The path continues past several well-marked ruins, including **ancient sanctuaries** to gods. At the end, turn right to the enormous **city walls**. Excavations continue.

MACEDONIA DIRECTORY

ACCOMMODATION

Skopje's hotels are expensive; agencies find private rooms. Ohrid and villages have budget and midrange choices; book ahead for July–August, Orthodox Christmas (7 January), and Orthodox Easter, and during major festivals or carnivals elsewhere.

ACTIVITIES

Zare Lazarevski ski centre in Mavrovo National Park is Macedonia's premier resort. Popova Šapka ski centre, near Tetovo, will hopefully resume operations – check locally.

Hiking is spectacular in Mavrovo, Galičica and Pelister National Parks, and in Bitola-area Mariovo. Lake Matka near Skopje has wooded walks, boating and caving. **Zoran 'Max' Stamboliski** (☎ 075 292928; zoke_medmax@ yahoo.com) is a very experienced guide who leads tours and trips including hiking, caving, canyoning, paragliding and horseback riding in some of Macedonia's most beautiful spots.

Lake Ohrid is perfect for swimming and boating. Birdwatch on Lake Prespa and Lake Tikveš. Paragliding's great on Mt Galičica near Ohrid and in Kruševo.

Travel agencies in Skopje, Ohrid and Bitola run outdoors tours. The website of the mountaineering association, **Korab Mountain Club** (www.korab.org.mk/indexen.html) details 14 mountain routes.

BOOKS

Who Are the Macedonians? by Hugh Poulton offers good background.

BUSINESS HOURS

Businesses operate 8am to 8pm weekdays and 8am to 2pm Saturday. Post offices operate 6.30am to 4pm, banks 7am to 5pm Monday to Friday.

DANGERS & ANNOYANCES

Macedonia's Albanian villages near Kosovo and Albania don't see tourists, and outsiders may be suspiciously scrutinised (sheepdogs are usually more dangerous, however, and the locals friendly enough). Avoid Skopje's avaricious bus/train station taxis. Some visitors are alarmed by Roma children's begging and occasional pickpocketing attempts. Littering still vexes, but for many it's the new 'Europeanising' law forbidding sale of alcohol in shops and kiosks after 7pm that represents Macedonia's greatest annoyance.

EMBASSIES & CONSULATES

All missions below are in Skopje.
Albania (off Map p508; ☎ 02-2614 636; ambshqip@ mt.net.mk; HT Karpoš 94a)
Australia (off Map p508; ☎ 02-3061 114; austcon@ mt.net.mk; Londonska 11b)
Bulgaria (Map p508; ☎ 02-3229 444; bgemb@unet .com.mk; Ivo Ribar Lola 40)
Canada (Map p508; ☎ 02-3225 630; honcon@unet.com .mk; bul Partizanski Odredi 17a)
France (off Map p508; ☎ 02-3118 749; www.amba france-mk.org; Salvador Aljende 73)
Germany (off Map p508; ☎ 02-3093 900; dt.boskop@ mol.com.mk; Lerinska 59)
Greece (Map p508; ☎ 02-3219 260; grfyrom@unet.com .mk; Borka Taleski 6)

Montenegro (off Map p508; ☎ 02-3227 277; mail@
montenegroembassy.org.mk; Vasil Stefanovski 7)
Netherlands (Map p508; ☎ 02-3129 319; www.nl
embassy.org.mk; Leninova 69-71)
Russia (Map p508; ☎ 02-3117 160; embassy@russia.org
.mk; Pirinska 44)
Serbia (off Map p508; ☎ 02-3129 298; yuamb@unet
.com.mk; Pitu Guli 8)
UK (Map p508; ☎ 02-3299 299; beskopje@mt.net.mkl;
Dimitrie Čupovski 26)
USA (off Map p508; ☎ 02-3116 180; www.skopje.us
embassy.gov; Samoilova bb)

HOLIDAYS
New Year 1 and 2 January
Orthodox Christmas 7 January
International Women's Day 8 March
Orthodox Easter Week March/April
Labour Day 1 May
SS Cyril and Methodius Day 24 May
Ilinden Day 2 August
Republic Day 8 September
1941 Partisan Day 11 October

INTERNET RESOURCES
Balkanalysis (www.balkanalysis.com) Politics and cur-
rent events, with archives covering Macedonia and other
Balkan countries.
Culture in Macedonia (www.culture.in.mk) Cultural
info and festival listings.
Exploring Macedonia (www.exploringmacedonia.com)
Useful travel website.
Macedonia Loves You (www.macedonialovesyou.eu)
Informative, photo-rich site.
Macedonian Wine Route (www.macedonianwine
route.com) Macedonian wineries information.
Skopje Online (www.skopjeonline.com.mk) Updated city
info, plus nightclub listings.
Tikves Wine Region (www.tikveswineregion.com) More
information on Macedonia's wine country.

MONEY
There are Macedonian denar (MKD) 10, 50,
100, 500, 1000 and 5000 notes, and one-, two-
and five-denar coins. Denars are nonconvert-
ible abroad. Euros are usually accepted. Some

EMERGENCY NUMBERS

- Ambulance ☎ 194
- Fire ☎ 193
- Police ☎ 192
- Roadside assistance ☎ 196

---

hotels quote rates in euros, but payment in
denars is always accepted.
 Macedonian exchange offices (*menuvačnici*)
work commission-free. ATMs are widespread, except in villages. Avoid travellers
cheques. Credit cards aren't always accepted –
carry cash.

POST
Mail to Europe and North America takes
seven to 10 days. Certified mail (*preporačeno*)
is more expensive. The small green form you
fill out should be kept as proof. Letters to
the USA cost 38MKD, to Australia 40MKD
and to Europe 35MKD. Skopje has global
shipping companies.

TELEPHONE & FAX
The country code for Macedonia is ☎ 389.
Internet cafes offer cheap international
phone service. Public-telephone cards sold
in kiosks or post offices in units of 100
(200MKD), 200 (300MKD), 500 (650MKD)
or 1000 (1250MKD) offer good value for
domestic calls. Drop the initial zero in
city codes and mobile prefixes (three-digit
numbers starting with ☎ 07) when calling
from abroad.
 Macedonia's largest provider is T-Mobile,
followed by Cosmofon and VIP.
 Major post offices do international faxing,
though lawyers' offices do it more cheaply.

TOURIST INFORMATION
Travel agencies are best, though some towns
have information offices; see the information
section of specific towns.

TRAVELLERS WITH DISABILITIES
City streets' random holes can challenge
the wheelchair-bound, and most historical
sites and old quarters aren't wheelchair-
friendly. Expensive hotels may provide
wheelchair ramps. Buses and trains have no
disabled access.

VISAS
Passport holders from Australia, Canada, the
EU, Iceland, Israel, New Zealand, Norway,
Switzerland, Turkey and the USA do not need
a visa and can stay for three months. Visas are
required for most others. Visa fees average
US$30 for a single-entry visa and US$60 for
a multiple-entry visa. Check www.mfa.gov
.mk for updated information.

MACEDONIA

TRANSPORT IN MACEDONIA

GETTING THERE & AWAY

Air

Macedonia flights mostly go to **Alexander the Great Airport** (☎ 02-3148 651), 21km from Skopje. Ohrid's **St Paul the Apostle Airport** (☎ 046-252 820) sees little action. See www.airports.com.mk for information, including timetables and weather conditions. Exchange offices and hotel-booking and car-rental services are at Skopje's airport.

Airlines flying to/from Macedonia include the following:

Adria Airways (JP; ☎ 02-117 009; www.adria.si)
Croatia Airlines (OU; ☎ 02-3115 858; www.croatiaairlines.hr)
JAT (JU; ☎ 02-3116 532; www.jat.com)
Macedonian Airlines (MAT; IN; ☎ 02-3292 333; www.mat.com.mk).

Land

The two most used of four border crossings between Macedonia and Albania are along Lake Ohrid: Kafasan–Qafa e Thanës, 12km southwest of Struga, is busiest, followed by Sveti Naum–Tushëmishti, 29km south of Ohrid. There's also Blato, 5km northwest of Debar, and Stenje, on Lake Prespa's southwestern shore.

Of three border crossings to Bulgaria, the most-frequented is Deve Bair (90km from Skopje, just after Kriva Palanka) which leads to Sofia. The Delcevo crossing (110km from Skopje) leads to Blagoevgrad, while the Novo Selo crossing, 160km from Skopje beyond the southeastern city of Strumica, accesses Petrich.

For Kosovo, the Blace border crossing is 20 minutes north from Skopje. Another crossing is Tetovo's Jazince.

Tabanovce is the major road and rail border crossing for Serbia. Pelince, 25km northeast, is less frequently used.

BUS

Regular buses serve all Balkan cities. See the boxed text, p513, for details of international services from Skopje.

CAR & MOTORCYCLE

A Green Card endorsed for Macedonia is required; see p982 for more.

TRAIN

The north–south train line serving Macedonia starts in Thessaloniki, and heads south to Serbia, Croatia and Slovenia; there's also an international train service to Kosovo. See p512 for details.

Find international-route timetables on the website for **Euro Railways** (www.eurorailways.com).

GETTING AROUND

Bicycle

Cycling is popular, and out of cities traffic is light, though mountains and reckless drivers are common.

Bus

Skopje is well-connected to domestic destinations. Buses vary from old and rickety to new and air-conditioned. During summer, book ahead for Ohrid buses. (For service details, see the boxed text, p512.) Baggage fees (10MKD) are encountered. People ship parcels or letters by bus, paying the driver about 100MKD. The recipient waits to retrieve the item upon the bus's arrival.

Car & Motorcycle

Police at checkpoints randomly stop cars. If you have the correct documentation and aren't violating laws, don't worry.

AUTOMOBILE ASSOCIATIONS

AMSM (Avto Moto Soyuz na Makedonija; ☎ 02-3181 181; www.art.com.mk, in Macedonian; Ivo Ribar Lola 51, Skopje) offers road assistance, towing services and information (in German, English and Macedonian), and has branches nationwide.

DRIVING LICENCE

National driver's licences are respected, though an international driving permit is best.

FUEL & SPARE PARTS

Petrol stations are prevalent except in rural areas, where they often close after dark. Unleaded and regular petrol cost about 60MKD per litre, while diesel costs around 44MKD per litre. Spare parts and sometimes service are available at the fantastically named 'vulkanizer' shops.

HIRE

Skopje's rental agencies include international biggies and local companies. Ohrid has many agencies, other cities fewer. Sedans average €50 daily, including insurance. Bring your passport, driver's licence and credit card.

INSURANCE

Rental agencies provide insurance (€15 to €25 a day, depending on vehicle type; the nonwaivable excess is €1000 to €2500). Green-Card insurance is accepted; third-party insurance is compulsory.

ROAD RULES

Drive on the right. Speed limits are 120km/h (motorways), 80km/h (open road) and 50km/h to 60km/h (in towns). Speeding fines start from 1500MKD. Seat belts and headlights are compulsory. Cars must carry replacement bulbs, two warning triangles, a first-aid kit and (15 November to 15 March) snow chains. Motorcyclists and their passengers must wear helmets. Police are vigilant on speeding, drink driving and headlights. Fines are payable immediately. The legal blood-alcohol limit is 0.05%.

Taxi

Macedonian taxis are inexpensive. Skopje base rates are 50MKD, in smaller cities 30MKD to 40MKD. For intercity routes, some taxis wait to fill up with four people before going – the individual cost is barely more than the bus-ticket rate.

Train

Macedonia's trains are living museums, and hopefully the government won't follow through on its threat to modernise them.

The major lines are Tabanovce (on the Serbian border) to Gevgelija (on the Greek border), via Kumanovo, Skopje, Veles, Negotino and Demir Kapija; and Skopje to Bitola, via Veles and Prilep. Smaller Skopje–Kičevo and Skopje–Kočani lines exist. See p512 for details of services from Skopje.

MACEDONIA

Moldova

Moldo-who? Only vaguely known in Europe and all but anonymous to the rest of the world, travel blogs about Moldova – consistently ranked near the bottom of the World Database of Happiness – are more often written by melancholy Peace Corps volunteers rather than tipsy revellers enjoying what is arguably the best wine drinking (ad)venture on the planet. More sober tourist attractions are few, but outstanding, such as the dramatic and beautiful setting of the Orheiul Vechi cave monastery or the breakaway republic of Transdniestr, still plugging along as one of Europe's top (and most notorious) idiosyncratic wonders. Chişinău's unexpectedly superb dining and clubbing options have been known to extend a few visits as well.

A veritable melee of cultural, political and economic turmoil ensued after the country's 1991 independence – eye-popping even by post-Soviet standards. As the former USSR collapsed, the Turkic Gagauz and the Soviet-bent Transdniestr areas recognised the opportunity and declared their respective independences almost simultaneously. A bloody civil war ensued, leaving hundreds of people dead. Today, Gagauz maintains a calm truce with Moldova, while alleged transgressions of Transdniestr continue to aggravate Chişinău and generate the occasional statement of concern from the European Union. Though news briefs about Moldova's corruption, organised crime, arms dealing, human trafficking and shaky return to communism have subsided, the country's recently stated EU membership aspirations haven't exactly gotten Brussels sharpening its pencils.

Although Moldova is a perpetual contender for the 'Poorest Country in Europe' designation, prices here, particularly for accommodation, can be surprisingly high. Coming from Romania, expect to pay about the same for almost everything.

FAST FACTS

- **Area** 33,843 sq km
- **Capital** Chişinău
- **Currency** leu; €1 = 14.83 lei; US$1 = 10.87 lei; UK£1 = 15.75 lei; A$1 = 7.52 lei; ¥100 = 11.30 lei; NZ$1 = 6.09 lei
- **Famous for** wine, folk art, breakaway regions
- **Official languages** Moldovan, Russian
- **Phrases** bună (hello); *merci* (thank you); *cum vă numiţi?* (what's your name?)
- **Population** 4.3 million
- **Telephone codes** country code ☎ 373; international access code ☎ 22
- **Visas** required for Australian and New Zealand passport holders; see p551 for details

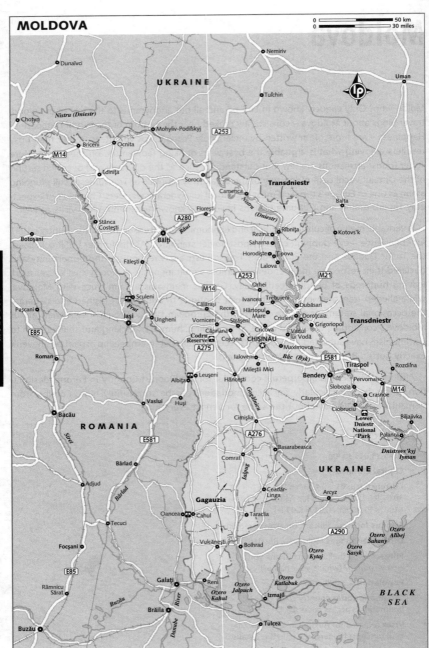

MOLDOVA

0 ———————— 50 km
0 ———————— 30 miles

UKRAINE

Dunaïvci

Nemiriv

Tuľčin

Uman

Chotyn

Nistru (Dniestr)

Mohyliv-Podiľskyj

A253

Briceni
Ocnita

M14

Edinița

Soroca

Transdniestr

Camenca

Balta

*Nistru
(Dniestr)*

Floreşti

A280

Stânca
Costeşti

Rezina
Rîbnița

Kotovs'k

Bălți

Răut

Saharna

Horodişte
Tipova

Botoşani

Fălești

Lalova

A253

Orhei

M21

Sculeni

M14

Ivancea
Trebujeni

Dubăsari

Prut

Călăraşi
Recea

Hârtopul
Mare

Criuleni

Paşcani

Iaşi

Ungheni

Vornicen

Strășeni
Cricova

Dorotcaia

Grigoriopol

Transdniestr

Căpriana
Cojușna

CHIȘINĂU

Vadul
lui Vodă

E85

Codru
Reserve

A275

Ialoveni

Maximovca

Bâc (Byk)

E581

Roman

Mileştii Mici

Tiraspol

Rozdiľna

Albița
Leuşeni

Hâncești

Bendery
Pervomajsc

Slobozia

M14

Vaslui

Huşi

Căuşeni

Crasnoe

Bacău

Cimişlia

Ciobruciu

Lower
Dniestr
National
Park

Biljajivka

ROMANIA

A276

Basarabeasca

Palanca

E581

Bărlad

Comrat

UKRAINE

*Dnistrovs'kyj
lyman*

Adjud

Bârlad

Ceadâr-
Linga

Arcyz

Gagauzia

Oancea
Cahul

Taraclia

A290

*Ozero
Alibej*

Tecuci

Vulcăneşti
Bolhrad

*Ozero
Sahany*

*Ozero
Kytaj*

*Ozero
Sasyk*

Focşani

E85

*Ozero
Katlabuk*

Râmnicu
Sărat

Galați
Reni

*Ozero
Jalpuch*

Izmajil

BLACK
SEA

Buzău

Brăila

Danube River

*Ozero
Kahul*

Buzău

Tulcea

MOLDOVA

HIGHLIGHTS

- Stroll the admirably green streets and parks, then sample the religion-changing nightlife of **Chişinău** (p534).
- Designate a driver for tours of the world-famous wine cellars at **Mileştii Mici** (p542) and **Cricova** (p541).
- Detox at the fantastic cave monastery, burrowed by 13th-century monks, at **Orheiul Vechi** (p542).
- Go *way* off-the-beaten-path in the self-styled 'republic' of **Transdniestr** (p543), a surreal, living homage to the Soviet Union.
- Gorge on the many **dining** (p538) gems found in Chişinău.

ITINERARIES

- **One week** Arrive in Chişinău – buy and uncork several bottles of wine to fuel partying… erm, civilised wine tasting. Use Chişinău as your base, making a trip out to the cave monastery at Orheiul Vechi. Take a tour around a big-name vineyard.
- **Two weeks** Follow the one-week itinerary, then spend a few memorably surreal days in Transdniestr, the country that doesn't officially exist. Tack on a few smaller vineyard tours around Chişinău, purchasing your customs limit, before returning home.

CLIMATE & WHEN TO GO

Moldova has moderate winters and warm summers. Hikers and wine enthusiasts would do well to travel between May and September, when you have more guarantees that camping grounds and attractions will be open. As there is little tourism in Moldova, there's no real low or high season.

HISTORY

Moldova today straddles two historic regions divided by the Nistru (Dniestr) River. Historic Romanian Bessarabia incorporated the region west of the Nistru, while tsarist Russia governed the territory east of the river (Transdniestr).

Bessarabia, part of the Romanian principality of Moldavia, was annexed in 1812 by the Russian empire. In 1918, after the October Revolution, Bessarabia declared its independence. Two months later the newly formed Democratic Moldavian Republic united with Romania. Russia never recognised this union.

Then in 1924 the Soviet Union created the Moldavian Autonomous Oblast on the eastern banks of the Nistru River, and incorporated Transdniestr into the Ukrainian Soviet Socialist Republic (SSR). A few months later the Soviet government renamed the oblast the Moldavian Autonomous Soviet Socialist Republic (Moldavian ASSR). During 1929 the capital was moved to Tiraspol from Balta (in present-day Ukraine).

In June 1940 the Soviet army, in accordance with the terms of the secret protocol associated with the Molotov-Ribbentrop Pact, occupied Romanian Bessarabia. The Soviet government immediately joined Bessarabia with the southern part of the Moldavian ASSR – specifically, Transdniestr – naming it the Moldavian Soviet Socialist Republic (Moldavian SSR). The remaining northern part of the Moldavian ASSR was returned to the Ukrainian SSR (present-day Ukraine). Bessarabia suffered terrifying Sovietisation, marked by the deportation of 300,000 Romanians.

During 1941 allied Romanian and German troops attacked the Soviet Union, and Bessarabia and Transdniestr fell into Romanian hands. Consequently, thousands of Bessarabian Jews were sent to labour camps and then deported to Auschwitz. In August 1944 the Soviet army reoccupied Transdniestr and Bessarabia. Under the terms of the Paris Peace Treaty of 1947, Romania had to relinquish the region and Soviet power was restored in the Moldavian SSR.

Once in control again the Soviets immediately enforced a Sovietisation program on

---

CONNECTIONS: MOVING ON FROM MOLDOVA

International connections from Moldova are little better than provincial-calibre. Daily trains from Chişinău head to Iaşi and Bucharest, as well as branching out into Ukraine, some continuing to Minsk, St Petersburg and Moscow (p541). Buses run similar routes (p540), though transiting Transdniestr when going to Odesa (Ukraine) is strongly discouraged. Buses from Chişinău to Transdniestr are frequent, but the 'border' crossing can be hair-raising; see p544 for details.

MOLDOVA

HOW MUCH?

- Bottle of Cricova table wine €2 to €3
- Museum admission (adult) €1
- Short taxi ride €2
- Local bus ticket €0.15
- Internet access €0.50 per hr

LONELY PLANET INDEX

- 1L petrol €0.82
- 1L bottled water €0.50
- Beer in a bar (Chişinău) €1 to €2
- Souvenir T-shirt €3 to €5
- Street snack (pizza slice) €0.50

the Moldavian SSR. The Cyrillic alphabet was imposed on the Moldovan language (a dialect of Romanian) and Russian became the official state language. Street names were changed to honour Soviet communist heroes, and Russian-style patronymics were included in people's names.

In July 1949, 25,000 Moldovans were deported to Siberia and Kazakhstan. And in 1950–52 Leonid Brezhnev, then first secretary of the central committee of the Moldovan Communist Party, is said to have personally supervised the deportation of a quarter of a million Moldovans.

Mikhail Gorbachev's policies of *glasnost* (openness) and *perestroika* (restructuring) from 1986 paved the way for the creation of the nationalist Moldovan Popular Front in 1989. Moldovan written in the Latin alphabet was reintroduced as the official language in August 1989. In February and March 1990 the first democratic elections to the Supreme Soviet (parliament) were won by the Popular Front. Then in April 1990 the Moldovan national flag (the Romanian tricolour with the Moldavian coat of arms in its centre) was reinstated. Transdniestr, however, refused to adopt the new state symbols and stuck to the red banner.

In June 1990 the Moldovan Supreme Soviet passed a declaration of sovereignty. After the failed coup attempt against Gorbachev in Moscow in August 1991, Moldova declared its full independence and Mircea Snegur became the democratically elected president in December 1991. Moldova was granted 'most-favoured nation' status by the USA in 1992, qualifying for International Monetary Fund (IMF) and World Bank loans the same year.

Counteracting these nationalist sentiments was an emerging desire for autonomy among ethnic minority groups. In Transdniestr, the Yedinstivo-Unitatea (Unity) movement was formed in 1988 to represent the interests of the Slavic minorities. This was followed in November 1989 by the creation of the Gagauz Halki political party in the south of Moldova, where the Turkic-speaking Gagauz minority was centred. Both ethnic groups' major fear was that an independent Moldova would reunite with Romania.

The Gagauz went on to declare the Gagauz Soviet Socialist Republic in August 1990. A month later the Transdniestrans declared independence, establishing the Dniestr Moldovan Republic. In presidential elections, Igor Smirnov came out as head of Transdniestr, Stepan Topal head of Gagauzia.

Whereas Gagauzia didn't press for more than autonomy within Moldova, Transdniestr settled for nothing less than outright independence. In March 1992 Moldovan president Mircea Snegur declared a state of emergency. Two months later full-scale civil war broke out in Transdniestr, when Moldovan police clashed with Transdniestran militia in Bendery (then called Tighina), who were backed by troops from Russia. An estimated 500 to 700 people were killed and thousands wounded in events that shocked the former Soviet Union.

A ceasefire was signed by the Moldovan and Russian presidents, Snegur and Boris Yeltsin, in July 1992. Provisions were made for a Russian-led, tripartite peacekeeping force comprising Russian, Moldovan and Transdniestran troops to be stationed in the region. Troops remain there today, maintaining an uneasy peace.

Moldova took a step forward in its bid for a place in the EU when Deputy Prime Minister Ion Sturza signed a Partnership and Cooperation Agreement with the EU in May 1999. But while Moldova is keen to join the ranks of the EU, two major obstacles still block its path: the country's mounting foreign debt and its inadequate economic growth.

Widely regarded as the poorest and one of the most corrupt nations in Europe, Moldova is endeavouring to shake these stigmas. In late 2005 the country signed agreements committing itself to combat corruption and lock down people-trafficking. Average household income remains low, and with roughly one-third of the country's GDP comprised of monies sent home from emigrants working abroad, an unproductive economic dependency is developing, which will require long-term domestic cultivation to counteract. Even nationalists grudgingly admit that Moldova's economy may never flourish unless it's anchored to a stronger economic entity (ie Romania).

Romania's 2007 entrance into the EU means that the Moldovan border is the EU's eastern frontier. Moldovans that once freely crossed into Romania for school, shopping or visiting relatives now find themselves standing in demoralising lines to get visas, causing understandable feelings of heightened isolation and dwindling opportunities.

The Russian–Georgian conflict of 2008 was deeply felt in Moldova due to their similar predicament with Russian-occupied Transdniestr. Though no such confrontation seemed forthcoming in Moldova at the time of writing, the government continues to be understandably cautious. Meanwhile, citizens who watch Russian-language (and therefore Russian-oriented) news tend to side with Russia on such matters.

PEOPLE

With 4.3 million inhabitants, Moldova is the most densely populated region of the former Soviet Union. Moldovans make up 78.2% of the total population, Ukrainians constitute 8.4%, Russians 5.8%, Gagauz 4.4%, Bulgarians 1.9%, and other nationalities such as Belarusians, Poles and Roma compose 1.3%.

Most Gagauz and Bulgarians inhabit southern Moldova. In Transdniestr, Ukrainians and Russians make up 58% of the region's population; Moldovans make up 34%. It is one of the least urbanised countries in Europe.

RELIGION

Moldova stays on course with the region's religious leanings; the vast majority being Eastern Orthodox (98%), with the recovering Jewish community (1.5%) at a distant second. Baptists and 'other' make up the remaining 0.5%.

ARTS

There is a wealth of traditional folk art in Moldova, with carpet making, pottery, weaving and carving predominating.

Traditional dancing in Moldova is similar to the traditional dances of other Eastern European countries. Couples dance in a circle, a semicircle or a line to the sounds of bagpipes, flutes, panpipes and violins.

Two of Moldova's most prolific modern composers are Arkady Luxemburg and Evgeny Doga, who have both scored films and multimedia projects, as well as written songs, concertos, suites and symphonies. Dimitrie Gagauz has for over three decades been the foremost composer of songs reflecting the folklore of the Turkic-influenced Gagauz population of southern Moldova.

The biggest name in Moldovan painting is Mihai Grecu (1916–98), who cofounded the National School of Painting and was also a poet and free love advocate. In sculpture, Anatol Coseac today produces some highly original woodworks.

ENVIRONMENT

Moldova is tiny and landlocked. It's a country of gently rolling steppes, with a gradual sloping towards the Black Sea. With one of the highest percentages of arable land in the world, Moldova is blessed with rich soil. Fields of grains, fruits and sunflowers are characteristic of the countryside. Moldova counts some 16,500 species of animals (460 of which are vertebrates) as its citizens.

There are five scientific reserves (totalling 19,378 hectares) and 30 protected natural sites (covering 22,278 hectares). The reserves protect areas of bird migration, old beech and oak forests, and important waterways. The Codru reserve, Moldova's oldest, boasts 924 plant species, 138 kinds of birds and 45 mammals; this is the most frequently visited reserve.

A great effort has been made by environmental groups to protect Moldova's wetland regions along the lower Prut and Nistru Rivers.

Never heavily industrial, Moldova faces more issues of protection and conservation than pollution. The majority of its 3600 rivers and rivulets were drained, diverted or dammed, threatening ecosystems.

FOOD & DRINK

The concept of 'health food' in Moldova is still scarce. Indeed, you'll do more physiological damage fretting about calories and arteries than simply giving in and enjoying. Run it off when you get home.

MOLDOVA

In Moldova, some Russian influences have seen that pickled fruits and vegetables are popular, as are Russian meals such as *pelmeni* (Russian-style ravioli stuffed with meat). A Turkic influence has arguably been strong here; in the south you may find the delicious Gagauz *sorpa*, a spicy ram soup.

Though slightly improved in recent years, vegetarians will find their meals limited. Locally grown fresh fruit and veg is always a bonus, but expect to find few vegetarian choices. We've pointed them out when we've found them.

Moldova produces excellent wines and brandies. Red wines are called *negru* and *roşu*, white wine is *vin alb*, while *sec* means dry, *dulce* is sweet and *spumos* translates as sparkling.

Across the country, restaurants can be expected to stay open until at least 11pm nightly. Outside of Chişinău, where the choice of eateries is astounding, you'll be lucky to find a decent restaurant and will be stuck with hotel dining rooms, bars or cafeterias.

Nonsmoking awareness has yet to gain serious traction in Moldvoa. Some restaurants will offer nonsmoking sections, but in general it's still a carcinogenic free-for-all.

CHIŞINĂU

☎ 22 / pop 785,000

In Chişinău (*kish*-i-now in Moldovan, *kish*-i-nyov in Russian), fleets of luxury cars rivalling Monaco dominate traffic, while fashionably dressed inhabitants strut down boutique-lined avenues, talking into state-of-the-art mobile phones, before retiring for lunch in fancy restaurants. How did this improbable wealth find its way to the capital of Europe's poorest country? Answer: you don't wanna know and we ain't asking.

Sizeable incoming cash-flow from emigrants working abroad accounts for some of this dubious affluence, but the contrast between the merely well-off and the truly well-connected is blatantly underscored by individuals who are clearly above the law and shamelessly conduct themselves as such. While this dodginess may be distracting for alarmed visitors, citizens of this vibrant, good-natured city have long since dismissed these oddities in favour of what really counts: having a good time.

CHIŞINĂU IN TWO DAYS

Sightseeing options are engaging but thin and easily covered in a half-day amble. Spend both nights ensconced in Chişinău's legendary nightlife.

On your first day eat at the **Beer House** (p538), sampling its home-brew before moving on to cocktails at **Déja Vu** (p539). Dance the night away at **Galant** (p540).

On your second day get a hearty breakfast at **Cactus Café** (p538). Wander through the **National Archaeology & History Museum** (p537) and **National Museum of Fine Arts** (p537), then find a nice spot in one of the city's excellent parks until recovered. Finally, do it all again until 6am at **Star Track** (p540).

First chronicled in 1420, Chişinău became a hotbed of anti-Semitism in the early 20th century. Later Chişinău was the headquarters of the USSR's southwestern military operations during Soviet rule. Between 1944 and 1990 the city was called Kishinev, its Russian name, which is still used by some of the few travel agencies abroad who actually know where it is.

In 2007, Chişinău elected 28-year-old Liberal Party vice-president Dorin Chirtoacă as their mayor, a small victory for the anti-communist coalition, which simultaneously tipped the city council majority to their side. However, at the time of writing, a dubious party-switch by a former Chirtoacă ally has returned the city council majority to communist hands.

ORIENTATION

Chişinău's street layout is a typically Soviet grid system of straight streets.

The train station is a five-minute walk from the city centre on Aleea Gării. Exit the train station, turn right along Aleea Gării to Piaţa Negruzzi, then walk up the hill to Piaţa Libertăţii. From here the main street, B-dul Ştefan cel Mare, crosses the city from southeast to northwest. The city's main sights and parks cluster around this street.

INFORMATION
Bookshops

Cartea Academica (B-dul Ştefan cel Mare 148; ⏰ 9am-6pm Mon-Sat) Your best bet for English-language titles.
Librărie Eminescu (B-dul Ştefan cel Mare 180; ⏰ 9am-6pm Mon-Fri, to 5pm Sat) Much larger, but devoid of English.

MOLDOVA

Cultural Centres

Alliance Française (☎ 234 510; Str Sfatul Ţării 18; 8am-6.10pm Mon-Fri, to 4pm Sat) Has a well-equipped *mediathèque* (media centre) and hosts regular cultural events.

Internet Access

Internet (Hotel Cosmos, Piaţa Negruzzi 2; per hr 7 lei; 24hr)

Left Luggage

The **train station** (☎ 252 737; Aleea Gării; per day 8 lei; 24hr) has a 24-hour left-luggage service, 100m north of the main entrance alongside the platform.

Medical Services

Contact the US embassy (p550) for a list of English-speaking doctors.
Felicia (☎ 223 725; B-dul Ştefan cel Mare 62; 24hr) Well-stocked pharmacy.
Municipal Clinical Emergency Hospital (☎ 903; www.ournet.md/~scmu; Str Toma Ciorba 1; 24hr) Provides a variety of emergency services and a good likelihood of finding English-speaking staff.

Money

There are ATMs all over the city centre, in all the hotels and in shopping centres. Currency exchanges are concentrated around the bus and train stations, and also along B-dul Ştefan cel Mare.
Eximbank (☎ 270 287; B-dul Ştefan cel Mare 6; 9am-5pm Mon-Fri) Can give you cash advances in foreign currency.
Victoriabank (☎ 576 425; Str 31 August 1989, 141; 9am-4pm Mon-Fri) Amex's representative in Moldova.

Post

Central post office (☎ 227 737; B-dul Ştefan cel Mare 134; 8am-7pm Mon-Sat, to 6pm Sun) There is also a post office on Aleea Gării (open to 8pm).

Telephone

Central telephone office (B-dul Ştefan cel Mare 65; 24hr) Book international calls inside the hall marked 'Convorbiri Telefonice Internaţionale'. Faxes and telegrams can also be sent from here. Receive faxes at ☎ 549 155.

Travel Agencies

There's no tourist information centre in Moldova, but there are plenty of agencies where you can get information. Most offer discounted rates in some hotels.

Sometimes travel agencies take a while to reply to emails (if ever). A better bet for pre-trip contact is independent operators like **Radu Sargu** (☎ 0691-389 53; www.moldova-travel .com), for apartment rentals, local information and assistance.

Solei Turism (☎ 271 314; www.solei.md; B-dul Negruzzi 5; 8am-6pm Mon-Sat, 9am-5pm Sun), a very efficient organisation, can book accommodation and transport tickets, but is known for its multiday excursions into remote Moldova, taking in monasteries, places of interest and incorporating rural homestays.

DANGERS & ANNOYANCES

The odd Bucharest-style restaurant pricing scam has been reported. Never order anything, particularly wine, without confirming the price *in writing* (eg on the menu) to avoid surprises on the bill. If you've been victimised, keep all receipts and report it to the police.

Cross streets with care – according to locals, hapless pedestrians are mowed down by recklessly driven ministers' cars on an almost weekly basis.

Travellers are required to have their passports with them *at all times*. Cheeky police are prone to random checks.

SIGHTS

Lacking in pulse-quickening 'must-sees', Chişinău is simply a pleasant city to wander about and discover as you go – with frequent cafe breaks and all-you-can-carry wine and champagne shopping sprees. Heavily bombed during WWII, little remains of its historic heart. Still, there are some great museums and parks, and the communist iconography merging with symbols of Moldovan nationalism is intriguing.

Start smack in the city centre, where Chişinău's best-known parks diagonally oppose each other, forming two diamonds at the city's core. The highlights here are the Holy Gates (1841), also known as Chişinău's own **Arc de Triomphe**. To its east sprawls **Parcul Catedralei** (Cathedral Park), dominated by the city's main **Orthodox Cathedral**, with its lovely bell tower (1836). On the northwestern side of the park is a colourful 24-hour **flower market**.

Government House, where cabinet meets, is the gargantuan building opposite the Holy Gates. The parliament convenes in **Parliament House** (B-dul Ştefan cel Mare 123) further north. Opposite this is the ominous **Presidential Palace**, conspicuous photography of which will elicit a security response.

CENTRAL CHIŞINĂU

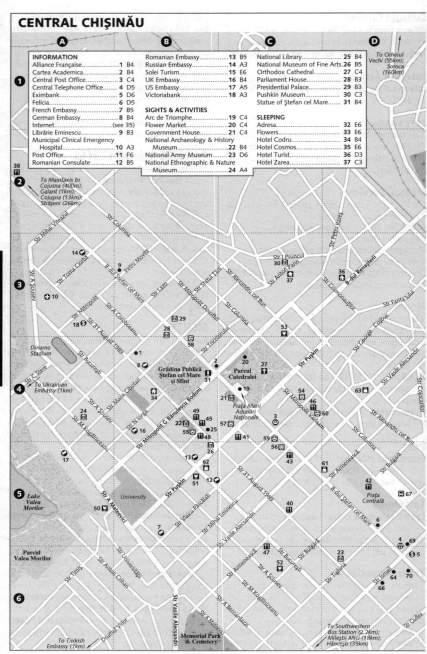

INFORMATION
Alliance Française....................**1** B4
Cartea Academica...................**2** B4
Central Post Office..................**3** C4
Central Telephone Office........**4** D5
Eximbank................................**5** D6
Felicia....................................**6** D5
French Embassy......................**7** B5
German Embassy.....................**8** B4
Internet..............................(see 35)
Librărie Eminescu...................**9** B3
Municipal Clinical Emergency
    Hospital.........................**10** A3
Post Office............................**11** F6
Romanian Consulate..............**12** B5

Romanian Embassy................**13** B5
Russian Embassy....................**14** A3
Solei Turism...........................**15** E6
UK Embassy...........................**16** B4
US Embassy............................**17** A5
Victoriabank..........................**18** A3

SIGHTS & ACTIVITIES
Arc de Triomphe....................**19** C4
Flower Market........................**20** C4
Government House..................**21** C4
National Archaeology & History
    Museum.........................**22** B4
National Army Museum...........**23** D6
National Ethnographic & Nature
    Museum.........................**24** A4

National Library......................**25** B4
National Museum of Fine Arts..**26** B5
Orthodox Cathedral...............**27** C4
Parliament House...................**28** B3
Presidential Palace.................**29** B3
Pushkin Museum....................**30** C3
Statue of Ştefan cel Mare.......**31** B4

SLEEPING
Adresa...................................**32** E6
Flowers..................................**33** E6
Hotel Codru...........................**34** B4
Hotel Cosmos........................**35** E6
Hotel Turist............................**36** D3
Hotel Zarea...........................**37** C3

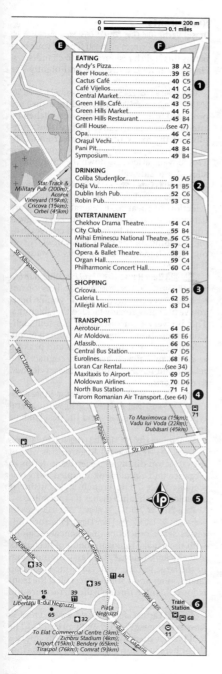

Grădina Publică Ştefan cel Mare şi Sfînt (Ştefan cel Mare Park) is a first-rate strolling and people-watching area. Ştefan was Moldavia's greatest medieval prince and ubiquitous symbol of Moldova's brave past. His **statue** (1928) lords it over the entrance.

Museums

The grandaddy of Chişinău's museums, the **National Archaeology & History Museum** (☎ 240 426; Str 31 August 1989 nr 121a; admission/photo/video 15/15/40 lei; ☒ 9am-6pm Tue-Sat) has archaeological artefacts from Orheiul Vechi, including Golden Horde coins, Soviet-era weaponry and a huge WWII diorama on the 1st floor.

Opposite the **National Library** is the **National Museum of Fine Arts** (Muzeul de Arte Plastice; ☎ 241 730; Str 31 August 1989, 115; admission 10 lei; ☒ 10am-6pm Tue-Sun), which has an interesting collection of contemporary European (mostly Romanian and Moldovan) art, folk art, icons and medieval knick-knacks.

The highlight of the massive and wonderful **National Ethnographic & Nature Museum** (☎ 244 002; Str M Kogălniceanu 82; adult/child 15/10 lei; ☒ 10am-6pm Tue-Sun) is a life-size reconstruction of a mammal skeleton, discovered in the Rezine region in 1966. Allow at least an hour to see the museum's pop art, taxidermied animals and exhibits covering geology, botany and zoology. An English-language tour – arranged in advance – costs 100 lei.

The small open-air military exhibition known as the **National Army Museum** (cnr Str 31 August 1989 & Str Tighina; admission/photo 2/3 lei; ☒ 9am-8pm Tue-Sun) displays Soviet-made tanks, fighter planes and other military toys inherited by Moldova's armed forces.

Northeast of the central parks is the **Pushkin Museum** (☎ 292 685; Str Anton Pann 19; admission 15 lei; ☒ 10am-4pm Tue-Sun), where Russian poet Alexander Pushkin (1799–1837) spent an exiled three years between 1820 and 1823. It was here that he wrote *The Prisoner of the Caucasus* and other classics – that is, when he wasn't involved in the amorous intrigues, hard-drinking and occasional violence of his social circles in what was then a distant rough-around-the-edges outpost of the Russian empire. You can step in and view his tiny cottage, filled with original furnishings and personal items. An English-language tour costs 100 lei. If the gate is locked, knock on the nearby window.

MOLDOVA

SLEEPING

Check out **Marisha** (www.marisha.net) for cheap homestays and apartments in Chişinău.

Hotel Zarea (☎ 227 625; Str Anton Pann 4; s/d with shared bathroom 270-390 lei, d with private bathroom 560-700 lei) This drab high-rise has dour, smoky rooms that are appropriately priced. There's a bar and billiard club. Breakfast isn't included.

Hotel Turist (☎ 220 637; B-dul Renaşterii 13; s 500-700 lei, d 500 lei) For a kitsch blast of the Soviet past, try this place, overlooking a giant Soviet memorial to communist youth. The socialist mural on its facade is prime photo-op material. The low-end singles are in tatty condition; the doubles are all unrenovated.

our pick Adresa (☎ 544 392; www.adresa.md; B-dul Negruzzi 1; 1-room apt 613-1227 lei; ⊙ 24hr) For short- or long-term stays, this reliable agency is a great alternative to hotels, renting out one- to three-room apartments throughout the city. It's a memorable way to live as the locals do, using rusty lifts (elevators) or climbing disagreeable staircases. Still, they're all safe, comfortable and clean. Most aren't right in the city centre but are a short taxi ride away.

Hotel Cosmos (☎ 542 757; www.hotel-cosmos.com; Piaţa Negruzzi 2; s/d 613/789 lei, with air-con 841/1104 lei; ✕) Rooms are reasonably priced in this concrete hulk, with decent beds, newish baths and grubby balconies overlooking the bedlam in Piaţa Negruzzi. Downstairs there's a shopping centre, full-service desk and internet cafe.

Hotel Codru (☎ 208 104; www.codru.md; Str 31 August 1989, 127; s 1253-1488 lei, d 1410-2193 lei, ste 2350-3133 lei) Get through the ho-hum lobby and enjoy paradoxically nice rooms that become downright luxurious when you reach 'eurostandard' classification. Wi-fi, balconies and immaculate bathrooms complete the package.

Flowers (☎ 277 262; www.hotelflowers.md; Str Anestiade 7; s/d 2193/2506 lei; ✕ ✕ 🖵) This 18-room boutique hotel is a good splurge. Enormous wi-fi and minibar-equipped rooms with high ceilings are exquisitely decorated with tasteful restraint, incorporating paintings by local artists and, of course, a small jungle's worth of plants and flowers.

EATING

The assortment of great places to eat in Chişinău far exceed this section's word-count limit. These are some of our favourites, but we encourage you to explore others that look interesting.

Restaurants

Oraşul Vechi (Old City; ☎ 225 063; Str Armenească 24; mains 45-300 lei; ⊙ noon-midnight) One of your best bets is this stylish restaurant with chandeliers, classic paintings, a fireplace and nightly live piano. Its speciality is the fish.

Grill House (☎ 224 509; Str Armenească 24; mains 50-300 lei; ⊙ noon-midnight) Outstanding dishes are produced from the open, fire-oven kitchen by attentive servers. Creative pasta dishes compliment the array of hearty meat and fish. Skip the outrageously priced foreign wine for a Moldovan variety. Go down the atmospheric alley off the sidewalk.

Green Hills Café (☎ 220 114; B-dul Ştefan cel Mare 77; mains 55-130 lei; ⊙ 9am-midnight) Though the large selection of meat and vegetable dishes are delicious, most come for a quick fix – great coffee, cocktails or beer, and, of course, people-watching on the city's main drag. A second branch, named Green Hills Restaurant, is at Str 31 August 1989, 76.

our pick Beer House (☎ 275 627; B-dul Negruzzi 6/2; mains 60-150 lei; ⊙ 11am-midnight) 'To beer or not to beer' says the menu, but if you're here, you've probably already tackled that dilemma. This brewery-cum-restaurant has four delicious home-brewed beers and a superb menu, warming up with chicken wings and peaking at rabbit or chicken grilled in cognac. The relaxed ambience and impeccable service add to the charm.

Opa (☎ 221 862; Str Mitropolit Varlaam 88; mains 79-220 lei; ⊙ 9am-11pm) A Greek grill with several types of souvlaki, salads and the best baklava in Chişinău.

Symposium (☎ 211 318; Str 31 August 1989, 78; mains 80-170 lei; ⊙ 11am-midnight) Regarded as one of the city's top dining experiences in terms of elegance and refinement, coupled with reasonable prices. The French-style cuisine is succulent, with lamb dishes its speciality.

Pani Pit (☎ 240 127; 31 August 1989, 115; www.ten.md; mains 80-180 lei; ⊙ 11am-11pm) Peasant waitresses serve omelettes and pancakes, along with the usual Moldovan menu of beef, pork and chicken. Choose the classy dining room or the large terrace, with cushioned cast iron chairs, vines and a small waterfall. If the front is locked, enter through the terrace around the side.

our pick Cactus Café (☎ 502 394; www.cactus.md; Str Armenească 41; mains 95-175 lei; ⊙ 9am-11pm; 🖵) The Wild West meets urban bohemian interior decor here will stun wine-fogged patrons into

MAKE NEW FRIENDS

What with their friendly, outgoing disposition, you shouldn't have any trouble winning acquaintances in Moldova. However, if you want to be instantly embraced, and possibly kissed, steer the conversation towards music, then casually drop these names: Zdob şi Zdub and Gândul Mâţei.

Zdob şi Zdub (zdob-shee-zdoob; www.zdob-si-zdub.com) have been together since 1995, working Moldovan audiences into a lather with their Romanian-folk-meets-the-Red-Hot-Chili-Peppers sound fusion. In 2005 the group achieved a stunning sixth-place finish in the Eurovision Song Contest. These days they tour so ferociously that poor Moldova hardly hears from them. You're more likely to catch a show in Romania.

Gândul Mâţei (gun-dool muts-ehee; www.myspace.com/gandulmatei) nimbly run the gamut from lounge music to Coldplay-esque ballads to rocking *hard*. They're starting to break out of the Moldovan market, but still gig regularly in Chişinău.

Both bands have a very strong following in Moldova, and locals between the ages of 15 and 35 are guaranteed to become unwound with breathless reverence at the mere mention of their names. Moreover, their shows are fabulous and a highly recommended experience.

thinking they've been zapped to Brooklyn during the night. Extravagant breakfasts, vegetarian meals and daring plates like 'turkey jam rolls wrapped in aubergines' don't help to dull the sensation. Free wi-fi.

Cafes

The voracious outdoor cafe movement has swelled, contemptuous of adjacent, deafening traffic. More serene terraces can be found flanking the Opera & Ballet Theatre, opposite the main entrance to the university on Str A Mateevici and in the courtyard leading to Parcul Valea Morilor.

Café Vijelios (Str Puşkin 22; mains 10-22 lei; ✷ 11am-11pm) This cafeteria serves surprisingly succulent food priced for the impoverished university crowd.

Quick Eats

For cheap, questionably appetising eats, there are kiosks and small 'cafes' around the bus station and central market, where a dish of mystery meat or meat-filled pastries costs about 15 lei.

Andy's Pizza (☎ 210 210; B-dul Ştefan cel Mare 169; mains 45-55 lei; ✷ 7.30am-11pm) This alleged pizzeria, the flagship location of a popular chain, only serves eight different pizzas, filling the remainder of the menu with spaghetti, chicken wings and unlikely zingers like steak, herring and (admittedly delicious) chocolate cake.

Self-Catering

Central market (Piaţa Centrală; ✷ 7am-5pm) Since 1825 this market has been the scene of lively price haggling for fresh meat and produce.

Brave the crowds for its fresh food and singular ambience. It sprawls out around the central bus station on Str Tighina and Str Armeneasca.

Green Hills Market (B-dul D Cantemir 6; ✷ 7am-9pm) The newest and most central location of the Green Hills Market chain. Sprawling and modern, it's comparable to any Western supermarket chain.

DRINKING

Coliba Studenţilor (Str A Mateevici; ✷ 8am-11pm) This student hangout is opposite the university, just above the park. The terrace is a good place to bump into eager English speakers.

Déja Vu (☎ 227 693; Str Bucureşti 67; ✷ 11am-2am) A true cocktail bar, with a tantalising drinks menu. There's also a small dining hall serving meals, but most come here to lounge about with multicoloured cocktails perched in their hands. FYI – friendly women here are not always friendly for free.

Robin Pub (Str Alexandru cel Bun 83; mains 42-195 lei; ✷ 11am-midnight) A friendly, affordable local-pub feel reigns in this tastefully decorated hang-out. The extravagant menu includes delectable crêpes Suzette for dessert. It's an ideal place to forget about the world in an unpretentious atmosphere.

Dublin Irish Pub (☎ 245 855; Str Bulgară 27; mains 46-180 lei; ✷ noon-11pm) Rather expensive, but one of the few places in town where you can get a pint of the good stuff (70 lei).

ENTERTAINMENT

Posters listing 'What's On' are displayed on boards outside the city's various theatres.

MOLDOVA

Nightclubs

Chişinău parties in earnest every weekend, but in some of the larger clubs be prepared for body searches, metal detectors and tough-guy posturing from goonish doormen.

City Club (Str 31 August 1989, 121; 10pm-6am) In the alley next to the Licurici Puppet Theatre, this 2nd-floor club consistently ranks as one of the hippest places in town.

Galant (717 407; Calle leşilor 49; 10pm-4am) In the Buiucani neighbourhood, Galant is a favourite for fans of dance music and charitable bartenders. Though the club is refreshingly nonposeur-ish and uncrowded, the petit dance floor gets a little tight.

Star Track (496 207; Str Kiev 7; 10pm-4am Tue-Sun) The epicentre of Rîşcani's nightlife, the dark interior offers comfortable sofas and make-out booths where one can ogle dance performances by scantily clad men and women. Under Star Track is the less titillating but equally popular Military Pub.

Performing Arts

Opera & Ballet Theatre (245 104; B-dul Ştefan cel Mare 152; box office 10am-2pm & 5-7pm) This venue is home to the esteemed national opera and ballet company. Grab a bite at the Andy's Pizza location outside the entrance before the show.

Mihai Eminescu National Theatre (221 177; B-dul Ştefan cel Mare 79; box office 11am-6.30pm) Contemporary Romanian productions can be seen at this theatre, founded in 1933.

National Palace (Palatul Naţional; 213 544; Str Puşkin 21; box office 11am-5pm) Various cabarets, musicals and local theatre group productions are performed here.

Organ Hall (Sala cu Orgă; 225 528; B-dul Ştefan cel Mare 79) Classical concerts and organ recitals are held at this hall, next to the Mihai Eminescu National Theatre. Performances start at 6pm; tickets are sold at the door.

Philharmonic Concert Hall (224 505; Str Mitropolit Varlaam 78) Moldova's National Philharmonic is based here.

Chekhov Drama Theatre (Teatrul Dramatic A Cehov; 223 362; Str Pârcălab 75) Plays in Russian are performed at the Chekhov Drama Theatre, situated where Chişinău's choral synagogue was located until WWII.

Sport

Moldovans are big football fans and Chişinău has three stadiums to prove it. The new **Zimbru** **Stadium** is the city's first European regulation football stadium, located in the Botanica district. **Dinamo Stadium** (Stadionul Dinamo) is north of the city centre on Str Bucureşti. Moldovans like football so much, in fact, there's an American football team called the Chişinău Barbarians, who hold occasional matches, in full gear.

SHOPPING

Cricova (222 775; B-dul Ştefan cel Mare 126; 10am-7pm Mon-Fri, to 6pm Sat, to 4pm Sun) One of several outlets for the Cricova wine factory. It stocks numerous types of shockingly affordable wines and champagnes (only 23 lei to 70 lei each), plus the crystal glasses to drink them in.

Mileştii Mici (211 229; www.milestii-mici.md; Str Vasile Alecsandri 137; 9am-8pm Mon-Fri) The outlet store for the Mileştii Mici wine cellars. It also has outlets on the 1st floor of the Elat Commercial Centre (4km southeast of the city centre) and at the airport.

Galeria L (221 975; Str Bucureşti 64; 10am-6pm Mon-Fri, to 5pm Sat, to 4pm Sun) Holds temporary art exhibitions, and sells small works of art and souvenirs crafted by local artists.

GETTING THERE & AWAY
Air

Moldova's only airport of significance is in Chişinău, **Chişinău international airport** (KIV; 525 111), 15.5km southeast of the city centre. Obviously, it has only international flights. For more information on airlines servicing Chişinău, see p552.

Bus

Chişinău has three bus stations. The **North Bus Station** (Autogara Nord; 439 489; www.autogara .md) is where nearly all domestic and international lines depart, except Transdniestr-bound lines, which depart from the Central Bus Station. Services include 12 daily buses to Străşeni, and regular buses to Soroca, Bălţi, Recea, Ediniţa and Briceni. There are buses half-hourly between 9.15am and 10pm to Orhei.

There are daily buses to Moscow (520 lei, 30 hours), St Petersburg (770 lei, 33 to 36 hours) and Kyiv (235 lei, 11 hours). Avoid at all costs buses that transit bribe-hungry Transdniestr through to Odesa (89 lei, five to six hours): opt instead for the longer, but less problematic, route through Palanca. You can buy advance tickets here or from a tiny office at the train station. The information booth charges 1 leu per question.

Domestic and international maxitaxis operate from the **Central Bus Station** (Autogara Centrală; ☎ 542 185; Str Mitropolit Varlaam), behind the central market. Maxitaxis go to Tiraspol (32 lei, 1½ hours) and Bendery (27 lei) every 20 to 35 minutes from 6.30am to 6.30pm, with reduced services until 10pm. Buses to Bucharest are 200 lei (12 hours). There are buses half-hourly from 9.15am to 10pm to Orhei (21 lei), leaving from the 'Casele Suburbane' terminal about 100m west of Central Station.

Bus services to/from Comrat, Hânceşti and other southern destinations use the less crowded **Southwestern Bus Station** (Autogara Sud-vest; ☎ 723 983; cnr Şoseaua Hânceşti & Str Spicului), located approximately 2.2km from the city centre. Daily local services include five buses to Comrat (45 lei) in Gagauzia and six to Hânceşti. A fleet of private maxitaxis to Iaşi, Romania (120 lei, four hours) also departs from here.

Eurolines (☎ 222 827; www.eurolines.md), with an office at the train station, operates a few buses to Western Europe, including Berlin (three weekly), Munich (twice weekly), Paris (twice weekly), Potsdam (twice weekly) and Saabrucken (twice weekly) via Stuttgart and Munich. **Atlassib** (☎ 229 551; www.atlassib.ro; Str Ismail 561) goes to Italy and Spain.

Train
International routes departing from Chişinău's sparkling new **train station** (☎ 252 737; Aleea Gării) include three daily trains to Moscow (600 lei, 28 to 33 hours), three daily trains to Kyiv (400 lei, 12 hours), one each to St Petersburg (400 lei, 40 hours), Bucharest (488 lei, 14 hours), and three to Lviv (400 lei, eight hours), and three weekly services to Minsk (550 lei, 25 hours). To get to Budapest, you must change in Bucharest.

GETTING AROUND
To/From the Airport
Maxitaxi 65 departs every 20 minutes from Str Ismail, across from UNIC mall near the corner of B-dul Ştefan cel Mare for the airport (3 lei).

Car & Motorcycle
Hire cars are available from **Loran Car Rental** (Hotel Codru; ☎ 243 710; www.turism.md/loran; Str 31 August 1989, 127) from €34 (or 542 lei) per day

(Dacia Logan), including insurance. Payments can be made in cash (euros or lei) or by credit card; a deposit is required.

Public Transport
Bus/maxitaxi 45 runs from the Central Bus Station to the Southwestern Bus Station, as well as maxitaxi 117 from the train station. Bus 1 goes from the train station to B-dul Ştefan cel Mare.

Trolleybuses 1, 4, 5, 8, 18 and 22 go to the train station from the city centre. Buses 2, 10 and 16 go to the Southwestern Bus Station. Maxitaxis 176 and 191 go to the North Bus Station from the city centre. Tickets costing 2 lei for buses and 1 leu for trolleybuses are sold onboard.

Most bus routes in town and to many outlying villages are served by nippy maxitaxis (3 lei per trip, pay the driver). Maxitaxis run regularly between 6am and 10pm, some with reduced service until midnight.

Taxi
Many official and unofficial taxis do not have meters or prices listed on the door and taxi-stand drivers may try to rip you off. Ordering a **taxi** (☎ 1448, 1433, 1422, 1407) is best. If you decide to hop in off the street, agree on a price to your destination before getting in the car.

AROUND CHIŞINĂU

Even the furthest reaches of Moldova are a reasonable day-trip from Chişinău, though that's not to say an overnight somewhere isn't a good idea. Get out of the capital and you'll find a far more tranquil atmosphere.

CRICOVA
Of Moldova's many fine wineries, **Cricova** (☎ 22-441 204; www.cricova.md; Str Ungureanu 1; ☺ 8am-4pm) is arguably the best known. Its underground wine kingdom, 15km north of Chişinău, is one of Europe's biggest. Some 60km worth of the 120km-long underground limestone tunnels – dating from the 15th century – are lined wall-to-wall with bottles. The most interesting part of the tour is the wineglass-shaped cellar of collectible bottles, including 19 bottles of Gerhing's wines, a 1902 bottle of Becherovka, a 1902 bottle of Evreiesc de Paşti from Jerusalem and pre-WWII French red wines.

MOLDOVA

Cricova wines and champagnes enjoy a high national and international reputation. Legend has it that in 1966 astronaut Yuri Gagarin entered the cellars, re-emerging (with assistance) two days later. Russian president Vladimir Putin celebrated his 50th birthday here.

You must have private transport and advance reservations to get into Cricova. Your one-hour tour (500 lei per person) includes a short wine tasting with *placinte* (pastries) and gift bottles of wine and champagne.

Once you've finished at Cricova, head to the much-awarded **Acorex vineyard** (www.acorex .net; ☺ 9am-6pm), just down the hill. There's no tour, but their shop sells limited lines not available in most stores or outside Moldova.

MILEŞTII MICI

While Cricova has the hype, **Mileştii Mici** (☎ 382 333; www.milestii-mici.md; 2hr tour, tasting & lunch 500 lei per person; ☺ 9am-5pm Mon-Fri) has the goods. Also housed in a limestone mine, these are *the* largest cellars in Europe (over 200km of tunnels). They were recognised by Guinness in 2005 for having the largest wine collection in the world (1.5 million bottles), though the collection has now surpassed the two million bottle mark.

Excellent value tours, done by car, wind down through the cellars with stops at notable collections and artistically executed tourist points, terminating at the elegantly decorated restaurant, with a sea-bottom motif, 60m below ground. These tours, which include, naturally, wine tasting, are stunning, while being refreshingly informal and hilarious. Tours can be arranged directly with the winery. Tour groups must have a minimum of four people – this is negotiable – while a Saturday/Sunday tour must have a minimum of 15 people.

COJUŞNA

Just 13km northwest of Chişinău, **Cojuşna** (☎ 22-615 329; Str Lomtadze 4; ☺ 8am-6pm) offers spunky, friendly and affordable tours, though the setting is moribund in comparison to Cricova and Mileştii Mici.

Cojuşna will need advance warning if you want a hot meal and/or a tour in English (two- to three-hour tour per person 246 lei, with meal 377 lei). Drop-ins are possible, but staff aren't always free (or willing) to open the very worthwhile wine-tasting rooms, decorated with wooden furniture carved by a young local and his father. However, you can always buy wines (20 lei to 280 lei per bottle) from the shop.

Catch one of the frequent maxitaxis leaving from Calea Eşilor (take trolleybus 1, 5 or 11 up B-dul Ştefan cel Mare to the Ion Creangă university stop), get off at the Cojuşna stop. Ignore the fork on the left marked 'Cojuşna' and walk or hitch the remaining 2km along the main road to the vineyard entrance, marked again by a 'Cojuşna' sign and a white-washed Jesus-on-the-cross. The winery is about 200m from the road.

ORHEIUL VECHI

Ten kilometres southeast of Orhei lies Orheiul Vechi ('Old Orhei', marked on maps as the village of Trebujeni), unquestionably Moldova's most fantastic sight. It's certainly among its most picturesque places.

The **Orheiul Vechi Monastery Complex** (Complexul Muzeistic Orheiul Vechi; ☎ 235-34 242; adult/student 10/5 lei; ☺ 9am-6pm Tue-Sun), carved into a massive limestone cliff in this wild, rocky, remote spot, draws visitors from around the globe.

The **Cave Monastery** (Mănăstire în Peştera), inside a cliff overlooking the gently meandering Răut River, was dug by Orthodox monks in the 13th century. It remained inhabited until the 18th century, and in 1996 a handful of monks returned to this secluded place of worship and are slowly restoring it. You can enter the cave via an entrance on the cliff's plateau.

Ştefan cel Mare built a fortress here in the 14th century, but it was later destroyed by Tartars. In the 18th century the cave-church was taken over by villagers from neighbouring Butuceni. In 1905 they built a church above ground dedicated to the Ascension of St Mary. The church was shut down by the Soviets in 1944 and remained abandoned throughout the communist regime. Services resumed in 1996.

Ancillary attractions include remnants of a 15th-century defence wall surrounding the monastery complex, an ethnographic museum in the nearby village of Butuceni and newly opened caves across the valley.

You'll find the headquarters on the main road to the complex where you park and purchase your tickets for the complex. You can also arrange guides and get general information.

It's forbidden to wear shorts and women must cover their heads while inside the monastery.

WORTH THE TRIP: VADU LUI VODA

When Moldovans on a budget want to get away from it all, they head for Vadu lui Voda and retire to **Zimbit Camping** (☎ 0692-005 70, 416 049; 4-bed cabin with shared bathroom 130 lei, r with private bathroom 618 lei). Fresh air, sports, walking, river excursions and enthusiastic beer-drinking are the main pursuits here. Three square meals are available in the bar-restaurant and there's ample eating in the village – or bring your own food and grill out. The cabins are bare, but for the cots, and the shared bathhouse is reminiscent of summer camp, but you'll be in good company, with droves of like-minded Moldovans. Bond with nature, water-ski on the river, kick around on the nearby football pitch or just retreat to a shady tree with a book and a bottle of Moldovan wine. Maxitaxis for Vadu lui Voda leave from Chişinău's Central Bus Station (Autogară Centrală) regularly throughout the day, departing from the street one block north of the station by the factory on Str Tighina. Pay the driver.

Orheiul Vechi Monastery Headquarters (☎ 235-56 912; d 400-500 lei) has six pleasant rooms and a small restaurant. The rooms facing the monastery have spine-tingling balcony views. Spending the night here is highly recommended.

From Chişinău, daily buses depart from the Central Bus Station for Butuceni or Trebujeni (20 lei, about one hour) at 10.20am, 3pm and 6.15pm. Returns trips run daily at 6am and 4.45pm, with an additional bus at noon Friday to Sunday.

SOROCA

pop 38,492

Soroca is the Roma 'capital' of Moldova, but people come here to see the outstanding **Soroca fortress** (☎ 230-24 873; admission/guided tour 2/50 lei; ⌚ 9am-4pm Wed-Sun May-Oct, low season by appointment). Part of a medieval chain of military fortresses built by Moldavian princes between the 14th and 16th centuries to defend Moldavia's boundaries, the fortress was founded by Ştefan cel Mare and rebuilt by his son, Petru Rareş, in 1543–45.

The fortress is administered by the **Soroca Museum of History and Ethnography** (☎ 230-22 264; Str Independentei 68; admission 2 lei; ⌚ 10am-4pm Tue-Sun, low season by appointment). This well-designed museum is a real treat; its 25,000 exhibits cover archaeological finds, weapons and ethnographic displays.

The simple, but clean and bright rooms at the **Nistru Hotel** (☎ 230-23 783; Str Mihiel Malmut 20; d 350 lei) are your best bet in Soroca. The hotel is hidden down an improbable side street one block east of the red-roofed Soroca city council building, which faces the park.

There are 12 daily buses to Soroca from Chişinău's North Bus Station (2½ hours).

TRANSDNIESTR

pop 555,500

The self-declared republic of Transdniestr (Pridnestrovskaia Moldavskaia Respublica, or PMR in Russian), a narrow strip of land covering 3567 sq km on the eastern bank of the Nistru River is, according to them, one of the world's last surviving bastions of communism.

Political jibba-jabba and historic ethnic boundaries notwithstanding, Moldova maintains that Transdniestr was illegally grabbed from their sovereign territory. With Russia's support, Transdniestr effectively won its 'independence' during a bloody civil war in the early 1990s. A tenuous, bitter truce has ensued ever since.

Travellers will be stunned by this idiosyncratic region that has developed its own currency, police force, army and borders, controlled by Transdniestran border guards. Russian is the predominant language. Transdniestrans boycott the Moldovan independence day and celebrate their own independence day on 2 September.

Although as recently as 2007 we were sternly informed that western visitors are officially 'not welcome' in Transdniestr, its tourism website (www.visitpmr.com) paradoxically woos all comers, painting the area as 'Europe's hidden jewel' and giving a decidedly abridged version of the region's recent history and independence.

In truth, visits here can be quite pleasant, and the surreal atmosphere is admittedly unforgettable, though increasingly aggressive (and expensive) bribe shake-downs at the border leave many visitors too traumatised to notice.

BORDERS SANS BOREDOM

We receive continuous reader feedback reporting disturbing hijinks at Transdniestran border crossings, where organised intimidation is used to separate travellers from their money. Accusations of incomplete paperwork or invented transgressions (such as carrying a camera) lead to ludicrous 'fines' starting as high as €200. Some alleged offences border on the absurd, such as not having visas (unnecessary) or letters of invitation, acquired at the 'Transdniestran Embassy' (nonexistent).

Being invited into a hut with several looming, armed guards is not uncommon, where your infraction(s) is (are) grimly pointed out in a farcically massive, ancient tome, written in indecipherable Cyrillic script. Then the haggling about your fine begins. You will be directed 'by law' to show them all of your money – a brazen way for them to gauge the size of the fine they can impose. If you resist, a theatrical performance designed to heighten anxiety and break your will commences: ominous forms are filled out, your bags will be pulled off your bus, presumably leaving you stranded. Anyone without passable fluency in Russian is in for a hard time.

There are ways to visit Transdniestr with reduced border drama. It's strongly recommended that you travel in private transport with Moldovan plates and bring a fluent Russian speaker, preferably someone with experience travelling in the region. Also, you're strongly advised to avoid the hectic, bribe-factory border crossing near Bendery. Going through the virtually deserted crossing at Grigoropol is a comparative breeze and only adds 30 minutes to your driving time, however you *cannot* transit Transdniestr to Ukraine using this crossing. You can also take a maxitaxi to Grigoropol from Chișinău's North Bus Station, though you'll have to wait for a connecting maxitaxi onward to Tiraspol at the Grigoropol bus station – and you'll likely need Transdniestran rubles in hand to pay for that maxitaxi.

Transiting the republic during a Moldova–Ukraine journey verily invites a bribe stare-down. Unless you intend to stop and visit Transdniestr, you should circumnavigate the region by passing through the southeast village of Palanca.

If you enter Transdniestr on public transport and are detained, often your best defence is calm and patience. Let the maxitaxi leave you behind. Another will be along shortly. Even the most persistent guards will eventually get tired of dealing with you, particularly if their tactics don't appear to be working. Worst case scenario, you'll be stonewalled at a mirthfully small bribe offer (say €5 or 80 Moldovan lei) or you're sent back to where you came from.

Entry permit prices/requirements change frequently. At the time of writing, permits were 'officially' 12 lei (about US$1), available *at the border* no matter what the guys on duty playfully tell you. For stays of less than 10 hours, you don't need to pay this fee.

If you're staying for over 24 hours, you'll need to register with **OVIR** (☎ 533-55 047; ul Kotovskogo 2a; 9am-noon Mon, 9am-noon & 1-4pm Tue & Thu, 1-3pm Fri). Registration costs about 18 Moldovan lei or 16 Transdniestran roubles. Go down the alley and inquire at the rear white building with the red roof. Oh, and 'men must wear pants'! Seriously. Outside OVIR business hours go to the **Tiraspol Militia Office** (☎ 533-34 169; Roza Luxemburg 66; 24hr) where registration is possible, but you'll probably be asked to check in at the OVIR office the following working day anyway. Some top-end hotels will register you automatically.

Leif Pettersen

History

Igor Smirnov was elected president of Transdniestr in 1991, following the region's declaration of independence four months prior. Most of the time the region pushes for the creation of a Moldovan federation, with proportionate representation between Moldova, Transdniestr and Gagauzia.

Neither Smirnov's presidency nor the Transdniestran parliament is recognised by the Moldovan – or any other – government. The Russian 14th army, headquartered in Tiraspol since 1956, covertly supplied Transdniestran rebels with weapons during the civil war. The continued presence of the 5000-strong Russian 'operational group' in Transdniestr today is seen by locals as a guarantee of their security.

The Ministry of State Security (MGB), a modern-day KGB, has sweeping powers, and has sponsored the creation of a youth wing, called the Young Guard, for 16- to 23-year-olds.

Alongside a number of agreements between Moldova and Transdniestr since 1991, there have been countless moves by both sides designed to antagonise or punish the other. In 2003 alone, a piqued Smirnov slapped exorbitant tariffs on all Moldovan imports, instantly halting trade over the 'border' and making life more difficult for ordinary people on both sides. He later had phone connections severed between the two regions for a few weeks.

While Smirnov is becoming increasingly mistrusted by his 'electorate', a large subsection of locals still refuse to criticise their government. Political and economic attitudes aside, popular opinion still strongly supports independence from Moldova.

On 6 July 2006, a bomb blast on a local bus in Tiraspol killed eight people. Transdniestran politicians were quick to blame 'Moldovan provocateurs', though it was eventually revealed that an amateur bomb-maker had lost control of his merchandise.

After hastily abolishing the presidential term limit that he himself established, Smirnov was elected to a fourth five-year term as president with a 'reported' 82.4% of the vote in December 2006.

For more practical details about visiting the country, see p551.

TIRASPOL

☎ 533 / pop 183,700

The sights are ho-hum and the accommodation iffy; nevertheless, this is one of the most mind-bending, surreal and distinctly memorable places in Europe.

Tiraspol (from the Greek, meaning 'town on the Nistru'), 70km east of Chişinău, is the second-largest city in Moldova – sorry – make that the largest city and capital of Transdniestr! Glorifying all things Soviet, this veritable Lenin-loving theme park is starting to show capitalist cracks. Meanwhile, questionable business dealings from the tiny elite widen the divide between the haves and the have-nots.

The city was founded in 1792 following Russian domination of the region. According to the 2004 Transdniestran census, its inhabitants consist of Moldovans (32%), Russians

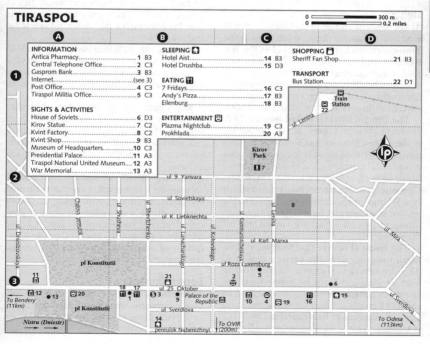

(30%), and ethnic Ukrainians (29%), with groups of Bulgarians, Poles, Gagauz, Jews, Belarusians and others making up the final 9%.

Orientation & Information

The train and bus stations are next to each other at the end of ul Lenina. Exit the train station and walk down ul Lenina, past Kirov Park, to ul 25 Oktober (the main street). Ul 25 Oktober, Tiraspol's backbone, is also its commercial strip, with most of the shops and restaurants located here.

Antica Pharmacy (ul 25 October; ☽ 24hr)

Central telephone office (cnr ul 25 Oktober & ul Kommunisticheskaya; ☽ 24hr) Through the far-left door, you can buy phonecards (10 rubles to 22 rubles) to use in the modern pay telephones and use internet (per hour 3.50 rubles). You can also buy phone cards at any Sheriff Market.

Gasprom Bank (ul 25 Oktober 76; ☽ 9am-8pm Mon-Sat) Changes money.

Internet (ul 25 October 76; per hr 4.50 rubles; ☽ 9am-11pm) Below Gasprom Bank.

Post office (ul Karl Marx 149; ☽ 7.30am-7pm Mon-Fri) Won't be of much use to you unless you want to send postcards to all your friends in Transdniestr.

Sights

At the western end of ul 25 Oktober stands a Soviet armoured tank, from which the Transdniestran flag flies. Behind is the **War Memorial** with its Tomb of the Unknown Soldier, flanked by an eternal flame in memory of those who died on 3 March 1992 during the first outbreak of fighting. On weekends, it's covered in flowers left by wedding day brides.

The **Tiraspol National United Museum** (ul 25 Oktober 42; admission 4 rubles; ☎ 9am-5pm Sun-Fri) is the closest the city has to a local history museum, with an exhibit focusing on poet Nikolai Dimitriovich Zelinskogo, who founded the first Soviet school of chemistry. Opposite is the **Presidential Palace**, from which Igor Smirnov rules his mini-empire. Loitering and/or photography here is likely to end in questioning and a guard-escorted trip off the property.

The **House of Soviets** (Dom Sovetovul; ul 25 Oktober), towering over the eastern end of ul 25 Oktober, has Lenin's angry-looking bust peering out from its prime location. Inside is a **memorial** to those who died in the 1992 conflict. Close by is the military-themed **Museum of Headquarters** (☎ 95 382; ul Kommunisticheskaya 34; admission/photo 2/5 rubles;

☽ 8.30am-5pm Mon-Sat), who can also arrange city tours (Russian only).

The **Kvint factory** (☎ 37 333; http://kvint.biz; ul Lenina 38) is one of Transdniestr's pride and joys – since 1897 it's been making some of Moldova's finest brandies. Buy the least expensive cognac in Europe (starting at less than €2!) either near the front entrance of the plant or at the **Kvint shop** (ul 25 Oktober 84; ☽ 24hr).

Further north along ul Lenina, towards the bus and train stations, is **Kirov park**, with a **statue** of the Leningrad boss who was assassinated in 1934, conveniently sparking mass repressions throughout the USSR.

Sleeping & Eating

You must register at **OVIR** (ul Kotovskogo No 2A; ☽ Mon-Fri) if staying more than 24 hours (see the boxed text, p544). Visit www.marisha.net to arrange a homestay.

Hotel Drushba (☎ 34 266; ul 25 Oktober 116; r 170-340 rubles) Under total renovation during our visit, expect this place to be markedly more expensive when it re-opens.

Hotel Aist (☎ 73 776; pereulok Naberezhnyi 3; d 240-300 rubles) Despite a derelict exterior, this is a decent hotel. The more expensive rooms have luxuries such as hot water, private toilet and TV.

7 Fridays (☎ 92 210; ul 25 Oktober 112; mains 14-60 rubles; ☽ 11am-midnight) A popular cafe serving all manner of meat, salads and soups. Menus are Russian-only, but there are pictures to point at.

Andy's Pizza (ul 25 Oktober 72; mains 17-38 rubles; ☽ 9am-11pm) The Andy's Pizza chain has done what the Moldovan and Transdniestran governments can't: establish smooth cross-border business. The familiar pizzas and pastas are all here.

Eilenburg (☎ 73 011; pereulok Naberezhnyi 1; mains 25-100 rubles; ☽ 11am-midnight) A medieval-themed German restaurant, with girls in dirndl dresses, stone walls, a suit-of-armour and, coincidentally, some excellent food. Choose from beef stroganoff, quail, rabbit, salmon, quail-egg omelettes, and pancakes topped with caviar (25 rubles).

Entertainment

Prokhlada (☎ 34 642; ul 25 Oktober 50; ☽ 4pm-6am) This cavernous, sombre (but friendly) space is the best place in town for a lazy drink or hot dancing session.

Plazma Nightclub (ul Lenina; ☺ terrace 9am-midnight, club 9pm-4am Tue-Sun) More terrace bar than club, but you can dance here till late.

Shopping

Sheriff Fan Shop (ul 25 October 69; ☺ 10am-7pm) Buy jerseys and memorabilia if you're a fan of the Moldovan league champions – or a fan of total monopolies.

Getting There & Away
BUS

You can only pay for tickets to destinations in Transdniestr with the local currency, but will be allowed to pay in Moldovan lei/Ukrainian hryvnia for tickets to Moldova/Ukraine. Buy tickets inside the left-hand door of the station.

From Tiraspol there is one daily buses to Bălţi (Moldova; 71.60 rubles, six hours), 24 daily to Odesa (Ukraine; 37.25 rubles, three hours), one daily to Kyiv (Ukraine; 185 rubles, 14 hours) and once weekly to Berlin (Germany). Buses/maxitaxis go to Chişinău (26.70 rubles) nearly every half-hour from 5.50am to 8.50am, and maxitaxis run regularly from 6.30am to 8.05pm.

Trolleybus 19 (1.50 rubles) and quicker maxitaxis 19 and 20 (2.50 rubles) cross the bridge over the Dniestr to Bendery.

TRAIN

One daily train goes to Moscow, via Kyiv, leaving promptly at 2.06am (3rd/2nd class R700/1000, 26 hours). All other train services have been discontinued indefinitely.

BENDERY
☎ 552 / pop 123,000

Bendery (sometimes called Bender, and previously known as Tighina), on the western banks of the Dniestr River, is the greener, more aesthetically agreeable counterpart to Tiraspol. Despite civil war bullet-holes still decorating several buildings – Bendery was hardest hit by the 1992 military conflict with Moldova – the city centre is a breezy place.

During the 16th century Moldavian prince Ştefan cel Mare built a large defensive fortress here on the ruins of a fortified Roman camp. In 1538 the Ottoman sultan, Suleiman the Magnificent, conquered the fortress and transformed it into a Turkish *raia* (colony), renaming the city Bendery, meaning 'belonging to the Turks'. During the 18th century Bendery was seized from the Turks by Russian troops who then massacred Turkish Muslims in the city. In 1812 Bendery fell permanently into Russian hands. Russian peacekeeping forces remain here to this day.

Information

Central department store (cnr ul Lenina & ul Kalinina; per hr 4 rubles; ☺ 9am-8pm) Has two internet clubs on the top floor.
Currency exchange (ul Sovetskaya) Change money here; located next to the Central Market.
Pharmacy (cnr ul Suvorova & ul S Liazo; ☺ 8am-9pm)
Telephone office (cnr ul S Liazo & ul Suvorova; ☺ 24hr) International telephone calls can be booked from here. It also has internet (per hour 3.50 rubles; available between 7am and 10pm).

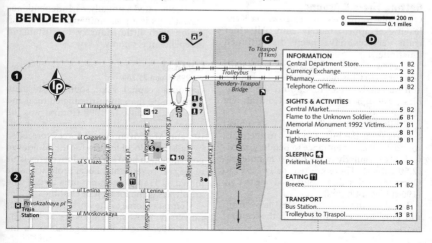

BENDERY

INFORMATION
Central Department Store......................1 B2
Currency Exchange.................................2 B2
Pharmacy...3 B2
Telephone Office....................................4 B2

SIGHTS & ACTIVITIES
Central Market..5 B2
Flame to the Unknown Soldier...............6 B1
Memorial Monument 1992 Victims.........7 B1
Tank..8 B1
Tighina Fortress......................................9 B1

SLEEPING
Prietenia Hotel......................................10 B2

EATING
Breeze..11 B2

TRANSPORT
Bus Station...12 B1
Trolleybus to Tiraspol..........................13 B1

Sights

Bendery's main sight is the great Turkish **Tighina fortress**, built in the 1530s to replace a 12th-century fortress built by the Genovese. Until recently an off-limits Transdniestran military training ground, at the time of writing plans were in motion to open it to the public in time for the 600th anniversary of Tighina in October 2008. At the entrance to the city, close to the famous **Bendery–Tiraspol bridge**, is a **memorial park** dedicated to local 1992 war victims. An eternal flame burns in front of an armoured **tank**, from which flies the Transdniestran flag. Haunting **memorials** to those killed during the civil war are scattered throughout many streets in the city centre.

Sleeping & Eating

A three-tier pricing system is intact here, with different prices for locals; Moldovans, Ukrainians and Belarusians; and all other foreigners.

Prietenia Hotel (☎ 29 660; ul Tkachenko 10; r without/with hot water 360/600 rubles) The large rooms and thin beds here are overpriced. The complex includes a sauna, billiards room and 'nightclub'.

Breeze (cnr ul Kalinina & ul Lenina; mains 23 rubles; ⏰ 8am-11pm) Located in the park across from the department store, this small restaurant has a popular terrace, where grilled-meat dishes are the favourite. It also doubles as a hangout and bar.

Getting There & Around

One daily train goes to Moscow, via Kyiv, leaving at approximately 2am. All other train services have been discontinued indefinitely.

There are buses and maxitaxis every half-hour or so to Chişinău (35 rubles, 1½ hours), and one daily direct to Comrat (56.30 rubles), though others go to Comrat, via several stops.

Trolleybus 19 for Tiraspol (1.50 rubles) departs from the bus stop next to the main roundabout at the entrance to Bendery; maxitaxis also regularly make the 20-minute trip (2.50 rubles). There are two daily buses to Odesa (41 rubles, three hours) and one to Kyiv (190 rubles, 14 hours).

Local maxitaxis (2.50 rubles) leave from the currency exchange near the central market.

GAGAUZIA

pop 171,500

The region of Gagauzia (Gagauz Yeri) covers 1832 sq km of noncontiguous land in southern Moldova. Far less militant than the separatists in Transdniestr, this Turkic-influenced Christian ethnic minority forfeited full independence for autonomy, being subordinate to Moldova constitutionally and for foreign relations and defence. There's still disagreement over language and economic issues, however.

Gagauzia is comprised of three towns and 27 villages dotted throughout three broken-up districts. Gagauzi Muslim antecedents fled here from the Russo-Turkish wars in the 18th century. They were allowed to settle in the region in exchange for their conversion to Christianity. Their language is a Turkish dialect, with its vocabulary influenced by Russian Orthodoxy, as opposed to the Islamic influences inherent in Turkish. Gagauz look to Turkey for cultural inspiration and heritage.

The republic has its own flag (blue, white and red stripes with three white stars in the upper left corner), its own police force, its own newspapers (*Sabaa Ildyzy, Gagauz Vesti* and *Guneshhik*), and its own university. The official languages here are Gagauzi, Moldovan and Russian, though Russian is used almost everywhere, including the university. Gagauz autonomy was officially recognised by the Moldovan government on 23 December 1994; now celebrated annually as Independence Day. Theirs is a predominantly agricultural region with little industry to sustain an independent economy.

COMRAT

☎ 298 / pop 25,200

Gagauzia's capital, 92km south of Chişinău, is little more than an intriguing cultural and provincial oddity. In 1990 Comrat was the scene of clashes between Gagauz nationalists and Moldovan armed forces, preceded by calls from local leaders for the Moldovan government to hold a referendum on the issue of Gagauz sovereignty. Local protesters were joined by Transdniestran militia forces, who are always game for a bit of clashing.

Comrat is home to the world's only Gagauz university. Most street signs are in Russian; some older ones are in Gagauzi but in the

Cyrillic script. Since 1989, Gagauzi, alongside Moldovan, has used the Latin alphabet.

From the bus station, walk south along the main street, Str Pobedy, past the market to pl Pobedy (Victory Sq). St John's Church stands on the western side of the square, behind which lies the central park. Pr Lenina runs parallel to Str Pobedy, west of the park.

You can make international calls at the **post office** (Str Pobedy 55; ☉ 8am-6pm Mon-Fri, to 5pm Sat).

The captivating **Comrat Museum** (☎ 238-22 694; pr Lenina 164; admission 5 lei; ☉ 9am-4pm Tue-Sat) is a dizzying hotchpotch of mundane to fascinating items, seemingly collected from townspeoples' attics. Items include photos of noteworthy locals, books, historical newspaper clippings, costumes, tools, weapons, musical instruments, foreign currency, gifts from visiting dignitaries, furniture, models and a very enthusiastic woman watching the infrequently opened front door who will insist on guiding you, despite the lack of a common language.

The regional **başkani** (assembly) is on pr Lenina. The Gagauzi and Moldovan flags fly from the roof.

Next to the assembly is the **Gagauz Culture House**, in front of which stands a statue of Lenin. West of pr Lenina at Str Galatsăna 17 is the **Gagauz University** (Komrat Devlet Üniversitesi), founded in 1990. Four faculties (national culture, agronomy, economics and law) serve 1500 students, who learn in Russian and Gagauz. The main foreign languages taught are Romanian, English and Turkish.

There are five daily return buses from Chişinău to Comrat (45 lei). From Comrat there is one daily direct bus via Bendery to Tiraspol, and others that make frequent stops.

MOLDOVA DIRECTORY

ACCOMMODATION

Chişinău has a good range of hotels. Most towns have small hotels that have survived from communist days. Basic singles or doubles with a shared bathroom cost €25 to €35 per room in Chişinău, but outside the capital rooms will usually be €12 to €20. Midrange rooms cost €44 to €80, and top-end rooms are €90 to €180. Unless noted otherwise, all accommodation options have private bathrooms and include breakfast in the price. Some hotels

may offer nonsmoking rooms, but in general smoking occurs anywhere and everywhere.

You will be asked to briefly present your passport upon registration; they may keep it for several hours in order to register it.

Camping grounds (*popas turistic*) are practically nonexistent in Moldova. The good news is that wild camping is allowed anywhere unless otherwise prohibited.

The idea of homestays in Moldova is in its infancy. Check **Marisha** (www.marisha.net) for a growing list of options. The few places calling themselves 'hostels' are merely converted apartments with four to six beds in a room.

BOOKS

Playing the Moldovans at Tennis is Tony Hawks' dated but nevertheless hilarious account of his visit to a much bleaker Moldova in the mid-'90s to satisfy a drunken bet, challenging him to defeat the entire Moldovan football team at tennis. Moldova took a mild PR hit in *The Geography of Bliss*, by Eric Weiner, who recounts his visit to the alleged 'least happy nation on the planet'. *The Moldovans: Romania, Russia and the Politics of Culture* by Charles King is a more recent, textbook snapshot of this 'intriguing East Europe borderland'.

BUSINESS HOURS

Banks can be expected to open from 9am to 3pm, with many closing for an hour around noon. Most shops are open from 9am or 10am to 6pm or 7pm, some closing on Sunday. Post offices are open from 8am to 7pm Monday to Friday, until 4pm Saturday and closed Sunday. Museums are usually open from 9am to 5pm, with most closing on Monday. Restaurants can be expected to stay open until at least 11pm nightly. Theatrical performances and concerts usually begin at 7pm.

EMBASSIES & CONSULATES

Following is a list of countries with embassies or consulates in Chişinău:

France (Map pp536-7; ☎ 22-200 400; www.amba france.md; Str Vlaicu Pircalab 6)

Germany (Map pp536-7; ☎ 22-200 600; ambasada -germana@riscom.md; Str Maria Cibotari 35)

Romania embassy (Map pp536-7; ☎ 22-228 126; ambrom@moldnet.md; Str Bucureşti 66/1); consulate (Map pp536-7; ☎ 22-237 622; Str Vlaicu Pircalab 39)

Russia (Map pp536-7; ☎ 22-234 942; www.moldova .mid.ru; B-dul Ştefan cel Mare 153)

MOLDOVA

Turkey (off Map pp536–7; ☎ 22-242 608; tremb@
moldova.md; Str V Cupcea 60)
UK (Map pp536–7; ☎ 22-251 818; www.britishembassy
.md; Str Nicolae Iorga 18)
Ukraine (off Map pp536–7; ☎ 22-582 151; www.mfa
.gov.ua, in Ukrainian; Str V Lupu 17)
USA (Map pp536–7; ☎ 22-408 300; http://moldova
.usembassy.gov; Str A Mateevici 103)

FESTIVALS & EVENTS

Moldova is not a festival-heavy country,
perhaps because her citizens find any excuse to party anytime throughout the year.
Their major festival is the **Wine Festival** on the
second Sunday in October (and for several
wine-drenched days preceding and following it). The government has even instituted
a visa-free regime for this period. Chişinău's
City Day is 14 October.

GAY & LESBIAN TRAVELLERS

Before Moldova repealed its Soviet antigay
law in 1995, it was one of only four European
countries to still criminalise homosexuality.
Now Moldova has among the most progres-
sively liberal laws on the continent: homosexual activity is legal for both sexes at 14,
the same age as for heterosexual sex. In 2003
the government adopted a National Human
Rights Plan which would see the prohibition
of discrimination against homosexuals en-
shrined in law. In reality homosexual persecution is largely ignored. Chişinău's annual
Gay Pride parade (theoretically in May) was
banned for five years straight, and in 2008 it
was cancelled on the eve of the event citing
safety concerns for the participants.

Needless to say, homosexuality is still a
hushed topic, and politicians still get away
with antigay rhetoric. While most people take
a laissez-faire attitude towards the notion of
homosexuality, being visibly out is likely to
attract unwanted attention. For more information, visit www.gay.md.

HOLIDAYS

The following national holidays are celebrated
in Moldova.
New Year's Day 1 January
Orthodox Christmas 7 January
International Women's Day 8 March
Orthodox Easter April/May
Victory (1945) Day 9 May
Independence Day 27 August
National Language Day 31 August

INTERNET RESOURCES

Get your everyday Moldova news and information at **Moldova Azi** (www.az i.md).

MONEY

We've quotde most prices in this chapter in
Moldovan lei to make on-the-ground price references easier. At the time of writing, US$1 =
11.24 lei, €1 = 17.84 lei.

Moldovan lei come in denominations of 1,
5, 10, 20, 50, 100, 200 and 500 lei. There are
coins for 1, 5, 10, 25 and 50 bani (there are
100 bani in a leu).

Note that the breakaway Transdniestran
republic has its own currency, which is useless
anywhere else in the world (see opposite).

It's easy to find ATMs in Chişinău, but not
in other towns in Moldova. Eximbank will
cash travellers cheques and give cash advances
on major credit cards. Shops and restaurants
will not accept travellers cheques. While credit
cards won't get you anywhere in rural areas,
they are widely accepted in larger department
stores, hotels and most restaurants in cities
and towns.

POST

From Moldova, it costs 5 lei to 7 lei to send
a postcard or letter under 20g to Western
Europe, Australia and the USA.

DHL (www.dhl.com) is the most popular international courier service in the region. It
has offices in Chişinău and Tiraspol. See its
website for details.

TELEPHONE

Moldtelecom, the wonderfully named state-
run telephone company, sells pay cards
that can be used to dial any number within
Moldova only. These are sold at any telephone
centre in the country. To make an international call using a prepaid card, you need to
use a private company like Treitelecom. These
are good for local calls too. Cards are available
at any Moldpressa newspaper stand.

Mobile phone service in Moldova is provided by Chişinău-based Moldcell (run by

---

EMERGENCY NUMBERS

- Ambulance ☎ 903
- Fire ☎ 901
- Police ☎ 902

TRANSDNIESTR DIRECTORY

Language

The official state languages in Transdniestr are Russian, Moldovan and Ukrainian. Students in schools and universities are taught in Russian and the local government and most official institutions operate almost solely in Russian. All street signs are written in Russian and sometimes Ukrainian.

Money

The only legal tender is the Transdniestran rouble (TR). Officially introduced in 1994, it quickly dissolved into an oblivion of zeros. To keep up with inflation, monetary reforms introduced in January 2001 slashed six zeros from the currency, with a new TR1 banknote worth one million roubles in old money. Some taxi drivers, shopkeepers and market traders will accept payment in US dollars – or even Moldovan lei or Ukrainian hryvnia, but generally you'll need to get your hands on some rubles (US$1 = 8.50 rubles, €1 = 13.40 rubles).

Spend all your roubles before you leave, as no one honours or exchanges this currency outside Transdniestr, though you might find takers in Chişinău, from where Transdniestr-bound maxitaxis depart if you get stuck with a large amount.

Media

The predominantly Russian Transdniestran TV is broadcast in the republic between 6am and midnight. Transdniestran Radio is on air during the same hours. Bendery has a local TV channel that airs 24 hours.

The two local newspapers are in Russian. The *Transdniestra* is a purely nationalist affair advocating the virtues of an independent state; *N Pravda* is marginally more liberal.

Post

Transdniestran stamps featuring local hero General Suvorov can only be used for letters sent within the Transdniestran republic and are not recognised anywhere else. For letters to Moldova, Romania and the West, you have to use Moldovan stamps (available in Transdniestr, but less conveniently than in Moldova).

Moldtelecom) and the ubiquitous **Orange** (www.orange.md). Moldova's country code is ☎ 373.

VISAS

Since 1 January 2007 citizens of EU member states, USA, Canada and Japan no longer need visas. Everyone else is still on the hook though. Furthermore, Australians, New Zealanders and South Africans all require an invitation from a company, organisation or individual. When acquiring a visa in advance, payments to the consulates are usually in the form of a bank deposit at a specified bank.

Visas can be easily acquired on arrival at Chişinău airport or, if arriving by bus or car from Romania, at three border points: Sculeni (north of Iaşi); Leuşeni (main Bucharest–Chişinău border); and Cahul. Visas are not issued at any other border crossings, nor when entering by train. Citizens of countries requiring an invitation must present the original

document (copies/faxes not accepted) at the border if buying a visa there.

In 2002 Moldova generously started instituting a visa-free regime for all foreigners wishing to partake in its Wine Festival (second Sunday in October). These visa-free visits cannot exceed 10 days. However, those nationalities ordinarily needing invitation letters must still acquire them.

An HIV/AIDS test is required for foreigners intending to stay in Moldova longer than three months. Certificates proving HIV-negative status must be in Russian and English.

See **Welcome to Moldova!** (www.turism.md) and follow the links to check for the latest news on the visa situation.

Costs & Registration

The price of a single-/double-entry tourist visa valid for one month is US$60/75 or 674/843 lei. Single-/double-entry transit visas valid for 72 hours are US$30/60 or 337/674 lei. Special

MOLDOVA

rates apply for tourist groups of more than 10 persons, and for children, the handicapped and the elderly.

Visas can be processed within a day at the **Moldovan consulate** (☎ 40-21-410 9827; B-dul Eroilor 8, Bucharest) in Romania. Applications must be made between 8.30am and 12.30pm Monday to Friday. After paying for the visa at a specified bank in the city centre, you then collect your visa between 3pm and 4pm the same day.

TRANSPORT

GETTING THERE & AWAY

Entering and leaving Moldova is usually a breeze. Moldovan border guards are no longer genuinely surprised to see foreign tourists – though they still haven't learned how to smile. Any potential complications are often easily resolved on the spot with a monetary 'gift', though use this option with caution, as bribes are technically illegal.

MOLDOVA

Air

Moldova's only airport of significance is **Chişinău International** (KIV; ☎ 22-525 111), 15.5km south of the city centre. **Voiaj Travel** (www.voiaj.md) in Chişinău publishes the latest airport schedules.

There are two national airlines. **Moldavian Airlines** (2M; ☎ 22-549 339; www.mdv.md; B-dul Ştefan cel Mare 3, Chişinău), located in the **Air Service** (www.airservice.md) travel centre, offers 12 weekly flights to Timişoara (Romania) and two daily flights to Budapest (Hungary), from where it has connections to other European destinations. **Air Moldova** (9U; ☎ 22-272 715; www.airmoldova.md; B-dul Negruzzi 10, Chişinău) has daily flights between Chişinău and Bucharest (Romania), and to Timişoara.

Also in the Air Service travel centre is **Carpatair** (V3; ☎ 22-549 339; www.carpatair.com), which flies to Timişoara six times weekly. **Aerotour** (UN; ☎ 22-542 454; www.transaero.md; B-dul Ştefan cel Mare 3, Chişinău) has two flights daily to Budapest, one or two flights daily to Bucharest and two flights weekly to Prague.

Tarom Romanian Air Transport (RO; ☎ 22-541 254; www.tarom.ro; B-dul Ştefan cel Mare, 3, Chişinău; 🕑 9am-5pm) flies to Bucharest eight times weekly.

The following airlines also fly to Moldova:

Austrian Airlines (OS; ☎ 22-244 083; www.austrianair.com)

Transaero (UN; ☎ 542 454; www.transaero.md) Flies between Chişinău and Bucharest.

Turkish Airlines (TK; ☎ 22- 27 85 25; www.turkishairlines.com)

Land

BUS

Moldova is well linked by bus lines to central and Western Europe; for more details, see p541. While not as comfortable as the train, buses tend to be faster, though not always cheaper.

For bus journeys between Chişinău and Odesa, we strongly advise taking the route going through the southeast Palanca border crossing, circumnavigating Transdniestr.

CAR & MOTORCYCLE

The Green Card (a routine extension of domestic motor insurance to cover most European countries) is valid in Moldova. Extra insurance can be bought at the borders.

TRAIN

From Chişinău, there are three daily trains to Lviv (Ukraine) and Moscow. Westbound, there are nightly trains to Romania and beyond.

There's an overnight service between Bucharest and Chişinău; at 12 hours, the journey is longer than taking a bus or maxitaxi (the train heads north to Iaşi, then south again), but is more comfortable if you want to sleep. For more details, see p541.

GETTING AROUND

Bicycle

Moldova is mostly flat, making cycling an excellent way of getting around. That is, it would be if it weren't for the bad condition of most of the roads, and for the lack of infrastructure – outside of Chişinău, you'll have to rely on your own resources or sense of adventure (and trying to enlist help from friendly locals) if you run into mechanical trouble.

Bus & Maxitaxi

Moldova has a good network of buses running to most towns and villages. Maxitaxis, which follow the same routes as the buses, are quicker and more reliable.

Car & Motorcycle

In Chişinău, travel agencies can arrange car hire or try Loran Car Rental (see p541).

Be wary, however, as the roads are in poor condition. EU and US driving licences are accepted here; otherwise, bring both your home country's driving licence and your International Driving Permit (IDP), which is recognised in Moldova.

The intercity speed limit is 90km/h and in built-up areas 60km/h; the legal blood alcohol limit is 0.03%. For road rescue, dial ☎ 901. The **Automobile Club Moldova** (ACM; ☎ 22-292 703; www.acm.md) can inform you of all regulations and offer emergency assistance (this is a members-only service).

Local Transport

In Moldova, buses cost about 2 lei, trolley-buses 1 leu and city maxitaxis 3 lei.

Taxi

In Moldova, there are official (and unofficial) taxis, often without meters, both of which may try to rip you off. It's best to call a taxi. A taxi ride to anywhere inside Chişinău is unlikely to cost more than 64 lei. You should agree upon a price before getting in the car.

Montenegro
Црна Гора

Imagine a place with sapphire beaches as spectacular as Croatia's, rugged peaks as dramatic as Switzerland's, canyons nearly as deep as Colorado's, *palazzi* as elegant as Venice's and towns as old as Greece's and then wrap it up in a Mediterranean climate and squish it into an area two-thirds the size of Wales and you start to get a picture of Montenegro.

Going it alone is a brave move for a nation of this size – its entire population of 678,000 would barely fill a medium-sized city – but toughing it out is something these gutsy people have had plenty of experience in. Their national identity is built around resisting the Ottoman Empire for hundreds of years in a mountainous enclave much smaller than the current borders.

Given its natural assets, tourism is vitally important to Montenegro's future. In that respect it's done spectacularly well filling its tiny coast with Eastern European sunseekers for two months of each year, while serving up the rest of the country as bite-sized day trips. The upshot for intrepid travellers is that you can easily sidestep the hordes in the rugged mountains of Durmitor, the primeval forest of Biogradska Gora National Park or in the many towns and villages where ordinary Montenegrins go about their daily lives. This is, after all, a country where wolves and bears still lurk in forgotten corners.

Montenegro, Crna Gora, Black Mountain: the name itself conjures up romance and drama. There are plenty of both on offer as you explore this perfumed land, bathed in the scent of wild herbs, conifers and Mediterranean blossoms. Yes, it really is as magical as it sounds.

MONTENEGRO

FAST FACTS

- **Area** 13,812 sq km
- **Capital** Podgorica
- **Currency** euro (€); US$1 = €0.73; UK£1 = €1.06; A$1 = €0.50; ¥100 = €0.76; NZ$1 = €0.41
- **Famous for** being really beautiful
- **Key phrases** *zdravo* (hello); *doviđenja* (goodbye); *hvala* (thanks)
- **Official language** Montenegrin
- **Population** 678,000
- **Telephone codes** ☎ 382; international access code ☎ 00
- **Visas** not required by Australian, British, Canadian, New Zealand, US or most EU citizens; see p579

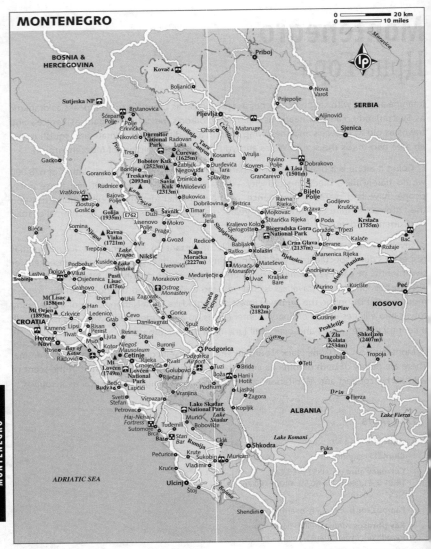

MONTENEGRO

HIGHLIGHTS

- Marvel at the majesty of the **Bay of Kotor** (p561) and explore the historic towns hemmed in by the region's limestone cliffs.
- Drive the vertiginous route from Kotor to the Njegoš Mausoleum at the top of **Lovćen National Park** (p570).

- Enjoy the iconic island views while lazing on the uncrowded sands of **Sveti Stefan** (p567).
- Seek the spiritual at peaceful **Ostrog Monastery** (p575).
- Float through paradise, rafting between the kilometre-plus-high walls of the **Tara River** (p576).

HOW MUCH?

- **Bottle of Vranac (local red wine) from market** €2.50
- **Internet access** per hour €1
- **Cup of coffee** €1
- **Short taxi ride** €5
- **Postcard** €0.50

LONELY PLANET INDEX

- **1L petrol** €0.99
- **1L bottled water** €1
- **500mL beer** €1.50
- **Souvenir T-shirt** €12
- **Street snack (burek)** €1

ITINERARIES

- **One week** Base yourself in the Bay of Kotor for two nights. Drive through Lovćen to Cetinje, then the next day continue to Šćepan Polje via Ostrog Monastery. Go rafting the following morning and spend the night in Podgorica. Head to Virpazar for a boat tour of Lake Skadar and then take the scenic lakeside road to Ulcinj. Finish in Sveti Stefan.

- **Two weeks** Follow the itinerary above, but allow extra time in Kotor, Lake Skadar and Sveti Stefan. From Šćepan Polje head instead to Žabljak and then Biogradska Gora National Park before continuing to Podgorica.

CLIMATE & WHEN TO GO

Like most of the Mediterranean, the coast enjoys balmy summers and mild winters. The warmest months are July and August, when the temperature ranges from 19°C to 29°C (average lowest to average highest), while the coldest is January (4°C to 12°C).

You're best to avoid the height of the tourist season in July and August and aim instead for May, June, September and October. You'll still get plenty of sunshine and an average water temperature over 20°C. The ski season is roughly from December to March.

HISTORY
Before the Slavs

Historians record the Illyrians inhabiting the region by 1000 BC, establishing a loose federation of tribes across much of the Balkans. By around 400 BC the Greeks had established some coastal colonies and by AD 10 the Romans had absorbed the entire region into their empire. In 395 the Roman Empire was split into two halves, the Western half retaining Rome as capital, the Eastern half, which eventually became the Byzantine Empire, centred on Constantinople. Modern Montenegro lay on the fault line between the two entities.

In the early 7th century, the Slavs arrived from north of the Danube. Two main Slavic groups settled in the Balkans: the Croats along the Adriatic coast and the Serbs in the interior. With time most Serbs accepted the Orthodox faith, while the Croats accepted Catholicism.

First Kingdoms

In the 9th century the first Serb kingdom, Raška, arose near Novi Pazar (in modern Serbia) followed shortly by another Serb state, Duklja, which sprang up on the site of the Roman town of Doclea (present-day Podgorica). Initially allied with Byzantium, Duklja eventually shook off Byzantine influence and began to expand. Over time Duklja came to be known as Zeta, but from 1160 Raška again became the dominant Serb entity. At its greatest extent it reached from

MONTENEGRO

CONNECTIONS: MOVING ON FROM MONTENEGRO

Many travellers make the most of the proximity of Dubrovnik's Čilipi airport to Herceg Novi to tie in a visit to Croatia with a Montenegrin sojourn. At the other end of the coast, Ulcinj is the perfect primer for exploring Albania and is connected by bus to Shkodra. Likewise, Rožaje both captures elements of Kosovar culture and is well connected to Peć. A train line and frequent bus connections make a trip to Montenegro's closest cousins in Serbia a breeze. Montenegro shares a longer border with Bosnia and Hercegovina (BiH) than any of its neighbours. There are plenty of crossings for drivers, as well as regular bus services from towns.

Towns with onward international transport include Herceg Novi (p562), Kotor (p565), Bar (p569), Ulcinj (p570), and Podgorica (p574).

the Adriatic to the Aegean and north to the Danube.

Expansion was halted in 1389 at the battle of Kosovo Polje, where the Serbs were defeated by the Ottoman Turks. Thereafter the Turks swallowed up the Balkans and the Serb nobility fled to Zeta, on Lake Skadar. When they were forced out of Zeta by the Ottomans in 1480 they established a stronghold and built a monastery at Cetinje on the foothills of Mt Lovćen.

Montenegro & the Ottomans

This mountainous area became the last redoubt of Serbian Orthodox culture when all else fell to the Ottomans. It was during this time that the Venetians, who ruled Kotor, Budva and much of the Adriatic Coast, began calling Mt Lovćen the Monte Negro (Black Mountain) which lends its name to the modern state. Over time the Montenegrins established a reputation as fierce and fearsome warriors. The Ottomans opted for pragmatism, and largely left them to their own devices.

With the struggle against the Ottomans, the previously highly independent tribes began to work collaboratively by the 1600s. This further developed a sense of shared Montenegrin identity and the *vladika*, previously a metropolitan position within the Orthodox Church, began mediating between tribal chiefs. As such, the *vladika* assumed a political role, and *vladika* became a hereditary title: the prince-bishop.

While Serbia remained under Ottoman control, in the late 18th century the Montenegrins under *vladika* Petar I Petrović began to expand their territory, doubling it within the space of a little over 50 years.

A rebellion against Ottoman control broke out in Bosnia and Hercegovina (BiH) in 1875. Montenegrins joined the insurgency and made significant territorial gains as a result. At the Congress of Berlin in 1878 Montenegro and Bosnia officially achieved independence.

In the early years of the 20th century there were increasing calls for union with Serbia and rising political opposition to the ruling Petrović dynasty. The Serbian king Petar Karadjordjević attempted to overthrow King Nikola Petrović and Montenegrin-Serbian relations reached their historical low point.

The Balkans Wars of 1912–3 saw the Montenegrins joining the Serbs, Greeks and Bulgarians and succeeded in throwing the Ottomans out of southeastern Europe. Now that Serbia and Montenegro were both independent and finally shared a border, the idea of a Serbian-Montenegrin union gained more currency. King Nikola pragmatically supported the idea on the stipulation that both the Serbian and Montenegrin royal houses be retained.

The Two Yugoslavias

Before the union could be realised WWI intervened. The Serbs quickly entered the war and the Montenegrins followed in their footsteps. Austria-Hungary invaded Serbia shortly afterwards and swiftly captured Cetinje, sending King Nikola into exile in France. In 1918 the Serbian army reclaimed Montenegro, and the French, keen to implement the Serbian-Montenegrin union, refused to allow Nikola to leave France. The following year Montenegro was incorporated in the Kingdom of the Serbs, Croats and Slovenes, the First Yugoslavia.

Throughout the 1920s some Montenegrins put up spirited resistance to the union with Serbia. This resentment was increased by the abolition of the Montenegrin church, which was absorbed by the Serbian Orthodox Patriarchate.

During WWII the Italians occupied the Balkans. Tito's Partisans and the Serbian Chetniks engaged the Italians, sometimes lapsing into fighting each other. Ultimately, the Partisans put up the best fight and with the diplomatic and military support of the Allies, the Partisans entered Belgrade in October 1944 and Tito was made prime minister. Once the Communist federation of Yugoslavia was established, Tito decreed that Montenegro have full republic status and the border of the modern Montenegrin state was set. Of all the Yugoslav states, Montenegro had the highest per-capita membership of the Communist party and it was highly represented in the armed forces.

The Union & Independence

In the decades following Tito's death in 1980, Slobodan Milošević used the issue of Kosovo to whip up a nationalist storm in Serbia and ride to power on a wave of nationalism. The Montenegrins largely supported their Orthodox co-religionists. In 1991 Montenegrin paramilitary groups were responsible for the shelling of Dubrovnik and parts of the Dalmatian littoral. In 1992, by which point Slovenia, Croatia and BiH had opted for independence, the Montenegrins voted overwhelmingly in support of a plebiscite to remain in Yugoslavia with Serbia.

In 1997 Montenegrin leader Milo Djukanović broke with an increasingly isolated Milošević and immediately became the darling of the West. As the Serbian regime became an international pariah, the Montenegrins increasingly wanted to re-establish their distinct identity.

In 2000 Milošević lost the election in Serbia. Meanwhile Vojislav Koštunica came to power in Montenegro. With Milošević now toppled, Koštunica was pressured to vote for a Union of Serbia and Montenegro. In theory this union was based on equality between the two republics, however in practice Serbia was such a dominant partner that the union proved unfeasible from the outset. In May 2006 the Montenegrins voted for independence. Since then the divorce of Serbia and Montenegro has proceeded relatively smoothly. Montenegro has rapidly opened up to the West, in particular welcoming many holidaymakers, and has instituted economic, legal and environmental reforms with a view to becoming a member of the EU.

PEOPLE

In the last census (2003) 43% of the population identified as Montenegrin, 32% as Serb, 8% as Bosniak (with a further 4% identifying as Muslim), 5% as Albanian, 1% as Croat and 0.4% as Roma. Montenegrins are the majority along most of the coast and the centre of the country, while Albanians dominate in the southeast (around Ulcinj), Bosniaks in the far east (Rožaje and Plav), and Serbs in the north and Herceg Novi.

To get an idea of the population shifts caused by the recent wars you need only look at the changes since the 1981 census, when Montenegrins made up 69% of the population and Serbs only 3%.

RELIGION

Religion and ethnicity broadly go together in these parts. Over 74% of the population is Orthodox (mainly Montenegrins and Serbs), 18% Muslim (mainly Bosniaks and Albanians) and 4% Roman Catholic (mainly Albanians and Croats).

In 1993 the Montenegrin Orthodox Church (MOC) was formed, claiming to revive the autocephalous church of Montenegro's bishop-princes that was dissolved in 1920 following the formation of the Kingdom of Serbs, Croats and Slovenes in 1918. The Serbian Orthodox Church (SOC) doesn't recognise the MOC and still control most of the country's churches and monasteries.

ARTS

Montenegro's visual arts can be divided into two broad strands: religious iconography and Yugoslav-era painting and sculpture. The nation's churches are full of wonderful frescos and painted iconostases (the screen that separates the congregation from the sanctuary in Orthodox churches). Of the modern painters, an early great was Petar Lubarda (1907–1974), whose stylised oil paintings included themes from Montenegrin history.

Towering over Montenegrin literature is Petar II Petrović Njegoš (1813–51); towering so much, in fact, that his mausoleum overlooks the country from the top of the black mountain itself. This poet–prince-bishop, produced the country's most enduring work of literature *Gorski vijenac (The Mountain Wreath)*, a verse play romanticising the brutal struggle with the Ottomans.

Archbishop Jovan of Duklja was producing religious chants in the 10th century, making him the earliest known composer in the region. Traditional instruments include the flute and the one-stringed *gusle,* which is used to accompany epic poetry.

The unusual *oro* is a circle dance accompanied by the singing of the participants as they tease each other and take turns to enter the circle and perform a stylised eagle dance. For a dramatic conclusion, the strapping lads form a two-storey circle, standing on each other's shoulders.

ENVIRONMENT
The Land

Montenegro is comprised of a thin strip of Adriatic coast, a fertile plain around Podgorica and a whole lot of mountains. The highest peak is Kolac (2534m) in the Prokletije range near the Albanian border. Most of the mountains are limestone and karstic in nature and they shelter large swathes of forest and glacial lakes. Rivers such as the Tara, Piva and Morača have cut deep canyons through them.

MONTENEGRO

The oddly shaped Bay of Kotor is technically a drowned river canyon although it's popularly described as a fjord. Lake Skadar, the largest in the Balkans, spans Montenegro and Albania in the southeast.

Wildlife

Among the mammals that live in Montenegro are otters, badgers, roe deer, chamois, foxes, weasels, moles, groundhogs and hares. Bears, wolves, lynxes and jackals are a much rarer sight. Tortoises, lizards and snakes are easier to find and you might spot golden and imperial eagles, white-headed vultures and peregrine falcons above the peaks. The rare Dalmatian pelican nests around Lake Skadar, along with pygmy cormorants, yellow heron and whiskered tern.

National Parks

Sometime during the lifetime of this book it's possible that Montenegro will declare a section of the Prokletije Mountains bordering Albania its fifth national park, joining Lovćen, Durmitor, Biogradska Gora and Lake Skadar. The current parks cover an area of 90,870 hectares.

Environmental Issues

For a new country, especially one recovering from a recent war, Montenegro has made some key moves to safeguard the environment, not the least declaring itself an 'ecological state' in its constitution. Yet in the rush to get bums on beaches, the preservation of the nation's greatest selling point sometimes plays second fiddle to development.

Water shortages continue to affect the coast and in 2008 high salinity levels rendered Tivat's supply undrinkable. A new desalination plant has been constructed near Budva but these operations are notoriously energy intensive.

The country currently imports 40% of its electricity and ideas mooted for increasing supply have included new hydro projects, requiring the flooding of river canyons, or potentially nuclear energy.

There's little awareness of litter as a problem. It's not just the ubiquitous practice of throwing rubbish out of car windows; we've seen waitresses clear tables by throwing refuse straight into a river and we've heard reports of train employees doing the same. Along the coast, fly-tipping of rubble from building sites is a problem. On an encouraging note, recycling is being trialled in Herceg Novi.

FOOD & DRINK

Loosen your belt, you're in for a treat. Eating in Montenegro is generally an extremely pleasurable experience. By default, most of the food is local, fresh and organic, and hence very seasonal. The only downside is a lack of variety. By the time you've been here a week, menu déjà vu is likely to have set in.

The food on the coast is virtually indistinguishable from Dalmatian cuisine: lots of grilled seafood, garlic, olive oil and Italian dishes. Inland it's much more meaty and Serbian-influenced.

Staples & Specialities

The village of Njeguši in the Montenegrin heartland is famous for its *pršut* (dried ham) and cheese. Anything with Njeguški in its name is going to be a true Montenegrin dish and stuffed with these goodies.

In the mountains, meat roasted *ispod sača* (under a metal lid covered with hot coals) comes out deliciously tender. Lamb is also slowly cooked in milk. You might eat it with *kačamak,* a cheesy, creamy cornmeal or buckwheat dish – heavy going but comforting on those long winter nights.

On the coast, be sure to try the fish soup, grilled squid (served plain or stuffed with *pršut* and cheese) and black risotto (made from squid ink). Whole fish are often presented to the table for you to choose from and are sold by the kilogram.

Montenegro's domestic wine is eminently drinkable and usually the cheapest thing on the menu. Vranac and Krstač are the indigenous red and white grapes, respectively. Nikšićko Pivo (try saying that after a few) is the local beer and a good thirst-quencher. Many people distil their own *rakija* (brandy), made out of just about anything (grapes, pears, apples etc). They all come out tasting like rocket fuel, although the plum variety (*šljivovica*) is the most lethal.

The coffee is universally excellent. In private houses it's generally served Turkish-style, 'black as hell, strong as death and sweet as love'.

Where to Eat & Drink

Fast-food outlets and bakeries (*pekara*), serving *burek* (meat- or spinach-filled pastries), pizza slices and *palačinke* (pancakes), are easy to find. Anywhere that attracts tourists will have a selection of restaurants and *konoba* (small family-run affairs). There is generally no distinction between a cafe and bar. Restaurants open at around 8am and close around midnight, while cafe-bars may stay open until 2am or 3am.

Nonsmoking sections are a rumour from distant lands that have yet to trouble the citizens of Montenegro.

Vegetarians & Vegans
Eating in Montenegro can be a trial for vegetarians and almost impossible for vegans. Pasta, pizza and salad are the best options.

Habits & Customs
Lunch has traditionally been the main family meal but with Western working hours catching on, this is changing. Bread is served free of charge with most meals.

BAY OF KOTOR

Coming from Croatia, the Bay of Kotor (Boka Kotorska) starts simply enough, but as you progress through fold upon fold of the bay and the surrounding mountains get steeper and steeper, the beauty meter gets close to bursting. It's often described as Southern Europe's most spectacular fjord and even though the label's not technically correct, the sentiment certainly is.

HERCEG NOVI ХЕРЦЕГ НОВИ
☎ 031 / pop 12,700

It's easy to drive straight through Herceg Novi without noticing anything worth stopping for, especially if you've just come from Croatia with visions of Dubrovnik still dazzling your brain. However, just below the uninspiring roadside frontage hides an appealing Old Town with ancient walls, sunny squares and a lively at-

---

BAY OF KOTOR IN TWO DAYS

Drive around the Bay, stopping where the mood takes you. Start with breakfast in **Herceg Novi** (above), check out the mosaics in **Risan** (p563) and allow plenty of time to visit **Perast** (p563) and its islands. Stop for the night near **Kotor** (p563) and spend the next day exploring the **Stari Grad** (p563).

---

mosphere. The water's cleaner here near the mouth of the bay, so the pebbly beaches and concrete swimming terraces are popular.

Information
There's a cluster of banks with ATMs around Trg Nikola Đurkovića, while the main street Njegoševa has the post office and an internet cafe. The **tourist office** (☎ 350 820; www.hercegnovi .travel; Jova Dabovica 12; ☻ 8am-3pm Mon-Fri) is on the 1st floor above a house.

Sights
The big fort visible from the main road is the **Kanli-Kula** (Bloody Tower; admission €1; ☻ 8am-midnight), a notorious prison during Turkish rule (roughly 1482–1687). You can walk around its sturdy walls and enjoy views over the town. The bastion at the town's seaward edge, **Fortemare**, was rebuilt by the Venetians during their 110-year stint as overlords.

The elegant crenulated **clocktower**, built in 1667, was once the main city gate. Just inside the walls is Trg Herceg Stjepana (commonly called Belavista Sq), a gleaming white piazza that's perfect for relaxing, drinking and chatting in the shade. At its centre is the Orthodox **Archangel Michael's Church** (built 1883–1905), its lovely proportions capped by a dome and flanked by palm trees. Its Catholic counterpart, **St Jerome's** (1856), is further down the hill, dominating Trg Mića Pavlovića.

From its hillside location in the town's eastern fringes, **Savina Monastery** (☎ 345 300; Manastirska 21; ☻ 6am-8pm) enjoys wonderful coastal views. This peaceful complex is dominated by the elegant 18th-century Church of the Dormition, carved from pinkish stone. Inside there's a beautiful gilded iconostasis but you'll need to be demurely dressed to enter (no shorts, singlets or bikinis). The smaller church beside it has the same name but is considerably older (possibly from the 14th century) and has the remains of frescos. The monastery is well signposted from the highway.

Apart from the building itself (a fab bougainvillea-shrouded baroque palace with absolute sea views), the highlight of the **Regional Museum** (☎ 322 485; www.rastko.org .yu/rastko-bo/muzej; Mirka Komnenovića 9; admission €1.50; ☻ 9am-6pm Mon-Sat winter, 9am-8pm Tue-Sun summer) is its impressive icon gallery.

High above the town, on the other side of the main road, is the **Španjola fortress**, which was started and finished by the Turks but

MONTENEGRO

named after the Spanish (yep, in 1538 they had a brief stint here as well). If the graffiti and empty bottles are anything to go by, it's now regularly invaded by local teenagers.

Activities

Herceg Novi is shaping up as the best base for arranging active pursuits, largely due to a network of expats running professional, customer-focused, environmentally-aware businesses. A good place to start is **Black Mountain** (☎ 321 968; www.montenegroholiday.com; Šetalište Pet Danica 41), an agency that can arrange pretty much anything, including diving, rafting, hiking and paragliding. They offer mountain bike tours (about €20 per person), rent out bikes (€15 per day) and have a second office at the bus station.

Another excellent outfit run by British expats, **Kayak Montenegro** (☎ 067-887 436; www.kayakmontenegro.com; Šetalište Pet Danica bb; hire 1-/4-/8-hr €5/15/25) rents kayaks and offers paddling tours across the bay (€45, including equipment), as well as day trips to explore Lake Skadar from Rijeka Crnojevića (price on application). In October they work with Black Mountain to stage the **Adventure Race Montenegro** (p578).

From May to September **Diving Center Marina** (☎ 069-637 915; www.dcmarina.com) organises dives to about 20 sites in the vicinity of the bay and Budva, including various wrecks and caves. A two-dive trip costs €55 including tanks, weights and the boat trip.

Yachting Club 32 (☎ 069-333 011; Šetalište Pet Danica) offers parasailing (single/double €40/60 per 10 minutes) and hires jet skis (€50 per 20 minutes), paddleboats (per hour €8) and mountain bikes (hour/three hours/day €3/6/15).

Sleeping

In summer there are often people around the bus station touting private accommodation. Black Mountain (above) can fix you up with rooms starting from around €15 per person, although most of their apartments are at a higher level.

Hotel Perla (☎ 345 700; www.perla.cg.yu; Šetalište Pet Danica 98; s €61-104, d €76-130, tr €111-189, apt €140-210; 🖳) It's a fair stroll from the centre but if it's beach you're after, Perla's possie is perfect. The helpful staff speak excellent English and the front rooms of this medium-sized modern block have private terraces and sea views.

our pick **Hotel Aurora** (☎ 321 620; www.auroramontenegro.com; Šetalište Pet Danica 42; tw €70-100, d €80-100, tr €105-120; 🖳) You'd never suspect that this handsome stone building was once the railway station, especially given its prime waterfront location at the foot of the Old Town. Oscar-nominated filmmaker Emir Kusturica was behind its loving transformation into a chic and comfortable eight-room boutique hotel, hence the three tiny cinemas of the Aurora Artplex (admission €3) on the ground floor.

Eating & Drinking

If you want to take on the local women in a tussle for the best fresh fruit and vegetables, get to the **market** (Trg Nikole Đurkovića) by around 8am.

Konoba Hercegovina (☎ 322 800; Trg Nikole Đurkovića; mains €2-6) A firm favourite with the locals, this all-year-long eatery serves everything from burgers and *ćevapčići* to traditional meat and fish grills and more-exotic dishes like Hungarian goulash.

our pick **Portofino** (Trg Herceg Stjepana; breakfast €2.50-5, mains €6-16) Its blissful location in Herceg Novi's prettiest square makes it tempting to linger here all day, which is exactly what the town's expat community seems to do. The Italianate menu features creamy pastas and juicy steaks.

Konoba Feral (Šetalište Pet Danica 47; mains €7.50-15) Feral is a local word for a ship's lantern, so it's seafood (not wild cat) that takes pride of place on the menu. The grilled squid is amazing and comes with a massive serving of seasonal vegetables and salads.

Getting There & Around

BUS

At the time of research the **bus station** (☎ 321 225; Jadranska Put; 🕒 6am-9pm) was on the main highway above the centre, but there were plans to move international services to the western approach to town. Hopefully through-services will continue to stop at the old station. There are frequent buses to Kotor (€3.50, one hour), Budva (€5, 1¾ hours) and Podgorica (€9, three hours).

From Herceg Novi there are buses to Dubrovnik (€8, two hours, two daily), Sarajevo (€22, seven hours, four daily) and Belgrade (€30, 13 hours, nine daily).

CAR

A tortuous, often grid-locked, one-way system runs through the town, so you're best to park on the highway. If you're driving to Tivat or Budva it's usually quicker to take the **ferry**

MONTENEGRO

(car/motorcycle/passenger €4/1.50/free; 24hr) from Kamenari (15km northeast of Herceg Novi) to Lepetane (north of Tivat). Queues can be horrendously long in summer.

Budget (321 100; www.budget.com; Njegoševa 90) Rents cars from €68 for one day. If you need a taxi, call **Taxi More** (9730).

BOAT

Taxi boats ply the coast during summer, charging about €10 for a trip to the beaches on the Luštica Peninsula.

PERAST ПЕРАСТ

Looking like a chunk of Venice has floated down the Adriatic and anchored itself onto the bay, Perast's streets hum with melancholy memories of the days when it was rich and powerful. This tiny town boasts 16 churches and 17 formerly grand *palazzi*, one of which has been converted into **Perast Museum** (373 519; admission €2.50; 9am-6pm Mon-Sat, to 2pm Sun) and showcases the town's proud seafaring history.

The 55m belltower belongs to **St Nicholas' Church**, which also has a **museum** (admission €1; 10am-6pm) containing bits of saints and beautifully embroidered vestments.

Just offshore are two peculiarly picturesque islands. The smaller **Sv Đorđe** (St George's Island) rises from a natural reef and houses a Benedictine monastery shaded by cypresses. Its big sister, **Gospa od Škrpjela** (Our-Lady-of-the-Rock Island), was artificially created in the 15th century and every year on 22 July the locals row over with stones to continue the task. Its magnificent church was erected in 1630. Boats regularly ply to the islands for around €3.

Perast makes an atmospheric and peaceful base from which to explore the bay. Several houses rent rooms or you can try the **Hotel Conte** (032-373 687; www.hotel-conte .com; apt €90-250;), a series of delux studio to two-bedroom sea-view apartments in historic buildings scattered around St Nicholas' Church. It has wi-fi and its wonderful restaurant, **Conte Nautilus** (mains €6.50-14), serves fresh fish with lashings of romance on its waterside terrace.

Not far from Perast, **Risan** is the oldest town on the bay, dating to at least the 3rd century BC. Signposts point to some superb **Roman mosaics** (admission €2; 8am-8pm 15 May-15 Oct), discovered in 1930.

KOTOR КОТОР

032 / pop 13,500

Those prone to operatic outbursts may find themselves launching into Wagner at their first glimpse of this dramatically beautiful town. Its sturdy walls – started in the 9th century and tweaked until the 18th – arch steeply up the slopes behind it. From a distance they're barely discernable from the mountain's grey hide but at night they're spectacularly lit, reflecting in the water to give the town a golden halo. Within those walls lie labyrinthine marbled lanes, where churches, shops, bars and restaurants surprise you on hidden piazzas.

Orientation

Kotor's funnel-shaped Stari Grad (Old Town) sits between the bay and the lower slopes of Mt Lovćen. Newer suburbs surround the town, linking up to the old settlements of Dobrota to the north, Muo to the west and, beyond this, Prčanj. The main road to Tivat and Budva turns off the waterfront road at a baffling uncontrolled intersection south of the Stari Grad and heads through a long tunnel.

Information

You'll find a choice of banks with ATMs, an internet cafe called **Forza** (304 352; Trg od Oružja; 7am-midnight), and the post office on the main square, Trg od Oružja. There's a **tourist information booth** (325 950; www.kotor.travel; outside Vrata od Mora; 8am-8pm) just outside the main gate

Sights

The best thing to do in Kotor is to get lost and found again in the maze of streets. You'll

---

FREE THRILLS

Many of Montenegro's most memorable experiences can be had for free:

- Wander the marbled lanes of **Kotor's Stari Grad** (above).
- Take the **back road** (p565) from Kotor to Lovćen.
- Enjoy the iconic view of **Sveti Stefan** (p567) from the highway.
- Call into either of the Centre for Contemporary Art's two **Podgorica galleries** (p573).
- Visit **Ostrog Monastery** (p575).

MONTENEGRO

soon know every corner, as the town is quite small, but there's plenty of old churches to pop into and many coffees to be drunk in the shady squares.

Stepping through the main entrance, **Vrata od Mora** (Sea Gate, 1555), onto Trg od Oružja (Square of Arms) you'll see the strange stone pyramid in front of the **clock tower** (1602) that was once used as a pillory to shame wayward citizens.

Kotor has a proud history as a naval power and the **Maritime Museum** (☎ 069-045 447; Trg Bokeljske Mornarice, Stari Grad; admission €4 incl audioguide; ⏰ 8am-11pm Jul-Aug, 8am-7pm Mon-Sat & 9am-1pm Sun Apr-Jun & Sep, 8am-2pm Mon-Sat & 9am-1pm Sun Oct-Mar) celebrates it with three storeys of displays housed in a wonderful early 18th-century palace.

The town's most impressive building is the Catholic **St Tryphon Cathedral** (Trg Sv Tripuna, Stari Grad; admission €1.50; ⏰ 8.30am-7pm), originally built in the 12th century but reconstructed after several earthquakes. The Cathedral's gently hued interior is a masterpiece of Romanesque-Gothic architecture, with slender Corinthian columns alternating with

pillars of pink stone, thrusting upwards to support a series of vaulted roofs. Its gilded silver-relief altar screen is considered Kotor's most valuable treasure.

The energetic can make the 1200m ascent via 1350 steps up the **fortifications** (admission €2, charged May to Sep) for unforgettable views and a huge sense of achievement. There are entry points near the North Gate and Trg od Salata.

Sleeping

Although the Stari Grad is a charming place to stay, you'd better pack earplugs. In summer the bars blast music onto the streets until 1am every night and rubbish collectors clank around at 6am. Some of the best options are just out of Kotor in quieter Dobrota, Muo and Prčanj.

Enquire about private accommodation at the city's information booth (p563). **Meridian Travel Agency** (☎ 323 448; www.tameridian.cg.yu; ⏰ 9am-3pm & 6-9pm Mon-Sat), near Trg od Oružja, in the lane behind the clock tower, has rooms on their books at around €15 to €30 per person and can also book hotels.

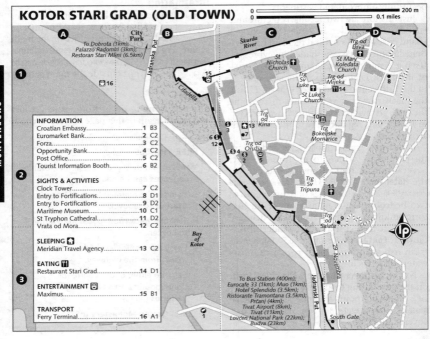

KOTOR STARI GRAD (OLD TOWN)

0 — 200 m
0 — 0.1 miles

INFORMATION
Croatian Embassy............................1 B3
Euromarket Bank.............................2 C2
Forza...3 C2
Opportunity Bank............................4 C2
Post Office.......................................5 C2
Tourist Information Booth...............6 B2

SIGHTS & ACTIVITIES
Clock Tower......................................7 C2
Entry to Fortifications......................8 D1
Entry to Fortifications......................9 D2
Maritime Museum...........................10 C1
St Tryphon Cathedral......................11 D2
Vrata od Mora..................................12 C2

SLEEPING 🛏
Meridian Travel Agency...................13 C2

EATING 🍴
Restaurant Stari Grad......................14 D1

ENTERTAINMENT 🎭
Maximus...15 B1

TRANSPORT
Ferry Terminal..................................16 A1

DETOUR: BACK ROAD TO MT LOVĆEN

Looming above Kotor is **Mt Lovćen**. The journey to this ancient core of the country is one of the world's great drives. Take the road heading towards the Tivat tunnel and turn right just past the graveyard (there's no sign). After 5km, follow the sign to Cetinje on your left opposite the fort. From here there's 17km of good but narrow road snaking up 25 hairpin turns, each one revealing a vista more spectacular than the last. Take your time and keep your wits about you; you'll need to pull over and be prepared to reverse if you meet oncoming traffic. From the top the views stretch over the entire bay to the Adriatic. At the entrance to Lovćen National Park you can continue straight ahead for the shortest route to Cetinje or turn right and continue on the scenic route through the park.

Eurocafe 33 (☎ 069-047 712; lemaja1@cg.yu; Muo 33; r €20-25 per person; ✴) On the Muo waterfront, this traditional stone building with a small private beach enjoys possibly the best views of Kotor. The top two floors have a scattering of differently configured rooms, some of which share bathrooms. The owner's an ex-footballer turned assistant coach for the national side and speaks excellent English. If there are a few of you, enquire about booking a floor.

ourpick Palazzo Radomiri (☎ 333 172; www.palaz zoradomiri.com; Dobrota; s €60-160, d €100-200, ste €60-280; ✴ 🖥) Exquisitely beautiful, this honey-coloured early 18th-century *palazzo* has been transformed into a first-rate boutique hotel. Some rooms are bigger and grander than others (hence the variation in prices), but all 10 have sea views and luxurious furnishings. Guests can avail themselves of a small workout area, sauna, pool, private jetty, bar and restaurant; half-board is included in the summer prices and wi-fi is available.

Hotel Splendido (☎ 301 700; www.splendido-hotel .com; Prčanj; s €65-116, d €93-166, apt €119-199; ✴ 🖥 🖥) Negotiating the 4km drive along the narrow waterfront road from Kotor can be stressful, but aside from that Splendido is magnifico. Completely gutted and fitted with comfortable modern rooms, this large stone *palazzo* still surveys the bay as solidly as it's ever done, although there's now a blissful terrace and swimming pool separating it from the water's edge. Wi-fi is available.

Eating & Drinking

There are tons of small bakeries and takeaway joints on the streets of Kotor.

This town is full of cafe-bars that spill into the squares and are abuzz with conversation during the day. All chitchat stops abruptly in the evening, when speakers are dragged out onto the ancient lanes and the techno cranked up to near ear-bleeding volumes.

ourpick Ristorante Tramontana (☎ 301 700; Prčanj; mains €4-16) It's hard to top the romantic setting of this Italian restaurant on the terrace of the Hotel Splendido. The food is equally memorable, from sublime pasta to perfectly tender grilled squid.

Restaurant Stari Grad (☎ 322 025; Trg od Mlijeka; mains €8-18) Head straight through to the stone-walled courtyard, grab a seat under the vines and prepare to get absolutely stuffed full of fabulous food – the serves are huge. Either point out the fish that takes your fancy or order from the traditional à la carte menu.

Restoran Stari Mlini (☎ 333 555; Jadranska Put, Ljuta; meals €11-21) It's well worth making the 7km trip to Ljuta for this magical restaurant set in and around an old mill by the edge of the bay. If you've got time to spare and don't mind picking out bones, order the Dalmatian fish stew with polenta for two. The steaks are also excellent, as are the bread, wine and service.

Entertainment

Maximus (☎ 334 342; admission €2-5; ⊙ 11pm-5am Thu-Sat, nightly summer) Montenegro's most pumping club comes into its own in summer, hosting big name international DJs and local starlets.

Getting There & Away

The **bus station** (☎ 325 809, ⊙ 6am-9pm) is to the south of town, just off the road leading to the Tivat tunnel. Buses to Herceg Novi (€3.50, one hour), Budva (€3, 40 minutes) and Podgorica (€7, two hours) are at least hourly.

A taxi to Tivat airport costs around €8.

Azzurra Lines (www.azzurraline.com) ferries connect Kotor and Bar with Bari, Italy (€65, nine hours, weekly in summer).

MONTENEGRO

TIVAT ТИВАТ
☎ 032 / pop 9,450

Big things are planned for this town, which is not a bad thing, as Tivat doesn't have a lot to lose from development. At present it's the airport that's the drawcard, although there are a lot of sweet villages and beaches to explore on the coast between here and Kotor and on the Luština Peninsula. The helpful **tourist office** (☎ 671 324; www.tivat.travel; Palih Boraca 8; ☽ 8am-3pm Mon-Sat, to 2pm Sun) can point you in the direction of some terrific walks.

If you've got an early flight, the **Hotel Villa Royal** (☎ 675 310; www.hotelvillaroyal.cg.yu; Kalimanj bb; s €42-65, d €68-102, apt €102-141; ☒ ☐) is a bright modern block with clean rooms and friendly staff.

From the **bus station** (Palih Boraca bb) there are frequent buses to Budva (€2) via the airport (€0.50), as well as services to Kotor (€1, six daily) and Herceg Novi (€3, seven daily).

Tivat Airport is 3km south of town and 8km through the tunnel from Kotor. Airport minibuses leave when full and head to Budva (€3.50) and Herceg Novi (€8).

ADRIATIC COAST

Much of Montenegro's determination to re-invent itself as a tourist mecca has focused on this gorgeous stretch of beaches. In July and August it seems that the entire Serbian world and a fair chunk of its Orthodox brethren can be found crammed onto this less-than-100km-long stretch of coast. Avoid these months and you'll find a charismatic set of small towns and fishing villages to explore, set against clear Adriatic waters and Montenegro's mountainous backdrop.

BUDVA БУДВА
☎ 033 / pop 10,100

The poster child of Montenegrin tourism, Budva – with its atmospheric Old Town and numerous beaches – certainly has a lot to offer. Yet the child has quickly moved into a difficult adolescence, fuelled by rampant development that has leeched much of the charm from the place. In the height of the season the sands are blanketed with package holidaymakers from Russia and the Ukraine, while by night you'll run the gauntlet of glorified strippers attempting to cajole you into the beachside bars.

It's the buzziest place on the coast so if you're in the mood to party, bodacious Budva will be your best buddy.

Orientation & Information

Apart from the Old Town, hardly any streets have names and even fewer have signs. The main beachside promenade is pedestrianised Slovenska Obala, which in summer is lined with fast-food outlets, beach bars, travel agencies hawking tours, internet cafes and a fun park. The post office and a cluster of banks are on and around ulica Mediteranska. The **tourist office** (☎ 452 750; Njegoševa bb, Stari Grad; ☽ 9am-9pm May-Oct) has brochures on sights and accommodation.

Sights & Activities

Budva's best feature and star attraction is the Stari Grad – a mini Dubrovnik with marbled streets and Venetian walls rising from the clear waters below. Much of it was ruined in two earthquakes in 1979 but it has since been completely rebuilt and now houses more shops, bars and restaurants than residences. At its seaward end, the **Citadel** (admission €2; ☽ 8am-midnight May-Nov) offers striking views, a small museum and a library full of rare tomes and maps. In the square in front of the citadel are a cluster of interesting churches. Nearby is the **entry to the town walls** (admission €1; ☽ 9am-5pm Mon-Sat).

The **Archaeological Museum** (☎ 453 308; Petra I Petrovića 11, Stari Grad; adult/child €2/1; ☽ 9am-10pm) shows off the town's ancient and complicated history – dating back to at least 500 BC – over three floors of exhibits. Also in the Old Town is the **Museum of Modern Art** (☎ 451 343; Cara Dušana 19; admission free; ☽ 8am-2pm & 5-8pm), an attractive gallery staging temporary exhibitions.

The **Montenegro Adventure Centre** (☎ 067-580 664; www.montenegrofly.com; Lapčići) offers plenty of action from its perch high above Budva. Rafting, hiking, mountain biking, diving and accommodation can all be arranged, as well as paragliding from launch sites around the country. An unforgettable tandem flight landing 750m below at Bečići beach costs €65.

Sleeping & Eating

The tourist office (above) produces an excellent hotel directory and private accommodation booklet.

Hotel Kangaroo (☎ 458 653; www.kangaroo.cg.yu; Velji Vinogradi bb; s €29-69, d €39-69, tr €59-104; ☒ ☐)

Bounce into a large clean room with a desk, terrace and excellent bathroom at this mid-sized hotel that's a hop, skip and jump from the beach and has wi-fi. The owners once lived in Perth, hence the name and the large mural of Captain Cook's *Endeavour* in the popular restaurant below.

Hotel Astoria (☎ 451 110; www.hotelastoria.cg.yu; Njegoševa 4; s €130-190, d €170-230, ste €180-380; 🔀 🖳) Water shimmers down the corridor wall as you enter this chic boutique hotel hidden in the Old Town's fortifications. The rooms are on the small side but they're beautifully furnished; the seaview suite is spectacular. The wonderful guest-only roof terrace is Budva's most magnificent dining area.

Knez Konoba (Mitrov Ljubiše bb; mains €9-15) Hidden within Stari Grad's tiny lanes this atmospheric eatery only sports two outdoor tables and a handful inside. Try the black risotto – it's more expensive than most (€10) but they present it beautifully, with slices of lemon and orange, along with tomato, cucumber and olives.

Getting There & Away

The **bus station** (☎ 456 000; Ivana Milutinovića bb) has regular services to Herceg Novi (€5, 1¾ hours), Kotor (€3, 40 minutes) and Cetinje (€3, 40 minutes). **Meridian Rentacar** (☎ 454 105; www.meridian-rentacar.com; Mediteranski Sportski Centar) is opposite the bus station.

You can flag down the Olimpia Express (€1.50) from the bus stops on Jadranska Put to head to Bečići (five minutes) or Sveti Stefan (20 minutes). They depart every 30 minutes in summer and hourly in winter.

SVETI STEFAN СВЕТИ СТЕФАН
☎ 033

Impossibly picturesque Sveti Stefan, 5km south of Budva, provides the biggest 'wow' moment on the entire coast. From the 15th century to the 1950s this tiny island – connected to the shore by a narrow isthmus and crammed full of terracotta-roofed dwellings – housed a simple fishing community. That was until someone had the idea to nationalise it and turn it into a luxury hotel. Until the wars of the 1990s it was a big hit with both Hollywood and European royalty.

Over the last few years tradesmen have replaced screen goddesses on its exclusive streets, but the resort will reopen during the lifetime of this book. When it does, it's likely that a day

rate will once again be charged for mere mortals to wander around. In the meantime, make the most of the lovely beaches facing the island while they're comparatively uncrowded.

Sveti Stefan is also the name of the new township that's sprung up onshore. From its slopes you get to look down at that iconic view all day – which some might suggest is even better than staying in the surreal enclave below.

From the beach there's a very pleasant walk north to the cute village of **Pržno** where there are some excellent restaurants and another attractive beach.

Sleeping & Eating

Levantin Travel Agency (☎ 468 206; www.geocities.com /levantin88/levantin; Vukice Mitrović 3) Not only does the charming, helpful owner bear a striking likeness to Michael Palin in the *Life of Brian*, he can sort you out with private accommodation, apartments and other travel arrangements.

our pick **Vila Drago** (☎ 468 477; www.viladrago.com; Slobode 32; d €34-68, tr €58-100, apt €103-170; 🔀) The only problem with this place is that you may never want to leave your terrace, as the views are so sublime. The supercomfy pillows and fully stocked bathrooms are a nice touch, especially at this price. Watch the sunset over the island from the grapevine-covered terrace restaurant (mains €4 to €11) and enjoy specialities from the local Paštrovići clan, like roast suckling pig (€15 per kilogram).

Getting There & Away

Olimpia Express buses head to and from Budva (€1.50, 20 minutes) every 30 minutes in summer and hourly in winter, stopping on Ulica Slobode near the Vila Drago.

PETROVAC ПЕТРОВАЦ
☎ 033

The Romans had the right idea, building their summer villas on this lovely bay. The pretty beachside promenade is perfumed with the scent of lush Mediterranean plants and a picturesque 16th-century **Venetian fortress** guards a tiny stone harbour. This is one of the best places on the coast for families: the accommodation is reasonably priced, the water's clear and kids roam the esplanade at night with impunity.

In July and August you'll be lucky to find an inch of space on the town beach but wander south and there's cypress and oleander-lined

---

TAKING THE BAR EXAM

One of the legacies of the former Yugoslavia's communist years is a rigorous education system. We asked English teacher Daniela Đuranović to teach us a thing or two about her home town and country.

Where's a good place to begin? First swim in the sea. Bar's most beautiful beaches are a little out of town. For me, Montenegro's best beach is Pržno, near Sveti Stefan.

What else shouldn't be missed? You must visit the mountains. They're beautiful in summer but I like them at winter covered in snow. I don't ski, though. I just drink coffee and tea and enjoy the nature.

You seem to have a good life here. I see TV programs about Provence (France), talking about the nature, the cheese, the produce. I can eat that food every day. In summer I have everything I need right here.

Lučice Beach and beyond it the 2.5km-long sweep of **Bulgarica Beach**.

Sleeping & Eating
Mornar Travel Agency (☎ 033-461 410; www.mornar -travel.com; ☽ 8am-8pm summer, to 2pm winter) An excellent local agency offering private accommodation from €23 per person.

Hotel W Grand (☎ 033-461 703; www.wgrandpetrovac .com; s €41-71, d €54-94, tr €81-141; P ☒ ☐) The colour scheme simulates the effect of waking up inside an egg-yolk but this modern mid-sized hotel has roomy rooms with comfy beds and puts on a brilliant breakfast buffet on its view-hungry terrace. Wi-fi is available too.

Konoba Bonaca (☎ 069-084 735; mains €8-15) Set back slightly from the main beach drag, this traditional restaurant focuses mainly on seafood but the local cheeses and olives are also excellent. Grab a table under the grapevines on the terrace and gaze out to sea.

Getting There & Away
Petrovac's **bus station** (☎ 068-838 184) is near the top of town. Regular services head to Budva and Bar (both €2, 30 minutes).

BAR БАР
☎ 030 / pop 13,800
Dominated by Montenegro's main port and a large industrial area, Bar is unlikely to be anyone's highlight, but it is a handy transport hub welcoming trains from Belgrade and ferries from Italy. More interesting are the ruins of Stari Bar (Old Bar) in the mountains behind.

Orientation & Information
Bar's centre is immediately east of the marina and ferry terminal. Beaches stretch north from here, while the port and industrial area are to the south. There are several banks with ATMs around ulica Maršala Tita and ulica Vladimira Rolovića.

Accident & Emergency Clinic (☎ 124; Jovana Tomeševića 42)

Post office (☎ 301 300; Jovana Tomeševića bb)

Tourist information centre (☎ 311 633; Obala 13 Jula bb; ☽ 7am-9pm Jul & Aug, to 2pm Mon-Fri Sep-Jun) Helpful staff with good English; stocks useful brochures listing sights and private accommodation.

Sights
Presenting an elegant facade to the water, **King Nikola's Palace** (☎ 314 079; Šetalište Kralje Nikole; admission €1; ☽ 8am-3pm) has been converted into a museum housing a collection of antiquities, folk costumes and royal furniture. Its shady gardens contain plants cultivated from seeds and cuttings collected from around the world by Montenegro's sailors.

Impressive **Stari Bar** (adult/child €1/0.50; ☽ 8am-8pm), Bar's original settlement, stands on a bluff 4km northeast off the Ulcinj road. A steep cobbled hill takes you past a cluster of old houses and shops to the fortified entrance where a short dark passage pops you out into a large expanse of vine-clad ruins and abandoned streets overgrown with grass and wild flowers. A small **museum** just inside the entrance explains the site and its history. The Illyrians founded the city in around 800 BC. It passed in and out of Slavic and Byzantine rule until the Venetians took it in 1443 and held it until it was taken by the Ottomans in 1571. Nearly all the 240 buildings now lie in ruins, a result of Montenegrin shelling, when the town was captured in 1878.

Buses marked Stari Bar depart from the centre of new Bar every hour (€1).

Sleeping & Eating

Hotel Princess (☎ 300 100; www.hotelprincess-monten egro.com; Jovana Tomaševića 59; s €80-140, d €100-200, apt €150-450; ✖ ▢ ▣) It's pricey and generic but this resort-style hotel is the only decent option in town. Make the most of your money at the private beach, swimming pool and spa centre. Wi-fi available.

Konoba Spilja (☎ 340 353; Stari Bar bb; mains €3-15) So rustic you wouldn't be surprised if a goat wandered through, this is a terrific spot for a traditional meal after exploring Stari Bar.

Getting There & Away

The **bus station** (☎ 346 141) and adjacent **train station** (☎ 301 622; www.zeljeznica.cg.yu) are 1km southeast of the centre. Destinations include Podgorica (€5, seven daily) and Ulcinj (€2.50, six daily). Trains to Podgorica (€3, one hour, 14 daily) also stop at Virpazar (€2).

Montenegro Line (www.montenegrolines.net) ferries to Bari (€60, nine hours, three weekly) and Ancona (€71, 11 hours, twice weekly in summer) in Italy, and **Azzurra Lines** (www.azzurraline .com) ferries to Bari (€65, nine hours, weekly in summer) leave from the **ferry terminal** (Obala 13 Jula bb) near the centre. You can book your Montenegro Lines ferry tickets here and there's a post office and ATM. Azzura Line can be booked at **Mercur** (☎ 313 617; Vladimir Rolovića bb).

ULCINJ УЛЦИНЬ
☎ 030 / 10,850

If you want a feel for Albania without actually crossing the border, buzzy Ulcinj's the place to go. The population is 72% Albanian and in summer it swells with Kosovar holidaymakers for the simple reason that it's a hell of a lot nicer than any of the Albanian seaside towns. The elegant minarets of numerous mosques give Ulcinj a distinctly Eastern feel, as does the music echoing out of the kebab stands.

For centuries Ulcinj had a reputation as a pirate's lair. By the end of the 16th century as many as 400 pirates, mainly from Malta, Tunisia and Algeria, made Ulcinj their main port of call – wreaking havoc on passing vessels and then returning to party up large on Mala Plaža. Ulcinj became the centre of a thriving slave trade, with people – mainly from North Africa – paraded for sale on the town's main square.

You'll find banks, internet cafes, supermarkets, pharmacies and the post office on Rr Hazif Ali Ulqinaku.

Sights & Activities

The ancient Stari Grad overlooking Mali Plaža is still largely residential and somewhat dilapidated – a legacy of the 1979 earthquake. A steep slope leads to the **Upper Gate**, where there's a small **museum** (☎ 421 419; admission €1; ☼ 6am-noon & 5-9pm) containing Roman and Ottoman artefacts just inside the walls.

Mala Plaža may be a fine grin of a cove but it's hard to see the beach under all that suntanned flesh in July and August. You're better to stroll south, where a succession of rocky bays offer a little more room to breathe. **Ladies' Beach** (admission €1.50) has a strict women-only policy, while a section of the beach in front of the Hotel Albatross is clothing-optional.

The appropriately named **Velika Plaža** (Big Beach) starts 4km southeast of the town and stretches for 12 sandy kilometres. Sections of it sprout deckchairs but there's still plenty of space to lose yourself. To be frank, this large flat expanse isn't as picturesque as it sounds and the water is painfully shallow – great for kids but you'll need to walk a fair way for a decent swim.

On your way to Velika Plaža you'll pass the murky **Milena canal**, where local fishermen use nets suspended from long willow rods attached to wooden stilt houses. The effect is remarkably redolent of South East Asia. There are more of these contraptions on the banks of the **Bojana River** at the other end of Veliki Plaža.

Divers wanting to explore various wrecks and the remains of a submerged town should contact the **D'olcinium Diving Club** (☎ 067-319 100; www.uldiving.com; introductory dive €30, 2 dives incl equipment €40). They also hire snorkelling (€3) and diving (€15) gear.

Sleeping

Real Estate Travel Agency (☎ 421 609; www.real estate-travel.com; Hazif Ali Ulqinaku bb; ☼ 8am-9pm) This strangely named agency has obliging English-speaking staff who can help you find private rooms (from €10 per person), apartments or hotel rooms. They also rent cars, run tours and sell maps of Ulcinj.

Hotel Dolcino (☎ 422 288; www.hoteldolcino.com; Hazif Ali Ulqinaku bb; s/d/q/ste €40/50/60/70; ✖) You can't quibble over the exceptionally reasonable prices of this modern business-orientated minihotel in the centre of town. The quieter rooms at the back have spacious terraces, although the small front balconies are great for watching the passing parade.

MONTENEGRO

Dvori Balšića & Palata Venecija (☎ 421 457; www .realestate-travel.com; Stari Grad; s/d/d/apt €75/100/140/190; 🖳) If you've ever fancied being king of the castle, these grand stone *palazzi* in the Old Town should satisfy the urge. The sizeable rooms all have kitchenettes, romantic sea views, wi-fi and stucco and dark wooden interiors.

Eating & Drinking

Restaurant Pizzeria Bazar (☎ 421 639; Hazif Ali Ulqinaku bb; mains €4-10) An upstairs restaurant that's a great idling place when the streets below are heaving with tourists. People-watch in comfort as you enjoy a plate of *Lignje na žaru* (grilled squid), the restaurant's speciality.

Riblja Čorba (☎ 401 720; Bojana River; mains €6-10) Not actually in Ulcinj but well worth the 14km drive, this memorable fish restaurant is one of several that jut out over the Bojana River just before the bridge to Ada Bojana. The name means fish soup and their broth is indeed sublime: thick with rice and served in a metal pot that will fill your bowl twice over.

Getting There & Away

The **bus station** (☎ 413 225) is on the northeastern edge of town just off Bul Vëllazërit Frashëri. Services head to Bar (€2.50, 30 minutes, six daily), Podgorica (€7, one hour, daily), Shkodra (Albania; €4.50, 90 minutes, daily) and Pristina (Kosovo; €22.50, eight hours, three daily).

Minibuses head to Shkodra at 9am and 3pm (or when they're full) from the carpark beside Ulcinj's market (about €5).

CENTRAL MONTENEGRO

The heart of Montenegro – physically, spiritually and politically – is easily accessed as a day trip from the coast but it's well deserving of a longer exploration. Two wonderful national parks separate it from the coast and behind them lie the two capitals, the ancient current one and the newer former one.

LOVĆEN NATIONAL PARK ЛОВЋЕН

Directly behind Kotor is **Mt Lovćen** (1749m), the black mountain that gave *Crna Gora* (Montenegro) its name (*crna/negro* means 'black', *gora/monte* means 'mountain' in Montenegrin and Italian respectively). This locale occupies a special place in their hearts of all Montenegrins. For most of its history it

represented the entire nation – a rocky island of Slavic resistance in an Ottoman sea. The old capital of Cetinje nestles in its foothills.

The national park's 6220 hectares are home to 85 species of butterfly, 200 species of birds and mammals, including brown bears and wolves. It's criss-crossed with well-marked hiking paths.

The **National Park Office** (☎ 033-761 128; www .nparkovi.cg.yu; Ivanova Korita bb; 🕙 9am-5pm Apr-Oct, less in winter) is near its centre and offers accommodation in four-bedded bungalows (€40). If you're planning some serious walking, buy a copy of the *Lovćen Mountain Touristic Map* (scale 1:25,000), available from the office and park entries.

Lovćen's star attraction is the magnificent **Njegoš Mausoleum** (admission €3) at the top of its second-highest peak, Jezerski Vrh (1657m). Take the 461 steps up to the entry, where two granite giantesses guard the tomb. Inside, under a golden mosaic canopy, a 28-ton Vladika Petar II Petrović Njegoš rests in the wings of an eagle, carved from a single block of black granite. The actual tomb lies below and a path at the rear leads to a dramatic circular viewing platform. A photographer stationed near the entrance has a stash of folk costumes for a quirky souvenir photo (€5).

If you're driving, the park can be approached from either Kotor or Cetinje (entry fee €2). The back route between the two shouldn't be missed (see p565).

CETINJE ЦЕТИЊЕ
☎ 041 / pop 15,150

Rising from a green vale surrounded by rough, grey mountains, Cetinje is an odd mix of former capital and overgrown village, where single-storey cottages and stately mansions share the same street. Pretty Njegoševa is a partly pedestrianised thoroughfare lined with interesting buildings, including the **Presidential Palace** and various former embassies marked with plaques. Everything of significance is in the immediate vicinity. There's not much English spoken at the **tourist information centre** (☎ 078-108 788; Novice Cerovića bb; 🕙 8am-8pm Mon-Sat, 9am-5pm Sun) but you can buy souvenirs and Cetinje guidebooks (€10).

Sights
MUSEUMS

The **National Museum of Montenegro** (Narodni muzej Crne Gore; all museums adult/child €8/4; 🕙 9am-5pm, last admission 4.30pm) is actually a collection of five museums housed in a clump of important buildings. A joint ticket will get you into all of them or you can buy individual tickets.

Two are housed in the former parliament (1910), Cetinje's most imposing building. The fascinating **History Museum** (Istorijski muzej; ☎ 230 310; Novice Cerovića 7; adult/child €3/1.50) is very well laid out, following a timeline from the Stone Age to 1955. There are few English signs but the enthusiastic staff will walk you around and give you an overview, before leaving you to your own devices.

Upstairs is the equally excellent **Art Museum** (Umjetnički muzej; adult/child €3/1.50). There's a small collection of icons, the most important being the precious 9th-century *Our Lady of Philermos*, which was traditionally believed to be painted by St Luke himself. Elsewhere in the gallery all of Montenegro's great artists are represented, with the most famous having their own separate spaces. Expect a museum staff member to be hovering as you wander around.

While the hovering at the Art Museum is annoying, the **King Nikola Museum** (Muzej kralja Nikole; ☎ 230 555; Trg Kralja Nikole; adult/child €5/2.50) can be downright infuriating. Entry is only by guided tour, which the staff will only give to a group, even if you've pre-paid a ticket and they've got nothing else to do. Still, this 1871 palace of Nikola I, last soverign of Montenegro, is worth the hassle.

Opposite the National Museum, the castle-like **Njegoš Museum** (Njegošev Muzej; ☎ 231 050; Trg Kralja Nikole; adult/child €3/1.50) was the residence of Montenegro's favourite son, prince-bishop–poet Petar II Petrović Njegoš. The hall was built and financed by the Russians in 1838 and housed the nation's first billiard table, hence the museum's alternative name, Biljarda. The bottom floor is devoted to military costumes, photos of soldiers with outlandish moustaches and exquisitely decorated weapons. Njegoš's personal effects are displayed upstairs.

When you leave the museum turn right and follow the walls to the glass pavilion housing a fascinating large scale **relief map** (adult/child €1/0.50) of Montenegro created by the Austrians in 1917.

Occupying the former Serbian Embassy, the **Ethnographic Museum** (Etnografski muzej; Trg Kralja Nikole; adult/child €2/1) is the least interesting of the five but if you've bought a joint ticket you may as well check it out. The collection

of costumes and tools is well presented and has English notations.

CETINJE MONASTERY

It's a case of three times lucky for **Cetinje Monastery** (☎ 231 021; ☉ 8am-6pm), having been repeatedly destroyed during Ottoman attacks and rebuilt after. This sturdy incarnation dates from 1785, with its only exterior ornamentation being the capitals of columns recycled from the original building, founded in 1484.

The chapel to the right of the courtyard holds the monastery's proudest possessions: a shard of the 'true cross' and the mummified right hand of St John the Baptist. The hand's had a fascinating history, having escaped wars and revolutions and passing through the hands of Byzantine emperors, Ottoman sultans, the Knights Hospitalier, Russian tsars and Serbian kings. It's now housed in a bejewelled golden casket by the chapel's window, draped in heavy fabric. The casket's only occasionally opened for veneration, so if you miss out you can console yourself that it's not a very pleasant sight.

The monastery **treasury** (admission €2; ☉ 8am-4pm) is only open to groups, but if you are persuasive enough and prepared to wait around, you may be able to get in. It holds a wealth of fascinating objects that form a blur as you're shunted around the rooms by one of the monks. These include jewel-encrusted vestments, ancient handwritten texts, icons, royal crowns and a copy of the 1494 *Oktoih* (Book of the Eight Voices), the first book printed in Serbian.

If your legs, shoulders or cleavage are on display you'll either be denied entry or given a smock to wear.

Sleeping & Eating

Accommodation in Cetinje is limited and there are only a few proper restaurants.

Hotel Grand (☎ 242 400; hotelgrand@cg.yu; Njegoševa 1; s €45-60, d €64-80, apt €120) 'Fading grandeur' would be a more apt description than 'Grand', but aside from a few pigeons roosting in the walls, Cetinje's only hotel is a pleasant place to stay. The comfy beds, new linen and spongy carpet strips certainly help.

Vinoteka (☎ 068-555 771; Njegoševa 103; mains €2.20-5) The wood-beamed porch looking onto the garden is such a nice spot that the excellent and reasonably priced pizza and pasta feels like a bonus – the decent wine list even more so.

MONTENEGRO

Getting There & Away

Cetinje's on the main highway between Budva and Podgorica and can also be reached by a glorious back road from Kotor via Lovćen National Park; see p565. The **bus station** (Trg Golootočkih Žeta) is only two blocks from the main street but it doesn't have a timetable, ticket counter or even a phone. Buses leave every 30 minutes for Podgorica (€3) and hourly for Budva (€3).

LAKE SKADAR NATIONAL PARK
СКАДАРСКО ЈЕЗЕРО

The Balkans' largest lake, dolphin-shaped Lake Skadar has its tail and two-thirds of its body in Montenegro and its nose in Albania. Covering between 370 and 550 sq km (depending on the time of year), it's one of the most important reserves for wetland birds in the whole of Europe. The endangered Dalmatian pelican nests here, along with 256 other species, while 48 known species of fish lurk beneath its smooth surface. On the Montenegrin side, an area of 400 sq km has been protected by a national park since 1983. It's a blissfully pretty area, encompassing steep mountains, hidden villages, historic churches, clear waters and floating meadows of waterlilies.

The **National Park Visitors' Centre** (☎ 020-879 100; www.skadarlake.org; Vranjina bb; admission €2; ☼ 8am-4pm) is on the opposite side of the causeway heading to Podgorica from Virpazar. This modern facility has excellent displays about all the national parks, not just Lake Skadar, and sells park entry tickets (per day €4) and fishing permits (per day €5).

In the busy months, various tour operators set up kiosks in the vicinity. **Kings Travel** (☎ 020-202 800) hires rowboats (per hour/day €25/100) and speed boats with drivers (per hour/day €60/300).

Just along the causeway are the remains of the 19th-century fortress **Lesendro**. The busy highway and railway tracks prevent land access to the site.

Rijeka Crnojevića Ријека Црнојевића

The northwestern end of the lake thins into the serpentine loops of the Rijeka Crnojevića (Crnojević River) and terminates near the pretty village of the same name. It's a charming, tucked-away kind of place, accessed by side roads that lead off the Cetinje–Podgorica highway. Occupying four wooden huts that jut out over the river on stilts is a **National Park**

Visitors' Centre (admission €1; ☼ 8am-4pm), which houses a historical display.

You wouldn't expect it but this sleepy place is home to one of Montenegro's best restaurants. **Stari Most** (☎ 033-239 505; fish per kg €25-45, 5-course set menu €40-50) is well located on the marble riverside promenade, looking towards the photogenic arched stone bridge (1854) from which it derives its name. Fish, particularly eel, is the speciality here and the fish soup alone is enough to justify a drive from Podgorica.

Virpazar Вирпазар

This sweet little town serves as the main gateway to the national park. It's centred on a pretty town square and a river blanketed with waterlilies. Most of the boat tours of the lake depart from here, so the tranquillity is briefly shattered at around 10.30am, when the tour buses from the coast pull in. There's a **National Park kiosk** by the marina that sells entry tickets and fishing permits but doesn't offer much information.

The **Pelikan Hotel** (☎ 020-711 107; pelikanzec@ cg.yu; r €52-75; 🏠) is a well-run one-stop shop offering accommodation, an excellent traditional restaurant (main €5 to €12) and 2½-hour boat tours that explore the lake's northern reaches (€30). The rooms are clean and have nice views over the square, although some of them are tiny.

Virpazar doesn't have a bus station but buses on the Bar–Podgorica route stop here. The decrepit **train station** (☎ 020-441 435) is off the main road, 800m south of town. There are regular services to Bar (€2) and Podgorica (€2.50).

Murići Мурићи

The southern edge of the lake is the most dramatic, with the Rumija Mountains rising precipitously from the water. From Virpazar there's a wonderful drive following the contours of the lake through the mountains towards the border before crossing the range and turning back towards Ulcinj. About halfway, a steep road descends to the village of **Murići**. This is one of the lake's best swimming spots. Local boatmen offer trips to the monasteries on the nearby islands for around €10 per hour.

The **Murići Vacation Resort** (☎ 069-688 288; www .nacionalnipark-izletistemurici.com; per person €35) has simple log cabins nestled within an olive grove. A decent ablutions block is shared and the price includes three meals in the shady outdoor

restaurant (mains €5-9). They also organise **lake tours** (€16) that visit the islands and Virpazar.

PODGORICA ПОДГОРИЦА
☎ 020 / pop 136,480

Podgorica's never going to be Europe's most happening capital but if you can get past the sweltering summer temperatures and concrete apartment blocks you'll find a pleasant little city with lots of green space and some decent galleries, restaurants and bars.

The city sits at the confluence of two rivers. West of the broad Morača is what passes for the business district. The smaller Ribnica River divides the eastern side in two. To the south is Stara Varoš, the heart of the former Ottoman town. North of the Ribnica is Nova Varoš, an attractive, mainly low-rise precinct of late 19th-/early 20th-century buildings housing a lively mixture of shops and bars. At its centre is the attractive main square, Trg Republika.

Information

You'll find plenty of ATMs scattered around the inner city.

Accident & Emergency clinic (Hitna Pomoć; ☎ 124; Vaka Djurovića bb)

Montenegro Adventures (☎ 202 380; www.mon tenegro-adventures.com; Moskovska 63-4) The commercial wing of the nonprofit Centre for Sustainable Tourism Initiatives (www.cstimontenegro.org), with whom they share an office. They organise tours, accommodation and the like.

Tourist Organisation Podgorica (TOP; ☎ 667 535; www.podgorica.travel; Slobode 47)

www.club (Bokaška 4; per hr €1.50; ☉ 8am-2am) Decent cafe-bar with internet terminals.

Sights

Despite Cetinje nabbing most of the national endowment, the new capital is well served by the **Podgorica Museum & Gallery** (☎ 242 543; Marka Miljanova 4; adult/child €5/1; ☉ 9am-8pm). There's an interesting section on the city's history, including antiquities surviving from its Roman incarnation, Doclea. The gallery features local big hitters such as Dado Đurić and Petar Lubarda, whose large canvas *Titograd* (1956) takes pride of place in the foyer.

The Centre for Contemporary Art operates two galleries in Podgorica. The bottom two floors of the once-royal palace **Dvorac Petrovića** (☎ 243 513; Kruševac bb; admission free; ☉ 8am-2pm & 4-9pm Mon-Fri & 10am-4pm Sat summer, 8am-8pm Mon-Fri & 8am-2pm Sat winter) are given over to high-profile exhibitions, while the top floor has an oddball collection of miscellanea. Temporary exhibitions are also staged in the small **Galerija Centar** (☎ 665 409; Njegoševa 2; admission free; ☉ 9am-2pm & 5-9pm Mon-Fri, 10am-2pm Sat).

An indicator of the healthy state of Orthodoxy in Montenegro is the immense **Hram Hristovog Vaskrsenja** (Temple of Christ's Resurrection; Bul Džordža Vašingtona). It's still incomplete after 15 years' construction, but its large dome, white stone towers and gold crosses are a striking addition to Podgorica's skyline.

Sleeping

Most visitors to Podgorica are here for business, either commerce or government-related. Hotels set their prices accordingly and private accommodation isn't really an option.

Hotel Evropa (☎ 623 444; www.hotelevropa.cg.yu; Orahovačka 16; s €55-70, d/tr €90/120; ☒ 🖳) It's hardly a salubrious location, but Evropa is handy to the train and bus station and offers clean rooms with comfortable beds, writing desks and decent showers. Despite its diminutive size there's a sauna, fitness room, wi-fi and ample parking.

Hotel Eminent (☎ 664 646; eminent@cg.yu; Njegoševa 25; s/d/tr €80/130/160, apt €90-140; ☒) Given its location and excellent facilities, the Eminent seems to be set up for business people keen on an after-work tipple. The front rooms can be noisy but the funky mezzanine apartments open on to a covered veranda at the back. Wi-fi is available.

Eating & Drinking

Head to the **little market** (Moskovska bb) or the **big market** (Bratstva Jedinstva bb) for fresh fruit and vegetables.

Laterna (☎ 232 331; Marka Miljanova 41; mains €4-13; ☉ 9am-midnight Mon-Sat) Farm implements hang from the rough stone walls, creating a surprisingly rustic ambience in the centre of the city. A selection of meat and fish grills is offered but it's hard to go past the crispy-based pizza – it's quite possibly Montenegro's best.

Leonardo (☎ 242 902; Svetozara Markovića bb; mains €4-13) Leonardo's unlikely position at the centre of a residential block makes it a little tricky to find but the effort's well rewarded by accomplished Italian cuisine. The pasta dishes are delicious and reasonably priced, given the upmarket ambience, while the €4 pizzas should leave even those on a budget with a Mona Lisa smile.

Buda Bar (☎ 067-344 944; Stanka Dragojevića 26; ☉ 8am-2am) A golden Buddha smiles serenely

PODGORICA

0   500 m
0   0.3 miles

INFORMATION			
Accident & Emergency Clinic.....1	C1	Hram Hristovog Vaskrsenja.......13	A1
Bosnia & Hercegovina Embassy...2	D1	Montenegro Adventures............14	A1
French Embassy........................3	D1	Podgorica Museum & Gallery....15	C2
German Embassy.......................4	C1		
Italian Embassy.........................5	A1	SLEEPING	
Serbian Embassy.......................6	B2	Hotel Eminent.........................16	C1
Tourist Organisation Podgorica...7	C1	Hotel Evropa..........................17	D3
UK Embassy..............................8	A1		
US Embassy..............................9	B2	EATING	
www.club...............................10	C1	Big market.............................18	C3
		Laterna.................................19	D2
SIGHTS & ACTIVITIES		Leonardo...............................20	B1
Dvorac Petrovića....................11	B2	Little Market...........................21	A1
Galerija Centar........................12	C2		

DRINKING	
Buda Bar...............................22	C1

ENTERTAINMENT	
Kino Kultura...........................23	D2

TRANSPORT	
Adria Airlines.........................24	B1
Bus station.............................25	D3
Croatia Airlines....................(see 24)
JAT Airways.........................(see 16)
Meridian Rentacar.................26	A1
Montenegro Airlines...............27	C2

as you meditate over your morning coffee or search for the eternal truth at the bottom of a cocktail glass. This is one slick watering hole; the tent-like semi-enclosed terrace is the place to be on balmy summer nights.

Entertainment

Kino Kultura (IV Proleterske Brigade 1; admission €2.50) The screenings aren't as regular as you might expect for the city's only cinema but you might luck upon an English-language movie with Montenegrin subtitles.

Getting There & Away
BUS

Podgorica's **bus station** (☎ 620 430; Trg Golootočkih Žrtava; ⏰ 5am-10pm) has a left-luggage service,

ATM and services to all major towns, including Herceg Novi (€9, three hours), Kotor (€7, two hours) and Ulcinj (€7, one hour).

TRAIN

Don't expect any English or a lot of help from the information desk at the **train station** (☎ 441 211; www.zeljeznica.cg.yu; Trg Golootočkih Žrtava 13; ⏰ 5am-11pm). Thankfully, timetables are posted. Destinations include Bar (€3, one hour, 14 daily), Virpazar (€2.50, 40 minutes, 14 daily), Kolašin (€4.50, 1½ hours, three daily) and Belgrade (€22, 7½ hours, four daily).

CAR

The major rental car agencies all have counters at Podgorica airport. Excellent local agency

Meridian Rentacar (☎ 234 944, 069-316 666; www.meridian-rentacar.com; Bul Džordža Vašingtona 85) also has a city office.

Getting Around

It's not difficult to get around town on foot but if you fancy trying a local bus they cost €0.60 for a short journey. **Podgorica Airport** (☎ 020-872 016) is 9km south of the city. Montenegro Airlines runs a shuttle bus (€3) between the airport and Trg Republika, timed around their flights. Airport taxis have a standard €15 fare to the centre but ordinary taxis should only charge about €8.

OSTROG MONASTERY МАНАСТИР ОСТРОГ

Resting in a cliff-face 900m above the Zeta valley, the gleaming white **Ostrog Monastery** is the most important site in Montenegro for Orthodox Christians. Even with its masses of pilgrims, tourists and trashy souvenir stands, it's a strangely affecting place.

Leaving the main Podgorica–Nikšić highway 19km past Danilovgrad, a narrow road twists uphill for 7km before it reaches the **Lower Monastery** (1824). In summer you'll be greeted with sweet fragrances emanating from the mountain foliage. The church has vivid frescos and behind it is a natural spring, where you can fill your bottles with deliciously fresh water and potentially benefit from an internal blessing as you sup it. From here the faithful, many of them barefoot, plod up another two steep kilometres to the main shrine. Nonpilgrims and the pure of heart may drive to the upper carpark.

The **Upper Monastery** (the really impressive one) is dubbed 'Sv Vasilije's miracle', because no-one seems to understand how it was built. Constructed in 1665 within two large caves, it gives the impression that it has grown out of the very rock. Sv Vasilije (St Basil), a bishop from Hercegovina, brought his monks here after the Ottomans destroyed Tvrdos Monastery near Trebinje. Pilgrims queue to go into the atmospheric shrine where the Saint's fabric-wrapped bones are kept. To enter you'll need to be wearing a long skirt or trousers (jeans are fine) and cover your shoulders.

One of the only nonsmoking establishments in the country, the **guest house** (☎ 067-405 258; dm €4) near the Lower Monastery offers tidy single-sex dorm rooms, while in summer

many pilgrims lay sleeping mats in front of the Upper Monastery.

There's no public transport but numerous tour buses head here from all of the tourist hot spots. Expect to pay about €15 to €20 for a daytrip from the coast.

NORTHERN MOUNTAINS

This really is the full Monte: soaring peaks, hidden monasteries, secluded villages, steep river canyons and a whole heap of 'wild beauty', to quote the tourist slogan. It's well worth hiring a car for a couple of days to get off the beaten track – some of the roads are truly spectacular.

DURMITOR NATIONAL PARK ДУРМИТОР

☎ 052 / pop 4900

Magnificent scenery ratchets up to the stupendous in this national park, where ice and water have carved a dramatic landscape from the limestone. Some 18 glacial lakes known as *gorske oči* (mountain eyes) dot the Durmitor range, with the largest, **Black Lake** (Crno Jezero), a pleasant 3km walk from Žabljak. The rounded mass of **Međed** (The Bear, 2287m) rears up behind the lake flanked by others of the park's 48 peaks over 2000m, including the highest, **Bobotov Kuk** (2523m). In winter (December to March) Durmitor is Montenegro's main ski resort; in summer it's a popular place for hiking, rafting and other active pursuits.

The park is home to enough critters to cast a Disney movie, including 163 species of bird, about 50 types of mammals and purportedly the greatest variety of butterflies in Europe.

Žabljak, at the eastern edge of the range, is the park's principal gateway and the only town within its boundaries. It's not very big and nor is it attractive, but it has a supermarket, post office, bank, hotels and restaurants, all gathered around the parking lot that masquerades as the main square.

Information

Durmitor National Park Visitor Centre (☎ 360 228; www.nparkovi.cg.yu; ⏱ 7am-2pm autumn & spring, 8am-6pm winter & summer) On the road to the Black Lake, this centre includes a wonderful micromuseum focusing on the park's flora and fauna. The knowledgable English-speaking staff sells local craft, fishing permits (river/lake €15/10), maps (€8) and hiking guidebooks.

MONTENEGRO

Summit Travel Agency (☎ 361 502; anna.grbovic@ cg.yu; Njegoševa bb, Žabljak) Owner Anna Grbović speaks good English and can arrange jeep tours (€100 for up to three people), rafting trips and mountain bike hire (per hour/day €2/10).

Activities

RAFTING

Slicing through the mountains at the northern edge of the national park like they were made from the local soft cheese, the **Tara River** forms a canyon that at its peak is 1300m deep. By way of comparison, Colorado's Grand Canyon is only 200m deeper.

Rafting along the river is one of the country's most popular tourist activities, with various operators running trips daily between May and October. The river has a few rapids but don't expect an adrenaline-fuelled white-water experience. You'll get the most excitement in May, when the last of the melting snow still revs up the flow.

The 82km section that is raftable starts from Splavište, south of the impressive 150m high Tara Bridge, and ends at Šćepan Polje on the Bosnian border. The classic two-day trip heads through the deepest part of the canyon on the first day, stopping overnight at Radovan Luka. Most of the day-tours from the coast traverse only the last 18km – this is outside the national park and hence avoids hefty fees. You'll miss out on the canyon's depths but it's still a beautiful stretch, including most of the rapids. The buses follow a spectacular road along the Piva River, giving you a double dose of canyon action.

If you've got your own wheels you can save a few bucks and avoid a lengthy coach tour by heading directly to Šćepan Polje. **Tara Tour** (☎ 069-086 106; www.tara-tour.com) offers an excellent half-day trip (with/without breakfast and lunch €40/30) and has a cute set of wooden chalets with squat toilets and showers in a separate block; accommodation, three meals and a half-day's rafting costs €55. Another good operator is **Kamp Grab** (☎ 083-200 598; www .tara-grab.com), with lodgings blissfully located 18km upstream at Brstanovica.

Summit Travel Agency (above) offers a range of tours from Žabljak starting from Splavište (half-/one-/two-day tour €50/110/200).

HIKING

Durmitor is one of the best-marked mountain ranges in Europe. Some suggest it's a little too

well labelled, encouraging novices to wander around seriously high altitude paths that are prone to fog and summer thunderstorms. Check the weather forecast before you set out, stick to the tracks and prepare for sudden drops in temperature. You'll be charged €2 per day to enter the park and paths can be as easy as a 4km stroll around the Black Lake.

SKIING

On the slopes of **Savin Kuk** (2313m), 5km from Žabljak, you'll find the main ski centre. Its 3.5km run starts from a height of 2010m and is best suited to advanced skiers. On the outskirts of town near the bus station, **Javorovača** is a gentle 300m slope that's good for kids and beginners. The third centre at **Mali Štuoc** (1953m) should have reopened by the time you read this; it has terrific views over the Black Lake, Međed and Savin Kuk, and slopes to suit all levels of experience.

One of the big attractions for skiing here is the cost: day passes are around €15, weekly passes €70 and ski lessons between €10 and €20. You can rent ski and snowboard gear from **Sport Trade** (☎ 069-538 831; Vuka Karadžića 7, Žabljak) for €10 per day.

Sleeping & Eating

Summit Travel Agency (left) can help you source private accommodation, starting from around €10 per person. Most of the giant Yugoslav-era hotels were either closed for renovation when we visited or deserved to be.

Autokamp Mlinski Potok Mina (☎ 069-497 625; camp sites per person €3, bed €10) With a fabulously hospitable host (there's no escaping the *rakija* shots), this camping ground above the National Park Visitors Centre is an excellent option. The owner's house can sleep 12 guests in comfortable wood-panelled rooms and he has another house sleeping 11 by the Black Lake.

MB Hotel (☎ 361 601; www.mb-hotel.com; Tripka Đakovića bb, Žabljak; s/d/villa €30/57/100) In a quiet backstreet halfway between the town centre and the bus station, this little hotel offers modern rooms, English-speaking staff and an attractive restaurant and bar. The restaurant even has a nonsmoking section – something even less likely to be seen in these parts than wolves. Wi-fi available.

Eko-Oaza Suza Evrope (☎ 067-511 755; eko-oaza@ cg.yu; Dobrilovina; cottage €50) Situated 25km west of Mojkovac at the beginning of the arm of the park that stretches along the Tara River, this 'eco oasis' consists of four comfortable wooden cottages, each sleeping five people. From here you can hike up the mountain and stay overnight in a hut near the glacial Lake Zaboj (1477m).

National Eco Restaurant (☎ 361 337; Božidara Žugića 8, Žabljak; mains €3-10) A great place to try traditional mountain food, such as lamb or veal roasted 'under the pan' (€24 per kilogram). It's all locally sourced and hence organic, without trying very hard.

Getting There & Away

The most reliable road to Žabljak follows the Tara River west from Mojkovac. In summer this 70km route takes about 90 minutes. If you're coming from Podgorica the quickest route is through Nikšić and Šavnik, but the road can be treacherous in winter. The main highway north from Nikšić follows the dramatic Piva Canyon to Šćepan Polje.

There's a petrol station near the **bus station** (☎ 361 318) at the southern end of Žabljak on the Nikšić road. Buses head to Belgrade (€25, nine hours, two daily) and Podgorica (€9.50, 3½ hours, three daily).

BIOGRADSKA GORA NATIONAL PARK
БИОГРАДСКА ГОРА

Nestled in the heart of the Bjelasica Mountain Range, this pretty national park has as its heart 1600 hectares of virgin woodland – one of Europe's last three remaining primeval forests. The main entrance to the park is between Kolašin and Mojkovac on the Podgorica–Belgrade route. After paying a €2 entry fee you can drive the further 4km to the lake.

You can hire rowboats (per hour €5) and buy fishing permits (per day €20) from the **park office** (☎ 020-865 625; www.nparkovi.cg.yu) by the carpark. If you're planning to tackle the excellent hiking tracks it's worth buying a copy of the *Mountains of Bjelasica* booklet (€3).

Nearby there's a **camping ground** (small/large tent €3/5) with basic squat toilets and a cluster of 11 new windowless log cabins, each with two beds (€20). The ablutions block for the cabins is much nicer. **Restoran Biogradsko Jezero** (mains €5.50-9.20) has a wonderful terrace where you can steal glimpses of the lake through the trees as you tuck into a traditional lamb or veal dish.

The nearest bus stop is an hour's walk away at Kraljevo Kolo and the nearest train station is a 90-minute walk at Štitarička Rijeka. The next major town with decent hotels and an excellent **tourist office** (☎ 020-865 110; Trg Borca 2; ⊗ 8am-4pm) is Kolašin, 15km south of the park entrance.

MONTENEGRO DIRECTORY

ACCOMMODATION

A tidal wave of development has seen hotels large and small spring up in the popular destinations. Prices are very seasonal, peaking in July and August on the coast. Where the prices vary according to the season we've listed a range from the cheapest low-season price through to the most expensive high-season rate for each room category. Budget rooms can cost up to €30 per night, and you should be able to find a midrange option for less than €90. Top-end rooms start from this mark and head into the hundreds. Unless otherwise mentioned the rooms have bathrooms and the tariff usually includes breakfast.

The cheapest option is private accommodation and apartment rentals. These can be arranged through travel agencies or, in season, you may be approached at the bus stop or see signs hanging outside of houses. Some local tourist offices publish handy guides.

Facilities at camp grounds tend to be basic, often with squat toilets and limited water. The national parks have cabin-style accommodation.

An additional tourist tax (less than €2 per night) will be added to the rate for all accommodation types.

ACTIVITIES

Hooking up with activity operators can be difficult due to language difficulties, lack of permanent offices and out-of-date websites. Luckily there are some excellent travel agencies who will do the legwork for you, including Black Mountain (p562), Montenegro Adventures (p573), and the London-based agency **So Montenegro** (☎ in the UK 20-3039 5651; www.somonte gro.co.uk).

The National Tourist Office, in association with mountain clubs, has developed the resource *Wilderness Hiking & Biking* which outlines five magical routes (downloadable from

MONTENEGRO

www.montenegro.travel/xxl/en/brochures
/index.html). At the same web address you can
download the *Wilderness Biking Montenegro*
pamphlet, outlining five 'top trails' and the
mother of all mountain biking routes, the
14-day, 1276km Tour de Montenegro.

For diving, head to Herceg Novi (p562) and
Ulcinj (p569). Kayaking is possible at Herceg
Novi (p562), and Budva offers paragliding
(p566). For rafting, try the Tara River (p576)
and for skiing head to Durmitor (p576).

BUSINESS HOURS

Business hours in Montenegro are a relative
concept. Even if hours are posted on the doors
of museums or shops, don't be surprised if
they're not heeded. Banks are usually open
from 8am to 5pm Monday to Friday and until
noon Saturday. Shops in busy areas often
start at around 8am or 9am and close at a
similar time in the evening. Sometimes they'll
close for a few hours in the late afternoon.
Restaurants open at around 8am and close
around midnight, while cafe-bars may stay
open until 2am or 3am.

CUSTOMS REGULATIONS

In a bid to stop tourists from neighbouring
countries bringing all their holiday groceries
with them, Montenegro now restricts what
food can be brought into the country. For
other customs information, see p965.

DANGERS & ANNOYANCES

Montenegro's towns and villages are generally safe places. Montenegro's roads, on the
other hand, can be treacherous, due to some
kamikaze-style local driving habits.

Chances are you'll see some snakes if
you're poking around ruins during summer.
Montenegro has two types of venomous viper,
but they'll try their best to keep out of your
way. If bitten you should head to a medical
centre for the antivenom.

EMBASSIES & CONSULATES

For a full list, see www.vlada.cg.yu/eng/mini
nos/. The following are all in Podgorica, unless
otherwise stated:

Albania (off Map p574; ☎ 020-652 796; Zmaj Jovina 30)
Bosnia and Hercegovina (Map p574; ☎ 020-618 105;
Atinska 58)
Croatia Podgorica (off Map p574; ☎ 020-269 760;
Vladimira Ćetkovića 2); Kotor (☎ 032-323 127;
Šušanj 248)

France (Map p574; ☎ 020-655 348; Atinska 35)
Germany (Map p574; ☎ 020-667 285; Hercegovačka 10)
Italy (Map p574; ☎ 020-234 661; Bul Džordža
Vašingtona 83)
Serbia (Map p574; ☎ 020-402 500; Hotel Podgorica, Bul
Svetog Petra Cetinjskog 1)
UK (Map p574; ☎ 020-205 460; Bul Svetog Petra
Cetinjskog 149)
USA (Map p574; ☎ 020-225 417; Ljubljanska bb)

FESTIVALS & EVENTS

Most of the coastal towns host summer festivals and the former Venetian towns have a
tradition of masked carnivals.

Active types should enter the awesome
Adventure Race Montenegro (www.adventurerace
montenegro.com; 1-/2-day entry €120/200). This two-day
event in early October combines kayaking,
mountain biking, trekking and orienteering
with brilliant scenery, environmental awareness and fundraising for local charities.

GAY & LESBIAN TRAVELLERS

Although homosexuality was decriminalised
in 1977, you won't find a single gay or lesbian
venue in Montenegro. Attitudes to homosexuality remain hostile and life for gay people is
extremely difficult, exacerbated by the fact
that most people are expected to live at home
until they're married.

Many gay men resort to online connections (try www.gayromeo.com) or take their
chances at a handful of cruisy beaches.

HOLIDAYS

Public holidays in Montenegro include:
New Year's Day 1 January
Orthodox Christmas 7 January
Orthodox Easter Monday April/May
Labour Day 1 May
Independence Day 21 May
Statehood Day 13 July

MONEY

Montenegro uses the euro (€). You'll find
banks with ATMs in all the main towns, most
of which accept Visa, MasterCard, Maestro
and Cirrus. Don't rely on restaurants, shops
or smaller hotels accepting credit cards.

Tipping isn't expected although it's common to round up to the nearest euro.

POST

Every town has a post office, which locals use
for paying their bills: be prepared for horren-

EMERGENCY NUMBERS

- Ambulance ☎ 124
- Fire ☎ 123
- Police ☎ 122

dous queues. Parcels should be taken unsealed
for inspection. You can receive mail, addressed
poste restante, in all towns for a small charge.
International postal services are slow.

TELEPHONE

Montenegro has recently been given its own
country code (☎ 382) and a new set of local
codes. Partly because of the changes, many
businesses advertise their mobile numbers
(starting with ☎ 06) instead of land lines.

The international access prefix is ☎ 00 or +
from a mobile phone. Post offices are the best
places to make international calls.

Local SIM cards are a good idea if you're
planning a longer stay. The main providers
are T-Mobile, M:tel and Promonte; they have
storefronts in most towns.

VISAS

Visas are not required for citizens of most
European countries, Australia, New Zealand,
Canada, UK and the USA. In most cases this
allows a stay of up to 90 days.

WOMEN TRAVELLERS

Other than a cursory interest shown by men
towards solo women travellers, travelling is
hassle-free and easy. In Muslim areas a few
women wear a headscarf but most adopt
Western fashions.

TRANSPORT IN MONTENEGRO

GETTING THERE & AWAY
Air

Both **Tivat** (TIV; ☎ 032-617 337) and **Podgorica** (TGD;
☎ 020-872 016) have airports and Dubrovnik's
airport (p258) is very near the border. The
following airlines fly to/from Montenegro:

Adria Airlines (JP; Map p574; ☎ 020-201 201; www
.adria-airways.com; Ivana Vujoševića 46, Podgorica) Flies
from Ljubljana and Sarajevo to Podgorica.

Aerosvit (VV; ☎ 380-44-496 7975; www.aerosvit.com)
Flies from Kiev to Tivat.

Atlant-Soyuz Airlines (3G; ☎ 7-495-436 7045; www
.atlant-soyuz.ru) Flies from Moscow to Tivat.

Austrojet (AUJ; www.austrojet.at) Flies from Banja Luka
to Tivat.

Croatia Airlines (OU; Map p574; ☎ 020-201 201; www
.croatiaairlines.com; Ivana Vujoševića 46, Podgorica) Flies
from Zagreb to Podgorica.

JAT Airways (JU; www.jat.com) Budva (☎ 033-451 641;
Mediteranska 2); Podgorica (Map p574; ☎ 020-664 750;
Njegoševa 25) Flies from Belgrade and Niš (summer only)
to Tivat and from Belgrade to Podgorica.

Malév Hungarian Airlines (MA; ☎ 36-1-235 3888;
www.malev.hu) Flies from Budapest to Podgorica.

Montenegro Airlines (YM; www.montenegroairlines
.com) Budva (☎ 033-454 900; Slovenska Obala bb);
Podgorica (Map p574; ☎ 020-664 411; Slobode 23) Flies
from Belgrade, Moscow and Niš (summer only) to Tivat.
Also from Belgrade and Ljubljana to Podgorica.

Moskovia Airlines (3R; ☎ 033-455 967; www.ak3r.ru;
Mediteranska 23, Budva) Flies from Moscow to Tivat and
Podgorica.

Rossiya Airlines (FV; ☎ 7-495-995 2025; www.rossiya
-airlines.ru) Flies from St Petersburg to Tivat.

S7 Airlines (S7; ☎ 033-459 706; www.s7.ru) Flies from
Moscow to Tivat and Podgorica.

Ukraine International Airlines (PS; ☎ 380-44-581
5050; www.flyuia.com) Flies from Kiev to Tivat (summer
only).

Ural Airlines (U6; ☎ 7-343-345 3645; www.uralairlines
.ru) Flies from Yekaterinburg to Tivat (summer only).

Land

There are two main crossings between Albania
and Montenegro, linking Shkodra to Ulcinj
(Sukobin) and to Podgorica (Hani i Hotit).

For Bosnia, two checkpoints link Nikšić
to Trebinje (Dolovi) and to Srbinje (Šćepan
Polje). There's a more remote crossing halfway
between the two at Vratkovići and another in
the Kovač Mountains in the far north.

There's a busy checkpoint on the Adriatic
highway between Herceg Novi and Dubrovnik,
Croatia; expect delays.

There's only one crossing between Kosovo
and Montenegro, on the road between Rožaje
and Peć.

If you're heading to Serbia, the busiest crossing is north of Bijelo Polje near Dobrakovo,
followed by the checkpoint northeast of
Rožaje and another east of Pljevlja.

BUS

There's a well-developed bus network linking Montenegro with the major cities of the
region. Podgorica is the main hub but buses

MONTENEGRO

stop at many coastal towns as well. For details of bus travel from specific towns see p562 and p570.

CAR & MOTORCYCLE

Drivers need an International Driving Permit (IDP) and vehicles need Green Card insurance or insurance must be bought at the border.

TRAIN

Montenegro's only working passenger train line starts at Bar and heads into Serbia. For details on the train to Belgrade, see p574.

SEA

For details on ferries to Italy from Kotor and Bar, see p565 and p569.

GETTING AROUND
Bicycle

Cyclists are a rare species, even in the cities. Don't expect drivers to be considerate. Wherever possible, try to get off the main roads. The National Tourist Office has been developing a series of wilderness mountain biking trails (p577).

Bus

The local bus network is extensive and reliable. Buses are usually comfortable, air conditioned and rarely full. It's slightly cheaper to buy your ticket on the bus rather the station, but a station-bought ticket theoretically guarantees you a seat. Luggage carried below the bus is charged at €1 per piece.

Car & Motorcycle

Independent travel by car or motorcycle is an ideal way to gad about and discover the country; some of the drives are breathtakingly beautiful. Traffic police are everywhere, so stick to speed limits and carry an IDP. Allow more time than you'd expect for the distances involved, as the terrain will slow you down.

The major European car-hire companies have a presence in various centres, but **Meridian Rentacar** (☎ 454 105; www.meridian-rentacar.com), which has offices in Budva, Bar and Podgorica (Map p574), is a reliable local option; one-day hire starts from €45.

Train

Željeznica Crne Gore (☎ 441 211; www.zeljeznica.cg.yu) runs the only passenger train line, heading north from Bar. The trains are old and stiflingly hot in summer but they're priced accordingly and the route through the mountains is spectacular. Useful stops include Virpazar, Podgorica and Kolašin.

MONTENEGRO

REGIONS WITHIN THE REGION

Eastern Europe is a vast region, incorporating millions of square kilometres in land area and 21 independent nations. The cultures and landscapes are so varied that it can be difficult to create a cohesive picture of the region – but expansive coasts, voluminous rivers and sharp political boundaries (past and present) can help connect the dots. Explore the regions within the region to find commonalities among the diversity.

Along the Adriatic

If you think of Eastern Europe as a cold, colourless destination, think again – and then head directly to the eastern coast of the Adriatic. Here the rugged rocky mountains drop straight into the crystalline waters, yachties hop from island to idyllic island, and Roman ruins, medieval cities and quaint fishing villages dot the tantalising landscape.

❶ Dubrovnik, Croatia
Walking around the city walls of Dubrovnik (p249) offers expansive vistas of rocky islands, grassy mountains and shimmering seas, along with views of people pegging out their washing on lines running between buildings.

❷ Piran, Slovenia
Surrounded by the sparkling Adriatic on three sides, picturesque Piran (p900) is the highlight of the slim Slovenian coast, with Gothic architecture and seafood delicacies that are reminiscent of Venice.

❸ Zadar, Croatia
This Croatian chocolate box (p233) offers all of the Dalmatian treats, from Roman ruins and medieval churches to quaint cafes and sun-bleached beaches. Sample them all, but don't miss the maraschino cherry.

❹ Kotor, Montenegro
Fifteen hundred steps lead up to the old fort that overlooks the sleepy town of Kotor (p563). The reward? A cooling dip in the emerald-coloured fjord.

❺ Sveti Stefan, Montenegro
Once a fishermen's village and now a luxury island hotel, Sveti Stefan (p567) is one big vehicle-free zone – perfect for a leisurely stroll taking in all its charms: rustic stone buildings, narrow streets, small churches and shops...

Baltic Bliss

A land of extremes, this northern corner of Eastern Europe is known for its silent, stoic population, who brave the deep, dark winters. But their reward comes in summer months, when the sky stays light around the clock, the Baltic waters warm to a bearable (and bare-able) frigid and the cities' old towns come to life.

❶ Vilnius, Lithuania
With Europe's largest medieval Old Town, Vilnius (p472) is a maze of cobbled streets punctuated by church spires, quaint courtyards, cosy cafes and Jewish-heritage sights.

❷ Gdańsk, Poland
From the Teutonic takeover to the collapse of communism, this vibrant port (p643) has played a crucial role in Polish history. Explore the colourful Old Town before heading to the seaside resort at Sopot or the pristine beaches of Hel for a cooling Baltic dip.

❸ Rīga, Latvia
Foodies visiting Rīga (p443) should head straight to the Central Market. Old ladies haggle over prices for shiny berries, big bunches of sorrel and pickled garlic, while containers overflow with fresh sour cream, hearty black bread and every cut of meat imaginable.

❹ Tallinn, Estonia
Explore the gorgeous Old Town in Tallinn (p334), or escape the crowds and leg it to lovely Kadriorg Park for some space, a breath of fresh air and wonderful people-watching.

❺ St Petersburg, Russia
Russia's 'northern capital', St Petersburg (p771) is at its most enticing during the magical white nights, when the sun never sets and the whole town celebrates. Locals and visitors stay out to drink champagne and watch the parade of ships that passes through when the Neva bridges are raised.

❻ Lahemaa National Park, Estonia
Follow the coastline of this national park (p349) out of Käsmu, once a village for sea captains and now a burgeoning colony of artists. Discover Estonia's past at the park's manor houses, but don't bypass the Bronze Age archaeological sites.

❼ Jūrmala, Latvia
With pine forest descending to meet wide, white-sand beaches, Jūrmala (p456) provides a perfect escape from the city. Pack a picnic and watch the sunset after a long summer day.

Beautiful Blue Danube

Contrary to popular opinion (most notably held by Johann Strauss II), the Danube is not blue; it's really more of a murky greenish brown. But it *is* beautiful, stringing together some of Eastern Europe's most precious urban and natural jewels before splaying out into the Danube Delta and the Black Sea.

❶ Danube Delta, Romania

As the mighty Danube approaches the Black Sea, it splits into three, creating the Danube Delta (p735). Rich in birdlife and fish species, this wetlands habitat is home to Europe's largest pelican colony.

❷ Belgrade, Serbia

Boasting beautiful river views, the Serbian capital (p807) surrounds a fantastic fairytale castle. The Belgrade population knows how to have a good time, and you'll find people crowding into cafes and getting carried away on river cruises every day of the week.

❸ Budapest, Hungary

Looking for pampering in Budapest (p373)? Relax in the glory of the Gellért Baths (Gellért Fürdő), which combine serious spa treatments with extravagant architectural excesses, then retire to a Viennese-style coffee house for tokay and excellent cherry strudels.

❹ Bratislava, Slovakia

Wander the historic cobblestone centre of this charming city (p836), which is preserving its past even as it embraces its Euro-centric future. Climb up Castle Hill for an overview of the city.

❺ Novy Sad, Serbia

Visit Novy Sad (p819) in July to be part of the Exit Festival, where wildly eclectic sounds and amazing views enchant and exhilarate revellers. Described as the place where 'hedonism meets activism', Novy Sad really becomes a State of Exit.

❻ Rusenski Lom Nature Park, Bulgaria

The rocky cliffs of this ever expanding nature reserve (p178) house the intriguing Ivanovo Rock Monastery; for the claustrophobic, there are miles of walking trails providing fresh air and expansive river views.

❼ Vidin, Bulgaria

Centuries-old walls surround this historic city (p191), which is topped by a 10th-century fortress. Enjoy the city's riverside setting in the leafy park or at one of many floating fish restaurants.

Red Ramble

The Soviet Union is gone but not forgotten. No trip to Eastern Europe is complete without a visit to one of the former republics to remember the regime that so shaped the region in the 20th century.

❶ Moscow, Russia

Not only the capital of Russia and the capital of the USSR, Moscow (p753) was the capital of communism. Stepping onto Red Sq never ceases to inspire: the towers of the Kremlin, the colours adorning St Basil's Cathedral, and the elaborate edifice of the State History Museum all encircle a vast stretch of cobblestones.

❷ Yalta, Ukraine

The events of 1945 at the Great Livadia Palace in Yalta (p947) changed the course of history. Here – in the wake of the Allied victory – Churchill, Roosevelt and Stalin divvied up Europe and inadvertently launched the Cold War.

❸ Minsk, Belarus

Meander down the grandiose main thoroughfare in Minsk (p76), where the ghost of Stalinism still lurks amid the monolithic communist-era architecture. Remember dark days and witness the city cautiously moving towards a brighter future.

❹ Transdniestr, Moldova

Step back in time when you enter this idiosyncratic and anachronistic region (p543), which claims to be one of the last bastions of communism. There are plenty of Lenin statues – and even a Kirov! – ready for photos.

Poland

If they were handing out prizes for 'most eventful history', Poland would be sure to get a gong. The nation has spent centuries at the pointy end of history, grappling with war and invasion. Nothing, however, has succeeded in suppressing the Poles' strong sense of nationhood and cultural identity, as exemplified by the ancient royal capital of Kraków, with its breathtaking castle, and bustling Warsaw, with its postwar reconstruction of its Old Town.

For the time being, at least, the time for resistance to oppressive regimes is over, as Poles enjoy the peaceful space provided by their membership of the EU. As investment flows into the country and the economy grows, Poles are visiting and working overseas like never before. The product is a younger generation that's more cosmopolitan and 'European' than its predecessors. As a result, regional centres such as urbane Gdańsk, cultured Wrocław and lively Poznań exude a sophisticated energy that's a heady mix of old and new.

Away from the cities, Poland is a diverse land, from its northern sandy beaches and magnificent southern mountains to the lost-in-time forest of Białowieża National Park in the east. And everywhere there are seldom-visited towns to discover, with their own ruined castles, picturesque squares and historic churches.

Although prices are rising as its economy gathers strength, Poland is still good value for travellers. As the Polish people work on combining their distinctive national identity with their place in the heart of Europe, it's a fascinating time to visit this beautiful country.

FAST FACTS

- **Area** 312, 685 sq km
- **Capital** Warsaw
- **Currency** złoty; €1 = 4.58zł; US$1 = 3.36zł; UK£1 = 4.87zł; A$1 = 2.33zł; ¥100 = 3.50zł; NZ$1 = 1.87zł
- **Famous for** Chopin, Copernicus, Marie Curie, Solidarity, vodka
- **Official language** Polish
- **Phrases** *dzień dobry* (good morning/afternoon); *dziękuję* (thank you); *proszę* (please)
- **Population** 38 million
- **Telephone codes** country code ☎ 48; international access code ☎ 00
- **Visas** not required for EU citizens; US, Canadian, New Zealand and Australian citizens do not need visas for stays of less than 90 days, see p666

POLAND

HIGHLIGHTS

- Experience the beauty and history of Kraków's **Wawel Castle** (p609).
- Meet European bison and other magnificent fauna at **Białowieża National Park** (p607).
- Soak up the cosmopolitan vibe of **Gdańsk** (p643) and take a dip in the Baltic at nearby **Sopot** (p649).
- Enjoy the skiing or hiking life of the **Tatra Mountains** (p629).
- Discover Warsaw's tragic wartime history at the **Warsaw Rising Museum** (p600).

ITINERARIES

- **One Week** Spend a day exploring Warsaw with a stroll round the Old Town and a stop at the Warsaw Rising Museum. The next day, head to Kraków for three days, visiting the Old Town, Wawel Castle, the former Jewish district of Kazimierz, and Wieliczka. Take a day trip to Oświęcim, then head on to Zakopane for two days.
- **Two Weeks** Follow the above itinerary, then on the eighth day travel to Wrocław for two days. Progress north to Toruń for a day, then onward to Gdańsk for two days, exploring the Old Town and visiting Westerplatte. Wind down with a couple of days at the seaside in Sopot.

CLIMATE & WHEN TO GO

Poland's weather can be unpredictable. Summer is usually warm and sunny, with July the hottest month, but it's also the season with the highest rainfall. Spring and autumn are pleasantly warm but can also be wet. Snow can fall anywhere in Poland between December and March, lingering until April or even May in the mountains.

The tourist season runs roughly from May to October, peaking in July and August. Many Polish families go on holidays during these two months, so transport is crowded and accommodation limited. From mid-autumn to mid-spring, outdoor activities are less prominent and many camping grounds and youth hostels are closed.

HISTORY

Poland's history started with the Polanians (People of the Plains). During the early Middle Ages, these Western Slavs moved into the flatlands between the Vistula and Odra Rivers. Mieszko I, Duke of the Polanians, adopted Christianity in 966 and embarked on a campaign of conquest. A papal edict in 1025 led to Mieszko's son Bolesław Chrobry (Boleslaus the Brave) being crowned Poland's first king.

Poland's early success proved fragile, and encroachment from Germanic peoples led to the relocation of the royal capital from Poznań to Kraków in 1038. More trouble loomed in 1226 when the Prince of Mazovia invited the Teutonic Knights to help convert the pagan tribes of the north. These Germanic crusaders used the opportunity to create their own state along the Baltic coast. The south had its own invaders to contend with, and Kraków was attacked by Tatars twice in the mid-13th century.

The kingdom prospered under Kazimierz III 'the Great' (1333–70). During this period, many new towns sprang up, while Kraków blossomed into one of Europe's leading cultural centres. When the daughter of Kazimierz's nephew, Jadwiga, married the Grand Duke of Lithuania, Jagiełło, in 1386, Poland and Lithuania were united as the largest state in Europe, stretching from the Baltic to the Black Sea.

The Renaissance was introduced to Poland by the enlightened King Zygmunt during the 16th century, as he lavishly patronised the arts and sciences. By asserting that the earth travelled around the sun, Nicolaus Copernicus revolutionised the field of astronomy in 1543.

The 17th and 18th centuries produced disaster and decline for Poland. First it was subject to Swedish and Russian invasions, and eventually it faced partition by surrounding empires. In 1773 Russia, Prussia and Austria seized Polish territory in the First Partition; by the time the Third Partition was completed in 1795, Poland had vanished from the map of Europe.

Although the country remained divided through the entire 19th century, Poles steadfastly maintained their culture. Finally, upon the end of WWI the old imperial powers dissolved, and a sovereign Polish state was restored. Very soon, however, Poland was again at war. Under the command of Marshal Jozef Piłsudski, Poland defended its eastern territories from long-time enemy Russia, now transformed into the Soviet Union and determined to spread its revolution westward. After two years of impressive fighting by the outnumbered Poles, an armistice was signed, retaining Vilnius and Lviv within Poland.

Though Polish institutions and national identity flourished during the interwar period, disaster soon struck again. On 1 September 1939, a Nazi blitzkrieg rained down from the west; soon after, the Soviets invaded Poland from the east, dividing the country with Germany. This agreement didn't last long, as Hitler soon transformed Poland into a staging ground for the Nazi invasion of the Soviet

CONNECTIONS: MOVING ON FROM POLAND

Due to its central position, Poland offers plenty of possibilities for onward travel. The country is well-connected by train: there are direct connections to Berlin from both Warsaw (via Poznań) and Kraków; to Prague from Warsaw and Kraków; and to Kyiv from Warsaw and Kraków (via Przemyśl and Lviv). Trains also link Warsaw to Minsk and Moscow, and Gdańsk to Kaliningrad. International buses head in all directions, including eastward to the Baltic States, Belarus and Ukraine; see p605 for information on buses from Warsaw. From southern Zakopane (p629), it's easy to hop to Slovakia via bus, or even minibus. And from the Baltic coast ports of Gdańsk (p648), Gydania (p650) and Świnoujscie (p667), ferries head to various ports in Denmark and Sweden.

POLAND

HOW MUCH?

- **Night in a hostel** 50zł
- **Night in a midrange double room** 250zł
- **Three-course restaurant meal for two** 150zł
- **Postcard** 1zł
- **Postage stamp** 3zł

LONELY PLANET INDEX

- **1L petrol** 3.80zł
- **1L bottled water** 2zł
- **Beer** 6zł to 8zł
- **Souvenir T-shirt** 35zł
- **Street snack (zapiekanka)** 4zł to 5zł

Union. Six million Polish inhabitants died during WWII (including the country's three million Jews), brutally annihilated in death camps. At the war's end, Poland's borders were redrawn yet again. The Soviet Union kept the eastern territories and extended the country's western boundary at the expense of Germany. These border changes were accompanied by the forced resettlement of more than a million Poles, Germans and Ukrainians.

Peacetime brought more repression. After WWII, Poland endured four decades of Soviet-dominated communist rule, punctuated by waves of protests, most notably the paralysing strikes of 1980–81, led by the Solidarity trade union. Finally, in the open elections of 1989, the communists fell from power and in 1990 Solidarity leader Lech Wałęsa became Poland's first democratically elected president.

The post-communist transition brought radical changes, which induced new social hardships and political crises. But within a decade Poland had built the foundations for a market economy, and reoriented its foreign relations towards the West. In March 1999, Poland was granted full NATO membership, and it joined the EU in May 2004.

In the 2007 parliamentary elections, Poles decisively rejected the Eurosceptic policies of the Law and Justice party's government, eccentrically headed by the twin Kaczyński brothers as president (Lech) and prime minister (Jarosław). The new centrist government of prime minister Donald Tusk's Civic Platform is steering a pro-business, pro-EU course, although Lech Kaczyński's term as president runs to 2010.

PEOPLE

For centuries Poland was a multicultural country, home to large Jewish, German and Ukrainian communities. Its Jewish population was particularly large, and once numbered more than three million. However, after Nazi genocide and the forced resettlements that followed WWII, the Jewish population declined to 10,000 and Poland became an ethnically homogeneous country, with some 98% of the population being ethnic Poles.

More than 60% of the citizens live in towns and cities. Warsaw is by far the largest urban settlement, followed by Łódź, Kraków, Wrocław, Poznań and Gdańsk. Upper Silesia (around Katowice) is the most densely inhabited area, while the northeastern border regions remain the least populated.

Between five and 10 million Poles live outside Poland. This émigré community, known as 'Polonia', is located mainly in the USA (particularly Chicago).

Poles are friendly and polite, but not overly formal. The way of life in large urban centres increasingly resembles Western styles and manners. In the countryside, however, a more conservative culture dominates, evidenced by traditional gender roles and strong family ties. In both urban and rural settings, many Poles are devoutly religious.

The Poles' sense of personal space may be a bit cosier than you are accustomed to – you may notice this trait when queuing for tickets or manoeuvring along city streets. When greeting each other, Polish men are passionate about shaking hands. Polish women often shake hands with men, but the man should always wait for the woman to extend her hand first.

RELIGION

Roman Catholicism is the dominant Christian denomination, adhered to by more than 80% of Poles. The Orthodox church's followers constitute about 1% of the population, mostly living along a narrow strip on the eastern frontier.

The election of Karol Wojtyła, the archbishop of Kraków, as Pope John Paul II in 1978, and his triumphal visit to his homeland a year later, significantly enhanced the status of the church in Poland. The country was proud of the late Pope: even now his image can be seen in public places and private homes throughout the country.

The overthrow of communism was as much a victory for the Church as it was for democracy. The fine line between the Church and the state is often blurred in Poland, and the Church is a powerful lobby on social issues. Some Poles have grown wary of the Church's influence in society and politics, but Poland remains one of Europe's most religious countries, and packed-out churches are not uncommon.

ARTS
Literature

Poland has inherited a rich literary tradition dating from the 15th century, though its modern voice was shaped in the 19th century, during the long period of foreign occupation. It was a time for nationalist writers such as the poet Adam Mickiewicz (1798–1855), and Henryk Sienkiewicz (1846–1916), who won a Nobel Prize in 1905 for *Quo Vadis?* This nationalist tradition was revived in the communist era when Czesław Miłosz was awarded a Nobel Prize in 1980 for *The Captive Mind*.

At the turn of the 20th century, the avant-garde 'Young Poland' movement in art and literature developed in Kraków. The most notable representatives of this movement were writer Stanisław Wyspiański (1869–1907), also famous for his stained-glass work; playwright Stanisław Ignacy Witkiewicz (1885–1939), commonly known as Witkacy; and Nobel laureate Władysław Reymont (1867–1925). In 1996 Wisława Szymborska (b 1923) also received a Nobel Prize for her poetry.

Music

The most famous Polish musician was undoubtedly Frédéric Chopin (1810–49), whose music displays the melancholy and nostalgia that became hallmarks of the national style. Stanisław Moniuszko (1819–72) injected a Polish flavour into 19th-century Italian opera music by introducing folk songs and dances to the stage. His *Halka* (1858), about a peasant girl abandoned by a young noble, is a staple of the national opera houses.

On a more contemporary note, popular Polish musicians you might catch live in concert include the controversial Doda (pop singer); Feel (pop-rock band); Łzy (pop-rock band); Indios Bravos (reggae band); and Kasia Cerekwicka (pop singer). Poland's equivalent of the Rolling Stones is Lady Pank, a rock band formed in 1982 and still going strong.

Visual Arts

Poland's most renowned painter was Jan Matejko (1838–93), whose monumental historical paintings hang in galleries throughout the country. Wojciech Kossak (1857–1942) is another artist who documented Polish history; he is best remembered for the colossal painting *Panorama of Racławicka,* on display in Wrocław (p633).

A long-standing Polish craft is the fashioning of jewellery from amber. Amber is a fossil resin of vegetable origin that comes primarily from the Baltic region, and appears in a variety of colours from pale yellow to reddish brown. The best places to buy it are Gdańsk, Kraków and Warsaw.

Polish poster art has received international recognition; the best selection of poster galleries is in Warsaw and Kraków.

Cinema

Poland has produced several world-famous film directors. The most notable is Andrzej Wajda, who received an Honorary Award at the 1999 Academy Awards. *Katyń*, his moving story of the Katyń massacre in WWII, was nominated for Best Foreign Language Film at the 2008 Oscars. Western audiences are probably more familiar with the work of Roman Polański, who directed critically acclaimed films such as *Rosemary's Baby* and *Chinatown*. In 2002 Polański released the incredibly moving film *The Pianist,* which was filmed in Poland and set in the Warsaw Ghetto of WWII. The film went on to win three Oscars and the Cannes Palme d'Or. The late Krzysztof Kieślowski is best known for the *Three Colours* trilogy. The centre of Poland's movie industry, and home to its prestigious National Film School, is Łódź.

ENVIRONMENT

Poland covers an area of 312,685 sq km, approximately as large as the UK and Ireland put together, and is bordered by seven nations and one sea.

The northern edge of Poland meets the Baltic Sea. This broad, 524km-long coastline is spotted with sand dunes and seaside lakes. Also concentrated in the northeast are many postglacial lakes – more than any country in Europe, except Finland.

The southern border is defined by the mountain ranges of the Sudetes and Carpathians. Poland's highest mountains are the rocky Tatras, a section of the Carpathian Range it shares with Slovakia. The highest peak of the Polish Tatras is Mt Rysy (2499m).

The area in between is a vast plain, sectioned by wide north-flowing rivers. Poland's longest river is the Vistula (Wisła), which winds 1047km from the Tatras to the Baltic.

About a quarter of Poland is covered by forest. Some 60% of the forests are pine trees, but the share of deciduous species, such as oak, beech and birch, is increasing.

Poland's fauna includes hare, red deer, wild boar and, less abundantly, elk, brown bear and wildcat. European bison, which once inhabited Europe in large numbers, were brought to the brink of extinction early in the 20th century and a few hundred now live in Białowieża National Park (p607). The Great Masurian Lakes district (p659) attracts a vast array of bird life, such as storks and cormorants. The eagle, though rarely seen today, is Poland's national bird and appears on the Polish emblem.

Poland has 23 national parks, but they cover less than 1% of the country. No permit is necessary to visit these parks, but most have small admission fees. Camping in the parks is sometimes allowed, but only at specified sites. Poland also has a network of less strictly preserved areas called 'landscape parks', scattered throughout the country.

FOOD & DRINK
Staples & Specialities
Various cultures have influenced Polish cuisine, including Jewish, Ukrainian, Russian, Hungarian and German. Polish food is hearty and filling, abundant in potatoes and dumplings, and rich in meat.

Poland's most famous dishes are *bigos* (sauerkraut with a variety of meats), *pierogi* (ravioli-like dumplings stuffed with cottage cheese, minced meat, or cabbage and wild mushrooms) and *barszcz* (red beetroot soup, better known by the Russian word *borscht*).

Hearty soups such as *żurek* (sour soup with sausage and hard-boiled eggs) are a highlight of Polish cuisine. Main dishes are made with pork, including *golonka* (boiled pig's knuckle

served with horseradish) and *schab pieczony* (roast loin of pork seasoned with prunes and herbs). *Gołąbki* (cabbage leaves stuffed with mince and rice) is a tasty alternative.

Placki ziemniaczane (potato pancakes) and *naleśniki* (crepes) are also popular dishes.

Poles claim the national drink, *wódka* (vodka), was invented in their country. It's usually drunk neat and comes in a number of flavours, including *myśliwska* (flavoured with juniper berries), *wiśniówka* (with cherries) and *jarzębiak* (with rowanberries). The most famous variety is *żubrówka* (bison vodka), flavoured with grass from the Białowieża Forest. Other notable spirits include *krupnik* (honey liqueur), *śliwowica* (plum brandy) and *goldwasser* (sweet liqueur containing flakes of gold leaf).

Poles also appreciate the taste of *zimne piwo* (cold beer); the top brands, found everywhere, include Żywiec, Tyskie, Lech and Okocim, while regional brands are available in every city.

Where to Eat & Drink
The cheapest place to eat Polish food is a *bar mleczny* (milk bar), a survivor from the communist era. These no-frills, self-service cafeterias are popular with budget-conscious locals and backpackers alike. Up the scale, the number and variety of *restauracja* (restaurants) has ballooned in recent years, especially in the big cities. Pizzerias have also become phenomenally popular with Poles. And though Polish cuisine features plenty of meat, there are vegetarian restaurants to be found in most cities.

Menus usually have several sections: *zupy* (soups), *dania drugie* (main courses) and *dodatki* (accompaniments). The price of the main course may not include a side dish – such as potatoes and salads – which you choose (and pay extra for) from the *dodatki* section. Also note that the price for some dishes (particularly fish and poultry) may be listed per 100g, so the price will depend on the total weight of the fish or meat.

Poles start their day with *śniadanie* (breakfast); the most important and substantial meal of the day, *obiad*, is normally eaten between 2pm and 5pm. The third meal is *kolacja* (supper). Most restaurants, cafes and cafe-bars are open from 11am to 11pm. It's rare for Polish restaurants to serve breakfast, though milk bars and snack bars are open from early morning. In the Eating sections of this chapter, only nonstandard restaurant hours are listed.

Smoking is common in bars and restaurants, though there have been unsuccessful proposals to ban it from public spaces. It's becoming more common for hotels and restaurants to offer nonsmoking options.

WARSAW

pop 1.7 million

Warsaw (Warszawa in Polish, var-*shah*-va) may not be the prettiest of Poland's cities, but there's no mistaking its dynamism. As the bustling capital and business centre of the nation, Warsaw is home to an array of

dining and nightlife that's the equal of any European city its size.

It's true, however, that Warsaw can be hard work. The city centre sprawls across a wide area, quite separate from the attractive but tourist-heavy Old Town, and its traffic-choked streets lined with massive concrete buildings can be less than enthralling.

However, look at Warsaw with a historic perspective and you'll see the capital in an entirely new light. As a city that's survived everything fate could throw at it – including the complete destruction of its historic heart in WWII – Warsaw is a place with an extraordinary back story.

When you factor in its entertainment options; the beauty of its reconstructed Old

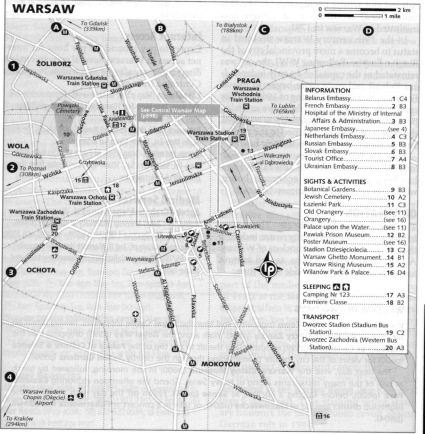

WARSAW

INFORMATION	
Belarus Embassy	**1** C4
French Embassy	**2** B3
Hospital of the Ministry of Internal Affairs & Administration	**3** B3
Japanese Embassy	(see 4)
Netherlands Embassy	**4** C3
Russian Embassy	**5** B3
Slovak Embassy	**6** B3
Tourist Office	**7** A4
Ukrainian Embassy	**8** B3

SIGHTS & ACTIVITIES	
Botanical Gardens	**9** B3
Jewish Cemetery	**10** A2
Łazienki Park	**11** C3
Old Orangery	(see 11)
Orangery	(see 16)
Palace upon the Water	(see 11)
Pawiak Prison Museum	**12** B2
Poster Museum	(see 16)
Stadion Dziesięciolecia	**13** C2
Warsaw Ghetto Monument	**14** B1
Warsaw Rising Museum	**15** A2
Wilanów Park & Palace	**16** D4

SLEEPING	
Camping Nr 123	**17** A3
Premiere Classe	**18** B2

TRANSPORT	
Dworzec Stadion (Stadium Bus Station)	**19** C2
Dworzec Zachodnia (Western Bus Station)	**20** A3

CENTRAL WARSAW

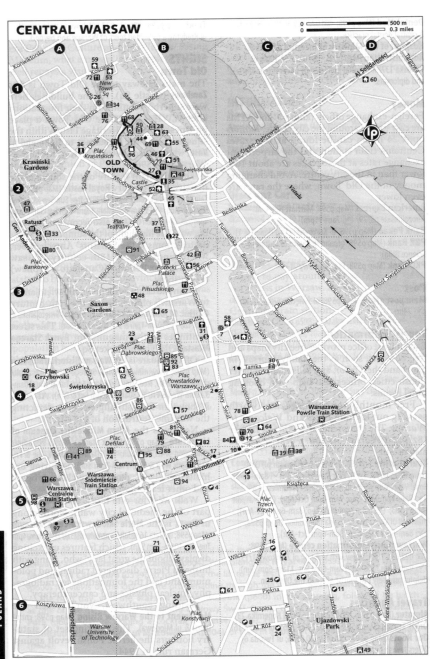

from early morning. In the Eating sections of this chapter, only nonstandard restaurant hours are listed.

Smoking is common in bars and restaurants, though there have been unsuccessful proposals to ban it from public spaces. It's becoming more common for hotels and restaurants to offer nonsmoking options.

WARSAW

pop 1.7 million

Warsaw (Warszawa in Polish, var-*shah*-va) may not be the prettiest of Poland's cities, but there's no mistaking its dynamism. As the bustling capital and business centre of the nation, Warsaw is home to an array of

dining and nightlife that's the equal of any European city its size.

It's true, however, that Warsaw can be hard work. The city centre sprawls across a wide area, quite separate from the attractive but tourist-heavy Old Town, and its traffic-choked streets lined with massive concrete buildings can be less than enthralling.

However, look at Warsaw with a historic perspective and you'll see the capital in an entirely new light. As a city that's survived everything fate could throw at it – including the complete destruction of its historic heart in WWII – Warsaw is a place with an extraordinary back story.

When you factor in its entertainment options; the beauty of its reconstructed Old

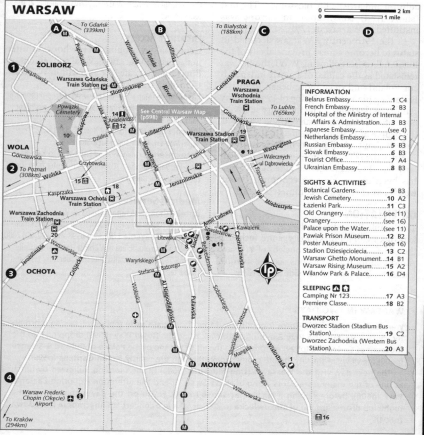

Town, Royal Way and former Royal Parks; and the history represented by the Stalinist-era Palace of Culture and the Warsaw Rising Museum, what emerges is a complex city that well repays a visit.

HISTORY

The Mazovian dukes were the first rulers of Warsaw, establishing it as their stronghold in the 14th century. The city's strategic central location led to the capital being transferred from Kraków to Warsaw in 1596, following the earlier union of Poland and Lithuania.

Although the 18th century was a period of catastrophic decline for the Polish state, Warsaw underwent a period of prosperity during this period. Many magnificent churches, palaces and parks were built, and cultural and artistic life blossomed. The first (short-lived) constitution in Europe was instituted in Warsaw in 1791.

In the 19th century Warsaw declined in status to become a mere provincial city of the Russian Empire. Following WWI, the city was reinstated as the capital of a newly independent Poland and once more began to thrive. Following the Warsaw Rising of 1944, the city centre was devastated, and the entire surviving population forcibly evacuated. Upon war's end, the people of Warsaw returned to the capital, and set about rebuilding its historic heart.

Since the fall of communism, and particularly since Poland's entry into the EU, Warsaw has been undergoing an economic boom, which has reshaped its commercial heart.

ORIENTATION

The Vistula River divides the city. The western left-bank sector features the city centre, including the Old Town, the historic nucleus of Warsaw. Almost all tourist attractions, as well as most tourist facilities, are on this side of the river.

If arriving by train, Warszawa Centralna station is, as the name suggests, within walking distance of the city centre and major attractions. If you arrive by bus at either major PKS bus station, you can take a train from an adjoining station into the centre.

INFORMATION

Bookshops

American Bookstore (Map p598; ☎ 022 827 4852; ul Nowy Świat 61) Books, including guidebooks, and maps.
EMPiK Galeria Centrum (Map p598; ul Marszałkowska 116/122); Royal Way (Map p598; ul Nowy Świat 15/17) Foreign books, newspapers and magazines.

Discount Cards

Warsaw Tourist Card (1/3 days 35/65zł) Free or discounted access to museums, public transport and some theatres, sports centres and restaurants. Available at the tourist office.

Internet Access

Expect to pay around 5zł per hour for internet access in Warsaw. Several convenient but dingy internet cafes are also within Warszawa Centralna train station.
Casablanca (Map p598; ul Krakowskie Przedmieście 4/6; 9am–1am Mon-Fri, 10am–2am Sat, 10am–midnight Sun) Enter from ul Oboźna.
Internet Café (Map p598; ul Nowy Świat 18/20; 9am–11pm Mon-Fri, 10am–10pm Sat & Sun)
Verso Internet (Map p598; ul Freta 17; 8am–8pm Mon-Fri, 9am–5pm Sat, 10am–4pm Sun) Enter from the rear, off ul Świętojerska.

Medical Services

Apteka Grabowskiego (Map p598; Warszawa Centralna; 24hr) Nonstop pharmacy at the train station.
Centrum Medyczne LIM (Map p598; ☎ 022 458 7000; www.cm-lim.com.pl; 3rd fl, Marriott Hotel, Al Jerozolimskie 65/79) Offers specialist doctors, laboratory tests and house calls.

WARSAW IN TWO DAYS

Wander through the **Old Town** (opposite) and tour the **Royal Castle** (opposite), having lunch afterwards at **Restauracja Przy Zamku** (p604). Walk along the **Royal Way** (p599) dropping into the **Museum of Caricature** (p599) en route. Take the lift to the top of the **Palace of Culture & Science** (p600) for views of the city, before promenading through the nearby **Saxon Gardens** (p599).

The next day, visit the **Warsaw Rising Museum** (p600) in the morning, followed by lunch at one of the many restaurants along ul Nowy Świat. Spend the afternoon exploring **Łazienki Park** (p600), before sipping a cocktail at **Sense** (p604). Finish off the day with a visit to the nightclub district around **ul Mazowiecka** (p604), or take in a concert at **Filharmonia Narodowa** (p604).

POLAND

Dental-Med (Map p598; ☎ 022 629 5938; ul Hoża 27)
A central dental practice.
**Hospital of the Ministry of Internal Affairs &
Administration** (Map p595; ☎ 022 508 2000; ul
Wołoska 137) A hospital preferred by government officials
and diplomats.

Money
Foreign-exchange offices *(kantors)* and ATMs
are easy to find around the city centre. *Kantors*
open 24 hours can be found at Warszawa
Centralna train station and the airport, but
exchange rates at these places are about 10%
lower than in the city centre. Avoid changing
money in the Old Town, where the rates are
even lower.
American Express (Map p598; Marriott Hotel, Al
Jerozolimskie 65/79; ☒ 7am-11pm)
Bank Pekao (Map p598; ul Krakowskie Przedmieście 1)
PBK Bank (Map p598; ground fl, Palace of Culture &
Science Bldg)
PKO Bank (Map p598; Plac Bankowy 2)

Post
Main post office (Map p598; ul Świętokrzyska 31/33;
☒ 24hr)

Tourist Information
Each tourist office provides free city maps and
free booklets, such as the handy *Warsaw in
Short* and the *Visitor*, and sells maps of other
Polish cities; offices also help with booking
hotel rooms.

Free monthly tourist magazines worth
seeking out include *Faces* and *Welcome to
Warsaw*. The comprehensive *Warsaw Insider*
(8zł) and *Warsaw in Your Pocket* (5zł) are
also useful.
Tourist office (☎ 9431; www.warsawtour.pl) Old
Town (Map p598; 1st fl, Plac Zamkowy 10; ☒ 8am-4pm);
Royal Way (Map p598; ul Krakowskie Przedmieście 39;
☒ 9am-8pm May-Sep, 9am-6pm Oct-Apr); Okęcie airport
(Map p595; ☒ 8am-8pm May-Sep, 8am-6pm Oct-Apr);
main hall of Warszawa Centralna train station (Map p598;
☒ 8am-8pm May-Sep, 8am-6pm Oct-Apr).
Warsaw tourist information centre (Map p598;
☎ 022 635 1881; www.wcit.waw.pl; pl Zamkowy 1/13;
☒ 9am-6pm Mon-Fri, 10am-6pm Sat, 11am-6pm Sun)
Helpful privately run tourist office in the Old Town.

Travel Agencies
Almatur (Map p598; ☎ 022 826 2639; ul Kopernika 23)
Orbis Travel (Map p598; ☎ 022 827 7265; ul Bracka 16)
Our Roots (Map p598; ☎ 022 620 0556; ul Twarda 6)
Offers Jewish heritage tours.

Trakt (Map p598; ☎ 022 827 8068; www.trakt.com.pl;
ul Kredytowa 6) Guided tours of Warsaw and beyond.

SIGHTS
Old Town
The main gateway to the Old Town is **Plac
Zamkowy** (Castle Sq). All the buildings here
were superbly rebuilt from their foundations
after WWII, earning the Old Town a place
on Unesco's World Heritage List. Within the
square stands the **Monument to Sigismund III
Vasa**, who moved the capital from Kraków to
Warsaw in 1596.

The dominant feature of the square is the
massive 13th-century **Royal Castle** (Map p598; Plac
Zamkowy 4; adult/concession 20/13zł, free Sun Sep-May, free
Mon Jun-Aug; ☒ 11am-4pm Mon, 10am-4pm Tue-Sat, 11am-
4pm Sun, closed Mon Oct-Apr), also reconstructed after
the war. The highlight of the sumptuously decorated rooms is the Senators' Antechamber,
where landscapes of 18th-century Warsaw
by Bernardo Bellotto (Canaletto's nephew)
are on show.

From the castle, walk down ul Świętojańska
to Warsaw's oldest church, the 15th-century
Gothic **St John's Cathedral** (Map p598; ul Świętojańska 8;
crypt 1zł; ☒ 10am-1pm & 3-5.30pm Mon-Sat). This street
continues to the magnificent **Rynek Starego
Miasta** (Old Town Market Sq).

Off the square is the **Warsaw Historical Museum**
(Map p598; www.mhw.pl; Rynek Starego Miasta 42; adult/
concession 6/3zł, free Sun; ☒ 11am-6pm Tue & Thu, 10am-
3.30pm Wed & Fri, 10.30am-4.30pm Sat & Sun). At noon
it shows an English-language film depicting
the wartime destruction of the city.

Nearby is the **Adam Mickiewicz Museum of
Literature** (Map p598; Rynek Starego Miasta 20; adult/
concession 5/4zł, free Sun; ☒ 10am-3pm Mon, Tue & Fri,
11am-6pm Wed & Thu, 11am-5pm Sun), featuring exhibits on Poland's most revered literary figure
and other leading writers.

Walk west for one block to the **Barbican**,
part of the medieval city walls. North along
ul Freta is the **Marie Skłodowska-Curie Museum**
(Map p598; ul Freta 16; adult/concession 8/3zł; ☒ 10am-4pm
Tue-Sat, 10am-3pm Sun), which features unexciting
displays about the great lady, who, along with
husband Pierre, discovered radium and polo-
nium, and laid the foundations for radiogra-
phy, nuclear physics and cancer therapy.

Heading southwest, you'll reach the
Monument to the Warsaw Rising (Map p598; cnr ul
Długa & ul Miodowa). This striking set of statu-
ary honours the heroic Polish revolt against
German rule in 1944.

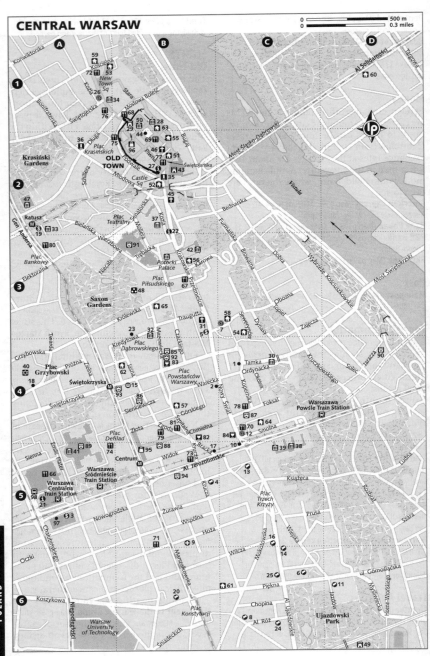

CENTRAL WARSAW

0 | 500 m
0 | 0.3 miles

INFORMATION
Almatur.......................................**1** C4
American Bookstore..................**2** B4
American Express.......................**3** A5
Apteka Grabowskiego............(see 21)
Australian Embassy.....................**4** B5
Bank Pekao..................................**5** B3
Canadian Embassy.....................**6** C6
Casablanca..................................**7** C3
Centrum Medyczne LIM..........(see 3)
Czech Embassy............................**8** C6
Dental-Med.................................**9** B5
EMPiK......................................(see 95)
EMPiK...**10** C5
German Embassy........................**11** D6
Internet Café.............................**12** C4
Irish Embassy.............................**13** C5
Lithuanian Embassy..................**14** C6
Main Post Office........................**15** B4
New Zealand Embassy..............**16** C5
Orbis Travel...............................**17** B5
Our Roots...................................**18** A4
PBK Bank..................................(see 41)
PKO Bank...................................**19** A2
South African Embassy.............**20** B6
Tourist Office............................**21** A5
Tourist Office............................**22** B2
Trakt...**23** B3
UK Embassy...............................**24** C4
US Embassy................................**25** C6
Verso Internet...........................**26** A1
Warsaw Tourist Information
  Centre.....................................**27** B2

SIGHTS & ACTIVITIES
Adam Mickiewicz Museum of
  Literature................................**28** B1
Barbican.....................................**29** B1
Centre for Contemporary Art..(see 49)
Chopin Museum.........................**30** C4
Church of the Holy Cross **31** B3
Ethnographic Museum...............**32** B3

Jewish Historical Institute.........**33** A2
Marie Skłodowska-Curie
  Museum...................................**34** A1
Monument to Sigismund III
  Vasa...**35** B2
Monument to the Warsaw
  Uprising...................................**36** B2
Museum of Caricature.............**37** B2
Museum of the Polish Army.....**38** C5
National Museum.......................**39** C5
Nożyk Synagogue.......................**40** A4
Palace of Culture & Science......**41** A5
Radziwiłł Palace.........................**42** B3
Royal Castle................................**43** B2
Rynek Starego Miasta................**44** B2
St Anne's Church........................**45** B2
St John's Cathedral....................**46** B2
State Archaeological Museum....**47** A2
Tomb of the Unknown Soldier..**48** B3
Ujazdów Castle..........................**49** D6
Warsaw Historical Museum......**50** B1

SLEEPING 🏠
Castle Inn...................................**51** B2
Dom Literatury...........................**52** B2
Dom Przy Rynku Hostel............**53** A1
Hostel Helvetia..........................**54** C3
Hostel Kanonia..........................**55** B2
Hotel Bristol..............................**56** B3
Hotel Gromada Centrum...........**57** B4
Hotel Harenda...........................**58** C3
Hotel Le Regina.........................**59** A1
Hotel Praski................................**60** D1
Nathan's Villa Hostel................**61** C6
Oki Doki Hostel.........................**62** B4
Old Town Apartments................**63** B1
Smolna Youth Hostel.................**64** C4
Sofitel Victoria..........................**65** B3

EATING 🍴
Albert Supermarket...................**66** A5
Bar Bistro Bez Kantów.............**67** B3

Bar Pod Barbakanem.................**68** B1
Bazliszek Restauracja.................**69** B2
Cô Tú..**70** C4
Dżonka.......................................**71** B5
Gospoda Pod Kogutem............**72** A1
Green Way...............................(see 71)
London Steakhouse...................**73** B5
MarcPol Supermarket................**74** A5
Podwale Piwna Kompania.........**75** B2
Restauracja Pod Samsonem......**76** A1
Restauracja Przy Zamku............**77** B2
Tam Tam.....................................**78** C4
Taqueria Mexicana....................**79** B4
Tukan Salad Bar.........................**80** A3
Zgoda Grill Bar..........................**81** B4

DRINKING 🍷 🍸
Między Nami..............................**82** B4
Paparazzi....................................**83** B4
Sense..**84** C4

ENTERTAINMENT 🎭
Enklawa......................................**85** B4
Filharmonia Narodowa..............**86** B4
Foksal 19....................................**87** C4
Kino Atlantic..............................**88** B5
Kinoteka.....................................**89** A5
Teatr Ateneum...........................**90** D4
Teatr Wielki................................**91** B3
Tygmont......................................**92** B4
Underground Music Café...........**93** B4
ZASP Kasy Teatralne.................**94** B5

SHOPPING 🛍
Galeria Centrum........................**95** B5
Lapidarium.................................**96** B1

TRANSPORT
LOT Office..................................**97** A5
Polski Express Bus Stop............**98** A5

Not far from there, the **State Archaeological Museum** (Map p598; ul Długa 52; adult/concession 8/4zł, free Sun except 3rd Sun of month; 🕑 9am-4pm Mon-Wed & Fri, 11am-6pm Thu, 10am-4pm Sun, closed 1st & 3rd Sun each month) is located in a 17th-century former arsenal.

Royal Way (Szlak Królewski)

This 4km route links the Royal Castle with Łazienki Park (see p600) via ul Krakowskie Przedmieście, ul Nowy Świat and Al Ujazdowskie. Bus 180 runs along or near this route and continues south to Wilanów Park (Map p595). Bus 100 also runs on Saturday and Sunday from May to September, between Plac Zamkowy and Łazienki Park.

Just south of the Royal Castle is the ornate 15th-century **St Anne's Church** (Map p598; ul Krakowskie Przedmieście 68; 🕑 daylight hr), with impressive views from its **tower** (adult/concession 3/2zł; 🕑 10am-6pm Tue-Sun).

Along nearby ul Kozia is the quirky **Museum of Caricature** (Map p598; www.muzeumkarykatury.pl; ul Kozia 11; adult/concession 5/3zł, free Sat; 🕑 11am-5pm Tue-Sun), exhibiting numerous original works by Polish and foreign caricaturists, created from the 18th century onwards.

Further south along ul Krakowskie Przedmieście you'll find **Radziwiłł Palace** (Map p598; not open to the public), the residence of the Polish president. To the west, beyond Plac Piłsudskiego, are the **Saxon Gardens** (admission free; 🕑 24hr). At the entrance is the small but poignant **Tomb of the Unknown Soldier** (Map p598), which stands within the only surviving remnant of the Saxon Palace that once stood here and was destroyed by the Nazis. The ceremonial changing of the guard takes place at noon on Sunday. At time of research, work had begun on rebuilding the palace, so access to the area may be limited when you visit.

Oki Doki Hostel (Map p598; ☎ 022 826 5112; www
.okidoki.pl; Plac Dąbrowskiego 3; dm 55-73zł; s/d 142/220zł)
There are no drab dorms here. Each is deco-
rated thematically using the brightest paints
available; try the communist (red with a big
image of Lenin). Lower bunks have good
headroom, and the shared bathrooms are
clean and bright. The hostel also has a bar,
free washing machine and kitchen, and hires
out bikes (25zł per day).

Midrange

Hotel Praski (Map p598; ☎ 022 818 4989; www.praski
.pl; Al Solidarności 61; s/d from 150/230zł) The rooms of
this inexpensive hotel vary in size, but have
attractive high ceilings and comfortable beds.
Bathrooms are clean, red carpets add old-
fashioned charm, and some rooms have views
of Praski Park. It's an easy walk across the
river to the Old Town.

Premiere Classe (Map p595; ☎ 022 624 0800; www
.campanile.com.pl; ul Towarowa 2; r 189zł) If you're not
bothered too much by room size, this modern
hotel makes a good base. Rooms are small but
bright, and neatly set up with modern furnishings. Friendly staff is a plus. Guests can use
the restaurants, bars and fitness centre in the
neighbouring sister hotels.

Dom Literatury (Map p598; ☎ 022 828 3920;
www.fundacjadl.com/hotele.html, in Polish; ul Krakowskie
Przedmieście 87/89; s/d 220/370zł) Within a grand
historic building, this accommodation features rambling halls and staircases bedecked
with pot plants and sizeable paintings. There
is a maze of comfortable rooms, many of
which have excellent views of the Old Town
and the Vistula. You're paying for the location, however, rather than the standard, and
you can't expect too much English from the
friendly staff.

Castle Inn (Map p598; ☎ 022 425 0100;
www.castleinn.pl; ul Świętojańska 2; s 250zł, d from 270zł)
Progress up the stairs to the striking purple
decor and shiny tiles of this Old Town accommodation, situated in a 17th-century
tenement house. All rooms overlook either
Castle Sq or St John's Cathedral, and come
in a range of playful styles.

Hotel Gromada Centrum (Map p598; ☎ 022 582 9900;
www.gromada.pl; Plac Powstańców Warszawy 2; s/d from
320/350zł) Centrally located, the Gromada is a
big concrete box but also a great launching
pad for exploring the central city. Upstairs
from the funky green foyer, the featureless
brown-carpeted corridors stretch out into the

distance like an optical illusion. The rooms are
plain, but clean and spacious.

Hotel Harenda (Map p598; ☎ 022 826 0071; www
.hotelharenda.com.pl; ul Krakowskie Przedmieście 4/6; s/d/ste
from 320/360/460zł) Boasting a great location just
off the Royal Way, the Harenda's rooms are
neat and clean, with solid timber furniture.
There's an old-fashioned feel to the hotel's interiors, and an expensive antique shop just off
the foyer if retail therapy is required. Breakfast
is an additional 25zł.

Top End

Sofitel Victoria (Map p598; ☎ 022 657 8011; www.sofitel
.com; ul Królewska 11; d/ste from €150/250; 🖳) The very
model of a modern business hotel, with a spacious marble foyer, and a lounge area housing
a small library of books on Polish culture and
history. The rooms are conservatively decorated, with gleaming bathrooms. The cheaper
doubles are great value.

Hotel Le Regina (Map p598; ☎ 022 531 6000; www
.leregina.com; ul Kościelna 12; d/ste from €180/450; 🖾) It's
not cheap, but the Le Regina is a jaw-dropping
combination of traditional architecture and
contemporary design. The enormous rooms
feature king-size beds with headboards of
dark, polished wood. Deluxe rooms also have
timber floors, and terraces with courtyard
views. All rooms sport spectacular bathrooms
with marble benchtops.

Hotel Bristol (Map p598; ☎ 022 551 1000; www.war
saw.lemeridien.com; ul Krakowskie Przedmieście 42/44; r from
750zł; 🖳) Established in 1899 and restored to
its former glory after a massive renovation, the
Bristol is touted as Poland's most luxurious
hotel. Its neoclassical exterior houses a feast
of original art nouveau features, and huge,
traditionally decorated rooms. Attentive staff
cater to your every whim.

EATING

The most recent revolution to conquer the
Polish capital has been a gastronomic one.
A good selection of restaurants can be found
in the Old Town and New Town, and in the
area between ul Nowy Świat and the Palace
of Culture & Science.

Budget

Tukan Salad Bar (Map p598; ☎ 022 531 2520; Plac
Bankowy 2; mains from 5zł; 🕑 8am-8pm Mon-Fri, 10am-
6pm Sat) This place has several outlets around
the capital offering a wide choice of salads. As
the name suggests, look for the toucan on the

Not far from there, the **State Archaeological Museum** (Map p598; ul Długa 52; adult/concession 8/4zł; free Sun except 3rd Sun of month; 🕑 9am-4pm Mon-Wed & Fri, 11am-6pm Thu, 10am-4pm Sun, closed 1st & 3rd Sun each month) is located in a 17th-century former arsenal.

Royal Way (Szlak Królewski)
This 4km route links the Royal Castle with Łazienki Park (see p600) via ul Krakowskie Przedmieście, ul Nowy Świat and Al Ujazdowskie. Bus 180 runs along or near this route and continues south to Wilanów Park (Map p595). Bus 100 also runs on Saturday and Sunday from May to September, between Plac Zamkowy and Łazienki Park.

Just south of the Royal Castle is the ornate 15th-century **St Anne's Church** (Map p598; ul Krakowskie Przedmieście 68; 🕑 daylight hr), with impressive views from its **tower** (adult/concession 3/2zł; 🕑 10am-6pm Tue-Sun).

Along nearby ul Kozia is the quirky **Museum of Caricature** (Map p598; www.muzeumkarykatury.pl; ul Kozia 11; adult/concession 5/3zł, free Sat; 🕑 11am-5pm Tue-Sun), exhibiting numerous original works by Polish and foreign caricaturists, created from the 18th century onwards.

Further south along ul Krakowskie Przedmieście you'll find **Radziwiłł Palace** (Map p598; not open to the public), the residence of the Polish president. To the west, beyond Plac Piłsudskiego, are the **Saxon Gardens** (admission free; 🕑 24hr). At the entrance is the small but poignant **Tomb of the Unknown Soldier** (Map p598), which stands within the only surviving remnant of the Saxon Palace that once stood here and was destroyed by the Nazis. The ceremonial changing of the guard takes place at noon on Sunday. At time of research, work had begun on rebuilding the palace, so access to the area may be limited when you visit.

POLAND

South of the tomb is the **Ethnographic Museum** (Map p598; ul Kredytowa 1; adult/concession 8/4zł, Wed free; 9am-4pm Tue, Thu & Fri, 11am-6pm Wed, 10am-5pm Sat & Sun). It displays Polish folk costumes, and regional arts and crafts.

Back along the Royal Way is the 17th-century **Church of the Holy Cross** (Map p598; ul Krakowskie Przedmieście 3; erratic). Chopin's heart is preserved in the second pillar on the left-hand side of the main nave. It was brought from Paris, where he died of tuberculosis aged only 39. If you want to know more, head along ul Tamka to the small **Chopin Museum** (Map p598; ul Okólnik 1; adult/concession 8/4zł, free Wed; 10am-6pm Tue-Sat). On show are letters, hand-written musical scores and the great man's last piano.

East of the junction of ul Nowy Świat and Al Jerozolimskie is the **National Museum** (Map p598; www.mnw.art.pl; Al Jerozolimskie 3; adult/concession 12/7zł, incl temporary exhibitions 17/10zł, Sat free; 10am-4pm Tue-Fri, 10am-6pm Sat & Sun), with an impressive collection of Greek and Egyptian antiquities, Coptic frescos, medieval woodcarvings and Polish paintings; look out for the surrealistic fantasies of Jacek Malczewski. Next door is the **Museum of the Polish Army** (Map p598; Al Jerozolimskie 3; museum adult/concession 8/4zł, free Wed; 10am-5pm Wed-Sun May-Sep, 10am-4pm Wed-Sun Oct-Apr), with army vehicles outside and miscellaneous militaria within.

Go south along Al Ujazdowskie and cross busy ul Armii Ludowej. Over the road is the cutting-edge **Centre for Contemporary Art** (Map p598; www.csw.art.pl; Al Ujazdowskie 6; adult/concession 12/6zł, free Thu; 11am-7pm Tue-Sun). It's housed in the reconstructed **Ujazdów Castle** (Map p598), originally built during the 1620s. Further down (towards the south) are the small **Botanical Gardens** (Map p595; adult/concession 5/2.50zł; 10am-8pm Apr-Aug, 10am-6pm Sep-Oct).

Łazienki Park

This large, shady and popular **park** (admission free; daylight hr) is best known for the 18th-century **Palace upon the Water** (Map p595; adult/concession 12/9zł; 9am-4pm Tue-Sun). It was the summer residence of Stanisław August Poniatowski, the last king of Poland, who was deposed by the Russian army and confederation of Polish magnates in 1792. The park was once a royal hunting ground attached to Ujazdów Castle.

The **Old Orangery** (Map p595; adult/concession 6/4zł) contains a sculpture gallery and an 18th-century theatre. Between noon and 4pm every Sunday from May to September, piano recitals are held among the nearby rose gardens.

Wilanów Park

Another magnificent **park** (Map p595; ul Wisłostrada; adult/concession 5/3zł; 9am-dusk) lies 6km south-east of Łazienki Park. Its centrepiece is the splendid **Wilanów Palace** (Map p595; www.wilanow-palac.art.pl; adult/concession 16/8zł, free Sat; 9.30am-4.30pm Sun-Fri, 10.30am-6.30pm Sat), the summer residence of King Jan III Sobieski, who ended the Turkish threat to Central Europe by defeating the Turks at Vienna in 1683. In summer, be prepared to wait. The last tickets are sold one hour before closing time.

In the well-kept park behind the palace is the **Orangery** (Map p595; admission fee varies with exhibitions; 10am-6.30pm), which houses an art gallery. The **Poster Museum** (Map p595; adult/concession 9/5zł, free Wed; noon-4pm Mon, 10am-4pm Tue-Sun) in the former royal stables is a repository of Poland's world-renowned poster art.

To reach Wilanów, take bus 116 or 180 from ul Nowy Świat or Al Ujazdowskie.

Palace of Culture & Science

Massive, brooding and inescapable, this **towering structure** (Map p598; www.pkin.pl; Plac Defilad 1; 9am-8pm daily Sep-May, 9am-8pm Mon-Thu, to 11pm Fri-Sun Jun-Aug) has become an emblem of the city, as it's slowly rehabilitated from its Stalinist past. It has a particularly sinister aspect at dusk, though it's also a handy landmark. The palace was built in the early 1950s as a 'gift of friendship' from the Soviet Union (the kind of unwanted gift that's hard to hide away), and is still one of Europe's tallest buildings (over 230m). The clock faces were added to the building in the postcommunist period.

The **observation terrace** (adult/concession 20/15zł) on the 30th floor provides a panoramic view, though it can be very cold and windy.

Warsaw Rising Museum

This impressive **museum** (Map p595; ul Grzybowska 79; adult/concession 4/2zł, free Sun; 8am-6pm Mon, Wed & Fri, 10am-8pm Thu, 10am-6pm Sat & Sun) commemorates Warsaw's insurrection against its Nazi occupiers in 1944, which was destined to end in defeat and the destruction of much of the city and its population. The Rising was viciously suppressed by the Germans (while the Red Army stood by on the opposite bank of the Vistula), with more than 200,000 Poles dying by its conclusion.

The moving story of the Rising is retold here via photographs, exhibits and audiovisual displays. The centrepiece is a massive memorial wall emitting a heartbeat and selected audio recordings. At the end of the journey there's a replica 1944 cafe, underlining the fact that life went on, even in the worst days of the struggle. Captions are in Polish and English. Catch trams 8, 22 or 24 from Al Jerozolimskie, heading west.

Jewish Heritage

The suburbs northwest of the Palace of Culture & Science were once predominantly inhabited by Jewish Poles. During WWII the Nazis established a Jewish ghetto in the area, but razed it to the ground after crushing the Warsaw Ghetto Uprising in April 1943.

The **Warsaw Ghetto Monument** (Map p595; cnr ul Anielewicza & ul Zamenhofa) remembers the Nazis' victims via pictorial plaques. The nearby **Pawiak Prison Museum** (Map p595; ul Dzielna 24/26; admission free; 10am-4pm Wed-Sun) was a Gestapo prison during the Nazi occupation. Moving exhibits include letters and other personal items.

The most poignant remainder is Europe's largest **Jewish Cemetery** (Map p595; ul Okopowa 49/51; admission 4zł; 10am-5pm Mon-Thu, 9am-1pm Fri, 9am-4pm Sun). Founded in 1806, it has more than 100,000 gravestones. Visitors must wear a head-covering to enter, and it's accessible from the Old Town on bus 180, heading north from ul Nowy Świat.

The **Jewish Historical Institute** (Map p598; 022 827 9221; www.jewishinstitute.org.pl; ul Tłomackie 3/5; adult/concession 10/5zł; 9am-4pm Mon-Wed & Fri, 11am-6pm Thu) has permanent exhibits about the Warsaw Ghetto, as well as local Jewish artworks. Further south is the neo-Romanesque **Nożyk Synagogue** (Map p598; ul Twarda 6; admission 6zł; 9am-5pm Mon-Fri, 11am-4pm Sun), Warsaw's only synagogue to survive WWII.

FESTIVALS & EVENTS

International Book Fair (www.bookfair.pl) May
Mozart Festival (www.operakameralna.pl) June/July
Warsaw Summer Jazz Days (www.adamiakjazz.pl) July
Art of the Street Festival (www.sztukaulicy.pl) July
Warsaw Autumn International Festival of Contemporary Music (www.warsaw-autumn.art.pl) September
International Frédéric Chopin Piano Competition (www.konkurs.chopin.pl) October five-yearly, next due in 2010
Warsaw Film Festival (www.wff.pl) October

SLEEPING

Not surprisingly, Warsaw is the most expensive Polish city for accommodation, though there's a number of reasonably priced hostels around town. The tourist offices (p597) can help find a room.

Budget

Camping Nr 123 (Map p595; 022 822 9121; www.astur.waw.pl; ul Bitwy Warszawskiej 1920r 15/17; per person/tent 24/10zł;) Set in extensive grounds near the Dworzec Zachodnia bus station. Cabins (90zł) are also available from mid-April to mid-October and there's a tennis court nearby.

Smolna Youth Hostel (Map p598; 022 827 8952; www.hostelsmolna30.pl; ul Smolna 30; dm 36zł, s/d 65/120zł) Very central and very popular, though there's a midnight curfew (2am in July and August) and reception is closed between 10am and 4pm. It's simple but clean, and there's a lounge and kitchen area. Note that guests are separated into dorms according to gender, and reception is up four flights of stairs.

Hostel Helvetia (Map p598; 022 826 7108; www.hostel-helvetia.pl; ul Kopernika 36/40; dm 45-65zł, r 150-190zł) Bright hostel with an attractive combined lounge and kitchen. Dorms have lockers available, and there's one small women-only dorm. Bike hire is 25zł per day. Enter from the street behind, ul Sewerynów.

Nathan's Villa Hostel (Map p598; 022 622 2946; www.nathansvilla.com; ul Piękna 24/26; dm 45-65zł, r 170-180zł, apt 220zł) Nathan's sunlit courtyard leads to well-organised dorms, while private rooms are comfortable and decorated with monochrome photographs of Polish attractions. The kitchen is well set up, and there's a free laundry, a book exchange, and games to while away rainy days.

Hostel Kanonia (Map p598; 022 635 0676; www.kanonia.pl; ul Jezuicka 2; dm 50zł, r 190-240zł) Housed in a historic building in the heart of the Old Town, accommodation is mostly in dorms, with only one double and one triple. Some rooms have picturesque views onto the cobblestone streets, and there's a dining room with basic kitchen facilities.

Dom Przy Rynku Hostel (Map p598; 022 831 5033; www.cityhostel.net; Rynek Nowego Miasta 4; dm 55zł; Jul-Sep) Located in a quiet corner of the busy New Town, Przy Rynku is a neat, clean and friendly hostel occupying a 19th-century house. Its rooms accommodate two to five people, and there's a kitchen and laundry for guest use.

Oki Doki Hostel (Map p598; ☎ 022 826 5112; www
.okidoki.pl; Plac Dąbrowskiego 3; dm 55-73zł, s/d 142/220zł)
There are no drab dorms here. Each is deco-
rated thematically using the brightest paints
available; try the communist (red with a big
image of Lenin). Lower bunks have good
headroom, and the shared bathrooms are
clean and bright. The hostel also has a bar,
free washing machine and kitchen, and hires
out bikes (25zł per day).

Midrange

Hotel Praski (Map p598; ☎ 022 818 4989; www.praski
.pl; Al Solidarności 61; s/d from 150/230zł) The rooms of
this inexpensive hotel vary in size, but have
attractive high ceilings and comfortable beds.
Bathrooms are clean, red carpets add old-
fashioned charm, and some rooms have views
of Praski Park. It's an easy walk across the
river to the Old Town.

Premiere Classe (Map p595; ☎ 022 624 0800; www
.campanile.com.pl; ul Towarowa 2; r 189zł) If you're not
bothered too much by room size, this modern
hotel makes a good base. Rooms are small but
bright, and neatly set up with modern furnishings. Friendly staff is a plus. Guests can use
the restaurants, bars and fitness centre in the
neighbouring sister hotels.

Dom Literatury (Map p598; ☎ 022 828 3920;
www.fundacjadl.com/hotele.html, in Polish; ul Krakowskie
Przedmieście 87/89; s/d 220/370zł) Within a grand
historic building, this accommodation features rambling halls and staircases bedecked
with pot plants and sizeable paintings. There
is a maze of comfortable rooms, many of
which have excellent views of the Old Town
and the Vistula. You're paying for the location, however, rather than the standard, and
you can't expect too much English from the
friendly staff.

ourpick Castle Inn (Map p598; ☎ 022 425 0100;
www.castleinn.pl; ul Świętojańska 2; s 250zł, d from 270zł)
Progress up the stairs to the striking purple
decor and shiny tiles of this Old Town accommodation, situated in a 17th-century
tenement house. All rooms overlook either
Castle Sq or St John's Cathedral, and come
in a range of playful styles.

Hotel Gromada Centrum (Map p598; ☎ 022 582 9900;
www.gromada.pl; Plac Powstańców Warszawy 2; s/d from
320/350zł) Centrally located, the Gromada is a
big concrete box but also a great launching
pad for exploring the central city. Upstairs
from the funky green foyer, the featureless
brown-carpeted corridors stretch out into the

distance like an optical illusion. The rooms are
plain, but clean and spacious.

Hotel Harenda (Map p598; ☎ 022 826 0071; www
.hotelharenda.com.pl; ul Krakowskie Przedmieście 4/6; s/d/ste
from 320/360/460zł) Boasting a great location just
off the Royal Way, the Harenda's rooms are
neat and clean, with solid timber furniture.
There's an old-fashioned feel to the hotel's interiors, and an expensive antique shop just off
the foyer if retail therapy is required. Breakfast
is an additional 25zł.

Top End

Sofitel Victoria (Map p598; ☎ 022 657 8011; www.sofitel
.com; ul Królewska 11; d/ste from €150/250; ☒) The very
model of a modern business hotel, with a spacious marble foyer, and a lounge area housing
a small library of books on Polish culture and
history. The rooms are conservatively decorated, with gleaming bathrooms. The cheaper
doubles are great value.

Hotel Le Regina (Map p598; ☎ 022 531 6000; www
.leregina.com; ul Kościelna 12; d/ste from €180/450; ☒) It's
not cheap, but the Le Regina is a jaw-dropping
combination of traditional architecture and
contemporary design. The enormous rooms
feature king-size beds with headboards of
dark, polished wood. Deluxe rooms also have
timber floors, and terraces with courtyard
views. All rooms sport spectacular bathrooms
with marble benchtops.

Hotel Bristol (Map p598; ☎ 022 551 1000; www.war
saw.lemeridien.com; ul Krakowskie Przedmieście 42/44; r from
750zł; ☒) Established in 1899 and restored to
its former glory after a massive renovation, the
Bristol is touted as Poland's most luxurious
hotel. Its neoclassical exterior houses a feast
of original art nouveau features, and huge,
traditionally decorated rooms. Attentive staff
cater to your every whim.

EATING

The most recent revolution to conquer the
Polish capital has been a gastronomic one.
A good selection of restaurants can be found
in the Old Town and New Town, and in the
area between ul Nowy Świat and the Palace
of Culture & Science.

Budget

Tukan Salad Bar (Map p598; ☎ 022 531 2520; Plac
Bankowy 2; mains from 5zł; ☺8am-8pm Mon-Fri, 10am-
6pm Sat) This place has several outlets around
the capital offering a wide choice of salads. As
the name suggests, look for the toucan on the

door. This branch is hidden from the street in the arcade running parallel.

Bar Pod Barbakanem (Map p598; ul Mostowa 27/29; mains 5-8zł; 8am-5pm Mon-Fri, 9am-5pm Sat & Sun) Near the Barbican, this popular former milk bar that survived the fall of the Iron Curtain continues to serve cheap, unpretentious food in an interior marked by tiles: on the floor, walls and tabletops. Fill up while peering out through the lace curtains at the passing tourist hordes.

our pick **Cô tú** (Map p598; Hadlowo-Usługowe 21; mains 10-14zł; 10am-9pm Mon-Fri, 11am-7pm Sat & Sun) The wok at this simple Asian diner never rests, as hungry Poles can't get enough of the excellent dishes coming from the kitchen. The menu is enormous, covering seafood, vegetable, beef, chicken and pork, and you'll never have to wait more than 10 minutes for your food despite the queues. Duck through the archway at Nowy Świat 26 to find it.

Green Way (Map p598; 022 696 9321; ul Hoża 54; mains 10-13zł; 10am-8pm Mon-Fri, 11am-7pm Sat & Sun) Slicker than the usual outlets of this chain, with a cafe ambience and a good outdoor dining zone. Take your pick of the international menu, which includes goulash, curry, samosas and enchiladas. Portions are hefty, and there's no table service.

Dżonka (Map p598; 022 621 5015; ul Hoża 54; mains 10-30zł; 11am-7pm Mon-Fri, 11am-5pm Sat & Sun) This hidden gem serves a range of Asian dishes, covering Chinese, Japanese, Korean and Thai cuisine. Though small (just six tables), it has loads of personality, with dark timber surfaces, bamboo place mats and Japanese newspapers plastering the walls. There's some spicy food on the menu, including Sichuan cuisine, though it's been toned down a little for Polish palates.

Restauracja Pod Samsonem (Map p598; 022 831 1788; ul Freta 3/5; mains 10-30zł) Situated in the New Town, and frequented by locals looking for inexpensive and tasty meals with a Jewish flavour. Interesting appetisers include Russian pancakes with salmon, and 'Jewish caviar'. Spot the bas relief of Samson and the lion above the next door along from the entrance.

The most convenient places for groceries are the **MarcPol Supermarket** (Map p598; Plac Defilad) in front of the Palace of Culture & Science building, and the **Albert Supermarket** (Map p598; ul Złota 59) in the Złote Tarasy shopping centre behind Warszawa Centralna train station.

Midrange & Top End

Bar Bistro Bez Kantów (Map p598; 022 892 9800; ul Krakowie Przedmieście 11; mains 15-45zł; 6am-11pm) Informal, sunlit eatery on the Royal Way, with timber tables beneath sleek wooden panelling. Dishes involve pork, duck, veal and fish. Unusually for a Polish restaurant, it also serves breakfast.

Gospoda Pod Kogutem (Map p598; 022 635 8282; ul Freta 50; mains 17-40zł) Cosy eatery at the top of the New Town, presenting quality versions of Polish classics in a soothing dark green interior. Eat outside in summer. If you're game, try pig's trotters 'the Polish way'.

Bazyliszek Restauracja (Map p598; 022 831 1841; Rynek Starego Miasta 1/3; mains 19-40zł) Step beneath the basilisk into this restaurant in a prime spot on the Old Town Market Sq. It serves mainly Polish-style dishes, with forays into foreign cuisine like Argentinian steak.

Zgoda Grill Bar (Map p598; 022 827 9934; ul Zgoda 4; mains 22-45zł) A bright, informal place serving up a range of tasty Polish standards. There's also a decent salad bar available.

Podwale Piwna Kompania (Map p598; 022 635 6314; ul Podwale 25; mains 21-49zł; 11am-1am Mon-Sat, noon-1am Sun) The restaurant's name (The Company of Beer) gives you an idea of the lively atmosphere in this eatery just outside the Old Town's moat. The menu features lots of grilled items and dishes such as roast duck, Wiener schnitzel, pork ribs and steak. There's a courtyard for outdoor dining.

Tam Tam (Map p598; 022 828 2622; ul Foksal 18; mains 25-39zł) Housed in a colourful 'African-style' place with outdoor seating in the warmer months. The varied menu includes pasta, soups and salads, and a big list of teas and coffees. Pull up a bongo drum as a seat, and tuck in.

London Steakhouse (Map p598; 022 827 0020; Al Jerozolimskie 42; mains 28-78zł) You'll find it hard to convince yourself you're in London, but it's fun to spot the UK memorabilia among the cluttered decor, while being served by waitresses wearing Union Jack neckties and miniskirts. Steaks dominate the menu, which also includes fish and chips. A full English breakfast is served daily until 2pm.

Taqueria Mexicana (Map p598; 022 556 4720; ul Zgoda 5; mains 29-52zł) Brightly-hued place festooned with Mexican rugs, featuring a central bar. Varieties of tacos, enchiladas and fajitas adorn the menu, and there's a 22zł set lunch.

Restauracja Przy Zamku (Map p598; ☎ 022 831 0259; Plac Zamkowy 15; mains 38–85zł) An attractive, old-world kind of place with hunting trophies on the walls and attentive, white-aproned waiters. The top-notch Polish menu includes fish and game and a bewildering array of entrées – try the excellent hare pâté served with cranberry sauce.

DRINKING

our pick **Sense** (Map p598; ul Nowy Świat 19; ☺ noon–late) A very modern venue with a mellow atmosphere. Comfortable banquettes sit beneath strings of cube-shaped lights, and there's an extensive wine and cocktail list, with some drinks measured in a 'Palace of Culture' (a tall scientific beaker). Try the house speciality, ginger rose vodka. There's also an impressive food menu if you're hungry.

Paparazzi (Map p598; ul Mazowiecka 12) This is one of Warsaw's flashest venues, where you can sip a bewildering array of cocktails under blown-up photos of Hollywood stars. It's big and roomy, with comfortable seating around the central bar.

Między Nami (Map p598; ul Bracka 20) A mix of bar, restaurant and cafe, 'Between You & Me' attracts a trendy set with its designer furniture, whitewashed walls, and excellent vegetarian menu. There's no sign over the door; look for the white awnings and chilled crowd.

ENTERTAINMENT
Nightclubs

There's no shortage of good clubs in Warsaw. Explore ul Mazowiecka, ul Sienkiewicza and the area around ul Nowy Świat for more nightclub action.

Enklawa (Map p598; www.enklawa.com, in Polish; ul Mazowiecka 12; ☺ 9pm–4am Tue–Sat) Funky red-and-orange space with comfy plush seating, mirrored ceilings, two bars and plenty of room to dance. Check out the long drinks list, hit the dance floor or observe the action from a stool on the upper balcony. Wednesday night is 'old school' night, with music from the '70s to '90s.

Foksal 19 (Map p598; ul Foksal 19; ☺ bar 5pm–1am Mon–Thu, 5pm–3am Fri & Sat, nightclub 11pm–5am Fri & Sat) Ultramodern playpen for Warsaw's bright young things. Downstairs is a cool drinking zone with a backlit bar, subdued golden lighting and comfy couches. Upstairs is the nightclub – a blue-lit contemporary space with DJs playing a variety of sounds.

Underground Music Café (Map p598; www.under .pl, in Polish; ul Marszałkowska 126/134) A swarm of students and backpackers pour into this basement club for its cheap beer, dark lighting and selection of music that varies from '70s and '80s to house, R&B and hip hop. Enter via the below-ground staircase facing McDonald's.

Tygmont (Map p598; ☎ 022 828 3409; www.tygmont .com.pl; ul Mazowiecka 6/8; ☺ 6pm–late) Hosting both local and international acts, the live jazz here is both varied and plentiful. Concerts start around 8pm but the place fills up early, so either reserve a table or turn up at opening time. Dinner is also available.

Free jazz concerts also take place in the Old Town's Rynek Starego Miasta on Saturday at 7pm in July and August.

Performing Arts

Advance tickets for most theatrical events can be bought at **ZASP Kasy Teatralne** (Map p598; ☎ 022 621 9454; Al Jerozolimskie 25; ☺ 9am–7pm Mon–Fri) or **EMPiK** Galeria Centrum (Map p598; ul Marszałkowska 116/122); Royal Way (Map p598; ul Nowy Świat 15/17) in the city centre.

Teatr Ateneum (Map p598; ☎ 022 625 7330; www .teatrateneum.pl, in Polish; ul Jaracza 2) This place leans towards contemporary Polish-language productions.

Teatr Wielki (Map p598; ☎ 022 692 0200; www.teatr wielki.pl; Plac Teatralny 1) The Grand Theatre hosts opera and ballet in its aptly grand premises.

Filharmonia Narodowa (Map p598; ☎ 022 551 7111; www.filharmonia.pl; ul Jasna 5) Classical-music concerts are held here.

Cinemas

To avoid watching Polish TV in your hotel room, catch a film at the central **Kino Atlantic** (Map p598; ul Chmielna 33) or enjoy a flick in socialist-era glory at **Kinoteka** (Map p598; Plac Defilad 1) within the Palace of Culture & Science.

SHOPPING

Galeria Centrum (Map p598; ul Marszałowska 104/122) is a sprawling modern shopping mall in the city centre.

There are also plentiful antique, arts and crafts shops around Rynek Starego Miasta in the Old Town, so brandish your credit card and explore. One of the most interesting is **Lapidarium** (Map p598; ☎ 022 635 6828; www.lapidarium .pl; ul Nowomiejska 15/7), which offers jewellery and communist-era collectibles.

GETTING THERE & AWAY
Air
The **Warsaw Frédéric Chopin airport** (Map p595; www.lotnisko-chopina.pl) is more commonly called Okęcie airport. The separate Etiuda terminal mostly handles discount airline departures. The useful tourist office (p597) is on the arrivals level of Terminal 2.

At the arrivals level there are ATMs and several *kantors*. There are also car-rental companies, a left-luggage room and a newsagent where you can buy public transport tickets.

Domestic and international flights can be booked at the **LOT office** (Map p598; ☎ 0801 703 703; Al Jerozolimskie 65/79), or at any travel agency. Other airlines are listed on p666.

Bus
Warsaw has two major bus terminals for PKS buses. **Dworzec Zachodnia** (Western Bus Station; Map p595; Al Jerozolimskie 144) handles domestic buses heading south, north and west of the capital, including up to nine daily to Częstochowa (41zł, four hours), 10 to Gdańsk (50zł, six hours), nine to Kraków (43zł, six hours), 11 to Olsztyn (30zł, five hours), five to Toruń (37zł, four hours), four to Wrocław (51zł, seven hours), and five to Zakopane (57zł, eight hours). This complex is southwest of the city centre and adjoins the Warszawa Zachodnia train station. Take the commuter train that leaves from Warszawa Śródmieście station.

Dworzec Stadion (Stadium Bus Station; Map p595; ul Sokola 1) adjoins the Warszawa Stadion train station. It is also easily accessible by commuter train from Warszawa Śródmieście. Dworzec Stadion handles some domestic buses to the east and southeast, including 20 daily to Lublin (26zł, three hours), four to Białystok (30zł, 3½ hours) and three to Zamość (35zł, 4¾ hours).

Polski Express (Map p598) operates coaches from the airport, but passengers can also get on or off and buy tickets at the kiosk along Al Jana Pawła II, next to the Warszawa Centralna train station. Useful Polski Express services include those to Lublin (31zł, 3½ hours, five daily), Szczecin (63zł, 9½ hours, two daily) and Toruń (41zł, 3½ hours, eight daily).

International buses depart from and arrive at Dworzec Zachodnia or, occasionally, outside Warszawa Centralna. Tickets are available from the bus offices at Dworzec Zachodnia, from agencies at Warszawa Centralna or from any of the major travel agencies in the city,

including Almatur (p597). **Eurolines Polska** (www .eurolinespolska.pl) operates a huge number of buses to destinations throughout Eastern and Western Europe; some sample routes include Amsterdam (20 hours, daily), Cologne (20½ hours, daily), London (27 hours, four weekly), Paris (24 hours, daily), Rome (28 hours, four weekly) and Vienna (13 hours, five weekly).

Train
Warsaw has several train stations, but the one that most travellers will use is **Warszawa Centralna** (Warsaw Central; Map p598; Al Jerozolimskie 54). Refer to the relevant destination sections in this chapter for information about services to/from Warsaw.

Warszawa Centralna is not always where trains start or finish, so make sure you get on or off promptly; and guard your belongings against pickpocketing and theft at all times.

The station's main hall houses ticket counters, ATMs and snack bars, as well as a post office, newsagents and a tourist office. Along the underground mezzanine level leading to the platforms are a dozen *kantors* (one of which is open 24 hours), a **left-luggage office** (⏰ 7am–midnight), lockers, eateries, outlets for local public transport tickets, internet cafes and bookshops.

Tickets for domestic and international trains are available from counters at the station (but allow at least an hour for possible queuing) or, in advance, from any major Orbis Travel office (p597). Tickets for immediate departures on domestic and international trains are also available from numerous, well-signed booths in the underpasses leading to Warszawa Centralna.

Some domestic trains also stop at Warszawa Śródmieście station, 300m east of Warszawa Centralna, and Warszawa Zachodnia, next to Dworzec Zachodnia bus station.

GETTING AROUND
To/From the Airport
The cheapest way of getting from the airport to the city centre is bus 175, which leaves every 10 to 15 minutes for the Old Town, via ul Nowy Świat and Warszawa Centralna train station. If you arrive in the wee hours, night bus N32 links the airport with Warszawa Centralna every 30 minutes.

The taxi fare between the airport and the city centre is from 35zł to 40zł. Official taxis displaying a name, telephone number and fares can be arranged at the official taxi counters at the international arrivals level.

Car

Warsaw traffic isn't fun, but there are good reasons to hire a car for jaunts into the countryside. Major car-rental companies are listed in the local English-language publications, and include **Avis** (☎ 022 650 4872; www.avis.pl), **Hertz** (☎ 022 500 1620; www.hertz.com.pl) and **Sixt** (☎ 022 511 1550; www.sixt.pl). For more details about car hire see p668.

Public Transport

Warsaw's public transport operates from 5am to 11pm daily. The fare (2.80zł) is valid for one ride only on a bus, tram, trolleybus or metro train travelling anywhere in the city.

Warsaw is the only place in Poland where ISIC cards get a public-transport discount (of 48%).

Tickets are available for 60/90 minutes (4/6zł), one day (9zł), three days (16zł), one week (32zł) and one month (78zł). Buy tickets from kiosks (including those marked 'RUCH') before boarding, and validate them on board.

A metro line operates from the Ursynów suburb (Kabaty station) at the southern city limits to Słodowiec in the north, via the city centre (Centrum), but is of limited use to visitors. Local commuter trains head out to the suburbs from the Warszawa Śródmieście station.

Taxi

Taxis are a quick and easy way to get around – as long as you use official taxis and drivers use their meters. Beware of unauthorised 'Mafia' taxis parked in front of top-end hotels, at the airport, outside Warszawa Centralna train station and in the vicinity of most tourist sights.

MAZOVIA & PODLASIE

After being ruled as an independent state by a succession of dukes, Mazovia shot to prominence during the 16th century, when Warsaw became the national capital. The region has long been a base for industry, the traditional mainstay of Poland's second largest city, Łódź. To the east of Mazovia, toward the Belarus border, lies Podlasie, which means 'land close to the forest'. The main attraction of this region is the impressive Białowieża National Park.

ŁÓDŹ

pop 767,000

Little damaged in WWII, Łódź (pronounced woodge) is a lively, likeable place with a wealth of attractive art nouveau architecture, and the added bonus of being off the usual tourist track. It's also an easy day trip from Warsaw. Łódź became a major industrial centre in the 19th century, attracting immigrants from across Europe. Though its textile industry slumped in the post-communist years, the centrally-located city has had some success in attracting new investment in more diverse commercial fields.

Many of the attractions are along ul Piotrkowska, the main thoroughfare. You'll find banks and *kantors* here, and on ul Kopernika, one street west. You can't miss the bronze statues of local celebrities along ul Piotrkowska, including pianist Artur Rubenstein, seated at a baby grand. The helpful **tourist office** (☎ 042 638 5955; www.cityoflodz.pl; ul Piotrkowska 87; ☯ 8am-7pm Mon-Fri, 9am-2pm Sat May-Oct, 8am-6pm Mon-Fri, 9am-2pm Sat Nov-Apr) hands out free tourist brochures.

As Łódź is famous for being the centre of Poland's cinema industry (giving rise to the nickname 'Holly-Woodge'), film buffs will find some attractions of interest here. Along ul Piotrkowska near the Grand Hotel, you can see **star-shaped plaques** honouring Polish stars and directors such as Roman Polański, and the **Cinematography Museum** (www.kinomuzeum.pl; Plac Zwycięstwa 1; adult/concession 5/3zł; ☯ 9am-4pm Wed & Fri-Sun, 11am-5pm Tue & Thu) three blocks east of ul Piotrkowska's southern pedestrian zone is worth a look both for its collection of old cinema gear and its mansion setting.

The **Historical Museum of Łódź** (ul Ogrodowa 15; adult/concession 7/4zł, free Sun; ☯ 10am-2pm Mon, 10am-4pm Tue & Thu, 2-6pm Wed, 10am-2pm Sat & Sun) is 200m northwest of Plac Wolności, at the northern end of the main drag. Close by is the fascinating **Manufaktura** (www.manufaktura.com; ul Karskiego 5), a shopping mall and entertainment centre constructed within a massive complex of historic red-brick factory buildings. **Dętka** (Plac Wolności 2; adult/concession 4/2zł; ☯ noon-8pm Wed, Sat & Sun, Jun-Sep) is a new attraction operated by the Historical Museum, which features guided tours every half-hour through the old brick sewer system beneath the city's streets, with exhibits en route.

Herbst Palace (ul Przędzalniana 72; adult/concession 7/4.50zł, free Thu; ☯ 10am-5pm Tue, noon-5pm Wed & Fri, noon-7pm Thu, 11am-4pm Sat & Sun) has been converted into an appealing museum. It's accessible by bus 55 heading east from the cathedral at the southern end of ul Piotrkowska. The **Jewish Cemetery** (www.jewishlodzcemetery.org; ul Bracka 40; admission 4zł, free first Sun of month; ☼ 9am-5pm Sun-Thu, 9am-3pm Fri Apr-Oct, 9am-3pm Sun-Fri Nov-Mar) is one of the largest in Europe. It's 3km northeast of the city centre and accessible by tram 1 or 6 from near Plac Wolności. Enter from ul Zmienna.

The tourist office can provide information about all kinds of accommodation. The **youth hostel** (☎ 042 630 6680; www.yhlodz.pl; ul Legionów 27; dm 18-30zł, s/d/tr 45/71/120zł) is excellent, so book ahead. It features nicely decorated rooms in a spacious old building, with free laundry and a kitchen. It's 250m west of Plac Wolności.

The **Hotel Savoy** (☎ 042 632 9360; www.hotelsavoy .com.pl; ul Traugutta 6; s/d from 119/249zł) is well positioned just off central ul Piotrkowska. Don't be put off by the scuffed corridors and stencilled door numbers: they conceal spacious, light-filled rooms with clean bathrooms.

Around the corner, the **Grand Hotel** (☎ 042 633 9920; www.orbis.pl; ul Piotrkowska 72; s/d from 289/339zł) offers a touch of faded, if overpriced, fin de siècle grandeur.

Opposite the Grand, **Chłopska Izba** (☎ 042 630 8087; ul Piotrkowska 65; mains 15-39zł; ☼ noon-11pm) is a restaurant with folksy decor, serving up tasty versions of all the Polish standards. **Esplanada** (☎ 042 630 5989; ul Piotrkowska 100; mains 19-39zł) is an excellent belle époque–style eatery serving quality Polish cuisine in a colourful venue.

From the **airport** (www.airport.lodz.pl), which can be reached by city buses 55, 65 and L (2.40zł, 20 minutes), there are flights via Ryanair to several British and Irish destinations, including London (at least daily) and Dublin (three weekly). Jet Air connects to other European cities, including Vienna (twice daily). The only domestic flights are twice-daily Jet Air services to Bydgoszcz, from where you can connect to other Polish and international cities.

From the convenient Łódź Fabryczna station, 400m east of the city centre, you can travel to Warsaw (31zł, 1½ hours, 15 daily) and Częstochowa (33zł, 2½ hours, three daily). From the Łódź Kaliska train station, 1.2km southwest of central Łódź, trains go to Warsaw (33zł, two hours, three daily), Wrocław (43zł, four hours, three daily), Poznań (43zł, 4½ hours, seven daily), Częstochowa (33zł, two hours, six daily), Toruń (34zł, three hours,

10 daily) and Gdańsk (51zł, seven hours, five daily). Buses head in all directions from the bus terminal, next to the Fabryczna train station.

BIAŁOWIEŻA NATIONAL PARK

Once a centre for hunting and timber-felling, Białowieża (Byah-wo-*vyeh*-zhah) is now Poland's oldest national park. Its significance is underlined by Unesco's unusual recognition of the reserve as both a Biosphere Reserve *and* a World Heritage site. The forest contains over 100 species of birds, along with elk, wild boars and wolves. Its major drawcard is the magnificent European bison, which was once extinct outside zoos, but has been successfully reintroduced to its ancient home.

The logical visitor base is the charming village of **Białowieża**. The main road to Białowieża from Hajnówka leads to the southern end of Palace Park (the former location of the Russian tsar's hunting lodge), then skirts around the park to become the village's main street, ul Waszkiewicza. At the western end of this street is the **post office** (☼ 7am-7pm Mon-Fri, 7am-2pm Sat).

Money can be changed at the Hotel Żubrówka; the hotel also has an ATM by the entrance and offers public internet access in its foyer.

You'll find the **PTTK** (Polskie Towarzystwo Turystyczno-Krajoznawcze, Polish Tourist Country Lovers Society; ☎ 085 681 2295; www.pttk.bialowieza.pl; ul Kolejowa 17; ☼ 8am-4pm) at the southern end of Palace Park. Serious hikers should contact the **National Park office** (☎ 085 682 9700; www.bpn .com.pl, in Polish; ☼ 9am-4pm) inside Palace Park. Most maps of the national park (especially the one published by PTOP – Północnopodlaskie Towarzystwo Ochrony Ptaków, North Podlasian Bird Protection Society) – detail several enticing hiking trails.

Sights & Activities

The elegant **Palace Park** (admission free; ☼ daylight hr) is only accessible on foot, bicycle or horse-drawn cart across the bridge from the PTTK office. Over the river is the excellent **Natural & Forestry Museum** (adult/concession 12/6zł; ☼ 9am-4.30pm Apr-Sep, 9am-4pm Tue-Sun Oct-Mar), with displays on local flora and fauna, and beekeeping.

The **European Bison Reserve** (Rezerwat Żubrów; adult/concession 6/3zł; ☼ 9am-5pm May-Sep, 8am-4pm Tue-Sun Oct-Apr) is an open-plan zoo containing many of these mighty beasts, as well as

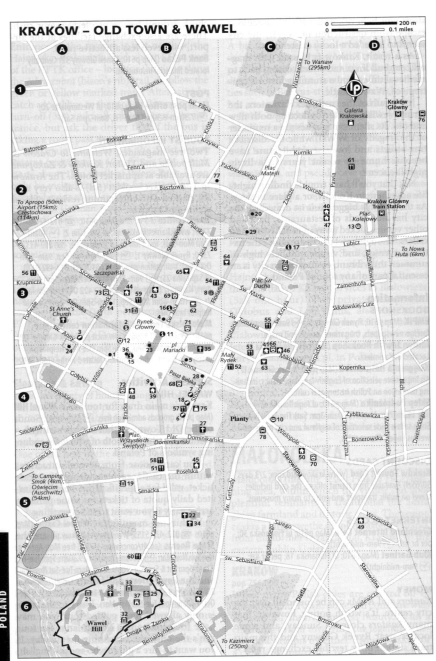

KRAKÓW – OLD TOWN & WAWEL

wolves, strange horse-like tarpans and mammoth żubroń (hybrids of bison and cows). Entrance to the reserve is just north of the Hajnówka–Białowieża road, about 4.5km west of the PTTK office – look for the signs along the *żebra żubra* (bison's rib) trail, or follow the green or yellow marked trails. Alternatively, catch a local bus to the stop at the main road turn-off (3zł) and walk a kilometre to the entrance, but ask the driver first if the bus is taking a route past the reserve.

The main attraction is the **Strict Nature Reserve** (adult/concession 6/3zł; ☺ 9am-5pm), which starts about 1km north of Palace Park. It can only be visited on a three-hour tour with a licensed guide along an 8km trail (165zł for an English- or German-speaking guide). Licensed guides (in many languages) can be arranged at the PTTK office or any travel agency in the village. Note that the reserve does close sometimes due to inclement weather.

A comfortable way to visit the nature reserve is by horse-drawn cart, which costs 160zł in addition to guide and entry fees (three hours) and holds four people. Otherwise, it may be possible (with permission from the PTTK office) to visit the reserve by bicycle (with a guide). The Dom Turysty PTTK hires out bikes (25zł per day), as do several other hotels and pensions.

Sleeping & Eating

There are plenty of homes along the road from Hajnówka offering private rooms for about 40/70zł for singles/doubles.

Paprotka Youth Hostel (☎ 085 681 2560; www .paprotka.com.pl; ul Waszkiewicza 6; dm from 19zł, s/d 30/50zł) One of the best in the region. The rooms are light and spruce, with high ceilings and potted plants; the newly renovated bathrooms are clean, and the kitchen is excellent. There's a washing machine as well.

Dom Turysty PTTK (☎ 085 681 2505; dm from 25zł, d/tr/q from 80/105/128zł) Inexpensive accommodation inside Palace Park. It's seen better days, but the position and rates are hard to beat. It has a pleasant restaurant with a bison-head motif.

Pension Gawra (☎ 085 681 2804; www.gawra.bialow ieza.com; ul Polecha 2; d/tr from 60/90zł) A quiet, homely place with large rooms lined with timber in a hunting lodge–style, overlooking a pretty garden just behind the Hotel Żubrówka. The doubles with bathrooms are much more spacious than those without.

Pensjonacik Unikat (☎ 085 681 2774; www.unikat.bi alowieza.com; ul Waszkiewicza 39; s/d/tr/q 90/100/120/140zł) A bit too fond of dead creatures' hides as decor, but good value with its tidy wood-panelled rooms, one of which is designed for disabled access. The restaurant offers specialities such as Belarus-style potato pancakes, and has a menu in both German and English.

Hotel Żubrówka (☎ 085 681 2303; www.hotel -zubrowka.pl; ul Olgi Gabiec 6; s/d/ste from 340/380/500zł) Just across the way from the PTTK office, this is the town's best hotel. It's eccentrically decorated with animal hides, a working miniature water wheel, and pseudo cave drawings along the corridors. Rooms are predictably clean and comfortable, and there's a cafe, restaurant and nightclub on the premises.

Getting There & Away

From Warsaw, take the express train from Warszawa Centralna to Siedlce (1½ hours), wait for a connection on the slow train to Hajnówka (two hours), and then catch one of the nine daily PKS bus services to Białowieża (5zł, one hour). Two private companies, Oktobus and Lob-Trans, also run fairly squeezy minibuses between Hajnówka and Białowieża (5zł, one hour, 10 daily). For the latest timetable information, check out www .turystyka.hajnowka.pl, in Polish.

Four buses a day travel from the Dworzec Stadion station in Warsaw to Białystok (30zł, 3½ hours), from where two buses travel to Białowieża, at 6.30am and 3.10pm (15zł, 2½ hours). You may need to stay overnight in Białystok to catch these connecting services.

MAŁOPOLSKA

Małopolska (literally 'lesser Poland') is a stunning area, within which the visitor can spot plentiful remnants of traditional life amid green farmland and historic cities. The region covers a large swathe of southeastern Poland, from the former royal capital, Kraków, to the eastern Lublin Uplands.

KRAKÓW
pop 756,000

While many Polish cities are centred on an attractive Old Town, none can compare with Kraków for sheer, effortless beauty. With a charming origin involving the legendary defeat of a dragon by either Prince Krakus or a cobbler's apprentice (depending on which

POLAND

story you believe), and with a miraculous escape from destruction in WWII, the city seems to have led a lucky existence.

As a result, Kraków is blessed with magnificent buildings and streets dating back to medieval times, and a stunning historic centrepiece, Wawel Castle.

Just south of the castle lies Kazimierz, the former Jewish quarter, reflecting both new and old. Its silent synagogues are a reminder of the tragedy of WWII, while the district's tiny streets and low-rise architecture have become home in recent years to a lively nightlife scene.

Not that you'll have trouble finding nightlife anywhere in Kraków, or a place to sleep. As the nation's biggest tourist drawcard, the city has hundreds of restaurants, bars and other venues tucked away in its laneways and cellars. Though hotel prices are above the national average, and visitor numbers high in summer, this vibrant, cosmopolitan city is an essential part of any tour of Poland.

Information
BOOKSHOPS
EMPiK (Map p610; Rynek Główny 5; 9am-10pm) Sells foreign newspapers, magazines, novels and maps.
Jarden Jewish Bookshop (Map p612; ul Szeroka 2) Located in Kazimierz.
Księgarnia Hetmańska (Map p610; Rynek Główny 17) An impressive selection of English-language books, including nonfiction on Polish history and culture.
Sklep Podróżnika (Map p610; ul Jagiellońska 6; 11am-7pm Mon-Fri, 10am-3pm Sat) The Traveller's Shop sells a wide selection of regional and city maps, as well as Lonely Planet titles.

DISCOUNT CARDS
Kraków Tourist Card (www.krakowcard.com; 2/3 days 50/65zł) Available from tourist offices, the card includes travel on public transport and entry to many museums.

INTERNET ACCESS
Greenland Internet Café (Map p610; ul Floriańska 30; per hr 4zł; 9am-midnight)
Klub Garinet (Map p610; ul Floriańska 18; per hr 4zł; 9am-midnight)

MONEY
Kantors and ATMs can be found all over the city centre. It's worth noting, however, that many *kantors* close on Sunday, and some located near Rynek Główny and the main train station offer terrible exchange rates –

check around before proffering your cash. There are also exchange facilities at the airport, with even less attractive rates.
Bank Pekao (Map p610; Rynek Główny 32) Centrally located financial institution.

POST
Main post office (Map p610; ul Westerplatte 20; 7.30am-8.30pm Mon-Fri, 8am-2pm Sat)

TOURIST INFORMATION
Two free magazines, *Welcome to Cracow & Małopolska* and *Visitor: Kraków & Zakopane* are available at upmarket hotels. The *Kraków in Your Pocket* booklet (5zł) is also very useful, packed with entertaining reviews of local sights and eateries.
Tourist office ul Św. Jana (Map p610; ☎ 012 421 7787; www.karnet.krakow.pl; ul Św. Jana 2; 10am-6pm Mon-Sat); town hall tower (Map p610; ☎ 012 433 7310; Rynek Główny 1; 9am-7pm Apr-Sep, 9am-5pm Oct-Mar); train station area (Map p610; ☎ 012 432 0110; ul Szpitalna 25; 9am-7pm May-Oct, 9am-5pm Nov-Apr); Kazimierz (Map p612; ☎ 012 422 0471; ul Józefa 7; 10am-6pm May-Sep, 11am-5pm Oct-Apr) Several helpful branches.
Małopolska tourism information centre (Map p610; ☎ 012 421 7706; www.mcit.pl; Rynek Główny 1/3; 9am-8pm May-Sep, 9am-5pm Oct-Apr) Helpful privately run tourist office centrally located in the Cloth Hall.

Sights & Activities
WAWEL HILL
Kraków's main draw for tourists is **Wawel Hill** (Map p610; grounds admission free; 6am-dusk). South of the Old Town, the hill is crowned with a castle and cathedral, both of which are enduring symbols of Poland.

You can choose from several attractions within the castle, each requiring a separate ticket, valid for a specific time. There's a limited daily quota of tickets for some parts, so arrive early if you want to see everything.

Within the magnificent **Wawel Castle** (Map p610; ☎ 012 422 5155; www.wawel.krakow.pl) are the **State Rooms** (adult/concession 15/8zł, free Mon Apr-Oct, free Sun Nov-Mar; 9.30am-1pm Mon, 9.30am-5pm Tue-Fri, 11am-6pm Sat & Sun Apr-Oct, 9.30am-4pm Tue-Sat Nov-Mar) and the **Royal Private Apartments** (adult/concession 20/15zł; 9.30am-5pm Tue-Fri, 11am-6pm Sat & Sun Apr-Oct, 9.30am-4pm Tue-Sat Nov-Mar). Entry to the latter is only allowed on a guided tour; you may have to accompany a Polish language tour if it's the only one remaining for the day. If you want to hire a guide who speaks English,

POLAND

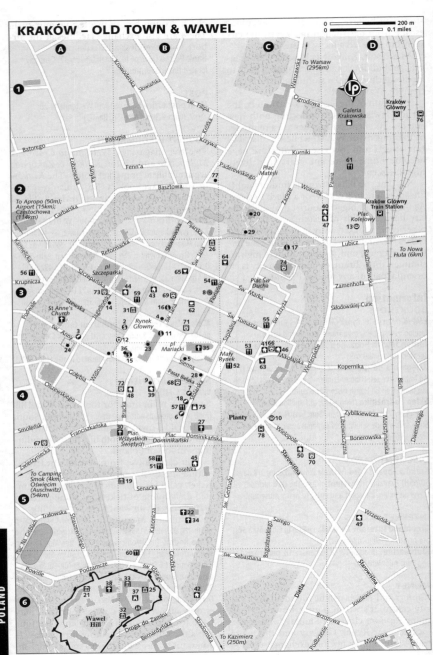

KRAKÓW – OLD TOWN & WAWEL

French or German, contact the onsite **guides office** (☎ 012 422 1697).

The 14th-century **Wawel Cathedral** (Map p610; adult/concession 10/5zł; 9am-5pm Mon-Sat, 12.15-5pm Sun) was the coronation and burial place of Polish royalty for four centuries, and houses **Royal Tombs**, including that of King Kazimierz Wielki. The **bell tower** of the golden-domed **Sigismund Chapel** (1539) contains the country's largest bell (11 tonnes).

Ecclesiastical artefacts are displayed in the small **Cathedral Museum** (Map p610; adult/concession 5/2zł; 10am-3pm Tue-Sun).

Other attractions include the **Museum of Oriental Art** (adult/concession 7/4zł; 9.30am-5pm Tue-Fri, 11am-6pm Sat & Sun Apr-Oct, 9.30am-4pm Tue-Sat Nov-Mar); the **Crown Treasury & Armoury** (adult/concession 15/8zł, free Mon; 9.30am-5pm Tue-Fri, 11am-6pm Sat & Sun Apr-Oct, 9.30am-4pm Tue-Sun Nov-Mar); the **Lost Wawel** (adult/concession 7/4zł, free Mon Apr-Oct, free Sun Nov-Mar; 9.30am-1pm Mon, 9.30am-5pm Tue-Fri, 11am-6pm Sat & Sun Apr-Oct, 9.30am-4pm Tue-Sat Nov-Mar), a well-displayed set of intriguing archaeological exhibits; and the atmospheric **Dragon's Cave** (Map p610; admission 3zł; 10am-5pm Apr-Oct). Go here last, as the exit leads out onto the riverbank.

OLD TOWN

The focus of the Old Town is **Rynek Główny** (Main Market Sq), Europe's largest medieval town square (200m by 200m). At its centre is the 16th-century Renaissance **Cloth Hall** (Sukiennice; Map p610), housing a large souvenir market. The upstairs **Gallery of 19th-Century Polish Painting** is closed for a renovation expected to take several years; if you're keen to see its works, you can catch a minibus from ul Starowiślna near the post office to its **temporary exhibition** (ul Zamkowa 2, Niepołomice; adult/concession 8/5zł; 10am-6pm) outside Kraków at the Royal Castle in Niepołomice.

The 14th-century **St Mary's Church** (Map p610; Rynek Główny 4; adult/concession 6/4zł; 11.30am-6pm Mon-Sat, 2-6pm Sun) fills the northeastern corner of the square. The huge main altarpiece by Wit Stwosz (Veit Stoss in German) of Nuremberg is the finest Gothic sculpture in Poland, and is opened ceremoniously each day at 11.50am. Every hour a *hejnał* (bugle call) is played from the highest tower of the church. The melody, played in medieval times as a warning call, breaks off abruptly to symbolise the moment when, according to legend, the throat of a 13th-century trumpeter was pierced by

POLAND

a Tatar arrow. Between May and August you can climb the **tower** (adult/concession 5/3zł).

Just south of St Mary's, the **English Language Club** (ul Sienna 5; admission 1.50zł; ☾ 6-8pm Wed) has met weekly since the dying days of communism, when local students wanted to make contact with foreign visitors. Their meetings are a fun way to meet a mixed bunch of Poles, expats and tourists in a relaxed setting.

West of the Cloth Hall is the 15th-century **town hall tower** (Map p610; adult/concession 6/4zł; ☾ 10.30am-6pm May-Oct), which you can climb. A little further west is the **Collegium Maius** (p610; ul Jagiellońska 15; adult/concession 12/6zł; Sat 6zł; ☾ 10am-2.20pm Mon-Fri, 10am-1.20pm Sat), the oldest surviving university building in Poland. Guided tours of its fascinating academic collection run half-hourly and there's usually a couple in English, at 11am and 1pm. Even if you don't go on a tour, step into the magnificent arcaded courtyard for a glimpse of the beautiful architecture.

On the northwest corner of the Rynek, the **Historical Museum of Kraków** (Map p610; www.mhk.pl; Rynek Główny 35; adult/concession 8/6zł, free Sat; ☾ 10am-5.30pm Wed-Sun May-Oct, 9am-4pm Wed & Fri-Sun, 10am-5pm Thu Nov-Apr) has paintings, documents and oddments relating to the city.

From St Mary's Church, walk up (northeast) ul Floriańska to the 14th-century **Florian Gate**. This is a tourism hotspot, with crowds, buskers, and artists selling their work along the remnant section of the old city walls. Beyond it is the **Barbican** (Map p610; adult/concession 6/4zł; ☾ 10.30am-6pm Apr-Oct), a defensive bastion built in 1498. Nearby, the **Czartoryski Museum** (Map p610; ul Św Jana 19; adult/concession 10/5zł, free Sun May-Oct, free Thu Nov-Apr; ☾ 10am-6pm Tue-Sat, 10am-4pm Sun May-Oct, 10am-3.30pm Tue-Sun Nov-Apr) features an impressive collection of European art, including Leonardo da Vinci's *Lady with an Ermine*. Also on display are Turkish weapons and artefacts, including a campaign tent from the 1683 Battle of Vienna.

South of Rynek Główny, Plac Wszystkich Świętych is dominated by two 13th-century monastic churches: the **Dominican Church** (Map p610; ul Stolarska 12; admission free; ☾ 9am-6pm) to the east and the **Franciscan Church** (Map p610; Plac Wszystkich Świętych 5; admission free; ☾ 9am-5pm) to the west. The latter is noted for its stained-glass windows.

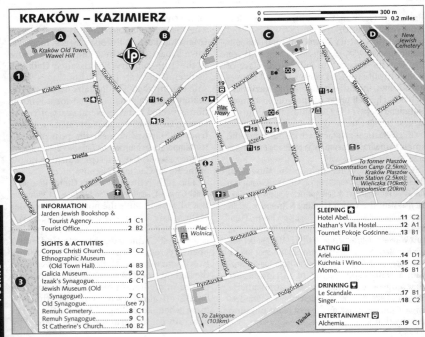

KRAKÓW – KAZIMIERZ

0 _____ 300 m
0 _____ 0.2 miles

INFORMATION
Jarden Jewish Bookshop & Tourist Agency................1 C1
Tourist Office..............................2 B2

SIGHTS & ACTIVITIES
Corpus Christi Church.............3 C2
Ethnographic Museum (Old Town Hall)..............4 B3
Galicia Museum.......................5 D2
Izaak's Synagogue..................6 C1
Jewish Museum (Old Synagogue)........................7 C1
Old Synagogue.................(see 7)
Remuh Cemetery.....................8 C1
Remuh Synagogue..................9 C1
St Catherine's Church............10 B2

SLEEPING 🛏
Hotel Abel.................................11 C2
Nathan's Villa Hostel............12 A1
Tournet Pokoje Gościnne......13 B1

EATING 🍴
Ariel..14 D1
Kuchnia i Wino......................15 C2
Momo......................................16 B1

DRINKING 🍷
Le Scandale............................17 B1
Singer.....................................18 C2

ENTERTAINMENT 🎭
Alchemia................................19 C1

POLAND

FREE THRILLS

If you're short of cash, take advantage of these *gratis* Kraków attractions:

- Visit the beautiful courtyard of the **Collegium Maius** (opposite).

- Soak up the heady historical atmosphere of the grounds of **Wawel Castle** (p609).

- Examine the intriguing collection of the **Czartoryski Museum** (opposite) for free on certain weekdays.

- Catch the historic *hejnał* (bugle call) being played from the tower of **St Mary's Church** (p611) each hour.

- Take a walk from the bus 134 terminus through the Las Wolski woods to the monumental **Piłsudski Mound**.

To the south, you'll find the **Archaeological Museum** (Map p610; ul Poselska 3; adult/concession 7/5zł, free Sun; ☻ 9am-2pm Mon-Wed, 2-6pm Thu, 10am-2pm Fri & Sun), with displays on local prehistory and ancient Egyptian artefacts, including animal mummies.

Continuing south along ul Grodzka is the early 17th-century Jesuit **Church of SS Peter & Paul** (Map p610; ul Grodzka 64; ☻ dawn-dusk), Poland's first baroque church. The Romanesque 11th-century **St Andrew's Church** (Map p610; ul Grodzka 56; ☻ 9am-6pm Mon-Fri) was the only building in Kraków to withstand the Tatars' attack of 1241.

KAZIMIERZ

Founded by King Kazimierz the Great in 1335, Kazimierz was originally an independent town. In the 15th century, Jews were expelled from Kraków and forced to resettle in a small prescribed area in Kazimierz, separated by a wall. The Jewish quarter later became home to Jews fleeing persecution from throughout Europe.

By the outbreak of WWII there were 65,000 Jewish Poles in Kraków (around 30% of the city's population), and most lived in Kazimierz. During the war the Nazis relocated Jews to a walled ghetto in Podgórze, just south of the Vistula River. They were exterminated in the nearby **Płaszów Concentration Camp**, as portrayed in Steven Spielberg's haunting film *Schindler's List*.

Kazimierz's western Catholic quarter includes the 14th-century Gothic **St Catherine's Church** (Map p612; ul Augustian 7; admission free; ☻ only during services), with an imposing 17th-century gilded high altar, while the 14th-century **Corpus Christi Church** (Map p612; ul Bożego Ciała 26; admission free; ☻ 9am-7pm Mon-Sat) is crammed with baroque fittings. The **Ethnographic Museum** (Map p612; Plac Wolnica 1; adult/concession 8/4zł, free Sun; ☻ 11am-7pm Tue-Sat, 10am-3pm Sun May-Sep, 10am-6pm Mon, 10am-3pm Wed-Fri, 10am-2pm Sat & Sun Oct-Apr) in the Old Town Hall has a collection of regional crafts and costumes.

The eastern Jewish quarter is dotted with synagogues. The 15th-century **Old Synagogue** is the oldest Jewish religious building in Poland. It now houses the **Jewish Museum** (Map p612; ul Szeroka 24; adult/concession 7/5zł; ☻ 10am-2pm Mon, 9am-5pm Tue-Sun Apr-Oct, 10am-2pm Mon, 9am-4pm Wed-Sun Nov-Mar), with exhibitions on Jewish traditions.

Not far away, the **Galicia Museum** (Map p612; www.galiciajewishmuseum.org; ul Dajwór 18; adult/concession 12/6zł; ☻ 9am-7pm Mar-Oct, 10am-6pm Nov-Feb) features an impressive photographic exhibition, depicting modern-day traces of southeastern Poland's once thriving Jewish community.

A short walk north is the small 16th-century **Remuh Synagogue** (Map p612; ul Szeroka 40; adult/concession 5/2zł; ☻ 9am-4pm Sun-Fri), still used for religious services. Behind it, the **Remuh Cemetery** (admission free; ☻ 9am-4pm Mon-Fri) boasts some extraordinary Renaissance gravestones. Nearby, the restored **Izaak's Synagogue** (Map p612; ul Kupa 18; admission 5/2zł; ☻ 10am-4pm Sun-Fri) is decorated with impressive frescos from the 17th century.

It's easy to take a self-guided walking tour around Kazimierz with the *Jewish Kazimierz Short Guide* booklet, available from the Jarden Jewish Bookshop (see p609).

WIELICZKA SALT MINE

Wieliczka (vyeh-*leech*-kah), 15km southeast of the city centre, is famous for the **Wieliczka Salt Mine** (www.kopalnia.pl; ul Daniłowicza 10; adult/concession 64/49zł; ☻ 7.30am-7.30pm Apr-Oct, 8am-5pm Nov-Mar). It's an eerie world of pits and chambers, and every single element from chandeliers to altarpieces was hewn by hand from solid salt. The mine is included on Unesco's World Heritage list.

The highlight of a visit is the richly ornamented **Chapel of the Blessed Kinga**, a church measuring 54m by 17m, and 12m high. Construction of this underground temple took more than 30 years (1895–1927), resulting in the removal of 20,000 tonnes of rock salt.

POLAND

614 MAŁOPOLSKA •• Kraków

Book your stay at lonelyplanet.com/hotels

WORTH THE TRIP: NOWA HUTA

There's another side to Kraków that few tourists see. Catch tram 4, 15 or 22 east from Kraków Główny train station to Plac Centralny in Nowa Huta. This suburb was a 'workers' paradise' district built by the communist regime in the 1950s to counter the influence of the city's religious and intellectual traditions. Its immense, blocky concrete buildings stretch out along broad, straight streets, a fascinating contrast to the Old Town's delicate beauty.

The obligatory guided tour through the mine takes about two hours (a 2km walk). Tours in English operate approximately hourly between 9am and 5pm, increasing to half-hourly from 8.30am to 6pm in July and August. If you're visiting independently, you must wait for a tour to start. Last admission to the mine is shortly before closing time.

The best way to get to Wieliczka is by minibus (look for the 'Salt Mine' sign on the windscreen), departing frequently between 6am and 8pm from a location on ul Starowiślna, near the main post office in Kraków (2.50zł).

Tours

The following companies operate tours of Kraków and surrounding areas:

Almatur (Map p610; ☎ 012 422 4668; http://en .almatur.pl; Rynek Główny 27) Arranges various outdoor activities during summer.

Cracow Tours (Map p610; ☎ 012 619 2447; www .cracowtours.pl; Rynek Główny 41) Inside Orbis Travel, offering city tours, and tours of Auschwitz and the salt mines.

Crazy Guides (☎ 0500 091 200; www.crazyguides.com) Offers entertaining tours of the city's communist-era suburbs, in restored East German cars.

Jarden Jewish Bookshop & Tourist Agency (Map p612; ☎ 012 421 7166; www.jarden.pl; ul Szeroka 2) The best agency for tours of Polish Jewish heritage. Its showpiece, 'Retracing Schindler's List' (two hours by car), costs 60zł per person. All tours require a minimum of three and must be booked in advance. Tours are in English, but other languages can be arranged.

Festivals & Events

Organ Music Festival March

Krakow International Film Festival (www.cracow filmfestival.pl) May

Lajkonik Pageant In May/June, seven days after Corpus Christi.

Jewish Culture Festival (www.jewishfestival.pl) June/July

International Festival of Street Theatre (www .teatrkto.pl, in Polish) July

Summer Jazz Festival (www.cracjazz.com) July

Kraków Christmas Crib Competition December

Sleeping

Kraków is unquestionably Poland's major tourist destination, with prices to match. Booking ahead in the busy summer months is recommended.

BUDGET

Camping Smok (☎ 012 429 8300; ul Kamedulska 18; per person/tent 22/15zł) It's small, quiet and pleasantly located 4km west of the Old Town. To get here from outside the Kraków Główny train station building, take tram 2 to the end of the line in Zwierzyniec and change for any westbound bus (except bus 100).

Cracow Hostel (Map p610; ☎ 012 429 1106; www.cracow hostel.com; Rynek Główny 18; dm 35-80zł, ste 300zł) This place is perched high above the Rynek, with an amazing view of St Mary's Church from the roomy but comfortable lounge. There's also a kitchen and washing machine.

Stranger Hostel (☎ 012 432 0909; www.thestranger hostel.com; ul Dietla 97; dm 45-60zł, d/tr/q 140/210/240zł) This popular place is always jumping, via live music gigs, parties, barbecues and DVD films on a large screen. Most dorms have eight to 12 beds, though there are some private rooms available.

Greg & Tom Hostel (Map p610; ☎ 012 422 4100; www .gregtomhostel.com; ul Pawia 12; dm from 50zł, d 150zł) This well-run hostel is spread over two locations; the private rooms are a 10-minute walk away on ul Warszawska. The staff are friendly, the rooms are clean, and laundry facilities are included.

Mama's Hostel (Map p610; ☎ 012 429 5940; www .mamashostel.com.pl; ul Bracka 4; dm 50-65zł, d 200zł) Centrally located red-and-orange lodgings with a beautiful sunlit lounge overlooking a courtyard, with the aroma of freshly roasted coffee drifting up from a cafe below in the mornings. There's also table soccer and a washing machine.

our pick **Nathan's Villa Hostel** (Map p612; ☎ 012 422 3545; www.nathansvilla.com; ul Św. Agnieszki 1; dm/d from 50/160zł) Comfy rooms, sparkling bathrooms, free laundry and a friendly atmosphere make this place a big hit with backpackers, and its cellar bar, mini-cinema, beer garden and pool

table add to the appeal. Conveniently located between the Old Town and Kazimierz.

MIDRANGE

An agency offering decent rooms around town is **Jordan Tourist Information & Accommodation Centre** (Map p610; ☎ 012 422 6091; www.jordan.krakow .pl; ul Pawia 8; 🕑 8am-6pm Mon-Fri, 9am-2pm Sat; s/d around 130/150zł)

Apropo (☎ 0665 277 676; www.apropo.info; ul Karmelicka 36; d/tr 150/210zł) Set of comfortable rooms within a fully renovated old apartment, with access to shared bathrooms, a light-filled kitchen and laundry facilities. It's in a convenient location not far from the Old Town.

Tournet Pokoje Gościnne (Map p612; ☎ 012 292 0088; www.accommodation.krakow.pl; ul Miodowa 7; s/d/tr from 150/200/220zł) This is a neat pension in Kazimierz, offering simple but comfortable and quiet rooms. The bathrooms, however, are tiny.

AAA Kraków Apartments (☎ 012 426 5121; www .krakow-apartments.biz; apt from 180zł) Agency renting out renovated apartments in the vicinity of the Old Town, with a smaller selection in Kazimierz. Cheaper rates are available for longer stays.

Hotel Abel (Map p612; ☎ 012 411 8736; www.hotel abel.pl; ul Józefa 30; s/d/tr 180/250/270zł) Reflecting the character of Kazimierz, this hotel has a distinctive personality, evident in its polished wooden staircase, arched brickwork and age-worn tiles. The comfortable rooms make a good base for exploring the historic Jewish neighbourhood.

Hotel Royal (Map p610; ☎ 012 421 3500; www.royal .com.pl; ul Św. Gertrudy 26-29; s/d/ste from 180/330/460zł) Impressive art nouveau edifice with loads of old-world charm, just below Wawel Castle. It's split into two sections: the higher-priced two-star rooms are cosy, and far preferable to the fairly basic one-star rooms at the back.

Wielopole Guest Rooms (Map p610; ☎ 012 422 1475; www.wielopole.pl; ul Wielopole 3; s/d 250/378zł, ste 438-538zł) Smart and simple modern rooms in a renovated block on the eastern edge of the Old Town, with narrow beds but spotless bathrooms. The tariff includes an impressive buffet breakfast.

Hotel Wit Stwosz (Map p610; ☎ 012 429 6026; www.wit-stwosz.com.pl; ul Mikołajska 28; s/d/tr/ste 295/370/450/550zł) In a historic town house belonging to St Mary's Church, and decorated in a suitably religious theme. Rooms are compact and simply furnished, but tasteful and attractive.

TOP END

Hotel Amadeus (Map p610; ☎ 012 429 6070; www .hotel-amadeus.pl; ul Mikołajska 20; s/d/ste €190/200/300) Everything about this hotel says 'class'. The rooms are tastefully furnished, though singles are rather small given the price. One room has wheelchair access, and there's a sauna, a fitness centre, and a well-regarded restaurant. While hanging around the Amadeus' foyer, you can check out photos of famous guests.

Hotel Saski (Map p610; ☎ 012 421 4222; www.hotel saski.com.pl; ul Sławkowska 3; s/d/tr/ste 330/410/460/490zł) The Saski occupies a historic mansion, complete with a uniformed doorman, rattling old lift and ornate furnishings. The rooms themselves are comparatively plain.

Hotel Wawel (Map p610; ☎ 012 424 1300; www .hotelwawel.pl; ul Poselska 22; s/d/ste 330/460/580zł; 🐾) Ideally located just off busy ul Grodzka, this is a pleasant place offering tastefully decorated rooms with timber highlights. It's far enough from the main drag to minimise noise.

Hotel Stary (Map p610; ☎ 012 384 0808; www.stary .hotel.com.pl; ul Szczepańska 5; s/d 800/900zł, ste from 1140zł; 🐾 🛗) Setting new standards for accommodation in Poland, the Stary is housed in an 18th-century aristocratic residence that exudes charm. The fabrics are all-natural, the bathroom surfaces Italian marble, and there's a fitness centre, swimming pool and rooftop terrace to enjoy.

Eating

Kraków is a food paradise, tightly packed with restaurants serving a wide range of international cuisines.

One local speciality is *obwarzanki* (ring-shaped pretzels powdered with poppy seeds, sesame seeds or salt) available from street vendors dozing next to their barrows.

Self-caterers can stock up at the **supermarket** within the Galeria Krakowska shopping mall next to the main train station.

BUDGET

our pick **Momo** (Map p612; ☎ 0609 685 775; ul Dietla 49; mains 4-13zł; 🕑 11am-8pm) Vegans will cross the doorstep of this Kazimierz restaurant with relief – the majority of the menu is completely animal-free. The space is decorated with Indian craft pieces, and serves up subcontinental soups, stuffed pancakes and rice dishes, with a great range of cakes. The Tibetan dumplings are a treat worth ordering.

Green Way (Map p610; ☎ 012 431 1027; ul Mikołajska 14; mains 7-15zł; ☺ 10am-10pm Mon-Fri, 11am-9pm Sat & Sun) The Green Way offers good value vegetarian fare such as vegie curry, enchiladas and salads.

Ariel (Map p612; ☎ 012 421 7920; ul Szeroka 18; mains 9-48zł) Atmospheric Jewish restaurant packed with old-fashioned timber furniture and portraits, serving a range of kosher dishes. Try the Berdytchov soup (beef, honey and cinnamon) for a tasty starter. There's often live music here at night.

Kuchnia i Wino (Map p612; ☎ 012 430 6710; ul Józefa 13; mains 11-49zł; ☺ noon-10pm) The name – 'Cuisine and Wine' – may not suggest this bistro has a lot of imagination, but just try one of its delightfully inspired Mediterranean dishes, such as veal with basil, and you'll be impressed. There's fresh seafood available from Thursday to Saturday.

Gruzińskie Chaczapuri (Map p610; ☎ 012 429 1131; ul Floriańska 26; mains 12-22zł) Cheap and cheerful place serving up tasty Georgian dishes. Grills, salads and steaks fill out the menu, and there's a separate vegetarian selection with items such as the traditional Georgian cheese pie with stewed vegetables.

Restauracja Pod Gruszką (Map p610; ☎ 012 422 8896; ul Szczepańska 1; mains 12-55zł; ☺ noon-midnight) A favourite haunt of writers and artists, this upstairs establishment is the eatery that time forgot, with its elaborate old-fashioned decor featuring chandeliers, lace tablecloths, age-worn carpets and sepia portraits. The menu covers a range of Polish dishes, the most distinctive being the soups served within small bread loaves.

MIDRANGE & TOP END

Ipanema (Map p610; ☎ 012 422 5323; ul Św. Tomasza 28; mains 14-115zł; ☺ 5pm-midnight Mon-Thu, 1pm-midnight Sat & Sun) A banana palm as decor may seem out of place in Poland, but this bright place pulls it off. The Brazilian menu features steaks, grills and a range of interesting Afro-Brazilian dishes.

Smak Ukraiński (Map p610; ☎ 012 421 9294; ul Kanonicza 15; mains 15-30zł; ☺ noon-10pm) This Ukrainian restaurant presents authentic dishes in a cosy little cellar decorated with provincial flair. Expect lots of dumplings, *borscht* and waiters in waistcoats.

Orient Ekspres (Map p610; ☎ 012 422 6672; ul Stolarska 13; mains 15-39zł) Hercule Poirot might be surprised to find this elegant eatery here,

well off the route of its railway namesake. The food is mainly Polish, with some international additions, accompanied by wine by the glass. Mellow music and candlelight make it a good place for a romantic rendezvous.

Casa della Pizza (Map p610; ☎ 012 421 6498; Mały Rynek 2; mains 16-46zł) This unpretentious place is away from the bulk of the tourist traffic, with a menu of pizzas and pasta. The downstairs bar section is the Arabian-styled Shisha Club, serving Middle Eastern food.

Nostalgia (Map p610; ☎ 012 425 4260; ul Karmelicka 10; mains 18-37zł; ☺ noon-11pm) A refined version of the traditional Polish eatery, Nostalgia features a fireplace, overhead timber beams, uncrowded tables and courteous service. Wrap yourself around Russian dumplings, a 'Hunter's Stew' of cabbage, meat and mushrooms, or vegie options such as potato pancakes. In warm weather there's an outdoor dining area.

Pod Aniołami (Map p610; ☎ 012 421 3999; ul Grodzka 35; mains 20-58zł; ☺ 1pm-midnight) This eatery 'under the angels' offers high-quality Polish food in a pleasant cellar atmosphere, though it can get a little smoky. Specialities include the huntsman's smoked wild boar steak.

Balaton (Map p610; ☎ 012 422 0469; ul Grodzka 37; mains 20-58zł; ☺ noon-10pm) Balaton, with its shabby decor and uninspired wait staff, may not look inviting, but it's a very popular place for simple Hungarian food and seems to fill up quickly every night.

Metropolitan Restaurant (Map p610; ☎ 012 421 9803; ul Sławkowska 3; mains 22-68zł; ☺ 7.30am-midnight Mon-Sat, 7.30am-10pm Sun) Attached to Hotel Saski, this place has nostalgic B&W photos plastering the walls, and is a great place for breakfast. It also serves pasta, grills and steaks, including luxurious items such as beef fillet flambé in a cognac sauce.

Drinking

There are hundreds of pubs and bars in Kraków's Old Town, many housed in ancient vaulted cellars, which get very smoky. Kazimierz also has a lively bar scene, centred on Plac Nowy and its surrounding streets.

Paparazzi (Map p610; ul Mikołajska 9; ☺ 11am-1am Mon-Fri, 4pm-4am Sat & Sun) If you haven't brought any reading material with you to this bar, look up – the ceiling is plastered with pages from racy tabloid newspapers. It's a bright, modern place, with B&W press photos covering the walls. The drinks menu includes cocktails

POLAND

such as the Polish martini, built around bison grass vodka. There's also inexpensive bar food.

Le Scandale (Map p612; Plac Nowy 9; 8am-3am) Smooth Kazimierz drinking hole with low black leather couches, ambient lighting and a gleaming well-stocked bar. Full of mellow drinkers sampling the extensive cocktail list.

Singer (Map p612; ul Estery 20; 9am-4am Sun-Thu, 9am-5am Fri & Sat) Laidback hang-out of the Kazimierz cognoscenti, this relaxed cafe-bar's moody candlelit interior is full of character. Alternatively, sit outside and converse over a sewing machine affixed to the table.

Pod Papugami (Map p610; Św. Jana 18; 1pm-2am Mon-Sat, 3pm-2am Sun) This is a vaguely Irish cellar pub decorated with old motorcycles and other assorted odds and ends. A good place to hide from inclement weather, with its pool table and tunnel-like maze of rooms.

Piwnica Pod Złotą Pipą (Map p610; ul Floriańska 30; noon-midnight) Less claustrophobic than other cellar bars, with lots of tables for eating or drinking. Decent bar food and international beers on tap.

Café Camelot (Map p610; Św Tomasza 17; 9am-midnight) For coffee and cake, try this genteel haven hidden around an obscure street corner in the Old Town. Its cosy rooms are cluttered with lace-covered candlelit tables, and a quirky collection of wooden figurines featuring spiritual or folkloric scenes.

Entertainment

The comprehensive Polish-English booklet *Karnet* (4zł), published by the tourist information centre (see p609), lists almost every event in the city.

NIGHTCLUBS

our pick Piano Rouge (Map p610; 012 431 0333; www.thepianorouge.com; Rynek Główny 46; 11am-2am) A sumptuous cellar venue decked out with classic sofas, ornate lampshades and billowing lengths of colourful silk. There's a dizzying array of nightly live jazz acts, and an in-house restaurant.

Łubu-Dubu (Map p610; ul Wielopole 15; 6pm-late) The name of this place (*wooboo-doo*boo) is as funky as its decor. It's a grungy upstairs joint that's an echo of the past, from the garish colours to the collection of objects from 1970s Poland. DJs spin 'old school' tracks, and a series of rooms creates spaces for talking or dancing as the mood strikes.

Alchemia (Map p612; ul Estery 5; 9am-3am) This Kazimierz venue exudes a shabby-is-the-new-cool look with rough-hewn wooden benches, candlelit tables and a companionable gloom. It hosts regular live music gigs and theatrical events through the week.

Black Gallery (Map p610; ul Mikołajska 24; 5pm-late) Underground pub-cum-nightclub with a modern aspect: split levels, exposed steel frame lighting and a metallic bar. It really gets going after midnight. It also has a more civilised courtyard, open from 2pm.

Rdza (Map p610; www.rdza.pl; ul Bracka 3/5; 7pm-late) This basement club attracts some of Kraków's more sophisticated clubbers, with its Polish house music bouncing off exposed brick walls and comfy sofas. Guest DJs start spinning at 9pm Friday and Saturday.

PERFORMING ARTS

Stary Teatr (Map p610; 012 422 4040; www.stary-teatr.pl, in Polish; ul Jagiellońska 5) This accomplished theatre company offers quality productions. To overcome the language barrier, pick a Shakespeare play you know well from the repertoire, and take in the distinctive Polish interpretation.

Teatr im Słowackiego (Map p610; 012 422 4022; www.slowacki.krakow.pl, in Polish; Plac Św. Ducha 1) This grand place, built in 1893, focuses on Polish classics and large productions.

Filharmonia Krakowska (Map p610; 012 422 9477; www.filharmonia.krakow.pl; ul Zwierzyniecka 1) Hosts one of the best orchestras in the country; concerts are usually held on Friday and Saturday.

CINEMAS

Two convenient cinemas are **Kino Sztuka** (Map p610; cnr Św. Tomasza & Św. Jana), and the tiny **Kino Pasaż** (Map p610; Rynek Główny 9).

Shopping

The place to start (or perhaps end) your Kraków shopping is at the large **souvenir market** within the Cloth Hall, selling everything from fine amber jewellery to tacky plush dragons.

Fascinating examples of Polish poster art can be purchased at **Galeria Plakatu** (Map p610; 012 421 2640; www.cracowpostergallery.com; ul Stolarska 8; noon-5pm Mon-Fri, 11am-2pm Sat).

Getting There & Away

For information on travelling from Kraków to Zakopane, Częstochowa or Oświęcim (for Auschwitz), refer to the relevant destination sections later.

POLAND

AIR

The **John Paul II International airport** (www.lotnisko -balice.pl) is more often called Balice airport, after the suburb in which it's located, about 15km west of the Old Town. The airport terminal hosts several car-hire desks, along with currency exchanges offering unappealing rates. To get to the Old Town by public transport, step aboard the shuttle bus to the nearby train station, from the sign marked 'PKP' outside the airport. A conductor on board the train will sell you a ticket (8zł, 16 minutes) for the short journey to Kraków Główny station.

LOT flies between Kraków and Warsaw several times a day, and offers direct connections from Kraków to Frankfurt, Munich, Paris, Vienna and Tel Aviv, with flights to New York and Chicago during the summer months. Bookings for all flights can be made at the **LOT office** (Map p610; ☎ 0801 703 703; ul Basztowa 15). There are also domestic flights via Jet Air to Poznań (six times a week).

A range of other airlines, including several budget operators, connect Kraków to cities in Europe, including an array of destinations across Britain and Ireland. There are direct flights at least daily to and from London via British Airways, Centralwings, easyJet and Ryanair. Dublin is serviced daily by Ryanair and Aer Lingus.

BUS

If you've been travelling by bus elsewhere in Poland, Kraków's modern main **bus terminal** (Map p610; ul Bosacka 18) will seem like a palace compared to the usual facility. It's located on the other side of the main train station from the Old Town. Taking the train will generally be quicker, but buses of interest to visitors run to Lublin (38zł, five hours, hourly), Zamość (40zł, seven hours, five daily) and Cieszyn (17zł, three hours, 10 daily) on the Czech border.

TRAIN

The lovely old **Kraków Główny train station** (Map p610; Plac Dworcowy), on the northeastern outskirts of the Old Town, handles all international trains and most domestic rail services. The railway platforms are about 150m north of the station building, and you can also reach them from the adjacent Galeria Krakowska shopping mall.

Each day from Kraków, 22 trains head to Warsaw (48zł, three hours). There are also 14 trains daily to Wrocław (45zł, 4½ hours), 11 to Poznań (53zł, 7½ hours), two to Lublin (49zł, 5¼ hours), and 11 to Gdynia, via Gdańsk (62zł, 8¾ hours).

Advance tickets for international and domestic trains can be booked directly at the station or from Cracow Tours (p614).

OŚWIĘCIM
pop 40,800

Few place names have more impact than Auschwitz, which is seared into public consciousness as the location of history's most extensive experiment in genocide. Every year hundreds of thousands visit Oświęcim (osh-*fyen*-cheem), the Polish town that gave its German name to the infamous Nazi death camp, to learn about its history and to pay respect to the dead.

Established within disused army barracks in 1940, Auschwitz was initially designed to hold Polish prisoners, but was expanded into the largest centre for the extermination of European Jews. Two more camps were subsequently established: Birkenau (Brzezinka, also known as Auschwitz II), 3km west of Auschwitz; and Monowitz (Monowice), several kilometres west of Oświęcim. In the course of their operation, between one and 1.5 million people were murdered in these death factories – about 90% of these were Jews.

GETTING THERE & AWAY

For most visitors, Auschwitz and Birkenau are an easy day trip from Kraków.

From Kraków Główny station, 13 mostly slow trains go to Oświęcim (11zł, 1½ hours) each day, though more depart from Kraków Płaszów station.

Far more convenient are the approximately hourly buses each day to Oświęcim (11zł, 1½ hours) departing from the bus station in Kraków, which either pass by or terminate at the museum. The return bus timetable to Kraków is displayed at the Birkenau visitors centre.

Every half-hour from 11.30am to 4.30pm between 15 April and 31 October, buses shuttle passengers between the visitor centres at Auschwitz and Birkenau (buses run to 5.30pm in May and September, and until 6.30pm from June to August). Otherwise, follow the signs for an easy walk (3km) or take a taxi. Auschwitz is also linked to the town's train station by buses 24, 25, 28 and 29 every 30 to 40 minutes.

Most travel agencies in Kraków offer organised tours of Auschwitz (including Birkenau), from 100zł to 130zł per person. Check with the operator for exactly how much time the tour allows you at Auschwitz, as some run to a very tight schedule.

Auschwitz

Auschwitz was only partially destroyed by the fleeing Nazis, so many of the original buildings remain as a bleak document of the camp's history. A dozen of the 30 surviving prison blocks house sections of the **State Museum Auschwitz-Birkenau** (☎ 033 844 8100; www .auschwitz.org.pl; admission free; ☑ 8am-7pm Jun-Aug, 8am-6pm May & Sep, 8am-5pm Apr & Oct, 8am-4pm Mar & Nov, 8am-3pm Dec-Feb).

About every half-hour, the cinema in the **visitors centre** at the entrance shows a 15-minute documentary film (adult/concession 3.50/2.50zł) about the liberation of the camp by Soviet troops on 27 January 1945. It's shown in several languages throughout the day; check the schedule at the information desk as soon as you arrive. The film is not recommended for children under 14 years old. The visitors centre also has a cafeteria, bookshops, a *kantor* and a left-luggage room.

Some basic explanations in Polish, English and Hebrew are provided on site, but you'll understand more if you buy the small *Auschwitz Birkenau Guide Book* (translated into about 15 languages) from the visitors centre. English-language tours (adult/concession 39/30zł, 3½ hours) of Auschwitz and Birkenau leave at 10am, 11am, 1pm and 3pm daily, and can also occur when a group of 10 people can be formed. Tours in a range of other languages can be arranged in advance.

Auschwitz is an easy day trip from Kraków. However, if you want to stay overnight, **Centre for Dialogue and Prayer** (☎ 033 843 10 00; www.cent rum-dialogu.oswiecim.pl; ul Kolbego 1; camping per person 23zł, s/d/tr/ste 95/190/285/270zł) is 700m southwest of Auschwitz. It's comfortable and quiet, and the price includes breakfast. Most rooms are en suite, and full board is also offered.

Birkenau

Birkenau (admission free; ☑ 8am-7pm Jun-Aug, 8am-6pm May & Sep, 8am-5pm Apr & Oct, 8am-4pm Mar & Nov, 8am-3pm Dec-Feb) was actually where the murder of huge numbers of Jews took place. This vast (175 hectares), purpose-built and grimly efficient camp had more than 300 prison barracks and four huge gas chambers complete with crematoria. Each gas chamber held 2000 people and electric lifts raised the bodies to the ovens. The camp could hold 200,000 inmates at one time.

Although much of the camp was destroyed by retreating Nazis, the size of the place, fenced off with barbed wire stretching almost as far as the eye can see, provides some idea of the scale of this heinous crime. The viewing platform above the entrance provides further perspective. In some ways, Birkenau is even more shocking than Auschwitz and there are fewer tourists.

CZĘSTOCHOWA
pop 245,000

Częstochowa (chen-sto-*ho*-vah), 114km northwest of Kraków, is an attractive pilgrimage town, dominated by the graceful Jasna Góra monastery atop a hill at its centre. The monastery, founded by the Paulites of Hungary in 1382, is the home of the Black Madonna, and owes its fame to a miracle. In 1430 a group of Hussites stole the holy icon, slashed it and broke it into three pieces. Legend has it that the picture bled, and the monks cleaned the retrieved panel with the aid of a spring, which rose miraculously from the ground. Though the picture was restored, the scars on the Virgin's face were retained in memory of the miracle.

The Madonna was also credited with the fortified monastery's resistance to the Swedish sieges of the 1650s. In 1717 the Black Madonna was crowned Queen of Poland.

From the train station, and adjacent bus terminal, turn right (north) up Al Wolności – along which are several internet cafes – to the main thoroughfare, Al Najświętszej Marii Panny (simplified to Al NMP). At the western end of this avenue is the monastery and at the eastern end is Plac Daszyńskiego. In-between you'll find the **tourist office** (☎ 034 368 2250; Al NMP 65; ☑ 9am-5pm Mon-Sat) and banks.

Sights

The **Paulite Monastery on Jasna Góra** (☎ 034 365 3888; www.jasnagora.pl; admission free; ☑ dawn-dusk) retains the appearance of a hilltop fortress. Inside the grounds are three **museums** (donations welcome; ☑ 9am-5pm May-Oct, 9am-4pm Nov-Apr): the **Arsenal**, with a variety of old weapons;

POLAND

the **600th-Anniversary Museum** (Muzeum Sześćsetlecia), which contains Lech Wałęsa's 1983 Nobel Peace Prize; and the **Treasury** (Skarbiec), featuring offerings presented by the faithful.

The **tower** (☼ 8am-4pm May-Oct) is the tallest (106m) historic church tower in Poland. The baroque church beneath is beautifully decorated. The image of the Black Madonna is on the high altar of the adjacent chapel, entered from the left of the church aisle. It's hard to see, so a copy is on display in the **Knights' Hall** (Sala Rycerska) in the monastery. Note that the Madonna is sometimes concealed by a silver cover; if so, check with the onsite information office for the next scheduled uncovering. It's quite an event, as priests file in, music plays and the image slowly emerges.

On weekends and holidays expect long queues for all three museums. The crowds in the chapel may be so thick that you're almost unable to enter, much less get near the icon.

In the town hall the **Częstochowa Museum** (Al NMP 45; adult/concession 4/3zł; ☼ 11am-5pm Tue-Sun Jun-Sep, 9am-3.30pm Tue, Thu & Fri, 11am-5.30pm Wed, 10am-4pm Sat & Sun Oct-May) features an ethnographic collection and modern Polish paintings.

Festivals & Events

The major Marian feasts at Jasna Góra are 3 May, 16 July, 15 August (especially), 26 August, 8 September, 12 September and 8 December. On these days the monastery is packed with pilgrims.

Sleeping & Eating

Dom Pielgrzyma (☎ 034 377 7564; ul Wyszyńskiego 1/31; dm 25zł, s/d/tr from 70/100/135zł) A huge place behind the monastery, it offers numerous quiet and comfortable rooms, and is remarkably good value.

Youth Hostel (☎ 034 324 3121; ul Jasnogórska 84/90; dm 27zł; ☼ 15 Jun-15 Sep) This hostel, two blocks north of the tourist office, has modest facilities. Look for the triangular green sign on the building's wall.

Plenty of eateries can be found near the Dom Pielgrzyma. Better restaurants are dotted along Al NMP.

Bar Viking (☎ 034 324 5768; ul Nowowiejskiego 10; mains 4-40zł; ☼ 10am-10pm) About 200m south of the Częstochowa Museum, this friendly place has a good range of dishes, including vegetarian choices.

Restaurant Cleopatra (☎ 034 368 0101; Al NMP 71; mains 15-20zł) The cheerfully out-of-place Cleopatra, near the tourist office, serves pizzas, kebabs and sandwiches among pillars painted with ancient Egyptian designs.

Getting There & Away

The **bus terminal** (Al Wolności 45) is next to the train station, but train travel is the superior option to most destinations.

From **Częstochowa Osobowa train station** (Al Wolności 21), 13 trains a day go to Warsaw (41zł, three hours). There are eight daily trains to Gdynia via Gdańsk (60zł, 9½ hours), six to Łódź (33zł, two hours), three to Olsztyn (56zł, seven hours), three to Zakopane (45zł, seven hours), nine to Kraków (31zł, 2½ hours) and four to Wrocław (34zł, three hours).

LUBLIN
pop 353,000

If the crowds are becoming too much in Kraków, you could do worse than jump on a train to Lublin. This attractive eastern city has many of the same attractions – a beautiful Old Town, a castle, good bars and restaurants – but is less visited by international tourists.

Though today the city's beautifully preserved Old Town is a peaceful blend of Gothic, Renaissance and baroque architecture, Lublin has an eventful past. In 1569 the Lublin Union was signed here, uniting Poland and Lithuania; and at the end of WWII, the Soviet Union set up a communist government in Lublin, prior to the liberation of Warsaw.

Information

Bank Pekao Old Town (ul Królewska 1); City centre (ul Krakowskie Przedmieście 64)

EMPiK (Galeria Centrum, 3rd fl, ul Krakowskie Przedmieście 16) Bookshop.

Main post office (ul Krakowskie Przedmieście 50)

Net Box (ul Krakowskie Przedmieście 52; per hr 4.50zł; ☼ 9am-9pm Mon-Fri, 10am-9pm Sat, 2-9pm Sun) Internet access in a courtyard off the street.

Tourist office (☎ 081 532 4412; www.lublin.pl; ul Jezuicka 1/3; ☼ 9am-6pm Mon-Fri, 10am-4pm Sat, 10am-3pm Sun May-Sep, 9am-5pm Mon-Fri, 10am-3pm Sat Oct-Apr) Lots of free brochures, including the city walking-route guide *Tourist Routes of Lublin*.

Sights
CASTLE

The substantial **castle**, standing on a hill northeast of the Old Town, has a dark history. It was

POLAND

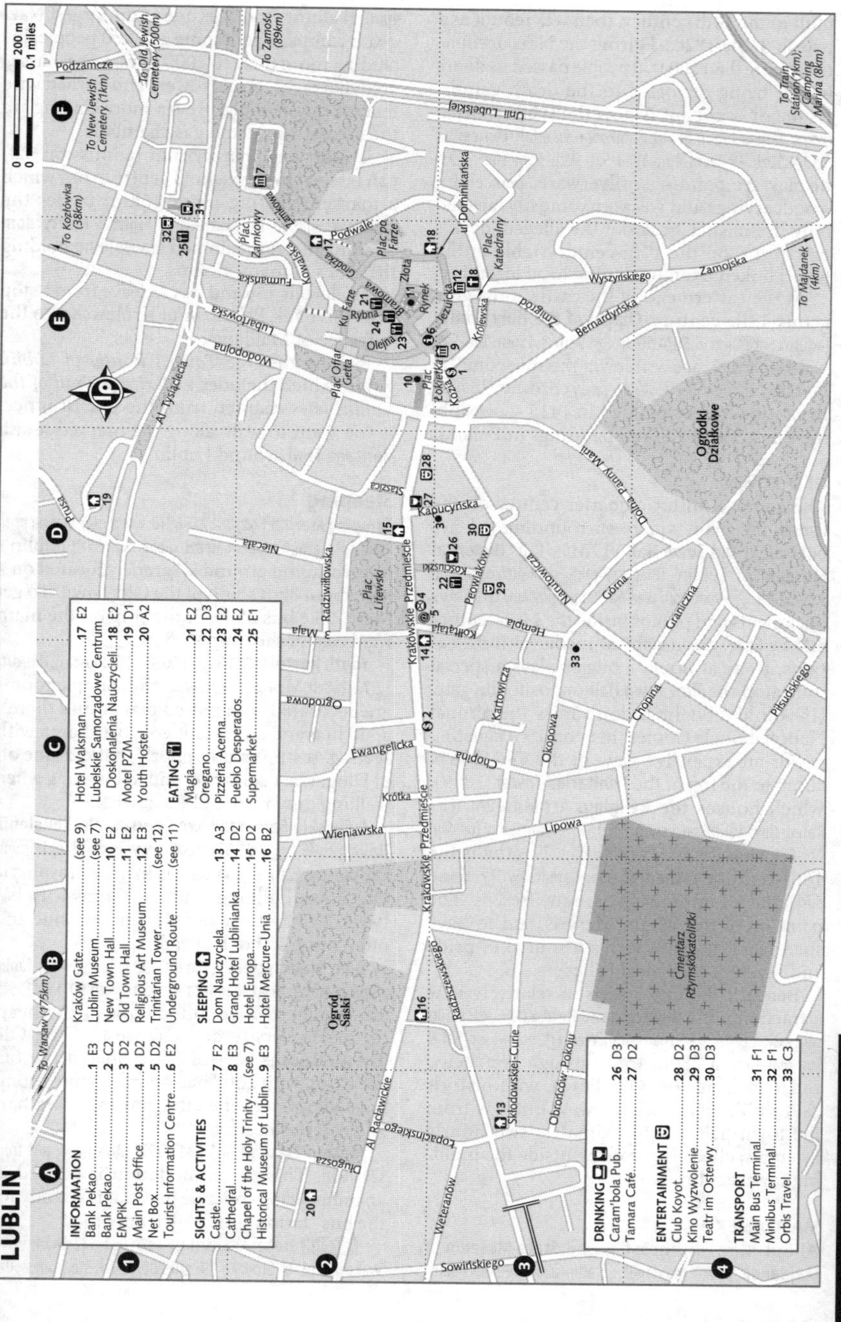

LUBLIN
INFORMATION
Bank Pekao 1 E3
Bank Pekao 2 C2
EMPiK 3 D2
Main Post Office 4 D2
Net Box 5 D2
Tourist Information Centre 6 E2
SIGHTS & ACTIVITIES
Castle 7 F2
Cathedral 8 E3
Chapel of the Holy Trinity (see 7)
Historical Museum of Lublin 9 E3
Kraków Gate (see 9)
Lublin Museum (see 7)
New Town Hall 10 E2
Old Town Hall 11 E2
Religious Art Museum 12 E3
Trinitarian Tower (see 12)
Underground Route (see 11)
SLEEPING
Dom Nauczyciela 13 A3
Grand Hotel Lublinianka 14 D2
Hotel Europa 15 D2
Hotel Mercure-Unia 16 B2
Hotel Waksman 17 E2
Lubelskie Samorządowe Centrum Doskonalenia Nauczycieli 18 E2
Motel PZM 19 D1
Youth Hostel 20 A2
EATING
Magia 21 E2
Oregano 22 D3
Pizzeria Acerna 23 E2
Pueblo Desperados 24 E2
Supermarket 25 E1
DRINKING
Caram'bola Pub 26 D3
Tamara Café 27 D2
ENTERTAINMENT
Club Koyot 28 D2
Kino Wyzwolenie 29 D3
Teatr im Osterwy 30 D3
TRANSPORT
Main Bus Terminal 31 F1
Minibus Terminal 32 F1
Orbis Travel 33 C3
0 200 m
0 0.1 miles
To Warsaw (175km)
To Kozłówka (38km)
To New Jewish Cemetery (1km)
To Old Jewish Cemetery (500m)
To Zamość (89km)
To Majdanek (4km)
To Train Station (1km); Camping Marina (8km)
Podzamcze
Ogród Saski
Plac Litewski
Ogródki Działkowe
Cmentarz Rzymskokatolicki
Krakowskie Przedmieście
Al Racławickie
Al Tysiąclecia
Lubartowska
Lipowa
Narutowicza
Unii Lubelskiej
Zamojska
Rynek

built in the 14th century, then was rebuilt as a prison in the 1820s. During the Nazi occupation, more than 100,000 people passed its doors before being deported to the death camps. Its major occupant is now the **Lublin Museum** (www.zamek-lublin.pl; ul Zamkowa 9; adult/concession 6.50/4.50zł; 9am-4pm Wed-Sat, 9am-5pm Sun). On display are paintings, silverware, porcelain, woodcarvings and weaponry, mostly labelled only in Polish. Check out the alleged 'devil's paw-print' on the 17th-century table in the foyer, linked to an intriguing local legend.

At the eastern end of the castle is the gorgeous 14th-century **Chapel of the Holy Trinity** (adult/concession 6.50/4.50zł; 9am-3.45pm Tue-Sat, 9am-4.45pm Sun), accessible via the museum. Its interior is covered with polychrome Russo-Byzantine frescos painted in 1418 – possibly the finest medieval wall paintings in Poland.

OLD TOWN
The compact historic quarter centres on the **Rynek**, the main square surrounding the neoclassical **Old Town Hall** (1781). The **Historical Museum of Lublin** (Plac Łokietka 3; adult/concession 3.50/2.50zł; 9am-4pm Wed-Sat, 9am-5pm Sun) displays documents and photos inside the 14th-century **Kraków Gate**, a remnant of medieval fortifications. Daily at noon, a bugler plays a special tune atop the **New Town Hall** opposite the gate. (If you like bugling, don't miss the annual National Bugle Contest here on 15 August.)

For an expansive view of the Old Town, climb to the top of the **Trinitarian Tower** (1819), which houses the **Religious Art Museum** (Plac Katedralny; adult/concession 7/5zł; 10am-5pm Tue-Sun Apr-Oct, 10am-3pm Sat & Sun Nov-Mar). Nearby is the 16th-century **cathedral** (Plac Katedralny; dawn-dusk) and its impressive baroque frescos. The painting of the Virgin Mary is said to have shed tears in 1949, so it's a source of pride and reverence for local believers.

Beneath the city streets, a relatively new attraction is the **Underground Route** (Rynek 1; adult/concession 6/4zł; 10am-4pm Wed-Fri, noon-5pm Sat & Sun May-Oct), a 280m trail through connected cellars beneath the Old Town, with historical exhibitions along the way. Entry is from the town hall at approximately two-hourly intervals; check the notice outside the building for exact times.

MAJDANEK
About 4km southeast is the **State Museum of Majdanek** (www.majdanek.pl; admission free; 9am-4pm). It commemorates one of the largest Nazi death camps, where some 235,000 people, including more than 100,000 Jews, were massacred. Barracks, guard towers and barbed wire fences remain in place; even more chilling are the crematorium and gas chambers.

A short explanatory film (admission 3zł) can be seen in the visitors centre, from which a marked 'visiting route' (5km) passes the massive stone **Monument of Fight & Martyrdom** and finishes at the domed **mausoleum** holding the ashes of many victims.

Trolleybus 156 and bus 23 leave from a stop near the Bank Pekao on ul Królewska, to the entrance of Majdanek.

Pick up the free *Tourist Routes of Lublin* guide, which includes a *Heritage Trail of the Lublin Jews* chapter, from the tourist office, if you want to walk along the marked **Jewish Heritage Trail** around Lublin.

Sleeping
Camping Marina (081 745 6910; www.graf-marina.pl, in Polish; ul Krężnicka 6; per tent 8zł, cabins from 55zł) Lublin's only camping ground is serenely located on a lake about 8km south of the Old Town. To get there, take bus 25 from the stop on the main road east of the train station.

Youth Hostel (081 533 0628; ul Długosza 6; dm/d/tr 32/72/108zł) Modest but well run. Simple rooms are decorated with potted plants, and there's a kitchen and a pleasant courtyard area with seating. It's 100m up a poorly marked lane off ul Długosza; take the second left turning when walking down from ul Racławickie.

Lubelskie Samorządowe Centrum Doskonalenia Nauczycieli (081 532 9241; www.lscdn.pl; ul Dominikańska 5; dm 52zł) This place is in an atmospheric Old Town building, and has rooms with between two and five beds. It's good value and often busy, so book ahead.

Dom Nauczyciela (081 533 8285; www.lublin.oupis.pl/hotel; ul Akademicka 4; s/d/tr from 90/110/195zł) Value-packed accommodation in the heart of the university quarter, west of the Old Town. Rooms have old-fashioned decor but are clean, with good bathrooms. Some rooms have views over the city, and there are bars and eateries nearby.

Motel PZM (081 533 4232; ul Prusa 8; s/d from 120/160zł) This accommodation is housed in an uninspiring concrete pile, but it's handy for the bus station. It's car-friendly too.

our pick Hotel Waksman (081 532 5454; www.waksman.pl; ul Grodzka 19; s/d 200/220zł, ste from 260zł)

This small gem is excellent value for its quality and location. Just within the Grodzka Gate in the Old Town, it offers elegantly appointed rooms with different colour schemes, and an attractive lounge with tapestries on the walls. One room has a waterbed.

Hotel Mercure-Unia (☎ 081 533 2061; www.orbis .pl; Al Racławickie 12; s/d from 265/295zł; ☒) This business hotel is big, central and convenient, and offers all modern conveniences, though it's lacking in atmosphere. There's a gym, bar and restaurant on the premises. Breakfast is 35zł extra per person.

Grand Hotel Lublinianka (☎ 081 446 6100; www .lublinianka.com; ul Krakowskie Przedmieście 56; s/d from 300/360zł; ☒) The swankiest place in town includes free use of a sauna and spa. The cheaper (3rd floor) rooms have skylights but are relatively small, while 'standard' rooms are spacious and have glitzy marble bathrooms. One room is designed for wheelchair access, and there's a good restaurant onsite.

Hotel Europa (☎ 081 535 0303; www.hoteleuropa .pl; ul Krakowskie Przedmieście 29; s/d from 380/420zł, ste 1150zł; ☒) Central hotel offering smart, thoroughly modernised rooms with high ceilings and elegant furniture, in a restored 19th-century building. Two rooms are designed for wheelchair access, and there's a nightclub downstairs.

Eating & Drinking

Pueblo Desperados (☎ 081 534 6179; Rynek 5; mains 6-24zł; ☒ 9am-10pm Mon-Thu, 9am-midnight Fri & Sat, 10am-10pm Sun) Takes a reasonable stab at Mexican cuisine in its tiny sombrero-decorated premises off the Old Town's central square. The usual suspects (burritos, tacos) are on the menu, along with so-called Mexican pizzas.

Pizzeria Acerna (☎ 081 532 4531; Rynek 2; mains 11-41zł) The Acerna is a popular eatery on the main square, serving cheap pizzas and pasta in dazzling variations.

our pick Magia (☎ 081 532 3041; ul Grodzka 2; mains 16-70zł; ☒ noon-midnight) Charming, relaxed restaurant with numerous vibes to choose from within its warren of dining rooms and large outdoor courtyard. Dishes range from tiger shrimps and snails to deer and duck, with every sort of pizza, pasta and pancake between.

Oregano (☎ 081 442 5530; ul Kościuszki 7; mains 20-45zł; ☒ noon-11pm) This pleasant, upmarket restaurant specialises in Mediterranean cuisine, featuring pasta, paella and seafood. There's a well-organised English menu, and the chefs aren't scared of spice.

Tamara Café (ul Krakowskie Przedmieście 36) This cafe-bar takes its *vino* very seriously. Whether you're a cultured wine connoisseur, a courtyard cocktail fancier, or a hungry tippler who wants some vodka with (or in) your meal, pull up a chair.

Caram'bola Pub (ul Kościuszki 8; ☒ 10am-late Mon-Fri, noon-late Sat & Sun) This pub is a pleasant place for a beer or two. It also serves inexpensive bar food, including Lublin's ubiquitous pizzas.

There's a **supermarket** located near the bus terminal.

Entertainment

Club Koyot (ul Krakowskie Przedmieście 26; ☒ noon-late Mon-Fri, 4pm-late Sat & Sun) This club is concealed in a courtyard and features live music or DJs most nights.

Kino Wyzwolenie (ul Peowiaków 6; adult/concession 15/13zł) If you'd prefer a movie to music, this is a classic 1920s cinema in a convenient location.

Teatr im Osterwy (☎ 081 532 4244; ul Narutowicza 17) Lublin's main theatrical venue, which features mostly classical plays.

Getting There & Away

From the **bus terminal** (Al Tysiąclecia), opposite the castle, buses head to Białystok (27zł, three daily), Kraków (38zł, hourly), Olsztyn (72zł, one daily), Przemyśl (16zł, four daily) and Zakopane (63zł, one daily). Buses also leave approximately hourly to Zamość (15zł) and various destinations within Warsaw (26zł). From the same terminal, Polski Express offers five daily buses to Warsaw (31zł, three hours). Private minibuses head to various destinations, including Warsaw (30zł, every half-hour), from bus stops north and west of the bus terminal.

The **train station** (Plac Dworcowy) is 1.2km south of the Old Town and accessible by bus 1 or 13. When leaving the station, look for the bus stop on ul Gazowa, to the left of the station entrance as you walk down the steps (not the trolleybus stop). Alternatively, trolleybus 150 from the station is handy for the university area and the youth hostel. A dozen trains go daily to Warsaw (34zł, 2½ hours) and two travel to Kraków (49zł, 5¼ hours). Buy tickets from the station or **Orbis Travel** (☎ 081 532 2256; www.orbistravel.com.pl; ul Narutowicza 33a).

AROUND LUBLIN

The hamlet of **Kozłówka** (koz-*woof*-kah), 38km north of Lublin, is famous for its sumptuous late-baroque **palace**, which houses the **Museum of the Zamoyski Family** (☏ 081 852 8310; www.muzeum zamoyskich.lublin.pl; adult/concession for entry to all sections 24/12zł; ☉ 10am-4pm Tue-Sun 15 Mar-Oct, 10am-3pm Nov-15 Dec). The collection in the **main palace** (adult/concession 16/8zł) features original furnishings, ceramic stoves and a large collection of paintings. You must see this area on a Polish-language guided tour, whose starting time will be noted at the top of your ticket. An English-language tour (best organised in advance) costs an extra 50zł. The entrance fee to this section also includes entry to the 1907 **chapel**.

Even more interesting is the incongruous **Socialist-Realist Art Gallery** (adult/concession 6/3zł; ☉ 10am-4pm Tue-Sun 15 Mar-Oct), decked out with numerous portraits and statues of communist-era leaders. It also features many idealised scenes of farmers and factory workers striving for socialism. These stirring works were originally tucked away here in embarrassment by the communist authorities, after Stalin's death led to the decline of this all-encompassing artistic style.

You can stay in some **palace rooms** and on an 'agrotourist' farm, **Agro Kozłówkie Rządcówke** (☏ 081 852 8220). Contact staff in advance about availability and current costs.

From Lublin, there's one morning bus to Kozłówka at 8.30am (7.50zł, 50 minutes). Alternatively, you can catch one of the frequent buses from Lublin to Lubartów, then take one of the regular minibuses that pass Kozłówka from there.

A bus heads back to Lublin from Kozłówka around 3.30pm, and another around 6.30pm. Double-check bus timetables before you visit the museum so you can plan your departure accordingly. If you get stuck, take a minibus to Lubartów, from where there is regular transport back to Lublin.

ZAMOŚĆ

pop 66,500

While most Polish cities' attractions centre on their medieval heart, Zamość (*zah*-moshch) is pure Renaissance. The streets of its attractive, compact Old Town are perfect for exploring, and its central market square is a symmetrical delight, reflecting the city's glorious 16th-century origins.

Zamość was founded in 1580 by Jan Zamoyski, the nation's chancellor and commander-in-chief. Designed by an Italian architect, the city was intended to be a prosperous trading settlement between Western Europe and the region stretching east to the Black Sea.

In WWII, the Nazis earmarked the city for German resettlement, sending the Polish population into slave labour or concentration camps. Most of the Jewish population of the renamed 'Himmlerstadt' was exterminated.

The splendid architecture of Zamość's Old Town was added to Unesco's World Heritage list in 1992. Since 2004, EU funds have been gradually restoring Zamość to its former glory.

Information

Bank Pekao (ul Grodzka 2)
K@fejka Internetowa (Rynek Wielki 10; per hr 3zł; ☉ 7.30am-5pm Mon-Fri, 9am-2pm Sat) Internet access.
Main post office (ul Kościuszki)
Tourist office (☏ 084 639 2292; Rynek Wielki 13; ☉ 8am-6pm Mon-Fri, 10am-5pm Sat & Sun May-Sep, 8am-5pm Mon-Fri, 9am-2pm Sat Oct-Apr) Sells *Along the Streets of Zamość* (2zł) and the glossy *Zamość – A Short Guidebook* (8.50zł).

Sights

The **Rynek Wielki** (Great Market Sq) is the heart of Zamość's attractive Old Town. The impressive Italianate Renaissance square (exactly 100m by 100m) is dominated by the lofty, pink **town hall** and surrounded by colourful arcaded burghers' houses, many adorned with elegant designs. The **Museum of Zamość** (ul Ormiańska 30; adult/concession 6/3zł; ☉ 9am-4pm Tue-Sun) is based in two of the loveliest buildings on the Rynek and houses interesting exhibits, including paintings, folk costumes, archaeological finds and a scale model of the 16th-century town.

Southwest of the square is the mighty 16th-century **cathedral** (ul Kolegiacka; ☉ dawn-dusk), which hosts the tomb of Jan Zamoyski in the chapel to the right of the high altar. The **belfry** (admission 1.50zł; ☉ May-Sep) can be climbed for good views of the historic cathedral bells and the Old Town. In the grounds, the **Sacral Museum** (admission 1.50zł; ☉ 10am-4pm Mon-Fri, 10am-1pm Sat & Sun May-Sep, 10am-1pm Sun Oct-Apr) features various robes, paintings and sculptures.

Zamoyski Palace (closed to the public) lost much of its character when it was converted into a military hospital in the 1830s. Today it's used for government offices. Nearby, the

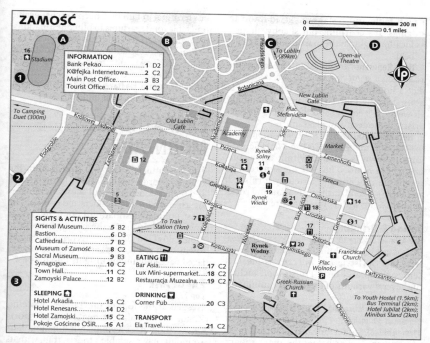

ZAMOŚĆ

| | | 0 | 200 m |
| | | 0 | 0.1 miles |

INFORMATION
Bank Pekao.....................1 D2
K@fejka Internetowa.........2 C2
Main Post Office...............3 B3
Tourist Office...................4 C2

SIGHTS & ACTIVITIES
Arsenal Museum..............5 B2
Bastion............................6 D3
Cathedral.........................7 B2
Museum of Zamość..........8 C2
Sacral Museum.................9 B3
Synagogue......................10 C2
Town Hall.......................11 C2
Zamoyski Palace..............12 B2

SLEEPING
Hotel Arkadia..................13 C2
Hotel Renesans...............14 D2
Hotel Zamojski................15 C2
Pokoje Gościnne OSiR......16 A1

EATING
Bar Asia...........................17 C2
Lux Mini-supermarket......18 C2
Restauracja Muzealna......19 C2

DRINKING
Corner Pub......................20 C3

TRANSPORT
Ela Travel.........................21 C2

Arsenal Museum (ul Zamkowa 2; adult/concession 6/3zł; ☯ 9am-4pm Tue-Sun) holds an unremarkable collection of cannons, swords and firearms. To the north of the palace stretches a beautifully landscaped **park**.

Before WWII, Jewish citizens accounted for 45% of the town's population (of 12,000) and most lived in the area north and east of the palace. The most significant Jewish architectural relic is the Renaissance **synagogue** (ul Pereca 14; adult/concession 5/2zł; ☯ 9am-5pm Tue-Sat), built in the early 17th century. For some years it was used as a public library, but is now empty and awaiting transformation into a cultural centre. In the meantime you can visit and see its original wall and ceiling decoration, and a simple photo exhibition of Jewish life in the region.

On the eastern edge of the Old Town is the antiquated **Market Hall** (Hala Targowa), closed until 2010 due to a major renovation. Behind it is the best surviving **bastion** from the original city walls.

Sleeping

Youth Hostel (☎ 084 638 9500; ul Zamoyskiego 4; dm 15zł; ☯ Jul-Aug) You can find this hostel in a school

building 1.5km east of the Old Town, not far from the bus terminal. It's basic but functional and very cheap.

Pokoje Gościnne OSiR (☎ 084 638 6011; ul Królowej Jadwigi 8; dm 24zł, s/d/tr 90/125/150zł) Located in a sprawling sporting complex, a 15-minute walk west of the Old Town, and packed with old trophies and students playing table tennis. Rooms are plainly furnished, clean and comfortable, although the bathrooms fall short of the ideal.

Camping Duet (☎ 084 639 2499; ul Królowej Jadwigi 14; s/d/tr/q 75/90/120/150zł; ☒) West of the Old Town, Camping Duet has neat bungalows, tennis courts, a restaurant, sauna and jacuzzi. Larger bungalows sleep up to six.

Hotel Jubilat (☎ 084 638 6401; www.hoteljubilat.pl; ul Kardynała Wyszyńskiego 52; s/d/tr from 136/177/292zł) An acceptable, if slightly drab, place to spend the night, right beside the bus station. It couldn't be handier for late arrivals or early departures, but it's a long way from anywhere else. It has a restaurant and fitness club.

Hotel Arkadia (☎ 084 638 6507; www.arkadia.zamosc .pl; Rynek Wielki 9; s/d/tr/ste from 140/160/200/250zł) With just nine rooms, this compact place offers a pool table and restaurant in addition to lodgings. It's charming but shabby, though its location right on the market square is hard to beat.

Hotel Renesans (☎ 084 639 2001; www.hotelrenesans .pl; ul Grecka 6; s/d/ste from 140/205/216zł) It's ironic that a hotel named after the Renaissance is housed in the Old Town's ugliest building. However, it's central and the rooms are surprisingly modern and pleasant.

Hotel Zamojski (☎ 084 639 2516; www.orbis.pl; ul Kołłątaja 2/4/6; s/d/ste 227/335/475zł; 🔲) The best joint in town is situated within three connected old houses, just off the square. The rooms are modern and tastefully furnished, and there's a good onsite restaurant and cocktail bar, along with a fitness centre.

Eating & Drinking
Bar Asia (ul Staszica 10; mains 5-9zł; 🕐 8am-5pm Mon-Fri, 8am-4pm Sat) For hungry but broke travellers, this old-style *bar mleczny* is ideal. It serves cheap and tasty Polish food including several variants of *pierogi*, in a minimally decorated space.

Restauracja Muzealna (☎ 084 638 7300; ul Ormiańska Ormianska 30; mains 10-25zł; 🕐 11am-10pm Mon-Sat, 11am-9pm Sun) Subterranean restaurant in an atmospheric cellar below the main square, bedecked with ornate timber furniture and portraits of nobles. It serves a better class of Polish cuisine at reasonable prices, and has a well-stocked bar.

Corner Pub (ul Żeromskiego 6) This cosy Irish-style pub is a good place to have a drink. It has comfy booths and the walls are ornamented with bric-a-brac such as antique clocks, swords and model cars.

For self-caterers, there's the handy **Lux mini-supermarket** (ul Grodzka 16; 🕐 7am-8pm Mon-Sat, 8am-6pm Sun) near the Rynek.

Getting There & Away
Buses are usually more convenient and quicker than trains. The **bus terminal** (ul Hrubieszowska) is 2km east of the Old Town and linked by frequent city buses, primarily buses 0 and 3. Daily, buses go to Kraków (40zł, seven hours, five daily), Warsaw (35zł, 4¾ hours, three daily) and Lublin (15zł, two hours, hourly).

Quicker and cheaper are the minibuses that travel every 30 minutes between Lublin and Zamość (10zł, 1½ hours). They leave from the minibus stand opposite the bus terminal in Zamość and from a corner northwest of the

bus terminal in Lublin. Check the changeable timetable for departures to other destinations, including Warsaw and Kraków.

From the train station, about 1km southwest of the Old Town, one train heads to Lublin (28zł, 1½ hours) every day, and one to Warsaw (48zł, 5½ hours). **Ela Travel** (☎ 084 638 5775; ul Grodzka 18) sells international bus and air tickets.

CARPATHIAN MOUNTAINS

The Carpathians (Karpaty) stretch from the southern border with Slovakia into Ukraine, and their wooded hills and snowy mountains are a beacon for hikers, skiers and cyclists. The most popular destination here is the resort town of Zakopane in the heart of the Tatra Mountains (Tatry). Elsewhere, historic regional towns such as Przemyśl and Sanok offer a relaxed pace and unique insights into the past.

ZAKOPANE
pop 27,300
Nestled at the foot of the Tatra Mountains, Zakopane is Poland's major winter sports centre, though it's a popular destination year-round. It may resemble a tourist trap, with its overcommercialised, overpriced exterior, but it also has a relaxed, laid-back vibe that makes it a great place to chill out for a few days, even if you're not intending to ski or hike.

Zakopane also played an important role in keeping Polish culture alive during the long years of foreign rule in the 19th century. Many artistic types settled in the town, including composer Karol Szymanowski and the writer and painter, Witkacy. Witkacy's father, Stanisław Witkiewicz, was inspired by traditional local architecture to create the famous Zakopane style. Some of his buildings still stand.

Information
Bank Pekao (ul Krupówki 19)
Centrum Przewodnictwa Tatrzańskiego (Tatra Guide Centre; ☎ 018 206 37 99; ul Chałubińskiego 42a; 🕐 9am-3pm) Arranges English- and German-speaking mountain guides.
Księgarnia Górska (ul Zaruskiego 5) Bookshop in the reception area of the Dom Turysty PTTK, sells regional hiking maps.
Main post office (ul Krupówki; 🕐 7am-8pm Mon-Fri, 8am-2pm Sat)

POLAND

Orbis Travel (☎ 018 201 5051; ul Krupówki 22) Offers the usual services, as well as accommodation in hotels and pensions. Also has an in-house *kantor*.

Tourist office (☎ 018 201 2211; ul Kościuszki 17; ⏰ 9am–5pm daily Jul & Aug, 9am–5pm Mon–Fri Sep–Jun) Offers advice, and sells hiking and city maps. The centre can also arrange rafting trips down the Dunajec River.

Widmo (ul Galicy 6; per hr 5zł; ⏰ 7.30am–midnight Mon–Fri, 9am–midnight Sat & Sun) Internet access.

Sights & Activities

Check out exhibits about regional history, ethnography and geology at the **Tatra Museum** (ul Krupówki 10; adult/concession 7/5.50zł, free Sun; ⏰ 9am–5pm Tue–Sat, 9am–3pm Sun), along with displays on local flora and fauna. Head southwest to **Villa Koliba** (ul Kościeliska 18), the first design (1892) by Witkiewicz in the Zakopane style. Fittingly, it now houses the **Museum of Zakopane Style** (adult/concession 7/5.50zł; ⏰ 9am–5pm Wed–Sat, 9am–3pm Sun).

About 350m southeast is **Villa Atma** (ul Kasprusie 19) with its **Szymanowski Museum** (adult/concession 6/3zł, free Sun; ⏰ 10am–3.30pm Wed, Thu, Sat & Sun, 10am–6pm Fri), dedicated to the great musician who once lived there. There are piano recitals here in summer.

The **Tatra National Park Natural Museum** (ul Chałubińskiego 42a; admission free; ⏰ 8am–3pm Mon–Sat), near the Rondo en route to the national park, has some mildly interesting exhibits about the park's natural history.

A short walk northeast up the hill leads to **Villa Pod Jedlami** (ul Koziniec 1), another splendid house built in the Zakopane style (the interior

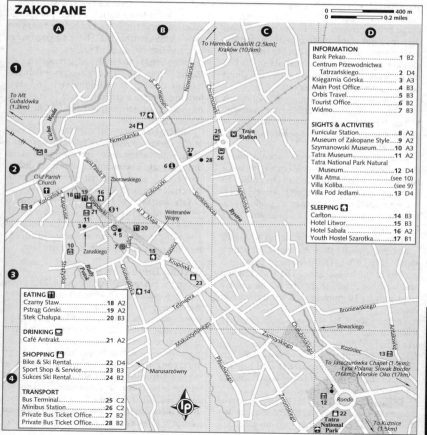

ZAKOPANE

0   400 m
0   0.2 miles

INFORMATION
Bank Pekao.............................**1** B2
Centrum Przewodnictwa
  Tatrzańskiego.....................**2** D4
Księgarnia Górska....................**3** A3
Main Post Office.......................**4** B3
Orbis Travel.............................**5** B3
Tourist Office..........................**6** B2
Widmo....................................**7** B3

SIGHTS & ACTIVITIES
Funicular Station......................**8** A2
Museum of Zakopane Style......**9** A2
Szymanowski Museum.............**10** A3
Tatra Museum........................**11** A2
Tatra National Park Natural
  Museum.............................**12** D4
Villa Atma.........................(see 10)
Villa Koliba........................(see 9)
Villa Pod Jedlami..................**13** D4

SLEEPING
Carlton..................................**14** B3
Hotel Litwor...........................**15** B3
Hotel Sabała..........................**16** A2
Youth Hostel Szarotka.............**17** B1

EATING
Czarny Staw...........................**18** A2
Pstrąg Górski..........................**19** A2
Stek Chałupa.........................**20** B3

DRINKING
Café Antrakt...........................**21** A2

SHOPPING
Bike & Ski Rental....................**22** D4
Sport Shop & Service...............**23** B3
Sukces Ski Rental....................**24** B2

TRANSPORT
Bus Terminal..........................**25** C2
Minibus Station.......................**26** C2
Private Bus Ticket Office...........**27** B2
Private Bus Ticket Office...........**28** B2

To Harenda Chairlift (2.5km);
Kraków (103km)

To Mt Gubałówka (1.2km)

Old Parish Church

Train Station

Weteranów Wojny

Broniewskiego

Słowackiego

Koziniec

To Jaszczurówka Chapel (1.5km);
Łysa Polana; Slovak Border
(16km); Morskie Oko (17km)

Marusarzówny

Rondo

Tatra National Park

To Kuźnice (1.5km)

POLAND

cannot be visited). Perhaps Witkiewicz's greatest achievement is the **Jaszczurówka Chapel**, about 1.5km further east along the road to Morskie Oko.

Mt Gubałówka (1120m) offers excellent views over the Tatras and is a popular destination for tourists who don't feel overly energetic. The **funicular** (adult/concession one-way 10/8zł, return 16/12zł; ☉ 8am-10pm Jul & Aug, 8.30am-7.20pm Apr-Jun & Sep, 8.30am-6pm Oct & Nov) covers the 1388m-long route in less than five minutes, climbing 300m from the funicular station just north of ul Krupówki.

Sleeping

Given the abundance of private rooms and decent hostels, few travellers actually stay in hotels. The tourist office usually knows of great bargains in guest houses.

Some travel agencies in Zakopane can arrange private rooms, but in the peak season they may not want to offer anything for less than three nights. Expect a double room (singles are rarely offered) to cost about 70zł in the peak season in the town centre, and about 50zł for somewhere further out.

Locals offering private rooms may approach you at the bus or train stations; alternatively, just look out for signs posted in the front of private homes – *noclegi* and *pokoje* both mean 'rooms available'.

Like all seasonal resorts, accommodation prices fluctuate considerably between low season and high season (December to February and July to August). Always book accommodation in advance at peak times, especially on weekends. The following rates are for high season.

Youth Hostel Szarotka (☎ 018 201 3618; www .szarotkaptsm.republika.pl; ul Nowotarska 45; dm/d/tr 40/100/150zł) This friendly, homely place gets packed in the high season. There's a kitchen and washing machine on site. It's on a noisy road about a 10-minute walk from the town centre.

Carlton (☎ 018 201 4415; www.carlton.pl; ul Grun-waldzka 11; s/d/tr 100/200/300zł) Good value pension in a grand old house away from the main drag, featuring light-filled rooms with modern furniture. There's an impressive shared balcony overlooking the road, and a big comfy lounge lined with potted plants.

ourpick **Hotel Sabała** (☎ 018 201 5092; www.sabala .zakopane.pl; ul Krupówki 11; s/d/ste from 310/400/520zł; ⬚) Built in 1894 but thoroughly up-to-date, this

striking timber building has a superb location overlooking the picturesque pedestrian thoroughfare. It offers cosy, attic-style rooms, and there's a sauna and solarium on the premises. A candlelit restaurant has views of street life.

Hotel Litwor (☎ 018 202 4200; www.litwor.pl; ul Krupówki 40; s/d/ste 488/613/838zł; ⬚) This sumptuous four-star place, with large, restful rooms, has all the usual top-end facilities, including a gym and sauna. A 20% discount applies to advance bookings. It also has an excellent restaurant serving classy versions of traditional dishes.

Eating & Drinking

The main street, ul Krupówki, is lined with all sorts of eateries.

Czarny Staw (☎ 018 201 3856; ul Krupówki 2; mains 10-46zł; ☉ 10am-1am) Offers a tasty range of Polish dishes, including a variety of dumplings, and much of the menu is cooked before your very eyes on the central grill. There's a good salad bar, and live music most nights.

Pstrąg Górski (☎ 018 206 4163; ul Krupówki 6; mains 16-30zł; ☉ 9am-10pm) This self-service fish restaurant, done up in traditional style and overlooking a narrow stream, serves some of the freshest trout, salmon and sea fish in town. It's excellent value.

Stek Chałupa (☎ 018 201 5918; ul Krupówki 33; mains 18-40zł; ☉ 8am-midnight) Big friendly barn of a place, with homely decor and waitresses in traditional garb. The menu features meat dishes, particularly steaks, though there are vegetarian choices among the salads and *pierogi*.

Café Antrakt (☎ 018 201 73 02; ul Krupówki 6; ☉ 11am-midnight) A mellow venue for an alcoholic or caffeine-laden drink, hidden away above the street with an ambient old-meets-new decor. It occasionally hosts live jazz.

Getting There & Away

From the **bus terminal** (ul Chramcówki), PKS buses run to Kraków every 45 to 60 minutes (16zł, two hours). Two private companies, **Trans Frej** (www.trans-frej.com.pl, in Polish) and **Szwagropol** (www .szwagropol.pl, in Polish), also run comfortable buses from here (18zł) at the same frequency. At peak times (especially weekends), you can buy your tickets for the private buses in advance from offices a short distance west of the bus station in Zakopane. Tickets are also available in Kraków for Trans Frej buses from **Biuro Turystyki i Zakwaterowania Waweltur** (Map p610; ul Pawia 8) and for Szwagropol buses from **Fogra Travel** (Map p610; ul Pawia 12). The minibus station opposite the bus terminal is most useful for journeys to towns within the Tatra Mountains.

From Zakopane, PKS buses also go once daily to Lublin (63zł, six hours), Sanok (39zł, 6½ hours), Przemyśl (42zł, 4½ hours) and Warsaw (60zł, eight hours). Two daily buses head to Poprad in Slovakia (21zł). PKS buses – and minibuses from opposite the bus terminal – regularly travel to Lake Morskie Oko and on to Polana Palenica. To cross into Slovakia, get off this bus/minibus at Łysa Polana, cross the border on foot and take another bus to Tatranská Lomnica and the other Slovak mountain towns.

From the **train station** (ul Chramcówki), trains for Kraków (33zł, 3½ hours) leave every two hours or so. Three trains a day go to Częstochowa (45zł, seven hours), three to Gdynia via Gdańsk (64zł, 13 hours), two to Łódź (53zł, nine hours), two to Poznań (56zł, 12 hours), and six head to Warsaw (53zł, nine hours).

TATRA MOUNTAINS

The Tatras, 100km south of Kraków, are the highest range of the Carpathian Mountains, providing a dramatic range of rugged scenery that's a distinct contrast to the rest of Poland's flatness. Roughly 60km long and 15km wide, this mountain range stretches across the Polish–Slovak border. A quarter is in Poland and is mostly part of the Tatra National Park (about 212 sq km). The Polish Tatras contain more than 20 peaks over 2000m, the highest of which is Mt Rysy (2499m).

Sights & Activities

CABLE CAR TO MT KASPROWY WIERCH

The **cable car** (adult/concession return 38/28zł; 7am-9pm Jul & Aug, 7.30am-5pm Apr-Jun, Sep & Oct, 8am-4pm Nov) from Kuźnice (3km south of Zakopane) to the summit of Mt Kasprowy Wierch (1985m) is a classic tourist experience enjoyed by Poles and foreigners alike. At the end of the trip, you can get off and stand with one foot in Poland and the other in Slovakia. The one-way journey takes 20 minutes and climbs 936m. The cable car normally shuts down for two weeks in May and November, and won't operate if the snow and, particularly, the winds are dangerous. Note that ticket prices are discounted significantly outside July and August.

The view from the top is spectacular (clouds permitting). Two chairlifts transport skiers to and from various slopes between December and April. A restaurant serves skiers and hikers alike. In summer, many people return to Zakopane on foot down the Gąsienicowa Valley, and the most intrepid walk the ridges all the way across to Lake Morskie Oko via Pięciu Stawów, a strenuous hike taking a full day in good weather.

If you buy a return ticket, your trip back is automatically reserved for two hours after your departure, so buy a one-way ticket to the top (28zł) and another one down (20zł), if you want to stay longer. Mt Kasprowy Wierch is popular; so in summer, arrive early and expect to wait. PKS buses and minibuses to Kuźnice frequently leave from Zakopane.

LAKE MORSKIE OKO

The emerald-green Lake Morskie Oko (Eye of the Sea) is among the loveliest lakes in the Tatras. PKS buses and minibuses regularly depart from Zakopane for Polana Palenica (30 minutes), from where a road (9km) continues uphill to the lake. Cars, bikes and buses are not allowed up this road, so you'll have to walk, but it's not steep (allow about two hours one way). Alternatively, take a horse-drawn carriage (35/20zł uphill/downhill, but very negotiable) to within 2km of the lake. In winter, transport is by horse-drawn four-seater sledge, which is more expensive. The last minibus to Zakopane returns between 5pm and 6pm.

HIKING

If you're doing any hiking in the Tatras get a copy of the *Tatrzański Park Narodowy* map (1:25,000), which shows all hiking trails in the area. Better still, buy one or more of the 14 sheets of *Tatry Polskie*, available at Księgarnia Górska (p626) in Zakopane. In July and August these trails can be overrun by tourists, so late spring and early autumn are the best times. Theoretically you can expect better weather in autumn, when rainfall is lower.

Like all alpine regions, the Tatras can be dangerous, particularly during the snow season (November to May). Remember the weather can be unpredictable. Bring proper hiking boots, warm clothing and waterproof rain gear – and be prepared to use occasional ropes and chains (provided along the trails) to get up and down some rocky slopes. Guides are not necessary because many of the trails are marked, but can be arranged in Zakopane (see p626) for about 230zł per day.

POLAND

There are several picturesque valleys south of Zakopane, including the **Dolina Strążyska**. You can continue from the Strążyska by the red trail up to **Mt Giewont** (1909m), 3½ hours from Zakopane, and then walk down the blue trail to Kuźnice in two hours.

Two long and beautiful forested valleys, the **Dolina Chochołowska** and the **Dolina Kościeliska**, are in the western part of the park, known as the Tatry Zachodnie (West Tatras). These valleys are ideal for cycling. Both are accessible by PKS buses and minibuses from Zakopane.

The Tatry Wysokie (High Tatras) to the east offer quite different scenery: bare granite peaks and glacial lakes. One way to get there is via cable car to **Mt Kasprowy Wierch**, then hike eastward along the red trail to Mt Świnica (2301m) and on to the Zawrat pass (2159m) – a tough three to four hours from Mt Kasprowy. From Zawrat, descend northwards to the Dolina Gąsienicowa along the blue trail and then back to Zakopane.

Alternatively, head south (also along the blue trail) to the wonderful **Dolina Pięciu Stawów** (Five Lakes Valley), where there is a mountain refuge 1¼ hours from Zawrat. The blue trail heading west from the refuge passes **Lake Morskie Oko**, 1½ hours from the refuge.

SKIING

Zakopane boasts four major ski areas (and several smaller ones) with more than 50 ski lifts. **Mt Kasprowy Wierch** (p629) and **Mt Gubałówka** (p628) offer the best conditions and the most challenging slopes in the area, with the ski season extending until early May. Lift tickets cost 8zł for one ride at Mt Kasprowy Wierch, and 5zł on the smaller lift at Mt Gubałówka. Alternatively, you can buy a day card (90zł) at Mt Kasprowy Wierch, which allows you to skip the queues. Purchase your lift tickets on the relevant mountain.

Another alternative is the **Harenda chairlift** (☎ 018 206 4029; www.harendazakopane.pl; ul Harenda 63; ☽ 9am-6pm) just outside Zakopane, in the direction of Kraków. A one-way/return ticket is 4/6zł, and a day card is 70zł.

Ski equipment rental is available at all facilities except Mt Kasprowy Wierch. Otherwise, stop off on your way to Kuźnice at the **ski rental** place near the Rondo in Zakopane. Other places in Zakopane, such as **Sukces Ski Rental** (☎ 018 206 4197; ul Nowotarska 39) and **Sport Shop & Service** (☎ 018 201 5871; ul Krupówki 52a), also rent ski gear.

Sleeping

Tourists are not allowed to take their own cars into the park; you must walk in, take the cable car or use an official vehicle owned by the park or a hotel or hostel.

Camping is also not allowed in the park, but eight PTTK mountain refuges/hostels provide simple accommodation. Most refuges are small and fill up fast; in midsummer and midwinter they're invariably packed beyond capacity. No one is ever turned away, however, though you may have to crash on the floor if all the beds are taken. Do not arrive too late in the day, and bring along your own bed mat and sleeping bag. All refuges serve simple hot meals, but the kitchens and dining rooms close early (sometimes at 7pm).

The refuges listed here are open all year, but some may be temporarily closed for renovations or because of inclement weather. Check the current situation at the Dom Turysty PTTK in Zakopane or the regional **PTTK headquarters** (☎ 018 443 8610) in Nowy Sącz.

Dolina Pięciu Stawów Hostel (☎ 018 207 7607; dm 25-30zł) This is the highest (1700m) and most scenically located refuge in the Polish Tatras.

Hala Kondratowa Hostel (☎ 018 201 9114; dm 28zł) This place is about 30 minutes beyond Kalatówki on the trail to Giewont. It's in a terrific location and has a great atmosphere, but it is small.

Roztoka Hostel (☎ 018 207 7442; dm 28-30zł) Hikers wishing to traverse the park might want to begin here. It's accessible by the bus or minibus to Morskie Oko.

Morskie Oko Hostel (☎ 018 207 7609; dm 32-42zł) An early start from Zakopane would allow you to visit Morskie Oko in the morning and stay here at night.

Kalatówki Hotel (☎ 018 206 3644; s/d/tr/ste from 48/94/117/132zł) This large and decent refuge is the easiest to reach from Zakopane. It's a 40-minute walk from the Kuźnice cable-car station.

DUNAJEC GORGE

An entertaining and leisurely way to explore the Pieniny Mountains is to go **rafting** on the Dunajec River, which winds along the Polish–Slovak border through a spectacular and deep gorge.

The trip starts at the wharf (Przystan Flisacka) in Kąty, 46km northeast of Zakopane, and you can finish either at the spa town of

Szczawnica (adult/concession 39/19.50zł, 2¼ hours, 18km), or further on at Krościenko (adult/concession 48/24zł, 2¾ hours, 23km). The raft trip operates between April and October, but only starts when there's a minimum of 10 passengers.

The gorge is an easy day trip from Zakopane. Catch a regular bus to Nowy Targ (4zł, 30 minutes, hourly) from Zakopane to connect with one of five daily buses (10zł, 45 minutes) to Kąty. From Szczawnica or Krościenko, take the bus back to Nowy Targ (7zł, one hour, hourly) and change for Zakopane. Krościenko has frequent bus links with Szczawnica, and five buses travel daily between Szczawnica and Kraków (14zł, 2½ hours). You can also return to the Kąty car park by bus with the raftsmen.

To avoid waiting around in Kąty for a raft to fill up, organise a trip at any travel agency in Zakopane or at the tourist office. The cost is around 75zł to 80zł per person, and includes transport, equipment and guides.

SANOK
pop 39,400

Nestled in a picturesque valley in the foothills of the Bieszczady Mountains, Sanok has been subject to Ruthenian, Hungarian, Austrian, Russian, German and Polish rule in its eventful history. Although it contains an important industrial zone, it's also a popular base for exploring the mountains.

The helpful **tourist office** (☎ 013 464 4533; www .sanok.pl; Rynek 14; ⏰ 9am-5pm Mon-Fri year-round, 9am-3pm Sat & Sun Oct-Apr) on the market square is the best place to find brochures on Sanok's attractions. The **PTTK office** (☎ 013 463 2512; www.pttk .avx.pl; ul 3 Maja 2; ⏰ 8am-5pm Mon-Fri) also provides visitor information. There's a **Bank Pekao** (cnr ul Grzegorza & ul Kościuszki) nearby, and you can

check email at **Prox** (ul Kazimierz Wielkiego 6; per hr 3zł) further west.

Sanok is noted for its unique **Museum of Folk Architecture** (www.skansen.mblsanok.pl; ul Rybickiego 3; adult/concession 9/6zł; ⏰ 8am-6pm May-Oct, 8am-2pm Nov-Apr), which features architecture from regional ethnic groups. Walk north from the town centre for 2km along ul Mickiewicza and ul Białogórska, then cross the bridge and turn right. The **Historical Museum** (ul Zamkowa 2; adult/concession 10/7zł; ⏰ 9am-3pm Tue-Sun, 8-10am Mon) is housed in a 16th-century castle and contains an impressive collection of Ruthenian icons, along with a modern art gallery.

Sanok's surrounding villages are attractions in their own right, as many have lovely old churches. The marked **Icon Trail** takes hikers or cyclists along a 70km loop, passing by 10 village churches, as well as attractive mountain countryside. Trail leaflets and maps (in English, German and French) are available from the tourist office, as well as information on other themed trails including a Jewish heritage route.

Convenient budget accommodation is available at **Hotel Pod Trzema Różami** (☎ 013 463 0922; www.podtrzemarozami.pl; ul Jagiellońska 13; s/d/tr/ste 80/100/120/140zł), about 300m south of the main square. Further south (another 600m) and up the scale is **Hotel Jagielloński** (☎ 013 463 1208; www.hoteljagiellonski.bieszczady24.pl; ul Jagiellońska 49; s/d/tr/ste 115/150/195/230zł), with distinctive wooden furniture, parquetry floors and a very good restaurant. Sanok's most comfortable option is **Hotel Sanvit** (☎ 013 465 5088; www.sanvit.sanok.pl; ul Łazienna 1; s/d/tr/ste 110/150/190/250zł), just west of the square, with bright, modern rooms, shining bathrooms, spa treatments and a restaurant.

Karczma Jadło Karpackie (☎ 013 464 6700; Rynek 12; mains 8-25zł) is an amenable, down-to-earth bar and restaurant on the main square. A good

---

WORTH THE TRIP: LAKE SOLINA

In the far southeastern corner of Poland, wedged between the Ukrainian and Slovak borders, lies **Lake Solina**. This sizeable reservoir (27km long and 60m deep) was created in 1968 when the San River was dammed. Today it's a popular centre for water sports and other recreational pursuits.

Polańczyk is the best place to base yourself. This pleasant town on the lake's western shore offers a range of attractions, including sailing, windsurfing, fishing and beaches. There are also numerous hotels and sanatoriums offering spa treatments.

There are regular buses from Sanok to Polańczyk each day. For more details, check out Lonely Planet's Poland country guide, visit www.karpaty.turystyka.pl or step into the local **tourist office** (☎ 013 470 3028; ul Wiejska 2).

place to have a drink, alcoholic or otherwise, is **Weranda Caffe** (ul 3 Maja 14; 10am-10pm), a cosy cafe-bar with a fireplace, and outdoor seating in summer.

The bus terminal and adjacent train station are about 1km southeast of the main square. Six buses go daily to Przemyśl (11zł, two hours), and one to Zakopane (39zł, 6½ hours). Buses also head regularly to Kraków and Warsaw. Train journeys to these destinations, however, may require multiple changes.

PRZEMYŚL
pop 67,100

Everything about Przemyśl (*psheh*-mishl) feels big: its sprawling market square, the massive churches surrounding it, and the broad San River flowing through the city.

Luckily the area of most interest to visitors – around the sloping **Rynek** (Market Sq) – is compact and easily explored. The **tourist office** (016 675 2164; www.przemysl.pl; ul Grodzka 1; 10am-6pm Mon-Fri, 9am-5pm Sat & Sun Apr-Sep, 9am-5pm Mon-Fri, 10am-2pm Sat Oct-Mar) is situated above the southwest corner of the square. Check your emails at the **public library** (ul Słowackiego 15; per hr 2zł; 10am-6pm Mon-Fri, 10am-4pm Sat), on the main road along the eastern edge of the Old Town.

About 350m southwest of the Rynek are the ruins of a 14th-century **castle** (ul Zamkowa), built by Kazimierz Wielki. In a modern building just northeast of Rynek, you can learn about the history of the surrounding region at the **National Museum of the Przemyśl Lands** (Plac Joselewicza; adult/concession 5/2.50zł; 9.30am-4.30pm Tue & Fri, 10am-2.30pm Wed, Thu & Sat, noon-6pm Sun).

For variety, visit the curious **Museum of Bells and Pipes** (ul Władycze 3; adult/concession 5/2.50zł; 9.30am-4.30pm Tue & Fri, 10am-2.30pm Wed, Thu & Sat, noon-6pm Sun) in the old Clock Tower, where you can inspect several floors worth of vintage bells, elaborately carved pipes and cigar cutters (the city has long been famous across Poland for manufacturing these items). From the top of the tower there's a great view.

Przemyśl has a selection of inexpensive accommodation, including the central **Dom Wycieczkowy Podzamcze** (016 678 5374; ul Waygarta 3; dm 23zł, d/tr/q 64/81/108zł), on the western edge of the Old Town. Its rooms have seen some wear, but it's pleasant enough for the price. **Hotelik Pod Basztą** (016 678 8268; www.hotelik-pod-baszta.w.interia.pl; ul Królowej Jadwigi 4; s/d/tr from 39/59/79zł) is

just below the castle. Rooms are a little old-fashioned, with shared bathrooms, but many have castle or city views.

More comfort is available at **Hotel Europejski** (016 675 7100; www.hotel-europejski.pl; ul Sowińskiego 4; s/d/tr/ste 110/140/170/210zł) in a renovated old building facing the attractive facade of the train station. An impressive staircase leads to simple, light rooms with high ceilings.

A worthy place to eat is **Restauracja Piwnica Mieszczańska** (016 675 0459; Rynek 9; mains 6-25zł), on Rynek. It must be Poland's only cellar restaurant with access to a skylight, and is decorated with mini-chandeliers and lace tablecloths. The bourgeoisie platter (three kinds of meat) will interest ardent carnivores, and there's a reasonable selection of soups and fish dishes.

Restauracja Karpacka (016 678 9057; ul Kościuszki 5; mains 10-30zł; 10am-10pm), just west of the tourist office, is an old-fashioned eatery featuring bow-tied waiters, a timber ceiling and yellow stucco walls. It serves a good range of Polish standards, and Ukrainian *borscht* as a nod to the neighbours just down the road.

If you fancy a drink, **Bistro Absynt** (Plac Dominikański 4), on the northwest corner of Rynek, is a relaxed space from which to sip and people-watch.

From Przemyśl, buses run to Lviv (95km) in Ukraine several times a day and regularly to all towns in southeastern Poland, including Sanok (11zl, two hours, six daily). Trains run to Lublin (41zł, four hours, two daily), Kraków (43zł, 3¾ hours, 11 daily) and Warsaw (53zł, 6¾ hours, four daily), and stop here on the way to/from Lviv. The bus terminal and adjacent train station in Przemyśl are about 1km northeast of the Rynek.

SILESIA

Silesia (Śląsk) is a fascinating mix of landscapes. Though the industrial zone around Katowice has limited attraction for visitors, beautiful Wrocław is a historic city with lively nightlife, and the Sudeten Mountains draw hikers and other nature lovers.

The history of the region is similarly diverse, having been governed by Polish, Bohemian, Austrian and German rulers. After two centuries as part of Prussia and Germany, the territory was largely included within Poland's new borders after WWII.

WROCŁAW
pop 640,000

When citizens of beautiful Kraków enthusiastically encourage you to visit Wrocław (*vrots-wahf*), you know you're onto something good. The city's delightful Old Town is a gracious mix of Gothic and baroque styles, and its large student population ensures a healthy number of restaurants, bars and nightclubs.

Wrocław has been traded back and forth between various rulers over the centuries, but began life in the year 1000 under the Polish Piast dynasty and developed into a prosperous trading and cultural centre. In the 1740s it passed to Prussia, under the German name of Breslau. Under Prussian rule, the city became a major textile manufacturing centre, greatly increasing its population.

Upon its return to Poland in 1945, Wrocław was a shell of its former self, having sustained massive damage in WWII. Though 70% of the city was destroyed, sensitive restoration has returned the historic centre to its former beauty.

Information

Bank Pekao (ul Oławska 2)

EMPiK (Rynek 50) Bookshop.

Internet Netvigator (ul Igielna 14; per hr 3zł; 9am-midnight)

Księgarnia Świat Podróżnika (ul Wita Stwosza 19/20) Maps and guidebooks.

Main post office (Rynek 28; 6.30am-8.30pm Mon-Sat)

Tourist office (☎ 071 344 3111; www.wroclaw.pl; Rynek 14; 9am-9pm Apr-Oct, 9am-8pm Nov-Mar)

Tourist & Cultural Information Centre (☎ 071 342 0185; www.wroclaw-info.pl; ul Sukiennice 12; 8am-7pm Mon-Fri, 9am-5pm Sat & Sun Apr-Oct) Handles cultural ticket sales and offers internet access.

W Sercu Miasta (ul Przejście Żelaźnicze 4; per hr 4zł; 9am-midnight Mon-Sat, noon-midnight Sun) Internet access down a laneway in the middle of Rynek.

Sights

In the centre of the Old Town is the **Rynek**, Poland's second-largest old market square (after Kraków). The beautiful **town hall** (built 1327–1504) on the southern side plays host to the **City Dwellers' Art Museum** (adult/concession 7/5zł, free Wed; 11am-5pm Tue-Sat, 10am-6pm Sun), with stately rooms on show, and exhibits featuring the art of gold and the stories of famous Wrocław inhabitants.

In the northwestern corner of the Rynek are two attractive small houses linked by a baroque gate. They're called **Jaś i Małgosia** (ul Św. Mikołaja), a couple better known to English speakers as Hansel and Gretel.

See if you can spot the diminutive statue of a gnome at ground level, just to the west of these houses; he's one of over 70 **Gnomes of Wrocław**, which are scattered through the city. Whimsical as they are, they're attributed to the symbol of the Orange Alternative, a communist-era dissident group that used ridicule as a weapon, and often painted gnomes where graffiti had been removed by the authorities.

Behind gate and gnome is the monumental 14th-century **St Elizabeth's Church** (ul Elżbiety 1; admission 5zł; 9am-7pm Mon-Fri, 11am-5pm Sat, 1-6pm Sun May-Oct, 10am-5pm Mon-Sat, 1-5pm Sun Nov-Apr) with its 83m-high tower, which you can climb for city views. The southwestern corner of the Rynek opens into **Plac Solny** (Salt Sq), once the site of the town's salt trade and now home to a 24-hour flower market.

West of the Rynek is the **Arsenal**, a remnant of the town's 15th-century fortifications. It now houses the **Military Museum** (ul Cieszyńskiego 9; adult/concession 7/5zł; 11am-5pm Wed-Sat, 10am-6pm Sun), with the usual collection of old weapons.

One block east of the Rynek is the Gothic **St Mary Magdalene's Church** (ul Łaciarska; admission free; 9am-4pm Mon-Sat) with a Romanesque portal from 1280 incorporated into its southern external wall. Climb the 72m high tower and its connected **bridge** (adult/concession 4/3zł, 10am-8pm Apr-Oct) for a lofty view. Further east, the 15th-century former Bernardine church and monastery encompasses the **Museum of Architecture** (ul Bernardyńska 5; adult/concession 7/5zł; 10am-4pm Tue, Wed, Fri & Sat, noon-6pm Thu, 11am-5pm Sun).

Slightly further east is Wrocław's pride and joy (and major tourist attraction), the giant **Panorama of Racławicka** (www.panoramaraclawicka.pl; ul Purkyniego 11; adult/concession 20/15zł; 9am-5pm Tue-Sun May-Oct, 9am-4pm Tue-Sun Nov-Apr), a 360-degree painting of the 1794 Battle of Racławice, in which the Polish peasant army, led by Tadeusz Kościuszko, defeated Russian forces intent on partitioning Poland. Created by Jan Styka and Wojciech Kossak for the centenary of the battle in 1894, the painting is an immense 114m long and 15m high, and was brought here by Polish immigrants displaced from Lviv after WWII. Due to the communist government's uneasiness about glorifying a famous Russian defeat, however, the panorama wasn't re-erected until 1985, in a circular building east of the Old Town. Obligatory tours (with audio in

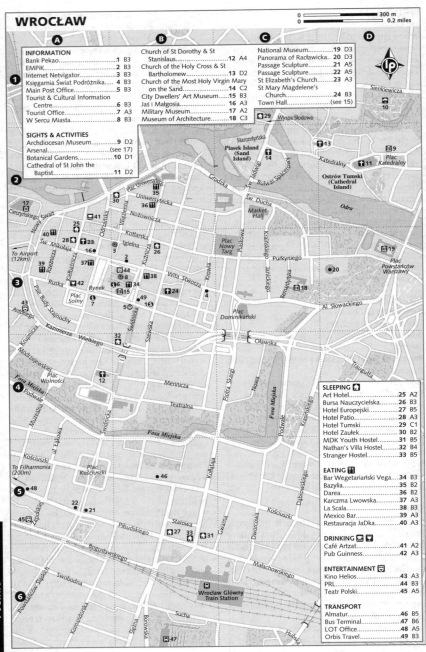

WROCŁAW

0 — 300 m
0 — 0.2 miles

POLAND

English, French, German, Spanish, Russian and other languages) run every 30 minutes between 9am and 4.30pm from April to November, and 10am and 3pm from December to March. The ticket also allows entry to the National Museum on the same day.

Located nearby, the **National Museum** (www .mnwr.art.pl; Plac Powstańców Warszawy 5; adult/concession 15/10zł, free Sat; 9am-4pm Wed-Fri & Sun, 10am-6pm Sat) exhibits Silesian medieval art, and a fine collection of modern Polish painting. Entry is included with a ticket to the Panorama.

North of the river is **Piasek Island** (Sand Island), where you'll find the 14th-century **Church of the Most Holy Virgin Mary on the Sand** (ul Św. Jadwigi; erratic) with lofty Gothic vaults and a year-round nativity scene. Cross the small bridge to **Ostrów Tumski** (Cathedral Island), a picturesque area full of churches, though it's no longer an island (an arm of the Odra River was reclaimed during the 19th century), and walk to the two-storey Gothic **Church of the Holy Cross & St Bartholomew** (Plac Kościelny; 9am-6pm), built between 1288 and 1350. Classical music concerts are often held in these two churches.

Further east is the Gothic **Cathedral of St John the Baptist** (Plac Katedralny; 10am-6pm Mon-Sat, except during services). Uniquely, there's a lift to whisk you to the top of the **tower** (adult/concession 5/4zł) for superb views. Next door is the **Archdiocesan Museum** (Plac Katedralny 16; adult/concession 3/2zł; 9am-3pm Tue-Sun). Nearby are the charming **Botanical Gardens** (ul Sienkiewicza 23; adult/concession 7/5zł; 8am-6pm Apr-Oct), where you can chill out among the chestnut trees and tulips.

To the south of the Old Town is the **Church of St Dorothy & St Stanislaus** (ul Świdnicka; dawn-dusk), a massive Gothic complex built in 1351. About 500m south of the church on the corner of ul Świdnicka and ul Piłsudskiego is a fascinating sculpture called **Passage** (Przejście), which depicts a group of pedestrians being swallowed by the pavement, only to re-emerge on the other side of the street.

Festivals & Events
Musica Polonica Nova Festival (www.musicapolonica nova.pl, in Polish) February
Jazz on the Odra International Festival (www .jnofestival.pl) April
Wrocław Non Stop (www.wroclawnonstop.pl) June/July
Wratislavia Cantans (www.wratislaviacantans.pl) September
Wrocław Marathon (www.wroclawmaraton.pl) September

Sleeping
BUDGET
MDK Youth Hostel (071 343 8856; www.mdk.kopernik .wroclaw.pl; ul Kołłątaja 20; dm/d from 22/29zł) Not far from the train station, this is a basic place, located in a grand mustard-coloured building. Some dorms are huge and beds are packed close together. It's almost always full, so book ahead.

Stranger Hostel (071 344 1206; www.thestranger hostel.com; ul Kołłątaja 16; dm 40-55zł) A tatty old staircase leads up to pleasant budget accommodation. Dorms are set in renovated apartment rooms with ornate lamps and decorative ceilings. Bathrooms are shiny clean, and guests have free access to a kitchen and washing machine. There's a games console and a DVD projector for rainy days.

Nathan's Villa Hostel (071 344 1095; www.nathans villa.com; ul Świdnicka 13; dm/r from 45/150zł) Sister to the successful Kraków hostel (p614), this comfortable 96-bed place is conveniently placed 150m south of the Rynek. It does accept noisy Polish school groups in addition to backpackers, so check before you check in.

Bursa Nauczycielska (071 344 3781; www.dodn .wroclaw.pl/bursa; ul Kotlarska 42; s/d/tr/q 65/110/105/120zł) A basic but clean hostel with shared bathrooms, ideally located just one block northeast of the Rynek. There's a lot of brown in the colour scheme, but the rooms are quite cosy.

MIDRANGE & TOP END
Old Town Apartments (Map p598; 022 351 2260; www .warsawshotel.com; Rynek Starego Miasta 12/14, Warsaw; apt from €85) Warsaw-based agency with modern, fully furnished one-bedroom apartments around Wrocław's main square. Weekly rates are available.

Hotel Zaułek (071 341 0046; www.hotel.uni.wroc .pl; ul Garbary 11; s/d from 260/330zł) Run by the university, this guest house accommodates just 18 visitors in a dozen homely rooms. The 1pm checkout is a plus for heavy sleepers, and weekend prices are a steal. Half and full board is available.

Hotel Tumski (071 322 6099; www.hotel-tumski .com.pl; Wyspa Słodowa 10; s/d/tr/ste from 260/380/420/530zł) This is a neat hotel in a peaceful setting overlooking the river, offering reasonable value for money. It's ideal for exploring the lovely ecclesiastical quarter, and there's a good restaurant attached.

Hotel Europejski (071 772 1000; www.silfor.pl; ul Piłsudskiego 88; s/d/ste 269/309/349zł) Apparently a leopard can change its spots – the formerly drab Europejski has recently been transformed into a smart business hotel. Rooms are clean and bright, and very handy for the train station.

Art Hotel (☎ 071 787 7100; www.arthotel.pl; ul Kiełbaśnicza 20; s/d/ste from 270/290/340zł; ☒) Elegant but affordable accommodation in a renovated apartment building. Rooms feature tastefully restrained decor, quality fittings and gleaming bathrooms. Within the arched brick cellar is a top-notch restaurant, and there's a fitness room to work off the resultant calories.

Hotel Patio (☎ 071 375 0400; www.hotelpatio.pl; ul Kiełbaśnicza 24; s/d/ste from 300/330/500zł) Pleasant lodgings a short hop from the main square, housed within two buildings linked by a covered sunlit courtyard. Rooms are clean and light, sometimes small but with reasonably high ceilings. There's a restaurant, bar and hairdresser on site.

Eating & Drinking

Bar Wegetariański Vega (☎ 071 344 3934; Rynek 1/2; mains 5-6zł; ☒ 8am-7pm Mon-Fri, 9am-5pm Sat) This is a cheap cafeteria in the centre of the Rynek, offering vegie dishes in a light green space. Good choice of soups and crepes. Upstairs there's a vegan section, open from noon.

Bazylia (Plac Uniwersytecki; mains 5-10zł; ☒ 8am-8pm) Inexpensive and bustling modern take on the classic *bar mleczny*, in a curved space with huge plate-glass windows overlooking the venerable university buildings. The menu has a lot of Polish standards such as *bigos* and *gołąbki*, and a decent range of salads and other vegetable dishes. Order and pay at the till before receiving your food.

La Scala (☎ 071 372 5394; Rynek 38; mains 12-140zł) Offers authentic Italian food and particularly good desserts. Some dishes are pricey, but you're paying for the location. The cheaper trattoria at ground level serves good pizza and pasta.

Mexico Bar (☎ 071 346 0292; ul Rzeźnicza 34; mains 13-38zł; ☒ noon-midnight) Compact, warmly lit restaurant featuring sombreros, backlit masks and a chandelier made of beer bottles. There's a small bar to lean on while waiting for a table. All the Tex-Mex standards are on the menu, but book at least two days ahead for a table on weekends.

Karczma Lwowska (☎ 071 343 9887; Rynek 4; mains 15-41zł; ☒ noon-midnight) Has a great spot on the main square, with outdoor seating in summer, and offers the usual meaty Polish standards in a space with a rustic rural look. It's worth stopping by to try the beer, served in ceramic mugs.

Darea (☎ 071 343 5301; ul Kuźnicza 43/45; mains 25-100zł; ☒ 11am-10pm) With management at the LG Electronics factory in nearby Kobierzyce top-heavy with Koreans, it was inevitable that Wrocław would produce a place serving dishes like *bibimbab* and *bulgogi*. You won't find better Korean anywhere in Poland.

Restauracja JaDka (☎ 071 343 6461; www.jadka.pl; ul Rzeźnicza 24/25; mains 38-81zł; ☒ noon-11pm) Arguably the best restaurant in town, presenting impeccable modern versions of Polish classics amid elegant table settings in delightful Gothic surrounds. The set lunch available Monday to Saturday is a snip at 35zł.

Pub Guinness (Plac Solny 5; ☒ noon-2am) No prizes for guessing what this pub serves. A lively, fairly authentic Irish pub, spread over three levels on a busy corner. The ground-floor bar buzzes with student and traveller groups getting together, and there's a restaurant and beer cellar as well. A good place to wind down after a hard day's sightseeing.

Café Artzat (ul Malarska 30) This low-key cafe just north of the Church of St Elizabeth is one of the best places in town to recharge the batteries over coffee or tea and a good book.

Entertainment

Check out the bimonthly *Visitor* (free and in English) for details of what's on in this important cultural centre. It's available from the tourist office and upmarket hotels.

PRL (Rynek Ratusz 10; ☒ noon-late) The dictatorship of the proletariat is alive and well in this tongue-in-cheek venue inspired by communist nostalgia. Disco lights play over a bust of Lenin, propaganda posters line the walls, and red menace memorabilia is scattered through the maze of rooms. Descend to the basement – beneath the portraits of Stalin and Mao – if you'd like to hit the dance floor. Tuesday is karaoke night.

Teatr Polski (☎ 071 316 0777; www.teatrpolski .wroc.pl, in Polish; ul Zapolskiej 3) Wrocław's main theatrical venue stages classic Polish and foreign drama.

Filharmonia (☎ 071 342 2001; www.filharmonia .wroclaw.pl; ul Piłsudskiego 19) This place hosts concerts of classical music, mostly on Friday and Saturday nights.

Kino Helios (www.heliosnet.pl; ul Kazimierza Wielkiego 19a) If you're after a movie, head to this modern multiplex screening English-language films.

Getting There & Away

Orbis Travel (☎ 071 344 4408; Rynek 29) and **Almatur** (☎ 071 343 4135; ul Kościuszki 34) offer the usual services. If you're travelling to/from Wrocław at the weekend, you'll be in competition with thousands of itinerant university students, so book your ticket as soon as possible.

AIR

From **Copernicus airport** (www.airport.wroclaw.pl), LOT flies frequently between Wrocław and Warsaw. It also heads daily to Brussels, and twice daily to Frankfurt and Munich. Tickets can be bought at the **LOT office** (☎ 0801 703 703; ul Piłsudskiego 36).

A range of budget carriers connect Wrocław with other European cities, including a range of British and Irish regional destinations. Ryanair and Wizz Air fly daily to London; Ryanair heads five times a week to Dublin; and Cimber Air operates five flights a week to Copenhagen.

The airport is in Strachowice, about 12km west of the Old Town. The half-hourly bus 406 and infrequent night bus 249 link the airport with Wrocław Główny train station and the bus terminal.

BUS

The **bus terminal** (ul Sucha 11) is south of the main train station, and offers four daily buses to Warsaw (51zł, seven hours). For most other travel, however, the train is more convenient.

TRAIN

The **Wrocław Główny station** (ul Piłsudskiego 105) was built in 1856 and is a historical monument in itself. Every day, trains to Kraków (45zł, 4½ hours) depart every one or two hours, with similarly frequent services to Warsaw (102zł, 5¾ hours), usually via Łódź. Wrocław is also linked by train to Poznań (34zł, 2½ hours, at least hourly), Częstochowa (34zł, three hours, four daily) and Szczecin (51zł, five hours, eight daily).

SUDETEN MOUNTAINS

The Sudeten Mountains (Sudety) run for over 250km along the Czech–Polish border.

The Sudetes feature dense forests, amazing rock formations and deposits of semiprecious stones, and can be explored along the extensive network of trails for **hiking** or **mountain biking**. The highest part of this old eroded chain is Mt Śnieżka (1602m).

Szklarska Poręba, at the northwestern end of the Sudetes, offers superior facilities for **hiking** and **skiing**. It's at the base of Mt Szrenica (1362m), and the town centre is at the upper end of ul Jedności Narodowej. The small **tourist office** (☎ 075 754 7740; www.szklarskaporeba .pl; ul Pstrowskiego 1) has accommodation info and maps. Nearby, several trails begin at the intersection of ul Jedności Narodowej and ul Wielki Sikorskiego. The red trail goes to **Mt Szrenica** (two hours) and offers a peek at **Wodospad Kamieńczyka**, a spectacular waterfall.

Karpacz to the southeast has more nightlife on offer, though it attracts fewer serious mountaineers. It's loosely clustered along a 3km road winding through Łomnica Valley at the base of Mt Śnieżka. The **tourist office** (☎ 075 761 8605; www.karpacz.com.pl; ul Konstytucji 3 Maja 25a) should be your first port of call. To reach the peak of Mt Śnieżka on foot, take one of the trails (three to four hours) from Hotel Biały Jar. Some of the trails pass by one of two splendid postglacial lakes: **Mały Staw** and **Wielki Staw**.

The bus is the fastest way of getting around the region. Every day from Szklarska Poręba, about five buses head to Wrocław (29zł, three hours) and one train plods along to Warsaw (60zł, 11 hours). From Karpacz, get one of hourly buses to Jelenia Góra (7zł, one hour), where buses and trains go in all directions.

For the Czech Republic, take a bus from Szklarska Poręba to Jakuszyce (4zł, 15 minutes), cross the border on foot to Harrachov (on the Czech side) and take another bus from there.

WIELKOPOLSKA

Wielkopolska (Greater Poland) is the region where Poland came to life in the Middle Ages, and is referred to as the Cradle of the Polish State. As a result of this ancient eminence, its cities and towns are full of historic and cultural attractions.

The royal capital moved from Poznań to Kraków in 1038, though Wielkopolska remained an important province. Its historic significance didn't save it from international

POLAND

conflict, however, and the region became part of Prussia in 1793. Wielkopolska rose against German rule at the end of WWI and became part of the reborn Poland. The battles of WWII later caused widespread destruction in the area.

POZNAŃ
pop 565,000

No one could accuse Poznań of being too sleepy. Between its regular trade fairs, student population and visiting travellers, it's a vibrant city with a wide choice of attractions. There's a beautiful Old Town at its centre, with a number of interesting museums, and a range of lively bars, clubs and restaurants. The surrounding countryside is also good for cycling and hiking.

Poznań grew from humble beginnings, when 9th-century Polanian tribes built a wooden fort on the island of Ostrów Tumski. From 968 to 1038 Poznań was the de facto capital of Poland. Its position between Berlin and Warsaw has always underlined its importance as a trading town, and in 1925 a modern version of its famous medieval trade fairs was instituted. The fairs, filling up the city's hotels for several days at a time, are the lynchpin of the city's economy.

As it's at the heart of Wielkopolska, Poznań makes a good transport hub from which to explore the region.

Information
Bank Pekao Old Town (ul 23 Lutego); ul Św. Marcin (ul Św. Marcin 52/56)
City Information Centre (☎ 061 851 9645; ul Ratajczaka 44; ☺ 10am-7pm Mon-Fri, 10am-5pm Sat) Handles bookings for cultural events.
E24 (ul Półwiejska 42; per hr 4.50zł; ☺ 24hr) Inside the massive Stary Browar shopping centre.
EMPiK (Plac Wolności) Bookshop.
Globtroter Turystyczna (Stary Rynek 98/100) Sells maps and guidebooks. Enter from ul Żydowska.
Main post office (ul Kościuszki 77; ☺ 7am-8pm Mon-Fri, 8am-3pm Sat)
Tourist office (☎ 061 852 6156; Stary Rynek 59; ☺ 9am-8pm Mon-Sat, 10am-6pm Sun May-Sep, 9am-5pm Mon-Fri Oct-Apr)

Sights
If you're in the attractive **Stary Rynek** (Old Market Sq) at noon, keep an eye out for the goats in the Renaissance **town hall** (built 1550–60). Every midday two metal goats above its clock butt

their horns together 12 times, echoing an improbable centuries-old legend of two animals escaping a cook and fighting each other in the town hall tower. Inside the building, the **Poznań Historical Museum** (adult/concession 5.50/3.50zł, free Sat; ☺ 9am-4pm Tue, Thu & Fri, 11am-6pm Wed, 10am-3pm Sat & Sun) displays splendid period interiors.

Also within the square are the **Wielkopolska Military Museum** (Stary Rynek 9; adult/concession 3.50/2.20zł, free Sat; ☺ 9am-4pm Tue-Sat, 10am-3pm Sun) and the **Museum of Musical Instruments** (Stary Rynek 45; adult/concession 5.50/3.50zł, free Sat; ☺ 11am-5pm Tue-Sat, 10am-3pm Sun), along with the **Museum of the Wielkopolska Uprising** (Stary Rynek 3; adult/concession 4/2zł, free Sat; ☺ 10am-5pm Tue, Thu & Fri, 10am-6pm Wed, 10am-3pm Sat & Sun), which details the conflict in the region between German and Polish fighters after WWI.

The **Archaeological Museum** (ul Wodna 27; adult/concession 6/3zł, free Sat; ☺ 10am-4pm Tue-Fri, 10am-6pm Sat, 10am-3pm Sun) contains Egyptian mummies and displays on the prehistory of western Poland.

The 17th-century **Franciscan Church** (ul Franciszkańska 2; ☺ 8am-8pm), one block west of the Rynek, has an ornate baroque interior, complete with wall paintings and rich stucco work. Above the church, on a hill, is the **Museum of Applied Arts** (Gora Przemysła 1; adult/concession 5.50/3.50zł, free Sat; ☺ 10am-4pm Tue-Sat, 10am-3pm Sun), featuring glassware, ceramics, silverware and clocks.

The nearby **National Museum: Paintings & Sculpture Gallery** (Al Marcinkowskiego 9; adult/concession 10/6zł, free Sat; ☺ 10am-6pm Tue, 9am-5pm Wed, 10am-4pm Thu, 10am-5pm Fri & Sat, 10am-3pm Sun) displays mainly 19th- and 20th-century Polish paintings.

Two blocks south of Stary Rynek is the large, pink, baroque **Parish Church of St Stanislaus** (ul Gołębia 1; ☺ erratic) with monumental altars built in the mid-17th century. A short stroll southeast is the **Ethnographic Museum** (☎ 061 852 30 06; ul Grobla 25; adult/concession 5.50/3.50zł, free Sat; ☺ 10am-4pm Tue, Wed, Fri & Sat, 10am-3pm Sun), presenting a collection of woodcarving and traditional costumes.

The 19th-century Prussian **Poznań Citadel**, where 20,000 German troops held out for a month in February 1945, lies about 1.5km north of the Old Town. The fortress was destroyed by artillery fire but a park was laid out on the site, which incorporates both the **Poznań Army Museum** (Al Armii Poznań; admission free; ☺ 9am-4pm Tue-Sat, 10am-4pm Sun) and the nearby **Poznań Citadel Museum** (Al Armii Poznań; adult/concession 4/2zł, free Fri; ☺ 9am-4pm Tue-Sat, 10am-4pm Sun).

In a park in the area west of Stary Rynek, the emotive **Monument to the Victims of June 1956** commemorates the dead and injured of the massive 1956 strike by the city's industrial workers, which was crushed by tanks. Next door in the Cultural Centre, there's more detail to be uncovered in the **Museum of Poznań June 1956** (ul Św. Marcin 80/82; adult/concession 4/2zł, free Sat; ☼ 10am-6pm Tue-Fri, 10am-4pm Sat & Sun).

In **Park Wilsona**, 1km southwest of the train station, you'll find **Palm House** (ul Matejki 18; adult/concession 5.50/4zł; ☼ 9am-5pm Tue-Sat, 9am-6pm Sun). This huge greenhouse (built in 1910) contains 17,000 species of tropical and subtropical plants.

Ostrów Tumski is 1km east of the Old Town (take any eastbound tram from Plac Wielkopolski). This river island is dominated by the monumental, double-towered **Poznań Cathedral** (ul Ostrów Tumski), originally built in 968. The Byzantine-style **Golden Chapel** (1841) and the **mausoleums** of Mieszko I and Boleslaus the Brave are behind the high altar. Opposite the cathedral is the 15th-century Gothic **Church of the Virgin Mary** (ul Panny Marii 1/3).

Some 1.6km east of the Old Town is **Lake Malta**, a favourite weekend destination for Poles. It holds sailing regattas, outdoor concerts and other events in summer, and in winter there's a ski slope in operation.

A fun way to visit the lake is to take tram 3, 4 or 8 from Plac Wielkopolski to the Rondo Śródka stop on the other side of Ostrów Tumski. From the nearby terminus, you can catch a miniature train along the **Malta Park Railway** (ul Jana Pawła II; adult/concession 4.50/3zł; ☼ 10am-6.45pm Mon-Fri, 10am-6pm Sat & Sun May-15 Oct), which takes the lake's shore to the **New Zoo** (ul Krańcowa 81; adult/concession 9/6zł; ☼ 9am-7pm Apr-Sep, 9am-4pm Oct-Mar). This sprawling institution houses diverse species, including Baltic grey seals, in a pine forest environment.

Festival & Events

The largest trade fairs take place in January, June, September and October.

Poznań Jazz Festival (www.jazz.pl) March
St John's Fair Cultural event in June.
Malta International Theatre Festival (www.malta-festival.pl) June

Sleeping

During trade fairs, the rates of Poznań's accommodation dramatically increase. A room may also be difficult to find, so it pays to book

ahead. Prices given here are for outside trade fair periods.

Check out **Biuro Zakwaterowania Przemysław** (☎ 061 866 3560; www.przemyslaw.com.pl; ul Głogowska 16; s/d from 53/85zł, apt from 170zł; ☼ 8am-6pm Mon-Fri, 10am-2pm Sat), an accommodation agency not far from the train station. Rates for weekends and stays of more than three nights are cheaper than the prices quoted here.

Youth Hostel No 3 (☎ 061 866 4040; ul Berwińskiego 2/3; dm 30zł) Cheap lodgings about a 15-minute walk southwest of the train station along ul Głogowska, adjacent to Park Wilsona. It's a basic 'no frills' option, but fills up fast with students and school groups. There's a 10pm curfew.

Frolic Goats Hostel (☎ 061 852 4411; www.frolicgoatshostel.com; ul Wrocławska 16/6; dm/d/tr from 50/140/250zł) Named after the feisty goats who fight above the town hall clock, this hostel is aimed squarely at the international backpacker. There's a washing machine on the premises, bike hire is available for 25zł per day, and room rates are unaffected by trade fairs. Enter from ul Jaskółcza.

Mini Hotelik (☎ 061 633 1416; Al Niepodległości 8a; r 129-161zł) Like it says on the label, this is a small place in an old building between the train station and the Old Town. It's basic but clean, with colourfully painted chambers. Some rooms share a bathroom. Enter from ul Taylora.

Hotel Lech (☎ 061 853 0151; www.hotel-lech.poznan.pl; ul Św. Marcin 74; s/d/tr 172/264/366zł) Hotel Lech has standard three-star decor, but rooms are relatively spacious and the bathrooms are modern. Flash your ISIC card for a discount.

our pick Rezydencja Solei (☎ 061 855 7351; www.hotel-solei.pl; ul Szewska 2; s/d/ste 199/299/389zł) Temptingly close to Stary Rynek, this tiny hotel offers small but cosy rooms in an old-fashioned residential style, with wallpaper and timber furniture striking a homely note. The attic suite is amazingly large and can accommodate up to four people.

Hotel Stare Miasto (☎ 061 663 62 42; www.hotelstaremiasto.pl; ul Rybaki 36; s/d 215/340zł; ☒) Elegant, value-for-money hotel with a tasteful chandeliered foyer and spacious breakfast room. Rooms can be small, but are clean and bright with lovely starched white sheets. Some upper rooms have skylights in place of windows.

Hotel Rzymski (☎ 061 852 8121; www.rzymskihotel.com.pl; Al Marcinkowskiego 22; s/d/tr from 245/300/405zł)

POLAND

POLAND

POZNAŃ

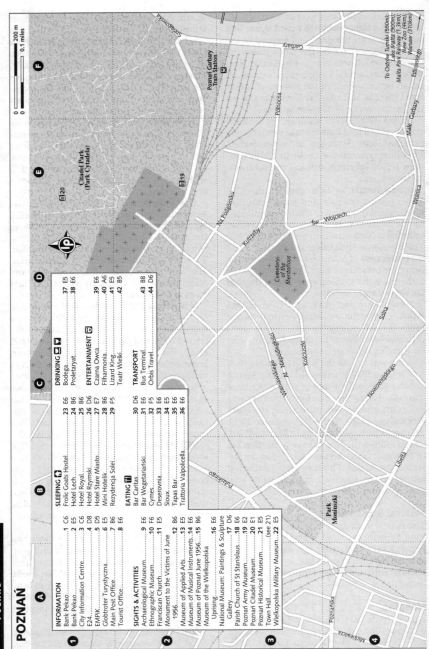

INFORMATION
Bank Pekao..............................**1** C6
Bank Pekao..............................**2** E5
City Information Centre..............**3** C6
E24..**4** D8
EMPiK..**5** D5
Globtroter Turystyczna..............**6** E5
Main Post Office.......................**7** B6
Tourist Office............................**8** E6

SIGHTS & ACTIVITIES
Archaeological Museum.............**9** E6
Ethnographic Museum..............**10** F6
Franciscan Church.....................**11** E5
Monument to the Victims of June
1956.....................................**12** B6
Museum of Applied Arts...........**13** E5
Museum of Musical Instruments..**14** E6
Museum of Poznań June 1956....**15** B6
Museum of the Wielkopolska
Uprising................................**16** E6
National Museum: Paintings & Sculpture
Gallery..................................**17** D6
Parish Church of St Stanislaus....**18** E6
Poznań Army Museum................**19** E2
Poznań Citadel Museum............**20** E1
Poznań Historical Museum.........**21** E5
Town Hall.................................(see 21)
Wielkopolska Military Museum...**22** E5

SLEEPING
Frolic Goats Hostel....................**23** E6
Hotel Lech................................**24** B6
Hotel Royal...............................**25** B6
Hotel Rzymski...........................**26** D6
Hotel Stare Miasto....................**27** E7
Mini Hotelik.............................**28** B6
Rezydencja Solei.......................**29** F5

EATING
Bar Caritas...............................**30** D6
Bar Wegetariański.....................**31** E6
Cymes......................................**32** F5
Deserownia...............................**33** E6
Sioux.......................................**34** E5
Tapas Bar..................................**35** E6
Trattoria Valpolicella..................**36** E6

DRINKING
Bodega.....................................**37** E5
Proletaryat................................**38** E6

ENTERTAINMENT
Czarna Owca.............................**39** E6
Filharmonia...............................**40** A6
Lizard King...............................**41** E5
Teatr Wielki..............................**42** B5

TRANSPORT
Bus Terminal.............................**43** B8
Orbis Travel..............................**44** D6

Citadel Park
(Park Cytadela)

Poznań Garbary
Train Station

Cemetery
of the
Meritorious

Park
Moniuszki

To Ostrów Tumski (550m);
Lake Malta (900m);
Malta Park Railway (1.3km);
New Zoo (4km);
Warsaw (310km)

200 m
0.1 miles

WORTH THE TRIP: GNIEZNO

If you're staying in Poznań, it's worth checking out historic Gniezno, one of Poland's oldest set-tlements. It was probably here that Poland's Duke Mieszko I was baptised in 966, the starting point of Catholicism's major role in the nation's story. In 1025, Bolesław Chrobry was crowned in the city's cathedral as the first Polish king. Gniezno probably also functioned as Poland's first capital before Poznań achieved that honour, though history is murky on this point.

Whatever the case, Gniezno makes a good day trip from Poznań, or a short stopover. Setting out from its attractive broad **market square**, you can investigate its historic **cathedral**, dating from the 14th century, and a **museum** dedicated to Poland's origins, situated on the nearby lakeside.

An hour north of Gniezno is the Iron Age village of **Biskupin**, unearthed in the 1930s and partly reconstructed. Passing by it is a **tourist train** that links the towns of Żnin and Gąsawa, both of which have regular bus transport to Gniezno. Gniezno itself is linked to Poznań by frequent trains and buses throughout the day.

For more details, check out Lonely Planet's Poland country guide, visit www.turystyka.powiat -gniezno.pl, or drop into Gniezno's **tourist office** (☎ 061 428 4100; ul Tumska 12).

Offers the regular amenities of three-star comfort, and overlooks Plac Wolności. The decor has a lot of brown, and rooms aren't quite as grand as the elegant facade suggests, but they're a decent size.

Hotel Royal (☎ 061 858 2300; www.hotel-royal.com .pl; ul Św. Marcin 71; s/d 320/420zł) This is a gorgeous place set back from the main road. Rooms have huge beds and sparkling bathrooms.

Eating & Drinking

Bar Wegetariański (☎ 061 821 1255; ul Wrocławska 21; mains 5-10zł; 11am-6pm Mon-Fri, 11am-3pm Sat) This cheap eatery is in a cellar off the main road, bedecked with plant life around the walls, and offers tasty meat-free dishes. Mind the decaying concrete steps.

Bar Caritas (Plac Wolności 1; mains 8-15zł; 8am-7pm Mon-Fri, 10am-5pm Sat, noon-5pm Sun) You can point at what you want without resorting to your phrasebook at this cheap and convenient milk bar. There are many variants of *naleśniki* (crepes) on the menu. Lunchtimes get crowded, so be prepared to share a table.

Cymes (☎ 061 851 6638; ul Woźna 2/3; mains 18-26zł; 11am-10pm) If you're tired of pork for dinner, this ambient Jewish restaurant is the logical place to go. The interior is warm and cosy, done out like a residential dining room with ceramic plates on the walls. On the menu are various poultry and fish dishes, including a whole goose for eight people, to be ordered 24 hours beforehand.

Deserovnia (☎ 061 852 5029; ul Świętosławska 12; mains 19-55zł) One side of this split-personality venue is a sporty bar, all dark timber, beer and photos of sports stars. The other side is a gracious restaurant serving classy Polish cuisine. Heads or tails?

Sioux (☎ 061 851 6286; Stary Rynek 93; mains 20-100zł; noon-11pm) As you'd expect, this is a 'Western'-themed place, complete with waiters dressed as cowboys. Bizarrely named dishes such as 'Scoundrels in Uniforms from Fort Knox' (chicken legs) are on the menu, along with lots of steaks, ribs, grills and enchiladas.

Trattoria Valpolicella (☎ 061 855 7191; ul Wrocławska 7; mains 21-66zł; 1-11pm) Serves a wide variety of pasta and other Italian specialities, well suited to a glass of vino, in convincingly rustic Mediterranean surroundings.

our pick Tapas Bar (☎ 061 852 8532; Stary Rynek 60; mains 32-62zł; noon-midnight) Atmospheric place dishing up authentic tapas and Spanish wine, in a room lined with intriguing bric-a-brac including jars of stuffed olives, Mediterranean-themed artwork and bright red candles. Most tapas dishes cost 14zł to 22zł, so forget the mains and share with friends.

Proletaryat (ul Wrocławska 9; 1pm-2am Mon-Sat, 3pm-2am Sun) Small red communist nostalgia bar with an array of socialist-era gear on the walls, including the obligatory bust of Lenin in the window, and various portraits of the great man and his comrades. Play 'spot the communist leader' while sipping a boutique beer from the Czarnków Brewery.

Bodega (ul Żydowska 4) On a street populated with cafes, Bodega's sleek modern lines stand out. The geometrically sharp interior is com-

POLAND

posed of mellow chocolate and gold tones, with candles on the tables. Good coffee is accompanied by sweet temptations.

Entertainment
Lizard King (Stary Rynek 86; ☽ noon-2am) Simultaneously happening and laid-back, this venue is in prime position on Stary Rynek. Friendly crowds sit drinking and eating in the split-level space, casting the occasional glance at the lizard over the bar. There's live music later in the week, mostly rock, jazz or blues, usually from 9pm.

Czarna Owca (ul Jaskółcza 13; ☽ noon-2am Mon-Fri, 5pm-2am Sat) Literally 'Black Sheep', this is a popular club with nightly DJs playing a mix of genres including R&B, house, rock, Latin, soul and funk. There's a disco night on Friday and a retro night on Tuesday.

Teatr Wielki (☎ 061 659 0280; www.opera.poznan.pl; ul Fredry 9) is the main venue for opera and ballet, while not far away, the **Filharmonia** (☎ 061 853 6935; www.filharmonia.poznan.pl; ul Św. Marcin 81) offers classical concerts at least weekly.

Getting There & Away
From **Poznań airport** (www.airport-poznan.com.pl), LOT flies at least six times a day to Warsaw, twice daily to Frankfurt, and at least three times daily to Munich. Tickets are available from the **LOT office** (☎ 0801 703 703) at the airport or from **Orbis Travel** (☎ 061 851 2000; Al Marcinkowskiego 21).

There are also domestic flights via Jet Air to Kraków (six times a week). A vast array of other European cities are serviced from Poznań, including London via British Airways, Wizz Air and Ryanair (at least daily); Dublin via Ryanair (three times a week); and Copenhagen via SAS (daily). The airport is in the western suburb of Ławica, 7km from the Old Town and accessible by buses 59 and L.

The **bus terminal** (ul Towarowa 17) is a 10-minute walk east of the train station. However, most destinations can be reached more comfortably and frequently by train.

The busy **Poznań Główny train station** (ul Dworcowa 1) offers services to Kraków (53zł, 7½ hours, 11 daily), Szczecin, some of which continue to Świnoujście (39zł, 2½ hours, 15 daily), Gdańsk and Gdynia (48zł, 5½ hours, seven daily), Toruń (33zł, 2½ hours, six daily) and Wrocław (34zł, 2½ hours, at least hourly). Nearly 20 trains a day head to Warsaw (95zł, 3½ hours).

POMERANIA

Pomerania (Pomorze) is an attractive region with diverse drawcards, from beautiful beaches to architecturally pleasing cities. It covers a large swathe of territory along the Baltic coast, from the German border in the west, to the lower Vistula Valley in the east. A sandy coastline stretches from Gdańsk to western Szczecin, and Toruń lies inland. Pomerania was fought over by Germanic and Slavic peoples for a millennium, before being incorporated almost fully within Poland after WWII.

GDAŃSK
pop 457,000
Port cities are usually lively places with distinctive personalities, and Gdańsk is no exception. From its busy riverside waterfront to the Renaissance splendour of its charming narrow streets, there's plenty to like about this coastal city.

And few Polish cities occupy such a pivotal position in history as Gdańsk. Founded more than a millennium ago, it became the focus of territorial tensions when the Teutonic Knights seized it from Poland in 1308. The city joined the Hanseatic League in 1361, and became one of the richest ports in the Baltic through its membership of the trading organisation. Finally, the Thirteen Years' War ended in 1466 with the Knights' defeat and Gdańsk's return to Polish rule.

This to-and-fro between Germanic and Polish control wasn't over, however – in 1793 Gdańsk was incorporated into Prussia, and after the German loss in WWI it became the autonomous Free City of Danzig. The city's environs are where WWII began, when the Nazis bombarded Polish troops stationed at Westerplatte. Gdańsk suffered immense damage during the war, but upon its return to Poland in 1945, its historic centre was faithfully reconstructed.

In the 1980s, Gdańsk achieved international fame as the home of the Solidarity trade union, whose rise paralleled the fall of communism in Europe. Today it's a vibrant city and a great base for exploring the Baltic coast.

Information
BOOKSHOPS
EMPiK (ul Podwale Grodzkie 8) Opposite the main train station.

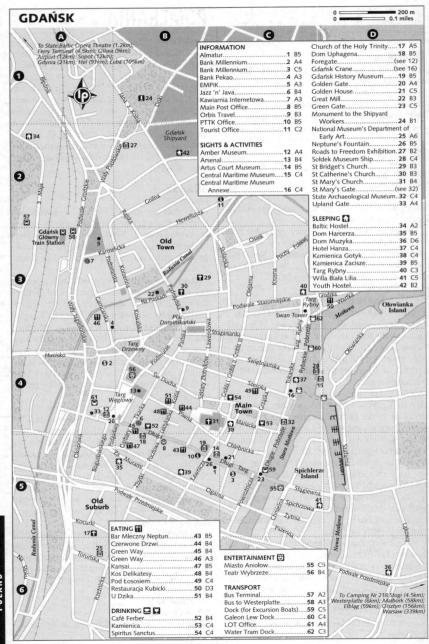

GDAŃSK

0 ————— 200 m
0 ————— 0.1 miles

INFORMATION

Almatur	1 B5
Bank Millennium	2 A4
Bank Millennium	3 C5
Bank Pekao	4 A3
EMPiK	5 A3
Jazz 'n' Java	6 B4
Kawiarnia Internetowa	7 A3
Main Post Office	8 B5
Orbis Travel	9 B3
PTTK Office	10 B5
Tourist Office	11 C2

SIGHTS & ACTIVITIES

Amber Museum	12 A4
Arsenal	13 B4
Artus Court Museum	14 B5
Central Maritime Museum	15 C4
Central Maritime Museum Annexe	16 C4

Church of the Holy Trinity	17 A5
Dom Uphagena	18 B5
Foregate	(see 12)
Gdańsk Crane	(see 16)
Gdańsk History Museum	19 B5
Golden Gate	20 A4
Golden House	21 C5
Great Mill	22 B3
Green Gate	23 C5
Monument to the Shipyard Workers	24 B1
National Museum's Department of Early Art	25 A6
Neptune's Fountain	26 B5
Roads to Freedom Exhibition	27 B2
Sołdek Museum Ship	28 C4
St Bridget's Church	29 B3
St Catherine's Church	30 B3
St Mary's Church	31 B4
St Mary's Gate	(see 32)
State Archaeological Museum	32 C4
Upland Gate	33 A4

SLEEPING

Baltic Hostel	34 A2
Dom Harcerza	35 B5
Dom Muzyka	36 D6
Hotel Hanza	37 C4
Kamienica Gotyk	38 C4
Kamienica Zacisze	39 B5
Targ Rybny	40 C3
Willa Biała Lilia	41 C5
Youth Hostel	42 B2

EATING

Bar Mleczny Neptun	43 B5
Czerwone Drzwi	44 B4
Green Way	45 B4
Green Way	46 A3
Kansai	47 B5
Kos Delikatesy	48 B4
Pod Łososiem	49 C4
Restauracja Kubicki	50 D3
U Dzika	51 B4

DRINKING

Café Ferber	52 B4
Kamienica	53 C4
Spiritus Sanctus	54 C4

ENTERTAINMENT

Miasto Aniołów	55 C5
Teatr Wybrzeże	56 B4

TRANSPORT

Bus Terminal	57 A2
Bus to Westerplatte	58 A3
Dock (for Excursion Boats)	59 C5
Galeon Lew Dock	60 C4
LOT Office	61 A4
Water Tram Dock	62 C3

To State Baltic Opera Theatre (1.2km);
Ferry Terminal (4.5km); Oliwa (9km);
Airport (12km); Sopot (12km);
Gdynia (21km); Hel (93km); Łeba (105km)

Gdańsk Shipyard

Old Town

Gdańsk Główny Train Station

Main Town

Ołowianka Island

Spichlerze Island

Old Suburb

To Camping Nr 218 Stogi (4.5km);
Westerplatte (6km); Malbork (58km);
Elbląg (59km); Olsztyn (156km);
Warsaw (339km)

POLAND

INTERNET ACCESS

Jazz 'n' Java (ul Tkacka 17/18; per hr 5zł; ☯ 10am-10pm)

Kawiarnia Internetowa (Cinema City, ul Karmelicka 1; per hr 6zł; ☯ 9am-1am Mon-Sat, 9.30am-1am Sun) Free coffee over 30 minutes access.

MONEY

Bank Millennium Old Town (ul Wały Jagiellońskie 14/16); Main Town (ul Długi Targ 14/16)

Bank Pekao (ul Garncarska 23)

POST

Main post office (ul Długa 22; ☯ 8am-8pm Mon-Fri, 9am-3pm Sat)

TOURIST INFORMATION

PTTK office (☎ 058 301 1343; www.pttk-gdansk.pl; ul Długa 45; ☯ 9am-6pm Mon-Fri, 8.30am-4.30pm Sat & Sun)

Tourist office (☎ 058 301 4355; www.got.gdansk.pl; ul Heweliusza 29; ☯ 8am-4pm Mon-Fri) Well-concealed from the casual tourist, but helpful.

TRAVEL AGENCIES

Almatur (☎ 058 301 2424; Długi Targ 11)

Orbis Travel (☎ 058 301 4544; ul Podwale Staromiejskie 96/97)

Sights

MAIN TOWN

The beautiful ul Długa (Long Street) and Długi Targ (Long Market) form the city's main historic thoroughfare, and are known collectively as the **Royal Way**. Polish kings traditionally paraded through the **Upland Gate** (built in the 1770s on a 15th-century gate), onward through the **Foregate** (which once housed a torture chamber) and **Golden Gate** (1614), and proceeded east to the Renaissance **Green Gate** (1568).

Following the royal lead and starting from the Upland Gate, walk east to the Foregate. Within this structure, you can visit the **Amber Museum** (www.mhmg.gda.pl/bursztyn; adult/concession 10/5zł, free Tue; ☯ 10am-2.30pm Tue, 10am-3.30pm Wed-Sat, 11am-3.30pm Sun), wherein you can marvel at the history of so-called 'Baltic gold'.

Further along ul Długa is the 18th-century **Dom Uphagena** (ul Długa; adult/concession 8/5zł, free Tue; ☯ 10am-3pm Tue, 10am-4pm Wed-Sat, 11am-4pm Sun), featuring ornate furniture.

Proceed to the **Gdańsk History Museum** (ul Długa 47; adult/concession 8/5zł, free Tue; ☯ 10am-3pm Tue, 10am-4pm Wed-Sat, 11am-4pm Sun), inside the towering Gothic **Main Town Hall**. On show are

photos of old Gdańsk, and the damage caused during WWII.

Not far past this point, behind **Neptune's Fountain** (1633), is the **Artus Court Museum** (ul Długi Targ 43/44; adult/concession 8/5zł, free Tue; ☯ 10am-3pm Tue, 10am-4pm Wed-Sat, 11am-4pm Sun), where merchants used to congregate. The adjacent **Golden House** (1618) has a strikingly rich facade.

When you reach the Green Gate, step through and follow the riverside promenade north to the 14th-century **St Mary's Gate**, which houses the **State Archaeological Museum** (ul Mariacka 25/26; adult/concession 6/4zł, free Sat; ☯ 10am-4pm Tue-Sun). It features an overly generous number of formerly diseased ancient human skulls, displays of amber, and river views from the adjacent **tower** (admission 3zł).

Through this gate, stroll along picturesque **ul Mariacka** (St Mary's St), lined with 17th-century burgher houses and amber shops. At the west end of ul Mariacka is the gigantic 14th-century **St Mary's Church** (admission free; ☯ 8.30am-6pm, except during services). Watch little figures troop out at noon from its 14m-high astronomical clock, adorned with zodiacal signs. Climb the 405 steps of the **tower** (adult/concession 4/2zł) for a giddy view over the town. West along ul Piwna (Beer St) is the Dutch Renaissance **Arsenal** (1609), particularly attractive when its gilt is caught by the rays of the sun.

Back on the waterfront north of St Mary's Gate, you'll find the 15th-century **Gdańsk Crane**, the largest of its kind in medieval Europe and capable of hoisting loads of up to 2000kg. It's now part of the **Central Maritime Museum** (ul Ołowianka 9-13; one section adult/concession 6/4zł, all four sections 15/9zł; ☯ 10am-6pm May-Oct, 10am-4pm Tue-Sun Nov-Apr). The museum offers a fascinating insight into Gdańsk's seafaring past, including the **Sołdek Museum Ship**, built here just after WWII.

OLD TOWN

Almost totally destroyed in 1945, the Old Town has never been completely rebuilt. However, among its gems are **St Catherine's Church** (ul Wielkie Młyny; ☯ 8am-6pm Mon-Sat), Gdańsk's oldest church (begun in the 1220s). Opposite, the **Great Mill** (ul Wielkie Młyny) was built by the Teutonic Knights around 1350. It used to produce 200 tonnes of flour per day and continued to operate until 1945.

Right behind St Catherine's is **St Bridget's Church** (ul Profesorska 17; ☯ 10am-6pm Mon-Sat).

Formerly Lech Wałęsa's place of worship, the church was a strong supporter of the shipyard activists in the 1980s.

At the north end of the Old Town is the evocative **Roads to Freedom Exhibition** (ul Wały Piastowskie 24; adult/concession 6/4zł; ☺ 10am-4pm Tue-Sun). This excellent museum charts the decline and fall of Polish communism and the rise of the Solidarity trade union, and is a place that anyone interested in Gdańsk's history should visit.

A short walk further north, the soaring **Monument to the Shipyard Workers** (Plac Solidarności) stands at the entrance to the Gdańsk Shipyards. It was erected in late 1980 in memory of 44 workers killed during the riots of December 1970, and was the first monument in a communist regime to commemorate the regime's victims.

OLD SUBURB

The **National Museum's Department of Early Art** (ul Toruńska 1; adult/concession 10/6zł; ☺ 10am-5pm May-Sep, 9am-4pm Oct-Apr) is famous for its Dutch and Flemish paintings, especially Hans Memling's 15th-century *Last Judgment*.

Adjoining the museum is the former Franciscan **Church of the Holy Trinity** (ul Św. Trójcy; ☺ 10am-8pm Mon-Sat), built at the end of the 15th century.

OLIWA

Some 9km northwest is the lovely **Park Oliwski** (ul Cystersów), surrounding the towering **Oliwa Cathedral** (☺ 8am-8pm), built in the 13th century with a Gothic facade and a long, narrow central nave. The famous baroque organ is used for recitals each hour between 10am and 3pm Monday to Saturday in July and August. Nearby is the **Ethnographic Museum** (ul Cystersów 19; adult/concession 8/5zł; ☺ 10am-5pm Tue-Sun) in the Old Granary, and the **Modern Art Gallery** (adult/ concession 9/6zł; ☺ 10am-5pm Tue-Sun) in the former Abbots' Palace.

To reach the park, take the commuter train to the Gdańsk Oliwa station (3.10zł). From there, it's a 10-minute walk; head (west) up ul Poczty Gdańsk, turn right (north) along the highway and look for the signs (in English) to 'Ethnographic Museum' and 'Cathedral'.

WESTERPLATTE

WWII began at 4.45am on 1 September 1939, when the German battleship *Schleswig-Holstein* began shelling the Polish naval post at Westerplatte, 7km north of Gdańsk's Main Town. The 182-man Polish garrison held out against ferocious attacks for a week before surrendering.

The enormity of this event is marked by a hilltop **memorial** (admission free; ☺ 24hr), a small **museum** (ul Sucharskiego 1; adult/concession 3/2zł; ☺ 9am-4pm May-Sep) and **ruins** remaining from the Nazi bombardment.

Bus 106 (25 minutes) goes to the park every 15 minutes from a stop outside the main train station in Gdańsk. Alternatively, excursion boats (22/45zł one way/return) to and around Westerplatte leave from a dock near the Green Gate in Gdańsk between April and November.

Festivals & Events

International Organ Music Festival (www.gdanskie -organy.com, under Concerts) June to August.
International Street & Open-Air Theatre Festival (www.feta.pl) July
Sounds of the North Festival (www.nck.org.pl) July/August
St Dominic's Fair (www.mtgsa.pl, under Jarmark Św Dominika) Annual shopping fair in August.
International Shakespeare Festival (www.teatr -szekspir.gda.pl) August

Sleeping

Accommodation can be tight in the warmer months. If you're having trouble finding accommodation, check with the PTTK office. Also consider staying in nearby Sopot (p649) or Gdynia (p650).

BUDGET

Camping Nr 218 Stogi (☎ 058 307 3915; www.camping -gdansk.pl; ul Wydmy 9; per person/tent 12/6zł, cabins 60-110zł; ☺ May-Sep) This camping ground is only 200m from the beach in the seaside holiday centre of Stogi, about 5.5km northeast of the Main Town. Tidy cabins sleep between two and five people, and facilities include a volleyball court and children's playground. Take tram 8 or 13 from the main train station in Gdańsk.

Youth Hostel (☎ 058 301 2313; www.mokf.com.pl; ul Wałowa 21; dm/s/d/tr/q 18/31/62/63/84zł) Old-style hostel in a quiet, old building on the doorstep of the Gdańsk Shipyards, Lech Wałęsa's old stamping ground. Rooms are brown and basic, but clean. Book ahead, particularly in summer. Smoking and drinking are strictly forbidden and there's a midnight curfew.

POLAND

Dom Harcerza (☎ 058 301 3621; www.domharcerza
.pl; ul Za Murami 2/10; dm 34zł, s/d/tr/q 50/120/150/160zł)
The rooms are small but cosy at this place,
which offers the best value and location
for any budget-priced hotel. It's popular
(so book ahead), and can get noisy when
large groups are staying here. There's a
charming old-fashioned restaurant on the
ground floor.

Baltic Hostel (☎ 058 721 9657; www.baltichostel.com
.pl; ul 3 Maja 25; dm 40zł, r 120zł) Readers have given
mixed reviews of this hostel aimed at the international budget traveller. The dorms are a
bit crowded, but the lounge is good and it's
handy to the bus and train stations. Save it for
when the other hostels are full. The entrance is
right at the end of the long brown apartment
block, around to the right.

Apartments Poland (☎ 058 346 9864; www.apart
mentpoland.com; apt €30-65) An agency with renovated properties scattered through the Tri-
City Area (Gdańsk/Sopot/Gdynia), including
a number in central Gdańsk. Some are big
enough for families or other groups. Be aware
of the additional electricity charge when
checking out, based on a meter reading.

Targ Rybny (☎ 058 301 5627; www.gdanskhostel.com
.pl; ul Grodzka 21; dm 50zł, d/tr/q 150/180/240zł) A popular modern hostel in a great central location
overlooking the quay. It's a little cramped, but
clean and sociable, with a comfy lounge area.
It also offers bike rental (20zł per day).

MIDRANGE & TOP END

Kamienica Zacisze (☎ 0508 096 221; www.apartments
.gdansk.pl; ul Ogarna 107; apt €105-155) Set within a
quiet courtyard off the street, this communist-era workers' dormitory building has been
transformed into a set of light, airy apartments for up to six people. Each apartment
has high ceilings, a fully equipped kitchen
and loads of space. Excellent value for the
location and quality.

our pick **Dom Muzyka** (☎ 058 326 0600; www
.dom-muzyka.pl; ul Łąkowa 1/2; s/d/ste 220/310/460zł;
🖭) Gorgeous white rooms with arched ceilings and quality furniture, inside the Music
Academy some 300m east of the city centre.
From July to August, a second wing of the
building offers cheaper student-style accommodation. It's hard to spot from the street;
head for the door on the city end of the courtyard within the big yellow-brick building.

Willa Biała Lilia (☎ 058 301 7074; www.bialalilia
.pl; ul Spichrzowa 16; s/d/apt 260/320/420zł) The White

Lily Villa is an attractive accommodation
choice a short walk east of the Main Town on
Spichlerze Island. Rooms are neat and clean,
and the staff are helpful.

Kamienica Gotyk (☎ 0602 844 535; www.gotykhouse
.eu; ul Mariacka 1; s/d 280/310zł) This Gothic guest
house claims to be Gdańsk's oldest residence.
Inside, the rooms are compact but neat, with
clean bathrooms. The location is impressive,
with St Mary's Church and the cafes and shops
of ul Mariacka just outside the door.

Hotel Hanza (☎ 058 305 3427; www.hanza-hotel.com
.pl; ul Tokarska 6; s/d/ste from 695/745/985zł; 🖭) The
Hanza is attractively perched along the waterfront near the Gdańsk Crane, and offers
elegant, tasteful rooms in a modern building. Some rooms have enviable views over
the river.

Eating

Bar Mleczny 'Neptun (ul Długa 33/34; mains 2-13zł;
🕑 7.30am-7pm Mon-Fri, 10am-6pm Sat & Sun) This joint
is a cut above your run-of-the-mill milk bar,
with potted plants, lace curtains, decorative
tiling and old lamps for decor.

Green Way (☎ 058 301 4121; ul Garncarska 4/6; mains 7-
10zł; 🕑 10am-7pm Mon-Fri, noon-7pm Sat & Sun) Popular
with local vegetarians, this eatery serves everything from soy cutlets to Mexican goulash
in an unfussy blue-and-yellow space. There's
another, more central, branch at ul Długa 11.

U Dzika (☎ 058 305 2676; ul Piwna 59/61; mains
7-39zł; 🕑 11am-10pm) Pleasant eatery with a
nice outdoor terrace, specialising in *pierogi*
(dumplings). If you're feeling adventurous, try
the Fantasy Dumplings, comprising cottage
cheese, cinnamon, raisins and peach.

Kansai (☎ 058 324 0888; ul Ogarna 124/125; mains
8-99zł; 🕑 noon-9pm Tue-Sat, noon-8pm Sun) You'd expect fish to be served in a seaport, but Kansai
adds an exotic twist by serving sushi in full-on
Japanese ambience. Waiters are dressed in
traditional robes, there's a samurai sword on
the counter, and the menu has dishes made
from tuna, salmon and butterfish, along with
classic California rolls.

Czerwone Drzwi (☎ 058 301 5764; ul Piwna 52/53;
mains 18-55zł; 🕑 noon-10pm) Step through the
Red Door into a relaxed, refined cafe atmosphere, which helps you digest the small
but interesting menu of *pierogi*, pasta and
Polish classics.

Restauracja Kubicki (☎ 058 301 0050; ul Wartka 5;
mains 24-80zł) The Kubicki is a decent mid-priced
place to try Polish food, especially seafood. It's

POLAND

one of the oldest eateries in Gdańsk, established in the Danzig days of 1918, and offers appropriately old-fashioned decor and service off a scenic laneway next to the river.

Pod Łososiem (☎ 058 301 7652; ul Szeroka 52/54; mains 55-90zł; ❤ noon-10pm) This is one of Gdańsk's oldest and most highly regarded restaurants, and is particularly famous for its salmon dishes and the gold-flecked liqueur *goldwasser*, which was invented here. Red leather seats, brass chandeliers and a gathering of gas lamps fill out the posh interior.

For self-catering, visit **Kos Delikatesy** (ul Piwna 9/10) in the Main Town.

Drinking

Spiritus Sanctus (ul Grobla I 13; ❤ 3-10pm) If you're tired of beer and vodka, head for this stylish wine bar opposite St Mary's Church. While you're enjoying your Slovenian white or Croatian red, you can marvel at the amazing decor, a jumble of abstract art and classic objets d'art.

our pick Café Ferber (ul Długa 77/78; ❤ 8am-late) It's startling to step straight from Gdańsk's historic main street into this very modern cafe-bar, dominated by bright red panels, a suspended ceiling and boxy lighting. Partake of breakfast, well-made coffee, international wines, and cocktail creations such as the *szary kot* (grey cat). On weekends, DJs spin house and chill-out music into the wee small hours.

Kamienica (ul Mariacka 37/39) The best of the bunch on Mariacka is this excellent two-level cafe with a calm, sophisticated atmosphere and the best patio on the block. It's as popular for daytime coffee and cakes as it is for a sociable evening beverage.

Entertainment

Miasto Aniołów (www.miastoaniolow.com.pl, in Polish; ul Chmielna 26; admission 10zł; ❤ 9pm-late) The City of Angels covers all the bases – late-night revellers can hit the spacious dance floor, crash in the chill-out area, or hang around the atmospheric deck overlooking the Motława River. Nightly DJs play disco and other dance-oriented sounds.

State Baltic Opera Theatre (☎ 058 763 4912; www.operabaltycka.pl; Al Zwycięstwa 15) This place is in the suburb of Wrzeszcz, not far from the train station at Gdańsk Politechnika.

Teatr Wybrzeże (☎ 058 301 1328; ul Św. Ducha 2) Next to the Arsenal is the main city theatre. Both Polish and foreign classics (all in Polish) are part of the repertoire.

Getting There & Away

AIR

From **Lech Wałęsa airport** (www.airport.gdansk.pl), LOT has at least five daily flights to Warsaw, and at least three daily to Frankfurt and Munich. Tickets can be bought at the **LOT office** (☎ 0801 703 703; ul Wały Jagiellońskie 2/4).

Gdańsk is also connected to a plethora of other European cities, including London via Ryanair and Wizz Air (at least daily); Dublin via Ryanair and Centralwings (daily); and Copenhagen via SAS (up to three daily).

BOAT

Polferries (www.polferries.pl) offers services between Gdańsk and Nynäshamn (18 hours) in Sweden every other day in summer (less frequently in the low season). The company uses the **ferry terminal** (ul Przemysłowa) in Nowy Port, about 5km north of the Main Town and a short walk from the local commuter train station at Gdańsk Brzeżno. Orbis Travel and the PTTK Office in Gdańsk provide information and sell tickets.

Between April and October, excursion boats leave regularly from the dock near the Green Gate in Gdańsk for Westerplatte (adult/concession return 45/22/zł). Further north along the dockside, you can board the **Galeon Lew** (adult/concession return 35/20zł), a replica 17th-century galleon, for hourly cruises to Westerplatte. Just north of the galleon is the **Water Tram**, a ferry which heads to Sopot (adult/concession 10/5zł, three daily) and Hel (16/8zł, three daily) each weekend during May and June, then daily from July to August. Bicycles cost an extra 2zł to transport.

BUS

The **bus terminal** (ul 3 Maja 12) is behind the main train station and connected to ul Podwale Grodzkie by an underground passageway. Useful bus destinations include Warsaw (50zł, six hours, 10 daily) and Świnoujście (58zł, 8½ hours, one daily).

TRAIN

The city's main train station, **Gdańsk Główny** (ul Podwale Grodzkie 1), is conveniently located on the western outskirts of the Old Town. Most long-distance trains actually start or finish at Gdynia, so make sure you get on/off quickly here.

Each day nearly 20 trains (mainly express) head to Warsaw, (88zł, 4½ hours). There are trains to Olsztyn (34zł, three hours, seven daily), Kraków (62zł, 8¾ hours, 11 daily), Poznań (48zł, 5½ hours, seven daily), Toruń (39zł, four hours, six daily) and Szczecin (51zł, 5½ hours, four daily). Trains also head to Białystok (53zł, 7½ hours, three daily) and Lublin (56zł, eight hours, four daily).

Getting Around

The airport is in Rębiechowo, about 12km northwest of Gdańsk. It's accessible by bus 110 from the Gdańsk Wrzeszcz local commuter train station, or bus B from outside the Gdańsk Główny train station. Taxis cost 45zł to 55zł one way.

The local commuter train – the SKM – runs every 15 minutes between 6am and 7.30pm, and less frequently thereafter, between Gdańsk Główny and Gdynia Główna stations, via Sopot and Gdańsk Oliwa stations. (Note: the line to Gdańsk Nowy Port, via Gdańsk Brzeźno, is a separate line that leaves less regularly from Gdańsk Główny.) Buy tickets at any station and validate them in the yellow boxes at the platform entrance, or purchase them pre-validated from vending machines on the platform.

AROUND GDAŃSK

Gdańsk is part of the so-called Tri-City Area including Gdynia and Sopot, which are easy day trips from Gdańsk.

Sopot

pop 39,600

Sopot, 12km north of Gdańsk, has been one of the Baltic coast's most fashionable seaside resorts since the 19th century. It has an easy-going atmosphere, good nightlife, and long stretches of sandy beach.

INFORMATION

The **tourist office** (☎ 058 550 3783; www.sopot.pl; ul Dworcowa 4; ☑ 9am-8pm Jun-Aug, 10am-6pm Sep-May) is about 50m from the main train station. A short walk to the east of the station is **Gamer** (ul Chopina 1; per hr 4.50zł; ☑ 9am-10pm), an internet cafe.

SIGHTS & ACTIVITIES

From the tourist office, head down ul Bohaterów Monte Cassino, one of Poland's most attractive pedestrian streets, past the surreal **Crooked House** (Krzywy Domek; ul Bohaterów Monte Cassino 53) shopping centre to Poland's longest pier (515m), the famous **Molo** (www .molo.sopot.pl; adult/concession 3.80/2zł; ☑ 8am-8pm Apr-Sep). Various attractions and cultural events can be found near and along the structure.

Opposite Pension Wanda, **Museum Sopotu** (☎ 058 551 2266; ul Poniatowskiego 8; adult/concession 7/5zł; ☑ 10am-4pm Tue-Fri, noon-5pm Sat & Sun) has displays recalling the town's 19th-century incarnation as the German resort of Zoppot.

SLEEPING & EATING

There are no real budget options in Sopot, and prices increase during the busy summer season. Bistros and cafes serving a wide range of cuisines sprout up in summer along the promenades.

Willa Karat II (☎ 058 550 0742; ul 3 Maja 31; s/d/tr 150/270/290zł) Cosy budget lodgings a few blocks from the beach, with light, spacious rooms and clean bathrooms, and plants decorating the corridors. There's a kitchen and dining area for guest use. From the train station, walk right along ul Kościuszki, then left along ul 3 Maja towards the coast.

Hotel Eden (☎ 058 551 1503; www.hotel-eden.com .pl; ul Kordeckiego 4/6; s/d/tr/q/ste 200/300/360/420/480zł) One of the less expensive places in town. It's a quiet, old-fashioned pension with high ceilings, classic furniture and recently renovated bathrooms, overlooking a park one street from the beach.

Pension Wanda (☎ 058 550 3038; ul Poniatowskiego 7; s/d/tr 240/330/420zł, ste from 390zł) The Wanda is a homely place with light, airy rooms, in a handy location about 500m south of the pier. Some rooms have sea views.

Zhong Hua Hotel (☎ 058 550 2020; www.hotel chinski.pl; Al Wojska Polskiego 1; s/d 510/550zł, ste from 680zł) Attractive accommodation in a striking wooden pavilion on the seafront. The foyer is decked out in Chinese design, with hanging lanterns and beautiful timber furniture. The theme extends to the small but pleasant rooms, with views of the water.

Café del Arte (ul Bohaterów Monte Cassino 53) This classy cafe, within the Crooked House, is a great place to enjoy coffee, cake and ice cream surrounded by artistic objects in the combined cafe-gallery.

Mandarynka (ul Bema 6; ☑ noon-10pm) One street south of the main drag, this is a very cool confection of timber tables, scarlet lampshades and huge orange cushions. There's a food menu, and a DJ in action upstairs most nights.

GETTING THERE & AWAY

From the **Sopot train station** (ul Dworcowa 7), local SKM commuter trains run every 15 minutes to Gdańsk Główny (4.50zł, 15 minutes) and Gdynia Główna (3.10zł, 10 minutes) stations. Excursion boats leave several times a day (May to September) from the Sopot pier to Gdańsk and Hel. The Water Tram also links Sopot with Gdańsk (adult/concession 10/5zł, three daily) and Hel (12/6zł, three daily) each weekend during May and June, then daily from July to August.

Gdynia
pop 252,000

As a young city with a busy port atmosphere, Gdynia, 9km north of Sopot, is less atmospheric than Gdańsk or Sopot. It was greatly expanded as a seaport after this coastal area (but not Gdańsk) became part of Poland following WWI. However, it's worth dropping into on a day trip.

SIGHTS & ACTIVITIES

From the main Gdynia Główna train station on Plac Konstytucji, where there is a **tourist office** (☎ 058 721 2466; www.gdynia.pl; ☼ 8am-6pm Mon-Fri, 9am-4pm Sat, 9am-3pm Sun May-Sep, 10am-5pm Oct-Apr), follow ul 10 Lutego east for about 1.5km to the **Southern Pier**.

Moored on the pier's northern side are two interesting museum ships. First up is the curiously sky-blue destroyer **Błyskawica** (adult/concession 8/4zł; ☼ 9.45am-5pm Tue-Sun), which escaped capture in 1939 and went on to serve successfully with Allied naval forces throughout WWII.

Beyond it is the beautiful three-masted frigate **Dar Pomorza** (adult/concession 8/4zł; ☼ 9am-6pm daily Jul-Sep, 10am-4pm Tue-Sun May & Jun & Oct), built in Hamburg in 1909 as a training ship for German sailors. There's information in English on the dockside.

A 20-minute walk uphill (follow the signs) from Teatr Muzyczny on Plac Grunwaldzki (about 300m southwest of the start of the pier) leads to **Kamienna Góra**, a hill offering wonderful views.

SLEEPING & EATING

Gdynia is probably best visited as a day trip, but there are some reasonable accommodation options. There are several cheap eateries in the city centre, and upmarket fish restaurants along the pier.

China Town Hotel (☎ 058 620 9221; www.chinahotel .pl; ul Dworca 11a; s/d/tr/q 100/140/240/280zł) Inexpensive lodgings can be found here, opposite the train station. The rooms are plain but serviceable for a night, though singles are very small. There's a Chinese restaurant in the same building.

Hotel Antracyt (☎ 058 620 1239; ul Korzeniowskiego 19; www.hotel-antracyt.pl; s/d 200/280zł) This place is further south, on a hill in an exclusive residential area, with fine views over the water.

our pick **Willa Lubicz** (☎ 058 668 4740; ul Orłowska 43; www.willalubicz.pl; s/d/ste 380/410/690zł) If you're looking for style you could try this quiet, upmarket place with a chic 1930s ambience at the southern end of town; Gdynia Orłowo is the nearest train station. Third-floor rooms have views of the sea.

Bistro Kwadrans (☎ 058 620 1592; Skwer Kościuszki 20; mains 8-17zł; ☼ 9am-10pm Mon-Fri, 10am-10pm Sat, noon-10pm Sun) One block north of the median strip along ul 10 Lutego, this is a great place for tasty Polish food. It also serves up pizzas, including an improbable variant involving banana and curry.

GETTING THERE & AWAY

Local commuter trains link Gdynia Główna station with Sopot (3.10zł) and Gdańsk (4.50zł) every 15 minutes. From the same station, trains run hourly to Hel (13zł, two hours) and half-hourly to Lębork (12zł, one hour), where you can change for Łeba. From the small bus terminal outside, minibuses also go to Hel (12zł, two hours, six daily).

Stena Line uses the **Terminal Promowy** (ul Kwiatkowskiego 60), about 5km northwest of Gdynia. It offers services between Gdynia and Karlskrona (10½ hours) in Sweden. Take bus 150 from ul Władysława IV.

Between May and September, excursion boats leave Gdynia's Southern Pier to Hel (adult/concession one way 45/30zł, return 60/42zł), from a point beyond the Dar Pomorza. The Water Tram also links Gdynia with Hel (adult/concession 10/5zł, four daily) and Jastarnia (adult/concession 10/5zł, three daily). Bikes cost 2zł extra to transport.

Hel
pop 3900

Never was a town more entertainingly named – English speakers can spend hours creating amusing twists on 'to Hel and back', or 'a cold day in Hel'. In fact, this old fishing village at the tip of the Hel Peninsula north of Gdańsk is an attractive place to visit, and a popular beach resort. The pristine, windswept **beach** on the Baltic side stretches the length of the peninsula. On the southern side, the sea is popular for **windsurfing**; equipment can be rented in the villages of **Władysławowo** and **Jastarnia**.

The **Fokarium** (ul Morska 2; admission 2zł; 🕑 8.30am-dusk), off the main road along the seafront, is home to endangered Baltic grey seals. It also has a good souvenir shop for those 'I'm in Hel' postcards to send to friends back home. The 15th-century **Gothic church**, further along the esplanade, houses the **Museum of Fishery** (ul Nadmorksi 2; adult/concession 5/3zł; 🕑 10am-4pm Tue-Sun).

Visitors often stay in **private rooms** offered within local houses (mostly from May to September), at about 90zł per double. **Captain Morgan** (☎ 058 675 00 91; www.captainmorgan.hel.org.pl; ul Wiejska 21; d/tr 100/140zł) also offers plain, clean rooms, and good seafood in a quirky pub stuffed with maritime memorabilia.

To Hel, minibuses leave every hour or so from the main train station in Gdynia (12zł, two hours). Several trains depart from Gdynia daily (13zł, two hours, hourly), and from May to September from Gdańsk (20zł, three hours, hourly). Hel is also accessible by excursion boat from Gdańsk, Sopot and Gdynia – see the Getting There & Away section for each of these destinations for details.

Malbork
pop 38,300

The magnificent **Malbork Castle** (☎ 055 647 0800; www.zamek.malbork.pl; adult/concession 30/20zł; 🕑 9am-7pm Tue-Sun May-Aug, 10am-5pm Tue-Sun Apr & Sep, 10am-3pm Tue-Sun Oct-Mar) is the centrepiece of this town, 58km southeast of Gdańsk. It's the largest Gothic castle in Europe, and was once known as Marienburg, headquarters of the Teutonic Knights. It was constructed by the Order in 1276 and became the seat of their Grand Master in 1309. Damage sustained in WWII has been repaired since the conflict's end, and it was placed on the Unesco World Heritage List in 1997. The entry fee includes a compulsory Polish language tour; tours in English and other languages are available on request (195zł). On Mondays there's a limited tour for a bargain basement 5zł.

The **Youth Hostel** (☎ 055 272 2408; www.ssm malbork.webpark.pl, in Polish; ul Żeromskiego 45; dm/d 22/55zł) is a reasonable budget option in a local school about 500m south of the castle.

Hotel Zamek (☎ 055 272 3367; www.hotelprodus .pl; ul Starościńska 14; s/d/ste €63/72/170) is inside a restored medieval building in the Lower Castle. The rooms are a bit old-fashioned, but the bathrooms are up-to-date. The restaurant has character, but can be crowded with tour groups.

our pick **Hotel Grot** (☎ 055 646 9660; www.grothotel .pl; ul Kościuszki 22d; s/d/tr/ste 199/289/379/399zł) is classy for its price range, with contemporary furniture and an impressive restaurant. It's down an unnamed dead-end laneway opposite the unrecommended Hotel Zbyszko.

Restauracja Piwniczka (☎ 055 273 3668; ul Starościńska 1; mains 10-80zł; 🕑 10am-7pm) is an atmospheric cellar restaurant beneath the west wall of the castle.

The castle is 1km west of the train and bus stations. Leave the train station, turn right, cut across the highway, head down ul Kościuszki and follow the signs. Malbork is an easy day trip by train from Gdańsk (12zł, 50 minutes, at least hourly). From Malbork, trains also go to Olsztyn (31zł, two hours, seven daily).

TORUŃ
pop 207,000

The first thing to strike you about Toruń, south of Gdańsk, is its massive red-brick churches, looking more like fortresses than places of worship. The city is defined by its striking Gothic architecture, which gives its Old Town a distinctive appearance and its promotional slogan: *gotyk na dotyk* (Touch Gothic). The city is a pleasant place to spend a few days, offering a nice balance between a relaxing slow pace and engaging entertainment diversions.

Toruń is also famous as the birthplace of Nicolaus Copernicus, a figure you cannot escape as you walk the streets of his home town – you can even buy gingerbread men in his likeness. The renowned astronomer spent his youth here, and the local university is named after him.

Historically, Toruń is intertwined with the Teutonic Knights, who established an outpost here in 1233. Following the Thirteen Years' War (1454–66), the Teutonic Order and Poland signed a peace treaty here, which returned to Poland a large area of land stretching from Toruń to Gdańsk.

Toruń was fortunate to escape major damage in WWII, and as a result is the best-preserved Gothic town in Poland. The Old

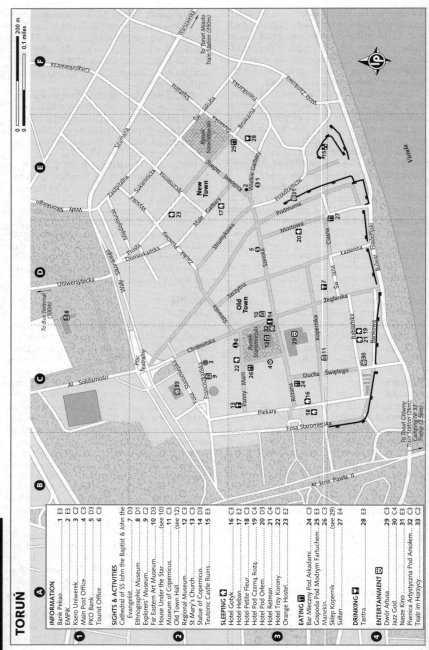

POLAND

TORUŃ

INFORMATION
Bank Pekao...................................1 E3
EMPIK...2 E3
Ksero Uniwerek..............................3 C3
Main Post Office...........................4 C3
PKO Bank..5 D3
Tourist Office.................................6 C3

SIGHTS & ACTIVITIES
Cathedral of SS John the Baptist & John the
  Evangelist...................................7 D3
Ethnographic Museum................8 D1
Explorers' Museum........................9 C2
Far Eastern Art Museum............10 D3
House Under the Star...........(see 10)
Museum of Copernicus...............11 C3
Old Town Hall.......................(see 12)
Regional Museum.........................12 C3
St Mary's Church..........................13 C3
Statue of Copernicus..................14 D3
Teutonic Castle Ruins.................15 E3

SLEEPING 🛏
Hotel Gotyk...................................16 C3
Hotel Heban..................................17 E2
Hotel Petite Fleur........................18 C4
Hotel Pod Czarną Różą...............19 C4
Hotel Pod Orłem..........................20 D3
Hotel Retman...............................21 C4
Hotel Trzy Korony........................22 C3
Orange Hostel...............................23 E2

EATING 🍴
Bar Mleczny Pod Arkadami........24 C3
Gospoda Pod Modrym Fartuchem..25 E3
Manekin..26 C3
Sklep Kopernik....................(see 29)
Sułtan...27 E4

DRINKING 🍷
Tantra..28 E3

ENTERTAINMENT 🎭
Dwór Artusa...................................29 C3
Jazz God...30 C4
Nasze Kino......................................31 E3
Piwnica Artystyczna Pod Aniołem...32 C3
Teatr im Horzycy..........................33 C2

0   200 m
0   0.1 miles

Town was added to Unesco's World Heritage List in 1997.

Information

Bank Pekao (ul Wielkie Garbary 11)

EMPiK (ul Wielkie Garbary 18) Bookshop.

Ksero Uniwerek (ul Franciszkańska 5; per hr 3zł; 8am-7pm Mon-Fri, 9am-4pm Sat) Internet access.

Main post office (Rynek Staromiejski; 6am-9pm)

PKO Bank (ul Szeroka)

Tourist office (056 621 0931; www.it.torun.pl; Rynek Staromiejski 25; 9am-4pm Mon & Sat, 9am-6pm Tue-Fri, 9am-1pm Sun)

Sights

The starting point for any exploration of Toruń is the **Rynek Staromiejski** (Old Town Market Sq), the focal point of the Old Town. The **Regional Museum** (www.muzeum.torun.pl; Rynek Staromiejski 1; adult/concession 10/6zł; 10am-6pm Tue-Sun May-Sep, 10am-4pm Tue-Sun Oct-Apr) sits within the massive 14th-century **Old Town Hall**, featuring a fine collection of 19th- and 20th-century Polish art. Other displays recall the town's guilds, and there's an exhibition of medieval stained glass and religious paintings. Climb the 40m-high **tower** (adult/concession 10/6zł; 10am-4pm Tue-Sun Apr, 10am-8pm Tue-Sun May-Sep) for great views.

In front of the town hall is an elegant **statue** of Copernicus. Look for other interesting items of statuary around the square, including a dog and umbrella from a famous Polish comic strip, a donkey that once served as a punishment device, and a fabled violinist who saved Toruń from a plague of frogs.

The richly decorated, 15th-century **House Under the Star**, with its baroque facade and spiral wooden staircase, contains the **Far Eastern Art Museum** (Rynek Staromiejski 35; adult/concession 7/4zł; 10am-6pm Tue-Sun May-Sep, 10am-4pm Tue-Sun Oct-Apr).

Just off the northwestern corner of the square is the late-13th-century **St Mary's Church** (ul Panny Marii; dawn-dusk), a Gothic building with magnificent 15th-century stalls.

Just around the corner is the **Explorers' Museum** (ul Franciszkańska 11; adult/concession 8/5zł; 11am-6pm Tue-Sun May-Sep, 10am-4pm Tue-Sun Oct-Apr), a small but interesting institution showcasing artefacts from the collection of inveterate wanderer Antonio Halik. There are hats, travel documents, and souvenirs of his journeys – including a vast array of hotel keys!

In 1473, Copernicus was allegedly born in the brick Gothic house (there's some doubt) that now contains the fairly dull **Museum of Copernicus** (ul Kopernika 15/17; adult/concession 10/7zł; 10am-6pm Tue-Sun May-Sep, 10am-4pm Tue-Sun Oct-Apr), presenting replicas of the great astronomer's instruments. More engaging, if overpriced, is the museum's short **audiovisual presentation** (adult/concession 12/7zł) regarding Copernicus' life in Toruń; and the extravagantly titled **World of Toruń's Gingerbread** (adult/concession 10/6zł). Visitors are guided by a costumed medieval townswoman and given the chance to bake their own *pierniki* (gingerbread). A combined ticket to any two of the three attractions costs 18/11zł.

One block east is the **Cathedral of SS John the Baptist & John the Evangelist** (ul Żeglarska; adult/concession 3/2zł; 9am-5.30pm Mon-Sat, 2-5.30pm Sun Apr-Oct), founded in 1233 and completed more than 200 years later, with its massive **tower** (adult/concession 6/4zł) and bell. There's no sightseeing allowed during services.

Further east are the ruins of the **Teutonic Castle** (ul Przedzamcze; adult/concession 4/2zł, free Mon; 10am-6pm), destroyed in 1454 by angry townsfolk protesting against the knights' oppressive regime.

In a park just north of the Old Town is the **Ethnographic Museum** (ul Wały Sikorskiego 19; adult/concession 8.50/4.50zł; 9am-4pm Wed & Fri, 10am-5pm Tue, Thu-Sun), showcasing traditional customs, costumes and weapons.

Sleeping

Toruń is blessed with a plentiful number of hotels within converted historic buildings in its Old Town; but as they're fairly small, it pays to book ahead.

Camping Nr 33 Tramp (056 654 7187; www.tramp.mosir.torun.pl; ul Kujawska 14; camping per person 8.50zł, tents 5.50-11zł, d/tr/q 50/70/90zł; May-Sep) There's a choice of cabins or hotel-style rooms at this camping ground on the edge of the train line, along with an onsite snack bar. It's a five-minute walk west of the main train station.

Orange Hostel (056 652 0033; www.hostelorange.pl; ul Prosta 19; dm/s/d/tr 30/50/90/120zł) The wave of Polish hostels for the international backpacker has finally swept over sleepy Toruń. Orange is in a handy location, its decor is bright and cheerful, and its kitchen is an impressive place to practise the gentle art of self-catering.

Hotel Trzy Korony (056 622 6031; www.hotel3korony.pl; Rynek Staromiejski 21; s/d/tr/ste from 100/140/180/260zł) This budget hotel is by no means luxurious, but the simple rooms are neatly furnished with pine furniture, blue sofas and sunny yellow wallpaper. The hotel's glorious history includes stopovers by three distinguished monarchs (hence the 'three crowns' in the name).

Hotel Pod Orłem (☎ 056 622 5024; www.hotel.torun .pl; ul Mostowa 17; s/d/apt from 120/150/215zł) This hotel is great value, and although the rooms are smallish, have squeaky wooden floors, and some contain poky bathrooms, the service is good and it's central. The foyer and corridors are fun with their jumble of framed pop-art images and old photos.

Hotel Pod Czarną Różą (☎ 056 621 9637; www.hotel czarnaroza.pl; ul Rabiańska 11; s/d/tr/ste 170/210/250/320zł) 'Under the Black Rose' is spread between a historic inn and a new wing facing the river, though its interiors present a uniformly clean up-to-date look. Some doubles come with small but functional kitchens.

Hotel Retman (☎ 056 657 4460; www.hotelretman .pl; ul Rabiańska 15; s/d 190/250zł) Attractively decorated accommodation offering spacious, atmospheric rooms with red carpet and solid timber furniture. Downstairs is a good pub and restaurant.

Hotel Gotyk (☎ 056 658 4000; www.hotel-gotyk .com.pl; ul Piekary 20; s/d 190/270zł) Housed in a fully modernised 14th-century building just off the main square, rooms are very neat, with ornate furniture and high ceilings, and all come with sparkling bathrooms.

Hotel Heban (☎ 056 652 1555; www.hotel-heban .com.pl; ul Małe Garbary 7; s/d/ste from 190/300/350zł) This is a stylish, upmarket hotel occupying a historic 17th-century building in a quiet street. It also has a good restaurant, situated off a lavish foyer with painted wooden ceilings and a 24-hour bar.

Hotel Petite Fleur (☎ 056 621 5100; www.petite fleur.pl; ul Piekary 25; s/d 210/270zł) Just opposite the Gotyk, the Petite Fleur offers fresh, airy rooms in a renovated old town house, some with exposed original brickwork and rafters. It also has a French cellar restaurant.

Eating & Drinking

Bar Mleczny Pod Arkadami (ul Różana 1; mains 3-8zł; ☺ 9am-7pm Mon-Fri, 9am-4pm Sat) This classic milk bar is just off the Old Town Sq, with a range of low-cost dishes. It also has a takeaway window serving a range of tasty *zapiekanki* (toasted rolls with cheese, mushrooms and ketchup) and sweet waffles.

Sułtan (☎ 056 621 0607; ul Mostowa 7; mains 8-12zł; ☺ noon-midnight) A splash of Middle Eastern cuisine in northern Poland, in a cheerful venue decorated with colourful lanterns and Arabic script. The menu contains many variants of kebabs, along with soups, salads and pizzas.

Gospoda Pod Modrym Fartuchem (☎ 056 622 2626; Rynek Nowomiejski 8; mains 10-35zł; ☺ 10am-10pm) This pleasant, unpretentious 15th-century pub on the New Town Sq has been visited by Polish kings and Napoleon. The usual meat-and-cabbage Polish dishes are joined by an array of Indian food, including a good vegetarian selection.

Manekin (☎ 056 621 0504; Rynek Staromiejski 16; mains 11-13zł) Vaguely Wild West decor adorns this inexpensive central restaurant specialising in *naleśniki* (crepes). It offers a variety of filled pancakes, including vegetarian options.

Tantra (ul Ślusarska 5) This astonishingly decorated bar is done out in an Indian and Tibetan theme and layered with cloth and other artefacts from the subcontinent. Sit on the cushion-strewn divans, order a drink from the long list, and meditate on the infinite.

Toruń is famous for its *pierniki*, which come in a variety of shapes, and can be bought at **Sklep Kopernik** (☎ 056 622 8832; Rynek Staromiejski 6).

Entertainment

Piwnica Artystyczna Pod Aniołem (Rynek Staromiejski 1) Set in a splendid spacious cellar in the Old Town Hall, this bar offers live music some nights. Check the posters outside for the latest gigs.

Jazz God (ul Rabiańska 17; ☺ 5pm-2am Sun-Thu, 5pm-4am Fri & Sat) This is a lively cellar club with rock DJs most nights from 9pm.

Teatr im Horzycy (☎ 056 622 5222; Plac Teatralny 1) The main stage for theatre performances.

Dwór Artusa (☎ 056 655 4929; Artus Court, Rynek Staromiejski 6) This place often presents classical music.

Nasze Kino (www.naszekino.pl, in Polish; ul Podmurna 14; admission 12zł) Cool little art-house cinema embedded within part of the old city wall, its single screen showing a range of non-Hollywood films.

Getting There & Away

The **bus terminal** (ul Dąbrowskiego) is a 10-minute walk north of the Old Town. Polski Express has eight buses a day to Warsaw (41zł, 3½ hours) and two a day to Szczecin (59zł, six hours).

The **Toruń Główny train station** (Al Podgórska) is on the opposite side of the Vistula River and linked to the Old Town by bus 22 or 27 (get off at the first stop over the bridge). Some trains stop and finish at the more convenient Toruń Miasto train station, about 500m east of the New Town.

From the Toruń Główny station, there are trains to Poznań (33zł, 2½ hours, six daily), Gdańsk and Gdynia (39zł, four hours, six daily), Kraków (53zł, 7½ hours, three daily), Łódź (34zł, three hours, 10 daily), Olsztyn (34zł, 2½ hours, seven daily), Szczecin (49zł, five hours, up to three daily), Wrocław (48zł, 5½ hours, three daily) and Warsaw (41zł, three hours, nine daily). Trains travelling between Toruń and Gdańsk often change at Bydgoszcz, and between Toruń and Kraków you may need to get another connection at Inowrocław.

ŁEBA
pop 3800

Heading west from Gdańsk along the Pomeranian coast, Łeba (*weh*-bah) is the first major beach resort you encounter. Between May and September, this quiet fishing village transforms into a lively seaside destination.

The **tourist office** (☎ 059 866 2565; www.leba.pl; ul 11 Listopada 5a; ☯ 8am-8pm Mon-Fri, 8am-6pm Sat, 10am-4pm Sun Jul-Aug, 8am-4pm Mon-Fri Sep-Jun) is between the train station and the main street, ul Kościuszki. There are eateries on ul Kościuszki.

To reach the wide sandy **beach** from the train station, or adjacent bus stop, walk north along ul Kościuszki, ul Wojska Polskiego and ul Nadmorska for about 1.5km to the better eastern beach; if in doubt, follow the signs to the beachside Hotel Neptun.

SIGHTS

Beginning just west of Łeba, **Słowiński National Park** stretches along the coast for 33km. It contains a diversity of habitats, including forests, lakes, bogs and beaches, but the main attraction is the huge number of massive (and shifting) **sand dunes** that create a desert landscape. The wildlife and birdlife is also remarkably rich.

From Łeba to the sand dunes, follow the signs from near the train station northwest along ul Turystyczna and take the road west to the park entrance in the hamlet of Rąbka.

Minibuses ply this road in summer from Łeba (5zł); alternatively, it's a pleasant walk or bike ride (8km). No cars or buses are allowed beyond the park entrance.

SLEEPING & EATING

Many houses offer private rooms all year round, but finding a vacant room during summer can be tricky. There are plenty of decent eateries in the town centre and along ul Nadmorska.

Camping Nr 41 Ambre (☎ 059 866 2472; www.ambre .leba.pl; ul Nadmorska 9a; camping per adult/concession 13/8zł, cabins 240-400zł) This is a decent camping ground, but bring mosquito repellent if you don't want to be eaten alive.

Hotel Gołąbek (☎ 059 866 2175; www.hotel-golabek .leb.pl; ul Wybrzeże 10; s/d/tr/ste 240/350/410/700zł) This hotel exudes style on the edge of the wharf, with views of charming old fishing boats and the port. In summer the hotel hires out bicycles (5zł per hour).

GETTING THERE & AWAY

The usual transit point is Lębork, 29km south of Łeba. In summer there are several daily trains between the two destinations (8zł, 50 minutes). To Lębork, slow trains run every hour or two from Gdańsk, via Gdynia (16zł, 1½ hours). In summer (June to August), two trains run directly between Gdynia and Łeba (20zł, 2¼ hours), and four trains travel daily to/from Wrocław (55zł, eight hours).

SZCZECIN
pop 412,000

Szczecin (*shcheh*-cheen) is the major city and port of northwestern Poland. Massive damage in WWII accounts for the unaesthetic mishmash of new and old buildings in the city centre, but enough remains to give a sense of the pre-war days. The broad streets and massive historic buildings bear a strong resemblance to Berlin, for which Szczecin was once the main port as the German city of Stettin. Szczecin may not have the seamless charm of Toruń or Wrocław, but it's worth a visit if you're travelling to/from Germany.

Information

The **tourist office** (☎ 091 434 0440; Al Niepodległości 1; ☯ 9am-5pm Mon-Fri, 10am-2pm Sat) is helpful, as is the **cultural & tourist information office** (☎ 091 489 1630; ul Korsazy 34; ☯ 10am-6pm) in the castle. The **post office** and banks can be found along

---

WORTH THE TRIP: BALTIC BEACHES

Between Łeba and the German border, there are numerous seaside towns with unpolluted waters, offering fine sandy beaches during summer. Here are a few places for a sunbathing detour on your way west between Gdańsk and Szczecin:

■ **Ustka** Once the summer hang-out of German Chancellor Otto von Bismarck, this fishing port is full of atmosphere.

■ **Darłowo** A former medieval trading port with an impressive castle, and two beaches linked by a pedestrian bridge over a river.

■ **Kołobrzeg** This coastal city offers historic attractions, spa treatments and Baltic cruises.

■ **Międzyzdroje** A popular seaside resort and the gateway to Wolin National Park.

■ **Świnoujście** On a Baltic island shared with Germany, this busy port town boasts a long sandy shore and pleasant parks.

For more details, check out Lonely Planet's *Poland* country guide, or www.poland.travel.

Al Niepodległości, the main street. There's a handy internet cafe, **Portal** (Plac Zwycięstwa 3; per hr 5zł; ☺ 9am-11pm), in a big orange building 200m west of the tourist office.

Sights

The huge and austere **Castle of the Pomeranian Dukes** (ul Korsarzy 34; admission free; ☺ dawn-dusk) lies 500m northeast of the tourist office. Originally built in the mid-14th century, it was enlarged in 1577 and rebuilt after major damage from airborne bombing in WWII. Its **Castle Museum** (adult/concession 6/3zł, free Thu; ☺ 10am-6pm Tue-Sun) explains the building's convoluted history, with special exhibitions mounted from time to time.

A short walk down (south) from the castle is the 15th-century **Old Town Hall** (ul Mściwoja 8), which contains the **Museum of the City of Szczecin** (adult/concession 6/3zł, free Thu; ☺ 10am-6pm Tue, 4pm Wed-Sun). Nearby is the charmingly rebuilt **Old Town** with its cafes, bars and clubs. Three blocks northwest of the castle is the **National Museum** (ul Staromłyńska 27; adult/concession 6/3zł, free Thu; ☺ 10am-6pm Tue, Wed & Fri, 10am-4pm Thu, Sat & Sun), housing a historic art collection.

At the train station you can explore the city's newest attraction, **Szczecin Underground** (☎ 091 434 0801; www.schron.szczecin.pl; ul Kolumba 1/6; admission 15zł; ☺ noon). This guided tour takes you through a German-built bomb shelter that later became a Cold War fallout shelter. Pay at the Centrum Wynajmu i Turystyki office.

Sleeping & Eating

Camping PTTK Marina (☎ 091 460 1165; www.campingmarina.pl; ul Przestrzenna 23; per person/tent 15/9zł, s/d cabins 80/120zł) On the shore of Lake Dąbie –

get off at the Szczecin Dąbie train station and ask for directions (2km).

Youth Hostel PTSM (☎ 091 422 4761; www.ptsm.home.pl; ul Monte Cassino 19a; dm/d 24/50zł) This hostel has clean, spacious rooms and is 2km northwest of the tourist office. Catch tram 1 north to the stop marked 'Piotr Skargi', then walk right one block.

Hotelik Elka-Sen (☎ 091 433 5604; www.elkasen.szczecin.pl; Al 3 Maja 1a; s/d 140/180zł) Simple, light-filled rooms in a basement location in the centre of town. Just south of the tourist office, enter from the side street.

Hotel Podzamcze (☎ 091 812 1404; www.podzamcze.szczecin.pl; ul Sienna 1/3; s/d/ste 190/240/295zł) This hotel is in a charming location near the Old Town Hall. Its rooms are compact and its bathrooms tiny, but it's in a great location for the castle, the town hall and the train station.

Haga (☎ 091 812 1759; ul Sienna 10; mains 11-24zł) This informal place in the Old Town produces excellent Dutch-style filled pancakes from a menu listing more than 400 combinations.

Karczma Polska Pod Kogutem (☎ 091 434 6873; Plac Lotników 3; mains 12-62zł) Northwest of Al Niepodległości, this restaurant serves topnotch traditional Polish food. Roast rabbit in hazelnut sauce, anyone?

Getting There & Away

The **airport** (www.airport.com.pl) is in Goleniów, 45km northeast of the city. A shuttle bus (14zł) operated by **Interglobus** (☎ 091 485 0422; www.interglobus.pl) picks up from stops outside the LOT office and the train station before every flight, and meets all arrivals. Alternatively, a taxi should cost around 120zł.

LOT flies between Szczecin and Warsaw four times a day. Book at the **LOT office** (☎ 0801 703 703; ul Wyzwolenia 17), about 200m from the northern end of Al Niepodegłości. International flights on Ryanair include London (at least daily) and Dublin (three weekly). Oslo (five weekly) is reached via Norwegian.

The **bus terminal** (Plac Grodnicki) and the nearby **Szczecin Główny train station** (ul Kolumba) are 600m southeast of the tourist office. Bus departures are of limited interest, though Polski Express operates two services each day to Toruń (59zł, six hours) and Warsaw (63zł, 9½ hours) from a stand at the train station. Trains travel regularly to Poznań (39zł, 2½ hours, 15 daily), Gdańsk (51zł, 5½ hours, four daily) and Warsaw (56zł, seven hours, eight daily). Trains also head north to Świnoujście (28zł, two hours, hourly).

Another way to reach Świnoujście is via **ferry** (☎ 091 488 5564; www.wodolot-szczecin.pl; ul Jana z Kolna 7; adult/concession 50/25zł; ☼ mid-Jun–Oct), which travels daily from a quay north of the castle across the waters of the Szczeciński Lagoon (1¼ hours).

Advance tickets for trains and ferries are available from **Orbis Travel** (☎ 091 434 2618; Plac Zwycięstwa 1), about 200m west of the main post office.

WARMIA & MASURIA

The dominant feature of Warmia and Masuria is its beautiful postglacial landscape dominated by thousands of lakes, linked to rivers and canals, which host aquatic activities like yachting and canoeing. This picturesque lake district has little industry, and as a result remains unpolluted and attractive, especially in summer. Like much of northern Poland, the region has changed hands between Germanic and Polish rulers over the centuries.

ELBLĄG–OSTRÓDA CANAL

The longest navigable canal still used in Poland stretches 82km between Elbląg and Ostróda. Constructed between 1848 and 1876, this waterway was used to transport timber from inland forests to the Baltic. To overcome the 99.5m difference in water levels, the canal utilises an unusual system of five water-powered slipways so that boats are sometimes carried across dry land on rail-mounted trolleys.

Usually, **excursion boats** (☼ mid-May–Sep) depart from both Elbląg and Ostróda daily at 8am (adult/concession 85/65zł, 11 hours), but actual departures depend on available passengers. For information, call the **boat operators** (☎ Elbląg 055 232 4307, Ostróda 089 646 3871; www.zeglug a.com.pl).

Pensjonat Boss (☎ 055 239 3728; www.pensjonatboss .pl; ul Św Ducha 30; s/d/tr/ste 160/230/300/300zł) is one of several small hotels in Elbląg's Old Town, offering comfortable rooms above its own bar. **Camping Nr 61** (☎ 055 641 8666; www.camping61.com.pl; ul Panieńska 14; per person/tent 12/5zł; cabins d/q 60/100zł; ☼ May-Sep), right at Elbląg's boat dock, is a pleasant budget option. In Ostróda, try **Hotel Promenada** (☎ 089 642 8100; ul Mickiewicza 3; s/d/tr/ste from 140/180/240/300zł), 500m east of the bus and train stations.

Elbląg is accessible by frequent trains and buses from Gdańsk, Malbork, Frombork and Olsztyn. Ostróda is regularly connected by train to Olsztyn (8zł, 30 minutes, hourly) and Toruń (31zł, two hours, seven daily), and by bus to Olsztyn and Elbląg.

FROMBORK
pop 2500

It may look like the most uneventful town in history, but Frombork was once home to the famous astronomer Nicolaus Copernicus. It's where he wrote his ground-breaking *On the Revolutions of the Celestial Spheres,* which established the theory that the earth travelled around the sun. Beyond the memory of its famous resident, it's a charming, sleepy settlement that was founded on the shore of the Vistula Lagoon in the 13th century. It was later the site of a fortified ecclesiastical township, erected on Cathedral Hill.

The hill is now occupied by the extensive **Nicolaus Copernicus Museum** (ul Katedralna 8), with several sections requiring separate tickets. Most imposing is the red-brick Gothic **cathedral** (adult/concession 4/2zł; ☼ 9.30am-5pm Mon-Sat May-Sep, 9am-4pm Mon-Sat Oct-Apr), constructed in the 14th century. The nearby **Bishop's Palace** (adult/concession 4/2zł; ☼ 9am-4pm Tue-Sun) houses various exhibitions on local history, while the **belfry** (adult/concession 5/3zł; ☼ 9.30am-5pm May-Sep, 9am-4pm Oct-Apr) is home to an example of Foucault's pendulum. A short distance from the main museum, the **Hospital of the Holy Ghost** (adult/concession 4/2zł; ☼ 9am-4pm Tue-Sat) exhibits historical medical instruments and manuscripts.

Camping Nr 12 (☎ 055 243 7744; ul Braniewska 14; per person/tent 7/10zł, dm/d/tr 25/58/87zł; ☯ May-Sep) is a privately owned camping ground at the eastern end of town, on the Braniewo road. It has basic cabins and a snack bar on the grounds.

Dom Familijny Rheticus (☎ 055 243 7800; www .domfamilijny.pl; ul Kopernika 10; s/d/ste 88/120/240zł) is a small, quaint old place with cosy rooms and good facilities, a short walk to the east of the bus stop. Breakfast is an extra 7zł.

The bus station is on the riverfront about 300m northwest of the museum. Frombork can be directly reached by bus from Elbląg (8zł, 40 minutes, hourly) and Gdańsk (18zł, three hours, two daily). The best place to get on and off is the bus stop directly below the museum on ul Kopernika.

OLSZTYN
pop 175,000

Olsztyn (*ol*-shtin) is a pleasant, relaxed city whose rebuilt Old Town is home to cobblestone streets, art galleries, cafes, bars and restaurants. As a busy transport hub, it's also the logical base from which to explore the region, including the Great Masurian Lakes district (opposite).

It's also another city on the Copernicus trail, as the great astronomer once served as administrator of Warmia, commanding Olsztyn Castle from 1516 to 1520. From 1466 to 1772 the town belonged to the kingdom of Poland. With the first partition of the nation, Olsztyn became Prussian Allenstein, until it returned to Polish hands in 1945.

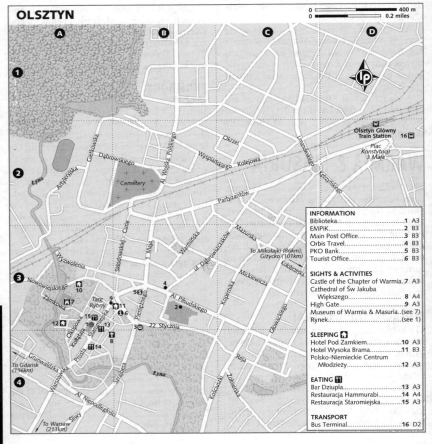

| OLSZTYN | | 0 | 400 m |
| | | 0 | 0.2 miles |

INFORMATION
Biblioteka...........................1 A3
EMPiK..................................2 B3
Main Post Office.................3 B3
Orbis Travel.........................4 B3
PKO Bank.............................5 B3
Tourist Office......................6 B3

SIGHTS & ACTIVITIES
Castle of the Chapter of Warmia.7 A3
Cathedral of Św Jakuba
Większego........................8 A4
High Gate............................9 A3
Museum of Warmia & Masuria.(see 7)
Rynek..................................(see 1)

SLEEPING 🏠
Hotel Pod Zamkiem...........10 A3
Hotel Wysoka Brama.........11 B3
Polsko-Niemieckie Centrum
Młodzieży......................12 A3

EATING 🍴
Bar Dziupla........................13 A3
Restauracja Hammurabi.....14 A4
Restauracja Staromiejska...15 A3

TRANSPORT
Bus Terminal......................16 D2

The **tourist office** (☎ 089 535 3565; ul Staromiejska 1; ☯ 8am-4pm Mon-Fri) is next to the High Gate. Regarding money matters, try the **PKO Bank** (ul Pieniężnego).

For snail mail, go to the **main post office** (ul Pieniężnego); for cybermail, visit the **Biblioteka** (Library; ul Stare Miasto 33; per hr 3zł; ☯ 10am-7pm Mon-Fri, 9am-2pm Sat) in the centre of the Rynek, which offers internet access on its first floor. Books and maps are sold at **EMPiK** (ul Piłsudskiego 16) inside the Alfa Centrum shopping mall.

Sights

The **High Gate** is the remaining section of the 14th-century city walls. Further west, the 14th-century **Castle of the Chapter of Warmia** (ul Zamkowa 2) contains the **Museum of Warmia & Masuria** (adult/concession 9/7zł; ☯ 9am-5pm Tue-Sun May-Aug, 10am-4pm Tue-Sun Sep-Apr). Its exhibits star Copernicus, who made some astronomical observations here in the early 16th century, along with coins and art.

The **Rynek** (Market Sq) was rebuilt after WWII destruction. To the east, the red-brick Gothic **Cathedral of Św. Jakuba Większego** (ul Długosza) dates from the 14th century. Its 60m tower was added in 1596.

Sleeping

Hotel Wysoka Brama (☎ 089 527 3675; www.hotel wysokabrama.olsztyn.pl; ul Staromiejska 1; s/d/ste from 55/70/160zł) Offers cheap but basic rooms in a very central location next to the High Gate.

Hotel Pod Zamkiem (☎ 089 535 1287; www .hotel-olsztyn.com.pl; ul Nowowiejskiego 10; s/d/tr/ste from 160/220/260/250zł) Charmingly old-fashioned pension, featuring an extravagant stairwell constructed of dark timber carved with German text; but avoid the damp ground floor rooms. It's near the castle.

Polsko-Niemieckie Centrum Młodzieży (☎ 089 534 0780; www.pncm.olsztyn.pl; ul Okopowa 25; s/d/ste from 190/210/350zł) This place is situated next to the castle. The rooms (some with views of the castle) are plain, but have gleaming bathrooms. There's a sunlit restaurant off the foyer.

Eating

Bar Dziupla (☎ 089 527 5083; Rynek 9/10; mains 7-24zł; ☯ 8.30am-10pm) This small place is renowned among locals for its tasty Polish food, such as *pierogi*. It also does a good line in soups.

Restauracja Hammurabi (☎ 089 534 9467; ul Prosta 3/4; mains 10-32zł; ☯ 11am-11pm Fri & Sat, 11am-9pm Sun-Thu) The Hammurabi offers some inexpensive Middle Eastern choices in a cheerful Arabian setting, along with pizzas and steaks.

Restauracja Staromiejska (☎ 089 527 5883; ul Stare Miasto 4/6; mains 18-32zł; ☯ 10am-10pm) In classy premises on the Rynek, this restaurant serves quality Polish standards at reasonable prices. There's a range of *pierogi* and *naleśniki* on the menu.

Getting There & Away

From the **bus terminal** (ul Partyzantów), useful buses travel to Białystok (44zł, five hours, five daily) and Warsaw (30zł, five hours, 11 daily).

Trains depart from the **Olsztyn Główny train station** (ul Partyzantów) to Kętrzyn (20zł, 1½ hours, eight daily), Białystok (45zł, 4½ hours, three daily), Warsaw (41zł, four hours, seven daily), Gdańsk (34zł, three hours, seven daily) and Toruń (34zł, 2½ hours, seven daily). **Orbis Travel** (☎ 089 522 0613; Al Piłsudskiego) sells advance train tickets.

GREAT MASURIAN LAKES

The Great Masurian Lakes district east of Olsztyn has more than 2000 lakes, which are remnants of long-vanished glaciers, and surrounded by green hilly landscape. The largest lake is Lake Śniardwy (110 sq km). About 200km of canals connect these bodies of water, so the area is a prime destination for yachties and canoeists, as well as those who love to hike, fish and mountain-bike.

The detailed *Wielkie Jeziora Mazurskie* map (1:100,000) is essential for anyone exploring the region by water or hiking trails. The *Warmia i Mazury* map (1:300,000), available at regional tourist offices, is perfect for more general use.

ACTIVITIES

The larger lakes can be sailed from Węgorzewo to Ruciane-Nida, while canoeists might prefer the more intimate surroundings of rivers and smaller lakes. The most popular kayak route takes 10 days (106km) and follows rivers, canals and lakes from Sorkwity to Ruciane-Nida. Brochures explaining this route are available at regional tourist offices. There's also an extensive network of **hiking** and **mountain-biking** trails around the lakes.

Most travellers prefer to enjoy the lakes in comfort on **excursion boats**. Boats run daily (May to September) between Giżycko and Ruciane-Nida, via Mikołajki; and daily (June

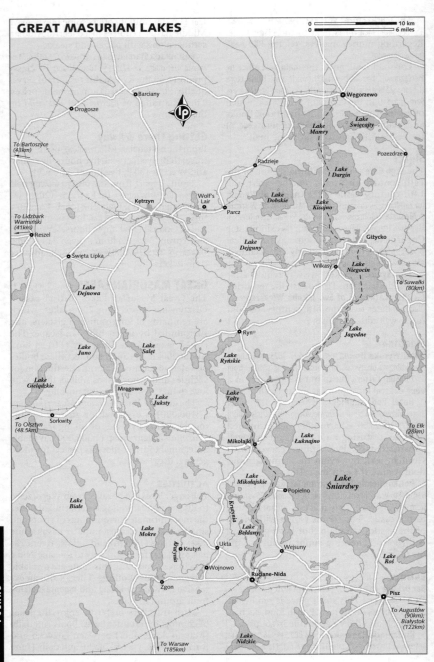

GREAT MASURIAN LAKES

0 — 10 km
0 — 6 miles

Barciany

Drogosze

Węgorzewo

Lake Mamry

Lake Święcajty

To Bartoszyce (43km)

Radzieje

Pozezdrze

Lake Dargin

Wolf's Lair

Kętrzyn

Parcz

Lake Dobskie

Lake Kisajno

To Lidzbark Warmiński (41km)

Giżycko

Reszel

Lake Dejguny

Wilkasy

Lake Niegocin

Święta Lipka

To Suwałki (80km)

Lake Dejnowa

Ryn

Lake Jagodne

Lake Juno

Lake Sałęt

Lake Ryńskie

Lake Gielądzkie

Mrągowo

Lake Juksty

Lake Tałty

To Olsztyn (48.5km)

Sorkwity

Mikołajki

Lake Łuknajno

To Ełk (28km)

Lake Śniardwy

Lake Mikołajskie

Popielno

Lake Białe

Krutynia

Lake Mokre

Lake Bełdany

Krutyń

Ukta

Wejsuny

Lake Roś

Wojnowo

Ruciane-Nida

Pisz

Zgon

To Augustów (90km); Białystok (122km)

Lake Nidzkie

To Warsaw (185km)

to August) between Węgorzewo and Ruciane-Nida, via Giżycko and Mikołajki. However, services are more reliable from late June to late August. Schedules and fares are posted at the lake ports.

Święta Lipka

This village boasts a superb 17th-century **church** (☼ 7am-7pm), one of the purest examples of late-baroque architecture in Poland. Its lavishly decorated organ features angels adorning the 5000 pipes, and they dance to the organ's music. This mechanism is demonstrated several times daily from May to September, and recitals are held Friday nights from June to August.

Ask any of the regional tourist offices for a list of homes in Święta Lipka offering private rooms. There are several eateries and places to drink near the church.

Buses run to Kętrzyn every hour or so, but less often to Olsztyn.

Wolf's Lair

An eerie attraction at Gierłoż, 8km east of Kętrzyn, is the **Wolf's Lair** (Wilczy Szaniec; ☎ 089 752 4429; www.wolfsschanze.home.pl; adult/concession 10/5zł; ☼ 8am-dusk). This was Hitler's wartime headquarters for his invasion of the Soviet Union, and his main residence from 1941 to 1944.

In 1944 a group of high-ranking German officers tried to assassinate Hitler here. The leader of the plot, Claus von Stauffenberg, arrived from Berlin on 20 July for a regular military staff meeting. A frequent guest, he entered the meeting with a bomb in his briefcase. He placed it near Hitler and left to take a prearranged phone call, but the briefcase was then unwittingly moved by another officer. Though the explosion killed and wounded several people, Hitler suffered only minor injuries. Von Stauffenberg and some 5000 people allegedly involved in the plot were subsequently executed.

On 24 January 1945, as the Red Army approached, the Germans blew up Wolfsschanze (as it was known in German), and most bunkers were at least partly destroyed. However, huge concrete slabs – some 8.5m thick – and twisted metal remain. The ruins are at their most atmospheric in winter, with fewer visitors and a thick layer of snow.

A large map is posted at the entrance, with features of interest clearly labelled in English (Hitler's personal bunker, perhaps aptly, is unlucky number 13). Booklets outlining a self-

guided walking tour are available in English and German at the kiosk in the car park. The services of English- and German-speaking guides are also available for 50zł.

Hotel Wilcze Gniazdo (☎ 089 752 4429; kontakt@wolfsschanze.pl; s/d/tr 70/80/130zł), situated in original buildings within the complex, is fairly basic but adequate for one night. A restaurant is attached.

Catch one of several daily PKS buses (3.50zł, 15 minutes) from Kętrzyn to Węgorzewo (via Radzieje, not Srokowo) and get off at the entrance. Between 10am and 4pm in July and August, a special bus marked *zielona linia* (green line) also runs from the train station in Kętrzyn to Wolf's Lair (Wilczy Szaniec; 3.50zł, 25 minutes, five daily). Contact the Kętrzyn **tourist office** (☎ 089 751 4765; Plac Piłsudskiego 1; ☼ 8.30am-3pm Mon-Fri) for updated transport details.

Giżycko
pop 29,600

Giżycko (ghee-*zhits*-ko) is the largest lakeside centre in the region, set on the northern shore of Lake Niegocin. A notable historic site is the 19th-century **Boyen Fortress** (ul Turystyczna 1; adult/concession 6/3zł; ☼ 9am-5pm), built by the Prussians to defend the border with Russia.

Near the main square (Plac Grunwaldzki) is the very helpful **tourist office** (☎ 087 428 5265; www.gizycko.turystyka.pl; ul Wyzwolenia 2; ☼ 9am-6pm Mon-Fri, 10am-4pm Sat & Sun Jul-Aug, 8am-5pm Mon-Fri, 10am-2pm Sat May & Jun & Sep, 9am-5pm Mon-Fri Oct-Apr) and **Bank Pekao** (ul Olsztyńska 15a). There are some *kantors* in the town centre, including one at **Orbis Travel** (☎ 087 428 3598; ul Dąbrowskiego 3), about 250m east of the main square.

Sailing boats are available from **Almatur** (☎ 087 428 5971; ul Moniuszki 24), 700m west of the fortress, and at **Centrum Mazur** (☎ 087 428 3871; ul Moniuszki 1) at Camping Nr 1 Zamek.

Wama Tour (☎ 087 429 3079; ul Konarskiego 1) rents out bicycles (30zł per day), and Hotel Zamek has kayaks (8zł per hour). **Żegluga Mazurska** (☎ 087 428 2578; ul Kolejowa 8) operates excursion boats, and you can arrange car rental through **Fiat Autoserwis** (☎ 087 428 5986; ul 1 Maja 21).

SLEEPING & EATING

Hotel Zamek (☎ 087 428 2419; www.cmazur.pl; camping per person 7.50zł; dm 25zł; r from 160zł; ☼ May-Sep) This combined hotel and camping ground provides a decent standard of accommodation for the price, and hires out bikes for 10zł per hour.

Boyen Fortress Youth Hostel (☎ 087 428 2959; www
.festeboyen.pl; dm 16-20zł) Has a character-packed
location within the battlements, and offers the
usual basic but clean facilities.

our pick **Hotel Cesarski** (☎ 087 428 1514; www
.cesarski.pl; Plac Grunwalszki 8; s/d/ste 160/250/350zł)
Formerly the German Kaiserhof, this newly
renovated hotel is great value for its quality
and central location.

Kuchnie Świata (☎ 087 429 2255; Plac Grunwaldzki 1;
mains 9-39zł; ❍ 11am-11pm) A good dining choice
is this cheery red-and-orange space serving
up an eclectic range of dishes including pizza
and pasta, along with *placki ziemniaczane* and
other Polish favourites.

GETTING THERE & AWAY
From the train station, on the southern edge
of town near the lake, trains run to Kętrzyn
(8zł, 40 minutes, 11 daily), Olsztyn (28zł,
two hours, eight daily) and Gdańsk (48zł, 4½
hours, four daily).

From the adjacent bus terminal, buses
travel regularly to Mikołajki (10zł, one hour,
hourly) and Olsztyn (20zł, three hours, at least
hourly). Buses head to Warsaw every hour or
two (39zł, five hours).

Mikołajki
pop 3800
Mikołajki (Mee-ko-*wahy*-kee), 86km east
of Olsztyn, is a great base for exploring the
lakes, and it's a picturesque little village in
its own right. The **tourist office** (☎ 087 421 5507;
www.mikolajki.pl; Plac Wolności 3; ❍ 9am-8pm Jul & Aug,
9am-5pm Tue-Sun May & Jun, Sep & Oct) is in the town
centre. Nearby are *kantors* and ATMs.

Sailing boats and kayaks can be hired
from **Cicha Zatoka** (☎ 087 421 5011; Al Spacerowa 1)
at the waterfront on the other side of the
bridge from the town centre, and also from
the appropriately named **Fun** (☎ 087 421 6277;
ul Kajki 82).

Lake Śniardwy and **Lake Łuknajno** are ideal
for cycling. The tourist office can provide details and maps, and bikes can be rented from
Pensionjat Mikołajki (30zł per day).

SLEEPING & EATING
You'll find pensions and homes offering private rooms dotted along ul Kajki, the main
street leading around Lake Mikołajskie;
more pensions can be found along the
roads to Ruciane-Nida and Ełk. There are
plenty of eateries situated along the water-

front and around the town square to cater
for high-season visitors.

Camping Nr 2 Wagabunda (☎ 087 421 6018; www
.wagabunda-mikolajki.pl; ul Leśna 2; per person/tent 13/13zł,
cabins d/tr/q from 100/130/150zł; ❍ May-Oct) Across
the bridge, this camping ground is 1km
southwest of the town centre.

Pensjonat Mikołajki (☎ 087 421 6437; www.pens
jonatmikolajki.prv.pl; ul Kajki 18; s/d/ste from 120/180/360zł)
An attractive place to stay, with timber
panelling and a prime lakefront location.
Some rooms have balconies overlooking
the water.

Pizzeria Królewska (☎ 087 421 6323; ul Kajki 5;
mains 10-25zł; ❍ noon-10pm) A reasonable pizza
restaurant open year-round, in cos cellar
premises.

GETTING THERE & AWAY
From the bus terminal, next to the bridge
at Plac Kościelny, up to seven buses go to
Olsztyn (15zł, two hours) each day. Otherwise,
get a bus (7zł, 40 minutes, hourly) to
Mrągowo and change there for Olsztyn. Buses
also go hourly to Giżycko (10zł, one hour),
and four daily to Warsaw (38zł, 4½ hours). A
private company, **Agawa** (☎ 0698 256 928) runs an
express service daily to Warsaw year-round,
departing from the bus terminal.

From the dozy train station, two slow
trains shuttle along daily to Olsztyn (14zł,
two hours), and two to Ełk (11zł, 1½ hours).
In quiet times, the ticket office only opens
30 minutes (or less) before departures.

POLAND DIRECTORY

ACCOMMODATION
In this chapter, budget accommodation is
defined as any place offering dorm beds, or
hotels with double rooms costing up to 150zł
per night. Midrange denotes accommodation
offering doubles for between 150zł and 400zł
per night; top-end is anything above that.
All prices quoted are high season rates.

Unless otherwise noted, rooms have private
bathrooms. Nearly every accommodation in
every budget level offers internet access of
some sort, even if it's just the computer in reception when the receptionist isn't too busy.
Though there have been (so far unsuccessful)
proposals to ban smoking from public spaces,
it is becoming more common for hotels to
offer nonsmoking options.

Camping

Poland has hundreds of camping grounds, and many offer good-value cabins and bungalows. Most open May to September, but some only open their gates between June and August.

Hostels

Schroniska młodzieżowe (youth hostels) in Poland are operated by Polskie Towarzystwo Schronisk Młodzieżowych (PTSM), a member of Hostelling International. Most only open in July and August, and are often very busy with Polish students; the year-round hostels have more facilities. Youth hostels are open to all, with no age limit. Curfews are common, and many hostels close between 10am and 5pm.

A growing number of privately-operated hostels operate in the main cities, and are geared towards international backpackers. They're open 24 hours and offer more modern facilities than the old youth hostels, though prices are higher. These hostels usually offer free use of washing machines, in response to the near-absence of laundromats in Poland.

A dorm bed can cost anything from 15zł to 75zł per person per night. Single/double rooms, if available, cost from about 80/100zł.

Hotels

Hotel prices often vary according to season, and are posted at hotel reception desks. Top-end hotels sometimes quote prices in euros, and discounted weekend rates are often available. Rooms with a private bathroom can be considerably more expensive than those with shared facilities. Most hotels offer 24-hour reception.

If possible, check the room before accepting. Don't be fooled by hotel reception areas, which may look great in contrast to the rest of the establishment. On the other hand, dreary scuffed corridors can sometimes open into clean, pleasant rooms.

Accommodation (sometimes with substantial discounts) can be reliably arranged via the internet through www.poland4u.com and www.hotels poland.com.

Mountain Refuges

PTTK runs a chain of *schroniska górskie* (mountain refuges) for hikers. They're usually simple, with a welcoming atmosphere, and serve cheap, hot meals. The more isolated refuges are obliged to accept everyone, so can be crowded in the high season. Refuges are normally open all year, but confirm with the nearest PTTK office before setting off.

Private Rooms & Apartments

Some destinations have agencies (usually called *biuro zakwaterowania* or *biuro kwater prywatnych*), which arrange accommodation in private homes. Rooms cost about 80/110zł per single/double. The most important factor to consider is location; if the home is in the suburbs, find out how far it is from reliable public transport.

During the high season, home owners also directly approach tourists. Prices are open to bargaining, but you're more likely to be offered somewhere out in the sticks. Also, private homes in smaller resorts and villages often have signs outside their gates or doors offering a *pokoje* (room) or *noclegi* (lodging).

In Warsaw, Kraków, Wrocław and Gdańsk, some agencies offer self-contained apartments, which are often an affordable alternative to hotels.

ACTIVITIES

Hikers and long-distance trekkers can enjoy marked trails across the Tatra Mountains (p629), where one of the most popular climbs is up the steep slopes of Mt Giewont (1894m). The Sudeten Mountains (p637) and the Great Masurian Lakes district (p659) also offer good walking opportunities. National parks worth hiking through include Białowieża National Park (p607), Kampinos National Park just outside Warsaw, Wielkopolska National Park outside Poznań, and the compact Wolin National Park east of Świnoujście. Trails are easy to follow and detailed maps are available at most larger bookshops.

As Poland is fairly flat, it's ideal for cyclists. Bicycle routes along the banks of the Vistula River are popular in Warsaw, Toruń and Kraków. Many of the national parks – including Wolin, Tatra (near Zakopane) and Słowinski (near Łeba) – offer bicycle trails, as does the Great Masurian Lakes district. For more of a challenge, try cycling in the Bieszczady ranges around Sanok (p631). Bikes can be rented at most resort towns and larger cities.

Zakopane (p630) will delight skiers from December to March, and facilities are cheaper than the ski resorts of Western Europe. Other sports on offer here include hang-gliding and paragliding. Another place to hit the snow is Szklarska Poręba (p637) in Silesia.

POLAND

Throngs of yachties, canoeists and kayakers enjoy the network of waterways in the Great Masurian Lakes district (p659) every summer; boats are available for rent from all lakeside towns, and there are even diving excursions. Windsurfers can head to the beaches of the Hel Peninsula (p651).

BOOKS

God's Playground: A History of Poland, by Norman Davies, offers an in-depth analysis of Polish history. The condensed version, *The Heart of Europe: A Short History of Poland*, also by Davies, has greater emphasis on the 20th century. *The Polish Way: A Thousand-Year History of the Poles and their Culture*, by Adam Zamoyski, is a superb cultural overview. The wartime Warsaw Rising is vividly brought to life in Norman Davies' *Rising '44*, and *The Polish Revolution: Solidarity 1980-82*, by Timothy Garton Ash, is entertaining and thorough. *Jews in Poland* by Iwo Cyprian Pogonowski provides a comprehensive record of half a millennium of Jewish life. Evocative works about rural life in interwar Poland include Bruno Schultz's *Street of Crocodiles* and Philip Marsden's *The Bronski House*.

BUSINESS HOURS

Most shops are open from 10am to 6pm Monday to Friday, and until 2pm on Saturday. Supermarkets and larger stores often have longer opening hours. Banks in larger cities are open from about 8am to 5pm weekdays (sometimes until 2pm on Saturday), but have shorter hours in smaller towns. *Kantors* generally follow shop hours.

Most restaurants, cafes and cafe-bars are open from 11am to 11pm. Nightclubs are often open from 9pm to the wee small hours of the next day.

DANGERS & ANNOYANCES

Poland is a relatively safe country, and crime has decreased significantly in recent years. Be alert, however, for thieves and pickpockets around major train stations, such as Warszawa Centralna. Robberies have been a problem on night trains, especially on international routes. Try to share a compartment with other people if possible.

Theft from cars is a widespread problem, so keep your vehicle in a guarded car park whenever possible. Heavy drinking is com-

mon and drunks can be disturbing, though rarely dangerous.

As Poland is an ethnically homogeneous nation, travellers who look racially different may attract curious stares from locals in outlying regions. Football (soccer) hooligans are not uncommon, so avoid travelling on public transport with them (especially if their team has lost!).

EMBASSIES & CONSULATES

All diplomatic missions listed are in Warsaw unless stated otherwise.

Australia (Map p598; ☎ 022 521 3444; www.australia .pl; ul Nowogrodzka 11)

Belarus (Map p595; ☎ 022 742 0990; www.belembassy .org/poland; ul Wiertnicza 58)

Canada (Map p598; ☎ 022 584 3100; www.canada.pl; ul Matejki 1/5)

Czech Republic (Map p598; ☎ 022 525 1850; www .mzv.cz/warsaw; ul Koszykowa 18)

France (Map p595; ☎ 022 529 3000; www.ambafrance -pl.org; ul Puławska 17); Kraków (Map p610; ☎ 012 424 5300; ul Stolarska 15)

Germany (Map p595; ☎ 022 584 1700; www.amba sadaniemiec.pl; ul Jazdów 12); Kraków (Map p610; ☎ 012 424 3000; ul Stolarska 7)

Ireland (Map p598; ☎ 022 849 6633; www.irlandia.pl; ul Mysia 5)

Japan (Map p595; ☎ 022 696 5000; www.pl.emb-japan .go.jp; ul Szwoleżerów 8)

Lithuania (Map p595; ☎ 022 625 3368; www.lietuva.pl; ul Ujazdowskie 14)

Netherlands (Map p595; ☎ 022 559 1200; www.nl embassy.pl; ul Kawalerii 10)

New Zealand (Map p598; ☎ 022 521 0500; www .nzembassy.com; Al Ujazdowskie 51)

Russia (Map p595; ☎ 022 621 3453; http://warsaw .rusembassy.org; ul Belwederska 49)

Slovakia (Map p595; ☎ 022 528 8110; emb.warsaw@ mzv.sk; ul Litewska 6)

South Africa (Map p598; ☎ 022 625 6228; warsaw .consular@foreign.gov.za; ul Koszykowa 54)

Ukraine (Map p595; ☎ 022 622 4797; www.ukraine -emb.pl; Al Szucha 7)

UK (Map p598; ☎ 022 311 0000; www.britishembassy .pl; Al Róż 1); Kraków (Map p610; ☎ 012 421 7030; ul Św. Anny 9)

USA (Map p598; ☎ 022 504 2000; http://poland.us embassy.gov; Al Ujazdowskie 29/31); Kraków (Map p610; ☎ 012 424 5100; ul Stolarska 9)

GAY & LESBIAN TRAVELLERS

Since the change of government in 2007, overt homophobia from state officials has declined;

though with the Church remaining influential in social matters, gay acceptance in Poland is still a work in progress. The gay community is becoming more visible, however, and in 2010 Warsaw is hosting **EuroPride** (www.europride .com), the first time this major gay festival has been held in a former communist country.

In general though, the Polish gay and lesbian scene remains fairly discreet. Warsaw and Kraków are the best places to find gay-friendly bars, clubs and accommodation. The free tourist brochure, the *Visitor,* lists a few gay nightspots, as do the **In Your Pocket** (www.inyourpocket.com) guides.

The best sources of information on gay Warsaw and Kraków are online at www .gayguide.net and www.gaypoland.pl. **Lambda** (☎ 022 628 5222; www.lambda.org.pl) is a national gay rights and information service.

HOLIDAYS
Poland's official public holidays:

New Year's Day 1 January
Easter Sunday March or April
Easter Monday March or April
State Holiday 1 May
Constitution Day 3 May
Pentecost Sunday Seventh Sunday after Easter
Corpus Christi Ninth Thursday after Easter
Assumption Day 15 August
All Saints' Day 1 November
Independence Day 11 November
Christmas 25 and 26 December

INTERNET ACCESS
Internet access is near-universal in Polish accommodation, from hostels through to every class of hotel: either as wireless access, via on-site computers, or both. As a result, individual accommodation with internet access has not been denoted as such in this chapter.

In the unlikely event that your lodgings are offline, you'll likely find an internet cafe nearby; expect to pay between 3zł and 5zł per hour. Also, some forward-thinking city councils have set up wireless access in their main market squares (eg Warsaw's Rynek Starego Miasta).

INTERNET RESOURCES
Commonwealth of Diverse Cultures (www.common wealth.pl) Outlines Poland's cultural heritage.
Poland.pl (www.poland.pl) News and a website directory.
Poland Tourism Portal (www.poland.travel) Useful travel site.

Polska (www.poland.gov.pl) Comprehensive government portal.
VirtualTourist.com (www.virtualtourist.com) Poland section features postings by travellers.
Visit.pl (www.visit.pl) Accommodation booking service.

MEDIA
The glossy, English-language *Poland Monthly* and the *Warsaw Business Journal* are aimed at the business community, while *Warsaw Insider* has more general-interest features, listings and reviews.

The free *Welcome to…* series of magazines covers Poznań, Kraków, Zakopane and Warsaw monthly. The free magazine *Poland: What, Where, When* covers Warsaw, Kraków and Gdańsk.

Recent newspapers and magazines from Western Europe and the USA are readily available at EMPiK bookshops, which are *everywhere,* and at news-stands in the foyers of upmarket hotels.

Poland has a mix of privately-owned TV channels, and state-owned nationwide channels. Foreign-language programs are painfully dubbed with one male voice covering all actors (that's men, women and children) and no lip-sync, so you can still hear the original language underneath. Most hotels offer English-language news channels.

Cinemas are present in all city centres, including modern multiplexes. English-language films are usually subtitled rather than dubbed into Polish, with the exception of children's movies.

MONEY
The Polish currency is the złoty (*zwo*-ti), abbreviated to zł. (The currency is also sometimes referred to by its international currency code, PLN). It's divided into 100 groszy (gr). Denominations of notes are 10, 20, 50, 100 and 200 złoty (rare), and coins come in one, two, five, 10, 20 and 50 groszy, and one, two and five złoty.

Bankomats (ATMs) accept most international credit cards and are easily found in the centre of all cities and most towns. Banks without an ATM may provide cash advances over the counter on credit cards.

Private *kantors* (foreign-exchange offices) are everywhere. *Kantors* require no paperwork and charge no commission. Rates at *kantors* in the midst of major tourist attractions, in top-end hotels and at airports are generally poor.

The most widely accepted currencies are the euro, the US dollar and the pound sterling (in that order), though most *kantors* will change a range of other currencies. Foreign banknotes should be in good condition or *kantors* may refuse to accept them.

Travellers cheques are more secure than cash, but *kantors* rarely change them, and banks that do will charge 2% to 3% commission. A better option is a stored value cash card, which can be used in the same manner as a credit card; ask your bank about this before leaving home.

POST

Postal services are operated by Poczta Polska. Most cities have a dozen or more post offices, of which the Poczta Główna (main post office) has the widest range of services.

Letters and postcards sent by air from Poland take a few days to reach a European destination and a week or so to anywhere else. The cost of sending a normal-sized letter (up to 20g) or a postcard to other European countries is 3zł, rising to 3.50zł for North America and 4.50zł for Australia.

TELEPHONE

At the time of writing, landlines had 10 digits, incorporating the former three-digit area codes; however, the initial '0' will be phased out during the life of this book. To call Poland from abroad, dial the country code ☎ 48, then the last nine digits of the Polish number, dropping the initial '0'. The international access code from Poland is ☎ 00. For help, try the operators for local numbers (☎ 913), national numbers and codes (☎ 912) and international codes (☎ 908), but don't expect anyone to speak English.

The three mobile telephone providers are Orange, Era and Plus GSM. Prepaid accounts are cheap by Western European standards, and are quick and easy to set up at local offices of these companies. Reception is generally good and covers the whole country. Mobile numbers are often quoted as nine digits, but require an initial zero to be dialled from landline phones.

EMERGENCY NUMBERS

- Ambulance ☎ 999
- Fire ☎ 998
- Police ☎ 997
- Police (from mobile phones) ☎ 112

Most public telephones use magnetic phonecards, available at post offices and kiosks in units of 15 (9zł), 30 (15zł) and 60 (24zł) – one unit represents one three-minute local call. The cards can be used for domestic and international calls.

TRAVELLERS WITH DISABILITIES

Poland is not well set-up for people with disabilities, although there have been significant improvements over recent years. Wheelchair ramps are only available at some upmarket hotels, and public transport will be a real challenge for anyone with mobility problems. However, many top-end hotels now have at least one room specially designed for disabled access – book ahead for these. There are also some low-floor trams now running on the Warsaw and Kraków public transport networks. Information on disability issues is available from **Integracja** (☎ 022 635 1330; www.integr acja.org).

VISAS

EU citizens do not need visas to visit Poland and can stay indefinitely. Citizens of Australia, Canada, Israel, New Zealand, Switzerland and the USA can stay in Poland up to 90 days without a visa.

However, since Poland's entry into the Schengen zone in December 2007, the 90 day visa-free entry period has been extended to all the Schengen countries; so if travelling from Poland through Germany and France, for example, you can't exceed 90 days in total. Once your 90 days is up, you must leave the Schengen zone for a minimum 90 days before you can once again enter it visa-free.

South African citizens do require a visa. Other nationals should check with Polish embassies or consulates in their countries for current visa requirements. Updates can be found at the website of the Ministry of Foreign Affairs, www.msz .gov.pl.

TRANSPORT IN POLAND

GETTING THERE & AWAY
Air

The majority of international flights to Poland arrive at Warsaw's Okęcie airport, while other important airports include Kraków Balice, Gdańsk, Poznań and Wrocław. The national carrier **LOT** (LO; www.lot.com; ☎ from mobiles 0801 703 703, 22 9572) flies to all major European cities.

Other major airlines flying to Poland:

Aeroflot (SU; ☎ 022 621 1611; www.aeroflot.com)
Air France (AF; ☎ 022 556 6400; www.airfrance.com)
Alitalia (AZ; ☎ 0801 107 700; www.alitalia.it)
British Airways (BA; ☎ 00 800 441 1592; www.ba.com)
Centralwings (C0; ☎ 022 420 5775; www.central wings.com)
easyJet (U2; ☎ 0044 870 6 000 000; www.easyjet.com)
KLM (KL; ☎ 022 556 6444; www.klm.pl)
Lufthansa (LH; ☎ 022 338 1300; www.lufthansa.pl)
Malév (MA; ☎ 022 697 7472; www.malev.hu)
Ryanair (FR; ☎ 0300 703 007; www.ryanair.com)
SAS (SK; ☎ 022 850 0500; www.flysas.com)
SkyEurope (NE; ☎ 00 421 2 3301 7301; www.sky europe.com)
Wizz Air (W6; ☎ 0300 503 010; www.wizzair.com)

Land

Since Poland is now within the Schengen zone, there are no border posts or border crossing formalities between Poland and Germany, the Czech Republic, Slovakia and Lithuania. Below is a list of major road border-crossings with Poland's non-Schengen neighbours that accept foreigners and are open 24 hours.

Belarus (South to north) Terespol, Kuźnica Białostocka.
Russia (West to east) Gronowo, Bezledy.
Ukraine (South to north) Medyka, Hrebenne, Dorohusk.

If you're heading to Russia or Lithuania and your train/bus passes through Belarus, be aware that you need a Belarusian transit visa and you must obtain it in advance; see p96 for details.

BUS

International bus services are offered by dozens of Polish and international companies. They're cheaper than trains, but not as comfortable or fast.

One of the major operators is **Eurolines Polska** (☎ 032 351 2020; www.eurolinespolska.pl), which operates to a range of European destinations, including eastern cities such as Minsk, Brest, Vilnius, Tallinn and Riga.

CAR & MOTORCYCLE

To drive a car into Poland, EU citizens need their driving licence from home, while other nationalities must obtain an International Drivers Permit in their home country. Also required are vehicle registration papers and liability insurance (Green Card). If your insurance is not valid for Poland you must buy an additional policy at the border.

TRAIN

Trains link Poland with every neighbouring country and beyond, but international train travel is not cheap. To save money on fares, investigate special train tickets and rail passes (see p984). Domestic trains in Poland are significantly cheaper, so you'll save money if you buy a ticket to a Polish border destination, then take a local train.

Do note that some international trains to/from Poland have become notorious for theft. Keep a grip on your bags, particularly on the Berlin–Warsaw, Prague–Warsaw and Prague–Kraków overnight trains, and on *any* train travelling to/from Gdańsk.

Sea

For ferry services from Gdańsk and Gdynia see p648 and p650, respectively. There are also car and passenger ferries from the Polish town of Świnoujście, operated by the following companies:

Polferries (www.polferries.pl) Offers daily services from Świnoujście to Ystad (eight hours) in Sweden, every Saturday to Rønne (5¼ hours) in Denmark, and five days a week to Copenhagen (nine to 10½ hours).
Unity Line (www.unityline.pl) Runs ferries between Świnoujście and Ystad (6¾ hours).

Any travel agency in Scandinavia will sell tickets for these services. In Poland, ask at any Orbis Travel office. In summer, passenger boats ply the Baltic coast from Świnoujście to Ahlbeck, Heringsdorf, Bansin and Zinnowitz in Germany.

GETTING AROUND
Air

LOT (☎ 0801 703 703, from mobiles 22 9572; www.lot .com) flies several times a day from Warsaw to Gdańsk, Kraków, Poznań, Szczecin and Wrocław. Another Polish airline, **Jet Air** (☎ 022 846 8661; www.jetair.pl) serves Warsaw, Łódź, Kraków, Poznań and Zielona Góra from its hub in Bydgoszcz.

Bicycle

Cycling is not great for getting around cities, but is often a good way to travel between villages. Major roads are busy but generally flat, while minor roads can be bumpy. If you get tired, it's easy to place your bike in the special luggage compartment of a train. These compartments are at the front or rear of slow passenger trains, but rarely found on fast

POLAND

or express trains, and never on InterCity or EuroCity services. You'll need a special ticket for your bike from the railway luggage office.

Bus

Buses can be useful on short routes and through the mountains in southern Poland; but usually trains are quicker and more comfortable, and private minibuses are quicker and more direct.

Most buses are operated by the state bus company, PKS. It provides two kinds of service from its bus terminals (dworzec autobusowy PKS): ordinary buses (marked in black on timetables), and fast buses (marked in red), which ignore minor stops.

Timetables are posted on boards inside or outside PKS bus terminals. Additional symbols next to departure times may indicate the bus runs only on certain days or in certain seasons. Terminals usually have an information desk, but it's rarely staffed with English speakers. Tickets for PKS buses are usually bought at the terminal, but sometimes from drivers. Note that the quoted bus frequencies in this chapter are as per the summer schedule.

The largest private bus operator is **Polski Express** (www.polskiexpress.net), which operates long-distance routes to/from Warsaw (p605). Polski Express buses normally arrive and depart from PKS bus terminals – exceptions are mentioned in the relevant destination sections.

The price of bus tickets is determined by the length, in kilometres, of the trip. Prices start at roughly 3zł for a journey of up to 5km. Minibuses charge set prices for journeys, and these are normally posted in their windows or at the bus stop.

Car & Motorcycle
FUEL & SPARE PARTS

Petrol stations sell several kinds of petrol, including 94-octane leaded, 95-octane unleaded, 98-octane unleaded and diesel. Most petrol stations are open from 6am to 10pm (from 7am to 3pm Sunday), though some operate around the clock. Garages are plentiful. Roadside assistance can be summoned by dialling ☎ 981 or 022 9637.

HIRE

Major international car-rental companies, such as **Avis** (www.avis.pl), **Hertz** (www.hertz.pl) and **Europcar** (www.europcar.com.pl), are represented in larger cities and have smaller offices at airports. Rates are comparable to full-price rental in Western Europe.

Some companies offer one-way rentals, but no agency will allow you to drive their precious vehicle into Russia, Ukraine or Belarus.

Rental agencies will need to see your passport, your local driving licence (which must be held for at least one year) and a credit card (for the deposit). You need to be at least 21 or 23 years of age to rent a car; sometimes 25 for a more expensive car.

It's usually cheaper to prebook a car in Poland from abroad, rather than to front up at an agency inside the country.

ROAD RULES

The speed limit is 130km/h on motorways, 100km/h on two- or four-lane highways, 90km/h on other open roads and 50km/h in built-up areas. If the background of the sign bearing the town's name is white you must reduce speed to 50km/h; if the background is green there's no need to reduce speed (unless road signs indicate otherwise). Radar-equipped police are very active, especially in villages with white signs.

Unless signs state otherwise, cars may park on pavements as long as a minimum 1.5m-wide walkway is left for pedestrians. Parking in the opposite direction to traffic flow is allowed. The permitted blood alcohol level is a low 0.02%, so it's best not to drink if you're driving. Seat belts are compulsory, as are helmets for motorcyclists. All drivers must use headlights during the day (and night!).

Train

Trains will be your main means of transport. They're cheap, reliable and rarely overcrowded (except for July and August peak times). **Polish State Railways** (PKP; www.pkp.pl) operates trains to almost every place listed in this chapter.

InterCity trains operate on major routes out of Warsaw, including Gdańsk, Kraków, Poznań, Wrocław and Szczecin. They only stop at major cities and are the fastest way to travel by rail. These trains require seat reservations.

Down the pecking order but still quick are pociąg ekspresowy (express trains) and the similar but cheaper pociąg TLK (TLK trains). Pociąg pospieszny (fast trains) are a bit slower and more crowded, but will most likely be the type of train you most often catch. *Pociąg osobowy* (slow passenger trains) stop at every tree at the side of the track and should be used only for short trips. Express and fast trains do not normally require seat reservations except at peak times; seats on slow trains cannot be reserved.

Almost all trains carry two classes: *druga klasa* (2nd class) and *pierwsza klasa* (1st class), which is 50% more expensive. The carriages on long-distance trains are usually divided into compartments: 1st-class compartments have six seats; 2nd-class ones contain eight seats.

Note that the quoted train fares in this chapter are for a second class ticket on a *pospieszny* train, or the most likely alternative if the route is mainly served by a different type of train. Frequencies are as per the summer schedule.

In a couchette on an overnight train, compartments have four/six beds in 1st/2nd class. Sleepers have two/three people (1st/2nd class) in a compartment fitted with a washbasin, sheets and blankets. Most 2nd-class and all 1st-class carriages have nonsmoking compartments.

Train *odjazdy* (departures) are listed on a yellow board and *przyjazdy* (arrivals) on a white board. Ordinary trains are marked in black print, fast trains in red. An additional 'Ex' indicates an express train, and InterCity trains are identified by the letters 'IC'. The letter 'R' in a square indicates the train has compulsory seat reservation. The timetables also show which *peron* (platform) it's using. Be aware that the number applies to *both* sides of the platform. If in doubt, check the platform departure board or route cards on the side of carriages, or ask a fellow passenger.

Be aware that signage is very poor at Polish train stations – there's often only one sign in the middle of the platform, making it hard to spot if you're at the rear of the train as it pulls in. If in doubt about your location, ask a fellow passenger.

Timetable and fare information in English is on the PKP website. *Miejsca sypialne* (sleepers) and *kuszetki* (couchettes) can be booked at special counters in larger train stations or from Orbis; pre-booking is recommended.

If a seat reservation is compulsory on your train, you will automatically be sold a *miejscówka* (reserved) seat ticket. If you do not make a seat reservation, you can travel on *any* train (of the type requested, ie slow, fast or express) to the destination indicated on your ticket on the date specified.

Your ticket will list the *klasa* (class); the *poc* (type) of train; where the train is travelling *od* (from) and *do* (to); the major town or junction the train is travelling *prez* (through); and the total *cena* (price). If more than one place is listed under the heading *prez* (via), find out from the conductor *early* if you have to change trains at the junction listed or be in a specific carriage (the train may separate later).

If you get on a train without a ticket, you can buy one directly from the conductor for a small supplement (8zł) – but do it right away. If the conductor finds you first, you'll be fined for travelling without a ticket. You can always upgrade from 2nd to 1st class for a small extra fee (about 8zł), plus the additional fare.

Romania

After decades – centuries in some cases – of an unseen hand leaning on Romania's 'pause' button, breathtaking change and development are under way. Formerly the 'Wild West of Eastern Europe', Romania has found EU membership ushering in the good (repaired roads, reliable utilities, economic reform), the bad (stupefying inflation, bans on horse carts, rules, rules, rules) and the ugly (when will giant bug-eye sunglasses go out of style?).

Leave the big cities, however, and you'll hardly notice the transformation. Predominantly rural Romania has a singular beauty, beguiling simplicity and fascinating history that remain untouched. Aesthetically stirring hand-ploughed fields, sheep stampedes straight down countryside roads, and homemade-plum-brandy stills endure. The antics of an infinitesimal number of con artists and beggars have birthed exaggerated stories about Romanians, but in truth you're far less likely to be the victim of crime here than in much of Western Europe. Instead, enjoy the friendliness of a generation with no vivid memories of Nicolae Ceauşescu.

The boomerang-shaped Carpathian Mountains offer exceptional and relatively uncrowded hiking, biking and skiing options. Towns like Braşov, Sibiu and Sighişoara are time-warp strolling grounds for fans of Gothic architecture, Austro-Hungarian legacy and Vlad 'Ţepeş' Dracula shtick. The fishies – and the birds that chomp them – play host in the Danube Delta. Bucolic and wooden Maramureş has the 'merry cemetery', while Unesco-listed painted monasteries dot southern Bucovina – and, for the record, big cities such as Cluj and Timişoara are a blast too.

FAST FACTS

- **Area** 237,500 sq km
- **Capital** Bucharest
- **Currency** new leu; €1 = 4.32 lei; US$1 = 3.17 lei; UK£1 = 4.59 lei; A$1 = 2.19 lei; ¥100 = 3.30 lei; NZ$1 = 1.78 lei
- **Famous for** Dracula, Transylvania, Nadia Comaneci's 10.0 in the 1976 Olympics
- **Official language** Romanian
- **Phrases** *bună* (hello); *da* (yes); *nu* (no); *mulţumesc* (thank you)
- **Population** 22.3 million
- **Telephone codes** country code ☎ 40; international access code ☎ 00
- **Visas** citizens of the USA, Canada, Japan, Australia and New Zealand visa-free for up to 90 days. Many others require a visa; see p741

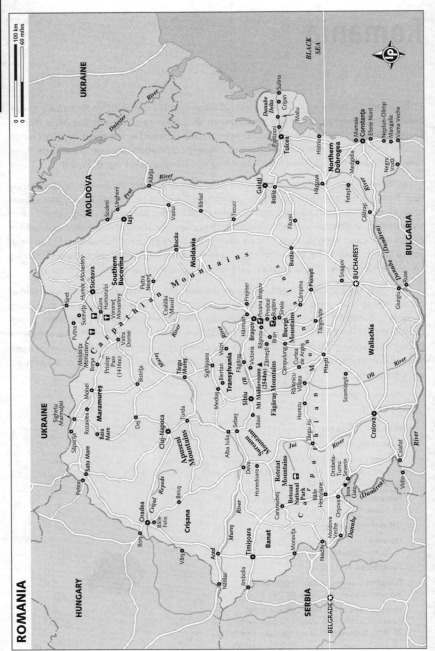

ROMANIA

HIGHLIGHTS

- Ascend castles, mountains and castles on top of mountains using the Gothic, medieval town of **Braşov** (p694) as a base.
- Follow the Unesco World Heritage conga-line of painted monasteries in **southern Bucovina** (p724).
- Rewind a few centuries and immerse yourself in **Maramureş** (p716), Europe's last thriving peasant society.
- Trace the heroic 1989 revolution to tenacious **Timişoara** (p713).
- Row through the tributaries and the riot of nature in the **Danube Delta** (p735).

ITINERARIES

- **10 days** Devote appropriate time to the parts of Bucharest that did and did not survive Ceauşescu, then train to Sinaia for Peleş Castle and hiking or biking the Bucegi Mountains. Braşov is Transylvania's main event for castles, activities and beers at sidewalk cafes. Spend a day in Sighişoara's medieval citadel, then train back to Bucharest or on to Budapest.
- **One month** Arrive in Bucharest (plane) or Timişoara (train), then head into Transylvania, stopping off for a day or two each at Sinaia, Braşov, Sighişoara and Sibiu. Head up to the student town of Cluj-Napoca and rent a car for a four- to five-day excursion into Maramureş – make it six days if you go by (slower) public transport. Continue on to southern Bucovina's painted monasteries, stopping in Iaşi if time allows. If driving, return the car to Cluj-Napoca and fly out from there.

CLIMATE & WHEN TO GO

Romania is a year-round destination, though winter can be a challenge in terms of closures and accessibility of certain attractions: the average annual temperature in the south is 11°C, 7°C in the north and only 2°C in the mountains. In the summer months, temperatures have risen to above 40°C in recent years in Bucharest and along the Black Sea coast, while winter chills of below -35°C are not unknown in the Braşov depression.

HISTORY
Ancient Romania & Dracula

Ancient Romania was inhabited by Thracian tribes, more commonly known as Dacians. The Greeks established trading colonies along the Black Sea from the 7th century BC, and the Romans conquered in AD 105–06. The slave-owning Romans brought with them their civilisation and the Latin language.

From the 10th century the Magyars (Hungarians) expanded into Transylvania, and by the 13th century all of Transylvania was under the Hungarian crown.

The Romanian-speaking principalities of Wallachia and Moldavia offered strong resistance to the Ottomans' northern expansion in the 14th and 15th centuries. Mircea the Old, Vlad Ţepeş and Ştefan cel Mare (Steven the Great) were legendary figures in this struggle.

Vlad Drăculea, ruling prince of Wallachia from 1456 till 1462 and 1476 till 1477, posthumously gained the moniker 'Ţepeş' (Impaler) after his favoured form of punishing his enemies – impaling. A dull wooden stake was carefully inserted into the anus, driven slowly through the body avoiding vital organs, until it emerged from the mouth, resulting in hours, even days, of agony before death. He is perhaps more legendary as the inspiration for 19th-century novelist Bram Stoker's Count Dracula. (Vlad's surname, Drăculea, means 'son of the

---

CONNECTIONS: MOVING ON FROM ROMANIA

Trains, buses and maxitaxis swarm around every available border crossing.

Trains depart Bucharest (p687) heading for destinations including Sofia, Budapest, Chişinău, İstanbul, Belgrade, Kyiv, Minsk and Moscow – the latter three via Suceava. Bucharest also has long-haul buses (p686) to Western European destinations, and daily maxitaxi service to Sofia.

Budapest can be easily reached by bus or train from Oradea (p713), Timişoara (p716) and Cluj-Napoca (p710).

Suceava (p727) has one daily bus to Chernivtsi, Ukraine, as well as Chişinău, though entering Moldova is easier from Iaşi (p723). Timişoara buses go all over Western Europe (p716), including Spain, Italy and Sweden. Nearly every major city has bus service to İstanbul. Somewhat expensive summertime-only catamarans go weekly from Constanţa (p732) to Odesa and Varna.

dragon', after his father, Vlad Dracul, a knight of the Order of the Dragon.)

When the Turks conquered Hungary in the 16th century, Transylvania became a vassal of the Ottoman Empire. In 1600 the three Romanian states – Transylvania, Wallachia and Moldavia – were briefly united under Mihai Viteazul (Michael the Brave). In 1687 Transylvania fell under Habsburg rule.

In 1859 Alexandru Ioan Cuza was elected to the thrones of Moldavia and Wallachia, creating a national state, which in 1862 took the name Romania. The reformist Cuza was forced to abdicate in 1866, and his place was taken by the Prussian prince Karl of Hohenzollern, who took the name Carol I. Romania declared independence from the Ottoman Empire in 1877, and, after the 1877–78 War of Independence, Dobrogea became part of Romania.

Romania in WWI & WWII

In 1916 Romania entered WWI on the side of the Triple Entente (Britain, France and Russia) with the objective of taking Transylvania – where 60% of the population was Romanian – from Austria-Hungary. The Central Powers (Germany and Austria-Hungary) occupied Wallachia. With the defeat of Austria-Hungary in 1918, the unification of Banat, Transylvania and Bucovina with Romania was finally achieved.

In the years leading to WWII, Romania, under foreign minister Nicolae Titulescu, sought security in a French alliance. On 30 August 1940 Romania was forced to cede northern Transylvania to Hungary by order of Nazi Germany and fascist Italy.

To defend the interests of the ruling classes, General Ion Antonescu forced King Carol II to abdicate in favour of his son Michael. Then Antonescu imposed a fascist dictatorship. In June 1941 he joined Hitler's anti-Soviet war with gruesome results: 400,000 Romanian Jews and 36,000 Roma were murdered at Auschwitz and other camps.

On 23 August 1944 Romania suddenly changed sides, captured 53,159 German soldiers and declared war on Nazi Germany. By this act, Romania salvaged its independence and shortened the war.

Ceauşescu

After the war, the Soviet-engineered return of Transylvania enhanced the prestige of the left-wing parties, which won the parliamentary elections of November 1946. A year later the monarchy was abolished and the Romanian People's Republic was proclaimed.

Soviet troops withdrew in 1958, and after 1960 Romania adopted an independent foreign policy under two leaders, Gheorghe Gheorghiu-Dej (leader from 1952 to 1965) and his protégé, Nicolae Ceauşescu (1965 to 1989).

Ceauşescu's domestic policy was chaotic and megalomaniacal. In 1974 the post of president was created for him. He placed his wife, Elena, son Nicu and three brothers in important political positions during the 1980s. Some of Ceauşescu's expensive follies were projects like the Danube Canal from Agigea to Cernavo, the disruptive redevelopment of southern Bucharest (1983–89) and the 'systemisation' of agriculture by the resettlement of rural villagers into concrete apartment blocks.

The late 1980s saw workers' riots in Braşov and severe food shortages in the winter of 1988–89. But the spark that ignited Romania came on 15 December 1989, when Father László Tökés publicly condemned the dictator from his Hungarian church in Timişoara. Police attempts to arrest demonstrating parishioners failed and civil unrest quickly spread.

On 21 December in Bucharest, an address by Ceauşescu during a rally was cut short by anti-Ceauşescu demonstrators. They booed him, then retreated to the boulevard between

READING LIST

There's surprisingly little coverage of Romania in English-language publishing. One of the best history books on Romania, Lucian Boia's excellent *Romania*, surveys Romania's past and present in a colourful, if philosophical, way. Robert Kaplan's *Balkan Ghosts* devotes a couple of key chapters to post-revolutionary Romania. Some of Isabel Fonseca's fascinating *Bury Me Standing* follows the Roma population in Romania. Of course, the most famous 'Romanian' book is Bram Stoker's *Dracula*, which begins and ends in Transylvania.

Piaţa Universităţii and Piaţa Romană, only to be crushed hours later by police gunfire and armoured cars. The next morning thousands more demonstrators took to the streets. At midday Ceauşescu reappeared with his wife on the balcony of the Central Committee building to speak, only to be forced to flee by helicopter. The couple were arrested in Târgovişte, taken to a military base and, on 25 December, executed by a firing squad.

The National Salvation Front (FSN) swiftly took control. In May 1990 it won the country's first 'democratic' elections – some European observers reported voter coercion and intimidation in rural areas – placing Ion Iliescu at the helm as president and Petre Roman as prime minister. In Bucharest, student protests against this former communist ruler were ruthlessly squashed by 20,000 coal miners shipped in courtesy of Iliescu. Ironically, when the miners returned in September 1991, it was to force the resignation of Petre Roman, who was blamed for worsening living conditions.

Modern Romania

Romania's birth as a modern nation was a difficult one. In December 1999 President Constantinescu dismissed Radul Vasile and replaced him with former National Bank of Romania governor, Mugur Isărescu. But by mid-2000 Isărescu was fighting for his political life after the opposition accused him of mismanagement of the State Property Fund. This was followed in May 2000 by the collapse of the National Fund for Investment (NFI), which saw thousands of investors lose their savings.

Romania joined the Council of Europe in 1993. The EU started accession talks with Romania in March 2000, and the country joined NATO in 2004. All this came as Romania chummed up with the USA, allowing its Iraq-bound military to set up bases and granting lucrative construction projects to American companies – something some EU members weren't happy with. In 2006, the EU granted Romania membership in 2007 – though Brussels warned it would continue to monitor Romania's progress in fighting corruption and organised crime. Romania has since been threatened with EU sanctions after reviews in both 2007 and 2008 cited a lack of progress, though at the time of writing none had been handed down.

PEOPLE

Romanians make up 89% of the population; Hungarians are the next largest ethnic group (7%), followed by Roma (2%), and smaller populations of Ukrainians, Germans, Russians and Turks. Germans and Hungarians live almost exclusively in Transylvania, while Ukrainians and Russians live mainly near the Danube Delta, and Turks along the Black Sea coast.

The government estimates that only 400,000 Roma live in Romania, although other sources estimate between 1.5 and 2.5 million. A good site to learn more about the Roma is the Budapest-based **European Roma Rights Centre** (http://e rrc.org).

RELIGION

The majority of Romania's population (87%) is Eastern Orthodox Christian. The rest is made up of Protestants (6.8%), Catholics (5.6%) and Muslims (0.4%), along with some 39,000 Jehovah's Witnesses and 10,000 Jews.

ARTS

Painting on glass and wood remains a popular folk art. Considered to be of Byzantine origin, this traditional peasant art was widespread in Romania from the 17th century onwards. Superstition and strong religious beliefs surrounded these icons, which were painted to protect a household from evil spirits.

The paintings of Nicolae Grigorescu (1838–1907) absorbed French Impressionism, and his canvases are alive with the colour of the Romanian countryside.

Romania's most famous sculptor is Constantin Brâncuşi (1876–1957), whose polished bronze and wood works are held by museums in Paris, New York and Canberra, as well as in Romania at the Museum of Art in Craiova and Bucharest's National Art Museum (p682).

Modern literature emerged in the mid-19th century in the shape of romantic poet Mihai Eminescu (1850–89), who captured the spirituality of the Romanian people in his work.

The Romanian classical-music world is nearly synonymous with George Enescu (1881–1955), whose Romanian Rhapsodies Nos 1 and 2 and opera *Odeipe* are generally considered classics.

Most Romanians and world residents are less charitable of the Cheeky Girls, Cluj-Napoca-born twins who made the big time (or at least a hit single) after leaving for the UK.

New regard for Romanian cinema has emerged, starting with hits like Nae Caranfil's comedy *Filantropica* (2002) and Cristi Puiu's *The Death of Mr Lăzărescu* (2005). In 2007, director Cristian Mungiu won the Cannes Film Festival's top prize with *4 Months, 3 Weeks and 2 Days*, a disturbing tale of illegal abortion in communist-era Romania, while the late Cristian Nemescu's film *California Dreamin'* also took honours.

ENVIRONMENT
The Land
Covering 237,500 sq km, Romania – shaped a bit like an agitated pufferfish – is made up of three main geographical regions, each with its particular features. The mighty Carpathian Mountains run down into the country's centre from the Ukraine, before curling northwards. West of this are large plateaus where villages and towns lie among the hills and valleys. East of the mountains are the low-lying plains (where most of the country's agricultural output comes from), which end at the Black Sea, and Europe's second-largest delta region where the Danube spills into the sea.

Wildlife
Rural Romania has thriving animal populations that include chamois, lynx, fox, deer, wolf, bear and badger. There are 33,792 species of animals here (707 of which are vertebrates; 55 of these are endangered) as well as 3700 species of plants (39 of which are endangered).

Bird life in the Danube Delta is unmatched. It is a major migration hub for numerous bird species and home to 60% of the world's small pygmy cormorant population.

National Parks
Romania has nearly 600 protected areas – including 13 national parks, three biosphere reserves and one Natural World Heritage site (the Danube Delta) – totalling over 12,000 sq km.

Environmental Issues
Romania may very well have more rubbish bins than any country on earth (look around, it's stunning) – the problem is getting people to use them. NGOs such as **Pro Natura** (www .pronatura.ro) and the **Transylvania Ecological Club** (www.greenagenda.org) work to spread word about how to diminish the impact of tourism on the country's environment.

Romania has the ongoing problem of cleaning up the pollution left by communist-era chemical plants. If you're on the train between Sighişoara and Cluj-Napoca, look out for the dilapidated, blackened plants in Copşa Mică, which until the early 1990s were so dangerous to the local community that some two-thirds of children showed signs of mental illness.

FOOD & DRINK
Romanian cuisine, in all its porky, potato-y, cabbage-y glory, shares many similarities with that of its neighbours and borrows liberally from the cultures that have occupied its land. It's mainly hearty, simple food laden with winter-insulating butter, cream and grease, though new, upmarket Romanian restaurants are toying with the old formulas in interesting ways. You're on a diet, you say? Best of luck!

Mămăligă is essentially cornmeal mush that's boiled or fried, sometimes topped with cream and/or cheese, and proudly served to sceptical visitors at every meal. *Ciorbă* (soup) is the other mainstay of the Romanian diet and a powerful hangover remedy. Favourites include *ciorbă de burta* (tripe soup served with a dollop of sour cream) and *ciorbă de legume* (vegetable soup cooked with meat stock).

Other common dishes are *muşchi de vacă/ porc/miel* (cutlet of beef/pork/lamb), *ficat* (liver), *piept de pui* (chicken breast) and *cabanos prajit* (fried sausages). Typical desserts include *plăcintă* (turnovers), *clătite* (crêpes) and *cozonac* (brioche).

Thanks to the Orthodox diet, you can always find some vegetarian dishes, unexciting and repetitious as they will come to be. If a plate of *mămăligă* does not turn you on, try *cașcaval pâine* (cheese covered in breadcrumbs and fried), *salată roșii* (tomato salad), *salată castraveți* (cucumber salad) and *salată asortată* (mixed salad, usually just a mix of – guess what? – tomatoes and cucumbers). When you're really lucky, you'll find vegetable soup or stew, or a dish made from aubergine.

Among the best Romanian wines are Cotnari, Murfatlar, Odobești, Târnave and Valea Călugărească.

Țuică is a once-filtered clear brandy made from fermented fruit (the tastiest and most popular is plum *țuică*). It's usually 30-proof, but can reach an ear-smoking 60-proof and higher.

Restaurants are generally open from 10am to midnight. Bars usually open at 10am and close anywhere from 1am to 5am, depending on the day of the week.

Smoking awareness is gaining ground in large cities. Many restaurants will offer nonsmoking sections, though they're sometimes only a few nonpartioned centimetres away from the smoking section. Bars and clubs are still a smoker's delight, as are many rural areas.

BUCHAREST

☎ 021/031 / pop 2.1 million

Many Romanians slam it, some travellers depart visibly stunned after a couple of days (or a single drive through the increasingly gridlocked centre), but Bucharest is an intriguing and evolving mix of eras. Wide boulevards with century-old villas, which once earned it the debatable moniker 'Paris of the East', mingle with deviously hidden 18th-century monasteries, unsightly communist-built housing blocks and statement-making government headquarters – some riddled with statement-making bullet holes from the 1989 revolution. Just two decades after his demise, in a transformation that is rich in poetic justice, Ceaușescu's intended legacy is being smothered by stylish people, fast cars and a nightlife scene that's as happening as any in Western Europe. The country's top museums are here, and there are plenty of green parks providing escape from encroaching capitalism and the repellent effects of newly available car loans. Ongoing development and gen-

trification of the crumbling historic centre is encouraging and hints at a modernised return to classiness.

ORIENTATION

Bucharest's main train station, Gara de Nord, is a few kilometres northwest of Bucharest's centre. The station is connected by the metro to Piața Victoriei on the northern side of the centre and to Piața Unirii on the southern side. Bus 133 will take you just north of the centre to Piața Romană; bus 85 goes to Piața Universității.

Bucharest's most historic areas spread to either side of the main boulevard B-dul Bălcescu, which changes its name to B-dul General Mageru to the north, and B-dul IC Brătianu south of Piața Universității.

Maps

By far the best Bucharest map, available at bus ticket stands, is the *100% Planul Orașului București Map* (1:200,000; 11 lei), with all transport routes.

INFORMATION
Bookshops

Anthony Frost English Bookshop (Map p680; ☎ 311 5138; Calea Victoriei 45; www.librariaengleza.ro; ☺ 10am-7pm Mon-Sat, 10am-2pm Sun) Fiction, nonfiction, travel, comics, biographies and more, all in English.
Librăria Noi (Map p680; ☎ 311 0700; B-dul Nicolae Bălcescu 18; ☺ 9.30am-8.15pm Mon-Sat, 11am-6.45pm Sun) Huge bookshop, with English-language novels, LP guides, maps and a fab antiques section.

Cultural Centres

British Council Library (Map p678; ☎ 307 9600; www.britishcouncil.ro; Calea Dorobanților 14; ☺ 9am-7pm Mon-Fri, to 1.30pm Sat) Library, internet access and cafe.
French Institute (Map p678; ☎ 316 0224; www.culture-france.ro; B-dul Dacia 77; ☺ 9am-6.30pm Mon-Thu, 9am-4.30pm Fri, 10am-2.30pm Sat) Film screenings at the on-site cinema, plus internet and a bistro.

Emergency

Ambulance ☎ 973
Police (☎ 955, central station 311 2021)

Internet Access

Nearly all hotels and hostels have internet access. Cafes with wi-fi are common.
Access Internet (Map p678; ☎ 317 4153; B-dul Lascăr Catargiu 6; per hr 4 lei; ☺ 24hr) International calls start at 0.12 lei per minute.

GREATER BUCHAREST

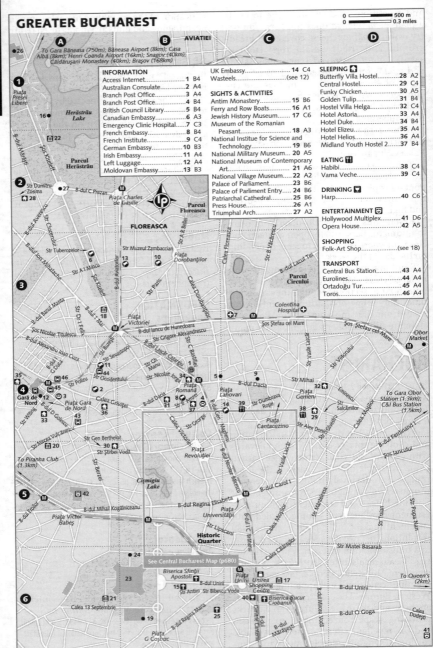

INFORMATION
Access Internet..................1	B4
Australian Consulate..........2	A4
Branch Post Office.............3	A4
Branch Post Office.............4	B4
British Council Library........5	B4
Canadian Embassy..............6	A3
Emergency Clinic Hospital...7	C3
French Embassy..................8	B4
French Institute.................9	C4
German Embassy................10	B3
Irish Embassy....................11	A4
Left Luggage....................12	A4
Moldovan Embassy.............13	B3
UK Embassy.....................14	C4
Wasteels.....................(see 12)	

SIGHTS & ACTIVITIES
Antim Monastery................15	B6
Ferry and Row Boats...........16	A1
Jewish History Museum.......17	C6
Museum of the Romanian	
Peasant.........................18	A3
National Institue for Science and	
Technology....................19	B6
National Military Museum.....20	A5
National Museum of Contemporary	
Art...............................21	A6
National Village Museum......22	A2
Palace of Parliament............23	B6
Palace of Parliment Entry.....24	B6
Patriarchal Cathedral...........25	B6
Press House......................26	A1
Triumphal Arch...................27	A2

SLEEPING
Butterfly Villa Hostel...........28	A2
Central Hostel....................29	C4
Funky Chicken...................30	A5
Golden Tulip.....................31	B4
Hostel Villa Helga..............32	C4
Hotel Astoria....................33	A4
Hotel Duke......................34	B4
Hotel Elizeu.....................35	A4
Hotel Helios.....................36	A4
Midland Youth Hostel 2......37	B4

EATING
Habibi............................38	C4
Vama Veche.....................39	C4

DRINKING
Harp.............................40	C6

ENTERTAINMENT
Hollywood Multiplex...........41	D6
Opera House....................42	A5

SHOPPING
Folk-Art Shop.................(see 18)	

TRANSPORT
Central Bus Station.............43	A4
Eurolines.........................44	A4
Ortadoğu Tur....................45	A4
Toros.............................46	A4

See Central Bucharest Map (p680)

Internet & Games (Map p680; ☎ 0721 877 886; B-dul Regina Elisabeta 25; per hr 4 lei; ⏱ 24hr)

Left Luggage
There's **left luggage** (Map p678; Piaţa Gara de Nord 1; per day small/big bag 3/6 lei; ⏱ 24hr) at the train station, in the hallway leading to the front exit.

Medical Services
Emergency Clinic Hospital (Map p678; ☎ 317 0121; Calea Floreasca 8; ⏱ 24hr) Bucharest's best state hospital.
Finesse (Clinica Stomatologica; Map p680; ☎ 313 4781; www.finesse-dent.ro; Str Hristo Botev 7; ⏱ 10am-8pm Mon-Fri, to 4pm Sat)
Sensi-Blu (Map p680; ☎ 305 7314; B-dul Nicolae Bălcescu 7; ⏱ 24hr) Reliable pharmacy chain with countless locations.

Money
Currency-exchange bureaux are everywhere, though it's better to change money at a bank or stick to the ATM. Avoid the currency-exchange counters at the airport; there are ATM machines in the arrivals hall.
Banca Comercială Română (Map p680; B-dul Regina Elisabeta 5; ⏱ 8.30am-5.30pm Mon-Fri, to 12.30pm Sat)

Post
Central post office (Map p680; ☎ 315 9030; Str Matei Millo 10; ⏱ 7.30am-8pm Mon-Fri) Collect poste restante mail here.

Telephone
RomTelecomm cards (from 10 lei) are available at news-stands. Most phone booths are neglected, but still work. You'll have no problem finding a shop selling Orange or Vodaphone SIM cards for your mobile phone – try a central street like B-dul Magheru.

Access Internet (p677) can help with international calls too.

Tourist Information
Bucharest continues to ignore its baffling absence of tourism resources. The overabundance of travel agencies in the centre focus primarily on getting you *out* of the country. Hostels and hotels are your best bet for domestic information and leads for car rental and day trips to Snagov or even Bran Castle.
Wasteels (Map p678; ☎ 317 0370; www.wasteelstravel .ro; Gara de Nord; ⏱ 8am-7pm Mon-Fri, to 2pm Sat) Conveniently located on the left side of the exit hallway of the train station, Wasteels can provide car rental, help with train reservations, and possibly call you a reliable taxi.

Nova Tour (Map p680; ☎ 315 0131; B-dul Nicolae Bălcescu 21) Has limited domestic tour info.

DANGERS & ANNOYANCES
Bucharest's stray dogs (aka 'community dogs') not-so-coincidentally disappeared right before the 2008 NATO summit, returning to the streets soon afterward tagged and in seemingly fewer numbers. Though the dogs are largely docile, people are occasionally bitten – in 2006 a Japanese businessperson bled to death following a freak bite that severed an artery. If bitten, go to a hospital within 36 hours for antirabies injections. Avoid packs of dogs, which occasionally occupy empty lots behind buildings.

The odd encounter with fake police (aka 'tourist police') is still being reported. If accosted by dubious officials, insist on being escorted to the nearest station before producing passports, money etc.

Another 'danger' is the taxi drivers who charge extortionately high prices. Worst are those in and around Gara de Nord and to a lesser extent at the airports. We've heard of travellers paying 500 lei for a 17-lei ride! Legit taxis will have prices printed on the side of the car, usually the door, ranging from 1.70 to 3.30 lei per kilometre. Wasteels (left) can usually call for a taxi from the train station if you don't have a phone to call one of the reliable companies listed on p688.

SIGHTS
Bucharest's museums, some of the best in Romania, will delight those with the requisite stamina. Historic Calea Victoriei roars with heavy vehicles and aspirant street racers, but it's a scenic thoroughfare and it connects the two main squares of the city: Piaţa Victoriei in the north, and Piaţa Revoluţiei in the centre. Follow the river east to where it goes under the sprawling Piaţa Unirii.

Ceauşescu's Bucharest
An entire suburb of historic buildings was smashed when Nicolae Ceauşescu returned from tours of Pyongyang and Beijing in the 1980s, suffering from some righteous reverse-culture shock. Feverish reconstruction ensued in Bucharest (and eventually all of Romania) which is particularly evident along **Bulevardul Unirii** in southern Bucharest. Romania's 'Champs-Élysées' is a chaotic, fountain-lined 3.2km boulevard – deliberately pipping Paris' by a resounding 6m (take that Frenchies!).

ROMANIA

CENTRAL BUCHAREST

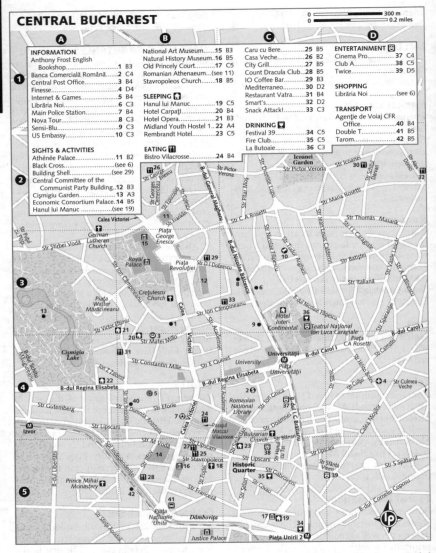

INFORMATION
Anthony Frost English
　Bookshop..........................1　B3
Banca Comercială Română....2　C4
Central Post Office................3　B4
Finesse.................................4　D4
Internet & Games.................5　B4
Librăria Noi.........................6　C3
Main Police Station...............7　B4
Nova Tour...........................8　C3
Sensi-Blu.............................9　C3
US Embassy........................10　C3

SIGHTS & ACTIVITIES
Athénée Palace..................11　B2
Black Cross.....................(see 6)
Building Shell.................(see 29)
Central Committee of the
　Communist Party Building..12　B3
Cişmigiu Garden................13　A3
Economic Consortium Palace.14　B5
Hanul lui Manuc...........(see 19)

National Art Museum.......15　B3
Natural History Museum..16　B5
Old Princely Court..........17　C5
Romanian Athenaeum....(see 11)
Stavropoleos Church........18　B5

SLEEPING
Hanul lui Manuc.............19　C5
Hotel Carpaţi..................20　B4
Hotel Opera...................21　B3
Midland Youth Hostel 1...22　A4
Rembrandt Hotel............23　C5

EATING
Bistro Vilacrosse.............24　B4

Caru cu Bere...................25　B5
Casa Veche....................26　B2
City Grill........................27　B5
Count Dracula Club........28　B5
IO Coffee Bar.................29　B3
Mediterraneo.................30　D2
Restaurant Vatra............31　B4
Smart's..........................32　D2
Snack Attack!.................33　C3

DRINKING
Festival 39.....................34　C5
Fire Club........................35　C5
La Butoaie.....................36　C3

ENTERTAINMENT
Cinema Pro....................37　C4
Club A...........................38　C5
Twice............................39　D5

SHOPPING
Librăria Noi................(see 6)

TRANSPORT
Agenţie de Voiaj CFR
　Office...........................40　B4
Double T........................41　B5
Tarom............................42　B5

Stroll just north into the historic centre (see opposite) to get a sense of what was once here.

From central **Piaţa Unirii** (under which the city's crippled Dâmboviţa River flows), look southwest, where the **Patriarchal Cathedral** (Catedrala Patriahală; Map p678; Str Dealul Mitropoliei) – the centre of Romanian Orthodox faith, built between 1656 and 1658. It triumphantly peeks

over once-grand housing blocks on B-dul Unirii designed to 'hide' the city's churches. One such fatality is the **Antim Monastery** (Mănăstirea Antim; Map p678; Str Antim), which is south, just one block before the boulevard ends; it dates from 1715.

Anchoring B-dul Unirii is the mother of all white elephants, the **Palace of Parliament** (Palatul

---

FREE THRILLS

Bucharest's sprawl means worthwhile free activities are prohibitively distant from one another, but if you happen to be in the area, here are a few you can add to your un-free itinerary:

- Wander the **historic centre** (below), admiring the crumbling, restored and under-restoration streets and buildings.
- Take a break in the atmospheric courtyard at **Stavropoleos Church** (p682), dating from 1724 and possibly central Bucharest's most serene spot.
- Escape the car-horn refrain at the **Triumphal Arch** (p683) and in the exquisite walking and picnicking grounds of **Herăstrău Park** (p683).
- Pay your disrespects to the final resting places of Nicolae and Elena Ceauşescu at **Ghencea Civil Cemetery** (below).
- Enjoy the heat retreat and Bucharestian-watching in the heroically tended **Cişmigiu Garden** (p682) .

Parlamentului; Map p678; ☎ 311 3611; B-dul Naţiunile Unite; adult/student with ID 22 lei/free; ☑ 10am-4pm), the world's second-largest administrative building (after the US Pentagon). Built in 1984 (and still unfinished), the building's 12 storeys and 3100 rooms cover 330,000 sq metres, and cost an estimated €3.3 billion. The hefty ticket price doesn't buy you a particularly informative or inspiring tour, but the hourly 45-minute tours are the only way to see a handful of the opulent marble rooms, finishing at the balcony that Ceauşescu didn't live long enough to speak from. Facing the Palace of Parliament from B-dul Unirii, the entrance is around to the right (a 12-minute walk).

At the back of the Palace of Parliament is the superb **National Museum of Contemporary Art** (Muzeul Naţionalde Arta Contemporana; Map p678; ☎ 318 9137; www.mnac.ro; Calea 13 Septembrie; adult/student 8 lei/free; ☑ 10am-6pm Wed-Sun), which opened in 2004. The four-floor exhibition space features eclectic European art – including installation and video – and is easily one of Eastern Europe's most provocative spaces. There's a top-floor open-air cafe. As you make your way back to B-dul Unirii, note the half-finished **National Institute for Science & Technology** (Map p678; cnr B-dul Libertăţii & Calea 13 Septembrie), one of several half-done or abandoned buildings in Bucharest.

Alternatively, a 45-minute lacklustre walk west (or take bus 385 from outside the Parliament ticket office on B-dul Naţiunile Unite) leads to **Ghencea Civil Cemetery** (Cimitriul Civil Ghencea; Map p678; ☎ 413 8590; Calea 13 Septembrie; ☑ 8am-8pm), where you can morbidly seek out the final resting spots of Nicolae Ceauşescu (row I-35, marked with a red cross, to the left of the entry path) and his wife Elena (H25, to

the right of the entry path), both executed on Christmas Day in 1989.

Historic Centre

Some of the most heart-wrenching and gutless antiprotester violence of the 1989 revolution took place at **Piaţa Universităţii** (Map p680), which straddles Bucharest's most evocative, historic streets. Horrified journalists watched tanks roll over Romanian freedom fighters and soldiers shoot into crowds of protestors from their viewpoint inside Hotel Inter-Continental. Scour the area and you'll find bullet marks in some buildings and 10 stone crosses commemorating those killed. A **black cross** and plaque on the wall at B-dul Nicolae Bălcescu 18 marks the spot where the first protestor, Mihai Gătlan, died at 5.30pm on 21 December 1989.

Much of the historic centre lies in the blocks to the southwest. A good access way is along **Calea Victoriei**, built in 1692 under Brâncoveanu's orders to link the centre with his summer palace in Mogoşoaia, 14km northwest. Three blocks south is **Stradă Lipscani**, the newly cobblestoned eastern portion of which is one of the early benefactors of central Bucharest's long-awaited gentrification efforts. Smart shops, restaurants and cafes have duly followed. At the time of writing, intriguing Roman ruins uncovered during street resurfacing stood fenced-off, but sadly exposed to people with rubbish-disposal deficiencies.

Another block south is the ritzy **Economic Consortium Palace** (Casa de Economii şi Consemnaţiuni), designed by French architect Paul Gottereau between 1894 and 1900. Across the street is the **National History Museum**

(Muzeul National de Istorie a Romaniei; Map p680; ☎ 311 3356; Calea Victoriei 12; adult/student 7/2 lei; ☺ 10am-6pm Wed & Fri-Sun, noon-8pm Thu), housed in the neoclassical former Post Office Palace (1894). Despite ongoing, snail-paced renovations, it's worth seeing for the dismantled replica of the 2nd-century 40m Trajan's Column; its 2500 characters retell the Dacian Wars against Rome. (Go to panel 18 to see decapitated heads.) There's also a gold-crammed treasury.

A block east of the museum, the **Stavropoleos Church** (Map p680; Str Stavropoleos), on a street meaning 'town of the cross', dates from 1724 and is one of Bucharest's most atmospheric churches. The ornate courtyard, full with tombstones and relics from the city's demolished churches, is the most peaceful spot in central Bucharest.

The heart of the historic centre is the **Old Princely Court** (Palatul Voievodal; Map p680; Curtea Veche; ☎ 314 0375; Str Franceza 21-23; admission 3 lei; ☺ 10am-5pm), a busted-up court from the 15th century with a Vlad Țepeș statue out front. Classic Romanian bureaucracy and opportunism suffered by travel TV show host Anthony Bourdain at this site ignited a bitter hissy fit by the celebrity chef that lingered for the remainder of his Romania visit.

Just southeast, the historic **Hanul lui Manuc** (Manuc's Inn) was built in 1808 to shelter and feed travelling merchants and is one of the few remaining buildings of that era. The hotel and courtyard restaurant-bar (p684) were under extensive refurbishment at the time of writing.

To the southeast, just beyond Piața Unirii, the interesting **Jewish History Museum** (Muzeul de Istorie al Comunitaților Evreiești din România; Map p678; ☎ 311 0870; admission by donation; ☺ 9am-1pm Sun-Fri) is housed in a colourful synagogue that dates from 1836 (but was rebuilt in 1910). Exhibits (in English and Romanian) outline Jewish contributions to Romanian history, which not all Romanians know about. In 1941, 800,000 Jews lived in Romania; today only 10,000 remain. You need your passport to enter.

Piața Revoluției

The scene of Ceaușescu's infamous last speech of 21 December 1989 was on the balcony of the former **Central Committee of the Communist Party building** (Map p680), a few blocks northwest of Piața Universității. Sensing irreparable doom amid cries of 'Down with Ceaușescu', he briefly escaped in a helicopter from the

roof. Meanwhile, the crowds were riddled with bullets, and many died.

The **building shell** (Map p680; cnr Str DI Dobrescu & Str Boteanu) is all that remains of the former home of the hated Securitate after it was destroyed by protestors in 1989. Now a modern glass structure stands inside it; you can see striking Revolution photos while sipping hipster coffee in the basement IO Coffee Bar (p684).

Housed in the early-19th-century Royal Palace, the **National Art Museum** (Muzeul Național de Artă; Map p680; ☎ 313 3030; http://art.museum.ro; Calea Victoriei 49-53; combination ticket 15 lei, Romanian or European collection 10 lei, 1st Wed of month free; ☺ 11am-7pm Wed-Sun) is a super three-part museum. The north door leads to the **Gallery of Romanian Art** (adult/student 10/5 lei), with hundreds of icons saved from communist-destroyed churches and many paintings, including arresting portraits by Nicolae Grigorescu. Also in the building is the small **Treasures of Roman Art** (adult/student 10/5 lei). The south door leads to the absorbing **Gallery of European Art** (adult/student 8/4 lei), a 12,000-piece collection, largely assembled from Tsar Carol I's collection, which covers all things from Rembrandt and Bartolomeo to Rodin and Monet.

Just to the north is the **Athénée Palace** (Str Episcopiei 1-3), so evocatively captured in its postrevolutionary, prostitute-teeming state by Robert Kaplan in *Balkan Ghosts*. Designed to outdo Paris in 1918, the hotel later served as a hotbed for Romania's 'KGB', the Securitate. Now Hilton has cleaned it up – and priced rooms beyond their worth.

Just east is the grand domed **Romanian Athenaeum** (Ateneul Român; Map p680; ☎ 315 6875; admission 6 lei), which hosts prestigious concerts. Built in 1888, this is where George Enescu made his debut in 1898. Today it's home to the George Enescu Philharmonic Orchestra. Hours vary.

Just west is the locally loved **Cișmigiu Garden**, with shady walks, cafes and a ridiculous number of benches on which to sit and stare at Bucharestians going by.

Northern Bucharest

Bucharest's most luxurious villas and parks line the grand avenue **Șoseaua Kiseleff**, which begins at **Piața Victoriei** (Map p678). A leafy walk north of the Piața are two wonderful museums that pay tribute to Romania's rural heart.

About 200m north, the **Museum of the Romanian Peasant** (Muzeul Țăranului Român; Map p678;

317 9661; Şos Kiseleff 3; adult/student 6/2 lei; 10am-6pm Tue-Sun) is so good you may want to hug it. Chosen as Europe's best museum in 1996, it makes the best of little money. Handmade cards (in English) personalise exhibits, such as a full 19th-century home located upstairs, a heartbreakingly sweet room devoted to grandmas, and 'hidden' rooms that hand-scrawled directions usher you to. Don't miss the (rare) communism exhibit downstairs, with Lenin busts and portraits of Romanian leader Gheorghiu-Dej. An 18th-century Transylvanian church is in the back lot, as is the museum's gift shop.

About a kilometre north is the 1935–36 **Triumphal Arch** (Arcul de Triumf; Map p678), based on the Paris monument and devoted to WWI and the reunification of Romania in 1918. Traffic roars by, so it's tricky to reach; the arch was covered in scaffolding and the viewing platform closed at the time of writing.

Pathways just east lead to the lovely **Herăstrău Park** (Parcul Herăstrău), which hugs the chain of lakes that stripe northern Bucharest. There are plenty of cafes around. On the east side, about 500m north, a **ferry** (5 lei one way) crosses the lake regularly, and you can rent **pedal boats and rowboats** (6 lei per person per hour). Adjoining the park, but best accessed from Şos Kiseleff, is the **National Village Museum** (Muzeul Naţional al Satului; Map p678; 317 9110; www.muzeul-satului.ro; Şos Kiseleff 28-30; adult/student 6/3 lei; 9am-7pm Mon May-Sep, 9am-5pm Tue-Fri, to 4pm Mon Oct-Apr), a terrific open-air collection of several dozen homesteads, churches, mills and windmills that have been relocated from rural Romania. At times in July and August artisans in traditional garb show off various rural trades.

At the north end of Şos Kiseleff is the Stalinesque **Press House** (Casa Presei Libre), built in 1956. Note the hammer and sickle imprint midway up the tower.

Western Bucharest

Not far from the train station, the pinky-peach **National Military Museum** (Muzeul Militar Naţional; Map p678; 319 6015; Str Mircea Vulcănescu 125-127; adult/student 5/2.5 lei; 9am-5pm Tue-Sun) doubles nicely as a Romanian history museum. Note the 1988 communist mural in the entry; in back is a superb hangar with Aurel Vlaicu's famed 1911 plane, which Romanians attest made the first 'real' flight.

FESTIVALS & EVENTS

Bucharest's Carnival is held from late May to early June.

SLEEPING

Budget options in the centre have improved, though the tranquillity of staying out of the centre may be worth the commute. The grotty Gara de Nord area has some cheaper options. Breakfast is included unless otherwise noted.

Budget

Casa Albă (off Map p678; 230 4525; Alea Privighetorilor 1-3; camp sites per person 30 lei, bungalows with shared/private showers 78/90 lei) This camping ground is in way-north Bucharest. Take bus 301 north from Piaţa Romană; get off at 'Restaurant Baneasa' stop. The entrance is across the road. Driving from the centre, pass IKEA, exit before the next bridge and take the second right on Alea Privighetorilor. It's down 600m on the left. Bungalows share toilets.

Funky Chicken (Map p678; 312 1425; www.funkychickenhostel.com; Str Gen Berthelot 63; dm 30 lei) Just a couple of blocks from Cişmigiu Garden, this bare-bones, but pleasant, hostel occupies a historic home on a shady street. Its three dorm rooms sleep 18. No breakfast, but there's a kitchen and free cigarettes.

Butterfly Villa Hostel (Map p678; 0747 032 644; www.villa-butterfly.com; Str Dumitru Zosima 82; dm/d 44/103 lei;) One of Bucharest's best hostels. Run by a German-Romanian couple, Butterfly is not necessarily the best located, but there's free laundry, a roof terrace, all-day breakfasts and a leafy courtyard. Bus 282 heads here from the train station, and bus 300 from Piaţa Romana.

Hostel Villa Helga (Map p678; 0741 127 514, 212 0828; Str Mihei Einesci 184; dm 45 lei, d with shared/private bathroom 130/210 lei;) The location and amenities are superb. This completely refurbished villa has several private rooms, a large kitchen, a small library, tourist information and train station/airport pick-up. Your seventh night here is free.

Central Hostel (Map p678; 610 2214; www.centralhostel.ro; Str Salcâmilor 2; dm/d from 48/140 lei;) A converted villa in a quiet neighbourhood east of the centre has clean rooms with new beds, a kitchen, laundry (8 lei), lockers and patio seating under a vine shade. Prices drop in low season.

our pick Midland Youth Hostel 1 (Map p680; 317 0362; www.themidlandhostel.com; B-dul Regina Elisabeta 44,

Apt 32; dm/d 60/150 lei; 🖳) It doesn't get any more central or affordable than this. Bathrooms are a little tight, but amenities include the combo TV room/kitchen, free internet/wi-fi, lockers, laundry (5 lei) and a view over Cişmigiu Garden. Enter through the building's side door on Str Ion Z Zalomit. A second location, Midland Youth Hostel 2 (Map p678), at Str Biserica Amzei 22, was opening at the time of writing.

Midrange

Hotel Carpaţi (Map p680; ☎ 315 0140; www.hotelcarpati bucuresti.ro; Str Matei Millo 16; s/d with shared bathroom 118/180 lei, d with private bathroom 220-261 lei; 🖳) This popular central option has 40 recently renovated rooms – some rather tiny and creaky – and a great breakfast served with a little pomp in the Paris-style lobby lounge. All rooms have TV and sink. Wi-fi in the lobby only.

Hotel Astoria (Map p678; ☎ 318 9989; B-dul Dinica Golescu 27; s/d 129/183 lei) Facing the station, Astoria's yesteryear grace is fading rapidly, though the location is ideal for layovers and early departures. Scenes were shot here for Cannes top prize winner *4 Months, 3 Weeks and 2 Days*.

Hanul lui Manuc (Manuc's Inn; Map p680; ☎ 313 1415; hmanuc@rnc.ro; Str Franceză 62-64; s/d 162/260 lei) Renovations at this 19th-century *caravanserai* (inn) should be completed by the time you visit. It's one of the city's oldest buildings and has a colourful guest list from its past that includes prostitutes, criminals and Lonely Planet authors. Sculpted wooden balconies line the terrace overlooking the courtyard and restaurant. Expect notably higher postrenovation prices.

Hotel Helios (Map p678; ☎ 310 7083; Calea Griviţei 91; contact@hotelhelios.ro; s/d 242/283 lei; 🞰) This 15-room hotel is only a few blocks from the train station, but feels far away – it faces a quaint Orthodox church. Rooms are rather simple, but stylish, with floor-to-ceiling wardrobes. Prices drop 20% Saturday and Sunday. Cable internet only.

Hotel Elizeu (Map p678; ☎ 319 1734; www.hotelelizeu .ro; Str Elizeu 11-13; s/d 300/334 lei; 🞰) This 54-room hotel is comfortable and modern, with quiet rooms, 100 channels of satellite TV, one hour of free wi-fi daily, minibar and lavish Swedish complimentary buffet breakfast.

Rembrandt Hotel (Map p680; ☎ 313 9315; www .rembrandt.ro; Str Smârdan 11; s/d from 330/371 lei; 🞰 🖳) Stylish beyond its three-star rating, this 15-room, Dutch-owned hotel faces the landmark National Bank in the historic centre. Rooms have polished wood floors, wall-size timber headboards and DVD players. Book way in advance as the few cheaper 'tourist class' rooms go quickly.

Top End

Golden Tulip (Map p678; ☎ 212 5558; www.goldentulip bucharest.com; Calea Victoriei 166; s/d 477/569 lei; 🞰 🖳) Rooms here are wood, with a splash of red furniture and strong IKEA influences. Full-wall glass windows provide great views of the street bustle, though vehicle noise is audible. Enjoy top-end hotel amenities like slippers, toiletry baskets and in-room coffee/tea. Rates drop 20% Friday to Sunday.

Hotel Opera (Map p680; ☎ 312 4857; www.hotelopera .ro; Str Ion Brezoianu 37; s/d 488/569 lei; 🞰 🖳) Set on a backstreet corner, this 33-room, faintly art deco music-themed hotel enjoys membership in Top Hotels Group, and offers, among other things, Mercedes airport transfer. The rooms are small but nicely arranged. Rates don't include 9% VAT.

Hotel Duke (Map p678; ☎ 317 4186; www.hotelduke .ro; B-dul Dacia 33; s/d 550/661 lei; 🞰 🖳) At Piaţa Romana, the 38-room Duke is a pleasant business-style hotel with attentive staff, priced for people with expense accounts. Rooms are smallish, but modern and very clean. There's a business centre, wi-fi throughout the hotel, a casual bar where suits chat, and several nearby restaurants.

EATING
Budget

[our pick] IO Coffee Bar (Map p680; ☎ 315 6098; Str Demetru I Dobrescu 5) Looking out from a blown-out ruin of the 1989 clash at nearby Piaţa Revoluţi, this cafe has backlit wall-length B&W prints of the 1989 scene and candles on the table. Nights and weekends the volume rises with jazz and dance music. Free wi-fi.

Snack Attack! (Map p680; ☎ 312 7664; Str Ion Câmpineanu 10; sandwiches 8 lei; ⏰ 7.30am-8pm Mon-Fri, to 2pm Sat) Fresh, cheap takeaway panini and salads (including hummus and tabouli with tortillas).

Bistro Vilacrosse (Map p680; ☎ 315 4562; Pasajul Macca/Vilacrosse; mains 9-20 lei) The small Vilacrosse borrows its style heavily from Parisian side streets, with sepia tones, wood floors and gingham tablecloths, though paradoxically, the service here is friendly and quick! The food's good too, including a wine-splat-tered Transylvania pork fillet on a bed of (French!) fries and roasted cabbage. A few vegetarian options.

Habibi (Map p678; ☎ 805 5498; Str Vasile Lascar 98; wissam_nasser75@hotmail.com; mains 9-35 lei) The Lebanese tradition for food, class and at-tentive service punctuates the atmosphere here. The huge menu covers a lot of culi-nary territory, but stick with the theme, like the 'starter plate' (30 lei) to sample chef Ahmad's faves.

Midrange

ourpick Caru cu Bere (Map p680; ☎ 313 7560; www .carucubere.ro; Str Stavropoleos 3-5; mains 12-40 lei; ☺ 8am-midnight; 🖫) Despite a decidedly tourist-leaning atmosphere, with servers in peasant costumes and sporadic Roma song-and-dance numbers, Bucharest's oldest beer house continues to draw in a strong local crowd. The colour-ful belle époque interior and stained-glass windows dazzle, as does the mixed sausage platter (for two!), which, while delicious, is enough grease for a month. Dinner reserva-tions recommended.

Casa Veche (Map p680; ☎ 312 5816; Str George Enescu 15; pizzas 16-23 lei) With courtyard seats under vines, and traditional upstairs seating, this place offers great-quality crispy pizzas and a winner setting near the centre.

City Grill (Map p680; ☎ 314 2489; www.citygrill .ro; Str Lipscani 12; mains 16-44 lei; ☺ 10am-10pm) Enviably situated in the increasingly pleas-ant Lipscani area, requisite terrace included, City Grill defies the chain stereotype with great Romanian food, wi-fi and likeable staff. Some vegetarian options.

Restaurant Vatra (Map p680; ☎ 315 8375; www .vatra.ro; Str Ion Brezoianu 23-25; mains 17-28 lei; ☺ noon-midnight) While Bucharest restaurant decor gets schlockier, thankfully the food here remains excellent. We almost spun around and left upon eyeing the rustic folk interior, ceramics, weavings and servers in peasant micro-dresses, but the homemade dishes, including a tasty plate of *sarmale* (cabbage or vine leaves stuffed with spiced meat and rice) with *mămăligă*, are filling and reasonably priced.

Vama Veche (Map p678; ☎ 211 6446; Str Cristofor Columb 13; fixed-price menus 18-30 lei) Lunch service slows to a maddening crawl, but the fixed menus are delicious and the apple strudel is worth the wait.

Top End

Smart's (Map p680; ☎ 211 9035; Str Alex Donici 14; mains 20-80 lei; ☺ 11am-late) On a shady lane, this popu-lar pub serves (rather Romanian) pub fare, with a selection of salads (11 to 14 lei) and pastas (15 to 20 lei) out on its peaceful side-walk tables. It's a relaxing spot to sit with a bottle of Leffe.

Mediterraneo (Map p680; ☎ 211 5308; Str Icoanei 20; mains 22-45 lei) This great little corner restaurant on a cobbled back lane draws expats and locals for Turkified Mediterranean fare (fish, kebabs, pastas). Sunday brunch (35 lei) is a big deal.

Count Dracula Club (Map p680; ☎ 312 1353; www .count-dracula.ro; Splaiul Independenţei 8a; mains 22-88 lei; ☺ 4pm-midnight) Even the hardest backpacker has to occasionally submit to kitsch like this: a spooky home with blood-dripping walls, Transylvania-themed rooms, impaled heads, hands reaching through walls, and blood red lights. Plus, Drac himself shows up for a show at 9.30pm on Tuesdays and Fridays. Pull the bell chain to enter.

DRINKING

Bucharest's budding bar scene is liveliest in the Str Lipscani area. Piaţas Universităţii and Unirii bustle with revellers at the weekend.

Piranha Club (off Map p678; ☎ 315 9129; www.club piranha.ro; Spl Independenţei 313; ☺ 10am-late) About 2.5km west of the centre, this unique jungle lodge–type place has piranhas in aquariums, gazebos decked out like country homes, and pretty good food. There are live shows often. It's south of the river, a couple of hundred metres west of the Grozăveşti metro station.

Festival 39 (Cafeneaua Bucuestiului d'Altadata; Map p680; ☎ 0743 333 9909; www.festival39.com; Str Franceza 64) A swanky preclub staging zone, with dark, cosy seating, live piano, a full menu, and scenes of 1930s Bucharest on the wall. Men dressed too casually will be turned away.

Harp (Map p678; ☎ 335 6508; Bibescu Vodă 1) The Irish friendliness of the bouncer won us over at this busy place, adorned with front pages of Irish newspapers. Though pub food is curi-ously absent on the menu (mains 19 to 25 lei), the nicely reproduced pub interior is spot on. Reservations recommended at the weekend.

Fire Club (Map p680; ☎ 0722 390 946; Str Gabroveni 12) This big red-brick room usually has groups of students crouching on stools around small tables with bottles of Tuborg in hand. Rock and punk shows are staged in the basement.

La Butoaie (Map p680; B-dul Nicolae Bălcescu 2) Huge and priced for uni students (meaning cheap beer), this lively open-deck bar on the 5th floor of the Ion Luca Caragiale National Theatre fits hundreds, with benches and big pillows in seating areas. It fills early on warm days. Live music and movies shown on weekends.

ENTERTAINMENT
Şapte Seri (Seven Evenings; www.sapteseri.ro) and *24-Fun* are free, weekly entertainment listings magazines (in Romanian).

Cinemas
Bucharest is fond of the movies, and plays foreign-language films in their original language. A few options:
Cinema Pro (Map p680; B-dul IC Brătianu 6; tickets 11 lei)
Hollywood Multiplex (Map p678; ☎ 327 7020; Bucureşti Mall, Calea Vitan 55-59; tickets 13-21 lei) Multiscreen jobbie.

Nightclubs
Club A (Map p680; ☎ 315 6853; Str Blănari 14; 9pm-5am Thu-Sun) Run by students, this club is a classic and is beloved by all who go there. Cheap beer and rock tunes fill the house until 5am Friday and Saturday nights.

Twice (Map p680; ☎ 313 5593; Str Sfânta Vineri 4, Sect 3; 9pm-5am) DJs and amateur stripping are part of the hip-to-hip youth dancing across two rooms. As one candid local put it, 'go there if you're desperate and drunk'.

Gay & Lesbian Venues
Bucharest's first and most popular gay disco is **Queen's** (off Map p678; Str Juliu Barach 13; noon-3am).

For more information on Romania's gay and lesbian community, see p740.

Performing Arts
For information on seeing the philharmonic at the Romanian Athenaeum, see p682.

At the **Opera House** (Opera Română; Map p678; ☎ 313 1857; B-dul Mihail Kogălniceanu 70) you can enjoy a full-scale opera in a lovely building for 8 to 16 lei.

SHOPPING
For beautifully made woven rugs, table runners, national Romanian costumes, ceramics and other local crafts, don't miss the excellent folk-art shop inside the Museum of the Romanian Peasant (p682).

Librăria Noi (Map p680; ☎ 311 0700; B-dul Nicolae Bălcescu 18; 9.30am-8.15pm Mon-Sat, 11am-6.45pm Sun) has a great collection of antique books and maps.

GETTING THERE & AWAY
Air
International flights use the **Henri Coanda airport** (formerly Otopeni; ☎ 204 1000; www.otp-airport.ro; Şos Bucureşti-Ploieşti), 16.5km north of Bucharest on the road to Braşov. Arrivals and departures use marked side-by-side terminals (arrivals are to the north). There are **information desks** (☎ 204 1220; 24hr) in both terminals.

Băneasa airport (off Map p678; ☎ 232 0020; Şos Bucureşti-Ploieşti 40), 8km north of the centre, is used for some internal and charter flights.

Romania's national airline is **Tarom** (Transporturile Aeriene Române; www.tarom.ro; airport ☎ 317 4444; centre Map p680; ☎ 337 0400; Spl Independenţei 17; 8.30am-7.30pm Mon-Fri, 9am-2pm Sat).

See p742 for details of international flights to Romania, and p743 for domestic-flight information.

Bus
DOMESTIC DESTINATIONS
Bucharest's bus system is frankly a mess, scarred by ever-changing departure locations, companies and schedules. Try checking www.cdy.ro or asking your hotel to help with the latest. Or stick with the train.

The most popular routes are the maxitaxis to Braşov (21 lei, 2½ hours), which stop in Sinaia (17 lei), Buşteni and Predeal on the way. Some continue on to Sighişoara (35 lei, five hours). **C&I** (off Map p678; ☎ 256 8039; Str Ritmului 35) runs these from its office 3.25km east of Piaţa Romana: from metro station Piaţa Iancului, go south for one block on Şoseaua Mihei Bravu (toward Maxbet Casino) and right on B-dul Ferdinand. It's up two blocks on the left. Buses 69 and 85 go there from Gara de Nord.

Every 45 minutes or so, maxitaxis head for Constanţa (33 lei, 3½ hours) from the so-called **Central Bus Station** (Autogara; Map p678), which is located about 350m southeast of the train station.

INTERNATIONAL BUSES
The biggest name in international buses is **Eurolines** (☎ 316 3661; www.eurolines.ro; Str Buzeşti 44; 24hr), which links many Western European destinations with Bucharest. Services include four weekly buses to Athens (293 lei,

22 hours), three weekly to Berlin (458 lei, 32 hours) and to Rome (330 lei, 37 to 40 hours), a daily bus to Vienna (253 lei, 25 hours) and four weekly to Paris (403 lei, 39 hours). Working with Eurolines, **Atlassib** (www.atlassib .ro) handles Italian destinations.

Daily maxitaxis to Sofia, Bulgaria (66 lei) depart at 3.44pm from **Double T** (Map p680; ☎ 313 3642; Calea Victoriei 2; ☺ 6am-9pm).

Those who are Turkey-bound have several options leaving from around Gara de Nord, including **Ortadoğu Tur** (Map p678; ☎ 318 7538; Str Gara de Nord 6-8) and **Toros** (Map p678; ☎ 233 1898; Calea Griviţei 134-136). The 12-hour trip costs about 150 lei one way.

Car & Motorcycle
Bucharest offers some of the country's cheapest car-rental rates. Major car-rental agencies can be found at the Henri Coanda airport arrivals hall. Cheapest are **C&V** (☎ 201 4611, 0788-998 877; www .dvtouring.ro) and **Autonom** (www.autonom.com), offering the Dacia Logan for 126 lei per day (including unlimited mileage and insurance, minimum two days); it falls to 104 lei per day if you rent for more than a week. The tinier Daewoo Matiz goes for 90 lei and 72 lei, respectively.

Hourly parking rates apply in the centre, particularly off Piaţa Victoriei and Piaţa Universităţii – look for the wardens in yellow-and-blue uniforms. In many places you can just pull onto the sidewalk.

Train
Gara de Nord (Map p678; ☎ 319 9539; Piaţa Gara de Nord 1) is the central station for national and international trains. Call ☎ 021 9521 or ☎ 021 9522 for telephone reservations. It has two halls, where same-day tickets can be purchased. Facing the station, the one to the right sells 1st- and 2nd-class domestic tickets; the one to the left sells international (marked 'casa internaţionale') and 1st-class domestic tickets. At night, if you don't have a ticket, you have to pay 1 leu to enter the station.

Tickets can also be purchased at **Agenţie de Voiaj CFR office** (Map p680; ☎ 313 2643; www.cfr.ro; Str Domnita Anastasia 10-14; ☺ 7.30am-7.30pm Mon-Fri, 9am-1.30pm Sat). A seat reservation is compulsory if you are travelling with an Inter-Rail or Eurail pass. Wasteels agency on the platform (see p679) can help out too. International tickets must be bought in advance.

Some local trains to/from Constanţa use Gara Obor station (off Map p678),

DOMESTIC TRAINS FROM BUCHAREST

Sample direct daily service:

Destination	Price (lei)	Duration (hr)	Daily departures
Braşov	37	2½	frequent
Cluj-Napoca	69	7½	five
Constanţa	44	2-4	seven
Iaşi	71	7	six
Sibiu	57	5	four
Sighişoara	53	4½	eight
Suceava	71	8	six
Timişoara	86	8	seven
Tulcea	39	6	one

east of the centre. Bus 85 goes between the two stations.

Check the latest train schedules on either www.cfr.ro or the reliable German site www.bahn.de.

Daily international services include four trains to Budapest's Keleti station (13 to 15 hours); two trains to Sofia (11 hours) and Gorna Oryakhovitsa (near Veliko Târnovo, Bulgaria; 6½ hours); and one train each to Belgrade (12 hours), Chişinău (12 hours), Vienna (16 to 17 hours), İstanbul (20 hours), Kyiv (31 hours) and Moscow (47 hours).

GETTING AROUND
To/From the Airport
BUS
To get to Henri Coanda (Otopeni) or Băneasa airport, take bus 783 from the city centre, departing every 15 minutes between 5.37am and 11.23pm (every half-hour at weekends) from Piaţas Unirii and Victoriei and every *piaţa* in between. The Piaţa Unirii stop is on the south side.

Buy a ticket, valid for a round trip or two people one way, for 7 lei at any RATB (Régie Autonome de Transport de Bucureşti) bus-ticket booth near a bus stop. Once inside the bus remember to feed the ticket into the stamping machine.

Băneasa is 40 to 100 minutes from the centre, depending on traffic; get off at the 'aeroportul Băneasa' stop.

Henri Coanda is about 60 to 120 minutes from the centre. The bus stops outside the departures hall then continues to arrivals.

To get to the centre from Henri Coanda, catch bus 783 from the downstairs ramp outside the arrivals hall; you'll need to buy a ticket

TAXI

Taking a reputable taxi from the centre to Otopeni should cost no more than 50 to 70 lei. Fly Taxi monopolises airport transfers to the centre, though at 3.3 lei per km, they're the most expensive. Alternatively, cross the street, enter the parking ramp and enquire at the taxis waiting there. Look for prices on the door (about 1.7 lei) or agree on a fixed price. Avoid the illegal taxis with no posted prices or meters.

TRAIN

At the time of writing, in a long-awaited response to the increasingly slow and unpredictable journey by road, train service to Henri Coanda had just begun, leaving hourly from Gara de Nord from 5am to 11pm. The journey (6 lei, 45 minutes) includes a short shuttle-bus ride from the train terminus to the airport.

Public Transport

You can buy tickets (1.30 lei) for buses, trams and trolleybuses at any **RATB** (www.ratb.ro) street kiosk, marked 'casa de bilete' or simply 'bilete'. Punch your ticket on board or risk an on-the-spot fine.

Public transport runs from 5am to about 11pm (reduced service on Sunday). There's some info online. The *100% Planul Oraşului Bucureşti Map* is a good map with routes.

Bucharest's metro dates from 1979 and has four lines and 46 stations. Trains run every five to seven minutes during peak periods and about every 20 minutes off-peak between 5.30am and 11.30pm.

To use the metro, buy a magnetic-strip ticket at the subterranean kiosks inside the main entrance to the metro station. Tickets valid for two/10 journeys cost 2.20/8 lei. A one-month unlimited travel ticket costs 23 lei. A one-day unlimited-ride ticket is 4 lei.

Taxi

Opt for a cab with a meter, and avoid the guys outside Gara de Nord. It's best to call one, or have a restaurant or hotel call for you. Reputable companies include **Cobalcescu** (☎ 021 9451), **CrisTaxi** (☎ 021 9461) and **Taxi Sprint** (☎ 021 9495). Check that the meter is on; rates are posted on the door.

AROUND BUCHAREST

The tomb of infamous tyrant Vlad Ţepeş lures visitors to **Snagov** (about 40km north of Bucharest) – as much as the large lake and leisure complex. Devour the legend of Dracula by visiting the grave where his headless torso is said to lie, buried in the famous 16th-century **church and monastery**, on an island in Snagov Lake.

Most visitors go by organised day trip – and hostels like Butterfly Villa Hostel (p683) in Bucharest arrange these, usually dropping by **Căldăruşani Monastery.**

It's possible to go by maxitaxi; they leave hourly from Piaţa Universităţii via Piaţa Romana, Piaţa Presei and the Press House in Bucharest (5 lei each way). Once there, a good destination is **Complex Astoria** (☎ 316 7550; s/d 128/186 lei; ⊗), which has tennis courts and rents boats to take to the church. It has three- and four-star rooms too. It's on the south side of the lake a few kilometres east of the town centre. There are no signs directing drivers: go through Snagov, then left at the railroad tracks.

WALLACHIA

Wallachia (Ţara Românească) is regularly omitted by travellers eager to pounce on Romania's marquee destinations. This leaves copious elbow room for you, the intrepid nonconformer, to tour some of the country's most beautiful and peaceful monasteries, take in some of Romania's more obscure but very special sights and delve into the heart of the sizeable Roma community.

That personal space evaporates when you approach the heart-stopping and relatively popular Transfăgărăşan Rd. In the summer months (roughly from June to September), fearless drivers and nervous passengers can navigate one of the highest roads in Europe, cutting dramatically across the Făgăraş Mountains from its starting point north of Curtea de Argeş.

CURTEA DE ARGEŞ

☎ 0248 / pop 33,400

Curtea de Argeş has a humble, likeable charm, enriched by the captivating treasures left over from being a princely seat in the 14th century. Its church is considered to be the oldest monument preserved in its original form in Wallachia. The city's storied monastery, home to the Episcopal cathedral, sculpted from white stone, is unique for its chocolate-box architecture and the important royal tombs it hides.

The historic town is a gateway to the Făgăraş Mountains.

Orientation

The train station, a 19th-century architectural monument, is 50m north of the bus station on Str Albeşti. The centre is a 10-minute walk along Str Albeşti then up the cobbled Str Castanilor and along Str Negru Vodă. Continue on until you reach a statue of Basarab I, from where all the major sights, a camping ground and hotels (signposted) are a short walk.

Information

Raiffeisen Bank (B-dul Basarabilor; 🕑 8.30am-6.30pm Mon-Fri) is next to Hotel Posada.

The **post office** (B-dul Basarabilor 17-19; 🕑 7am-8pm Mon-Fri) and the telephone office are in the same building.

There is a **tourist office** (☎ 721 451; B-dul Basarabilor 27-29; 🕑 9am-5pm Mon-Fri) at Hotel Posada.

Sights

PRINCELY COURT

The ruins of the **Princely Court** (Curtea Domnească; 🕑 10am-6pm; adult/student 3/1 lei, camera 5 lei), which originally comprised a church and palace, are in the city centre. The church was built in the 14th century by Basarab I, whose statue stands in the square outside the entrance to the court.

Basarab died in 1352. His burial place near the altar in the princely church at Curtea de Argeş was discovered in 1939. The princely court was rebuilt by Basarab's son, Nicolae Alexandru Basarab (r 1352-68), and completed by Vlaicu Vodă (r 1361-77). While precious little remains of the palace today, the 14th-century church (built on the ruins of a 13th-century church) is almost perfectly intact.

HISTORIC CENTRE

The **County Museum** (Muzeul Orăşenesc; ☎ 711 446; Str Negru Vodă 2; adult/student 3/1 lei; 🕑 9am-4pm Tue-Sun) charts the history of the region. If it's locked, enquire upstairs. Rising on a hill are the ruins

of the 14th-century **Biserica Sân Nicoară** (Sân Nicoară Church).

CURTEA DE ARGEŞ MONASTERY

This fantastical **Episcopal cathedral** (Mănăstirea Curtea de Argeş; adult/child 2/1 lei; 🕑 8am-7pm) was built between 1514 and 1526 by Neagoe Basarab (r 1512-21) with marble and mosaic tiles from Constantinople. Legend has it that the wife of Manole, the master stonemason, was embedded in the church's walls, in accordance with a local custom obliging the mason to bury a loved one alive within the church to ensure the success of his work. Manole told his workers that the first wife to bring their lunch the next day would be entombed. The workers duly went home and warned their women – and so Manole's wife arrived first.

The current edifice dates from 1875 when French architect André Lecomte du Nouy was brought in to save the monastery, which was in near ruins.

The white marble tombstones of King Carol I (1839-1914) and his poet wife Elizabeth (1853-1916) lie to the right of the entrance. To the left of the entrance are the tombstones of King Ferdinand I (1865-1927) and British-born Queen Marie (1875-1938) whose heart, upon her request, was put in a gold casket and buried in her favourite palace in Balcic in southern Dobrogea. Following the ceding of southern Dobrogea to Bulgaria in 1940, however, her heart was moved to a marble tomb in Bran. Neagoe Basarab and his wife are also buried in the *pronaos*.

In the park across the road lies **Manole's Well**. Legend has it that Manole tried – and failed – to fly from the monastery roof when his master, Neagoe, removed the scaffolding to prevent him building a more beautiful structure for anyone else. The distant natural spring marks the hapless, and apparently aerodynamic, stonemason's supposed landing pad.

Sleeping

our pick **Pensiunea Ruxi** (☎ 0727 827 675; Str Negru Vodă 104; www.pensiunea-ruxi.ro; r 90 lei; 🖳) Across from Hotel Confarg. While the rooms are new and comfortable, the real treat is the homey atmosphere; the family will go to heart-warming lengths to make sure you're taken care of. Daughter Ruxandra's computer is available for quick email checks for those who ask nicely. Breakfast costs 12 lei.

Hotel Confarg (☎ 728 020; Str Negru Vodă 5; s/d/ste 95/140/180 lei) Rooms are large and modern. Doubles have huge tubs and the suites are relatively swanky for the price.

Hotel Posada (☎ 721 451; www.posada.ro; B-dul Basarbilor 27-29; d 160 lei) Under massive renovations at our visit, so expect prices for updated rooms to rise. Try to get a front room to watch the sunset over the mountains. Wi-fi included.

Eating & Drinking

Restaurant Capra Neagră (☎ 721 619; Str Alexandru Lahovary; mains 6-9 lei) Sit on the terrace here and enjoy Romanian dishes.

Crema Basarbilor (☎ 0744 653 750; B-dul Basarbilor 106; mains 8-32 lei; ⏰ 11.30am-11pm) The summer camp–inspired terrace is nice, but sit inside to enjoy the full menu of classic Romanian fare, with a few 'international' dishes for pizazz, including an 'English Breakfast'. There's a short vegetarian menu. The restaurant is just 20m from the Princely Court, toward the centre. Free wi-fi.

Montana Pizzerie (☎ 722 364; B-dul Basarbilor 72; pizzas 9-15 lei; ⏰ 7am-11pm) This place serves up fresh pizzas and beer. Most nights there is live music. It has a few decent rooms (doubles 125 lei) upstairs.

Getting There & Away

There are nine daily trains running to/from Piteşti (3.90 lei, one hour). Change at Piteşti for all train routes.

State buses run from the bus station to/from Braşov (one daily at 10am), stopping at Arefu and Câmpulung Muscel. Bucharest service runs five times a day on weekdays and three per day on weekends.

A daily maxitaxi to Bucharest via Piteşti leaves at 8am from outside Hotel Posada. Other maxitaxis go to/from Arefu and Piteşti from an unofficial **maxitaxi stop** (cnr Str Mai 1 & Str Lascăr Catargiu).

TRANSYLVANIA

After a century of being name-checked in literature and cinema, the word 'Transylvania' enjoys instant, worldwide recognition. The mere mention of it conjures waves of imagery: mind-bending mountains, Gothic castles, fortified churches, dusty peasant villages, spooky moonlight and a roll-call of bloodthirsty, shape-shifting creatures with wicked overbites.

Unexplained puncture wounds to the neck notwithstanding, Transylvania is all those things and more. The Carpathian Mountains are indeed spectacular, with hiking and skiing cited as being second only to Switzerland. Valleys are dotted with Saxon towns and fortified churches from the Middle Ages. The well-beaten paths up to Bran and Peleş Castles are absolutely worth the crowd-rage. And Dracula's face will stare back at you from a variety of coffee mugs and T-shirts.

Ancient walls, cobblestones, singular architecture and trendy sidewalk cafes pepper the towns of Braşov, Sighişoara and Sibiu – Transylvania's 'Big Three' – the latter of which is still aglow from its tenure as an EU 'Cultural Capital' in 2007. For a little less 'ahhhh', and a little more 'aiii!!', the booming student town Cluj-Napoca is where you'll find the country's most agreeable nightlife.

However, it's said that true Romania begins only when you get to the villages. Try to get some wheels and venture out on your own to the more remote Saxon villages, where two horse carts equals a traffic jam.

SINAIA
☎ 0244 / pop 14,600

Build an eye-popping castle and they will come. Little did King Carol I know that Peleş Castle, his decadent summer residence doubtlessly designed to invoke wretched envy in visiting royal counterparts, would eventually be overrun by busloads of gawking tourists. Situated on the Bucharest–Braşov highway, it's difficult to avoid this defining sight, evidenced by the state of the car park. There are plenty of supplementary century-old buildings throughout town, too, a few now serving as hotels.

Sinaia is set among an exquisite, fir-clad scrap of the towering Bucegi Mountains, offering ski runs and hiking trails for year-round fun. It's a little hectic, but wait for the buses to leave or time a mid-autumn or spring visit, and you'll find the resort's peaceful side.

Sinaia is alleged to have gained its name from Romanian noble Mihai Cantacuzino, who, following a pilgrimage to Mt Sinai in Israel in 1695, founded the Sinaia Monastery. It developed into a major resort after King Carol I selected the area for his summer residence in 1870.

BUCEGI MOUNTAINS

Sinaia and Bușteni, 5km north, are the principal gateways to this stunning (and popular) mountain range of dizzying skiing, mountain-biking and hiking fun on a plateau situated high up on the border of Transylvania and Wallachia. Hikes are well marked – some make for great biking. Things get harsh when winds and weather rush over the plateau. There are cabanas up here, but most visitors go as a day trip. Talk to Snow (below) in Sinaia about ski runs and biking trails, or to get equipment.

From Sinaia, the 30-person **cable car** (☎ 311 764/872; to Cota 1400/Cota 2000 one way 13/23.50 lei, return 26/47 lei; ☽ 9am-5pm) leaves half-hourly to two station points (Cota 1400 and Cota 2000), but lines stack for a couple of hours in summer (roughly mid-June to mid-September); get there by 7am. **Bușteni's cable-car station** (☎ 320 306; one way/return 23.50/47 lei; ☽ 8.30am-5pm Wed-Mon, 10.30am-5pm Tue) is another access point.

It's possible to hike from the top to Bran – it's about five hours' hike from atop Cota 2000 to Cabana Omul, and another five downhill into Bran. It's a *very* rough hike going up from Bran. Day or overnight trips require the 1:70,000 Dimap trail map of Bucegi, which has trail-marker details.

Orientation & Information

The train station is directly downhill from the centre of town. From the station climb up the stairway across the street to busy B-dul Carol I. The centre and cable car are to the left, the palace is uphill to the right.

Amco's *Ploiești* map includes a so-so city map. Better is the SunCart *Sinaia* map (10 lei), which also includes Bușteni.

Banca Transilvania (B-dul Carol I nr 14; ☽ 9am-5pm Mon-Fri, 9.30am-12.30pm Sat) Has a 24-hour ATM; foreign-exchange service is next door.

Central post office (☎ 311 591; B-dul Carol I 3; ☽ 7am-8pm Mon-Fri, 8am-1pm Sat)

Dracula's Land (☎ 311 441; mihneasutu@yahoo.com; B-dul Carol I nr 14; ☽ 9am-5pm) It hides its tacky name for the street (its sign merely says 'Tourist Office'), but some chummy blokes inside can help find a villa or hotel room for you, arrange hiking guides or change money.

Eco Laundry (☎ 0788 660 788; B-dul Carol I 31; ☽ 7am-4pm) Drop-off laundry behind the big grey building. It's 3 to 10 lei per article of clothing. Try to cut a whole-load deal.

Flower Power (B-dul Carol I; ☽ 9am-7pm Mon-Fri) Bookshop carrying area maps, man.

Salvamont (☎ 313 131, nationwide 0-SALVAMONT; Primărie, B-dul Carol I) Inside the tourist information centre and at Cota 2000 chairlift station; 24-hour mountain-rescue service.

Sinaia tourism information centre (☎ 315 656; www.info-sinaia.ro; B-dul Carol I 47; ☽ 8.30am-4.30pm Mon-Fri) Lots and lots of information and brochures and maps, but it can't book rooms.

Telephone office (☽ 10am-6pm Mon-Fri, to 2pm Sat) In the same building as the central post office. Their public fax line is 314 010.

Sights

Romania's new monarchy debuted in a blaze of pomp with **Peleș Castle** (☎ 310 205; compulsory tours adult/child 15/5 lei; ☽ 11am-5pm Tue, 9am-4.15pm Wed-Sun), a 20-minute walk up from the centre. King Carol I's vision of fairy-tale turrets rising above acres of green meadows and grand reception halls in alternating Moorish, Florentine and French styles is still awe-inspiring a century later. Endless heavy woodcarved ceilings and gilded pieces induce crossing eyes. Worthwhile tours take in the 1st floor only – note the ground-breaking central vacuuming system.

About 100m up the hill from the castle, the German-medieval **Pelișor Palace** (☎ 310918; compulsory tours adult/child 10/3 lei; ☽ 9am-5pm Wed-Sun) has a hard time competing with its neighbour. Built by King Carol to house his nephew (and future king) Ferdinand (1865–1927) and wife Marie (who didn't get on well with King C and loathed Peleș; its art nouveau style is certainly less showy. The popular Marie died in the arched gold room upstairs.

Activities

Near the cable car, **Snow** (☎ 311 198; Str Cuza Voda 2a; ☽ 9am-6pm) rents out skis and snowboards for 35 lei per day, and bikes for 12/60 lei per hour/day.

Skis can also be rented at Cota 1400; mountain bikes can be rented at the **bike outlet** (☎ 314 906; Str Octavia Goga 1; per hr 16 lei; ☽ 8am-6pm).

Sleeping

Travel agencies around town can find you a room in one of the countless pensions starting

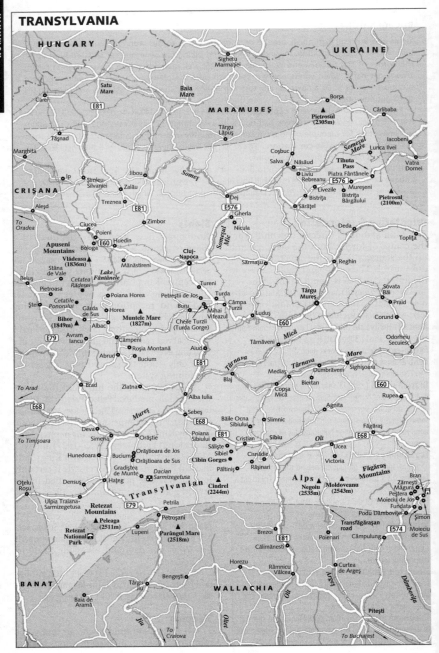

TRANSYLVANIA

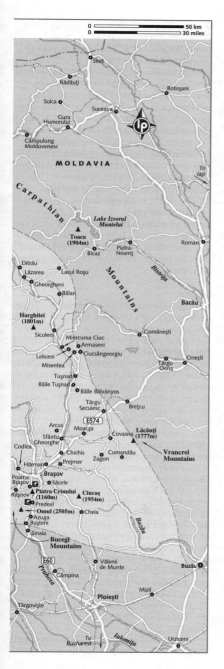

at 100 lei. In the Bucegi Mountains there are several cabanas that, purportedly, always have a space for a hiker in need of winks. Some have no electricity.

Hotel Economat (☎ 311 151; srpsinaia@apps.ro; Aleea Peleşului 2; s/d from 90/180 lei) Just outside the Peleş gate, this place has decent rooms in a setting lovely enough that first-time visitors have been known to mistake it for the castle! There are a few 'Villa Turistica' choices here, the best being the two-star Corpul Villa (doubles with shared/private bathroom 100/160 lei).

Hotel Caraiman (☎ 313 551; B-dul Carol I nr. 4; palace@rdslink.ro; s/d/apt 135/180/235 lei) Of the faded-glory century-old hotels – and Sinaia teems with them – we like the large rooms at the 1881 red-and-white Caraiman most, for being less royal ball and more rustic and laid-back. Free wi-fi.

Marami Hotel (☎ 315 560; www.marami.ro; Str Furnica 52; s/d/ste 200/220/240 lei; 🐾) The chalet-style frame looks a little cheap, but this is probably Sinaia's best midrange option. The vibe is slightly art deco and dorm-y with a hint of IKEA. Request a balcony room. Wi-fi, sauna and jacuzzi available.

Eating

There are a few fast-food stands and pizza places along B-dul Carol I.

Irish House (☎ 310 060; www.irishhouse.ro; B-dul Carol I nr 80; mains 10-30 lei; 🕙 8am-midnight) There's Guinness on tap (9 lei), green ceilings, and a few token Irish dishes on the menu, including an 'Irish Breakfast' (11 lei). But this place fills for its good Romanian food and reasonably priced pizzas.

Snow (☎ 311 198; Str Cuza Voda; mains 15-47 lei; 🕙 9am-11pm) Snow gets busiest with ski and bike rentals, but its outdoor-indoor Romanian restaurant does decent fare, including a few vegetarian dishes.

La Brace (☎ 310 348; Str Coştilei 27; mains 15-48 lei; 🕙 11am-midnight Mon-Fri, 9.30am-midnight Sat & Sun) You'll have earned a good meal by the time you hike up here – it's a 15-minute walk from the centre (follow the signs). Amid trees, near passing cable cars, this place is popular for its pizza and pastas.

Getting There & Away

Sinaia is on the Bucharest–Braşov rail line – 126km from the former and 45km from the latter – so jumping on a train to Bucharest (24 lei, 1½ hours) or Braşov (16.1 lei, one hour) is a cinch.

Buses and maxitaxis run every 45 minutes between roughly 7am and 10pm from the central bus stop on B-dul Carol I to Azuga (10 minutes) and Buşteni (3 lei, 20 minutes); some go all the way to Bucharest or Braşov. Rates are less than the train, and the trip is quicker, but there's little room for luggage. Pay the driver.

BRAŞOV

☎ 0268/0368 / pop 284,600

Braşov (Brassó in Hungarian) is Romania's ground-zero tourist destination for very good reason. Ringed by perfect mountains and verdant hills (never mind the faux-Hollywood 'Braşov' sign up there), the city is adorned with baroque facades, bohemian outdoor cafes and the lovely Piaţa Sfatului – one of Romania's finest squares. The agreeable locals are seemingly impervious to the increasing number of visitors each summer. The city is a joy to wander, good food is easy to find and innumerable day trips can be launched from here: hiking or skiing in the Bucegi Mountains, castling in Bran, Râşnov and Sinaia and more.

Braşov started out as a German mercantile colony named Kronstadt. At the border of three principalities, it became a major medieval trading centre. The Saxons built some ornate churches and town houses, protected by a massive wall that still remains.

Orientation

Several brick pedestrian lanes lead from central Piaţa Sfatului, including Str Republicii, which leads north to B-dul Eroilor and Parcul Central. B-dul Eroilor also links two other main thoroughfares, Str Mureşenilor to its west and Str Nicolae Bălcescu to its east.

The train station is 3km northeast of the city centre. Braşov has a few bus stations – Autogara 1, next to the train station, is the most active.

Information

You'll find numerous ATMs, banks and exchange offices on and around Str Republicii and B-dul Eroilor.

Aventours (☎ 472 718; www.discoveromania.ro; Str Paul Richter 1; ⏰ 10am-3pm Mon-Fri) This small agency, led by English-speaking guides, offers great tailor-made tours (particularly mountain-based ones) and oodles of information on the area.

Central post office (☎ 411 609; Str Iorga Nicolae 1; ⏰ 7am-8pm Mon-Fri, 8am-1pm Sat)

County Hospital (☎ 333 666; Calea Bucureşti 25-27; ⏰ 24hr)

Extreme Adventure (☎ 0723 990 776; www.extreme adventure.ro) As advertised, hiking, mountain-biking, climbing, skiing and heliskiing adventures are on offer.

Left luggage (per day 6 lei; ⏰ 24hr) At the train station, it's located in the underpass that leads out from the tracks.

Librărie George Coşbuc (☎ 444 395; Str Republicii 29; ⏰ 9am-7pm Mon-Fri, 10am-4pm Sat) Bookshop.

Raiffeisen Bank (Piaţa Sfatului; ⏰ 9am-6.30pm Mon-Fri, 10am-2pm Sat) Gives cash advances on Visa and MasterCard.

Salvamont (☎ 0725 826 668, nationwide 0-SALVAMONT) Emergency rescue for the mountains.

Tibi (☎ 410 185; Str Gheorghe Bariţiu 8; per hr 3 lei; ⏰ 24hr) Internet access.

Tourist information centre (☎ 419 078; www .brasovcity.ro; Piaţa Sfatului 30; ⏰ 9am-5pm) In the gold city council building, the English-speaking staff can point you to tour services, offer free brochures and track down hotel vacancies.

Sights

Though sorely lacking in decent museums, drifting through Braşov's medieval glory is arresting enough.

A good starting point for a walk is central **Piaţa Sfatalui**, where witches were once burned and prisoners tortured in the gold **Council House** (Casa Sfatului), which dates from 1420; listen closely when passing (we hear that a caretaker hastily quit after hearing 'ghostly screams' from the tower at night). The building also houses the good tourist information centre and unmemorable **Braşov Historical Museum** (☎ 472 350; adult/student 5/1 lei; ⏰ 10am-6pm Tue-Sun Jun-Sep, 9am-5pm Tue-Sun Oct-May).

Looming from the south, the Gothic **Black Church** (Biserica Neagră; admission 4 lei; ⏰ 10am-5pm Mon-Sat), built between 1384 and 1477, gained its name after a 1689 fire blackened its walls. It's noticeably less black these days after an over-ambitious scrub-down. Inside the church (supposedly the largest Gothic place of worship between Vienna and İstanbul) you can view apse statues moved from outside and 120 fabulous Turkish rugs – merchants' gifts after Ottoman shopping sprees. Organ recitals on the 4000-pipe instrument are usually held in July and August, at 6pm on Tuesdays, Thursdays and Saturdays (5 lei).

A couple of blocks east, cobblestone **Stradă Sforii** is one of Europe's narrowest 'streets',

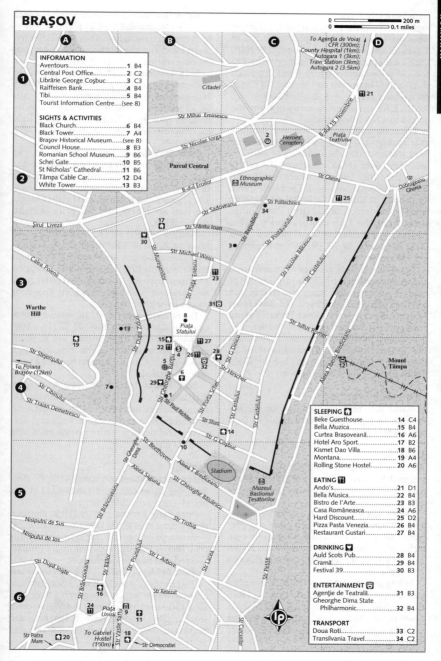

BRAŞOV

Citadel

Str Mihai Eminescu

To Agenţia de Voiaj
CFR (300m);
County Hospital (1km);
Autogara 1 (3km);
Train Station (3km);
Autogara 2 (3.5km)

21

Str Nicolae Iorga

2

Heroes'
Cemetery

Piaţa
Teatrului

Parcul Central

Ethnographic
Museum

Str Gherea

B-dul Eroilor

Str
Dobrogeanu
Gherea

Şirul Livezii

Str Sadoveanu

Str Politechnicii
34

25

17

Str Sfântu Ioan

30

Str Republicii

33

Calea Poienii

Str Michael Weiss

3

Str Poştavarilor

Str Nicolae Bălcescu

Str Castelului

23

Warthe
Hill

Str Piaţa Enescu

Str Mureşenilor

31

8

13

Piaţa
Statului

Str Julius Romer

Aleea Tiberiu Brediceanu

**Mount
Tâmpa**

12

19

Str Stejerişului

15
22

27

28

32

Str C Diniu

To Poiana
Braşov (12km)

5

4

26

Str Hirscher

Str Gheorghe Bariţiu

Str Castelului

Str Cerbului

Str Cibinului

7

6

29

Str Paul Richter

Str Porta Schei

1

Str Traian Demetrescu

Str Sforii

Str G Coşbuc

Str Gheorghe Dima

Str Beethoven

14

Aleea T Brediceanu

10

Stadium

Aleea Saguna

Str Gheorghe Bălulescu

Muzeul
Bastionul
Teşătorilor

Str Brâncoveanu

Nisipului de Sus

Nisipului de Jos

Str După Inişte

Str Prundului

Str L Arbore

Str Lacea

Str Bailor

Str Petofi

Str Trotuş

Str Retezat

16

Str Curcanilor

24

9

11

Piaţa
Unirii

Str Vasile Saftu

18

Str Piatra
Mare

20

To Gabriel
Hostel
(150m)

Str Democraţiei

0 _____ 200 m
0 _____ 0.1 miles

with perfectly framed views of the 'Braşov' sign that looks over town from Mt Tâmpa. This regrettable publicity ploy appeared in 2004 and was enlarged (and floodlit) in 2007. One local laughed it off, 'Do they think I'm too old to remember where I am?' To reach it, take the **Tâmpa cable car** (Telecabina; ☎ 478 657; one way/return 10/20 lei; ⊙ 9.30am-5pm Tue-Sun), well worth it for the stunning views of town and access to a few hiking trails.

From the cable-car station, you'll notice that a substantial portion of the original town wall still encircles the centre. The neoclassical **Schei Gate** (1828) separates the centre from the Schei District, where – in Saxon days – the Romanians lived. The black-spired Orthodox **St Nicholas' Cathedral** (St Nicolae din Scheii; ⊙ 6am-9pm), accessed from Piaţa Unirii, dates from the 14th century and is home to the small **Romanian School Museum** (Prima Scoala Romaneasca; ☎ 511 411; adult/student 5/3 lei; ⊙ 9am-5pm Tue-Sun).

Leave time to look out over the centre from the two towers on the hillside just west of the centre – it's popular when the setting sun puts a golden hue on Braşov. The **Black Tower** (Turnul Neagru) and **White Tower** (Turnul Alba), which are both rather white actually, are reached by a lovely promenade alongside the western city walls and a rushing stream. A side road leads to the promenade from about 200m south of the Black Church.

Festivals & Events

If you're here in April, look out for the **Juni Pageant**. In December Braşov holds its **De la Colind la Stea** festival.

Sleeping

All three hostels are near Piaţa Unirii, and reached by bus 51 from the train station. Each offers a variety of similarly priced castle/village tours.

Gabriel Hostel (☎ 0744 844 223; Str Vasile Saftu 41a; dm/d 35/100 lei; 🖳) This 50-bed place was preparing for a major overhaul during our visit; it should be completed by the time you arrive. Take bus 51 to the last stop; the hostel is just across the street.

Rolling Stone Hostel (☎ 0744 816 970; www.rolling stone.ro; Str Piatra Mare 2a; dm/r from 36/120 lei; 🖳) Run by the high-energy Bolea family, the Stone is a welcoming hostel spot, with an on-site bar and bike rental. There are also off-site private apartments.

Kismet Dao Villa (☎ 514 296; www.kismetdao.ro; Str Democratiei 2b; dm/d 40/130 lei; 🖳) This dorm-y, four-floor, six-room hostel has a DVD library, playful staff and one free beer/soda to get your evening started.

Beke Guesthouse (☎ 511 997; Str Cerbului 32; r with shared bathroom per person 40-50 lei) A lovely Hungarian-speaking couple runs this handful of spartan rooms that overlook a vine-covered courtyard. Often they'll bring by a jug of homemade wine. No breakfast, no sign, no English.

Hotel Aro Sport (☎ 478 800; Str Sfântu Ioan 3; s/d with shared bathroom 56/78 lei) These boxy rooms evoke classic Eastern Europe travel – a sink in the corner and a shower down the hall. They're surprisingly clean and bright though, the staff are lovely, and the price is right. No breakfast.

Montana (☎ 0723 614 534; info@montana.ro; Calea Poienii; s/d 190/230 lei) This super Brady Bunch–style, Kermit-green six-room hillside guest house is up the hill, past the White Tower on a hairpin driveway. It has slanted cedar roofs and seriously pastel room themes. Top-floor rooms have great balconies.

Curtea Braşoveană (☎ 472 336; www.curteabrasov eana.ro; Str Băilor 16; s/d 210/260 lei; 🕱 🖳) In a 100-year-old house, these rooms are modern and immaculate, some with exposed brick and wood ceilings. Buffet breakfast and sauna included.

Bella Muzica (☎ 477 956; www.bellamuzica.ro; Piaţa Sfatului 19; s/d 220/270 lei; 🕱) The terrific 22-room Muzica has very stylish rooms with soft lighting, textured orange walls and old-style wood desks to write poems on. Cable internet only.

Eating

Ando's (B-dul 15 Noiembrie 4; mains 6-11 lei; ⊙ 10am-10pm) Big shawarmas and sandwiches at low prices – and zero character.

Pizza Pasta Venezia (☎ 470 511; Str Hirscher 2; pastas & pizzas 10-24 lei; ⊙ 10am-10pm) Wall-sized Venetian paintings and soft lighting help this cosy Italian restaurant fill before its similar-themed and named neighbours.

Bistro de l'Arte (☎ 0722 219 980; www.bistrodelarte .ro; Piaţa Enescu 11; mains 12-28 lei; ⊙ 9am-1am Mon-Sat, noon-midnight Sun) On the ground floor of a cosy 15th-century building, the Bistro serves small meals – sandwiches, fish, spaghetti and breakfasts. There are excellent loose teas and wi-fi access.

Casa Româneasca (Piaţa Unirii; mains 12-26 lei; noon-midnight) Deep in the Schei district, away from trolling tourists, this *casa* serves tasty *sarmalute cu mamaliguta* (boiled beef rolled with vegetables and cabbage; 15 lei).

our pick **Bella Musica** (☎ 477 956; Str Gheorghe Bariţu 2; mains 12-46 lei) Pretty much everyone's local favourite, this lovely cavernous basement restaurant of red brick and candlelight serves up a few Mexican dishes, but keeps the focus on very tasty Romanian fare. Staff bring a welcome shot of *ţuică*, excellent chips and salsa and a 'music menu' for requests – the list includes 'best ballads' by Uriah Heap, Celine Dion, the Boss and Floyd.

Restaurant Gustari (☎ 475 365; Piaţa Sfatului 14; mains 13-29 lei; 8am-11pm) Despite the questionable tourist-trap location, Gustari keeps it simple – no flashiness, just savoury Romanian food at correct prices. The terrace view is fantastic. It does great *sarmale* (15 lei).

Hard Discount (Str Nicolae Bălcescu; 24hr) is a fully stocked supermarket next to the indoor-outdoor fruit and vegetable market.

Drinking

Cramă (Str Gheorghe Bariţa 20; 9.30am-8pm Mon-Fri, 9am-5pm Sat) A well-hidden alley/basement joint, selling wine from 5 lei per litre for red, and 4.50 lei for white. *Ţuică* is 29.50 lei for 1L – enough to flatten the whole hostel.

Auld Scots Pub (☎ 470 183; Str Hirscher 10; 4pm-2am Tue-Fri, noon-2am Sat & Sun) The kilts and Connery on the walls and seriously overpriced drinks of this inviting bar can be forgiven because of its tasteful sitting areas, three-board dart room and better-than-average pub fare.

Festival 39 (☎ 478 664; Str Mureşenilor 23; 10am-midnight) Cosy, dimly lit, and with stylishly distressed decor. Happy locals fill the tables here when other bars are empty.

Entertainment

The **Gheorghe Dima State Philharmonic** (☎ 473 058; Str Hirscher 10) performs mainly between September and May. Tickets can be purchased at the **Agenţie de Teatrală** (☎ 471 889; Str Republicii 4; 10am-5pm Tue-Fri, to 2pm Sat).

Getting There & Around
BICYCLE
Doua Roti (☎ 470 207; Str Nicolae Bălcescu 55; 8.30am-5pm Mon-Fri, 9am-1pm Sat) is a bike shop selling used bikes from 200 lei.

BUS
Maxitaxis and microbuses are the best way to reach places near Braşov, including Bran, Râşnov and Sinaia. Otherwise it's generally better to go by train.

The most accessible station is **Autogara 1** (☎ 427 267), next to the train station, a ramshackle lot with a booming maxitaxi business (hourly jobs ply the Târgu Mureş–Sighişoara–Braşov–Buşteni–Bucharest route) and some long-distance buses. From 6am to 7.30pm, maxitaxis leave every half-hour for Bucharest (28 lei, 2½ hours), stopping in Buşteni and Sinaia. About four or five maxitaxis leave daily for Sibiu (20 lei, 2½ hours), stopping in Făgăraş town, and Iaşi (48 lei, six to seven hours). Bus 51 goes to/from the centre (pre-buy ticket). In the centre, catch it in Piaţa Unirii or anywhere on Str Nicolae Bălcescu.

Autogara 2 (Bartolomeu; ☎ 426 332; Str Avram Iancu 114), 1km west of the train station, sends half-hourly buses to Râşnov (2.50 lei, 25 minutes) and Bran (4 lei, 40 minutes) from roughly 6.30am to 11.30pm. A dozen daily buses go to Zărneşti (3.50 lei, one hour), fewer on weekends. Take bus 12 to/from the centre (it stops at the roundabout just north of the station).

CAR & MOTORCYCLE
Car-rental rates are higher than in Bucharest, Sibiu or Cluj. **Transilvania Travel** (☎ 477 623; www.transilvaniatravel.com; Str Republicii 62; 10am-6pm Mon-Fri, to 2pm Sat) rents cars from 105 lei daily; prices drop if you rent for a week or more.

TAXI
Taxi drivers seem pretty honest in Braşov. A couple of good agencies are **Martax** (☎ 313 040) and **Tod** (☎ 321 111). Taking a taxi to the 'Three Castles' in Bran, Râşnov and Sinaia costs about 253 lei, including waiting time.

TRAIN
Advance tickets are sold at the **Agenţie de Voiaj CFR** (Str 15 de Noiembre 43; 8am-7.30pm Mon-Fri).

Daily domestic train service includes the following (prices are for 2nd-class seats on rapid trains): at least hourly to Bucharest (32 lei, 2½ hours), a dozen to Sighişoara (34 lei, 2½ hours), nine to Sibiu (29 lei, 2¾ hours), five to Cluj-Napoca (36 lei, six hours), one to Iaşi (54 lei, 8½ hours).

International links include three daily trains to Budapest (seat/sleeper 144/194 lei,

14 hours), one to Vienna (234 lei, 18 hours) and one daily train each to Prague (337 lei, 21 hours) and İstanbul (224 lei, 19 hours).

From the station, take bus 51 to the centre.

AROUND BRAŞOV
Bran & Râsnov
☎ 0268

Though Vlad Ţepeş only dropped by once in the 15th century (maybe), it's hard to skip this so-called 'Dracula's castle', 30km south of Braşov. The atmospheric **Bran Castle** (☎ 238 333; www.brancastlemuseum.ro; adult/student 12/6 lei; 9am-7pm Tue-Sun, noon-7pm Mon May-Sep, 9am-5pm Tue-Sun Oct-Apr) dates from 1378. At first look, the 60m-high castle, set on a rocky outcrop between facing hills, certainly seems like a Hilton for the undead, but the inside – full of tour groups – is somewhat anticlimactic. Queen Marie summered here frequently in the 1920s, as highlighted by exhibits inside.

Bran's **Sâmbra Oilor** festival is held in September.

Râsnov, 12km toward Braşov, doubles the castle intake with the tempting ruins of the 13th-century **Râsnov fortress** (Cetatea Râsnov; ☎ 230 255; admission 12 lei; 9am-8pm May-Oct, to 6pm Nov-Apr). From the central square, steps lead up the hill where inclined alleys and a museum await.

SLEEPING

Generally Bran is a less appealing base than Braşov or other villages in the area. **Antrec** (☎ 236 340, 0788 411 450; www.antrec.ro; Str Principală 509; 9am-5pm Mon-Fri, to 1pm Sat) arranges private accommodation in the area.

Pensiunea Stefi (☎ 0721 303 009; www.hotel stefi-ro.com; Piaţa Unirii 5; r 100 lei;) This five-room guest house, behind the giant red gate in the main square, has carpeted rooms, sauna, fitness centre and a wading pool. Breakfast is 14 lei.

Vila Bran (☎ 236 866; www.vilabran.ro; Str Principală 238; r 100-160 lei) This 103-room, 12-building complex is unflinchingly touristy – three restaurants, tennis court, fitness centre, billiards, flying fox, indoor basketball court – but the view of the hills is worth it. No breakfast. Free wi-fi.

GETTING THERE & AWAY

Buses marked 'Bran-Moeciu' (4 lei, one hour) depart every 40 minutes from Braşov's Autogara 2. Return buses to Braşov leave Bran from roughly 7am to 6pm in winter, to 10pm in summer. All buses to and from Braşov stop at Râsnov.

From Bran there are about a dozen buses daily to Zărneşti (4 lei, 40 minutes).

Poiana Braşov

Braşov's skiers prefer this **mountain** (www.poi ana-brasov.ro), 14km from Braşov and reached by an easy bus trip, over Sinaia's. Ski rental starts at 26 lei per day, an all-day pass is about 250 lei and a five-trip pass is 120 lei. There are good intermediate runs, and a couple of advanced slopes, plus hiking trails in summer.

Just at the bottom of the lift, **Club Rossignol** (☎ 0721 200 470; r 240 lei) has cheap ski rental and large, kid-fort-like loft rooms (mattresses on the floor) with balconies. You can stuff up to four people in a room at no extra charge. Reserve several days in advance in winter. Prices are drastically reduced in summer. No breakfast.

Vila Violeta (☎ 0744 484 441; Str Poiana Doamnei 3; d 140-180 lei) is a humble red-roofed white house hidden off the town's only four-way intersection. Its five rooms range from simple to moderate. No breakfast, but there's a kitchen for guest use.

Bus 20 leaves from B-dul Eroilor in front of the County Library in Braşov every half-hour for Poiana Braşov (4 lei), from where it's a 20-minute walk to the slopes.

Zărneşti
☎ 0268

This windswept town at the edge of the lovely, rugged Piatra Craiului National Park can seem *Twilight Zone*–calibre eerie, but locals are particularly nice, and Zărneşti provides an excellent springboard to nearby hikes.

ORIENTATION & INFORMATION

Buses stop at a roundabout near the post office and about 100m past the city hall along Str Metropolit Ion Meţianu. The train station is about 1km east of city hall.

The **Piatra Craiului National Park Office** (☎ 223 165; www.pcrai.ro; Str Topliţei 150; 8am-4pm Mon-Thu, to 2.30pm Fri) is in a bizarrely located but gorgeously set structure about 2km towards the mountains (west) from the centre of town; follow the 'Plaiu Foii' sign at the bus stop roundabout, then go left at the fork. It has excellent maps and guides available (from 82 lei per day).

ACTIVITIES

The 14,800-hectare Piatra Craiului and its twin-peaked Piatra Mică (Stone of the Prince; no jokes) rise southwest of town. The National Park Office has outstanding maps detailing hiking loops. The yellow-vertical-stripe signs leading from the road either west or south of town mark a four- or five-hour trip that goes through the gorge where Jude Law got shot in *Cold Mountain*. A 30km multiday hike goes along the ridge for about 25km (there are shelters, but no food), finishing at Podul Dambovitei.

SLEEPING

Cabana Gura Raului (☎ 0722 592 375; per person 25 lei) A bit wobbly, but set at the outset of Zărneşti Canyon at the east end of town, this fading cabana offers 17 boxy rooms and food. Breakfast is 7.50 lei.

Pensuine Fabius (☎ 0742 010 498, 0722 523 199; Str Dr Senchea 7; r 75 lei) Run by a lovely family (that includes *two* priests), the five-room Fab offers semirustic rooms with TV and private bath. From the bus stop, go a block on Str Baiulescu, then right on Str Dr Senchea.

GETTING THERE & AWAY

There are 14 daily buses leaving weekdays to Autogara 2 in Braşov (3.5 lei, one hour), and about half that at weekends. About five or six daily buses head to Bran (2.50 lei, 40 minutes).

SIGHIŞOARA

☎ 0265 / pop 32,300

Most famously known as the spot where Vlad 'Ţepeş' Dracula scampered about when impaled Turks were just a twinkle in his eye, this dreamy, medieval citadel town is a destination in its own right. Sighişoara (Schässburg in German, Segesvár in Hungarian) has brightly coloured, half-a-millennium-old town houses bordering hilly cobbled streets, and church bells that clang atmospherically in the early hours. Cute museums uncover the colourful local history. Over the low hills flanking the town are pastures and forests leading to traditional Saxon villages. Bus tours and tacky souvenir carts overwhelm the citadel in summer, often prompting backpackers to flee after one day, but a night here is highly recommended.

Good day trips from here include Saxon Land towns or a day (or two) in the half-Hungarian town of Târgu Mureş.

Information

There are numerous exchange offices lining the city's main street, Str 1 Decembrie 1918. Banca Transilvania has a 24-hour ATM in the citadel, between Piaţa Cetăţii and Muzeulul.

Blink and you'll miss the tiny sign announcing that you can visit the History Museum, the medieval arms collection, and the Torture Room Museum for a combo ticket price of 10 lei (about the same price as the student discounts for all three).

There are internet points in Burg Hostel.

Café International & Family Centre (☎ 777 844; Piaţa Cetăţii 8; internet per hr 3 lei; ☼ 8am-8pm Mon-Sat Jun-Sep; 1-7pm Mon-Sat Oct-May) Internet access. Volunteer staff of this nonprofit agency double as a tourist office (in summer only); they arrange walking tours, rent bikes, and can point you to area hikes.

Eye Tours (☎ 0721 176 299; www.eye-tours.com) Offers day trips to nearby villages and hiking tours.

Post office (Str 1 Decembrie 1918 nr 17; ☼ 7.30am-7.30pm Mon-Fri) In a funny yellow-panel building.

Steaua Agenţie de Turism (☎ 772 499; Str 1 Decembrie 1918 nr 10; ☼ 9.30am-5pm Mon-Fri) Can find private accommodation (starting at 55 lei per person per night) in the residential area northwest of the citadel.

Tourist Information (☎ 770 415; Str O Goga; ☼ 10am-4pm Mon-Fri, 9am-1pm Sat) Can book beds.

Sights

Sighişoara's primary sights are clustered in the compact, delightfully medieval **citadel** – perched on a hillock and fortified with a 14th-century wall, to which 14 towers and five artillery bastions were later added. Today the citadel, which is on the Unesco World Heritage list, retains just nine of its original towers (named for the guilds in charge of keeping them up) and two of its bastions.

Entering the citadel, you pass under the massive **clock tower** (Turnul cu Ceas), which dates from 1280. Inside the great little **History Museum** (☎ 771 108; Piaţa Muzeului 1; adult/child 5/2.50 lei; ☼ 10am-4.30pm Mon, 9am-6.30pm Tue-Fri, 9am-4.30pm Sat & Sun mid-May–mid-Sep, 9am-3.30pm Tue-Fri, 10am-3.30pm Sat & Sun mid-Sep–mid-May), Sighi's tale is told in small rooms off the steps winding up to the 7th-floor lookout, which has superb panoramic views.

Under the clock tower on the right (if heading out of the Old Town) is the small, dark **Torture Room Museum** (admission 3 lei; ☼ 10am-4.30pm Mon, 9am-6.30pm Tue-Fri, 9am-4.30pm Sat & Sun mid-May–mid-Sep, 9am-3.30pm Tue-Fri, 10am-3.30pm Sat & Sun mid-Sep–mid-May), which shows how fingers were

SIGHIŞOARA

smashed and prisoners burned with coals. If it's closed, ask at the medieval arms collection for entry.

Towards Piaţa Cetăţii on the left, the small **Collection of Medieval Arms** (adult/student 4/2 lei; 10am-4.30pm Mon, 9am-6.30pm Tue-Fri, 9am-4.30pm Sat & Sun mid-May–mid-Sep, 9am-3.30pm Tue-Fri, 10am-3.30pm Sat & Sun mid-Sep–mid-May) has four rooms devoted to medieval helmets, shields, crossbows and maces.

Hidden away behind the 15th-century **Church of the Dominican Monastery** (Biserica Mănăstirii), across from the museum, is a **Vlad Ţepeş statue**, showing the legend with his trademark 1980s porno moustache.

Speaking of, continuing west towards Piaţa Cetăţii, you come to the renovated **Casa Dracula** (now a restaurant; see opposite), in which Vlad Ţepeş reputedly lived until the age of four.

The quiet, minuscule **Piaţa Cetăţii** is the heart of old Sighişoara. It was here that markets and public executions were held.

From the square, turn left up Str Şcolii to the 172 steps of the **covered stairway** (scara acoperit), to the 1345 Gothic **Church on the Hill** (Biserica din Deal; Bergkirche; mid-Apr–Oct), a 429m-high Lutheran church with an atmospheric German cemetery just behind.

Escape the crowds and visit the **Breite Ancient Oak Tree Reserve** (506 024; www.breite.ro), recently saved from being catastrophically developed into a Dracula theme park. Managed by the Mihai Eminescu Trust and the Sighisoara Local Council, it's currently 70 hectares (with expansion to 133 hectares pending). The oldest oaks are roughly 800 years old, with circumferences of 400cm to 600cm. Follow Str Ilarie Chendie southwest for about 2km (it changes to Str Ana Ipatescu after the bridge), then turn right onto Str Vasile Lucaci. Take the unsigned left or right forks (the middle is a dead end).

Festivals & Events
Sighişoara's **Medieval Festival of the Arts** happens in July.

Sleeping
Burg Hostel (☎ 778 489; www.ibz.ro; Str Bastionului 4-6; dm 30 lei, s/d with shared bathroom 50/78 lei, s/d with private bathroom 70/86 lei; 🖳) This slightly sterile hostel has functional rooms with various bed counts. Breakfast is 12 lei. Net extra, wi-fi free.

Gia Hostel (☎ 772 486; hotelgia@gmail.com; Str Libertăţii 41; dm/r from 35/95 lei; 🖳) Backing the railway line (about a 15-minute walk to the citadel), these rooms recently enjoyed a complete and thoughtful redecoration. There's lots of good services: bike rental, bar, an hour's free internet and kitchen/grill access.

Nathan's Villa (☎ 772 546; www.nathansvilla.com; Str Libertăţii 8; dm/d 37/85 lei; 🖳) This popular choice (with free laundry and a bar) is efficiently run and usually the best (and only) nightlife in town. It's open from April to November only.

Hostel Ellen Villa (☎ 776 402; www.elenvillahostel.com; Str Libertăţii 10; dm/r 37/100 lei; 🖳) This homey place, next to Nathan's, feels more like a guest house than a hostel. Breakfast is 8 lei.

ourpick Bed & Breakfast Coula (☎ 777 907; Str Tâmplarilor 40; r per person 54 lei) This homey, unsigned 400-year-old home in the citadel has large rooms with classic ceramic wood-fire heaters. It's run by a heart-warmingly kind English-speaking family, who can help arrange Saxon church trips and rent you a bike (25 lei). There are six rooms (only one's in use in winter). Dinner's available with advance notice.

Casa Cu Cerb (Stag House; ☎ 774 625; Str Şcolii 1; s/d 160/215 lei; 🖳) First thing you see walking into this all-restored 1693 building is Prince Charles' mug – he stayed here a few days in 2002. It's a good choice, with cast-iron bed frames and rattan rugs by the TV sitting area. No breakfast.

Casa Wagner (☎ 506 014; www.casa-wagner.com; Piaţa Cetăţii 7; s/d/ste from 179/215/304 lei; 🖳) This 22-room, 350-year-old beauty on the main square has a mix of rooms, some with balconies; sin-gles are a bit cramped, but others sprawl. The ground-floor restaurant (mains 15 to 30 lei) has interesting takes on Romanian cuisine.

Eating
Café International & Family Centre (☎ 777 844; Piaţa Cetăţii 8; mains 5-11 lei; ☯ 8.30am-7.30pm Mon-Sat Jun-Sep, 9am-6pm Mon-Sat Oct-May) This two-room cafe, with chairs in the square, is an ideal lunch spot with daily-made mostly vegetarian fare, including quiches and lasagne, plus desserts.

Rustic (Str 1 Decembrie 1918 nr 7; mains 6-18 lei; ☯ 8am-midnight Mon-Sat, noon-midnight Sun) Rustic indeed. This wood-and-brick 'man's man' bar-restaurant is down from the citadel. The *ciorba ţaraneasca de porc* (countryside pork soup) will erase the hangover acquired at Nathan's Villa. Eggs served all day.

Casa Dracula (☎ 771 596; Str Cositorarilor 5; mains 13-60 lei) This three-room, candlelit restaurant is too tempting to pass by – juicy meats in Dracula's first home. It's OK to come for a red wine only (3 lei).

Getting There & Away
About a dozen trains daily connect Sighişoara with Braşov (27 lei, two hours), nine of which continue on to Bucharest (55 lei, 4½ hours). Five daily trains go to Cluj-Napoca (46 lei, 3½ hours). You'll need to change trains in Mediaş to reach Sibiu (10 lei, 2½ hours). Three daily trains go to Budapest (140 lei, nine hours); the night one has a sleeper (from 200 lei). Buy tickets at the **train station** (☎ 771 886), or at the central **Agenţie de Voiaj CFR** (☎ 771 820; Str O Goga 6a; ☯ 8.30am-3.30pm Mon-Fri).

Next to the train station on Str Libertăţii, the **bus station** (☎ 771 260) sends buses of various sizes and colours to Budapest (72 lei, eight hours, two weekly), Făgăraş (14 lei, three hours, one daily) and Sibiu (15 lei, 2½ hours, five daily).

SAXON LAND
Sighişoara, Sibiu and Braşov – the 'Saxon Triangle' if you will – enclose an area loaded with undulating hills and cinematic villages. These yesteryear villages, some sitting at the ends of rather nasty dirt roads, frequently have outstanding fortified churches dating from the 12th century. Even just a kilometre or two off the Braşov–Sibiu highway you'll find a world where horse carriages and walking are generally the only ways anyone gets around, and where a car – any car – gets stares.

Popular destinations include **Biertan** (28km southwest of Sighişoara) and **Viscri** (about 40km east). The former has the added attraction of the Cramă Biertan (wine cellar) on Richiş Rd just outside of town selling bottles starting at 5 lei, while the latter misses most tour buses, as the road south of Buneşti is quite rough. Call **Carolina Fernolend** (☎ 0740 145 397) to arrange private accommodation in Viscri (about 90 lei per person including breakfast and dinner) and a look at the church.

Bus service is infrequent and unreliable. Renting a car is cheapest from Sibiu (p705). Gia Hostel (p701) in Sighişoara also rents a car, or you can arrange a taxi.

SIBIU
☎ 0269/0369 / pop 154,900

Crumbling, car-rattling old Sibiu, despite being the capital and most culturally active of the Transylvanian Saxon towns, was once frequently overshadowed by Braşov, Sighişoara and Cluj-Napoca. Then the EU designated it as a 'Capital of Culture' for 2007. Now freshly scrubbed, painted and cobblestoned, the pedestrian areas are frame-worthy from any angle and every third building has been declared a historic monument. Unique 'eyelid' rooftop windows wink from pastel buildings as you sip drinks in Romania's most serene, car-free squares. Some locals liked the old Sibiu better – falling roof tiles, ankle-twisting cobblestones and all – but there's no arguing that new Sibiu is ready to dance in the spotlight.

Founded in the 12th century on the site of the former Roman village of Cibinium, Sibiu (Hermannstadt to the German Saxons, Nagyszében to Hungarians) served as the seat of the Austrian governors of Transylvania under the Habsburgs from 1703 to 1791, and again from 1849 to 1867.

Orientation
The adjacent bus and train stations are near the centre of town. Exit the station and stroll up Str General Magheru four blocks to Piaţa Mare, the historic centre.

Information
ATMs are located all over the centre as well as in most hotels.

Banca Comercială Română (Str Nicolae Bălcescu 11; ☽ 8.30am-5.30pm Mon-Fri, to 12.30pm Sat) Changes travellers cheques and gives cash advances.

Casa Luxemburg (☎ 216 854; www.kultours.ro; Piaţa Mică 16; ☽ 8am-9pm) Travel agent offering loads of city tours (23 to 51 lei, minimum four people) and day trips (about 200 lei), bike rental (35 lei per day), audioguides (23 to 51 lei) and a useful free Sibiu map.

Central post office (Str Mitropoliei 14; ☽ 7am-8pm Mon-Fri, 8am-1pm Sat)

Internet (Str Nicolae Bălcescu 29; per hr 2.5 lei; ☽ 24hr) Down the alley and upstairs.

Left luggage (Piaţa 1 Decembrie 1918; per day 4 lei; ☽ 24 hr) At the train station.

Librăria Humanitas (☎ 211 434; Str Nicolae Bălcescu 16; ☽ 10am-7pm Mon-Sat, from 11am Sun) Good map selection and some books in English.

Salvamont (☎ 0745 140 144, 0-SALVAMONT) Provides 24-hour mountain-rescue service.

Tourist information centre (☎ 208 913; www.sibiu .ro; Piaţa Mare 2; ☽ 9am-5pm Mon-Sat) This superb 'can-do' office is on the ground floor of the new city hall. Staff can help with bus schedules and book accommodation.

Sights
TOWN CENTRE
The expansive Piaţa Mare was the very centre of the old walled city. A good start for exploring the city is to climb to the top of the 1588 **Turnul Sfatului** (Council Tower; admission 2 lei; ☽ 10am-8pm), which links Piaţa Mare with its smaller sister square, Piaţa Mică.

The **Brukenthal Museum** (☎ 217 691; www .brukenthalmuseum.ro; Piaţa Mare 5; adult/student 12/3 lei; ☽ 10am-6pm) is the oldest and probably finest art gallery in Romania. Founded in 1817, the museum is in the baroque palace (1785) of Baron Samuel Brukenthal (1721–1803), former Austrian governor. There are excellent collections of 16th- and 17th-century Flemish, Italian, Dutch, French, Austrian and Romanian paintings, including a giant painting of Sibiu from 1808. Admission is free for kids.

The square's most impressive building, however, is the **Banca Agricola** (Piaţa Mare 2), which now houses the town hall and tourist information centre. Just west of here is the lovely Primăriă Municipiului (1470), now the newly reopened **History Museum** (Str Mitropoliei 2; adult/child 17/5 lei; ☽ 10am-5pm). Serious coin went into the swanky new displays, some behind glass in moody corridors. They start at the Palaeolithic age and sweep through all the epochs, displaying tools, ceramics, bronze, jewellery, life-sized home scenes, costumes and furniture. Other sections hold exhibits of guild work (including glassmaking, brasswork

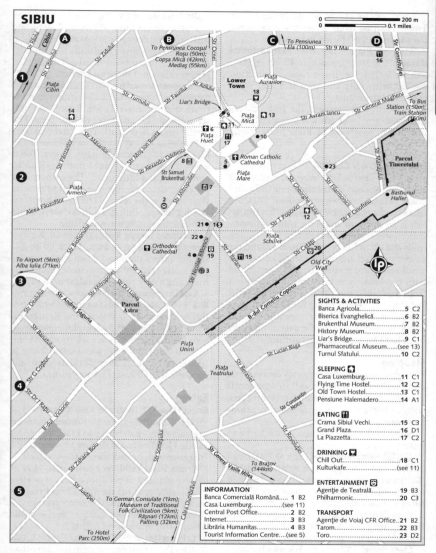

SIBIU

SIGHTS & ACTIVITIES
Banca Agricola.....................**5** C2
Biserica Evanghelică...............**6** B2
Brukenthal Museum................**7** B2
History Museum....................**8** B2
Liar's Bridge........................**9** C1
Pharmaceutical Museum........(see 13)
Turnul Sfatului.....................**10** C2

SLEEPING
Casa Luxemburg...................**11** C1
Flying Time Hostel................**12** C2
Old Town Hostel..................**13** C1
Pensiune Halemadero............**14** A1

EATING
Crama Sibiul Vechi................**15** C3
Grand Plaza........................**16** D1
La Piazzetta........................**17** C2

DRINKING
Chill Out............................**18** C1
Kulturkafe.........................(see 11)

ENTERTAINMENT
Agenţie de Teatrală..............**19** B3
Philharmonic......................**20** C3

TRANSPORT
Agenţie de Voiaj CFR Office....**21** B2
Tarom...............................**22** B3
Toro................................**23** D2

INFORMATION
Banca Comercială Română..... **1** B2
Casa Luxemburg.................(see 11)
Central Post Office................**2** B2
Internet.............................**3** B3
Librăria Humanitas................**4** B3
Tourist Information Centre...(see 5)

and carpentry), an armoury, Roman artefacts and a treasury.

Nearby, on Piaţa Huet, is the Gothic **Biserica Evanghelică** (Evangelical Church; Piaţa Huet; 9am-8pm Mon-Sat, 11am-8pm Sun), built from 1300 to 1520. For renovations lasting until 2011, there's scaffolding covering the four magnificent baroque funerary monuments and the 1772

organ with 6002 pipes (the largest in southeast Europe). The tomb of Mihnea Vodă cel Rău (Prince Mihnea the Bad), son of Vlad Ţepeş, is in a closed-off section behind the organ (ask for entry). This prince was murdered in front of the church in 1510. You can climb the **church tower** (admission 4 lei); ask for entry at Casa Luxemburg (opposite).

North of the centre is interesting Lower Town, reached from under the photogenic **Liar's Bridge** (1859) facing Piaţa Mică.

Also on Piaţa Mică, the **Pharmaceutical Museum** (☎ 218 191; adult/child 4/2 lei; ☺ 10am-6pm Tue-Sun) is a three-room collection packed with pills and powders and scary medical instruments.

It's worth walking along the 16th-century **city walls** and watchtowers, accessible a few blocks southeast of Piaţa Mare, along Str Cetăţii.

OUTSIDE TOWN CENTRE

Sibiu's highlight is 5km from the centre. The sprawling **Museum of Traditional Folk Civilization** (Muzeul Civilizaţiei Populare Tradiţionale Astra; ☎ 242 599; Calea Răşinarilor 14; adult/child 15/4 lei; ☺ 10am-6pm Tue-Sun) is an open-air museum with a growing collection of over 120 traditional dwellings, mills and churches brought from around the country and set among two small lakes and a small zoological garden. There's a restaurant with creekside bench seating. Trolleybus 1 from the train station goes here (get off at the last stop and keep walking for less than 1km, or take the hourly Răşinari tram). A taxi is about 10 lei one way. The museum may stay open until 8pm weather permitting.

Sleeping

New pensions are popping up everywhere, and they're all full. Book well in advance. If you get caught without a bed, pick up a free copy of Şapte Seri for a full list of pensions and hotels.

Much of the hotel boom is on the highway outside town.

ourpick Flying Time Hostel (☎ 0369-730 179; www.sibiuhostel.ro; Str Gheorghe Lazar 6; dm/d from 40/145 lei; ☐) In an 18th-century building designed to stay naturally cool, this place has 'classic' furniture and decor courtesy of an interior designer's brain splatter. There's great beds, a flowery inner courtyard cafe and a downstairs pub with live music. Laundry is 7 lei.

Chess Hostel (☎ 0740 096 920; www.chesshostel sibiu.ro; Ştefan Cel Mare 6; dm 40-50 lei; ☐) The airy dorms in this restored 1930s yellow/brown house have lockers, clothes hooks, hangers and lights on every bed. The owners live on-site and will arrange bike/car hire and onward hostel bookings. No breakfast, but there's a self-catering kitchen with coffee and tea all day. Laundry is 7 lei.

Old Town Hostel (☎ 216 445; www.hostelsibiu.ro; Piaţa Mică 26; dm 45 lei) In a 450-year-old building with crowded dorms overlooking Piaţa Mică, this bare-bones hostel boasts the most atmospheric location in Sibiu – and not much else. No breakfast, but there's a kitchen.

Pensiune Halemadero (☎ 212 509; Str Măsarilor 10; d/tr with shared bathroom 80/120 lei) Family-run four-room deal in Lower Town. Rooms are old-school, with TV and three or four beds. The family runs a beery patio cafe. No breakfast.

Pensiunea Ela (☎ 215 197; www.ela-hotels.ro; Str Nova 43; s/d 100/120 lei; ☐) This Lower Town guest house has just eight rooms, all clean and comfy, if a little small. The owners care for every detail (and you're asked to remove your shoes in the room). The 15-lei breakfast is a bit disappointing. Laundry service and self-catering kitchen are available.

Pensiunea Cocoşul Roşu (☎ 0369-427 482; www.cocosulrosu.ro; Str Ocnei 19; s/d/tr 120/130/150 lei; ☐) Behind a thick door and down a long atmospheric alley are eight immaculate rooms surrounding a nice patio. Breakfast is 10 lei.

Casa Luxemburg (☎ 216 854; www.kultours.ro; Piaţa Mică 16; s/d/tr 160/270/330 lei) It's a little dorm-y, but this six-room job overlooks the Evangelical Church and Piaţa Mică. Complimentary fruit, water and wine awaits in each room. Wi-fi.

Hotel Parc (☎ 424 455; www.hotelparcsibiu.ro; Str Şcoala de Înot 1-3; s/d 225/280 lei; ☐) Sixty-nine fully modern, if slightly unexciting, rooms.

Eating

Grand Plaza (☎ 210 427; Str 9 Mai 60; mains 9-13 lei; ☺ 9am-10.30pm) No-nonsense Romanian cuisine at great prices – meats are 9 to 13 lei, soups 6 lei, salads 3 lei. The ciolan de porc pe varză călită, (pig knee with beans) is quite the spectacle.

Crama Sibiul Vechi (Str P Ilarian; mains 14-28 lei; ☺ noon-midnight) This popular, evocative brick-cellar spot off the main crawl reels in locals for its tasty Transylvanian armoury of ciorba (soup), mutton, sausages, beef and fish. There's live music most nights.

La Piazzetta (☎ 230 879; Piaţa Mică 15; pizzas & pastas 16-22 lei) This square pizza shop is livelier than most, with smoking couples eating pizza at red-chequered tables.

Drinking

Piaţa Mică is the drinking headquarters.

Kulturkafe (Piaţa Mică 16; ☺ 10am-3am Mon-Fri, 1pm-3am Sat, 3pm-3am Sun) Good table spots on the square, slightly more adult-like inside.

Chill Out (Piaţa Mică 23; ☾ lounge 11am-midnight, club 10pm-6am Wed, Fri, Sat & Sun) Local students hightail it to this fun, loud, enigmatic spot. Themed nights include Jell-O Shots (Saturday), Retro (Sunday) and Ladies' Night (Wednesday).

Entertainment

Sibiu's **International Astra Film Festival** is held in May.

Agenţie de Teatrală (☎ 0369-101 578; Str Nicolae Bălcescu 17; ☾ 11am-6pm Mon-Fr, to 3pm Sat) Tickets for major events are sold here.

Philharmonic (☎ 210 264; www.filarmonicasibiu.ro; Str Cetăţii 3-5) A big cultural player that's hosted classical orchestral concerts since 1949.

Getting There & Around

AIR

Sibiu airport (☎ 229 161; Sos Alba Iulia 73) is 5km west of the centre. Trolleybus 8 runs between the airport and the train station.

Tarom (☎ 211 157; Str Nicolae Bălcescu 10; ☾ 9am-12.30pm & 1.30-5pm Mon-Fri) has daily flights to Bucharest (from 169 lei one way), Munich (683 lei) and Vienna (1349 lei). **Carpatair** (☎ 229 161; www.carpatair.com), which has an office at the airport, flies to Germany and Italy via Timişoara. Budget airline **Blue Air** (www.blueair-web.com) flies to Madrid, Cologne and Stuttgart.

BUS

The **bus station** (☎ 217 757; Piaţa 1 Decembrie 1918) is opposite the train station. Bus and maxitaxi services include Braşov (20 lei, 2½ hours, four daily), Bucharest (48 lei, 5½ hours, five to seven daily), Cluj-Napoca (28 lei, 3½ hours, nine daily) and Timişoara (43 lei, six hours, two daily).

CAR & MOTORCYCLE

Toro (☎ 232 237, 0745 425 441; Str Filarmonicii 5; ☾ 8am-4pm Mon-Fri, to 1pm Sat) rents Dacias for 108 to 136 lei per day.

TAXI

To call a taxi dial ☎ 0269 953.

TRAIN

Sibiu lies at an awkward rail junction; sometimes you'll need to change trains. But there are 10 daily direct trains to Braşov (29 lei, 2½ hours), four to Bucharest (44 lei, five hours) and three to Timişoara (44 lei, five hours). Buy tickets at the station or at **Agenţie de Voiaj CFR office** (☎ 216 441; Str Nicolae Bălcescu 6; ☾ 7am-8pm Mon-Fri).

Trolleybus 1 connects the train station with the centre, but it's only a 450m walk along Str General Magheru.

FĂGĂRAŞ MOUNTAINS
☎ 0268/0368

The Făgăraş Mountains cut a serrated line south of the main Braşov–Sibiu road, sheltering dozens of glacial lakes. The famed **Transfăgăraşan Road** (generally open only from June to September due to snow) cuts north–south through the range. No buses ply the route.

Despite its name, Făgăraş town (pop 43,900) is not the prime access point to the Făgăraş Massif. Most hikers head south to the mountains from the town of Victoria.

TÂRGU MUREŞ (MAROSVÁSÁRHELY)
☎ 0265/0365 / pop 170,000

The biggest map-dot in Transylvania's Székely Land, and home to Romania's ethnic

---

HIKING FROM VICTORIA

The Făgăraş Massif is regarded as the most dazzling section of the Carpathian Mountains, and holds arguably some of the best hiking in Europe. The rocky wilderness, featuring well-trodden paths and excellent cabins, is enriched by wildlife and more than 40 glacial lakes. Plan trips for August and September to rule out heavy snow encounters – though a dusting is always possible.

Alight at Ucea train station (59km from Sibiu), from where you can catch a bus (or walk the 7km) to **Victoria**. From here you can hike to **Cabana Turnuri** (1520m; 20 beds) in about six hours. The scenery is stunning once you start the ascent. The next morning head for **Cabana Podragu** (2136m; 68 beds), four hours south.

Cabana Podragu makes a good base if you want to climb **Mt Moldoveanu** (2544m), Romania's highest peak. It's a tough uphill climb, but the views from the summit are unbeatable. Otherwise, hike eight hours east, passing by Mt Moldoveanu, to Cabana Valea Sambetei (1407m). From Cabana Valea Sambetei you can descend to the railway in Ucea, via Victoria, in a day.

Hungarian population, Târgu Mureş' worn Habsburg-style architecture and Hungarian accent gives it a distinctive feel from surrounding towns. Its lengthy central square begs to be strolled with a camera at the ready.

Orientation & Information

Central Piaţa Trandafirilor runs for several blocks in the busy commercial heart, where you can find ATMs, bars and food. At its northeastern end stands the landmark Orthodox church. Str Bernady György leads east from there past the 14th-century citadel. The train station is 1km south, the bus station 1.5km south.

Two blocks west of the Orthodox church, **PC House** (cnr Str Arany Ianoş & Str Aurel Filmon; per hr 3 lei; ⏱ 9am-9pm Mon-Fri, from 3pm Sat, from 6pm Sun) has a slick reading room with computers where you can check email.

Tourism information centre (☎ 0365-404 934; www.cjmures.ro/turism; cnr Piaţa Trandafirilor & Str Enescu; ⏱ 8am-8pm Tue-Thu, to 4pm Mon & Sat), in the Culture Palace, is a superbly run centre offering free maps and information on the region.

Sights

At the southwestern end of Piaţa Trandafirlor, the **Culture Palace** (Palatul Culturii; cnr Piaţa Trandafirilor & Str Enescu; adult/student 7/2 lei, camera 3 lei; ⏱ 9am-6pm Tue-Sun) is Târgu Mureş' beloved landmark and top attraction. Inside its glittering, tiled, steepled roof is an often-used concert hall and several worthwhile museums (all admission included in the entry price). The best is the **Hall of Mirrors** (Sala Oglinzi), with 12 stained-glass windows lining a 45m hallway – a lengthy tape in various languages explains the folk tales portrayed in each. The **History Museum** (1st floor) houses many large late-19th- and early-20th-century paintings; the **Archaeological Museum** (2nd floor) explains, in English, Dacian pieces found in the region.

Sleeping & Eating

MS Hostel (☎ 0752 243 536; Piaţa Trandafirilor 61; www .mshostel.ro; dm/d 36/43 lei) Superbly central, this just-opened 20-bed hostel is often unstaffed, so call ahead. Enter and cross the courtyard to the left-side door. No breakfast, but cafes are just downstairs.

Hotel Transylvania (☎ 265 616; Piaţa Trandafirilor 46; rezervari.mures@unita-turism.ro; d with shared bathroom 85 lei, s/d with private bathroom from 95/130 lei) Dead centre with decent rooms overlooking the square. Renovated rooms (singles 180 lei, doubles 236 lei) have cable internet only. Call ahead to schedule your arrival as it's sometimes unstaffed.

Pensiune Ana Maria (☎ 264 401; Str AL Papui Ilarian 17; s/d/apt 120/140/150 lei; 🖳) Possibly where cousin Elvis Habsburg was exiled for his suggestive hip-shaking, this playful eight-room guest house mixes a bit of green Vegas garishness and Austrian tradition – breakfasts are huge and superb. To get here, go past the citadel and turn right at Str AL Papui Ilarian.

Hotel Concordia (☎ 260 602; Piaţa Trandafirilor 45; s/d 395/466 lei; 🍴 🖳 🖥) One of Romania's most chic boutique hotels; splurgers love the stark and giant rooms (with zebra-print chairs and fashion prints on the walls) and glass-roofed pool.

Kebab (Str Bolyai 10; kebabs 7 lei; ⏱ 6.30am-10pm) A block north of the square, this budget spot has curt service but good kebab specials.

Leo (Piaţa Trandafirilor 36-38; mains 12-35 lei; ⏱ 24hr) On the eastern side of the square, this outdoor-indoor spot gets busy with families and young couples enjoying pizzas and tasty Romanian food.

Getting There & Away

Daily bus and maxitaxi services from the **bus station** (☎ 237 774; Str Gheorghe Doja) include 18 or so to Sighişoara (9 lei, 1½ hours); five to Cluj-Napoca (16 lei, 2½ hours); and two to Sibiu (15 lei, three hours). Bus 18 connects the centre with the station.

The **Agenţie de Voiaj CFR** (☎ 266 203; Piaţa Teatrului 1; ⏱ 7am-8pm Mon-Fri), facing Piaţa Trandafirilor near its northwestern corner, sells tickets for trains. Trains go to Bucharest (53 to 80 lei, 8½ hours, two daily), Sibiu (21 lei, 5½ hours, two daily), Cluj-Napoca (21 lei, 2½ hours, one daily), Timişoara (46 lei, 6½ hours, one daily) and Budapest (150 lei, 7½ hours, two daily). Bus 5 connects the station with the centre.

CLUJ-NAPOCA

☎ 0264 / pop 318,000

'Club-Napoca' isn't as picturesque as its Saxon neighbours, but it's famed for its dozens of cavernous, unsnooty discos filled with agreeable students. Even outside the clubs, Cluj is one of Romania's most energised and welcoming cities – our dentist invited us to live music later that evening. Its attractions aren't staggering, and the screaming traffic ruins that which is attractive, but it's a 'real' city where everything's going on (football, opera, espresso, heated politics, trams), with a few surprise nuggets. It's a great base for renting a car – far cheaper than Braşov – and serves as a perfect staging area for excursions into Maramureş.

Cluj-Napoca holds the **International Folk Music & Dance Festival of Ethnic Minorities in Europe** in August.

History
In AD 124, Roman Emperor Marcus Aurelius elevated the Dacian town of Napoca to a colony. From 1791 to 1848 and again after the union with Hungary in 1867, Cluj-Napoca served as the capital of Transylvania.

In the mid-1970s the old Roman name of Napoca was added to the city's official title to emphasise its Daco-Roman origin. In the 1990s, then-mayor Gheorghe Funar furthered that Romanian nationalist swipe (painting rubbish bins in Romanian colours), embarrassing many locals.

Orientation
The *gara* (train station) is located 1.5km north of the city centre. Walk left out of the station and cross the street to catch tram 101 or a trolleybus south down Str Horea. Most buses arrive at and depart from Autogara 2, north of town. City information and an excellent interactive map are at www.cluj4all.com.

CLUJ-NAPOCA

0   200 m
0   0.1 miles

INFORMATION	
Banca Comercială Română..	1 A2
Blade Net	2 C3
Central Post Office	3 B2
Diverta	4 B3
Gaudeamus	5 B3
Net Zone	6 A2

SIGHTS & ACTIVITIES	
Emil Racoviţa Insitute of Speleology	7 B3
Ethnographic Museum of Transylvania	8 A3
Hungarian Cemetery (Entrance)	9 B4
National Art Museum	10 B3
National History Museum of Transylvania	11 A2
Pharmaceutical Museum	12 B3
St Michael's Church	13 B3

SLEEPING	
Fulton	14 B2
Hotel Agape	15 C3
Hotel Meteor	16 C3
Retro Hostel	17 B4

EATING	
Cafeteria Nicola	18 B2
Central Market	19 C2
Hotel Agape	(see 15)
Oncos	20 C2
Restaurant Matei Corvin	21 B3
Roata	22 A3
Speed/Alcatraz	23 B4

DRINKING	
Diesel Club	24 B3

Music Pub	25 A1

ENTERTAINMENT	
Agenţie de Teatrală	26 D3
Cinema Arta	27 B4
National Theatre Cluj-Napoca	28 D3

TRANSPORT	
Agenţie de Voiaj CFR...	29 C2
Autonom	30 A4
Tarom	31 B2

MAPS

The best map for the city is Stiefel's *Cluj-Napoca* (10 lei), though perfectly good maps are freely available at hotels/hostels.

Information

Cluj still has no tourist information centre. See www.cjnet.ro for general information on the city, or try one of the travel agencies listed below.

Most cafes have free wi-fi.

Banca Comercială Română (Str Gheorghe Barițiu 10-12; ☾ 8.30am-6pm Mon-Fri, 8.30am-12.30pm Sat) Gives cash advances and changes travellers cheques.

Blade Net (Str Iuliu Maniu 17; per hr 2.40 lei; ☾ 8am-midnight) Internet access.

Central post office (Str Regele Ferdinand 33; ☾ 7am-8pm Mon-Fri, 8am-1pm Sat)

Diverta (Str Universității 1; ☾ 8am-8pm Mon-Fri, 9am-4pm Sat) Has contemporary books in English.

Gaudeamus (☎ 439 281; Str Iuliu Maniu 3; ☾ 9am-7pm, 10am-2.30pm Sat) A bookshop with some maps and many Hungarian titles.

Green Mountain Holidays (☎ 0744 637 227; www.greenmountainholidays.ro) Terrific ecotourism agency providing activity-filled trips in the Apuseni Mountains.

Net Zone (Piața Muzeului 5; per hr 2 lei; ☾ approx 24hr) Internet access.

Pan Travel (☎ 420 516; www.pantravel.ro; Str Grozavescu 13; ☾ 9am-5pm Mon-Fri) This top-notch outfit can book accommodation, car rental (from 108 lei per day), provide guides and arrange Maramureș trips. It's best to make contact ahead of time.

Transylvania Ecological Club (Clubul Ecologic Transilvania; ☎ 431 626; www.greenagenda.org) Grassroots environmental group focusing on ecotravel in the region.

Sights

TOWN CENTRE

The vast 14th-century **St Michael's Church** dominates Piața Unirii. The neo-Gothic tower (1859) topping the Gothic hall church creates a great landmark. Outside is a huge equestrian statue (1902) of the famous Hungarian king Matthias Corvinus (r 1458–90), who was born here. (At night compare the half-hearted lighting on this with the elaborate lighting of the namesake Romanian hero on **Piața Avram Iancu** three blocks east.)

Facing Piața Unirii is the interesting **National Art Museum** (☎ 496 952; Piața Unirii 30; adult/child 4.60/2.30 lei; ☾ 10am-5pm Wed-Sun), housed inside the baroque Banffy Palace (1791).

The small three-room **Pharmaceutical Museum** (☎ 597 567; Str Regele Ferdinand 1; adult/child 5/3 lei; ☾ 10am-4pm Mon-Sat) is in Cluj's first apothecary (1573). Old glass cases housing grounded mummy dust, 18th-century aphrodisiacs and medieval alchemy symbols are brought to life by the hilarious guide, who ushers you around as if showing off game-show prizes.

A block north, the museum of the **Emil Racovița Institute of Speleology** (Str Sextil Pușcariu 10) is finally settled in its new location, but it keepz whimsical hours. The much-travelled scientist Racovița opened the world's first cave institute in Cluj in 1920.

Just off lovely Piața Muzeului is the **National History Museum of Transylvania** (☎ 495 677; Str Constantin Daicoviciu 1; adult/child 6/3 lei; ☾ 10am-4pm Tue-Sun), filled with ghoulish remains of ancient tombs and many Roman pieces – the modern sections are under ongoing renovation.

Freshly renovated, the **Ethnographic Museum of Transylvania** (Muzeul Etnografic al Transilvaniei; ☎ 592 344; www.muzeul-etnografic.ro; Str Memorandumului 21; adult/student 4/2 lei) has two floors of well-presented displays featuring tools, weapons, hand crafts, toys and household items with detailed descriptions in English. It also runs an **open-air ethnographic museum** (adult/student 4/2 lei; ☾ 10am-6pm May-Sep, 8am-4pm Oct-Mar, closed Apr), with 14 traditional buildings; take bus 27 to Hoia forest from the train station or bus 30 from the centre.

OUTSIDE TOWN CENTRE

In the 'student ghetto' west of the centre, inside the Biology and Geology Faculty, you'll find the surprisingly rewarding **Museum of Zoology** (☎ 595 739; Str Clinicilor 5-7; adult/student 2/1 lei; ☾ 9am-3pm Mon-Fri, 10am-2pm Sat & Sun), an L-shaped lab that looks like it hasn't changed in five decades. From Str Clinicilor, veer left through the brick gate.

Just south, head past fast-food joints up Str Bogdan P Hașdeu to Str Pasteur to reach the fragrant 1930 **Alexandru Borza Botanic Gardens** (☎ 592 152; Str Republicii 42; adult/student 4/2 lei; ☾ 9am-6pm), with shaded green lawns and a super Japanese garden.

Just east of here, most easily reached from Str Avram Iancu down the hill, is an immense, memorable **Hungarian cemetery** (Házsongárdi temető).

For an overall view of Cluj-Napoca, climb up the 1715 **citadel** (*cetatea*), northwest of the centre.

Courses

Access (☎ 420 476; www.access.ro; Str Țebei 21, 3rd fl; ⏰ 10am-6pm Mon & Thu, 2-8pm Tue-Wed, 2-6pm Fri) offers Romanian-language courses.

Sleeping

Camping Făget (☎ 596 227; camp sites 28 lei, 2-person huts 58 lei) This hilltop collection of OK cabanas and tent spots is 7km south of the centre. Take bus 35 to the end of the line, from where it's a 2km marked hike.

our pick **Retro Hostel** (☎ 450 452; www.retro.ro; Str Potaissa 13; dm/s/d/tr from 39/77/116/165 lei; 🖳) On a quiet lane amid 16th-century citadel wall fragments, the newly expanded Retro is one of Romania's best hostels. Dorms are a little tight – there are only a couple of bathrooms. The chatty and tirelessly helpful staff offer good-value day trips. Breakfast is 14 lei.

Pensiunea Junior (☎ 432 028; www.pensiune-junior.ro; Str Cări Ferate 12; s/d 100/130 lei) This red building with simple rooms is on a loud, unappealing street 100m east of the train station. Rooms 1 and 7 are away from traffic noise, though. It's prohibitively distant from the centre, but it's perfect for layovers or early departures. Free wi-fi. No breakfast.

Vila 69 (☎ 591 592; vila69@email.ro; Str Hașden 69; s/d 115/150 lei) Seventeen rather simple but modern rooms in a happy little place near the university action. Take Str Clinicolor, turn left on Str Piezișă, and it's 200m up the street. Free wi-fi.

Hotel Meteor (591 060; www.hotelmeteor.ro; B-dul Eroilor 29; s/d 161/188 lei) Slightly worn, modern hotel. Some rooms are quite small, but staff are nice and there's laundry service. The restaurant's alley tables mean night-time noise in good weather.

Fulton (☎ 597 898; www.fulton.ro; Str Sextil Pușcariu 10; s 161-277 lei; d 182-298 lei; 🖳) This faded back-street central boutique inn has earth-tone striped walls, wrought-iron bed frames, and a laid-back covered patio bar. Plug-in and wi-fi internet free.

Hotel Agape (☎ 406 523; www.hotelagape.ro; Str Iuliu Maniu 6; s/d 244/279 lei; ⧆ 🖳) Run by Hungarian locals, this 40-room hotel has *six* restaurants. Giant rooms are so-so – you're paying for location. Request a nonsmoking room.

Eating

There are heaps of good pizza, hamburger and kebab options on Str Piezișă in the 'student ghetto' and more centrally on Piața Lucian Blaga and Str Napoca.

Cafeteria Nicola (Str Regele Ferdinand 13; pastries 1-3 lei; ⏰ 8am-10pm) A lazy coffee and sinful pastries can be enjoyed at this tiny place.

Speed/Alcatraz (Str Napoca 4-6; pizzas 13 lei, sandwiches 5 lei; ⏰ 24hr) Busy fast-food place with good seating options, including some in the 'Al Capone' jail cages.

Hotel Agape (Str Iuliu Maniu 6; mains 7 lei; ⏰ 10am-9pm) Has a Romanian-style, glass-roofed cafeteria on the ground floor.

Tokyo (☎ 0753 103 272; Str Marinescu 5; sushi & rolls from 15 lei; ⏰ 10am-10pm) Japanese pop on the stereo and the traditional Japanese gate out front are certainly a break from all the Romanian restaurants around town. Full meal prices are very high by Romanian standards. To get here go south on Str Babeș from the centre and turn right on Str Marinescu.

Restaurant Matei Corvin (☎ 597 496; Str Matei Corvin 3; mateicorvinrestaurant@gmail.com; mains 16-42 lei; ⏰ 10am-10pm) The hefty, leather-bound, multi-lingual menus could press pulp out of oranges, but these tourist-trap alarm bells will silence when you sample the competently prepared international cuisine. Relatively expensive, but worth the splurge. Nonsmokers are granted a tiny refuge in the main dining room.

Roata (☎ 592 022; Str Alexandru Ciura 6a; mains 17-35 lei; ⏰ noon-midnight Tue-Sat, from 1pm Sun-Mon) Housed in a back-alley house, with tasty traditional Romanian dishes served on clay plates.

For fresh produce, stroll through the quite colourful **central market**, behind the Complex Commercial Mihai Viteazul shopping centre on Piața Mihai Viteazul, which also houses supermarket **Oncos** (⏰ 7am-9pm Mon-Sat, 8am-8pm Sun).

Drinking

Piața Unirii is the site of many subterranean watering holes, but clubs and bars are spread out throughout the centre. It pays to explore.

Diesel Club (☎ 493 043; Piața Unirii 17) Walk past the hipsters in the all-glass entry and go down-stairs into a cavernous room with red-spotlit tables and 15-lei gin and tonics.

Music Pub (☎ 432 517; Str Horea 5; ⏰ 9am-3am Mon-Fri, noon-5am Sat, 5pm-5am Sun) A little Wild West up front, the sprawling pub is a great, more casual place for buddy blokes and indie-pop flirters. Live music Saturday and Sunday.

The 'student ghetto', southwest of Cluj-Napoca's centre (on and off Str Piezișă, – aka 'Puke Street' for reasons other than what you're thinking – reached by Str Clinicilor about 300m from Piața Lucian Blaga), teams with lively open-air bars, including **La Solas** (Str Piezișă-2am).

Entertainment

Șapte Seri (www.sapteseri.ro) and *24-Fun* are free biweekly booklets listing all the latest goings-on (in Romanian).

Cinema Arta (☎ 596 616; Str Universității 3) screens Hollywood films in English. Tickets cost about 8 lei.

The **Agenție de Teatrală** (☎ 595 363; Piața Ștefan cel Mare 14; ☒ 11am-5pm Tue-Fri) sells tickets for theatre, opera and the philharmonic, which hit the stage at the **National Theatre Cluj-Napoca** (☎ 590 272; Piața Ștefan cel Mare 2-4).

Getting There & Around

AIR

Tarom has at least three daily direct flights to Bucharest (one way/return from 202/352 lei). Tickets can be bought at the airport (8km east of town, reached by bus 8) or in town at **Tarom** (☎ 432 669; Piața Mihai Viteazul 11; ☒ 8am-6pm Mon-Fri, 9am-1pm Sat). Budget carrier **Wizz Air** (www.wizzair.com) flies to London, Paris, Rome, Barcelona and more.

BUS

Bus services from **Autogara 2** (Autogara Beta; ☎ 455 249), 350m northwest of the train station (take the overpass), include the following: Brașov (37 lei, two daily), Bucharest (48 lei, 7½ hours, two daily), Budapest (70 lei, several daily), Chișinău (70 lei, one daily), Suceava (42 lei, two daily) and Sibiu (20 lei, 3½ hours, several daily). There is no Autogara 1. Budapest-bound maxitaxis stop at the international bus station there and finish at the Budapest airport.

CAR

Pan Travel (p708) and **Autonom** (☎ 590 588; www.autonom.ro; Str Victor Babes 10) offer Dacias and Matiz for 108 lei per day. **Rodna** (☎ 416 773; www.rodna-trans.ro; Str Traian Vuia 62), towards the airport, rents Dacia Logans from 145 lei per day, and foreign cars for a bit more.

TAXI

Diesel Taxi (☎ 0264 953/946) is a well-regarded, meter-using local company.

TRAIN

The **Agenție de Voiaj CFR** (☎ 432 001; Piața Mihai Viteazul 20; ☒ 7am-7pm Mon-Fri) sells domestic and international train tickets in advance.

TRAINS FROM CLUJ-NAPOCA

Some sample fares for *accelerat* trains:

Destination	Price (lei)	Duration (hrs)	Daily departures
Brașov	44	4	6
Bucharest	53	7½	6
Budapest	110	5	2
Iași	53	9	3
Oradea	29	2¼-4	12
Sibiu	46	4	1
Sighișoara	37	3½	6
Suceava	44	7	3
Timișoara	44	7	6

CRIȘANA & BANAT

The areas of Crișana (north of the Mureș River) and Banat (to the south) once merged imperceptibly with Vojvodina (Serbia) and Hungary's Great Plain; until 1918 all three regions were governed jointly. This legacy can still be appreciated in spirit and in the weathered Habsburg architecture in Oradea, Arad and Timișoara, the latter of which is still brimming with pride after lighting the fuse that ignited the 1989 revolution.

The nearby Apușeni Mountains offer skiing, caving, gorges and waterfalls, while a pair of hot-spring resorts (Băile Felix and Băile Herculane) promise to undo damage done while partaking in the former. Zigzag between urban refinement, breathtaking excitement and recuperative leisure all within a few hours' drive.

ORADEA

☎ 0259 / pop 209,600

One deliberate 360-degree rotation in Oradea's Piața Unirii and you'll know why it's considered one of the best surviving representations of the Austro-Hungarian Empire's 19th-century romantic style.

The city, a few kilometres east of the Hungarian border, was ceded to Romania in 1920 and has since taken on an air of faded grandeur, but it's a lovely place to stop.

Orientation

The train station is a couple of kilometres north of the centre; trams 1 and 4 run south from Piața București (outside the train station) to Piața Unirii, Oradea's main square. Tram 4 also stops at the northern end of

Calea Republicii, a five-minute walk south to the centre.

The main square north of the river is Piaţa Republicii (also called Piaţa Regele Ferdinand I).

Information

24-hour pharmacy (☎ 418 242; cnr Str Libertăţii & Piaţa Republicii)
Alpha Bank (☎ 457 840; Piaţa Unirii 24; ⏰ 9am-4pm Mon-Fri) Has all services.
Internet cafe (Str George Enescu 24; per hr 1.80 lei; ⏰ 8.30am-midnight Mon-Fri, noon-midnight Sat & Sun)
Panda Tours (☎ 477 222; Str Iosif Vulcan 6; ⏰ 9am-5pm Mon-Fri) These guys can book domestic tours.
Post & telephone offices (☎ 431 342; Str Roman Ciorogariu 12; ⏰ 8am-8pm Mon-Fri, 8am-2pm Sat)

Sights

Oradea's most imposing sights are on its two central squares, Piaţa Unirii and Piaţa Republicii.

PIAŢA UNIRII

The 1784 Orthodox **Biserica cu Lună** (Moon Church; Piaţa Unirii) has an unusual lunar mechanism on its tower that adjusts position in accordance with the moon's movement.

In the centre of Piaţa Unirii stands an equestrian **statue of Mihai Viteazul**, the prince of Wallachia (r 1593–1601), who is said to have rested in Oradea in 1600. East of this statue, overlooking the Crişul Repede River, you'll find the magnificent **Vulturul Negru** (Black Vulture; 1908) hotel and covered arcade, which

links Piaţa Unirii with Str Independenţei and Str Vasile Alecsandri. A **statue of Mihai Eminescu**, the 19th-century Romantic poet, overlooks the river's southern bank.

Further east of Piaţa Unirii is **Parcul Central**, with a large monument, and a citadel, which was built in the 13th century and now houses government offices.

PIAŢA REPUBLICII & NORTH

Across the bridge the magnificent neoclassical **Teatrul de Stat** (State Theatre), designed by Viennese architects Fellner and Hellmer in 1900, dominates Piaţa Republicii. To the east is the long, pedestrianised Calea Republicii, lined with bookshops and cafes.

A block southwest of the train station is **Şirul Canonicilor** (Canon's Corridor), a series of archways that date back to the 18th century.

The **Catedrala Romano-Catolică** (Roman Catholic Cathedral; 1780) is the largest in Romania. The adjacent **Palatul Episcopia Ortodoxă** (Episcopal Palace; 1770), with 100 fresco-adorned rooms and 365 windows, was modelled after Belvedere Palace in Vienna. It houses the **Muzeul Ţării Crişului** (Museum of the Land of the Criş Rivers; ☎ 412 725; B-dul Dacia 1-3; admission 1.55 lei; ⏰ 10am-5pm Tue-Sun), with history and art exhibits relevant to the region.

Sleeping

Camping Venus (☎ 318 266; per person tents/bungalows 5/30 lei) This camping ground is in Băile 1 Mai, 9km southeast of Oradea. Bungalows sleep two or three. Take a southbound tram 4 (black number) from the train station, or an eastbound tram 4 (red number) from Piaţa Unirii to the end of the line, then bus 15 to the last stop.

Hostel Felix (☎ 437 011; tineret_bh@yahoo.com; Str Mihai Eminescu 11; dm 30 lei) This slapdash 'hostel' has 4-bed dorms with seatless toilets and zero ambience, but it's undeniably central and cheap. There's no immediate sign; enter and cross the courtyard, passing the tennis courts, and the door is on the left.

Oradea Hostel (☎ 0751 246 861; Tudor Vladimescu 40; www.oradeahostel.com; dm 35 lei; 🖳) Now *this* is a hostel! An amiably managed 20-bed jobbie with free laundry, self-catering kitchen, a terrace, wine-cellar bar and common room with foosball and TV.

Hotel Parc (☎ 411 699; Calea Republicii 5-7; s/d/tr with shared bathroom 49/83/98 lei, d/tr with private bathroom

93/109 lei) This two-star option has friendly staff and large, classic rooms that are worn and sometimes smoky, but reasonably clean. The bathroom upgrade is worth it.

Pension Gobe (☎ 414 845; Str Dobrogeanu Gherea 26; s/d/tr 106/142/248 lei) This family-owned pension has several charming rooms, a small restaurant and a bar.

our pick Hotel Atlantic (☎ 426 911; www.hotel atlantic.ro; Str Iosif Vulcan 9; s/d/ste 170/190/235 lei) These spacious, contemporary rooms sport *huge* marble bathrooms, some with spas, and your own private bar! The Blue Suite has a bed the size of a trampoline. Wi-fi in the lobby only.

Eating & Drinking

Calea Republicii is lined with cheap and cheerful eateries and cafes.

Restaurant Vegetarian Cris (☎ 441 593; Str George Enescu 30; mains 6-12 lei; ⏰ 9am-9pm Sun-Thu, to 5pm Fri, closed Sat) At Romania's first vegetarian restaurant, choose from a tantalisingly cheap menu featuring soups, stuffed peppers, minced-lentil balls, macaroni and cabbage, pumpkin schnitzel, walnut haggis, and a river of soy. Free wi-fi.

Capitolium (☎ 420 551; Str Avram Iancu 8; mains 14-30 lei; ⏰ 8am-midnight) You may have trouble getting over the chandeliers, Roman columns, plants and gaudy paintings, but you won't have the same concern with the menu, which includes a delicious steak with rice and mushroom sauce.

Cyrano (☎ 0740 163 943; Calea Republicii 7; mains 14-30 lei; ⏰ 8.30am-midnight Mon-Fri, 9.30am-midnight Sat, noon-midnight Sun) A popular hang-out with ideal people-watching from coveted terrace tables. Though the menu teems with Romanian favourites, the incredible *ciorbă de viţel cu tarhon in chiflă* (meat and vegie soup in a bread bowl; 10 lei) is all the food you need.

Most of Oradea's terrace cafes and restaurants double as bars in the evening. The glass-covered alley behind Hotel Vulturul Negru is poseur central.

Irish Kelly's Pub (☎ 413 419; Calea Republicii 2) Caters for a rowdy crowd on its outside terrace.

Lion Café (Str Independenţei 1; ⏰ 7am-1am) Small and smoky, this place has free wi-fi and little elbow room come night-time.

Entertainment

Tickets for performances at the **State Philharmonic** (Filarmonica de Stat; ☎ 430 853; Str Moscovei 5; tickets 10-20 lei) can be purchased from its **ticket**

office (🕑 8am-3pm Mon-Wed & Fri, 8am-3pm & 5-9pm Thu) or inside the **Teatrul de Stat** (State Theatre; ☎ 476 568; Piața Republicii 4-6; 🕑 10am-1pm & 5-7pm).

Getting There & Away

AIR
Tarom (☎ 431 918; Piața Republicii 2; 🕑 8am-6pm Mon-Fri, 10am-1pm Sat) has three weekly flights to Baia Mare, daily flights to Bucharest and one weekly flight to Satu Mare from **Oradea airport** (☎ 416 082; Calea Aradului km 6). The closest international airport is at Arad.

BUS
From Oradea **autogara** (☎ 418 998; Str Râzboieni 81), south of the centre, there are daily services to Beiuș, Deva and Satu Mare. More than 20 maxitaxis run daily to and from Băile Felix.

A daily state bus (55 lei, 10 hours), as well as faster maxitaxis (about 80 lei), go to Budapest, leaving from outside the train station. Purchase tickets from the driver.

CAR & MOTORCYCLE
The border crossing into Hungary for motorists is at Borș, 16km west of Oradea, and is open 24 hours.

TRAIN
The **Agenție de Voiaj CFR** (☎ 416 556; Calea Republicii 2; 🕑 7am-8pm Mon-Fri) sells advance tickets.

The train station is about 2km north of the centre. Take tram 1 (two-ride ticket 3 lei) to the centre of Piața Unirii. Daily fast trains from Oradea include three to Budapest (85 lei), two to Bucharest (71 lei), five to Băile Felix, three to Cluj-Napoca (29 lei), one to Brașov (54 lei) and three to Timișoara (32 lei).

TIMIȘOARA
☎ 0256 / pop 321,900
Tenacious Timișoara stunned the world – though not as much as it stunned the Ceaușescus – as the birthplace of the 1989 revolution. Beaming residents refer to it as 'Primul Oraș Liber' (First Free Town). A charming Mediterranean air pervades Romania's fourth-largest city, which is accentuated by regal Habsburg buildings and a thriving cultural and sports scene. Being in the west, and having infinitely better tourist resources than Bucharest, Timișoara is a far superior overland point of arrival for first-time Romania visitors.

Orientation
Old Town has retained its circular orientation, with major streets and boulevards jutting out, pinwheel-like. Confusingly, Timișoara-Nord (the northern train station) is west of the city centre. Walk east along B-dul Republicii to the Opera House and Piața Victoriei. To the north is Piața Libertății. Piața Unirii, the Old Town square, bookended by the Roman Catholic Cathedral and the Serbian Orthodox Church, is two blocks further north. Timișoara's bus station is beside the Idsefin Market, three blocks from the train station. Take B-dul General Drăgălina south to the canal, cross the bridge and head west to the next bridge. B-dul CD Loga, south of the centre, swoops past a series of lovely parks, as well as the Metropolitan Cathedral. To get to the Eastern Train Station and international bus terminal, follow Aleea Demetriade northeast of Old Town.

Information
Farmacie Remedia (B-dul Revoluției 1989; 🕑 7am-8pm Mon-Sat)
Farmado Pharmacy (Piața Victoriei 7; 🕑 8am-9pm Mon-Fri, from 9am Sat & Sun)
Info Centru Turistic (☎ 437 973, http://infocentru .onepoint.ro; Str Alba Iulia 2; 🕑 9am-8pm Mon-Fri, to 5pm Sat) This new tourism office can assist with accommodation and trains, and provide maps and Banat regional info.
Post office Central branch (☎ 491 999; B-dul Revoluției 2; 🕑 8am-7pm Mon-Fri, to noon Sat); Str Macieșilor branch (Str Macieșilor; 🕑 8am-7pm Mon-Fri) The central post office can get busy; if so, try the branch on Str Macieșilor.
Telephone office (Str N Lenau; 🕑 9am-6pm Mon-Fri, to 1pm Sat) Has fax facilities, plus free internet!
Unicredit Tiriac Bank (☎ 306 800; Piața Victoriei 2; 🕑 9am-4pm Mon-Fri)
Volksbank (☎ 406 101; Str Piatra Craiului 2; 🕑 9am-5.30pm)

Sights
Begging to be photographed with your widest lens is Piața Victoriei, a beautiful pedestrian mall with shops and cafes, the **National Theatre & Opera House** (p716) at its head, and bullseyed by a column topped with the classic scene of **Romulus and Remus** feeding from the mother wolf – a gift from the city of Rome – at its centre. This is where thousands of demonstrators gathered on 16 December 1989 following the siege on Lászlo Tökés' house. A memorial plaque on the front of the Opera House today reads: 'So you, who pass by this building, will dedicate a thought for free Romania.'

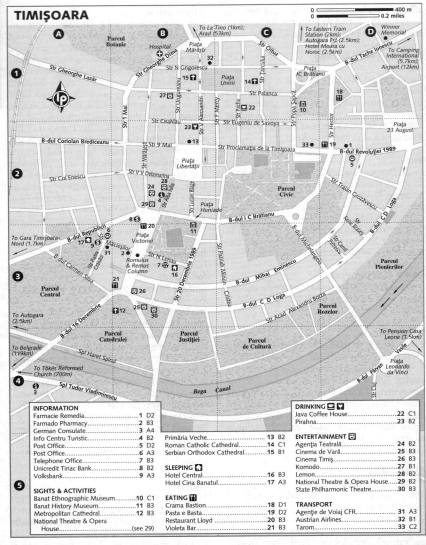

TIMIŞOARA

Just east of the *piaţa* is the 15th-century Huniades Palace, housing the **Banat History Museum** (Muzeul Banatului; ☎ 491 339; Piaţa Huniade 1; adult/student 2/1 lei; 10am-4pm Tue-Sun), which is worth visiting for its displays on natural history, geology, armour, weapons, archaeology, ceramics, tools and scale-model countryside shelters.

Towering over the mall's southwestern end is the 1946 Romanian Orthodox **Metropolitan Cathedral** with unique electrical bells. Next to the cathedral is Parcul Central, and just south of it the Bega Canal.

The 1989 revolution began on 15 December 1989 at the **Tökés Reformed Church** (Biserica Reformată Tökés; ☎ 492 992; Str Timotei Cipariu 1), off B-dul 16

Decembrie just southwest of the centre, where Father László Tökés spoke out against the dictator.

Piaţa Libertăţii and the **Primăria Veche** (Old Town Hall; 1734) lie north. Piaţa Unirii is Timişoara's most picturesque square, featuring a baroque 1754 **Roman Catholic Cathedral** and the 1754 **Serbian Orthodox Cathedral**. Housed in the city's oldest remaining 18th-century bastion, the **Banat Ethnographic Museum** was closed for renovations during our last pass.

Sleeping

Camping International (☎ 208 925; campinginternational@yahoo.com; Aleea Pădurea Verde 6; camp sites per tent 20 lei, chalets s/d/q 92/126/220 lei) Nestled in the Green Wood forest on the opposite side of town from Timişoara-Nord train station. The main entrance of this excellent camping ground is on Calea Dorobanţilor. From the station catch trolleybus 11 to the end of the line. The bus stops less than 50m from the camping ground. The site has a restaurant, and chalets have central heating.

Hotel Moara cu Noroc (☎ 214 203; Str Lirei 4; d 60 lei) No frills in a noncentral, residential neighbourhood. Take trolleybus 14, and alight at the first stop (with a blue 'Melinda Impex Steel' sign) after passing two consecutive cemeteries on the left (about 10 minutes from the centre, 20 from the train station). Cross the street and walk 100m down Str Lirei. The hotel is in a white and blue building. No breakfast.

Hotel Cina Banatul (☎ 490 130; B-dul Republicii 3-5; s/d 120/140 lei) Still the best-value pad in the centre, with clean, modern rooms. No breakfast.

our pick **Pension Casa Leone** (☎ 292 621; www.casaleone.ro; B-dul Eroilor 67; s/d/tr 134/159/212 lei; 🖳) This lovely seven-room pension offers exceptional service and individually decorated rooms. It gives a 5% discount to holders of this book. Take tram 8 from the train station and alight at the Deliblata station, or call ahead to arrange transport.

Hotel Central (☎ 490 091; www.hotel-central.ro; Str N Lenau 6; s/d 160/180 lei; 🞭) Modern and comfortable, this place offers a big breakfast and guarded parking.

Eating & Drinking

Bottles of the local Timişoreana Pils beer sell for about 4 lei at any of the lovely terrace cafes lining Piaţ Unirii and Piaţa Victoriei, where you can while away the time or plot the next revolution.

Crama Bastion (☎ 221 199; Str Hector 1; mains 9-22 lei; 🕙 11am-11pm) Classic Romanian dishes vie with the wine list for attention in this traditional restaurant in 18th-century fortifications.

Pasta e Basta (☎ 493 913; B-dul Revolutiei 1989 nr 7; mains 12-40 lei) A trendy place slinging pizzas that feed two (17 lei), pasta and meat entrées. Skip the overpriced wine. For food on the go, step into the 'Italian-German' pastry shop next door.

Restaurant Lloyd (☎ 294 949; www.lloyd.ro; Piaţa Victoriei 2; mains 15-40 lei; 🕙 11am-11pm) Exquisite international-Romanian menu of steaks, shark, smoked salmon and a spit-roast joint, served on a leafy terrace. Live music most nights.

La Tino (☎ 226 455; Calea Aradului 14; mains 17 lei; 🕙 noon-10pm) There's scrummy pizzas at this place north of the city centre.

Violeta Bar (Piaţa Victoriei; 🕙 10am-8pm) A popular sweets cafe.

Java Coffee House (☎ 432 495; Str Pacha 6; 🕙 24hr) A dark, cosy coffee shop. Sit in the back for less smoke with your coffee. Hot sandwiches (6 lei) are available across the street at Java Snack House.

Piranha (Str V Alecsandri 5; 🕙 7am-4am; 🖳) A full cafe-bar with house music and a 'whiskey red bull' special for only 7 lei. Arrive early on weekends to get one of the giant puffy couches fronting aquarium tables – filled with piranhas!

Entertainment
CINEMAS
Cinema Timiş (☎ 491 290; Piaţa Victoriei 7; tickets 6 lei) Movies are screened in their original language.

Cinema de Vară (B-dul CD Loga 2; tickets 6 lei) Tickets at this brilliant outdoor cinema cost the same but it's far more fun!

NIGHTCLUBS
Be seen in these funky haunts.

Lemon (Str Alba Iulia 2; 🕙 10pm-4am Thu-Sun) This club in the cellar of a piano bar has hip-hop and house DJs.

Komodo (Str Ungureanu 9) So trendy it hurts, this large, colourfully lit eclectic bar has techno-house DJs on weekends.

PERFORMING ARTS
Buy tickets (starting at 40 lei) from **Agenţia Teatrală** (☎ 499 908; Str Mărăşeşti 2; 🕙 10am-1pm

& 5-7pm Tue-Sun) for performances at the following venues.

Classical concerts are held most evenings at the **State Philharmonic Theatre** (Filharmonica de Stat Banatul; ☎ 492 521; B-dul CD Loga 2). Tickets can also be bought at the box office inside.

The **National Theatre & Opera House** (Teatrul Naţional şi Opera Română; ☎ 201 284; Str Mărăşeşti 2) is highly regarded.

Getting There & Away
AIR
The airport is 12km east of the centre. **Tarom** (☎ 200 003; B-dul Revoluţiei 1989 3-5; ☼ 8am-8pm Mon-Fri, 7am-1pm Sat) has four daily direct flights to Bucharest (starting at 212 lei) and several weekly international flights.

Timişoara is the hub of **Carpatair** (reservations@carpatair.com; www.carpatair.ro), Romania's thriving new airline, with direct service to nine key Romanian cities as well as a growing list of international destinations.

Austrian Airlines (☎ 490 320; all-tsr-to@aua.com; Piaţa Unirii 6) has daily flights to Vienna starting at €200 (about 700 lei) plus taxes.

BUS
The small, shabby **autogara** (☎ 493 471; B-dul Maniu Iuliu 54; ☼ 6am-8pm Mon-Fri) has six platforms where slow state buses depart daily for Campeni, Arad (10 lei, five daily), Sibiu (41 lei, six hours, two daily) and Rimincu Valcea.

International buses leave from the Autogara Est (East Bus Station), which is merely a few kiosks cluttered outside the east train station. **Atlassib** (☎ 226 486) goes to Rome (283 lei), Spain (300 lei) and even Sweden. **Eurolines** (☎ 288 132; timisoara.ag@eurolines.ro) goes to Budapest (124 lei, three weekly) and Madrid, among others. **Murat** (☎ 0744 144 326, no English) goes to İstanbul every Monday (165 lei).

TRAIN
All major train services depart from **Gara Timişoara-Nord** (Northern Train Station; ☎ 491 696; Str Gării 2). Purchase tickets in advance from the **Agenţie de Voiaj CFR** (☎ 491 889; cnr Str Măcieşilor & Str V Babeş; ☼ 7am-8pm Mon-Fri). Daily trains include five to Bucharest (82 lei, 8½ hours), one to Cluj-Napoca (64 lei, five to six hours), five to Băile Herculane (38 lei, three hours), one to Baia Mare (12 lei, six hours) via Arad and three sadistically slow runs to Iaşi (78 lei, 16 hours). Additionally, three go to Budapest (95 lei) and one to Belgrade (64 lei).

MARAMUREŞ

Dismount from the horse-drawn cart and tip your chauffer in cigarettes. You've found one of the last places where rural European medieval life remains intact, where peasants live off the land as countless generations did before them. Even Romanians joke that nothing has changed here for 100 years – welcome to Maramureş.

Having inconceivably flown under the radar during the collectivisation of the 1940s, systemisation of the '80s and the Westernisation of the '90s, the region is finding that newly imposed EU regulations are starting to cramp its medieval peasant style. Yet nothing short of an occupying force is going to touch the hand-built wooden churches, traditional music, colourful costumes and timeless festivals. Villagers' homes are still fronted with traditional, giant, ornately carved wooden gates. Ear-smoking, 100-proof *ţuică* stills percolate in the garden, usually tended by a rosy-cheeked patriarch. Mirthful sights of villagers with pitchforks in one hand and mobile phones in the other notwithstanding, sensations of time travel and escapism punctuate most visits here.

SIGHETU MARMAŢIEI
☎ 0262 / pop 44,200
Being the northernmost significant town in Romania, Sighet (as it's known locally) still gives off a whiff of provincial air, despite the area's nominally increasing tourism popularity and gentrification. Its name is derived from the Thracian and Dacian word *seget* (fortress).

The town is famed for its vibrant **Winter Festival**. Its former maximum-security prison is now open as a sobering and informative museum (see opposite).

Information
ATM (Piaţa Libertăţii 8) Outside Hotel Tisa.
Banca Română (Calea Ioan Mihaly de Apşa 24; ☼ 9am-5pm Mon-Fri) ATM, plus cash transfer and exchange facilities.
Fundaţia OVR Agro-Tur-Art (☎ 330 171; www .vaduizei.ovr.ro) In Vadu Izei (6km south), it's the region's best source of books and information; it can also book rooms in local homes.
MM Pangaea Project Turism (☎ 312 228; www .pangaeaturism.ro; Piaţa Libertăţii 15; ☼ 9am-4pm Mon-Fri) Offers simple maps and group tours.
Post & telephone office (Str Ioan Mihaly de Apşa 39) Opposite the Maramureş Museum.

SIGHET PRISON

In May 1947 the communist regime embarked on a reign of terror, slaughtering, imprisoning and torturing thousands of Romanians. While many leading prewar figures were sent to hard-labour camps, the regime's most feared intellectual opponents were interned in Sighetu Marmaţiei's maximum-security prison. Between 1948 and 1952, about 180 members of Romania's academic and government elite were imprisoned here.

Today four white marble plaques covering the barred windows of the prison list the 51 prisoners who died in the Sighet cells, notably the academic and head of the National Liberal Party (PNL), Constantin Brătianu; historian and leading member of the PNL, Gheorghe Brătianu; governor of the National Bank, Constantin Tătăranu; and Iuliu Maniu, president of the National Peasants' Party (PNŢ).

The prison, housed in the old courthouse, was closed in 1974. In 1989 it reopened as the **Muzeu al Gândirii Arestate** (Museum of Arrested Thought; ☎ 314 424; Str Corneliu Coposu 4; adult/student 6/3 lei; ☯ 9.30am-6.30pm mid-Apr–mid-Oct, to 4.30pm mid-Oct–mid-Apr). Photographs are displayed in the torture chambers and cells.

Sights

On Piaţa Libertăţii, the **Hungarian Reformed Church** was built during the 15th century. Close by is the 16th-century **Roman Catholic Church**.

Nearby, the **Maramureş Museum** (Piaţa Libertăţii 15; adult/student 4/2 lei; ☯ 10am-6pm Tue-Sun) displays colourful folk costumes, rugs and carnival masks.

Just off the square is Sighet's only remaining **synagogue** (Str Bessarabia 10). Before WWII there were eight synagogues serving a large Jewish community, which comprised 40% of the town's population.

The Jewish writer and 1986 Nobel Peace Prize winner, Elie Wiesel, who coined the term 'Holocaust', was born in (and later deported from) Sighet. His **house** is on the corner of Str Dragoş Vodă and Str Tudor Vladimirescu. Along Str Gheorghe Doja, there is a **monument** (Str Mureşan) to the victims of the Holocaust.

Allow at least half a day to wander through the incredible constructions at the open-air **Village Museum** (Muzeul Satului; ☎ 314 229; Str Dobăieş 40; adult/child 4/2 lei; ☯ 9am-7pm Jun-Sep, 10am-6pm Oct-May), southeast of Sighet's centre. Children love the wood dwellings, cobbled pathways and 'mini-villages'. You can even stay overnight in tiny wooden cabins (20 lei) or pitch a tent (5 lei).

Sleeping & Eating

For homestays in the area, check out www.ruraltourism.ro and www.pensiuni.info.ro. In Vadu Izei, **Fundaţia OVR Agro-Tur-Art** (☎ 330 171; www.vaduizei.ovr.ro) can also book private rooms.

Cobwobs Hostel (☎ 0745 615 173; www.cobwobs.com; Str 22 Decembrie 1989 nr) Run by an English/Romanian couple, this home-turned-hostel arranges tours of the area and offers dinners (24 lei) in its garden. Breakfast is 10 lei.

Motel Buţi (☎ 311 035; Str Ştefan cel Mare 6; s/d/tr 100/120/150 lei; 💻) Spotless rooms, but undersized for the price. There's a bar and pool table downstairs. Internet is 5 lei per hour.

Hotel Coroana (☎ 312 645; Piaţa Libertăţii 8; d/tr 105/125 lei) The long, dark hallways open into bright, basic rooms. Being smack-bang in the centre of Sighet, you're paying for location more than comfort.

our pick **Casa Iurca** (☎ 318 882; www.casaiurca.ro; Str Dragos Voda 14; r 155 lei; 😺) Charming, immaculate wood-trimmed rooms surround this private courtyard oasis. Easily the best value in the region. The on-site Romanian restaurant is exceptional (mains 10 to 32 lei). Free wi-fi throughout.

David's (Str Ioan Mihaly de Apşa 1; ☯ 7am-10pm; mains 6-23 lei) The bar-of-the-moment, with a menu of salads, pizza and meat.

Getting There & Away

A car/foot bridge from Sighet to Ukraine opened to foreigners in 2008. At the time of writing, there was no public transport using this crossing.

BUS

The **bus station** (☎ 312 488; Str Gării; ☯ closed Sun) is opposite the train station. There are several local buses daily to Baia Mare (10 lei, 65km), Satu Mare (12 lei, 122km), Borşa, Budeşti, Călineşti (all 5 lei) and Vişeu de Sus (7 lei),

MARAMUREŞ

and one bus daily to each of Bârsana, Botiza, Ieud and Mara.

TRAIN
Advance tickets are sold at the **Agenţie de Voiaj CFR** (☎ 312 666; Piaţa Libertăţii 25; ☼ 7am-8pm Mon-Fri). There's one daily fast train each to Timişoara (70 lei, 12 hours), Bucharest (70 lei, 12 hours), Cluj-Napoca (38 lei, six hours) and Arad (62 lei, 11½ hours).

SĂPÂNŢA
☎ 0262
Unassuming Săpânţa village has one of the most singular attractions in Romania: the **Merry Cemetery** (admission 5 lei, camera 5 lei), famous for the colourfully painted, epitaph-inscribed wooden crosses adorning its tombstones. Shown in art exhibitions across Europe, the crosses attract legions of visitors who marvel at the gentle humour and human warmth that created them.

Off the main road, a new wooden church claiming to be the **tallest wooden structure in Europe** (75m) has been built – with a stone base.

The village itself lies 12km northwest of Sighetu Marmaţiei, just 4km south of

Ukraine. Find rooms at **Pensiunea Stan** (☎ 372 337; d 60 lei), opposite the cemetery entrance, and **Pensiunea Ileana** (☎ 372 137; d 70 lei), to the right of Pensiunea Stan; breakfast at Ileana is 15 lei

Camping Poieni (☎ 372 228; www.camping-poieni.ro; camp sites 15 lei, cabins per person 50 lei, pension incl breakfast 130-180 lei), 3km south of Săpânţa and adjacent to an atmospheric river, has a variety of accommodation and an on-site restaurant.

Eight buses a day go to Sighetu Marmaţiei.

VALEA IZEI
☎ 0262 / pop 3000
The Valea Izei (Izei Valley) follows the Iza River eastward from Sighetu Marmaţiei to Moisei. A tight-knit procession of quintessential Maramureş peasant villages nestle in the valley, all featuring the region's famed elaborately carved wooden gates and tall wooden churches.

Gradually developing tourism in the region provides visitors the opportunity to sample traditional cuisine or try their hand at woodcarving, wool weaving and glass painting.

In mid-July, Vadu Izei, together with the neighbouring villages of Botiza and Ieud,

quired its first church in 1720 (its interior paintings were done by local artists). The Orthodox **Bârsana Monastery** is a popular pilgrimage spot in Maramureş. It was the last Orthodox monastery to be built in the region before Serafim Petrovai, head of the Orthodox church in Maramureş, converted to Greco-Catholicism in 1711.

Rozavlea

Continue south though Strâmtura to Rozavlea, first documented under the name of Gorzohaza in 1374. Its fine **church**, dedicated to the archangels Michael and Gabriel, was built between 1717 and 1720 in another village, then erected in Rozavlea on the site of an ancient church destroyed by the Tatars.

Botiza

From Rozavlea continue south for 3km to Şieu, then turn off for Botiza. Botiza's **old church**, built in 1694, is overshadowed by the large **new church** constructed in 1974 to serve the 500 or so devout Orthodox families.

Opération Villages Roumains (OVR) runs an efficient agrotourism scheme in Botiza. Bookings can be made with local representative **George Iurca** (☎ 0722 942 140; botizavr@sintec.ro; house 742; ☯ 8am-10pm), whose house is signposted. George also runs German-, French- and English-language tours of Maramureş and Transylvania (215 to 287 lei per group per day), rents out mountain bikes (18 lei per day) and organises fishing trips.

Ieud

The oldest wooden church in Maramureş, dating from 1364, is in Ieud, 6km south of the main road from Şieu, slightly hidden behind an overgrown cemetery. Ieud was first documented in 1365. Its fabulous Orthodox **Church on the Hill** was built from fir wood and used to house the first known document to be written in Romanian (1391–92), in which the catechism and church laws pertaining to Ieud were coded. The church was restored in 1958 and in 1997.

Ieud's second **church** is Greco-Catholic, and was built in 1717. It is unique to the region as it has no porch. At the southern end of the village, it houses one of the largest collections of icons on glass found in Maramureş.

OVR runs a small agrotourism scheme in Ieud. You can make advance bookings

hosts the **Maramuzical Festival**, a lively four-day international folk-music festival.

Vadu Izei

Vadu Izei, at the confluence of the Iza and Mara Rivers 6km south of Sighetu Marmaţiei, serves as the gateway to valley excursions and homestays.

Fundaţia OVR Agro-Tur-Art (☎ 330 171; www.vaduizei.ovr.ro; house No 161) is an unrivalled source of local information and has rooms for rent in private homes (per person 30 to 80 lei). **Florin Muntean** (☎ 0766 755 267; www.casamuntean.home.ro; Str Dumbrava 505; r with shared bathroom per person 33 lei; ☐) rents rooms and arranges tours starting at 180 lei per group per day. The lovely **Ramona Ardelean** (☎ 0744 827 829; www.pensiunea ardelean.ro; s/d 100/120 lei) also arranges guided tours in French or English (90 lei full day, plus 1 leu per kilometre), as well as picnics, woodcarving and icon-painting workshops, and homestays.

Bârsana

From Vadu Izei continue southeast for 12km to Bârsana. Dating from 1326, the village ac-

through the office in Vadu Izei (p719) or go straight to local representatives **Vasile Chindris** (☎ 336 197; house 201; per person with half-/full board 70/90 lei), **Liviu Ilea** (☎ 336 039; house 333; per person without/ with board 36/72 lei) or **Vasile Rişco** (☎ 336 019; House No 705; r with half-/full board 43/64 lei).

Moisei

Moisei lies 7km northeast of Săcel, at the junction of route 17C and route 18. A small town at the foot of the Rodna Massif, Moisei is known for its traditional crafts and customs. It gained regrettable fame in 1944 when retreating Hungarian (Horthyst) troops gunned down 31 people before setting fire to the village.

In 1944, following the news that the front was approaching Moisei, villagers started to flee, including those forced-labour detachments stationed in the village. Occupying Hungarian forces organised a manhunt to track down the deserters. Thirty-one were captured and detained in a small camp in nearby Vişeu de Sus without food or water for three weeks. On 14 October 1944 Hungarian troops brought the 31 prisoners to a house in Moisei, locked them inside, then shot them through the windows – 29 were killed. Before abandoning the village, the troops set it on fire, leaving all 125 remaining families homeless.

Only one house in Moisei survived the blaze: the one in which the prisoners were shot. Today it houses a small **museum** in tribute to those who died in the massacre. Opposite, on a hillock above the road and railway line, is a circular **monument** to the victims. The 12 upright columns symbolise sun and light. Each column is decorated with a traditional carnival mask, except for two that bear human faces based on the features of the two survivors.

The museum and monument are at the eastern end of the village. If the museum is locked, knock at the house next door and ask for the key.

BORŞA
☎ 0262

Ore has been mined at Borşa, 12km east of Moisei, since the mid-14th century. The area was colonised in 1777 by German miners from Slovakia; later, Bavarian-Austrian miners moved to Baia Borşa, 2km northeast of the town, to mine copper, lead and silver.

The **Complex Turistic Borşa**, a small ski resort and tourist complex 10km east of Borşa town,

is a main entry point to the **Rodna Mountains**, part of which form the Pietrosul Rodnei Nature Reservation (5900 hectares). For useful information on the hiking trails leading into the massif, talk to staff at the two-star **Hotel Cerbul** (☎ 344 199; Str Fântâna; s/d/tr without breakfast 80/100/130 lei).

In winter, you can ski down the 2030m-long ski run at the complex (beginner to intermediate). There's a **ski lift** (Str Brâdet 10; ☉ 7am-6pm), but ski hire is not available.

PRISLOP PASS

Famed for its remoteness and postcard-worthy beauty, Prislop Pass is the main route from Maramureş into Moldavia. The drive is spectacular. Hikers can trek east from Borşa across the pass into Moldavia and head northeast to Câmpulung Moldovenesc and on to the monasteries of southern Bucovina; or south to the natural mineral waters of Vatra Dornei and through to the fantastic Bicaz Lake.

At 1416m a **roadside monument** marks the site of the last Tartar invasion prior to their final flight from the region in 1717. Nearby is the Hanul Prislop, site of the **Hora de la Prislop**, the major Maramureş festival, held yearly on the second Sunday in August.

MOLDAVIA

The Romania postcards you buy showing cinematically perfect forested hills and undulating valleys were most likely taken in Moldavia. The topographical, pastoral and cultural love child of Transylvania and Maramureş, Moldavia nevertheless remains an idiosyncratic tourism option, usually only visited by travellers with abundant time on their hands. Roam between painted churches, urban excesses and village retreats all connected by train rides where the only book you'll crack open will be this one.

IAŞI
☎ 0232 / pop 402,800

Iaşi (pronounced 'yash'), Romania's second-largest city, is discreetly rich with fabulous buildings, important monasteries, sprawling parks and unpretentious cultural treasures. Tragically, municipal planners didn't invoke the same discretion with the ocean of cement that partitions it all.

Moldavia's capital since 1565, and Romania's capital briefly during WWI, Iaşi is a fun, eclectic city, teeming with beautiful people, restaurants, bars and nightspots. It's also the ideal staging area for incursions on the Moldovan border, 20km away.

Iaşi Days (second week in October) is an unhinged street party, fuelled by a river of *must* (a sweet, fermented not-quite-wine brew).

Orientation

Legend has it that Iaşi's street system was plotted by a blindfolded, three-legged donkey. OK, we made that up, but it's plausible. To reach Iaşi's bus station (Autogara Iaşi Vest) from Gara Centrală train station, walk northwest along Str Străpungerea Silvestru for about 1km. To reach Piaţa Unirii from Gara Centrală train station, walk northeast along Str Gării for two

blocks, then turn right on to Şos Arcu. From Piaţa Unirii, B-dul Ştefan cel Mare runs southeast past the Mitropolia Moldovei (Moldavian Metropolitan Cathedral) and the Church of the Three Hierarchs, ending at the Palatul Culturii (Palace of Culture). B-dul Carol I starts at Piaţa Mihai Eminescu and runs northwest, past the university, Parcul Copou and the Botanical Gardens.

Information

For any emergency within the city, dial ☎ 112.

Cliven Turism (☎ 258 326; www.reservation.ro; B-dul Ştefan cel Mare 8-12; ☺ 9am-6pm Mon-Fri, to 2pm Sat) As agents for Antrec, it can arrange rural accommodation and city tours.

IAŞI

INFORMATION	
Cliven Turism	1 C3
Forte Café	2 D3
Post Office	3 C3
Raiffeisen Bank	4 C3
Sfântu Spiridon University Hospital	5 C3
Telephone Centre	6 B2
Tourist Information Centre	7 B3

SIGHTS & ACTIVITIES	
Church of the Three Hierarchs	8 C4
Golia Monastery	9 D3

Hotel Unirea	10 C3
Moldavian Metropolitan Cathedral	11 C4
Palatul Culturii	12 D4
Vasile Alecsandri National Theatre	(see 28)

SLEEPING	
Casa Bucovineana Hostel	13 C3
Hotel Municipal	14 B2
Hotel Traian	15 B3

EATING	
Casa Lavric	16 C3
Casa Pogor	17 B2
Casa Universitatilor	18 B2

Central Market	19 D4
Family Pizza	20 C3
Ginger Ale	21 B3
Pub Baron	22 D4

DRINKING	
Terasa Corso	23 B3

ENTERTAINMENT	
Agenţia de Opera	24 C3
Cinema Victoria	25 B3
Filarmonica	26 C3
Opera Română	(see 27)
Vasile Alecsandri National Theatre	27 C3

TRANSPORT	
Agenţie de Voiaj CFR	28 B3
Autonom	(see 1)
Carpatair	29 C3
Maxitaxis to Chişinău	30 A2
Tarom	31 B3

Forte Cafe (B-dul Independenței 27; per hr 1.80 lei; ☼ 24hr) In a passage off the footpath.

Post office (☎ 212 222; Str Cuza Vodă 10; ☼ 8am-7pm Mon-Fri, to 1pm Sat)

Raiffeisen Bank (B-dul Ștefan cel Mare 2; ☼ 8.30am-6.30pm Mon-Fri, 9am-2pm Sat)

Sfântu Spiridon University Hospital (☎ 240 822, extension 193; B-dul Independenței 1) The city's largest hospital. Walk-ins go to 'Secretariat Arhiva' on first level.

Telephone centre (Str Alexandru Lăpușneanu; ☼ 8am-8pm Mon-Fri, to 3pm Sat) Has fax service.

Tourist information centre (☎ 261 990; www .turism-iasi.ro; Piața Unirii 12, ☼ 9am-6pm Mon-Fri, to 1pm Sat) A compulsory first stop, it offers excellent city maps and activity brochures for the region.

Sights
BULEVARDUL ȘTEFAN CEL MARE & AROUND

Start your tour on Piața Unirii, the main square, with a trip to the 13th-floor restaurant in **Hotel Unirea** for a bird's-eye view of Iași.

Eastwards, the tree-lined B-dul Ștefan cel Mare leads to the **Moldavian Metropolitan Cathedral** (Mitropolia Moldovei; 1833–39), with its cavernous interior painted by Gheorghe Tattarescu. In mid-October thousands of pilgrims flock here to celebrate the day of St Paraschiva, the patron saint of the cathedral and of Moldavia.

Opposite is a park, and at the northeastern end is the **Vasile Alecsandri National Theatre** (1894–96). In front of it is a statue of its founder Vasile Alecsandri (1821–90), a poet who single-handedly created the theatre's first repertoire with his Romanian adaptation of a French farce.

Under eternal restoration but nevertheless fabulous, is the **Church of the Three Hierarchs** (Biserica Sfinților Trei Ierarhi; 1637–39), unique for its mesmerising stone-patterned exterior. Built by Prince Vasile Lupu, the church was badly damaged by Tatar attacks in 1650 but later restored. Inside are the marble tombs of Prince Vasile Lupu and his family, as well as Prince Alexandru Ioan Cuza and Moldavian prince Dimitrie Cantemir.

At the southern end of B-dul Ștefan cel Mare stands the giant neo-Gothic **Palatul Culturii**, built between 1906 and 1925 on the ruins of the **old princely court**, founded by Prince Alexandru cel Bun (r 1400–32) in the early 15th century. Its four wonderful museums will be closed during a comprehensive five-year renovation project, due to be completed in 2013.

A few blocks north, past the central market, is the fortified **Golia Monastery** (admission free; Str Cuza Vodă), which was constructed in a late Renaissance style. The monastery's walls and the 30m Golia tower at the entrance shelter a 17th-century church, noted for its vibrant Byzantine frescos and intricately carved doorways.

PARCUL COPOU
To get to **Parcul Copou** (Copou Park), laid out between 1834 and 1848, catch tram 1 or 13 north from Piața Unirii. The park, which was established during the princely reign of Mihail Sturza, is famed for being a favourite haunt of the legendary poet Mihai Eminescu (1850–89). He allegedly penned some of his best works beneath his favourite linden tree in this park.

The tree is still standing, behind a 13m-tall **monument of lions**, and opposite the main entrance to the park. A bronze bust of Eminescu stands in front of it. Nearby is the **Mihai Eminescu Museum of Literature** (☎ 0747 499 405; adult/child 2.40/1.20 lei; ☼ 10am-5pm Tue-Sun), which recalls the life and loves of Romania's most cherished writer and poet.

Sleeping
Casa Bucovineana Hostel (☎ 222 913; Str Cuza Vodă 30; s/d/ste with shared bathroom 70/100/200 lei, d with bathroom 120 lei) Many rooms are dark and smoky, but shared bathrooms are, surprisingly, immaculate. Some doubles have in-room showers. Breakfast is not included, but the neighbouring restaurant will fill your void.

Hotel Municipal (☎ 267 832; B-dul Independenței Bloc D1-D2; s/d/tr 99/165/218 lei) Basic rooms in a building set back from the boulevard (the entrance is in the rear). The beds are a bit unforgiving, but the price, location and generous complimentary breakfast compensate.

Iași Apartment (☎ 0746 067 979; www.iasi-apt.com, s/d/tr from 105/105/195 lei; ✷) These guys maintain several modern apartments with air-con, internet and cable TV smack in the city centre. Discounts for long stays. No breakfast.

Hotel Traian (☎ 266 666; Piața Unirii 1; s/d/ste 295/365/795 lei) A friendly and elegant hotel designed by Gustave Eiffel of Paris tower fame. The high-ceilinged rooms are awash in old-world comfort, with large, modern bathrooms. Yes, there's a sumptuous 'Eiffel Room'.

Eating & Drinking

Casa Universitatilor (☎ 340 029; B-dul Carol I 9; mains 6-15 lei) The simple but tasty grilled dishes and pizzas are geared for destitute students and their grossly underpaid professors. The lime-tree-festooned terrace is great for a lazy beer.

Pub Baron (☎ 0752 066 885; Str Sfântu Lazăr 52; mains 8-16 lei; ☾ 24hr) This place has cosy wooden interiors and a great terrace. It's heavy on fresh grills, cooked in brick ovens in the dining room, but there are many salads and fish dishes too.

Family Pizza (☎ 262 400; Str Gl Brătianu; mains 8-20 lei; ☾ 8am-midnight) This lively, brightly lit parlour has 25 types of pizza, plus pasta and tons of pastries to choose from. It also delivers.

Casa Pogor (☎ 0747 258 892; Str Vasile Pogor 4; mains 12-29 lei) The last bastion of Iaşi's awful service has been purged and now has servers as lovely as its insanely cosy basement (formerly the famed Junimea wine cellar) and antique-y main dining hall. The multitiered terrace is beaut too.

Ginger Ale (☎ 276 017; Str Săulescu 23; mains 15-30 lei; ☾ 11am-1am) This place feels like an oversize, old-fashioned cafe with its antique furniture and warm dining room. A great place for fresh salads, drinks or a full meal. It also has 20% to 50% discounts on the long menu daily from noon to 4pm.

Casa Lavric (☎ 229 960; Str Sf Atanasie 21; mains 15-40 lei) Iaşi's best Romanian restaurant is owned by singer/musician Laura Lavric and decorated in classic musical instruments. The menu – including a short vegetarian page – is devoid of English, but the staff's language skills more than make up for this. Reservations required on weekends.

Central Market (☾ 8am-4pm) Get fresh fruit, vegetables, meat, cheeses and flowers at this underground market, with stairway entrances off Str Costache Negri and Str Anastasie Panu.

Terasa Corso (☎ 276 143; www.corsoterasa.ro; Str Alexandru Lăpuşneanu 11; ☾ 11am-midnight Mon, 10am-1am Tue-Sun) This huge, outdoor-indoor amphitheatre-shaped pub is scenester paradise and Iaşi's primary social hub. There's free wi-fi.

Entertainment

Viper Club (Iulius Mall; ☾ 24hr, disco 11pm-4am) This rainy-day entertainment option, about a kilometre out of the centre, features bowling alleys, billiards and video games. It transforms into a house-music haven come night-time.

Cinema Victoria (☎ 312 502; Piaţa Unirii 5; tickets 8 lei) Films shown in English with Romanian subtitles.

Filarmonica (Philharmonic; ☎ 212 509; www.filarmonicais.ro; Str Cuza Vodă 29; box office ☾ 10am-1pm & 5-7pm Mon-Fri) Be sure to see the much-revered Iaşi State Philharmonic Orchestra if it's in town; concerts are massively popular. Tickets cost from 13 to 21 lei, plus there are 50% student discounts.

Vasile Alecsandri National Theatre (☎ 316 778; Str Agatha Bârsescu 18) and the **Opera Română** (☎ 211 144) are located in the same impressive neo-baroque building. For advance bookings go to the **Agenţia de Opera** (☎ 255 999; B-dul Ştefan cel Mare 8; ☾ 10am-5pm Mon-Sat). Tickets cost 18 to 22 lei, with 50% student discounts.

Getting There & Around
AIR
Tarom (☎ 267 768; www.tarom.com; Şos Arcu 3-5; ☾ 9am-5pm Mon-Fri) has daily flights to Bucharest for 100 to 200 lei. **Carpatair** (☎ 215 295; www.carpatair.com; Str Cuza Vodă 2; ☾ 9am-6pm Mon-Fri) has flights to Timişoara Monday to Saturday, where you can catch connecting flights to Italy, Germany, Hungary, Austria, Ukraine and Greece.

BUS
The **central bus station** (Autogara Iaşi Vest; ☎ 214 720), behind the large building labelled 'Auto Centre', has seven daily maxitaxis to Târgu Neamţ (12 lei), five to Suceava (18 lei) and Bacau (20 lei) and two to Piatra Neamţ (22 lei). There's an overnight bus direct to Henri Coanda airport in Bucharest (64 lei); reserve one day in advance. Slower buses run to Vatra Dornei (13 lei), Sibiu (68 lei) and Braşov (48 lei).

Maxitaxis to Chişinău leave from outside the Billa supermarket three to four times daily, while up to six daily (slower) buses to Chişinău depart from the bus station.

CAR & MOTORCYCLE
Autonom (☎ 220 504; iasi@autonom.ro; B-dul Ştefan cel Mare 8-12; ☾ 9am-6pm Mon-Fri) has the best car-hire rates and 24hr assistance.

TRAIN
Trains arrive and depart from the Gara Centrală (also called Gara Mare and Gara du Nord) on Str Garii. The **Agenţie de Voiaj CFR** (☎ 242 620; Piaţa Unirii 10; ☾ 7.30am-8.30pm Mon-Fri) sells advance tickets.

There are six daily trains to Bucharest (71 lei, seven hours), one service daily each to Oradea, Galaţi and Mangalia, and four to Timişoara (via Oradea, affectionately called the 'horror train' by locals).

SOUTHERN BUCOVINA

Though southern Bucovina is inexorably associated with its trove of distinctive and ceaselessly hypnotic painted churches – collectively designated World Heritage sites by Unesco in 1993 – it's also a rural paradise on a par with Maramureş, with the advantage of better transport connections. Once you've absorbed some of Europe's greatest artistic monuments, sample Romania's signature folklore, picturesque villages, bucolic scenery and colourful inhabitants, leaving lasting memories that Transylvanian castles simply can't compete with.

Southern Bucovina comprises the northwestern region of present-day Moldavia; northern Bucovina is in Ukraine.

SUCEAVA

☎ 0230 / pop 118,200

Suceava, the capital of Moldavia from 1388 to 1565, was a thriving commercial centre on the Lviv–İstanbul trading route. Today it's the seat of Suceava county and gateway to the painted churches of Bucovina.

Orientation

Piaţa 22 Decembrie is the centre of town, with most sites of note being within a 400m radius. Suceava's main train station is easily reached by bus or maxitaxi. From Suceava station, cross the street and take bus 2 to the centre of town (buy ticket on board). From Piaţa 22 Decembrie, walk south along Str Ştefan cel Mare past Central Park and Bucovina Mall to the Bucovina History Museum. Or head north for St Dimitri's Church and the Central Market. The City of Residence citadel is east of the centre, down Str Cetăţii, over the creek and through Parcul Şipote.

Information

There are several ATMs on Piaţa 22 Decembrie and along Str Ştefan cel Mare. There's no longer a telephone office in Suceava, but you can buy payphone cards for international calls in any shop. Suceava is bursting with tourist resources.

Bilco (☎ 522 460; Str Nicolae Bălcescu 2; ☯ 8.30am-6.30pm Mon-Fri, 9am-1pm Sat) Can arrange monastery tours and car hire.

Ciprian Slemcho (☎ 0744 292 588; www.mtour.ro) This highly recommended private tour guide is a specialist in both religion and history. A two-person, five-monastery tour is €80.

Games Pit (Str Mihai Eminescu 13; per hr 2 lei; ☯ 24hr) Internet access.

Infoturism (☎ 551 241; infoturism@suceava.rdsnet .ro; Str Ştefan cel Mare 23; ☯ 8am-4pm Mon-Fri) Inside the Museum of Natural Sciences, this is the official tourism office of Suceava county.

Post office (☎ 531 872; Str Dimitrie Onciul; ☯ 8am-4pm Mon-Fri)

Raiffeisen Bank (Str Nicolae Bălcescu 2; ☯ 9am-6.30pm Mon-Fri)

Sights

The unsightly **Casa de Cultură** (House of Culture) is at the western end of Piaţa 22 Decembrie, the city's main square. West of Piaţa 22 Decembrie is Hanul Domnesc, a marvellous 16th-century guest house containing the **Ethnographic Museum** (☎ 214 081; Str Ciprian Porumbescu 5; adult/child 2/1 lei; ☯ 9am-5pm Tue-Sun), with a fine collection of folk costumes and typical household items.

North of the bus stop along B-dul Ana Ipătescu lie the foundations of the 15th-century **Princely Palace**, made nearly impossible to appreciate by the substantial fence that surrounds them. To the west is **St Dimitri's Church** (Biserica Sfântul Dumitru; 1535) built by Petru Rareş.

Return to Piaţa 22 Decembrie and follow Str Ştefan cel Mare south past Parcul Central (Central Park) to the informative **Bucovina History Museum** (Muzeul Naţional al Bucovinei; ☎ 216 439; Str Ştefan cel Mare 33; adult/child 3/1 lei; ☯ 9am-5pm Tue-Sun). Mildly neglected, the museum nevertheless has pictures and artefacts stretching for miles, starting at the Bronze Age, touching on the likes of Vlad Ţepeş, and lavishing justifiable attention on Moldavian prince/saint/Ottoman scourge/founder of painted monasteries, Ştefan cel Mare (Stephen the Great). The presentation comes to an abrupt end at 1945, and old paintings now hang in rooms that formerly glorified the communist era.

The **Monastery of St John the New** (Mănăstirea Sfântu Ioan cel Nou; 1522), off Str Mitropoliei, is well worth visiting. The paintings on the outside of the church are badly faded compared with most of the fantastical painted

SOUTHERN BUCOVINA

churches, but they're a good preview of what's to come on your trip.

Backtrack to McDonald's, follow the adjacent footpath along the stream, cross the little bridge and scale the 241 steps up to the **equestrian statue** (1966) of Ștefan cel Mare. Follow the footpath to the left of the statue up to the **City of Residence Citadel** (Cetatea de Scaun; admission 3 lei, camera 5 lei; ☉ 9am-6pm), a fortress that held off Mehmed II, conqueror of Constantinople (İstanbul) in 1476. It's much more attractive from a distance than from the inside.

Sleeping

ourpick High Class Hostel (☎ 0723 782 328; www.class hostel.ro; Str Mihai Eminescu 19; per person 50 lei) Run by Monika, a good-humoured, monastery-guid-ing, problem-solving force of nature, this tulip-fringed proverbial home-away-from-home is hidden on a quiet street near the centre. No breakfast, but there's a self-catering kitchen with tea and coffee all day. Free wi-fi.

Villa Alice (☎ 522 254; www.villaalice.ro; Str Simon Florea Marian 1; 2-star s/d 80/100 lei, 3-star s/d from 120/140 lei; 🖳) These small bright rooms have comfortable beds, refrigerators and very clean bathrooms. Some rooms have balconies.

ourpick Pensiunea Giardino (☎ 531778, www.giar dino.ro; Str Dobrogeanu Gherea 2; s/d 107/133 lei; 🖳) This immaculate three-star pension is one of the best-value options in Romania. The complimentary buffet breakfast is a thing to behold. Just 200m from the bus station. Psst! 'Prices are negotiable for backpackers'!

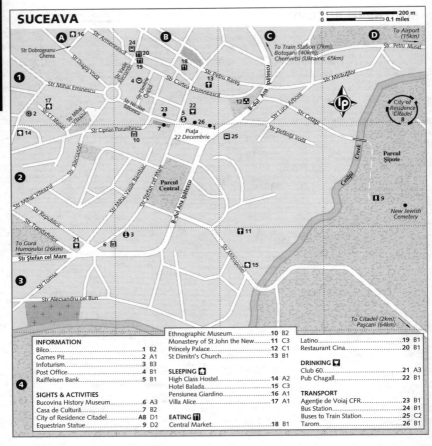

Hotel Balada (☎ 520 408; www.balada.ro; Str Mitropoliei 3; s/d/ste 210/255/400 lei; ❄ ▣) One of the top hotels in the region, this three-storey place offers elegance and comfort over pure luxury; rooms are simply furnished, but have unexpected flourishes like bars and exercise bikes. It's on a lovely, quiet street. Breakfast is 20 lei.

Eating & Drinking

Restaurant Cina (☎ 220 964; Str Vasile Alecsandri 10; mains 8-20 lei; ❨ 8am-10.30pm) A mildly upmarket Romanian menu, with salads and all your favourite chicken, pork, fish and beef dishes. Creative detours include the 'Elisée beef fillet' (beef with pineapple, pepper and salsa sauce). The terrace is a pleasant place to have a few drinks.

Latino (☎ 523 627; Str Curtea Domnească 9; mains 12-40 lei; ❨ 9am-11pm) The classy, subdued decor is accentuated by impeccable service and a dazzling, ever-changing menu that runs the gamut from 25 kinds of pizza – with real mozzarella! – to a dozen first-rate pasta dishes (15 lei) and steaming fresh fish dishes (24 to 40 lei).

Pub Chagall (☎ 0723 961 127; www.chagall.ro; Str Ştefan cel Mare; mains 10-25 lei; ❨ 11am-1am) A cosy, somewhat smoky cellar pub and restaurant. Though it has a thick menu of pizza, chicken, pork and beef, it's mostly used as a drinking hole. Enter by going through the tunnel and down the stairs in the alley.

Club 60 (☎ 209 440; Str Ştefan cel Mare; ❨ 1pm-1am) Enter here at your own risk! Emanating smooth vibes, this vast, loft-style lounge-bar has wooden floors, antique furnishings, comfy sofas and billiard tables. Entrance is in back of the Universal Department Store – climb the stairs to the 2nd floor.

If you're self-catering, the **central market** (cnr Str Petru Rareş & Str Ştefan cel Mare) is close to the bus station.

Getting There & Away

AIR
Suceava's **Ştefan cel Mare Airport** (www.aeroportsuceava.ro) is about 15km northeast of the centre.

Tarom (☎ 214 686; www.tarom.ro; Str Nicolae Bălcescu 2; ☺ 7am-5pm Mon-Fri) has four weekly flights to Bucharest starting at about 180 lei.

Carpatair (☎ 529 559; www.carpatair.com) flies to Timişoara three times a week.

BUS
The **bus station** (☎ 524 340) is in the centre of town at Str Armenească.

Bus and maxitaxi services include 20 daily to Gura Humorului (6 lei), 10 to Botoşani (6 lei), 10 to Rădăuţi (6 lei), 12 to Iaşi (20 lei), five to Vatra Dornei (15 lei), three to Bucharest (40 lei) and four to Târgu Neamţ (9 lei). One daily bus goes to Chernivtsi (Cernăuţi) in Ukraine (20 lei), and a daily 6am bus leaves for Chişinău, Moldova (50 lei).

TRAIN
The bus stop for the train station is east of Piaţa 22 Decembrie, across B-dul Ana Ipătescu, next to McDonald's. The **Agenţia de Voiaj CFR** (☎ 214 335; Str Nicolae Bălcescu 8; ☺ 7.30am-8.30pm Mon-Fri) sells advance train tickets.

Daily train services from the newly spruced-up Gara Burdujeni (also known as Gara Sud or Gara Principala) include nine to Gura Humorului (11 lei, 1¼ hours), seven to Vatra Dornei (21 lei, 3¼ hours), three each to Iaşi (27 lei, 2½ hours) and Timişoara (70 lei, 13½ hours), and one to Bucharest (79 lei, seven hours). To get to Moldoviţa, change at Vama.

BUCOVINA MONASTERIES
☎ 0230

Voroneţ
The *Last Judgment* fresco, which fills the entire western wall of the **Voroneţ Monastery** (adult/child 3/1 lei; ☺ 8am-7pm Apr-Sep, to 4pm Oct-Mar), could be one of the most marvellous frescos

in the world. At the top, angels roll up the signs of the zodiac to indicate that the time of sin is coming to an end. The middle fresco shows humanity being brought to judgment. On the left, St Paul escorts the believers, while on the right Moses brings forward the non-Christians. Souls are judged according to their deeds: good deeds are recorded by the angels, bad deeds by the devils. The souls are represented naked, because there is nothing material about them and they are unable to hide anything on Judgment Day. To the left is *Paradise* and the *Garden of Eden*. Opposite is the *Resurrection*.

On the northern wall is *Genesis*, from Adam and Eve to Cain and Abel. The southern wall features a tree of Jesse (see p728 for more on the Suceviţa Jesse tree) with the genealogy of biblical personalities. In the vertical fresco to the left is the story of Saint Nicholas and the martyrdom of St John the New (whose relics are in the Monastery of Sfântu Ioan cel Nou in Suceava). The vibrant, almost satiny blue pigment used throughout the frescos is known as 'Voroneţ blue', known for changing colour under different illumination.

In the narthex lies the tomb of Daniel the Hermit, the first abbot of Voroneţ Monastery. It was upon the worldly advice of Daniel, who told Ştefan cel Mare not to give up his battle against the Turks, that the Moldavian prince went on to win further victories against the Turks and then to build Voroneţ Monastery out of gratitude to God.

In 1785 the occupying Austrians forced Voroneţ's monks to abandon the monastery. Since 1991 the monastery has been inhabited by a small community of nuns.

SLEEPING & EATING
The town of Gura Humorului is a perfect base to visit Voroneţ. Every second house takes in tourists. The usual rate per person per night in a so-called *vila* is around 50 to 75 lei. There's wild camping possible on the south bank of the Moldova River, 500m south of the bus station; follow the only path and cross the river.

Pensiunea Lions (☎ 235 226; www.motel-lions.ro, in Romanian; Str Ştefan cel Mare 39; s/d 80/100 lei) This three-star pension-restaurant minicomplex is warm, homey and clean. Beds are decent and all rooms have a balcony. Request a room away from the noisy road.

Hotel Simeria (☎ 230 227; Mihail Kogalniceanu 2; s/d from 110/280 lei; 🖳) This is a modern, clean and pleasant hotel. Some rooms have balcony; all have refrigerator and TV. No breakfast.

Casa Elena (☎ 235 326; www.casaelena.ro; s/d 148/185 lei; 🖳) A quick 3.5km trip from Gura Humorului (2km from Voroneţ Monastery), this four-star option has 47 rooms in six different villas, all in a massive, lavish complex. Often bustling with groups, amenities include billiard room, sauna and two restaurants.

GETTING THERE & AWAY
See p727 for bus and train services from Suceava to Gura Humorului. A lovely option is to walk the 4km along a narrow village road to Voroneţ. The route is clearly marked and it's impossible to get lost.

Humor
Of all the Bucovina monasteries, **Humor Monastery** (Mănăstirea Humorului; adult/child 3/1 lei; ☿ 8am-7pm Apr-Sep, to 4pm Oct-Mar) has the most impressive interior frescos.

On the southern exterior wall of the 1530 church, you can see the life of Virgin Mary (on left), Saint Nicholas and the parable of the prodigal son (on right). On the porch is the *Last Judgment* and, in the first chamber inside the church, scenes of martyrdom.

Aside from hitching a ride the 6km from Gura Humorului, there are regular maxitaxis that depart from next to the towering Best Western Hotel, at the start of the road towards the monastery.

Moldoviţa
Moldoviţa Monastery (adult/child 3/1 lei; ☿ 8am-7pm Apr-Sep, to 4pm Oct-Mar) is in the middle of a quaint village. It's a fortified enclosure with towers and brawny gates, and a magnificent painted church at its centre. The monastery has undergone careful cleaning in recent years.

The fortifications here are actually more impressive than the frescos. On the church's southern exterior wall is a depiction of the Siege of Constantinople, while on the porch is a representation of the Last Judgment, all on a background of blue. Inside the narthex, on a wall facing the original carved iconostasis, is a portrait of Prince Petru Rareş (Moldoviţa's founder) and his family offering the church to Christ. All these paintings date from 1537. In the monastery's small museum is Petru Rareş' original throne and the 'Golden Apple',

awarded by Unesco for the uniqueness of Bucovina's painted monasteries.

SLEEPING & EATING
See www.ruraltourism.ro for some great homestays in Vama, a small village 14km south of Moldoviţa on the main Suceava–Vatra Dornei road.

Letitia Orsvischi Pension (☎ 0745 869 529; letita _orsivschi@yahoo.fr; Str Gării 20; s/d with shared bathroom 50/80; 🖳) This property in Vama has a painted-egg exhibit (5 lei for a guided tour) and an ethnographic museum. Rooms are simple but clean. Breakfast is 15 lei, dinner 30 lei. Follow the signs with painted eggs. No English.

Casa Alba (☎ 340 404; www.casa-alba.suceava.ro; s/d/ste 120/140/220 lei) You certainly won't feel a monastic asceticism in this modern villa with large rooms, couches and free wi-fi. Follow the one road heading south 5km west of Frasin about 3km east of Vama.

GETTING THERE & AWAY
Moldoviţa Monastery is right above Vatra Moldoviţei's train station (be sure to get off at Vatra Moldoviţei, not Moldoviţa). From Suceava there are eight daily trains to Vama (13.20 lei, 1 hour), and from Vama three trains leave daily for Vatra Moldoviţei (2.70 lei, 35 minutes).

Suceviţa
Suceviţa Monastery (adult/child 3/1 lei; ☿ 8am-7pm Apr-Sep, to 4pm Oct-Mar) is the largest of the Bucovina painted monasteries.

The church inside the fortified quadrangular enclosure (built between 1582 and 1601) is almost completely covered in frescos. As you enter you first see the *Ladder of Virtues* fresco covering most of the northern exterior wall, which depicts the 30 steps to paradise. On the southern exterior wall is Jesse's genealogical tree symbolising the continuity of the Old and New Testaments. The tree grows from the reclining figure of Jesse, who is flanked by a row of ancient Greek philosophers. To the left is the Virgin, with angels holding a red veil over her head. Mysteriously, the western wall remains blank. Legend has it that the artist fell off his scaffolding and died, leaving artists of the time too scared to follow in his footsteps.

SLEEPING & EATING
It's worth spending a night here and doing a little hiking in the surrounding hills. Wild camping is possible in the field across the

stream from the monastery, as well as along the road from Moldoviţa. The road from Marginea to Suceviţa is littered with *cazare* (room for rent) signs.

Pensiunea Emilia (☎ 0743 117 827; Str Bercheza 173; per person 60 lei) Of the handful of pensions in the immediate area, this one is most appealing. It has only five rooms, but all feel like home. Walk about 500m up the road opposite the monastery.

Pensiunea Silva (☎ 417 019; www.pensiunea silva.ro; Suceviţa 391; r per person incl full board 72 lei; 💻) The hunting-lodge motif here is punctuated by a gaggle of taxidermied critters inside the front door. Located on the western edge of nearby Suceviţa village by the Info-Tur office, it's an easy 3km walk to the monastery.

GETTING THERE & AWAY
Suceviţa is difficult to reach by public transport. There are only two daily buses from Rădăuţi, and six maxitaxis travel to Rădăuţi from Suceava daily (6 lei). Hitching or biking are your best bets.

NORTHERN DOBROGEA

In a prospective Romania photo essay, the northern Dobrogea region may very well have the least representation. There are no breathtaking mountains, ancient churches, striking castles or former princes with an unsettling bloodlust. Yet, despite being considered the 'least Romanian' part of the country, this is where you'll find the strongest evidence of Romania's proud connection to ancient Rome in the form of statues, busts, sarcophagi and other archaeological finds.

There are also extraordinary natural attractions here. You can soothe your body with sunshine and curative mud at the Black Sea coast (Marea Neagră). Alternatively there is the Danube Delta, a tangled web of canals, riverbeds and wetlands where fish leap out of the water to gulp the bugs, birds hover above to snatch the fish, humans lurk nearby to photograph the birds, and bugs converge to feast on the humans – the circle of life.

CONSTANŢA
☎ 0241/0341 / pop 304,300
Constanţa is the gateway to Romania's seaside activities. Sadly, EU membership–driven price hikes have made Black Sea vacations fairly expensive, even by Western European

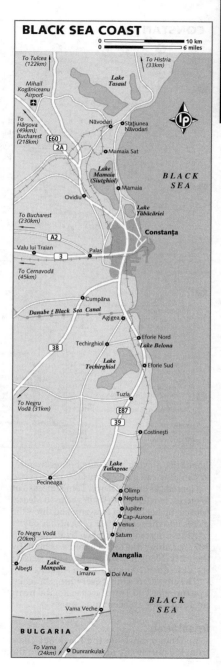

CONSTANŢA

0 — 200 m
0 — 0.1 miles

standards. Staying in private homes (cazare) or camping can ease expenses.

Constanţa's original name, Tomis, means 'cut to pieces', in reference to Jason's beloved Medea, who cut up her brother Apsyrtus and threw the pieces into the sea near the present-day city.

After Constanţa was taken by Romania in 1877, a railway line to Bucharest was built. By the early 1900s it was a fashionable seaside resort frequented by European royalty.

The city offers a bit of everything: beaches, a picturesque Old Town, archaeological treasures and a few excellent museums.

Orientation

Constanţa sprawls up the Black Sea coast from the port in the south to Mamaia in the north. The train station is about 2km west of the centre. To reach Constanţa's centre, exit the station, buy a ticket from the kiosk to the right and take bus 40, 41 or 43 down B-dul Ferdinand to Parcul Arheologic (Archaeological Park) or just walk along B-dul Ferdinand. North of B-dul Ferdinand is Constanţa's business district and many of its best restaurants. The area around Str Ştefan cel Mare is lined with shops, restaurants and theatres. South of B-dul Ferdinand are the tiny streets of Old Town, sporting the city's best museums, churches and neglected buildings.

Like Bucharest, Constanţa's lack of street signage will drive new arrivals into a singular rage. When seeking a specific address, sometimes there's nothing to be done but wander around and ask.

Information
Most hotels and travel agencies have exchange outlets. Avoid independent exchange offices offering too-good-to-be-true rates along B-dul Tomis, south of B-dul Ferdinand.

Banca Transilvania (☎ 619 116; B-dul Tomis 57; ⏱ 9am-5pm Mon-Fri, 9.30am-12.30pm Sat) Changes travellers cheques, gives unlimited cash advances on Visa and MasterCard and has an ATM.

Central post office & telephone office (☎ 552 222; B-dul Tomis 79-81; ⏱ 7am-8pm Mon-Fri, 8am-1pm Sat) The telephone office has free internet and wi-fi.

County Hospital (Spitalul Judeţean; ☎ 662 222; B-dul Tomis 145) North of the centre.

Latina Tourism (☎ 639 713; escapade@latina.ro; B-dul Ferdinand 70; ⏱ 9am-6pm Mon-Fri, to 1pm Sat) A recommended travel agency that can help find local accommodation.

Planet Games (☎ 552 377; cnr Str Ştefan cel Mare & Str Răscoala din 1907; per hr 3 lei; ⏱ 24hr) Internet.

Sights
Constanţa's leading nonbeach attraction is the **History & Archaeological Museum** (☎ 618 763; Piaţa Ovidiu 12; adult/child 10/5 lei; ⏱ 8am-8pm Jun-Sep, 9am-5pm Tue-Sun Oct-May). Cool that sunburn while admiring archaeological artefacts, the bones of a 2nd-century woman and mammoth tusks.

Roman-era Tomis archaeological fragments spill over onto the surrounding square. Facing these is a glass museum, which shelters a gigantic 3rd-century **Roman mosaic** discovered in 1959. The **statue of Ovid**, erected on Piaţa Ovidiu in 1887, commemorates the Latin poet who was exiled to Constanţa in AD 8; rumour has it that he hated the place.

A block south is **Mahmudiye Mosque** (Moscheia Mahmudiye; Str Arhiepiscopiei), dating from 1910, with a 140-step minaret you can climb when the gate is unlocked. Two blocks further down the same street is an Orthodox **Catedrala** (1885). Along the promenade is the **Genoese lighthouse** (1860) and pier, with a fine view of old Constanţa.

Another museum in town worth checking out is the **Folk Art Museum** (Muzeul de Artă Populară; ☎ 616 133; B-dul Tomis 32; adult/child 5/2.50 lei; ⏱ 9am-5pm Jul-Sep, 9am-5pm Oct-May), which has handicrafts, costumes and rotating temporary exhibitions. Further north along the boulevard is the **Art Museum & Gallery** (Muzeul de Artă Populară; ☎ 617 012; B-dul Tomis 84; adult/child

9/4.50 lei; ⏱ 9am-7.30pm Mon-Fri), with mostly still-life and landscape paintings and sculptures. Contemporary exhibitions are held in an adjoining art gallery. The newly renovated **Muzeul Marinei Române** (Naval History Museum; ☎ 619 035; Str Traian 53; adult/child 8/4 lei; ⏱ 9am-5pm Wed-Sun Jun-Sep, 9am-5pm Tue-Sun Oct-May), housed in the old Navy high school, has two floors of fantastic displays: recovered artefacts, costumes, ancient documents and naval items.

Near the city's main intersection, B-dul Ferdinand and B-dul Tomis, is Parcul Victoriei, which has remains of the 3rd-century **Roman city wall** and the 6th-century Butchers' Tower, loads of Roman sculptures and the modern **Victory monument** (1968).

Heading north towards Mamaia, you pass Constanţa's **Planetarium** (☎ 831 553; B-dul Mamaia; adult/child 10/5 lei; ⏱ 8am-9pm Jun–mid-Sep, to 4pm mid-Sep–May), on the southeastern shores of Lake Tăbăcăriei.

Activities
Delphi (☎ 0722 336 686; www.divingdelphi.ro) provides a range of scuba-diving opportunities.

Sleeping
A small legion of people meet every arriving train in Constanţa and line the roadside outside Mamaia in high season with *cazare* signs – some simply jangle their keys. Prices range from 60 to 120 lei. The rooms are usually plain, with shared bathroom and privacy is scant. Always agree on a price and view the room before handing over money.

The nearest camping ground is north of Mamaia (see p733).

Hotel Tineretului (☎ 613 590; fax 611 290; B-dul Tomis 24; s/d 89/100 lei) Cheap for good reason: the rooms are worn, the bedding half-heartedly laundered, the bathrooms woeful and the reception indifferent. However, the location is terrific.

Hotel Florentina (☎ 512 535; B-dul IC Brătianu 24; s 99-105 lei, d 138-148 lei) Walking distance from the bus/train station, and nothing else. Still, it's one of the better-value places in town, with clean rooms and a large breakfast.

Hotel Sport (☎ 611 009; Str Cuza Vodă 2; s 128-160 lei, d 160-200 lei; ▨) A popular two-star, central place. The more expensive rooms have a sea view. No breakfast.

Hotel Maria (☎ 611 711; B-dul 1 Decembrie 1918; s/d 160/200 lei; ▨) This modern, spotless option, across from the park facing the train station, has lots of glass, chrome and deep blue to soothe your sun-withered nerves. There are 48 rooms, yet it's cosy and quiet. Free wi-fi.

Hotel Class (☎ 660 766; www.hotelclass.ro; Str Răscoala din 1907 nr 1; s/d/ste 210/245/300 lei; ✿ ▯) One of the swankiest places in town, everything here is new or new-looking enough to make it worth the price.

Eating & Drinking

New Pizzico (☎ 615 555; www.newpizzico.ro; Piaţa Ovidiu 7; mains 11-50 lei; ✿ 9am-2am) While the wood-fired pizza and summer terrace are its main draw, Pizzico has a menu that offers truffles (by request), pasta, buffalo wings, fish (summer only) and salads. It also delivers. Free wi-fi.

Restaurant La Protap (☎ 639 843; www.restaurant-la-protap.ro; B-dul 1 Decembrie 1918 nr 12; mains 15-40 lei; ✿ 7.30-2am) Next to Hotel Balada, Romanian tat decor literally hangs from the rafters, but the incredible menu of fish, grills, barbecues and international food is worth the eyesore. The 'sufle surprise' (10 lei), served ablaze, is a mountain of meringue, pastry, raspberry sauce and ice cream – easily feeding two.

Café D'Art (☎ 612 133; B-dul Tomis 97; mains 16-30 lei; ✿ 9am-midnight) Tree trunks sprout through the dining room and the terrace is lovely. Food is available, but the long drinks menu (cocktails 15 lei) makes it especially popular as an evening drinking hole.

Marco Polo (☎ 617 537; www.marccopolo.ro; Str Mircea cel Bătrân 103; mains 16-33 lei) A swanky Italian restaurant where servers swarm to keep patrons happy. Portions are generous and the pizza, pasta, meat, fish and vegie dishes are all delicious.

our pick **Irish Pub** (☎ 550 400; www.irishpub.ro; Str Ştefan cel Mare 1; mains 20-40 lei; ✿ 9am-1am) The attractive, orderly wood interior and exceptional menu (one of the best in Romania) miss the true mark of an Irish pub, though you can get your pint of Guinness here. The popular terrace partially overlooks the sea.

Entertainment

Popular films are presented at **Cinema Studio** (☎ 611 358; www.ampmleisure.com; cnr B-dul Tomis & Str Negru Vodă). In summer, films are also screened at **Cinema Grădină Tomis** (B-dul Ferdinand), an outside cinema in Archaeological Park.

Tickets for the **Metamorfoze State Drama Theatre & Opera** (☎ 615 268; Str Mircea cel Bătrân 97) are

sold at the **ticket office** (www.opera-balet-constanta.ro, in Romanian; B-dul Tomis 97; ✿ 10am-4pm Mon-Sat). The theatre is also home to the Filarmonica Marea Neagră (Black Sea Philharmonic) and the **Oleg Danovski Ballet Theatre** (☎ 480 300).

Getting There & Away

AIR

In summer there are international flights from Athens and sometimes İstanbul to/from Constanţa's **Mihail Kogalniceanu Airport** (☎ 255 100; aeroport@aic.ro), 25km from the centre. At the time of writing, **Ryanair** (www.ryanair.com) was running flights here from Pisa.

Tarom (☎ 662 632; Str Ştefan cel Mare 15; ✿ 8am-6pm Mon-Fri, 8.30am-12.30pm Sat) no longer flies out of Constanţa, but can book flights from Bucharest. **Carpatair** (☎ 255 422; constanta@carpatair. com) flies to Timişoara six days a week. Its office is at Constanţa's airport.

BOAT

Catamarans go to Odesa, Ukraine (343 lei, six hours) on Saturdays, and Varna, Bulgaria (162 lei, 3½ hours) on Fridays from Constanţa Port, June to September. Visit or call the **Navlomar office** (☎ 611 970; agent@navlomar.com; Constantza Port, 4th fl, Navlomar Bldg). A scan of your passport is required for email booking.

BUS

Constanţa has two bus stations. From the **Autogara Sud** (Southern Bus Station; ☎ 665 289; B-dul Ferdinand), next to the train station, buses to İstanbul (100 lei, 17½ hours) depart daily. Tickets are sold in advance from **Condor Tour** (☎ 660 696) next to the general ticket office. Buses go to Chişinău Monday and Friday (60 lei, nine hours) at 7pm. Buses 100 and 40 go to Mamaia.

From Constanţa's **Autogara Nord** (Northern Bus Station; ☎ 641 379; Str Soveja 35) services include one daily maxitaxi to Iaşi (50 lei, eight hours) and three weekly to Chişinău (60 lei, 11 hours, summer only). Maxitaxis leave for Tulcea (24 lei, 2½ hours) every 30 minutes from 6am to 7.30pm.

If you're travelling south along the Black Sea coast, buses are infinitely more convenient than trains. From Constanţa's train station, turn right and walk 50m to the long queue of maxitaxis, buses and private cars destined for Mangalia, stopping at Eforie Nord, Eforie Sud, Neptun-Olimp, Venus and Saturn.

TRAIN

Constanţa's train station is near the southern bus station at the west end of B-dul Ferdinand.

The **Agenţie de Voiaj CFR** (☎ 617 930; Aleea Vasile Canarache 4; ☾ 7.30am-8.30pm Mon-Sat, to 2.30pm Sat) sells long-distance tickets only; for local train service (down the coast), buy tickets at the train station.

There are 11 to 15 daily trains to Bucharest (20 lei, 2½ to 4½ hours) and daily services to Suceava, Cluj-Napoca, Satu Mare, Galaţi, Timişoara and other destinations. As many as 19 trains a day head from Constanţa to Mangalia (3 lei, one to 1¼ hours).

MAMAIA
☎ 0241

Mamaia is where the real action is, if by 'action' you mean pretty beaches, pretty people and pretty dreadful hangovers. This 8km strip of golden sands, restaurants and nightclubs is Romania's most popular resort. Avoid visiting in July and August, when prices spike.

Information

Every hotel has a currency exchange, and ATMs are easy to find, but to change travellers cheques you have to go to Constanţa.

Info Litoral Tourist Information Centre (☎ 555 000; www.infolitoral.ro, www.romanianriviera.ro; Constanţa Chamber of Commerce Bldg, B-dul Alexandru Lăpuşneanu 185; ☾ 9am-4pm Mon-Fri), behind a blue-glass facade, is a highly informed and friendly group of people. The staff also give away maps and sell booklets.

The **post office and telephone office** (☾ 8am-8pm Mon-Fri) is 200m south of the Cazino complex on the promenade.

Sights & Activities

Mamaia's number-one attraction is its wide, golden **beach**, which stretches the length of the resort. The further north you go, the less crowded it becomes.

In summer, **boats** (☎ 252 494; return 20 lei; ☾ 9am-midnight) ferry tourists across Lake Mamaia to **Insula Ovidiu** (Ovidiu Island), where Ovid's tomb is located. They depart every 30 minutes from the Tic-Tac wharf opposite the Staţia Cazino bus stop.

The huge **Aqua Magic** (adult/under 12yr 60/40 lei; ☾ 9am-6pm mid-May–mid-Sep) amusement park is about 200m from Hotel Perla, beyond Mamaia's main entrance.

Some 50m north of Hotel Bucureşti, by the banks of Lake Mamaia, is a **water-sports school** (☎ 588 888), offering waterskiing, yachting, windsurfing and rowing.

Sleeping & Eating

For information about rooms in private homes, see p731. Most private homes will be a 10- to 20-minute maxitaxi ride from the beach. Camping is no longer allowed on the beach in Mamaia proper. **Centrul de Cazare Cazino** (☎ 831 200; ☾ 10am-9pm mid-Jun–mid-Sep) has lists of available accommodation.

Booking hotel rooms through travel agencies in Constanţa (see p731) can save you as much as 15% on the rack rate.

Popas Hanul Piraţilor (☎ tents 831 454, huts 0744 241 930; camp sites 16-20 lei, 2-bed huts 80 lei) A camping ground 3km north of Mamaia's northern limit, this has shabby huts, but an on-site cafe and stretches of fine sand nearby. Bus 23 and maxitaxi 23E stop in front of it.

Hotel Turist (☎ 831 006; B-dul Mamaia 288; s/d 170/220 lei) *Much* nicer conditions than similarly priced rooms on the beach, with fridges, good beds and new bathrooms. Close enough for those wanting the beach scene without the beach nightlife blaring through the walls. Take bus 40 from the train station.

Hotel Bulevard (☎ 831 533; www.complexbulevard .ro; B-dul Mamaia 294; s 280-380 lei, d 360-420 lei; ☒ ☒) Modern and posh, offering full services and free wi-fi. Next to Hotel Turist.

Hotel Perla (☎ 831 995; s/d/ste incl full board 380/480/580 lei; ☒) Stationed at the town's main entrance, this huge hotel is both a landmark and reliable service centre. Wi-fi in reception.

Hotel Ovidiu (☎ 831 590; d 220 lei) and nearby **Hotel Doina** (☎ 831 815; www.hoteldoina.ro; s 200 lei, d 180-220 lei) are, relatively speaking, the best deals on the beach. Rooms are basic but clean, with Doina being a slight step down in quality and not offering breakfast. Frugal university students often book a double room, then cram in eight people for an extreme budget weekend at the beach. Hint, hint.

Almost every hotel has an adjoining restaurant and there are numerous fast-food stands and self-serve restaurants lining the boardwalk – all meagre. Nightclubs start after Hotel Victoria and continue ad infinitum.

Getting There & Around

Tickets for trains departing from Constanţa (left) can be bought in advance at the **Agenţie de**

Voiaj CFR (☎ 617 930), adjoining the post and telephone office on the promenade in Mamaia.

The quickest way to travel between Constanţa and Mamaia is by maxitaxi. Maxitaxis 23, 23E and 301 depart regularly from Constanţa's train station, stopping at major hotels. Also, bus 40 goes to the entrance of Mamaia, and bus 100 takes you to the northern end of Mamaia.

In summer a 'train' runs up and down Mamaia's 5km-long boardwalk.

Vehicles not registered in Constanţa must pay a 3-lei road tax when entering Mamaia.

NEPTUN-OLIMP
☎ 0241

Before the 1989 revolution, the twin resort of Neptun-Olimp was the exclusive tourist complex of Romania's Communist Party. Olimp, a huge complex of hotels facing the beach, is the party place. Neptun, 1km south, is separated from the Black Sea by two small lakes amid some lush greenery. Together they form a vast expanse of hotels and discos.

Neptun-Olimp is perhaps the nicest and chicest of the Romanian Black Sea resorts. The Info Litoral Tourist Information Centre (p733) in Mamaia can provide detailed information about these resorts.

The resort complex offers a reasonable range of activities: tennis, windsurfing, jet-skiing, sailing, minigolf, bowling and discos.

Hotel Craiova (☎ 701 048; www.hotelurineptun.ro, in Romanian; per 100-140 lei; 🛋) is a two-star property just 75m from the beach. Rooms are a tad musty, but otherwise bright with good beds and surprisingly comfortable communist garage-sale furniture. All have refrigerator and some have balcony. Hotel Slatina (☎ 701 046; d 50-70 lei, 🛋), next to Craiova, is a definite step down in quality, but acceptable for the price. Neither property includes breakfast in the price.

All trains travelling from Bucharest or Constanţa to Mangalia stop at Halta Neptun station, midway between the two resorts and within walking distance of the hotels.

The CFR office (Str Plopilor) is inside Neptun's Hotel Apollo, northwest of Lake Neptun II.

Private maxitaxis run between the resort towns and Mangalia.

MANGALIA
☎ 0241 / pop 44,300

Formerly ancient Greek Callatis, Mangalia, founded in the 6th century BC, contains sev-

eral minor archaeological sites. With its many tour groups of elderly Europeans, it's not a party town.

Orientation & Information
Mangalia spreads like a beach town along the coast, with nothing of note further than a few blocks inland. The train station is 1km north of the centre. Turn right as you exit and follow Şos Constanţei (the main and only road you're ever likely to use, aside from the beachfront road) south. At the roundabout, turn left for Hotel Mangalia, the Izvor Hercules fountain and the beach, or go straight ahead for the pedestrianised section of Şos Constanţei and most facilities, including the Callatis Archaeological Museum and the Casă de Cultură. Private and city buses stop in front of the train station.

Most hotels have currency exchanges. Cash travellers cheques or get cash advances on Visa and MasterCard at the Banca Comercială Română, (Şos Constanţei 25; 🕑 8am-4pm Mon-Fri).

The telephone office (Str Ştefan cel Mare 14-15; 🕑 8am-8pm) and post office (🕑 7am-9pm Mon-Fri, 8am-4pm Sat, 11am-7pm Sun) are in the same building.

There is a small tourist information kiosk (🕑 8.30am-4pm) outside the train station; it gives out leaflets and can help with booking accommodation.

Sights
The Callatis Archaeological Museum (☎ 753 580; Str Şoseaua Constanţei 26; adult/child 5/2.50 lei; 🕑 8am-8pm) has a good collection of Roman sculptures and artefacts. Just past the high-rise building next to the museum are some remnants of a 4th-century Roman-Byzantine necropolis.

At the south side of Hotel Mangalia, along Str Izvor, are the ruins of a 6th-century Palaeo-Christian basilica and a fountain (Izvorul Hercules) dispensing sulphurous mineral water that, despite the smell, some people drink.

Cultural events take place in the Casă de Cultură, which has a large socialist mural on its facade. One block east of the post office is the Turkish Moscheea Esmahan Sultan (Sultan Esmahan Mosque; Str Oituz; 🕑 9am-8pm). Built in 1525, and surrounded by a lovely garden and well-kept cemetery, it was undergoing restoration during our visit.

From here, head east down Str Oituz to the beachfront, where, in the basement of Hotel

President, remains of the walls of the Callatis citadel dating from the 1st to the 7th centuries are open in the **Muzeul Poarta Callatiana** (Callatiana Archaeological Reservation; ☆ 24hr).

Sleeping & Eating

Antrec (☎ 759 473) arranges rooms in private homes in Mangalia, Doi Mai and other coastal resorts from 85 to 142 lei per night.

Hostel Sailor (☎ 753 492; Decembrie 1918 nr 7a; dm/d 20/110 lei; ⊠) At the south end of Ştefan cel Mare street, about 500m from the beach, these bright, clean rooms are good value. The nine-bed dorm room is in the attic and has no air-con. There's a bar with billiards downstairs. No breakfast.

Pensiune Oituz (☎ 0722 332 821; Str Oituz 11; r with shared bathroom 90 lei) About 150m up the road from the mosque away from the beach, this is a comfy two-star pension with six rooms. Reception closes from 2pm to 6pm daily.

Hotel President (☎ 755 861; www.hpresident.com; Str Treilor 6; s/d/ste from 210/360/580; ⊠) This four-star luxury hotel is the top place to stay south of Constanţa. Wi-fi in reception only.

Hotel Paradiso (☎ 752 052; www.hotelparadiso.ro; Str Rozelor 35; s/d 245/320 lei; ⊠ ▣) The flashy, marble-accented lobby outshines the rooms, which are simply nice. It's one of the few hotels on the coast with full wheelchair access; there are ramps onto the beach.

Hotel Zenit (☎ 751 645; Str Teilor 7; s 195-235 lei, d 210-250 lei) and **Hotel Astra** (☎ 751 673; Str Teilor 9) are surprisingly pleasant two-star options on the promenade with similar prices. Three-star **Hotel Corsa** (☎ 751 156; www.hotelcorsa.com; Str Teilor 11; s/d 296/312 lei; ⊠) has a bar-terrace and free wi-fi, balconies, good beds and minibar in rooms.

You can't go wrong at the **Cafe del Mar** (☎ 0723 356 610; Str Treilor 4; mains 12-30 lei; ☆ 24hr) There's a great double-decker terrace, stylish interiors and one of the most varied, fanciful menus around – it's the only place on the coast serving US-style buffalo wings (11 lei) and potato skins (14 lei)! It's next to Hotel President.

Getting There & Away
BUS

Maxitaxis running up the coast from Constanţa to Vama Veche (every 20 minutes) stop at Mangalia's train station, post office and all along Şos Constanţei. Maxitaxis to Constanţa (5 lei) run from 5am to 11pm.

TRAIN

The **Agenţie de Voiaj CFR** (☎ 752 818; Str Stefan cel Mare 14-15; ☆ 7.30am-8.30pm Mon-Sat, to 1.30pm Sun) adjoins the central post office.

Mangalia is at the end of the line from Constanţa. In summer there are 19 daily trains between Constanţa and Mangalia (5.10 lei, one to 1¼ hours), five of which are direct to/from Bucharest Nord (55 lei, 6 hours). In summer there are also express trains to/from Iaşi, Sibiu, Suceava, Cluj-Napoca and Timişoara.

DANUBE DELTA

After passing through 10 countries and absorbing countless lesser waterways, the mighty Danube River pours into the Black Sea just south of the Ukrainian border at an average of 6300 cubic metres of water per second. The Danube splits into three separate channels – Chilia, Sulina and Sfântu Gheorghe – that fan out and create a constantly evolving 4187-sq-km wetland of marshes, reed islets and sandbars, providing sanctuary for 300 species of birds and 160 species of fish. Reed marshes cover 156,300 hectares, constituting one of the world's largest single expanses of reed beds.

The Danube Delta (Delta Dunarii) is under the protection of the Administration of the Danube Delta Biosphere Reserve Authority (DDBRA), set up in response to the ecological disaster that befell the delta region during Ceauşescu's attempt to transform it into an agricultural area. Now there are 18 protected reserves (50,000 hectares) that are off limits to tourists or anglers, including the 500-year-old Leţea Forest and Europe's largest pelican colony. The areas open to visitors are a birdwatcher's paradise, with protected species such as the roller, white-tailed eagle, great white egret, mute and whooper swans, falcon and bee-eater.

The Delta is included on Unesco's World Heritage list.

GETTING AROUND

Beware touts at Tulcea's port peddling tours while claiming that regular ferries are cancelled and/or village accommodation is unavailable or ghastly. The Information & Ecological Education Centre (p737) in Tulcea can help book birdwatching trips.

In the Delta proper it's easy to hire boats into the delta's exotic backwaters. Look for signs saying *'plimbri cu barca'* (boat for rent).

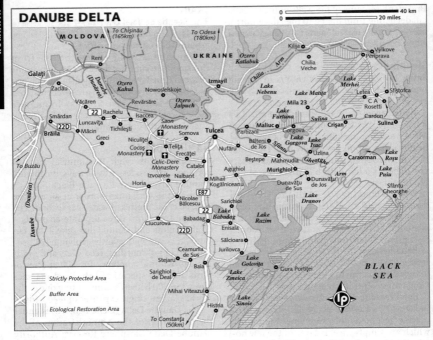

DANUBE DELTA

Strictly Protected Area

Buffer Area

Ecological Restoration Area

Hydrofoil

Hydrofoils (☎ 0755 080 370; www.naverapide.ro) de-part daily from the Hera Pontoon, 100m west of Hotel Delta in Tulcea to Sulina (noon, stop-ping in Crişan) and Sfântu Gheorghe (1.30pm, stopping in Mahmudia). Both journeys are 1½ hours and cost 45 lei each way. Purchase tickets at the pontoon or on board. In high season, to guarantee a seat, reserve the night before either at the boat or by phone.

Ferry

Navrom (☎ 0240-511 553; www.navrom.x3m.ro, in Romanian) operates passenger ferries year-round to towns and villages in the Delta. At the time of writing, Navrom had discontinued its weekend day-trip tours out of Tulcea, but these may resume. Check the website or the Information & Ecological Education Centre (opposite) for current information.

Navrom runs intermittent fast and slow ferries. To Sulina, the slow ferry (24 lei, four hours) departs Tulcea at 1.30pm Monday to Friday, returning at 7am on Tuesday, Wednesday, Thursday, Friday and Sunday. The fast ferry (30 lei, 2½ hours) leaves

Tulcea at 1.30pm on Saturday, returning at 7am Monday.

The slow ferry to Sfântu Gheorghe (26 lei, 5½ hours) departs from Tulcea at 1.30pm on Monday, Wednesday and Friday, return-ing at 7am Tuesday, Thursday and Saturday. The fast ferry (32 lei, three hours) departs Tulcea at 1.30pm on Thursday, returning at 7am on Friday.

Fast ferries to Periprava (29 lei, four hours) depart Tulcea at 1.30pm Monday to Wednesday, stopping at Chilia Veche. Return ferries leave Periprava at 6am Tuesday to Thursday.

Ferry tickets can be purchased at Tulcea's Navrom terminal from 11.30am to 1.30pm. There are also ticket counters on the ferries themselves.

Car

It's now possible, though not particularly cheap, to drive over the dike from Sulina to Sfântu Gheorghe. You'll have to arrange the journey through locals, as there's no public transport. This is best done from Sulina as there are few cars available in Sfântu Gheorghe.

Tulcea
☎ 0240 / pop 97,900

Tulcea (tool-*cha*), settled by Dacians and Romans from the 7th to 1st centuries BC, is a port town and the gateway to the Danube Delta. It's usually passed through quickly en route to the delta, but it has fine restaurants and nightclubs as well as a sizeable Turkish population, giving it a refreshing multicultural flavour.

Tulcea hosts the annual **International Folk Festival of Danubian Countries** in August, when local songs, games and traditional activities are played out against a Danubian backdrop.

ORIENTATION
With the hills to the south and the Danube to the north, getting oriented in Tulcea is a breeze. The bus and train stations and the Navrom ferry terminal are adjacent to one another, overlooking the Danube at the western end of the riverfront promenade. The promenade stretches for about a kilometre east along the river past Hotel Delta and into a residential area with museums and the Azizie Mosque. Most hotels and shops start a block back from the river and continue up the hill. Lake Ciuperca is west of the stations. Inland two blocks, between Str Păcii and Str Babadag, is Piaţa Unirii, the centre of Tulcea.

INFORMATION
Anason Pharmacy (☎ 513 352; Str Babadag 8) Has an all-night dispenser.

Future Games (Str Isaccei 12; per hr 3 lei; ☼ 10am-2am) Web browsing.

Ibis Tours (☎ 512 787; www.ibis-tours.ro; Str Dimitrie Sturza 6; ☼ 9am-6pm Mon-Sat) Arranges wildlife and birdwatching tours in the delta and Dobrogea, led by professional ornithologists, from 145 lei per day.

Information & Ecological Education Centre (☎ 519 214; www.deltaturism.ro; Str Portului 34a) A representative of Antrec and run by the Danube Delta Biosphere Reserve (DDBR), the centre can book accommodation in homes, hotels and pensions and assist in arranging tours. No fixed hours.

Tourism information centre (☎ 519 130; www .primaria-tulcea.ro; Str Gării 26) Mainly a Tulcea-only information centre, it also offers some Danube and boat tour assistance. It's hidden slightly back from the river promenade, next to the Capitania Portului building.

Post office (☎ 512 869; Str Babadag 5; ☼ 7am-8pm Mon-Fri, 8am-noon Sat)

Raiffeisen Bank (☼ 8am-5pm Mon-Fri) Directly across from Hotel Delta.

Telephone centre (☼ 7am-8pm) Same building as the post office.

SIGHTS
As you stroll along the river you'll see the **Independence Monument** (1904) on Citadel Hill at the far eastern end of town. You can reach this by following Str Gloriei from behind the Egreta Hotel to its end. The views are superb.

The **Natural History Museum & Aquarium** (☎ 515 866; Str Progresului 32; adult/child 4/2 lei; ☼ 10am-6pm) features stuffed delta fauna, a life-size model cave and a basement aquarium.

The minaret of **Moscheia Azizie** (Azizie Mosque; 1863) is down Str Independenţei.

The **Folk Art & Ethnographic Museum** (☎ 516 204; Str 9 Mai nr 4; adult/student 4/2 lei) has Turkish and Romanian traditional costumes, rugs and carpets, and fishing nets.

In front of the Greek Orthodox church is a **memorial** to the local victims of the 1989 revolution.

SLEEPING
No camping is allowed within Tulcea's city limits. However, there are many areas where wild camping is permitted on the banks of the canal within a few kilometres of the city; ask at the Information & Ecological Education Centre for details.

Multiday delta tours aboard floating hotels ('boatels') is a unique, albeit pricey, way to visit the delta. Prices start at 340 lei per person per day for two-star boats and rocket up to 2200 lei for four-star boats, including full board. Check www.ddbra.ro for a list of operators.

Casa Albastra Hotel (☎ 535 662; s/d 40/80 lei) A typical Romanian sport hotel, this place is about 300m past Insula Complex down a gravel road and a serious hike from the centre. Breakfast is not included in rates.

Mini Hotel Pelican (☎ 510 078; www.hotel-pelican .com; Str Trandafirilor 26; d 90) Up the hill from central Tulcea on a residential street, this hotel has basic rooms and friendly staff. Request tiny rooftop Room 7 for a sweeping view of the city out your door. Breakfast is 7 lei, and the hotel has wi-fi.

Hotel Europolis (☎ 512 443; www.europolis.ro; Str Păcii 20; s/d 95/140 lei; ☒) Value-conscious travellers will enjoy these simple rooms with huge bathrooms. For the same price, you can also stay at the hotel's Complexul Touristic Europolis, a resortlike place by Lake Câşla, 2km outside of Tulcea. Favoured by groups, the site is lovely, with walking trails in the thick of nature. Water bikes and small boats can be rented.

Insula Complex (☎ 530 908; Lake Ciuperca; s/d 100/130 lei) Seconds from the train station on Lake Ciuperca, this two-star option has an on-site restaurant and large rooms. Turn right out of the train station and cross the bridge to the island. Free wi-fi.

Hotel Delta (☎ 514 720; www.deltahotelro.com; Str Isaccei 2; s/d 190/240 lei; ✎ ▯ ▣) Dated, but still the most luxurious rooms in town. Some afford unimpeded views of the river. There's a restaurant and bar.

EATING & DRINKING

There's a string of cafes and kebab and fast-food joints along Str Unirii.

Restaurant Select (☎ 510 301; Str Păcii 6; mains 13-41 lei) The multilingual, varied menu offers fish, frog legs, pizza and the local speciality, *tochitura Dobrogeana* (pan-fried pork with spicy sauce).

Restaurant Faleza (☎ 511 517; Str Gării 34; mains 6-30 lei; ✆ 7am-11pm) Watch ferry traffic from this terrace fronting the promenade, serving pizza, fish, traditional Romanian fare and breakfast.

Trident Pizzeria (Str Babadag; mains 12-29 lei; ✆ 8am-11pm) An excellent spot for cheesy pizzas and fast pasta. Opposite the Winmarket Department Store.

GETTING THERE & AWAY

The **Agenţie de Voiaj CFR** (☎ 511 360; Str Unirii 4; ✆ 8am-3.30pm Mon-Fri) is on the corner of Str Babadag. The **train station** (Str Portului) has two slow trains a day to Constanţa (38 lei, five hours) and one daily train to Bucharest (59 lei, six hours).

The **bus station** adjoins the **Navrom ferry terminal** (Str Portului). As many as 15 daily buses and maxitaxis head to Bucharest (60 lei), at least nine to Galaţi (16 lei) and one to Iaşi (50 lei). Maxitaxis to Constanţa (24 lei) leave every half-hour from 5.30am to 8pm. One bus a day heads to İstanbul (180 lei).

Tulcea to Sulina
☎ 0240

Almost 64km down the shortest channel of the Danube sits Sulina, the delta's largest

---

> **DELTA PERMITS**
>
> Though locals scoff and dismiss the idea of permits (10 lei), there are occasional checks and you will be fined 100 lei if you don't have one. If on a group excursion of any kind, these are automatically handled by the operator. If you hire a local fisher, ask to see a valid permit. If you go boating or foraging independently or simply visit a village, legally you must have one. **AJVPS** (☎ 511 404, 515 411; Str Isaccei 10; ✆ 7am-8pm Mon-Fri, to 1pm Sat) in Tulcea issues permits. You need separate permits to fish or hunt.

---

town. Its once sleepy and dusty esplanade has been comprehensively overhauled and now features an ATM, well-stocked markets and smart restaurants. Those seeking tranquillity and traditional delta village life can find it in nearby **Cardon**, accessible from Sulina either by a boat trip or by a far less scenic maxitaxi ride.

The Navrom ferry's first stop is at **Partizani**, from where you can find a fisher to row you to the three lakes to the north – Tataru, Lung and Mester. Next stop is **Maliuc**, where there is a hotel and camping ground for 80 people. North of Maliuc is **Lake Furtuna**, a snare for birdwatchers.

The next stop for the ferry is the junction with Old Danube, 1km upstream from **Crişan**. There are several pensions in the village, all charging about 54 lei per person. Try **Pensiune Gheorghe Silviu** (☎ 511 279) or **Pensiune Pocora** (☎ 547 036). There is also the DDBR's **Crişan Centre for Ecological Information & Education** (☎ 519 214; office@delta turism.ro; ✆ 8am-4pm Tue-Sun), which has wildlife displays, a library and a video room. At the main Crişana ferry dock, ask about side trips to **Mila 23** or **Caraorman**.

There is a camping area on the road to the beach.

In Sulina, **Pensiunea Ana** (☎ 0742 421 976; pen siuneana@yahoo.com; r 80 lei) is run out of the home of a caring family. Breakfast is 10 lei. **Pensiune Delta Sulina** (☎ 0722 275 554; r 72-108 lei) is a comfortable three-star option, charging 11 lei for breakfast and 25 lei for dinner.

For information on ferries and hydrofoils see p736 at the start of this Danube Delta section.

ROMANIA DIRECTORY

ACCOMMODATION

Prices for Romanian accommodation have risen disproportionately since EU membership. Unfavourable price-versus-value shock isn't uncommon, particularly in high season. There are five root options: hostels, private homestays (*cazare*); family-style guest-house pensions (*pensiunes*); hotels (a grab-bag ranging from moribund communist leftovers to the burgeoning boutique hotel industry); and camping grounds that usually include simple wooden huts (*căsuţe*).

Budget permitting, aim for pensions, which are often lovingly run and offer insight into how Romanians live, costing 100 to 150 lei (about €25 to €35) per person, with an extra 30 to 45 lei (€7 to €10) for full board, and a little more in cities. The best online resource is www.ruraltourism.ro; otherwise contact **Antrec** (National Association of Rural, Ecological & Cultural Tourism; www.antrec.iiruc.ro), whose headquarters is in Bran.

You'll find budget rooms for under 130 lei (€30). Hostels cost around 50 to 60 lei (€12 to €14) for a dorm bed; sometimes private rooms (with shared bathroom) are available for 85 to 130 lei (€20 to €30). Hostels vary in quality, with Bucharest's topping in terms of travel-savvy hang-outs. **Youth Hostels Romania** (www.hihostels -romania.ro) has information on HI hostels.

A frantic hotel renovation boom has resulted in a glut of new three- and four-star hotels with a frustrating decline in one- and two-star options. The old stalwarts are hit-and-miss. Polished B&Bs are appearing, but still rare. Midrange hotels tend to cost 130 to 250 lei (€30 to €60), more so in Bucharest. Top-end places will generally cost more than 250 lei (€60).

In-town camping is often in less-than-ideal locations, and conditions are sometimes quite shoddy. In most mountain areas there's a network of cabanas (cabins or chalets) with restaurants and dormitories. Prices are much lower than those of hotels and no reservations are required, but arrive early if the cabana is in a popular location.

Apă caldă (hot water) is finally ubiquitous, but air-conditioning is still rare in budget places. Complimentary wi-fi is a fast-growing standard across all classes, though beware of hotels advertising 'internet connections' that are merely dial-up lines requiring a local ISP.

All reviews in this chapter include breakfast and private bathroom unless otherwise noted. Prices are for high season.

Hotels in cities will offer nonsmoking rooms, though not always in budget places. In rural areas, nonsmoking awareness is nascent at best.

ACTIVITIES

Most outdoor fun is related to Romania's Carpathians, which stripe the country impressively. Emergency rescue is provided by **Salvamont** (☎ 0-SALVAMONT; www.salvamont.org, in Romanian), a voluntary mountain-rescue organisation with 21 stations countrywide.

Birdwatching

Europe's greatest wetlands, the Danube Delta (p735), is home to the continent's largest pelican colony. Plus, most of the world's population of red-breasted geese (up to 70,000) winter here.

Cycling

Mountain biking has taken off in recent years. Some roads can be hair-rising to ride along as traffic zooms by. A great place to go is Sinaia, where you can rent a bike and take it to the plateau atop the Bucegi Mountains by lift. **Clubul de Cicloturism Napoca** (office@ccn.ro, Cluj-Napoca) can offer bike-rental advice. **Transylvania Adventure** (www.adventuretransylvania.com) offers eight-day trips (including bike, meals and accommodation) from mid-May to mid-October for about 3400 lei (approximately €800).

Hiking

Hiking is the number-one activity, which is not surprising considering the intensity of the Carpathians cutting across the country. The most popular places are in the Bucegi (p691), and Făgăraş and the Piatra Craiului (p699).

Trails are generally well marked, and a system of cabanas, huts and hotels along the trails on the mountain tops and plateaus make even a several-day trek more than comfortable. Guided hikes are offered by **Romanian Alpineguide** (www.alpineguide.ro) and **Green Mountain Holidays** (www.greenmounta inholidays.ro).

Skiing

Ski and snowboard centres are popular, but ski runs tend to be fewer (and costlier) than many Bulgarian slopes. Sinaia (p691) and Poiana Braşov (p698) are the most popular ski slopes.

ROMANIA

The ski season runs from December through March. Resorts rent skis and snowboards for 43 to 52 lei (about €10 to €12) per day; lift tickets are sometimes bundled by number of trips (five trips can run to €34).

BUSINESS HOURS
Banks can be expected to open from 9am to 5pm Monday to Friday, and 9am to noon on Saturday. Most museums open from 9am or 10am to 5pm or 6pm Tuesday to Sunday. Opening hours for many institutions change slightly following daylight saving. Restaurants can be expected to stay open roughly from 10am to midnight.

DANGERS & ANNOYANCES
Romania sometimes gets a rip-off reputation that's hardly justified. Taxi drivers at train stations are likely to overcharge, a few Bucharest restaurants add extra charges to some bills and pickpockets target wallets and mobile phones in busy areas such as buses. Another problem are the many stray dogs seen nationwide, particularly in Bucharest. Take the necessary precautions, though, and you're likely to have a trouble-free visit.

The biggest annoyances are trying to get someone to change a 50-lei note, museums that charge upwards of 65 lei (€15) to take photographs, and the lack of laundry facilities.

Also be sure to take some food and water and lots of mosquito repellent on any expedition into the Danube Delta outside of Sulina and Sfântu Gheorghe. Warning: do not drink Danube water!

EMBASSIES & CONSULATES
Unless stated otherwise, the following embassies are in Bucharest.

Australia (Map p678; ☎ 021-316 7558; Str Buzeşti 14-18, 5th fl)

Canada (Map p678; ☎ 021-307 5000; bucst@dfait -maeci.gc.ca; Str Tuberozelor 1-3)

France (Map p678; ☎ 021-303 1000; www.ambafrance -ro.org; Str Biserica Amzei 13-15)

Germany Bucharest (Map p678; ☎ 021-202 9830; www .bukarest.diplo.de; Str Gheorghe Demetriade 6-8); Sibiu (Map p703; ☎ 0269-211 133; Str Lucian Blaga 15-17); Timişoara (Map p714; ☎ 0256-309 800; www.temeswar .diplo.de; Spl Tudor Vladmirescu 10, Timişoara)

Ireland (Map p678; ☎ 021-310 2131; www.embassy ofireland.ro; Str Buzeşti 50-52)

Moldova (Map p678; ☎ 021-230 0474; consulat .bucuresti@msa.md; Aleea Alexandru 40)

UK (Map p678; ☎ 021-201 7200; www.ukinromania.fco .gov.uk; Str Jules Michelet 24)

USA (Map p680; ☎ 021-200 3300; www.us embassy.ro; Str Tudor Arghezi 7-9)

GAY & LESBIAN TRAVELLERS
In 2001, Romania became one of Europe's last countries to decriminalise homosexual activity. Bucharest has the most active gay and lesbian scene, including the emergence of GayFest in late May, which features events, films and disco nights. **Accept** (www.accept-romania.ro) is a gay-, lesbian- and transgender-rights group.

HOLIDAYS
Public holidays in Romania:
New Year 1 and 2 January
Catholic & Orthodox Easter Mondays March/April
Labour Day 1 May
Romanian National Day 1 December
Christmas 25 and 26 December

LEGAL MATTERS
If you are arrested, you can insist on seeing an embassy or consular officer straight away. It's not advisable to present your passport to people on the street unless you know for certain that they are authentic officials – cases of theft have been reported.

Romanians can legally drink, drive and vote (though not simultaneously!) at 18. The age of consent in Romania is 15.

MONEY
In Romania the only legal tender is the leu (plural: lei). From January 2007, the old lei was taken out of circulation, and the new lei (abbreviated 'RON') – with four fewer zeroes – took over. If someone offers an old note (say a 500,000-lei note instead of a 50-lei note), don't take it. The new lei notes come in denominations of one, five, 10, 50, 100, 200 and 500 – try to avoid the 200s and 500s as no one outside of hotels will give change for them. Coins come in one, five, 10, 20 and 50. People sometimes still quote prices in old lei, giving hapless travellers sticker shock.

Prices are frequently quoted in euros – especially at hotels. We've quoted most prices in this chapter in Romanian lei to make on-the-ground price references easier.

ATMs are everywhere and give 24-hour withdrawals in lei on your Cirrus, Plus, Visa, MasterCard and Eurocard. Some banks, such as Banca Comercială Română, give cash advances on credit cards in your home currency.

Moneychangers are ubiquitous (avoid changers with bodyguard goons out front), but you should change currency at banks whenever possible. Dollars and euros are easiest to exchange, though British pounds are widely accepted. You often must show a passport to change money. Some changers advertise juicy rates, but subtly disguise a '9' as a '0' etc. Count your money carefully.

Cashing travellers cheques is becoming increasingly difficult. Some branches of the Banca Comercială Română and Raiffeisen Bank, among others, will cash travellers cheques. Credit cards won't get you anywhere in rural areas, but they are widely accepted in larger department stores, hotels and most restaurants in cities and towns.

POST

A postcard or letter under 20g to Europe from Romania costs 2.70 lei and takes seven to 10 days. The postal system is reliable, if slow.

Poste restante is held for one month (addressed c/o Poste Restante, Poştă Romană Oficiul Bucureşti 1, Str Matei Millo 10, RO-70700 Bucureşti, Romania) at Bucharest's central post office (p679).

TELEPHONE

Romania's telephone centres are scaling down and public phones are increasingly neglected amid the mobile-phone revolution. Mobile phones are preferable to landlines for many Romanians.

Phonecards (10 lei) can be purchased at news-stands and used in phone booths for domestic or international calls.

European mobile phones with roaming work in Romania; otherwise you can get a Romania number from Orange or Vodaphone, which have shops everywhere. The SIM card

---

CHANGES TO TELEPHONE NUMBERS

As of 2008, you must use area codes, provided under our destination headings, when dialling any landline in Romania, even if you're just down the road. This goes for nonemergency three- and four-digit short numbers as well. Emergency numbers are still only three digits. Mobile-phone numbers are 10 digits, beginning with 07.

EMERGENCY NUMBERS

- Ambulance ☎ 112
- Fire ☎ 112
- Police ☎ 112

---

costs about 18 lei including credit; domestic calls are about 0.35 to 0.50 lei per minute.

Dial ☎ 971 for Romania's international operator. Going the other way, Romania's country code is ☎ 40.

TOURIST INFORMATION

State tourism information centres are slowly appearing in major cities around the country, though Bucharest remains a black hole of tourist information. Most travel agents are geared to get you *out* of Romania, but some can help, or will try to. The best information often comes from travel-oriented accommodation such as hostels or pensions that offer day trips.

The so-called **Romanian National Tourist Office** (www.romaniantourism.ro, in Romanian) amazingly has no offices in Romania but keeps an active **London office** (☎ 020 7224 3692; infoUK@RomaniaTourism.com; 22 New Cavendish St) and **New York City office** (☎ 212 545 8484; infoUS@RomaniaTourism.com; 19th fli, 355 Lexington Ave).

VISAS

Your passport must be valid for at least six months beyond the date you enter the country in order to obtain a visa.

Citizens of the USA, Canada, Australia, New Zealand, Japan and many other countries may travel visa-free for 90 days in Romania. EU citizens, obviously, may stay indefinitely. As visa requirements change frequently, check with the **Ministry of Foreign Affairs** (www.mae.ro) before departure.

Romania issues two types of visas to tourists: transit and single-entry. Transit visas (for those from countries other than the ones mentioned above) cannot be bought at the border.

To apply for a visa you need a passport, one recent passport photograph and the completed visa application form accompanied by the appropriate fee. Citizens of some countries (mainly African) need a formal invitation from a person or company in order to apply for a visa; see the Ministry of Foreign Affairs website for details.

Regular single-entry visas (US$25) are valid for 90 days from the day you arrive. Single-entry visas are usually issued within a week (depending on the consulate), but for an extra US$6 can be issued within 48 hours.

Transit visas can be either single-entry (US$15) – valid for three days and allowing you to enter Romania once – or double-entry (US$25), allowing you to enter the country twice and stay for three days each time.

Check your visa requirements for Serbia and Montenegro, Hungary, Bulgaria and Ukraine if you plan on crossing those borders. If you are taking the Bucharest–St Petersburg train, you need Ukrainian and Belarusian transit visas on top of the Russian visa.

TRANSPORT IN ROMANIA

GETTING THERE & AWAY
Air
Tarom (Transporturile Aeriene Române, RO; www.tarom.ro) is Romania's state airline. Bucharest's **Henri Coanda airport** (formerly Otopeni; OTP; ☎ 021-201 4788; www.otp-airport.ro; Şos Bucureşti-Ploieşti, Bucharest) is the country's largest.

Major airlines flying into the country:
Air France (AF; ☎ 021-319 2705; www.airfrance.com)
Air Moldova (9U; ☎ 021-312 1258; www.airmoldova.md)
Austrian Airlines (OS; ☎ 021-204 2208; www.austrian air.com)
British Airways (BA; ☎ 021-303 2222; www.british -airways.com)
ČSA (Czech Airlines; OK; ☎ 021-315 3205; www.csa.cz)
KLM (KL; ☎ 021-312 0149; www.klm.com)
LOT Polish Airlines (LO; ☎ 021-314 1096; www.lot.com)
Lufthansa (LH; ☎ 021-204 8410; www.lufthansa.com)
Swiss Airlines (LX; ☎ 021-312 0238; www.swiss.com)
Turkish Airlines (TK; ☎ 021-311 2410; www.turkish airlines.com)

Budget carriers have arrived en masse in Romania. **Carpatair** (☎ 0256-300 900; www.carpatair .com) connects Timişoara with Italy, Germany, Hungary, Austria, Moldova, Ukraine and Greece; it also runs flights from Budapest to Târgu Mureş and Cluj-Napoca, and from Bucharest to Kyiv. Air Moldova and Tarom operate daily flights between Chişinău and Bucharest. **Wizz Air** (www.wizzair.com) flies from Bucharest, Cluj, Timişoara and Târgu Mureş to Spain, Italy, Germany, Belgium and London. **easyJet** (www.easyjet.com) flies from Bucharest to Milan, Madrid and Gatwick. At the time of writing, **Ryanair** (www.ryanair.com) had announced cancellation of service to Arad, but was still

flying to Constanţa from Pisa. **Myair** (www.myair .com) flies from Bucharest to Italy and Paris, but it is prone to changing and cancelling flights at the last minute. **Blue Air** (www.blueair-web.com) flies from several Romanian cities to London, Italy, Germany, France, Spain, Belgium, Portugal and Cyprus. **germanwings** (www.germanwings .com) flies from Bucharest and Cluj to Bulgaria, Sweden, Switzerland, Germany, Italy, Spain, Austria, Poland and London.

Land
Expect long queues at checkpoints, particularly on weekends. Carry food and water for the wait. Don't try bribing a Romanian official and beware of unauthorised people charging dubious 'ecology', 'disinfectant' or other dodgy taxes at the border.

BUS
Romania is well linked by bus lines to central and Western Europe as well as Turkey; see p673 for popular routes. While not as comfortable as the train, buses tend to be faster, though not always cheaper.

Eurolines (www.eurolines.ro) has a flurry of buses linking numerous cities in Romania with Western Europe. Buses to Germany cost 440 lei (€125) one way, while buses to Paris and Rome cost 310 to 380 lei (€90 or €110).

Eurolines and other private companies have many daily buses to Budapest from cities throughout Romania, including Bucharest, Arad, Braşov and Cluj-Napoca.

Most major cities have intermittent service to İstanbul.

CAR & MOTORCYCLE
The best advice here is to ensure your documents (personal ID, insurance, registration and visas, if required) are in order before crossing into Romania. The Green Card (a routine extension of domestic motor insurance to cover most European countries) is valid in Romania. Extra insurance can be bought at the borders.

TRAIN
International train tickets are sometimes sold at train stations, but often you'll need to go to the CFR (Romanian State Railways) office in town (look for the Agenţie de Voiaj CFR signs) or Wasteels travel-agency offices. Tickets must be bought at least two hours prior to departure.

Those travelling on an Inter-Rail or Eurail pass still need to make seat reservations (14 lei, or 52 lei if using a couchette) on express trains within Romania. Even if you're not travelling with a rail pass, practically all international trains require a reservation (automatically included in tickets purchased in Romania). If you already have a ticket, you may be able to make reservations at the station an hour before departure, though it's preferable to do so at a CFR office at least one day in advance.

There are four Budapest–Bucharest trips daily; the trip takes 13 to 15 hours by way of Arad and Lököshaza. It's also possible to pick up the Budapest train from other Romanian cities including Braşov (p697), Timişoara (p716) and Cluj-Napoca (p710). Braşov also has trains to Vienna, Prague and İstanbul, while Timişoara has a train to Belgrade.

The two daily trains that run between Bucharest and Sofia (11 hours) are slow and crowded but cheap. Both services stop in Ruse.

There are also trains from Bucharest to Moldova, Turkey, Russia and Austria; see p687 for details of trains from the capital.

Sea
BOAT
Catamaran service departs once a week from Constanţa (p732) to Varna, Bulgaria, and Odesa, Ukraine, in summer only.

GETTING AROUND
Air
State-owned carrier **Tarom** (www.tarom.ro) is Romania's main carrier. **Carpatair** (www.carpat air.com) runs domestic routes from its hub in Timişoara. From Bucharest, **Blue Air** (www .blueair-web.com) flies to Arad and **Wizz Air** (www .wizzair.com) flies to Cluj-Napoca.

Bicycle
Cyclists have become a more frequent sight in Romania, particularly in Transylvania, Maramureş and Moldavia, but rental is not that widespread. There are generally bike and bike-repair shops in most major towns. A good place to rent one is Sinaia (p691).

Boat
Boat is the only way of getting around much of the Danube Delta; see p736.

Bus
A mix of buses, microbuses and maxitaxis combine to form the seriously disorganised Romanian bus system spread across a changing array of bus companies. Finding updated information can be tough without local help. The slick new website www.autogari.ro gives a snapshot of domestic and international bus schedules, but it is by no means comprehensive. Some maxitaxi routes – such as Braşov–Sinaia and Sibiu–Cluj-Napoca – are more useful than others, though departure points are prone to migrating without notice. Generally it's easier to plan train travel.

Fares are cheap, though, and calculated per kilometre – about 1 lei per 10km.

This chapter reflects the situation at research time; the routes should remain roughly the same.

Car & Motorcycle
Even if you're on a budget, it's well worth splitting the costs of a car – sometimes as low as 87 lei (€25) per day for short-term rental or 66 lei (€19) per day for long-term rental – and getting out into rural areas like Maramureş and Saxon Land. It's amazing how much things can change only 2km from a 'main' paved highway. Some roads are impassable without 4WD, though everything in this chapter can be reached by a Daewoo Matiz (the cheapest rental car, and a fine one), if you take extra precautions.

Braşov has some of the country's higher rental rates, whereas Bucharest, Sibiu, Iaşi and Cluj-Napoca have lower rates. Drop-off service is allowed by many companies, with an extra fee of about 175 lei (€50). **Autonom** (www.autonom.com) is a reliable and inexpensive agency with offices around the country. See destination sections for more car-rental recommendations.

Some tips:

- Give yourself time – Things go slower; flocks of sheep, horse carts, full-lane tractors, construction and giant potholes halt traffic.
- Get a map – A map is mandatory if you're planning to travel on back roads. Maps can be found in bookshops and some highway petrol stops. A good one is Amco Press' 1:750,000 *Romania* (about 10 lei).
- Hitchhiking – It's a part of life, and you'll see old women, even children, hailing rides. Generally there are no problems doing so, though we 'enjoyed' the company of an extremely drunk man looking to go 500m.

■ Parking – Even in central Bucharest, a sidewalk is fair game to park your car. Though they're easy to avoid, some areas are marked 'P cu plata', meaning payment is required. Pay the bloke in a vest trolling the area – or move 50m to a bare sidewalk spot. A local in one town explained what happens if they get a ticket: 'It's their job to ticket us, and ours to throw it away.'

Your country's driving licence will be recognised here. There is a 0% blood-alcohol tolerance limit. Seatbelts are compulsory in the front and back; children under 12 are forbidden to sit in the front.

Speed limits are 90km/h on major roads and 50km/h inside highway villages and towns unless otherwise noted. A few motorways allow faster driving. Speed traps – such as the video ones between Braşov and Bucharest – are common; drivers warn each other of lurking police with a flash of the headlights.

Local Transport

Buses, trams and trolleybuses provide transport within most towns and cities in Romania, although many are crowded. They usually run from about 5am to midnight, although services can get thin on the ground after 7pm in more remote areas. Purchase tickets at newspaper stands or kiosks marked *bilete* or *casă de bilete* before boarding, and validate them once aboard.

In many rural parts, the only vehicles around are horse-powered. Horse and cart, once the most popular form of transport in Romania, hit hard times in 2008 when a rash and short-sighted decision was made to ban them from major roads; they were blamed for causing up to 10% of accidents (curiously, omnipresent problems like frenzied speeding and incessant mobile phone use never came up). Where still in use, many carts will stop and give you a ride, the driver expecting no more than a few cigarettes or lei in return.

Bucharest is the only city in Romania to have a metro system.

Train

Rail has long been the most popular way of travelling around Romania. **Căile Ferate Române** (CFR; Romanian State Railways; www.cfr.ro) runs trains over 11,000km of track, providing service to most cities, towns and larger villages in the country. The *mersul trenurilor* (national train

timetable) is published annually and sold for about 10 lei at CFR offices, though they tend to sell out by April. Better (for times, but not prices) is the German site www.bahn.de.

Sosire means 'arrivals' and *plecare* is 'departures'. On posted timetables, the number of the platform from which each train departs is listed under *linia*.

CLASSES

In Romania there are four different types of train, which travel at different speeds, offer varying levels of comfort and charge different fares.

The cheapest trains are the sadistically slow local personal trains. *Accelerat* trains are faster, hence a tad more expensive and less crowded. Seat reservations are obligatory for all classes except personal, and are automatic when you buy your ticket. *Rapid* trains are faster still. Pricier Inter-City trains are the most comfortable but aren't much faster than rapid trains.

Vagon de dormit (sleepers) are available between Bucharest and Cluj-Napoca, Oradea, Timişoara, Tulcea and other points. First-class sleeping compartments generally have two berths, 2nd-class sleepers generally have four berths and 2nd-class couchettes have six berths. Book these in advance.

Fares listed in this chapter generally indicate one-way, 2nd-class seats on *rapid* or *accelerat* trains.

RESERVATIONS

Tickets for all but international trains can be purchased at the station right up until departure. Advance tickets are also sold at an Agenţie de Voiaj CFR, a train-ticket office found in every city centre. Theoretically you can buy tickets at CFR offices up to two hours before departure. Your reservation ticket lists the code number of your train along with your assigned *vagon* (carriage) and *locul* (seat).

If you have an international ticket right through Romania, you're allowed to make stops along the route but you must purchase a reservation ticket each time you reboard an *accelerat* or *rapid* train. If the international ticket was issued in Romania, you may also have to pay a supplement each time.

In a pinch you can leap aboard a departing train and pay the ticket-taker for the ride, but this may cost as much as 50% over the regular price. Best to arrive a little early and visit the ticket window.

Russia Россия

Home to Moscow and St Petersburg, Russia is a destination that every traveller should want to visit. That relatively so few do make it here has much to do with the country's bureaucratic approach to visas (and life in general). Stay in the EU if you want things easy, but venture east for one of the last truly adventurous and nonconformist destinations in Europe.

Much of Eastern Europe's history stems from decisions made by tsars and later by USSR commissars. Even today, the states neighbouring this vast, oil- and gas-rich country ignore Russia at their peril. For an insight into this tense, complex relationship from the Russian point of view, head straight to Moscow, the brash, exciting economic motor driving the nation's resurgence as a great power. The rich history, awe-inspiring architecture and infrastructure, and frenzied pace of development in Europe's largest city makes it a must on any trip to the region.

Easier on the eye and the soul is St Petersburg, Russia's former imperial capital and still its most beautiful and alluring city. With its colourful and often crumbling Italianate mansions, wending canals and enormous Neva River, it is one of the incontestable highlights of the continent.

Aiming to emulate the tourist-friendly nature of its Baltic neighbours is little Kaliningrad, a Russian exclave wedged between Poland and Lithuania on the Baltic Sea. Once the Germanic state of East Prussia, it's a fascinating destination, combining all the best elements of its enormous mother, and deserves more visitors.

FAST FACTS

- **Area** 16,995,800 sq km
- **Capital** Moscow
- **Currency** rouble (R); €1 = R46; US$1 = R33; UK£1 = R49; A$1 = R23; ¥100 = R35; NZ$1 = R19
- **Famous for** vodka, communism, oil, billionaires
- **Official language** Russian
- **Phrases** *privyet* (hi); *do svidaniya* (goodbye); *spasiba* (thanks); *izvinitye* (excuse me); *mozhno yesho stakanchik?* (may I have another little glassful?)
- **Population** 141.4 million
- **Telephone codes** country code ☎ 7; international access code ☎ 8 (wait for second tone), then 10
- **Visas** required by all and can be a real headache – begin preparing well in advance of your trip! For more details, see p797

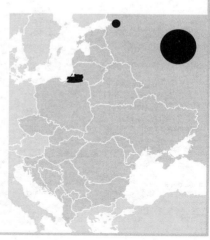

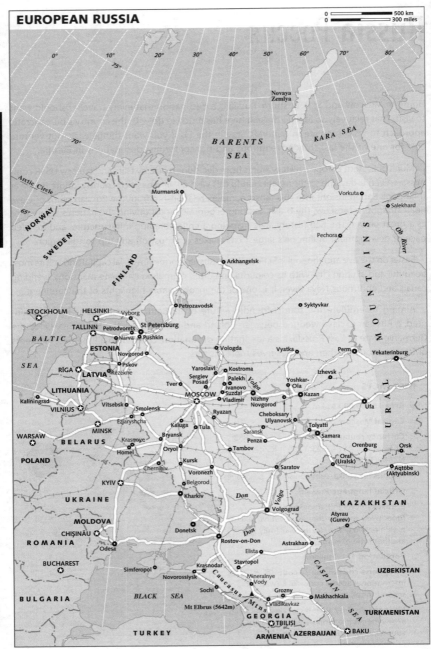

EUROPEAN RUSSIA

0 — 500 km
0 — 300 miles

RUSSIA

0° 10° 20° 30° 40° 50° 60° 70° 80°

75°

Novaya
Zemlya

70°

KARA SEA

BARENTS
SEA

Arctic Circle

65°

NORWAY

Murmansk

Vorkuta

Salekhard

SWEDEN

FINLAND

Pechora

Ob River

Arkhangelsk

STOCKHOLM   HELSINKI

Vyborg

Petrozavodsk

Syktyvkar

M
O
U
N
T
A
I
N
S

TALLINN   Petrodvorets
St Petersburg
Narva   Pushkin

BALTIC

ESTONIA   Novgorod

Vologda

Vyatka

Perm

Yekaterinburg

SEA

RĪGA   Pskov

Rézekne

LATVIA

Yaroslavl   Kostroma
Sergiev   Palekh
Posad   Ivanovo
Tver   Suzdal

Izhevsk

U
R
A
L

LITHUANIA

Yoshkar-
Ola

Kaliningrad

Vitsebsk

Smolensk

MOSCOW   Vladimir

Nizhny
Novgorod

Kazan

Ufa

VILNIUS

Ezjaryshcha

Ryazan

Cheboksary
Ulyanovsk

Tolyatti

WARSAW

MINSK

Krasnoye

Kaluga   Tula

Saransk

Penza

Samara

Orenburg

Orsk

BELARUS

Homel

Bryansk
Oryol

Tambov

Oral
(Uralsk)

POLAND

Chernihiv

Kursk

Saratov

Aqtobe
(Aktyubinsk)

Voronezh

Belgorod

Volga

KYIV

Kharkiv

Don

Volgograd

KAZAKHSTAN

UKRAINE

Atyrau
(Gurev)

MOLDOVA

Donetsk

Don

CHIŞINĂU

Rostov-on-Don

Astrakhan

ROMANIA

Odesa

Elista

Stavropol

CASPIAN

BUCHAREST

Simferopol

Krasnodar

Mineralnye
Vody

UZBEKISTAN

Novorossiysk

Caucasus

Grozny

Makhachkala

BULGARIA

BLACK   SEA

Sochi

Vladikavkaz

SEA

Mt Elbrus (5642m)

Mts

GEORGIA

TURKMENISTAN

TURKEY

TBILISI

ARMENIA   AZERBAIJAN   BAKU

HIGHLIGHTS

- March across **Red Square** (p758) and smell the power in the air at the **Kremlin** (p759), the nerve centre of the world's largest country.
- Explore the world-famous art collection of the **Hermitage** (p777) in magnificent St Petersburg.
- Marvel at the gilded palaces and estates of **Petrodvorets** and **Tsarskoe Selo** (p786).
- See the real Russia in the 'Golden Ring' – the historic towns of **Suzdal**, **Vladimir** and **Sergiev Posad** (p769), famed for their beautiful monasteries and churches and just a short trip from Moscow.
- Engage with the more Euro-friendly Russia in historic **Kaliningrad** (p787), the youthful capital of the country's westernmost exclave.

ITINERARIES

- **Three days in Moscow** For the first two days, see the boxed text, p754. On day three venture out to one of the delightful Golden Ring towns of Suzdal, Vladimir or Sergiev Posad.
- **Three days in St Petersburg** Wander up Nevsky Pr, see Palace Sq, the mighty Neva River and the unforgettable Hermitage, where you can lose yourself for hours in the magnificent collection. Day two allows time for the historic St Peter & Paul Fortress, the Church on Spilled Blood and the wonderful Russian Museum. On day three, take an excursion out of the city and visit either Petrodvorets or Tsarskoe Selo for a taste of how the tsars lived.
- **Two days in Kaliningrad** Admire the reconstructed Gothic Cathedral, then wander along the river to the excellent World Ocean Museum, where you can explore several boats and a submarine. The Amber Museum, inside one of the city's old fortification towers, is also impressive. Strike out for the coast on day two to enjoy either the old Prussian charm of the spa town of Svetlogorsk or the sand dunes and forests of the Kurshskaya Kosa National Park.

CLIMATE & WHEN TO GO

Winter temperatures can dip as low as -20°C in both Moscow and St Petersburg, but summers are hot and humid. Despite such extremes of weather, most times of year can be good for visiting Russia. The snows make the often grimy cities look quite magical. Avoid March and early April – the 'thaw' is the least pleasant time since the grey weather and general muddiness make walking about unpleasant. The best months to visit are May, June and September.

HISTORY

Russia's origins are rooted in countries it nowadays likes to think of as its satellites; it effectively sprang forth from Ukraine and Belarus in the Dark Ages, and took its alphabet from Bulgaria, from where Christianity also spread. The birth of the Russian state is usually identified with the founding of Novgorod in 862 AD, although from the early 13th century until 1480, Russia was effectively a colony of the Mongols.

Ivan the Terrible

The medieval period in Russia was a dark and brutal time, never more so than during the reign of Ivan the Terrible (r 1547–84), whose sobriquet was well earned through his fantastically cruel punishments, such as boiling his enemies alive. He also killed his son and heir in a fit of rage and is said to have blinded the architects who built St Basil's Cathedral on Red Sq.

Despite Ivan the Terrible's conquest of the Volga basin and obsession with reaching the Baltic (at that time controlled by the Lithuanians and Swedes), it was not until

---

CONNECTIONS: MOVING ON FROM RUSSIA

Bordering Belarus, Estonia, Latvia, Lithuania, Poland and Ukraine, Russia has excellent train and bus connections with the rest of Europe.

With all your various visas in order, a wide variety of itineraries is possible. Interesting routes linking Kaliningrad (p792) with St Petersburg (p785) will take you through the Baltic countries, while trains between Kaliningrad and Moscow (p768, p793) head through Belarus. Trains from Kharkiv in Ukraine transit via Kursk, Oryol and Tula to terminate in Moscow. From Novgorod there are direct trains to Kyiv twice a week, while Pskov, just 30km from Estonia, is a great place to either say goodbye or hello to Russia.

the Romanov dynasty (1613–1917) that Russia began absorbing sparsely populated neighbouring regions and filling them with Russians. Territorial expansion between the 17th and 19th centuries saw the country increase in size exponentially to include Siberia, the Arctic, the Far East, Central Asia and the Caucasus, a massive land grab that created the huge country Russia is today.

Peter, Catherine & Later Tsars

Peter the Great (r 1689–1725) began to modernise Russia by setting up a navy, educational centres and beginning the construction of St Petersburg in 1703. Russia's capital moved north to St Petersburg from Peter's hated Moscow in 1712, and remained there until the Bolsheviks moved it back to Moscow more than two centuries later.

Catherine the Great (r 1762–96) continued Peter the Great's legacy, in the process making Russia a world power by the mid-18th century. Her 'enlightened despotism' saw the founding of the art collection that was to become the Hermitage, a huge expansion in the sciences and arts, a correspondence with Voltaire, and the strengthening of the nation. However, it also saw her brutal suppression of a Cossack rebellion and intolerance for any institution that would threaten her authority.

The 19th century saw feverish capitalist development undermined by successively autocratic and backwards tsars. Alexander I (r 1801–25) was preoccupied with Napoleon, who invaded Russia and got as far as Moscow in 1812, but was eventually beaten by the Russian winter. Alexander II (r 1855–81) took the brave step of freeing the serfs in 1861, but baulked at political reform, thus sowing the seeds of a revolutionary movement.

The Bolsheviks & the USSR

Nicholas II, Russia's last tsar, ascended the throne in 1894. It was his refusal to countenance serious reform that precipitated the 1917 revolution. What began as a liberal revolution was hijacked later the same year in a coup led by the Bolsheviks under Vladimir Ulyanov, aka Lenin, which resulted in the establishment of the world's first communist state.

Between 1917 and 1920 the Bolsheviks fought a bloody civil war against the 'whites', who supported the monarchy. The tsar and his family were murdered in 1918 and eventually resistance to the communists trickled out.

HOW MUCH?

- Second-class overnight train between Moscow and St Petersburg R2060 to R2500
- Standard taxi fare R200
- Barack Obama novelty nesting doll R1000
- One hour online R50 to R100
- Meal in a midrange restaurant R600 to R1000

LONELY PLANET INDEX

- 1L petrol R21
- 1L bottled water R25
- Bottle of beer (Baltika) R70
- Souvenir T-shirt R750
- Street snack (blin) R50

By the time Lenin died in 1924, Russia had become the principal member of the Union of Soviet Socialist Republics (USSR), a communist superpower absorbing some 14 neighbouring states between 1922 and 1945. Lenin's successor Josef Stalin, with single-minded brutality, forced the industrialisation of the country. Millions were killed or imprisoned under his watch. However, he saw Russia through the devastation of WWII, and by the time Stalin died in 1953, the USSR had a full nuclear arsenal and half of Europe as satellite states.

The Collapse of Communism

After Stalin, Khrushchev (r 1957–64) began a cautious reform program and denounced Stalin before being removed and replaced by Leonid Brezhnev, whose rule (1964–82) was marked by economic stagnation and growing internal dissent. Mikhail Gorbachev's period of reform, known as perestroika, began in 1985, but it was too late to save the Soviet Union. Within six years the USSR had collapsed alongside communism, and reformer Boris Yeltsin was elected Russia's first-ever president in 1991.

Yeltsin led Russia into the roller-coaster world of cut-throat capitalism, which saw the creation of a new superclass of oligarchs – businesspeople who made billions from buying once state-owned commodities and running them as private companies – while prices soared and the rouble crashed, wiping out the meagre savings of the vast majority of the population.

On New Year's Eve 1999, with his health on the wane, Yeltsin resigned, stepping aside for Vladimir Putin, a steely-faced ex-KGB officer who was prime minister at the time. Elected president the following year, Putin's policy of steering a careful course between reform and centralisation made him highly popular. Russia began to recover the confidence it had lost during the Yeltsin years, and the economy boomed off the back of oil and gas exports. However, the West became alarmed at Putin's tightening of control over the media and political opponents, as well as his brutal clampdown on the independence movement in Chechnya following terrorist attacks in the capital and elsewhere in 2002 and 2004.

Russia Today

With no credible opponent, Dmitry Medvedev's election to president in March 2008 was never in doubt. Non-Russian observers worried about how 'democratic' this practically preordained outcome really was, and fretted even more in August of the same year when Russia came to blows with Georgia over the breakaway regions of Abkhazia and South Ossetia. A future flashpoint could be with Ukraine, over the continued stationing of the Russian navy in the Crimea.

With Putin, who is again back in the role of prime minister, Medvedev presides over a strong economy growing at an average 7% per year (although the economic crisis of 2008/9 put a big dent in that figure) and a nation awash with US-dollar billionaires that has become the world's number-one luxury goods market – Lenin is surely spinning in his mausoleum!

PEOPLE

There's some truth to the local saying 'scratch a Russian and you'll find a Tatar'. Over the centuries Russia has absorbed people from a huge number of nationalities including the Mongols, the Tatars, Siberian peoples, Ukrainians, Jews and Caucasians. This means that while the vast majority of people you meet will describe themselves as Russian, ethnic homogeneity is not always that simple.

On a personal level, Russians have a reputation for being dour, depressed and unfriendly. In fact, most Russians are anything but, yet find constant smiling indicative of idiocy, and ridicule pointless displays of happiness commonly seen in Western culture. Even though Russians can appear to be unfriendly and even downright rude when you first meet them (especially those working behind glass windows of any kind), their warmth is quite astounding as soon as the ice is broken. Just keep working at it.

RELIGION

The vast majority of Russians identify themselves as Orthodox Christians, although the proportion of those who actually practise their faith is small. The Russian Orthodox Church is led by Patriarch Alexei II. The church has become ever more vocal in recent years, virulently condemning homosexuality, contraception and abortion.

Religious freedom exists in Russia – St Petersburg boasts the world's most northerly mosque and Buddhist temple. There can be unbelievable residual prejudice against Jews, although this is very rarely exhibited in anything other than the odd negative comment and some deeply entrenched stereotypes. There is certainly no reason for Jewish travellers to worry about coming to Russia.

ARTS

Blame it on the long winter nights, the constant struggle against authoritarianism or the long-debated qualities of the mysterious 'Russian soul', but Russia's artistic contribution to the world is nothing short of gobsmacking.

Literature

Russia's formal literary tradition sprung to life with the poetic genius of Alexander Pushkin (1799–1837), whose epic *Yevgeny Onegin* stands out as one of Russian literature's greatest achievements, an enormous, playful, philosophical poem from which any Russian can quote at least a few lines.

Pushkin's life was tragically cut short by a duel, and though his literary heir, Mikhail Lermontov, had the potential to equal or even surpass Pushkin's contribution – his novel *A Hero of Our Time* and his poetry spoke of incredible gifts – only a few years later Lermontov, too, was senselessly murdered in a duel in southern Russia.

THE TRADITIONS OF THE BANYA

For centuries Russians have made it an important part of their week to visit a *banya* (hot bath) and you can't say you've really been to Russia unless you've done likewise.

The focus of the *banya* is the *parilka* (steam room). Here, rocks are heated by a furnace, with water poured onto them using a long-handled ladle. Often, a few drops of eucalyptus or pine oils (sometimes even beer) are added to the water, creating a scent in the burst of scalding steam that's released into the room; you'll note that even though people are naked in the *banya* some wear felt caps *(chapkas)* to protect their hair from the effects of the heat, and sandals *(tapki)* to protect their feet.

As they sweat it out, some bathers grab hold of a *venik* (a tied bundle of birch branches) and beat themselves or each other with it. Though it can be painful, the effect can also be pleasant and cleansing: apparently, the birch leaves (sometimes oak or, agonisingly, juniper branches) and their secretions help rid the skin of toxins. After the birch-branch thrashing, bathers run outside and, depending on their nerve, plunge into the *basseyn* (ice-cold pool) or take a cooling shower. The whole process is then repeated several times for anything up to two hours.

To take part, try Moscow's splendid Sanduny Baths (p763) or several *bani* in St Petersburg (p780).

By the late 19th century Russia was producing some of the world's great classics – Leo Tolstoy and Fyodor Dostoyevsky were the outstanding talents, the former bringing the world enormous tapestries of Russian life such as *War and Peace* and *Anna Karenina*, the latter writing dark and troubled philosophical novels, such as *Crime and Punishment* and *The Brothers Karamazov*.

The early 20th century saw a continued literary flowering. From what was widely known as the Silver Age came the poetic talents of Alexander Blok, Anna Akhmatova and Osip Mandelstam. By the late 1920s, with Stalin's grip on power complete, all writers not spouting the party line were anathematised. Dissenting writers were either shot, took their own lives, fled, or were silenced as Stalin revealed his socialist-realist model of writing, which brought novels with titles such as *Cement* and *How the Steel Was Tempered* to the toiling masses. Despite this, many writers wrote in secret, and novels such as Mikhail Bulgakov's *The Master and Margarita* and poems such as Anna Akhmatova's *Requiem* survived Stalinism to become classics.

Despite Khrushchev allowing some literary freedom (it was under his watch that Solzhenitsyn's *A Day in the Life of Ivan Denisovich* was published, a novella depicting life in one of Stalin's gulags), censorship continued until the mid-1980s when, thanks to Mikhail Gorbachev's policy of glasnost (openness), writers who had only been published through the illegal network of *samizdat* (the home printing presses), and were thus read only by the intelligentsia, suddenly had millions of readers.

Since the demise of the Soviet Union, Russian literature has bloomed and embraced the postmodernism that was proscribed by the Soviet authorities. Current literary big hitters, all of whose books have been translated into English, include the mystery writer Boris Akunin; the surrealist Viktor Pelevin; Tatyana Tolstaya, author of the symbolic sci-fi novel *The Slynx*; and Viktor Yerofeev. The France-based expat writer Andrei Makine is also widely respected.

Cinema

Russia has produced some of the world's most famous film images – largely thanks to the father of the cinematic montage, Sergei Eisenstein, whose *Battleship Potemkin* (1925) and *Ivan the Terrible* (1944–46) are reference points for anyone serious about the history of film. Despite constant headaches with authority, Andrei Tarkovsky produced complex and iconoclastic films in the 1960s and 1970s; *The Mirror* and *Andrei Rublev* are generally considered to be his two greatest works.

In recent times Nikita Mikhalkov and Alexander Sokurov have established themselves as internationally renowned Russian directors. Mikhalkov's *Burnt by the Sun* won the Oscar for best foreign film in 1994, and he seemed to find a more sentimental and Hollywood-friendly style for his underwhelming *The Barber of Siberia* (1999). Alexander

Sokurov has made his name producing art-house historical dramas, including *Taurus, Molokh* and 2002's astonishing *Russian Ark* – the only full-length film ever made using one long tracking shot. Andrei Zvyagintsev's stunning debut feature, *The Return* (2003), which scooped the Golden Lion at Venice, is a sublime visual treat.

The glossy vampire thriller *Night Watch* (2004), by Kazakhstan-born director Timur Bekmambetov, struck box office gold both at home and abroad, leading to an equally successful sequel, *Day Watch* (2006), and to Bekmambetov's being lured to Hollywood. *Twilight Watch,* the final part of the trilogy, was in production at the time of writing.

TV

With a population habituated for decades to receiving the party line through the tube, conventional wisdom has it that in Russia, they who control the TV, rule the country. Ex-president Putin grasped this fact and through a variety of takeovers and legal challenges succeeded in putting practically all TV channels under the Kremlin's direct or indirect control. In an effort to present Russia's viewpoint to the outside world, the state also set up the digital channel Russia Today (www.russiatoday.ru) in 2005, a CNN-like news-and-current-affairs station that even broadcasts in Arabic.

TV news and analysis plays it safe, avoiding pretty much any criticism of the government, while entertainment is dominated by crime series in which shaven-headed veterans of the war in Chechnya pin down conspiring oligarchs and politicians. That said, Russian TV provides a wide choice of programs, some unique, some modelled on Western formats. Perhaps it's a sign of the times, but there's a boom of sitcoms and comedy shows. The national channel Kultura, dedicated entirely to arts and culture, is always worth a look. For news, RenTV (www.ren-tv.com) has coverage that tends to be more objective than the norm.

Music

Russia is, of course, famous for composers such as Pyotr Ilyich Tchaikovsky, Nicolai Rimsky-Korsakov, Sergei Prokofiev and Dmitri Shostakovich, and despite the enormous and almost universally horrific output of the Russian pop-music industry, music is taken extremely seriously in modern Russia.

Indeed, on any night of the week in Moscow or St Petersburg, there's likely to be a good choice of concerts, gigs, ballet and opera to choose from.

The likes of techno-pop girl duo tATu and pretty-boy singer Dima Bilan, winner of 2008's Eurovision Song Contest, are the tame international faces of Russia's contemporary music scene. More-interesting music can be heard from groups like Leningrad (www.myspace.com/leningradru), Markscheider Kunst (www.mkunst.ru) and Deti Picasso (www.detipicasso.ru), as well as the jazz-rock singer Zemphira (www.zemfira.ru).

Painting

Internationally, the best-known Russian artists are the avant-garde painters of the early 20th century, such as Vasily Kandinsky and Kazimir Malevich. However, most Russians will quite rightly point you towards the 'greats' of the 19th century, such as Ilya Repin and the *peredvizhniki* (wanderers) – the generation of painters who rejected the strict formalism of the St Petersburg Academy and painted realistic rural scenes with deep social messages.

Anyone visiting Russia will want to see the collection of foreign art held at the Hermitage (p777). The best galleries for Russian art are the Russian Museum (p778) in St Petersburg and Moscow's State Tretyakov Gallery (p762).

Theatre & Dance

Theatre is one of the more vibrant art forms in Russia today. Since Chekhov revolutionised Russian drama in the late 19th century, Russia has seen countless innovations, from Constantin Stanislavsky, who created method acting, to Vsevolod Meyerhold, the theatrical pioneer whom Stalin had arrested and murdered. Among the most celebrated contemporary theatre directors today are Kama Ginkas, who works with the Moscow Art Theatre, Pyotr Fomenko, who heads up the Moscow's Pyotr Fomenko Workshop Theatre, and Lev Dodin at St Petersburg's Maly Drama Theatre.

Ballet in Russia evolved as an offshoot of French dance combined with Russian folk and peasant dance techniques. It stunned Western Europeans when it was first taken on tour during the late 19th century. The celebrated Bolshoi (p767) and Mariinsky (p784) Theatres have worked hard to reinvent themselves since the end of the Soviet Union, and their

RUSSIA

productions are regularly seen around the world on lucrative tours.

SPORT

Since Soviet times Russia has been honing its sporting prowess, and today it continues to invest heavily in sports, developing facilities, new training programs and offering fat fees to attract top overseas coaches. The most popular spectator sport is soccer, which is enjoying a boom pumped up by sponsorship deals with Russian big business. The bottomless pockets of state energy giant Gazprom enabled Zenit St Petersburg to gain not only the Russian league title in 2007 but also the UEFA Cup in 2008. CSKA Moscow, funded at the time by Roman Abramovich's Sibneft, also lifted the UEFA Cup in 2005.

ENVIRONMENT

While Russia as a country encompasses almost every conceivable type of landscape, European Russia is characterised by flat fields and forests. You can take the train from one city to the other and barely pass a hill or a valley. However, the Kaliningrad region sports half of the sandy Kurshskaya Kosa (Curonian Spit), the Curonian Lagoon and the world's largest supply of amber.

The disastrous environmental legacy of communism is enormous. As well as both Moscow and St Petersburg being polluted from traffic and heavy industry, the countryside is frequently blighted by eyesores of crumbling and abandoned factories and other industrial plants. Environmental consciousness remains relatively low, although things are slowly changing with the emergence of a small but vocal Russian environmental movement.

FOOD & DRINK

Russian food, while very good, can be bland: spices are not widely used and dill is overwhelmingly the herb of choice, sprinkled onto almost everything. That said, you can eat extremely well in Russia – Caucasian food is popular throughout the country and is delicious. All the major cities overflow with restaurants serving cuisine from all over the world as well as top-notch renditions of national dishes.

Staples & Specialities

Russian soups are excellent. Delicious borsch (beetroot soup), *solyanka* (a soup made from pickled vegetables) and *ukha* (fish soup) are always reliable. *Pelmeni* are Russian ravioli – meat or fish parcels wrapped in dough and served with *smetana* (sour cream) – and are the lowest common denominator in Russian cooking. Other, more interesting possibilities are *zharkoye* (literally 'hot' – meat stew in a pot), bliny, caviar, beef stroganoff, *goluptsy* (mincemeat wrapped in cabbage leaves) and fish specialities, such as sturgeon, salmon and pikeperch.

Where to Eat & Drink

The traditional cheap Soviet-style *stolovoya* (canteen) has been almost entirely edged out by slick fast-food chains and upmarket restaurants that serve the latest fashionable cuisine and tend to be quite formal. This said, there's an increasing number of relaxed diner-style eateries in evidence in the cities, and Western-style cafes have become extremely popular. Bars and beer halls are where most Russians prefer to drink. These relaxed, generally cheap places usually combine beer and hearty Russian fare, sometimes with live music.

Restaurants and bars typically open from noon to midnight, although there may be a break between afternoon and evening meals. However, they will often open later than their stated hours if the establishment is full.

Smoking is allowed in practically all restaurants and bars, with a few even offering nonsmoking sections; however, Russian lawmakers are pondering introducing a nationwide ban on smoking in public places.

Vegetarians & Vegans

Russia can be tough for vegetarians, and near impossible for vegans. Vegetarians will find themselves eating bliny with sour cream, mushrooms, cheese or savoury *tvorog* (whey); ordering mushroom julienne (mushrooms fried in garlic, cheese and cream); and visiting Georgian restaurants often. Vegans might be wishing they could go home.

Habits & Customs

Food etiquette is fairly straightforward. Symbolic of its importance in Russian culture, it's drinking that is full of unspoken rules. First of all, never drink vodka without *zakuski* (snacks) – you'll get drunk otherwise, whereas (according to any Russian) that will *never* happen if you consume pickled herring or gherkins with your vodka. Once a bottle (vodka or otherwise) has been finished, it's considered rude to put it back on the table – always put it on the floor instead. Don't talk during toasts, and always appear to drink to the toast (even if you dribble it down your chin or drink nothing at all). Men should always down a vodka shot in one. Women are let off this requirement, although being able to down a large shot will garner respect from all quarters.

MOSCOW MOCKBA

☎ 495 & 499 / pop 10.4 million

Intimidating in its scale, but also exciting and unforgettable, Moscow is many things to many people, a place that inspires extreme passion or loathing. History, power and wild capitalism hang in the air alongside an explosion of creative energy throwing up edgy art galleries and a dynamic restaurant, bar and nightlife scene with something for everyone. Tchaikovsky and Chekhov are well represented at the city's theatres, but you can also see world premieres by up-and-coming composers and choreographers.

Although much of its architectural heritage has been destroyed, the sturdy stone walls of the Kremlin continue to occupy the founding site of Moscow and remains of the Soviet state are scattered all around the city. History is being examined in innovative ways, as institutions such as the Gulag History Museum broach subjects that were long brushed under

GREATER MOSCOW

0 — 2 km
0 — 1.0 miles

the carpet. It's quite possible to find a quiet neighbourhood and create your own refuge from the chaos, or, alternatively, embrace the city and its infectious energy; few cities in the world have so much to spare.

HISTORY
In the mid-12th century Yury Dolgoruky constructed the first Kremlin at a strategic spot atop Borovitsky Hill. A century later the Mongol forces of the Golden Horde burned the city to the ground and began to use Moscow to monitor the river trade and road traffic to exact tribute. Moscow's Prince Ivan acted as tax collector, earning himself the moniker 'Moneybags' (Kalita). In the process, Moscow developed into a regional capital.

Towards the end of the 15th century, the once diminutive duchy emerged as an expanding state under the reign of Grand Prince Ivan III (the Great). To celebrate his successes, he imported a team of Italian artisans for a complete renovation of the Kremlin. The city developed in concentric rings outward from this centre. Under Ivan IV (the Terrible) in the 16th century, the city earned the nickname of 'Gold-Domed Moscow' because of its multitude of monastery fortresses and magnificent churches.

In 1712 Peter the Great relocated the capital to St Petersburg, and in the early 1800s Moscow suffered further at the hands of Napoleon Bonaparte. But after the Napoleonic Wars, Moscow was feverishly rebuilt and industry prospered.

When the Bolsheviks gained control of Russia in 1917, the capital returned to Moscow. Stalin devised an urban plan for the city: historic cathedrals and monuments were demolished; in their place appeared the marble-bedecked metro and neo-Gothic skyscrapers. In the following decades, Moscow expanded at an exponential rate.

Moscow was the scene of the most dramatic events of the political transition of the early 1990s. Boris Yeltsin led crowds protesting the attempted coup in 1991; and two years later he ordered the army to blast the parliament into submission. Within the Moscow city government, the election of Mayor Yury Luzhkov in 1992 set the stage for the creation of a big-city boss: his interests range from the media to manufacturing and from five-star hotels to shopping malls. While the rest of Russia struggled to survive the collapse of communism, Moscow emerged as an enclave of affluence.

> **MOSCOW IN TWO DAYS**
> **Red Square** (p758) and the **Kremlin** (p759) have to be your first stops, followed by the **Pushkin Museum** (p762) and the **Cathedral of Christ the Saviour** (p762) on the Moscow River. On day two go south of the river and enjoy the spectacular collection at the **State Tretyakov Gallery** (p762) and the magnificent **Novodevichy Convent** (p763) before hitting Moscow's legendary **nightlife scene** (p766).

Early in the new millennium, Moscow was a target for terrorist attacks linked to the ongoing crisis in Chechnya. Over the course of several years, hundreds of people in Moscow were wounded or killed when suicide bombers attacked a theatre, a rock concert, metro stations and airplanes.

In 2007, Mayor Luzhkov was reappointed to his fifth term in office. Under his oversight, the city continues to undergo a massive physical transformation, with skyscrapers shooting up along the Moscow River.

ORIENTATION
The medieval centre of the city, the Kremlin, is a triangle on the northern bank of the Moscow River. The modern city centre radiates around it, the main streets being Tverskaya ul and ul Novy Arbat. The very centre of the city is defined by the 'garden ring' – a vast eight-lane highway that rings Moscow's central district.

INFORMATION
Bookshops
Atlas (Map pp756-7; ☎ 495-928 6109; Kuznetsky most 9/10; ☁ 9am-8pm Mon-Fri, 10am-6pm Sat, 11am-5pm Sun; Ⓜ Kuznetsky Most) A map shop with city and regional maps covering the whole country.
Dom Inostrannoy Knigi (Map pp756-7; ☎ 495-628 2021; Kuznetsky most 18/7; ☁ 9am-9pm Mon-Fri, 10am-9pm Sat, 10am-8pm Sun; Ⓜ Kuznetsky Most) Has the widest selection of literature in foreign languages.

Internet Access
Wireless access (not always free) is ubiquitous. A listing of places with wi-fi is available in Russian at http://wifi.yandex.ru.
Cafemax Zamoskvorechie (Map pp756-7; ☎ 495-950 6050; Pyatnitskaya ul 25; per hr R50-90; ☁ 24hr; Ⓜ Novokuznetskaya); Tverskoy (Map pp756-7; ☎ 495-741 7571;

Novoslobodskaya ul 3; per hr R120; 24hr; Novoslobodskaya) Late-night and early-morning discounts available.
Pronto Internet Cafe (Map pp756-7; 495-692 5181; Tverskaya ul 10; per hr R130-160; 9am-10pm; Pushkinskaya) Computers and coffee on the second floor of the Tsentralnaya Hotel.
Time Online Okhotny Ryad (Map p760; 495-988 6426; per hr R70-100; 24hr; Okhotny Ryad); Komsomolskaya (Map pp756-7; 495-266 8351; Komsomolskaya pl 3; per hr R70-100; 24hr; Komsomolskaya) Offers copy and photo services, as well as over 100 zippy computers and free wi-fi access.

Internet Resources
www.moscowmaximum.blogspot.com An anonymous blog providing in-depth club reviews and insiders' info on Moscow nightlife.
www.moscow-taxi.com Viktor the virtual taxi driver provides extensive descriptions of sights inside and outside of Moscow, as well as hotel bookings and other tourist services.
www.redtape.ru Forums offer inside information on any question you might ask about the city.

Media
For those who can read Russian, *Afisha* and *Time Out* are reliable listings magazines, both available at any news-stand. The following English-language media are all free:
element (www.elementmoscow.ru) Weekly newsprint magazine with restaurant reviews and concert and art exhibition listings.
Moscow News (www.moscownews.ru) This longstanding news weekly focuses on domestic and international politics and business.
Moscow Times (www.themoscowtimes.com) Daily paper that is the undisputed king of the hill in locally published English-language news. The Friday edition is a great source for what's happening at the weekend.
Passport Magazine (www.passportmagazine.ru) An excellent monthly lifestyle magazine.

Medical Services
There are several expensive, foreign-run health services available in Moscow.
36.6 Basmanny (Map pp756-7; 495-923 2258; ul Pokrovka 1/13; Kitay-Gorod); Tverskoy (Map pp756-7; 495-623 4718; Kuznetsky most 18/7; Kuznetsky Most); Arbat (Map pp756-7; 495-203 0207; ul Novy Arbat 15; Arbatskaya) A chain of 24-hour pharmacies.
American Medical Centre (Map pp756-7; 495-933 7700; www.amcenter.ru; Grokholsky per 1; Pr Mira) Offers 24-hour emergency service, consultations and a full range of medical specialists, including paediatricians and dentists. Also has an on-site pharmacy with English-speaking staff.

Money
Banks, exchange counters and ATMs are ubiquitous and credit cards widely accepted.
American Express (Map p760; 495-543 9400; Vetoshny per 17; 10am-9.30pm; Teatralnaya) is the most reliable place to cash American Express travellers cheques and has an ATM, mail-holding and travel services for Amex cardholders.

Post
Main post office (Map pp756-7; Myasnitskaya ul 26; 8am-8pm Mon-Fri, 9am-7pm Sat & Sun; Chistye Prudy) Moscow's main post office is on the corner of Chistoprudny bul. The central telegraph (below) also offers postal facilities.

Telephone & Fax
Moscow payphones operate with cards that are available in shops, kiosks and metro stations. Most international mobile phones with roaming will automatically switch over to a local network. Alternatively, buy a local SIM card from any of the hundreds of mobile-phone shops around the city.
Central telegraph (Map p760; Tverskaya ul 7; post 8am-10pm, telephone 24hr; Okhotny Ryad) This convenient office offers telephone, fax and internet services.

Tourist Information
Moscow City Tourist Information Centre (Map p760; 495-232 5657; www.moscow-city.ru; ul Ilyinka 4; 9am-6pm Mon-Fri; Kitay-Gorod) Located in Gostinny Dvor, the capital's official tourist office does not answer the telephone, nor is it open on weekends.

Travel Agencies
Maria Travel Agency (Map pp756-7; 495-725 5746; ul Maroseyka 13; Kitay-Gorod) Offers visa support, apartment rental and some local tours, including to the Golden Ring.
Unifest Travel (Map p753; 495-234 6555; www.unifest.ru; Komsomolsky pr 13; Park Kultury) On-the-ball travel company offering rail and air tickets, visa support, and trans-Siberian and Central Asian packages.

DANGERS & ANNOYANCES
Unfortunately, street crime targeting tourists has increased in recent years, although Moscow is not as dangerous as paranoid locals may have you think. As in any big city, be on your guard against pickpockets and muggers. Be particularly careful at or around metro stations at Kursk Station and Partizanskaya, where readers have reported specific incidents.

RUSSIA

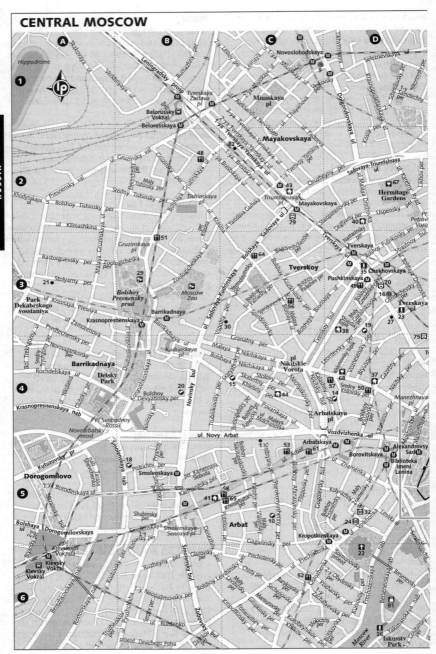

CENTRAL MOSCOW

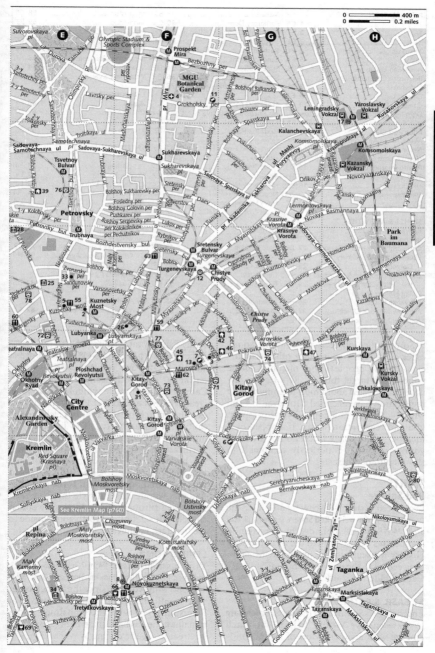

Some police officers can be bothersome, especially to dark-skinned or otherwise foreign-looking people. Other members of the police force target tourists. Reports of tourists being hassled about their documents and registration have declined. However, it's still wise to carry a photocopy of your passport, visa and registration stamp. If stopped by a member of the police force, do not give him your passport! It is perfectly acceptable to show a photocopy instead.

SIGHTS
Red Square

Begin your visit to Moscow by admiring the massively impressive **Red Square** (Krasnaya pl; Map p760; **M** Pl Revolyutsii), bounded by the Kremlin and Lenin's Mausoleum to the west, the State History Museum to the north, GUM shopping centre to the east and fabulous St Basil's Cathedral to the south.

ST BASIL'S CATHEDRAL
Entering Red Sq through the **Resurrection Gate** (Voskresenskiye Vorota; Map p760), you'll emerge with a superb view of the magnifi-

cently flamboyant **St Basil's Cathedral** (Sobor Vasilia Blazhennogo; Map p760; **☎** 495-698 3304; adult/student R100/50; **◯** 11am-5pm Wed-Mon; **M** Pl Revolyutsii) on the far side. Technically the Intercession Cathedral, this ultimate symbol of Russia was created between 1555 and 1561 (replacing an existing church on the site) to celebrate the capture of Kazan by Ivan the Terrible. The misnomer 'St Basil's' actually refers only to the northeastern chapel, which was added later. It was built over the grave of the barefoot holy fool Vasily (Basil) the Blessed, who predicted Ivan's damnation. Its design is the culmination of a wholly Russian style that had been developed through the building of wooden churches. It's definitely worth going inside to see the stark medieval wall paintings.

LENIN'S TOMB
Visit this granite **tomb** (Map p760; **☎** 495-623 5527; admission free; **◯** 10am-1pm Tue-Thu, Sat & Sun; **M** Pl Revolyutsii) while you can, since the former leader may eventually end up beside his mum in St Petersburg. For now, the embalmed leader remains as he has been since 1924 (apart from a retreat to Siberia during WWII).

CHANGING TELEPHONE NUMBERS

Moscow's telephone system is undergoing a modernisation and expansion, which may result in the changing of many numbers. There are now two area codes functioning within the city: ☎ 495 and ☎ 499. Gradually many old ☎ 495 numbers will be changed to ☎ 499 (with a slight change of number, in many cases). Note that dialling patterns for the two area codes are different:

- Within the ☎ 495 area code, dial seven digits, with no area code.
- Within the ☎ 499 area code, dial 10 digits (including ☎ 499).
- From ☎ 495 to ☎ 499 or vice versa, dial ☎ 8 + 10 digits (including appropriate area code). Although this looks like an intercity call, it is charged as a local call.

To call a mobile phone (usually numbers starting ☎ 915, 916 or 926) from a landline – or vice versa – dial ☎ 8 + 10 digits.

Before joining the queue at the northwestern corner of Red Sq, drop your camera at the left-luggage office in the State History Museum, as you will not be allowed to take it with you. After trooping past the embalmed, oddly waxy figure, emerge from his red-and-black stone tomb and inspect where Stalin, Brezhnev and many of communism's other heavy hitters are buried along the Kremlin wall.

STATE HISTORY MUSEUM & GUM

The **State History Museum** (Map p760; ☎ 495-692 3731; www.shm.ru; adult/student R150/60, audioguide R110; ⏰ 10am-5pm Wed-Sat & Mon, 11am-7pm Sun; Ⓜ Pl Revolyutsii) has an enormous collection covering the Russian empire from the Stone Age on. The building, dating from the late 19th century, is itself an attraction – each room is in the style of a different period or region. A joint ticket, which costs R230/115 (adult/student) and allows access to the State History Museum and St Basil's Cathedral, is available.

Finally, drop into **GUM** (see p768) to see the showpiece Soviet shopping centre turned designer mall for the new rich, with its stunning glass roof and centrepiece fountains.

The Kremlin

The apex of Russian political power and once the centre of the Orthodox Church, the **Kremlin** (Map p760; ☎ 495-202 3776; www.kremlin.museum.ru; adult/student R300/50, audioguide R200; ⏰ 9.30am-4pm Fri-Wed; Ⓜ Aleksandrovsky Sad) is not only the kernel of Moscow but of the whole country. It's from here that autocratic tsars, communist dictators and democratic presidents have done their best – and worst – for Russia.

Occupying a roughly triangular plot of land covering Borovitsky Hill on the north bank of the Moscow River, the Kremlin is enclosed by high walls 2.25km long, with Red Sq outside the east wall. The best views of the complex are from Sofiyskaya nab across the river.

Before entering the Kremlin, deposit bags at the left-luggage office (R60 per bag, open 9am to 6.30pm Friday to Wednesday), beneath the Kutafya Tower near the main ticket office. The main ticket office is in the Alexandrovsky Garden, just off Manezhnaya pl. The entrance ticket covers admission to all five church-museums, as well as Patriarch's Palace and exhibits in the Ivan the Great Bell Tower. It does not include the Armoury or the Diamond Fund Exhibition. In any case, you can and should buy tickets for the Armoury here.

Photography is not permitted inside the Armoury or any of the buildings on Sobornaya pl (Cathedral Sq). Visitors wearing shorts will be refused entry.

SOUTHWEST BUILDINGS

From the Kutafya Tower, which forms the main visitors' entrance, walk up the ramp and pass through the Kremlin walls beneath the **Trinity Gate Tower** (Troitskaya Bashnya; Map p760). The lane to the right (south) passes the 17th-century **Poteshny Palace** (Poteshny Dvorets; Map p760), where Stalin lived. The horribly out-of-place glass-and-concrete **State Kremlin Palace** (Kremlyovksy Dvorets Syezdov; Map p760) houses a concert and ballet auditorium (p767), where many Western pop stars play when they are in Moscow.

ARMOURY & DIAMOND FUND

In the Kremlin's southwestern corner is the **Armoury** (Map p760; adult/student R350/70, audioguide R200; ⏰ entry 10am, noon, 2.30pm & 4.30pm), a

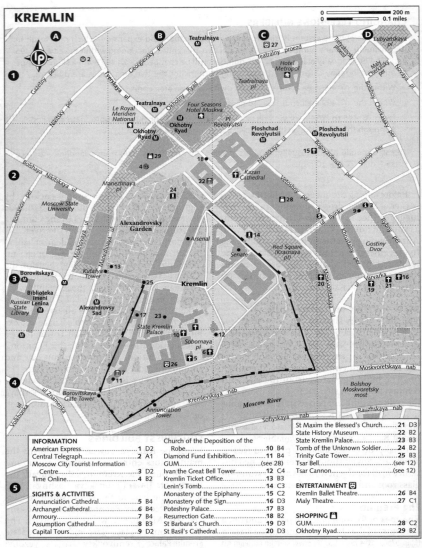

KREMLIN

mind-numbingly opulent collection of treasures accumulated over time by the Russian state and church. Tickets specify entry times. Highlights include Fabergé eggs and reams of royal regalia.

If the Armoury doesn't sate your diamond lust, there are more in the separate **Diamond Fund Exhibition** (Vystavka Almaznogo Fonda; Map p760;

☎ 495-629 2036; admission R500; ⏰ 10am-1pm & 2-5pm Fri-Wed; Ⓜ Aleksandrovsky Sad), in the same building. The lavish collection includes the largest sapphire in the world.

SOBORNAYA PLOSHCHAD
On the northern side of Sobornaya pl, with five golden helmet domes and four

semicircular gables facing the square, is the **Assumption Cathedral** (Uspensky Sobor; Map p760), built between 1475 and 1479. As the focal church of prerevolutionary Russia, it's the burial place of most heads of the Russian Orthodox Church from the 1320s to 1700. The iconostasis dates from 1652, but its lowest level contains some older icons, including the *Virgin of Vladimir* (Vladimirskaya Bogomater), an early-15th-century Rublyov-school copy of Russia's most revered image, the *Vladimir Icon of the Mother of God* (Ikona Vladimirskoy Bogomateri).

The delicate little single-domed church beside the west door of the Assumption Cathedral is the **Church of the Deposition of the Robe** (Tserkov Rizopolozheniya; Map p760), built between 1484 and 1486 by masons from Pskov.

With its two golden domes rising above the eastern side of Sobornaya pl, the 16th-century **Ivan the Great Bell Tower** (Kolokolnya Ivana Velikogo; Map p760) is the Kremlin's tallest structure. Beside the bell tower stands the **Tsar Bell**, a 202-tonne monster that cracked before it ever rang. North of the bell tower is the mammoth **Tsar Cannon**, cast in 1586 but never shot.

The 1508 **Archangel Cathedral** (Arkhangelsky Sobor; Map p760), at the square's south-eastern corner, was for centuries the coronation, wedding and burial church of tsars. The tombs of all of Russia's rulers from the 1320s to the 1690s are here bar one (Boris Godunov, who was buried at Sergiev Posad).

Finally, the **Annunciation Cathedral** (Blagoveshchensky Sobor; Map p760), at the southwest corner of Sobornaya pl and dating from 1489, contains the celebrated icons of master painter Theophanes the Greek. He probably painted the six icons at the right-hand end of the diesis row, the biggest of the six tiers of the iconostasis. *Archangel Michael* (the third icon from the left on the diesis row) and the adjacent *St Peter* are ascribed to Russian master Andrei Rublyov.

ALEKSANDROVSKY GARDEN

A good place to relax is this pleasant garden (Map p760) along the Kremlin's western wall. At the garden's northern end is the **Tomb of the Unknown Soldier**, containing the remains of a soldier who died in December 1941 at kilometre 41 of Leningradskoe sh – the nearest the Nazis came to Moscow. The changing of the guard happens every hour from 10am to 7pm in summer, and to 3pm during winter. Opposite the gardens is Manezhnaya pl and the underground Okhotny Ryad shopping mall.

Around Red Square

On the southwestern side of the square is the fine edifice of **Moscow State University** (Map p760), built in 1793. The classic Stalinist Hotel Moskva, once fronting the northeastern side of the square, was demolished in 2004 to make way for a huge underground car park. A replica of the original (now to be a Four Seasons Hotel) was under construction at the time of research.

Teatralnaya pl opens out on both sides of Okhotny Ryad, 200m north of Manezhnaya pl. The northern half of the square is dominated by the **Bolshoi Theatre** (see p767), where Tchaikovsky's *Swan Lake* was premiered (to bad reviews) in 1877. Look out for the stunning art nouveau **Metropol Hotel** (Map pp756–7), one of Moscow's most historic, on Teatralny proezd facing the Bolshoi at an angle across the road.

Tverskoy District

The streets around Tverskaya ul, Moscow's main avenue, comprise the vibrant Tverskoy District, characterised by old architecture and new commerce. Small lanes such as **Kamergersky per** and **Stoleshnikov per** are among Moscow's trendiest places to sip a coffee or a beer and watch the big-city bustle.

In the midst of the swanky shops on ul Petrovka, an archway leads to a courtyard strung with barbed wire and hung with portraits of political prisoners. This is the entrance to the **Gulag History Museum** (Map pp756-7; ☎ 495-621 7346; www.museum-gulag.narod.ru, in Russian; ul Petrovka 16; ⏰ 11am-4pm Tue-Sat; Ⓜ Chekhovskaya). Guides dressed like camp guards describe the vast network of labour camps that existed in the former Soviet Union and recount the horrors of camp life.

Nearby, the **Moscow Museum of Modern Art** (MMOMA; Map pp756-7; ☎ 495-694 2890; www.mmoma.ru; ul Petrovka 25; adult/student R200/100; ⏰ noon-7pm; Ⓜ Chekhovskaya) is housed in a classical 18th-century merchant's home. It contains 20th-century works by the likes of Marc Chagall, Natalia Goncharova and Vasily Kandinsky, as well as a whimsical sculpture garden.

Back on Tverskaya ul there's the **equestrian statue of Yury Dolgoruky** (Map pp756–7), the founder of the city, facing the **Moscow Mayor's Office** (Map pp756–7). Further still, on Pushkinskaya pl, there's a huge **statue of Alexander Pushkin** (Map pp756–7), a monument to Russia's national poet, behind which is the gaudy Rossiya cinema and casino complex.

Kitay Gorod

This 13th-century neighbourhood was the first in Moscow to grow up outside the Kremlin walls. While its name means China Town in modern Russian, do not expect anything Chinese – the name derives from an old Russian word meaning 'wattle', for the supports used for the walls that protected the suburb. This is the heart of medieval Moscow and parts of the suburb's walls are visible. The main places of interest are the collection of churches in the neighbourhood. Look out for the charming, brightly painted **Monastery of the Epiphany** (Map p760) opposite Ploshchad Revolyutsii metro station and the small churches along ul Varvarka. These are the 17th-century **Monastery of the Sign** (Map p760), the 1698 **St Maxim the Blessed's Church** (Map p760) and **St Barbara's Church** (1795–1804; Map p760).

Communist history can be seen on Staraya pl, where the western side of the square is taken up by the headquarters of the **Presidential Administration of Russia** (Map pp756–7); previously the Central Committee Building, it was once the most important decision-making organ of the Communist Party and thus the whole of the Soviet Union. The one-time **Lubyanka Prison** (Map pp756–7) crowning Lubyanka Hill was once the headquarters of the dreaded KGB; today it's the nerve centre of its successor, the FSB (Federal Sercurity Service) and is not open to the public.

Pushkin Museum of Fine Arts

Moscow's premier foreign-art museum is the **Pushkin Museum of Fine Arts** (Map pp756–7; ☎ 495-203 7998; www.museum.ru/gmii; ul Volkhonka 12; adult/student R300/150, audio tour R200; ☼ 10am-6pm Tue-Sun; Ⓜ Kropotkinskaya), showing off a broad selection of European works, mostly appropriated from private collections after the revolution. They include Dutch and Flemish masterpieces from the 17th century, several Rembrandt portraits, and the Ancient Civilisation exhibits, which include the impressive Treasures of Troy. The

Pushkin's amazing collection of Impressionist and post-Impressionist paintings can now be found next door at the new **Gallery of European & American Art of the 19th & 20th Centuries** (Map pp756–7; ☎ 495-203 1546; ul Volkhonka 14; adult/student R300/150; ☼ 10am-6pm Tue-Sun, to 8pm Thu; Ⓜ Kropotkinskaya).

Cathedral of Christ the Saviour

Dominating the skyline along the Moscow River, the gargantuan **Cathedral of Christ the Saviour** (Map pp756–7; ☎ 495-202 4734; www.xxc.ru; admission free; ☼ 10am-5pm; Ⓜ Kropotkinskaya), finished in 1997, sits on the site of an earlier and similar church of the same name, built from 1839 to 1883 to commemorate Russia's victory over Napoleon. The original was destroyed during Stalin's orgy of explosive secularism. Stalin planned to replace the church with a 315m-high 'Palace of Soviets' (including a 100m statue of Lenin), but the project never got off the ground – literally. Instead, for 50 years the site served an important purpose as the world's largest swimming pool.

State Tretyakov Gallery

Nothing short of spectacular, the **State Tretyakov Gallery** (Map pp756–7; ☎ 499-238 1378; Lavrushinsky per 10; adult/student R225/150; ☼ 10am-6.30pm Tue-Sun; Ⓜ Park Kultury) holds the world's best collection of Russian icons and an outstanding collection of other prerevolutionary Russian art, particularly the works of the 19th-century *peredvizhniki* (p751).

New Tretyakov & Art Muzeon

The premier venue for 20th-century Russian art is the new building of the State Tretyakov Gallery on Krymsky val, better known as the **New Tretyakov** (Map p753; ☎ 499-238 1378; adult/student R225/150; ☼ 10am-6.30pm Tue-Sun; Ⓜ Park Kultury). Besides the plethora of socialist realism, the exhibits showcase avant-garde artists like Kazimir Malevich, Vasily Kandinsky, Marc Chagall, Natalia Goncharova and Lyubov Popova.

Behind the complex is the wonderful, moody **Art Muzeon** (Map p753; ☎ 499-238 3396; ul Krymsky val 10; admission R100; ☼ 9am-9pm; Ⓜ Park Kultury). This open-air sculpture park started as a collection of Soviet statues put out to pasture when they were ripped from their pedestals in the post-1991 wave of anti-Soviet feeling. They have now been joined by fascinating and diverse contemporary work. A monumental but controversial **statue of Peter**

FREE THRILLS

Moscow can drain your wallet faster than an addiction to crack, so wise up to the following sights and activities that can all be enjoyed for free (or very little):

- March across **Red Square** (p758) and pay your respects to Lenin.
- Cruise the designer shops and arcades of **GUM** (p768).
- Watch the changing of the guard in the **Aleksandrovsky Garden** (p761).
- Ogle the bizarre **statue of Peter the Great** (below).
- Ride the **metro** – for R19 you could spend all day checking out magnificent stations. Among our favourites are: **Mayakovskaya**, Grand Prize winner at the 1939 World's Fair in New York; **Komsomolskaya**, a huge stuccoed hall, its ceiling covered with mosaics depicting military heroes; and **Prospekt Mira**, decorated in elegant gold-trimmed white porcelain with bas-reliefs of happy comrades.

---

the Great (Map pp756-7; Bersenevskaya nab; M Polyanka) by sculptor Zurab Tsereteli stands on the river bank overlooking the park.

Novodevichy Convent
A cluster of sparkling domes behind turreted walls on the Moscow River, **Novodevichy Convent** (Map p753; ☎ 499-246 8526; adult/student R150/60; ☻ grounds 8am-8pm daily, museums 10am-5pm Wed-Mon; M Sportivnaya) was founded in 1524 to celebrate the taking of Smolensk from Lithuania. This is where Peter the Great imprisoned his half-sister Sofia for her part in the Streltsy Rebellion. The oldest and most dominant building in the grounds is the white **Smolensk Cathedral**, its sumptuous interior covered in 16th-century frescos.

Adjacent to the convent, **Novodevichy Cemetery** (Map p753; admission free; ☻ 9am-5pm; M Sportivnaya) is among Moscow's most prestigious resting places – a veritable 'who's who' of Russian politics and culture. You will find the tombs of Chekhov, Gogol, Mayakovsky, Stanislavsky, Prokofiev, Eisenstein and many other Russian and Soviet notables. The most recent notable addition is former President Boris Yeltsin, who died in 2007.

ACTIVITIES
Moscow has some of the swankiest *bani* (hot baths) in the country (see the boxed text, p750), and it would be a shame to leave without trying one out.
Banya on Presnya (Map pp756-7; ☎ 495-253 8690; Stolyarny per 7; general admission R700-800; ☻ 8am-8pm Wed-Mon, from noon Tue; M Ulitsa 1905 Goda) Offers an excellent, segregated *banya* as well as spa services and an on-site cafe.

Sanduny Baths (Map pp756-7; ☎ private 495-628 4633, general 495-625 4631; www.sanduny.ru; Neglinnaya ul 14; private room per hr from R1300, general admission per 2hr R600-800; ☻ 8am-10pm; M Chekhovskaya) The oldest and most luxurious *banya* in the city.

TOURS
Some reliable operators:
Capital Tours (Map p760; ☎ 495-232 2442; www.capitaltours.ru; Gostiny Dvor, ul Ilyinka 4; M Kitay-Gorod) Offers city bus tours and twice-daily tours of the Kremlin.
Hop On Hop Off (Map pp756-7; ☎ 495-787 7335; www.hoponhopoff.ru; ul Shchipok 1; adult/child R750/400; ☻ 10am-5pm; M Serpukhovskaya) This bus circulates around the city, stopping at designated points. Hop on and off as many times as you like within a 24-hour period.
Patriarshy Dom Tours (Map pp756-7; ☎ 495-795 0927; http://russiatravel-pdtours.netfirms.com; Vspolny per 6, Moscow school No 1239; M Barrikadnaya) Provides English-language tours on just about any specialised subject.

SLEEPING
More hostels may have opened, but overall Moscow is still an expensive place to lay your head. Be sure to book hostels well ahead to secure the best deals, or consider renting a flat. The following online agencies offer good deals, some from as low as R2800 (€62) per night: www.cheap-moscow.com, www.flatmates.ru/eng, www.hofa.ru and www.moscowapartments.net

All hotels listed below offer nonsmoking rooms unless stated otherwise.

Budget
Trans-Siberian Hostel (Map pp756-7; ☎ 495-916 2030; www.transsiberianhostel.com; Barashevsky per 12;

dm R630-700, d R1750; **M** Kitay-Gorod; **🖳**) Snag one of the two double rooms in this tiny hostel, and you're getting one of the capital's best bargains: you won't find a private room at this price anywhere else in central Moscow. A train-themed decor brightens the place up.

Nova House (Map pp756-7; ☎ 495-623 4659; nova hostel@nm.ru; Apt 6, Devyatkin per 4; dm R680, d R2600-2800; **M** Kitay-Gorod; **🖳**) It's hard to say who at Nova House is friendlier: Oleg, the owner, or Vasya, the lovable resident cat. Both ensure a homey atmosphere, enhanced by the funky contemporary decor, mural-painted ceilings and walls, and a beautiful upright piano in the common living room. Bonus: bikes!

our pick **Home from Home Hostel** (Map pp756-7; ☎ 495-229 8018; www.home-fromhome.com; Apt 9, ul Arbat 49; dm R700-800, d R2000; **M** Smolenskaya; **🖳**) The spruced-up entryway, with comfy couches and potted plants on the landing, is rare indeed in Moscow! Inside, original art and mural-painted walls create a bohemian atmosphere. Enter the courtyard from Plotnikov per and look for entrance No 2.

Godzillas Hostel (Map pp756-7; ☎ 495-699 4223; www.godzillashostel.com; Bolshoy Karetny per 6; dm/d/tr R725/1740/2175; **M** Tsvetnoy bul; **🖳**) Moscow's biggest and most professionally run hostel, with 90 beds out over four floors. Rooms are spacious and light-filled and painted in different colours. There are also three kitchens and a big living room with satellite TV.

Napoleon Hostel (Map pp756-7; ☎ 495-628 6695; www .napoleonhostel.com; Maly Zlatoustinsky per 2, 4th fl; dm R800-1000; **M** Kitay-Gorod; **🖳**) Ignore the decrepit entryway and climb to the fourth floor, where you'll find a fully renovated hostel. The light-filled rooms have six to 10 wooden bunks, for a total of 47 beds (but only two toilets and two showers – do the maths!), plus a clean kitchen and a comfy common room.

Midrange

Kita Inn (Map pp756-7; ☎ 8-926-664 4118, 8-919-772 4002; www.kitainn.com; Apt 9-10, 2-ya Tverskaya-Yamskaya 6/7; r R3325; **M** Mayakovskaya; **🖳**) Finally, somebody opened a proper pension in Moscow. The private rooms are simple and sweet – IKEA beds, posters on the wall and windows overlooking a shady courtyard. The owner has a few flats in the neighbourhood all offering similar facilities; see also Flamingo B&B (www.flamingobed.com).

Hotel Sverchkov (Map pp756-7; ☎ 495-625 4978; Sverchkov per 8; sverchkov8@mail.ru; s/d from R3800/4400;

M Chistye Prudy) This tiny 11-room hotel in a graceful 18th-century building has hallways lined with plants, and paintings by local artists on the walls. Though rooms have old-style bathrooms and faded furniture, this place is a rarity for its intimacy and hominess. No nonsmoking rooms available.

Ozerkovskaya Hotel (Map p753; ☎ 495-951 7644; www.cct.ru; Ozerkovskaya nab 50; s/d from R5400/6300; **M** Paveletskaya; **🖳**) The 25 rooms here are simply decorated, but parquet floors and comfortable queen-size beds rank it above the standard post-Soviet fare. Also offers attentive service and a central location (convenient for the train to Domodedovo airport).

Melody Hotel (Map pp756-7; ☎ 495-723 5246; www.melody-hotel.ru, in Russian; Skatertny per 13; s/d R5500/6900; **M** Arbatskaya) Unique for its small size, Melodiya has only 46 small but comfortable rooms (none of them nonsmoking). Fantastic location on a residential street just off the Arbat.

our pick **Assambleya Nikitskaya Hotel** (Map pp756-7; ☎ 495-933 5001; www.assambleya-hotels.ru, in Russian; Bolshaya Nikitskaya ul 12; s R7110-7900, d R9450-10,500; **M** Okhotny Ryad; **🍴** **🖳**) This cosy, comfortable place offers a rare combination: superb location, reasonable prices and authentic Russian charm. While the building and rooms are freshly renovated, it preserves an anachronistic atmosphere, with heavy floral drapes and linens.

Sovietsky Hotel (Map p753; ☎ 495-960 2000; www .sovietsky.ru; Leningradsky pr 32/2; r from R7200; **M** Dinamo; **🍴** **🖳** **🖳**) Built in 1952, this preserved slice of Stalin-era architecture sports a gilded hammer and sickle and enormous Corinthian columns flanking the front door. Even the simplest rooms have ceiling medallions and other ornamentation. The legendary restaurant Yar – complete with old-fashioned dancers – is truly over the top.

East-West Hotel (Map pp756-7; ☎ 495-232 2857; www.eastwesthotel.ru; Tverskoy bul 14/4; s/d incl breakfast R9000/10,000; **M** Pushkinskaya; **🍴** **🖳**) Located on the loveliest stretch of the Boulevard Ring, this small hotel evokes the atmosphere of the 19th-century mansion it once was. It's a kitschy but charming place with 24 individually decorated rooms and a lovely fountain-filled courtyard. The price drops significantly on weekends.

Top End

Hotel Akvarel (Map pp756-7; ☎ 495-502 9430; www .hotelakvarel.ru; Stoleshnikov per 12; s/d R10,500/12,250;

Ⓜ Chekhovskaya; ⊠ 🖳) Set amid all the grandeur of Stoleshnikov per is this intimate business-class hotel, offering 23 simple but sophisticated rooms adorned with watercolour paintings. Reduced rates on weekends.

Golden Apple (Map pp756-7; ☎ 495-980 7000; www.goldenapple.ru; ul Malaya Dmitrovka 11; s/d from R12,000/12,500; Ⓜ Pushkinskaya; ⊠ 🖳) A classical edifice fronts the street, but the interior is sleek and sophisticated. The rooms are decorated in a minimalist, modern style accented with funky light fixtures. Comfort is paramount, with no skimping on luxuries.

EATING

Many restaurants, especially top-end eateries, accept credit cards, and almost all restaurants have English-language menus. Check out ultracool Kamergersky per for a huge range of cafes and restaurants.

Restaurants

Vostochny Kvartal (Map pp756-7; ☎ 499-241 3803; ul Arbat 45/24; meals R400-600; Ⓜ Smolenskaya) Vostochny Kvartal used to live up to its name, acting as the 'Eastern Quarter' of the Arbat. Uzbek cooks and Uzbek patrons assured that this was the real-deal place to get your *plov* (pilaf rice with diced mutton and vegetables). The place has since gone the way of the Arbat itself, drawing in more English speakers than anything else. Nonetheless, it still serves some of the best food on the block.

Skromnoe Obayanie Burzhuazii (Modest Charms of the Bourgeoisie; Map pp756-7; ☎ 495-623 0848; ul Bolshaya Lubyanka 24; meals R400-600; 🕑 24hr; Ⓜ Lubyanka) The main draw of 'Bourgeoisie' is the cool, casual setting. The menu is reasonably priced and wide-ranging, from pizza to sushi to sandwiches, but don't expect gourmet fare.

Botanika (Map pp756-7; ☎ 495-254 0064; Bolshaya Gruzinskaya ul 61; meals R500-700; 🕑 11am-10pm; Ⓜ Belorusskaya) Rare is the restaurant in Moscow that is both fashionable and affordable. Somehow Botanika manages to be both, offering light, modern fare, with plenty of soups, salads and grills.

Mayak (Map pp756-7; ☎ 495-291 7503; Bolshaya Nikitskaya ul 19; meals R600-800; Ⓜ Okhotny Ryad) Named for the Mayakovsky Theatre downstairs, this is a remake of a much beloved club that operated in this spot throughout the 1990s. More cafe than club, it still attracts actors, artists and writers, who come to see friendly faces and to eat filling European fare.

Genatsvale (Map pp756-7; meals R600-800) ul Novy Arbat (☎ 495-203 9453; ul Novy Arbat 11; Ⓜ Arbatskaya); ul Ostozhenka (☎ 495-202 0445; ul Ostozhenka 12/1; Ⓜ Kropotkinskaya) Moscow's favourite Georgian restaurant has a new outlet on the Arbat. But what better setting to feast on favourites like *khachipuri* (cheesy bread) and lamb dishes? For a more intimate atmosphere, head to the original location on ul Ostozhenka.

Correa's Bolshaya Gruzinskaya ul (Map pp756-7; ☎ 495-605 9100; Bolshaya Gruzinskaya ul 32; meals R600-1000; 🕑 8am-midnight; Ⓜ Belorusskaya); ul Bolshaya Ordinka (Map p753; ☎ 495-725 6035; ul Bolshaya Ordinka 40/2; Ⓜ Tretyakovskaya) Book ahead for this tiny space – there are only seven tables. The menu is simple – sandwiches (R200 to R300), pizzas and grills – but everything is prepared with the freshest ingredients and the utmost care. The outlet near the Tretyakov is roomier, but reservations are still recommended for Sunday brunch (R400 to R600).

Mari Vanna (Map pp756-7; ☎ 495-650 6500; Spiridonevsky per 10; meals R1000-1500; 🕑 9am-11pm; Ⓜ Pushkinskaya) Like you've stumbled into someone's apartment for dinner served on tiny mismatched plates, on a table cluttered with dried flowers in vases. Don't look for the sign (there is none), just ring the doorbell at No 10. You'll be ushered into these homey environs and served delicious Russian home cooking.

Café Pushkin (Map pp756-7; ☎ 495-739 0033; Tverskoy bul 26a; 'business lunches' R750, meals R1500-2000; 🕑 24hr; Ⓜ Pushkinskaya) The queen mother of *haute-russe* dining, with an exquisite blend of Russian and French cuisines. There's a different atmosphere on each floor, including a richly decorated library and a pleasant rooftop cafe.

Cafes

Volkonsky Keyser (Map pp756-7; ☎ 495-699 4620; Bolshaya Sadovaya ul 2/46; meals R200-400; Ⓜ Mayakovskaya) The queue often runs out the door here as loyal patrons wait their turn for the city's best fresh-baked breads, pastries and pies. It's worth the wait, especially if you decide on a fruit-filled croissant or to-die-for olive bread.

Stolle (Map p753; ☎ 499-246 0589; Malaya Pirogovskaya ul 16; meals R200-500; 🕑 9am-9pm; Ⓜ Sportivnaya) The selection of sweets and savouries sit on the counter, fresh from the oven. It may be difficult to decide (mushroom or meat? apricot or apple?), but you really can't go wrong.

Coffee Mania (Map pp756-7; ☎ 495-775 4310; Bolshaya Nikitskaya ul 13, Moscow Conservatory; meals

R600-800; 🕑 24hr; Ⓜ Alexandrovsky Sad) With all of Moscow's opportunities for fine dining and big spending, where is the most popular place for the rich and famous to congregate? Can you believe it's a place called Coffee Mania? The friendly, informal cafe is beloved for its homemade soups, fresh-squeezed juices and steaming cappuccino, not to mention its summer terrace overlooking the leafy courtyard of the conservatory.

Quick Eats

Grably (Map pp756-7; ☎ 495-545 0830; Pyatnitskaya ul 27; meals R200-300; 🕑 10am-11pm; Ⓜ Novokuznetskaya) The big buffet features an amazing array of fish, poultry and meat, plus salads, soups and desserts. After you run the gauntlet and pay the bill, take a seat in the elaborate wintergarden seating area.

Prime Star (Map pp756-7; meals R200-300; 🕑 7am-11pm) Basmanny (☎ 495-781 8080; ul Maroseyka 6/8; Ⓜ Kitay-Gorod); Tverskoy (☎ 495-692 1276; Kamergersky per; Ⓜ Teatralnaya); Arbat (☎ 495-290 4481; ul Arbat 9; Ⓜ Arbatskaya) Here's a novel concept: a sandwich shop. And not only that, a *healthy* sandwich shop, also serving soups, salads, sushi and other 'natural food'. Everything is pre-prepared and neatly packaged, so you can eat in or carry out.

Moo-Moo (meals R200-300; 🕑 9am-11pm) Basmanny (Map pp756-7; ☎ 495-623 4503; Myasnitskaya ul 14; Ⓜ Lubyanka); Khamovniki (Map p753; ☎ 495-245 7820; Komsomolsky pr 26; Ⓜ Frunzenskaya); Arbat (Map pp756-7; ☎ 495-241 1364; ul Arbat 45/24; Ⓜ Smolenskaya) You will recognise this place by its black-and-white Holstein-print decor. The cafeteria-style service offers an easy approach to all the Russian favourites.

Jagannath (Map pp756-7; ☎ 495-628 3580; Kuznetsky most 11; meals R300-500; 🕑 10am-11pm; Ⓜ Kuznetsky Most) If you are in need of vitamins, this is a funky vegetarian cafe, restaurant and shop with free wi-fi. Its Indian-theme decor is more New Age-y than ethnic. Service is slow but sublime, and the food is worth the wait.

DRINKING

Gravitate towards the **Hermitage Gardens** (Map pp756-7; Ⓜ Pushkinskaya Tverskaya) or the **Aleksandrovsky Garden** (Map pp756-7; Ⓜ Okhotny Ryad) during the summer months for relaxed beer drinking amid the greenery.

Kvartira 44 (🕑 noon-2am Sun-Thu, to 6am Fri & Sat) Bolshaya Nikitskaya ul (Map pp756-7; ☎ 495-291 7503; Bolshaya Nikitskaya ul 22/2; Ⓜ Okhotny Ryad); ul Malaya Yakimanka (Map p753; ☎ 495-238 8234; ul Malaya Yakimanka 24/8; Ⓜ Polyanka) Somebody had the brilliant idea to convert an old Moscow apartment into a crowded, cosy bar, with tables and chairs tucked into every nook and cranny. There is another apartment near the Tretyakov.

Apshu (Map pp756-7; ☎ 495-953 9944; Klimentovsky per 10; 🕑 24hr; Ⓜ Tretyakovskaya) With decor inspired by a little fishing village on the Baltic coast, this trendy place is a magnet for artists and other creative types. It offers inexpensive food and drinks, board games, art exhibitions, concerts…basically something for everyone.

Chaikhona No 1 (🕑 2pm to last customer) Hermitage Gardens (Map pp756-7; ☎ 495-971 6842; Ⓜ Chekhovskaya); Park of Culture (Map p753; ☎ 495-778 1756; Ⓜ Frunzenskaya) Housed in an inviting, exotic tent laid with oriental rugs and plush pillows, this cool Uzbek lounge and cafe is one of the best chill-out spots in the city. If you are hungry, there is *plov* and *shashlyk* on the menu.

ENTERTAINMENT

To find out what's on, see the weekly magazine *element* and the weekly entertainment section in Friday's *Moscow Times*.

Nightclubs

Propaganda (Map pp756-7; ☎ 495-624 5732; www.propagandamoscow.com; Bolshoy Zlatoustinsky per 7; 🕑 noon-6am; Ⓜ Kitay-Gorod) This long-time favourite looks to be straight from the warehouse district, with exposed-brick walls and pipe ceilings. It's a cafe by day (meals R500 to R700), but at night they clear the dance floor and let the DJ do his stuff. This is a gay-friendly place, especially on Sunday nights.

Krizis Zhanra (Map pp756-7; ☎ 495-623 2594; www.kriziszhanra.ru; ul Pokrovka 16/16; 🕑 concerts 9pm daily, 11pm Fri & Sat; Ⓜ Chistye Prudy) Everybody has something good to say about Krizis and what's not to love? Good cheap food, copious drinks and rockin' music every night, all of which inspires the gathered to get their groove on.

Simachyov Bar & Boutique (Map pp756-7; ☎ 495-629 8085; www.denissimachev.com; Stoleshnikov per 12/2; 🕑 11am to last customer; Ⓜ Chekhovskaya) By day, it's a boutique and cafe, owned and operated by the famed fashion designer of the same name. By night, it morphs into a hip-hop-happening nightclub that combines glamour and humour. Look sharp to pass face control.

Live Music

Moscow offers a great variety of gigs and concerts. The main venues are the Olimpiisky

Sports Complex (metro stop: Tsvetnoy Bulvar) and the State Kremlin Palace (p759). Following are more-intimate smaller venues where you can often see good Russian and foreign bands.

Art Garbage (Map pp756-7; ☎ 495-628 8745; www .art-garbage.ru; Starosadsky per 5; ☺ noon-6am; Ⓜ Kitay-Gorod) Enter this funky club-cafe through the courtyard, which is littered with sculpture. Inside, the walls are crammed with paintings of all genres, and there are DJs spinning or live music every night.

Chinese Pilot Dzhao-Da (Map pp756-7; ☎ 495-623 2896; www.jao-da.ru, in Russian; Lubyansky proezd 25; cover R300-500; ☺ concerts 10pm Thu, 11pm Fri & Sat; Ⓜ Kitay-Gorod) A relaxed and relatively inexpensive place to hear live music. This divey basement place hosts lots of different kinds of bands from around Europe and Russia, so check out the website in advance. Look out for free concerts on Monday nights.

Roadhouse (Map p753; ☎ 499-245 5543; www.road house.ru; ul Dovatora 8; ☺ noon-midnight, concerts 9pm; Ⓜ Sportivnaya) If your dog got run over by a pick-up truck, you can find some comfort at the Roadhouse Blues Bar, with down-and-out live music every night, plus cold beer and a whole menu of salty cured meats.

Gay & Lesbian Venues

As well as the venues listed here, there is a great gay night at Propaganda (opposite). For more information see www.gay.ru/english.

Tri Obezyani New Age (Map pp756-7; ☎ 495-916 3555; www.gaycentral.ru, in Russian; Nastavnichesky per 11/1; ☺ 10pm-7am Thu-Sun; Ⓜ Chkalovskaya) The biggest and best club on the gay scene. Besides the dance floor, which is hopping, the club has drag queens and go-go boys, an internet cafe and a cinema. Go in a group or take a taxi from the metro: there have been reports of attacks on the surrounding streets.

12 Volts (Map pp756-7; ☎ 495-933 2815; www.12voltclub .ru, in Russian; Tverskaya ul 12; meals R400-600; ☺ 6pm-6am; Ⓜ Mayakovskaya) The founders of Moscow's lesbian movement opened this welcoming cafe-cum-social-club, tucked in the courtyard off Tverskaya.

Performing Arts

Bolshoi Theatre (Map pp756-7; ☎ 495-250 7317, hot-line 8-800-333 1333; www.bolshoi.ru; Teatralnaya pl 1; tick-ets R200-2000; Ⓜ Teatralnaya) An evening at the Bolshoi is still one of Moscow's most romantic options. Both the ballet and opera compa-nies perform a range of Russian and foreign works. At the time of research, the Bolshoi was preparing to reopen its main stage after a multiyear renovation. In the meantime, the smaller New Stage (Novaya Stsena) has been hosting performances.

Kremlin Ballet Theatre (Map p760; ☎ 495-620 7729; www.kremlin-gkd.ru; ul Vozdvizhenka 1; Ⓜ Alexandrovsky Sad) The Bolshoi does not have a monopoly on ballet and opera in Moscow. Leading dancers also appear with the Kremlin Ballet, which performs in the State Kremlin Palace (inside the Kremlin).

Moscow International House of Music (Map p753; ☎ 495-730 1011; www.mmdm.ru; Kosmodamianskaya nab 52/8; tickets R200-2000; Ⓜ Paveletskaya) This venue for the Russian Philharmonic towers over the Moscow River. It has three halls, including Svetlanov Hall, which has the largest organ in Russia.

Tchaikovsky Concert Hall (Map pp756-7; ☎ 495-232 5353, box office 495-699 0658; www.classicalmusic.ru; Triumfalnaya pl 4/31; tickets R100-1000; Ⓜ Mayakovskaya) Home to the State Symphony Orchestra, which specialises in the music of its namesake composer and other Russian classics.

MKhAT (Map pp756-7; ☎ 495-629 8760; http://art.theatre .ru; Kamergersky per 3; Ⓜ Teatralnaya) Also known as the Chekhov Moscow Art Theatre, this is where method acting was founded more than 100 years ago. Watch for English-language versions of Russian classics performed by the American Studio.

Maly Theatre (Map p760; ☎ 495-623 2621; Teatralnaya pl 1/6; Ⓜ Teatralnaya) A lovely thea-tre founded in 1824, performing mainly 19th-century works.

Circus

Nikulin Circus on Tsvetnoy Bulvar (Map pp756-7; ☎ 495-625-8970; www.circusnikulin.ru; Tsvetnoy bul 13; tickets R250-2000; ☺ shows 7pm Thu-Mon & 2.30pm Sat; Ⓜ Tsvetnoy Bulvar) Named for the beloved actor, director and clown Yury Nikulin, this build-ing has housed the circus since 1880 (though it has been thoroughly modernised). Its the-matic shows are also acclaimed.

Sport

The premier football league has five Moscow teams: Spartak (www.spartak.com), Lokomotiv (www.fclm.ru), CSKA (www.pfc -cska.com), Dynamo (www.fcdynamo.ru) and FC Moskva (www.fcmoscow.ru), each with a loyal following.

RUSSIA

RUSSIA

You can buy tickets online at the club websites. Otherwise, it's usually possible to buy tickets immediately before games, which are played at the following venues:

Dynamo Stadium(Map p753; ☎ 495-612 7172; Leningradsky pr 36; M Dinamo) Hosts Dynamo and CSKA. However, at the time of research, a new state-of-the-art stadium was being constructed for CSKA.

Lokomotiv Stadium (off Map p753; ☎ 499-161 4283; Bolshaya Cherkizovskaya ul 125; M Cherkizovskaya)

Luzhniki Stadium (Map p753; ☎ 495-785 9717; www .luzhniki.ru; Luzhnetskaya nab 24; M Sportivnaya) Hosts Torpedo and Spartak.

SHOPPING

GUM (Map p760; ☎ 495-788 4343; www.gum.ru; Krasnaya pl 3; ☺ 10am-10pm; M Pl Revolyutsii) is packed with designer labels and good souvenir shops.

Izmaylovo Market (off Map p753; Izmaylovskoye shosse; admission R15; ☺ 9am-6pm Sat & Sun; M Partizanskaya) Jump on the metro to reach this sprawling area packed with art, handmade crafts, antiques, Soviet paraphernalia and just about anything you might want for a souvenir.

Art Strelka (Map pp756-7; ☎ 8916-112 7180; Bersenevskaya nab 14/5; ☺ 4-8pm; M Novokuznetskaya) The garages at the old Red October candy factory now serve as studio and gallery space and are worth exploring.

Artists set up their stalls on ul Krymsky val, opposite the entrance to the Park of Culture (Map p753), and in the underground walkway. There are also galleries within the Tsentralny Dom Khudozhnikov in the New Tretyakov (p762).

GETTING THERE & AWAY
Air
Moscow is served by three main international airports:

Domodedovo (off Map p753; ☎ 495-933 6666; www .domodedovo.ru) Located 48km south of the city.

Sheremetyevo (off Map p753; ☎ 495-232 6565; www .sheremetyevo-airport.ru) Located 30km northwest of the city.

Vnukovo (off Map p753; ☎ 495-436 2813; www .vnukovo-airport.ru) Located 30km southwest of the city.

For a list of carriers that serve the city, and for airport information, see p799.

Boat
The Moscow terminus for cruises to St Petersburg is 10km northeast of the city centre at **Severny Rechnoy Vokzal** (Northern River Station; off Map p753; Leningradskoe shosse 51; M Rechnoy Vokzal). Take the metro to Rechnoy Vokzal stop, then walk 15 minutes due west, passing under Leningradskoe shosse and through a nice park.

Bus
To book a seat, go to the long-distance bus terminal, the **Shchyolkovsky bus station** (off Map p753; M Shchyolkovskaya), 8km east of the city centre. Queues can be bad, so it's advisable to book ahead, especially for travel on Friday, Saturday or Sunday.

Buses tend to be crowded but are usually faster and more convenient than the *prigorodny* (suburban) trains to some Golden Ring destinations (opposite).

Train
Moscow has nine main stations. Be sure to check which Moscow station your train is using; even trains to/from the same destination may use different stations.

Belorussky vokzal (Belarus Station; Map p753; Tverskaya Zastava pl; M Belorusskaya) For Smolensk, Kaliningrad, Minsk, Warsaw, Vilnius, Berlin; some trains to/from the Czech Republic; and suburban trains to/from the west.

Kazansky vokzal (Kazan Station; Map p753; Komsomolskaya pl; M Komsomolskaya) For Vladimir, Nizhny Novgorod, the Ural Mountains, Siberia; the Volga; and suburban trains to/from the southeast.

Kursky vokzal (Kursk Station; Map p753; pl Kurskogo vokzala; M Kurskaya) For the Caucasus, eastern Ukraine, Crimea, Georgia, Azerbaijan. It also has some trains to/from Vladimir.

Kievsky vokzal (Kyiv Station; Map p753; Kievskaya pl; M Kievskaya) Serves Kyiv and Prague. Also has Aeroexpress services to Vnukovo airport.

Leningradsky vokzal (Leningrad Station; Map pp756-7; Komsomolskaya pl; M Komsomolskaya) Serves Novgorod, Pskov, St Petersburg, Tallinn, Helsinki.

Paveletsky vokzal (Pavelets Station; Map p753; Paveletskaya pl; M Paveletskaya) Serves trains heading south, including the Aeroexpress to Domodedovo airport.

Rizhsky vokzal (Riga Station; Map p753; Rizhskaya pl; M Rizhskaya) Serves Latvia.

Savyolovsky vokzal (Savyolov Station; Map p753; pl Savyolovskogo vokzala; M Savyolovskaya) Services to/from the north, including the Aeroexpress to Sheremetyevo airport.

Yaroslavsky vokzal (Yaroslavl Station; Map p753; Komsomolskaya pl; M Komsomolskaya) Serves most trains to Siberia, the Far East, China and Mongolia.

Tickets are sold at the train stations, but it is much easier to buy tickets from a travel agent

WORTH THE TRIP: GOLDEN RING TOWNS

To get some sense of how ordinary Russians live (and to escape the madness of the capital), head to one of the historic towns of the Golden Ring northeast of Moscow. Our pick is **Suzdal** (Суздаль), an idyllic village packed with old monasteries, convents, churches and intricately decorated *izby* (wooden cottages). You can easily combine this with a visit to nearby **Vladimir** (Владимир), where you can view the 12th-century **Assumption Cathedral** (Uspensky Sobor; ☎ 4922-325 201; admission R100; ☼ 7am-8pm Tue-Sun) containing magnificent frescos, and the **Cathedral of St Dmitry** (Dmitrievsky Sobor), where the art of Vladimir-Suzdal stone carving reached its pinnacle.

The daily express train between Moscow's Kursky vokzal (R340, 2½ hours) and Nizhny Novgorod (R400, 2½ hours) stops in Vladimir, as do many slower trains. Privately run buses (R200, 3½ hours) also leave regularly from Kursky and Kazansky vokzaly to Vladimir. For Suzdal there is one direct bus connection daily with Moscow's Shchyolkovskaya Avtovokzal (R250, 4½ hours); it's easier to take the train to Vladimir and then one of the regular buses to Suzdal (R40, one hour).

Alternatively, the charming town of **Sergiev Posad** (Сергиев Посад), just 60km from central Moscow, is an easy day trip. The principal attraction here is the venerable 15th-century **Trinity Monastery of St Sergius** (Troitse-Sergieva Lavra; ☎ 496-544 5356; admission free, photos R150; ☼ 10am-6pm), one of the most important and active monasteries in the Russian Orthodox religion. The fastest transport option is the express train that departs from Moscow's Yaroslavsky vokzal (R293, one hour, twice daily). Suburban trains also run every half-hour (R110, 1½ hours).

(see p755) or *kassa zheleznoy dorogi* (railway ticket office). These are often conveniently found in hotel lobbies. Most local agencies charge a small service fee, but be careful of international travel agencies that may charge considerable mark-ups. One agency selling train (and airline) tickets with many outlets around town is **Glavagentstvo-Service** (Map pp756-7; ☎ 495-745 6548; 1-ya Tverskaya-Yamskaya ul 15; Ⓜ Belorusskaya).

GETTING AROUND
To/From the Airport
As of 2008, all airports are accessible by a convenient **Aeroexpress train** (☎ 8-800-700 3377; www.aero-express.ru); services leave from different stations depending on the airport they serve – see opposite for details. If you have a lot of luggage and you wish to take a taxi, it is highly recommended to book in advance (right) to take advantage of fixed rates offered by most companies (usually R1000 to R1500 to/from any airport).

Public Transport
The **Moscow metro** (www.mosmetro.ru) is the easiest, quickest and cheapest way of getting around Moscow. Many of the stations are marble-faced, frescoed, gilded works of art, and you will rarely wait on the platform for more than two minutes. But they do get packed during rush hour. The 176 stations are marked outside by 'M' signs. Magnetic

tickets (R19) are sold at ticket booths. It's useful to buy a multiple-ride ticket (10 rides for R155, 20 for R280), which saves you the hassle of queuing every time.

Buses, trolleybuses and trams are useful along a few radial or cross-town routes that the metro misses, and are necessary for reaching sights away from the city centre. Tickets (R25) are usually sold on the vehicle by a conductor.

Taxi
See p800 for information on hailing unofficial taxis. Expect to pay R150 to R200 for a ride around the city centre. Official taxis – which can be recognised by the draughtboard logo on the side and/or a small green light in the windscreen – charge higher rates. To book a cab by phone, call the **Central Taxi Reservation Office** (Tsentralnoe Byuro Zakazov Taxi; ☎ 495-627 0000; www.cbz-taxi.ru).

NOVGOROD НОВГОРОД
☎ 8162 / pop 240,000
Between Moscow and St Petersburg, Novgorod (New Town) is an even older capital of Russia. From its humble beginnings as a trading town on the route between Byzantium and the Baltics, Novgorod grew to become one of the most important political and cultural centres in northwest Russia in the early Middle Ages.

Although something of a backwater these days, Novgorod's magnificent cultural legacy can still be seen in its numerous churches and museums, many of them surrounded by the mighty walls of its kremlin.

Novgorod has two main centres: the kremlin on the west bank of the Volkhov River, and the old market district, Yaroslav's Court, on the east bank. The town's switched-on **tourist office** (☎ 773 074; www.visitnovgorod.ru; Sennaya pl 5; ☻ 9.30am-6pm) will help you get your bearings. City tours in English, French or German can be arranged. After hours, you can contact the 24-hour hotline at ☎ 8162-998 686.

SIGHTS
The Kremlin
Surrounded by a pleasant wooded park, the **kremlin** (☎ 773 608; ☻ 6am-midnight) is one of Russia's oldest, first built in the 9th century, then rebuilt with brick in the 14th century (the version that still stands today). It houses the city's most famous sites, the highlight of which is the handsome, Byzantine **Cathedral of St Sophia** (☻ 8am-8pm). Finished in 1050, it is one of the oldest buildings in Russia. Services usually take place between 6pm and 8pm daily. Close by, the 15th-century **belfry** and a leaning 17th-century **clock tower** poke above the city walls. In summer it opens as

a **museum** (admission R30; ☻ 9am-5pm); enter for the spectacular views from the observation platform.

The 16m-high, 300-tonne **Millennium of Russia Monument**, unveiled in 1862, is a who's who of Russian history, depicting some 127 figures – ranging from Mother Russia through to Catherine the Great. The Gothic **Chamber of Facets** (adult/student R110/60; ☻ 10am-6pm Thu-Tue, closed last Fri of month), part of a palace built in 1433, has a collection of icons and lavish church booty from throughout the region, including some beautiful illuminated manuscripts.

Yaroslav's Court
Across a footbridge from the kremlin is old Novgorod's market, with the remnants of an 18th-century arcade facing the river. Beyond that is the market gatehouse, an array of churches sponsored by 13th- to 16th-century merchant guilds, and a 'road palace' built in the 18th century as a rest stop for Catherine the Great.

The 12th-century Kyiv-style **Court Cathedral of St Nicholas** (Nikolo-Dvorishchensky sobor; ☎ 636 187; adult/student R100/60; ☻ 10am-6pm Wed-Sun, closed last Fri of month) is all that remains of the early palace complex of the Novgorod princes, from which Yaroslav's Court (Yaroslavovo

---

WORTH THE TRIP: SMOLENSK & PSKOV СМОЛЕНСК & ПСКОВ

Set on the upper Dnepr River, 360km southwest of Moscow, Smolensk is one of Russia's oldest cities and has ancient walls, onion-dome cathedrals and well-landscaped parks strewn across the undulating hills. The highlight is the magnificent Assumption Cathedral, but music lovers should also consider visiting for the renowned Glinka Festival, which runs from 1 to 10 June.

The recommended place to stay is **Hotel Tsentralnaya** (☎ 383 604; http://smolensk-otel.keytown .com; cnr pl Lenina & ul Konenkova; s 1100-1400, d 2200-2800), while a good place to eat is **Russky Dvor** (☎ 683 499; Glinka Garden; mains R80-130; ☻ 9am-11pm).

There are several daily trains between Smolensk and Minsk (R640, four hours) and Brest (R930, eight hours), as well as regular trains to Warsaw (R2536, nine hours), Prague (R4063, 24 hours), Berlin (R4163, 41 hours) and Moscow (platskartny/kupe R370/650, 5½ hours).

The medieval church-studded city of Pskov, dominated by its mighty riverside kremlin and just 30km from Estonia, makes for an impressive first sight if you are coming over from the Baltics; or a pleasant farewell from Russia should you be headed in the opposite direction. Lay your head at the **Hotel Rizhskaya** (☎ 462 223; Rizhsky pr 25; s/d R950/1700; 🖳) and dine at **Kafe V'Gorod N** (☎ 737 124; Oktyabrsky pr 19; dishes R120-200; ☻ 8am-1am).

Direct trains to St Petersburg (platskartny/kupe R440/650, five hours) depart at ungodly hours; you're better off taking the bus (R525, 5½ hours). Night trains go to Moscow (platskartny/kupe R1200/1900, 12 hours), Rīga (R1540, eight hours) and Vilnius (R1090, eight hours).

Two to three buses daily connect with Novgorod (R321, 4½ hours), and two buses a day go to Smolensk (R641, eight to 10 hours). If you are heading to Estonia, take the 8.20am bus to Tallinn (R700, six hours) or the 2pm bus to Tartu (R500, four hours).

dvorishche) gets its name. The cathedral holds church artefacts and temporary exhibitions of local interest. Downstairs you can see fragments from the church's original frescos.

SLEEPING

The tourist office keeps a list of local homestays. Expect to pay around R800 per person for a room.

Hotel Rossiya (☎ 634 185; nab Aleksandra Nevskogo 19/1; r from R1160) Enter the battered Rossiya around the back. Inside, things are still holding together. Most rooms have been renovated, but for those who don't mind roughing it a little, the unrenovated rooms are slightly cheaper. Some rooms have nice views of the river and the kremlin.

Hotel Novgorodskaya (☎ 772 260; www.novgorod skaya.nov.ru; ul Desyatinnaya 6a; s/d from R1250/1560) Resembling a dormitory, this low-key place has comfortable, well-maintained rooms and a good location.

Beresta Palace Hotel (☎ 940 910; www.fclnovgorod .ru; ul Studencheskaya 2; s/d incl breakfast from R3000/3500; 🖳) Novgorod's best hotel, with comfortable rooms, good service, a health club, sauna, tennis courts, and free wi-fi.

EATING & DRINKING

During summertime, several open-air cafes facing the kremlin's west side make pleasant spots for a drink.

Ilmen (☎ 778 374; ul Gazon 2; meals from R50; ⏲ bistro 10am-10pm, restaurant noon-midnight) The ground floor has a little deli for takeaway snacks, and a bistro for cheap sit-down eats. Upstairs, the more formal restaurant has fresh-roasted meats, a good wine selection and a menu packed with Russian and Scandinavian dishes.

Restoran Detinets (☎ 774 624; dishes R200-350; ⏲ noon-5pm & 7-11pm) Amid castle walls lit by iron chandeliers, sample classic Russian fare of pork chops, fish and stuffed bliny. The restaurant is on the top floor; at a little bar on the bottom floor you can sample *medovukha*, a honey-brewed mead. English menu available.

ourpick **Café Le Chocolat** (☎ 739 009; ul Lyudogoshcha 8; dishes R250-650; ⏲ 9am-11pm) This ubercool cafe, with a nonsmoking section, offers some tantalizing options, including Thai tuna, French duck and dozens of sushi platters. This is one place worth a splurge.

GETTING THERE & AROUND

The **train station** (☎ 739 380) is located 1.5km west of the kremlin, at the end of pr Karla Marksa. A fast *elektrichka* runs daily to St Petersburg's Moscow Station (R287; three hours). There's also a night-train connection with Moscow (*platskartny/kupe* R600/1000; eight hours). There are also trains twice a week to Kyiv.

The modern **bus station** (☎ 739 979), next to the train station, serves St Petersburg (R290, four hours) at least once an hour. There's also direct bus service to Pskov (R321, 4½ hours) at 8am and 4pm.

From the bus and train stations, take buses 4 and 20 (R10) into the city and 4 or 19 back. A taxi should cost about R100.

ST PETERSBURG
САНКТ ПЕТЕРБУРГ

☎ 812 / pop 4.6 million

'St Petersburg is Russia, but it is not Russian.' The opinion of Nicholas II, the empire's last tsar, on his one-time capital still resonates. The city is a fascinating hybrid where one moment you can be clapping along to a fun Russian folk-music show in a baroque hall or sniffing incense inside a mosaic-covered Orthodox church, the next grooving on the dance floor of an underground club or posing at a contemporary-art event in a renovated bakery.

Above all, Europe's fourth-largest city is a visual delight. The Neva River and surrounding canals reflect unbroken facades of handsome 18th- and 19th-century buildings that house a spellbinding collection of cultural storehouses, culminating in the incomparable Hermitage. It's easy to imagine how such an environment, warts and all, was the inspiration for many of Russia's greatest artists, including the writers Pushkin, Gogol and Dostoevsky, and musical maestros such as Rachmaninoff, Tchaikovsky and Shostakovich. This giant warehouse of Russian culture has more to offer the traveller than perhaps anywhere else in the country.

HISTORY

Starting with the Peter & Paul Fortress, founded on the marshy estuary of the Neva River in 1703, Peter the Great and his successors

RUSSIA

CENTRAL ST PETERSBURG

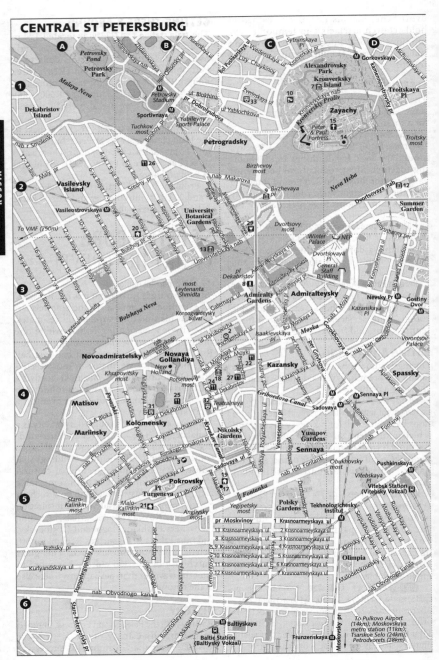

1 Krasnoarmeyskaya ul
2 Krasnoarmeyskaya ul
13 Krasnoarmeyskaya ul 3 Krasnoarmeyskaya ul
8 Krasnoarmeyskaya ul 4 Krasnoarmeyskaya ul
9 Krasnoarmeyskaya ul 5 Krasnoarmeyskaya ul
10 Krasnoarmeyskaya ul 6 Krasnoarmeyskaya ul
11 Krasnoarmeyskaya ul 7 Krasnoarmeyskaya ul
12 Krasnoarmeyskaya ul

To Pulkovo Airport
(14km); Moskovskaya
metro station (11km);
Tsarskoe Selo (24km);
Petrodvorets (28km)

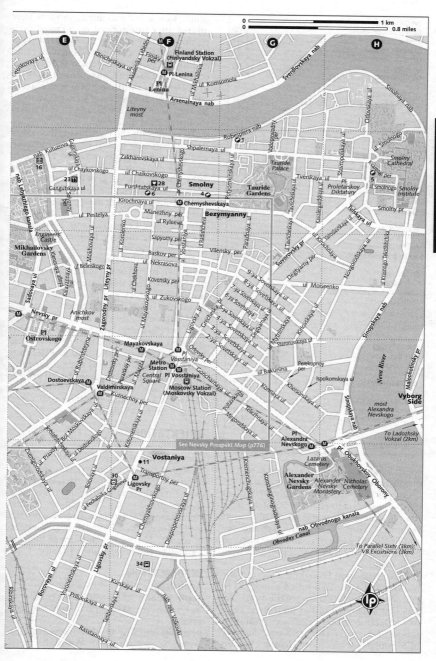

RUSSIA

commissioned a city built to grand design by mainly European architects. By the early 19th century, St Petersburg had firmly established itself as Russia's cultural heart. But at the same time as writers, artists and musicians – such as Pushkin, Turgenev and, later, Tchaikovsky and Dostoevsky – lived in and were inspired by the city, political and social problems were on the rise.

Industrialisation brought a flood of poor workers and associated urban squalor to St Petersburg. Revolution against the monarchy was first attempted in the short-lived coup of 14 December 1825. The next revolution was in 1905, sparked by the 'Bloody Sunday' of 9 January, when more than a hundred

people were killed and hundreds more were injured after troops fired on a crowd petitioning the tsar outside the Winter Palace. The tsar's government limped on, until Lenin and his Bolshevik followers took advantage of Russia's disastrous involvement in WWI to instigate the third successful revolution in 1917. Again, St Petersburg (renamed a more Russian-sounding Petrograd in 1914) was at the forefront of the action.

To break with the tsarist past, the seat of government was moved back to Moscow, and St Petersburg was renamed Leningrad after the first communist leader's death in 1924. The city – by virtue of its location, three million-plus population and industry – remained one of Russia's most important, thus putting it on the front line during WWII. For 872 days Leningrad was besieged by the Germans, and one million perished in horrendous conditions.

During the 1960s and 1970s Leningrad's bohemian spirit burned bright, fostering the likes of dissident poet Joseph Brodsky and underground rock groups such as Kino and Akvarium. In 1991, as the Soviet Union came tumbling down, the city reverted to calling itself St Petersburg. Millions of roubles were spent on restoration for the city's tricentenary celebrations in 2003, and St Petersburg looks better now probably than at any other time in its history – a source of great pride to two local boys made good: President Dmitry Medvedev and former president and current prime minister Vladimir Putin.

ORIENTATION

St Petersburg is spread out across many different islands, some real and some created through the construction of canals. The central street is Nevsky Pr, which extends for some 4km from the Lavra Alexandra Nevskogo (Alexander Nevsky Monastery) to the Hermitage. The vast Neva River empties into the Gulf of Finland, filtered through a number of islands. The most significant of these are Vasilevsky and Petrogradsky Islands.

INFORMATION
Bookshops

Anglia (Map p776; ☎ 579 8284; nab reki Fontanki 30; ☾ 10am-7pm; Ⓜ Gostiny Dvor) English-language bookshop.

Dom Knigi (Map p776; ☎ 448 2355; www.spbdk.ru; Nevsky pr 28; ☾ 9am-midnight; Ⓜ Nevsky Pr)

Internet Access

Internet cafes and wi-fi access are common across the city.

Café Max (Map p776; ☎ 273 6655; www.cafemax.ru; Nevsky 90/92; per hr R40; ⏰ 24hr; Ⓜ Mayakovskaya) Wi-fi available here. Also has a branch in the Hermitage.

FM Club (Map p776; ☎ 764 3674; ul Dostoevskogo 6a; per hr R35; ⏰ 10am-8am; Ⓜ Vladimirskaya)

Quo Vadis (Map p776; ☎ 333 0708; www.quovadis .ru; Nevsky pr 66; per hr R100; ⏰ 24hr; Ⓜ Gostiny Dvor) Enter from Liteyny pr.

Laundry

Stirka (Map p776; ☎ 314 5371; Kazanskaya ul 26; ⏰ 11am-11pm; Ⓜ Sadovaya/Sennaya Pl) Cafe-bar and launderette – what a good idea! A 5kg wash costs R140. The dryer is R90.

Media

The following English-language publications are available free at many hotels, hostels, restaurants and bars across the city:

St Petersburg in Your Pocket (www.inyourpocket .com/city/st_petersburg.html) Monthly listings booklet with useful up-to-date information and short features.

St Petersburg Times (www.sptimes.ru) Published every Tuesday and Friday (when it has an indispensable listings and arts review section), this plucky little newspaper has been fearlessly telling it like it really is for over 15 years.

Medical Services

The clinics listed here are open 24 hours and have English-speaking staff:

American Medical Clinic (Map p776; ☎ 740 2090; www.amclinic.ru; nab reki Moyki 78; Ⓜ Sadovaya)

Apteka Petrofarm (Map p776; ☎ 314 5401; Nevsky pr 22; ⏰ 24hr; Ⓜ Nevsky Pr) Pharmacy.

Medem International Clinic & Hospital (Map p776; ☎ 336 3333; www.medem.ru; ul Marata 6; Ⓜ Mayakovskaya)

Post

Post office branches are scattered throughout the city. All the major air-courier services are available in St Petersburg.

Central post office (Map pp772-3; ☎ 312 8302; www .spbpost.ru; Pochtamtskaya ul 9; ⏰ 24 hr; Ⓜ Sadovaya/ Sennaya Pl) Worth visiting just to admire its recently renovated, elegant Style Moderne (art deco) interior. The express mail service EMS Garantpost is available here.

Telephone & Fax

You can buy a local SIM card at any mobile-phone shop, such as **Dixis** (www.dixis.ru) or **Euroset** (www.spb.euroset.ru), both chains with several branches across the city, from as little as R150, including R100 of credit.

Local phonecards (taksfon karta) are available from shops, kiosks and metro stations and can be used to make local, national and international calls from any phone. Call centres are better value for international calls – look for the sign Mezhdunarodny Telefon.

Tourist Information

From May to September the city sponsors 'angels' (ie guides) who roam Nevsky Pr, Palace Square and the like ready to assist tourists.

City Tourist Information Centre (Map p776; www .visit-petersburg.com) main office (☎ 310 8262; Sadovaya ul 14/52; ⏰ 10am-7pm Mon-Sat; Ⓜ Gostiny Dvor); Hermitage booth (Map p776; Dvortsovaya pl 12; ⏰ 10am-7pm daily; Ⓜ Nevsky Pr) The English-speaking staff is vague about most things but will do their best to help. There are also branches at the Pulkova-1 and Pulkova-2 air terminals (open 10am to 7pm Monday to Friday).

Travel Agencies

The following agencies have English-speaking staff:

City Realty (Map p776; ☎ 570 6342; www.cityrealty .ru; Muchnoy per 2; tourist visas from US$25; Ⓜ Nevsky Pr) As well as arranging all types of accommodation and transport tickets, this very reliable agency can help sort out your visa, including business ones.

Ost-West Kontaktservice (Map p776; ☎ 327 3416; www.ostwest.com; Nevsky pr 105; ⏰ 10am-6pm Mon-Fri; Ⓜ Pl Vosstaniya) The multilingual staff here can find you an apartment to rent and organise tours and tickets.

Parallel Sixty (off Map pp772-3; ☎ 928 0739; www.par allel60.ru; ul Avtogennaya 6, office 415; Ⓜ Elizarovskaya) Friendly and efficient agency that can arrange visas, accommodation and tours. It also runs VB Excursions (p781).

Sindbad Travel (Map p776; ☎ 332 2020; www.sind bad.ru; 2-ya Sovetskaya ul 12; ⏰ 9am-10pm Mon-Fri, 10am-6pm Sat & Sun; Ⓜ Pl Vosstaniya). A genuine Western-style discount air-ticket office, staffed by friendly, knowledgeable people.

DANGERS & ANNOYANCES

Never drink tap water in St Petersburg as it could contain Giardia lamblia, a parasite that can cause horrific stomach cramps and nausea. Bring a water filter or stick to bottled water, which is available everywhere. If you must drink tap water, boil it for a good few minutes first.

The humidity and marshland location of St Petersburg makes it mosquito hell from May until October. Be prepared – bring repellent or

NEVSKY PROSPEKT

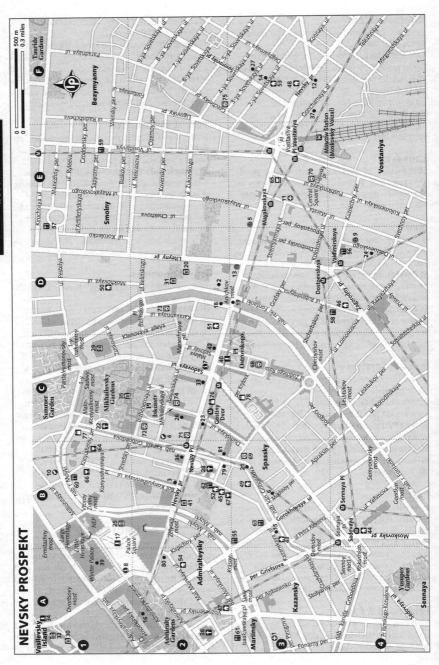

RUSSIA

the standard antimosquito tablets and socket plug. Alternatively you can buy these all over the city – ask for *sredstva protif kamarov*.

Human pests include the ever-present pickpockets on Nevsky pr – be vigilant and look out particularly for the infamous gangs of children who work the area around Griboedova Canal.

Sadly, racist attacks are a reality in the city. Skinhead gangs have killed an unprecedented number of mainly Caucasian and Central Asians in the past few years, and there's a climate of fear among ethnic minorities. That said, attacks in the city centre are rare, so we still encourage nonwhite travellers to visit, but suggest exercising far more caution here than anywhere else in the region. Avoid the suburbs whenever possible and try not to go out alone after dark.

SIGHTS
The Hermitage & Dvortsovaya Ploshchad
Mainly set in the magnificent Winter Palace, the **State Hermitage** (Map p776; ☎ 571 3465; www

.hermitagemuseum.org; Dvortsovaya pl 2; adult R350, student & under 17yr free; ☻ 10.30am-6pm Tue-Sat, to 5pm Sun; Ⓜ Nevsky Pr) fully lives up to its sterling reputation. You can be absorbed by its treasures – which range from Egyptian mummies and Scythian gold to early-20th-century paintings by Matisse and Picasso – for days and still come out wishing for more.

Queues for tickets, particularly from May to September, can be horrendous. The museum can also be very busy on the first Thursday of the month, when admission is free. Either go late in the day when the lines are likely to be shorter or book your ticket online through the Hermitage's website: US$17.95 gets you an entrance plus use of camera or camcorder to the main Hermitage buildings. You'll be issued with a voucher that allows you to jump the queue and go straight to the ticket booth.

Joining a tour is another way to avoid queuing: call the museum's **excursions office** (☎ 571 8446; ☻ 11am-1pm & 2-4pm); they will tell you what time to show up for the tours in English, German or French.

The museum's main entrance is from the **Palace Square** (Dvortsovaya pl), one of the city's most impressive and historic spaces. Stand back to admire the palace and the central 47.5m-high **Alexander Column**, named after Alexander I and commemorating the 1812 victory over Napoleon. Enclosing the square's south side is the **General Staff Building** (Map p776; ☎ 314 8260; Dvortsovaya pl 6-8; adult/student R200/free; ☼ 10am-6pm Tue-Sun; Ⓜ Nevsky Pr), which in its east wing has an excellent branch of the Hermitage where the crowds drop away.

Church of the Saviour on Spilled Blood

This multidomed dazzler of a **church** (Spas na Krovi; Map p776; ☎ 315 1636; http://eng.cathedral.ru /saviour; Konyushennaya pl; adult/student R300/150; ☼ 11am-7pm Thu-Tue Oct-Apr, 10am-8pm Thu-Tue May-Sep; Ⓜ Nevsky Pr), partly modelled on St Basil's in Moscow, was built between 1883 and 1907 on the spot where Alexander II was assassinated in 1881 (hence its gruesome name). The interior's 7000 sq metres of mosaics fully justify the entrance fee.

Russian Museum

Facing on to the elegant pl Iskusstv (Arts Sq) is the former Mikhailovsky Palace, now the **Russian Museum** (Russy Muzey; Map p776; ☎ 595 4248; www.rusmuseum.ru; Inzhenernaya ul 4; adult/student R350/150; ☼ 10am-5pm Mon, to 6pm Wed-Sun; Ⓜ Gostiny Dvor), housing one of the country's finest collections of Russian art. After the Hermitage you may feel you have had your fill of art, but try your utmost to make some time for this gem of a museum.

The museum owns three other city palaces, all worth visiting if you have time, where permanent and temporary exhibitions are held: the **Marble Palace** (Mramorny Dvorets; Map pp772-3; ☎ 312 9196; Millionnaya ul 5; adult/student R350/150; ☼ 10am-5pm Wed-Mon; Ⓜ Nevsky Pr); the **Mikhailovsky Castle** (Mikhaylovsky Zamok; Map p776; ☎ 595 4248; Sadovaya ul 2; adult/student R350/150; ☼ 10am-5pm Mon, to 6pm Wed-Sun; Ⓜ Gostiny Dvor), also known as the Engineer's Castle; and the **Stroganov Palace** (Map p776; ☎ 312 9054; Nevsky pr 17; adult/student R350/150; ☼ 10am-5pm Tue-Sun; Ⓜ Nevsky pr). A ticket for R600, available at each palace, covers entrance to all three within a 24-hour period.

St Isaac's Cathedral & Around

The golden dome of this **cathedral** (Isaakievsky Sobor; Map p776; ☎ 315 9732; http://eng.cathedral.ru/isaac; Isaakievskaya pl; adult/student R300/150; ☼ 10am-8pm Thu-Mon, closed last Mon of month; Ⓜ Sadovaya/Sennaya Pl) dominates the city skyline. Its lavish interior is open as a museum, but many visitors just buy the separate ticket to climb the 262 steps up to the **colonnade** (adult/student R150/100; ☼ 10am-7pm Thu-Mon, closed last Mon of month) around the dome's drum to take in panoramic views.

Behind the cathedral is **ploshchad Dekabristov** (Decembrists' Square; Map pp772–3), named after the Decembrists' Uprising of 14 December 1825. Falconet's statue of Peter the Great, the **Bronze Horseman** (Map pp772–3), stands at the end of the square towards the river.

THE CURATOR'S CHOICE

'I first visited the Hermitage when I was five or six years old. At that time what I liked the most were the **Egyptian mummies** (Room 100). They were displayed at a low height so I could see them well and read their names, such as Pa De Ist.

Visitors to the Hermitage shouldn't miss **Raphael's Loggia** (Room 227) – Catherine the Great commissioned Giacomo Quarrengi in the 1780s to create this copy of a gallery she admired at the Vatican. It was made exactly to scale, so not only is it a great event of art but also of technique and design.

The Hermitage has lots of works by Rubens, many of them from his studio – he was like the Damien Hirst of his day, presiding over a factory of artists. One piece that undoubtedly was done by his hand, though, is **Perseus and Andromeda** (Room 246). It's a masterpiece. You look at Medusa's eyes and you feel afraid, and the horse looks so real you feel you could touch it.

From the 20th-century works, I recommend Matisse's **Dance and Music** (Room 344), a magnificently vibrant pair of paintings commissioned by his patron Sergei Shchukin. Originally the genitalia of the nude male dancers were shown, but [they were later] painted over. If the light is right, it's possible to see the painting as Matisse intended. It's a dilemma for the Hermitage whether to restore it to the way it was.'

Dr Dimitri Ozerkov, Chief Curator, Hermitage 20/21 Project

Nevsky Prospekt

Walking Nevsky Pr (Map p776) – Russia's most famous street – is an essential St Petersburg experience. Starting at Dvortsovaya pl, notice the gilded spire of the **Admiralty** to your right as you head southeast down Nevsky towards the Moyka River. Across the Moyka, Rastrelli's baroque **Stroganov Palace** houses a branch of the Russian Museum (opposite), as well as a couple of restaurants and a chocolate shop masquerading as a 'museum'.

A block beyond the Moyka, on the southern side of Nevsky pr, see the great arms of the **Kazan Cathedral** (Kazansky Sobor; ☎ 571 4826; Kazanskaya pl 2; admission free; ☿ 10am-7pm, services 10am & 6pm; Ⓜ Nevsky pr) reach out towards the avenue. It's a working cathedral, so please show some respect for the local customs if you enter.

Opposite the cathedral is the **Singer Building**, a Style Moderne beauty recently restored to all its splendour when it was the headquarters of the sewing-machine company; inside is the bookshop Dom Knigi and a coffee shop with a great view over the street.

A short walk south of the cathedral, along Griboedova Canal, sits one of St Petersburg's loveliest bridges, the **Bankovsky most**. The cables of this 25.2m-long bridge are supported by four cast-iron gryphons with golden wings.

View the lavish **Grand Hotel Europe** (☎ 329 6000; www.grandhoteleurope.com; Mikhaylovskaya ul 1/7; Ⓜ Nevsky Pr/Gostiny Dvor), built between 1873 and 1875, redone in Style Moderne in the 1910s and completely renovated in the early 1990s. Across Nevsky pr, the historic department store **Bolshoy Gostiny Dvor** (see p784) is another Rastrelli creation dating from 1757–85. Beside it stands the **clock tower** of the former Town Duma, seat of the prerevolutionary city government.

At 48 Nevsky pr, the **Passazh** department store has a beautiful arcade (note the glass ceilings), while on the corner of Sadovaya ul is the Style Moderne classic **Yeliseyevsky**, once the city's most sumptuous grocery store. At the time of research the building was closed, but its grand exterior is well worth a look.

An enormous **statue of Catherine the Great** stands at the centre of **Ploshchad Ostrovskogo**, commonly referred to as the Catherine Gardens; at the southern end of the gardens is **Aleksandrinksy Theatre**, where Chekhov's *The Seagull* premiered in 1896.

Nevsky pr crosses the Fontanka Canal on the **Anichkov most**, with its famous 1840s statues

(sculpted by the German Pyotr Klodt) of rearing horses at its four corners.

Summer Garden

St Petersburg's loveliest park, the **Summer Garden** (Letny Sad; Map p772-3; admission free; ☿ 10am-10pm May-Sep, to 8pm Oct–mid-Apr, closed mid-late Apr; Ⓜ Gostiny Dvor) is a great place to relax. In its northeast corner is the modest, two-storey **Summer Palace** (Muzey Letny Dvorets Petra 1; ☎ 314 0374; adult/student R300/150; ☿ 10am-5pm Wed-Mon early May-early Nov), built for Peter from 1710 to 1714. Inside it's stocked with early-18th-century furnishings of limited appeal.

Sheremetyev Palace

Facing the Fontanka Canal, the splendid **Sheremetyev Palace** (1750–55) houses two lovely museums. The **Museum of Music** (Map p776; ☎ 272 3898; www.theatremuseum.ru/eng; nab reki Fontanki 34; adult/student R180/90; ☿ noon-6pm Wed-Sun; Ⓜ Gostiny Dvor) contains a collection of beautifully decorated instruments. The upstairs palace rooms have been wonderfully restored; you get a great sense of how cultured life must have been here.

In a separate wing of the palace, reached from Liteyny pr, is the charming **Anna Akhmatova Museum at the Fountain House** (Map p776; ☎ 579 7239; www.akhmatova.spb.ru; Liteyny pr 53; adult/student R120/80; ☿ 10.30am-6.30pm Tue-Sun, 1-9pm Wed, closed last Wed of month; Ⓜ Mayakovskaya), filled with mementos of the poet and her family, all persecuted during Soviet times.

Yusupov Palace

In a city of glittering palaces, the dazzling interiors of the **Yusupov Palace** (Map pp772-3; ☎ 314 9883; www.yusupov-palace.ru; nab reki Moyki 94; adult/student R500/280; ☿ 11am-5pm; Ⓜ Sadovaya/Sennaya Pl) more than hold their own. Best known as the place where Rasputin met his untimely end, the palace sports a series of richly decorated rooms culminating in a gilded jewel box of a theatre, where performances are still held. Admission includes an audio tour in English or one of several other languages. Places are limited to 20 daily for each of the two English-language *Murder of Rasputin* tours (adult/student R300/150).

Contemporary-Art Galleries

The best places to see examples of St Petersburg's thriving contemporary-art scene are at the galleries occupying **Pushkinskaya 10**

(Map p776; ☎ 764 5371; www.p10.nonmuseum.ru; Ligovsky pr 53; admission free; ⏰ 3-7pm Wed-Sun; Ⓜ Pl Vosstaniya) and **Loft Project Floors** (Loft Proekt Etazhi; Map pp772-3; Ligivosky pr 74; admission free; ⏰ 2-10pm Tue-Sat; Ⓜ Ligovsky pr).

The former dates back to an artists' squat established in 1988. Now a fully legit non-profit organisation, this legendary locale also houses the cool music clubs **Fish Fabrique** (p784) and **Experimental Sound Gallery** (p784). While the art centre commonly goes by the name 'Pushkinskaya 10', note that the entrance is through the archway at Ligovsky pr 53.

Hidden away off the main road in the former Smolensky Bread Bakery, Loft Project Floors consists of four large and industrial-looking gallery spaces, the main one being **Globe Gallery** (www.globegallery.ru).

The Petrograd Side

The term 'Petrograd Side' refers to the cluster of delta islands located between the Malaya Neva and the Bolshaya Nevka channels, including the large Petrogradsky Island and little Zaychy Island, home to the Peter & Paul Fortress.

The principal attraction here is the **Peter & Paul Fortress** (Petropavlovskaya krepost; Map pp772-3; ☎ 238 4550; www.spbmuseum.ru/peterpaul; ⏰ grounds 6am-10am; exhibitions 11am-6pm Thu-Mon, to 5pm Tue; Ⓜ Gorkovskaya). Founded in 1703 as the original military fortress for the new city, it was mainly used as a political prison up to 1917: famous residents include Peter's own son Alexei, as well as Dostoyevsky, Gorky and Trotsky. Individual tickets are needed for each of the fortress' attractions, so the best deal is the combined entry ticket, which costs R250/130 (adult/student) and allows access to all the exhibitions on the island (except the bell tower). It's valid for 10 days.

At noon every day a cannon is fired from the **Naryshkin Bastion** (Map pp772-3), scaring the daylights out of tourists. It's fun to walk along the **battlements** (adult/student R100/60). Most spectacular of all is the **SS Peter & Paul Cathedral** (Map pp772-3; adult/student R170/80), with its landmark needle-thin spire and magnificent baroque interior. All Russia's tsars since Peter the Great have been buried here. The latest addition was Nicholas II and his family, finally buried here by Yeltsin in 1998 – you'll find them in an anteroom to your right as you enter. Also look out for the famously ugly

pinhead **statue of Peter the Great** in the centre of the fortress.

Vasilevsky Island

Some of the best views of St Petersburg can be had from Vasilevsky Island's eastern 'nose', known as the **Strelka**. The two **Rostral Columns** (Map p776) on the point, studded with ships' prows, were oil-fired navigation beacons in the 1800s; on some holidays, such as **Victory Day**, gas torches are still lit on them.

The best of many museums gathered on Vasilevsky Island is the riverside **Menshikov Palace** (Menshikovsky Dvorets; Map pp772-3; ☎ 323 1112; www.hermitagemuseum.org; Universitetskaya nab 15; adult/student R200/100; ⏰ 10.30am-6pm Tue-Sat, to 5pm Sun; Ⓜ Vasileostrovskaya), built in 1707 for Peter the Great's confidant Alexander Menshikov. Now a branch of the Hermitage, the palace's impressively restored interiors are filled with period art and furniture.

The **Museum of Anthropology & Ethnography** (Kunstkamera; Map p776; ☎ 328 1412; www.kunstkamera.ru; Tamozhenny per; adult/student R200/100; ⏰ 11am-6pm Tue-Sat, to 5pm Sun; Ⓜ Vasileostrovskaya) was established in 1714 by Peter the Great, who used it to display his ghoulish collection of monstrosities, notably preserved freaks, two-headed mutant foetuses and odd body parts: they still draw the crowds today.

Housed in what was once the Stock Exchange, the **Central Naval Museum** (Tsentralny Voenno-Morskoi Muzey; Map p776; ☎ 328 2502; Birzhevoy proezd 4; adult/student R320/110; ⏰ 11am-6pm Wed-Sun, closed last Thu of month; Ⓜ Vasileostrovskaya), is a must for naval enthusiasts. Next door, the **Museum of Zoology** (Zoologichesky Muzey; Map pp772-3; ☎ 328 0112; www.zin.ru/mus_e.htm; Universitetskaya nab 1; adult/child R150/50, Thu free; ⏰ 11am-6pm Sat-Thu; Ⓜ Vasileostrovskaya) has some amazing exhibits, including a complete woolly mammoth, thawed out of the Siberian ice in 1902, and a live insect zoo.

ACTIVITIES

Good, centrally located *bani* include **Coachmen's Banya** (Yaskiye Bani; Map p776; ☎ 312 5836; www.yamskie.ru; ul Dostoevskogo 9; admission R150-500; ⏰ men 8am-10.30pm Mon & Wed-Sun, women 8am-10.30pm daily; Ⓜ Vladimirskaya) and **Usachovskie Bani** (Map pp772-3; ☎ 714 3984; Makarenko per 12; admission R100-360; ⏰ women 9am-9pm Tue & Thu, 8am-10pm Sat, men 9am-9pm Wed & Fri, 8am-8pm Sun; Ⓜ Sadovaya/Sennaya Pl).

For swimming try the **VMF** (off Map pp772-3; ☎ 322 4505; Sredny pr 87, Vasilyevsky Island; admission R350; ⏰ 7am-9pm; Ⓜ Vasileostrovskaya) – a 50m pool on

Vasilevsky Island. In winter head down to Zaychy Island and watch the famous ice swimmers, or 'walruses', who start the day with a bracing dip in the water through a hole carved into the ice.

Bikes can be rented from **Skatprokat** (Map p776; ☎ 717 6836; www.skatprokat.ru; Goncharnaya ul 7; rental per day R500; ⏰ 24hr; Ⓜ Pl Vosstaniya).

TOURS

A boat tour in the city is highly recommended, and during the main tourist season (May to October) there are plenty of boats for hire. For a guided tour in English, try **Anglo Tourismo** (Map p776; ☎ 921 989 4722; anglotourismo@yahoo.com; nab reki Fontanki 21; adult/student R450/350; Ⓜ Gostiny Dvor), which also runs walking tours.

The brilliant band of guides at **Peter's Walking Tours** (☎ 943 1229; www.peterswalk.com) can give you an insight into the city like no one else. The standard walking tour (R500) departs from the HI St Petersburg Hostel (Map p776) at 10.30am. Also on offer are lots of cool itineraries, around themes such as Dostoevsky, Rasputin, the Great October Revolution, and food, as well as a regular bike tour, which leaves from Skatprokat (above).

Another excellent walking tour operator is **VB Excursions** (off Map pp772-3; ☎ 911 999 5678; www .vb-excursions; ul Avtogennaya 6, office 415; Ⓜ Elizarovskaya). It's 'Back in the USSR' tour (R925 per person) includes a visit to a typical Soviet apartment for tea and bliny.

FESTIVALS & EVENTS

St Petersburg celebrates **City Day** on 27 May, which marks the founding of the city with mass festivities. The **white nights** (around the summer solstice in late June) are truly unique. The city comes alive and parties all night as the sun only barely sinks below the horizon, leaving the sky a magical grey-white throughout the night.

SLEEPING

Room prices are at a premium between May and September. Outside this period, rates may be up to 30% lower than those quoted here.

As well as City Realty (p775), Ost-West Kontaktservice (p775) and Zimmer Nice (right), the following can arrange apartment rentals and homestays:

Andrey & Sasha's Homestay (Map p776; ☎ 315 3330; asamatuga@mail.ru; nab kanala Griboedova 49; r with shared bathroom from €60; Ⓜ Sadovaya/Sennaya Pl)

Host Families Association (HOFA; ☎ 901 305 8874; www.hofa.ru; s/d/apt from €29/44/118) The most established and reliable agency for homestays and rental of private flats.

Budget

Seven Bridges Hostel (Map pp772-3; ☎ 572 5415; http://7bridges.night.lt; Apt 34, ul Labutina 36; dm/s/d US$18/24/26; Ⓜ Sennaya Pl/Sadovaya; 💻) This convivial place is named after the seven bridges that tether Pokrovsky Ostrov – the hostel's location – to the rest of St Petersburg. The two dorm rooms have four beds each, and there's a very comfy lounge well stocked with books and videos.

our pick **Cuba Hostel** (Map p776; ☎ 921 7115, 315 1558; www.cubahostel.ru; Kazanskaya 5; dm R550; Ⓜ Nevsky Pr; 💻) This funky hang-out presses all the right buttons in terms of atmosphere, friendliness, price and location. Each of the dorms – with four to 10 beds – is painted a different colour, and arty design is used throughout.

Hostel Pilau (Map p776; ☎ 572 2711; www.hostelpilau .ru; Apt 12, ul Rubinshteyna 38; dm/r from R550/2100; Ⓜ Vladimirskaya/Dostoevskaya; 💻) Occupying a renovated 19th-century flat, the 10-bed dorm is in the best-appointed room at Hostel Pilau, with beautiful plaster mouldings on the walls and ceiling. Smaller dorm rooms are simpler in design, but all rooms have newly polished parquet flooring, high ceilings and big windows.

Crazy Duck (Map p776; ☎ 310 1304; www.crazyduck.ru; Apt 4, Moskovsky pr 4; dm from R750; Ⓜ Sadovaya/Sennaya Pl; 💻) This cheery newcomer to the city's hostel scene offers plenty of home comforts to supplement its eight-, six- and four-bed dorms, including a fab lounge, kitchen with top-notch facilities, and jacuzzi.

Zimmer Nice (Map p776; ☎ 973 3757; www.zimmer .ru; Apt 7, Malaya Morskaya ul 8; dm/s/d from R750/1300/2000; Ⓜ Nevsky Pr; 💻) This place is indeed nice, but if it's full, it has another very similar hostel located at Sovetskaya 2ya 19, Apt 86, as well as several centrally located apartments available for rent.

Midrange

our pick **Art Hotel Terezinni** (Map pp772-3; ☎ 332 1035; www.trezzini-hotel.com; Bolshoy pr 8; s/d incl breakfast from R2500/3360; Ⓜ Vasileostrovskaya; 💻) All the rooms at this arty hotel are very appealing, even the compact economy singles. Standouts are rooms 201 and 214, which have little

balconies and overlook the neighbouring St
Andrew's Cathedral.

Hotel Repin (Map p776; ☎ 717 9976; www.repin
-hotel.ru; Nesky pr 136; s/d incl breakfast R2800/3700; Ⓜ Pl
Vosstaniya; 🖵) The Repin's flower-bright colours make it one of the city's more pleasant
minihotels, with bigger-than-usual rooms
(some of them nonsmoking), preserved
original features including antique ceramic
wall stoves, and a spacious lounge area hung
with reproductions of the illustrious Russian
artist's most famous works.

Polikoff Hotel (Map p776; ☎ 314 7925; www.polikoff
.ru; Nevsky pr 64/11; r incl breakfast from R3000; Ⓜ Gostiny
Dvor; 🗷 🖵) Tricky to find (the entrance is
through the brown door on Karavannaya ul,
where you'll need to punch in 26 for reception) the Polikoff Hotel is worth hunting out
for its rooms brimming with contemporary
cool decor, quiet but central location and
pleasant service.

Pio on Mokhovaya (Map p776; ☎ 273 3585; www
.hotelpio.ru; Apt 10 & 12, Mokhovaya ul 39; s/d/tr/q incl breakfast
€100/120/150/170; Ⓜ Chernyshevskaya; 🖵) Split across
two apartments, the rooms at this appealing
guest house are named after Italian towns.
They're simply but elegantly furnished, with
modern fixtures and dusky pastel-coloured
walls. There's a sister property, the Pio on
Griboedov (Map p776; Apt 5, nab kanala
Griboedova 35), with canal views and a few
cheaper rooms sharing bathrooms.

Rachmaninov Antique-Hotel (Map p776; ☎ 327
7466; www.hotelrachmaninov.com; Kazanskaya ul 5, 3rd fl;
s/d/ste incl breakfast R4400/4550/12,680; Ⓜ Nevsky Pr;
🗷 🖵) Superstylish minihotel, where minimalist decor is offset by antiques.

Top End

ourpick **AlexanderHouse**(Mappp772-3; ☎ 5753877; www
.a-house.ru; nab Krukova kanala 27; s/d from R7140/7820, apt
s/d R12,920/13,600, all incl breakfast; Ⓜ Sadovaya/Sennaya
Pl; 🗷 🖵) The 19 spacious rooms at this lovely
boutique hotel are each named and tastefully
styled after the world's top cities. It also has
a comfortable lounge area with an attached
kitchen for guests' use, a library, *banya*, restaurant and lush garden.

Hotel Astoria (Map p776; ☎ 494 5757; www.rocco
fortecollection.com; Bolshaya Morskaya ul 39; s/d/ste from
R17,150/19,250/24,500; Ⓜ Nevsky Pr; 🗷 🖵) This
long-established hotel is the very essence of
old-world class and the choice of visiting VIPs –
their names are listed on plaques next to the
elevator. Some rooms are nonsmoking.

EATING

St Petersburg is one of the best places to eat
in Russia. Those on a budget should look
out for bliny kiosks throughout the city,
where a quick snack will not cost you more
than R50.

Restaurants

Schaste (Happiness; Map p776; ☎ 572 2675; www.schaste
-est.com; ul Rubinshteyna 15/17; mains R250-400; 🕙 9am-
midnight Mon-Thu, 9am-7am Fri, 10am-7am Sat, 10am-mid-
night Sun; Ⓜ Dostoevskaya/Vladimirskaya) Romantic
cherubs are the motif of this charming cafe-
bar, even on the dot-to-dot puzzles that
are printed on the place mats. The vaguely
Russian food is tasty and the three-course
lunch for R250 is a steal.

Teplo (Map pp772-3; ☎ 570 1974; Bolshaya Morskaya
ul 45; mains R260-500; Ⓜ Sadovaya/Sennaya Pl) You'll
instantly warm to Teplo's cosy living-room
atmosphere; it's liberally scattered with
cuddly soft toys. The food – roast chicken,
salmon in savoy cabbage, sweet and savoury
pies and pastries baked daily – is equally
comforting.

ourpick **Sadko** (Map pp772-3; ☎ 920 8228; www
.probka.org; ul Glinki 2; mains R260-650; Ⓜ Sa-
dovaya/Sennaya Pl) This impressive restaurant
serves all the Russian favourites, while its
decor applies traditional floral designs to
a slick contemporary style. It has a great
children's room and is ideal as a pre– or
post–Mariinsky Theatre dining option. The
waiters, many of whom are music students
at the local conservatory, give impromtu
vocal performances.

Terrassa (Map p776; ☎ 337 6837; www.terrassa.ru;
Kazanskaya ul 3; mains R300-700; Ⓜ Nevsky Pr) Atop the
Vanity shopping centre, this cool bistro has
unbelievable views towards Kazan Cathedral.
In the open kitchen, chefs busily prepare fu-
sion cuisine, exhibiting influences from Italy,
Asia and beyond.

Makarov (Map p776; ☎ 327 0053; www.makarov
-rest.com; Manezhny per 2; mains R400-500; 🕙 noon-
11pm Sun & Mon, 8am-11pm Tue-Fri, 11am-midnight Sat;
Ⓜ Chernyshevskaya) Charming place overlooking
the Cathedral of the Transfiguration of our
Saviour and serving traditional Russian with
a twist in a relaxed setting.

Cafes

ourpick **Stolle** (www.stolle.ru; pies R60-100; 🕙 8am-
10pm); Konyushennaya per (Map p776; Konyushennaya per
1/6; Ⓜ Nevsky Pr); ul Vosstaniya (Map p776; ul Vosstaniya

32; ⓜ Chernyshevskaya); ul Dekabristov 19 (Map pp772-3; ul Dekabristov 19; ⓜ Sadovaya/Sennaya Pl); ul Dekabristov 33 (Map pp772-3; ul Dekabristov 33; ⓜ Sadovaya/Sennaya Pl); Vasilyevsky Island (Map pp772-3; 1-ya linii 50; ⓜ Vasileostrovskaya) We can't get enough of the traditional Russian savoury and sweet pies at this expanding chain of cafes, and we guarantee you'll also be back for more. It's easy to make a meal of it with soups and other dishes that can be ordered at the counter.

Zoom Café (Map p776; www.cafezoom.ru; Gorokhovaya ul 22; mains R200-400; ⓜ Nevsky Pr) Popular boho/student hang-out with regularly changing art exhibitions. Serves unfussy tasty European and Russian food and has wi-fi access, a very relaxed ambience, and a nonsmoking zone.

Café Idiot (Map pp772-3; ☎ 315 1675; nab reki Moyki 82; meals R400; ⏱ 11am-1am; ⓜ Sennaya Pl) This long-running vegetarian cafe charms with its prerevolutionary atmosphere. It's an ideal place to visit for a nightcap or late supper. It also has free wi-fi and a nonsmoking area.

Quick Eats

Herzen Institute Canteen (Map p776; Herzen Institute courtyard, nab reki Moyki 48; mains R50-100; ⏱ noon-6pm Mon-Sat; ⓜ Nevsky Pr) This no-frills Chinese outlet caters to the students from the Herzen Institute, who arrive here in droves at lunchtime.

Olyushka & Russkye Bliny (Map pp772-3; Gagarinskaya ul 13; mains R70-100; ⏱ 11am-6pm Mon-Fri; ⓜ Chernyshevskaya) The students at the nearby university quite rightly swear by these authentic canteens that hark back to the simplicity of Soviet times. Olyushka serves only *pelmeni*, all handmade, while Russkye Bliny does a fine line in melt-in-the-mouth pancakes.

Self-Catering

Out of the city's food markets, **Kuznechny Market** (Map p776; Kuznechny per 3; ⏱ 8am-8pm; ⓜ Vladimirskaya) should not be missed. It's the most colourful and pricey of the city's food halls, and although you can taste delicious fruit, honey and cheese here, you'll inevitably be charmed into making some purchases.

DRINKING

our pick **Achtung Baby** (Map p776; Konyushennaya pl 2; entry after 10pm Fri & Sat R300; ⏱ 6pm-6am; ⓜ Nevsky Pr) The best of several bars and clubs that have taken over the old tsarist-era stables, this place makes great use of the vast, high ceil-

ing space. We love the furry globes that hang over the bar.

Sochi (Map p776; Kazanskaya ul 7; ⏱ 6pm-6am; ⓜ Nevsky Pr) Occupying one half of the same building as the microbrewery Tinkoff is this new venture by the woman who launched St Petersburg's DJ-bar scene. Prop yourself at the long bar or groove along with the hipsters to bands and eclectic selections from the DJs.

Other Side (Map p776; www.theotherside.ru; Bolshaya Konyushennaya ul 1; ⏱ noon to last customer, concerts 8pm Sun-Thu, 10pm or 11pm Fri & Sat; ⓜ Nevsky Pr) There's live music most nights at this fun and funky bar, as well as decent food (mains R200 to R500), but most people turn up to enjoy its seven beers on tap.

City Bar (Map pp772-3; www.citybar.ru; Furshtatskaya ul 20; ⏱ 11am-2am; ⓜ Chernyshevskaya) Always busy with expats, travellers and the locals who enjoy their company. Has free wi-fi access, fine food and live entertainment. Music, poetry readings and stand-up comedy are all on the agenda, depending on the day.

Die Kneipe (Map pp772-3; Grad Petrov; ☎ 326 0137; Universitetskaya nab 5; ⏱ noon to last customer; ⓜ Vasileostrovskaya) The refreshing ales and German-style sausages are reason enough to stop by this fine microbrewery with a view across the Neva from its outdoor tables.

ENTERTAINMENT
Nightclubs

Griboedov (Map pp772-3; ☎ 764 4355; www.griboedovclub.ru; Voronezhskaya ul 2a; cover R100-400, free noon-8pm; ⏱ 5pm-6am; ⓜ Ligovsky Pr) This eternally hip club in an artfully converted bomb shelter is a fun place most nights. It has recently extended above ground with the groovy cafe-bar Griboedov Hill, which hosts live music performances in the evenings.

Underground Club (Map pp772-3; ☎ 572 1551; www.undergroundclub.ru; cnr Lyubansky per & Zverinskaya ul; cover R250-350; ⏱ midnight-6am Fri & Sat; ⓜ Gorkovskaya) Quite literally underground, since this club's four dance floors occupy a sprawling bomb shelter. DJs spin hardcore electronic dance music.

Purga (Map p776; ☎ 570 5123; www.purga-club.ru; nab reki Fontanki 11; cover R100-300; ⏱ 4pm-6am; ⓜ Gostiny Dvor) Every night in one room of this intimate fun-packed club you can celebrate the new year Russian-style, while in the other a traditional wedding celebration is in full flow.

Gay & Lesbian Venues

Check out **Excess** (www.xs.gay.ru) for the latest
city-specific information. The main club is
Central Station (Map p776; ☎ 312 3600; www.central
station.ru; ul Lomonosova 1/28; cover after midnight R100-300;
⏰ 6pm-6am; Ⓜ Gostiny Dvor), featuring two dance
floors, several bars, a cafe and souvenir shop.
Open-minded straights will feel very comfortable here as most people just want to dance.

Performing Arts

The main season is September to the end of
June. In summer many companies are away
on tour, but plenty of performances are
still staged.

Mariinsky Theatre (Map pp772-3; ☎ 326 4141; www
.mariinsky.ru; Teatralnaya pl 1; box office ⏰ 11am-7pm;
Ⓜ Sadovaya/Sennaya Pl) Home to the world-
famous Kirov Ballet and Opera company.
A visit here is a must, if only to wallow in
the sparkling glory of the interior. Use the
website to book and pay for tickets in advance – either for the theatre or the acousti-
cally splendid new concert hall (ul Pisareva
20) nearby.

Mikhailovsky Opera & Ballet Theatre (Map p776;
☎ 585 4305; www.mikhailovsky.ru; pl Iskusstv 1; Ⓜ Nevsky
Pr) Challenging the Mariinksy in terms of
the standards and range of its performances is this equally historic and beautifully
restored theatre.

The St Petersburg Philharmonica's
Symphony Orchestra is particularly renowned,
and the grand **Shostakovich Philharmonia Bolshoy
Zal** (Big Hall; Map p776; ☎ 710 4257; www.philharmonia
.spb.ru; Mikhailovskaya ul 2; Ⓜ Gostiny Dvor) is one of its
two concert halls, the other being the **Maly Zal
imeni Glinki** (Small Hall; Map p776; ☎ 571 8333; Nevsky
pr 30; Ⓜ Nevsky Pr).

Live Music

Bands also play at the Other Side (p783) and
Sochi (p783).

Fish Fabrique (Map p776; ☎ 164 4857; www.fishfab
rique.spb.ru; Ligovsky pr 53; cover R100-150; ⏰ 3pm-late;
Ⓜ Pl Vosstaniya) Legendary bar set in the building that's the focus of the avant-garde art
scene, thus attracting an interesting crowd
that gives this cramped space its edge.

Mod Club (Map p776; ☎ 881 8371; modclub.spb.ru;
Konyushennaya pl 2; cover Fri & Sat R200; ⏰ 6pm-6am;
Ⓜ Nevsky Pr) There's a groovy mix of live and
spun music at this fun, invariably packed
place with two bars and little balconies for a
prime view of the stage.

Zoccolo (Map p776; ☎ 274 9467; www.zoccolo.ru; 3-ya
Sovetskaya ul 2/3; cover R200-300; ⏰ 7pm-midnight Sun-Thu,
7pm-6am Fri & Sat, concerts 8pm; Ⓜ Pl Vosstaniya) Has a
very positive vibe and a great line-up of sounds
including indie rock, Latin-hip-hop-reggae
and even, 'if-Radiohead-played-punk'.

Experimental Sound Gallery (GEZ-21; Map p776;
☎ 764 5258; www.tac.spb.ru; Ligovsky pr 53, 3rd fl; cover
R100-150; ⏰ concerts from 9pm; Ⓜ Pl Vosstaniya)
You know that a place called 'experimental' is going to be out there. Also catch film
screenings, readings and other expressions
of creativity. The attached cafe is a very
groovy hang-out.

Sport

Petrovsky Stadium (Map pp772-3; ☎ 328 8903; www
.petrovsky.spb.ru; Petrovsky ostrov 2; Ⓜ Sportivnaya)
Petersburgers are fanatical about the fortunes
of local soccer team **Zenit** (www.fc-zenit.ru), who
usually play here. Tickets (R100 to R800) can
be purchased at theatre ticket booths or at the
stadium three days before a game.

SHOPPING

Bolshoy Gostiny Dvor (Map p776; www.bgd.ru; Nevsky
pr 35; Ⓜ Gostiny Dvor) The granddaddy of all St
Pete's department stores is looking mighty
fine after years of restoration. You'll find a
great selection of nearly everything here, including fashion and souvenirs, at reasonably
competitive prices.

Souvenir Market (Map p776; Konyushennaya pl;
⏰ 10am-dusk; Ⓜ Nevsky Pr) This very well-
stocked souvenir market is diagonally across
the canal from the Church of the Saviour on
Spilled Blood.

Tovar dlya Voennikh (Map p776; Sadovaya ul 26;
⏰ 10am-7pm Mon-Sat; Ⓜ Gostiny Dvor) The best
place to buy cool Russian military clothes and
memorabilia. Look out for the circular green-
and-gold sign with Military Shop written in
English; the entrance is inside the courtyard.

GETTING THERE & AWAY
Air

Pulkovo-1 (☎ 704 3822) and **Pulkovo-2** (☎ 704 3444)
are, respectively, the domestic and international terminals of St Petersburg's **Pulkovo airport** (off Map pp772-3; www.pulkovoairport.ru/eng). For
carriers that fly to Russia, see p799.

Tickets for all airlines can be purchased
from travel agencies and from the **Central
Airline Ticket Office** (Map p776; ☎ 315 0072; Nevsky pr
7; ⏰ 8am-8pm Mon-Fri, to 6pm Sat & Sun; Ⓜ Nevsky Pr),

which also has counters for train and international bus tickets.

Boat

From June to August **DFDS Lisko** (☎ 4012-660 404; www.dfdslisco.ru) runs a weekly ferry service on the *George Ots*, travelling between Baltiysk in Russia's Kaliningrad region and St Petersburg. **Trans-Eksim** (☎ 4012-660 468; www .transexim.ru) also runs weekly car ferries between Baltiysk and Ust-Luga, 150km west of St Petersburg. Tickets can be purchased at **Baltic Tours** (Map p776; ☎ 320 6663; www.baltictours.ru; Sergei Tyulenina per 4-13; Ⓜ Nevsky Pr).

Bus

St Petersburg's main bus station, **Avtovokzal No 2** (Map pp772-3; ☎ 766 5777; www.avokzal.ru, in Russian; nab Obvodnogo kanala 36; Ⓜ Ligovsky Pr) – there isn't a No 1 – has both international and European Russia services.

Tickets can be purchased here and at the **Central Airline Ticket Office** (Map p776; ☎ 315 0072; Nevsky pr 7; Ⓨ 8am-8pm Mon-Fri, to 6pm Sat & Sun; Ⓜ Nevsky Pr).

Buses are the cheapest way to travel to Tallinn (R900, 7½ hours, seven daily) and Rīga (R700 to R1050, 11 hours, two daily), but for Moscow the train is a better option. There are regular buses from St Petersburg to Helsinki, Finland (eight hours, four to six daily).

Train

Trains to/from Moscow go from **Moskovsky vokzal** (Moscow Station; Map p776; ☎ 768 4597; pl Vosstaniya; Ⓜ Pl Vosstaniya), while direct services to/from the Baltics, Belarus, the Czech Republic, Germany, Hungary, Poland and Ukraine run from **Vitebsky vokzal** (Vitebsk Station; Map pp772-3; ☎ 768 5807; Zagorodny pr 52; Ⓜ Pushkinskaya). Trains to/from Helsinki run from **Finlyandsky vokzal** (Finland station; Map pp772-3; ☎ 768 7687; pl Lenina 6; Ⓜ Ploshchad Lenina) and **Ladozhsky vokzal** (Ladoga station; Map pp772-3; ☎ 768 5304; Zhanevsky pr 73; Ⓜ Ladozhskaya), which also has services to/from the far north of Russia and towards the Urals.

Tickets can also be purchased at the train stations, the **Central Train Ticket Office** (Map p776; ☎ 762 3344; nab kanala Griboedova 24; Ⓨ 8am-8pm Mon-Sat, to 4pm Sun; Ⓜ Nevsky Pr), the **Central Airline Ticket Office** (Map p776; ☎ 315 0072; Nevsky pr 7; Ⓨ 8am-8pm Mon-Fri, to 6pm Sat & Sun; Ⓜ Nevsky Pr) and many travel agencies around town.

GETTING AROUND
To/From the Airport

Pulkovo airport, about 17km south of the centre, is easily and (very) cheaply accessed by metro and bus. From Moskovskaya metro station, bus 39 runs to Pulkovo-1, the domestic terminal, and bus 13 runs to Pulkovo-2, the international terminal. There are also plenty of *marshrutky*. The trip takes about 15 minutes and costs just R16 to R22. Or you can take the buses and *marshrutky* K3 all the way from the airport to Sennaya pl in the city centre or K39 to pl Vosstaniya (R35). Buses stop directly outside each of the terminals.

By taxi you should be looking at around R600 to get to the city (R400 is the price from the city to the airport). Most taxi drivers will request more from foreigners, so be prepared to haggle or take the bus.

Public Transport

The **metro** (Ⓨ 5.30am-midnight) is usually the quickest way around the city and you'll rarely wait more than three minutes for a train. *Zhetony* (tokens; R17) can be bought from booths in the stations. If you are staying more than a day or two, however, it's worth buying a 'smart card' (a plastic card that the machine reads when you touch the circular light), which is good for multiple journeys over a fixed time period. There's around a R30 deposit for the card, on top of which you'll pay a minimum of R140 (10 trips/seven days).

Marshrutkas are a quick alternative to the slower buses and trolleybuses. Costs vary with the route, but the average fare is R20 and fares are displayed prominently inside each van.

Taxi

Holding your arm out will cause unofficial taxis to stop very quickly. The standard rate for a short distance (1km to 2km) is R50, R100 for a journey roughly between 2km and 5km, and whatever you can negotiate for trips longer than about 5km. As a foreigner, expect to have the price raised. Always agree on a price before getting into the taxi.

To book a taxi in advance try **Peterburgskoe taksi 068** (Petersburg Taxi; ☎ 068, 324 7777), **Taxi Blues** (☎ 271 8888) or **Taxi-Million** (☎ 700 0000). For more information about taxis in Russia, see p800.

WORTH THE TRIP: PETRODVORETS & TSARSKOE SELO

Among the several palace estates that the tsars built around St Petersburg as country retreats, the ones not to miss are **Petrodvorets** (☎ 427 0073; www.peterhof.ru, in Russian; ul Razvodnaya 2), 29km west of St Petersburg, and **Tsarskoe Selo** (Tsar's Village; ☎ 465 2281; http://eng.tzar.ru; Sadovaya ul 7), 25km south of the city in the town of Pushkin.

If time is limited, Petrodvorets, also known as Peterhof, is the one to opt for, mainly because of its **Grand Cascade & Water Avenue**, a symphony of over 140 fountains and canals located in the **Lower Park** (Nizhny Park; adult/student R300/150; ☯ 9am-8pm Mon-Fri, to 9pm Sat & Sun). The fountains only work from mid-May to early October (from 11am to 5pm Monday to Friday and 11am to 6pm Saturday and Sunday), but the gilded ensemble still looks marvellous at any time of the year.

Tsarskoe Selo's big draw is the baroque **Catherine Palace** (Yekaterininsky dvorets; adult/student R500/250; ☯ 10am-6pm Wed-Mon, closed last Mon of month), built between 1752 and 1756, but almost destroyed in WWII. The exterior and 20-odd rooms, including the dazzling Great Hall and Amber Room, have been expertly restored.

Buses and *marshrutky* (minibuses) to Petrodvorets (R45, 30 minutes) run frequently from outside metro stations Avtovo, Leninsky Pr and Pr Veteranov. There's also the K404 bus from outside the Baltisky vokzal (R50, 40 minutes). All stop near the main entrance to the Upper Garden.

From May to September, the *Meteor* hydrofoil (one-way/return R400/700, 30 minutes) goes every 20 to 30 minutes from 9.30am to at least 7pm from the jetty in front of St Petersburg's Hermitage.

Marshrutky (R30, 30 minutes) regularly shuttle to Pushkin from outside metro Moskovskaya. Infrequent suburban trains run from St Petersburg's Vitebsk station. For Tsarskoe Selo, get off at Detskoe Selo station (R36) from where *marshrutky* (R15) run to the estate.

KALININGRAD REGION
КАЛИНИНГРА
ДСКАЯ ОБЛАСТЬ

pop 955,281

Sandwiched by Poland to the south and Lithuania to the east and north, and with 148km of Baltic coastline to the west, the Kaliningrad region is a Russian exclave that's intimately attached to the Motherland yet also a world apart. In this 'Little Russia' – only 15,100 sq km – you'll find plenty of fine hotels and restaurants, a youthful outlook plus all the traditions of the big parent, wrapped up in a manageable package of beautiful countryside, splendid beaches and fascinating historical sights.

The Teutonic Knights ruled the Baltic in the Middle Ages from the city of Königsburg (now Kaliningrad). While Stalin ethnically cleansed the land of all Germans, centuries of Germanic culture and architecture were not as easily removed. In the go-ahead capital Kaliningrad, beside glitzy new shopping malls, the old cathedral has been rebuilt, and there are plans to resurrect the castle and obliterated medieval core of the city. An hour's drive north lies the Baltic coast and the pine forests and Sahara-style dunes of the Kurshskaya Kosa National Park, a Unesco World Heritage site.

The region's airport offers plenty of connections from points around Europe. Friendly, open-minded locals will only be too happy to assist you once you arrive – anyone familiar with the insular ways of big Russia will be amazed. Everyone else will be equally delighted to discover this Russian gem.

See p798 for information on visas for Kaliningrad.

History

The indigenous pagan population of the region was conquered in the 13th century by Teutonic Knights. By 1525 the area, famous since Roman times for its amber deposits, had become the Duchy of Prussia, Europe's first Protestant state, with its capital at Königsberg. The city's liberal atmosphere attracted scholars, artists, scientists and entrepreneurs from across Europe; in 1697 Peter the Great visited as part of Russia's Grand Embassy, and the 18th-century philosopher Immanuel Kant spent all his life there.

After WWI, East Prussia was separated from the rest of Germany when Poland regained statehood. The three-month campaign by which the Red Army took it in 1945 was one of the fiercest of WWII, with hundreds of thousands of casualties on both sides. In 1946 the region was renamed Kaliningrad in honour of the recently deceased Mikhail Kalinin, one of Stalin's more vicious henchmen. The surviving German population was either killed, relocated to far-flung corners of the Soviet Union or deported to Germany. The population is now predominantly Russian.

In the early 1990s, following the breakup of the Soviet Union, the region struggled through extreme economic difficulties. The discovery of oil off the coast and the granting of special economic zone status has helped it turn the corner. There has been talk of Kaliningrad becoming an independent fourth 'Baltic state'. The prospects for this are highly unlikely, as Russia would have much to lose by granting autonomy to this resource-rich region. The Baltic fleet is headquartered in Baltiysk (off limits to Western tourists unless on a specially arranged tour), and the area's strategic importance is key, particularly in light of recent EU expansion east. Most importantly, the vast majority of Russians living here are proud of their Slavic heritage and ties to the Motherland.

KALININGRAD КАЛИНИНГРАД
☎ 4012 / pop 423,000

A fascinating, affluent city that's clearly going places, Kaliningrad is an excellent introduction to Russia's most liberal region. Interesting museums and historical sights sprout in between the shiny new shopping centres and multitude of leafy parks that soften vast swaths of brutal Soviet architecture. Plentiful transport options and good hotels mean you can use the city as a base to see the rest of the region.

Founded as a Teutonic fort in 1255, Königsberg joined the Hanseatic League in 1340, and from 1457 to 1618 was the residence of the grand masters of the Teutonic order and their successors, the dukes of Prussia. The first king of Prussia, Frederick I, was crowned here in 1701. For the next couple of centuries the city flourished, producing citizens such as the philosopher Immanuel Kant (1724–1804).

RUSSIA

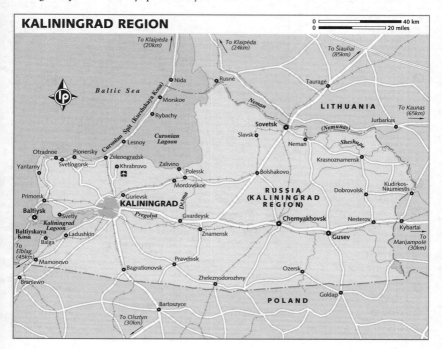

KALININGRAD REGION

0 _____ 40 km
0 _____ 20 miles

RUSSIA

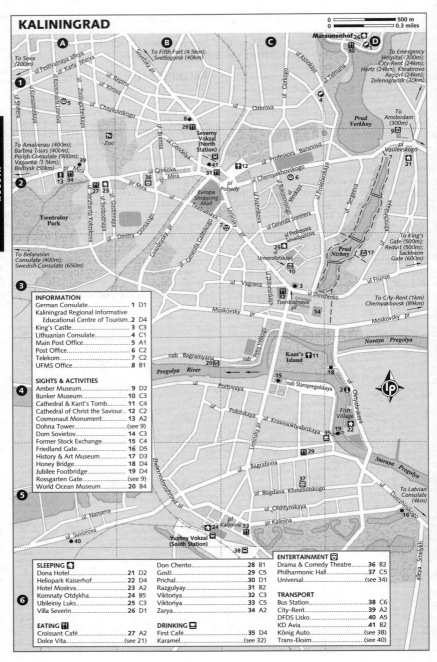

KALININGRAD

0 ——— 500 m
0 ——— 0.3 miles

INFORMATION

German Consulate.............................1 D1
Kaliningrad Regional Informative
  Educational Centre of Tourism.....2 D4
King's Castle......................................3 C3
Lithuanian Consulate........................4 C1
Main Post Office...............................5 A1
Post Office..6 C2
Telekom..7 C2
UFMS Office.....................................8 B1

SIGHTS & ACTIVITIES

Amber Museum.................................9 D2
Bunker Museum..............................10 C3
Cathedral & Kant's Tomb...............11 C4
Cathedral of Christ the Saviour.....12 C2
Cosmonaut Monument...................13 A2
Dohna Tower............................(see 9)
Dom Sovietov..................................14 C3
Former Stock Exchange..................15 C4
Friedland Gate.................................16 D5
History & Art Museum.....................17 D3
Honey Bridge...................................18 D4
Jubilee Footbridge...........................19 D4
Rossgarten Gate.......................(see 9)
World Ocean Museum.....................20 B4

SLEEPING

Dona Hotel.......................................21 D2
Heliopark Kaiserhof.........................22 D4
Hotel Moskva...................................23 A2
Komnaty Otdykha............................24 B5
Ubileiniy Luks..................................25 C3
Villa Severin....................................26 D1

EATING

Croissant Café.................................27 A2
Dolce Vita..................................(see 21)

Don Chento......................................28 B1
Gosti...29 C5
Prichal..30 D1
Razgulyay...31 B2
Viktoriya...32 C3
Viktoriya...33 C5
Zarya..34 A2

DRINKING

First Café...35 D4
Karamel.....................................(see 32)

ENTERTAINMENT

Drama & Comedy Theatre.............36 B2
Philharmonic Hall...........................37 C5
Universal.....................................(see 34)

TRANSPORT

Bus Station......................................38 C6
City-Rent..39 A2
DFDS Lisko......................................40 A5
KD Avia..41 B2
König Auto.................................(see 38)
Trans-Eksim..............................(see 40)

Old photos attest that the former Königsberg was once an architectural gem equal to Prague or Kraków. The combined destruction of WWII and the Soviet decades put paid to all that. However, there are lovely prewar residential suburbs that evoke the Prussian past, and following the successful reconstruction of the war-damaged cathedral (mainly thanks to donations from Germany), the authorities also have big plans to remodel Kaliningrad with a mix of futuristic and heritage-inspired building projects.

Orientation

Leninsky pr, a north–south avenue, is the city's main artery, running over 3km from the bus and main train station, Yuzhny vokzal (South Station), to Severny vokzal (North Station). About halfway it crosses the Pregolya River and passes the cathedral, the city's major landmark. The city's modern heart is further north, around pl Pobedy.

Information

Russkaya Evropa (www.russeuropa.com) publishes the free quarterly listings magazine *Welcome to Kaliningrad*, available in hotel lobbies, which has useful information in English on the city and region; see its website for more information.

Baltma Tours (☎ 931 931; www.baltma.ru; pr Mira 94, 4th fl) The efficient, multilingual staff here can arrange visas, accommodation and a surprising array of local excursions – including one to Yantarny, home of what was once the world's largest amber mine, and another to the military port city of Baltiysk (formerly Pillau), which requires a special permit to enter.

Emergency Hospital (☎ 466 989; ul Nevskogo 90; ☯ 24hr)

Kaliningrad Regional Informative Educational Centre of Tourism (☎ 655 055; www.tourismkalinin grad.ru; Fish Village, ul Oktyabrskaya 2; ☯ 10am-8pm) Staffed by a helpful, English-speaking crew; you can buy guides to the region here.

King's Castle (☎ 350 782; www.kaliningradinfo.ru; Hotel Kaliningrad, Leninsky pr 81; ☯ 8am-8pm Mon-Fri, 9am-4pm Sat) A private tourist agency that also operates as a tourist information centre. You can access the internet here and book tours of the city and to the Kurshskaya Kosa.

Königsberg.ru (www.konigsberg.ru) Web-based tour agency through which you can book hotels and arrange visas, including the 72-hour express visa.

Main post office (ul Kosmonavta Leonova 22; ☯ 9am-8pm Mon-Fri, 10am-6pm Sat & Sun) Located about 600m north of pr Mira. It also has internet access.

Post office (ul Chernyakhovskogo 32; ☯ post office 10am-2pm & 3-7pm Mon-Fri, 10am-2pm & 3-6pm Sat, internet room 10am-2pm & 3-10pm Mon-Sat) Internet access (R50 per hour) and postal services.

Telekom (ul Teatralnaya 13; ☯ 9am-7pm) For long-distance calls, fax and internet access (R50 per hour).

University Guides (foreign.lit.dep@gmail.com) Send an email to these guys if you're looking for a student guide to show you around town.

Sights

CATHEDRAL & AROUND

A Unesco World Heritage site, the majestic red-brick Gothic **cathedral** (☎ 646 868; adult/ student R100/50; ☯ 9am-5pm) dates back to 1333. For decades after WWII, its ruins rose above the once densely populated Kant Island – now all parkland dotted with sculptures. Rebuilt during the 1990s, the cathedral is occasionally used for concerts, and its ground floor has both small Lutheran and Orthodox chapels. Upstairs you'll find the reconstructed carved-wood Wallenrodt Library, interesting displays of old Königsberg and objects from archaeological digs. On the top floor is an austere room with the death mask of Immanuel Kant, whose rose-marble **tomb** lies outside on the outer north side.

Crossing the nearby **Honey Bridge**, the oldest of the city's bridges, you'll arrive at the half-timber riverside development known as **Fish Village** (Ribnaya Derevnya). Disneyland-ish it may be, but this collection of hotels, tourist information office, shops and restaurants is a laudable attempt to reprise some of the city's destroyed architectural heritage. The village's first phase included the handsome new **Jubilee Footbridge**.

Across the river south of the cathedral is the **Former Stock Exchange** (Leninsky pr 83), a fine Renaissance-style building built in the 1870s; it now houses a disco and various community clubs.

WORLD OCEAN MUSEUM

Two boats and a sub can be explored at this excellent **museum** (☎ 538 915; www.vitiaz.ru; nab Petra Velikogo 1; adult/student R200/120, individual vessels R120/80; ☯ 11am-6pm Wed-Sun Apr-Oct, 10am-5pm Wed-Sun Nov-Mar), strung along the banks of the Pregolya River. The highlight is the handsome former expedition vessel, *Vityaz*, which during its heyday conducted many scientific studies around the world. Also part of the complex is the Maritime Hall in a newly restored old warehouse building; it has interesting displays on fishing and the sea-connected history of Kaliningrad, as well as rare archaeological finds of the remains of a 19th-century wooden fishing boat.

AMBER MUSEUM

On the edge of the Prud Verkny (Upper Pond), this **museum** (☎ 466 888; www.amber museum.ru; pl Marshala Vasilevskogo 1; adult/student R90/60; ✆ 10am-6pm Tue-Sun) has some 6000 examples of amber artworks, the most impressive being from the Soviet period. In addition to enormous pieces of jewellery containing prehistoric insects suspended within, some of the more fascinating works include an amber flute and a four-panelled amber and ivory chalice depicting Columbus, the *Niña*, the *Pinta* and the *Santa Maria*.

CITY FORTIFICATIONS & GATES

The Amber Museum is housed in the attractive **Dohna Tower**, a bastion of the city's old defensive ring. The adjacent **Rossgarten Gate**, one of Königsberg's city gates, contains a decent restaurant.

Several other bits of the fortifications and gates remain scattered around the city. The impressively renovated **King's Gate** (☎ 581 272; ul Frunze 112; adult/student R80/40; ✆ 11am-6pm Wed-Sun) houses a museum with cool models of old Königsberg and exhibits on the personalities who shaped the region's history. A little south of here is the twin-towered **Sackheim Gate** (cnr pr Moscovsky & Litovsky Val).

The **Friedland Gate** (pr Kalinina 6; adult/child R20/10; ✆ 10am-5pm Tue-Sun) contains a small museum with a great map plotting the locations of the 13 original city gates. There's an intriguing

arms display, and the original cobblestone road that ran through the gate is visible inside.

AMALIENAU & MARAUNENHOF

Casual strolls through the linden-scented, tree-lined neighbourhoods of Amalienau to the city's west along pr Mira and Maraunenhof at the north end of the Prud Verkhny are the best way to get an idea of genteel pre-WWII Königsberg. Amalienau is particularly lovely, with an eclectic range of villas; many along ul Kutuzova and the streets connecting pr Pobedy and Mira were designed by the architect Friedrich Heitmann. In Maraunenhof you'll find several appealing small hotels, as well as the German consulate, with its strikingly colourful visa section.

OTHER MUSEUMS

The **History & Art Museum** (☎ 453 844; ul Klinicheskaya 21; adult/student R70/50; ✆ 10am-6pm Tue-Sun), housed in a reconstructed 1912 concert hall by the banks of the pretty Prud Nizhny (Lower Pond), is worth a visit. Though it mainly focuses on Soviet rule, the German past is not ignored in the many interesting displays. There are chilling posters of the castle's destruction.

Cross the footbridge over Prud Nizhny and walk west towards the university to discover the fascinating **Bunker Museum** (Muzei Blindazh; ☎ 536 593; Universitetskaya ul 2; adult/student R70/50; ✆ 10am-4pm Tue-Sun), the buried German command post in 1945, where the city's last German commander, Otto van Lasch, capitulated to the Soviets.

PLOSHCHAD POBEDY & PROSPEKT MIRA

Ploshchad Pobedy is the site of several modern shopping centres and the new **Cathedral of Christ**

THE RETURN OF THE CASTLE?

Königsberg's majestic castle, dating from 1255, once stood on Tsentralnaya pl. Severely damaged during WWII and dynamited out of existence in the late 1960s, it was replaced by the outstandingly ugly **Dom Sovietov** (House of Soviets). During the eyesore's construction it was discovered that the land below it was hollow, with a (now flooded) four-level underground passage connecting to the cathedral. The decaying half-finished building has never been used.

Now Kaliningrad's chief planner, Alexander Bazhin has put forward a plan, endorsed by no less a figure than former President Putin, to rebuild the castle and some of the historical streets once surrounding it, as part of a scheme that also includes a clutch of modern skyscrapers and a convention centre to mask Dom Sovietov. The estimated US$100 million needed for the project has yet to be raised. In the meantime, it's possible to peer down at the archeological dig that has revealed the **castle's foundations** (☎ 350 782; 81 Leninsky pr; admission free; ✆ noon-3pm Sat & Sun).

the **Saviour** (Kafedralny Sobor Khrista Spasitelya), its gold domes visible from many points in the city.

Extending west of the square is pr Mira, lined with shops and cafes leading to some of the city's prettiest areas. Along here you'll find the **zoo** (Zoopark; ☎ 218 924; pr Mira 26; adult/student R100/40; ☼ 9am-9pm Jun-Aug, 10am-5pm Sep-May), which before WWII was considered the third best in the world, but is now in a sorry state (donations accepted – and needed!).

Further west is the striking **Cosmonaut Monument**, a gem of Soviet iconography. It honours the several cosmonauts who hail from the region. Just west, as pr Pobedy branches out from pr Mira, is the entrance to **Tsentralny Park** (Central Park), a splendid, forestlike park on the grounds of an old German cemetery.

Festivals & Events
The **Baltic Season** (www.baltseasons.ru) is an international festival of arts that offers up a range of musical and theatrical productions from June to November each year. In August there's also the **Don Chento Jazz Festival** (www.en.jazzfestival.ru).

Sleeping
Kaliningrad is well served with midrange and top-end hotels, but it's crying out for a decent hostel or budget accommodation.

Komnaty Otdykha (☎ 586 447; pl Kalinina; r R800) Inside the south train station, the resting rooms are surprisingly quiet and clean, with OK shared bathrooms. Find them by turning right down the corridor after the ticket hall and walking up to the third floor.

our pick **Villa Severin** (☎ 365 373; www.villa-severin.ru; ul Leningradskaya 9a; s/d from R950/1900; ✦ ▣) There's a very homely atmosphere at this pretty villa, set back from the Prud Verkny, with nine comfortably furnished rooms including simple student rooms. It also has a small sauna and cafe.

Hotel Moskva (☎ 352 300; www.hotel.kaliningrad.ru; pr Mira 19; s/d from R1950/2400) Kaliningrad's oldest hotel has been reborn after extensive renovations and has bright spacious rooms, friendly atmosphere and a good location. Under the same management are the Hotel Kaliningrad and Chaika Hotel.

Ubileiniy Luks (☎ 519 024; www.ubilejny-lux.ru; ul Universitetskaya 2; r/apt from R2500/3800; ✦ ▣) Atop a business centre, this hotel's central quiet location is ideal. Its 13 rooms are all enormous, and most have kitchens. Wi-fi internet is available.

Dona Hotel (☎ 351 650; dona.kaliningrad.ru; pl Marshala Vasilevskogo 2; s/d incl breakfast from R2550/3050; ✦ ▣) Featuring design touches worthy of a Philippe Starck protégé, the Dona is a tribute to sleek modernism. It has friendly English-speaking staff, pleasant buffet breakfasts, and Dolce Vita, one of the city's best restaurants.

Heliopark Kaiserhof (☎ 592 222; www.heliopark.ru; ul Oktyabrskaya 8; s/d incl breakfast from R3350/4150; ✦ ▣) Anchoring Fish Village, this is a very nicely designed and furnished hotel, with a central atrium and superstylish rooms.

Eating
our pick **Croissant Café** (pr Mira 24; meals R100; ☼ 9am-11pm Sun-Thu, 24hr Fri & Sat) A chic baked-goods heaven. Indulge in flaky pastries, quiches, muffins, biscuits and cakes, as well as omelettes and bliny for breakfast.

Don Chento (☎ 937 672; www.donchento.ru; Sovetsky pr 9-11; meals R100-200) No need to endure depressing Soviet throwback *stolovye* (canteens) for budget meals when you can dig in at the self-serve salad bar or pick a slice of pizza at this stylish chain with several branches across the city. It sponsors a jazz festival each August (left).

Razgulyay (☎ 533 689; pl Pobedy 1; meals R100-200) The extensive buffet here features roasted meats, salads, fresh juices and many other tasty selections in a cheery, folk-style setting. There's also a more formal restaurant.

Zarya (☎ 213 929; pr Mira 43; meals R200-300; ☼ 10am-3am) Fashionable brasserie in the lobby of the Scala cinema that also has an attractive outdoor area. Service can be hit-and-miss, but the food is reliable.

Prichal (☎ 703 030; ul Verkhneozyornaya 2a; meals R200-500; ☼ noon-1am Sun-Thu, to 2am Fri & Sat) Private huts in a pretty garden overlooking the Prod Verkhny make this spruced-up Soviet-era Georgian restaurant a memorable dining experience.

our pick **Gosti** (☎ 384 747; Maliy per 32; meals R400-800; ☼ noon-midnight) Attached to the city's technical college, this charming restaurant has a wonderful homey atmosphere, inventive food and attentive service. At lunchtime everything is half-price.

Dolce Vita (☎ 351 612; pl Marshala Vasilevskogo 2; mains R500-1000; ☼ noon-midnight) Bust your budget for the fantastic food at this elegant restaurant next to the Dona Hotel. The melon-and-mint gazpacho is inspired.

RUSSIA

Self-caterers should visit the lively central market on ul Chernyakhovskogo or **Viktoriya** (Kaliningrad Plaza, Leninsky pr 30; 10am-10pm), a large Western-style supermarket; it also has a handy branch opposite the bus and train station at pl Kalinina.

Drinking

First Café (644 829; ul Yepronovskaya 21) Kaliningrad's answer to Starbucks has three other locations in the city other than this branch opposite Fish Village. It's a stylish cafe-bar operation with a wide range of drinks, snacks and free wi-fi.

Karamel (Kaliningrad Plaza, Leninsky pr 30; 24hr) On the 7th floor of a shopping centre, Karamel offers splendid city views, a DJ spinning top sounds, and a wide range of drinks and dishes.

Reduit (461 951; Litovsky Val 27) Endure desultory service at this beer hall and restaurant to sample the tasty selection of ales brewed on the premises.

Entertainment

NIGHTCLUBS

Major DJs from Russia and Western Europe jet in for gigs at Kaliningrad's many clubs, which open around 9pm but typically don't get going until well after midnight. Top picks:

Universal (952 996; www.club-universal.com; pr Mira 43; admission from R300) Kaliningrad's classiest club.

Vagonka (956 677; www.vagonka.net; Stanochnaya ul 12; admission from R150) Best option for the under-21 crowd and drinks are cheap.

Amsterdam (353 306; www.amsterdam-club.ru; 38/11 Litovsky Val; admission R100-400; 7pm-2am Sun-Thu, until 6am Fri & Sat) Hidden 200m down an unnamed side street off Litovsky Val, Kaliningrad's sole gay club is best visited on weekends.

PERFORMING ARTS

Drama & Comedy Theatre (212 422; pr Mira 4; tickets R150-200) Plays, ballets and classical concerts are staged in this handsomely restored building.

Philharmonic Hall (448 890; ul Bogdana Khmelnitskogo 61a; tickets from R180) This beautifully restored neo-Gothic church, which has excellent acoustics, hosts organ concerts, chamber-music recitals and the occasional symphony orchestra.

Classical concerts are also occasionally held at the cathedral.

Getting There & Away

There are three border crossings from Poland and four from Lithuania.

AIR

Kaliningrad's **Khrabrovo airport** (459 426) 24km north of the city, is the hub of **KD Avia** (355 815; www.kdavia.eu; pl Pobedy 4), which has flights to Moscow (around R1645 one-way) and St Petersburg (R3100 one-way), as well as to France, Germany, Italy, Spain, the UK and Ukraine.

BOAT

DFDS Lisko (660 404; www.dfdslisco.ru; ul Suvorova 45) is the agent for the weekly ferry service on the *George Ots*, travelling between Baltiysk and St Petersburg, the *Vilnius* ferry between Baltiysk and Sassnitz in Germany, and the *Lisco Patria* ferry between Baltiysk and Klaipéda. **Trans-Exim** (660 468; www.transexim .ru; ul Suvorova 45) also runs weekly car ferries between Baltiysk and Ust-Luga, 150km west of St Petersburg. Check the websites for the latest prices and schedules.

BUS

The **bus station** (643 635; ul Zheleznodorozhnaya 7) is next to Yuzhny vokzal. Buses depart from here to every corner of the region, including Svetlogorsk (R50, one hour, every 30 minutes). International destinations served include Klaipéda (R240, three hours, four daily), Kaunas/Vilnius (R465/640, six/eight hours, two daily), Rīga (R660, nine hours, two daily), Tallinn (R1192, 14 hours, one daily), Olshtyn/Gdansk (R350/500, four/five hours, twice daily) and Warsaw (R650, nine hours, one daily). **König Auto** (460 304) has several buses weekly to Berlin (R2300) and many other German cities.

The best way to Svetlogorsk (R50, one hour) and Zelenogradsk (R45, 45 minutes) is via *mashrutky* from the bus stop next to Severny vokzal (North Station) on Sovetsky pr. They run about every 15 minutes or so until about 8pm.

TRAIN

There are two stations in the city: **Severny vokzal** (North Station; 601 838) and the larger **Yuzhny vokzal** (South Station; 600 888). All long-distance and many local trains go from Yuzhny vokzal, passing through but not always stopping at Severny vokzal. It's important to note that *all* trains, including local ones, run on Moscow time, so if a train is scheduled to depart at 10am on the timetable it will leave at 9am Kaliningrad time.

Local trains include around 12 a day to Svetlogorsk (R45, 1¼ hours) and seven to Zelenogradsk (R37, 30 minutes).

Services to greater Russia and elsewhwere in Europe include four daily trains to Vilnius (R1700, six hours), one daily to Berlin (R2900, 14 hours), three daily to Moscow (R2700, 23 hours) and one daily to St Petersburg (R3000, 26 hours). A train goes every other day to Kyiv (R2500, 25 hours).

Getting Around

Tickets for trams, trolleybuses, buses and minibuses are sold on board (R10). To get to the domestic airport, take bus 138 from the bus station (R30, 30 minutes). Taxis ask at least R700 from the airport, and less to the airport.

If you're planning on touring the region, Kaliningrad is a good place to rent a car. Agencies include **City-Rent** (☎ 509 191; www.city -rent39.ru; pr Mira 46 & Moskovsky pr 182a). It also has a branch at the airport, as does **Hertz** (☎ 761 555; www.hertz.ru; Sovetsky pr 21a). Rates start at R800 per day.

SVETLOGORSK СВЕТЛОГОРСК
☎ 40153 / pop 10,950

Developed in the early 20th century as a spa resort, this pleasant, slow-placed town 35km northwest of Kaliningrad has a narrow beach backed by steep sandy slopes, pretty old German houses, revamped sanatoriums, top-class hotels, a delightful shady forest setting scattered with artful sculptures, and a well-maintained promenade. However, if beaches are your thing, the ones at the Kurshskaya Kosa are far nicer and cleaner.

Svetlogorsk is quite spread out. Svetlogorsk II, the train terminus, is on ul Lenina, the town's major street running east–west and bisected by ul Oktyabskaya. To the south, Kaliningradskiy pr runs past the tranquil Tikhoe pond.

The **Svetlogorsk tourist information centre** (☎ 22098; www.tourism.svetlagorsk.org; ul Karl Marksa 7a; ☼ 9am-7pm Mon-Fri, 10am-7pm Sat, 10am-4pm Sun) has helpful English-speaking staff who can assist with hotel bookings, tours and car rental, among other things. There's also internet access here (R35 per hour).

Sights

A 15-minute walk west of the town centre in the village of Otradnoe is the charming **Herman Brachert House Museum** (Doma-Muzei Germana Brakheta; ☎ 21166; www.brachert.ru; ul Tokareva 7; admission R100; ☼ 10am-5pm Sat-Thu), the former home of the sculptor whose work can be spotted all around Svetlogorsk; his bronze *Nymph* statue resides in a mosaic-decorated shell on the promenade.

Ul Oktyabrskaya is lined with handsome buildings, including the striking 25m-high **water tower** built in Jugendstil (art nouveau) style; take a peep inside the sanatorium beneath to see the colourful wall murals. Nearby, at the attractive wooden **Organ Hall** (Organniy Zal; ☎ 21761; organ-makarov.narod.ru; ul Kurortnaya 3; tickets R300), concerts are held throughout the week.

The east end of the promenade is graced by an impressive **sundial**, decorated with an eye-catching mosaic of the zodiac.

Sleeping & Eating

Stary Doktor (☎ 21362; www.alter-doctor.ru; ul Gagarina 12; s/d R2200/2400) In an old German home, this is one of Svetlogorsk's more charming options. Rooms are simple and cosy.

Hotel Universal (☎ 743 658; www.hotel-universal .ru; ul Nekrasova 3; s/d R2200/2600) Conveniently close to the train station and set in its own quiet grounds, this modern small hotel is nicely designed and has a variety of spacious rooms.

Falke Hotel Resort (☎ 21605; www.falke-hotel.ru; ul Lenina 16; s/d from R4700/7000;) With its tasteful luxury style, the Falke is a good choice for pampering. Its indoor pool, in a balmy winter garden, is big enough for a decent swim.

Kafe Blinnaya (Oktyabrskaya ul 22; bliny R20-30; ☼ 9am-6pm) It's self-serve for inexpensive bliny, salads etc at this simple cafe with streetside seating. The neighbouring bar (open noon to 3am) offers table service at higher prices.

Korvet (☎ 22040; Oktyabrskaya ul 36; pizza R200-300) This pizzeria and cafe based in the 1901 Kurhaus is a lovely place for a meal. Lounge in comfy sofas, listening to chill-out music; there are rugs to keep warm if it gets too chilly. On Friday and Saturday nights it morphs into party central, with DJs keeping things going into the early hours.

Getting There & Around

From Kaliningrad you can either take a train (R45, 1¼ hours, 12 daily) to Svetlogorsk II or

RUSSIA

the faster and far more frequent buses and taxi buses (R50, 45 to 60 minutes), which leave from Kaliningrad's bus station and stop outside Severny vokzal on Sovetsky pr. Buses arrive and depart from either in front of the Svetlogorsk II station or along Kaliningradskiy pr.

Svetlogorsk is easy to navigate on foot or by bicycle: rent bikes from **Eksi Tur** (ul Oktyabskaya 10; per hr/day R50/350; ⏰ 10am-5pm Mon-Sat).

KURSHSKAYA KOSA NATIONAL PARK
КУРШСКАЯ КОСА
☎ 40150

Tall, windswept sand dunes and dense pine forests teeming with wildlife lie along the 98km-long Curonian Spit, which divides the tranquil Curonian Lagoon from the Baltic Sea and is a Unesco World Heritage site. The 50 kilometres of the spit that lie in Russian territory are protected within the **Kurshskaya Kosa National Park** (www.kurshskayakosa.ru, in Russian; admission per person/car R30/200), a fascinating place to explore or to relax on pristine beaches.

Tranquil fishing and holiday villages dot the eastern coast. From south to north they are: Lesnoy, Rybachy (the largest, with a population of 1200), and Morskoe, which has spectacular views of the dunes from raised platforms at nearby **Vistota Efa** (42km mark; admission free). Also don't miss the **Dancing Forest** (Tantsuyushchiy Les; 37km mark; admission free), where wind-sculpted pines do indeed appear to be frozen mid-boogie.

To learn more about the park, drop by the **museum** (☎ 45119; 14km mark; admission R30; ⏰ 9.30am-4.30pm Tue-Sun May-Sep, 10am-4pm Tue-Sun Oct-Apr), where you can also see some deer and cute woodcarvings by a local artist. Call the museum to pre-arrange an excursion at the **Fringilla Field Station** (23km mark; tours R50; ⏰ 9am-6pm Apr-Oct) a bird-ringing centre in operation since 1957, where enormous funnelled nets can trap an average of 1000 birds a day.

In Lesnoy, **Kurshskaya Kosa** (☎ 45242; www .holiday39rus.ru; Tsentralnaya ul 17; s/d incl breakfast from R1800/1900; 🖵) is one of the Spit's best deals for accommodation and dining. It also has internet access and a cash machine and rents bicycles (R100 per hour). Also worth checking out is **Morskoe** (☎ 41330; www.morskoe.org; ul Dachnaya 6; r from R2350) in Morskoe.

With an early start it's possible to see most places on the Korshskaya Kosa by public transport. Four buses a day from Kaliningrad (via

Zelenogradsk) head up the spit en route to Klaipėda in Lithuania. There are at least three others that shuttle between Zelenogradsk and Morskoe (R57, 50 minutes). All stop in Lesnoy and Rybachy.

For more flexibility rent a car or arrange a tour in either Kaliningrad or Zelenogradsk, where a car and driver for half a day should cost around R1500.

RUSSIA DIRECTORY

ACCOMMODATION
Prices in this chapter are listed in budget order (from cheapest to most expensive). Budget accommodation is still hard to come by in Russia, and it is strongly recommended to book ahead for summer. During the white nights in St Petersburg in late June, booking early is essential.

For a dorm bed in Moscow or St Petersburg, rates run between R550 and R750. A double room with bathroom in a budget hotel will cost anything up to R3000. Elsewhere budget hotels can be as cheap as R500 a night with shared facilities, although R700 to R1500 is a more realistic minimum. You'll pay R1500 to R4000 for a midrange double (except in Moscow and St Petersburg, where midrange rooms start above R3000). For top-end accommodation expect to pay upwards of R4000 (R10,000 for Moscow and St Petersburg). Rooms in this chapter come with private bathroom unless otherwise stated. Some but not all hotels have nonsmoking rooms and/or floors.

BUSINESS HOURS
Russians work from early in the morning until mid-afternoon. Shops generally open between 9am and 11am and stay open until 8pm or 9pm. Banks have more traditional opening hours – usually 9am to 6pm Monday to Friday. Restaurants and bars are generally open from noon to midnight, except for a break between afternoon and evening meals, but they'll often work later than their stated hours if the establishment is full. In fact, many simply say that they work *do poslednnogo klienta* (until the last customer leaves).

CHILDREN
Russians love children and travelling there with them can be fun as long as you have a relaxed attitude and a degree of patience. In

Moscow, at Gorky Park, officially the **Park of Culture** (Map p753; ☎ 495-237 1266; ul Krymsky val; adult/child R80/20; ☺ 10am-10pm; Ⓜ Park Kultury), there's always plenty to entertain kids, including fairground rides and boats on the small lakes. The big cats and polar bears at the **Moscow Zoo** (Map pp756-7; ☎ 499-255 5375; www.moscowzoo.ru; cnr Barrikadnaya & Bolshaya Gruzinskaya uls; adult/child R150/free; ☺ 10am-7pm Tue-Sun May-Sep, to 5pm Tue-Sun Oct-Apr; Ⓜ Barrikadnaya) make it worth a visit.

In St Petersburg the Museum of Anthropology & Ethnography (p780) is an all-time favourite, with its display of mutants in jars, as are the Museum of Zoology (p780), with its stuffed animals, and the **Artillery Museum** (Voyenno-istorichesky Muzey Artilerii; Map p772-3; ☎ 232 0296; Alexandrovsky Park 7; adult/student courtyard R50/20, museum R300/150, camera R100; ☺ 11am-6pm Wed-Sun; Ⓜ Gorkovskaya), with its collection of tanks. For live animals there's the **Leningradsky Zoo** (Leningradsky Zoopark; Map p772-3; ☎ 232 4828; www.spbzoo.ru; Aleksandrovsky park 1; adult/child R250/60; ☺ 10am-5pm).

DANGERS & ANNOYANCES
Despite the media fascination with gangland killings and the 'Russian mafia', travellers have nothing to fear on this score – the increasingly respectable gangster classes are not interested in such small fry. Travellers need to be very careful of pickpockets, though. Also be aware that there are some local gangs that can surround and rob travellers quite brazenly in broad daylight, although these are rare.

Bear in mind that, while things have improved slowly, many police officers and other uniformed officials are on the make – some are not much better than the people they are employed to protect the public from. If you feel you are being unfairly treated or if the police try to make you go somewhere with them, pull out your mobile phone and threaten to call your embassy ('ya pozvonyu svoyu posolstvu'). This will usually be sufficient to make them leave you alone. However, if they still want you to go somewhere, it's best to call your embassy immediately.

Sadly, racism is a problem in Russia. Be vigilant on the streets around Hitler's birthday (20 April), when bands of right-wing thugs have been known to roam around spoiling for a fight with anyone who doesn't look Russian. It's a sure thing that if you look like a foreigner you'll be targeted with suspicion by many (the police, in particular) at any time of year. Although far from a daily occurence, Moscow and St Petersburg have all seen violent attacks on non-Russians, particularly people from the Caucasus. If you stick to the main tourist areas and stay aware of what's going on around you, you should be fine.

EMBASSIES & CONSULATES
Check out www.russianembassy.net for a full list of Russian embassies overseas.
Australia Moscow (Map pp756-7; ☎ 495-956 6070; www.russia.embassy.gov.au; Podkolokolny per 10a/2; Ⓜ Kitay Gorod); St Petersburg (Map p776; ☎ 812-315 1100; ul Italyanskaya 1; Ⓜ Nevsky pr)
Belarus Moscow (Map pp756-7; ☎ 495-924 7031; www.embassybel.ru; Maroseyka ul 17/6, 101000; Ⓜ Kitay Gorod); Kaliningrad (off Map p788; ☎ 4012-214 412; ul Dm Donskogo 35a); St Petersburg (Map p772-3; ☎ 812-274 7212; ul Bonch-Bruevicha 3a; Ⓜ Chernyshevskaya)
Canada (Map pp756-7; ☎ 495-925 6000; www.dfait-maeci.gc.ca/missions/russia-russie/menu-eng.asp; Starokonyushenny per 23, Moscow; Ⓜ Kropotkinskaya)
France Moscow (Map p753; ☎ 495-937 1500; www.ambafrance.ru; ul Bolshaya Yakimanka 45; Ⓜ Oktyabrskaya); St Petersburg (Map p776; ☎ 812-332 2270; nab reki Moyki 15; Ⓜ Nevsky Pr)
Germany Moscow (Map p753; ☎ 495-937 9500; www.moskau.diplo.de; Mosfilmovskaya ul 56; Ⓜ Universitet, then bus 119); Kaliningrad (Map p788; ☎ 4012-326 923; www.kaliningrad.diplo.de; ul Demyana Bednogo 13a); St Petersburg (Map pp772-3; ☎ 812-320 2400; Furshtatskaya ul 39; Ⓜ Chernyshevskaya)
Latvia (Map p788; ☎ 4012-706 755; Englesa ul 52a, Kaliningrad)
Lithuania (Map p788; ☎ 4012-959 486; Proletarskaya ul 133, Kaliningrad)
Netherlands (Map pp756-7; ☎ 495-797 2900; www.netherlands-embassy.ru; Kalashny per 6, Moscow; Ⓜ Arbatskaya)
New Zealand (Map pp756-7; ☎ 495-956 3579; www.nzembassy.msk.ru; Povarskaya ul 44, Moscow; Ⓜ Arbatskaya)
Poland (Map p788; ☎ 4012-950 419; www.polkon-kaliningrad.ru; Kashtanovaya Alleya 51, Kaliningrad)
Sweden (Map p788; ☎ 4012-959 400; Kutuzova ul 29, Kaliningrad)
UK Moscow (Map pp756-7; ☎ 495-956 7200; www.britemb.msk.ru; Smolenskaya nab 10; Ⓜ Smolenskaya); St Petersburg (Map p772-3; ☎ 812-320 3200; pl Proletarskoy Diktatury 5; Ⓜ Chernyshevskaya)
Ukraine (Map pp756-7; ☎ 495-629 9742; www.mfa.gov.ua; Leontevsky per 18, Moscow; Ⓜ Pushkinskaya)
USA Moscow (Map pp756-7; ☎ 495-728 5000; www.moscow.usembassy.gov; Bol Devyatinsky per 8; Ⓜ Barrikadnaya); St Petersburg (Map p772-3; ☎ 812-331 2600; ul Furshtatskaya 15; Ⓜ Chernyshevskaya)

GAY & LESBIAN TRAVELLERS

Homosexuality was legalised in Russia in the early 1990s but remains a divisive issue throughout the country. Not everyone goes as far as Moscow's mayor, Yury Luzhkov, who sided with ultraconservative protestors who broke up a gay parade in the capital in 2008, calling such events 'satanical'. But in general this is a conservative country, and being gay is frowned upon.

This said, there are active and relatively open gay and lesbian scenes in both Moscow and St Petersburg, and newspapers such as the *Moscow Times* and *St Petersburg Times* feature articles on gay and lesbian issues and listings for clubs, bars and events (although you shouldn't expect anything nearly as prominent as you might find in other major world centres). Away from these two major cities, the gay scene tends to be pretty much underground.

For a good overview, visit http://english .gay.ru, which has up-to-date information, good links and a resource for putting you in touch with personal guides for Moscow and St Petersburg.

HOLIDAYS

Russia's main public holidays:
New Year's Day 1 January
Russian Orthodox Christmas Day 7 January
Defender of the Fatherland Day 23 February
International Women's Day 8 March
International Labour Day/Spring Festival 1 May
Victory Day (1945) 9 May
Russian Independence Day (1991) 12 June
Unity Day 4 November

Many businesses are also closed from 1 to 7 January. Other widely celebrated holidays are Defenders of the Motherland Day (23 February) and Easter Monday.

INTERNET RESOURCES

Written and maintained by Russian backpackers, **Way to Russia** (www.waytorussia.net) is highly informative and on the ball. However, we've received complaints about buying train tickets through third parties associated with the site.

Also dip into **Russian Beyond the Headlines** (www.rbth.rg.ru), a wide-ranging online magazine with interesting features, sponsored by the daily paper *Rossiyskaya Gazeta*.

See p755 for a list of other useful internet resources.

MEDIA

Russia is a TV country, with radio and newspapers sidelined to a greater extent than elsewhere in Europe or the US. The internet has exploded in recent years with all manner of blogs on **LiveJournal** (www.livejournal.com), the main platform for free political and cultural debate in Russia, with both the opposition and progovernment forces broadly represented. So far, the censorship prominent in the old media (mainly in the form of self-censorship to avoid any potential clashes with the authorities) hasn't significantly affected the web, but there are fears that this freedom-of-speech loophole may also come to be plugged.

Magazines

There are scores of magazines on all topics, with respected news magazines including the weeklies *Kommersant Vlast* (www.kommersant.ru/vlast.aspx), *Russian Newsweek* (www.runewsweek.ru, in Russian), *Ogonyok* (www.ogoniok.com/) and *Expert* (http://eng. expert.ru).

Newspapers

Kommersant (www.kommersant.com), the leading paper and one of the most respected, and its main rival, *Izvestia* (http://izvestia .com), have financial ties with Gazprom, the state-owned gas monopoly, and so are muted in their criticism of the government. *Vedomosti* (www.vedomosti.ru/eng/), a joint venture by the *Financial Times* and *Wall Street Journal,* is a highly professional business daily.

The most famous anti-establishment newspaper is the tabloid *Novaya Gazeta* (http://en.novayagazeta.ru), which the crusading journalist Anna Politkovskaya wrote for before her murder in 2006. Other tabloid-type (but not necessarily -format) papers include *Komsomolskaya Pravda* (www .kp.ru, in Russian) and the weekly *Argumenty i Fakty* (www.aif.ru, in Russian), both very pro-government.

The *Moscow Times,* a free English-language daily, has built its reputation on healthy scepticism of the Kremlin and pioneering investigative writing. It's twice-weekly sister paper, the *St Petersburg Times,* is the best source of local news from Russia's second city.

Radio

Radio is broken into three bands: AM, UKV (66MHz to 77MHz) and FM (100MHz to

107MHz). A Western-made FM radio usually won't go lower than 85MHz. BBC's World Service short-wave (SW) frequencies in the morning, late evening and night are near 9410kHz, 12,095kHz (the best) and 15,070kHz, though exact settings vary depending on your location; see www.bbc.co.uk/worldservice.

TV
TV channels include Channel 1 (Pervy Kanal; www.1tv.ru), NTV (www.ntv.ru) Rossiya (www.rutv.ru), Kultura, Sport, RenTV (www.ren-tv.com), MTV-Russia, and Russia Today (http://RussiaToday.ru), an English-language satellite channel. Each region has a number of local channels, while in many hotels you'll have access to CNN and BBC World, plus several more satellite channels in English and other languages. For more on Russian TV, see p751.

MONEY
The Russian currency is the rouble, written as 'рубль' and abbreviated as 'ру' or 'р'. There are 100 kopecks in a rouble, and these come in coin denominations of one (rarely seen), five, 10 and 50. Also issued in coins, roubles come in amounts of one, two, five and 10, with banknotes in values of 10, 50, 100, 500, 1000 and 5000 roubles.

You can use all major credit and debit cards in ATMs, and in good restaurants and hotels. It's possible to exchange travellers cheques, although at a price. Euro or US-dollar cash is the best to bring, and should be in pristine condition – crumpled or old notes are often refused. Most major currencies can be exchanged at change booths all over any town in Russia. Look for the sign *obmen valyut*. You may be asked for your passport.

POST
The Russian post service **Potcha Rossia** (www.russianpost.ru/portal/en/home/posta) gets an unfair rap. Postcards, letters and parcels sent abroad usually arrive within a couple of weeks, but there are occasional lapses. To send a postcard or letter up to 20g anywhere in the world by air costs R19 or R16.10, respectively.

TELEPHONE
The international code for Russia is ☎ 7. The international access code from landline

EMERGENCY NUMBERS
- Ambulance ☎ 03
- Fire ☎ 01
- Police ☎ 02

phones in Russia is ☎ 8, followed by 10 after the second tone, followed by the country code. From mobile phones, however, just dial + before the country code to place an international call.

TRAVELLERS WITH DISABILITIES
Travellers using wheelchairs aren't well catered for in Russia; there's a lack of access ramps and lifts. However, attitudes are enlightened, and things are slowly changing. Major museums, such as the Hermitage and the Russian Museum, offer very good disabled access.

VISAS
Everyone needs a visa to visit Russia, and it will probably be your biggest single headache, so allow yourself at least a month before you travel to secure one. There are several types of visa, but most travellers will apply for a tourist visa, valid for 30 days from the date of entry. The process has three stages: invitation, application and registration.

Russia Visas
INVITATION
To obtain a visa, you first need an invitation. Hotels and hostels will usually issue anyone staying with them an invitation (or 'visa support') free or for a small fee (typically around €20 to €30). If you are not staying in a hotel or hostel, you will need to buy an invitation – costs typically range from €15 to €35 for a tourist visa depending on whether you require a single- or double-entry type and how quickly you need the invitation, and €45 to €270 for the various types of business visas. This can be done through most travel agents, via specialist agencies and online (see p798).

APPLICATION
Invitation in hand, you can then apply for a visa at any Russian embassy. Costs vary – anything from US$50 to US$450 – depending on the type of visa applied for and how quickly you need it. Rather frustratingly, Russian embassies

---

VISA AGENCIES

Several agencies specialise in getting visas. In the US, try **Zierer Visa Services** (☎ 1-866 788 1100; www.zvs.com), which also has affiliates in the UK (www.uk.cibt.com), France (www.action-visas .com/cibt), Germany (www.visum-centrale.de), Australia (https://visalink.com.au), the Netherlands (http://visumdienst.nl), Sweden and Denmark (www.cometconsular.com). Other agencies include the US-based **Russia-visa.com** (www.russia-visa.com) and the UK- and Russian-based **Real Russia** (www.realrussia.co.uk).

Invitations can also be procured online. Some recommended sites:

Express to Russia (www.expresstorussia.com)
Russian Business Visa (www.russian-business-visa.com)
Russia Direct (www.russiadirect.co.uk)
Visa Able (www.visaable.com)
Way to Russia (http://waytorussia.net)

---

are practically laws unto themselves, each with different fees and slightly different application rules. Avoid potential hassles by checking well in advance what these rules might be.

We highly recommended applying for your visa in your home country rather than on the road. Indeed, the rule is that you're supposed to do this, although we know from experience that some embassies and consulates can be more flexible than others.

REGISTRATION

On arrival, you should fill out an immigration card – a long white form issued by passport control; often these are given out in advance on your flight. You surrender one half of the form immediately to the passport control, while the other you keep for the duration of your stay and give up only on exiting Russia. Take good care of this as you'll need it for registration and could face problems while travelling in Russia – and certainly will on leaving – if you cannot produce it.

You must register your visa within three working days of arrival. If you're staying at a hotel, the receptionist should be able to do this for you for free or a small fee (typically around R900 to R1000). Once registered, you should receive a separate slip of paper confirming the dates you'll be staying at that particular hotel. Keep this safe – that's the document that any police who stop you will need to see.

If staying in a homestay or rental apartment, you'll either need to pay a travel agency (anything from R900 to R3200) to register your visa for you (most agencies will do this through a hotel) or make arrangements with the landlord or a friend to register you through the post office. See http://waytorussia.net/RussianVisa

/Registration.html for how this can be done, as well as a downloadable form that needs to be submitted at post offices.

Kaliningrad Visas

Citizens of Schengen countries, the UK, Switzerland and Japan can enter Kaliningrad with an on-demand 72-hour tourist visa. These need to be arranged via local tourist agencies, such as those listed, p789.

Unless you're flying, to reach the Kaliningrad region from anywhere else in Russia you must have either a double- or multiple-entry Russian visa, and/or visas for its neighbouring countries. Multiple-entry visas need to be arranged in advance.

If you have any questions or problems regarding Russian visas during your stay in the region, contact the main **UFMS office** (former PVU; ☎ 4012-563 809, 4012-563 804; Sovetsky pr 13, Room 9) in Kaliningrad.

WOMEN TRAVELLERS

The most common problem faced by foreign women in Russia is sexual harassment. It can be quite common to be propositioned in public, especially if you are walking alone at night. Unpleasant as it may be, this is rarely dangerous and a simple 'kak vam ne stydno' ('you should be ashamed of yourself') delivered in a suitably stern manner should send anyone on their way.

That said, Russian men can also be extremely chivalrous, and will open doors, give up their seats and wherever possible help any female out to a far greater degree than their Western counterparts. Women are also very independent, and you won't attract attention by travelling alone as a female.

10

TRANSPORT IN RUSSIA

GETTING THERE & AWAY

Air

Moscow's **Sheremetyevo-2** (SVO; ☎ 495-232 6565; www.sheremetyevo-airport.ru) and the much more congenial **Domodedovo** (DME; ☎ 495-933 6666; www.domodedovo.ru) airports host the bulk of Russia's international flights. There are also many daily international services to St Petersburg's **Pulkovo-2** (LED; ☎ 812-704 3444; www.pulkovoairport.ru/eng) airport and Kaliningrad's **Khrabrovo airport** (☎ 459 426).

Airlines flying into Russia include the following. Phone numbers are given for the Moscow office, where applicable.

Aeroflot Russian International Airlines (SU; ☎ 495-223 5555; www.aeroflot.ru/eng)
Air France (AF; ☎ 495-937 3839; www.airfrance.com)
Austrian Airlines (OS; ☎ 495-995 0995; www.aua.com)
Belavia (B2; ☎ 017-210 4100; www.belavia.by)
bmi (BD; ☎ in the UK 0870 6070 555; www.flybmi.com)
British Airways (BA; ☎ 495-363 2525; www.britishairways.com)
ČSA (Czech Airlines; OK; ☎ 495-973 1847, 978 1745; www.csa.cz/en/)
Delta Air Lines (DL; ☎ 800-700 0990; www.delta.com)
Finnair (AY; ☎ 495-933 0056; www.finnair.com)
Japan Airlines (JL; ☎ 495-730 3070; www.jal.co.jp/en)
KD Avia (KD; ☎ 495-641 1074; www.kdavia.eu)

KLM (KL; ☎ 495-258 3600; www.klm.com)
LOT Polish Airlines (LO; ☎ 800-5082 5082; www.lot.com)
Lufthansa (LH; ☎ 495-980 9999; www.lufthansa.com)
Rossiya (FV; ☎ 495-995 2025; http://eng.pulkovo.ru/en/)
SAS (SK; ☎ 495-775 4747; www.flysas.com)
S7 Airlines (S7; ☎ in Moscow 495-777 9999, in Novosibirsk 383-298 9090; www.s7.ru)
Transaero Airlines (UN; ☎ 495-788 8080; www.transaero.com)

Land

Adjoining some 13 countries, the Russian Federation has a huge number of border crossings. From Eastern Europe you are most likely to enter from Finland near Vyborg, Estonia at Narva, Latvia at Rēzekne, Belarus at Krasnoye or Ezjaryshcha, and Ukraine at Chernihiv. You can enter Kaliningrad from Lithuania and Poland at any of seven border posts.

If you're travelling to or from Russia via Belarus, note that you do need a transit visa and you must obtain it in advance; see p96 for details. See p97 for more information about crossing between Russia and Belarus.

Sea

The main opportunity to reach Russia by sea is from Sassnitz (Germany) or Klaipėda (Lithuania) to Kaliningrad (p792).

TRAVEL AGENCIES

Independent travellers may need to use travel agents to secure visa invitations (see p797) and to book internal travel; without Russian-language skills, it can sometimes be tricky to organise more than a simple train or plane ticket. The following agencies are recommended:

Australia

Eastern Europe/Russian Travel Centre (☎ 02-9262 1144; www.eetbtravel.com)
Passport Travel (☎ 03-9500 0444; www.travelcentre.com.au)
Russian Gateway Tours (☎ 02-9745 3333; www.russian-gateway.com.au)

UK

Go Russia (☎ 020-3355 7717; www.justgorussia.co.uk) Cultural and adventure-holiday specialist.
Regent Holidays (☎ 0845-277 3317; www.regent-holidays.co.uk)
Russia Experience (☎ 020-8566 8846; www.trans-siberian.co.uk) Very experienced and reliable.

USA

Exeter International (☎ 813-251 5355; www.russiatours.com) Specialises in luxury tours to Moscow and St Petersburg.
Go to Russia Travel (☎ 404-827 0099; www.gotorussia.com) Has offices in Atlanta, San Francisco and Moscow; offers full range of travel services.
Mir Corporation (☎ 206-624 7289; www.mircorp.com) Award-winning operation with many different tours, including one by steam train from Kyiv and Murmansk.

RUSSIA

GETTING AROUND

Air

Flying in Russia is like the country itself – a unique experience. Fights can be delayed, often for hours and with no or little explanation.

A few of Russia's airlines allow you to book over the internet (see below). Otherwise it's no problem buying a ticket at ubiquitous *aviakassa* (ticket offices). Generally, you're better off booking internal flights once you arrive in Russia, where more flights and flight information are available and where prices may be lower. Fares are generally 30% cheaper (60% on major Moscow routings) for advance bookings or evening departures.

Flights between Moscow and St Petersburg go every hour; a seat costs around R3000 including taxes (one-way) for a ticket bought two weeks in advance.

Boat

One of the most pleasant ways of travelling around Russia is by river. The season runs from late May through to mid-October, Numerous cruise boats ply the routes between Moscow and St Petersburg, many stopping at some of the Golden Ring cities on the way. Some cruises are specifically aimed at foreign tourists; for lower prices, sail on a boat aimed at Russian holidaymakers. Some recommended boat operators and agencies:

Infoflot (Map pp756-7; ☎ 495-684 9188; www.infoflot .com; ul Shchepkina 28, Moscow; Ⓜ Pr Mira) The market leader with a second office in St Petersburg.

Mosturflot (☎ 495-221 7222; www.mosturflot.ru)

Vodohod (☎ 495-223 96 11; www.vodohod.com/eng)

Ferries also link Kaliningrad with St Petersburg (p785).

AIR TICKETS VIA THE WEB

Online agencies with English interfaces specialising in Russian air tickets include **Avantix** (☎ 495-787 7272; www.avantix.ru) and **Pososhok.ru** (☎ 495-234 8000; http:// avia.waytorussia.net).

Sky Express (XW; ☎ 495-580 9360; www .skyexpress.ru/en) is a Russian low-cost carrier with services between Moscow, St Petersburg and Kaliningrad as well as several other major Russian cities. Its hub is Vnukovo airport, Moscow.

Bus

Long-distance buses complement rather than compete with the rail network. They generally serve areas with no railway or routes on which trains are slow, infrequent or overloaded. The St Petersburg–Novgorod route, for example, has 10 buses daily (R220, four hours).

There's almost no need to reserve a seat – just arrive a good 30 minutes to one hour before the scheduled departure and buy a ticket. Prices are comparable to 2nd-class train fares; journey times depend on road conditions. A sometimes hefty fee is charged for larger bags.

Marshrutky are minibuses that are quicker than the rusty old buses. Where roads are good and villages frequent, *marshrutky* can be twice as fast as buses, and are well worth the double fare.

Car & Motorcycle

It's perfectly possible to bring your own vehicle into Russia, but expect delays, bureaucracy and the attention of the roundly hated GAI (traffic police), who take particular delight in stopping foreign cars for document checks.

To enter Russia with a vehicle you will need a valid International Driving Permit, your passport, and the insurance and ownership documents for your car.

Hiring a car is far preferable to bringing your own vehicle into Russia. As you don't really need a car to get around big cities, they are mainly of use when making trips out of town where public transport may not be so good. All the major agencies have offices in Moscow and St Petersburg.

Petrol comes in four main grades: 76-, 93-, 95- and 98-octane. Prices range from R22.50 to R30 per litre. Unleaded gas is available in major cities; BP gas stations usually sell it.

Driving in Russia is on the right-hand side, and at an intersection traffic coming from the right has the right of way. The speed limit is generally 60km per hour in towns. The maximum legal blood-alcohol content is 0.03%. This rule is strictly enforced, so don't drink and drive.

Hitching & Unofficial Taxis

Hitching for free is something of an alien concept in Russia, but paying a small amount to be given a lift is a daily reality for millions. The system's honour code is so ingrained that drivers will often go to extraordinary lengths

---

BUYING TRAIN TICKETS ONLINE

There are several sites where you can book train tickets online, including that of **RZD** (www.rzd .ru, in Russian), which has plans to launch an English-language booking service. The sites below are in English:

- **Bilet.ru** (☎ 495-925 7571; www.bilet.ru) Partners with **Your Train** (www.poezda.net/en), a railway timetable search system for the Commonwealth of Independent Sates (CIS).
- **Russian Rails** (☎ 916-202 6070; www.russianrails.com)
- **Trains Russia.com** (☎ in the US 1-888-263 0023, in Moscow 495-225 5012; www.trainsrussia.com/en /travels) Authorised US agent for RZD; tickets are issued in its Moscow office. They can then be picked up there or they can be delivered for US$15 to any address in Moscow or for US$30 to any Moscow airport or rail station, or sent via international DHL delivery to your home address.
- **VisitRussiacom** (☎ in the US 800 755 3080; www.visitrussia.com)

---

to get you to your destination. In cities you'll see people flagging down cars all the time; long-distance hitching is less common, but it's still acceptable if the price is right. Simply state your destination and ask 'skolko?' (how much?). Obviously, use common sense: don't get into a car with more than one passenger and be careful if travelling alone at night.

Train

Russia is criss-crossed by an extensive train network efficiently run by **Russian Railways** (www.eng.rzd.ru/wps/portal/rzdeng/fp). Suburban or short-distance trains are called elektrichkas and do not require advance booking: you can buy your ticket at the prigorodny poezd kassa (suburban train ticket offices) at train stations.

For long-distance trains, unless otherwise specified we quote 2nd-class (kupe) fares. Expect 1st-class (SV) fares to be double this, and 3rd class (platskartny) to be about 40% less. Children under five travel free if they share a berth with an adult; otherwise, children under 10 pay a reduced fare for their own berth. On the better-class skory (fast) and firmeny (name) trains it's also possible to

have two grades of kupe fare: with or without meals. Fares quoted in this chapter should be used as a guide only.

You're advised to reserve at least 24 hours in advance for any long-distance journey, although bookings cannot be made any earlier than 45 days before the date of departure. You'd be wise to buy well in advance over the busy summer months and holiday periods such as New Year's and early May, when securing berths at short notice on certain trains can be difficult. Tickets for key trains on the busy Moscow–St Petersburg route can also be difficult to come by, but those with flexible options should be able to find something.

Bring your passport (or a photocopy), as without it you'll be unable to buy tickets. You can buy tickets for others if you bring their passports or photocopies. Queues can be very long and move with interminable slowness. If you're in a hurry, go to the service centres that exist in most big train stations. Here you pay a R200 surcharge and avoid the queues. Alternatively, most travel agents will organise the reservation and delivery of train tickets for a substantial mark-up.

Serbia Србија

Newsflash: Serbia is no longer the Bad Boy of the Balkans. Some former territory has stepped out on its own in recent years, but what remains has much to offer independent travellers who want to form their own opinion of this misunderstood and misrepresented state.

Serbia has been a melting pot of colliding and complementary cultures for centuries. Up north, Hungarian influences cross the border into the Vojvodinian region; the art nouveau town of Subotica is as much Hungarian as it is Serbian. The town of Novi Sad, presided over by the Petrovarian Citadel, hosts an edgy music festival that reverberates through Eastern Europe, except perhaps in the nearby pocket of Fruska Gora National Park, where monastic life has endured for generations.

Pressed against the border of Bosnia and Hercegovina (BiH), village traditions and sincere hospitality make the Zlatibor region one of the most special places in the country. Below the mountainous ski resort of Kopaonik, is the eclectic town of Novi Pazar where Ottoman stylings show how modern-day Islam evolved from Turkish Rule in the Sanžak region.

Beating at the heart of all this is Belgrade. Once dismissed as drab, this dynamic capital is now being hailed by travellers as an urban highlight. Vivid museums, creative restaurants and nightlife of every pace for every taste make this all-hours town a visitors' playground.

SERBIA

FAST FACTS

- **Area** 77,474 sq km
- **Capital** Belgrade
- **Currency** dinar (DIN); €1 = 95DIN; US$1 = 70DIN; UK£1 = 101DIN; A$1 = 48DIN; ¥100 = 72DIN; NZ$1 = 39DIN
- **Famous for** winning the Eurovision Song Contest, tennis (think Ana Ivanovic, Monica Seles, Novak Djokovic, Jelena Jankovic…)
- **Official language** Serbian
- **Phrases** *zdravo* (hello); *doviđenja* (goodbye); *hvala* (thanks)
- **Population** 7.5 million
- **Telephone codes** country code ☎ 381; international access code ☎ 00
- **Visa** generally not needed; see p829

HIGHLIGHTS

- Marvel at Belgrade's mighty **Kalemegdan Citadel** (p811).
- Witness the quiet town of **Novi Sad** (p819) as it morphs into the State of Exit every July.
- Ponder the contrasting architecture and cultural fusions in Turkish-toned **Novi Pazar** (p824) in Southern Serbia.
- Gape at splendid surprises bursting from the Vojvodinian plains, like the art nouveau architecture of **Subotica** (p821).
- Explore the villages in the gently rolling plains of **Zlatibor** (p824).

ITINERARIES

- **One week** Enjoy two days of cultural and culinary exploration in Belgrade, then move on to Novi Sad for day trips into Fruška Gora.
- **Two to three weeks** Follow the above then head north to Hungarian-influenced Subotica, before slicing south for mountain air in Zlatibor on your way to Ottoman-influenced Novi Pazar.

CLIMATE & WHEN TO GO

The north has a Continental climate with cold winters and humid summers, hottest in July and August. Ski season is generally from late November to late March or early April. Festivals and events (such as the hedonistic Exit Festival; see p820) can make accommodation scarce.

HISTORY

Early Invasions

Serbian history has been punctuated by foreign invasions from the time the Celts supplanted the Illyrians in the 4th century BC, through to the arrival of the Romans 100

HOW MUCH?

- **Short taxi ride** 150DIN
- **Internet access** per hour 80DIN to 150DIN
- **Cup of coffee** 100DIN
- **Bottle of plum brandy** 500DIN
- **Postcard** 30DIN

LONELY PLANET INDEX

- **1L petrol** 88DIN
- **1L bottled water** 80DIN
- **500mL beer (Lav/Jelen)** 80DIN
- **Souvenir T-shirt** 600DIN
- **Street snack (burek)** 60DIN

---

years later, the Slavs in the 6th century AD, the Turks in the 14th century, the Austro-Hungarians in the late 19th and early 20th centuries, and the Germans briefly in WWII. A pivotal event occurred in AD 395 when the Roman Emperor Theodosius I divided his empire giving Serbia to the Byzantines, locking the country into Eastern Europe. This was cemented in 879 when Saints Cyril and Methodius converted Serbs to the Orthodox religion.

Enter the Ottomans

Independence briefly flowered from 1217 with a 'golden age' during Stefan Dušan's reign as emperor (1346–55). Serbia declined after his death and at the pivotal Battle of Kosovo in 1389 the Turks defeated Serbia, ushering in 500 years of Islamic rule. Early revolts were crushed but one in 1815 led to de facto independence that became complete in 1878.

CONNECTIONS: MOVING ON FROM SERBIA

Serbia is landlocked by accessible neighbours. From the northern art nouveau town of Subotica (p822) you can travel over the Hungarian border and onwards to Budapest. The town of Vršac is only 10km from the Romanian border, and the Bulgarian border is 45 minutes from the small town of Pirot. When things are calm on the Kosovar border, €5 and three hours get you from the Ottoman-influenced Serbian town of Novi Pazar (p826) into the Kosovoan capital of Pristina. The enchanting Zlatibor region stretches to Bosnia and Hercegovina, allowing travellers with wheels the opportunity to take a day trip to the Bridge on the River Drina. In short, the whole of Eastern Europe feels accessible from Belgrade; Bucharest, Budapest, Ljubljana, Moscow, Sofia and Zagreb are a railride away (see p817) and regular buses serve destinations including Banja Luka, Llubljana, Sarajevo and Split (see p817).

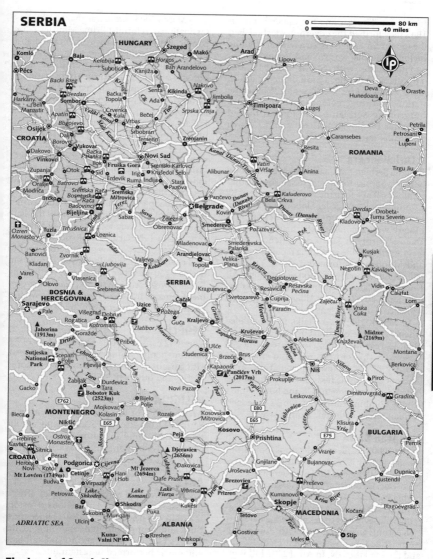

SERBIA

HUNGARY

Komló • Baja • Kelebija • Horgoš • Szeged • Makó • Arad • Lipova • Deva • Hunedoara • Orăştie
Pécs • Bački Breg • Bezdan • Subotica • Kanjiža • Ban Arandelovo • Timişoara • Lugoj • Petrila • Petroşani • Lupeni
Harkany • Beli • Manastir • Apatin • Bogojevo • Sombor • Bačka Topola • Crvenka • Kula • Vrbas • Bečej • Srpska Crnja • Kikinda • Nakovo • Jimbolia • ROMANIA
Osijek • CROATIA • Dalj • Borovo • Vukovar • Bačka Palanka • Ilok • Novi Sad • Fruška Gora • Sremski Karlovci • Krušedol Selo • Irig • Ruma • Indija • Stara Pazova • Alibunar • Vatin • Vršac • Anina • Tirgu Jiu
Zupanja • Otok • Sid • Erdevik • Sremska Rača • Bosanska Rača • Badovci • Bijeljina • Sremska Mitrovica • Jerez • Sabac • Pančevo • Dunav (Danube River) • Bela Crkva • Kaluderovo • Derdap • Drobeta-Turnu Severin
Modrica • Orašje • Batrovci • Brčko • Ozren Monastery • Tuzla • Trbušnica • Loznica • Sava • Železnik • Obrenovac • Belgrade • Kovin • Dunav (Danube River) • Kladovo
Banovići • Vareš • Zvornik • Kladanj • Ljubovija • Kolubara • Valjevo • Mladenovac • Smederevo • Pozarevac • Pek • Kusjak • Negotin • Kavilovo • Vidin • Calafat • Lom
Olovo • Vlasenica • Srebrenica • Jadar • Topola • Velika Plana • Smederevska Palanka • Resava • Despotovac • Resavica • Bor • Zaječar • Vrska Cuka
BOSNIA & HERCEGOVINA • Sarajevo • Pale • Višegrad • Dobrun • Užice • Požega • Čačak • Kragujevac • Svetozarevo • Ćuprija • Paraćin • Resavska Pećina
Jahorina (1913m) • Rogatica • Kotroman • Zlatibor • Guča • Kraljevo • Zapadna Morava • Kruševac • Aleksinac • Knjaževac • Midžor (2169m) • Montana • Berkovica
Foča • Goražde • Pribol • Studenica • Ušče • Brzeće • Brus • Rasina • Južna Morava • Niš • Nišava • Pirot
Sutjeska National Park • Šcepan Polje • Pljevlja • Kapaonik • Pančićev Vrh (2017m) • Prokuplje • Leskovac • Dimitrovgrad • Gradina
Gacko • Žabljak • Đurđevica Tara • Bobotov Kuk (2523m) • Bijelo Polje • Novi Pazar • Ibar • Toplica • E80 • Jablanica • Veternica • E65 • Klisura Vrla • BULGARIA
Bieca • MONTENEGRO • Mojkovac • Kolašin • Berane • Rožaje • Kosovska Mitrovica • Kosovo • Prishtina • E75 • Pernik
Nikšić • Ostrog Monastery • Zeta • Morača • Peja • Vranje • Bujanovac
Trebinje • Cavtat • Sitnica • Djeravica (2656m) • Gnjilane • Kjustendil • Blagoevgrad
CROATIA • Herceg Novi • Perast • Podgorica • Cijevna • Mt Jezerca (2694m) • Đakovica • Uroševac • Brezovica • Preševo • Kumanovo • Kriva River • MACEDONIA
Mt Lovćen (1749m) • Cetinje • Hani Hoti • Qafe Prush • Vrbnica • Prizren • Skopje • Kočani • Stip
Budva • Petrovac • Virpazar • Lake Shkodra • Lake Komani • Lake Fierza • Kukësi • Drini • Tetovo
Bar • Sukobin • Muriqani • Puka • Kuna-Valni NP • Rreshen • Peshkopi • ALBANIA • Gostivar • Veles

ADRIATIC SEA • Ulcinj • Shkodra

0 ——— 80 km
0 ——— 40 miles

SERBIA

The Land of South Slavs

On 28 June 1914 Austria-Hungary used the assassination of Archduke Franz Ferdinand by a Bosnian Serb to invade Serbia, sparking WWI. In 1918 Croatia, Slovenia, BiH, Vojvodina, Serbia and its Kosovo province, Montenegro, and Macedonia were joined into the Kingdom of Serbs, Croats and Slovenes. This lengthy title remained until 1929 when the countries became Yugoslavia (Southern Slavs).

In March 1941 Yugoslavia joined the fascist Tripartite Alliance, sparking a military coup and withdrawal from the alliance; Germany reacted by bombing Belgrade. Rival resistance movements fought the Germans and each other, with communist partisans led by

Josip Broz Tito gaining the upper hand. In 1945 they formed the government, abolished the monarchy and declared a federal republic including Serbia, Kosovo and Vojvodina.

Tito broke with Stalin in 1948 and Yugoslavia became a nonaligned nation, albeit bolstered by Western aid. Within the nation, growing regional inequalities and burgeoning Serbian expansionism fuelled demands by Slovenia, Croatia and Kosovo for greater autonomy.

A Turbulant Era

By 1986 Serbian nationalists were espousing a 'Greater Serbia' to encompass Serbs in other republics. This doctrine was appropriated by Communist Party leader Slobodan Milošević, horrifying other republics, which fought bloody wars against the Serbian-controlled Yugoslav army to gain independence.

In April 1992 the remaining republics, Serbia and Montenegro, formed a 'third' Yugoslav federation without provision of autonomy for Kosovo; the latest event in a series of brutal repressions of the majority Albanians in Kosovo. Violence erupted in January 1998.

In March 1999 peace talks in Paris failed when Serbia rejected a US-brokered peace plan. In response to organised resistance in Kosovo, Serbian forces moved to empty the country of its Albanian population; hundreds of thousands fled into Macedonia and Albania, galvanising the US and NATO into a 78-day bombing campaign. On 12 June 1999 Serbian forces withdrew from Kosovo.

European Dawn

In the 2000 presidential elections, opposition parties led by Vojislav Koštunica declared victory but their claim was denounced by Milošević. Opposition supporters from all over Serbia swarmed to Belgrade and stormed parliament. When Russia recognised Koštunica's win, Milošević had to acknowledge defeat.

Koštunica restored ties with Europe, acknowledged Yugoslav atrocities in Kosovo and rejoined the UN. In April 2001 Milošević was arrested and extradited to the international war-crimes tribunal in The Hague.

In April 2002 a loose union of Serbia and Montenegro replaced Yugoslavia. The EU-brokered deal was intended to stabilise the region by accommodating Montenegrin demands for independence, allowing for a referendum after three years.

In March 2003 Serbia was shaken by the assassination of reformist Prime Minister Zoran Đinđić, who had been instrumental in handing Milošević to The Hague. Parliamentary elections in December 2003 were inconclusive but saw a worrying resurgence of nationalism. Power-sharing deals installed Koštunica as head of a centre-right coalition relying on support from Milošević's Socialist Party. Finally, in June 2004, Serbia gained a new president in pro-European Boris Tadić.

On 11 March 2006 Milošević was found dead in his cell, ending a chapter in the region's history. In May, 55% of Montenegrins voted for independence from Serbia which was formally declared the following month. The following May, 12 people (several of whom were former members of the paramilitary wing of the state security police) were found guilty of Đinđić's murder. In February 2008, Kosovo declared its independence; a move that Serbia held to be illegal. In May 2008, Tadić won 102 seats in Serbia's 250-member parliament, reaffirming Serbia's pro-European future, but the government remains fractured over how Kosovo impacts on Serbia's future with the EU.

PEOPLE

The 2002 census revealed a population of 7.5 million people comprising Serbs (82.9%), Hungarians (3.9%), Bosniaks (1.8%), Roma (1.4%) and others (8.9%).

RELIGION

Around 85% of the population identify as Serbian Orthodox. The 5% Roman Catholic population are Vojvodinian Hungarians. Muslims (Albanians and Slavic) comprise around 3% of the population.

ARTS

The survival and active rebellion of artistic expression throughout dark periods of history is a source of pride. Today creative juices flow thick and strong, with films spawning idyllic villages (see p826), art sold in cocktail bars and music performed in restaurants.

Literature

Bosnian-born, but a past Belgrade resident, Ivo Andrić was awarded the Nobel prize for his *Bridge over the Drina*.

Internationally acclaimed word wizard Milorad Pavić writes in many dimensions; *The Inner Side of the Wind* can be read from the back or the front, and you can read a male or female edition of Pavić's lyrical lexicon *Dictionary of the Khazars*.

Cinema

World-renowned director Emir Kusturica sets the bar on Serbian cinema with his raucous approach to story-telling. Look out for *Underground* (1995), the surreal tale of seemingly never-ending Balkan conflicts, *Time of the Gypsies* (1989), *Black Cat, White Cat* (1998), *Zavet* (2007), and *Life is a Miracle* (2004) about an optimistic Serbian engineer working on the Mokra Gora railway (p826).

Music

Blehmuzika (brass music influenced by Turkish and Austrian military music) is the national music. A popular example is the soundtrack to the film *Underground* and albums by trumpet player Boban Marković.

Cross ethnic folk music with techno and you get 'turbofolk'; controversial during the Milošević era for nationalist overtones but now more mainstream fun.

Modern music covers anything from wild Romani music to house, jazz, drum 'n' bass, funk, reggae, rock or hip hop. Nightlife follows suit, offering every type of soundtrack. Don't miss Novi Sad's Exit Festival (p820).

Marija Šerifovi's triumph at the 2007 Eurovision Song Contest gave Serbia the honour of hosting the event in 2008.

Architecture

Architecture is a living record of who has been and gone. Ottoman, Austro-Hungarian, and Serbian-Byzantine styles have fought for dominance, often over the same buildings, which have been stripped, redressed and modified over the years depending on who was in power. On top of this is the concrete layer of post-WWII buildings.

ENVIRONMENT

Serbia-proper comprises 77,474 sq km. Midzor (2169m) is its highest mountain. Zlatibor and Kopaonik are winter playgrounds.

Vojvodina is pancake-flat agricultural land. South of the Dunav (Danube River) the landscape rises through rolling green hills, which crest where the eastern outpost of the Dinaric Alps slices southeastwards across the country.

Major national parks are Kapaonik and Fruška Gora. Among Serbia's mammals are wild boar, wildcat, beaver, otters, suslik, lynx and mouflon. Around 40% of Serbia's 360 bird species are of European Conservation Concern.

Serbia faces air pollution around Belgrade and dumping of industrial waste into the Sava. Some remnants of the 1999 NATO bombings, such as factories outside Belgrade, are ecological hazards.

FOOD & DRINK

The ubiquitous snack is *burek,* a filo-pastry pie made with *sir* (cheese), *meso* (meat), *krompir* (potato) or occasionally *pečurke* (mushrooms), commonly consumed with yoghurt.

Serbia is famous for grilled meats such as *ćevapčići* (kebab), *pljeskavica* (spicy hamburger) and *ražnjići* (pork or veal kebabs). Karađorđe's schnitzel is a tubular roll of veal, stuffed with *kajmak* (curdled, salted milk).

Regional cuisines range from spicy Hungarian goulash in Vojvodina to Turkish kebabs in Novi Pazar.

The further from major cities you are, the more baffled waiters look at requests for vegetarian food. There's always vegetarian pizza, *Srpska salata* (raw peppers, onions and tomatoes, seasoned with oil, vinegar and maybe chilli) and *šopska salata* (tomatoes, cucumber and onion, topped with grated white cheese). Also try *gibanica* (cheese pie), *zeljanica* (cheese pie with spinach) or *pasulj prebranac* (cooked spiced beans).

Lav and Jelen are popular brews of *pivo* (beer). Many people distil *rakija* (brandy) from plums or other fruit. A traditional Serbian dessert wine is *bermet* – try it in Vojvodina where family recipes are passed down through generations. Pretend it's not so, but Serbian coffee is Turkish coffee.

Restaurants are generally open from 8am to 11pm or midnight, and bars from 9pm until around 3am. Smoking is as ubiquitous as breathing in Serbia.

BELGRADE БЕОГРАД

☎ 011 / pop 1.58 million

Edgy, adventurous, dignified and audacious Belgrade evolves before your eyes, creating what is quickly gaining repute as a Balkan melting pot. This chaos shows in the architecture; socialist blocks are squeezed between art nouveau masterpieces, and remnants of the Habsburg legacy contrast with Ottoman relics.

SERBIA

BELGRADE

| 0 | 1 km |
| 0 | 0.6 miles |

INFORMATION	
Albanian Embassy	1 B4

SIGHTS & ACTIVITIES	
Maršal Tito's Grave	2 B4
Sveti Sava	3 C3

SLEEPING	
Arka Barka	4 A1

ENTERTAINMENT	
Sava Centar	5 A2

It is here where the Sava River meets the Dunav (Danube River), where East meets West, where old-world culture gives way to new-world nightlife.

Belgrade's cafe culture is second to none; grandiose coffee houses, funky sidewalk ice-creameries and tatty smokey dens all find rightful place along the pedestrian street of Knez Mihailova which is flanked by fascinating historical buildings all the way to ancient Kalemegdan Citadel crowning the city. Deeper in Belgrade's bowels are museums which guard the cultural, religious and military heritage of the country. Josip Broz Tito and other ghosts of the past have been laid to rest here.

Its name, Beograd, means 'White City' but this colourful capital is anything but.

HISTORY

As its mishmash of architecture shows, Belgrade has been destroyed and rebuilt countless times in its 2300-year history. Celts first settled on the lumpy hill at the confluence of the Sava River and the Dunav, the Romans came in the 1st century and havoc was wreaked by Goths and Huns until the area was colonised by Slavic tribes in the 6th century. In 1403 Hungary gave Belgrade to Stefan Lazarević, making it the Serbian capital. The 1400s saw waves of Turkish attacks; Sultan Suleiman the Magnificent (and 300,000 soldiers) conquered Belgrade in 1521 and shipped its population to İstanbul. Belgrade continued to be fought over by Austrians, Turks and Serbs themselves. The Karađorđević dynasty began in 1807 when Belgrade was liberated from the Turks. The Obrenović dynasty followed when Miloš Obrenović staged the Second Serbian uprising and ordered the murder of Karađorđević. Turkey finally relinquished control in 1867. In 1914, the Austro-Hungarian empire captured Belgrade but was soon driven out, returning more triumphantly with German help in 1915, and staying for three years. In 1918, Belgrade became the capital of Yugoslavia after Serbs, Croats and Slovenes united. Belgrade was bombed by both Nazis and Allies during WWII.

In the 1990s, Belgrade became the stage of strong resistance against Slobodan Milošević, both underground and in the open; protestors took to the streets on numerous occasions. In 1999, NATO forces bombed Belgrade for three months after Milošević refused to cease the ethnic cleansing of Albanians. Belgrade's power of protest was displayed in 2000, when citizens stormed Parliament against Miloševićs electoral fraud. People took to the streets again in 2008 in opposition to Kosovo's declaration of independence.

ORIENTATION

The central train station and the two major bus stations are all near each other on the southern side of the city centre. A couple of blocks northeast, Terazije runs to Trg Republike, from where Knez Mihailova, Belgrade's lively pedestrian boulevard, leads to Kalemegdan Citadel.

INFORMATION
Bookshops

Guidebooks, novels, CDs and DVDs are available at the following places:

IPS (Map pp810-11; ☎ 328 18 59; Trg Republic 5; ⌚ 9am-9pm Mon-Fri, 10am-5pm Sat)
Mamut (Map pp810-11; ☎ 0645 152 248; cnr Knez Mihailova & Sremska; ⌚ 9am-10pm Mon-Sat, noon-10pm Sun)
Plato (Map pp810-11; ☎ 262 4751; Knez Mihailova 48; ⌚ 9am-midnight Mon-Sat, noon-midnight Sun)

Internet Access

Click 011 (Map pp810-11; ☎ 263 0024; Rajicéva 14; per hr 100DIN; ⌚ 9am-9pm Mon-Fri, 11am-7pm Sat & Sun)
Mamut (Map pp810-11; ☎ 0645 152 248; cnr Knez Mihailova & Sremska; per hr 100DIN; ⌚ 9am-10pm Mon-Sat, noon-10pm Sun) Offers internet access or free wireless if you BYO laptop. Internet calls cost 25DIN per minute.
Net Hol (Map pp810-11; ☎ 323 9853; Nusiceva 3; ⌚ 10am-2am; 100DIN per hr) Late-night internet off the passageway behind Kasina Hotel.

Internet Resources

Belgrade City (www.beograd.org.yu)
Belgrade in Your Pocket (www.inyourpocket.com /serbia/city/belgrade.html)
Tourist Organisation of Belgrade (www.tob.co.yu)

Medical Services

Boris Kidrič Hospital Diplomatic Section (Map pp810-11; ☎ 643 839; Miloša Porcerca Pasterova 1; ⌚ 7am-7pm Mon-Fri)
Klinički Centar (Map pp810-11; ☎ 361 7777; Miloša Porcerca Pasterova 2; ⌚ 24hr) Medical clinic.
Prima 1 (Map pp810-11; ☎ 361 0999; Nemanjina 2; ⌚ 24hr) All-hours pharmacy.

Money

Banca Intesa (Map pp810-11; Knez Mihailova 30; ⌚ 8am-8pm Mon-Fri, 9am-3pm Sat)
Erste Bank (Map pp810-11; Knez Mihailova 36; ⌚ 8am-6pm Mon-Fri, 9.30am-1.30pm Sat)

SERBIA

BELGRADE IN TWO DAYS

Brunch at **Que Pasa?** (p815) before exploring **Kalemegdan Citadel** (p811). Promenade leisurely down architecturally eclectic Knez Mihailova, stopping at **Russian Tsar** (p815) for opulent coffee and cake. Soak up the meeting-point atmosphere at nearby **Trg Republike** and check whether the **National Museum** (p812) is open, or spend the afternoon in the **Ethnographic Museum** (p812). When hunger sets in, wander through cobblestoned **Skadarska** (p812) to enjoy traditional Serbian fare accompanied by energetic Roma violins. Leave bohemia behind and return to 'real' Belgrade with a live gig at **Akademija** (p816) or a cocktail at **Ben Akiba** (p815).

The next day, ponder the past at **Maršal Tito's grave** (p813) before heading to **Zemun** (p818) for a seafood lunch.

Back in the big smoke, enjoy dinner at historical **?** (p814) before heading to nearby **Andergraund** (p816) for a heady Belgrade clubbing experience. If clubbing's not for you, opt instead for a leisurely meal at **Little Bay** (p814) for fine dining and live opera.

CENTRAL BELGRADE

INFORMATION

Australian Embassy	1 C3
Banca Intesa	2 B3
Boris Kidrič Hospital Diplomatic Section	3 C6
Bosnian Embassy	4 F5
Bulgarian Embassy	5 C6
Canadian Embassy	6 B6
Central Post Office	7 D5
Click 011	8 B3
Croatian Embassy	9 B6
Dutch Embassy	10 C3
Erste Bank	11 B3
French Embassy	12 B3
German Embassy	13 B6
Hungarian Embassy	14 E6
IPS	15 C4

Klinički Centar	16 C6
KSR Beograd Tours	17 C5
Mamut	18 C4
Net Hol	19 C4
Plato	20 B3
Prima 1	21 B5
Raiffeisen Bank	22 C4
Tourist Organisation of Belgrade	23 C3
Tourist Organisation of Belgrade	24 B5
Tourist Organisation of Belgrade	25 C4
UK Embassy	26 B6
US Embassy	27 B6

SIGHTS & ACTIVITIES

Bayrakli Mosque	28 B2
Burial Chamber of Sheikh Mustafa	29 C3
City Zoo	30 B2
Ethnographic Museum	31 B3
Gallery of Frescoes	32 B2
Kalemegdan Citadel	33 A2
Military Museum	34 A2

Raiffeisen Bank (Map pp810–11; Terazije 27; 8am-7pm Mon-Fri, 9am-3pm Sat) In the walkway linking Terazije with Trg Nikola Pašića.

Post

Central post office (Map pp810–11; ☎ 633 492; Takovska 2; 8am-7pm Mon-Sat)

Tourist Information

Tourist Organisation of Belgrade (Map pp810–11; www.tob.co.yu); Central Railway Station (☎ 361 2732; 9am-8pm Mon-Fri, 9am-5pm Sat, 10am-4pm Sun); Makedonska (☎ 334 3460; Makedonska 5; 9am-9pm Mon-Fri, 10am-4pm Sat & Sun); Terazije Underpass (☎ 635 622; fax 635 343; 9am-8pm Mon-Fri, 9am-5pm Sat) Cheery and friendly with brochures, city maps and events listings.

SIGHTS
Kalemegdan Citadel

Some 115 battles have been fought over imposing Kalemegdan (Map pp810–11). Fortifications began in Celtic times. The Romans extended it onto the flood plains during the settlement of 'Singidunum', Belgrade's Roman name. Much of what stands today is the product of 18th-century Austro-Hungarian and Turkish reconstructions.

Entering from Knez Mihailova brings you to the Upper Citadel. Through **Stambol Gate** (Map pp810–11), built by the Turks around 1750, you'll find yourself in the firing line of canons and tanks; welcome to the **Military Museum** (Map pp810–11; ☎ 334 4408; adult/child 100/50DIN; 10am-5pm Tue-Sun) presenting a complete military history of former Yugoslavia right up to the 1999 NATO bombings. Captured Kosovo Liberation Army (KLA) weapons and bits of a downed American stealth fighter are on display.

The nearby **City Zoo** (Map pp810–11; ☎ 262 4526; adult/child 300/200DIN; 8am-8pm) comes with an interesting anecdote reminiscent of *Twelve Monkeys*; when Nazi bombs damaged enclosures, several dangerous occupants were freed to wander the streets of Belgrade.

Stari Grad

South of the citadel along Knez Mihailova street is Stari Grad (Old Town). This jigsaw of architecture covers two centuries, beginning when Belgrade was snatched from the dying Ottoman empire and given a boost by the Habsburgs. People promenade along pedestrian **Knez Mihailova** (Map pp810–11) where

SERBIA

cafes spill onto pavements. Fine buildings include the elegant pink and white, neo-Renaissance **School of Fine Arts** (Map pp810-11; cnr Knez Mihailova & Rajićeva). Further down is the **Serbian Academy of Arts & Sciences** (Map pp810–11), an early-20th-century art nouveau building with the goddess Nike at its helm.

At the other end of Knez Mihailova is Trg Republike (Republic Sq), a meeting point and outdoor exhibition space. On the square is the **National Museum** (Map pp810-11; ☎ 330 6000; www.narodnimuzej.org.yu; Trg Republike 1A), closed for renovations at the time of writing.

A few blocks away, the **Ethnographic Museum** (Map pp810-11; ☎ 328 1888; Studentski Trg 13; adult/student 150/60DIN; 🕙 10am-5pm Tue-Sat, 9am-2pm Sun) contains traditional costumes, working utensils, mountain-village interiors and ćilim (pileless woven rugs).

The 1831 **Palace of Princess Ljubica** (Map pp810-11; ☎ 263 8264; Kneza Sime Markovića 8; adult/child 100/50DIN; 🕙 10am-5pm Tue, Wed, Fri & Sat, noon-8pm Thu, 10am-2pm Sun) is a Balkan-style palace built for the wife of Prince Miloš. Rooms are filled with period furniture, and ćilim carpets. The most authentic area is the hammam (Turkish bath) where Ljubica would have been steamed and massaged.

Adjacent, the Patriarchate (Patrijaršija) building contains the small **Museum of the Serbian Orthodox Church** (Map pp810-11; ☎ 263 8875; Kralja Petra 5; adult/child 50/20DIN; 🕙 8am-3pm Mon-Fri, 9am-noon Sat, 11am-1pm Sun). Objects here were passed between many hands (including its first collector, Saint Sava) before finally being displayed together here in the 1940s.

Dorćol

Named from the Turkish dört yol (four roads), Dorćol stretches from Stedentski Trg (Student Sq) to the Dunav, and from Skadarska to Kalemegdan Citadel. Once upon a time, Turks, Greeks, Jews, Germans, Armenians and Vlachs lived side-by-side here and bartered in a mix of languages. These days Dorćol is a pleasant residential area, but little remains of its former cosmopolitanism.

The area has been nipped and tucked by a tug-of-war over the years; the Turks gave it the Ottoman characteristic of cobbled, winding streets, the Austrians 'straightened' them and the curves later returned with the Turks.

One of the few remaining pieces of Ottoman architecture is the 18th-century **Burial Chamber of Sheik Mustafa** (Map pp810-11; cnr Braće Jugovića &

Višnjićeva), a dervish sheik from Baghdad. The last remaining mosque in Dorćol – and indeed Belgrade – is **Bayrakli Mosque** (Map pp810-11; cnr Kralja Petra & Gospodar Jevremova). Dating back to around 1575, the mosque remains a functional place of worship, even after being damaged in the March 2004 riots (a backlash against the anti-Serb pogroms in Kosovo at the time); it's still guarded against further retaliation.

St Aleksandar Nevski church (Map pp810-11; Cara Dušana 63) is the first Christian place of worship to have been built in the area.

Opened in 1953, the **Gallery of Frescoes** (Map pp810-11; ☎ 262 1491; www.narodnimuzej.org.yu; Cara Uroša 20; admission free; 🕙 10am-5pm Tue, Wed, Fri & Sat, noon-8pm Thu, 10am-2pm Sun) gives a good idea of Byzantine Serbian church art. Full-size replicas of church and monastery paintings are exact down to the last detail, even reproducing scratches and wear.

Skadarska

Skadarska (Map pp810–11), or Skadarlija is Belgrade's answer to Montmarte. This cobblestoned strip east of Trg Republike was the bohemian heartland at the turn of the 20th century. You may find yourself dining next to a writer, poet, philosopher or film star, but old-fashioned charm is more forced these days. Drop your cynicism and enjoy Serbian cuisine while roving Roma bands provide the ambience.

Central Belgrade

Belgrade hustles and bustles along Terazije. The jewel on this crown is Hotel Moscow (p814) built between 1906 and 1907.

From here, towards the Sava River (downhill from the Balkan Hotel), you come to **Zeleni Venac market** (Map pp810-11; 🕙 7am-4pm), a place of trade since the 19th century and a hub for city buses.

From Terazije, walk through to adjacent Trg Nikola Pašića to the **Musuem of the History of Serbia** (Map pp810-11; ☎ 328 7242; Trg Nikola Pašića; adult/child 100/50DIN; 🕙 noon-6pm Tue-Sat). At the time of research, slow-going renovations meant only a temporary (but enthralling) exhibition about assassinations was accessible.

Behind the post office is **Sveti Marko church** (Map pp810-11; ☎ 323 1940; Bulevar Kralja Aleksandra 17), based on the design of Gračanica Monastery (p435) in Kosovo. The church contains the grave of Emperor Dušan (1308–55). Behind is the tiny white **Russian church** (Map pp810–11), erected by Russian refugees who fled the October Revolution.

The **Museum of Automobiles** (Map pp810-11; ☎ 303 4625; Majke Jevrosime 30; adult/child 100/80DIN; 🕑 11am-7pm) is a compelling collection of cars and motorcycles. The pick for our garage would be the '57 Cadillac convertible: only 25,000km and one careful owner – President Tito.

One of Belgrade's best museums is **Nikola Tesla Museum** (Map pp810-11; ☎ 243 3886; www.tesla-museum.org; Krunska 51; admission 200DIN; 🕑 10am-6pm Tue-Fri, 10am-1pm Sat & Sun) where you can meet the man on the 100DIN note. The museum has some wondrously sci-fi-ish interactive elements.

Outer Belgrade

South down Kraja Milan across Trg Slavija, **Sveti Sava** (Map p808; Svetog Save) is the world's biggest Orthodox church; a fact entirely obvious looking at the city skyline from a distance or standing under its dome. The church is built on the site where the Turks apparently burnt relics of St Sava (the founder of the independent Serbian Orthodox church). Work on the church (frequently interrupted by wars) continues today.

Further south, a visit to **Maršal Tito's grave** (Kuća Cveća, House of Flowers; Map p808; ☎ 367 1485; Bulevar Mira; admission free; 🕑 10am-5pm Tue-Sat, 10am-1pm Sun) is obligatory. Among the collection of gifts presented to him over the years, is a Rolls Royce from Queen Elizabeth of Britain, a writing set from JFK and a bowl given 'with great admiration and affection' by Elizabeth Taylor and Richard Burton. Take trolleybus 40 or 41 at the south end of Parliament on Kneza Miloša. It's the second stop after it turns into Bulevar Mira.

FREE THRILLS

The best things in Belgrade are still free:

- Wander around **Kalemegdan Citadel** (p811).
- Explore **Stari Grad** (p811), the evocative Old Town.
- Visit the **Gallery of Frescoes** (opposite), where timeless art has been recreated down to the last scratch.
- Gasp at the size of **Sveti Sava** (above).
- Promenade along the Dunav (Danube River) to **Zemun** (p818).

For aircraft enthusiasts, the **Aviation Museum** (off Map p808; ☎ 267 0992; Suračin; admission 400DIN; 🕑 8.30am-6.30pm Tue-Sun summer, 9am-3pm Tue-Sun winter) at the airport contains rare planes, a WWII collection, and bits of the infamous American stealth fighter shot down in 1999.

SLEEPING

Accommodation in Belgrade is the worst value for money in the country. Hostels are thankfully getting their act together but few midrange options stand out.

Budget

The **Youth Hostel organisation** (Ferijalni Savez Beograd; Map pp810-11; ☎ 324 8550; www.hostels.org.yu; 2nd fl, Makedonska 22; 🕑 9am-5pm) does deals with local hotels. You need HI membership (500/700DIN under/over 26) or an international student card.

UniTurs Hostel (Map pp810-11; ☎ 334 6241; www.uni-turs.com; Andrićev Venac 12/3; dm 800-960DIN, tw 1200DIN; 💻) A sparkling surprise at the southern tip of Piornirksi Park, with fresh parquet floors, lockable cupboards, computers, breezy kitchen and in-built radio in the shower.

Yellowbed Hostel (Map pp810-11; ☎ 262 8220; www.yellowbed.net; Višnjećeva 3; dm from 1000DIN) Balconies, wireless, a terrace, good-humoured staff and a central location behind Studentski Trg make this a great budget base.

Arka Barka (Map p808; ☎ 064 200 4445; www.arkabarka.net; Bulevar Nikole Tesle bb; dm €15; ❄ 💻) Floating off Usće Park (within stumbling distance of Dunav barges), Arka Barka offers Ikea-fresh furniture, wireless, and a breezy verandah. A couple of private rooms cater for up to four people. The hostel is a moderate walk, or a short ride on bus 15 or 84 to the centre.

Hostel City Center (Map pp810-11; ☎ 264 4055; www.hostelcitycenterbelgrade.com; Savski trg 7; dm 850-1020DIN, s/d with shared bathroom from 1890/2520DIN, s/d with private bathroom from 2460/3280DIN, apt 3925DIN) Immediately opposite the train station, this hotel-hostel hybrid is perfect for late or early connections. Rooms without bathrooms have a private sink and are airy, though perhaps a little loud.

Hotel Royal (Map pp810-11; ☎ 263 4222; www.hotelroyal.co.yu; Kralja Petra 56; s 2640-3600DIN, d 3600DIN; 💻) The Royal books up fast because it's cheap, clean, central and has character. Rooms are pleasant and tidy and the reception buzzes around a glass-mosaic staircase.

SERBIA

Hotel Astoria (Map pp810-11; ☎ 360 5100; www
.astoria.co.yu; Milovana Milovanovića 1; s/d 2970/4620DIN,
d with shared bathroom 2970DIN, d with air-con 5170DIN;
☒) Conveniently near the train station,
the Astoria offers light airy rooms with
cable TV and minibars. Linen is crisp and
staff helpful.

Midrange
Hotel Excelsior (Map pp810-11; ☎ 323 1381; www.hotel
excelsior.co.yu; Kneza Miloša 5; s/d from €33/50; ☐) This
is a great-value authentic oldie with an evocative history; former guests include Ivo Andrić,
Josephine Baker and German staff during
WWII. Some spacious creaky rooms have
balconies overlooking Piornirski Park.

Kasina Hotel (Map pp810-11; ☎ 323 5575; www.kasina
.stari-grad.co.yu; Terazije 25; s/d standard €42/€81, comfort
€81/103; ☒ ☐) Depending on your choice of
'comfort' or 'standard' you get air-conditioning and a minibar, or neither and slightly
darker rooms.

Hotel Palace (Map pp810-11; ☎ 263 7222; www.palace
hotel.co.yu; Topličin Venac 23; s/d/ste €70/105/130; ☐) A
grand oldie that has kept up with the times,
Hotel Palace books up quickly for freshly
furnished rooms, large bathrooms and
wireless.

Not particularly pretty but well-facilitated
options include **Hotel Prag** (Map pp810-11; ☎ 361
0422; www.hotelprag.co.yu; Kraljice Natalije 27; s/d with air-
con 4700/6500DIN, without air-con 4100/5900DIN; ☒ ☐)
and **Hotel Union** (Map pp810-11; ☎ 324 8022; www.hotel
unionbelgrade.com; Kosovska 11; s/d from €49/79; ☒ ☐).

Cross your fingers that **Hotel Splendid** (Map
pp810-11; ☎ 323 5444; www.splendid.co.yu; D Jovanovića
5) reopens in this price category (and lives up
to its name) when renovations are finished.

Top End
ourpick Hotel Moscow (Hotel Moskva; Map pp810-11;
☎ 268 6255; hotelmoskva@absolutok.net; Balkanska 1; s/d
from €100/€143; ☒ ☐) A source of city pride
since it opened in 1906, the art nouveau
Moscow has not made a move to modernise.
Despite some single rooms persecuting you
for not being a double and prices that mock
the common man, this is the place to scrib-
ble your memoirs at a big old desk.

Le Petit Piaf (Map pp810-11; ☎ 303 5252; www.petitpiaf
.com; Skadarska 34; ste €120-170; ☒ ☐) This hotel fits
right into Skadarska – Belgrade's answer to
Montmartre. Loft rooms evoke Parisian apartments with split levels and sloping ceilings.

Balkan Hotel (Map pp810-11; ☎ 3636 000; www
.balkanhotel.net; Prizrenska 2; s/d from 9020/10,660DIN, ste
12,000-18,400DIN; ☒ ☐) Renovations have made
the Balkan's modern rooms incongruous
with the old-world exterior. The attached
old-world Orient Express cafe is an asset.

Aleksandar Palas (Map pp810-11; ☎ 330 5300; www
.aleksandarpalas.com; Kralja Petra 13-15; apt €250; ☒ ☐)
Exclusive but unpretentious, this place offers
nine suites with king-sized beds, home entertainment systems, and blinged-up showers. Prices drop on weekends.

EATING
The choice is particularly overwhelming
along Knez Mihailova, 29 Novembra and
Makedonska.

Skadarska
Šešir Moj (My Hat; Map pp810-11; ☎ 322 8750;
Skadarska 21; meals 300-500DIN; ☺ 9am-2am) Roma
bands swirl past your alcove, playing heart-
tugging music as you hoe into a *punjena bela
vešalica* (pork fillet stuffed with *kajmak*).

Writers' Club (Klub Književnika; Map pp810-11; ☎ 262
7931; Francuska 7; meals 400-600DIN; ☺ 8pm-2am) Once
frequented by state-approved literati of the
Tito era, locals still come here for stuffed
courgettes and roast lamb. Things get busy
around 10pm.

Guli (Map pp810-11; ☎ 323 7204; Skadarska 13; meals
400-800DIN; ☺ noon-11am Mon-Sat, 2-11pm Sun) A
modern rebel in old-world Skadarska, Guli
offers pizza, pasta and international wine
selections acclaimed by A-list clientele.

Central Belgrade
? (Map pp810-11; ☎ 635 421; Kralja Petra 6; meals 250-
500DIN; ☺ 8am-midnight) An essential albeit hit-
and-miss dining experience, this old-style
tavern (in both atmosphere and flavour) offers tender lamb or veal *ispod sača* (which is
more enticing than the young bull's sex glands
on offer). Its quizzical name is the result of a
dispute with the adjacent church, which ob-
jected to the tavern naming itself in relation
to a house of god.

ourpick Little Bay (Map pp810-11; ☎ 328 4163; www
.little-bay.co.uk; Dositejeva 9A; meal 400DIN; ☺ 9am-1am)
Inexplicably cheap and one of the finest dining experiences you'll have in Serbia, here you
can enjoy carpaccio with blue-cheese mousse
and mustard pear (240DIN) or a traditional
roast (295DIN) in a private opera box or

under the marquee or on the tree-lined street, while an opera singer belts out Puccini in the middle of it all.

allo allo (Map pp810-11; ☎ 323 8888; Svetozara Markovića 19A; meals 350-600DIN; ☯ 9am-midnight) If you're sick of *šopska salata*, come here for a nuanced salad like rocket and pine-nut laden 'Le Cler' (550DIN) or sesame sprinkled 'Lili' (350DIN). Pizzas aren't the cheapest, but are up there with the best. Black-tied waiters bring a blanket if you get chilly on the terrace.

Trattoria Košava (Map pp810-11; ☎ 262 7344; www .trattoriakosova.com; Kralja Petra 36; meals 400-800DIN; ☯ 8am-1am Mon-Fri, noon-1am Sat & Sun) Sit upstairs in lamp-lit nostalgia and enjoy an enormous plate of wildberry pancakes (250DIN).

Iguanaćošku (Iguana at the Corner; Map pp810-11; ☎ 744 8690; www.iguanacosku.com; Beogradska 37; meals 800-1200DIN; ☯ noon-11am Mon-Sat, 1-5pm Sun). After 15 years in Melbourne, husband and wife Goran and Bata brought the kids and Australian fusion food back to Belgrade. Thai, French and Indian highlights have class and kick. Try salmon steak with sweet chilli sauce and coconut milk (880DIN).

Jevrem (Map pp810-11; ☎ 328 4746; www.restoran -jevrem.com; Gospodar Jevrema 36; meals 800DIN; ☯ 11am-1am Mon-Sat) Decorated to 1920s tastes with plush armchairs and white umbrellas in the courtyard Jevrem offers elegant food and live music (8pm Thursday to Saturday).

Que Pasa? (Map pp810-11; ☎ 330 5377; www.ale ksandarpalas.com; Kralja Petra 13-15; meals 600-1300DIN; ☯ 10am-2am Tue-Sat, 10am-1am Sun-Mon) Spacious, luminous and chic, this restaurant attracts highrollers from the 30+ bracket. Like the music, the menu leans decidedly towards Mexico. Have a burrito brunch with multi-vitamin juice (420DIN), turkey in hazelnut sauce (720DIN, 912 calories) or 'Steak My Love' (1250DIN, 1066 calories).

Post or pre-clubbing munchies can be satiated around Trg Republike for under 100DIN. Follow your nose to **Pekara Toma** (Map pp810-11; Kolarčeva 10; snacks 50-200DIN; ☯ 24hr) for freshly baked pizzas, pastries, bread or salads.

Zeleni venac market (Map pp810-11; cnr Brankova Prizrenska & Narodnog Fronta; ☯ 7am-4pm) is scrounging ground for DIY food.

Outer Belgrade

Priroda (off Map p808; ☎ 241 1890; sneskapriroda@ yahoo.com; Batutova 11; meals 250-400DIN; ☯ noon-7pm) Despite odd opening hours, Priroda, about 6km east of the central train station, is a

superb vegetarian restaurant where even carnivores will appreciate the break from Serbian staples.

Dačo (off Map p808; ☎ 278 1009; www.kafana-daco .com; Patrisa Lumumbe 49; meals 250-700DIN; ☯ 10am-midnight Tue-Sun) A village experience on steroids, at Dačo chillies hang from ceilings, bits and bobs clutter walls, and musicians bully diners into sing-alongs. It's a few kilometres from the centre, but the food is well worth the haul; get going before you get hungry. Reservations recommended.

DRINKING

There's a fine line between a cafe, bar and club in Belgrade. Quiet cafes morph into drinking dens at night and thumping clubs in early hours. In spring and summer, action spills onto terraces and pavements.

Bars

our pick **Federal Association of Globe-Trotters** (Map pp810-11; ☎ 324 2303; www.aur.org.yu; Bul Despota Stefana 7/1; ☯ 1pm-midnight Mon-Fri, 3pm-late Sat & Sun) Through the black gate, past the lazy cats and down the dingy staircase is an oasis of eclectic cool. Trust us.

Ben Akiba (Map pp810-11; ☎ 323 7775; Nušićeva 8; ☯ 9am-late) Belgrade's worst-kept secret is a converted 1st-floor flat which began as a haven for liberals to drink and deplore Milošević. Now Belgrade's chic come for cocktail conversations. Walls often exhibit local art.

Three Carrots (Map pp810-11; ☎ 683 748; www .threecarrots.co.yu; Kneza Milosa 16; ☯ 9am-1am) Fast-flowing Guinness and occasional live music draws cosmopolitan crowds to Belgrade's Irish offering.

Pastis Bistro (☎ 328 8188; Strahinjića bana 52B; ☯ 8am-late) Less pretentious than its neighbours, this is the place to go if you're feeling sociable. The mood is mild, the tunes smooth, and the people suave.

Crveni Petao (Map pp810-11; ☎ 262 0050; Cara Lazana 16; ☯ 9am-2am) The place locals come for their post-work-week wind-down and pre-weekend rev-up, Crveni Petao is an outdoor bar pleasantly plonked where two streets intersect.

Cafes

Russian Tsar (Ruski Car; Map pp810-11; ☎ 633 628; Obilićev venac 28; ☯ 8am-1am) Renovated to look like it hasn't changed for 100 years, Russian Tsar has gold trimmings and dripping chandeliers that

SERBIA

add dollars to decadent cakes. If you're indecisive, grab the surprise dessert (325DIN).

Try a mocha at **Greenet** (Map pp810-11; ☎ 323 8474; Nušićeva 3; ☒ 8am-midnight), *the* place for local coffee connoisseurs.

ENTERTAINMENT
Nightclubs

The club scene in Belgrade is limited only by imagination and hours in the day. The music is a smorgasbord of well-known European and local DJs playing house, R&B, hip hop, drum 'n' bass, Balkan beats of turbofolk or lurid tones of jazz.

CITY NIGHTCLUBS

Andergraund (Underground; Map pp810-11; ☎ 063 407070; www.andergraund.com; Pariška 1A; ☒ 10am-4am) The city's most legendary nightspot, Andergraund has spaces on a tiered terrace on the citadel walls, but most of it is underneath in an old cavern where sweaty crowds gyrate.

White (Map pp810-11; ☎ 063 308 039; Pariška 1A; ☒ 11am-4am) Next door to Andergraund, this place pulls a colourful crowd of disco and house fans.

Akademija (Art Kafe 'Fleka'; Map pp810-11; ☎ 627 846; www.akademija.net, in Serbian; Rajićeva 10; ☒ 10pm-4am Mon-Sat, noon-2am Sun) This is a basement institution where alternative crowds and student activists have been rocking for two decades; anything from funk and punk to reggae, electro or fetish happens here.

Oh! Cinema! (Map pp810-11; ☎ 328 4000; Kalemegdan Citadel; ☒ 11pm-4am) During the day, upbeat tunes here coax you into early alcohol, and the views from the eastern bulwarks of the citadel keep you drinking till dawn. This terrace bar is open in summer only.

Plastic (Map pp810-11; ☎ 064 640 3956; www.club-plastic.com; cnr Dalmatinska & Takovska; ☒ 10pm-late Thu-Sat) A slick venue where DJs spin house, trance and techno, Plastic offers an electric atmosphere with plenty of chill-out space to rest your dance-slammed bones.

Bitef Art Cafe (Map pp810-11; ☎ 063 594 294; www.bitefartcafe.co.yu; Skver Mire Trailović 1; ☒ 7pm-4am) Beloved particularly by funk, soul and jazz aficionados, this cafe offers pop one night, a string quartet the next or even a straight-up, sit-down performance.

DUNAV BARGES

Adjacent to Hotel Jugoslavija in Novi Belgrade is a 1km-long strip of some 20 barges. Most are closed in winter. Get there with bus 15 or 84 from Zeleni Venac or 68, 603 or 701 from Trg Republike. Get out at Hotel Jugoslavija.

Blaywatch (off Map p808; ☎ 064 477 771; www.blaywatch.net.yu; ☒ midnight-4am) This throbbing, fleshy place gets crowded and dress codes may be enforced (sneakers bad on boys, skimpy good on girls). The crowd at this party palace is a mix of locals and foreigners, all occupied with each other, and the dance and turbo tunes.

Bibis (off Map p808; ☎ 319 2150; www.bibis.co.yu; ☒ 10am-2am) Bibis is a pleasant place to eat during the day before it morphs into a club after dark. This is a good choice to sample a splav (see below), with a diverse crowd you can blend into. The music changes from night to night (though turbofolk is rarely played), but on the whole it's a good place for a chat and a drink before you hit its larger, louder neighbours.

Akapulco (off Map p808; ☎ 778 4760; ☒ noon-3am) Where blinged-up boys come to flaunt their money and she-accessories. Stay away if you have a low turbofolk threshold.

SAVA RIVER BARGES

On the western bank of the Sava River is a 1.5km strip of floating bars, restaurants and discos known as 'splavs'. Most are only open in summer.

Leading the pack at the moment, enormous **Freestyler** (☎ 063 300 839; www.splavfree.rs; Brodaska bb; ☒ 1am-5am Thu-Sun) churns out house, techno and R&B to packed-in patrons. Nearby, **Exile** (☎ 063 819 0855; Savski kej bb; ☒ midnight-3am) pounds out techno and **Sound** (Savski kej bb; ☒ midnight-3am) plays house and disco. Others are **Babilon** (☎ 318 0232; Savski kej bb) and **Cruise** (☎ 215 7210; Savski kej bb).

Walk over Brankov Most or take tram 7, 9 or 11.

Performing Arts

For concert and theatre tickets, go to **Bilet Servis** (Map pp810-11; ☎ 303 3311; www.biletservis.co.yu; Trg Republike 5; ☒ 9am-11pm Mon-Sat, noon-10pm Sun).

During winter, the **National Theatre** (Map pp810-11; ☎ 262 0946; www.narodnopozoriste.co.yu; Trg Republike; ☒ box office 10am-2pm Tue-Sun) has opera performances, or you can see the Belgrade Philharmonia at the **Kolarčev University Concert Hall** (Map pp810-11; ☎ 630 550; Studentski Trg 5; ☒ box office 10am-noon & 6-8pm). **Dom Omladine** (Map pp810-11;

324 8202; www.domomladine.org; Makedonska 22; box office 10am-10pm) hosts a range of cultural events, while **Serbian Academy of Arts & Sciences** (Map pp810-11; 334 2400; www.saisu.ac.yu; Knez Mihailova 35; concerts 6pm Mon & Thu) has free concerts and exhibitions. For larger exhibitions and visiting stars, look to **Sava Centar** (Map p808; 220 6060; www.savacentar.com; Milentija Popovića 9, Novi Beograd; box office 10am-8pm Mon-Fri, 10am-3pm Sat).

Cinemas

For Hollywood blockbusters in English or with English subtitles try **Tuckwood Cineplex** (Map pp810-11; 323 6517; www.tuck.co.yu; Kneza Miloša 7; tickets 150-280DIN) or **Dom Sindikata** (Map pp810-11; 323 4849; www.dds.co.yu; Trg Nikole Pašića 5; tickets 200-250DIN).

SHOPPING

Belgrade's main street, Knez Mihailova, is lined with global brands. Souvenir supplies can be bought from vendors in Kalemegdan Park and the **craft street market** (Map pp810-11; cnr Kralja Milana & Njegoševa; 8am-5pm Mon-Sat), and there's Belgrade-themed stationary at **IPS** (Map pp810-11; 328 1859; Trg Republic 5; 9am-9pm Mon-Fri, 10am-5pm Sat). See p809 for bookshops.

GETTING THERE & AWAY
Bus

Belgrade has two adjacent bus stations: **BAS** (Map pp810-11; 636 299; Železnička 4) serves the region, while **Lasta** (Map pp810-11; 625 740; Železnička bb) deals with destinations around Belgrade.

Sample services are Subotica (440DIN, three hours), Niš (460DIN, three hours), Podgorica (940DIN, nine hours), Budva (1160DIN, 12 hours) and Novi Pazar (580DIN, three hours) for Kosovo.

International routes include Banja Luka (1665DIN, 7½ hours, daily), Bratislava (2600DIN, 12 hours, Wednesday and Sunday), Ljubljana (3000DIN, 7½ hours, daily), Milan (4920DIN, 17½ hours, Wednesday and Saturday), Paris (7600DIN, 28 hours, Monday, Tuesday, Wednesday, Friday and Saturday), Sarajevo (1640DIN, eight hours, daily), Split (3800DIN, 12½ hours, Monday to Saturday), Vienna (2560DIN, 9½ hours, Monday to Thursday) and Zürich (5700DIN, 23 hours, Tuesday and Saturday).

Car & Motorcycle

Several car-hire companies have offices at Nikola Tesla Beograd Airport:
AVIS (209 7062; www.avis-serbia.co.yu; 8am-8pm)
Budget (228 6361; www.budget.co.yu; 8am-8pm Mon-Fri, 8am-6pm Sat, 8am-5pm Sun)
Europcar (228 9028; www.europcar.co.uk; 8am-9pm Mon-Fri, noon-9pm Sat & Sun)
Hertz (228 6017; www.hertz.co.yu; 8am-8pm)

Train

The **central train station** (Map pp810-11; 629 400; Savski Trg 2) has an **information office** (361 8487; platform 1; 7am-7pm), **tourist office** (361 2732; 9am-8pm Mon-Fri, 9am-5pm Sat, 10am-4pm Sun), **exchange bureau** (6am-10pm) and **sales counter** (/fax 265 8868; 9am-4pm Mon-Sat).

Frequent trains go to Novi Sad (199DIN, 1½ hours) and Subotica (420DIN, three hours).

International daily departures (prices include sleeper) from Belgrade include Bucharest (4200DIN, 14 hours), Budapest (2780DIN, seven hours), İstanbul (5190DIN, 26 hours), Ljubliana (4150DIN, 10 hours), Moscow (10,000DIN, 50 hours), Munich (9000DIN, 17 hours), Sofia (2600DIN, 11 hours), Thessaloniki (4200DIN, 16 hours), Vienna (6950DIN, 11 hours), and Zagreb (3100DIN, seven hours).

GETTING AROUND
To/From the Airport

Nikola Tesla Airport is 18km from Belgrade. **JAT bus** (675 583) connects the airport with the **JAT bus terminal** (Trg Slavija) via the railway station (200DIN, hourly 7am to 10pm from airport, hourly 5am to 9pm from town, or coordinated with scheduled JAT flights). Alternatively, bus 72 connects the airport with Zaleni Venac (46DIN to 60DIN, half-hourly from 5am to midnight from airport, 4.40am to 11.40pm from town); the cheapest tickets must be purchased from news-stands.

Don't fall in the taxi shark pit outside the airport (where you could be charged up to €30 for a 30-minute ride which shouldn't be more than €15); ask the tourist office in the arrivals hall to call one for you. A taxi from the airport to Knez Mihailova should be around 1100DIN.

Car & Motorcycle

Parking in Belgrade is regulated by three parking zones – red (one hour), yellow (two hours)

SERBIA

and green (three hours). Tickets must be bought from kiosks or via SMS (best avoided if you don't read Serbian).

See p817 for car-hire companies.

Public Transport

Trams and trolleybuses serve limited routes, but buses ply all over town. Tickets cost 29DIN from a street kiosk or 40DIN from the driver.

Tram 2 connects Kalemegdan Citadel with Trg Slavija, the bus stations and the central train station.

Taxi

Whatever experience you have with taxi drivers at transport hubs, don't hold it against all of them. Move away from hubs and flag down a distinctly labelled cruising cab. A 5km trip costs around 200DIN.

AROUND BELGRADE

It's easy to get waylaid in Belgrade, but you can get a glimpse of the country beyond the capital with suprisingly little effort. Even southern Serbian towns such as Topola and Despotovac can be visited as day trips from Belgrade.

ZEMUN ЗЕМУН

Some 6km northwest of central Belgrade, Zemun was the most southerly point of the Austro-Hungarian empire when the Turks ruled Belgrade.

Above the market area, up the narrow cobbled street of Grobnjačka, remnants of the old village lead uphill towards **Gardoš** fortress dating to the 9th century. Walls from the 15th-century remain, as does the **Tower of Sibinjanin Janko**, built in 1896 to celebrate the millennial anniversary of the Hungarian state and to keep an eye on the Turks.

Descending from the tower is **Nikolajevska church** (Njegoševa 43), dating to 1731, with some astoundingly beautiful baroque iconostasis.

At the time of writing, **Zemun Museum** (☎ 316 5234; Glavna 9) was closed for extensive renovations which will hopefully be worth the wait.

Zemun is a laid-back accommodation alternative to Belgrade. Floating between Zemun and Belgrade is Arka Barka (p813) hostel. The lobby of the more upmarket **Hotel Skala** (☎ 307 5032; Bežanijska 3; s/d/apt 6300/8100/9000DIN;

🖥 ❄) has homely wi-fi–equipped rooms and a basement restaurant.

Among the many venues serving fish and fun along the Dunav:

Aleksandar (☎ 199 462; Kej Oslobođenja 49; meals 500DIN; ☺ 9am-midnight)

Venecija (☎ 307 7611; Kej Oslobeđja bb; meals from 600DIN; ☺ 9am-midnight)

Reka (☎ 261 1625; www.reka.co.yu; Kej Oslobođenja 73B; fish mains 600-1000DIN)

Zemun is a 45-minute walk from Belgrade (across Brankov Most, along Nikole Tesle and the Kej Oslogođenja waterside walkway) or take bus 15 or 64 from Zeleni Venac market, or bus 83 from the main train station.

SMEDEREVO СМЕДЕРЕВО

The shockingly large **Smederevo Fortress** (admission 50DIN; ☺ 8am-8pm), 46km southwest of Belgrade, is a 25-tower triangular fort, built impressively quickly by despot Đurađ Brankovic. The fortification was conquered by the Turks in 1459 (after 20 years of trying). Immense damage was caused by an explosion of a German ammunition train in WWII.

Lovingly maintained **Smederevo Museum** (☎ 026 222 138; admission 70DIN; ☺ 10am-5pm Tue-Fri, 10am-3pm Sat & Sun) records town history with artefacts dating from Roman times. There is little English, but walking around (probably by yourself) is pleasant.

Regular buses (330DIN, 1½ hours, every 15 minutes) leave from Belgrade's Lasta station. The museum is a block left of the bus station. If you can't see the fortress just beyond across the train tracks, you're beyond help.

VOJVODINA ВОЈВОДИНА

Some of Serbia's highlights spring forth from the level plains of Vojvodina, a rich mix of Hungarian and Serbian cultures and traditions. Its capital, Novi Sad, hosts the Exit Festival – one of the freshest festivals in the Balkans. Nearby the rolling hills of Fruška Gora are pierced by monasteries and the enchanting town of Sremski Karlovci; once the home of the Serbian Orthodox Patriarchate. Closer to Hungary in both distance and character is Subotica; an art deco dream.

NOVI SAD НОВИ САД
☎ 021 / pop 299,000

When it's not hosting Serbia's biggest music festival, Novi Sad is an upbeat town just for the hell of it. Cafes spill onto the main thoroughfare which locals prowl for ice cream, and atmospheric alleyways are social centres after dark. All of this is presided over by Petrovaradin Citadel atop a mighty volcanic rock.

Orientation

A 2.5km walk down Bulevar Oslobođenja from the bus or train station, and left on Pavla Papa leads to the centre. Alternatively take bus 11A to the city bus station and find Zmaj Jovina, the heart of Novi Sad, one block south. Leading off here, cobbled Dunavska is a hub of shops and cafes, while Laze Telečkog is the place to drink the night away.

Glavni Most bridge delivers you to the foot of the citadel.

Information
BOOKSHOPS

IPS Megastore (☎ 421 302; Zmaj Jovina 16; ☼ 9am-9pm Mon-Sat) CDs, DVDs and guidebooks.

INTERNET ACCESS

Internet Club Net 21 (☎ 064 223 5010; Zmaj Jovina 14; per hr 50DIN; ☼ 24hr)

Kym Internet Club (☎ 423 161; cnr Laze Telečkog & Mite Tuzica; per hr 65DIN; ☼ 24hr)

INTERNET RESOURCES

Tourist Organisation of Vojvodina (www.vojvodina online.com)

MEDICAL SERVICES

Apoteka Pharmacy (☎ 402 820; www.apoteka novisad.co.rs; Mihajla Pupina 7; ☼ 7.30am-9pm Mon-Fri, 7am-9pm Sat) Art deco drugery!

MONEY

Raiffeisen Bank (☎ 488 0200; Trg Slobode 3; ☼ 8am-7pm Mon-Fri, 9am-3pm Sat)

UniCredit Bank (www.unicreditbank.co.yu; Trg Slobode 3; ☼ 9am-4.30pm Mon-Wed & Fri, 9am-6pm Thu)

POST

Main post office (☎ 614 708; Narodnih Heroja 2; ☼ 9am-9pm Mon-Sat, 10am-6pm Sun) Also telephone centre.

SERBIA

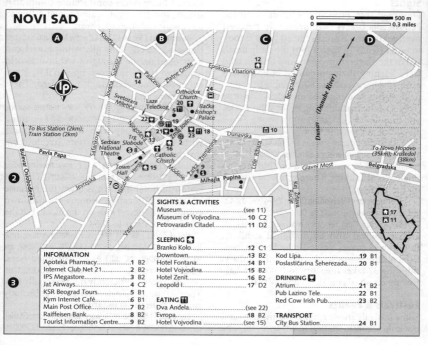

NOVI SAD

0 ___ 500 m
0 ___ 0.3 miles

SIGHTS & ACTIVITIES
Museum	(see 11)
Museum of Vojvodina	10 C2
Petrovaradin Citadel	11 D2

SLEEPING 🛏
Branko Kolo	12 C1
Downtown	13 B2
Hotel Fontana	14 B1
Hotel Vojvodina	15 B2
Hotel Zenit	16 B2
Leopold I	17 D2

EATING 🍴
Dva Anđela	(see 22)
Evropa	18 B2
Hotel Vojvodina	(see 15)

INFORMATION
Apoteka Pharmacy	1 B2
Internet Club Net 21	2 B2
IPS Megastore	3 B2
Jat Airways	4 C2
KSR Beograd Tours	5 B1
Kym Internet Café	6 B1
Main Post Office	7 B2
Raiffeisen Bank	8 B2
Tourist Information Centre	9 B2

Kod Lipa	19 B1
Poslastičarina Šeherezada	20 B1

DRINKING 🍸
Atrium	21 B2
Pub Lazino Tele	22 B2
Red Cow Irish Pub	23 B2

TRANSPORT
City Bus Station	24 B1

ENTERING THE STATE OF EXIT

Every July, people unite around Petrovaradin Citadel (below) for the epic **Exit Festival** (www.exitfest .org; 4 days approx €90, camping €18). The first festival, in 2000, lasted 100 days and is remembered for having energised a generation of young Serbs against Milošević. Since then it has grown to attract musicians and audiences from around the region and beyond. In 2006, rather than tickets, revellers were issued with passports to the State of Exit – the 'newest Balkan State' and a decidedly peaceful one. The star-studded 2007 line-up included the Beastie Boys, Groove Armada, Lauryn Hill, Robert Plant, Snoop Dogg and the Prodigy. The likes of Manu Chau, Primal Scream, the Sex Pistols and The Hives attended Exit in 2008... along with more than 100,000 audience members.

TOURIST INFORMATION

Tourist information centre (☎ 421 811; www .novisadtourism.org.yu; Mihajla Pupina 9; ⊗ 8.30am-8pm Mon-Thu, 7.30am-8pm Fri, 7.30am-2pm Sat) Professional people to direct you in and around Novi Sad.

TRAVEL AGENCIES

Autoturist (☎ 523 863; www.autoturist.co.yu; Mite Ruzica 2; ⊗ 8am-8pm Mon-Fri, 8am-2pm Sat) Bus tickets and local tours.
KSR Beograd Tours (☎ 527 455; Svetozara Miletića 4; ⊗ 7am-7pm Mon-Fri, 7am-1pm Sat) Train tickets.

Sights

Designed by French architect Vauban, **Petrovaradin Citadel** is impressively perched overlooking the river. In the 88 years it took to build (from 1692 to 1780) the daily death toll of the slaves, murderers and thieves who were 'earning their purgatory' building it is estimated between 70 to 80. Notable prisoners held within its dungeons include Karađorđe (leader of the first uprising against the Turks, and founder of a dynasty) and a young Tito – albeit not at the same time.

Within the citadel's walls the **museum** (☎ 433 613, 433 145; muzgns@eunet.yu; admission 100DIN; ⊗ 9am-5pm Tue-Sun) is beautifully laid out but lacking English explanations. There's striking artwork on the 1st floor.

The **Museum of Vojvodina** (Muzej Vojvodine; ☎ 420 566; www.muzejvojvodine.org.yu; Dunavska 35-7; admission 100DIN; ⊗ 9am-5pm Tue-Sun) houses historical, archaeological and ethnological exhibits. Building 35 covers Vojvodinian history from Palaeolithic times to the late 19th century. Building 37 takes the story to 1945 with harrowing emphasis on WWI and WWII.

Festivals & Events

Some festivals are worth making the trip (and booking accommodation in advance) for. The biggest is July's Exit Festival (above) which secures a stellar line-up each year. **Cinema City Festival** (www.cinemacity.org) in June may do for movies what Exit has done for music. September's **International Festival of Street Musicians** (www.cekans.org.yu) turns Novi Sad into an open-air stage. **Novi Sad Jazz Festival** (www.kcns .org.yu), held each November since 1979, gets better every year.

Sleeping

Brankovo Kolo (☎ 528 623; www.hostelns.com; Visarionova 3; d/tr/q per person €8/7/6; 🖳) A centrally located hostel with comfortable communal spaces, this is a great option (open 1 July to 25 August only). Book ahead.

Downtown (☎ 64 192 0342; www.hotelsnovisad.com; Njegoševa 2; dm €10) This glistening hostel can be booked online through www.hostelworld .com, but if you just rock up you'll be given coffee and conversation, if not a bed. There is one twin room.

Hotel Fontana (☎ 621 779; www.fontana-ns.com; Pašićeva 27; s/d/tr 2800/3300/4000DIN; ⊠) Fontana is casual and cosy with well-sized rooms with slanting wooden roofs overlooking the courtyard.

Hotel Vojvodina (☎ 622 122; www.hotelvojvodina .co.yu; Trg Slobode 2; s/d from 3100/4400DIN) The last state-run hotel in town is often full because of its central location. Rooms are rundown compared to newer kids on the block, but the atmosphere dates to 1854.

Hotel Zenit (☎ 621 444; www.hotelzenit.co.yu; Zmaj Jovina 8; s 4700-5700DIN; d 5700-6500DIN, tr 8200DIN, apt 10,000-15,100DIN; ⊠ 🖳) A glass-fronted hotel with cosy rooms in a prime location, this popular place is efficiently but personally run. The two cheaper single rooms are significantly smaller than the standard rooms.

Leopold I (☎ 488 7878; www.leopoldns.com; Citadel; s 9900-10,725DIN, d 7425-14,025DIN, apt 15,680-29,700DIN)

Renovated a year ago, the infinite corridors here are lined with 60 rooms in Gothic, Renaissance or the more economical modern style. The cherry on the cake is the Leopold I apartment, fit for a Kaiser or a family of four.

Eating

Kod Lipa (☎ 615 259; Svetozara Miletića 7; meals from 250DIN; ⏰ 8am-11pm) Old photographs show that little has changed at Kod Lipa since it started serving Vojvodinian cooking in the 19th century.

Restaurant Fontana (☎ 064 351 7914; www .restoranfontana.com; meals from 400DIN; ⏰ 9am-late) This tucked-away place is where local gastronomes eat in the ambient dining room or around the courtyard fountain.

Dva Anđela (☎ 662 4989; Laze Telečkog 14; mains 500DIN; ⏰ 9am-11pm Mon-Thu, 9am-1am Fri & Sat, 11am-11pm Sun) A slick new place with iPod-cool interiors. Nab a people-watching position along Laze Talečkog and try penne with porcini (440DIN).

Go to **Evropa** (Dunavska 6; cakes 50-100DIN; ⏰ 8am-midnight) for *žito*, traditional dessert made of crushed wheat and walnuts. For cold calorie bombs, try **Poslastičarnica Šeherezada** (☎ 623 280; Zmaj Jovina 19; desserts 140DIN; ⏰ 8am-1am).

Drinking

Laze Telečkog is lined with bars of different moods and characters. There's **Atrium** (atrium@ bomar.co.yu; Laze Telečkog 2; ⏰ 9am-midnight), serving drinks in a faux library, on balconies, or on the main thoroughfare, and **Pub Lazino Tele** (Laze Telečkog 16; www.lazinotele.com; ⏰ 8am-1am), with an eclectic atmosphere making it a good choice on a street of endless choices. Also popular, **Red Cow Irish Pub** (cnr Dunavska & Zmaj Jovina; ⏰ 8am-1am) is on the 1st floor off the courtyard opposite the city library on Zmaj Jovina.

Getting There & Away

You can arrange flights with the national carrier **JAT Airways** (☎ 456 397; www.jat.com; Mihajla Pupina 18; ⏰ 9am-5pm Mon-Fri) here.

Frequent trains leave the **train station** (☎ 443 200; Bulevar Jaše Tomića 4) for Belgrade (330DIN, 1½ hours) and Subotica (290DIN, 1½ hours).

The **bus station** (☎ 442 021; Bulevar Jaše Tomića 6; ⏰ information counter 6am-11pm) next door has frequent services to Belgrade (590DIN, one hour, every 10 minutes) and Subotica (690DIN, two hours, hourly), but these are more expensive and slower than trains. Buses also go to Uzice (950DIN, five hours) and Zlatibor (1060DIN, six hours).

SUBOTICA СУБОТИЦА
☎ 024 / pop 148,400

Serbian and Hungarian languages mingle in the streets, the smell of goulash laces the air and art nouveau buildings (1908–12) sparkle in this proud, provincial town.

SERBIA

WORTH THE TRIP: FRUŠKA GORA & SREMSKI KARLOVCI
ФРУШКА ГОРА & СРЕМСКИ КАРЛОВЦИ

Fruška Gora is an 80km stretch of rolling hills where monastic life has continued for centuries. Thirty-five monasteries were built here between the 15th and 18th centuries to protect Serbian culture and religion from the Turks. With your own wheels you can flit freely between the 16 remaining monasteries. Otherwise, ask about tours at tourist offices in Novi Sad (opposite) and Sremski Karlovci (below). Public transport gets you to villages within the park from where you can walk between sights. An easy outing is done with a bus from Novi Sad bound for Irig; ask to be let out at the **Novo Hopovo Monastery** (150DIN, 30 minutes), an easy five-minute walk. From here walk or catch local buses to other points such as **Vrdnik**. Get a local map such as the Geokarta 1:60,000 *Fruška Gora* map (210DIN) and visit www.npfruskagora.co.yu.

At the edge of Fruška Gora on the banks of the Dunav (Danube River) is the misplaced town of Sremski Karlovci, layered in historical significance. Lined with stunning structures like the **Orthodox cathedral** (1758–62), the baroque **Four Lions fountain** and the **Chapel of Peace** at the southern end of town (where the Turks and Austrians signed the 1699 Peace Treaty), Sremski Karlovci is also at the heart of a famed wine region. Visit the **Museum of Beekeeping & Wine Cellar** (☎ 881 071; muzpcela@eunet.yu; Mitropolita Stratimirovića 86) to try famous bermet wine.

Take frequent buses 61 or 62 from Novi Sad (100DIN, 30 minutes) and visit the **tourist organisation** (☎ 882 128, 883 855; www.karlovci.co.yu; Branka Radičevića 7; ⏰ 9am-5pm Mon-Sat) in the main square.

Orientation

The art nouveau Modern Art Gallery is through the park opposite the train station on Đure Đakovića, and is one of the most beautiful buildings in the country. The bus station is 1km left (southeast) of here. About 100m left of the museum is the pedestrian street (Korzo) on the right, leading to the clock tower, under which is the tourist information centre.

Information

Bookshop (☎ 551 845; 7.30am-7pm Mon-Fri, 7.30am-1pm Sat) Old-world bookshop through the park opposite the clock tower.

Exchange office (Train station; 8am-6.30pm Mon-Sat, 8am-7pm Sun)

Left-luggage office (Train station; per item 60DIN; 24hr)

Pireus Bank (9am-5pm Mon-Fri, 9am-1pm Sun)

Raiffeisen Bank (8am-7pm Mon-Fri, 9am-3pm Sat)

Tourist information office (☎ 670 350; ticsu@subotica.net; town hall; 8am-8pm Mon-Sat, to noon Sun) On the park side of the town hall.

Sights

Subotica's main attraction is its art nouveau architecture. Most sights are along Korzo and on the main square, Trg Republike.

The **town hall** (Trg Republike) built in 1910, is a curious mix of art nouveau and something Gaudí may have had a playful dab at. It houses an engaging **historical museum** (admission 50DIN; 10am-2pm Tue-Fri, 10am-1pm Sat). If the exquisitely decorated council chambers are open, don't miss them.

One of the most stunning buildings in Serbia, the graceful **Modern Art Gallery** (☎ 552 651; liksus@tippnet.co.yu; Trg Lenjina 5; admission 50DIN; 8am-6pm Mon-Fri, 9am-noon Sat) is adorned with mosaics, floral patterns, ceramic tiles and stained-glass windows.

The 1854 **National Theatre** on the main square is a Romanesque terracotta structure resting on six heavy pillars; it's Serbia's oldest theatre.

The first art nouveau building to have sprung up in Subotica, the magnificent **synagogue** is in a tattered state, which renovations will hopefully remedy.

Sleeping

Well hidden behind the Ekonomski Fakultet at Segedinksi put 11, **Hostel Bosa Milećević** (☎ 548 290; Marije Vojnić Tošinice 7; per person 930DIN) saves some tidy top-floor rooms for budget travellers.

One of few midrange options in town, **Hotel PBG** (☎ 556 542; www.pbghotel.co.yu; Harambašićeva 21; s/d from 2320/4000DIN;) is located just out of the centre. Hopefully renovations to **Hotel Patria** (a few hundred metres left on leaving the train station) will help fill the city's midrange gap.

At the end of cafe-lined Matije Korvina, the four-star **Hotel Galleria** (☎ 647 111; www.galleria-center.com; Matije Korvina 17, s/d standard 4800/6400DIN, s apt 8000-18,000DIN, d apt 9600-24,000DIN;) offers spacious rooms (two of which are wheelchair-equipped) decked in warm mahogany-look furniture, with bookshelves framing the bed.

Eating

Immediately behind the Modern Art Gallery, **Boss Caffe** (☎ 551 111; www.bosscaffe.com; Matije Korvina 8; 7am-midnight Mon & Wed-Sat, 7am-1am Sun & Tue) offers art nouveau surrounds and a range of food, including tacos (195DIN to 375DIN). Many dishes are offered in entree and main sizes.

Tea must be taken at time-frozen, art nouveau **Ravel** (☎ 554 670; Nušićeva 2; cakes 50-100DIN; 9am-10pm Mon-Sat, 11am-10pm Sun).

Getting There & Away

It's possible to take a day trip to Subotica from Belgrade. From Subotica's **train station** (☎ 555 606) there are two trains to Szeged, Hungary (240DIN, 1¾ hours). Trains to Belgrade (480DIN, 3½ hours) call at Novi Sad (400DIN, 1½ hours).

The **bus station** (☎ 555 566; Marksov Put) has hourly buses to Novi Sad (650DIN, two hours) and Belgrade (900DIN, 3½ hours).

PALIĆ ПАЛИЋ

The centrepiece of Palić, 8km from Subotica and 10km from the Hungarian border, is the 5-sq-km lake for boating, swimming and fishing. In mid-July Palić hosts a **European film festival** (☎ 554 600; www.palicfilmfestival.com).

The **tourist information office** (☎ 753 111; www.palic.co.yu; Kanjiški put 17A; 8am-6pm) can help filter through accommodation options.

From Subotica, take bus 6 from diagonally opposite Hotel Patria (40DIN, 20 minutes).

SOUTHERN SERBIA

Great adventures await south of Belgrade. Zlatibor's rolling hills are a peaceful privilege to explore anytime of year. Dramatic Kopoanik is a popular ski destination for Europeans in the know. Pressed against Balkan neighbours are the melding cultural heritages of the Raška region (known interchangeably by the Turkish 'Sandžak'), the last to be liberated from Ottoman rule in 1912.

The town of Novi Pazar feels more Turkish than some pockets of İstanbul with minarets and Ottoman streets, but nearby are some of the country's most revered Orthodox monasteries.

TOPOLA ТОПОЛА
☎ 034 / pop 25,000

Tiny Topola, 65km from Belgrade, is where Karađorđe pitched the Serbian insurrection against the Turks in 1804 and where his grandson, King Petar I, built one of the most jaw-dropping churches in the country.

One ticket (200DIN) grants access to three impressive sights. Karađorđe led his rebellion from a building that is now a **museum** (Kralijice Marije; �9am-5pm); it's one of the surviving remnants of the old fortified town. The canon at the entrance could be heard all the way to Belgrade, summoning leaders to the very room now housing the bulk of the museum's collection. The missing handle was removed by King Petar I, who made it into a crown for his 1904 coronation.

Atop Oplenac hill, the white-marble, five-domed **Church of St George** (Avenija Kralja Petra I; �8am-7pm) was built by King Petar between 1904 and 1912. Vibrant frescos are magnificently rendered on every inch of the church with over 40 million mosaic pieces. Millions more grace the Karađorđe family mausoleum under the church.

Opposite, **Petar House** (Avenija Kralja Petra I; �8am-7pm) was used by workmen building the church, and by King Petar during his visits to inspect progress. Some humanising portraits of the royal family are exhibited here.

Your ticket also lets you visit the Wine Grower's House at the park entrance.

The **Tourist Organisation of Topola** (☎ 811 172; www.topolaoplenac.org.rs; Kneginje Zorke 13; �8am-5pm Mon-Fri, 10am-5pm Sat) can provide a town map.

Day-trippers can use frequent buses to and from Belgrade (500DIN, 1½ hours).

DESPOTOVAC ДЕСПОТОВАЦ
☎ 035 / pop 25,500

The reasons to come to this idyllic southern Serbian town are nearby Manasija Monastery and Resava Cave.

Manasija monastery, 2km north of Despotovac is fortified by 11 looming towers. A refuge for artists and writers fleeing the Turkish invasion of Kosovo in the first half of the 15th century, the monastery was burnt by the Turks in 1456 and further damaged in 1718 by an explosion of gunpowder stored on the premises by the Austrians. Many consider the Manasija frescos to be predecessors of the Serbian equivalent of Renaissance art.

A winding 20km beyond Despotovac, **Resavska Pećina** (Resava Cave; ☎ 611 110; www .resavska-pecina.co.yu; adult/child 220/170DIN; �9am-5pm Apr-Oct) was discovered in 1962. The guided tour through impressive halls takes around 40 minutes. Brace yourself for camera-happy school groups and temperatures of just 7°C.

A taxi will take you to both the cave and the monastery for around 1600DIN, including waiting time.

Belgrade buses leave four times a day to Despotovac (580DIN, 2½ hours).

NIŠ НИШ
☎ 018 / pop 250,000

Niš is a lively city of curious contrasts, where horse-drawn carriages trot alongside new cars, and cocktails are sipped in cobblestoned alleys.

Niš was settled in pre-Roman times and flourished during the time of local-boy-made-good Emperor Constantine (AD 280–337). Turkish rule lasted from 1386 until 1877 despite several Serb revolts; the tower of Serbian skulls and Tvrđava Citadel are reminders of Turkish dominion. The Nazis built one of the country's most notorious concentration camps here, ironically named 'the Red Cross'.

Orientation & Information

Tvrđava Citadel shelters the adjacent market and bus station. The train station is west on Dimitrija Tucovića. The main pedestrian boulevard, Obrenovićeva, stretches before the citadel. Crossing Nikole Pašića, cobblestoned Kopitareva (Tinker's Alley) was once populated by merchants and is now a trendy eating and drinking area.

SERBIA

Internet cafe (☎ /fax 501 800; Trg Oslobođenja bb; per hr 30DIN; ☺ 7am-11pm) Four computers in the foyer of Hotel Ambassador.

KSR Beograd (☎ /fax 523 808; Trg Oslobođenja 9; ☺ 8am-4pm Mon-Fri, 9am-2pm Sat) Train tickets at station prices.

Post office (Voždova Karađorđa 13A; ☺ 8am-8pm) Internet access for 50DIN per hour.

Tourist Organisation of Niš (☎ 523 118; www .nistourism.org.yu; Voždova Karađorđa 7; ☺ 7.30am-7pm Mon-Fri, 9am-1pm Sat) Maps and domestic bus bookings.

Sights

Built by the Turks in the 18th century, **Tvrđava Citadel** (Jadranska; ☺ 24hr) is now a recreational area with restaurants, cafes, trinket shops and miniature train rides (40DIN). The citadel hosts a blues, rock and pop festival in July and a jazz festival in October.

The **Tower of Skulls** (Ćele Kula; ☎ 222 228; Braće Tankosić bb; adult/child 120/100DIN; ☺ 8am-8pm Tue-Sun Apr-Oct, 9am-4pm Tue-Sat, 10am-4pm Sun Nov-Mar) is an eerie sight. With Serbian defeat imminent at the 1809 Battle of Čegar, the duke of Resava kamikazeed towards the Turkish defences, firing at their gunpowder stores. In doing so, he killed himself, 4000 of his men, and 10,000 Turks. The Turks still triumphed and to deter future acts of rebellion, beheaded, scalped and embedded the skulls of the dead Serbs in this tower. Only 58 of the initial 952 skulls remain. Contrary to Turkish intention, the tower serves as a proud monument of Serbian resistance.

Mediana (☎ 550 433; Bulevar Cara Konstantina bb; admission free; ☺ 8am-4pm Tue-Sat, 10am-6pm Sun, closed Nov-Apr), on the eastern outskirts of Niš, is what remains of Constantine's 4th-century Roman palace. Archaeological digging has so far revealed a palace, forum and an expansive grain-storage area with some almost intact pottery vessels. There's an archaeology collection at the small **museum** (☎ 511 531; Nikole Pašića 59; adult/child 100/80DIN; ☺ 10am-8pm Tue-Sun).

Sleeping

The few choices in Niš are good ones.

More hostels should be like **Hostel Niš** (☎ 515 703; www.hostelnis.com; Dobrička 3A; dm 1050DIN, tw per person 1550DIN; ▯), which is central, clean, friendly, has wireless, lockable trundle draws and is a five-minute walk (towards the river and a block left) from the bus station.

A relic of another era, rooms at **Hotel Ambassador** (☎ /fax 501 800; Trg Oslobođenja bb; s/d 2685/3680, with air-con & TV 3110/4100; ▯ ▯) are

stale but liveable. Photos of Elizabeth Taylor greet you in the foyer (the poor thing was a guest in 1971).

Hidden in an arcade of travel agents, **Regent Club** (☎ 524 924; www.regentclub.com; Obrenovićeva 10; s/d/tr 5450/7400/9450DIN, apt 11,280DIN; ▯ ▯) offers enormous rooms with complimentary coffee-making facilities, large desks, spa-showers and wi-fi. Prices plummet on weekends.

Modern **Hotel Niški Cvet** (☎ 297 700; www.niski cvet.com; Kej 29 Decembra 2; s/d 5450/7800DIN, apt 10,300-13,850; ▯ ▯) offers views over Nišava River and the citadel.

Eating & Drinking

A crumbling Turkish bathhouse outside, and an elegant multialcove dining space inside, **Hamam** (☎ 513 444; Tvrđava; meals 200-2000DIN; ☺ 11am-midnight) offers national fare like *dim-ljena vešalica* (a roll of smoked pork stuffed with cream cheese and almonds) and pizzas. Other diverse choices:

Tramvaj (Tramway; ☎ 257 909; Pobede 20; ☺ 8am-midnight) Ice-cream concoctions served in a tram.

Restoran Sindjelić (☎ 512 550; Nikole Pasića 36; ☺ 8am-1am Sun-Fri, 8am-2am Sat; meals from 400DIN) Hearty traditional fare.

Broz (Obrenovićeva bb; ☺ 10am-late). Cheers to Broz Tito.

There are many fast-paced options in the cobblestoned Kopitareva area on the south side of Nikole Pašića, such as generous **Pleasure Caffe** (☎ 231 466; St Sava Park 31B; ☺ 7.30am-11.30pm Mon-Fri, 7.30am-1am Sat & Sun; mains 200-500DIN).

Getting There & Away

The **bus station** (☎ 355 177; Kneginje Ljubice) has frequent services to Belgrade (800DIN, three hours), Brzeće (550DIN, 1½ hours) for Kopaonik, four daily to Novi Pazar (940DIN, four hours) and three to Užice (900DIN, five hours) for Zlatibor. There are three daily buses to Topola (630DIN, 2½ hours).

From the **train station** (☎ 364 625), there are eight trains to Belgrade (800DIN, 4½ hours) and two to Bar (2400DIN, 11½ hours).

NOVI PAZAR НОВИ ПАЗАР
☎ 020 / pop 54,000

Novi Pazar is the cultural heartland of the Sandžak region. Here, the mostly Muslim locals don't even try to pretend that the Turkish coffee is Serbian. Besides its tapestry of Turkishness, some idyllic Orthodox sights are in the vicinity.

Orientation & Information

The Turkish quarter is on the south side of the river. On the other side are 28 Novembar's numerous cafes, bars and restaurants. Nouveau-wacko Hotel Vrbak is a curious central landmark straddling the barely wet Raška River.

A taxi ride into town from the bus station costs around 90DIN. There are internet cafes and several banks around the bus station.

Sights

The Old Town is lined with cafes and shops peddling Turkish desserts, meat, nuts or copperware. Attempts to restore the ruined **hammam** (just off Maj street) have failed dismally, leaving it at the mercy of coffee-drinking men.

The following sights are accessible by taxi; a return trip to a single site should cost around 800DIN.

Unesco-protected **Sopoćani Monastery** was built in the mid-13th century by King Uroš (who is buried here), destroyed by the Turks at the end of the 17th century and restored in the 1920s. Frescos inside the Romanesque church are prime examples of medieval art which miraculously (or perhaps divinely) survived more than two centuries exposed to the elements. The *Assumption of the Mother of God* fresco is one of the most renowned in Serbia.

Three kilometres from town on a bluff on the Kraljevo road, the small stone **Church of St Peter** (Petrova Crkva) is the oldest in Serbia and its only pre-Nemanjić church; parts date to the 8th century. In the late 1950s, the ancient cemetery around the church was discovered to hold the grave of a 5th-century Illyrian prince. If it's locked, ask at the nearby house to be let in.

Visible from the Church of St Peter and dating from 1170, **St George Monastery** (Đurđevi Stupovi, Pillars of St George) is the result of a promise to God by Stefan Nemanja (founder of the medieval Nemanjić dynasty) that he would endow a monastery to St George if he was released from Turkish captivity. Veracious efforts to restore the monastery after extensive WWII damage are resurrecting monastic life.

Sleeping & Eating

Suffering an architectural identity crisis, window trimmings, ottomans, and the glass onion-dome capping the foyer of **Hotel Vrbak** (☎ 314 548, 314 844; Maršala Tita bb; s/d from 1200/2200DIN) hint at the East, but the dilapidated state of things suggests that Vrbak fell with Yugoslavia. This friendly, freaky place deserves patronage for its quirkiness; just check that everything turns on, closes, flushes and smells as it should.

Opposite Vrbak, small oriental-style **Hotel Kan** (Cannes; ☎ /fax 315 300; Rifata Burdžovića 10; s 1914-2395DIN, d 2870DIN, tr 3830DIN) offers simple but clean rooms with cable TV and minibars. Walls feel makeshift and windows could be bigger, but it's secure and central.

The best hotel in town for wi-fi-equipped rooms and a high-quality restaurant offering some respite is **Hotel Tadž** (☎ 311 904; www.hoteltadz.co.yu; Rifata Burdževića 79; ▣).

Behind the market area is budget-friendly **Hotel Palma** (☎ 335 400; Jošanićki Kej bb; s/d 1000/2000DIN) and more upmarket **Hotel Atlas** (☎ 316 352; Jošanićki Kej bb; s/d/tr/apt 3000/5000/5800/6800DIN; ✼ ▣) next door.

Down-to-earth **Ukus** (1 Maj 59; meals 110-190DIN; ☾ 8am-11pm) serves home-cooked meals.

Getting There & Away

Frequent buses leave the **bus station** (☎ 318 354) to Belgrade (1000DIN, four hours). An

---

WORTH THE TRIP: STUDENICA MONASTERY

One of the most sacred sites in Serbia, Studenica was established in the 1190s by Stefan Nemanja and developed by his sons Vukan and Stefan. Active monastic life was cultivated by much-revered St Sava and continues today. Studenica is a fully functioning monastery, but members of this thriving little community don't mind the occasional visitor.

There are three churches within impressive oval walls. **Bogorodičina crkva** (The Church of Our Lady), contains the tomb of Stefan Nemanja, brought here by his brother, Sava. Smaller **Kraljeva crkva** (King's Church), houses the acclaimed *Birth of the Virgin* fresco.

From Novi Pazar, getting to Studenica without your own transport means travelling via Užiće (every 15 to 30 minutes from 5am) and catching a local bus from there, or negotiating a return taxi journey.

overnight bus goes to Sarajevo (€15, seven hours) and four daily buses to Pristina (€5, three hours) in Kosovo.

KOPAONIK КОПАОНИК
☎ 036

Situated around Pančićev Peak (Pančićev Vrh, 2017m) overlooking Kosovo, Serbia's prime ski resort has 44km of ski slopes served by 23 lifts and is a pleasant base for hiking. Prices plummet off season, though many places open arbitrarily or close completely.

Orientation & Information
Kopoanik sits 1770m above sea level. The smaller sub-village of Brzeće is 14km below. In the centre of the resort are ATMs, a post office, shops and restaurants.

Balkan Holidays (www.balkanholidays.co.uk)
Crystal (www.crystalski.co.uk) British outfit that books ski holidays in 'Kop'.
Ski Centre Kopaonik (☎ 471 203; ☽ 8am-3pm Mon-Thu, 8am-8pm Fri-Sun) Ski passes at the base of Hotel Grand.
Tourist Centar Kopaonik (International CG; ☎ 471 977; www.kopaonik-genex.com/eng) Persons interested in monastery tours are pooled here.

Sleeping & Eating
Large-scale hotels with restaurants, gym facilities, pizzerias, discos and shops cost between 1500DIN and 3000DIN for a single and 1660DIN to 4000DIN per double.

Options include **JAT Apartments** (☎ 471 043; www.jatapartmani.com; Kopaonik; apt per 1/2/3/4/5 persons from 1520/1680/2160/2960/3520DIN plus tax; ☐), **Hotel Grand** (☎ 471 037; www.kopaonik-genex.com; s €56-130, d €88-213; ☐ ☒) with a swimming pool, fitness centre, tennis courts and ski slopes on your doorstep, and **Hotel Junior** (☎ 037-823 344; Brzeće; s/d from €40/50).

Simple salads and decadent meat platters are available at **Gril Andreja** (☎ 471 977; meals 300-800DIN; ☽ 8am-midnight). Uphill from the centre, down the unpaved road, **Etno Club Sunce** (☎ 063 771 994; meals 200-700DIN; ☽ 8am-midnight) serves home cooking by the fire. Also try **Koala Restaurant** (☎ 471 977; ☽ 8.30-midnight) attached to Villa Bianca.

Getting There & Away
In season, there are three daily buses from Belgrade (1200DIN, six hours) and one from Niš (800DIN, four hours). From Novi Pazar, pick up an infrequent connection in Raška. For Raška bus information, call ☎ 737 555. Taxis from Raška cost around 1200DIN.

ZLATIBOR ЗЛАТИБОР
☎ 031 / pop 156,000

A special region of rolling plains, prophecies, traditions and hospitality, Zlatibor stretches from the Tara and Šargan mountains in the north, east to the Murtenica hills bordering BiH.

WORTH THE TRIP: ZLATIBOR EXCURSIONS

If it weren't for the ticket counter and school groups, you'd swear you'd stepped straight into a 19th-century Serbian village at the **Open-Air Museum** (☎ 031-802 291; www.sirogojno.org.au; adult/child 120/70DIN; ☽ 9am-4pm Oct-Apr, 9am-7pm May-Sep) in the village of Sirogobjo. High-roofed, fully-furnished wooden houses are spread across a pleasant mountainside and are open for your exploration.

Mokra Gora is home to the village of **Drvengrad** (Küstendorf; ☎ 031-800 686; www.mecavnik.info; Mećavnik hill; adult/child 180/100DIN; ☽ 9am-9pm), built by enigmatic film-maker Emir Kusturica in 2002 for his film *Life is a Miracle*. Quirky, colourful flourishes give the village a fantastical feel. The Stanley Kubrick cinema shows Kusturica's films. Take Bruce Lee Street down past the church for prime panoramas and indulge at the **restaurant** (☎ 031-800 688), where you can breakfast on bacon and eggs (150DIN) with Che Guevara biorevolution juice (130DIN), or lunch on veal in *kaymak* (500DIN).

The **Šargan 8 railway** (☎ 031-800 505; bookings 510 288; www.zeleznicesrbije.com; adult 500DIN; ☽ 10.30am & 1.25pm daily, 8am & 4.10pm when necessary) tourist train was once part of a narrow-gauge railway linking Belgrade with Sarajevo and Dubrovnik; it runs April to September. The joy of the 2½-hour journey is in its disorienting twists, turns and tunnels.

Without your own wheels, reach these sights via bus from Užice or on a tour with **Zlateks** (☎ 031-841 244; www.zlateks.co.yu; bus station, Tržni centar; ☽ 7am-8pm).

Orientation & Information

The Tržni town centre has everything you could need, but not far beyond are quaint villages where locals are oblivious to nearby ski slopes.

Anitours (☎ /fax 841 855; www.anitours.co.yu; Tržni centar; ⏰ 8am-7pm) Accommodation and tours for upwards of €10.

Igraonica Internet Caffe (Tržni centar; per hr 120DIN; ⏰ 9am-midnight) Two internet cafes with fast connections.

Komercijalna Bank (☎ 845 182; Tržni centar; ⏰ 8am-8pm Mon-Fri, 9am-3pm Sat Jan, Feb, Jul & Aug, 8am-4pm Mon-Fri, 9am-1pm Sat Mar-Jun & Sep-Dec)

Post office (☎ 841 337; Tržni centar; ⏰ 7am-7pm) Also has phones and maps.

Zlateks (☎ 841 244; www.zlateks.co.yu; bus station, Tržni centar; ⏰ 7am-8pm) Tourist agency at the bus station organises tickets, accommodation and tours.

Sights & Activities

Zlatibor's slopes are mostly mild. Major skiing hills are Tornik and Obudovica. The **nordic skiing trail** at the northern foothill of Šumatno Brdo is 1042m at its highest point.

Several walking trails start, end or pass the Tržni centre. In easy reach is the **monument** in memory of local victims of German aggression in 1941; head south along Ul Sportova, cross the footbridge and follow the footpath to the monument and its spectacular views.

If your dignity is expendable, take a **miniature train** from the car park behind the bus station (250DIN for a return trip into lush surrounds).

Sleeping & Eating

Private rooms and apartments offer more space, facilities and privacy for less money than resorts. In season they typically cost €30 to €80 for two to six people and €10 to €30 less out of season. Find them through travel agents.

Out of the centre, **Olimp** (☎ 842 555; www .hotelolimp.com; Naselje Sloboda bb; s/d/tr B&B from 2200/3600/4500DIN, s/d/tr half-board 3000/4800/7500DIN; 🖳) offers expansive balcony views. Rooms are dark but spacious at **Hotel Vis** (☎ 841 467; snezana.teodosic@ozone-hotels.com; s/d standard 3200/5400DIN, s/d/tr apt 3700/6200/8400DIN); choose your view when you check in. New, sleek **Hotel Mona Zlatibor** (☎ 841 021; www.monazlatibor .com; Naselje Jezero 26; s/d from 5980/8000DIN, apt from 7000DIN; 🖳 🖳 🖳) opposite the bus station has a wellness centre.

The best meals are found in local villages, but good central options include **Grand Zlatibor** (☎ 848 123; www.grand-zlatibor.co.yu; meals from 400DIN; ⏰ 11am-midnight) or more traditional **Zlatiborska Koliba** (☎ 841 638; meals 250-600DIN; ⏰ 8am-midnight) at the foot of the ski slopes. Locals enjoy *burek* breakfasts and fresh pastries from **Cafe Dukat** (☎ 514 753; pastries 40-100DIN; ⏰ 7am-4pm).

For DIY supplies, head to **TP Palisad supermarket** (⏰ 7am-8pm), at the town end of the lake.

Getting There & Around

Express buses leave the **bus stand** (☎ 841 244, 841 587) for Belgrade (700DIN, four hours), Novi Sad (1005DIN, 6½ hours) and almost hourly to Užice (120DIN, 45 minutes, between 5.50am and 11.10pm), the nearest railhead.

Without your own wheels, the easiest way to explore the region is to join locally organised tours (left). A return taxi from Tržni to the edge of the region costs around 2000DIN.

SERBIA DIRECTORY

ACCOMMODATION

More hostels have opened here in recent years; **Hostel World** (www.hostelworld.com) is a key website for hostel bookings.

Private rooms and apartments offer superb value and can be organised through tourist offices. 'Wild' camping is possible outside national parks.

You'll find budget rooms for less than €15 per person, midrange ranges for between €20 to €50, and top-end rooms for more than €50.

Unless otherwise stated, prices include breakfast and private bathrooms. If you depend on internet access, check that wireless actually works. Where a room is 'nonsmoking', this does not mean that the room has not been smoked in, only that you are free not to smoke in it.

ACTIVITIES

If you enjoy hiking, national parks offer quiet respite; Tara National Park has almost 20 marked paths ranging from a couple to 18 kilometres. The cultural sites of Zlatibor (left) are ideally explored on foot. Climbers will enjoy the canyons of the Drina River.

It is possible to kayak and raft at Tara National Park along the Drina River; con-

SERBIA

tact the **Drina-Tara Rafting Club** (www.raftingtara
.com in Serbian) or **Era Rafting Club** (☎ 064 413 1752;
azara@ptt.yu). Rafting club **Bodo** (www.tarabodo.com)
organises rafting on the Tara.

The main ski resorts are Zlatibor (p827)
and Kopaonik (p826), both of which are also
popular for summer hiking.

Several spots in Serbia have rich
birdlife, including areas around Belgrade.
Keen birdwatchers should contact the
League for Ornithological Action of Serbia
(www.ptica.org) for more information.

BUSINESS HOURS
Banks are open from around 8am to 5am
Monday to Friday and 8am to 2pm Saturday.
On weekdays many shops open at 8am to
6pm, and some open until early afternoon
on Saturdays. Restaurants are generally open
from 8am to 11pm or midnight, and bars from
9pm until around 3am. Take all of this with
a grain of salt.

DANGERS & ANNOYANCES
Travelling around Serbia is generally safe for
travellers who exercise the usual cautions.
The exceptions can be border areas, particularly the southeast Kosovo border where
Serb-Albanian tensions remain. Check the
situation before attempting to cross overland,
and think twice about driving there with
Serbian-plated cars.

Smoking is a hard-to-avoid annoyance,
even in nonsmoking zones.

EMBASSIES & CONSULATES
A complete list of embassies and consulates
in Serbia, as well as Serbian embassies around
the world is available at www.mfa.gov.yu/
Worldframe.htm. Countries are represented
in Belgrade (area code ☎ 011):

Albania (Map p808; ☎ 306 6642; embassy.belgrade@
mfa.gov.al; Bulevar Mira 25A)
Australia (Map pp810-11; ☎ 330 3400; belgrade
.embassy@dfat.gov.au; Čika Ljubina 13)
Bosnia & Hercegovina (Map pp810-11; ☎ 329 1995;
ambasadabih@sbb.co.yu; Milana Tankosića 8)
Bulgaria (Map pp810-11; ☎ 361 3980; bulgamb@
eunet.yu; Birčaninova 26)
Canada (Map pp810-11; ☎ 306 3000; bgrad@
international.gc.ca; Kneza Miloša 75)
Croatia (Map pp810-11; ☎ 367 9150; crobg@mvpei.hr;
Kneza Miloša 62)
France (Map pp810-11; ☎ 302 3500; ambafr_1@Eunet
.yu; Pariska 11)

Germany (Map pp810-11; ☎ 306 4300; germany@sbb
.co.yu; Kneza Miloša 74-6)
Hungary (Map pp810-11; ☎ 244 0472; mission.blg@
kum.hu; Krunska 72)
Netherlands (Map pp810-11; ☎ 2023 900; bel@
minbuza.nl; Simina 29)
UK (Map pp810-11; ☎ 264 5055; ukembbg@eunet.yu;
Resavska 46)
USA (Map pp810-11; ☎ 361 9344; http://belgrade
.usembassy.gov; Kneza Miloša 50)

HOLIDAYS
Public holidays in Serbia:
New Year 1 January
Orthodox Christmas 7 January
St Sava's Day 27 January
Nation Day 15 February
Orthodox Good Friday April/May
Orthodox Easter Monday April/May
International Labour Days 1 and 2 May
Victory Day 9 May
Republic Day 29 November
St Vitus's Day 28 June

St Sava's Day, Victory Day and St Vitus's Day
are working days revered as holidays.

Orthodox churches celebrate Easter
between one and five weeks later than
other churches.

MONEY
Serbia retains the dinar though some hotels
may want payment in euros.

ATMs are widespread in major towns and
cards are accepted by established businesses.
Exchange offices readily change hard currencies into dinars and back again; look for
yellow diamond 'Menjačica' signs. Exchange
machines accept euros, US dollars, and
British pounds. Commission is charged for
travellers cheques.

POST
Parcels should be taken unsealed to the
main post office for inspection. You can
receive mail, addressed poste restante, for a
small charge.

TELEPHONE
The country code is ☎ 381. Press the *i* button on public phones for dialling commands
in English. Calls to Europe/Australia/North
America cost around 50/100/80DIN per
minute. Long-distance calls can also be
made from booths in post offices.

Phonecards can be bought in post offices and tobacco kiosks for 300DIN (for local cards) and 600DIN (for international cards). Halo Plus cards allow longer calls locally, in the former Yugoslav Republic region or internationally, depending on which category you buy. Calls to Europe/Australia/USA cost 13/40/40DIN per minute.

Mobile-phone numbers can be purchased at branches for around 200DIN, and recharge cards at supermarkets and kiosks.

TOURIST INFORMATION
Novi Sad and Belgrade have plenty of English material and friendly fountains of knowledge behind the desk.

In addition to the **National Tourist Office of Serbia** (www.serbia.travel), the **Tourist Organisation of Belgrade** (www.tob.co.yu) is a useful starting point.

VISAS
Tourist visas for stays of less than 90 days aren't required by citizens of most European countries, Australia, New Zealand, Canada and the USA. The **Ministry of Foreign Affairs** (www.mfa.gov.yu/Visas/VisasR.htm) has full details.

If you're not staying at a hotel or private home, you must register with the police within 24 hours of arrival and subsequently on changing address.

TRANSPORT IN SERBIA

GETTING THERE & AWAY
Air
Belgrade's **Nikola Tesla Beograd Airport** (☎ 011-209 444, 064 848 5402, 063 255 066; www.airport-belgrade .co.yu) handles most international flights. Office telephone numbers below are for Belgrade:
Aeroflot (SU; ☎ 011-328 6071; www.aeroflot.com)
Aerosvit (VV; ☎ 011-328 3430; www.aerosvit.ua/eng)

Air France (AF; ☎ 011-638 378; www.airfrance.com)
Alitalia (AZ; ☎ 011-676 692; www.alitalia.com)
Austrian Airlines (OS; ☎ 011-324 8077; www.aua.com)
British Airways (BA; ☎ 011-328 1303; www.british airways.com)
ČSA (OK; ☎ 011-361 4592; www.csa.cz)
Germanwings (4U; ☎ 011-526 7005; www.german wings.com)
JAT (JU; ☎ 011-311 4222; www.jat.com)
Kuban Airlines (KIL; ☎ 011-303 7106; www.alk.ru)
Lufthansa (LH; ☎ 011-303 4944; www.lufthansa.com)
Montavia (GZP; ☎ 011-362 0690; www.montavia.com)
Montenegro Airlines (YM; ☎ 011-262 1122; www .montenegro-airlines.cg.yua)
Norwegian Air Shuttle (DY; www.norwegian.no)
Olympic Airways (OA; ☎ 011-303 6850; www.olympic -airlways.gr)
Swiss International Air Lines (LX; ☎ 011-303 0140; www.swiss.com)
Tunisair (TU; ☎ 011-323 3174; www.tunisair.com)
Turkish Airlines (TK; ☎ 011-303 6195; www.turkishairlines.com)

Land
Serbia can be entered from any of its neighbours. Make sure you are registered with the police (it is the duty of your hotel/host to do this) and have registration paper(s) with you when leaving.

Because Serbia does not acknowledge crossing points into Kosovo as international border crossings, it may not be possible to enter Serbia from Kosovo unless you first entered Kosovo from Serbia.

Some northern border points were temporarily closed after damage was caused by angry mobs in February 2008 following Kosovo's declaration of independence. Check the situation with your embassy before attempting to cross. Also see p432.

BUS
Bus services to Western Europe and Turkey are well developed; see p817 for details of services from Belgrade.

CAR & MOTORCYCLE
Drivers need International Driving Permits (available from your home motoring association). Vehicles need Green Card insurance, or insurance purchased at the border (from €80 a month).

Driving Serbian-plated cars into Kosovo is not advised, and often not permitted by rental agencies or insurers.

TRAIN

International rail connections leaving Serbia originate in Belgrade; see p817 for details. Heading north and west, most call at Novi Sad and Subotica and east via Niš.

Several trips from Serbia offer a nice slice of scenery; the route to Bar (1000DIN plus three-/six-berth couchette 1000/564DIN, 11½ hours) on the Montenegrin coast is one. For more information visit **Serbian Railways** (www.serbianrailways.com).

GETTING AROUND
Bicycle

Bicycle paths are improving in larger cities like Belgrade and Novi Sad. Vojvodina is relatively flat, but main roads make for dull days. Mountainous regions such as Zlatibor offer mountain biking in summer months. Picturesque winding roads come with the downside of narrow shoulders.

Bus

Bus services are extensive, though outside major hubs sporadic connections may leave you in the lurch for a few hours. In southern Serbia particularly, you may have to double back to transport hubs.

Reservations are only worthwhile for international buses and during festivals. Receipts are given for luggage stowed below (between 20DIN to 50DIN per piece). Fares vary depending on which company is running the route.

Car & Motorcycle

The **Automobile & Motorcycle Association of Serbia** (Auto-Moto Savez Srbije; Map pp810–11; ☎ 011-333 1200; www.amss.org.yu; Kneginje Zorke 58) provides extensive information on its website and roadside assistance (☎ 987); the association's temporary office is at Ruzveltova 18 (Map pp810–11). Drivers need International Driving Permits (available from your home motoring association).

Several car-hire companies have offices at Nikola Tesla Beograd Airport in Belgrade; see p817. Small-car hire typically costs €50 per day. Check where you are *not* able to take the car.

Outside main cities, parking is no problem; most hotels offer guests free parking. In Belgrade and other large towns you may have to purchase tickets from machines, kiosks or via SMS (in Serbian only).

Traffic police are everywhere and accidents happen frequently. Buckle up, drive on the right, don't drink (the limit is 0.05%) and stick to speed limits (120km/h on motorways, 100km/h on dual carriageways, 80km/h on main roads and 60km/h in urban areas).

Train

Serbian Railways (☎ 011-361 4811; www.serbianrailways.com) serves Novi Sad, Subotica and Niš from Belgrade. Enthusiasts will enjoy the Šargan 8 railway in Mokra Gora (p826).

Generally trains aren't as regular and reliable as buses. Tickets can be booked through Serbian Railways or travel agents.

Slovakia

Yee! ha! yip! Exuberant, high-pitched squeals burst forth from folk dancers as they stomp 'round the floor. A field of fresh heather blooms on a Tatra mountain hillside once dominated by pine forest. A little old *babka* waits at the train station wearing kerchief and full village dress. Visiting Slovakia is not about earth-shattering sights or superlatives, it's more about experiencing the every day in a place where folkways and nature still hold sway.

That's not to say Bratislava doesn't bustle. As investment pours in, building cranes dominate the cityscape and a new and oh-so-trendy restaurant or hotel seems to open every second minute. The compact, rabbit-warren Old Town has to a certain extent gone commercial, but it's worth a day or two of distraction wandering the back streets.

Just make sure you also venture outside the capital to explore the ancient castles, traditional villages and national parks. Dense forests cover the low hills and fortress ruins top the cliffs of central Slovakia. Further east, medieval towns sit beneath the High Tatras peaks and a gondola swoops up to 2000m. You can hike beside a gorge waterfall one day and search out nail-less wooden churches in tiny villages the next.

Unfortunately, all is not pastoral bliss. You'll still see traces of the communist legacy – heavy industry and truly ugly concrete buildings. Thankfully the country's folksy spirit remains intact. So pull up a plate of *halušky* (dumplings) with *bryndza* (sheep's cheese) and drink a glass of *slivovice* (firewater-like plum brandy) for us – *nazdravie!*

FAST FACTS

- **Area** 49,035 sq km
- **Capital** Bratislava
- **Currency** euro (€); US$1 = €0.73; UK£1 = €1.06; A$1 = €0.50; ¥100 = €0.76; NZ$1 = €0.41
- **Famous for** ice hockey, beautiful women, mountain hiking, folk traditions
- **Official Language** Slovak
- **Phrases** *ahoj* (hello); *dovidenia* (goodbye); *ďakujem* (thank you); *este pivo prosím* (another beer please), *kde je WC* (veyt-say)? (where's the loo?)
- **Population** 5.44 million
- **Telephone Codes** country code ☎ 421; international access code ☎ 00
- **Visas** citizens of the UK, USA, Canada, Australia, New Zealand and Japan can enter Slovakia for 90 days without a visa; see p871

SLOVAKIA

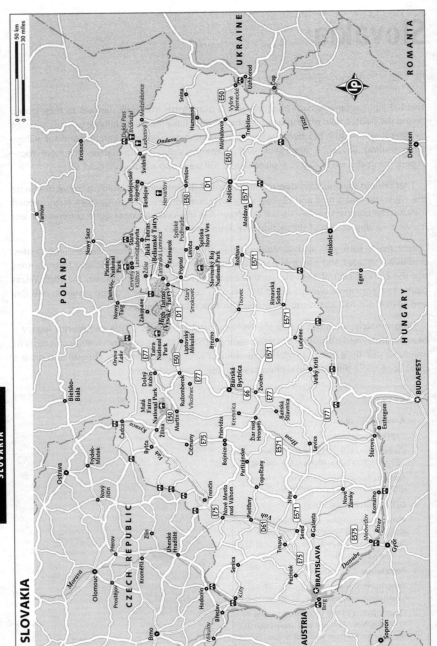

SLOVAKIA

HIGHLIGHTS

- Hike between mountain huts among the crests of one Europe's smallest alpine mountain ranges, the 12km-long **High Tatras** (p851).
- Linger with friends over cake, coffee and drinks at one of the myriad sidewalk cafes in Old Town **Bratislava** (p836).
- At 4 hectares long, the ruins of **Spiš Castle** (p860) are among the biggest in Europe.
- Go rural by staying in one of the traditional log-cottage villages like **Vlkolinec** (p847) or **Čičmany** (p848).
- Stay in a medieval burgher's house and visit the nation's most beautiful Gothic altar in **Levoča** (p858).

ITINERARIES

- **Three days** Entering from the east, either take the bus in from Kraków or fly to Poprad to get to the High Tatras. If rural bliss is your thing, make Ždiar your two-day mountain-hiking base, if you like more pampering after your exertion, stay in Tatranská Lomnica. On day three ride the rails west to the country's capital, Bratislava.
- **One week** Spend four nights in the Tatras, taking a day trip or two to see Spiš Castle, medieval Levoča or Kežmarok. Stop for a night in Trenčín to catch a torchlight tour of the hilltop fortress before venturing on to Old Town Bratislava for the last two nights.

CLIMATE & WHEN TO GO

Slovakia's moderate climate averages -2°C in January and 25°C in August. Spring floods are quite common, but autumn can be rainy, too. Snow blankets the mountains into April and the upper elevations of the High Tatras are covered well into June.

The tourist season runs from May through September. Lodging prices are lower outside those months, but many sights in outlying areas aren't open. September is still quite warm, young wine is being harvested and the mountains are snow-free (usually), making it one of the best times to visit. Rates skyrocket nationwide during the Easter and Christmas holidays.

HISTORY

Slavic tribes wandered west into what would become Slovakia sometime round about the 5th century; by the 9th, the territory was part of the short-lived Great Moravian empire. It was about then that the Magyars (Hungarians) set up shop next door and subsequently laid claim to the whole territory. In the early 16th century, the Turks moved into Budapest pushing the Hungarian monarchs to take up residence in Bratislava (known then as Pressburg, in German, or Pozsony, in Hungarian). Because Slovakia was the Hungarian frontierland, many fortresses were constructed during the Middle Ages, and can still be seen today.

At the turn of the 20th century, Slovak intellectuals cultivated ties with the Czechs and took their nation into the united Czechoslovakia post-WWI. A brief period of independence transpired when leaders declared Slovakia a German ally – the day before Hitler's troops invaded Czechoslovakia in March 1939. It was not a populist move and in August 1944 Slovak partisans instigated the ill-fated Slovak National Uprising (Slovenské Národné Povstanie, or SNP), a source of ongoing national pride (and innumerable street names).

After the communist takeover in 1948, power was again centralised in Prague until 1989, when the Velvet Revolution brought down the curtains on the communists. Elections in 1992 saw the left-leaning Movement for a Democratic Slovakia (HZDS) come to power with Vladimír Mečiar, a former boxer, as prime minister. By that summer the Slovak parliament had voted to declare sovereignty, and the federation dissolved peacefully on 1 January 1993.

Despite changing government leadership that first rejected and then embraced economic and social reforms, Slovakia was accepted into NATO and the EU by 2004,

SLOVAKIA

CONNECTIONS: MOVING ON FROM SLOVAKIA

Though few airlines fly into Slovakia itself, Bratislava is just 60km from the well-connected Vienna International Airport. By train from Bratislava (p844), Budapest (three hours) and Prague (five hours) are easy to reach. Heading further east, buses become your best bet. You can connect to Zakopane, Poland (2½ hours) from Poprad (p857) near the Tatra Mountains, and to Uzhgorod, Ukraine (2½ hours) through Kosice (p867).

HOW MUCH?

- **Night in hostel** €32
- **Double room in pension** €85
- **Day's ski hire** €10
- **Bicycle** €140
- **Postcard** €0.30

LONELY PLANET INDEX

- **1L petrol** €0.98
- **1L bottled water** €0.50
- **Beer** €1
- **Souvenir T-shirt** €10
- **Street snack (ice-cream scoop)** €0.40

and the Schengen member states in 2007. Amid some consternation over rising prices, the euro became the national currency in January 2009.

PEOPLE

A deeply religious and familial people, Slovaks have strong family circles and a deep sense of folk traditions. The young are warm and open, but there can be a reserve about older generations. Show interest in their country, or ask for help, and the shell cracks. Generosity and warmth lurk just behind the stoicism. Thankfully, surly service is now the exception rather than the rule in the tourist industry.

With such great scenery, it's not surprising that most Slovaks spend their weekends outdoors. *Isť na prechadsku* (going for a walk) is a national pastime so you will doubtless run into a backpack-toting Slovak wherever you trek in nature. About a quarter of the population lives in the five largest cities.

Government statistics estimate that Slovakia's population is 86% Slovak, 10% Hungarian and 1.7% Roma. This last figure is in some dispute as some groups estimate the Roma population as high as 3.5%. The minority Roma are still viewed with an uncompromising suspicion – at best.

RELIGION

Slovakia's first Christian church was founded in Nitra in AD 833 after SS Cyril and Methodius visited the Great Moravian empire. Despite 50 years of communist sup-

pression, the majority of Slovaks retained their strong beliefs. Today Roman Catholics form the majority (about 69%), but evangelicals are also numerous; East Slovakia has many Greek Catholic and Orthodox believers.

ARTS

Some city dwellers may have been put off by the clichéd image of the communist-era 'happy peasant', but traditional folk arts, from music to architecture, are still celebrated – especially during summer festivals.

Cinema

Slovak cinema first made its mark as part of the Czechoslovak New Wave of the 1960s, with classic films like *Smrt si rika Engelchen* (Death Calls Itself Engelchen, 1963) directed by Ján Kádar, and *Obchod na korze* (The Shop on the Main Street, 1965) by Elmar Klos. Martin Sulík was one of Slovakia's most promising new directors, winning an Oscar nomination for *Všetko, čo mám rád* (Everything I Like, 1992), and international acclaim for *Krajinka* (The Landscape, 2000). Unfortunately, lack of funding and the closing of the Koliba movie studios has meant there has been no serious Slovak movie-making since 2000, though there have been a few collaborations.

Music

Traditional Slovak folk instruments include the *fujara* (a 2m-long flute), the *gajdy* (bagpipes) and the *konkovka* (a strident shepherd's flute). Folk songs helped preserve the Slovak language during Hungarian rule, and in East Slovakia musical folk traditions are an integral part of village life.

In classical music, the 19th-century works of Ján L Bela and the symphonies of Alexander Moyzes receive world recognition. Slovakia's contemporary music scene is small, but vibrant. Modern musicians combine traditional lyrics or rhythms with a modern beat. Zuzana Mojžišová's music seems to have an almost Romany-like vibrancy, but stems from Slovak folk music. Marián Varga riffs on classical themes and the Peter Lipa band is the granddaddy of the Bratislava Jazz Days festival (p841).

Architecture

The wooden churches of East Slovakia, easily accessible from Bardejov (see p869) are some of the most interesting architectural gems in the country. You can see transplanted versions at a *skanzen* (open-air museum), like the one in Martin (p848), where vernacular village architecture is preserved. Levoča is known for its nearly complete medieval town walls and for the Gothic Church of St Jacob, and its 18m-high altar carved by Master Pavol. Of course you can't miss the brutal socialist-realist architecture of the communist epoch, as evidenced by the New Bridge (Nový most, p840) in Bratislava. Yes, it does resemble a UFO on a stick.

SPORT

Enter any bar or restaurant during puck-pushing season (September to April) and 12 large men and an ice rink will never be far from the TV screen, even at nice restaurants. Local club rivalries are heated, but the Olympic team showing has flagged in recent years. The announcement that Slovakia will host the 2011 World Championships surely perked up fans.

Slovak athletes did capture an Olympic slalom canoeing gold in 2008. But it's football that fills the summer months for most. The Slovaks have yet to attain the rabid fanaticism found elsewhere in Europe, but club games are a reliable source of red-blooded bravado. SK Slovan Bratislava is the nation's most successful team.

ENVIRONMENT
The Land

Slovakia sits in the heart of Europe, straddling the northwestern end of the Carpathian Mountains. This hilly country forms a clear physical barrier between the plains of Poland and Hungary. Almost 80% of Slovakia is more than 750m above sea level, and forests, mainly beech and spruce, cover 40% of the country.

Southwestern Slovakia is a fertile lowland stretching from the foothills of the Carpathians down to the Danube River, which, from Bratislava to Štúrovo, forms the border with Hungary.

Northern Slovakia is dominated by the High Tatras (Vysoké Tatry) mountains along the Polish border; Gerlachovský štít (2654m) being the highest peak. The forested ridges of the Low Tatras (Nízke Tatry) and the Malá Fatra are national park playgrounds. South are the gorges and waterfalls of Slovenský raj and the limestone caves of Slovenský kras. The longest river, the Váh, rises in the Tatras

and flows 390km west and south to join the Danube at Komárno.

Wildlife

Slovakia's national parks contain bears, marmots, wolves, lynxes, chamois, mink and otters, though they're rarely seen. Deer, pheasants, partridges, ducks, wild geese, storks, grouse, eagles and other birds of prey can be seen across the country.

National Parks

National parks and protected areas make up 20% of Slovakia. The parks in the High Tatras, Slovenský raj and Malá Fatra regions should not be missed.

Environmental Issues

Slovakia is a mixed bag in environmental terms. No doubt due to most Slovaks' penchant for all things outdoorsy, large swathes of the countryside are technically protected parkland. Watchdog groups like the International Union for the Conservation of Nature have protested that more and more development in the Tatras has put its national park status in question. And the communist legacy left more than its fair share of grimy, industrial factories. Big centres such as Bratislava and Košice do suffer from air pollution.

The controversial Gabčíkovo hydroelectric project, on the Danube west of Komárno, produces enough power to cover the needs of every home in Slovakia. But some believe it exacerbates the damage caused by annual floods and has damaged bird habitats.

Tens of thousands of hikers pass through Slovakia's parks and protected areas every year – try to do your bit to keep them pristine. Wherever possible, carry out your rubbish, avoid using detergents or toothpaste in or near watercourses, stick to established trails (this helps prevent erosion), cook on a kerosene stove rather than an open fire and do not engage in or encourage – by purchasing goods made from endangered species – unlawful hunting.

FOOD & DRINK
Staples & Specialities

Slovak cuisine is basic central European fare: various fried meat schnitzels with fries and hearty stews with potatoes. Soups like *cesnaková polievka* (garlic soup), either creamy or clear with croutons and cheese, and *kapustnica*

SLOVAKIA

(cabbage soup), with a paprika and pork base, start most meals. Slovakia's national dish is *bryndzové halušky*, gnocchi-like dumplings topped with soft sheep's cheese and bits of bacon fat. Don't pass up an opportunity to eat in a *salaš* or a *koliba* (rustic log-cabin eateries), where these traditional specialities are the mainstay.

For dessert, try *palacinka* (crepes) stuffed with jam or chocolate. *Ovocné knedličky* (fruit dumplings) are round balls filled with fruit and coated with crushed poppy seeds or breadcrumbs, dribbled with melted butter and sometimes accompanied by fruit purée and ice cream – yum.

Slovak wine is...what do oenophiles say...highly drinkable (ie good and cheap). The Modra region squeezes dry reds, like Frankovka and Kláštorné. Slovak Tokaj, a white dessert wine from the southeast, is trying to give the Hungarian version a run for its money (though it falls short).

Slovak *pivo* (beer) is as good as the Czech stuff – try full-bodied Zlatý Bažant or dark, sweet Martiner. *Borovička* (a potent berry-based clear liquor) and *slivovice* (plum-based) are consumed as shots and are said to aid digestion.

Where to Eat & Drink

Restaurants nationwide are generally open from 10am to 10pm. Self-service cafeterias (called *samoobsluha reštaurácie, jedáleň* or *bufet*) cater to office workers and are great places to eat during the day (but close early). Look for food stands near train and bus stations.

All manner of trendy world food has found a foothold in Bratislava, but most Slovak towns only have a pizzeria or a Chinese takeaway in addition to local staples. Cafes (spelled in English) are often as much bar and restaurant as coffee shop; *kaviareň* (cafes) may only serve beverages, but that includes alcohol; a *cukráreň* (pastry or sweet shop) is where you go to get cakes and ice creams with your java.

Most restaurants across the country have nonsmoking sections, but don't be surprised if these tables are right next to the smoking ones. Bars are definitely not nonsmoking.

Vegetarians & Vegans

It ain't easy being green in Slovakia. In this meat-lovers' haven even vegetable soups are made with chicken stock, and *bezmäsa* (meatless) dishes aren't always meatless (those bacon crumbles on the dumplings apparently don't count). Most menus have a pasta or a rice dish, and there's always the ubiquitous *vyprážaný syr* (fried cheese). Other than that, pizzerias are always an option.

Habits & Customs

Small tips (10%) are expected from foreigners, but your friends are likely to say you're spoiling the waiter. At least round up the bill to the next 10, like the locals do.

BRATISLAVA

☎ 02 / pop 426,091

Bratislava? Isn't that the town where some hostelling horror movies were set? Indeed. But the only scary things about Slovakia's capital are the no-longer-bargain-basement lodging prices, and the fact that the first international chain stores have appeared on the scene. Bath and Body Works – *gasp*!

The capital city is a host of contrasts – a charming Old Town across the river from a communist concrete-block city, an age-old castle sharing the skyline with the 1970s, UFO-like New Bridge. Still, narrow pedestrian streets, pastel 18th-century rococo buildings and sidewalk cafes galore make for a supremely strollable – if miniscule – historic centre. You may want to pop into a museum if it's raining, but otherwise the best thing to do is meander the mazelike alleys, stopping regularly for coffee or drinks. There's sure to be some chichi restaurant just opened. Try to ignore the gangs of inebriated English-speaking blokes roaming about on weekends. Ok, it's a little scary.

HISTORY

Founded in AD 907, Bratislava was already a large city in the 12th century. In 1467 the Hungarian Renaissance monarch Matthias Corvinus founded a university here, Academia Istropolitana. The city flourished during the reign of Maria Theresa of Austria (1740–80), when many of the imposing baroque palaces you see today were built. From the Turkish invasion until 1830, Hungarian monarchs were crowned in St Martin's cathedral, and Hungarian parliament met in Bratislava (then known as Pressburg or Poszony in German or Hungarian) until 1848.

GREATER BRATISLAVA

INFORMATION	
Bratislava Culture & Information	
Centre.........................	1 B2
Dutch Embassy.................	2 A3
Poliklinika Ružinov...........	3 D3

SIGHTS & ACTIVITIES	
Chair Lift.........................	4 A1
Chatam Sofer's Grave Site..5	A4
Sad Janka Krála Park........	6 B4
TV Tower..........................	7 A1

SLEEPING	
Hostel Possonium..............	8 B3
Hotel-Penzión Arcus.........	9 B3
Penzión Zlatá Noha.........	10 B2

EATING	
Krishna............................	11 A4

ENTERTAINMENT	
Dopler..............................	12 D3
HC Slovan Stadium...........	13 C2
SK Slovan Stadium............	14 C2
State Puppet Theatre........	15 B3

TRANSPORT	
Koliba (Bus 203	
Terminus).......................	16 B2
Main Bus Station..............	17 C3
Main Train Station Bus Stop.18	B2
Main Train Station Tram	
Stop...............................	19 B2

The communists did a number on the town's architecture and spirit, razing a large part of the Old Town (including the synagogue) to make way for the modern new second city of Czechoslovakia. Today, as the capital of one of the newer euro-currency members of the EU, Bratislava is a city under construction. Business complexes rise faster than mushrooms after a spring rain. Look for a new (and not cheap) hotel opening on a corner near you.

ORIENTATION

Bratislava's pedestrian centre starts south of Hodžovo nám. Follow Poštová south and you cross Obchodná (Shopping St) before getting to Nám SNP and the heart of the Old

Town, bounded by the castle in the west and Tesco department store in the east. The large, plaza-like Hviezdoslavovo nám is a convenient reference point, with the Old Town to the north, the Danube to the south, and the Slovak National Theatre on its east end.

The main train station, Hlavná stanica, is located just 1km north of the centre. The main bus station, called Mlynské Nivy by locals because of the street it's on, is a little over 1km east of the Old Town.

INFORMATION
Bookshops

Interpress Slovakia (Map p838; Sedlárska 2; ☼ 9am-10pm Mon-Sat, 2-10pm Sun) Foreign newspapers and local periodicals in English.

Next Apache (Map p838; Panenská 28; ⊙ 9am-10pm Mon-Fri, 10am-10pm Sat & Sun) Loads of used English books and a comfy cafe.

Discount Cards
Bratislava City Card (1/2/3 days €6/10/12) Provides discounted museum admission and city transport; it's sold at the Bratislava Culture & Information Centre (opposite).

Emergency
Main police station (Map p838; ☎ 159; Gunduličova 10)

Internet Access
Hlavné and Hviezdoslavovo nám are free wi-fi zones.

Wifi Café (Map p838; ground fl, Tatracentrum, Hodžovo nám; ⊙ 8.30am-9.30pm Mon-Fri, 10am-8pm Sat, 11am-8pm Sun) Six flat-screen terminals; wi-fi for the price of a beverage.

Internet Kaviaren (Map p838; ☎ 095248208; 1st fl, Tesco, Kamenné nám 1; per 15min €1; ⊙ 9am-9pm Mon-Fri, 9am-7pm Sat & Sun) Ten terminals hidden behind the garden department in Tesco.

Left Luggage
Main bus station (autobusova stanica; Map p837; Mlynské Nivy; per bag per day €1.25; ⊙ 5.30am-10pm Mon-Fri, 6am-6pm Sat & Sun)

Main train station (hlavná stanica; Map p837; per bag per day €1.50; ⊙ 6.30am-11pm)

Media
Slovak Spectator (www.slovakspectator.sk) English-language weekly with current affairs and event listings.

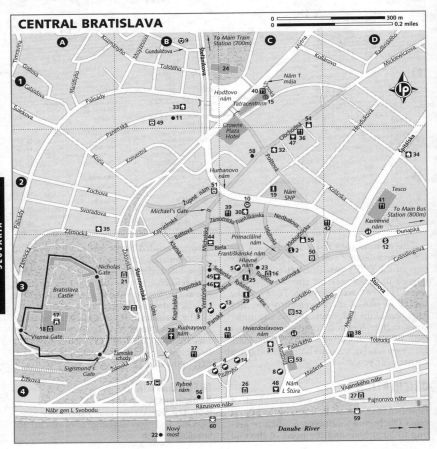

BRATISLAVA IN TWO DAYS

Spend a day roaming the pedestrian streets, stopping for nibbles at one of Bratislava's many eateries like **Prašná Bašta** (p842). Ascend castle hill or the New Bridge, for a citywide view, contrasting the charming old town with the ugly new. The next day, trip out to **Devín Castle** (p844) at the confluence of two rivers and three countries.

Medical Services

Poliklinika Ruzinov (Map p837; ☎ 4823 4113; Ružinovská 10) Hospital with emergency services and a 24-hour pharmacy.

Money

Bratislava has an excess of banks and ATMs in the Old Town, with several branches on Poštova and around Kamenné nám. There are also ATMs and exchange booths in the train and bus stations, and at the airport.

Tatra Banka (Map p838; Dunajská 4) Has staff that speak exceptional English.

Post

Main post office (Map p838; Nám SNP 34-35)

Tourist Information

Bratislava Culture & Information Centre (BKIS; ☎ 16 186; www.bkis.sk) Airport (MR Štefánika; ☒ 8am-

7.30pm Mon-Fri, 10am-6pm Sat); Centre (Map p838; Klobučnícka 2; ☒ 8.30am-7pm Mon-Fri, 10am-5pm Sat); Main train station (Map p837; Hlavná stanica; ☒ 8am-4.30pm Mon-Fri, 10am-2pm Sat) Staff hide brochures behind the central tourist office counter and seem uninterested, but keep pressing and they'll help – a little.

Bratislava Tourist Service (BTS; Map p838; ☎ 2070 7501; www.bratislava-info.sk; Ventúrska 9; ☒ 10am-8pm) A tiny, tiny place, but it has a much more obliging staff than BKIS, and lots of maps and knick-knacks.

SIGHTS & ACTIVITIES
Old Town

Bratislava Castle (Bratislavský hrad; Map p838; admission free; ☒ 9am-9pm Apr-Sep, to 6pm Oct-Mar) lords over the west side of the Old Town on a hill above the Danube. Winding ramparts provide a great vantage point for comparing ancient and communist Bratislava. The castle looks a bit like a four-poster bed, a shape that was well established by the 15th century. During the Turkish occupation of Budapest, this was the seat of Hungarian royalty. A fire devastated the fortress in 1811; what you see today is a reconstruction from the 1950s. Except for a small archaeology exhibit, most of the interiors that make up the **Historical Museum** (Historické múzeum; Map p838; ☎ 5441 1441; www.snm.sk; adult/concession €3/1.50; ☒ 9am-5pm Tue-Sun) are closed for reconstruction until 2011. To see a more historically complete castle, take the bus beneath the New Bridge to Devín (p844), 8km outside the city.

SLOVAKIA

INFORMATION	
Austrian Embassy	**1** B3
Bratislava Culture & Information	
Centre	**2** C3
Bratislava Tourist Service	**3** B3
Czech Embassy	**4** C4
French Embassy	**5** C3
German Embassy	**6** B4
Internet Kaviaren	(see 41)
Interpress Slovakia	**7** B3
Irish Embassy	**8** C4
Main Police Station	**9** B1
Main Post Office	**10** C2
Next Apache	**11** B1
Tatra Banka	**12** D3
UK Embassy	**13** C3
US Embassy	**14** C4
Wifi Café	**15** C1

SIGHTS & ACTIVITIES	
Apponyi Palace	**16** C3
Bratislava Castle	**17** A3
Historical Museum	**18** A3
Monument to the Slovak National	
Uprising	**19** C2
Museum of Clocks	**20** B3
Museum of Jewish Culture	**21** B3

New Bridge	**22** B4
Old Town Hall	**23** C3
Presidential Palace	**24** C1
Reduta Palace	(see 53)
Roland's Fountain	**25** C3
Slovak National Gallery	**26** C4
Slovak National Museum	**27** D4
St Martin's Cathedral	**28** B3
Watcher	**29** C3

SLEEPING	
Arcadia Hotel	**30** C2
Carlton Hotel	**31** C4
City Hostel	**32** C2
Downtown Backpackers	**33** B1
Hostel Blues	**34** D2
Penzión Chez David	**35** A2

EATING	
City Vegetarian	**36** C2
El Gaucho	**37** B4
Pizza Mizza	**38** D3
Prašná Bašta	**39** C2
Presto	**40** C1
Tesco	**41** D2
U Jakubu	**42** D2

U Remeselníka	(see 54)
Verne	**43** C3

DRINKING	
Čokoládovňa	**44** B3
Dubliner	**45** B3
Greenwich Cocktail Bar	**46** B3
Kréma Gurmánov Bratislavy	**47** C2
Malecón	**48** C4

ENTERTAINMENT	
Apollon Club	**49** B1
Café Štúdio Club	**50** C3
Channels	**51** B2
Slovak National Theatre	**52** C3
Slovak Philharmonic	**53** C4

SHOPPING	
Úľuv	**54** C1
Vinotéka sv Urbana	**55** C3

TRANSPORT	
Avis	**56** B4
Bus to Devín Castle	**57** B4
DPB Office	**58** C2
Hydrofoil Terminal	**59** D4
Propeller Terminal	**60** B4

A series of old homes winds down the castle hill along Židovská in what was once the Jewish quarter. The **Museum of Clocks** (Múzeum hodín; Map p838; ☎ 5441 1940; Židovská 1; adult/concession €2/0.70; ☼ 10am-5pm Tue-Sun) is housed in the skinniest house in Slovakia. Further down, the **Museum of Jewish Culture** (Múzeum Židovskej kultúry; Map p838; ☎ 5441 8507; Židovská 17; adult/concession €6.70/2; ☼ 11am-5pm Sun-Fri) displays moving exhibits about the community lost during WWII. Black-and-white photos show the old ghetto and synagogue ploughed under by the communists to make way for a highway and bridge. The staff can help arrange a visit to **Chatam Sofer's grave site** (Map p837; www .chatamsofer.com; Žižkova at tram tunnel; donations accepted; ☼ by appointment only), the resting place of the much revered 19th-century rabbi.

A relatively modest interior belies the elaborate history of **St Martin's Cathedral** (Dóm sv Martina; Map p838; ☎ 5443 1359; Rudnayovo nám; admission €1.50; ☼ 8-11.30am & 1.30-4.30pm Mon-Sat). Eleven ruling monarchs (10 kings and one queen, Maria Theresa) were crowned in this 14th-century church. The busy motorway almost touching St Martin's follows the moat of the former city walls and is shaking the building to its core.

Further east along the Danube, the 1st-floor exhibits of the **Slovak National Museum** (Slovenské Národné múzeum; Map p838; ☎ 5934 9122; www.snm.sk; Vajanského nábr 2; adult/concession €3.30/1.70; ☼ 9am-5pm Tue-Sun) provide a super overview of the folk cultures and customs of Slovakia. Skip the tired natural-history stuff upstairs.

An 18th-century palace and a Stalinist-modern building make interesting co-hosts

MAN AT WORK

The most photographed sight in Bratislava is a bronze statue called the **Watcher** (Čumil; Map p838). He peeps out of an imaginary manhole at the intersection of Panská and Rybarska, below a 'Man at Work' sign. But he's not alone. There are other quirky statues scattered around the pedestrian old town. Can you find them? The **Frenchman** leans on a park bench, the **Photographer** stalks his subject paparazzi-style around a corner and the **Schöner Náci** tips his top hat on a square. Look up for other questionable characters, like a timepiece-toting monk and a rather naked imp, decorating building facades.

for the **Slovak National Gallery** (Slovenská Národná Galéria; Map p838; ☎ 5443 4587; www.sng.sk; Rázusovo nábr 2; adult/concession €3.30/1.70; ☼ 10am-5pm Tue-Sun). The nation's eclectic art collection ranges from Gothic to graphic design.

Two of Old Town's opulent theatres are off Hviezdoslavovo nám, a broad, tree-lined plaza. The gilt, neobaroque 1914 **Reduta Palace** hosts the nation's philharmonic orchestra (see p843), and the ornate 1886 Slovak National Theatre (p843) is the city's opera house. Neither is open for tours, but ticket prices aren't prohibitive.

Bustling, narrow **Rybárska brána** (Fisherman's Gate) street runs from Hviezdoslavovo nám to Hlavné nám, a main square which is filled with cafe tables in summer and a craft market that grows exponentially at Easter and Christmas times. **Roland's Fountain** (Map p838) at the centre may have been built in 1572 as an old-fashioned fire hydrant. Flanking one side of the square is the 1421 **old town hall** (Stará radnica; Map p838), and the city museum contained within, under indefinite reconstruction at the time of writing. The renovation of the nearby **Apponyi Palace** (Map p838; ☎ 5920 5112; Radničná 1; adult/concession €6.60/1.30; ☼ 10am-5pm Tue-Fri, 11am-6pm Sat & Sun) is complete, and it now serves as a museum of 18th- and 19th-century decorative arts.

Communist Bratislava

Forty-five years of communist rule was bound to leave its mark on Bratislava. Case in point: **Petržalka** (Map p837), the ugly, concrete-jungle housing estate across the river from the Old Town. (Can't you imagine going to the wrong flat in an identical adjacent building after drinking a few too many? Believe us, it happens.)

A sizeable chunk of the old city, including the synagogue, was demolished to create **New Bridge** (Nový most; Map p838; ☎ 6252 0300; www.u-f-o.sk; Viedenská cesta; observation deck adult/concession €6.70/3.30; ☼ 10am-11pm), colloquially called the UFO (pronounced ew-fo) bridge. This modernist marvel from 1972 has a viewing platform, an overhyped nightclub and a restaurant with out-of-this-world prices.

The communist-realist **Monument to the Slovak National Uprising** (Map p837; Nám SNP) actually celebrates partisans who fought Nazi fascism in WWII. The namesake square is where at midnight on 31 December 2002 hundreds of thousands danced – this author included – as Slovakia became an independent nation.

Still nostalgic for the good old days? Down a brewsky or two with Stalin, Lenin and the boys (or at least their statues) at Kréma Gurmánov Bratislavy (p842).

Hiking

To get out of the city and into the forest, take trolleybus 203 northeast from Hodžovo nám to the end of the line at Koliba, then walk up the road for about 20 minutes to the **TV tower** (Map p837) on Kamzík Hill (440m). Posted maps outline the many hiking possibilities in the forest surrounds and there are a couple of hotels with restaurants in the park. A **chair lift** (lanovka; Map p837; ☎ 5479 2503; adult/concession return €4/2.70; 🕙 10am-5pm Thu-Sun Oct-May) makes the 15-minute journey downhill to the picnic areas and playgrounds of Železná studienka and back.

FESTIVALS & EVENTS

Bratislava's best events are arts related. From June to September the **Cultural Summer Festival** (Kultúrne leto; ☎ 5441 3063; www.bkis.sk) brings a smorgasbord of operas, plays and performances to the streets and venues around town. Classical music takes centre stage at the **Bratislava Music Festival** (Bratislavské hudobné slávnosti; ☎ 5443 4546; www.bhsfestival.sk), which runs from late September to mid-October. **Bratislava Jazz Days** (Bratislavských jazzových dní; ☎ 5293 1572; www.bjd.sk) makes music for three days in September. The 26th of November is the usual start to the **Christmas market** with even more crafts and edibles for sale on Hlavné nám (Map p838). Try the *varene vino* (hot spiced wine), yum!

SLEEPING

Bratislava's lodging market is giving nearby Vienna's rates a run for its money these days, but don't expect comparable services. To book an apartment, check out www.bratislavahotels.com and www.apartmentsbratislava.com.

All hostels listed have free wi-fi, kitchens, laundries, and beer and wine for sale.

Hostel Possonium (Map p837; ☎ 2072 0007; www.possonium.sk; Šancová 20; dm €17-18, d €51; 🖳) Mixed reviews have come in for Bratislava's newest hostel. Drawbacks include street noise and a 2km walk to the centre. Pluses: being across from the train station and having the lowest prices.

Hostel Blues (Map p838; ☎ 09204020; www.hostelblues.sk; Špitálska 2; dm €20, d €63; 🖳) Friendly, professional staff not only help you plan your days, they offer free city sightseeing tours weekly. Jazz bands play some nights in the coffee house–like communal space (with free internet computers). Choose from single sex or mixed dorms, or those with double bunk beds. Apartments sleep four to six (from €108).

Downtown Backpackers (Map p838; ☎ 5464 1191; www.backpackers.sk; Panenská 31; dm €16-25, d €66; 🖳) A boozy Bohemian classic (you enter through a bar). Red brick walls and tapestries add character, as does the fact you have to walk through some dorm rooms to get to others.

City Hostel (Map p838; ☎ 5263 6041; www.cityhostel.sk; Obchodná; s/d €40/60; 🖳) More hotel than hostel really, cubicle-like singles and doubles all have their own bathrooms and TV. The super mod (leather and lime green) reception area has coffee and internet access, both of which are free.

Penzión Zlatá Noha (Map p837; ☎ 5477 4922; www.zlata-noha.sk; Bellova 2, Koliba hill; s/d €67/83; 🖳) Tranquillity and family-run attention make up for distance at this comfy modern guest house above town. It's a great place for those with vehicles, and bus 203 regularly runs the 4km to the Old Town. For €7 you can add a buffet breakfast, and they'll cook other meals to order. Free wi-fi.

Hotel-Penzión Arcus (Map p837; ☎ 5557 2522; www.hotelarcus.sk; Moskovská 5; s/d incl breakfast €68/100) Because this family-run hotel was once an apartment building, rooms are quite varied in size (some with balcony, some with courtyard views). Flowery synthetic chairs seem a little outdated but bathrooms are new and sparkly white. Communal kitchens are available and some rooms have internet access.

Penzión Chez David (Map p838; ☎ 5441 3824; www .chezdavid.sk; Zámocká 13; s/d incl breakfast €74/102; ☒) With the cool blue colour scheme, great old photos of synagogues on the walls, and primo old-town location, you'll hardly even notice the building's boxiness (though the rooms are small). Kosher restaurant on site; free wi-fi in restaurant and garden.

Carlton Hotel (Map p838; ☎ 5939 0000; www.bratislava .radissonsas.com; Hviezdoslavovo nám 3; r €150-250; ☒ ☐) The Carlton, currently owned by Radisson, has been cruising like a luxury liner on one of the town's main squares since 1837. Walk from here across the street to the opera or symphony. Unfortunately some rooms have been outfitted in a jarringly modern aesthetic; ask for the classic if you prefer.

Arcadia Hotel (Map p838; ☎ 5949 0500; www.arcadia -hotel.sk; Františkánska 3; s/d incl breakfast €250/280; ☒ ☒) Pains were taken when turning a 13th-century palace into Bratislava's first five-star hotel: an ornate stained-glass skylight tops the interior courtyard, hand-painted designs grace the dining room's vaulted arches... Why not cuddle into the luxe robe and relax on a red-and-gold silk settee, or dip into the wellness whirlpool, before you dress for a decadent dinner?

EATING

The Old Town certainly isn't lacking for dining options or international cuisines. Most cater to visitors, and are priced accordingly. What's harder to find is reasonable Slovak food.

Student-oriented cheap eats, both sit-down and takeaway, are available all along Obchodná (Map p838). Cafeterias catering to workers (ie not open late, but you can order to go) are a great resource for budgeteers.

U Jakubu (Map p838; ☎ 5441 7951; Nám SNP 24; mains €2-5; ☽ 8am-6pm Mon-Fri) Pile on the hearty fried and stewed classics in standard Slovak self-service style.

Presto (Map p838; ☎ 5464 8057; ground fl, Tatracentrum, Hodžovo nám 3; mains €3-6; ☽ 8am-3pm Mon-Fri) Owned by the upscale Italian restaurant next door, this modern cafeteria has an international flavour – and lots of vegetables.

Verne (Map p838; ☎ 5443 0514; Hviezdoslavovo nám 18; mains €5-8; ☽ 8.30am-midnight Mon-Fri, 11am-midnight Sat & Sun) Thoroughly reasonable prices, long hours (breakfast, too) and sidewalk seating attract expats and locals alike. Slovak-international food served.

U Remeselníka (☎ 5273 1357; Obchodná 64; mains €5-10) This folksy cafe, associated with the traditional craft store upstairs (see opposite), is a great place to try a trio of *halušky* – dumplings with sheep's cheese and bacon, with *klobasa*, and with cabbage.

Pizza Mizza (Map p838; ☎ 5296 5034; Tobrucká 5; mains €5-11) Word is the cooks might be resting on their accolades as of late, but Pizza Mizza is still a pleasant house-like restaurant with a long list of wood-fired options and pastas.

our pick **Prašná Bašta** (Map p838; ☎ 5443 4957; Zámočnicka 11; mains €8-15) The round, vaulted interior oozes old-Bratislava charm, but the hidden courtyard seating with a view of Michael's Gate is even better. Dishes range from traditional (potato dough–crusted schnitzel) to modern Eastern European (pork medallions with cream, leak and mustard sauce).

Also recommended:

City Vegetarian (Map p838; ☎ 5273 1381; Obchodná 58; mains €2-5; ☽ 11am-4pm Mon-Fri) Vegetarian self-service.

Tesco (Map p838; ☎ 4446 4057; Kamenné nám 1; ☽ 8am-9pm Mon-Fri, 9am-7pm Sat & Sun) Big supermarket for self-catering.

Of the many, many spiffy global food alternatives in Old Town – none priced for the average Slovak – **El Gaucho** (Map p838; ☎ 3212 1212; Hviezdoslavovo nám 13; mains €15-22) is one worth the dough. The Argentinian spices are good, but beef's really the thing here. You might also try **Krishna** (Map p837; ☎ 5464 1804; Botel Marina, Nábr arm gen L Svobodu; mains €10-18) for some decent tandoori.

DRINKING

From mid-April to October, sidewalk tables fill with friends settling in for a cocktail or two. Any one will do for a drink.

Čokoládovňa (Map p838; ☎ 5433 3945; Michalská 6; ☽ 9am-9pm) This tiny 'chocolate cafe' has liqueurs, coffees and desserts made with the dark ambrosia.

Kréma Gurmánov Bratislavy (KGB; Map p838; ☎ 5273 1279; Obchodná 52; ☽ 10am-2am Mon-Fri, 4pm-3am Sat, 4pm-midnight Sun) Drink a dark and smoky toast to a statue of Stalin under a Soviet flag at the cellar KGB bar.

Malecón (Map p838; ☎ 0910274583; Nám L Štúra 4) Where the pretty people go to sip and swill – mainly mojitos. Could owning a Beemer be a prerequisite for entry?

British themes are all the rage, but unless you want to only meet English speakers, steer clear of the touristy **Dubliner** (Map p838; ☎ 5441 0706; Sedlárska 6; ⏳ 11am-3am Mon-Sat, to 1am Sun) and head to the more mixed crowd at **Greenwich Cocktail Bar** (Map p838; ☎ 0910760222; Zelená 10; ⏳ 4pm-2am).

ENTERTAINMENT

Check **What's On** (www.whatsonslovakia) and **Kam do Mesta** (www.kamdomesta.sk) for the latest live bands and theatre events. We know of a few Brits who've been turned away by bouncers; backlash from stag party antics. Just be respectful, and know that Bratislavans themselves are pretty conservative.

Nightclubs

Café Štúdio Club (Map p838; ☎ 5443 1796; cnr Laurinská & Radničná; ⏳ 10am-1am Mon-Wed, to 3am Thu & Fri, 4pm-3am Sat) Bop to the oldies, or chill out to jazz; most nights there's live music of some sort.

Channels (Map p838; ☎ 0911447323; Župné nám 2; ⏳ 9.30am-4am) Each of two stories has a bar and a dance floor for grooving to a techno DJ beat.

Dopler (Map p837; ☎ 0903686707; Prievozská 18; ⏳ 8pm-5am Fri & Sat) The city's biggest dance club, a taxi ride from the centre, draws in a college-age (and younger) crowd.

Apollon Club (Map p838; ☎ 091548031; www.apollon -gay-club.sk; Panenská 24; ⏳ 6pm-3am Mon-Thu & Sun, 6pm-5am Fri & Sat) The only gay disco in town has two bars and three stages. Monday is karaoke; Sunday, boys only.

Sport

Home games of Bratislava's hallowed ice-hockey team are held at **HC Slovan stadium** (Map p837; ☎ 4445 6500; www.hcslovan.sk, in Slovak; Odbojárov 3), while the hometown football team plays at **SK Slovan stadium** (Map p837; ☎ 4437 3083; www.slovan futbal.sk in Slovak; Viktora Tegelhoffa 4). You can buy tickets for both teams online at www.eventim.sk.

Performing Arts

Slovak National Theatre (Slovenské Národné Divadlo, SND; Map p838; www.snd.sk; Hviezdoslavovo nám; ⏳ 8am-5.30pm Mon-Fri, 9am-1pm Sat) The local company stages both Slavic and international operas, along with ballets, at the state theatre. Buy tickets online, or at the ticket office around the back of the building.

Slovak Philharmonic (Slovenská Filharmónia; Map p838; ☎ 5920 8233; www.filharmonia.sk; cnr Nám L Štúra & Medená; ⏳ ticket office 1-7pm Mon, Tue, Thu & Fri, 8am-2pm Wed) Listen to the state opera in gilt splendour at its Reduta Palace theatre home.

State Puppet Theatre (Štátne Bábkové Divadlo; Map p837; ☎ 5292 3668; www.babkovedivadlo.sk; Dunajská 36) Puppet shows here cater to the younger generation; some are even Shakespeare-inspired (age seven and older).

Folk dance and music ensembles, like **Sluk** (☎ 6285 9125; www.sluk.sk) and **Lúčnica** (☎ 5292 0068; www.lucnica.sk), perform at various venues around town. Look for the schedules online.

SHOPPING

There are several crystal, craft and jewellery stores, as well as souvenir booths, in and around Hlavné nám. More and more artisan galleries are popping up in old-town alleys; check out the side streets.

Úľuv (Map p838; ☎ 5273 1351; www.uluv.sk; Obchodná 64) For serious folk-art shopping head to Úľuv, where there are two stores and a courtyard filled with artisans' studios.

Vinotéka Sv Urbana (Map p838; ☎ 5433 2573; Klobučnícka 4) Slovak and international wines for sample and sale.

GETTING THERE & AWAY

Slovakia's capital city, Bratislava is the main hub for trains, buses and airplanes heading into and out of the country. The best source for both domestic and international train and bus schedules is http://cp.atlas.sk.

Air

Most of the destinations from **MR Štefánika airport** (BTS; ☎ 3303 3353; Ivanska cesta 1; www.airportbrati slava.sk), 7km northeast of the centre, are outside the region. You can fly between Bratislava and Košice, on **SkyEurope Airlines** (☎ 4850 1000; www.skyeurope.com), with up to five flights daily.

Boat

Plying the waters is a cruisy way to get to Bratislava from neighbouring Danube cities. From mid-April to September, **Slovenská plavba a prístavy** (☎ 5293 2226; www.lod.sk) runs one or two daily hydrofoils to Vienna (€22 one way, 1½ hours) and to Budapest (€79 one way, four hours) from the **hydrofoil terminal** (Map p838; Fajnorovo nábr 2). From June to October the **Twin City Liner** (☎ 0903610716; www.twincityliner.com) operates up to six boats a day between Vienna (€28 one way, 1½ hours) and the Bratislava **propeller terminal** (Map p838; Rázusovo nábr).

Bus

The **main bus station** (autobusová stanica, AS; Map p837; ☎ reservations 5556 7349; www.slovaklines.sk; Mlynské Nivy) is 1.5km east of the Old Town. Buses leave from here heading to towns across Slovakia, including Žilina (€9, three hours, seven daily), Poprad (€15, seven hours, four daily) and Košice (€17, eight hours, nine daily).

Eurolines (☎ 5556 7349; www.eurolines.sk) runs direct buses between Bratislava and Prague (€12, four hours, daily) and Budapest (€19, 3½ hours, daily). It also connects Bratislava with many major Western European cities including Geneva, London (23 hours, five weekly), Munich, Paris (20 hours, three weekly), Rotterdam, Strasbourg and Vienna (one hour, hourly).

Train

At least 12 daily trains depart the **main train station** (Hlavná stanica; www.zsr.sk), 1km north of the centre, for Košice (€19, 5½ hours), most via Trenčín, (€6, two hours), Žilina (€10, 2¾ hours) and Poprad (€14, 4¾ to eight hours).

Direct trains connect Bratislava with Prague (€27, 4½ hours, six daily), Budapest (€21, three hours, seven daily) and Vienna (€9, one hour, 30 daily). Night departure trains link Bratislava with Kraków (€36, 7½ hours, daily) and Warsaw (€40, 8¼ hours, daily) in Poland.

GETTING AROUND
To/From the Airport

Bus 61 links the airport with the main train station (€0.75, 20 minutes). To get to the centre by taxi costs up to €15, services that operate out of the airport legitimately charge more than in town.

Public Transport

The main train station, Hlavná stanica, is located just 1km north of the centre. Tram 13 runs from the station to Nám L Štúra, immediately south of Hviezdoslavovo nám, and bus 93 stops at Hodžovo nám. The main bus station, called Mlynské Nivy by locals because of the street it's on, is a little over 1km east of the Old Town. If you arrive by bus, you can take bus 206 to Hodžovo nám, or bus 210 to the train station.

Dopravný Podnik Bratislava (DPB; ☎ 5950 5950; www.dpb.sk) runs an extensive tram, bus and trolleybus network. You can buy tickets (€0.50/0.60/0.75 for 10/30/60 minutes) at

news-stands and at the **DPB office** (Map p838; Obchodná 14; ☺ 9am-5.30pm Mon-Fri). Validate on board. One-/two-/three-/seven-day *turistické cestovné lístky* (tourist travel tickets) cost €3/6/7/10 and are sold by the DPB office and train and bus stations. Check routes and schedules at www.imhd.sk.

The Bratislava City Card (one/two/three days for €6/10/12) includes all city transport, among other benefits. It's sold by Bratislava Culture & Information Centres; see p839 for details.

Car

Numerous international rental agencies have offices at the airport; **Alimex** (☎ 5564 1641; www .alimex.sk) is usually the most reasonable.

Taxi

Bratislava's taxis have meters, but there still seems to be a slight English-speaking surcharge. Within the Old Town a trip should cost no more than €10. Try **ABC Taxi** (☎ 16 100) or **Fun Taxi** (☎ 16 777).

AROUND BRATISLAVA

Hard-core castle aficionados should don their daypack and head to **Devín Castle** (☎ 02-6573 0105; Muranská; adult/concession €3/1.50; ☺ 10am-5pm Tue-Fri, to 6pm Sat & Sun mid-Apr–Oct), 9km west of Bratislava. Once the military plaything of 9th-century warlord Prince Ratislav, the castle withstood the Turks but then was blown up in 1809 by the French. Peer at the older bits that have been unearthed and tour a reconstructed palace museum. Bus 29 links Devín with Bratislava's New Bridge stop, under the bridge. Austria is just across the river.

WEST SLOVAKIA

Snaking along the Small Carpathians on the main route northeast of Bratislava, watch for hilltop castle ruins high above the Váh River. Trenčín's magnificent, reconstructed castle is one of the most impressive along this once heavily fortified stretch.

TRENČÍN
☎ 032 / pop 56,850

The pretty pedestrian plazas and lively nightlife in this university town are attractive enough. But it's the mighty castle looming above the 18th- and 19th-century buildings that's really worth seeing. The form of today's fortress dates from around the 15th century but the city is much older than that. Trenčín Castle was first noted in a Viennese chronicle of 1069, and Roman legionnaires fancied the town's site (they called it Laugaricio) and stationed here in the 2nd century AD.

Orientation

From the adjacent bus and train stations walk west through Park MR Štefánika and beneath the highway past the Hotel Tatra, where a street bears left uphill to Mierové nám, the main square. The whole centre is easily walkable.

Information

Cultural Information Centre (☎ 161 86; www .trencin.sk; City Office, Sládkovičova; ☺ 10am-5pm Mon-Fri, 10am-noon Sat) Helpful, well-informed staff sell event tickets as well as giving out gobs of info.
Main post office (Mierové nám 21)
Mike Studio (Mierové nám 31; per 30min €1; ☺ 9am-10pm Mon-Sat, 10am-10pm Sun;) Just internet terminals, no cafe.
VUB Banka (Mierové nám 37) ATM and exchange.

Sights

Sitting high atop a rocky crag, **Trenčín Castle** (Trenčiansky hrad; ☎ 7435 657; www.muzeumtn.sk; adult/concession €4/2; ☺ 9am-5.30pm May-Sep, to 4.30pm Apr & Oct, to 3.30pm Nov-Mar) overshadows the town, as any good fortress should. Climb ever-more stairs to reach the lowest level of the castle fortifications, from there you already have commanding views of the Váh River plain. Two levels higher, you can enter the towers and palaces with one of the frequent tours. A complete visit of the reconstructed rooms takes about 75 minutes (in Slovak only, call two days ahead to arrange an English-speaking guide). At night, the green and purple spots light the exterior; the most evocative time to visit is summer evenings during a two-hour, torch-light tour, complete with medieval sword fighting, minstrels and staged frolics.

The town's unique claim to fame is the **Roman inscription** of AD 179, soldier's graffiti commemorating a battle against Germanic tribes. It is actually carved into the cliff behind the **Hotel Tatra** (☎ 6506 111; www.hotel-tatra .sk; Ul gen MR Štefánika 2) and can only be viewed through a window in the hotel's staircase; ask

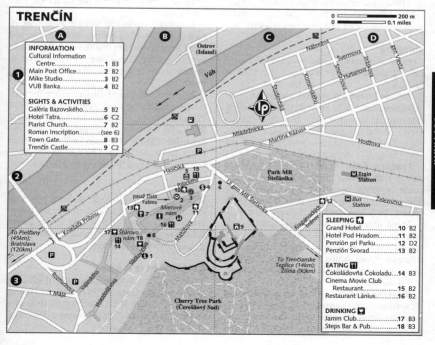

WORTH THE TRIP: PIEŠŤANY

Thermal waters bubble under much of the country. Slovakia's premier spa site, **Piešťany** (☎ 33-775 7733; www.spa-piestany.sk), is only 87km northeast of Bratislava. A few years back Slovak spas were medical facilities requiring a doctor's note. Not so today. OK, there's still a slightly antiseptic look to some treatment rooms, but many of Piešťany's lovely 19th-century buildings sport a new coat of Maria-Theresa-yellow paint and others are under reconstruction. On Kúpele ostrov (Spa Island) you can swim in thermal pools, breathe seaside-like air in a salt cave and be wrapped naked in hot mud. Head to the *kasa* (cashier) at Napoleon 1 to book a service, or go online. There are several island hotels, which can be reserved on the spa website, and many more in town across the river. Trains from Bratislava take 1¼ hours (€4, 12 daily) and you can continue on the same line to Trenčín (€2, 45 minutes).

---

at reception. The translation reads: 'To the victory of the emperor and the army which, numbering 855 soldiers, resided at Laugaricio. By order of Maximianus, legate of the 2nd auxiliary legion'.

Temporary exhibits at the **Galéria Bazovského** (☎ 7436 858; www.gmab.sk, in Slovak; Palackého 27; adult/concession €1/0.80; ❧ 9am-5pm Tue-Sun) represent some of the best of 20th-century Slovak and Czech art. The main collection contains works by local painter Miloš Bazovský (1899–1968).

At the western end of Mierové nám are the baroque **Piarist Church** (Piaristický kostol) and a 16th-century **town gate** (*mestská brána*).

Sleeping

Trenčín has many more pensions than we can list, ask at the tourist office if those below are full.

Penzión Svorad (☎ 7430 322; www.svorad-trencin .sk; Palackého 4; dm €19-26) Frayed curtains, peeling linoleum, thin mattresses – but oh, the castle views. This dormitory-like pension resides in part of an old grammar school; maybe that's why the staff is so rule-obsessed.

Penzión pri Parku (☎ 7434 377; www.penzionpriparku .sk; Kragujevackých hrdinov 7; r €25-38) Ignore the mishmash of 1990s furnishings and admire the Victorian building in city park. Here you're close to both train and bus stations. Free wi-fi.

Grand Hotel (☎ 7434 353; www.grand-hotel.sk; Palackého 34; s/d €62/70; 🖳) Soft contemporary rooms are awash in dark woods and upscale neutrals. Perks at this modern hotel include free bike rental, and whirlpool and sauna use. Wi-fi included.

Hotel Pod Hradom (☎ 7442 507; www.podhradom .sk; Matúšova 12; r incl breakfast €86-98; 🖳) On a wee, winding street en route to the castle; a prime location and patio view are the main draws

at this 10-room lodging. Sloped ceilings and skylights add character to spartan rooms. Free broadband access.

Eating & Drinking

Čokoládovňa Čokoladu (☎ 0903480318; Štúrovo nám 7; cakes €1-3; ❧ 9am-8pm Mon-Sat, 1-8pm Sun) With a name like 'Chocolate Cafe Chocolate', what do you think they serve?

Cinema Movie Club Restaurant (☎ 0902898533; Palackého 33; mains €5-8) Chicken and risotto dishes are quite good here, but the real steal is the weekday lunch set menu for under €4. Free wi-fi zone.

Restaurant Lánius (☎ 7441 978; Mierové nám 20; mains €5-13) Creaking beams, wood floors and stone fireplaces make this the cosiest of places serving hearty Slovak fare. The dining room up the stairs at the rear of the courtyard is most fun.

Numerous cafes and drinkeries line the pedestrian plazas; check out **Steps Bar & Pub** (☎ 7446 252; Sládkovičova 4-6; ❧ 10.30am-1am Sun-Thu, to 4am Fri & Sat), which attracts a college-age crowd, and **Jamm Club** (Štúrovo nám 5; ❧ noon-1am Mon-Thu, noon-3am Fri, 2pm-3am Sat, 2pm-1am Sun), which hosts occasional live jazz and blues (other nights are disco).

Events

World music, jazz, rock, techno, hip hop, alternative; what kind of music isn't represented one weekend in July at the **Bazant Pohoda Festival** (www.pohodafestival.sk), the largest music festival in Slovakia.

Getting There & Away

Trains are the quickest and most cost-efficient way to get here from Bratislava (€6, two hours, at least 12 daily). Most continue on to Košice (€14, four hours). Twenty trains a day travel to Žilina (€6, 1½ hours).

CENTRAL SLOVAKIA

The rolling hills and forested mountain ranges of central Slovakia are home to the shepherding tradition that defines Slovak culture. Watch roadside for farmers selling local sheep's cheese. The beautiful Malá Fatra mountain range is where this nation's Robin Hood, Juraj Jánošík, once roamed.

ŽILINA

☎ 041 / pop 85,655

A Slavic tribe in the 6th century was the first to recognise Žilina's advantageous location at the intersection of several important trade routes, on the Váh River. Today it's still a convenient base for exploring the Malá Fatra National Park, surrounding fortresses and folk villages. That said, there isn't much to see in town besides the old palace-like castle on the outskirts.

Orientation

The train station is on the northeastern side of the Old Town, near the Váh River. A 700m walk along Národná takes you past Nám A Hlinku up to Mariánské nám, the main square. From the south end of the bus station, follow Jána Milca northeast to Národná.

Information

Net Café Pohoda (☎ 5640 099; Kukučínova 8; per hr €1.30; ⏰ 9am-10pm Mon-Fri, 2-10pm Sat)
Main post office (Sládkovičova 1)
Tatra Banka (cnr Mariánské nám & Farská) ATM.
Tourist Information Office (TIK; ☎ 7233 186; www .zilina.sk\tik; Republiky 1; ⏰ 9am-5pm Mon-Fri, 9am-2pm Sat & Sun) Loaded with info.

Sights

North across the Váh River, **Budatín Castle** (Budatínsky zámok; ☎ 5620 033; Topoľová 1; adult/concession €1.30/0.70; ⏰ 9am-4.30pm Tue-Sun May-Aug, to 3.30pm Sep & Oct, to 1.30pm Nov-Apr) is more mansion than stronghold. The museum inside contains exhibits of 18th- and 19th-century decorative arts as well as wire figures made by area tinkers.

Other than that, you're left to stroll through the somewhat plain pedestrian squares.

Sleeping

The tourist office books accommodation, including private rooms, for a fee.

Kompas Cafe (☎ 0918481319; http://kompascafe .wordpress.com; Vojtecha Spanyola 37; dm €11) Two- to five-bed worker hostel rooms have wood beds, striped curtains, and not much else. At least there's a convivial cafe and a small kitchen here; 1km from the centre.

Penzión Majovey (☎ 5624 152; www.slovanet.sk /majovey in Slovak; Jána Milca 3; s/d €36/62) A deep coral exterior is more interesting than the clean white room interiors, but the bathrooms are huge and tile floors keep things cool throughout. Very convenient.

Hotel Dubna Skala (☎ 5079 100; www.hoteldubna skala.sk; Hurbanova 8; s/d €119/144; 🞐) Hyper-modern lighted-glass murals as headboards seems an unlikely choice for a neoclassical building, but this stylish boutique hotel pulls it off. Check out the contemporary wine-cellar restaurant.

Eating & Drinking

Interchangeable bars and cafes lie around Mariánske and Hlinka squares.

Voyage Voyage (☎ 5640 230; Mariánske nám 191; mains €4-11) If the sleek neon and chrome don't convince you this isn't your typical Slovak eatery, menu items like chicken sauté with honey and chillis will.

O2 (☎ 5640 320; Na Priekope 39; mains €5-11) Start with broccoli soup and move on to one of

---

WORTH THE TRIP: VLKOLÍNEC

The folksy mountain village of **Vlkolínec** (☎ 4321 023; www.vlkolinec.sk in Slovak; adult/student €2/1; ⏰ 9am-3pm), about 71km east and south of Žilina, has long been considered a national treasure (and not just by Unesco). The pastel paint and steep roofs on the 45 traditional plastered log cabins are remarkably well maintained. It's easy to imagine a *vlk* (wolf) wandering through this wooded mountainside settlement arranged along a small stream. You pay entry to walk around, and one of the buildings has been turned into a small house museum, but this is still a living village – if just barely. Of the 35 residents, 12 are school children.

Driving or hiking the 6km up hill from Ružomberok is the only way to get to the village. Five direct trains a day stop in Ružomberok on their way from Bratislava (€12, 3½ hours) and Žilina (€3, 1½ hours) to Košice (€8, 2½ hours).

WORTH THE TRIP: BOJNICE CASTLE

Bojnice Castle (Bojnice zámok; ☎ 046-5430 633; www.bojnicecastle.sk; adult/child €5.30/2.70; ☺ 9am-5pm daily Jul & Aug, 9am-5pm Tue-Sun Sep & May, 10am-3pm Tue-Sun Oct-Apr) comes straight out of a fairy-tale dream filled with towers and turrets and crenulated mouldings. The original 12th-century fortification got an early 20th-century redo by the Pálffy family, who modelled it on French romantic castles. (Original Gothic and Renaissance parts do survive within.) The time to visit is during the **International Festival of Ghosts & Ghouls** in May, which attracts thousands. Costumed guides re-enact legends and put on shows throughout the castle and grounds. The palace also gets decked out for Christmas, Valentine's Day and medieval events, among others; check the website. Bojnice, 3km from Prievidza (via local bus 3), is not on a main train line. A bus from Žilina to Prievidza takes 1½ hours (€2.60, eight daily), from Bratislava it's 3½ hours (€6.50, eight daily).

---

the traditional pork dishes, such as the cutlet grilled with bacon and topped with smoked sheep's cheese.

And then there's **Palacinkáreň** (☎ 0907297413; Dolný Val 9; mains €2-5; ☺ 9am-8pm Mon-Fri, 9am-2pm Sun) with savoury and sweet crêpes to order.

Pizzeria Carolina (☎ 5003 030; Národná 5; pizzas €3-8) is especially popular with university students.

Getting There & Away
Žilina is on the main railway line from Bratislava to Košice. At least 12 trains daily head to Trenčín (€6, one hour), Bratislava (€9, 2¾ hours), Poprad (€7, two hours) and Košice (€10, three hours).

AROUND ŽILINA
As well as nearby Malá Fatra National Park, a few folk culture sights within an hour of Žilina are well worth exploring.

The nearby town of **Martin** is an industrial centre with a **tourist information office** (☎ 4234 776; www.tikmartin.sk; Štefánika 9A) and the country's largest *skanzen* (open-air village museum). The **Museum of the Slovak Village** (Múzeum Slovenské Dediny; ☎ 043-4239 491; www.snm-em.sk; adult/concession €1.70/0.80; ☺ 9am-6pm Jul & Aug, 10am-5pm Tue-Sat Sep, Oct, May & Jun, 10am-2.30pm Tue-Sat Nov-Apr) comes complete with working *krčma* (village pub). Traditional buildings from all over the region have been moved here. Take the bus to Martin (€150, 40 minutes, half-hourly), 35km south of Žilina. The village museum is 4km southeast of the city. Take bus 10 from the bus station to the last stop, Ľadovaň, and walk the remaining 1km up through the forest (or hail a taxi).

Dark log homes painted with white geometric patterns fill the traditional village of **Čičmany** (www.cicmany.viapvt.sk, in Slovak), which is

50 minutes south of Žilina by bus (€1.80, five daily). If you've seen a brochure or postcard of Slovakia, you've probably seen a photograph of a Čičmany. Most houses are private residences, but **Radenov House** (No 42; adult/concession €1.60/0.80; ☺ 10am-4pm Tue-Sun) is a museum and there's a small restaurant in the long, narrow settlement. Return bus times allow hours to wander and photograph.

MALÁ FATRA NATIONAL PARK
☎ 041
Sentinel-like formations stand watch at the rocky gorge entrance to the valley filled with pine-clad slopes above. The Malá Fatra National Park (Národný park Malá Fatra) incorporates a chocolate box–pretty, 200-sq-km swathe of its namesake mountain range. The Vrátna Valley (Vrátna dolina), 25km east of Žilina, lies at the heart of the park. From here you can access the trailheads, ski lifts and a cable car to start your exploration. The long, one-street town of Terchová is at the lower end of the valley, Chata Vrátna is at the top. The small cluster of buildings in Štefanová lie east of the main valley road, 1km uphill from Terchová.

Information
For basic trails and ski runs, check out www.vratna.sk. For serious hiking, VKÚ's 1:50,000 *Malá Fatra – Vrátna* map (No 110) is best.
Mountain Rescue Service (Horská Záchranná služba; ☎ 5695 232; http://his.hzs.sk/; Štefanová)
Terchová tourist information centre (☎ 5695 307; www.ztt.sk; Sv Cyrila a Metoda 96, Terchová; ☺ 8am-5pm Mon-Fri, 9am-4pm Sat, 10am-3pm Sun) ATM next door.
Vrátna Infocentrum (☎ 5695 648; www.vratna.sk; Sv Maritina 294, Terchová; ☺ 8am-4pm) Focuses on Vrátna Valley.

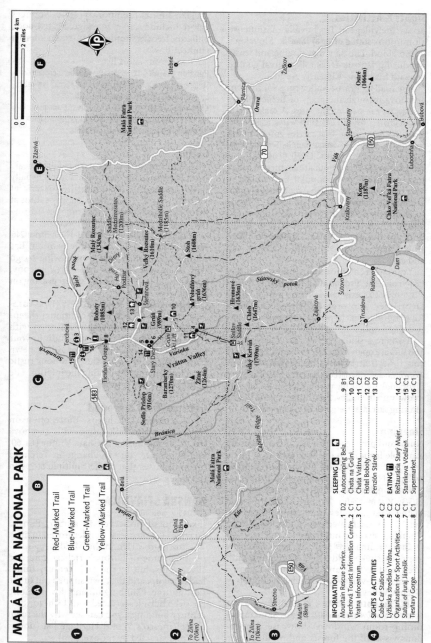

MALÁ FATRA NATIONAL PARK

Red-Marked Trail
Blue-Marked Trail
Green-Marked Trail
Yellow-Marked Trail

INFORMATION
Mountain Rescue Service.....1 D2
Terchová Tourist Information Centre.2 C1
Vrata Infocentrum.....3 C1

SIGHTS & ACTIVITIES
Cable Car Station.....4 C2
Lyžiarska stredisko Vrátna.....5 C2
Organization for Sport Activities.....6 C2
Statue of Juraj Jánošík.....7 C1
Tiesňavy Gorge.....8 C1

SLEEPING
Autocamping Belá.....9 B1
Chata na Grúni.....10 D2
Chata Vrátna.....11 C2
Hotel Boboty.....12 D2
Penzión Starek.....13 D2

EATING
Reštaurácia Starý Majer.....14 C2
Starinkova Vzeláreň.....15 C1
Supermarket.....16 C1

Sights & Activities

Above the village of Terchová is an immense aluminium **statue of Juraj Jánošík**, Slovakia's Robin Hood. The dancing, singing and feasting during Jánošík Days folk festival go one beneath his likeness in early August.

The road to Vrátna Valley runs south from Terchová through the crags of **Tiesňavy Gorge** (Tiesňavy roklina), past picnic sites. A **cable car** (kabínkova lanovka; ☎ 5993 049; Chata Vrátna; return adult/concession €10/7; ☼ 8am-4pm) carries you from the top of the valley to **Snilov Saddle** (Snilovské sedlo; 1524m) below two peaks, **Chleb** (1647m) and **Velký Kriváň** (1709m). Both are on the red, ridge trail, one of the most popular in the park. A hike northeast from Chleb over **Poludňový grúň** (1636m), **Hromové** (1636m) and **Stoh** (1608m) to **Medziholie Saddle** (1185m) takes about 5½ hours. From there you can descend for an hour on the green trail to **Štefanová** village where there's a bus stop, and places to stay and eat.

You can rent mountain bikes (per day €8) from the **Organization for Sport Activities** (☎ 0903546600; www.splavovanie.sk) hut at Starý Dvor; they also organise two-hour Orava River rafting trips (from €15 per person) with two days' notice.

If you're a skier, the Vrátna Valley's tows and lifts are open from December to April. Buy your ticket from **Lyžiarska stredisko Vrátna** (☎ 5695 055; www.vratna.sk; day lift ticket adult/child €22/15) at Starý Dvor, look for the big parking lot on the left side midway up the valley. Nearby are several shacks offering **ski rental** (per pair €15; ☼ 8am-4pm).

Sleeping

Numerous private apartments and cottages are available for rent in the Terchová area, many are listed with pictures on the tourist-office website. No camping is allowed in the park.

Autocamping Bela (☎ 5621 478; per person/tent/car €3/3/3; ☼ May-mid-Oct; 🏊) Five kilometres west of the Vrátna Valley, this camping ground has 300 sites, a heated pool and a food stand. There's a bus stop out front.

Chata Vrátna (☎ 5695 739; http://chata.vratna .org; d/tr €23/30) Muddy hikers, giggling children and a fragrant wood-smoke aroma fill this well-worn, basic chalet at the top of Vrátna Valley.

our pick **Hotel Boboty** (☎ 5695 228; www.hotel boboty.sk; Nový Dvor; s/d €56/102; 🖳 🏊) Skyscraping dining-room windows showcase tremendous vistas of the forests and mountains in a clean-line contemporary style. Services galore include sauna, massage, heated pool, billiards, free ski shuttle and in-room internet connections.

Also on our short list:

Penzión Stárek (☎ 5695 359; www.penzionstarek.sk; Štefanová 124; d incl breakfast €39; 🖳) Small log-cabin inn with good pizza restaurant and wi-fi.

Chata na Grúni (☎ 5695 324; www.chatanagruni.sk; dm €11) Hiker's hut at the top of Paseky chairlift; four- to six-bed dorms and self-service restaurant.

Eating

The food situation in the park is fairly bleak; most Slovaks bring their own. Hotels usually have restaurants, including the pizzeria at Penzión Stárek. There are takeaway stands at Starý Dvor and there's a supermarket (potraviny) at the valley turn-off in Terchová.

Starinkova Včeláreň (☎ 5993 130; A Hlinku 246, Terchová; snacks €1-4) This friendly tearoom has scones and homemade honey wine to go with its brew. From the 2nd-storey balcony, sip your cup and watch the sheep grazing on the hillside.

Reštaurácia Starý Majer (☎ 5695 419; mains €5-10; ☼ 10am-9pm) Tuck into traditional sheepherders' dishes surprisingly seasoned with fresh herbs. They even serve lemon in your water, a refreshing twist. Sit at rough-hewn picnic tables in the courtyard or among rustic farm implements decorating the interior. The best of the valley eateries.

Getting There & Around

At least every two hours, more often on weekdays, buses link Žilina with Terchová (€1.40, 45 minutes) and Chata Vrátna (€1.60, one hour). Or you can change in Terchová for local buses that make multiple stops in the valley.

BANSKÁ ŠTIAVNICA

☎ 045 / pop 10,674

Like a fossil preserved in amber, Banská Štiavnica is a medieval wonder frozen in time. The town grew rich in the Middle Ages, exploiting some of Europe's richest gold and silver veins, but by the 19th century mines had dried up, and the town slipped out of the flow of time. Climbing up and down among the steep hillsides terraced with 15th- to 18th-century buildings, you can see why the town made Unesco's World Heritage list (unless you're distracted by the exertion).

Orientation & Information

From the train station it's a 2km climb uphill through the factories and housing blocks to Nám sv Trojice, the main square in the Old Town. Buses stop 500m closer, at Križovatka. The **City Tourist Information Office** (☎ 6949 653; www.banskastiavnica.sk; Nám sv Trojice 3; ☼ 8am-5.30pm May-Sep, 8am-4pm Mon-Fri, 8am-2pm Sat Oct-Apr) doubles as a two-terminal internet cafe.

Sights

Wandering the steep streets gazing at old burghers' houses is the main attraction. Buildings aren't all in pristine condition, but the overall effect is still arresting. **Slovak Mining Museum** (Slovenské banské múzeum; ☎ 6949 422; ☼ 8am-5pm May-Aug, to 4pm Tue-Sun Sep-Apr) has several branches; most interesting is the **Open-air Mining Museum** (JK Hella 12; adult/concession €4/2; ☼ 8am-5pm May-Aug, to 4pm Tue-Sun Sep-Apr) where you can take a trip down into a former working mine. The umbrella organisation also manages the town history exhibits in the 16th-century **Old Castle** (Starozámocká 1; adult/concession €3/1.50; ☼ 8am-5pm May-Aug, to 4pm Tue-Sun Sep-Apr) and the 'History of the Struggle against the Turks' display at the **New Castle** (Novozámocká 1; adult/concession €3/1.50; ☼ 8am-5pm May-Aug, to 4pm Tue-Sun Sep-Apr) on an opposite hill. All are accessed by Slovak language tour, with English text available.

Sleeping & Eating

The info office keeps a long list of private rooms. There's a grocery store across from the bus stop.

Hostel 6 (☎ 0905106706; www.hostel6.sk; Andreja Slackovica 6; dm €13.30; 💻) Book ahead to snag one of the 14 beds in this tiny, hospitable backpackers hostel. The bathroom, kitchen and common room are similarly small but cosy; laundry available.

Penzión Príjemný Oddych (☎ 6921 301; www.prijemnyoddych.sk, in Slovak; Starozámocká 3; r €40) Yellow walls and framed folk embroidery keep the 17th-century building feeling light and, indeed, *prijemný* (pleasing). On-site restaurant, playground and a sauna.

For homemade Slovak food at its finest, try the *kapustnica* (cabbage and sausage soup) at **U Böhmna** (☎ 0903525022; Strieborná 7; mains €4-8) or anything on the menu at **Matej** (☎ 6912 051; Akademická 4; mains €5-10), not the grand hotel, but the little restaurant across the way from it.

Getting There & Away

Banská Štiavnica is not the easiest place to get to without your own transport. Only one direct bus daily departs from Bratislava (€7.60, 3½ hours), at 1pm. Otherwise, all bus and train arrivals require a change in Zvolen or Banská Bystrica. Check schedules at http://cp.atlas.sk.

EAST SLOVAKIA

Alpine peaks in Slovakia? As you look upon the snow-strewn jagged mountains rising like an apparition east of Liptovský Mikuláš, you may think you're imagining things, but there they are. Hiking the High Tatras is undoubtedly the highlight of the region, but in eastern Slovakia you can also admire ancient architecture, explore castle ruins, visit the second city and seek out small villages. Though it's a distance from Bratislava, once you get here, the area is fairly compact And Poland is just the other side of the mountains.

HIGH TATRAS

☎ 052

OK, this isn't exactly Switzerland, but the High Tatras (Vysoké Tatry) is the tallest range in the Carpathian Mountains. The massif is only 25km wide and 78km long, about 600 of the 726 sq km area falls within Slovakia. Photo opportunities at higher elevations might get you fantasising about a career with *National Geographic* – pristine snowfields, ultramarine mountain lakes and crashing waterfalls. Lower elevations are still recovering from a massive windstorm in late 2004 that uprooted trees and turned a once-dense pine forest into meadow.

Since 1949 most of this jagged range has been included in the Tatra National Park (Tanap), complementing a similar park in Poland. But that hasn't arrested development (much to the chagrin of watchdog groups like International Union for Conservation of Nature). The three main resort towns – Štrbské Pleso, Starý Smokovec and Tatranská Lomnica – continue to grow. A €250-million project is underway to add four luxury hotels and new ski runs by 2011.

When planning your trip, keep in mind that the higher trails are closed from November to mid-June, and avalanches may close lower portions as well. There's snow by November,

HIGH TATRAS

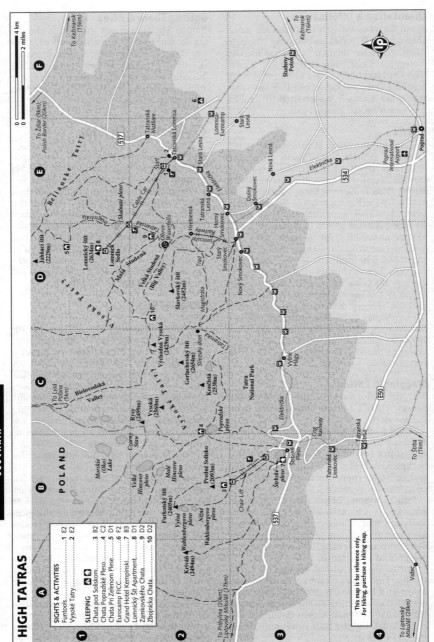

SIGHTS & ACTIVITIES

Funtools	1 E2
Vysoké Tatry	2 E2

SLEEPING

Chata pod Soliskom	3 B2
Chata Popradské Pleso	4 C2
Chata Pri Zelenom Plese	5 D1
Eurocamp FICC	6 F2
Grand Hotel Kempinski	7 B3
Lommický Štít Apartment	8 D1
Zamkovského Chata	9 D2
Zbojnícka Chata	10 D2

SLOVAKIA

This map is for reference only.
For hiking, purchase a hiking map.

which lingers at least until May. June and July are especially rainy. July and August are the warmest (and most crowded) months. Hotel prices and crowds are at their lowest from October to April.

Orientation

Poprad is the nearest sizeable town (with main-line train station and airport), 15km south of Starý Smokovec. Tatranská Lomnica, the smallest and quaintest resort, lies 5km to the east of Smokovec and the bustling lakeside Štrbské Pleso is 11km west. A narrow-gauge electric train connects Poprad with Štrbské Pleso via Starý Smokovec, where you have to change to get to Tatranská Lomnica. Roads lead downhill from the resorts to less expensive villages.

MAPS

Our High Tatras map (Map p852) is intended for orientation only, not as a hiking guide. Buy the widely available, 1:25,000 VKÚ *Vysoké Tatry* (No 2) map. Green maps list summer hiking trails, blue ones show winter ski routes.

Information

All three main resort towns have ATMs.

Hotel FIS (☎ 4492 221; Areál FIS, Štrbské Pleso; per hr €4; ♥ 24hr) Two lobby computers available for public rental.

Post office (off Cesta Slobody) Above Starý Smokovec train station.

Slovenská Sporiteľňa (☎ 4424 261; Cesta Slobody 24, Starý Smokovec) Central, with ATM and exchange.

Tatra Information Office (TIK) Starý Smokovec (☎ 4423 440; www.tatry.sk; Starý Smokovec 23; ♥ 8am-8pm Mon-Fri, to 1pm Sat); Štrbské Pleso (☎ 4492 391; Hotel Toliar; ♥ 8am-4pm); Tatranská Lomnica (☎ 4468 118; Cesta Slobody; ♥ 10am-6pm Mon-Fri, 9am-1pm Sat) The Štrbské Pleso branch is good for trail information, Smokovec has the largest office, and overall, the staff in Lomnica are the most helpful.

T-Ski Travel (☎ 4423 200; www.slovakiatravel.sk; Starý Smokovec 46, Starý Smokovec; ♥ 9am-4pm Mon-Thu, to 5pm Fri-Sun) Books lodging, including some hikers' huts, in person and online. Can arrange ski and mountain-bike programs. Located at the funicular station.

Townson Travel (☎ 4782 731; Tatranská Lomnica 94; per hr €3; ♥ 9am-5pm Mon-Fri) A travel agency with one public computer.

U Michalka Café (Starý Smokovec 4; per hr €3; ♥ 9am-midnight) Four terminals, great desserts (breakfast too).

Sights & Activities

A 600km network of trails reaches all the alpine valleys and some peaks, with mountain huts for hikers to stop at along the way. Routes are colour coded and easy to follow. Park regulations require you to keep to the marked trails and to refrain from picking flowers. Always wear hiking boots and layer clothing. Know that the assistance of the Mountain Rescue Service is not free and beware of sudden thunderstorms on ridges and peaks where there's no protection. For the latest weather and trail conditions stop by the **Mountain Rescue Service** (Horská Záchranná Služba; ☎ emergency 18 300; http://his.hzs.sk/; Starý Smokovec 23, Starý Smokovec).

STARÝ SMOKOVEC

From Starý Smokovec a **funicular railway** (☎ 4467 618; www.vt.sk; adult/concession return €7/5.50; ♥ 7.30am-7pm), or a 55-minute hike on the green trail, takes you up to **Hrebienok** (1280m). From here you have a great view of the Velká Studená Valley and a couple of hiking options. Following the red trail, past the restaurant and lodging at Bilíkova chata, to **Obrov Waterfalls** (Obrovsky vodopad) takes about an hour. Continuing on from the falls, it's a 35-minute hike to Zamkovského chata, and Skalnaté pleso (see below), with its cable car and trails down to Tatranská Lomnica. An excellent day hike, this is part of the **Tatranská Magistrála Trail** that follows the southern slopes of the High Tatras for 65km.

Rent mountain bikes at **Tatrasport** (☎ 4425 241; www.tatry.net/tatrasport; per day €15; ♥ 8am-noon & 1-6pm), above the bus-station parking lot.

TATRANSKÁ LOMNICA

While in the Tatras, you shouldn't miss the ride to the precipitous 2634m summit of **Lomnický štít** (bring a jacket!). From Lomnica, a large **gondola** (☎ 0903112200; www.vt.sk; adult/concession return €12/6; ♥ 8.30am-7pm Jul & Aug, to 3.30pm Sep-Jun) stops at mid-station Štart before it takes you to the winter sports area, restaurant and lake at **Skalnaté pleso**. From there, a smaller **cable car** (☎ 0903112200; www.vt.sk; adult/concession return €20/16; ♥ 8.30am-7pm Jul & Aug, to 3.30pm Sep-Jun) goes on to the summit where there's a viewing platform and Warhol-esque cafe-bar. Queues form early and timed tickets sometimes sell out.

Alternatively, you can yomp it up to Skalnaté by foot (2½ hours), where there's also a **chairlift** (☎ 0903112200; www.vt.sk; adult/concession €5/4; ♥ 8.30am-5.30pm Jul & Aug, 8.30am-4.30pm Sep-Jun) running up to **Lomnické sedlo**, a 2190m saddle and ski area and trailhead below the summit.

SLOVAKIA

Get off the cable car at Štart and you're at **Funtools** (☎ 0903112200; www.vt.sk; cable car plus 1 ride €9; ☺ noon-6.30pm May-Sep), from where you can take a fast ride down the mountain on a two-wheeled scooter, a luge-like three-wheel cart or on a four-wheel modified skate board.

ŠTRBSKÉ PLESO

Talk about development, if it's not a new condo-hotel going up, it's an old one being revamped. The big news is that in early 2009 Kempinski opened a five-star resort on the shores of Štrbské pleso, the glacial lake at 1346m. Day hikes are extremely popular here where you can follow the red-marked **Magistrála Trail** (uphill from the train station) for 3km (about an hour) to **Popradské pleso**, an even more idyllic pond at 1494m. From Popradské pleso the Magistrála zigzags steeply up the mountainside then traverses east towards **Sliezsky dom** and the Hrebienok funicular above Starý Smokovec (four hours).

There is also a year-round **chairlift** (☎ 4492 343; www.parksnow.sk; adult/concession return €7.50/5; ☺ 8am-3.30pm) up to Chata pod Soliskom, from where it's a 2km (one hour) walk north along the red trail to the 2093m summit of **Predné Solisko**.

CLIMBING

You can reach the top of **Slavkovský štít** (2452m) via the blue trail from Starý Smokovec (7.5km; seven to eight hours return), but to scale the peaks without marked hiking trails (Gerlachovský štít included), you must hire a mountain guide. Contact the **Mountain Guides Society Office** (☎ 4422 066; www.tatraguide.sk; Starý Smokovec 38, Starý Smokovec; ☺ 10am-6pm Mon-Fri, noon-6pm Sat & Sun Jun-Sep, 10am-6pm Mon-Fri Oct-May), by the Hotel Smokovec. Guides cost from €150, and the society runs classes too.

WINTER SPORTS

Park Snow (☎ 4492 343; www.parksnow.sk; Areál FIS; day lift ticket adult/concession €26/18; ☺ 8.30am-3.30pm) in Štrbské pleso is the most poplar ski and snowboard area, with two chairlifts, four tow lines, 12km easy to moderate runs, one jump and a snow -tubing area.

But Tatranská Lomnica's ski resort, **Vysoké Tatry** (☎ 0903112200; www.vt.sk; Tatranská Lomnica 7, Tatranská Lomnica; day lift ticket adult/concession €27/22; ☺ 9am-3.30pm) is competing with a new high-speed quad lift that links to 6km of runs

---

SPLURGE

Ever slept on top of the world? You can approximate the feeling in the **Lomnický Šít apartment** (☎ 0903112200; info@vt.sk; r €428) at the 2600m observatory atop Lomnický Šít. Accommodation for up to four includes return cable-car rides, a peep through the telescope, three-course dinners at the cafe, and breakfasts down at Skalnaté Pleso.

(1300m drop). That brings the total to 8km of easy to moderate runs, two chairlifts, two cable cars and a tow line for beginner slopes. You can hire skis and snowboards at both resorts for about €15 per day.

Tow-assist snow sledging and tubing is to be had at **Snow Funpark** (☎ 0903112200; Hrebienok; per ride €1.50; ☺ 10.30am-4.30pm), at the top of the funicular above Starý Smokovec.

Sleeping

For the quintessential Slovak mountain experience, you can't beat hiking from one *chata* (a mountain hut, could be anything from shack to chalet) to the next, high up among the peaks. Food (optional meal service or restaurant) is always available. Beds in these hikers' huts fill up fast; reserve ahead.

No wild camping is permitted: there is a camping ground near Tatranská Lomnica. If you're looking for cheap sleeps, Ždiar (p856), east over the ridge, is a good option. It's best to reserve private rooms (per person €15 to €20) ahead of time via the internet (www.tatry .sk and www.tanap.sk/homes.html) as tourist offices don't do bookings and rooms fill fast.

STARÝ SMOKOVEC & AROUND

Penzion Gabriel (☎ 4422 332; www.jmg.sk; Nový Smokovec 68, Nový Smokovec; r €50-52) Steep dormer rooflines give alpine flare to this geodesic guest house. Inside rooms are just as mod, with cobalt blues and oranges. Refrigerators in-room, shared kitchen.

Bilíkova chata (☎ 4422 439; www.bilikovachata.sk, in Slovak; Hrebienok; r with shared bathroom €53) A 10 minute walk down hill from the upper funicular station brings you to the closest of the higher elevation (1220m) *chaty*. Stay among the clouds at this basic log-cabin hotel with a full-service restaurant.

Grand Hotel (☎ 4870 000; www.grandhotel.sk; Starý Smokovec 38; s/d €86/112; ☒) More than 100 years of history are tied up in the most prominent lodging in Starý Smokovec. For full effect, splash out in the imperial grandeur of the royal suite (€230).

Other mountain huts:

Zbojnícka chata (☎ 0903638000; www.zbojnicka chata.sk; dm incl breakfast €15) Sixteen dorm-style beds, self-service eatery and small kitchen; at 1960m.

Zamkovského chata (☎ 4422 636; www.zamka.sk, in Slovak; dm €15-20) Twenty-eight beds in two- to four-bed rooms; full board available; at 1475m.

TATRANSKÁ LOMNICA & AROUND

Look for private room (*privat* or *zimmer frei*) signs on the back streets south and east of the train station.

Penzión Encian (☎ 4467 520; www.tatry.sk/encian; Tatranská Lomnica 36; s/d €33/66) Owners Zdenka and Štefan Unák have created a warm and welcoming main-street inn. The small restaurant has a fire in the hearth and antique skiing memorabilia on display.

Grandhotel Praha (☎ 4467 941; www.grandhotel praha.sk; s/d incl breakfast €105/145; 🖳 🍴) Remember when travel was elegant and you dressed for dinner? No? Well the 1899 Grandhotel does. Rooms are appropriately classic, if uninspired, and there's a snazzy spa.

From Skalnaté pleso above Tatranská Lomnica you could hike west 2½ hours to the huts listed under Starý Smokovec (opposite), or 2½ hours east to **Chata pri Zelenom plese** (☎ 4467 420; www.zelenepleso.sk; dm €13), a 50-bed lakeside lodge at 1540m.

ŠTRBSKÉ PLESO & AROUND

Rabid development and crowds make staying in Štrbské pleso a last choice, with one grand exception.

Grand Hotel Kempinski (☎ 3262 222; www.kemp inski-hightatras.com; Kupelna 6; r €255-300; 🛇 🖳 🍴) After seamlessly blending several remodelled villas and new buildings, Kempinski opened its lap-of-luxury chateau lakeside in spring of 2009. Far and away the swankiest Tatra accommodation, the chain is hoping to entice high-end travellers into Poprad-Tatry airport with their Zen spa awaiting after the limousine service to the hotel.

Mountain huts above Štrbské pleso:

Chata pod Soliskom (☎ 0905652036; www.chata solisko.sk; dm €10) Nine beds, ugly concrete building, nice

terrace. No hiking required – it's next to the chairlift; at 1800m.

Chata Popradské pleso (☎ 4492 177; www.poprad skepleso.sk; dm €15, d €53) Sizeable log lodge with restaurant and bar. Reserve ahead and you can drive here (road requires permission); at 1500m.

Eating & Drinking

The villages are close enough that it's easy to sleep in one and eat in another, but the restaurant offerings in general aren't great. All of the hotels, and some of the guest houses, have OK eateries; the grand ones have bars and discos. Look for the local *potraviny* (supermarket) on the main road in each village.

Samoobslužná Reštaurácia (☎ 4781 011; Hotel Toliar, Štrbské pleso 21; mains €2.50-6; 🕑 7am-10pm) This self-service cafeteria has one-dish meals (goulash, chicken stir-fry etc) and a few vegetarian options.

Reštaurácia Stará Mama (☎ 4467 713; shopping centre Sintra, Tatranská Lomnica; mains €5-12) Substantial soups and homemade *halušky* are the main reason to frequent this rustic fave; but the menu is actually quite extensive.

Tatry Pub (☎ 4422 448; Tatra Komplex, Starý Smokovec; 🕑 1pm-midnight) Refresh yourself at the official watering hole of the Mountain Guide Club. A full schedule of events includes DVD presentations, karaoke and DJ nights; pub food, too.

Scattered among the villages are numerous, often touristy, *koliba* restaurants. Our favourites are **Koliba Patria** (☎ 4492 591; Southern lake shore, Štrbske pleso; mains €6-15), for it's lakeside terrace, and **Zbojnícka Koliba** (☎ 4467 630; road to Grand Hotel Praha, Tatranská Lomnica; mains €10-20; 🕑 4pm-midnight), where some weekend evenings musicians play gypsy songs on the cimbalom while your chicken roasts over the open fire (it'll take an hour to cook).

Getting There & Around

The main road through the Tatras resorts is Rte 537, or Cesta Slobody (Freedom Way). Connect to it from the E50 motorway through Tatranská Štrba, Poprad or Velká Lomnica. To reach the Tatras by public transport from most destinations you need to switch in Poprad to an electric train that makes numerous stops along the main Tatra road, or buses that go to off-line destinations as well.

SLOVAKIA

BUS

Buses from Poprad travel to Starý Smokovec
(€0.80, 20 minutes, every 30 minutes),
Tatranská Lomnica (€1.20, 35 minutes, every
60 minutes) and Štrbské pleso (€1.50, 50 minutes, every 45 minutes).

At least every 1½ hours buses connect
Tatranská Lomnica with Kežmarok (€1, 30
minutes) and Ždiar (€1, 25 minutes).

Local buses run between the resorts every
20 minutes and tend to be quicker than the
train. Starý Smokovec to Tatranská Lomnica
(€0.30) takes 10 minutes, and to Štrbské pleso
(€1) takes 35 minutes.

TRAIN

A narrow-gauge electric train connects
Poprad and the main High Tatra resort towns
at least hourly. One line runs from Poprad
via Starý Smokovec (30 minutes) to Štrbské
Pleso (one hour), with frequent stops in between. Another line connects Starý Smokovec
to Tatranská Lomnica (15 minutes). A third
route from Tatranská Lomnica through
Studeny Potok (15 minutes) loops south to
Poprad (25 minutes). A €1.50 ticket covers
up to a 29km ride, but it's easier to buy a one-
/three-/seven-day pass for €3.30/6.70/12. If
there's not a ticket window, buy tickets from
the conductor; validate on board.

A cog railway runs between Tatranská Štrba
(on the main Žilina–Poprad railway line) and
Štrbské pleso (€1, 15 minutes, hourly).

BELÁ TATRAS
☎ 052

Travel east over the High Tatra mountain
ridges and you start to hear Slovak spoken
with a Polish accent. The Goral folk culture is
an intricate part of the experience in the small
Belianské Tatry (Belá Tatras). Traditional
wooden cottages are still the building method
of choice in the main village of Ždiar, giving
the place a rustic, laid-back quality that the
toney resort villages have always lacked. From
here it's an easy day trip or journey on to
Poland; heck, you can walk there!

Ždiar

Decorated timber cottages line long and narrow Ždiar, the only mountain settlement
inhabited since the 16th century. Goral traditions have both been bolstered and eroded by
tourism. Several sections of the village are historical reservations, including the **Ždiar House**

Museum (Ždiarsky dom; ☎ 4498 142; adult/concession
€3/1.50; ☺ 10am-4pm Tue-Sun), a tiny place with
colourful local costumes and furnishings.

Cross over the main road from the museum and a green trail skirts the river through
Monkova Valley (880m) for a 2½-hour return
hike with very little elevation change. You
could also veer off to **Širkové sedlo** (1826m)
and continue on to **Kopské sedlo** (1750m) in
about three hours. At this point return, or
cross over into the High Tatras. Chata pri
Zelenom plese (p855) is an hour away, the
cable car to Tatranská Lomnica (p853) is 2½
hours beyond that.

SLEEPING & EATING

Ždiar has a huge number of *privaty* (here
they are large lodgings with shared facility
rooms for rent, about €11 per person), so
odds are good if you just show up and knock.
Otherwise, check www.zdiar.sk (in Slovak),
under *ubytovanie*. Pictures, prices and contact
info is pretty straightforward.

ourpick Ginger Monkey Hostel (☎ 4498 0844; www
.gingermonkey.eu; Ždiar 294; dm/d €13/30; 🖳) Crushing
mountain views from an old Goral-style
house, hot tea at any hour, laundry, wi-fi, a
surprising sense of community among adventurous English-speakers… There's been some
talk that this sort of writing will ruin things
(remember the movie *The Beach*?) But how
could we not mention the Monkey? There's a
full kitchen, but most evenings the host leads
the whole crew to a local restaurant for rousing conversations about social systems, life's
purpose and what superhero could whoop
which. Don't just book one night, you'll end
up extending.

Goral Krčma (☎ 4498 138; Ždiar 460; mains €3-6) A
traditional 'village pub' restaurant associated
with an inn, this *krčma* serves all the regional
specialities, like potato pancakes stuffed with
a spicy sauté.

Other good eats:

Rustika Pizzeria (☎ 0908575050; Ždiar 334; pizza €4-6)
Wood-fired pizza served in an old log house.

U Veroniky (☎ 0908575050; Ždiar 351; mains €5-10)
Cute little romantic restaurant.

GETTING THERE & AWAY

There are up to six buses daily between Ždiar
and Poprad (€1.80, 50 minutes) via Starý
Smokovec (€1.10, 45 minutes) and Tatranská
Lomnica (€1, 30 minutes). At least four daily
buses travel between Ždiar and the Polish

border, Tatranská Javorina, Lysá Poľana stop (€1, 30 minutes). From there you can walk across the bridge to the Polish side, where there are regular public buses and private minibuses to Zakopane (26km).

POPRAD
☎ 052 / pop 55,185

Poprad is an important air and land transfer point for the High Tatras. Otherwise, the modern, industrial city's attraction is limited. Oh, there is a HUGE water park here. From the adjacent train and bus stations, the central pedestrian square, Nám sv Egídia, is a five-minute walk south on Alžbetina.

Information

City Information Centre (☎ 7721 700; www.poprad .sk; Dom Kultúry Štefánikova 72; ☉ 8am-5pm Mon-Fri, 9am-noon Sat) Town info only.

Ex Cafe (J Curie 17; per hr €2; ☉ 8am-10pm Mon-Sat, from 1pm Sun) Internet terminals, no wi-fi.

Activities

Poprad's thermal water park, **Aqua City** (☎ 7851 222; www.aquacitypoprad.sk; Športová 1397; ☉ 9am-9pm), is admirably green. Among other initiatives, the water, heat and electricity here come from geothermal and solar sources. Prices for sauna, swim and slide zones differ; access to the outdoor thermal complex is €18/15 per day for adult/concession.

Sleeping & Eating

Numerous restaurants and cafes line Nám sv Egídia. The old Germanic village of Spišská Sobota, 2km northeast of the centre, is now part of Poprad. There are more than 10 lodging options on or near its medieval square.

Hotel Cafe Razy (☎ 7764 101; www.hotelcaferazy .sk; Nám Sv Egídia 58; s/d €36/56) Simple rooms with wood lofts are pretty sane (two have wi-fi), it's weekend evenings when the pizza cafe downstairs crowds up that get a little CRazy.

Caffe Filicori (☎ 0915962358; Nám Sv Egídia 42; small dishes €2-6) A modern cafe facade hides an excellent, vegetable-rich light menu. Try the 'zucchini' – baked mozzarella wrapped in the grilled green vegetable, sprinkled with balsamic vinegar and real shaved mozzarella on a bed of rocket lettuce. Free wi-fi zone.

Getting There & Away

Bus 12 travels between Poprad city centre and **Poprad-Tatry International airport** (☎ 7763 875; www.airport-poprad.sk; Na Letisko 100), 5km west of the centre. **SkyEurope** (☎ 02-3301 7301; www.skyeurope .com) runs three flights per week between here and London's Luton Airport.

Intercity (IC) or Eurocity (EC) trains are the quickest way to get in and out of Poprad; four a day run to Bratislava (€16, four hours) and Košice (€6.50, one hour). For more on the electric trains that traverse the 13km or so to the High Tatras resorts, see opposite.

To reach Poland, you can take a bus from Poprad to Tatranská Javorina, Lysá Poľana stop (€2.50, 1½ hours, four daily). Walk across to the buses waiting to take you to Zakopane.

KEŽMAROK
☎ 052 / pop 17,383

Snuggled beneath the broody peaks of the High Tatras, Kežmarok's pocket-sized old-town square with resident castle seems especially quaint. The influence of the original 13th-century German settlers is evident in the architecture even today. Numerous distinct churches, and all those ice-cream shops, make it well worth an afternoon; and in July, the European Folk Craft Market comes to town.

Orientation & Information

Kežmarok is 14km east of Tatranská Lomnica and 16km northeast of Poprad – easy day-tripping distances. The bus and train stations are side by side, northwest of the Old Town; follow Dr Alexandra to the main square, Hlavné nám.

Alter Ego (☎ 4525 432; Hlavné nám 3) Great bookstore and map collection.

Kežmarok Information Agency (☎ 4524 047; www .kezmarok.net; Hlavné nám 46; ☉ 8am-5pm Mon-Fri, 9am-2pm Sat & Sun) Stocks heaps of brochures and souvenirs.

Sights

The imposing red-and-green, pseudo-Moorish **New Evangelical Church** (☎ 4526 314; cnr Toporcerova & Hviezdoslavovo; ☉ 10am-noon & 2-4pm Tue-Sat May-Oct), c 1894, dominates the south end of town. A €1.50 ticket also covers entry to the **Old Wooden Evangelical Church** (cnr Toporcerova & Hviezdoslavovo; ☉ 10am-noon & 2-4pm Tue-Sat May-Oct), next door. Built in 1717 without a single nail, it has an amazing interior of carved and painted wood.

The small, mansionlike **Kežmarok Castle** (☎ 4522 618; Hradné nám 45; adult/concession €2.30/1; ☉ by tour 9am-4pm Apr-Oct) dates back to the 15th century and is now a museum with period furniture and archaeology exhibits.

The second weekend in July, the **European Folk Craft Market** attracts traditional and modern artisans demonstrating and vending their wares. Plenty of food, drink and entertainment is to be had among the crowds then.

Sleeping & Eating

Penzión U Jakubu (☎ 4526 315; www.penzionujakuba.sk; Starý trh 39; mains €4-8) Take a seat at a big wooden bench near the open fire and be waited on by servers in traditional costume. An authentic, folksy Slovakness pervades both restaurant and guest house (rooms €30 to €40).

Sidewalk cafes abound in the pedestrian area around Hlavné nám. There are no fewer than six *cukráreň* (pastry cafes) serving cakes and ice cream, or you could stop at the tables on the square run by **Pizza Classica** (☎ 4523 693; cnr Hviezdoslavova & Hlavné nám; pizzas €3-8).

Getting There & Away

Buses are the way to get around locally; services run direct to Poprad (€1, 30 minutes, 16 daily), Tatranská Lomnica (€1, 30 minutes, 12 daily), Starý Smokovec (€1.30, 35 minutes, six daily) and Ždiar (€1.30, 40 minutes, three daily).

PIENINY NATIONAL PARK
☎ 052
With gently bubbling waters flowing between impressive 500m-tall cliffs, the 21-sq-km **Pieniny National Park** (Pieninský Národný Park) was created to protect the 9km **Dunajec Gorge**. The park combines with a similar one on the Polish side of the river and extends between the Slovak village of **Červený Kláštor** and Szczawnica, Poland. River floating is the main attraction here, but there's a riverside hiking trail and an ancient monastery, too.

At the mouth of the gorge is the fortified 14th-century **Red Monastery** (Červený Kláštor; ☎ 4822 955; adult/concession €2/1; ☒ 10am-5pm May-Oct). Mostly a park administrative centre, the monastery contains a fairly disappointing museum with statuary and old area prints. Two kilometres west, look for the small **information centre** (☎ 4822 122; www.pieniny.sk; Rte 543; ☒ 9am-5pm May-Oct).

There are two departure points along Rte 243 for a **river float trip** (☎ 4282 840; www.pltnictvo.sk; adult/concession €8.50/4; ☒ daylight May-Oct) in a *pltě* (shallow, flat-bottom wood rafts): one

opposite the monastery, and another 1km upriver west of the village. Don't be expecting white-water thrills – the Dunajec is a rather sedate 1½-hour experience terminating near the Slovak village of Lesnica.

To return to Červený Kláštor you can hike back the way you came, along the riverside trail through the gorge, in a little over an hour. It's an interesting walk even if you don't do water. Or, 500m southeast of the river drop off is Chata Pieniny in Lesnica. The lodging rents out bicycles (one way €4) and buses depart from there. Follow the yellow trail north of Lesnica (1.5km) and you reach a pedestrian border crossing into Poland.

Sleeping & Eating

Copious *privaty* and *zimmer frei* line the one road in Červený Kláštor. Food stalls stand between the monastery and the river launch.

Hotel Pltník (☎ 4822 525; www.hotelpltnik.sk; Červený Kláštor; per person/tent €2/1.70) Skip the ragged hotel and pitch your tent in the big river-front field next door.

Chata Pieniny (☎ 4397 530; www.chatapieniny.sk; Lesnica; dm €10) What a cheap and cheerful log lodge. Stay in a two- to six-bed dorm near the terminus of the raft trip. On-site restaurant, minimarket and bike rental (€4 per day).

Getting There & Away

Getting here is a challenge unless you have a car. Buses run to Červený Kláštor from Poprad (€3, two hours), via Kežmarok (€2, 1¼ hour) only two times a day Monday to Saturday and once on Sunday. From Košice (€6, three hours), there's one direct afternoon bus, otherwise you have to change in Stará Ľubovňa. Check schedules at http://cp.atlas.sk.

LEVOČA
☎ 053 / pop 14,677
High medieval walls surround ancient town buildings and cobblestone streets – so this is what Slovakia looked like in the 13th century. Today Levoča is one of the few Slovak cities to have its historic defences largely intact. At the old-town centre is the pride of the country's religious art and architecture collection, the Gothic Church of St Jacob and its 18m-high alter by Master Pavol. During the Middle Ages the king of Hungary invited Saxon Germans to colonise the eastern frontiers and Levoča became central to the resulting Slavo-Germanic Spiš cultural region.

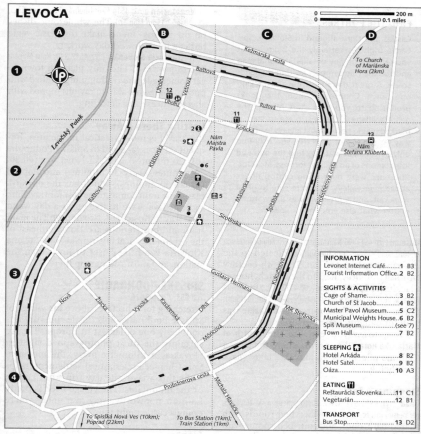

LEVOČA

INFORMATION	
Levonet Internet Café........1	B3
Tourist Information Office.2	B2

SIGHTS & ACTIVITIES	
Cage of Shame....................3	B2
Church of St Jacob..............4	B2
Master Pavol Museum.........5	C2
Municipal Weights House..6	B2
Spiš Museum................(see 7)	
Town Hall..........................7	B2

SLEEPING	
Hotel Arkáda.....................8	B2
Hotel Satel.........................9	B2
Oáza.................................10	A3

EATING	
Reštaurácia Slovenka.......11	C1
Vegetarián.......................12	B1

TRANSPORT	
Bus Stop..........................13	D2

SLOVAKIA

Orientation & Information

Levoča is on the main E50 motorway between Poprad (28km) and Košice (94km). The centre is 1km north of the train and bus stations. Both banks and post are on the small main square, Nám Majstra Pavla.

Levonet Internet Café (☎ 0908478700; Nám Majstra Pavla 38; per hr €2.50; ⏰ 10am-10pm)

Tourist information office (☎ 4513 763; www .levoca.sk; Nám Majstra Pavla 58; ⏰ 9am-6pm May-Sep, 9am-4pm Mon-Fri, 10am-2pm Sat Oct-Apr) Ask for the free photocopied map.

Sights

The spindles-and-spires **Church of St Jacob** (Chrám sv Jakuba; ☎ 4512 347; www.chramsvjakuba.sk; Nám Majstra Pavla; adult/concession €2/1; ⏰ 1pm, 2pm,

3pm & 4pm Apr-Oct), built in the 14th and 15th centuries, elevates your spirit with its soaring arches, precious art and rare furnishings. Everyone comes to see the splendid golden Gothic altar (1517) created by Master Pavol of Levoča. On it the mysterious master carved and painted cherubic representations of the Last Supper and the Madonna and Child. (This Madonna's face appeared on the original 100Sk banknote.) Buy tickets at the **cashier** (kasa; ⏰ 11am-5pm) inside the **Municipal Weights House** across the street from the north door. Entry is limited to certain hours, so check online or in person for additional times in the high season, we've listed the minimum.

Gothic and Renaissance eye candy abound on the main square, No 20 is the **Master Pavol**

FIND THE FORTRESS

Castles and ruins abound in Slovakia. Spiš Castle (right) is certainly the biggest, but you can pick up any detailed national map and see the ruin symbols dotting the landscape. A great day's adventure is tracking one down. Choose a symbol that looks promising to you, and start hiking. The nearest village is the best place to start, a marked hiking path almost always leads the way. At the top of your trek you may find only a hearth, or you may find the outlined foundations of an ancient fortress. Most fortifications were built along clifftop ridges above river valleys, so you're sure to get a work out, and a great view as a reward no matter what else you find.

Museum (☎ 4513496; Nám Majstra Pavla 20; adult/concession €1.40/0.80; ☒ 9am-5pm Tue-Sun) dedicated to the city's most celebrated son. The 15th-century **town hall** (*radnica*), next to the church, houses a lacklustre **Spiš Museum** (☎ 4512 449; Nám Majstra Pavla; adult/concession €2.50/1.60; ☒ 9am-5pm Tue-Sun). The adjacent 16th-century **cage of shame** was built for naughty boys and girls.

From town you can see the **Church of Mariánska hora**, 2km north, where the largest Catholic pilgrimage in Slovakia takes place in early July.

Sleeping & Eating

Oáza (☎ 4514 511; www.ubytovanieoaza.sk; Nová 65; per person incl breakfast €10) Two-bed rooms with shared bathroom, and four-bed rooms with bathroom and kitchen, are just what the budget doctor ordered. There's a big shared garden (with lawn, caged chickens and vegetables) between the two parts of the house.

Hotel Arkáda (☎ 4512 372; www.arkada.sk; Nám Majstra Pavla 26; s/d €35/53; ☐) Pine timbers and furnishings are the norm, but you can upgrade to an apartment with antiques for just €67. The hotel restaurant (mains €5 to €8) serves heaping grilled meat platters and fondue for two among its offerings. Free wi-fi.

Hotel Satel (☎ 4512 943; www.hotelsatel.com; Nám Majstra Pavla 55; s/d €36/53) Vaulted arches come standard in any respectable 14th-century building, and the Hotel Satel is no exception. Just don't expect ornate – the Middle Ages were austere, as are the hotel's contemporary furnishings. Limited wi-fi available.

Vegetarián (☎ 4514 576; Uhoľná 137; mains €3-5; ☒ 10am-3.15pm Mon-Fri) The wholesome dishes on the no-fuss menu make this basic vegie buffet a hit with weekday workers.

Reštaurácia Slovenka (☎ 4512 339; Nám Majstra Pavla 66; mains €3-7) The only place in town to get homemade *pirohy* (dumplings stuffed with potato, somewhat akin to ravioli) topped with sheep's cheese and crackling.

Getting There & Away

Bus travel is most practical in the area; frequent services take you to Spišské Podhradie (€1, 20 minutes), Spišská Nová Ves (€0.80, 20 minutes, every 30 minutes) and Poprad (€1.60, 30 minutes), which has the onward, main-line train connections best for travelling to Bratislava. Two to five buses a day wend their way to Košice (€4, two hours). The main train and bus stations are 1km southeast of the centre; the local bus stop at Nám Štefana Kluberta is a little closer to town than the station, and most routes stop there.

SPIŠSKÉ PODHRADIE
☎ 053 / pop 3826

Stretching for 4 hectares above the village of Spišské Podhradie, Spiš Castle ruins are undoubtedly one of largest in Europe. They're certainly the most photographed sight in Slovakia. A kilometre away, the medieval Spiš Chapter ecclesiastical settlement, helps make this a favourite day trip from Levoča or the mountains. The village itself is pretty ho-hum, not worth a stay-over unless you're doing a castle night tour.

Sights

From the E50 motorway you catch glimpses of eerie outlines and stony ruins crowning the ridge on the eastern side of Spišské Podhradie. Can it really be that big? Indeed, **Spiš Castle** (Spišský hrad; ☎ 4541 336; www.spisskyhrad .com; adult/concession €4.50/2.50; ☒ 9am-5pm May-Oct) seems to go on forever. If the reconstructed ruins are this impressive, imagine what the fortress once was.

Chronicles first mention Spiš Castle in 1209, and the remaining central residential tower is thought to date from that time. From there defenders are said to have repulsed the Tatars in 1241. Rulers and noble families kept adding fortifications and palaces during the 15th and 16th centuries, but by 1780 the site had already lost military significance and much was destroyed in a fire that year. It wasn't until the 1970s that efforts were made to salvage and reconstruct what remained. Few structures are whole, but there's a cistern, a chapel and a rectangular Romanesque palace, which holds the museum. Descend to the dungeon to see the meaty bits; scary torture devices the human mind has invented. Night tours are available some summer weekends.

From the spur line train station, the castle is a healthy hike up. Cross the tracks near the station and follow the yellow markers. One kilometre south is Spišské Podhradie's bus stop. If you're driving or cycling, the easiest access is off the Prešov highway east of the castle.

On the west side of Spišské Podhradie, you'll find the still active **Spiš Chapter** (Spišská Kapitula; adult/concession €2/1), a 13th-century Catholic complex encircled by a 16th-century wall. Charming Gothic houses line the single street running between the two medieval gates. Buy tickets from the **information office** (☎ 0907388411; ☺ 11.15am-2.45pm), where you can also pick up a guide. At the upper end is the magnificent **St Martin's Cathedral**, built in 1273, with twin Romanesque towers and a Gothic sanctuary. Inside are several trifold painted Gothic altars from the 15th century – quite impressive. On either side of the cathedral are the **seminary** and the Renaissance **bishop's palace** (1652). If you're travelling to Spiš Chapter by bus from Levoča, get off one stop before Spišské Podhradie, at Kapitula.

Sleeping & Eating

The castle has a food stand, and the village, a little grocery store.

Penzión Podzámok (☎ 4541 755; www.penzion podzamok.sk; Podzámková 28; s/d with shared bathroom €12/24; ☒) Three family houses have been cobbled together to create a simple 42-bed guest house with a backyard view of the castle. Follow the street next to the bridge north. Full board available.

Spišsky Salaš (☎ 4541 202; www.spisskysalas.sk; Levočská cesta 11; mains €3-7) You can tell this is a local rustic specialities fave by the number of kids on the playground and the long wait for a table at the log restaurant and terrace on summer weekends. In addition to tasty lamb stew, the Salaš offers three simple wood-panel lodging rooms for rent (per person €13). It's on the road between E50 and Spišské Podhradie, 3km west of Spiš Chapter.

Getting There & Away

Buses connect with Levoča (€1, 20 minutes) and Poprad (€2.20, 50 minutes) at least hourly, services to Košice (€3, 1½ hours, 12 daily) are only slightly less frequent. A spur railway line heads to Spišské Podhradie from Spišské Vlachy (€0.50, 10 minutes), a station on the main line from Poprad to Košice, only three (inconvenient) times a day.

SLOVENSKÝ RAJ & AROUND

☎ 053

With rumbling waterfalls, steep gorges, sheer rockfaces, thick forests and hilltop meadows, Slovenský raj is a national park for the passionately outdoorsy. A few easier trails exist, but the one-way, ladder-and-chain ascents are the most dramatic. You cling to a metal rung headed straight up a precipice while an icy waterfall splashes and sprays you from a metre away. Oh, that's after you've scrambled horizontally across a log ladder to cross the stream down below. Pure exhilaration.

Orientation

The nearest town of any size is the lacklustre Spišská Nová Ves, 23km southeast of Poprad. The main trailheads on the northern edge of the national park are at Podlesok, on the outskirts of Hrabušice (16km southwest of Poprad), and Čingov, 5km west of Spišská Nová Ves. There are lodgings and eateries near northern trailheads. For full town services, you'll have to go into Spišská Nová Ves or Hrabušice. Dedinky, at the south end of the park, is a regular village with pub, supermarket, a lake and houses. Before you trek, make sure to buy VKÚ's 1:25,000 *Slovenský raj* hiking map (No 4), available at many tourist offices and bookshops countrywide.

Information

Your lodging place is often the best source of information; orientation maps are posted near trailheads. Procure money before you get to the park; there's an ATM and exchange at the Spišska Nová train station.

Internet Café (☎ 4299 402; Drevárska 2, Spišská Nová Ves; per hr €2; ☺ 10am-10pm)

Mountain Rescue Service (Horská Záchranná Služba; ☎ emergency 183 00; http:// his.hzs.sk)

Tourist information centre (☎ 4428 292; www .slovenskyraj.sk; Letná 49, Spišská Nová Ves; ☺ 8am-6pm Mon-Fri, 9am-1pm Sat, 2pm-6pm Sun May-Sep, 8am-5pm

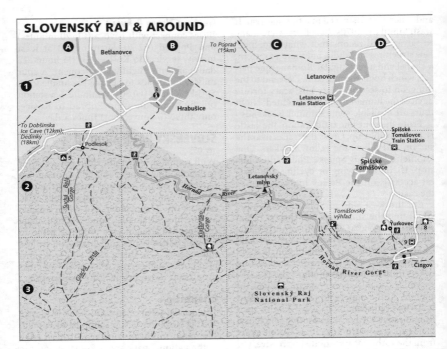

SLOVENSKÝ RAJ & AROUND

Mon-Fri Oct-May) Hit-or-miss help with area accommodation and info.

Tourist information (☎ 4299 854; Hlavná 171, Hrabušice; ☉ 8am-6pm Jun-Aug) Small, summertime office.

Sights & Activities

Slovenský raj National Park (Slovak Paradise; www.sloven skyraj.sk; admission €1), has numerous trails that include a one-way *roklina* (gorge) sections and take at least half a day. The shortest, **Zejmarská Gorge** hike, on a blue trail, starts at Biele Vody (15 minutes northeast of Dedinky via the red trail). The physically fit can run, clamber and climb up in 50 minutes; others huff and puff up in 90 minutes. To get back, you can follow the green trail down to Dedinky, or there's a **chairlift** (adult/concession €1/0.50; ☉ 9am-5pm) that works sporadically.

From Čingov a green trail leads up the **Hornád River Gorge** to **Letanovský mlyn** (1½ hours), from there the blue trail continues along the river to the base of the green, one-way, technically aided **Kláštorisko Gorge** hike (one hour). At the top, you can take a break at the lodge and restaurant, **Kláštorisko chata**

(☎ 4493 307; klastorisko@infosk.sk) before following another green trail back along the ridge towards Čingov. Allow at least six hours for the circuit, including lunch at Kláštorisko.

From Podlesok, an excellent day's hike (six to seven hours) heads up the **Suchá Belá Gorge** (with several steep ladders), then east to Kláštorisko on a yellow then red trail. From here, take the blue trail down to the Hornád River, then follow the river gorge upstream to return to Podlesok.

Six kilometres west of Dedinky is **Dobšinská Ice Cave** (Dobšinská Ľadová Jaskyňa; ☎ 7881 470; adult/concession €7/5; ☉ 9am-4pm Tue-Sun Jun-Aug, 9.30am-2pm Tue-Sun May & Sep). The frozen formations are most dazzling in May, before they start to melt. Tours leave every hour or so.

Sleeping & Eating

Surrounding towns have private rooms (many listed at www.slovenskyraj.sk). All the park's hotels and pensions have restaurants. From May to September food stands open near the Podlesok trailhead. Stock up on provisions at the supermarket next to the bus station in Spišska Nová Ves.

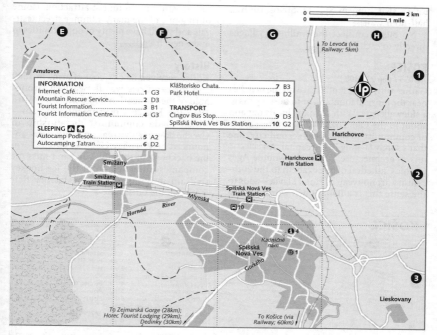

INFORMATION
Internet Café...1 G3
Mountain Rescue Service.....................2 D3
Tourist Information.................................3 B1
Tourist Information Centre...................4 G3

SLEEPING 🏕 🏠
Autocamp Podlesok................................5 A2
Autocamping Tatran...............................6 D2

Kláštorisko Chata....................................7 B3
Park Hotel...8 D2

TRANSPORT
Čingov Bus Stop......................................9 D3
Spišská Nová Ves Bus Station............10 G2

Autocamp Podlesok (☎ 4299 165; atcpodlesok@ gmail.com; Podlesok; per person/tent €2/2, huts per person €9) Pitch a tent in the big field (600 capacity) or choose from A-frame cabins, small huts and cottages with two to 12 beds and a bathroom. Full restaurant on-site.

Autocamping Tatran (☎ 4297 105; www.durkovec .sk; per person/tent €3/2, dm €10, 2-person hut with shared bathroom €20; 🐾) Tents crowd together in the pasture surrounded by tiny huts and two big dormitories, neither are exactly new. Restaurant, game room and bike rental (per day €5) are available here, 2km west of Čingov.

Horec Tourist Lodging (☎ 0905742996; www.horec .xf.cz; Dobšinska Masa 62, Dedinky; s/d with shared bathroom €12/24) Eight clean, bright and basic two-bed rooms share two bathrooms, a common room and a kitchen. On the west side of the lake.

Park Hotel (☎ 4422 022; www.hotelfloraslovenskyraj.sk; Hradisko, Čingov; s/d €55/34) Each of the renovated-in-'07 rooms has its own balcony overlooking a landscaped lawn, with plenty of chairs for lounging. Active types can appreciate the tennis court and sauna for post-hike recovery. A big summer terrace and even bigger menu selection (mains €4 to €10) make this a good stop even if you're not sleeping over.

Getting There & Around

Off season especially, you may consider springing for a hire car in Košice; public transport connections can be a chore. Check schedules at http://cp.atlas.sk carefully. Four buses a day travel from Poprad to Dedinky (€2, 1¼ hours) and one (at 3.06pm) from Košice (€5, two hours).

Year-round from Spišska Nová Ves, six buses run weekdays and one on weekends (9.20am) to Čingov (€0.60, 12 minutes); two buses run weekdays only (6.35am and 2.30pm) to Hrabušice/Podlesok (€1.30, 35 minutes). You can reach Spišska Nová Ves by train from Poprad (€1.50, 25 minutes, 12 daily) and Košice (€4, 1½ hours, 12 daily), and by bus from Levoča (€0.80, 25 minutes, every half-hour). More buses (up to six) run from Spišská Nová Ves to the villages on weekends in July and August.

Weekdays there are two good connections from Poprad (6.25am and 2.25pm) to Hrabusice/Podlesok (€1.70, 50 minutes total), switching in Spišský Štrtok (only a half-hour wait).

No buses connect the trailhead villages directly to each other.

KOŠICE

☎ 055 / pop 235,300

Gather with the rest of Košice on the benches near the musical fountain, or to raise a glass at a sidewalk cafe. With so many locals out and about in the Old Town, you get a real sense of community in Slovakia's second city, one that's sorely lacking in the capital. An eclectic mix of architecture – from the Middle Ages Gothic Cathedral of St Elizabeth to the 20th-century art nouveau of Hotel Slávia – adds to the sense this is a living town worth getting

to know, not just a tourist attraction. Come during one of the many summer street festivals and you'll have plenty of opportunities to make new friends.

History

Košice received its city coat of arms in 1369 and for centuries was the eastern stronghold of the Hungarian kingdom. On 5 April 1945 the Košice Government Program – which made communist dictatorship in Czechoslovakia a virtual certainty – was announced here. Today US Steel girders form the backbone of the city; you can't miss the company's influence, from the ice-hockey stadium it sponsored to the factory flair stacks on the outskirts.

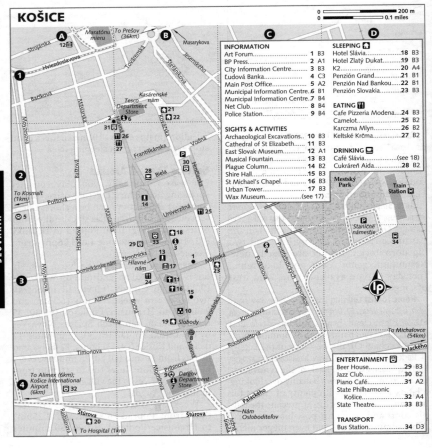

KOŠICE

INFORMATION	
Art Forum	**1** B3
BP Press	**2** A1
City Information Centre	**3** B3
Ľudová Banka	**4** C3
Main Post Office	**5** A2
Municipal Information Centre	**6** B1
Municipal Information Centre	**7** B4
Net Club	**8** B4
Police Station	**9** B4

SIGHTS & ACTIVITIES	
Archaeological Excavations	**10** B3
Cathedral of St Elizabeth	**11** B3
East Slovak Museum	**12** A1
Musical Fountain	**13** B3
Plague Column	**14** B2
Shire Hall	**15** B3
St Michael's Chapel	**16** B3
Urban Tower	**17** B3
Wax Museum	(see 17)

SLEEPING	
Hotel Slávia	**18** B3
Hotel Zlatý Dukát	**19** B3
K2	**20** A4
Penzión Grand	**21** B1
Penzión Nad Bankou	**22** B1
Penzión Slovakia	**23** B3

EATING	
Cafe Pizzeria Modena	**24** B3
Camelot	**25** B2
Karczma Mlyn	**26** B2
Keltské Krčma	**27** B2

DRINKING	
Café Slávia	(see 18)
Cukráreň Aida	**28** B2

ENTERTAINMENT	
Beer House	**29** B3
Jazz Club	**30** B2
Piano Café	**31** A2
State Philharmonic Košice	**32** A4
State Theatre	**33** B3

TRANSPORT	
Bus Station	**34** D3

Orientation

The adjacent bus and train stations are just east of the Old Town. A five-minute walk along Mlynská brings you into Hlavná, which broadens to accommodate the squares of Nám Slobody and Hlavné nám.

Information

BOOKSHOPS

Art Forum (☎ 6232 677; Mlynská 6) Coffee-table pictorials and fiction in English; good selection by Slovak authors.
BP Press (☎ 6228 280; Hlavná 102) Foreign magazines and newspapers.

EMERGENCY

Police station (☎ 159; Pribinova 6)

INTERNET ACCESS

The City Information Centre (below) has five terminals at a cheap €0.50 per 20 minutes. Fast connections can be found at **Net Club** (☎ 6221 933; Hlavná 9; per hr €1.60; ☉ 9am-10pm).

MEDICAL SERVICES

Hospital (Fakultná Nemocnica L Pasteura; ☎ 6153 111; Rastislavova 43)

MONEY

Ľudová Banka (Mlynská 29) ATM and exchange; between the centre and transport stations.

POST

Main post office (Poštová 18)

TOURIST INFORMATION

City Information Centre (☎ 6258 888; www.kosice .sk; Hlavná 59; ☉ 9am-6pm Mon-Fri, 9am-1pm Sat, 1-5pm Sun Jun-Sep, closed Sun Oct-May) Large and official info office (read: less personable); internet access available.
Municipal Information Centre (MIC; ☎ 16 168; www.mickosice.sk) Dargov Department Store (Hlavná 2; ☉ 9am-7pm Mon-Sat, 9am-1pm Sun); Tesco Department Store (Hlavná 111; ☉ 8.30am-8.30pm Mon-Fri) Tiny info stands with a vibrant young staff and oodles of knick-knacks for sale.

Sights

Landscaped flower beds surround the **musical fountain** in the middle of Hlavná nám, across from the 1899 State Theatre. To the north stands a large baroque **plague column** from 1723.

The dark and brooding 14th-century **Cathedral of St Elizabeth** (Dóm sv Alžbety; ☎ 0908667093; adult/concession €4/2; ☉ 1-5pm Mon, 9am-5pm Tue-Fri,

9am-1pm Sat) wins the prize for sight most likely to grace your Košice postcard home. You can't miss Europe's easternmost Gothic cathedral dominating the square. Below the church, a **crypt** contains the tomb of Duke Ferenc Rákóczi, who was exiled to Turkey after the failed 18th-century Hungarian revolt against Austria. Don't forget to climb the church's **tower** for city views. To the south of the cathedral is the 14th-century **St Michael's Chapel** (adult/concession €1/0.50; ☉ 1-5pm Mon, 9am-5pm Tue-Fri, 9am-1pm Sat).

To check out the **Urban Tower** (originally built in the 14th century, rebuilt in the 1970s) you have to buy entry to the cheesy (and overpriced) **Wax Museum** (Múzeum voskových figurín; ☎ 6232 534; www.waxmuseum.sk; Hlavná 3; adult/concession €4/2.60; ☉ 11am-3pm Mon-Fri, noon-3pm Sat, 1-3pm Sun).

Get lost in the mazelike passages and tunnels of the **archaeological excavations** (☎ 6228 393; adult/concession €1/0.60; ☉ 10am-6pm Tue-Sun). The underground remains of medieval Košice – defence chambers, fortifications and waterways – weren't discovered until building work in 1996.

The 1945 Košice Government Program was proclaimed from the 1779 **Shire Hall** (Župný dom; Hlavná 27); today there's a minor art gallery inside.

The most intriguing part of the **East Slovak Museum** (Východoslovenské múzeum; ☎ 6220 309; Hviezdoslavova nám 3; adult/concession €1.30/0.70; ☉ 9am-5pm Tue-Sat, 9am-1pm Sun) is the gold treasure on display in the basement vault. During the renovation of the house at Hlavná 68 in 1935, this secret stash of 2920 gold coins dating from the 15th to 18th centuries was discovered. Anyone have a shovel?

Sleeping

The City Information Centre usually puts together a list of accommodation that includes summer dorms.

K2 (☎ 6230 909; Štúrova 32; s/d with shared bathroom €12/24) It's just a room, and a rather dowdy one at that. But what more do you want for this price in Old Town? No common room, no kitchen, no laundry.

ourpick Penzión Slovakia (☎ 7289820; www.penzion slovakia.sk; Orliá 6; s/d €48/54) A small, city guest house with loads of charm: guest quarters have wood-panelled ceilings, skylights and a mid-century mod aesthetic. Each room is named for a Slovak city. Free broadband connections, plus an excellent grill restaurant downstairs.

Penzión Grand (☎ 6337 546; www.penzionslovakia
.sk; Kováčska 65; s/d/tr €46/52/66) These 2nd- and
3rd-floor lodgings (no elevator) ring an inviting interior courtyard with skylights above
and a ground-floor cafe below (tasty salads).
Furnishings are oddly mismatched. Wi-fi in
some rooms.

Hotel Zlatý Dukat (☎ 7279 333; www.hotelzlatydukat
.sk; Hlavná 16; s/d €121/131; ▨) You'd never know
from the classic contemporary design (dark
wood and light linen, flat-screen TVs) that the
building's history traces to the 13th century.
Look through the glass floor near the reception desk to see the foundations of this story.
Free wi-fi; room service available.

Yet more choices:

Penzión Nad Bankou (☎ 6838 221; Kováčska 63;
s/d/tr €40/53/60) Three travelling together get quite a
bargain at this guest house above a reasonable cafe.

Hotel Slávia (☎ 6224 395; www.hotelslavia.sk; Hlavná
63; s €78-80, d €90-125; ▨ ▨) Flower-shape lights and
candy-coloured pastels inside a 1902 art nouveau hotel
and cafe.

Eating & Drinking

The 2nd floor of the train station has a surprising array of low-cost food options in a
brightly lit, modern setting: sandwich bar,
self-service Slovak food, pizza restaurant and
pastry cafe. Any of the sidewalk cafes on the
main square is a fine place to drink on a warm
summer evening.

Cafe Pizzeria Modena (☎ 6222 788; Hlavná 40;
pizza €2.50-5) A university crowd hangs out at
the courtyard cafe tables here. You can also
descend to the cellar restaurant to try the
personal-sized pizzas and fresh salads.

Camelot (☎ 6854 039; Kováčka 19; mains €8-17)
Cellar vaults and wooden trenchers certainly
evoke the knightly spirit, but the food here is
also darn good. Try the whole roast chicken
or duck.

Practically next door each other, both
Keltské Krčma (☎ 6225 328; Hlavná 80; mains €7-12;
☽ 10am-11.30pm Mon-Thu, to 1am Fri & Sat, 3-11.30pm Sun)
and **Karczma Mlyn** (☎ 6220 547; Hlavná 82; mains €3-8;
☽ 11am-midnight Sun-Thu, to 1am Sun) are pubs good
for a pint, and for heaping portions of hearty
food. The latter is more local-frequented;
enter through the courtyard.

For coffee and sweets try turn-of-the-20th-
century **Café Slaviá** (☎ 6233 190; Hotel Slaviá, Hlavná 63;
☽ 7am-11pm). For the most popular ice cream
and cakes in town, head to **Cukráreň Aida**
(☎ 6256 649; Hlavná 81; cakes €1-3; ☽ 8am-10pm).

Entertainment

The monthly publication **Kam do Mesta** (www
.kamdomesta.sk) lists in Slovak the whats, wheres
and whens of Košice's entertainment scene.

State Theatre (Štátne Divadlo Košice; ☎ 6221 231;
www.sdke.sk; Hlavná 58; ☽ box office 9am-5.30pm Mon-Fri,
10am-1pm Sat) Local opera and ballet companies
stage performances in the 1899 neobaroque
theatre from September to May.

State Philharmonic Košice (Štátna Filharmónia Košice;
☎ 6224 514; www.sfk.sk; House of the Arts, Moyzesova 66)
The spring musical festival is a good time to
catch performances of the city's philharmonic
at the House of the Arts, but concerts take
place year-round.

Beer House (☎ 0918807999; Hlavná 54; ☽ 11am-
midnight Mon-Thu, 11am-2am Fri, 4pm-2am Sat, 4pm-
midnight Sun) A regular schedule of live music
includes rock, funk and '70s and '80s pop.

DJs spin house music most nights at both
the **Jazz Club** (☎ 6224 237; Kováčska 39; ☽ 11am-
midnight Mon-Thu, 11am-2am Fri, 4pm-2am Sat, 4pm-
midnight Sun) and the **Piano Café** (☎ 0915517339;
Hlavná 92; ☽ 10am-midnight Mon-Thu, 10am-1am Fri,
3pm-1am Sat, 3pm-midnight Sun). Watch for the occasional live jazz concert at each.

Shopping

Wander onto the alleylike 'Craftsman St'
(*Hrnčiarska*) for some truly unique shopping – at a potter's workshop, an iron-works
master, a herbalist and a gemstone studio. The
leathermaker is around the corner and north
on Kovačka street.

Getting There & Away

Check bus, plane and train schedules at http://
cp .atlas.sk.

AIR

Košice International airport (KSC; ☎ 6221 093; www
.airportkosice.sk) is about 6km southwest of the
centre. **SkyEurope** (☎ reservations 02-4850 4850; www
.skyeurope.com) has up to four daily flights to/from
Bratislava (one hour), one to Prague and several weekly flights to London. **ČSA** (Czech Airlines,
OK; ☎ 6782 490; www.czechairlines.com) has up to five
daily flights to and from Prague. **Austrian Airlines**
(☎ 02-4940 2100; www.austrianairlines.com) runs a flight
to Vienna every day except Saturday.

BUS

The **bus station** (☎ 6789 250; Staničné nám) sits beside the train station east of town. Buses are
most efficient for getting to Levoča (€4, two

hours, eight daily) or Bardejov (€3.60, two hours, 12 daily).

Eurobus (☎ 055-680 7306; www.eurobus.sk, in Slovak) handles routes in eastern Slovakia. There is one bus a day from Košice to Prague (€28, 11 hours), and one to Uzhhorod, Ukraine (€6, 2½ hours); a second, early morning bus runs from Friday to Sunday. Another option for getting to Uzhhorod is transferring to a bus in Michalovce (€2.50, one hour, four daily). Poland-bound by bus is not so easy: getting to Zakopane, for example, requires transfers in Poprad and Tatranská Javorina.

CAR

There are several big international car-rental representatives at the airport, but **Alimex** (☎ 7290 100; www.alimex.sk; Košice International Airport) is cheapest, if you're willing to drive around with adverts painted on the car.

TRAIN

The **train station** (☎ 2292 175; Staničné nám) is an easy walk from Hlavná nám. Express trains (R) run to/from Poprad (€6.50, 1¼ hours, up to 10 daily) and Žilina (€10.50, three hours, up to 14 daily). If you're commuting all the way to/from Bratislava, an IC or EC train (€19, five hours, four daily) is your best bet; even on an express train you could crawl along for more than seven hours with no dining car.

You can ride the rails from Košice to Miskolc (€4, 1½ hours, four daily) and Budapest (€25, four hours, four daily) in Hungary, and Kraków (€25, six hours, one daily). A sleeper train leaves Košice every night for Moscow (€57, 36 hours – ugh!) stopping in Lviv (€18, 12 hours) and Kyiv (€32, 22½ hours) in Ukraine. It also stops at Čop (€4, 2½ hours), 14km from Uzhhorod (not on the main train line), but arriving at 1am and finding a taxi isn't fun. It's easier to take a bus.

Getting Around

Transport tickets (€0.60, one zone) are good for buses and trams in most of the city; buy them from news-stands and public transport kiosks and validate on board. Bus 23 between the airport and the train station requires a two-zone ticket (€1).

BARDEJOV

☎ 054 / pop 33,374

Muted hues and intricately painted facades set apart each of Bardejov's Gothic-Renaissance burgher houses. And yet the remarkable homogeneity of uniformly steep roofs and flat fronts helps make the main square the prettiest in Slovakia. Bardejov has been enthusiastically well preserved since the 15th century (there's always some scaffolding signalling upkeep) and deservedly made Unesco's World Heritage list in 2000. Today the quiet square is the tourist draw, but there are a few museums, including one that sheds light on this region's Eastern-facing religious art. Venture a couple of kilometres north of town to Bardejovské Kúpele, and you can take a cure at a thermal spa or explore traditional culture at an open-air village museum. Wooden churches in the area reflect the Carpatho-Rusyn heritage that the area shares with neighbouring parts of Ukraine and Poland.

History

Bardejov received its royal charter in 1376, and grew rich on trade between Poland and Russia. After an abortive 17th-century revolt against the Habsburgs, Bardejov's fortunes declined. In late 1944 heavy WWII fighting took place at the Dukla Pass on the Polish border, 54km northeast of Bardejov.

Orientation

The main square, Radničné nám, is a 600m walk southwest of the bus and train station. Some old town walls still encircle the city, enter through the gate off Slovenská at Baštová.

Information

ČSOB (Radničné nám 7) Exchange and ATM.
Golem Internet Café (Radničné nám 35; per hr €1; ⊗ 9am-11pm Mon-Fri, 1-11pm Sat & Sun)
Main post office (Dlhý rad 14)
Tourist information centre (☎ 4723 013; www .bardejov.sk; Radničné nám 21; ⊗ 9am-6.30pm Mon-Fri & 9am-4pm Sat & Sun May-Sep, 9am-5pm Mon-Fri, 9am-4pm Sat & 1-4pm Sun Oct-Apr) Loads of info, souvenirs and guide services.

Sights

There are two branches of the **Šariš Museum** (☎ 4724 966; www.muzeumbardejov.sk; ⊗ 8am-noon & 12.30-4pm Tue-Sun) Icon Exposition (Expozícia ikony; Radničné nám 27; adult/concession €2/1); town hall (radnica; Radničné nám 48; adult/concession €2/1) worth seeing. In the centre square, the town hall contains altarpieces and a historical collection. Built in 1509, it was the first Renaissance building in

Slovakia. At the Icon Exposition more than 130 dazzling icons from the 16th to 19th centuries are on display. The religious art originally decorated Greek Catholic and Orthodox churches east of Bardejov.

The interior of the 15th-century **Basilica of St Egídius** (Bazilika Sv Egídia; Radničné nám; adult/concession €1/0.80; ☻ 10am-3.30pm Mon-Fri, to 2.30pm Sat) is packed with no fewer than 11 Gothic altarpieces, built from 1460 to 1510.

Sleeping & Eating

Penzión Semafor (☎ 0905830984; www.penzion semafor.sk; Kellerova 13; s/d €24/32, apt s/d €28/38) The five bright doubles in this family-run guest house share a communal kitchen and laundry; two more-spacious 'apartment' rooms have small kitchens of their own.

Hotel Bellevue (☎ 4728 404; www.bellevuehotel.sk; Mihalov 2503; s/d €64/84; ☻ 🖳 🏊) Glass-enclosed pool, landscaped gardens and leafy surrounds are the main selling points for this hotel on a hill, 3km south of centre. There is a special-evening-out restaurant and great views.

el. Restaurant & Lodging (☎ 4728 404; www.el -restaurant.sk; Stöcklova 43; mains €3-9) An emphasis on fine ingredients make even the traditional Slovak dishes here seem fresh. The large variety of salads and vegetarian dishes is novel too. Access to room service is one of the best things about the three modern rooms for rent upstairs (single/double including breakfast €24/40).

Other eats:

Maja Sendvič (☎ 091941064; Radničné nám 15; sandwiches €1.50-3; ☻ 8am-9pm Mon-Fri, 1-11pm Sat, 3-9pm Sun) Big baguette sandwiches to go.

Reštaurácia Hubert (Radničné nám 4; mains €4-12) Game dishes and meaty fare.

Getting There & Away

Bardejov is on a spur train line from Prešov, so buses are most convenient. They run between Bardejov and Košice (€4, 1¾ hours, 13 daily) and to/from Poprad (€5, 2½ hours, eight daily). You can bus it to Bardejovské Kúpele (€0.40, five to 10 minutes) every half-hour or so.

Though you're close to Poland here, you're not near a main bus route. For those with a car, the E371 crosses into Poland north of Svidník, a town 35km east of Bardejov.

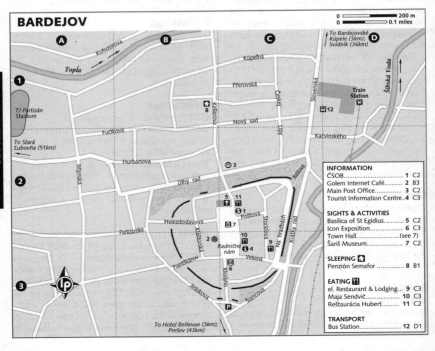

BARDEJOV

WORTH THE TRIP: WOODEN CHURCHES

Travelling east from Bardejov, you come to the crossroads of Western and Eastern Christianity. The Greek Catholic (or Uniate) and Orthodox faithful living in the region in the 17th to 19th centuries built intricate onion-domed wooden churches (many without nails) and decorated them with elaborate icon screens and interior paintings. In July of 2008, eight eastern Slovak wooden churches were added to the Unesco World Heritage list, including one Catholic and two Protestant, but there are many more to see than that. (The Greek Catholic Presov Diocese website, www .grkatpo.sk/drevenecerk, has an extensive list.) Most of the churches are in isolated villages with limited bus connections and fewer services. Buy a *Wooden Churches Around Bardejov* booklet at the Bardejov tourist information centre (p867) for a self-driving tour of vernacular architecture in that area, including the oldest listed church at **Hervatov** (c 1500). Others, such as the listed churches at **Ladomirá** and **Bodružal** are closer to Svidník.

AROUND BARDEJOV

Three short kilometres to the north, with frequent local bus connections, you'll find the parklike spa town of **Bardejovské Kúpele**. If you want to book a service (mineral bath €10, 15-minute massage €7), you have to go in person to the **Spa House** (Kúpelny dom; ☎ 4774 225; ⏱ 8am-noon & 1-5pm Mon-Sat) at the top of the main pedestrian street. Across the way is the **Museum of Folk Architecture** (Múzeum Ľudovej Architektúry; ☎ 4722 070; adult/concession €1.30/0.70; ⏱ 9am-5pm Tue-Sun, to 3pm Oct-Apr), the oldest *skanzen* (open-air museum) in Slovakia. One of the Unesco-listed wooden churches is among the many traditional buildings relocated here. If you have a car, park in the lot by the bus station at the base of the village and walk up; the whole village is pedestrian-only.

SLOVAKIA DIRECTORY

ACCOMMODATION

For every season there is a price: May to September is considered tourist season, but prices top out around Christmas/New Year and Easter holidays. From October to April, rates drop dramatically (10% to 50%). We quote tourist-season prices. A midrange double room in Bratislava will run from €60 to €150, luxury digs upwards of that (often in the €250 range), and a dorm bed costs around €25. Reviews in this chapter are ordered according to price; a tourist tax of at least €1 is not included. Breakfast can usually be added for €4 to €8 and parking is widely available outside Bratislava. Rooms in this chapter include private bathroom unless otherwise stated. These days most lodgings have at least some nonsmoking rooms, though you'll still come across a few smoking-only accommodations.

Most camping grounds open from May to September and are accessible on public transport. Many have a restaurant and assorted cheap cabins. Wild camping is prohibited in national parks.

Outside Bratislava there are few backpacker-style hostels in Slovakia. Student dormitories throughout the country open to tourists in July and August. If you're looking for cheap sleeps outside those months, *ubytovňa* is the word to know. These are hostels for workers (in cities) or Slovak tourists (near natural attractions) that usually have basic, no-nonsense shared-bathroom singles and doubles or dorms.

Tourist towns outside the capital usually have private rooms, usually with shared facilities, for rent; look for signs reading '*privat*' or '*zimmer frei*' (from €10 per person). Information offices and websites sometimes have lists of renters.

Pensions are guest houses, with en-suite bathrooms, that have fewer services but more character than hotels.

ACTIVITIES

Slovakia is one of Eastern Europe's best areas for hiking. You can take it relatively easy in the low mountains of Malá Fatra National Park (p850), hike higher elevation trails in the High Tatras (p853) or climb up ladders and foot holds through a challenging gorge ascent in Slovenský raj (p862). For even more adrenalin, sign up with one of the local mountain guides (p854) to scale the tallest peaks.

The High Tatras ski resorts (www.vt.sk and www.parksnow.sk) have some of Europe's cheapest alpine skiing, a day's lift ticket costs about €25. The season runs from December to April. See p854 for more.

BUSINESS HOURS

Restaurants nationwide are generally open from 10am to 10pm. Stand-alone shops open around 9am and close at 5pm or 6pm weekdays and at noon on Saturdays. The local *potraviny* (supermarket) hours are from 6.30am or 7am until 5pm or 6pm Monday to Friday and from 7am to noon on Saturday. Big-name chain grocery and department stores (Tesco, Billa etc) have longer hours, typically until 9pm for downtown branches and 24 hours for suburban hyper-markets.

Bank hours are from about 8am to 5pm Monday to Thursday, and until 4pm Friday. Post offices work from 8am to 7pm Monday to Friday and until 11am Saturday.

Most museums and castles are closed on Monday. Many tourist attractions outside the capital open only from May to September.

DANGERS & ANNOYANCES

Crime is low compared with Western Europe, but pickpocketing does happen. Just be aware. Never leave anything on the seat of an un-attended vehicle, even a locked one; apparently that's advertising you don't want it any more.

EMBASSIES & CONSULATES

Australia and New Zealand do not have embassies in Slovakia; the nearest are in Vienna and Berlin respectively. The following are all in Bratislava:

Austria (Map p838; ☎ 02-5443 1334; www.embassy austria.sk; Ventúrska 10)
Czech Republic (Map p838; ☎ 02-5920 3303; www.mzv.cz/bratislava/; Hviezdoslavovo nám 8)
France (Map p838; ☎ 02-5934 7111; www.france.sk; Hlavné nám 7)
Germany (Map p838; ☎ 02-5920 4400; www.pressburg.diplo.de; Hviezdoslavovo nám 10)
Ireland (Map p838; ☎ 02-5930 9611; www.dfa.ie; Carlton Savoy Bldg, Mostová 2)
Netherlands (Map p837; ☎ 02-5262 5081; www.holandskoweb.com; Frana Krála 5)
UK (Map p838; ☎ 02-5998 2000; www.britishembassy.sk; Panská 16)
USA (Map p838; ☎ 02-5443 0861; http://slovakia.usembassy.gov; Hviezdoslavovo nám 4)

FESTIVALS & EVENTS

During summer months folk festivals take place all over Slovakia. In late June, early July, folk dancers and musicians gather at the biggest, **Východná Folklore Festival** (www.obec-vychodna .sk, in Slovak), 32km west of Poprad. Weeks-long musical festivals with daily concerts are big in both Bratislava (p841) and Košice. The **Slovak Spectator** (www.slovakspectator.sk) newspaper lists events countrywide.

HOLIDAYS

New Year's & Independence Day 1 January
Three Kings Day 6 January
Good Friday & Easter Monday March/April
Labour Day 1 May
Victory over Fascism Day 8 May
SS Cyril & Methodius Day 5 July
SNP Day 29 August
Constitution Day 1 September
Our Lady of Sorrows Day 15 September
All Saints' Day 1 November
Christmas 24 to 26 December

INTERNET RESOURCES

Kompas (www.kompas.sk) Searchable countrywide map site.
Lodge Yourself (www.ubytujsa.sk) Places to stay in Slovakia.
Slovak Tourism Board (www.slovakiatourism.sk) Comprehensive overview and practicalities: history, culture, accommodation and restaurant listings.
Slovakia Document Store (www.panorama.sk) Great online bookstore, plus countrywide info.
What's On Slovakia (www.whatsonslovakia.com) Event listings.

MONEY

As of January 2009, Slovakia's currency is the euro. You'll still hear reference to the former currency, the Slovak crown, or Slovenská koruna (Sk).

Almost all banks have exchange desks and there are usually branches in or near the town square. ATMs are quite common even in smaller towns, but shouldn't be relied upon in villages. In Bratislava, credit cards are widely accepted. Elsewhere, Visa and MasterCard are accepted at most hotels and at higher category restaurants (though only if you announce before requesting the bill that you plan to pay with credit).

If you stay in a hostel in Bratislava, eat your meals in local pubs and use local transport, you can expect to spend €40 a day, if you're looking to bed down in pensions and dine in smarter eateries, count on €100 per day. You can get by on less out in the provinces, but there aren't many hostels. Concession admission prices are generally good for children younger than 12, students with ID, and seniors older than 65.

POST

Poste restante sent to Bratislava (c/o Poste restante, 81000 Bratislava 1), can be picked up at the **main post office** (Map p838; Nám SNP 34-35, Bratislava) and will be kept for one month.

TELEPHONE

Slovakia's country code is ☎ 421. Landline numbers can have either seven or eight digits. Mobile phone numbers are often used for business; they start with ☎ 09. When dialling from abroad, you need to drop the zero from both city area codes and mobile phone numbers.

To dial internationally from inside Slovakia, dial ☎ 00, the country code and the number.

Payphones require *telefónna karta* (telephone cards), purchased from newsagents, for local calls. International phone cards, like **EZ Phone** (www.ezcard.sk; per min to UK & USA €0.60) can also be bought.

TOURIST INFORMATION

The **Association of Information Centres of Slovakia** (AICES; ☎ 16 186; www.aices.sk) is an extensive network of city information centres. There's no Slovakia-wide information office; your best bet is to go online to the **Slovak Tourist Board** (www.slovakiatourism.sk).

TRAVELLERS WITH DISABILITES

Slovakia is behind many EU countries in terms of facilities for travellers with disabilities. Few hotels and restaurants have ramps or barrier-free rooms. **Slovak Union for the Disabled** (Slovenský zväz telesne postihnutých; ☎ 02-6381 4478; www.sztp.sk) works to change the status quo.

VISAS

Citizens of other EU countries do not require visas. Visitors from Australia, New Zealand, Canada, Japan and the US can enter visa-free for up to 90 days. South Africans need a visa. For a full list, see www.mzv.sk (under 'Ministry' and then 'Travel'). If you do require

---

EMERGENCY NUMBERS

- Ambulance ☎ 112
- Fire ☎ 112
- Police ☎ 112

---

a visa, it must be bought in advance – they are not issued on arrival.

TRANSPORT IN SLOVAKIA

GETTING THERE & AWAY

Air

Between June and September, SkyEurope runs flights from Bratislava to Split and Dubrovnik in Croatia. Czech Airlines shuttles regularly between Prague and both Bratislava and Košice.

Most of the other cities you can reach by air from Bratislava are within Western Europe; British destinations are particularly well represented by Ryanair and SkyEurope. SkyEurope also flies to London from Košice and Poprad.

Vienna International airport (VIE; www.viennaairport.com), 60km from Bratislava, is served by a vast range of flights. Buses connect to Bratislava's bus station and airport almost hourly.

Airlines flying to and from Slovakia:
Austrian Airlines (OS; ☎ 02-4940 2100; www.austrian airlines.com)
Czech Airlines (cOK; ☎ 02-5720 0710; www.czech airlines.com)
Ryanair (FR; ☎ 353-1 249 7791; www.ryanair.com)
SkyEurope Airlines (NE; ☎ 02-4850 1000; www.sky europe.com)

Land

After Slovakia became a member of the Schengen Agreement within the EU in 2007, land border crossings with other member states (Austria, Czech Republic, Poland and Hungary) were eliminated. This makes the check coming into Slovakia (and the EU) at the Ukraine border even more strenuous. Expect a delay as guards search for contraband cigarettes and vodka.

BUS

The best search engine for international and domestic bus schedules is http://cp.atlas.sk. The major hubs for departures to Eastern and Western Europe destinations are Bratislava (p836) and Košice (p864). There are also buses to Poland from Poprad (p857).

CAR & MOTORCYCLE

As well as your vehicle's registration papers, you need a 'green card', which shows you are covered by at least third-party liability insurance. Your vehicle must display a nationality sticker and carry a first-aid kit and warning triangle.

TRAIN
Direct trains connect Bratislava (p844) with the Czech Republic, Austria, Poland and Hungary, while trains from Košice (p867) head to Hungary, Poland, Russia and Ukraine. The website http://cp.atlas.sk has international and domestic schedules.

River
During spring and summer, Danube riverboats offer an alternative way to get between Bratislava and neighbouring Danube cities. See p843 for details.

GETTING AROUND
Bicycle
Roads are often narrow and potholed, and in towns cobblestones and tram tracks can prove dangerous for bike riders. Theft's a problem, so a lock is a must. Bike rental is uncommon outside the mountains. The cost of transporting a bike by rail is usually 10% of the train ticket.

Bus
National buses run by **Slovenská autobusová doprava** (SAD; www.sad.sk) are comparably priced to trains, but less convenient for most cities in this chapter. Search schedules at http://cp.atlas.sk. When looking at bus timetables in terminals, beware of the footnotes (fewer buses may go on weekends). It's helpful to

know that *premáva* means 'it operates' and *nepremáva* means 'it doesn't operate'.

Car & Motorcycle
All foreign driving licences with photo ID are valid in Slovakia.

In order to use Slovakia's motorways (denoted by green signs), all vehicles must have a motorway sticker (*nálepka*), which should be displayed in the windscreen. Rental cars come with them. You can buy stickers at petrol stations.

Parking restrictions are eagerly enforced with bright orange tyre boots. Always buy a ticket, either from a machine, or from the attendant wandering around with a waist pack, and put it on your dashboard.

Both Bratislava and Košice airports have international car-rental agencies.

Local Transport
City buses and trams operate from around 4.30am to 11.30pm daily. Tickets are sold at public transport offices and at news-stands. In Bratislava, some stops have ticket-vending machines. Validate tickets in the red machines on board or you could face a fine of up to €50.

Train
Slovak Republic Railways (Železnice Slovenskej Republiky or ŽSR; ☎ 18 188; www.zsr.sk) provides a cheap and efficient rail service. Most of the places covered in this chapter are on or near the main railway line between Bratislava and Košice. Check schedules at http://cp.atlas.sk.

Slovenia

It's a tiny place, about half the size of Switzerland, and counts just over two million people. But the only way to describe pint-sized Slovenia (Slovenija), an independent republic bordering Italy, Austria, Hungary, Croatia and the Adriatic Sea, is that it's 'a mouse that roars'.

Slovenia has been dubbed a lot of things since independence in 1991 – 'Europe in Miniature', 'The Sunny Side of the Alps', 'The Green Piece of Europe' – and, though they may sound like blurbs, they're all true. From beaches, snow-capped mountains, hills awash in grapevines and wide plains blanketed in sunflowers, to Gothic churches, baroque palaces and art nouveau civic buildings, Slovenia offers more diversity than countries many times its size. Its incredible mixture of climates brings warm Mediterranean breezes up to the foothills of the Alps, where it can even snow in summer. With more than half of its total area covered in forest, Slovenia truly is one of the greenest countries in the world – and in recent years it has also become Europe's activities playground.

Among Slovenia's greatest assets, though, are the Slovenes themselves – welcoming, generous, multilingual, broad-minded. As far as they are concerned, they do not live emotionally, spiritually or even geographically in 'Eastern' Europe – their home is the very heart of the continent.

FAST FACTS

- **Area** 20,273 sq km
- **Capital** Ljubljana
- **Currency** euro (€); US$1 = €0.73; UK£1 = €1.06; A$1 = €0.50; ¥100 = €0.76; NZ$1 = €0.41
- **Famous for** hiking and skiing, Lake Bled, Lipizzaner horses, *pršut* (air-dried ham)
- **Official language** Slovene
- **Phrases** *dober dan* (hello); *živijo* (hi); *prosim* (please); *hvala* (thank you); *oprostite* (excuse me); *nasvidenje* (goodbye)
- **Population** 2.018 million
- **Telephone codes** country code ☎ 386; international access code ☎ 00
- **Visas** not required for most nationalities; see p908

SLOVENIA

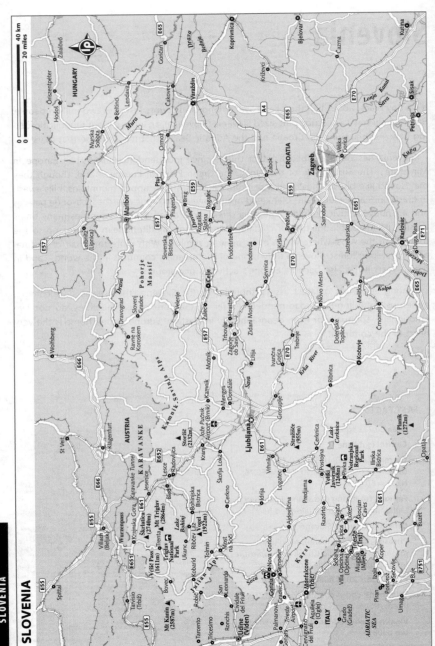

HIGHLIGHTS

- Experience the architecture, hilltop castle, green spaces and cafe life of **Ljubljana** (p877), Slovenia's capital.
- Wax romantic at the picture-postcard setting of **Bled** (p889): the lake, the island, the hilltop castle.
- Get into the outdoors or in the bluer-than-blue Soča in the majestic mountain scenery at **Bovec** (p894), arguably the country's best outdoor activities centre.
- Explore the series of karst caves at **Škocjan** (p897) a scene straight out of Jules Verne's *A Journey to the Centre of the Earth*.
- Swoon at wonderful Venetian architecture in the romantic port of **Piran** (p900).

ITINERARIES

- **Three days** Enjoy a long weekend in Ljubljana, sampling the capital's museums and nightlife, with an excursion to Bled.
- **One week** Spend a couple of days in Ljubljana, then head north to unwind in Bohinj or romantic Bled beside idyllic mountain lakes. Depending on the season take a bus or drive over the hair-raising Vršič Pass into the valley of the vivid blue Soča River and take part in some extreme sports in Bovec or Kobarid before returning to Ljubljana.

CLIMATE & WHEN TO GO

The ski season generally lasts from December to March, though heavy snowfall can keep the Vršič Pass closed as late as May. Spring is a great time to be in the lowlands, though it can be pretty wet in May and June. At the same time, the days are getting longer and off-season rates apply. Hotel prices rise in summer, peaking in August, when rooms can be hard to come by on the coast. Warm September days are calm and ideal for hiking and climbing, while October and November can be rainy.

HISTORY

Slovenes can make a credible claim to have invented democracy. By the early 7th century their Slavic forebears had founded the Duchy of Carantania (Karantanija), based at Krn Castle (now Karnburg in Austria). Ruling dukes were elected by ennobled commoners and invested before ordinary citizens. This model was noted by the 16th-century French political theorist Jean Bodin, whose work was a key reference for Thomas Jefferson when he wrote the American Declaration of Independence in 1775–76. Carantania (later Carinthia) was fought over by Franks and Magyars from the 8th to 10th centuries, and later divided up among Austro-Germanic nobles and bishops. By 1335 Carantania and most of present-day Slovenia, with the exception of the Venetian-controlled coastal towns, were dominated by the Habsburgs.

Indeed, Austria ruled what is now Slovenia until 1918, apart from a brief interlude between 1809 and 1813 when Napoleon created six 'Illyrian Provinces' from Slovenian and Croatian regions and made Ljubljana the capital. Napoleon proved a popular conqueror as his relatively liberal regime de-Germanised the education system. Slovene was taught in schools for the first time, leading to a blossoming of national consciousness. In tribute, Ljubljana still has a French Revolution Sq (Trg Francoske Revolucije) with a column bearing a likeness of the French emperor.

Fighting during WWI was particularly savage along the Soča Valley – what would later become known as the Isonzo Front, which was occupied by Italy then dramatically retaken by German-led Austrian-Hungarian forces. The war ended with the collapse of Austria-Hungary, which handed western Slovenia to Italy as part of postwar reparations. Northern Carinthia, including the towns of Beljak and Celovec (now Villach and Klagenfurt), voted

---

CONNECTIONS: MOVING ON FROM SLOVENIA

As wonderful as Slovenia is, it is extremely well placed to leave. Border formalities with Slovenia's three European Union neighbours – Italy, Austria and Hungary – are almost nonexistent and all are accessible by train (p908) and (less frequently) bus (p908), as are many other European nations. Venice can also be reached by boat from Izola (p900) and Piran (p903). As a member state that forms part of the EU's external frontier, Slovenia must implement the strict Schengen border rules, so expect a somewhat closer inspection of your documents – national ID (for EU citizens) or passport and, in some cases, visa – when travelling by train or bus to/from Croatia.

SLOVENIA

HOW MUCH?

- 100km by bus/train €9/6
- Bicycle rental (one day) €5 to €15
- Bottle of ordinary/quality Slovenian wine €4/8
- Cup of coffee in a cafe €1 to €2.50
- Daily ski pass (adult/child) €26/16

LONELY PLANET INDEX

- 1L petrol €0.96
- 1L bottled water €0.35 to €1
- 500mL local beer (shop/bar) €1/3
- Souvenir T-shirt €10 to €15
- Street snack (burek) €2 to €3

---

to stay with Austria in a 1920 plebiscite. What remained of Slovenia joined fellow south (*jug*) Slavs in forming the Kingdom of Serbs, Croats and Slovenes, later Yugoslavia.

Nazi occupation in WWII was for the most part resisted by Slovenian partisans, though after Italy capitulated in 1943 the anti-partisan Slovenian Domobranci (Home Guards) were active in the west and, in a bid to prevent the communists from taking political control in liberated areas, threw their support behind the Germans. The war ended with Slovenia regaining Italian-held areas from Piran to Bovec, but losing Trst (Trieste) and part of divided Gorica (Gorizia).

Slovenia, with only 8% of the national population, was the economic powerhouse of Tito's Yugoslavia, producing up to 20% of the national GDP. By the 1980s the federation was becoming increasingly Serb-dominated, and Slovenes, who already felt taken for granted economically, feared losing their political autonomy. After free elections, Slovenia broke away from Yugoslavia on 25 June 1991. A 10-day war that left 66 people dead followed; rump Yugoslavia swiftly signed a truce in order to concentrate on regaining control of coastal Croatia. Slovenia was admitted to the UN in May 1992 and, together with nine other 'accession' countries, became a member of the EU in May 2004. In January 2007 Slovenia replaced the tolar with the euro as the national currency.

Slovenia shared the presidency of the EU Council with France in 2008, the same year

that saw the death of President Janez Drnovšek of cancer at age 57. In the national elections of October of that year, Janez Janša's coalition government was defeated by the Social Democrats under Borut Pahor, who was able to form a coalition with three minority parties.

PEOPLE

The population of Slovenia is largely homogeneous. More than 87% are ethnic Slovenes, with the remainder being Croats, Serbians, Bosnians and Roma; there are also small enclaves of Italians and Hungarians, who have special deputies looking after their interests in parliament. Slovenes are ethnically Slavic, typically multilingual and extroverts. Just under 58% of Slovenes identify themselves as Roman Catholics.

ARTS

Slovenia's most cherished writer is the Romantic poet France Prešeren (1800–49), whose statue commands Ljubljana's central square. Prešeren's patriotic yet humanistic verse was a driving force in raising Slovene national consciousness. Fittingly, a stanza of his poem *Zdravljica* (A Toast) comprise the lyrics of the national anthem.

Many of Ljubljana's most characteristic architectural features, including its recurring pyramid motif, were added by celebrated Slovenian architect Jože Plečnik (1872–1957), whose work fused classical architectural principles and folk-art traditions.

Slovenia has some excellent modern and contemporary artists, including Rudi Skočir, whose style reflects a taste for Viennese art nouveau. A favourite sculptor-cum-designer is Oskar Kogoj, whose work has become increasingly commercial in recent years.

Postmodernist painting and sculpture were more or less dominated from the 1980s by the multimedia group Neue Slowenische Kunst (NSK) and the artists' cooperative Irwin. It also spawned the internationally known industrial-music group Laibach, whose leader, Tomaž Hostnik, died tragically in 1983 when he hanged himself from a *kozolec*, the traditional (and iconic) hayrack found almost everywhere in Slovenia. Slovenia's vibrant music scene embraces rave, techno, jazz, punk, thrash-metal and *chanson* (torch songs from the likes of Vita Mavrič); the most popular local rock group is Siddharta, the only Slovenian band ever to appear on MTV. There's also a folk-music revival: listen for the groups Katice, Brina and Katalena, who play traditional Slovenian music with a modern twist. Terra Folk is the quintessential world music band.

Another way to hear traditional music is to attend the fun-filled Ljubljana-based 'Slovenian Evening' of folk music and dancing (audience participation mandatory) along with a four-course meal of Slovenian specialities plus wine run by an outfit called **Židana Marela** (☎ 040-363 272; www.zidanamarela.si; €33). Groups depart from the Prešeren monument at 7.15pm on Wednesday and Friday year-round and proceed to the Skriti Kot (Hidden Corner), a restaurant in the shopping mall below Trg Ajdovščina. Just follow the guide with the red umbrella.

Well-received Slovenian films in recent years include *Kruh in Mleko* (Bread & Milk, 2001), the tragic story of a dysfunctional small-town family by Jan Cvitković, and Damjan Kozole's *Rezerni Deli* (Spare Parts, 2003) about the trafficking of illegal immigrants through Slovenia from Croatia to Italy by a couple of embittered misfits living in the southern town of Krško, site of the nation's only nuclear power plant. Much lighter is *Petelinji Zajtrk* (Rooster's Breakfast, 2007), a romance by Marko Naberšnik set in Gornja Radgona on the Austrian border in northeast Slovenia.

ENVIRONMENT

Slovenia is amazingly green; indeed, just under 57% of its total surface area is covered in forest. It is home to almost 3200 plant species – some 70 of which are indigenous. Triglav National Park is particularly rich in native flowering plants. Among the more peculiar endemic fauna in Slovenia is a blind salamander called *Proteus anguinus* that lives deep in karst caves, can survive for years without eating and has been called a 'living fossil'.

FOOD & DRINK

It's relatively hard to find such archetypal Slovenian foods as *žlikrofi* ('ravioli' filled with cheese, bacon and chives), *brodet* (fish soup) from the coast, *ajdovi žganci z ocvirki* (buckwheat 'porridge' with savoury pork crackling/scratchings) and salad greens doused in *bučno olje* (pumpkinseed oil); generally these are dishes eaten at home. A *gostilna* or *gostišče* (inn) or *restavracija* (restaurant), which are generally open 10am or 11am to 10pm or 11pm, more frequently serves *rižota* (risotto), *klobasa* (sausage), *zrezek* (cutlet/steak), *golaž*

(goulash) and *paprikaš* (piquant chicken or beef 'stew'). *Riba* (fish) is usually priced by the *dag* (100g). *Postrv* (freshwater trout) generally costs half the price of sea fish, though grilled squid *(lignji na žaru)* doused in garlic butter is usually a bargain.

Common in Slovenia are such Balkan favourites as *cevapčiči* (spicy meatballs of beef or pork), *pljeskavica* (spicy meat patties) and *ražnjiči* (shish kebabs), often served with *krompir* (potatoes).

You can snack cheaply on takeaway pizza slices or pieces of *burek* (€2 to €3), flaky pastry sometimes stuffed with meat, cheese or apple. Alternatives include *štruklji* (cottage-cheese dumplings) and *palačinke* (thin sweet pancakes).

Some restaurants have *dnevno kosilo* (set lunches), including *juha* (soup) and *solata* (salad), for as low as €5. This can be less than the price of a cheap main course, and usually one option will be vegetarian.

Tap water is safe to drink everywhere. Distinctively Slovenian wines include peppery red Teran made from Refošk grapes in the Karst region, Cviček, a dry light red – almost rosé – *vino* (wine) from eastern Slovenia and Malvazija, a straw-colour white wine from the coast that is light and dry. Slovenes are justly proud of their top vintages, but cheaper bar-standard 'open wine' (*odprto vino*) sold by the decilitre (0.1L) is often rot-gut.

Pivo (beer), whether *svetlo* (lager) or *temno* (dark), is best on *točeno* (draught).

There are dozens of kinds of *žganje* (fruit brandy) available, including *češnjevec* (made with cherries), *sadjevec* (mixed fruit), *brinjevec* (juniper), *hruška* (pears, also called *viljamovka*) and *slivovka* (plums).

Like many other countries in Europe, Slovenia bans smoking across the board in all public places, including restaurants, bars and hotels.

LJUBLJANA

☎ 01 / pop 216,200

Ljubljana is by far Slovenia's largest and most populous city. It is also the nation's political, economic and cultural capital. As such, virtually everything of national importance begins, ends or is taking place in Ljubljana.

But it can be difficult to get a grip on the place. In many ways the city whose name *almost* means 'beloved' (*ljubljena*) in Slovene

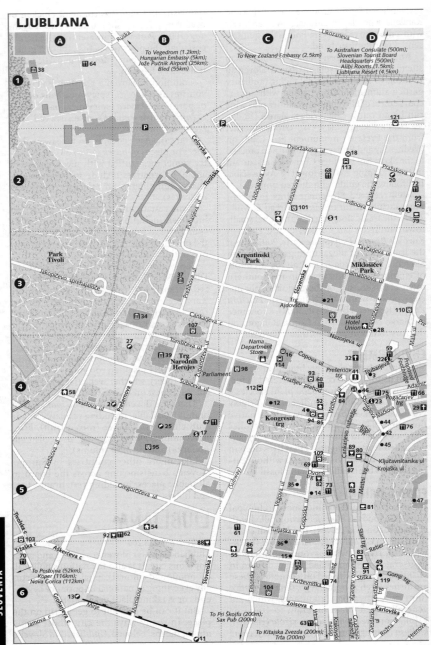

LJUBLJANA

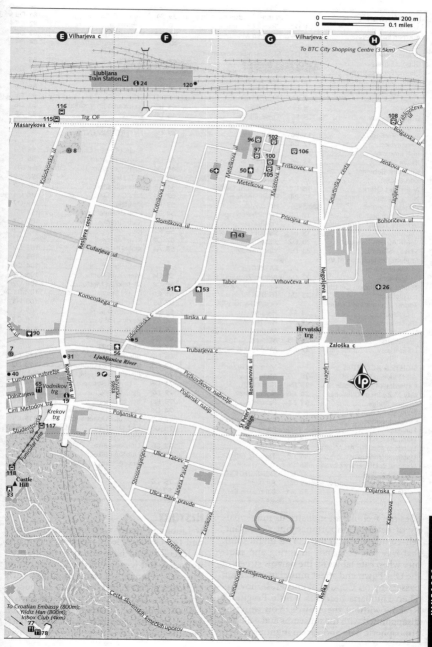

does not feel like an industrious municipality of national importance but a pleasant, self-contented small town. You might think that way too, especially in spring and summer when cafe tables fill the narrow streets of the Old Town and street musicians entertain passers-by on Čopova ul and Prešernov trg. Then Ljubljana becomes a little Prague or Kraków without the crowds. You won't be disappointed with the museums and galleries, atmospheric bars and varied nightlife either.

HISTORY

If Ljubljana really was founded by Jason and the Golden Fleece–seeking Argonauts as legend would have you believe, they left no proof. But legacies of the Roman city of Emona – remnants of walls, dwellings, early churches, even a gilded statuette – can be seen everywhere. Ljubljana took its present form as Laibach under the Austrian Habsburgs, but it gained regional prominence in 1809, when it became the capital of Napoleon's short-lived

'Illyrian Provinces'. Some fine art nouveau buildings filled up the holes left by a devastating earthquake in 1895, and architect Jože Plečnik continued the remake of the city up until WWII.

ORIENTATION

Prešernov trg, on the left bank of the Ljubljanica River, is the heart of Ljubljana. Just across delightful Triple Bridge is the picturesque – if bite-sized – Old Town, which follows the north and west flanks of Castle Hill. The bus and train stations are 800m northeast of Prešernov trg up Miklošičeva c.

Ljubljana's Jože Pučnik Airport, at Brnik near Kranj, is 27km north of the city.

Maps

Excellent free maps, some of which show the city's bus network, are available from the tourist offices (see p882). The more detailed 1:20,000-scale *Mestni Načrt Ljubljana* (Ljubljana City Map; €7.70) from Kod & Kam is available at news-stands and bookshops.

INFORMATION
Bookshops

Geonavtik (☎ 252 70 27; www.geonavtik.com; Kongresni trg 1; ☺ 8.30am-8.30pm Mon-Fri, 8.30am-4pm Sat) Stocks guides and books about Slovenia.

Knjigarna Behemot (☎ 251 13 92; www.behemot .si; Židovska steza 3; ☺ 10am-8pm Mon-Fri, 10am-3pm Sat) Pint-size English-language bookshop for bibliophiles.

Kod & Kam (☎ 200 27 32; www.gzs-dd.si/kod&kam; Trg Francoske Revolucije 7; ☺ 8am-8pm Mon-Fri, 8am-1pm Sat) Map specialists.

Discount Cards

The Ljubljana Card (€12.50), valid for three days (72 hours) and available from the tourist offices (p882), offers free admission to many museums, unlimited city bus travel and dis-counts on organised tours, accommodation and restaurants, hire cars etc.

Internet Access

Web connection is available at virtually all hostels and hotels, the Slovenia Tourist Information Centre (p882; €1 per half-hour), STA Ljubljana (p882; €1 per 20 minutes) and Student Organisation of the University of Ljubljana (p882; free). In addition:

Cyber Café Xplorer (☎ 430 19 91; Petkovškovo nabrežje 23; per 30min/hr/5hr €2.50/4/12; ☺ 10am-10pm Mon-Fri, 2-10pm Sat & Sun) Ljubljana's best internet cafe, with 10 superfast computers, wi-fi and international phone calls at €0.10 per minute.

DrogArt (☎ 439 72 70; Kolodvorska ul 20; 1st 15min free, then per 30min/hr €1/1.80; ☺ 10am-4pm Mon-Fri) Opposite the train station.

Portal.si Internet (☎ 234 46 00; Trg OF 4; per hr €3.80; ☺ 7am-8.30pm) In the bus station (get code from window No 4).

Internet Resources

City of Ljubljana (www.ljubljana.si) Comprehensive information portal on every aspect of life and tourism.

Laundry

Washing machines (€5 per load) are available, even to nonguests, at the Celica Hostel (p884). Commercial laundries, including **Chemo Express** (☎ 251 44 04; Wolfova ul 12; ☺ 7am-6pm Mon-Fri); Tabor (☎ 23107 82; Vidovdanska ul 2), charge from €4.20 per kg.

Left Luggage

Bus station (Trg OF 4; per day €2; ☺ 5.30am-10.30pm Sun-Fri, 5am-10pm Sat) Window No 3.

Train station (Trg OF 6; per day €2-3; ☺ 24hr) Coin lockers on platform No 1.

Medical Services

Central Pharmacy (Centralna Lekarna; ☎ 244 23 60; Prešernov trg 5; ☺ 7.30am-8pm Mon-Fri, 8am-1pm Sat)

LJUBLJANA IN TWO DAYS

Take the funicular up to **Ljubljana Castle** (p882) to get an idea of the lay of the land. After a seafood lunch at **Ribca** (p886), explore the Old Town then cross the Ljubljanica River via St James Bridge and walk north along bust-lined Vegova ul to Kongresni trg and **Prešernov trg** (p882). Over a fortifying libation at **Kavarna Tromostovje** (p886), plan your evening: low key at **Jazz Club Gajo** (p887), chichi at **Ultra** (p887) or alternative at **Metelkova Mesto** (p887).

On your second day check out some of the city's excellent **museums and galleries** (p883), and then stroll or cycle through Park Tivoli, stopping for a oh-so-local horse burger at **Hot Horse** (p886) along the way.

Community Health Centre Ljubljana (Zdravstveni Dom Ljubljana; www.zd-lj.si; ☎ 472 37 00; Metelkova ul 9; ⓨ 7.30am-7pm) For nonemergencies.

University Medical Centre Ljubljana (Univerzitetni Klinični Center Ljubljana; ☎ 522 50 50; www3.kclj.si; Zaloška c 2; ⓨ 24hr) Accident and emergency service.

Money

There are ATMs at every turn, including a row of them outside the main tourist information centre (TIC) office. At both the bus and train stations you'll find **bureaux de change** (ⓨ 7am-8pm) changing cash for no commission but not travellers cheques.

Abanka (☎ 300 15 00; Slovenska c 50; ⓨ 9am-5pm Mon-Fri)

Nova Ljubljanska Banka (☎ 476 39 00; Trg Republike 2; ⓨ 8am-6pm Mon-Fri)

Post

Main post office (Slovenska c 32; ⓨ 8am-7pm Mon-Fri, to 1pm Sat) Holds poste restante for 30 days and changes money.

Post office branch (Pražakova ul 3; ⓨ 8am-7pm Mon-Fri, to noon Sat) Just southwest of the bus and train stations.

Tourist Information

Slovenia Tourist Information Centre (STIC; ☎ 306 45 76; www.slovenia.info; Krekov trg 10; ⓨ 8am-9pm Jun-Sep, 8am-7pm Oct-May) Internet and bicycle hire also available.

Student Organisation of the University of Ljubljana (Študentska Organizacija Univerze Ljubljani; ŠOU; ☎ 433 01 76; www.sou-lj.si; Trubarjeva c 7; ⓨ 9am-6pm Mon-Thu, 9am-3pm Fri) Information and free internet.

Tourist Information Centre Ljubljana Old Town (TIC; ☎ 306 12 15; www.visitljubljana.si; Kresija Bldg, Stritarjeva ul; ⓨ 8am-9pm Jun-Sep, 8am-7pm Oct-May); Train station (☎ 433 94 75; Trg OF 6; ⓨ 8am-10pm Jun-Sep, 10am-7pm Oct-May)

Travel Agencies

Erazem (☎ 430 55 37; www.erazem.net; basement, Miklošičeva c 26; ⓨ 10am-5pm Mon-Fri Jun-Sep, noon-5pm Mon-Fri Oct-May) Staff make flight and train bookings and sell student and hostel cards.

STA Ljubljana (☎ 439 16 90; www.staljubljana.com; 1st fl, Trg Ajdovščina 1; ⓨ 10am-1pm & 2-5pm Mon-Fri) Discount airfares for students; go online at their internet cafe (open 8am to midnight Monday to Saturday).

SIGHTS

Ljubljana Castle (☎ 232 99 94; www.ljubljanafestival .si; admission free; ⓨ 9am-11pm May-Sep, 10am-9pm Oct-

Apr) crowns a wooded hill that is the city's focal point. It's an architectural mishmash, including fortified walls dating from the early 16th century, a late-15th-century chapel and a 1970s concrete cafe. The best views are from the 19th-century **watchtower** (adult/student/child €3.50/2/2; ⓨ 9am-9pm May-Sep, 10am-6pm Oct-Apr); admission includes a visit to the **Virtual Museum** below, a 23-minute, 3-D video tour of Ljubljana though the centuries. The fastest way to reach the castle is via the **funicular** (vzpenjača; adult/student/child return €3/2/2; ⓨ 9am-11pm May-Sep, 10am-9pm Oct-Apr), which ascends from Krekov trg every 10 minutes, though you can also take the hourly **tourist train** (adult/child €3/2; ⓨ up 9am-9pm, down 9.20am-9.20pm) from just south of the TIC on Stritarjeva ul. It takes about 15 minutes to walk to the castle from the Old Town.

Central Prešernov trg is dominated by the salmon pink, 17th-century **Franciscan Church of the Annunciation** (ⓨ 6.40am-noon & 3-8pm) and the **Prešeren monument** (1905), in honour of the national poet France Prešeren. Coyly observing Prešeren from a terracotta window at Wolfova ul 4 is a bust of his unrequited love (and poetic inspiration), Julija Primic. Wander north of the square along Miklošičeva c to admire the fine **art nouveau buildings**, including the landmark Grand Hotel Union at No 1, built in 1905, and the colourful former Cooperative Bank (1922) at No 8.

Leading southward from Prešernov trg is the small but perfectly formed **Triple Bridge**; prolific architect Jože Plečnik added two side bridges to the 19th-century span in 1931 to create something truly unique. The renovated baroque **Robba Fountain** stands before the Gothic **town hall** (1718) in **Mestni trg**, the 'City Square', that leads into two more: **Stari trg** (Old Sq) and **Gornji trg** (Upper Sq).

East of the Triple Bridge, the 18th-century **Cathedral of St Nicholas** (Dolničarjeva ul 1; ⓨ 10am-noon & 3-6pm) is filled with pink marble, white stucco, gilt and a panoply of baroque frescoes. North and east of the cathedral is a lively open-air market (p886) selling both foodstuffs and dry goods, the magnificent riverside **Plečnik Colonnade** and the **Dragon Bridge** (Zmajski Most; 1901), a span guarded by four of the mythical creatures that are now the city's mascots.

The main building of **Ljubljana University** (Kongresni trg 12) was erected as a ducal palace in 1902. The more restrained Philharmonic Hall (p888) dates from 1898. South of the university building is the **National & University Library** (Gosposka ul 14; ✆ 9am-6pm Mon-Fri, 9am-2pm Sat), Plečnik's masterpiece completed in 1941, with its stunning main reading room. Diagonally opposite is the excellent **City Museum of Ljubljana** (☎ 241 25 00; www.mm-lj.si; Gosposka ul 15; adult/student & child €4/2.50; ✆ 10am-6pm Tue-Sun). The reconstructed Roman street dating back to the 1st century AD is worth a visit in itself.

Of several major galleries and museums west of Slovenska c, the best are the impressive **National Gallery** (☎ 241 54 18; www.ng-slo.si; Prešernova c 24 & Cankarjeva c 20; permanent collection free, temporary exhibits adult/student €7/3.50; ✆ 10am-6pm Tue-Sun), which contains the nation's historical art collection and the fascinating **National Museum of Contemporary History** (☎ 300 96 10; www.muzej -nz.si; Celovška c 23; adult/student €3.35/2.50; ✆ 10am-6pm) in Park Tivoli, with its imaginative look at 20th-century Slovenia through multimedia and artefacts. The inwardly vibrant (but outwardly drab) 1940s **Ljubljana Modern Art Museum** (☎ 241 68 00; www.mg-lj.si; Cankarjeva c 15) was undergoing extensive renovation at the time of research.

The **National Museum of Slovenia** (☎ 241 44 00; www.nms.si; Muzejska ul 1; adult/student €3/2.50, admission 1st Sun of month free; ✆ 10am-6pm Fri-Wed, 10am-8pm Thu), in an elegant 1888 building, has rich archaeological and coin collections, including a Roman lapidarium and a Stone Age bone flute discovered near Cerkno in western Slovenia in 1995. Joint entry to the National Museum and the attached **Slovenian Museum of Natural History** (☎ 241 09 40; www2.pms-lj.si; Muzejska ul 1; adult/student €3/2.50), which keeps the same hours, costs €5/4/10 per adult/student/family.

The **Slovenian Ethnographic Museum** (☎ 300 87 00; www.etno-muzej.si; Metelkova ul 2; adult/student €4.50/2.50; ✆ 10am-6pm Tue-Sun), housed in the 1886 Belgian Barracks on the southern edge of Metelkova, has a permanent collection on the top floor with traditional Slovenian trades and crafts – everything from beekeeping and blacksmithing to glass-painting and pottery making.

TOURS

Two-hour **walking tours** (adult/child 4-12yr €10/5; ✆ 10am, 2pm & 5pm Apr-Oct) that are combined with a ride up to the castle on the funicular or the tourist train or a cruise on the Ljubljanica are organised by the TIC (opposite). They depart daily from the town hall on Mestni trg in season.

FESTIVALS & EVENTS

There is plenty going on in and around the capital, including **Druga Godba** (www.drugagodba .si), a festival of alternative and world music at the Križanke in late May/early June; the **Ljubljana Festival** (www.ljubljanafestival.si), the nation's premier cultural event (music, theatre and dance) held from early July to late August; and the **Ljubljana Marathon** (www.ljubljanskimaraton .si) in late October.

SLEEPING

Ljubljana is not overly endowed with accommodation choices, though it has gained several new places in the budget and midrange levels in recent years.

Budget

The TIC (opposite) has comprehensive details of **private rooms** (€20-30 per person) and **apartments** (€50-95) though only a handful are what could be called central.

Ljubljana Resort (☎ 568 39 13; www.ljubljanaresort .si/eng; Dunajska c 270; camping adult €7.50-13.50, child €5.75-10.25; ✆ year-round; 🖳 🛋) Wait till you see the facilities at this attractive 6-hectare camping ground–cum-resort 4km north of the city centre. Along with a 50-room hotel (singles €71 to €111, doubles €112 to €152) and five bungalows (€105 to €150) accommodating up to five people, there's Laguna (www.laguna.si, admission adult/child from €8/10, open June to September), a 'city beach club' (read water park) with outdoor swimming pools, fitness studio with sauna, and badminton and volleyball courts. Take bus 6 or 8 to the Ježica stop.

Dijaški Dom Tabor (☎ 234 88 40; www.d-tabor.lj.edus .si; dm/s/d €11/26/38; ✆ late Jun–late Aug; 🖳) In summer five colleges in Ljubljana open their halls of residence (*dijaški dom*) to visitors, but only this 300-bed one, a 10-minute walk southeast of the bus and train stations, is really central. Accommodation is in rooms with one to 10 beds. Enter from Kotnikova ul.

Simbol Castle Hostel (☎ 041-720 825; www.simbol.si; Petkovškovo nabrežje 47; dm/d/tr/q €16/50/54/68; 🖳) A favourite new place in Ljubljana, this five-room hostel wraps around a tiny courtyard bordering the Ljubljanica, and one room has views of the castle. Rooms, with two to six beds, have their own kitchens. Internet is free.

Alibi Hostel (☎ 251 12 44; www.alibi.si; Cankarjevo nabrežje 27; dm/d €20/50; 🖳 🖳) This well-situated 106-bed hostel on the Ljubljanica has brightly painted, airy dorms with four to 12 wooden bunks and five doubles. One room is air-conditioned and there's a private suite at the top for six people. Farther afield to the north in Bežigrad (bus 14 to Podmilščakova stop), Alibi Rooms (☎ 433 13 31; Kolarjeva ul 30) has eight rooms with between two and six beds (dorms €18, doubles €46) in an old villa with a lovely garden.

our pick **Celica Hostel** (☎ 230 97 00; www.hostel celica.com; Metelkova ul 8; dm €21, s/d/tr cell €47/54/66, 4-to 5-bed room per person €27, 6-to 7-bed room per person €22; 🖳) This stylishly revamped former prison (1882) in Metelkova has 20 'cells', designed by as many different architects and complete with original bars; it also has nine rooms and apartments with three to seven beds; and a packed, popular 12-bed dorm. The ground floor is home to three cafes (set lunch €5 to €7; open 7.30am to midnight) and the hostel boasts its own gallery where everyone can show their own work.

Vila Veselova (☎ 059-926 721; www.v-v.si; Veselova ul 14; dm €21, d/q €68/102; 🗶 🖳) This very attractive bright yellow villa, with its own garden and 42 beds in the centre of the museum district, offers mostly hostel accommodation in five colourful rooms with four to eight beds. A double and two apartments with attached facilities and access to a kitchen make it an attractive midrange option, however. Some rooms face Park Tivoli across busy Tivolska c.

Midrange

Penzion Pod Lipo (☎ 031-809 893; www.penzion-podlipo .com; Borštnikov trg 3; d/tr/q €59/72/96; 🖳) Sitting atop one of Ljubljana's oldest *gostilne* and by a 400-year-old linden tree, this 10-room inn offers excellent value in a part of the city that is filling up with bars and restaurants. Fall in love with the communal kitchen, the original hardwood floors and the east-facing terrace that catches the morning sun.

Hotel Emonec (☎ 200 15 20; www.hotel-emonec.com; Wolfova ul 12; s €59-72, d €67-77, tr/q €90/105; 🖳) The decor is simple and functionally modern at this 39-room hotel and the staff is less than welcoming, but everything is spotless and you can't beat the central location.

Slamič B&B (☎ 433 82 33; www.slamic.si; Kersnikova ul 1; s €65-80, d €95-107; 🗶 🖳) It's a titch away from the action but Slamič, a B&B above a famous cafe and teahouse, offers 11 bright rooms with antique(ish) furnishings and parquet floors. Choice rooms include quiet No 1 looking on to a back garden and No 9 just

off an enormous terrace used by the cafe and made for smokers.

Pri Mraku (☎ 421 96 00; www.daj-dam.si; Rimska c 4; s €69-77, d €102-112, tr €121-131; 🗶 🖳) Although it calls itself a *gostilna*, 'At Twilight' is really just a smallish hotel (36 rooms) in an old building with no lift and a garden. Rooms on the 1st and 4th floors have air-con.

Hotel Park (☎ 300 25 00; www.hotelpark.si; Tabor 9; s €75-80, d €104-110; 🖳) A partial facelift inside and out has made this tower-block hotel an even better-value midrange choice in central Ljubljana. The 200 pleasant, well-renovated standard and comfort rooms are bright and unpretentiously well equipped. Cheaper 'hostel' rooms, some of which have shared facilities and others en-suite shower, cost €22/26 per person with shared/private bathroom in a double and €17/19 in a quad. Students with ISIC cards get a 10% discount.

Top End

Antiq Hotel (☎ 421 35 60; www.antiqhotel.si; Gornji trg 3; s €113-164, d €144-204; 🗶 🖳) Ljubljana's first (and still only) boutique hotel was cobbled together from a series of townhouses and on the site of a Roman workshop. It has 16 rooms and apartments, most of which are very spacious, a small wellness centre next door and multitiered back garden. The decor is kitsch with a smirk and there are fabulous little nooks and touches everywhere: glassed-in medieval courtyard; vaulted ceilings; two noncarpeted, antiallergenic floors; and bath towels trimmed with Slovenian lace. Among our favourite rooms are enormous No 8 on the 2nd floor, with swooningly romantic views of the Hercules Fountain, and No 10, an even bigger two-room suite on the top floor with a terrace and glimpses of Ljubljana Castle. The two cheapest rooms (singles/doubles €61/77), Nos 2 and 9, have their own bathrooms but they're on the corridor.

EATING

The Old Town has a fair number of appealing restaurants, but the majority of the venues here are cafes. For cheaper options, try the dull but functional snack bars around the bus and train stations, and both on and in the shopping mall below Trg Ajdovščina.

Restaurants

Harambaša (☎ 041-843 106; Vrtna ul 8; dishes €3.50-6; 🕑 10am-10pm Mon-Fri, noon-10pm Sat, noon-6pm Sun)

Here you'll find authentic Bosnian – Sarajevan to be precise – dishes like *čevapčiči* (spicy meatballs of beef or pork) and *pljeskavica* (meat patties) served at low tables in a charming modern cottage.

Kitajska Zvezda (☎ 425 88 24; Hrenova ul 19; mains €4.10-12.30; ✆ 11am-11pm) If you're looking for a fix of rice or noodles, try the 'Chinese Star' on the river just south of the Old Town. Szechuan dishes, including the *ma po doufu* (tofu with garlic and chilli), are good; they also do Cantonese and Shanghainese food.

Vegedrom (☎ 513 26 42; Vodnikova c 35; mains €5.60-12.60; ✆ 11am-10pm Mon-Fri, noon-10pm Sat) This appealing, if somewhat pricey, vegan restaurant at the northeastern edge of Park Tivoli now also dibble-dabbles (or is that nibble-nabbles?) in Indian food. The set lunch is good value at €6.90 and there's a salad bar (from €3.40).

Pri Škofju (☎ 426 45 08; Rečna ul 8; mains €7-15; ✆ 10am-midnight Mon-Fri, noon-midnight Sat & Sun) Still our off-the-beaten track favourite, this wonderful little place in tranquil Krakovo, south of the city centre, serves some of the best prepared local dishes and salads in Ljubljana, with an ever-changing menu. Weekday set lunches are good value at €5.30 to €6.90.

Sokol (☎ 439 68 55; Ciril Metodov trg 18; mains €7-20; ✆ noon-11pm) In this old vaulted house, traditional Slovenian food is served on heavy tables by costumed waiters. Along with traditional dishes like *obara* (veal stew, €7) and Krvavica sausage with cabbage and turnips (€8.50), there are the more esoteric deep-fried bull's testicles with tartare sauce and grilled stallion steak (€16).

Namasté (☎ 425 01 59; Breg 8; mains €7.50-15.50; ✆ 11am-midnight Mon-Sat, to 10pm Sun) Should you fancy a bit of Indian, head for this place on the left bank of the Ljubljanica. You won't get high street–quality curry but the thalis (from €7.50) and tandoori dishes (from €12.30) are good. The choice of vegetarian dishes is better than average and the set lunch is €8.

Cantina Mexicana (☎ 426 93 25; Knafljev prehod 3; mains €7.90-16.80; ✆ 10am-1am Sun-Tue, 10am-3am Wed-Fri, 9am-3am Sat) This stylish Mexican restaurant has an eye-catching red and blue exterior and hacienda-like decor inside. The fajitas (€7.90 to €12.90) are good.

Yildiz Han (☎ 426 57 17; Karlovška c 19; mains €8.50-15; ✆ noon-midnight Mon-Sat) If Turkish is your thing, head for authentic (trust us) 'Star House', which features belly dancing on Friday nights. Lunches are a snip at €5.

Taverna Tatjana (☎ 421 00 87; Gornji trg 38; mains €8.50-22; ✆ 3pm-midnight Mon-Sat) A wooden-beamed cottage pub with a nautical theme (think nets and seascapes), this is actually a rather exclusive fish restaurant with a lovely (and protected) back courtyard for the warmer months.

Gostilna Rimska XXI (☎ 425 20 29; Rimska c 21; mains €10-24; ✆ 12.30pm-1am Mon-Fri) This sleek new *gostilna* that changes its menu twice a day serves Mediterranean-inspired dishes till late. Set lunch is €16.

Špajza (☎ 425 30 94; Gornji trg 28; mains €14.60-22; ✆ noon-11pm Mon-Sat, to 10pm Sun) A welcome return to the Old Town is the 'Pantry', nicely decorated with its rough-hewn tables and chairs, wooden floors, frescoed ceilings and nostalgic bits and pieces. Try the 'Špajza filet' (€22), which is actually horseflesh, or a bit of *kozliček iz pečiče* (oven-roasted kid; €14.60); wines from a dozen different Slovenian producers are served. A three-course set lunch is only €10.

Pri Vitezu (☎ 426 60 58; Breg 18-20; mains €18-30; ✆ noon-11pm Mon-Sat) Located directly on the left bank of the Ljubljanica, 'At the Knight' is the place for a special meal (Mediterranean-style grills and Adriatic fish dishes), whether in the brasserie, the salon or the very cosy Knight's Room.

Ljubljana is awash in pizzerias, where pizza routinely costs €4 to €8.50. The pick of the crop includes **Foculus Pizzeria** (☎ 251 56 43; Gregorčičeva ul 3; ✆ 10am-midnight Mon-Fri, noon-midnight Sat & Sun), which boasts a vaulted ceiling painted with spring and autumn leaves; **Trta** (☎ 426 50 66; Grudnovo nabrežje 21; ✆ 11am-10.30pm Mon-Fri, noon-10.30pm Sat), on the right bank of the Ljubljanica; and **Mirje** (☎ 426 60 15; Tržaška c 5; ✆ 10am-10pm Mon-Fri, noon-5pm Sat), southwest of the city centre, which does some excellent pasta dishes, too.

Quick Eats

Nobel Burek (Miklošičeva c 30; burek €2, pizza slice €1.40; ✆ 24hr) This hole-in-the-wall serves Slovenian-style fast food round-the-clock.

Restavracija 2000 (☎ 476 69 25; Trg Republike 1; dishes €1.50-3, set lunch €6.50; ✆ 9am-7pm Mon-Fri, 9am-3pm Sat) In the basement of the Maximarket department store, this glass and chrome self-service eatery is surprisingly upbeat, and just the ticket if you want something quick while visiting the main museums.

Ajdovo Zrno (☎ 041-690 478; Trubarjeva c 7; soups & sandwiches €1.80-2, set lunch €6; 🕑 10am-7pm Mon-Fri) Vegetarian 'Buckwheat Grain' serves soups, sandwiches, fried vegetables and lots of different salads (self-service, €3 to €6). And they have terrific, freshly squeezed juices, including the unusual rose-petal juice with lemon. Enter from little Mali trg.

Paninoteka (☎ 041-529 824; Jurčičev trg 3; soups & toasted sandwiches €2.40-6; 🕑 8am-1am Mon-Sat, 9am-11pm Sun) Healthy sandwich creations on a lovely little square by the river.

Hot Horse (☎ 521 14 27; Park Tivoli; snacks & burgers €2.80-6; 🕑 9am-6am Mon, 10am-6am Tue-Sun) This place in a kiosk in the city's largest park supplies Ljubljančani with their favourite treat: horse burgers (€4). It's just down the hill from the National Museum of Contemporary History.

Ribca (☎ 425 15 44; Adamič-Lundrovo nabrežje 1; dishes €3-7.50; 🕑 8am-4pm Mon-Fri, 8am-2pm Sat) This basement seafood bar below the Plečnik Colonnade in Pogačarjev trg serves tasty fried squid, sardines and herrings to hungry market-goers. Set lunch is €7.50.

Self-Catering

Handy supermarkets include a large **Mercator** (Slovenska c 55; 🕑 7am-9pm) southwest of the train and bus stations and a smaller, more central **Mercator branch** (Kongresni trg 9; 🕑 7am-8pm Mon-Fri, 8am-3pm Sat & Sun) just up from the river.

The **Maximarket supermarket** (☎ 476 68 00; basement, Trg Republike 1; 🕑 9am-9pm Mon-Fri, 8am-5pm Sat) below the department store of the same name has the largest selection of food and wine in the city centre.

The open-air **market** (Pogačarjev trg & Vodnikov trg; 🕑 6am-6pm Mon-Fri, 6am-4pm Sat Jun-Sep, 6am-4pm Mon-Sat Oct-May), held across two squares north and east of the cathedral, sells mostly fresh fruit and vegetables.

DRINKING

Few cities of this size have central Ljubljana's concentration of inviting cafes and bars, the vast majority with outdoor seating.

Bars & Pubs

Kavarna Tromostovje (☎ 430 12 18; Prešernov trg 1; 🕑 7am-1am Apr-Oct) This cafe-bar on the southern side of Prešernov trg seems to change its name on an annual basis but remains one of the most popular places for a drink if you just want to sit outside and watch the passing parade.

Maček (☎ 425 37 91; Krojaška ul 5; 🕑 9am-1am) *The* place to be seen in Ljubljana on a sunny summer afternoon, the 'Cat' is Kavarna Tromostovje's rival on the right bank of the Ljubljanica. Happy hour is between 4pm and 7pm on weekdays.

Salon (☎ 439 87 64; Trubarjeva c 23; 🕑 9am-1am Mon-Wed, 9am-3am Thu-Sat, 3pm-1am Sun) Salon is a dazzling designer-kitsch cocktail bar featuring gold ceilings, faux leopard armchairs, heavy purple velvet drapes and excellent cocktails (€4.50 to €6.50).

Sax Pub (☎ 283 14 57; Eipprova ul 7; 🕑 noon-1am Mon, 10am-1am Tue-Sat, 4-10pm Sun) Two decades in Trnovo and decorated with colourful murals and graffiti inside and out, the Sax has live jazz at 9pm or 9.30pm on Thursdays from late August to December and February to June. Canned stuff rules at other times.

Dvorni Bar (☎ 251 12 57; Dvorni trg 2; 🕑 8am-1am Mon-Sat, 8am-midnight Sun) This wine bar is an excellent place to taste Slovenian vintages; it stocks more than 100 varieties and has wine tastings every second Wednesday of the month.

Pr' Skelet (☎ 252 77 99; Ključavničarska ul 5; 🕑 10am-3am) It might sound like a one-joke wonder, but you'll shake, rattle and roll at this skeleton-themed basement bar, where cocktails are two for one throughout the day.

Žmavc (☎ 251 03 24; Rimska c 21; 🕑 7.30am-1am Mon-Fri, 10am-1am Sat, 6pm-1am Sun) A superpopular student hang-out west of Slovenska c, with comic-strip scenes and figures running half-way up the walls.

Pr' Semaforju (☎ 040-893 664; Slovenska c 5; 🕑 7am-midnight Mon-Fri) Student (and we're talking spotty teens here) hang-out par excellence, 'At the Traffic Light' (the name is translated into a dozen languages outside) is a slightly grotty cafe-bar that rocks later in the evening.

Cafes & Teahouses

Kavarna Zvezda (☎ 421 90 90; Kongresni trg 4 & Wolfova ul 14; 🕑 7am-11pm Mon-Sat, 10am-8pm Sun) The 'Star Café' is celebrated for its shop-made cakes, especially *skutina pečena* (€2.60), an eggy cheesecake.

Le Petit Café (☎ 251 25 75; Trg Francoske Revolucije 4; 🕑 7.30am-midnight) Just opposite the Križanke, this pleasant, studenty place offers great coffee and a wide range of breakfast goodies (€2.60 to €6.50).

Ambient (☎ 430 27 56; Čufarjeva ul 5; 🕑 7am-1am Mon-Fri, 9am-1am Sat, 6pm-1am Sun) This stylish cafe-cum-bistro hidden down a narrow side street just east of Miklošičeva c caters to a diverse crowd throughout the day.

Kafeterija Lan (Gallusovo nabrežje 27; 10am-midnight Mon-Thu, 10am-1am Fri, 11am-midnight Sat & Sun) A little greener-than-green cafe-bar on the river below Cobbler Bridge, Lan is something of a hipster gay magnet. There's a nice terrace under a spreading chestnut street.

Čajna Hiša (421 24 44; Stari trg 3; 9am-10.30pm Mon-Fri, 9am-3pm & 6-10pm Sat) If you take your cuppa seriously, come here; the appropriately named 'Teahouse' offers a wide range of green and black teas and fruit tisanes for €1.80 to €3.40 a pot.

Babo Juice Bar (040-533 334; Krojaška ul 4; juices & smoothies €1.95-4.40; 9am-9pm) Of the crop of juice bars that have sprouted all over Ljubljana, Babo is the best, with some excellent fruit and vegetable combinations.

Slaščičarna Pri Vodnjaku (425 07 12; Stari trg 30; 8am-midnight) For all kinds of chocolate of the ice cream and drinking kind, the 'Confectionery by the Fountain' will surely satisfy – there are almost three-dozen flavours (€1 per scoop), as well as teas (€1.60) and fresh juices (€0.80 to €3.35).

ENTERTAINMENT

The free quarterly **Ljubljana Life** (www.ljubljanalife.com) has practical information and listings. **Ljubljana in Your Pocket** (www.inyourpocket.com; €2.90), another quarterly, will cost you, but it's a thousand times more useful. *Where to? in Ljubljana*, available from the tourist offices (p882), lists cultural and sporting events.

Nightclubs

Inbox Club (428 96 90, 428 75 01; www.inbox-club.com; Jurčkova c 224; 9pm-dawn Thu-Sat) Ljubljana's biggest club is hidden in a shopping centre opposite the Leclerc Hypermarket (take bus 27 to NS Rudnik, the last stop) in the far southeastern suburbs.

Klub K4 (438 02 61; www.klubk4.org; Kersnikova ul 4; 8pm-2am Tue, 8pm-4am Wed & Thu, 9pm-6am Fri & Sat, 10pm-4am Sun) This evergreen venue in the basement of the Student Organisation of Ljubljana University (ŠOU) headquarters features rave-electronic music on Fridays and Saturdays, with other styles of music on weeknights, and a popular gay and lesbian night on Sundays. It closes in July and August.

Bachus Center Club (241 82 44; www.bachus-center.com; Kongresni trg 3; 9pm-5am Mon-Sat) This place has something for everyone, including

a restaurant and bar-lounge, and attracts a pretty tame, pretty mainstream crowd.

As Lounge (425 88 22; www.gostilnaas.si; Čopova 5A but enter from Knafljev prehod; 9am-3am Wed-Sat) DJs transform this candlelit basement bar into a pumping, crowd-pulling nightclub four nights a week. The way the name sounds in Slovene might have you thinking you're going to get lucky. It just means 'ace', ace.

Ultra (070 818 979; www.ultra-club.si; Nazorjeva ul 6; 10pm-6am Wed-Sat) Ultra is a popular dance venue with four different theme nights and a switched-on, somewhat chichi crowd.

KMŠ (425 74 80; www.klubkms.si; Tržaška ul 2; 8am-5am Mon-Fri, 9pm-5am Sat) Located in the deep recesses of a former factory complex, the 'Maribor Student Club' is a raucous place with music and dancers all over the shop.

Metelkova Mesto (www.metelkova.org; Masarykova c 24) 'Metelkova Town', an ex-army garrison taken over by squatters after independence, is now a free-living commune – a miniature version of Copenhagen's Christiania. In this two-courtyard block, a dozen idiosyncratic venues hide behind brightly tagged doorways, coming to life generally after midnight, daily in summer and on Fridays and Saturdays the rest of the year. Entering the main 'city gate' from Masarykova c, the building to the right houses **Gala Hala** (www.galahala.com), with live bands and club nights, and **Klub Channel Zero** (www.ch0.org), with punk and hardcore. Easy to miss in the first building to the left are **Klub Tiffany** (www.ljudmila.org/siqrd/tiffany) for gay men and **Klub Monokel** (www.klubmonokel.com) for lesbians. Due south is the ever-popular **Jalla Jalla Club** (www.myspace.com/jallajallaclub), a congenial pub with concerts. Beyond the first courtyard to the southwest, **Klub Gromka** (www.metelkova.org/gromka) in the building with the conical roof has folk, live concerts, theatre and lectures. Next door is **Menza pri Koritu** (www.menzaprikoritu.org) under the strange E.T.-like figures with performances and concerts.

Live Music

Orto Bar (232 16 74; www.orto-bar.com; Graboličeva ul 1; 8am-4am Mon-Wed, 8am-5am Thu-Sat, 6-9pm Sun) A popular bar-club for late-night drinking and dancing with occasional live music, Orto is just five minutes' walk from Metelkova.

Jazz Club Gajo (425 32 06; www.jazzclubgajo.com; Beethovnova ul 8; 11am-2am Mon-Fri, 7pm-midnight Sat & Sun) Now in its 15th year, Gajo is the city's premier venue for live jazz and attracts both local and international talent (jam sessions 9pm Mondays).

Roxly Café Bar (☎ 430 10 21; www.roxly.si; Mala ul 5; ☺ 7am-2am Mon-Wed, to 3am Thu & Fri, 10am-3am Sat) New venue north of the Ljubljanica; there's live rock music from 10pm two or three nights a week.

Performing Arts

Philharmonic Hall (Filharmonija; ☎ 241 08 00; www.filhar monija.si; Kongresni trg 10) This century-old concert hall is home to the Slovenian Philharmonic Orchestra, founded in 1701.

Opera House (☎ 241 17 40; www.opera.si; Župančičeva ul 1) Opera and ballet are performed at the neo-Renaissance Opera House dating back to 1882.

Križanke (☎ 241 60 00, box office 241 60 26; Trg Francoske Revolucije 1-2) Hosts concerts of the Ljubljana Festival (p883) and other events both inside and out what was a sprawling monastic complex dating back to the 13th century.

Cankarjev Dom (☎ 241 71 00; www.cd-cc.si; Prešernova c 10) is Ljubljana's premier cultural centre and has two large auditoriums (the Gallus Hall has perfect acoustics) and a dozen smaller performance spaces offering a remarkable smorgasbord of performance arts. The **ticket office** (☎ 241 72 99; ☺ 11am-1pm & 3-8pm Mon-Fri, 11am-1pm Sat & 1hr before performances) is in the subway below Maximarket Supermarket.

Cinema

Kinoteka (☎ 434 25 20; www.kinoteka.si; Miklošičeva c 28) The 'Slovenian Cinematheque' screens archival art and classic films in their original languages.

GETTING THERE & AWAY
Bus

The **bus station** (☎ 234 46 00, information 090 93 42 30; www.ap-ljubljana.si; Trg OF 4; ☺ 5.30am-10.30pm Sun-Fri, 5am-10pm Sat) opposite the train station has bilingual info-phones; just pick one up and wait for the connection. Frequent buses serve Bohinj (€8.30, two hours, 86km, hourly) via Bled (€6.30, 1¼ hours, 57km). Most buses to Piran (€12, three hours, 140km, up to seven daily) go via Koper (€11.10, 2½ hours, 122km, up to 16 daily) and Postojna (€6, one hour, 53km, up to 36 daily).

International services from Ljubljana include Belgrade (€35, 7¾ hours, 536km, 10am and 10.25pm daily); Budapest (€8, six hours, 442km, 1pm Wednesday, Friday and Sunday), Frankfurt (€83, 12½ hours, 777km, 7.30pm Sunday to Friday, 9.30pm Saturday) via Munich (€48, 6¾ hours, 344km); Poreč (€17.50, 4½ hours, 162km, 1.45pm daily), Sarajevo (€38, 9½ hours, 570km, 3.15pm daily 4pm Wednesday and Sunday); Skopje (€50, 15 hours, 960km, 3pm Sunday to Friday); Split (€44, 10½ hours, 528km, 7.40pm daily) via Rijeka (€17, 2½ hours, 136km); Trieste (€11.60, 2¾ hours, 105km, 2.25pm Monday to Saturday); and Zagreb (€13.60, 2½ hours, 154km, 2.25am daily).

Train

Ljubljana's **train station** (☎ 291 33 32; www.slo -zeleznice.si; Trg OF 6; ☺ 5am-10pm) has daily services to Koper (€7.75 to €13, 2½ hours, 153km, up to five times daily). Alternatively you can take one of the more frequent Sežana-bound trains and change at Divača (€6.25 to €7.75, 1¾ hours, 104km).

Ljubljana–Vienna trains (€61.80, 6¼ hours, 385km, twice daily) via Graz (€31.40, 200km, three hours) are expensive, although Spar Schiene fares as low as €29 apply on certain trains at certain times. Otherwise save a little bit of money by going first to Maribor (from €7.70, 2½ hours, 156km, up to two dozen daily), where you can buy a Maribor–Graz ticket (€13, one hours, three daily) and then continue on domestic tickets from Graz to Vienna (€31.40, 2¾ hours, 214km). Similar savings apply via Jesenice and Villach and/or Klagenfurt.

Three trains depart daily from Ljubljana for Munich (€71.40, 6½ hours, 405km). The 11.50pm departure has sleeping carriages available.

Ljubljana–Venice trains (€25 to €47, four hours, 244km) via Sežana depart at 2.22am and 10.35am. It's cheaper to go first to Nova Gorica (€7.75, 3½ hours, 153km, five daily), cross over to Gorizia and then take an Italian train to Venice (€8.75, 2¼ hours).

For Zagreb there are seven trains daily from Ljubljana (€12.20, 2½ hours, 154km) via Zidani Most. Two trains from the capital serve Rijeka (€12.60, 2½ hours, 136km) via Postojna.

Ljubljana–Budapest trains (€57.80, 8¾ hours, 451km, twice daily) go via Ptuj and Hodoš; there are Budapest Special fares available for as low as €29 on certain trains at certain times. Belgrade (€25 to €44, 10 hours, 535km) is served by four trains a day.

GETTING AROUND

The cheapest way to Ljubljana's recently re-named **Jože Pučnik Airport** (LJU; www.lju-airport.si) at Brnik is by city bus from stop 28 (€4.10, 50 minutes, 27km) at the bus station. These run at 5.20am and hourly from 6.10am to 8.10pm Monday to Friday; on weekends there's a bus at 6.10am and then one every two hours from 9.10am to 7.10pm. A **private airport van** (☎ 041-792 865; €5) also links Trg OF near the bus station with the airport (30 minutes) up to 10 times daily between 5.20am and 10.30pm. A **taxi** (☎ 031-311 311, 041-445 406) from downtown Ljubljana will cost you about €38.

Ljubljana has an excellent network of city buses. Most operate every five to 15 minutes from 5am to 10.30pm, though some start as early as 3.15am and run till midnight. The central area is perfectly walkable, though, so buses are really only necessary if you're staying out of town. Buy metal tokens (*žetoni*; €0.80) from news-stands, or pay €1 on board.

Ljubljana Bike (per 2hr/day €1/5; ⏰ 8am-7pm or 9pm Apr-Oct) has two-wheelers available from 10 locations around the city, including the train station, the STIC office (p882), Celica Hostel (p884) and opposite Antiq Hotel.

JULIAN ALPS

The Julian Alps – named in honour of Caesar himself – form Slovenia's dramatic north-west frontier with Italy. Triglav National Park, established in 1924, includes almost all of the Alps lying within Slovenia. The centre-piece of the park is, of course, Mt Triglav (2864m), Slovenia's highest mountain, but there are many other peaks here reaching above 2000m. Along with an embarrassment of fauna and flora, the area offers a wide range of adventure sports.

KRANJ

☎ 04 / pop 34,950

At the foot of the Kamnik-Savinja Alps, with the snow-capped peak of Storžič (2132m) and others looming to the north, Kranj is Slovenia's fourth-largest city. The attractive Old Town, perched on an escarpment above the confluence of the Sava and Kokra Rivers, barely measures 1km by 250m.

The frequent weekday buses between Kranj and Ljubljana airport at nearby Brnik make it possible to head straight to the Julian Alps without first going to the capital. While waiting for your onward bus to Bled (€3.60, 30 minutes, 23km), have a look at the Old Town, starting with the art nouveau **former post office** (Koroška c 2) facing Maistrov trg and its rooftop cafe, a 600m walk south from the bus station. On your way you'll pass the 87-room **Hotel Creina** (☎ 281 75 00; www.hotel-creina.si; Koroška c 5; s/d €81/102; 🖥 🔲), the only game in town and now getting a much needed refit. The **tourist office** (☎ 238 04 50; www .tourism-kranj.si; Glavni trg 2; ⏰ 8am-7pm Mon-Sat, 9am-4pm Sun) can find you a private room from €25 or, in summer, a bed in a student dormitory (€15).

Most places of interest are along just three streets – pedestrianised Prešernova ul, Tavčarjeva ul and Tomišičeva ul – the first two of which lead to the **Church of St Cantianus**, with impressive frescoes and stained glass. Another 300m farther south, the Old Town dead-ends at the Serbian Orthodox **Plague Church**, built during a time of pestilence in 1470, and the 16th-century **defence tower** behind it. **Mitnica** (☎ 040-678 778; Tavčarjeva ul 35; ⏰ 7am-11pm Mon-Wed, 7am-1am Thu, 7am-2am Fri & Sat, 3-11pm Sun) is a relaxing cafe-bar in the basement of a 16th-century toll house with a huge terrace backing on to the river.

From Kranj it's an easy excursion to **Škofja Loka** (population 12,275) whose main square, **Mestni trg**, contains beautifully painted houses and a **tourist office** (☎ 512 02 68; www.skofjaloka.info; Mestni trg 7). The fine **castle** (Grajska pot 13) has the **Loka Museum** (☎ 517 04 00; adult/child €3/2.10; ⏰ 9am-6pm Tue-Sun Apr-Oct, 9am-5pm Sat & Sun Nov-Mar) with one of the best ethnographical collections in Slovenia. Buses for Škofja Loka (€2.30, 25 minutes, 13km) depart hourly from Kranj between 5.10am and 9.10pm.

BLED

☎ 04 / pop 5415

With an emerald-green lake, a picture-postcard church on a tiny island, a medieval castle clinging to a rocky cliff, and some of the highest peaks of the Julian Alps and the Karavanke as backdrops, Bled seems to have been designed by some god of tourism. As it is Slovenia's most popular destination, it can get pretty crowded in summer, but it's small, convenient and a delightful base from which to explore the mountains.

Information

À Propos Bar (☎ 574 40 44; Bled Shopping Centre, Ljubljanska c 4; per 15/30/60min €1.25/2.10/4.20; ⏰ 8am-midnight) Internet access.

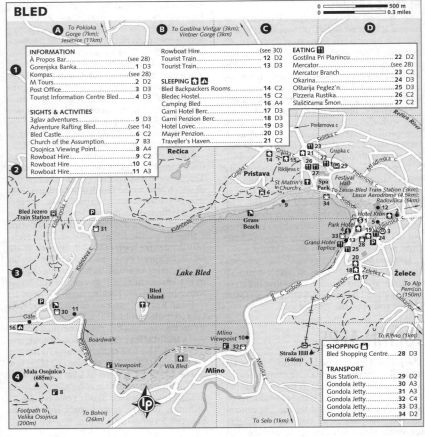

BLED

Gorenjska Banka (C Svobode 15; ☼ 9-11.30am & 2-5pm Mon-Fri, 8-11am Sat) North end of Park Hotel shop complex.

Kompas (☎ 572 75 00; www.kompas-bled.si; Bled Shopping Centre, Ljubljanska c 4; ☼ 8am-8pm Mon-Sat, 8am-noon & 4-8pm Sun Jul & Aug, 8am-7pm Mon-Sat Sep-Jun) Rents private rooms and bicycles.

M Tours (☎ 575 33 00; www.mtour.net; Ljubljanska c 7; ☼ 8am-8pm Mon-Sat, 8am-noon & 4-8pm Sun) Has private rooms.

Post office (Ljubljanska cesta 10; ☼ 8am-7pm Mon-Fri, 8am-noon Sat)

Tourist Information Centre Bled (☎ 574 11 22; www .bled.si; C Svobode 10; ☼ 8am-9pm Mon-Sat, 9am-5pm Sun Jul & Aug, 8am-7pm Mon-Sat, 11am-5pm Sun Mar-Jun & Sep-Oct, 9am-6pm Mon-Sat, noon-4pm Sun Nov, 8am-6pm Mon-Fri, 8am-1pm Sun Dec-Feb) Internet access is free for 15 minutes or pay €2.50/4 per 30/60 minutes

Sights

Sitting on its very own islet, the baroque **Church of the Assumption** (☼ 8am-dusk) is Bled's icon. Getting there by a piloted **gondola** (pletna; ☎ 041-427 155; per person €12) is the archetypal tourist experience. Gondola prices are standard from any jetty, and you'll stay on the island long enough to ring the 'lucky' bell; all in all, it's a 1½-hour trip. Ordinary row-yourself boats for three to four people cost €10 to €13 per hour.

Perched atop a 100m-high cliff, **Bled Castle** (☎ 572 9780; Grajska c 25; adult/student/child €7/6/3.50; ☼ 8am-8pm May-Oct, 8am-5pm Nov-Apr) is the perfect backdrop to a lake view. One of many access footpaths leads up from behind the Bledec Hostel. Admission includes entry to the recently revamped **museum collection**.

SLOVENIA

A short distance southeast of Bled and well served by bus (€1.80, 15 minutes, 7.5km, half-hourly), the sleepy town of **Radovljica** (population 6000) has a particularly delightful square called **Linhartov trg** in its Old Town, where there are restored and painted **manor houses**, an interesting **gallery**, the fascinating **Beekeeping Museum** (☎ 532 05 20; Linhartov trg 1; adult/student €3/2.50; ☉ 10am–1pm & 3–6pm Tue–Sun May–Oct, 10am–noon & 3–5pm Wed, Sat & Sun Mar, Apr, Nov & Dec) and, on the edge of the square, a **tourist office** (☎ 531 53 00; www.radovljica.si; Gorenjska c 1). The square lies 400m southeast of the bus station via Gorenjska c or just 100m up narrow Kolodvorska ul from the train station to the south.

Activities

The best way to see Lake Bled is on foot; the 6km stroll around the lake shouldn't take more than a couple of hours, including the short (but steep) climb to the brilliant **Osojnica viewing point** in the southwest. If you prefer, jump aboard the **tourist train** (adult/child €3/2; ☉ 9am–9pm May–mid-Oct, Sat & Sun Nov–Apr) for the 45-minute twirl around the lake, which departs from in front of the Sport Hall and, more centrally, from just north of the tourist office.

A popular and easy walk is to **Vintgar Gorge** (adult/student/child €4/3/2; ☉ 8am–7pm mid-May–Oct) 4km to the northwest. The highlight is the 1600m-long wooden walkway (1893) that criss-crosses the swirling Radovna River for the first 700m or so. Thereafter the scenery becomes tamer, passing a tall railway bridge and a spray-spouting weir, and ending at the anticlimactic 13m-high **Šum Waterfall**. The easiest way to get to the gorge is via the appealing Gostilna Vintgar, an inn just three well-signed kilometres away on quiet, attractive roads from the Bledec Hostel. From early June to September, a daily bus (€3.50) leaves Bled bus station for Vintgar at 10am daily, arriving at 10.30am and returning at noon.

For something tougher, join one of the rafting or kayaking (€25 to €44) or paragliding (€85) trips on offer from **3glav adventures** (☎ 041-683 184; www.3glav-adventures.com; Ljubljanska c 1; ☉ 9am–7pm Apr–Oct); **Adventure Rafting Bled** (☎ 574 40 41, 051-676 008; www.adventure-rafting.si; Bled Backpackers Rooms, Grajska c 21; ☎ Apr–Oct) organises rafting and canyoning. Both the tourist office (opposite) and Kompas (opposite) rent **bikes** for €3.50/6 for one-/three-hours, or €8/11 for a half-/full day.

Sleeping

Bled is now blessed with several hostels, all within spitting distance of one another. Kompas (opposite) and M Tours (opposite) in the Hotel Krim have lists of private rooms, with singles/doubles starting at €24/38.

Camping Bled (☎ 575 20 00; www.camping-bled .com; Kidričeva c 10c; adult €8.50-11.50, child €5.95-8.05; ☉ Apr–mid-Oct) This popular 6.5-hectare site fills a small valley at the western end of the lake and boasts a popular restaurant.

Bled Backpackers Rooms (☎ 574 40 41, 051-678 008; www.bled-backpackersrooms.com; Grajska c 21; per person €17; 🖳) With the attached George Best Bar open till at least midnight daily, this five-room place with 20 beds is Bled's party hostel. We love the room with the huge balcony and the storage lockers that open from the top.

Bledec Hostel (☎ 574 52 50; www.mlino.si; Grajska c 17; HI members/nonmembers dm €18/20, d €24/26; 🖳) This official, somewhat old-fashioned hostel has dorms with four to seven beds and private bathrooms, a bar and an inexpensive restaurant. Laundry service (€8.50) and internet access (€2.10 per half-hour) is available.

Traveller's Haven (☎ 031-704 455, 041-396 545; www .travellers-haven.com; Riklijeva c 1; per person €19; 🖳) This stunning new facility in a converted old villa (c 1909) has six rooms with between two and six beds, a great kitchen, free internet and laundry, and a chilled vibe.

Alp Penzion (☎ 576 74 50; www.alp-penzion.com; Cankarjeva c 20a; s €41, d €54-72) About 750m south of the town centre, the Alp is a bit away from the action but can be recommended for its tranquil location and lovely garden.

Garni Hotel Berc (☎ 576 56 58; www.berc-sp.si; Pod Stražo 13; s €40-45, d €65-70; 🖳) This purpose-built place, reminiscent of a Swiss chalet, has 15 rooms on two floors in a quiet location above the lake. Just opposite is a second branch, Garni Penzion Berc (☎ 574 18 38; Želeška c 15; singles €35 to €40, doubles €60 to €55), with simpler rooms and cheaper rates.

Mayer Penzion (☎ 576 57 40; www.mayer-sp.si; Želeška c 7; s €45, d €70-75, apt €100; 🖳) This delightful, flower-bedecked 12-room inn in a renovated 19th-century house is in the same neighbourhood as Garnic Hotel Berc. It's equally celebrated for its in-house restaurant.

Hotel Lovec (576 86 15; www.lovechotel.com; Ljubljanska c 6; s €110-151, d €128-225, ste from €245; 🏊 🖳 🍽) A new favourite, the Lovec has been completely overhauled and now boasts 60 of some of the most attractive rooms in Bled. We love the rooms with blonde-wood walls, red carpet and bath with jacuzzi in front of a massive window facing the lake.

Eating

Slaščičarna Šmon (☎ 574 16 16; Grajska c 3; ☯ 7.30am-10pm) Bled's sweet of choice is *kremna rezina* (cream cake; €2.20), a layer of vanilla custard topped with whipped cream and sandwiched neatly between two layers of flaky pastry.

Gostilna Pri Planincu (☎ 574 16 13; Grajska c 8; mains €5-20.50; ☯ 10am-10pm) 'At the Mountaineers' is a homey pub-restaurant just down the hill from the hostels, with Slovenian mains like sausage and *skutni štruklji* (cheese curd pastries) and grilled Balkan specialities such as *čevapčiči* (spicy meatballs of beef or pork; €7.40) and *pljeskavica z kajmakom* (Serbian-style meat patties with mascarpone-like cream cheese; €8.40).

Ostarija Peglez'n (☎ 574 42 18; C Svobode 19A; mains €8.50-22; ☯ 11am-midnight) The best restaurant in Bled, the 'Iron Inn' is just opposite the landmark Grand Hotel Toplice, with attractively retro decor and some of the best fish dishes in town.

Okarina (☎ 574 14 58; Ljubljanska c 8; mains €9.80-24.80; ☯ noon-midnight) This very upmarket restaurant has lots of colourful art spread over a modern dining room and serves both international favourites and decent Indian dishes like chicken *masala* and tandoori bass. There's a good choice of vegetarian options.

Pizzeria Rustika (☎ 576 89 00; Riklijeva c 13; pizza €5.70-9.50; ☯ noon-midnight Tue-Sun) A marble-roll down the hill from the hostels, this place has its own wood-burning oven and seating on two levels plus an outside terrace.

You'll find a **Mercator** (Ljubljanska c 4; ☯ 7am-8pm Mon-Sat, 8am-noon Sun) at the eastern end of Bled Shopping Centre. There's a smaller **Mercator branch** (Prešernova c 48; ☯ 7am-8pm Mon-Sat, 8am-4pm Sun) close to the hostels.

Getting There & Around

Frequent buses to Bohinj (€3.60, one hour, 26km, hourly), Ljubljana (€6.30, 1¼ hours, 57km, hourly) and Kranj (€3.60, 30 minutes, 23km, half-hourly) via Radovljica (€1.80, 15 minutes, 7.5km) leave from the central bus station.

Bled has no central train station. Trains to Bohinjska Bistrica (€1.50, 20 minutes, 18km, seven daily) and Nova Gorica (€5.35, two hours, 79km, seven daily) use little Bled Jezero train station, which is 2km west of central Bled – handy for the camping ground but little else. Trains for Ljubljana (€4.10 to €7.60, 45 minutes to one hour, 51km, up to 17 daily) use Lesce-Bled train station, 4km to the east of town.

Book a taxi on ☎ 031-705 343.

BOHINJ
☎ 04 / pop 5275

Lake Bohinj, a larger and much less-developed glacial lake 26km to the southwest, is a world apart from Bled. Mt Triglav is visible from the lake and there are activities galore – from kayaking and mountain biking to hiking up Triglav via one of the southern approaches.

Bohinjska Bistrica, the area's largest village, is 6km east of the lake and only interesting for its train station. The main tourist hub on the lake is **Ribčev Laz** at the eastern end. Its miniscule commercial centre contains a supermarket, a post office (which changes money), an ATM and the **Bohinj tourist office** (☎ 574 60 10; www.bohinj-info.com; Ribčev Laz 48; ☯ 8am-8pm Mon-Sat, to 6pm Sun Jul & Aug, 8am-6pm Mon-Sat, 9am-3pm Sun Sep-Jun), which can help with accommodation and sells **fishing licences** (€25 per day for the lake, €38.50 catch and release). Central **Alpinsport** (☎ 572 34 86; www.alpinsport.si; Ribčev Laz 53; ☯ 9am or 10am-6pm or 8pm) organises a range of activities, and hires out kayaks, canoes, mountain bikes (per hour/day €4/14) and other equipment from a kiosk near the stone bridge. Next door is the delightful **Church of St John the Baptist**, which contains splendid 15th- and 16th-century frescoes, but is undergoing a protracted renovation.

The nearby village of **Stara Fužina** has an appealing little **Alpine Dairy Museum** (☎ 041-564 904; Stara Fužine 181; adult/child €2.10/1.60; ☯ 11am-7pm Tue-Sun Jul & Aug, 10am-noon & 4-6pm Tue-Sun Jan-Jun, Sep & Oct). Just opposite is a cheesemonger called **Planšar** (☎ 572 30 95; Stara Fužina 179; ☯ 1am-7pm Tue-Sun Jul & Aug, 10am-noon & 4-6pm Tue-Sun Jan-Jun, Sep & Oct), which specialises in homemade dairy products such as hard Bohinj cheese, cottage cheese and curd pie. Just 2km east is **Studor**, a village famed for its *toplarji*, the double-linked hayrack with barns or storage areas at the top, some of which date from the 18th and 19th centuries.

From June to late September, the inventively named **Tourist Boat** (☎ 041-434 986; adult/child/family one-way €8.50/6/18, return €10/7/23; ☯ 10am-6pm) departs from the pier just opposite the Alpinsport kiosk every 30 to 40 minutes

HIKING MT TRIGLAV

The Julian Alps offer some of Europe's finest hiking. In summer some 170 mountain huts *(planinska koča* or *planinski dom)* operate, none more than five hours' walk from the next. These huts get very crowded, especially on weekends, so booking ahead is wise. If the weather turns bad, however, you won't be refused refuge.

At €27 per person in a room with up to four beds or €18 in a dormitory in a Category I hut (Category II huts charge €20 and €12 respectively), the huts aren't cheap, but as they serve meals (a simple meal should cost between €4.70 and €6.20 in a Category I hut, and €3.50 and €5 in a Category II hut) you can travel light. Sturdy boots and warm clothes are indispensable, even in midsummer. Trails are generally well marked with a white-centred red circle, but you can still get lost and it's very unwise to trek alone. It's best to engage the services of a qualified (and licensed) guide, who will cost from €50/150 per two-/eight-hour period.

The tourist offices in Bled (p890), Bohinj (opposite), Kranjska Gora (p894) and Bovec (p895) all have lots of hiking information, sell maps in a variety of scales and can help book huts and guides in their regions. You might also contact the Alpine Association of Slovenia (p906) directly.

(between four and six times a day at other times), terminating a half-hour later at the Ukanc jetty at the lake's far western end. Just 300m up from the Ukanc jetty and 5km west of Ribčev Laz, a **cable car** (☎ 572 97 12 adult/child one-way €8/6, return €12/8; 🕑 8am-6pm) whisks up half-hourly to 1540m; from here, paths continue up **Mt Vogel**.

In September, the **Cows' Ball** (www.bohinj.si) at Bohinj is a zany weekend of folk dance, music, eating and drinking to mark the return of the cows from their high pastures down to the valleys.

Sleeping & Eating

Private rooms (per person €10-15) and **apartments** (d €33-44, q €48.50-70) are available through the tourist office.

Autokamp Zlatorog (☎ 572 34 82; www.aaturizem.com; Ukanc 2; per person €7-12; 🕑 May-Sep) This pine-shaded 2.5-hectare camping ground accommodating 500 guests is at the lake's western end, 4.5km from Ribčev Laz.

Hostel Pod Voglom (☎ 572 34 61; www.hostel-podvoglom.com; Ribčev Laz 60; per person with shared bathroom €19-21, with private bathroom €22-24, dm €16-18; 💻) This welcome addition to Bohinj's budget accommodation scene some 3km west of the centre has 119 beds in 46 somewhat frayed rooms in two buildings. The so-called Hostel Building has doubles, triples and dormitory accommodation with shared facilities; rooms in the Rodica Annexe, with between one and four beds, are with en suite.

Penzion Gasperin (☎ 572 36 61; www.bohinj.si/gasperin; Ribčev Laz 36A; per person €22-33; ❄ 💻) This positively spotless chalet-style guest house with 20 rooms (nine of which are spanking new) is just 350m east of the tourist office and run by a friendly British/Slovenian couple. Some rooms (eg Nos 1, 2 and 3) have balconies.

Hotel Bellevue (☎ 572 33 31; www.hoteli-bohinj.si; Ribčev Laz 65; s €48-57, d €56-74; 💻) The shabby Bellevue has a beautiful (if somewhat isolated) and atmospheric location on a hill about 700m south of the lake. Whodunit fans take note: Agatha Christie stayed in room No 204 for three weeks in 1967. Thirty-eight of the hotel's 59 rooms are in the unattractive Savica Annexe.

Gostilna Rupa (☎ 572 34 01; Srednja Vas 87; mains €7-15; 🕑 10am-midnight Jul & Aug, 10am-midnight Tue-Sun Sep-Jun) If you're under your own steam, head for this country-style restaurants in the next village over from Studor and about 5km from Ribčev Laz. Among the excellent home-cooked dishes are *ajdova krapi*, crescent-shaped dumplings made from buckwheat and cheese, various types of local *klobasa* (sausage) and Bohinj trout.

Getting There & Around

Buses run regularly from Ukanc ('Bohinj Zlatorog' on most schedules) to Ljubljana (€8.70, two hours, 91km, hourly) via Ribčev Laz, Bohinjska Bistrica and Bled (€4.10, one hour, 34km), with six extra buses daily between Ukanc and Bohinjska Bistrica (€2.70 20 minutes, 12km). From Bohinjska Bistrica, passenger trains to Nova Gorica (€4.70, 1¼ hours, 61km, up to seven daily) make use of a century-old tunnel under the mountains that provides the only direct option for reaching the Soča Valley. In addition there are daily auto trains (*avtovlaki*) to Podbrdo (€7.50, eight minutes, 7km, five daily) and Most na Soči (€11.50, 25 minutes, 28km, three daily).

KRANJSKA GORA

☎ 04 / pop 1490

Nestling in the Sava Dolinka Valley, Kranjska Gora is Slovenia's largest and best-equipped ski resort. It's at its most perfect under a blanket of snow, but its surroundings are wonderful to explore at other times as well. There are endless possibilities for hiking and mountaineering in Triglav National Park, which is right on the town's doorstep to the south, and few travellers will be unimpressed by a trip over Vršič Pass (1611m), the gateway to the Soča Valley.

Kranjska Gora has lots of places offering ski tuition and hiring out equipment, including **ASK Kranjska Gora Ski School** (☎ 588 53 02; www.ask-kg.com; Borovška c 99A) in the same building as SKB Banka. Rent bikes from one of the **Sport Point** (☎ 588 48 83; www.sport-point.si; Borovška c 74; per hr/4hr/day €3.50/6.50/10; 9am-9pm) outlets. To watch the experts, the men's slalom and giant slalom **Vitranc Cup** (www.pokal-vitranc.com) is held in Kranjska Gora in late February and early March, and the **Ski-Jumping World Cup Championships** (www.planica.info) at nearby Planica (also in March).

Borovška c, 400m south of the bus stops, is the heart of the village, with the endearing **Liznjek House** (☎ 588 19 99; Borovška 63; adult/child €2.50/2; 10am-8pm Tue-Sat, 10am-5pm Sun May-Oct & Dec-Mar), an 18th-century museum house with a good collection of household objects and furnishings peculiar to Gorenjska province. At its western end is the **Tourist Information Centre Kranjska Gora** (☎ 580 94 40; www.kranjska-gora.si; Tičarjeva c 2; 8am-8pm Mon-Sat, 9am-6pm Sun Jun-Sep & mid-Dec–Mar, 8am-3pm Mon-Fri, 8am-4pm Sat, 9am-1pm Sun May, 8am-3pm Mon-Fri, 9am-4pm Sat Apr & Oct–mid-Dec).

Sleeping & Eating

Accommodation costs peak from December to March and in midsummer. **Private rooms** (per person €12-24) and **apartments** (d €34-50, q €68-108) can be arranged through the tourist office.

Hostel Pr' Tatko (☎ 031-479 087; Podkoren 72; www.prtatko.com; dm €13-17, q €56-76;) One of Slovenia's nicest small hostels is in Podkoren, just 3km to the northwest of Kranjska Gora. It's a four-room affair in a traditional old farmhouse, each with between four (one en suite) and eight beds. There's a decent-sized kitchen and common room. They'll teach you how to collect mushrooms in season.

Pension Borka (☎ 031-536 288; darinka2007@gmail.com; Borovška c 71; per person €20-30) Not a patch (operative word) on the Tatko but a lot more central, this very frayed property has some three-dozen rooms – mostly doubles and triples – crying out for a refit. There's a large cellar restaurant.

Hotel Kotnik (☎ 588 15 64; www.hotel-kotnik.si; Borovška c 75; s €50-59, d €60-78;) If you're not into big high-rise hotels with hundreds of rooms, choose this charming, bright yellow low-rise property. It has 15 cosy rooms, a great restaurant and pizzeria, and it couldn't be more central.

Gostilna Pri Martinu (☎ 582 03 00; Borovška c 61; mains €4-12.50; 10am-11pm) This atmospheric tavern-restaurant in an old house opposite the fire station is one of the best places in town to try local specialities, such as *telečja obara* (veal stew; €4) and *ričet* (barley stew with smoked pork ribs; €5.90).

Getting There & Away

Buses run hourly on the half-hour to Ljubljana (€8.70, two hours, 91km) via Jesenice (€3.10, 30 minutes, 23km), where you should change for Bled (€2.70, 20 minutes, 16km). There's just one direct departure to Bled (€5.20, one hour, 40km) on weekdays at 9.05am. A service to Bovec (€6.70, two hours, 46km) via Vršič Pass departs five times daily (six on Sunday) in July and August, and on Saturday and Sunday at 8.27am in June and September.

SOČA VALLEY

The Soča Valley region is defined by the 96km-long Soča River coloured a deep, almost artificial turquoise. The valley has more than its share of historical sights, most of them related to one of the costliest battles of WWI, but the majority of visitors are here for rafting, hiking, skiing and other active sports.

Bovec

☎ 05 / pop 1760

Effectively the capital of the Soča Valley, Bovec has a great deal to offer adventure-sports enthusiasts. With the Julian Alps above, the Soča River below and Triglav National Park all around, you could spend a week here hiking, kayaking, mountain biking and, in winter, skiing at Mt Kanin (2587m), Slovenia's highest ski station, without ever doing the same thing twice.

The compact village square, **Trg Golobarskih Žrtev**, has everything you'll need. There are cafes, a hotel, the helpful **Tourist Information Centre Bovec** (☎ 389 64 44; www.bovec.si; Trg Golobarskih Žrtev; ⏲ 8.30am-8.30pm Jul & Aug, 9am-5pm Mon-Fri, 9am-noon & 4-6pm Sat, 9am-noon Sun Sep-Jun) and a half-dozen adrenalin-raising adventure-sports companies.

ACTIVITIES
There's no shortage of activities on offer in and around Bovec. Possibilities include **canyoning** (€43 to €45 for two hours) at Sušec, or **caving** (€35 per person with guide). Or you could try your hand at **hydrospeed** (like riding down a river on a boogie board); you'll pay €45 to €55 for a 6km to 8km ride. A guided 10km **kayaking** tour costs from €39.50 to €41.50 per person, or a one-day training course from €45 to €53.50.

From April to October, you can go **rafting** (€35/45 for a 10/20km trip). And in winter you can take a tandem paraglider flight (ie as a passenger accompanied by a qualified pilot) from atop the Kanin cable car, 2000m above the valley floor. A flight costs from €110; ask Avantura for details.

Recommended operators:

Avantura (☎ 041-718 317; www.avantura.org)
Bovec Rafting Team (☎ 388 61 28, 041-338 308; www.bovec-rafting-team.com)
Outdoor Freaks (☎ 389 64 90, 041-553 675; www.outdoorfreaks.si)
Soča Rafting (☎ 389 62 00, 041-724 472; www.soca-rafting.si)
Sport Mix (☎ 389 61 60, 031-871 991; www.sportmix.traftbovec.si)
Top Extreme (☎ 041-620 636; www.top.si)

SLEEPING & EATING
Alp Hotel (☎ 388 40 00; www.alp-chandler.si; Trg Golobarskih Žrtev 48; s €48-60, d €66-90; 🖥 🏊) This 103-room hotel is fairly good value and as central as you are going to find in Bovec. Guests get to use the swimming pool at the nearby Hotel Kanin.

Dobra Vila (☎ 389 64 00; www.dobra-vila-bovec.com; Mala Vas 112; s €58-105, d €88-135; 🖥) This positive stunner of a 12-room boutique hotel is housed in an erstwhile telephone-exchange building. It has its own small cinema, library, restaurant and wine cellar.

Martinov Hram (☎ 388 62 14; Trg Golobarskih Žrtev 27; mains €6.90-19.50; ⏲ 10am-10pm Tue-Thu, to midnight

Fri & Sat) Traditional restaurant in an attractive inn specialising in game, Soča trout and mushroom dishes. During the winter, pizza rears its ugly head.

Private rooms (per person €15-30) are easy to come by in Bovec through the TIC.

Camping facilities are generally better in Kobarid (p896), but **Kamp Polovnik** (☎ 388 60 69; www.kamp-polovnik.com; Ledina 8; adult €5-7, child €3.75-5.25; ⏲ Apr–mid-Oct) about 500m southeast of the town centre is much more convenient.

GETTING THERE & AWAY
Buses to Nova Gorica (€7.50, two hours, 77km, up to five a day) go via Kobarid (€3.10, half-hour, 21km). A service to Kranjska Gora (€6.70, two hours, 46km) via the spectacular Vršič Pass departs five times daily (six on Sunday) in July and August, and on Saturday and Sunday at 3.35pm in June and September.

Kobarid
☎ 05 / pop 1235
Some 21km south of Bovec, quaint Kobarid (Caporetto in Italian) lies in a broad valley on the west bank of the Soča River. Although it's surrounded by mountain peaks higher than 2200m, Kobarid somehow feels more Mediterranean than alpine. The Italian border is just 9km to the west.

The **Tourist Information Centre Kobarid** (☎ 380 04 90; www.lto-sotocje.si; Gregorčičeva ul 8; ⏲ 9am-8pm Jul & Aug, 9am-12.30pm & 1.30-7pm Mon-Fri, 9am-1pm Sat Sep-Jun) is next door to the award-winning **Kobarid Museum** (☎ 389 00 00; Gregorčičeva ul 10; adult/student/child €4/3/2.50; ⏲ 9am-6pm Mon-Fri, 9am-7pm Sat & Sun Apr-Sep, 10am-5pm Mon-Fri, 9am-6pm Sat & Sun Oct-Mar), devoted almost entirely to the Isonzo (Soča) Front of WWI, which formed the backdrop to Ernest Hemingway's *A Farewell to Arms*. A free pamphlet and map titled *The Kobarid Historical Trail* outlines a 5km-long route that will take you past remnant WWI troop emplacements to the impressive **Kozjak Stream Waterfalls**. More ambitious is the hike outlined in the *Pot Miru/Walk of Peace* brochure.

Kobarid is beginning to give Bovec a run for its money in extreme sports, and you'll find several outfits on or off the town's main square that can organise rafting, canyoning, canoeing and paragliding from April to October. They include the long-established

XPoint (☎ 388 53 08, 041-692 290; www.xpoint.si; Trg Svobode 6); the new and enthusiastic **Positive Sport** (☎ 040-654 475; www.positive-sport.com; Markova ul 2); and Apartma-Ra, which also organises two-hour quad-bike trips for €45.

The oldest (and, some would say, friendliest) camping ground in the valley, **Kamp Koren** (☎ 389 13 11; www.kamp-koren.si; Drežniške Ravne 33; per person €8.50-10; mid-Mar–Oct;) is a small site about 500m northeast of Kobarid on the left bank of the Soča River and just beyond the Napoleon Bridge, built in 1750.

The welcoming little **Apartma-Ra** (☎ 041-641 899; apartma-ra@siol.net; Gregorčičeva ul 6C; per person €15-25;) lies between the museum and Trg Svobode and has five rooms and apartments, some with terraces. The best place in town is the **Hotel Hvala** (☎ 389 93 00; wwww.hotelhvala.si; Trg Svobode 1; s €59-72, d €82-108;), which has 31 rooms – some recently renovated to a level unseen in provincial Slovenia – linked by a snazzy new lift, a bar, a superb Restavracija Topli Val restaurant and a Mediterranean-style cafe in the garden.

In the centre of Kobarid you'll find two of Slovenia's best restaurants, both of which specialise in fish and seafood: the incomparable **Restavracija Topli Val** (☎ 389 93 00; Trg Svobode 1; mains €9.50-25; noon-10pm) and **Restavracija Kotlar** (☎ 389 11 10; Trg Svobode 11; mains €8.50-20; noon-11pm Thu, Sun & Mon, to midnight Fri & Sat).

Buses, which arrive at and depart from in front of the Cinca Marinca bar on Trg Svobode, link Kobarid with Nova Gorica (€6, 1½ hours, 55km, up to five daily) and Ljubljana (€11.50, three hours, 130km, up to four daily) passing Most na Soči train station, which is good for Bled and Bohinj. Buses that cross over the spectacular Vršič Pass to Kranjska Gora (€7.85, three hours, 68km) depart three times a day in July and August.

Nova Gorica
☎ 05 / pop 12,585

When the town of Gorica, capital of the former Slovenian province of Goriška, was awarded to the Italians after WWII, the new socialist government in Yugoslavia set itself to building a model town on the eastern side of the border. They called it 'New Gorica' and erected a chain-link barrier between the two towns. This rather flimsy 'Berlin Wall' was pulled down to great fanfare in 2004, leaving Piazza della Transalpina (or Trg z Mozaikom on this side) straddling the border right behind Nova

Gorica's train station. There you'll now find the esoteric **Museum of the Border in Gorica 1945–2004** (☎ 333 44 00; admission free; 1-5pm Mon-Fri, 9am-7pm Sat, 10am-7pm Sun). Nova Gorica is an easy way to get to/from Italy; Italian bus 1 (€0.98) will whisk you from Via G Caprin opposite the museum to Gorizia train station.

The helpful **Tourist Information Centre Nova Gorica** (☎ 330 46 00; www.novagorica-turizem.com; Bevkov trg 4; 8am-8pm Mon-Fri, 9am-1pm Sat & Sun Jul & Aug, 8am-6pm Mon-Fri, 9am-1pm Sat Sep-Jun) is in the lobby of the Kulturni Dom (Cultural House).

One of the few inexpensive accommodation options, **Prenočišče Pertout** (☎ 330 75 50, 041-624 452; www.prenociscepertout.com; Ul 25 Maja 23; s/d/tr €24/34/51) is a five-room B&B in Rožna Dolina, south of the town centre and scarcely 100m northeast of the Italian border. The Italian restaurant **Marco Polo** (☎ 302 97 29; Kidričeva ul 13; mains €8-17; 11am-11pm Mon-Thu, 11am-midnight Fri & Sat, noon-midnight Sun), with a delightful back terrace 250m east of the tourist office, is one of the town's best places to eat, serving pizza (€4.40 to €7.80), pasta (€5.50 to €10) and more ambitious dishes.

Buses travel hourly between Nova Gorica and Ljubljana (€10.70 2½ hours, 116km) via Postojna (€6.30, one hour, 53km), and up to five times daily to Bovec (€7.50, two hours, 77km) via Kobarid (€6, 1½ hours, 55km).

Trains link Nova Gorica with Bohinjska Bistrica (€4.70, 1¼ hours, 61km, up to seven daily), a springboard for Bled, with Postojna (€5.65, two hours, 61km, six daily) via Sežana and Divača, and with Ljubljana (€7.75, 3½ hours, 153km, five daily) via Jesenice.

KARST & COAST

Slovenia's short coast (47km) is an area of both history and recreation. Three important towns full of Venetian Gothic architecture – Koper, Izola and Piran – are the main drawcards here and the southernmost resort of Portorož has some decent beaches. En route from Ljubljana or the Soča Valley, you'll cross the Karst, a huge limestone plateau and a land of olives, ruby-red Teran wine, *pršut* (air-dried ham), old stone churches and deep subterranean caves. In fact, Slovenia's two most famous caverns – Postojna and Škocjan – are here.

POSTOJNA
☎ 05 / pop 8850

Slovenia's single most popular tourist attraction, **Postojna Cave** (☎ 700 01 00; www.postojnska-jama.si;

Jamska c 30; adult/student/child €20/16/13; ☻ tours hourly 9am-6pm Jul & Aug, to 5pm May, Jun & Sep, 10am, noon, 2pm & 4pm Apr & Oct, 10am, noon & 3pm Nov-Mar) is about 2km northwest of the town of that name. The 5.7km-long cavern is visited on a 1½-hour tour, but about 4km of it is covered by an electric train and the rest on foot. Inside, impressive stalagmites and stalactites stretch almost endlessly in all directions, as do the chattering crowds who pass them.

Close to the cave's entrance is the **Proteus Vivarium** (adult/student/child €7/6/4, with cave €24/19/14; ☻ 9.30am-5.30pm May-Sep, 10.30am-3.30pm Oct-Apr), a speliobiological research station with a video introduction to underground zoology. A 45-minute tour then leads you into a small, darkened cave to peep at some of the endemic *Proteus anguinus*, shy (and miniscule) creatures you've just learned about in the Postojna Cave.

Predjama (population 85), a village 9km northwest of Postojna, can claim the remarkable **Predjama Castle** (☎ 751 60 15; Predjama 1; www .turizem-kras.si; adult/student/child €8/7/5; ☻ 9am-7pm Jul & Aug, to 6pm May, Jun & Sep, 10am-5pm Apr & Oct, to 4pm Nov-Mar), which appears to grow out of a yawning cave. The partly furnished interior spread over four floors boasts costumed wax mannequins, one of which dangles from the dripping rock-roofed torture chamber. Beneath are stalactite-adorned **caves** (adult/student/child €7/6/4, cave & castle combination ticket €13/11/8; ☻ tours 11am, 1pm, 3pm & 5pm May-Sep), which lack Postojna's crowds but also much of its grandeur; tours last an hour.

Sleeping & Eating

Kompas Postojna (☎ 721 14 80; www.kompas-postojna .si; Titov trg 2A; r per person €18-20; ☻ 8am-7pm Mon-Fri, 9am-1pm Sat Jun-Aug, 8am-6pm Mon-Fri, 9am-1pm Sat May, Sep & Oct, 8am-5pm Mon-Fri, 9am-1pm Sat Nov-Apr) Has private rooms.

Hotel Sport (☎ 720 22 44; www.sport-hotel.si; Kolodvorska c 1; dm €20, s €55-65, d €70-90, tr €96-125, q €120-160; ▣) A much more expensive proposition than when it opened a few short years ago, the Sport still offers reasonable value for money, with 32 spick-and-span and very comfortable rooms, including 40 hostel beds. It's just 300m north of the centre of Postojna. It rents mountain bikes (half-/full day €9/15) for exploring nearby Notranjska Regional Park.

Pizzeria Minutka (☎ 720 36 25; Ljubljanska c 14; pizza €4.90-7.10; ☻ noon-11pm) A pizzeria with a terrace, Minutka is a favourite with locals and is just south of the Hotel Sport.

Getting There & Away

Buses from Ljubljana to Koper, Piran and Nova Gorica all stop in Postojna (€6, one hour, 54km, half-hourly). The train is less useful, as the station is 1km east of town (ie almost 3km from the caves).

As close as you'll get by local bus from Postojna to Predjama (€2.30, 15 minutes, 9km, five daily Monday to Friday) and during the school year only is Bukovje, a village about 2km northeast of Predjama. A taxi from Postojna, including an hour's wait at Predjama Castle, will cost €30, which staff at Kompas Postojna can organise.

ŠKOCJAN CAVES
☎ 05

The immense system of **Škocjan Caves** (☎ 708 21 00; www.park-skocjanske-jame.si; Škocjan 2; adult/ student/child €14/10/6), a Unesco World Heritage site since 1986, is far more captivating than the larger one at Postojna, and for many travellers a visit here will be a highlight of their trip to Slovenia. With relatively few stalactites, the attraction is the sheer depth of the awesome underground chasm, which you cross by a dizzying little footbridge. To see this you must join a shepherded walking tour, lasting 1½ to two hours and involving hundreds of steps and a funicular ride at the end. Tours depart hourly from 10am to 5pm from June to September, at 10am, 1pm and 3.30pm in April, May and October, and at 10am and 1pm Monday to Saturday, and 10am, 1pm and 3pm Sunday from November to March.

The nearest town with accommodation is **Divača** (population 1330), 5km to the northwest. **Gostilna Malovec** (☎ 763 12 25; Kraška 30a; per person €20) has a half-dozen basic but renovated rooms in a building beside its traditional **restaurant** (mains €5-15; ☻ 8am to 10pm). For something a bit more, well, 21st century, cross the road to **Orient Express** (☎ 763 30 10; Kraška c 67; pizza €4.60-14; ☻ 11am-11pm Sun-Fri, 11am-2am Sat), a lively pizzeria and pub.

Bus services running from Ljubljana to Koper and the coast stop at Divača (€8, 1½ hours, 82km, half-hourly), as do trains (€6.25, 1½ hours, 104km, hourly). Staff at the train station ticket office can provide you with a photocopied route map for walking to the caves and there is a copy posted outside. Alternatively, a courtesy van meets incoming trains at 10am, 11.04am, 2pm and 3.35pm and will transport those with bus or train tickets to the caves.

LIPICA

☎ 05 / pop 95

Lipica is where Austrian Archduke Charles, son of Ferdinand I, established a stud farm to breed horses for the Spanish Riding School in Vienna in 1580. The snow-white beauties are still born and raised at the **Lipica Stud Farm** (☎ 739 15 80; www.lipica.org; Lipica 5; adult/student & child from €9/4.50), which offers equestrian fans a variety of tours, as well as riding and lessons. Tour times are complex; see the website for details.

Good value is the 80-room **Hotel Klub** (☎ 739 15 70; s/d €32/49; 🖳) near the stud farm with a sauna and fitness centre. The nearby **Hotel Maestoso** (☎ 739 15 80; s/d €80/120; 🖳 🖳) has 66 more modern rooms.

A van meets incoming trains at Divača, 9km to the northeast, at 10.19am, 11.24am, 2.24pm and 3.59pm and transports ticket holders to the stud farm.

KOPER

☎ 05 / pop 24,630

Coastal Slovenia's largest town, Koper (Capodistria in Italian and Aegida to the Greeks) at first glance appears to be a workaday city that scarcely gives tourism a second thought. Yet its central core is delightfully medieval and far less overrun than its ritzy cousin Piran, 17km down the coast. Koper grew rich as a key port trading salt, and was the capital of Istria under the Venetian Republic during the 15th and 16th centuries. It remains Slovenia's most important port.

Orientation

The joint bus and train station is about 1.5km southeast of central Titov trg. To walk into town, just head north along Kolodvorska c in the direction of the cathedral's distinctive campanile (bell tower). Alternatively, take bus 1 or 2 to Muda Gate.

Information

Banka Koper (Kidričeva ul 14; 🕑 8.30am-noon & 3-5pm Mon-Fri, 8.30am-noon Sat)
Kompas (☎ 663 05 81; Pristaniška ul 17; 🕑 8am-7pm Mon-Fri, 8am-1pm Sat) Private rooms.
Palma Travel Agency (☎ 663 36 60; Pristaniška ul 21; 🕑 8am-7pm Mon-Fri, 9am-noon Sat) Private rooms.
Pina (☎ 627 80 72; Kidričeva ul 43; adult/student per hr

€4.20/1.20; 🕑 4-10pm) Central internet cafe with 10 terminals.
Post office (Muzejski trg 3; 🕑 8am-7pm Mon-Fri)
Tourist Information Centre Koper (☎ 664 64 03; www.koper.si; Praetorian Palace, Titov trg 3; 🕑 9am-9pm Jul & Aug, 9am-5pm Mon-Fri, to 7pm Sat & Sun Sep-Jun)

Sights

You'll change centuries abruptly as you pass through **Muda Gate** (1516) leading into Prešernov trg. Continue north past the bridge-shaped **Da Ponte Fountain** (1666), and up Župančičeva ul and Čevljarska ul, the narrow commercial artery, to reach **Titov trg**. This fine central square is dominated by the 15th-century **City Tower** (adult/child €2/1.50; 🕑 9am-2pm & 4-9pm), which can be climbed, attached to the part-Gothic, part-Renaissance **Cathedral of the Assumption**. The Venetian Gothic and Renaissance **Praetorian Palace** (Titov trg 3; admission free) contains the town hall, with an old pharmacy and the tourist office on the ground floor and a ceremonial hall with exhibits on the 1st floor. Opposite, the splendid 1463 **Loggia** is now an elegant cafe (p900) and gallery. To the east of it is the circular Romanesque **Rotunda of St John the Baptist**, a baptistery dating from the second half of the 12th century.

The **Koper Regional Museum** (☎ 663 35 70; Kidričeva ul 19; adult/child €2.50/1.50; 🕑 9am-1pm & 6-9pm Tue-Sun Jul & Aug, 10am-6pm Tue-Fri, 9am-1pm Sat & Sun Sep-Jun), inside the Belgramoni-Tacco Palace, contains an Italianate sculpture garden. Kidričeva ul also has a few multicoloured **medieval houses** with beamed overhangs. It leads west into Carpacciov trg, the former fish market with a 15th-century **salt warehouse** and the stone **Column of St Justina** dating from 1571.

Sleeping

Both Kompas (left) and the Palma Travel Agency (left) can arrange **private rooms** (per person r €20-31) and **apartments** (2-person €32-40, 4-person €56-70), most of which are in the new town beyond the train station.

Motel Port (☎ 639 32 60; www.port-turizem.si; Ankaranska c 7; dm €15-17, s €29-40, d €43-48, tr €54-60; 🗷 🖳) Hidden on the 2nd floor of a shopping centre southeast of the Old Town, this place has 30 rooms, some of them en suite and air-conditioned and others dorm rooms with four to six beds. There's a breezy cafe-bar here as well.

Museum Hostel (☎ 626 18 70, 041-504 466; bozic .doris@siol.net; Muzejski trg 6; per person €20-25) This

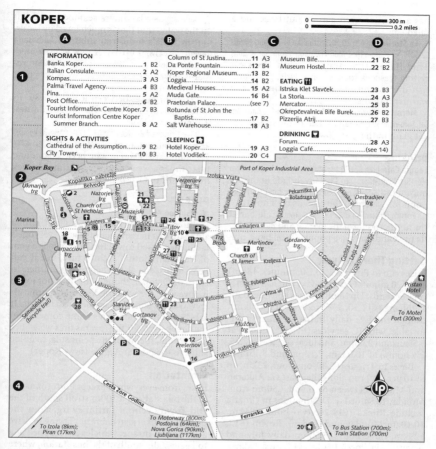

KOPER

---

good-value place is more a series of bright apartments with modern kitchens and bathrooms than a hostel. Reception is at the little Museum Bife, a cafe-bar on Muzejski trg; the rooms are actually at Mladinska ul 7.

Hotel Vodišek (☎ 639 24 68; www.hotel-vodisek.com; Kolodvorska c 2; s €45-60, d €68-90, tr €83-110; 🅿 🖵) This hotel, with 32 small but reasonably priced rooms, is in a shopping centre halfway between the Old Town and the train and bus stations. Guests get to use the hotel's bicycles for free.

Hotel Koper (☎ 610 05 00; www.terme-catez.si; Pristaniška ul 3; s €76, d €120; 🅿 🖵) This pleasant, 65-room property on the very edge of the historic Old Town is the only central hotel in Koper.

Eating

Okrepčevalnica Bife Burek (☎ 271 347; Kidričeva ul 8; snacks €1.70-2.50; ⏰ 7am-10pm) Buy good-value *burek* here and enjoy it at Titov trg for a take-away snack.

Istrska Klet Slavček (☎ 627 67 29; Župančičeva ul 39; dishes €2.50-14; ⏰ 7am-10pm Mon-Fri) This 'Istrian Cellar', situated below the 18th-century Carli Palace, is one of the most colourful places for a meal in Koper's Old Town. Filling set lunches go for less than €7, and there's local Malvazija and Teran wine from the barrel.

Pizzerija Atrij (☎ 627 22 55; Triglavska ul 2; pizza €3-6.70; ⏰ 9am-10pm Mon-Fri, 10am-10pm Sat) This popular pizzeria down an alleyway no wider than your average quarterback's shoulder spread has a small covered garden out back and a salad bar.

La Storia (☎ 626 20 18; Pristaniška ul 3; mains €9.90-22.50; ⌚ 11am-11pm Mon-Fri, noon-11pm Sat & Sun) This Italian-style trattoria with sky-view ceiling frescoes focuses on salads, pasta and fish dishes and has outside seating in the warmer months.

Mercator (Titov trg 2; ⌚ 7am-8pm Mon-Fri, 7am-1pm Sat, 8am-noon Sun) Small branch of the supermarket giant in the Old Town.

Drinking

Loggia Café (☎ 621 32 13; Titov trg 1; ⌚ 7.30am-10pm Mon-Sat, 10am-10pm Sun) This lovely cafe in the exquisite 15th-century Loggia is the best vantage point for watching the crowds on Titov trg.

Forum (Pristaniška ul 2; ⌚ 7am-11pm) Cafe-bar at the northern side of the market and facing a little park and the sea; a popular local hang-out.

Getting There & Away

Buses run to Piran (€3.10, 30 minutes, 18km) every 20 minutes on weekdays and half-hourly on weekends. Up to nine buses daily head for Ljubljana (€11.10, 1¾ to 2½ hours, 120km), though the five daily trains are more comfortable, with IC services (€13, 2¼ hours) at 5.55am and 2.45pm, and local services (€7.75, 2½ hours) at 10.03am, 7.12pm and 8.13pm.

Buses to Trieste (€2.80, one hour, 23km, up to 10 per day) run along the coast via Ankaran and Muggia between 6am and 7.30pm from Monday to Saturday. Destinations in Croatia include Rijeka (€11.20, two hours, 84km, 10.10am Monday and Friday), Rovinj (€12, 129km, three hours, 3.50pm daily July and August) via Poreč (€10, two hours, 88km), plus three more to Poreč only at 7.30am, 2pm and 3.55pm Monday to Friday.

IZOLA

☎ 05 / pop 11,270

Overshadowed by more genteel Piran, Izola (Isola in Italian) has a certain Venetian charm, narrow old streets, and nice waterfront bars and restaurants. Ask the helpful **Tourist Information Centre Izola** (☎ 640 10 50; www.izola.eu; Sončno nabrežje 4; ⌚ 9am-9pm Mon-Sat, 10am-5pm Sun Jun-Sep, 9am-5pm Mon-Fri, 10am-5pm Sat Oct-May) about **private rooms** (s €18-26, d €26-36) or, in July and August, check out the 174-bed **Riviera** (☎ 662 1740; branko.miklobusec@guest.arnes.si; Prekomorskih Brigad ul 7; dm €24), a student dormitory overlooking the marina. **Ribič** (☎ 641 83 13; Veliki trg 3; mains €8-18; ⌚ 8am-1am) is a landmark seafood restaurant on the waterfront that is much loved by locals. Out in Izola's industrial suburbs, **Ambasada Gavioli** (☎ 641 8212, 041-353 722; www.ambasada-gavioli.com; Industrijska c; ⌚ 8pm or 11pm-6am Fri & Sat) remains Slovenia's top club, showcasing a procession of international and local DJs.

Frequent buses between Koper (€1.80, 15 minutes, 6km) and Piran (€2.30, 20 minutes, 9.5km) go via Izola.

The **Prince of Venice** (☎ 05-617 80 00; www.kompas-online.net) catamaran serves Venice (€47 to €70, 2½ hours) at 7.30am or 8am between one and three times a week, and several times a week from April to October.

PIRAN

☎ 05 / pop 4430

Picturesque Piran (Pirano in Italian), sitting at the tip of a narrow peninsula, is everyone's favourite coastal town. Its Old Town is a gem of Venetian Gothic architecture, but it can be a mob scene at the height of summer. In April or October, though, it's hard not to fall in love with the winding Venetian Gothic alleyways and tempting seafood restaurants. It is believed that the town's name comes from the Greek word for fire *(pyr)* as fires were once lit at Punta, the tip of the peninsula, to guide ships to the port at Aegida (now Koper).

Orientation

Buses from everywhere except Portorož arrive at the bus station, a 300m stroll south of the Old Town's central Tartinijev trg, along the portside Cankarjevo nabrežje. Trying to drive a car here is insane; vehicles are stopped at a toll gate 200m south of the bus station, where the sensible choice is to use the huge Fornače car park (per hour/day €1/10) and ride the very frequent shuttle bus into town.

Information

Banka Koper (Tartinijev trg 12; ⌚ 8.30am-noon & 3-5pm Mon-Fri, 8.30am-noon Sat)

Caffe Neptun (☎ 041-724 237; www.caffeneptun.com; Dantejeva ul 4; per 15min €1; ⌚ 7am-1am Mon-Sat, 8am-10pm Sub) Modern cafe near bus station with internet access.

Maona Tourist Agency (☎ 673 45 20; www.maona.si; Cankarjevo nabrežje 7; ⌚ 9am-8pm Mon-Sat, 10am-1pm & 5-7pm Sun) Rents private rooms and bikes, organises activities and cruises.

Post office (Cankarjevo nabrežje; ⌚ 8am-7pm Mon-Fri, 8am-noon Sat)

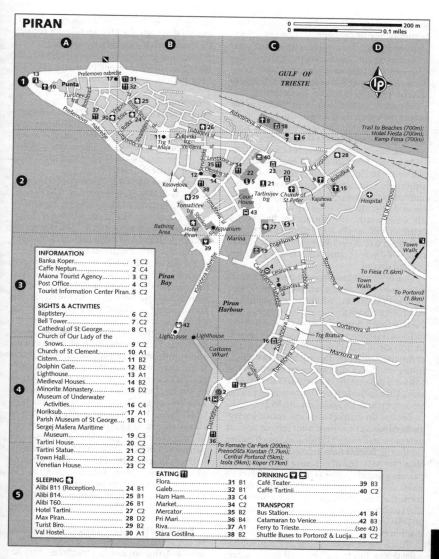

PIRAN

GULF OF TRIESTE

Trail to Beaches (700m);
Hotel Fiesta (700m);
Kamp Fiesa (700m)

Punta

Piran Bay

Piran Harbour

To Fiesa (1.6km)
Town Walls
To Portorož (1.8km)

Lighthouse

Customs Wharf

To Fornače Car Park (200m);
Prenočišča Korotan (1.7km);
Central Portorož (5km);
Izola (9km); Koper (17km)

INFORMATION
Banka Koper	1 C2
Caffe Neptun	2 C4
Maona Tourist Agency	3 C3
Post Office	4 C3
Tourist Information Center Piran	5 C2

SIGHTS & ACTIVITIES
Baptistery	6 C2
Bell Tower	7 C2
Cathedral of St George	8 C1
Church of Our Lady of the Snows	9 C2
Church of St Clement	10 A1
Cistern	11 B2
Dolphin Gate	12 B2
Lighthouse	13 A1
Medieval Houses	14 B2
Minorite Monastery	15 D2
Museum of Underwater Activities	16 C4
Noriksub	17 A1
Parish Museum of St George	18 C1
Sergej Mašera Maritime Museum	19 C3
Tartini House	20 C2
Tartini Statue	21 C2
Town Hall	22 C2
Venetian House	23 C2

SLEEPING
Alibi B11 (Reception)	24 B1
Alibi B14	25 B1
Alibi T60	26 B1
Hotel Tartini	27 C2
Max Piran	28 D2
Turist Biro	29 B2
Val Hostel	30 A1

EATING
Flora	31 B1
Galeb	32 B1
Ham Ham	33 C4
Market	34 C2
Mercator	35 B2
Pri Mari	36 B4
Riva	37 A1
Stara Gostilna	38 B2

DRINKING
Café Teater	39 B3
Caffe Tartinii	40 C2

TRANSPORT
Bus Station	41 B4
Catamaran to Venice	42 B3
Ferry to Trieste	(see 42)
Shuttle Buses to Portorož & Lucija	43 C2

Tourist Information Center Piran (☎ 673 44 40; www.portoroz.si; Tartinijev trg 2; ⏰ 9am-7pm Jul-Sep, 9am-5pm Oct-Jun) In the impressive town hall.

Sights & Activities
Piran is watched over by the **Cathedral of St George** (Adamičeva ul 2) dating from the 16th and 17th centuries. If time weighs heavily on your hands, visit the attached **Parish Museum of St George** (☎ 673 34 40; admission €1; ⏰ 10am-1pm & 3-5pm Mon & Wed-Fri, 10am-6pm Sat & Sun), which contains church plate, paintings and a lapidary. The cathedral's free-standing **bell tower** (admission €2; ⏰ 10am-1pm & 6-9pm) dates back to 1608 and can be climbed. It was clearly modelled on the campanile at San Marco's Basilica in

Venice, and its octagonal mid-17th-century **baptistery** has imaginatively recycled a 2nd-century Roman sarcophagus as a baptismal font. To the east runs a 200m stretch of the 15th-century **town walls** complete with loopholes. The **Minorite Monastery** (☎ 673 44 17; Bolniška ul 30) on the way down to Tartinijev trg has a delightful cloister, and in the **Church of Our Lady of the Snows** almost opposite is a superb 15th-century arch painting of the Crucifixion. The **Sergej Mašera Maritime Museum** (☎ 671 00 40; Cankarjevo nabrežje 3; adult/student/child €/3.50/2.50/2.10; ☽ 9am-noon & 6-9pm Tue-Sun Jul & Aug, 9am-noon & 3-6pm Tue-Sun Sep-Jun) has 2000-year-old Roman amphorae beneath the glass ground floor, and lots of impressive antique ships' models and ex-voto offerings upstairs. A short distance south, the **Museum of Underwater Activities** (☎ 041-685 379; Župančičeva ul 24; adult/student/child €/3/2/2; ☽ 9.30am-10pm Jun-Sep) makes much of Piran's close association with the sea and diving.

One of Piran's most eye-catching structures is the red 15th-century **Venetian House** (Tartinijev trg 4), with its tracery windows and stone lion relief. When built this would have overlooked Piran's inner port, which was filled in 1894 to form Tartinijev trg. The square is named in honour of the 18th-century violinist and composer Giuseppe Tartini; his **statue** stands in the middle of the square and **Tartini House** (☎ 663 35 70; Kajuhova ul 12; adult/child €1.50/1; ☽ 9am-noon & 6-9pm Tue-Sun Jul & Aug, 11am-noon & 5-6pm Tue-Sun Sep-Jun) is where he was born in 1692.

Behind the market north of Tartinijev trg, **medieval houses** have been built into an ancient defensive wall along Obzidna ul, which passes under the **Dolphin Gate** erected in 1483. **Trg 1 Maja** (1st May Sq) may sound like a socialist parade ground, but in fact it's one of Piran's most attractive squares, with a **cistern** dating from the late 18th century. Rainwater from the surrounding roofs flow into it through at least one of the fish borne by the stone putti in back.

Punta, the historical 'snout' of Piran, still has a **lighthouse**, but today's is small and modern. Attached to it, the round, serrated tower of 18th-century **Church of St Clement** evokes the ancient beacon from which Piran got its name.

Most water-related activities take place in Portorož, but if you want to give diving a go, **Noriksub** (☎ 673 22 18, 041-746 153; www.skupina noriksub.si; Prešernovo nabrežje 24; shore/boat dive €30/40; ☽ 9am-noon & 1-6pm Tue-Sun Jun–mid-Sep, 10am-4pm

Sat & Sun mid-Sep–May) organises shore and boat-guided dives, gives PADI open-water courses (beginners €240) and hires equipment.

The Maona Tourist Agency (p900) rents **bikes** for €6/9/15/20 per two-/five-/10-/24-hour period.

Sleeping

Private rooms (s €16-30, d €23-42, tr €32-55) and **apartments** (d €38-50, q €60-84) are available through the Maona Tourist Agency (p900) and the central **Turist Biro** (☎ 673 25 09; www.turistbiro-ag.si; Tomažičeva ul 3; ☽ 9am-1pm & 4-7pm Mon-Sat, 10am-1pm & 4-6pm Sun), opposite the Hotel Piran.

Kamp Fiesa (☎ 674 62 30; autocamp.fiesa@siol.net; adult €8.50-10, child €3.25; ☽ May-Sep) The closest camping ground to Piran is at Fiesa, 4km by road but less than 1km if you follow the coastal trail (*obalna pešpot*) east from the Cathedral of St George. It's tiny and becomes very crowded in summer, but is right on the beach.

Val Hostel (☎ 673 25 55; www.hostel-val.com; Gregorčičeva ul 38A; per person €22-25; ⌨) This central, partially renovated hostel has 22 rooms, with two to four beds, shared shower, kitchen and washing machine. It's a great favourite with backpackers.

Alibi B11 (☎ 673 01 41; 031-363 666; www.alibi.si; Bonifacijeva ul 11; per person €20-22; ⌨) The newest addition to the ever-expanding Alibi stable is not their nicest property but has mostly doubles in eight rooms over four floors in an ancient (and rather frayed) townhouse on a narrow street. Reception for all three hostels is here. Diagonally opposite is Alibi B14 (Bonifacijeva ul 14), an upbeat and colourful four-floor party place with six rooms (per person €20 to €22), each with two to six beds, bath and kitchenette. There's also a washing machine here. More subdued is Alibi T60 (Trubarjeva ul 60; per person €25 to €27.50) to the east with a fully equipped double on each of five floors. The view terrace of the top room is priceless.

Hotel Fiesa (☎ 671 22 00; www.hotelfiesa.com; Fiesa 57; park view d €58-78, tr €68-85, d sea view €69-98, tr €82-110) Although not in Piran itself, this 22-room pink-coloured hotel overlooking the sea near the Kamp Fiesa camping ground is one of the most atmospheric places to stay in the area.

Max Piran (☎ 673 34 36, 041-692 928; www.maxpiran .com; Ul IX Korpusa 26; s €35-40, d €60-70; ⌨) Piran's most romantic accommodation option has just six rooms – each bearing a woman's name rather than a number – in a delightful coral-coloured 18th-century townhouse. It's just down from the cathedral.

Hotel Tartini (☎ 671 10 00; www.hotel-tartini-piran .com; Tartinijev trg 15; s €56-86, d €76-112, ste €128-192; ❇ 🖳) This attractive, 45-room property faces Tartinijev trg and manages to catch a few sea views from the upper floors. The staff are especially friendly and helpful. If you've got the dosh, splash out on suite No 40a; we're suckers for eyrie-like round rooms with €1-million views.

Eating & Drinking

One of Piran's major attractions is its plethora of fish restaurants, especially along Prešernovo nabrežje, though don't expect any bargains there.

Flora (☎ 673 12 58; Prešernovo nabrežje 26; pizza €4-7.50; ❇ 10am-1am Jul & Aug, 10am-10pm Sep-Jun) The terrace of this simple pizzeria east of the Punta lighthouse has uninterrupted views of the Adriatic.

Galeb (☎ 673 32 25; Pusterla ul 5; mains €8-11; ❇ 11am-4pm & 6pm-11pm or midnight Wed-Mon) This excellent family-run restaurant with seafront seating is east of the Punta lighthouse. The food is good but takes no risks.

Pri Mari (☎ 673 47 35, 041-616 488; Dantejeva ul 17; mains €7.50-16; ❇ 10am-11pm Tue-Sun Jul & Aug, noon-10pm Tue-Sat, noon-6pm Sun Sep-Jun) This stylish Italian-owned restaurant south of the bus station serves the most inventive Mediterranean and Slovenian dishes in town. Try the fish paté and mussels in wine.

Stara Gostilna (☎ 673 31 65; Savudrijska ul 2; mains €7.50-17; ❇ 9am-11pm) This delightful bistro in the Old Town serves both meat and fish dishes, and offers some of the best and most welcoming service in town.

Riva (☎ 673 221 80; Prešernovo nabrežje; mains €8-24; ❇ 11.30am-midnight) The only seafood restaurant on Prešernovo nabrežje worth patronising is this classy place with the strip's best decor and sea views.

Café Teater (☎ 051-694 100; Stjenkova ul 1; ❇ 7am-3am Mon-Fri, 9am-3am Sat & Sun) Anyone who's anyone in Piran can be found at this cafe with a waterfront terrace and troppo furnishings.

Caffe Tartini (☎ 673 33 81; Tartinijev trg 3; ❇ 7am-3am) This cafe, housed in a classical building opposite the Venetian House, is a wonderful place for a cup of something hot and a slice of something sweet at almost any time of the day.

There's an outdoor **market** (Zelenjavni trg; ❇ 7am-2pm Mon-Sat) in the small square behind the town hall. **Mercator** (Levstikova ul 5; ❇ 7am-8pm Mon-Sat, 8am-noon Sun) has a branch in the Old Town. **Ham Ham** (Tomšičeva ul 41; ❇ 7am-midnight) is a convenience store opposite the bus station.

Getting There & Away

From the bus station, buses run every 20 to 30 minutes to Koper (€3.10, 30 minutes, 18km) via Izola, while five head for Trieste in Italy (€10, 1¾ hours, 36km) between 6.45am and 6.55pm Monday to Saturday. Between three and five daily buses go to Ljubljana (€12, 2½ to three hours, 140km) via Divača and Postojna.

From the southern end of Tartinijev trg, a shuttle bus (€1) goes every 15 minutes to Lucija via Portorož.

Venezia Lines (☎ 05-674 71 61; www.venezialines .com) catamarans sail to Venice (one way/return €46/89, 2¼ hours) at 8.30am on Wednesday from May to mid-September. A new service run by **Trieste Lines** (www.triestelines.it) links Piran and Trieste twice a day Tuesday to Sunday from late April to late September. Buy tickets (one way/return €6.80/12.60) from the TIC in Piran.

PORTOROŽ
☎ 05 / pop 2900

Portorož (Portorose in Italian), the biggest resort in Slovenia, is actually quite classy for a seaside town, even along Obala, the main drag. And with the recent reopening of the 185-room Palace, the art nouveau hotel that put Portorož on the map, it may even start to relive its glory days. Portorož's sandy beaches are relatively clean, and there are pleasant spas and wellness centres where you can take the waters or cover yourself in curative mud.

At the same time, the vast array of accommodation options makes Portorož a useful fall back if everything's full in Piran. Full listings are available at the **Tourist Information Center Portorož** (☎ 674 22 20; www.portoroz.si; Obala 16; ❇ 9am-7pm Jul & Aug, 9am-5pm Mon-Sat, 10am-2pm Sun Sep-Jun). Just off the main road between Piran and the centre of Portorož, the summer-only hostel **Prenočišča Korotan** (☎ 674 54 00; www.sd.sd .si/sdp/prenocisca; Obala 11; s €30-33, d €43-46, tr €57-60, q €69-73; ❇ Jul & Aug; 🖳) has en-suite rooms. Be warned, though, that there is a 40/20% supplement for stays of just one/two nights. At the other end of the scale, the 48-room **Hotel Marko** (☎ 617 40 00; www.hotel-marko.com; Obala 28; s €56-96, d €70-120), with lovely gardens just opposite Portorož Bay is delightful.

There are dozens of decent pizzerias along Obala, but the place of choice is **Pizzeria Figarola** (☎ 674 22 00; Obala 14A; pizza €6.50-10.50; 🕙 10am-10pm), with a huge terrace just up from the main pier.

Papa Chico (☎ 677 93 10; Obala 26; mains €5.80-11.30; 🕙 9am-2am Mon-Sat, 10am-2am Sun) serves 'Mexican fun food' (go figure), including fajitas (€9.40 to €11.30).

Kavarna Cacao (☎ 674 10 35; Obala 14; 🕙 8am-1am Sun-Thu, to 3am Fri & Sat) wins the award as the most stylish cafe-bar on the coast and boasts a fabulous waterfront terrace.

Every 20 minutes, a shuttle bus (€1) from Piran trundles along Obala on its way to Lucija, passing by Prenočišča Korotan.

EASTERN SLOVENIA

The rolling vine-covered hills of eastern Slovenia are attractive but much less dramatic than the Julian Alps or, indeed, the coast. If you're heading by train to Vienna via Graz in Austria it saves money to stop in lively Maribor, Slovenia's second-largest city; international tickets are very expensive per kilometre, so doing as much travelling as possible on domestic trains saves cash. While there, consider visiting postcard-perfect Ptuj just down the road.

MARIBOR
☎ 02 / pop 89,450
Slovenia's light-industrial second city really has no unmissable sights but oozes with charm thanks to its delightfully patchy Old Town. Pedestrianised central streets buzz with cafes and student life, and in late June/early July the old, riverside Lent district buzzes with the two-week **Lent International Summer Festival** (http://lent.slovenija.net) extravaganza of folklore and culture.

Maribor Castle (Grajski trg 2), on the main square's northeast corner, contains a magnificent 18th-century **rococo staircase** visible from the street and the **Maribor Regional Museum** (☎ 228 35 51; adult/student & child €3/2.50; 🕙 9am-4pm Tue-Sat, 9am-2pm Sun), one of Slovenia's richest archaeological and ethnographical collections but undergoing a protracted renovation.

Two cafe-packed blocks to the southwest, the **Cathedral** (Slomškov trg) sits in an oasis of fountain-cooled calm. Follow little Poštna ul southward into **Glavni trg** with its extravagant **town hall** (Glavni trg 14) and **plague pillar**, a lovely column of saints erected by townspeople in gratitude for having survived the plague. A block farther south down Mesarski prehod is the Drava River's north bank, where you'll find the **Stara Trta** (Vojašniška 8), the world's oldest living grapevine. It's been a source of a dark red wine called Žametna Črnina (Black Velvet) for more than four centuries.

The helpful **Tourist Information Centre Maribor** (☎ 234 66 10; www.maribor.si; Partizanska c 6A; 🕙 9am-7pm Mon-Fri, to 6pm Sat & Sun Jul & Aug, 9am-6pm Mon-Sat, to 1pm Sun Sep-Jun) has a complete listing of places to stay. At the budget end of the spectrum, try the new **Alibi C2** (☎ 051-663 555; www.alibi.si; Cafova ul 2; dm €17-20, d per person €20-25; 🖳), a superswanky hostel with seven doubles and six dorms with six beds each in a beautifully renovated 19th-century building. Just around the corner is the **Grand Hotel Ocean** (☎ 234 36 73; www.hotelocean .si; Partizanska c 39; s €70-75, d €100; 🎧 🖳), a stunning 23-room boutique hotel named after the first train to pass through the city in 1846 (and, well, the most exciting thing to happen here since).

Gril Ranca (☎ 252 55 50; Dravska ul 10; dishes €3-6; 🕙 8am-11pm Mon-Sat, noon-9pm Sun) serves simple but scrumptious Balkan grills in full view of the Drava. For something more, ahem, cosmopolitan try **Toti Rotovž** (☎ 228 76 50; Glavni trg 14 & Rotovški trg 9; mains €6-18; 🕙 9am-midnight Mon-Thu, 9am-2am Fri & Sat), a peculiar place behind the town hall that serves up just about every cuisine under the sun – from Slovenian to Thai and Greek to Mexican.

Buses run to Ljubljana (€12, three hours, 127km) two to four times a day. Also served are Celje (€6.30, 1½ hours, 55km, up to 10 a day) and Ptuj (€3.60, 45 minutes, 27km, hourly). There are daily buses to Munich (€46, 7½ hours, 453km) at 6.50pm and 9.50pm, and one to Vienna (€29, 4½ hours, 258km) at 5.45pm. Of the two-dozen daily trains to/from Ljubljana (€7.75, 2½ hours, 156km), five are IC express trains costing €19.60 and taking just under two hours.

PTUJ
☎ 02 / pop 18,950
Rising gently above a wide, almost flat valley, compact Ptuj (Poetovio to the Romans) forms

a symphony of red-tile roofs best viewed from across the Drava River. Its pinnacle is the well-preserved **Ptuj Castle** (Na Gradu 1), containing the fine **Regional Museum Ptuj** (☎ 787 92 30; adult/student/child €4/2.50/2.50; ☉ 9am-6pm Mon-Fri, 9am-8pm Sat & Sun Jul & Aug, 9am-6pm daily May-Jun & Sep–mid-Oct, 9am-5pm mid-Oct–Apr).

For 10 days before Mardi Gras crowds come from far and wide to spot the shaggy Kurent straw men at Slovenia's foremost traditional carnival, **Kurentovanje** (www.kurentovanje.net). A 'rite of spring', it is celebrated for 10 days up to Shrove Tuesday (February or early March); the museum has some excellent Kurentovanje-related exhibits. The **Tourist Information Centre Ptuj** (☎ 779 60 11; www.ptuj-tourism.si; Slovenski trg 3; ☉ 9am-8pm May–mid-Oct, 9am-6pm mid-Oct–Apr), facing a medieval tower in the Old Town, has reams of information and lists of places to stay. If you're looking for budget accommodation, look no further than **Hostel Eva** (☎ 771 24 41, 040-226 522; info@bikeek.si; Jadranska 22; per person €12-17), a welcoming, up-to-date hostel connected to a bike shop (per day €10) with six rooms containing two to four beds and a large, light-filled kitchen. If you'd like more comfort, continue walking west on Prešernova ul past a parade of cafes and bars to the new **Park Hotel Ptuj** (☎ 749 33 00; www.parkhotel-ptuj.si; Prešernova ul 38; s €81-98, d €108-122, ste €110-126; 🖳), a lovely new boutique hotel in an 18th-century townhouse with 15 individually designed rooms and lots of original artwork on the walls.

Eat next door at **Amadeus** (☎ 771 70 51; Prešernova ul 36; mains €6.50-20; ☉ noon-10pm Mon-Thu, noon-11pm Fri & Sat, noon-4pm Sun), a very pleasant *gostilna* above a cafe-bar serving *štruklji* (dumplings with herbs and cheese; €3.50), steak and pork dishes. More pleasant in the warmer months is **Ribič** (☎ 749 06 35; Dravska ul 9; mains €9-18; ☉ 10am-11pm Sun-Thu, to midnight Fri & Sat), the best restaurant in Ptuj, with a great riverside terrace and the ideal spot to have a fish dinner. Next to the town's open-air **market** (Novi trg; ☉ 7am-3pm) you'll find a large **Mercator** (Novi trg 3; ☉ 7.30am-7.30pm Mon-Fri, 7.30am-1pm Sat) supermarket.

Buses to Maribor (€3.60, 45 minutes, 27km) run at least hourly on weekdays but are less frequent on weekends. A half-dozen IC trains from Ljubljana (€9.20 to €13, 2½ hours, 155km) pass through Ptuj daily, two of which (10.08am and 7.03pm) are on their way to Budapest (€38.60, 4¼ hours, 313km).

SLOVENIA DIRECTORY

ACCOMMODATION

Accommodation listings throughout this guide have been ordered by price. Very roughly, budget accommodation means a double room under €50, midrange is €51 to €100 and top end is anything over €101. Accommodation is a little bit more expensive in Ljubljana. Unless otherwise indicated, rooms include en-suite toilet and bath or shower and breakfast. Smoking is banned in hotels.

Camping grounds generally charge per person, whether you're in a tent or caravan. Almost all sites close from mid-October to mid-April. Camping 'rough' is illegal in Slovenia, and this law is enforced, especially around Bled. Seek out the Slovenian Tourist Board's *Camping in Slovenia*.

Slovenia's growing stable of hostels includes Ljubljana's trendy Celica and the Alibi chain of hostels found in the capital, at Piran and now in Maribor. Throughout the country there are student dormitories (residence halls) moonlighting as hostels for visitors in July and August. Unless stated otherwise hostel rooms share bathrooms. Hostels usually cost from €15 to €22; prices are at their highest in July and August and during the Christmas break, when it can sometimes be difficult to find accommodation at any price.

Tourist information offices can help you access private rooms, apartments and tourist farms, or they can recommend private agencies that will. Such accommodation can appear misleadingly cheap if you overlook the 30% to 50% surcharge levied on stays of less than three nights. Also be aware that many such properties are in outlying villages with minimal public transport, and that the cheapest one-star category rooms with shared bathroom are actually very rare, so you'll usually pay well above the quoted minimum. Depending on the season you might save a little money by going directly to any house with a sign reading *sobe* (rooms). For more information check out the Slovenian Tourist Board's **Friendly Countryside** (www.slovenia.info/touristfarms) pamphlet listing upwards of 200 farms with accommodation.

Guest houses, known as a *penzion, gostišče,* or *prenočišča*, are often cosy and better value than full-blown hotels. Nonetheless it can be difficult to find a double room in a hotel for under €50. Beware that locally listed rates are usually quoted per person assuming double occupancy. A tourist tax – routinely €0.50 to €1 (hotel) per person per day – is usually not included.

ACTIVITIES
Extreme Sports
Several areas specialise in adrenalin-rush activities, the greatest range being available at Bovec (p895), famous for rafting, hydro-speed, kayaking and canyoning, and increasingly at Bled (p891). Bovec is also a great place for paragliding; in winter you ascend Mt Kanin via ski lift and then jump off. Gliding costs are very reasonable from Lesce near Bled. Scuba diving from Piran (p902) is also good value.

Hiking
Hiking is extremely popular, with the **Alpine Association of Slovenia** (www.pzs.si) counting some 55,000 members and Ljubljančani flocking in droves to Triglav National Park (p893) on weekends. There are more than 7000km of marked trails and paths, and in summer as many as 170 mountain huts offer comfortable trailside refuge. Several treks are outlined in Lonely Planet's more comprehensive *Slovenia*.

Skiing
Skiing is a Slovenian passion, with slopes particularly crowded over the Christmas holidays and in early February. See the Slovenian Tourist Board's **Ski Centers of Slovenia** (www.slovenia.info/skiing) for more details.

Kranjska Gora (up to 1291m; p894) has some challenging runs, and the world record for ski-jumping was set at nearby Planica, 4km to the west. Above Lake Bohinj, Vogel (up to 1800m) is particularly scenic, as is Kanin (up to 2300m) above Bovec, which can have snow as late as May. Being relatively close to Ljubljana, Krvavec (up to 1971m), northeast of Kranj, can have particularly long lift queues.

Just west of Maribor in eastern Slovenia is a popular choice and the biggest downhill skiing area in the country. Although relatively low (336m to 1347m), the Mariborsko Pohorje is easily accessible, with very varied downhill pistes and relatively short lift queues.

Other Activities
Mountain bikes are available for hire from travel agencies at Bled, Bohinj, Bovec, Kranjska Gora and Postojna.

The Soča River near Kobarid and the Sava Bohinjka near Bohinj are great for fly-fishing April to October. Licences for the latter cost €55/38 (catch/catch and release) and are sold at the tourist office and certain hotels.

Spas and wellness centres are very popular in Slovenia; see **Slovenia Spas** (www.spa-slovenia.com) website for more information. Most towns have some sort of spa complex, and hotels often offer free or bargain-rate entry to their guests.

BUSINESS HOURS
All businesses post their opening times (*delovni čas*) on the door. Many shops close Saturday afternoons. A handful of grocery stores open on Sundays, including some branches of the ubiquitous Mercator supermarket chain. Most museums close on Mondays. Banks often take lunch breaks from 12.30pm to 2pm and only a few open on Saturday mornings.

Restaurants typically open for lunch and dinner until at least 10pm, and bars until midnight, though they may have longer hours on weekends and shorter ones on Sundays.

EMBASSIES & CONSULATES
Following are among the embassies and consulates in Slovenia. Unless noted otherwise, they are all in Ljubljana.

Australia (off Map pp878–9; ☎ 01-425 42 52; Dunajska c 50; ☼ 9am-1pm Mon-Fri)

Austria (Map pp878–9; ☎ 01-479 07 00; Prešernova c 23; ☼ 8am-noon Mon-Thu, 8-11am Fri) Enter from Veselova ul.

Canada (Map pp878–9; ☎ 01-252 44 44; 12th fl, Trg Republike 3; ☼ 9am-noon Mon-Fri)

Croatia Ljubljana (Map pp878–9; ☎ 01-425 62 20; Gruberjevo nabrežje 6; ☼ 9am-1pm Mon-Fri); Maribor (☎ 02-234 66 86; Trg Svobode 3; ☼ 10am-1pm Mon-Fri)

France (Map pp878–9; ☎ 01-479 04 00; Barjanska c 1; ☼ 8.30am-12.30pm Mon-Fri)

Hungary (off Map pp878–9; ☎ 01-512 18 82; ul Konrada Babnika 5; ☼ 8am-5pm Mon-Fri)

Ireland (Map pp878–9; ☎ 01-300 89 70; Palača Kapitelj, Poljanski nasip 6; ☼ 9.30am-12.30pm & 2.30-4pm Mon-Fri)

Italy Ljubljana (Map pp878–9; ☎ 01-426 21 94; Snežniška ul 8; ☼ 9-11am Mon-Fri); Koper (Map p899; ☎ 05-627 37 49; Belvedere 2; ☼ 8.30am-noon Mon-Fri)

Netherlands (Map pp878–9; ☎ 01-420 14 61; Palača Kapitelj, Poljanski nasip 6; ☼ 9am-noon Mon-Fri)

New Zealand (off Map pp878–9; ☎ 01-580 30 55; Verovškova ul 57; ☼ 8am-3pm Mon-Fri)

South Africa (☎ 01-200 63 00; Pražakova ul 4; ☼ 3-4pm Tue) In Kompas building.
UK (Map pp878-9; ☎ 01-200 39 10; 4th fl, Trg Republike 3; ☼ 9am-noon Mon-Fri)
USA (Map pp878-9; ☎ 01-200 55 00; Prešernova c 31; ☼ 9-11.30am & 1-3pm Mon-Fri)

FESTIVALS & EVENTS

Major cultural and sporting events are listed under 'Events' on the website of the **Slovenian Tourist Board** (www.slovenia.info) and in the STB's comprehensive *Calendar of Major Events in Slovenia*, issued annually.

Slovenia's biggest open-air rock concert **Rock Otočec** (www.rock-otocec.com) is a three-day event held in late June/early July at Prečna airfield, 5km northwest of Novo Mesto in southeastern Slovenia.

GAY & LESBIAN TRAVELLERS

Roza Klub (☎ 01-430 47 40; Kersnikova ul 4) in Ljubljana is made up of the gay and lesbian branches of ŠKUC (Študentski Kulturni Center or Student Cultural Centre).

GALfon (☎ 01-432 40 89; ☼ 7-10pm Mon-Fri) is a hotline and source of general information for gays and lesbians. The websites of **Slovenian Queer Resources Directory** (www.ljudmila.org/siqrd) and **Out in Slovenia** (www.outinslovenija.com) are both extensive and partially in English.

HOLIDAYS

Slovenia celebrates 14 holidays (*prazniki*) a year. If a holiday falls on a Sunday, then the following Monday becomes the holiday.
New Year 1 and 2 January
Prešeren Day (Slovenian Culture Day) 8 February
Easter March/April
Insurrection Day 27 April
Labour Days 1 and 2 May
National Day 25 June
Assumption Day 15 August
Reformation Day 31 October
All Saints Day 1 November
Christmas Day 25 December
Independence Day 26 December

INTERNET ACCESS

Virtually every hostel and hotel now has internet access – a computer for guests' use (free or for a small fee), wi-fi, or both. Most cities and towns have at least one cyber cafe but they usually only have a handful of terminals. Be advised that Slovenian keyboards are neither qwerty nor azerty but qwertz, reversing the y and z keys, but otherwise following the Anglophone norm.

INTERNET RESOURCES

The website of the **Slovenian Tourist Board** (www.slovenia.info) is tremendously useful, as is that of **Mat'Kurja** (www.matkurja.com), a directory of Slovenian web resources. Most Slovenian towns and cities have a website accessed by typing www.town.si (or sometimes www.town-tourism.si). Especially good are **Ljubljana** (www.ljubljana.si), **Maribor** (www.maribor.si) and **Piran-Portorož** (www.portoroz.si).

MONEY

Slovenia uses the euro as its official currency. Exchanging cash is simple at banks, major post offices, travel agencies and *menjalnice* (bureaux de change), although some of the latter don't accept travellers cheques. Major credit and debit cards are accepted almost everywhere, and ATMs are ubiquitous.

POST

Local mail costs €0.27 for up to 20g, while an international airmail stamp costs €0.45. Poste restante is free; address it to and pick it up from the main post office at Slovenska c 32, 1101 Ljubljana.

TELEPHONE

Slovenia's country code is ☎ 386. Public telephones require a phonecard (*telefonska kartica* or *telekartica*), available at post offices and some news-stands. The cheapest card (€4, 25 units) gives about 20 minutes' calling time to other European countries; the highest value is €14.60 with 300 units. Local SIM cards with €5 credit are available for €12 from **SiMobil** (www.simobil.si) and for €15 from **Mobitel** (www.mobitel.si). Mobile numbers in Slovenia are identified by the prefix ☎ 031-, 040-, 041- and 051-.

TOURIST INFORMATION

The Ljubljana-based **Slovenian Tourist Board** (off Map pp878-9; ☎ 01-589 18 40; www.slovenia.info; Dunajska

---

EMERGENCY NUMBERS

■ Ambulance ☎ 112
■ Fire ☎ 112
■ Police ☎ 113
■ Roadside assistance ☎ 1987

SLOVENIA

c 156) has dozens of tourist information centres (TICs) in Slovenia, and overseas branches in a half-dozen European countries; see 'STB Representative Offices Abroad' on its website for details.

VISAS

Citizens of virtually all European countries, as well as Australia, Canada, Israel, Japan, New Zealand and the USA, do not require visas to visit Slovenia for stays of up to 90 days. Holders of EU and Swiss passports can enter using a national identity card.

Those who do require visas (including South Africans) can get them for up to 90 days at any Slovenian embassy or consulate – see the website of the **Ministry of Foreign Affairs** (www.mzz.gov.si) for a full listing. They cost €35 regardless of the type of visa or length of validity. You'll need confirmation of a hotel booking plus one photo, and you may have to show a return or onward ticket.

WOMEN TRAVELLERS

In the event of an emergency call the **police** (☎ 113) any time or the **SOS Helpline** (☎ 080 11 55; www.drustvo-sos.si; ☽ noon–10pm Mon-Fri, 6-10pm Sat & Sun).

TRANSPORT IN SLOVENIA

GETTING THERE & AWAY
Air

Slovenia's only international airport receiving regular scheduled flights at present – Aerodrom Maribor does limited charters only – is Ljubljana's recently renamed **Jože Pučnik Airport** (LJU; www.lju-airport.si) at Brnik, 27km north of Ljubljana. From its base here, the Slovenian flag-carrier, **Adria Airways** (JP; ☎ 080 13 00, 01-369 10 10; www.adria-airways.com), serves some 28 European destinations on regularly scheduled flights, with just as many holiday spots served by charter flights in summer. Adria can be remarkably good value and includes useful connections to İstanbul, Ohrid (Macedonia), Pristina (Kosovo) and Tirana (Albania).

Other airlines with regularly scheduled flights to and from Ljubljana:

Air France (AF; ☎ 01-244 34 47; www.airfrance.com/si) Daily flights to Paris (CDG).

Austrian Airlines (OS; ☎ 01-202 01 00; www.aua.com) Multiple daily flights to Vienna.

Brussels Airlines (SN; ☎ 04-206 16 56; www.brussels airlines.com) Daily flights to Brussels.

ČSA Czech Airlines (OK; ☎ 04-206 17 50; www.czech airlines.com) Flights to Prague.

easyJet (EZY; ☎ 04-206 16 77; www.easyjet.com) Low-cost flights to London Stansted.

Finnair (AY; ☎ 080 13 00, 01-369 10 10; www.finnair .com) Flights to Helsinki.

JAT Airways (JU; ☎ 01-231 43 40; www.jat.com) Daily flights to Belgrade.

Malév Hungarian Airlines (MA; ☎ 04-206 16 76; www.malev.hu) Daily flights to Budapest.

Turkish Airlines (TK; ☎ 04-206 16 80; www.turkish airlines.com) Flights to İstanbul.

Land
BUS

International bus destinations from Ljubljana include Serbia, Germany, Hungary, Croatia, Bosnia and Hercegovina, Macedonia and Italy; see p888 for details. You can also catch buses to Italy and Croatia from coastal towns, including Piran (p903) and Koper (p900). Maribor (p904) also has buses to Germany and Austria.

TRAIN

It is possible to travel to Italy, Austria, Germany and Croatia by train; Ljubljana (p888) is the main hub, although you can, for example, hop on a train to Budapest at Ptuj (p905).

Train travel can be expensive. It is sometimes cheaper to travel as far as you can on domestic routes before crossing any borders. For example, you can travel on a Ljubljana–Vienna service but you will save a little bit of money by going first to Maribor; see p904 for details.

Seat reservations, compulsory on trains to and from Italy and on InterCity (IC) trains, cost €3.50, but it is usually included in the ticket price.

Sea

Piran despatches ferries to Trieste a couple of times a day and catamarans to Venice at least once a week; see p903 for details. There's also a catamaran between nearby Izola and Venice in summer months; see p900.

GETTING AROUND
Bus

It's worth booking long-distance buses ahead of time, especially when travelling on Friday afternoons. If your bag has to go in the luggage compartment below the bus, it will cost €1.50 extra. The online bus timetable, **Avtobusna Postaja Ljubljana** (www.ap-ljubljana.si), is extensive, but generally only lists buses that use Ljubljana as a hub.

Bicycle

Bicycles may be hired at some train stations, tourist offices, travel agencies and hotels.

Car

Hiring a car is recommended, and can even save you money as you can access cheaper out-of-centre hotels and farm or village homestays. Daily rates usually start at around €40/210 per day/week, including unlimited mileage, collision-damage waiver and theft protection. Unleaded petrol *(bencin)* costs €1.21 (95 octane) and €1.25 (98 octane), with diesel at €1.31. You must keep your headlights illuminated throughout the day. If you'll be doing a lot of driving consider buying Kod & Kam's 1:100,000 *Avtoatlas Slovenija* (€27).

A new law requires all cars to display a *vinjeta* (road-toll sticker) on the windscreen. They cost €35/55 for a half-/full year and are available at petrol stations, post offices and some kiosks; for a complete list consult the website www.cestnina.si. These will already be in place on a rental car but if you are driving your own vehicle, failure to display such a sticker risks a fine of €300 to €800.

Further information is available from the **Automobile Association of Slovenia** (☎ 01 530 53 00; www.amzs.si)

Hitching

Hitchhiking is fairly common and legal, except on motorways and a few major highways. Even young women hitch in Slovenia, but it's never totally safe and Lonely Planet doesn't recommend it.

Train

Slovenian Railways (Slovenske Železnice; ☎ 01-291 33 32; www.slo-zeleznice.si) has a useful online timetable that's easy to use. Buy tickets before boarding or you'll incur a €2.50 supplement. Be aware that EuroCity (EC) and InterCity (IC) trains carry a surcharge of €1.50 on top of standard quoted fares, while InterCity Slovenia ones cost €8.80/5.70 extra in 1st/2nd class.

Ukraine Україна

Since the exciting days of 2005's Orange Revolution, this latecomer to the European party has now opened its doors unreservedly to the west. And while progress has not been without its pitfalls, it's hard not to be broadly optimistic about Ukraine's future as it continues to emerge from Russia's shadow and looks forward to entering its third decade of independence.

'The land on the edge' is how Ukraine's name translates into English, and you'll immediately notice how the country is simultaneously familiar and foreign, predictable and surprising, the last stop on the continent before the great enigma of Russia. While many travellers stop off solely in Kyiv on their way through to the east, it's well worth taking your time to see this preconception-challenging land: gorgeous Lviv, much-touted as 'the new Prague', the Carpathian mountains across the country's southwest and the magical Black Sea port of Odesa, where Eurasian cultures click with enviable ease. All these are accessible and largely backpacker-free destinations. Going even deeper into the country, the mountainous landscapes and 'Russian Riviera' of Crimea await. Here, in a land of myth and great natural beauty, cultural clashes between Europe and Asia, Christianity and Islam, communism and capitalism play out, whether it's on the promenade of Yalta, the ultimate Soviet holiday resort, or in the Crimean Tatar capital of Bakhchysaray, home to the perfectly preserved Kahn's Palace and one of Ukraine's most beguiling towns. Ukraine is changing all the time, so get here as soon as possible while it remains a land apart.

FAST FACTS

- **Area** 603,628 sq km
- **Capital** Kyiv (Kiev)
- **Currency** hryvnia (hry); €1 = 10.90hry; US$1 = 7.99hry; UK£1 = 11.60hry; A$1 = 5.53hry; ¥100 = 8.32hry; NZ$1 =4.49hry
- **Famous for** Orange Revolution, a poisoned president, Chornobyl, football striker Andriy Shevchenko
- **Official Language** Ukrainian
- **Phrases** *dobry dyen* (hello); *ya nye rahzumyeyu* (I don't understand); *dyakuyu* (thanks)
- **Population** 46.4 million
- **Telephone codes** country code ☎ 380; international access code ☎ 8 + 10
- **Visa** not required for EU, US, Swiss or Canadian citizens, but needed for Australians and New Zealanders; see p956

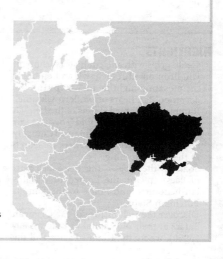

UKRAINE

HIGHLIGHTS

- Get to grips with ancient history, shop till you drop on Khreshchatyk and embrace the pulsating nightlife in **Kyiv** (p916), the cosmopolitan heart of modern Ukraine.
- Ramble the cobbled streets of the Unesco World Heritage–listed Old Town in **Lviv** (p926), the deeply Ukrainian city quickly being discovered by travellers in search of the next big thing.
- Soak up the vibe in the Black Sea port of **Odesa** (p936), the hotbed of Ukrainian hedonism and home to the famous Potemkin Steps.
- Discover the rich history of the Crimean Tatars at their old capital in **Bakhchysaray** (p950), where the Khan's Palace and the scenery of Chufut-Kale can't fail to astound you.
- Take a trip deep into Ukraine's heartland and discover **Kamyanets-Podilsky** (p935), a perfectly preserved old town set on a towering island of rock surrounded by a deep ravine.

ITINERARIES

- **One week** Begin by sampling the charms of Kyiv before heading either south to party in Odesa or west for a more refined and relaxed time in Lviv.
- **Two weeks** Spend three days in Kyiv, two in Lviv, then pass through rocking Odesa to Crimea, making Yalta your base and being sure to visit Bakhchysaray.

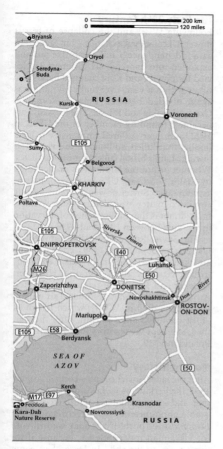

CLIMATE & WHEN TO GO

Ukraine's climate may surprise you – the summer months are usually hot, especially in July and August, where you can expect temperatures in the 20s almost every day. The country has a long, freezing winter, although Yalta and Odesa enjoy a marginally subtropical climate and are much milder than the rest of the country, even in December.

Near Odesa and in Crimea, tourism is at its peak from June to August, and accommodation is priciest then. The country basically comes to a halt during the first two weeks of May for a series of holidays, making a visit at that time both interesting and frustrating. For weather and crowds, May, June and September are the best times to visit.

HISTORY
Kyivan Rus

In 882 Oleh of Novgorod – of the Varangians (a Scandinavian civilisation) – declared himself ruler of Kyiv. The city prospered and grew into a large, unified Varangian state that, during its peak, stretched between the Volga River, the Danube River and Baltic Sea. By the 11th and 12th centuries, the Varangian state began to splinter into 10 rival princedoms. When prince of Suzdal Andriy Bogolyubov sacked Kyiv in 1169, the end of the Varangian era was complete.

Prince Roman Mstyslavych regained control of Kyiv in 1203 and united the regions of present-day western, central and northern Ukraine. There was a period of relative prosperity under his dynamic son, King Danylo, and grandson Lev. During this time, much of eastern and southern Ukraine came under the control of the Volga-based, Mongol Golden Horde. Its empire was emasculated, however, in the 14th century by the Black Death, as well as by the growing military strength of Russian, Polish and Lithuanian rulers.

Cossacks & Russian Control

By the turn of the 15th century, the uncontrolled steppe in southern Ukraine began to attract runaway serfs, criminals, Orthodox refugees and other outcasts from Poland and Lithuania. Along with a few semi-independent Tatars, the inhabitants formed self-governing militaristic communities and became known as *kazaki* (Cossacks), from the Turkic word meaning 'outlaw, adventurer or free person'.

CONNECTIONS: MOVING ON FROM UKRAINE

Ukraine is well linked to its neighbours, particularly Russia and Belarus, with whom it shares the Soviet rail system. Kyiv (p924) is connected by bus or train to Moscow, St Petersburg, Minsk, Warsaw and Budapest, as well as other Eastern European capitals. Odesa is the hub for travelling to Moldova, with many daily buses (p943) to Chişinău (both going via and avoiding Tiraspol); the city also has ferries (p943) to Bulgaria, Romania and Turkey. From Uzhhorod it's a short journey to the international mainline into Europe at Chop, connecting Ukraine with Slovakia and Hungary.

Ukrainian Cossacks eventually developed the self-ruling Cossack Hetmanate, which to some degree reasserted the concept of Ukrainian self-determination.

In 1648 Hetman Bogdan Khmelnytsky (aided by Tatar cavalry) overcame the Polish rulers at the battle of Pyliavtsi. He was forced to engage in a formal but controversial military alliance with Muscovy in 1654, but in 1660 a war broke out between Poland and Russia over control of Ukraine. This ended with treaties that granted control over Kyiv and northern Ukraine to Russia and territory to the west of the Dnipro River to the Poles.

During the course of the 18th century Russia expanded into southern Ukraine and also gained most of Western Ukraine from Poland, except for the far west, which went to the Habsburg Empire.

The 19th century saw a slow growth of nationalist sentiment, which became significant in Kyiv from the 1840s. When the tsarist authorities banned the use of Ukrainian as an official language in the capital, the movement's focus shifted to Austrian-controlled Lviv.

Shortly afterwards in 1854, Britain and France attacked Russia in the Crimean War, fearing the empire's creep to the Mediterranean Sea. The two-year war resulted in an estimated 250,000 dead on each side, but failed to check Russia's encroachment on the Mediterranean. In 1876 Russian influence over Ukraine was further cemented by Tsar Alexander II's banning of Ukrainian in print and on the stage.

The Early 20th Century

Following WWI and the collapse of tsarist power, Ukraine had a chance – but failed – to gain independence. Civil war broke out and exploded into anarchy: six different armies vied for power, and Kyiv changed hands five times within a year. Eventually Ukraine was again divided between Poland, Romania, Czechoslovakia and Russia. The Russian part became a founding member of the USSR in 1922, and later suffered immensely from a famine that killed millions in the years following Stalin's brutal collectivisation policies. Whether or not the famine was orchestrated by Stalin, who saw Ukrainian nationalism as a threat to Soviet power, remains a hotly contested matter in academic circles. What is in no doubt is that millions died of starvation in Ukraine between 1932 and 1933.

The Soviet Red Army rolled into Polish Ukraine in September 1939. The Germans attacked in 1941 and by the year's end controlled virtually all of Ukraine. However, Kharkiv and Kyiv were retaken by the Red Army two years later. An estimated six million Ukrainians died in WWII, which left most of the country's cities in ruin. After the war, the USSR kept the territory it had taken from Poland in 1939.

Modern History

After the failed Soviet counter-coup in August 1991, the Verkhovna Rada (Supreme Council) met, and speaker Stanyslav Hurenko's memorable announcement was recorded by the *Economist* for posterity: 'Today we will vote for Ukrainian independence, because if we don't we're in the shit.' In December, some 84% of the population voted in a referendum to back that pragmatic decision, and Leonid Kravchuk was elected president.

The economy foundered, things seemed chaotic and people were largely dissatisfied with the results of their move for independence. Finally, the hryvnia, Ukraine's currency, was introduced in 1996, and a process of privatisation kick-started the economy. It wasn't until 1997, under President Leonid Kuchma, that inflation fell from an inconceivable 10,000% to 10%. The economy strengthened but not enough: the hryvnia felt the ripple effects hard from the 1998 Russian financial crisis, dipping 51% in value.

President Kuchma was returned to power in October 1999 after what were widely regarded as dubious elections. His credibility shrivelled further in November 2000 when a tape emerged of Kuchma having an alleged 'rid me of this turbulent priest' moment regarding Georgy Gongadze, a journalist highly critical of Kuchma's presidency, whose beheaded corpse had been discovered in a forest outside Kyiv a few months earlier.

The Orange Revolution

Kuchma was limited to two terms in power, and so he backed Viktor Yanukovych to run for office in the October 2004 presidential elections. But both the international press and the Ukrainian public were all about Viktor Yushchenko, who was poisoned (but not killed) a week before the elections, allegedly by political foes, turning his ruggedly handsome face into…well, just rugged.

Because no-one carried more than 50% of the votes in the first round of elections, a runoff was scheduled for 21 November. The official results of this run-off had Yanukovych ahead by 3%, but exit polls showed Yushchenko ahead by 11%. Something wasn't quite right and by the next day, about 500,000 people had peacefully gathered on Kyiv's maydan Nezalezhnosti (Independence Sq), bearing flags, setting up tents, chanting, singing and having a good time. Kyiv citizens took complete strangers into their homes, and the media reported a marked drop in city crime during the span of the protest. The world was watching and officials had no choice but to annul the run-off results.

But the protesters stayed on, sometimes numbering more than one million and often withstanding freezing temperatures, until 26 December 2004, when a second run-off took place under intense international scrutiny. Yushchenko won with 52% and was inaugurated 23 January 2005, the climax to the surprisingly peaceful, but massively significant 'Orange Revolution', so called as it was the colour of choice for the crowds supporting Yushchenko.

Ukraine Today

Since Yushchenko's victory, his popularity has declined enormously, and the sclerotic institutions of Ukraine's lumbering body politic have done little to address the massive across-the-board reforms needed by the country.

One-time Yushchenko ally Yulia Tymoshenko, Ukraine's prime minister in 2005 and then again from 2007, is now Yushchenko's number-one rival in the 2010 presidential elections. Having toned down her anti-Russian rhetoric, built bridges with Moscow over gas prices and notably restrained her criticism of the Russian actions during the Russia–Georgia conflict in 2008, Tymoshenko has skilfully positioned herself as the Kremlin's favoured candidate for the Ukrainian presidency.

With an election held every year since the Orange Revolution, thanks to the various political parties' inability to form stable coalitions, Ukraine is still lacking the political stability it so needs to bring about real reform. NATO and EU membership are both probably a decade away, and neither is wanted by the majority of the population at present. But it's not all bad, especially when compared with neighbouring Belarus and Russia; Ukraine today enjoys a vibrant political scene, genuine debate and a largely free press.

PEOPLE

Ukraine's population has been steadily declining since independence. About 66% of the population live in urban areas. Some 78% are Ukrainian and another 17% are ethnic Russians. The remainder includes Belarusians, Moldovans, Bulgarians, Poles, Hungarians, Romanians, Tatars and Jews. Almost all of the country's Tatar population (less than 250,000) lives in Crimea.

RELIGION

Almost 97% of Ukrainians are Christian, and most of those follow some sort of orthodoxy. Orthodoxy in Ukraine has a complex history of its own, but basically, central and southern Ukraine mostly follow the Ukrainian Orthodox Church (UOC; with a Moscow patriarch), while the rest of the country follows the Ukrainian Autocephalous Orthodox Church (UAOC; with a Kyiv patriarch). To make matters more confusing, the UOC split in 1992, with a breakaway new church called the Ukrainian Orthodox Church of Kyiv and All-Ukraine, which recognises the Kyiv patriarch.

But wait, there's more. The Uniate Church, which is also referred to as the Ukrainian-Greek Catholic Church, follows Orthodox worship and ritual but recognises the Roman pope as its leader. Uniate priests are the only Catholic priests in the world allowed to marry.

UKRAINE

There are some very small Jewish minorities in all cities, while Muslim communities, primarily Tatars, live in Crimea.

ARTS

Many Ukrainians believe that to understand their heritage you must appreciate the significance of Taras Shevchenko, who was punished by exile in 1847 for his satirical poems about Russian oppression. Arguably the most talented and prolific Ukrainian writer of the early 20th century was Ivan Franko, whose scholarly and moving works shed light on the issues that plague Ukrainian society. He was, of course, imprisoned by the Russians. Lesia Ukrainka, a wealthy young woman whose frail health kept her indoors writing moody poetry, could be considered the Emily Dickinson of Ukraine.

In the cinema world, Aleksandr Dovzhenko's 1930 silent film *Earth* is considered by some critics to be one of the most significant films of all time. The most notable contemporary Ukrainian director (although she was born in a part of Romania that's now in Moldova) is Odesa-based Kira Muratova. Her absurdist, cruel style and fascination with the repulsive have earned her films much critical acclaim, if not a huge fan base. Check out her 1971 avant-garde classic *Dolgiye Provody* (*A Long Goodbye* in English) for a taste.

The art of creating *pysanky* (brightly coloured, detailed eggshells), is uniquely Ukrainian. During Easter you will be able to find some for sale (great souvenirs but hard to pack safely), and there are year-round wooden-egg samples for purchase.

Okean Elzy (www.okeanelzy.com) is one of the country's bigger music sensations. The well-respected rock group sounds a little like the Clash and has a charismatic lead singer. Sofia Rotaru, the queen of Ukrainian pop, has just turned 60 and is much loved throughout the country.

ENVIRONMENT

The largest country wholly within Europe, Ukraine has a topography consisting almost completely of steppe: gently rolling, partially wooded plains, bisected by the Dnipro River. The only serious mountains are the Carpathians, in the west, and the Crimeans, in the south. A central belt of fertile, thick, humus-rich soil in Ukraine spawned the term *chernozem* (meaning 'black earth') and is what

gave the country the nickname 'the breadbasket of Europe'.

Visitors don't come for rare-wildlife watching, but there is a good amount of diversity, including elk, deer, wild boars, brown bears and wolves. Lots of geese and ducks, and small furry mammals such as rabbits and muskrats, can be seen from trains. Ukraine has a few national parks, the most significant of which is the Carpathian National Natural Park.

In addition to the destructive Soviet industrialisation of the countryside, Ukraine still suffers from the effects of Chornobyl (Chernobyl in Russian), the worst nuclear accident in history (see p926).

FOOD & DRINK

Grim and stodgy? That's the stereotype of food from Ukraine, but in fact there's much to be said for Ukrainian cooking, especially with the good restaurants now open in most large towns and the resurgence of Crimean Tatar cuisine in the south bringing some much needed spice to the country's palates.

Some tasty Ukrainian dishes are *varenyky* (traditional dumplings made with rolled dough), *borshch* (beet soup) and *holubtsi* (stuffed cabbage rolls). Chicken Kiev *(kotleta po-Kiyvsky)*, is a deep-fried butter-stuffed ball of chicken.

Crimea produces sweet wines, and champagne from around Odesa is surprisingly palatable. The most popular Ukrainian beers are Slavutych, Chernihivsky and Obolon. Vegetarians can have a hard time outside the larger cities here, although the concept at least is understood these days, if not always catered for. Fish eaters will have no problem at all, save a rather repetitive diet of fish. Most bars and restaurants tend to open from 10am until 11pm or midnight.

KYIV КИЇВ

☎ 044 / pop 2.7 million

If Ukraine is a fragmented union of different Slavic nationalities, then Kyiv is its ideal cosmopolitan capital. The city just about manages to straddle the vast Dnipro River, which effectively splits Ukraine into its eastern Russian-speaking population and its western Ukrainian-speaking one, uniting the two, however precariously, in the birthplace of both cultures.

Kyiv is a city changing fast. A national capital for less than two decades, it has taken on the role with aplomb and can comfortably compare to long-established seats of government elsewhere in Europe, with its extraordinary history, dramatic geography and developmental frenzy.

Home of Ukraine's still-fragile democracy and seat of the Orange Revolution, Kyiv is a busy, exciting party town. Take a walk down the Stalinist Khreshchatyk, now the city's premiere shopping district, see centuries of faith at the Caves Monastery and join young Kyivans out at one of the city's hot nightspots – you won't be bored in this post-revolutionary boom town.

ORIENTATION

Kyiv's main street is vul Khreshchatyk, which heads northeast towards maydan Nezalezhnosti, the main square. On weekends Khreshchatyk is closed to traffic, and citizens flood the street.

North of here is the Old Town, on a steep hill overlooking Podil, the historic merchants' quarter and river port. Across the river, on the more working-class 'left' (east) bank, is a cluster of islands hugged by beaches and parkland.

INFORMATION
Bookshops

Dinternal (☎ 278 1362; prov Muzeyny 2; ⌚ 10am-7pm Mon-Sat; Ⓜ Maydan Nezalezhnosti) An English-language bookshop located through the arch.

Entresol (☎ 235 8342; Bul Tarasa Shevchenko 2; ⌚ 10am-midnight; Ⓜ Teatralna) There's a good selection of English books at this upmarket cafe.

Internet Access

Free wi-fi access can be had across town at many smarter restaurants, look for the wi-fi logo displayed in the window.

Orbita (☎ 234 1693; 2nd fl, vul Khreshchatyk 29; per hr 6hry; ⌚ 8am-1am; Ⓜ Teatralna) The handiest internet cafe in the city centre.

Laundry

There are no self-service laundries, but hotel floor maids will do a good job for a reasonable rate. Many apartment rentals offer a washing machine.

Left Luggage

Possible for a small fee at the train and bus stations. Also, your hotel will hold it for you for several hours, usually for free.

KYIV IN TWO DAYS

Muse over mummies at the **Caves Monastery** (p919), then scoot to the nearby **Museum of the Great Patriotic War** (p920) and **Rodina Mat** (p920). Finish up with a slap-up Ukrainian meal at **Pervak** (p923).

Wander down Khreshchatyk (on a Sunday if possible, when it's pedestrian-only) and see the maydan Nezalezhnosti, the seat of the Orange Revolution. Climb the hill to **St Sophia's Cathedral** (p919) and **Andriyivsky uzviz** (p920) and catch a live show at **Art Club 44** (p923) or go boozing.

Medical Services

American Medical Centre (☎ 490 7600; www.amcenters.com; vul Berdychivska 1; Ⓜ Lukyanivska) Handles routine and emergency medical and dental. Staff members speak English.

Money

Both ATMs and exchange booths signposted обмін валют (obmin valyut) are ubiquitous. Rates offered by exchange booths in hotels are not necessarily worse, but in general they vary hugely, so shop around. Larger banks will cash travellers cheques and give cash advances on credit cards.

Post & Telephone

Central post office (☎ 065; vul Khreshchatyk 22; ⌚ 8am-9pm Mon-Fri, to 7pm Sun; Ⓜ Khreshchatyk) Has a 24-hour phone office.

Travel Agencies

There are no tourist information centres, but there are plenty of travel agencies, which do city tours as well as day trips to the Chornobyl Exclusion Zone. Three of the most reliable and popular:

New Logic (☎ 206 2200; www.newlogic.ua; Leonardo Business Centre, vul Bohdana Khmelnytskoho; Ⓜ Teatralna) Offers an excellent range of city sightseeing tours. Can also book hotels and railway tickets.

Sam Travel (☎ 238 6020; vul Ivana Franko 40b; Ⓜ Universitet) Organise tours throughout Ukraine, including the Carpathians, Chornobyl and Crimea visits.

SoloEast Travel (☎ 985 3115; www.tourkiev.com) A Canadian-Ukrainian venture, with friendly English-speaking service. A popular choice for Chornobyl, but also good for private apartments, train and hotel bookings throughout the country.

CENTRAL KYIV

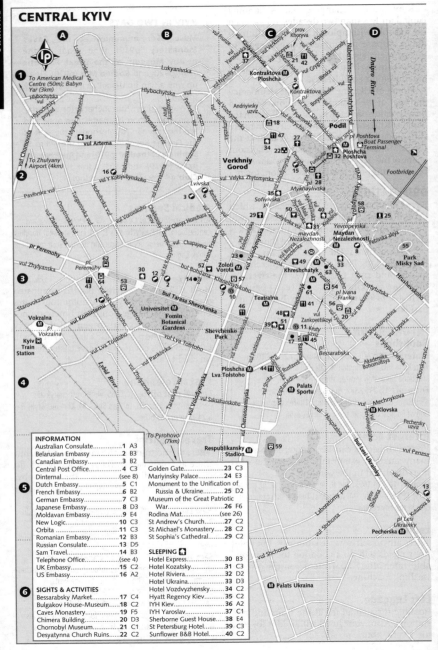

To American Medical
Centre (50m); Babyn
Yar (3km)

To Zhulyany
Airport (4km)

To Pyrohovo
(7km)

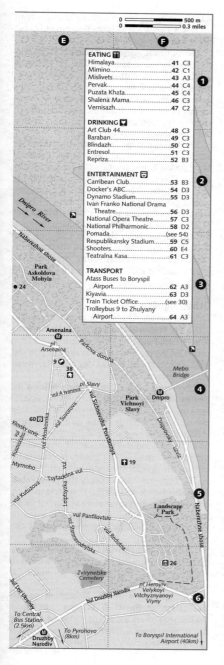

SIGHTS
Caves Monastery

Rolling across 28 hectares of wooded slopes above the Dnipro River, the **Caves Monastery Complex** (☎ 290 3071; www.lavra.kiev.ua; vul Sichnevoho Povstannya 21; adult/child incl map 16/8hry; ☿ Upper Lavra 9am-7pm summer, 9.30am-6pm winter, Lower Lavra sunrise-sunset, caves 9am-4.30pm), also known as the Kyiv-Pechersk Lavra, deserves at least a half-day. It is the most popular tourist site in the city, a highlight of visiting Ukraine and arguably the spiritual heart of the Ukrainian people. The site is divided into the Upper Lavra (a complex of churches and museums for which entry is charged) and the Lower Lavra (the caves themselves, for which entry is free).

Entering through the Upper Lavra's Trinity Gate takes you onto a square dominated by the Trinity Gate Church and the Dormition Cathedral. Further into the complex, there are a large number of museums – many of which are of marginal interest – and the superb Refectory Church of St Antoniy and St Feodosiy, which contains beautifully painted frescos. There's a great view across the Dnipro from behind the church.

Continuing past the church and down under the flying buttresses will take you to the two sets of **caves** in the Lower Lavra, a few minutes' walk away; buy a candle to light your way at a kiosk before you enter. Inside the caves, dozens of niches contain glass-topped coffins holding the blanketed bodies of the monks; believers kneel and pray at the coffins, and kiss the glass tops as well. It's all very spooky, although it can be claustrophobic on a busy day (weekends are best avoided if possible).

The **excursion bureau** (☎ 291 3171; tours per person 15hry) is on the left just past the entrance, but lingering unofficial guides offer better two-hour tours in English for 50hry to 75hry per small group.

St Sophia Cathedral Complex

The city's oldest standing church and one of its most famous tourist attractions is the magnificent **St Sophia's Cathedral** (Sofiysky Sobor; ☎ 278 2083; Sofiyivska pl; grounds 2hry, adult/child 22/5hry, bell tower 5hry; ☿ grounds 9am-7pm, cathedral 10am-6pm Fri-Tue, to 5pm Wed; Ⓜ Maydan Nezalezhnosti). Built from 1017 to 1031 and named after Hagia Sofia (Holy Wisdom) Cathedral in İstanbul, its Byzantine plan and decoration announced the new religious and political authority of Kyiv. Prince Yaroslav, the 10th-century prince

UKRAINE

under whom Kyiv reached the height of its cultural and military strength, is buried here. Perhaps the most memorable aspect of a visit is the cathedral's interior, where there are 11th-century mosaics and frescos.

Andriyivsky Uzviz

Your visit to Kyiv wouldn't be complete without a walk along steep, cobblestoned Andriyivsky uzviz (Andrew's Descent), one of the oldest streets in town. Avoid the incline by taking the **funicular** (tickets 50 kopeks; 🕑 6.30am-11pm; Ⓜ Poshtova Ploscha) to the top of the hill, where you'll find the **St Michael's Monastery**, with its seven-cupola, periwinkle cathedral. Further down the street is the baroque **St Andrew's Church** (adult/student & child 6/2hry), built in 1754 in St Petersburg with its over-the-top decoration, including gaudy domes covered in gold baubles. Across from St Andrew's, up a small flight of stairs and on the ground before the National Museum of Ukrainian History are the **Desyatynna Church ruins**. Prince Volodymyr, who converted Kievan Rus to Christianity in the 10th century, ordered it built in 989 and used 10% of his income for it, hence the name (*desyatyn* means one-tenth). In 1240 it collapsed under the weight of people who took refuge on its roof during a Tatar siege.

From here, take souvenir-stall-lined Andriyivsky uzviz down the hill to start your descent into the realm of *matryoshki* (nesting dolls) and McLenin T-shirts.

Museums

Kyiv has a huge range of museums, but the following stand out as the ones to visit on a short stay.

The **Chornobyl Museum** (🕿 417 5422; prov Khoryva 1; adult/student & child 10/3hry, pre-ordered English language excursion 50hry; 🕑 10am-6pm Mon-Sat, closed last Mon of month; Ⓜ Kontraktova Ploscha) is a harrowing must-see for anyone wanting to know more about the world's worst nuclear accident. It very effectively combines two rooms of exhibits with a room of artwork and photography by those affected by the disaster. Book an English tour in advance, as there is no English signage.

Bulgakov House-Museum (🕿 425 3188; Andriyivsky uzviz 13; adult/student 5/3hry, obligatory excursion 12/6hry; 🕑 10am-5pm Thu-Tue; Ⓜ Kontraktova Ploscha) is where the beloved author of *The Master and Margarita* lived in the early 20th century, and his childhood home has been turned into a museum. The house and location will be in-

stantly recognisable to anyone familiar with his novel *The White Guard*. You can only visit the house on a guided tour.

The outdoor museum **Pyrohovo** (🕿 526 2416; vul Chervonopraporna; admission 10hry; 🕑 10am-5pm) holds 17th- to 20th-century wooden cottages, churches, farmsteads and windmills. Take *marshrutka* (shared minibus) 24, trolleybus 11 or bus 27 from the Lybidska metro station; the entrance is hard to miss. A taxi will cost about 75hry each way.

The **Museum of the Great Patriotic War** (🕿 285 9452; www.warmuseum.kiev.ua; vul Sichnevoho Povstannya 44; adult/child 4/1hry; 🕑 10am-4pm Tue-Sun) documents Ukrainian suffering during WWII and most memorably includes a gruesome pair of gloves made from human skin. Visible from miles around is the nearby **Rodina Mat** (Defence of the Motherland Monument), known variously as the 'Iron Lady' or 'Tin Tits'. You can take a lift from the museum right into the head of this fine looking 62m-high titanium statue of a woman with shield and sword.

Other Sights

Originally erected in 1037 but reconstructed in 1982, the **Golden Gate** (Zoloti Vorota; vul Volodymyrska 40a; Ⓜ Zoloti Vorota) was the original entrance into Old Kyiv. The new version of the old gate is a focal point for the city and a favoured meeting place for locals.

The very Gaudí-esque **Chimera Building** (vul Bankova 10; Ⓜ Khreshchatyk), with its demonic-looking animals and gargoyles, is probably the weirdest building in the city. It was constructed at the beginning of the 20th century by architect Vladislav Gorodetski, an eccentric genius who made it his home. It's currently part of the presidential administration.

The baroque, 18th-century **Mariyinsky Palace** (vul Hrushevskoho 5; Ⓜ Arsenalna) is surrounded by a lovely park with great river views but as it's a government building it remains closed to the public. It was being refurbished at the time of research.

The **Bessarabsky Market** (pl Bessarabska; Ⓜ Ploscha Lva Tolstoho) is a large covered hall that sells fresh produce, meats and honey; it can make for nice photos.

The metal-rainbow **Monument to the Unification of Russia & Ukraine** (Ⓜ Maydan Nezalezhnosti) offers excellent vistas of the city along the Dnipro; there's also a good viewpoint at Mariyinsky Palace (above).

KYIV METRO

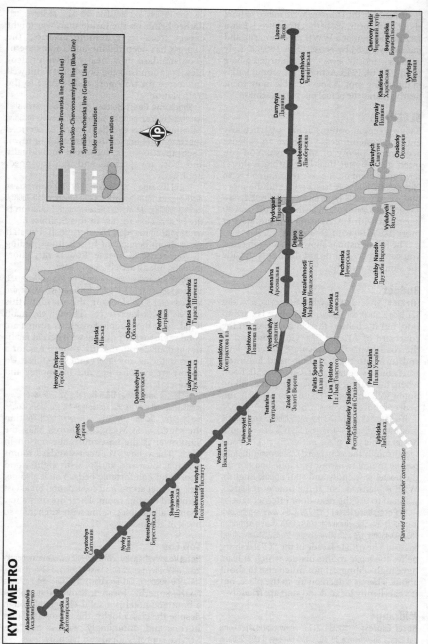

Syatoslhyno-Browarska line (Red Line)
Kurenivsko-Chervonoarmiyska line (Blue Line)
Syretsko-Pecherska line (Green Line)
Under construction
Transfer station

Akademmistechko Академмістечко
Zhytomyrska Житомирська
Syyatoshyn Святошин
Nyvky Нивки
Beresteyska Берестейська
Shulyavska Шулявська
Politekhnichny Instytut Політехнічний інститут
Universytet Університет
Vokzalna Вокзальна

Syrets Сирець
Dorohozhychi Дорогожичі
Lukyanivska Лук'янівська

Heroyiv Dnipra Героїв Дніпра
Minska Мінська
Obolon Оболонь
Petrivka Петрівка
Tarasa Shevchenka Тараса Шевченка
Kontraktova pl Контрактова пл
Poshtova pl Поштова пл

Teatralna Театральна
Zoloti Vorota Золоті Ворота
Palats Sportu Палац Спорту
Pl Lva Tolstoho Пл Льва Толстого
Respublikansky Stadion Республіканський Стадіон
Lybidska Либідська

Khreshchatyk Хрещатик
Arsenalna Арсенальна
Maydan Nezalezhnosti Майдан Незалежності
Klovska Кловська
Pecherska Печерська
Palats Ukraina Палац Україна
Druzhby Narodiv Дружби Народів

Hydropark Гідропарк
Dnipro Дніпро
Livoberezhna Лівобережна
Darnytsya Дарниця
Chernihivska Чернігівська
Lisova Лісова

Vydubychi Видубичі
Slavutych Славутич
Osokorky Осокорки
Pozniaky Позняки
Kharkivska Харківська
Vyrlytsya Вирлиця
Boryspilska Бориспільська
Chervony Hutir Червоний хутір

Planned extension under construction

UKRAINE

Just outside the Dorohozhychi metro station, about 4km northwest of the city centre, is **Babyn Yar**, the location of a WWII execution site and mass grave used by Nazis. Over 100,000 Kyiv citizens – mostly Jews – were murdered here from 1941 till 1943. Actually, the monument is in the wrong spot. A small marble monument nearby marks the actual place of execution.

SLEEPING

Kyiv's sleeping options aren't a particularly enticing bunch unless you have an expense account or plenty of spare cash. You can often get a better deal by renting a short-term apartment online. We recommend **Teren Plus** (☎ 428 1010; www.teren.kiev.ua) and the more budget-minded **UA Apartments** (☎ 205 9292; www.uaapartments.com). Rates can be as little as €20 per night with UA Apartments, but start at more like €100 with Teren Plus.

The follow listings show high-season rates; you can expect significant discounts outside the summer months.

Budget

IYH Kiev (☎ 481 3838; www.hihostels.com.ua; vul Artema 52a, Bldg 2, 5th fl; dm 125hry). This place is hard to find, but it's behind the US consulate in the courtyard of Artema 52a. Go to the end of the road (with the consulate on your left) and turn into the last right-hand entrance, where there's a guard post. Go to the 5th floor, where the staff of this Gogolian place will no doubt welcome you. There's no kitchen and bedrooms are very basic, but clean.

IYH Yaroslav (☎ 417 3189; www.hihostels.com.ua; vul Yaroslavska 10; dm/tw 140/150hry) Kyiv's other youth hostel is this tiny place in the district of Podil (go through the courtyard). Sleeping just 10 people in one twin and two four-bed dorms, the hostel is friendly and staff speak English. Wi-fi is planned, but at the time of research, you had to use the next-door internet cafe.

St Petersburg Hotel (☎ 279 7364; www.s-peter.com.ua; bul Tarasa Shevchenka 4; s/d/tr with shared bathroom 180/290/450hry, s/d with private bathroom 430/580hry, all incl breakfast) The ornate facade of the St Petersburg belies the basic rooms inside, which at least have high ceilings, if not much else to shout about. There's a decrepit air to the place, but it's excellently located and staff are friendly.

Midrange

Hotel Express (☎ 234 2113; www.expresskiev.com; bul Tarasa Shevchenka 38/40; s 450-600hry, d 698-990hry,

ste 1500-1980hry, incl breakfast; 🗷 🖵 ; Ⓜ Universitet) Rather better on the inside than you might expect from its gruesome exterior, the Express has been redone and rooms are of good standard now, nearly all with balconies. Location isn't the best but it's still well connected for transport and is close to the train station.

Sherborne Guest House (☎ 490 9693; www.sherbornehotel.com.ua; provulok Sichneviy 9; apt 450-1425hry; Ⓜ Arsenalna) This excellent block of serviced apartments is one of the best deals in town. Each apartment is decorated individually and most are spacious and well equipped. Book early.

Hotel Ukraina (☎ 278 6675, 279 0347; www.ukraine-hotel.kiev.ua; vul Instytutska 4; s 490-610hry, d 650-760hry, ste 990-1900hry; Ⓜ Maydan Nezalezhnosti) Location is the best reason to stay in this Stalinist hotel overlooking maydan Nezalezhnosti. The staff varies from belligerent to solicitous, adding to your sense of unease. Rooms vary enormously, but all are clean and safe.

Hotel Kozatsky (☎ 279 4914; vul Mykhaylivska 1/3; s/d from 586hry, ste 652-1064hry, incl breakfast; Ⓜ Maydan Nezalezhnosti) Overlooking the maydan, this is Kyiv's best-kept secret. Though the main building is thoroughly Soviet, its rooms are good value for the price, all with decent facilities and air-con in the 'lux' rooms. Ask for a room in the nearby *fligel* (annexe) – these two rooms are even better value for money and share a kitchen.

our pick **Sunflower B&B Hotel** (☎ 279 3846; www.sunflowerhotel.kiev.ua; vul Kostolna 9-41; s/d 965/1100hry, incl breakfast; 🗷 🖵 ; Ⓜ Maydan Nezalezhnosti) Within the sound of St Michael's Church bells, the Sunflower is the best midrange option in town. The yellow, Western-standard rooms are spacious and quiet, with light-wood floors and comfortable beds. You'll also get free internet access and continental breakfast delivered to your room. There are only a few rooms (all doubles, some with kitchens), so book in advance.

Top End

Hotel Vozdvyzhensky (☎ 531 9900; www.vozdvyzhensky.com; vul Vozdvyzhenska 60; s 1300-1580hry, d 1300-2000hry, ste 2500-3000hry, incl breakfast; 🗷 🖵 ; Ⓜ Poshtova Ploscha) Superbly located, Kyiv's first stab at a boutique hotel is a solid choice, although despite the classy lobby, the rooms are fairly normal and, annoyingly, wi-fi is not free. Service is professional and friendly.

Hotel Riviera (☎ 581 2888; www.rivierahotel.com.ua; vul Sagaydachnogo 15; r 1517-2528hry, ste 2126-5498hry, incl breakfast; ✲ 🖳 ; Ⓜ pl Poshtova) Located in bustling Podil, this new addition to the top-end hotels in Kyiv has a distinct boutique feel, with huge flat-screen TVs, free wi-fi and breakfast served in your room. It could go all out and be properly boutique, but given the vagaries of Ukrainian taste, it was probably safer to go for the neutral decor in the rooms, which are elegant without being exciting.

Hyatt Regency Kiev (☎ 581 1234; www.kiev.regency .hyatt.com; vul Tarasova 5; r from 3300hry, ste from 4800hry; ✲ 🖳 ; Ⓜ Maydan Nezalezhnosti) Opposite St Sophia's Cathedral, the glass-fronted Hyatt is home from home to visiting presidents, rock stars and the business elite. The hotel has all the amenities you'd expect in this price range, and offers a range of elegant, understated rooms.

EATING

Kyiv's eating scene has changed beyond recognition in the past few years, and there are a huge number of good restaurants. Even so it's best to read up before trying new places – standards are very uneven.

Puzata Khata (☎ 246 7245; vul Baseyna 1/2a; mains 5-15hry; ⌚ 8am-11pm; Ⓜ Teatralna) This ubiquitous chain is cheap and offers cafeteria-style dining; the food isn't spectacular but it's reliably OK and makes for an easy lunch stop.

Pervak (☎ 235 0952; vul Rognedynska 2; mains 30-80hry; ⌚ 11am-last customer; Ⓜ Ploscha Lva Tolstoho) Soviet style is superhip at Pervak, which serves high-quality Ukrainian food and has a popular and fun bar scene, as well as live music. The set lunches are great (43hry) and there's a buzz about the whole place.

Shalena Mama (Crazy Mama; ☎ 234 1751; vul Tereshchenkivska 4a; mains 40-100hry; ⌚ 24hr; Ⓜ Teatralna) This handy 24-hour diner with a Rolling Stones theme (each dish is a Stones anthem) features red upholstered booths and red glitter tables, as well as a predictable soundtrack. Food is tasty – a range of Ukrainian and international dishes, from gazpacho to *deruni* (potato pancakes).

Vernisazh (☎ 425 2403; Andriyivsky Uzviz 30; mains 50-90hry; Ⓜ pl Poshtova) This friendly and atmospheric eatery on Kyiv's most famous street is clad in local art and serves up decent meals despite the touristy nature of the area. There's also a small outside terrace – fight for a table.

Himalaya (☎ 270 5437; vul Khreshchatyk 23; mains 50-100hry; ⌚ 11.30am-11.30pm; Ⓜ Maydan Nezalezhnosti) A well-translated English menu and plenty of vegetarian options make Himalaya a firm favourite. The menu is enormous, and even includes Chinese dishes, as well as its large Indian selection. If you can't enter from Khreshchatyk, go through the huge arch just north of the restaurant, walk uphill, take the first right, and go about 100m.

our pick **Mimino** (☎ 417 3545; vul Spaska 10a; mains 60-170hry; ⌚ 11am-1am; Ⓜ pl Kontraktova) This stellar Georgian restaurant is great for a splurge. As Georgian meals are comprised of many dishes, the prices soon add up, but the traditional cooking is Kyiv's best, served in an atmospheric, dark setting.

Mislivets (☎ 236 3735; vul Saksaganskogo 147/5; mains 80-200hry; ⌚ noon-10pm; Ⓜ Universitet) A good choice for trying traditional Ukrainian food, this place has plenty of charm, whether you choose to eat outside on the terrace or inside, where there's a dark taverna feel. The menu encompasses Ukrainian classics and so is heavy on game, grilled meats, soups and salads.

DRINKING
Bars

Art Club 44 (☎ 279 4137; vul Khreshchatyk 44b; cover varies; Ⓜ Teatralna) This underground place may have lost its alternative credentials a little since the Orange Revolution, but it's still a great venue, with live music every night, making it a good place to meet young locals.

Baraban (☎ 229 2355; vul Prorizna 4a; ⌚ 11am-11pm; Ⓜ Maydan Nezalezhnosti) Popular with a colourful range of journalists, artists and intellectuals, 'the Drum' is hidden away but repays the effort to find it (it's at the back of a courtyard). There's bar food here too.

Blindazh (☎ 228 1511; Mala Zhytomirska 15; Ⓜ Maydan Nezalezhnosti) This dive bar is decked out with war paraphernalia and Soviet-era posters. People come for the moody atmosphere and inexpensive libations, not for the food, which makes army rations seem preferable.

Cafes

Kyiv's cafe society is well-established now, and you'll find decent coffee shops all over the city. Our favourites include **Entresol** (☎ 235 8347; Bul Tarasa Shevchenko 2; ⌚ 11am-11pm; Ⓜ Teatralna) where you'll find a playful layout, free wi-fi and a great little bookshop, and any of the classy chain **Repriza** (☎ 235 8347; Vul Bogdana Khmelnytskoho 40/25; ◷ 10am-11pm; Ⓜ Universitet) where delicious cakes are served up, as well as great coffee.

ENTERTAINMENT
Nightclubs
Inventive small concerts are held at Art Club 44 (p923). The following are some fun clubs that don't focus on gambling and stripping (which are well marketed and need no review here). Most charge a cover that varies (probably 30hry to 100hry) depending on what's on.

Caribbean Club (☎ 288 1290; vul Kominternu 4; ◷ 4pm-last customer Mon-Fri, from 6pm Sat & Sun; Ⓜ Universitet/Vokzalna) Injecting some much needed Latino sass into Kyiv's nightlife, this hugely popular disco is a place to find great dancers showing off on the dance floor.

Docker's ABC (☎ 278 1717; www.docker.com.ua; vul Zankovetskoyi 15/4a; ◷ 24hr; Ⓜ Khreshchatyk) By day a cafe-bar, Docker's is best once the sun goes down, when it opens up as a popular nightclub where live acts often perform. The decor has a nautical theme.

Pomada (☎ 279 5552; Zankovetskoyi 6; ◷ 10pm-4am; Ⓜ Khreshchatyk) Kyiv's most popular gay club is slap-bang in the heart of the capital, and very much geared to the 'elite'. It's a fun place with high prices.

Shooters (☎ 254 2024; www.shooters.kiev.ua; vul Moskovska 22; ◷ 24hr; Ⓜ Arsenalna) This Kyiv mainstay is the pick-up joint of choice, where rich expats and gorgeous young women hang out together and dance the night away.

Performing Arts
Kyiv has a large theatre and music scene. Tickets can be purchased in advance at the **Teatralna Kasa** (vul Khreshchatyk 21; Ⓜ Khreshchatyk). Same-day tickets can be purchased at the venue.

National Opera Theatre (☎ 279 1169; www.opera.com.ua; vul Volodymyrska 50; Ⓜ Zoloti Vorota) Performances at this lavish opera house are a grandiose affair. The schedule changes nightly.

Ivan Franko National Drama Theatre (☎ 279 5921; www.franko-theatre.kiev.ua, in Ukrainian; pl Ivana Franka 3; Ⓜ Khreshchatyk) Highly respected performances are put on here, but they're usually only in Ukrainian.

National Philharmonic (☎ 278 1697; www.filarmonia.com.ua; Volodymyrska uzviz 2; Ⓜ Maydan Nezalezhnosti) Housed in a beautiful white building, while inside is a phenomenal organ.

Sport
Dynamo Stadium (☎ 229 0209; vul Hrushevskoho 3; Ⓜ Maydan Nezalezhnosti) is Ukraine's most beloved stadium, named after Ukraine's most beloved football team. Dynamo itself plays all its important matches at the newer 100,000 seater **Respublikansky Stadium** (vul Chervonoarmiyska 55; Ⓜ Respublikansky Stadion) where the Euro 2012 football final will also be held.

SHOPPING
Without a doubt, the place to shop for souvenirs is along Andriyivsky uzviz. Western-style malls and shopping centres are fast becoming ubiquitous in the town centre, even though the number of people who can shop there hasn't quite justified the sheer quantity of them.

GETTING THERE & AWAY
Air
The **Boryspil international airport** (☎ 490 4777; www.airport-borispol.kiev.ua) is 35km from central Kyiv. All international flights use Terminal B; Terminal A is used for internal flights. In 2008, **Wizzair** (www.wizzair.com) began operating cheap internal flights from Terminal A to Odesa, Simferopol and Lviv. These were by far the best deals for internal air travel in the country at the time of research.

Other domestic flights and some charters to other CIS countries arrive and leave from **Zhulyany Airport** (☎ 242 2308; www.airport.kiev.ua); it's close to the centre (about 8km away).

Kiyavia (☎ 490 4901; vul Horodetskoho 4; www.kiyavia.com) works well for booking domestic flights.

Bus
Almost all long-distance buses, including Autolux, use the **Central Bus Terminal** (☎ 265 0430; pl Moskovska 3; Ⓜ Lybidska). To get there from Lybidska metro station, take minibus 457 (1.50hry), trolleybus 4, 11 or 12, or tram 9 or 10 one stop.

Trains are more comfortable than buses. If it must be bus, try the privately owned **Autolux** (www.autolux.ua), which goes between Kyiv and Ivano-Frankivsk, Lviv, Odesa, Simferopol and Uzhhorod. All routes stop at Boryspil Airport and the Kyiv train station. The website allows for online booking.

From the central bus station there are buses to Chişinău (Moldova; 80hry to 130hry, 9½ hours, three daily) and Moscow (140hry to 180hry, 20 hours, one daily), as well as some nonregular buses to Minsk (110hry, 12½ hours).

State-run buses go to Odesa (90hry to 120hry, eight hours, hourly), Simferopol (105hry, 16 hours, one daily), Yalta (170hry, 18 hours, two daily), Sevastopol (200hry, 18 hours, one daily), Lviv (95hry, 11 hours, up to six daily) and Kamyanets-Podilsky (100hry, 12 hours, two daily).

Train

The modern **train station** (☎ 005; pl Vokzalna 2) is located right next to the Vokzalna metro station. The **train ticket office** (☎ 050; bul Tarasa Shevchenka 38/40; ✆ 7am-9pm), next to the Hotel Express, is usually less hectic for ticket purchases. For non-CIS destinations, go to Hall No 1, down a hallway on the left as you enter the main area.

Trains from Kyiv go to Uzhhorod, (110hry, 17 hours, four daily), Chernivsti (85hry, 15 hours, two daily), Kamyanets-Podilsky (55hry, 4½ hours or 12 hours overnight, two daily), Lviv (70hry to 110hry, 6½ to 12 hours, six daily), Odesa (110hry, nine to 15 hours, five daily), Sevastopol (120hry, 17 hours, two daily) and Simferopol (110hry to 155hry, 15 hours, two daily).

Internationally there are daily trains to Moscow, St Petersburg, Minsk, Warsaw, Brest and Budapest. There are also frequent services to Prague, Belgrade, Sofia, Chişinău and Berlin.

GETTING AROUND
To/From the Airport

The usual way to Boryspil airport (10hry, 45 minutes) is on an **Atass bus** (☎ 296 7367). Buses depart from the bus stop at pl Peremohy (4am to midnight) and from the train station (5am to 3.30am) every 15 to 30 minutes, although they leave once an hour until 6am. At Boryspil, buses arrive/depart from in front of the international terminal. In both directions all Atass buses stop at Kharkhovska metro station, allowing you to buy the cheapest possible ticket (20hry) and connect to/from the much faster metro as soon as possible. A taxi will set you back about 150hry to 200hry.

To get to Zhulyany airport, take trolley-bus 9 from either pl Peremohy or the train station's south terminal (30 to 40 minutes). Alternatively you can call a taxi (about 50hry for a 20-minute ride).

Boat

Cruises from the south arrive from May to October at the **Boat Passenger Terminal**, near metro Ploscha Poshtova. There are no scheduled ferry services from here at present. For cruise bookings, contact **Chernova Ruta** (☎ 253 9247; www.ruta-cruise.com).

Public Transport

Kyiv's metro is clean, efficient, reliable and easy to use, especially if you read Cyrillic. Trains run frequently between around 6am and midnight on all three lines. Single-ride tokens (*zhetony*) cost 50 kopeks and are sold at entrances; there are also token-vending machines that only sometimes work.

Tickets for buses, trams and trolleybuses cost 60 kopeks and are sold at street kiosks or directly from the driver or conductor. Minibuses (*marshrutky*) cost 1hry to 2hry; pay the driver upon entering.

Taxi

Catching a taxi from the train station, on pl Peremohy and outside hotels, inevitably incurs a higher price, so try to find one elsewhere on the street. From the train station to the centre may cost 50hry. Try to look for newer, official-looking cars, which are more likely to have a meter and hence won't rip you off. Catching metered cabs on the street is rare. By phone, try ☎ 200 0200. You can also flag down a private car and negotiate a price if you speak the language.

WESTERN UKRAINE

You haven't really been to Ukraine until you've been to the country's western flank, the Ukrainian heartland where the country's culture and language are cradled with equal amounts of pride and vigilance. Here the gentle sound of Ukrainian reverberates in the medieval towns and speaking Russian will attract (not always positive) attention. The region wasn't annexed by the USSR until 1939, and somehow escaped bombing during WWII, so both the architecture and the attitudes have, for the most part, managed to avoid the Soviet influence, leaving it with a relaxed, central European look and feel.

This land of brave Cossack feats and earthy peasant humour straight out of Gogol offers some wonderful attractions to travellers, from the Unesco World Heritage site of Lviv's Old Town to the rolling scenery of the Carpathians. Don't miss out on wonderful

CHORNOBYL

On 26 April 1986 reactor No 4 at Chornobyl nuclear power station, 100km north of Kyiv, exploded and nearly 9 tons of radioactive material (90 times as much as in the Hiroshima bomb) spewed into the sky. An estimated 4.9 million people in northern Ukraine, southern Belarus and south-western Russia were affected. Some people – especially the elderly, who cannot conceive of the dangers of this invisible stuff called radiation – have returned to the area since the evacuation, and even live off the small gardens they've planted by their homes. For more information about the situation and how to help, visit www.childrenofchornobyl.org, and watch the Oscar-winning documentary *Chernobyl Heart*.

Western monitors now conclude that radioactivity levels at Chornobyl are negligible, so organised tours of the site and surrounding 'ghost' villages have thrived, as travellers undertake extreme tourism to 'the zone'. But consider the risks before signing up – although the half-life of the thyroid-attacking iodine isotopes is long past, the dangerous plutonium ones will not decompose for another 20,000 or so years. (Although tour agencies may claim they won't go to plutonium-affected areas, it's hard to imagine how an explosion of radioactive particles could be contained into certain zones.)

If you do decide to go, the standard price for a six-hour visit is about €100, as long as there are other takers. Trips for just one or two people are much more expensive, but the various travel agencies often pool their takers to keep the prices down. Sam Travel (p917) is a long-established company that organises trips. If you opt to play it safe and eschew Chornobyl itself, do pay a visit to the riveting Chornobyl Museum (p920) in Kyiv.

Kamyanets-Podilsky either, a dramatically located settlement straddling a jaw-dropping ravine topped with an impressive fortress that, for many, is the highlight of the region.

LVIV ЛЬВІВ
☎ 032 (7 digits), 0322 (6 digits) / pop 745,000
Whether you're arriving from the east, with its Soviet cities and concrete architecture, or from the west, where tourist numbers can sometimes feel out of control, you'll be extremely glad to have arrived in Lviv, Ukraine's loveliest city. This fabulous relic of Galicia's cosmopolitan past feels distinctly un-Soviet, with its central European flavour and charismatic population. Best of all, despite the extraordinary architectural wealth here, tourists remain a small minority, even in the Unesco World Heritage–listed Old Town in midsummer.

While tourism is still in its infancy here, entrepreneurial locals have filled the gap, meaning that today Lviv boasts Ukraine's best established English-speaking tourist industry. With new hotels opening all the time, cheap airlines are beginning to make Lviv an easily accessible weekend break from Western Europe. But for the moment it remains one of the continent's best-kept secrets – come and enjoy it while you can.

Information
Budinok Knigi (☎ 722 550; pl Mitskevycha; ☼ 10am-6pm Mon-Fri, to 3pm Sat) Lviv's oldest bookshop has maps, guides and some novels in English.
Central post office (☎ 065; vul Slovatskoho 1; ☼ 8am-8pm Mon-Fri, 8am-4pm Sat, 9am-3pm Sun)
Chorna Medea (☎ 261 0250; vul Petra Doroshenka 50; per hr 6hry; ☼ 24hr) Very popular internet cafe.
Internet Klub (☎ 242 4210; vul Dudaeva 12; per hr 4-6hry; ☼ 24hr) Twenty terminals; can connect laptops.
Internet Service (☎ 294 8204; vul Shevska 6; per hr 6hry; ☼ 10am-9pm) Small internet cafe off the main square on 2nd floor of Litera Bookshop.
Tourist information centre (☎ 201 8666, 948 204; www.tourinfo.lviv.ua; pl Rynok 2; ☼ 10am-1pm & 2-6pm Mon-Fri) English-speaking staff are helpful and there's lots of information available.

Sights
OLD TOWN
Any tour of Lviv should begin with **ploscha Rynok** (Market Square), the excellently preserved hub of the city's political and commercial life from the Middle Ages. In 1998 it was declared a Unesco World Heritage site. The town hall (*ratusha*), which takes up most of the square itself, was originally built in the 14th century, and has been rebuilt several times since then: once in the 16th century when it was demolished by fire and most recently in 1851.

LVIV

0 — 200 m
0 — 0.1 miles

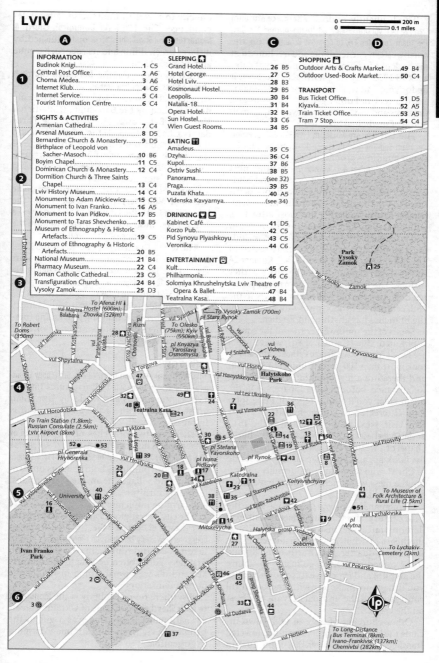

INFORMATION	
Budinok Knigi	1 C5
Central Post Office	2 A6
Chorna Medea	3 A6
Internet Klub	4 C6
Internet Service	5 C4
Tourist Information Centre	6 C4

SIGHTS & ACTIVITIES	
Armenian Cathedral	7 C4
Arsenal Museum	8 D5
Bernardine Church & Monastery	9 D5
Birthplace of Leopold von Sacher-Masoch	10 B6
Boyim Chapel	11 C5
Dominican Church & Monastery	12 C4
Dormition Church & Three Saints Chapel	13 C4
Lviv History Museum	14 C4
Monument to Adam Mickiewicz	15 C5
Monument to Ivan Franko	16 A5
Monument to Ivan Pidkov	17 B5
Monument to Taras Shevchenko	18 B5
Museum of Ethnography & Historic Artefacts	19 C4
Museum of Ethnography & Historic Artefacts	20 B5
National Museum	21 B4
Pharmacy Museum	22 C4
Roman Catholic Cathedral	23 C4
Transfiguration Church	24 B4
Vysoky Zamok	25 D3

SLEEPING	
Grand Hotel	26 B5
Hotel George	27 C5
Hotel Lviv	28 B3
Kosmonaut Hostel	29 B5
Leopolis	30 B4
Natalia-18	31 B4
Opera Hotel	32 B4
Sun Hostel	33 C6
Wien Guest Rooms	34 B5

EATING	
Amadeus	35 C5
Dzyha	36 C4
Kupol	37 B6
Ostriv Sushi	38 B5
Panorama	(see 32)
Praga	39 B5
Puzata Khata	40 A5
Videnska Kavyarnya	(see 34)

DRINKING	
Kabinet Café	41 D5
Korzo Pub	42 C5
Pid Synoyu Plyashkoyu	43 C5
Veronika	44 C6

ENTERTAINMENT	
Kult	45 C6
Philharmonia	46 C6
Solomiya Khrushelnytska Lviv Theatre of Opera & Ballet	47 B4
Teatralna Kasa	48 B4

SHOPPING	
Outdoor Arts & Crafts Market	49 B4
Outdoor Used-Book Market	50 C4

TRANSPORT	
Bus Ticket Office	51 D5
Kiyavia	52 A5
Train Ticket Office	53 A5
Tram 7 Stop	54 C4

The brilliantly oddball **Pharmacy Museum** (☎ 722 041; vul Drukarska 2; adult/student/child 3/2/1hr; ⏰ 10am-7pm Mon-Fri, to 6pm Sat & Sun) is on the northwestern corner of the square, housed at the back of a functioning pharmacy that dates back to 1735. Pay the pharmacists to open it up for you, and walk into a world of containers, drawers and other gadgets for herbs and tinctures and salves. You can even buy a small bottle of medicinal 'iron wine'.

The **Lviv History Museum** (☎ 720 671; pl Rynok; ⏰ 10am-5pm Thu-Tue) is spread out between different buildings around the square, at Nos 4, 6 and 24. **Number 4** (admission 2hry) is the most interesting, covering the city's 19th- and 20th-century history, including two floors dedicated to the Ukrainian nationalist movement. **Number 6** (admission 3hry) is the most attractive, with an Italian-Renaissance inner courtyard and an exquisitely decorated interior, including a wood-cut parquet floor constructed of 14 different kinds of hardwood. **Number 24** (admission 2hry) expounds on the city's earlier history. The highlight is an enormous painting depicting the old walled city of Lviv in the 18th century. Pr Svobody was a moat! None of the branches has anything in English.

South of the southwest corner of the square is pl Katedralna (Cathedral Sq), where you'll see Lviv's impressive **Roman Catholic Cathedral**. It took more than 100 years to build (1370–1480) and therefore a few different styles (Gothic, Renaissance, baroque) are apparent. On the north side, you'll find a relief of Pope John Paul II, erected to commemorate his 2001 Lviv visit. Next to the cathedral is the 1617 **Boyim Chapel** (admission 2hry; ⏰ 9am-6pm), the burial chapel of a wealthy Hungarian merchant family. Look up, and you'll see an atypical statue of Christ, who seems to be mournfully observing the mess we wretched sinners have made of this world.

Armenians have lived in Ukraine since the 11th century, and the 1363 **Armenian Cathedral** demonstrates the historical continuity at the heart of what is still considered Lviv's Armenian quarter, just north of pl Rynok. If the cathedral is open, go inside to admire the atypical and evocative frescos. Otherwise you'll have to make do with the beautiful courtyard and the unusual carving of Christ on the cross.

Other churches of note in Old Town include the late-17th-century, twin-bell towered **Transfiguration Church** (vul Krakivska), the first in

the city to revert to Catholicism after independence. The 1745–64 **Dominican Church & Monastery** (vul Stavropihiyska) is distinguished by its large green dome and its rococo, baroque and classical features.

Also look out for the **Dormition Church & Three Saints Chapel** (vul Ruska), which was constructed between 1591 and 1629 and is easily distinguished by the 65m-high, triple-tiered Kornyakt Bell Tower (1572–78). The Three Saints Chapel (1578–91) is nestled beneath the tower and built into the north side of the church, in a wonderful little courtyard. Together, the two structures are considered to be the historic centre of the city.

South of here is 17th-century **Bernardine Church & Monastery** (vul Pidvalna), now the Ukrainian Catholic Church of St Andrew – a major Lviv landmark, considered to have the finest baroque interior in the city.

The Royal Arsenal, built between 1639 and 1646, once held weapons to be used in wars against the Turks; it now holds a **museum** (admission 5hry, ⏰ 10am-5.45pm), which houses weapons, armour and other artefacts. The statue on the square outside is of Federov, a 16th-century monk who brought printing to Ukraine (perhaps why there's an outdoor used-book market here as well).

NEW TOWN

The **National Museum** (☎ 742 280; pr Svobody 20; admission 14hry; ⏰ 10am-6pm Sat-Thu) features 15th- to 19th-century icons and works by Ukrainian artists. The interior of the building itself is impressive as well.

There are two branches of the **Museum of Ethnography & Historic Artefacts** (☎ 727 808; pl Rynok 10 & pr Svobody 15; adult/student 5/2hry; ⏰ 11am-5.30pm Tue-Sun). Both buildings hold exhibits on farm culture and village life in the Carpathians, including furniture, woodcarvings, ceramics and farming implements.

The city's prestigious **Solomiya Khrushelnytska Lviv Theatre of Opera & Ballet** (☎ 728 672; www.lviv opera.org; pr Svobody 28; admission 10hry) allows you to take a peak inside during the day if there's no matinee. You'll often be able to see rehearsals, and it's well worth going inside for the beautiful interiors.

Elsewhere on pr Svobody is the **Monument to Taras Shevchenko**, a statue of Ukraine's greatest nationalist writer that was a gift to the people of Lviv from the Ukrainian diaspora in Argentina.

OTHER SIGHTS

The city's enormous **Lychakiv Cemetery** (vul Mechnikova; adult/student 10/5hry; � 9am-5pm) is a very worthy detour – it's one of the loveliest cemeteries in Eastern Europe. If you get on tram 2 or 7 in Old Town, you'll arrive right in front of the cemetery five stops later (if you get confused, ask for the *klad-bee-sheh*).

The **Museum of Folk Architecture & Rural Life** (☎ 718 017; vul Chernecha Hora 1; adult/child 1.50/0.75hry; � 11am-7pm Tue-Sun Apr-Oct, to 6pm Nov-Mar) is a large park that holds more than 100 old wooden homes and churches. Take tram 7 for four stops from vul Pidvalna, continue in same direction and turn left on vul Krupyarska (Крупярська), and follow the signs.

Lviv's **Vysoky Zamok** (High Castle) gives you a fantastic vista over the city's sublime cupola-strewn skyline from the city's highest point, although you may have to squint through some trees; good times to visit are sunset and winter, when there are no leaves to obstruct the view. The 14th-century ruined stone fort at the summit was Lviv's birthplace and offers the best vantage point of the modern city.

There are several ways to reach Vysoky Zamok. The easiest method is to make your way to the corner of vul Vynnychenka and vul Kryvonosa and just head up the hill towards the TV tower. The castle is east of the tower; follow the steel stairs behind the restaurant at the first crest of the hill. If you're feeling lazy you can take a taxi most of the way up, approaching from the east via vul Vysoky Zamok.

One final quirky sight is the **birthplace of Leopold von Sacher-Masoch** (vul Kopernyka 22), the world's original 'masochist'. The author of *Venus in Furs* came into the world here in 1835, although he spent most of his subsequent 60 years begging to be whipped in Austria, Germany and Italy.

Sleeping

The best-value option for anyone planning to stay for more than a couple of nights here is to rent an apartment. We recommend **In Lviv** (☎ 728 001; www.inlviv.info), **Rent in Lviv** (☎ 50-432 7638; www.rentinlviv.com) and **Lviv Apartments** (☎ 67-672 5161; www.lviv-apartments.com), where prices start at around €25 per day.

BUDGET

Sun Hostel (☎ 291 1970; www.sun.lviv.ua; pr Shevchenko 16; dm/d from 50/100hry) Inside the travel agency of the same name, this centrally located but rather chaotically run hostel has unbeatably low prices that include free wi-fi and access to a washing machine. The place is rather cramped, with a crowded, labyrinthine floorplan, but rooms are decent with wooden floors in quirky layouts.

Kosmonaut Hostel (☎ 274 0274; www.thekosmonaut.com; vul Sichovykh Striltsiv 8; dm 70-90hry; s/d/apt 100/200/210hry; ☐) The most centrally located, best run and friendliest hostel in town, the Gagarin-themed Kosmonaut is great fun, with free guest wi-fi, a shared kitchen, four dorms, one apartment with en suite facilities and a twin room (that can be booked as a single). The hostel also offers visa support for those who need it.

Hotel Lviv (☎ 423 555; hotel_lviv@svitonline.com; pr V Chornovola 7; s/d from 130/200hry) Just behind the opera house, this ageing behemoth presents a number of options, from the very basic rooms with a basin and shared facilities to surprisingly spacious 'lux' rooms. A few words of Ukrainian work wonders on the floor ladies, who turn instantly from dragons to mothers. There's only hot water in the mornings and evenings.

MIDRANGE

our pick **Hotel George** (☎ 725 952; www.georgehotel.com.ua; pl Mitskevycha 1; s/tw with shared bathroom 190/220hry, with private bathroom 370/400hry) Look no further for old-world Lviv – the famous colonnaded lobby gives this place an atmosphere that money alone just can't buy. The 'tourist class' rooms here are a great deal and share facilities on the corridor, while the more expensive options are en suite, yet surprisingly simple.

Natalia-18 (☎ 242 2068; www.natalia18.ho.com.ua; pl K Yaroslava Osmomysla 7; s 360hry, d 520-700hry, tr 770-900hry; ☒ ☐) A welcome addition to the midrange hotels in Lviv, Natalia is a cosy, central place with rather dark (but perfectly comfortable) rooms, all of which have a safe, phone, TV and minibar. There's no wi-fi, but there's a terminal in reception with a web hookup (per hour 5hry).

Wien Guest Rooms (☎ 444 314; www.wienhotel.lviv.ua; pl Svobody 12; s 450-640hry, d 500-690hry, ste 820-870hry; ☒ ☐) Hidden away from casual passers-by, despite being moments from pl Rynok, the Wien has the air of a private club. That's not to say it's pretentious in any way – quite the opposite, in fact – the staff is delightful and

UKRAINE

the simple, comfortable rooms are great value. There's free wi-fi throughout.

TOP END

Opera Hotel (☎ 225 9000; www.hotel-opera.lviv.ua; pr Svobody 45; s 570-680hry, d 800-920hry, ste 1100-1840hry, incl breakfast; ✕ 💻) Overlooking the opera house, this excellent option has friendly and professional staff, a great rooftop restaurant and very comfortable rooms with all the amenities you'd expect.

Grand Hotel (☎ 272 4042; www.ghgroup.com.ua; pr Svobody 13; s 690hry, d 885-975hry, ste 1075-2000hry, incl breakfast; ✕ 💻 🏊) The Grand's unbeatable location, coupled with the old-world feel in its well-appointed lobby, makes this a great top-end option. The rooms have some grand touches, such as pattered wooden floors and ceiling mouldings, although they lack the extra flair of a true five-star hotel. Rates include the use of a nearby fitness centre and swimming pool.

Leopolis (☎ 295 9500; www.leopolishotel.com; vul Teatralna 16; r 1250-1550hry, ste 2500-3200hry, incl breakfast; ✕ 💻) Having opened in 2007 as the first luxury hotel in Old Town, the dazzling Leopolis is now the city's best address. With 43 rooms open at present, and a new wing being built to double that number, the hotel also plans to add a pool, gym and sauna. Rooms are airy and stylish, all with king-size beds. Service is friendly and there are two excellent restaurants to boot.

Eating

There are a few culinary gems in Lviv, although overall the city seems to run on coffee and cake far more than haute cuisine.

Puzata Khata (☎ 240 3265; vul Sichovykh Striltsiv; mains 5-15hry; ✕ 8am-11pm) This popular cafeteria-style chain serves up Ukrainian staples in a rowdy setting popular with students from the nearby university. Unlike the one in Kyiv, there is plenty of seating.

Videnska Kavyarnya (☎ 722 021; www.wienkaffe .lviv.ua; pr Svobody 12; mains 8-60hry; ✕ 10am-11pm) One of many popular restaurants with spring and summer sidewalk seating; this charming place is split between a relaxed cafe and a formal dining room. This is a great place to try innovative Ukrainian food.

Ostriv Sushi (☎ 722 972; pr Svobody 6-8; mains 12-30hry; ✕ 8am-11pm Mon-Fri, 10am-10pm Sat & Sun) This well-designed steel-and-glass space makes a welcome break from Old Town Lviv.

Describing itself as a 'democratic Japanese restaurant', the restaurant offers a range of Japanese food and is great in the summer, when it opens up to the busy main avenue.

Dzyha (☎ 297 5010; vul Virmenska 35; mains 25hry; ✕ 8am-11pm) This great option is a relaxed bar outside, with a decent yet informal restaurant inside. The place attracts an arty crowd, who order food from the newspaper-style menu, including delicious Galician toast, *nasylniki* (pancakes) and even stuffed piglet. This is also a good breakfast spot.

Kupol (☎ 261 1454; vul Chaykovskoho 37; mains 25-85hry; ✕ 11am-11pm) One of Lviv's most celebrated restaurants, Kupol is a gorgeously attired two-room affair where time has stood still since 1938 (the year before the Soviets arrived). Old-world charm works a treat here, with mementos, sepia photographs and antiques sprinkled about the place. Even better, the sumptuous food is no afterthought – try the fried liver with apple and calvados or the trout cooked with almonds.

Praga (☎ 274 1220; vul Hnatyuka 8; mains 30-70hry; ✕ 8am-11pm) Split into two parts, the elegant Praga contains both a coffee and cake shop, where beers and light meals are also served up, and a much classier restaurant serving classic Czech fare. It's also one of the few places in town with free wi-fi.

our pick Amadeus (☎ 261 5022; pl Katedralna 7; mains 30-100hry; ✕ 11am-11pm) Lviv's most enduringly popular eatery is rightly Amadeus, where you can relax in the sunshine on a stylish wicker chair or snuggle up inside the grand cafe itself, always confident that the modern European cuisine will be excellent, the traditional music kept at a pleasant volume and the staff delightful.

Panorama (☎ 225 9011; pr Svobody 45; mains 40-150hry) On the roof of the Opera Hotel, Panorama enjoys impressive views of the city's cupolas from its terrace, although the ambitious and excellent food is just as much of a reason to dine here. Inside is glacially cool, while the small terrace is perfect for lunch on a summer's day.

Drinking

Drinking in Lviv revolves more around coffee than alcohol, although that's not to say locals don't love beer, they just like coffee even more!

Kabinet Café (vul Vynnychenka 12; ✕ 10am-11pm) Definitely one of the city's more interesting spots for a drink, Kabinet serves up hot and cold bevies in a stylish library setting complete with billiards table.

Korzo Pub (☎ 296 7092; vul Brativ Rohatyntsiv 10; ☽ noon-midnight Sun-Thu, to 2am Fri & Sat) This is the best pub in town, with a lovely wooden interior. There's a wide range of beers, decent food and a crowd of regulars.

Pid Synoyu Plyashkoyu (vul Ruska 4; ☽ 11.30am-10pm) This charmer of a cafe's name means 'Under the Bluebottle' and it's a clue to finding it – go through the door under the bluebottle and head through the courtyard to escape the crowds on pl Rynok and enjoy a sublime coffee in refined, dark surroundings. There's also free wi-fi here and a small food menu that includes fondue.

our pick **Robert Doms** (☎ 292 2593; vul Kleparivska 18; ☽ noon-midnight) Look no further for Lviv's most atmospheric drinking venue – Robert Doms is a converted beer storage vault once used by the neighbouring Lvivske brewery, and it's a gem. The three subterranean rooms have the feel of a German Bier Keller, with big banqueting tables, live music, superb platters of Ukrainian cooking and an endless supply of sweet, sweet beer. It's a hike from the centre, past the Kraichevsky Market, but well worth the walk!

Veronika (☎ 297 8128; pr Shevchenka 21; ☽ 10am-midnight) Run by the folks who brought you Amadeus, the best restaurant in town, Veronika is an equally brilliant place for cake and coffee in the grand surrounds. Bag a table outside in the sun.

Entertainment

A performance at the beautiful **Solomiya Khrushelnytska Lviv Theatre of Opera & Ballet** (☎ 728 672; www.lvivopera.org; pr Svobody 28; tickets 50-400hry) is a must. For concerts, the **Philharmonia** (☎ 741 086; vul Chaykovskoho 7; tickets 40-100hry) is also highly recommended. Tickets are sold on-site or at the **teatralna kasa** (☎ 233 3188; pr Svobody 37; ☽ 10am-1pm & 3-5pm Mon-Sat).

For something more alternative, head to **Kult** (☎ 242 2242; vul Chaykovskoho 7; admission varies; ☽ noon-2am), a basement venue next to the Philharmonia that reverberates with live Ukrainian rock music every night of the week.

Shopping

There's a lively **outdoor arts and crafts market** (☽ morning-sunset) off pr Svobody that is excel-lent for souvenirs and gifts of all sorts. If you're into old books, there's a quirky **outdoor used-book market** (☽ morning-sunset) by the Arsenal Museum.

Getting There & Away

AIR

Lviv airport (☎ 298 112; www.avia.lviv.ua) is about 9km west of the centre. It's small and basic (no ATM or currency exchange). There are domestic flights, as well as international flights to Vienna with Austrian Airlines, and Warsaw with LOT Polish Airlines. There are daily flights to/from Kyiv, for which prices vary enormously, but the best offers at the time of writing were from budget airline **Wizzair** (www.wizzair.com).

BUS

Lviv has eight bus terminals, but only one is of use to most travellers – the **long-distance bus terminal** (Holovny Avtovokzal; ☎ 632 473; vul Stryska 271), about 8km south of the city centre (take *marshrutka* 71 or 180 from pr Svobody or trolleybus 5 from pl Petrushevycha).

Advance tickets for public buses to Kyiv (100hry, 11 hours, six daily), Kamyanets-Podilsky (73hry, eight hours, twice daily), Chernivtsi (55hry, 7½ hours, twice daily) and Uzhhorod (48hry, six hours, four daily), as well as international destinations, are sold at the **bus ticket office** (vul Vynnychenka 8; ☽ 9am-6pm Mon-Sat). Bus information (not in English) can be had at ☎ 004 until 8pm.

Privately run **Autolux** (www.autolux.com.ua) also operates from the long-distance terminal, sending nice, modern buses regularly to Kyiv and other cities. See the website for up-to-date details.

From Lviv, there are buses to Warsaw (137hry, 11 hours, three daily), Kraków (115hry, one daily, nine hours) and Przemyśl (55hry, three hours, 12 daily), but we do not recommend using them, as the delays at the busy border can be huge, something alleviated on a train.

TRAIN

The **train station** (☎ 005; pl Dvirtseva) is 1.75km west of the city centre and connected to town by trams 1 and 9. Tickets can also be obtained from the **train ticket office** (☎ 226 5276; vul Hnatyuka 20; ☽ 8am-2pm & 3-8pm Mon-Sat, to 6pm Sun); be prepared to stand in line, especially in spring and summer. Each window

UKRAINE

closes for 10 minutes an hour – check before joining when a window is closing if a line is short.

From Lviv, there are trains to Kyiv (70hry to 110hry, 6½ to 12 hours, six daily), Odesa (105hry, 12 hours, three daily) Uzhhorod (60hry, eight hours, twice daily), Chernivtsi (50hry, 5½ to 11 hours, three daily) and Simferopol (153hry, 25 hours, three daily).

Getting Around

Unless you're going somewhere off the map provided here, walking is the best option.

Marshrutka 95 links the airport and the centre, as does trolleybus 9 from the university building on vul Universytetska. A taxi there will cost from 25hry to 35hry.

Tram 1 or 9, or *marshrutka* 66, 67 or 68 link the train station with pr Svobody and pl Rynok.

Marshrutka 71 and 180 from pr Svobody or trolleybus 5 from pl Petrushevycha go to the long-distance bus terminal.

There are multitudes of *marshrutky* marked Центр (Centre), and any of these should traverse the main part of pr Svobody.

UZHHOROD УЖГОРОД

☎ 03122 (5 digits), ☎ 0312 (6 digits) pop 118,000

The border town of Uzhhorod (Uzhgorod in Russian) is a mercantile place with plenty of ready charm and a good introduction to Ukraine for those arriving from the EU. Split in half by the Uzh River, which separates the New and Old Towns, the town is an ideal staging post for anyone travelling to/from Slovakia or Hungary, but is otherwise a bit of a backwater, and not worth the significant detour from Lviv.

Information

Banks, exchange offices and ATMs are easy to find in the town centre. For internet access, try **A Club** (vul Korzo 2; per hr 3hry; ☯ 24hr), a gaming centre where you can also get online. For local help with hiking, cycling and general tours of the area, contact **Turkul** (www.turkul.com), an excellent grass-routes sustainable tourism group based in Uzhhorod.

Sights

First built in 1241 and added to throughout the Middle Ages, **Uzhhorod Castle** (vul Kapitulna; adult/child 5/2hry; grounds only 1hry; ☯ 9am-5pm Tue-Sun) is on a hill 400m northeast of the main square.

It has a museum, but best is the sweeping view of the region from its grounds. Across from the castle is the open-air **Museum of Folk Architecture & Rural Life** (adult/child 4/1hry; ☯ 10am-5pm Wed-Mon). Transcarpathian abodes, tools and crafts are on display. Downhill from the castle is the twin-towered, yellow 1640 **cathedral** (vul Kapitulna).

You can explore the ruins of the **Nevitsky Zamok** (Bride-to-Be Castle), 12km from the city (taxi 60hry return). The castle was first mentioned in chronicles in the 14th century, and rumour has it villagers used to hide women during enemy attacks. Views from the castle are jaw-dropping.

Sleeping & Eating

Hotel Atlant (☎ 614 095; www.atlant-hotel.com; pl Koryatovicha 27; s 180hry, d 260-330hry, ste 4300hry; ✖ 💻) These modern rooms are as sweet as can be and awesome value – especially the singles, which are on the top floor (no lift) and have skylights and slanted ceilings. It's a small place though; book ahead if you can. There's free wi-fi here.

Hotel Uzhhorod (☎ 619 050; www.hoteluzhgorod .com; pl Khemlnitskoho 2; s 279-319hry, d 399hry, tw 439hry, unrenovated s 169-239hry, d 289hry, incl breakfast; ✖ 💻) This friendly modernised Soviet hotel knows the meaning of service and features very smart rooms that have all been fully refurbished. The exception is the 4th-floor rooms, which are untouched, but cost much less and are a good choice for those on a budget. It's a pleasant 10-minute walk along the river to the centre of town.

Cafe Da Da (☎ 32 346; vul Kapitulna 5; mains 3-20hry; ☯ 7am-10pm) This funky-arty-bohemian establishment is a lifeline for vegetarians and has an incense-infused atmosphere that you'll either love or hate. It's just down the hill from the Uzhhorod Castle.

Kaktus Kafe (☎ 32 515; vul Korzo 7; mains 8-25hry; ☯ 10am-11pm) Probably the most popular hang-out in town, this smoky, noisy joint is full of beer- and coffee-drinkers. The theme is decidedly Wild West upstairs; downstairs it seems to be Aztec. The food is pretty good, but the service can be slow.

Uzhgorod Castle (☎ 443 668; www.uzhgorod castle.com; vul Kapitulna 33; mains 20-100hry, ☯ 11am-11pm) Located in the walls of the castle, this atmospheric place offers some excellent cooking, and is a good place to try local Carpathian cooking.

Getting There & Away

The bus and train stations are across the street from each other at the end of pr Svobody. For a taxi, call ☎ 051.

BUS

Buses go from the **bus terminal** (pr Svobody) to Chernivtsi (64hry, 10 to 12 hours, twice daily) and Lviv (48hry, six hours, four daily). From Uzhhorod, there are one or two uncomfortable daily buses to the Slovak city of Košice (44hry, three hours), and to the Hungarian city of Nyiregyhaza (45hry, three hours).

TRAIN

Uzhhorod has a modern train station, but no cross-border trains from Hungary or Slovakia stop here – they all go through Chop instead. From Uzhhorod itself trains go to Kyiv (110hry, 17 hours, four daily), Lviv (60hry, eight hours, twice daily) and Odesa (128hry, 20 hours, one daily).

CHERNIVTSI ЧЕРНІВЦІ

☎ (8-)03722 (5 digits), (8-)0372 (6 digits) / pop 260,000

Chernivsti is an attractive town only slowly beginning to realise its potential and make progress towards smartening itself up and attracting visitors. The glorious town centre, though still rough and ready, has many Habsburg gems from the 19th century. It's a great stopover for those passing through, to or from nearby Romania, and offers a laid-back introduction to Ukraine for new arrivals.

Orientation

The centre of town is around pl Tsentralna, and the main thoroughfare vul Holovna which runs north towards the train station on vul Gagarina. The bus station is on vul Holovna, a good 4km southeast of the centre. Trolleybuses 3 and 5 run between the two through the centre.

Information

Post office (vul Khydyakova 6) A block north of pl Tsentralna, there's also a telephone office next door.
Tourist Information Centre (☎ 553 684; www.city .cv.ua; vul Holovna 16; ☽ 10am-1pm & 2-6pm Mon-Fri) Staff speak no English but can offer a couple of English-language pamphlets.
VIP Internet (Basement, vul Universytetska 36; per hr 3hry; ☽ 9am-9pm Mon-Sat) Downstairs from the Anmaliya (анмалія) hair salon.

Sights

Chernivtsi is best enjoyed by wandering the streets aimlessly. The only must-see in town is **Chernivtsi University** (vul Kotsyubynskoho), a fantastic red-brick ensemble with coloured tiles decorating its pseudo-Byzantine, pseudo-Moorish and pseudo-Hanseatic wings. The architect responsible was Czech Josef Hlavka, who was also behind Chernivtsi's Armenian Cathedral (vul Ukrainska 30), as well as large chunks of Vienna. He completed it in 1882 for the Metropolitans – or Orthodox Church leaders – of Bukovyna as their official residence. The Soviets later moved the university here. The university is 1.5km northwest of the town centre; any trolleybus heading down vul Universytetska will take you there.

The city's most unusual church is **St Nicholas Cathedral** (vul Ruska 35). It's called the 'drunken church', because of the four twisted turrets surrounding its cupola. Painted blue with golden stars, these create an optical illusion, much like an Escher painting. The church is a 1930s copy of a 14th-century royal church in Curtea de Arges (Romania).

To plunge headlong into capitalist Ukraine today, visit the 33-hectare **Kalynivsky Market** (☽ 8am-2pm), a conduit into Ukraine for goods from neighbouring countries, which attracts 50,000 shoppers a day. It's a frenetic, wonderful people-watching phenomenon, even if you don't buy anything. Take any of the numerous *marshrutky* to калинівський рунок; many leave from in front of the train station.

Sleeping & Eating

Chernivtsi Backpackers (☎ 525 533; www.hihostels .com.ua; apt 4, Zankovetska 25; dm 90hry, incl breakfast; ▯) Tiny and more like a private apartment than a hostel, Chernivtsi Backpackers has room for one six-person dorm, a shared shower, toilet and kitchen. Reception is friendly though, and trips into the Carpathians can be arranged.

Hotel Kyiv (☎ 580 856; vul Holovna 46; s/d 130/240hry) The surprisingly comfy Kyiv has high ceilings, decently remodelled rooms and friendly floor staff, despite the fact that it's still very Soviet. The real boon is its location, just moments from the centre of town.

Knaus (☎ 510 255; www.knaus.cv.ua; vul Holovna 26a; mains 35-55hry; ☽ noon-4am) Expensive by local standards, this rather kitschy faux-Bavarian Bierstube offers a large, meaty selection of dishes, many of which are heated at your table by candles.

our pick **Reflection** (☎ 526 682; vul Holovna 66; mains 25-80hry; ⏱ 9am-11pm) Breaking some sort of immutable law of physics that such restaurants can't exist in rural Ukraine, Reflection is a godsend to the hungry traveller, with its sophisticated interior and wonderful menu (including bruschetta, chicken curries, steaks and teriyaki salad). There's even a full breakfast menu too. We may have dreamt it.

Getting There & Away

The **bus station** (☎ 416 35; vul Holovna 219) is 4km southeast of the centre, where services leave to Kyiv (140hry, nine to 12 hours, three every evening), Kamyanets-Podilsky (25hry, two hours, roughly every two hours), Odesa (172hry, 14 hours, one daily) and Lviv (55hry, 7½ hours, twice daily), among others. There is one scheduled bus a day to Suceava (Romania; 45hry, 4½ hours), but there are also private *marshrutky* throughout the day from Chernivtsi's bus station.

The **train station** (☎ 592 190; vul Gagarina 38) is 1.5km north of the centre. Advance train tickets are also sold in town at the **train ticket office** (☎ 429 24, 055; vul Holovna 128; ⏱ 9am-7pm). Trains serve Kyiv (85hry, 12½ hours to 15 hours, two or three daily), Odesa (108hry, 17 hours, daily), Uzhhorod (63hry, six hours, even dates) and Lviv (50hry, 5½ to 11 hours, three daily). There is also a daily service to Sofia (470hry) that passes through Suceava and Bucharest.

CARPATHIAN MOUNTAINS

One of the least-developed areas in all of Europe is the easternmost section of the Carpathian Mountains, which cut through the lower corner of Western Ukraine. Among the undulating ridges lives a cluster of various ethnic groups, including the Hutsuls, who, despite their clear Romanian ties, have turned out to be a source of pride to the Ukrainian national identity.

In addition to the Hutsuls, many other mountain dwellers still live traditional lifestyles and speak in dialects coloured by the tongues of neighbouring Poland, Slovakia, Hungary and Romania. Roads are still bad and the economy is still quite poor, so in most areas, the only vehicles you see may be old Soviet military off-road vehicles and horse-drawn carts.

The Carpathians are home to Ukraine's highest peak, Mt Hoverla (2062m) and its largest national park, and there are opportunities for camping, homestays, hiking, mountain biking and, most of all, skiing in some of the wildest natural areas on the continent.

Carpathian National Natural Park

The Carpathian National Natural Park (CNNP) is Ukraine's largest at 503 sq km. Despite the status of the land, industrial logging still takes place, and only about 25% of the park area is actually protected. Founded in 1980, the CNNP shelters wolves, brown bears, lynx, bison and deer. Hutsuls still live in the park, and the country's highest peak, Mt Hoverla, is here as well, and most people come here for hiking in the summer and skiing in the winter. Wild camping is allowed, although you have to pay an entrance fee (adult/child 6/2hry). Fires are also prohibited, although this is largely ignored.

Yaremcha is a touristy Hutsul village, with lots of folk crafts on sale and several 'Hutsul' restaurants. It is probably the most obvious place for a home base, as it's easy to reach and makes a good staging point for a Mt Hoverla ascent. From the gateway town of Ivano-Frankivsk, there are dozens of buses and *marshrutky* to Yaremcha (13hry, 1½ hours). There is a good range of accommodation, from rented rooms and cottages to hotels. You can book in advance via their websites.

Ski Resorts

The area is still largely undeveloped, but Ukraine's small collection of ski resorts offers one European-standard resort and several inexpensive options, with both hotel and homestay accommodation on-site or nearby. Rentals are no problem, although except for Bukovel, the equipment might be older. The season lasts usually until early May. You can arrange package ski trips through **Piligrim** (www.piligrim.lviv.ua) and **Lviv Ecotour** (www.lvivecotour.com), or book your own accommodation online through www.skiukraine.info, which also provides transport details. Homestays can be arranged in advance via **Rural Green Tourism** (www.greentour.co m.ua/en/orders).

Bukovel (☎ 03434 372 89; www.bukovel.com; lift tickets weekday/weekend 170/190hry), not far from Ivano-Frankivsk, is Ukraine's biggest and best resort and meets European standards. A huge amount of investment is being made here, and plans to bid for the 2018 Winter Olympics have been announced.

Lines are rarely longer than five minutes for the modern chairlifts, and night skiing, snow machines, a ski school, medical centre and new rental equipment are all on offer. Accommodation in cottages is pricey, but discounts are generous for advance booking, and there are some more economical triples as well. Cheaper accommodation can be found in Yarmecha, 30km away, which has buses to/from the resort. Transfers can also be organised by the Bukovel resort itself.

Just 130km from Lviv, **Slavske** (☎ 38 0322 42 242; www.slavsko.com.ua, in Ukrainian; lift tickets 65-120hry), called Slavsko in Russian, is the most popular and easiest to reach. There are four mountains here, making up the country's greatest variety of slopes. The downside? There's only one chairlift (the rest are tows), large moguls can be a problem, rentals are not so new and there are sometimes long lines on weekends and holidays. If you're willing to fork out 120hry though, you'll get VIP status and go right to the front. Three well-priced **hotels** (www .skiukraine.info) are nearby and at the train station people offer cottages for rent. There are at least three daily trains between Uzhhorod and Kyiv that stop in Slavsko.

A favourite for hard-core skiers and snowboarders, **Drahobrat** (☎ 03132-42 009; www.ski.lviv .ua/drahobrat; per lift 4hry) is the tallest, longest slope (base at 1300m, elevation drop up to 350m). As such, it gets the most snow and longest season but has more inclement weather. Since it's hard to get to (a two- to three-hour bus or car ride), it's worthwhile only if you stay a few days. There are only tow lifts, but slopes are well groomed, and lines are not much of a problem. Take a bus or taxi from Ivano-Frankivsk train station to Yasinya. At the bottom of the road in Yasinya, old Soviet vehicles wait to take you 18km to the resort (80hry to 120hry per car). Homestays aren't available, but well-priced accommodation can be booked online at www.skiukraine.info.

KAMYANETS-PODILSKY
КАМ'ЯНЕЦЬ-ПОДІЛЬСЬКИЙ
☎ 03849 / pop 100,000

In a country with no shortage of impressive fortresses, the unique town of Kamyanets-Podilsky still stands out for its gorgeous castle and dramatic natural beauty. The name Kamyanets refers to the massive stone island created by a sharp bend in the river Smotrych, and the resulting verdant canyon rings a charming old town guarded by a fortress straight out of a fairy tale. If Český Krumlov in the Czech Republic or Bulgaria's Veliko Târnovo were your thing, don't miss this equally stunning double-barrelled delight.

History

Old Town is broken into different quarters, and under the medieval Magdeburg Law, the main settlers – Ukrainians, Poles, Armenians and Jews – each occupied a different one. In the town's heyday, during the interwar period, there were five Roman Catholic churches, 18 Orthodox churches and a Jewish community of 23,500 served by 31 prayer houses. During WWII the Germans used the Old Town as a ghetto, and an estimated 85,000 people died there. Intensive fighting and air raids destroyed some 70% of Old Town, and only 13 churches survived.

Orientation & Information

The Old Town is on a rock island, accessible by two bridges – the western bridge takes you to the castle and the 'new' eastern bridge to the Soviet new town, where you'll find both the bus station and train station. The bus station is six blocks east of the new bridge, while the train station is 1km north of the bus station. The two bridges are joined by vul Starobulvarna that runs through pl Virmensky, the Old Town's main square.

The **post and phone office** (vul Soborna 9) offers internet access from terminals. Use the side entrance on vul Ohiyenka. Banks and ATMs can be found around pl Virmensky.

Sights & Activities

The walk across the new bridge into Old Town is probably one of the best parts of visiting Kamyanets-Podilsky. Once you're there, enjoy wandering around the well-preserved streets, and then head across the old bridge to the town's main sight, the **old castle** (vul Zamkova; adult/student 5/3hry; ⏰ 9am-6.30pm, to 5pm Mon), which was originally built of wood in the 10th century but reconstructed of stone some 500 years later. You can order a tour in English by calling **Valera** (09-75403966; up to 25 people 40hry). Much of the fun here comes from the total freedom you have to climb all over the ramparts. Behind the castle, to the west, is the **new castle**, a series of earth ramparts and 17th-century stone walls.

UKRAINE

The faded salmon-coloured **Dominican Monastery & Church** (pl Virmensky) features a tall bell tower. It was founded in the 14th century but was expanded in baroque style in the 18th century. In a park just to the north is the 14th-century **town hall**, recently renovated.

Another 500m further the north is the 16th-century **Cathedral of SS Peter & Paul** (vul Tatarska). About two minutes' walk further north is the 16th-century **Porokhovi Gate** and the seven-storey stone **Kushnir Tower**.

Festivals & Events

In Kamyanets-Podilsky, there's a national hot-air balloon competition, complete with stunts, in mid-May; in September is the 'Tournament of Knights', complete with jousting and sword-fighting.

Sleeping

Hotel Ksenia (☎ 20 379; Zhvanetske shosse 3; s/d/tr 100/160/250hry, ste 300-550hry; ☒) Located beyond the fortress outside the town itself is this whimsical castle-style folly, which surprisingly makes for the best budget option. All normal rooms share bathrooms and are clean and simple. The 'lux' options all have bathrooms and feature four-poster beds and air-con, not to mention interior-design choices from the Saddam Hussein school. There's a cavernous restaurant here too, but for anything else, it's a 10-minute walk to the Old Town.

Hotel Taras Bulba (☎ 90 633; www.tarasbylba.com; vul Starobulvarna 6; r 250hry, ste 350-400hry, incl breakfast; ☒) Kamyanets' latest hotel offering is this friendly Old Town place that opened in 2008. With just 18 simply furnished but comfortable rooms, each with TV, fridge and phone, the location and the relative interior-design purgatory make this the best option in town.

Hotel Syem Dney (☎ 30 392, 30 322; vul Soborna 4; s/d 360/450hry, incl breakfast; ☒ ☐ ☒) Once a Soviet behemoth, the renamed 'Seven Days' hotel in the new town has been fully remodelled as an upmarket option and, despite some garish colour choices in the rooms, this is a smart, friendly and comfortable place to stay.

Hotel Hetman (☎ 067-588 2215; www.hetman-hotel.com.ua; Polski rynok 8; r 385-450hry, ste 600hry, incl breakfast; ☒) Almost unspeakably tasteless design in the rooms is the only real gripe about the otherwise very good ye olde Ukraine-style Hetman, located in the middle of the Old Town. Rooms are large and comfortable but may give you nightmares.

Eating & Drinking

New York Street Pizza (☎ 8 097 581 9300; vul Dominikanska 26; pizzas from 5hry) The irony of the name will be lost on nobody given NYSP's location on a lovely baroque town square, but this place is popular with younger locals, who create their own pizzas and drink cold beers on the terrace here.

Kafe Pid Bramoyu (☎ 21 588; vul Zamkova 1a; mains 10-25hry) On the bridge and overlooking the castle and canyon, the view from this atmospheric old-style tavern is outstanding. With Ukrainian and Armenian dishes on the menu, there's plenty of choice, although the Caucasian-style selection of meat and fish *shashlyk* is fail-safe.

Taras Bulba (☎ 90 533; vul Starobulvarna 6; mains 15-20hry) Sepulchral and rather damp it may be, but Taras Bulba's designers would no doubt argue that was intentional at this medieval-styled place full of nooks and crannies to eat in. The simple menu features old favourites such as kebabs and chicken cutlets.

Hostinny Dvir (☎ 22 228; vul Trotiyska 1; mains 20-30hry) This perennial grand Soviet favourite for tour groups seems rather left behind these days amid the newer competition, but still serves up hardy traditional fare in its pleasant main hall.

Getting There & Away

The train station is 1km north of the bus terminal. A taxi into town should be about 10hry, or you can take bus 1 into the new or Old Town. The only direct long-distance trains are to/from Kyiv (52hry, six hours on the day train, 12 hours on the overnight train, two daily).

The **bus terminal** (☎ 31 251; vul Koriatovychiv) is 500m east of the new town, and about 1km from the bridge that leads into the Old Town. There are direct bus services to/from Kyiv (111hry, 12 hours, five daily), Chernivtsi (25hry, two hours, every one to two hours), Lviv (73hry, eight hours, two daily) and Odesa (157hry, 12 hours, two daily).

ODESA ОДЕСА

☎ 0482 (6 digits), 048 (7 digits) / pop 1 million
With its back turned to the rest of the country, admiring itself in the sparkling waters of the Black Sea, Odesa is its own world – one rather amused that the rest of Ukraine even dares border it. One part narcissist, one part humorist, Odesa cannot help making an impression on

anyone lucky enough to visit. And yet despite this, there are few tangible sights to see or activities to engage in. Odesa is all about atmosphere, attitude and action.

In Odesa cultural fusing has become an art form – the cosmopolitan city's melting pot of Eurasian cultures has created the lively Odesan patter that serves as a wellspring of slang throughout the Russian-speaking world. And then there's the joking. When you live in a city this wild, you better learn to laugh about it. Odesans do; they seem to have a hereditary talent for brassy wisecracks and snappy witticisms, and their sense of humour is legendary.

HISTORY

Before it became part of the Russian Empire, modern-day Odesa was, among others, a part of the Greek Empire, the Roman Empire, and the Golden Horde. In the second half of the 15th century, the Turks founded a settlement named Hadjibey here, building a fortress around it.

In the 18th century, Catherine the Great was eyeing the place, imagining it as 'the St Petersburg of the South' and in 1789, her dutiful lover, General Potemkin, captured the fortress for her. In 1815, things really began to boom when the city became a duty-free port, and a huge demand for labour arose. Newcomers were encouraged with free land and a five-year tax-free status, and soon the city became a refuge – 'Odesa Mama' – for runaway serfs, criminals, renegades and dissidents.

Odesa was the crucible of the early 1905 workers' revolution, with a local uprising and the mutiny on the battleship *Potemkin Tavrichesky*. Between 1941 and 1944, Odesa sealed its reputation as one of Stalin's 'hero' cities, when partisans sheltering in the city's catacombs (see p942) during WWII put up a legendary fight against the occupying Romanian troops (allies of the Nazis).

Jews initially came to Odesa to escape persecution, but suffered the same fate here. In the early 20th century, they accounted for one-third of the city's population, but after horrific pogroms in 1905 and 1941, hundreds of thousands emigrated. Many emigrated to America, settling around Brooklyn's Brighton Beach, now nicknamed 'Little Odesa'.

INFORMATION

Banks with ATMs and Western Union offices are all over the place and easy to spot.

Bukva (☎ 358 404; vul Derybasivska 14; ☼ 10am-6pm Mon-Sat) Well-stocked bookshop that includes a section of English-language literature.

Central post office (☎ 266 467; vul Sadova10)

Eugenia Travel (☎ 220 331; www.eugeniatours.com.ua; vul Rishelevska 23) English-speaking Janna offers the best tours in the city at decent prices.

European Business Centre (vul Preobrazhenska 34; per hr 6hry; ☼ 9am-midnight) Large internet centre on the ground floor of the Hotel Passazh.

London Sky Travel (☎ 729 3196; www.lst.com.ua; Sea Passenger Terminal, vul Prymorska 6) Does visas, tours and hotel bookings, as well as Black Sea ferries.

Salix (☎ 487 289 737; www.salix.od.ua; vul Torhovo 14) This Anglo-Ukrainian outfit is authentically 'green', offering responsible tours to the Danube delta, as well as Crimea and other southern destinations.

SIGHTS & ACTIVITIES

Odesa is surprisingly thin on must-sees. Most agree that just a couple of days is plenty to spend here, as it's far more about atmosphere than activity. The first stop on everyone's itinerary will of course be the world-famous **Potemkin Steps** (see the boxed text, p940). These 192 waterfront steps (1837–41) spill down the hillside from a statue of the Duc de Richelieu towards the Black Sea; they are best viewed from the bottom, where they seem higher than they are, thanks to a gradual narrowing from bottom (21m wide) to top (13m wide). A free funicular runs up the side of the steps (from 8am to 11pm) for those who don't fancy the walk back up.

Running along the top of the Potemkin Steps is **Prymorsky bulvar**, a shady promenade that stretches from pl Dumska, home of Odesa's **City Hall** as well as its main **Pushkin Statue**, to the magnificent 1826 **Vorontsov Palace**, the residence of a former governor of the same name. Sadly it's not usually open to the public, but you can still wander right up to its exterior and see the vivid Arabic tiling on the otherwise neoclassical facade, or check out its graffiti-strewn colonnades that command fantastic views of the city's busy port.

To the left, leading to a park and the pleasing pedestrian extension of the promenade, is the 'Mother-in-Law Bridge', supposedly built on the order of a communist official to make it easier for his wife's mother to go home at night, leaving him in peace. The bridge is today home to hundreds of engraved or painted padlocks locked onto the railings – each representing a relationship. When a

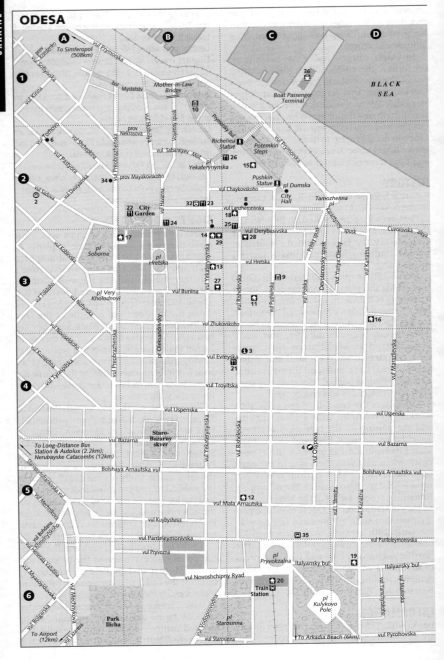

ODESA

A — B — C — D

BLACK
SEA

To Simferopol
(508km)

Mother-in-Law
Bridge

Boat Passenger
Terminal

Mystetstv

vul Prymorska

prov Korolenko

vul Sofiyivska

vul Kirina

prov Nekrasova

vul Shchepkina

vul Tornovo

vul Pastyora

vul Preobrazhenska

Voyensky spusk

vul Sabaneyev Mist

Prymorsky bul

Richelieu
Statue

Potemkin
Steps

vul Yekaterynynska

Pushkin
Statue

vul Chaykovskoho

pl Dumska

City
Hall

Tamozhenna
pl

vul Sidora

vul Dvoryanska

prov Mayakovskoho

vul Havanna

City
Garden

vul Lanzheronivska

vul Derybasivska

Kozelnytska spusk

Cuvorovska aleya

pl
Soborna

pl
Hretska

vul Hretska

Polsky spusk

Devolanovsky spusk

vul Yuriya Olesha

vul Kanatna

vul Marazlievska

vul Kobleska

vul Tolstoho

vul Nizhynska

vul Novoselskoho

pl Very
Kholodnoy

vul Bunina

vul Yekaterynynska

vul Rishelievska

vul Pushkinska

vul Polska

vul Kuznechna

vul Tyraspilska

pr Oleksandrivsky

vul Zhukovskoho

vul Preobrazhenska

vul Evreyska

vul Troyitska

vul Uspenska

vul Uspenska

To Long-Distance Bus
Station & Autolux (2.2km);
Nerubayske Catacombs (12km)

vul Bazarna

Staro-
Bazarany
skver

vul Yekaterynynska

vul Rishelievska

vul Osypovi

vul Bazarna

vul Staroportofrankivska

Bolshaya Arnautska vul

Bolshaya Arnautska vul

vul Mechnikova

vul Bohdana Khmelnytskoho

vul Hennadia Vatutina

vul Myasoyedovska

vul Mechnikova

vul Mala Arnautska

vul Kuybysheva

vul L Smidta

vul Kanatna

vul Panteleymonivska

vul Panteleymonivska

vul Pryvozna

pl
Pryvokzalna

Italyansky bul

Italyansky bul

vul Yamchytskoho

vul Novoshchipny Ryad

Train
Station

vul Bolgarska

vul Tarasa

Park
Ilicha

To Airport
(12km)

vul Vodoprovodna

pl
Starosinna

vul Starosinna

pl
Kulykovo
Pole

To Arkadia Beach (6km);

vul Pyrohovska

vul Pyrohovska

6 • 34 • 2 ⊘

10 🏛 36

26 🏛 15 🏛 8 • 18 🏛 25 🏛

22 🏛 32 🏛 23 14 🏛 29 1 • 28 🏛 9 🏛 24 🏛 17 🏛 13 🏛 27 🏛 11 🏛

3 🏛 21 🏛 16 🏛

4 •

12 🏛

35 🏛

19 🏛

20 🏛

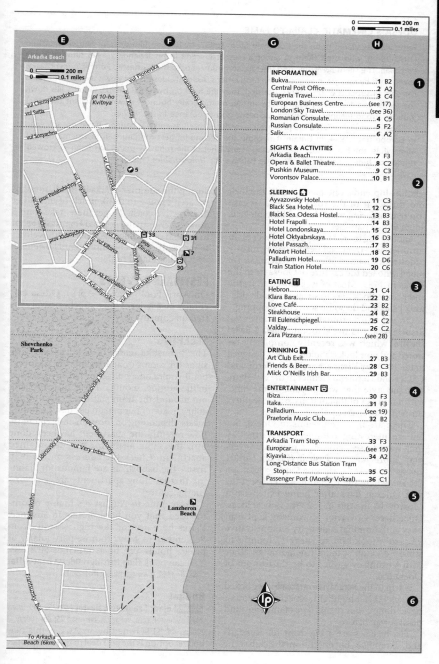

INFORMATION
Bukva...**1** B2
Central Post Office..........................**2** A2
Eugenia Travel...............................**3** C4
European Business Centre............(see 17)
London Sky Travel......................(see 36)
Romanian Consulate......................**4** C5
Russian Consulate..........................**5** F2
Salix...**6** A2

SIGHTS & ACTIVITIES
Arkadia Beach...............................**7** F3
Opera & Ballet Theatre..................**8** C2
Pushkin Museum............................**9** C3
Vorontsov Palace.........................**10** B1

SLEEPING
Ayvazovsky Hotel.........................**11** C3
Black Sea Hotel............................**12** C5
Black Sea Odessa Hostel..............**13** B3
Hotel Frapolli...............................**14** B3
Hotel Londonskaya.......................**15** C2
Hotel Oktyabrskaya......................**16** D3
Hotel Passazh..............................**17** B3
Mozart Hotel................................**18** C2
Palladium Hotel............................**19** D6
Train Station Hotel.......................**20** C6

EATING
Hebron...**21** C4
Klara Bara....................................**22** B2
Love Café.....................................**23** B2
Steakhouse..................................**24** B2
Till Eulenschpiegel........................**25** C2
Valday...**26** C2
Zara Pizzara..............................(see 28)

DRINKING
Art Club Exit................................**27** B3
Friends & Beer..............................**28** C3
Mick O'Neills Irish Bar...................**29** B3

ENTERTAINMENT
Ibiza..**30** F3
Itaka...**31** F3
Palladium..................................(see 19)
Praetoria Music Club.....................**32** B2

TRANSPORT
Arkadia Tram Stop........................**33** F3
Europcar...................................(see 15)
Kiyavia..**34** A2
Long-Distance Bus Station Tram
 Stop..**35** C5
Passenger Port (Morsky Vokzal).......**36** C1

ODESA'S CINEMATIC CLAIM TO FAME

Fame was showered upon the Potemkin Steps (p937) by Russian film director Sergei Eisenstein (1898–1948), who used them to shoot a massacre scene in his legendary 1925 film *Battleship Potemkin*. The silent B&W epic told the tale of mutiny aboard the battleship *Potemkin Tavrichesky*, sparked off by meagre, maggot-ridden food rations. As local Odesans run down the steps towards the ship in support of the sailors' uprising, they are fired on by tsarist troops. Blood spills down the steps, and a runaway pram, baby inside, methodically bounces down; a brilliant trick that induces strong feelings of tension, suspense and impotence in the viewer.

The film was considered too provocative by the authorities and was banned. It was not screened in Europe until 1954. In Britain it became the second-longest-running ban in cinema history. Meanwhile, the film's most spellbinding scene (that of the runaway pram) has been 'borrowed' numerous times, including in Brian de Palma's *The Untouchables* (1987).

relationship ends, one party breaks the lock and throws it to the road below – in case you're wondering what that sobbing bloke is doing with a hammer.

Another big tourist hot spot is Odesa's main commercial street, **vul Derybasivska** (mostly pedestrian), named after the Frenchman De Ribas, who led the capture of Odesa from the Turks in 1789. Most of it is closed to traffic and people flock here to stroll alongside sidewalk cafes and do some souvenir shopping.

On vul Lanzheronivska, facing down vul Rishelevska, sits the elaborate **Opera & Ballet Theatre**, which was recently completely restored and now looks fabulous. It was designed in the 1880s by Viennese architects Ferdinand Fellner and Hermann Helmer in the Habsburg baroque style that was popular at the time, with a number of Italian Renaissance features thrown in to liven up the ensemble.

There are many museums in Odesa, but few are interesting to foreigners – it's the city they want to see. However, literature-lovers may appreciate the **Pushkin Museum** (☎ 251 034; vul Pushkinska 13; admission 5hry; ☉ 10am-5pm Mon-Sat), where the romantic writer spent his first Odesan days after being exiled from Moscow by the tsar in 1823 for radical ideas. Once here, Governor Vorontsov kept him busy with humiliatingly petty administrative jobs, so it took him an entire 13 months to stir up enough scandal (including an affair with Vorontsov's wife) to be thrown out of Odesa too.

A trip to the **Nerubayske catacombs** (see boxed text, p942) is a highlight, especially if you've never done a tour of this type of underground passageway before.

The beaches are a big draw for Russians and Ukrainians, but apart from the club scene

during the summer at **Arkadia Beach**, foreigners aren't going to think much of the rather unattractive coast. To get there, take tram 5 down lovely, sanatoria-lined **Frantsuzsky bulvar** to the end of the line. **Lanzheron Beach** is closer to the centre and a bit more family oriented, with a dilapidated funfair.

FESTIVALS & EVENTS

On April Fool's Day (1 April), Odesa celebrates **Humourina**, a huge street carnival centred on comedy.

SLEEPING

The 'babushka mafia' of old dears carrying signs for rooms or apartments are your best bet if you're on a budget or haven't reserved in the summer months. The babushkas hang out around the train station. Expect to pay 40hry to 80hry per person per day, including meals, depending on location and *remont* (ie how recently the apartment has been done up), the same again for a self-contained apartment. Check the address on the map first – the babushkas are famous for claiming that far-flung apartments are '*v tsentre*' (in the centre).

From June to August it's highly recommended that you book hotels in advance. Prices here are for the high season; from September to May, rooms, particularly at pricier hotels, can be as much as 50% less. You can book flats through **Odessa Rent-A-Flat** (☎ 787 3444; www.odessarentaflat.com).

Budget

ourpick **Black Sea Odessa Hostel** (☎ 252 200; www .blackseahostels.com; vul Yekaterynynska 25; dm 100hry, d 200hry; ✿ 🖳) Owned by an Aussie, this new budget option is the best deal in town – a proper hostel with all the frills: free wi-fi, laundry, massive dorm rooms and two flat-screen satellite TVs. Enter through the courtyard and find the entrance immediately on your right. The even cheaper Duke hostel, run by the same management, is located on the floor above.

Train Station Hotel (☎ 727 1368/69; dm 120hry, r 250hry; 🔀) The rooms at Odesa's *vokzal* are spacious, newly renovated and great value.

Hotel Passazh (☎ 728 5500/01/02; www.passage .odessa.ua; vul Preobrazhenska 34; s 110-309hry, d 140-440hry, ste 558hry; 🖳) There's an enormous range of rooms available here, and you can usually find something even in the high season. It's undeniably shabby, but comes with a great location, plenty of faded grandeur and more atmosphere than you'll find anywhere else at this price. Passazh does offer one touch of modernity: a good internet centre on the ground floor.

Midrange

Hotel Oktyabrskaya (☎ 728 8863; info@oktyabrskaya .od.ua; vul Kanatna 31; s 200-300hry, d 250-300hry, ste 400-700hry, incl breakfast; 🔀) In an elegant, worn building, Hotel Oktyabrskaya thankfully evokes only a little of the proletariat revolution its name refers to. Think red marble walls, polished old parquet floors, wide, banistered staircases, and soaring ceilings. Rooms waver between tacky and cute, differing mostly in hue. It's a fantastic deal.

Hotel Frapolli (☎ 356 800; www.odessapassage.com /frapoli; vul Derybasivska 13; s 430-833hry, d 612-1015hry, ste 1015-1315hry, incl breakfast; 🔀 🖳) The 26-room Frapoli is right at the heart of the action on Odesa's main drag. The most basic standards are much smaller than the 'improved' rooms and suites, but all are comfortable, if a tad sterile in decoration, and reception is friendly. There's free wi-fi in the lobby.

Ayvazovsky Hotel (☎ 728 9777; www.ayvazovsky .com.ua; vul Bunina 19; s/d from 490/650hry, ste 750-890hry, incl breakfast; 🔀 🖳) This new 27-room hotel is designed in the local understanding of 'British style' (think surprisingly funky Victoriana with the odd modern touch) and is a winner. It's a short walk from vul Derybasivska.

Black Sea Hotel (☎ 300 904; www.bs-hotel.com.ua; vul Rishelevska 59; s/d from 520/955hry, incl breakfast; 🖳 🖳) This ugly 1970s concrete tower shelters generic but surprisingly well-appointed and spacious rooms, most of which have been smartly renovated (the exceptions are the shabby and

far-from-chic singles). The once-surly staff is now friendly, helpful and English-speaking.

Palladium Hotel (☎ 728 7730; www.hotel-palladium .com.ua; bul Italyansky 4; r from 585-1680hry, incl breakfast; 🔀 🖳) The attractive, pastel-hued rooms here feature minimalist decor and fine-textured carpets, as well as their own silly names – the Octavian Suite anyone? It definitely qualifies as a good deal for Odesa. The popular downstairs nightclub is free for hotel guests, as is summer club Itaka (p943).

Top End

Hotel Londonskaya (☎ 738 0110; www.londred.com; Primorsky bulvar 11; s 780-962hry, d 963-1145hry, ste 1456-3900hry, incl breakfast; 🔀 🖳) It's hard not to love this old dame through whose doors everyone who is anyone in Odesa must surely have passed, and even if the 1990s refit is feeling a little tired in some rooms (while the suites remain classic and exquisite), the iron-lace balustrades, stained-glass windows, crystal chandeliers and parquet flooring all ooze grand Regency charm.

Mozart Hotel (☎ 377 777; www.mozart-hotel.com; vul Lanzheronivska 13; s 800-965hry, d 1150-1300hry, ste 1650-2100hry, incl breakfast; 🔀 🖳 🔉) The location here is perfect, but while the rooms may be a tad more up-to-date than the Londonskaya's, there's no comparison for atmosphere. Staff seemed rather snippy when we last visited too. There's a small pool, fitness centre and free wi-fi, and the building at least enjoys an attractive neoclassical facade.

EATING

Hebron (☎ 150 374; vul Rishelevska 30; mains 30-75hry; closed Sat) There may be very few Jews left in Odesa, but this restaurant, located downstairs in the city's synagogue, is the best place to come for a taste of Odesa's rich Jewish heritage.

Till Eulenschpiegel (☎ 429 046; vul Derybasivska 12; mains 40hry; 8am-11pm Mon-Fri, noon-midnight Sat & Sun) This friendly, laid-back place on Odesa's main street has a decent selection of Ukrainian standards on its menu, but is also open for breakfast (weekdays only) – a rarity among the restaurants in Odesa.

Zara Pizzara (☎ 728 8888; vul Rishelevska 5; mains 40-60hry) This pizzeria has an enviously located summer terrace, real Italian-style thin-crust pizza loaded with toppings, and hefty calzones on offer. But what sets it apart is that it actually opens before 9am for breakfast. For that we'll overlook the overpriced beer.

UKRAINE

Valday (☎ 722 6737; pl Yekaterynynskaya 3; mains 50-85hry) This grand-style brasserie is a great option for breakfast, lunch or dinner. Outside is a super sun terrace under the gaze of Catherine the Great, while the inside is seriously smart – all white tablecloths and high-end European food.

Love Café (☎ 784 0203; vul Yekaterynynska 12; mains 50-90hry) The tacky decor may be hilarious: the theme is Hollywood romance, and rather out of date pictures – of Brad and Jen and even more hilariously, siblings Jake and Maggie Gyllenhaal – deck the walls. Yet not all is lost – the moneyed Moscow crowd eat to be seen on the terrace, while very good food, from sushi to chicken Kiev is served up inside. There's also free wi-fi.

Steakhouse (☎ 348 782; vul Derybasivska 20; mains 50-100hry) Despite a few inevitably garish touches in a place overwhelmingly favoured by wealthy Russian tourists, this fantastic steakhouse is stylishly decked out in painted wood and distressed walls. The best steak in town – just take your choice from the large menu. There's also free wi-fi.

Klara Bara (☎ 375 108; Gorodskoy Sad; mains 70hry) Tucked away off vul Derybasivska in a quiet corner of the city garden, this modern ivy-covered cafe and restaurant has a cosy atmosphere and makes for one of the best outside tables in town. It serves European fare with Thai touches, a range of freshly caught fish and local *shashlyk*, plus brilliant Turkish coffee.

DRINKING

our pick Friends & Beer (Druzya i Pivo; ☎ 760 1998; vul Derybasivska 9) This recreated charming USSR-era living room is proof that 'Retro Soviet' doesn't have to mean political posters and constructivist art. The staff is charming, the food and drink selection excellent and there's free wi-fi.

Mick O'Neills Irish Bar (☎ 268 437; vul Derybasovskaya 13; ☼ 24hr) Two storeys of wooden railings and all the trappings of pub decor (paper money from all over the world, billiards, pinball machines) set the scene for this restaurant and hang-out. There's a busy outside terrace open day and night.

Art Club Exit (vul Bunina 24; ☼ 5pm-late) For something a lot more local, try this often-rowdy basement bar. The entrance is near a hard-to-spot 'Exit' sign.

ENTERTAINMENT

Odesa's raucous club scene is divided into two seasons: summer (June to August) and the rest of the year. In the summer all action shifts to Arkadia Beach, which boasts two huge, Ibiza-style nightclubs that produce heightened levels of madness seven days a week. At other times the action is closer to the city centre. Unless otherwise noted, the following clubs

---

THE ODESA UNDERGROUND

The limestone below Odesa is riddled with more than 1000km of catacombs (hence the sinking status of some buildings in the city). They weren't used as cemeteries, but were formed by Cossacks and other residents who mined the land for the limestone, which was used for local buildings. The resulting network of tunnels turned out to be a great place for smugglers, revolutionaries and fugitives throughout history.

One network of tunnels in Nerubayske, 12km northwest of Odesa, sheltered a group of partisans during WWII. This event is explained at the **Museum of Partisan Glory** (☎ 8-067 729 2485; admission 6hry, guided tour 50hry; ☼ 9am-4pm), which includes a fascinating, flashlight tour of the catacombs, with exhibits showing what life was like for the underground fighters who hid and lived here when they weren't derailing Nazi trains or otherwise thwarting the fascists.

You can just show up in Nerubayske in a taxi (80hry return trip) or by *marshrutka* 84 (2hry, 35 minutes) which leaves from outside Odesa's Pryvoz bus station. You may have to rustle up staff to open the doors if they're not expecting you, and tours will be in Russian only. In summer, Russian-language tour groups tout trips from the train station. If you don't know Russian, it's still interesting to visit, although Eugenia Travel (p937) and other agencies do tours in English and other languages (about 175hry).

Keep in mind that it will be dark and close in the catacombs (claustrophobes beware), as well as chilly – no matter how warm the day is. Each year at least one person wanders into a catacomb entrance they discover around Odesa and never comes out. Don't be one of them. Stick to the tour.

charge 50hry to 100hry on weekends (much less on weekdays). Steeply discounted or free admission for women is the norm.

Ibiza (☎ 777 0205; Arkadia Beach; ☼ summer) This white, free-form open cave structure is Arkadia's most upmarket and most expensive club. European DJs and big-ticket Russian and Ukrainian pop bands often play here.

Itaka (☎ 349 188; Arkadia Beach; ☼ summer) It's slightly more downmarket than Ibiza and consequently often rowdier (in a good way). The Greek columns and statues are a tad much but you'll hardly care when it's 5am and you are out of your gourd. Like Ibiza it also draws big regional pop acts.

Palladium (☎ 728 6566; bul Italyansky 4; ☼ Sep-May) Itaka's sister club takes up the slack downtown when Itaka shuts in September. There's a nightly show program around 11pm, followed by general debauchery.

Praetoria Music Club (☎ 726 6484; vul Lanzheronivska 26) This is one of the few city centre-clubs that has a pulse in the summer.

GETTING THERE & AWAY
Air
The Odesa **airport** (☎ 006, 658 186, 213 576; www .airport.od.ua) is located about 12km southwest of the city centre. There are several daily flights to/from Kyiv (one hour). There are also air connections to Simferopol (40 minutes) several times a week with **Southern Airlines** (Pivdenny Avialinii; ☎ 376 600). There are international flights from all over Eastern Europe, including Moscow, Warsaw, Prague, Budapest, Rīga and Timişoara. For schedules and to buy air tickets go to **Kiyavia** (☎ 276 259; www.kiyavia .com; vul Preobrazhenska 15).

Boat
From the **passenger port** (vul Prymorska), there are twice-weekly **London Sky Travel** (☎ 729 3196; www .lst.com.ua) catamarans between Odesa and Varna in Bulgaria (740hry, eight hours), as well as ferries to Constanta in Romania (560hry, six hours, once weekly June to September); London Sky Travel has an office at the Odesa passenger port. The car passenger ferry *Caledonia*, operated by **UKR Ferry** (www .ukrferry.com) runs three times a week between Odesa and İstanbul (US$190, 36 hours).

There are also ferries to other Ukrainian Black Sea destinations, such as Yalta and Sevastopol.

Bus
Most international and long-haul domestic buses leave from the **long-distance bus station** (☎ 004; vul Kolontaevska 58), 3km west of the train station. Frequent **Gunsel** (☎ 326 212) and **Autolux** (☎ 716 4612; www.autolux.com.ua) buses are the most comfortable and quickest way to travel to Kyiv (90hry to 120hry, 7½ hours). Other companies serve Simferopol (100hry, 12 hours, six daily), Yalta (115hry, 14 hours, three daily), Lviv (120hry, 15 hours, twice daily) and Chernivtsi (120hry, 13 hours, twice daily) via Kamyanets-Podilsky.

There are at least 10 daily buses to Chişinău via Tiraspol, and two via Palanka (50hry to 60hry, five to seven hours). The latter avoid Transdnistr.

Train
The **train station** (☎ 273 357, 272 4242; pl Pryvokzalna) is a big busy place. Tickets for future dates or with non-CIS (Commonwealth of Independent States) destinations must be purchased at the **Service Centre** (☼ 7am-9.30pm), which can be found inside the station; look for the sign 'Сервисний Центр'. To find it from the main entrance of the station, go right and walk to the end, turn left past the pharmacy and look for the signed double doors. Once you're there, go to **window 5** (☼ 8am-7pm) for non-CIS destinations. All other windows will be able to help with train tickets for future dates.

There are train connections between Odesa and Kyiv (110hry, nine to 15 hours, five daily, Uzhhorod (128hry, 20 hours, one daily), Lviv (105hry, 12 hours, three daily) and Simferopol (85hry, 11 to 13 hours, twice daily). On odd dates there are *platskartny*-only trains to Kamyanets-Podilsky (85hry, 18 hours).

GETTING AROUND
From the airport, bus 129 goes to the train station; buses 101 and 117 go between the airport and pl Hretska, in the centre southwest of vul Derybasivska. The going rate for a taxi to/from the airport is 50hry. The drivers waiting outside the terminal will insist on 150hry for a ride to the town centre – do not be duped, they will fold eventually.

To get to the centre from the train station (about a 20-minute walk), go to the stop near the McDonald's and take any bus saying 'Площа Грецка' (ploshcha Hretska), such as bus 148. Bus 155 or 109, plus trolleybus 4 or 10, go up vul Pushkinska before curving around to vul Prymorska past the passenger port and the foot of the Potemkin Steps.

Bus 208 and trolleybus 8 go from the train station to the long-distance bus station. From Pryvoz market/bus station to pl Hretska, take bus 220.

Taxis in Odesa charge incredibly high prices, as the city's taxi drivers are stubborn when it comes to fleecing tourists. When taking a taxi from your hotel, ask the front desk to call one for you, and ask them to agree on a price over the phone. You're more likely to pay the right price that way than if you just flag one down from in front of the hotel by yourself. **Elit-Taxi** (☎ 371 030) has reliable service.

Rental cars can be hired through **Europcar** (☎ 777 4011; www.europcar.ua), located in the Hotel Londonskaya.

CRIMEA КРИМ

Rip up what you think you know about Ukraine and start from scratch – Crimea will confound any generalisations you've made about the country so far and take you into a new world of astonishing scenery, rich cultural foment and a semitropical climate kept balmy by the winds coming off the warm Black Sea. No wonder this peninsula has been fought over by the Greeks, Khazars, Tatars, Mongols, Huns, Genoese, Ottomans, Russians, French and British over the centuries.

The most attractive and interesting part of the peninsula is the so-called 'Russian Riviera' – you'll understand the accuracy of the name if you're here in the summer months, when much of Moscow descends on the resorts here. In addition to the seedy resort towns of Yalta and Alupka, you'll find the fascinating palaces where modern European history was shaped in 1945 by the 'Big Three' (Stalin, Churchill and Roosevelt), not to mention the attractive Russian naval headquarters of Sevastopol. But the highlight of the entire peninsula is without doubt tiny Bakhchysaray, the old Crimean Tatar capital with the dramatic setting and the perfectly preserved Khan's Palace.

History

While Crimea's early history is a palimpsest of cultural annexations from the Greeks and Scythians to the Genoese and Jews, the real crucible of the peninsula's history has been the conflict between the Turkic and the Slavic peoples for control.

The Mongols arrived in 1240 as they shattered Kyivan Rus, and their descendents, the Crimean Tatars, formed a khanate here, which in later years became a vassal state of the Ottoman Empire.

While a Turkish vassal state, Crimea enjoyed much autonomy. The same was not true when the Russians arrived in 1783 and began a campaign of 'revenge' for the Tatars' slave-trading raids into Russia over past centuries. Most of the peninsula's four to five million Tatars fled to Turkey, while Russians, Ukrainians, Bulgarians and even some Germans were invited to resettle Crimea.

Much to the chagrin of its rival empires, Russia wanted to take over the faltering Ottoman Empire, and when Tsar Nicholas I sent troops into the Ottoman provinces of Moldavia and Wallachia (ostensibly to protect the Christians there) in 1854, the British and French assembled in Varna (now in Bulgaria) to protect İstanbul. Both sides lost about 250,000 soldiers in the war, many from bad medical care – to which British nurse Florence Nightingale drew attention.

By the 1860s, however, Crimea had became a chic leisure spot, thanks to Russia's imperial family building a summer estate at Livadia, on the outskirts of Yalta.

During the civil war that followed the Russian Revolution, Crimea was one of the last 'white' bastions. The Germans occupied the peninsula for three years during WWII and Crimea lost nearly half its inhabitants. The population was drained once again by Stalin (see the boxed text, p951).

Throughout the Soviet era, millions came each year to Crimea, attracted by the warmth, beauty, beaches and mountain air. In 1954 Khrushchev transferred control of the peninsula to Ukraine, a sticking point today, as the Crimean population have more in common with Russia, and have been working to make Russian the official language. More importantly, the peninsula is a geopolitical time bomb, as Russia uses Sevastopol as its Black Sea Naval Base. While there's a lease running until 2017, there's no telling how things will pan out with a resurgent Russia and a largely pro-Russian local population.

SIMFEROPOL СІМФЕРОПОЛЬ
☎ 0652 / pop 345,000

In the centre of the peninsula, Crimea's capital, largest city and transport hub is a place most people pass through rather than stay in. While Simferopol (sim-fer-OP-ul) has some things going for it, not for nothing did one expat in nearby Sevastopol dub Simferopol 'simply awful' when we mentioned it.

Despite an underwhelming reputation, the city boasts plenty of accommodation options, decent eateries and a small smattering of sights if you have to spend a few hours or overnight here. In recent years, a lot of money has been spent on renovating the city, which you'll see in the rowdy construction areas and freshly painted facades.

Information

24-hour Pharmacy (☎ 546 911; pr Kirova 22)
Bukva Books (☎ 273 153; vul Sevastopilska 6; ⏲ 9am-8pm Mon-Fri, to 7pm Sat, to 6pm Sun) Offers a small selection of English-language classics.
Central post office (☎ 272 255; vul Rozy Lyuxemburg 1) Also has a telephone office and internet centre, both 24 hours.

Ferrari Internet café (☎ 278 159; vul Pushkina 11; ⏲ 24hr) Through the courtyard in office 18.
Pro-Internet Centre (☎ 549 805; Basement, vul Karla Marksa 1; per hr 4hry; ⏲ 9am-8pm)

Sights

The attractions of Simferopol aren't going to leave much of an impression. Most enjoyable during a visit is a tranquil walk along the Salhir River, which is dotted with willow trees. Also, strolling the pedestrian zone of vul Pushkina makes for good window shopping and people-watching, especially because there are benches on which to rest along the way.

Three Saints Church (vul Hoholya 16), **Holy Trinity Cathedral** (vul Odeska 12) and **Church of Sts Peter & Paul** (vul Oktyabrska) are three Orthodox churches in town and worth a gander because of the ornate mosaic iconography on the facades. East of the centre, up the quaint vul Kurchatova, is the restored 1502 **Kebi-Jami Mosque**, which was reconstructed in the 17th century and is the oldest building in the city. Today it's the centre of a rundown Tatar neighbourhood – wander up here to appreciate how different life is for Crimean

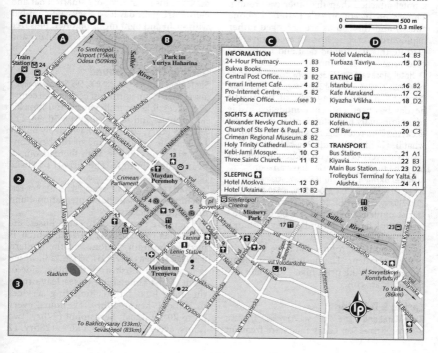

Tatars here on the margin of society. Locals are surprisingly friendly, especially if they hear you speaking English.

Right in the heart of the city is the **Alexander Nevsky Church** (Maydan Peremohy), a splendid white stone neo-Byzantine structure that was being rebuilt at the time of our last visit.

The town's **Crimean Regional Museum** (☎ 276 347; vul Hoholya 14; adult/student 10/5hry; ☼ 9am-5pm Wed-Mon) features a geology room with mastodon jaws, a natural history (read: taxidermy) room, a Christian history room and a WWII history room.

Sleeping

Turbaza Tavriya (☎ 232 024; vul Bespalova 21; s 120-180hry, d 170-250hry) This tranquil, hillside place is popular despite being a bit far from the centre, so call ahead. Of two buildings, one has been fully renovated, the other partially so (no lift or in-room phone, but otherwise similar). *Marshrutky* 15 and 17 go here from pl Sovietskaya.

Hotel Valencia (☎ 510 606; www.valencia.crimea.ua; vul Odeska 8; r 150-600hry; ☒) This oddball place in the centre of town is more of a restaurant with a hotel attached than the other way round. There's no reception (it's better to phone ahead) and the rooms are arranged rather haphazardly, each in its own eccentric style. Despite this it's a good deal and rooms are comfortable, with bathrooms and TV.

Hotel Moskva (☎ 237 389; www.moskva-hotel.com; vul Kyivska 2; s 263-328hry, d 396-496hry, ste 576-796hry; ☒ ▯) This crumbling relic of Intourist's heyday has been entirely remodelled inside to an unusually high standard, with only the decaying concrete balconies giving any hint of what lies behind the building's cladding. The rooms are very decent now, although note that only the higher categories have air-con.

Hotel Ukraina (☎ 510 165; www.ukraina-hotel.biz; vul Rozy Lyuxemburg 7; s 350-440hry, d 540-640hry, ste 1020-2100hry, incl breakfast; ☒ ▯) The deeply faux-tsarist opulence here will not be everyone's taste (think dark green and gold everything), but this is definitely the smartest place in town, even if the rooms don't live up to the lobby's grandeur. The business-class rooms are not worth the price hike – the only difference is air-con.

Eating & Drinking

Kafe Marakand (☎ 524 698; vul Vorovskoho 17; mains 8-20hry; ☼ closed Sun) Local Tatars are frequent

patrons here, where you can sit on a traditional bed and sup from the many fine dishes on offer such as *plov* (meat and rice), *lagman* (beef noodle soup), *shashlyk* and *lepyoshky* (flat, round bread). Staff veer between solicitous and indifferent, but this is one of the best places in town to taste Tatar cooking.

Istanbul (vul Horkoho 5; mains 10-30hry; ☼ 11am-11pm) This Turkish place has a small, not-very-Turkish menu – including Siberian *manti* (Tatar dumplings) and Greek moussaka, although its kebabs are great and the family-run establishment is very friendly. A good pit stop for lunch.

Kiyazha Vtikha (☎ 291 489; vul Turgeneva 35; mains 18-40hry) This rustic Ukrainian whimsy is a silly place by the river, but the Ukrainian food is excellent. There's a sunflower-stuffed outdoor eating area where you can eat in your own *izba* (wooden hut).

Kofein (☎ 505 990; vul Pushkina 8; ☼ 9am-11pm) The decor here is one big Benetton ad, but there's an amazing array of coffees from all over the world at this fun cafe, as well as good cakes and light meals.

Off Bar (☎ 620 494; vul Proletarska; ☼ 11am-midnight) This is Simferopol's smartest bar and club. During the day it's a sleek cafe-cum-bar with sushi and light meals on offer, plus free wi-fi. After dark it becomes a cocktail bar and even a night club at weekends.

Getting There & Around

Simferopol airport (SIP; ☎ 006, 595 545; www.airport.crimea.ua) is 15km northwest of the town centre and accessible by trolleybus 9 (50 kopeks, 30 minutes) and *marshrutky* 49, 50, 98, 113 and 115 (1hry, 20 minutes), which ply bulvar Lenina.The airport is one of the best connected in the country, with flights from all over Eastern Europe. The airport's website has an up-to-date schedule.

Kiyavia (☎ 272 116; vul Sevastopilska 22; ☼ 9am-6pm Mon-Fri, to 5pm Sat) sells both international and domestic air tickets.

There are two places to catch buses: the **bus station** (☎ 252 560; pl Vokzalna), which is next to the train station, and the modern **main bus station** (☎ 275 211; vul Kyivska 4), which is near Hotel Moskva on the other side of town. Most timetabled buses leave from the main bus station, including services to Yalta (17hry to 19hry, 1½ hours, every 10 to 20 minutes), Sevastopol (22hry, two hours, every 20 minutes), Odesa (28hry, 12 hours, five daily) and Bakhchysaray (9hry, one hour, hourly).

For local transport around town, *marshrutky* are the way to go – in fact, the city is clogged with them, so walking is another good option. *Marshrutky* usually leave from the bus station by the train station, where you'll find touts offering regular fast services to Yalta (25hry) and Bakhchysaray (15hry).

The **train station** (☎ 005, 243 418) is at the end of bulvar Lenina. Most trains to/from Simferopol are very busy, especially from June to August, so book your tickets as early as possible. Services link Simferopol with Kyiv, (110hry to 155hry, 15 hours, two daily) Lviv (103hry to 153hry, 25 hours, three daily) and Odesa (85hry, 11 to 13 hours, twice daily). There are also regular connections to Minsk, Moscow and St Petersburg during the summer months.

Local *elektrychka* run regularly along the Crimean peninsula to/from Sevastopol (6hry, two hours, eight daily) stopping en route in Bakhchysaray (3hry, 40 minutes).

From 5am to 8pm, the world's longest – and slowest! – trolleybus ride leaves from the **trolleybus terminal** (vul Gagarina), next to the train station, for Yalta (12hry, 2½ hours, every 20 minutes), stopping in Alushta. It's not the most time-efficient method of transport, but it's definitely a novelty. The views along the way are spectacular, but if you don't want to dawdle, the Yalta-bound *marshrutky* take the same route and zip by the trolleys.

YALTA ЯЛТА
☎ 0654 / pop 80,500

Like dark matter, Yalta exerts a poorly understood yet irresistible force on people in Crimea, and it seems almost anyone you meet will be heading to or escaping from the peninsula's most famous and tackiest resort town, once the preserve of tsars and artists and now…well, not.

While the city enjoys a spectacular setting with the vast Crimean Mountains rising sharply from the sea, once you start to descend towards the overdeveloped town centre, you'll soon realise that the journey to Yalta was one of the greatest aspects of a visit here.

In town, you'll find a lively waterfront promenade, lined with tiny flashing casinos,

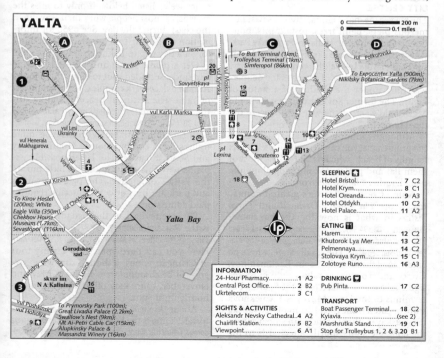

YALTA

0 ___ 200 m
0 ___ 0.1 miles

SLEEPING 🛏	
Hotel Bristol......................	7 C2
Hotel Krym........................	8 C1
Hotel Oreanda..................	9 A3
Hotel Otdykh....................	10 C2
Hotel Palace.....................	11 A2

EATING 🍴	
Harem...............................	12 C2
Khutorok Lya Mer............	13 C2
Pelmennaya......................	14 C2
Stolovaya Krym................	15 C1
Zolotoye Runo..................	16 A3

INFORMATION	
24-Hour Pharmacy................	1 A2
Central Post Office..............	2 B2
Ukrtelecom..........................	3 C1

SIGHTS & ACTIVITIES	
Aleksandr Nevsky Cathedral.	4 A2
Chairlift Station....................	5 B2
Viewpoint.............................	6 A1

DRINKING 🍷	
Pub Pinta............................	17 C2

TRANSPORT	
Boat Passenger Terminal....	18 C2
Kyiavia.............................(see 2)
Marshrutka Stand...............	19 C1
Stop for Trolleybus 1, 2 & 3.	20 B1

To Bus Terminal (1km);
Trolleybus Terminal (1km);
Simferopol (86km)

To Expocenter Yalta (500m);
Nikitsky Botanical Gardens (7km)

Yalta Bay

To Kirov Hostel (200m); White Eagle Villa (350m); Chekhov House-Museum (1.7km); Sevastopol (116km)

To Prymorsky Park (100m);
Great Livadia Palace (2.2km);
Swallow's Nest (9km);
Mt Ai-Petri Cable Car (15km);
Alupkinsky Palace &
Massandra Winery (16km)

touristy restaurants, touts beseeching you to touch their monkey while they take your picture and desperate artists offering to draw an unflattering caricature of you. In fact, especially after recent renovations, Yalta seems like a caricature of itself – sort of a painted-up, exaggerated version of what a resort town is supposed to look like. Despite this, it makes a good base for operations in Crimea and can be fun in small doses.

Information

24-hour pharmacy (cnr vul Morska & vul Chekhova; 🕑 24hr)

Central post office (☎ 312 073; pl Lenina 1; 🕑 8am-9pm Mon-Fri, to 6pm Sat, to 4pm Sun in summer, reduced hr winter)

Expocenter Yalta (☎ 272 546, 8-050-324 2350; www .travel2crimea.com; Hotel Massandra, vul Drazhynskogo 48; 🕑 9am-5pm Mon-Sat May-Sep, Mon-Fri Oct-Apr) With years of experience, excellent English and a helpful manner, owner Ihor Brudny runs a superior travel service.

Ukrtelecom (vul Moskovskaya 9; per hr 5hry; 🕑 24hr) Internet access and phone calls.

Sights
CITY CENTRE

The **promenade**, nab Lenina, stretches past numerous piers, palm trees, restaurants, boutiques and souvenir stalls to **Prymorsky Park**, where there are some carnival-type rides. It starts at **ploscha Lenina**, the centre of activity. Here there are plenty of benches for people-watching under the shadow of a statue of Lenin. The former Soviet leader gawks at the McDonald's across the way as if it were the devil himself.

Although swimming isn't an option along the promenade, you can descend to a few short lengths of beach, which is all rocks – most of them flat and perfect for skipping along the placid, rather plain waterfront.

Anton Chekhov, Russia's greatest dramatist, wrote *The Cherry Orchard* and *Three Sisters* in what is now the **Chekhov House-Museum** (☎ 394 947; www.chekhov.com.ua; vul Kirova 112; adult/student 15/10hry; 🕑 10am-5pm Tue-Sun Jun-Sep, Wed-Sun Sep-May). The small estate, where he entertained the likes Chaliapin, Rachmaninov, Gorky and Tolstoy, is Yalta's only must-see sight. Take *marshrutka* 8 from the Spartak bus terminus to the Dom-Muzey A P Chekhova stop, or catch trolleybus 1 from pl Radyanska (Sovietskaya), alight at the sixth stop, walk up the concrete stairs shortly afterwards to the

right at Krayniy (крайний) pereulok and turn left into vul Kirova at the top. To walk takes 15 to 20 minutes from the Spartak Cinema. Included in the price of admission is a tour (in Russian only) from women who are obviously passionate about the place, and the grounds are lovely. Last entry is at 4.30pm.

The 1903 **Aleksandr Nevsky Cathedral** (vul Sadova 2) is a beautiful example of neo-Byzantine architecture. The architect was Nikolai Krasnov, who designed many palaces on Crimea's southern coast.

There is a mediocre **chairlift** (return 20hry; 🕑 11am-5pm Apr-Sep, to 11pm Jul & Aug). Buy your ticket, step into a big dented bucket, and you're off, swinging above dilapidated rooftops to a bizarre pseudo-Greek temple and **viewpoint**, called Darsan. The boarding point is behind nab Lenina 17, along vul Kirova.

OTHER SIGHTS

Many travellers hang in Yalta not because they're into the resorty Yalta vibe, but because it makes an excellent base from which to see Crimea's spectacular historic and natural sights. It makes sense to do the tour in the order we've listed below, if only to miss the crowds, as most people work their way down the coast during the day. See p950 for information on getting to these places. And don't forget a day trip to Bakhchysaray is possible.

Get a picnic lunch and a bottle of wine and find a secluded spot to enjoy them in the Alupka palace-park complex, 16km southwest of Yalta. The setting is peaceful and beautiful, and the majestic **Alupkinsky Palace** (adult/child 30/15hry; 🕑 8am-8pm summer, 9am-5pm winter), built for Count Mikhail Vorontsov, is quite impressive, a combination of Moorish fancy and Scottish castle. The latter possibly explains why this was Churchill's base during the Yalta Conference. The palace grounds and park are free; only the interior requires paid admission.

Fifty metres back up the road towards Yalta is the **Massandra winery** (☎ 721 198; admission 30-35hry; 🕑 tours Tue-Sat May-Nov, Tue, Thu & Sat Dec-Apr). Here you can participate in a tasting tour of Crimean wines, although dry-wine lovers will be disappointed. Between May and November, tours kick off at 11am, and run hourly until 5pm.

About 1km east of Alupka, on the way back toward Yalta, is the **Mt Ai-Petri cable car** (kanatnaya doroga; return trip 40hry; 🕑 10am-5pm, cars every 20 min).

It's a truly dizzying ride across the foothills and up the mountain's sheer face, during which you overlook the coast and the sea. At the summit, there are expansive views inland, too. The lines can be huge in summer – so get here in good time. This is the best chance most visitors have to see much of Crimea's landscape.

Possibly the most internationally famous landmark on the peninsula is the cliff-side castle known as the **Swallow's Nest** (Lastochkino Gnizdo; viewing platform 5hry; ☺ 8am-6pm Tue-Sun). Honestly, although it looks great on a postcard or a travel brochure, the Swallow's Nest is weirdly small, unimpressive and fake-looking. Inside it's a bad Italian restaurant with a strict no gawping policy – you'll have to brave mediocre pizza to see inside. Be prepared for a lot of stairs and big crowds. There are regular fast boats to/from Yalta from the small pier at the bottom of the Swallow's Nest (30hry).

In February 1945 Stalin, Roosevelt and Churchill shaped the face of postwar Europe at the Yalta Conference in the **Great Livadia Palace** (☎ 315 579; adult/child 30/15hry; ☺ 10am-5pm Thu-Tue April-Oct, Wed-Sun Nov-Mar), 3km southwest of central Yalta. Included in the price is a one-hour Russian-language tour, although you're welcome to stroll through on your own. It features photos and memorabilia about this historic event, as well as displays about the palace's original owner, the last Russian emperor, Nicholas II. He spent just four seasons here with his family before they were all arrested by the Bolsheviks and eventually shot. The stories behind the Yalta conference are fascinating, though unless you speak Russian, it's best to read up before you come, unless you can find an English-speaking guide. The famous photograph of the 'Big Three' was taken in the Italian courtyard, which costs an extra 10hry to enter.

If you go by *marshrutka,* cross the street where it stops for you, and make your descent. Go down stairs on the left by the orange building. You'll eventually find it if you keep descending.

Sleeping

Hotel prices fluctuate seasonally, peaking in July and August and during the new-year season, when reservations for all hotels are recommended. We've listed the highest rates. Yalta is crawling with hotels; the ones reviewed here are most recommended. You will never be homeless though – babushkas hang around the main bus terminal offering private rooms (see p954). There are signs all over town with phone numbers of people offering rooms; look for variations containing the words 'сдам, жильё, квартира'.

Hotel Krym (☎ 271 703; baza@hotelkrim.yalta.crimea .ua; vul Moskovskaya 1/6; s 50-130hry, d 50-260hry; ⊠) You'll have to step up the charm to crack a smile from the staff at Hotel Krym, designed by architect Krasnov (who also did the Livadia Palace, among others), but you can't beat the prices or the location (expect noise, especially in summer). The cheaper rooms for each category have a shared bathroom, and the priciest doubles and triples have air-con.

Kirov Hostel (☎ 326 480; hostel.kirov@gmail.com; vul Kirova 1/6; s 150hry, d 300hry) Yalta finally has a hostel of sorts; it's housed in a tiny part of a once elite Soviet sanatorium, so don't expect any signs. Walk through the main gate and continue straight on to the main building, where the hostel manager will be called. At present just 12 rooms form the 'hostel' (one tiny part of a huge accommodation block), although there are plans for expansion. All rooms have new furnishings and decent bathrooms. There's also free wi-fi and for 15hry breakfast can be had in the vast main cafeteria. The young team is enthusiastic and slowly finding its way – something we're keen to support. This place is a must for the sheer novelty of its location.

Hotel Otdykh (☎ 353 069; vul Drazhynskoho 14; s 190hry, d 250-520hry, incl breakfast; ⊠) Once a 19th-century brothel for visiting government dignitaries, Hotel Otdykh perches high on the oldest street in town, removed from the carnival of the promenade and in an area where life is relatively normal. The rooms here are a great deal – from the newly renovated pricier ones to the few that remain untouched and together form a museum of Soviet tourism. All rooms have air-con and 24-hour hot water, and it's just a two-minute walk to a small beach.

Hotel Bristol (☎ 271 606; www.hotel-bristol.com.ua; vul Ruzvelta 10; s 530-645hry, d 600-715hry, ste 975-2515hry; ⊠ ▣ ▣) Prices have shot up here in recent years, and it has to be admitted, if you're here for the seafront, you can't get a much better location. Rooms are comfortable, if lacking any style, although ones overlooking the street can be loud at night. There's a pool, gym and business centre, as well as paid internet access from the 107 rooms.

UKRAINE

our pick **White Eagle Villa** (☎ 327 702, 8-050 972 8986; prov Krutoy 4; s/d incl breakfast 600/650hry; ✖) This hidden villa is the perfect refuge from Yalta's unrelenting chaos. In pastel tones, the refitted villa plays host to six comfortable rooms, all individually attired and all with private facilities. The English-speaking staff make great efforts to help foreigners. Book in advance, especially in winter, when the hotel is only open for group bookings.

Hotel Oreanda (☎ 274 250; www.hotel-oreanda.com; nab Lenina 35/2; s 1250-1450hry, d 1850-2485hry, ste 3245-8475hry, incl breakfast & dinner; ✖ 🖥 🖳) Not only the best location, reputation and service in town, but also the best coffee – the Oreanda is hard to beat. Favoured by Russian millionaire types, the place is all you'd expect from a five-star hotel in a big resort town. The large rooms all have in-room internet access and there are two pools and a Turkish bath to relax in.

Eating & Drinking

Pelmennaya (☎ 323 932; vul Sverdlova 8; mains 10hry; ⏲ 8am-10pm) Not far from Hotel Otdykh, this hole-in-the-wall place is great for a quick hot bite with Yalta's working class. *Pelmeni* (Russian-style ravioli stuffed with meat), of course, is the main offering, but bliny and a few other dishes can be had here too.

our pick **Harem** (☎ 326 318; pl Ignatenko 6; mains 40-80hry; ⏲ 10am-midnight) This stellar addition to the Yalta dining scene should not be missed, not least as it serves up some of the best Tatar cuisine in Crimea. Harem enjoys a relaxed, trendy vibe, as diners eat and smoke hookahs on the large terrace overlooking a small square. Sample dishes include chicken hearts with vegetables in plum sauce and baked lamb in sultanas. There's also free wi-fi.

Khutorok Lya Mer (☎ 271 815; vul Sverdlova 9; mains 60-150hry; ⏲ 11am-2am) One of Yalta's best eating experiences, this nautical-themed space may look a bit cheesy, but the food is of a great standard, including fresh fish (try the sturgeon *shashlyk* with pomegranate sauce). Service is friendly and there's a menu in English, but book ahead, especially if you want a sea view table on the terrace.

Pub Pinta (☎ 272 442; vul Ignatenko 7) This place is one of Yalta's more pleasant places to have a pint – even though it's in the centre of the action, there's great bar food, good beer and a friendly crowd.

The waterfront walkway is dotted with several cute little places to eat, and there are many well-signed supercheap cafeterias (столовая) around town as well. One is **Stolovaya Krym** (mains 5hry; ⏲ 8am-7pm), associated with the budget hotel next door.

Getting There & Away

There are no trains or flights to Yalta – the only way in is by bus. Trolleybuses to/from Simferopol (p947) start/finish at the **trolleybus terminal** (vul Moskovskaya). Opposite that is the **bus terminal** (☎ 342 325) where buses leave for Bakhchysaray (28hry, 2½ hours, five daily), Sevastopol (20hry, two hours, every 15 to 30 minutes) and Simferopol (18hry, two hours, every 10 to 20 minutes). There's also a daily Odesa-bound bus (115hry, 14 hours), and two daily buses to Kyiv (170hry, 18 to 20 hours).

There is a **boat passenger terminal** (morskoy vokzal; ☎ 320 094; vul Ruzvelta 5), but it sees little use. However, it is possible to reach Odesa on London Sky Travel's speed ferry (see p943), as well as İstanbul and Varna during the season.

Getting Around

A trolleybus ride is 50 kopeks. *Marshrutky* within the town are 1.50hry. Taxis within the town are relatively expensive (10hry on average), and drivers are not particularly eager for your business. **Avka-Trans Taxis** (☎ 231 085, 8-067 563 0444) are metered and cost half as much around town. They're often found at the intersection of vul Ruzvelta and nab Lenina.

To get to/from the terminals, take trolleybus 1, 2 or 3 along vul Moskovskaya/Kyivskaya; most *marshrutky* along those streets also go to/from the terminals.

Just off vul Moskovskaya, there is a *marshrutka* stand where these minibuses go to sights just outside of Yalta. *Marshrutka* 32 and bus 27 serve Livadia, Swallow's Nest, and the Mt Ai-Petri cable car, stopping and turning around at Alupka (where Massandra Winery is). The conductor will ask if there are any '*wanters*' for the each stop (shout back '*yest!*' – 'there are' – and the bus will pull over).

BAKHCHYSARAY БАХЧИСАРАЙ
☎ 06554 / pop 33,000

A world away from the glitz and noise of the resort towns on the coast, the former capital of the Crimean khanate is an absolute must-see on any trip to the peninsula. With three

---

CRIMEA'S TATAR POPULATION

On 18 May 1944 Stalin accused Crimea's Tatars of collaborating with the Nazis, and deported the entire Muslim population to Central Asia and Siberia. The Tatar language was banned and all traces of the culture were obliterated. Crimea was repopulated with Ukrainians, Russians, Bulgarians and Germans. It is estimated that more than 46% percent of the Tatars died during deportation.

Since the late 1980s, about 260,000 Tatars have returned to their lost homeland and have been trying to re-establish themselves and their culture. It hasn't been easy. Few speak their Turkic mother tongue and many still live in poor, slumlike conditions, with no water or electricity. However, the Ukrainian government has started giving money to the cause of the returning deportees, and conditions are improving. You will probably see new Tatar homes being constructed in the foothills and restaurants serving Tatar cuisine make for one of the region's highlights.

---

stellar attractions: the Khan's Palace (which dates back to the 16th century), the still-working Uspensky Monastery built into sheer cliff walls and the 6th-century cave city of Chufut-Kale, it's worth doing an overnight trip here, not least because there are some great accommodation options and plenty of chances to taste Crimean Tatar cuisine.

Sights

Bakhchysaray's sights can be done on a day trip, from Sevastopol or Yalta, but it's worth staying overnight to see the town once the tourist buses have left. Starting at the Khan's Palace, the sights are in a line ending up at Chufut-Kale. Stop any *marshrutka* heading down vul Lenina for a ride towards the Uspensky Monastery, or it's a 20-minute walk through the town.

The remarkable **Khan's Palace** (☎ 42 881; www.hansaray.org.ua; vul Lenina 129; adult/student 30/15hry; ☷ 8am-5.30pm Jul & Aug, to 4.30pm Wed-Mon May, Jun, Sep & Oct, to 4.30pm Thu-Mon Nov-Apr) was built by Russian and Ukrainian slaves in the 16th century and has been remarkably well maintained since it was spared destruction on the whim of Catherine the Great in the 18th century. Apparently the scourge of the Crimean Tatars thought the palace 'romantic', and it's hard to disagree with her. The palace has a special place in Russian hearts, as Pushkin wrote a famous poem about the small fountain inside, and so it's become a focal point for the tours. A Russian-language tour is included in the price of the ticket, but you're allowed to wander around the palace yourself.

Even visitors who have had enough of visiting churches and monasteries will not regret visiting the **Uspensky Monastery** (admission free). Built into the side of a cliff (note the frescos high up above on the cliff walls), the working

monastery has such a lovely and romantically devout feel, you may even consider signing up for monkhood yourself. The water there is said to have miraculous healing properties, and you'll see visitors filling their plastic Coca-Cola bottles with the stuff. Look across to the opposite cliffs for wild peacocks – you're likely to hear their persistent calls before you see them.

Next up is the 6th-century cave city of **Chufut-Kale** (admission 20hry; ☷ 8am-6pm). It's a 1.5km uphill walk (much of it shady) – along the way you'll see the entrance to a Dervish and Muslim cemetery that is in ruins; only a couple of tombstones are still legible. Chufut-Kale, a honeycomb of caves and structures where, for hundreds of years, people took refuge, is an exciting and breathtaking place to explore. Although the joint entrance to the Uspensky Monastery and Chufut-Kale looks a bit touristy, the 1.5km uphill (but shady) walk to the cave city ensures it's not too overrun with people.

Sleeping & Eating

our pick Hotel Usta (☎ 47 343, 8-050 647 7188; www.usta.rcf.crimea.ua; vul Rechnaya 125; s/d 100/180hry; ☐) This fantastic small hotel a short walk from the Khan's Palace is out through the backyard of a Crimean Tatar crafts collective of the same name. Spick-and-span rooms, many with balconies overlooking the valley, all have bathrooms (though singles share bathrooms) and there's free wi-fi and use of a communal kitchen. On our last visit, they were building an extension, such is this venture's well-earned popularity.

Prival (☎ 47 846, 8-050 497 6691; www.prival.crimea.com; vul Shmidta 43; dm 60hry, d 230-250hry, 2- to 4-person cottages 250-450hry) Offers breathtaking vistas of the limestone cliffs, a sauna, pool, jacuzzi and

UKRAINE

a tennis court, with cheap dorms and smart cottages available too. It's a well-signed 500m from the entrance to the Khan's Palace.

Musafir (☎ 8-050 6697526; off vul Lenina 106; mains 6-25hry) On the hillside above the loud V Gosti u Khana restaurant, this lovely Crimean Tatar place serves up good traditional food, while guests sit on beds and soak up the exotic atmosphere.

Pushkin Le Café (☎ 474 61; www.pushkin.crimea.ua; vul Lenina 106A; mains 30-50hry; ⏰ 10am-11pm) This excellent restaurant combines a charming 19th-century drawing-room atmosphere with a skilfully executed menu that runs the gamut from Russian to Crimean Tatar, via French and Italian. There's also a shady garden perfect for lunch on a hot day.

Getting There & Around

Because buses and trains connect Bakhchysaray with Simferopol and Sevastopol very frequently all day, it's more feasible to do a day trip here from those cities than from further afield Yalta.

From Bakhchysaray's crumbling **bus station** (☎ 42 972), buses go to Sevastopol (7hry, one hour, every 40 minutes) and Simferopol (9hry, 40 minutes, every 10 to 20 minutes). Outside the bus station there are two *marshrutka* stops – one for the old town, and one for new town. Any *marshrutka* going to the old town will drop you outside the Khan's Palace.

Trains are another option: they run to Simferopol (3hry, 40 minutes, eight daily) and Sevastopol (3.20hry, 1½ hours, seven daily).

SEVASTOPOL СЕВАСТОПОЛЬ
☎ 0692 / pop 330,000

Sevastopol has enjoyed a rich and dramatic history – whether as the venue for one of the Crimean War's most gruesome sieges, as the scene of another brutal siege by German forces during WWII, or as a closed city and home to the Soviet Union's Black Sea Fleet during the Cold War – this naval citadel has seen a lot of action. Today Sevastopol remains Crimea's most Russian town, with the Russian Black Sea Fleet having a lease on its base until 2017 and the town filled with sailors. While 2017 remains a way off yet, there's much speculation about whether the Russians will definitely be leaving or not, even though President Yushchenko has said that this must happen. If you canvas local opinion

though, you'll find few people in favour of Russians leaving.

Today Sevastopol is a prosperous, clean and attractive town that takes great pride in its history and strategic importance. While there are limited sights here, a visit here is a must for any military-history buffs.

History

Modern Sevastopol (see-va-*stop*-all in Russian) has an attractive appearance, but it was a different story when the city was making international headlines during the Crimean War. After 349 days of bombardment by the British, French and Turks in 1854–55, it lay devastated by the time of its defeat. Arriving 10 years later, Mark Twain still felt moved to remark, 'In whatsoever direction you please, your eye scarcely encounters anything but ruin, ruin, ruin!'

History repeated itself in 1942, when the city fell to the Germans after a brutal 250-day siege. Stalin promptly proclaimed it a 'hero city' for holding out so long. Today only 10 buildings in town date from before 1945.

Information

There are 24-hour ATMs along pr Nakhimova and vul Bolshaya Morskaya.

Central post office (☎ 544 881; vul Bolshaya Morskaya 21; ⏰ 8am-6pm Mon-Fri, to 5pm Sat) Internet access available too at 4.60hry per hour.

Kiyavia (☎ 542 829; vul Lenina 13; ⏰ 9am-2pm & 3-7pm Mon-Fri) Plane tickets.

Odyssey Internet Club (☎ 544 965; vul Bolshaya Morskaya 27; ⏰ 24hr) With 25 computers at 6hry per hour. In the courtyard opposite the church.

Sevram Travel (☎ 555 878; office@sevram.com; Office 63, Palace of Childhood, pr Nakhimova 4) City tours with Crimean War specialists in English and other languages. Located in the building's eastern rotunda.

Telephone office (⏰ 9am-10pm) Near the post office.

Sights

The major Crimean War sight in town is the **Panorama** (Istorichesky bulvar; adult/student 20/10hry; ⏰ 10am-5pm Tue-Sun), a massive painting with 3-D elements depicting the defence of Sevastopol. The **Black Sea Fleet Museum** (☎ 542 289; vul Lenina 11; admission 15hry; ⏰ 10am-5pm Wed-Sun, closed last Fri of month) provides colourful displays about the controversial Russian fleet; though no English assistance is on hand. The Crimean War and naval history aside, the ruins of the ancient Greek city of **Chersonesus** (admission 15hry; ⏰ 9am-7pm May-Oct, to 4pm Nov-Apr) are fun

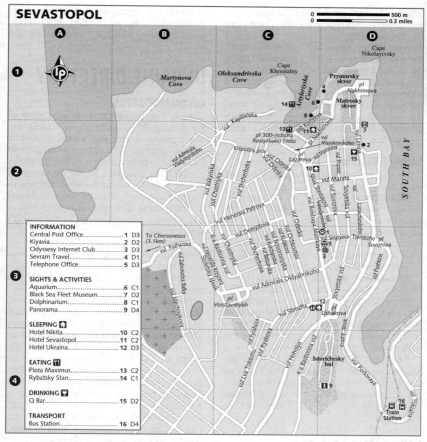

SEVASTOPOL

to explore. Founded in 422 BC, Chersonesus (Khersones locally) is the spot where Volodymyr the Great was famously baptised as a Christian in AD 989, thus launching what would become the Russian Orthodox Church. Local bus/*marshrutka* 22 goes directly there. Alternatively, you can catch trolleybus 2 or 6 westwards to the Rossiya (Россия) stop; turn back to the first street (vul Eroshshenko), and it's at the end, a 20-minute walk away.

Sevastopol is known for its **Dolphinarium** (☎ 930 730; nab Kornilova 2; adult/child 50/25hry; ⏰ 9am-7pm Tue-Sun) and nearby **Aquarium** (☎ 543 892; www.sevaquarium.com; adult/child 35/15hry; ⏰ 9am-7pm May-Oct, Tue-Sun Nov-Apr), the latter of which was recently refitted and now contains a large shark pool.

Sleeping

Hotel Ukraina (☎ 542 127; www.ukraine-hotel.com.ua; vul Hoholya 2; s 240-400hry, d 300-560hry, incl breakfast; 🐕) This newly redone hotel is a halfway house between a fusty Soviet establishment and a modern hotel. There are lots of different room categories, but all rooms have bathrooms, balconies, telephone and TV. There's air-con in most rooms, and while the refit has been slapdash in places, the staff is friendly and welcoming.

Hotel Sevastopol (☎ 539 071; www.sevastopol-hotel.com.ua; pr Nakhimova 8; s 450-550hry, d 750hry, ste 900-5000hry; 🖳) This magnificent slice of Stalinist pomp right in the heart of town definitely makes for Sevastopol's most striking accommodation, evocative as it is of Cold War grandeur. Rooms are divided into 'economy' and 'improved' – both are decent and spacious, the economies are simply much older. There's free wi-fi in the lobby.

Hotel Nikita (☎ 549 066; www.elite-apartments .biz; spusk Shestakova 1a; apt incl breakfast 450-1200hry; ✗ 🖳 🖳) This newly built elite residence is excellently located and despite being horribly nouveau riche, it's frustratingly hard to fault – the 'modern' room is particularly good value. All rooms are self-contained apartments, with questionable taste but a modern feel. There's paid wi-fi access. Book in advance.

Eating & Drinking

Cafes and restaurants abound in the main waterfront area.

Pizza Maximus (☎ 948 888; nab Kornylova; mains 30-55hry; ✹ 10am-11pm) On the harbour, this friendly and popular pizza joint serves up good food to the masses in its large outdoor eating area. There's free wi-fi and a full menu, including the option to make your own. A delivery service is also available.

Rybatsky Stan (☎ 557 278; nab Klokacheva 15; mains 140-220hry; ✹ 11-3am) Quite unlike anywhere else in town, this excellent seafood restaurant enjoys a national reputation and a great setting, with two outdoor terraces giving great views over the harbour. There's an expansive menu with plenty of nonseafood dishes.

Q Bar (☎ 679 3130; vul Lenina 8a; ✹ 10am-11pm) Tucked away in a courtyard, this bar is an unexpected surprise for Sevastopol, a trendy, gay-friendly cocktail bar and coffee lounge, perfect for an evening drink. There's free wi-fi here too.

Getting There & Around

The bus station and train station are within visible walking distance of each other – you can take a shortcut across the train tracks as locals do, or walk around on the road. Any *marshrutka* (1.50hry, pay on exit) or trolleybus from the stations will take you to the centre (pr Nakhimova).

From the **bus station** (vul Vokzalna), you can catch a ride to Simferopol (17hry, two hours, 32 daily), Yalta (20hry, two hours, 20 daily) and Bakhchysaray (11hry, 1½ hours, 22 daily). Once-daily buses to Odesa (73hry, 13 hours) are available for hard-core kopek-pinchers who can sleep in a chair.

From the Sevastopol **train station** (vul Portovaya), there are trains to Bakhchysaray (3.20hry, 1½ hours, seven daily), Simferopol (4.90hry, two hours, seven daily) and Kyiv (166hry, 17 hours, twice daily), and international trains to Moscow, St Petersburg and Minsk.

UKRAINE DIRECTORY

ACCOMMODATION

Ukraine's accommodation is improving all the time, as old Soviet hotels are refurbished, new ventures started and a small hostelling culture develops. The strangest thing about Ukrainian accommodation is that it's totally normal to be charged a fee for a reservation. This is actually worth doing in Crimea in summer or anywhere in the country during the early May slew of holidays, as you're guaranteed a room. The rest of the year it's probably not.

Organised camping grounds are rare anywhere in Ukraine and are usually at least 10km from the city centre. Wild camping is allowed, but fires are prohibited, although this is largely ignored.

Hostels are just starting up in Ukraine, check www.hihostels.com.ua/en for information on top of what's provided in this book.

Most budget hotels are unsightly Soviet monstrosities built in the 1960s and '70s; rooms are old, but are reasonably comfortable, clean and cheap. Many budget hotels have cheaper rooms with a shared bathroom. Midrange hotels or more expensive rooms in budget hotels may have more polite staff and remodelled, Western-style bathrooms. Top-end hotels usually meet most Western standards of service and aesthetics.

Private rooms in family homes are a popular option in Crimea and Odesa, especially in the summer. Look for people with signs around their necks reading комнаты (*komnaty*, 'rooms' in Russian). However, before deciding, always check the exact location and proximity to public transport. The cost ranges from 50hry to 100hry per person per night.

You'll find budget doubles for under 400hry, midrange doubles will cost between 400hry and 1000hry, while top-end doubles will generally cost more than 1000hry. Unless otherwise stated, all rooms in this chapter have private bathroom. Prices given throughout are for high season; there are considerable savings of between 20% and 50% to be made outside of this time, particularly in the Crimea.

ACTIVITIES

Hiking opportunities are richest in the Carpathian National Natural Park and around Crimea. Before arrival, try to buy the *Hiking Guide to Poland & Ukraine*, by Tim Burford, which describes hikes in Ukraine. The detailed Topograficheskaya Karta maps are available in Kyiv, though hiking trails are poorly marked on the maps or not at all. The virtually untouched slopes of the Carpathians (p934) are starting to become popular for snow sports between November and May.

BUSINESS HOURS

Official working hours are 9am (or 10am) to 5pm (or 6pm) Monday to Friday, with an hour-long break anywhere between noon and 2pm. Shops often open until about 8pm on weekdays and all day Saturday. Most bars and restaurants tend to open from 10am until 11pm or midnight.

EMBASSIES & CONSULATES

The following are in Kyiv unless otherwise noted.

Australia (Map pp918-19; ☎ 044-246 4223; vul Kominternu 18/137; Ⓜ Vokzalna) Honorary consulate.

Belarus (Map pp918-19; ☎ 044-537 5200; www.bel embassy.org.ua; vul Kotsyubynskoho 3; Ⓜ Universitet)

Canada (Map pp918-19; ☎ 044-590 3100; www.kyiv .gc.ca; vul Yaroslaviv Val 31; Ⓜ Zoloti Vorota)

France (Map pp918-19; ☎ 044-590 3600; www .ambafrance-ua.org; vul Reitarska 39; Ⓜ Zoloti Vorota)

Germany (Map pp918-19; ☎ 044-247 6800; www. german-embassy.kiev.ua; vul Khmelnytskoho 25; Ⓜ Zoloti Vorota)

Japan (Map pp918-19; ☎ 044-490 5500; www.ua.emb -japan.go.up; prov Muzeyny 4, 7th fl; Ⓜ Maydan Nezalezhnosti)

Moldova (Map pp918-19; ☎ 044-280 7721; moldoukr@ sovamua.com; vul Sichnevoho Povstannya 6; Ⓜ Arsenalna)

Netherlands (Map pp918-19; ☎ 044-490 8200; www .netherlands-embassy.com.ua; Kontraktova pl 7; Ⓜ Kontraktova Ploscha)

Romania Kyiv (Map pp918-19; ☎ 044-234 5261; www .kiev.mae.ro; vul Kotsyubynskoho 8; Ⓜ Universitet); Odesa (Map pp938-9; ☎ 048-725 0399; vul Bazarna 31, Odesa)

Russia Kyiv (Map pp918-19; ☎ 044-296 4504; www .embrus.org.ua; vul Kutuzova 8; Ⓜ Pecherska); Odesa (Map pp938-9; ☎ 048-296 4504; Gagarinskoe Plato 14)

UK (Map pp918-19; ☎ 044-490 3600; www.ukinukraine. fco.gov.uk; vul Desyatynna 9; Ⓜ Maydan Nezalezhnosti)

USA (Map pp918-19; ☎ 044-490 0000/4000; www.usemb.kiev.ua; vul Yuriya Kotsyubynskoho 10; Ⓜ Lukyanivska)

FESTIVALS & EVENTS

International Labour Day (1 May) is always a big deal, no matter where you are in the former Soviet Union; bigger cities have fireworks, concerts and other performances. On 24 August, **Independence Day** sees each city in Ukraine hosting a festival and parade.

HOLIDAYS

New Year's Day 1 January
Orthodox Christmas 7 January
International Women's Day 8 March
Orthodox Easter (Paskha) April
Labour Day 1 and 2 May
Victory Day 9 May
Constitution Day 28 June
Independence Day 24 August
Catholic Christmas 25 December

GAY & LESBIAN TRAVELLERS

Homosexuality is legal in Ukraine, but as with much of the rest of the region, it's far better to remain discreet, as homophobia is rife. Despite this there are small gay scenes in Kyiv and Odesa, while in the rest of the country most gay life happens on the internet. Check out www.gayua.com and www.gay.ru for the latest listings and events.

In most hotels you'll be fine asking for a double room as a gay couple, although that's largely due to the utter indifference of hotel staff to everything, rather than a liberal streak developing in the country's accommodation sector.

LANGUAGE

Ukrainian (see p1012) was adopted as the sole official language at independence. However, apart from the population in the west of the country, most Ukrainians (especially in the south and east), speak Russian as a first language. A hybrid of the two languages, called Surzhyk, is spoken in Kyiv and other major cities. All over the country it's common to hear conversations in which one party speaks in Russian and the other in Ukrainian. For native speakers of either language, the other is relatively easy to understand – this is not the case for foreigners who have learned Russian; you'll quickly be mystified! Speaking English, especially in Western Ukraine, is a better move.

In the Carpathians, some people living outside of city centres speak a Ukrainian dialect that is influenced by Polish, Slovak and Russian; they usually understand

Russian, but it may be difficult to understand their accent.

MONEY

The hryvnia (hry) is divided into 100 units, each called a kopek. Coins come in denominations of one, two, five, 10, 25 and 50 kopeks, as well as one hryvnia, while there are one, two, five, 10, 20, 50, 100, 200 and 500 hryvnia notes.

Although many hotels give prices in US dollars or euros, you will expected to pay in hryvnia.

ATMs and foreign-exchange offices (euros and US dollars only) are easily found even in small cities in Ukraine, and Western Union seems to have a desk in most banks. Exchanging money on the black market is unnecessary and illegal. Avoid bringing travellers cheques – they're hard to change.

POST

Post is reliable from Ukraine, but if you're sending something valuable, use the state-run International Express Mail (EMS), available at post offices. There are offices of DHL and FedEx in many cities if you need to transport something fast.

Normal-sized letters or postcards cost 3.50hry to anywhere outside Ukraine by ordinary mail or a bit more for express service. Domestic services take three days to a week; international takes a week to 10 days.

TELEPHONE

Ukraine's country code is sometimes listed as ☎ 380 and sometimes as ☎ 38. Although the former is the officially correct version, the latter makes more practical sense, so we've chosen it for the Quick Reference on the inside front cover of this book. Using ☎ 38 as the country code, you don't have to remember to drop the initial 0 of the city code when dialling from abroad. To call Kyiv from London, for example, you would just dial ☎ 00 38 044, instead.

As the Ukrainian telephone system slowly migrates from analogue to digital, many cities and towns now have two area codes. The longer one (eg ☎ 0482 for Odesa) is used with the shorter, old numbers. The shorter area code (eg ☎ 048) just drops the last digit and will be used with longer, new numbers.

For interstate calls within Ukraine, dial ☎ 8, wait for a tone, then dial the city code (with its first zero) and number – there should always be a 10-digit combination.

> ### EMERGENCY NUMBERS
>
> ■ Ambulance ☎ 03
> ■ Fire ☎ 01
> ■ Police ☎ 02

Anyone with an unlocked GSM mobile phone can simply buy a Ukrainian SIM card from any dealer and slot it in their handset to make cheap calls locally. To dial a local mobile-phone number within Ukraine, you must always prefix it with an ☎ 8, as if calling another town. Common codes for mobiles include ☎ 050 and ☎ 067. The main network operators are **Kyivstar** (www.kyivstar.net) and **MTS** (www.mts.com.ua). Recharge cards are sold absolutely everywhere.

VISAS

For stays of up to 90 days, visas are no longer required for EU, US, Norwegian, Swiss, Canadian and Japanese citizens. Australians, Israelis, New Zealanders and South Africans still need them. Point-of-entry visas are not issued. Comprehensive information about application forms and fees can be found at www.ukrconsul.org.

Visas are available from your local embassy. See the Ministry of Foreign Affairs of Ukraine (www.mfa.gov.ua) for a complete list of embassies, including contact details (click on 'About the Ministry' and choose 'Diplomatic Missions of Ukraine').

There are several types of visa, including business, tourist and private, with single, double and multiple entries available. Detailed explanations are found via the Embassy of Ukraine in Australia (www.mfa.gov.ua/australia). Letters of invitation are technically needed for all visas, although these can usually be provided with no problem by a hotel or travel agency for no fee, and is not always asked for. Single and double-entry visas can be bought for one to six months. Multiple-entry visas are valid for three to 12 months.

TRANSPORT IN UKRAINE

GETTING THERE & AWAY
Air

Most international flights use Kyiv's **Boryspil international airport** (KBP; ☎ 490 4777; www.airport-boris

pol.kiev.ua). Odesa and Lviv both receive some international flights from nearby countries; Simferopol gets some in the summer months. There's no departure tax in the Ukraine.

Ukraine's international airline carriers are **AeroSvit** (☎ 490 3490; www.aerosvit.com) and **Ukraine International Airlines** (☎ 461 5050; www .flyu ia.com).

The following are the main international airlines with offices in Kyiv.

Aeroflot (SU; ☎ 234 7638; www.ua.aeroflot.aero/eng)
Air Baltic (BT; ☎ 238 2649/68; www.airbaltic.com)
Air France (AF; ☎ 496 3575; www.airfrance.com)
Austrian Airlines (OS; ☎ 289 2032, 492 7232; www.aua.com)
British Airways (BA; ☎ 585 5050; www.ba.com)
Delta Airlines (DL; ☎ 246 5656; www.delta.com)
Dniproavia (Z6; ☎ 239 5311; www.dniproavia.com)
El Al (LY; ☎ 230 6993; www.elal.co.il)
Estonian Air (OV; ☎ 289 0520; www.estonian-air.ee)
Finnair (AY; ☎ 247 5777; www.finnair.com)
KLM (KL; ☎ 490 2490; www.klm.com)
LOT (LO; ☎ 288 1054/55; www.lot.com)
Lufthansa (LH; ☎ 490 3800; www.lufthansa.com)
Malév (MA; ☎ 490 7342/43; www.malev.com)
Transaero (UN; ☎ 490 6565, 286 7913; www.transaero.ru/english)
Turkish Airlines (code TK; ☎ 490 5933)

Land
BUS
Buses are far slower, less frequent and less comfortable than trains for long-distance travel.

See the relevant cities' and towns' Getting There and Away listings for bus transport details on fares and schedules to places outside Ukraine.

CAR & MOTORCYCLE
Always drive across official border stations to avoid complications. Foreign drivers must have an International Driving Permit (IDP) and must sign a declaration that they will be leaving the country with the car by a given date (no more than two months later). You'll also need vehicle insurance valid for the former Soviet Union. Policies bought at the border often prove useless, so buy beforehand.

TRAIN
Ukraine lends itself well to train travel. The rolling stock may not be in its first flush of

youth and still quite slow, but train travel here is punctual, cheap and a great way to see the country. Overnight rides are also a great way to save the expense of a hotel.

To be safe, try to get tickets at least a day in advance; if you're travelling during the New Year or May holidays, or going to Odesa or Crimea any time in summer, get tickets as early as possible.

The entire country is well connected by train to many places in Russia, and less so to major places in Belarus. See p925 for international trains from Kyiv.

Sea
There are ferries between Odesa and destinations including Varna (in Bulgaria), Constanta (in Romania) and İstanbul (in Turkey). See p943 for details.

GETTING AROUND
Air
In Kyiv, there are several offices of **Kiyavia** (☎ 044-490 4901; www.kiyavia.com; vul Horodetskoho 4; Ⓜ Khreshchatyk), which can book tickets on all flights. On its useful website you can get timetables and prices for all domestic and international flights.

Airlines flying domestic routes include **Ukraine International Airlines** (☎ 044-461 5050; www.flyuia.com) and **Aerosvit** (☎ 044-235 8710; www .aerosvit.com) and budget airline **Wizzair** (www .wizzair.com), which between them have flights between Kyiv, Lviv, Odesa, Simferopol and Uzhhorod. In Kyiv, domestic flights arrive at and depart from both **Boryspil international airport** (KBP; ☎ 490 4777; www.airport-borispol.kiev.ua) and **Zhulyany Airport** (☎ 242 2308; www.airport.kiev .ua; 92 Provitroflotsky pr).

Bicycle
Despite zero biking infrastructure, cycling is becoming more popular in Ukraine, even as a means of intracity travel. City roads are too congested and crumbling to make riding in them really enjoyable, but in Kyiv you'll see people doing it anyway and there are a few places to get away. The website www .tryukraine.com/info/cycling.shtml is a good resource.

Boat
Dnipro River cruises, from Kyiv to the Black Sea, can be booked through many travel agencies, but the principal operator is **Chervona Ruta**

(☎ 8-044 253 9247; www.ruta-cruise.com). Check its very comprehensive website for details.

Ukrferry (☎ 8-048 234 4059; www.ukrferry.com) has Black Sea cruises in Crimea, where, depending on availability, you might be able to nab a berth for just one leg, say from Sevastopol to Yalta. **London Sky Travel** (☎ 048 729 3196; www .lst.com.ua) in Odesa offers overnight ferries between Odesa and Sevastopol (600hry including meals, 17 hours) between May and early October.

Bus

Most public buses are decrepit and are recommended only when trains aren't running the route you want to travel, although a few private bus companies, such as **Autolux** (www .autolux.com.ua), offer comfortable services between points in Crimea, Kyiv, Odesa and Lviv. Schedules and price information are available on the website, and you can book by email.

Larger cities often have several *avtovokzal* (bus stations) but only one normally handles long-distance routes of interest to travellers. Tickets can be bought one or two days in advance at the major bus terminal and sometimes at separate ticket offices in the city centres.

Car & Motorcycle

To drive a private or rented vehicle to and around Ukraine you'll need an IDP and acceptable insurance. Ukraine participates in the Green Card System, so procure one in advance, as border guards have been known to sell useless policies.

Drive on the right. Unless otherwise indicated, speed limits are 60km/h in towns, 90km/h on major roads and 110km/h on highways. Speed traps are common, although traffic police will often wave you down without obvious reason.

It's a criminal offence to drive after consuming alcohol or without wearing a seat belt. Legally you must always carry a fire extinguisher, first-aid kit and warning triangle.

Avis (www.avis.com), **Europcar** (www.europcar .com) and **Hertz** (www.hertz.com.ua) have offices in Ukraine, including Kyiv, Lviv, Odesa, Simferopol and Yalta.

Local Transport

Cheap but crowded trolleybuses, trams and buses operate in all cities and major towns. Tickets can be bought on board and *must* be punched to be validated – look for others doing this to see how.

The fare for any given *marshrutka* (a privately run minibus serving a bus route) is displayed prominently at the front inside each bus; payment is usually taken upon entry but sometimes upon exit. To stop a *marshrutka*, simply hold out your hand and it will stop. Jump in, sit down, pass cash to the driver (a human chain operates if you are not sitting close enough) and then call out '*ostano*-vee-*tyes po*-zhal-*sta!*' when you want to get out and the driver will pull over.

Although it's often possible to hire an official taxi in larger towns, private taxis are a popular and surprisingly safe alternative, but difficult if you don't speak Ukrainian or Russian. Negotiate a price before you get in, and never get into a car if there's already a passenger.

Train

Train travel is normally frequent, cheap and efficient. An overnight train is an economical way to get around, and many services are timed to depart at dusk and arrive in the morning (after dawn). If you will be travelling during the 1 May holidays, or into or out of the Crimea in the summer, book tickets well in advance.

Regional Directory

This chapter provides an overview of conditions, and includes information that applies to the whole of Eastern Europe. Given the vast size of the region, this has meant some generalisation. For specifics on any given topic, see the individual country directories.

ACCOMMODATION

In this book, accommodation prices are quoted in the currency used by the establishment being reviewed. This means that some hotel prices are given in local currency, while others are listed in euros.

The accommodation options in each city or town are listed in ascending price order, starting with budget options, then midrange and top end. Prices listed are for high season and include private bathroom, unless otherwise indicated.

If you are travelling in summer – or if you intend to visit any particular country during a festival, event or other peak holiday period – you will do well to book your accommodation in advance. Hostels and cheap hotels fill up very quickly, especially in popular backpacker destinations such as Prague, Budapest and Kraków. In most cities, there is a shortage of good-value midrange accommodation options. In any case, it's worth a three-minute international phone call (or an email) to avoid wasting your first day in town searching for a place to stay.

If you arrive in a country by air, there is often an accommodation-booking desk at the airport, although it rarely covers the lower strata of hotels. Tourist offices often have extensive accommodation lists, and the more helpful ones will go out of their way to find you something suitable. In most countries the fee for this service is very low and, if the accommodation market is tight, it can save you a lot of running around.

In some countries – primarily Belarus, Moldova, Russia and Ukraine – it's still necessary to give up your passport for 'registration', supposedly so the local authorities know where you are staying.

See the individual country directories for an overview of local accommodation options.

Camping

The cheapest way to stay in Eastern Europe is to camp, and there are many camping grounds throughout the region. That said, a large proportion of the region's attractions are found in cities, where there often simply aren't any camping grounds. Most camping grounds near urban areas are large

---

BOOK YOUR STAY ONLINE

For more accommodation reviews and recommendations by Lonely Planet authors, check out the online booking service at www.lonelyplanet.com/hotels. You'll find the true, insider low-down on the best places to stay. Reviews are thorough and independent. Best of all, you can book online.

sites, intended mainly for motorists, though they're usually accessible by public transport and there's almost always space for backpackers with tents. Many camping grounds in Eastern Europe rent small on-site cabins, bungalows or caravans for double or triple the regular camping fee; in the most popular resorts all the bungalows are usually full in July and August.

The standard of camping grounds in Eastern Europe varies from country to country. They're unreliable in Romania, crowded in Slovenia and Hungary (especially on Lake Balaton), and variable in the Czech Republic, Poland, Slovakia and Bulgaria. Some countries, including Moldova and Belarus, have very few official camping grounds, though you can usually find somewhere to pitch your tent. Croatia's coast has nudist camping grounds galore (signposted FKK, the German acronym for 'naturist'); they're excellent places to stay because of their secluded locations, although they can be a bit far from other attractions.

Camping grounds may be open from April to October, May to September, or perhaps only June to August, depending on the category of the facility, the location and demand. A few private camping grounds are open year-round. Camping in the wild is usually illegal; ask local people about the situation before you pitch your tent on a beach or in an open field.

In Eastern Europe you are sometimes allowed to build a campfire; ask first, however.

See p966 for information on camping discount cards.

Farmhouses

'Village tourism', which means staying at a farmhouse, is highly developed in Estonia, Latvia, Lithuania and Slovenia, and popular in Hungary. It's like staying in a private room or pension, except that the participating farms are in picturesque rural areas and may have activities nearby such as horse riding, kayaking, skiing and cycling. See **Worldwide Opportunities on Organic Farms** (www.wwoof.org) for information about working on organic farms in exchange for room and board.

Guest Houses & Pensions

Small private pensions are now very common in parts of Eastern Europe. Priced somewhere between hotels and private rooms, pensions typically have fewer than a dozen rooms, and

may sometimes have a small restaurant or bar on the premises. You'll get much more personal service at a pension than you would at a hotel, though there's a wee bit less privacy. Pensions can be a lifesaver if you arrive at night or on a weekend, when the travel agencies assigning private rooms are closed. Call ahead to check prices and ask about reservations – someone will usually speak some halting English, German or Russian.

Homestays & Private Rooms

Homestays are often the best and most authentic way to see daily life in Eastern Europe. It's perfectly legal to stay with someone in a private home, although in countries such as Russia, where visa registration is necessary, you'll probably have to pay a travel agency to register your visa with a hotel.

In most Eastern European countries, travel agencies can arrange accommodation in private rooms in local homes. In Hungary you can get a private room almost anywhere, but in the other countries only the main tourist centres have them. Some rooms are like mini apartments, with cooking facilities and private bathrooms for the sole use of guests. Prices are low but there's often a 30% to 50% surcharge if you stay fewer than three nights. In Hungary, the Czech Republic and Croatia, higher taxation has made staying in a private room less attractive than before, but it's still good value and cheaper than a hotel.

People will frequently approach you at train or bus stations in Eastern Europe offering a private room or a hostel bed. This can be good or bad – it's impossible to generalise. Just make sure it's not in some cardboard-quality housing project in the outer suburbs and that you negotiate a clear price. Obviously, if you are staying with strangers, you shouldn't leave your valuables behind when you go out; certainly don't leave your money, credit cards or passport.

You don't have to go through an agency or an intermediary on the street for a private room. Any house, cottage or farmhouse with *zimmer frei* (German), *sobe* (Slovak) or *szoba kiadó* (Hungarian) displayed outside is advertising the availability of private rooms; just knock on the door and ask if any are available.

Staying with Eastern European friends will almost certainly be a wonderful experience, thanks to the full hospitality the region is justly famous for. Make sure you bring some small gifts for your hosts – it's a deeply ingrained cultural tradition throughout the region.

Hostels

Hostels offer the cheapest roof over your head in Eastern Europe, and you don't have to be a youngster to take advantage of them. Most hostels are part of the national Youth Hostel Association (YHA), which is affiliated with the **Hostelling International** (HI; www.hihostels.com) umbrella organisation.

Hostels affiliated with HI can be found in most Eastern European countries. A hostel card (see p966) is seldom required, though you sometimes get a small discount if you have one. To join HI you can ask at any hostel or contact your local or national hostelling office.

At a hostel, you get a bed for the night plus use of communal facilities; there's often a kitchen where you can prepare your own meals. You may be required to have a sleeping sheet – simply using your sleeping bag is often not allowed. If you don't have a sleeping sheet, you can sometimes hire one for a small fee.

Hostels vary widely in their character and quality. The hostels in Poland tend to be extremely basic but they're inexpensive and friendly. In the Czech Republic and Slovakia, many hostels are actually fairly luxurious junior hotels with double rooms, and are often fully occupied by groups. A number of privately run hostels in Prague and Budapest are serious party venues, while many Hungarian hostels outside Budapest are student dormitories that are open to travellers for six or seven weeks in summer only.

There are many hostel guides and websites with listings, including the hostel bible, HI's *Europe*. Many hostels accept reservations by phone, fax or email, but not always during peak periods (though they might hold a bed for you for a couple of hours if you call from the train or bus station). You can also book hostels through national hostel offices.

Hotels

At the bottom end of the scale, cheap hotels may be no more expensive than private rooms or guest houses, while at the other extreme you'll find beautifully designed boutique hotels and five-star hotels with price tags to match.

Single rooms can be hard to find in Eastern Europe, as you are generally charged by the room and not by the number of people in it. The cheapest rooms sometimes have a washbasin but no bathroom, which means you'll have to go down the corridor to use the toilet and shower. Breakfast may be included in the price of a room, or it may be extra – and mandatory.

University Accommodation

Some universities rent out space in student halls in July and August. This is quite popular in the Baltic countries, Croatia, the Czech Republic, Hungary, Macedonia, Poland, Slovakia and Slovenia. Accommodation will sometimes be in single rooms (but is more commonly in doubles or triples), and cooking facilities may be available. Enquire at the college or university, at student-information services or at local tourist offices.

ACTIVITIES
Birdwatching

The countries of Eastern Europe may not be the world's best destination for spotting our feathered friends, but birders will certainly get a look at some unusual species in Albania (p65), the Danube Delta (p735) in Romania, and several locations around Serbia (p828).

Canoeing & Kayaking

Those travelling with folding kayaks will want to launch them on waterways including Poland's Great Masurian Lakes (p659), the Soča River (p895) in Slovenia, the Vltava (p307) in the Czech Republic, Latvia's Gauja River (p461); the Elafiti and Kornati Islands (p256) in Croatia; and the Bay of Kotor (p562) in Montenegro.

Cycling

Along with hiking, cycling is one of the best ways to get close to the scenery and the people, and keep fit in the process. It's also a good way to get around many cities and towns, and to see remote corners of the country that you wouldn't ordinarily get to.

The hills and mountains of Eastern Europe can be heavy going, but this is offset by the abundance of things to see. Physical fitness is *not* a major prerequisite for cycling on the plains of eastern Hungary, but the persistent wind might slow you down. Popular holiday cycling areas in Eastern Europe include the Šumava region (p309) and the Moravian wine country (p309) in the Czech Republic; various routes in Hungary (p426), Montenegro (p577) and Poland (p663); and Curonian Spit (p496) in western Lithuania. In Romania, Sinaia (p739) is a great place to go mountain biking across the plateau atop the Bucegi Mountains.

See p979 for more information on bicycle touring, and the individual country chapters for rental outfits, routes and tips on places to go.

Diving

It's not the Caribbean, but the Adriatic offers its own rewards. Explore caves and shipwrecks along the coast in Croatia (p256), Montenegro (p562, p569) and Slovenia (p902).

Extreme Sports

If medieval Old Towns, castle-topped peaks and communist monuments don't get your blood pumping, never fear – you can still get your adrenalin rush in Eastern Europe. In Sigulda (p460), Latvia, you'll find bungee jumping, bobsledding and skydiving; while Bovec (p894), Slovenia, is famous for hydrospeeding, canyoning and paragliding.

Hiking

Almost every country in Eastern Europe offers excellent hiking, with well-marked trails through forests, mountains and national parks. Chalets or mountain huts in Poland, Bulgaria, Slovakia, Romania and Slovenia offer dormitory accommodation and basic meals; public transport will often take you to the trailheads. In this book we include information about hiking in the High Tatras of Poland (p629) and Slovakia (p853), the Malá Fatra of Slovakia (p850), the Făgăraş Mountains (p705) in Romania, the Rila Mountains (p156) of Bulgaria and the Julian Alps (p893) of Slovenia. There are also many other hiking areas that are less well known, including Theth (p55) in Albania; various destinations in the Czech Republic (p321); a number of national parks in Macedonia (p524); the Bieszczady Mountains (p631) in Poland; Risnjak National Park (p256) in Croatia; Tara National Park (p827) in Serbia; and Carpathian National Natural Park (p934) in Ukraine. The best months for hiking are from June to September, especially late August and early September, when the summer crowds will have largely disappeared.

Horse Riding

Though horse riding is possible throughout Eastern Europe, the sport is best organised – and cheapest – in Hungary, whose people, it is said locally, 'were created by God to sit on horseback'. The best horse-riding centres are on the Great Plain (Nagyalföld), though you'll also find riding schools in Transdanubia (Dunántúl) and northern Hungary; see p426 for more information. Horse riding is also very popular (and affordable) in the Baltic countries, the Czech Republic, Poland and Slovenia.

Rafting

Exciting white-water rafting is possible in spring and summer on some of Eastern Europe's most scenic rivers: the Vrbas River (p134) and the River Una (p135) in Bosnia and Hercegovina (BiH), the Tara River (p576) in Montenegro, the Drina (p827) in Serbia, and the Soča River (p895) in Slovenia. Rafting on the Dunajec River (p630, p858) along the border of Poland and Slovakia is fun, but it's not a white-water experience.

Sailing

Eastern Europe's most famous yachting area is the passage between the long, rugged islands off Croatia's Dalmatian coast. Yacht tours and rentals are available, although this is certainly not for anyone on a budget. If your means are more limited, the Great Masurian Lakes of northeastern Poland are a better choice, as small groups can rent sailing boats by the day for very reasonable rates; try the towns of Giżycko (p661) and Mikołajki (p662). Hungary's Lake Balaton is also popular among sailing enthusiasts; p404 for information on hiring boats.

Skiing

Eastern Europe's premier skiing areas are the High Tatras of Slovakia (p854) and Poland (p630); the Carpathian Mountains in Romania (p698) and Ukraine (p934); Borovets (p158) and Bankso (p158) in the Rila Mountains and Pamporovo (p165) in the Rodopi Mountains, all located in Bulgaria; and Slovenia's Julian Alps (p894, p894). The Bosnian capital Sarajevo (p119), which hosted the 1984 Winter Olympics, is a growing place for skiing and you'll find some of the best-value slopes in Europe within an hour of the city. There are less well-known ski areas in Belarus (p93), Macedonia (p513), Montenegro (p576) and Serbia (p826, p827).

The skiing season generally lasts from early December to late March, though at higher altitudes it may extend an extra month either way. Snow conditions can vary greatly from year to year and region to region, but January and February tend to be the best (and busiest) months. Snowboarding is especially popular in Slovakia, as is cross-country skiing in the Czech Republic and Ukraine.

Thermal Baths & Saunas

There are hundreds of thermal baths in Eastern Europe open to the public. The most affordable are in the Czech Republic, Hungary and Slovenia, and along the Black Sea in Romania. Among the best are the thermal lake at Hévíz (p409), the Turkish baths of Budapest (p378) and the spa town of Harkány (p413), all of which are in Hungary; and the fin de siècle spas of Karlovy Vary (Karlsbad; p298) in the Czech Republic.

The Baltic countries are famous for their proliferation of saunas – both the traditional 'smoke' variety, and the clean and smokeless modern sauna. The traditionalist will find many opportunities to take in an old-style sauna in Lithuania. Another must for lovers of heat and sweat is the traditional Russian *banya* (hot bath; p763), where you can be beaten into cleanliness with birch twigs!

BUSINESS HOURS

Eastern Europe tends to have similar working patterns to Western Europe and North America. Saturday and Sunday are official days off, although only banks and offices are shut; most shops, restaurants and cafes are open every day of the week.

Banks and offices are usually open from 9am to 5pm Monday to Friday, often with an hour or two off for lunch. They may also be open on Saturday mornings. Shops usually stay open until 7pm or later.

During the hot summer months, some enterprises will shut for two or three hours in the early afternoon, reopening at 3pm or 4pm and working into the evening. See the individual country directories for more specific details.

CHILDREN

Travelling with your children in Eastern Europe will be a treat and a challenge for the whole family. Entire amusement parks operate on the premise of allowing guests to visit representations of foreign countries –

how much more exciting and exotic to visit the real countries in person!

The number-one guideline for travelling with children is to avoid packing too much activity into the available time. (Actually, this should be the number-one guideline for travelling without children too.)

The second guideline is to allow your children to help plan the trip. Sure, they may not have an opinion about Macedonia versus Montenegro or Latvia versus Lithuania, but once you arrive, they will certainly have an opinion about how they would like to spend the day. Furthermore, if your kids have helped to plan the itinerary, they will know what to look forward to and will be more engaged upon arrival.

In Eastern Europe most car-rental firms have children's safety seats for hire at a small cost, but it is essential that you book them in advance. The same goes for high chairs and cots; they're standard in many restaurants and hotels but numbers are limited. The choice of baby food, infant formulas, soy and cows' milk, disposable nappies and the like is often as great in the Eastern European supermarkets as it is back home.

A good resource is Lonely Planet's *Travel with Children* by Cathy Lanigan and Maureen Wheeler.

CLIMATE CHARTS

Eastern Europe enjoys a continental climate, which means – simply – hot in summer and cold in winter. These hots and colds can go to extremes, but rarely so much so as to prevent travel. Eastern Europe is a fascinating place to visit any time of year – just as long as you pack the proper gear!

Winter is particularly daunting in Belarus, Russia, Ukraine and the Baltic countries: temperatures sink well below freezing and stay there for several months. But if you come prepared with warm boots and a furry hat, you will enjoy snow-covered landscapes and cities filled with a magical frosty charm.

At the other end of the spectrum, July and August can be uncomfortably hot in the cities and throughout the Balkans. This is the time to visit alpine areas such as the High Tatras, the Carpathian Mountains and the Rila Mountains. Alternatively, pack your swimsuit and boogie on down to the beaches.

If you prefer moderation, you will enjoy Eastern Europe in late spring (May, June)

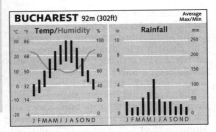

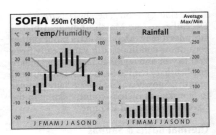

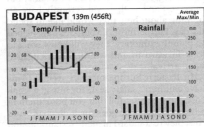

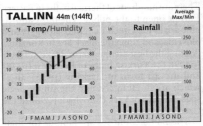

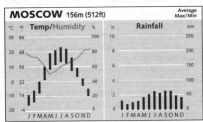

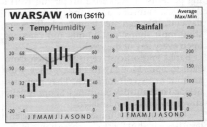

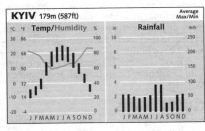

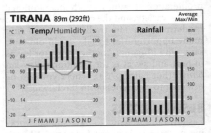

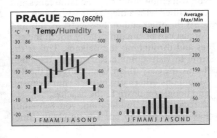

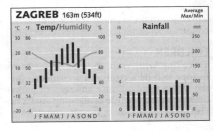

or early autumn (September) – throughout the region these months are not too hot and not too cool.

CUSTOMS REGULATIONS

You should have no problem with bringing in and taking out personal effects. That said, be aware that antiques, antiquarian books (printed before 1945), crystal glass, gemstones, lottery tickets, philatelic materials, precious metals (gold, silver, platinum), securities and valuable works of art may have to be declared in writing or even accompanied by a 'museum certificate' (available from the place of purchase) in many Eastern European countries.

Most countries allow the import and export of hard currency up to a value of €10,000 without a declaration. Some countries – such as Montenegro (€2000) and Russia (US$3000) – have stricter limits, so take precautions to complete a declaration form upon entry if necessary.

Throughout most of Eastern Europe, the usual allowances for tobacco (eg 200 to 250 cigarettes, but a lung-busting 1000 cigarettes in Belarus), alcohol (2L of wine, 1L of spirits) and perfume (50g) apply to duty-free goods purchased at airports or on ferries. Customs checks are pretty cursory and you probably won't even have to open your bags, but don't be lulled into a false sense of security.

DANGERS & ANNOYANCES

Eastern Europe is as safe – or unsafe – as any other part of the developed world. If you can handle yourself in the big cities of Western Europe, North America or Australia, you'll have little trouble dealing with the less pleasant side of Eastern Europe. Look purposeful, keep alert and you'll be OK.

Some locals will regale you with tales of how dangerous their city is and recount various cases of muggings, break-ins, kidnappings etc, often involving Roma or other popular scapegoats (most Eastern Europeans will tell you horror stories about the Romanians and Albanians). Most of these stories are overblown and exaggerated and you are unlikely to have any threatening encounters.

Corruption

Low-level corruption is disappearing fast, as the back-scratching system – so common during the communist regimes – claims its rightful place in the dustbin of history. Do not pay bribes to people in official positions, such as police, border guards, train conductors and ticket inspectors.

Be aware, however, that these anachronistic systems still exist in Belarus, Moldova, Russia and Transdniestr. If corrupt cops want to hold you up because some obscure stamp is missing from your documentation or on some other pretext, just let them and consider the experience an integral part of your trip. Insisting on calling your embassy is always a good move; officers are likely to receive some grief if their superiors learn they are harassing tourists.

If you're taken to the police station for questioning, you'll have the opportunity to observe the quality of justice in that country from the inside. In most cases, the more senior officers will eventually let you go (assuming, of course, you haven't committed a real crime). If you do have to pay a fine or supplementary charge, insist on a proper receipt before turning over any money; this is now law in Hungary, for example, where traffic police were once notorious for demanding 'gifts' from motorists guilty of some alleged infraction. In all of this, try to maintain your cool, as any threats from you will only make matters worse.

Drugs

Always treat drugs with a great deal of caution. There are a lot of drugs available in the region, but that doesn't mean they are legal. The continual fighting in the former Yugoslavia in the 1990s forced drug traffickers to seek alternative routes from Asia to Western Europe, sometimes crossing through Hungary, Slovakia, the Czech Republic and Poland. Now EU members, these countries do not look lightly upon drug abuse.

Landmines

BiH (p136) and Kosovo (p437) still have landmines. It's the only time Lonely Planet will ever advise you *not* to venture off the beaten track.

Scams

A word of warning about credit cards: fraudulent shopkeepers have been known to make several charge-slip imprints with your credit card when you're not looking and then simply copy your signature from the authorised slip. There have also been reports of these unscrupulous people making quick and very hi-tech duplicates of credit- or debit-card information with a machine. If your card leaves your possession for longer than you think necessary, consider cancelling it.

Now that most Eastern European currencies have reached convertibility, there is no longer a black market for currency exchange in this region. The days of getting five times the official rate for cash on the streets of Warsaw and Bucharest are well and truly over. Anyone who approaches you offering such a deal (an uncommon occurrence these days) is an outright thief, trying to get their hands on your money, either by scamming you or by simply taking it.

Theft

Theft is definitely a problem in Eastern Europe, and the threat comes from both local thieves and fellow travellers. The most important things to guard are your passport, other documents, tickets and money – in that order. It's always best to carry these items in a sturdy pouch on your belt or under your shirt. Train-station lockers or luggage-storage counters are useful to store your luggage (but not valuables) while you get your bearings in a new town. Be very suspicious of people who offer to help you operate your locker.

Always be wary of snatch thieves and lessen your risk by taking simple precautions. Cameras and shoulder bags are great for these people, who sometimes operate from motorcycles or scooters, slashing the strap before you have a chance to react. A small day pack is better, but watch your rear and don't keep valuables in the outside pockets. Loop the strap around your leg while seated at bars or cafes. Carrying a backpack on your front may prevent pickpockets, but it will also let everyone know you are a tourist (and one who thinks everyone is a thief).

Pickpockets are most active in dense crowds, especially in busy train stations and on public transport during peak hours. A common ploy in the Budapest and Prague metros has been for a group of well-dressed young people to surround you, chattering away while one of the group zips through your pockets or purse.

Be careful even in hotels: don't leave valuables lying around in your room. Carry your own padlock for hostel lockers and always use them.

Parked cars containing luggage or other bags are prime targets for petty criminals in most cities, and cars with foreign number plates and/or rental-agency stickers attract particular attention. While driving in cities, beware of snatch thieves when you pull up at the lights – keep doors locked and windows rolled up.

In the case of theft or loss, always report the incident to the police and ask for a statement; otherwise your travel-insurance company won't pay up.

Violence

It's unlikely that travellers will encounter any violence while in Eastern Europe. Be aware, however, that many countries in the region have thriving neo-Nazi movements, which tend to target resident Roma, blacks and Asians. Foreigners have been attacked in Hungary and the Czech Republic. Russian neo-Nazis have developed a charming tradition of seeking out fights with nonwhite people on Hitler's birthday (20 April); St Petersburg in particular has seen an extraordinary amount of violence against ethnic minorities, and not only on birthdays. We do not discourage anyone from travelling to these places, but we do urge anyone with dark skin to exercise a great deal of caution: travel with friends, avoid the suburbs and don't go out at night alone.

DISCOUNT CARDS
Camping Card International

The Camping Card International (CCI) is a camping-ground ID valid for a year. It can be used instead of a passport when checking in to camping grounds and includes third-party insurance. As a result, many camping grounds will offer discounts of up to 25% for cardholders. CCIs are issued by automobile associations, camping federations and, sometimes, on the spot at camping grounds. See **Camping Card International** (www.campingcardinternational.org) for links to local organisations and lists of participating camping grounds.

Hostel Cards

No hostels in Eastern Europe require that you be a hostelling association member, but they sometimes charge less if you have a card. Some hostels will issue one on the spot or after a few days' stay, though this might cost a bit more than getting it at home.

Senior Cards

Many attractions offer reduced-price admission for people over 60 or 65 (or sometimes 55 for women). EU residents, especially, are eligible for discounts in many EU countries. Make sure you bring proof of age.

For a fee of around €20, European residents aged 60 and over can get a Railplus Card as an add-on to their national rail senior pass. It entitles the holder to train-fare reductions of around 25%.

Before leaving home, check with an agency that caters to senior travel – such as Elder Hostel (p984) – for age-related travel packages and discounts.

Student, Youth & Teacher Cards

An International Student Identity Card (ISIC) is a plastic ID-style card that provides discounts on many forms of transport (including airlines and local transport), cheap or free admission to museums and sights, and inexpensive meals in some student cafeterias and restaurants.

If you're under 26 but not a student, you are eligible to apply for an International Youth Travel Card (IYTC, formerly GO25), issued by the Federation of International Youth Travel Organisations, or the Euro26 card; however, the latter card may not be recognised in Albania, Moldova, Romania, Serbia and Montenegro. Both cards go under different names in different countries and give much the same discounts and benefits as an ISIC.

An International Teacher Identity Card (ITIC) identifies the holder as an instructor and offers similar deals.

All these cards are issued by student unions, hostelling organisations or youth-oriented travel agencies; alternatively see the **International Student Travel Confederation** (www.isic.org).

ELECTRICITY

Eastern European countries run on 220V, 50Hz AC. Most appliances set up for 240V will quite happily handle 220V without modification (and vice versa), but it's preferable to adjust your appliance to the exact voltage if you can; some modern battery chargers and radios will do this automatically. Don't mix 110/125V with 220/240V without a transformer.

Several countries outside Europe (the USA and Canada, for instance) have 60Hz AC, which will affect the speed of electric motors even after the voltage has been adjusted. This means that CD and tape players (where motor speed is all-important) will be useless, but appliances such as electric razors, hairdryers, irons and radios will work fine.

Plugs in Eastern Europe are the standard round two-pin variety, sometimes called the europlug. If your plugs are of a different design, you'll need an adapter.

EMBASSIES & CONSULATES

See the individual country directories for the addresses of embassies and consulates in Eastern Europe.

It's important to realise what your embassy can and cannot do to help if you get into trouble while travelling abroad. Remember that you are bound by the laws of the country you are visiting. Generally speaking, your embassy cannot help much if your emergency is of your own making. It will not post bail or otherwise act to get you out of jail.

If your documents are lost or stolen, your embassy can assist you in obtaining a new passport; this is greatly simplified if you have a photocopy of your passport. Your embassy may refer you to a lawyer or a doctor, but it is highly unlikely to provide any financial assistance, no matter what your emergency. (That's what insurance is for.)

GAY & LESBIAN TRAVELLERS

Consensual homosexual sex is legal in all of the countries of Eastern Europe. The laws on the books do not signal an open-minded approach to sexual minorities, however. You are unlikely to raise any eyebrows by sharing a room (or a bed) with your same-sex partner. But in many countries, society frowns on overt displays of affection in any case – and even more so when it's between members of the same gender. As long as you are discreet on the street, you are unlikely to attract attention or trouble.

Many countries have online forums and gay advocacy groups. Latvia, Hungary, Poland and Russia have all had gay-pride events in recent years. Unfortunately, on most occasions, marchers were outnumbered by antigay protesters, which often ended in arrests on both sides. Many gays and lesbians in Eastern Europe actually oppose such parades as they provoke the majority into taking an antigay stance when they would otherwise pay no heed to the gay and lesbian population.

Despite this don't-ask-don't-tell situation, most Eastern European capitals have small, lively gay scenes, usually centred on one or two bars and clubs. Exceptions to this rule are Tirana, Skopje, Sarajevo and Chişinău, where there is nothing gay- or lesbian-specific that is accessible to visitors. Outside large towns, gay and lesbian life is almost nonexistent. See the individual country directories for more info.

HOLIDAYS

Throughout Eastern Europe, children get the summer months (usually July and August) off from school, which is one reason why this is the busiest time to go to the beach and other resorts. There are also usually breaks for Easter and Christmas; keep in mind that dates for Orthodox Christmas and Easter are different to those of their Catholic and Protestant counterparts. Even in countries with a large Muslim population, such as BiH and Albania, school holidays generally follow these guidelines. See the individual country directories for details of local public holidays and festivals.

INSURANCE

A travel-insurance policy to cover theft, loss and medical problems is always a good idea. The policies written by STA Travel and other student-travel organisations are usually good value. Some insurance policies will specifically exclude 'dangerous activities', which can include scuba diving, motorcycling and even trekking. Some policies even exclude certain countries, so read your fine print. Also check that your policy covers ambulances and an emergency flight home.

You may prefer a policy that pays doctors or hospitals directly rather than reimbursing your claims after the fact. Some policies ask you to call back (reverse charges) to a centre in your home country, where an immediate assessment of your problem is made. If you have to file a claim, make sure you keep all documentation. For more information on health insurance, see p988. For details on car insurance, see p982.

Worldwide cover to travellers from over 44 countries is available online at www.lonely planet.com/travel_services.

INTERNET ACCESS

With few exceptions, any decent-sized town in Eastern Europe has internet access in some shape or form. Connections may be slow, there might not be coffee and you might be sitting in a smelly room full of teenage boys playing war games – but one way or another you'll never be far from your email account, even in less developed nations such as Albania and Moldova. Indeed, in some cities, internet cafes can be a social hub and a great way of meeting locals as well as other travellers.

If you are travelling with a laptop, there is good news for you too. Wi-fi has taken off in Eastern Europe, with hot spots in cafes, bars, libraries, hotels, hostels and even public places. The Baltics are particularly good – Tallinn alone has more than 300 wi-fi spots, most of them free. It's increasingly common for any high-standard or boutique hotel to have wi-fi in the rooms. Sadly, most business hotels charge for this service, while boutique hotels are more likely to offer it for free.

MAPS

Bringing a good regional map will make things a great deal easier if you are planning a long trip taking in more than a couple of countries. There's a huge range available, but we recommend *Eastern Europe,* produced by Latvian publishers Jana Seta, and *Eastern Europe* from Freytag and Berndt.

In general, buying city maps in advance is unnecessary, as nearly all large towns produce them locally for a fraction of the price you'll pay at home. However, maps of Eastern European capitals and other major towns are widely available from travel bookshops if you want a particularly detailed map in advance.

MONEY

Things have simplified in Eastern Europe, and there are no real worries about 'soft' and 'hard' currencies. The main problem you'll face is constant currency changes as you flit between the crown, złoty, rouble, lei, lev, lek, dinar and various other national currencies. There is no longer any particular desire for 'hard' currency (the days when hoteliers would slash the rates if you paid in US dollars are long gone), and the convertibility of almost all Eastern European currencies makes them a stable and reliable way to carry cash. The euro remains the easiest currency to change throughout the region, particularly in light of the US dollar's weakness over the past few years.

With the accession of half of the region to the EU, there's a move for some countries to adopt the euro themselves. At the time of research, Slovakia and Slovenia were the only Eastern European countries that are part of the eurozone. Kosovo and Montenegro have also adopted the euro, as they have no currency of their own. Bulgaria, BiH, Estonia, Latvia and Lithuania all have currencies pegged to the euro; indeed the three Baltic countries are expected to officially adopt the euro in 2010 (or, in the case of Latvia, 2013). Other countries with longer-term intentions to adopt the euro include Bulgaria, the Czech Republic, Hungary, Poland and Romania.

ATMs

Rip-off exchange offices and the hassle of trying to change travellers cheques at the weekend have mostly become things of the past with the arrival of ATMs that accept most credit and cash cards. Nearly all Eastern European countries have plenty of ATMs in their capitals, and sometimes in smaller towns too. Check the specific situation in your destination before setting out from the big city.

Cash or debit cards can be used throughout Eastern Europe at ATMs linked to international networks such as Cirrus and Maestro. The major advantage of using ATMs is that you don't pay commission charges to exchange money, although you might pay a bank fee. The exchange rate is usually at a better rate than that offered for travellers cheques or cash exchanges.

If you choose to rely on plastic, go for two different cards – this allows one to be used as backup in the case of loss, or more commonly, if a bank does not accept one card. Better still is a combination of cards and travellers cheques so you have something to fall back on if there are no ATMs in the area, or they accept local cards only.

Cash

Of course, cash is the easiest way to carry money, but if you lose it you're out of luck. The two most favoured currencies throughout Eastern Europe are the euro and the US dollar. Although it's not difficult to exchange other major world currencies in big cities, you are at the mercy of the exchange office and its rates. A far better option is to change your money into euros or US dollars before you leave home.

Credit Cards

As purchase tools, credit cards are still not as commonly used as they are in Western Europe, but cards such as Amex, Visa and MasterCard are gaining ground. You'll be able to use them at upmarket restaurants, shops, hotels, car-rental firms, travel agencies and many petrol stations.

Bear in mind that if you use a credit card for purchases, exchange rates may have changed by the time your bill is processed, which can work out to your advantage or disadvantage.

Charge-card companies such as Amex, and to a lesser extent Diners Club, have offices in most countries in Eastern Europe and, because they treat you as a customer of the company rather than of the bank that issued the card, they can generally replace a lost card within 24 hours. The cards' major drawback is that they're not widely accepted off the beaten track. Credit cards such as Visa and MasterCard are more widely accepted because they tend to charge merchants lower commissions.

There are also a couple of tricky scams involving credit cards; see p965.

Moneychangers

Never exchange your hard-earned cash without first shopping around for a decent rate. If you happen to be in a tourist area, you can take comfort knowing you'll be offered crappy rates everywhere; examples include around the Charles Bridge in Prague or Rynek Główny (Main Market Sq) in Kraków. In this case, don't bother shopping around – just leave for a less touristed neighbourhood. Border crossings, airports and train stations are typically places where rates aren't great, but many people change money out of necessity.

Tipping

Tipping practices vary from country to country, and often from place to place. In general, you can't go wrong if you add 10% onto your bill at a restaurant. Porters at upmarket hotels will appreciate a few euros for their efforts. In fashionable venues in urban centres, the wait staff will expect this; in rural locations you might astonish your server. See the individual country chapters for specific advice.

Travellers Cheques

The benefit of using travellers cheques rather than cash is the protection they offer from theft. But this old-school travel tool has lost its once enormous popularity, as more and more travellers prefer to withdraw cash from ATMs as they go along.

Keep in mind that banks usually charge from 1% to 2% commission to change travellers cheques (up to 5% in Bulgaria, Estonia, Latvia, Lithuania and Romania), and opening hours are sometimes limited.

The privately owned exchange offices in Albania, Bulgaria, Poland, Romania and Slovenia change cash at excellent rates without commission. Not only are their rates sometimes higher than those offered by the banks for travellers cheques, but they stay open much longer, occasionally even 24 hours. However, do take care in Belarus, the Czech Republic, Estonia, Hungary, Latvia, Lithuania, Moldova, Slovakia and Ukraine, as some big moneychangers take exorbitant commissions unless you cash a small fortune with them. Always check the commission and rate before signing a travellers cheque or handing over any cash.

Amex and Thomas Cook representatives cash their own travellers cheques without commission, but both give poor rates of exchange. If you're changing more than US$20, you're usually better off going to a bank and paying the standard 1% to 2% commission to change there.

Western Union

If everything goes horribly wrong – your money, travellers cheques and credit cards are all stolen – don't despair. While it's a terrible (and highly unusual) situation, a friend or relative back home will be able to wire money to you anywhere in Eastern Europe via Western Union (WU). We don't bother listing WU representatives in this guide as there are literally thousands of them; just look for the distinctive yellow and black sign. The sender is given a code that they communicate to you, then you take the code to the nearest office, along with your passport, to receive your cash.

PHOTOGRAPHY & VIDEO

Eastern Europe was once notorious for its photographic restrictions – taking shots of anything 'strategic', such as bridges or train stations, was strictly forbidden. These days local officials are much less paranoid, but you need to use common sense when it comes to taking photos; photographing military installations, for example, is never a good idea anywhere in the world. Most importantly, have the courtesy to ask permission before taking close-up photos of people. Be aware that museums often demand that you buy permission to photograph or video their displays.

If you are using a digital camera, be sure you have enough memory to store your snaps. If you do run out of memory space you can burn your photos onto a CD; even if you don't have your laptop with you, an increasing number of processing labs now offer this service. To download your pics at an internet cafe you'll need a USB cable and a card reader, but be warned that some internet cafes may not let you plug your gear into their computers.

Film and camera equipment is available everywhere in Eastern Europe, though you'll have a better selection in larger towns. Avoid buying film at tourist sites in Europe, such as the Castle District in Budapest or by Charles Bridge in Prague, as it will certainly be more expensive than in normal photography shops.

It is easy to obtain videotapes and memory cards in most towns and cities, though you may wish to bring them from home to ensure that there are no compatibility issues with your camcorder. It is usually worth buying at least a few at home at the start of your trip.

POST

Both the efficiency and cost of the national postal systems in Eastern Europe vary enormously. There seems to be no set rules, but EU countries are likely to be faster, more reliable and more expensive than the non-EU states.

Postal service from Belarus, Moldova, Montenegro, Russia and Ukraine is slow, but the mail usually reaches its destination eventually. For added assurance and speed, most of these countries offer an express service. The only country where it is not advised to use the state-run postal service to send parcels is Albania.

To send a parcel from Eastern Europe you usually have to take it unwrapped to a main post office; parcels weighing over 2kg often must be taken to a special customs post office. The post-office staff will usually wrap the parcels for you. The staff may ask to see your passport and note the number on the form; if you don't have a return address within the country put the address of any large tourist hotel.

Poste restante is an unreliable, not to mention increasingly unnecessary, communication method. If you desperately need something posted to you, do your research – find a friend of a friend who could receive the mail at their address, or ask nicely at a hotel you plan to stay at. You can also have mail sent to you at Amex offices if you have an Amex card or are carrying its travellers cheques.

Details of post offices are given for cities and towns in the individual country chapters, and postage costs given in the country directories.

SOLO TRAVELLERS

Travelling alone is an exciting and fulfilling experience: you do exactly what you want to do and see what you want to see. Most rewardingly, solo travellers are more likely to meet locals and socialise with new people. On the flip side, travelling alone can be lonely. And when things don't work out, it's more frustrating if there is no one to share your pain.

The best place for solo travellers to find some company is at hostels, which are set up to allow the guests to mix and mingle. Indeed, you may pick up a travelling companion who is heading in your direction. Other places to meet fellow travellers are internet cafes and expat bars (usually the ubiquitous Irish pubs).

TELEPHONE

Telephone service has throughout the region improved in a very short time. Cities in Eastern Europe have a huge number of call centres; they're increasingly the domain of entrepreneurs who offer discounted rates, although there are also state-run call centres, which are often in the same building as the main post office. Here you can often make your call from one of the booths inside an enclosed area, paying the cashier as you leave. Public telephones are almost always found at post offices.

Mobile Phones

Today you'll see farmers travelling by horse and cart in rural Romania chatting on their mobile, while old grannies selling sunflower seeds on a quiet Moscow side street write text messages to their grandchildren. The expansion of mobile-phone use in Eastern Europe has been phenomenal, and this can be great for travellers too. If you plan to spend more than a week or so in any one country, consider buying a SIM card to slip

> ### EMERGENCY NUMBERS
>
> The phone number ☎ 112 can be dialled for emergencies in all EU states; at the time of writing, the EU states in Eastern Europe were Bulgaria, the Czech Republic, Estonia, Hungary, Latvia, Lithuania, Poland, Romania, Slovakia and Slovenia. See the individual country directories for country-specific emergency numbers.

into your phone, although you'll need to check with your provider at home that your handset has been unlocked. SIM cards can cost as little as €10 and can be topped up with cards available at supermarkets and mobile-phone dealers. Alternatively, if you have roaming, your phone will usually switch automatically over to a local network. This can be expensive if you use the phone a great deal, but can be very useful for ad hoc and emergency use.

Phone Codes

Every country's international dialling code and international access code is given in the Fast Facts section at the beginning of each chapter. If area codes are used within a country, they are listed directly under each town's name.

To call abroad from a landline you simply dial the international access code for the country you are calling from (most commonly ☎ 00 in Eastern Europe, but ☎ 8-10 in Belarus, Moldova, Russia and Ukraine). From a mobile phone simply dial the country acccess code, the city code and the local number.

To make a domestic call to another city in the same country, you generally need to dial the area code (with the initial zero) and the number; however, in some countries the area code is an integral part of the phone number, and must be dialled every time – even if you're just calling next door.

Phonecards

Local telephone cards – available from post offices, telephone centres, news-stands or retail outlets – are used everywhere in the region. In any given country, there's a wide range of local and international phonecards available. For local calls you're usually better off with a local phonecard.

TIME

Eastern Europe spans three time zones: Central European Time (GMT+1), Eastern European Time (GMT+2) and Moscow Time (GMT+3). At noon in New York, it's 6pm in Warsaw, 7pm in Minsk and 8pm in Moscow.

Central European Time (GMT+1 hour) Albania, BiH, Croatia, Czech Republic, Hungary, Kosovo, Macedonia, Montenegro, Poland, Serbia, Slovakia and Slovenia.

Eastern European Time (GMT+2 hours) Belarus, Bulgaria, Estonia, Kaliningrad, Latvia, Lithuania, Moldova, Romania and Ukraine.

Moscow Time (GMT+3 hours) Moscow and St Petersburg.

All countries employ daylight savings. Clocks are put forward an hour at the start of daylight savings, usually on the last Sunday in March. They are set back one hour on the last Sunday in October.

TOURIST INFORMATION

The provision of tourist information varies enormously. While countries that have successfully realised their potential as holiday destinations have developed a network of excellent tourist information centres (TICs), there are still many countries that take little or no interest in the economic benefits tourism can bring. Countries in the latter category are Ukraine, Belarus and Moldova. Russia is similarly badly organised, although there are unhelpful TICs in both Moscow and St Petersburg. Among the best prepared are Slovakia, Slovenia, Croatia, the Czech Republic, Hungary, Poland and Bulgaria, many of which have tourist offices abroad as well as throughout the country. The Baltic countries, Montenegro, Romania, Albania and Macedonia fall in a middle category of places actively trying to encourage tourism, but whose efforts remain rather obscure at the moment. See individual country chapters for details of local TICs.

TRAVELLERS WITH DISABILITIES

Cobblestone streets and medieval Old Towns are charming indeed – but they can also be awkward for travellers with disabilities. In general, wheelchair-accessible rooms are available only at top-end hotels (and are limited, so be sure to book in advance). Rental cars and taxis may be accessible, but public transport rarely is. Most major museums and sites have disabled access, although there are many exceptions. It's fair to say that access for those with disabilities has not been a priority in the past two decades of rapid reform.

If you have a physical disability, get in touch with your national support organisation (preferably the travel officer if there is one) and ask about the countries you plan to visit. The organisations often have libraries devoted to travel, including access guides, and staff can put you in touch with travel agencies who specialise in tours for the disabled. The **Royal Association for Disability & Rehabilitation** (Radar; ☎ in the UK 020-7250 3222; www.radar.org.uk) is a very helpful association and sells a number of publications for people with disabilities.

VISAS & DOCUMENTS
Copies

The hassles created by losing your passport can be considerably reduced if you have a record of its number and issue date or, even better, photocopies of the relevant data pages. A photocopy of your birth certificate can also be useful.

Also note the serial numbers of your travellers cheques (cross them off as you cash them) and take photocopies of your credit cards, air ticket and any other travel documents. Keep all this emergency material separate from your passport, cheques and cash, and leave extra copies with a reliable party at home. Add some emergency money (€50 to €100 in cash) to this separate stash as well. If you do lose your passport, notify the police immediately to get a statement, and contact your nearest consulate.

Passport

Your most important travel document is your passport, which should remain valid until well after you return home. Most countries require three or six months of validity before they will grant a visa. More importantly, you may have some difficulty re-entering your home country if your visa has expired while you were away.

Once you start travelling, carry your passport (or a copy of it) at all times and guard it carefully. Camping grounds and hotels sometimes insist that you hand over your passport for the duration of your stay, which is inconvenient. If you offer to pay upfront, there is no reason for the establishment to keep your visa for longer than one night for registration purposes.

LIFE TAKES VISA (IN SOME PLACES)

Visa regulations vary throughout Eastern Europe: for most countries you won't need a visa at all, while for others obtaining a visa is a trial of skill, patience and planning. This table outlines visa requirements in the relevant countries at the time of writing; see individual country chapters for more detail. Be aware, however, that visa regulations can and do change, so you should always check with the individual embassies or a reputable travel agency before travelling.

	Visa on arrival	EU citizens	US citizens	Canadian citizens	Australian citizens	NZ citizens
Albania	No*	No	No	No	No	No
Belarus	Yes**	Yes	Yes	Yes	Yes	Yes
Moldova	Varies**	No	No	No	Yes	Yes
Russia	No	Yes	Yes	Yes	Yes	Yes
Ukraine	No	No	No	No	Yes	Yes

*Compulsory €10 entry fee payable on arrival.
**Visa invitation still required in advance.

Registration

Some countries require visitors to register with the local authorities within 48 hours of arrival, supposedly so they know where you are staying. If you're staying at a hotel or other official accommodation, the administration will take care of this registration for you.

If you're staying with friends, relatives or in a private room, you're supposed to register with the police yourself. In some cases, this is a formality that is never enforced, so you can skip it. In other cases (such as Russia), you can be fined if you do not go through the motions. Obtaining registration through the proper channels is a major hassle, often requiring fluent language skills, a pile of documents and several hours of negotiation. You are better off paying a local travel agency for the registration instead of trying to do it yourself. This loophole defeats the whole purpose of registration, as the agency will likely register you at some hotel or address where you will never set foot. But it technically fulfils your legal requirements and protects you from sticky-fingered policemen.

Consult individual country directories for more information.

Visas

A decade ago a trip through Eastern Europe would result in visas filling several passport pages; today you'll be lucky to get an entry stamp in many cases.

If you have your heart set on stamps in your passport, head to Belarus or Russia, where all travellers require a visa (see p95 or p797, respectively); Australians and New Zealanders will also need visas to enter Moldova (p551)

and Ukraine (p956). All other countries covered in the book are accessible without visas to Australian, New Zealand, EU and US passport holders, as long as they are staying for 90 days or less. See the individual country directories for specific requirements.

With a valid passport and visa (if required) you'll be able to visit most Eastern European countries for up to three (and sometimes even six) months, provided you have some sort of onward or return ticket and/or 'sufficient means of support'.

In line with the Schengen Agreement, there are no longer strict passport controls at the borders between most EU countries, but procedures between EU and non-EU countries can still be fairly thorough. See p978 for further details about the Schengen zone.

If you do get a visa, it's important to remember that it has an expiration date, and you'll be refused entry after that period has elapsed. Consulates sometimes issue visas on the spot, although some levy a 50% to 100% surcharge for 'express service'. If there's a choice between getting a visa in advance and on the border, go for the former option if you have the time. They're often cheaper in your home country and this can save on bureaucratic procedure. Decide in advance if you want a tourist or transit visa; transit visas, usually valid for just 48 or 72 hours, are often cheaper and issued faster, but it's usually not possible to extend a transit visa or change it to a tourist visa.

WOMEN TRAVELLERS

Women travellers will find that Eastern Europe is a safe and welcoming place to travel, whether you're in a group, with a mate, or on your own. It is always wise to take some basic precautions: avoid walking on the streets alone after dark; avoid taking a taxi alone after dark; and avoid accepting drinks from strangers or consuming too much alcohol if you are out by yourself. Taking these precautions, most women will enjoy safe, hassle-free travel throughout the region.

That is not to say that sexual harassment does not exist, however. It is not unusual for women to be propositioned by strangers on the street. As a rule, foreigners are still a little exotic and therefore attract more attention, but this attention is rarely dangerous, and is easily deflected with a shake of the head and a firm 'no'. (Use the local language if you can, but English usually works fine too.)

In Muslim countries, women travelling solo will certainly be of interest or curiosity to both local men and women. In Albania and BiH, women may feel self-conscious in bars and cafes, which are usually populated only by men. Unmarried men rarely have contact with women outside their family unit, and so may shower travelling women with too much attention. (In such areas, women travelling with a male companion will often experience the opposite, and may need to pinch themselves as a reminder that yes, they actually exist.)

Many Eastern European women like to get dolled up, often donning high heels, short skirts and plenty of make-up. In fact, some clubs require these fancy duds to get past the bouncer, so you may wish to trade your sneakers for stilettos for that night out on the town.

WORK

The massive expansion of the EU in recent years has meant that EU citizens have free rein to work in many countries in the region. However, with unemployment still a problem, Eastern European countries aren't always keen on handing out jobs to foreigners. If you're not an EU citizen, the paperwork involved in arranging a work permit can be almost impossible, especially for temporary work.

That doesn't prevent enterprising travellers from topping up their funds occasionally – and they don't always have to do this illegally. If you do find a temporary job in Eastern Europe, though, the pay is likely to be abysmally low. Do it for the experience, not to earn your fortune. Teaching English is the easiest way to make some extra cash, but the market is saturated in places such as Prague and Budapest. You'll probably be much more successful in less popular places such as Sofia and Bucharest.

If you play an instrument or have other artistic talents, you could try working the streets. As every Peruvian pipe player (and his fifth cousin) knows, busking is fairly common in major Eastern European cities such as Prague, Budapest and Ljubljana. Some countries may require municipal permits for this sort of thing, so talk to other street artists before you start.

There are several references and websites that publicise specific positions across Eastern Europe. **Transitions Abroad** (www.transitionsabroad .com) publishes *Work Abroad: the Complete Guide to Finding a Job Overseas* and the *Alternative Travel Directory: the Complete Guide to Work, Study and Travel Overseas,* as well as a colour magazine, *Transitions Abroad.* Its website lists paid positions and volunteer and service programs. **Action Without Borders** (www.idealist.org) and **Go Abroad** (www.go abroad.com) list hundreds of jobs and volunteer opportunities.

Work Your Way Around the World by Susan Griffith gives good, practical advice on a wide range of issues. The publisher Vacation Work has some useful titles, including *The Directory of Summer Jobs Abroad,* edited by David Woodworth. *Working Holidays* by Ben Jupp (Central Bureau for Educational Visits & Exchanges in the UK) is another good source, as is *Now Hiring! Jobs in Eastern Europe* by Clarke Canfield (Perpetual Press).

Organising a volunteer-work placement is another great way to gain a deeper insight into local culture. In some instances volunteers are paid a living allowance, sometimes they work for their keep, and sometimes they are required to pay to undertake the program.

Several websites can help you search for volunteer work opportunities in Eastern Europe. The **Coordinating Committee for International Voluntary Service** (www.unesco.org/ccivs) is an umbrella organisation, with over 140 member organisations worldwide. It's useful if you want to find out about your country's national volunteer placement agency. Check the Transitions Abroad website and **Serve Your World** (www.serveyourworld.com) to search for vacancies and other volunteering opportunities in Eastern Europe.

Transport in Eastern Europe

CONTENTS

GETTING THERE & AWAY

The revolution in cheap air travel, so long confined to Western Europe, has spread to the eastern end of the continent, opening up the region as never before. Travellers from Western Europe can pop over for €100 or less; even if you are coming from further afield, you can connect to almost any part of Eastern Europe from a major Western European hub. There are more than 2000 low-cost air routes criss-crossing Europe at the moment, run by 50 budget airlines serving almost 300 airports. There has never been a better time to take advantage of these bargains and explore Europe's fastest-changing region.

Keep in mind, of course, that air travel unfortunately releases an enormous amount of carbon dioxide into the atmosphere, making it the most environmentally detrimental form of transport. Some travellers choose to ease their conscience by travelling to Eastern Europe by train – a far more atmospheric and environmentally sound way to enter the region. A particularly thrilling option is to approach Eastern Europe from Asia on the legendary Trans-Siberian, Trans-Mongolian or Trans-Manchurian Railways. Taking the train from Western Europe may not be quite such an experience, but it is cheaper and quicker, and railway riders will feel the geographic, economic and political transition that takes place when crossing the boundary from East to West. The Iron Curtain may have been torn down, but its shadow still hangs across the continent.

There are many ferry services operating in the Baltic Sea, linking Scandinavia and Germany with countries such as Poland, Lithuania, Latvia and Estonia. Other routes cross the Adriatic from Italy to Slovenia, Croatia, Macedonia and Albania. This is a romantic, old-world way to travel.

Of course, bus, bicycle and car are also possible ways to enter the region.

Flights, tours and rail tickets can be booked online at www.lonelyplanet.com /travel_services.

ENTRY REQUIREMENTS

All countries obviously require non-EU travellers to have a valid passport, preferably with at least six months between the time of departure and the passport's expiration date. EU travellers from countries that issue national identity cards are increasingly using these to travel within the EU, although it's impossible to use these as the sole travel documents outside of the EU.

Visas are another thing to consider. Some countries still require some nationalities to buy a document that allows entry between certain dates. Specifically, Belarus and Russia require all nationalities to obtain visas, while Aussie and Kiwi travellers also need visas to enter Moldova and Ukraine. Other nationalities may have additional requirements; see p973 or the individual country directories for details.

THINGS CHANGE...

The information in this chapter is particularly vulnerable to change. Check directly with the airline or a travel agent to make sure you understand how a fare (and ticket you may buy) works and be aware of the security requirements for international travel. Shop carefully. The details given in this chapter should be regarded as pointers and are not a substitute for your own careful, up-to-date research.

CLIMATE CHANGE & TRAVEL

Climate change is a serious threat to the ecosystems that humans rely upon, and air travel is the fastest-growing contributor to the problem. Lonely Planet regards travel, overall, as a global benefit, but believes we all have a responsibility to limit our personal impact on global warming.

Flying & Climate Change

Pretty much every form of motor travel generates CO_2 (the main cause of human-induced climate change) but planes are far and away the worst offenders, not just because of the sheer distances they allow us to travel, but because they release greenhouse gases high into the atmosphere. The statistics are frightening: two people taking a return flight between Europe and the US will contribute as much to climate change as an average household's gas and electricity consumption over a whole year.

Carbon Offset Schemes

Climatecare.org and other websites use 'carbon calculators' that allow jetsetters to offset the greenhouse gases they are responsible for with contributions to energy-saving projects and other climate-friendly initiatives in the developing world – including projects in India, Honduras, Kazakhstan and Uganda.

Lonely Planet, together with Rough Guides and other concerned partners in the travel industry, supports the carbon offset scheme run by climatecare.org. Lonely Planet offsets all of its staff and author travel.

For more information check out our website: lonelyplanet.com.

AIR

Moscow, Prague, Budapest and Warsaw are the region's best-connected air hubs: they all have transatlantic flights, as well as plenty of flights from Western Europe; all except Moscow have plenty of budget airlines serving them. Other smaller hubs are Rīga, Timişoara, Zagreb, Kyiv and Bratislava, all of which have regular flights to many European cities. Most of the small hubs also have budget-airline connections, although as a rule the further east you go the fewer there are.

Airlines

Only Moldova and Montenegro are not served by direct flights from Western Europe and further abroad.

NATIONAL AIRLINES

Almost every country in Eastern Europe has its own national carrier. Most of these airlines provide direct flights to major cities across Western Europe.

Adria Airways (JP; www.adria-airways.com) Slovenia's national airline serves some 28 European destinations from Ljubljana; also offers seasonal charters.

Aeroflot (SU; www.aeroflot.ru) Russia's national airline; flights from Moscow go all over the world, including Europe, Asia and North America.

Aerosvit Ukrainian Airline (VV; www.aerosvit.com) Has flights to European destinations, plus direct flights to Bangkok, Beijing, Dubai, Delhi, New York, Shanghai and Toronto.

Air Baltic (BT; www.airbaltic.com) Latvia's national airline; flies from Rīga to some 50 destinations around Europe.

Belavia (B2; www.belavia.by) Belarus' national airline; has flights from Minsk to Berlin, Frankfurt, Hanover, London, Manchester, Milan, Rome and Vienna.

BH Airlines (JA; www.bhairlines.ba) The national airline for Bosnia and Hercegovina (BiH); flies directly from Sarajevo to Frankfurt, Cologne, İstanbul, Skopje, Stuttgart and Zürich.

Bulgaria Air (FB; www.air.bg) Operates flights from Sofia to Amsterdam, Athens, Barcelona, Beirut, Berlin, Brussels, Frankfurt, İstanbul, Larnaca, Paris, London, Madrid, Manchester, Tel Aviv, Tripoli, Vienna and Zürich.

Croatia Airlines (OU; www.coratiaairlines.hr) Operates flights from five Croatian airports to most of the European capitals, as well as to Bologna, Catania, Dusseldorf, Frankfurt, Hanover, İstanbul, Lyon, Munich, Palermo, Turin and Zürich. Additional flights in summer.

Czech Airlines (ČSA, OK; www.csa.cz) Flies from Prague to most European cities.

Estonian Air (OV; www.estonian-air.ee) Links Tallinn with some 20 cities in Europe and Russia, including Barcelona, Brussels, Copenhagen, Dublin, Frankfurt, Hamburg, Helsinki, London, Milan, Munich, Oslo, Paris, Rome, Stockholm and Vienna.

JAT (JU; www.jat.com) Serbia's national airline services many European cities, as well as Dubai and İstanbul.

Kosova Airlines (KOS; www.kosovaairlines.com) Flies from Pristina to Dusseldorf, Frankfurt, Geneva, Munich, Stuttgart and Zürich.

Macedonian Airlines (IN; www.mat.com.mk) Flies from Skopje to Berlin, Dusseldorf, Hamburg, İstanbul, Rome, Vienna and Zürich; also flies between Ohrid and Vienna.

Malév (MA; www.malev.hu) Hungary's national airline; offers flights from Budapest to all the major European capitals, as well as to New York and Toronto.

Moldavian Airlines (2M; www.mdv.md) Has flights from Chişinău to Budapest and Timişoara.

Polish LOT Airlines (LO; www.lot.com) Flies from Warsaw to all major European cities, plus Chicago, New York, Tel Aviv and Toronto.

Tarom (RO; www.tarom.ro) Romania's national airline; flies from Bucharest to destinations all over Europe, plus Cairo, Dubai, Damascus and Tel Aviv.

Ukraine International Airlines (PS; www.flyuia.com) Operates flights to many European cities, as well as Dubai and Tbilisi.

BUDGET AIRLINES

The invaluable travellers website **Fly Cheapo** (www.flycheapo.com) is a great resource to see which budget airlines fly where.

Look out for some of the following airlines, which provide the biggest selection of flights to/from Eastern Europe:

Air Berlin (AB; www.airberlin.com) Flights mainly originate in Germany, and travel to Bulgaria, Croatia, Hungary and Russia.

Baboo (F7; www.flybaboo.com) Based in Geneva, this airline services Bulgaria, Croatia and Romania.

Blue Air (0B; www.blueair-web.com) Romania's first budget airline.

bmibaby (WW; www.bmibaby.com) The budget arm of BMI; flies to Prague, Kraków and Warsaw.

Carpatair (V3; www.carpatair.com) Another Romania cheapie, this one flies out of Timişoara.

Click4Sky (OK; www.click4sky.com) A division of Czech Airlines; flies to a slew of Eastern European cities.

clickair (XG; www.clickair.com) A Spanish carrier that services Bucharest, Budapest, Dubrovnik, Moscow, Prague and Warsaw.

easyJet (U2; www.easyjet.com) One of Europe's biggest low-cost carriers, with hubs across the continent and flights to many Eastern European cities.

germanwings (4U; www.germanwings.com) Offers flights from four German cities to destinations across Eastern Europe.

Jet2.com (LS; www.jet2.com) A UK airline servicing Croatia, the Czech Republic, Hungary and Poland.

Meridiana (IG; www.meridiana.it) An Italian carrier flying to the Czech Republic, Hungary, Moldova, Russia and Serbia.

Norwegian Air Shuttle (DY; www.norwegian.no) An Oslo-based airline that flies to 20 different Eastern European destinations.

Ryanair (FR; www.ryanair.com) One of the largest low-cost carriers, Ryanair flies to at least eight countries in Eastern Europe.

SkyEurope (NE; www.skyeurope.com) Services Bulgaria, Croatia, the Czech Republic, Hungary, Romania and Slovenia.

Smart Wings (QS; www.smartwings.net) Based in the Czech Republic; flies to destinations in Western Europe, plus Hungary and Russia.

Wind Jet (IV; www.volawindjet.it) Italian airline going to the Czech Republic, Latvia, Poland, Romania and Russia.

Wizz Air (W6; www.wizzair.com) Whizzes you to Bulgaria, Croatia, Hungary, Poland, Romania and Ukraine.

Asia & Australia

Most travellers from Asia or Australia will need to head to Western Europe first, as there are relatively few direct flights from the region to cities in Eastern Europe. The exception is Moscow, which is a destination for flights from all of the major Asian cities. Unfortunately, Sheremetyevo Airport does not make for the most pleasant stopover – not to mention the fact that you'll need a transit visa if your layover is more than 24 hours or you want to leave the international airport. So a direct flight to Moscow is not really recommended unless you intend to spend some time in Russia.

Aerosvit has direct flights to Kyiv from Bangkok, Beijing and Shanghai. Another option is **Korean Airlines** (KE; www.koreanair.com), which operates a direct flight from Seoul to Prague.

Middle East

Dubai has direct flights to Belgrade, Bucharest, Kyiv and Moscow.

Tel Aviv has many direct flights to Eastern European cities, including Bucharest, Budapest, Kraków, Kyiv, Minsk, Odesa, Prague, Sofia and Warsaw. The flights are

---

THE SCHENGEN AGREEMENT

The EU treaty known as the Schengen Agreement removes border controls between states that are signatory to the treaty. As a result, there are no longer strict passport controls between Schengen states, although border-crossing formalities may be stricter when entering the Schengen zone. If you're travelling by land or sea to Eastern Europe, Austria, Denmark, Germany, Greece, Finland, Italy and Sweden all belong to the Schengen zone; within Eastern Europe, the Czech Republic, Estonia, Hungary, Latvia, Lithuania, Poland, Slovakia and Slovenia have signed the agreement. Bulgaria and Romania are expected to implement the Schengen Agreement in 2011.

---

operated by the national carriers and by **El Al** (LY; www.elal.co.il).

North America

Most travellers from Canada and the USA will probably find that they have to make a connection in Western Europe before they arrive at their Eastern European destination.

There are many flights to Moscow from New York, Chicago, Washington, DC, and Toronto, making this a reasonable option if you intend to spend time in Russia.

Delta (DL; www.delta.com) is the only North American airline that provides direct service to Eastern Europe (Russia aside), flying from Atlanta to Prague. Malév services New York and Toronto from Budapest, while Aerosvit does the same from Kyiv. Polish LOT Airlines has direct flights to Warsaw from both Chicago and New York.

Western Europe

There are countless flights from Western Europe to almost every country in Eastern Europe, and with the proliferation of low-cost carriers, it is increasingly easy to fly straight to your destination. See p977 for a list of budget airlines.

UK & Ireland

The UK is connected by direct flights to every country in Eastern Europe except Moldova and Montenegro – **British Airways** (BA; www.britishair ways.com) even offers a direct flight to Albania. Furthermore, the UK is at the centre of the budget-airline network, meaning that low-cost carriers operate flights from four airports in London, as well as Belfast, Bristol, Glasgow, Liverpool, Manchester and more. EasyJet and Ryanair are the biggest operators.

LAND
Border Crossings

With the expansion of the EU, crossing into Eastern Europe has never been simpler.

At all points of entry and exit, staff are likely to be polite and efficient, and you should be able to cross with minimal hassle or confusion.

The region can be entered from all sides, including from Germany and Austria into the Czech Republic; from Turkey or Greece into Bulgaria, Macedonia or Albania; from Italy and Austria into Slovenia; and from Finland into Russia.

Bus

Never a great option for long-distance travel, buses have recently been undercut even by airlines in prices. However, not all places are served by budget airlines, so buses are always a useful fallback if travelling from Western Europe, and are reliably cheap. **Eurolines** (www .eurolines.com) has a vast network with member companies in many Eastern European countries and offers innumerable routes across the continent. **Ecolines** (www.ecolines.net) also runs buses between Eastern and Western Europe.

See individual country chapters for details of specific bus services.

Car & Motorcycle

Travelling by car or motorcycle into Eastern Europe gives travellers an immense amount of freedom and is generally worry-free.

If you're driving a car into Eastern Europe, keep in mind that some insurance packages, especially those covering rental cars, do not include all European countries. Hiring a car in Italy, for example, and driving it to Croatia will be problematic unless you have the correct insurance stamp. Be sure to ask the agency to insure the car in all of the countries where you plan to travel.

See p981 for more on travelling by car or motorcycle throughout Europe.

Train

There are numerous routes into Eastern Europe by train, mostly from Western Europe. The big railway hubs in Eastern Europe are Prague, Budapest, Bucharest, Belgrade and Moscow. Albania is unique in Eastern Europe, as it has no international train services at all, while Montenegro has a single line that heads into Serbia. See individual country chapters for train services to Western Europe and Turkey.

From Asia, the Trans-Siberian, Trans-Mongolian and Trans-Manchurian Railways connect Moscow to the Russian far east, Ulaanbaatar (Mongolia) and Beijing (China). Central Asian cities such as Tashkent, Almaty and Dushanbe are also regularly connected by long-distance trains to Moscow.

SEA

The expansion of budget airlines into Eastern Europe has made travelling by sea into the region far less attractive. Back in the day, a good way to arrive in the region would be to catch a cheap flight to Italy, Greece or Finland, followed by a boat connection to the Western Balkans or Estonia. It's rather unnecessary these days, but boat is still an atmospheric and inexpensive way to travel.

Regular boats from several companies connect Italy with Croatia, Slovenia, Montenegro and Albania; there are also services between Greece and Albania. A car-passenger ferry links Odesa and İstanbul.

From Scandinavia, ferries ply the Gulf of Finland and the wide Baltic Sea, connecting Helsinki with Tallinn, and Stockholm with Rīga. Gdańsk and Gdynia are also linked to Sweden and Denmark.

See individual country chapters for details.

GETTING AROUND

The borders between Serbia and Kosovo, and Russia and Belarus can be problematic; see p438 and p97, respectively, for details.

See opposite for information on the Schengen Agreement.

AIR

The major Eastern European cities are connected by a full schedule of regular flights, and with the advent of low-cost airlines, prices are seriously competitive with trains and even buses; see p976 for a list of airlines around the region. Particularly well-connected regional airports include Moscow, St Petersburg, Prague, Budapest, Warsaw, Rīga, Timişoara and Zagreb.

Many countries offer domestic flights, although there is rarely a need to fly internally unless you are in a particular rush. Russia is the exception: flying from either Moscow or St Petersburg to Kaliningrad saves the trouble of getting a double-entry Russian visa. (If you travel to Kaliningrad by boat or land, you are given an exit stamp, thus invalidating your single-entry visa.)

In 2006 more than 90 airlines were banned from operating in the EU, due to unsafe practices. Ukraine Cargo Airways, Ukrainian Mediterranean Airlines and Volare Aviation Entreprise were all banned, so you may want to avoid their flights even if they are cheap.

BICYCLE

Eastern Europe is compact enough to make it ideal for a cycling trip, and mountainous enough to ensure that it will be challenging. If you are planning a tour of the region by bike, contact one of these helpful cycling clubs:

Cyclists' Touring Club (CTC; ☎ in the UK 0870 873 0060; www.ctc.org.uk) Offers its members an information service on all matters associated with cycling, including maps, cycling conditions, itineraries and detailed routes).

European Cyclists' Federation (☎ in Belgium 02 234 38 74; www.ecf.com) Advocates bike-friendly policies and organises tours. Also manages EuroVelo, a project to create bike routes across the continent.

The key to a successful bike trip is to travel light. That said, it's always worth carrying the tools necessary for repairing a puncture. You might want to consider packing spare brake and gear cables, spanners, Allen keys, spare spokes and strong adhesive tape. Before you set off, ensure that you are competent at carrying out basic repairs (there's no point in loading up with equipment that you haven't got a clue how to use!). Always check your bike thoroughly each morning and again at night when the day's touring is over. Take a good lock and always use it when you leave your bike unattended. The wearing of helmets is not compulsory but is certainly advised.

A seasoned cyclist can average about 80km a day, but this depends on the terrain and how much weight is being carried. Don't overdo it – there's no point burning yourself out during the initial stages.

One major drawback to cycling in Eastern Europe is the disgusting exhaust fumes put out by Eastern European vehicles, especially buses and trucks. You'll often find yourself gasping in a cloud of blue or black smoke as these vehicles lumber along quiet country roads. Roads in the southern Balkans – particularly Albania, BiH, Serbia, Macedonia and Montenegro – can be terrible, and there's also the risk of landmines and unexploded ordnance in Kosovo and BiH. For popular cycling spots, see p961.

Hire

Except in a few of the more visited regions, it can be difficult to hire bikes in Eastern Europe. The best spots are often camping grounds and resort hotels during the summer months, or travel agencies in the major cities.

Purchase

For major cycling tours, it's best to have a bike you're familiar with, so consider bringing your own rather than buying on arrival. If you can't be bothered with the hassle then there are places to buy in Eastern Europe (shops selling new and secondhand bicycles or you can check local papers for private vendors), but you'll need a specialist bicycle shop for a machine capable of withstanding touring. CTC (p979) can provide members with a leaflet on purchasing.

Transporting a Bicycle

You should be able to take your bicycle on plane trips. You can either take it apart and pack all the pieces in a bike bag or box, or simply wheel it to the check-in desk, where it should be treated as a piece of check-in luggage. You may have to remove the pedals and turn the handlebars sideways so that it takes up less space in the aircraft's hold; check all this with the airline well in advance, preferably before you pay for your ticket. If your bicycle and other luggage exceed your weight allowance, ask about alternatives, as you may otherwise find yourself being charged a fortune for excess baggage.

Within Europe, bikes can usually be transported on trains as luggage, subject to a fairly small supplementary fee. If it's possible, book your tickets in advance.

Tours

Plenty of companies offer organised cycling tours of Eastern Europe. These specialised companies generally plan the itinerary, organise accommodation and transport luggage, making life a lot simpler for cyclists:

BaltiCCycle (www.balticcycle.eu) A club promoting cycling in the Baltic countries. Includes information on routes, maps and bike rental.

Experience Plus (www.experienceplus.com) Runs cycling tours throughout the region, including cycling and cruising Croatia, cycling the Danube from Budapest to the Black Sea, and cycling through the heart of the Balkans.

First Light Bicycle Tours (www.firstlightbicycletours .com) Offers several cycling tours in the Czech Republic, as well as one epic journey from Kraków to Budapest. Self-guided tours also available.

Top Bicycle (www.topbicycle.com) This Czech company offers cycling tours of the Czech Republic and Slovakia, as well as more-extensive tours around the region.

Velo Touring (www.velo-touring.hu) Based in Budapest, this company offers tours of Austria and Hungary, as well as bike rentals for those who want to go it alone.

BOAT

Eastern Europe's massive rivers, and myriad canals, lakes and seas provide rich opportunities for boat travel, although in almost all cases these are very much pleasure cruises rather than particularly practical ways to get around. Boat travel is usually far more expensive than the equivalent bus or train journey, but that's not necessarily the point.

BUS

Buses are a viable alternative to the rail network in most Eastern European countries. Generally they tend to complement the rail system rather than duplicate it, though in some countries – notably Hungary, the Czech Republic and Slovakia – you'll almost always have a choice between the two options.

In general, buses are slightly cheaper and slower than trains; in Russia, Poland, Hungary, the Czech Republic and Slovakia they cost about the same. Buses tend to be best for shorter hops, getting around cities and reaching remote rural villages. They are often the only option in mountainous regions. The ticketing system varies in each country, but advance reservations are rarely necessary. On long-distance buses you can usually pay upon boarding, although it's safest to buy your ticket in advance at the station.

The only company covering the majority of the region is **Eurolines** (www.eurolines.com). See also the individual country chapters for more details about long-distance buses.

FIVE GREAT BOAT JOURNEYS IN EASTERN EUROPE

- Budapest–Bratislava (Hungary–Slovakia; p388, p843) – From one gorgeous capital to another, this journey takes in the magnificent Danube Bend, Szentendre and lovely Esztergom.
- Split–Dubrovnik (Croatia; p260) – This great day trip cruises along the dramatic, stunning Croatian coastline; some ferries stop at Mljet as well as Hvar and Korčula.
- Danube Delta (Romania; p735) – Watch the wildlife or snag some fish amid the amazing marshy wetlands where the Danube empties into the Black Sea.
- Moscow–St Petersburg (Russia; p800) – This slow meander traverses the winding waterways and rustic villages that dot the landscape between Russia's two biggest cities.
- Great Masurian Lakes (Poland; p659) – Explore as many as 2000 lakes by canoe, kayak or sailboat, or sit back and relax while the captain steers your excursion boat into the sunset.

CAR & MOTORCYCLE

Travelling with your own vehicle allows you increased flexibility and the option to get off the beaten track. However, cars can be inconvenient in city centres when you have to negotiate strange one-way systems or find somewhere to park in the narrow streets of Old Towns. Also, theft from vehicles is a problem in many parts of the region – never leave valuables in your car.

Due to high theft levels and terrible roads, Albania remains something of a no-go area for many, although the situation is improving. Russia, Belarus and Ukraine still remain tediously difficult places to drive into – border controls can take a long time and bribes are often the order of the day. It is not recommended to drive a rental car from Serbia into Kosovo, and vice versa.

Driving Licence & Documentation

Proof of ownership of a private vehicle (a Vehicle Registration Document for British-registered cars) should always be carried when touring Europe. An EU driving licence may be used throughout most of Eastern Europe, as may North American and Australian ones. If you want to be extra cautious – or if you have any other type of licence – you should obtain an International Driving Permit (IDP) from your local motoring organisation. Technically, you need a certified Russian translation for driving in Russia, though this is rarely enforced. Always double-check which type of licence is required in your chosen destination before departure.

Every vehicle travelling across an international border should display a sticker that shows the country of registration.

Fuel & Spare Parts

The problems associated with finding the right kind of petrol – or petrol of any kind – are all but over in Eastern Europe. Fuel prices still vary considerably from country to country, however, and may bear little relation to the general cost of living. Relatively affluent Slovenia, for example, has very cheap fuel while the opposite is true in inexpensive Hungary. Savings can be made if you fill up in the right place. Russia is the cheapest spot, followed by Romania, which has prices half those of neighbouring Hungary. Motoring organisations in your home country can give more details.

Unleaded petrol of 95 or 98 octane is now widely available throughout Eastern Europe, though it may not be stocked at the odd station on back roads, or outside main cities in Russia. To be on the safe side in Russia, bring a 20L can to carry an extra supply, especially if your car is fitted with a catalytic converter, as this expensive component can be ruined by leaded fuel. Unleaded fuel is usually slightly cheaper than super (premium grade). Look for the pump with green markings and the word *Bleifrei*, German for 'unleaded'. Diesel is usually significantly cheaper in Eastern Europe.

Good-quality petrol is easy to find in the Baltic countries, but stations seem to be placed somewhat erratically. Several may be located within a few kilometres of each other, then there may not be any for incredibly long stretches. Make sure you fill up your tank wherever possible – especially if you are travelling off the main highways.

Spare parts for Western cars are widely available from garages and dealerships around the region, although this is less the case in

Belarus, Moldova and Ukraine, and of course in more-rural areas.

Hire
Hiring a car is now a relatively straightforward procedure. The big international firms will give you reliable service and a good standard of vehicle. Prebooked rates are generally lower than walk-in rates at rental offices, but either way you'll pay about 20% to 40% more than in Western Europe.

Local companies will usually offer lower prices than the multinationals, but be wary of printed tariffs intended only for local residents, which may be lower than the prices foreigners are charged. The big chain companies sometimes offer the flexibility of allowing you to pick up the vehicle from one place and drop it off at another at no additional charge.

If you're coming from North America, Australia or New Zealand, ask your airline if it has any special deals for rental cars in Europe, or check the ads in the weekend travel sections of major newspapers. You can often find very competitive deals.

You should be able to make advance reservations online. Check out the following websites:

Avis (www.avis.com)
Budget (www.budget.com)
Europcar (www.europcar.com)
Hertz (www.hertz.com)

Bear in mind that many companies will not allow you to take cars into certain countries. Russia, Belarus, Moldova and Albania all regularly feature on forbidden lists – there's usually a way around this, but check in advance with the car-hire firm you're planning to use.

Insurance
Third-party motor insurance is compulsory throughout the EU. For non-EU countries make sure you check the requirements with your insurer. For further advice and more information contact the **Association of British Insurers** (☎ in the UK 020-7600 3333; www.abi.org.uk).

In general you should get your insurer to issue a Green Card (which may cost extra), an internationally recognised proof of insurance, and check that it lists all the countries you intend to visit. The European Accident Statement is available from your insurance company and allows each party at an accident to record information for insurance

purposes. The Association of British Insurers has more details. Never sign accident statements you cannot understand or read – insist on a translation and sign that only if it's acceptable.

If the Green Card doesn't list one of the countries you're visiting and your insurer cannot (or will not) add it, you will have to take out separate third-party cover at the border of the country in question. This may be the case for Bulgaria, Russia and the Baltic countries. Allow extra time at borders to purchase insurance, as this can slow you down by several hours.

Taking out a European breakdown-assistance policy, such as the Five Star Service with **AA** (☎ in the UK 0870 550 0600) or the Eurocover Motoring Assistance with **RAC** (☎ in the UK 0800 550 055; www.rac.co.uk), is a good investment. Non-Europeans might find it cheaper to arrange for international coverage with their own national motoring organisation before leaving home. Ask your motoring organisation for details about reciprocal services offered by affiliated organisations around Europe.

Road Rules
Motoring organisations are able to supply their members with country-by-country information on motoring regulations, or they may produce motoring guidebooks for general sale.

According to statistics, driving in Eastern Europe is much more dangerous than in Western Europe. Driving at night can be particularly hazardous in rural areas as the roads are often narrow and winding, and you may encounter horse-drawn vehicles, cyclists, pedestrians and domestic animals. In the event of an accident you're supposed to notify the police and file an insurance claim.

If your car has significant body damage from a previous accident, point this out to customs upon arrival in the country and have it noted somewhere, as damaged vehicles may only be allowed to leave the country with police permission.

Standard international road signs are used throughout all of Eastern Europe. You drive on the right-hand side of the road throughout the region and overtake on the left. Keep right except when overtaking, and use your indicators for any change of lane or when pulling away from the kerb. You're not allowed to overtake more than one car at a time.

Speed limits are posted, and are generally 110km/h or 120km/h on motorways, 100km/h on highways, 80km/h on secondary and tertiary roads, and 50km/h or 60km/h in built-up areas. Motorcycles are usually limited to 90km/h on motorways, and vehicles with trailers to 80km/h. In towns you may only sound the horn to avoid an accident.

Everywhere in Eastern Europe the use of seatbelts is mandatory, and motorcyclists (and their passengers) must wear a helmet. In most countries, children under 12 and intoxicated passengers are not allowed in the front seat. Driving after drinking *any* alcohol is a serious offence – most Eastern European countries have a 0% blood-alcohol concentration (BAC) limit.

Throughout Eastern Europe, when two roads of equal importance intersect, the vehicle coming from the right has right of way unless signs indicate otherwise. In many countries this rule also applies to cyclists, so take care. On roundabouts vehicles already in the roundabout have the right of way. Public transport vehicles pulling out from a stop also have right of way. Stay out of lanes marked 'bus' except when you're making a right-hand turn. Pedestrians have right of way at marked crossings and whenever you're making a turn. In Europe it's prohibited to turn right against a red light even after coming to a stop.

It's usually illegal to stop or park at the top of slopes, in front of pedestrian crossings, at bus or tram stops, on bridges or at level crossings. Almost everywhere in Europe it is compulsory to carry a red warning triangle, which you must use when parking on a highway in an emergency. If you don't use the triangle and another vehicle hits you from behind, you will be held responsible.

A first-aid kit and a fire extinguisher are also required in most Eastern European countries, while a spare-bulb kit and headlamp converters are also recommended. Contact the RAC or the AA for more information.

Be aware of trams as these have priority at crossroads and when they are turning right. Don't pass a tram that's stopping to let off passengers until everyone is out and the doors have closed again. Never pass a tram on the left or stop within 1m of tram tracks. A police officer who sees you blocking a tram route by waiting to turn left will flag you over.

Traffic police administer fines on the spot; always ask for a receipt.

HITCHING

Hitching is never entirely safe in any country, and we don't recommend it. Travellers who decide to hitch should understand that they are taking a small but potentially serious risk. People who do choose to hitch will be safer if they travel in pairs and let someone know where they plan to go.

As long as public transport remains cheap in Eastern Europe, hitching is more for the adventure than for the transport. In Russia, Albania and Romania, drivers expect riders to pay the equivalent of a bus fare. In Romania traffic is light, motorists are probably not going far, and you'll often face small vehicles overloaded with passengers. If you want to give it a try, though, make yourself a small, clearly written cardboard destination sign, remembering to use the local name for the town or city (Praha not Prague, or Warszawa not Warsaw). Don't try to hitch from the city centres; city buses will usually take you to the edge of town. Hitching on a motorway is usually prohibited.

Women will find hitching safer than in Western Europe, but the standard precautions should be taken: never accept a ride with two or more men, don't let your pack be put in the boot, only sit next to a door you can open, ask drivers where they are going before you say where you're going etc. Don't hesitate to refuse a ride if you feel at all uncomfortable, and insist on being let out at the first sign of trouble. Best of all, try to find a travelling companion.

Travellers considering hitching as a way of getting around Eastern Europe may find the following websites useful: for general facts, destination-based information and rideshare options visit **BUG – the Backpackers Ultimate Guide to Europe** (www.bugeurope.com); the useful **Hitchhikers** (www.hitchhikers.org) connects hitchhikers and drivers worldwide.

LOCAL TRANSPORT

Public transport in Eastern Europe has been developed to a far greater extent than in Western Europe. There are excellent metro networks in Moscow, St Petersburg, Warsaw, Prague, Kyiv, Minsk, Budapest and Bucharest. It is a great way to cover distances for a small fare.

One form of transport that doesn't exist in Western Europe is the shared minibus (*marshrutka* in the former Soviet Union, *furgon* in the Balkans). These quick but cramped minibuses are used throughout Eastern Europe as both inter- and intracity transport. St Petersburg would cease to function without them, and it's also the most likely way you'll travel between mountain towns in Albania.

Trolleybuses are another phenomenon of Eastern Europe. Although slow, they are environmentally friendly (being powered by electricity and having no emissions in the city) and can be found throughout the former Soviet Union; the world's longest trolleybus route runs between Simferopol and Yalta in Ukraine (see p947).

Trams are popular throughout Eastern Europe, though they vary greatly in their speed and modernity. Those in Russia are borderline antiques that seem to derail on a daily basis, while Prague's fleet of sleek trams have everything from electronic destination displays to pickpockets.

TOURS

A package tour is generally worth considering only if your time is very limited or you have a special interest such as skiing, canoeing, sailing, horse riding, cycling or spa treatments. Cruises on the Danube are an exciting and romantic way to see Europe's most famous river, although they tend to be on the expensive side.

Most tour prices are for double occupancy, which means singles have to share a double room with a stranger of the same sex or pay a supplement to have the room to themselves.

Probably the British company most experienced in booking travel to Eastern Europe is **Regent Holidays** (☎ in the UK 0845 277 3317; www.regent-holidays.co.uk). Its comprehensive individual and group tours take in everything from a two-week Hanseatic Baltic tour to city breaks in Minsk and tours of Albania.

Other recommended travel agents in the UK include **Baltic Holidays** (☎ in the UK 0845 070 5711; www.balticholidays.com), which exclusively runs tours of the Baltic region and northwest Russia, including weekend city breaks, family holidays, spa breaks and activity tours. Custom itineraries follow themes such as Soviet heritage and Jewish heritage.

In Australia you can obtain a detailed brochure outlining dozens of upmarket tours (including to Russia) from the **Eastern Europe Russian Travel Centre** (☎ in Australia 02-9262 1144; www.eetbtravel.com).

Exodus (www.exodus.co.uk) and **Explore!** (www.exploreco.uk) are also recommended. A good-value, environmentally active tour operator that includes Eastern Europe is **Intrepid Travel** (www.intrepidtravel.com), which offers 'comfort trips', 'active trips' and everything in between.

Young revellers can party on Europe-wide bus tours. **Contiki** (http://contiki.com) and **Top Deck** (www.topdecktravel.co.uk) offer camping- and hotel-based bus tours for the 18-to-35 age group. Both offer a great variety of routes, and trips run from one to three weeks, or even longer. **Beetroot Experience** (www.beetroot.org) is a cool backpackers travel organisation offering specialised trips in Russia. The signature offering is the Beetroot Express, a seven-day introduction to Moscow and St Petersburg.

For people aged over 50, **Elder Hostel** (☎ in the USA 800 454 5768; www.elderhostel.org) offers educational tours all over the world, including Russia, the Baltic countries, the Balkans and central Europe.

National tourist offices in most Eastern European countries offer trips to points of interest. These may range from one-hour city tours to excursions of several days' duration into regional areas. They are often more expensive than going it alone, but are sometimes worth it if you are pressed for time. A short city tour will give you a quick overview of the place and can be a good way to begin your visit.

TRAIN

Trains are the most atmospheric, comfortable and fun way to make long overland journeys in Eastern Europe. All major cities are on the rail network, and it's perfectly feasible for train travel to be your only form of intercity transport. In general trains run like clockwork, and you can expect to arrive pretty much to the timetabled minute.

Overnight trains also have the benefit of saving you a night's accommodation. It's a great way to meet locals – and it's not unusual to be invited to stay for a night or two with people who shared your cabin. If you're travelling overnight (which is nearly always the case when you're going between countries), you'll get a bed reservation included in the price of your ticket, although you may have to pay a few euros extra for the bedding once on board.

Each wagon is administered by a steward, who will look after your ticket and – crucially,

TRANSPORT
IN EASTERN EUROPE

FIVE GREAT TRAIN RIDES IN EASTERN EUROPE

- Moscow–St Petersburg (Russia; p785) – The overnight sleeper train won't afford you great views of flat central Russia, which is fairly dull even during the daytime, but you can pitch up in the dining car at midnight and drink vodka with your fellow passengers for a truly fun train trip.
- Septemvri–Bansko (Bulgaria; p159) – This train clanks along a narrow gauge through the valley where the Rila and Rodopi Mountains meet; get ready for some lovely mountain scenery and chain-smoking shepherds jumping on and off the train.
- Belgrade–Bar (Serbia–Montenegro; p830, p574) – Take the day train on this charming route that passes through the Morača canyon north of Podgorica.
- Gdynia–Hel (Poland; p650, p651) – This gentle train ride along the Hel Peninsula stops at a number of sleepy villages on the way, then as the peninsula narrows towards its destination you get alternating views of the Baltic Sea on one side and the Gulf of Gdańsk on the other.
- Jesenice–Nova Gorica (Slovenia; p893) Travelling via Bohinjska Bistrica, this 89km route beneath the Julian Alps and Soča Valley celebrated its centennial in 2006; if you are travelling south, sit on the right-hand side of the train to see the cobalt blue Soča at its most sparkling.

---

if you arrive during the small hours – who will make sure that you get off at the correct stop. Each wagon has a toilet and washbasin at either end, although their state of cleanliness varies. Be aware that toilets may be closed while the train is at a station and a good 30 minutes before you arrive in a big city, so go to the toilet while you can.

If you plan to travel extensively by train, it might be worth getting hold of the *Thomas Cook European Timetable,* which gives a complete listing of train schedules and indicates where supplements apply or where reservations are necessary. It is updated monthly and is available from **Thomas Cook** (www.thomascook.com) outlets in the UK and in Australia; bigger bookstores in Australia can also order in copies if they don't have any in stock. Elsewhere you'll have to order through **Rail Europe** (www.raileurope.com). Rail Europe also has train fares, schedules for the most popular routes in Europe and information on train passes.

A particularly useful online resource for timetables in Eastern Europe is the **DeutscheBahn** (www.bahn.de), which includes schedules and fares for trains all across Europe.

If you intend to stick to one or a handful of countries, consider purchasing the national timetable published by the state railway.

Classes

The system of classes in Eastern Europe is similar to that in Western Europe. Short trips, or longer ones that don't involve sleeping on the train, are usually seated like a normal train – benches (on suburban trains) or aeroplane-style seats (on smarter intercity services).

There are generally three classes of sleeping accommodation on trains – each country has a different name for them, but for the sake of simplicity, we'll call them 3rd, 2nd and 1st class.

Third-class accommodation, which generally consists of six berths in each compartment, is the cheapest option, although you may feel your privacy has been slightly invaded. In the former Soviet Union, 3rd class is called *platskartny* and does not have compartments; instead, there's just one open carriage with beds everywhere. Third-class accommodation is not available everywhere.

Second class (known as *kupeyny* in the former Soviet Union) has four berths in a closed compartment. If there are two of you, you will share your accommodation with two strangers. However, if there are three of you, you'll often have the compartment to yourselves.

First class (SV in the former Soviet Union) is a treat, although you are paying for space rather than decor. Here you'll find two berths in a compartment, usually adorned with plastic flowers to remind you what you've paid for.

Costs

While it's reasonably priced, train travel costs more than bus travel in some countries. First-class tickets are double the price of 2nd-class tickets, which are in turn approximately twice the price of 3rd-class tickets.

Reservations

It's always advisable to buy a ticket in advance. Seat reservations are also advisable, but are only necessary if the timetable specifies one is required. On busy routes and during the summer, however, always try to reserve a seat several days in advance. For peace of mind, you may prefer to book tickets via travel agencies before you leave home, although this will be more expensive than booking on arrival in Eastern Europe. You can book most routes in the region from any main station in Eastern Europe.

Safety

Be aware that trains, while generally safe, can attract petty criminals. Carry your valuables on you at all times – don't even go to the bathroom without taking your cash, wallet and passport. If you are sharing a compartment with others, you'll have to decide whether or not you trust them. If there's any doubt, be very cautious about leaving the compartment. At night, make sure your door is locked from the inside. If you have a compartment to yourself, you can ask the steward to lock it while you go to the dining car or go for a wander outside when the train is stopped. However, be aware that most criminals strike when they can easily disembark from the train, and on rare occasions the stewards are complicit.

In the former Soviet Union, the open-plan 3rd-class accommodation is by far the most vulnerable to thieves.

Train Passes

Not all countries in Eastern Europe are covered by rail passes, but passes do include a number of destinations and so can be worthwhile if you are concentrating your travels on a particular part of the region. These are available online or through most travel agents.

Check out the excellent summary of available passes, and their pros and cons, at **Seat 61** (www.seat61.com/Railpass.htm). Keep in mind that all passes offer discounted 'youth' prices for travellers who are under 26 years of age on the first day of travel. Children are aged four to 11. Also note that discounted fares are available if you are travelling in a group of two to five people (although you must always travel together).

In the USA, you can buy passes through **Rail Europe** (www.raileurope.com); in Australia you can use either **Rail Plus** (www.railplus.com.au) or Rail Europe.

BALKAN FLEXIPASS

The Balkan Flexipass includes Bulgaria, Romania, Greece, Serbia, Montenegro, Macedonia and Turkey. This pass is not available to anyone who is a resident of Europe, the UK, Morocco, Turkey, or any of the countries of the former Soviet Union. It is valid for 1st-class travel only. In the USA, Rail Europe charges US$256/153/128 per adult/youth/child for five days of 1st-class travel within one month; passes with 10 or 15 days of travel are also available. In Australia, Rail Plus offers the same pass for A$377/303/225 per adult/youth/child.

EURAIL GLOBAL

The famous Eurail pass allows the greatest flexibility for 'overseas' visitors only – if you are a resident of Europe or the UK, check out the InterRail Pass. The Eurail Global pass allows unlimited travel in 21 countries, including Croatia, the Czech Republic, Hungary, Romania and Slovenia. The pass is valid for a designated period of time, ranging from 15 days (adult/youth/child US$700/455/351 or A$1118/695/476) to three months (adult/youth/child US$1962/1278/982 or A$3131/1951/1568).

Alternatively, if you don't plan to travel quite so intensively but you still want the range of countries, consider the Eurail Global Flexi, which allows for 10 or 15 travel days over the course of two months. The Flexi is suitably more affordable: the 10-day pass goes for US$826/545/414 per adult/youth/child from Rail Europe or A$1319/824/662 from Rail Plus.

EURAIL SELECT

Again, non-Europe residents can purchase this pass, which covers travel in three, four or five neighbouring countries, which you choose from the 18 available. Your Eastern European options include Bulgaria, Croatia, Czech Republic, Hungary, Montenegro, Romania, Serbia and Slovenia. Note that Bulgaria, Serbia and Montenegro count as one country for Eurail pass purposes, as do Croatia and Slovenia, so the clever traveller can get six countries for the price of three. From Rail Europe this would be US$443/289/223 per adult/youth/child for five days of travel in two months; from Rail Plus you'll pay A$710/442/357. Adult and child fares are for 1st class, while the youth fare is only for 2nd class. Again, additional countries and additional days of travel are available for higher cost.

Alternatively, the Eurail regional passes cover two countries, although this generally limits you to one Eastern European country and one Western European country. The exception is the Hungary-Croatia-Slovenia pass, which is available for US$239/168/121 per adult/youth/child or A$385/258/195.

EUROPEAN EAST PASS

The European East Pass can be purchased by anyone not permanently resident in Europe, the UK and the former Soviet Union. The pass is valid for travel in Austria, the Czech Republic, Hungary, Slovakia and Poland, and offers five days of travel in a one-month period. It also includes bonuses such as Danube River cruises.

European East is sold in North America, Australia and the UK. In the US, Rail Europe charges US$299/209 for 1st-/2nd-class travel (half-price for children), with extra rail days available for purchase. In Australia, **Rail Tickets** (www.railtickets.com.au) sells the same pass for A$438/307.

INTERRAIL GLOBAL

These passes are available to European residents of more than six months' standing (passport identification is required), although residents of Turkey and parts of North Africa can also buy them. Terms and conditions vary slightly from country to country, but the InterRail pass is not valid for travel within your country of residence. For complete information, see **InterRail** (www.interrail.net).

InterRail Global allows for unlimited travel in 30 European countries, including BiH, Bulgaria, Croatia, the Czech Republic, Hungary, Macedonia, Montenegro, Poland, Romania, Serbia, Slovakia and Slovenia. The consecutive pass is valid for unlimited travel within a period of 22 days or one month. The Flexi version of InterRail allows for five or 10 rail days within a designated time period.

Rail Choice (www.railchoice.co.uk) offers 22 days of unlimited travel for £603/306/312 per adult/youth/child. Ten rail days in the same time period go for £485/237/243.

INTERRAIL & EURAIL COUNTRY PASSES

If you are intending to travel extensively within any one country, you might consider purchasing a Country Pass (InterRail if you are an EU resident, Eurail if not). The Eurail Country Pass is available for Bulgaria, Croatia, Czech Republic, Hungary, Poland, Romania and Slovenia. The InterRail Country Pass is available for all of those countries, plus Serbia and Slovakia. The passes and prices vary for each country, so check out the websites above for more information. You'll probably need to travel extensively to recoup your money, but the passes will save you the time and hassle of buying individual tickets that don't require reservations. Some of these countries also offer national rail passes; see individual country chapters for more information.

TRANSPORT
IN EASTERN EUROPE

Health

CONTENTS

Travel health largely depends on your pre-departure preparations, your daily health care while travelling and how you handle any medical problem that does develop. Eastern Europe is generally an exceptionally safe place to visit from a medical point of view, with no tropical diseases and an extensive, if sometimes basic, health-care system throughout the region.

BEFORE YOU GO

Prevention is the key to staying healthy while abroad. A little planning, particularly for pre-existing illnesses, will save trouble later: see your dentist before a long trip, carry spare contact lenses or glasses, and take your optical prescription with you. Bring medications in their original, clearly labelled, containers, along with a signed and dated letter from your physician describing your medical conditions and medications, including generic names. If carrying syringes or needles, be sure to have a physician's letter documenting their medical necessity.

INSURANCE

In 2004 the European Health Insurance Card (EHIC) was introduced for all EU citizens, replacing the E111 form that was previously necessary to receive free or reduced-price treatment. With large numbers of Eastern European countries now EU members, this is a very useful card, although it will not cover you for nonemergencies or emergency repatriation.

Other travellers should find out if there is a reciprocal arrangement for free medical care between their country and the destination country. If you do need health insurance, strongly consider a policy that covers you for the worst-possible scenario, such as an accident requiring an emergency flight home. Find out if your insurance plan will make payments directly to providers or reimburse you later for overseas health expenditures. The former option is generally preferable, as it doesn't require you to pay out-of-pocket expenses in a foreign country.

RECOMMENDED VACCINATIONS

The World Health Organization (WHO) recommends that all travellers be covered for diphtheria, tetanus, measles, mumps, rubella and polio, regardless of their destination. Since most vaccines don't produce immunity until at least two weeks after they're given, visit a physician at least six weeks before departure.

INTERNET RESOURCES

The WHO's publication **International Travel and Health** (www.who.int.ith/) is revised annually and is available online. Some other useful websites include the following.

Age Concern (www.ageconcern.org.uk) Advice on travel for the elderly.

Fit For Travel (www.fitfortravel.scot.nhs.uk) General travel advice for the layperson.

TRAVEL-HEALTH WEBSITES

It's usually a good idea to consult your government's travel health-website before departure, if one is available:

Australia (www.dfat.gov.au/travel/)
Canada (www.travelhealth.gc.ca)
UK (www.doh.gov.uk/traveladvice/)
US (www.cdc.gov/travel/)

Marie Stopes International (www.mariestopes
.org.uk) Information on women's health and
contraception.

MDtravelhealth.com (www.mdtravelhealth.com)
Travel-health recommendations for every country. Updated
daily.

FURTHER READING

Health Advice for Travellers (currently called
the *T7.1* leaflet) is an annually updated leaflet by the UK's Department of Health, available free in post offices. It contains some
general information, recommended vaccines for different countries and information on reciprocal health agreements. Lonely
Planet's *Travel with Children* includes
advice on travel health for younger children.
Other recommended references include
Travellers' Health by Dr Richard Dawood
and *The Traveller's Good Health Guide* by
Ted Lankester.

IN TRANSIT

DEEP VEIN THROMBOSIS (DVT)

Blood clots may form in the legs during plane
flights, chiefly because of prolonged immo-
bility. The longer the flight, the greater the
risk. The chief symptom of DVT is swelling
or pain of the foot, ankle, or calf, usually but
not always on just one side. When a blood clot
travels to the lungs, it may cause chest pain
and breathing difficulties. Travellers with any
of these symptoms should immediately seek
medical attention.

To prevent the development of DVT
on long flights, you should walk about the
cabin, contract the leg muscles while sitting,
drink plenty of fluids, and avoid alcohol
and tobacco.

JET LAG & MOTION SICKNESS

To avoid becoming jet lagged (common
when crossing more than five time zones),
try drinking plenty of nonalchoholic fluids and only eating light meals. On arrival,
get exposure to sunlight and readjust your
schedule (for meals, sleep and so on) as soon
as possible.

Antihistamines such as dimenhydrinate
(Dramamine) and meclizine (Antivert,
Bonine) are usually the first choice for treat-
ing motion sickness. A herbal alternative
is ginger.

IN EASTERN EUROPE

AVAILABILITY & COST OF HEALTH CARE

Good basic health care is readily available,
and pharmacists can give valuable advice and
sell over-the-counter medication for minor
illnesses. They can also advise when more
specialised help is required and point you in
the right direction. The standard of dental
care is usually good, but it is sensible to have
a dental check-up before a long trip.

Medical care is not always readily available outside of major cities, but embassies,
consulates and five-star hotels can usually
recommend doctors or clinics. In some
cases, medical supplies required in hospital
may need to be bought from a pharmacy
and nursing care may be limited. Note that
there can be an increased risk of hepatitis B and HIV transmission via poorly
sterilised equipment.

In general health-care costs are still relatively low in Eastern Europe, and tend to be
more expensive in EU member states than
in non-EU member states; bear in mind,
however, that in most non-EU states you'll
probably want to go to a private clinic for
anything more than a doctor's consultation,
and therefore comprehensive health insurance
is essential.

INFECTIOUS DISEASES
Poliomyelitis

Poliomyelitis is spread through contaminated food and water. Its vaccine is one of
those given in childhood and should be
boosted every 10 years, either orally or as
an injection.

Rabies

Spread through bites or licks from an infected
animal on broken skin, rabies is always fatal
unless treated promptly. Animal handlers
should be vaccinated, as should those travelling to remote areas where a reliable source
of postbite vaccine would not be available
within 24 hours. To be vaccinated, three injections are needed over a month. If you are
bitten and have not been vaccinated, you will
need a course of five injections starting 24
hours or as soon as possible after the injury.
If you have been vaccinated, you will need
fewer injections and have more time to seek
medical help.

HEALTH

Tickborne Encephalitis

Spread by tick bites, tickborne encephalitis is a serious infection of the brain. Vaccination is advised for those in risk areas who are unable to avoid tick bites (such as campers, forestry workers and walkers). Two doses of vaccine will provide protection for year, while three doses provide up to three years' protection. Anyone walking in the Baltics and Russia for any length of time should consider vaccination, as cases have been steadily rising.

Typhoid & Hepatitis A

Both of these diseases are spread through contaminated food (particularly shellfish) and water. Typhoid can cause septicaemia; hepatitis A causes liver inflammation and jaundice. Neither is usually fatal but recovery can take a long time. Typhoid vaccine (Typhim Vi, Typherix) will give protection for three years. In some countries, the oral vaccine Vivotif is also available. Hepatitis A vaccine (Avaxim, VAQTA, Havrix) is given as an injection; a single dose will give protection for up to a year, and a booster after a year gives 10 years' protection. Hepatitis A and typhoid vaccines can also be given as a single-dose vaccine (Hepatyrix, Viatim).

TRAVELLER'S DIARRHOEA

To prevent diarrhoea, only eat fresh fruits or vegetables if they've been cooked or peeled; be wary of dairy products that might contain unpasteurised milk. Avoid buffet-style meals. If a restaurant is full of locals, the food is probably safe.

If you develop diarrhoea, be sure to drink plenty of fluids, preferably an oral rehydration solution (eg Dioralyte). A few loose stools don't require treatment, but if you start having more than four or five stools a day, you should start taking an antibiotic (usually a quinolone drug) and an antidiarrhoeal agent (such as loperamide). If diarrhoea is bloody, persists for more than 72 hours or is accompanied by fever, shaking, chills or severe abdominal pain, you should seek medical attention.

ENVIRONMENTAL HAZARDS
Heat Exhaustion & Heatstroke

Heat exhaustion occurs after excessive fluid loss is combined with inadequate replacement of fluids and salt. Symptoms include headaches, dizziness and tiredness. Dehydration is already happening by the time you feel thirsty,

so aim to drink sufficient water to produce pale, diluted urine. To treat heat exhaustion, replace lost fluids by drinking water and/or fruit juice, and cool the body with cold water and fans. Treat salt loss with salty fluids such as soup or Bovril, or add a little more table salt to foods than usual.

Heatstroke is much more serious, resulting in irrational and hyperactive behaviour, and may eventually lead to loss of consciousness and death. Rapid cooling by spraying the body with water and fanning is ideal. Emergency fluid and electrolyte replacement by intravenous drip is recommended.

Insect Bites & Stings

Mosquitoes are found in most parts of Europe. They may not carry malaria but can cause irritation and infected bites. Use a DEET-based insect repellent.

Bees and wasps cause real problems only to those with a severe allergy. If you have a severe allergy to bee or wasp stings, carry an EpiPen or a similar adrenalin injection.

Sandflies are found around the Mediterranean beaches. They usually cause only a nasty itchy bite, but can occasionally carry a rare skin disorder called cutaneous leishmaniasis.

Bed bugs lead to very itchy, lumpy bites. Spraying the mattress with crawling-insect killer after changing the bedding will get rid of them.

Scabies are tiny mites that live in the skin, particularly between the fingers. They cause an intensely itchy rash. Scabies are easily treated with lotion from a pharmacy.

Snake Bites

Avoid getting bitten: do not walk barefoot, or stick your hand into holes or cracks. If bitten by a snake, do not panic. Immobilise the bitten limb with a splint (eg a stick) and apply a bandage over the site firmly; do not apply a tourniquet, or cut or suck the bite. Get the victim to medical help as soon as possible so that antivenene can be given if necessary. Half of those bitten by venomous snakes are not actually injected with poison.

Water

Tap water may not be safe to drink, so it is best to stick to bottled water or boil water for 10 minutes, use water purification tablets or a filter. Do not drink water from rivers or lakes, as it may contain bacteria or viruses that can cause diarrhoea or vomiting. St Petersburg is a particular hot spot for dangerous water – *never* drink from the tap here. Brushing your teeth with tap water is very unlikely to lead to problems, but use bottled water if you want to be ultrasafe.

TRAVELLING WITH CHILDREN

All travellers with children should know how to treat minor ailments and when to seek medical treatment. Make sure the children are up to date with routine vaccinations, and discuss possible travel vaccines with your doctor well before departure. Some vaccines are not suitable for children less than one year old.

If your child is vomiting or has diarrhoea, lost fluid and salts must be replaced. It may be helpful to take rehydration powders that can be reconstituted with boiled water.

The risk of rabies and other diseases means that children should be encouraged to avoid and mistrust dogs or other mammals. Any bite, scratch or lick from a warm-blooded, furry animal should immediately be thoroughly cleaned. If there is any possibility that the animal is infected with rabies, immediate medical assistance should be sought; see p989 for more.

WOMEN'S HEALTH

Emotional stress, exhaustion and travelling through different time zones can all contribute to an upset in the menstrual pattern. If using oral contraceptives, remember some antibiotics, diarrhoea and vomiting can stop the pill from working and lead to the risk of pregnancy – take condoms with you just in case. Time zones, gastrointestinal upsets and antibiotics do not affect injectable contraception.

Travelling during pregnancy is usually possible but there are important things to consider. The most risky times for travel are during the first 12 weeks of pregnancy and after 30 weeks. Antenatal facilities vary greatly between countries, and you should think carefully before travelling to a country with poor medical facilities or where there are major cultural and language differences from home.

Illness during pregnancy can be more severe, so take special care to avoid contaminated food and water, and insect and animal bites. A general rule is to only use medications, including vaccines, if the risk of infection is substantial. Some vaccines are best avoided (eg those that contain live organisms), but there is very little evidence that damage has been caused to an unborn child when vaccines have been given to a woman before pregnancy was suspected.

Take written records of the pregnancy with you. Ensure your insurance policy covers pregnancy delivery and postnatal care, but remember that insurance policies are only as good as the facilities available. Always consult your doctor before you travel.

SEXUAL HEALTH

Emergency contraception is most effective if taken within 24 hours after unprotected sex. The **International Planned Parent Federation** (www.ippf.org) can advise about the availability of contraception in different countries.

Condoms are available throughout the region. When buying condoms, look for a European CE mark, which means they have been rigorously tested; keep them in a cool dry place, as they may otherwise crack and perish.

HEALTH

Language

CONTENTS

This language guide offers basic vocabulary to help you get around Eastern Europe. For more extensive coverage of the languages included in this guide, pick up a copy of Lonely Planet's *Eastern Europe Phrasebook* or *Baltic Phrasebook*.

Some of the languages in this chapter use polite and informal modes of address (indicated by the abbreviations 'pol' and 'inf' respectively). Use the polite form when addressing older people, officials or service staff.

ALBANIAN

PRONUNCIATION

Written Albanian is phonetically consistent and pronunciation shouldn't pose too many problems for English speakers. Each vowel in a diphthong is pronounced, and the **rr** is trilled. However, Albanians possesses certain letters that are present in English but rendered differently. These include the following:

ë	often silent; at the beginning of a word it's like the 'a' in 'ago'
c	as the 'ts' in 'bits'
ç	as the 'ch' in 'church'
dh	as the 'th' in 'this'
gj	as the 'gy' in 'hogyard'
j	as the 'y' in 'yellow'
q	between 'ch' and 'ky'; similar to the 'cu' in 'cure'
th	as in 'thistle'
x	as the 'dz' in 'adze'
xh	as the 'j' in 'jewel'

ACCOMMODATION

camping ground	kamp pushimi
double room	një dhomë më dy krevat
hotel	hotel
single room	një dhomë më një krevat

Do you have any rooms available?	A keni ndonjë dhomë të lirë?
How much is it per night/person?	Sa kushton për një natë/njeri?
Does it include breakfast?	A e përfshin edhe mëngjesin?

CONVERSATION & ESSENTIALS

Hello.	Tungjatjeta/Allo.
Goodbye.	Lamtumirë. (pol)
	Mirupafshim. (inf)
Yes.	Po.
No.	Jo.
Please.	Ju lutem.
Thank you.	Ju falem nderit.
That's fine.	Eshtë e mirë.
You're welcome.	S'ka përse.
Excuse me.	Me falni. (to get past)
	Më vjen keq. (before a request)
I'm sorry.	Më falni, ju lutem.
Do you speak English?	A flisni anglisht?
How much is it?	Sa kushton?
What's your name?	Si quheni ju lutem?
My name is ...	Unë quhem .../Mua më quajnë ...

EMERGENCIES – ALBANIAN

Help!	Ndihmë!
Call a doctor!	Thirrni doktorin!
Call the police!	Thirrni policinë!
Go away!	Zhduku!/Largohuni!
I'm lost.	Kam humbur rrugë.

SHOPPING & SERVICES

bank	*bankë*
chemist/pharmacy	*farmaci*
the ... embassy	*... ambasadën*
market	*treg*
newsagency	*agjensia e lajmeve*
post office	*postë*
public toilet	*banjë*
tourist office	*zyrë turistike*
What time does it open/close?	*Në ç'ore hapet/mbyllet?*

TIME, DAYS & NUMBERS

What time is it?	*Sa është ora?*
today	*sot*
tomorrow	*nesër*
in the morning	*në mëngjes*
in the afternoon	*pas dreke*
Monday	*e hënë*
Tuesday	*e martë*
Wednesday	*e mërkurë*
Thursday	*e ënjte*
Friday	*e premte*
Saturday	*e shtunë*
Sunday	*e diel*
1	*një*
2	*dy*
3	*tre*
4	*katër*
5	*pesë*
6	*gjashtë*
7	*shtatë*
8	*tetë*
9	*nëntë*
10	*dhjetë*
100	*njëqind*
1000	*njëmijë*

TRANSPORT

What time does the ... leave/arrive?	*Në ç'orë niset/arrin ...?*
boat	*barka/lundra*
bus	*autobusi*
tram	*tramvaji*
train	*treni*
I'd like ...	*Dëshiroj ...*
a one-way ticket	*një biletë vajtje*
a return ticket	*një biletë kthimi*
(1st/2nd) class	*klas (i parë/i dytë)*
bus stop	*stacion autobusi*
timetable	*orar*

SIGNS – ALBANIAN

Hyrje	Entrance
Dalje	Exit
Informim	Information
Hapur	Open
Mbyllur	Closed
E Ndaluar	Prohibited
Policia	Police
Stacioni I Policisë	Police Station
Nevojtorja	Toilets
Burra	Men
Gra	Women

DIRECTIONS

Where is ...?	*Ku është ...?*
Go straight ahead.	*Shko drejt.*
Turn left.	*Kthehu majtas.*
Turn right.	*Kthehu djathtas.*
near/far	*afër/larg*

BULGARIAN

Bulgarian uses the Cyrillic alphabet and it's definitely worth familiarising yourself with it (see p1009).

ACCOMMODATION

camping ground
къмпингуване   *kâmpinguvane*

double room
двойна стая   *dvoyna staya*

guest house
пансион   *pansion*

hotel
хотел   *khotel*

private room
стоя в частна квартира   *stoya v chastna kvartira*

single room
единична стая   *edinichna staya*

youth hostel
общежитие   *obshtezhitie*

Do you have any rooms available?
Имате ли свободни стаи?
imateh li svobodni stai?

How much is it?
Колко струва?
kolko struva?

Is breakfast included?
Закуската включена ли е?
zakuskata vklyuchena li e?

EMERGENCIES – BULGARIAN

Help!
Помош! — *pomosh!*

Call a doctor!
Повикайте лекар! — *povikayte lekar!*

Call the police!
Повикайте полиция! — *povikayte politsiya!*

Go away!
Махайте се! — *mahayte se!*

I'm lost.
Загубих се. — *zagubih se*

CONVERSATION & ESSENTIALS

Hello.
Здравейте. (pol) — *zdraveyte*

Hi.
Здрасти. (inf) — *zdrasti*

Goodbye.
Довиждане. (pol) — *dovizhdane*
Чао. (inf) — *chao*

Yes.
Да. — *da*

No.
Не. — *ne*

Please.
Моля. — *molya*

Thank you.
Благодаря. (pol) — *blagodarya*
Мерси. (inf) — *mersi*

I'm sorry.
Съжалявам. — *sâzhalyavam*

Excuse me.
Извинете ме. — *izvinete me*

I don't understand.
Аз не разбирам. — *az ne razbiram*

What's it called?
Как се казва това? — *kak se kazva tova?*

How much is it?
Колко струва? — *kolko struva?*

SHOPPING & SERVICES

bank
банка — *banka*

church
църква — *tsârkva*

hospital
болница — *bolnitsa*

market
пазар — *pazar*

museum
музей — *muzey*

post office
поща — *poshta*

tourist office
бюро за туристическа информация — *byuro za turisticheska informatsiya*

TIME, DAYS & NUMBERS

What time is it?	Колко е часът?	*kolko e chasât?*
today	днес	*dnes*
tonight	довечера	*dovechera*
tomorrow	утре	*utre*
in the morning	сутринта	*sutrinta*
in the evening	вечерта	*vecherta*
Monday	понеделник	*ponedelnik*
Tuesday	вторник	*vtornik*
Wednesday	сряда	*sryada*
Thursday	четвъртък	*chetvârtâk*
Friday	петък	*petâk*
Saturday	събота	*sâbota*
Sunday	неделя	*nedelya*
0	нула	*nula*
1	едно	*edno*
2	две	*dve*
3	три	*tri*
4	четири	*chetiri*
5	пет	*pet*
6	шест	*shest*
7	седем	*sedem*
8	осем	*osem*
9	девет	*devet*
10	десет	*deset*
20	двайсет	*dvayset*
100	сто	*sto*
1000	хиляда	*hilyada*

TRANSPORT

What time does the ... leave/arrive?
В колко часа заминава/пристига ...?
v kolko chasa zaminava/pristiga ...?

city bus
градският автобус — *gradskiyat avtobus*

intercity bus
междуградският автобус — *mezhdugradskiyat avtobus*

plane
самолетът — *samolehtât*

train
влакът — *vlakât*

tram
трамваят — *tramvayat*

arrival	пристигане	*pristigane*
departure	заминаване	*zaminavane*
timetable	разписание	*razpisanie*

LANGUAGE

Where is the bus stop?
Къде е автобусната спирка?
kâde e avtobusnata spirka?

Where is the train station?
Къде е железопътната гара?
kâde e zhelezopâtnata gara?

Where is the left-luggage office?
Къде е гардеробът?
kâde e garderobât?

DIRECTIONS

left/right	ляво/дясно	*lyavo/dyasno*
straight ahead	направо	*napravo*

Please show me on the map.
Моля покажете ми на картата.
molya pokazhete mi na kartata

CROATIAN & SERBIAN

PRONUNCIATION

The writing systems of Croatian and Serbian are phonetically consistent: every letter is pronounced and its sound will not vary from word to word. With regard to the position of stress, only one rule can be given: the last syllable of a word is never stressed. In most cases the accent falls on the first vowel in the word.

Serbian uses both the Cyrillic and Roman alphabet, so it's worth familiarising yourself with the former (see p1009). Croatian uses a Roman alphabet.

The principal difference between Serbian and Croatian is in the pronunciation of the vowel 'e' in certain words. A long **e** in Serbian becomes **ije** in Croatian (eg *reka*, *rijeka* (river), and a short **e** in Serbian becomes **je** in Croatian, eg *pesma*, *pjesma* (song).

Sometimes, however, the vowel '**e**' is the same in both languages, as in *selo* (village). There are also a number of variations in vocabulary between the two languages. We haven't marked these differences in pronunciation in the following words and phrases, but you'll still be understood, even with a Croatian lilt to your language. Where significant differences occur, we've included both, with Croatian marked 'C' and Serbian marked 'S'.

ACCOMMODATION

camping ground	
kamping	кампинг
guest house	
privatno prenoćište	приватно преноћиште
hotel	
hotel	хотел
youth hostel	
omladinsko prenoćište	омладинско преноћиште

Do you have any rooms available?
Imate li slobodne sobe?
Имате ли слободне собе?

How much is it per night/per person?
Koliko košta za jednu noć/po osobi?
Колико кошта за једну ноћ/по особи?

Does it include breakfast?
Da li je u cijenu uključen i doručak?
Да ли је у цену укључен и доручак?

I'd like ...	
Želim ...	Желим ...
a double-bed room	
sobu sa duplim krevetom	собу са дуплим креветом
a single room	
sobu sa jednim krevetom	собу са једним креветом

CONVERSATION & ESSENTIALS

Hello.	
Zdravo.	Здраво.
Goodbye.	
Doviđenja.	Довиђења.
Yes.	
Da.	Да.
No.	
Ne.	Не.
Please.	
Molim.	Молим.
Thank you.	
Hvala.	Хвала.
You're welcome. (as in 'don't mention it')	
Nema na čemu.	Нема на чему.

EMERGENCIES – CROATIAN & SERBIAN

Help!
Upomoć! — Упомоћ!
Call a doctor!
Pozovite (lekara) (S)/ lijecnika! (C) — Позовите лекара!
Call the police!
Pozovite miliciju (S)/ policiju (C)! — Позовите милицију!
Go away!
Idite! — Идите!
I'm lost.
Izgubljen/Izgubljena sam se. (m/f) — Изгубио/Изгубила сам сам се. (m/f)

Excuse me.
Oprostite. — Опростите.
Sorry. (excuse me, forgive me)
Pardon. — Пардон.
Do you speak English?
Govorite li engleski? — Говорите ли енглески?
How much is it ...?
Koliko košta ...? — Колико кошта ...?
What's your name?
Kako se zovete? — Како се зовете?
My name is ...
Zovem se ... — Зовем се ...

SHOPPING & SERVICES

I'm looking for ...
Tražim ... — Тражим ...
  a bank
  banku — банку
  the ... embassy
  ... ambasadu — ... амбасаду
  the market
  pijacu — пијацу
  the post office
  poštu — пошту
  the tourist office
  turistički biro — туристички биро

TIME, DAYS & NUMBERS

What time is it? *Koliko je sati?* — Колико је сати?
today *danas* — данас
tomorrow *sutra* — сутра
in the morning *ujutro* — ујутро
in the afternoon *popodne* — поподне

Monday *ponedjeljak* — понедељак
Tuesday *utorak* — уторак
Wednesday *srijeda* — среда
Thursday *četvrtak* — четвртак

SIGNS – CROATIAN & SERBIAN

Ulaz/Izlaz Улаз/Излаз	Entrance/Exit
Informacije Информације	Information
Otvoreno/Zatvoreno Отворено/Затворено	Open/Closed
Slobodne Sobe Слободне Собе	Rooms Available
Nema Slobodne Sobe Нема Слободне Собе	Full/No Vacancies
Milicija (S)/Policija (C) Милиција	Police
Stanica Milicije (S)/ Policije (C) Станица Милиције	Police Station
Zabranjeno Забрањено	Prohibited
Toaleti (S)/Zahodi (C) Тоалети	Toilets

Friday *petak* — петак
Saturday *subota* — субота
Sunday *nedjelja* — недеља

1	*jedan*	један
2	*dva*	два
3	*tri*	три
4	*četiri*	четири
5	*pet*	пет
6	*šest*	шест
7	*sedam*	седам
8	*osam*	осам
9	*devet*	девет
10	*deset*	десет
100	*sto*	сто
1000	*hiljadu (S) tisuću (C)*	хиљаду

TRANSPORT

What time does the ... leave/arrive?
Kada ... polazi/dolazi? — Када ... полази/долази?
  boat
  brod — брод
  bus (city)
  autobus (gradski) — аутобус (градски)
  bus (intercity)
  autobus (međugradski) — аутобус (међуградски)
  train
  voz (S)/vlak (C) — воз
  tram
  tramvaj — трамвај

1st class
prvu klasu   прву класу
2nd class
drugu klasu   другу класу
one-way ticket
kartu u jednom pravcu   карту у једном правцу
return ticket
povratnu kartu   повратну карту

DIRECTIONS
Where is the bus/tram stop?
Gdje je autobuska/tramvajska stanica (S)/*postaja* (C)?
Где је аутобуска/трамвајска станица?
Can you show me (on the map)?
Možete li mi pokazati (na karti)?
Можете ли ми показати (на карти)?

Go straight ahead.
Idite pravo naprijed.   Идите право напред.
Turn left.
Skrenite lijevo.   Скрените лево.
Turn right.
Skrenite desno.   Скрените десно.
far
daleko   далеко
near
blizu   близу

CZECH

PRONUNCIATION
Many Czech letters are pronounced as per their English counterparts. An accent lengthens a vowel and the stress is always on the first syllable. Words are pronounced as written, so if you follow the guidelines below you should have no trouble being understood. When consulting indexes on Czech maps, be aware that **ch** comes after **h**.

c	as the 'ts' in 'bits'
č	as the 'ch' in 'church'
ch	as in Scottish 'loch'
ď	as the 'd' in 'duty'
ě	as the 'ye' in 'yet'
j	as the 'y' in 'you'
ň	as the 'ni' in 'onion'
ř	as the sound 'rzh'
š	as the 'sh' in 'ship'
ť	as the 'te' in 'stew'
ž	as the 's' in 'pleasure'

EMERGENCIES – CZECH
Help!	*Pomoc!*
Call a doctor/	*Zavolejte doktora/*
ambulance/police!	*sanitku/policii!*
Go away!	*Běžte pryč!*
I'm lost.	*Zabloudil jsem.* (m)
	Zabloudila jsem. (f)

ACCOMMODATION
camping ground	*kemping*
double room	*dvoulůžkový pokoj*
guest house	*penzión*
hotel	*hotel*
private room	*privát*
single room	*jednolůžkový pokoj*
youth hostel	*ubytovna*

Do you have any	*Máte volné pokoje?*
rooms available?	
Does it include	*Je v tom zahrnuta snídaně?*
breakfast?	

CONVERSATION & ESSENTIALS
Hello/Good day.	*Dobrý den.* (pol)
Hi.	*Ahoj.* (inf)
Goodbye.	*Na shledanou.*
Yes.	*Ano.*
No.	*Ne.*
Please.	*Prosím.*
Thank you.	*Děkuji.*
That's fine/You're	*Není zač/Prosím.*
welcome.	
Sorry.	*Promiňte.*
I don't understand.	*Nerozumím.*
What's it called?	*Jak se to jmenuje?*

SHOPPING & SERVICES
How much is it?	*Kolik to stojí?*
bank	*banka*
chemist	*lékárna*
church	*kostel*
market	*trh*
museum	*muzeum*
post office	*pošta*
tourist office	*turistické informační centrum*
travel agency	*cestovní kancelář*

TIME, DAYS & NUMBERS
What time is it?	*Kolik je hodin?*
today	*dnes*
tonight	*dnes večer*
tomorrow	*zítra*

SIGNS – CZECH	
Vchod	Entrance
Východ	Exit
Informace	Information
Otevřeno	Open
Zavřeno	Closed
Zakázáno	Prohibited
Policie	Police Station
Telefon	Telephone
Záchody/WC/ Toalety	Toilets

in the morning	ráno
in the evening	večer

Monday	pondělí
Tuesday	úterý
Wednesday	středa
Thursday	čtvrtek
Friday	pátek
Saturday	sobota
Sunday	neděle

1	jeden
2	dva
3	tři
4	čtyři
5	pět
6	šest
7	sedm
8	osm
9	devět
10	deset
100	sto
1000	tisíc

TRANSPORT
What time does the ... leave/arrive?	Kdy odjíždí/přijíždí ...?
boat	loď
city bus	městský autobus
intercity bus	meziměstský autobus
train	vlak
tram	tramvaj

arrival	příjezdy
departure	odjezdy
timetable	jízdní řád

Where is the bus stop?	Kde je autobusová zastávka?
Where is the station?	Kde je nádraží?
Where is the left-luggage office?	Kde je úschovna zavazadel?

DIRECTIONS
Where is it?	Kde je to?
left	vlevo
right	vpravo
straight ahead	rovně
Please show me on the map.	Prosím, ukažte mi to na mapě.

ESTONIAN

ALPHABET & PRONUNCIATION
The letters of the Estonian alphabet: **a, b, d, e, f, g, h, i, j, k, l, m, n, o, p, r, s, š, z, ž, t, u, v, õ, ä, ö, ü**.

a	as the 'u' in 'cut'
ä	as the 'a' in 'cat'
ai	as the 'ai' in 'aisle'
b	similar to English 'p'
ei	as in 'vein'
g	similar to English 'k'
j	as the 'y' in 'yes'
õ	somewhere between the 'e' in 'bed' and the 'u' in 'fur'
ö	as the 'u' in 'fur' but with rounded lips
oo	as the 'a' in 'water'
öö	as the 'u' in 'fur'
š	as 'sh'
ü	as a short 'you'
uu	as the 'oo' in 'boot'
ž	as the 's' in 'pleasure'

CONVERSATION & ESSENTIALS
Hello.	Tere.
Goodbye.	Head aega/Nägemiseni.
Yes.	Jah.
No.	Ei.
Excuse me.	Vabandage.
Please.	Palun.
Thank you.	Tänan/Aitäh. (pol/inf)
Do you speak English?	Kas te räägite inglise keelt?

SHOPPING & SERVICES
Where?	Kus?
How much?	Kui palju?
bank	pank
chemist	apteek
currency exchange	valuutavahetus
market	turg
toilet	tualett

TIME, DAYS & NUMBERS
today	täna
tomorrow	homme

Monday	*esmaspäev*
Tuesday	*teisipäev*
Wednesday	*kolmapäev*
Thursday	*neljapäev*
Friday	*reede*
Saturday	*laupäev*
Sunday	*pühapäev*

1	*üks*
2	*kaks*
3	*kolm*
4	*neli*
5	*viis*
6	*kuus*
7	*seitse*
8	*kaheksa*
9	*üheksa*
10	*kümme*
100	*sada*
1000	*tuhat*

TRANSPORT

airport	*lennujaam*
bus	*buss*
bus station	*bussijaam*
compartment (class)	*kupee*
port	*sadam*
sleeping carriage	*magamisvagun*
soft class/deluxe	*luksus*
stop (eg bus stop)	*peatus*
taxi	*takso*
ticket	*pilet*

ticket office	*piletikassa/kassa*
train	*rong*
train station	*raudteejaam*
tram	*tramm*
trolleybus	*trollibuss*

HUNGARIAN

PRONUNCIATION

The pronunciation of Hungarian consonants can be simplified by pronouncing them more or less as in English; the exceptions are listed below. Double consonants **ll**, **tt** and **dd** aren't pronounced as one letter as in English, but are instead lengthened so you can almost hear them as separate letters. Also, **cs**, **zs**, **gy** and **sz** (consonant clusters) are separate letters in Hungarian and appear that way in telephone books and other alphabetical listings. For example, the word *cukor* (sugar) appears in the dictionary before *csak* (only).

c	as the 'ts' in 'hats'
cs	as the 'ch' in 'church'
gy	as the 'j' in 'jury'
j	as the 'y' in 'yes'
ly	as the 'y' in 'yes'
ny	as the 'ni' in 'onion'
r	like a slightly trilled Scottish 'r'
s	as the 'sh' in 'ship'
sz	as the 's' in 'set'
ty	as the 'tu' in British English 'tube'
w	as 'v' (found in foreign words only)
zs	as the 's' in 'pleasure'

Vowels are a bit trickier, and the semantic difference between **a**, **e** or **o** with and without an accent mark is great. For example, *hát* means 'back' while *hat* means 'six'.

a	as the 'o' in hot
á	as in 'father'
e	short, as in 'set'
é	as the 'e' in 'they' with no 'y' sound
i	as in 'hit' but shorter
í	as the 'i' in 'police'
o	as in 'open'
ó	a longer version of **o** above
ö	as the 'u' in 'burst' without the 'r' sound
ő	a longer version of **ö** above
u	as in 'pull'
ú	as the 'ue' in 'blue'

LANGUAGE

ü   similar to the 'u' in 'flute'; purse your
     lips tightly and say 'ee'
ű   a longer, breathier version of **ü**
     above

ACCOMMODATION

camping ground	kemping
guest house	fogadót
hotel	szálloda
private room	fizetővendég szoba
single/double room	egyágyas/kétágyas szoba
youth hostel	ifjúsági szálló

Do you have rooms available?	Van szabad szobájuk?
How much is it per night/person?	Mennyibe kerül éjszakánként/személyenként?
Does it include breakfast?	Az ár tartalmazza a reggelit?

CONVERSATION & ESSENTIALS

Hello.	Szia/Szervusz. (inf/pol)
Good afternoon/day.	Jó napot kívánok. (pol)
See you later.	Viszontlátásra.
Goodbye.	Szia/Szervusz. (inf/pol)
Yes.	Igen.
No.	Nem.
Please.	Kérem.
Thank you.	Köszönöm.
Sorry.	Sajnálom.
Excuse me.	Bocsánat. (to get past)
	Elnézést. (to get attention)
What's your name?	Hogy hívják? (pol)
	Mi a neved? (inf)
My name is ...	A nevem ...
I don't understand.	Nem értem.
Do you speak English?	Beszél angolul?
What's it called?	Hogy hívják?

SHOPPING & SERVICES

Where is ...?	Hol van ...?
a bank	bank
a chemist	gyógyszertár
the market	a piac
the museum	a múzeum
the post office	a posta
a tourist office	idegenforgalmi iroda

How much is it?	Mennyibe kerül?
What time does it open?	Mikor nyit ki?
What time does it close?	Mikor zár be?

EMERGENCIES – HUNGARIAN	
Help!	Segítség!
Call a doctor!	Hívjon egy orvost!
Call an ambulance!	Hívja a mentőket!
Call the police!	Hívja a rendőrséget!
Go away!	Menjen el!
I'm lost.	Eltévedtem.

TIME, DAYS & NUMBERS

What time is it?	Hány óra?
today	ma
tonight	ma este
tomorrow	holnap
in the morning	reggel
in the evening	este

Monday	hétfő
Tuesday	kedd
Wednesday	szerda
Thursday	csütörtök
Friday	péntek
Saturday	szombat
Sunday	vasárnap

1	egy
2	kettő
3	három
4	négy
5	öt
6	hat
7	hét
8	nyolc
9	kilenc
10	tíz
100	száz
1000	ezer

TRANSPORT

What time does the ... leave/arrive?	Mikor indul/érkezik a ...?
boat/ferry	hajó/komp
city bus	helyi autóbusz
intercity bus	távolsági autóbusz
plane	repülőgép
train	vonat
tram	villamos

Where is ...?	Hol van ...?
the bus stop	az autóbuszmegálló
the station	a pályaudvar
the left-luggage office	a csomagmegőrző

SIGNS – HUNGARIAN

Bejárat	Entrance
Kijárat	Exit
Információ	Information
Nyitva	Open
Zárva	Closed
Tilos	Prohibited
Rendőrőr- Kapitányság	Police Station
Toalett/WC	Toilets
Férfiak	Men
Nők	Women

arrival	*érkezés*
departure	*indulás*
timetable	*menetrend*

DIRECTIONS

(Turn) left.	*(Forduljon) balra.*
(Turn) right.	*(Forduljon) jobbra.*
(Go) straight ahead.	*(Menyen) egyenesen elore.*
Please show me on the map.	*Kérem, mutassa meg a térképen.*
near/far	*közel/messze*

LATVIAN

ALPHABET & PRONUNCIATION

The letters of the Latvian alphabet: a, b, c, č, d, e, f, g, ģ, h, i, j, k, ķ, l, ļ, m, n, ņ, o, p, r, s, š, t, u, v, z, ž.

ā	as the 'a' in 'barn'
ai	as in 'aisle'
c	as the 'ts' in 'bits'
č	as the 'ch' in 'church'
ē	as the 'e' in 'where'
ei	as in 'vein'
ģ	as the 'j' in 'jet'
ī	as the 'i' in 'marine'
ie	as in 'pier'
j	as the 'y' in 'yes'
ķ	as the 'tu' in 'tune'
ļ	as the 'lli' in 'billiards'
ņ	as the 'ni' in 'onion'
o	as the 'a' in 'water'
š	as the 'sh' in 'ship'
ū	as the 'oo' in 'boot'
ž	as the 's' in 'pleasure'

CONVERSATION & ESSENTIALS

Hello.	*Labdien/Sveiki.*
Goodbye.	*Uz redzēšanos/Atā.*

EMERGENCIES – LATVIAN

Help!	*Palīgā!*
I'm ill.	*Es esmu slims/slima.* (m/f)
I'm lost.	*Es esmu apmaldījies/ apmaldījusies.* (m/f)
Go away!	*Ejiet projam!*
Call ...!	*Izsauciet ...!*
a doctor	*ārstu*
an ambulance	*ātro palīdzību*
the police	*policiju*

Yes.	*Jā.*
No.	*Nē.*
Excuse me.	*Atvainojiet.*
Please.	*Lūdzu.*
Thank you.	*Paldies.*
Do you speak English?	*Vai jūs runājat angliski?*

SHOPPING & SERVICES

bank	*banka*
chemist	*aptieka*
currency exchange	*valūtas maiņa*
hotel	*viesnīca*
market	*tirgus*
post office	*pasts*
toilet	*tualete*

Where?	*Kur?*
How much?	*Cik?*

TIME, DAYS & NUMBERS

today	*šodien*
tomorrow	*rīt*
yesterday	*vakar*
Monday	*pirmdiena*
Tuesday	*otrdiena*
Wednesday	*trešdiena*
Thursday	*ceturtdiena*
Friday	*piektdiena*
Saturday	*sestdiena*
Sunday	*svētdiena*
1	*viens*
2	*divi*
3	*trīs*
4	*četri*
5	*pieci*
6	*seši*
7	*septiņi*
8	*astoņi*
9	*deviņi*

10	desmit
100	simts
1000	tūkstots

TRANSPORT

airport	lidosta
arrival time	pienākšanas laiks
bus	autobuss
bus station	autoosta
departure time	atiešanas laiks
port	osta
stop (eg bus stop)	pietura
taxi	taksometrs
ticket	biļete
ticket office	kase
train	vilciens
train station	dzelzceļa stacija
tram	tramvajs

LITHUANIAN

ALPHABET & PRONUNCIATION

The letters of the Lithuanian alphabet: **a, b, c, č, d, e, f, g, h, i/y, j, k, l, m, n, o, p, r, s, š, t, u, v, z, ž**. In some circumstances the **i** and **y** are interchangeable.

c	as 'ts'
č	as 'ch'
ei	as the 'ai' in 'pain'
ie	as the 'ye' in 'yet'
j	as the 'y' in 'yes'
š	as 'sh'
ui	as the 'wi' in 'win'
y	between the 'i' in 'tin' and the 'ee' in 'feet'
ž	as the 's' in 'pleasure'

Accent marks above and below vowels (eg **ā, ė** and **į**) all have the general effect of lengthening the vowel:

ā	as the 'a' in 'father'
ę	as the 'e' in 'there'
ė	as the 'e' in 'they'
į	as the 'ee' in 'feet'
ų	as the 'oo' in 'boot'
ū	as the 'oo' in 'boot'

CONVERSATION & ESSENTIALS

Hello.	Labas/Sveikas.
Goodbye.	Sudie/Viso gero.
Yes.	Taip.
No.	Ne.
Excuse me.	Atsiprašau.
Please.	Prašau.
Thank you.	Ačiū.
Do you speak English?	Ar kalbate angliškai?

SHOPPING & SERVICES

bank	bankas
chemist	vaistinė
currency exchange	valiutos keitykla
hotel	viešbutis
market	turgus
post office	paštas
toilet	tualetas
Where?	Kur?
How much?	Kiek?

TIMES, DAYS & NUMBERS

today	šiandien
tomorrow	rytoj
Monday	pirmadienis
Tuesday	antradienis
Wednesday	trečiadienis
Thursday	ketvirtadienis
Friday	penktadienis
Saturday	šeštadienis
Sunday	sekmadienis
1	vienas
2	du

<table>
<tr><td colspan="2">SIGNS – LITHUANIAN</td></tr>
<tr><td>Įėjimas</td><td>Entrance</td></tr>
<tr><td>Išėjimas</td><td>Exit</td></tr>
<tr><td>Informacija</td><td>Information</td></tr>
<tr><td>Atidara</td><td>Open</td></tr>
<tr><td>Uždara</td><td>Closed</td></tr>
<tr><td>Nerūkoma</td><td>No Smoking</td></tr>
<tr><td>Patogumai</td><td>Public Toilets</td></tr>
</table>

3	*trys*
4	*keturi*
5	*penki*
6	*šeši*
7	*septyni*
8	*aštuoni*
9	*devyni*
10	*dešimt*
100	*šimtas*
1000	*tūkstantis*

TRANSPORT

airport	*oro uostas*
arrival time	*atvykimo laikas*
bus	*autobusas*
bus station	*autobusų stotis*
departure time	*išvykimo laikas*
port	*uostas*
stop (eg bus stop)	*stotelė*
taxi	*taksi*
ticket	*bilietas*
ticket office	*kasa*
train	*traukinys*
train station	*geležinkelio stotis*
tram	*tramvajus*

MACEDONIAN

There are 31 letters in the Macedonian Cyrillic alphabet and it's well worth familiarising yourself with it (see p1009). Stress usually falls on the third syllable from the end in words with three syllables or more. If the word has only two syllables, the first is usually stressed. There are exceptions, such as new borrowings and other foreign loan words – eg литература is 'li·te·ra·*tu*·ra', not 'li·te·*ra*·tu·ra' (literature).

ACCOMMODATION
camping ground
кампинг — *kamping*
guest house
приватно сметување — *privatno smetuvanje*

hotel
хотел — *hotel*
youth hostel
младинско преноќиште — *mladinsko prenočište*

a double room
соба со брачен кревет
soba so bračen krevet
a single room
соьа со еден кревет
soba so eden krevet
for one/two nights
за една/два вечери
za edna/dva večeri

Do you have any rooms available?
Дали имате слободни соби?
dali imate slobodni sobi?
How much is it per night/per person?
Која е цената по ноќ/по особа?
koja e cenata po noč/po osoba?
Does it include breakfast?
Дали е вклучен ројадок?
dali e vključen pojadok?

CONVERSATION & ESSENTIALS
Hello.
Здраво. — *zdravo*
Goodbye.
Приатно. — *priatno*
Yes.
Да. — *da*
No.
Не. — *ne*
Excuse me.
Извинете. — *izvinete*
Please.
Молам. — *molam*
Thank you.
Благодарам. — *blagodaram*
You're welcome.
Нема зошто/ — *nema zošto/*
Мило ми е. — *milo mi e*
Sorry.
Опростете ве молам. — *oprostete ve molam*
Do you speak English?
Зборувате ли англиски? — *zboruvate li angliski?*
What's your name?
Како се викате? — *kako se vikate?*
My name is ...
Јас се викам ... — *jas se vikam ...*

EMERGENCIES – MACEDONIAN

Help!
Помош! *pomoš!*
Call a doctor!
Повикајте лекар! *povikajte lekar!*
Call the police!
Викнете полиција! *viknete policija!*
Go away!
Одете си! *odete si!*
I'm lost.
Јас загинав. *jas zaginav.*

SIGNS – MACEDONIAN

Влез	Entrance
Излез	Exit
Отворено	Open
Затворено	Closed
Информации	Information
Полиција	Police
Полициска Станица	Police Station
Забането	Prohibited
Клозети	Toilets
Машки	Men
Женски	Women

SHOPPING & SERVICES

bank
банка *banka*
chemist/pharmacy
аптека *apteka*
embassy
амбасада *ambasada*
market
пазар *pazar*
newsagency
киоск за весници *kiosk za vesnici*
post office
пошта *pošta*
stationers
книжарница *knižarnica*
telephone centre
телефонска *telefonska*
централа *centrala*
tourist office
туристичко биро *turističko biro*

How much is it?
Колку чини тоа?
kolku čini toa?
What time does it open/close?
Кога се отвора/затвора?
koga se otvora/zatvora?

TIME, DAYS & NUMBERS

What time is it?	Колку е часот?	*kolku e časot?*
today	денес	*denes*
tomorrow	утре	*utre*
morning	утро	*utro*
afternoon	попладне	*popladne*
Monday	понеделник	*ponedelnik*
Tuesday	вторник	*vtornik*
Wednesday	среда	*sreda*
Thursday	четврток	*četvrtok*
Friday	петок	*petok*
Saturday	сабота	*sabota*
Sunday	недела	*nedela*

1	еден	*eden*
2	два	*dva*
3	три	*tri*
4	четири	*četiri*
5	пет	*pet*
6	шест	*šest*
7	седум	*sedum*
8	осум	*osum*
9	девет	*devet*
10	десет	*deset*
100	сто	*sto*
1000	илада	*ilada*

TRANSPORT

**What time does the next
... leave/arrive?**
Кога доаѓа/заминува идниот ...?
koga doagja/zaminuva idniot ...?
boat
брод *brod*
city bus
автобус градски *avtobus gradski*
intercity bus
автобус меѓуградски *avtobus megjugradski*
train
воз *voz*
tram
трамвај *tramvaj*

bus stop
автобуска станица *avtobuska stanica*
timetable
возен ред *vozen red*
train station
железничка станица *zheleznička stanica*

I'd like ...
Сакам ...
sakam ...
1st class
прва класа *prva klasa*

2nd class
втора класа   *vtora klasa*
a one-way ticket
билет во еден правец   *bilet vo eden pravec*
a return ticket
повратен билет   *povraten bilet*

I'd like to hire a car/bicycle.
Сакам да изнајмам кола/точак.
sakam da iznajmam kola/točak

DIRECTIONS
Where is ...?
Каде је ...?   *kade je ...?*
Go straight ahead.
Одете право напред.   *odete pravo napred*
Turn left/right.
Свртете лево/десно.   *svrtete levo/desno*
near/far
блиску/далеку   *blisku/daleku*

POLISH

PRONUNCIATION
Written Polish is phonetically consistent, which means that the pronunciation of letters or clusters of letters doesn't vary from word to word. The stress almost always falls on the second-last syllable.

Vowels
a	as the 'u' in 'cut'
e	as in 'ten'
i	similar to the 'ee' in 'feet' but shorter
o	as in 'lot'
u	a bit shorter than the 'oo' in 'book'
y	similar to the 'i' in 'bit'

There are three vowels unique to Polish:

ą	a nasal vowel sound like the French *un*, similar to 'own' in 'sown'
ę	also nasalised, like the French *un*, but pronounced as 'e' in 'ten' when word-final
ó	similar to Polish **u**

Consonants
In Polish, the consonants **b**, **d**, **f**, **k**, **l**, **m**, **n**, **p**, **t**, **v** and **z** are pronounced more or less as they are in English. The following consonants and clusters of consonants sound very different to their English counterparts:

c	as the 'ts' in 'its'
ch	similar to the 'ch' in the Scottish 'loch'
cz	as the 'ch' in 'church'
ć	much softer than Polish **c** (as 'tsi' before vowels)
dz	similar to the 'ds' in 'suds' but shorter
dź	as **dz** but softer (as 'dzi' before vowels)
dż	as the 'j' in 'jam'
g	as in 'get'
h	as **ch**
j	as the 'y' in 'yet'
ł	as the 'w' in 'wine'
ń	as the 'ny' in 'canyon' (as 'nee' before vowels)
r	always trilled
rz	as the 's' in 'pleasure'
s	as in 'set'
sz	as the 'sh' in 'show'
ś	as **s** but softer (as 'si' before vowels)
w	as the 'v' in 'van'
ź	softer version of **z** (as 'zi' before vowels)
ż	as **rz**

ACCOMMODATION
camping ground	*kemping*
hotel	*hotel*
youth hostel	*schronisko młodzieżowe*

Do you have any rooms available?	*Czy są wolne pokoje?*
Does it include breakfast?	*Czy śniadanie jest wliczone?*

double room	*pokój dwuosobowy*
private room	*kwatera prywatna*
single room	*pokój jednoosobowy*

CONVERSATION & ESSENTIALS
Hello.	*Cześć.* (inf)
Hello/Good morning.	*Dzień dobry.* (pol)
Goodbye.	*Do widzenia.*
Yes/No.	*Tak/Nie.*
Please.	*Proszę.*

Thank you.	Dziękuję.
Excuse me/Sorry.	Przepraszam.
I don't understand.	Nie rozumiem.
What's it called?	Jak to się nazywa?

SHOPPING & SERVICES

bank	bank
chemist	apteka
church	kościół
city centre	centrum miasta
market	targ/bazar
museum	muzeum
post office	poczta
tourist office	informacja turystyczna

| How much is it? | Ile to kosztuje? |
| What time does it open/close? | O której otwierają/zamykają? |

TIME, DAYS & NUMBERS

What time is it?	Która jest godzina?
today	dzisiaj
tonight	dzisiaj wieczorem
tomorrow	jutro
in the morning	rano
in the evening	wieczorem

Monday	poniedziałek
Tuesday	wtorek
Wednesday	środa
Thursday	czwartek
Friday	piątek
Saturday	sobota
Sunday	niedziela

1	jeden
2	dwa
3	trzy
4	cztery
5	pięć
6	sześć
7	siedem
8	osiem
9	dziewięć
10	dziesięć
100	sto
1000	tysiąc

TRANSPORT

What time does the ... leave/arrive?	O której godzinie przychodzi/odchodzi ...?
boat	statek
bus	autobus
plane	samolot
train	pociąg
tram	tramwaj

SIGNS – POLISH	
Wejście	Entrance
Wyjście	Exit
Informacja	Information
Otwarte	Open
Zamknięte	Closed
Wzbroniony	Prohibited
Posterunek Policji	Police Station
Toalety	Toilets
Panowie	Men
Panie	Women

arrival	przyjazd
departure	odjazd
timetable	rozkład jazdy

Where is the bus stop?	Gdzie jest przystanek autobusowy?
Where is the station?	Gdzie jest stacja kolejowa?
Where is the left-luggage office?	Gdzie jest przechowalnia bagażu?

DIRECTIONS

left	lewo
right	prawo
straight ahead	prosto
Please show me on the map.	Proszę pokazać mi to na mapie.

ROMANIAN

PRONUNCIATION

Until the mid-19th century, Romanian was written in the Cyrillic alphabet. Today Romanian employs 28 Latin letters, some of which bear accents. At the beginning of a word, e and i are pronounced 'ye' and 'yi', while at the end of a word i is virtually silent. At the end of a word ii is pronounced 'ee'. Word stress is usually on the second last syllable.

| ă | as the 'a' in 'ago' |
| î | as the 'i' in 'river' |

c	as 'k', except before e and i, when it's as the 'ch' in 'chip'
ch	always as the 'k' in 'king'
g	as in 'go', except before e and i, when it's as in 'gentle'
gh	always as the 'g' in 'get'
ş	as 'sh'
ţ	as the 'tz' in 'tzar'

ACCOMMODATION

camping ground	camping
double room	o cameră pentru două persoane
guest house	casa de oaspeţi
hotel	hotel
private room	cameră particulară
single room	o cameră pentru o persoană
youth hostel	camin studentesc

Do you have any rooms available?	Aveţi camere libere?
How much is it?	Cît costă?
Does it include breakfast?	Include micul dejun?

CONVERSATION & ESSENTIALS

Hello.	Bună.
Goodbye.	La revedere.
Yes.	Da.
No.	Nu.
Please.	Vă rog.
Thank you.	Mulţumesc.
Sorry.	Iertaţi-mă.
Excuse me.	Scuzaţi-mă.
I don't understand.	Nu înţeleg.
What's it called?	Cum se cheamă?

SHOPPING & SERVICES

| How much is it? | Cît costă? |

bank	banca
chemist	farmacistul
city centre	centrum oraşului
the ... embassy	ambasada ...
market	piaţa
museum	muzeu
post office	poşta
tourist office	birou de informatii turistice

TIME, DAYS & NUMBERS

What time is it?	Ce oră este?
today	azi
tonight	deseară
tomorrow	mîine
in the morning	dimineaţa
in the evening	seară

Monday	luni
Tuesday	marţi
Wednesday	miercuri
Thursday	joi
Friday	vineri
Saturday	sîmbătă
Sunday	duminică

1	unu
2	doi
3	trei
4	patru
5	cinci
6	şase
7	şapte
8	opt
9	nouă
10	zece
100	o sută
1000	o mie

TRANSPORT

What time does the ... leave/arrive?	La ce oră pleacă/soseşte ...?
boat	vaporul
bus	autobusul
plane	avionul
train	trenul

Where is the bus stop?	Unde este staţia de autobuz?
Where is the station?	Unde este gară?
Where is the left-luggage office?	Unde este biroul pentru bagaje de mînă?

arrival	sosire
departure	plecare
timetable	mersul/orar

DIRECTIONS

left	stînga
right	dreapta
straight ahead	drept înainte
Please show me on the map.	Vă rog arătaţi-mi pe hartă.

LANGUAGE

RUSSIAN

THE CYRILLIC ALPHABET

The Russian Cyrillic alphabet, with Roman-letter equivalents and common pronunci-ations, is shown on the chart, opposite.

PRONUNCIATION

The sounds of **a**, **o**, **e** and **я** are 'weaker' when the stress in the word does not fall on them; eg in вода (*voda*, water) the stress falls on the second syllable, so it's pro-nounced 'va-DA'. The vowel **й** only follows other vowels in so-called diphthongs, eg **ой** 'oy', **ей** 'ey/yey'. Russians usually print **ё** without the dots, a source of confusion in pronunciation.

The 'voiced' consonants **б**, **в**, **г**, **д**, **ж** and **з** are not voiced at the end of words or be-fore voiceless consonants. For example, хлеб (*hleb*, bread) is pronounced 'khlyep'. The **г** in the common adjective endings '-ero' and '-oro' is pronounced 'v'.

ACCOMMODATION

breakfast	завтрак	*zaftrak*
hotel	гостиница	*gastinitsa*
room	номер	*nomer*

How much is a room?
Сколько стоит номер? *skol'ka stoit nomer?*

CONVERSATION & ESSENTIALS

Hello.
Здравствуйте. *zdrastvuyte*
Good morning.
Доброе утро. *dobraye utra*
Good afternoon.
Добрый день. *dobryy den'*
Good evening.
Добрый вечер. *dobryy vecher*
Goodbye.
До свидания. (pol) *da svidaniya*
Bye!
Пока! (inf) *paka!*
How are you?
Как дела? *kak dila?*
Yes.
Да. *dat*
No.
Нет. *net*
Please.
Пожалуйста. *pazhalsta*
Thank you (very much).
(Большое) спасибо. *(bal'shoye) spasiba*

Pardon me.
Простите/Пожалуйста. *prastite/pazhalsta*
No problem/Never mind. (literally, 'nothing')
Ничего. *nichevo*
Do you speak English?
Вы говорите *vy gavarite*
   по-английски? *pa angliyski?*
What's your name?
Как вас зовут? *kak vas zavut?*
My name is ...
Меня зовут ... *minya zavut ...*

SHOPPING & SERVICES

How much is it?
Сколько стоит? *skol'ka stoit?*
bank
банк *bank*
market
рынок *rynak*
pharmacy
аптека *apteka*
post office
почтам *pochta*
telephone booth
телефонная будка *tilifonnaya budka*

TIME, DAYS & NUMBERS

What time is it?
Который час? *katoryy chas?*
today
сегодня *sivodnya*
tomorrow
завтра *zaftra*
am/in the morning
утра *utra*
pm/in the afternoon
дня *dnya*
in the evening
вечера *vechira*

THE CYRILLIC ALPHABET

CYRILLIC	ROMAN	PRONUNCIATION
А а	a	as in 'father'; also as in 'ago' when unstressed in Russian
Б б	b	as in 'but'
В в	v	as in 'van'
Г г	g	as in 'go'
Ѓ ѓ	gj	as the 'gu' in 'legume' (Macedonian only)
Д д	d	as the 'd' in 'dog'
Е е	ye	as in 'yet' when stressed; as in 'year' when unstressed (Russian)
	e	as in 'bet' (Bulgarian); as in 'there' (Macedonian)
Ё ё	yo	as in 'yore' (Russian only)
Ж ж	zh	as the 's' in 'measure'
З з	z	as in 'zoo'
Ѕ ѕ	zj	as the 'ds' in 'suds' (Macedonian only)
И и	i	as the 'ee' in 'meet'
Й й	y	as in 'boy'
Ј ј	j	as the 'y' in 'young' (Macedonian only)
К к	k	as in 'kind'
Ќ ќ	kj	as the 'cu' in 'cure' (Macedonian only)
Л л	l	as in 'lamp'
Љ љ	lj	as the 'lli' in 'million' (Macedonian only)
М м	m	as in 'mat'
Н н	n	as in 'not'
Њ њ	nj	as the 'ny' in 'canyon' (Macedonian only)

CYRILLIC	ROMAN	PRONUNCIATION
О о	o	as the 'a' in 'water' when stressed; as the 'a' in 'ago' when unstressed (Russian); as in 'hot' (Bulgarian & Macedonian)
П п	p	as in 'pick'
Р р	r	as in 'rub' (but rolled)
С с	s	as in 'sing'
Т т	t	as in 'ten'
У у	u	as in 'rule'
Ф ф	f	as in 'fan'
Х х	kh	as the 'ch' in 'Bach' (Russian)
	h	as in 'hot' (Macedonian)
Ц ц	ts	as in 'bits'
Џ џ	dz	as the 'j' in 'judge' (Macedonian only)
Ч ч	ch	as in 'chat'
Ш ш	sh	as in 'shop'
Щ щ	shch	as 'shch' in 'fresh chips' (Russian)
	sht	as the '-shed' in pushed' (Bulgarian)
Ъ ъ	â	as the 'a' in 'ago' (Bulgarian only)
ъ		'hard' sign (Russian only)
Ы ы	y	as the 'i' in 'ill' (Russian only)
ь		'soft' sign (Russian only)
Э э	e	as in 'end' (Russian only)
Ю ю	yu	as the word 'you'
Я я	ya	as in 'yard

1	один	adin
2	два	dva
3	три	tri
4	четыре	chityri
5	пять	pyat'
6	шесть	shest'
7	семь	sem'
8	восемь	vosim'
9	девять	devit'
10	десять	desit'
100	сто	sto
1000	тысяча	tysyacha

TRANSPORT

What time does the ... arrive/leave?

В котором часу отправляется/прибывает ...?
f katoram chasu atpravlyaetsa/pribyvaet ...?

bus
автобус · *aftobus*

fixed-route minibus
маршрутное такси · *marshrutnaye taksi*

steamship
пароход · *parakhot*

train
поезд · *poyezt*

tram
трамвай · *tramvay*

hard/2nd-class (compartment)
купейный · *kupeyny*

one-way ticket
билет в один конец · *bilet v adin kanets*

pier/quay
причал/пристань · *prichal/pristan'*

SIGNS – RUSSIAN

Вход	Entrance
Выход	Exit
Открыто	Open
Закрыто	Closed
Справки	Information
Касса	Ticket Office
Больница	Hospital
Милиция	Police
Туалет	Toilets
Мужской (М)	Men
Женский (Ж)	Women

c as the 'ts' in 'its'
č as the 'ch' in 'church'
dz as the 'ds' in 'suds'
dž as the 'j' in 'judge'
ia as the 'yo' in 'yonder'
ie as the 'ye' in 'yes'
iu as the word 'you'
j as the 'y' in 'yet'
ň as the 'ni' in 'onion'
ô as the 'wo' in 'won't'
ou as the 'ow' in 'know'
š as the 'sh' in 'show'
y as the 'i' in 'machine'
ž as the 'z' in 'azure'

reserved-place/3rd-class (carriage)
плацкартный — *platskartny*
return ticket
билет в оба конца — *bilet v oba kantsa*
soft/1st-class (compartment)
мягкий — *myahkiy*
stop (bus/trolleybus/tram)
остановка — *astanofka*
train station
железно дорожный — *zhilezna darozhnyy*
(ж. д.) вокзал — *vagzal*
two tickets
два билета — *dva bilety*

DIRECTIONS
Where is ...?
Где ...? — *gde ...?*
straight on
прямо — *pryama*
to/on the left
налево — *naleva*
to/on the right
направо — *naprava*

Can you show me (on the map)?
pakazhite mnye pazhalsta (na karte)
Покажите мне, пожалуйста (на карте).

SLOVAK

PRONUNCIATION
In Slovak words of three syllables or less the stress falls on the first syllable. Longer words generally also have a secondary accent on the third or fifth syllable. There are thirteen vowels (a, á, ä, e, é, i, í, o, ó, u, ú, y, ý), three semi-vowels (l, ĺ, r) and five diphthongs (ia, ie, iu, ou, ô). Letters and diphthongs that may be unfamiliar to native English speakers include the following:

ACCOMMODATION
camping ground	kemping
double room	dvojlôžková izba
guest house	penzión
hotel	hotel
private room	privat
single room	jednolôžková izba
youth hostel	mládežnícka ubytovňa

Do you have any rooms available? — *Máte voľné izby?*
How much is it? — *Koľko to stojí?*
Is breakfast included? — *Sú raňajky zahrnuté v cene?*

CONVERSATION & ESSENTIALS
Hello.	Ahoj.
Goodbye.	Dovidenia.
Yes.	Áno.
No.	Nie.
Please.	Prosím.
Thank you.	Ďakujem.
Excuse me.	Prepáčte mi.
I'm sorry.	Ospravedlňujem sa.
I don't understand.	Nerozumiem.
What's it called?	Ako sa do volá?

SHOPPING & SERVICES
How much is it?	Koľko to stojí?
bank	banka
chemist	lekárnik
church	kostol
city centre	centrum mesta
market	trh
museum	múzeum
post office	pošta
tourist office	turistické informačné centrum

TIME, DAYS & NUMBERS
What time is it?	Koľko je hodín?
today	dnes
tonight	dnes večer

EMERGENCIES – SLOVAK

Help!	*Pomoc!*
Call a doctor!	*Zavolajte doktora/lekára!*
Call an ambulance!	*Zavolajte záchranku!*
Call the police!	*Zavolajte políciu!*
Go away!	*Chod preč/*
	Chodte preč! (sg/pl)
I'm lost.	*Nevyznám sa tu.*

---

tomorrow	*zajtra*
in the morning	*ráno*
in the evening	*večer*

Monday	*pondelok*
Tuesday	*utorok*
Wednesday	*streda*
Thursday	*štvrtok*
Friday	*piatok*
Saturday	*sobota*
Sunday	*nedeľa*

1	*jeden*
2	*dva*
3	*tri*
4	*štyri*
5	*päť*
6	*šesť*
7	*sedem*
8	*osem*
9	*deväť*
10	*desať*
100	*sto*
1000	*tisíc*

TRANSPORT

What time does	*Kedy odchádza/prichádza ...?*
the ... leave/arrive?	
boat	*loč*
city bus	*mestský autobus*
intercity bus	*medzimestský autobus*
plane	*lietadlo*
train	*vlak*
tram	*električka*

arrival	*príchod*
departure	*odchod*
timetable	*cestovný poriadok*

Where's the bus stop?	*Kde je autobusová zastávka?*
Where's the station?	*Kde je vlaková stanica?*
Where's the left-	*Kde je úschovňa batožín?*
luggage office?	

SIGNS – SLOVAK

Vchod	Entrance
Východ	Exit
Informácie	Information
Otvorené	Open
Zatvorené	Closed
Zakázané	Prohibited
Polícia	Police Station
Telefón	Telephone
Záchody/WC/Toalety	Toilets

DIRECTIONS

left	*vľavo*
right	*vpravo*
straight ahead	*rovno*
Please show me on	*Prosím, ukážte mi to na mape.*
the map.	

SLOVENE

PRONUNCIATION

Slovene pronunciation isn't difficult. The alphabet consists of 25 letters, most of which are very similar to English. It doesn't have the letters 'q', 'w', 'x' and 'y', but you will find **ê**, **é**, **ó**, **ò**, **č**, **š** and **ž**. Each letter represents only one sound, with very few exceptions. At the end of syllables and before vowels, the letters **l** and **v** are both pronounced like the English 'w'. Though words like *trn* (thorn) look unpronounceable, most Slovene dialects add a short vowel like an 'a' or the German 'ö' in front of the **r** to give a Scot's pronunciation of 'tern' or 'tarn'. Here is a list of letters specific to Slovene:

c	as the 'ts' in 'its'
č	as the 'ch' in 'church'
ê	as the 'a' in 'apple'
e	as the 'a' in 'ago' (when unstressed)
é	as the 'ay' in 'day'
j	as the 'y' in 'yellow'
ó	as the 'o' in 'more'
ò	as the 'o' in 'soft'
r	a rolled 'r' sound
š	as the 'sh' in 'ship'
u	as the 'oo' in 'good'
ž	as the 's' in 'treasure'

ACCOMMODATION

camping ground	*kamping*
guest house	*gostišče*
hotel	*hotel*

EMERGENCIES – SLOVENE

Help!	*Na pomoč!*
Call a doctor!	*Pokličite zdravnika!*
Call the police!	*Pokličite policijo!*
Go away!	*Pojdite stran!*

Do you have a ...?	*Ali imate prosto ...?*
bed	*posteljo*
cheap room	*poceni sobo*
double room	*dvoposteljno sobo*
single room	*enoposteljno sobo*

How much is it ...?	*Koliko stane ...?*
for one/two nights	*za eno noč/za dve noči*
per night/person	*za eno noč/osebo*

Is breakfast included?	*Ali je zajtrk vključen?*

CONVERSATION & ESSENTIALS

Hello.	*Pozdravljeni.* (pol)
	Zdravo/Živio. (inf)
Good day.	*Dober dan!*
Goodbye.	*Nasvidenje!*
Yes.	*Da/Ja.* (pol/inf)
No.	*Ne.*
Please.	*Prosim.*
Thank you (very much).	*Hvala (lepa).*
You're welcome.	*Prosim/Ni za kaj!*
Excuse me.	*Oprostite.*
What's your name?	*Kako vam je ime?*
My name is ...	*Jaz sem ...*
Where are you from?	*Od kod ste?*
I'm from ...	*Sem iz ...*

SHOPPING & SERVICES

Where is the/a ...?	*Kje je ...?*
bank/exchange	*banka/menjalnica*
consulate/embassy	*konzulat/ambasada*
post office	*pošta*
telephone centre	*telefonska centrala*
tourist office	*turistični informacijski urad*

TIME, DAYS & NUMBERS

Monday	*ponedeljek*
Tuesday	*torek*
Wednesday	*sreda*
Thursday	*četrtek*
Friday	*petek*
Saturday	*sobota*
Sunday	*nedelja*

in the morning	*zjutraj*
in the evening	*zvečer*

today	*danes*
tonight	*nocoj*
tomorrow	*jutri*

1	*ena*
2	*dve*
3	*tri*
4	*štiri*
5	*pet*
6	*šest*
7	*sedem*
8	*osem*
9	*devet*
10	*deset*

UKRAINIAN

Because of Ukraine's history of domination by outside powers, the language was often considered inferior or subservient to the dominant languages of the time – Russian in the east, Polish in the west. Today, the Ukrainian language is slowly being revived, and in 1990 it was adopted as the official language. Russian is understood everywhere by everyone, and it still remains the principal language travellers will need.

Alphabet & Pronunciation

Around 70% of the Ukrainian language is identical or similar to Russian and Belarusian. The Cyrillic alphabet chart (p1009) covers the majority of letters used in the Ukrainian alphabet. Ukrainian has three additional letters not found in Russian, **i**, **ï**, and **є**, all of which are neutral vowel sounds (the Russian letter **o** is often replaced by a Ukrainian **i**). The Ukrainian **г** usually has a soft 'h' sound. The Ukrainian alphabet doesn't include the Russian letters **ё**, **ы** and **э**, and has no hard sign, **ъ**, although it does include the soft sign, **ь**. These differences between the two languages are sometimes quite simple in practice: for example, the town of Chernigov in Russian is Chernihiv in Ukrainian. Overall, Ukrainian is softer sounding and less guttural than Russian.

The **-я** *(-ya)* ending for nouns and names in Russian (especially in street names) is dropped in Ukrainian, and the letter **и** is transliterated as *y* in Ukrainian, whereas in Russian it's transliterated as *i*, eg a street named *Deribasovskaya* in Russian would be *Derybasivska* in Ukrainian.

| 100 | sto |
| 1000 | tisoč |

TRANSPORT
What time does ...   *Kdaj odpelje/pripelje ...?*
the leave/arrive?
   boat/ferry   *ladja/trajekt*
   bus   *avtobus*
   train   *vlak*

bus station	*avtobusno postajališče*
one-way (ticket)	*enosmerna (vozovnica)*
return (ticket)	*povratna (vozovnica)*
timetable	*spored*
train station	*železniška postaja*

SIGNS – SLOVENE

Vhod	Entrance
Izhod	Exit
Informacije	Information
Odprto	Open
Zaprto	Closed
Prepovedano	Prohibited
Stranišče	Toilets

DIRECTIONS
left	*levo*
right	*desno*
straight ahead	*naravnost naprej*
Can you show me	*A mi lahko*
on the map?	*pokažete na mapi?*

LANGUAGE

The Authors

MARA VORHEES
Coordinating Author

It was 1988 when Mara took her first trip to Eastern Europe, riding a bus from Helsinki to Leningrad, then ditching her tour group for friendly black marketeers. She has since travelled throughout the region, acting as au pair in Ukraine, bussing through the Baltics, journeying by train across Russia and drifting down the Danube. Her first assignment for Lonely Planet was the 6th edition of this very book, and she authored the *Moscow City Guide, St Petersburg City Guide* and *Russia*. When not in the east, she lives in a pink house in Somerville, Massachusetts. Follow her adventures at www.maravorhees.com. Mara wrote Destination Eastern Europe, Getting Started, Itineraries, Regions within the Region, Regional Directory and Transport in Eastern Europe.

BRETT ATKINSON
Czech Republic

Brett has been travelling to Eastern Europe for more than 20 years, and has honeymooned in Slovenia and Bosnia, written about Hungary's communist past, and island-hopped in Croatia. On his second extended research trip to the Czech Republic, he attempted to really get off the beaten track, especially if this meant seeking out interesting out-of-the-way microbreweries. When he's not on the road for Lonely Planet, Brett lives with Carol in Auckland, New Zealand. Fortunately his local microbrew emporium produces a damn fine Bohemian pilsner, ensuring the world's best beer is never far away.

CAROLYN BAIN
Estonia

Melbourne-born Carolyn got her first glimpse behind the Iron Curtain in Poland in early 1989, while she was a student in Denmark. It was the year communism unravelled throughout Eastern Europe, and thus began her fascination. In 1991, while studying Russian and politics at university, she was overjoyed when her Soviet Politics class had to change its name to the Soviet Union and Beyond. Since then she has applauded the renewed independence and flourishing creativity of the Baltic countries on regular visits to the region. She has covered Sweden and Denmark for Lonely Planet, but Estonia holds a special place in her heart for combining the best of Eastern Europe and Scandinavia into something heartwarmingly unique.

LONELY PLANET AUTHORS

Why is our travel information the best in the world? It's simple: our authors are passionate, dedicated travellers. They don't take freebies in exchange for positive coverage so you can be sure the advice you're given is impartial. They travel widely to all the popular spots, and off the beaten track. They don't research using just the internet or phone. They discover new places not included in any other guidebook. They personally visit thousands of hotels, restaurants, palaces, trails, galleries, temples and more. They speak with dozens of locals every day to make sure you get the kind of insider knowledge only a local could tell you. They take pride in getting all the details right, and in telling it how it is. Think you can do it? Find out how at **lonelyplanet.com**.

THE AUTHORS

NEAL BEDFORD   Hungary, Lithuania

A trip to the northeastern corner of Poland some summers ago saw Neal come into more contact with Lithuania than he'd expected. Many locals affiliated themselves with Vilnius rather than Warsaw, and whenever he read about Poland's history, up would pop that country just across the border. His interest sparked, he decided to explore Lithuania. He found paganism and Catholicism comfortably sleeping in the same bed; dense, mysterious forests and glistening lakes; sweeping sand dunes; and curious, friendly people (once you broke the ice). He also found some of the most challenging restaurant service he'd ever experienced. Neal has travelled through much of Eastern Europe from his base in Vienna, Austria.

JAYNE D'ARCY   Albania

Ever since she watched Celtic Tigers eat up and commercialise Irish culture in the mid-'90s, Jayne's been attracted to countries with more character and lower GDPs. Albania hit her radar in 2006, when she joined her first-ever package tour; although she complained about her fellow travellers, she was pretty stoked to get a new passport stamp and see some amazing ruins in relative peace. The changes in Albania since then are astonishing, but while the similarities to the 'old Ireland' are huge (homemade spirits, dodgy roads), the Albanian Tiger is yet to emerge. As well as writing about travel, Jayne produces features on design, people and the environment.

CHRIS DELISO   Macedonia

Chris Deliso's long experience of seductive Macedonia began a decade ago and, since 2002, has evolved to full-fledged residential status. As a travel writer and journalist, he has covered almost everything there is to cover here, but still delights in uncovering the country's many hidden places, which range from mountain wilds and ancient ruins shrouded by vineyards to rustic village eateries and secret lakeshore beaches. For Chris, researching the present guide involved off-roading in remote locales, swimming in four lakes and rivers, handling real ancient Macedonian gold, eating plenty of grilled meats, and sampling one superb wine after another in the Tikveš wine region. He has also cowritten Lonely Planet's *Greece*, *Bulgaria* and *Western Balkans* guides.

PETER DRAGICEVICH   Montenegro

After a dozen years working for newspapers and magazines in both his native New Zealand and Australia, Peter finally gave into Kiwi wanderlust, giving up staff jobs to chase his diverse ancestral roots around much of Europe. While it was family ties that first drew him to the Balkans, it's the history, natural beauty, convoluted politics, cheap *rakija* (fruit brandy) and, most importantly, the intriguing people that keep bringing him back. He's contributed to 12 Lonely Planet titles, including writing the Macedonia and Albania chapters for the previous edition of the *Eastern Europe* guide. He's just completed Lonely Planet's first guidebook to *Montenegro*.

LISA DUNFORD
Hungary, Slovakia

Lisa has been fascinated with Eastern Europe since childhood, probably because her grandfather came from a part of the Carpathian region that was Hungary, then Czechoslovakia and now Ukraine. She studied in Budapest during university, and after graduation worked at the US Agency for International Development in Bratislava. She learned the language, danced on the main square the night Slovakia became an independent nation, and made lifelong friends. Though she returns to Eastern Europe often, Lisa, her husband, and their dog currently call a riverfront in East Texas home.

MARK ELLIOTT
Bosnia & Hercegovina

British-born travel writer Mark Elliott was only 11 when his family first dragged him to Sarajevo and stood him in the now defunct concrete footsteps of Gavrilo Princip. Fortunately no Austro-Hungarian emperors were passing at the time. He has since visited virtually every corner of Bosnia and Hercegovina, supping Hercegovinian wines with master vintners, talking philosophy with Serb monks and Sufi mystics, and drinking more Bosnian coffee than any healthy stomach should be subjected to. When not travel writing he lives a blissfully quiet life in suburban Belgium with the lovely Danielle, who he met while jamming blues harmonica in a Turkmenistan club.

STEVE FALLON
Hungary, Slovenia

Steve has been travelling to Slovenia since the early 1990s, when a travel-publishing company initially refused his proposal to write a guidebook to the country because of 'the war going on' (it had ended two years before) and a US newspaper of record told him that their readers weren't interested in 'Slovakia'. Never mind, it was his own private Idaho for over a decade. Though he *still* hasn't reached the top of Mt Triglav (next time – *domen*, promise!), Steve considers at least part of his soul Slovenian and returns to the country as often as he can for a glimpse of the Julian Alps, a dribble of *bučno olje* (pumpkin-seed oil) and a dose of the dual.

VESNA MARIC
Croatia

Vesna was born in Bosnia and Hercegovina while it was still a part of Yugoslavia and, as a result, she has never been able to see Croatia as a foreign country. A lifelong lover of Dalmatia's beaches, pine trees, food and wine, she expanded her knowledge during this book by exploring Zadar and Zagreb, two cities she discovered anew. Researching Croatia was a true delight.

TOM MASTERS   Belarus, Ukraine

Tom enjoyed getting to grips with Belarus and Ukraine after years of passing through them on the way to Russia, where he has studied and worked on and off for more than a decade. His main surprise was how little Belarus lived up to its consistently negative portrayal in the press – the people were some of the friendliest he's ever met, and Minsk was a ball of pent-up positive energy. Travelling through Crimea in August was another unforgettable experience, although in future he'll avoid the crowds at Yalta and head immediately for romantic Bakhchysaray. Tom lives and works in London, and more of his work can be seen at www.mastersmafia.com.

MARIKA McADAM   Kosovo, Serbia

Marika is an Australian writer and lawyer currently based on the precipice of Eastern Europe in Vienna. Marika has explored Europe as far north as Sweden, as far west as Spain and as far south as Italy, but the further east she goes, the more at home she feels. Her memories of Serbia as being grim and grumpy were completely eclipsed on this research trip by experiences with fun and friendly Serbs, with whom she laughed about nothing and everything. And whatever its international status, resolutely determined and unfailingly hospitable Kosovo has marked her forever (literally – she burnt her arse in a jacuzzi).

LEIF PETTERSEN   Moldova, Romania

In 2003, after nine years of feigning interest in electronic payments for the US Federal Reserve System, Leif – originally from Minneapolis, Minnesota – was 'Kramered' into being a homeless, shameless, godless freelance travel writer by an unbalanced friend. Leif's weakness for pretty girls brought him in 2004 to Romania, where he's lived and travelled for nearly two cumulative years. He's repeatedly visited every notable patch of grass in Romania and Moldova, making priceless friends – except for Romania's neo-Nazi party, which publicly denounced him in 2008, calling him a 'slimeball' and 'human piece of garbage' (yes, really). Leif writes an almost award-winning, 'slightly caustic' blog, KillingBatteries.com.

BRANDON PRESSER   Latvia

With his wanderlust bigger than his wallet, Brandon earned his backpacker stripes after an epic overland adventure from Morocco to Finland. He was delighted to revisit Eastern Europe for the Latvia chapter, especially since he's got a bit of Baltic blood in him. After savouring several blissful beach days on the Kurzeme coast, Brandon put his Harvard art-history degree to good use while checking out Rīga's surplus of evocative art nouveau architecture. Brandon has contributed to a handful of Lonely Planet guides, including *Estonia, Latvia & Lithuania 5*, and when he's not writing his way across the globe he enjoys crossword puzzles, scuba diving and vintage Bond flicks – especially the ones with crafty KGB agents.

THE AUTHORS

ROBERT REID
Bulgaria

Brooklyn-based Robert (www.reidontravel.com) likes Bulgaria. He returned for the third time to update the chapter for *Eastern Europe*, and experienced thrilling, unexpected things – stumbling into Roman roads, being forced to do a Bulgarian traditional dance (and liking it), being cornered by sheep. He's written for Lonely Planet since 2003, and has updated over a dozen guidebooks, including *Romania & Moldova, Russia, Trans-Siberian Railway* and *New York City Guide*.

TIM RICHARDS
Hungary, Poland

Having transferred with an international teaching organisation from a two-year stint in Egypt, Tim spent a year teaching English in Kraków in 1994–95. He was fascinated by the massive postcommunist transition affecting every aspect of Polish life, and by the surviving remnants of the Cold War days. He's since returned to Poland repeatedly for Lonely Planet, and has been delighted by his reacquaintance with this beautiful, complex country. When he's not on the road for Lonely Planet, Tim is a freelance journalist living in Melbourne, Australia, and writes on various topics: travel, lifestyle, the arts, technology and pets. You can see more of his writing at www.iwriter.com.au.

SIMON RICHMOND
Russia

After studying Russian history and politics at university, Simon's first visit to the country was in 1994, when he wandered goggle-eyed around gorgeous St Petersburg, and peeked at Lenin's mummified corpse in Red Sq. He's since travelled the breadth of the nation, from Kamchatka in the far east to Kaliningrad in the far west, stopping off at many points between. An award-winning writer and photographer, Simon has written about Russia for several publications, including the Russian edition of *Newsweek*. He's the coauthor of the 1st and subsequent editions of Lonely Planet's *Trans-Siberian Railway*, as well as editions 3, 4 and 5 of *Russia*. Catch him online at www.simonrichmond.com.

THE AUTHORS

Behind the Scenes

THIS BOOK

Eastern Europe is part of Lonely Planet's Europe series, which also includes *Western Europe, Mediterranean Europe, Central Europe, Scandinavian Europe* and *Europe on a Shoestring*. Lonely Planet also publishes phrasebooks to these regions. This guidebook was commissioned in Lonely Planet's London office, and produced by the following:

Commissioning Editors Fiona Buchan, William Gourlay, Clifton Wilkinson

Coordinating Editors Susan Paterson, Laura Stansfeld

Coordinating Cartographer Csanad Csutoros

Coordinating Layout Designer Cara Smith

Managing Editor Imogen Bannister

Managing Cartographers Mark Griffiths, Herman So

Managing Layout Designers Laura Jane, Indra Kilfoyle

Assisting Editors Nigel Chin, Jessica Crouch, Chris Girdler, Carly Hall, Kim Hutchins, Amy Karafin, Helen Koehne, Rosie Nicholson, Sally O'Brien, Helen Yeates

Assisting Cartographers Fatima Basic, Barbara Benson, Owen Eszeki, Tony Fankhauser, Tadhgh Knaggs, Valentina Kremenchutskaya

Cover Designer Jane Hart

Colour Designer Vicki Beale

Project Manager Glenn van der Knijff

Language Content Coordinator Quentin Frayne

Thanks to Lucy Birchley, Sally Darmody, Ryan Evans, Mark Germanchis, Katie Lynch, John Mazzocchi, Wayne Murphy, Trent Paton, Lyahna Spencer, Gina Tsarouhas, Branislava Vladisavljevic

THANKS
MARA VORHEES

Many thanks to Will Gourlay for bringing me on board for this project. How we miss you already! Thankfully, Fiona Buchan and Jo Potts stepped up to fill the hole left by Will's departure. I am also grateful for the watchful eye of Laura Stansfeld. Of course it is my 17 coauthors who did the real heavy lifting for this book, and they deserve all the credit.

BRETT ATKINSON

Hi and special thanks to Greg and Francie in Olomouc, and Tomáš in Wallachia – you all make returning to the Czech Republic a pleasure. Thanks also to Oldřiška and family in Český Krumlov, and to Doug in Loket. I'm sorry I wasn't around to see Jethro Tull under the castle; it looked pretty cool on YouTube. Thanks to Mara Vorhees for her hard work as coordinating author. In Lonely Planet–ville, thanks to Mark Griffiths and the cartography team for making sense of my multicoloured maps, and special thanks to the wonderfully tireless Will Gourlay for his undying energy and passion for

---

THE LONELY PLANET STORY

Fresh from an epic journey across Europe, Asia and Australia in 1972, Tony and Maureen Wheeler sat at their kitchen table stapling together notes. The first Lonely Planet guidebook, *Across Asia on the Cheap,* was born.

Travellers snapped up the guides. Inspired by their success, the Wheelers began publishing books to Southeast Asia, India and beyond. Demand was prodigious, and the Wheelers expanded the business rapidly to keep up. Over the years, Lonely Planet extended its coverage to every country and into the virtual world via lonelyplanet.com and the Thorn Tree message board.

As Lonely Planet became a globally loved brand, Tony and Maureen received several offers for the company. But it wasn't until 2007 that they found a partner whom they trusted to remain true to the company's principles of travelling widely, treading lightly and giving sustainably. In October of that year, BBC Worldwide acquired a 75% share in the company, pledging to uphold Lonely Planet's commitment to independent travel, trustworthy advice and editorial independence.

Today, Lonely Planet has offices in Melbourne, London and Oakland, with over 500 staff members and 300 authors. Tony and Maureen are still actively involved with Lonely Planet. They're travelling more often than ever, and they're devoting their spare time to charitable projects. And the company is still driven by the philosophy of *Across Asia on the Cheap:* 'All you've got to do is decide to go and the hardest part is over. So go!'

the region and for this book. Finally, thanks to Carol for holding the fort in Auckland for a long 10 weeks, and for actually recognising me when I (eventually) got home. I promise to take you to Prague next time, OK?

CAROLYN BAIN

In Estonia (and beyond), a huge *aitäh* to Steve Kokker for his friendship, kindness and immense local wisdom. Others who generously helped out with tips and company around the country include Pille Petersoo, Liina Laar, Geli Lillemaa, Hugo and Tim, Maido Rüütli, Sergei Iarovenko, Malcolm Russell, Madis Mutso and Varje Papp. Big bouquets and heartfelt thanks to friends who shared with me the pleasure of their company on parts of this trip: Sally O'Brien and George Dunford for the memorable weekend in Tallinn; Brandon Presser and Neal Bedford for making work fun in Rīga and Vilnius; and Amanda Harding and Graham Harris for the incredible Baltic City Blitz. Cheers guys!

NEAL BEDFORD

A low bow of gratitude to Nicola Williams for all her tips, hints, and contacts in the country. In the country, a huge thank you to Andrew Quested, the man in the know in Lithuania, for all his suggestions and shouts; Nomeda Navickaite and friends for their knowledge of the capital and the coast; Hans Bastian Hauck for the sailing trip of a lifetime and good company; Cornelis Oskamp and Lena Björkenor for evenings out and random meetings; and the Lithuanian tourist office, bus station, and train station staff for all the help they gave. Lastly, thanks to Karin, for spending a beautiful week with me, giving up her precious holiday time, and keeping me sane when the workload gets too much. Much love.

JAYNE D'ARCY

Thanks to Sharik Billington for taking on Albania with me and my three year old; to Miles for coping with all the cheek pinching; to Will Gourlay for sending me up the Accursed Mountains in the first place; and to Orieta Gliozheni in Korça, Stavri Cifligu in Tirana, Marius Qytyku in Berat, Yolanda Kebo in Saranda and Edward Shehi and his Italian tourists in Voskopoja. Thanks to Dr Shannon Woodcock at La Trobe University, Australia; Mada at Sunrock, Corfu; and everyone else along the way who had the keys and let us in.

CHRIS DELISO

It would be impossible to thank everyone who deserves recognition here, since my gratitude is great and goes back 10 years. For this specific book, then,

I would like to mention the following: Jason Miko, Aleksandar Konevski, Aleksandar Danilovski and Ivo Marussi (Skopje); Nikola Kiselinov, Danijel Medaroski, Vilijam Hristovski, Risto and Anita Stojoski, Dimitri, and Cobi and Darko (Ohrid and around); Kiril Jonovski (Prespa); Patrice Koerper, Elena Petkovska, Gorki Baloyannis, Nesad Azenovski and Petar Cvetkovski (Bitola and around); Saško Atanasov, Aleksandar Panov, Divna Jordanovska, Violeta Jankova, Efrem Ristov, Konstantin and Stevo (Tikveš wine region); Stevče Donevski (Kratovo); Anne Withers, Saško Dončovski, Ace Stojanov and Dragi Pop-Stojanov (Strumica). My biggest gratitude goes to Buba and Marco. Extra thanks go to Lonely Planet's editorial, production and mapmaking teams for their hard work throughout.

PETER DRAGICEVICH

A huge thanks to all the wonderful people who helped me along the way, especially my beloved Dragičević cousins, Hayley and Jack Delf, Goran and Jadranka Marković, Dragana Ostojić, Slavko Marjanović, Danica Ćeranić, Kirsi Hyvaerinen and David Mills. Extra special thanks to Milomir Jukanović and to my enthusiastic editor Will Gourlay.

LISA DUNFORD

Dearest Saša, always being welcomed as a part of your family means more to me than I can say. Fero, Šimi, Sari Petriska – thank you, too. I appreciate the help of everyone who made suggestions and helped me along my way, including Martin Latal, Karen and Matuš Sulek, Zuzana Bielikova, Jimbo Holden and the Monkey. Mara, Will, Fee – thanks for the hard work pulling Eastern Europe together!

MARK ELLIOTT

Many thanks to Will Gourlay and the Lonely Planet team, and to Edis Hodžić, Guillaume Martin, Olivier Janoschka, Snezhan in Trebinje, Vlaren at Tvrdoš Monastery, Semir in Blagaj, Narmina in Mostar, Branislav Andrić in Višegrad and so many more, including the mysterious 'angel' who provided me with such insights to the Belašnica highland villages then disappeared without my ever knowing his name. As ever my greatest thanks go to my endlessly inspiring wife Dani Systermans and to my unbeatable parents who, three decades ago, had the crazy idea of driving me to Bosnia in the first place.

STEVE FALLON

A number of people assisted in the research and writing of the Slovenia chapter, in particular my dear friends and fonts of all knowledge at the

Ljubljana Tourist Board: Verica Leskovar, Tatjana Radovič and Petra Stušek. Others to whom I'd like to say *najlepša hvala* for assistance, inspiration, sustenance and/or a few laughs along the way include the boys (Miha Anzelc, Luka Esenko and Tomaž Marič) of Žtdana Marela in Ljubljana; Brina Čehovin and Tina Križnar of the Slovenian Tourist Board, Ljubljana; Marino Fakin of Slovenian Railways, Ljubljana; Aleš and Tanja Hvala of the Hotel Hvala and Restavracija Topli Val, Kobarid; Lado Leskovar of UNICEF, based in Ljubljana; Tomaž Škofic of Adria Airways in Ljubljana; Robert Stan of Adventure Rafting Bled; and the staff at the Tourist Information Centre Ptuj for assistance (way beyond the call of duty) in helping me find an industrial-strength *klopotec* (wind rattle) on short notice as I whizzed in on a rainy morning from southwest Hungary. Goodbye pigeons! As always, my efforts here are dedicated to my partner, Michael Rothschild, who is way overdue a visit to God's own country.

VESNA MARIC

Hvala to Maja Gilja, my mother, Toni and Marina Ćavar, Ružica, Stipe, Ante, Dana and Loreta Barać. Also *hvala* to Kristina Hajduka, and Janica and Matej. Thanks to Gabriel and all the travellers I chatted to along the way. Thanks also to Anja Mutić and William Gourlay.

TOM MASTERS

I owe a big debt of gratitude to my dear friend Gabriel Gatehouse in Kiev (not Kyiv), who kindly lent me his home, helped me enormously with tackling Ukraine and with whom discussing the finer nuances of Ukrainian politics never gets boring. Thanks also to Will Gourlay at Lonely Planet for sending me to Eastern Europe again, and to the various people who helped me on my way in Belarus and Ukraine – especially Nina in Brest, Dima in Minsk, Dima 2 in Odessa (not Odesa) and Svetlana in Yalta.

MARIKA McADAM

As always, the folk I met on the road are what make this job the best one in the world. Thank you for agreeing with me that different languages, culture, history and religion don't have to get in the way of a shared sense of humour. It was an honour to be a part of the army of authors assembled to put this book together, and a girl could have no finer colleague than a Lonely Planet commissioning editor. Thanks also to my sister Lorina, who was up for anything in Serbia, and to Jo, who came along to Kosovo and always makes wherever he is my favourite place in the world.

LEIF PETTERSON

Thanks goes to Gruia Badescu and Cristiana Groza, who helped me find the oft-well-hid beauty in Bucharest. In Chișinău, Marina Waters and Vitale Eremia once again provided valuable and speedy follow-up fact checking. Monica Zavoianu's expertise helped fortify the Bucovina monastery sections. Direction provided by Daniela and Florentina at the Info Litoral Tourist Information Centre in Mamaia saved me hours of pavement pounding. Thanks to Sebastian Muntean in Sibiu for last second warnings about telecom changes. In London, I'm indebted again to Will 'Power' Gourlay whose poised direction and advice are like an email Valium every time. Finally, thanks to the precious few who convinced me to stop working for a few minutes and get drunk.

BRANDON PRESSER

A heartfelt *paldies* to Aleks Karlsons and Ellie Schilling for adding me to their Rīga posse, to Ojars and Irma Kalnins for an unforgettable trip to Kolkasrags, and to Inese Loce – you were a lifesaver (literally!). To my wonderful Baltic coauthors, Carolyn and Neal – it was such a treat to work with you both. Also a big thank you to Mara Vorhees, Lane Levine, Vaira Vīķe-Freiberga, Aleks Čakste, Jānis Jenzis, Karlis Celms, Richards Baerug, Jūlija Minkeviča, Jānis Rutka, Richard Kalnins, Greg Bloom, my parents and the ab fab Lonely Planet production staff.

ROBERT REID

Thanks to Lonely Planet for sending me three times now to Bulgaria, and to the many many Bulgarians for their generous help, particularly Assen and Ira in Sofia, but also Georgi in Sofia, Sofia's wine-drinking club for letting me crash at Vinopolis, Bendida in Plovdiv, the Rodopi Smile hostel guys in Kârdzhali, the mayor of Kavarna for putting up Uriah Heap murals on the housing blocks, Boris at Ruse's great information centre, and the drunk guy who led me and Assen to the hardest 300m walk of all time at a tomb-raider Roman site near Bulgaria's reluctant northernmost village, Vrâv.

TIM RICHARDS

As always, I'm indebted to the professional staff of Poland's tourist offices, who perform their jobs with enthusiasm and skill. The staff at the Australian embassy in Warsaw also provided useful information. I also give thanks to the national train company PKP; their *pospieszny* trains aren't fast, but they're frequent and usually on time. Thanks also to my Polish fellow passengers who struck up conversations, and learned far more about Australia and light packing than they'd bargained for in return. Much love to my Polish friends – particularly Ewa, Magda, Gosia and Andrzej – for your thoughts on Poland's history and society (and also for those tip-offs about local musicians). And to Magda again for inviting me to a groovy soirée at her Warsaw apartment, packed with cool and interesting guests. Thanks to Coffee Heaven for keeping my seat warm in their Warszawa Centralna outpost. And a final thanks to all the waitresses who were amused by my dodgy Polish – there's more where that came from!

SIMON RICHMOND

My fellow Lonely Planet editors and authors Will Gourlay, Leonid Ragozin, Mike Kohn and Mara Vorhees were a great help – *bolshoi spasibo* all round. It's always a pleasure returning to St Petersburg and catching up with old friends such as Peter, Sasha and Andrey. Cheers also to Matt Brown, for being on the ball about all things Piter, and to Jennifer Fell, Ilya Gurevich, Dr Dimitri Ozerkov, Andrei Dmitriev, Vyacheslav Bochkov, Valery Katsuba, Sergei Politovsky, marathon train-traveller Ed Greig, Chris Hamilton, and Paul and Veronica at Express to Russia for assistance with my visa. In Kaliningrad Elmira Khaimourzina and Marina Drutman both presented the friendly face of Russian tourism, while Harry Potter fans Ksenia Prasolava and Irina Yegorava were charming company and provided a local perspective on their precious piece of Russia.

OUR READERS

Many thanks to the travellers who used the last edition and wrote to us with helpful hints, useful advice and interesting anecdotes:

Sarah Amies, Mark Anderson, Audrey Baills, Rui Bebiano, Jo Bertram, Emma Biasini, Markus Bierl, Linda Bradshaw, David Brocklesby, Molly Brookfield, Rita Bulusu, Simon Century, Marie Cochrane, John Cooke, Dan Coplan, Julie Cowan, Justin Curran, Nicolae Dandis, Assen Davidov, Clement Delplanque, Valeri Dimitrov, Helen Douglas, Chelsea Downing, Tony Duffy, Olivia Faul, Laura Fermann, Tom Ferrington, Michael Fischer, Robert Foitzik, Tobias Franke-Polz, Ludovica Galeazzi, Alex Galloway, Diane Gasner, Astrid Glatz, Gary Goldberg, Laura Gonzalez Gomez, Denise Green, Glenn Havelock, Kristy Henney, Petra Heylen, Alison Hood, Tom Humphrey, Joshua James, Verena Jasper, Betty and Gene Jemail, Kent Johnson, Wayne Jones, Adam Jones, Mirka Kartano, Melinda Kent, Raffi Kojian, Leo Koolhoven, Sasu Laitinen, Robert Leger, George Lerchs, Daniela

Longobardi, Diego Lopez Lopez, Xingkai Loy, Helena Makkonen, Juli Mallett, Craig Martin, Thomas Maurer, Greg Mcelwain, Anthony Mcgowan, Cale Mclellan, Helen Mills, Janet Morrissey, Cathy Nemmert, Kathleen Neumann, Krista Niles, Katie Nixon, Michael Pass Pass, Matt Pepe, Maria Perez, Madalina Phillips, Mike Poblete, Sasha Savic, Ted Schumacher, Paul Seaver, Julia Smith, Pierre St-Jacques, Thomas Sternagel, Ryan Taylor, Mike Thomson, Harm Jan Timmer, Lukas Tinguely, Pippa Tizzard, Job Van Der Geest, Jens Verlinde, Nancy Wagner, Michael Wheeler, Jonathan Wickens, Bob Withington

ACKNOWLEDGMENTS
Many thanks to the following for the use of their content:

Globe on title page ©Mountain High Maps 1993 Digital Wisdom, Inc.

Internal photographs by Lonely Planet Images, and by Andrew Bain p583 (#4); Glenn Beanland p587 (#4); Krzysztof Dydynsk p585 (#4); John Elk III p582 (#2); Greg Elms p586 (#2); Roberto Gerometta p587 (#3); Richard I'Anson p581; Rachel Lewis p582 (#1), p583 (#3); Diana Mayfield p586 (#1); Martin Moos p588 (#1); Witold Skrypczak p585 (#3); Jonathan Smith p588 (#2); Wayne Walton p584 (#2); Brent Winemaker p584 (#1).

Index

Index

INDEX

INDEX

INDEX

INDEX

1044

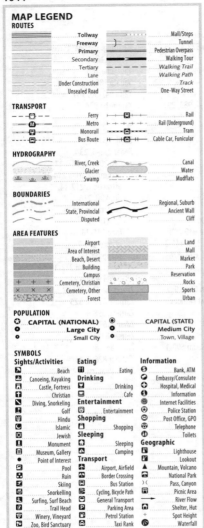

MAP LEGEND

ROUTES

- Tollway
- Freeway
- Primary
- Secondary
- Tertiary
- Lane
- Under Construction
- Unsealed Road
- Mall/Steps
- Tunnel
- Pedestrian Overpass
- Walking Tour
- Walking Trail
- Walking Path
- Track
- One-Way Street

TRANSPORT

- Ferry
- Metro
- Monorail
- Bus Route
- Rail
- Rail (Underground)
- Tram
- Cable Car, Funicular

HYDROGRAPHY

- River, Creek
- Glacier
- Swamp
- Canal
- Water
- Mudflats

BOUNDARIES

- International
- State, Provincial
- Disputed
- Regional, Suburb
- Ancient Wall
- Cliff

AREA FEATURES

- Airport
- Area of Interest
- Beach, Desert
- Building
- Campus
- Cemetery, Christian
- Cemetery, Other
- Forest
- Land
- Mall
- Market
- Park
- Reservation
- Rocks
- Sports
- Urban

POPULATION

- CAPITAL (NATIONAL)
- Large City
- Small City
- CAPITAL (STATE)
- Medium City
- Town, Village

SYMBOLS

Sights/Activities
- Beach
- Canoeing, Kayaking
- Castle, Fortress
- Christian
- Diving, Snorkeling
- Golf
- Hindu
- Islamic
- Jewish
- Monument
- Museum, Gallery
- Point of Interest
- Pool
- Ruin
- Skiing
- Snorkelling
- Surfing, Surf Beach
- Trail Head
- Winery, Vineyard
- Zoo, Bird Sanctuary

Eating
- Eating

Drinking
- Drinking
- Cafe

Entertainment
- Entertainment

Shopping
- Shopping

Sleeping
- Sleeping
- Camping

Transport
- Airport, Airfield
- Border Crossing
- Bus Station
- Cycling, Bicycle Path
- General Transport
- Parking Area
- Petrol Station
- Taxi Rank

Information
- Bank, ATM
- Embassy/Consulate
- Hospital, Medical
- Information
- Internet Facilities
- Police Station
- Post Office, GPO
- Telephone
- Toilets

Geographic
- Lighthouse
- Lookout
- Mountain, Volcano
- National Park
- Pass, Canyon
- Picnic Area
- River Flow
- Shelter, Hut
- Spot Height
- Waterfall

LONELY PLANET OFFICES

Australia
Head Office
Locked Bag 1, Footscray, Victoria 3011
☎ 03 8379 8000, fax 03 8379 8111
talk2us@lonelyplanet.com.au

USA
150 Linden St, Oakland, CA 94607
☎ 510 250 6400, toll free 800 275 8555
fax 510 893 8572
info@lonelyplanet.com

UK
2nd fl, 186 City Rd,
London EC1V 2NT
☎ 020 7106 2100, fax 020 7106 2101
go@lonelyplanet.co.uk

Published by Lonely Planet Publications Pty Ltd
ABN 36 005 607 983

© Lonely Planet Publications Pty Ltd 2009

© photographers as indicated 2009

Cover photograph: House facades, Telč, Czech Republic, Izzet Keribar/
Lonely Planet Images. Many of the images in this guide are available for licensing from Lonely Planet Images: www.lonelyplanet
images.com.

Mixed Sources
Product group from well-managed
forests and other controlled sources
www.fsc.org Cert no. SGS-COC-005002
© 1996 Forest Stewardship Council
FSC